Legalease is a leading independent publisher of information for law firms and their clients. Established in 1987, Legalease is the publisher of *The Legal 500* series which today provides analysis and information on law firms in over 75 countries around the world through *The European Legal 500*, *The UK Legal 500* and *The Asia Pacific Legal 500*. Legalease is the publisher of *Legal Business* magazine, *The In-House Lawyer* magazine, *Der Syndikus*, *The Practical Lawyer*, *The Employment Law Journal*, *The Trusts and Estates Law & Tax Journal*, *The Property Law Journal*, *The Family Law Journal*, *The Personal Injury Law Journal* and *Wills and Trusts Law Reports*. Additionally, Legalease runs the leading legal website – **www.legal500.com** – where visitors are able to access many of our publications and find information regarding international commercial legal developments. The site has nearly 500,000 users a month.

The EUROPEAN LEGAL 500

JOHN PRITCHARD

LAW FIRMS IN EUROPE

AND THE MIDDLE EAST

Published annually by Legalease, Kensington Square House, 12-14 Ansdell Street, London W8 5BN
Phone: +44 20 7396 9292, Fax: +44 20 7396 9300

Editor-in-chief John Pritchard
Editor Mairead Keohane
Editorial research Jim Banks, Gill Booles, Andrew Burnyeat, Chris Crowe, Rachael Doeg, Stephen Doggett, Richard Freeland, Perry Gourley, Lucy Hickman, David Kelly, Sam Kenworthy, Martin Keuneman, Alan Lamb, Nicola Laver, Debbie Legall, James Lewis, Kate Mansey, Adrienne Margolis, Anthony Notaras, Laurent Pompanon, Nick Reader, Maria Shahid, Ian Skillicorn, Jessica Smerin, Catherine Smith, Camilla Sutton, Caroline Thorpe, Luke Walton
Group sales manager Catherine Wallen
Publishing assistants James Chatterley, George Forth, Mark Gibbins, Sam Holdsworth, Janet Isokariari, Asim Shirwani, Amy Taylor, Toni Wyatt
Managing editors Rosie McGechie, Annette Sheppard
Production editors Michael Diver, Stephen Jones, Victoria Lennon, Andrew Mackie, Monica Matthews, Rachel Morrison, Eleanor Perry, Laura Sharp, Helen Smith
Data management Nick Amanovic, Andrew Chiakle, Mick Cotham, Peter Gough, Flora Samuels, Jitka Taborska
Technical assistant Femi James
Website and electronic publishing Brian Kavanagh
Business development director Joe Bell
Chief executive Mark Cusick
Printed and bound by Butler & Tanner, Frome

First published 1991
Fourteenth edition 2004

ISBN 1 903927 27 7

Enquiries about inclusion in the directory sections of *The European Legal 500* should be directed to Catherine Wallen;
enquiries about the editorial sections should be addressed to Mairead Keohane.

Further copies can be ordered from Marie Kraus
phone: +44 20 7396 9313, fax: +44 20 7396 9302,
e-mail: subscriptions@legalease.co.uk

CONTENTS

THE EUROPEAN LEGAL MARKET

From the publisher

I am pleased to send you a copy of the 2004 edition of ***The European Legal 500***. This 14th edition reports on and analyses the practices of thousands of law firms in 55 jurisdictions in Europe and the Middle East. I would like to thank all those firms and clients who assisted our researchers in their task.

New this year are chapters on Iran, Jordan and Qatar – we extend a particularly warm welcome to the lawyers in those countries and welcome them to ***The European Legal 500***.

I hope that you will find the book useful in making contact with lawyers throughout the region. We are committed to providing our readers with fair and accurate reporting and analysis. As always, we welcome your feedback on our research.

We wish you a happy and successful 2004.

John Pritchard

INTRODUCTION
How to use this book

The European Legal 500 is a guide to commercial law firms in Europe and the Middle East. Countries throughout western, central, and eastern Europe are included, as are Bahrain, Egypt, Iran, Israel, Jordan, Kuwait, Lebanon, Oman, Qatar, Saudi Arabia and the UAE.

Each chapter falls into two distinct parts: the editorial section and the directory section. The editorial section is a mixture of factual information and commentary. This commentary consists of a general review of which firms do what types of work, and which firms are generally reckoned by their peers to have a 'good name' within the national, and international, legal community. The editorial is based largely on the combined opinions of the many lawyers and law firm clients who co-operated in the research in each country. Accordingly, it is important to appreciate that the editorial lists should not be taken as a definitive statement on law firms, but rather as a starting point for discussion.

All editorial comments and listings are completely independent and no firm has been able to secure its inclusion within the editorial sections through payment.

The directory section for each country is made up of professional cards based on information supplied by the firms and approved by them prior to publication.

THE EDITORIAL

The editorial sections consist largely of our own opinions. The views expressed represent the opinions of the editors, with no assumption of legal liability or responsibility for mistakes or inaccuracies. The research for the editorial is based on the combined opinions of the many lawyers interviewed in each jurisdiction, commentary from clients and analysis of deals or contentious issues reported. It is important to note that the editorial is therefore a subjective overview based on systematic research.

Once again, in this edition we have included a table showing the largest firms, according to the number of lawyers in the firm, in each particular country (except Liechtenstein). As always, we rely on the integrity of the firms to supply the correct figures. British and American readers should note that there are relatively few really large continental firms (with more than 50 lawyers, for example) and that many of the leading firms within particular areas of practice will be found to be comparatively small. Many of the larger offices today are those of the international firms of UK and US origin.

In certain jurisdictions some of the larger firms will dominate several categories of work. The research is not, however, limited to these firms only; smaller firms and specialist boutique practices are included where appropriate.

The tables of recommendations are divided into groups: firms are listed in groups in order of priority, and alphabetically within groups. Furthermore, the firms have been sorted alphabetically by using the first name or initial of the firm and not by terms such as *Advokatfirmaet* or *Law Office*. Sole practitioners are listed in the same way as firms alphabetically by initial or first name.

Readers should also note the differences between local Bar regulations within different jurisdictions. In a number of countries, the local Bar rules on advertising and publicity are a matter of delicacy. In such jurisdictions, no comments have been made with regard to the expertise of particular firms. Instead, lists have been made of firms known to be involved in commercial work – with the proviso that no significance should be attached to the inclusion or non-inclusion of a firm. It should not be inferred in such cases that one firm is 'better' than another; the tables serve only as an indication of suitability.

✪ This symbol in the tables denotes that a law firm has a professional card at the end of that chapter.

England and Wales, Scotland, Guernsey, Jersey, and the Isle of Man

The editorial for England and Wales, Scotland and Offshore Britain (ie Guernsey, Isle of Man, and Jersey) is a digest of the information contained in ***The Legal 500 (2003 UK edition)***. However, we have requested details of the number of lawyers in each firm in order to bring the size tables for these areas in line with those in the rest of the book. As always, we rely on the integrity of the firms to supply the correct figures.

THE DIRECTORY

The directory sections of the book contain professional cards placed by firms within each jurisdiction. The full-page professional cards have profiles based on information provided by the participating firms. These profiles, having been approved by the firms prior to publication, are completely separate and different from the editorial. The professional cards are designed for use by lawyers and clients in different jurisdictions.

We should also emphasise that taking an entry in the directory section does not necessarily mean that a firm will be mentioned in the editorial section.

Within the directory sections, firms are listed in alphabetical order within each town. Thus, in Spain, for example, the listing for firms in Barcelona will precede that for firms in Madrid. As mentioned above, the alphabetical listing uses the first name or initial of the firm and not generic terms such as *Advokatfirmaet* or *Law Office*.

Firm names: There is often a surprising amount of confusion about the correct name for a law firm. To the outsider, it can often be difficult to identify the correct firm. In some jurisdictions, it is virtually mandatory to include the names of all partners within the full firm name. Thus the retirement of an individual partner can result in a change in the firm name. Similarly, some firms operate as the local offices of major international law practices, such as *Baker & McKenzie*. In certain jurisdictions, the correct name of the parent firm can be used; in other jurisdictions local Bar rules mean that the foreign name cannot be used. Thus, it is not always easy to identify whether a firm is independent or the local office of an international practice.

A further complication is that local tradition may require that a phrase such as *Law Office of...* (or equivalent) has to be used at the beginning of the name of the firm. Thus many firms in Italy begin with *Studio Legale*; similarly, in Sweden many firms start with the title

Advokatfirman. All of this means that some care has to be taken in identifying particular firms.

Addresses of firms: We list only one address for each firm within a particular city. This is for reasons of space and simplicity (as well as clarity). Many firms have more than one office, however, and these are listed under '**Other offices**' (see below).

Phone numbers: Most firms will, of course, have many phone lines and several different phone numbers. For reasons of space and clarity, we have restricted ourselves to the main phone number.

All phone numbers are quoted in their international form. Thus we have included the country code in a firm's telephone number (for use when dialling that number from outside the country – the relevant international dialling-out code has to be inserted in place of the + sign).

Fax numbers: Once again, we have quoted only one fax number (despite the fact that many firms will have more than one fax line). It should also be noted that some countries continue to use phrases such as telefax and telecopier when referring to fax machines.

Languages: The languages spoken in the office are generally listed alphabetically – the native language is not usually included (for example, a German firm in Germany would not include German as one of the languages spoken). However, for bilingual or trilingual countries all the native languages spoken in that country may be listed. Additionally, we do include mention of local language capability for firms' foreign offices.

Other offices: Many firms have other offices; these are generally listed in alphabetical order. Some firms have indicated that particular offices are 'associated' offices, and we have marked those with an asterisk (*). However, many of these other offices are not, in practice, genuine offices. Instead, they may amount to a correspondent relationship with a local firm, or merely the displaying of a nameplate in another law firm's office. These are also denoted by *.

Number of lawyers: Most firms have supplied us with the total number of lawyers in the firm and, where applicable, the total number at the office which appears on the professional card. The definition of 'lawyers' includes partners, assistants, associates, attorneys, solicitors, and so on; it does not include consultants, paralegals, trainees, and notaries. (It should be noted, however, that in some countries the title of lawyer cannot be assumed when the person is employed by someone else; for example a *Rechtsanwalt* in Austria.)

However, it is important not to place too much emphasis on these figures. Firstly, a few firms have refused to supply this information and, secondly, we would repeat the point that the size of a law practice will often not be a significant factor. There are many very small firms in most countries that are strong within particular areas of law.

Categories of work: Each professional card lists categories of work that the firm undertakes (generally with the name of the person to be contacted for each category).

WHO'S WHO IN THE LAW

Professional contacts: In this section we include biographies of selected partners and contacts in the firms. The information has been provided by the firms themselves. Please note that the partners listed for each firm do not necessarily represent the whole of the partnership. For the total number of lawyers in a firm, please refer to the firm's professional card.

INDEX OF PROFESSIONAL CARDS

Each professional card is listed at the back of the book alphabetically by firm name, followed by the location and the page number on which the professional card appears.

AUSTRIA

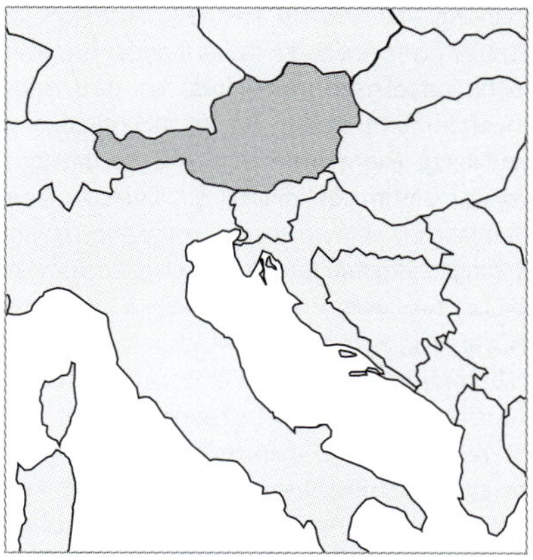

Population	**8.1 million**
Number of lawyers	**4,100**
Professional title	**Rechtsanwalt; Rechtsanwältin**
Currency	**Euro (€)**

Index

Austria is a small country that is an EU member and benefits from its location right in the centre of Europe. It borders Germany, the Czech Republic, Slovakia, Hungary, Slovenia, Italy, Switzerland and Liechtenstein. Germany is Austria's most important trading partner, followed by Italy and the neighbouring former eastern bloc states. Austrian businesses regard the latter as their home market. Austria is a federal republic with nine autonomous provinces, of which Vienna is the wealthiest. The government is a coalition between the far-right Freedom Party (FPÖ) and the dominant conservative People's Party (ÖVP), led by Chancellor Wolfgang Schussel.

BILLING

Billing rates are governed by the Austrian Lawyers' Scale of Fees Act. The Austrian Bar Association also issues guidelines on fees. Most foreign clients are billed on an hourly basis to spare them the intricacies of the Act. Fixed-fee lump sums are popular in litigation, but if a party agrees to pay more than the rate, the additional fees are not recoverable from the losing party. Contingency or success-related fees are prohibited, but a fixed percentage of the claim can be negotiated as a bonus in advance.

MARKETING

Austrian lawyers are now able to publish a client's name with approval. Currently, however, few firms use external PR agencies or have in-house marketing teams.

IN-HOUSE LAWYERS

Lawyers registered with the Austrian Bar Association may work directly – and even exclusively – for individual companies, on the condition that they are not paid a salary. Salaried in-house lawyers are not classified as independent professionals and therefore may not join the Bar Association, and must use the title *jurist* instead of *rechtsanwalt*. They cannot represent their employers in court and their activity is limited to those tasks not requiring a full *rechtsanwalt*. Many medium-sized Austrian companies do not have in-house lawyers, but will instead employ a person with legal education who also has responsibility for areas such as insurance, property or human resources. Some large Austrian companies have recently been downscaling their in-house legal teams.

ECONOMIC CLIMATE

In 2000, Austria sparked protests, culminating in a six-month EU freeze on bilateral political contacts, when it formed the first government in Europe to include a far-right populist party. The anti-immigration, eurosceptical Freedom Party (FPÖ), formed a coalition of almost equal partners with the conservative People's Party (ÖVP), replacing the longstanding 'grand coalition' between the conservatives and the Social Democrats (SPÖ).

However, in the general election of 2002 the Freedom Party lost considerable voter share to the People's Party. Though the Freedom Party is still part of the coalition, conservative chancellor Wolfgang Schussel is now in a dominant position. Regional elections in March 2004 are expected to be an important test for the Freedom Party and its figure-head Jorg Haider, currently governor of the southern Austrian province of Carinthia. The Social Democrats and the environmentalist Green Party, which is also strong in Austria, are currently growing, due to dissatisfaction with the government.

The Austrian economy has recovered, and managed to grow at about the average rate for the EU in 2003. This is largely due to its growing participation in the economies of its Eastern European neighbours. Austria has traditionally leaned heavily on Germany, a country which buys 40% of Austrian exports. However, with Germany in a state of economic stagnation and nearby Switzerland in recession, Austria has been turning towards the Czech Republic, Slovakia, Hungary and Slovenia, where economic growth has been running at double the EU average. Austria's national corporate giants OMV, Erste Bank and Wienerberger are investing heavily in Eastern Europe. When the former eastern bloc countries join the EU, Austria – for many years simply regarded as the cheap version of Germany – will find itself not on the fringes but in the heart of Europe, a place it has not occupied since it lost its empire nearly a century ago.

Chancellor Schussel, has been working hard, against considerable opposition, to shake up the stable consensus culture – where the state is still more powerful and has more spending power than private industry – to which Austria has been accustomed for 40 years. Chancellor Schussel has pushed through several unpopular reform packages, including a cut in pension benefits and the privatisation of the steel group, Voestalpine. There were major strikes in 2003, and the Austrian economy remained weak in the third quarter, with domestic and foreign demand for goods and

The largest firms

1	Schönherr Rechtsanwälte	71
2	Wolf Theiss	69
3	Dorda Brugger Jordis	60
4	Freshfields Bruckhaus Deringer	56
5	CMS Strommer Reich-Rohrwig Karasek Hainz	50
	Cerha Hempel Spiegelfeld Hlawati	50
7	Binder Grösswang Rechtsanwälte	47
8	Saxinger Chalupsky Weber & Partners Rechtsanwälte GmbH	46
9	DLA Weiss-Tessbach	41
10	Baier Lambert	30
11	Haarmann Hügel Attorneys at Law	26
	Lansky, Ganzger & Partner Rechtsanwälte GmbH	26
13	Fiebinger, Polak, Leon & Partners Rechtsanwälte	25
	Hausmaninger Herbst Rechtsanwälte GmbH	25
15	Baker & McKenzie	24
	Hasch & Partner Anwaltsgesellschaft mbH	24
	Preslmayr Attorneys at Law	24
18	Haslinger/Nagele & Partner Rechtsanwälte GmbH	23
19	Eiselsberg Natlacen Walderdorff Cancola	21
20	Graf, Maxl & Pitkowitz	20
	Kunz Schima Wallentin	20
22	Fellner Wratzfeld & Partner Rechtsanwälte	17
23	Greiter Pegger Kofler & Partners	16
	Wietrzyk Dullinger Rechtsanwälte GmbH	16
25	Brauneis, Klauser & Prändl	15
	Neudorfer, Griensteidl, Hahnkamper, Stapf & Partner	15
	Siemer-Siegl-Füreder & Partner	15

These figures represent the total number of lawyers in this country only, and have been supplied by the firms themselves. The figures should be accurate as at 1 January 2004.

services stagnant. However, government policy has focused on boosting growth through tough direct investment incentives, and the country's strong public sector infrastructure spending has benefited industry, particularly the construction. Despite Austria's high taxes and red tape, the economy seems likely to perform well throughout 2004.

LEGAL MARKET

Many Austrian companies still prefer to use one law firm for all their legal work, but the market is slowly becoming more international and competitive, and there are high-quality, international standard legal services on offer.

The leading heavyweight corporate law firms in the Austrian market are **Wolf Theiss**, **Freshfields Bruckhaus Deringer** and **Schönherr Rechtsanwälte**. **Schönherr Rechtsanwälte**, a very old and well-established firm, has made great strides in brushing the dust off its image and re-establishing itself as a major corporate player. *Weiss Tessbach*, one of the oldest firms in Austria, suffered a blow in 2003 when six partners left, reportedly over differences of opinion on the firm's strategy in central and eastern Europe. In October 2003, the firm merged with UK-based **DLA** to become **DLA Weiss-Tessbach**, and the market is still waiting to see how this will affect the practice.

There has not yet been the tide of major Anglo-American tie-ups in Austria that have swept some comparably small European jurisdictions. **Wolf Theiss** was in intensive merger discussions with **Clifford Chance LLP** two years ago, but decided not to go ahead with the international tie-up. Mergers with German firms have so far been more important than those with Anglo-American firms. *Heller Löber Bahn & Partners* merged with German firm *Bruckhaus Westrick Stegemann* and then, in 2000, became part of UK-based **Freshfields Bruckhaus Deringer** through merger. **Haarmann Hügel Attorneys at Law** is a co-operation – to all intents and purposes a merger – with Germany-based **Haarmann Hemmelrath**.

In early 2003, US-based **Skadden, Arps, Slate, Meagher & Flom LLP** opened a greenfield office Vienna, having had a longstanding Austrian desk. Also in 2003, **Baker & McKenzie** tied up with local firm *Kerres & Diwok*. UK-based **Lovells** has a long-standing association in Austria, operating as **Lovells in association with Mondl, Trummer, Thomas & Partner Rechtsanwälte GmbH**. The *Denton International* network, of which **Baier Lambert** was a member, has now dissolved.

The fate of another international network member, **CMS Strommer Reich-Rohrwig Karasek Hainz**, has been much discussed in the Austrian press, amid rumours that the firm was breaking up. All that is currently certain is that name partner Georg Karasek is leaving – probably to set up his own firm – and name partner Alfred Strommer is retiring. Apart from this, it is business as usual at the Vienna-based firm.

BANKING AND FINANCE

The Austrian market for business financing is dominated by three large native commercial banks: Bank Austria – which is now owned by HVB in Germany; Erste Bank; and RZB. There are no Austrian-based investment banks, and investment banking activity in the country comes from London, Frankfurt, and to some extent Swiss banks, some of which have offices in Vienna. Traditionally, companies have looked to banks for loans for financing, and it is still relatively innovative for Austrian companies to issue bonds. However, sophisticated financial products are now being imported from foreign banks, securitisation is beginning, and private equity is becoming a popular form of financing. Interest from international venture capital companies is just starting to return to Austria, following the slump of the last two years. There have been a number of IPOs as Austrian companies, which initially decided to become listed in Brussels or Frankfurt, return to the reviving Vienna Stock Exchange (VSE).

As the financial markets in Vienna become increasingly sophisticated, a handful of law firms that are able to handle the new products are surging ahead of the pack of traditional banking firms.

Cerha Hempel Spiegelfeld Hlawati is active in assisting foreign banks – such as Société Générale, HVB subsidiary BAWAG, Citibank and Scholler Bank – in developing products for the Austrian market, and acts on most of the groundbreaking transactions in the capital markets. The practice is led by the highly regarded Edith Hlawati. The firm advised state privatisation and holding agency ÖIAG on its issuance of notes worth €30bn that were exchangeable into Telekom Austria shares, the first ever issue of exchangeable bonds by an Austrian issuer. Other key transactions were acting as Austrian counsel to underwriters JPMorgan and Goldman Sachs in the €110bn IPO of Bank Austria, the largest IPO in Europe in 2003, and as Austrian counsel to Telekom Austria on the largest (€72bn) corporate bond of an Austrian issuer to date. The firm also has considerable experience in asset finance transactions.

Dorda Brugger Jordis has a large banking department headed by Andreas Mayr, who has been working on some high-profile corporate bonds, notably advising arrangers Bank Austria Creditanstalt/HVB on offerings of €200m of bonds by the Austrian Federal Railway Company, and €250m of bonds by OMV AG. On the capital markets side, Andreas Zahradnik has been working for RCB Raiffeisen Centrobank in the listing of shares on the VSE. Tibor Varga is recommended for syndicated loans. He advised the Austrian arrangers of a €800m revolving credit facility, the largest syndicated loan transaction in Austria. Winfried Schwarz is recommended for cross-border and US lease transactions. In structured finance, Florian Kresleher has a good reputation.

BANKING AND FINANCE

CERHA HEMPEL SPIEGELFELD HLAWATI ✪
DORDA BRUGGER JORDIS ✪
WOLF THEISS ✪

BINDER GRÖSSWANG RECHTSANWÄLTE ✪
FRESHFIELDS BRUCKHAUS DERINGER ✪
KUNZ SCHIMA WALLENTIN & PARTNER
ORTNER PÖCH FORAMITTI ✪
SAXINGER CHALUPSKY WEBER & PARTNERS RECHTSANWÄLTE GMBH ✪
SCHÖNHERR RECHTSANWÄLTE ✪

CMS Strommer Reich-Rohrwig Karasek Hainz ✪
DLA Weiss-Tessbach ✪
Eiselsberg Natlacen Walderdorff Cancola ✪
Fellner Wratzfeld & Partner Rechtsanwälte ✪
Fiebinger, Polak, Leon & Partners Rechtsanwälte ✪
Haarmann Hügel Attorneys at Law ✪
Hauser Partners Rechtsanwälte GmbH ✪
Hausmaninger Herbst Rechtsanwälte GmbH ✪
Preslmayr Attorneys at Law J

ARNOLD Rechtsanwalts-Partnerschaft
Baier Lambert ✪
Baker & McKenzie ✪
Brauneis, Klauser & Prändl ✪
Graf, Maxl & Pitkowitz ✪
Griss & Partner
Hasch & Partner Anwaltsgesellschaft mbH ✪
Neudorfer, Griensteidl, Hahnkamper, Stapf & Partner ✪

Alix Frank Rechtsanwälte KEG
Dallmann & Juranek ✪
Giger, Ruggenthaler & Simon Rechtsanwälte KEG
Greiter Pegger Kofler & Partners ✪
Haslinger/Nagele & Partner Rechtsanwälte GmbH ✪
Held Berdnik Astner & Partner, Rechtsanwälte ✪
Lovells in association with Mondl, Trummer, Thomas & Partner Rechtsanwälte GmbH ✪
Skadden, Arps, Slate, Meagher & Flom LLP
Zirngibl Langwieser

Firms are listed A-Z in tiers which are ranked in order of priority
✪ Indicates firm displays contact details at the end of this chapter.

Wolf Theiss is strong in capital markets, where it has been advising Erste Bank on the secondary public offering of shares worth €650m, the largest capital increase ever in Austria. Another key transaction was advising Voestalpine AG, a leading Central European steel manufacturer, on the secondary public offering of shares worth €330m, in a high-profile privatisation project. General banking clients include ABN Amro, Barclay Capital and Deutsche Bank, whom the firm has been advising on a €372m syndicated multi-currency term loan and revolving facility agreement.

Binder Grösswang Rechtsanwälte has an excellent reputation for asset finance, structured finance and cross-border leasings. The firm recently worked on a €500m syndicated loan facility for arranger Bank Austria Creditanstalt, and on the €125m refinancing of the Xerium Group. It also has capital markets experience, having advised the dealers on the €5bn debt issuance programme of Hypo Vorarlberg. Christian Klausegger is recommended for structured finance and cross-border leasing, and Michael Kutschera is recommended for capital markets.

Freshfields Bruckhaus Deringer offers a strong combination of tax and legal advice on asset finance transactions. It also advised the Austrian government on the sale, through a securitisation, of a real estate portfolio worth €2bn. Friedrich Jergitsch is recommended for asset and structured finance, and for his expertise in Russian markets. In capital markets, the firm has been advising the Carlyle Group on a secondary public offering. In the general bank finance arena, it has acted for Bank Austria Creditanstalt AG on the €2.755m financing of an acquisition through a bridge facility, and subsequent refinancing into a syndicated loan term.

Kunz Schima Wallentin & Partner's finance partner Veronika Kozak has an outstanding reputation for cross-border leasing, particularly in relation to financing, and her clients include some of the largest US banks and insurance companies. Her asset finance practice grew out of aircraft leasing where, despite the down market, she has still been acting for Austrian Airlines and subsidiaries in leasing out superfluous planes. She has also been acting for the Vienna waste water network in the $609m leasing and lease-back of part of its system to a US investor, a complex tax driven lease financing transaction.

Ortner Pöch Foramitti is a banking boutique which has an excellent reputation for complex cross-border credit or note issuance facilities, and for leasing transactions. Peter Pöch is recommended for banking regulatory and capital markets work.

Saxinger Chalupsky Weber & Partners Rechtsanwälte GmbH's Stefan Weber is known for his capital markets expertise, while Franz Mittendorfer and Dietmar Huemer have advised on a number of cross-border leases and also on lease and lease-back transactions all over Austria. Recent projects include acting for the issuer on the IPO of Bank Austria Creditanstalt, the largest IPO in Europe in 2003.

Schönherr Rechtsanwälte's Peter Feyl has a strong securitisation practice, and has worked on the first synthetic securitisation in Austria. Key clients of the firm include JPMorgan, Deutsche Bank and Veronis Suhler Stevenson. The firm was the Austrian counsel on the €300m post-acquisition financing of Uralita's acquisition of Pfleiderer, and also advised the AIG Emerging Europe Infrastructure Fund on a €23m mezzanine financing.

CMS Strommer Reich-Rohrwig Karasek Hainz has a solid banking practice, which recently advised Westdeutsche Immobilien Bank on the financing of the €360m acquisition of the Millennium Tower in Vienna. Alexander Russ is recommended for bank regulatory work. On the capital markets side, the firm has advised the Austrian Federal Railway Corporation and BNP Paribas on the international private placement of a €500m corporate bond.

DLA Weiss-Tessbach has a leading practice in project finance, where it advises many prominent German and Austrian Banks, including Bank Austria and HVB. Stefan Eder is highly recommended. The firm has also worked for an Austrian private bank on a short-term, revolving financing securitisation, and on a €1bn bond issue.

Eiselsberg Natlacen Walderdorff Cancola has handled syndicated loan work for a major Italian bank with subsidiaries in Vienna. It has also been advising a US bank on the implementation of a central clearing unit for a worldwide customer. Georg Walderdorff is recommended.

Fellner Wratzfeld & Partner Rechtsanwälte's Markus Fellner has a good reputation for project finance. On the bank finance side, it has been advising some major Austrian banks, including Bank Austria, on restructurings and insolvencies.

Fiebinger, Polak, Leon & Partners Rechtsanwälte acts for several multinational and Austrian banks, who it advises on all aspects of banking law and capital markets.

Haarmann Hügel Attorneys at Law is strong on tax advice for institutions that are developing financial products in the capital markets, particularly financial products in the public sector. Recent work includes advising OMB on the $320m inaugural US private placement transaction in Austria, and advising the State of Lower Austria and NÖ Hypobank on a €2.5bn ABS transaction, the largest securitisation so far. The firm also handles major banking litigation. Florian Gibitz is recommended.

Wulf Gordian Hauser at **Hauser Partners Rechtsanwälte GmbH** is a well regarded banking lawyer. Recent work includes advising Deutsche Bank on a €65m securitised facility agreement and collateral pooling agreements, advising a UK bank a €2.9bn credit agreement, and advising a consortium of European banks on a syndicated facility of €1bn.

Preslmayr Attorneys at Law is acting for some major Austrian banks, including Bank für Arbeit und Wirtschaft, in cartel investigations by the European Commission. The firm also represents banks in litigation with consumer groups over interest rates on loans. In addition, it acts for a number of medium-sized US venture capital funds.

ARNOLD Rechtsanwalts-Partnerschaft advises Austrian and international banks on questions of banking secrecy and stamp duty issues in contracts. It also regularly assists banks in implementing Internet banking facilities.

Baier Lambert works for a number of investment funds and foundations, with a focus on Eastern Europe and Russia. It is currently advising the Austrian subsidiaries of a large Russian bank on regulatory issues and syndicated loan transactions. Peter Lambert is recommended.

Baker & McKenzie has good experience in syndicated loans and asset-backed securities. Clients include Société Générale and Deutsche Bank. Georg Diwok is recommended.

Brauneis, Klauser & Prändl has particular expertise in hedge funds. Stefan Geppert, together with top-flight Irish law firm **Arthur Cox**, has been working to set up a new convertible hedge fund domiciled in Ireland and managed by Nicholas Applegate Capital Management LLC, with shares distributed mainly in Austria and Germany.

Graf, Maxl & Pitkowitz has been acting for the borrower in a €200m PPP financing in the infrastructure area. Otto Waechter is recommended.

Griss & Partner has been acting for an Austrian bank in the structuring of an equity and debt participation in a US high-yield bond fund. Gunter Griss and Gabriele Krenn are recommended.

Hasch & Partner Anwaltsgesellschaft mbH focuses on advising companies on reorganisations of their financial structures. It has recently advised the Austrian branch of a multinational company on a new debt structure worth €350m.

Neudorfer, Griensteidl, Hahnkamper, Stapf & Partner's Michael Steiner has been acting for investors in investment disputes. The firm has also advised a major Austrian bank on the refinancing of a cross-border time-sharing complex.

CENTRAL AND EASTERN EUROPE

Austrian companies have always had extremely important business relations with Central and Eastern Europe, even during the communist era. Ever since the fall of the Iron Curtain, Austrian law firms have considered the region to be their home market. With the imminent accession of ten former eastern bloc countries to the EU, Austrian law firms are jostling to position themselves as the gateway between the new member states and the West, particularly for Anglo-American firms. Croatia is a particularly interesting jurisdiction for Austrian law firms, with a strong tourism business on the Mediterranean coast, and a plethora of recent privatisations. Privatisation and large transactions have almost dried up in Serbia since prime minister Zoran Djindjic was shot dead in March 2003. Austrian law firms are therefore concentrating their new office openings on Zagreb. Ljubljana, the Slovenian capital, and Bratislava, the Slovakian capital, are also increasingly on their radar. Hungary is less important to Austrian law firms, as it has its own highly developed legal market. Some Austrian law firms are looking as far afield as Sofia and the markets of south-eastern Europe.

The corporate practice at **DLA Weiss-Tessbach** has a longstanding focus on Central and Eastern Europe, and the firm has offices in Bratislava, Budapest, Prague, Zagreb and Sarajevo. It has recently worked on the restructuring of an Austrian bank with interests in Central and Eastern Europe, and on a large acquisition in Slovenia.

Freshfields Bruckhaus Deringer has access to a worldwide network with offices in Hungary, Slovakia and Russia. From Vienna, it acts for a number of major international clients in the Eastern European region. These include German media group Bertelsmann, and the largest magazine publisher in Europe, Gruner & Jahr. A major project was acting for Ruhrgas and Gaz de France on the $2.7bn purchase of 49% of SPP. Another large project was acting for major German, French and Italian gas companies in relation to the €2.7bn privatisation of the entire Slovakian gas industry.

Schönherr Rechtsanwälte is strong in Romania – where it was the first German-speaking firm to establish an office – and in Croatia, where its real estate practice is very strong. The firm also has offices in Serbia and Slovenia, where it is one of the largest firms. It has a Bulgarian lawyer on its staff and handles Bulgarian work out of Romania. The firm is particularly strong in project finance and in the oil industry, and has been acting for OMV in the acquisition of petrol stations in Eastern Europe. Other pan-Eastern European clients include UNIQA International, the largest Austrian insurer.

Wolf Theiss is extremely strong in the region. About half the firm's heavyweight corporate work has an Eastern European component. It has offices in Prague, Belgrade, Bratislava, Ljubljana and Zagreb, and is handling a considerable amount of property work in Hungary. Key clients in the region are HVB, Erste Bank and IMB. The firm has been advising Novartis on the €870m acquisition of a 99.1% interest in the listed Slovenian pharmaceutical company Lek.

CMS Strommer Reich-Rohrwig Karasek Hainz has a well-established office in Belgrade and a new office in Zagreb, while other Central and Eastern European jurisdictions are served through member firms of the international *CMS* network. It has recently advised Interbrew on the €360m acquisition of leading Serbian brewery Apatinska Pivara, the largest private deal ever completed in Serbia. Peter Huber is recommended.

Cerha Hempel Spiegelfeld Hlawati stands out from the pack because of its Budapest office, which is particularly strong on commercial property advice. Many of its clients in Hungary are German funds who were active in Vienna and moved further east as the Austrian property market consolidated. The firm has recently acted for Immofinanz on a real estate acquisition in Budapest. The firm also has an office in Zagreb.

Eiselsberg Natlacen Walderdorff Cancola has offices in Budapest and Prague, and is an extremely strong player in Hungary and the Czech Republic. Some of the lawyers in its Prague office are also qualified in Slovakia, and the firm has a close relationship with a local legal practice in Zagreb. The practice was substantially strengthened when Thomas Brandstatter joined from **Schönherr Rechtsanwälte** in 2003. Recent work includes advising on a railway project in the Czech Republic, and advising an international company on investments in Eastern European retail units.

Haarmann Hügel Attorneys at Law's co-operation with **Haarmann Hemmelrath** gives it access to offices in Budapest, Bucharest, Moscow, Prague and Warsaw. The Austrian clients that it advises in Central and Eastern Europe include OMV, for whom it has acted, with the support of the Bucharest office, on a number of acquisitions in the region.

Despite the demise of the *Denton International* network of which it was part, **Baier Lambert** has maintained the sub-network of firms in Central and Eastern Europe, which it now co-ordinates from Austria, and with which it works very closely. Magda Svobodal has been acting for one of the largest banks in the Czech Republic in a tracing and recovery action worth €150m.

Dorda Brugger Jordis is the only leading corporate Austrian firm that has chosen not to open offices in Central and Eastern Europe, but to establish its own network of 'best friends', which comprises one leading local firm in each of the following jurisdictions; Bosnia, Bulgaria, Croatia, Czech Republic, Estonia, Hungary, Latvia, Lithuania, Poland, Romania, Russia, Serbia, Slovakia and Slovenia. Recent work through the network has included advising an Austrian-based paper trading company on its acquisition of a stake in an Eastern European company, and advising the Sarejevo Privatisation Venture on the €19m sale of the Central Profit Bank in Serbia.

Griss Partner has considerable projects expertise while **Hasch & Partner Anwalts-**

CENTRAL AND EASTERN EUROPE

DLA WEISS-TESSBACH ✪
FRESHFIELDS BRUCKHAUS DERINGER ✪
SCHÖNHERR RECHTSANWÄLTE ✪
WOLF THEISS ✪

CMS Strommer Reich-Rohrwig Karasek Hainz ✪
Cerha Hempel Spiegelfeld Hlawati ✪
Eiselsberg Natlacen Walderdorff Cancola J
Haarmann Hügel Attorneys at Law ✪

Baier Lambert ✪
Dorda Brugger Jordis ✪
Griss & Partner
Hasch & Partner Anwaltsgesellschaft mbH ✪
Haslinger/Nagele & Partner Rechtsanwälte GmbH ✪
Saxinger Chalupsky Weber & Partners Rechtsanwälte GmbH ✪

Firms are listed A-Z in tiers which are ranked in order of priority
✪ Indicates firm displays contact details at the end of this chapter.

gesellschaft mbH has an office in Prague and a close co-operation with a local firm in Zagreb. The firm is particularly strong in mid-tier real estate transactions in the region, where it acts for a number of private investors and trade organisations. It has also worked on the merger of the Czech subsidiaries of two major publishers.

Haslinger/Nagele & Partner Rechtsanwälte GmbH has a Prague office and Czech Republic-qualified lawyers based in Austria.

In 2003, **Saxinger Chalupsky Weber & Partners Rechtsanwälte GmbH** opened in an office in the Czech Republic following a longstanding relationship with Czech lawyer Monika Wetzlerova, who is now a partner in the firm. The firm has a strong practice in the energy sector.

CORPORATE AND COMMERCIAL

Corporate activity has been picking up in Austria over the last year, but transactions have been moving slowly, and potential acquirers have been cautious and aggressive. The largest transaction of 2003 was the €1.9bn acquisition by Heineken of BBAG. A voluntary corporate governance code was introduced in October 2002 and is already considered to be a success, with the number of Austrian listed companies acting in conformity with the code currently between 65% and 70%. The Vienna Stock Exchange may soon make adherence to the code mandatory.

Public private partnerships (PPPs) are still in their teething phase in Austria, but a motorway currently being planning through the north of the country, to Prague, is likely to be constructed through a PPP. Privatisations, and part privatisations of state-owned companies, also continue apace.

Binder Grösswang Rechtsanwälte is a heavyweight player with a strong corporate/commercial team. The firm recently advised IT company Pixelpark AG on the increase of its participation in PXP Software AG. On the privatisation side, the firm has recently acted for ÖIAG on the €540m privatisation of Voestalpine AG. Michael Kutschera is recommended.

CMS Strommer Reich-Rohrwig Karasek Hainz advised US insurance company AIG in connection with the €1.2bn acquisition of the Norwegian pharmaceuticals group Nycomet. One of the firm's most important and longstanding corporate clients is Telekom Austria. On the projects side, the firm has been advising Westdeutsche Immobilien Bank on the financing of its €360m acquisition of the Millennium City in Vienna. Johannes Reich-Rohrwig and Peter Huber are recommended.

Cerha Hempel Spiegelfeld Hlawati's Edith Hlawati advised Heineken on its successful bid and subsequent €1.9bn acquisition of 100% of the shares of Getränkebeteiligungs, the holding company of BBAG and Brau Union, one of the largest brewers in Austria, and its seven subsidiaries in Eastern Europe, the deal described above. Benedikt Spiegelfeld is recommended for his strong practice in distribution and franchising, where clients include McDonald's and Hewlett-Packard.

DLA Weiss-Tessbach, through is recent merger with the UK-based firm, now benefits from an international network. The firm's corporate practice within Austria is very active in Central and Eastern Europe, where it has recently been involved in the cross-border restructuring of a Hungarian group containing a German entity. Ivo Deskovich, whose clients include Deutsche Telekom, is recommended for general corporate work, and Stefan Eder is recommended for infrastructure and project finance.

Dorda Brugger Jordis advised major client Verbund, the Austrian electricity producer, on its multi-billion euro merger with the Energie Allianz – which consists of five Austrian regional power suppliers – to create the tenth largest supplier of electricity to industrial clients in the EU. The firm also advised the vendor in the sale of Austrian food producer Inzersdorfer to a German acquirer. Martin Brodey is recommended.

A major corporate client described the Vienna office of **Freshfields Bruckhaus Deringer** as 'outstanding'. He added: 'They provide state-of-the-art work. Their efforts are stamped by utmost seriousness and the personal integrity of their partners, and I would rate them as the absolute number one law firm in Austria.' The firm has been involved in some major transactions in the energy sector. It is currently advising Energie Allianz in the transaction described above, and is also advising EVN AG and WIENGAS GmbH on the establishment of a £500m joint venture in the gas sector with OMV and other utilities companies. Privatisation work includes advising the Austrian government on the securitisation of a real estate portfolio worth €2bn. Willibald Plesser is recommended.

The corporate practice at **Haarmann Hügel Attorneys at Law** has particular strength on tax advice, with a large number of in-house tax advisers working on the structuring of M&A transactions. The firm also has a leading position in advising companies on corporate governance issues. It advised the management of the Herold group on the biggest MBO so far in Austria. Florian Gibitz is recommended.

Major corporate player **Schönherr Rechtsanwälte** acted on the only large public takeover that occurred in 2003, representing General Electric in the €200m takeover of listed gas turbine manufacturer Jenbacher AG, a transaction which broke new legal ground by using a material advisers charge clause in a public offer. The firm also acted for Andritz AG in a secondary public offering, and advised one of the bidders for BBAG, in the deal described above. Christian Herbst is recommended.

Wolf Theiss has a very large corporate practice. The firm advised BBAG and its 600 core shareholders in the sale of a majority stake to Heineken, in the transaction described above, and in the negotiation of the Central European brewers' agreement between BBAG and Heineken. Another key transaction was advising Erste Bank on the secondary public offering of shares worth €650m, the largest capital increase in Austrian history. On the privatisation front, the firm has been advising Gallaher Ltd on the €768m acquisition of Austria Tabak AG from ÖIAG. Christian Hoenig is recommended.

Baier Lambert is particularly strong in the banking and insurance sectors. Arthur Wolff also has significant experience in transactions involving China. He has recently been advising an Austrian company that is an international market

CORPORATE AND COMMERCIAL

BINDER GRÖSSWANG RECHTSANWÄLTE
CMS STROMMER REICH-ROHRWIG KARASEK HAINZ
CERHA HEMPEL SPIEGELFELD HLAWATI
DLA WEISS-TESSBACH
DORDA BRUGGER JORDIS
FRESHFIELDS BRUCKHAUS DERINGER
HAARMANN HÜGEL ATTORNEYS AT LAW
SCHÖNHERR RECHTSANWÄLTE
WOLF THEISS

Baier Lambert
Baker & McKenzie
Eiselsberg Natlacen Walderdorff Cancola
Fellner Wratzfeld & Partner Rechtsanwälte
Fiebinger, Polak, Leon & Partners Rechtsanwälte
Hauser Partners Rechtsanwälte GmbH
Hausmaninger Herbst Rechtsanwälte GmbH
Kunz Schima Wallentin & Partner
Ortner Pöch Foramitti
Preslmayr Attorneys at Law
Saxinger Chalupsky Weber & Partners Rechtsanwälte GmbH
Skadden, Arps, Slate, Meagher & Flom LLP

Alix Frank Rechtsanwälte KEG
ARNOLD Rechtsanwalts-Partnerschaft
Brauneis, Klauser & Prändl
Draxler & Partner Rechtsanwälte
Foglar-Deinhardstein & Brandstätter KEG
Gassauer-Fleissner Rechtsanwälte
Graf, Maxl & Pitkowitz
Greiter Pegger Kofler & Partners
Hasch & Partner Anwaltsgesellschaft mbH
Haslinger/Nagele & Partner Rechtsanwälte GmbH
Lovells in association with Mondl, Trummer, Thomas & Partner Rechtsanwälte GmbH
Neudorfer, Griensteidl, Hahnkamper, Stapf & Partner
Petsch, Frosch & Klein
Siemer-Siegl-Füreder & Partner

continued

CORPORATE AND COMMERCIAL (continued)

Dallmann & Juranek ✪
Deissenberger & Partners
Griss & Partner
Held Berdnik Astner & Partner, Rechtsanwälte ✪
Höhne, In der Maur & Partner Rechtsanwälte OEG
Jakobljevich, Grave & Vetter
Kaan Cronenberg & Partners
Kammerlander, Piaty, Mueller-Mezin, Schoeller ✪
Kosch & Partner
Pallauf Pullmann Meißnitzer & Partner, Rechtsanwälte OEG
Renate Weinberger (Dr), Rechtsanwaltskanzlei
Schramm Partner Rechtsanwälte ✪
Zeiner & Zeiner
Zirngibl Langwieser

Firms are listed A-Z in tiers which are ranked in order of priority
✪ *Indicates firm displays contact details at the end of this chapter.*

leader in fire fighting equipment for airports on its investments in China.

Baker & McKenzie has a strong M&A practice led by Christoph Kerres. The firm acted for US group General Dynamics in its acquisition of the Austrian Steyr group, a transaction with a value of over €100m. It has also worked on some large pharmaceutical industry transactions. Christoph Kerres is recommended for M&A, and Gerhard Eichberger for restructuring work.

Eiselsberg Natlacen Walderdorff Cancola has an Italian desk staffed by native Italian speakers and an Italy-qualified lawyer. The desk gives ongoing corporate advice to some major Italian companies. The corporate department also has particular expertise in logistics, where the firm has been advising on a major sale and leaseback of railway carriages. The firm's client base includes international insurance companies. Maximilian Eiselsberg is recommended.

Fellner Wratzfeld & Partner Rechtsanwälte has a strong IT company client base. The firm is also currently acting for an oil supplier that is purchasing parts of a network of gas stations from a competitor in Eastern Europe.

Fiebinger, Polak, Leon & Partners Rechtsanwälte has been advising a large multinational insurance group on the divestment of its Austrian, Hungarian, Czech and Liechtenstein activities to another insurance group. It also acted as lead counsel to an Austrian listed group in the setting up of a joint venture with a French listed company.

Hauser Partners Rechtsanwälte GmbH's recent international work includes representing a large Austrian flexible packaging group in the acquisitions of Danish and German flexible packaging businesses. It has also advised radio group GWR plc in its divestiture of a major Austrian radio network. Wulf Gordian Hauser is recommended.

Hausmaninger Herbst Rechtsanwälte GmbH is particularly strong in the e-commerce and Internet start-up sectors, where Christian Hausmaninger has a good reputation.

Kunz Schima Wallentin & Partner has a strong reputation with clients from the US and Italy, and the firm has a native Italian speaker on its staff. It has been handling a considerable amount of work on corporate governance matters, and on directors' and officers' liability. Georg Schima recently assisted a major Swiss bank in establishing its Vienna branch, and the firm has also worked on the restructuring of the Austrian Railways Corporation. Peter Kunz has a niche in advising private hospitals.

Ortner Pöch Foramitti is a banking firm that specialises in finance transactions. Corporate clients are mainly credit institutions, security houses, financing institutions, venture capitalists and private equity fund managers. Heinz Rindler is recommended.

Preslmayr Attorneys at Law has a corporate practice oriented towards Western Europe, with clients from the UK, Scandanavia and the US. It is a member of the international *TAGLaw* network. The firm's corporate practice has a focus on deals involving IT companies. It has been acting on the acquisition by international legal publisher LexisNexis of Austrian publisher Orac. Martin Preslmayr is recommended.

Saxinger Chalupsky Weber & Partners Rechtsanwälte GmbH advised Scottish & Newcastle on its second place bid for BBAG, in the deal mentioned above. The firm has core expertise in the PPP arena. Stefan Weber has been advising a public financing company on the multi-billion-euro project to renew the mountain railway line across Austria to Ljubljana. Other clients include IBM and KPMG. Gerald Schmidsberger is recommended for corporate restructuring work.

Skadden, Arps, Slate, Meagher & Flom LLP's Rainer Wachter handles cross-border M&A work for Austrian and international clients. He advised OMV on its $565m bid for refinery assets in several Eastern European jurisdictions, and Comdisco Inc in its $538m sale of its operations in Western Europe.

Alix Frank Rechtsanwälte KEG is known for its work on restructurings. Franz Heidinger is also an expert on cross-border deals involving Anglo-American law.

ARNOLD Rechtsanwalts-Partnerschaft also has good restructuring expertise, and has been advising on the transfer of the activities of a Germany-based medical devices company to Austria, and the reorganisation of a shopping centre corporation. Wolf-Dieter Arnold is recommended.

At **Brauneis, Klauser & Prändl**, Felix Prändl and Stefan Geppert have been advising a Singapore listed company in an Austrian acquisition. The firm has also advised an Austrian think tank on the restructuring of its group through a three-way spin-off. In addition, the firm has considerable expertise in PPPs and privatisation. Arno Brauneis has been advising on the privatisation of a utilities company.

Draxler & Partner Rechtsanwälte has some strong clients in the energy sector, and Italian language capability. Peter Draxler is recommended

Foglar-Deinhardstein & Brandstätter KEG has particular expertise in franchise and distribution agreements, and a number of key clients in property administration and the water and chemical industries.

Gassauer-Fleissner Rechtsanwälte has been working on the acquisition of several parcel courier companies for a state-owned infrastructure entity. It also acts exclusively for an Austrian investment bank whose activities are focused on Eastern Europe. Hanno Schatzmann is recommended.

Graf, Maxl & Pitkowitz has been doing substantial work in the projects arena, notably ongoing work for the Federation of Austrian Industry in the preparation of a feasibility study for a high speed connection between Vienna and Bratislava. The firm has also been advising EUROPPASS LKW-Mautsyste GmbH on a €180m infrastructure maintenance agreement for toll roads.

Greiter Pegger Kofler & Partners has an excellent reputation in the transport sector, and also acts for insurers. Stefan Kofler is recommended.

Hasch & Partner Anwaltsgesellschaft mbH has been advising an Austrian client on its €16m acquisition of all the Austrian assets of KPNQwest, which included Austrian-based EUNET, a European-wide network of small Internet providers. Clients include a number of Austrian venture capitalists.

Haslinger/Nagele & Partner Rechtsanwälte GmbH has a number of prominent public authorities among its clients, and expertise in advising on public procurement and privatisations.

Lovells in association with Mondl, Trummer, Thomas & Partner Rechtsanwälte GmbH, which has an association with UK-based **Lovells**, has been acting for Austria Haustechnick AG in a de-listing and reorganisation following the company's takeover, and for Brain Force Software AG in its acquisition of NSE Software AG. Gregor Trummer is recommended.

At **Neudorfer, Griensteidl, Hahnkamper, Stapf & Partner** Helmut Neudorfer has been advising the shareholder of one of Austria's leading personnel companies on its restructuring and refinancing. The firm is also handling the Austrian component of a European-wide acquisition in the technical/medical industries by a US-based company.

Petsch, Frosch & Klein has a Milan office and a Spanish lawyer, Isabel-Clara Canals, on its staff. It has a number of prominent Italian clients on its books.

Siemer-Siegl-Füreder & Partner's international clients include Siemens, Scania Österrech and Sonepar. Austrian clients include Böhlerit GbH & Co KG, for whom the firm acts worldwide and is currently advising, together with a Mexican law firm, on the restructuring of its Mexican subsidiaries. Hannes Füreder and Markus Fellner are recommended.

DISPUTE RESOLUTION

Vienna is one of the most important arbitration centres in Europe, and has a popular central location. Most firms still have their litigators and arbitrators spread around various departments, though some have recently formed dedicated dispute resolution departments. It is still rare to find a lawyer who only handles contentious business. Mediation for commercial disputes is starting to become accepted in Austria, and an act is expected to be passed in September 2004 to create an official qualification for mediators.

Andreas Reiner of **Andreas Reiner & Partner** is Austria's leading arbitrator. He handles arbitrations – both advising parties to arbitration and sitting as an arbitrator – for major international clients, who are often nation states involved in international public law disputes. He has a worldwide practice, arbitrating in jurisdictions far beyond the borders of Austria, and in many cases that have no link to Austria. He has recently been working outside Austria on an energy industry arbitration involving questions of public law, in which one of the parties is a state and the amount in dispute is over $100m. The firm often acts as co-counsel to other law firms involved in arbitrations, giving specialist advice on specific aspects of the case. It has recently been advising the lawyers of a major Swedish corporate group on its arbitration against an Eastern European group. The firm also has a respectable domestic litigation practice.

Baier Lambert has an outstanding practice in arbitrations involving banking, petroleum, telecoms and construction. Erhard Boehm is currently representing a European conglomerate in an arbitration and is a highly experienced arbitrator. The firm is also strong in domestic litigation. The practice has been strengthened by the arrival from **Freshfields Bruckhaus Deringer** of Marie-Therese Trofaier, who has significant experience in arbitration and as a mediator.

Brauneis, Klauser & Prändl's Alexander Klauser has been acting for Austrian consumers and the largest Austrian consumer protection agency, VKI, against banks and travel agencies, in national and ECJ proceedings and an Austrian Supreme Court appeal.

Cerha Hempel Spiegelfeld Hlawati is one of the only firms to have a discrete contentious business department. It has been acting for Vienna Airport Security Systems in a matter concerning procurement proceedings. At €67m, this was the largest Austrian service contract to date. Other contentious business clients include Telekom Austrian – for whom it has just acted in a large arbitration – the Austrian Mint, and the general hospital in Vienna, for whom it has acted in a media-related dispute. Irene Welser and Benedikt Spiegelfeld are recommended, and Felix Stortecky is an experienced mediator.

Freshfields Bruckhaus Deringer also has a distinct litigation department, which has been acting for US-based EDS in a major piece of litigation against the Austrian Social Security Agency. This was one of the largest cases of 2003. It has also been representing a global industrial engineering company, with headquarters in Austria, in national court proceedings and an ICC arbitration. Thomas Kustor is recommended for litigation and Jenny Power for arbitration, while James Costello benefits from being US-qualified.

Schönherr Rechtsanwälte has a strong reputation for arbitration. Hellwig Torggler is a leading arbitrator, and is also increasingly handling high-level mediations. The focus of his practice is on cross-border disputes. Gerold Zeiler is recommended for litigation.

Wolf Theiss also has a litigation practice group consisting of highly specialised lawyers who are full-time litigators. The group has been acting for UK investment fund Duke Street Capital, which is involved as a shareholder in one of Austria's largest insolvency and fraud cases, involving liabilities worth €90m. The firm has also been acting for a Scandinavian group in a €750m UNCITRAL arbitration proceeding relating to a joint venture involving a major portion of Poland's telecoms infrastructure.

DLA Weiss-Tessbach has been handling litigation arising out of debt collection, a €200m piece of litigation for a large Austrian mortgage bank, and a €70m piece of real estate litigation concerning acid rain pollution. Gerhard Benn-Ibler and Stefan Eder are recommended.

Dorda Brugger Jordis has been acting for the UN's International Atomic Energy Agency in a UNICITRAL arbitration. It has also been acting for Austrian industrial clients in employment-related litigation in the US and Austria. Florian Kremslehner and Thomas Angermair are recommended.

Engin-Deniz Reimitz Schönherr Hafner Rechtsanwälte KEG has a focus on litigation relating to intellectual property, media, entertainment and unfair competition. Clients include Procter & Gamble.

Fiebinger, Polak, Leon & Partners Rechtsanwälte has a strong focus on litigation and arbitration. Rudolf Fiebinger is recommended.

Greiter Pegger Kofler & Partners has an experienced mediator in Ivo Greiter, while at **Griss & Partner**, Gunter Griss has been sitting as an arbitrator in three ICC cases, one of which involved a Japanese claimant and an Italian respondent. The firm has also been acting for a bank in a dispute over liability in securities investment transactions, and for a leading Austrian company in connection with litigation in France over the construction of a manufacturing facility. Edwin Mächler has good experience in litigation involving finance transactions.

Haarmann Hügel Attorneys at Law has been advising Bank Austria on a number of pieces of litigation concerning commercial transactions. Generally, it handles a substantial amount of litigation on construction, public procurement and competition matters. Arnold Gerscha, Gregor Schett and Herbert Schrittesser are recommended.

At **Haslinger/Nagele & Partner Rechtsanwälte GmbH** both Norbert Nagele and Dietmar Lux are well known arbitrators, while at **Hauser**

DISPUTE RESOLUTION

Andreas Reiner & Partner
Baier Lambert ✪
Brauneis, Klauser & Prändl ✪
Cerha Hempel Spiegelfeld Hlawati ✪
Freshfields Bruckhaus Deringer ✪
Schönherr Rechtsanwälte ✪
Wolf Theiss ✪

DLA Weiss-Tessbach ✪
Dorda Brugger Jordis ✪
Engin-Deniz Reimitz Schönherr Hafner Rechtsanwälte KEG
Fiebinger, Polak, Leon & Partners Rechtsanwälte ✪
Greiter Pegger Kofler & Partners ✪
Griss & Partner
Haarmann Hügel Attorneys at Law ✪
Haslinger/Nagele & Partner Rechtsanwälte GmbH ✪
Hauser Partners Rechtsanwälte GmbH ✪
Preslmayr Attorneys at Law ✪
Sattler & Schanda
Siemer-Siegl-Füreder & Partner ✪

ARNOLD Rechtsanwalts-Partnerschaft
Baker & McKenzie ✪
Binder Grösswang Rechtsanwälte ✪
CMS Strommer Reich-Rohrwig Karasek Hainz ✪
Deissenberger & Partners
Draxler & Partner Rechtsanwälte
Eiselsberg Natlacen Walderdorff Cancola ✪
Gassauer-Fleissner Rechtsanwälte ✪
Graf, Maxl & Pitkowitz ✪
Hausmaninger Herbst Rechtsanwälte GmbH ✪
Lovells in association with Mondl, Trummer, Thomas & Partner Rechtsanwälte GmbH ✪
Neudorfer, Griensteidl, Hahnkamper, Stapf & Partner ✪
Ortner Pöch Foramitti ✪
Pallauf Pullmann Meißnitzer & Partner, Rechtsanwälte OEG
Petsch, Frosch & Klein
Zandl & Grundei (Dres), Rechtsanwälte

Firms are listed A-Z in tiers which are ranked in order of priority
✪ Indicates firm displays contact details at the end of this chapter.

Partners Rechtsanwälte GmbH Wulf Gordian Hauser has been handling a large number of ICC arbitrations. The firm has also handled some specialised institutional arbitrations, such as cases before the WIPO Arbitration and Mediation Centre.

Preslmayr Attorneys at Law focuses on arbitration. Karl Preslmayr is a well regarded arbitrator, and also represents parties to arbitrations. Reinhard Schanda at **Sattler & Schanda** is also a respected arbitrator.

At **Siemer-Siegl-Füreder & Partner**, Heinrich Siegl is a strong arbitrator and litigator, who has been acting for Siemens SGP Verkehrstechnik GmbH is an arbitration involving claims arising from the construction of high-speed rail construction elements. Markus Fellner, who has been representing a Swiss subsidiary of Bouygues in an ICC arbitraion, is also recommended.

ARNOLD Rechtsanwalts-Partnerschaft has been advising clients in the Austrian Supreme Court on cases concerning telecoms site sharing and private radio law. Nikolaus Arnold is recommended.

Baker & McKenzie's practice has been strengthened by the recruitment of Alice Fremuth, who joined from **Wolf Theiss**, and is an experienced arbitrator and mediator. Her workload is primarily international. She is currently working on the mediation of a large shareholder dispute.

Binder Grösswang Rechtsanwälte is acting as counsel to arbitrations in the ICC in Zürich concerning corporate and labour law, and in an ad hoc arbitration in Zürich concerning contract and energy law.

CMS Strommer Reich-Rohrwig Karasek Hainz's Johannes Reich-Rowrig is a well known construction arbitrator. He has been representing the equipment procurement and service company, master-talk, in an arbitration against the Austrian Federal Ministry of the Interior over a €120m contract. In litigation, the firm has been defending a client in a bank guarantee claim against US-based Georgia Pacific. It also has experience in litigation involving Islamic Shari'a law.

Deissenberger & Partners has a good reputation for litigation, while **Draxler & Partner Rechtsanwälte** is well regarded for arbitration.

Eiselsberg Natlacen Walderdorff Cancola is strong in arbitrations in Central and Eastern Europe, and in banking litigation. It is acting for a France-based group in a concrete industry arbitration, and is also handling unfair competition litigation on behalf of an Austrian postal company. Dieter Natlacen is recommended.

Gassauer-Fleissner Rechtsanwälte has been working on litigation surrounding a high volume supply contract for raw materials. Bettina Baar-Baarenfels is a mediator, while Christian Gassauer-Fleissner sits as an arbitrator.

Graf, Maxl & Pitkowitz has been acting in arbitral board proceedings under UNCITRAL rules and Viennese rules, in a €80m dispute. Nikolaus Pitkowitz is recommended.

At **Hausmaninger Herbst Rechtsanwälte GmbH**, Christian Hausmaninger and Christoph Stippl have good reputations, while at **Neudorfer, Griensteidl, Hahnkamper, Stapf & Partner** Wolfgang Hahnkampter acts as an arbitrator in Austria and Slovenia, and regularly serves in large ICC and UNCITRAL arbitrations.

Other recommended practitioners are Thomas Mondl of **Lovells in association with Mondl, Trummer, Thomas & Partner Rechtsanwälte GmbH** for litigation; Peter Pöch of **Ortner Pöch Foramitti** and Günther Frosch of **Petsch, Frosch & Klein** for arbitration; and Brigitta Pallauf of **Pallauf Pullmann Meißnitzer & Partner, Rechtsanwälte OEG** and Andreas Grundei of **Dres Zandl & Grundei, Rechtsanwälte** for mediation.

EU AND COMPETITION

Austria joined the EU in 1995, and Austrian law is still in the process of being fully harmonised with EU standards. New regulations governing cartel procedures come into force in the spring of 2004, and a competition authority has recently been established to advise Austria's Cartel Court. There is also a new Competition Tribunal, which is doing particularly important work on public procurement, handling complaints that the Austrian government – which spends €22bn each year on pubic procurement projects – has fallen foul of the EU competition regime. Public procurement, usually handled by competition lawyers as it has a strong regulatory element, is relatively new in Austria but is becoming increasingly popular. All the larger law firms now have a public procurement expert, but those with particularly developed experience are **CMS Strommer Reich-Rohrwig Karasek Hainz**, **Siemer-Siegl-Füreder & Partner** and boutique public procurement practice **Schramm Partner Rechtsanwälte**.

Electricity regulation is now a more pressing topic than telecoms regulation in Austria. A new telecoms act is expected in the summer of 2004, and the telecoms competition environment is becoming more technically sophisticated, particularly in relation to network and site sharing.

Cerha Hempel Spiegelfeld Hlawati is acting for Mobilkom Austria before the ECJ, the Austrian Cartel Court and the Austrian Supreme Court. On the merger control side, it has recently advised on the acquisition of retail stores owned by Julius Meinl – part of the Austria-based Meinl group – by SPAR and LÖWA, and on the acquisition of Stock Austria by Germany-based Eckes. Claudine Vartian and Benedikt Spiegelfeld are recommended.

Freshfields Bruckhaus Deringer has been working to obtain an exemption for three leading Austrian banks, including Erste Bank, to establish a joint venture for payment systems. It has also been acting for two regional telecoms operators in price review proceedings. Axel Reidlinger has an outstanding reputation.

EU AND COMPETITION

CERHA HEMPEL SPIEGELFELD HLAWATI ✪
FRESHFIELDS BRUCKHAUS DERINGER ✪
HAARMANN HÜGEL ATTORNEYS AT LAW ✪
SCHÖNHERR RECHTSANWÄLTE ✪
SCHRAMM PARTNER RECHTSANWÄLTE ✪
WOLF THEISS ✪

Brauneis, Klauser & Prändl ✪
CMS Strommer Reich-Rohrwig Karasek Hainz ✪
DLA Weiss-Tessbach ✪
Dorda Brugger Jordis ✪
Eiselsberg Natlacen Walderdorff Cancola ✪
Fiebinger, Polak, Leon & Partners Rechtsanwälte ✪
Georg Legat (Dr)
Graf, Maxl & Pitkowitz ✪
Hauser Partners Rechtsanwälte GmbH ✪
Preslmayr Attorneys at Law ✪
Siemer-Siegl-Füreder & Partner ✪

Alix Frank Rechtsanwälte KEG
Fellner Wratzfeld & Partner Rechtsanwälte ✪
Gassauer-Fleissner Rechtsanwälte ✪
Greiter Pegger Kofler & Partners ✪
Griss & Partner
Gugerbauer & Partner Rechtsanwälte KEG
Hasch & Partner Anwaltsgesellschaft mbH ✪
Haslinger/Nagele & Partner Rechtsanwälte GmbH ✪
Hausmaninger Herbst Rechtsanwälte GmbH ✪
Held Berdnik Astner & Partner, Rechtsanwälte ✪
Kammerlander, Piaty, Mueller-Mezin, Schoeller ✪
Ortner Pöch Foramitti ✪
Saxinger Chalupsky Weber & Partners Rechtsanwälte GmbH ✪

Firms are listed A-Z in tiers which are ranked in order of priority
✪ *Indicates firm displays contact details at the end of this chapter.*

Haarmann Hügel Attorneys at Law has a strong practice and has recently been handling some tough merger filings, including two at the European Commission. It has been advising Essilor France on the merger control aspects of its acquisition of the Ruppe + Hubrach Group. It has also been acting for Österreichische Volksbanken AG, NÖ Landesbank and Hypothekenbank in competition proceedings before the European Court of First Instance. The firm also handles a considerable amount of public procurement work, particularly for the State of Lower Austria. Rainer Roniger has an outstanding reputation.

Schönherr Rechtsanwälte's Hanno Wollmann is a market leader for merger control. The firm is handling some extremely complex cases, including advising on the Austrian review of the merger of two leading publicly owned Austrian bus companies, and on the EU review of a merger between electricity producers which consolidated half the Austrian market.

Schramm Partner Rechtsanwälte is a public procurement boutique, highly specialised and highly regarded, which acts for national and local government and federal agencies. Clients include the Austrian social security system, a state-owned housing association – which it has been advising on a €1bn procurement – the state of Tyrol – which it has been advising on a PPP project relating to waste management – Postbus, the state owned bus company, and the Austrian government department responsible for IT procurement. In the private sector, it is advising Mobile.com and a Vienna-based transport company. Johannes Schramm is recommended.

Wolf Theiss has been acting for Novartis in Central and Eastern Europe, co-ordinating merger filings in 11 jurisdictions. It has also advised energy and gas companies BEWAG and BEGAS on merger control issues involved in the formation of the Energy Allianz (see **Corporate and commercial** section).

Brauneis, Klauser & Prändl's Bernhard Girsch has been advising Ruhrgas Austria AG on the Austrian Competition Authority's clearance of its acquisition of a gas distribution operation in Salzburg, and on the clearance of the merger between Arthur Andersen, Austria, and Deloitte & Touche, Austria.

CMS Strommer Reich-Rohrwig Karasek Hainz's Bernst Elsner specialises in pubic procurement work, and also has a strong practice in competition and merger control. He has been advising leading Austrian waste management company ASA Abfall Service AG and Viennese electricity producer and distributor Wienstrom on public procurement issues.

DLA Weiss-Tessbach is working for the Austrian Chamber of Commerce to develop an EU accession product, which will be used to test the extent to which the Eastern European subsidiaries of Austrian companies are fit to join the EU in 2004. Through its recent merger, the firm now has access to a large Brussels office. Max Becker is recommended.

Dorda Brugger Jordis' Stephan Polster has been advising Austrian energy giant VERBUND on complex EU merger control proceedings. On the public procurement side, the firm has been working on the €3m procurement of an alarm system for the Salzburg fire brigade.

Eiselsberg Natlacen Walderdorff Cancola is acting for Italy-based Tecnica on filing notification of its merger with Nordica in Austria, the most important market for the companies' sky equipment. It has also been acting for Red Mail, a competitor of Austrian Post, in lodging a complaint about the latter's abuse of a market-dominant position.

Fiebinger, Polak, Leon & Partners Rechtsanwälte has acted on EU level merger clearances, and also gives competition law advice to multinational companies in the energy, insurance, life sciences and electronic industries. Johannes Willheim is recommended.

Sole practitioner **Dr Georg Legat** has an excellent reputation for his work on distribution and franchises.

Graf, Maxl & Pitkowitz has experience in advising bidding companies on public procurement projects.

Hauser Partners Rechtsanwälte GmbH is known for its work on the competition aspects of M&A transactions, and for its international connections, particularly with France. It has been acting for a multinational group, led by an Austrian pulp and paper company, in merger filings before the German Bunkeskartellamt, relating to the €280m acquisition of the largest paper mill in Russia.

Preslmayr Attorneys at Law is strong in public procurement, and also has good experience on merger notifications. Public procurement clients include Air Liquide, Austria. It acts for General Electric on merger control matters relating to the company's acquisitions in Austria, and internationally. Dieter Hauk is recommended.

Siemer-Siegl-Füreder & Partner's Michael Breitfeld is strong in public procurement, and has ECJ experience. Clients include the Vienna Harbour. Markus Fellner is recommended for competition work, and handles many Austrian merger filings for Siemens.

Alix Frank Rechtsanwälte KEG's Wolfgang Punz has been handling several merger task force control cases, some involving transactions with a value over €1bn. The firm also has public procurement experience.

Fellner Wratzfeld & Partner Rechtsanwälte has advised ministries and government institutions on the implementation of EU regulations.

Gassauer-Fleissner Rechtsanwälte's Richard Regner is the permanent adviser to a major Austrian city council on public procurement questions, and is also advising an IT company on a major Austrian IT public procurement project. The firm also has regulatory experience, and advises on merger control.

Greiter Pegger Kofler & Partners is strong in public procurement, while **Griss & Partner**'s Edwin Mächler has been handling a number of pieces of unfair competition litigation.

Norbert Gugerbauer of **Gugerbauer & Partner Rechtsanwälte KEG** is a well regarded competition lawyer, while **Hasch & Partner Anwaltsgesellschaft mbH** has a strong practice focusing on pan-European distribution and franchising matters, where clients include MoneyPoint.

At **Haslinger/Nagele & Partner Rechtsanwälte GmbH**, Martin Stempkowski is recommended, while Christoph Herbst of **Hausmaninger Herbst Rechtsanwälte GmbH** also has a good reputation.

Held Berdnik Astner & Partner, Rechtsanwälte has public procurement experience, while **Ortner Pöch Foramitti** has experience in advising on state aid.

Saxinger Chalupsky Weber & Partners Rechtsanwälte GmbH's Stefan Weber and Karl Weinhäupl have experience in public procurement, state aid, abuse of market power and merger notifications in Austria. They have been working for Scottish & Newcastle on Austrian competition issues.

EMPLOYMENT

Most firms in Austria, even those with large commercial practices, still tend to act for both employers and employees.

Leading labour and employment boutique **Burgstaller & Preyer, Partnerschaft von Rechtsanwälten OEG** has an impressive Austrian and international client base spanning the telecoms, IT, pharmaceuticals, transport, logistics and banking industries. In the last year it has been focusing on advice to companies that are reducing their workforces, closing plants, transferring groups of employees to plants located in other countries, outsourcing IT and other departments, dissolving pension plans and changing collective labour agreements. Helmut Preyer and Gerald Burgstaller are recommended.

CMS Strommer Reich-Rohrwig Karasek Hainz's Bernhard Hainz is one of the strongest

EMPLOYMENT

BURGSTALLER & PREYER, PARTNERSCHAFT VON RECHTSANWÄLTEN OEG
CMS STROMMER REICH-ROHRWIG KARASEK HAINZ ✪
KUNZ SCHIMA WALLENTIN & PARTNER
ZANDL & GRUNDEI (DRES), RECHTSANWÄLTE

Cerha Hempel Spiegelfeld Hlawati ✪
Dorda Brugger Jordis ✪
Draxler & Partner Rechtsanwälte
Eiselsberg Natlacen Walderdorff Cancola ✪
Fellner Wratzfeld & Partner Rechtsanwälte ✪
Freshfields Bruckhaus Deringer ✪
Gassauer-Fleissner Rechtsanwälte ✪
Neudorfer, Griensteidl, Hahnkamper, Stapf & Partner ✪
Preslmayr Attorneys at Law ✪
Siemer-Siegl-Füreder & Partner ✪

DLA Weiss-Tessbach ✪
Greiter Pegger Kofler & Partners ✪
Hasch & Partner Anwaltsgesellschaft mbH ✪
Hauser Partners Rechtsanwälte GmbH ✪
Saxinger Chalupsky Weber & Partners Rechtsanwälte GmbH ✪
Schönherr Rechtsanwälte ✪
Wolf Theiss ✪

Firms are listed A-Z in tiers which are ranked in order of priority
✪ Indicates firm displays contact details at the end of this chapter.

employment lawyers in Austria. His practice has a corporate focus, and recent work includes advising the EC in legal proceedings at the ECJ on the establishment of works councils. He has also acted for Austrian banking giant BA-CA in litigation relating to company pensions and the employer's liability for stock market risks.

Kunz Schima Wallentin & Partner is a market leading firm in employment matters. The firm has been involved in drafting the legislation that divides the Austrian Railways Corporation into several companies, and aligns the employment regulations specific to the company with general Austrian employment law. In the last year, Georg Schima has also advised a major Swiss bank on establishing its Vienna branch, numerous companies and pension funds on pension payments, and been involved in significant employment litigation.

Zandl & Grundei (Dres), Rechtsanwälte has particular expertise in advising on employers' insurance. Andreas Grundei is recommended.

Cerha Hempel Spiegelfeld Hlawati is the permanent counsel to Flughafen Wien and its subsidiary, Vienna International Airport Security Systems. Irene Welser is recommended.

Dorda Brugger Jordis has particular expertise in advising international investors on the law governing civil servants working for publicly owned companies. In Austria, these are notoriously difficult to lay off following privatisation. Clients include former state-owned auctioneers Dorotheum. Thomas Angermair is recommended.

Draxler & Partner Rechtsanwälte has a focus on collective labour agreements and on pensions. Peter Stock is recommended.

Eiselsberg Natlacen Walderdorff Cancola has been acting for many companies that are being sued for pensions mis-selling. It is also advising the Austrian branch of a major international company on an outsourcing project for employees, and advising some subsidiaries of another international group on employment issues in its direct selling unit. Wolfgang Kapek is recommended.

Fellner Wratzfeld & Partner Rechtsanwälte's Kurt Wratzfeld also has significant specialisation in the law governing civil servants. He acts for many publicly owned companies, and is an expert on social plans and mass redundancies.

Freshfields Bruckhaus Deringer has been representing an international retailer in model litigation before the Austrian Supreme Court and the ECJ. Stefan Köck is recommended.

Gassauer-Fleissner Rechtsanwälte's Michael Nocker advises companies on management service contracts and pension planning, and is a market leader in claims for compensation by commercial agents.

Neudorfer, Griensteidl, Hahnkamper, Stapf & Partner's Wolfgang Hahnkamper has been advising on prominent industrial action in the public transport sector.

Preslmayr Attorneys at Law has been working on the labour law aspects of the Nauticast deal. Andrea Futterknecht is recommended.

Siemer-Siegl-Füreder & Partner's labour law clients include a major airline, one of Austria's leading private security firms, Subway Austria and the Austrian Managers' Association. Hannes Füreder and Gerald Gries are recommended.

DLA Weiss-Tessbach has been working on the closing of a mid-sized Austrian business, and has a substantial number of labour law clients in the telecoms sector.

At **Greiter Pegger Kofler & Partners**, Ralf Geymayer has a good reputation.

Hasch & Partner Anwaltsgesellschaft mbH's clients include investment bankers and the coach of a major football team. The firm, strong in private client work, also advises private foundations on employment matters.

Hauser Partners Rechtsanwälte GmbH has a solid employment law practice, while at **Saxinger Chalupsky Weber & Partners Rechtsanwälte GmbH**, Johannes Michael Blätterbinder is an expert on stock option plans, pension matters and cross-border matters relating to restructurings. He recently acted for the owner on the closing down of Carrera Optyl Brillen Vertribes und Erzeugunggesellschaft.

Schönherr Rechtsanwälte has recently worked on restructurings for the Austrian operations of Pfizer Corporation, State Street Bank's custody business, Johnson Controls and AXA insurance. Gerold Zeiler is recommended.

Wolf Theiss has been advising Bank Austria on labour disputes and on the implementation of new terms and conditions affecting over 1000 employees in Croatia.

IT AND E-COMMERCE

E-commerce is starting to become popular in Austria, although local consumers are still cautious and not entirely comfortable with making payments via the Internet. Electronic signatures have recently been introduced, but take-up has so far been slow. However an E-Government Act, which is due to be passed in 2004, is expected to generate significant Internet activity. There has been a dampening of Internet start-ups in the last two years, but this is expected to change due to the upturn in the private equity markets.

Baier Lambert is a leader in computer and Internet law, particularly on regulatory issues. It has been advising companies on issues surrounding applications for radio licences in Austria. Arthur Wolff and Georg Röhsner are recommended.

Brauneis, Klauser & Prändl has a market leading IT lawyer in Felix Prändl. He has been advising the Austrian Regulatory Authority for Telecommunications and Broadcasting on setting up a digital terrestrial television channel in co-operation with Siemens and Telekom Austria. He also acts for HP Austria, Oracle Austria and T-Online.at.

Dorda Brugger Jordis acts for a major Austrian software producer, and handles considerable work for private equity firms that are investing in technology or new economy companies. It is has expertise in software litigation and software licensing, and recently acted for a US producer of gaming machinery in a sale and licensing of software to an Austrian company. Stefan Polster is recommended.

Höhne, In der Maur & Partner Rechtsanwälte OEG acts for some major database producers, multi-media manufacturers and ISPs.

DDr Meinhard Ciresa has recently been focusing on advising companies on IT security.

Sattler & Schanda has recently been acting for a software producer in significant litigation relating to the unlawful use of a software package. Reinhard Schanda has a leading reputation in the market.

Alix Frank Rechtsanwälte KEG is strong on licensing, outsourcing and domain name

IT AND E-COMMERCE

Baier Lambert ✪
Brauneis, Klauser & Prändl ✪
Dorda Brugger Jordis ✪
Höhne, In der Maur & Partner Rechtsanwälte OEG
Meinhard Ciresa, DDr
Sattler & Schanda

Alix Frank Rechtsanwälte KEG
ARNOLD Rechtsanwalts-Partnerschaft
Fellner Wratzfeld & Partner Rechtsanwälte ✪
Fiebinger, Polak, Leon & Partners Rechtsanwälte ✪
Preslmayr Attorneys at Law ✪
Saxinger Chalupsky Weber & Partners Rechtsanwälte GmbH ✪
Schönherr Rechtsanwälte ✪
Wolf Theiss ✪

Freshfields Bruckhaus Deringer ✪
Gassauer-Fleissner Rechtsanwälte ✪
Graf, Maxl & Pitkowitz ✪
Greiter Pegger Kofler & Partners ✪
Haarmann Hügel Attorneys at Law ✪
Hasch & Partner Anwaltsgesellschaft mbH ✪
Hauser Partners Rechtsanwälte GmbH ✪
Ortner Pöch Foramitti ✪
Schmidt, Kornfeld, Wukoschitz, Windhager
Siemer-Siegl-Füreder & Partner ✪

Firms are listed A-Z in tiers which are ranked in order of priority
✪ Indicates firm displays contact details at the end of this chapter.

disputes. Stephan Novotny and Franz Heidinger are recommended.

ARNOLD Rechtsanwalts-Partnerschaft is strong in e-commerce, and has been working on the establishment of a partner/franchise programme for a company active in pan-European content management systems. Nikolaus Arnold is recommended.

At **Fellner Wratzfeld & Partner Rechtsanwälte**, Sabine Fehringer has a good reputation for outsourcing.

Fiebinger, Polak, Leon & Partners Rechtsanwälte recently advised a major Austrian publishing house on the setting up and maintenance of its web portal. It also has experience in the implementation of online payment systems, and on data protection.

Preslmayr Attorneys at Law's Rainer Knyrim is an expert on data protection, with companies advised including Air Liquide.

Saxinger Chalupsky Weber & Partners Rechtsanwälte GmbH has a strong reputation for advising traditional companies, notably banks, on the outsourcing of their IT departments and the creation of Internet platforms and online auctions. Dietmar Huemer is recommended.

Schönherr Rechtsanwälte was lead counsel for Frantschach Packaging in connection with the worldwide introduction of a b2b e-commerce model. It also worked on IT aspects of the entries of Blackberry and eBay into the Austrian market. Peter Madl has a good reputation.

Wolf Theiss has been advising Raiffeisen Bausparkasse GmbH on a new database system, and a group of US investors on their investment in an Austrian software company.

In e-commerce, **Freshfields Bruckhaus Deringer** has been advising Hutchison 3G Austria GmbH on end-user pricing models for 3G telecoms services. Alex Reidlinger is recommended.

Gassauer-Fleissner Rechtsanwälte has been doing significant work in outsourcing. It has advised a leading multinational outsourcing company on public tenders, and worked on the largest Austrian outsourcing deal of 2003, which spanned 16 jurisdictions. In the field of e-commerce, it has been involved in online auctions, and has advised on data protection and spamming. In addition, it advised on the establishment of a major Austrian payment platform for m-commerce applications.

Graf, Maxl & Pitkowitz has been negotiating a €15m IT installation agreement and a €40m IT maintenance agreement for EUROPASS LKW-Mautsystem GmbH.

Greiter Pegger Kofler & Partners has expertise in advising on e-commerce contracts and data security.

Haarmann Hügel Attorneys at Law has been advising the Austrian diners' club, Air Plus, on IT contracts. It is also giving ongoing IT advice to one of the largest management consultants in Austria.

Hasch & Partner Anwaltsgesellschaft mbH has been advising the Internet service provider EUNET on establishing a structure for work with domains, and on how to collect and utilise its IP rights, in advance of its sale to an Italian company. Joachim Janezic is recommended.

Hauser Partners Rechtsanwälte GmbH, **Ortner Pöch Foramitti** and **Schmidt, Kornfeld, Wukoschitz, Windhager**, all have good IT practices. Rainer Kornfeld at **Schmidt, Kornfeld, Wukoschitz, Windhager** is particularly recommended for his deep knowledge of the computer industry.

Siemer-Siegl-Füreder & Partner has been acting for a leading Austrian mineral water producer in a domain dispute over the use of its name in Hungary. Reinhard Brunar is recommended.

INSOLVENCY AND CORPORATE RECOVERY

The Austrian insolvency regime is weighted in favour of the creditor, as the debtor has to pay legal costs. Some smaller practices have outstanding reputations as court appointed receivers, while the larger corporate practices that advise banks and companies on insolvencies often choose not to act as receivers because of perceived conflicts.

Brauneis, Klauser & Prändl is a leading receiver which does also advise companies. This has included representing American and Dutch members of the Babcock Borsig Power Group in the bankruptcy proceedings of their Austrian subsidiary. Alexander Klauser, who also has strong experience in restructurings, is recommended.

Graf, Maxl & Pitkowitz also advises debtors. It has been acting on the composition proceedings of Austrian shipbuilder Kneissel, and for Elektra Bregenz in negotiations surrounding the closure of production operations. It has also advised Bank Burgenland on litigation relating to the Howe bankruptcy. Alexander Isola is recommended.

Held Berdnik Astner & Partner, Rechtsanwälte is a specialist practice whose partners are all well known for acting as receivers in major bankruptcies, and also advises creditors and debtors in insolvencies.

Kosch & Partner is another firm of receivers that is highly recommended for work in Lower Austria. Norbert Kosch has retired, but his successors are well regarded receivers, who have been acting on the bankruptcy of a major company in the bakery business.

Preslmayr Attorneys at Law's Florian Gehmacher is appointed as a court receiver or represents the bank in many major cases. He recently acted as receiver in the insolvency of Hofmann & Maculan, and advised the creditors in the insolvencies of Trigon Bank and Diskontbank.

Schulyok Unger & Partner Rechtsanwälte OEG acts for banks in insolvency proceedings and also works as debtors' counsel and as an official receiver.

INSOLVENCY AND CORPORATE RECOVERY

BRAUNEIS, KLAUSER & PRÄNDL ✪
GRAF, MAXL & PITKOWITZ ✪
HELD BERDNIK ASTNER & PARTNER, RECHTSANWÄLTE ✪
KOSCH & PARTNER
PRESLMAYR ATTORNEYS AT LAW ✪
SCHULYOK UNGER & PARTNER RECHTSANWÄLTE OEG

Abel & Abel
Baier Lambert ✪
CMS Strommer Reich-Rohrwig Karasek Hainz ✪
Cerha Hempel Spiegelfeld Hlawati ✪
Eiselsberg Natlacen Walderdorff Cancola ✪
Freshfields Bruckhaus Deringer ✪
Haarmann Hügel Attorneys at Law ✪
Wolf Theiss ✪

DLA Weiss-Tessbach ✪
Dorda Brugger Jordis ✪
Fellner Wratzfeld & Partner Rechtsanwälte ✪
Hasch & Partner Anwaltsgesellschaft mbH ✪
Haslinger/Nagele & Partner Rechtsanwälte GmbH ✪
Kunz Schima Wallentin & Partner
Neudorfer, Griensteidl, Hahnkamper, Stapf & Partner ✪
Saxinger Chalupsky Weber & Partners Rechtsanwälte GmbH ✪
Schönherr Rechtsanwälte ✪
Siemer-Siegl-Füreder & Partner ✪

Firms are listed A-Z in tiers which are ranked in order of priority
✪ Indicates firm displays contact details at the end of this chapter.

Insolvency boutique **Abel & Abel** has the well regarded receivers Johanna Abel-Winkler and Norbert Abel on its team.

Baier Lambert's Andreas Alzinger acts as a receiver, and also advises companies and a number of banks.

CMS Strommer Reich-Rohrwig Karasek Hainz has a practice focused on restructurings. Clients recently advised include Styria Medien AG, EPN Europromet Telekon AG, and Austrian management consultants Neumann Holding, on the restructuring of its international network.

Cerha Hempel Spiegelfeld Hlawati is also strong on restructuring. Edith Hlawati and Benedikt Spiegelfeld are recommended.

Eiselberg Natlacen Walderdorff Cancola regularly advises banking clients in insolvency-related matters.

Freshfields Bruckhaus Deringer advises major creditors and assists large companies with restructurings. It has been acting for a consortium of international lending banks – whose agent is Bank of America Securities Ltd – on the €175m bankruptcy of the Austrian Steiner Industries group. It has also advised a creditor, a major computer manufacturer, on the bankruptcy of an Austrian listed ISP. Maria Pflügl is recommended.

Haarmann Hügel Attorneys at Law is a major corporate firm that also acts as a receiver. It also advises companies on restructuring. In 2001 it acted for RHI on its restructuring and subsequent capital markets offering. Romana Weber-Wilfert is recommended.

Wolf Theiss is advising Stora Enso, one of Europe's largest paper companies, in connection with the €20m insolvency of a major supplier. The firm also acts for Erste Bank.

DLA Weiss-Tessbach has been advising major banks on the receiverships of a technology company and an Austrian hotel, and is working on the silent restructuring of a large real estate investor which has holdings in Austria and the Czech Republic.

Dorda Brugger Jordis has been advising Austin International on its acquisition of the business of Wien GmbH from the receiver, in the course of the bankruptcy proceedings of Dynamit Nobel. Nikolaus Vogt and Andreas Zahradnik are recommended.

Fellner Wratzfeld & Partner Rechtsanwälte does not act as a receiver, but has significant experience in monitoring corporate recoveries for banks. Clients include Bank Austria. Markus Fellner is recommended.

At **Hasch & Partner Anwaltsgesellschaft mbH**, Alexander Hasch has been working as a receiver on a major international case concerning Austrian subsidiaries of UK companies, and involving the transfer of many patents and trade marks to the UK and the Czech Republic. The firm also advises debtors, particularly on rehabilitation procedures.

Haslinger/Nagele & Partner Rechtsanwälte GmbH has a solid practice led by Norbert Nagele and Thomas Kurz, who both act as receivers and advisers to debtors.

Kunz Schima Wallentin & Partner is one of the leading labour law practices in Austria, and is also strong on insolvency matters. Eberhard Wallentin acted on the €24m bankruptcy of Dynamit-Nobel.

Neudorfer, Griensteidl, Hahnkamper, Stapf & Partner's Christof Sapf acted on the Austrian part of the KPNQwest insolvency.

Saxinger Chalupsky Weber & Partners Rechtsanwälte GmbH's Ernst Chalupsky concentrates on corporate restructuring. Clients include Obst Huber and a number of banks.

Schönherr Rechtsanwälte works for banks, particularly foreign banks such as Deutsche Bank and ABN Amro, and for corporate clients. Wolfgang Höller has been advising the Salzburg Airport developer in connection with the bankruptcy of a construction firm.

Siemer-Siegl-Füreder & Partner has been acting for the largest company in Austria's electronics industry in relation to subsidiary liability cases about joint ventures with a now insolvent company.

INTELLECTUAL PROPERTY AND MEDIA

In Austria patent attorneys are a separate profession. They practise on their own or in small firms, and need to be employed for the registration of patents. Experienced clients can instruct patent attorneys directly. Patent attorneys cannot, however, appear in court on their own, they must be accompanied by a lawyer. Sohn Pauvloy is the leading firm of patent attorneys; both Peter Pauvloy and Helmut Hohn are highly regarded. Sole practitioner Dr Haffner also has a good reputation, and has worked on patents for Gillette. Austrian IP lawyers have traditionally also handled unfair trade matters, as until recently trade mark infringement in Austria was governed by the country's Unfair Competition Act. This changed in 2002, and specialisms in either IP or competition law are starting to becoming apparent in the market. It is also common for counterfeiters from the East to use Austria as an entry point into Europe, and product piracy advice is therefore very important.

Dr Michel Walter is Austria's leading copyright boutique. Michel Walter acts for some prominent artists and international clients. Felix Daum has a particular niche in piracy matters, while Albrecht Haller specialises in multimedia and Internet-related IP law.

Schönherr Rechtsanwälte is the only major corporate firm in Austria to be a market leader in both IP and media, though its practice has suffered a blow with the recent departure of Lathar Wiltscheck. However, Guido Kucszko is considered by many to be the best IP lawyer in Austria, while Christian Hauer is also very highly regarded. Both act at an EU level on trade mark and patent litigation. Clients include Microsoft, Red Bull and some major pharmaceutical companies.

Dorda Brugger Jordis' IP practice has an IT focus, advising on software-related copyright matters and litigation. Winfried Schwarz is recommended for copyright law.

Eiselsberg Natlacen Walderdorff Cancola has just been appointed permanent counsel in IP matters to the Nestlé group, having recently won a Supreme Court victory for the client over trade mark protection for the Smarties tube. The firm has a strong practice in the protection of luxury goods from product piracy. On the media side, the firm has been advising on transmission rights for the 2005 ice-hockey world championship.

Important new clients at IP boutique **Engin-Deniz Reimitz Schönherr Hafner Rechtsanwälte KEG** include Procter & Gamble, Oakley, Replay and Hexal Pharma GmbH, for whom it is acting in an important patent case in Vienna's Commercial Court. The firm also acts for Starbucks and Hugo Boss on trade mark issues, and for Cassina, Vitra and Wittman on copyright issues. Georg Schönherr is recommended.

Freshfields Bruckhaus Deringer has been advising individuals involved in an MBO on well-known trade marks. It has also been representing Porsche Design in contentious design matters against German, US, Taiwanese and Dutch defendants. Christoph Pöchhacker is particularly recommended for trade mark matters. On the media law side, the firm has been advising the European Handball Federation on TV rights.

Gassauer-Fleissner Rechtsanwälte has a market leader in Christian Gassauer-Fleissner. He is particularly strong in patent litigation and the pharmaceutical sector. He has recently been working to obtain a preliminary injunction against a generic drug producer on behalf of one of the world's largest pharmaceutical companies, and working on cases involving world-leading drug brands.

INTELLECTUAL PROPERTY AND MEDIA

MICHEL WALTER (DR)
SCHÖNHERR RECHTSANWÄLTE ✪

Dorda Brugger Jordis ✪
Eiselsberg Natlacen Walderdorff Cancola ✪
Engin-Deniz Reimitz Schönherr Hafner Rechtsanwälte KEG
Freshfields Bruckhaus Deringer ✪
Gassauer-Fleissner Rechtsanwälte ✪
Giger, Ruggenthaler & Simon Rechtsanwälte KEG
Höhne, In der Maur & Partner Rechtsanwälte OEG
Kunz Schima Wallentin & Partner
Meinhard Ciresa, DDr
Sattler & Schanda

Baier Lambert ✪
CMS Strommer Reich-Rohrwig Karasek Hainz ✪
Cerha Hempel Spiegelfeld Hlawati ✪
Griss & Partner
Haslinger/Nagele & Partner Rechtsanwälte GmbH ✪
Saxinger Chalupsky Weber & Partners Rechtsanwälte GmbH ✪
Schmidt, Kornfeld, Wukoschitz, Windhager
Wolf Theiss ✪
Zeiner & Zeiner

Brauneis, Klauser & Prändl ✪
DLA Weiss-Tessbach ✪
Fiebinger, Polak, Leon & Partners Rechtsanwälte ✪
Foglar-Deinhardstein & Brandstätter KEG ✪
Greiter Pegger Kofler & Partners ✪
Haarmann Hügel Attorneys at Law ✪
Kammerlander, Piaty, Mueller-Mezin, Schoeller ✪
Lovells in association with Mondl, Trummer, Thomas & Partner Rechtsanwälte GmbH ✪
Ortner Pöch Foramitti ✪
Petsch, Frosch & Klein
Siemer-Siegl-Füreder & Partner ✪

Firms are listed A-Z in tiers which are ranked in order of priority
✪ *Indicates firm displays contact details at the end of this chapter.*

Giger, Ruggenthaler & Simon Rechtsanwälte KEG is a media firm that has an excellent reputation for litigation, and acts for a number of prominent publishing houses and newspaper companies.

Höhne, In der Maur & Partner Rechtsanwälte OEG is very strong in both IP and media work. Its client bases include publishing houses, broadcasters, producers and advertising agencies.

Kunz Schima Wallentin & Partner's Thomas Wallentin has a leading reputation for IP work in the film industry. He has advised some major multinational film productions, including Cannes Film Festival prize winners, on copyright issues and financing structure. The firm also has a strong general patent and trade mark practice.

DDr Meinhard Ciresa is a well regarded IP lawyer who has recently been working on disputes about geographic domains and a dispute regarding the trade marking of yellow as an abstract colour. Manpower is an IP litigation client.

Sattler & Schanda has a well respected practitioner in Reinhard Schanda, who is an expert in trade marks, and acts for a number of large pharmaceutical clients.

Baier Lambert has been advising a number of German newspapers on Austrian competition matters. The firm also has a strong IP practice, with particular experience in the pharmaceutical and brewery sectors.

CMS Strommer Reich-Rohrwig Karasek Hainz has been advising the CineStar Group, a leading German multiplex provider, on the licensing of IP rights, including the licensing of its trade mark in Croatia. On the media side, the firm has been advising the German Pay TV Corporation on its expansion of private TV licensing in Austria.

Cerha Hempel Spiegelfeld Hlawati has been advising a leading US entertainment corporation on trade mark proceedings surrounding the screening of its films in Austria. It also has good experience in handling domain name, patent and copyright disputes. Irene Welser is recommended.

Haslinger/Nagele & Partner Rechtsanwälte GmbH has a good reputation for trade mark work. Klaus Haslinger is recommended.

Saxinger Chalupsky Weber & Partners Rechtsanwälte GmbH has a solid IP practice, and administers many major brands in Austria. It manages the largest trade mark portfolio in the country, which spans the food, medical, pharmaceutical and sports sectors. Maximilian Gumpoldsberger is recommended.

Schmidt, Kornfeld, Wukoschitz, Windhager's Harald Schmidt is a well-regarded patent infringement lawyer.

Wolf Theiss has been defending Colgate-Palmolive in litigation, and advising the company on international trade mark applications. Other IP clients include Reed Elsevier, Novartis Pharma GmbH and Erste Bank. On the media side, the firm has been defending Constantin Film-Holding GmbH, the largest film distributor in Austria, in proceedings relating to alleged abuse of a market dominant position.

Zeiner & Zeiner is a small firm with some important international, particularly US, clients in the IP field.

PRIVATE CLIENT

Private client work in Austria means acting for family owned companies, of which there are many important players in the Austrian market, particularly in the machinery, car supply, car manufacture and packaging industries. Private client work is therefore considered an important area of practice to the country's top commercial law firms, and there is some excellent advice on offer. Austrian law allows for the establishment of the private foundation, an entity that is mid-way between a company and a trust. It is an extremely tax efficient vehicle, and a popular choice for those seeking to transfer their assets. The Private Foundations Act dates from 1993, but only in the last three years have there been the first significant decisions by the Austrian High Court in the field of private foundations, and a number of important re-organisations are consequently being worked on at the moment.

Eiselsberg Natlacen Walderdorff Cancola is the leading private client firm in Austria. Founding partner Maximilian Eiselsberg is known as an outstanding specialist who is particularly strong on private foundations. The firm has been working for clients who are selling or restructuring their assets in Austrian industry, using the private foundation as a tool by which to allocate and administer these assets.

At **Jakobljevich, Grave & Vetter**, Jörg Jakobljevich has outstanding experience in private foundations, on which he acts for clients internationally. Christian Grave is also extremely highly recommended.

Schönherr Rechtsanwälte's Hellwig Torggler was one of the pioneers of Austrian private foundation law. He now sits on the boards of many private foundations. The firm is known for its connections to the paper industry.

Baker & McKenzie's Christoph Kerres is an excellent M&A lawyer who also advises a number of private foundations and family entrepreneurs.

Cerha Hempel Spiegelfeld Hlawati has acted for many leading families with interests in Austrian and foreign industry.

The name of **Dorda Brugger Jordis**' Theresa Jordis is, for many, synonymous with private client work in Austria. She is vice-president of the supervisory board of Erste Bank, and also sits on the boards of Wolford AG and Generali. Her work includes the setting up of major private trusts, inheritance and tax issues, and general property management.

PRIVATE CLIENT

EISELSBERG NATLACEN WALDERDORFF CANCOLA ✪
JAKOBLJEVICH, GRAVE & VETTER
SCHÖNHERR RECHTSANWÄLTE ✪

Baker & McKenzie ✪
Cerha Hempel Spiegelfeld Hlawati ✪
Dorda Brugger Jordis ✪
Greiter Pegger Kofler & Partners ✪
Haarmann Hügel Attorneys at Law ✪
Hasch & Partner Anwaltsgesellschaft mbH ✪
Siemer-Siegl-Füreder & Partner ✪

ARNOLD Rechtsanwalts-Partnerschaft
Brauneis, Klauser & Prändl ✪
Freshfields Bruckhaus Deringer ✪
Gassauer-Fleissner Rechtsanwälte ✪
Griss & Partner
Haslinger/Nagele & Partner Rechtsanwälte GmbH ✪
Saxinger Chalupsky Weber & Partners Rechtsanwälte GmbH ✪

Firms are listed A-Z in tiers which are ranked in order of priority
✪ Indicates firm displays contact details at the end of this chapter.

Greiter Pegger Kofler & Partners has a policy of not allowing its lawyers to sit on company boards, to avoid conflicts of interest. The firm has a good reputation for advising on private foundations, and Ivo Greiter is recommended.

Haarmann Hügel Attorneys at Law is a tax-focused firm whose leading tax partner, Hanns Hügel, also has an excellent reputation for private client work. He is currently advising one of the richest families in Austria on using new tax provisions to protect its estates. Florian Gibitz is also recommended.

Hasch & Partner Anwaltsgesellschaft mbH has an excellent reputation for private client work. Few lawyers in Austria act for more private foundations than Alexander Hasch. He has been handling many of the re-organisations of private foundations required by the High Court decisions referred to above.

Siemer-Siegl-Füreder & Partner is particularly strong in property advice to private clients. It is currently advising one wealthy individual on the sale of half of a stately home and the re-investment of this money, and also acts for a client who is a shareholder of one of the leading breweries in Bavaria. Mario Schiavon is recommended for estate planning, and Hannes Füreder for the corporate structuring of private wealth.

ARNOLD Rechtsanwalts-Partnerschaft is a leading tax boutique which also has a solid private client practice. Nikolaus Arnorld is recommended.

At **Brauneis, Klauser & Prändl**, Arno Brauneis and Bernhard Girsch advise on estate administration, while Felix Prändl and Brigitte

Sammer are currently setting up a major private foundation for a client who is restructuring a business.

Freshfields Bruckhaus Deringer advises the Porsche family, and has also advised the Roth Fund on waste disposal business, the Steinleitner Fund in relation to shopping centres, and the Berghofer family on the powder coating business. Günther Horvath is recommended for corporate advice, and Michael Sedlaczek for tax advice.

Gassauer-Fleissner Rechtsanwälte's Christian Gassauer-Fleissner regularly advises family owned business and private foundations. His work often involves the administration of bankable assets.

Griss & Partner's Gunter Griss is working on the restructuring of corporate pension plans for a large private foundation and a leading regional bank.

Haslinger/Nagele & Partner Rechtsanwälte GmbH acts for family enterprises in the establishment and administration of property management private foundations.

Saxinger Chalupsky Weber & Partners Rechtsanwälte GmbH's Wolfgang Lauss has a solid practice in private foundation work. Franz Mittendorfer is also recommended.

REAL ESTATE AND CONSTRUCTION

Though the planning restrictions in Vienna are very strict and becoming stricter, the Millennium Tower, the only skyscraper on the historic city bank of the Danube, was successfully built. With a shopping centre and cinema complex in its lower levels, this is one of the prime pieces of real estate in the country. Property is cheap in Austria at the moment, and international buyers regard it as a safe investment. When selecting a law firm it is often important to look at the quality of environmental law advice on offer, as Austria also has extremely strict regulations for the protection of the environment.

Cerha Hempel Spiegelfeld Hlawati is Austria's leading real estate firm. Recent work for investors in Austria includes advising Henderson Global Investors on the €45m acquisition of a shopping centre in Burgenland, advising the largest open-ended German fund, Deka Immobilien Investment Gesellschaft mbH, on the €80m acquisition of a shopping centre in Vienna, and advising WestInvest Gesellschaft für Investmentfonds on the €39.4m acquisition of another shopping centre in Vienna. Alfred Nemetschke is recommended.

Real estate clients say that they particularly value **Wolf Theiss**' international capability and its network of offices in Eastern Europe. The firm has recently advised DB Real Estate on the €70m acquisition of the first phase of the Europlaza office complex in Vienna, and Portugal-based Sona Imobiliairia on the intended €150m development of a shopping centre in Vienna. Peter Oberlechner is recommended.

REAL ESTATE AND CONSTRUCTION

CERHA HEMPEL SPIEGELFELD HLAWATI ✪
WOLF THEISS ✪

CMS STROMMER REICH-ROHRWIG KARASEK HAINZ ✪
DLA WEISS-TESSBACH ✪
DORDA BRUGGER JORDIS ✪
SCHÖNHERR RECHTSANWÄLTE ✪
SIEMER-SIEGL-FÜREDER & PARTNER ✪

Alix Frank Rechtsanwälte KEG
Baier Lambert ✪
Brauneis, Klauser & Prändl ✪
Eiselsberg Natlacen Walderdorff Cancola ✪
Fiebinger, Polak, Leon & Partners Rechtsanwälte ✪
Freshfields Bruckhaus Deringer ✪
Haarmann Hügel Attorneys at Law ✪
Neudorfer, Griensteidl, Hahnkamper, Stapf & Partner ✪
Saxinger Chalupsky Weber & Partners Rechtsanwälte GmbH ✪

Deissenberger & Partners
Gassauer-Fleissner Rechtsanwälte ✪
Hasch & Partner Anwaltsgesellschaft mbH ✪
Held Berdnik Astner & Partner, Rechtsanwälte ✪
Höhne, In der Maur & Partner Rechtsanwälte OEG
Kaan Cronenberg & Partners
Kammerlander, Piaty, Mueller-Mezin, Schoeller ✪
Lovells in association with Mondl, Trummer, Thomas & Partner Rechtsanwälte GmbH ✪
Zirngibl Langwieser

Firms are listed A-Z in tiers which are ranked in order of priority
✪ Indicates firm displays contact details at the end of this chapter.

CMS Strommer Reich-Rohrwig Karasek Hainz suffered a blow with the departure of construction guru and name partner Georg Karasek. However the firm is still very strong in commercial property. Nikolaus Weselik has a well-regarded practice and considerable expertise in construction-related litigation. He has advised Westdeutsche Immobilien Bank on the €350m financing of the acquisition of the Millennium Tower, and WestFonds Immobilien Anlage-gesellschaft on the €60m acquisition of the Real Estate Opernringhof in Vienna.

DLA Weiss-Tessbach is handling litigation for one of the largest construction companies in Austria. Gerhard Benn-Ibler has a good reputation for construction arbitration.

Dorda Brugger Jordis is advising a state-owned company on its planned €120m-€160m sale, by auction, of a real estate portfolio. It has also advised MIBA Sinter-Reibebeläge on a €40m construction project, and is currently acting for Verbund in a €5m construction dispute. Stefan Artner is recommended.

Schönherr Rechtsanwälte has been advising Deutsche Bank on the €6.6m sale and lease-back of its office building in Vienna. It has also been working on the granting of a €22m option in the sale of an Austrian business park.

Siemer-Siegl-Füreder & Partner has been working on the review of lease agreements for a 5000 sq m property, and on an agreement to lease space in a designer outlet on the Czech border. Reinhard Bruner is recommended.

Alix Frank Rechtsanwälte KEG acts for Wienerberger Baust offindustrie AG, Pipelife and the Bramac-Group. It is advising on construction matters in Austria and Hungary. Wolfgang Punz is recommended.

Baier Lambert has been working on the €400m sale of a shopping centre in one of Vienna's most important shopping streets, and on the €700m development of an office and business park. Clients include the largest listed Austrian property developer.

Brauneis, Klauser & Prändl has been working on a construction project for a tunnel in Salzburg. Arno Brauneis is recommended.

Eiselsberg Natlacen Walderdorff Cancola has been advising Austria's largest construction company on a restructuring and squeeze-out matter, and working on a real estate project in Prague.

Fiebinger, Polak, Leon & Partners Rechtsanwälte has advised major Austrian companies and private clients in the development and construction of residential buildings, and on the construction of a large office complex. It also has experience in advising on underground infrastructure projects.

Freshfields Bruckhaus Deringer has been advising the Austrian government on the sale of the Bundeswohnbaugesellschaften, which mainly consists of a €2bn real estate portfolio. The firm also has environmental expertise, and has been advising a large German manufacturer on issues of parent company liability for environmental damage. Georg Bahn is recommended.

Haarmann Hügel Attorneys at Law has been acting for a number of companies and business parks in Lower Austria, including developer EcoPlus, which is owned by the State of Lower Austria, in developing sites in Salzburg. Herbert Schrittesser is recommended.

Neudorfer, Griensteidl, Hahnkamper, Stapf & Partner's Stefan Probst has a strong niche practice in advising agriculture and forestry clients, including country estates. Klaus Voithofer has been handling litigation for a company running a project to build a music hall.

Saxinger Chalupsky Weber & Partners Rechtsanwälte GmbH regularly represents a company from the health sector in commercial property projects, including the development of a spa in Upper Austria. It has worked for a number of hospitals, and on Linz Central Station. Eduard Saxinger is recommended.

TAX

The largest tax matter currently at stake in Austria is the challenge of the Austrian beverage tax in the European courts. This is effectively a class action, though these are not officially allowed in Austria.

Not all of the major corporate firms in Austria have developed strong tax practices, and there are some excellent tax law boutiques on the market. In 2003, international tax specialist Robert Schneider left **Wolf Theiss** to set up his own boutique **SchneideR's Rechtsanwalts – KEG**.

ARNOLD Rechtsanwalts-Partnerschaft is a market leading tax focused firm. It regularly handles tax litigation before the Austrian Administrative Court and the Austrian Constitutional Court, and takes tax cases to the ECJ. The firm is currently working on cases concerning the taxation of zero bonds, the interpretation of double taxation treaties, refund issues in energy tax, and stamp duty. It also has a strong practice in the specialist field of transfer taxes. Wolf-Dieter Arnold is recommended.

Freshfields Bruckhaus Deringer is particularly strong on the tax aspects of the structuring of M&A transactions and capital markets products, and on the taxation of investment funds. The tax department has a substantial client base in the energy, telecoms and e-commerce sectors. Recent work includes advising a US-based multinational group on the €1.5bn refinancing structure of its European group activities. Michael Sedlaczek and Claus Staringer are recommended.

Haarmann Hügel Attorneys at Law also has a reputation for strong tax support on corporate transactions. Hanns Hügel has an outstanding reputation as a tax lawyer, while Clemens Hasenauer is also recommended for the international tax expertise that he brings to the re-organisation of international companies.

TAX

ARNOLD RECHTSANWALTS-PARTNERSCHAFT
FRESHFIELDS BRUCKHAUS DERINGER ✪
HAARMANN HÜGEL ATTORNEYS AT LAW ✪

Dorda Brugger Jordis ✪
Wolf Theiss ✪

Brauneis, Klauser & Prändl ✪
Cerha Hempel Spiegelfeld Hlawati ✪

Baker & McKenzie ✪
CMS Strommer Reich-Rohrwig Karasek Hainz ✪
DLA Weiss-Tessbach ✪
Greiter Pegger Kofler & Partners ✪
Hausmaninger Herbst Rechtsanwälte GmbH ✪
Saxinger Chalupsky Weber & Partners Rechtsanwälte GmbH ✪
SchneideR's Rechtsanwalts – KEG

Firms are listed A-Z in tiers which are ranked in order of priority
✪ Indicates firm displays contact details at the end of this chapter.

The tax practice at **Dorda Brugger Jordis** has a corporate and financial focus. It has advised the Austrian Railway Corporation on tax aspects of corporate bonds, and advised Citibank on tax aspects of cross-border lease transactions. The firm is also defending a number of banks in substantial tax litigation by the tax authorities, and is acting for Wein & Co in the European beverage tax cases.

Wolf Theiss has been advising major clients, including Deutsche Bank and UBS, on tax issues related to the structuring of complex financial products, including index-linked bonds that allow investment into a foreign fund. The firm is also strong on tax support for M&A transactions, property investment funds, infrastructure and project finance work. Christian Hoenig is recommended.

Brauneis, Klauser & Prändl has a co-operation with Deloitte & Touche which allows it to provide strong tax advice on M&A transactions and restructuring.

Cerha Hempel Spiegelfeld Hlawati's Johannes Prinz and Peter Knobl enjoy good reputations on structured finance matters.

At **Baker & McKenzie**, Imke Gerdes is acting for telephone companies against the Austrian State in an attempt to reclaim up to €500m in VAT. This is a test case which, if successful, is expected to generate claims worth €7bn in Germany.

CMS Strommer Reich-Rohrwig Karasek Hainz has been giving tax advice to AIG on its €1.2bn acquisition of the Nycomed Group. Gerhard Rettenbacher is recommended.

DLA Weiss-Tessbach has good tax lawyers supporting its projects, corporate and commercial property departments.

Greiter Pegger Kofler & Partners' Franz Pegger is well regarded, while **Hausmaninger Herbst Rechtsanwälte GmbH** also has a solid reputation.

Saxinger Chalupsky Weber & Partners Rechtsanwälte GmbH's Werner Minihold has a good practice in corporate reorganisations, appellate procedures and international tax structures, such as tax sparing and ABS structures. Tax structuring clients include the Borealis Group and IBM. He has also handled significant tax litigation for insurance companies.

SchneideR's Rechtsanwalts – KEG is a new tax boutique headed by Robert Schneider. He specialises in international tax matters and also has significant experience in the Austrian energy markets. Recent work includes handling Austrian tax issues for the beneficiaries of a Bermudan trust.

HELD BERDNIK ASTNER & PARTNER, RECHTSANWÄLTE

SCHLÖGELGASSE 1
KAISER-JOSEF-PLATZ
8016 GRAZ

Telephone: +43 316 83 25 270
Fax: +43 316 81 43 15
E-mail: graz@hba.at
Website: www.hba.at

Languages
Croatian, English, French, Italian

Other offices
Vienna

Number of lawyers 13
at this office 11

CATEGORIES OF WORK

- Contract and commercial law
- Mergers and acquisitions
- Law of construction, building and real estate
- Law of fair trade and antitrust
- Law of intellectual property (general), copyright, patent and trade marks
- Company and corporation law
- Banking, securities and finance law
- Labour and social law
- Family law (general), law of divorce and maintenance
- Litigation and arbitration law
- Trust and foundation law
- Insolvency law
- South eastern Europe
- Private client

KAMMERLANDER, PIATY, MUELLER-MEZIN, SCHOELLER

GLACISSTRASSE 27
8010 GRAZ

Telephone: +43 316 80 68 0
Fax: +43 316 80 68 21
E-mail: office@pmsp.at

Languages
English, German

Number of lawyers 4

CATEGORIES OF WORK

Commercial law (general)
Dr Martin Piaty

Company law
Dr Martin Piaty

Intellectual property and trade marks
Dr Stefan Schoeller

New media and Internet
Dr Stefan Schoeller

Media law
Dr Martin Piaty, Dr Stefan Schoeller

Law regulating radio and television broadcasting
Dr Martin Piaty

Antitrust and competition
Dr Martin Piaty, Dr Stefan Schoeller

Real estate
Mag Michael Mueller-Mezin

Hospital law
Dr Martin Piaty

Public procurement
Dr Martin Piaty

EC law (general)
Dr Martin Piaty, Dr Stefan Schoeller

Arbitration and litigation
Mag Michael Mueller-Mezin

BINDER GRÖSSWANG RECHTSANWÄLTE

KAISERJÄGERSTRASSE 1
6020 INNSBRUCK

Telephone: +43 512 579 973 0
Fax: +43 512 579 973 8
E-mail: tirol@bgnet.at
Website: www.bgnet.at

Languages
Croatian, English, French, German, Italian, Spanish

Other offices
Vienna

Number of lawyers 47
at this office 6

CATEGORIES OF WORK

Asset finance, securitisation
Dr Tibor Fabian, Dr Stefan Tiefenthaler

Banking, finance
Dr Michael Binder, Dr Michael Kutschera

Capital markets
Dr Michael Binder, Dr Ivo Rungg

Competition
Dr Raoul Hoffer, Dr Johannes Barbist

Corporate and commercial
Dr Michael Binder,
Mag Alexander Kramer

Cross-border leases
Dr Christian Klausegger,
Dr Thomas Schirmer

E-commerce
Dr Ivo Rungg, Dr Norbert Wiesinger

Government business, regulatory
Dr Christian Klausegger,
Dr Stefan Tiefenthaler

Dispute resolution, litigation, arbitration
Dr Michael Kutschera,
Dr Christian Klausegger

Intellectual property
Dr Ivo Rungg, Dr Hellmut Buchroithner

Labour law
Dr Klaus Grösswang, Mag Horst Lukanec

M&A
Dr Michael Binder, Dr Michael Kutschera

Privatisation
Dr Michael Kutschera, Dr Florian Khol

Tax
Dr Andreas Hable, Dr Michael Binder

Telecommunications
Dr Norbert Wiesinger,
Dr Christian Klausegger,

Trusts and estates
Dr Tibor Fabian, Mag Laetizia Riedel

GREITER PEGGER KOFLER & PARTNERS

MARIA-THERESIEN-STRASSE 24
6020 INNSBRUCK 158

Telephone: +43 512 57 18 11
Fax: +43 512 58 49 25
E-mail: info@greiter.lawfirm.at
Website: www.greiter.lawfirm.at

Languages
English, French, German, Italian

Number of lawyers 16

CATEGORIES OF WORK

Personal injury

Companies, corporations

Banking, securities and finance

Mergers and acquisitions

Competition, antitrust

Commercial law (general)

Employment, labour

Tax

Insurance

Intellectual property, trade marks

Commercial agency/distribution agreements

Real property

Inheritance

Environment

Establishment of companies, subsidiaries

HASLINGER/NAGELE & PARTNER RECHTSANWÄLTE GMBH

ROSEGGERSTRASSE 58
4020 LINZ

Telephone: +43 732 78 43 310
Fax: +43 732 77 43 31
E-mail: office@haslinger-nagele.com
Website: www.haslinger-nagele.com

Languages
Czech, English, French, German

Other offices
Prague, Vienna

Number of lawyers 25
at this office 14

Contacts
Dr Norbert Nagele, Dr Klaus Haslinger, Dr Christoph Szep, Mag Thomas Kurz, Dr Wilhelm Bergthaler, Dr Dietmar Lux, Mag Karin Niedermair, Mag Martin Oder, Mag Martin Stempkowski, Mag Martin Niederhuber

CATEGORIES OF WORK

- Commercial law and corporate law
- Mergers and acquisitions
- Insolvency, corporate restructuring
- Competition law and intellectual property
- Environment
- Dispute resolution, litigation and international arbitration
- Banking and finance
- Commercial property, real estate
- Energy and natural resources
- Antitrust
- Labour and employment

BAIER LAMBERT

KÄRNTNERRING 12
1010 VIENNA

Telephone: +43 1 515 50
Fax: +43 1 515 50 50
E-mail: blr@baierlambert.com
Website: www.baierlambert.com

Languages
Czech, English, French, German, Hungarian

Number of lawyers 30

Contact
Dr Erhard Böhm

CATEGORIES OF WORK

Banking	Litigation and arbitration
Company and commercial law	Mergers and acquisitions
Central and eastern European law	Real estate and property law
EU law	Telecommunications
Energy and natural resources	Distribution and agency
Franchising law	Capital markets
Intellectual property	Insolvency and restructuring
International transactions	Employment and labour law

BAKER & McKENZIE

SCHUBERTRING 2
1010 VIENNA

Telephone: +43 1 516 60
Fax: +43 1 516 60 60
E-mail: vienna.info@bakernet.com
Website: www.bakernet.com

Languages
English, French, German, Spanish

Other offices
For a list of all offices and other information regarding the firm please consult Baker & McKenzie's Frankfurt office entry

Number of lawyers 3,380
at this office 24

Contacts
Christoph Kerres, Georg Diwok

Member
IBA; Technology Lawyers Consortium

Baker & McKenzie is a global law firm with 66 offices in 36 countries.

CATEGORIES OF WORK

Business law	Employment and labour law
Corporate law	Litigation and arbitration law
Mergers and acquisitions	EU law
Private foundations (trust)	Antritrust and competition law
Banking, securities and finance law	Joint ventures
Public law, environment and energy law	Intellectual property law
Media law and unfair competition law	Distribution and franchise law

BINDER GRÖSSWANG RECHTSANWÄLTE

STERNGASSE 13
1010 VIENNA

Telephone: +43 1 534 800
Fax: +43 1 534 808
E-mail: bg@bgnet.at
Website: www.bgnet.at

Languages
Croatian, English, French, German, Italian, Spanish

Other offices
Innsbruck

Number of lawyers 47
at this office 41

CATEGORIES OF WORK

Asset finance, securitisation
Dr Tibor Fabian, Dr Stefan Tiefenthaler

Banking, finance
Dr Michael Binder, Dr Michael Kutschera

Capital markets
Dr Michael Binder, Dr Ivo Rungg

Competition
Dr Raoul Hoffer, Dr Johannes Barbist

Corporate and commercial
Dr Michael Binder,
Mag Alexander Kramer

Cross-border leases
Dr Christian Klausegger,
Dr Thomas Schirmer

Government business, regulatory
Dr Christian Klausegger,
Dr Stefan Tiefenthaler

E-commerce
Dr Ivo Rungg, Dr Norbert Wiesinger

Dispute resolution, litigation, arbitration
Dr Michael Kutschera,
Dr Christian Klausegger

Intellectual property
Dr Ivo Rungg, Dr Hellmut Buchroithner

Labour law
Dr Klaus Grösswang, Mag Horst Lukanec

M&A
Dr Michael Binder, Dr Michael Kutschera

Privatisation
Dr Michael Kutschera, Dr Florian Khol

Tax
Dr Andreas Hable, Dr Michael Binder

Telecommunications
Dr Norbert Wiesinger,
Dr Christian Klausegger

Trusts and estates
Dr Tibor Fabian, Mag Laetizia Riedel

THE FIRM

Binder Grösswang Rechtsanwälte is one of the leading law firms in Austria. As a team of specialists, the members of the firm aspire to meet the clients' needs on an outstanding level by pooling both the individual experience and the collective know-how of the firm. Thus, the best reference of the firm is the high quality of its work and services provided.

Binder Grösswang Rechtsanwälte was founded by Dr Martin Binder in Vienna in 1962. Today it consists of 17 partners and approximately 30 associates.

Committed to the highest level of legal expertise, the firm advises both major Austrian corporate, banking and industry clients and has established a strong international competence in various areas during the last four decades.

In September 1999, the firm established a new office in Innsbruck to meet the needs of enterprises doing business in the western parts of Austria for counselling on the spot. As the office consists of a team of local lawyers, headed by Ivo Rungg, the economic circumstances in the western part of Austria are well known, and a close connection to clients is guaranteed. Moreover, this office assists the firm's presence in the economic area of northern Italy and southern Germany because of its geographical location.

AREAS OF PRACTICE

The major areas of the firm's practice comprise all legal aspects involved in the establishment, merger and acquisition, running and divestiture of business, privatisation, banking and financing transactions, all kinds of cross-border business activities, IPOs, securities, telecommunications, antitrust and competition, distribution, public procurement, subsidies, labour, litigation and arbitration.

The firm advises on all issues of business and commercial law that may arise in the running of a business. This includes the negotiation and drafting of agreements for sales contracts, distribution systems, leases, indemnities, suretyships, security in interests or other commercial transactions and assistance in case of disputes.

BRAUNEIS, KLAUSER & PRÄNDL
RECHTSANWÄLTE OEG

BAUERNMARKT 2
1010 WIEN

Telephone: +43 1 532 12 10 0
Fax: +43 1 532 12 10 20
E-mail: viennalaw@bkp.at
Website: www.bkp.at

Languages
English, French, German, Italian

Number of lawyers 15

CATEGORIES OF WORK

EU and competition law
Dr Alexander Klauser,
Dr Bernhard Girsch

IT and telecommunications law
Dr Felix Prändl,
Dr Arno Brauneis

Intellectual property
Dr Arno Brauneis,
Dr Bernhard Girsch

International distribution law
Dr Arno Brauneis

Companies, corporations, tax
Dr Felix Prändl,
Mag Brigitte Sammer

Mergers and acquisitions
Dr Felix Prändl,
Mag Stefan Geppert

Real estate
Dr Arno Brauneis, Dr Orlin Radinsky

Insolvency
Dr Alexander Klauser

Litigation and arbitration
Dr Alexander Klauser

Banking law and securities
Mag Stefan Geppert

Labour and employment
Dr Arno Brauneis, Dr Orlin Radinsky

CMS STROMMER REICH-ROHRWIG KARASEK HAINZ

EBENDORFERSTRASSE 3
1010 WIEN

Telephone: +43 1 404 43 0
Fax: +43 1 404 43 90 00
E-mail: office@cmslegal.at
Website: www.cmslegal.at

Languages
Croatian, Czech, English, French, Russian, Serbian, Slovakian, Slovenian, Spanish

Other offices
Belgrade, Brussels, Prague, Zagreb

Number of lawyers 65
at this office 50

Contacts
Bernt Elsner, Peter Huber

Member
CMS Transnational Legal and Tax Services; World Law Group

CATEGORIES OF WORK

Banking and finance
Peter Huber, Alexander Russ

Capital markets
Martin Zuffer,
Johannes Reich-Rohrwig

Central and Eastern Europe
Radivoje Petrikic, Gregor Famira

Commercial property, real estate and construction
Georg Karasek, Nikolaus Weselik

Competition and EU
Bernt Elsner, Jörg Zehetner

Corporate and commercial
Johannes Reich-Rohrwig,
Peter Huber

Dispute resolution
Johannes Reich-Rohrwig, Thomas Frad

Energy and national resources
Daniela Karollus-Bruner, Thomas Rabl

Public procurement, regulatory
Bernt Elsner

Fraud and white-collar crime
Wolfgang Brandstetter

Infrastructure
Peter Huber, Nikolaus Weselik

Insolvency and corporate restructuring
Johannes Reich-Rohrwig,
Nikolaus Weselik

Intellectual property, media
Egon Engin-Deniz,
Daniela Karollus-Bruner

Labour and employment
Bernhard Hainz, Christoph Wolf

M&A, transactions
Peter Huber, Günther Hauslik

CERHA HEMPEL SPIEGELFELD HLAWATI
PARTNERSCHAFT VON RECHTSANWÄLTEN

PARKRING 2
1010 WIEN

Telephone: +43 1 514 35 0
Fax: +43 1 514 35 39
E-mail: office@chsh.at
Website: www.chsh.at

Languages
Croatian, English, French, German, Hungarian, Italian, Norwegian, Polish, Romanian, Russian, Spanish

Other offices
Brussels, Budapest, Zagreb

Number of lawyers 65
at this office 50

CATEGORIES OF WORK

Mergers and acquisitions
Edith Hlawati, Benedikt Spiegelfeld

Banking
Edith Hlawati, Karl Hempel

Capital markets
Edith Hlawati, Volker Glas

Companies, corporations
Karl Hempel, Oskar Winkler

Arbitration and litigation
Karl Hempel, Irene Welser

Commercial law (contracts)
Benedikt Spiegelfeld, Irene Welser

Franchising and distribtution
Benedikt Spiegelfeld

Information technology
Volker Glas, Johannes Fuchs

Real estate, construction, building
Alfred Nemetschke

Competition, antitrust, intellectual property
Claudine Vartian, Julian Feichtinger

Privatisation, telecommunications
Edith Hlawatl, Claudine Vartian

Labour law
Irene Welser, Julian Feichtinger

Eastern Europe
Karl Hempel, Alfred Nemetschke

Regulation, administrative, constitutional law
Peter Lewisch, Claudine Vartian

Energy
Benedikt Spiegelfeld

DALLMANN & JURANEK
ATTORNEYS AT LAW

GUSSHAUSSTRASSE 2
1040 VIENNA

Telephone: +43 1 504 41 42
Fax: +43 1 504 41 42 43
E-mail: office@dallmann.cc
Website: www.dallmann.cc

Languages
English, French, German, Russian, Spanish

Other offices
Paris

Number of lawyers 9
at this office 8

Contact
Dr Armin Dallmann LLR

CATEGORIES OF WORK

Banking
Dr Armin Dallmann

Mergers and acquisitions
Dr Armin Dallmann,
Dr Johannes Juranek

Intellectual property
Dr Johannes Juranek

New media and Internet
Dr Johannes Juranek

Capital markets
Dr Armin Dallmann,
Dr Thomas Zivny

Project finance
Dr Armin Dallmann,
Dr Thomas Zivny

Company
Dr Armin Dallmann,
Dr Johannes Juranek

Litigation
Dr Johannes Juranek

Arbitration
Dr Johannes Juranek,
Laurence Yansouni JD

Employment
Dr Johannes Juranek

Trusts and estates
Dr Armin Dallmann,
Dr Johannes Juranek

DLA WEISS-TESSBACH

ROTENTURMSTRASSE 13
1010 WIEN

Telephone: +43 1 531 78 0
Fax: +43 1 533 52 52
E-mail: wien@dla.com
Website: www.dla.com

Languages
Czech, English, French, Hungarian, Italian, Slovak

Other offices
Amsterdam, Antwerp, Bangkok, Bergen, Berlin, Birmingham, Bradford, Bratislava, Brussels, Budapest, Cologne, Copenhagen, Edinburgh, Essen, Frankfurt, Glasgow, Hamburg, Hong Kong, Leeds, Liverpool, London, Madrid, Manchester, Milan, Moscow, Oslo, Paris, Prague, Rotterdam, Salzberg, Sarajevo, Shanghai, Sheffield, Singapore, Stockholm, Zagreb

Number of lawyers 82
at this office 40

Contacts
Stefan Eder, Ivo Deskovic

Member
DLA Group

CATEGORIES OF WORK

General corporate	Intellectual property
Commercial (general) and contract	Property, real estate
Competition	Mergers and aquisitions
Project finance, financing	Environmental
EU law	Labour
Eastern Europe	Telecoms, IT
Litigation	Public procurement
Banking	

THE FIRM

Weiss-Tessbach was established in 1878 and is one of the longest-established law firms in Austria. 15 years ago, the firm decided on an extremely dynamic development. Since 1990, the number of lawyers at the firm has increased more than four times from 15 to over 80, and the number of offices from one to seven. On October 1st 2003, Weiss-Tessbach was integrated with DLA on the basis of a shared vision to become a top five full-service European law firm. With its current offices in six central and eastern European countries, DLA Weiss-Tessbach will continue to expand into the region at a time of EU accession for many countries.

DLA Weiss-Tessbach is part of DLA Group. DLA Group is an exclusive alliance of international full-service law firms with a shared vision. Established in 1999, DLA Group now has over 2,200 lawyers across 21 countries, who deliver expert local know-how and international solutions. DLA Group provides legal advice in 37 major cities across Europe, Singapore, Thailand, Hong Kong and the People's Republic of China.

AREAS OF PRACTICE

The firm has strengthened its core areas of expertise (commercial and corporate, M&A, banking and finance, intellectual property, real estate), and has expanded into other areas of law (administrative, employment, telecoms, technology, venture capital). Today, the firm is able to assist its corporate clients in all aspects of their activities.

DLA Weiss-Tessbach has well-established relations with clients of various backgrounds. The firm advises small and medium-sized enterprises as well as leading (often publicly listed) international and domestic industrial groups, service providers, banks and other financial institutions and individuals.

DLA Weiss-Tessbach has established a particular reputation for its ability to handle cases in international cross-border contexts. It carefully views the ongoing developments in central Europe with the aim of combining the needs of the constantly changing international legal market and industry, whilst also upholding the high standard of service that the firm has always been able to offer to its clients.

DORDA BRUGGER JORDIS

DR KARL LUEGER-RING 10
1010 VIENNA

Telephone: +43 1 533 47 95 0
Fax: +43 1 533 47 97
E-mail: office@dbj.at
Website: www.dbj.at

Languages
English, French, Italian, Spanish

Number of lawyers 60

CATEGORIES OF WORK

Companies, corporations
Theresa Jordis, Tibor Varga

Tax
Tibor Varga

Mergers and acquisitions
Christian Dorda, Martin Brodey

Commercial law (general)
Theresa Jordis, Christoph Brogyányi

Banking, securities and finance
Florian Kremslehner,
Andreas Zahradnik

Copyright
Winfried Schwarz

Trade marks
Walter Brugger, Martin Reinisch

Arbitration and litigation
Christian Dorda, Florian Kremslehner

Insolvency
Andreas Zahradnik, Nikolaus Vogt

Telecommunications
Martin Brodey, Stephan Polster

Competition, antitrust
Walter Brugger, Stephan Polster

Administrative law
Stefan Günther, Florian Keschmann

Employment, labour
Thomas Angermair, Alexandra Knell

EU law
Stefan Günther

Real estate
Stefan Artner, Johannes Hysek

Capital markets
Andreas Mayr, Andreas Zahradnik

THE FIRM

The law firm of Dorda Brugger Jordis was established in 1976 and has developed into one of the major law firms in Austria. The firm is composed of 60 lawyers, several of whom have university degrees from and work experience in the US. Dorda Brugger Jordis offers advice on Austrian law to international and domestic clients. The firm has links with large accountancy firms and has also built up a strong and effective network of contacts worldwide. This includes major law firms in the US, UK, Germany and France, and is particularly strong in such areas as banking and financial law, mergers and acquisitions, and corporate law.

Recently, the firm has also established a 'best-friends' program with top-tier local law firms in many central and eastern European countries. The program has been designed to provide a full range of legal and related services and to assure true quality work in terms of expertise and efficiency for any given transaction for clients. In addition, the program has also been developed to identify together with the respective 'best-friend' strategic business opportunities for clients.

AREAS OF PRACTICE

Endeavouring to meet the needs of corporate clients, it is the stated objective of Dorda Brugger Jordis to provide the professional services that the business community expects from an efficient law firm with an international practice. The firm covers all areas of corporate, civil and commercial law (including labour law, banking, mergers and acquisitions, unfair competition law, and commercial litigation), which are relevant to its corporate clients. It is constantly seeking to maintain its up-to-date legal expertise and all of its lawyers participate regularly in training programmes within specific areas of law.

The firm is well known for quick, detailed and reliable legal counsel in international business transactions. Clients range from the largest US-based and international corporations and their Austrian subsidiaries to large- and medium-sized Austrian business entities such as banks and industrial and commercial enterprises. The firm does not practise criminal or divorce law.

EISELSBERG NATLACEN WALDERDORFF CANCOLA

RECHTSANWÄLTE

SCHWARZENBERGPLATZ 7
1030 WIEN

Telephone: +43 1 716 55
Fax: +43 1 716 55 99
E-mail: wien@enwc.com
Website: www.enwc.com

Languages
Czech, English, French, Hungarian, Italian, Turkish

Other offices
Budapest, Prague

Number of lawyers 39
at this office 25

Contacts
Dr Maximilan Eiselsberg, Dr Raimund Cancola

CATEGORIES OF WORK

- Corporate and commercial law
- EU and competition
- Banking and finance
- Labour and employment
- Private client
- Intellectual property
- Central and Eastern Europe
- Telecommunications
- Tax
- Litigation and arbitration
- Commercial property
- Real estate
- Capital markets
- Construction and building

FELLNER WRATZFELD & PARTNER

RECHTSANWÄLTE – ATTORNEYS AT LAW

WIPPLINGERSTRASSE 23
1010 VIENNA

Telephone: +43 1 537 70
Fax: +43 1 537 70 70
E-mail: office@fwp.at
Website: www.fwp.at

Languages
English, French, German

Number of lawyers 23

CATEGORIES OF WORK

Mergers and acquisitions
Markus Fellner

Companies and corporations
Markus Fellner

Antitrust and competition
Markus Fellner

Arbitration and litigation
Kurt Wratzfeld

Real estate
Markus Kajaba, Michael Achleitner

Agricultural, food, drugs
Michael Hecht

Public law, environment
Michael Hecht, Markus Kajaba

IP, IT
Sabine Fehringer

Employment, labour
Kurt Wratzfeld

Damage and liability, product liability, insurance
Kurt Wratzfeld

Telecoms
Sabine Fehringer, Michael Hecht

Trusts and foundations, inheritance
Markus Fellner, Kurt Wratzfeld

Trade marks, intellectual property
Sabine Fehringer

Tax
Markus Fellner

Media, unfair competition
Sabine Fehringer

Public sector
Michael Hecht

Banking, securities and finance
Markus Fellner, Michael Hecht

FIEBINGER, POLAK, LEON & PARTNERS RECHTSANWÄLTE

AM GETREIDEMARKT 1
1060 VIENNA

Telephone: +43 1 58 25 80
Fax: +43 1 58 25 82
Email: fplp@fplp.at
Website: www.fplp.at

Languages
English, French, German, Spanish

Number of lawyers 25

CATEGORIES OF WORK

Corporate law and M&A
P Polak, B Ortner

Banking law
P Polak, B Ortner

Unfair competition
C Leon, C Kletzer

Intellectual property and media law
C Leon, C Kletzer

International arbitration
R Fiebinger, C Leon

Real estate
M Maurer-Kollenz, S Kirchdorfer

Competition and distribution
J Willheim, P Polak

Energy law
K Kossuth, P Polak

Administrative law
K Kossuth

Environmental law
K Kossuth

Labour law
B Ortner, R Fiebinger

Project finance
P Polak, B Ortner

EU matters and competition
J Willheim, P Polak

IT and telecoms
B Ortner

Pharmaceutical law
M Maurer-Kollenz, P Polak

General contract law
R Fiebinger, P Polak

Patent law
C Kletzer

Private client
K Mueller

FOGLAR-DEINHARDSTEIN & BRANDSTÄTTER KEG

PLANKENGASSE 7
1010 VIENNA

Telephone: +43 512 15 71
Fax: +43 513 43 42
E-mail: office@fdblawyers.com
Website: www.fdblawyers.com

Languages
English, French, German, Italian

Number of lawyers 11

CATEGORIES OF WORK

Mergers and acquisitions
Dr Foglar-Deinhardstein,
Dr Brandstätter

Commercial and company law
Dr Foglar-Deinhardstein,
Mag Hoffmann

EU and antitrust law
Dr Brandstätter, Mag Görg

Competition law
Mag Hoffmann, Mag Görg

Intellectual property
Dr Ankershofen, Mag Görg

Litigation
Mag Aberham, Dr Ankershofen

Arbitration
Dr Foglar-Deinhardstein,
Dr Brandstätter

Banking and finance
Dr Brandstätter

Real estate and construction, public procurement
Mag Aberham, Mag Hinteregger

Employment
Mag Hinteregger, Dr Ankershofen

Telecommunications
Dr Foglar-Deinhardstein,
Mag Hoffmann

Environmental
Mag Hinteregger, Mag Maybach

Food and drug
Dr Ankershofen, Mag Maybach

Administrative
Mag Hoffmann, Mag Hinteregger

Product liability
Mag Maybach, Dr Ankershofen

Tax law
Dr Goschler

FRESHFIELDS BRUCKHAUS DERINGER

SEILERGASSE 16
1010 VIENNA

Telephone: +43 1 51 51 50
Fax: +43 1 512 63 94
E-mail: email@freshfields.com
Website: www.freshfields.com

Languages
Extensive language capabilities

Other offices
Amsterdam, Bangkok, Barcelona, Beijing, Berlin, Bratislava, Brussels, Budapest, Cologne, Düsseldorf, Frankfurt, Hamburg, Hanoi, Ho Chi Minh City, Hong Kong, London, Madrid, Milan, Moscow, Munich, New York, Paris, Rome, Shanghai, Singapore, Tokyo, Washington

Number of lawyers 2,504
at this office 56

Contact
Günther Horvath

CATEGORIES OF WORK

Corporate	**Tax**
Finance	**Real estate**
Antitrust, competition and trade	**Employment, pensions and benefits**
Intellectual property and IT	**Dispute resolution (including environment, planning and regulatory)**

GASSAUER-FLEISSNER
RECHTSANWÄLTE GmbH

WALLNERSTRASSE 4
1010 WIEN

Telephone: +43 1 205 206 0
Fax: +43 1 205 206 207
E-mail: office@gassauer.at
Website: www.gassauer.at

Languages
English, French, German, Italian, Portuguese, Spanish

Number of lawyers 12

Other offices
Salzburg

CATEGORIES OF WORK

M&A, corporate	**Real estate**
IP/IT	**Competition law**
Labour law	**Distribution and agency**
Private client	**Public procurement**
Public law	**State aid**

GRAF, MAXL & PITKOWITZ

ATTORNEYS AT LAW

STADIONGASSE 2
1010 WIEN

Telephone: +43 1 401 17
Fax: +43 1 401 17 40
E-mail: office@gmp.at
Website: www.gmp.at

Languages
English, French, German, Russian

Other offices
Graz

Number of lawyers 22

Contacts
Dr Nikolaus Pitkowitz MBL-HSG,
Dr Martin Maxl,
Dr Ferdinand Graf LLM (NYU),
Dr Otto Wächter LLM (NYU) MBL-HSG,
Dr Alexander Isola MCJ (NYU)

CATEGORIES OF WORK

Corporate and commercial
All partners

Mergers and acquisitions
Martin Maxl, Ferdinand Graf

Intellectual property
Ferdinand Graf

Unfair competition
Ferdinand Graf

Antitrust
Ferdinand Graf

Media
Nikolaus Pitkowitz

Real estate
Martin Maxl, Nikolaus Pitkowitz

Eastern Europe (joint venture and privatisation)
Nikolaus Pitkowitz

Infrastructure
Otto Waechter

Telecoms
Ferdinand Graf, Otto Waechter

Arbitration
Nikolaus Pitkowitz

Litigation
Nikolaus Pitkowitz

Food law
Martin Maxl

Distribution law
Martin Maxl

Insolvency and restructuring
Alexander Isola

Project finance
Otto Waechter

Public procurement
Otto Waechter

HAARMANN HÜGEL ATTORNEYS AT LAW

IN CO-OPERATION WITH HAARMANN HEMMELRATH

ARES-TOWER
DONAU-CITY-STRASSE 11
1220 VIENNA

Telephone: +43 1 260 50 0
Fax: +43 1 260 50 133
E-mail:
vienna@haarmannhemmelrath.com
Website: www.haarmannhuegel.com

Languages
Bulgarian, Croatian, Czech, Dutch, English, French, German, Hungarian, Italian, Japanese, Mandarin, Norwegian, Polish, Portuguese, Romanian, Russian, Slovak, Spanish, Vietnamese

Other offices
Berlin, Bielefeld, Brussels, Bucharest, Budapest, Cologne, Dusseldorf, Frankfurt, Hamburg, Leipzig, London, Moscow, Milan, Munich, Paris, Prague, Rome, Shanghai, Stuttgart, Singapore, Tokyo, Warsaw

Number of lawyers 281
at this office 26

CATEGORIES OF WORK

Commercial law (general)
Univ Prof Dr Hanns F Hügel,
Mag René Schneider

Company law, M&A
Univ Prof Dr Hanns F Hügel,
Dr Florian Gibitz

Tax law
Univ Prof Dr Hanns F Hügel,
Dr Clemens Hasenauer

Banking
Dr Florian Gibitz, Dr Gregor Schett

Labour law
Mag René Schneider, Dr Florian Gibitz

Competition – antitrust, distribution law
Dr Rainer Roniger, Dr Astrid Ablasser

Litigation
Dr Gregor Schett, Mag Dominik Leiter

EU law, public procurement, energy
Dr Rainer Roniger,
Dr Christian Schneider

Real estate
Mag René Schneider

Intellectual property law, media law
Mag Dominik Leiter

Public law, environment
Dr Christian Schneider

Capital markets
Univ Prof Dr Hanns F Hügel,
Dr Clemens Hasenauer

HASCH & PARTNER ANWALTSGESELLSCHAFT MBH

BÖRSEGASSE 12
1010 VIENNA

Telephone: +43 1 532 12 70
Fax: +43 1 532 12 70 230
E-mail: wien@hasch.co.at
Website: www.hasch.co.at

Languages
Czech, English, French, Russian

Other offices
Ceske Budejovice, Linz, Graz, Prague

Number of lawyers 31
at this office 7

Contacts
Dr Alexander Hasch, Dr Franz Guggenberger, Dr Kurt-Heinrich Wolfmair, Mag Thomas Riedler, Mag Veronika Feichtinger-Burgstaller, Mag Wilhelm Deutschmann, Mag Joachim J Janezic, Mag Robert Schgör, Dr Gerhard Hochedlinger, Dr Wolfgang Luschin LLM, Dr Gerald Amandowitsch

CATEGORIES OF WORK

- Corporate and commercial
- Banking and secured financing
- Capital markets and IPOs
- Liquidation and reorganisation
- Corporate law
- Tax law
- Private client, trusts and estates
- Trade and distribution
- Antitrust and EC competition law
- Intellectual property and unfair competition
- Tort and product liability
- Administrative law and public tendering
- Litigation and dispute resolution
- Labour and employment
- Criminal law (tax disputes and white-collar crime)
- Real estate
- Environmental law
- Internet and e-commerce

HAUSER PARTNERS RECHTSANWÄLTE GMBH

RECHTSANWALTSKANZLEI, ATTORNEYS AT LAW PC

SEILERSTÄTTE 18–20
1010 VIENNA

Telephone: +43 1 512 29 00 14
Fax: +43 1 513 77 42
E-mail: hauser@hauserpartners.com
Website: www.hauserpartners .com

Languages
English, French, German

Number of lawyers 7

Contacts
Dr Wulf Gordian Hauser LLM (admitted in Austria, New York and Washington DC); Dr Kordula Fleiß (admitted in Austria); Dr Mathias Ettel (admitted in Austria); Mag Peter Blaschke (admitted in Austria); Associate: Mag Jan Gruszkiewicz LLM (admitted in Austria); Mag Bernhard Priemayer (admitted in Austria)

CATEGORIES OF WORK

- Mergers and acquisitions
- Corporate and commercial
- International commercial arbitration and litigation
- Antitrust and competition
- Commercial real estate
- Banking and finance
- International transactions and joint ventures
- Foreign investment in Austria and central and eastern Europe
- Distribution and agency
- Labour
- Foundations and trusts

HAUSMANINGER HERBST RECHTSANWÄLTE GMBH

FRANZ JOSEFS-KAI 3
1010 VIENNA

Telephone: +43 1 513 95 40
Fax: +43 1 513 95 40 12
E-mail: office@hhw.at
Website: www.hhw.at

Languages
English, French, German, Italian

Number of lawyers 25

CATEGORIES OF WORK

Banking and finance
Christian Hausmaninger, Christoph Herbst

Commercial and company law
Christian Hausmaninger, Mark Kletter

Mergers and acquisitions
Christian Hausmaninger, Mark Kletter

EU and merger control
Christoph Herbst, Mark Kletter

Arbitration
Christian Hausmaninger

Corporate governance
Christian Hausmaninger, Mark Kletter

Litigation
Robert Leitner, Jürgen Zouplna

Capital markets
Christian Hausmaninger, Mark Kletter

Public procurement
Claus Casati, Christoph Herbst

Labour law
Jürgen Zouplna

Energy law
Christoph Herbst

Competition law
Claus Casati, Christoph Herbst

LANSKY, GANZGER & PARTNER
RECHTSANWÄLTE GMBH

ROTENTURMSTRAßE 29/9
1010 WIEN

Telephone: +43 1 533 33 300
Fax: +43 1 532 84 83
E-mail: office@lansky.at
Website: www.lansky.at

Languages
English, German

Other offices
Sarajevo

Number of lawyers 29
at this office 26

Contacts
Dr Gabriel Lansky, Dr Gerald Ganzger

Member
Euro Defi

CATEGORIES OF WORK

Administrative

Banking and finance

Capital markets

Commercial property, real estate

Competition and state aids

Construction

Corporate and commercial

Dispute resolution – litigation and arbitration

Employment

Energy and natural resources

Environment

Foreign direct investment

Fraud and white-collar crime

Information technology

Infrastructure and project finance – public-private partnerships

Insolvency, corporate restructuring

Insurance

Intellectual property

Media and entertainment

Mergers and acquisitions

Private client

Privatisation

Public procurement

Regulatory

Tax

Telecommunications

LOVELLS

IN ASSOCIATION WITH MONDL, TRUMMER, THOMAS & PARTNERS RECHTSANWÄLTE GmbH

GRABEN 29A
1010 WIEN
(SPRECHSTELLE)

Telephone: +43 1 53 55 744
Fax: +43 1 53 50 649
E-mail: information@lovells.com
Website: www.lovells.com

Languages
English

Other offices
Alicante, Amsterdam, Beijing, Berlin, Brussels, Budapest*, Chicago, Düsseldorf, Frankfurt, Hamburg, Ho Chi Minh City, Hong Kong, London, Milan, Moscow, Munich, New York, Paris, Prague, Rome, Shanghai, Singapore, Tokyo, Warsaw, Zagreb*

Number of lawyers 1,600
at this office 8

Contact
Dr Thomas Mondl

CATEGORIES OF WORK

Mergers and acquisitions

Banking, securities and finance

Commercial law (general)

Competition, antitrust

Companies, corporations

Contract

Construction, building

EC law

Trade marks, intellectual property

Arbitration and litigation

NEUDORFER GRIENSTEIDL HAHNKAMPER STAPF & PARTNER

ESSLINGGASSE 9
1010 VIENNA

Telephone: +43 1 536 50
Fax: +43 1 536 50 12
E-mail: officewien@aaa–law.at
Website: www.aaa–law.at/wien

Languages
Croatian, English, German, Italian, Spanish

Other offices
Graz*, Salzburg*

Number of lawyers 15

Member
In association with Kaan Cronenberg & Partner (Graz); Pallauf Pullmann Meissnitzer & Partner (Salzburg) – AAA Austrian Advocates Alliance

International groupings
IAG International; DIRO Eine Europäische Rechtanwaltsorganisation

CATEGORIES OF WORK

Banking and finance, capital markets and securities
Helmut Neudorfer, Michael Steiner

Mergers and acquisitions
Wolfgang Hahnkamper, Michael Steiner

Distribution, trade agencies and franchising
Wolfgang Hahnkamper

Antitrust, unfair competition
Stephan Probst

Liability and insurance
Klaus Voithofer, Wolfgang Zacherl

Employment and labour
Wolfgang Hahnkamper

EU law, tenders
Klaus Voithofer

Insolvency and restructuring
Christof Stapf, Michael Neuhauser

Debt collection
Wolfgang Zacherl, Michael Steiner

Property and agriculture
Stephan Probst

Food and drug law
Michael Neuhauser

Foundations, inheritance and wills (private client)
Helmut Neudorfer

Media
Stephan Probst

Commercial litigation
(all partners)

Cross-border litigation/arbitration
Wolfgang Hahnkamper

IP, patent and trade mark, licensing and copyright
Helmut Neudorfer

ORTNER PÖCH FORAMITTI
RECHTSANWÄLTE GMBH

STRAUCHGASSE 1-3
1010 VIENNA

Telephone: +43 1 535 37 21
Fax: +43 1 533 15 55
E-mail: office@opf.at
Website: www.opf.at

Languages
English, French, Spanish

Number of lawyers 9

Contacts
Dr Peter Pöch, Dr Michael Krassnigg, Dr Marie Helen Pichler, Dr Heinz Rindler, Mag Katrin Hanschitz

CATEGORIES OF WORK

Banking law, securities
Dr P Pöch, Dr H Rindler

Corporate law
Dr M Krassnigg, Dr H Rindler

Energy, deregulatory
Dr P Pöch, Dr H Rindler

Litigation
Mag K Hanschitz

Investment funds
Dr MH Pichler, Dr P Pöch

M&A
Dr H Rindler, Dr M Krassnigg

Copyright, media, software
Dr P Pöch, Dr MH Pichler

Arbitration
Dr P Pöch

Trade marks
Dr MH Pichler

Project, asset and structured finance
Dr M Krassnigg, Dr H Rindler

Aviation
Dr H Rindler, Mag K Hanschitz

Antitrust
Dr P Pöch, Dr M Krassnigg

Unfair competition, advertising
Dr P Pöch, Dr MH Pichler

EU law
Dr M Krassnigg, Dr P Pöch

Telecommunications, e-commerce
Dr MH Pichler

Capital markets, regulatory
Dr P Pöch, Dr H Rindler

Venture capital, private equity
Dr M Krassnigg, Mag K Hanschitz

PRESLMAYR ATTORNEYS AT LAW

DR KARL LUEGER-RING 12
1010 VIENNA

Telephone: +43 1 533 16 95
Fax: +43 1 535 56 86
E-mail: office@preslmayr.at
Website: www.preslmayr.at

Languages
English, French, German, Italian

Number of lawyers 24

Member
TAGlaw; ICC

CATEGORIES OF WORK

Companies, corporations
Dr Rainer Herzig,
Dr Martin Bartlmä

Mergers and acquisitions
Dr Martin Preslmayr, Dr Karl Preslmayr

Venture capital, private equity
Dr Martin Preslmayr

Antitrust and competition
Mag Dieter Hauck, Dr Rainer Herzig

EU law
Mag Dieter Hauck, Dr Rainer Herzig

Banking, securities, finance
Dr Karl Preslmayr,
Dr Florian Gehmacher

Public procurement
Mag Dieter Hauck, Dr Raymond Madl

Contract
Dr Karl Preslmayr, Mag Erland Pirker

Telecommunications
Mag Dieter Hauck, Dr Rainer Knyrim

Advertising
Dr Rainer Herzig, Dr Karl Preslmayr

Arbitration and litigation
Dr Karl Preslmayr, Dr Martin Preslmayr

Insolvency
Dr Florian Gehmacher,
Dr Matthias Schmidt

Food and drug law
Dr Rainer Herzig

Employment, labour
Dr Karl Preslmayer,
Dr Barbara Kurz

Trade marks, intellectual property
Dr Rainer Herzig, Dr Karl Preslmayr

Data protection
Dr Rainer Knyrim

SAXINGER CHALUPSKY WEBER & PARTNERS

RECHTSANWÄLTE GmbH

RATHAUSPLATZ 4
1010 VIENNA

Telephone: +43 1 427 2000
Fax: +43 1 427 2010
E-mail: vienna@scwp.at
Website: www.scwp.at

Languages
Czech, English, French, German, Italian, Russian, Spanish

Other offices
Graz, Linz., Pilsen, Prague, Wels

Number of lawyers 51
at this office 12

CATEGORIES OF WORK

Administrative law
Markus Nußbaumer

Antitrust
Wolfgang Lauss, Karl Weinhäupl

Arbitration
Eduard Saxinger

Banking and secured financing
Stefan Weber, Franz Mittendorfer

Capital markets
Stefan Weber

Commercial and company law
Ernst Chalupsky, Gerald Schmidsberger

Corporate law
Wolfgang Lauss, Gerald Schmidsberger

Cross-border leases
Franz Mittendorfer, Dietmar Huemer

Energy and environmental law
Markus Nußbaumer

EU and competition law
Stefan Weber, Karl Weinhäupl

Insolvency and restructurings
Ernst Chalupsky, Alexander Anderle

Labour and industrial relations
Johannes Blätterbinder

Litigation and dispute resolution
Eduard Saxinger, Daniela Witt-Dörring

Mergers and acquisitions
Wolfgang Lauss, Gerald Schmidsberger

Tax law
Werner Minihold

Intellectual property
Peter Baumann, Maximilian Gumpoldsberger

Public private partnerships
Stefan Weber, Franz Mittendorfer

Public procurement
Franz Mittendorfer, Dietmar Huemer

Real estate and construction
Eduard Saxinger, Daniela Witt-Dörring

THE FIRM

Saxinger Chalupsky Weber & Partners is one of the leading Austrian law firms. Its lawyers are highly specialised and committed to the highest standards of legal service and proficiency.

The firm resulted from a merger of three leading Austrian firms, the roots of which date back to 1919. On the basis of its longstanding tradition, Saxinger Chalupsky Weber & Partners offers legal services in all areas of law relevant to businesses. Through its offices in Vienna, Linz, Wels and Graz, as well as Pargue and Pilsen, the firm is in the unique position to directly cover the most important Austrian and Czech industrial regions, locally-connected to the relevant authorities.

The firm's approach is creative and pragmatic, helping its clients to assess and effectively manage legal risks and to find practical solutions in the relevant legal, business and, when necessary, political environments.

Saxinger Chalupsky Weber & Partners has extensive experience in the legal management of projects in Austria and in foreign jurisdictions. Partners of the firm have authored numerous articles and books on domestic and international business law, and they teach in leading European law schools. They are regularly consulted by the Austrian legislature on legislative matters.

AREAS OF PRACTICE

Partners of Saxinger Chalupsky Weber & Partners are leading experts in their areas of law. Saxinger Chalupsky Weber & Partners provides legal services in all areas of law relevant to businesses and, in particular, when clearance with public authorities is necessary. Services range from general advice on legal matters to conducting complex national and international transactions.

In addition to their experience in Austria, the firm's lawyers have practised, studied or trained abroad. Their areas of specialisation include corporate and commercial matters, mergers and acquisitions involving special financial structures and multi-jurisdictional issues, corporate finance, securities (public offerings), banking and financial services, energy law, production facilities and business permits, environmental law, insolvency, inward investments, privatisation projects, litigation and arbitration

Saxinger Chalupsky Weber & Partners advises Austrian and foreign, large and medium-sized, public and private companies, as well as Austrian and international governments and governmental organisations.

The firm's partners have a wide range of experience in providing legal advice in the implementation of cross-border transactions, as well as in the structuring and legal co-ordination of companies' activities in foreign countries. Through its network of excellent partner firms, Saxinger Chalupsky Weber & Partners regularly assists clients in their business strategies throughout Central and Eastern Europe.

International companies who operate businesses or branches or provide services directly in Austria can rely on comprehensive legal services through the firm's offices in Austria's primary industrial regions.

SCHÖNHERR RECHTSANWÄLTE

TUCHLAUBEN 17
1010 WIEN

Telephone: +43 1 53 43 70
Fax: +43 1 53 43 76 100
E-mail: office@schoenherr.at
Website: www.schoenherr.at

Languages
English, French, Italian

Other offices
Belgrade, Brussels, Bucharest, Ljubljana, Zagreb

Number of lawyers 96
at this office 71

CATEGORIES OF WORK

Antitrust and competition
Hanno Wollmann

Public law, regulatory
Christian Schmelz

Companies, corporations, tax
Hellwig Torggler, Peter Feyl

Corporate reorganisations
Stephan Frotz

Mergers and acquisitions
Christian Herbst, Christoph Lindinger

EU law
Hanno Wollmann

Banking, securities and finance
Peter Feyl, Stephan Frotz

Real estate, construction
Peter Madl, Thomas Wenger

Contract and commercial law
Peter Madl, Thomas Wenger

Employment, labour
Gerold Zeiler

Media, unfair competition
Guido Kucsko, Christian Hauer

Tax
Peter Feyl

Trade marks, intellectual property
Christian Hauer, Guido Kucsko

Arbitration and litigation
Hellwig Torggler, Gerold Zeiler

THE FIRM

Schönherr Rechtsanwälte was founded in 1950 and is one of the leading law firms in Austria. It is also among Austria's largest law firms with 25 partners and over 70 other fee-earners. The firm has offices in Vienna, Brussels, Belgrade, Bucharest, Ljubljana and Zagreb.

AREAS OF PRACTICE

The firm is a full-service commercial and corporate law firm covering all areas of corporate, civil and commercial law. Principal areas include corporate, banking, international transactions, (cross-border) M&A, privatisations, capital markets, intellectual property, unfair competition, antitrust, public, including environmental law, labour law, EU law, media, information technology, telecoms, energy, commercial litigation and arbitration.

The firm serves international and Austrian corporate clients ranging from US-based and international corporations and their Austrian subsidiaries, large and medium-sized enterprises to governmental agencies. Clients come from the financial, industrial and service sectors including banking, insurance, information technology, media, food, pharmaceuticals, energy, construction, automotive, and paper and packaging.

The firm's first priority is to provide top quality efficient and responsive legal work to its international and Austrian clients.

SCHRAMM PARTNER RECHTSANWÄLTE

BARTENSTEINGASSE 2
1010 WIEN

Telephone: +43 1 409 76 09
Fax: +43 1 409 76 09 30
E-mail: kanzlei@schramm-partner.at
Website: www.schramm-partner.at

Languages
English, French, German

Number of lawyers 14

CATEGORIES OF WORK

Public procurement
Dr Johannes Schramm,
Dr Matthias Öhler

Privatisation
Dr Johannes Schramm,
Mag Horst Fössl

Subsidies
Dr Johannes Schramm,
Dr Georg Zellhofer

EC law and competition
Dr Matthias Öhler,
Dr Johannes Schramm

Administrative law
Mag Horst Fössl

Contracts and commercial
Mag Alexander Singer,
Mag Bernd Jahnel

Corporate
Mag Alexander Singer

SIEMER-SIEGL-FÜREDER & PARTNER

DOMINIKANERBASTEI 10
1010 WIEN

Telephone: + 43 1 512 14 45
Fax: + 43 1 513 79 84
E-mail: office@ra-siefur.at
Website: www.ra-siefur.at

Languages
English, French

Number of lawyers 15

Contact
Hannes Füreder, Markus Fellner

Member
MERITAS

CATEGORIES OF WORK

M&A, corporate and commercial law, trusts and foreign investments
Hannes Füreder, Markus Fellner

Public procurement
Michael Breitenfeld

Public law, government business, regulatory, telecommunications
Michael Breitenfeld, Markus Fellner

Litigation, arbitration and mediation
Heinrich Siegl, Gerald Gries

Unfair competition
Heinrich Siegl, Reinhard Brunar

Real estate and construction
Reinhard Brunar, Mario Schiavon

Aviation law
Hannes Füreder, Gerald Gries

Transport law
Hannes Füreder, Gerald Gries

Banking, securities and finance
Hannes Füreder, Markus Fellner

Competition and antitrust
Markus Fellner

Distribution, franchise and commercial agents
Hannes Füreder, Markus Fellner

EU law
Markus Fellner

Labour and employment law
Hannes Füreder, Gerald Gries

Industrial and IP, IT and media law
Reinhard Brunar

Biotechnology law
Mario Schiavon, Reinhard Brunar

WOLF THEISS
ATTORNEYS AT LAW

SCHUBERTRING 6
1010 VIENNA

Telephone: +43 1 515 10
Fax: +43 1 515 10 25
E-mail: wien@wolftheiss.com
Website: www.wolftheiss.com

Languages
Czech, English, French, German, Hungarian, Italian, Spanish

Other offices
Prague, Belgrade, Bratislava, Ljubljana, Zagreb

Number of lawyers 98
at this office 69

Contacts
Markus Heidinger, Christian Hoenig, Peter Oberlechner, Andreas Schmid, Richard Wolf

CATEGORIES OF WORK

- Antitrust and competition
- Corporate and M&A
- Banking, capital markets, securities, project finance, investment funds
- Litigation and arbitration
- Employment and labour
- Tax and insurance
- Real estate, construction and leases
- Distribution and franchising
- IP and trade marks
- Infrastructure
- Contracts and commercial
- European law
- Telecoms and energy
- Public procurement
- Pharmaceuticals
- Eastern Europe

THE FIRM

Wolf Theiss, founded in 1957, stands among the leading law firms in Central Europe, with a concentration on Austrian, European and international business law, and additional expertise in the legal regimes of Central and Eastern Europe.

At its six locations, in Vienna, Prague, Belgrade, Bratislava, Ljubljana and Zagreb, a total of 200 people, including 98 lawyers (42 of whom are partners), work for Austrian and international client companies in industry, trade and services, as well as banking and insurance. At the point of contact between law and business, Wolf Theiss develops innovative solutions on the basis of legal, tax and business know-how.

BAHRAIN

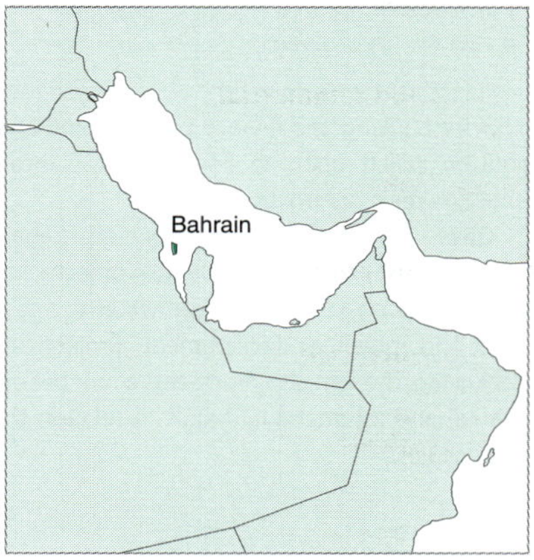

Population	667,238
Number of lawyers	n/a
Professional title	Advocate
Currency	Bahraini Dinar (BD)

Index

The Middle East Kingdom of Bahrain is an archipelago made up of 36 small islands in the Persian Gulf. About one-fifth of its inhabitants live in the capital, Manama, which is linked by road and causeway to Saudi Arabia.

Bahrain has undergone a prolonged period of constitutional reform since the Emir, Sheikh Hamad bin Isa Al Khalifa, came to power. He has presided over political and economic reforms, and attempted to improve relations between the Shia Muslims and the ruling Sunni minority. In 2002 Sheikh Hamad declared himself king and proposed that Bahrain should become a constitutional monarchy with an elected parliament and independent judiciary.

The country's bicameral legislature was reconstituted in October 2002. Bahrainis were able to vote in the first parliamentary elections for a lower house since the National Assembly had been dissolved in 1975.

With only modest oil reserves of its own, Bahrain acts as a regional hub for the shipping and refining of petroleum products. Now that local oil reserves are declining it has begun to diversify, particularly into financial services and tourism.

BILLING

The average hourly fee for lawyers in Bahrain ranges from €150 to €300 for an associate and €300 to €500 for a partner. Local clients often prefer lawyers to work for them on a capped or fixed-fee basis.

MARKETING

All of the international firms have websites, as well as individual email addresses for their partners and associates. Few local firms have an Internet presence although their use of email is growing.

IN-HOUSE LAWYERS

Large financial institutions and banks in Bahrain frequently employ in-house lawyers. Other commercial entities rarely do so.

ECONOMIC CLIMATE

Oil continues to be Bahrain's main source of revenue; petroleum revenues account for about 60% of government revenue and 65% of exports. Although the country has enjoyed a sound economy in recent years, unemployment, especially among the young, is an increasing problem.

The newly liberalised economy has helped turn Bahrain into an international finance centre, specialising in offshore banking. New commercial laws are coming into force to meet the WTO criteria of member states by 2005. It is hoped that this will attract more foreign investment into the country.

Other measures to boost the economy have been introduced in recent years. In 2003 a new law granted land and property ownership rights to non-Bahrainis in numerous areas in Manama and other parts of the country. There are also plans to allow foreign nationals to own 100% of any business by 2005.

Bahrain is negotiating to become the first Gulf state country to sign a Free Trade Agreement (FTA) with the US. The FTA would abolish customs duties between the two countries and establish Bahrain as a regional centre for the movement of North American goods. This is seen as a first step towards the creation of a Middle East Free Trade Area.

The relatively liberal social environment in Bahrain has made it a popular tourist destination in the region. A new draft law aims to protect the environment and Bahrain's growing tourism industry.

A law has been drafted to replace the Bahrain Monetary Agency (BMA) law of 1973. It will expand the BMA's authority to include stock exchange and insurance operations. To reflect this new role, the BMA will change its name to the Central Bank of Bahrain.

The country is continuing its commitment to privatisation. In mid-2003 it retained Ernst & Young as financial consultants for the proposed privatisation of Bahrain's electricity sector. As a result of the 2002 Telecommunications Law, the Bahrain telecoms company, Batelco has lost its monopoly over Internet services. New licences are now being offered to the private sector.

LEGAL MARKET

The Bahrain legal market has suffered in recent years. In 2002 some foreign firms closed their Manama offices, and **Norton Rose**'s decision to open in nearby Dubai in 2003 indicates that Bahrain is facing stiff competition for professional services.

Trowers & Hamlins continues its policy of attacking the Middle East market through a

The largest firms

1	Al Mahmood & Zu'Bi	9
2	Norton Rose	8
3	Qays H. Zu'bi, Attorneys & Legal Consultants	6
4	Hassan Radhi & Associates	5
	Taqi & Mohammad Ahmed	5
	Trowers & Hamlins	5
7	Baker & McKenzie	2
8	Reid Minty Middle East Legal Consultants	1

These figures represent the total number of lawyers in this country only, and have been supplied by the firms themselves. The figures should be accurate as at 1 January 2004.

patchwork of local offices, while **Baker & McKenzie** continues to thrive in nearby Saudi Arabia as well as Bahrain. Other firms that regularly work in Bahrain prefer to base their Middle East practices in the UAE; a notable one being **Clyde & Co**.

Qays H. Zu'bi, Attorneys & Legal Consultants continues its co-operation agreement with the Dubai Office of **Clifford Chance LLP**. **Clifford Chance LLP** has seconded Ayman Khaleq to the firm, with two further secondees expected by early 2004.

There have been a number of top-level changes among some of the international firms in Bahrain. In March 2003, Neale Downes joined **Trowers & Hamlins**, taking over Roger Clarke's role as head of the banking and finance practice. At **Norton Rose**, Carol Roberts took over from John Inglis as managing partner, her second posting in Bahrain. Meanwhile, Patrick Watson-Thorp joined the corporate department from the firm's London office.

The new laws aimed at encouraging foreign investment in Bahrain should lead to a growing need for legal advice from companies worldwide that are looking to invest in the country.

BANKING AND FINANCE

Bahrain has been regarded as the Middle East's financial capital for 30 years. It has the region's largest concentration of banks and other financial institutions, although the development of the UAE as a financial centre may affect work in the long term.

Norton Rose has a formidable client list in Bahrain, with a team of three lawyers dealing with banking and finance work. Carol Roberts returned to Bahrain in December 2002 to assume John Inglis's role as managing partner. Among several financings in the past year, she advised on the $500m sovereign bond issue by the Kingdom of Bahrain. Roberts also advised the Saudi National Commercial Bank as manager of the subscription by the Kingdom of Saudi Arabia of $700m floating rate notes issued by the Lebanese Republic. The firm also gave advice to a number of other banks, including Gulf International Bank as arranger of a $150m syndicated acquisition for an Omani borrower.

Baker & McKenzie's Bahrain office has a strong reputation for its banking and finance expertise. It advised a large, privately owned Saudi petrochemicals complex on a $280m loan.

Trowers & Hamlins advised a number of banks in 2003 and continues to act as retained counsel to the National Bank of Bahrain, providing advice on a full range of legal issues. The firm is led by Dominic O'Neil, who is widely recognised as a leading figure in the local banking and finance market. A client praised the 'very high quality' of the firm's work.

Both **Al Mahmood & Zu'Bi** and **Hassan Radhi & Associates** are well known for their excellent banking and finance practices and are regularly called upon to advise on the local aspects of major international deals.

Qays H. Zu'bi, Attorneys & Legal Consultants represented the Bahrain branch of a regional bank on a $62m bond connected to a gas plant and pipeline development project in Kazakhstan. The firm also represents a number of regional and international banks in relation to loan facilities.

BANKING AND FINANCE

NORTON ROSE

Baker & McKenzie
Trowers & Hamlins

Al Mahmood & Zu'Bi
Hassan Radhi & Associates
Qays H. Zu'bi, Attorneys & Legal Consultants ✪

Firms are listed A-Z in tiers which are ranked in order of priority
✪ Indicates firm displays contact details at the end of this chapter.

CORPORATE AND COMMERCIAL

Norton Rose works for major international clients, providing commercial advice on M&A, investment funds and private equity. The firm's regional presence was strengthened in September 2003 by the opening of a long-awaited Dubai office. Corporate head Zubair Mir continues to work for Kuwait Finance House, a leading Islamic investment bank in the Middle East, and is retained by the Bahrain Telecommunications Company (Batelco) to undertake all its corporate and commercial work. In 2003 this included advising a consortium led by Batelco on the acquisition of a mobile phone licence in Iraq. **Norton Rose** is also retained by Mellon Global Investments, and by retail group Fucom. It has worked on a number of investment funds, including advising the government of Iran on establishing the first-ever investment fund into Iran, which was structured to adhere to the principles of Islamic banking. The firm also advised Abraaj Capital, which is the first professional vehicle for an MBO investment into the Gulf region, with a target capitalisation of $150m.

Al Mahmood & Zu'Bi maintains its position as a top local firm for commercial work and inward investment, and partner Hugh Stokes is highly regarded for his work in the insurance and energy sectors. The firm regularly receives referral instructions from international law firms.

Hassan Radhi & Associates enjoys an excellent reputation for its corporate and commercial work. Name partner Hassan Radhi is widely respected.

Trowers & Hamlins has an excellent record in corporate and commercial work; partner Dominic O'Neil is noted in particular. In 2003 the firm acted for Group 4 Securitas on its acquisition of a

CORPORATE AND COMMERCIAL
NORTON ROSE
Al Mahmood & Zu'Bi
Hassan Radhi & Associates
Trowers & Hamlins
Baker & McKenzie
Qays H. Zu'bi, Attorneys & Legal Consultants ✪

Firms are listed A-Z in tiers which are ranked in order of priority
✪ Indicates firm displays contact details at the end of this chapter.

DISPUTE RESOLUTION
AL MAHMOOD & ZU'BI
HASSAN RADHI & ASSOCIATES
Haya Rashed Al Khalifa Law Firm
Norton Rose
Qays H. Zu'bi, Attorneys & Legal Consultants ✪

Firms are listed A-Z in tiers which are ranked in order of priority
✪ Indicates firm displays contact details at the end of this chapter.

PROJECT FINANCE
NORTON ROSE
Baker & McKenzie
Trowers & Hamlins
Qays H. Zu'bi, Attorneys & Legal Consultants ✪

Firms are listed A-Z in tiers which are ranked in order of priority
✪ Indicates firm displays contact details at the end of this chapter.

controlling interest in a security services company. **Trowers & Hamlins** continues to provide ongoing advice to the company on contractual and regulatory matters. The firm also advises a number of regional and multinational corporations on restructuring, registration and distribution agreements.

Baker & McKenzie has an eminent corporate practice in Saudi Arabia and a good record on large-scale regional transactions. In 2003 the firm advised a leading US manufacturer in connection with the financial lease of a commercial aircraft to a Bahrain-based company.

Qays H. Zu'bi, Attorneys & Legal Consultants has a thriving association with **Clifford Chance LLP**, and in 2003 represented a Bahrain government body in connection with negotiating promoters and television rights related to the staging of the Bahrain Grand Prix. The firm was also involved in the drafting of the Telecommunications Law.

DISPUTE RESOLUTION

International firms are not permitted to represent clients in local courts unless they employ a lawyer of Bahraini origin. As a result of the regulations that control rights of audience in Bahraini courts, restricting them to locally qualified lawyers, local firms continue to dominate in litigation while the international firms are better known for their banking and corporate transactions.

Al Mahmood & Zu'Bi is considered to have a very strong litigation practice. It has represented several international corporations in proceedings. International firms in Bahrain often refer litigation work to **Al Mahmood & Zu'Bi**.

Hassan Radhi & Associates and **Haya Rashed Al Khalifa Law Firm** are highly regarded by both local and international law firms for litigation.

Abdullah Mutawi is the head of **Norton Rose**'s dispute resolution department. He joined the GCC Commercial Arbitration Centre's panel of arbitrators in 2001. **Norton Rose** acted for Bahrain-based Shamil Bank in the Commercial Court in London on a successful $50m claim brought by the bank against a Bangladeshi conglomerate. This was the largest Islamic finance dispute to be litigated to date and set a precedent for banks wishing to transact according to shari'a principles while also being governed by English law. The firm also acts for a number of companies on insurance issues and public liability policy.

Qays H. Zu'bi, Attorneys & Legal Consultants is experienced in both domestic and international disputes. The firm handles litigation for the Dubai office of **Clifford Chance LLP**.

ISLAMIC FINANCE

The most significant development in the legal market for 2003 has been the rapid growth of the Islamic finance market. The year saw many firms acting on complex Islamically financed transactions. Furthermore, the integration of Islamic tranches in projects is becoming increasingly common.

Norton Rose maintains an excellent record in Islamic finance, and has an eminent Islamic finance practice in London. Nadim Khan leads the Islamic finance practice in Bahrain and is one of the leading Islamic banking and finance lawyers in the region. In 2003 the firm advised a Bahrain-based bank on facilities connected to a Brazilian entity for the acquisition of oil and petroleum products. The firm also advised on a $250m Islamic facility as part of its work for the Aluminium Bahrain Line 5 expansion financing.

Qays H. Zu'bi, Attorneys & Legal Consultants has a leading Islamic banking and investment practice. The firm served as legal counsel to a leading Islamic bank and an international fund manager in connection with a $100m Islamic private equity fund which will invest in New Zealand and Australia.

Baker & McKenzie's lawyers have extensive experience of general banking and finance, including Islamic finance. In 2003 they advised a leading regional bank on a shari'a-compliant home ownership scheme.

Trowers & Hamlins has also advised clients on compliance with shari'a law, both from Bahrain and its other offices in the region and in London.

ISLAMIC FINANCE
NORTON ROSE
Qays H. Zu'bi, Attorneys & Legal Consultants ✪
Baker & McKenzie
Trowers & Hamlins

Firms are listed A-Z in tiers which are ranked in order of priority
✪ Indicates firm displays contact details at the end of this chapter.

PROJECT FINANCE

The Aluminium Bahrain Bond was one of the largest financings in the Middle East in 2003. It integrates conventional loans, bonds and both Islamic and ECA financing. A number of international and local firms have been providing advice on either side of the transaction.

Norton Rose continued to advise Aluminium Bahrain in relation to the $1.5bn financing of its Line 5 expansion. The firm advised on Saudi Arabia's first privatisation of power and water utilities, drafting a shari'a-compliant $2.2bn capital lease. It also acted for a number of other corporations on power projects. The firm also advised ANZ Investment Bank on project financing worth $600m.

Baker & McKenzie advised the bank syndicate on provision of the financing to Aluminium Bahrain. The firm also advised Arab Banking Corporation on the provision of a $1bn loan for the construction of a petrochemical plant in Jabail in Saudi Arabia.

Trowers & Hamlins is retained counsel to the $1.5bn IDB Infrastructure Fund. In 2003, the firm advised on the fund's $150m acquisition of a major shareholding in AES Oasis Limited, a new company which owns power and water generation plants in Oman and Pakistan. This was the first ever change of ownership in privately funded power and water assets in the Middle East region.

Qays H. Zu'bi, Attorneys & Legal Consultants acted as local counsel to the banking syndicate in connection with the Aluminium Bahrain bond.

SHIPPING

The Dubai office of **Clyde & Co** is involved in shipping work throughout the Middle East. This includes acting on behalf of Bahrain-based entities, particularly on marine insurance matters.

The Dubai office of **Hill Taylor Dickinson** represents shipping clients throughout the region, including Bahrain. It is well known for its maritime insurance practice and disputes work, and is currently representing shipyard ASRI in a major dispute.

Abdullah Mutawi of **Norton Rose** is a leading expert on international maritime labour law and trade union issues. In 2003 he advised a number of major shipowners and P&I clubs on insurance and labour law matters.

Other local and international firms offer maritime and shipping legal services. These include **Baker & McKenzie**; **Clifford Chance LLP**; **Hassan Radhi & Associates**; and **Haya Rashed Al Khalifa Law Firm**.

SHIPPING

CLYDE & CO

Hill Taylor Dickinson

Baker & McKenzie
Clifford Chance LLP
Norton Rose

Hassan Radhi & Associates
Haya Rashed Al Khalifa Law Firm

Firms are listed A-Z in tiers which are ranked in order of priority

QAYS H. ZU'BI, ATTORNEYS & LEGAL CONSULTANTS

IN CO-OPERATION WITH CLIFFORD CHANCE LLP

PO BOX 2397
MANAMA

Telephone: +973 17 538 600
Fax: +973 17 532 342
E-mail: qzubi@qayszubilaw.com
Website: www.qayszubilaw.com

Languages
Arabic, English, French

Other offices
Dubai

Number of lawyers 6

Member
International Bar Association; AIPPI; GCC Commercial Arbitration Centre

CATEGORIES OF WORK

Banking
Qays H Zu'bi, Chris Johnstone

Islamic finance structures
Qays H Zu'bi, Rasha Sabkar

Securities
Qays H Zu'bi, Chris Johnstone

Investment funds
Qays H Zu'bi

Company listing and formation
Qays H Zu'bi, Samer AmrO

Infrastructure
Qays H Zu'bi, Rasha Sabkar

Mergers and acquisitions
Qays H Zu'bi, Rasha Sabkar

Telecommunications
Qays H Zu'bi

Construction
Qays H Zu'bi, Chris Johnstone

Intellectual property
Qays H Zu'bi, Samer Amro

Joint ventures
Qays H Zu'bi, Samer Amro

Distribution and licensing
Qays H Zu'bi, Mamoon Eltayeb

Franchise and agencies
Qays H Zu'bi, Mamoon Eltayeb

Procurement and tenders
Qays H Zu'bi, Jihad Ghoury

Insurance
Qays H Zu'bi, Jihad Ghoury

Labour and employment
Qays H Zu'bi, Mamoon Eltayeb

Litigation and arbitration
Qays H Zu'bi, Mamoon Eltayeb

BELGIUM

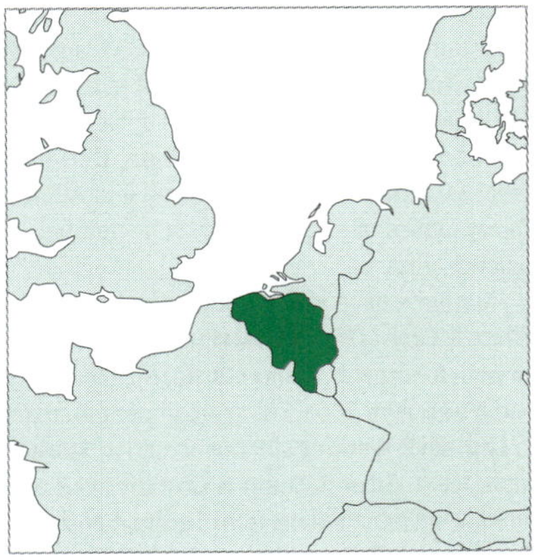

Population	10.4 million
Number of lawyers	13,050
Professional title	Avocat; advocaat
Currency	Euro (€)

Index

Belgium's economy, identity, and legal market are very closely linked to its status as the home to the institutions of the European Union. Its position as a central player in the drive towards greater integration masks the fact that Belgium is a devolved state, where regional governments have much power. Since 1993, the country has been split into three distinct regions: Brussels, Flanders and Wallonia, with a small German-speaking community in the east.

Under the current constitutional arrangements, there are six federal, regional and communal governments and even issues such as agriculture and trade promotion are the responsibility of the regions rather than a central state. In the context of legal services, this divide influences differences in structure, billing rates, client base and professional rules.

Flanders and Wallonia have quite different economies, with Flanders now dominating the national economy. Wallonia is home to more traditional and declining industries. Maritime and transport specialists are to be found in Antwerp, which is also an important hub for the diamond industry.

The most important economic development in recent years has been the announcement that the government intends to float about half the shares in Belgacom, which is valued at about €10bn. This is a courageous step, as there is little appetite for privatisation in Europe, especially of a telco. But Belgacom is well-run and not saddled with debt like many other operators are, having declined to invest in 3G licences. It could be Europe's largest flotation since Orange in 2001.

Belgium's relationship with the US has also hit the rocks in the last year. Attempts to use Belgium's now repealed laws covering crimes against humanity irritated Washington, to the extent that it may have caused prevarication over building a new Brussels Nato HQ.

BILLING

The diversity of firms in Brussels means it is difficult to generalise about billing. Cost and billing methods will vary between Belgian and international firms, and between EU and Belgian law matters.

Billing has become a sore point in many firms as the invasion of Anglo-Saxon firms has disrupted the status quo, and lawyers absorbed into international firms will have to bill so highly their local client base will desert them. General commercial law advice from a reputable Belgian law firm will cost the client between €200 to €250 for a partner, going up to around €370 for a senior partner. Quality advice in other commercial centres like Antwerp is not significantly less expensive. International firms usually charge similar rates to their home jurisdictions, and as such, prices could double. EU work done by both international and local firms is usually charged at a higher rate. Transfer and registration fees can also be added, as can the use of a notary to authenticate legal documents.

MARKETING

There are 29 Bars in Belgium, a mixture of French and Flemish-speaking, but all of them share a very restrictive approach. Brussels-based lawyers generally have to adhere to both the French and Belgian Bar rules, which restrict all forms of active marketing. Even brochures and websites have to be approved by the local Bar. Reform plans remain tentative and cautious, though some progress is being made.

IN-HOUSE LAWYERS

In-house lawyers are often referred to as *juristes* in French, a term used to describe legal professionals not fully-qualified as *avocats*. Most of the larger companies employ significant teams of *juristes* to handle day-to-day corporate housekeeping and some litigation in the lower courts. In-house lawyers can make written submissions to the higher courts, but are not members of the Bar. Major litigation, or difficult corporate deals, will require the services of an experienced lawyer.

LIMITING LIABILITY

Professional indemnity rules vary a great deal between individual Bars in Belgium, to the extent that some Bars do not require it at all. The Brussels Bar Association has an insurance policy, which members can subscribe to, usually as part of their annual Bar Council subscription fee. The premium is roughly €175. In Brussels, individual claims under the professional indemnity insurance cover are capped at €370,000, but policies can vary in the amount and extent of cover. Some policies do not cover fraud and misappropriation of funds, and the excess can vary a great deal. Clients should

The largest firms

1	Linklaters De Bandt	180
2	Allen & Overy	135
3	Lawfort	120
4	Loyens	112
	Stibbe	112
6	Liedekerke Wolters Waelbroeck Kirkpatrick	107
7	ELEGIS (Buyle Dieryck Maingain)	104
8	Coudert Brothers LLP – Coppens, Van Ommeslaghe & Faurès	102
9	Laga & Philippe	100
10	Freshfields Bruckhaus Deringer	93
11	DLA Caestecker	80
12	Baker & McKenzie	72
13	Janson, Baugniet	70
14	Cleary Gottlieb Steen & Hamilton	68
15	Eubelius	65
16	Claeys & Engels, member of ius laboris	63
	NautaDutilh	63
18	Monard – D'Hulst	62
19	Clifford Chance LLP	54
20	Van Bael & Bellis	50
21	Simont Braun	44
22	Van Eeckhoutte, Taquet & Clesse	42
23	Lontings & Partners	41
24	ALTIUS	40
	Tiberghien Advocaten	40

These figures represent the total number of lawyers in this country only, and have been supplied by the firms themselves. The figures should be accurate as at 1 January 2004.

check the policies if instructing a firm in an unfamiliar town.

A, B AND C LIST

Belgium's list system relates to the standing of individual lawyers, their rights of audience in court, and which individuals can advise on Belgian law.

Most Belgian lawyers are on the A list, which is for practising Belgian lawyers who are entitled to give advice on Belgian law and have full rights of audience in all courts except the Court of Cassation.

Non-Belgian lawyers can register on the B list, and can only advise on Belgian law in conjunction with an A-list lawyer. The activities of B-list lawyers are subject to the control of the Belgian Bar.

The C list is similar to the B list, but is a common list between the French and Flemish Bars in Brussels. Foreign lawyers are allowed to register, but the list has become increasingly unpopular.

However, Belgium is the heart of the EU and European law provides for the free movement of workers between member states. As such, lawyers from other member states must be admitted to the A list, but have to pass aptitude tests in practice areas where their training is different to that in Belgium. Unsurprisingly, these exams are difficult and few have passed.

COURT STRUCTURE

In civil law matters, the first court stage is one of the 27 courts of first instance in Belgium. The next stage up is one of the five courts of appeal. Finally, the highest domestic court before the European Court of Justice, is the Court of Cassation, or Supreme Court.

Only 20 lawyers in Belgium have rights of audience in the Court of Cassation, appointed by Royal Decree. Some of those individuals are listed in the **Dispute resolution** section of this chapter.

LEGAL MARKET

The structure of this chapter reflects the division between the legal markets operating in Belgium, taking both the domestic market and the EU market into account. There is a certain amount of overlap between the two and there are a number of firms active in both. Most of the international firms practise both domestic and EU law and certainly these firms tend to dominate the EU side.

In 2002, domestic firms experienced dramatic changes. **Liedekerke Wolters Waelbroeck Kirkpatrick** fragmented, its Antwerp office taken over by **Baker & McKenzie**, and several leading names joined **Ashurst** and **NautaDutilh**. Belgo-Dutch firm **Stibbe** also suffering significant losses, its alliance with UK firm **Herbert Smith** and German firm **Gleiss Lutz** leading to internal debates over strategy, and a host of departures. Both firms have fought back impressively in 2003.

Loyens built on its success in recruiting former **Linklaters De Bandt** managing partner Roel Nieuwdorp, with a substantial corporate team. In 2003, the firm opened a new Luxembourg office, established an IP practice, and took on more than 20 further lawyers from **Linklaters De Bandt** and the former *Bogaert & Vandemeulebroeke*.

International firms have enjoyed another successful year. **Linklaters De Bandt** remains the market leader in a number of fields but it is closely followed by **Freshfields Bruckhaus Deringer**, **Cleary Gottlieb Steen & Hamilton** and **Allen & Overy** which are all top-tier in a number of practice areas.

US firms have had a good year. **Jones Day**, **White & Case LLP** and **Shearman & Sterling LLP** all went for growth. **Wilmer Cutler Pickering LLP** had a turbulent 2002, losing a competition team to **Latham & Watkins LLP** but acquiring **Stibbe**'s trade team. **Gibson, Dunn & Crutcher LLP** also hired some practitioners from **Squire, Sanders & Dempsey L.L.P.**. **Oppenheimer Wolff & Donnelly LLP** hived off its local practice to focus on EU law, and a new firm **Olislaegers De Creus** has been formed in association with the Americans to handle local law.

A host of US firms have opened new offices in Belgium to focus on antitrust. **Latham & Watkins LLP** has entered the Brussels market for the first time, and like other newcomers **Shearman & Sterling LLP** and **Howrey Simon Arnold & White, LLP**, it is vying for its position in the market. Other parvenus in 2003 are **Willkie Farr & Gallagher LLP**, and **Arnold & Porter LLP**, which recruited Marleen Van Kerckhove from **Clifford Chance LLP**.

Sidley Austin Brown & Wood LLP opened in August 2003, recruiting a trade team from **Hogan & Hartson L.L.P.**, which also lost much of its local law capability as well over the summer.

One would expect such an influx of brilliant antitrust practices to send a shiver down the spines of those already in the city, but most of the settled players are optimistic that the US firms will be restricted to merger filings for their own clients. Unlike in the US, most European clients prefer to give competition work to larger international outfits than antitrust boutiques, and the timing looks unfortunate for the Americans as the Commission will farm out much competition work to a local level from next year, favouring those firms with a pan-European capability.

THE BIG FOUR

The success of one-stop-shops in Belgium came to a shuddering halt with Enron and new laws in Belgium designed to guarantee auditor independence. All the associations between accountants and law firms in Belgium have formally disintegrated, although it is currently unclear how much informal allegiance the firms will have with their old partners in the future.

Worst-hit was *Bogaert & Vandemeulebroeke*. As the alliance with **Landwell** collapsed, amongst others, name partner Geert Bogaert left for **Loyens**, leaving the firm in disarray. In November 2003 it re-launched as **Lawfort**.

Lontings & Partners, linked to KPMG; *Peeters Advocaten*, linked to Ernst & Young; and **Laga & Philippe**, linked to Deloitte & Touche, have all terminated their associations. Ernst & Young re-launched its legal practice as **EY Law**.

The biggest success story has been **DLA Caestecker**, the product of a merger in 2002 between *Andersen Legal* firm *Caestecker & Partners* and UK firm **DLA**, which has so far paid dividends.

AVIATION

Brussels does not have many specialist aviation lawyers but the sector is becoming more important for several firms.

Allen & Overy is not known as an aviation firm but has acted for Swiss Air on several matters; for KLM on several passenger claims under the Warsaw Convention; and for Saudi Arabian Airlines on whether it is subject to Belgian social security rules.

Catherine Erkelens handles IT as well as aviation at **Bird & Bird**, so much aviation work is IT-related, such as e-commerce and computer reservation systems. The firm created the Brussels Air Law Forum, and mainly deals with ground-handling for the likes of Lufthansa.

DLA Caestecker has recently been working on the Sabena bankruptcy.

Freshfields Bruckhaus Deringer has a very strong aircraft finance and leasing practice, working for International Lease Finance Corporation on the repossession of three aircraft leased to VG Airlines.

Liedekerke Wolters Waelbroeck Kirkpatrick acts for Brussels Airlines on general commercial matters as well as aviation law.

Wilmer Cutler Pickering LLP has a strong historical presence in aviation law in the US, and counts United Airlines amongst its clients.

AVIATION

- Allen & Overy ✪
- Bird & Bird ✪
- DLA Caestecker ✪
- Freshfields Bruckhaus Deringer ✪
- Liedekerke Wolters Waelbroeck Kirkpatrick ✪
- Wilmer Cutler Pickering LLP ✪

Firms are listed A-Z

✪ Indicates firm displays contact details at the end of this chapter.

BANKING, FINANCE AND CAPITAL MARKETS

Allen & Overy has built a top-tier finance practice in Brussels, even though *Loeff Claeys Verbeke* was a corporate firm. In 2003 it acted for Barclays Capital on the financing of the acquisition of Ontex by Candover, Belgium's largest LBO.

Clifford Chance LLP undertakes lots of plain syndicated loans, with experience on the more sophisticated matters as well. It is one of the few firms to handle securitisation, and is also very active on Belgian equity offerings. It will be Belgian counsel to the global co-ordinators (Goldman Sachs, Morgan Stanley, Lehman Brothers, UBS, Dexia and KBC) on the IPO of Belgacom. Yves Herinckx is a very well-respected practitioner.

Ivan Peeters of **Freshfields Bruckhaus Deringer** is one of the country's top names for finance. The firm enjoyed award-winning equity work in 2002, and is also pioneering international securitisation work in Belgium. It is acting for HeidelbergCement on various rights issues and delistings.

Linklaters de Bandt has broad finance capability, acting on loans for the likes of Bank of America, KBC Bank and UBS.

Baker & McKenzie undertakes much advice to Fortis Bank on various loans; and is Belgian counsel to Argenta Spaarbank on a securitisation

Coudert Brothers LLP – Coppens, Van Ommeslaghe & Faurès does a lot of banking work in Ghent for the likes of ING, BNP Paribas. Pierre Van Ommeslaghe is a good lawyer.

A good choice for local matters, **NautaDutilh** is close to ING, and is local counsel to Euroclear Bank. Marc van der Haegen is an expert on regulatory banking matters, and Benoit Feron is also a respected name.

Stibbe is regularly instructed by ABN Amro, and in 2003 also advised UBS on establishing operations in Belgium. Another major piece of work was advising Industrial Commercial Bank of China on the takeover and restructuring of Fortis Bank in Hong Kong.

ELEGIS (Buyle Dieryck Maingain)'s Jean-Pierre Buyle has a good banking practice, acting for many local banks on advice and litigation.

Willkie Farr & Gallagher LLP's Xavier Dieux is a high-profile name in the finance field, especially disputes.

Liedekerke Wolters Waelbroeck Kirkpatrick acted for Credibe on the €2.8bn sale of its mortgage portfolio, part of the ongoing privatisation process the firm has been involved in for some time.

A new addition is **Loyens**, which has worked hard in recent years to build credible finance capability. Antwerp-based Wilfrid Goris heads the department, which has experience in aircraft finance and cross-border insolvency.

Another new name in the list is **Simont Braun**. One group of partners led by banking star Lucien Simont has joined forces with *Braun Bigwood* to create a new firm called **Simont Braun**, which will focus on corporate, banking, IP, competition and commercial arbitration.

BANKING, FINANCE AND CAPITAL MARKETS

- ALLEN & OVERY ✪
- CLIFFORD CHANCE LLP
- FRESHFIELDS BRUCKHAUS DERINGER ✪
- LINKLATERS DE BANDT ✪

- Baker & McKenzie ✪
- Coudert Brothers LLP – Coppens, Van Ommeslaghe & Faurès ✪
- NautaDutilh ✪
- Stibbe ✪

- ALTIUS ✪
- Cleary Gottlieb Steen & Hamilton ✪
- ELEGIS (Buyle Dieryck Maingain) ✪
- Eubelius
- Lawfort ✪
- Willkie Farr & Gallagher LLP ✪

- Hunton & Williams ✪
- Liedekerke Wolters Waelbroeck Kirkpatrick ✪
- Loyens ✪
- Simont Braun ✪

Firms are listed A-Z in tiers which are ranked in order of priority

✪ Indicates firm displays contact details at the end of this chapter.

CORPORATE AND COMMERCIAL: ANTWERP

Antwerp is a very important industrial and commercial centre, accounting for a significant proportion of Belgium's GDP. Flanders has its own government and parliament, and the city is also home to important insurance clients such as ING. Several international firms have offices there, and tend to use Antwerp as an extension of their Brussels' office.

Allen & Overy's managing partner Wim Dejonghe is one of Belgium's heavyweight corporate stars, and the office works seamlessly with Brussels.

Linklaters de Bandt focuses on corporate work in Antwerp, with top names Jean-Pierre Blumberg and Jan van Lancker receiving strong peer and client recommendation.

Baker & McKenzie has settled well after taking **Liedekerke Wolters Waelbroeck Kirkpatrick**'s Antwerp office in 2002, including IT partner Koen De Winter; environmental expert Pascal Mallien; and corporate finance partner Jan Cerfontaine.

Coudert Brothers LLP – Coppens, Van Ommeslaghe & Faurès has three partners in Antwerp: Alexandre Diercxsens; Francis Marck; and Bernard Insel. The office does a lot of insurance, such as for AXA, and also maritime and transport law.

CORPORATE AND COMMERCIAL: ANTWERP

ALLEN & OVERY ✪
LINKLATERS DE BANDT

Baker & McKenzie ✪
Coudert Brothers LLP – Coppens, Van Ommeslaghe & Faurès
ELEGIS (Buyle Dieryck Maingain) ✪
ELEGIS (Huybrechts Engels Craen and Partners) ✪
Loyens
Roosendaal Keyzer

Firms are listed A-Z in tiers which are ranked in order of priority
✪ Indicates firm displays contact details at the end of this chapter.

Also prominent in transport and shipping is **ELEGIS (Buyle Dieryck Maingain)**, led by partner Hugo Callens.

Antwerp is home to **Loyens**' litigation practice, headed by Martine De Roeck. Wilfred Goris is also a well-known commercial lawyer.

Roosendaal Keyzer is better known for shipping, but has experience of more mainstream commercial matters as well. Partners Dirk Berckmans and Peter Buntinx are recommended.

CORPORATE AND COMMERCIAL: BRUSSELS

Allen & Overy's entry into the market has been very successful, with fewer departures than other Magic Circle firms. Some 26 partners and 125 associates handle all types of big-ticket commercial work, and are especially good on banking and finance. In 2003 the firm acted for Barclays Capital in the largest LBO ever in Belgium; and also for Koramic Building Product on the sale of a 50% stake in its subsidiary Koramic Roofing.

Linklaters de Bandt is an exceptionally good full-service firm, outstanding on corporate and finance, especially major M&A. It has a history acting on flotations, having worked on Interbrew and Agfa, and will act for Belgacom on its offering. With 150 local lawyers and 30 EU practitioners, the firm has downsized after its merger, but the biggest hitters are still there: Jean-Marie Nelissen Grade, Jean-Pierre Blumberg and Paul Van Hooghten.

Ashurst goes up in the rankings this year for its strength in M&A and corporate finance, and the firm also has capability in employment and IP. Carl Meyntjens is a very good corporate lawyer, and acted for Vivendi on the largest BOOT project in Belgium, relating to water purification.

Baker & McKenzie's Brussels office is part of one of the world's largest networks, and in partner Koen De Winter has a very experienced and able practitioner.

Nearly half of **Cleary Gottlieb Steen & Hamilton**'s workload is local law. Since 1960 the Belgian government has been a major client, and the office is strong on privatisation and competition. It will act for the government on the sale of Belgacom. Jan Meyers and Jean-Louis Joris are two of the most eminent names in Brussels for corporate transactions.

Clifford Chance LLP has dropped the 'Pünder' name in its drive to harmonise the European brand. Xavier Remy and Laurent Legein are notable partners, who work along with six other partners and about 50 other lawyers. The firm is a first port of call for big corporate and capital markets deals, such as acting for ABN Amro as buyer on the €2.8bn Credibe privatisation.

Coudert Brothers LLP – Coppens, Van Ommeslaghe & Faurès' core business is EU law, but it has a historical presence for mid-ticket work in the local market. The firm is seen less than in previous years, but still has big instructions, such as the Lafarge restructuring. Other major clients include the Walloon government and Canal+. Eric Deltour is considered a very good lawyer by clients.

DLA Caestecker is a full-service practice with pockets of excellence in areas like environment, property and IT. Its profile was enhanced when insolvency heavyweight Christian Van Buggenhout arrived from **Stibbe**, bringing with him the Sabena bankruptcy work.

Corporate boutique **Eubelius** is a stable and impressive collection of academically minded lawyers, which counts Belgacom amongst its clients.

Freshfields Bruckhaus Deringer has not quite made the impact in Belgium it has elsewhere in Europe, but Chris Sunt is a well-regarded lawyer. The firm represented Essent on a power plant operation in Antwerp.

NautaDutilh is expanding aggressively, and posted 25% growth in 2003. Partners Peter Callens and Dirk van Gerven are well-respected lawyers.

Stibbe's Jan Peeters is an eminent name in the market. The firm has good contacts with banks, and the alliance with **Herbert Smith** kept them busy in a lean year. A full-service firm with many strengths, such as local government, it has had a year of consolidation after some departures last year. It has been very active for Carrefour on distribution around Europe.

Expanding from its IP roots, **ALTIUS** is now a full-service outfit with seven partners and 30 assistants. Recent highlights include an acquisition for Dutch groups Van Nieuwpoort Beheer BV and De Hoop Temeuzen BV of Readymix Belgium from RMC plc.

Paul Hermant leads four partners and 19 associates at **Bird & Bird**. Serving the firm's major clients like BT, the office also handles matters for local SMEs, with a focus in the IT sector. Across Europe, the firm had a good 2003, and in Belgium has been busy in insolvency and litigation. Other major areas include commercial spin-off work for the University of Brussels.

CORPORATE AND COMMERCIAL: BRUSSELS

ALLEN & OVERY ✪
LINKLATERS DE BANDT ✪

Ashurst ✪
Baker & McKenzie ✪
Cleary Gottlieb Steen & Hamilton ✪
Clifford Chance LLP
Coudert Brothers LLP – Coppens, Van Ommeslaghe & Faurès ✪
DLA Caestecker ✪
Eubelius
Freshfields Bruckhaus Deringer ✪
NautaDutilh ✪
Stibbe ✪

ALTIUS ✪
Bird & Bird ✪
CMS Lexcelis ✪
ELEGIS (Buyle Dieryck Maingain) ✪
Jones Day ✪
Lawfort ✪
Liedekerke Wolters Waelbroeck Kirkpatrick ✪
Lontings & Partners ✪
Loyens ✪
Tiberghien Advocaten ✪
White & Case LLP

Bertouille & Partners ✪
Berwin Leighton Paisner
De Backer & Partners
De Wolf & Partners
Dechert LLP
EY Law
Eversheds
Gérard & Associés
Hunton & Williams ✪
Janson, Baugniet ✪
Laga & Philippe ✪
McGuireWoods LLP ✪
McKenna Long & Aldridge LLP ✪
Monard – D'Hulst ✪
Olislaegers De Creus
Simmons & Simmons ✪
Van Bael & Bellis ✪

Firms are listed A-Z in tiers which are ranked in order of priority
✪ Indicates firm displays contact details at the end of this chapter.

CMS Lexcelis is particularly experienced in compulsory takeovers, and in 2003 also advised an operator on the creation of a European-wide lottery.

ELEGIS (Buyle Dieryck Maingain) is a good mid-size national firm, with a notable litigation practice. Examples of recent work include lobbying for European Tugowners' Association, and representing Belgium in the legal committees of the European Franchising Federation.

Jones Day has a solid local practice, especially in the telecoms sector.

Lawfort is the re-launched *Bogaert & Vandemeulebroeke*. Corporate name partner Geert Bogaert left after the alliance with Landwell collapsed.

Liedekerke Wolters Waelbroeck Kirkpatrick is Belgium's largest independent local firm since the disintegration of the *Association of European Lawyers* in 2001. Traditionally strong on M&A and tax, and making a push in employment and environment, the firm has been on a hiring spree since losing notable partners in 2002. The corporate team acted for Credibe in the largest domestic deal of 2003, the sale of its state-owned portfolio of mortgage loans.

Dirk Lontings at **Lontings & Partners** is a recognised expert in non-profit and trade associations. His 43-lawyer firm has been promoted in the table this year, although it is no longer associated with KPMG. Corporate and labour are core areas, and the firm is also a top name for insurance.

Traditionally known for tax, **Loyens** is trying to be more full-service. Aggressive growth has been aided by attrition from the Magic Circle, with another notable addition being Geert Bogaert and several others from *Bogaert & Vandemeulebroeke*, who has great experience, especially in car distribution. The firm now numbers 65 corporate lawyers and 30 tax lawyers.

Tiberghien Advocaten has a small corporate department, derived from its historic tax practice.

White & Case LLP's Thierry Lohest is trying to build a local practice. The firm has an emphasis on public transactions in Europe, and is also acting for Agfa on restructuring its European operations.

Bertouille & Partners received strong client recommendation for advice on EU telecoms regulatory issues, and also recently handled an MBO of three companies at Siemens.

Berwin Leighton's old public procurement practice has been re-launched as a pure corporate finance boutique with **Berwin Leighton Paisner**. Much work is mid-ticket, especially for Israeli clients.

De Backer & Partners is a cost-effective alternative for clients seeking a full-service local outfit.

Part of the **Osborne Clarke** alliance network, **De Wolf & Partners** has ten partners and 15 assistants covering all aspects of corporate and commercial law.

Two partners and eight assistants at **Dechert LLP** handle cross-border transactional work, with expertise in asset-backed finance and international M&A.

EY Law, formerly, *Peeters Advocaten*, lost several members of its finance team to **Simmons & Simmons**, where Frank De Baepe has already carved out a good name for himself.

Eversheds has grown from an EU practice into a more general firm in recent years. Ten fee-earners cover commercial advice and employment.

Hunton & Williams has a solid corporate, environmental and technology practice, mainly for multinationals on cross-border deals. The firm acted for Navigant on acquisitions of Transcap in France, and ITC in Belgium.

With seven partners and nine assistants in Brussels, and two regional offices, **Monard – D'Hulst** handles commercial work for local clients, especially distribution and trade, and has a strong client base in construction.

Oppenheimer Wolff & Donnelly LLP no longer offers local law services, which have been taken over by new associated local outfit **Olislaegers De Creus**.

Van Bael & Bellis is mainly known as an EU boutique but has corporate clients such as AstraZeneca, Coca-Cola and Honda Motor. In 2003 it advised SABIC on its acquisition of shares in the petrochemical business of DSM.

DISPUTE RESOLUTION

Unlike in many countries, historically litigation has not been a core area for many Belgian firms as most lawyers would all do their own litigation.

Only 20 lawyers can litigate in Belgium's highest court, the Court of Cassation. They are hand-picked by the King of Belgium, and spread amongst several firms.

Allen & Overy has a highly experienced team, including the esteemed Luc Demeyere. He represented SAirGroup in its litigation against Sabena, at €3bn the largest case in Belgium, and is also advising Transliq AG on proceedings relating to Swiss Cargo's bankruptcy.

Coudert Brothers LLP – Coppens, Van Ommeslaghe & Faurès has years of experience in the market, and a pair of leading names in Pierre van Ommeslaghe and Isabelle Heenan. Name partner André Faurès is also a noted arbitrator.

Litigation boutique **Hanotiau & Van Den Berg** boasts the talents of three of Belgium's top disputes lawyers: Bernard Hanotiau, Paul Lefebvre and Pascal Hollander. The firm has more experience in arbitration than most local outfits.

Linklaters de Bandt has two excellent litigators in Jean-Marie Nelissen Grade and Johan Verbist, and François Lefèvre is an admired arbitrator. The team is acting for two bankers indicted in the Pineau-Valencienne case; for Dexia Bank on its dispute with some diamond trading companies; and for De Beers in a series of disputes as a result of reorganising its distribution network.

Ludovic Degryse of **Stibbe** is one of the few lawyers qualified to appear in the Belgian Supreme Court. Big recent cases include acting for Thomas Cook on a successful arbitration; and for KBC on a parent-subsidiary directive case.

Dal & Veldekens' Patrick Van Leynseele is a good lawyer for court work, while **Eubelius**' partners have a reputation for being academically-minded, and the firm is very popular with peers as well as clients.

DISPUTE RESOLUTION

ALLEN & OVERY ✪
COUDERT BROTHERS LLP – COPPENS, VAN OMMESLAGHE & FAURÈS ✪
HANOTIAU & VAN DEN BERG ✪
LINKLATERS DE BANDT ✪
STIBBE ✪

Baker & McKenzie ✪
Dal & Veldekens
De Backer & Partners
De Schrijver Van de Gehuchte & Partners
ELEGIS (Buyle Dieryck Maingain)
Eubelius
Freshfields Bruckhaus Deringer ✪
Gérard & Associés
Janson, Baugniet ✪
Liedekerke Wolters Waelbroeck Kirkpatrick ✪
Matray, Matray et Hallet
Van Bael & Bellis ✪
Willkie Farr & Gallagher LLP ✪
White & Case LLP

Firms are listed A-Z in tiers which are ranked in order of priority
✪ *Indicates firm displays contact details at the end of this chapter.*

Freshfields Bruckhaus Deringer received a boost in 2003 when arbitrator Alain Zenner returned to the Brussels office. The firm acted for Swiss International Air Lines on various claims brought by the French company Air Lib.

Liedekerke Wolters Waelbroeck Kirkpatrick has made notable progress in this field in the last two years. Claude Verbraeken has retired, but managing partner Aimery de Schoutheete and Joe Sepulchre remain as leading names. Examples of top cases in 2003 are acting for a Far East car manufacturer in a large ICC arbitration against three former European distributors.

Van Bael & Bellis is mainly known as an EU boutique, but also acts for blue-chip clients on matters before the Belgian courts, especially in the pharmaceutical sector.

Xavier Dieux at **Willkie Farr & Gallagher LLP** undertakes some work for the Belgian government, for example on cases before the Constitutional Court relating to the status of the National Bank of Belgium.

A new addition is **White & Case LLP**, which is building on its EU disputes practice. In 2003 it acted for Crédit Lyonnais Suisse on an international arbitration; and for the Ukraine government in an arbitration against Norsk Hydro.

Clifford Chance LLP recruited Sébastien Ryelandt from **Hanotiau & van den Berg** to head its litigation department.

ENVIRONMENT

Environmental practice is a very important area in Belgium as liabilities for companies are huge.

ENVIRONMENT

DLA CAESTECKER ✪
HAUMONT SCHOLASSE & PARTNERS
LIEDEKERKE WOLTERS WAELBROECK KIRKPATRICK ✪
STIBBE ✪

Allen & Overy ✪
Hunton & Williams ✪
Linklaters De Bandt ✪
Ryckbost & Ryckbost Ostende

Firms are listed A-Z in tiers which are ranked in order of priority
✪ *Indicates firm displays contact details at the end of this chapter.*

Readers should cross-refer with the **EU regulatory** section later in the chapter, for firms with expertise in EU environmental law.

Bob Martens at **DLA Caestecker** is a well known name in environmental law and public procurement. Apart from litigation concerning flight paths around Brussels, he has been involved in brownfield redevelopment and soil pollution cases, including drafting the regulatory framework for the Flemish government.

Haumont Scholasse & Partners has been raised in the rankings this year, and is considered an excellent niche firm. Francis Haumont and Michael Scholasse have very good reputations for environmental work.

Liedekerke Wolters Waelbroeck Kirkpatrick's Dirk Lindemans has a strong regulatory and litigation practice; and the firm also boasts the talents of Bernard Deltour. The firm has been involved in landmark litigation relating to soil pollution; as well as advice on compliance with EU waste management and defending criminal prosecutions.

Stibbe's partner Jan Bouckaert and two other partners are assisting the Flemish regional government on the development of Antwerp Airport, and on a series of other multi-billion euro regional projects.

Allen & Overy is not as high profile as it used to be for environmental law, but Jan Schamp is a fine lawyer. Work includes acting for the Flemish government on various developments, and for Recticel on an acquisition of a brownfield site.

A new addition to the table is US firm **Hunton & Williams**, which gives health and safety advice to electronics producers, and on liability issues in relation to biotechnology.

Linklaters De Bandt's partner Patrick Peeters has good experience in the sector and is recommended by clients.

Ostende-based **Ryckbost & Ryckbost** is a niche environmental and town and country planning firm, led by partner Donatienne Ryckbost. The team has particular experience in soil contamination issues.

FRAUD AND WHITE-COLLAR CRIME

EUBELIUS
LINKLATERS DE BANDT ✪
STIBBE ✪

Allen & Overy ✪
Dumont Sablon & Vanheeswijck
Hanotiau & van den Berg ✪
Johan Scheers
Liedekerke Wolters Waelbroeck Kirkpatrick ✪
Simont Braun ✪
Vanderveeren & Associés

Firms are listed A-Z in tiers which are ranked in order of priority
✪ *Indicates firm displays contact details at the end of this chapter.*

FRAUD AND WHITE-COLLAR CRIME

Under Belgian law a company may be charged with a criminal offence, so white-collar fraud is central to many law firms' practices.

Raf Verstraeten at **Eubelius** is one of the country's top fraud experts, and is assisted by 11 other specialist lawyers.

Other notable names are **Linklaters de Bandt** partner Johan Berbist, and Hans van Bavel at **Stibbe**.

Allen & Overy has an experienced team led by Leo Neels, covering the high-end fraud market.

Hanotiau & van den Berg remains a top name for litigation generally despite Sébastien Ryelandt leaving for **Clifford Chance LLP**.

Simont Braun's Jean-François Terlinden is a notable presence in the market.

Dumont Sablon & Vanheeswijck is a fraud boutique with a good track record, as is **Vanderveeren & Associés**, where Pascal Vanderveeren is considered a reputable expert.

INFORMATION TECHNOLOGY

Allen & Overy is very strong internationally on IT, and in Geert Glas has a major player in the Belgian market. In 2003 he worked for EDS on outsourcing; and for the Belgian government on a dispute with an IT service provider over the court's computer system.

Baker & McKenzie is very well-known on the litigation side of IT, and partner Daniel Fesler is also experienced in a range of matters such as outsourcing and software development.

Catherine Erkelens at international IT powerhouse **Bird & Bird** undertakes a lot of outsourcing, contracts, litigation, and data protection for a range of clients. The firm is advising Mastercard on IT contract drafting; and Cap Gemini Ernst & Young on litigation.

DLA Caestecker's managing partner Steven De Keyser leads one of Belgium's broadest and most focused IT practices. Maintaining the old *Andersen Legal* associations, it has advised Accenture on several projects.

INFORMATION TECHNOLOGY

Allen & Overy ✪
Baker & McKenzie ✪
Bird & Bird ✪
DLA Caestecker ✪
Linklaters De Bandt ✪
Stibbe ✪
White & Case LLP

Firms are listed A-Z
✪ *Indicates firm displays contact details at the end of this chapter.*

Linklaters De Bandt can draw on an enviable local and international client base, with three specialist IT lawyers led by Carl De Mayer.

Erik Valgaeren is a young IT practitioner at **Stibbe**, focusing on outsourcing, contracts, general corporate law as it relates to IT, as well as privacy.

White & Case LLP undertakes corporate matters in the telecoms sector, such as acting for Sonera on its massive merger with Telia AB.

INTELLECTUAL PROPERTY

National trade mark laws are being harmonised and new EU patent laws are coming into force in spring 2004. The market has been fluid, with lots of lateral hires, at junior level especially.

Allen & Overy's Geert Glas is one of the country's top experts, and Thierry Van Innis is also recommended. They have undertaken a lot of work recently for Diageo, for example on parallel imports of J&B and Smirnoff Ice. Other major cases include representing Cubatabaco & Habanas in a denomination infringement claim.

Originally an IP boutique, **ALTIUS** retains its reputation for quality advice and litigation. Much recent work has been domain name disputes, and also trade mark issues for Gallup Organisation, Bose, Dell, and Red Bull. Paul Maeyaert is a well-respected practitioner.

Bird & Bird has an excellent pan-European presence in IP, and Bruno Vandemeulen is a top lawyer. He leads a full service IP department with a focus on hard IP. The firm is also growing its patent litigation practice as well. In 2003 the team represented Electrolux in a multi-jurisdictional dispute on robot-mowers.

Linklaters de Bandt has an excellent IP practice, including the eminent Carl De Meyer and Jean-Christophe Troussel. The team is especially good for complex patent litigation.

NautaDutilh has a strong life sciences practice and is very strong on pharmaceuticals, rather than the mechanical side. Probably the largest team in Brussels includes Jean-Jo Evard, Philippe Péters and Benoît Strowel. One of the top firms for patents, for the likes of GSK, the team also undertakes a lot of trade mark matters.

One group of partners led by banking star Lucien Simont has joined forces with *Braun*

INTELLECTUAL PROPERTY

ALLEN & OVERY ⭘
ALTIUS ⭘
BIRD & BIRD ⭘
LINKLATERS DE BANDT ⭘
NAUTADUTILH ⭘
SIMONT BRAUN ⭘
STIBBE ⭘

Alain Berenboom
Covington & Burling ⭘
Crowell & Moring
DLA Caestecker ⭘
Liedekerke Wolters Waelbroeck Kirkpatrick ⭘

DCH (De Caluwé & Horsmans) ⭘
Marx, Van Ranst, Vermeersch & Partners ⭘
Van Bael & Bellis ⭘
Van Bunnen Remiche Ferrant & Kileste

Firms are listed A-Z in tiers which are ranked in order of priority
⭘ *Indicates firm displays contact details at the end of this chapter.*

Bigwood to create a new firm called **Simont Braun**, which will focus on corporate, banking, IP and competition and commercial arbitration. Fernand de Visscher and Laurent de Brouwer are very good patent litigators.

Stibbe's Ludovic de Gryse is an eminent litigator, and is assisted by Bridget Dauwe. Three members of the team are members of the High Council for Intellectual Property, which advises the government on IP. Much work is biotechnology and pharmaceuticals, especially for universities.

Alain Berenboom is a sole practitioner specialising in copyright.

One partner and two associates at **Covington & Burling** undertake regulatory work in hi-tech sectors. The firm has experience on anti-piracy campaigns, and is well-known for public policy work in relation to IP as well as conventional IP.

Washington, DC-based **Crowell & Moring** has expanded its IP practice recently. Kristof Roox is a rising star, with experience on the international side of IP.

Benoît Michaux at **DLA Caestecker** is seen a lot in the market. The firm handles high-profile projects for the likes of regional governments, and has specific expertise in technology transfer.

DCH (De Caluwé & Horsmans) is experienced on soft IP, and is working hard to get more patents instructions. Clients include the likes of AstraZeneca.

At **Marx, Van Ranst, Vermeersch & Partners** 24 lawyers focus on IP, media and employment law. It has a reputation for copyright litigation, with growing capability in patent litigation. The arrival of Liesbeth Lemeur adds trade mark and patent litigation strength.

A new addition is **Van Bael & Bellis**, which has good experience on IP litigation. The firm represents one of the world's largest pharmaceutical groups, and also acts for Chiron in the 'Torpedo' litigation in Belgium.

Van Bunnen Remiche Ferrant & Kileste is experienced on soft IP, especially litigation.

LABOUR AND EMPLOYMENT

Claeys & Engels, member of Ius Laboris is considered the leading national labour practice, with experience acting for employers and employees on all aspects of labour law. Thierry Claeys, Chris Engels and Jean-Louis Davain are all excellent practitioners.

Formerly *Bogaert & Vandemeulebroeke*, **Lawfort** has suffered a tumultuous 2003, but in Véronique Pertry has a very good employment specialist.

Alexander Vandenbergen specialises in pensions and restructurings at **Lontings & Partners**, and was joined in 2003 by Professor Marc De Vos. The firm has one of the largest departments with 15 lawyers, acting on litigation, dismissals, contracts and transfer of undertakings.

Loyens recruited Christian Willems from **Linklaters De Bandt**, so with department head Carl Bevernage, the firm now has over ten specialist lawyers.

Niche local firm **Van Eeckhoutte, Taquet & Clesse** is a first port of call for individuals requiring reliable and reputable litigation specialists.

Much of **Allen & Overy**'s employment work is related to corporate reorganisation, such as for Bayer and Reilly Chemicals. The firm also has a strong pensions team, acting for the likes of Colgate-Palmolive. Pieter De Koster has a very good reputation amongst clients.

Bird & Bird took some employment practitioners from **Allen & Overy** early in 2003 to start a labour department, with a focus on the IP sector and data protection.

Stanislas van Wassenhove leads five other lawyers in the labour department at **CMS Lexcelis**. The firm is very active in pensions law, and collective dismissals.

DLA Caestecker now has 14 lawyers in its labour law department, and is targeting it as a specific growth area. Much work is advice on diversity issues and collective dismissal rather than litigation.

Employment is one of **Eversheds**' core areas. Three fee-earners are busy on restructurings, for example for Scoot. The team also acted for Unisys on the employment law implications of its acquisition of KPMG in Belgium.

Liedekerke Wolters Waelbroeck Kirkpatrick is trying to grow its labour practice. It is currently advising NMBS on its negotiations with Wagons-Lits on costs of night train activity; and successfully defended a French temp agency against Temporary Employers Social Fund.

Linklaters De Bandt lost Christian Willems to **Loyens**, but still has Luc Vananerbeke as a leading name in the field.

LABOUR AND EMPLOYMENT

CLAEYS & ENGELS, MEMBER OF IUS LABORIS ⭘

LAWFORT ⭘
LONTINGS & PARTNERS ⭘
LOYENS ⭘
VAN EECKHOUTTE, TAQUET & CLESSE

Allen & Overy ⭘
Bird & Bird ⭘
CMS Lexcelis ⭘
DLA Caestecker ⭘
De Schrijver Van de Gehuchte & Partners
Eversheds
Liedekerke Wolters Waelbroeck Kirkpatrick ⭘
Linklaters De Bandt ⭘
Marx, Van Ranst, Vermeersch & Partners ⭘
NautaDutilh ⭘
Stibbe ⭘
Tilleman van Hoogenbemt *Antwerp* ⭘

Firms are listed A-Z in tiers which are ranked in order of priority
⭘ *Indicates firm displays contact details at the end of this chapter.*

Marx, Van Ranst, Vermeersch & Partners' employment team, led by Rafaël Claes, was boosted with the arrival of Dylan Casaer from *Peeters Advocaten*.

NautaDutilh has a solid labour practice, for likes of General Motors on plant closures.

Stibbe's Herman Craeninckx has a good name in the market. He acts almost exclusively for employers on matters like transfer of undertakings, and was busy on restructurings in 2003.

Popular with clients and peers alike, Antwerp-based **Tilleman van Hoogenbemt** is a niche employment practice, with respected practitioners.

MEDIA AND ENTERTAINMENT

Allen & Overy boasts an impressive client base in the media sector, such as the press agency Belga, and also De Persgroep and Roularta Media Group. Highlights in 2003 included acting for Zomba Records on a successful copyright dispute over a song on Michael Jackson's *Thriller* album.

The loss of **Bird & Bird**'s media team two years ago meant a drop in regulatory work, but the firm still does the commercial side of media work. In 2003 it acted for Turner Broadcasting

MEDIA AND ENTERTAINMENT

Allen & Overy ⭘
Bird & Bird ⭘
Cleary Gottlieb Steen & Hamilton ⭘
Liedekerke Wolters Waelbroeck Kirkpatrick ⭘
NautaDutilh ⭘

Firms are listed A-Z
⭘ *Indicates firm displays contact details at the end of this chapter.*

Europe in litigation related to broadcast fees for CNN; and for Winterthur Europe in advertising litigation.

From its competition department, **Cleary Gottlieb Steen & Hamilton** acts for one of Belgium's main media players, and is also active for film studios.

Liedekerke Wolters Waelbroeck Kirkpatrick lost Denis Waelbroeck to **Ashurst** but maintains a presence in the field.

NautaDutilh's Fabienne Brison has a good reputation with media clients, and regularly represents Dutch broadcaster NOS.

MERGERS AND ACQUISITIONS

New laws in 2003 to facilitate private equity investments have not kick-started the M&A market as some hoped.

Exploiting the old *Loeff Claeys Verbeke* client base, **Allen & Overy** appeared on a number of large deals in 2003, the most in the Benelux region in 2003 by volume and value. Examples are acting for Koramic Building Product on the sale of 50% of its subsidiary Koramic Roofing to Wienberger AG for €210m to create the second largest tile producer in Europe; and for Royal Vendex KBB on its acquisition of the Belgian activities of Leroy Merlin Group.

Clifford Chance LLP has a smaller corporate team than other leading players, but comes out top for total deal value in 2003 in Belgium. The firm acted for GE Aircraft Engines on its acquisition of Agfa-Gevaert's non-destructive testing business; and for AGF Belgium on the sale of its banking subsidiary to ING.

Linklaters de Bandt is unquestionably a leading name for big-ticket deals, doing more of the massive deals than any other firms. In 2003 it advised Ontex on the sale of its majority stake to Candover; and Dexia Bank on the sale on a one-third stake in Credit Agricole Belgique.

Koen Vanhaerents at **Baker & McKenzie** is a leading name in the field, acting for Deceuninck on its acquisition of Thyssen Polymer business of Thyssen Krupp.

Cleary Gottlieb Steen & Hamilton is less well known for pure M&A than other areas, but has a very high quality practice. In 2003 it represented Coca-Cola on its acquisition of a local bottler.

In Thierry Tilquin and Philippe Malherbe, **Liedekerke Wolters Waelbroeck Kirkpatrick** has two highly experienced M&A lawyers.

A new addition is **White & Case LLP**, where three partners and seven assistants represented Swedish multinational Sapa AB on its acquisition of Remi Claes Aluminium, involving due diligence in 14 countries.

Another new addition is **Ashurst**, which has a very strong top-end European M&A practice. In 2003 the firm acted for Candover on its £630m bid for a 75% stake in Belgian hygiene products manufacturer Ontex, Belgium's largest deal of 2003.

MERGERS AND ACQUISITIONS

ALLEN & OVERY ✪
CLIFFORD CHANCE LLP
LINKLATERS DE BANDT ✪

Baker & McKenzie ✪
Cleary Gottlieb Steen & Hamilton ✪
Liedekerke Wolters Waelbroeck Kirkpatrick ✪
Stibbe ✪
White & Case LLP

Ashurst ✪
Coudert Brothers LLP – Coppens, Van Ommeslaghe & Faurès ✪
Eubelius
Freshfields Bruckhaus Deringer ✪
NautaDutilh ✪

ALTIUS ✪
Bird & Bird ✪
CMS Lexcelis ✪
DLA ✪
Jones Day ✪
Lontings & Partners ✪

Firms are listed A-Z in tiers which are ranked in order of priority
✪ Indicates firm displays contact details at the end of this chapter.

Coudert Brothers LLP – Coppens, Van Ommeslaghe & Faurès has a lot of M&A work in the hotel industry. A new client is Elia, the Belgian grid operator.

Freshfields Bruckhaus Deringer's Chris Sunt is a top name for M&A. He acted for Lafarge on an acquisition from BPB plc.

Bird & Bird acted for the buyer on its acquisition of Proton; and is also advising the shareholders of De Schutter Group on the selling of their interest in De Brouwer Group.

Cedric Guyot at **CMS Lexcelis** is a respected name for mid-market deals.

Jones Day represented Bridgestone Europe on the acquisition of an interest in Nokian Tyres; and is also representing Konika on its merger with Minolta.

Lontings & Partners name partner Dirk Lontings acted for Lekkerland group on its acquisition of Caritas and Tabaccomat, two Belgian subsidiaries of Imperial Tobacco.

REAL ESTATE

Belgium is enjoying a boom in property work, and lawyers are taking advantage. This is partly motivated by a poor economy in other areas, as investors flock to a safer investment, but accession is bringing ten new countries to the EU and this is stimulating a lot of real estate work in Brussels.

Allen & Overy has a renewed commitment to property work after an internal reorganisation. In 2003 the firm was advising Skidmore, Owings & Merrill Inc on their negotiation with Nato over the design and construction of the new Nato HQ in Brussels.

REAL ESTATE

Allen & Overy ✪
Baker & McKenzie ✪
Linklaters De Bandt ✪
Stibbe ✪

CMS Lexcelis ✪
DLA Caestecker ✪
De Wolf Law Firm *Maarkedal* ✪
Lawfort ✪
Liedekerke Wolters Waelbroeck Kirkpatrick ✪

Firms are listed A-Z in tiers which are ranked in order of priority
✪ Indicates firm displays contact details at the end of this chapter.

Baker & McKenzie's Dimonique Lechien leads a team including Pascal Mallien, which is considered one of the most serious players in the property market. Much work is property finance, and the firm is advising AXA Belgium on the sale and leaseback of a Tractebel property portfolio.

Jacques Périlleux and Yves Moreau at **Linklaters De Bandt** offer a range of property advice to the firm's broad commercial client base.

With 41 fee-earners, **Stibbe** has the largest administrative and real estate department in Brussels. Traditionally a core area, partner Rudy Nauwelaerts has been involved in many important property deals in Belgium in the last decade, and is currently representing 60 clients on cross-border leasing matters, with major clients including Belgacom, Fortis and ING.

CMS Lexcelis has been developing its property capability in recent years, and recently acted for a large French institutional investor in a programme of property acquisitions.

DLA Caestecker acts for the government on real estate issues and PPP projects. Much work is corporate real estate transactions for the likes of Intervest Group and Oppenheim.

Liedekerke Wolters Waelbroeck Kirkpatrick has Claude Gonthier and Yves Delacroix handling tax matters. The firm advised on a sale and leaseback for Alstom; and acted for IKEA on real estate expansion in Belgium.

SHIPPING AND TRANSPORT

Much of Belgium's maritime work is Antwerp-based, and is now dominated by niche firms as the international practices have decided to pull out of what is for them an unprofitable area.

Wim Fransen at **Fransen Advocaten** is president of the Belgian Maritime Organisation, and mainly focuses on acting for vessel owners.

Kegels & Co Advocaten operates more on the cargo side and has a good record on international elements in shipping. Tony Kegels undertakes insurance-related matters, André Kegels for P&I clubs, and Dirk Noels is experienced on the dry side.

SHIPPING AND TRANSPORT

FRANSEN ADVOCATEN
KEGELS & CO ADVOCATEN *Antwerp* ✪
ROOSENDAAL KEYZER

AntwerpLaw *Antwerp* ✪
Coudert Brothers LLP – Coppens, Van Ommeslaghe & Faurès ✪
DLA Caestecker ✪
ELEGIS (Buyle Dieryck Maingain) ✪
ELEGIS (Huybrechts Engels Craen and Partners) ✪
Liedekerke Wolters Waelbroeck Kirkpatrick ✪
Stibbe ✪
Van Doosselaere Advocaten
Wijffels, Geuens, De Paep

Firms are listed A-Z in tiers which are ranked in order of priority
✪ *Indicates firm displays contact details at the end of this chapter.*

Roosendaal Keyzer is another leading practice, with Frank Roosendaal, Luke Keyzer and Gerald Straatman all notable names in the shipping market.

A new addition is **AntwerpLaw**, a niche transport and insurance firm of three partners and two assistants handling cargo claims and bills of lading disputes on the cargo side for local clients. Current work includes defending a fishing vessel on a collision dispute with the *Ms Mare Lycium*.

Bernard Insel at **Coudert Brothers LLP – Coppens, Van Ommeslaghe & Faurès** is experienced on maritime insurance, while Peter Van de Vijner has a general transport practice at **DLA Caestecker**.

ELEGIS (Buyle Dieryck Maingain)'s partner Christian Dieryck is professor of maritime insurance, and Paul Verguts sits as a judge in the court of appeal and is experienced in transport matters.

Van Doosselaere Advocaten is a small practice with a good reputation amongst shipowners. Luc Maes is a respected practitioner.

Wijffels, Geuens, De Paep is another good outfit, with name partners Luc Wijffels and Rudiger De Paep standing out.

TAX

AFSCHRIFT ✪
BAKER & McKENZIE ✪
FRESHFIELDS BRUCKHAUS DERINGER ✪
LIEDEKERKE WOLTERS WAELBROECK KIRKPATRICK ✪
LINKLATERS DE BANDT ✪
LOYENS ✪
TIBERGHIEN ADVOCATEN ✪

Allen & Overy ✪
Clifford Chance LLP
Dumont Sablon & Vanheeswijck
Jones Day ✪
NautaDutilh ✪
Stibbe ✪

CMS Lexcelis ✪
Morgan Lewis ✪

Firms are listed A-Z in tiers which are ranked in order of priority
✪ *Indicates firm displays contact details at the end of this chapter.*

Afschrift is a tax boutique, specialising in litigation. Thierry Afschrift is a well known expert in the market, and the firm is also a member of *Trans Europe Law Firm Alliance (TELFA)*.

Alain Huyghe leads ten tax lawyers at **Baker & McKenzie**, and the firm was bolstered by the arrival in 2003 of Philippe Lion as a partner from PwC, who specialises in tax structuring. Recent highlights include restructuring for Telenet Group following its acquisition of Mixed Intercommunales.

Freshfields Bruckhaus Deringer gives tax advice on a range of corporate-related matters, led by partner Axel Haelterman.

Liedekerke Wolters Waelbroeck Kirkpatrick's tax practice is mainly M&A-related, capital markets, projects and real estate matters related to tax. Litigation has included recent landmark judgments in the Court of Cassation. John Kirkpatrick is one of Brussels' top tax lawyers, he is assisted by the up-and-coming Daniel Garabedian.

Linklaters de Bandt places less emphasis on its tax capability than it used to, but has an excellent reputation for M&A-related advice and tax planning. Six partners and 18 other lawyers advise a wide client base, including the government.

Loyens used to be a niche tax firm specialising in consultancy, and still has over 30 tax lawyers in various specialised sub-groups. Matters covered include corporate tax, estate tax, financial litigation, VAT and labour benefits, and the team recently advised on the tax implications of building Belgium's second biggest shopping mall. Head of tax is Christian Chéruy.

Tiberghien advocaten is a mid-size local firm with good name, and partner Bernard Peeters is experienced in tax matters.

Philippe Hinnekens is a respected specialist at **Allen & Overy**, which advised Acasa Esana on the new tax shelter regulations; and advised AON Belgium on tax planning.

Thanks to the efforts of the excellent Thierry Blockerye, **Clifford Chance LLP** goes up in the rankings this year. Known for real estate tax and restructuring, the firm acted for Pricoa in the acquisition of the Heytens retail portfolio; and for Atenor on the optimisation of its real estate portfolio.

Litigation boutique **Dumont Sablon & Vanheeswijck** has also risen in the rankings this year on the basis of its excellent tax work.

Jones Day's corporate partner Howard Liebman handles mainly corporate-related tax matters for the firm, while **NautaDutilh**'s Werner Heyvaert has a broad tax practice.

At **Stibbe**, Luc de Broe and Jacques Malherbe lead another partner and 17 other fee-earners on tax related to financial services, corporate, PPP, employee benefits, and a lot of real estate. Examples of work include acting for 52 Flemish municipalities on cross-border leasing.

CMS Lexcelis has acted on several large property refinancing operations, and various other real estate-related tax matters. As part of the Europe-wide network, the firm advised a pharmaceutical group on various tax matters. André Bailleux is a respected practitioner.

EU AND COMPETITION

Competition: With the accession of ten new states in May 2004, there promises to be a radical change in competition practice. Competition law will undergo a process of 'modernisation,' by which more investigations will be conducted on a national level. Firms will have to examine their competition strategies, perhaps focusing more on pan-European capability. Merger control work is significantly down, with the Commission only dealing with about one-fifth the number of the cases it was a couple of years ago. Mario Monti has made it clear he sees cartels and state aid as priority areas.

Cleary Gottlieb Steen & Hamilton has been involved in many of the most important EU merger control cases in recent years, and has unquestionably the finest transatlantic practice. 2003 highlights include the Shneider Indemnity case against the Commission, and the team also handles national competition work for various countries from Brussels, such as for the Mayor of London on the London Underground PPP. Partner Robbert Snelders is a very important player in the market, and the firm boasts a host of impressive names such as Maurits Dolmans, Romano Subiotto and Nicholas Levy. Added to these in 2003 was Francisco Enrique González Diaz, former head of the Commission's Merger Task Force, who specialises in competition and state aid.

Frank Montag is head of the global competition practice at **Freshfields Bruckhaus Deringer**, while leading names John Davies and Rachel Brandenburger split their time with London. With strong pan-European capability, especially in Germany, it also has perhaps the largest Brussels competition practice. Major deals in 2003 included for P&O Cruises on six investigations in Germany, the UK, US and Brussels; and for EnergieAllianz on the Phase II investigation into its joint venture with Verbund.

Allen & Overy is also strong around Europe and enjoys an enviable US client base. Michael Reynolds and David Harrison lead 22 full-time competition lawyers. The focus is merger control, and although the firm has been seen less than in previous years it still has major work, for example

COMPETITION

CLEARY GOTTLIEB STEEN & HAMILTON ✪
FRESHFIELDS BRUCKHAUS DERINGER ✪

- Allen & Overy ✪
- Clifford Chance LLP
- Linklaters ✪
- Wilmer Cutler Pickering LLP ✪

- Ashurst ✪
- Herbert Smith ✪
- Lovells ✪
- Skadden, Arps, Slate, Meagher & Flom LLP
- Slaughter and May ✪
- Van Bael & Bellis ✪
- White & Case LLP

- Arnold & Porter LLP ✪
- Baker & McKenzie ✪
- Coudert Brothers LLP – Coppens, Van Ommeslaghe & Faurès ✪
- Gide Loyrette Nouel ✪
- Gleiss Lutz ✪
- Hengeler Mueller ✪
- Howrey Simon Arnold & White, LLP ✪
- Latham & Watkins LLP ✪
- Morgan Lewis ✪
- Norton Rose
- Squire, Sanders & Dempsey L.L.P. ✪

- Akin Gump Strauss Hauer & Feld
- Bird & Bird ✪
- Bredin Prat ✪
- CMS EU Law Office ✪
- Covington & Burling ✪
- DLA ✪
- Dechert LLP
- Eversheds
- Garrigues
- Haarmann Hemmelrath ✪
- Hammonds
- Heuking Kühn Lüer Wojtek ✪
- Hogan & Hartson L.L.P. ✪
- Jones Day ✪
- Kemmler Rapp Böhlke
- Morrison & Foerster LLP ✪
- Oppenheimer Wolff & Donnelly LLP
- SJ Berwin ✪
- Shearman & Sterling LLP
- Stanbrook & Hooper
- Stibbe ✪
- Taylor Wessing ✪
- Weil, Gotshal & Manges LLP ✪

Firms are listed A-Z in tiers which are ranked in order of priority
✪ Indicates firm displays contact details at the end of this chapter.

for Sun Microsytems on the Microsoft case. The team also advised French manufacturer Schneider Electric on its successful appeal against the Commission's block on its acquisition of Legrand.

Smaller than many other leading competition practices, **Clifford Chance LLP** nonetheless pulls in the biggest deals. Having advised GE on its blocked merger with Honeywell, in 2003 the firm advised GE Medical Systems on its $2bn acquisition of Instrumentarium Oy of Finland, obtaining Phase II clearance. Other headline deals include acting for Pfizer on its acquisition of Pharmacia Corp, the largest deal worldwide by value in 2002, which received clearance in 2003. Simon Baxter leads a team including Charles van Sasse van Ysselt and Martin Bechtold.

A premier local practice and pre-eminence in many countries gives **Linklaters** a strong client base. Clients consider Gerwin Van Gerven a terrific lawyer, amongst stellar names such as Bernard van de Walle de Ghelcke, Alec Burnside and Olivier d'Ormesson who are all excellent all-round competition lawyers. A merger-driven practice is bound to be affected by the lack of M&A work, but there has been a significant rise in cartel instructions.

A formidable transatlantic antitrust practice, mainly based on merger control, allows **Wilmer Cutler Pickering LLP** to mix it with the best in Brussels. Despite losing some partners to **Latham & Watkins LLP**, the firm still has Thomas Meuller, Claus Deiter Ehlermann and John Ratcliff, and has brought in Charles Stark from Washington, DC, a former head of the international office of the antitrust division of the US Department of Justice.

Ashurst has moved up in the rankings this year. An excellent European M&A practice provides a steady stream of merger control work, and the firm is also involved in a high proportion of cartel cases. Julian Ellison and Mark Clough have a low-key but very busy practice, with perhaps more litigation than any other firm.

Herbert Smith has a leading London competition practice and has made great strides in Brussels in recent years, drawing on its alliance with **Gleiss Lutz** and **Stibbe**. Lord Brittan is a consultant and Craig Pouncey has a good name too, but the star is undoubtedly Stephen Kinsella. Examples of work are acting for Aberdeen Journals on an appeal concerning a fine for predatory pricing; and for Gannett UK Ltd on competition clearance for the purchase of SMG Scottish Titles.

As part of a broader European competition group, **Lovells** has nearly 30 lawyers in Brussels, including Nick Bromfield, Philip Collins, and office managing partner Tom McQuail. The team undertakes a lot of behavioural work, and boasts an enviable record of winning on big cases. For example, for Mars against Unilever in a 14-year landmark case over Mars' access to freezer outlets, culminating in the Court of First Instance announcing its decision for Mars in late 2003. The firm was also principal adviser to 17 shipping lines on the Atlantic Conference Agreement's (Taca) judgment, in which a €270m fine was overturned by the ECJ.

Skadden, Arps, Slate, Meagher & Flom LLP has a reputation for merger regulation filings generated by M&A in New York, with major deals in 2003 including for Amgen on its merger with Immunex Corporatio; and for Ball on its merger with Schmalbach-Lubeka. The firm made a strong statement of intent last year by plucking James Venit from **Wilmer Cutler Pickering LLP**.

Slaughter and May has two partners in Brussels: John Boyce and Michael Rowe. The office may lack numbers, but shares a building with best friends **Hengeler Mueller**, and **Bredin Prat** is also present in the city. **Hengeler Mueller** partners Hans-Jörg Niemeyer and Bernhard Maessen have good names, as does **Bredin Prat**'s Hughes Calvet. The network advised on Bae's acquisition of 30% of tank manufacturer Alvis. **Slaughter and May** also undertakes domestic UK work from Brussels, such as advising Walmart on its bid to acquire Safeway.

EU boutique **Van Bael & Bellis** is more known on the trade side, but Jean-François Bellis and Kris von Hove have a good record across the board on all EU matters. Merger control work includes acting for Bemis Company and Morgan Adhesives Company on Commission proceedings. Cartel advice for Gyproc Benelux and article 82 defences for IBM and United Brands demonstrate a wide range of skills.

White & Case LLP has an experienced 40-strong team devoted to all aspects of EU law, with notable experience on litigation, state aid, public affairs and international trade. A top name for cartel defence cases, the very highly regarded Ian Forrester QC is currently representing a major software company in a huge Competition Commission case. Other headline deals include for Sonera on its multi-billion euro merger with Telia AB, the largest ever in the Nordic region; and for Vestar Capital Partners in its acquisition of SAB Wabco, Europe's leading manufacturer of train brakes.

In 2003 Marleen Van Kerckhove moved from **Clifford Chance LLP** to newly opened **Arnold & Porter LLP**. One of the top antitrust practices in the US, with blue-chip clients like Pfizer, it has opened to cater for domestic US clients on European competition matters, especially merger control. Much work is in the telecoms sector and healthcare, and it is acting for France Télécom in one of the major current state aid cases.

Baker & McKenzie has a specialist European Law Centre to handle all aspects of EU law. Ross Denton returned to London, while partner Thomas Lampert has moved to Brussels from Frankfurt. The team has strength in cartels, especially referrals from the US, such as for Cabot on cartel investigation.

Coudert Brothers LLP – Coppens, Van Ommeslaghe & Faurès is seen as less of a force in competition law than it used to be, but Stephen Spinks is considered a great lawyer. Many clients are French and Scandinavian, and also Asian, such as Toyota. An example of recent work is representing Cascades on cartonboard products cartel litigation before the ECJ.

Gide Loyrette Nouel has 20 people in Brussels, including Dominique Voillemot, working on competition, trade and with a specialism in the agri-food sector. A major instruction at present is the state aid case for France Télécom, and merger advice for SEB on its acquisition of Moulinex.

Howrey Simon Arnold & White, LLP is certainly a firm to watch after a lot of investment and publicity surrounding its opening in 2003. Initial indications are positive for partners Trevor Soames and Julian Joshua, but will its superb US client base follow them in Europe?

Another newcomer is **Latham & Watkins LLP**, which hired **Wilmer Cutler Pickering LLP** partners Andreas Weitbrecht and Jean Paul Poitras. **Morgan Lewis** is a more established presence, with Izzet Sinan handling competition matters.

Norton Rose has been thriving recently, especially in the transport and energy sectors. Riccardo Celli has a good name, as does John Cook. The firm acted for Honeywell on two major transactions with BASF; and also advised Norsk Hydro on the sale of its FlexPac business to Alcan.

Brian Hartnett leads three partners and nine associates at **Squire, Sanders & Dempsey L.L.P.**, which has been active on state aid advice to the Czech government; as well as work for Saatchi & Saatchi, Expedia and Eli Lilly.

Bird & Bird recruited Wilko van Weert from **Stanbrook & Hooper**, who has strong experience with Japanese clients. The firm works more on the cartel side, and is hoping to exploit the large increase in IP-related competition work.

Led by David Hull, **Covington & Burling** has particular expertise on competition as it affects intellectual property, such as licensing and distribution agreements.

For a largely US client base, **Dechert LLP** works on cartel investigations and merger control, especially in the technology and chemical sectors.

Eversheds undertakes cartel work, and some state aid for UK regional development agencies. The firm is strong on public sector work and also the transport industry. Examples of work include for a UK carbonless paper producer on cartel work.

Spanish firm **Garrigues** and German outfit **Haarmann Hemmelrath** have reputable offices, as does **Heuking Kühn Lüer Wojtek**.

Hogan & Hartson L.L.P.'s Catriona Hatton is a recognised name in the market, and the firm hired George Metaxas from **Weil, Gotshal & Manges LLP** in October 2003. The team represented Fairchild in the sale of its aerospace fasteners business to Alcoa on merger filing; and obtained clearance for Umicore's acquisition of OMG's precious metals business.

Eric Morgan de Rivery of **Jones Day** splits his time between Brussels and Paris. In 2003 the firm represented MMO2 on its European mobile phone network; and Mastercard on the Commission investigation into interchange fees.

SJ Berwin has experience on litigation, especially in the food and fisheries sectors. Clients include FENIN and Electricidade de Portugal. Ramon Garcia Gallardo is a good competition practitioner.

Stanbrook & Hooper lost Wilko van Weert to **Bird & Bird**, but name partner Clive Stanbrook is not to be underestimated. He has a history of major cases but will probably focus more on trade and anti-dumping in the future. One of the only other remaining EU boutiques is **Kemmler Rapp Böhlke**.

Peter Willis has joined **Taylor Wessing**'s Brussels office from London, which has a good technology and pharmaceuticals practice, a strong presence in Germany and a new emphasis on regulatory matters as well.

George Metaxas left **Weil, Gotshal & Manges LLP**, but the firm still has a good telecoms practice, especially in Eastern Europe. The firm acted on the Konika/Minolta merger clearance.

Customs, trade, WTO and anti-dumping: **Hammonds** is historically one of the leading anti-dumping practices in Brussels, defending exporters outside Europe as well as inside the EU. Partners Konstantinos Adamantopolous and Edward Borovikov have been joined by Rudi Leleu, DG Trade at the Commission, who has extensive experience in anti-dumping.

Sidley Austin Brown & Wood LLP took the entire trade team from **Hogan & Hartson L.L.P.**, including eminent names Richard Weiner and Laurent Reussmann. Seven lawyers have a pre-eminent WTO practice, appearing in more than half of the total WTO cases in the last decade. A recent example is for the European shipbuilders on the huge WTO trade barriers case against South Korea. The firm is also representing the Commission in the US Supreme Court on a crucial case concerning discoverability of documents relating to whistleblowing.

Ivo van Bael and Jean-François Bellis at **Van Bael & Bellis** lead the largest trade practice in Brussels. It is the only Brussels trade firm with a Geneva office specialising in WTO issues. The firm represented Egypt in the WTO challenge bought by Turkey against Egypt's anti-dumping measures; and is also representing Sony on the customs classification of the PlayStation2.

Vermulst Waer & Verhaeghe is an anti-dumping boutique, especially for Asian respondents, and the firm also does some WTO work. Edwin Vermulst is regarded as a major player, and Paul Waer is also recommended.

White & Case LLP places more emphasis on state aid and cartels, but also boasts a prominent WTO practice, led by Alastair Sutton. De Pont de Nemours is being represented in an anti-dumping case; and the Hong Kong mission to the EU is being advised on trade issues. Thomas Tindemans handles public affairs and regulatory matters.

Covington & Burling handles state aid and public procurement, with notable experience in relation to PPP and its compatibility with procurement rules. In 2003 the firm represented a European ferry company as a complainant before the Commission.

Freshfields Bruckhaus Deringer is the only Magic Circle firm to continue with a committed trade team. Michael Schütte is managing partner of the Brussels office, while partner Hans-Joachim Preiss spends much of his time in Berlin. The firm acted for Degussa, Cabot, and Columbia Chemicals on antidumping proceedings concerning imports of carbon black from Egypt.

Rien van Oueveren at **Lovells** is acting for Alstrom on the state aid investigation, which started in August 2003.

Stanbrook & Hooper's Fred Lukoff works extensively in the trade area and is considered by peers an excellent lawyer. Philip Bentley QC is another prominent name.

In 2002, **Wilmer Cutler Pickering LLP** took on the whole team from **Stibbe**, including Marco Bronckers, Frédéric Louis and Yves Van Gerven. Since then, the trade practice has flourished, and is one of most active on WTO matters. It is acting for the ANDEAN countries in the trade preferences litigation.

Robert Maclean at **CMS EU Law Office** is a recommended lawyer, and **Coudert Brothers**

CUSTOMS, TRADE, WTO AND ANTI-DUMPING

HAMMONDS
SIDLEY AUSTIN BROWN & WOOD LLP ✪
VAN BAEL & BELLIS ✪
VERMULST WAER & VERHAEGHE
WHITE & CASE LLP

Covington & Burling ✪
Freshfields Bruckhaus Deringer ✪
Lovells ✪
Stanbrook & Hooper
Wilmer Cutler Pickering LLP ✪

CMS EU Law Office ✪
Cleary Gottlieb Steen & Hamilton ✪
Clifford Chance LLP
Coudert Brothers LLP – Coppens, Van Ommeslaghe & Faurès ✪
Crosby Renouf ✪
Herbert Smith ✪
Kemmler Rapp Böhlke
Mayer, Brown, Rowe & Maw Gaedertz
Oppenheimer Wolff & Donnelly LLP

Eversheds
Gide Loyrette Nouel ✪
Linklaters ✪

Firms are listed A-Z in tiers which are ranked in order of priority
✪ Indicates firm displays contact details at the end of this chapter.

LLP – Coppens, Van Ommeslaghe & Faurès' Paulette Vander Schueren represented the Korean side in the Korean Shipbuilders case.

Cleary Gottlieb Steen & Hamilton and **Clifford Chance LLP** have experienced customs and anti-dumping practices.

Crosby Renouf's Ursula O'Dwyer is also highly experienced.

Herbert Smith partner Craig Pouncey is acting for the government of Antigua and Barbuda on its WTO action against the US ban on cross-border gambling and betting.

Eversheds has a good regulatory and international trade team, with experience of ten anti-dumping cases for the Chinese government.

Gide Loyrette Nouel is active on anti-subsidy and anti-dumping. The firm is acting for the Chinese government on the WTO steel dispute with the US; and for ACP on sugar subsidies dispute with the EU.

EU regulatory – Agriculture: O'Connor and Company is one of the few firms to have a genuine specialism in this area, and Bernard O'Connor is well known for his expertise on CAP. **Gide Loyrette Nouel** also has experience in the agri-food sector.

EU regulatory – Energy: Norton Rose is a major player for energy work internationally, and has advised Eni and Naturkraft on regulatory matters in 2003. Most of the big international players have experience in the energy sector, so the following are all recommended: **Allen & Overy**; **Baker & McKenzie**; **Clifford Chance LLP**; **Coudert Brothers LLP – Coppens, Van Ommeslaghe & Faurès**; **Covington & Burling**; **Freshfields Bruckhaus Deringer**; **Herbert Smith**; **Norton Rose**; **Skadden, Arps, Slate, Meagher & Flom LLP**; and **Slaughter and May**. **Willkie Farr & Gallagher LLP** has also acted for oil majors on regulatory investigations.

EU regulatory – Environment: Allen & Overy, **Linklaters** and **Simmons & Simmons** are known in the UK for their expertise in environmental work. **Heuking Kühn Lüer Wojtek**'s Gabrielle Williamson is a well-known name in the field. A new addition is **DLA Caestecker**, which includes amongst its clients for environmental regulatory advice the Flemish government, which it has advised on brownfield development and noise pollution. **White & Case LLP** has a strong international environmental practice, as well as its strength at national level. **Covington & Burling** is also renowned for its strength in this area, and in 2003 advised various technology clients on environmental restrictions on electronic equipment. Also recommended are **Crosby Renouf** and **Oppenheimer Wolff & Donnelly LLP**.

EU regulatory – Food and drugs: Covington & Burling's Peter Bogaert and **Keller & Heckman**'s Jean-Phillipe Montfort are two eminent names in this area, and **Oppenheimer Wolff & Donnelly LLP**; **Lovells** and **Stanbrook & Hooper** all have experience as well. Jacqueline Mailly left **Hogan & Hartson** for **Sidley Austin Brown & Wood LLP**.

EU regulatory – Information technology: Allen & Overy is acting for the NHS on a multi-billion euro IT public procurement project. **DLA Caestecker** has advised various companies and bodies on electronic signatures and data protection regulation. A firm with a strong technology focus, **Taylor Wessing** will also be strengthened by the arrival of Klaus-Heiner Lehne and Andreas Haak. Other leading individuals include Catherine Erkelens at **Bird & Bird**; **Covington & Burling**'s David Harfst; and **Coudert Brothers LLP – Coppens, Van Ommeslaghe & Faurès**' Geoffrey de Foestraets. Other firms with a good record in this field are **Jones Day**; **Morrison & Foerster LLP**; **Squire, Sanders & Dempsey L.L.P.**; **Weil, Gotshal & Manges LLP**; **Freshfields Bruckhaus Deringer**; **Olswang** and **Sidley Austin Brown & Wood LLP**.

EU regulatory – Pharmaceuticals and biotechnology: Arnold & Porter LLP is a new entry to the market in 2003, bringing a great international reputation for pharmaceuticals. It may provide competition to more established players like **Covington & Burling**, which has been busy in 2003 on various matters concerning new medicines and general compliance. **Cleary Gottlieb Steen & Hamilton** has advised various pharmaceutical companies on the incorrect application of EU pharmaceuticals directives by a number of states. **Keller & Heckman** is a small firm with a good name, and other large firms with international presence are **Bird & Bird**; **Oppenheimer Wolff & Donnelly LLP**; **Simmons & Simmons**; **Freshfields Bruckhaus Deringer**; **Hengeler Mueller**; **Herbert Smith**; **Taylor Wessing**; **NautaDutilh**; and **Squire, Sanders & Dempsey L.L.P.**.

EU regulatory – Telecoms: Squire, Sanders & Dempsey L.L.P.'s Tom Ramsey and Peter Alexiadis are two of the leading lights in Brussels. Other names that clients will turn to first are **Jones Day**'s Bernard Armory; and **Weil, Gotshal & Manges LLP**' David Cantor. **Wilmer Cutler Pickering LLP** has been active in the aviation as well as telecoms, and the team includes the well-respected Christian Duvernoy. **Taylor Wessing** has a great international presence in the sector, as does **Freshfields Bruckhaus Deringer**. Otrher recommended firms are **Olswang**; **Bird & Bird**; **Cleary Gottlieb Steen & Hamilton**; **Coudert Brothers LLP – Coppens, Van Ommeslaghe & Faurès**; **Dechert LLP**; **Sidley Austin Brown & Wood LLP** and niche outfit **Stanbrook & Hooper**.

EU REGULATORY

Akin Gump Strauss Hauer & Feld
Allen & Overy ✪
Arnold & Porter LLP ✪
CMS Lexcelis ✪
Cleary Gottlieb Steen & Hamilton ✪
Clifford Chance LLP
Coudert Brothers LLP – Coppens, Van Ommeslaghe & Faurès ✪
Covington & Burling ✪
Crosby Renouf ✪
Freshfields Bruckhaus Deringer ✪
Hengeler Mueller ✪
Herbert Smith ✪
Jones Day ✪
Keller & Heckman
Linklaters ✪
Lovells ✪
McKenna Long & Aldridge LLP ✪
NautaDutilh ✪
Norton Rose
Olswang
Oppenheimer Wolff & Donnelly LLP
Sidley Austin Brown & Wood LLP ✪
Slaughter & May ✪
Squire, Sanders & Dempsey L.L.P. ✪
Stanbrook & Hooper
Stibbe ✪
Van Bael & Bellis ✪
Weil, Gotshal & Manges LLP ✪
White & Case LLP
Willkie Farr & Gallagher LLP ✪
Wilmer Cutler Pickering LLP ✪

Baker & McKenzie ✪
Bird & Bird ✪
DLA Caestecker ✪
Dechert LLP
Gide Loyrette Nouel ✪
Gleiss Lutz ✪
Hammonds
Heuking Kühn Lüer Wojtek ✪
Morrison & Foerster LLP ✪
O'Connor and Company
SJ Berwin ✪
Simmons & Simmons ✪
Skadden, Arps, Slate, Meagher & Flom LLP
Taylor Wessing ✪
Vermulst Waer & Verhaeghe

Firms are listed A-Z in tiers which are ranked in order of priority
✪ Indicates firm displays contact details at the end of this chapter.

EU regulatory – Transport: A core area for **Norton Rose**, the firm has unsurpassed expertise, for example acting for the UK rail regulator. Other players are **Clifford Chance LLP**; **Coudert Brothers LLP – Coppens, Van Ommeslaghe & Faurès**; and **Freshfields Bruckhaus Deringer**.

ALLEN & OVERY

UITBREIDINGSTRAAT 80
2600 ANTWERPEN

Telephone: +32 3 287 7222
Fax: +32 3 287 7244
E-mail: information@allenovery.com
Website: www.allenovery.com

Languages
Dutch, English, French, German, Italian, Spanish

Other offices
Amsterdam, Bangkok, Beijing, Brussels, Bratislava, Budapest, Dubai, Frankfurt, Hamburg, Hong Kong, London, Luxembourg, Madrid, Milan, Moscow, New York, Paris, Prague, Rome, Shanghai, Singapore, Tokyo, Turin, Warsaw

Number of lawyers 2,305
at this office 38

Contact
Wim Dejonghe

CATEGORIES OF WORK

Corporate and M&A
Wim Dejonghe, Pierre-Olivier Mahieu

Employment and incentives
Karin Rasschaert

Public and administrative
Christian Lesaffer

Banking, finance and capital markets
Sylvia Kierszenbaum

Litigation and ADR
Luc Demeyere

Environment and planning
Els Desair

Media and entertainment
Filip Van Elsen

Insolvency and restructuring
Luc Demeyere

IT, Internet and telecoms
Filip Van Elsen

ANTWERPLAW

DE NATIE
VLAAMSE KAAI 76
2000 ANTWERP

Telephone: +32 3 232 6888
Fax: +32 3 232 6943
E-mail: info@antwerplaw.com
Website: www.antwerplaw.com

Languages
Dutch, English, French, German, Spanish

Other offices
Brasschaat, Paarl

Number of lawyers 13
at this office 6

Contact
Patricia Leers (managing partner)

Member
CLA; BELCLIV-CLUSIB; IMC; MLA; KKNAW; Cape Chamber (Cape Regional Chamber); Cercle (study committee of marine insurers); Universha (Universiteit en Haven)

CATEGORIES OF WORK

Arbitration

Banking, finance and tax law

Competition and general EC law

Environmental and administrative law

General corporate/commercial law and contracts

IT and computer law

Intellectual property

International trade

Media and entertainment

Real estate

Shipping and transport

P&I, charterparties, arrest, customs, cargo, liabilities

Tort, liability and insurance law (marine and non-marine)

Traffic and road accidents

Social law

Legal audit

Outsourcing (defence and recoveries, claim and risk management)

BAKER & McKENZIE

MEIR 24
2000 ANTWERP

Telephone: +32 3 213 40 40
Fax: +32 3 213 40 45
E-mail: baker.br@bakernet.com
Website: www.bakernet.com

Languages
Dutch, English, French, German

Other offices
For a full list of offices and other information regarding the firm please consult Baker & McKenzie's Brussel's office entry

Number of lawyers 3,380
at this office 15

Contacts
Koen Vanhaerents, François Gabriel

CATEGORIES OF WORK

Banking and finance
J Cerfontaine

Corporate
J Cerfontaine

Dispute resolution
K De Winter, J Cerfontaine

Intellectual property
K De Winter

International/commercial
K De Winter

IT/communications
K De Winter

Real estate, construction, environment and tourism
P Mallien

ELEGIS
BUYLE DIERYCK MAINGAIN

KORTE LOZANASTRAAT 20-26
2018 ANTWERPEN

Telephone: +32 3 238 78 50
Fax: +32 3 237 98 99
E-mail: bdm@elegis.be
Website: www.elegis.be

Languages
Dutch, English, French, German

Other offices
Brussels, Eupen, Liege

Number of lawyers 104
at this office 11

Member
AIJA; AEDB; Euro Franchise Lawyers; IBA; ICC; UIA

CATEGORIES OF WORK

Commercial litigation
Werner Van der Veeken, Hugo Callens

Corporate
Hugo Callens

Banking and finance
Christian Dieryck

Labour law
Marina Van der Auweraert

Competition, antitrust
Christian Dieryck, Werner Van der Veeken

Maritime and marine insurance
Paul Verguts, Christian Dieryck

Transportation
Paul Verguts, Christian Dieryck

Construction and project development
Hugo Callens

Arbitration
Christian Dieryck, Paul Verguts

Distribution
Christian Dieryck

Environment
Werner Van der Veeken

Real estate
Hugo Callens

ELEGIS

HUYBRECHTS ENGELS CRAEN AND PARTNERS

AMERIKALEI 73
2000 ANTWERPEN

Telephone: +32 3 244 15 60
Fax: +32 3 238 41 40
E-mail: hec-law@ping.be
Website: www.elegis.be

Languages
Dutch, English, French, German, Italian

Other offices
Brussels, Eupen, Liege

Number of lawyers 104
at this office 23

Member
TerraLex; ECBA; Belgium Maritime Law Association

CATEGORIES OF WORK

Corporate and commercial litigation
Peter Engels, Annemie Cox

Banking and finance
Marc A Huybrechts, Edmond J Brondel

Shipping and transport
Marc A Huybrechts, Wouter Den Haerynck

Employment
MC Craen, Dominique Neirynck

Criminal law
Peter Engels

Insurance
Wouter Den Haerynck, Dominique Neirynck

Construction and project development
Luc Janssens, Peter Engels

Arbitration
Marc A Huybrechts

Distribution
Peter Engels, Edmond J Brondel

Real estate and environment
Peter Engels, Wim Slosse

Administrative law
Wim Slosse, Peter Engels

EU and competition
Annemie Cox, Wouter Den Haerynck

KEGELS & CO

ADVOCATEN

MECHELSESTEENWEG 196
2018 ANTWERPEN

Telephone: +32 3 257 17 71
Fax: +32 3 257 14 74
E-mail: info@kegels-co.be
Website: www.kegels-co.be

Languages
Dutch, English, French, German, Spanish

Number of lawyers 12

CATEGORIES OF WORK

Maritime
Tony Kegels, André Kegels

Inland waters
Tony Kegels

Road and air carriage
Dirk Noels, Valerie Diercken

Transport intermediaries
Dirk Noels, Koen Kerstens

EU and competition
Laurent de Scheemaecker, André Kegels

Agency/distribution
Dirk Noels, Valerie Diercken

Arbitration
Tony Kegels, Patricio Diaz Gavier

Banking and finance
Benoît Goemans, Kristin Verhaegen

Litigation
André Kegels, Dirk Noels

General contracts
Tony Kegels, Dirk Noels

Insurance
Tony Kegels, Tom Valckx

Customs
André Kegels, Mathieu Verly

Employment and labour
Dirk Noels, Koen Kerstens

Liability
Kristin Verhaegen, Sarah Stas

TILLEMAN VAN HOOGENBEMT

MEIR 24, BUS 6
2000 ANTWERP

Telephone: +32 3 220 64 00
Fax: +32 3 220 64 19
E-mail: filip.tilleman@tvh-law.be

Languages
Dutch, English, French, German

Other Offices
Brussels, Paris*

Number of Lawyers 11
at this office 9

Contact
Filip Tilleman

CATEGORIES OF WORK

Labour law
Filip Tilleman,
Herman van Hoogenbemt

Restructuring and transfer of undertakings
Filip Tilleman,
Herman van Hoogenbemt

National and international social security law
Herman van Hoogenbemt,
Yves Jorens

Discrimination and harassment
Filip Tilleman

European labour law
Yves Jorens

Pension plans
Herman van Hoogenbemt

Criminal law
Michael Verhaeghe

Commercial law
Ann De Wael

THE FIRM

Tilleman van Hoogenbemt (TVH) is a niche firm specialising in all legal matters related to national and international employment. Its founders, Filip Tilleman and Herman van Hoogenbemt, were partners in the labour department of the former Benelux firm Loeff Claeys Verbeke. Both have published numerous books and articles on all aspects of labour law and are frequent speakers at conferences.

Yves Jorens is professor of national and international social security law in the faculty of law at the universities of Gent and Antwerp. He is an expert in, and has written many books and articles on European social law and international employment. He is also project director of an European Observatory for the Social Security of Migrant Workers, commissioned by the European Commission, which gives him wide access to social security authorities throughout the EU.

AREAS OF PRACTICE

The firm mainly focuses its interest on all topics of labour law, both individual (dismissals, working time, remuneration, harassment, etc) and collective (collective redundancies, negotiations with unions, transfer of undertakings, strikes, etc), social security law, international employment, and any other employment-related branch of the law (tax law, criminal law, privacy, unfair competition of former employees, intellectual property, etc).

In order to support its activities in its major field of interest, the firm also conducts a general business law practice, as well as a criminal law practice, focused on social criminal law.

Although the firm has a strong academic background, its main purpose is to provide its clients with concrete solutions, based on a thorough knowledge of a client's business and needs and a no-nonsense approach. TVH lawyers are strongly committed to providing clients with workable and clear solutions without entering into legal details if these are not relevant for business people. If necessary, clients' interests are strongly defended before all possible courts.

The firm as a whole is strongly committed to a cost-effective approach, thus aiming at giving more value for money. As a result, the firm has succeeded in keeping its fees substantially below market average.

TVH serves all kinds of business clients, including both global and local companies. In order to serve its internationally orientated clients, the firm has established an informal network of correspondents in a number of European countries, thus avoiding the additional costs of setting up a formal organisation, while having recourse to specialised services abroad. However, due to its frequent involvement in cases related to cross-border employment between Belgium and its neighbouring countries, the firm has set up formal links with like-minded firms in France (Pierre-Phillippe Franc in Paris) and the Netherlands (Houben Advocaten in Breda).

AFSCHRIFT

AVENUE LOUISE 208
1050 BRUSSELS

Telephone: +32 2 646 46 36
Fax: +32 2 644 38 00
E-mail: avocats@afschrift.com
Website: www.afschrift.com

Languages
Croatian, Dutch, English, French, German, Hebrew, Italian, Slovenian, Spanish

Other offices
Geneva, Madrid

Number of lawyers 20

Member
TELFA (Trans European Law Firms Alliance)

CATEGORIES OF WORK

Tax
Thierry Afschrift, Sophie Vanhaelst

VAT
Muriel Igalson

Joint venture, M&A
Thierry Afschrift, Martin van Beirs

Estate planning
Pascale Hautfenne, Sylvie Leyder

Corporate, finance
Martin van Beirs, Ines Wouters

Litigation, arbitration
Sylvie Leyder, Anne Rayet

Intellectual property
Anne Rayet, Thierry Afschrift

ALLEN & OVERY

AVENUE DE TERVUEREN 268 A
1150 BRUSSELS

Telephone: +32 2 780 2222
Fax: +32 2 780 2244
E-mail: information@allenovery.com
Website: www.allenovery.com

Languages
Dutch, English, French, German, Italian, Spanish, Russian

Other offices
Amsterdam, Antwerp, Bangkok, Beijing, Bratislava, Brussels, Budapest, Dubai, Frankfurt, Hamburg, Hong Kong, London, Luxembourg, Madrid, Milan, Moscow,New York, Paris, Prague, Rome, Shanghai, Singapore, Tirana, Tokyo, Turin, Warsaw

Number of lawyers 2,305
at this office 118

Contact
Wim Dejonghe,
Michael Reynolds (EU and competition law)

CATEGORIES OF WORK

Aviation
Werner Eyskens

Banking and finance
Pieter Bienenstock

Capital markets
Philippe Hamer, Dirk Meeus

Corporate and M&A
Louis-H Verbeke

Employment and incentives
Pieter De Koster

Environment and planning
Jan Schamp

EU and competition law
David Harrison, Francis Herbert

Insolvency and restructuring
Koen Van den Broeck, Werner Eyskens

Intellectual property
Thierry van Innis

IT, Internet and telecoms
Geert Glas

Litigation and ADR
Joost Everaert, Koen Van den Broeck

Media and entertainment
Geert Glas

Property
Bruno de Duve, Daniel Gillet

Public and administrative
Véronique Vanden Acker

State aids
David Harrison, Jacques Steenbergen

Taxation
Bruno de Duve, Philippe Hinnekens

Trade law and antidumping
Francis Herbert

ALTIUS

AVENUE DU PORT, 16
1080 BRUSSELS

Telephone: +32 2 426 1414
Fax: +32 2 426 2030
E-mail: info@altius.com
Website: www.altius.com

Languages
Dutch, English, French, German, Italian, Spanish

Number of lawyers 40

Contact
Johan De Bruycker
(johan.debruycker@altius.com)

CATEGORIES OF WORK

Commercial contracts and IT
Herman De Bauw

Commercial litigation
Christophe Ronse

Banking and finance
Johan De Bruycker

Capital markets
Johan De Bruycker

Intellectual property
Paul Maeyert

Competition law
Carmen Verdonck

Employment law
Sylvie Dubois

Property/environment
William Timmermans

Mergers and acquisitions
Philippe Jadoul,
Carine van Regenmortel

ARNOLD & PORTER LLP

11 RUE DES COLONIES
KOLONIËNSTRAAT 11
1000 BRUSSELS

Telephone: +32 2 517 6600
Fax: +32 2 517 6603
Website: www.arnoldporter.com

Languages
Arabic, Bengali, Chinese, Ebrou, Estonian, Farsi, Filipino, French, German, Greek, Hebrew, Hindustani/Punjabi/Urdu, Hungarian, Italian, Japanese, Konkani (Indian), Latin, Marathi, Portuguese, Russian, Sesotho, Spanish, Turkish, Vietnamese

Other offices
Washington DC, Century City, Denver, London, Los Angeles, New York, McLean (Virginia)

Number of lawyers 724
at this office 9

International groupings
The World Law Group

CATEGORIES OF WORK

Antitrust, competition and trade regulation
Marleen Van Kerckhove (Brussels),
Bill Baer (DC)

Bankruptcy
Daniel Lewis (DC)

Corporate and commercial
Jeremy Willcocks (London),
Steve Kaplan (DC)

Environmental
Thomas Milch (DC)

EU regulatory
Ian Dodds-Smith (London)

Financial institutions
Patrick Doyle (DC)

Food, drug and medical devices
John Bentivoglio (DC)

Intellectual property and technology
Joel Freed (DC), David Apatoff (DC)

International arbitration
Jean Kalicki (DC)

International trade
Larry Schneider (DC)

Life sciences, biotech
Richard Johnson (DC),
Julian Thurston (London)

Litigation
Robert Weiner (DC)

Product liability
Ian Dodds-Smith (London)

Tax
Dick Hubbard (DC)

Telecoms/media and Internet
Michael Ryan (London),
Patrick J Grant (DC)

Real estate
George Covucci (DC),
Lee Narrow (London)

ASHURST

AVENUE LOUISE 489
1050 BRUXELLES

Telephone: +32 2 626 1900
Fax: +32 2 626 1901
Website: www.ashurst.com

Languages
Dutch, English, French, Greek, Italian, Spanish

Other offices
Frankfurt, London, Madrid, Milan, Munich, New Delhi*, New York, Paris, Singapore, Tokyo

Number of lawyers 813
at this office 30

Contacts
Julian Ellison, Carl Meyntjens

CATEGORIES OF WORK

EU law

Competition, information technology, telecommunications, energy, transport, insurance and financial services

International trade law, dumping, subsidies and origin rules

Litigation and representation before the European Courts in Luxembourg

Public procurement

State aid

Belgian law

Cross-border M&A/MBO/LBO

Banking/capital markets/ EASDAQ listings

Company/commercial

Employment

BECH-BRUUN DRAGSTED

AVENUE DE TERVUEREN 155
1150 BRUXELLES

Telephone: +32 2 736 05 23
Fax: +32 2 736 20 51
E-mail:
bruxelles@bechbruundragsted.com
Website: www.bechbruundragsted.com

Languages
English, French, German

Other offices
Aarhus, Copenhagen, Moscow

Number of lawyers 261
at this office 4

Contact
Morten Lau Smith

CATEGORIES OF WORK

General EU law practice

Competition law

Public procurement

The internal market

Telecommunications and media

Air and maritime transport

Cases before the European Court of Justice and the Court of First Instance

BAKER & McKENZIE

AVENUE LOUISE 149
EIGHTH FLOOR
1050 BRUSSELS

Telephone: +32 2 639 36 11
Fax: +32 2 639 36 99
E-mail: baker.br@bakernet.com
Website: www.bakernet.com

Languages Dutch, English, French, German, Greek, Italian

Other offices Almaty, Amsterdam, Antwerp, Bahrain, Baku, Bangkok, Barcelona, Beijing, Berlin, Bogotá, Bologna, Brasilia, Brussels, Budapest, Buenos Aires, Cairo, Calgary, Caracas, Chicago, Dallas, Düsseldorf, Frankfurt, Geneva, Guadalajara, Hanoi, Ho Chi Minh City, Hong Kong, Houston, Juarez, Kyiv, London, Madrid, Manila, Melbourne, Mexico City, Miami, Milan, Monterrey, Moscow, Munich, New York, Palo Alto, Paris, Porto Alegré, Prague, Rio de Janeiro, Riyadh, Rome, St Petersburg, San Diego, San Francisco, Santiago, São Paulo, Shanghai, Singapore, Stockholm, Sydney, Taipei, Tijuana, Tokyo, Toronto, Valencia, Vienna, Warsaw, Washington DC, Zürich

Number of lawyers 3,380
at this office 50

Contacts
Koen Vanhaerents, François Gabriel

CATEGORIES OF WORK

Banking and finance
I Maes, A De Raeve

Corporate finance
K Vanhaerents, P Leys

Dispute resolution
P Sculier

Employment
J Slootmans, F Gabriel

Intellectual property
P Sculier

International/commercial
P Herten, A Gutermann

IT/communications
A Gutermann, D Fesler

Real estate, construction, environment and tourism
D Lechien, P Herten

Tax
A Huyghe, P Lion

THE FIRM

Baker & McKenzie is a leading global law firm with 66 offices in 36 countries. A multinational network of over 4,400 legal professionals offers clients resources and knowledge in every area of business law in virtually every important financial and commercial centre in the world.

Baker & McKenzie has been established in Europe for over 40 years, having opened its first European offices in 1957. Since then, the European and Middle Eastern network has grown to 29 offices, giving it unparalleled geographical coverage.

The Brussels office opened in 1957. In 1998, Baker & McKenzie set up a dedicated European Law Centre in Brussels, which serves as the firm's centre of expertise on all issues of European Union law.

In March 2002, Baker & McKenzie merged with the Antwerp-based law practice of Jan Cerfontaine, Pascal Mallien and Koen De Winter.

Baker & McKenzie aims to provide clients with practical solutions by combining technical excellence with a creative and results-oriented approach.

AREAS OF PRACTICE

Baker & McKenzie co-ordinates its core practice areas on local, regional and global levels, giving most of its lawyers experience in more than one jurisdiction, as well as providing multinational teams of specialists.

Utilising a global practice group structure and groundbreaking technology coupled with a personal, detailed understanding of a client's specific business, Baker & McKenzie is able to organise its extensive resources to provide focused and strategic counsel to clients.

Baker & McKenzie in Brussels has advised on the structuring of transactions and the conduct of business in conformity with both local and European Community law, in a broad range of practice areas, including corporate and commercial; banking and finance; securities and capital markets transactions; international taxation; pensions and executive compensation; commercial litigation and arbitration; mergers and acquisitions; real estate; environmental law; intellectual property and information technology; and employment law.

BAKER & McKENZIE

EUROPEAN LAW CENTRE

AVENUE LOUISE 149
EIGHTH FLOOR
1050 BRUSSELS

Telephone: +32 2 639 37 66
Fax: +32 2 538 77 26
E-mail: elc@bakernet.com
Website: www.bakernet.com

Languages
Dutch, English, French, German, Greek, Italian, Portuguese, Spanish

Other offices Almaty, Amsterdam, Antwerp, Bahrain, Baku, Bangkok, Barcelona, Beijing, Berlin, Bogotá, Bologna, Brasilia, Brussels, Budapest, Buenos Aires, Cairo, Calgary, Caracas, Chicago, Dallas, Düsseldorf, Frankfurt, Geneva, Gudalajara, Hanoi, Ho Chi Minh City, Hong Kong, Houston, Juarez, Kyiv, London, Madrid, Manila, Melbourne, Mexico City, Miami, Milan, Monterrey, Moscow, Munich, New York, Palo Alto, Paris, Porto Alegré, Prague, Rio de Janeiro, Riyadh, Rome, St Petersburg, San Diego, San Francisco, Santiago, São Paulo, Shanghai, Singapore, Stockholm, Sydney, Taipei, Tijuana, Tokyo, Toronto, Valencia, Vienna, Warsaw, Washington DC, Zürich

Number of lawyers 3,380
at this office 7

Contacts
Fiona Carlin, Thomas Lampert

CATEGORIES OF WORK

Customs and trade law (including EU and WTO)
K Katsoulis

Enlargement (advice concerning aspects resulting from the accession of the new member states to the EU)
F Carlin, K Katsoulis

EU constitutional law
Prof CO Lenz

European cartels and transatlantic investigations
F Carlin, Th Lampert

European merger control and co-ordination of multinational merger control
Th Lampert, N Niejahr

General European competition law (including competition law advice in distribution systems and competition law compliance)
F Carlin, Th Lampert

Internal market
N Niejahr, K Katsoulis

Litigation
Prof CO Lenz

Public Affairs
K Katsoulis

Public procurement
K Katsoulis, N Niejahr

State aids
N Niejahr, K Haegeman

Telecommunications, energy and regulated industries
F Carlin, Th Lampert

THE FIRM

Baker & McKenzie is a leading global law firm with 66 offices in 36 countries. A multinational network of over 4,400 legal professionals offers clients resources and knowledge in every area of business law in virtually every important financial and commercial centre in the world.

Baker & McKenzie has been established in Europe for over 40 years, having opened its first European offices in 1957. Since then, the European and Middle Eastern network has grown to 29 offices, giving it unparalleled geographical coverage.

The Brussels office opened in 1957. In 1998, Baker & McKenzie set up a dedicated European Law Centre (ELC) in Brussels, which serves as the firm's centre of expertise on all issues of European Union law.

In March 2002, Baker & McKenzie merged with the Antwerp-based law practice of Jan Cerfontaine, Pascal Malien and Koen De Winter.

Baker & McKenzie aims to provide clients with practical solutions by combining technical excellence with a creative and results-oriented approach.

The ELC brings together lawyers from different legal and linguistic backgrounds (EU) who specialise in EU law and policy, whilst being fully integrated within Baker & McKenzie's global and European network. Among its leading lawyers, the ELC counts: Professor Dr Carl Otto Lenz (Of Counsel, former Advocate General at the European Court of Justice); Fiona Carlin (managing partner of the European Law Centre with over ten years' experience in Brussels and chair of the Competition Law Subcommittee of the American Chamber of Commerce); Dr Thomas Lampert (partner and specialist in EU and German competition law); Ross Denton (partner and competition lawyer, and also head of the firm's WTO law practice); and Carla Hamburger (Of Counsel, a well known and highly respected Dutch and EU competition law specialist).

AREAS OF PRACTICE

Baker & McKenzie co-ordinates its core practice areas on local, regional and global levels, enabling it to provide clients with a multinational team of specialists where appropriate. The European Law Centre (ELC) is the focal point of Baker & McKenzie's European Competition Law Practice Group, comprising more than 85 lawyers.

As such, the ELC regularly provides advice on the competition law implications of mergers, joint ventures and other complex transactions. When transactions are required to be notified to national regulators, the ELC co-ordinates such notifications, in unison with members of the firm's global antitrust group, which is present in every major antitrust centre around the world.

The ELC is also regularly engaged in cartel work dealing with both the European Commission and national competition authorities. It regularly prepares tailored competition compliance programmes for its clients and offers targeted competition audits.

The ELC has extensive experience in advising clients, including governments, on EU state aid matters, such as the implications of being recipents of state subsidies, preferential tax treatment and other forms of state aid, and also helps clients who are at a competitive disadvantage in comparison to their competitors who have received state aid.

The ELC frequently monitors and advises on other areas of EU legislation, such as internal market issues, telecommunications and e-commerce law, environmental and energy law, the public procurement rules, financial services, and constitutional matters and legislative procedures. The ELC has in-depth expertise in international trade matters, and represents clients in anti-dumping investigations initiated by the European Commission. It advises on customs legislation, as well as on EU export controls, trade sanctions and WTO rules. The ELC's litigation team and public affairs unit are both very experienced and successful in a variety of EU-related matters.

BERTOUILLE & PARTNERS

RUE DE LA VALLEÉ 43
1000 BRUSSELS

Telephone: +32 2 647 97 00
Fax: +32 2 647 98 99
E-mail: info@bertouille-law.be
Website: www.bertouille-law.be

Languages
English, French, Dutch, German

Other offices
Prague

Number of lawyers 18
at this office 15

Contact
Stéphane Bertouille

Member
World IT Lawyers; Moore Stephens Legal Network; Interjurist

CATEGORIES OF WORK

Mergers and acquisitions
Stéphane Bertouille, Phillipe Van den Broecke

Tax planning
Stéphane Bertouille, Catherine Sbille

Personal income tax (international)
Catherine Sbille, Philippe Willemsens

Litigation
Peter Bax, Mario Van Santvoort

General commercial law
Phillipe Van den Broecke, Damien Joos de ter Beerst

Employment law
Bénédicte Tilmant, Naima Es-Samri

Corporate law
Guy Rulkin, Judith Swerts

Establishment in Belgium
Bénédicte Tilmant

Intellectual property
Véronique Marien

Telecoms
Stéphane Bertouille, Bie Heyninck

BIRD & BIRD

RUE DE LA LOI 15
1040 BRUSSELS

Telephone: +32 2 282 6000
Fax: +32 2 282 6011
E-mail: brussels@twobirds.com
Website: www.twobirds.com

Languages
English, Dutch, French, German, Italian, Spanish

Other offices
Düsseldorf, Hong Kong, London, Milan, Munich, Paris, Stockholm, The Hague

Number of lawyers 358
at this office 23

Contact
Paul Hermant

CATEGORIES OF WORK

Aviation

Banking and financial services

Communications

Competition and EU law

Corporate

Employment

Internet and e-commerce

Information technology

Intellectual property

Media and sport

Life sciences

BREDIN PRAT

6 AVENUE LLOYD GEORGE
1000 BRUXELLES

Telephone: +32 2 639 2710
Fax: +32 2 646 0311

Languages
Dutch, English, French

Other offices
Paris

Number of lawyers 57
at this office 4

CATEGORIES OF WORK

General EU law	**European litigation**
EC competition	**State aid**
Merger control	

THE FIRM

Bredin Prat is a Paris-based law firm specialised in business law and in particular high-level mergers and acquisitions (including major French privatisations) and litigation. The Paris office has acquired a widely recognised expertise in the field of domestic and EU competition law with its highly respected partners Robert Saint-Esteben and Hugues Calvet.

The Brussels Office was founded in 1999. In 2003, Marc Pittie became the Brussels-based partner in charge of the office, heading a team of four EU specialised lawyers, members of the Paris or the Brussels Bar.

Through previous experience in private practice and as a clerk at the Court of First Instance in Luxembourg, Marc Pittie has wide experience of international transactions as well as behavioural cases before the European Commission and the European courts. The Brussels office has also developed an in-depth understanding of the internal politics of the Commission and good working relationships with its officials, as well as a strong insight of litigation in front of the European Community courts.

The Brussels practice is fully integrated within the Paris office's competition law practice group with a total number of 11 lawyers dedicated to EU and national competition.

AREAS OF PRACTICE

The firm advises on all aspects of competition law including merger control, abuse of a dominant position, cartels, state aids, regulatory matters and commercial transactions, both at a counselling and litigation stage. Its Brussels based lawyers are able to give advice and opinions on EU, French and/or Belgian law in French, English and Dutch, and appear in front of European as well as national jurisdictions.

Having been involved in many major cases involving both French and multinational companies, the firm has gained special expertise in complex and highly sensitive transactions and litigation cases.

The Brussels office has acquired specific experience in the fields of telecoms, the entertainment industry, banking facilities and also various industrial sectors.

Through the Paris office, the firm is able to offer a full range of services, advising on M&A and corporate as well as tax aspects. Relying on its 'Best-Friends' network, Bredin Prat also offers assistance on an international basis, especially as regards international antitrust filings and clearances in the context of multi-jurisdictional transactions and multi-jurisdictional cartel investigations.

CMS EU LAW OFFICE

AVENUE LOUISE 200
1050 BRUXELLES

Telephone: +32 2 650 04 20
Fax: +32 2 650 04 22
E-mail: eulawoffice@cmslegal.com
Website: www.cmslegal.com

Languages
English, French, German, Dutch, Italian

Other CMS offices advising on EU law
Aberdeen, Düsseldorf, Frankfurt, Hamburg, London, Lyon, Milan, Munich, Paris, Rome, Stuttgart, Vienna, Utrecht, Zurich

Number of lawyers 1,800
at this office 8

CMS law firms
CMS Adonnino Ascoli & Cavasola Scamoni; CMS Bureau Francis Lefebvre; CMS Cameron McKenna; CMS Derks Star Busmann; CMS von Erlach Klainguti Stettler Wille; CMS Hasche Sigle; CMS Lexcelis; CMS Strommer Reich-Rohrwig Karasek Hainz

Contacts
M Bauer, R Bosman

CATEGORIES OF WORK

Competition and antitrust

Merger control

State aid

Anti-dumping and subsidies

WTO regulation

EU customs law

Free movement of goods and services

Distribution and franchising

EU litigation

Lobbying of EU institutions

CMS LEXCELIS

AVENUE LOUISE 200
1050 BRUSSELS

Telephone: +32 2 626 22 00
Fax: +32 2 626 22 51
E-mail: firstname.name@cmslegal.be
Website: www.cmslegal.be

Languages
English, Dutch, French, German, Italian

Number of lawyers 29

Contacts
Stanislas van Wassenhove, Bruno Duquesne

Member
CMS is a transnational legal and tax organisation established by eight European law firms with the express aim of providing integrated cross-border services. Other members include: CMS Adonnino Ascoli & Cavasola Scamoni, Italy; CMS Bureau Francis Lefebvre, France; CMS Cameron McKenna, UK; CMS Derks Star Busmann, The Netherlands; CMS Hasche Sigle, Germany; CMS Strommer Reich-Rohrwig Karasek Hainz, Austria; CMS von Erlach Klainguti Stettler Wille, Switzerland.

CATEGORIES OF WORK

Mergers and acquisitions

Banking, securities and finance

Corporate restructuring

Bankruptcy and insolvency

Distribution, IT and IP

Dispute resolution

Employment and pensions

Real estate

Taxation

CHIOMENTI STUDIO LEGALE

41 AVE R VANDENDRIESSCHE
1150 BRUSSELS

Telephone: +32 2 775 9900
Fax: +32 2 775 9927
E-mail: bruxelles@chiomenti.net

Languages
English, French, German, Italian

Other offices
London, Milan, New York, Rome, Turin

Number of lawyers 140
at this office 4

Member
Lex Mundi

CATEGORIES OF WORK	
Corporate and M&A	**IP, media and IT**
Banking and finance	**Litigation and arbitration**
Capital markets	**Insolvency and corporate restructuring**
Regulatory and financial services	**Employment and labour**
Tax	**Telecommunications**
European, competition and international law	**Energy**
Administrative and environmental law	**Real estate**

THE FIRM

Chiomenti Studio Legale continues the practice started by Pasquale Chiomenti in the late 1940s as one of the first Italian law firms with international capabilities, advising Italian and foreign clients in the progressive expansion of post-war economy.

Since then Chiomenti Studio Legale has steadily consolidated its initial position as one of Italy's leading law firms, meeting the challenge of increasing globalisation of business. Today the firm is composed of more than 150 lawyers and tax advisers and has offices in Rome, Milan, Turin, London, Brussels and – since September 2003 – New York.

Chiomenti has always been a leader in tailoring legal techniques developed in an international context for implementation in Italy and specifically in developing Italian legal techniques in order to accommodate the requirements of international business clients. This is of increasing importance today when the majority of business transactions in Europe have a cross-border dimension and a growing proportion of legal disputes have an international aspect.

In 2001, Chiomenti Studio Legale and Skadden, Arps, Slate, Meagher & Flom entered into a strategic alliance that combines their respective strengths in US, Italian and English law.

AREAS OF PRACTICE

Corporate and M&A: friendly and hostile takeovers, leveraged and management buy-outs, privatisations, joint ventures, company restructuring, general corporate and commercial transactions.

Banking and finance: debt and equity instruments, international and domestic loans, real estate loans, debt restructuring and rescheduling etc.

Capital markets: IPOs and other public offerings, equity offerings, financial products private and public placements.

Regulatory and financial services: rules and regulations applying to banks, financial intermediaries, investment funds and insurance companies. Representing clients before Bank of Italy, CONSOB and ISVAP, formations, mergers, spin-offs, purchases and sales.

Tax: corporate and individual taxation, mergers and acquisitions and corporate reorganisation, international and EU taxation.

European law, competition and international law: advice in connection with antitrust matters, public subsidies, telecoms, power, transportation, free circulation of goods and services, agriculture, concentration and consolidation of joint ventures and unfair competition.

Administrative law and environmental law: contracts and concessions of public works, service and supply contracts, legal assistance to administrative authorities and to private and public entities operating in the utilities sector.

IP, media and IT: copyrights, trade marks, trade secrets, patents, new communication and transmission systems and media and communications rules and regulations.

Litigation and arbitration: financial and commercial disputes before civil and administrative courts and administrative authorities and national supervisory authorities.

Insolvency and corporate restructuring: assistance in connection with bankruptcy procedures, pre-packaged bankruptcies, bankruptcy administration and liquidations.

Employment and labour: national, European and international employment and labour law.

Telecommunications and energy: regulatory issues, licensing, interconnection, telecoms securities offering and project financing.

Energy: regulatory issues, project finance, mergers and acquisitions, sales and joint venture.

Real estate: acquisition and sale, mergers and spin-offs, rentals, construction, bids, development, asset management services, leasing, credit over pledge securitisation, and credits from rentals.

DCH (DE CALUWÉ & HORSMANS)

AVENUE LOUISE 283/21
1050 BRUSSELS

Telephone: +32 2 639 26 26
Fax: +32 2 639 26 27
E-mail: law@horsmans.be
Website: www.dch-lawyers.com

Languages
Dutch, English, French, German, Spanish

Number of lawyers 24

CATEGORIES OF WORK

Corporate	**White-collar crime**
Banking and finance	**Competition law**
Employment and incentives	**Intellectual property**
EU-WTO law	**Real estate**
Litigation and arbitration	**Medical and pharmaceutical law**
Tax law	**Administrative law**
Bankruptcy	

ELEGIS

BUYLE DIERYCK MAINGAIN

RUE AUGUSTE DE BOECK 54
1140 BRUXELLES

Telephone: +32 2 240 15 20
Fax: +32 2 240 15 30
E-mail: bdm@elegis.be
Website: www.elegis.be

Languages
Dutch, English, French, German

Other offices
Antwerp, Eupen, Liege

Number of lawyers 104
at this office 35

Member
AIJA; AEDBF; Euro Franchise Lawyers; IBA; ICC; UIA

CATEGORIES OF WORK

Commercial litigation André Lombart, Daniel De Jaeger	**Distribution and franchising** André Lombart, Daniel De Jaeger
Corporate Jean Pierre Renard	**Computer law** Christophe Steyaert
Banking and finance Jean-Pierre Buyle, Christophe Steyaert	**Tax** Marc Marlière
Labour law Bernard Maingain	**Mergers and acquisitions** Jean Pierre Renard, Bernard Maingain
Competition, antitrust Christophe Steyaert	**Bankruptcy and insolvency** Jean-Pierre Renard, Philippe Colle
Intellectual property Daniel De Jaeger	**Financial criminal law** Jean-Pierre Buyle, Jean-Pierre Renard
Contracts Philippe Colle	**Insurance law** Philippe Colle
Real estate and construction Françoise Balon	**Patrimony rights** Françoise Balon

DLA CAESTECKER

106 AVENUE LOUISE
1050 BRUSSELS

Telephone: +32 2 500 1 500
Fax: +32 2 500 1 600
E-mail: steven.de.keyser@dla.com
Website: www.dla.be

Languages
Danish, Dutch, English, French, German, Greek, Spanish, Swedish

Other offices
Amsterdam, Antwerp, Bangkok, Bergen, Berlin, Birmingham, Bradford, Bratislava, Budapest, Cologne, Copenhagen, Edinburgh, Essen, Frankfurt, Glasgow, Hamburg, Hong Kong, Leeds, Liverpool, London, Madrid, Manchester, Milan, Moscow, Oslo, Paris, Prague, Rotterdam, Salzberg, Sarajevo, Shanghai, Sheffield, Singapore, Stockholm, Vienna, Zagreb

Number of lawyers 95
at this office 80

Contact
Steven De Keyser (regional managing partner)

Member
DLA Group

CATEGORIES OF WORK

Banking and finance
Yves Brosens

Business support and restructuring
Christian Van Buggenhout

Competition
Charles Price

Commercial and projects
Catherine Grisart

Corporate, mergers and acquisitions
Dirk Caestecker

Environmental and administrative
Bob Martens

EU and competition
David Cox, Frank Fine

Labour law
Eddy Lievens

Litigation and arbitration
Catherine Grisart, Charles Price

Public-private partnership and outsourcing
Steven De Keyser

Real estate
Els Empereur

Sports law
Catherine Grisart

Technology, media and communications (IT/IP)
Benoît Michaux, Patrick Van Eecke

Trade, anti-dumping and WTO
Prof Geert Van Calster

Transport and logistics

THE FIRM

DLA Caestecker is a law firm with origins that go back to January 1997 and that was quickly recognised as one of the fastest-growing law firms in Belgium.

Today, 95 lawyers (including 18 partners) work for DLA Caestecker in Belgium. DLA Caestecker offers a full-service, locally led law firm with international capability to national and international clients.

DLA is the founding member of DLA Group. DLA Group is an exclusive alliance of international full-service law firms with a shared vision. Established in 1999, DLA Group now has over 2,200 lawyers across 21 countries, who deliver expert local know-how and international solutions. DLA Group provides legal advice in 37 major cities across Europe, Singapore, Thailand, Hong Kong and the People's Republic of China.

DLA Caestecker has offices in Brussels and Antwerp. DLA Caestecker's clients are medium-sized and large national and international companies as well as local governments.

DLA is already one of the world's largest law firms and is keen to maintain its reputation for providing quality advice on all the day-to-day issues faced by medium and large businesses.

AREAS OF PRACTICE

DLA Caestecker invests in its clients to understand what their needs really are and how value can be added to their business. A team typically consists of lawyers able to really understand and empathise with client's commercial needs, both locally and on a broader international level. Lawyers of DLA Caestecker differentiate themselves by their speed of response and their desire to put the client first.

DLA Caestecker's lawyers specialise in all aspects of business law and regularly transact on a cross-border basis. DLA Caestecker is organised to provide a range of essential business legal advice including: banking and finance; business support and restructuring; commercial and projects; corporate and M&A; environment and administrative; EU and competition; human resources; litigation and arbitration; public-private partnership and outsourcing; real estate; sports; technology, media and communications; transport and logistics.

A brochure providing more details is available upon request or at www.dla.be.

FRESHFIELDS BRUCKHAUS DERINGER

BASTION TOWER
PLACE DU CHAMP DE MARS/
MARSVELDPLEIN 5
1050 BRUSSELS

Telephone: +32 2 504 7000
Fax: +32 2 504 7200
E-mail: email@freshfields.com
Website: www.freshfields.com

Languages
Extensive language capabilities

Other offices
Amsterdam, Bangkok, Barcelona, Beijing, Berlin, Bratislava, Budapest, Cologne, Düsseldorf, Frankfurt, Hamburg, Hanoi, Ho Chi Minh City, Hong Kong, London, Madrid, Milan, Moscow, Munich, New York, Paris, Rome, Shanghai, Singapore, Tokyo, Vienna, Washington

Number of lawyers 2,504
at this office 93

Contact
Michael Schütte

CATEGORIES OF WORK

- Corporate
- Finance
- Antitrust, competition and trade
- Intellectual property and IT
- Dispute resolution (including environment, planning and regulatory)
- Employment, pensions and benefits
- Real estate
- Tax

GIDE LOYRETTE NOUEL

VIEW BUILDING
RUE DE L'INDUSTRIE, 26-38
1040 BRUSSELS

Telephone: +32 2 231 11 40
Fax: +32 2 231 11 77
E-mail: gln.brussels@gide.com
Website: www.gide.com

Other offices
Algiers, Beijing, Bucharest, Budapest, Casablanca, Hanoi, Istanbul, London, Moscow, New York, Paris, Prague, Riyadh, Shanghai, Tunis, Warsaw

Number of lawyers 480
at this office 20

Contacts
Dominique Voillemot (voillemot@gide.com),
Antoine Gosset-Grainville (gossetgrainville@gide.com),
Olivier Prost (prost@gide.com),
Michel Jacquot (jacquot@gide.com),
Jean Naslin (naslin@gide.com)

CATEGORIES OF WORK

- EU and competition
- International trade
- Anti-dumping and countervailing duty proceedings
- GATT/WTO regulations
- Customs law
- Free movement of individuals, capital, goods and services
- Distribution and franchising
- Litigation
- Information technology
- Telecommunications
- E-commerce and the Internet
- Public procurement
- Agriculture and food processing industry law

GLEISS LUTZ
RECHTSANWÄLTE

RUE GUIMARD 7
1040 BRUSSELS

Telephone: +32 2 551 10 20
Fax: +32 2 512 15 68
E-mail: info@gleisslutz.com
Website: www.gleisslutz.com

Languages
Dutch, German, English, French, Italian, Mandarin, Cantonese, Polish, Portuguese, Spanish, Russian, Czech, Slovak

Other offices
Berlin, Frankfurt, Munich, Stuttgart, Prague, Warsaw

Number of lawyers 200
at this office 5

Contact
Dr Ulrich Soltesz

Not authorised to appear before the Belgian courts

CATEGORIES OF WORK

German and international law

General EU law

Competition, antitrust

Mergers control

Anti-dumping and subsidies law

State aid

EU litigation

International trade law

German antitrust and commercial law

HAARMANN HEMMELRATH

118 AV DE CORTENBERGH
1000 BRUSSELS

Telephone: +32 2 74 01 100
Fax: +32 2 74 01 133
E-mail: brussels@haarmannhemmelrath.com
Website: www.haarmannhemmelrath.com

Languages
Dutch, English, French, German, Italian, Mandarin, Spanish, Vietnamese

Other offices
Berlin, Bielefeld, Bucharest, Budapest, Cologne, Dusseldorf, Frankfurt, Hamburg, Leipzig, London, Milan, Moscow, Munich, Paris, Prague, Rome, Shanghai, Singapore, Stuttgart, Tokyo, Vienna, Warsaw

Number of lawyers 281
at this office 7

CATEGORIES OF WORK

Antitrust law (including co-ordination of multi-jurisdiction antitrust proceedings)
Dr Rainer Roniger, Dr Astrid Ablasser

Public procurement law
Dr Rainer Roniger, Dr Matthias Lang

State aid law
Martina Maier, Dr Rainer Roniger

Merger control law (including co-ordination of multi-jurisdiction filings)
Dr Rainer Roniger, Martina Maier

International trade
Dr Rainer Roniger, Michael Hundebeck

Distribution
Dr Rainer Roniger, Dr Astrid Ablasser

Energy
DDr Christian Schneider, Dr Rainer Roniger

Transport
Martina Maier, DDr Christian Schneider

EC litigation
Martina Maier, Dr Rainer Roniger

General EU law
Martina Maier, Dr Rainer Roniger

HANOTIAU & VAN DEN BERG

AVENUE LOUISE 480/9
1050 BRUSSELS

Telephone: +32 2 290 39 00
Fax: +32 2 290 39 39
E-mail: info@hvdb.com
Website: www.hvdb.com

Languages
Dutch, English, French, German, Portuguese

Other offices
Paris

Number of lawyers 17

CATEGORIES OF WORK

International arbitration and litigation, including:

Competition

Construction and engineering

Corporate

Distribution and franchising

Energy and natural resources

Banking and finance

Information and communication technology

Intellectual property

Joint ventures, consortia and co-operation

Sales and purchasing

Transport and air law

Post M&A litigation

HENGELER MUELLER

AVENUE DE CORTENBERGH 118
BOITE 2
1000 BRUXELLES

Telephone: +32 2 7885 500
Fax: +32 2 7885 599
E-mail: hmbrx@hengeler.com
Website: www.hengeler.com

Other offices
Düsseldorf, Frankfurt, Berlin, London, Budapest, Prague

Number of lawyers 195
at this office 7

Contacts
Dr Bernhard Maassen, Dr Hans-Jörg Niemeyer, Dr Christoph Stadler

CATEGORIES OF WORK

EU and German competition law

Merger control

European regulatory affairs

State aid

Healthcare and life sciences

HERBERT SMITH

15 RUE GUIMARD
1040 BRUXELLES

Telephone: +32 2 511 7450
Fax: +32 2 511 7772
E-mail: contact@herbertsmith.com
Website: www.herbertsmith.com

Languages
Dutch, English, Finnish, French, German, Greek, Italian, Spanish, Swedish

Other offices
Bangkok, Beijing, Hong Kong, London, Moscow, Paris, Shanghai, Singapore, Tokyo

Number of lawyers 1,108
at this office 11

Contacts
Stephen Kinsella, Craig Pouncey

CATEGORIES OF WORK

Competition
Stephen Kinsella, Craig Pouncey

Customs, trade and WTO
Craig Pouncey, Lode Van Den Hende

Intellectual property
Stephen Kinsella

Mergers
Stephen Kinsella, Craig Pouncey

Media and telecoms
Stephen Kinsella, Hanna Anttilainen

Public procurement
Craig Pouncey, Adrian Brown

State aids
Craig Pouncey

Regulatory
Stephen Kinsella

Sport
Stephen Kinsella, Ken Daly

HOGAN & HARTSON LLP

VIEW BUILDING
RUE DE L'INDUSTRIE 26
1040 BRUSSELS

Telephone: +32 2 505 09 11
Fax: +32 2 505 09 96
E-mail: chatton@hhlaw.com
Website: www.hhlaw.com

Languages
English, Dutch, French, German, Italian, Russian, Spanish, Greek, Hungarian

Other offices
Baltimore, Beijing, Berlin, Boulder, Budapest, Colorado Springs, Denver, London, Los Angeles, McLean, Miami, Moscow, Munich, New York, Paris, Prague, Tokyo, Warsaw, Washington DC

Number of lawyers 1,018
at this office 10

Contact
Catriona Hatton

CATEGORIES OF WORK

EU regulatory and policy issues

International trade

European and international competition law

Food and agriculture

Healthcare/pharmaceuticals

Technology transfer and licensing

Communications

Energy liberalisation

Environment

Data protection

State aids

HEUKING KÜHN LÜER WOJTEK

AVENUE LOUISE 140
1050 BRUSSELS

Telephone: +32 2 646 2000
Fax: +32 2 646 2040
E-mail: brussels@heuking.de
Website: www.heuking.de

Languages
German, English, French, Dutch, Italian

Other offices
Berlin, Chemnitz, Cologne, Düsseldorf, Frankfurt, Hamburg, Munich

Number of lawyers 5

Contact
Dr Gabrielle H Williamson

CATEGORIES OF WORK

- General EC law
- EC competition law and merger control
- State aids
- EC and WTO trade and customs law
- Environmental, health and safety regulation
- Energy regulation
- Product regulation and liability
- Telecoms, media and IT law
- Transportation and postal services law
- Aviation law
- Intellectual property rights
- Labour law and social policy
- German and European M&A transactions

THE FIRM

Heuking Kühn Lüer Wojtek was founded in Düsseldorf, Germany, in 1971. Since then, the firm has spread geographically, and Heuking Kühn now has seven significant offices in Germany, as well as an office in Brussels.

The firm has an extensive international network of law firms, enabling it to provide its clients with seamless 'one-stop shopping', on international transactions and regulatory matters. Since its formation, Heuking Kühn Lüer Wojtek has specifically chosen to remain an independent law firm. It is Heuking Kühn Lüer Wojtek's philosophy that, to provide the best possible service to its clients, the firm must be able to co-operate with various other law firms which are at the top of the profession in their respective countries. This gives the firm the ability to make alternative counsel suggestions to its clients, giving the clients a choice of the best suitable law firm or lawyer in each country and for each matter. Over the last 30+ years, Heuking Kühn Lüer Wojtek has developed excellent relationships with the key firms in all of the major jurisdictions worldwide.

Heuking Kühn Lüer Wojtek is a name which is synonymous with legal competence. The firm is one of the largest commercial law firms in Germany, with more than 140 specialised lawyers and tax advisers, representing the interests of national and international clients. Included in the client list are large and medium-sized German and international companies in all areas of the manufacturing industry, as well as trade and service industries, associations, governmental and public sector organisations and private clients and trusts.

The firm prides itself on substantive legal competence and on the excellent education and continuing legal education of its lawyers. Moreover, virtually all of the lawyers are German-English bilingual.

Extensive specialisation and comprehensive knowledge of specific industry sectors provide the basis of all of Heuking Kühn Lüer Wojtek's legal counselling. Experienced partners and carefully selected associate lawyers develop innovative solutions to complex legal problems. The lawyers regularly work in their specific practice area groups and also in multi-group and multi-disciplinary teams with clients and outside consultants or advisers. Entrepreneurial thinking on behalf of firm clients, as well as efficient, quality, cost-effective and timely work and the highest personal dedication are key components of Heuking Kühn Lüer Wojtek's culture.

AREAS OF PRACTICE

Heuking Kühn Lüer Wojtek is a full-service commercial law firm. Cross-border and cross-sector knowledge in combination with a deep understanding of business reasoning enables service to clients with the broadest possible support in all their negotiations and business decisions. This applies equally to M&A transactions, to legal advice on company structure, business risk management, negotiations and negotiation tactics, training, crisis and insolvency counselling, corporate financial matters, and complex litigation and arbitration. Thanks to a variety of strong business clients, the firm has built long-term relationships with its clients and can assist them, beginning with the establishment of a business, followed by implementing business goals, including day-to-day legal work, reorganisations, acquisitions and divestitures.

Heuking Kühn Lüer Wojtek is actively involved with its clients in providing regulatory counselling in all areas of commercial law, as well as assisting them in organising and implementing their M&A transactions in Germany, throughout Europe, and internationally. Heuking Kühn Lüer Wojtek has particular expertise in German and EU company law; competition law, merger control and state aids; international investment, trade, and taxation matters; banking and finance; labour law; intellectual property rights; environmental, health, and safety regulation; product-specific regulation; real estate and construction law; telecoms, IT and media law; transport, postal services and shipping law; public procurement; family law; and private clients and family office matters.

HOUTHOFF BURUMA

KEIZERSLAAN 5
1000 BRUSSELS

Telephone: +32 2 507 9800
Fax: +32 2 507 9898
E-mail: info@houthoff.com
Website: www.houthoff.com

Languages
Dutch, English, French, German

Other offices
Amsterdam, London, Rotterdam, The Hague

Number of lawyers 323
at this office 10

Contacts
Weijer VerLoren van Themaat,
Gerard van der Wal

CATEGORIES OF WORK

Competition law

International trade and custom law

Trade with non-member countries

Intellectual property law

EU law

Agricultural law

European litigation

Pharmaceutical law

HOWREY SIMON ARNOLD & WHITE LLP

AVENUE DES NERVIENS 9-31
1040 BRUSSELS

Telephone: +32 2 741 1011
Fax: +32 2 741 1012
Website: www.howrey.com

Languages
Dutch, English, French, German, Greek, Italian, Portuguese, Spanish, Swedish

Other offices
Amsterdam, Chicago, Houston, Irvine, London, Los Angeles, Menlo Park, San Franscico, Washington DC

Number of lawyers 543
at this office 18

Contact
Trevor Soames

CATEGORIES OF WORK

European and national merger control: clearance of M&A and joint ventures
Trevor Soames, Geert Goeteyn

European cartels, private antitrust litigation and arbitration, and transatlantic investigations
Julian Joshua, Geert Goeteyn

General European competition
David Wood, Paris Anestis

Financial services competition regulation
David Wood

Global counselling
Michael J O'Neill

State aid
Paris Anestis, Trevor Soames

Aviation
Trevor Soames, Paris Anestis

Maritime transport
Trevor Soames, David Wood

Intellectual property, information technology and telecoms law
David Wood

Media and broadcasting
Trevor Soames, David Wood

HUNTON & WILLIAMS

AVENUE LOUISE 326, BOX 6
1050 BRUXELLES

Telephone: +32 (0)2 643 58 00
Fax: +32 (0)2 643 58 22
E-mail: info@hunton.com
Website: www.hunton.com

Languages
Dutch, English, French, German, Italian, Spanish

Other offices
Atlanta, Austin, Bangkok, Charlotte, Dallas, Hong Kong, Knoxville, London, McLean, Miami, New York, Norfolk, Raleigh, Richmond, Washington DC

Number of lawyers 850
at this office 7

Contacts
Prof Lucas Bergkamp, Hervé Cogels, Christopher Kuner

CATEGORIES OF WORK

Biotechnology/FDA/healthcare
Lucas Bergkamp

Chemical
Lucas Bergkamp

Consumer protection
Lucas Bergkamp

Corporate and commercial
Hervé Cogels, Charles Ashton

Corporate finance
Hervé Cogels, Peter Kavanagh

E-commerce
Christopher Kuner

Environmental
Lucas Bergkamp

Internet
Christopher Kuner

Labour law
Hervé Cogels, Lucas Bergkamp

Liability
Lucas Bergkamp

Privacy/data protection
Christopher Kuner

Product and trade regulation
Lucas Bergkamp

JANSON BAUGNIET

187 CHAUSSÉE DE LA HULPE
1170 BRUXELLES

Telephone: +32 2 675 30 30
Fax: +32 2 675 30 31
E-mail: email@janson-baugniet.be
Website: www.janson-baugniet.be

Languages
Dutch, English, French, German

Number of lawyers 70

Contacts
Henri-Paul Lemaitre, Rosine Périer

CATEGORIES OF WORK

Administrative law

Banking and finance

Bankruptcy and insolvency

Commercial law

Contracts

Corporate law

Employment and labour

Intellectual property/information

Technology

Litigation/dispute resolution

Mergers and acquisitions

Tax

JONES DAY

AVENUE LOUISE 480
BOX 7
1050 BRUXELLES

Telephone: +32 2 645 14 11
Fax: +32 2 645 14 45
Website: www.jonesday.com

Languages
Dutch, English, French, German, Italian, Spanish

Other offices
Atlanta, Chicago, Cleveland, Columbus, Dallas, Frankfurt, Hong Kong, Houston, Irvine, London, Los Angeles, Madrid, Menlo Park, Milan, Mumbai*, Munich, New Delhi*, New York, Palo Alto, Paris, Pittsburgh, Shanghai, Singapore, Sydney, Taipei, Tokyo, Washington DC

Number of lawyers 2,100
at this office 24

*In association with Pathak & Associates

CATEGORIES OF WORK

Banking, securities and finance
Thierry Buytaert

Corporate law
Luc Houben

EC competition law
Bernard Amory, Alexandre Verheyden
Eric Morgan de Rivery

Intellectual property
Mireille Buydens

Labour law
Luc Houben

Litigation
Sebastien Champagne

Mergers and acquisitions
Luc Houben, Howard Liebman

Real estate
Luc Houben, Thierry Buytaert

Tax law
Howard Liebman

Telecommunications law
Bernard Amory, Alexandre Verheyden

Commercial contracts
Sebastien Champagne, Luc Houben

KROMANN REUMERT

3 RUE DE LUXEMBOURG
1000 BRUXELLES

Telephone: +32 2501 0700
Fax: +32 2501 0701
E-mail: bru@kromannreumert.com
Website: www.kromannreumert.com

Languages
English, Dutch, French, German, the Scandinavian languages

Other offices
Aarhus, Copenhagen, London

Number of lawyers 232
at this office 2

Member
Lex Mundi; Scandinavian Law Alliance

CATEGORIES OF WORK

Banking and finance

Commercial and company

Competition

Employment and labour

Energy

Insolvency

Insurance and tort law

Intellectual property, media and marketing law

IT and telecommunications

Litigation and arbitration

Maritime and transportation

Mergers and acquisitions

Real property, environmental and construction law

Shipping

Stock exchange regulation

Tax law

LAGA & PHILIPPE

AVENUE LOUISE 240
1050 BRUSSELS

Telephone: +32 2 600 52 00
Fax: +32 2 600 52 01
E-mail: info@laga-philippe.com
Website: www.laga-philippe.com

Languages
Dutch, English, French, German, Italian, Spanish, Russian, Slovak

Other offices
Diegem, Ghent, Kortrijk, Luxembourg

Number of lawyers 103
at this office 25

CATEGORIES OF WORK	
Arbitration	Insolvency and reorganisation
Banking and finance	Insurance law
Commercial law	Intellectual property
Contract law	Medical and pharmaceutical law
Contractor law	Public law
Corporate, M&A	Real estate
Employment	Tax law
Estate planning	Torts and liabilities
European law	Trade practices

THE FIRM

With over 100 lawyers and an extensive specialisation, Laga & Philippe is one of the most prominent law firms in Belgium. Partners and senior lawyers at the firm include lawyers with over 20 years' experience at the Bar, as well as lawyers from a wide range of professional backgrounds including academia, tax and legal consultancy, industry and the banking world.

Laga & Philippe has offices in Brussels, Diegem, Ghent, Kortrijk and Luxembourg and works with top law firms throughout Europe with which it has built up privileged relationships.

AREAS OF PRACTICE

Laga & Philippe offers a full-service and international approach with specialists for each area of practice. Arbitration is entrusted to specialist lawyers and professors with sound experience in procedures before domestic and international Courts of Arbitration.

The banking and finance team provides advice on financial services, hybrid financing, assets, securities, cross-border leasing, venture capital, project financing, investment funds, advice for institutional investors and regulatory advice.

Commercial law work includes commercial distribution (agency, distributorships and franchise), sale of goods, bills of exchange, commercial leases, sureties and transport.

The contract law department is made up of a team of specialist lawyers who combine academic expertise in the field of Belgian and international contract law with a sound commercial practice.

The corporate law/mergers and acquisitions department specialises in group restructuring, corporate governance, acquisitions, divestitures, management buy-outs and joint ventures, IPOs, delistings, and mergers and due diligences.

The firm's experts provide advice and assistance in many areas of employment law and social security law, from drawing up and terminating contracts and drafting collective agreements to creating work regulations and pension schemes. They have also acquired extensive experience in dealing with mass redundancies and restructuring measures.

The firm's estate planning practice has extensive knowledge and experience in domestic and international estate planning, encompassing family law, property and security, income tax, hybrid financing structures, offshore planning and wealth tax.

The European law department provides a wide range of high-quality services on competition, state aids, public procurement and EU funding and has an extensive track record of working for the European Commission.

The insolvency and reorganisation department is made up of commercial law practitioners with extensive experience advising distressed companies and the creditors of distressed companies and devising and implementing corporate recovery plans.

The intellectual property expertise and information society services cover trade mark law, design patents and utility models, copyrights, patent and trade marks infringement proceedings, data protection, media, telecommunications, e-commerce and e-government.

The biomed group is specialised in pharmaceutical and medical law, tort and malpractice, contract and e-health.

Active in public law, the firm also deals with construction, environment and public procurement.

The real estate team has extensive experience in civil property law and contract law relating to property, as well as town planning and finance structuring.

The tax practice offers clients creative, multi-jurisdictional tax planning and high-quality personalised advisory services in a broad range of tax matters including M&A, international and local corporate restructuring.

The torts and liability team provides advice on risk and liability issues and defends its clients' interests in all types of court proceedings and alternative conflict resolving procedures.

LATHAM & WATKINS LLP

BOULEVARD DU RÉGENT, 43-44
1000 BRUSSELS

Telephone: +32 2 788 6000
Fax: +32 2 788 6060
Website: www.lw.com

Languages
Danish, English, Finnish, French, German, Italian, Spanish

Other offices
Boston, Chicago, Frankfurt, Hamburg, Hong Kong, London, Los Angeles, Milan, Moscow, New Jersey, New York, Northern Virginia, Orange County, Paris, San Diego, San Francisco, Silicon Valley, Singapore, Tokyo, Washington DC

Number of lawyers 1,500
at this office 19

CATEGORIES OF WORK

European competition law – articles 81 and 82 EC Treaty (cartels, other restrictions of competition and abuse of dominance), merger control, state aid

European trade law (including customs law and anti-dumping)

Litigation before European courts

European regulatory and legislative practice (including telecommunications)

LAWFORT

WOLUWEDAL 20
SINT-STEVENS-WOLUWE
1932 BRUSSELS

Telephone: +32 2 710 78 11
Fax: +32 2 710 78 53
E-mail: firstname.name@lawfort.be
Website: www.lawfort.be

Languages
Dutch, French, English, German

Other offices
Antwerp, Ghent, Liège

Number of lawyers 120

Contact
Marc Vandemeulebroeke (managing partner)

CATEGORIES OF WORK

Administrative and energy law
Rusen Ergec, Guy Block

Arbitration and mediation
Herman Verbist

Business criminal law
Patrick Waeterinckx

Commercial, distribution, IP/IT law
Wilfred Van Looveren, Annick Mottet

Corporate structuring, M&A, business recovery
Marie Evrard, Erwin Destuyver

Employment and human resources
Véronique Pertry, Frank Ruelens

Financial services
Marc Vandemeulebroeke, Guy Schrans

International projects and EU law
Marc Picat

Real estate, environment
François de Montpellier

Tax law
Jean Van Steenwinckel, Daniel De Crem

LIEDEKERKE WOLTERS WAELBROECK KIRKPATRICK

3 BOULEVARD DE L'EMPEREUR
1000 BRUXELLES

Telephone: +32 2 551 15 15
Fax: +32 2 551 14 14
E-mail: info@liedekerke-law.be
Website: www.liedekerke-law.be

Languages
French, Dutch, English, German, Danish, Italian, Spanish

Number of lawyers 107

CATEGORIES OF WORK

Banking
Jan Vincent Lindemans

Finance – capital markets
Thierry Tilquin, Piet van Overbeke

Corporate – M&A
Philippe Malherbe

Intellectual property
Martine Demeur

Taxation
Daniel Garabedian

Competition
Jules Stuyck

International law – WTO law
Nicolas Angelet

Insolvency
Paul Vandepitte

Employment law
Paul Geerebaert, Vincent Busschaert

Real estate
Yves Delacroix, Valérie Simonart

Environment
Bernard Deltour, Dirk Lindemans

Administrative law
Dirk Lindemans, Bernard Deltour

Aviation and transport
Marc Godfroid

Commercial litigation
Aimery de Schoutheete, Joe Sepulchre

Arbitration
Joe Sepulchre

Insurance
Pol Glineur

THE FIRM

Established in 1965, Liedekerke Wolters Waelbroeck Kirkpatrick is one of the oldest law firms in Belgium. It is also one of the largest Belgian independent law firms with over 100 lawyers. A number of them teach or have taught in renowned law faculties in Belgium or abroad, and are well-known figures in the legal world. The firm offers a broad range of services in the principal areas of expertise in business law and possesses a great deal of competence and a high reputation in general commercial law, including contract drafting and litigation, both nationally and internationally.

In each area, Liedekerke's aim is to offer high-quality, personalised services in which legal rigour is allied to solid practical experience and consideration of the economic need of its clients. Its approach is very much client-focused, always looking for the balance between good knowledge of the environment in which the client operates, and effective and creative legal advice. The firm works in French, Dutch and English, and several of its partners and associates are fluent in other languages as well. Relations with clients are built on a long-term perspective and the development of personal relationships.

The firm advises and represents domestic, foreign and multinational companies in the financial, property, industrial and service sectors, public authorities and international organisations, charitable organisations and private individuals. Liedekerke has long been developing relations with top-grade world corporations and foreign law firms of the first order.

AREAS OF PRACTICE

Liedekerke Wolters Waelbroeck Kirkpatrick advises on a wide range of areas in business law including the various branches of civil and commercial law; tax, accountancy and estate planning; finance and corporate; social security and labour law; public and administrative law; real estate; transport and insurance; intellectual and industrial property; white collar crime; European law and competition; international law including international economic law, human rights law and international criminal law. The firm has advised in numerous M&A and financial transactions in Belgium. It provides a full range of corporate and M&A services, including: advice on creation of undertakings, operations of companies, transfer of shares and assets, co-operation between undertakings; choice of the most appropriate form of reorganisation, negotiating and drafting documents, domestic and European Union merger control units.

The firm's activity covers all aspects of legal practice: consultations, negotiation and drafting of agreements; advice and assistance in the operations conducted by its clients or with which they are confronted, mediation; dispute resolution; participation in the drafting of legislative texts. The firm conducts proceedings before the national, European and international jurisdictions, both judicial and arbitral, the Court of Cassation, the Council of State and the Belgian Constitutional Court. Liedekerke Wolters Waelbroeck Kirkpatrick has always regarded the experience and handling of disputes as an essential complement to its advising activity.

LINKLATERS DE BANDT

RUE BREDERODE 13
1000 BRUSSELS

Telephone: +32 2 501 94 11
Fax: +32 2 501 94 94
Website: www.linklaters.com

Languages
All commercial and local languages in the countries where Linklaters operates

Other offices
Alicante, Amsterdam, Antwerp, Bangkok, Beijing, Berlin, Bratislava, Bucharest, Budapest, Cologne, Frankfurt am Main, Hong Kong, Lisbon, London, Luxembourg, Madrid, Milan, Moscow, Munich, New York, Paris, Prague, Rome, São Paulo, Shanghai, Singapore, Stockholm, Tokyo, Warsaw

Number of lawyers 2,000 worldwide

Contact
Jean-Pierre Blumberg

CATEGORIES OF WORK

Mergers and acquisitions
Jean-Pierre Blumberg, Jean-Marie Nelissen Grade

Capital markets
François De Bauw

Banking
Jacques Richelle

Tax
Ivo Onkelinx

Real estate
Jacques Pérîlleux

Intellectual property
Carl De Meyer

IT and communications
Tanguy Van Overstraeten

EU and competition
Gerwin Van Gerven

Employment, pensions and benefits
Luc Vanaverbeke

Public, administrative
Patrick Peeters

Litigation, arbitration
Johan Verbist

Projects
Jean-Pierre Blumberg, Frédéric Falla

THE FIRM

Linklaters advises the world's leading companies, financial institutions and governments on their most challenging transactions and assignments. With 2,000 lawyers, including 470 partners, and offices in major business and financial centres, its clients choose the firm for its distinctive combination of technical skill, commercial experience and outstanding service.

Linklaters has built a formidable global practice through organic growth and a series of mergers, joint ventures and co-operations with other respected law firms. In 2001, Linklaters merged with three of Europe's leading law firms to form Linklaters Oppenhoff & Rädler in Germany, Linklaters in Sweden, Linklaters De Bandt in Belgium and Linklaters Loesch in Luxembourg. In the same year, the firm formed a co-operation with Brazilian firm Goulart Penteado, Iervolino e Lefosse. This co-operation combines Linklaters' international capability with GPIL's extensive knowledge of the Brazilian market. In Singapore, the firm practises as Linklaters Allen & Gledhill, a joint venture with the premier Singapore practice of Allen & Gledhill, while in Italy, Linklaters has an exclusive relationship with Italian law firm Gianni, Origoni, Grippo & Partners.

LONTINGS & PARTNERS

BOURGETLAAN 40
AVENUE DU BOURGET 40
1130 BRUSSELS

Telephone: +32 2 708 40 00
Fax: +32 2 708 40 99
E-mail: lontings.partners@lontings.be
Website: www.lontingsandpartners.be

Languages
Dutch, English, French, German

Number of lawyers 41

CATEGORIES OF WORK

Corporate and commercial
Dirk Lontings, Vincent Dirckx

Banking, financial services and insurance
Hugo Keulers

Non-profit and trade associations
Dirk Lontings

ICT and IP
Jean-Paul Triaille

Regulatory, environment and real estate
Wouter Neven

Employment, pensions and benefits
Alexander Vandenbergen, Jan Hofkens

Tax litigation
Alain Claes

THE FIRM

Lontings & Partners maintains, with some pride, that it is a law firm with a distinct vision, believing not only in legal professionalism, but also in enthusiasm, commitment and involvement.

All specialists in their own fields, the firm's lawyers offer high-quality services to organisations in all necessary areas of the law. Lontings & Partners maintains the expertise, structure and commitment necessary to collaborate closely with clients, assisting them in achieving their business objectives, both in Belgium and abroad.

Lontings & Partners operates on an interpersonal level with key figures in clients' organisations, making time for the managing director, general manager, sales director, human resources director, finance and administration director, or any professional who appreciates clear and comprehensive legal advice. The firm strives to establish long-term professional relationships with clients and contacts. Throughout the changes that affect organisations, the firm endeavours to maintain steadfast counsel so that loyalty and mutual trust can grow.

Meticulous recruiting is a priority. Lawyers at Lontings & Partners, a number of whom hold university posts, have excellent academic credentials and a wealth of experience.

AREAS OF PRACTICE

Lontings & Partners believes that a comprehensive service to its clients is essential. Its seven departments, listed above, cover all relevant areas of the law.

More information can also be obtained on the firm's website: www.lontingsandpartners.be.

LOVELLS

AVENUE LOUISE 523
BOÎTE 24
1050 BRUXELLES

Telephone: +32 2 647 0660
Fax: +32 2 647 1124
E-mail: information@lovells.com
Website: www.lovells.com

Languages
Dutch, English, French, German, Italian, Spanish

Other offices
Alicante, Amsterdam, Beijing, Berlin, Budapest*, Chicago, Düsseldorf, Frankfurt, Hamburg, Ho Chi Minh City, Hong Kong, London, Milan, Moscow, Munich, New York, Paris, Prague, Rome, Shanghai, Singapore, Tokyo, Vienna*, Warsaw, Zagreb*

Number of lawyers 1,600
at this office 26

Contact
Nick Bromfield

CATEGORIES OF WORK

Competition, antitrust and merger control

Trade law and regulation

Dumping, customs and tariffs

Internal market legislation, regulatory issues and public policy

Telecommunications and energy

Company and commercial law

Mergers and acquisitions

Banking, finance and securities law

Real estate and intellectual property

Employment law

MANNHEIMER SWARTLING

AVENUE DE TERVUEREN 13
1040 BRUXELLES

Telephone: +32 2 732 22 22
Fax: +32 2 736 96 52
Website: www.mannheimerswartling.se

Languages
Dutch, English, Finnish, French, German, Swedish

Other offices
Berlin, Frankfurt, Gothenburg, Helsingborg, Malmö, New York, St Petersburg, Stockholm

Number of lawyers 330
at this office 4

Contact
Johan Coyet

CATEGORIES OF WORK

Competition law, merger control

EC law

Free movement of goods, services, persons and capital

Public procurement

State aid

Trade law

Telecommunications and media

Energy

LOYENS
ATTORNEYS AT LAW

WOLUWE ATRIUM
NEERVELDSTRAAT 101-103
1200 BRUSSELS

Telephone: +32 2 743 43 43
Fax: +32 2 743 43 10
E-mail: information@loyens.com
Website: www.loyens.be

Languages
Dutch, English, French, German, Italian, Spanish, Hebrew, Polish

Other offices
Amsterdam, Arnhem, Eindhoven, Rotterdam, Antwerp, Aruba, Curaçao, Frankfurt, Geneva, London, Luxembourg, New York, Paris, Singapore, Tokyo

Number of lawyers 744
at this office 96

Contact
Christian Chéruy (christian.chéruy@loyens.com)

CATEGORIES OF WORK

General and corporate tax
Christian Chéruy, Enrico Schoonvliet

Estate tax, personal income tax
Saskia Lust

Tax litigation
Reinhold Tournicourt

VAT and excise duties
Thierry Charon

Labour law, health law
Carl Bevernage

Commercial law, contracts, litigation, IP
Martine De Roeck, Dominique Janssen

Financial services, banking and financial law
Wilfred Goris

Corporate law, M&A
Roel Nieuwdorp

European law, energy
Koen Platteau

Real estate, environment
Wilfred Goris

THE FIRM
Loyens is a Belgian law firm and is part of Loyens & Loeff, an independent firm of lawyers, tax advisers and notaries which is the result of a merger between Loyens and a large number of lawyers and public notaries of the former Loeff Claeys Verbeke Nederland. The Belgian law firm has a well-established tax and general business law practice with 86 lawyers, of which 73 are in Brussels and 13 in Antwerp. With Loyens & Loeff in the Netherlands and in its own offices in the most important financial centres in Europe, the United States, the Caribbean and the Far East, the law firm counts approx 700 lawyers, tax advisers and notaries in total.

In addition to a strong position on the Belgian market, Loyens has a broad international scope due to the Loyens & Loeff offices. Furthermore, Loyens has an excellent relationship with leading law firms in Europe and elsewhere in the world. In this way, clients in Belgium and abroad can obtain top-level advice provided by lawyers and independent tax advisers. Thanks to this broad national and international expertise, Loyens is able to effectively and efficiently supervise transactions both within Belgium and across the borders.

AREAS OF PRACTICE
Loyens offers a broad range of integrated legal and tax advice, including corporate law, business and commercial law and litigation, banking and financial law, labour law, tax law, energy law, European law and antitrust, focusing on corporate clients. The firm differs from other national and international providers of legal services because of the combination of tax and business law as equally important components and in an integrated way. For Loyens, the priority is to provide a high standard of legal services in an efficient and creative way.

MARX, VAN RANST, VERMEERSCH & PARTNERS

TERVURENLAAN 270
270 AVENUE DE TERVUEREN
1150 BRUXELLES

Telephone: +32 2 285 01 00
Fax: +32 2 230 33 39
E-mail: info@mvvp.be
Website: www.mvvp.be

Languages
English, Dutch, French, German, Italian

Number of lawyers 25

CATEGORIES OF WORK

Corporate law
Kristoffel Vermeersch, Nicole Van Ranst

Mergers and acquisitions
Nicole Van Ranst, Kristoffel Vermeersch

Commercial law
Jan Ravelingien, Bernard Caris

Intellectual property
Peter Marx, Herman Croux

Media and entertainment law
Peter Marx, Herman Croux

Trade practices and competition
Jan Ravelingien

Labour and employment law
Rafaël Claes

Business migration
Rafaël Claes, Bernard Caris

Real estate
Stefaan Verbouwe

Regulatory affairs and public law
Stefaan Verbouwe

Tax and finance
Kristoffel Vermeersch

Litigation and arbitration
Herman Croux, Jan Ravelingien

McGUIREWOODS LLP

250 AVENUE LOUISE
BTE 64
1050 BRUSSELS

Telephone: + 32 2 629 42 11
Fax: + 32 2 629 42 22
Website: www.mcguirewoods.com

Languages
Dutch, English, French, German, Spanish

Other offices
Almaty, Atlanta, Baltimore, Charlotte, Charlottesville, Chicago, Detroit, Jacksonville, New York, Norfolk, Pittsburgh, Richmond, Tysons Corner, Washington DC

Number of lawyers 764
at this office 17

CATEGORIES OF WORK

Administrative law, product liability
Emmanuel de Cannart d'Hamale, Wouter Van Cutsem

Advertising
Xavier Van der Mersch

Agency, distribution and franchising
Emmanuel de Cannart d'Hamale, Xavier Van der Mersch

Aviation, competition and antitrust, eastern Europe
John Barnum

Banking and finance
Hubert André-Dumont, Christiane Zuniga

Corporate and commercial, corporate finance, M&A and joint ventures
Hubert André-Dumont, Xavier Van der Mersch

Project finance
Hubert André-Dumont, Christiane Zuniga

E-commerce and Internet, computer and information technology
Emmanuel de Cannart d'Hamale, Wouter Van Cutsem

Employment and benefits, transnational tax matters
Xavier Van der Mersch

Inward investment
Hubert André-Dumont, Xavier Van der Mersch

Litigation and arbitration
Wouter Van Cutsem, Emmanuel de Cannart d'Hamale

Mining and Africa
Hubert André-Dumont, Emmanuel de Cannart d'Hamale

Real estate and construction
Hubert André-Dumont, Wouter Van Cutsem

MCKENNA LONG & ALDRIDGE LLP

56 RUE DES COLONIES (BOX 14)
1000 BRUSSELS

Telephone: +32 2 278 1211
Fax: +32 2 278 1200
E-mail: brussels@mckennalong.com
Website: www.mckennalong.com

Languages
Dutch, English, French, German, Italian, Romanian, Spanish

Other offices
Atlanta, Denver, Los Angeles, Philadelphia, San Francisco, San Diego, Washington DC

Number of lawyers 375
at this office 7

Contacts
Koen Van Maldegem,
Robert A Matthews

CATEGORIES OF WORK

Environmental
Ursula Schliessner,
Robert A Matthews

European business and regulatory
Koen Van Maldegem,
Claudio Mereu

European litigation
Robert A Matthews,
Claudio Mereu

European competition law
Claudio Mereu,
Koen Van Maldegem

Food and drug
Ursula Schliessner

International arbitration and litigation
Philippe Logelain

Coporate and commercial
Philippe Logelain

MONARD – D'HULST

TERVURENLAAN 270
1050 BRUSSELS

Telephone: +32 2 234 67 10
Fax: +32 2 280 47 79
Website: www.monard-d'hulst.be

Languages
Dutch, English, French, German

Other offices
Hasselt*, Kortrijk*

Number of lawyers 60

Member
Nomos Alliance

CATEGORIES OF WORK

Commercial
Erik Monard, Tillo Mestdagh

Corporate,
Tillo Mestdagh, Frank Cleeren

M&A
Ortwin Carron, Frank Cleeren

Property, construction
Luc Linders

Environment and public
Xavier D'Hulst, Koen Geelen

Tax
Stefaan Lettens, Jan Sandra

White-collar crime
Reinhold Tournicourt, Chris Barbier

Insolvency
Marleen Verfallie, Piet Carlier

Labour, employment
Piet Carlier, Carl Vereecke

Liability, insurance
Katrien Seynaeve, Koen Geelen

Private
Lieven Decaluwé, Hedwig Thury

Media
Marleen Verfaillie

MORGAN LEWIS

7 RUE GUIMARD
1040 BRUXELLES

Telephone: +32 2 507 75 00
Fax: +32 2 507 75 55
E-mail: info@morganlewis.com
Website: www.morganlewis.com

Languages
Dutch, English, French, German, Spanish, Swedish, Turkish

Other offices
Boston, Chicago, Frankfurt, Harrisburg, Irvine, London, Los Angeles, Miami, New York, Palo Alto, Philadelphia, Pittsburgh, Princeton, San Francisco, Tokyo, Washington DC

Number of lawyers 1,150+
at this office 4

CATEGORIES OF WORK

EC and national merger control, joint ventures, distribution and IP licensing
Izzet M Sinan, Jonathan Uphoff

Telecommunications and technology
Izzet M Sinan

THE FIRM

Morgan Lewis, with more than 1,150 lawyers in 17 offices in the US, Europe and Asia, ranks among the top ten law firms in the world.

Every area of the firm's practice – from antitrust to litigation – has a strong international component. Morgan Lewis represents clients in mergers and acquisitions, technology and emerging business all over the world, resolving differing and sometimes conflicting laws in a number of jurisdictions to produce optimum results. Additionally, the firm's lawyers understand the problems and complexities of transactional litigation and can advise on US and EU regulatory matters.

The firm's clients are diverse and include Fortune 250 companies, leading financial services and investment banking organisations, as well as pioneers in the e-commerce and Internet sector. The firm also represents high-net-worth individuals. All clients receive the same high levels of care, and the firm recognises why clients choose Morgan Lewis – because they want a professional firm with experienced, quality people who are as internationally minded as they are.

The firm handles a vast diversity of legal work including antitrust, business and commercial litigation, business and finance, corporate transactions, employment, labour and benefits, energy and utilities, intellectual property, investment management, life sciences, personal law, mergers and acquisitions, real estate, securities, tax, and technology.

AREAS OF PRACTICE

Founded in 1989, the Brussels office of Morgan Lewis is an important element of one of the world's largest and most sophisticated antitrust practices. The firm provides clients with the full spectrum of antitrust services, from preventive counselling and merger control to advice on cutting-edge antitrust issues to defence of 'bet your company' antitrust litigation, including particularly international cartel cases. The firm focuses on effective strategies, careful structuring and skilled implementation to provide clients with tailored, cost-effective and innovative solutions to enable them to meet their business objectives. Morgan Lewis antitrust lawyers work as one worldwide, integrated team, irrespective of office location, and are particularly experienced in addressing complex multi-jurisdictional issues.

The Brussels office is routinely involved in cross-border mergers and acquisitions, international joint ventures and the structuring and restructuring of multinational groups. In this context, the firm's expertise in global tax strategy and European company law and formation has enabled Morgan Lewis to provide material assistance to colleagues and clients in the timely conception and execution of such complex transactions.

The office is fully integrated with the firm's 16 other client offices located in the US and the Far East, and particularly with its other European offices in London and Frankfurt. The firm's clients have often found it particularly useful to deal with the same law firm to co-ordinate their business, acquisition and growth strategies over three continents.

MORRISON & FOERSTER LLP

AVENUE MOLIÈRE 262
1180 BRUSSELS
BELGIUM

Telephone: +32 2 347 0400
Fax: +32 2 347 1824
Website: www.mofo.com

Languages
Dutch, French, German, Italian, Swedish

Other offices
Beijing, Century City, Denver, Hong Kong, London, Los Angeles, New York, Northern Virginia, Orange County, Palo Alto, Sacramento, San Diego, San Francisco, Shanghai, Singapore, Tokyo, Walnut Creek, Washington DC

Number of lawyers 975
at this office 5

Contact
Claire Smith Yamauchi (cyamauchi@mofo.com)

CATEGORIES OF WORK

Competition
Christopher Norall, Rony Gerrits

Intellectual property
Karin Retzer

Internet/e-commerce
Karin Retzer

Privacy/data protection
Karin Retzer

Licensing
Karin Retzer

Trade
Christopher Norall

THE FIRM

Morrison & Foerster was founded in 1883 and is now one of the world's largest international law firms, with almost 1,000 attorneys located in 19 offices in key business centres around the world.

The firm represents clients from a growing number of mature and emerging industries. The firm's primary focus over the last few years has been on the hi-tech sector, serving clients from the following areas: biotechnology and pharmaceuticals; chemicals; communications; computers and electronics technology; energy; entertainment and sports; healthcare; Internet and new media; securities and venture capital; and software development and distribution. The firm also has long-standing clients in fields including banking and financial services, insurance, mining, publishing, manufacturing, real estate and transportation.

Morrison & Foerster's Brussels office was established in 1991 and plays a key role in the firm's highly-integrated global technology practice. The office has a full-service EU practice, providing counselling and litigation services. The office has lawyers qualified to practise under national laws in Belgium, Germany, Sweden and the US.

AREAS OF PRACTICE

The services provided by the Brussels office include:

Intellectual property: the office's services include the preparation of licensing and joint venture agreements, negotiating and obtaining clearance for complex technology transfer arrangements and corporate partnerships, and defending intellectual property rights in judicial litigation or complex international mediation and arbitration. Additionally, the office has been involved in the establishment and advising of standardisation forums for industry players, ensuring interoperability of new generations of products, and legislative advocacy on EU developments affecting IP rights, including initiatives on copyright, trade marks, patents, design rights and databases.

Competition and merger regulation: the firm provides a cutting-edge service, particularly in the technology sector, including representing companies on compliance with EU and national merger regulation, the preparation of internal company programs designed to ensure compliance with EU law, representation in investigations and litigation before the European Commission, the preparation and presentation of anti-competitive behaviour complaints to the Commission, and counselling on the formulation of contracts including licensing, distribution and franchising agreements.

E-commerce: The office's lawyers have unsupassed expertise in e-commerce issues, ranging from traditional intellectual property work to new areas of law including Internet liability, privacy, digital signatures and taxation of Internet transactions. The Brussels office covers matters including the drafting and negotiating of licensing, service and collaboration agreements, and the adoption of policies relating to e-commerce products and services, including the distribution of music or news and providing certification services.

Privacy: the firm advises clients on compliance with EU and member state privacy laws, and assist with questions regarding the international processing of personal data. Lawyers have experience in consulting and negotiating with the European Commission, the European Parliament and with national data protection authorities throughout Europe.

Telecommunications: Morrison & Foerster assists clients in matters related to EU and national telecommunications regulation and competition law applicable to the sector.

Trade: the Brussels office has experience in anti-dumping, anti-subsidy, customs and WTO-related issues. The firm's attorneys have advised governments on GATT/WTO dispute resolution proceedings.

NAUTADUTILH

CHAUSSÉE DE LA HULPE 177/6
1170 BRUSSELS

Telephone: +32 2 566 80 00
Fax: +32 2 566 80 01
E-mail: ndbru@nautadutilh.com
Website: www.nautadutilh.com

Languages
Dutch, English, French, German, Italian, Korean, Spanish

Other offices
Amsterdam, London, Luxembourg, New York, Rotterdam

Number of lawyers 503
at this office 63

Contact
Benoît Strowel

CATEGORIES OF WORK

Capital markets Benoît Feron	**Life sciences** Maarten Meulenbelt
Construction/property Didier De Vliegher	**Private equity** Peter Callens
Commercial litigation/arbitration Marc van der Haegen	**Projects/project finance** Didier De Vliegher
Restructuring and insolvency Dirk van Gerven	**Public M&A** Benoît Feron
Employment Phillippe François	**EU, regulatory and competition** Maarten Meulenbelt
Energy and utilities Peter Callens	**Structured finance and securitisation** Yvette Verleisdonk
Finance litigation Dirk van Gerven	**Taxation** Werner Heyvaert
Intellectual property and ICT Philippe Péters	**Telecoms and media** Philippe Péters

THE FIRM

NautaDutilh enjoys a strong reputation throughout the Benelux. With more than 500 attorneys, civil law notaries and tax advisers, and offices in Amsterdam and Rotterdam, NautaDutilh is one of the largest law firms in the Netherlands and its Brussels office has grown quickly to become a recognised player in the Belgian market. The firm's core businesses are corporate, banking, finance and tax law, but it has chosen to maintain a broader, market-focused practice than some of its peers.

The position established by the firm in its domestic market – and the interests of the clients it serves there – convinced it to resist the advances of global law firms and remain clearly and publicly independent. Nevertheless, it has invested in maintaining close but non-exclusive relationships with other market-leading (or specialist) law firms throughout the world, especially in the UK and the US. Today, over half of the firm's revenue comes from international business and it acts for many global corporations and (investment) banks. By nurturing its 'best friends' relationships, NautaDutilh has become the preferred Benelux referral firm for many leading overseas law firms, and it is convinced that it can offer each individual client a service tailor-made to their specific requirements. The firm's experience operating in the major financial centres of the world helps it to be even more effective in its domestic Benelux markets. Its offices in London and New York (which practise only Dutch and Belgian law) play an important role in supporting its corporate, banking and finance practice, and its Luxembourg office provides specialist support to its tax practice elsewhere.

AREAS OF PRACTICE

By listening carefully to its clients and studying the market place, NautaDutilh has recognised the need to focus its expertise in particular markets or business sectors. The firm has therefore organised itself in a range of market-driven practice groups, such as life sciences, energy and utilities, and shipping and logistics. Drawing their talents from throughout the firm, these groups offer clients a powerful concentration of legal and business skills tailored to their specific business needs and complement the firm's established areas of legal work.

Besides corporate, banking, finance and tax – NautaDutilh's core practices – the firm offers high-level advice on: construction/property; intellectual property and ICT; EU, regulatory and competition; employment; litigation; insurance and liability; and maritime law. The firm also offers its services to private clients.

PESTALOZZI LACHENAL PATRY

165 AVENUE LOUISE
1050 BRUXELLES

Telephone: +32 2 646 60 10
Fax: +32 646 75 34
E-mail: bru@plplaw.ch
Website: www.plplaw.ch

Languages
English, French, German

Other offices
Geneva, Zurich

Number of lawyers 111
at this office 3

Member
Lex Mundi

CATEGORIES OF WORK

Swiss and EC competition law
Christophe Rapin

EC and WTO trade law and regulations
Christophe Rapin

EC corporate and commercial law
Christophe Rapin

SJ BERWIN

SQUARE DE MEEÛS 19
BOÎTE 3
1050 BRUXELLES

Telephone: +32 2 511 53 40
Fax: +32 2 511 59 17
E-mail: brussels@sjberwin.com
Website: www.sjberwin.com

Languages
English, French, German, Italian, Portuguese, Spanish

Other offices
Berlin, Frankfurt, London, Madrid, Munich, Paris

Number of lawyers 411
at this office 13

Contact
Ramon Gallardo

CATEGORIES OF WORK

Competition

Consumer and sanitary

Energy and national resources

Environment

International litigation/dispute resolution and arbitration

Corporate law

Mediation/bilateral

Private clients

Funding

Mergers and acquisitions

Shipping and transport

Trade laws

Major Article 85 notifications (restrictive practices)

EC merger regulation notifications

State aid

Agriculture and fisheries law

EU trade law

EU and national aspects of biotech regulation

Agrochemicals

EU litigation

EU customs law

Consulting and lobbying (EU public affairs)

SIDLEY AUSTIN BROWN & WOOD LLP

SQUARE DE MEEUS 35
1000 BRUSSELS

Telephone: +32 2 504 6400
Fax: +32 2 504 6401
Website: www.sidley.com

Languages
Dutch, English, French, Greek, Spanish

Other offices
Beijing, Chicago, Dallas, Geneva, Hong Kong, London, Los Angeles, New York, San Francisco, Shanghai, Singapore, Tokyo, Washington DC

Number of lawyers 1,500+
at this office 7

Contacts
Richard LA Weiner, Laurent A Ruessmann, Maurits Lugard, Arnoud Willems

CATEGORIES OF WORK

Global and EU trade policy	**EU trade remedies**
WTO law and negotiations	**Customs**
Dispute resolution	**Financial services**
State aid	**Regulatory**

THE FIRM

In May 2001, the law firms of Sidley & Austin and Brown & Wood merged to become Sidley Austin Brown & Wood. The combination of these two legal authorities creates a new kind of law firm. The two firms meld a 235-year combined legacy of service and legal innovation, creating a firm of more than 1,500 attorneys worldwide.

Members of Sidley's Brussels office represent EU and foreign-based companies before the European Commission, Council and Parliament, EU member state authorities, and the European courts. Its lawyers have also served as counsel to the European Commission on WTO and other matters and represent companies, trade associations, and governments in a variety of WTO disputes.

AREAS OF PRACTICE

The lawyers practising in the Brussels office are particularly experienced in: trade policy decisions involving the European Union institutions, as well as European national trade administrations; trade negotiations under the WTO and other multilateral, bilateral, and association agreements; trade remedies under European Union laws; customs issues under European, third-country, bilateral, and multilateral arrangement; export licensing and enforcement matters; international standards and technical barriers to trade including the operation of mutual recognition agreements between the European Union and its trading partners; information privacy policy, regulation, and enforcement matters affecting the use of private and corporate information in the European Union; market access initiatives, assisting governments, companies, and trade associations to overcome tariff and non-tariff barriers; and international arbitration, including claims under bilateral investment treaties.

Global and EU trade policy: the firm helps clients identify the opportunities and avoid the pitfalls in multilateral and bilateral trade and investment regimes, as well as in national trade and customs legislation. It advises clients on international trade negotiations, including WTO negotiations.

Dispute resolution: the firm's WTO dispute settlement practice is unsurpassed among private law firms: lawyers in the international trade and dispute resolution group have advised governments, trade associations, and companies in 200 WTO disputes.

State aid: the firm serves as legal counsel on many of the most sensitive state aid issues in the EU. It assists industries that face subsidy challenges in markets around the globe, assessing the compatibility of national practices with applicable international trade rules. It also counsels clients on the formalities of privatisation and the effect of privatisation on the countervailability of subsidies.

EU trade remedies: the Brussels office lawyers handle high-profile EU anti-dumping, anti-subsidy, and safeguards investigations, representing complainants, respondents, trade associations, importers, users, and consumers of imported products, and advising clients affected either by the activities targeted by trade remedies or by the remedies themselves. These investigations require a combination of political sophistication and technical expertise.

Also, Brussels office lawyers have successfully invoked the EU's trade barriers regulation for clients, challenging foreign market access barriers, violations of trade agreements, and inadequate protection of intellectual property rights. The firm represents clients on the full range of EU customs issues, assisting in connection with the EU position in WTO rules of origin negotiations, European Anti-Fraud Office (OLAF) investigations, and the development and application of special tariff preference arrangements.

The affiliated firms, Sidley Austin Brown & Wood LLP, a Delaware limited liability partnership, Sidley Austin Brown & Wood LLP, an Illinois limited liability partnership, Sidley Austin Brown & Wood, an English general partnership, and Sidley Austin Brown & Wood, a New York general partnership, are referred to herein collectively as Sidley Austin Brown & Wood.

SIMMONS & SIMMONS

AVENUE LOUISE 149 B 16
1050 BRUXELLES

Telephone: +32 2 542 0960
Fax: +32 2 542 0961
E-mail: enquiries@simmons-simmons.com
Website: www.simmons-simmons.com

Languages
English, French, Dutch, German

Other offices
London, Rotterdam, Paris, Milan, Rome, Düsseldorf, Frankfurt, Madrid, Padua, Oporto, Madeira, Abu Dhabi, Qatar, Hong Kong, Shanghai, Tokyo, New York

Number of lawyers 754
at this office 15

Contact
Anthony Orr

CATEGORIES OF WORK

Corporate

Banking

Capital markets

Taxation

Projects, PFI

EU, competition

Dispute resolution

Intellectual property

Employment

Financial markets

Pharmaceutical and biotechnology

Energy and utilities

TMT

Aerospace and defence

Transport

Real estate and construction

Consumer goods

SIMONT BRAUN

AVENUE LOUISE 149
PO BOX 20
1050 BRUSSELS

Telephone: +32 2 543 70 80
Fax: +32 2 543 70 90
E-mail: info@simontbraun.be
Website: www.simontbraun.be

Languages
Danish, Dutch, English, French, German, Greek, Hebrew, Italian, Polish, Portuguese

Number of lawyers 44

CATEGORIES OF WORK

Arbitration and litigation
John Bigwood, Paul Alain Foriers

Commercial law
Alain Vandemeulebroeke, Béatrice Thieffry

Company law
Lucien Simont, Paul Alain Foriers

Criminal financial law
Jean-François Terlinden

Finance and banking
Sandrine Hirsch, Michèle Grégoire

Intellectual property and competition law
Fernand de Visscher, Eric De Gryse

Labour law
Sylvie Lacombe, Stéphane Baltazar

Mergers and acquisitions
Sandrine Hirsch, Baudouin Paquot

Real estate and construction
Thomas Braun, Michèle Borgers

Administrative law
Kate Lijne Ronse

Supreme Court
Lucien Simont

Tax law
Baudouin Paquot, Anne-Véronique Stainier

Trade practices, e-commerce and distribution
Laurent de Brouwer, Emmanuel Cornu

SLAUGHTER AND MAY

AVENUE DE CORTENBERG 118
1000 BRUSSELS

Telephone: +32 2 737 94 00
Fax: +32 2 737 94 01
E-mail: brussels@slaughterandmay.com
Website: www.slaughterandmay.com

Other offices
London, Paris, Singapore, Hong Kong, New York

Number of lawyers 569
at this office 10

Contacts
John Boyce, Michael Rowe

CATEGORIES OF WORK

Competition law including merger control, antitrust, cartel investigations
John Boyce, Michael Rowe

Litigation and representation before national courts and the European Courts in Luxembourg
John Boyce, Michael Rowe

State aid
John Boyce, Michael Rowe

Public procurement
John Boyce, Michael Rowe

Internal market issues
John Boyce, Michael Rowe

International trade law, dumping, subsidies
John Boyce, Michael Rowe

General corporate and commercial

Mergers and acquisitions

Financing

Litigation and arbitration

Taxation

Technology, media and telecoms

Pensions and employment

Commercial real estate

THE FIRM

Slaughter and May has an extensive international practice covering a wide range of corporate, commercial and financial work, with offices in London, Brussels, Paris, Singapore, Hong Kong and New York. It provides a comprehensive and integrated service covering all the areas in which corporate and other clients look for advice in order to implement their business decisions.

The firm's approach to international work places quality of advice and a longstanding in-depth knowledge of the jurisdiction at the heart of its strategy. It has close working relationships with leading independent law firms in all the major jurisdictions. These relationships allow the firm to provide the best legal advice worldwide in a seamless and integrated manner.

Established in 1989, the Brussels office focuses on EU and competition law matters. The Brussels team is led by two resident partners, John Boyce and Michael Rowe, and comprises in total about ten lawyers operating as an integral part of the firm's Competition Group.

The Slaughter and May Competition Group has close working relationships with leading competition specialists in independent law firms in existing EU Member States and the New Accession Countries, as well as outside Europe. It is able to draw on these relationships to assemble tailor-made integrated teams of lawyers who have the best expertise and contacts in each jurisdiction for particular cases (from multi-jurisdictional merger cases to international cartel proceedings). A number of the European firms with whom the firm works also have offices in Brussels. This further facilitates the close working relationships and contacts between the firm's competition practices and extends to joint training, secondments, and know-how and technology exchanges.

AREAS OF PRACTICE

The Brussels office advises on all aspects of competition law. In particular, it advises on merger control notifications to the European Commission and to national competition authorities. It also represents clients on complaints and investigations under Article 81 and 82 of the EC Treaty (and equivalent national laws) and the rules of State aid. The office also monitors other EU developments (such as internal market issues and trade issues) and maintains regular contact with Commission officials.

The relationships the firm has with other leading EU competition practices mean that it is particularly well-placed to respond to the proposed regime of increased co-operation within the European Competition Network (the network established between the European Commission and the 25 EU Member States' national competition authorities) as from 1 May 2004.

Further details on other areas of practice within the firm are provided in the London office entry of this publication.

SQUIRE, SANDERS & DEMPSEY L.L.P.

165, AVENUE LOUISE, BOX 13-14
1050 BRUSSELS

Telephone: +32 2 627 1111
Fax: +32 2 627 1100
E-mail: bhartnett@ssd.com
Website: www.ssd.com

Languages
Dutch, English, French, German, Italian, Spanish

Other offices
Beijing, Bratislava, Budapest, Cincinnati, Cleveland, Columbus, Hong Kong, Houston, London, Los Angeles, Madrid, Miami, Milan, Moscow, New York, Palo Alto, Phoenix, Prague, Rio de Janeiro, San Francisco, Taipei, Tampa, Tokyo, Tysons Corner, Washington DC, Bucharest*, Dublin*, Kyiv*

Number of lawyers 710
at this office 10

Contact
Brian Hartnett

Member
American Chamber of Commerce

CATEGORIES OF WORK

Belgian commercial
Anthony Van der Hauwaert

Computer technology, multimedia services
Anthony Van der Hauwaert, Alexander Benczek

Environmental
Cristiana Spontoni

EU competition law
Brian Hartnett, Rebecca O'Donnell

EU state aid
Brian Hartnett, Oliver Geiss

Food and drugs, pharmaceuticals
Cristiana Spontoni

Hospitality and leisure
Kenneth Hatton

Intellectual property
Brian Hartnett, Alexander Benczek

International transactions
Kenneth Hatton, Anthony Van der Hauwaert

Mergers and acquisitions/joint ventures
Brian Harnett, Rebecca O'Donnell

Power generation, energy
Rebecca O'Donnell

Telecoms
Thomas Ramsey, Jeff Ryen

THE FIRM

Founded in 1890, Squire, Sanders & Dempsey is a multi-jurisdictional law firm with 710 lawyers practising in offices in Europe, the Americas and Asia. The firm's practice covers most substantive areas of the law, with an emphasis on business and finance matters.

The firm operates as a single global partnership, which ensures client accountability and the seamless delivery of uniformly high-quality legal services throughout the world. The firm's lawyers come from many countries and cultures, are licensed to practise in both common law and civil law jurisdictions, and communicate with clients in their native languages. Today, the firm remains committed to the fundamental principles ordained by its founders: to serve clients effectively and maintain the professional standards that distinguish both the firm and its people.

AREAS OF PRACTICE

The firm is organised around four major practice areas: advocacy, business, capital markets and regulated industries. Within these practice areas, the firm's work can be divided into numerous areas of specialisation, including banking, bankruptcy and restructuring, biotechnology and pharmaceuticals, communications, competition law, converging technologies, corporate, energy, environmental, health care, intellectual property, international dispute resolution, labour and employment, litigation, mergers and acquisitions, privatisations, project finance, real estate, securities and taxation.

Since its opening in 1975, the Brussels office has been engaged primarily in the practice of European Community (EC) law, representing a wide range of multinational companies.

The Brussels office regularly represents clients before the European Commission on competition law matters, energy and environmental regulation, trade and customs law, intellectual property law, telecoms regulations, pharmaceutical regulations and other areas of EC law. The office also regularly represents clients before the Court of Justice challenging the decisions of the European Commission.

Regular contact with the EC keeps attorneys apprised of new and emerging regulatory policies and practices relating to sectoral or topical issues impacting on clients. In addition, the Brussels lawyers have spearheaded a number of key regulatory projects for the European Commission and other national regulatory bodies relating to the implementation of EU regulation.

The Brussels office functions bilingually in English and French and many of the attorneys are European nationals qualified to advise on their respective national laws. Clients receive advice not only on their rights and obligations at the EC level, but also on the laws of the major member states (France, Germany, Italy, Spain, Belgium, Ireland and the UK) and the implementation of the Community Law into those national legal systems. In addition, European and other clients are represented in all legal aspects of investments in the United States as well as cross-country mergers and acquisitions, privatisation matters, and other international business transactions. Similarly, American clients are advised on their legal matters throughout the European Community and Central and Eastern Europe.

Many of the Brussels office attorneys are acknowledged leaders in their fields of expertise.

STIBBE

RUE H WAFELAERTSSTRAAT 47-51
1060 BRUSSELS

Telephone: +32 2 533 5211
Fax: +32 2 533 5212
E-mail: info@stibbe.be
Website: www.stibbe.com

Languages
Dutch, English, French, German, Italian, Spanish

Other offices
Amsterdam, London, New York

Number of lawyers 309
at this office 112

Contact
Rudy Nauwelaerts

CATEGORIES OF WORK

Litigation and arbitration
Jean-Pierre Fierens

Mergers and acquisitions
Marc Fyon

Equity, capital markets
Jan Peeters

Finance and banking
Jan Peeters

Telecoms and IT
Erik Valgaeren

Employment
Herman Craeninckx

Tax
Luc De Broe

Administrative and public law, real estate
David D'Hooghe

EU, competition and regulation
Peter Wytinck

Intellectual property
Ludovic De Gryse

TAYLOR WESSING

TRÔNE HOUSE
4 RUE DU TRÔNE
1000 BRUSSELS

Telephone: +322 289 6060
Fax: +322 289 6070
E-mail: brussels@taylorwessing.com
Website: www.taylorwessing.com

Languages
Dutch, English, French, German, Russian

Other offices
Alicante*, Berlin, Brussels, Cambridge, Dubai*, Düsseldorf, Frankfurt, Hamburg, Munich, London, Paris, Shanghai*

Number of lawyers 550
at this office 10

Contacts
Peter Willis, Martin Baker, Marco Hartmann-Rüppel, Markus Wirtz

Member
Interlex; Unilaw

CATEGORIES OF WORK

Competition and merger control

Intellectual property

E-commerce/Internet/telecoms

Free movement – capital, people, products and services

Energy

Environment

EU legislation

Financial services

Life sciences and healthcare

Public procurement

Regulatory affairs

State aid

Trade and WTO

THOMPSON HINE LLP

GALLIERSLAAN 33
AVENUE DES GAULOIS
1040 BRUSSELS

Telephone: +32 2 737 70 67
Fax: +32 2 736 16 02
E-mail: ludo.deklerck@thompsonhine.com
Website: www.thompsonhine.com

Languages
Cantonese, Chinese, Dutch, English, French, German, Greek, Gujarati, Hebrew, Hindi, Italian, Japanese, Korean, Latin, Lithuanian, Polish, Portuguese, Russian, Sign Language, Spanish, Yiddish

Other offices
Cincinnati, Cleveland, Columbus, Dayton, New York, Washington DC

Number of lawyers 350
at this office 2

Member
United States Law Firm Group;
American Corporate Counsel Association

CATEGORIES OF WORK

Bankruptcy
Alan Lepene

Business litigation
Steven Kaufman

Business regulation and government affairs
Thomas Wilcox

Commercial and public finance
Katherine Brandt

Competition, antitrust and white-collar crime
Thomas Collin

Construction
Jeffrey Appelbaum

Corporate transactions and securities
Sharen Neuhardt

Employee benefits and executive compensation
Timothy Brown

Environmental
Andy Kolesar

Healthcare
Jane Garfinkel

Intellectual property
Mark Levy

Labour and employment
Keith Spiller

Personal and succession planning
Crofford Macklin Jr

Product liability litigation
Robert Monnin

Real estate
Thomas Coyne

Taxation
Thomas Callahan

THE FIRM

Established in 1911, Thompson Hine LLP today is among the largest business law firms in the United States. For the last three years, the firm has been named as one of the Best Corporate Law Firms in the United States (in an annual survey of 32,000 corporate directors conducted by the *Corporate Board Member* magazine). With more than 360 lawyers, Thompson Hine serves some of the premier businesses in the world, including: Ford, Toyota, Goodrich, Goodyear, Alltel, Verizon, KeyCorp, Bank One, Toro and Whirlpool.

AREAS OF PRACTICE

The firm represents US clients on matters in all regions of the world, as well as foreign clients with interests in the United States and in the Benelux countries. In addition to advising these clients, the firm participates and engages in administrative proceedings, arbitration and both civil and criminal litigation on a variety of matters.

Thompson Hine's extensive experience in international work enables it to help clients achieve their global business objectives. The firm provide counsel relative to matters in virtually all countries located in the biggest trading areas around the world, including Western Europe, Central and South America and the Far East. In addition, the firm has provided counsel to less traditional places of business such as Algeria, Antigua, Barbados, Bulgaria, the Cayman Islands, Granada, India, Israel, Lebanon, Macau, New Zealand, Oman, Pakistan, the Philippines, Poland, Romania, Russia, Saudi Arabia, St Kitts and Nevis, St Lucia, South Africa and the former Yugoslavia.

Areas of practice include: commercial agreements; competition law; customs and duty matters; distribution; foreign investment; immigration; importing and exporting issues; intellectual property protection; joint ventures; licensing; mergers and acquisitions; NAFTA matters; trade regulation issues; transportation.

Lawyers work with an international network of over 200 correspondent counsel in more than 60 countries, including the major international business centres of Amsterdam, Berlin, Frankfurt, London, Madrid, Mexico City, Milan, Paris and Tokyo. The firm regularly handles a wide range of corporate matters with local counsel around the world.

The international group works through the firm's Brussels office to represent clients in Belgium and the Netherlands and to co-ordinate legal work through Europe, as well as working and collaborating with firms around the world, including: an Asian network of law firms including Chinese firms in Hong Kong and Beijing; British firms in Hong Kong and Shanghai; Indian firms in New Delhi, Mumbai, Calcutta and Bangalore; and a corporate law boutique in Brazil, and with a large general business firm in Brazil that maintains a liaison office in New York, among other locations.

The group also works with Chinese banks on various commercial financing matters including secured transactions and commercial contracts; frequently meets with contacts from the Chinese Consulate in New York; and works extensively with two law firms in Thailand.

The international group handles substantial joint venture work between US and foreign investors, including projects in Australia, Brazil, the Czech Republic, Germany, Indonesia, Italy, Japan, Kenya, Korea, Nigeria, Poland, Taiwan, Thailand and the UK; negotiates licenses and develops distribution and sales agency agreements; and handles taxable and tax-free mergers and acquisitions, spin-offs and restructuring, joint ventures, partnerships, LLCs, leveraged buy-outs, financings, sale and leaseback transactions, tax planning and workouts.

Also, the group represents domestic and foreign clients in a wide variety of matters before courts throughout the US, and represents clients before federal administrative agencies, the Court of International Trade and congressional committees regarding trade policies, agency determination and legislative matters.

TIBERGHIEN

ADVOCATEN – AVOCATS – LAWYERS

GEMEENSCHAPPENLAAN 2
AVENUE DES COMMUNAUTES
1140 BRUSSELS

Telephone: +32 2 773 40 00
Fax: +32 2 773 40 55
Email: info@tiberghien.be
Website: www.tiberghien.com

Languages
Dutch, English, French, German

Number of lawyers 42

Contact
Bernard Peeters

CATEGORIES OF WORK

Tax (direct taxes, indirect taxes)

Litigation (tax and corporate)

Capital markets, banking and finance, financial instruments

Benefits and compensation

Corporate and commercial

M&A and corporate finance

Estate planning

Real estate

UGGC & ASSOCIÉS

AVENUE ALBERT ELISABETH 46
BOÎTE 1
1200 BRUSSELS

Telephone: +32 2 736 6614
Fax: +32 2 736 6818
E-mail: avocats@uggc-law.be
Website: www.uggc-law.be

Languages
Arabic, Dutch, English, French, German, Italian, Portuguese, Spanish

Other offices
Casablanca, Paris

Number of lawyers 90
at this office 8

CATEGORIES OF WORK

Tax and corporate law
Jean-Nicolas Goossens

Commercial law
Philip Van Doorn,
Willem-Henri van Rijckevorsel

Competition and EC law
Philip Van Doorn

Real estate and construction
Willem-Henri van Rijckevorsel

Arbitration and mediation
Philip Van Doorn

VAN BAEL & BELLIS

AVENUE LOUISE 165
1050 BRUSSELS

Telephone: +32 2 647 73 50
Fax: +32 2 640 64 99
Email: info@vanbaelbellis.com
Website: www.vanbaelbellis.com

Languages
Arabic, Danish, Dutch, English, Finnish, French, German, Italian, Japanese, Polish, Russian, Spanish, Ukrainian

Other offices
Geneva

Number of lawyers 52

CATEGORIES OF WORK

EC and national competition law

EC and international trade law (anti-dumping and other trade protection measures; customs law; WTO)

Regulatory law (pharmaceuticals, aviation, telecommunications, energy)

Belgian business law:

Arbitration and litigation

Mergers and acquisitions and corporate law

Intellectual property and IT

Employment

Pharmaceutical law

Tax

ADVOKATFIRMAN VINGE

RUE DU LUXEMBOURG 3
1000 BRUSSELS

Telephone: +32 2 501 07 00
Fax: +32 2 501 07 07
Website: www.vinge.se

Languages
English, French, German, Swedish

Other Offices
Gothenburg, Helsingborg, Hong Kong, London, Malmö, Paris, Shanghai, Stockholm

Number of lawyers 262
at this office 4

Contact
Olle Rislund

Member
Scandinavian Law Alliance with Kromann Reumert (Denmark) and Thommessen (Norway); Lex Mundi

CATEGORIES OF WORK	
Corporate finance	Telecoms
Mergers and acquisitions	Litigation
Corporate	Environmental
Capital markets	Real estate
EU and antitrust	Tax
Intellectual property	Insolvency and restructuring
IT	Insurance
Media	Employment
Marketing	Transport

THE FIRM

Established through a merger between leading Swedish firms in 1983, Vinge is today one of the largest firms in Scandinavia, with some 262 lawyers in nine Swedish and overseas offices. In 1991, the firm set up the Scandinavian Law Alliance together with the Danish law firm Kromann Reumert and the Norwegian firm Thommessen. Vinge is also a member of Lex Mundi.

AREAS OF PRACTICE

Vinge has a substantial international practice, with a strategic focus on M&A and corporate finance. The firm has acted in most of the major mergers and acquisitions in Sweden in recent years, and has consistently achieved top positions on *Merger Market*'s list of M&A advisers in the Nordic market. The firm regularly represents clients in connection with large international financing transactions, including project financing and structured finance arrangements. Vinge's competition law team is one of the most distinguished and experienced in the Nordic markets. A full-service firm, Vinge also advises domestic and international clients within a number of specialist areas such as employment, intellectual property, IT, media marketing, property, telecom, litigation and arbitration, insolvency, insurance, tax, and transport. In addition to four offices in Sweden, the firm has a presence in London, Paris, Brussels, Hong Kong and Shanghai.

WEIL, GOTSHAL & MANGES

81 AVENUE LOUISE
BTE 9-10
1050 BRUXELLES

Telephone: +32 2 543 7460
Fax: +32 2 543 7489
Website: www.weil.com

Other offices
Austin, Boston, Budapest, Dallas, Frankfurt, Houston, London, Miami, Munich, New York, Paris, Prague, Silicon Valley, Singapore, Warsaw, Washington DC

Number of lawyers 1,000
at this office 6

Contact
Jon Filipek

CATEGORIES OF WORK

EU and international competition law

IP, technology and communications

Corporate and commercial

Mergers and acquisitions

Telecom regulatory

Data protection

THE FIRM

Established in 1931 in New York, Weil, Gotshal & Manges combines lawyers worldwide to meet clients' needs in recognition of the benefits of broad industry and regional experience. The lawyers in the firm's practice groups work together to provide full-service legal advice to clients in sectors as diverse as energy, financial services and hi-tech.

The firm developed a network of offices across the US in the 1970s and 1980s to cater for its expanding client base, and was one of the first international law firms to establish a major presence in central Europe. The firm now has established offices in Brussels, Budapest, Frankfurt, London, Paris, Prague, Singapore and Warsaw.

The firm advises a broad and diverse group of clients, including many of the largest and most prominent corporations and government agencies around the globe, and leading financial institutions.

AREAS OF PRACTICE

The firm's US and European antitrust practice advises on international M&A regulatory notifications, antitrust distribution counselling, cartels, litigation and government and state competition policy. Expertise includes software and computer, healthcare, telecommunications and media, transportation, utilities, heavy industry, consumer goods, financial services and sports.

The corporate department is the firm's largest. The department advises international financial institutions and corporate clients in complex public and private M&As, private equity deals and strategic alliances.

The firm's corporate governance practice is recognised as one of the pre-eminent counsellors of corporate boards, management and institutional investors on the full range of governance issues, including board composition, structure and processes; executive and director compensation; director responsibilities; internal and governmental investigations of alleged accounting or other corporate misconduct; and shareholder initiatives. The firm has advised the World Bank, the OECD, the European Commission and various stock exchanges and regulatory bodies, and is a leader in providing director training programmes worldwide.

The firm advises on a wide range of financing activities and has particular expertise in acquisition finance, asset-based finance, debt restructuring and insolvency, debt and equity capital markets, derivatives, high-yield debt, securitisation, structured finance and telecoms and multimedia financing.

The firm has a leading IP and technology practice and advises some of the world's major technology, media and telecommunications companies. It also acts for investors in technology, media and communications entities. The practice handles patent infringements, outsourcing transactions, strategic alliances, cross-border mergers and acquisitions, investments and IPOs, and advises on the protection and exploitation of IP and on a wide range of e-commerce matters, including data protection. It has expertise in regulatory telecoms matters.

The litigation practice advises international clients on all major areas of the law and has extensive experience in all aspects of dispute resolution. It advises clients in jury trials and appeals, arbitration and alternative dispute forums.

The firm's real estate practice handles complex real estate transactions (including finance, securitisations, development, leasing, sales, acquisitions and debt restructurings) across the US and Europe. It also advises clients on real estate M&A transactions involving real estate investment trusts.

The firm has one of the largest bankruptcy and business reorganisation practices in the world. It includes attorneys in New York, Boston, Dallas, Frankfurt, Houston, London and Miami. The department has been involved in virtually all of the major chapter 11 reorganisation cases in the US and in major national and international out-of-court debt restructurings.

The tax department provides advice on international and domestic taxation, covering many different economic sectors. The department works with the firm's other departments to find innovative solutions to problems that present various and competing multi-disciplinary considerations.

WILLKIE FARR & GALLAGHER LLP

AVENUE LOUISE 480/3B
1050 BRUSSELS

Telephone: +32 2 290 1820
Fax: +32 2 290 1821
Website: www.willkie.com

Languages
French, English, Dutch, German, Norwegian

Other offices
New York, Washington DC, Paris, London, Milan, Rome, Frankfurt

Number of lawyers 560
at this office 8

Contacts
Xavier Dieux, Marc van der Woude

CATEGORIES OF WORK

Mergers and acquisitions	**Litigation and arbitration**
Corporate finance	**Aviation**
Banking law	**Competition**
Business reorganisation/ restructuring	**Energy law**

WILMER CUTLER PICKERING LLP

RUE DE LA LOI 15
1040 BRUXELLES

Telephone: +32 2 285 49 00
Fax: +32 2 285 49 49
Email: law@wilmer.com
Website: www.wilmer.com

Languages
Dutch, English, French, German, Italian, Spanish, Swedish

Other offices
Berlin, Baltimore, London, N Virginia, New York, Washington DC

Number of lawyers 545
at this office 22

Contacts
Claus-Dieter Ehlermann, John Ratliff, Charles S Stark, Paul A von Hehn, Marco Bronckers, Thomas Mueller, Christian Duvernoy, Yves van Gerven, Sven B Völcker, Frédéric Louis, Eric J Mahr

CATEGORIES OF WORK

Competition	**Information technology and intellectual property**
Merger control	**Media and sports law**
Cartel investigations	**Financial services**
State aids	**Litigation**
International trade	**EU regulatory**
Aviation	**Environment**
Telecommunications and regulated industries	**Public procurement**
Transactions, corporate	

ELEGIS

HANNEQUART & RASIR

PLACE DES NATIONS-UNIES 7
4020 LIÈGE

Telephone: +32 4 342 30 50
Fax: +32 4 341 41 50
E-mail: hrl@elegis.be
Website: www.elegis.be

Languages
Dutch, English, French, German

Other offices
Antwerp, Brussels, Eupen, Namur

Number of lawyers 104
at this office 30

CATEGORIES OF WORK

Banking and finance
François Moises

Employment
Michel Strongylos

Administrative
André Delvaux, Patrick Henry

Sport
Martin Hissel, Jean-Louis Dupont

Construction and real estate
André Delvaux, Frédéric Pottier

Information technology and e-commerce
Jean-François Henratte

Environment
Patrick Henry

Insurance
Noël Simak, Joëlle Tinant

Tax
François Delobbe

Dispute resolution – litigation and arbitration
Patrick Henry

Mergers and acquisitions
Luc Herve

EU and competition
François Moises, André Delvaux

DE WOLF LAW FIRM

ETIKHOVESTRAAT 6
9680 MAARKEDAL

Telephone: +32 55 235 200
Fax: +32 55 300 651
E-mail: dewolf@lawfirmdewolf.com
Website: www.lawfirmdewolf.com

Languages
English, French, German

Number of lawyers 6

CATEGORIES OF WORK

Public procurement (including EU law)
Carlos De Wolf, Jozef Timmermans

Construction law
Carlos De Wolf, Jozef Timmermans

Project finance
Carlos De Wolf, Catherine Peeters

Environmental law
Konstantijn Roelandt, Leen De Smet

Insurance law
Hilde Van Parys, Catherine Peeters

Real estate law
Leen De Smet, Carlos De Wolf

Company law (including public law companies)
Jozef Timmermans, Carlos De Wolf

Planning and zoning
Konstantijn Roelandt

BOSNIA-HERZEGOVINA

Population	4.1 million
Number of lawyers	1,049
Professional title	Advokat
Currency	Marka

Index

Eight years on from the bloody civil war that left 250,000 dead, Bosnia-Herzegovina (BiH) remains divided but forward-looking. For the first time since peace was effected, BiH is beginning to resemble a single country. The two 'entities' that comprised the post-war BiH, the Republika Sprska and the Federation of Bosnia-Herzegovina, no longer enjoy the full and separate autonomy that was the result of the peace accord. Gradually the jurisdictions of each are being replaced by one central administration. The 13,000-strong international peacekeeping force, in place since the war, is due to be halved in 2004.

Following nationwide elections in October 2002, a new central government has embarked on a package of EU-backed reforms with the long-term goal of meeting the requirements of EU membership.

BILLING

The Bar Association in each entity dictates the fees charged. Domestic firms typically charge between €50 and €100 per hour. International firms charge approximately twice that rate. A flat fee can sometimes be negotiated for larger instructions.

MARKETING

Each Bar Association governs law firm marketing. Limited advertising (for example a website) is permitted, providing permission has first been granted by the Bar. At present marketing by law firms is virtually non-existent.

IN-HOUSE LAWYERS

In-house lawyers are members of a separate Bar. As well as representing their employers in commercial matters, in-house lawyers have rights of audience.

ECONOMIC CLIMATE

Since the five-year foreign aid package ceased in 2000, the once-high rate of economic growth has plummeted. Current economic growth of 5% per annum is stable, but far less than the 12% per annum that the World Bank judges to be necessary for evidence of long-term sustainable growth.

Nevertheless, economic reform is visibly underway. A short-term strategy to boost exports has been implemented and privatisation of state assets is well underway in both entities. Progress has been made in corporate governance and accountancy.

Though the time for investment may not yet be here, it is a healthy sign that international companies are now beginning to seriously consider BiH. VW, Coca-Cola, KPMG, Deloitte & Touche and various foreign banks are among a number of companies with long-term plans in BiH. Further opportunities for investment exist in the wood, tourism and metal industries and in the privatisation of power and telecoms companies.

LEGAL MARKET

In accordance with EU legislation, the prohibition against the establishment of large law firms has been abolished. That said, at present there are no large domestic firms; most firms continue to operate very traditionally, with one named attorney-at-law assisted by one or two junior lawyers. Different laws in the two entities create difficulties for firms working in both. Many smaller firms prefer to communicate in German rather than English.

International law firms are generally positive about the potential in BiH but only **DLA Weiss-Tessbach**, **IKRP Rokas & Partners Ltd** and **Lansky, Ganzger & Partner d.o.o.** have set up offices there; other firms opting to work from offices in neighbouring countries instead. Though there are 1,049 lawyers admitted in BiH, few have experience of working beyond their own city or province. Our recommendations focus on those firms that have the experience and capability of advising on large-scale deals across the whole of BiH. A number of London-based firms are actively considering work in the country.

LEGISLATIVE DEVELOPMENTS

Establishment of an effective rule of law is paramount if BiH is to become a fully functioning European state. In this respect BiH has come on in 'leaps and bounds' according to the Office of the High Representative, the international community's interim-appointed governor. There is still much to be done, but very specific and significant steps have been taken. In particular, a State Court with special chambers for tackling economic crime and corruption has been established. The criminal code has been rewritten and new criminal procedures have been introduced. Unlike elsewhere in the region, BiH has taken great care to establish an entirely new judiciary and, importantly, it is effective across both entities.

The largest firms

1	Bojana Tkalcic-Dulic Attorney at Law	3
	Lansky, Ganzger & Partner d.o.o.	3
3	DLA Weiss-Tessbach	2
	IKRP Roka & Partners Ltd	2
5	Advokati Karabdic Salih & Kerim	1

These figures represent the total number of lawyers in this country only, and have been supplied by the firms themselves. The figures should be accurate as at 1 January 2004.

CORPORATE AND COMMERCIAL

Bojana Tkalcic-Dulic Attorney at Law enjoys the highest reputation of any lawyer within BiH. With the aid of two associates and three trainee lawyers, the office of **Bojana Tkalcic-Dulic Attorney at Law** is able to advise on all aspects of corporate, commercial, banking, investment, privatisation and labour law. Clients include several foreign embassies, and the IFC and EBRD on local company financing projects. Ms Tkalcic-Dulic has represented foreign investors during some of BiH's largest bank, insurance and manufacturing privatisations.

UK and Austrian firm **DLA Weiss-Tessbach** has doubled its Bosnian presence; practice head, Nedzida Slihbegovic-Whalen (who has studied corporate law in the US), has been joined by new lawyer, Sanel Karaduz. With a network of other larger offices in Eastern Europe (Croatia, Slovakia, the Czech Republic and Hungary), the firm is well placed to carry out major corporate, commercial and finance work, including privatisation.

Amila Ferizovic Kunosic, Attorney at Law heads a team of two other lawyers in Tuzla in the north-east of the Federation. Specialising in commercial and property advice, she has carried out work for international companies in both entities. She has also worked for Frankfurt-based bank, LHB, in the troubled Brcko district of the Federation. Much of the firm's work is conducted in Sarajevo where the team collaborates with a number of other practices, including **Bojana Tkalcic-Dulic Attorney at Law**. Major clients include German-owned companies Alba International and TBG Concrete.

Branko Maric, Attorney at Law is highly spoken of by domestic and international colleagues alike. Assisted by trainee lawyers, Branko Maric has represented a number of major clients and is legal adviser to the World Bank. Clients regard him as being 'very capable'. He specialises in advising foreign clients on investments into BiH.

Greek firm **IKRP Rokas & Partners Ltd** opened a representative office in Sarajevo in 2002. Two local lawyers run the office, which is headed by Athanassios Kyriakopoulos in Athens. The firm has experience in dispute resolution, privatisation and advising on foreign investment, particularly in the insurance and banking sectors. Clients are usually referred through the firm's Athens office and include Greek, Italian and Swedish companies.

Vienna-based **Lansky, Ganzger & Partner d.o.o.** was the first foreign firm to open an office in the independent BiH. With six other offices in Central and Eastern Europe, attorneys Sasa Jovanovic and Nikola Jankovic are well supported regionally. The office offers experience in banking and privatisation. Clients include Avon Cosmetics, Bank Austria Creditanstalt, and the European investment company, DEG.

Based in Banja Luka, Republika Sprska, **Ruzica Topic, Attorney at Law** is supported by a team of six others. The firm advises on all aspects of commercial law. With various partners in the Bosnian Federation, the office is at an advantage when carrying out work in both entities. An impressive client roster includes British American Tobacco, Deloitte & Touche, EPIC Wien, and Lithuanian bank, Ikio. Ruzica Topic was previously a colleague of Bojana Tkalcic-Dulic.

Emir Kovacevic, Attorney at Law is based in Sarajevo and has carried out local commercial work for foreign law firms, and companies such as British American Tobacco.

Sole practitioner, **Zlatko Sehovic, Attorney at Law** has represented German, Austrian, and Swiss insurance companies in the Federation of Bosnia-Herzegovina since 1988.

CORPORATE AND COMMERCIAL

Bojana Tkalcic-Dulic Attorney at Law
DLA Weiss-Tessbach ✪

Amila Ferizovic Kunosic, Attorney at Law
Branko Maric, Attorney at Law
IKRP Rokas & Partners Ltd
Lansky, Ganzger & Partner d.o.o.
Ruzica Topic, Attorney at Law

Emir Kovacevic, Attorney at Law
Karabdic Salih & Kerim, Advokati ✪
Zlatko Sehovic, Attorney at Law

Firms are listed A-Z in tiers which are ranked in order of priority
✪ *Indicates firm displays contact details at the end of this chapter.*

DLA WEISS-TESSBACH

FRA ANDJELA ZVIZDOVICA 1/10
71000 SARAJEVO

Telephone: +387 33 295 236
Fax: +387 33 295 242
E-mail: sarajevo@dla.com
Website: www.dla.com

Languages
English

Other offices
Amsterdam, Antwerp, Bangkok, Bergen, Berlin, Birmingham, Bradford, Bratislava, Brussels, Budapest, Cologne, Copenhagen, Edinburgh, Essen, Frankfurt, Glasgow, Hamburg, Hong Kong, Leeds, Liverpool, London, Madrid, Manchester, Milan, Moscow, Oslo, Paris, Prague, Rotterdam, Salzberg, Shanghai, Sheffield, Singapore, Stockholm, Vienna, Zagreb

Number of lawyers 82
at this office 2

Contact
Peter Solt (Vienna)

Member
DLA Group

CATEGORIES OF WORK

General corporate	Corporate
Banking and finance	Mergers and aquisitions
Insolvency	Litigation
Privatisation	

THE FIRM

Weiss-Tessbach was established in 1878 and is one of the longest-established law firms in Austria. 15 years ago, the firm decided on an extremely dynamic development. Since 1990, the number of lawyers at the firm has increased more than four times from 15 to over 80, and the number of offices from one to seven. On October 1st 2003, Weiss-Tessbach was integrated with DLA on the basis of a shared vision to become a top five full-service European law firm. With its current offices in six central and eastern European countries, DLA Weiss-Tessbach will continue to expand into the region at a time of EU accession for many countries.

DLA Weiss-Tessbach is part of DLA Group. DLA Group is an exclusive alliance of international full-service law firms with a shared vision. Established in 1999, DLA Group now has over 2,200 lawyers across 21 countries, who deliver expert local know-how and international solutions. DLA Group provides legal advice in 37 major cities across Europe, Singapore, Thailand, Hong Kong and the People's Republic of China.

AREAS OF PRACTICE

The firm has strengthened its core areas of expertise (commercial and corporate, M&A, banking and finance, intellectual property, real estate), and has expanded into other areas of law (administrative, employment, telecoms, technology, venture capital). Today, the firm is able to assist its corporate clients in all aspects of their activities.

DLA Weiss-Tessbach has well-established relations with clients of various backgrounds. The firm advises small and medium-sized enterprises as well as leading (often publicly listed) international and domestic industrial groups, service providers, banks and other financial institutions and individuals.

DLA Weiss-Tessbach has established a particular reputation for its ability to handle cases in international cross-border contexts. It carefully views the ongoing developments in central Europe with the aim of combining the needs of the constantly changing international legal market and industry, whilst also upholding the high-standard services that the firm has always been able to offer to its clients.

ADVOKATI KARABDIC SALIH & KERIM

BRAVADZILUK 8
71000 SARAJEVO

Telephone: +387 61 177 527
Fax: +387 33 531 500
E-mail: karabdic@bih.net.ba

Languages
English, German

Number of lawyers 3

Member
Juritax

CATEGORIES OF WORK

General commercial practice
Kerim Karabdic, Salih Karabdic

Business law
Kerim Karabdic, Salih Karabdic

Property law
Kerim Karabdic, Salih Karabdic

Privatisation
Kerim Karabdic, Salih Karabdic

Investments
Kerim Karabdic, Salih Karabdic

Charitable organisations
Kerim Karabdic, Salih Karabdic

International arbitration
Kerim Karabdic, Salih Karabdic

Criminal law
Kerim Karabdic, Salih Karabdic

Family law
Kerim Karabdic, Salih Karabdic

BULGARIA

Population	7.8 million
Number of lawyers	8,900
Professional title	Attorney
Currency	Lev (BGL)

Index

After the fall of communism in 1989, Bulgaria weathered a fairly rapid succession of governments, a series of strikes and, in the mid-90s, a severe financial crisis. Yet today the country enjoys relative stability and is attracting increasing international attention.

Politically, Bulgaria's multi-party democracy meets EU standards, and in 2003 the EU declared that Bulgaria now has a 'functioning market economy'. Bulgaria expects to become a full member of Nato in May 2004.

The ruling party's domestic outlook is less positive. The coalition government, led by former king and technocratic reformer, Simeon Saxe-Coburg, won 43% of the vote in the 2001 general election. But last October the government limped to third place behind the Socialist Party and right-wing United Democratic Forces, with a woeful 11% of the electorate behind them. Saxe-Coburg's government is reportedly unsettled and divided. Furthermore, voters are clearly displeased with their prime minister's failure to fulfil ambitious election promises, such as his pledge to improve living standards within 800 days of taking office.

However, the Bulgarian electorate is historically fickle, and the prime minister deserves credit for competent management of the economy and a recent decline in unemployment. EU accession, pencilled in for 2007, remains Bulgaria's priority, and may provide the government with the cohesiveness it needs to survive. If it does not, the nation's EU focus would nevertheless provide a stabilising influence for the new government.

Situated at the crossroads of Europe, Asia and the Middle East, Bulgaria borders Serbia and Macedonia to the west; Greece and Turkey to the south; and the Black Sea to the east. The northern border with Romania follows the Danube. Romania is faring less well than its southern neighbour in its bid to join the EU in 2007. Some fear that the EU, currently absorbing a glut of new member countries, may use Romania's ill-preparedness as an excuse to postpone Bulgaria's accession until 2010.

BILLING

Firms are becoming more flexible in their approach to billing, and will often design a pricing package tailored to the client's wishes and the type of work involved. Where hourly rates are used, they range from €50-€120 for an associate and €120-€170 for a senior associate. The maximum charged by senior partners is around €300 an hour. Many firms charge international clients more than their domestic counterparts, and US and UK pockets are often hit the hardest. It is not uncommon for firms to charge new international clients up to three times the normal fee, a rate which will drop once the firm and client have established a relationship.

MARKETING

The advertising of legal services is restricted by the 1991 Advocacy Act, leaving foreign legal directories and magazines, and the Internet as the only legitimate marketing forums. Most firms have a website, many of which are slickly produced and informative. The emergence of a rash of young firms has further intensified an already competitive market, and some firms complain of rivals overselling themselves.

IN-HOUSE LAWYERS

In-house lawyers are common in larger companies. They do not have to be members of the Bar, but must have passed the Ministry of Justice's legal examination in order to provide legal opinion. The terms of Article 20 of Bulgaria's Civil Proceedings Code allow in-house lawyers to represent clients in court.

ECONOMIC CLIMATE

The EU's announcement in 2003 that Bulgaria is 'a functioning market economy', reflected the progress of Bulgaria's economic reform programme over the past 12 months. The country's currency board arrangement, wage moderation and a strict fiscal stance have provided a high degree of macroeconomic stability. Real GDP is expected to grow at a rate of 4.7% in 2004.

The country also boasts falling unemployment, an expanding private sector and improvements in regulatory services. As markets have been liberalised, FDI has increased and entrepreneurs have made use of newly available bank credits.

Yet problems remain, and further economic development is vital. Commentators have expressed concern at the sharp widening of Bulgaria's current account deficit; it accounted for 6.5% of GDP in 2003, a figure expected to dip only slightly this year. Product and labour markets must

The largest firms

1	Djingov, Gouginski, Kyutchukov & Velichkov	39
	LIC-Penkov, Markov & Partners	38
3	Georgiev, Todorov & Co	33
4	Borislav Boyanov & Co	29
5	Batkov, Stoev, Botev & Associates	19
6	Novel Consult	16
7	LEGACOM Antov & Partners	15
	Landwell Bulgaria	15
	Studio Legale Sutti	15
10	Arsov, Natchev, Ganeva	13
11	Simeonov & Dermendjiev	12
12	Kambourov & Partners	11
	O.R.A.C. Dimitrov, Petrov & Co	11
14	Dobrev, Kinkin, Lyutskanov & Partners	10
	KPMG Bulgaria OOD	10
	Seplex Law Offices	10
17	Hayhurst Robinson	9
18	DIA Consult – Law Office	8
	PI Partners	8
20	IKRP Rokas and Partners OOD	7
	InterLex Consult	7
	Modus Consult	7
23	Chernev, Komitova & Partners	6
	Eastlaw	6
	Totev & Ivanov	6
	Yalnazov & Dzhikov	6

These figures represent the total number of lawyers in this country only, and have been supplied by the firms themselves. The figures should be accurate as at 1 January 2004.

enhance their flexibility, and administrative and judicial frameworks require sharper definition in order to reassure potential investors of their rights. If Bulgaria fails to attract higher levels of investment, it will be unable to sustain EU standards of growth and competitiveness. Current predictions foresee Bulgaria's GDP growth slowing to 4.5% in 2005.

LEGAL MARKET

The relatively youthful Bulgarian market continues to develop at some pace, and competition among firms is rife. A number of young, aggressive firms have entered the market, and established firms are considering their future directions in a post-privatisation era, in which competition for foreign investment clients is expected to be fierce.

The telecoms sector has already seen an increase in foreign investors, following the introduction of a new telecoms law in 2003. This regulated and liberalised the industry. Many firms are now keen to be viewed as major players in this area.

In spite of such progress, much remains to be done. Though some estimates put the market's level of EU compliance at 80%, with full harmonisation achievable by May 2004, other reports suggest that such forecasts are overly optimistic.

In reality, the legal system is adapting sluggishly to EU standards. For example, the country's new advocacy act, which will regulate law firms, has been with parliament for two years. Critics hope that significant changes to the country's commercial law, due to take effect in July 2004, will not meet the same fate.

Another obstacle to EU compliance is the judiciary, which is resisting much-needed reform. Until such problems are remedied, Bulgaria's legal market will remain immature.

Borislav Boyanov & Co continues to command respect at the top end of the market, and it is widely considered that **Georgiev, Todorov & Co** has had an impressive year. **Djingov, Gouginski, Kyutchukov & Velichkov** continues to merit its position as a leading heavyweight firm. **LIC – Penkov, Markov & Partners** and **LEGACOM Antov & Partners** have strong practices in most areas. **Seplex Law Offices** and **Landwell Bulgaria** also feature on some of the bigger transactions.

FOREIGN FIRMS

The major foreign firms have yet to enter the Bulgarian market. Nonetheless, UK and US firms will be engaged on a case-by-case basis on the top deals. **CMS Cameron McKenna**, **Debevoise & Plimpton** and **Linklaters** were among such firms in 2003.

A few smaller European firms have Bulgarian offices. These include Greek firm **IKRP Rokas & Partners** (which also has outposts in Belgrade, Bucharest, Budapest, Skopje and Zagreb). Milan-based **Studio Legale Sutti** is present in Sofia, while **Hayhurst Robinson** offers a blend of US, Canadian, British and Bulgarian lawyers, and also has offices in Hungary, Bulgaria and Romania. **Coeler & Partners** has a main office in Hamburg, and a branch office in Milan. **Niesar & Diamond LLP and Todorova Law Offices Business Banking Corporate Environmental Legal Consultancy** is linked to San Francisco firm **Niesar & Diamond LLP**.

BANKING AND FINANCE

The hire of banking specialist Svetlina Kortenska in 2003 further consolidated **Borislav Boyanov & Co**'s position as a leading banking and finance firm. Clients include the Bulgarian government, which received advice on its entry into the ISDA Master Agreement with the World Bank. The firm acts for a number of local and international banks on all necessary matters, including the establishment of banks and branches, regulatory compliance, and day-to-day operations. It also represents the interests of a number of insurance companies.

At **Djingov, Gouginski, Kyutchukov & Velichkov**, the 'brilliant' Zdravka Ugrinova is experienced in foreign banking matters, while name partner Stephan Kyutchukov wins praise for 'technical strength in finance'. A key deal was the privatisation of the State Savings Bank, on which the firm joined JPMorgan in advising the Bulgarian government. An impressive client list includes the EBRD, IFC, Commerzbank, IMI, DEG, Bank Austria AG and HVB. Work last year ranged from establishing a micro-financing bank, to bank mergers and restructuring, to the transfer of ownership.

Hayhurst Robinson's strong banking and finance practice was boosted further in 2003 by the hire of experienced banking lawyer, Renete Petkova. As well as advising OTP Bank on the acquisition of the former National Savings Bank, the firm assisted two multilateral investment banks with a large project financing deal. The firm recently checked loan security for AngloIrish Bank. Clients praise the firm for 'looking for solutions rather than just highlighting problems'.

LIC – Penkov, Markov & Partners represents a number of financial and investment intermediaries and investment companies, several of which are owned by the TBI group. The firm recently advised on the establishment of new financial companies, obtaining clearances from the relevant financial authorities. The EBRD is an ongoing client, and recently sought advice on the restructuring of a paper factory. Name partner Ivan Markov is well-reputed.

BANKING AND FINANCE

BORISLAV BOYANOV & CO
DJINGOV, GOUGINSKI, KYUTCHUKOV & VELICHKOV ✪
HAYHURST ROBINSON ✪
LIC – PENKOV, MARKOV & PARTNERS ✪

DIA Consult – Law Office
Deloitte & Touche EOOD ✪
Eastlaw
Landwell Bulgaria ✪

Boteva & Kantutis
Dobrev, Kinkin, Lyutskanov & Partners ✪
Dospevsky & Partners, Law Office
Georgiev, Todorov & Co
IKRP Rokas & Partners
Interius
KPMG Bulgaria OOD
Kambourov & Partners ✪
LEGACOM Antov & Partners
Novel Consult
Seplex Law Offices
Simeonov & Dermendjiev
Spasov & Bratanov

Modus Consult
Stoyanov Mittov Tanev
Sutti, Studio Legale ✪
Vladimirov Law Office

Firms are listed A-Z in tiers which are ranked in order of priority
✪ *Indicates firm displays contact details at the end of this chapter.*

Insurance company Allianz Bulgaria Life consulted **DIA Consult – Law Office** over the signing of an insurance agency agreement with Bulbank JSCo. The firm also advised Commercial Bank Bulgaria Invest. Clients find the firm experienced, knowledgeable and professional.

Eastlaw's clients include three Bulgarian banks and several pension funds. The firm is currently representing ING Pension Fund Group before the Bulgarian Commission on Protection of Competition. Angel Kalaidjiev has an excellent reputation among lawyers and clients alike.

Nikolay Bebov heads the finance team at **Landwell Bulgaria**, which is building a sound reputation for itself. The team won key clients in 2003; First Investment Bank received advice on cross-border subordinated term debt and day-to-day business matters; the team also acted as Bulgarian counsel for Landesbank, Hamburg on the structuring of a marine mortgage facility. Galina Bunkova is also recommended.

As an internationally recognised legal expert in anti-corruption and money laundering, Nina Boteva at **Boteva & Kantutis** occupies a unique niche in the Bulgarian market. National Bank of Greece, Commercial Bank of Greece and United Bulgarian Bank are among the clients she has advised on compliance with anti-money laundering legislation.

Dobrev, Kinkin, Lyutskanov & Partners advised DePfa Investment Bank on providing credit to several Bulgarian banks. Corporate Commercial Bank in Sofia is another client.

Law Office Dospevsky & Partners successfully recovered $200,000 from UBB, the third largest Bulgarian bank, on behalf of an Italian company.

Georgiev, Todorov & Co's client list comprises several international banks. As part of their ongoing work on the rehabilitation of Bulgaria's second largest thermal power plant, the firm's lawyers are advising the Japanese Bank of International Cooperation.

Interius acts for several banks, financial institutions and pension funds.

Name partner Yavor Kambourov at **Kambourov & Partners** is experienced in banking matters, having acted for HSBC, Biochim, Bulbank and First Private Bank among others. The EBRD is an ongoing client.

LEGACOM Antov & Partners counted CA-IB Corporate Finance and Erste Bank AG among its banking and finance clients in 2003.

Novel Consult's lawyers are equipped to offer advice on permit arrangements, status regulations, capital adequacy and all bank transactions and operations. The team has experience of debt restructuring, guarantees, bankruptcy and litigation.

Seplex Law Offices advised Mizuho Corporate Bank on energy matters and power sector privatisation. The firm was also consulted by Deutsche Bank, London in 2003.

Simeonov & Dermendjiev is advising on a $10m trade and export finance agreement between the Bulgarian Electricity Company and Irish-based VA-Tech Finance Ltd. DSK Bank is also a client. According to clients, the firm has a well-developed western perspective.

Spasov & Bratanov bolstered its banking and finance practice by hiring Vassil Hadjov, former legal adviser to the EBRD in London. Following a referral from **Allen & Overy**, the firm advised the foreign lenders on an acquisition finance facility to an international consortium of investment banks. The firm conducted acceleration and insolvency proceedings for a foreign-controlled Bulgarian bank on a $6m claim. Several local banks are among its regular clients.

Modus Consult has provided the World Bank office in Sofia with advice on local legislation for the last three years. The firm also represented Kapitalbank plc in the first bank bankruptcy case under Bulgaria's new Banking Act.

Stoyanov Mittov Tanev advised the Geneva-based Catholic Relief Service on an innovative micro-financing deal. Partner Ventsislav Tanev previously worked at **Borislav Boyanov & Co**, and clients appreciate his 'strong communication skills'.

In 2003, **Studio Legale Sutti** assisted various international clients with bank loan documentation.

ING, Hill Samuel and Lloyds TSB have all sought advice from maritime law firm **Vladimirov Law Office** regarding financial contracts with western shipowners. Vladimir Vladimirov has an excellent reputation, both as a lawyer and a 'fixer'.

CAPITAL MARKETS

Borislav Boyanov & Co acted for Microsoft in connection with its 2003 options exchange, General Electric regarding its grant of restricted stock units, and for Monsanto on the company's long term incentive plan. The firm advised Oracle on its 2003 ESPP and Abbot Labs on its stock option plan. The firm's client list boasts a number of international investment banks, which were most recently advised on entry into the ISDA Master Agreement.

Though it was a relatively quiet year for the Bulgarian Stock Exchange, 2003 saw **Djingov, Gouginski, Kyutchukov & Velichkov** advise a French food producer on the acquisition of a major equity stake in a Bulgarian public company. Carlsberg Breweries also received advice from the firm on a share acquisition. The 'western-minded' team provided assistance on the enforceability of the ISDA Master Agreement to, among others, Citibank and UBS. TBIH Ltd received advice on restructuring, and an IPO. 'All of the firm's lawyers are pretty fluent in English', according to one client.

The finance team at **Landwell Bulgaria** was a visible presence in 2003. It advised First Investment Finance and First Investment Bank, as issuer and guarantor respectively, on three consecutive, high-value bond issues. Alpha Broker, Italy, received advice on share transfers among multiple shareholders, while the Balkan Advisory Company received brokerage licensing assistance. The firm provides ongoing advice to Pioner Investments, managers of the first non-Bulgarian mutual fund to be publicly offered in Bulgaria. Nikolay Bebov is a finance specialist, whose 'thoroughness and promptness' impresses clients.

DIA Consult – Law Office advised Commercial Bank Bulgaria Invest on the issuance of

CAPITAL MARKETS

BORISLAV BOYANOV & CO
DJINGOV, GOUGINSKI, KYUTCHUKOV & VELICHKOV ✪
LANDWELL BULGARIA ✪

DIA Consult – Law Office
Eastlaw
Georgiev, Todorov & Co
KPMG Bulgaria OOD
Kambourov & Partners ✪
Novel Consult
Spasov & Bratanov

Firms are listed A-Z in tiers which are ranked in order of priority
✪ *Indicates firm displays contact details at the end of this chapter.*

mortgage bonds worth €7m. Clients value the firm's flexibility.

Eastlaw assisted ING Bank Sofia on the public offering of bonds issued by Petrol AD, a Bulgarian petroleum company. The firm advised on all stages of the $7.5m deal, which involved multiple bond issues.

Georgiev, Todorov & Co's practice benefits from partner Alexander Katzarsky's knowledge of stock market legislation.

Kambourov & Partners advised a client on securities and share trading.

Novel Consult's clients include capital markets brokers CapMan International and Elana Inc. Joint managing partner Petya Kolcheva heads the capital markets team.

Spasov & Bratanov hired Natalia Koumpikova, ex-vice-president of the Bulgarian State Securities Committee, last summer. Ms Koumpikova has undertaken a substantial part of the firm's securities advice. Clients include one of the top blue-chip companies in Bulgaria.

CORPORATE AND COMMERCIAL

Borislav Boyanov & Co recently advised the Canadian group, Dundee Precious Metals Inc on the acquisition of the concessionaire of the biggest working copper/gold mine in south-east Europe. The team also represented UK-based Gort Securities on the successful acquisition of the prestigious Radisson SAS Grand Hotel in Sofia. Yordan Naydenov heads an experienced M&A team, which also acted on three separate merger clearances for Dupon, Philip Morris and a large Bulgarian bank. German company Heidelberg Cement received full legal advice regarding the divestment of its Bulgarian operations. The firm also provided competition advice to IBM. Meanwhile the tax practice was busy representing a leading Bulgarian bank in a $20m dispute. Name partner Borislav Boyanov is consistently named as one of Bulgaria's most impressive lawyers. The firm is a member of several legal networks and alliances, including *TerraLex*.

Six recent middle-ranking hires at **Djingov, Gouginski, Kyutchukov & Velichkov** have seen the firm swell to 39 lawyers. Despite the much-publicised collapse of the Bulgar Tabac privatisation on which the firm was advising, its lawyers acted on some of the country's top deals last year. The firm assisted Estée Lauder and Denvya Cement with corporate restructuring; performed due diligence in advance of a possible joint venture for a precious metals business; and advised numerous well-known businesses on the establishment of local subsidiaries and representative offices. Partner Marius Velichkov is recommended by clients for his 'very good commercial sense'. The M&A team has an enviable reputation, with clients including Carlsberg Breweries and Michigan Magnetics.

CORPORATE AND COMMERCIAL

BORISLAV BOYANOV & CO
DJINGOV, GOUGINSKI, KYUTCHUKOV & VELICHKOV ✪
LIC – PENKOV, MARKOV & PARTNERS ✪

DIA Consult – Law Office
Georgiev, Todorov & Co
Hayhurst Robinson ✪
Landwell Bulgaria ✪
LEGACOM Antov & Partners
Seplex Law Offices

Boteva & Kantutis
Braykov's Legal Office
Deloitte & Touche EOOD ✪
KPMG Bulgaria OOD
Kambourov & Partners ✪
Novel Consult
Simeonov & Dermendjiev
Sutti, Studio Legale ✪
Totev & Ivanov ✪

Arsov, Natchev, Ganeva
Batkov, Stoev, Botev & Associates ✪
Dobrev, Kinkin, Lyutskanov & Partners ✪
Eastlaw
Goleminov & Goleminov
IKRP Rokas & Partners
Interius
Modus Consult
Niesar & Diamond LLP and Todorova Law Offices Business Banking Corporate Environmental Legal Consultancy
O.R.A.C. Dimitrov, Petrov & Co
PI Partners ✪
Spasov & Bratanov

A & M Partners
Bazlyankov Stanoev & Tashev
Chernev, Komitova & Partners
Coeler & Partners
Dardov, Assenov & Partners
Dospevsky & Partners, Law Office
Dimitrov, Deevska, Vitanova & Antonov
Interjures Bulgaria Ltd
InterLex Consult
Kazakov & Kazakov & Co
Sabev & Partners ✪
Stoyanov Mittov Tanev
Vladimirov Law Office
Yalnazov & Dzhikov

Firms are listed A-Z in tiers which are ranked in order of priority
✪ Indicates firm displays contact details at the end of this chapter.

With 36 lawyers **LIC – Penkov, Markov & Partners** is one of Bulgaria's largest firms. Its network of 11 offices enables the firm to react quickly and provide local expertise, and the firm has fingers in most legal pies. Recent work included providing restructuring advice to the TBIH group, and acquisition advice to Lines Holding. Hewlett-Packard and Thomas Cook are also clients. The firm is a member of *Lex Mundi*, and was the first Bulgarian law firm admitted to the Bulgarian International Business Association (BIBA).

DIA Consult – Law Office's eight-lawyer team assisted a long-term client, Industrial Holdings Bulgaria, with the purchase of the majority interest in a major pharmaceutical company. The firm also advised Private Engineering JSCo on the acquisition of real estate and developing tourism investment projects. The firm belongs to *Consulegis*, an international network of law firms and other professional advisers.

Georgiev, Todorov & Co recently moved to new premises in Sofia, and has offices in all of Bulgaria's major cities. The firm's 41 lawyers offer a wide range of expertise, with particularly strong litigation, insolvency and taxation practices. Microsoft, Heineken and Turner Broadcasting Europe are just a few of the firm's well-known international clients.

Hayhurst Robinson advised OTP Bank on its €311m acquisition of the former Bulgarian National Savings Bank. The firm has a network of offices in Budapest, Bucharest and Belgrade, and considerable experience of privatisation, investment, banking, energy and project finance matters. Clients find the firm 'extremely thorough', and welcome its blend of foreign and well-known local lawyers.

In 2003, **Landwell Bulgaria** advised Alpha Broker, Italy on corporate reorganisation. As part of its ongoing legal services to Hilton International, the firm provided company and contract advice. A number of other significant clients have received M&A and other legal advice from the firm. Managing partner Irina Tsvetkova specialises in M&A and commercial law, while Maria Urmanova has good knowledge of company law. The ten-lawyer firm is a correspondent law firm of PwC.

LEGACOM Antov & Partners has a well-reputed 15-lawyer practice. Clients in 2003 included property company Urban 3000, CA-IB Corporate Finance, Erste Bank AG and Eurocom Cable, one of Bulgaria's largest cable operators.

Seplex Law Offices has a strong client list, including AT&T, USAID and HIT hypermarkets. Three new German-speaking hires last year joined the firm's German team, formed in response to an increase in German corporate clients. All of the firm's 14 lawyers speak English, and clients say they provide a 'very professional' service. Last year's workload included advising on the establishment of a joint-venture company between the local Playboy International subsidiary and Balkan News Corporation.

Boteva & Kantutis continues to advise the Dutch and Finnish embassies in Sofia on labour, commercial, taxation and real estate issues as well as legislative changes. The firm is working alongside **Linklaters** to provide ongoing advice to BP on employee and international sharesave schemes. Frank Orban at **deKieffer & Horgan** in Washington DC acts as the firm's international counsel, providing a point of contact for US clients. Name partner Nina Boteva is recommended.

Braykov's Legal Office is headed by the 'charismatic, extremely able and highly-principled' Valentin Braykov. The firm acts for ten multinationals, including IBM, BAT, Xerox and Diageo. Clients say the firm offers a combination of impressive legal skills, excellent local connections, and a strong awareness of western business culture.

KPMG Bulgaria OOD acted on several M&A transactions last year, and continued to work for Belvedere SA, France on the acquisition of two wineries. The firm is providing ongoing corporate and commercial advice to US oil company, Vintage Petroleum International. In November 2003, the firm terminated its alliance with the **KLegal** network of law firms.

Kambourov & Partners is an experienced firm, bullishly seeking to increase its market share. Stefan Tzakov joined the corporate and commercial team from rival **LIC – Penkov, Markov & Partners** last year, and tax specialist Emil Emanuilov further enhanced the practice's skills set. The firm advised Afin Bulgaria on leasing contracts and payment recovery, and assisted the buyer in the establishment of retail businesses throughout Bulgaria. Nu Image and Universal Studios, California received contract and tax advice from the team. A recent coup for the firm was winning the pitch to advise Nokia on all corporate and administrative matters in Bulgaria. The firm was also retained as general legal counsel by Koc Holdings, following its work for the company on the state telecoms privatisation.

Novel Consult provides a full range of corporate services. Clients include Centillion Ltd, ICL Bulgaria and Reuters. The firm has nine lawyers, and offices in Sofia, Plovdiv, Varna and Rousse.

Both clients and lawyers testify that **Simeonov & Dermendjiev** provides an 'excellent service' in international arbitration. Name partner Ivaylo Dermendjiev is 'highly regarded in the international world', according to peers; he is the only Bulgarian member of the London Court of International Arbitration. In 2003 the firm won a case for the Privatisation Agency of Bulgaria against Arthur Andersen, and is currently representing the Bulgarian government in a $230m case against Zeevi Holdings. The firm also advises several large foreign manufacturing and commercial companies, and recently opened a second Sofia office dedicated to international arbitration cases.

Studio Legale Sutti represented Austrian Airlines, Czech Airlines and Alitalia during the insolvency proceedings of Balkan AD. Its lawyers advised the US buyer of Cable Bulgaria, and act as legal counsel to Sofia Film. The firm has good links with the US, and a flexible outlook. Partner Yavor Varadinov is an established player in the market.

Totev & Ivanov is run by two former PwC lawyers, Dimtar Totev and Ilian Totev. Founded in 2001, the firm's clients range from medium-sized local companies to multinationals. The firm has an established relationship with **Watson, Farley & Williams**, and aims to provide quality work at better value than the larger firms.

Arsov, Natchev, Ganeva is a boutique firm with an international client base. Specialist areas are concessions, infrastructure, insolvency and administrative law. Its lawyers also have good knowledge of EU legislation. The firm assisted Shell with debt recovery, and is involved in PHARE-financed projects worth €2m. Other clients include IATA, Air France and the French Embassy. Name partner Svetlana Ganeva is recommended for her knowledge of aviation law; the firm represents some of the largest European airports, including Sofia Airport in the Balkan Airlines insolvency case. Partners Svetlana Ganeva and Vladimir Natchev are fluent French speakers.

Batkov, Stoev, Botev & Associates focuses on corporate and commercial, contract and administrative law, as well as civil rights. The firm's most significant client is Austrian-owned Mobiltel, Bulgaria's first GSM operator. The firm has provided permanent legal counsel to the company since 1997, and is currently engaged in negotiations to secure a strategic investor on behalf of the company's shareholders. Pharmaceutical business Sopharma is another ongoing client.

Dobrev, Kinkin, Lyutskanov & Partners provides a full range of advice to a good number of local and foreign clients, including German company Sparky, and a Bulgarian chemical business. The ten-lawyer team also advised GlobalSoft Consolidator Ltd on the acquisition of several Bulgarian IT companies.

In 2003, **Eastlaw** advised the investor on the $40m acquisition of a Bulgarian bank, and provided restructuring advice to a Bulgarian newspaper and its shareholders. The 'well-organised, professional and fairly priced' firm is experienced in competition matters, and clients include several insurance companies.

Goleminov & Goleminov is an international business law firm covering a range of practice areas, predominantly serving clients across Europe and North America.

IKRP Rokas & Partners is the Sofia branch of a Greek firm which has built up a network of offices throughout southern and eastern Europe. The firm has been active in providing M&A advice to both foreign and local clients, in particular the Bulgarian subsidiaries of Greek companies.

Interius handles corporate, employment, taxation, finance and customs matters for both foreign and local clients.

Having traditionally advised large Bulgarian companies, **Modus Consult** is now expanding its client base by targeting small to medium-sized international clients. In 2003 the firm conducted due diligence on Bulgarian oil refinery, Plama JSCo. Ongoing clients include a German cosmetics company, the Bulgarian concession of coffee producer Elite International, and Whirlpool Bulgaria. English-speaking lawyer Svilina Dinitrova is recommended.

The lawyers at **Niesar & Diamond LLP and Todorova Law Offices Business Banking Corporate Environmental Legal Consultancy** boast a varied skills set including knowledge of money-laundering issues and environmental law. The firm advises numerous European and US clients, and benefits from its affiliation with San-Francisco firm **Niesar & Diamond LLP**.

Though primarily known as IT and media specialists, the 12 lawyers at **O.R.A.C. Dimitrov, Petrov & Co** also provide general corporate and commercial services. Recent work includes advising an Italian company on the restitution of several textile plants.

PI Partners provided ongoing legal support to a Greek-owned, Bulgarian listed company operating a five-star international hotel. The team of four lawyers also advised several international clients on acquisition and post-acquisition matters. The firm has other offices in Greece and Romania, giving it regional stretch. It also belongs to **EY Law**, the network of independently practising law firms associated with Ernst & Young. Clients find the firm 'very professional and reliable', and 'open to new challenges'.

Spasov & Bratanov is a boutique firm of four partners and four independent lawyers with whom the firm has exclusive relationships. Six of these lawyers are based in Sofia, where the firm has its office, with the remaining two working in Plovdiv and Varna. The firm recently advised foreign lenders on acquisition finance, and completed due diligence for a client involved in the acquisition of a Bulgarian telecommunications company. The firm also negotiated a $1.5m claim settlement for a Bulgarian client.

With offices in Sofia and Plovdiv, **Bazlyankov Stanoev & Tashev** recently assisted an Israeli company with the $3m purchase of over 95% of a Bulgarian business.

Coeler & Partners offers advice on all corporate and commercial matters. The firm's main office is in Hamburg, and there is another branch office in Milan.

Law Office Dospevsky & Partners is a small firm which advises on corporate and commercial matters. Clients include Shoenefeld Airport in Berlin, and several German insurance companies.

Kazakov & Kazakov & Co is a six-lawyer firm based in the northern city of Rousse, concentrating on corporate and commercial law.

Stoyanov Mittov Tanev's clients recommend the firm to NGOs. Its lawyers advised the Catholic Relief Service on corporate and tax issues, and represented it in court. Other clients include Eli Lilli, the American Red Cross, the Bulgarian American Chamber of Commerce and the American University in Bulgaria. Partner Ivan Mittov is experienced in tax matters, while Ventsislav Tanev speaks excellent English.

Vladimirov Law Office has represented health insurance company Bulstrad on all corporate and commercial matters for ten years. Alliance is another longstanding client.

IP, IT, TELECOMS AND MEDIA

With partner Damien Simeonov at the helm, **Borislav Boyanov & Co**'s media and communications practice was busy in 2003. It performed due diligence of leading Bulgarian mobile operator Mobiltel, on behalf of a potential investor, and also of Internet company, Orbitel. The team continued to advise the EBRD on the seemingly interminable OTC privatisation. In the media arena, the firm acted for a US conglomerate on the acquisition of several Bulgarian radio stations. The firm's IP practice is run by Natasha Andreeva, and includes specialised patent attorneys. IT clients include IBM and Oracle.

Djingov, Gouginski, Kyutchukov & Velichkov advises a slew of international and local clients on trade mark and patent matters. The firm has a number of medium-sized IT clients, while Warner Bros and Reuters are among the media clients who have sought advice from the firm. Representing the government in the Bulgaria Telecom privatisation has given the firm telecoms experience, and Austria Telecom, and Mobikom received advice from the team on the acquisition of shares in the leading Bulgarian GSM operator.

As well as advising the preferred bidder in the ongoing privatisation of BTC, the national telecoms company, **Georgiev, Todorov & Co** also represents Motorola UK and Cosmo Bulgaria Mobile. The firm offers full IP services, and IT clients include Microsoft.

US company Ador Industries is one of several foreign investors which **LIC – Penkov, Markov & Partners** assisted with trade mark protection last year. Dimitar Lozanov has expertise in this field. The firm's IT lawyers continued to advise Hewlett-Packard on all legal matters, and Akamai Technologies, ProSoft and Ebox Holdings have all used the firm on a case-by-case basis.

O.R.A.C. Dimitrov, Petrov & Co is one of very few Bulgarian firms with real expertise and a lofty reputation in ICT, e-commerce and broadcast law. The firm also has considerable IP experience. A highlight in 2003 was advising the national Communications Regulation Commission, a regular client, on the tender procedure for

IP, IT, TELECOMS AND MEDIA

BORISLAV BOYANOV & CO
DJINGOV, GOUGINSKI, KYUTCHUKOV & VELICHKOV ✪
GEORGIEV, TODOROV & CO
LIC – PENKOV, MARKOV & PARTNERS ✪
O.R.A.C. DIMITROV, PETROV & CO
SEPLEX LAW OFFICES

Deloitte & Touche EOOD ✪
Hayhurst Robinson ✪
Kambourov & Partners ✪
Landwell Bulgaria ✪
TelecomLex Consult

Arsov, Natchev, Ganeva
Batkov, Stoev, Botev & Associates ✪
Braykov's Legal Office
Boteva & Kantutis
Dobrev, Kinkin, Lyutskanov & Partners ✪
Interius
LEGACOM Antov & Partners
Patent Universe ✪

Sabev & Partners ✪
Simeonov & Dermendjiev
Spasov & Bratanov
Sutti, Studio Legale ✪

Firms are listed A-Z in tiers which are ranked in order of priority
✪ *Indicates firm displays contact details at the end of this chapter.*

the third national television licence. Satellite operator Neterra is another significant broadcast client. The firm boasts a substantial number of IT clients, including Bankservice plc, Nexcom Bulgaria and ProLink Ltd, an ISP. Telecoms clients include Mobikom. Name partner George Dimitrov is an electronic signature expert.

Seplex Law Offices was involved in negotiations with more than ten banks on behalf of ongoing client AT&T, regarding the provision of SWIFT services. The firm has significant telecoms experience, and recently advised Koc Holdings on the BTC privatisation. The firm's IP practice attracted new clients from Japan and Australia. The firm boasts a newly established public procurement team, which is currently drafting amendments to the Public Procurement Law for Bulgaria's Parliamentary Commission. IT clients include Cisco.

Hayhurst Robinson partner David Butts has extensive licensing experience, and acts on multi-jurisdictional deals throughout Europe.

Kambourov & Partners' work advising second bidder Koc Holdings in the BTC privatisation has consolidated the firm's telecoms experience. Nokia has recently become a regular client, receiving advice on all corporate and administrative matters. Media clients include Nu Image and Universal Studios, California. The firm has provided trade mark protection advice for existing clients.

Galina Bunkova heads the comprehensive IP practice at **Landwell Bulgaria**, while Lilia Andonova is in charge of advising the firm's telecoms clients. Clients appreciate the firm's responsiveness.

TelecomLex Consult concentrates on telecoms and Internet issues, with clients including the Bulgarian Ministry of Transport and Communications, France Télécom, Ericsson and BTC-Net. IP work includes advising a Bulgarian mobile telecoms business on trade marks.

In July 2003, **Arsov, Natchev, Ganeva** represented the national Communication Regulation Commission on the award of the third national TV licence tender. The firm worked alongside **O.R.A.C. Dimitrov, Petrov & Co** on the deal.

Batkov, Stoev, Botev & Associates permanently advises Austrian-owned GSM operator, Mobiltel. The firm is 'very well educated' in telecoms law, say clients.

Braykov's Legal Office's clients include IBM. The firm undertakes IP work for its core group of MNC clients.

At **Boteva & Kantutis**, name partner Nina Boteva utilised her anti-corruption expertise to represent software companies offering transaction monitoring products to banks. The firm is also advising *Cosmopolitan* on trade mark matters.

Having provided privatisation advice to Incoms Telecom Holding, **Dobrev, Kinkin, Lyutskanov & Partners** now advises the telecoms company on all legal matters. The firm also provided M&A advice to software company GlobalSoft Consolidator Ltd.

Interius advises mostly international clients on all IP matters. Olga Sirakova is the firm's main IP lawyer.

LEGACOM Antov & Partners is acting as legal adviser to Eurocom Cable EAD, one of the main players in the Bulgarian cable arena. The firm has advised on a number of transactions regarding the acquisition of various local cable television networks.

Patent Universe comprises one technically educated patent lawyer, one other lawyer, and ten patent experts. The firm specialises solely in patent and trade mark work. Clients include Bass, Unilever, Siemens, ExxonMobil and Pfizer.

Sabev & Partners assisted ai informatics with the drafting of a commercial contract with the largest Bulgarian coal mining company.

Simeonov & Dermendjiev has a nine-strong patent and trade mark bureau consisting of lawyers and technical experts. It is headed by IP specialist Julian Varbanov.

Spasov & Bratanov completed due diligence and advised on the acquisition of a Bulgarian telecommunications company.

Studio Legale Sutti represented the US purchasers of Cable Bulgaria, and advises Sofia Film JSCo on all legal matters. The firm also provides patent and trade mark advice.

MARITIME

Vladimirov Law Office has offices in both Sofia and the port town, Varna. The firm specialises in maritime law, with Vladimir Vladimirov considered by peers to be one of the foremost shipping lawyers in Bulgaria. Clients include Bulgaria's largest shipowner, Navigation Maritime Bulgaria, and Cosmos Shipping. The firm works with several international law firms, including **Ince & Co** and **Hill Taylor Dickinson**.

PRIVATISATION AND FOREIGN INVESTMENT

As part of a team led by JPMorgan, **Djingov, Gouginski, Kyutchukov & Velichkov** advised the Bulgarian government on the €320m privatisation of the State Savings Bank. The firm is again representing the state, this time with Deutsche Bank, in the long-running Bulgaria Telecom privatisation. The firm also acted for the buyers in the privatisations of the Vazov military industrial plant, and a hydro-power operation. The firm also advised the potential purchaser in the collapsed Bulgar Tabac privatisation.

In the ongoing BTC privatisation, **Georgiev, Todorov & Co** is one of several firms advising preferred bidder, Advent International. Work includes negotiation, draft agreement consultation and legislative analysis, as well as litigation. The firm is also providing Greek-based bidder, Piraeus Bank, with ongoing advice on the sale of the National Bulgarian Savings Bank. In early 2003, lawyers from the firm's Sofia and Rousse offices teamed up to assist Rompetrol, the Romanian oil operator, in implementing a substantial investment, and establishing a local subsidiary.

Kambourov & Partners is one of the firms advising Koc Holding in the high-profile BTC privatisation, working in conjunction with US firm **Debevoise & Plimpton**. The firm has been retained by Koc Holdings to advise on general legal matters. Work is about to begin advising a large international energy company in the upcoming privatisation of the Bulgarian energy sector. Clients find the firm 'honest, reliable and competent in Bulgarian law', and recommend Yavor Kambourov and Vladimir Rangeloff in particular.

Having participated in over 30 privatisations, **LIC – Penkov, Markov & Partners**' experience in this area is extensive. The firm is working alongside **CMS Cameron McKenna** in advising the preferred bidder, Advent International, on the controversial BTC privatisation. The firm has also been appointed by the Privatisation Agency as a consultant and intermediary in the sale of the Bulgarian Commercial Sea Fleet and River Navigation Fleet. An 18-strong team has been formed for the job, which involves performing due diligence and strategy preparation.

LEGACOM Antov & Partners is experienced in privatisation matters. It recently advised CA-IB Corporate Finance, Austria, on the Bulgar Tabac privatisation. It also provided advice to another Austrian client, Erste Bank, one of the bidders for a Bulgarian state savings bank. In addition the team is currently acting for a potential bidder in the tender procedure for the privatisation of the Bulgarian electricity distribution sector.

Seplex Law Offices has continued to strengthen its practice. The 'competent and quick response' firm provided administrative and litigation advice to the Turkish-led consortium and second bidder in the Bulgarian Telecom privatisation. It was also consulted by Turkish glass producers Sisecam on a $150m greenfield investment in Bulgaria.

Borislav Boyanov & Co continues to advise the Bulgarian government on the privatisation of the state's seven electricity distribution companies. The firm is also representing the Italian company acting as principal sponsor in the €580m modernisation of the Maritsa East 3 power plant, the largest foreign investment in Bulgaria thus far.

KPMG Bulgaria OOD survived a rigorous selection process to act as legal adviser to Vintage Petroleum International, the US company shooting for gas in the Black Sea. Work has so far included securing permits, negotiating with the government, and advising on work plan drafts. Other FDI work includes advising on the €50m Mall of Sofia project, and providing comprehensive legal assistance to a German construction company engaged in constructing a €50m printing facility.

Studio Legale Sutti has acted in the privatisation of a number of Bulgaria's mines, and two cement plants. The firm recently completed work on the privatisation of the Interhotel Grand Hotel in Sofia. A number of potential foreign investors received advice from the firm last year. Name partner Yavor Varadinov has a sound reputation.

Arsov, Natchev, Ganeva is advising the National Bank of Greece in London on the privatisation of state minority stakes in several Bulgarian companies. These include Navigation Maritime Bulgare, BTC and the State Insurance Institute. Name partner Marin Arsov is the firm's FDI lawyer.

Dobrev, Kinkin, Lyutskanov & Partners advised Incoms Telecom Holding in several privatisation transactions.

Eastlaw is currently assisting a potential buyer in the privatisation of Balkancar – a complex and sizeable deal. The firm recently advised a possible investor in the cancelled Diplomatic Real Estates Agency privatisation.

Landwell Bulgaria extended its foreign investment experience by advising Bulgaria's National Electricity Company on the €580m rehabilitation of the Maritsa East 3 power plant.

Niesar & Diamond LLP and Todorova Law Offices Business Banking Corporate Environmental Legal Consultancy continues to advise the Bulgarian American Enterprise Fund, a US Congress institution which supplies promising Bulgarian businesses with loans and equity investments.

Novel Consult worked on the privatisation of a major industrial building and reconstruction enterprise; this work involved voucher privatisation, management buyout, and debt to equity swap. The team, led by Valeri Koev, also carried out due diligence for a significant number of clients. The firm has wide-ranging foreign investment capabilities, including experience of agriculture and industry.

PI Partners provided complete legal support for all stages of an estimated $150m greenfield foreign investment project in the glass industry. Clients appreciate the firm's 'professionalism and loyalty'.

Sabev & Partners' four-lawyer team advised Tobacco Capital Partners in the attempted privatisation of Bulgar Tabac. The firm also represented the Bulgarian Post-Privatisation Control Agency in arbitration proceedings against the buyer of Balkan Airlines; this work was carried out alongside **Freshfields Bruckhaus Deringer** and Israeli-firm **I Gornitzky & Co**.

MARITIME

VLADIMIROV LAW OFFICE

PRIVATISATION AND FOREIGN INVESTMENT

DJINGOV, GOUGINSKI, KYUTCHUKOV & VELICHKOV ✪
GEORGIEV, TODOROV & CO
KAMBOUROV & PARTNERS ✪
LIC – PENKOV, MARKOV & PARTNERS ✪
LEGACOM ANTOV & PARTNERS
SEPLEX LAW OFFICES

Borislav Boyanov & Co
KPMG Bulgaria OOD
Sutti, Studio Legale ✪

Arsov, Natchev, Ganeva
DIA Consult – Law Office
Dobrev, Kinkin, Lyutskanov & Partners ✪
Deloitte & Touche EOOD ✪
Eastlaw
Landwell Bulgaria ✪
Niesar & Diamond LLP and Todorova Law Offices Business Banking Corporate Environmental Legal Consultancy
Novel Consult
PI Partners ✪
Sabev & Partners ✪
Spasov & Bratanov

Firms are listed A-Z in tiers which are ranked in order of priority
✪ Indicates firm displays contact details at the end of this chapter.

Spasov & Bratanov provided acquisition finance advice to the foreign lenders in a privatisation deal last year. The firm also advised a foreign lender on the financing of a state-backed, power plant rehabilitation project.

PROJECT FINANCE AND CONSTRUCTION

Borislav Boyanov & Co is acting as local counsel to the principal sponsor of the €580m Maritsa East 3 project to modernise the Maritsa East power plant. The deal constitutes the largest single foreign investment to date in Bulgaria. The firm's wide-ranging experience of project finance and construction includes providing advice on oil, gas, water and nuclear energy matters.

Djingov, Gouginski, Kyutchukov & Velichkov advised clients on ten separate projects in 2003. These included advising BNP Paribas on structured finance, and the AIG Emerging Europe Infrastructure Fund on mezzanine finance for the Galata gasfield development project. A further highlight was providing advice on the securitisation of a financing facility for the mining industry, to NM Rothschild & Sons.

Last year, **Hayhurst Robinson** continued to advise two investment banks in connection with the €80m project financing of the Galata gasfield development. The team also provided a multilateral financial institution with advice on the financing of several Bulgarian companies.

Anticipating a surge in FDI, **KPMG Bulgaria OOD** has set up a team dedicated to construction, real estate and infrastructure issues. The team is providing full assistance to the developers of the €50m Mall of Sofia, one of the largest privately financed infrastructure projects in Bulgaria. It is also advising the German building company constructing a €50m printing facility, and is assisting a US petroleum company on all legal matters relating to its Black Sea exploration project. Hristo Andonov speaks good English and heads a western-orientated practice.

Landwell Bulgaria advised Bulgaria's National Electricity Company and Maritsa East Mines on the rehabilitation of the Maritsa 3 thermal power plant.

Totev & Ivanov is acting as local counsel alongside **Skadden, Arps, Slate, Meagher & Flom LLP** in London, on the largest single foreign investment in Bulgaria. The firms are advising US-based Entergy on a complex investment covering the takeover, rehabilitation, exploitation and transfer back of a coal-fired power station. Other work includes providing financing advice on the construction of a thermal power plant with London firm **Watson, Farley & Williams**, and advising a US investor on a gas exploration project.

Georgiev, Todorov & Co is acting for a consortium of Mitsui & Co, Toshiba and the Japanese Bank of International Cooperation in the rehabilitation of a thermal power plant. The project requires the team to draw on its energy, construction, project finance and contract experience.

Kambourov & Partners advised SMA Group on its involvement with a thermo power plant, and advised on various hydro-electric plants. The team provided Italian firm Sallini Gruppo with advice on the financing and construction of roads in Bulgaria. Clients consider the firm 'professional, competent and decent'.

LEGACOM Antov & Partners advised Urban 3000 and Colliers Continental Properties on the construction, sale and lease of luxury apartments at the 'Sofia Gardens' residential complex in the Bulgarian capital.

LIC – Penkov, Markov & Partners advised Thomas Cook on the financing and construction of hotels on the Black Sea coast. The firm's tourism knowledge was again employed in advising IFA Hotel and Touristik on closing a contract for managing a Black Sea resort.

Novel Consult was involved with a variety of projects, including the acquisition of the TBS Hotel Ambassador, and the incorporation and restructuring of Bulgarian Cheese. The firm advised on numerous aspects of the development of a privately-owned airport and pilot school.

Seplex Law Offices saw off stiff competition to win client HIT Hypermarkets, the German retailer. The firm is advising on the construction and operation of shopping malls throughout Bulgaria.

Bazlyankov Stanoev & Tashev advised clients on the construction of a €34m trade and shopping centre, and a €53m housing project.

IKRP Rokas & Partners advises a number of Greek construction companies.

Sabev & Partners advised US company BearingPoint Inc on the concession for the Bulgarian Airports Project. Work included the drafting of tender documents and a concession agreement. The firm advised the same client on its USAID-funded Commercial Law Reform Project.

Simeonov & Dermendjiev has a long-term contract to advise the Kozlodui nuclear power plant on loan agreements and the rehabilitation of the plant.

Stoyanov Mittov Tanev advised a US company on the construction of a $1.5m conference centre in Sofia.

Studio Legale Sutti is in the early stages of advising the constructors of a new highway.

PROJECT FINANCE AND CONSTRUCTION

BORISLAV BOYANOV & CO
DJINGOV, GOUGINSKI, KYUTCHUKOV & VELICHKOV ✪
HAYHURST ROBINSON ✪
KPMG BULGARIA OOD
LANDWELL BULGARIA ✪
TOTEV & IVANOV ✪

Georgiev, Todorov & Co
Kambourov & Partners ✪
LEGACOM Antov & Partners
LIC – Penkov, Markov & Partners ✪
Novel Consult
Seplex Law Offices

Arsov, Natchev, Ganeva
Bazlyankov Stanoev & Tashev
Boteva & Kantutis
Dobrev, Kinkin, Lyutskanov & Partners ✪
IKRP Rokas & Partners
Sabev & Partners ✪
Simeonov & Dermendjiev
Stoyanov Mittov Tanev
Sutti, Studio Legale ✪

Firms are listed A-Z in tiers which are ranked in order of priority
✪ Indicates firm displays contact details at the end of this chapter.

BATKOV, STOEV, BOTEV & ASSOCIATES

48 ALABIN STREET
1000 SOFIA

Telephone: +359 2 986 4774
Fax: +359 2 986 3497
E-mail: office@batkov.com
Website: www.batkov.com

Languages
English, French, German, Russian

Number of lawyers 27

Member
Interlegal

CATEGORIES OF WORK

Administrative
Todor Batkov, Georgi Georgiev

Banking
Boyko Botev, Georgi Georgiev

Civil law
Boyko Botev, Alexander Angelov

Corporate and commercial
Georgi Georgiev,
Radostina Konstantinova

Labour and social security
Anna Avramova, Rossen Stoyanov

Litigation and arbitration
Boyko Botev, Stoyan Yakimov

Privatisation and foreign investments
Ventsislav Stoev,
Radostina Konstantinova

Tax
Ventsislav Stoev, Rossen Stoyanov

Telecommunications
Todor Batkov, Martin Yordanov

THE FIRM

Batkov, Stoev, Botev & Associates was founded in 1991. Since then it continues growing steadily – today it is one of the major law companies in Bulgaria. Nowadays it numbers 19 lawyers working in almost all practice areas, nine trainees and office staff.

The new and the larger office of the company is situated in the centre of the city of Sofia – near the building of the Courts of Justice.

The firm's main task is to provide creative, practical advice at the highest quality level based not only on the knowledge of the matters, but also on understanding the clients' businesses and needs, and the industries in which they operate. The result: creative, prompt, cost-effective, satisfactory and value-added solutions to its clients.

Lawyers work both individually and in teams created for the single purpose of delivering solutions for the firm's clients.

In order to render quality services, the firm is constantly involved in its members' enhancing their knowledge in specific areas of practice.

The nature of the firm's clients varies from multinational companies through the entire range of privately owned companies, and commercial entities to individuals.

AREAS OF PRACTICE

Batkov, Stoev, Botev & Associates understand that it is impossible for a lawyer to specialise in all legal matters. But the breadth of its experience and the diversity of its knowledge enables the firm to handle multiple matters demanding large numbers of lawyers on tight deadlines – while producing the highest quality legal work. The firm works extensively with a broad range of industries, including: telecommunications; software; Internet services; banking; financial services; pharmaceutical; healthcare; media; intellectual property; manufacturing; real estate; retail; energy, oil, and gas; technology; transportation.

Batkov, Stoev, Botev & Associates represents clients in proceedings before national agencies and governmental bodies. Several attorneys have also represented state agencies in specialised matters. Batkov, Stoev, Botev & Associates is ready to assist clients in all types of government and regulatory matters.

Batkov, Stoev, Botev & Associates helps forward its clients in: loan and finance agreements; estate and trust administration; counselling investors in obtaining and closing financial agreements; increase or reduction of capital; advice on the setting up and running of business in Bulgaria; mergers and acquisitions counselling; negotiation, drafting and enforcement of all kinds of commercial contracts.

The telecommunications sector is unique and dynamic in nature. Batkov, Stoev, Botev & Associates is a leading adviser on the financing, regulatory and commercial aspects of national telecoms financings and projects. Whether a bank, a telecoms operator, an investor, a state agency or a government, the firm can assist on the full spectrum of transactions and activities in the telecommunications sector.

During the last few years the firm's lawyers have been actively involved in the privatisation and foreign investment processes in Bulgaria. The law firm has represented investors and investment companies alike for more than ten years.

Litigation is one of the firm's largest practice areas. Batkov Stoev, Botev & Associates represent clients at both trial, appellate and supreme court levels throughout the country. Experience includes almost every type of general civil, administrative, and commercial litigation.

With colleagues in other countries, the firm can give co-ordinated cross-border advice on all tax issues.

Batkov, Stoev, Botev & Associates is the first Bulgarian law company to have been elected a member of Interlegal – the international network of law firms.

DELOITTE & TOUCHE EOOD

55 ALEXANDER STAMBOLIJSKI BOULEVARD
1000 SOFIA

Telephone: +359 2 980 8500
Fax: +359 2 980 0436
Website: www.deloitte.bg

Languages
English, French, Macedonian, Russian

Other offices
Varna; Skopje, Macedonia

Number of lawyers 10

Member
Deloitte & Touche Integrated and Allied Services Practices

CATEGORIES OF WORK

Banking and finance
Borislav Stratev

Commercial contracts
Borislav Stratev, Milena Rizova

Concessions
Borislav Stratev

Consumer protection
Milena Rizova

Corporate and commercial
Borislav Stratev, Milena Rizova

Energy
Milena Rizova

EU and competition
Peter Boyukliev

Foreign investments
Borislav Stratev

Government contracts
Borislav Stratev

Insurance law
Milena Rizova

Intellectual property, IT and media
Milena Rizova

Labour law
Milena Rizova

Mergers and acquisitions
Borislav Stratev, Milena Rizova

Privatisation
Borislav Stratev

Procurement
Borislav Stratev

Tax law
Borislav Stratev, Svetlana Yordanova

DJINGOV, GOUGINSKI, KYUTCHUKOV & VELICHKOV

10 TSAR OSVOBODITEL BOULEVARD
1000 SOFIA

Telephone: +359 2 932 11 00
Fax: +359 2 980 35 86
E-mail: dgkv@dgkv.com
Website: www.dgkv.com

Languages
English, French, German, Russian

Other offices
Frankfurt, Germany

Number of lawyers 39

Contacts
Assen Djingov, Marius Velichkov

CATEGORIES OF WORK

Privatisation
Marius Velichkov

General corporate
Assen Djingov

Banking
Stephan Kyutchukov

Securities
Vessela Stancheva

Project finance
Stephan Kyutchukov

Mergers and acquisitions
Georgi Gouginski

Tax
Marius Velichkov

Construction
Stephan Kyutchukov

Litigation
Irina Stoeva

Telecommunications
Zdravka Ugrinova

Secured transactions
Stephan Kyutchukov

Energy
Georgi Gouginski

Competition
Nikolai Gouginski

Environmental law
Stephan Kyutchukov

Commercial property
Stephan Kyutchukov

Commercial contracts
Georgi Gouginski

IP, IT and media
Kalina Tchakarova

Labour law
Kalina Tchakarova

THE FIRM

Djingov, Gouginski, Kyutchukov & Velichkov was established in 1994 and is now one of Bulgaria's largest and most prominent law firms, with a diverse legal service and strong emphasis on foreign investment.

AREAS OF PRACTICE

The firm's leading position in the field of project finance and corporate finance is founded on high expertise in all aspects of lending, debt finance, securitisation, security/offshore agreements and guarantees. The firm is counsel to EBRD, IFC, JBIC and BSTDB on the financing of various infrastructure, construction and financial projects.

In the energy and infrastructure sector, the firm has advised AES, Entergy, EnergoPro and Rolls-Royce Power Ventures on their major investment projects, and Rheinbraun in its joint venture with NEK. The firm is the principal counsel to OMV for the construction of a nationwide network of petrol stations and advises CEZ for the recently launched privatisation of the Bulgarian electricity distribution companies. The firm has also represented Anglian Water and Thames Water for Varna, Shumen and Burgas water concessions.

The firm acts as legal adviser for global commercial banks, such as HVB, BNP Paribas, Citibank, Biochim, Société Générale and TC Ziraat Bank in relation to their operations in Bulgaria. It has represented IFC and AIG for the acquisition of shares in large Bulgarian banks. The firm has acted as counsel to EBRD, IFC, Commerzbank and two major German funds for the establishment of ProCredit Bank, a Bulgarian micro finance bank, and to Paribas in relation to the first Euro Bond issue for Sofia, for the amount of DEM100m. It advised UBS, Citibank, Rabobank, JP Morgan and BNP Paribas on various regulatory matters. The firm also advises numerous US and European investment banks and securities firms about their interests and operations on the Bulgarian market of stocks, bonds and T-bills.

The firm's leading role in the privatisation process has received strong international recognition. The firm has been involved in Bulgaria's largest privatisation deals: Bulgarian Telecommunications Company and State Savings Bank, as counsel to the government, Bulgartabac Holding, where the firm represented Deutsche Bank as a potential purchaser. The firm also represented: OMV in the acquisition of the state-owned gasoline retail company; Deutsche Bank for its acquisition of the three main domestic pharmaceutical companies; Nomura, Société Générale and KBC Bank in their acquisitions of Bulgaria's three largest banks; and SKF in the privatisation of a bearings plant.

In the field of telecommunications and media, the firm has a steadily growing practice. The firm has represented: Sanoma Magazines for the acquisition of a Bulgarian publishing business; Playboy with regard to publishing of Playboy magazine in Bulgaria; Warner Bros with regard to the hiring of Bulgarian extras; Reuters and Bloomberg for their Bulgarian activity; Broadnet for setting up of a national cable operator; a consortium of investors for MobilTel acquisition – the largest M&A transaction in Bulgaria; and Gazprombank in relation to acquisition of shares in a media holding structure. The firm also advised Telecom Italia in a tender for a GSM licence.

In the field of labour law, the firm advises on all aspects of employer/employee relationships, including layouts and employment of foreign personnel. Major clients include SKF, Carlsberg, OMV, etc.

The list of clients includes, among others: Abbot, Accor, Alcatel, AndersenLegal IP, BP, Bristol Myers Squibb, Cable & Wireless, Carlsberg, Chase Manhattan, Chevron Texaco, Coca-Cola, Conoco UK, DMG, Dyno Industries, Eli Lilly, Enron, Ford, Estee Lauder, GE International, Hilton, ING Barings, Japan Tobacco, Kempinski Hotels, Merill Lynch, Morgan Stanley, Nokia, Nomura International, Shell, Schroder Salomon Smith Barney, Cercol, Standard Bank London, Volvo, Whirlpool, and Western Union.

DOBREV, KINKIN, LYUTSKANOV & PARTNERS

8 TSAR IVAN SHISHMAN STREET
1000 SOFIA

Telephone: +359 2 980 34 75
Fax: +359 2 980 42 61
E-mail: lawfirm-office@lawfirm-bg.org
Website: www.lawfirm-bg.com

Languages
English, German, Russian

Number of lawyers 10

Contact
Grozdan Dobrev

Member
Associated member European Law Firm (ELF)

CATEGORIES OF WORK

Banking and finance
Roumen Lyutskanov, Theodore Bojinov

Finance and construction
Vladimir Kinkin, Theodore Bojinov

Infrastructure projects
Ventsislav Nizamski, Elissaveta Gangalova

Commercial and company law
Vladimir Kinkin, Alexander Georgiev

Capital markets
Grozdan Dobrev, Theodore Bojinov

Competition law
Grozdan Dobrev, Elissaveta Gangalova

Shipping and transport
Vladimir Kinkin, Alexander Georgiev

Insurance law
Theodore Bojinov, Alexander Georgiev

Privatisation and foreign investment
Vladimir Kinkin, Grozdan Dobrev

Securities
Elissaveta Gangalova, Theodore Bojinov

Mergers and acquisitions
Gozdan Dobrev, Ventsislav Nizamski

Litigation
Alexander Georgiev, Elissaveta Vukovska

Arbitration
Vladimir Kinkin, Alexander Georgiev

THE FIRM

Dobrev, Kinkin, Lyutskanov & Partners was established in its original form in 1989 and now comprises senior partners, partner lawyers and legal assistants. The firm is a registered company and operates in compliance with the Bar Act.

The firm offers legal services and assistance to corporate clients, covering the full range of their activities. External consultants are employed if necessary. The firm's major specialisms are commercial and company law and litigation, and some of the firm's lawyers are qualified in the field of international economic relations.

AREAS OF PRACTICE

Dobrev, Kinkin, Lyutskanov & Partners provides legal assistance and services mainly for the business operations of clients working in the fields of commercial and company law, financial, banking and tax law, including privatisation deals, securities, transport, insurance, litigation and so on.

The firm's activities include: incorporation, mergers, acquisitions, spin-offs, divisions, structuring and winding up of companies and enterprises; preparation and implementation of transactions involving property and rights management; participation in litigation and bankruptcy proceedings; collateral and guarantees; preparation and servicing of notarial transactions and certifications; preparation of commercial contracts; legal services in connection with taxation and legal defence with regard to tax liability statements; legal assistance in the execution and implementation of insurance, transport and forwarding contracts; preparation of due diligence reports; preparation and conclusion of privatisation deals and legal assistance in their implementation.

The main principles underlying the work of the firm are the specialisations of its individual lawyers and team work. Teams of experts in various aspects of law are established to work on specific legal issues, with the basic rule being to keep clients informed about the development of their cases.

The firm's lawyers provide legal assistance and defence in the preparation and conduct of lawsuits and arbitration cases in Bulgaria and abroad.

HAYHURST ROBINSON

24 VASSIL LEVSKI BLVD
SOFIA 1000

Telephone: +359 2 963 0378
Fax: +359 2 963 0398
E-mail: hrsofia@hrintlaw.com
Website: www.hrintlaw.com

Languages
Bulgarian, English, French, Hungarian, Romanian, Russian, Serbian

Other offices
Belgrade, Bucharest, Budapest

Number of lawyers 40
at this office 9

Contact
Barbara Mendler (bmendler@hrintlaw.com)

International groupings
Interlex Group; IBA

CATEGORIES OF WORK

Foreign investment
Robert Hayhurst, David Butts

Privatisation
David Butts, Reneta Petkova

Energy and natural resources
Robert Hayhurst, George Georgiev

Real estate
David Butts

Project and corporate finance
Robert Hayhurst, David Butts

Banking
Reneta Petkova

Private equity
Neil Berlad, Robert Hayhurst

Mergers and acquisitions
Robert Hayhurst, Reneta Petkova

Telecoms
Todd Robinson, John Fitzpatrick

Pharmaceutical
David Butts, Teodora Ivanova

Licensing and hi-tech
David Butts, John Fitzpatrick

Insurance
George Georgiev

Shipping
George Georgiev

Transport infrastructure
Todd Robinson, Robert Hayhurst

General corporate
Reneta Petkova

Corporate insolvency and bankruptcy
Reneta Petkova, David Butts

KAMBOUROV & PARTNERS

55 NEOFIT RILSKI STREET
SOFIA 1000

Telephone: +359 2 986 9999
Fax: +359 2 986 9995
E-mail: office@kambourov.biz
Website: www.kambourov.biz

Languages
English, French, German, Italian, Russian

Number of lawyers 11

Contacts
Yavor Kambourov, Vladimir Rangeloff

CATEGORIES OF WORK

Foreign investments
Yovor Kambourov, Vladimir Rangeloff

Privatisation
Yavor Kambourov, Vladimir Rangeloff

Litigation and arbitration
Yavor Kambourov, Vladimir Rangeloff

Banking law and bank insolvency
Yavor Kambourov, Plamen Borissov

Insolvency proceedings
Yavor Kambourov

Intellectual property and copyright
Yavor Kambourov, Mitko Karushkov

Taxation and customs issues
Emil Emanuilov, Vladimir Rangeloff

Employment and social security issues
Emil Emanuilov

Commercial law (including mergers and acquisitions)
Yavor Kambourov, Vladimir Rangeloff

Corporate law
Kiro Kirov

Telecommunications, TV, movie industry
Mitko Karushkov, Yavor Kambourov

Energy sector, mining
Vladimir Rangeloff

Concessions
Stefan Tzakov

Competition and consumer protection
Mitko Karushkov

THE FIRM

Kambourov & Partners is a legal and tax firm dedicated to providing a high-quality service. The firm is organised as a multi-disciplinary practice – legal, tax, accounting, customs and litigation. The firm maintains the core values of the legal profession – independence of professional judgement, protection of confidential client information, and loyalty.

The firm has experienced professionals with national and international reputations for delivering legal, tax, accountancy and customs services, both in a transactional and advisory context, in combination with equivalent advice from professionals working in other areas. The team consists of two partners and nine lawyers.

AREAS OF PRACTICE

Kambourov & Partners advises on all issues relating to foreign investment (including greenfield investments), commercial, competition and consumer protection law, corporate, personal and turnover taxation, employment law, social, unemployment and health security, insurance law, accountancy, banking, customs law and litigation. The firm provides more than just legal advice, it assists its clients in international tax matters, as well as in legal and tax litigation.

Kambourov & Partners provides a comprehensive range of legal and tax services across the following areas.

Foreign investments advice related to legal and business issues in Bulgaria including: incentives for financing in different sectors; establishing business representation; greenfield investments; working out, establishing and maintaining effective legal, financial, taxation, customs and accountancy systems for foreign investors in Bulgaria.

Advice in all corporate law-related issues (setting up companies, and the restructuring of companies, capital and shareholders structure). Also advises on the management and legal representation of companies.

Commercial transactions: advice on contracts for suppliers and customers, general conditions applied to clients; drafting sale, distributor, loan, financial lease, rent and agency agreements; collateral arrangements – pledge assessments including registered pledge agreements without transfer of possession, mortgage agreements, guarantees; commercial papers (bills of exchange, promisory notes).

Consumer protection: preliminary and operative advice as to the liabilities related to consumer protection; representation and assistance before the relevant authorities; providing legal services as to warranty liabilities; legal assistance in litigation related to consumer protection.

Competition advice covers abuse of majority market share position, co-ordinated practice, cartels, dumping, unlawful advertisement, prohibition of exclusivity of supplying sources, etc).

Administrative services advice includes: obtaining work and stay permits for foreigners; establishing the legal status of foreigners working in Bulgaria (such as accommodation, benefits, personal taxation, social, health and unemployment insurance, etc).

Advice on customs-related issues, including establishing and maintaining different import and export regimes.

Taxation: personal tax advice for Bulgarian and foreign employees, managers and members of the managing corporate bodies); corporate tax advice includes profits tax treaties, avoidance of double taxation; VAT and excises advice; tax planning; and tax protection (includes tax audits, protection before tax authorities and tax litigation).

Advice in accountancy law and auditing services, in particular Bulgarian accounting standards.

Advice on employment-related issues including social security and health insurance (coverage, contributions, benefits, medical assistance, etc).

A full litigation service includes representation before the Bulgarian state courts, institutional arbitration courts and ad hoc arbitrations.

LIC-PENKOV, MARKOV & PARTNERS

BL 22, ENTR A
IZTOK DISTRICT
1113 SOFIA

Telephone: +359 2 971 3935
Fax: +359 2 971 1191
E-mail: lega@bulnet.bg
Website: www.legainterconsult.com

Languages
Bulgarian, English, French, German, Russian

Other offices
Bourgas, Dobrich, Lovech (2), Pleven (and Troyan), Rousse, Sofia (2), Stara Zagora, Targovishte, Varna, Vratsa

Number of lawyers 39
at this office 23

International groupings
Lex Mundi; Eurojuris (Germany); Bulgarian International Business Association; Business Club of German Economy

CATEGORIES OF WORK

Commercial and business
Vladimir Penkov, Ivan Markov

Privatisation
Vladimir Penkov, Roussin Yordanov

Foreign investment
Vladimir Penkov

Joint venture
Vladimir Penkov

Banking and financial
Ivan Markov

Mergers and acquisitions
Vladimir Penkov, Svetlin Adrianov

Antitrust and competition
Svetlin Adrianov

Consumer protection
Svetlin Adrianov

Telecoms
Pavel Velchev

Labour
Dimitar Chorbadjiev

Tax
Dimitar Slavchev

Real estate
Todorin Pakerov

Commercial (international)
Vladimir Penkov

Licensing
Vladimir Penkov

Litigation
Todorin Pakerov

Arbitration (international)
Vladimir Penkov

Customs
Roman Stoyanov

Maritime
Krastio Georgiev

THE FIRM

Established in 1990, Lega InterConsult is now one of the largest law firms in Bulgaria, with offices in Sofia and nine other major Bulgarian cities. The firm employs 39 lawyers and a comprehensive team of support staff. The firm has strong co-operative links with Lansky, Gauzger & Partners (Vienna), Niebaum, Kohler, Punge, Söder (Dortmund). Lega InterConsult was the first domestic firm to be admitted to the Bulgarian International Business Association (BIBA), an association of foreign investors in the country. Since 2003 it has been a member of the Business Club of German Economy in Bulgaria.

The firm is noted for its commitment to research. It has published articles on: the harmonisation of Bulgarian and EU corporate and commercial law for the Bulgarian Centre for the Study of Democracy; *The EU: Towards an Institutional Infrastructure*; tax and development; Customs Acts and regulation. The firm contributes to specialised publications such as the *International Privatisation Law Review*. Lega InterConsult also publishes its own newsletter, the first of its kind in Bulgaria and with a circulation of 2,200, that provides up-to-date legal information to governmental and non-governmental institutions, embassies, businesses and individual experts in the legal and economic sectors. The firm is active in the preparation of bills and legal regulations concerning issues including concessions, privatisations and electronic signature.

Lawyers at the firm regularly take part in international legal and business forums, including in recent years: the 1999 UN forum on new trends in competition law in Brno; the 2000 international conference of the Centre for Energy Efficiency in Sofia; the Fourth Session of the Bulgarian-German Committee Conference for Economic Co-operation in Hanover.

AREAS OF PRACTICE

The firm's main areas of practice are commercial and business law with particular emphasis on corporate law, privatisation, foreign investment, joint ventures, banking and financial law, mergers and acquisitions, antitrust and competition, consumer protection, telecoms, labour law, tax law, real estate, international commercial law, licensing, litigation and international arbitration. Lega InterConsult are specialists in the provision of legal advice on the international aspects of commercial, company and civil law. Lawyers at the firm are recognised experts in many of the fields mentioned.

One of the firm's main activities is advising overseas clients on investment opportunities in Bulgaria. Lega InterConsult advises on the legal regulations relating to taxation, customs procedures, export and import, currency, employment and social security and their relation to the contemporary investment climate.

The recognised strength of Lega InterConsult's legal presence in the investment sector has led to its involvement in some of the largest investment projects in the region. The firm's major international clients include: The Coca-Cola Company, directly and through Leventis Group and Clarina; Heineken, in Brewinvest and Brewmasters' investment in Bulgarian breweries; Hewlett-Packard; the European Bank for Reconstruction and Development (EBRD); DaimlerChrysler AG; Siemens AG; Willi Betz Group in its distribution of Mercedes-Benz and Chrysler; Bayer AG; Sumitomo Corporation; National Bank of Greece; Cargill; Salini; Advent International; Titan Cement; Galagher Int; Telefonica; Enichem; Karelia Tobacco; Laufen; Knauf; Chimco (Bulgaria); Lafarge, Autotechnica (authorised importer of Audi and Seat); Frech; Sega Corporation; Akamai Technologies Inc; Oiltanking; Cammell Laird Plc; Alu Koenig Stahl; BASF AG; Velux A/S. The firm also advises the governments of Bulgaria and the Swiss Federation with regard to financing projects in Bulgaria.

LANDWELL BULGARIA

7TH FLOOR
9-11 MARIA LOUISA BLVD
1000 SOFIA

Telephone: +359 2 9355 100
Fax: +359 2 9355 166
E-mail:
irina.tsvetkova@bg.landwellglobal.com
Website: www.landwellglobal.com/bg

Languages
English, French, German, Italian, Spanish, Russian

Number of lawyers 15

Contact
Irina Tsvetkova (partner)

International groupings
Landwell, correspondent law firms of PricewaterhouseCoopers

CATEGORIES OF WORK

Commercial and competition
Galina Bunkova, Polina Ganeva

Corporate structuring
Irina Tsvetkova, Lilia Andonova

Dispute resolution and litigation
Irina Tsvetkova, Nikolay Bebov

Technology, media and communications
Lilia Andonova, Irina Tsvetkova

Employment and human resources
Polina Ganeva, Lilia Andonova

Financial services
Nikolay Bebov, Galina Bunkova

Intellectual property
Galina Bunkova, Polina Ganeva

Mergers and acquisitions
Nikolay Bebov, Maria Urmanova

Public law
Maria Urmanova, Dimitar Ivanov

Real estate and construction
Lilia Andonova, Maria Urmanova

Tax law
Lilia Andonova

Energy and mining
Nikolay Bebov, Galina Bunkova

Foreign direct investment
Irina Tsvetkova

International private law
Tsvetan Krumov

THE FIRM

Effective as from August 2002, the legal practice PricewaterhouseCoopers Legal and Tax Consultants was transformed into the law firm Landwell Bulgaria.

Landwell Bulgaria is part of the Landwell global network of law firms. Landwell's main focus is cross-border M&A transactions and corporate transformation projects. Landwell works closely on a number of projects with PricewaterhouseCoopers and is a market leader in the design and delivery of complex corporate change.

Landwell Bulgaria achieves a synergy of strong local capabilities with, being part of the global Landwell network, a global outlook.

AREAS OF PRACTICE

Landwell Bulgaria provides a full range of business law services. It focuses particularly on the following areas of practice: commercial and corporate law; M&A and privatisation projects; corporate structuring; financial services and banking; technology, media and communications; energy law and regulations; tax law; litigation and dispute resolution; and real estate and construction law.

PI PARTNERS
EY LAW

NATIONAL PALACE OF CULTURE
1 BULGARIA SQUARE
1463 SOFIA

Telephone: +359 2 986 26 22
Fax: +359 2 980 15 36
E-mail: pi.partners@bg.eylaw.com
Website: www.eylaw.com/bulgaria

Languages
English, French, German, Greek, Italian, Romanian, Spanish

Other offices
Athens, Bucharest, Thessaloniki

Number of lawyers 49
at this office 4

Contact
Anelia Dinova (anelia.dinova@bg.eylaw.com)

Member
EY Law

CATEGORIES OF WORK

Banking, finance and securities
Diana Volkova

M&A and privatisations
Anelia Dinova

Commercial and corporate
Milen Rusev

Human capital services and labour
Boyan Kirtshev

Litigation and arbitration
Milen Rusev

Real estate
Diana Volkova

PATENT UNIVERSE

26 KHAN ASPARUKH STREET
PO BOX 558
1000 SOFIA

Telephone: +359 29 89 79 82
Fax: +359 29 80 79 45
E-mail: patentuni@omega.bg
Website: www.patentuni.com

Languages
English, French, German, Russian, Spanish

Number of lawyers 2

International groupings
AIPPI; INTA; ABA

CATEGORIES OF WORK

Patents for inventions and unitily models
P Boykova, V Nesheva

Trade and service marks
M Markova, V Nesheva

Industrial designs
M Markova

Geographic indications
M Markova

BG domain names
M Markova

License agreements and assignments
V Nesheva

Border measures
V Nesheva

Specialised litigation relating to industrial property protection infringements, unfair competition
V Nesheva

Specialised translation of patent specifications
P Boykova, V Nesheva

SABEV & PARTNERS LAW FIRM

59 SOLUNSKA STREET
1000 SOFIA

Telephone: +359 2 953 1273
Fax: +359 2 953 1767
E-mail: office@sabevandpartners.com
Website: www.sabevandpartners.com

Languages
English, French, German, Russian

Number of lawyers 8

Contact
Mrs Boryana Boteva

CATEGORIES OF WORK

Corporate and commercial
George Sabev, Assen Alexiev

Capital markets and securities
George Sabev, Boryana Boteva

Taxation
B Boteva, Nevena Stoeva

Competition
Assen Alexiev

Intellectual property
Assen Alexiev

Property and construction law
Katilin Popov, K Kavaldsieva

Employment and social security
B Boteva, Kostya Karaivanov

Environment
Katilin Popov

Litigation and dispute resolution
A Alexiev, Stefan Stefanov

Public procurement
Boryana Boteva, Nevena Stoeva

Privatisation and concessions
Boryana Boteva, Nevena Stoeva

Telecommunications and IT
Assen Alexiev

International commercial
George Sabev, Katilin Popov

EU law
Katilin Popov

International arbitration
B Boteva, Stefan Stefanov

Bankruptcy
George Sabev, Assen Alexiev

Foreign investments
Boryana Boteva, Nevena Stoeva

Mergers and acquisitions
Stefan Stefanov, B Boteva

STUDIO LEGALE SUTTI

50 A LYUBEN
KARAVELOV STR
1000 SOFIA

Telephone: +359 2 963 5007
Fax: +359 2 963 2792
E-mail: maildesk@sutti.com
Website: www.sutti.com

Languages
Bulgarian, Dutch, English, French, German, Italian, Japanese, Portuguese, Romanian, Serbian, Spanish

Other offices
Belgrade, Bucharest, Genoa, London, Milan, Rome, Tokyo

Number of lawyers 130
at this office 15

Contact
Tzvetelina Mitkova Dimitrova

CATEGORIES OF WORK

Company, commercial law

Banking and finance

Mergers and acquisitions

Distribution, agency and franchising

Debt collection and insolvency

Commercial property law

Intellectual property

Patent and trade mark agency service

White-collar crime

EC, competition and antitrust law

IT and TLC law

Litigation and arbitration

Employment, labour law

Administrative law

Environmental law

TOTEV & IVANOV

16 VITOSHA STREET
1000 SOFIA

Telephone: +359 2 981 4331
Fax: +359 2 986 4652
E-mail: office@totevivanov.com
Website: www.totevivanov.com

Languages
English, French, German

Number of lawyers 6

CATEGORIES OF WORK

Project finance
Dimitar Totev, Ilian Ivanov

Securities regulations
Dimitar Totev

Corporate and commercial
Dimitar Totev

Real estate
Dimitar Totev

Tax
Ilian Ivanov

Mergers and acquisitions
Dimitar Totev, Ilian Ivanov

Employment
Ilian Ivanov

CROATIA

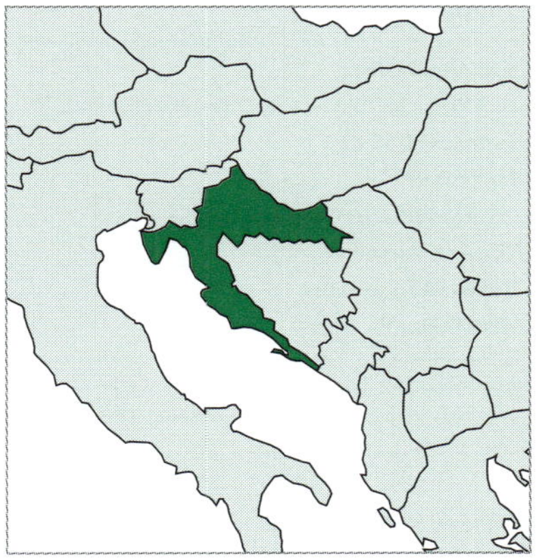

Population	4.4 million
Number of lawyers	2,500
Professional title	Odvjetnik
Currency	Croatian Kuna (HVK)

Index

The independent state of Croatia (or Republika Hrvastska) was formed in 1991. Nearly 780,000 Croatians live in the capital, Zagreb, the focus of much of the country's commercial activity.

Situated on the east Adriatic coast, Croatia's biggest earner is tourism, though traditional industries such as shipping still dominate the manufacturing sector.

Croatia is neighboured by Hungary, Slovenia, the autonomous Yugoslav province of Vojvodina, the Yugoslav Republic of Montenegro, and Bosnia-Herzegovina, which shares Croatia's longest border.

BILLING

Court work is charged according to a strict tariff set by the Croatian Bar Association. Non-contentious work is billed at €100 to €300 per hour depending on the type of work and seniority of the lawyer. Once a client has developed a relationship with a firm it is common for parties to agree on a billing package rather than continue with hourly rates.

MARKETING

The Croatian Bar Association's Code of Professional Ethics prohibits Croatian law firms from advertising in Croatia, in foreign newspapers, and from having websites. Many firms will not make overt references to clients.

IN-HOUSE LAWYERS

In-house lawyers may not join the Croatian Bar due to their perceived partiality.

POLITICAL AND ECONOMIC CLIMATE

Both Croatia's political and economic regimes have undergone significant change in recent years.

The country has steadily moved towards a fully-fledged democratic system, and formally applied to join the European Union in February 2003, raising the country's international profile. Meeting membership criteria is Croatia's overriding focus. Provided it does so, it will join the EU in a few years' time. Obstacles to membership include a judiciary in need of reform and the inevitable legislation overhaul and implementation required to meet EU benchmarks.

In November 2003, the nationalist Croatian Democratic Union Party won the general election, ousting the Social Democrats from power. Despite the change in government, it is expected that EU accession will remain the ruling party's priority.

With 4% average GDP growth since 2000, Croatia has one of the fastest-growing economies in Central Europe. Recent membership of the WTO and CEFTA demonstrate a more outward-looking stance, as does a 90% foreign-owned banking sector. However, unemployment sits at 15% and enterprise is hampered by an ill-equipped labour force. Though outmoded legislation is being replaced, the challenge of implementing the new laws contributes to a generally slow pace of reform in which sustainable growth cannot be guaranteed.

Though the tourism-dominated services sector generates 70% of GDP, shipping, clothing, chemicals, fertilisers and cement are also important industries.

LEGAL MARKET

Croatian Bar rules changed in 1994 to allow the formation of law firms. That said, 90% of Croatian lawyers are sole practitioners and firms that have been set up tend to be small. Most lawyers are generalists, and though the bigger firms do offer specialists, they are often encouraged to cover a variety of areas.

Bogdanóvic & Dolicki (in association with Lovells), **Porobija & Porobija** and **Zuric i Partneri** are consistently singled out by lawyers and clients alike as market leaders with distinguished reputations. **Markovic & Pliso** and **Hanzekovic, Radakovic and Partners** are also highly regarded.

Savoric & Partners, headed by the charismatic Boris Savoric, is an expanding firm aggressively seeking a share of the leaders' market. The firm worked on some attractive deals last year, and is considered by rivals to be 'up and coming'. Of the smaller firms, **Law Office Babic** and **Juric Law Offices** win praise for high-quality service. **DLA Weiss Tessbach / Law Office Natalija Peric** is well-established.

Despite increased international interest in Croatia following its application for EU membership, the Croatian legal market remains a 'closed shop'. The Croatian Bar prohibits foreign law firms from setting up permanent offices in Croatia, and it is forbidden for foreign lawyers to practise Croatian law. However, co-operation with international firms is permitted and leading local firms often have informal ties with foreign firms whose representatives may travel to Croatia to advise clients, as is the case with **Bogdanóvic & Dolicki (in association with Lovells)**.

The largest firms

1	Zuric i Partneri	22
2	Bogdanóvic & Dolicki (in association with Lovells)	19
3	Vukic, Jelusic, Sulina Stankovic, Jurcan & Jabuka	17
4	Markovic & Pliso	15
5	Vukmir & Associates	12
6	Hanzekovic, Radakovic and Partners	11
7	Mirjana Boric in co-operation with Cerha Hempel Spiegelfeld Hlawati	6
	Porobija & Porobija	6
	Savoric & Partners	6
	Schönherr Rechtsanwälte OEG in co-operation with Croatian Attorneys At Law	6
	Travas & Partners	6
12	DLA Weiss Tessbach / Law Office Natalija Peric	5
	Vedris & Partners	5
14	CMS d.o.o.	4
	KPMG Croatia d.o.o.	4
	Law Office Babic	4
	Law Offices Miroljub Macesic	4
	Pliso Rajic Milicic	4
	Wolf Theiss	4
20	Juric Law Offices	3
	Law Office Dragicevic	3
	Law Office Ljubenko	3
	Law Office Modrusan	3
	Matic-IKRP	3
25	Deissenberger & Partners d.o.o.	2
	Law Office Sebetic	2

These figures represent the total number of lawyers in this country only, and have been supplied by the firms themselves. The figures should be accurate as at 1 January 2004.

The top lawyers have excellent knowledge of Croatian law combined with a highly developed international legal perspective. Most Croatian lawyers speak good English, and several individuals have an impeccable grasp of the language. They include Boris Babic of **Law Office Babic**, Sanja Juric of **Juric Law Offices**, Dr Neven Cirkveni and Boris Porobija from **Porobija & Porobija** and Aleksej Miskovic of **Travas & Partners**. It is generally acknowledged that the legal market will eventually open up, but when this might happen continues to be debated.

Arbitration has become a popular method of dispute resolution as it can take several years for a case to pass through the congested Croatian court system. Arbitration takes place in the Croatian Chamber of Commerce.

The past year has seen unspectacular yet steady growth in the Croatian legal market, with increased activity reported in tourism, foreign investment and mergers and acquisitions work.

LEGISLATIVE DEVELOPMENTS

There has been a flurry of new legislation in Croatia of late. The Companies Act alone underwent over 200 amendments last summer. The pace of change was driven by the need to harmonise with the EU, and a desire to push legislation through Croatia's parliament before the general election in November 2003.

Though the legal profession welcomes the advent of a more liberal and logical system, there are concerns that the authorities may struggle to implement such considerable legislative reform. Some firms could be challenged by the need to keep up with the volume and speed of developments.

The most significant changes in 2003 include new laws concerning foreign exchange, civil litigation, companies and bankruptcy.

Much of the law is based on German and/or Austrian models, though English law is gaining influence as major finance deals are brokered through London.

BANKING, FINANCE AND CAPITAL MARKETS

BANKING, FINANCE AND CAPITAL MARKETS

HANZEKOVIC, RADAKOVIC AND PARTNERS
MARKOVIC & PLISO
POROBIJA & POROBIJA ✪
ZURIC I PARTNERI

BOGDANÓVIC & DOLICKI (IN ASSOCIATION WITH LOVELLS) ✪
SAVORIC & PARTNERS ✪

Babic, Law Office
DLA Weiss Tessbach / Law Office Natalija Peric ✪
Juric Law Offices
Matic-IKRP ✪
PricewaterhouseCoopers
Travas & Partners
Vukmir & Associates
Wolf Theiss ✪

Firms are listed A-Z in tiers which are ranked in order of priority
✪ Indicates firm displays contact details at the end of this chapter.

Hanzekovic, Radakovic and Partners has a very good reputation for banking, finance and loan advice, with notable activity in syndicated loans and foreign securities.

Markovic & Pliso has a strong reputation for banking and finance. In 2003 the firm advised on loan transactions for clients such as the Republic of Croatia, Bank of Tokyo and Chase Manhattan Bank. It acted for Citibank on a $5m promissory note purchase. The firm works with several high-profile international law firms.

Porobija & Porobija advised the Singapore branch of Deutsche Bank AG on a €250m loan, and represented Croatia's largest bank, Zagrebecka Banka and SEPFA Investment Bank Ltd on a €150m loan. 'First-rate' name partner Boris Porobija and his team worked to an extremely tight deadline to complete a €280m project bond transaction for UBS Warburg, and advised the issuing managers of a government bond.

Zuric I Partneri advised the seller on the €137m sale of 25% of Privredna Banka. The firm also advised on the sale of the largest bank in the Republic of Montenegro, acted for the seller in the acquisition of Rijeka Banka by ERSTE Bank, and for the majority shareholder in the merger of HVB Bank Croatia dd and Splitska Banka dd.

Bogdanóvic & Dolicki (in association with Lovells) acts for several Croatian banks and lists Chase Manhattan among its international banking clients. The firm has particular expertise in stock exchange listings.

Growing firm **Savoric & Partners** acted for the EBRD on the acquisition of a €137m share in one of Croatia's largest banks. The firm advised the EBRD, Accession Mezzanine Capital LC and a German financing firm on an equity investment in a leading Croatian dairy company. Other work includes multi-million euro loan advice and advising Privredna Banka Zagreb on the share listing of Croatia Insurance. Team head Boris Savoric is recommended for his experience, knowledge and professionalism.

Law Office Babic advised a major international bank on the acquisition financing of a Croatian company. Name partner Boris Babic is highly regarded and has excellent English.

DLA Weiss Tessbach / Law Office Natalija Peric provided financial and banking advice to Austrian-based Erste Bank and Hypo Alpe Adria Bank. The firm continues to represent bank consortiums in developing the Hilton Hotel, Dubrovnik and the Branimorova Commercial Centre.

Juric Law Offices deals frequently with the IFC, and current clients include a large German financing company.

Matic-IKRP advised a number of banks in 2003, while **PricewaterhouseCoopers**' Croatian legal department acted for EXIM Bank on concessions and guarantees and advised Heidelberg Cement on promissory notes, stocks and other securities. The office has ties with the **Landwell** law firm network.

Travas & Partners advised UniBanka on an €8m long-term loan facility. Zagrebacka Banka, Croatia's largest commercial bank, is a permanent client and the firm has advised a number of foreign banks on a deal-to-deal basis.

Austrian newcomer **Wolf Theiss** advised Splitska Banka on co-operation agreements and the sale of its stake in a pension company. Partner Christian Hoenig plans to double the five-strong team's capacity within the next two years.

CORPORATE AND COMMERCIAL

CORPORATE AND COMMERCIAL

BOGDANÓVIC & DOLICKI (IN ASSOCIATION WITH LOVELLS) ✪
MARKOVIC & PLISO
POROBIJA & POROBIJA ✪
ZURIC I PARTNERI

DLA WEISS TESSBACH / LAW OFFICE NATALIJA PERIC ✪
HANZEKOVIC, RADAKOVIC AND PARTNERS

Babic, Law Office
Juric Law Offices
Matic-IKRP ✪
PricewaterhouseCoopers
Savoric & Partners ✪
Travas & Partners
Vukmir & Associates

Cipcic-Bragadin
Divjak, Topic & Bahtijarevic
KPMG Croatia d.o.o.
Mirjana Boric in co-operation with Cerha Hempel Spiegelfeld Hlawati ✪
Law Offices Miroljub Macesic ✪
Neven Cirkveni (Dr)
Petrak Law Offices
Schönherr Rechtsanwalte OEG in co-operation with Croatian Attorneys At Law ✪
Vukic, Jelusic, Sulina Stankovic, Jurcan & Jabuka
Wolf Theiss ✪

Firms are listed A-Z in tiers which are ranked in order of priority
✪ Indicates firm displays contact details at the end of this chapter.

Bogdanóvic & Dolicki (in association with Lovells) includes the €100m merger of Dom fond and Korifej dd, and an €8m insurance company merger among its corporate work over the year. Name partner Tin Dolicki has 'fantastic' legal and commercial knowledge and clients find him 'a pleasure to work with'. The firm employs 23 lawyers, and one client describes it as 'easily the best law firm in Croatia'.

Markovic & Pliso advises Bechtel International on all corporate matters, and completed due diligence for a Croatian bank last year. Other clients include Bosch, McDonald's, Siemens and the EBRD. Partners Zoran Markovic and Miroslav Pliso head a 16-associate team.

Porobija & Porobija advised on bank and pension fund mergers. Other clients include the second-largest mobile phone operator in Croatia, Mars, ENI and Benetton. The firm has worked with **Linklaters** for seven years. Name partner Boris Porobija has an excellent reputation among clients and lawyers.

Zuric I Partneri acted for the winning party in a €500m acquisition, considered to have been Croatia's largest deal last year. Clients include General Motors, IBM, Cisco and BAT. Partner Branimir Skurla is recommended for corporate advice.

DLA Weiss Tessbach / Law Office Natalija Peric formed in October 2003, following the integration of UK-based international firm **DLA** and Austrian firm *Weiss-Tessbach*. The firm continues to assist Croatia Telecom with restructuring, has advised Deutsche Telekom on employment law and procurement issues, and has seen an increase in IP work. Vienna-based Peter Stolt works closely with the office which plans to expand over the coming year.

There was a reorganisation at **Hanzekovic, Radakovic and Partners**–Marijan Hanzekovic became managing partner, and five new partners were appointed through internal promotion. Two new lawyers were also hired, taking the firm total to ten. The team advises foreign and local clients on corporate and commercial matters, and experienced an increase in litigation and arbitration work during 2003.

The four-lawyer team at **Law Office Babic** is 'young and enthusiastic', according to clients, and headed by the 'excellent' Boris Babic. The team specialises in corporate and commercial advice for Fortune 100 and 500 companies, with expertise in competition and antitrust. The firm is currently advising a top multinational on branding strategy, and has ties to a number of top-tier US and UK firms. Clients report that Boris Babic is 'very considerate and very intelligent'.

Former business consultancy *Consensus d.o.o.* is now **Juric Law Offices**. Recent projects include advising a foreign client on the purchase of core assets from a bankrupt Croatian company, and advising on equity investment. The firm is recommended for mergers and acquisitions work, with name partner Sanja Juric singled out by clients for 'her commitment and excellent awareness of international clients' requirements'. Juric is a Bar member in Croatia and New York, practising in the latter for six years.

Matic-IKRP assisted the Croatian government in drafting Croatia's e-commerce law and is working with USAID on secondary legislation. Tin Matic heads a team of three and works closely with Greek firm **IKRP Rokas & Partners**, which has a network of offices in the region.

PricewaterhouseCoopers advised a French motorway maintenance company on corporate, commercial and labour issues. The firm acted for a Spanish energy company setting up in Croatia. Other clients include Motorola. The firm works closely with **Law Office Modric** on corporate, commercial and labour law, and with **Law Office Modrusan** on IP. Australian Don Markusic heads the legal department at PwC. He has worked in Croatia for eight years and is well known.

Savoric & Partners has a new partner and two new junior partners, increasing the number of fee-earners from six to nine. The team advised an international consortium on the high-profile start-up of Croatia's first private television station, has conducted litigation for the American Insurance Group, and also acts for L'Oréal France, Bang & Olufsen and McDonald's.

Travas & Partners provides permanent counsel to food company Agrokor, the largest private enterprise in Croatia, and offers a full range of corporate and commercial services. Partner Aleksej Miskovic speaks good English and works with the firm's international clients. The firm plans to hire one or two additional lawyers.

Vukmir & Associates' 12-lawyer team advises blue-chip clients, particularly on IP enforcement and technology issues. Led by the 'extremely conscientious' Mladen Vukmir, the firm is considered the market-leader in IP. The firm works with several high-profile international law firms including US firm **Covington & Burling** and UK firm **Lovells**. Clients include Mars, Microsoft and Business Software Alliance.

Cipcic-Bragadin opened a year ago. In 2003 the firm advised on the liquidation and restructuring of a paper product company, and on public-to-private transactions.

Divjak, Topic & Bahtijarevic advised a US media company on a successful bid for a Croatian advertising agency in 2003.

KPMG Croatia d.o.o. offers 'one-stop-shop' services which target clients seeking both tax, and corporate and commercial legal advice. In 2003, the firm advised Swiss International Airlines on restructuring its Croatian operations. Other clients include Thomas Cook, which received share purchase and post-acquisition advice from the firm. **KPMG Croatia d.o.o.** works closely with **Law Firm Simunovic & Batur**.

In its first year **Mirjana Boric in co-operation with Cerha Hempel Spiegelfeld Hlawati** handled transactions with an approximate total value of €100m. The firm focuses on commercial property, and is currently advising international clients on developing a Zagreb business centre, a shopping centre in the capital and a golf course on the Adriatic coast.

Law Offices Miroljub Macesic is a corporate and commercial firm specialising in maritime law, with a number of international shipping clients.

Dr Neven Cirkveni represented a local company in the €53m takeover of a major retail chain.

Petrak Law Offices acts for foreign companies setting up in Croatia. The three-lawyer firm advised Asian and German motor businesses and mutual bond buyers over the last year.

Schönherr Rechtsanwalte OEG in co-operation with Croatian Attorneys At Law acted on a number of acquisitions last year, advising businesses in the pharmaceutical, entertainment and energy sectors. Vienna-based Michael Lagler heads the three-lawyer team in Zagreb.

Vukic, Jelusic, Sulina Stankovic, Jurcan & Jabuka has grown by four lawyers, bringing the firm total to 17. Based in the port town Rijeka, the firm advises on corporate, maritime and transport law, and commercial litigation.

Wolf Theiss opened its Zagreb office in June 2003. The new office has two Austrian partners and works in conjunction with three Croatian lawyers. Clients include a major Austrian construction company and major European retail chain.

FOREIGN INVESTMENT, PROJECTS AND PRIVATISATION

Bogdanóvic & Dolicki (in association with Lovells) acted for the Croatian government on the privatisation of the national oil company, one of the country's biggest deals in 2003, and on various other projects. The firm also acted for Southern Breweries on an $88m brewery sale to Heineken.

With clients throughout Europe, **Hanzekovic, Radakovic and Partners** is providing ongoing advice on the construction of a major Croatian motorway. The firm works with several international firms, including **Clifford Chance LLP**.

Markovic & Pliso prepared the privatisation of Croatia Osiguranka for Chase Manhattan Bank and completed the privatisation of Privredna Banka Zagreb. Zoran Markovic is recommended.

Last year **Porobija & Porobija** acted for NewsCorp and Croatia Telecom on a public tender bid for a national TV channel. The firm also represented a Croatian tour operator on the privatisation of two hotels. Boris Porobija has excellent English and a reputation to match. The firm works closely with **Linklaters**.

Zuric I Partneri acted for the winning bidder in the €500m privatisation of INA, the national oil company. The team, which has an excellent reputation, drafted Croatia's secondary energy legislation and advised on several mid-range projects including a €70m hospital development and a €50m office development. The firm has five partners and 16 associates.

DLA Weiss Tessbach / Law Office Natalija Peric advises construction company Strabag, and is working on a significant retail project.

Juric Law Offices represented a bidder in the privatisation of Croatia's oil company, working closely with **Allen & Overy**. Sanja Juric is 'impressive', say clients, providing a good bridge between the international marketplace and Croatian law.

Savoric & Partners has advised several US and UK investment funds, including George Soros, on investments totalling $10m. The team acted for the winning bidder on the tender for the first privatised Croatian television channel, and acted for Coalco International and AIG/Lincoln on the purchase of land for prime development in Zagreb's city centre. The firm is recommended for its understanding of international business clients' requirements.

Divjak, Topic & Bahtijarevic advised the Croatian government on a concession contract for a national pipeline terminal.

Matic-IKRP acts for an Italian company developing three shopping centres in Croatia, is advising on Croatian energy sector reforms, and is working on secondary legislation for USAID.

Travas & Partners has acted on various projects for the American College of Management and Technology in Dubrovnik, and worked with **Baker & McKenzie** on IT procurement for Cap Gemini Ernst & Young.

FOREIGN INVESTMENT, PROJECTS AND PRIVATISATION

BOGDANÓVIC & DOLICKI (IN ASSOCIATION WITH LOVELLS) ✪
HANZEKOVIC, RADAKOVIC AND PARTNERS
MARKOVIC & PLISO
POROBIJA & POROBIJA ✪
ZURIC I PARTNERI

DLA WEISS TESSBACH / LAW OFFICE NATALIJA PERIC ✪
JURIC LAW OFFICES
SAVORIC & PARTNERS ✪

Babic, Law Office
Divjak, Topic & Bahtijarevic
Dragicevic, Law Office
Matic-IKRP ✪
PricewaterhouseCoopers
Travas & Partners
Wolf Theiss ✪

Firms are listed A-Z in tiers which are ranked in order of priority
✪ *Indicates firm displays contact details at the end of this chapter.*

SHIPPING

Law Offices Miroljub Macesic is a leading international maritime law firm based in the port town of Rijeka. Name partner Miroljub Macesic has a strong reputation for ship finance and litigation.

Also in Rijeka, **Vukic, Jelusic, Sulina Stankovic, Jurcan & Jabuka** advises on corporate and banking transactions for shipping clients.

Juric Law Offices is working with **Clifford Chance LLP** representing the major lenders and shareholders in the financing and restructuring of a shipyard.

Schönherr Rechtsanwalte OEG in co-operation with Croatian Attorneys At Law provided counsel for US equity investors, Great Circle Capital in relation to the privatisation of a Croatian maritime transport company.

SHIPPING

LAW OFFICES MIROLJUB MACESIC ✪
VUKIC, JELUSIC, SULINA STANKOVIC, JURCAN & JABUKA

Juric Law Offices
Schönherr Rechtsanwalte OEG in co-operation with Croatian Attorneys At Law ✪

Firms are listed A-Z in tiers which are ranked in order of priority
✪ *Indicates firm displays contact details at the end of this chapter.*

LAW OFFICES MIROLJUB MAĆEŠIĆ

POD KASTELOM NO 4
PO BOX 366
51000 RIJEKA

Telephone: +385 51 213 118
Fax: +385 51 215 030
E-mail: macesic@macesic.hr

Languages
English, German, Italian

Number of lawyers 9
at this office 6

Other offices
Zagreb

CATEGORIES OF WORK

Banking and finance

Commercial property, real estate

Corporate and commercial

Dispute resolution – litigation and arbitration

Foreign direct investment

Infrastructure and project finance

Insolvency/corporate restructuring

Insurance

Intellectual property

Mergers and acquisitions

Private client

Privatisation

Shipping and transport

BOGDANOVIĆ & DOLIČKI
IN ASSOCIATION WITH LOVELLS

UL ALEXANDERA VON HUMBOLDTA 4B/III
10000 ZAGREB

Telephone: +385 1 615 9595
Fax: +385 1 615 7733
E-mail: information@lovells.com
WWW: www.lovells.com

Languages
English, German

Other offices
Alicante, Amsterdam, Beijing, Berlin, Brussels, Budapest*, Chicago, Düsseldorf, Frankfurt, Hamburg, Ho Chi Minh City, Hong Kong, London, Milan, Moscow, Munich, New York, Paris, Prague, Rome, Shanghai, Singapore, Tokyo, Vienna*, Warsaw

Number of lawyers 1,600
at this office 19

Contact
Tin Dolicki

CATEGORIES OF WORK

- Mergers and acquisitions
- Banking, securities and finance
- Commercial law (general)
- Competition, antitrust
- Companies, corporations
- Contract
- Construction, building
- EU law
- Trade marks, intellectual property
- Arbitration and litigation

CMS D.O.O.

JURIŠIĆEVA 24
10000 ZAGREB

Telephone: +385 1 4825 600
Fax: +385 1 4825 601
E-mail: office@cmslegal.hr

Languages
English, German

Other offices
Belgrade, Brussels, Prague, Vienna

Number of lawyers 4

Contacts
Peter Huber, Gregor Famira

Member
CMS Transnational Legal and Tax Services; World Law Group

CATEGORIES OF WORK

- Banking and finance
- Capital markets
- Commercial property, real estate and construction
- Competition
- Corporate and commercial
- Dispute resolution
- Intellectural property
- Labour and employment
- Mergers and acquisitions
- Privatisation
- Regulatory/public procurement

DLA WEISS-TESSBACH/LAW OFFICE NATALIJA PERIC

MIHANOVICEVA 36
10000 ZAGREB

Telephone: +385 1 4854 200
Fax: +385 1 4854 241
E-mail: zagreb@dla.com
Website: www.dla.com

Languages
English, German

Other offices
Amsterdam, Antwerp, Bangkok, Bergen, Berlin, Birmingham, Bradford, Bratislava, Brussels, Budapest, Cologne, Copenhagen, Edinburgh, Essen, Frankfurt, Glasgow, Hamburg, Hong Kong, Leeds, Liverpool, London, Madrid, Manchester, Milan, Moscow, Oslo, Paris, Prague, Rotterdam, Salzberg, Sarajevo, Shanghai, Sheffield, Singapore, Stockholm, Vienna

Number of lawyers 82
at this office 5

Contact
Peter Solt (Vienna)

Member
DLA Group

CATEGORIES OF WORK

General commercial	**Corporate**
Banking and finance	**Mergers and aquisitions**
Insolvency	**Litigation**
Privatisation	

THE FIRM

Weiss-Tessbach was established in 1878 and is one of the longest-established law firms in Austria. 15 years ago, the firm decided on an extremely dynamic development. Since 1990, the number of lawyers at the firm has increased more than four times from 15 to over 80, and the number of offices from one to seven. On October 1st 2003, Weiss-Tessbach was integrated with DLA on the basis of a shared vision to become a top five full-service European law firm. With its current offices in six central and eastern European countries, DLA Weiss-Tessbach will continue to expand into the region at a time of EU accession for many countries.

DLA Weiss-Tessbach is part of DLA Group. DLA Group is an exclusive alliance of international full-service law firms with a shared vision. Established in 1999, DLA Group now has over 2,200 lawyers across 21 countries, who deliver expert local know-how and international solutions. DLA Group provides legal advice in 37 major cities across Europe, Singapore, Thailand, Hong Kong and the People's Republic of China.

Services in Croatia: DLA Weiss-Tessbach maintains a representative office in Zagreb. Legal services in Croatia are provided on the basis of an accredited co-operation agreement with the law office of Natalija Peric.

AREAS OF PRACTICE

The firm has strengthened its core areas of expertise (commercial and corporate, M&A, banking and finance, intellectual property, real estate), and has expanded into other areas of law (administrative, employment, telecoms, technology, venture capital). Today, the firm is able to assist its corporate clients in all aspects of their activities.

DLA Weiss-Tessbach has well-established relations with clients of various backgrounds. The firm advises small and medium-sized enterprises as well as leading (often publicly listed) international and domestic industrial groups, service providers, banks and other financial institutions and individuals.

DLA Weiss-Tessbach has established a particular reputation for its ability to handle cases in international cross-border contexts. It carefully views the ongoing developments in central Europe with the aim of combining the needs of the constantly changing international legal market and industry, whilst also upholding the high-standard services that the firm has always been able to offer to its clients.

LAW OFFICE LJUBENKO

BRANIMIROVA 9
10000 ZAGREB

Telephone: +385 1 4852 091
Fax: +385 1 4876 901
E-mail: ljubenko@inet.hr

Languages
Czech, English, French, German, Italian

Number of lawyers 3

CATEGORIES OF WORK

Invoice collecting
Mićo Ljubenko

Real estate
Ines Calusic

Tourism investments
Mićo Ljubenko

Banking and finance
Mićo Ljubenko

Construction
Jasmin Avdagic

Corporate finance
Jasmin Avdagic

Commercial and company law
Ines Calusic

EU and competition law
Vlatka Ljubenko

MATIĆ-IKRP

BEDNJANSKA 14
10000 ZAGREB

Telephone: +385 1 617 0791
Fax: +385 1 617 0792
Email: tin.matic@zg.tel.hr
Website: www.rokas.com

Languages
English, German, Italian, Spanish

Other offices
Athens, Belgrade, Bucharest, Piraeus, Skopje, Sofia

Number of lawyers 53
at this office 3

Member
IBA

CATEGORIES OF WORK

Arbitration
Tin Matić

Investment
Tin Matić

Banking and finance
Tin Matić

Transport
Iskra Bubas

Bankruptcy
Tin Matić

Real estate
Sonja Bobovec

Civil litigation
Iskra Bubas

Export/import
Tin Matić

Commercial
Iskra Bubas

Mediation
Tin Matić

Company
Iskra Bubas

Competition
Tin Matić

Franchising
Tin Matić

Family
Sonja Bobovec

E-commerce
Tin Matić

MIRJANA BORIC IN CO-OPERATION WITH

CERHA HEMPEL SPIEGELFELD HLAWATI

PARTNERSCHAFT VON RECHTSANWÄLTEN

A HEBRANGA 36/II
10000 ZAGREB

Telephone: +385 1 485 47 90
Fax: +385 1 487 18 90
E-mail: office.chsh@boric.hr
Website: www.chsh.at

Languages
Croatian, German, Russian

Other offices
Brussels, Budapest, Vienna

Number of lawyers 65
at this office 6

Contact
Mirjana Boric

CATEGORIES OF WORK

- Corporate law
- Real estate and construction law
- Civil law, litigation
- Labour law
- Insolvency law
- Business and administrative law
- Privatisations
- International private law
- Arbitration
- European Community law

LAW OFFICES MIROLJUB MAĆEŠIĆ

MIHANOVIĆEVA 16
10000 ZAGREB

Telephone: +385 1 45 77 248
Fax: +385 1 45 50 443
E-mail: macesic@macesic.hr

Languages
English, German, Italian

Number of lawyers 9
at this office 3

Other offices
Rijeka

CATEGORIES OF WORK

- Banking and finance
- Commercial property, real estate
- Corporate and commercial
- Dispute resolution – litigation and arbitration
- Foreign direct investment
- Infrastructure and project finance
- Insolvency/corporate restructuring
- Insurance
- Intellectual property
- Mergers and acquisitions
- Private client
- Privatisation
- Shipping and transport

POROBIJA & POROBIJA

GALLERY IMPORTANNE
IBLEROV TRG 10/VII
PO BOX 92
10000 ZAGREB

Telephone: +385 1 4693 999
Fax: +385 1 4693 900
E-mail: porobija@porobija.hr
Website: www.porobija.hr

Languages
English, French, German, Hungarian

Number of lawyers 14

CATEGORIES OF WORK

- Administrative and regulatory law
- Banking and finance and capital markets
- Bankruptcy
- Capital markets
- Commercial law
- Company law
- Competition law
- Concessions
- Construction law
- Energy and infrastructure
- Litigation and arbitration
- Mergers and acquisitons
- Privatisation
- Project financing
- Public utilities
- Real estate
- Telecommunications

SCHÖNHERR RECHTSANWÄLTE OEG
IN CO-OPERATION WITH CROATIAN ATTORNEYS AT LAW

JURISICEVA 19
10000 ZAGREB

Telephone: +385 1 488 38 39
Fax: +385 1 481 30 73
E-mail: office@schoenherr.hr
Website: www.schoenherr.at

Languages
Croatian, English, French, German

Other offices
Belgrade, Brussels, Bucharest, Ljubljana, Vienna

Number of lawyers 96
at this office 5

Contacts
Michael Lagler (m.lagler@schoenherr.at), Arijana Petres

CATEGORIES OF WORK

- International and Croatian practice
- International contracts and foreign investment
- Banking securities and finance
- M&A
- Privatisations
- Public private partnership
- Real estate and commercial property
- EU law

ŠAVORIĆ & PARTNERS

ANDRIJE HEBRANGA 27
10000 ZAGREB

Telephone: +385 1 4855 900
Fax: +385 1 4856 232
E-mail: boris.savoric@savoric.com

Languages
English, German

Number of lawyers 9

Member
American Chamber of Commerce, Croatia

CATEGORIES OF WORK

Banking and finance
Boris Savoric, Danijel Antun Banic

Mergers and acquisitions
Boris Savoric, Ivan Simac

Corporate and commercial, insurance
Boris Savoric, Helena Sjaus

Telecommunications
Boris Savoric, Ivan Simac

Litigation and arbitration
Boris Savoric, Helena Sjaus

Competition
Boris Savoric, Ivan Simac

Securities, project finance
Boris Savoric, Ivan Einwalter

Corporate finance
Boris Savoric, Danijel Antun Banic

Shipping and transport
Helena Sjaus, Vedrana Cikovic

Real estate
Helena Sjaus, Vedrana Cikovic

Employment
Helena Sjaus, Ana Janusic

Tax
Danijel Antun Banic, Ivan Einwalter

Cross-border transactions
Boris Savoric, Danijel Antun Banic

Information technology
Daniel Antun Banic, Ana Janusic

Insolvency, corporate restructuring
Danijel Antun Banic, Vedrana Cikovic

Intellectual property
Ivan Simac, Vedrana Cikovic

Media, entertainment, privatisation
Boris Savoric, Ana Janusic

Private client
Helena Sjaus, Ana Janusic

THE FIRM

Boris Savoric worked for a number of years for reputable and leading Croatian law firms and, in 2001, started his own practice with a number of associates. Since the firm was growing in terms of clients, transactional work and reputation in the Croatian market, as of January 2004, the firm hired two new associates, and Helena Sjaus joined the firm (now to be called Savoric & Partners) as partner. The firm advises international clients in major corporate and financial transactions, and assists foreign investors in joint ventures and mergers and acquisitions in Croatia. Boris Savoric specialises in international corporate and commercial law, cross-border transactions, project finance, mergers and acquisitions, and consulting the capital venture and other investment funds while doing business in Croatia.

Savoric & Partners is recognised as having young and dynamic yet experienced lawyers, offering a full range of quality legal services. The firm has been constantly growing from the day it was established. The office operates as a team of nine lawyers offering a complete solution to problems arising while doing business in Croatia. Savoric & Partners has established good relations, and often operates, with a number of reputable international law firms such as Baker & McKenzie, Squire, Sanders & Dempsey, Cadwalader, Wickersham & Taft, Weil, Gotshal & Manges, Leboef, Lamb, Greene & MacRae and Freshfields.

AREAS OF PRACTICE

The firm's client base consists of some of the largest Croatian companies and clients from the US and Europe: European bank for Reconstruction and Development, RTL Group, Henkel, AIG, UBS, McDonald's, L'Oreal France, Schering-Plough, SAS Rezidor hotels, Generali, Enron Corp, Croatia Osiguranje, Iskon Internet, DCM, Elka, Croatian Bank for Reconstruction and Development, Medika etc.

Significant projects and transactions for the firm include advising the European Bank for Reconstruction and Development, and DEG in equity investment in leading Croatian dairy producer Lura. The firm acted as legal advisor to Privredna Banka Zagreb (as sponsor) and Croatia Insurance d.d. (as issuer) in listing of all ordinary and preference shares of Croatia Insurance d.d. into the Quotation I of Zagreb Stock Exchange. The firm advises German/Luxembourg television and media group RTL and a consortium of leading Croatian companies Agrokor, Podravka, Atlantic group and HVB (Splitska) bank in winning the tender for the first privatised Croatian television channel and the starting-up of a TV station in Croatia. The firm also advised the European Bank for Reconstruction and Development in financing (with Zagrebacka Bank) one of the largest Croatian cement industries, Nasicecement in a syndicated loan of €40m. The firm advised European Bank for Reconstruction and Development in a €36m financing of the City of Zagreb solid waste programme The firm advised the investment fund SOROS in a recent US$8m investment in DCM, the cable TV operator, as well as acting as legal adviser to the sellers (capital venture funds) of Overseas, the largest parcel delivery company in Croatia, in the sale of shares to the strategic purchaser Austrian Post. Partner Boris Savoric was appointed by Enron Corp and Weil, Gotshal & Manges as legal adviser for the restructuring and liquidation of Enron business operations in Croatia.

The firm represents AIG (American Insurance Group), which has been insuring all UN vehicles and operations in Croatia, in several multi-million dollar litigation cases for compensation of damage. The firm is also very active in a number of MBO and LBO projects as well as in real estate development projects.

WOLF THEISS

PRASKA 10
10000 ZAGREB

Telephone: +385 1 492 5400
Fax: +385 1 492 5450
E-mail: zagreb@wolftheiss.com
Website: www.wolftheiss.com

Languages
Croatian, English, German, Italian

Other offices
Belgrade, Bratislava, Ljubljana, Prague, Vienna

Number of lawyers 98
at this office 4

CATEGORIES OF WORK

Mergers and acquisitions	**Information technology**
Banking	**Retail law**
Project finance	**Intellectual property**

THE FIRM
Wolf Theiss, founded in 1957, stands among the leading law firms in Central Europe, with a concentration on Austrian, European and international business law, and additional expertise in the legal regimes of Central and Eastern Europe.

At its six locations, in Vienna, Prague, Belgrade, Bratislava, Ljubljana and Zagreb, a total of 200 people, including 98 lawyers (42 of whom are partners), work for Austrian and international client companies in industry, trade and services, as well as banking and insurance. At the point of contact between law and business, Wolf Theiss develops innovative solutions on the basis of legal, tax and business know-how.

CYPRUS

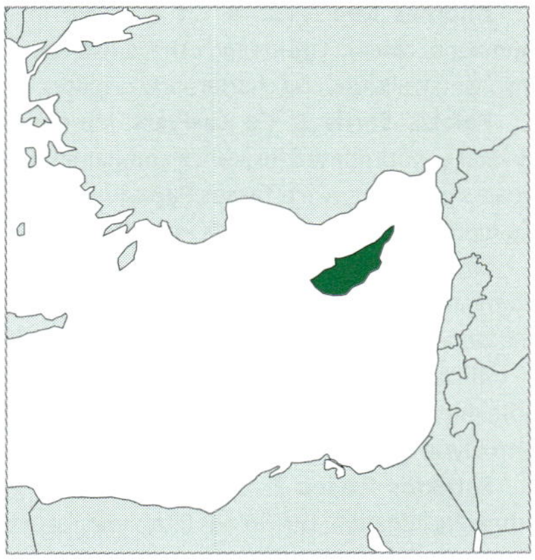

Population	802,000
Number of lawyers	1,200
Professional title	Dikigoros
Currency	Cyprus pound (CY£)

Index

Cyprus is situated in the Mediterranean Sea on the trade routes of Africa, Asia, Europe and the Middle East. This location has established the island's reputation as a commercial centre but also contributed to problems of sovereignty. Cyprus has been divided since 1974 following an aggressive Turkish response to a Greece-backed military coup, with the more prosperous and westernised southern two-thirds populated by Greek Cypriots, and the northern area by Turkish Cypriots. In 1983, the northern area was declared to be the Turkish Republic of Northern Cyprus, a denomination only recognised by Turkey, and unless reunification is achieved before formal membership is granted in May 2004, the accession to the EU will only apply to southern Cyprus. As such, this chapter is concerned only with law firms in the south. However, the likelihood of reunification is growing ever more likely, and the 'Green Line' which divided the island and was manned by UN troops was recently opened allowing free passage between the two territories for the first time in 30 years. Business activity is mostly located in the capital, Nicosia and the main port, Limassol.

BILLING

Contingency fees are not permitted, though this may change following accession to the EU. Legal advice is charged at between €170 and €510 per hour depending on the complexity and predicted timescale of the work, as well as the experience and standing of the lawyer. Senior partners' rates start at around €340.

MARKETING

Whilst regulations exist restricting law firm advertising, most of the larger firms have websites up and running or under construction, all in English.

IN-HOUSE LAWYERS

In-house lawyers are uncommon and do not have rights of audience in court.

ECONOMIC CLIMATE

Cyprus will finally become a member of the European Union on 1 May 2004, and the government has made amendments to meet European tax requirements, raising VAT to the minimum 15%. A single corporation tax rate of 10% for local companies and International Business Companies was introduced in 2003. Interest rates have been cut by the Central Bank of Cyprus to help improve the short-term prospects of the economy as the country adjusts to the changes. The liberalisation of the public utility markets was the start of changes in competition policy in line with EU *acquis communautaire*. Efforts to pre-empt problems with accession to the EU are being made, for example the establishment of a Cypriot consulate in Moscow airport to issue visas to Russian business representatives. Cypriot law firms are expecting the level of overseas investment to increase thanks to 'increased credibility' in light of the tax reforms and regulation of the stock market. Tourism is still the primary industry and Cyprus is keen to rebrand itself as an upmarket tourist destination.

LEGAL SYSTEM

The legal system mirrors that of English Common Law. Most of the laws are officially translated into English. However, Cyprus does have a constitution.

LEGAL MARKET

Tassos Papadopoulos, latterly of **Tassos Papadopoulos & Co**, was elected as President of Cyprus in February 2003. His resignation and move into political office has been followed by several established name partners of other leading firms who have taken positions as ministers and advisers. However, opinion on the island is that these figures have been occupied in politics more than law in recent years, and their departures will not weaken the firms or the legal market as a whole. Although foreign firms have been allowed to practise law in Cyprus since 2002, international law firms have yet to follow the example of major accountancy firms and establish themselves on the island. Overseas firms continue to instruct Cypriot lawyers as local counsel, such is the limited nature of the market at present. Most Cypriot firms currently prefer to remain independent and receive instructions from numerous overseas firms rather than tie themselves into exclusive associations. The top firms are instructed primarily on matters which encompass banking, tax, corporate and competition law, so most will practise in all of these areas rather than specialise. Complete departmentalisation is rare and many lawyers are active in more than one area.

The largest firms

1	Andreas Neocleous & Co	44
	Chrysses Demetriades & Co Law Office	44
3	L Papaphilippou & Co	20
4	George L Savvides & Co	17
	Patrikios Pavlou & Co	17
6	Tassos Papadopoulos & Co	16
7	Dr K Chrysostomides & Co	14
	George Y Yiangou & Co	14
9	Papacharalambous & Angelides	13
	Scordis, Papapetrou & Co	13
11	Georgiades & Pelides	12
12	Antis Triantafyllides & Sons	11
13	Michael Kyprianou & Associates	10
14	Lellos P Demetriades Law Office	9
15	Christos M Triantafyllides Law Firm	8
	Kyriacos Th Michaelides & Co Law Office	8
	Polakis Sarris & Co Lawyers	8
18	Markides, Markides & Co	7
19	Cacoyannis & Demetriou	6
	Chryssafinis & Polyviou	6
	Eliades, Paschalides, Hadjianistasiou & Co	6
22	Karides, Karides & Georghiades	4
	Law Office of Andrew Demetriou & Co	4
	Michaelides & Michaelides	4
	Yiannos G Georgiades and Co.	4

These figures represent the total number of lawyers in this country only, and have been supplied by the firms themselves. The figures should be accurate as at 1 January 2004.

Andreas Neocleous & Co maintains its position as the largest Cypriot firm with offices in seven locations across Cyprus and Eastern Europe, and boasts a multinational collection of lawyers. **Tassos Papadopoulos & Co**, **Antis Triantafyllides & Sons** and **Chrysses Demetriades & Co Law Office** are very well respected among legal professionals in Cyprus.

FOREIGN OFFICES

Overseas expansion is traditionally in the direction of Eastern Europe and Russia. **Andreas Neocleous & Co** has the widest representation, with offices in Budapest, Prague, Kiev and Moscow. **L Papaphilippou & Co** has offices in Athens and Warsaw. **Scordis, Papapetrou & Co** is represented in Athens and Moscow. Other firms with offices abroad include **Georgiades & Pelides** in Budapest, **Antis Triantafyllides & Sons** in Paris, and **Dr K Chrysostomides & Co** in Brussels.

Chrysses Demetriades & Co Law Office has a shipping-orientated office in the Greek port of Piraeus, and **Kyriacos Th. Michaelides & Co Law Office** has established a branch in Athens. **Patrikios Pavlou & Co** opened an office in Moscow in September 2003, and a representative office in Athens, and is seeking to expand further into Europe.

ADMIRALTY

Although this is a declining area (the number of cases brought before the Cyprus Admiralty Court has dropped to around 100 per year), most firms on the island will offer some form of admiralty advice. Only the top-ranked firms would claim to specialise in this area.

ADMIRALTY

CHRYSSES DEMETRIADES & CO LAW OFFICE
L PAPAPHILIPPOU & CO
MONTANIOS & MONTANIOS

Andreas Neocleous & Co ✪
Polakis Sarris & Co Lawyers
Tassos Papadopoulos & Co

George L Savvides & Co
Michaelides & Michaelides
Patrikios Pavlou & Co ✪

Antis Triantafyllides & Sons
Chryssafinis & Polyviou
Emilios Lemonaris
Georgiades & Pelides
K Chrysostomides (Dr) & Co
Kyriacos Th. Michaelides & Co Law Office ✪

Firms are listed A-Z in tiers which are ranked in order of priority
✪ Indicates firm displays contact details at the end of this chapter.

Chrysses Demetriades & Co Law Office remains in the top tier for admiralty advice. It is particularly recommended for its expertise in shipping insurance.

L Papaphilippou & Co represents major international ship owners and insurance companies.

Montanios & Montanios is reckoned to take the lion's share of admiralty work. Name partner Acis Montanious is well known.

Andreas Neocleous & Co is active in a number of cases in Cyprus and other jurisdictions, involving collisions and charterparty disputes.

Polakis Sarris & Co Lawyers represents several London-based insurance companies and Spain's Euler Siac, while **Tassos Papadopoulos & Co** represents the Cyprus Ports Authority.

Smaller firm **George L Savvides & Co** handles admiralty work from its Nicosia office, mostly for the owners of shipping fleets.

Michaelides & Michaelides has an active admiralty practice, taking instructions from UK firm **Clyde & Co**.

Patrikios Pavlou & Co has experience of admiralty litigation with Soteris Pittas and Stavros Pavlou. Clients include UK P&I clubs including the West of England.

Emilios Lemonaris represents several Greek shipping companies which dock in Cyprus, while **Kyriacos Th. Michaelides & Co Law Office** advises Cypriot insurance brokers.

Georgiades & Pelides has advised the UK and West of England P&I clubs.

BANKING AND FINANCE

With impending accession to the EU, Cyprus is bringing its financial services legislation into line with European legislation, which is increasing instructions to the leading firms with strong international client rosters. As with most areas of law on the island, there are recurring links with shipping, offshore company registration and debt collection.

The banking department of **Andreas Neocleous & Co**, headed by name partner Andreas Neocleous, retains a formidable client list, including JPMorgan Chase, Bank of America, Goldman Sachs and ING Barings. The firm also advised a UK Magic Circle law firm on a multi-tranche facility and interim facility, as local counsel, and was active in various debt issues. The department has been increased to ten fee-earners as a response to increased workload.

Chryssafinis & Polyviou acts for some of the largest international banks in the region. The department is headed by Polis Polyviou who is considered a leader in his field.

Georgiades & Pelides counts several major international financial institutions and credit ratings agencies amongst its clients, as well as the Capital Markets Commission and local regulators. Marcos Georgiades is the head of a team which negotiated the largest syndicated loan to

BANKING AND FINANCE

ANDREAS NEOCLEOUS & CO ✪
ANTIS TRIANTAFYLLIDES & SONS
CHRYSSAFINIS & POLYVIOU
GEORGIADES & PELIDES

CHRYSSES DEMETRIADES & CO LAW OFFICE
K CHRYSOSTOMIDES (DR) & CO
L PAPAPHILIPPOU & CO
TASSOS PAPADOPOULOS & CO

George L Savvides & Co
Kyriacos Th. Michaelides & Co Law Office ✪
Montanios & Montanios
Patrikios Pavlou & Co ✪

Christos M Triantafyllides Law Firm
Eliades, Paschalides, Hadjianistasiou & Co
Michaelides & Michaelides
Michael Kyprianou & Associates ✪
Papacharalambous & Angelides ✪
Polakis Sarris & Co Lawyers
Scordis, Papapetrou & Co
Yiannos G Georgiades and Co.

Firms are listed A-Z in tiers which are ranked in order of priority
✪ Indicates firm displays contact details at the end of this chapter.

corporate entities in Cypriot history last year, with a value of CY£34.2m (€58.8m).

Chrysses Demetriades & Co Law Office is instructed by various banks from Germany, the UK and the US, including Credit Suisse First Boston. The firm's strong shipping practice deals mainly with ship finance.

Dr K Chrysostomides & Co represents clients including Barclays Bank Plc, Universal Bank Cyprus, and French bank Société Générale.

L Papaphilippou & Co is instructed by the National Bank of Greece and the Cyprus Popular Bank, among others.

Pambos Ioaniddes leads a reputable banking practice at **Tassos Papadopoulos & Co**. The Cyprus Popular Bank is a client.

George L Savvides & Co represents both Cypriot and international banks on various matters including shipping finance.

Kyriacos Th. Michaelides & Co Law Office has a banking and finance team led by Christiana Michealides.

Montanios & Montanios advises banks from the UK, US, France and Israel. The firm specialises in aviation and shipping finance advice.

Patrikios Pavlou & Co acts for various banks including HSBC, Bank of Cyprus and Alpha Bank and specialises in cross-border securities.

Christos M Triantafyllides Law Firm advises in particular overseas clients on all aspects of offshore banking.

Eliades, Paschalides, Hadjianistasiou & Co acts for Cyprus Popular Bank and Hellenic Bank.

Michaelides & Michaelides advises the Hellenic Bank on a variety of banking matters, including litigation and debt recovery.

Michael Kyprianou & Associates has advised several overseas financial institutions over the past twelve months. The department is also particularly active in Russia.

Papacharalambous & Angelides is instructed by various banks on the island, including the Cyprus Popular Bank.

Polakis Sarris & Co Lawyers advises the Cyprus Popular Bank and the Hellenic Bank, mainly on contentious issues. Partner Christina Sarris leads the firm's finance practice.

Yiannos G Georgiades and Co. represents the Cyprus Popular Bank.

CONSTRUCTION

The forthcoming entry into the EU has effected widescale liberalisation of public utilities, which has in turn led to an increase in the number and scale of private finance projects. The island is also undergoing major infrastructure renewal comprising hospitals, road networks and new airports.

Law Office of Andrew Demetriou & Co is 'held in the highest regard' and continues to show strongly in all areas of construction, notably in litigation matters. Clients include various major Cypriot construction companies. Name partner Andrew Demetriou is also an active partner in the firm **Cacoyannis & Demetriou**, whose principal client is the Electricity Authority of Cyprus.

Kyriacos Th. Michaelides & Co Law Office is advising the JMP Group and the Archbishopric of Cyprus on various construction matters.

Andreas Neocleous & Co has advised the Alterra/Bechtel Consortium on BOT tenders for the new international airports in Cyprus, and is involved in various Public Private Partnership projects in Russia.

Tassos Papadopoulos & Co was among the first Cypriot law firms to specialise in construction law and retains a high level of expertise.

CONSTRUCTION

ANDREW DEMETRIOU & CO, LAW OFFICE OF ✪
KYRIACOS TH. MICHAELIDES & CO LAW OFFICE ✪

Andreas Neocleous & Co ✪
Chrysses Demetriades & Co Law Office
Tassos Papadopoulos & Co

George L Savvides & Co
L Papaphilippou & Co
Michaelides & Michaelides
Papacharalambous & Angelides ✪

Firms are listed A-Z in tiers which are ranked in order of priority
✪ Indicates firm displays contact details at the end of this chapter.

Michaelides & Michaelides, **George L Savvides & Co** and **L Papaphilippou & Co** advise several local construction companies.

Papacharalambous & Angelides is currently involved in several construction projects around Cyprus.

CORPORATE AND COMMERCIAL

Offshore investment into Cyprus provides much of the legal work on the island, and reforms to the competition laws are predicted to increase this area further. While tax regulations have been stiffened to lend the market more legitimacy, the tax levels are still generous to the overseas investor.

Elias A Neocleous heads the well-established commercial practice at **Andreas Neocleous & Co**, which continues to attract the highest-profile clients including de Beers, Dell, Thomas Cook, Volvo, Heineken, Rothschild, and is also instructed as local counsel by several leading UK firms. Most notably, the firm last year advised Gossard, Imperial Tobacco and Travelex Plc on the expansion and establishment of retail operations in Cyprus. Clients describe the firm as having an 'international flavour' and a 'good understanding of European issues'.

Chrysses Demetriades & Co Law Office is highly regarded. Christos Mavrellis heads a team which acts for various international clients. The

CORPORATE AND COMMERCIAL

ANDREAS NEOCLEOUS & CO ✪
CHRYSSES DEMETRIADES & CO LAW OFFICE
TASSOS PAPADOPOULOS & CO

ANTIS TRIANTAFYLLIDES & SONS
GEORGE L SAVVIDES & CO
GEORGIADES & PELIDES
K CHRYSOSTOMIDES (DR) & CO
PATRIKIOS PAVLOU & CO ✪

Andrew Demetriou & Co, Law Office of ✪
Chryssafinis & Polyviou
L Papaphilippou & Co
Scordis, Papapetrou & Co

Christos M Triantafyllides Law Firm
Kyriacos Th. Michaelides & Co Law Office ✪
Lellos P Demetriades ✪
Michael Kyprianou & Associates ✪
Montanios & Montanios
Papacharalambous & Angelides ✪

Eleni Vrahimi & Co, Law Office
John Clerides & Sons
Markides, Markides & Co
Polakis Sarris & Co Lawyers
Yiannos G Georgiades and Co.

Firms are listed A-Z in tiers which are ranked in order of priority
✪ Indicates firm displays contact details at the end of this chapter.

merger with *PL Cacoyannis & Co* has enlarged the department, despite the unfortunate passing away in 2003 of the enormously popular and respected George Cacoyannis.

Tassos Papadopoulos & Co has had its already stellar profile raised by the election of former name partner Tassos Papadopoulos to President of Cyprus. The commercial and corporate department is identified by fellow lawyers as a very competent outfit.

Antis Triantafyllides & Sons includes British American Tobacco and PepsiCo Inc among its clients. The department is managed by Stelios Triantafyllides.

George L Savvides & Co advises overseas clients on expansion into Cyprus and local and international clients on M&A issues.

Georgiades & Pelides receives the cream of its work from UK firms, acting as local counsel for **Herbert Smith**, **Linklaters**, **Allen & Overy** and **Clifford Chance LLP**, among others, on the Cypriot elements of global operations involving major international financial institutions. Name partner Marios Pelides handles international M&A work and joint ventures using Cyprus-based vehicles.

Dr K Chrysostomides & Co continues to impress in this field. Clients include Hellenic Petroleum AG and BP Cyprus.

Patrikios Pavlou & Co has reinforced strong links to Russia with the recent opening of the firm's Moscow office. The firm has advised the majority shareholders of a Russian manufacturing conglomerate on the Cyprus set-up of its operations. The department specialises in international trading matters.

Law Office of Andrew Demetriou & Co moves up the rankings having established a strong presence in telecommunications, negotiating a number of joint venture agreements between Greek and Cypriot telecoms companies.

Chryssafinis & Polyviou has a good reputation for its general commercial expertise, acting as external counsel to Cyprus Airways.

L Papaphilippou & Co advises various banks and public listed companies. The firm is also instructed by five major insurance companies.

Scordis, Papapetrou & Co advises a number of foreign investors on moving into Cyprus. Contacts in Eastern Europe are expanded and maintained through international offices in Moscow and Athens.

Christos M Triantafyllides Law Firm advises offshore companies and international investors. The firm's corporate practice is headed by managing partner Christos Triantafyllides.

Kyriacos Th. Michaelides & Co Law Office has taken instructions from the distillery subsidiary of the Diageo Group on distribution agreements, and from Danone on the Cypriot arm of a global restructuring exercise.

Lellos P Demetriades offers commercial advice under the leadership of senior managing partner, Lellos Demetriades. Clients include telecommunications, insurance, and electricity companies.

Michael Kyprianou & Associates is acting as legal counsels for Henyep Investments (Europe) Ltd, as well as for groups from Hong Kong and Russia on the establishment of financial services companies in Cyprus. The firm has also acted as local counsel for various UK law firms in the past year.

Montanios & Montanios offers investment advice to offshore companies under department heads Acis and Adam Montanios.

Papacharalambous & Angelides advises Porsche and Mercedes Benz on distribution agreements within Cyprus and general commercial issues, as well as various local and offshore companies on registration matters.

Polakis Sarris & Co Lawyers specialises in company registration and accompanying matters.

DISPUTE RESOLUTION

Disputes are still ongoing following the collapse of the Cyprus Stock Exchange in 1999 and are providing plenty of work for the island's litigators.

Antis Triantafyllides & Sons' George Triantafyllides heads one of the strongest litigation practices in Cyprus. The firm represents major international companies.

Kyriacos Th. Michaelides & Co Law Office has a respected litigation department receiving instructions from overseas and locally, with demanding work in the oil and telecoms industries.

New senior partner at **Tassos Papadopoulos & Co**, Pambos Ioannides, is regarded as one of the most widely knowledgeable lawyers on the island. Nicos Papaefstathiou, president of the Cyprus Bar Association, is another heavyweight member of the team.

Andreas Neocleous & Co acts for the Association of Investors as well as other individual investors, and advises primarily on debt recovery. The 'efficient, competent and responsive' litigation department, headed by Takis Christoforou, has increased to 15 fee-earners, and is split into four specialist teams each concentrating on different areas.

Chrysses Demetriades & Co Law Office claims to have represented every bank on the island. The department is currently involved in work relating to the resurrected stock exchange.

L Papaphilippou & Co is handling two of the biggest stock exchange-related cases in Cyprus, advising Global Soft Company and CNH Capital, in matters arising from the crash. Andreas Haviaras is the key litigator at the firm.

The litigation department at **Patrikios Pavlou & Co** is led by Soteris Pittas and Chrysostomos Nicolaou and claims a success rate of around 90%. Significant instructions in the past twelve months have come from a Middle Eastern distributor of tobacco products, Travelworld Vacations Ltd and Privat Bank of Ukraine. The firm advised the P&I clubs of the UK and West of England, and is also now receiving instructions directly from UK clients rather than being referred by UK firms.

Law Office of Andrew Demetriou & Co recently concluded two successful arbitrations against the Government of the Republic of Cyprus on construction matters, obtaining substantial damages in the process. Name partner Andrew Demetriou heads a team of four with particular expertise in construction, telecommunications and competition.

George L Savvides & Co remains an active presence in litigation on the island.

Led by partner Marcos Georgiades, **Georgiades & Pelides** has defended a variety of financial institutions against investor law suits, following the 1999 stock market crash. The firm is seen as a specialist in stock market work.

Dr K Chrysostomides & Co is instructed on arbitration matters by several local and overseas companies. Liexis Taliadoros heads the department.

Led by well-known Michael Kyprianou, **Michael Kyprianou & Associates** has been instructed by KPMG Cyprus. Medical negligence and personal injury cases are also a strength of this department. The firm is now acting on behalf of a US firm in a high-profile, $30m money-laundering lawsuit.

Michaelides & Michaelides represents mostly Cyprus-based corporations, banks, shipping and construction companies including Hellenic Bank.

DISPUTE RESOLUTION

ANTIS TRIANTAFYLLIDES & SONS
KYRIACOS TH. MICHAELIDES & CO LAW OFFICE ✪
TASSOS PAPADOPOULOS & CO

ANDREAS NEOCLEOUS & CO ✪
CHRYSSES DEMETRIADES & CO LAW OFFICE
L PAPAPHILIPPOU & CO
PATRIKIOS PAVLOU & CO ✪

Andrew Demetriou & Co, Law Office of ✪
Chryssafinis & Polyviou
George L Savvides & Co
Georgiades & Pelides
K Chrysostomides (Dr) & Co

Lellos P Demetriades ✪
Scordis, Papapetrou & Co

Emilios Lemonaris
Michael Kyprianou & Associates ✪
Michaelides & Michaelides
Montanios & Montanios
Papacharalambous & Angelides ✪
Polakis Sarris & Co Lawyers
Yiannos G Georgiades and Co.

Firms are listed A-Z in tiers which are ranked in order of priority
✪ Indicates firm displays contact details at the end of this chapter.

Montanios & Montanios is mainly active in shipping litigation, although it is also equipped to handle more general matters.

Papacharalambous & Angelides has a very active litigation department, particularly in family law, and also acts for Porsche and Mercedes Benz on litigation and arbitration matters as well as for local businesses. The Cypriot Co-operative Society is a longstanding client.

Polakis Sarris & Co Lawyers is particularly active in debt collection.

Litigator Yiannos G Georgiades of **Yiannos G Georgiades and Co.** has advised a large number of shareholders since the 1999 stock market crash.

EU AND COMPETITION

An increasingly busy field as the Cyprus judiciary gets to grips with the new raft of EU legislature. The fact that the laws will be brand new to the businesses of Cyprus rather than updated versions of old laws means that firms in this practice area are braced for a massive upsurge in complexity and quantity of work.

Andreas Neocleous & Co has advised a blue-chip European pharmaceutical company, a major European industrial company and various Cypriot government authorities on competition matters.

Patrikios Pavlou & Co advises on European tax structures and strategies to existing corporate clients. Andria Andreou is the head of the Cyprus Franchise Association, and accordingly the firm is well placed to advise on the competition aspects of franchising. The firm is establishing a network of European alliances in order to penetrate the market more effectively.

Law Office of Andrew Demetriou & Co has a growing presence in the burgeoning telecommunications sector, advising, among others, Callsat Telecom Ltd.

Kyriacos Th. Michaelides & Co Law Office is advising local and offshore businesses on the effects of the legislative changes and bringing them up to speed with emerging issues.

EU AND COMPETITION

ANDREAS NEOCLEOUS & CO ✪
PATRIKIOS PAVLOU & CO ✪

Andrew Demetriou & Co, Law Office of ✪
Chrysses Demetriades & Co Law Office
K Chrysostomides (Dr) & Co
Kyriacos Th. Michaelides & Co Law Office ✪
Lellos P Demetriades ✪

George L Savvides & Co
Georgiades & Pelides
L Papaphilippou & Co

Firms are listed A-Z in tiers which are ranked in order of priority
✪ Indicates firm displays contact details at the end of this chapter.

Lellos P Demetriades offers advice on competition law through ex-vice president of the Cypriot Monopolis Commission, Joanna Lozidou.

Georgiades & Pelides advises local companies on competition matters in light of the increased activity of the Cyprus Competition Commission.

INTELLECTUAL PROPERTY

The majority of the intellectual property law practised on the island is registration of company names and trade marks, and associated litigation.

Name partner Achilleas Demetriades at **Lellos P Demetriades** is well known for anti-piracy work in what is an untapped market. The practice was also active in reacting to the amendment to copyright law in Cyprus in 2002.

Andreas Neocleous & Co has taken instructions from Hewlett-Packard and a major global pharmaceutical company, as well as others, on general intellectual property matters. The department, headed by Elias Neocleous, is also advising the Planning Bureau of the Republic of Cyprus on the formulation of a legal framework and national strategy for e-commerce.

The IP specialists at **Chrysses Demetriades & Co Law Office** represent pharmaceuticals companies from the US and European all IP matters including infringements and registration.

Law Office Eleni Vrahimi & Co advises the Cyprus Performing Rights Society on all IP-related matters including an action for alleged breach of copyright against one of the island's largest television companies.

Dr K Chrysostomides & Co has three lawyers specialising in IP matters, led by Mrs E Chrysostomides.

Kyriacos Th. Michaelides & Co Law Office offers a strong IP practice headed by intellectual property specialist Renos Michaelides. The firm advises on all aspects of trade marks and patents, including IP matters relating to the marketing of The *Lord of the Rings* films in Cyprus.

Michael Kyprianou & Associates reports a major increase of instructions in IP related matters over the past year, in particular relating to trade mark and patent protection. The firm manages trade mark portfolios for companies with activities in Europe and Asia.

Polakis Sarris & Co Lawyers was instructed by Nokia during a trade mark dispute in Cyprus.

INTELLECTUAL PROPERTY

LELLOS P DEMETRIADES ✪

Andreas Neocleous & Co ✪
Chrysses Demetriades & Co Law Office
Eleni Vrahimi & Co, Law Office
K Chrysostomides (Dr) & Co
Kyriacos Th. Michaelides & Co Law Office ✪
Michael Kyprianou & Associates ✪

George L Savvides & Co
Polakis Sarris & Co Lawyers

Antis Triantafyllides & Sons
Georgiades & Pelides
Tassos Papadopoulos & Co
Yiannos G Georgiades and Co.

Firms are listed A-Z in tiers which are ranked in order of priority
✪ Indicates firm displays contact details at the end of this chapter.

MARITIME

Shipping law is traditionally a major practice area in Cyprus as many ship owners seek to reap the various tax benefits of having vessels registered under the Cyprus flag. This, and the strategic location of the island, are reasons why Cyprus holds the fifth biggest shipping register internationally.

Acis Montanios leads the renowned shipping department at **Montanios & Montanios** which has five lawyers specialising in ship finance.

Chrysses Demetriades & Co Law Office is widely regarded as having one of the leading maritime departments in Cyprus. The firm represents the majority of ship management companies on the island.

L Papaphilippou & Co has one of the strongest shipping practices in Cyprus, led by name partner Loukis Papaphilippou. The firm exclusively represents international clients.

Andreas Neocleous & Co continues to advise the Cypriot Ship Owners Association.

George L Savvides & Co receives shipping work from UK-based **Norton Rose** and represents major ship owners, Stelmar.

Tassos Papadopoulos & Co advises major ship owner Louis Group, while **Antis Triantafyllides & Sons** offers ship finance advice under partner George Triantafyllides.

MARITIME

MONTANIOS & MONTANIOS
CHRYSSES DEMETRIADES & CO LAW OFFICE
L PAPAPHILIPPOU & CO

Andreas Neocleous & Co ✪
George L Savvides & Co
Karides, Karides & Georghiades
Tassos Papadopoulos & Co

Antis Triantafyllides & Sons
K Chrysostomides (Dr) & Co
Kyriacos Th. Michaelides & Co Law Office ✪
Polakis Sarris & Co Lawyers

Emilios Lemonaris
Michaelides & Michaelides

Firms are listed A-Z in tiers which are ranked in order of priority
✪ Indicates firm displays contact details at the end of this chapter.

Kyriacos Th. Michaelides & Co Law Office has recently advised on the establishment of a flagging agency in Cyprus. The firm has also advised on the establishment of funds for a floating dock facility.

Polakis Sarris & Co Lawyers has longstanding client relationships with German and Greek ship owners.

TAX

Cyprus has adjusted its tax legislation in line with EU requirements, and the demand for specialist tax advice has increased as a result, from both local businesses and offshore companies. Cyprus also has a number of double taxation treaties with other countries.

Andreas Neocleous & Co advises a major US financial institution on taxation issues relating to acquisitions abroad and a multinational media and entertainment group on the Cypriot element of a global restructuring exercise. Other clients include Estée Lauder and the gas producer, Itera SA.

TAX

ANDREAS NEOCLEOUS & CO ✪
ANTIS TRIANTAFYLLIDES & SONS
CHRYSSES DEMETRIADES & CO LAW OFFICE
PATRIKIOS PAVLOU & CO ✪
TASSOS PAPADOPOULOS & CO

George L Savvides & Co
K Chrysostomides, (Dr) & Co
L Papaphilippou & Co

Georgiades & Pelides
Lellos P Demetriades ✪
Papacharalambous & Angelides ✪
Polakis Sarris & Co Lawyers
Scordis, Papapetrou & Co

Firms are listed A-Z in tiers which are ranked in order of priority
✪ Indicates firm displays contact details at the end of this chapter.

Antis Triantafyllides & Sons is well known for its tax practice and takes instructions on tax planning from both international and local clients.

Chrysses Demetriades & Co Law Office offers advice on all facets of financial and tax matters to international companies.

Patrikios Pavlou & Co advises on European tax structures in what is a growing market due to continued generous tax levels and the new-found credibility of EU membership. Several longstanding clients of the firm are moving operations to Cyprus to take advantage of the beneficial tax legislation and new trading opportunities. Stavros Pavlou heads the department.

George L Savvides & Co advises local companies on tax matters. Clients include the Cyprus-based PepsiCo bottling plant.

Dr K Chrysostomides & Co advised numerous companies on tax matters during the past year.

L Papaphilippou & Co and **Tassos Papadopoulos & Co** offer advice on international tax planning as part of their corporate service.

ANDREAS NEOCLEOUS & CO

NEOCLEOUS HOUSE
199 ARCH MAKARIOS III AVENUE
3608 LIMASSOL

Telephone: +357 25 36 28 18
Fax: +357 25 35 92 62
E-mail: info@neocleous.com
Website: www.neocleous.com

Languages
Czech, English, French, German, Greek, Hungarian, Italian, Russian, Ukrainian

Other offices
Budapest, Kiev, Moscow, Nicosia, Paphos, Prague

Number of lawyers 60
at this office 44

CATEGORIES OF WORK

Companies, corporate management, trustee and fiduciary services
Andreas Neocleous, Elias Neocleous

Tax law and international tax planning
Andreas Neocleous, Elias Neocleous

Admiralty and international trade law
Panayiotis Neocleous, Maria Ioannou

Banking law, finance, insolvency
Anna Panayiotidou, Christina Hadjigiorki

Administrative law
Christos Melides

Real estate, wills, land law and administration of estates
Lefkios Tsikkinis, George Christoforou

Internet, e-commerce and information technology law
Elias Neocleous, George Yiannoulakis

Shipping companies, ship registration, ship finance and aviation
Panayiotis Neocleous, Benjamin Maltby

Corporate finance, capital markets, securities
Elias Neocleous, Kyriakos Georgiades

Matrimonial and family law
Christos Melides, Anna Panayiotidou

European law
Andreas Neocleous, Elias Neocleous

General litigation
Takis Christoforou, Antonis Glykis

Arbitration (local and international)
Christos Melides, Kleopas Stylianou

Intellectual property and trade marks
Nicholas Ktenas, Elena Papachristoforou

PATRIKIOS PAVLOU & CO

4 RIGA FEREOU STREET
OMEGA COURT, 3RD & 5TH FLOORS
PO BOX 54543
3725 LIMASSOL

Telephone: +357 25 87 15 99
Fax: +357 25 34 45 48
E-mail: info@pavlaw.com
Website: www.pavlaw.com

Languages
English, French, Greek, Italian, Russian, Ukrainian

Other offices
Nicosia, Athens*, Moscow*

Number of lawyers 17
at this office 12

Member
International Tax Planning Association; International Bar Association; Association of International Tax Consultants

CATEGORIES OF WORK

Corporate and commercial law
Stavros Pavlou, Soteris Pittas

International tax planning
Stavros Pavlou, Andria Andreou

Banking and finance
Stavros Pavlou, Stella Louka Pavlou

Litigation and arbitration
Soteris Pittas, Chrysostomos Nicolaou

European law
Stavros Pavlou, Andria Andreou

Shipping
Patrikios Pavlou, Andria Andreou

Intellectual property
Patrikios Pavlou, Andria Andreou

Real estate, wills and probate
Patrikios Pavlou, Andria Andreou

Information technology
Stavros Pavlou, Andria Andreou

Internet and e-commerce
Stavros Pavlou, Andria Andreou

LAW OFFICE OF ANDREW DEMETRIOU & CO

31 EVAGORAS AVENUE
1ST FLOOR, EVAGORAS COMPLEX
1066 NICOSIA

Telephone: +357 22 67 50 90
Fax: +357 22 67 58 65
E-mail: reception@ademetriou.com
Website: www.ademetriou.com

Languages
English, French, German, Greek, Italian

Number of lawyers 4

Contact
Andrew Demetriou (managing partner)

Member
Cyprus Bar Association; International Bar Association; Chartered Institute of Arbitrators; World e-Business Law Report (panel members); Roster of UN Center on Transnational Corporations (panel members)

CATEGORIES OF WORK

Construction
Andrew Demetriou, Elena Michail-Pikis

Arbitration
Andrew Demetriou, Christos Frakalas

Litigation
Andrew Demetriou, Stella J Stephani

Telecommunications
Andrew Demetriou, Elena Michail-Pikis

EU and competition
Elena Michail-Pikis, Christos Frakalas

Commercial
Andrew Demetriou, Elena Michail-Pikis

Family law
Stella J Stephani

Consumer law
Christos Frakalas

Energy and natural resources
Andrew Demetriou, Elena Michail-Pikis

Quality manager
Nadja Phasoulli

KYRIACOS TH MICHAELIDES & CO

66 IPPOKRATOUS STREET
1015 NICOSIA
PO BOX 21548
1510 NICOSIA

Telephone: +357 22 452 400
Fax: +357 22 761 878
E-mail: online@ktmlaw.com
Website: www.ktmlaw.com

Languages
English, German, Greek

Other offices
Athens

Number of lawyers 9
at this office 8

CATEGORIES OF WORK

General litigation/civil litigation
Kyriacos Th Michaelides

Company law (incorporating management, trustee services)
Christiana K Michaelides, Renos K Michaelides

Commercial law
Christiana K Michaelides

Arbitration
Kyriacos Th Michaelides

Intellectual property
Renos K Michaelides

Banking, finance and capital markets
Christiana K Michaelides

Construction
Kyriacos Th Michaelides

Property and administration of estates
Christiana K Michaelides, Renos K Michaelides

Administrative
Kyriacos Th Michaelides

LELLOS P DEMETRIADES
LAW OFFICE

THE CHANTECLAIR HOUSE
9TH FLOOR
2 SOPHOULIS STREET
PO BOX 21646
NICOSIA 1511

Telephone: +357 22 676 060
Fax: +357 22 676 061
E-mail: info@ldlaw.com.cy
Website: www.ldlaw.com.cy

Languages
Dutch, English, French, German, Spanish

Number of lawyers 9

CATEGORIES OF WORK

Company law
Lellos Demetriades

Offshore companies (tax and trust)
Lellos Demetriades

Insurance
Joanna Loizidou

Competition
Olga Georgiades-Van der Pol

Copyright
Achilleas Demetriades

Commercial contracts
Jennifer Savvopoulos

Telecommunications
Olga Georgiades-Van der Pol

Trade marks
Aliki Charalambidou

Patents
Aliki Charalambidou

Anti-piracy (intellectual property)
Achilleas Demetriades

Arbitration
Achilleas Demetriades

General commercial and litigation
Joanna Loizidou

Employment law
Joanna Loizidou

MICHAEL KYPRIANOU & ASSOCIATES

6TH FLOOR
2 AGIAS ELENIS STREET
PO BOX 28765
1060 NICOSIA

Telephone: +357 227 51 800
Fax: +357 227 67 880
E-mail: m.kypri@cytanet.com.cy
Website: www.kyprianou.com.cy

Languages
English, French, German, Greek, Russian

Other offices
Limassol, Paphos

Number of lawyers 11
at this office 7

Contact
Menelaos Kyprianou

Member
Multilaw (Multinational Association of Independent Law Firms); Eurolink for Lawyers; ITPA; IBA

CATEGORIES OF WORK

Company law (incorporation of companies, trustee and fiduciary services)
Pavlos Aristodemou, Anna Grigorieva

Tax law and international tax planning
Pavlos Aristodemou

Ship registration and finance
Tonia Antoniou, Pavlos Aristodemou

Admiralty and international trade law
Menelaos Kyprianou

Franchising, mergers and acquisitions
Menelaos Kyprianou, Pavlos Kyprianou

Litigation and arbitration
Michael Kyprianou, Menelaos Kyprianou

Banking law, finance and insolvency
Demos Christodoulou, Margarita Liasi

Law of e-commerce
Tonia Antoniou, Margarita Liasi

Real estate, wills and administration of estates
Michael Kyprianou, Michael Hasikos

European law
Menelaos Kyprianou, Pavlos Kyprianou

Intellectual property
Tonia Antoniou

PAPACHARALAMBOUS & ANGELIDES

10 THEMISTOKLI DERVI STREET
1ST FLOOR
PO BOX 24901
NICOSIA 1305

Telephone: +357 22 670 189
Fax: +357 22 676 976
Email: office@palaw.com.cy
Website: www.palaw.com.cy

Languages
English, French, Greek, Romanian

Other offices
Athens*, Brussels*, Bucharest*, Larnaca*, Limassol*, London*, Moscow*, New York*, Paphos*, Paralimni*, Sofia*

Number of lawyers 13
at this office 10

CATEGORIES OF WORK

Litigation

Company law (registering local companies' trade marks, patents, trade names)

Offshore company registration and administration

Banking

Public and administrative law

Intellectual property

Trusts

Family

Registration of companies into the Cyprus Stock Exchange

Commercial law

Civil and criminal proceedings

Labour law

Consultancy

THE FIRM

Papacharalambous & Angelides was founded by Andreas Papacharalambous and Pavlos Angelides in 1983 and is based in the centre of Nicosia, the capital of Cyprus. However, prior to this, Andreas Papacharalambous and Pavlos Angelides maintained their own offices, begun in 1976 and 1977 respectively.

AREAS OF PRACTICE

Papacharalambous & Angelides began as a small office with two partners and has now expanded and evolved into a large firm consisting of ten in-house qualified lawyers and has association with lawyers in all the main towns in Cyprus including Larnaca, Limassol and Paphos. It covers a wide range of areas of practice and the members of the firm are very experienced in all these areas, being able to offer advice with particular emphasis on general litigation, company law, family law, public and administrative law, and civil and criminal proceedings.

Moreover, the firm covers all areas concerning athletic and sports law together with any rights and regulations within this area. In addition, the law firm offers consultation to many semi-governmental organisations. Papacharalambous & Angelides also specialises in stock exchange activities both within Cyprus and Greece. The firm also has an extensive international client base and has associate offices including permanent representation in Greece, Romania, Bulgaria, Belgium and the UK. The firm has recently expanded to Israel and France, and has strong links with many other European countries.

The firm tries to keep up with all current developments in the law so as to be more effectively and efficiently able to serve its clients. It has recently set up a website, providing information and updates on the firm.

CZECH REPUBLIC

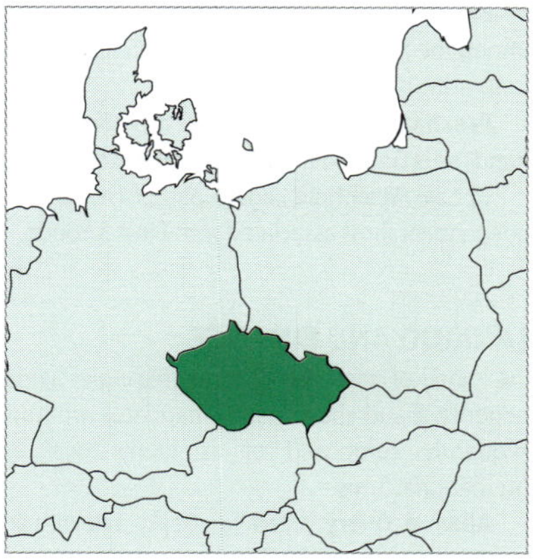

Population	**10.2 million**
Number of lawyers	**6,000**
Professional title	**Advokat**
Currency	**Koruna (Kc)**

Index

This beautiful Central European republic boasts one of the finest cities on the continent, Prague, as its capital, and a rich cultural heritage. But Bohemian life is losing its seedy side as the country cleans up its streets in advance of its impending accession to the EU.

EU membership began on 1 May 2004 and the prospect is increasingly influencing the Czech legal market and its clients.

Another era in Czech history ended in February 2003 with the end of Vaclav Havel's term as president. He took the country from the old Eastern Bloc into Nato and to the brink of joining the EU. The duty of completing that task falls to his successor, Vaclav Klaus.

The country has borders with Slovakia, from which it separated amicably in 1993, Austria, Germany and Poland. Relations with neighbouring countries have been fractious at times, but EU membership should bring about new incentives and methods for resolving disputes.

BILLING

The gap between rates charged by local firms and those charged by international firms are narrowing, at least in areas such as M&A. But the gaps are still large, with international firms charging up to €500 and local firms charging as little as €80 per hour. Firms are facing pressure from clients to move from hourly to fixed fees. It is also possible to find contingency fees, percentages and success fees.

Partners at Czech firms commonly charge between €200 and €300.

MARKETING

Until September 2003, all marketing was subject to extremely tight restrictions. But the law has been changed to allow limited advertising, and many firms are setting budgets for this purpose.

This benefits smaller and local firms who may be less well known than their larger, international counterparts. However, **Glatzová & Co** sees itself as aggressive in this regard and has set up a formal budget to take advantage of the new marketing opportunities as it seeks to challenge the Western firms present.

IN-HOUSE LAWYERS

Lawyers in the Czech Republic aspire to work in private firms, although the status of in-house lawyers remains high in comparison to other countries in the region. This is likely to change as the Czech market becomes more closely integrated with the international legal community.

ECONOMIC CLIMATE

The Czech Republic's accession to the EU is set for 1 May. Eyes are already being turned to membership of the euro. There is much less controversy here than within some existing EU member states, and some have commented that it is ironic that the Czech Republic may adopt the euro before the UK.

EU membership is expected to confer great benefits through increased trade and access to new funds for projects.

Yet in many cases, clients have only belatedly begun to ask their lawyers what they should be doing. Firms such as **Baker & McKenzie V.O.S.** have produced some highly detailed guidance for clients and have held seminars on the subject. Such seminars have been remarkably well attended.

CMS Cameron McKenna v.o.s. is among many firms which has been training its lawyers on the impact of EU accession.

Gleiss Lutz is one of a number of firms which has set up or expanded an EU desk in the last year.

The EU team at **Squire, Sanders & Dempsey, v.o.s., advokátní kancelár** visits the firm's Brussels office on a rotational basis.

Taxation and employment are areas on which lawyers have spent much time with clients, explaining the changes they may need to make.

Also, real estate prices are likely to rise considerably after EU accession, and numerous deals are being rushed through in advance of the May deadline.

Failed privatisations and BOT projects may resurface after May, albeit in a different form. The government faced criticism for the way it handled the D27 and other major national projects. Many of the groundbreaking projects hailed in 2002 fell flat in 2003, though there were some successes.

As with existing EU members, there will be tensions between the EU and the Czech Republic. Issues of concern include agricultural subsidies. Eurosceptics also fear their country will have little bargaining power, but europhiles suggest this situation would be worse still outside the EU.

There is also a big question mark over the readiness of the country's judiciary, one-third of which have experience of 'the old days', to adapt to

The largest firms

1	Linklaters	43
2	Kocián Solc Balastík	40
3	White & Case	37
4	Balcar, Polansky & spol.	30
	EY Law / Weinhold Legal	30
6	Brzobohaty Broz & Honsa	29
	Kríz and Belina	29
8	Allen & Overy	28
	Weil, Gotshal & Manges	28
10	Peterka & Partners v.o.s	27
	Procházka Randl Kubr	27
	Salans	27
13	Glatzová & Co	26
	Sodomka Soucek Jindra Mokry & Partners	26
15	CMS Cameron McKenna v.o.s.	24
16	Clifford Chance LLP	21
17	Baker & McKenzie V.O.S.	20
	Cermák Horejs Myslil	20
	Fiala, Profous, Maisner & Spol	20
	Rödl & Partner V.O.S.	20
	Squire, Sanders & Dempsey, v.o.s., advokátní kancelár	20
	Vejmelka & Wünsch, v.o.s.	20
23	Nörr Stiefenhofer Lutz	18
24	Haarmann Hemmelrath	17
25	Giese & Partner	16
	Havel & Holásek v.o.s., attorneys-at-law	16

These figures represent the total number of lawyers in this country only, and have been supplied by the firms themselves. The figures should be accurate as at 1 January 2004.

the new systems and procedures EU accession will bring.

Being a new country, Czech law has little in the way of precedent, unlike EU law. One suggestion is that judges be advised by professionals in the first few years. The prospect is that lower courts will issue a lot of decisions which will be incompatible with EU law and easily overturned by a higher court.

Economic growth is hovering around 2-3%, which is healthy enough for the region. There has been no downturn, and Czech companies have picked up business from neighbouring Germany in recent times. However, while inflation has fallen sharply to 2.8%, there has been a dramatic increase in unemployment to around 10%.

LEGAL MARKET

The Czech Republic's increasing convergence with Western economies and policies such as privatisation have brought in many international firms, some of which now have very close ties with local firms.

However, the vagaries and predicted short lifespan of the privatisation programme have created a fluid situation, resulting in a number of departures, lateral hires and predictions of downsizing in the future. In addition, local firms may be said to be entering a watershed period which may even result in mergers. Already, *Altheimer & Gray* has been swallowed up by **Salans**.

Weil, Gotshal & Manges reports that the value of legal work is increasingly appreciated by commercial and state clients, who are showing more willingness, in some cases, to pay higher fees or go to more prestigious firms.

There is some evidence that local firms want to have a bilateral presence. **Safár & Spol** set up a Bratislava office this year to improve its service to clients with bilateral interests.

Brzobohatý Broz & Honsa has worked with **Simmons & Simmons**, while **Glatzová & Co** regularly receives referrals from **Freshfields Bruckhaus Deringer**.

Gleiss Lutz has an alliance relationship with **Herbert Smith** in the UK and Belgium/Dutch firm **Stibbe**.

CMS Cameron McKenna v.o.s. was selected to represent the European Venture Capital Association and sees the development as a sign of growth to come as Western investors look to exploit opportunities in the Czech Republic.

Balcar Polanský Norton Rose was formed in 1998, the product of a highly successful working relationship between the local and international firms. As well as enjoying permanent representation from both firms, joint teams of varying sizes work together under this banner on an ad hoc basis. Last year it advised Honeywell on regulatory issues concerning various transactions.

The firm is not alone in predicting a surge of regulatory and competition work in the light of (impending) EU accession. Dozens of seminars and hundreds of client meetings have taken place on this issue.

Gide Loyrette Nouel also reports an increase in competition work and has represented various state bodies seeking to implement WTO decisions in the Czech Republic.

Many agree that the proportion of Czech lawyers within all firms is rising because of the increasing quality of their work; others remain to be convinced.

Balcar Polanský Norton Rose is recognised among the leading firms, especially in real estate, bankruptcy and banking.

Procházka Randl Kubr is a member of *Lex Mundi*, as is German firm **Nörr Stiefenhofer Lutz**.

EY Law / Weinhold Legal is part of a network of independent firms associated with Ernst & Young.

BANKING AND FINANCE

The work of local firms is increasingly being recognised and shortlists for mandates are now frequently composed of as many local as international firms.

Allen & Overy acted for Cesky Telekom in connection with an €850m syndicated loan, and advised the national lottery, Sazka, on the €200m lottery funding of its new sports arena to be opened in time for the 2004 World Ice Hockey Championships. Nic Bottomley continues to advise ISDA and the EBRD in an effort to promote statutory amendments and improve the enforceability of close-out netting legislation in the Czech Republic. Partner Mikulas Touska is recommended.

Balcar Polanský Norton Rose is best known for its banking and finance work, though it can also provide a high level of expertise in the areas of forced administration, insolvency and asset tracing. Dr Balcar Polansky, a partner in the Czech firm, is recognised in this field. The high-profile liquidation of Union Banka helped the firm develop its expertise in this area in 2003. Further clients include Komercni Banka, which it advised on software contracts. It also advised HSBC on the restructuring of its investment banking business, and advised Commerzbank's structured finance team on its lending and restructuring activities. There was also advice for ABC International Bank on a €15m finance and security package.

Clifford Chance LLP acted for the mandated lead/arrangers (Citibank, BACA, JPMorgan, KBC, CSOB, SANPAOLO and IMI) on the largest syndicated loan in Central Europe to date, an €850m euro credit facility to Ceske Telekom, the incumbent fixed line telephone operator, to buy the remaining 49% of mobile phone operator, Eurotel Praha. The practice is headed by highly-rated managing partner Vlad Petrus, and also acted for WestLB and SOB, among others.

Procházka Randl Kubr has the strongest reputation of all the Czech firms in the area of finance. Marek Prochazka is highly spoken of, and work in the last year includes the sale of a loan

BANKING AND FINANCE

ALLEN & OVERY ✪
BALCAR POLANSKY NORTON ROSE
CLIFFORD CHANCE LLP
PROCHÁZKA RANDL KUBR ✪
WEIL, GOTSHAL & MANGES ✪
WHITE & CASE

CMS Cameron McKenna v.o.s.
EY Law / Weinhold Legal
Linklaters ✪
Nörr Stiefenhofer Lutz ✪
Squire, Sanders & Dempsey, v.o.s., advokátní kancelár ✪

Baker & McKenzie V.O.S. ✪
Brzobohatý Broz & Honsa ✪
Dewey Ballantine v.o.s ✪
Gide Loyrette Nouel ✪
Giese & Partner
Glatzová & Co ✪
Gleiss Lutz ✪
Haslinger/Nagele & Partner, v.o.s.
Salans
Sodomka Soucek Jindra Mokry & Partners ✪
Vejmelka & Wünsch, v.o.s. ✪
Vyskocil, Kroslak a Spol
Wolf Theiss ✪

Firms are listed A-Z in tiers which are ranked in order of priority
✪ *Indicates firm displays contact details at the end of this chapter.*

portfolio for Komercni Banka. The firm is highly rated by others.

Weil, Gotshal & Manges is a top line firm and represented the Czech Airport Authority over its €300m financing of the new Prague-Ruzyne terminal. Other clients include Lehman Brothers, the EBRD and Citibank. Managing partner Karel Muzikar and partner Ken Schiff are very well-known.

White & Case was strengthened by the arrival of Jiri Tomola, who was previously an in-house lawyer with a Czech bank. Banks have been defending their right to state aid in advance of EU accession, and the firm has been assisting Ceskoslovenska Obchodni Banka, and others, in this regard.

Partner Paul Stallebrass of **CMS Cameron McKenna v.o.s.** heads a team of five and handled the TES/ICZ leveraged buy-out. The team specialises in structuring. Client TES Media/Karneval was advised along with investors AIG, JPMorgan Partners and GMT Communications on the multi-million euro deal.

The practice of **EY Law / Weinhold Legal** was boosted last year by the arrival of financial specialist Vera Filkukova from **Procházka Randl Kubr**. Work last year included advising a leading US investment bank over a potential transaction involving Union Banka. It also advised Erste Bank AG on the acquisition of Primalex by Riverside, valued at €16m.

Linklaters is known for the work of managing partner Francis Kucera, and Lukas Sevcik, although its third big name in this field, Alexandr Mares, has left the firm and has been working independently.

Nörr Stiefenhofer Lutz conducts bank audits, and is one of few firms to specialise in this field. It advises foreign investors on various banking and finance matters. It has an impressive list of German and Austrian clients but has also represented other companies and organisation, including the EBRD.

Squire, Sanders & Dempsey, v.o.s., advokátní kancelár, led by its experienced and respected managing partner Vladimira Papirnik, structured the financing on the hockey stadium deal. The firm has a very high level of expertise in finance and is developing its work in the area of non-performing loans. It handled an €8m syndicated loan financing for Ceska rafinerska.

Baker & McKenzie V.O.S. advised Ceskoslovenska Obchodni Banka on the transfer of €1.6bn of underlying assets held through foreign fund structures, established by the former Investicni a Postovni Banka to the Czech Consolidation Agency.

CAPITAL MARKETS

The Czech Republic is ripe for development in terms of the introduction of more sophisticated products, yet many firms report a quiet year in this sector in 2003.

Allen & Overy advised Cesky Telekom in the second bond issue under its €600m programme.

A lot of international work is handled by **Clifford Chance LLP**, which also acted for Deutsche Bank, the lead manager in the creation of a €1bn euro EMTN programme for the City of Prague.

Linklaters advised the City of Prague on the deal, the largest securities issue from a Czech issuer in the last year.

Procházka Randl Kubr is well known in this area and advised CSOB on a debt issue programme. It has been said that the firm has the domestic capital markets scene 'sewn up'.

Balcar Polanský Norton Rose has developed its private equity work through the work it undertakes for Genesis Capital. It also advised Ceske Radiokomunikace on the listing of shares on the Prague Stock Exchange, and helped international mutual funds group, MFS to sell its products on the Czech market. Komercni Banka was advised on the derivatives and other products including legal aspects of CDO investments, and also on how state aid might be affected by EU law.

Brzobohatý Broz & Honsa acted as exclusive Czech legal counsel to leading consumer finance provider, Home Credit Finance on the first ever rated and completed securitisation within Central Europe, involving €130m of its credit card receivables. The deal took a painstaking 11 months, and also involved **Simmons & Simmons**

CAPITAL MARKETS

ALLEN & OVERY ✪
CLIFFORD CHANCE LLP
LINKLATERS ✪
PROCHÁZKA RANDL KUBR ✪

Balcar Polanský Norton Rose
Brzobohatý Broz & Honsa ✪
Havel & Holásek v.o.s., attorneys-at-law ✪
Weil, Gotshal & Manges ✪
White & Case

Squire, Sanders & Dempsey, v.o.s., advokátní kancelár ✪

Firms are listed A-Z in tiers which are ranked in order of priority
✪ *Indicates firm displays contact details at the end of this chapter.*

and **Clifford Chance LLP**, which advised Credit Suisse First Boston (Europe). It is widely recognised that this deal will pave the way for future securitisations and **Brzobohatý Broz & Honsa** now has a desk to handle such work. It also advised Skoda on listing shares on the Prague Stock Exchange. Dresdner Bank was advised by the firm on negotiation of cross-border agreements. The firm has therefore widened its services in this area, and has joined the International Swaps and Derivatives Association.

Havel & Holásek v.o.s., attorneys-at-law advised a security brokerage firm on the public offer of a €10m bond issue.

Marek Vojáček was appointed to the partnership in January 2004; he is the firm's fifth partner.

Weil, Gotshal & Manges represented Argus Capital over a cross-border share offer in Svoboda on the Warsaw Stock Exchange. It also represented Ceska konsolidacni agentura in the first Czech MTN programme, worth €600m, and two bond issues within the programme worth €150m and €300m respectively. Karolina Horakova and Karel Devinek are recommended.

White & Case advised Czech electricity generator CEZ in connection with a €1bn bond programme.

CORPORATE AND COMMERCIAL

Several firms report a dry year in this field, at the same time predicting a large increase in activity.

Allen & Overy advised Bankgesellschaft Berlin in the sale of its 85.16% stake in Ivnostenska Banka to UniCredito Italiano. Other clients include Heinz, KPN Royal Dutch Telecom, Komercni Banka, Conoco and Shell. Led by Jane Townsend, the practice continues to offer an excellent service. Assistant Tomas Richter is also recommended.

Linklaters advised Credit Suisse First Boston and Morgan Stanley as joint arrangers of Telesource's 27% stake in Cesky Telekom by way of an accelerated book build offering. The firm has reorganised its Central and Eastern European offices and some recent departures are explained by this. **Linklaters** has suffered a number of losses and is 10% smaller than it was a year ago. Departures include corporate specialist partner Christopher Bremme, who moved to the Warsaw office, tax partner Henk Goosen, who went to Budapest, and banking partner Alexandr Mares. Three senior assistants have also left the firm, including Petr Guth, to **Allen & Overy** and Pavel Skopovy, who joined **Kocián Solc Balastík**. It nevertheless remains highly active and boasts a 21-strong team in this field with a client list that includes, for the first time, BMW and Sony.

Nike, Sotheby's, Estée Lauder and McKinsey are among the corporate clients of **Weil, Gotshal & Manges**. The firm was involved in at least five of the biggest deals of 2003. In the competition sphere, in which the firm is highly capable and experienced, the team represented Pilsner Urquell/SAB in a Czech competition investigation regarding vertical agreements in the Czech on-trade and off-trade markets. Other clients include TetraPak and Vitkovice Steel. Assistant Karel Drevinek is recommended.

White & Case advised Honeywell on the structuring of its operations in the Czech Republic. The firm is well-versed in utilities and manufacturing and has a Japanese practice to service the needs of the nation which has now become the Czech Republic's biggest single inward investor.

Baker & McKenzie V.O.S. expanded its fee-earning personnel by 25% over the year and has a strong employment practice. Less dependent on privatisation work, the firm has not suffered from the vagaries of that area in recent months. The firm recruited labour lawyer Karin Konstantinova, formerly with **EY Law / Weinhold Legal**. She is also experienced in M&A. **Baker & McKenzie V.O.S.** lists Hewlett-Packard and Motorola as clients in this area.

The practice of **Balcar Polanskỳ Norton Rose** was tipped to lose work following the departure of Benedict Coleman. However, it was boosted in 2002 by the arrival of Simon Renton. The firm is looking to expand its EU desk. Respected partner Dr Ludmila Neusptupna recently advised Belgian industrial concern NV Beckaert SA. The firm has advised Gerling NCM on establishing a Czech branch.

CMS Cameron McKenna v.o.s. advised Deutsche Bank in the restructuring of its portfolio in the Czech Republic. The firm has taken on a German team to provide clients from that country with a German-language service backed by international resources.

Clifford Chance LLP hired Tomos Krcil as a senior associate for its corporate and finance practice. Last year the firm helped WestLB Panmure successfully apply to the NPF for the role of financial adviser in the Unipetrol privatisation.

Gleiss Lutz has a five-strong team and lists Invensys and DaimlerChrysler as clients.

On the international front, **Lovells** and **Nörr Stiefenhofer Lutz** also provide good corporate advice. Some 70% of the latter firm's clients are German-based, though the practice has seven French-speakers and expects to attract more French clients this year. It is one of several firms predicting a surge in competition and regulatory work, especially in the area of antitrust. Clients include Volkswagen, Walter Bau, Credit Suisse Life & Pensions and Commerzbank.

Salans seems to have kept disruption to a minimum as it took over *Altheimer & Gray* and highly respected partner Petr Kotab has stayed on, helping to ensure that the firm's high-profile international clients have stayed on board.

Squire, Sanders & Dempsey, v.o.s., advokátní kancelár lists Anheuser-Busch, Du Pont and Conoco among its clients.

Brzobohatỳ Broz & Honsa was involved in analysing the structure of private Czech broadcaster, TV Nova Group. This quality local outfit receives valuable referrals from international firms.

Cermák Horejs Myslil provides a high quality service and has seven fee-earners in this area, led by Dr Richard Myslil. The team arranges leases for McDonald's and also represents Velux, Riverside and Novartis. On the competition side, it attracted supermarket chain Lidl as a new client in 2003, and continues to represent Lego. The firm is one of a very few to specialise in pharmaceuticals to any degree, and lists Merck, Pfizer and Novartis among its clients, with recent addition Roche.

Dewey Ballantine v.o.s is now headed solely by Petr Kotrlik, following the departure of former joint managing partner Michael Kroft. The firm advised Eurotel Praha on general corporate and commercial matters, and continues to advise SAB Miller following its acquisition of Miller Breweries.

The practice of **EY Law / Weinhold Legal** was known for partners Joel Schemmel and Pav Younis. Schemmel has left the firm to return to the US, but Younis continues to be highly recommended.

Fiala, Profous, Maisner & spol is a sizeable firm of 20 fee-earners and provides sound advice in many aspects of law within this area. Martin Maisner is a solid commercial lawyer.

Gide Loyrette Nouel represented Eurocopter in the sale of helicopters to the Czech government and commonly advises companies involved in start-ups or restructuring. Some 70% of the firm's clients are French-based. L'Oréal is a client and was recently advised on distribution agreements. The firm also advises on employment matters.

Glatzová & Co represents Cadbury-Schweppes, Bayer AG and Warburg in this area and was joined this year by former **Weil, Gotshal & Manges** associate Martin Randa, one of a number of lateral hires made by the firm in 2003.

Havel & Holásek v.o.s., attorneys-at-law advised Union Bank's bankruptcy administrator on the disposal of €250m of assets; and helped national rail operator, Ceske drahy separate into two entities.

CORPORATE AND COMMERCIAL

ALLEN & OVERY ✪
LINKLATERS ✪
WEIL, GOTSHAL & MANGES ✪
WHITE & CASE

Baker & McKenzie V.O.S. ✪
Balcar Polanskỳ Norton Rose
CMS Cameron McKenna v.o.s.
Clifford Chance LLP
Gleiss Lutz ✪
Lovells ✪
Nörr Stiefenhofer Lutz ✪
Salans
Squire, Sanders & Dempsey, v.o.s., advokátní kancelár ✪

Brzobohatỳ Broz & Honsa ✪
Cermák Horejs Myslil ✪
Dewey Ballantine v.o.s ✪
EY Law / Weinhold Legal
Fiala, Profous, Maisner & Spol
Gide Loyrette Nouel ✪
Glatzová & Co ✪
Haarmann Hemmelrath ✪
Havel & Holásek v.o.s., attorneys-at-law ✪
Hogan & Hartson Advokátní Kancelare, v.o.s. ✪
Kocián Solc Balastík
Procházka Randl Kubr ✪
Vejmelka & Wünsch, v.o.s. ✪
Vyskocil, Kroslak a Spol
Wolf Theiss ✪

Ambruz & Dark ✪
Holec & Partners ✪
Kríz and Belina
Peterka & Partners v.o.s ✪
Safár & Spol
Seddons
Sodomka Soucek Jindra Mokry & Partners ✪

Firms are listed A-Z in tiers which are ranked in order of priority
✪ *Indicates firm displays contact details at the end of this chapter.*

Hogan & Hartson Advokátní Kancelare, v.o.s. is outside counsel for Eurotel Praha, Eurotel Bratislava, Delphi Czech Republic and STE.

Procházka Randl Kubr handled sets of commercial export contracts for a leading technology exporter.

Vejmelka & Wünsch, v.o.s. recently appointed two new partners and concentrates mainly in the corporate, competition and M&A fields. New clients include Anheuser-Busch, Sony, the IFC and Debenhams.

Vyskocil, Kroslak a Spol has a five-strong team of employment lawyers. Tomas Rychly, who joined as a partner from **Allen & Overy** in January 2003 is well-known for his insolvency advice to creditors. Eastern Sugar is among its clients.

Other firms regularly receiving recommendations on the corporate front, include **Wolf Theiss**.

Ambruz & Dark claims to have pushed up gross revenues by 16% in the past year. It advised

Pepsi on the impact of EU accession and Shimizu on corporate issues.

Kríz and Belina lists Coca-Cola and German tobacco manufacturer, Reemtsma as clients. The firm has expanded through recruitment this year in an effort to boost its practice and has five new lawyers.

Peterka & Partners v.o.s picks up good local and some Western clients in this field.

Safár & Spol recruited Hana Sevelova last year from **Giese & Partner** and established a Bratislava office, attracting new clients with bilateral interests.

Sodomka Soucek Jindra Mokry & Partners has appointed four new, junior partners from within its ranks in the past year, including Dr Adam Batuna, responsible for general commercial practice. The firm advised on start-up issues for LG Philips Displays new picture tube technology plant in the Moravia district.

DISPUTE RESOLUTION

The dispute resolution department at **Balcar Polanský Norton Rose**, led by the able and experienced Dr Ludmila Neustupna, defended the former forced administrator of IP Banka in proceedings the bank brought against him in connection with the sale of the bank's banking business. The firm is also involved in the BCL fraud case, with **Norton Rose** partner Sam Eastwood heading things up.

Brzobohatý Broz & Honsa is currently involved in around $100m-worth of international arbitration. Jointly with **Freshfields Bruckhaus Deringer**, the firm is representing leading Czech television company, CET 21 in a dispute concerning a $1bn investment.

The four-strong team of **Cermák Horejs Myslil** picks up a good deal of work from its established IP practice. Partner Karel Cermak represented brewer, Budejovicky Budvar in its long-running trade mark battle with US brewer, Budweiser. Other clients include Tommy Hilfiger.

Salans lawyer Alena Banyaiova used to be a commercial judge and is among a number of registered arbitrators at the firm, which took over the *Altheimer & Gray* practice in 2003.

Squire, Sanders & Dempsey, v.o.s., advokátní kancelár successfully represented the Ministry of Finance in the so-called 'Nagel' case, where a British national brought as claim arising out of the abortive privatisation of telecoms. The decision came through on 10 September 2003. It is also involved in the continuing Nomura case, where again the client is the Ministry of Finance. The firm's counterparts are often international firms with no Czech branch, such as **Freshfields Bruckhaus Deringer**.

Weil, Gotshal & Manges is very strong in this area and represented Cepro, the largest Czech fuel pipeline operator, in a €100m VAT and excise tax case. The firm is also experienced in cases involving white-collar crime and fraud.

DISPUTE RESOLUTION

Balcar Polanský Norton Rose
Brzobohatý Broz & Honsa ✪
Cermák Horejs Myslil ✪
Salans
Squire, Sanders & Dempsey, v.o.s., advokátní kancelár ✪
Weil, Gotshal & Manges ✪

Baker & McKenzie V.O.S. ✪
Dewey Ballantine v.o.s ✪
Peterka & Partners v.o.s ✪

CMS Cameron McKenna v.o.s.
Clifford Chance LLP
Gide Loyrette Nouel ✪
Glatzová & Co ✪
Hogan & Hartson Advokátní Kancelare, v.o.s. ✪
Linklaters ✪
Nörr Stiefenhofer Lutz ✪
Procházka Randl Kubr ✪
Vyskocil, Kroslak a Spol

Firms are listed A-Z in tiers which are ranked in order of priority
✪ Indicates firm displays contact details at the end of this chapter.

Baker & McKenzie V.O.S. has been involved with disputes relating to the collapse of Investicni a Postovni Banka with a total value of €7bn, under ICC and LCIA rules.

Dewey Ballantine v.o.s advised CME Czech Republic as the Czech counsel for US firm **Debevoise & Plimpton**, against the Czech Republic in arbitration proceedings under the Treaty on Protection of Investment between the Netherlands and the Czech Republic. Other clients include CME Media Enterprises, Plze sky prazdroj as and CNTS over a contract breach claim.

Peterka & Partners v.o.s advised a Czech bank in a dispute worth tens of millions of euros against a major rival. Partner Ondrez Peterke is an experienced litigator who lived and worked in France for some years before returning to the Czech Republic. The firm has grown significantly over the past five years.

IP, IT AND E-COMMERCE

IT is another area into which the long arm of EU law is shortly to extend. **CMS Cameron McKenna v.o.s.** helped Warner Brothers protect the film rights to the *Harry Potter* movie. Other clients include Universal Studios and Twentieth Century Fox. The firm has an excellent reputation in this field and an eight-strong team is led by partner Peter Valert.

Cermák Horejs Myslil is best known for its work in this area, although there has been a change at the top in the last year, with the departure of respected senior partner Dr Karel Cermak to become Minister of Justice. He has been replaced by Dr Jan Matejka. That said, 17 of the firm's 22 lawyers continue to handle high-level IP work, representing Pfizer, Du Pont, Ford and Johnson & Johnson, among others. The firm recruited two new young lawyers in December 2003. Dr Andrea Povazanova, from the Slovak Justice Ministry, has also joined the firm to work on cases involving Slovak law. As well as trade marks, she also specialises in competition.

Linklaters continues to attract big name clients in this field, including Microsoft.

Allen & Overy advised British Telecom and Eurotel Praha in connection with regulatory issues.

Baker & McKenzie V.O.S. represents Hewlett-Packard in IT and Estée Lauder in IP.

Balcar Polanský Norton Rose helped verify that UUNET customer contracts comply with relevant Czech and EU law. The firm also helped the company apply for licences and advised Komercni Banka on a number of software contracts. It also defends the IP interests of adidas and EasyJet.

Weil, Gotshal & Manges represented a Czech brewery in a patent dispute settlement.

White & Case defends the intellectual property interests of the Ford Motor Company and also advises Pfizer. The firm is proud of its client base in the pharmaceutical sector.

MEDIA AND TELECOMS

Linklaters is known for its highly skilled telecoms practice and represents the Czech interests of BT.

Weil, Gotshal & Manges represented Cesky Telekom in its purchase of 40% of Eurotel for €865m, one of the largest telecoms deals in the Czech Republic. The firm also represented Cesky Telekom in a number of other matters, including the procurement of connectivity and communications infrastructure for state institutions.

Led by partner Michal Dlouhy, a **White & Case** team advised a consortium of composed of

IP, IT AND E-COMMERCE

CMS CAMERON MCKENNA V.O.S.
CERMÁK HOREJS MYSLIL ✪
LINKLATERS ✪

Allen & Overy ✪
Baker & McKenzie V.O.S. ✪
Balcar Polanský Norton Rose
Weil, Gotshal & Manges ✪
White & Case

Brzobohatý Broz & Honsa ✪
Clifford Chance LLP
Hogan & Hartson Advokátní Kancelare, v.o.s. ✪
Glatzová & Co ✪
Nörr Stiefenhofer Lutz ✪
Procházka Randl Kubr ✪
Squire, Sanders & Dempsey, v.o.s., advokátní kancelár ✪
Traplová Hakr Kubát Law and Patent Offices
Vyskocil, Kroslak a Spol
Vejmelka & Wünsch, v.o.s. ✪

Firms are listed A-Z in tiers which are ranked in order of priority
✪ Indicates firm displays contact details at the end of this chapter.

MEDIA AND TELECOMS

LINKLATERS ✪
WEIL, GOTSHAL & MANGES ✪
WHITE & CASE

Allen & Overy ✪
CMS Cameron McKenna v.o.s.
Squire, Sanders & Dempsey, v.o.s., advokátní kancelár ✪

Baker & McKenzie V.O.S. ✪
Balcar Polanský Norton Rose
Glatzová & Co ✪
Hogan & Hartson Advokátní Kancelare, v.o.s. ✪
Procházka Randl Kubr ✪
Vejmelka & Wünsch, v.o.s. ✪

Firms are listed A-Z in tiers which are ranked in order of priority
✪ *Indicates firm displays contact details at the end of this chapter.*

Spectrum Equity Investors, Lehman Brothers and GMT on a bid to purchase the assets of telecoms company, GTS from Dutch telecoms company, KPNQwest. Another client is Ceske Radiokomunikace. Practice head is Vaclav Jerman, who joined in 2002 and, together with senior associate Jakub Dostal, is credited with taking the department to new heights.

Allen & Overy has advised BT and Eurotel Praha on regulatory issues.

CMS Cameron McKenna v.o.s. is known for the work of telecoms specialist, Ian Parker.

Squire, Sanders & Dempsey, v.o.s., advokátní kancelár advised the NPF in connection with the privatisation of Cesky Telekom. Petr Slach is often requested by telecoms companies on regulatory matters.

Baker & McKenzie V.O.S. advised Nokia for the first time last year.

MERGERS AND ACQUISITIONS

Allen & Overy represented KPN NV in connection with the sale of its 6.5% shareholding in Cesky Telekom; the firm is usually involved in any high-profile Czech M&A deals.

Partner Helen Rodwell of **CMS Cameron McKenna v.o.s.** jointly leads a seven-strong team. The firm acted for Pojistovna Ceske Sporitelny AS in the €130m sale of its non-life insurance business. Other clients include Deutsche Bank, Credit Agricole and British Energy.

Linklaters helped Zurich Insurance transfer its business and insurance portfolio to Generali Insurance and advised on the subsequent closing of the branch of a foreign insurance company in the Czech Republic and elsewhere in CEE. The structure was unique and was later used as a template by others. The deal involved complex regulatory and corporate issues and merger control filing and certain co-ordination of the transaction throughout the CEE.

Weil, Gotshal & Manges represented OSINEK in the purchase of 51% of CEPS, the Czech monopoly high-voltage electricity grid operator, for €350m. Other big name clients include Invensys. The firm's privatisation work includes representing the Czech Consolidation Agency, which looks after non-performing loans, and the NPF in the sale of shares of Vitkovice.

White & Case offers top quality advice on M&A and partners Michal Dlouhy and Jan Matejcek are recommended. The firm was selected by the NPF to handle the latest attempt to privatise refining and petrochemicals giant Unipetrol. It also assisted in the Czech Republic's largest privatisation to date, that of Transgas, sold to client RWE Gas AG. The firm also advised Pfizer in connection with the worldwide merger of the Pharmacia Group into the Pfizer Group. Partner Ivo Barta advised long-standing client, Riverside on a $20m acquisition of paint manufacturer Primalex from Keramika Horni Briza. Other clients include Honeywell and JPMorgan Flemings. The work of the firm in this area has been recognised in previous years, and was further strengthened in 2003 by the return of Emil Nemec from a three-year secondment to the IFC. Zdenek Kabila joined the firm from the NPF. He works on public procurement transactions.

Baker & McKenzie V.O.S. represented Deutsche Bank/Morgan Grenfell in connection with the post-privatisation restructuring of Ceske Rediokomunikace, including a mandatory buy-out (squeeze-out) of minority shareholders. It also lists Czech Airlines and Siemens AG as clients in this area.

Balcar Polanský Norton Rose was tipped to lose work following the departure of Benedict Coleman but in fact has been handling some reasonable quality M&A, which, it expects, will increase, not least with the experienced Simon Renton now on board.

Clifford Chance LLP has 17 fee-earners capable of handling work in this area, led by partner William Knowles and senior associate Emil Holub, though few of that number work exclusively in this area due to the loose departmental structure adopted by this relatively small office. The team advised Blackstone Group on the Czech aspects of the worldwide acquisition of TRW Automotive.

Dewey Ballantine v.o.s has six fee-earners in its M&A department, headed by Petr Kotrlik and Martin Bourgeault. It acted as counsel to the EBRD in connection with its $6m investment in Czech tram manufacturer, Siemens Kolejova Vozidla.

EY Law / Weinhold Legal advised Obrascon Huarte Lain, on its acquisition of 61.1% of ŽPSV Uhersky Ostroh, the holding company of a Czech construction group.

Glatzová & Co acted as counsel for LNM Holdings in the largest merger and privatisation in the Czech steel sector to date, helping it to buy a $798m majority stake in the country's biggest steel manufacturer, Nova Hut.

Salans is the former office of *Altheimer & Gray*, which has now been incorporated as a result of a complete takeover. Its services have already been strengthened by the extra resources at the firm's disposal. The client base has remained loyal and appreciates the firm's cost-effective approach to smaller cases. Christopher Berlew is among the ex-*Altheimer & Gray* partners who have joined. Petr Kotab is very well respected in the commercial arena. The firm has also been involved in privatisations, advising Czech ministries.

Gide Loyrette Nouel is active in M&A and represented oil giant, Total in the sale of its Czech network to Shell.

Giese & Partner represented truck maker, Terex in the acquisition of Tatra. The firm has hired two new lawyers, including Pavlina Berenkova of **Gleiss Lutz**, to strengthen the M&A practice, and expanded its offices in the Myslbek building.

Gleiss Lutz has taken on three first-year associates, two of whom have been recruited to boost the M&A practice. Martin Nedelka has been made a partner. The firm helped Siemens/Alstrom buy a Czech industrial turbine business for €2bn and, with **Herbert Smith**, assisted Anglian Water in the sale of its Czech interests.

MERGERS AND ACQUISITIONS

ALLEN & OVERY ✪
CMS CAMERON MCKENNA V.O.S.
LINKLATERS ✪
WEIL, GOTSHAL & MANGES ✪
WHITE & CASE

Baker & McKenzie V.O.S. ✪
Balcar Polanský Norton Rose
Clifford Chance LLP
Dewey Ballantine v.o.s ✪
EY Law / Weinhold Legal
Glatzová & Co ✪
Salans

Gide Loyrette Nouel ✪
Giese & Partner
Gleiss Lutz ✪
Hogan & Hartson Advokátní Kancelare, v.o.s. ✪
Kocián Solc Balastík
Lovells ✪
Nörr Stiefenhofer Lutz ✪
Squire, Sanders & Dempsey, v.o.s., advokátní kancelár ✪
Vejmelka & Wünsch, v.o.s. ✪

Ambruz & Dark ✪
Brzobohatý Broz & Honsa ✪
Cermák Horejs Myslil ✪
Havel & Holásek v.o.s., attorneys-at-law ✪
Horák & Chvosta
Procházka Randl Kubr ✪
Vyskocil, Kroslak a Spol
Wolf Theiss ✪

Firms are listed A-Z in tiers which are ranked in order of priority
✪ *Indicates firm displays contact details at the end of this chapter.*

Libor Prokes of **Nörr Stiefenhofer Lutz** is recommended for M&A and due diligence work.

Squire, Sanders & Dempsey, v.o.s., advokátní kancelár has handled over 60 major privatisation transactions. Lubos Tichy is well-known and has advised the Czech Ministry of Privatisation and Industry on privatisation policies. The firm advised Du Pont in connection with the acquisition of a Czech company and has a solid reputation in this field.

Vejmelka & Wünsch, v.o.s. helped Taylor Nelson Sofres buy a local market research company in a $375m deal.

REAL ESTATE AND CONSTRUCTION

Allen & Overy advised TK Development on a number of transactions including leases and on a refinancing facility of €47m, provided by Eurohypo Aktiengesellschaft to three TK subsidiaries. Other clients included WestLB, Landesbank Kiel, Skanska and Grontmij Vastgoed Ontwikkeling.

Weil, Gotshal & Manges maintains its top-tier status, though other firms have been poaching its team, with **CMS Cameron McKenna v.o.s.** luring away two senior lawyers on the team, formerly led by the well-known Evan Lazar, who himself moved to **Salans** to head up real estate and property finance, along with Eric Rosedale, who was recruited in January 2004 from **Weil, Gotshal & Manges**'s Warsaw office. At **CMS Cameron McKenna v.o.s.**, the work of managing partner Hilary McDowell is respected and she jointly heads a team of nine with partner Petr Skacel. New clients in the last year include Black & Decker, which received advice on the establishment of new plant north of Prague. As well as advising on corporate due diligence in the Lighthouse matter, the firm also advised Mayfield Holdings in the development of the Prague Gate hotel and office project.

White & Case represented CSOB, the largest Czech bank, in tenders for the development of its new headquarters. Pfizer is another client. The firm has a solid background in greenfield developments and has expanded its client base and advises foreign investors, including Japanese business people, who often deal with partner Kvetodlav Krejci, who speaks fluent Japanese. Newly appointed partner Monika Rutland is well respected.

Baker & McKenzie V.O.S. recruited M&A/real estate specialist Paul Vrany, formerly with **EY Law/Weinhold Legal**, and David Simonek, who was with **Kocián Solc Balastík**.

Balcar Polanský Norton Rose is also highly active in this area. The firm advised the Quinlan Partnership following its acquisition of the Four Seasons Hotel Prague from the Four Seasons group.

Brzobohatý Broz & Honsa took part in one of the largest development projects in the Czech Republic for TK Development Group, a Czech subsidiary of a Danish company, involving the sale of four shopping malls and business centres.

REAL ESTATE AND CONSTRUCTION

ALLEN & OVERY ✪
WEIL, GOTSHAL & MANGES ✪
WHITE & CASE

Baker & McKenzie V.O.S. ✪
Balcar Polanský Norton Rose
Brzobohatý Broz & Honsa ✪
CMS Cameron McKenna v.o.s.
Clifford Chance LLP
Havel & Holásek v.o.s., attorneys-at-law ✪
Peterka & Partners v.o.s ✪
Salans

Ambruz & Dark ✪
EY Law / Weinhold Legal
Gide Loyrette Nouel ✪
Giese & Partner
Glatzová & Co ✪
Gleiss Lutz ✪
Hogan & Hartson Advokátní Kancelare, v.o.s. ✪
Nörr Stiefenhofer Lutz ✪
Procházka Randl Kubr ✪
Sodomka Soucek Jindra Mokry & Partners ✪
Squire, Sanders & Dempsey, v.o.s., advokátní kancelár ✪
Vejmelka & Wünsch, v.o.s. ✪
Wolf Theiss ✪

Firms are listed A-Z in tiers which are ranked in order of priority
✪ Indicates firm displays contact details at the end of this chapter.

The nine-strong team at **Clifford Chance LLP**, led by partner William Knowles, advised Pricoa Property Investment Management on the acquisition of a portfolio of retail warehouses in Prague and Budapest from Skanska. It is one of a number of significant deals in 2003 which justifies an improvement in the ranking of the firm in this area. Emil Holub is recommended.

Havel & Holásek v.o.s., attorneys-at-law advised the Czech Airport Authority on the construction of the North II terminal at Prague-Ruzyne worth €330m. The firm also helped UK mall operator, Freeport draft lease agreements with 90 tenants and advised the Czech Ministry of Transport on the €5-6bn PPP construction of the D47 motorway, and Sumitomo Light Metal Industries on the construction of a plant worth €10m in the Benatky nad Jizerou industrial zone The firm specialises in PPP and its ranks were boosted in 2003 by the arrival of Michael Mullen from **White & Case**, who brought several engineering and manufacturing clients with him. It boasts a good proportion of experienced US lawyers, which it sees as a competitive advantage, and its links with Deloitte Touche Tohmatsu have led to good representation within the Japanese business community in the Czech Republic. The firm is unusual in having a Japanese desk.

Peterka & Partners v.o.s advised a French developer and a Dutch supermarket chain on the acquisition of unrelated land plots in the centre of Prague for new offices and commercial premises. Some 80% of its fee-earners speak French and the firm has a high proportion of French clients. Unusually for a Czech firm, it also has a branch in the Slovak capital, Bratislava.

Salans moves up a tier thanks to the lateral hires described above.

TAX

LINKLATERS ✪
WHITE & CASE

Allen & Overy ✪
Baker & McKenzie V.O.S. ✪
Nörr Stiefenhofer Lutz ✪

Procházka Randl Kubr ✪
Salans

Firms are listed A-Z in tiers which are ranked in order of priority
✪ Indicates firm displays contact details at the end of this chapter.

TAX

A lot of work is being generated in this area as EU accession approaches. Specialist tax advisers are being recruited and trained.

Linklaters is trying to replicate the success of its tax practice in its other CEE offices, but has lost some senior personnel in this field in the process, including tax partner Henk Goosen. That said, the firm continues to offer market-leading tax capability.

Ales Cechel joined **White & Case** from Arthur Andersen along with ten colleagues and continues to provide an excellent service to clients in this area. Tax manager, Ales Zidek is highly regarded by clients and has recently advised Eurotel, the largest Czech mobile phone operator.

Allen & Overy has been boosted by the arrival of Petr Guth, a qualified Czech tax adviser formerly with **Linklaters**. He was seconded recently for three months to the Stuttgart office specifically to broaden his experience of the practical effects of EU law. This is part of the firm's wider strategic plan to develop its expertise in this area.

Baker & McKenzie V.O.S. has built up its tax practice with the recruitment of Martin Kopecky, formerly of Deloitte & Touche. Last year the firm attracted five high-profile new clients, including Wm Wrigley Jr Company, Lindab AB, France Télécom, Lucent Technology and Emerson Electric.

Nörr Stiefenhofer Lutz is another firm with a strong and respected tax practice, and regularly gets involved in major cross-border and local transactions.

Procházka Randl Kubr handled a complex tax driven demerger for a leading international real estate developer.

BAKER & McKENZIE V.O.S.

PRAHA CITY CENTRE
KLIMENTSKÁ 46
110 02 PRAGUE 1

Telephone: +420 236 045 001
Fax: +420 236 045 055
E-mail: borys.dackiw@bakernet.com
Website: www.bakernet.com

Languages
English, French, German, Russian
Slovak, Spanish, Ukrainian

Other offices
For a list of all offices and other information regarding the firm please consult Baker & McKenzie's London office entry

Number of lawyers 3,380
at this office 20

Contacts
Borys Dackiw, Alexandr César

Baker & McKenzie is a global law firm with 66 offices in 36 countries.

CATEGORIES OF WORK

Arbitration and dispute resolution

Banking and finance

Bankruptcy and corporate restructuring

Capital markets

Competition law

Derivatives

Employment

Environmental

EU law

Financial instruments and investment funds

General corporate and commercial

Intellectual property

Litigation

Mergers and acquisitions

Project finance

Privatisation

Real estate

Securities

Tax

Telecommunications

Venture capital

BRZOBOHATÝ BROŽ & HONSA

KLIMENTSKÁ 1207/10
110 00 PRAGUE 1

Telephone: +420 234 091 355
Fax: +420 234 091 366
E-mail: legal@bbh.cz
Website: www.bbh.cz

Languages
Czech, English, French, German, Russian, Slovak, Spanish

Number of lawyers 29

CATEGORIES OF WORK

Banking and finance
Tomáš Brzobohatý, Tomáš Otruba

Capital markets
Tomáš Otruba

Mergers and acquisitions
Josef Brož

Dispute resolution
František Honsa, Vladimír Uhde

Commercial property and real estate
Jan Petřík

Insurance
Tomáš Brzobohatý

Corporate and commercial
Hana Ižovská

Insolvency and corporate restructuring
Josef Brož

Information technology
Jan Petřík

Competition
Jiří Němec

Fraud and white-collar crime
František Honsa, Vladimír Uhde

Media and entertainment
Vladimír Uhde

Energy and natural resources
Jiří Němec

ČERMÁK HOŘEJŠ MYSLIL

LAWYERS AND PATENT ATTORNEYS

NÁRODNÍ 32
110 00 PRAHA 1

Telephone: +420 296 167 111
Fax: +420 224 946 724
E-mail: intelprop@apk.cz
Website: www.cermakhorejsmyslil.cz

Languages
English, French, German, Russian, Slovak, Swedish

Number of lawyers 20

Contact
Dr Karel Čermák

Member
Interleges; AIPPI; LIDC; INTA; LES; TAGLaw;

International groupings
In association with Bušvová Ursínyová Bušŏ Bratislava, Slovak Republic

CATEGORIES OF WORK

Intellectual property
Dr Karel Čermák, Dr Jan Matějka

Pharmaceuticals
Dr Karel Čermák Jr, Dr David Štros

Unfair competition
Dr Karel Čermák, Almut Rohnstock

Commercial/corporate
Dr Ing Richard Myslil,
Dr Stanislav Myslil

Construction and tax
Dr Karel Čermák Jr

Mergers and acquisitions
Dr Karel Čermák Jr, Dr Ing Richard Myslil

Competition
Dr Ing Richard Myslil

Commercial litigation
Mgr Michal Hanko, Dr Stanislav Myslil

Dispute resolution – litigation and arbitration
Dr Karel Čermák Jr, Dr Stanislav Myslil

E-commerce and Government business/regulatory
Dr Karel Čermák Jr

Environment
Dr Antonín Křížek

Foreign direct investment and privatisation
Dr Stanislav Myslil

Information technology
Dr David Štros

Insolvency, corporate restructuring
Dr Ing Richard Myslil

Labour law
Dr Ing Richard Myslil, Mgr Michal Hanko

Private client
Dr Jan Matějka

THE FIRM

The legal firm Čermák Hořejš Myslil was established in 1990 but for over 40 years some partners of the firm have specialised in the fields of industrial and intellectual property law and international commercial law. The firm compromises approximately 20 in-house lawyers, four patent attorneys and approximately 40 specialised and administrative employees, including legal and technical translators and a number of experienced and specially educated (through the Institute of Industrial-Legal Education and Industrial Property Office) trade mark and patent officers.

Through its Slovak associates Bušová Ursiínyová Bušo it provides all kinds of legal services in Slovakia.

AREAS OF PRACTICE

The firm has a long tradition and extensive experience in providing legal services in the fields of arbitration, industrial and other intellectual property law, commercial law, company law and foreign investment. In the patent area, it has experts in all technical fields, ranging from mechanical engineering to biotechnology. It also has experience in some specialised fields related to intellectual property, such as pharmaceuticals, foods tariffs, domain name disputes, and technical standards, including litigation. It is this tradition and experience that have made Čermák Hořejš Myslil one of the most highly demanded firms for representation within these legal fields by Czech and Slovak, as well as foreign and supranational, clientele.

DLA WEISS-TESSBACH

MÁNESOVA 5
120 00 PRAHA

Telephone: +420 2 2423 4413
Fax: +420 2 2224 6065
E-mail: praha@dla.com
Website: www.dla.com

Languages
English, French, German, Hungarian, Italian, Russian, Slovak

Other offices
Amsterdam, Antwerp, Bangkok, Bergen, Berlin, Birmingham, Bradford, Bratislava, Brussels, Budapest, Cologne, Copenhagen, Edinburgh, Essen, Frankfurt, Glasgow, Hamburg, Hong Kong, Leeds, Liverpool, London, Madrid, Manchester, Milan, Moscow, Oslo, Paris, Rotterdam, Salzberg, Sarajevo, Shanghai, Sheffield, Singapore, Stockholm, Vienna, Zagreb

Number of lawyers 82
at this office 11

Contact
Jörg Nürnberger

Member
DLA Group

CATEGORIES OF WORK

Corporate	Financing
Mergers and aquisitions	Real estate
Intellectual property	General commercial

THE FIRM

Weiss-Tessbach was established in 1878 and is one of the longest-established law firms in Austria. 15 years ago, the firm decided on an extremely dynamic development. Since 1990, the number of lawyers at the firm has increased more than four times from 15 to over 80, and the number of offices from one to seven. On October 1st 2003, Weiss-Tessbach was integrated with DLA on the basis of a shared vision to become a top five full-service European law firm. With its current offices in six central and eastern European countries, DLA Weiss-Tessbach will continue to expand into the region at a time of EU accession for many countries.

DLA Weiss-Tessbach is part of DLA Group. DLA Group is an exclusive alliance of international full-service law firms with a shared vision. Established in 1999, DLA Group now has over 2,200 lawyers across 21 countries, who deliver expert local know-how and international solutions. DLA Group provides legal advice in 37 major cities across Europe, Singapore, Thailand, Hong Kong and the People's Republic of China.

AREAS OF PRACTICE

The firm has strengthened its core areas of expertise (commercial and corporate, M&A, banking and finance, intellectual property, real estate), and has expanded into other areas of law (administrative, employment, telecoms, technology, venture capital). Today, the firm is able to assist its corporate clients in all aspects of their activities.

DLA Weiss-Tessbach has well-established relations with clients of various backgrounds. The firm advises small and medium-sized enterprises as well as leading (often publicly listed) international and domestic industrial groups, service providers, banks and other financial institutions and individuals.

DLA Weiss-Tessbach has established a particular reputation for its ability to handle cases in international cross-border contexts. It carefully views the ongoing developments in central Europe with the aim of combining the needs of the constantly changing international legal market and industry, whilst also upholding the high-standard services that the firm has always been able to offer to its clients.

DEWEY BALLANTINE VOS

ADRIA PALACE - 5TH FLOOR
JUNGMANNOVA 31
110 00 PRAHA 1

Telephone: +420 224 990 000
Fax: +420 224 990 001
E-mail: pkotrlik@deweyballantine.com
Website: www.deweyballantine.com

Languages
Czech, Danish, English, French, German, Slovak

Other offices
Austin, Budapest, East Palo Alto, Frankfurt, Houston, London, Los Angeles, Milan, New York, Rome, Warsaw, Washington DC

Number of lawyers 606
at this office 9

Contact
Petr Kotrlík

CATEGORIES OF WORK

- Mergers and acquisitions
- Competition
- Litigation
- General corporate law
- Privatisations
- Joint ventures
- Banking and capital markets
- Intellectual property
- Project finance
- International trade
- Energy and natural resources
- Telecommunications
- Environmental law
- Real estate

EISELSBERG NATLACEN WALDERDORFF CANCOLA V.O.S

U PRAŠNÉ BRÁNY 1
110 00 PRAHA 1

Telephone: +420 224 819 216
Fax: +420 224 819 217
E-mail: prag@enwc.com
Website: www.enwc.com

Languages
English, French, German, Hungarian, Italian

Other offices
Budapest, Vienna

Number of lawyers 39
at this office 7

Contacts
Dr Georg Walderdorff, Dr Erwin Hanslik

CATEGORIES OF WORK

- Company and commercial
- Banking and finance
- Intellectual property
- Labour and employment
- Mergers and acquisitions
- Real estate
- International arbitration and litigation
- Construction and building
- EU and competition

FELIX A SPOL

U NIKOLAJKY 5
150 00 PRAGUE 5

Telephone: +420 251 081 111
Fax: +420 251 081 122
E-mail: akfelix@akfelix.cz
Website: www.akfelix.cz

Languages
Czech, English, German, Polish, Russian, Slovak

Number of lawyers 20

Member
NOMOS Group

CATEGORIES OF WORK

- Banking, finance, securities
- Commercial property, real estate
- Competition and trade
- Corporate and commercial
- Construction and building
- Dispute resolution
- Employment, pensions, benefits
- Foreign direct investment
- Fraud and white-collar crime
- Insolvency, restructuring
- Intellectual property and IT
- Mergers and acquisitions
- Private client
- Shipping and transport
- Tax

GIDE LOYRETTE NOUEL

KRAKOVSKÁ 9
110 00 PRAGUE 1

Telephone: +420 222 871 111
Fax: +420 222 871 112
Website: www.gide.com
Email: gln.prague@gide.com

Other offices
Algiers, Beijing, Brussels, Bucharest, Budapest, Casablanca, Hanoi, Istanbul, London, Moscow, New York, Paris, Riyadh, Shanghai, Tunis, Warsaw

Number of lawyers 480
at this office 14

Contact
François Veit (veit@gide.com)

CATEGORIES OF WORK

- Foreign investment
- Company
- Mergers and acquisitions
- Restructuring
- Joint ventures
- Real estate transactions and financing
- Banking and finance
- Privatisation
- Intellectual property
- Labour
- Litigation and arbitration

GLATZOVÁ & CO

BETLÉMSKY PALÁC
HUSOVA 5
111 00 PRAGUE

Telephone: +420 224 401 440
Fax: +420 224 248 701-2
E-mail: office@glatzova.com
Website: www.glatzova.com

Languages
English, French, German, Russian

Number of lawyers 26

CATEGORIES OF WORK

Utility law
Vít Horácek, Renáta Zbranková

M&A
Vladimíra Glatzová,
Dana Schweigelová

Banking and financial markets
Vladimíra Glatzová,
Dana Schweigelová

Telecoms and IT
Vít Horácek

Real estate
Vít Horácek, Gabriel Archour

Anti-monopoly
Vít Horácek, Vlastilav Kusák

Labour
Vít Horácek, Renáta Zbranková

General commercial
Vladimíra Glatzová, Renáta Zbranková

Insurance
Vladimíra Glatzová,
Dana Schweigelová

Arbitration and litigation
Vít Horácek

THE FIRM

Glatzová & Co was founded in 1994 by Dr Vladimíra Glatzová as a solo practitionership. Since that time, the firm has expanded in size to 26 attorneys and has come to be regarded as one of the leading commercial law firms in the Czech Republic. In 1996, Dr Vit Horácek was appointed as a partner of the firm. In 2002, Renáta Zbranková LLM also became a partner of Glatzová & Co.

Glatzová & Co is recognised as a top law firm in a number of practice areas. In the online *European Legal 500* and *IFLR Guide to the World's Leading International Business Law Firms* as well as *Global Counsel 3000,* it is ranked as a recommended Czech firm in the areas of M&A, privatisation, real estate, joint ventures, banking and finance and capital markets. Its partners and senior associates are listed in other specialist publications among the world's leading lawyers in the areas of M&A, privatisation, real estate and corporate finance. The principal clients of the firm are major Western investors or their Czech subsidiaries across a large number of commercial sectors, including the pharmaceutical, steel, energy, technology, financial services, healthcare, real estate, global communications and manufacturing industries. The following companies are representative: Africa Israel Group, Arag, Allianz, Broadnet, Buderus, Cinergy, Citibank, DEPFA Bank (Aareal Bank), Deutsche Bank, EBRD, E. ON, Erste Bank, Ford, Gaz de France, Hermes, LIDL, LNM (Ispat), National Fuel Gas, ONDEO Services (formerly Lyonnaise des Eaux), Renault, Rockwool, Telekom Austria, Volvo and Warburg Pincus Venture Capital.

Glatzová & Co enjoys a reputation for the technical excellence of its lawyers, who are known for their sensitivity to clients' commercial objectives, their multi-jurisdictional experience and training and their strong links with major Western European and North American law firms.

AREAS OF PRACTICE

The firm offers advice on cross-border and domestic transactions and operations to businesses, financiers, governmental bodies, international organisations and private individuals. The principal areas of work are listed above with attorneys to contact. The firm has also recently established EU law specialist groups in all practice areas.

One of the chief areas of work is the handling of anti-monopoly/competition matters. The firm has co-ordinated the Czech approval of many significant multinational mergers and also participated in the filing and defence of complaints against competitors. In recent years, it has been instrumental in securing the domestic authorisation of mergers including LNM Steel Group/Nová Hut; Léčivá a.s/Slovakofarma a.s; E.ON/Ruhrgas A.S.; Bayer AG/Hoescht AG/BASF AG/RWE AG/VEW AG; and Brenntag AG/Stinnes AG. Glatzová & Co is also active in regulatory issues in the telecom and energy sectors, including representation of alternative telecoms against the legacy provider and the issue of public subsidies across many commercial areas.

Glatzová & Co's corporate practice is experienced in all stages of M&A transactions from due diligence through to transaction structuring, drafting and negotiation of complex purchase, off-take restructuring and relationship agreements, closure and post-closure requirements. It has acted in a wide range of utilities and terrestrial, cable and satellite broadcasting company transactions.

The firm's real estate practice represents international investors, architects, resort owners, construction companies, property developers and others in connection with the acquisition and sale of real estate, project development, architectural and construction work, retail and leisure schemes, joint ventures, greenfield projects, leasing and related litigation. The firm was the first to introduce a legal framework for time-sharing schemes in the Czech Republic.

Detailed brochures regarding individual practice areas are available.

GLEISS LUTZ
RECHTSANWÄLTE

JUGOSLÁVSKÁ 29
120 00 PRAGUE 2

Telephone: +420 224 007 500
Fax: +420 224 007 555
E-mail: info@gleisslutz.com
Website: www.gleisslutz.com

Languages
Cantonese, Dutch, English, French, German, Italian, Mandarin, Polish, Portuguese, Russian, Spanish, Slovak

Other offices
Berlin, Brussels, Frankfurt, Munich, Stuttgart, Warsaw

Number of lawyers 200
at this office 15

Contact
Dr Ivo Nesrovnal LLM

CATEGORIES OF WORK

Czech, Slovak and international practice

Banking, securities and finance

Commercial law (general)

Companies, corporations

Competition, antitrust

Employment, labour

Environment and pollution control

Mergers and acquisitions

Tax

Trade marks, intellectual property

HAARMANN HEMMELRATH

PALÁC MYSLBEK
OVOCNÝ TRH 8
110 00 PRAGUE 1

Telephone: +420 224 490 000
Fax: +420 224 490 033
E-mail:
prague@haarmannhemmelrath.com
Website:
www.haarmannhemmelrath.com

Languages
English, French, German, Italian, Russian, Slovak, Vietnamese

Other offices
Berlin, Bielefeld, Brussels, Bucharest, Budapest, Cologne, Dusseldorf, Frankfurt, Hamburg, Leipzig, London, Milan, Moscow, Munich, Paris, Rome, Shanghai, Singapore, Stuttgart, Tokyo, Vienna, Warsaw

Number of lawyers 281
at this office 17

CATEGORIES OF WORK

Corporate and business law
Pavel Vincík, Arthur Braun

Mergers and acquisitions, reorganisations
Arthur Braun, Dr Thu Nga Haškovcova

IP, antitrust, EU, media
Olga Cervinkova

Real estate transactions
Dr Thu Nga Haskovcova, Arthur Braun

Environmental and energy law
Olga Cervinkova

Labour law
Dr Stepanka Wiesnerova

International tax law
Ian Rowbotham

Czech tax law
Jitka Kolarova

Corporate finance, banking, leasing
Dr Thu Nga Haškovcova

Computer/Internet law
Hedvika Hartmanova

Litigation/arbitration
Hedvika Hartmanova

HAVEL & HOLÁSEK V.O.S., ATTORNEYS-AT-LAW

TYN 1049/3
110 00 PRAGUE 1

Telephone: +420 224 895 950
Fax: +420 224 895 980
E-mail: office@havelholasek.cz
Website: www.havelholasek.cz

Languages
English, Czech, French, German, Slovak

Number of lawyers 21

CATEGORIES OF WORK

Banking and finance
Jaroslav Havel, Robert Nešpůrek

Bankruptcy
Jaroslav Havel, Marek Vojáček

Corporate
Jaroslav Havel, Tomáš Kučírek

Commercial transactions
Jaroslav Havel, Robert Nešpůrek

Due diligence
Jaroslav Havel, Michael Mullen

EC law
Robert Nešpůrek

Economic competition
Tomaš Kučírek, Robert Nešpůrek

Employment
Jaroslav Havel, Daniel Zejda

Engineering and construction
Jan Holásek, Michael Mullen

Greenfield projects
Jan Holásek, Michael Mullen

Intellectual property
Robert Nešpůrek, Michael Mullen

Joint ventures and foreign investment
Jan Holásek, Michael Mullen

Mergers and acquisitions
Jaroslav Havel, Tomaš Kučirek

Public private partnerships
Jaroslav Havel, Robert Nešpůrek

Public tenders and procurement
Jan Holásek, Daniel Zejda

Real estate
Jan Holásek, Josef Hlavička

Securities
Robert Nešpůrek, Marek Vojáček

Telecommunications and media
Robert Nešpůrek

HOGAN & HARTSON
ADVOKÁTNÍ KANCELAŘE, V.O.S.

TRŽIŠTĚ 13
118 00 PRAGUE 1

Telephone: +420 222 117 111
Fax: +420 222 117 222
E-mail: mlovisek@hhlaw.com
Website: www.hhlaw.com

Languages
English, French, German, Russian, Slovak

Other offices
Baltimore, Beijing, Berlin, Boulder, Brussels, Budapest, Colorado Springs, Denver, London, Los Angeles, McLean, Miami, Moscow, Munich, New York, Paris, Tokyo, Warsaw, Washington DC

Number of lawyers 1,018
at this office 8

Contacts
Milan Lovisek, Jan Tanzer

CATEGORIES OF WORK

Mergers, acquisitions and divestitures

Company formation and corporate counselling

Privatisations

Corporate and project finance

Joint ventures and strategic alliances

Competition

Real estate

Intellectual property

E-commerce

Technology transfer

Telecommunications

Media

Not-for-profit organisations

HOLEC & PARTNERS

VÁCLAVSKÉ NÁMĚSTÍ 2-4
110 00 PRAHA 1

Telephone: +420 2 96 325 235
Fax: +42 0 296 325 240
E-mail: recepce@holec-advokati.cz
Website: www.holec-advokati.cz

Languages
English, German, Russian, Slovak

Number of lawyers 15

Contacts
Pavel Holec, Karel Zuska, Lubomir Lansky, Petr Holec

Holec & Partners is in co-operation with The Federation of Law Firms with over 3,000 lawyers worldwide.

CATEGORIES OF WORK

General corporate	Competition
Commercial transactions	Privatisations
Real estate law	Joint ventures
Construction law	Trade law
Insolvency and bankruptcy	Sports law
Financial products	Labour law
Banking law	Telecommunications law, IT
Capital markets	Project financing
Securities law	Administrative matters
International business	International and domestic dispute resolution
Mergers and acquisitions	

LINKLATERS

PALÁC MYSLBEK
NA PŘÍKOPĚ 19
117 19 PRAGUE 1

Telephone: +420 221 622 111
Fax: +420 221 622 199
Website: www.linklaters.com

Languages
Czech, Dutch, English, French, German

Other offices
Alicante, Amsterdam, Antwerp, Bangkok, Beijing, Berlin, Bratislava, Brussels, Bucharest, Budapest, Cologne, Frankfurt am Main, Hong Kong, Lisbon, London, Luxembourg, Madrid, Milan, Moscow, Munich, New York, Paris, Rome, São Paulo, Shanghai, Singapore, Stockholm, Tokyo, Warsaw

Number of lawyers 2,000 worldwide

Contacts
Francis Kucera

CATEGORIES OF WORK

Mergers and acquisitions/corporate
Luděk Vrána, Lukas Sevcik

Corporate reorganisations/privatisations
Luděk Vrána, Lukas Sevcik

Commercial
Luděk Vrána

Competition
Luděk Vrána

Banking and capital markets
Francis Kucera

Project finance
Francis Kucera

Private equity/venture capital and foreign investment
Lukas Sevcik

Real estate
Klára Štěpánková

Intellectual property
Luděk Vrána

Telecoms, media and entertainment
Luděk Vrána

Tax
Ton Kemp

Employment
Luděk Vrána

Energy
Luděk Vrána

Insolvency
Luděk Vrána

Arbitration
Luděk Vrána

THE FIRM

Linklaters advises the world's leading companies, financial institutions and governments on their most challenging transactions and assignments. With 2,000 lawyers, including 470 partners, and offices in major business and financial centres, its clients choose the firm for its distinctive combination of technical skill, commercial experience and outstanding service.

Linklaters has built a formidable global practice through organic growth and a series of mergers, joint ventures and co-operations with other respected law firms. In 2001 Linklaters merged with three of Europe's leading law firms to form Linklaters Oppenhoff & Rädler in Germany, Linklaters in Sweden, Linklaters De Bandt in Belgium and Linklaters Loesch in Luxembourg. In the same year, the firm formed a co-operation with Brazilian firm Goulart Penteado, Iervolino e Lefosse. This cooperation combines Linklaters' international capability with GPIL's extensive knowledge of the Brazilian market. In Singapore the firm practises as Linklaters Allen & Gledhill, a joint venture with the premier Singapore practice of Allen & Gledhill. While in Italy, Linklaters has a preferred relationship with the law firm Gianni, Origoni, Grippo & Partners.

LOVELLS

SLOVANSKÝ DŮM
NA PŘÍKOPĚ 22
110 00 PRAHA 1

Telephone: +420 221 411 700
Fax: +420 224 210 004
E-mail: information@lovells.com
Website: www.lovells.com

Languages
English, French, German, Russian, Spanish

Other offices
Alicante, Amsterdam, Beijing, Berlin, Brussels, Budapest*, Chicago, Düsseldorf, Frankfurt, Hamburg, Ho Chi Minh City, Hong Kong, London, Milan, Moscow, Munich, New York, Paris, Rome, Shanghai, Singapore, Tokyo, Vienna*, Warsaw, Zagreb*

Number of lawyers 1,600
at this office 14

Contact
Tomas Bettelheim

CATEGORIES OF WORK

- Banking and capital markets
- Dispute resolution
- Intellectual property and competition issues
- Mergers and acquisitions
- Project finance
- Technology transfers and franchising
- Commercial and other property-related services
- Environmental law and regulations
- Joint ventures
- Privatisation
- Public tenders

NÖRR STIEFENHOFER LUTZ

NA PŘÍKOPĚ 15
110 00 PRAGUE 1

Telephone: +420 233 112 111
Fax: +420 233 112 112
E-mail: nslprg@noerr.cz
Website: www.noerr.cz

Languages
English, French, German, Russian, Slovak, Spanish

Other offices
Berlin, Bucharest, Budapest, Dresden, Düsseldorf, Frankfurt, Moscow, Munich, Warsaw

Number of lawyers 237
(+ 53 tax advisers, public accountants and tax assistants)
at this office 18
(+ 14 tax advisers, public accountants and tax assistants)

Contacts
Jaroslav Melzer, Libor Prokes

CATEGORIES OF WORK

- Mergers and acquisitions, joint ventures, corporate reorganisations (MBO, MBI)
- General corporate practice
- Privatisation, greenfield investment
- Banking, project finance and capital markets
- Intellectual property and unfair competition
- Real estate, commercial property, construction
- Media and entertainment
- General commercial practice (agency, franchising, distribution, leasing)
- Labour and employment
- Telecoms and IT
- Pharmaceuticals
- Energy and mining
- Tax
- Litigation and arbitration

PETERKA & PARTNERS v.o.s

NA PŘÍKOPĚ 15
110 00 PRAGUE 1

Telephone: +420 272 143 400
Fax: +420 272 143 470
E-mail: office@cabinet.cz
Website: www.cabinet.cz

Languages
Czech, English, French, German, Slovak, Spanish, Russian

Other offices
Bratislava

Number of lawyers 40
at this office 27

Member
TerraLex®; International Lawyers Network (ILN)

CATEGORIES OF WORK

Company and commercial
Ondřej Peterka

Mergers and acquisitions
Ondřej Peterka

Competition law
Ondřej Peterka

Real estate development and construction
Pavla Přikrylova

Litigation and arbitration
Jiří Černý

Intellectual property
Hynek Peroutka

Labour law
Hynek Peroutka

Securities and finance
Jan Liška

Tax law
Magdaléna Vyškovská

Bankruptcy law
Hynek Peroutka

IT, finance
Jan Liška

International law
Ondřej Peterka

European law
Hynek Peroutka

THE FIRM

Peterka & Partners v.o.s was founded in 2000 by Mr Ondřej Peterka, attorney-at-law, and since then has grown into a respected and distinctive mid-sized, full-service Czech-origin law office on the emerging markets of central and eastern Europe. Its current two offices are based in Prague, the Czech Republic and Bratislava, Slovakia.

The firm's success, to a large degree, can be attributed to the leadership of Mr Ondřej Peterka, a member of the Paris Bar and the Czech Bar, and the team he has built and trained. The majority of the firm's lawyers have attended long-term studies abroad and practised within other national and international law offices, both in the Czech and Slovak Republics, as well as in countries of the European Union.
Peterka & Partners v.o.s attorneys' skills in providing legal services are greatly enhanced by their excellent knowledge of major world languages – particularly French and English – as well as persistent adherence to the shared vision of high work standards and ethics. The team at Peterka & Partners v.o.s is efficient and its goal is always to find an optimum solution for the clients' needs.

AREAS OF PRACTICE

The firm's areas of practice relate to activities of key foreign investors in the Czech and Slovak Republics. Fourteen of its clients are listed on the Paris, Frankfurt, London and New York stock exchanges, but the firm also advises many domestic clients – individuals, companies and institutions of major importance.

The firm specialises mainly in the following areas of law: mergers and acquisitions, corporate and commercial law, real estate development and construction law, litigation and arbitration, bankruptcy law, competition law, intellectual property law, labour law, securities, finance law and tax advising, IT, European and international law.

For detailed information about the law office, please see the following web sites: www.cabinet.cz or www.cabinet.sk. Different printed materials are available on request.

PROCHÁZKA RANDL KUBR

JÁCHYMOVA 2
110 00 PRAHA 1

Telephone: +42 221 430 111
Fax: +42 224 235 450
E-mail: office@prkadvo.cz
Website: www.prkadvo.cz

Languages
English, French, German, Russian

Number of lawyers 32

Contacts
Daniel Rosicky, Pavel Randl

Member
Lex Mundi

CATEGORIES OF WORK

Banking

Capital markets

Corporate

Intellectual property

Infrastructure

Merger control

Labour

Mergers and acquisitions

Joint ventures

Restructuring

Real estate

SODOMKA SOUČEK JINDRA MOKRÝ AND PARTNERS

U PRAŠNÉ BRÁNY 3
110 00 PRAHA 1

Telephone: +420 224 481 624
Fax: +420 222 328 205
E-mail: advokati@akssjm.cz
Website: www.akssjm.cz

Languages
English, French, German, Italian, Russian, Slovak

Other offices
Karlovy Vary

Number of lawyers 26

CATEGORIES OF WORK

Corporate and business law
Dr Tomáš Jindra, Dr Jan Souček

Intellectual property
Dr Jaroslav Sodomka,
Mrg Marek Bouček

Corporate acquisitions and mergers
Dr Jan Souček

Civil and commercial litigation
Dr Antonín Mokrý

Competition, antitrust
Dr Antonín Mokrý, Dr Adam Batuna

Unfair competition
Dr Jaroslav Sodomka,
Dr Tomáš Jindra

Banking and finance
Dr Jaroslav Sodomka,
Dr Tomáš Jindra

Contract law, joint ventures
Dr Jaroslav Sodomka,
Dr Tomáš Jindra

Real estate law
Dr Antonín Mokrý,
Mgr Kateřina Velková

Securities
Dr Jan Souček, Dr Adam Batuna

SQUIRE, SANDERS & DEMPSEY, V.O.S.,
ADVOKÁTNÍ KANCELÁŘ

VÁCLAVSKÉ NÁMĚSTÍ 57/813
110 00 PRAGUE 1

Telephone: +420 221 662 111
Fax: +420 221 662 222
E-mail: vpapirnik@ssd.com
Website: www.ssd.com

Languages
Danish, English, French, German, Russian, Slovak

Other offices
Beijing, Bratislava, Brussels, Budapest, Cincinnati, Cleveland, Columbus, Hong Kong, Houston, London, Los Angeles, Madrid, Miami, Milan, Moscow, New York, Palo Alto, Phoenix, Rio de Janeiro, San Francisco, Taipei, Tampa, Tokyo, Tysons Corner, Washington DC, Bucharest*, Dublin*, Kyiv*

Number of lawyers 710
at this office 20

Contact
Vladimira Papirnik

Member
American Chamber of Commerce; Association for Foreign Investment; Czech-French Chamber of Commerce

CATEGORIES OF WORK

Arbitration and litigation	Joint ventures
Banking and finance	International transactions
Bankruptcy and restructuring	Labour and employment
Competition law	Mergers and acquisitions
Corporate and commercial	Project finance
EU law	Real estate
Energy	Telecoms
Greenfield investments	Venture capital
Intellectual property	

THE FIRM

Founded in 1890, Squire, Sanders & Dempsey is a multi-jurisdictional law firm with 710 lawyers practising in offices in Europe, the Americas and Asia. The firm's practice covers most substantive areas of the law, with an emphasis on business and finance matters.

The firm operates as a single global partnership, which ensures client accountability and the seamless delivery of uniformly high-quality legal services throughout the world. The firm's lawyers come from many countries and cultures, are licensed to practise in both common law and civil law jurisdictions, and communicate with clients in their native languages. Today, the firm remains committed to the fundamental principles ordained by its founders: to serve clients effectively and maintain the professional standards that distinguish both the firm and its people.

Established in 1991, the Prague office provides a full range of legal services to Czech, foreign and multinational commercial clients. It maintains an extensive practice that utilises comprehensive international experience with essential local knowledge in a broad and varied transactional and financing practice. The office advises clients on complex transactions and restructurings in the Czech Republic and throughout Central and Eastern Europe, and works closely with the firm's Brussels and other Western European offices on matters involving EU law and the upcoming integration of the Czech Republic into the EU.

AREAS OF PRACTICE

The firm is organised around four major practice areas: advocacy, business, capital markets and regulated industries. Within these practice areas, the firm's work can be divided into numerous areas of specialisation, including banking, bankruptcy and restructuring, biotechnology and pharmaceuticals, communications, competition law, converging technologies, corporate, energy, environmental, healthcare, intellectual property, international dispute resolution, labour and employment, litigation, mergers and acquisitions, privatisations, project finance, real estate and securities.

The Prague office has extensive experience with foreign investment in the Czech Republic. It is one of the founding members of the Association for Foreign Investments, an organisation whose primary goal is to promote the Czech Republic abroad and to support CzechInvest, the Czech agency for foreign direct investment, in attracting foreign ventures. The office handles a variety of corporate matters and has extensive experience in the areas of privatisation transactions, mergers and acquisitions and greenfield investments, handling some of the most prominent transactions in the Czech Republic. In addition, the office's expansive real estate practice includes counselling foreign and domestic investors on a range of matters including acquisitions, financings and foreclosures.

In the financing field, the Prague office places a strong emphasis on lending and capital markets and represents clients including international lenders, borrowers, trustees, underwriters, credit enhancers and national and multinational development organisations in transactions ranging from commercial loans to project financing and asset-backed financing.

The Prague office specialises in international litigation and arbitration, representing clients in bilateral investment treaty arbitrations as well as in commercial disputes under all leading institutional rules including the ICC, UNCITRAL, LCIA, Stockholm and the Vienna Rules.

The firm's Prague lawyers are an integral part of the Czech legal community and are active in civic and business organisations including the American Chamber of Commerce in the Czech Republic.

VEJMELKA & WÜNSCH V.O.S.

ITALSKÁ 27
120 00 PRAHA 2

Telephone: +420 222 253 050
Fax: +420 222 253 090
E-mail: prague@vejwun.cz
Website: www.vejmelkawuensch.cz

Languages
Czech, English, German, Russian, Slovak
Swedish

Number of lawyers 25

Contacts
Josef Vejmelka, Peter Wünsch

CATEGORIES OF WORK

Corporate and M&A

Finance, banking and securities

Competition and trade

Intellectual property and IT

Tax

Real estate

Environmental planning and regulatory

Employment, pensions and benefits

Dispute resolution and arbitration

WEIL, GOTSHAL & MANGES

CHARLES BRIDGE CENTER
KRIZOVNICKÉ NÁM. 1
110 00 PRAGUE 1

Telephone: +420 221 407 300
Fax: +420 221 407 310
Website: www.weil.com

Other offices
Austin, Boston, Budapest, Brussels, Dallas, Frankfurt, Houston, London, Miami, Munich, New York, Paris, Silicon Valley, Singapore, Warsaw, Washington DC

Number of lawyers 1,000
at this office 28

Contact
Karel Muzikar

CATEGORIES OF WORK	
Banking	Mergers and acquisitions
Bankruptcy and restructuring	Private equity and venture capital
Capital markets	Privatisation
Litigation, dispute resolution	Real estate
IP and technology	Telecoms

THE FIRM

Established in 1931 in New York, Weil, Gotshal & Manges combines lawyers worldwide to meet clients' needs in recognition of the benefits of broad industry and regional experience. The lawyers in the firm's practice groups work together to provide full-service legal advice to clients in sectors as diverse as energy, financial services and hi-tech.

The firm developed a network of offices across the US in the 1970s and 1980s to cater for its expanding client base, and was one of the first international law firms to establish a major presence in central Europe. The firm now has established offices in Brussels, Budapest, Frankfurt, London, Paris, Prague, Singapore and Warsaw.

The firm advises a broad and diverse group of clients, including many of the largest and most prominent corporations and government agencies around the globe, and leading financial institutions.

AREAS OF PRACTICE

The firm's US and European antitrust practice advises on international M&A regulatory notifications, antitrust distribution counselling, cartels, litigation and government and state competition policy. Expertise includes software and computer, healthcare, telecommunications and media, transportation, utilities, heavy industry, consumer goods, financial services and sports.

The corporate department is the firm's largest. The department advises international financial institutions and corporate clients in complex public and private M&As, private equity deals and strategic alliances.

The firm's corporate governance practice is recognised as one of the pre-eminent counsellors of corporate boards, management and institutional investors on the full range of governance issues, including board composition, structure and processes; executive and director compensation; director responsibilities; internal and governmental investigations of alleged accounting or other corporate misconduct; and shareholder initiatives. The firm has advised the World Bank, the OECD, the European Commission and various stock exchanges and regulatory bodies, and is a leader in providing director training programmes worldwide.

The firm advises on a wide range of financing activities and has particular expertise in acquisition finance, asset-based finance, debt restructuring and insolvency, debt and equity capital markets, derivatives, high-yield debt, securitisation, structured finance and telecoms and multimedia financing.

The firm has a leading IP and technology practice and advises some of the world's major technology, media and telecommunications companies. It also acts for investors in technology, media and communications entities. The practice handles patent infringements, outsourcing transactions, strategic alliances, cross-border mergers and acquisitions, investments and IPOs, and advises on the protection and exploitation of IP and on a wide range of e-commerce matters, including data protection. It has expertise in regulatory telecoms matters.

The litigation practice advises international clients on all major areas of the law and has extensive experience in all aspects of dispute resolution. It advises clients in jury trials and appeals, arbitration and alternative dispute forums.

The firm's real estate practice handles complex real estate transactions (including finance, securitisations, development, leasing, sales, acquisitions and debt restructurings) across the US and Europe. It also advises clients on real estate M&A transactions involving real estate investment trusts.

The firm has one of the largest bankruptcy and business reorganisation practices in the world. It includes attorneys in New York, Boston, Dallas, Frankfurt, Houston, London and Miami. The department has been involved in virtually all of the major chapter 11 reorganisation cases in the US and in major national and international out-of-court debt restructurings.

The tax department provides advice on international and domestic taxation, covering many different economic sectors. The department works with the firm's other departments to find innovative solutions to problems that present various and competing multi-disciplinary considerations.

WOLF THEISS
ATTORNEYS AT LAW

KLIMENTSKÁ 10
110 00 PRAHA 1

Telephone: +420 251 018 611
Fax: +420 251 018 625
E-mail: praha@wolftheiss.com
Website: www.wolftheiss.com

Languages
English, French, German, Russian

Other offices
Bratislava, Vienna, Belgrade, Ljubljana, Zagreb

Number of lawyers 98
at this office 11

Contacts
Paul Sestak, Erik Steger

CATEGORIES OF WORK

- Antitrust and competition
- Corporate and M&A
- Banking, capital markets, securities, project finance, investment funds
- Litigation and arbitration
- Employment and labour
- Tax and insurance
- Real estate, construction and leases
- Distribution, franchising
- IP and trade marks
- Infrastructure
- Contract and commercial
- European law
- Telecoms and energy
- Public procurement
- Pharmaceuticals
- Eastern Europe

THE FIRM

Wolf Theiss, founded in 1957, stands among the leading law firms in Central Europe, with a concentration on Austrian, European and international business law, and additional expertise in the legal regimes of Central and Eastern Europe.

At its six locations, in Vienna, Prague, Belgrade, Bratislava, Ljubljana and Zagreb, a total of 200 people, including 98 lawyers (42 of whom are partners), work for Austrian and international client companies in industry, trade and services, as well as banking and insurance. At the point of contact between law and business, Wolf Theiss develops innovative solutions on the basis of legal, tax and business know-how.

DENMARK

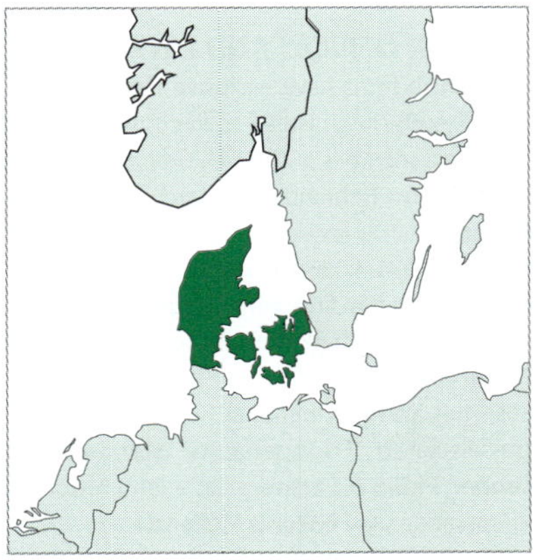

Population	5.37 million
Number of lawyers	4,300
Professional title	Advokat
Currency	Danish krone (DKr)

Index

In terms of area and population, Denmark is one of the smallest countries in Western Europe. Lying just North of Germany, it is the geographical gateway between continental Europe and the rest of Scandinavia. This link was made even stronger since the completion of the Øresund road and rail bridge in 2000, connecting Denmark with mainland Sweden. Flanked to the West by the North Sea and to the East by the Baltic, the Jutland peninsula makes up most of Denmark, of which the remainder stretches across more than 400 islands, Funen and Zealand being the two largest. While Jutland is the main industrial zone and home to the country's second city, Aarhus, Copenhagen, the capital, and main commercial centre, is on the island of Zealand. Denmark's third city, Odense, is on Funen Island.

Historically, Denmark is Europe's oldest kingdom, and its rulers held sway over much of Scandinavia for long periods of time. Its influence over the Nordic region may have diminished but Denmark still holds strong cultural, economic and political links with both Norway and Sweden.

BILLING

Billing rates in Denmark are generally quite reasonable, with hourly rates ranging from about €350 for a senior partner, down to around €150 for an assistant. Rates vary from firm to firm, and most clients agree that Denmark's largest law firms, collectively known as the Big Four, are more expensive than their smaller rivals.

MARKETING

The Danish Bar Association forbids direct marketing to clients, though firms are allowed to advertise how they wish. Generally the Danish legal market is still quite conservative and many firms do not put a very high emphasis on marketing, though this is slowly starting to change.

IN-HOUSE LAWYERS

Denmark has over 450 in-house lawyers and most of its largest companies have sizeable in-house teams. It is not uncommon for in-house lawyers to move into private practice and vice versa, and many firms will second lawyers to favoured clients.

ECONOMIC AND POLITICAL CLIMATE

Denmark has a minority coalition government, which lies firmly to the right of centre. Principally made up of the Liberal Party and the Conservative People's Party, the coalition is heavily influenced by the populist Danish People's Party, which enjoys a lot of leverage within Denmark's unicameral parliament (Folketing). This has led to stricter immigration policies, but also a greater investment in the welfare state and increased fiscal spending. The next general election can be held no later than November 2005.

The majority of Denmark's commercial sector is made up of small to medium-sized companies, which are often family owned. Of the country's largest companies, only a handful have more than 1,000 employees. For its part, the public sector remains the largest single employer, accounting for around one-third of its workforce. The service industry accounts for about 73% of GDP, while the industrial sector makes up a quarter. Agriculture, on the other hand, accounts for just 2% of the economy.

Denmark's economy is very dependent on foreign trade. The country has close links with mainland Europe and is a founding member of the European Free Trade Association and a member of the EU, although a national referendum in 2000 decided against adopting the euro.

The impact of the global economic downturn has not been as evident in Denmark as it has in other European countries. Nevertheless, growth has slowed quite considerably and is not expected to exceed 2.1% in 2004. The markets have been extremely quiet and M&A work has been minimal, although this is slowly starting to turn the corner. On the whole, it is consumer confidence that is the main impetus for growth.

LEGAL SYSTEM

While the English legal system is based on common law, Denmark's is based on statute. Before becoming lawyers, law school graduates must go through a three-year traineeship at a firm, followed by a Bar exam that must be passed before trainees are granted admission by the Minister of Justice. There is no distinction between barristers and solicitors in Denmark, though to gain rights of audience before the High Court, lawyers must have experience in the District Courts. To appear before the Supreme Court requires at least five years of experience in the High Court, and an exam must also be passed.

The largest firms

1	Bech-Bruun Dragsted	249
2	Kromann Reumert	230
3	Plesner Svane Grønborg	130
4	Gorrissen Federspiel Kierkegaard	122
5	Advokatfirmaet Dahl, Koch & Boll	95
6	Advokaterne Vingardshus	90
	Poul Schmith Law Firm	90
8	Lett & Co	63
9	DLA Nordic	62
10	De La Cour	47
11	Lind & Cadovius	40
	Plougmann & Vingtoff	40
13	Norsker & Jacoby	37
14	Jonas Bruun Advokatfirma	36
15	Mazanti-Andersen, Korsø Jensen & Partnere	35
	Philip & Partners	35
17	Focus Advokater LLP	34
	Hjejle, Gersted & Mogensen	34
19	Accura Advokataktieselskab	30
	Bang & Regnarsen	30
	Lett, Vilstrup & Partnere	30
	Magnusson Wahlin Qvist Stanbrook	30
23	Rønne & Lundgren	28
24	Advokatfirmaet Tommy V Christiansen	26
25	Johan Schlüter Advokatfirma	21

These figures represent the total number of lawyers in this country only, and have been supplied by the firms themselves. The figures should be accurate as at 1 January 2004.

LEGAL MARKET

The Danish legal market is dominated by the Big Four law firms: **Bech-Bruun Dragsted**; **Gorrissen Federspiel Kierkegaard**; **Kromann Reumert**; and **Plesner Svane Grønborg**. With over 240 fee-earners; **Bech-Bruun Dragsted** is the largest of the four, having come together after a series of mergers. Indeed, relative to Denmark's small size, the Big Four hold disproportionate sway over the market and employ a large percentage of its lawyers. Relatively speaking, **Bech-Bruun Dragsted** is much larger within Denmark than the largest of Magic Circle firms would ever hope to be in London. This in turn leads to a large number of conflicts, which are often to the advantage of the smaller mid-tier firms, such as **Jonas Bruun Advokatfirma** and **Hjejle, Gersted & Mogensen**. The perception is that most of the largest firms have reached their optimum size, and it is unlikely that the market could actually sustain any further growth.

While it is inevitable that the Big Four retain most of the largest corporate clients, a firm's brand is not necessarily the driver behind where a client chooses to go for legal advice. Individual lawyers still command a strong following and although the Big Four have many of the best practitioners, the smaller firms also have their fair share and corporate clients will regularly use them.

Lawyers in Denmark tend to take a more general approach to commercial law, though this is slowly starting to change. Thanks to their large size, the Big Four offer clients an array of specialised lawyers, whereas lawyers in mid-tier firms will work across a range of practice areas. Other than the full service law firms, there are several smaller niche practices. For employment law **Norrbom & Vinding Law Firm, member of ius laboris**, **Advokatfirmaet Elmer & Partnere** and **Advokatfirmaet Schebye & Jacobsen** are all recommended. Other specialised boutiques include: **Advokatfirmaet Bender.dk** and **von Haller Law Firm** for IT; **Lassen Ricard** for media and entertainment; and **Advokatfirmaet Tommy V Christiansen** for tax law.

REGIONAL FIRMS

All of the Big Four have regional offices in Aarhus, Denmark's second city, which is also home to **De La Cour** and **Abel & Skovgård Larsen Advokatfirma**. **Focus Advokater LLP** is the largest firm in Odense, while **Advokatfirmaet Dahl, Koch & Boll** has five offices across the Jutland peninsula, though not in Aarhus.

ACCOUNTANCY-LINKED FIRMS

Since **Accura Advokataktieselskab** parted ways with PwC on 1 January 2003, there are now no accountancy-linked firms in Denmark.

FOREIGN FIRMS

The lure of the Danish market has not been strong enough to attract many Western firms, which tend to opt for Sweden if they are going to set up base in Scandinavia. There are only two UK firms in the country: **Osborne Clarke** and **Eversheds Advokataktieselskab**, and with their small offices, neither have made much of an impression on the Danish market.

FOREIGN OFFICES AND LINKS

Few Danish firms have exclusive ties with firms abroad, preferring instead to keep their options open. As a member of the *DLA Group*, only *Lindh Stabell Horten* (rebranded in March 2004 as **DLA Nordic**) can truly lay claim to having exclusive ties with one firm. It also markets itself as a pan-Scandinavian law firm, with integrated offices in Norway and Denmark. **Magnusson Wahlin Qvist Stanbrook** has an office in Sweden, as well as close ties with UK national firm **Pinsents** and Brussels-based EU specialists **Stanbrook & Hooper**. **Philip & Partners** has a long history of co-operation with **Baker & McKenzie**

As part of the *Scandinavian Law Alliance*, **Kromann Reumert** has strong links with fellow members **Thommessen Krefting Greve Lund** and **Vinge**, two of the top firms in Norway and Sweden respectively. This is by no means an exclusive relationship, and if a client requires it they will work with other Scandinavian firms. The Alliance also benefits from shared offices in Brussels and London. Meanwhile, **Bech-Bruun Dragsted** has offices in Brussels and Moscow. **Dania Advokater A/S (Dania Law Firm Ltd)** is a smaller firm with offices in Greenland, Moscow and the Faroe Islands.

Several mid-sized firms have offices in Germany. **Bang & Regnarsen** boasts a five-lawyer office in Hamburg, as well as a strategic alliance with German firm **Schlawein Naab Partnerschaft**. Odense firm **Focus Advokater LLP** also has a Hamburg practice called **Dänische Advokaten**. **Norsker & Jacoby** has offices in Berlin and Cologne, while **Nebelong & Partnere Advokatfirma** also has an office in Berlin.

BANKING AND FINANCE

Banking and finance work in Denmark is not as complex as it is in other financial centres, although things are slowly starting to change. Mezzanine-backed lending is on the increase, though high-yield bond issues remain rare.

Bech-Bruun Dragsted moves to the top tier after recruiting **Herbert Smith** partner Ian Tokley to its finance practice. Tokley, who arrived in early 2004 and is a Danish speaker, has strong experience in finance and capital markets work and gives the practice a more international dimension. For acquisition finance the firm's work is largely borrower led and it acted for Nyco

BANKING AND FINANCE

BECH-BRUUN DRAGSTED ✪
GORRISSEN FEDERSPIEL KIERKEGAARD
KROMANN REUMERT ✪
PLESNER SVANE GRØNBORG ✪

Accura Advokataktieselskab ✪
DLA Nordic ✪
Eversheds Advokataktieselskab
Jonas Bruun Advokatfirma ✪
Lett, Vilstrup & Partnere ✪
Lind & Cadovius ✪
Nielsen & Nørager ✪

Firms are listed A-Z in tiers which are ranked in order of priority
✪ Indicates firm displays contact details at the end of this chapter.

Holdings 3 ApS on a €730m facility, though it is regularly instructed by lenders on refinancings. Partner Steen Halmind specialises principally in securities packages and restructurings, while Jørgen Reimer Jensen primarily focuses on EMTN programmes and advises companies on their borrowings through the European Investment Bank. Partner Steen Jensen is experienced in project finance and structured loans, advising, amongst others, Amagerbanken and Mezzanin Kapital.

Historically **Gorrissen Federspiel Kierkegaard** has always had a strong presence in banking and finance, and this is unlikely to change, even though experienced partner Thomas Federspiel is taking more of a back seat role. The firm still boasts some top of the range practitioners, and Herman Federspiel and Michael Steen Jensenare are two of its leading lights. Recently it has been highly active in securitisation and bond issues, while partner Henrik Lind is recommended for aviation finance and other areas of asset finance. Among its large host of banking clients, the firm includes Nordea Bank, Goldman Sachs, Dresdner Bank and Citibank, to name but a few.

Kromann Reumert has a strong tradition in banking and finance, maintaining strong links with an array of international banks, including Credit Suisse First Boston, Goldman Sachs and UBS Warburg. Partners Jørgen Kjegaard Madsen and Kim Rasmussen are both well known for their work in this area, which has seen an increase in complex transactions and highly structured deals. The team advises on asset finance, acquisition finance, regulatory work and derivatives for a healthy mix of banks, private equity funds, pension funds and corporate borrowers.

Plesner Svane Grønborg advises a mix of lenders and borrowers on a range of finance matters including refinancings, asset and acquisition based finance, shipping finance and derivatives. Recently it advised Nyco Holdings 2, a holding company in the Nycomed Group, on its €295m offering of ten-year senior and mezzanine notes. As well as acting for several major Scandinavian banks and financial institutions, it also advises several international clients including Goldman Sachs and Deutsche Bank.

Claus Bennetsen heads **Accura Advokataktieselskab**'s banking and finance practice, which acts for several medium-sized Scandinavian investment banks, such as Enskilda Secruities, Carnegie and Alfred Berg. The firm also handles some work for JP Morgan.

DLA Nordic is developing its banking and finance practice, which already undertakes a lot of investment fund work. Barclays Bank is one of the firm's major clients.

Banking and finance is **Eversheds Advokataktieselskab**'s strongest practice area. Recently the firm advised HSH Nordbank on a $250m export credit facility for the construction of a cement production plant. It also acted for BI Asset Management on several bond issues, totalling more than €269m. Managing partner Troels Askerud who regularly advises ABN Amro, is well known for his work.

Jonas Bruun Advokatfirma does a lot of syndicated loan and derivatives work for major Danish insurance companies and pension funds. One of the firm's largest instructions was from ABN Amro, as the senior lender on the group financing of CVC's €592m takeover of Danske Trælast. Partner Per Magid has recently acted for Danske Bank on a major banking dispute.

Esben Kjær is the banking specialist at **Lett, Vilstrup & Partnere**, which regularly gives loan advice to Nykredit, Denmark's largest mortgage provider. The firm also acts for Alm Brand Bank on loan procurements.

Frantz Palludan is the top banking partner at **Lind & Cadovius**, which acts for a number of international banks, including BNP Paribas and NM Rothschild.

Nielsen & Nørager is regularly instructed by Nordea Bank and JPMorgan. The firm also handles finance work for several major private equity funds. Arne Gerlyng-Hansen is strong on regulatory advice, while Morten Eldrup-Jørgensen is good on transactional matters.

CAPITAL MARKETS

Capital markets work has been low to non-existent in Denmark over the past few years, and most firms with expertise in the area have kept busy with private placements and de-listings, as well as a number of bond issues. In 2003 there was not a single IPO on the Copenhagen Stock Exchange (XCSE).

For **Bech-Bruun Dragsted**, the state of the market ensured that 2003 was a quiet year for Steen Jensen's well-regarded capital markets team. Nevertheless a number of private placements and significant securities-related instructions helped keep the wolves at bay. One highlight was advising the lenders, Secured Asset Funding Europe BV, on over €134m worth of credit linked notes, due in 2008.

CAPITAL MARKETS

BECH-BRUUN DRAGSTED ✪
GORRISSEN FEDERSPIEL KIERKEGAARD
KROMANN REUMERT ✪
PLESNER SVANE GRØNBORG ✪

Nielsen & Nørager ✪

Firms are listed A-Z in tiers which are ranked in order of priority
✪ Indicates firm displays contact details at the end of this chapter.

Gorrissen Federspiel Kierkegaard's capital markets expertise is second to none, and partner Klaus Søgaard is one of Denmark's leading lawyers in securities law. The state of the market has limited work to a number of bond issues for banks such as Nordea, though the firm is also recommended for large-scale IPOs and share listings, both at home and abroad.

Partner Jørgen Kjegaard Madsen is one of the top capital markets lawyers at **Kromann Reumert**, which has remained busy advising on the flotations of a number of small investment funds.

Plesner Svane Grønborg did its fair share of derivatives work in 2003, and represented Deutsche Bank on a convertible bond issue. The firm also advised on a number of de-listings and public to private deals. Finn Lernø and Jørgen Permin are both noted practitioners.

Outside of the Big Four, **Nielsen & Nørager** is the only firm with a strong line in capital markets work. It has acted on a number of private placements both within and outside of the biotech sector. It also represents several private equity funds.

CORPORATE AND COMMERCIAL

Having grown over the past decade through a series of mergers, **Bech-Bruun Dragsted** remains Denmark's largest law firm with over 240 fee-earners. Benefiting from offices in Brussels and Moscow, as well as Aarhus, its size brings clients distinct advantages. It offers high standard, full-service capabilities to its multinational and domestic clients and has teams specialising in a number of niche areas. Nonetheless, size has its downsides: high fees, fee-earner departures and variable quality. These problems are commonplace in larger legal markets, but in Denmark they are far more apparent, and all of the Big Four have suffered to varying degrees.

Of the top tier firms **Gorrissen Federspiel Kierkegaard** has arguably found the best balance between quality and size. With 125 fee-earners it hasn't expanded at such a rapid rate as some of its rivals, but this has in no way impacted on its popularity with international firms, which remains extremely high. It has always had a large

CORPORATE AND COMMERCIAL

BECH-BRUUN DRAGSTED ✪
GORRISSEN FEDERSPIEL KIERKEGAARD
KROMANN REUMERT ✪
PLESNER SVANE GRØNBORG ✪

Hjejle, Gersted & Mogensen
Jonas Bruun Advokatfirma ✪
Lett & Co ✪
Lett, Vilstrup & Partnere ✪
Lind & Cadovius ✪
Nielsen & Nørager ✪
Philip & Partners ✪

Accura Advokataktieselskab ✪
DLA Nordic ✪

Magnusson Wahlin Qvist Stanbrook
Mazanti-Andersen, Korsø Jensen & Partnere ✪
Norsker & Jacoby ✪

Focus Advokater LLP ✪
Lund Elmer Sandager
Rønne & Lundgren ✪

Dania Advokater A/S (Dania Law Firm Ltd)
Eversheds Advokataktieselskab
Osborne Clarke

Firms are listed A-Z in tiers which are ranked in order of priority
✪ *Indicates firm displays contact details at the end of this chapter.*

international following among its clients and it is seeing an increasing amount of work from within Denmark. In 2003 it represented over half the companies listed on the Danish Stock Exchange in some capacity. Within the partnership, Tomas Haagen Jensen is considered to be one of the firm's rising stars for corporate work. Major clients include FLS Industries, Elsam and Nykredit.

Praised for its 'excellent service', **Kromann Reumert**'s corporate department enjoys a sterling reputation, benefiting from the firm's membership of the *Scandinavian Law Alliance*, which offers its clients top-notch representation across the whole of Scandinavia. The firm, has started to shed its somewhat conservative reputation, and has recently expanded to 58 partners, which it feels is near its optimum size. It has seen growth in corporate activity from both mid-size and larger international clients, including Arla Foods, TDC and Carlsberg.

Plesner Svane Grønborg's 'excellent' 12-partner corporate practice had an active 2003. It gained Danfoss, one of Denmark's largest industrial groups, as a new client, and advised Ford, Mazda and the Scandinavian Motor Company on the overall restructuring of their respective dealership networks. Partner Steen Christensen is chairman of the board of directors of Nykredit, Denmark's second largest financial institution. Having worked in separate offices for some time, the firm finally moved into its new headquarters at the start of 2004.

11-partner **Hjejle, Gersted & Mogensen**, once one of Denmark's most prestigious firms, has been left behind by the Big Four in terms of size and modernity. Nevertheless, it still carries plenty of weight in the market and remains popular with clients as a high-quality alternative to the top tier. The firm advises a mix of public sector and private clients and has been active in the biotechnology sector for venture capitalists. It is also well known for its tax work.

Despite being considerably smaller than the top tier firms, what **Jonas Bruun Advokatfirma** lacks in size it doesn't lack in quality. The 11-partner firm offers a full service practice and is particularly strong in energy, telecoms and general M&A work. Recently it advised Naturgas Fyn on its formation of a joint venture, Statoil Gazelle, with Statoil Danmark, to sell natural gas and other energy products in Denmark. As well as international joint ventures, the firm is active in de-listings and share buyback programmes. Partners Mogens Ebeling, Jeppe Skadhauge and Christian Sinding all come highly recommended, while senior partner Arne Madsen has retired to become a consultant. Energy and telecoms specialist Christine Jansby was recently made up to partner.

17-partner **Lett & Co** has mapped out an ambitious growth strategy which it hopes will set it apart from the rest of the mid-tier and bring it closer to the Big Four. Its modernising approach includes appointing a non-fee earning managing director, Jan Hornsberg. The firm, which has an expanding office in Aarhus, is well known for its insurance, litigation and public sector work, but is also strong in areas such as EU and competition. Clients include Nordea Bank, Arla Foods and Aarhus County.

Lett, Vilstrup & Partnere has a strong name for public sector work, particularly for one of its largest clients, Danish State Railways (DSB). The firm is also popular with private sector clients, advising Group 4 Falck and Belgium's Etex Group on their Danish interests. For specialist environmental law, Vivi Bruhn Knudsen's practice comes highly recommended.

One of Denmark's more conservative firms, **Lind & Cadovius** has enjoyed a good reputation for commercial law, particularly on the disputes side, as well as in public procurement. However, the departure of Jon Stokholm to become a Supreme Court Judge in January 2003 was a definite setback for the firm.

Nielsen & Nørager has significantly strengthened its corporate capabilities with the recruitment of partner Eigil Lego Anderson from **Bech-Bruun Dragsted**. The firm is particularly experienced in the biotech and pharmaceuticals industry. It also advises several private equity funds, including the Scandinavian Life Science Fund.

Philip & Partners' commercial practice benefits from a close relationship with **Baker & McKenzie**. The firm has a good reputation but needs to bring in some new blood if it is to sustain its position in the market. Nonetheless, partner Henning Hansen comes highly recommended.

Accura Advokataktieselskab split from PwC and the **Landwell** network on 1 January 2003. The firm has since established a strong reputation. Marketing itself as a corporate boutique it has started to pick up several impressive clients, including Carlsberg, which it advised on a recent JV with Coca-Cola, FLS Industries, Merck and Alcatel. Kåre Stolt, Thomas Weincke and Karsten Kielland are the firm's top corporate partners. The firm also boasts strong tax and real estate practices.

Christian Scherfig and Casper Moltke head **DLA Nordic**'s solid corporate and commercial group, which also has offices in Norway and Sweden. The firm benefits greatly from its membership of the *DLA Group*, with which it works closely on pitches and transactions. Traditionally the firm has had a strong public sector role, advising the Municipality of Copenhagen, but its corporate team has started to attract several impressive clients, including DHL, Nordic Biotech and Credit Suisse First Boston.

Magnusson Wahlin Qvist Stanbrook has offices in Sweden, Estonia and Poland, and benefits from its association with **Stanbrook & Hooper**, the Brussels-based EU and competition specialist. In Copenhagen, the firm's strongest sectors are in EU and IT.

Mazanti-Andersen, Korsø Jensen & Partnere is more of a collective of partners rather than a fully integrated law firm. Nonetheless, lawyers do work together on major transactions and the firm boasts several first-rate partners, including Philip Thorsen, who is an expert on the Baltic region. Anders Cold and J Korsø Jensen are also rated.

Norsker & Jacoby represents numerous Danish small- to medium-sized enterprises, as well as international clients from the US and Europe. The 18-partner firm has a strong link with Germany, with offices in Berlin and Cologne.

Based primarily in Odense, Denmark's third-largest city, **Focus Advokater LLP** also has offices in Copenhagen and Hamburg. The 15-partner firm advises a mix of Danish clients, including Micro Matic Group, Amtssparekassen (a regional bank) and Marius Petersen (a waste management company), as well as a number of German banks and insurance groups.

With 22 fee-earners, **Lund Elmer Sandager** offers its clients, including Fiat and Bonniers, full service capabilities. Hans Christoffersen and Jørn Thaysen are two of the firm's top corporate partners.

Formerly part of *Andersen Legal*, **Rønne & Lundgren** benefits from strong links with former member firms. The firm acts for a mix of domestic and international clients, as well as some municipalities, such as the Municipality of Farum.

DISPUTE RESOLUTION

Danish society as a whole remains fairly non-litigious, and when commercial disputes do arise, arbitration has become an increasingly popular form of dispute resolution.

The Danish court system roughly breaks down into three tiers: the District Courts, the High Courts, including the Eastern High Court (Østre Landsret) and the Western High Court (Vestre Landsret), and at the top, the Supreme Court (Højesteret). Only about 100 lawyers have rights of audience in the Supreme Court. Added to these there are specialised courts such as the Labour Court and the Maritime and Commercial Court.

For most Danish lawyers and firms, dispute resolution isn't a specific focus, although some of the largest firms, such as **Gorrissen Federspiel Kierkegaard** have started setting up separate litigation departments. The reputations of numerous firms, however, still come largely down to one or two star individuals.

Bech-Bruun Dragsted boasts specialised litigators in employment, insurance, maritime, taxation and IT law and has acted for clients in 15 Supreme Court cases in the past two years. The firm is also experienced in arbitration, which makes up 50% of its dispute resolution work.

Gorrissen Federspiel Kierkegaard was the first Danish law firm to establish a specialised disputes practice, and its three leading partners Arne Bierfreund, Axel Kierkegaard and Henrik Christrup can more than hold their own. Bierfreund is particularly strong in international arbitrations, while Kierkegaard recently represented the defendants in a major insider trading case. Recently made up partner Christian Alsøe is considered to be a bright prospect.

Hjejle, Gersted & Mogensen is best known for its tax litigation, but can also offer clients top-notch representation in most commercial disputes, including arbitration. Among its host of Supreme Court-qualified lawyers, Oluf Engell, in particular, stands out. The firm is also strong for EU and Competition-related disputes.

Name checked by most of his peers, **Jonas Bruun Advokatfirma**'s partner Per Magid is one of the 'pre-eminent' figures on the Danish litigation scene. Recently he represented the Danish Bankers' Association in a major dispute before the Supreme Court. Partners Christian Sinding and Jeppe Skadhauge are also very active in disputes work.

Kromann Reumert handles a good mix of litigation and arbitration, which is a particular strength for Mogens Skipper-Pedersen. Based in Aarhus, Jørgen Jepsen is one of the firm's leading litigators.

Lett & Co has an active and well-respected group of disputes lawyers. For insurance disputes there are few who can match up to George Lett, while Jesper Lett is particularly good for tax matters. Regular clients include PwC, Nordea, TDC and Alm. Brand.

DISPUTE RESOLUTION

BECH-BRUUN DRAGSTED ✪
GORRISSEN FEDERSPIEL KIERKEGAARD
HJEJLE, GERSTED & MOGENSEN
JONAS BRUUN ADVOKATFIRMA ✪
KROMANN REUMERT ✪
LETT & CO ✪
MAZANTI-ANDERSEN, KORSØ JENSEN & PARTNERE ✪
PHILIP & PARTNERS ✪
PLESNER SVANE GRØNBORG ✪
TOMMY V CHRISTIANSEN, ADVOKATFIRMAET ✪

Dahl, Koch & Boll, Advokatfirmaet
Johan Schlüter Advokatfirma ✪
Lind & Cadovius ✪
Lett, Vilstrup & Partnere ✪
Nielsen & Nørager ✪
Norrbom & Vinding Law Firm, member of ius laboris ✪
Norsker & Jacoby ✪
Osborne Clarke
Poul Schmith Law Firm
Viltoft & Høberg-Petersen ✪

Firms are listed A-Z in tiers which are ranked in order of priority
✪ *Indicates firm displays contact details at the end of this chapter.*

Considered 'one of the best', J Korsø Jensen is the best known litigator at **Mazanti-Andersen, Korsø Jensen & Partnere**. He is active in construction-related disputes, and regularly acts for Alstom in litigation and arbitration. The firm is also strong for banking and tax disputes.

Name partner Dr Allan Philip of **Philip & Partners** is extremely well regarded for arbitrations.

Plesner Svane Grønborg boasts an impressive crop of partners who dedicate a substantial part of their time to dispute resolution. Jørgen Grønborg and Michael Rekling are representing the Port of Copenhagen before the Danish Supreme Court in a case against the Danish State regarding its nationalisation of the port. The total value of the case is estimated at €225m. Mikael Rosenmejer continues to act for the Scandinavian Tobacco Company in litigation throughout Scandinavia. Partners Torben Bondrop, Peter Fogh and Karen Dyekjær are also recommended.

Name partner Tommy Christiansen at **Advokatfirmaet Tommy V Christiansen** is arguably Denmark's leading tax litigator.

Based in Aalborg and with four other offices across the Jutland peninsula, **Advokatfirmaet Dahl, Koch & Boll** offers clients a strong, localised litigation practice.

Johan Schlüter Advokatfirma comes highly recommended for IP-related disputes.

Mads Berendt, Håkon Djurhuus and Nicolai Westergaard of **Lind & Cadovius** are all experienced in arbitration and litigation.

Lett, Vilstrup & Partnere appeared before the Supreme Court three times in 2003. Partner Ulf Anderson is the firm's best-known litigator.

At **Nielsen & Nørager**, Eigil Lego Anderson who recently arrived from **Bech-Bruun Dragsted** has a good name for disputes work. The firm is also recommended for insurance litigation.

Norrbom & Vinding Law Firm, Member Of ius laboris is the number one recommendation for employment related disputes, and both name partners Mariann Norrbom and Jørgen Vinding have excellent reputations. Recently the firm defended a major Danish supermarket in a discrimination case regarding the wearing of Muslim headscarves at work.

Norsker & Jacoby's main disputes lawyers are John Kahlke and Tove Meurs-Gerken, who has represented German clients in arbitration and litigation. Nils-Erik Norsker is also recommended.

Viltoft & Høberg-Petersen should be the first port of call for Danish construction-related disputes.

EU AND COMPETITION

Kromann Reumert's formidable EU and competition team boasts an enviable line up of star partners including the 'highly knowledgeable' Morten Kofmann, described by one client as 'the best for competition' in Denmark. The group undertakes a significant amount of merger control and Erik Bertelsen played an important role in Arla Foods' recent acquisition of Express Dairies. Other leading players within the department include the experienced Erik Mohr Mersing and Jens Munk Plum. Major clients include Carlsberg, SAS and TDC. The firm shares an office in Brussels with its partners in the *Scandinavian Law Alliance*.

Bech-Bruun Dragsted boasts one of the largest dedicated EU and competition groups in Denmark. The firm is used by a plethora of international clients, from a wide range of sectors, including telecoms, construction, maritime and media. Group head Peter Stig Jakobsen led his team through an active 2003, representing clients before the European Commission and the Danish Competition Council, as well as on a number of dawn raids. Another string to the firm's bow is its Brussels office, which is headed by dedicated partner Morten Lau Smith.

EU expert Jan-Erik Svensson is the main point of contact at **Gorrissen Federspiel Kierkegaard**, which is recommended for its merger and compliance related work. The firm advised Nykredit on competition issues regarding its acquisition of Totalkredit. It is active in the energy sector and continues to advise Elsam on issues relating to its proposed purchase of NESA.

Partners Katja Høegh and Karen Dyekjær-Hansen are two of the leading lights in **Plesner Svane Grønborg**'s well-regarded EU and competition group. One of its most significant

EU AND COMPETITION

KROMANN REUMERT ✪

BECH-BRUUN DRAGSTED ✪
GORRISSEN FEDERSPIEL KIERKEGAARD
PLESNER SVANE GRØNBORG ✪

Hjejle, Gersted & Mogensen
Jonas Bruun Advokatfirma ✪
Lett & Co ✪
Lett, Vilstrup & Partnere ✪
Lind & Cadovius ✪
Magnusson Wahlin Qvist Stanbrook
Nielsen & Nørager ✪
Viltoft & Høberg-Petersen ✪

Mazanti-Andersen, Korsø Jensen & Partnere ✪
Philip & Partners ✪

Firms are listed A-Z in tiers which are ranked in order of priority
✪ Indicates firm displays contact details at the end of this chapter.

cases was for Aalborg Portland, Denmark's largest cement manufacturer, before the ECJ, which recommended the annulment of a decision and the return of a paid fine. It has also advised the Scandinavian Motor Company, one of Denmark's largest car dealerships, as well as Levi-Strauss, Siemens and Telenor, among others.

Hjejle, Gersted & Mogensen has a lot of experience in competition law and merger notifications before the Danish Competition Authority. One of its largest ongoing cases is for the Danish Insurance Association at the ECJ. The firm regularly represents clients in Europe, before the ECJ and the EC.

Jeppe Skadhauge and Olaf Koktvedgaard are the two EU and competition experts at **Jonas Bruun Advokatfirma**. Skadhauge advised Naturgas Fyn and Statoil Danmark on the Danish merger clearance for their JV, Statoil Gazelle. Meanwhile Koktvedgaard was instructed by TV2/Denmark on competition issues regarding two JVs it had with national newspaper groups Berlingske and Jyllands-Posten/ Politiken.

Lett & Co has established a strong name in public procurement law, and one of its experts in this area is Jesper Fabricius. Usually the firm acts on behalf of Danish counties and local authorities such as Aarhus County and Copenhagen County. It has also established itself an extremely strong niche in EU law, particularly on food related matters. Partners Susie Ekstrand and George Lett were recently appointed by the EU Commission to educate new EU entrants on its food laws. The firm has acted on significant cases both in Brussels and Denmark, for a range of clients, including the Danish Dairy Board, Arla Foods and Renoflex.

Lett, Vilstrup & Partnere advised DSB on competition and public procurement aspects of its involvement in Rejsekort, a project to develop an electronic travel card for the whole of Denmark. Other than DSB the firm also represents several public municipal clients. Ulrik Lett, Mette Herskind and Anette Ryde are the main practitioners here.

Lotte Hummelshøj heads **Lind & Cadovius**' well-regarded competition practice. The firm is experienced in public procurement law, and has advised an impressive range of clients, including DONG, Post Denmark and DR, Denmark's largest TV station. Søren Zinck is also active in this area.

Magnusson Wahlin Qvist Stanbrook benefits greatly from its association with Brussels-based EU and competition specialists **Stanbrook & Hooper**. The firm advises both claimants and defendants, and is particularly experienced in the publishing sector. Anders Torbøl is one of the firm's leading practitioners.

Henrik Peytz is **Nielsen & Nørager**'s key EU and competition partner, with good experience before the ECJ. Peytz has done a lot of work in the media sector, and recently represented SBS and TV Danmark in a major case relating to state aid and government over-funding. The firm also carries out competition audits for its international clients.

Michael Gjedde-Nielsen and Jakob Juul at **Viltoft & Høberg-Petersen** are both experienced in EU and competition law, having represented a number of Danish municipalities, as well as the National Association of Danish Municipalities, on related matters.

EMPLOYMENT

Norrbom & Vinding Law Firm, member of ius laboris remains Denmark's leading employment law firm. The five-partner boutique is heavily involved in all aspects of employment and pensions law, advising only employers and employer's associations. Following the arrival of Karen Baggesen, the firm has started a specialised standalone training lab, which offers in-house training to old and new clients. Another major boost in 2003 was the recruitment of Hans Juhler, formerly head of **Poul Schmith Law Firm**'s employment group. With Juhler comes a host of new clients, including local authorities and state-owned companies. Name partners Mariann Norrbom and Jørgen Vinding both enjoy excellent reputations for both contentious and non-contentious work.

Amongst Denmark's full service law firms, it is **Bech-Bruun Dragsted** that has the best reputation for employment work, both in corporate support and standalone roles. The team, headed by Bjarke Vejby, has successfully represented numerous clients before the Danish Supreme and High Court, and recently won a Supreme Court case for Novo Nordisk regarding severance schemes. Other major clients include Maersk Data, TDC, SAS Commuter and the Danish Shipowners' Association. Managing Partner Lars Svenning Andersen also enjoys an extremely good reputation for employment law.

EMPLOYMENT

NORRBOM & VINDING LAW FIRM, MEMBER OF IUS LABORIS ✪

BECH-BRUUN DRAGSTED ✪

DLA Nordic ✪
Elmer & Partnere, Advokatfirmaet
Kromann Reumert ✪
Lind & Cadovius ✪
Schebye & Jacobsen, Advokatfirmaet

Gorrissen Federspiel Kierkegaard
Mazanti-Andersen, Korsø Jensen & Partnere ✪
Osborne Clarke
Poul Schmith Law Firm
Viltoft & Høberg-Petersen ✪

Firms are listed A-Z in tiers which are ranked in order of priority
✪ Indicates firm displays contact details at the end of this chapter.

The highly experienced Finn Schwarz heads **DLA Nordic**'s dedicated seven-lawyer employment team. About 70% of the group's work is standalone, though it also plays a support role to the corporate group. The firm represents an impressive range of employers including, GE Capital, Motorola, Velux and KLM.

Advokatfirmaet Elmer & Partnere solely represents unions and employees in labour cases.

Kromann Reumert's 'excellent' Helene Amsinck Boie and Claus Juel Hansen are both described as experts by their clients. Employment is a growing area for the firm, and the department's work is almost entirely standalone.

Lind & Cadovius is unique in that it acts for employers, employees and unions. Partner Birgitte Horn advises employers, while Nicolai Westergaard represents several unions, as well as being a judge in the Labour Court.

Advokatfirmaet Schebye & Jacobsen is another firm that enjoys a sound reputation for representing employees and unions. Name partners Ulla Jacobsen and Karen-Margrethe Schebye are recommended for their work in Aarhus and Copenhagen respectively.

Poul Schmith Law Firm represents the government and public sector in all its labour disputes, though the firm suffered a major blow when department head Hans Juhler left for **Norrbom & Vinding Law Firm, member of ius laboris**.

Viltoft & Høberg-Petersen offers employment advice to a number of unions and workers' associations. Jacob Juul is the firm's top practitioner.

ENERGY

In its bid to harmonise with the rest of the EU, Denmark's energy market has been an active source of work for many law firms. The electricity market was liberalised in 2000, and, with the

ENERGY

BECH-BRUUN DRAGSTED ✪
DLA NORDIC ✪
GORRISSEN FEDERSPIEL KIERKEGAARD
JONAS BRUUN ADVOKATFIRMA ✪
KROMANN REUMERT ✪

Lett, Vilstrup & Partnere ✪
Plesner Svane Grønborg ✪
Viltoft & Høberg-Petersen ✪

Firms are listed A-Z in tiers which are ranked in order of priority
✪ *Indicates firm displays contact details at the end of this chapter.*

proposed privatisation of DONG and the break-up of NESA, the gas and power sectors are moving in the same direction.

Formerly based in Aarhus, Per Hemmer has recently moved **Bech-Bruun Dragsted**'s energy group to Copenhagen, to focus on its growing international client base. The firm regularly advises on transactional and multi-utility issues. Clients include Eltra and Elkraft. Jens Auken and Jørgen Holst are both rated for their work in the energy sector.

Klavs V Gravesen's energy department at **DLA Nordic** advises national energy companies, municipalities and financial institutions on regulatory and corporate issues. The firm's largest clients are Energi E2 and Copenhagen Energy.

Jan-Erik Svensson and Henrik Christrup are the two main energy partners at **Gorrissen Federspiel Kierkegaard**. The bulk of the firm's work is on the competition and regulatory side, and it has seen a growth in instructions from electricity companies as the government looks to liberalise the sector. The firm is also advising Elsam on its proposed acquisition of NESA. Other major clients include RWE and Maersk oil and gas.

Jonas Bruun Advokatfirma remains extremely active in the energy sector, both on the regulatory and corporate side. Claus Høeg Madsen is recommended for his expertise in electricity, while Jeppe Skadhauge and Christian Sinding are strong in gas and renewables respectively. Høeg Madsen is currently representing the Danish Association of Electricity Companies in three test cases before the Danish Energy Complaints Board. Other major clients include NESA and Energi 2.

Rivals struggle to keep pace with **Kromann Reumert**'s highly-rated team, which advised the state-owned energy company, DONG, on the deregulation of the domestic gas market. International clients include Amerada Hess and Norsk Hydro. Anders Stubbe Arndal is recommended for his electricity work, while Michael Budtz is known for oil and gas.

Lett, Vilstrup & Partnere is the sole adviser to Shell in Denmark, advising it in all areas of the law. Vivi Bruhn Knudsen is recommended for her expertise in environmental law.

Plesner Svane Grønborg has eight lawyers with an interest in energy law. The practice has a strong corporate focus, and counts DONG Transmission among its clients.

Viltoft & Høberg-Petersen has good experience in wind power, and also acts for a number of municipalities on their related interests. Michael Gjedde-Nielsen is well regarded.

IT AND E-COMMERCE

Ole Horsfeldt heads **Bech-Bruun Dragsted**'s reputed IT group, which advises high-profile clients from across the spectrum. Recently it has become involved in IT outsourcing work and advised SAS on outsourcing to India, as well as the outsourcing of the Municipality of Copenhagen's payroll system. The firm regularly advises research and development houses and provides strong corporate support for venture capital groups. Partner Janne Glæsel is recommended for her IP expertise.

Kromann Reumert's core clients include major software vendors and systems integrators. The firm has seen a marked rise in outsourcing work and advised the facility services provider, ISS, on its outsourcing to CSC, the largest such project in Denmark. It also advised PFA, the Danish pensions and insurance company, on application development projects worth €100m. Partners Vagn Thorup and Lau Normann Jørgensen are recommended.

With offices in Jutland and Copenhagen, two-partner IT boutique **Advokatfirmaet Bender.dk** has established itself a very good name. Name partner Hanne Bender and Peter Lind Nielsen are both held in high regard by the rest of the legal market.

Boutique firm **Advokatfirmaet Elvang & Partnere** offers regulatory and commercial advice to its predominantly IT and biotech clients. Kristian Elvang-Gøransson is recommended for his work on licensing agreements and IT contracts. One of the firm's largest clients is SAP.

IT boutique **von Haller Law Firm** advises a healthy mix of public and private sector clients. It has acted for several municipalities on the procurement of IT systems. Venture capital work is picking up for the firm, and it represents a number of international VCs, as well as a large array of domestic start-ups. The firm has recently established strong relationships with IT consultancy Devoteam, and domain name provider Speednames, with which it has combined to offer a one-stop service to clients. Highly recommended name partner Martin von Haller Grønbæk sits on the board of the Danish IT Lawyer's Association.

With Jens Jakob Bugge at the helm, **DLA Nordic** has established itself an excellent name in IT work. The firm has acted for EDS on a number of outsourcing projects, and advises Motorola on its various e-commerce ventures. Further clients include Cognos, TNT and Den Blå Avis. Michael Goeskjaer is also recommended.

IT AND E-COMMERCE

BECH-BRUUN DRAGSTED ✪
KROMANN REUMERT ✪

Bender.dk, Advokatfirmaet
Elvang & Partnere, Advokatfirmaet
von Haller Law Firm

DLA Nordic ✪
Gorrissen Federspiel Kierkegaard
Lett & Co ✪
Lett, Vilstrup & Partnere ✪
Lind & Cadovius ✪
Magnusson Wahlin Qvist Stanbrook
Nielsen & Nørager ✪
Plesner Svane Grønborg ✪
Poul Schmith Law Firm

Firms are listed A-Z in tiers which are ranked in order of priority
✪ *Indicates firm displays contact details at the end of this chapter.*

Lett & Co has advised on several major outsourcings. Clients include TDC and Aarhus County, having represented the latter on a number of IT-related disputes.

Susanne Mark is **Lett, Vilstrup & Partnere**'s resident IT expert. Mark is experienced in issues regarding Internet portals. Recently the firm advised Krak, a major road map provider, on its expansion into the IT sector.

At **Lind & Cadovius**, Hans Madsen is the main expert in IT-related matters.

Nicolai Dragsted of **Magnusson Wahlin Qvist Stanbrook** is one of Denmark's top IT experts, and is well known for his expertise in outsourcing and IT contracts. One of the firm's largest deals was for Scandinavian IT, part of SAS, which it advised on an outsourcing deal with IBM. Other clients include Danish Payment System and DmData.

Jacob Norager Nielsen at **Nielsen & Nørager** is well versed in IT contracts, and regularly advises on purchases of large-scale IT systems. The firm acts for a number of venture capitalists in the IT sector.

Per Håkon Schmidt and Michael Rekling at **Plesner Svane Grønborg** are the two main points of contact for IT law. The firm has advised Hewlett-Packard on several large IT projects.

As well as advising the government, Henrik Berg of **Poul Schmith Law Firm** acts for a small number of private sector clients, particularly on IT contracts.

INSOLVENCY

Plesner Svane Grønborg's three-partner insolvency group is of the very highest order. Michael Zeigler, Peter Bang and Pernilla Bigaard are all held in extremely high regard by the rest of

INSOLVENCY

PLESNER SVANE GRØNBORG ✪

BECH-BRUUN DRAGSTED ✪
GORRISSEN FEDERSPIEL KIERKEGAARD
KROMANN REUMERT ✪

DLA Nordic ✪
Jonas Bruun Advokatfirma ✪
Lind & Cadovius ✪
Lund Elmer Sandager
Mazanti-Andersen, Korsø Jensen & Partnere ✪
Philip & Partners ✪
Poul Schmith Law Firm

Firms are listed A-Z in tiers which are ranked in order of priority
✪ *Indicates firm displays contact details at the end of this chapter.*

the legal community. Zeigler and Bigaard are both permanent trustees of the Bankruptcy Court.

Troels Tuxen heads **Bech-Bruun Dragsted**'s sizeable and highly experienced insolvency department. The 22-fee-earner team, which includes six partners, draws from a considerable pool of talent, including partners Ole Borch, Michael Serring and Karl Stephensen, all of whom are trustees of the Danish Bankruptcy Court. Borch was previously a chair of the International Bar Association's insolvency committee.

Axel Kierkegaard of **Gorrissen Federspiel Kierkegaard** is a court appointed trustee and is held in very high esteem by rival insolvency lawyers. One of his largest cases continues to be for Hafnia Holding on its insolvency and related issues. Anne Birgitte Gammeljord, who is assistant to the Commercial and Maritime Court, is also recommended.

Kromann Reumert's insolvency group enjoyed an extremely busy 2003. Highly rated partner Kurt Skovlund has been appointed trustee on some of Denmark's most high-profile insolvency cases, including Credit Finance Denmark, Imerco AmbA, the Danish ironmongers, and Teleglobe Danmark. Meanwhile Sven Rosenmeyer Paulsen was appointed trustee for KPNQwest.

DLA Nordic's Casper Moltke is a regular administrator at the Bankruptcy Court. The firm advised on the Danish aspects of Global Crossing's restructuring, it also advised on the restructuring of Copenhagen Electricity.

Partners Per Magid and Claus Høeg Madsen are the two main points of contact for insolvency work at **Jonas Bruun Advokatfirma**. Magid was recently appointed co-trustee by the court, for telecoms retailer Bluetel and its affiliates, which was declared bankrupt after Nokia terminated its co-operation with the group. Høeg Madsen, who is extremely well regarded in this field, was appointed, at the behest of the creditors, as trustee of Danish Steelworks, which has some 1,100 employees.

Lind & Cadovius has two strong insolvency partners within its ranks: Henrik Andersen, who is an administrator at the bankruptcy court, and Lars Skanvig.

Lund Elmer Sandager's highly experienced partner Jørgen Elmer is a court-appointed trustee, and very well regarded within the insolvency market.

Mazanti-Andersen, Korsø Jensen & Partnere has several court appointed trustees within its ranks, including the highly-rated J Korsø Jensen and Henrik Sanders, who acted for the bankrupt estate of computer company CRI, in arbitration proceedings against a former customer. The firm also helped in the restructuring of Farum Municipality, the largest such restructuring in Danish history.

Government advisers **Poul Schmith Law Firm**'s insolvency group does a large amount of work for the private sector. Finn Mejnertsen and Boris Frederiksen are two of the firm's leading partners.

INSURANCE

Headed by Henrik Valdorf-Hansen, **Bech-Bruun Dragsted**'s well regarded insurance department has seen a major increase in corporate work within the Danish insurance sector. It has advised a number of insurance clients on solvency strategies, following losses on investments and the negative effects of low interest rates. Significant Danish clients include Tryg, If and Codan, and the firm also represents a number of international insurance companies.

Kromann Reumert's impressive insurance team includes Morten Samuelsson, who is a professional liability expert, and personal injury specialist Christina Neugebauer. Praised for his experience and knowledge, Jens Rostock-Jensen recently advised airline carriers and aviation underwriters on insurance issues following September 11.

Lett & Co was one of the first Danish firms to specialise in insurance law, and it continues to boast an excellent reputation. The standing of George Lett alone would justify a top tier ranking, and the firm has several other high-quality insurance experts, including Pernille Sølling and Michael Grønbech. The firm successfully represented Alm. Brand in a major insurance case in the UK, it is also acting for clients in the first reinsurance case to go before the ordinary courts. Its domestic client list is second to none, and includes Tryg, Codan, PFA Pension and Danica.

Plesner Svane Grønborg is advising a number of insurers on major product and commercial liability cases. Highly rated partner Torben Bondrop is representing insurance companies before the Supreme Court on questions of cover and non-disclosure. Mikael Rosenmejer was recently elected honorary president of AIDA, the World Organisation for Insurance Law.

INSURANCE

BECH-BRUUN DRAGSTED ✪
KROMANN REUMERT ✪
LETT & CO ✪
PLESNER SVANE GRØNBORG ✪

Lett, Vilstrup & Partnere ✪
Nielsen & Nørager ✪

Gorrissen Federspiel Kierkegaard
Mazanti-Andersen, Korsø Jensen & Partnere ✪
Norsker & Jacoby ✪
Philip & Partners ✪
Rønne & Lundgren ✪

Firms are listed A-Z in tiers which are ranked in order of priority
✪ *Indicates firm displays contact details at the end of this chapter.*

Mark Thorsen heads **Lett, Vilstrup & Partnere**'s respected insurance practice. The firm advises insurers such as Tryg, more on regulatory issues rather than claims work.

Michael Wiisbye handles the majority of **Nielsen & Nørager**'s insurance workload, acting for insurers on all manner of claims and disputes. One of the firm's largest clients is If, one of Denmark's major insurers.

Alex Laudrup at **Gorrissen Federspiel Kierkegaard** has solid expertise in shipping and transport insurance.

INTELLECTUAL PROPERTY

The arrival of **Bech-Bruun Dragsted**'s top IP partner Ole Damsbo was a major boost for **Johan Schlüter Advokatfirma**'s young IP practice, which moves into the top tier. Set up in 2002, the firm has made a swift impact on the market and further added to its ranks with eight fee-earners from the patent and trade mark attorneys Plougmann & Vingtoft, with which the firm has a strategic alliance. The firm is experienced in anti-piracy, parallel imports, and patent and trade mark infringement, and advises a range of clients including Novartis and Johnson & Johnson.

Plesner Svane Grønborg has an excellent reputation, particularly in the pharmaceutical sector where it advises a host of blue-chip clients in patent and trade mark law. Peter-Ulrik Plesner one the firm's top patent specialists has been particularly active issuing successful injunctions for Lundbeck, AstraZeneca and GlaxoSmithKline. On top of its impressive expertise in pharmaceuticals it also represents several household names including Coca-Cola, Lego, adidas and Nike. Recently a team headed by Per Håkon Schmidt was appointed by Danske Bank to handle all its IP matters.

For **Bech-Bruun Dragsted**, the departure of Ole Damsbo to **Johan Schlüter Advokatfirma**, undoubtedly comes as a significant blow. Remaining partners include Janne Glæsel, who is

INTELLECTUAL PROPERTY

JOHAN SCHLÜTER ADVOKATFIRMA ✪
PLESNER SVANE GRØNBORG ✪

Bech-Bruun Dragsted ✪
DLA Nordic ✪
Kromann Reumert ✪
Lett & Co ✪

Bender.dk, Advokatfirmaet
Elvang & Partnere, Advokatfirmaet
Gorrissen Federspiel Kierkegaard
Lett, Vilstrup & Partnere ✪
Norsker & Jacoby ✪

Accura Advokataktieselskab ✪
Jonas Bruun Advokatfirma ✪
Osborne Clarke
Philip & Partners ✪
Rønne & Lundgren ✪
Viltoft & Høberg-Petersen ✪

Firms are listed A-Z in tiers which are ranked in order of priority
✪ *Indicates firm displays contact details at the end of this chapter.*

well known for her IT and telecommunications-related IP work, though she also acts for major brands including Mars and Gillette. Klaus Ewald Madsen also has strong expertise in the pharmaceutical sector.

Considered to be 'excellent on patent and IP issues', **Kromann Reumert** is very well regarded within the legal community. The firm is well known for its expertise in the pharmaceutical sector, where Olaf Eskildsen holds sway. Partners Erling Borcher, Nicolai Lindgreen and Frank Bøggild are also recommended. Clients praise its 'very service oriented' approach.

Lett & Co's strong practice acts for an impressive range of domestic and international clients, including ANR Productions, Invensys and Arla Foods. Recently the firm represented the Danish Dairy Board in its high-profile trade mark dispute with Fanoe Mejeri, over its rights to use the Lurpak brand. Jesper Fabricius and Aarhus-based Jan Bech are two of the firm's top practitioners.

Jens Jakob Bugge is **DLA Nordic**'s resident IP expert. The firm recently had a major victory for Tivoli amusement park in the commercial courts, to protect its trade mark from use by third parties. Other clients include GE Capital, BMW and Invensys.

For more specific advice in the field of IT and e-commerce, specialist firms such as **Advokatfirmaet Bender.dk** and **Advokatfirmaet Elvang & Partnere** come highly recommended.

Gorrissen Federspiel Kierkegaard is expanding its IP department by establishing an in-house patent and trade mark agency: GFK Designs and Trademarks. Jacob Ørndrup is the firm's IP expert.

IT expert Susanne Mark is the main IP practitioner at **Lett, Vilstrup & Partnere**, which offers advice on trade mark infringement and patent law. The group suffered a blow with the departure of media specialist Nina Henningsen to **Bech-Bruun Dragsted**.

Mads Marstrand-Jørgensen heads **Norsker & Jacoby**'s well regarded IP team, which is particularly strong on the litigation side, having appeared before the Supreme Court on a number of occasions.

MEDIA AND ENTERTAINMENT

Niels Andersen's media and entertainment group at **Bech-Bruun Dragsted** continues to enjoy a top-notch reputation, despite increasingly stiff competition from smaller boutique practices. Partner Bjarke Vejby is strong on the litigation side and has taken a number of test cases regarding music rights before the Copyright Licence Tribunal. Other notable practitioners include Per Neumann who is experienced within the film industry, and Strange Beck for his work with domestic and international TV and radio broadcasters. Major clients include Sky, EMI, Universal and the Motion Picture Association of America. The firm received a boost with the arrival of Nina Henningsen from **Lett, Vilstrup & Partnere** who brings with her a number of major clients including CNN, Canal+ and the Cartoon Network.

Four-partner firm, **Lassen Ricard** is one of the undoubted leaders in Danish broadcasting. The firm advises a host of major names, including TV2, BBV, DR (the National Danish Broadcasting Organisation) and Sony Music. Recent highlights include successfully representing DR twice before the Supreme Court against IFPI, the International Record Company Organisation, regarding copyright and broadcasting disputes. Partners Steen Lassen and Peter Lambert are both leaders in their field.

Set up in 2002, IT/IP and media boutique **Johan Schlüter Advokatfirma** has quickly established itself on the Danish legal scene. The firm recently acted for IFPI in the two Supreme Court hearings against DR, and although these were both unsuccessful, the firm is still considered to be one of the best in its field, particularly on the IP and rights side, and on general anti-piracy law.

Media and entertainment has traditionally been a strong area for **Nielsen & Nørager**, and Ole Finn Nielsen is very well respected within the sector. The firm is active in the film industry, advising on contracts and financing, and also represents a number of individuals including the director Bille August. The firm also acts for TV-Danmark.

DLA Nordic's impressive media and entertainment team covers a broad range of sectors, including publishing, music, sports, film and radio. Christian Scherfig is vice-chairman of TV2, which the firm is advising on its impending privatisation. In other areas it advised Clear Channel Inc and Aller AS on their sale of Radio 2 to SBS. It also assisted Nordic Open in setting up the first PGA golf tournament in Denmark.

MEDIA AND ENTERTAINMENT

BECH-BRUUN DRAGSTED ✪
LASSEN RICARD ✪

Johan Schlüter Advokatfirma ✪
Nielsen & Nørager ✪

DLA Nordic ✪
Kromann Reumert ✪
Plesner Svane Grønborg ✪
Viltoft & Høberg-Petersen ✪

Bang & Regnarsen
Brix Jensen Havemann Djurhuus
Jonas Bruun Advokatfirma ✪
Lett, Vilstrup & Partnere ✪

Firms are listed A-Z in tiers which are ranked in order of priority
✪ *Indicates firm displays contact details at the end of this chapter.*

Kromann Reumert is recommended for its expertise in the publishing industry. Erik Mohr Mersing advises the Danish Publishers Association, as well as several major publishing houses, including Gyldenhal, the largest in Denmark. Meanwhile, Martin Dahl Pedersen has acted for the Danish Newspaper Publishers' Association in a number of high-profile cases involving printed and electronic news. The firm also advises TDC on its cable TV interests.

Plesner Svane Grønborg's Per Håkon Schmidt is representing the Danish Football Association and the Premier League Federation before the Supreme Court in a case against telecoms operator TDC. Major clients include Canal Digital, Warner/Chappell Music Denmark and Broadcast Service Denmark.

Bjørn Høberg-Petersen of **Viltoft & Høberg-Petersen** has developed a strong niche representing actors, having advised the Danish Actors' Association (DAA) for over 25 years, as well as the International Federation of Actors.

Managing partner Kim Egegaard of **Bang & Regnarsen** is an undisputed heavyweight in boxing-related matters. As well as acting for the European Boxing Association, he has advised promoters on money transfers, contracts and transmission rights.

At **Brix Jensen Havemann Djurhuus**, partner Michael Christiani Havemann is experienced in media and film law.

As well as advising TV2, Denmark's second-largest TV company, **Jonas Bruun Advokatfirma** also acts for several newspapers and magazines in the Berlingske Group on content-based press law.

Lett, Vilstrup & Partnere's media and entertainment practice suffered the departure of

Nina Henningsen to **Bech-Bruun Dragsted**. Susanne Mark is now the main point of contact at the firm.

MERGERS AND ACQUISITIONS

For the largest and most complex M&A deals it is the Big Four that get most of the work, as they are the only ones with the size and resources to handle such transactions. Nevertheless, there are a number of smaller firms with some excellent practitioners, who are regularly referred work when the Big Four are conflicted out.

Bech-Bruun Dragsted is one of the most active firms in the Danish M&A market, having advised on several of 2003's largest transactions. One of the undoubted highlights for group head Søren Meisling and partner Philip Risbjørn was acting for AP Møller – Mærsk on its multi-million euro acquisition of Dampskibsselskabet af 1912, making it the largest shipping group in Denmark. The firm has a broad practice and is particularly experienced in venture capital work and advised CVC Capital Partners on its €800m acquisition of Danske Trælast A/S. Partner NE Nielsen also enjoys a good name.

In 2003 **Gorrissen Federspiel Kierkegaard** acted on two of the largest acquisitions in Denmark. The firm advised Danish bank Nykredit, on its highly complex acquisition of the 51.8% controlling share in Totalkredit, which was owned by 101 separate banks. It is also representing Danish energy giant Elsam on its proposed acquisition of NESA, which awaits approval from the competition authorities. A large proportion of the partnership is highly experienced in M&A, and managing partner Niels Heering and partner Klaus Søgaard are particularly well known for their work.

Kromann Reumert's esteemed M&A team is regularly praised for its high-quality advice and level of service. Of late it has been seeing a lot of mid- to high-level private M&A and equity work. A major instruction came from Arla Foods, Europe's largest dairy co-operative, on its acquisition of a 51% shareholding in Express Dairies, in a transaction worth £150m. The firm also advised DONG on its aborted takeover bid for NESA. Partners Poul Pedersen, Jørgen Kjegaard Madsen and Marianne Philip merit mention.

Plesner Svane Grønborg's top tier M&A team capped off the end of 2002 with one of Denmark's largest private equity exit transactions. This involved two of the firm's leading partners, Finn Lernø and Jacob Bier, who advised Nordic Capital on its disposal of Nycomed Holding to an investor group including Credit Suisse First Boston Private Equity, Blackstone Capital Partners and NIB Capital Private Equity. 2003 also presented the firm with a raft of venture capital and traditional M&A work. One of its newest clients, Danfoss, instructed it on the acquisition of DEVI, a global supplier of electronic floor heating systems.

MERGERS AND ACQUISITIONS

BECH-BRUUN DRAGSTED ✪
GORRISSEN FEDERSPIEL KIERKEGAARD
KROMANN REUMERT ✪
PLESNER SVANE GRØNBORG ✪

Jonas Bruun Advokatfirma ✪

Accura Advokataktieselskab ✪
Hjejle, Gersted & Mogensen
Lett, Vilstrup & Partnere ✪
Lind & Cadovius ✪
Nielsen & Nørager ✪
Philip & Partners ✪

DLA Nordic ✪
Eversheds Advokataktieselskab
Focus Advokater LLP ✪
Lassen Ricard ✪
Lett & Co ✪
Lund Elmer Sandager
Magnusson Wahlin Qvist Stanbrook
Mazanti-Andersen, Korsø Jensen & Partnere ✪
Rønne & Lundgren ✪

Firms are listed A-Z in tiers which are ranked in order of priority
✪ Indicates firm displays contact details at the end of this chapter.

Of the smaller firms, **Jonas Bruun Advokatfirma** is widely regarded by those in the Big Four to have the best M&A practice. Generally the quality of work and expertise is more than a match for those in the top tier, but the firm's size puts a limit on how much it can do. The undoubted highlight of the year has been advising NESA on its proposed €1.4bn sale to Elsam. It also acted for Højgaard Holding and FLS Industries on the €309m sale of their 41% shareholding in the Portuguese company Secil to its majority shareholder SEMAPA. Mogens Ebeling and Christian Sinding are the two leading partners here. Generally when the Big Four is conflicted out of work, **Jonas Bruun Advokatfirma** is one of the first ports of call.

Kåre Stolt and Thomas Weincke head **Accura Advokataktieselskab**'s up-and-coming M&A practice. The firm sees itself as an M&A boutique and acts for an impressive list of private equity investors and corporate clients, including 3i, Montague Private Equity, Merck, ChevronTexaco and Cable & Wireless. Recently it advised a consortium led by Axcel, on its acquisition of NetTest from Great Nordic. It is also well-versed in hostile takeovers and public-to-private bids, having recently advised CW Obel Consortium on its proposed bid to takeover Sjælsø Gruppen.

Like **Jonas Bruun Advokatfirma**, **Hjejle, Gersted & Mogensen** enjoys a strong reputation in M&A work, and regularly finds itself up against the Big Four. Most recently it acted for Gentoft Municipality and Copenhagen County on the sale of shares in NESA to Elsam, in a deal that has an overall value of €1.4bn. The firm also advises venture capitalists, particularly on investments in the biotech sector.

Lett, Vilstrup & Partnere's solid practice advised Falck Denmark on its purchase of Varde public hospital and the establishment of its own private hospital. It also acted for Alm. Brand, one of Denmark's largest insurers, on its sale of a portfolio of claims to DAI. Søren Jenstrup is rated.

Lind & Cadovius has a sound reputation in M&A, where partners Frantz Palludan and Hans Madsen are the main practitioners. The firm has, however, lost valuable fee-earners, and the demise of *Denton International*, from which it got numerous referrals, is a disappointment.

Nielsen & Nørager has established a good name for itself in M&A work, particularly in the pharmaceutical and biotech industries, where it represents several major venture capitalists. Recent highlights include advising Telmore on its sale to TDC. Morten Eldrup-Jørgensen is recommended, as is Eigil Lego Anderson who recently arrived from **Bech-Bruun Dragsted**.

DLA Nordic advised on an impressive range of transactions in 2003, including Credit Suisse First Boston on the €800m acquisition of Sigma Coating. It also acted for Roskilde County and Frederiksborg County on the sale of shares in NESA to Elsam. Partner Jakob Kornerup is recommended for his investment fund work, for clients such as Dania Capital, Nordic Biotech, Symbion Capital and Northzone IV.

Eversheds Advokataktieselskab regularly advises lenders on the financing of M&A deals. Managing partner Troels Askerud and partners Jens Arnesen and Mikael Lunøe are all experienced in M&A work.

Ib Thrane heads **Focus Advokater LLP**'s M&A group, which advises on small-to-medium sized acquisitions in and around Funen.

Primarily known for media and entertainment, **Lassen Ricard** also has a strong M&A practice, headed by name partner Lennart Ricard. Recently it acted for Sakata on its acquisition of L Dæhnfeldt's worldwide flower seed division. It also advised Bayer on its purchase of Tectrade, a leading supplier of raw materials in the European polyurethane processing industries. The firm also represents a number of VCs including VT Holding.

Jesper Fabricius and Finn Overgaard are the main M&A partners at **Lett & Co**, which focuses on small- to medium-sized transactions. A recent highlight was advising Aalborg Portland, one of the world's leading cement producers, on its acquisition of Mørchs Cement.

Philip Baruch is one of **Lund Elmer Sandager**'s leading M&A partners, with particularly good experience in advising Swedish companies on their various transactions in Denmark.

Lars Lokdam heads **Magnusson Wahlin Qvist Stanbrook**'s M&A practice, which advised on a number of sizeable transactions in 2003, for corporate and venture capital clients.

Mazanti-Andersen, Korsø Jensen & Partnere has a number of highly experienced partners in M&A. Anders Cold advised Cerealia on its acquisition of Schulstad, Denmark's largest bread producer. Meanwhile J Korsø Jensen, Jens Ahrendt and Kirsten Frijs advised EMI Group on the mergers of a number of its subsidiaries.

Finn Rønne heads **Rønne & Lundgren**'s seven-strong M&A group, which mainly acts for Danish companies, on their investments at home and abroad.

REAL ESTATE AND CONSTRUCTION

Leif Djurhuus, **Plesner Svane Grønborg**'s head of commercial property enjoys enormous popularity with clients, who think he delivers 'good quality work at a high level.' He is particularly experienced in shopping centre-related issues. One of the firm's largest transactions was for Nordea on the €175m sale of its real estate portfolio to Danish PKA Pension Funds. Partner Poul Flemming Hansen is also praised by clients for his 'focus, quality and performance'. On the construction side Peter Fogh enjoys a good contractor-based following, for which he does mainly contentious work. Recently he acted for contractors on disputes arising out of the much-maligned Copenhagen metro.

Viltoft & Høberg-Petersen's first-rate construction practice is headed by Michael Gjedde-Nielsen and Hans Lykke Hansen, both of whom are well-known construction experts. The firm advises clients from across the spectrum, including public sector bodies, private developers and contractors. One of its largest clients is ØSS, which developed the Copenhagen Metro. Partner Claus Berg is also recommended.

Accura Advokataktieselskab's leading real estate practice is headed by Henrik Goos. The firm regularly acts for the international real estate group Lend Lease. One of the firm's largest transactions was for Keops Ejendomme, which it advised on the sale and lease-back of SAS's Danish real estate holdings. It also advised the Keops Group on a bond issue and listing.

With over 30 real estate lawyers **Bech-Bruun Dragsted** needs a raft of instructions to justify its size, and on the acquisition front, 2003 didn't disappoint. Headed by highly rated partner Torben Schøn, the team advised on some of Denmark's largest transactions. Stand-out deals include advising PFA on its €1bn internal portfolio sale to one of its subsidiaries, the largest such transaction of its kind within Denmark. It also acted for PKA on its €250m purchase of Nordea's property portfolio. The firm is also experienced on the finance side and regularly advises banks and pension funds on major transactions.

Gorrissen Federspiel Kierkegaard advises both domestic and international clients on acquisitions and leasing arrangements in Denmark. Recently the firm advised CGI, Commerzbank's Equity Fund, on its €201.6m acquisition of CK Development's 50% shareholding in the Fields shopping centre in Copenhagen. The firm has several strong practitioners practising out of Aarhus, including Troels Andersen and Peter Sjøgreen.

A major highlight for **Hjejle, Gersted & Mogensen** was advising Magasin on its €148m sale of Illum, Copenhagen's most prestigious department store, to an American buyer. It also acts for Doughty Hanson & Co Real Estate Fund on its various investments in Denmark. The firm represents several Danish pension funds on their real estate investments and is praised for its 'great competence in procedural law'.

Jonas Bruun Advokatfirma boasts several experienced real estate lawyers, including partners Poul Heidmann and Christian Sinding.

Headed by Niels Balslev, **Kromann Reumert**'s quality real estate team is expanding and has recently added former corporate partner Thomas Albrechtsen to its ranks. The firm advises a mix of pension funds, developers and investors, including GE Capital Real Estate, SAS, Ikea, Marriott Hotel and Babcock & Wilcox Vølund ApS.

Lind & Cadovius has a solid and experienced real estate practice. Mads Berendt and CK Knudsen are two of the firm's leading partners in this sector.

Lund Elmer Sandager has a strong real estate practice, which acts for developers and investors. Partners Steen Raagaard Andersen and Kjeld Jørgensen are two of the firm's leading practitioners.

Westergaard & Alstrøm is a real estate and construction boutique that mainly advises local municipalities, though it does have a number of private clients as well.

DLA Nordic's real estate team regularly advises Copenhagen Municipality on its properties, it also acted for Copenhagen Energy on the sale of its headquarters.

Lett & Co partner Pernille Sølling is recommended for her expertise in risk insurance, and has acted for insurance companies on construction disputes. Clients included Copenhagen County, as well as insurers Tryg, Codan and Alm. Brand.

Real estate makes up for about 10% of **Lett, Vilstrup & Partnere**'s practice. Recent highlights include advising DSB on the development and sale of some of its substantial landholdings.

J Korsø Jensen at **Mazanti-Andersen, Korsø Jensen & Partnere** has a strong reputation for construction disputes. Alongside Philip Thorsen and Anne Videsen, he advised Alstom Power Danmark in a dispute regarding the construction of its water treatment and waste incineration plants. The firm also offers non-contentious advice to a number of construction companies.

REAL ESTATE AND CONSTRUCTION

PLESNER SVANE GRØNBORG ✪

VILTOFT & HØBERG-PETERSEN ✪

Accura Advokataktieselskab ✪
Bech-Bruun Dragsted ✪
Gorrissen Federspiel Kierkegaard
Hjejle, Gersted & Mogensen
Jonas Bruun Advokatfirma ✪
Kromann Reumert ✪
Lind & Cadovius ✪
Lund Elmer Sandager
Westergaard & Alstrøm

DLA Nordic ✪
Lett & Co ✪
Lett, Vilstrup & Partnere ✪
Mazanti-Andersen, Korsø Jensen & Partnere ✪

Magnusson Wahlin Qvist Stanbrook
Nielsen & Nørager ✪
Norsker & Jacoby ✪

Firms are listed A-Z in tiers which are ranked in order of priority
✪ Indicates firm displays contact details at the end of this chapter.

SHIPPING AND TRANSPORT

Alex Laudrup heads **Gorrissen Federspiel Kierkegaard**'s superb shipping and transport group. The practice boasts years of experience across the entire range of shipping law, both contentious and non-contentious. It acts for major Danish shipowners, including Norden and Scandlines, and several P&I clubs. The firm works closely with UK shipping firms such as **Watson, Farley & Williams** and **Richards Butler**. It has also acted for airlines including Maersk Air. Peter Appel is recommended on the transactional side.

Kromann Reumert's shipping department is highly recommended. Bent Neilsen, Lars Rosenberg Overby and Henrik Thal Jantzen advise most of Denmark's cargo and hull underwriters, as well as P&I and defence clubs such as Gard. Christian Hennings is well known for ship finance, while Anders Hedetoft is

SHIPPING AND TRANSPORT

GORRISSEN FEDERSPIEL KIERKEGAARD
KROMANN REUMERT ✪

Bang & Regnarsen
Bech-Bruun Dragsted ✪
DLA Nordic ✪
Focus Advokater LLP ✪
Lett, Vilstrup & Partnere ✪
Mazanti-Andersen, Korsø Jensen & Partnere ✪
Philip & Partners ✪
Plesner Svane Grønborg ✪
Viltoft & Høberg-Petersen ✪

Firms are listed A-Z in tiers which are ranked in order of priority
✪ Indicates firm displays contact details at the end of this chapter.

experienced in freight forwarding and customs issues. Recently the firm represented owners of the ship *Gdynia* following its high-profile collision with the *Fu Shan Hai*.

Ulla Fabricius heads **Bang & Regnarsen**'s shipping group, which advises domestic and international shipping companies, carriers and transport operators in contracts and liability matters.

Bech-Bruun Dragsted's shipping and transport group offers expertise across a range of related areas. It is currently involved in a major oil pollution case following the collision of the Chinese ship, *Fu Shan Hai*, and the Polish ship, *Gdynia*, in the Baltic Sea. It handles cargo claims and represents a number of shipowners, such as Torm and J Poulsen Shipping, and P&I clubs, including COSCO and West of England P&I Club. Group head Henrik Valdorf-Hansen also helms the firm's insurance department.

Through its membership of the *DLA Group*, **DLA Nordic** receives valuable referral work. In 2003 it advised an international oil company regarding a transporter's pollution of onshore facilities. It also provides transport liability advice to the insurer Vesta. One of the firm's main clients is the Mediterranean Shipping Company.

Peter Ringsted heads **Focus Advokater LLP**'s shipping group, which advised on the registration of over 25 foreign vessels in 2003. The firm represents a mix of owners, bareboat charterers and banks.

Lett, Vilstrup & Partnere is arguably Denmark's leading firm for railway transportation issues, and is the main adviser to the Danish State Railways (DSB).

Plesner Svane Grønborg concentrates mainly on shipping and aircraft finance and advised a Danish shipowner on the purchase of two Canadian tugboats. Peter Fogh is the main practitioner and has represented clients in the Supreme Court on shipping and transport cases.

Viltoft & Høberg-Petersen has particularly strong expertise in maritime penal law and maritime pollution. The firm has also represented crews on several salvage disputes. Bjørn Høberg-Petersen, who acts for the Danish Navigators' Association, and Niels Kjægaard are both recommended.

TAX

Group head Hans Severin Hansen of **Plesner Svane Grønborg** is the undisputed legal heavyweight of the Danish tax scene. Praised for his 'personal and dedicated approach and the ability to win tax court cases', Severin, who is a member of the permanent advisory board to the Ministry of Taxation, sets a 'high professional standard always ending at the right solutions'.

TAX

PLESNER SVANE GRØNBORG ✪

HJEJLE, GERSTED & MOGENSEN
TOMMY V CHRISTIANSEN, ADVOKATFIRMAET ✪

Accura Advokataktieselskab ✪
Bech-Bruun Dragsted ✪
Kromann Reumert ✪
Lett & Co ✪
Lind & Cadovius ✪
Nielsen & Nørager ✪

Dania Advokater A/S (Dania Law Firm Ltd)
Gorrissen Federspiel Kierkegaard
Mazanti-Andersen, Korsø Jensen & Partnere ✪
Norsker & Jacoby ✪
Osborne Clarke
Rønne & Lundgren ✪

Firms are listed A-Z in tiers which are ranked in order of priority
✪ Indicates firm displays contact details at the end of this chapter.

Recently the team represented Coloplast and Novo Nordisk in a test case before the Supreme Court, which ended in the court overruling 30 years of administrative practices on tax matters regarding employee share issues, at a cost to the state of €125-€250m.

Hjejle, Gersted & Mogensen has always enjoyed a superb reputation for tax work, particularly on the contentious side. Recently, however, its star has slightly diminished, since the retirement of one of its most esteemed senior partners, Aage Spang-Hanssen. The feeling is that the firm might struggle to replace him, although there are some strong practitioners in this area, including partners Søren Nielsen and Jan Steen Hansen.

Based in Aarhus, **Advokatfirmaet Tommy V Christiansen** is a tax boutique with a top-notch reputation, particularly on the litigation front. Name partner Tommy Christiansen carries an excellent name.

Accura Advokataktieselskab boasts a sound tax practice, which provides strong support for the firm's impressive corporate team. The practice, which is headed by Lars Fogh, has very strong expertise in tax structuring work.

Partner Kurt Siggaard heads **Bech-Bruun Dragsted**'s tax department from the firm's Aarhus office. The ten-fee-earner group handles a mixture of standalone and corporate support work, both on the contentious and non-contentious side. Partner Nikolaj Bjørnholm has been particularly active on the litigation front and in 2003 won several cases brought against the Danish tax authorities, including one before the Supreme Court and three in the High Court. Major clients include Northrop Grumman, JPMorgan, Credit Suisse First Boston and Gillette.

Kromann Reumert boasts a dedicated tax team, which offers both standalone and support advice. Partners Flemming Andersen, Jan Børjesson and Arne Ottosen are the firm's main practitioners.

Lett & Co's strong tax practice mainly focuses on litigation matters, such as customs duties and indirect taxation, though it also represents commercial clients on non-contentious issues. The firm is often instructed by the government when **Poul Schmith Law Firm** is conflicted out, and recently it represented the Ministries of Taxation and Defence before the Supreme Court, on tax issues surrounding their land holdings. It also acted for the Municipality of Høje-Tåstrup regarding the division of tax revenue between municipalities. The firm's two main tax experts are Claus Holberg and Jesper Lett, who is chairman of the Danish Tax Lawyers Association.

Lind & Cadovius has a sound tax litigation practice, where Jess Thiersen has a following. Jørgen Cadovius has experience in tax planning.

Henrik Peytz at **Nielsen & Nørager** is known for his expertise in EU-related tax law, and has appeared before the European Court of Justice in a case relating to Danish VAT rules and their compatibility with EU law.

TELECOMS

Bech-Bruun Dragsted offers its telecommunications clients a wealth of experience in regulatory and commercial matters, and is backed up by strong IT and IP teams. Of late it has advised clients on a variety of issues including UMTS licences, infra-sharing agreements and antitrust matters. Major clients include Orange, Telia, debitel and Colt Telecommunications.

Mogens Ebeling of **Jonas Bruun Advokatfirma** is highly recommended for his expertise in the telecoms sector, where the recently made up Christine Jansby also has a strong interest. Denmark's second largest telecoms company, Sonofon, is a major client, while the firm also acts for BT and AT&T. The firm regularly works alongside UK firms **Taylor Wessing**, **Bird & Bird** and **Olswang**.

TELECOMS

BECH-BRUUN DRAGSTED ✪
JONAS BRUUN ADVOKATFIRMA ✪
LETT & CO ✪
KROMANN REUMERT ✪

DLA Nordic ✪
Gorrissen Federspiel Kierkegaard
Lind & Cadovius ✪

Firms are listed A-Z in tiers which are ranked in order of priority
✪ Indicates firm displays contact details at the end of this chapter.

Lett & Co continues to be regularly instructed by TDC, which it is representing in the High Court against the Danish Data Association, Dansk IT, regarding the implementation of telecoms legislation. The litigation side to the firm's telecoms practice remains extremely busy.

Torben Waage is one of the leading practitioners at **Kromann Reumert**, which regularly acts for TDC. It was also appointed a trustee for KPNQwest.

Michael Goeskjær is the main telecoms partner at **DLA Nordic**, which advises Motorola on all its related issues. Other clients include Colt, MCI WorldCom and Global Crossing.

Gorrissen Federspiel Kierkegaard acts for several major telecoms clients including Orange and Hutchison 3G. Managing partner Niels Heering also sits on the board of TDC.

Hans Madsen heads **Lind & Cadovius**' practice, which has acted for several major telecoms players.

BECH-BRUUN DRAGSTED

FRUE KIRKEPLADS 4
8100 AARHUS C

Telephone: +45 89 31 00 00
Fax: +45 89 31 01 01
E-mail: info@bechbruundragsted.com
Website: www.bechbruundragsted.com

Languages
English, French, German, Russian, the Scandinavian languages

Other offices
Copenhagen, Brussels, Moscow

Number of lawyers 261
at this office 51

CATEGORIES OF WORK

- Banking, securities, finance and capital markets
- Construction law, environmental law and real property
- Corporate law
- Employment and labour law
- Energy law
- EU and competition
- Insolvency
- Intellectual property
- IT and telecommunications law
- Litigation and arbitration
- Maritime law, transport and insurance law
- Media and entertainment, sports law
- Mergers and acquisitions, venture capital
- Public law
- Reconstruction
- Tax law

DE LA COUR

LILLE TORV 6
PO BOX 505
8100 AARHUS C

Telephone: + 45 70 11 11 22
Fax: + 45 70 11 11 33
E-mail: delacour@delacour.dk
Website: www.delacour.dk

Languages
English, French, German, the Scandinavian languages

Other offices
Copenhagen

Number of lawyers 47
at this office 39

Member
Advoc, an international network of independent law firms

CATEGORIES OF WORK

- Arbitration and litigation
- Banking and finance
- Business set-up in China and eastern Europe
- Company and commercial
- Directorship
- Employment and labour
- Environmental law
- EU and competition
- Insolvency
- Insurance
- Intellectual property and IT
- Mergers and acquisitions
- Real estate and construction
- Sale and purchase of horses
- Tax
- Transport and maritime law

KROMANN REUMERT

3 RAADHUSPLADSEN
8000 AARHUS

Telephone: +45 70 12 12 11
Fax: +45 70 12 14 11
E-mail: arh@kromannreumert.com
Website: www.kromannreumert.com

Languages
Dutch, English, French, German, the Scandinavian languages

Other offices
Brussels, Copenhagen, London

Number of lawyers 232
at this office 52

Member
Lex Mundi; Scandinavian Law Alliance

CATEGORIES OF WORK

- Banking and finance
- Commercial and company
- Competition
- Employment and labour
- Energy
- Insolvency
- Insurance and tort law
- Intellectual property, media and marketing law
- IT and telecommunications
- Litigation and arbitration
- Maritime and transportation
- Mergers and acquisitions
- Real property, environmental and construction law
- Shipping
- Stock exchange regulation
- Tax law

LETT & CO

ÅBOULEVARDEN 31
8100 AARHUS C

Telephone: +45 86 12 86 00
Fax: +45 86 12 86 56
E-mail: lettco@lettco.dk
Website: www.lettco.dk

Languages
English, German, the Scandinavian languages

Other offices
Copenhagen

Number of lawyers 45
at this office 9

CATEGORIES OF WORK

- Mergers and acquisitions
- Company and commercial
- Competition/antitrust
- Insolvency
- Insurance and liability
- International trade
- Litigation and arbitration

ADVOKATFIRMAET TOMMY V CHRISTIANSEN

FRICHSPARKEN
SØREN FRICHS VEJ 42 A
8230 ÅRHUS

Telephone: +45 70 11 08 00
Fax: +45 70 11 08 01
E-mail: tvc@tvc.dk
Website: www.tvc.dk

Languages
English

Other offices
Copenhagen

Number of lawyers 26
at this office 24

Member
IBA (International Bar Association);
IFA (International Fiscal Association)

CATEGORIES OF WORK

Tax
Tommy V Christiansen, Lars Henriksen

Dispute resolution, litigation and arbitration
Tommy V Christiansen, Torben Bagge

Corporate restructuring
Tommy V Christiansen, Michael Serup

Corporate and commercial
Michael Serup, Søren Tonnesen

Mergers and acquisitions
Søren Tonnesen

Commercial property, real estate
Niels Kaiser

Construction
Niels Kaiser

Insolvency
Flemming Bastholm

Labour law
Flemming Bastholm

ACCURA
ACCURA ADVOKATAKTIESELSKAB

STRANDVEJEN 60
2900 HELLERUP
COPENHAGEN

Telephone: +45 39 45 39 50
Fax: +45 39 45 39 60
E-mail: info@accura.dk
Website: www.accura.dk

Languages
English, French, German,
the Scandinavian languages

Number of lawyers 30

Contacts
Kåre Stolt, Thomas Weincke

CATEGORIES OF WORK

Commercial and competition
Karsten Kielland,
Annemette Thorgaard

Company law
Kåre Stolt, Karsten Kielland

Corporate structuring
Lars Fogh, Kåre Stolt

Dispute resolution
Henrik Groos

Technology, media and communications
Claus Bennetsen,
Niels Christian Wedell-Wedellsborg

Employment and human resources
Anne Kathrine Schøn,
Nicole Offendal

Financial services
Claus Bennetsen,
Kim Toftgaard

Insolvency law/ financial restructuring
Jesper Trommer-Volf,
Peter Møller Nielsen

Intellectual property
Thomas Weincke, Karsten Kielland

Mergers and acquisitions
Kåre Stolt, Thomas Weincke

Public law
Henrik Groos

Real estate
Henrik Groos, Lars Bruun

Tax
Lars Fogh, Henriette la Cour

BECH-BRUUN DRAGSTED

LANGELINIE ALLÉ 35
2100 COPENHAGEN

Telephone: +45 72 27 00 00
Fax: +45 72 27 00 27
E-mail: info@bechbruundragsted.com
Website: www.bechbruundragsted.com

Languages
English, French, German, Italian, the Scandinavian languages

Other offices
Aarhus, Brussels, Moscow

Number of lawyers 261
at this office 198

CATEGORIES OF WORK

Aviation

Banking, securities, finance and capital markets

Construction law, environmental law and real property

Corporate law

Employment and labour law

Energy law

EU and competition

Insolvency

Intellectual property

IT and telecommunications law

Litigation and arbitration

Maritime law, transport and insurance law

Media and entertainment, sports law

Mergers and acquisitions, venture capital

Public law

Reconstruction

Tax law

DLA NORDIC

VED STRANDEN 18
P O BOX 2034
1012 COPENHAGEN

Telephone: +45 77 30 40 50
Fax: +45 77 30 40 77
E-mail: info@dlanordic.dk
Website: www.dlanordic.com

Languages
English, French, German, Hebrew, the Scandinavian languages

Other offices
Bergen, Oslo, Stockholm
and 33 offices across Europe and Asia

Number of lawyers 199
at this office 63

Contacts
Torsten Hoffmeyer, Finn Schwarz, Jens Jakob Bugge

Member
DLA Group

CATEGORIES OF WORK

Transport and energy
Hans Abildstrøm, Klavs V Gravensen

TIME
Jens Jakob Bugge, Michael Goeskjaer

Construction and real estate
Michael Neumann, Nicolai Horten

Public law (including competition law and consumer law)
Lars Carstens, Lise Groesmeyer

Tax and duty
Bjarne Becher Jensen, Anne Krebs

Commercial law (including administration of estates and insolvency)
Casper Moltke, Steen Klein

Corporate
Christian Scherfig, Torsten Hoffmeyer

Employment
Finn Schwarz,
Erik Wendelboe Christiansen

Criminal law
Jakob S Arrevad,
Finn Walther Petersen

THE FIRM

DLA Nordic is the only Nordic law firm, with offices in Copenhagen, Oslo, Bergen and Stockholm. The firm ranks among the leading law firms in its respective home markets in Denmark, Norway and Sweden. Each office provides a complete range of integrated legal services across borders, both in the local market and on a global basis.

DLA Nordic is is part of DLA Group. DLA Group is an exclusive alliance of international full-service law firms with a shared vision. Established in 1999, DLA Group now has over 2,200 lawyers across 21 countries, who deliver expert local know-how and international solutions. DLA Group provides legal advice in 37 major cities across Europe, Singapore, Thailand, Hong Kong and the People's Republic of China.

DLA Nordic's vision is to be the leading Nordic law firm, and is based on the observation that many clients hold operations in all three countries. DLA Nordic is a modern, growing practice with distinct client service focus; legal advice is based on a proactive approach and an understanding of the client's business. The firm offers a thorough and cost-effective mode of work, knowledge and insight in the local business environment, seamless Scandinavian and international legal services, and commercially based solutions.

Providing a full service in all major practice areas, the firm is organised into eight cross-border legal departments, concerning the practice areas. The departments work together making sure that legal expertise is exchanged and shared, utilising legal resources fully and providing optimal service to the client.

Clients include public and private companies in a variety of sectors: commerce; industry; manufacturing services; property; construction; finance; IT, telecoms, media and entertainment; transport; shipping; and oil, gas and electricity. The firm also serves a large number of international clients, including large corporations, banks, investment firms and venture capital funds.

AREAS OF PRACTICE

Transport and energy: specialised legal services in all fields of energy, transport and maritime law, over the European land transport law, based upon the CMR Convention, to the complex and still-developing laws on combined and multi-modual transports.

TIME: specialists in law related to IT, telecoms, IP and media, and marketing and entertainment. Represents IT companies of every kind.

Commercial property/real estate: all matters concerning purchase, sale and financing of non-residential properties and private housing properties. The division has a solid competence in dealing with sale and leaseback arrangements.

Public: DLA Nordic has a large department for public law that continues to expand, not least as a result of DLA Nordic's many years of acting for and providing legal services to a number of local governments.

Litigation: litigation continues as a central part of DLA Nordic's practice. The firm's integrated work method plays an important role, since litigation skills must often be combined with specialist knowledge.

Tax and duty: reviews and optimises clients' corporate structures and transactional documents ensuring full compliance with and utilisation of present applicable tax law. DLA Nordic also acts on behalf of clients in negotiations and disputes with tax authorities.

Commercial and insolvency: experience relating to all company matters including: company reconstruction; flotations; shareholders agreements and partnership agreements; liquidation and incorporations; and commercial contracts.

Corporate: provides all services within corporate law, both with transaction services as advice on specific matters.

Employment: years of in-depth experience in labour and employment law and practical knowledge of industry.

Criminal: all activities, including option/future fraud, asset stripping and injury.

DE LA COUR

HAMMERENSGADE 1
1267 KØBENHAVN K

Telephone: +45 70 11 11 22
Fax: + 45 70 11 11 33
E-mail: delacour@delacour.dk
Website: www.delacour.dk

Languages
English, German, French, Russian, Bulgarian, the Scandinavian languages

Other offices
Aarhus

Number of lawyers 47
at this office 8

Member
Advoc, an international network of independent law firms

CATEGORIES OF WORK

Arbitration and litigation

Banking and finance

Biotechnology

Company and commercial

Employment and labour

EU and competition

Insurance

Intellectual property and IT

Mergers and acquisitions

Real estate and construction

JOHAN SCHLÜTER ADVOKATFIRMA

SUNDKROGSGADE 9
2100 COPENHAGEN

Telephone: +45 33 63 96 50
Fax: +45 33 6396 60
E-mail: info@jschluter.com
Website: www.jschluter.com

Languages
English, German, French, the Scandinavian languages

Other offices
Aarhus

Number of lawyers 21

Contact
Johan Schlüter

CATEGORIES OF WORK

Commercial and company law
J Schlüter, M Lavesen

Litigation
T Steffensen, A Valentin

Arbitration
J Schlüter, T Steffensen

Copyright
J Schlüter, NB Jørgensen

Trademarks
L Karnøe

Patent
A Valentin, O Damsbo

Sports
L Halgreen

Media and entertainment
J Schlüter, KS Schierbeck

IT – Internet
NB Jørgensen

EU and competition
J Schlüter, L Halgreen

JONAS BRUUN ADVOKATFIRMA

BREDGADE 38
1260 COPENHAGEN K

Telephone: +45 33 47 88 00
Fax: +45 33 47 88 88
E-mail: jb@jblaw.dk
Website: www.jonasbruun.dk

Languages
Arabic, English, French, German, Spanish, Dutch

Number of lawyers 37

CATEGORIES OF WORK

Arbitration and litigation	Energy
Banking and finance	Environment
Commercial property	Intellectual property
Company and commercial	Mergers and acquisitions
Construction	Telecommunications, media and entertainment
EU and competition	

KROMANN REUMERT

5 SUNDKROGSGADE
2100 COPENHAGEN

Telephone: +45 70 12 12 11
Fax: +45 70 12 13 11
E-mail: cph@kromannreumert.com
Website: www.kromannreumert.com

Languages
English, Dutch, French, German, the Scandinavian languages

Other offices
Aarhus, Brussels, London

Number of lawyers 232
at this office 177

Member
Lex Mundi; Scandinavian Law Alliance

CATEGORIES OF WORK

Banking and finance	IT and telecommunications
Commercial and company	Litigation and arbitration
Competition	Maritime and transportation
Employment and labour	Mergers and acquisitions
Energy	Real property, environmental and construction law
Insolvency	Shipping
Insurance and tort law	Stock exchange regulation
Intellectual property, media and marketing law	Tax law

LASSEN RICARD

LAW FIRM

31 AMALIEGADE
1256 COPENHAGEN

Telephone: +45 33 32 20 12
Fax: +45 33 32 24 74
E-mail: lrlaw@lrlaw.dk
Website: www.lassenricard.dk

Languages
English, French, German, Norwegian, Swedish

Number of lawyers 10

CATEGORIES OF WORK	
Banking and finance	**IT**
Company and commercial	**Litigation and arbitration**
Construction	**Media and entertainment**
EU and competition	**Mergers and acquisitions**
Intellectual property	**Telecommunications**

THE FIRM

Lassen Ricard is an international law firm advising mainly on commercial law issues, and in particular, on cases relating to international matters.

Lassen Ricard attach importance to the personal contact between the client and the attorneys, or team of attorneys, who advise the client, to ensure an essential relationship of trust.

It is crucial for the firm to offer legal service of the highest professional standard. Lassen Ricard has a close, non-exclusive co-operation with distinguished law firms abroad.

In addition to their legal degrees from Danish universities, several of the firm's attorneys hold degrees from foreign universities, such as Harvard Law School, University of Delaware, Duke Law School, University of Chicago Law School, City of London College and George Washington University.

The attorneys of Lassen Ricard are authorised to appear before all Danish courts, including the Danish Supreme Court. They have extensive experience pleading before arbitral tribunals and also act as judges in arbitration tribunals. In addition, the firm has experience in pleading before the European Court of Justice.

AREAS OF PRACTICE

Lassen Ricard provides a full range of services within corporate and commercial law, media, entertainment and intellectual property law, mergers and acquisitions, EU and competition law, IT, telecoms and litigation. Among Lassen Ricard's clients within said areas are a large number of international companies, as well as large and mid-size Danish companies. The firm also assists some of their clients by being appointed board members.

Lassen Ricard has extensive knowledge within intellectual property and is the leading Danish law firm within media and entertainment representing a large number of broadcasters and broadcasting organisations, as well as record companies, theatres, artists etc.

Representative clients include: Agfa; Banctec; Bayer; British Broadcasting Corporation; Biomet; Discovery Communications Europe; Danish Radio and Television; Danish TV2; Eurosport; Matsushita; Nord-Deutscher Rundfunk; Norwegian Radio and Television; TV2 Norway; Rai; Seiko; Sony Music Entertainment; Zweites Deutsches Fernsehen; Maxxium (Remy Martin, Jim Beam, Highland Distillers); RTL Plus; Sakata; Sat-1; Swedish Radio and Television; The Union of Broadcasting Organisations regarding Denmark, Norway, Sweden and Iceland; The Presidium of the Danish Parliament; The EU Environment Agency; and Turner Broadcasting System.

LETT & CO

RÅDHUSPLADSEN 4
1550 COPENHAGEN V

Telephone: +45 33 77 00 00
Fax: +45 33 77 00 01
E-mail: lettco@lettco.dk
Website: www.lettco.dk

Languages
English, French, German, the Scandinavian languages

Other offices
Aarhus

Number of lawyers 45
at this office 36

CATEGORIES OF WORK

- Administrative law
- Mergers and acquisitions
- Company and commercial
- Competition/antitrust
- Tax
- Litigation and arbitration
- Insurance and liability
- Food law
- Public procurement
- Intellectual property
- IT and telecommunications
- Employment and labour
- EU Law

LETT, VILSTRUP & PARTNERE

ADVOKATER

BREDGADE 3
3 SAL
1260 KØBENHAVN K

Telephone: +45 33 15 48 00
Fax: +45 33 15 59 95
E-mail: info@lvp-law.dk
Website: www.lvp-law.dk

Languages
English, French, German, Russian, the Scandinavian languages

Number of lawyers 30

CATEGORIES OF WORK

- Mergers and acquisitions
- Maritime and transportation law
- Taxes and duties
- Company law
- Financial services
- Public law
- Environmental law
- IT, e-commerce and telecommunications
- Intellectual property, media and entertainment law
- EU and competition law
- Law of torts and insurance law
- Energy law
- Employment and labour law

LIND & CADOVIUS

38 ØSTERGADE
PO BOX 2256
1019 KØBENHAVN K

Telephone: +45 33 33 81 00
Fax: +45 33 33 81 01
E-mail: law.office@lindcad.dk
Website: www.lindcad.dk

Languages
English, German, French,
the Scandinavian languages

Number of lawyers 40

CATEGORIES OF WORK

Company and commercial
Jørgen Cadovius, Frantz Palludan

Mergers and acquisitions
Frantz Palludan, Hans Madsen

Banking and finance
Frantz Palludan

Telecommunications
Hans Madsen

Intellectual property
Mads Berendt

Insolvency law
Henrik Andersen, Lars Skanvig

Construction and real estate
CK Knudsen, Mads Berendt

Media and entertaiment
Jens Krogh Petersen

Insurance
Nicolai Westergaard

Arbitration and litigation
Mads Berendt, Håkun Djurhuus,
Nicolai Westergaard

Employment, labour law
Nicolai Westergaard, Birgitte Horn

Tax
Jess Thiersen

Family, matrimonial
Povl Holm-Jørgensen

Energy
Hans Madsen

Competition and EU law
Lotte Hummelshøj, Sørel Zinck

Environment
Håkun Djurhuus

White-collar crime
Mads Berendt

NIELSEN & NØRAGER

METROPOL
FREDERIKSBERGGADE 16
1459 COPENHAGEN K

Telephone: +45 33 11 45 45
Fax: +45 33 11 80 81
E-mail: info@nnlaw.dk
Website: www.nnlaw.dk

Languages
English, French, German,
the Scandinavian languages

Number of lawyers 17

Member
Unilaw

CATEGORIES OF WORK

Arbitration and litigation
Jacob Nørager-Nielsen,
Eigil Lego Andersen

Banking and finance
Arne Gerlyng-Hansen

Company and commercial
Ole Finn Nielsen,
Morten Eldrup-Jørgensen

Construction
Arne Gerlyng-Hansen,
Halfdan Krag Jespersen

Corporate finance, M&A
Morten Eldrup-Jørgensen,
Eigil Lego Andersen

EC and competition
Henrik Peytz

Insurance
Michael S Wiisbye

Information technology
Jacob Nørager-Nielsen

Media and entertainment
Ole Finn Nielsen

Real estate
Marianne Kjær Stolt,
Arne Gerlyng-Hansen

Taxation
Henrik Peytz, Jan Presfeldt

Employment
Marianne Kjær Stolt

Telecoms
Henrik Peytz

Biotech
Morten Eldrup-Jørgensen,
Jan Presfeldt

MAZANTI-ANDERSEN, KORSØ JENSEN & PARTNERE

69 ST KONGENSGADE
1264 KØBENHAVN K

Telephone: +45 33 14 35 36
Fax: +45 33 19 37 37
E-mail: info@mazanti.dk
Website: www.mazanti.dk

Languages
English, French, German, Italian, the Scandinavian languages

Number of lawyers 35

CATEGORIES OF WORK

Mergers and acquisitions
J Korsø Jensen, Anders Cold

Bankruptcy, liquidation
Henrik B Sanders, Peter Krarup

Company and commercial
J Korsø Jensen, Anders Cold

Distributorship, agency, and franchising law
Kirsten Frijs, Michael Jacobsen

Litigation and arbitration
J Korsø Jensen, Philip S Thorsen

Employment, labour law
Georg Dedichen, Mette Ravn Steenstrup

Marketing – trade marks
Lise Høgh, Hanne Magnussen

Finance and banking
Georg Dedichen, Jørgen Kjældgaard

International contract
J Korsø Jensen, Philip S Thoren

Intellectual property
Lise Høgh, Kirsten Frijs

Tax
Hanne Magnussen, Flemming Otzen

EU and competition
Lise Høgh, Philip Thorsen

Family, matrimonial
Hans Henrik Gamborg, Bente Lund Poulsen

Environment
Birgitte Refn Wenzel

THE FIRM

The firm was initially formed in 1853 by CCV Liebe, a prominent Danish lawyer and politician, whose lead was followed by his son, Otto Liebe, who was both the first chairman of the Danish Bar Association and, in 1920, prime minister of Denmark. From 1932 the firm was headed by Leif Gamborg, and from 1958 by J Mazanti-Andersen who, together with Jørgen and Hans Henrik Gamborg, has continued the firm's tradition in relation to corporate and procedural law and furthermore established its international basis and developed its tax practice. Following two mergers, the firm has now expanded its practice to cover international commercial and corporate law, reconstruction of companies and bankruptcies.

It is the opinion of the firm that legal services in relation to clients' activities outside Denmark are best provided for by use of local counsel in the country in question. Consequently, the firm, instead of setting up branch offices outside Denmark, has chosen to participate in an international network of business-oriented law firms in Europe, North America, Asia and Australia.

The international network – still expanding – is basically established through personal relations between the participating law firms, developed over many years. Due to these relations the firm's clients are assured that legal problems in individual foreign countries are solved by local lawyers with a satisfactory degree of personal involvement and competence.

Today, the firm is one of the largest, best-known and respected law firms in Denmark, representing major national and international clients in all areas of business-related matters.

AREAS OF PRACTICE

The firm has extensive expertise in company and commercial law combined with expertise in international tax matters. It is the stated objective of Mazanti-Andersen, Korsø Jensen & Partnere to provide the high-quality professional services that the business community expects from an efficient law firm with an international practice. The firm is constantly seeking to maintain its up-to-the-minute legal expertise and all its lawyers participate on a regular basis in an extensive legal training programme within specific areas of law. Many of the firm's lawyers also lecture on different areas of corporate and commercial law at universities both in Denmark and abroad.

It has been the experience of the firm that most clients prefer a consistent personal service. Consequently, it is a fundamental objective of the firm's operation to charge one lawyer with the sole responsibility for monitoring and co-ordinating all the affairs of each client to ensure that they have a clear line of contact with the firm.

Naturally, the firm is not restricted by this principle. If complicated projects demand the expertise from different parts of the firm, it will always make available the necessary resources to any client at short notice.

The active promotion of specialisations within the firm ensures that it is able to adapt its practice to meet developments in the business community together with the future needs and requirements of its clients. The firm has at its disposal all the necessary technical facilities, including an extensive computer-based legal library connected to a number of external databases.

NORRBOM & VINDING, member of ius laboris

LAW FIRM

DAMPFÆRGEVEJ 26
2100 COPENHAGEN

Telephone: +45 35 25 39 40
Fax: +45 35 25 39 50
E-mail: nv@nv-law.dk
Website: www.nv-law.dk

Languages
English, French, Italian, Spanish, the Scandinavian languages

Number of lawyers 20

Contacts
Mariann Norrbom, Jørgen Vinding, Morten Langer, Yvonne Frederiksen, Hans Juhler

Member
ius laboris, International Employment Law Pensions and Employee Benefits Alliance

CATEGORIES OF WORK

All aspects of labour law

All aspects of employment law

Company staff policies

Compensation and benefits

European labour law

Criminal aspects of labour law

Restructuring and transfer of undertakings

Social security

Employee participation

Pension schemes

Tax issues relating to employment law

THE FIRM

Norrbom & Vinding is a niche law firm dealing with all aspects of labour and employment law, exclusively for the management side. Although the firm is relatively new, it has 25 years of experience within its area of expertise, and a core of the firm's attorneys have worked together for more than 15 years. The firm is one of the first specialist offices in Denmark with a full service to both national and international clients on all aspects of law related to human resources.

Norrbom & Vinding is a member of ius laboris, International Employment Law Pensions and Employee Benefits Alliance. The alliance was formed in January 2001 and today numbers more than 1,000 lawyers in Europe, North and South America.

AREAS OF PRACTICE

Labour law: the firm advises managements in both public and private companies on the negotiation, interpretation and termination of collective agreements, and it frequently participates in industrial disputes procedures. The firm also advises companies on the establishment of European works councils.

Norrbom & Vinding offers advice on, and assistance with, both collective and individual aspects in connection with transfer of undertakings, restructuring, redundancies and outsourcing.

Pensions: pensions are an element of human resources attracting increasing interest. The firm assists on the drafting and implementation of company-based pension plans, pension issues relating to termination of employment and expatriation. The firm also offers advice on taxation aspects in relation to pensions.

Individual employment law: even within the very traditional area of employment law – the individual employment relationship – various developments in recent years have led to more complex legal problems. The firm's advice and sparring with HR departments within this area includes: recruitment procedures, employment contracts, material changes in existing employment conditions, severance agreements, discrimination, equal treatment, maternity/paternity leave, freedom of association and data protection.

Company policies: HR departments base their work on company policies to quite a large extent. Such policies may deal with issues ranging from alcohol policies, anti-harassment measures, the use of e-mail, and distribution of anniversary bonuses, to rules on absence due to sickness. The firm's advice on such aspects includes assessment of policies in relation to collective agreements and legislation, possible legal action in relation to non-compliance with company policies and review of policies with regard to sustainable development issues.

Benefits: today, pay is often a combination of many different elements, leading to an increase in the need for advice in relation to both the pay concept as such and to tax issues. In this area, Norrbom & Vinding assists on the composition of individual payroll packages and the development, implementation and subsequent administration of bonus, incentive and employee share programmes.

NORSKER & JACOBY

3 KVÆSTHUSGADE
1251 KØBENHAVN K

Telephone: +45 33 11 08 85
Fax: +45 33 93 75 30
E-mail: mmj@norsker-jacoby.dk
Website: www.norsker-jacoby.dk

Languages
English, French, German, Italian, Spanish, the Scandinavian languages

Other offices
Berlin, Cologne

Number of lawyers 43
at this office 37

Contacts
Mr M Marstrand-Jorgensen, Mr NE Norsker

CATEGORIES OF WORK

Patents, trade marks, designs, copyright

Companies, corporations

Commercial (general)

Banking, securities and finance

Family

German law

Insurance

Mergers and acquisitions

Arbitration and litigation

Insolvency

Commercial property

Tax

EU law

PHILIP & PARTNERS

VOGNMAGERGADE 7
1120 KØBENHAVN K

Telephone: +45 33 13 11 12
Fax: +45 33 32 80 45
E-mail: lawoffice@philip.dk
Website: www.philip.dk

Languages
English, French, German, Italian, Norwegian, Swedish

Number of lawyers 35

CATEGORIES OF WORK

Banking, securities and finance
Erik Malberg, Henning Hansen

Contract
Allan Philip, Claus Kaare Pedersen

Companies, corporations
Mogens Gaarden, Peer B Petersen

Mergers and acquisitions
Henning Hansen, Jesper Rothe

Tax
Mogens Gaarden, Peer B Petersen

Commercial law
Mogens Gaarden, Claus Kaare Pedersen

Arbitration and litigation
Allan Philip, Mogens Gaarden

Insurance
Jesper Hjetting, Mogens Gaarden

Trade marks, intellectual property, telecoms
Jesper Rothe, Jens Hjortskov

Admiralty, maritime
Allan Philip, Jens Hjortskov

Insolvency and reconstruction
Erik Malberg, Henning Hansen

EU and competition law
Jesper Rothe, Jens Hjortskov

Construction
Claus Kaare Pedersen, Peer B Petersen

PLESNER SVANE GRØNBORG

37 AMERIKA PLADS
2100 COPENHAGEN

Telephone: +45 33 12 11 33
Fax: +45 33 12 00 14
E-mail: psg@psglaw.dk
Website: www.psglaw.dk

Languages
English, French, German, Icelandic, Italian, Norwegian, Polish, Portuguese, Spanish, Swedish

Number of lawyers 130

CATEGORIES OF WORK

Commercial law and companies	Energy and mining law
Intellectual property	Corporate finance
Telecommunications and media	Insurance
Information technology	Mergers and acquisitions
Commercial property	Litigation and arbitration
Tax	Bankruptcy, insolvency
EU law	Competition law and unfair marketing
Banking, securities and finance	Product liability and consumer law
Construction law, environmental and building law	

RØNNE & LUNDGREN

TUBORG HAVNEVEJ 18
POSTBOX 90
2900 COPENHAGEN HELLERUP

Telephone: +45 35 25 25 35
Fax: +45 35 25 25 36
E-mail: info@rl.dk
Website: www.ronnelundgren.com

Languages
English, German, Italian, Norwegian, Swedish

Number of lawyers 27

Contacts
Finn Rønne, Jesper Lundgren

CATEGORIES OF WORK	
Corporate and commercial	Litigation and arbitration
Administrative	Media and entertainment
Employment	Mergers and acquisitions
EU and competition	Real property and construction
Insolvency and reorganisation	Financing and securities regulation
Insurance and tort	Succession
IP and marketing	Tax (including international tax)
IT	

THE FIRM

Rønne & Lundgren is based in Copenhagen. The firm was established in 1996 by senior partners from leading law firms in Copenhagen. Since 1996, the firm has grown each year, and today Rønne & Lundgren is one of the larger law firms in Copenhagen.

The firm is a business law practice and its lawyers have a reputation of combining legal excellence and innovation with a strong commercial focus.

Rønne & Lundgren has a wide international network covering Scandinavia, Europe and other countries throughout the world. The strong international profile has made Rønne & Lundgren a preferred choice for foreign entities that want to set up business in Denmark.

AREAS OF PRACTICE

Rønne & Lundgren is highly recognised for its corporate work, including international M&A work. However, the firm covers all areas of commercial law, including the following areas: administrative, company, employment, EU and competition, insolvency and reorganisation, insurance and tort, IP and marketing, IT, litigation and arbitration, media and entertainment, mergers and acquisitions, real property and construction, financing and securities regulation, succession, and tax law including international tax.

For further details about Rønne & Lundgren's practice areas and contact persons, please see www.ronnelundgren.com.

VILTOFT & HØBERG-PETERSEN

ADVOKATAKTIESELSKAB

GOTHERSGADE 109
1123 KØBENHAVN K

Telephone: +45 33 14 93 00
Fax: +45 33 14 32 56
E-mail: vhp@vhp.dk
Website: www.vhp.dk

Languages
English, French, German, Icelandic, the Scandinavian languages

Number of lawyers 11

CATEGORIES OF WORK

Construction law
Michael Gjedde-Nielsen, Hans Lykke Hansen

Labour and employment law
Bjørn Høberg-Petersen, Jakob Juul

Copyright/entertainment law
Bjørn Høberg-Petersen

Contract law
Claus Berg, Michael Gjedde-Nielsen

Public procurement law
Hans Lykke Hansen, Michael Gjedde-Nielsen

Arbitration
Hans Lykke Hansen, Michael Gjedde-Nielsen

Energy law
Jakob Juul

Computer law
Claus Berg, Jakob Juul

Environmental law
Michael Gjedde-Nielsen, Claus Berg

Criminal law
Bjørn Høberg-Petersen

FOCUS ADVOKATER LLP

FISKETORVET 3
POSTBOX 906
5100 ODENSE C

Telephone: +45 63 14 20 20
Fax: +45 63 14 20 30
E-mail: mail@focus-advokater.dk
Website: www.focus-advokater.dk

Languages
English, French, German, Spanish

Other offices
Copenhagen, Hamburg

Number of lawyers 35

Contacts
Peter Ringsted, Michael Clemmensen

CATEGORIES OF WORK

Arbitration and litigation

Banking, securities and finance

Companies, commercial law (general)

Construction

EU and competition

Environmental law

Family law (wills and estates)

Insolvency

Intellectual property

Mergers and acquisitions

Ship and aircraft finance

Sports and entertainment law

Tax

Transport

EGYPT

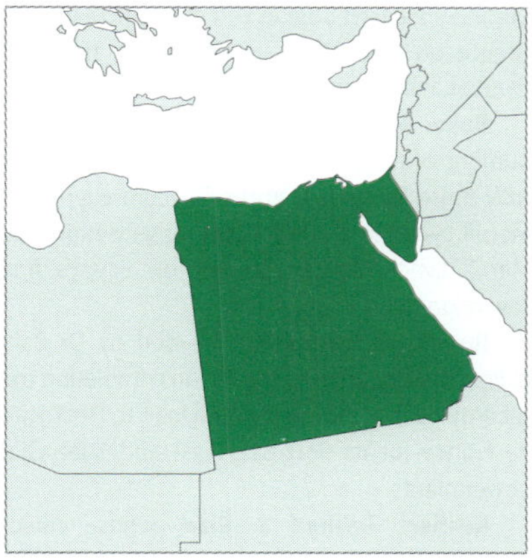

Population	**71.9 million**
Number of lawyers	**2,000**
Professional title	**Attorney at law**
Currency	**Egyptian pound (E£)**

Index

With the largest population in the Arab world, Egypt has played a pivotal role in the politics and economics of the Middle East in modern times. Situated on the north-east tip of Africa, it borders Sudan, Libya and Israel.

As a limited democratic state, much of the power in the country lies with President Hosni Mubarak who was re-elected for his fourth, six-year term in October 1999. He has presided over a process of gradual economic liberalisation that has brought domestic growth and significant foreign investment.

Arabic is the official language although English and French are widely spoken. Cairo is the main commercial centre and administrative heart of the country, while the key port of Alexandria is an important legal centre, particularly for maritime law.

Based on the constitution of 1971, the Egyptian legal system draws on Islamic, English and French law and features a hierarchy of courts from the Supreme Constitutional Court down to primary tribunals in each of the country's 26 governorates (*muhafazat*).

BILLING

Rates for legal services vary considerably depending on the seniority of the lawyer employed and the type of work undertaken.

Typical rates for associates working for international clients range from €120 to €220 per hour, while a partner may charge up to €320 an hour. For local clients, the fees charged by associates can fall to between €80 and €100.

IN-HOUSE LAWYERS

Larger companies, especially in the banking and finance sector, are moving towards increased use of in-house legal departments and have recruited from domestic law firms in recent years.

MARKETING

Egyptian firms are able to market themselves freely. Domestic law firms are increasingly establishing websites as part of marketing activities that include promotional literature and entries in legal directories.

ECONOMIC CLIMATE

The swift conclusion to the war in Iraq in 2003 led to a faster than expected recovery in Egypt's tourism industry – a key contributor to GDP. The economy, which is the second-largest in the Middle East after Saudi Arabia, is still seeing the benefits of a significant boost following the end of the Gulf War in 1991 when the country's allies wrote off more than $15bn of Egyptian debt.

Since then, President Mubarak has introduced a series of measures to strengthen the economy including privatisation of state enterprises, relaxation of trade barriers and deregulation of the business environment.

Exports are dominated by petroleum and natural gas, worth $1.9bn in 2002, while agriculture accounts for one-third of employment.

In September 2003, the National Democratic Party (NDP) approved an extensive economic reform package to encourage more foreign investment and privatisation.

LEGAL MARKET

Along with long-established names such as **Zaki Hashem & Partners** and **Shalakany Law Office** which have more than 140 years' experience between them, Egypt has a strong contingent of younger firms; these include **Al Kamel Law Office**; **Kosheri, Rashed & Riad**; **Law Office of Dr Hazem Gomaa**; and **Sarwat A. Shahid Law Firm**.

During 2003, **Ibrachy & Dermarkar** opened an associated office in Baghdad to take advantage of changes which mean foreign businesses can invest in Iraqi companies for the first time.

A number of Egyptian firms are members of international alliances, including **Ibrachy & Dermarkar** which is a member of *TAG Law*; **Shalakany Law Office**, a member of *Lex Mundi* and **Nadoury & Nahas**, a member of *Terralex*.

During the year **Mena Associates in association with Krauss Amereller Henkenborg** changed its name from *Soliman Law Office* to bring it in line with the other Middle Eastern offices – including those in Damascus, Baghdad and Dubai - which operate in association with the German firm.

FOREIGN FIRMS

Foreign firms can only operate in Egypt if they have an association with a domestic firm. In order to advise on Egyptian law a practitioner must be a member of the Egyptian Bar Association.

A number of foreign firms have managed to penetrate the Egyptian market and forge alliances with local firms over the past two decades.

The largest firms

1	Zaki Hashem & Partners	46
2	Al Kamel Law Office	44
3	Sarwat A. Shahid Law Firm	29
4	Ibrachy & Dermarkar	25
5	Denton Wilde Sapte	22
	Kosheri, Rashed & Riad	22
7	Baker & McKenzie	21
8	Sherif Saad Law Offices	14
9	Hilmy Law Firm	12
10	Adel Kamel Law Office	11
	Nadoury & Nahas	11
12	Mena Associates in association with Krauss Amereller Henkenborg	5
	Trowers & Hamlins	5
14	Bin Mahfouz International Law Firm	2

These figures represent the total number of lawyers in this country only, and have been supplied by the firms themselves. The figures should be accurate as at 1 January 2004.

The Cairo office of **Baker & McKenzie**, which operates in association with **Helmy & Hamza**, was established in 1985, making it the longest established formal international affiliation in the Egyptian legal market.

Others include **Denton Wilde Sapte** which has a local association with **El Oteifi Law Office**, and **Trowers & Hamlins** which works with **Nour Law Office**. **Mena Associates** operates in association with German law firm **Krauss Amereller Henkenborg** which also has offices in Baghdad and Dubai. **Sarwat A. Shahid Law Firm** is associated with international firm **Weil, Gotshal & Manges**.

In addition, several large international firms operate in Egypt on a project-by-project basis including **Clifford Chance LLP** and **Freshfields Bruckhaus Deringer**.

BANKING, FINANCE AND CAPITAL MARKETS

Egypt's new banking law came into effect in July 2003, heralding significant moves to strengthen the sector and stimulate foreign investment. The legislation, which applies to all registered banks in the country, introduced minimum capital requirements, more rigorous standards of credit and solvency controls and a provision allowing foreign companies to own more than 50% of local banks.

There have also been recent moves to raise the profile of the Cairo and Alexandria stock exchanges and increase trading in the 1,200 companies listed.

Denton Wilde Sapte assisted Pfizer on the Egyptian tranche of its divestment of the Adams business to Cadbury, including the regulatory elements with the Capital Market Authority in Egypt and the Cairo and Alexandria stock exchanges.

Shalakany Law Office, whose well-regarded banking team is led by Ashraf Ihab, has a team of five lawyers handling both litigation and non-contentious matters for clients including Credit Suisse First Boston, American Express Bank and the Arab Banking Corporation. The firm handled the first six Global Depositary Receipt issues offered by Egyptian entities on the international markets and the first leveraged buyout. It has extensive experience in mergers and acquisitions and bond issues and advises the Capital Market Authority in Egypt on the development of the capital markets and related laws and regulations.

Al Kamel Law Office represents a number of large financial clients including Chase Manhattan, Credit Suisse First Boston and the Bank of Central Greece on their affairs in Egypt. The firm also handles aviation finance.

Baker & McKenzie has acted for clients in a number of major transactions. The firm advised ABN Amro Rothschild in the Telecom Egypt IPO, Merrill Lynch in the electricity privatisation and Merrill Lynch/Morgan Stanley on Egypt's first sovereign bond issue.

Ibrachy & Dermarkar, headed by Dr Bahi Eldin Elibrachy, advised the IFC on completing the security package for the $400m loan to Electricité de France for its Port Said East and Suez Gulf power plants.

Kosheri, Rashed & Riad, whose major transactions have included the sale of the Egyptian African Bank, represents international banks and financial institutions including Wells Fargo Bank, the Arab Monetary Fund and Bank of America.

Sarwat A. Shahid Law Firm represents Middle Eastern and international banking clients including Artesia Bank of Belgium, Banque Continentale de Luxembourg, and BNP Paribas.

Trowers & Hamlins' work has included advising lenders and creditors in respect of the corporate and financial restructuring of National Vegetable Oils Company. The firm advised lenders in respect of the $80m syndicated secured equity funding of the participation of EGAS and EGPC in Egypt LNG, and acted for a hotel group over funding for a new project including handling loan agreements with three separate foreign lenders.

Amir Marghany of **Zaki Hashem & Partners** provided advice for the planned formation of a joint venture between Moody's Investors Service and Egyptian company Finance and Banking Consultants International (FINBI) to provide credit rating and research services in Egypt.

BANKING, FINANCE AND CAPITAL MARKETS

DENTON WILDE SAPTE ✪
SHALAKANY LAW OFFICE

Al Kamel Law Office
Baker & McKenzie ✪
Ibrachy & Dermarkar
Kosheri, Rashed & Riad ✪
Sarwat A. Shahid Law Firm
Trowers & Hamlins
Zaki Hashem & Partners

Nadoury & Nahas

Firms are listed A-Z in tiers which are ranked in order of priority
✪ Indicates firm displays contact details at the end of this chapter.

CORPORATE AND COMMERCIAL

Baker & McKenzie's reputation was strengthened with the election in June 2003 of highly respected managing partner Taher M Helmy as president of the board of governors of the American Chamber of Commerce in Egypt. Helmy oversees a team which acts for clients including PepsiCo, Cemex, Al Ahram Beverages, Fiat Auto, Daewoo Motors and Lockheed Martin.

Denton Wilde Sapte's strong reputation for aviation work led to it assisting Airbus on a deal for seven aircraft with Egyptair Holding Company.

CORPORATE AND COMMERCIAL

BAKER & MCKENZIE ✪
DENTON WILDE SAPTE ✪
SHALAKANY LAW OFFICE
ZAKI HASHEM & PARTNERS

Adel Kamel Law Office
Al Kamel Law Office
Ibrachy & Dermarkar
Kosheri, Rashed & Riad ✪
Mena Associates in association with Krauss Amereller Henkenborg
Sarwat A. Shahid Law Firm
Sharkawy Law Office
Towers & Hamlins

Hilmy Law Firm
Nadoury & Nahas

Firms are listed A-Z in tiers which are ranked in order of priority
✪ Indicates firm displays contact details at the end of this chapter.

The transaction was led by the highly regarded John Matouk who was made up to partner at the firm during 2003. **Denton Wilde Sapte**'s team also assisted Barclays on structuring, negotiating and closing the management buyout of food products manufacturer El Rashidi Mizan – the first transaction of its kind in Egypt.

Shalakany Law Office acts for clients including adidas Egypt, General Motors Egypt and Hitachi Europe Limited. The firm has particular expertise in agency distribution, joint ventures and franchise transactions.

Zaki Hashem & Partners is widely regarded as an excellent local firm, with experience of providing wide-ranging commercial and corporate advice to an international client base.

Adel Kamel Law Office acted for debis International Trading, a subsidiary of Daimler-Chrysler in recovering bad debts from an Egyptian company.

Al Kamel Law Office provides general corporate advice to clients such as IBM France and Netherlands, Ford Motors, Procter & Gamble and CNN.

Ibrachy & Dermarkar acted for the Suez Canal Container Terminal on reorganising its shareholding and on the sale by public auction of the shares of certain minority shareholders. The firm also advised CDC Capital Partners, formerly the Commonwealth Development Corporation, in the management buyout of El Rashidi Mizan.

Kosheri, Rashed & Riad has solid and recognised expertise. The firm has advised on privatisations and the sale of a number of banks. It boasts a high-profile, multinational client base.

Mena Associates in association with Krauss Amereller Henkenborg advises several large and medium-sized international companies on the establishment and structuring of distribution channels in Egypt and around the Middle East.

Sharkawy Law Office, headed by partner Abd El-Aziz El-Sharkawy, handles corporate work on behalf of a number of Egyptian and international clients.

Trowers & Hamlins, led by senior partner Sara Hinton, advised a major international group on a potential listing on the Egyptian Stock Exchange. The firm also acted for the Gulf Arab Investment Company in its proposed acquisition of Bahrain International Bank.

DISPUTE RESOLUTION

For foreign investors into Egypt, disputes through the courts can take a long time to resolve. Alternative dispute resolution (ADR) is increasingly used to avoid the highly bureaucratic court system.

Baker & McKenzie has solid contentious experience, across litigation and ADR methods.

Kosheri, Rashed & Riad was closely involved with the development of Egypt's arbitration law. Under Dr Tarek F Riad, the firm enjoys a strong reputation in the field of WTO agreement disputes. Its work has included representing the Kuwaiti government in arbitration with Aminoil Company. It also represented the Egyptian government in arbitration over the TABA border dispute with Israel. Clients including Philip Morris and Caterpillar turn to the firm for assistance in commercial litigation. Partner Dr Ahmed El-Kosheri is current vice-chairman of the International Court of Arbitration

Law Office of Dr Hazem Gomaa has worked on cases involving a total of $1bn since its inception in 1967 and provides services including mediation and international commercial arbitration along with litigation expertise.

Mena Associates in association with Krauss Amereller Henkenborg has acted for large European and Egyptian companies in arbitrations of disputes involving sums up to $120m.

Nadoury & Nahas, which has offices in both Cairo and Alexandria, specialises in financial and commercial litigation for a number of large international clients.

Shalakany Law Office, one of the first law firms in Egypt to develop specialised expertise in commercial arbitration, has been involved in many of the major arbitration cases in Egypt, including the Pyramids Plateau, the Cairo Metro, the Ahmad Hamdy Suez Canal Tunnel and the Isna Barrage arbitrations.

Sharkawy Law Office has significant experience in dispute resolution on behalf of local and international clients.

DISPUTE RESOLUTION

BAKER & MCKENZIE ✪
KOSHERI, RASHED & RIAD ✪

Hazem Gomaa (Dr), Law Office of
Mena Associates in association with Krauss Amereller Henkenborg
Nadoury & Nahas
Shalakany Law Office
Sharkawy Law Office
Sherif Saad Law Offices

Firms are listed A-Z in tiers which are ranked in order of priority
✪ Indicates firm displays contact details at the end of this chapter.

INTELLECTUAL PROPERTY

Baker & McKenzie ✪
Denton Wilde Sapte ✪
Hazem Gomaa (Dr), Law Office of
Shalakany Law Office

Al Kamel Law Office
Kosheri, Rashed & Riad ✪
Nadoury & Nahas

Firms are listed A-Z in tiers which are ranked in order of priority
✪ Indicates firm displays contact details at the end of this chapter.

INTELLECTUAL PROPERTY

A comprehensive Intellectual Property Rights Law was passed in May 2003 designed to bring Egypt's legislation into line with the Trade-Related Aspects of Intellectual Property Rights (TRIPS) agreement. Egypt was also due to become party to the Patent Cooperation Treaty (PCT) by the end of 2003.

Baker & McKenzie has worked on cross-border IP matters. The firm has considerable experience in technology transfer and the enforcement and protection of all IPRs.

Denton Wilde Sapte has significant experience in filing trade marks and patents in Egypt and of advising clients on the IP aspects of corporate transactions.

The **Law Office of Dr Hazem Gomaa** has solid, all-round experience.

Shalakany Law Office's respected partner Sharif Shihata specialises in protection for intellectual property including drafting and negotiating commercial contracts for the transfer or licensing of intellectual property, and the enforcement of rights, including through litigation, across a range of industries.

OIL AND GAS

Falling oil production and increasing domestic demand have led to concerns that Egypt will become a net importer of oil over the next decade. The concerns have led the government to encourage more exploration and better recovery from existing reserves.

Adel Kamel Law Office worked on the acquisition by Petronas from Edison of its share of Egypt's West Delta Deep Marine gasfield.

International energy companies, such as ABB Electrical Engineering, are among the clients of **Al Kamel Law Office**.

OIL AND GAS

Adel Kamel Law Office
Al Kamel Law Office
Baker & McKenzie ✪
Ibrachy & Dermarkar
Denton Wilde Sapte ✪
Kosheri, Rashed & Riad ✪
Mena Associates in association with Krauss Amereller Henkenborg
Trowers & Hamlins
Zaki Hashem & Partners

Firms are listed A-Z in tiers which are ranked in order of priority
✪ Indicates firm displays contact details at the end of this chapter.

PRIVATISATION

BAKER & MCKENZIE ✪
DENTON WILDE SAPTE ✪

Ibrachy & Dermarkar
Kosheri, Rashed & Riad ✪
Mena Associates in association with Krauss Amereller Henkenborg
Sarwat A. Shahid Law Firm

Firms are listed A-Z in tiers which are ranked in order of priority
✪ Indicates firm displays contact details at the end of this chapter.

TELECOMS

BAKER & MCKENZIE ✪
DENTON WILDE SAPTE ✪

Ibrachy & Dermarkar
Shalakany Law Office
Trowers & Hamlins

Firms are listed A-Z in tiers which are ranked in order of priority
✪ Indicates firm displays contact details at the end of this chapter.

Denton Wilde Sapte, led by highly rated senior partner and energy lawyer, Bridget McKinney, assisted two foreign clients on financing facilities totalling $175m during 2003 as part of $850m worth of asset finance work it carried out in the energy market in Egypt during 2003. The firm also advised Apicorp with a $100m financing facility with Egyptian General Petroleum.

Ibrachy & Dermarkar acted for the Suez Canal Container Terminal on reorganising its shareholding and continues its longstanding arrangement acting as general counsel for Exxon Mobil in Egypt.

Clients of **Kosheri, Rashed & Riad** include various oil industry majors such as Amoco Corporation and Elf Oil Deutschland.

Mena Associates in association with Krauss Amereller Henkenborg advised on the execution of a major gas project, while **Trowers & Hamlins** advised a bidder in respect of the tender for the sale of Edison's interest in Egypt including in relation to Egypt LNG.

PRIVATISATION

Egypt's privatisation programme all but came to a halt in 2003 after a decade of strong activity which saw 192 companies privatised. General world economic conditions and the failure of tenders to reach expected levels on a number of transactions are cited as the main reasons for the lack of deals. The government has signalled its intention to kickstart the revival of the privatisation process as economic conditions improve and there are currently more than 800 companies scheduled for privatisation.

Baker & McKenzie, which was involved in the drafting of the Privatisation Law of 1991, acted in Egypt's first privatisation in 1994 when it represented PepsiCo. The firm later acted for ABN Amro Rothschild in the Telecom Egypt IPO and for Merrill Lynch in the electricity industry privatisation.

Denton Wilde Sapte has been involved in almost all of Egypt's major privatisation transactions, including the acquisition by Blue Circle Industries of a majority stake in Alexandria Portland Cement Company (APCC) from the Egyptian Holding Company for Chemical Industries. Following Lafarge's takeover of Blue Circle Industries it assisted the buyer in the corporate restructuring of its newly acquired APCC asset, including a divestment of APCC's shareholding in Suez Cement.

Ibrachy & Dermarkar has been involved in work including the Telecom Egypt IPO.

Other firms handling privatisation issues in Egypt include **Sarwat A. Shahid Law Firm**, **Mena Associates in association with Krauss Amereller Henkenborg** and **Kosheri, Rashed & Riad**.

PROJECTS AND INFRASTRUCTURE

In 2003 the government announced a $1bn investment plan involving 132 projects across a range of sectors. Preference will be given to private sector investments although the government will finance certain projects through the National Investment Bank.

Baker & McKenzie has an impressive record in projects in Egypt. The office's portfolio includes advice on development of a number of airports, container ports and handling facilities.

Shalakany Law Office has acted as Egyptian counsel for consortia of local and international companies awarded the first major infrastructure BOT projects in Egypt, including the InterGen Sidi Krir power plant and two EDF power plants. The firm is advising the project company in the first major BOT project in the water sector. **Shalakany Law Office** was involved in the drafting of the Northern Region of Cairo Governorate General Cleaning Service Contract on behalf of A.M.A. International S.P.A (Municipality of Rome).

Law Office of Dr Hazem Gomaa has extensive experience in drafting and revision of construction agreements in major projects.

Mena Associates in association with Krauss Amereller Henkenborg represents a number of larger international construction and engineering companies.

Trowers & Hamlins relocated Tim Armsby from the firm's London office to work on projects, particularly advising EATCO in respect of a $1.2bn gas-to-polymers project at Damietta. The firm is also acting for lenders on a major industrial project.

PROJECTS AND INFRASTRUCTURE

BAKER & MCKENZIE ✪
SHALAKANY LAW OFFICE

Denton Wilde Sapte ✪
Ibrachy & Dermarkar
Kosheri, Rashed & Riad ✪
Hazem Gomaa (Dr), Law Office of
Mena Associates in association with Krauss Amereller Henkenborg
Nadoury & Nahas
Trowers & Hamlins

Firms are listed A-Z in tiers which are ranked in order of priority
✪ Indicates firm displays contact details at the end of this chapter.

TELECOMS

The government and Telecom Egypt are currently building a state-of-the-art network to provide data connectivity across the country. The network will significantly increase the number of fixed telephone lines and develop the data communication backbone capacity of the country.

Baker & McKenzie was involved in the drafting of Egypt's telecommunications legislation and acts for a number of international clients in the field.

Denton Wilde Sapte has acted as adviser to the Egyptian government on regulatory reform of the telecoms market and has been involved in a number of project finance transactions in the telecoms sector in Egypt.

Ibrachy & Dermarkar advised Motorola on its sale of shares in MobiNil to Orascom Telecom, while **Shalakany Law Office** acts for clients including France Télécom, MobiNil, IBM and Orange.

Trowers & Hamlins advised a major international telecoms company on a possible stock exchange listing in Egypt and on inter-shareholder matters.

BAKER & McKENZIE

WORLD TRADE CENTER
1191 CORNICH EL NIL, 18TH FLOOR
CAIRO

Telephone: +20 2 579 1801-6
Fax: +20 2 579 1808
Website: www.bakernet.com

Languages
English, French, German

Other offices
Almaty, Amsterdam, Antwerp, Bahrain, Baku, Bangkok, Barcelona, Beijing, Berlin, Bogotá, Bologna, Brasilia, Brussels, Budapest, Buenos Aires, Calgary, Caracas, Chicago, Dallas, Düsseldorf, Frankfurt, Geneva, Guadalajara, Hanoi, Ho Chi Minh City, Hong Kong, Houston, Juarez, Kyiv, London, Madrid, Manila, Melbourne, Mexico City, Miami, Milan, Monterrey, Moscow, Munich, New York, Palo Alto, Porto Alegré, Paris, Prague, Rio de Janeiro, Riyadh, Rome, St Petersburg, San Diego, San Francisco, Santiago, São Paulo, Shanghai, Singapore, Stockholm, Sydney, Taipei, Tijuana, Tokyo, Toronto, Valencia, Vienna, Warsaw, Washington DC, Zurich

Number of lawyers 3,380
at this office 21

Contact
Taher Helmy

CATEGORIES OF WORK

Administrative law
Kamal Aboulmagd, Hazim Rizkana

Arbitration
Samir M Hamza, Hazim Rizkana

Banking and finance
Taher Helmy, Hazim Rizkana

BOOT projects
Samir M Hamza, Mohammad Talaat

Commercial law, general
Samir M Hamza, Mohammad Talaat

Environmental law
Samir M Hamza, Hatem Soliman

Intellectual property law
Hazim Rizkana, Mohammad Talaat

Labour law
Mohammad Talaat, Mohamed Abdallah

Litigation
Hazim Rizkana, Saber Soliman

Mergers and acquisitions
Taher Helmy, Mohammed Ghannam

Privatisation
Taher Helmy, Hazim Rizkana

Securities
Taher Helmy, Hazim Rizkana

Tax
Samir M Hamza, Suzan Farid

Telecommunications law
Samir M Hamza, Mohammed Ghannam

THE FIRM

Founded in Chicago in 1949, Baker & McKenzie is a leading law firm with 66 offices in 36 countries. A multinational network of over 4,400 legal professionals offers clients resources and knowledge in every area of business law, in virtually every important financial and commercial centre in the world.

Baker & McKenzie has been established in Europe for over 40 years, having opened its first European offices in 1957. Since then, the European and Middle Eastern network has grown to 29 offices, giving it unparalleled geographical coverage.

The Cairo office of Baker & McKenzie (Helmy, Hamza & Partners) was established in 1985. It is the only law firm in Egypt that combines a detailed knowledge of local law and the ability to offer the experience of an international law firm with access to a vast global network of resources and legal expertise.

The clients of the Cairo office include large multinational corporations and local businesses. Baker & McKenzie's worldwide network of offices enables the Cairo office to refer Egyptian clients wishing to do business abroad to its own offices located in that particular jurisdiction.

As part of the Baker & McKenzie international network, the Cairo office is deeply committed to furthering its clients' business both within the Middle East region and globally.

AREAS OF PRACTICE

Baker & McKenzie coordinates its core practice areas on local, regional and global levels, giving most of its lawyers experience in more than one jurisdiction, as well as providing multinational teams of specialists.

Utilising a global practice group structure and groundbreaking technology coupled with a personal, detailed understanding of a client's specific business, Baker & McKenzie is able to organise its extensive resources to provide focused and strategic counsel to clients.

The Cairo office can advise clients on all legal issues, from purely domestic issues to the most complex cross-border or multi-jurisdictional transactions, tax planning or disputes. More specifically, it provides legal services to both domestic and international companies in a diverse range of specialisation including corporate, banking and finance, commercial, taxation, privatisation, transfer of technology, intellectual property, telecommunications, capital markets, joint ventures, restructuring, mergers and acquisitions, debt-equity swaps, oil and gas. The firm also conducts a strong commercial litigation and international arbitration practice.

The Cairo office is heavily involved in the issuance of Global Depository Receipts (GDRs) of shares of Egyptian companies, including participating in the preparation of offering circulars. The scope of activities carried out in the corporate practice is widespread; from advising and assisting in the bidding for Egypt's first private power plant project on a 'BOOT' (build, own, operate, and transfer) basis, to advising on the legal issues of transporting Egyptian antiquities from Egypt for exhibition in various American cities.

The government called upon the firm's expertise in the recent amendments to the Copyright Law, as well as drafting the Telecommunications and Environmental Laws.

DENTON WILDE SAPTE

9 SHAGARET EL DOR STREET
ZAMALEK
CAIRO

Telephone: +20 2 736 5128
Fax: +20 2 736 7717
E-mail: cairo@dentonwildesapte.com
Website: www.dentonwildesapte.com

Languages
Arabic, Dutch, English, French, German

Other offices
Abu Dhabi, Almaty, Beijing, Dubai, Gibraltar, Hong Kong, Istanbul, London, Milton Keynes, Moscow, Muscat, Paris, Singapore, Tashkent, Tokyo

Number of lawyers 876
at this office 22

Contacts
Bridget McKinney, John Matouk

CATEGORIES OF WORK

Arbitration

Aviation

Banking, finance

Capital markets

Company establishment

Constitutional and administrative law

Construction

Intellectual property

Joint ventures

Labour law

Litigation

Mergers and acquisitions

Oil and gas

Privatisation

Projects

Telecommunications

KOSHERI, RASHED & RIAD

16 MAAMAL EL SOKKAR STREET
GARDEN CITY
CAIRO 11451

Telephone: +20 2 795 4795
Fax: +20 2 795 8521
E-mail: samiakr@link.net
Website: www.krr-law.com

Languages
English, French, Arabic

Other offices
Paris*

Number of lawyers 22

Contacts
Dr Tarek Riad, Dr Hatem Gabr, Hala Riad, Dr Ahmed El-Kosheri

CATEGORIES OF WORK

Banking and finance	Maritime matters
Corporate and commercial	Foreign direct investment and competition
Mergers and acquisitions	Telecommunications and media and entertainment
Privatisation and capital markets	Dispute resolution (litigation and arbitration)
Construction	Infrastructure and project finance
Labour law	Tax
Energy and natural resources	Commercial property, real estate
Government business/ regulatory and environment	Intellectual property
Asset finance and securitisation	Information technology and e-commerce
Insurance	World Trade Organisation agreements and dispute resolution
Aviation and maritime affairs	Up/down stream gas agreements
BOT projects	
Oil concessions	

THE FIRM

Kosheri, Rashed & Riad was established in 1977 by Dr Ahmed El-Kosheri and Dr Samia Rashed. Both were corporate lawyers and professors of private international law at Ain University and Cairo University, respectively.

AREAS OF PRACTICE

Kosheri, Rashed & Riad has established an enviable worldwide reputation for itself as one of the leading law firms in Cairo, with a real strength in commercial/corporate matters and dispute resolution. Bearing in mind the track record of the founding partners, Prof Dr Samia Rashed and Prof Dr Ahmed Sadek El-Kosheri (vice-president of the ICC International Court of Arbitration and ad hoc judge in the International Court of Justice in The Hague), the firm has a leading reputation for commercial/corporate and arbitration/litigation in Cairo. It was, inter alia, closely involved in the development of Egypt's arbitration law. Name partner Dr Tarek F Riad – the only practising Harvard Law School SJD in Egypt – has initiated the firm's expanding practice in World Trade Organisation agreements. The firm also has a top-rated general corporate practice, with particular expertise in regional MENA law issues, securities law and investment matters.

Major matters for the firm include working on the sale of 50% of Misr America International Bank; representing the Egyptian government in international arbitration proceedings concerning the TABA border dispute between Egypt and Israel; representing the Kuwaiti government in the Aminoil arbitration between Kuwait and the Aminoil Company; and representing Philips Company in the privatisation of NEEASAE, the national electrical goods manufacturer.

This is in addition to: commercial litigation work for Philip Morris and Caterpillar; representing World Com and Flag Corporation, in the Egyptian agreements concerning the installation of a fibre optic cable between New York and Japan; BOOT projects in the electrical and infrastructure fields; tax litigation; acting as special adviser to the parliamentary speaker; analysing all Egypt's oil and gas concessions between foreign companies and the Egyptian government, as well as work involving investment trusts.

ESTONIA

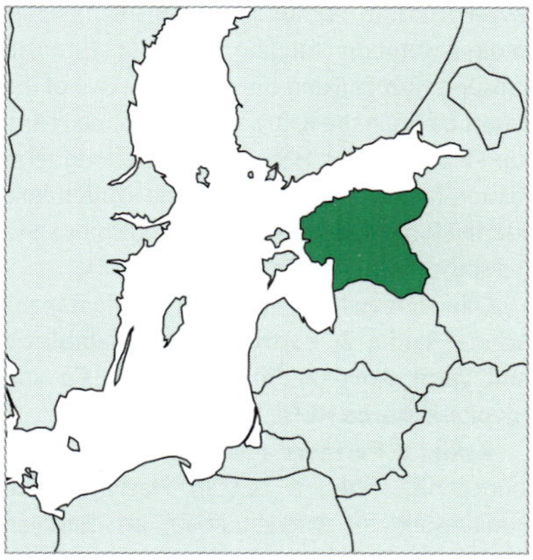

Population	1.4 million
Number of lawyers	417
Professional title	Advokaat
Currency	Estonian kroon (EEK)

Index

After centuries of Danish, Swedish, German and Russian rule, Estonia attained independence in 1918. Forcibly incorporated into the USSR in 1940, it regained its freedom in 1991, with the collapse of the Soviet Union. Since then, Estonia has been free to promote economic and political ties with Western Europe. In 2004 it will become a full member of the European Union and Nato. The country has one of the most open, progressive and fastest-growing economies of the future EU zone.

Estonia is the smallest and most northerly of the three Baltic States. It is bordered by the Baltic Sea, the Gulf of Finland, Latvia and Russia. Tallinn (population 411,600), the capital, is situated on the north-western tip of the country.

BILLING

Fees are commonly charged by the hour, although fixed and contingency fees may also be agreed. The hourly rate is between €100 and €200 for an associate, depending on the job in hand and up to €250 for a partner.

MARKETING

Marketing rules are among the most restrictive in Europe, and allow firms to publicise only very basic details about themselves, such as addresses and names of lawyers. Legitimate marketing is presently restricted to foreign legal directories and magazines, and the Internet.

IN-HOUSE LAWYERS

The banks and financial institutions undertake a range of work in-house and only outsource when specialist advice is required. In-house legal teams in some organisations, such as Hansapank, can be larger than Estonia's largest law firms.

ECONOMIC CLIMATE

Estonia's economy is one of the most open in Europe; the government welcomes foreign investment. It has a stable currency, a liberal foreign trade regime, and liberalisation of prices, abolition of state subsidies, fast privatisation and effective bankruptcy legislation. A decade after independence there are few legacies of the 50 years of Soviet occupation.

The government has followed a strategy designed to promote business and accelerate economic growth by making additional funds available for investment. The labour laws and the tax system have been reformed. Estonia has a system of low, flat-rate taxes with businesses exempt from corporate income tax.

The privatisation programme, a major priority, has been largely completed – only a few enterprises remain state controlled. The success of privatisation and an improved perception of the economic and political climate have led to a rise in foreign direct investment (FDI) which stood at €2.18bn by the end of 2000. FDI has financed greenfield investment, mergers and acquisitions. Companies partly or wholly owned by foreigners account for one-third of GDP.

Estonia has the most consolidated banking market within the Baltic region. The three major banks are Hansapank, Ühispank and Sampo Pank. Hansapank was sold to Swedbank in 1998, whilst Ühispank is fully owned by Swedish bank SEB, while a Finnish insurance consortium owns Sampo Pank.

The economy is greatly influenced by Sweden and Finland, which have replaced Russia as the major trading partners. Trade with these two Scandinavian neighbours accounts for nearly two-thirds of all exports and imports and large-scale investment has been experienced in every sector.

LEGAL MARKET

Considering the relatively small size of the Estonian legal market, it is not surprising that there are only a handful of firms large enough to handle corporate work. Internal division into specialist departments is rare, with most lawyers acting in more than one area. The majority of firms are sole practitioners handling criminal, family or litigation matters. Most Estonian commercial law firms are located in Tallinn, the commercial centre, although a few do have second offices in Tartu, home of the Supreme Court.

There is a trend amongst the corporate firms towards establishing a pan-Baltic presence through co-operation with firms in Latvia, Finland and Lithuania, both to expand their market and as a result of pressure from international clients who increasingly are looking to appoint a single firm for the region. Only two firms are truly pan-Baltic: **Sorainen Law Offices** and **Ernst & Young Baltic AS**. By contrast **Hedman Osborne Clarke Alliance**'s nine-strong Tallinn practice was

The largest firms

1	Raidla & Partners	26
2	Law Office Lepik & Luhaäär	19
3	Advokaadibüroo Tark & Co	17
4	Advokaadibüroo HETA	15
	Sorainen Law Offices	15
6	Law Office Aivar Pilv	12
7	Advokaadibüroo Paul Varul	10
	Teder & Partnerid	10
9	Hedman Osborne Clarke Alliance	9
	Luiga, Mugu & Borenius	9
	Mody Hääl & Partners	9
12	Lasvet Patent and Trademark Agency	8
13	Law Office Aavik, Arvisto & Partners trading as Baltic Commercial Law Office	7
14	Law Office Ots & Co	6
	Leppik & Partners	6
16	AAA Legal Services	5
	Ernst & Young Baltic AS	5
	Hough, Hübner, Hütt & Partners	5
	Law Office V Kaasik & Co	5
20	Jaanti DeBeck & Partners	2
	Magnusson Wahlin Qvist Stanbrook	2
22	Edith Sassian & Co	1
	Rödl & Partner	1

These figures represent the total number of lawyers in this country only, and have been supplied by the firms themselves. The figures should be accurate as at 1 January 2004.

established in 1992 but is legally classified as a branch of the Finnish firm. Since 2000 the firm has been associated with the UK's **Osborne Clarke**.

Estonia enjoys a stable legal market dominated by three firms: **Law Office Lepik & Luhaäär**, **Raidla & Partners** and **Advokaadibüroo A Jakobson & A Jaroslavski**.

Raidla & Partners and **Law Office Lepik & Luhaäär** are Estonia's largest firms in terms of fee-earners. Of the six lawyers who joined **Raidla & Partners** during the year, the most significant hire is Martin Käerdi, the former head of legal drafting at the Ministry of Justice. The firm enjoys an association with leading French firm **Moquet Borde & Associés**.

In the last few years a new generation of firms created by young lawyers has sprung up. **Luiga, Mugu & Borenius** at six years of age is older and slightly larger than **Mody Hääl & Partners**, which was established two years ago and has nine fee-earners. Both have quickly established themselves and are close to Finnish law firms who are important referrers of work. In 2000, **Luiga, Mugu & Borenius** signed a co-operation agreement with Finnish firm **Borenius & Kemppinen** which in turn has a joint venture with **Attorneys at Law Liepa, Skopina / BORENIUS** in Latvia. Meanwhile **Mody Hääl & Partners** has an informal relationship with **Castrén & Snellman** one of Finland's leading law firms.

Before the establishment of **Law Office Tehver & Partners** in early 2003, Partners Jaanus Tehver and Toomas Laanemaa worked for **Law Office V Kaasik & Co**.

LEXTAL Law Firm, the youngest firm, was established by former attorneys and partners of **Advokaadibüroo HETA**. At the time of going to print it was only recently formed, but had already attracted an impressive client list. The firm has four partners – Urmas Ustav, Ants Karu, Tarmo Sild and Ullar Talviste, perhaps best known as chairman of the Estonian Bar.

Law firm *BCLO Advokaadiburoo* has changed its name to **Law Office Aavik, Arvisto & Partners trading as Baltic Commercial Law Office**.

Law Office Aivar Pilv became the Estonian member of the 4,600-lawyer alliance, *TAGlaw*. The firm was founded by Aivar Pilv in 1993, and has an office in Tallinn with a smaller practice in Tartu.

Advokaadibüroo Paul Varul also has an office in Tartu where name partner and former Justice Minister Paul Varul is a professor at the university. Litigation accounts for two-thirds of the caseload for the firm, which is the Estonian member of the *Euro-American Lawyers Group*.

Law Office Keevallik & Partners is a member of two law firm alliances – *Baltic Law Alliance* and *Legal Skills*. **Edith Sassian & Co** provides general legal advice to clients from Estonia, Sweden, England, Latvia, Israel, France and Russia.

During 2003 Monika Mägi merged her firm with **Concordia Attorneys at Law**, a member of the *International Lawyers Group*.

BANKING AND FINANCE

Law Office Lepik & Luhaäär advises local and international institutions on structured finance and securities matters. The firm also has considerable insolvency experience. Name partner Peeter Lepik is well known.

Luiga, Mugu & Borenius name partner Sten Luiga is a member of the board of the Tallinn Stock Exchange Arbitration Court and has a reputation as one of Estonia's finest banking and finance lawyers. The firm recently assisted an international credit institution funding a major Estonian transport hub. Banking clients include two of the largest banks in the Baltic States, Hansapank and Suprema Securities. Hansapank has a long-term relationship with the firm. On the contentious side, the firm has advised many listed companies in disputes with the Stock Exchange

Other firms which regularly act for Hansapank include **Raidla & Partners**, **Advokaadibüroo Paul Varul**, **Advokaadibüroo Tark & Co** and **Advokaadibüroo HETA**.

Raidla & Partners advised Eesti Energia in connection with a €90m facility from Kreditanstalt für Wiederaufbau; an Estonian utilities company in connection with an €80m EBRD loan; and Linstow Tallin OÜ and NCC Ülemiste OÜ in connection with a loan from a bank syndicate led by Landesbank Schlewsig-Hostein Girozentrale. Partner Raino Paron is highly regarded.

Sorainen Law Offices successfully represented the State of Finland in a dispute with an Estonian insurance company over performance of a first demand guarantee. The firm's banking and finance practice has grown over the last two years and advises one of the major investment banks, the largest Latvian bank and a Scandinavian investment and development bank. Recently it provided business, taxation and licensing advice to a major

BANKING AND FINANCE

LEPIK & LUHAÄÄR, LAW OFFICE ✪
LUIGA, MUGU & BORENIUS ✪
RAIDLA & PARTNERS ✪
SORAINEN LAW OFFICES
TARK & CO, ADVOKAADIBÜROO ✪

Aivar Pilv, Law Office ✪
Hedman Osborne Clarke Alliance
HETA, Advokaadibüroo
Hough, Hübner, Hütt & Partners
Keevallik & Partners, Law Office
Lextal Law Firm
Mody Hääl & Partners ✪
Paul Varul, Advokaadibüroo
Teder & Partnerid
Tehver & Partners, Law Office
V Kaasik & Co, Law Office

Firms are listed A-Z in tiers which are ranked in order of priority
✪ Indicates firm displays contact details at the end of this chapter.

Russian oil company with regard to structuring its trading schemes.

Advokaadibüroo Tark & Co offers a wide range of banking and finance expertise. The firm recently advised the London branch of Deutsche Bank with regard to a €100m commercial paper programme as the result of a referral. Other clients over the year include JPMorgan, Sampo Pank, Barclays Bank, LHV Varahaldus and Westdeutsche Landesbank. Hannes Vallikivi is highly regarded.

Law Office Aivar Pilv advised AS Hansa Liising Eesti, a subsidiary of Hansapank, on leasing matters. Experience of extensive bankruptcy proceedings includes ERA Pank, RAS Ookean, insurance companies Polaris-Elu and Polaris-Vara. The firm acted for AS Pro Kapital in the Tallinn Stock Exchange Arbitration Court in a dispute.

Banking expert Üllar Talviste is one of four former **Advokaadibüroo HETA** lawyers who have formed **LEXTAL Law Firm**, Estonia's youngest firm. Talviste has a strong client base.

Mody Hääl & Partners is a young firm and a relative newcomer to the market but is already punching above its weight. The team advised a syndicate of foreign banks on a significant loan agreement for the purchase of a privatised Estonian railway company. Other clients include Tolaram Group, one of the largest textiles companies in the Baltics, and the Estonian Central Bank. The firm offers bankruptcy expertise.

Advokaadibüroo Paul Varul counts one of the largest Estonian banks among its clients, while **Teder & Partnerid** offers expertise in lending, securities, and disputes arising out of financial matters.

In **Law Office Tehver & Partners**' first year in practice, the firm represented international financial institutions and commercial banks in three loan agreements worth over €65m.

CORPORATE AND COMMERCIAL

Law Office Lepik & Luhaäär is highly regarded. The firm boasts an excellent local and international client base. Over the last year, the firm advised on the disposal of a majority shareholding in a local electricity distribution network, assisted a foreign telecoms company in the acquisition of a fibre optic submarine cable network and telecoms services, and advised a US-based manufacturer on the acquisition of an Estonian office equipment factory.

Of the few large mergers and acquisitions of the past year, the €150m acquisition by Stora Enso of the forestry group of companies Sylvester Group was by far the largest and was one of the largest transactions ever in Estonia. **Raidla & Partners** acted for Stora Enso. **Raidla & Partners** continues to build on its reputation as one of the best corporate and commercial teams. Sven Papp is highly recommended. (Priit Pahapill, **Mugu & Borenius**'s M&A and capital markets expert led negotiations on behalf of Sylvester Group.)

CORPORATE AND COMMERCIAL

LEPIK & LUHAÄÄR, LAW OFFICE ✪
RAIDLA & PARTNERS ✪
SORAINEN LAW OFFICES
TARK & CO, ADVOKAADIBÜROO ✪

Luiga, Mugu & Borenius ✪
Mody Hääl & Partners ✪
Paul Varul, Advokaadibüroo
Teder & Partnerid

A Jakobson & A Jaroslavski, Advokaadibüroo
Aavik, Arvisto & Partners trading as Baltic Commercial Law Office, Law Office
Aivar Pilv, Law Office ✪
Ernst & Young Baltic AS ✪
Hedman Osborne Clarke Alliance
HETA, Advokaadibüroo
Hough, Hübner, Hütt & Partners
Keevallik & Partners, Law Office
Ots & Co, Law Office
V Kaasik & Co, Law Office

Firms are listed A-Z in tiers which are ranked in order of priority
✪ Indicates firm displays contact details at the end of this chapter.

Sorainen Law Offices' ranks were bolstered by Ene Soop who joined from **Law Office Lepik & Luhaäär**, while the firm won several new clients including Coca-Cola and a global mobile phone operator. Foreign investment is almost 80% of **Sorainen Law Offices**' workload. During the last year the firm advised more than 35 foreign multinational companies on establishing subsidiaries in Estonia. Recent work includes advising Finnish investors on the acquisition of an important local port, assisting a Finnish energy company in divestment from the second-biggest heating company in Estonia and taking care of local closing matters of a cross-border acquisition by a Scandinavian construction company.

Minni-Trün Park has joined **Advokaadibüroo Tark & Co** from **Sorainen Law Offices**, further strengthening the former's M&A team. The firm continues to advise Microsoft, whilst new clients include a global mobile phone company. Aare Tark is recommended by peers and clients.

Luiga, Mugu & Borenius advised one of the world's major groups of institutional investors on the purchase of a 10% stake, worth €10m, in AS Tallink Group, the ferry operator and shipping company. (**Raidla & Partners** acted opposite.) Like many of the larger firms working in a relatively small market, **Luiga, Mugu & Borenius** has experience of advising all parties to M&A – buyers, sellers or funders. Name partner Margus Mugu is singled out for recommendation. Clients of the firm include Ober-Haus, Estonian Oil Service, one of the largest oil exporters in Estonia and AS Tallinn Cold Store. Additionally, the firm advised on the sale of shares in one of the country's largest producers of video tapes. About 10% of work is referrals from Finnish partner, **Borenius & Kemppinen**.

Mody Hääl & Partners counts Estonian Air, Olympus, McDonald's and Denmark's largest freight operator, DSB among its clients. Name partner Sanjay Jaanus Mody is recommended and is known for his punctuality and thoroughness. The firm recently advised Estonian Air on the leasing of a new aeroplane and, together with **Raidla & Partners**, represented the national carrier in one particularly long and complex piece of litigation. In an ongoing matter and as a result of referrals from Russian and Lithuanian firms, **Mody Hääl & Partners** is advising one of the world's largest oil companies on entry into the market.

Teder & Rask now operates as **Teder & Partnerid**, still under the guidance of Indrek Teder. The firm has extensive corporate experience and a track record in privatisations. Clients are drawn from diverse industry sectors, including telecoms, utilities and pharmaceuticals.

Four-partner **Advokaadibüroo A Jakobson & A Jaroslavski** advises corporate clients on transactional issues. Clients include Propaan Ltd, the largest propane supplier in Estonia.

Law Office Aavik, Arvisto & Partners trading as Baltic Commercial Law Office has a close relationship with a major Swedish private equity fund and has advised that client on the acquisition of two Estonian companies. Other cross-border work includes advising a Danish production company on the acquisition of an Estonian IT provider. The firm handles a range of corporate work along with public procurement.

Law Office Aivar Pilv advises on establishing companies, both locally and abroad, and on M&A. A recent highlight was representing the Competition Board in the landmark lawsuit against AS Elion regarding new price structures for telecoms services after termination of the Concession Agreement and opening of the Estonian telecoms market. Aivar Pilv and Ilmar-Erik Aavakivi advised. (**Raidla & Partners** represented AS Elion in appealing the decision.)

Ernst & Young Baltic AS is the Estonian member of the *EY Law* network whose other regional members include Latvia's **Kronbergs Law Office** and **Jurevicius, Balciunas & Partners EY Law** in Lithuania. The firm offers an all-round corporate service.

Hedman Osborne Clarke Alliance's corporate focus is on cross-border work, which is reflected in its roster of Scandinavian and German clients who include a major Scandinavian insurance group. In the M&A field, the firm's workload includes advising a major Estonian cleaning company on the acquisition of a local service company, and advising a German transit company planning to expand its Estonian interests via a local merger valued at EEK100m (€6.4m).

Law Office Keevallik & Partners specialises in commercial matters. The firm has experience of international mergers, obtaining approvals from the Estonian Competition Board and negotiating with the Estonian Privatisation Agency, insolvency and corporate restructuring. Clients of the firm include a subsidiary of one of the largest Scandinavian e-commerce companies, one of the largest broadcasting companies in the region and the biggest advertising company in Estonia, TBWA Guvatrak.

IP, IT AND TELECOMS

AAA Legal Services specialises in intellectual property. The firm, which is home to a number of qualified patent attorneys as well as lawyers, has offices in Estonia and Lithuania which have a stellar reputation in trade mark, patent and copyright matters.

In recent years **Law Office Aivar Pilv** has successfully settled several disputes related to trade marks and patents relating to music and entertainment, sport and various industrial sectors.

IP is a core practice of the **Hedman Osborne Clarke Alliance**. The firm registers trade marks and advises on licensing agreements for a variety of clients, including large software houses. IT-wise, it advises some of Estonia's leading IT and telecoms companies, a number of subsidiaries of Scandinavian IT companies and the UK's largest telco.

Law Office Keevallik & Partners is advising the Estonian Performers Association, one of the largest organisations representing record producers. The firm has experience in drafting software licensing agreements and other IP matters. Day-to-day, the firm assists one of the major telecoms companies in Estonia. Among other clients are a Swedish catalogue publishing company and one of the largest information companies in Estonia.

Lasvet Patent and Trademark Agency has eight patent attorneys, the majority of whom are European-qualified.

Luiga, Mugu & Borenius won a number of complex trade mark instructions. Vive Kaur is the firm's leading practitioner and helped prepare the draft Copyright Act. The firm is increasing its portfolio of IT clients. Monica Pihlak, who was previously in-house with AS Norma, is a rising star in IT/IP and taxation litigation.

Mody Hääl & Partners has been advising the second-largest telecoms group in Estonia on specific telecoms and competition matters.

Paul Varul of **Advokaadibüroo Paul Varul** provides trade mark and copyright advice. The firm has two large Estonian IT companies as clients and Aldo Kaljurand is helping draft the new telecoms laws.

Raidla & Partners is participating in drafting the new Telecoms Act to implement relevant EU directives. The firm has advised the Central Bank on software matters.

Sorainen Law Offices regularly handles enforcement matters. Recent work has included a number of trade mark disputes and representing a client in a dispute with the largest bank in Estonia.

Leading full-service firm, **Advokaadibüroo Tark & Co** advises Microsoft, Guinness UDV and Estonia Telecom on IT and IP issues. Partner Toomas Taube is recommended.

IP, IT AND TELECOMS

- AAA Legal Services
- Aivar Pilv, Law Office ✪
- Hedman Osborne Clarke Alliance
- Keevallik & Partners, Law Office
- Lasvet Patent and Trademark Agency
- Lepik & Luhaäär, Law Office ✪
- Luiga, Mugu & Borenius ✪
- Mody Hääl & Partners ✪
- Paul Varul, Advokaadibüroo
- Raidla & Partners ✪
- Sorainen Law Offices
- Tark & Co, Advokaadibüroo ✪

Firms are listed alphabetically
✪ Indicates firm displays contact details at the end of this chapter.

REAL ESTATE AND CONSTRUCTION

There is a great deal of foreign interest in the local real estate market. Indeed, real estate is a growth area as a result of relatively cheap land prices and the confidence of imminent EU accession. Many firms are developing this part of their practice as a result.

The development of a major real estate development in Tallinn is one of the biggest instructions currently occupying **Law Office Aavik, Arvisto & Partners trading as Baltic Commercial Law Office**

Law Office Aivar Pilv advises building contractors and local government on planning and construction matters including several projects in Tallinn. It counts a number of well-known real estate developers among its clients.

Law Office Keevallik & Partners provides a full range of property, real estate and construction legal services to clients including several leading Estonian building and construction companies. **Law Office Keevallik & Partners**' experience includes advising Scandinavian and Finnish construction companies on their entry into the market including setting up of subsidiaries. Name partner Toomas Keevallik is an expert in the field.

Law Office Lepik & Luhaäär advised a foreign bank in granting €20m funding for a shopping and business centre in Tallinn. The firm advised foreign investors in the construction of an oil terminal and development and construction of a grain silo in Estonia.

Mody Hääl & Partners is providing refinancing, restructuring and development advice to the owners of Mustamäe Shopping Centre, one of Estonia's largest retail schemes.

Raidla & Partners' clients include developers, investors and occupiers. The firm advised a foreign investor regarding the development of the largest shopping centre in Tallinn.

REAL ESTATE AND CONSTRUCTION

- Aavik, Arvisto & Partners trading as Baltic Commercial Law Office, Law Office
- Aivar Pilv, Law Office ✪
- Hedman Osborne Clarke Alliance
- Keevallik & Partners, Law Office
- Lepik & Luhaäär, Law Office ✪
- Luiga, Mugu & Borenius ✪
- Mody Hääl & Partners ✪
- Paul Varul, Advokaadibüroo
- Raidla & Partners ✪
- Tark & Co, Advokaadibüroo ✪
- Tehver & Partners, Law Office

Firms are listed alphabetically
✪ Indicates firm displays contact details at the end of this chapter.

TAX

Law Office Aavik, Arvisto & Partners trading as Baltic Commercial Law Office has the necessary tax expertise to advise international clients on all areas of tax planning. The firm has teamed up with an Estonian financial consultancy to provide financial and tax solutions to clients such as foreign investors.

Law Office Aivar Pilv has for the past decade advised both the Estonian Customs Board and the Tax Board. The firm has also advised several companies in settling tax disputes. Aivar Pilv, Erki Kergandberg, Marko Tiiman and Kristina Uuetoa-Tepper are the core tax team.

Ernst & Young Baltic AS has one of the largest tax practices, drawing on the resources of its wider

TAX

- Aavik, Arvisto & Partners trading as Baltic Commercial Law Office, Law Office
- Aivar Pilv, Law Office ✪
- Ernst & Young Baltic AS ✪
- Hedman Osborne Clarke Alliance
- HETA, Advokaadibüroo
- Hough, Hübner, Hütt & Partners
- Keevallik & Partners, Law Office
- Lepik & Luhaäär, Law Office ✪
- Luiga, Mugu & Borenius ✪
- Mody Hääl & Partners ✪
- Paul Varul, Advokaadibüroo
- Raidla & Partners ✪
- Rödl & Partner
- Sorainen Law Offices
- Tark & Co, Advokaadibüroo ✪
- Teder & Partnerid
- V Kaasik & Co, Law Office

Firms are listed alphabetically
✪ Indicates firm displays contact details at the end of this chapter.

pan-Baltic business unit. The Tallinn office advises companies on establishing a presence and assists in setting up in Estonia, drawing up agreements with a particular focus on tax matters.

Mody Hääl & Partners has a reputation for tax litigation. The firm's tax expert, name partner Marti Haal has secured several decisions against the Estonian Tax Board.

Advokaadibüroo Paul Varul has gained a number of significant tax clients. The firm carries out transactional work but the majority of its workload is litigation.

Sorainen Law Offices corners the market in cross-border work as a pan-Baltic firm with Helsinki-based Paul Künnap, the only lawyer specialising in Finnish-Estonian cross-border matters.

MARITIME AND TRANSPORT

Established as one of the 'Baltic capitals', Tallinn is an important port in the region. Most of the leading commercial firms have experience in advising on maritime and transport matters, both contentious and non-contentious. In addition, pockets of expertise can be found with certain individuals; Asko Pohla of **Pohla & Hallmägi** is one.

MARITIME AND TRANSPORT

- Aavik, Arvisto & Partners trading as Baltic Commercial Law Office, Law Office
- Hedman Osborne Clarke Alliance
- HETA, Advokaadibüroo
- Keevallik & Partners, Law Office
- Lepik & Luhaäär, Law Office ✪
- Luiga, Mugu & Borenius ✪
- Mody Hääl & Partners ✪
- Pohla & Hallmägi
- Raidla & Partners ✪
- Sorainen Law Offices
- Tark & Co, Advokaadibüroo ✪

Firms are listed alphabetically

✪ *Indicates firm displays contact details at the end of this chapter.*

LAW OFFICE AIVAR PILV

VABADUSE VÄLJAK 10
10146 TALLINN

Telephone: +372 6 404 650
Fax: +372 6 404 653
E-mail: info@apilv.ee
Website: www.apilv.ee

Languages
English, Finnish, German, Russian

Other offices
Tartu

Number of lawyers 12
at this office 9

Member
TAGLaw

CATEGORIES OF WORK

Bankruptcy law
Aivar Pilv, Margo Lemetti

Corporate law
Marko Tiiman, Margo Lemetti

Contracts
Ilmar-Erik Aavakivi, Kristina Uuetoa-Tepper

Banking and finance law
Eerik Entsik, Erki Kergandberg

Property law
Kristina Uuetoa-Tepper, Marko Tiiman

Intellectual property law
Eerik Entsik, Ilmar-Erik Aavakivi

Labour law
Kristina Uuetoa-Tepper, Piret Blankin

Valuation of business projects
Eerik Entsik, Paavo Paas

Land and ownership reform
Paavo Paas, Marko Tiiman

Administrative law
Aivar Pilv, Sven Sillar

Customs law
Kristina Uuetoa-Tepper, Erki Kergandberg

Taxation (tax law)
Aivar Pilv, Erki Kergandberg

Telecommunications
Paavo Paas, Piret Blankin

Competition law
Aivar Pilv, Ilmar-Erik Aavakivi

Copyright
Eerik Entsik, Sven Sillar

Constitutional law
Piret Blankin, Sven Sillar

Criminal law
Aivar Pilv, Tarmo Pilv

Arbitration and litigation
Aivar Pilv, Paavo Paas

ERNST & YOUNG BALTIC AS

TALLINN BUSINESS CENTER
HARJU 6, 4TH FLOOR
10130 TALLINN

Telephone: +372 6 310 610
Fax: +372 6 310 611
E-mail: advocate@ee.eylaw.com
Website: www.eylaw.com/ee

Languages
English, Estonian, Finnish, Russian

Number of lawyers 5

Contact
Heidi Wahtramae

Member
EY Law

CATEGORIES OF WORK

General practice
Company law
Corporate law
Mergers and acquisitions
Competition law
Real estate
Leases and leasing
Business law
Privatisation
Foreign investment
International commercial law
Intellectual property
Banking law
Securities
Finance
Telecommunications law
Energy law
Environmental law
Maritime law
Shipping
European Union law
Construction law
Debt collection
Labour and employment
Tax law
Civil litigation

LAW OFFICE LEPIK & LUHAÄÄR

DUNKRI 7
10123 TALLINN

Telephone: +372 6 306 460
Fax: +372 6 306 463
E-mail: info@abll.ee
Website: www.abll.ee

Languages
English, Estonian, Finnish, German, Russian, Swedish

Other offices
Riga*

Number of lawyers 20

Contacts
Peeter Lepik, Toomas Luhaäär

Member
Estonian Bar Association;
International Bar Association

International groupings
Lex Mundi; LAW

CATEGORIES OF WORK

Corporate and commercial
Toomas Luhaäär, Martin Simovart

Trade and investments
Peeter Lepik

Mergers and acquisitions
Martin Simovart, Martti Kalaus

Construction
Liina Linsi

Real estate
Liina Linsi

Banking and finance
Peeter Lepik, Martin Simovart

Competition
Martin Simovart, Martti Kalaus

Contracts
Peeter Lepik, Martin Simovart

Dispute resolution, litigation and arbitration
Liina Linsi, Vesse Võhma

Intellectual property
Mari-Ann Simovart

Tax
Toomas Luhaäär

Employment
Liina Linsi

Insolvency
Vesse Võhma

Privatisation
Toomas Luhaäär

LUIGA, MUGA & BORENIUS

PÄRNU MNT 15
10141 TALLINN

Telephone: +372 6 651 888
Fax: +372 6 651 899
E-mail: luiga@luiga.ee
Website: www.luiga.ee

Languages
English, Finnish, Russian

Number of lawyers 9

International groupings
In association with Borenius & Kemppinen (Helsinki), Liepa, Skopina/Borenius (Riga)

CATEGORIES OF WORK

Banking and finance
Sten Luiga, Priit Pahapill

Contracts
Margus Mugu, Karina Paatsi

Corporate and company
Margus Mugu, Monica Pihlak

EU and competition
Karina Paatsi

Intellectual property
Viive Kaur, Airi Hämmalov

Litigation, arbitration
Margus Mugu, Viive Kaur

Maritime and shipping
Margus Mugu, Airi Hämmalov

Mergers and acquisitions
Sten Luiga, Karina Paatsi

Privatisation
Margus Mugu, Monica Pihlak

Securities
Sten Luiga, Priit Pahapill

Tax
Margus Mugu, Priit Pahapill

MODY, HÄÄL & PARTNERS

PÄRNU MNT 10
10148 TALLINN

Telephone: +372 6 405 830
Fax: +372 6 405 831
E-mail: office@law.ee
Website: www.law.ee

Languages
English, Finnish, German, Russian

Number of lawyers 9

Contact
Sanjay Jaanus Mody

Member
Estonian Bar Association;
International Bar Association

CATEGORIES OF WORK

Banking and finance
Sanjay Jaanus Mody, Marti Hääl

Corporate and company
Peeter Kutman, Toomas Mälberg

Contracts
Marti Hääl, Peeter Kutman

Competition
Peeter Kutman

Energy and infrastructure projects
Peeter Kutman, Toomas Mälberg

Intellectual property
Silja Holsmer, Kairi Kurisoo

Insolvency
Sanjay Jaanus Mody

Litigation and arbitration
Sanjay Jaanus Mody, Marti Hääl

Mergers and acquisitions
Peeter Kutman

Real estate
Toomas Mälberg

Tax law
Marti Hääl

RAIDLA & PARTNERS

ROOSIKRANTSI 2
10119 TALLINN

Telephone: +372 6 407 170
Fax: +372 6 407 171
E-mail: email@raidla.ee
Website: www.raidla.ee

Languages
English, Finnish, German, Russian, Swedish

Number of lawyers 30

International groupings
Moquet Borde Associés

CATEGORIES OF WORK

Banking and finance, capital markets
Raino Paron

Corporate and commercial
Sven Papp

Dispute resolution, litigation and arbitration
Toomas Vaher

Energy and natural resources
Sven Papp, Jaanus Ikla

Insolvency/corporate restructuring
Toomas Vaher

Insurance
Raino Paron

Intellectual property
Reet Saks

Infrastructure
Jüri Raidla, Sven Papp

Mergers and acquisitions
Sven Papp, Raino Paron

Privatisation
Jüri Raidla

Shipping and transport
Toomas Vaher, Reet Saks

Tax
Monika Sehver, Maiu Fischer

Telecommunications
Sven Papp, Jaanus Ikla

Real estate development
Jüri Raidla, Sten Veidebaum

E-commerce
Raino Paron

Competition
Raino Paron

ADVOKAADIBÜROO TARK & CO

ROOSIKRANTSI 2
10119 TALLINN

Telephone: +372 6 110 900
Fax: +372 6 110 911
E-mail: tarkco@tarkco.ee
Website: www.tarkco.com

Languages
English, Finnish, French, German, Russian, Swedish

Number of lawyers 17

Member
Estonian Bar Association;
International Bar Association

CATEGORIES OF WORK

Banking and finance
Aare Tark, Hannes Vallikivi

Mergers and acquisitions
Risto Vahimets, Minni-Triin Park

Securities
Hannes Vallikivi, Risto Vahimets

Corporate finance
Hannes Vallikivi

Commercial and company law
Aare Tark, Jaan Lindmäe

EU and competition law
Toomas Taube, Kaja Leiger

Energy law and infrastructure projects
Risto Vahimets, Marit Savi

Intellectual property
Toomas Taube, Piret Luiga

Employment
Toomas Taube, Sille Allikmets

Tax
Aare Tark, Risto Vahimets

Insolvency
Maidu Kaasik, Andres Suik

Telecommunications
Maidu Kaasik, Allar Aru

Litigation and arbitration
Jaan Lindmäe, Andres Suik

Environment
Jaan Lindmäe, Kaja Leiger

Shipping and transport
Toomas Taube

FINLAND

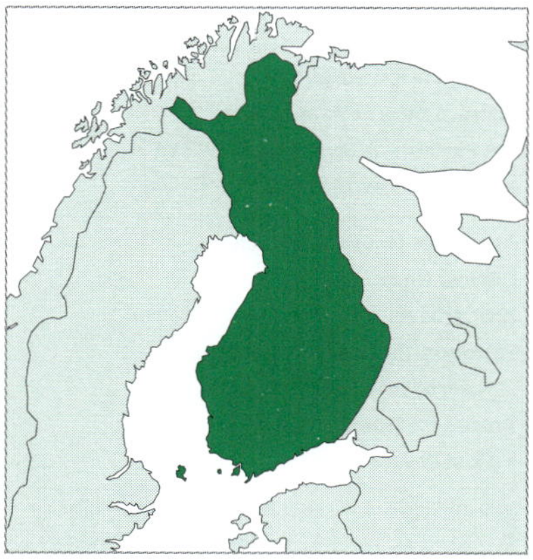

Population	5.19 million
Number of lawyers	1,640
Professional title	Asianajaja (Finnish); advocat (Swedish)
Currency	Euro (€)

Index

Although on the outskirts of the European Union, sharing a border with Russia, Finland is very much a central player in European matters. It is the only Nordic country to have adopted the euro as national currency, and the country also has strong political ties with the Baltic States. Finland's links to the Baltics are expected to strengthen after the Baltic States join the EU on 1 May 2004.

Finland gained independence in 1917, following hundreds of years of imperialist domination, firstly by the Swedes, then the Russians. Despite some communist participation in its government after independence, Finland maintained a Western model of democracy and peacefully co-existed with Russia.

The appointment of Anneli Jäätteemäki as prime minister at the beginning of 2003, meant Finland was the only European country to have women as both prime minister and president. However, Jäätteemäki resigned following a row dubbed 'Iraqgate' over allegations about leaked information used to secure her election victory only two months earlier. Her resignation came as quite a blow to Finns, who traditionally have been very politically stable. Maati Vanhanen took over as prime minister in June 2003.

BILLING

In Helsinki the bigger firms charge around €200 for an associate, while a partner would charge about €300. However, this figure can rise to €400 at some firms. Outside the Helsinki area, rates tend to be substantially lower. Over the past few years firms have increasingly been asked to bid for work, leading many of the larger firms to offer capped fees. However, hourly rates remain the most widely used form of billing.

MARKETING

Historically, Finnish law firms shied away from advertising their services, but as the legal market developed, firms became more aggressive in their marketing activities. All the large firms have websites, a trend now followed by the smaller firms. In addition, a number of firms have recently rebranded themselves.

IN-HOUSE LAWYERS

The majority of large Finnish banks, financial institutions and other large companies all have teams of in-house lawyers. Typically the bulk of the work will be carried out in-house, but specialist advice will be sought from law firms. In-house lawyers are not permitted to be members of the Bar.

ECONOMIC CLIMATE

Finland's economy has fallen on relatively hard times since the heady days of the technology boom. Since that time its economy has gradually weakened, but the summer of 2003 bore witness to a turnaround in economic fortunes. Analysts are now predicting GDP growth for 2003 to be around 1.4%. The new government is expected to continue tax cuts in 2004 in order to stimulate domestic demand. It is thought consumption will remain robust and consequently GDP is anticipated to increase by 2.8% in 2004.

Finland prides itself on its modern and competitive economy. Major exports include electronic and electrical products, pulp and paper, timber and wood, metal products, and chemicals. Around two-thirds of Finland is covered in forest which explains the country's long tradition of wood-based industries. It is estimated that every fifth Finn earns his or her livelihood from trees, either directly or indirectly. However, unemployment remains high in some areas, especially rural locations.

LEGAL MARKET

In November 2003 KPMG issued a statement saying that *KLegal* would be dissolved. At the time of going to press the Finnish office was unable to make a statement regarding its status. However, its managing partner and a number of key lawyers left to open **Borenius & Kemppinen**'s third domestic office in Tampere.

Throughout 2003 there were few other changes to the composition of the Finnish legal market. **Hannes Snellman** and **Roschier Holmberg, member of ius laboris** continue to dwarf rival firms in terms of both size and reputation. They are both top choices for clients wishing to carry out large deals. However, increasingly firms such as **Borenius & Kemppinen**, **Castrén & Snellman** and **Merilampi Marttila Laitasalo** are recognised as leading firms and continue to attract high-profile clients. In addition, the potential offered by the Baltic States, post-accession, has sparked a number of lawyers to contemplate the possibility of opening regional offices in one or more of the States.

With Finland's strong history in the telecoms market, it is unsurprising that a substantial number

The largest firms

1	Hannes Snellman	101
2	Roschier Holmberg, member of ius laboris	100
3	Castrén & Snellman	77
4	Borenius & Kemppinen	50
5	Krogerus & Co. Oy	40
6	Dittmar & Indrenius	26
7	Merilampi Marttila Laitasalo	22
	Veikko Palotie & Co	22
9	Fennica Attorneys-at-Law Ltd	21
10	Peltonen, Ruokonen & Itäinen Attorneys At Law	19
11	KLegal Oy	18
	Waselius & Wist	18
13	Juridia Ltd Attorneys-At-Law	17
	Mäkitalo Rämö Juutilainen Ltd, Attorneys-at-Law	17
15	Attorneys' House ANPR Ltd	16
	Ernst & Young	16
17	Susiluoto Attorneys-at-Law Ltd	15
18	Bützow Nordia	14
	Laakso, Lukander & Ruohola	14
	Luostarinen Mettälä Räikkönen	14
21	HH Partners, Attorneys-at-Law, Ltd	12
	Kallioinen, Tolppanen, Salminen & Co, Attorneys at Law, Ltd	12
	Sivenius, Suvanto & Co Oy	12
24	Procopé & Hornborg	11
	White & Case	11

These figures represent the total number of lawyers in this country only, and have been supplied by the firms themselves. The figures should be accurate as at 1 January 2004.

of Finnish niche IT and telecoms firms have recently emerged as strong players in the market. **Fennica Attorneys-at-Law Ltd** and **Susiluoto Attorneys-at-Law Ltd** both have excellent reputations.

Based on Swedish civil law, the Finnish legal system comprises a number of general courts, with the Supreme Court the highest authority. The Supreme Court modifies and interprets laws as necessary.

In order to become a member of the Bar, applicants are required to have a Master of Laws degree, and the appropriate level of legal experience. The professional title 'asianjaja' or 'advokat' applies only to those who have passed a professional examination and are members of the Bar. Competition for the country's best graduates remains immensely fierce as only around 400 law students graduate each year.

FOREIGN OFFICES

Only a few firms have offices abroad, but increasingly Russia and the Baltic States are seen as lucrative jurisdictions to tap into. **Castrén & Snellman St Petersburg Ltd** is the Russian office of the Finnish heavyweight. **Ahola & Sokka** also has a branch in St Petersburg. **Borenius & Kemppinen** has strengthened links with its successful joint venture office **Attorneys at law Liepa, Skopina / BORENIUS** in Riga, Latvia; in 2003 it reinforced its strategic alliance with **Attorneys at law Luiga, Mugu & Borenius**. **Heinonen & Co, Attorneys-at-Law, Ltd** has a Spanish office and **Hedman Osborne Clarke Alliance** has offices in Tallinn, St Petersburg and Frankfurt (the firm is a member of UK-based **Osborne Clarke**'s pan-European alliance). **Laakso, Lukander & Ruohola** has a German EEIG partner.

FOREIGN FIRMS

Finland remains largely unexplored by foreign law firms. US-based **White & Case** remains the most successful foreign firm in Finland, with an excellent reputation in the capital markets sector. **Asianajotoimisto Holland & Knight Oy** also maintains its presence in Helsinki.

BANKING AND FINANCE

Hannes Snellman's banking and finance team was greatly boosted in 2003 with the arrival of highly respected Matti Engelberg from Nordea Bank. Engelberg joins a 15-strong team which was extremely busy during 2003. The 'well-connected' firm was involved in a variety of Finnish law project financings, with particular focus on the Baltic countries. In addition, the firm arranged syndicated loans and advised an increasing number of Finnish companies on joining the bond market.

In 2003 the 'first-rate' specialist banking and finance firm **Luostarinen Mettälä Räikkönen** continued to increase in both size and stature. Clients praise Kimmo Mettälä for his 'commercial-awareness' and 'practical outlook'. A recent highlight for the firm was representing Sampo Bank plc and other lenders in connection with €100m multi-currency revolving facility to Nokian Tyres plc.

Highly prestigious **Roschier Holmberg, member of ius laboris** maintains its position as Finland's market leader in the banking and finance sector. Its superb banking team consistently receives quality instructions. At the end of 2002, the firm advised Morgan Stanley as the lead manager in Stora Enso Oyj's €370m forest asset securitisation through Tornator Finance plc. This was the first ever business securitisation of forest assets, and one of the very first public securitisations in Finland.

Petri Haussila at **White & Case** is one of the most revered lawyers in Finland. The office's banking and finance team continues to attract noteworthy instructions, working closely with the banking and finance teams in London, Paris and New York. Recently the firm was involved in a number of syndicated finance projects.

During 2003, the widely commended banking and finance team at **Borenius & Kemppinen** was kept extremely busy. The bulk of its finance work related to acquisition finance for banking syndicates.

Led by highly respected Pekka Lehtinen, the team at **Castrén & Snellman** continues to offer expertise in a wide range of financing issues. In 2003 this 'customer-focused' firm advised energy company Fortum on several large finance deals.

'High-quality' outfit **Waselius & Wist** maintains an excellent reputation for its banking

BANKING AND FINANCE

HANNES SNELLMAN ✪
LUOSTARINEN METTÄLÄ RÄIKKÖNEN ✪
ROSCHIER HOLMBERG, MEMBER OF IUS LABORIS ✪
WHITE & CASE

Borenius & Kemppinen ✪
Castrén & Snellman ✪
Waselius & Wist ✪

Dittmar & Indrenius ✪
Fennica Attorneys-at-Law Ltd ✪
HH Partners, Attorneys-at-Law, Ltd ✪
Merilampi Marttila Laitasalo ✪

Attorneys' House ANPR Ltd
Bützow Nordia
Krogerus & Co. Oy ✪
Peltonen, Ruokonen & Itäinen Attorneys At Law ✪
Procopé & Hornborg ✪
Veikko Palotie & Co ✪

Firms are listed A-Z in tiers which are ranked in order of priority
✪ Indicates firm displays contact details at the end of this chapter.

and finance work. During 2003 the firm acted as Finnish counsel to Scandinavian Beverage Group AB regarding its term loan agreement of SEK114m (€12.7m).

Dittmar & Indrenius lost one of its key lawyers in 2002, however in 2003 the firm proved itself to be a force to be reckoned with – it has maintained its excellent reputation in the banking and finance sector and is highly recommended.

Although relatively small, the banking and finance team at **Fennica Attorneys-at-Law Ltd** had an extremely successful year in 2003. The team, led by 'savvy' Jori Taipale, represented a number of leading banks. The firm also advised both borrowers and lenders on various domestic and international loan agreements and structured finance projects.

HH Partners, Attorneys-at-Law, Ltd's banking and finance expertise was strengthened by the arrival of Tuire Niemi. Previously legal counsel at two leading financial institutions, her experience within trade and export finance, as well as structured and project finance, will prove invaluable to the firm and its variety of clients.

At **Merilampi Marttila Laitasalo** 'thoroughly professional' Jukka Laitasalo has an excellent reputation in the field of banking. Ari Keinänen is also recommended in this area.

Attorneys' House ANPR Ltd has a good reputation for its work in the field of corporate and financial restructuring.

Bützow Nordia continues to be recognised as a thoroughly dependable firm in all matter of banking and finance issues.

Highly respected **Krogerus & Co. Oy** boasts several banks and financial institutions amongst its clients. Juha Wessman is an expert in project finance.

Hans Sundlad and Mikka Ojala at **Peltonen, Ruokonen & Itäinen Attorneys At Law** are widely respected for their banking and finance aptitude. The firm's clients include a number of banks and shipbuilders.

At **Procopé & Hornborg** Bjorn Nykvist is highly recommended for both his banking and finance expertise.

Veikko Palotie & Co's Mikko Pakarinen is experienced in the banking and finance sector.

CAPITAL MARKETS

For **Roschier Holmberg, member of ius laboris** 2003 yielded a great deal of activity within the capital markets sector, with a high volume of landmark deals. In September 2003 the firm advised on the public tender offer by Phoenix for Tamro Oyj, the leading pharmaceuticals wholesale company in the Nordic countries. Tomas Lindholm, Dimitrios Himonas and Petri Taivalkoski are all highly respected.

At **Waselius & Wist** 'seriously hard working' name partner Tarja Wist is praised by clients. One of the highlights in 2003 was advising CSFB in its issuance and listing of a programme of equity linked zero coupon notes, listed on the Helsinki Stock Exchange. Clients include a large number of important investment banks.

White & Case's Petri Haussila acts as co-head of the firm's securities practice group worldwide. The office acted as deal counsel in the offering of shares pursuant to pre-emptive subscription rights by Outokumpu, a mutlinational Finland-based metals and technology group.

During 2003 **Borenius & Kemppinen** was involved in numerous transactions in the capital markets sector. The firm maintains its reputation as one of the key players in the field.

At **Castrén & Snellman** 'highly focused' Johan Åkermarck played a crucial role in representing Hon Hai Precision Industry Ltd, one of the largest companies in the world, in its public tender offer to the shareholders at Eimo Oyj.

Despite the silence within the equity market, 'enthusiastic' and 'astute' Kari Lautijärvi led **Hannes Snellman**'s capital markets team on a variety of transactions. Highlights during 2003 included advising on a €4bn global MTN programme, and representing a number of banks on the issue of serial bonds, due in 2006.

HH Partners, Attorneys-at-Law, Ltd is praised for providing the 'right match in both capital markets knowledge and resources'. New arrival Tuire Niemi has extensive experience in the debt capital markets.

Although the IPO market was virtually non-existent during 2003 in Finland, **Krogerus & Co. Oy**'s capital markets activities remained high. The firm focused its attention on public tenders, plus merger and demerger transactions.

Merilampi Marttila Laitasalo's 'creative duo', Ari Keinaänen and Matti Ylä-Mononen, is lauded for its expertise, demonstrated by the involvement in the General Electric tender offer to the shareholders of Instrumentarium, a medical technology company, in January 2003.

CAPITAL MARKETS

ROSCHIER HOLMBERG, MEMBER OF IUS LABORIS ✪
WASELIUS & WIST ✪
WHITE & CASE

Borenius & Kemppinen ✪
Castrén & Snellman ✪
Hannes Snellman ✪

HH Partners, Attorneys-at-Law, Ltd ✪
Krogerus & Co. Oy ✪
Merilampi Marttila Laitasalo ✪

Fennica Attorneys-at-Law Ltd ✪
Luostarinen Mettälä Räikkönen ✪
Peltonen, Ruokonen & Itäinen Attorneys At Law ✪

Firms are listed A-Z in tiers which are ranked in order of priority
✪ Indicates firm displays contact details at the end of this chapter.

Although the capital markets sector was particularly slow in 2003, with no IPOs **Fennica Attorneys-at-Law Ltd** remained active in other aspects of capital markets in a variety of sectors, including IT and paper.

During 2003 highly respected **Luostarinen Mettälä Räikkönen** acted on a number of EMTN programmes, while **Peltonen, Ruokonen & Itäinen Attorneys At Law** is also recommended for its capital markets activities.

CORPORATE AND COMMERCIAL (INCLUDING M&A)

Year-on-year **Hannes Snellman** consistently emerges as Finland's pre-eminent firm for M&A transactions. Among a raft of high-profile transactions, the firm advised OM AB (Stockholm Stock Exchange) in its merger with HEX (Helsinki Stock Exchange). Clients praise the M&A practice's 'adept' and 'versatile' co-heads, Johan Aalto and Juhani Mäkinen.

The market leader for commercial expertise, **Roschier Holmberg, member of ius laboris** continues to make an impressive mark on the Finnish legal market. Figures suggest the total value of the firm's transactional work for 2002 accounted for 90% of the total value of all the transactions involving Finnish companies. One of the highlights of 2003 was representing General Electric in the public tender offer for Instrumentarium Corporation, a leading medical technology company – one of the few Finnish companies listed on Nasdaq. Not only was this the largest cash tender offer in Finland, it was also the largest Finnish tender offer by a US company.

Hot on the heels of opening its Espoo office, regional heavyweight **Borenius & Kemppinen** opened a third domestic office in Tampere at the end of 2003. Managed by former *KLegal* managing partner, Timo Seppälä, the office will greatly boost the firm's existing client base in the region.

Castrén & Snellman maintains its reputation as 'one of Finland's finest law firms'. The addition of Jari Sonninen, previously executive manager of financial and legal affairs at Aldata Solution Oyj is a significant bolster to the firm's M&A group. A recent highlight for the group was representing HEX in its merger with OM AB.

Renowned as an M&A boutique, **Dittmar & Indrenius** boasts a substantial share of Finland's high-value deals. The firm's client base includes a combination of domestic and foreign clients, including a number of household names. Widely respected partner Markus Troberg continues to augment the firm's profile with his outstanding reputation.

'Synonymous with IT expertise' **Fennica Attorneys-at-Law Ltd** extends its aptitude to corporate and commercial matters. 'Proactive' Harri Hynninen is regarded as a leading expert in M&A. The firm continues to act for a number of high-profile IT and telecoms clients in a variety of transactional matters.

In 2003 'highly dependable' **Krogerus & Co. Oy** opened a new office in Kuopio, signalling the success the firm has garnered since 2002. Not only has the size of the firm increased, its M&A activities have also grown significantly.

In January 2004 Niina Korppi-Tommola joined **Luostarinen Mettälä Räikkönen** as an associate from **Clifford Chance**. Prior to her arrival the 'excellent' firm had a successful year. Among a host of transactions it represented Helsinki Cooperative Society (HOK) in its merger with Ouusliike Elanto to create a new supermarket company with a substantial market share.

On the other side of the table in the HOK Elanto merger was 'impressive' **Merilampi Marttila Laitasalo**. The firm's transactional successes of 2003 do not end there – it was involved in a significant number of cross-border transactions. Pekka Merilampi maintains his reputation as one of Finland's leading company law experts.

During 2003 **Waselius & Wist** continued to grow organically. A highlight for the firm was acting as Finnish counsel in the sale of 45% of the issued shares in Atro Oyj by TXU Finland Holdings, a fully owned subsidiary of TXU Europe Group plc (in administration), to Savon Energiaholding Oy.

Although the first half of 2003 was relatively quiet for **White & Case**, and Finland as a whole, the latter picked up considerably. Highlights for Petri Haussila and his team included representing Botie Therapies in a complicated tri-partite merger.

With a background in the insolvency and bankruptcy sector **Attorneys' House ANPR Ltd** is recommended for corporate and commercial matters. The firm boasts a number of lawyers widely recognised as leading practitioners in the field.

Lauded for its 'accessible senior partners' **HH Partners, Attorneys-at-Law, Ltd** maintains strong relations with its new economy clients. Taino Tuohino continues to advise clients on a broad spectrum of contract, corporate and commercial law issues. The firm is also commended for the 'prompt service' rendered.

With 'one of the best reputations in the Turku area' **Laakso, Lukander & Ruohola** maintains its domination of south-west Finland. Clients praise the 'highly committed' lawyers at the largest firm based outside of Helsinki, and it continues to advise a number of major companies. Notable M&A transactions in 2003 reflect the firm's very strong regional status.

Widely praised **Peltonen, Ruokonen & Itäinen Attorneys At Law** boasts a number of major retail and energy companies as clients. In 2003 Ari Savela and Leif Itäinen were involved in a number of financing transactions and corporate restructurings.

Energy and telecoms companies make up the bulk of **Procopé & Hornborg**'s corporate and commercial client base, with a steady influx of domestic companies. The firm's managing partner Ismo Hentula is regarded as a leading specialist in both corporate and commercial work.

Highly regarded for its expertise in real estate matters **Veikko Palotie & Co** is also respected for M&A. Name partner Tauno Palotie is renowned as a specialist in the sector. During 2003 the firm was involved in a number of mergers and also joint venture consolidations.

CORPORATE AND COMMERCIAL (INCLUDING M&A)

HANNES SNELLMAN ✪
ROSCHIER HOLMBERG, MEMBER OF IUS LABORIS ✪

Borenius & Kemppinen ✪
Castrén & Snellman ✪
Dittmar & Indrenius ✪
Fennica Attorneys-at-Law Ltd ✪
Krogerus & Co. Oy ✪
Luostarinen Mettälä Räikkönen ✪
Merilampi Marttila Laitasalo ✪
Waselius & Wist ✪
White & Case

Attorneys' House ANPR Ltd
HH Partners, Attorneys-at-Law, Ltd ✪
Laakso, Lukander & Ruohola ✪
Peltonen, Ruokonen & Itäinen Attorneys At Law ✪
Procopé & Hornborg ✪
Veikko Palotie & Co ✪

Ahola & Sokka
Bützow Nordia
Gahmberg, Hästö & Co ✪
Hedman Osborne Clarke Alliance
Heinonen & Co, Attorneys-at-Law, Ltd ✪
Juridia Ltd Attorneys-At-Law ✪
Pirilä & Pöyhönen

ACE Law Ltd
Björkqvist & Björkqvist AB, Advokatbyrå
Heikkilä & Co Attorneys at Law Ltd.
Kallioinen, Tolppanen, Salminen & Co, Attorneys at Law, Ltd ✪
Kauttu & Sainio ✪
Lindblad
Mäkitalo Rämö Juutilainen Ltd, Attorneys-at-Law ✪
Malinen Moisio & Partners Ltd, Attorneys-at-Law
Pekka Pinomaa Oy, Asianajotoimisto
Reims & Co
Rödl & Partner
Sivenius, Suvanto & Co Oy ✪
Susiluoto Attorneys-at-Law Ltd
Teperi & Co Oy, Asianajotoimisto
Wrede & Co

Firms are listed A-Z in tiers which are ranked in order of priority
✪ Indicates firm displays contact details at the end of this chapter.

Among Finland's smaller firms is **Ahola & Sokka**. Name partner Juhani Ahola has an excellent reputation as a corporate adviser. The firm is also recommended for its commercial and bankruptcy advice.

Bützow Nordia is best known for its focus on business law, particularly cross-border work with a Russian element. The firm boasts a number of large multinational corporations, as well as small domestic companies amongst its clients.

Although principally a maritime and transport firm, **Gahmberg, Hästö & Co** also boasts an excellent corporate group, boosted in 2003 by the arrival of Veli-Matti Tarvainen, formerly general counsel at Partek, a leading engineering company. With the help of another new recruit, Max Jussila, the firm also advises Finnish and foreign companies on establishing business in China.

Harry Hedman is senior partner and head of **Hedman Osborne Clarke Alliance**'s Helsinki office. The firm is associated with UK firm **Osborne Clarke**. Hedman is recommended for his corporate and commercial expertise, in particular in relation to the retail sector.

Intellectual property boutique **Heinonen & Co, Attorneys-at-Law, Ltd** is widely praised by clients. Although its focus remains on IP, 2003 saw an increase in the number of commercial agreements drafted by the firm.

During 2003 **Juridia Ltd Attorneys-At-Law** was augmented by the arrival of well-respected Tero Routamo from **Veikko Palotie & Co**. Managing partner, 'knowledgeable' Hannu Rintala is praised by clients across the board. The firm also boasts Tim Williams, a qualified English solicitor who specialises in cross-border transactions.

Pirilä & Pöyhönen, a spin-off from **Krogerus & Co. Oy**, has continued to enjoy success in the field of M&A. In 2003 the firm represented one of Europe's largest electronics contract manufacturing companies in a high-profile transaction. Best known for his patent expertise, Kalle Pirilä is widely commended for his commercial nous.

Clients praise Mikko Rasaene at **ACE Law Ltd** for his 'business know-how'. During 2003 the firm attracted a number of large clients from the media and entertainment sector.

With offices in Turku, Helsinki, Huittinen and Tampere, **Heikkilä & Co Attorneys at Law Ltd.** has an excellent reputation and a wide range of domestic clients.

2003 was a highly successful year for **Kallioinen, Tolppanen, Salminen & Co, Attorneys at Law, Ltd**. This well-respected firm was involved in numerous transactions, advising buyers and sellers in the mid-size company sector, including on cross-border issues. Clients include companies in the healthcare industry.

Highly regarded for its technology and transport work, **Kauttu & Sainio** is also recommended for its corporate work. Its clients include a number of medium-sized companies involved in international transactions.

Best known for his experience in sports matters, Hannu Kalkas at **Lindblad** is highly recommended. The firm is involved in a variety of contract arrangements. Clients range from high-profile sports organisations, to small companies working in sports management.

With a strong domestic reputation **Mäkitalo Rämö Juutilainen Ltd, Attorneys-at-Law** continues to represent a wide range of clients, eight of whom are listed on the Helsinki Stock Exchange. In 2003 the firm was involved in a number of major M&A transactions.

Based in Turku **Attorneys-at-Law Malinen Moisio & Partners Ltd** has a good reputation for its corporate and commercial work.

At **Asianajotoimisto Pekka Pinomaa Oy** name partner Pekka Pinomaa is recommended for general corporate work, in particular in relation to the Baltic States.

With the majority of its lawyers based in Porvoo, **Reims & Co** enjoys a good regional reputation, while Petri Nykanen, at multidisciplinary firm **Rödl & Partner**, is known for both his corporate and commercial expertise.

Best known for its litigation work, **Sivenius, Suvanto & Co Oy** was successfully involved in representing a number of venture capital companies during 2003.

At **Susiluoto Attorneys-at-Law Ltd** Kalle Kyläkallio is renowned as a company law specialist. The firm's clients include a number of listed domestic and international companies.

Väinö Teperi at **Asianajotoimisto Teperi & Co Oy** is recommended for his corporate and commercial expertise.

Wrede & Co's main focus is on business law. The firm represents a number of foreign companies. One of its major clients is a large French energy company.

CORPORATE TAX

HH Partners, Attorneys-at-Law, Ltd's Arto Kukkonen is one of the leading tax advisers in Finland. The firm's clients include software, hardware and other IT companies. As well as Finnish companies, its clients include a number of big players from the US.

Hannes Snellman's tax department boasts high-profile partner Jarmo Ikkala. His team includes Leena Äärilä, a doyenne in the VAT arena, and up-and-coming specialist Antti Lehtimja.

Gunnar Westerlund at **Roschier Holmberg, member of ius laboris** leads the firm's corporate tax team. Renowned as one of the leaders in Finland, his work largely relates to the transactions the firm is involved with.

In terms of client relations few can match Leena Romppainen at **Castrén & Snellman**. Widely praised for her attention to detail, Romppainen remains a key player in the team's success.

Attorneys' House ANPR Ltd is highly regarded for its contentious tax work, while litigation partner Tom Vapaavuori is also recommended for his contentious expertise. He represented the victims in two groundbreaking industrial espionage cases.

HH Partners, Attorneys-at-Law, Ltd is replete with contentious talent in each of its practice areas. From tax to IP, the firm represents a number of major clients in both litigation and arbitration.

Previously chairman of the Finnish Bar, founder and name partner of **Peltonen, Ruokonen & Itäinen Attorneys At Law** Jukka Peltonen maintains an excellent reputation as a litigator. Throughout the firm, most of the lawyers are involved in litigation, as well as arbitration and mediation.

Jan Aminoff of **Aminoff & Weissenberg, Attorneys Ltd** is commended not only for his shipping expertise, but is also praised for his contentious talent.

Attorneys' House ANPR Ltd is recommended for insolvency and bankruptcy litigation.

Peter Anthoni at **Bützow Nordia** is renowned as a litigation and arbitration specialist.

Dittmar & Indrenius represents clients from a wide variety of industry sectors in all types of commercial disputes, both in Finland and abroad.

Krogerus & Co. Oy boasts several talented litigators and arbitrators. Among them is Marja Ramm-Schmidt who acts as a member of the Arbitration Board of the Finnish Central Chamber of Commerce.

In 2003 **Laakso, Lukander & Ruohola**'s Jarkko Ruohola represented several major telecoms companies in a range of litigious matters.

CORPORATE TAX

HH PARTNERS, ATTORNEYS-AT-LAW, LTD ✪
HANNES SNELLMAN ✪
ROSCHIER HOLMBERG, MEMBER OF IUS LABORIS ✪

Castrén & Snellman ✪

Attorneys' House ANPR Ltd
Borenius & Kemppinen ✪
Peltonen, Ruokonen & Itäinen Attorneys At Law ✪
Waselius & Wist ✪

Firms are listed A-Z in tiers which are ranked in order of priority
✪ Indicates firm displays contact details at the end of this chapter.

Borenius & Kemppinen assists both domestic and international clients on issues relating to direct and indirect taxation. In 2003 the firm was involved in a number of restructurings for private clients.

For **Peltonen, Ruokonen & Itäinen Attorneys At Law** 2003 was particularly active. The firm was involved in a variety of tax structurings.

Waselius & Wist is involved in a range of tax planning and structured tax. Niklas Thibblin, a specialist in the field, is recommended.

DISPUTE RESOLUTION

Partners Jouko Huhtala and Marko Hentunen spearhead **Castrén & Snellman**'s highly successful dispute resolution team. During 2003 the team represented a broad variety of clients, with a focus on commercial matters.

Highly regarded for their contentious aptitude **Hannes Snellman**'s Patrik Lindfors and Mika Savola co-head the firm's 15-strong dispute resolution team.

At **Merilampi Marttila Laitasalo** Jukka Laitasala and Ari Kantor are acknowledged for their enviable litigious talent. In 2003 both were involved in major domestic and international arbitration proceedings, as well as other commercial litigation.

Roschier Holmberg, member of ius laboris boasts a dispute resolution group of more than 20 lawyers, made up from specialists across the firm. Tomas Lindholm is widely praised by clients and peers alike for his arbitration skills. The firm is highly recommended for its IP litigation. The patent litigation team is led by partners Eva Nordman and Rainer Hilli. During 2003 the team appeared before Finnish courts in cases concerning supplementary patent protection for pharmaceuticals and in other fields of technology.

In 2003 **Borenius & Kemppinen** expanded its litigation and arbitration practice, which continues to be one of the core practices of the firm.

Known for his arbitration expertise, 'leading player' Marko Waino at **Fennica Attorneys-at-Law Ltd** was involved in a number of large arbitration proceedings and litigation during 2003. Fellow

DISPUTE RESOLUTION

CASTRÉN & SNELLMAN ✪
HANNES SNELLMAN ✪
MERILAMPI MARTTILA LAITASALO ✪
ROSCHIER HOLMBERG, MEMBER OF IUS LABORIS ✪

Borenius & Kemppinen ✪
Fennica Attorneys-at-Law Ltd ✪
HH Partners, Attorneys-at-Law, Ltd ✪
Peltonen, Ruokonen & Itäinen Attorneys At Law ✪

Aminoff & Weissenberg, Attorneys Ltd ✪
Attorneys' House ANPR Ltd
Bützow Nordia
Dittmar & Indrenius ✪
Krogerus & Co. Oy ✪
Laakso, Lukander & Ruohola ✪
Luostarinen Mettälä Räikkönen ✪
Pirilä & Pöyhönen
Procopé & Hornborg ✪
Susiluoto Attorneys-at-Law Ltd
Veikko Palotie & Co ✪
Waselius & Wist ✪

Firms are listed A-Z in tiers which are ranked in order of priority
✪ Indicates firm displays contact details at the end of this chapter.

Raimo Seppälä at **Luostarinen Mettälä Räikkönen** maintains his reputation as a leading litigator in banking and finance-related disputes.

Pirilä & Pöyhönen's Ilmari Pöyhönen is highly regarded for his commercial litigation skills. Fellow name partner Kalle Pirilä is also respected for his litigation work in the patent field, as well as in commercial disputes.

Procopé & Hornborg boasts three exceptional lawyers who are regularly involved in dispute resolution. They are partner Petri Kyllönen, as well as Satu Juurola and Mika Oksanen. Lotta Uusitalo is also recommended for competition litigation.

Name partner Tapio Susiluoto at **Susiluoto Attorneys-at-Law Ltd** is heavily involved in arbitration, and is also often instructed as counsel.

Veikko Palotie & Co maintains its reputation as a small but quality firm with its main focus on real estate matters. However, the firm also has an excellent reputation for dispute resolution. During 2003, the firm handled a significant amount of arbitration (both as arbitrator and as counsel) and litigation. Best known as a media and entertainment specialist, Mika Pakarinen is a highly respected litigator.

Name partner Jan Waselius at **Waselius & Wist** acted as chairman in the arbitration of Kone Finance Oy.

EU AND COMPETITION

In 2003 **Castrén & Snellman**'s respected practice took a blow, losing partner Petri Kuoppamäki to Nokia, after only a year. However, the firm's confidence should remain high, as the successful practice retained a number of high-profile clients, and continues to act on a number of complex competition projects.

Carl-Henrik Wallin heads the competition and EU law practice area within the M&A group at **Hannes Snellman**. He advises clients on all aspects of antitrust and trade regulation and European Union law.

Few Finnish lawyers can rival **Roschier Holmberg, member of ius laboris**' Christian Wik's magnificent reputation in the field of competition law. Along with colleague Mikko Alkio, Wik was involved with proceedings related to the alleged abuse of the dominant position held by four of Finland's largest commercial radio stations. For the widely praised firm, 2003 also saw an increase in the number of merger control feasibility studies it carried out.

Partner Janne Kairo leads the successful competition team at **Borenius & Kemppinen**. During 2003 the firm was extremely active, advising a number of foreign clients. One of the firm's main strengths is the recently formed Finnish-Baltic team, run from Helsinki but working closely with other experts in all the associated offices.

Although the firm has far fewer lawyers than other leading Finnish firms, comparatively **Fennica Attorneys-at-Law Ltd** holds a significant market share in this area. In 2003, a prominent achievement for Jori Taipale's competition team was representing Finland's low-cost airline, Flying Finn Ltd.

Katri Joenpolvi is one of **Krogerus & Co. Oy**'s key players within the competition team. In January 2003, the firm was boosted by the arrival of Marja-Liisa Järvinen, previously a sole practitioner. The firm represented a number of Finnish telecoms companies in cases before the competition authorities in Finland and Brussels.

Name partner Jukka Luostarinen at **Luostarinen Mettälä Räikkönen** is renowned for his competition expertise. In 2003 he represented a number of Finnish companies in cartel investigations.

Merilampi Marttila Laitasalo boasts one of Finland's finest competition practices. Arrtu Mentula and Ari Kantor are highly respected in the field.

White & Case's EU and competition practice has garnered a range of new instructions from clients, and in 2003 the firm also attracted a number of new clients. The practice was very active during the year, representing various clients before the competition authorities.

Peltonen, Ruokonen & Itäinen Attorneys At Law boasts a number of large Finnish enterprises as clients. In particular, the firm advises several important retail companies and assists clients from other industries with distribution arrangements.

Lotta Uusitalo at **Procopé & Hornborg** is widely acknowledged for her competition expertise. 2003 saw an increased workload in relation to competition issues stemming from business responsibilities in the Baltic States.

Waselius & Wist has extensive experience in the EU and competition sector. Mikka Eerola in particular is recommended.

A significant highlight for respected **HH Partners, Attorneys-at-Law, Ltd** in 2003 was representing one of the world's leading stainless steel producers before the European Court of Justice (ECJ).

Specialising in comparative European law, **Morini & Kiikeri International Law Firm** is largely focused on Finnish-Italian activities.

Reims & Co and **Veikko Palotie & Co** are also recommended for their EU and competition expertise.

EU AND COMPETITION

CASTRÉN & SNELLMAN ✪
HANNES SNELLMAN ✪
ROSCHIER HOLMBERG, MEMBER OF IUS LABORIS ✪

Borenius & Kemppinen ✪
Fennica Attorneys-at-Law Ltd ✪
Krogerus & Co. Oy ✪
Luostarinen Mettälä Räikkönen ✪
Merilampi Marttila Laitasalo ✪
White & Case

Peltonen, Ruokonen & Itäinen Attorneys At Law ✪
Procopé & Hornborg ✪
Waselius & Wist ✪

HH Partners, Attorneys-at-Law, Ltd ✪
Morini & Kiikeri International Law Firm
Reims & Co
Veikko Palotie & Co ✪

Firms are listed A-Z in tiers which are ranked in order of priority
✪ Indicates firm displays contact details at the end of this chapter.

IT AND TELECOMS

Known as 'Finland's Mr IT', Kimmo Rekola leads the widely commended IT and telecoms practice at **Castrén & Snellman**. Immensely respected by clients and contemporaries alike, his team continues to advise numerous clients, in particular in relation to outsourcing.

Fennica Attorneys-at-Law Ltd continues to go from strength to strength, thanks in no small part to 'unflappable' and 'responsive' Pekka Takki. Its client base widened further in 2003, and the firm now acts on an exclusive basis for various international companies. Amongst a raft of high-profile clients, the firm advised a leading banking group in the restructuring of its IT services.

Craig Thompson at **Roschier Holmberg, member of ius laboris** is renowned as an outstanding IT and telecoms lawyer. In 2003 the firms assisted domestic and international hi-tech enterprises with research and development agreements, licensing and other technology transfers. The firm was also involved in an

IT AND TELECOMS

CASTRÉN & SNELLMAN ✪
FENNICA ATTORNEYS-AT-LAW LTD ✪
ROSCHIER HOLMBERG, MEMBER OF IUS LABORIS ✪

HH Partners, Attorneys-at-Law, Ltd ✪
Hannes Snellman ✪
Krogerus & Co. Oy ✪
Susiluoto Attorneys-at-Law Ltd

Borenius & Kemppinen ✪
Luostarinen Mettälä Räikkönen ✪
Veikko Palotie & Co ✪

Dittmar & Indrenius ✪
Laakso, Lukander & Ruohola ✪
Peltonen, Ruokonen & Itäinen Attorneys At Law ✪

Firms are listed A-Z in tiers which are ranked in order of priority
✪ Indicates firm displays contact details at the end of this chapter.

increased amount of IT arbitration, the majority emerging from agreements made at the height of the IT boom. Niklas Östman is also recommended.

With over 20 years' experience in the IT field **HH Partners, Attorneys-at-Law, Ltd**'s 'thorough' and 'versatile' Alf-Ole Wanamo assists clients with outsourcing and public procurement issues. In 2003 the firm gained a number of extremely important IT companies as clients.

At **Hannes Snellman** Kaisa Fahlund is involved in a number of information technology-related transactions. A recent highlight for the firm was acting as legal adviser to Novo group. The firm is also highly recommended for telecoms.

Boasting one of the largest technology and media departments in Finland, **Krogerus & Co. Oy** maintains its position as one of the most successful firms in the field of technology procurement. Highly regarded and experienced Juha Pekka Katainen spearheads the firm's IT group.

Renowned as a quality technology boutique, **Susiluoto Attorneys-at-Law Ltd** maintained its reputation over the year. In 2003 Tappio Susci was deeply involved in advising on data security for one of the firm's largest clients, a major telco.

Janne Kairo and Pekka Tarkela at **Borenius & Kemppinen** head the firm's telecoms practice. The firm has worked with all of Finland's major telecoms companies.

In 2003 **Luostarinen Mettälä Räikkönen**'s Raimo Seppälä assisted a listed company with its investments in a number of IT-related companies.

Veikko Palotie & Co has an excellent reputation for its telecoms expertise. The firm also boasts a number up-and-coming associates with experience in the IT sector.

Dittmar & Indrenius acts as general local counsel and advisers for the Finnish operations of a leading international IT service and consultancy group, advising on technology, IT and intellectual property issues.

Veteran telecoms specialist, name partner Tapio Laakso at **Laakso, Lukander & Ruohola** has a strong reputation. Within the information technology sector, 'amiable' and 'knowledgeable' Jarkko Ruohola's clients include one of the most profitable IT companies in Finland.

Peltonen, Ruokonen & Itäinen Attorneys At Law has a good reputation for its IT work. The firm advises a number of major IT and telecoms companies.

INTELLECTUAL PROPERTY

With name partner Peter Backström at the helm, **Backström & Co** lives up to its reputation as a market leader in IP. Ongoing clients include a variety of household names.

Seppo Kemppinen, a patent lawyer, and Pekka Tarkela, a copyright expert lead **Borenius & Kemppinen**'s IP practice of 13 lawyers. The team's work covers the entire field of intellectual

INTELLECTUAL PROPERTY

BACKSTRÖM & CO ✪
BORENIUS & KEMPPINEN ✪
CASTRÉN & SNELLMAN ✪
HH PARTNERS, ATTORNEYS-AT-LAW, LTD ✪
HANNES SNELLMAN ✪
HEINONEN & CO, ATTORNEYS-AT-LAW, LTD ✪
ROSCHIER HOLMBERG, MEMBER OF IUS LABORIS ✪
SUSILUOTO ATTORNEYS-AT-LAW LTD

Fennica Attorneys-at-Law Ltd ✪
Luostarinen Mettälä Räikkönen ✪
Pirilä & Pöyhönen
Veikko Palotie & Co ✪

ACE Law Ltd
Dittmar & Indrenius ✪
Juridia Ltd Attorneys-At-Law ✪
Krogerus & Co. Oy ✪
Merilampi Marttila Laitasalo ✪
Peltonen, Ruokonen & Itäinen Attorneys At Law ✪
Procopé & Hornborg ✪
Waselius & Wist ✪

Firms are listed A-Z in tiers which are ranked in order of priority
✪ Indicates firm displays contact details at the end of this chapter.

property rights and IP litigation, with an emphasis on patents, trade marks and content-related IP.

Although best known for his work within IT, **Castrén & Snellman**'s Kimmo Rekola is also lauded by clients for his IP knowledge. In 2003 the firm advised a variety of clients on matters ranging from intellectual property rights to licensing arrangements.

HH Partners, Attorneys-at-Law, Ltd's extensive anti-piracy and anti-counterfeiting work was boosted during 2003 after taking on a major new game manufacturing client to combat anti-piracy activities.

At **Hannes Snellman** 'dynamic' senior associate Ella Mikkola has focused on IP for over ten years. The office has a strong reputation in the biotech and life sciences fields.

In 2003 **Heinonen & Co, Attorneys-at-Law, Ltd**'s domain name practice grew considerably. The 'professional' and 'customer oriented' firm is highly recommended in the field of trade marks and anti-counterfeiting. The firm's partner Hanna-Maija Elo is now chairman of the Finnish Anti-Counterfeiting Group.

Roschier Holmberg, member of ius laboris advises several domestic biotech companies on IP rights strategy in relation to venture capital investment rounds. Following a general increase in patent awareness, the firm has been involved in an increased amount of patent litigation. Among a host of landmark cases, it was involved with copyright cases involving Budweiser and Gillette, now subject to a ruling by the ECJ.

In one way or another, all of **Susiluoto Attorneys-at-Law Ltd**'s clients are linked to IP. Clients include a number of film producers, artists and record labels. Software copyright comprises 70% of the firm's caseload. The firm has also left its mark in the courts, having been involved in a significant number of precedent-setting cases.

At **Fennica Attorneys-at-Law Ltd** Pekka Raatikainen is widely recognised as a telecoms expert. Recent highlights for the firm include advising a number of high-profile clients in design right, trade mark and domain name matters, as well as in patent disputes.

Luostarinen Mettälä Räikkönen has a growing IP practice. The firm focuses on patents and licensing agreements.

Kalle Pirilä of **Pirilä & Pöyhönen** maintains his reputation as one of the most revered advisory and contentious patent lawyers in Finland. He is also known for his copyright and trade mark work.

Advising on intellectual property rights remains an important part of the work carried out by **Veikko Palotie & Co**. Although best known for its real estate work, the firm boasts a number of talented IP specialists.

ACE Law Ltd has a good reputation for intellectual property rights matters. Clients praise the firm for its 'prompt response to all manner of problems'.

Dittmar & Indrenius is highly recommended for its IP expertise, while **Juridia Ltd Attorneys-At-Law** boasts Kimmo Oila, a lawyer and engineer, specialising in software licensing and intellectual property rights.

In 2003 **Krogerus & Co. Oy** hired a number of senior specialist lawyers including in IP. The highly respected firm advises clients on a number of IP matters, *inter alia*, contentious and non-contentious trade mark matters.

Merilampi Marttila Laitasalo is becoming increasingly active in different patent matters. Led by the widely commended Tuomo Marttila, the team is involved in a range of patent disputes.

Peltonen, Ruokonen & Itäinen Attorneys At Law gained a number of new IP clients in 2003. Jussi Savonen is praised for his work in this area.

Petri Kyllönen at **Procopé & Hornborg** is recommended for his IP work.

Waselius & Wist boasts an extensive practice in trade mark registration and patent litigation. The firm acts as trade mark agent for a number of clients.

MARITIME AND TRANSPORT

Aminoff & Weissenberg, Attorneys Ltd remains an 'excellent niche firm' specialising in maritime and transport. Name partners Jan Aminoff and Ulla von Weissenberg represent the interests of vessel owners and underwriters in a variety of matters, and are praised for their 'high-quality work' and 'unrivalled expertise'.

MARITIME AND TRANSPORT

AMINOFF & WEISSENBERG, ATTORNEYS LTD ✪
CASTRÉN & SNELLMAN ✪
GAHMBERG, HÄSTÖ & CO ✪

Ahola & Sokka
HH Partners, Attorneys-at-Law, Ltd ✪
Hannes Snellman ✪
Kauttu & Sainio ✪
Veikko Palotie & Co ✪

Borenius & Kemppinen ✪
Bützow Nordia
Luostarinen Mettälä Räikkönen ✪
Procopé & Hornborg ✪
Roschier Holmberg, member of ius laboris ✪

Firms are listed A-Z in tiers which are ranked in order of priority
✪ Indicates firm displays contact details at the end of this chapter.

Widely considered as the leading maritime and transport lawyer in Finland, **Castrén & Snellman**'s Niklas Lagenskiöld routinely acts on behalf of P&I clubs and insurance companies. Senior associate Anna-Karin Mickwitz is also praised.

At **Gahmberg, Hästö & Co** name partner Henrik Gahmberg maintains his reputation as one of Finland's pre-eminent maritime and transport lawyers. Largely focused on maritime issues, the firm also boasts expertise in road transportation and freight forwarding claims.

Jukka Juunonen at **Ahola & Sokka** is a recommended road and transport expert.

'Attentive' John Bardy provides **HH Partners, Attorneys-at-Law, Ltd** with a key player in the maritime and transport field. Clients include both domestic and foreign shipowners, underwriters and P&I clubs.

Based in its Mariehamn office **Hannes Snellman** has a maritime practice with a magnificent reputation and considerable market share.

Despite its small size **Kauttu & Sainio** boasts an enviable reputation for shipping, in particular in cargo-related issues.

Veikko Palotie & Co handles stolen cargo claims, in particular those that are trafficked through Russia. The majority of its clients are carriers, but it also acts for insurers.

Borenius & Kemppinen has a long tradition of representing the biggest US-based cruise line companies in Finland, while **Bützow Nordia** has a strong transportation practice.

In 2003 **Luostarinen Mettälä Räikkönen** saw the development of its transport practice. The firm assisted on the outsourcing of transportation services by a large Finnish public sector client.

Procopé & Hornborg was dealt a blow in 2003 with the loss of Matti Hautakangas, who joined Fortum Oil and Gas.

Bernt Juthström at **Roschier Holmberg, member of ius laboris** has an excellent reputation in the field of maritime law. The firm is also recommended for its transport expertise.

REAL ESTATE AND CONSTRUCTION

With its widely respected and successful real estate group, **Castrén & Snellman** can lay claim to quality and expertise across all practice areas. Boasting major Finnish real estate companies as clients, as well as other domestic and foreign clients, the firm maintains an excellent reputation.

Veikko Palotie & Co's market-leading team consists of a number of extremely experienced and highly respected specialists. Veli Leinonen and Teemu Kauttu are two of the finest property lawyers in Finland.

Attorneys' House ANPR Ltd boasts a number of lawyers with in-depth environmental expertise in the real estate and construction sector.

Fennica Attorneys-at-Law Ltd's commercial property and construction team remained active during 2003. The firm undertook a major planning and construction project in the Helsinki metropolitan area, valued at €300m. Timo Korpiola and Marko Waino are both recommended.

At **HH Partners, Attorneys-at-Law, Ltd** 'pragmatic' Eero Kajander is a high-profile litigator and a well-known specialist in contract law, in particular relating to real estate matters.

Although **Hannes Snellman** does not have a dedicated real estate practice, the firm does continue to be active in the field, advising on property-related transactions.

At **Juridia Ltd Attorneys-At-Law** 'outstanding' Ilkka Koivisto and Matias Wallgren are highly recommended for their 'thorough' and 'accurate' work.

Kaj Swanljung at **Roschier Holmberg, member of ius laboris** is recommended for his expertise in the field of real estate.

Bützow Nordia is recommended for its construction expertise, while **Laakso, Lukander & Ruohola** boasts a substantial client base in south-west Finland, including a number of major building companies. The firm also represents a number of foreign investors and subsidiaries of foreign construction companies.

REAL ESTATE AND CONSTRUCTION

CASTRÉN & SNELLMAN ✪
VEIKKO PALOTIE & CO ✪

Attorneys' House ANPR Ltd
Fennica Attorneys-at-Law Ltd ✪
HH Partners, Attorneys-at-Law, Ltd ✪
Hannes Snellman ✪
Juridia Ltd Attorneys-At-Law ✪
Roschier Holmberg, member of ius laboris ✪

Bützow Nordia
Laakso, Lukander & Ruohola ✪

Firms are listed A-Z in tiers which are ranked in order of priority
✪ Indicates firm displays contact details at the end of this chapter.

AMINOFF & WEISSENBERG, ATTORNEYS LTD

RAUHANKATU 13A
00170 HELSINKI

Telephone: +358 9 6840 477
Fax: +358 9 6840 4740
E-mail: jan.aminoff@jaflaw.fi
Website: www.jaflaw.fi

Languages
English, Swedish

Number of lawyers 3

CATEGORIES OF WORK

Maritime law	General corporate and business law
Transport law	Contract law
Aviation law	Tort law
Insurance law	Insolvency
Sale and purchase of vessels	Litigation, arbitration and arrest proceedings

BACKSTRÖM & CO
ATTORNEYS AT LAW

ET MAKASIINIKATU 4
00130 HELSINKI

Telephone: +358 9 6689 940
Fax: +358 9 6689 9410
E-mail: info@backstromco.fi
Website: www.backstromco.fi

Languages
English, German, Swedish

Number of lawyers 3

Contacts
Peter Backström, Petri Eskola

Member
Eurojuris International EEIG

CATEGORIES OF WORK

Intellectual property	Corporate and commercial
Patents, trade marks	Commercial litigation, arbitration
Competition law	Contract law
Agency law, distribution	Damages and product liability

BORENIUS & KEMPPINEN

YRJÖNKATU 13A
00120 HELSINKI

Telephone: +358 9 615 333
Fax: +358 9 6153 3499
E-mail: info@borenius.com
Website: www.borenius.com

Languages
Swedish, English, Estonian, French, German, Latvian, Russian, Spanish

Number of lawyers 50

International groupings
Associated offices: Liepa, Skopina/Borenius (Riga), Luiga, Mugu & Borenius (Tallinn)

CATEGORIES OF WORK

Banking and finance	**Labour and employment**
Capital markets	**Life sciences**
Commercial contracts	**Mergers and acquisitions**
Corporate and commercial law	**Private equity and venture capital**
Dispute resolution	**Real estate and environment**
EU and competition	**Shipping**
Entertainment and media law	**Tax law**
Insolvency and bankruptcy law	**Telecoms**
Intellectual property rights	

THE FIRM

Established in 1911, Borenius & Kemppinen is one of the leading commercial law firms in Finland. The clientele includes both domestic and international listed and non-listed companies, authorities and sovereign states. Borenius & Kemppinen emphasises high quality of work and a business-minded approach to all legal issues.

Borenius & Kemppinen has a strong presence in the Baltic area through its associated offices in Tallinn, Estonia and Riga, Latvia.

AREAS OF PRACTICE

Borenius & Kemppinen has traditionally practised in the fields of domestic and international corporate law and general business law offering experienced service in all areas of business law.

The firm's main international areas of practice are:

Mergers and acquisitions: Borenius & Kemppinen's M&A practice is supported by an outstanding IP/IT, corporate, finance and labour capacity. The firm has advised investors, MBO and MBI teams, private equity and venture capital funds, and industrial buyers and sellers, in a broad spectrum of deals, from energy to Internet and mobile service providers.

Capital markets: Borenius & Kemppinen has been an adviser on several IPOs in Helsinki. The firm is a member of the APCIMS Legal Regulatory Committee and has New York law capacity in Helsinki.

The practice has been strengthened by the former managing director of the Helsinki Exchanges joining the firm.

Venture capital and private equity: Borenius & Kemppinen has advised private equity and venture capital fund management firms and investors in numerous fund documentations. Borenius & Kemppinen has acted for fund management firms in numerous acquisitions, MBOs and MBIs, and in exiting these through trade sale or IPOs.

Intellectual property rights: Borenius & Kemppinen strongly believes that its IPR team is second to none in Finland. The team has advised clients in the areas of IP law including patents, copyrights, trade marks, biotechnology, life sciences, IT, Internet and multimedia.

IT and telecoms: information technology, new media and digital content production are core areas of the firm's practice. Borenius & Kemppinen has been actively involved in the development and commercialisation of e- and m-commerce solutions in the technologically advanced Finnish market. The firm has gained extensive experience in IT-related legal issues such as data proctection, consumer protection, and Internet marketing regulation both in Finland and the EU. Clients of the firm include international and leading Finnish digital media publishers, telecoms, Internet and wireless service providers and IT equipment and infrastructure providers.

Litigation, arbitration and mediation: business-related litigation has always been one of the cornerstones of Borenius & Kemppinen, which has an impeccable record of major business clients. The lawyers in the litigation group also have thorough experience as arbitrators. Borenius & Kemppinen was one of the first firms to introduce mediation in Finland.

Insolvency: the firm's lawyers have acted as trustees in several of the biggest bankruptcies and corporate restructurings in Finland.

German practice: Borenius & Kemppinen has German law capacity in Helsinki advising clients in Finland and Finnish companies operating in German-speaking countries.

CASTRÉN & SNELLMAN

EROTTAJANKATU 5A
00130 HELSINKI

Telephone: +358 9 22 85 81
Fax: +358 9 60 19 61
E-mail: firstname.surname@castren.fi
Website: www.castren.fi

Languages
English, Estonian, Finnish, French, German, Italian, Russian, Swedish

Other offices
St Petersburg, Jyväskylä

Number of lawyers 72
at this office 67

CATEGORIES OF WORK

Mergers and acquisitions
Jan Kuhlefelt, Jan Örndahl

Corporate and acquisitions
Johan Åkermarck, Juha Väyrynen

Banking and finance
Pekka Lehitnen, Juha Väyrynen

Capital markets
Pekka Lehitnen, Merja Kivelä

Companies, corporations
Pekka Sirviö, Pauliina Tenhunen

Contract
Uwe Uusitalo, Jan Örndahl

Insolvency
Pekka Jaatinen, Claudio Busi

EU and competition
Johan Åkermarck, Hannu Pokela

Litigation and arbitration
Jouko Huhtala, Marko Hentunen

Environment and real estate
Elina Lampi-Fagerholm

Employment
Juha Väyrynen, Jan Kuhlefelt

Insurance
Mika Ilveskero, Pekka Jaatinen

IT, telecommunications and media
Kimmo Rekola, Johan Åkermarck

Intellectual property, trade mark
Jan Kuhlefelt, Hannu Pokela

Tax
Pekka Talari, Leena Romppainen

Energy
Juha Väyrynen, Merja Kivelä

Marketing, consumer law
Jan Kuhlefelt, Hannu Pokela

Maritime and transport
Niklas Langenskiöld

THE FIRM

Castrén & Snellman is known not only as one of the largest and leading law firms specialising in commercial and business law in Finland, but also as the oldest – the firm has been serving clients since 1888. The firm's client are Finnish, foreign and multinational corporations and financial institutions engaged in business activities in Finland and abroad. Currently, the firm has a staff of over 120 people including over 70 lawyers.

Castrén & Snellman St Petersburg was founded in 1994 to meet the increasing demand of western, high-class legal services in the neighbouring metropolis of Helsinki. The firm offers a full range of corporate, commercial, and contract law services mainly to foreign clients. Major assignments are carried out in full co-operation with the experts of the Castrén & Snellman in Finland.

Over the years, the firm has established relationships with leading law firms worldwide to enhance the legal services for international clients. Through contacts, the firm can offer modern legal expertise for today's global business operations.

AREAS OF PRACTICE

The types of work undertaken in the firm include mergers and acquisitions; banking and finance; capital markets; tax; insolvency; EU and competition; intellectual property; IT; telecommunications and Internet; litigation and arbitration; real estate environment; malpractice; healthcare and medical law; company law; contract law; Internet; transportation; product liability; consumer law; marketing; administrative procedures; entertainment; pharmaceutical; energy and chemical industry.

DITTMAR & INDRENIUS

POHJOISESPLANADI 25A
00100 HELSINKI

Telephone: +358 9 681 700
Fax: +358 9 652 406
E-mail: firstname.surname@dittmar.fi
Website: www.dittmar.fi

Languages
English, French, German, Swedish

Number of lawyers 26

Contacts
Markus Troberg, Antti Kuusimäki,
Jan Ollila, Petteri Uoti

CATEGORIES OF WORK

Mergers and acquisitions	**Dispute resolution**
Finance and capital markets	**Corporate and commercial**

THE FIRM

Dittmar & Indrenius is one of Finland's leading international law firms focused on mergers and acquisitions, finance and capital markets, dispute resolution and corporate and commercial.

Dittmar & Indrenius is frequently involved in large transactions, often with a cross-border dimension.

The firm provides its clients with a professional service of the highest calibre, combining technical excellence with commercial awareness and a practical, constructive approach to legal issues.

The firm maintains close contacts with leading law firms in the world, but is not tied to any formal network or association of firms.

The firm serves its clients in English, Finnish, French, German and Swedish.

AREAS OF PRACTICE

International work is an essential part of the firm's practice. Dittmar & Indrenius has a broad experience in cross-border mergers and acquisitions, and commercial and financial matters.

Dittmar & Indrenius represents leading international companies and institutions with various sectors, such as banking, finance, private equity, venture capital, insurance, information technology, telecommunications, manufacturers, automobiles, pharmaceuticals, consumer goods and services, aviation, consultancy, construction, energy, entertainment and media. Dittmar & Indrenius also acts for a number of governments and international organisations.

FENNICA ATTORNEYS AT LAW LTD

EROTTAJANKATU 15-17
00130 HELSINKI

Telephone: +358 9 6226 670
Fax: +358 9 6226 677
E-mail: contact@fennica.fi
Website: www.fennica.fi

Languages
English, French, German, Swedish

Number of lawyers 21

Contacts
Jori Taipale, Pekka Takki

CATEGORIES OF WORK

IT and telecommunications
Pekka Takki, Pekka Raatikainen

Intellectual property
Pekka Raatikainen, Tom Vapaavuori

General corporate and commercial
Tom Vapaavuori, Jaakko Hietala

Banking and finance
Jori Taipale, Jaakko Hietala

Mergers and acquisitions
Jori Taipale, Harri Hynninen

Capital markets
Harri Hynninen, Jori Taipale

Litigation and arbitration
Pekka Raatikainen, Marko Wainio

Real estate and construction
Marko Wainio, Jaakko Hietala

Competition
Jori Taipale

GAHMBERG, HÄSTÖ & CO

POHJOINEN MAKASIINIKATU 7 A 6
00130 HELSINKI

Telephone: +358 9 6869 880
Fax: +358 9 6869 8850
E-mail: ghetco@ghetco.com

Languages
English, German, the Scandinavian languages

Number of lawyers 9

Contact
Henrik Hästö

International groupings
Mackrell International

CATEGORIES OF WORK

Corporate
Henrik Hästö, Niclas Salingre

Real estate
Niclas Salingre

Mergers and acquisitions
Henrik Hästö, Henrik Gahmberg

Finance, securities
Henrik Gahmberg, Henrik Hästö

Maritime
Henrik Gahmberg, Herman Ljungberg

Tax
Henrik Hästö

Transport
Henrik Gahmberg, Herman Ljungberg

Litigation
Henrik Gahmberg, Niclas Salingre

Insurance
Henrik Gahmberg, Herman Ljungberg

Labour law
Niclas Salingre

HANNES SNELLMAN

ETELÄRANTA 8
00130 HELSINKI

Telephone: +358 9 22 88 41
Fax: +358 9 17 73 93
E-mail: hannes.snellman@hannessnellman.fi
Website: www.hannessnellman.fi

Languages
English, French, German, Swedish

Other offices
Turku, Mariehamn

Number of lawyers 101

Contact
Antti Heikinheimo (managing partner)

CATEGORIES OF WORK

M&A
Juhani Mäkinen, Johan Aalto

Technology
Tomas Holmberg

Competition and EU
Carl-Henrik Wallin

Finance and capital markets
Kari Lautjärvi

Tax
Jarmo Ikkala

Dispute resolution
Patrik Lindfors

THE FIRM

Founded in 1909 by Hannes Snellman, the firm is one of the two largest in Finland and continues to grow. The firm focuses on transactions and related corporate and commercial law and is organised into four practice groups (M&A; technology; finance and capital markets; dispute resolution).

Hannes Snellman has developed a broad network of international industrial and financial contacts. The firm regularly advises on international matters and maintains close ties with foreign law firms worldwide.

Hannes Snellman advises international clients on a regular basis, including leading financial institutions, major international corporations, industrial groups, leading investment banks and service companies. Geographically, the clients come mostly from the US, UK and continental Europe as well as Scandinavia.

AREAS OF PRACTICE

The M&A group represents the largest practice group within the firm, comprising some 50 lawyers. The group's activities encompass all areas of M&A work, including acquisitions, mergers and other corporate restructuring, MBOs, LBOs and general corporate work. Competition and EU matters as well as taxation are particularly strong complementary areas within the firm's M&A practice.

The technology group, with some 20 lawyers, covers industry sector requirements ranging from M&A, capital markets and other commercial transactions, to intellectual property, regulatory and commercial work. In addition to serving the IT, biotech and other technology sectors, the group also serves clients from non-technology sectors who are in need of highly specialised advice on matters relating to the dynamics of the hi-tech field.

The finance and capital markets group (with some 15 lawyers) is among the leading practices in Finland. The practice provides advice relating to syndicated or other bank loans, acquisition finance, asset and project finance, structured finance and derivatives, as well as credit institutions and related regulatory issues. The capital markets practice provides advice on public and private securities transactions and other corporate finance, such as offerings of debt and equity securities, convertibles, structured securities, or mutual funds, as well as investment firms and related regulatory issues. The group acts for various parties in respect to, among other matters, listings, de-listings, privatisations, tender offers, private equity and venture capital transactions.

The dispute resolution group deals with litigation, arbitration, mediation and matters concerning insolvency. The group comprises, for the time being, more than ten lawyers. Lawyers from other groups are also involved in litigation and arbitration coached by the dispute resolution group. The arbitration practitioners of the firm have extensive experience as counsels, chairmen and arbitrators in domestic and international arbitration proceedings, both ad hoc and institutional (eg under the Arbitration Rules of the Arbitration Institute of the Central Chamber of Commerce of Finland) and under the ICC Arbitration Rules). Many international proceedings have provided the arbitration practitioners of the firm with invaluable and wide-ranging experience. The firm is represented in the ICC International Court of Arbitration, the ADR/mediation work of the Finnish Bar Association as well as in the committees for international litigation, arbitration and ADR of the International Bar Association.

HH PARTNERS, ATTORNEYS-AT-LAW, LTD

MANNERHEIMINTIE 14 A
00100 HELSINKI

Telephone: +358 9 177 613
Fax: +358 9 653 873
E-mail: hhpartners@hhpartners.fi
Website: www.hhpartners.fi

Languages
English, Swedish

Number of lawyers 12

Contact
Mr Arto Kukkonen (managing partner)

CATEGORIES OF WORK

Capital market	Information technology and communications
Commercial	Intellectual property
Construction	Maritime and tranport
Contacts and competition	Media and marketing
Corporate and corporate finance	Mergers and acquisitions
Dispute resolution	Real estate
Environment	Taxation and employment
Insolvency	
Insurance	

HEINONEN & CO, ATTORNEYS-AT-LAW, LTD

FREDRIKINKATU 61A
PO BOX 671
00100 HELSINKI

Telephone: +358 9 2530 0600
Fax: +358 9 6944 352
E-mail: mail@heinonen.com
Website: www.heinonen.com

Languages
English, French, German, Swedish

Number of lawyers 6

Other offices
Alicante

Member
Eurofranchise Lawyers (an association of independent European franchise lawyers); Finnish Bar Association; AIPPI; INTA; ECTA; FICPI; IBA; representatives before OHIM

CATEGORIES OF WORK

Intellectual property	Trade marks
IPR agreements	Community trade marks
Copyright	Patents
Licensing	Designs
Franchises and franchising	Consumer law
Advertising and marketing	Data protection
Internet law (domain names)	Litigation
Anti-counterfeiting	

JURIDIA LTD ATTORNEYS-AT-LAW

MUNKKISAARENKATU 2
00150 HELSINKI

Telephone: +358 9 6841 230
Fax: +358 9 6225 400
E-mail: firstname.lastname@juridia.com
Website: www.juridia.com

Languages
English, French, German, Swedish

Number of lawyers 17

Contact
Hannu Rintala

Member
EuroLaw EEIG

CATEGORIES OF WORK

Company and securities
Olli Iirola

Mergers and acquisitions
Olli Iirola, Kimmo Oila

Corporate tax
Henri Steiner

Venture capital and private equity
Olli Iirola, Kimmo Oila

Commercial contract
Pekka Jäntti, Tim Williams

Construction
Ilkka Koivisto

Employment
Pekka Jäntti

Environment
Matias Wallgren

Competition and EU
Hannu Rintala

Insolvency and bankruptcy
Harri Lindfors, Antti Meriläinen

IPR and information technology
Kimmo Oila, Tero Routamo

Media and advertising
Hannu Rintala

Litigation and dispute resolution
Pekka Jäntti, Antti Meriläinen

English law, international transactions
Tim Williams

Damages and product liability
Tero Routamo

Telecommunications
Hannu Rintala

KALLIOINEN, TOLPPANEN, SALMINEN & CO
ATTORNEYS AT LAW

YRJÖNKATU 8 A 2
00120 HELSINKI

Telephone: +358 9 6126 090
Fax: +358 9 607 344
E-mail: helsinki@ktslaw.net
Website: www.ktslaw.net

Languages
English, German, Swedish

Other offices
Hämeenlinna, Tampere

Number of lawyers 12
at this office 5

Contact
Jari Salminen

CATEGORIES OF WORK

Banking and finance operations
Jukka Reilin, Jukka Soikkeli

Company law
Jari Salminen

Contract law
Jukka Soikkeli, Tuomo Kareila

Family law
Ruut Kallioinen

Insolvency and bankruptcy
Juha Kallioinen, Jarmo Muukkonen

Insurance law
Juha Kallioinen

Labour law
Timo Jarmas

Litigation and arbitration
Jari Maaranen

Mergers and acquisitions
Harri Tolppanen

Real estate and construction
Harri Tolppanen

KROGERUS & CO. OY

POHJOINEN MAKASIINIKATU 6A
PO BOX 143
00130 HELSINKI

Telephone: +358 9 6226 520
Fax: +358 9 631 811
E-mail: helsinki@krogerus.com
Website: www.krogerus.com

Languages
English, French, German, Spanish, Swedish

Other offices
Jyväskylä, Kuopio, Oulu

Number of lawyers 40

Contact
Hannu Krogerus

Member
IGL (International Grouping of Lawyers); ICC (Intercontinental Consultants); ICC (International Chamber of Commerce); TAGLaw; IBA (International Bar Association)

CATEGORIES OF WORK

Corporate and commercial law
Juha Pekka Katainen, Hannu Krogerus

Mergers and acquisitions
Hannu Krogerus, Mikko Mali

EU and competition
Katri Joenpolvi, Hannu Krogerus

Telecommunications and IT law
Katri Joenpolvi, Juha Pekka Katainen

Banking and finance (including project finance)
Juha Wessman, Mika Ståhlberg

Capital markets
Mika Ståhlberg, Mikko Mali

Intellectual property
Juha Pekka Katainen, Jari-Pekka Alho

Real estate
Pasi Kapanen, Juha Wessman

Litigation
Jari-Pekka Alho

Arbitration
Hannu Krogerus, Marja Ramm-Schmidt

Corporate restructuring and insolvency
Jarmo Makkonen, Jari-Pekka Alho

Labour law
Jari-Pekka Alho

Tax
Juha Regelin, Samuli Perttala

Technology and media law
Juha Pekka Katainen, Jari-Pekka Alho

Venture capital and private equity
Mika Ståhlberg, Mikko Mali

THE FIRM

Founded in 1992, Asianajotoimisto Krogerus & Co. Oy Attorneys-at-Law specialises in Finnish and international business law. The firm has offices in Helsinki, Jyväskylä, Kuopio and Oulu.

Krogerus & Co. Oy operates its business first and foremost on understanding the clients' businesses and their objectives. The firm's founders have long experience working as counsel for major Finnish industrial firms, banks and public administration, and they use this experience to its fullest extent when advising their clients.

The legal services offered to clients are tailored in co-operation with the clients themselves to suit their current needs. The firm's clients are large- and medium-sized domestic and foreign corporations and financial institutions. Krogerus & Co. Oy also serves smaller companies, especially internationally-orientated ones, in central, eastern and northern Finland. The firm also advises different sectors of public administration in Finland and abroad.

In order to offer the best possible services to its clients, the firm has established contacts with a number of investment and commercial banks, authorities and law firms, as well as auditing firms both in Finland and abroad.

AREAS OF PRACTICE

The firm's areas of practice are mergers and acquisitions, capital markets, venture capital and private equity, project finance, EU and competition law, technology and media, telecommunications, corporate restructuring, insolvency and litigation and arbitration.

M&A: The firm has advised various industrial buyers and sellers, private equity and venture capital funds, MBO and MBI teams and investors in numerous M&A transactions and investments in a broad variety of businesses ranging from IT, technology and telecoms sector to cosmetics. The firm has also advised the Finnish government in number of privatisation transactions.

Capital markets and finance: The firm and its partners have advised in various IPOs and public offerings, as well as mergers and demergers of listed companies. The firm has frequently acted as legal adviser in the field of project finance, as well as public-private-partnership (PPP) and real estate financing transactions.

Competition law: The firm has advised clients in dealing with the Finnish Competition Authority and the Commission of the European Union in issues concerning all fields of competition law, such as compliance work, negotiations with authorities (particularly M&A cases) and litigation.

EU law: Krogerus & Co. Oy has assisted clients in numerous assignments concerning European law. The assignments vary from litigation and negotiations with the Commission of the European Union to monitoring of the regulator developments in certain fields of EC law. The firm has been selected as the legal adviser for EU in Finland (Eurojus).

Technology and media: The firm has advised various major companies in their IT and technology procurement cases (including outsourcing agreements) and regularly advises leading Finnish IT, technology and media vendors on a full range of their commercial contractual issues. The firm constantly represents clients providing services and products to Nokia in their major framework and other contract negotiations with Nokia Corporation. The firm has especially worked on IT and technology projects in the field of banking and financing, telecommunications, e-business and contract manufacturing.

Corporate restructuring and insolvency: The firm's lawyers have wide experience in operating as official receivers in bankrupts' estates, voluntary and legal liquidation proceedings, acting as administrations in corporate restructurings and representing creditors in all such proceedings.

Dispute resolution: The firm serves major business clients in litigation and arbitration processes. Some of the firm's lawyers also act as mediators.

KAUTTU & SAINIO

BULEVARDI 6
00120 HELSINKI

Telephone: +358 9 6124 3930
Fax: +358 9 6127 233
E-mail: attorneys@kauttu-sainio.com
Website: www.kauttu-sainio.com

Languages
English, French, Spanish, Swedish

Number of lawyers 3

Contact
Tuomo Kauttu

Member
Euro-American Lawyers Group (EALG)

CATEGORIES OF WORK

- Corporate and commercial
- Mergers and acquisitions
- Intellectual property
- Commercial property and construction
- Maritime and transport
- Banking and finance
- Arbitration and litigation

ASIANAJOTOIMISTO LIUKSIALA & CO OY

MUSEOKATU 9 B
00100 HELSINKI

Telephone: +358 9 440 687
Fax: +358 9 408 807
E-mail: office@liuksiala
Website: www.liuksiala.com

Languages
English, German, Swedish

Number of lawyers 6

Contact
Aaro Liuksiala

CATEGORIES OF WORK

- Commercial (general)
- Corporate
- Mergers and acquisitions
- Litigation
- Arbitration
- Insolvency
- Transport
- Compensation claims
- Environmental
- Labour
- Banking, securities and finance
- Intellectual property
- Competition
- Insurance
- Construction

LUOSTARINEN METTÄLÄ RÄIKKÖNEN
ATTORNEYS AT LAW

MANNERHEIMINTIE 14 B
9TH FLOOR
00100 HELSINKI

Telephone: +358 9 5860 100
Fax: +358 9 5860 1060
E-mail: mail@lmrlaw.fi
Website: www.lmrlaw.fi

Languages
English, Finnish, French, German, Spanish, Swedish

Number of lawyers 15

CATEGORIES OF WORK

Banking and finance

Capital markets

Venture capital

Arbitration and litigation

Privatisation

Intellectual property

Mergers and acquisitions

Company and commercial

EU and competition

Energy

Telecommunications and IT

Labour law

MÄKITALO RÄMÖ JUUTILAINEN LTD
ATTORNEYS AT LAW

ETELÄESPLANADI 18
00130 HELSINKI

Telephone: +358 9 6844 410
Fax: +358 9 6844 4141
E-mail: attorneys@mrvlaw.fi
Website: www.mrvlaw.fi

Languages
English, French, German, Malay, Polish, Spanish, Swedish

Number of lawyers 15

CATEGORIES OF WORK

Banking and finance
Risto Rämö, Juha Mäkitalo

Mergers and acquisitions
Juha Mäkitalo, Risto Rämö

Corporate and commercial law
Juha Mäkitalo, Matti Kokko

Intellectual property
Risto Rämö, Matti Kokko

IT and telecoms
Jani Rantanen, Juho Lönnblad

Competition, EU
Juha Virolainen, Tuomas Kosonen

Distribution, agency and franchise
Jaana Virolainen, R Kamarul-Baharin

Environment
Jaana Juutilainen, Elina Männistö-Äimä

Real estate and construction
Matti Kokko, Mikko Pimiä

Life sciences
Risto Rämö, Heidi Ilvessalo

Litigation, arbitration
Mikko Pimiä, Jaana Juutilainen

Insolvency
Mikko Pimiä, Antti Korpela

Taxation
Mika Alanen, MikkoPimiä

Labour
Marcus Blomfelt, Mika Alanen

MERILAMPI MARTTILA LAITASALO

ETELÄESPLANADI 22 A
00130 HELSINKI

Telephone: +358 9 686 481
Fax: +358 9 6864 8484
E-mail: law.offices@mmllaw.fi
Website: www.mmllaw.fi

Languages
English, French, German, Swedish

Other offices
Tampere

Number of lawyers 22
at this office 18

Contacts
Ari Keinänen, Matti Ylä-Mononen, Arttu Mentula

CATEGORIES OF WORK

Mergers and acquisitions
Ari Keinänen, Matti Ylä-Mononen

Competition and EU
Arttu Mentula

Corporate law
Pekka Merilampi

Public procurement
Arttu Mentula

Banking and finance
Jukka Laitasalo

Intellectual property
Tuomo Marttila

Labour
Matti Ylä-Mononen

Insolvency
Jukka Laitasalo

Real estate
Ari Keinänen

Torts and product liability
Ari Kantor, Lassi Kettula

Capital markets
Matti Ylä-Mononen, Ari Keinänen

Dispute resolution
Jukka Laitasalo, Ari Kantor

THE FIRM

Merilampi Marttila Laitasalo Attorneys at Law Ltd was established in 1992 subsequent to the split of the biggest Finnish law firm at the time, and has grown steadily since then. The clientele consists of international and domestic companies.

The firm is recognised especially in the fields of mergers and acquisitions, company law and corporate governance, competition and EU, capital markets, litigation and arbitration as well as banking and finance.

AREAS OF PRACTICE

The firm is constantly involved in a number of major M&A and capital markets transactions. Pekka Merilampi, Ari Keinänen and Matti Ylä-Mononen represented Instrumentarium Corporation in the recent combination with General Electric. The value of this cross-border deal was approximately €2bn and was the second largest capital market transaction in Finland last year.

The firm advised Rautakirja Corporation and SanomaWSOY Corporation in the merger of these two listed media companies, a deal valued at approximately €320m. The firm also advised Kyro Corporation in a deal where Kyro acquired Z Bavelloni Immobiliare of Italy and Glasto Holding BV of the Netherlands as well as Suominen Corporation in its acquisition of the Dutch company Codi International BV. Furthermore, the firm represented the German real estate investment company IVG Immobilien AG in its acquisition of Polar Real Estate Corporation, the value of which was approximately €100m.

The firm is continuously involved in competition and EU law matters. Arttu Mentula and Ari Kantor are representing Skanska in the Asphalt Cartel case, the biggest competition law case ever in Finland. In addition, the firm is representing major breweries in a case concerning the establishment of a new recycling system for refillable beer and beverage bottles. The firm has handled many merger control filings and is providing advice on matters relating to the abuse of dominant position, distribution systems, cartels and other horizontal arrangements, compliance programs as well as public procurement.

The firm has a good track record in intellectual property. Tuomo Marttila has represented Tamglass Ltd, the world's leading manufacturer of safety glass machines and Rotex Ltd, which manufactures rock drilling systems, in high-profile patent litigations. In addition, the firm is regularly advising companies in the field of marketing and consumer law, including litigation before the Market Court.

The firm is continuously involved in international arbitration both as arbitrators and counsels related eg to mergers and acquisitions, distribution, telecom and the securities market. The firm has also been involved in damage cases based on competition law. Especially, Jukka Laitasalo and Ari Kantor are often involved in arbitration and complex litigation cases. Lassi Kettula, too, has strong litigation practice and is, among other things, acting as counsel in indemnification cases relating to an aircraft accident in Italy.

PELTONEN, RUOKONEN & ITÄINEN
ATTORNEYS AT LAW LTD

FREDRIKINKATU 48A
00100 HELSINKI

Telephone: +358 9 4176 0430
Fax: +358 9 4176 0417
E-mail: office@peltonenlaw.fi
Website: www.peltonenlaw.fi

Languages
English, French, German, Swedish

Number of lawyers 20

CATEGORIES OF WORK

Litigation and arbitration
Jukka Peltonen

Banking, financing and capital markets
Hans Sundblad, Mikko Ojala

Corporate law
Ari Savela

Mergers and acquisitions
Leif Itäinen

Trade and industry
Jukka Peltonen

Intellectual property
Jussi Savonen

IT, telecoms and media
Jussi Savonen, Kalevi Tervanen

Insurance, transportation and liability
Esa Salonen

Insurance regulatory issues and reinsurance
Kalevi Tervanen

Competition law
Anne Petäjäniemi-Björklund, Tero Kujala

Employment law
Pekka Ruokonen, Harriet Lagus

EU and international law
Ari Savela

Tax law
Leif Itäinen, Tuija Kaijalainen

Environment, real estate and construction
Jukka Peltonen

Insolvency and asset recovery
Leif Itäinen, Jussi Savonen

Private client
Harriet Lagus

THE FIRM
Peltonen, Ruokonen & Itäinen is a traditional, hands-on Finnish law firm founded in 1970 by Jukka Peltonen. The firm established its reputation as one of the leading commercial law firms in Finland in the 70s and has since then possessed strength in depth to handle complex transactions and disputes. In its practice, the firm has a focus on the professional skills and expertise of its attorneys and the firm is known to operate with an emphasis on client service of the highest quality.

The firm's clientele consists of major Finnish and international corporations, banks and other financial institutions, insurance companies, SMEs and growth business enterprises, family businesses, as well as private customers. Governmental agencies and municipalities use the firm's services on a regular basis.

Peltonen, Ruokonen & Itäinen is widely connected internationally and regularly serves clients outside Finland in matters of Finnish jurisdiction and law, and advise Finnish clients in their foreign operations.

AREAS OF PRACTICE
Peltonen, Ruokonen & Itäinen offers its services in all areas of business and commercial law. The firm's work covers various branches of business life and industries. Besides working closely with trade, industry, energy, communications, traffic, transport and construction businesses, Peltonen, Ruokonen & Itäinen specialises in the particular issues raised by banking, finance, insurance and securities markets.

The firm's litigation practice provides a comprehensive service to its clients. The firm's attorneys have experience in large-scale litigation in the general courts, administrative and special courts and governmental agency proceedings, including the Finnish Competition Authority and Market Court. The firm's practitioners represent clients regularly in domestic and international arbitration proceedings. The firm has extensive experience in handling complex multi-jurisdictional litigations. In addition to civil lawsuits, the firm has worked on several white-collar crime litigations.

Peltonen, Ruokonen & Itäinen is involved in mergers and acquisitions, capital financing arrangements, share and bond issues and corporate listings. The firm's attorneys advise in corporate financing arrangements, credit and equity issues, as well as project finance and capital market transactions for commercial banks and industrial companies. The firm's legal work in energy infrastructure and ship financing transactions are among the landmarks of this practice.

The firm's insurance and reinsurance law specialists advise on contentious and non-contentious matters, including contract drafting, facultative insurance and reinsurance coverage issues, policy interpretation, property damage, business interruption and liability insurance, errors and omissions and professional negligence. The firm also provides services in regulatory issues and insurance-related corporate transactions, captive insurance and reinsurance.

Peltonen, Ruokonen & Itäinen traditionally has wide-ranging expertise in bankruptcy, corporate restructuring and distraint affairs. The fraud and asset recovery work of the firm pursues asset tracing and recovery both in Finland and internationally.

The firm regularly advises both Finnish and foreign companies on Finnish employment law and practice.

In recent years, the firm has focused on strengthening its competence in EU and competition law, intellectual property rights and legal issues arising from the use of emerging technologies. Peltonen, Ruokonen & Itäinen also continue the tradition of attending to the legal affairs of private individuals.

ROSCHIER HOLMBERG, member of ius laboris

KESKUSKATU 7A
00100 HELSINKI

Telephone: +358 20 5066 000
Fax: +358 20 5066 100
E-mail: firstname.lastname@roschier.com
Website: www.roschier.com

Languages
English, French, German, Swedish

Other offices
Oulu, Tampere, Turku, Vaasa

Number of lawyers 100
at this office 85

Contacts
Tomas Lindholm (senior partner),
Lennart Simonsen (managing partner)

Member
ius laboris, International Employment Law Pensions and Employee Benefits Alliance

CATEGORIES OF WORK

Practice groups:

Corporate advisory and disputes
Tomas Lindholm, Petri Taivalkoski

Transactions and finance
Lennart Simonsen

Technology, media and communications
Rainer Hilli

Practice streams:

Corporate advisory
Carita Wallgren

EU and competition advisory
Christian Wik

Arbitration and ADR
Petri Taivalkoski

Litigation
Eva Nordman

General commercial and contracts
Jyrki Prusila

M&A
Lennart Simonsen

Private equity
Ulf-Henrik Kull

Equity capital markets
Dimitrios Himonas

Banking and finance
Gunnar Westerlund

Intellectual property rights
Rainer Hilli

IT and telecoms
Craig Thompson

Venture capital
Mika Alanko

Specialist teams:

Tax law
Gunnar Westerlund

Insurance law
Jyrki Prusila

Corporate law
Tomas Lindholm

Corporate restructuring and insolvency
Risto Ojantakanen

EU and competition law
Christian Wik

Real estate law
Kaj Swanljung

Environmental law
Mika Alanko

Media, entertainment and sports law
Rainer Hilli

Marketing and consumer law
Bernt Juthström

Pharmaceuticals and biosciences
Petri Myllyneva

Transport law
Bernt Juthström

Labour law
Eva Nordman

Liability issues
Petri Taivalkoski

PROCOPÉ & HORNBORG
LAW OFFICES

MANNERHEIMINTIE 20 B
PO BOX 1077
00101 HELSINKI

Telephone: +358 9 6944 466
Fax: +358 9 6948 651
E-mail: law.firm@procope-hornborg.fi
Website: www.procope-hornborg.fi

Languages
English, French, German, Swedish

Number of lawyers 11

CATEGORIES OF WORK

Arbitration and litigation
Petri Kyllönen, Satu Juurola

Banking and finance
Ismo Hentula

Capital markets, securities
Ismo Hentula, Björn Nykvist

Company and commercial
Ismo Hentula, Olavi Ylänkö

Competition, antitrust, EU law
Lotta Uusitalo, Martti Heinonen

E-commerce, new media
Petri Kyllönen

Employment, labour
Mika Oksanen

Energy
Ismo Hentula, Olavi Ylänkö

Maritime
Björn Nykvist

Mergers and acquisitions
Ismo Hentula

Trade marks, intellectual property and information technology
Lotta Uusitalo, Petri Kyllönen

Telecommunications law
Ismo Hentula

SIVENIUS, SUVANTO & CO OY

PACIUKSENKATU 21
00270 HELSINKI

Telephone: +358 9 5306 760
Fax: +358 9 5306 7699
E-mail: info@sisulaw.com
Website: www.sisulaw.com

Languages
English, Finnish, Swedish

Number of lawyers 12

CATEGORIES OF WORK

Commercial (general)
Juha Sivenius, Jukka Suvanto

Corporate
Juha Sivenius, Peter Bützow

Mergers and acquisitions
Juha Sivenius, Jukka Suvanto

Litigation
Juha Sivenius, Olli Hoppu

Arbitration
Juha Sivenius, Peter Bützow

Insolvency
Peter Bützow, Kari Huttunen

Transport
Olli Hoppu

Compensation claims
Jukka Suvanto, Olli Hoppu

Environmental
Olli Hoppu

Labour
Peter Bützow, Jarmo Henriksson

Banking, securities and finance
Peter Bützow, Jarmo Henriksson

Intellectual property
Jarmo Henriksson

Competition
Olli Hoppu

Insurance
Jukka Suvanto, Olli Hoppu

Construction
Juha Sivenius, Peter Bützow

VEIKKO PALOTIE & CO

ALEKSANTERINKATU 44 A
00100 HELSINKI

Telephone: +358 9 228 831
Fax: +358 9 2288 3300
E-mail: palotie@veikkopalotie.fi
Website: www.veikkopalotie.fi

Languages
English, French, German, Swedish

Number of lawyers 18

CATEGORIES OF WORK	
Arbitration	Employment, labour
Banking and finance	Environment
Commercial litigation	Insolvency/corporate restructuring
Competition and EU law	Insurance
Real estate and construction	IPR and information technology
Corporate and commercial	Media and entertainment
Damages and product liabilty	Mergers and acquisitions
Distribution, agency and franchise	Telecommunications

WASELIUS & WIST

ETELÄESPLANADI 24A
00130 HELSINKI

Telephone: +358 9 668 9520
Fax: +358 9 668 952 22
E-mail: ww@ww.fi
Website: www.ww.fi

Languages
English, French, German, Swedish, Russian

Number of lawyers 18

CATEGORIES OF WORK	
Finance law	EU law
Securities law	Antitrust and competition
Banking law	Labour law
Mergers and acquisitions	Litigation and arbitration
Industrial property	General corporate and business law

LAAKSO, LUKANDER & RUOHOLA

YLIOPISTONKATU 15 B
20100 TURKU

Telephone: +358 2 2733 777
Fax: +358 2 2337 777
E-mail: turku@laakso-lukander.fi
Website: www.laakso-lukander.fi

Languages
English, French, German, Spanish, Swedish

Other offices
Helsinki, Pori, Salo

Number of lawyers 14
at this office 10

Contacts
Harri Lukander, Jarkko Ruohola

CATEGORIES OF WORK

- **Agency and distribution**
- **Arbitration and litigation**
- **Company and commercial**
- **Construction**
- **Contract**
- **EC and competition**
- **Environment**
- **Extractable land resources**
- **Family**
- **Insolvency and bankruptcy**
- **Intellectual property and e-commerce**
- **Labour**
- **Licensing**
- **Mergers and acquisitions**
- **Tax**
- **IT and telecommunications**
- **Real estate**

FORMER YUGOSLAV REPUBLIC OF MACEDONIA

Population	2.1 million
Number of lawyers	1,300
Professional title	Advokat
Currency	Macedonian denar (MKD)

Index

The Former Yugoslav Republic Of Macedonia (FYROM) officially gained independence in 1991, following the break-up of Yugoslavia. The 25,333 sq km, land-locked country shares borders with Serbia and Montenegro to the north, Greece to the south, Albania to the west and Bulgaria to the east. It has a central position on the Balkan Peninsula.

The 2.1 million population is concentrated in a few urban areas. The capital, Skopje, situated in the north of the country has more than 600,000 inhabitants. Other major towns include Bitola, Tetovo, Kumanovo and Gostivar.

The ethnic make-up of the country is diverse, comprising 67% Macedonians, 22% Albanians and smaller numbers of Turks, Serbs and Romanies. Albanians are by far the largest ethnic minority in Macedonia.

BILLING

Hourly rates vary from €90 to €230 per hour depending on the complexity of the matter and seniority of the lawyer. Flat fees can be negotiated for larger projects.

MARKETING

The Macedonian Bar prohibits marketing by law firms.

POLITICAL AND ECONOMIC CLIMATE

FYROM obtained membership of the UN in 1993. Greece imposed trade restrictions on the country in 1992 due to its objection of the new state's use of what it regarded to be a Hellenic name and flag. The trade embargo was lifted in 1995.

Since the 2001 ethnic Albanian insurgency, FYROM has achieved greater political stability. In March 2003 the EU military mission, Concordia, took over peacekeeping duties from Nato.

In the past ten years privatisation has become a top priority. The country's privatisation programme has particularly concentrated on the privatisation of the banking sector. It is thought that this will aid FYROM's transition towards a free market economy, assisting it on the road to EU membership.

The country's main trading partners are Greece, Ukraine, Germany, Italy, Russia, and Serbia and Montenegro.

Unemployment remains high, with one-third of the population of Macedonia registered unemployed.

LEGAL MARKET

The legal market, though small, is developing. FYROM is gradually attracting foreign investment as it becomes more politically stable. Increasingly sophisticated road, rail and air links from all over Europe are creating opportunities for the country's commercial lawyers. As the market is small, the broader label of 'corporate and commercial' covers most legal practices of which privatisation plays a significant part.

FOREIGN LAW FIRMS

Foreign law firms are officially prohibited from practising in Macedonia. However, foreign firms, especially Greek firms are present. These are based mainly in the capital, Skopje, and are able to represent their clients' interests in the country without too much difficulty.

LEGISLATIVE DEVELOPMENTS

FYROM is working towards EU membership, though no date has been set for accession. During the past year the country has welcomed a closer association with the EU. Progress has been made to put in place the necessary administrative and legislative reforms to comply with the Stabilisation and Association Agreement (SAA).

In recent years steps have been taken to reform social security and improve business transparency by introducing legislation regarding bankruptcy. The government is looking to revise the tax system and reform price liberalisation in order to encourage more foreign investment.

Energy laws are being revised with plans underway to modernise some of Macedonia's older power plants. New hydroelectric power plants are being built.

CORPORATE AND COMMERCIAL

Of the eight firms recommended in this chapter, three stand out due to the quality of their work, the strength of client recommendations and their excellent reputations on both a domestic and international level.

Lawyers Antevski represented German media group WAZ in its investment in daily

The largest firms

1	Lawyers Antevski	9
	Mens Legis	9
3	IKRP Rokas and Partners	4
	Law & Patent Office Joanidis	4
5	Law Office Knezovic & Associates	3
	Peluso & Associates L.T.D.	3

These figures represent the total number of lawyers in this country only, and have been supplied by the firms themselves. The figures should be accurate as at 1 January 2004.

CORPORATE AND COMMERCIAL

ANTEVSKI, LAWYERS
KNEZOVIC & ASSOCIATES, LAW OFFICE
POLENAK, LAW OFFICE

IKRP Rokas & Partners
Joanidis, Law & Patent Office
Mens Legis
Monevski Law Firm
Peluso & Associates L.T.D.

Firms are listed A-Z in tiers which are ranked in order of priority
✪ Indicates firm displays contact details at the end of this chapter.

newspapers in FYROM, and acted for the World Bank Group and the CBI business and entertainment centre in Skopje in a corporate advisory capacity. The firm also represented manufacturer DSD of Saarbrucken, Germany, in litigation regarding unpaid damages of €562,000. Zlatko Antevski, the best known personality at the firm, is strongly recommended by long-term clients for his 'straightforward and professional' approach. The eight-lawyer firm is experienced in due diligence.

Law Office Knezovic & Associates has been acting for Bank Austria Creditanstalt in the acquisition of banks in FYROM. The firm, which comprises two partners and three associates, continues to represent Macedonian Telecom and British American Tobacco, and in 2003 advised Red Bull in relation to distribution within Macedonia. The head of the firm, Dejan Knezovic, has a strong following due to the 'quality and value' of his work.

Seven-lawyer **Law Office Polenak** represented the Coca-Cola Company regarding intellectual property rights. Clients also include the IFC, EBRD, Pro-Credit Bank AD Skopje and Philip Morris. The best known personalities at the firm are the two partners, Nikola and Kristijan Polenak and attorney-at-law Tatjana Popovski. Kristijan Polenak, known for his litigation expertise, is recommended for his 'sharp answers' and 'excellent English skills'.

Greek firm **IKRP Rokas & Partners** has three lawyers operating in its Skopje office, headed by local manager Theodoros Giannitsakis. The firm advises on a range of financial, corporate and dispute resolution matters.

Law & Patent Office Joanidis co-operates with firms across Europe and Japan. Three lawyers operate under the leadership of managing partner Jovan Joanidis to advise international clients on corporate, commercial, property, litigation, tax and privatisation matters.

Mens Legis operates over a range of practice areas. It has experience in due diligence and advised on the privatisation of a Macedonian telecommunications company and of Tutunski Kombinat, the biggest tobacco corporation in the country. Partners Biljana Cakmakova and Ljubica Ruben, and associate Anela Nikolic, recommended for her excellent English skills, are distinguished figures at the firm.

Monevski Law Firm acts for the EBRD and the IFC and advises on water supply and waste disposal projects in Macedonia. Sole partner Valerjan Monevski leads three lawyers. The firm has worked with international firm **Baker & McKenzie** and UK-based **Bird & Bird** on international transactions.

Giovanni Peluso heads **Peluso & Associates L.T.D.**. The firm advised the EU Treasury Unit on an annual loan to the Macedonian government. Practice strengths include financial, banking, privatisation, corporate, commercial matters and M&A. Clients include the European Commission. The firm works in close conjunction with its New York office.

FRANCE

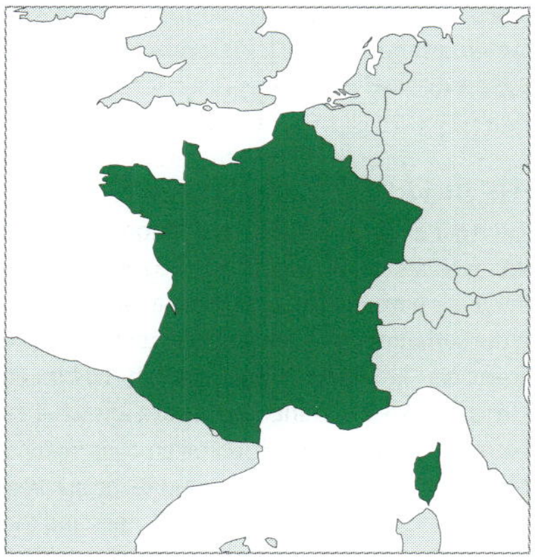

Population	61.3 million
Number of lawyers	35,000
Professional title	Avocat
Currency	Euro (€)

Index

France is divided into 96 metropolitan departments which are grouped into 22 regions. The heart of this centralised structure is Paris, the capital and epicentre of the country's business and legal community. As a result, Paris is home to both the country's leading indigenous law firms and a host of foreign law firms principally from the US and the UK.

Outside of Paris, Lyon, the capital of the Rhône-Alpes region, is France's second economic centre. The country's two other major centres of business are Lille and Marseille. Like Lyon, Lille is largely industrial while Marseille, the Mediterranean hub port, is the economic and maritime capital of the South. Other important cities include Nantes, Rennes, Bordeaux, Toulouse, Montpellier and Strasbourg. Law firms in the regions are dealt with at the end of the chapter.

BILLING

Fees are generally negotiated with the client in advance. The majority of firms work on an hourly rate basis. Hourly billing is quite a recent development for French firms, very much a result of the Anglo-Saxon firms' influence. Some firms prefer a flat fee. Contingency fees, which were officially prohibited, are now increasingly being used.

Hourly billing rates range from €155 for junior lawyers to €520 for senior partners, though in some cases more may be charged on particularly complex issues. Generally, rates outside Paris are lower, in general around one-third lower than in Paris.

MARKETING

The French legal profession is governed by a strict code of professional ethics (especially with regard to publicity). However, law firms are increasingly opening up to marketing, particularly in the Paris market where more than 50 foreign firms are represented.

IN-HOUSE LAWYERS

In-house lawyers are to be found in all larger companies. Most legal departments handle the majority of work themselves, seeking outside help only with regard to specific questions and, of course, litigation. In the case of certain small and medium-sized companies, a law firm might serve as an external legal department.

LEGAL MARKET

In 1992, the profession was modified by merging the *avocats* profession with that of the *conseils juridiques*. The resulting change was an important one: law firms were thus given an opportunity to provide a complete service adapted to the needs of business clients.

While the two professions are generally harmoniously intertwined in Paris, the picture is slightly different in the provinces where there is often still a distinction between firms engaged in court work and those supplying out-of-court legal services.

There are more than 35,000 avocats in France, of which approximately 40% are registered at the Paris Bar. In the regions, few firms boast more than ten avocats although there are some exceptions, notably in Lyon. The number of firms active on a national scale is small. The largest is **Fidal**, with 21 regional directorates and 107 offices. The other Big Four accountancy firms maintain offices in several cities outside Paris: **Landwell & Associés/ Partners** in Bordeaux, Grenoble, Lille, Lyon, Marseille, Montpellier, Nantes, Rennes, Strasbourg; **Deloitte & Touche Juridique et Fiscal**, Marseille, Lyon, Bordeaux, Tours, Lille, Nantes; **EY Law** in Bordeaux, Grenoble, Lille, Lyon, Marseille, Monaco, Montpellier, Nantes, Nice, Saint-Etienne, Strasbourg, Toulouse.

The other firm with a national spread is the labour law specialist **Barthélémy & Associés, member of ius laboris** with offices in 14 cities (Paris, Lille, Rennes, Strasbourg, Clermont-Ferrand, Lyon, Bordeaux, Toulouse, Nîmes, Montpellier, Marseille, Nice, Nantes, Saint-Etienne).

Compared to Anglo-Saxon firms, the size of French practices may appear modest. Where French firms have chosen expansion, this has often been done in order to add a broader international dimension (**Gide Loyrette Nouel** being the obvious example).

At the same time, there are also a number of medium-sized firms in Paris which do not compete in size but are regarded as centres of excellence (for example, **Bredin Prat**). Forty or so Anglo-Saxon firms are represented in Paris. Their contribution to the development of the legal market is undisputed and a number of these firms are well represented in our tables.

There are comparatively few other countries represented in the French legal market. German firms, for example, have tended to turn their expansion plans more towards Eastern Europe. Nonetheless, a handful of German firms have offices

The largest firms

1	Fidal	1,315
2	Landwell & Associés/Partners	660
3	EY Law	413
4	CMS Bureau Francis Lefebvre	363
5	Gide Loyrette Nouel	303
6	Deloitte & Touche Juridique et Fiscal	270
7	Freshfields Bruckhaus Deringer	245
8	Clifford Chance	198
9	Barthélémy & Associés, member of ius laboris	190
10	Linklaters	140
11	Lefèvre Pelletier & Associés	120
	Rambaud Martel	120
	Salans	120
14	Lovells	109
15	Allen & Overy	105
	Baker & McKenzie	105
17	Magellan	102
18	Lamy Ribeyre & Associés (Groupe)	97
19	Norton Rose	96
20	Latham & Watkins	95
21	Shearman & Sterling LLP	89
22	Cleary Gottlieb Steen & Hamilton	88
23	Bignon Lebray & Associés	82
	White & Case LLP	82
25	Herbert Smith	80
	UGGC & Associés	80

These figures represent the total number of lawyers in this country only, and have been supplied by the firms themselves. The figures should be accurate as at 1 January 2004.

in Paris: **Brandi Dröge Piltz Heuer & Gronemeyer**; **Haarmann Hemmelrath**; **Grützmacher Gravert Viegener**; and **BSR Rödl & Partners**. Dutch firm **Loyens & Loeff** is present, while **NautaDutilh** announced the closure of its Paris office in October 2002.

Scandinavia is represented in France by Swedish firm **Vinge**, and southern Europe by Italian firm **Carnelutti**, and Spanish firm **J A Cremades et Associés**.

LINKS ABROAD

Twenty-five French firms based in Paris maintain a presence abroad, varying from a small office staffed by one or two *avocats*, to a larger, structured office, often the result of a merger with a local firm.

Five firms have a strong foreign presence. At the end of the 1980s, **Gide Loyrette Nouel** took on an important strategic route to expansion in the international markets. Hence the setting up of offices in Riyadh, New York, and Brussels, followed by Warsaw, Moscow, Bucharest, Budapest, Prague, Istanbul, Hanoi, Beijing, Shanghai and, more recently, Tunis, Casablanca and Algiers (planned to open in early 2004). Finally, **Gide Loyrette Nouel** opened in London in 2003 with a 30-lawyer banking and finance team from **Sidley Austin Brown & Wood LLP**. Today one-third of the firm's lawyers are located abroad, in offices generally headed by a French partner.

Salans has a presence in London and the US, in Moscow and Warsaw as well as St Petersburg, Kyiv, Almaty, Baku and Atyrau. After taking over teams from *Altheimer & Gray* in 2003, the firm is now present in Prague, Bratislava, Bucharest, Istanbul and Shanghai.

CMS Bureau Francis Lefebvre is represented all over Europe, being part of the *CMS* network. But **CMS Bureau Francis Lefebvre** already had offices abroad, which have, in some cases, merged with the *CMS* offices in the same cities. To date, the firm is present in Berlin, Brussels, Bucharest, Buenos Aires, Casablanca, Düsseldorf, Madrid, Montevideo, Moscow, New-York, Sao Paulo, and Shanghai.

Vovan & Associés has offices in Italy, China, Vietnam and Thailand, while **DS Avocats** is well represented in Asia, Belgium and in Spain.

A number of other firms have successfully developed internationally in niche areas, often by accompanying particular clients. There are also firms that have developed special competence in EU law, such as **Coutrelis & Associés**, **Funck-Brentano Gewelbe Brousseau**, **UGGC & Associés** (the firm also opened an office in Casablanca in 2002), **Vogel & Vogel**, as well as specialists in environmental law **Huglo Lepage & Associés Conseil**. **Vogel & Vogel** is present in Frankfurt, while **Bignon Lebray & Associés** is represented in Madrid, **JP Karsenty & Associés** in London, Brussels and Milan, and **Ngo Miguérès & Associés** in Milan. In Eastern Europe, **Berlioz & Co** maintains a presence in Vilnius, and **Moquet Borde & Associés** is in Brussels, Tallinn, and Budapest. As for the US, **Sokolow Dunaud Carreras** has an office in New York, as has **Thieffry & Associés**. **Ngo Miguérès & Associés** is in Mexico. **Klein Goddard Associés** can be found in Singapore, **Lefèvre Pelletier & Associés** in Hong Kong, **Thieffry & Associés** in Shanghai, and **Adamas** in Beijing, Shanghai, Taipei, Canton. Finally, a few firms are represented in Africa: **EY Law** has offices in the Ivory Coast, Gabon, Senegal, Cameroon and Congo. **Klein Goddard Associés** is also established in the Ivory Coast.

THE BIG FOUR

The legal arms of the Big Four accountants had displayed grand ambitions in the 1990s. Those ambitions have been dampened by the follow-ups of the Sarbanes-Oxley law and the Loi de Sécurité Financière in France. Their growth has been particularly visible in the regions though where a few top local firms have been taken over. In Paris, they haven't reached the top, except in the tax area; the restrictions imposed to their activities and the subsequent moves of lawyers to traditional law firms have somewhat slowed their growth. Even if the Big Four firms now carry unquestionable weight, sustained by name as well as international connections, they are not competitors to traditional firms they would have hoped to become.

Fidal has the most extensive representation nationwide and is also largest in terms of number of lawyers.

Landwell & Associés/Partners is the combination of *Price Waterhouse Juridique et Fiscal* and *Coopers & Lybrand CLC Juridique et Fiscal* in 1999.

More recently, in September 2002, Brussels approved the merger between *HSD Ernst & Young* and *Archibald*, the legal arms of *Ernst & Young* and *Andersen Legal* in France to create **EY Law**. The merger wasn't processed without damage, various teams having left the firm to other Big Four or to traditional firms.

The other Big Four is **Deloitte & Touche Juridique et Fiscal**. At the time of writing the firm is in the process of becoming completely independent from the audit and accountancy activities and on the verge of adopting a new name.

MOVES, MERGERS AND SPLITS

There were no big mergers in Paris last year, although there were a few team moves. Five corporate partners from *Sokolow, Dunaud, Mercadier & Carreras* (now **Sokolow Dunaud Carreras**) left for **Norton Rose** when, at the same time, three partners and a team was leaving **Norton Rose** to create **Bouckaert Ormen Passemard Sportes**. In the environment field, **Pichavent Chétrit** is a split from **GAIA**. José Rosell became a partner of **Hughes Hubbard & Reed**; as a consequence, *Rosell & Associés* no longer exists.

Taylor Wessing arrived in France by hiring 30 lawyers from **Landwell & Associés/Partners**. Their work will focus on IT and media activities.

Bignon Lebray & Associés is the result of the demerger of *Bignon, Lebray, Delsol & Associés*; 18 partners left in June 2003, mostly to set up **Alerion** and **Delsol & Associés**.

Freshfields boosted its labour capacity by integrating highly-ranked labour boutique *Bélier & Associés*.

ADMINISTRATIVE AND PUBLIC LAW

Boivin & Associés has been active in administrative law for a long time and Jean-Pierre Boivin's doctrinal contribution to the matter is unrivalled. He is director of the IDPA (*Institut de Droit Public des Affaires du Barreau de Paris*). The firm has developed particular strength in administrative contracts, public markets, and delegation of public services, alongside a top environmental practice. The firm has advised Eurotunnel since 1985 in relation to its concession.

Two partners handle administrative law at **Gide Loyrette Nouel**: Laurent Deruy and Michel Guénaire. Their practice covers the major areas, primarily public contracts, public enterprises, public finances and local authorities. They assist the state, local authorities, public enterprises and numerous private companies and groups, both as advisers and on litigation. They have significant involvement in the issues relating to the enforcement of the new PPP contractual scheme, the reinforcement of the country's administrative decentralisation policy and continued endeavours to implement the provisions of the EU Gas Directives and foster the opening of the electricity market. Other teams are also involved in public law (privatisations, concessions): the corporate and the projects teams.

Even though the firm is now more visible in environmental law, for which it is a leader in France, **Huglo Lepage & Associés Conseil** has its origins in administrative litigation, and half of the work is still dedicated to the matter. Christian Huglo, Corinne Lepage and their teams advise and defend various local and regional authorities and departments. Their activities encompass administrative law, town planning, business public law, contracts, markets, delegation and PPP.

Allen & Overy has succeeded in establishing a strong reputation with partner Noël Chahid-Nouraï and recently recruited of counsel Frédéric Mion. The team offers a full range of advice on various matters including concessions and public works, regulatory and environmental issues, privatisation, litigation, public aspects of M&A, financings, tax and stock exchange transactions. The public law practice has been involved recently in the fields of infrastructure, telecommunications and energy.

In the construction and town-planning fields, **Claude Grangé** is undisputedly the best known specialist.

David Préat is the partner in charge at **Clifford Chance**. The team comprises seven lawyers, including Rémi Sermier, and adjoins strong projects, EU/competition and corporate practices. **Clifford Chance** advised the state in connection with various infrastructure projects; Sagem for the response to the call for tenders and the negotiation of a concession agreement for the construction and operation of high-speed telecommunications network infrastructure; and the Franco-Spanish intergovernmental commission in relation to the bid procedure for the concession of the international section of the Perpignan-Figueras high-speed rail link.

At **Freshfields Bruckhaus Deringer**, Thierry Laloum, along with five other associates, handles company and commercial public law-related cases. The firm is particularly strong in financial public law. The team advised a group of candidates in relation to the A19 and A41 motorways and the Perpignan-Figueras rail link projects; LD Com in the context of the concession for the construction and operation of a telecoms network; and Région Ile de France regarding the set up of a French commercial paper programme (*billets de trésorerie*) up to €500m.

Four-partner, eight-associate **Sur - Mauvenu et Associés** focuses on public company and commercial law (at a French and European level), particularly with regard to the provision of public services, such as transport and town planning, and with a sound knowledge of administrative contracts (including PPP, concessions, delegation of public services, etc.). Marie-Thérèse Sur-Le Liboux is considered an inventive practitioner.

UGGC & Associés' Jean-Nicolas Clément handles environmental issues; Bernard Lamorlette, former legal director of Lyonnaise des Eaux, is developing a town-planning practice; and Thierry dal Farra is a specialist in public contracts, public markets, public litigation and often works for the French State.

Adamas is based in Lyon and Paris and has developed expertise in public law over the last 40 years. The team now numbers four partners (including Romain Granjon) and ten associates, and offers services spanning environmental law, public markets, town planning and provision of public services.

Active for many years in public law with name partner Olivier Debouzy and Jean-Dominique Bloch, **August & Debouzy** reinforced its team in 2002 with the arrival of Christian Pierret, a former Ministre délégué de l'industrie, des PME, du commerce et de l'artisanat, and a specialist in regulation of public entities.

Baker & McKenzie is active in public law through Arnaud Cabanes, who is also an environmental law specialist, and Emmanuel Guillaume, on the telecoms side. The firm advised Conseil Général des Hauts-de-Seine, ADP and EADS (on PPP and PFI issues).

ADMINISTRATIVE AND PUBLIC LAW

BOIVIN & ASSOCIÉS
GIDE LOYRETTE NOUEL ✪
HUGLO LEPAGE & ASSOCIÉS CONSEIL ✪

Allen & Overy ✪
Claude Grangé
Clifford Chance
Freshfields Bruckhaus Deringer ✪
Sur - Mauvenu et Associés
UGGC & Associés ✪

Adamas ✪
August & Debouzy ✪
Baker & McKenzie ✪
Bignon Lebray & Associés
Brandford-Griffith Baverez Pasturel ✪
DS Avocats
De Castelnau
Darrois Villey Maillot Brochier ✪
GAIA
Klein Goddard Associés
Lafarge Flécheux Campana Le Blevennec
Linklaters ✪
Rambaud Martel ✪

Ader Amigues & Jolibois
Berlioz & Co
Bruno Kern Avocats
CMS Bureau Francis Lefebvre ✪
Carbonnier Lamaze Rasle & Associés
Denton Wilde Sapte ✪
EY Law ✪
Fidal
Franklin ✪
Goutal Alibert
JeantetAssociés ✪
Latournerie Wolfrom & Associés ✪
Lovells ✪
Lussan Brouillaud
Neveu Sudaka & Associés
Pichavent Chétrit
Salans
Sartorio & Associés
Vatier & Associés ✪
Veil Jourde La Garanderie ✪
White & Case LLP

Firms are listed A-Z in tiers which are ranked in order of priority
✪ Indicates firm displays contact details at the end of this chapter.

The commercial public law team at **Bignon Lebray & Associés** is led by Lionel Roche (in Lyon) who joins from **Adamas**. Arnaud Cazin left the firm.

At **Brandford-Griffith Baverez Pasturel**, Nicolas Baverez handles economic public law. He works for public entities including SNCF and GDF.

DS Avocats has a team of eight lawyers active in public business law. The three partners involved in this practice area are Daniel Chausse, Jean-François Bizet and Frédéric Lévy. They advise local communities, communes, public companies and construction companies regarding town planning, environmental or public markets issues and provision of public services.

Law firm **de Castelnau** specialises in local public law and decentralisation law and work for public or semi-public entities.

Darrois Villey Maillot Brochier practises public law, owing to François Sureau, a former member of the Conseil d'Etat. He handles public aspects of M&A and is equally involved in privatisation.

GAIA handles all types of public contracts, such as concession contracts and PPP. The team comprises two partners and five associates and combines expertise in public and environmental law.

At **Klein Goddard Associés**, the partner in charge is Laurent-Xavier Simonel, whereas Michel Bazex deals with administrative law at **Lafarge Flécheux Campana Le Blevennec**.

Linklaters recruited Paul Lignières from **Landwell & Associés/Partners** to set up the public law practice. He is a PPP specialist, deals with delegation of public services and handles public aspects of corporate transactions.

Rambaud Martel has an advisory and contentious public law practice. Areas covered include public markets (sometimes in relation with the strong construction practice of the firm), regulation, administrative responsibility, and capital opening of semi-public entities. Jean-Philippe Sorba, Frédéric Torron and Bruno Richard are involved.

AVIATION

Six-lawyer **Fernand Garnault** is undeniably the leading French aviation firm, acting for the national carrier and its insurers. The firm and its partners do, however, also work for other carriers and handle some matters for manufacturers, and services provided span finance, product and accident liability, insurance and regulatory issues. The firm enjoys a close relationship with reputed London aviation specialist **Beaumont and Son**.

Although there is some aviation activity in Paris, we would also recommend **Decker & Associés** in Toulouse, where the industry is well represented.

Gide Loyrette Nouel's aviation practice covers all air transport litigation, mortgages and insurance or reinsurance problems relating to such disputes. The team advises on a permanent basis major French aircraft manufacturers (as Aérospatiale, EADS, Eurocopter) on product liability and crash cases, and major aviation insurers such as La Réunion Aérienne, Axa and Allianz.

HPMBC Clyde & Co handles aviation issues arising from of its work for insurers. Gérard Honig is Airbus's lawyer and advised on the Airbus A320 crash in the UAE. He is also advising Aérospatiale in the Concorde case.

Holman Fenwick & Willan acts on a regular basis for Safair, Delta Airlines, American Airlines, RyanAir and Air Canada.

AVIATION

FERNAND GARNAULT

Decker & Associés
Gide Loyrette Nouel ✪
HPMBC Clyde & Co ✪
Holman Fenwick & Willan ✪
Norton Rose
Penningtons
Rappaport Hocquet
Rembauville-Nicolle & Bureau - Rbm2l
Soulez Larivière et Associés

Firms are listed A-Z in tiers which are ranked in order of priority
✪ Indicates firm displays contact details at the end of this chapter.

Norton Rose works mainly in aviation finance but is also involved in insolvencies, workouts and restructurings, insurance, repossessions and other contentious matters,

Penningtons has built a strong aviation practice in Paris. The firm regularly handles litigation and advisory work for Middle Eastern Airline, Sabena Technics and various US leasing corporations.

Rappaport Hocquet handles crash cases, generally advising the victims. The firm also works for pilots and air crew unions.

Rembauville-Nicolle & Bureau - Rbm2l's Patrice Rembauville-Nicolle maintains a strong reputation. He is Boeing's lawyer in France for all matters relating to accidents and, more generally, aviation litigation. He was representing Dunlop in the Concorde crash.

Soulez Larivière et Associés is well known for its aviation expertise. Clients include the Direction Générale de l'Aviation Civile and Snecma.

BANKING AND FINANCE

Allen & Overy's team consists of five partners, two French (Luc Rentmeesters, Christophe Jacquemin) and three English (Rod Cork, Adrian Mellor, Tim Scales). The client base features a number of large, international banks. The finance practice is international, covering acquisition finance, syndicated loans, structured finance, telecoms and asset finance and, less frequently, real estate finance. The firm has been particularly busy in activities relating to credit enhancement and corporate restructurings in the past year, being involved (on the banks' side) on Vivendi Universal's and Rhodia's restructurings. In other fields, **Allen & Overy** advised Qantas in relation to a double-dip financing of three A330s involving a French tax lease; CDC ixis and CIFGE on the refinancing of the Prado-Carénage tunnel; Mizuho Corporate Bank in the €420m LBO acquisition of Actaris by Montagu Private Equity; and Royal Bank of Scotland in the €156m acquisition of the Areva tower in La Défense.

BANKING AND FINANCE

ALLEN & OVERY ✪
CLIFFORD CHANCE
DE PARDIEU BROCAS MAFFEI & LEYGONIE ✪
FRESHFIELDS BRUCKHAUS DERINGER ✪
GIDE LOYRETTE NOUEL ✪
LINKLATERS ✪

ASHURST ✪
JONES DAY ✪
LATHAM & WATKINS ✪
ORRICK
SHEARMAN & STERLING LLP
WHITE & CASE LLP

Cleary Gottlieb Steen & Hamilton ✪
Herbert Smith ✪
JeantetAssociés ✪
Lovells ✪
Norton Rose
Simmons & Simmons ✪
Willkie Farr & Gallagher LLP ✪

August & Debouzy ✪
Bignon Lebray & Associés
Bredin Prat ✪
Chaintrier & Associés
Coudert Frères ✪
Debevoise & Plimpton ✪
Dechert
Denton Wilde Sapte ✪
Dubarry Le Douarin Veil ✪
EY Law ✪
Ince & Co ✪
Lefèvre Pelletier & Associés
Moquet Borde & Associés ✪
NomoS ✪
Rambaud Martel ✪
Salans
Slaughter and May ✪
Sokolow Dunaud Carreras
Sullivan & Cromwell LLP
UGGC & Associés ✪

Firms are listed A-Z in tiers which are ranked in order of priority
✪ Indicates firm displays contact details at the end of this chapter.

The **Clifford Chance** finance team works on complex structured finance transactions and securitisations on an international level (Richard Parolai and Jonathan Lewis). The firm is involved in acquisition finance, LBO finance and property financing for banks and investment funds in connection with managing debt portfolios, and is also well known for employee share plans (Olivier Bertin-Mourot), for Technip this year. **Clifford Chance** advised the French government in the debt restructuring of Alstom; Crédit Lyonnais, Crédit Agricole Indosuez and Royal Bank of Scotland acting as senior lenders to Vivendi Universal for the €4bn acquisition of a 26% stake in Cegetel Group from BT; UBS on its acquisition of Lloyds Bank SA from Lloyds TSB; and Merrill Lynch and HVB on the financing of the acquisition by Westbrook Partners of two real estate portfolios of Gecina and Simco and on the subsequent securitisation. The firm is also involved in regulatory work, advising London Clearing House on cross-border issues in relation to the coming together of a French clearing house and an English clearing house.

De Pardieu Brocas Maffei & Leygonie is regarded by many as the number one French banking firm and works closely with a few US firms. The practice covers regulatory, advisory and contentious matters (the latter being a traditional strength), with a strong activity in derivatives and structured finance (in connection with the externalisation of state assets) recently. The firm undertakes a wide range of finance work for clients who are banks and large insurance companies, as well as some investment companies. Antoine Maffei, Pierre Minor and Olivier Hubert are well-known specialists. Recent deals include advising Crédit Lyonnais in the financing of the acquisition by Nexity Topco of Nexity SAS and refinancing of an earlier facility (€575m); BNP Paribas in the financing of the purchase by GIE Vehiposte of vehicles to be leased to La Poste (€115m); and Wendel on a €500m syndicated loan.

Freshfields Bruckhaus Deringer's finance group boasts no less than ten partners. Although the firm's activities are diverse, certain practice areas merit special mention: structured finance and complex financing arrangements, property finance and transactions with an elaborate tax dimension. The firm is also involved in aviation and acquisition finance, and both syndicated and bank financing. The team also includes Anglo-Saxon members, three partners being solicitors. Among major work, we would mention the advice to 11 banks in connection with the restructuring of the Alstom Group debt; BNP Paribas, Crédit Agricole Indosuez, Crédit Commercial de France, Crédit Lyonnais, JPMorgan Plc and Société Générale, as arrangers in relation to the €2.5bn syndicated loan granted to Pinault Printemps Redoute; Bayern LB in relation to the financing of the acquisition of four buildings situated on avenue Montaigne in Paris; KKR on the financing of the €270m acquisition of Legrand; Deutsche Bank AG in connection with the refinancing of the acquisition of the property occupied by the Lido de Paris and UGC Normandie; and the Mezzanine Lenders in connection with the financing of the acquisition of Center Parcs Europe by Pierre & Vacances.

Gide Loyrette Nouel's 75-lawyer team is active in all areas of banking and finance. In addition to project finance, capital markets and securitisation (see corresponding chapters) the firm is also involved in structured finance (Eric Cartier-Millon, Kamel Ben Salah), and in financial institutions and services (Jean-Guillaume d'Hérouville). The team works closely with the London office which opened in June 2003 and is now made up of some 30 lawyers specialised in banking and finance. The firm advised the two lead arrangers, CIC and CAI, in the €600m LBO financing of the acquisition by Eurazeo of the Fraikin group, the first LBO financing based on an asset securitisation; the borrower in the €2.65bn LBO financing of the acquisition of Sophia by Société Foncière Lyonnaise SA; CCF and Crédit Lyonnais in the €850m multi-currency revolving facility granted to Zodiac SA; CB3 in the €126m financing by Natexis Banques Populaires of the acquisition of the 'CB3 tower' by a subsidiary of Colony from Technip; and Société Générale Asset Management for the setting up of the first French venture capital fund (*fonds commun de placement à risques*) dedicated to real estate investments (FCPR SGAM Immobilier).

Three types of activity are especially well developed at **Linklaters**: acquisition and LBO finance, structured finance and mainstream banking. Partners involved are Basil Zotiades (a CDO and high-yield structure specialist), Bertrand Andriani, Olivier Jauffret, Nathalie Hobbs and Jean-Jacque Essombè (a regulatory specialist). The firm is increasingly involved in syndicated loans and has started making a name for itself in jumbo deals (for EDF, Suez and Lafarge, advising the arrangers). On the LBO financing side, **Linklaters** has been busy with deals such as Actaris (on Montagu Private Equity's side), the Blini build-up by Labeyrie (acting for Barclays and Natexis Banques Populaires), and the Antargaz refinancing (advising AGZ). The banking team has also represented the lead presenting bank and senior debt arranger (Morgan Stanley) in the tender offer by Alcan for Pechiney; and Rémy Cointreau in a €500m credit facility.

Ashurst is certainly one of the premier firms in the acquisition finance field – with Jonathan Nabarro and Laurent Mabilat (Simon Thrower is back in London) – although it also carries out project, structured and asset finance work. The acquisition finance work principally involves LBO financing for French banks, as well as acting for foreign banks with operations in France and investment funds. A number of CDO deals have also been completed in the recent months. In 2003, the firm advised BNP Paribas, CADIF and Royal Bank of Scotland in the financing of the public-to-private deal of Trédi Environnement by Séché Environnement; Royal Bank of Scotland on the financing of the acquisition of Béghin Say by Origny Naples; ING on the financing of the acquisition of Terreal by Carlyle and Eurazeo from Saint Gobain; Groupe Figaro on the refinancing of its debt; Goldman Sachs and Natexis Banques on the financing of the acquisition by Apax Partners of Frans Bonhomme; and BNP Paribas on the financing of the acquisition by Axa PE of Tokheim International.

Jones Day's most developed area of activity is without doubt acquisition finance (Philippe Billot, Edward Nalbantian), but the firm also handles a significant number of asset and structured finance transactions, especially in the real estate field (François Bonteil), and tax driven financings. Moreover, the private equity sector is developing and the firm has recently been representing investment funds in LBOs. Pierre-Nicolas Ferrand relocated to the Paris Office after working in the Singapore office (Asian finance and restructuring matters). For example, the firm represented Société Générale in the financing of the acquisition of vessels by the French shipowner CMA CGM; Vivendi Environnement on a restructuring of a securitisation financing for the Tyseley waste energy facility in England; Royal Bank of Scotland in connection with the implementation of a €100m credit facility to the benefit of Carlyle European Real Estate Partners; and Crédit Agricole on a credit derivative risk-sharing structure over loan portfolio assets with another major French bank. Clients are mainly French banks, except in the property finance area, where there is a mix of banks (Morgan Stanley and Deutsche Bank to name two) and investors (US funds).

Latham & Watkins has a good name in banking, finance and capital markets, with a balanced clientele of banks and borrowers. The firm handles acquisition finance, LBO finance (Xavier Farde), debt restructuring and project or asset finance (Etienne Gentil), especially in the property area (Dominique Basdevant). Last year, the firm was involved in the refinancing by Rémy Cointreau through issues of €175m 6.5% senior notes due 2010 advising Bank of America Securities Ltd, BNP Paribas, Natexis Banques Populaires; the restructuring of the financing of the acquisition of some of Rhodia's business by Bain Capital, advising the senior and mezzanine lenders (Bear Stearns); the financing of the acquisition of Presses de la Vie Catholique, advising the purchaser Le Monde; and the €600m high-yield refinancing of mezzanine financing of the acquisition of Legrand by KKR/Wendel.

Orrick's reputation derives from its asset finance practice, which covers all industrial sectors and accounts for a third of the finance activity. The rest is made up of general banking (very often for borrowers), project finance, and financial disputes. The firm is one of few with a wide knowledge of cross-border leasing finance, hence the importance of having a link with the US and a tax capacity. The finance practice additionally covers property, shipping and trade finance. **Orrick** represented the French state-owned gas operator in connection with acquisition and French tax leasing of a liquefied natural gas carrier; lenders, lessors, and major airlines, for the sale and leaseback financings of Boeing and Airbus aircraft; a UK investment fund in venture-leasing investment and warrant issues; and an LBO fund in the acquisition of hi-tech companies.

Shearman & Sterling LLP is very active in acquisition and LBO finance (Martin Lebeuf works for French and US banks), but also handles property finance, syndicated loans and high-yield issues. The firm has expertise in derivatives instruments, and is very active in cross-border financings, handling structured and specialised finance work for a range of clients, including Vivendi and the French underground company RATP.

White & Case LLP is known for project finance, LBO and acquisition finance, structured and asset finance, very often on the banks' side but increasingly on the borrowers', and is developing high-yield and securitisation activities. Gilles Peigney is recommended. Thomas McDonald is in charge of asset finance (aviation and shipping) and Thierry Arachtingi is coming back from London. The firm is also active in the real estate, energy and commodities finance markets. **White & Case LLP** represented Apax in the €476m acquisition financing of the Frans Bonhomme Group; Eurazeo in the €500m acquisition financing of Fraikin; and advised on the $300m French tax lease/export credit financing (ECGD and Hermes) for the first three new Airbus aircraft to be operated by Qantas Airways Limited.

Cleary Gottlieb Steen & Hamilton has long assisted a range of international banks (for instance, Lazard and Rothschild) on all types of financings. The firm is involved in innovative financing products for French banks such as Tier 1 Preferred Securities. Structured financings, debt offerings and property financing are also handled by the firm.

Herbert Smith continues to grow with a team of two partners – Georges Dirani and Clotilde Dirnat – and some ten associates. Main areas of expertise include international debt finance, acquisition finance, structured finance, securitisations and derivatives. The client base is evenly split between banks and national and international borrowers, with a steady increase of instructions received from banks acting as arrangers.

The **JeantetAssociés** team is led by Jean-Marie Gaillard. The firm has developed particular expertise in financial aspects of M&A, complex structured financings, notably in the property area (Philippe Dubois) and tax-related cases, acting for borrowers and for financial institutions, for buyers and sellers.

Lovells is very active in banking as well as in finance. Its activities include acquisition finance (mainly for banks and investment funds), asset and aviation finance (on behalf of banks and aviation companies), international trade and commodities in emerging countries, project finance (water and harbour infrastructure), property and regulatory work, and syndicated loans (Alstom for example). PPP is also dealt with. Jacques Bertran de Balanda and Richard Jadot are the partners in charge.

Norton Rose's practice revolves around three types of work - asset finance, acquisition finance and project finance. The firm boasts a first-class reputation in shipping (Nigel Ward) and aviation finance (George Paterson, Alison Baxter) and is developing a trade finance activity (Bertrand Pellet has joined **Freshfields Bruckhaus Deringer**). The work centres on structured finance for banks of all nationalities (**Norton Rose** has been appointed to the Société Générale legal panel) and large French companies. The firm has advised SNCF on the largest ever QTE financing.

At **Simmons & Simmons** the structured finance team handles acquisition, asset and project financings. Notably, in acquisition finance, the firm undertakes a large amount of syndicated loans work, generally for the arranging banks (Colin Millar). In asset finance, the firm is notably involved in aircraft finance and repackaging (Matthieu de Varax and Jeremy Arscott). Regulatory work and financial services are also covered.

Daniel Payan and Annette Péron are active at **Willkie Farr & Gallagher LLP**. They deal with acquisitions and LBO finance on the issuer side.

CAPITAL MARKETS

CAPITAL MARKETS

ALLEN & OVERY ✪
CLEARY GOTTLIEB STEEN & HAMILTON ✪
CLIFFORD CHANCE
FRESHFIELDS BRUCKHAUS DERINGER ✪
GIDE LOYRETTE NOUEL ✪
LINKLATERS ✪
SHEARMAN & STERLING LLP

DE PARDIEU BROCAS MAFFEI & LEYGONIE ✪
JONES DAY ✪
LATHAM & WATKINS ✪
LOVELLS ✪
SULLIVAN & CROMWELL LLP
WILLKIE FARR & GALLAGHER LLP ✪

Brandford-Griffith Baverez Pasturel ✪
Bredin Prat ✪
Darrois Villey Maillot Brochier ✪
Davis Polk & Wardwell
Moquet Borde & Associés ✪
Orrick
Rambaud Martel ✪
Simmons & Simmons ✪
Skadden, Arps, Slate, Meagher & Flom LLP

Ashurst ✪
Baker & McKenzie ✪
Coudert Frères ✪
EY Law ✪
Fried, Frank, Harris, Shriver & Jacobson LLP ✪
Herbert Smith ✪
JeantetAssociés ✪
Landwell & Associés / Partners
Salans
Slaughter and May ✪
Veil Jourde La Garanderie ✪
White & Case LLP

Firms are listed A-Z in tiers which are ranked in order of priority
✪ Indicates firm displays contact details at the end of this chapter.

Allen & Overy has a leading practice in both France and Europe and the firm's partners devoted to capital markets work in Paris are principally Dan Lauder and François Poudelet, while Pierre Gissinger is well-known for his derivatives expertise. The firm is primarily active in the fields of debt, regulatory, warrants and derivatives, under French, English and US law, acting principally for French and international banks, although the firm is developing the equity side with a US securities law capacity. **Allen & Overy** carries out collateral work and has been active in a number of innovative products. A great deal of securitisations have also been handled lately. Highlights include advising Lehman Brothers in the first Tier 1 issue by a French bank (Cofinoga) utilising an English limited partnership; Alcatel in a €1bn convertible bond issue into new or existing shares followed by a cash tender offer of listed bonds; and UBS Warburg, BNP Paribas and Lazard in connection with the public listing in London and Paris of Kesa Electrical.

Cleary Gottlieb Steen & Hamilton enjoys an excellent reputation for its equities practice worldwide. In Paris, the firm's expertise manifests itself in French and US securities law with a complete range of international equity offerings, equity derivatives and other derivative transactions, structured financings, capital securities offerings and convertible, exchangeable and straight debt offerings. **Cleary Gottlieb Steen & Hamilton** advised the French Ministry of Finance and its adviser in connection with France Télécom's €15bn capital increase; Lafarge SA in its €1.3bn rights issue which included a public offering of new shares listed in France and the UK and a private placement in the US; Crédit Agricole SA in two Tier 1 preferred eurodollar offerings ($1.5bn and $550m); Gecina in connection with the establishment of a €1bn EMTN programme; and BNP Paribas in connection with the update of its $5bn US MTN programme. The French/US team includes Pierre-Yves Chabert, Robert Bordeaux-Groult and Andrew Bernstein.

Primarily involved in debt-related matters, **Clifford Chance**'s practice has extended to securitisations and equity offerings (with the arrival of Edward Kamman from **Skadden, Arps, Slate, Meagher & Flom LLP**). Other partners are Olivier Bertin-Mourot, Jonathan Lewis and Richard Parolai. The firm is active in both non-contentious (including employee share plans) and contentious equity work. **Clifford Chance** advised ERAP on the establishment of a €10bn EMTN programme and on the issue of €9.4bn notes; Veolia Environnement on the issue of two blocks of bonds (€1bn and €750m); the French Treasury on the accelerated auction sale of its 11% shareholding in Crédit Lyonnais; Deutsche Bank on the issue of Alcatel convertible bonds (€645m); Aventis on its buy-out offer for Rhodia's convertible bonds (€1,073m); Crédit Agricole/Indosuez as joint lead manager in a synthetic collateralised loan obligation transaction; and Merrill Lynch and HVB on the financing of the acquisition by Westbrook Partners of two real estate portfolios of Gecina and Simco and on the subsequent securitisation in the form of a CMBS.

Freshfields Bruckhaus Deringer retains its position as one of the leaders in both international (offshore) and domestic securitisations; for example, ABN Amro Bank NV and JPMorgan Securities Ltd were advised as joint lead managers in connection with the pan-European securitisation of 18 warehouse properties owned by the Prologis group; BNP Paribas was counselled in relation to the financing of the whole business securitisation set up by Chargeurs. Within the capital markets sector, the firm handles the placement of complex credit derivatives. Its client base is largely made up of banks.

Gide Loyrette Nouel has a leading practice in debt and equity issues, derivatives and structured products. The firm's main strength, however, rests in its expertise in securitisation (both domestic and offshore) with well-known Xavier de Kergommeaux and Gilles Saint Marc. The firm is also active in stock exchange introductions and dual listings. Work accomplished last year includes the €2.5bn ABCP securitisation of fixed phone invoices and rental system charges by France Télécom arranged by Société Générale and Deutsche Bank. The firm was also involved in Eros (European Loan Conduit) FCC for the purchase of mortgage loans granted by Morgan Stanley to Deutsche Bank's entities for the purchase of real estate properties previously owned by Thales. Also, **Gide Loyrette Nouel** represented Remy Cointreau in the issuing of €120m fixed rate senior notes, the first issue of fully dematerialised notes with a 144A placement without GDR; and HSBC on an EMTN Programme for the issue of notes by Crédit Commercial de France up to an amount of €10bn.

Linklaters' seven-partner specialised practice offers debt, equity, derivatives and growing securitisation expertise. The firm advises both lenders and borrowers and is developing both a high-yield and a US practice (Tom O'Neill). In the equity securities sector, the firm is primarily active with regard to pure stocks and shares and also handles the development of debt products convertible into and/or exchangeable for stocks and shares. Gilles Endréo is very well regarded and Basil Zotiades has developed CLO-CDO expertise. The team also has a good knowledge of credit derivatives, warrants, OTC products under French or English law for banks and companies, and EMTN programmes. Highlights over the year include acting for Rémy Cointreau on its French law-governed €175m high-yield bond refinancing; the arranger in connection with the establishment of a €10bn EMTN programme for ERAP (a public entity in the context of the recapitalisation of France Télécom); the lead managers on a number of equity linked transactions including the Oceanes initially developed for Valeo and PPR, exchangeable bonds (Suez/Fortis and Wendel/Cap Gemini); and pure equity transactions (Rexel, Wanadoo, Thales). **Linklaters** also handled three CDO transactions, the LFE Capital II CLO (for BNP Paribas), the Callisto I synthetic CDO (for CDC ixis Asset Management) and the Jazz II cash and synthetic CDO (for Axa Investment Managers).

Shearman & Sterling LLP is one of the top firms on the equity side, especially with regard to offerings with an international dimension. The firm has been involved in almost every privatisation since 1986, acting for issuers (Air France, Aérospatiale, Thomson Multimédia, Wanadoo), the Treasury or underwriters for listings in Paris and New York and other international offerings (Alcatel Câble, Alstom). Active partners are Hervé Letréguilly, Sami Toutounji and Manuel Orillac (Robert Treuhold is now the firm's managing partner in New York).

Alongside a traditional practice in share issues and derivatives, **De Pardieu Brocas Maffei & Leygonie** is distinguished by its expertise in payment systems, compensation and delivery rules (particularly the new European regulation on multi-product compensation instruments). Antoine Maffei and Pierre Minor have been particularly active in the implementation of a worldwide offer of shares for the employees of a major French banking Group and increased their presence in securitisation transactions of lease payments.

Jean-Marc Franceschi at **Jones Day** handles stock market introductions and all manner of capital transactions. The firm is experienced in pan-European securitisation projects involving non-standard products. For instance, the firm represented Aventis in connection with its issue of a €1.5bn bond, as part of its EMTN programme with a total value of €5bn; Lehman Brothers International and UBS Limited, the banks in charge of the issue of STMicroelectronics' $1.217bn zero coupon senior convertible bonds due 2013; OENEO in connection with its capital increase (€14m); and France Télécom SA on France Télécom's agreement to repurchase the loans granted by Nokia and Ericsson to MobilCom.

At **Latham & Watkins**, four partners are active alongside their M&A practice. Roberto Cristofolini (arrived from **Linklaters**) is entirely dedicated to capital markets with a focus on equity and equity linked issues, and Patrick Singer handles bond issues. The firm has been involved in a number of recent bond issues, acting primarily on behalf of the issuer and dealing with EMTN programmes for CADES, LVMH and Air Liquide. Equities work is often linked to the firm's M&A practice and includes privatisations, stock market introductions, capital increases and public bids, on behalf of both bidders and targets. The firm assisted LM Ericsson AB on the €5bn purchase by France Télécom of claims of banks in consideration for notes redeemable into shares.

Lovells is involved in major debt transactions with Philip Boys and Sharon Lewis who is also an international securitisation expert. The firms deals with equity issues, repackagings, derivatives, IPOs, financial services and funds work. **Lovells** advised Alstom on its refinancing arrangements for a principal amount of €3.2bn; Xerox on a French law whole-business securitisation of a loan of approximately €400m; EDF regarding a multi-currency revolving credit facility agreement for €6bn; Suez regarding the sale of Suez Group's 10% interest in Fortis including the issue of €1.19bn 4.5% exchangeable notes due 2006 exchangeable into shares; and CDC ixis on four simultaneous standalone bond issues listed in Luxembourg.

Sullivan & Cromwell LLP plays an important part in placing European operators on international markets, particularly in the US. The practice covers the whole range of products from IPOs and privatisations to private placements, including 144A placements. In 2003, the firm advised the underwriters in the capital increase of France Télécom; Goldman Sachs in the largest high-yield offering of the year by a European issuer (Vivendi Universal); UBS, global co-ordinator for an Axa warrants offering; and Scor in a French and international rights offering.

Willkie Farr & Gallagher LLP is active in stock market introductions, capital raising and secondary sales of share portfolios, usually acting for the issuer. In 2003, the team advised Elior on the €110m share capital increase and issuance of new shares on the Premier Marché; Teksid Aluminum on the €240m high-yield bond issue listed on the Luxembourg Stock Exchange; and BSN Glasspack on the €160m high-yield bond and €40m tender offer for existing high-yield bonds held by BSN Glasspack SA on the Luxembourg Stock Exchange.

Brandford-Griffith Baverez Pasturel is regularly involved in capital markets, advising issuers, banks and financial institutions on stock market listings or in the context of privatisations (Autoroutes du Sud de la France). The firm (Henri Brandford-Griffith, Diane Pasturel, Vanina Paolaggi, Laurent Sablé) also handles financial instruments issues and participates in the creation of new financial products (equity line) and new issuing structures (free granting of equity warrants). Recent deals include: advising Geodis on its capital increase; Rallye on the issuance of exchangeable bonds into Casino shares; and Deutsche Bank in connection with France Télécom's new equity issue.

Besides major privatisations (Air France, Aérospatiale, Crédit Lyonnais), **Bredin Prat** has expertise in various complex financial instruments and works on a regular basis with **Davis Polk & Wardwell** in the US for M&A related issues. The firm advised the underwriter JPMorgan Securities UK on securities aspects of the acquisition by institutional investors of a 8.5% stake in Renault from the French state, and took part in Crédit Agricole's capital increase.

Darrois Villey Maillot Brochier is also involved in capital markets issues. A privatisation specialist (François Sureau) and an expert in stock exchange-related transactions (Marie-Noëlle Dompé) are part of the firm. They advised Alcatel and Morgan Stanley in the implementation of the first tracker fund issued in Europe with listings in Paris, New York and Toronto, and handled the IPO of Autoroutes du Sud de la France in the context of its privatisation.

In the past five years, the Paris office of **Davis Polk & Wardwell** has represented the issuers or underwriters in numerous international securities offerings by French issuers, including Alstom, Axa, Dassault Systemes, Rhodia and Rhone Poulenc. French deals include the first global equity offering by a French company and the first offering under rule 144A by a French company. Recently, the firm acted on the €1.2bn rule 144A/regulation S secondary offering of common stock of a French automobile manufacturer by the French government as part of a privatisation and on the €1bn rule 144A/regulation S offering of high-yield senior and senior subordinated notes by a French chemical company.

Moquet Borde & Associés' capital markets team with Aline Poncelet worked on the introduction in France of equity lines and handled issues of OBSAR convertible debt securities. The firm is also recognised as an expert in the area of corporate governance.

Orrick has an increasingly important practice covering all aspects of capital markets, and particularly bond issues. The firm set up EMTN programmes for EADS and Renault and carried out a $170m private placement in the US for Imerys.

Rambaud Martel often deals with major transactions with stock exchange and capital markets aspects. The firm has a reputation for creativity in complex matters.

Simmons & Simmons' new capital market team is led by Arnauld Achard (from **Clifford Chance**) and focuses on structured securities, securitisation, CDOs (cash and synthetic), derivatives, funds and regulatory work.

The Paris office of **Skadden, Arps, Slate, Meagher & Flom LLP** handles privatisations with international placement aspects (Air France, Aérospatiale) and stock exchange introductions in Paris and New York (two hi-tech actors recently). The firm handled Air France's aircraft securitisation in 2003.

CONSTRUCTION

Bousquet's longstanding and close relationship with leading French construction company Bouygues has allowed this *généraliste* firm to develop a leading specialist construction practice, with seven dedicated lawyers. The firm also advises on property transactions.

The other top firm, **Rambaud Martel** lists major public contractors among its clientele (Roissy CDG airport, Ministry of Finance, Pompidou Centre among others). The construction department, led by Christophe Lapp, has attained a position of strength in recent years, being especially highly regarded for contract work and major construction projects, where the firm deals with the financing, building, maintenance and exploitation of the project. The firm also handles partnership contracts and disputes.

Claude Grangé is one of France's leading experts in public construction law and works for a variety of municipalities. Jean-Yves Le Mazou at **Le Mazou** has a comparable profile.

In construction insurance, **Karila & Associés** is our first choice. Jean-Pierre Karila advised on the Crédit Lyonnais fire case and is expert on the liability of builders, property developers, architects, and research consultancies.

Real estate accounts for a significant part of **Lefèvre Pelletier & Associés**' practice. Construction and town planning are frequent matters for the firm.

Gide Loyrette Nouel is well known for high-level construction litigation cases. Jean-Jacques Raquin and Eric Martin-Impératori are experts in the negotiation of acquisition contracts and in the processes required to obtain all related administrative authorisation.

White & Case LLP is well established in the construction sector. Partner Christopher Seppala undertakes significant projects and is sometimes involved in financing, advisory and litigation work.

The activity of **Caston Cabouche Gabrielli Marquet**, **Neveu Sudaka & Associés**, and **Naba et Associés**, is very much linked to insurance; **Charles Sirat - Jean-Paul Gilli** more to town planning. **Michel Tirard** is well known for advising property developers on planning matters. **Foucaud Tchekhoff Pochet & Associés** is also recommended.

CONSTRUCTION

BOUSQUET

RAMBAUD MARTEL ✪

CLAUDE GRANGÉ
KARILA & ASSOCIÉS
LEFÈVRE PELLETIER & ASSOCIÉS

Caston Cabouche Gabrielli Marquet
Charles Sirat - Jean-Paul Gilli
Foucaud Tchekhoff Pochet & Associés
Gide Loyrette Nouel ✪
Le Mazou
Michel Tirard
Naba et Associés
Neveu Sudaka & Associés
Vatier & Associés ✪
White & Case LLP

Firms are listed A-Z in tiers which are ranked in order of priority
✪ Indicates firm displays contact details at the end of this chapter.

CORPORATE AND COMMERCIAL

As in previous years, it is important to point out that we have omitted **Bredin Prat** and **Darrois Villey Maillot Brochier** from this section on the basis that their activity, high-level though it is, is largely transactional M&A and does not cover the full range of corporate and commercial work. See the separate **Mergers and acquisitions** section, below.

International firm **Cleary Gottlieb Steen & Hamilton** continues to enjoy the enviable position of being a US firm regarded locally as a fully-fledged French firm equipped with polyvalent lawyers working on non-standard issues. Traditionally known for its banking clientele, the firm has expanded its commercial practice, as evidenced by its evermore frequent incursions into high-level takeover bids. Equally, the firm has taken its place among the best firms in other practice areas, such as capital markets and privatisation, tax and European law and is getting more and more visible in litigation and arbitration.

Clifford Chance's origins in Paris are in finance and property. The practice is now vast: the main areas of activity remain financing (of acquisitions, projects and property), but other strengths include M&A, EU and competition, environmental law, tax, public law, litigation and arbitration. Over the last few years, the firm has been consistently growing, for example at a rate of 15.5% between 2002 and 2003 (April).

After several years of impressive growth and multiple lateral hires, **Freshfields Bruckhaus Deringer** is consolidating its structure and activity while on the verge of moving into bigger offices. Although the firm continues to be recognised for its banking, finance and capital markets work, its activities in cross-border M&A also rank highly. The firm's arbitration practice is recognised worldwide. Additional strengths include property, tax and EU law.

Gide Loyrette Nouel remains the benchmark French firm. With nearly 470 lawyers worldwide, the firm boasts some of the most renowned teams in the Paris market: M&A, banking and finance, capital markets, commercial property, public law, IP and litigation to mention a few. With 16 offices abroad, **Gide Loyrette Nouel** is also one of the few French firms with an international presence. In 2003, the firm opened an office in London with a 30-lawyer team from **Sidley Austin Brown & Wood LLP**.

Initially well known in Paris for corporate and finance law, **Linklaters** has increased its scope and become a full-service firm. This expansion is especially pronounced in the areas of tax, EU law, property, IP and M&A, including stock exchange issues and private equity. The historically well-developed capital markets practice is now

CORPORATE AND COMMERCIAL

CLEARY GOTTLIEB STEEN & HAMILTON ✪
CLIFFORD CHANCE
FRESHFIELDS BRUCKHAUS DERINGER ✪
GIDE LOYRETTE NOUEL ✪
LINKLATERS ✪
RAMBAUD MARTEL ✪

ALLEN & OVERY ✪
CMS BUREAU FRANCIS LEFEBVRE ✪
DE PARDIEU BROCAS MAFFEI & LEYGONIE ✪
JEANTETASSOCIÉS ✪
JONES DAY ✪
LATHAM & WATKINS ✪
LOVELLS ✪
MOQUET BORDE & ASSOCIÉS ✪
SALANS
SHEARMAN & STERLING LLP
VEIL JOURDE LA GARANDERIE ✪
WHITE & CASE LLP
WILLKIE FARR & GALLAGHER LLP ✪

Ashurst ✪
August & Debouzy ✪
Baker & McKenzie ✪
Denton Wilde Sapte ✪
Herbert Smith ✪
Norton Rose
Slaughter and May ✪
Simmons & Simmons ✪
Sullivan & Cromwell LLP
UGGC & Associés ✪

Bignon Lebray & Associés
Bird & Bird ✪
Brandford-Griffith Baverez Pasturel ✪
Caubet Chouchana Meyer
Coudert Frères ✪
DS Avocats
EY Law ✪
Fidal
Franklin ✪
Ginestié Paley-Vincent & Associés ✪
Granrut
Hughes Hubbard & Reed ✪
Kahn & Associés ✪
Lafarge Fléchеux Campana Le Blevennec
Landwell & Associés / Partners
Lefèvre Pelletier & Associés
NomoS ✪
SJ Berwin ✪
Skadden, Arps, Slate, Meagher & Flom LLP
Sokolow Dunaud Carreras
Vatier & Associés ✪
Weil, Gotshal & Manges ✪

continued

complemented by top banking and finance expertise, including project finance. In 2003, the firm added a public law capacity to its services.

Rambaud Martel is considered by some as the best possible combination of a high-level litigation practice and a top, high-quality advisory practice. The presence of the firm in the large stock exchange battles of the last few years is significant, but should not detract from similar expertise in EU law, labour, public and construction law, and insolvency. The firm regularly works with foreign practices including **Travers Smith Braithwaite** and **Macfarlanes**.

Allen & Overy hosts some 100 lawyers in Paris and has been expanding very quickly over recent years. The M&A, banking and finance and capital markets teams remain the pillars of the practice, but with a growing tax, competition, administrative and labour expertise. Also, **Allen & Overy** set up a first-tier intellectual property department in 2003. The firm boasts a highly international client base, acting in particular for a large number of major banks.

CMS Bureau Francis Lefebvre's activity is solid, supported by a wide client base. Belonging to the *CMS* network has strengthened the firm's international presence and its transactional practice. The firm remains the reference firm for tax in France. That said, **CMS Bureau Francis Lefebvre** now achieves half of its turnover from its other advisory activities with a strong employment law team and abilities in real estate and corporate/M&A (for mid-cap companies). The firm is also present in Lyon and Strasbourg.

Still considered one of the jewels in the banking and finance sector, **De Pardieu Brocas Maffei & Leygonie** is a multi-service firm, complementing its traditional activities in banking and finance with M&A, commercial property, insolvency, telecoms, litigation, insurance, labour and EU law expertise. Major transactions often combine corporate and finance work and the firm continues to grow at a moderate but regular pace, with a developing tax practice.

JeantetAssociés has decided to concentrate on practice areas with high added value and, after reducing its size considerably a few years ago and increasing its profitability at the same time, the firm is now growing again slowly in these areas, with three new partners in 2003 in corporate and banking. **JeantetAssociés** practises in areas related to M&A and litigation and is considering developments in public and labour law. The firm is determined to carry on as an independent player.

Jones Day's main practice areas in Paris include M&A, asset finance, acquisition finance and property. The firm's international arbitration and tax activities are also showing strong development, as well as the finance and IT practices. In 2003, EU and real estate departments have been reinforced with the arrival of two new partners. A commercial litigation department was also created.

Latham & Watkins is now present in Paris after taking over the local office of **Stibbe** in 2001. The merger appears to have been a success with no partner departures. **Latham & Watkins** is equipped with a well-established finance and capital markets practice (with one lateral hire in 2003). The firm has also developed strengths in M&A, LBOs, tax, EU law, labour law and IT.

Since the merger in 2001 with *Siméon & Associés*, **Lovells** is *de facto* a full-service firm, with now 23 partners working in eight practice groups. Development is centred on corporate activities (M&A, joint ventures, private equity), banking, finance and capital markets, but the firm is also active in IP/IT, competition and litigation with a desire to grow further in tax, restructurings and labour law.

In Paris, **Moquet Borde & Associés** is particularly active in M&A, litigation and related activities such as stock exchange law, corporate governance, competition and tax. New arrivals strengthened the tax, white-collar crime, litigation and M&A teams last year. At the same time, **Moquet Borde & Associés** has offices in Lyon, Brussels, and an Eastern European practice with a presence in Budapest and Tallinn.

Salans (formerly *Salans Hertzfeld & Heilbronn*) is well known for its Central and Eastern European practice but the firm is also present in London and in the US. The firm took over some 60 lawyers from *Altheimer & Gray* in September 2003 in London, New York, Prague, Bratislava, Bucharest, Istanbul and Shanghai. **Salans** now totals 450 lawyers with about 130 partners worldwide. A full-service firm, **Salans** is particularly prominent in pharma-pceuticals, luxury goods, aerospace, sport and venture capital. The firm's main areas of expertise are M&A, IT, labour law, arbitration and litigation (often with an East/West element).

Shearman & Sterling LLP has built its practice in Paris around international arbitration and equity capital markets expertise. The arbitration practice has expanded considerably into litigation, often with an international dimension, and the firm's knowledge of the stock markets complements a good practice in the financial markets and in M&A. The firm has recently set up a promising EU and competition team. The client base is mainly industrial and includes large international organisations.

Veil Jourde La Garanderie has two main areas of activity. In M&A, the firm is involved in large deals, such as public offerings, privatisations, LBOs and restructurings. Its reputation is equally well established in litigation, including criminal and commercial proceedings.

At **White & Case LLP**, the finance practice is large, covering acquisitions and all types of structured finance. The M&A practice, an all-round practice with a strong involvement in LBOs, is also recommended, as are the arbitration, litigation, real estate and construction teams.

US-based **Willkie Farr & Gallagher LLP** is renowned for M&A, being a leader in LBOs in Paris. The firm also enjoys a good reputation in tax, IT

CORPORATE AND COMMERCIAL (continued)

ASA Avocats Associés
Adamas ✪
Ader Amigues & Jolibois
Alerion ✪
Alexen Avocats ✪
Ayache Salama & Associés ✪
B.D.F.T.
BMH Avocats - Breitenstein Meillassoux Hauser Roth ✪
Barsi Doumith & Associés
Berlioz & Co
Bernard Hertz Béjot
Bertagna - Berrymans
Bousquet
Cahen & Associés
Carbonnier Lamaze Rasle & Associés
Chaintrier & Associés
Cornet Vincent Ségurel
Cotty Vivant Marchisio & Lauzeral ✪
Courtois Lebel
Curtis, Mallet-Prevost, Colt & Mosle ✪
De Gaulle Fleurance & Associés ✪
Dechert
Deloitte & Touche Juridique et Fiscal ✪
Delsol & Associés
Deprez Dian Guignot ✪
Dubarry Le Douarin Veil ✪
Eversheds-Frere Cholmeley
Falque & Associés
Farthouat Asselineau & Associés
Foucaud Tchekhoff Pochet & Associés
Gaillot, Bouchony & Associés
Hammonds Hausmann
Illouz Simonet Garcia
Klein Goddard Associés
Kramer Levin Naftalis & Frankel LLP
LMT Avocats
Lamy Lexel Avocats Associés ✪
Lamy Ribeyre & Associés ✪
Latournerie Wolfrom & Associés ✪
LeBoeuf, Lamb, Greene & Macrae L. L. P.
Lipworth, Cabinet ✪
Lussan Brouillaud
Magellan
Moisand Boutin & Associés
Neveu Sudaka & Associés
Ngo Miguérès & Associés
Normand Sarda & Associés
P.D.G.B.
Racine
Ratheaux ✪
Reinhart Marville Torre
Soulier
Thieffry & Associés
Vaisse & Associés
Vovan & Associés
Winston & Strawn

Firms are listed A-Z in tiers which are ranked in order of priority
✪ *Indicates firm displays contact details at the end of this chapter.*

and finance. Lately, the firm was strengthened by the arrival of an insolvency team.

Ashurst is known particularly for its M&A, LBO and acquisition finance expertise. The client base is mainly made up of banks and investment funds from around the globe. After having developed the tax and property practices, the firm is now developing into EU law and litigation/arbitration in order to offer an integrated practice across Europe.

August & Debouzy is a young, full-service firm founded in 1995 and comprising 80 lawyers. The firm's main practices include M&A, privatisation, administrative and economic law, employment, IT, IP and real estate. Clients include France Télécom, Vivendi, Philip Morris, Nexity, and Microsoft.

Baker & McKenzie's Paris office focuses on company law and M&A, particularly in the pharmaceutical and hi-tech sectors, but the firm also handles tax, IP/IT, capital markets, EU and competition, labour and litigation. The team expanded last year with the arrival of one tax partner and ten associates from *Archibald*, and more recently with two new partners specialising in competition and distribution.

Denton Wilde Sapte, the new name for *Denton Salès Vincent & Thomas* in France since January 2004, was born from teams from former firms *Salès Vincent & Associés* and *Thomas & Associés* joining with the English firm. Activity revolves around four areas: TMT; energy and infrastructure; property; financial institutions and insurance. The firm is active in M&A and joint ventures (notably in the venture capital sector), litigation, public law, tax and projects.

Herbert Smith is now well established in Paris after four years of considerable growth, and is consolidating in its core business: corporate work, finance, projects/energy, litigation/arbitration, the latter two being areas where the firm is particularly strong. The firm also enjoys an international alliance with **Stibbe** and **Gleiss Lutz**.

Norton Rose's reputation in EU and competition law as well as in finance work continues to rank it highly, particularly in shipping and aviation finance, projects and acquisition finance. Two important events for **Norton Rose** this year: the departure of the litigation/arbitration team, well known for their insurance capacity, to create an independent niche firm, and the arrival of five corporate partners from **Sokolow Dunaud Carreras** with experience in M&A, private equity and arbitration.

Although around half of **Slaughter and May**'s activity is in M&A and joint ventures, the firm nonetheless offers a full service. Unlike its English colleagues in Paris, the firm has opted for moderate growth, and now fields around 40 lawyers. **Slaughter and May** is also involved in tax, finance (including project finance) and litigation and works closely with leading local boutique **Bredin Prat**.

Simmons & Simmons is making a place for itself among Paris's multi-service firms and grew considerably in 2003 (+38% compared to 2002). The firm has developed a complete service, led by banking, finance (acquisition, asset and projects), company, commercial law and M&A. Its IP, capital markets, contentious and arbitration capabilities are also growing due to several lateral hires.

Sullivan & Cromwell LLP's practice centres on international securities offerings by French issuers, privatisation and M&A. The firm is also recognised for its project finance and tax expertise.

UGGC & Associés, with around 70 lawyers, is a commercial all-rounder, as active in M&A as it is in public law and insolvency.

Bignon Lebray & Associés is a general commercial firm, offering both advisory and contentious capability. It is the result of the splitting up of *Bignon, Lebray, Delsol & Associés* in June 2003 to form **Bignon Lebray & Associés** and **Delsol & Associés** in Paris and Lyon, and **Alerion** in Paris. **Bignon Lebray & Associés** is a founder member of *Meritas* and has offices in Madrid, Lyon, Lille and Aix-en-Provence, thus covering France from north to south. The firm's range of services includes company law, M&A, banking and finance, tax, labour, property, public and IP/media law.

Bird & Bird offers a service with a specialisation in the media, communications and information technology sectors, as well as an expertise in all aspects of business law: EU and competition law, IP, life sciences, tax, labour law, litigation, corporate and private equity.

With around 25 lawyers, **Brandford-Griffith Baverez Pasturel** mainly deals with M&A, litigation (including stock market cases), capital markets and public law. The firm recently added a tax capacity to its activity with the arrival of a new partner.

Mid-sized, **Caubet Chouchana Meyer** is active in five well-defined areas on an international level: M&A; property, notably advising foreign investment fund clients; litigation/arbitration; tax; and labour.

Coudert Frères retains an international clientele. The Paris practice covers practically the whole palette of commercial work, from litigation and arbitration to M&A, also being active in IT, capital markets, EU and competition, labour and tax. An M&A team arrived in 2003, while another one was leaving.

With about 80 lawyers, **DS Avocats** is a full-service firm known particularly for its EU and competition practice as well as business administrative law. Moreover, the firm is one of the few French firms with offices in Asia (China, South Korea and Vietnam), as well as in Brussels and Barcelona.

EY Law is the new entity formed after the two legal arms of the international MDPs merged in Paris at the end of 2002. Despite losses affecting the tax and the corporate practices, the new firm boasts 750 fee-earners, 500 of them in Paris. The core business revolves around corporate tax, labour law, human capital and corporate/M&A, but the firm is also present in indirect tax, IP/IT and litigation/arbitration.

National firm **Fidal** is best known for its tax expertise and for being the largest firm in the country. However, the Paris office is also extensively involved in labour law, company and commercial issues and competition, for a clientele of small and medium-sized companies and blue-chips. Additionally the firm offers niche practices such as health, tourism and sports law.

Franklin has expertise in M&A, projects, administrative law, litigation and IT. The 30-strong firm is also setting up tax and employment teams.

Ginestié Paley-Vincent & Associés' main focus is M&A, with specialisms in LBOs and risk capital. Other services offered include international tax and labour law. Its membership of the *DLA Group* has reinforced the firm's European presence.

Granrut is comprised of 20 lawyers and specialises in corporate, media, banking, environment and insurance law, mainly with a contentious angle (including arbitration and white-collar crime).

Hughes Hubbard & Reed's most visible practice area is international arbitration (with the arrival of a new partner). However, the firm remains active in M&A, IT, commercial property, pharmaceuticals law and labour law.

Kahn & Associés' practice is entirely dedicated to new technology and e-commerce. Clients include international IT companies with interests in France, investment funds and traditional French blue-chips embarking on e-commerce and start-up projects.

Lafarge Flécheux Campana Le Blevennec now has some 75 lawyers. The firm's main activities are labour, public, commercial, banking, environmental law, tax and property. The contentious dimension of the firm is worth pointing out.

Landwell & Associés/Partners now has about 650 lawyers across France, with the arrival of several lawyers from *Archibald* in 2002 and 2003. At the same time, 30 lawyers from the technologies/media department were leaving the firm to set up the Paris office of **Taylor Wessing**. Like the other Big Four firms, a good proportion of its work lies in corporate tax, but labour law, private tax and all other types of advisory work are also handled, and are growing more quickly than the tax activities.

Lefèvre Pelletier & Associés stands out for its expertise in commercial property, but is also diversifying into other areas of commercial practice. Notably, the firm is active in M&A, labour, tax, finance and insurance.

NomoS has more than 50 lawyers and is developing a complete range of services, with a focus on media/communications and IT/IP, private equity, consumer goods, distribution, food and health industries.

The Paris office of **SJ Berwin** opened in 2001 and has grown to a practice of more than 30 lawyers. A leading private equity firm in Paris, **SJ Berwin** now has expertise in creation of funds, LBOs and M&A, tax, EU and competition.

With 25 lawyers in Paris, **Skadden, Arps, Slate, Meagher & Flom LLP** is known for its M&A and corporate finance work. The firm particularly stands out in cross-border deals and investments abroad.

Sokolow Dunaud Carreras is a mid-sized firm. Its contentious practice is noted, as well as its company law and M&A work. Media and telecoms also account for a significant part of the firm's business and it benefits form an office in New York. Five corporate partners have left the firm to join **Norton Rose**.

With a litigation background, **Vatier & Associés** is active in arbitration, labour law, public and health law, and white-collar crime. The firm is growing in property and corporate.

Weil, Gotshal & Manges merged with *Serra, Leavy & Cazals* in January 2003. The structure, with about 30 lawyers, is active in corporate, LBO, tax and litigation and is growing quickly.

DISPUTE RESOLUTION: COMMERCIAL LITIGATION

In addition to its acknowledged expertise in stock exchange and European disputes, **Bredin Prat** also handles general commercial litigation. Issues covered include, merger or takeover-related litigation, liability guarantees, litigation between shareholders, or other types of commercial litigation such as distribution and price adjustment among other disputes.

Gide Loyrette Nouel's contentious capability is vast and each department undertakes litigation. In addition, eight partners are specifically in charge of litigation and are specialists in all kinds of disputes organised into four main areas: labour, business, crime and distribution.

At **Rambaud Martel**, every avocat has a litigation background and in fact litigation feeds the other practices within the firm. The contentious practice is broad, covering public, social and commercial law as well as construction, environmental and insolvency issues.

Darrois Villey Maillot Brochier handles sophisticated cases, often linked with M&A deals, shareholders and white-collar crime.

De Pardieu Brocas Maffei & Leygonie's contentious practice is traditionally focused on commercial, banking, finance and insurance law, although it also handles property disputes, insolvency, and white-collar crime.

Freshfields Bruckhaus Deringer's main activities in litigation are banking law, collective issues and liability guarantees, although the litigation team also covers a broader range of commercial litigation.

DISPUTE RESOLUTION: COMMERCIAL LITIGATION

BREDIN PRAT
GIDE LOYRETTE NOUEL
RAMBAUD MARTEL

DARROIS VILLEY MAILLOT BROCHIER
DE PARDIEU BROCAS MAFFEI & LEYGONIE
FRESHFIELDS BRUCKHAUS DERINGER
JEANTETASSOCIÉS
MOQUET BORDE & ASSOCIÉS

Cleary Gottlieb Steen & Hamilton
Clifford Chance
Granrut
Herbert Smith
Lafarge Flécheux Campana Le Blevennec
Salans
Vatier & Associés
Veil Jourde La Garanderie
White & Case LLP

Bouckaert Ormen Passemard Sportes
Coudert Frères
Latham & Watkins
Linklaters
Lovells
Shearman & Sterling LLP
Soulez Larivière et Associés
UGGC & Associés
Willkie Farr & Gallagher LLP

continued

Around 50% of **JeantetAssociés**' turnover springs from contentious work. Most of the partners handle litigation as it arises within their own area of expertise. **JeantetAssociés** is traditionally a strong litigation French firm.

Moquet Borde & Associés' contentious practice encompasses commercial litigation, banking and financial matters and insolvency. The team has been strengthened by the recent arrival of Stephen Montravers from **Coudert Frères**.

Cleary Gottlieb Steen & Hamilton's Jean-Marcel Cheyron and Jean-Yves Garaud handle litigation relating to product liability or post-M&A and restructuring cases, very often in an international context.

Clifford Chance's 22-lawyer team handles general commercial litigation, corporate, M&A and stock market litigation, one of the partners having a focus on the pharmaceuticals and luxury goods sectors.

Granrut's litigation practice is broad. In addition to criminal matters, the firm is also active in press law, media, public law and insolvency.

Herbert Smith undertakes a wide range of commercial litigation, a traditional strength of the firm globally. Competition, transport (maritime and haulage) and insurance (industrial and product liability) are the firm's strengths, with a growing banking and financial practice.

COMMERCIAL LITIGATION (continued)

- Ader Amigues & Jolibois
- Ashurst ✪
- August & Debouzy ✪
- Baker & McKenzie ✪
- Barbé Carpentier Thibault Groener & Associés ✪
- Barsi Doumith & Associés
- Berlioz & Co
- Bignon Lebray & Associés
- CMS Bureau Francis Lefebvre ✪
- Caubet Chouchana Meyer
- Deloitte & Touche Juridique et Fiscal ✪
- Denton Wilde Sapte ✪
- Dubarry Le Douarin Veil ✪
- EY Law ✪
- Fidal
- Franklin ✪
- Hauteclocque Larroumet
- Hughes Hubbard & Reed ✪
- Jones Day ✪
- Klein Goddard Associés
- Kramer Levin Naftalis & Frankel LLP
- LeBoeuf, Lamb, Greene & Macrae L. L. P.
- Lussan Brouillaud
- NomoS ✪
- Norton Rose
- Savin Martinet Associés ✪
- Simmons & Simmons ✪
- Slaughter and May ✪
- Sokolow Dunaud Carreras
- Thieffry & Associés
- Vaisse & Associés
- Weil, Gotshal & Manges ✪

Firms are listed A-Z in tiers which are ranked in order of priority
✪ Indicates firm displays contact details at the end of this chapter

Around 50% of **Lafarge Fléchеux Campana Le Blevennec**'s work is contentious, while **Salans**' litigation team numbers eight partners and covers the whole spectrum of disputes with an emphasis on international and cross-border matters.

Vatier & Associés is the other half of the former *Granrut Vatier Baudelot & Associés*. Particularly noteworthy is work relating to public law, insolvency and white-collar crime.

Veil Jourde La Garanderie's reputation rests on three fields: criminal financial matters and arbitration; insolvency; financial, stock market and commercial litigation.

While **White & Case LLP**'s litigation team is able to advise on all aspects of commercial litigation, it has a number of areas of particular expertise that include banking litigation, white-collar crime and administrative litigation.

Bouckaert Ormen Passemard Sportes is a split from **Norton Rose**. The firm handles commercial and financial litigation and half of the work is related to the insurance and reinsurance industries (Christian Bouckaert is very well known).

Coudert Frères is active in post-acquisition litigation, bank guarantees litigation, criminal and civil liability of company auditors and managers, trade regulation, advertising law, unfair competition, distribution agreements and oil productions sharing contracts.

Latham & Watkins fields a seven-lawyer litigation team that is mainly active in cross-border cases, very often for US clients. Commercial litigation, acquisition disputes and distribution issues are handled.

Numerous lawyers at **Linklaters** handle their own disputes. However, seven *avocats* are entirely dedicated to litigation, with strong skills in post-acquisition litigation. They also deal with commercial and distribution litigation, banking liability, white-collar crime, insolvency and real estate cases.

Two partners and ten associates at **Lovells** handle product liability and financial litigation among other issues.

Shearman & Sterling LLP's team is involved in post-arbitral matters. Some of the activity emanates from the M&A and corporate finance departments but this diverse international practice also handles related construction and environmental disputes.

At **Soulez Larivière et Associés**, Daniel Soulez Larivière is well known, while **UGGC & Associés**' litigation team numbers 13 lawyers. Areas of activity include transport and medical liability.

Five lawyers are dedicated to litigation at **Willkie Farr & Gallagher LLP**. The firm handles cases relating to administrative law, town planning and property, but also undertakes litigation in IP, banking and telecoms.

DISPUTE RESOLUTION: INTERNATIONAL ARBITRATION

The four-partner team at **Freshfields Bruckhaus Deringer** enjoys an enviable reputation and Jan Paulsson deserves special mention as a leading arbitrator. Of the other three partners, Eric Schwartz has solid experience in the construction sector and is currently handling two large arbitrations in the telecoms industry. Peter Turner and Nigel Blackaby's specialities are in investor/state cases, in South America for the latter. Typically, the firm has between 60 and 100 cases in progress.

Shearman & Sterling LLP's Paris team, led by Emmanuel Gaillard, comprises some 30 lawyers and four other partners (Peter Griffin, Philippe Pinsolle, Todd Wetmore and Fernando Mantilla-Serrano, a South America specialist arriving from **Garrigues** in Madrid). Current cases are in the construction and engineering, oil and gas, M&A and investment sectors. At present, the Paris office is handling around 40 cases.

At **Gide Loyrette Nouel**, Pierre Raoul-Duval heads up the arbitration practice. Philippe Nouel's status on the international arbitration scene in Paris also merits special mention, as well as Christian Camboulive and Carole Malinvaud's work. The arbitration cases handled by the team during 2003 (around 40) have concerned areas such as investments, joint venture contracts, construction projects, energy, mining, defence, M&A and IP matters, acting for governments, state-owned entities and corporations.

White & Case LLP also possesses an excellent reputation. Christopher Seppala and Stephen Bond are frequently mentioned; the latter is a former Secretary General of the ICC International Court of Arbitration. The areas in which the firm practises are construction, project finance, international joint ventures and investment, oil and gas, telecoms, banking and insurance, as well as litigation on behalf of or against governments.

Bredin Prat handles financial and commercial arbitrations, and those relating to investment. Jean-Denis Bredin is renowned for his role as an

DISPUTE RESOLUTION: INTERNATIONAL ARBITRATION

- FRESHFIELDS BRUCKHAUS DERINGER ✪
- SHEARMAN & STERLING LLP

- GIDE LOYRETTE NOUEL ✪
- WHITE & CASE LLP

- BREDIN PRAT ✪
- CLIFFORD CHANCE
- DARROIS VILLEY MAILLOT BROCHIER ✪
- DELVOLVÉ ROUCHE *
- DERAINS & ASSOCIÉS *
- JONES DAY ✪
- SALANS
- SERGE LAZAREFF *

- B Moreau - Lawyers
- Cleary Gottlieb Steen & Hamilton ✪
- Coudert Frères ✪
- Herbert Smith ✪
- Hughes Hubbard & Reed ✪
- Rambaud Martel ✪

- Curtis, Mallet-Prevost, Colt & Mosle ✪
- Denton Wilde Sapte ✪
- EY Law ✪
- Eversheds-Frere Cholmeley
- JeantetAssociés ✪
- Klein Goddard Associés
- Latham & Watkins ✪
- Linklaters ✪
- Lovells ✪
- Michael Lee
- Norton Rose
- Paul-A. Gélinas *
- Philippe Leboulanger
- Shadbolt & Co
- Simmons & Simmons ✪

* Firms mainly active as an arbitrator

continued

INTERNATIONAL ARBITRATION (continued)

Ader Amigues & Jolibois
Ashurst ✪
Augendre Fourment
August & Debouzy ✪
Baker & McKenzie ✪
Berlioz & Co
Bernards
Bertagna - Berrymans
Bouckaert Ormen Passemard Sportes
Bouloy Grellet & Godin
Brandford-Griffith Baverez Pasturel ✪
Castaldi Mourre Sprague
Caubet Chouchana Meyer
Holman Fenwick & Willan ✪
Lamy Ribeyre & Associés ✪
Moquet Borde & Associés ✪
Sokolow Dunaud Carreras
Thieffry & Associés
UGGC & Associés ✪

** Firms mainly active as an arbitrator*
Firms are listed A-Z in tiers which are ranked in order of priority
✪ Indicates firm displays contact details at the end of this chapter.

arbitrator. Christophe Delanoy, Robert Saint-Esteben and Tim Portwood also merit mention.

At **Clifford Chance** Jason Fry and Jean-Pierre Grandjean are the most active partners in this area with some ten lawyers working with them. Pierre Mayer has moved to **Clifford Chance** from **Coudert Frères**; he joins as a consultant.

At **Darrois Villey Maillot Brochier**, Matthieu de Boisseson has a first-class reputation in arbitration. He often acts as arbitrator for various international institutions and also advises multinational companies. Two young partners are also active, as counsels in matters relating to M&A.

Delvolvé Rouche handles a range of issues including finance, investment, joint ventures and construction. A large number of ICC arbitrations are undertaken by the firm, as are ad hoc proceedings. Jean-Louis Delvolvé acts mainly as an arbitrator.

Derains & Associés also has a good reputation; Yves Derains frequently appears before various international arbitration courts. The firm works with **Weil, Gotshal & Manges LLP** in the US and is known for its construction, energy, natural resources, international commerce and international finance expertise.

At **Jones Day**, German lawyer Michael Bühler and John Crawford head up the arbitration practice. Work includes cases in the fields of engineering, construction, oil and gas, trade, know-how transfer, joint ventures and shareholder agreements.

The three partners at **Salans** who regularly advise on arbitration matters are Bruno Leurent (particularly in relation to the Middle East), Carl Salans (who acts as an arbitrator), and Jeffrey Hertzfeld (who is involved in East-West arbitration, often in relation to investment, particularly concerning oil, in the republics of the former Soviet Union).

Serge Lazareff is considered one of the best arbitrators in France. He arbitrates in conflicts in various sectors, among them construction, international project finance and distribution contracts.

B Moreau - Lawyers' solid reputation is based largely on the expertise of Bertrand Moreau. He is president of the Comité Français de l'Arbitrage (CFA). He and his team advise on both domestic and international arbitrations.

At **Cleary Gottlieb Steen & Hamilton**, Jean-Yves Garaud and Jean-Marcel Cheyron handle an increasing volume of arbitration work.

At **Coudert Frères**, the international arbitration practice is led by William Craig. The other partners are Michael Polkinghorne, Philip Dunham and Xavier Nyssen. The firm's main activities centre on a specialisation in construction, investments and energy.

Herbert Smith's arbitration practice in Paris is headed up by Charles Kaplan. The group acts in matters covering a wide range of industries, including energy and natural resources, international investment and large-scale construction and engineering projects. Clients include governments, state-owned entities and multinational companies.

Hughes Hubbard & Reed's arbitration team operates under the leadership of Axel Baum (counsel) and José Rosell (financial and Latin America arbitrations), following the merger with *Rosell & Associés*. The firm undertakes arbitration work relating to multinational deals on behalf of manufacturers or governments in cases of investment, joint ventures, competition, environment, licences, etc.

Rambaud Martel's disputes strength extends to ADR and arbitration, notably in the construction sector. Jean-Pierre Martel acts as an arbitrator as well as counsel in the fields of infrastructure, energy, projects and company law (financial conflicts), with also the interventions of Christophe Lapp and Frédéric Torron in construction.

DISPUTE RESOLUTION: STOCK MARKET LITIGATION

Respected names at **Bredin Prat** include Paris legend Jean-François Prat who heads the team, Didier Martin and Sylvie Morabia.

Meanwhile, **Darrois Villey Maillot Brochier** boasts the considerable skills of Jean-Michel Darrois who is supported by Philippe Villey, Emmanuel Brochier, Hervé Pisani and Marie-Noëlle Dompé.

Rambaud Martel name partner Jean-Pierre Martel is outstanding, and Mathieu Rambaud is also recommended.

Other recommended firms and individuals include: **Brandford-Griffith Baverez Pasturel** (Henri-Brandford Griffith and Diane Pasturel); **Cleary Gottlieb Steen & Hamilton** (Pierre-Yves Chabert); **Clifford Chance** (Dominique Bompoint and Frédéric Peltier); **Freshfields Bruckhaus Deringer** (Patrick Bonvarlet); **Gide Loyrette Nouel** (Youssef Djehane); **Linklaters** (Thierry Vassogne); **Moquet Borde & Associés** (Dominique Borde); **Simmons & Simmons** (Thierry Gontard); and **Veil Jourde La Garanderie** (Jean Veil).

DISPUTE RESOLUTION: STOCK MARKET LITIGATION

BREDIN PRAT ✪
DARROIS VILLEY MAILLOT BROCHIER ✪
RAMBAUD MARTEL ✪

Brandford-Griffith Baverez Pasturel ✪
Cleary Gottlieb Steen & Hamilton ✪
Clifford Chance
Freshfields Bruckhaus Deringer ✪
Gide Loyrette Nouel ✪
Linklaters ✪
Moquet Borde & Associés ✪
Simmons & Simmons ✪
Veil Jourde La Garanderie ✪

Firms are listed A-Z in tiers which are ranked in order of priority
✪ Indicates firm displays contact details at the end of this chapter

EU AND COMPETITION

Robert Saint-Esteben of **Bredin Prat** is a leading practitioner and Hugues Calvet is also very well known. In Brussels, Marc Pittie joined from **Allen & Overy** (Chantal Momège is at **Ashurst** in Paris). Recent highlights include cases such as Pechiney/Alcan (counsel to Pechiney); Terreal/Carlyle and Eurazeo (counsel to Saint-Gobain); the appeal by Schneider against the European Commission (counsel to Schneider); and the appeal by Wanadoo of a Commission's decision for abuse of dominant position (counsel to Wanadoo).

While **Cleary Gottlieb Steen & Hamilton** is characterised by a long-established practice in Brussels, growth in the firm's Paris M&A practice has aided the development of competition capability. The Paris team now numbers five lawyers, including two partners: Antoine Winckler who divides his time equally between Brussels and Paris, and François Brunet. Recent deals include advising Crédit Lyonnais in the merger with Crédit Agricole SA; Lagardère in connection with the disposal of Vivendi Universal Publishing; and France Télécom and Lafarge in state aid matters.

Clifford Chance is a major player in EU and competition law with Claude Lazarus and younger partner Michel Debroux. The nine-lawyer team advises on all aspects of EU and French merger control, anti-competitive practices, state aid, and competition matters, in close link with the 38 antitrust partners worldwide. **Clifford Chance**

EU AND COMPETITION

BREDIN PRAT ✪
CLEARY GOTTLIEB STEEN & HAMILTON ✪
CLIFFORD CHANCE
NORTON ROSE
VOGEL & VOGEL ✪

FRESHFIELDS BRUCKHAUS DERINGER ✪
GIDE LOYRETTE NOUEL ✪
LATHAM & WATKINS ✪
LINKLATERS ✪
RAMBAUD MARTEL ✪

Coutrelis & Associés
Darrois Villey Maillot Brochier ✪
De Pardieu Brocas Maffei & Leygonie ✪
JeantetAssociés ✪
Jones Day ✪
Moquet Borde & Associés ✪

Ashurst ✪
Baker & McKenzie ✪
Bird & Bird ✪
DS Avocats
Fourgoux & Associés
Shearman & Sterling LLP

Avens Lehman & Associés
CMS Bureau Francis Lefebvre ✪
Coudert Frères ✪
Lovells ✪
Meffre & Grall ✪
NomoS ✪
Salans
Willkie Farr & Gallagher LLP ✪

Allen & Overy ✪
August & Debouzy ✪
Deprez Dian Guignot ✪
EY Law ✪
Fidal
Funck-Brentano Gewelbe Brousseau
Herbert Smith ✪
Landwell & Associés / Partners
SJ Berwin ✪
Sokolow Dunaud Carreras
Thieffry & Associés
UGGC & Associés ✪

Firms are listed A-Z in tiers which are ranked in order of priority
✪ Indicates firm displays contact details at the end of this chapter.

advised Vivendi Universal in increasing its share participation in Groupe Cegetel, in order to counter Vodafone's unsolicited bid; Crédit Agricole SA on the competition law aspects of its takeover bid for Crédit Lyonnais; the LFP (Ligue de Football Professionnel) for the allotment of the television broadcasting rights of the French Premier League; and GE Medical Systems taking over a major player in the medical equipment manufacturing sector.

At **Norton Rose**, Jean-Patrice de la Laurencie has a strong reputation in EU and competition law, and Laure Givry has expertise in distribution and consumer law. **Norton Rose** now has a strong team based in London, Brussels and Paris. The firm represented Canal + before the Court of First instance on appeal against a decision of the European Commission (merger control); the consortium Origny-Naples in multi-jurisdictional merger filings for the acquisition of Béghin Say; and several French independent publishers in relation to the proposed acquisition of Vivendi Universal Publishing by Lagardère.

Vogel & Vogel is a specialist EU and competition boutique. Founded in 1990, the firm currently numbers 36 lawyers with further offices in Brussels and Frankfurt. Its practice is particularly well developed in the automobile, audiovisual and telecoms sectors. Recently, the firm advised TPS in an action for abuse of a dominant position before the Competition Council against Canal + for the television rights for French football league 1 game; different car manufacturers in the context of the new European motor vehicle regulation and Renault and DaimlerChrysler France in merger notifications arising out of the acquisition of several independent motor vehicle dealerships; and SAUR in an abuse of a collective dominant position in the water treatment sector.

At **Freshfields Bruckhaus Deringer**, the team, consisting of two partners (Jacques-Philippe Gunther and Jérôme Philippe), plus some 12 associates, is active in merger regulation. It also handles French and European competition aspects as well as monopolies issues in the media and telecoms sectors. The French office works in close co-operation with the other offices in Europe which field a total of 170 lawyers, including 37 partners. Recent highlights include representing the banks in the Alstom case; Wanadoo in an abuse of dominant position case; a group of French banks (G3) on the antitrust aspects of the Alstom State aid plan; Wanadoo in front of the Court of First Instance for appeal against the European Commission's decision on predation on broad-band Internet access in France; BaByliss in an action before the French supreme administrative court for annulment of the Minister of Economy's decision approving the SEB/Moulinex concentration; and Gaz de France in relation to the notification to the European Commission, under state aid rules, of the reform of the energy pension scheme.

The EU and competition department of **Gide Loyrette Nouel** in Paris comprises five partners including Xavier de Roux and distribution specialists Antoine Choffel and Joëlle Salzmann. All work with a European dimension is handled in conjunction with the Brussels office (Dominique Voillemot, Antoine Gosset-Grainville); altogether the team is made of 50 lawyers between Paris and Brussels. They advise on all aspects of competition law including merger control, cartels, abuse of dominant position, state aids, vertical restraints and also specialise in distribution law, consumer protection, tobacco law, product liability, advertising, and unfair competition disputes. **Gide Loyrette Nouel** was involved in a large number of merger filings in various industries acting as counsel to: Natexis Banques Populaires which concluded a bearing agreement with Lagardère on all the VUP assets; Atofina within the frame of the creation of a joint venture with Samsung; and Casino, NMPP, Sony in connection with antitrust issues.

The Paris office of **Latham & Watkins** boasts three partners and around ten other lawyers devoted to competition law. The firm opened an office in Brussels in February 2002, while in the US, it fields a further 15 antitrust lawyers dealing regularly with EU-related matters. Alain Georges has a good knowledge of financial matters (including payment systems), the hotel industry (Accor), and hi-tech (CapGemini, Oberthur Card Systems); Christophe Clarenc is a deregulation expert (telecoms, gas, electricity, post) and represents France Télécom in most of its competition disputes; Hugues Vallette-Viallard has national and international expertise in structuring distribution networks and litigation between industrials and distributors (Apple, Campbell, Whirlpool).

Olivier d'Ormesson at **Linklaters** is now the second partner based in Paris (with Anne Wachsmann) and seven associates. They handle the French and European aspects of merger regulation and have been involved in some important state aid cases. Last year, the firm was active in the Air France/KLM merger and advised the national airline in different strategic alliances; in the automotive sector, advising Peugeot in relation to its worldwide development strategy; in the beer sector, with several ongoing matters before the French competition authorities; and in the private equity sector, advising several funds (Axa Private Equity, Montagu Private Equity, PAI) in merger control filings. The Paris office further benefits form the combined EU practice in Brussels which now numbers some 100 lawyers, including 25 partners.

Rambaud Martel has a recognised practice in EU and competition law. Claudine Maître-Devallon, Olivier de Juvigny and six associates handle this work. The firm's reputation, traditionally linked to construction and public law, has widened to include other sectors, such as transport, banking, distribution, media and computers. Apart from merger control law, the firm is also involved in criminal competition law, and is increasingly active in state aid. In abuse of a dominant position the team acted for clients like Lafarge, Plastic Omnium, Toshiba, Renault VI, Vinci, and advised, in their merger control process, Gecina in relation to the merger with Simco; BNP PARIBAS in connection with the acquisition of a stake in Crédit Lyonnais and intervention before CECEI; and Edison on the demerger of Béghin Say. To finish with, the firm was active in state aids cases relating to EDF, Bull and Alstom.

Coutrelis & Associés is well known for its expertise in counselling, lobbying and litigation. Its most developed practices are French and European antitrust law, food and drug law, and customs law. The firm has thus far appeared in more than 60 cases before the European Court of Justice or the Court of First Instance in Luxembourg.

Top M&A firm **Darrois Villey Maillot Brochier** launched its competition practice in 2002 with the recruitment of Didier Théophile from **Deprez Dian Guignot**.

At **De Pardieu Brocas Maffei & Leygonie**, Jean Leygonie handles EU and competition issues with younger partner Emmanuel Schulte. The firm acts in merger regulation but also in general antitrust, advising companies in the industrial, telecoms and banking sectors. Litigation and state aid are also handled. The firm advised on competition issues arising out of the restructuring of Alstom (advising banks); SNPE in the search of partnerships in the framework of its restructuring; and Batipart in the acquisition of various real estate portfolios.

At **JeantetAssociés**, Henry Lesguillons and Loraine Donnedieu de Vabres are recommended. The former has particular skills in concessions and public markets EU law as well as WTO issues; the latter handles contentious work, economic crime law but also advises in consumer and distribution matters.

With the arrival of Eric Morgan de Rivery in January 2003, **Jones Day** emerged onto the competition scene in Paris. Morgan de Rivery is a well-known specialist in deregulation, with a focus on telecoms matters, as well as gas, electricity, transport and media. The Paris group now numbers six lawyers, with teams in Brussels and all over Europe; the concentration of expertise in Washington, DC is another asset. **Jones Day** represented BP before the French Antitrust Authority and the Paris Court of Appeal in relation to a price fixing agreement; and Philip Morris and Reynolds regarding constitutional issues concerning the respective domain of intervention of the EC and the Member States.

Moquet Borde & Associés' competition practice is managed principally by Pierre Kirch who divides his time between the Paris and Brussels offices. Together with Béatrice Honorat, the firm provides services in the area of competition law relating both to advice and litigation. The expertise of Béatrice Honorat is to handle matters more specifically relating to markets (distribution, consumer protection and issues of EU law).

Other recommended players include Chantal Momège (**Ashurst**); Alex Dowding, Mireille Dany and Régis Fabre (**Baker & McKenzie**); Olivier Fréget (**Bird & Bird**); Hervé Lehman (**Avens Lehman & Associés**); Bernard Geneste (**CMS Bureau Francis Lefebvre**); Dominique Brault (**Coudert Frères**); Claude Lucas de Leyssac (**DS Avocats**); **Fourgoux & Associés**; Pierre de Montalembert (**Lovells**); Jean-Marie Meffre and Jean-Christophe Grall (**Meffre & Grall**); Christophe Pecnard (**NomoS**); Mélanie Thill-Tayara (**Salans**); Jean-Marie Cot (**Shearman & Sterling LLP**); and Dominique Berlin (**Willkie Farr & Gallagher LLP**).

EMPLOYMENT

With 180 lawyers spread across 14 offices, **Barthélémy & Associés, member of ius laboris** is the only large firm specialising in employment law. Jacques Barthélémy (founder of the firm), Alain Sauret (chairman), and Pascal Lagoutte (director of the Paris office), are well-known, and so are Michel Morand (acting for health and social trade associations) and Bruno Serizay (a social security expert). The firm covers all aspects of labour law and is particularly well known for its work in collective negotiations, acting for 70 employers federations, among them the largest employers.

CMS Bureau Francis Lefebvre has three specialised teams, each comprising about 14 lawyers. Nicolas de Sevin, Laurent Marquet de Vasselot, Pierre-Jean Sinibaldi and Jean-Claude Anisten are well known partners. The areas covered are restructurings (they worked on the Eridiana Beghin-Say demerger), collective dismissal, collective negotiations and remuneration strategies. Contentious work is developing.

Flichy & Associés, founded by Hubert Flichy who has an excellent reputation, comprises some 27 lawyers including seven partners. Very much a niche practice, the firm acts only on high-level issues for industrial companies like Pechiney or Moulinex, banks, and numerous pension funds. Restructurings, social plans and collective contentious matters constitute the bulk of its work. Hubert Flichy is president of EELA (European Employment Lawyers Association).

In January 2004, employment law boutique *Bélier & Associés* merged with **Freshfields**, the firm thus becoming a major player on the Paris labour law scene. Gilles Bélier is a leading lawyer in labour law and he joins other partner Pascale Lagesse to form a 21-lawyer team active in all areas of labour law, from international industrial restructurings to pension plans and dispute resolution.

Originally from Lyon, **Fromont Briens & Associés**, a partner firm of **Lamy Ribeyre & Associés**, developed a comprehensive practice in Paris with Gilles Briens in 1995. The firm is particularly renowned in social security matters but also handles employment law and has a strong disputes practice, including white-collar crime cases.

At **Gide Loyrette Nouel**, Joël Grange heads the employment department, backed up by Professor Couturier. The team is particularly involved in restructurings and M&A, collective redundancy plans, transfers of undertakings and collective disputes, with a strong litigation practice. The firm's labour and employment practice traditionally has an international outlook and, with 32 lawyers, offers significant resources. Health and safety regulations, and social security issues are also dealt with.

EMPLOYMENT

BARTHÉLÉMY & ASSOCIÉS, MEMBER OF IUS LABORIS ✪

CMS BUREAU FRANCIS LEFEBVRE ✪
FLICHY & ASSOCIÉS ✪
FRESHFIELDS
FROMONT BRIENS & ASSOCIÉS
GIDE LOYRETTE NOUEL ✪

August & Debouzy ✪
Fidal
Rambaud Martel ✪

Coblence & Associés
De Pardieu Brocas Maffei & Leygonie ✪
EY Law ✪
JeantetAssociés ✪
Landwell & Associés / Partners
Latham & Watkins ✪
Lefèvre Pelletier & Associés
Lovells ✪
Proskauer Rose ✪
Salans
Touati Henderson Selarl
Veil Jourde La Garanderie ✪

Alexen Avocats ✪
Allen & Overy ✪
Baker & McKenzie ✪
Bignon Lebray & Associés
Cariddi Mee Rué/Hogan & Hartson LLP ✪
Caubet Chouchana Meyer
Clifford Chance
Cleary Gottlieb Steen & Hamilton ✪
Courtois Lebel
Deloitte & Touche Juridique et Fiscal ✪
Eversheds-Frere Cholmeley
Herbert Smith ✪
Hughes Hubbard & Reed ✪
Kahn & Associés ✪
Lafarge Fléchеux Campana Le Blevennec
Lamy Lexel Avocats Associés ✪
Magellan
Moquet Borde & Associés ✪
NomoS ✪
Norton Rose
Simmons & Simmons ✪
Sokolow Dunaud Carreras
Sutra et Associés
Tuffal Nerson
UGGC & Associés ✪
VoxLaw
White & Case LLP

Firms are listed A-Z in tiers which are ranked in order of priority
✪ Indicates firm displays contact details at the end of this chapter.

August & Debouzy has a team of 21 lawyers dedicated to employment law, with Emmanuelle Barbara and Philippe Durand the partners in charge. The firm mostly handles general work, collective relations and procedures, M&A and restructurings, financial issues, pensions and benefits. Contentious work is also carried out. Clients are French and Anglo-Saxon and include Vivendi, Rhodia, Valeo, Canal + and Deutsche Bank.

At **Fidal**, Sylvain Niel is well known, while at **Rambaud Martel**, three partners handle labour issues full-time, together with a few others partially involved in labour matters. Anne le Bault de la Morinière heads the broad-based department which comprises of 15 associates and is notably strong in collective negotiations.

Chantal Giraud Van Gaver at **Coblence & Associés** is also recommended, and François Vergne is the partner in charge of the labour law department at **De Pardieu Brocas Maffei & Leygonie**. The firm advises clients on both individual and collective aspects of industrial reorganisations, social security and litigation closely connected with labour disputes (including in connection with M&A).

EY Law has a 90-lawyer team and covers the whole range of labour law with Alain Ménard and Roselyne Sands, the latter specialising in international issues.

At **JeantetAssociés**, Jean Néret is well known. The firm's speciality is contentious matters, accidents at work, major industrial incidents, working time and litigation against the URSSAF.

With a team of some 50 lawyers, **Landwell & Associés / Partners** covers all aspects of labour law, with William Phillips and Claudia Jonath the main partners (Jean-Marc Sainsard left for **Salans**). The firm is mostly involved in restructurings, social plans, relocation and stock option plans.

At **Latham & Watkins**, Agnès Cloarec, Marie-France Miserey-Saulgrain and a team of about 14 lawyers devote a large part of their time to labour aspects of company restructurings and outsourcings, with a particular focus on the banking, food, advertising, hotel and catering sectors. Half of the work is contentious.

Lefèvre Pelletier & Associés is active in labour law with a team of five associates, headed by Françoise Pelletier and Marie-Daphné Fishelson.

At **Lovells**, two partners focus on labour law. Among them, Christian Belloin has developed an expertise in complex social plans.

Yasmine Tarasewicz and five associates make up the labour team at US firm **Proskauer Rose**. Tarasewicz is notable for her expertise in labour law for US companies with operations in France.

Salans has an important labour and employment department, comprising 18 lawyers. Department heads, Jean-Louis Magnier and new partner Jean-Marc Sainsard (from **Landwell & Associés/Partners**) focus on advice in restructuring, collective negotiations and remuneration policies, contentious work, retirement and pension plans. Pascal Bathmanabane and Sophie Uettwiller left for **UGGC & Associés**. Amongst the clients are several large US companies, a major French bank, foreign banks present in France, hotel chains, pharmaceutical laboratories and several aviation and maritime companies.

The seven-fee-earner team at **Touati Henderson Selarl** is headed by partners Jean-Jacques Touati and Ming Henderson-Vu Thi. The practice advises on the full range of employment issues, from redundancy and employee benefits, to transfer of undertaking and works councils.

Finally, the names of Dominique de la Garanderie as well as Marie-Alice Jourde at **Veil Jourde La Garanderie** deserve mention for their expertise in labour law.

EMPLOYMENT: EMPLOYEES

Bouaziz Benamara
Florence Lyon-Caen
Grumbach & Associés
Henry Albouy Dudeffant
Lachaud Lepany Associés
Legrand & Associés
Wizenberg Cohen-Seat Grinsnir Peru

Firms are listed alphabetically

EMPLOYMENT: EMPLOYEES

The seven firms listed are active on behalf of employees. They act for trade unions and work councils, from giving legal advice including crisis management to litigation. The firms frequently work together in cases of collective redundancies. Some of the lawyers act for several unions.

ENVIRONMENT

BOIVIN & ASSOCIÉS
HUGLO LEPAGE & ASSOCIÉS CONSEIL ✪

Adamas ✪
Clifford Chance
Gide Loyrette Nouel ✪
Pichavent Chétrit
Savin Martinet Associés ✪
UGGC & Associés ✪
Winston & Strawn

Baker & McKenzie ✪
Brizay London
De Pardieu Brocas Maffei & Leygonie ✪
Granrut
Rambaud Martel ✪
Shearman & Sterling LLP
Soulez Larivière et Associés
Thieffry & Associés

Firms are listed A-Z in tiers which are ranked in order of priority
✪ Indicates firm displays contact details at the end of this chapter.

ENVIRONMENT

Environmental law makes up 50% of the work for **Boivin & Associés**' Jean-Pierre Boivin and his team of ten lawyers. The other partner is Manuel Pennaforte. The firm is increasingly active in projects in the oil, chemicals, water, waste, nuclear power, and iron and steel sectors, and also advises companies in the pharmaceuticals industry. Recent cases include: advising TotalFinaElf regarding the wreck of the *Erika*; AZF on the explosion of its chemical plant in Toulouse; Kodak in relation to pollution at a former site in Vincennes; BP France in important soil pollution matters; and well known waste companies regarding dioxin pollution cases.

Huglo Lepage & Associés Conseil's roots are in administrative litigation and the firm has now developed a pre-eminent name in environmental law. Many large cases over the years have contributed to the firm's reputation: *Amoco Cadiz*, the Alsace potash mines, Creys Malville and the pollution of the Rhine and, more recently, the *Erika* and the *Prestige*. Moreover, Corinne Lepage was Minister for the Environment from 1995 to 1997. The practice is split equally between advisory and contentious work and the firm handles all matters relating to the environment, including EU-related issues and M&A. Activities that are linked with the health and biotechnologies sectors are developing.

Adamas' practice in environmental law matters is mainly focused on five areas: handling of contaminated sites related issues, outsourcing of environmental industrial management, environmental audits in relation to M&A, water, waste and energy related public procurement, and servicing and risk management of closed minefields. Environmental law is now handled by a dedicated team of four full-time lawyers in Paris and two in Lyon, under the leadership of Yvan Razafindratandra. **Adamas** has offices in China and in Taiwan, and increasingly handles issues related to environmental law for foreign companies investing in China. Clients include the Communauté Urbaine de Lyon, an international luxury group, and a tyre manufacturer.

Four associates and one partner (Pierre Bechman), work full-time within **Clifford Chance**'s environmental practice which covers a broad range of matters relating to the environment. The work is mainly contentious. The firm successfully defended EDF in summary proceedings brought against it in connection with a nuclear power plant near Bordeaux; defended Cogema (nuclear fuel processing) against legal proceedings brought against one of its subsidiaries in connection with an alleged pollution of a lake in the south of France; and handled several litigation cases for mid-size industrial clients (TIM, ENAF) which all resulted in public authorities either withdrawing their demands on the clients before the court hearing (TIM) or losing the case.

At **Gide Loyrette Nouel**, environmental cases are dealt with by Laurent Deruy. The four-lawyer team is involved in major industrial acquisition and site restructuring operations. They have expertise in four segments of the environmental law: advice, litigation, contractual work and audit. Areas covered range from regulated industrial activities to air emissions, waste water, waste treatment, noise nuisance, mining and nuclear law, and polluted sites. A strong emphasis was recently put on the new regulation of air emissions allocation and trading. Banks, financial institutions and various types of industrials are advised.

Pichavent Chétrit is the result of a split up from **GAIA** in 2003. Jean-Daniel Chétrit is an environmental specialist whose work involves the redevelopment of urban and polluted sites, obtaining authorisations, planning permission for registered industrial plants and expropriation cases.

Savin Martinet Associés – a split from **De Pardieu Brocas Maffei & Leygonie** – deals with every type of environmental law issue. Its services include regulatory audits, purchase and sale audits, environmental risk analysis, the negotiation of environmental clauses in contracts (liability guarantees, etc), help with classified facilities, and case monitoring in conjunction with French authorities. Patricia Savin covers all aspects of pollution and nuisance law, including facilities classified for environmental protection, water, air, waste, all types of spills or releases, hazardous material transport and storage, etc. The problems associated with asbestos, termites, lead and VOCs, in particular in the real property field, are a speciality.

Jean-Nicolas Clément is the public/environment law specialist at **UGGC & Associés**. Aside from some town-planning activities, he devotes 90% of his time to environmental work (with a balanced advisory/contentious practice). Clément has built his reputation in the nuclear, quarry, waste and hydrocarbon sectors and was involved in the A28 motorway project, advising the Administration and the concessionary company on environmental issues.

Vincent Sol and Joëlle Herschtel head the environment practice at **Winston & Strawn**, supported by six associates. Sol is a member of the Conseil Supérieur des Installations Classées and an expert in polluted ground. The firm offers a global service encompassing civil, criminal and administrative litigation, as well as acquisition audits. Among the firm's clients are large manufacturers in the chemicals, pharmaceuticals, automotive, steel, energy and waste sectors. Some 40 dedicated lawyers span offices in Paris, Chicago and Washington, DC.

Caroline London at **Brizay London** carries out environmental work, largely from a local community perspective. She is also active in a national context, advising increasingly on environmental audits.

De Pardieu Brocas Maffei & Leygonie is active in environmental law. Lawyers involved include Jean Leygonie and Florence Guthfreund-Roland, Patricia Savin having left the firm to set up **Savin Martinet Associés**. Advisory work constitutes the major part of the practice, including environmental audits in relation to M&A and also in the context of property deals or telecoms issues. The firm acts mainly for industrial and insurance companies and banks.

Granrut merits a mention for the work of Christophe Bourdel in environmental law (industrial risk).

At **Rambaud Martel**, Guillaume Forbin and Jean-Philippe Sorba count manufacturers, paper makers and quarries among their clients. The firm has acted on major actions in the asbestos sector.

At **Shearman & Sterling LLP**, Françoise Labrousse has made a name for herself in environmental work, particularly in asbestos-related matters.

Daniel Soulez-Larivière at **Soulez Larivière et Associés** was appointed by TotalFinaElf to represent the company in two major environmental accidents – the sinking of *Erika* and the explosion of the AZF chemical plant in Toulouse. The firm is also involved in asbestos litigation.

Patrick Thieffry, at **Thieffry & Associés**, specialises in European environmental law. He acts for the Ministry of Environment in its relationships with Brussels, in the context of the water agencies and in cases like Metaleurop.

IT, TELECOMS AND THE INTERNET

Alain Bensoussan - Avocats is one of the leading IT specialist firms, Alain Bensoussan having been one of the first lawyer to specialise in the area some 20 years ago. The firm's practice centres on computing (which accounts for almost half of its activity), telecoms, communications and multimedia - traditionally the firm's three main areas of activity, to which the Internet, biotechnology and health, as well as space law are natural additions. About 90 lawyers work in the Paris, Lyon and Grenoble offices.

Bird & Bird is a sector-focused, full-service international firm specialising in the communications and IT industries and covering all aspects of business law. Having expanded rapidly, since it opened in Paris in January 2000, the firm now comprises 11 partners, plus 40 associates. Frédérique Dupuis-Toubol is the managing partner and she is considered an expert in the communications and IT field. Stéphane Lemarchand is another IT specialist. For **Bird & Bird**, contract negotiations and regulation (data protection for example) form the core of the firm's practice, but litigation, outsourcing and PPP issues are increasingly important. A life sciences practice has also developed under Paule Drouault-Gardrat. The client base comprises large users of computer technology and computer services companies.

IT, TELECOMS AND THE INTERNET

ALAIN BENSOUSSAN - AVOCATS
BIRD & BIRD ✪
KAHN & ASSOCIÉS ✪
SALANS

Baker & McKenzie ✪
Clifford Chance
De Pardieu Brocas Maffei & Leygonie ✪
Derriennic & Associés
Franklin ✪
Gide Loyrette Nouel ✪
Iteanu & Associés
Latham & Watkins ✪
Lovells ✪
Weil, Gotshal & Manges ✪
Willkie Farr & Gallagher LLP ✪

Alterman Benezra Leclerq
August & Debouzy ✪
BMH Avocats - Breitenstein Meillassoux Hauser Roth ✪
Cahen & Associés
Cariddi Mee Rué/Hogan & Hartson LLP ✪
DS Avocats
De Gaulle Fleurance & Associés ✪
Deprez Dian Guignot ✪
Dubarry Le Douarin Veil ✪
EY Law ✪
Hughes Hubbard & Reed ✪
Jones Day ✪
Latournerie Wolfrom & Associés ✪
LeBoeuf, Lamb, Greene & Macrae L. L. P.
NomoS ✪
Orrick
Rambaud Martel ✪
Sokolow Dunaud Carreras
Taylor Wessing ✪

Firms are listed A-Z in tiers which are ranked in order of priority
✪ Indicates firm displays contact details at the end of this chapter.

The firm also handles Internet issues (including IP work, contracts and corporate issues), and in the field of telecoms, the firm exclusively represents new entrants into the French market.

Ten partners and some 30 associates are active at **Kahn & Associés**. The firm traditionally acts for multinationals (mainly American, but also European and Israeli) and their French operations, but also for start-ups and venture capital funds. Among its clients are hardware manufacturers, software producers and distributors, makers of equipment and peripherals, computer goods and services providers, all sorts of hi-tech and telecoms companies and more traditional businesses. The firm's activity is structured around computer science (hardware and software), Internet, multimedia and telecoms. **Kahn & Associés** offers a wide range of expertise including corporate, M&A, IP, labour law and litigation. The firm has an office in Nice Sophia Antipolis, France's Silicon Valley.

Salans' IT team, consisting of four partners and 12 associates, is one of the leaders in the new technologies sector and is respected in the fields of computing, multimedia, Internet and telecommunications. Christiane Féral-Schuhl is particularly well known. Along with Bruno Grégoire Sainte-Marie, the firm has been active both in transactional work and litigation in the IT field since the 80s. Michael Hancock and Jeroen Luchtenberg both have telecoms backgrounds and now deal with a broad range of international and domestic telecoms, Internet, cable television and media transactions, reorganisations and disputes. In the last two years, the Paris group has become particularly active in French and international outsourcing contracts. The group represents a broad range of French and international clients including industry leaders, start-ups, software developers, service providers, media and telecommunications conglomerates, computer consultants, multimedia firms and inventors.

Baker & McKenzie's IT department is led by Emmanuel Guillaume, former head of the legal department at France Télécom, Christian Blomet and Rémy Bricard. While telecoms is a very important area for the firm, both nationally and internationally, **Baker & McKenzie** is also strong in computing and the Internet. The team has been particularly active recently in litigation, data protection and outsourcing.

Marc d'Haultfoeuille heads the seven-lawyer CMT team at **Clifford Chance** which covers computer law, multimedia and video games, hi-tech aspects of IP, and telecoms for French and foreign operators investing in France, advising Nokia for example. The firm is also involved in e-commerce and the Internet, data protection and cryptology, and also handles arbitration and litigation. It also dealt with outsourcing projects for EDS and Airbus.

De Pardieu Brocas Maffei & Leygonie has a team specialised in technology and is particularly known for its expertise in telecoms; Martine Georges-Naïm and Florence Guthfreund-Roland are the two partners in charge. Their telecoms practice is organised around five focal points: advice and assistance in regulatory matters, competition, contracts, M&A and project financing. The firm acts exclusively on behalf of new French (or some times US) entrants into the market. Besides the telecoms practice, the firm is increasingly involved in Internet and e-commerce issues, computer law and information technology.

Comprising ten lawyers, six of them partners, **Derriennic & Associés** is a leading firm in the new technologies sector. With 30 years' experience in the computing field, Jean-Noël Derriennic is particularly highly regarded, although the firm is now expanding into telecoms and Internet issues. The firm's client base spans software suppliers, as well as companies and administrative bodies using computer services.

At **Franklin**, Bradley Joslove leads the new technology department. The firm is very active in the cable industry and in the Internet (eBay) and handles outsourcing projects for big institutional French clients. Recently, a Japanese clientele has been developed.

On the telecoms side, **Gide Loyrette Nouel** is very active in international bids, handling both regulatory and transactional issues. The track record of the firm includes the assistance of over 20 national governments around the world. Highlights include handling the merger of TD and Cegetel, creating the second fixed telecoms operator in France; advising the French Army on the outsourcing of its telecoms networks; and advising several telecoms new entrants on all regulatory matters before the French Regulator ART. The firm is also active in the IT and Internet field, drafting for instance agreements for several US-based, worldwide groups for the transfer and the use outside the EU of personal data initially processed by subsidiaries established within the EU territory, and handles litigation on the user side. The partners in charge are Bertrand Nouel, Rémy Fekete and Olivier Cousi.

Iteanu & Associés has ten lawyers specialising in IT and e-commerce. The firm comprises three departments: corporate, contracts and litigation. Its activities include computing (service companies, publishers), telecoms (new service providers, equipment manufacturers) and a communications/audiovisual/Internet focus.

At **Latham & Watkins**, five lawyers devote themselves to IT full-time. The main facet of the firm's work is linked to its expertise in EU law - licences, relations with the regulatory authorities (ART) - although litigation (and arbitration) are also handled (Christophe Clarenc). As for Laurent Szuskin, he is active in telecoms (counsel and contracts), computing and new technologies, working for providers and users with an emphasis on outsourcing renegotiation contracts, and computer public markets litigation.

Lovells is active in IT. The firm handles advisory, regulatory and contentious aspects. The partners present in this field are Jean-Pierre Langlais and Pierre de Montalembert. Pierre-Menno de Girard deals with computing (contracts), databases, the Internet and CD-ROM production. Thomas Rouhette handles litigation. Among clients, the firm enjoys ongoing instruction from Colt.

At **Weil, Gotshal & Manges**, Claude Serra and Lucien Rapp regularly handle telecoms issues, both regulatory and commercial aspects. The firm advises on M&A transactions as well as on the formation of new companies.

At **Willkie Farr & Gallagher LLP**, François Bloch heads the TIME department. The multidisciplinary team comprises eight lawyers and is involved in corporate and financing issues as well as commercial and regulatory aspects. Lately, the firm handled the privatisation of telecoms in Morocco and litigation in the cable industry.

INSOLVENCY

Sonier & Associés is the market leader. A system of correspondents enables Gabriel Sonier's firm to maintain special relationships with banks (OBC, Crédit Foncier de France, Merrill Lynch, JPMorgan and Deutsche Bank), as well as other law firms that lack their own specialist. The firm acted in the main bankruptcies in France recently: Moulinex/Brandt, UBS (Valfond Group), Léon de Bruxelles, Complétel, Alcatel Réseaux d'Entreprises - Marine Communication, and Immobilière Hôtelière.

At **de Pardieu Brocas Maffei & Leygonie**, Jacques Henrot and Paul Talbourdet handle insolvency matters. They work mainly for lenders, and have been involved in several defective LBO financings and debt renegotiations (Vivendi, Alstom) recently. Other cases include Viatel, Valfond, CCMX and Royal Monceau. The firm is the French correspondent of US specialist **Bingham McCutchen LLP**.

At **Gide Loyrette Nouel**, Olivier Puech has a very good reputation and Jean-Michel Lucheux also deserves to be mentioned. They specialise in

INSOLVENCY

SONIER & ASSOCIÉS ✪

DE PARDIEU BROCAS MAFFEI & LEYGONIE ✪
GIDE LOYRETTE NOUEL ✪
JEANTETASSOCIÉS ✪
RAMBAUD MARTEL ✪
SANTONI PACCIONI & ASSOCIÉS
VEIL JOURDE LA GARANDERIE ✪
WILLKIE FARR & GALLAGHER LLP ✪

EY Law ✪
Fauvet, La Giraudière & Associés
Poulain & Associés
Saigne Sigrist
UGGC & Associés ✪
Vatier & Associés ✪

Allen & Overy ✪
Ashurst ✪
Bernard Lagarde, Cabinet
Cleary Gottlieb Steen & Hamilton ✪
Clifford Chance
Coudert Frères ✪
Denton Wilde Sapte ✪
Franklin ✪
Freshfields Bruckhaus Deringer ✪
Lovells ✪
Lussan Brouillaud
Moquet Borde & Associés ✪
Norton Rose
Olivier Pardo
Salans
Simmons & Simmons ✪
Sokolow Dunaud Carreras
White & Case LLP

Firms are listed A-Z in tiers which are ranked in order of priority
✪ Indicates firm displays contact details at the end of this chapter.

amicable restructurings (*'ad hoc mandates'* and *'conciliations'*) and the management of bankruptcy proceedings, as well as offering capability in all related litigation (banks' responsibility, management responsibility, etc.). The team was involved in the restructuring process of Metaleurop SA.

JeantetAssociés' Philippe Dubois is well regarded, with Yvon Dréano and Philippe Blaquier-Cirelli also involved in insolvency matters. The firm has experience of acting on all sides: for the companies (Bata and Métaleurop), for the creditors (Moulinex), or for the rescuers (Brandt and Air Liberté).

At **Rambaud Martel**, Michel Jockey works mainly for blue-chip companies and for banks. Valérie Lafarge-Sarkozy is also active. Most of their activity is directed towards prevention. Recently, the firm was involved in cases such as Bourgoin, Autodis-Autodistribution and Moulin Rouge.

Marc Santoni (**Santoni Paccioni & Associés**) is also very active, working for LBO funds for instance, and so are Georges Jourde – a highly-regarded litigant – and Guilhem Brémond (**Veil Jourde La Garanderie**).

Highly praised Jean-Dominique Daudier de Cassini has moved from **EY Law** to **Willkie Farr & Gallagher LLP** with four lawyers. The team numbers five dedicated lawyers and they work notably with the New York office where the practice is very strong, boasting a strong clientele of funds. The firm also advises companies on recovery procedures and risk management, and deals with strategies to safeguard against insolvency, as well as the resurrection of insolvent companies.

Jean-Yves Marquet and Hanker Sorensen (**EY Law**); François Fauvet (**Fauvet, La Giraudière & Associés**); Jean-Paul Poulain (**Poulain & Associés**); Philippe Saigne (**Saigne Sigrist**); Bernard Vatier (**Vatier & Associés**); and Jean-Jacques Uettwiller and Thierry Montéran (**UGGC & Associés**) are also recommended.

INSOLVENCY: RECEIVERS

Four firms are set apart due to their very well-defined activities. **Bigot Lyonnet**, **Poudenx Bayle**, **Oltramare Fourcault** and **Jean-Paul Petreschi** advise receivers and their representatives.

INSOLVENCY: RECEIVERS

BIGOT LYONNET
JEAN-PAUL PETRESCHI
OLTRAMARE FOURCAULT
POUDENX BAYLE

Firms are listed alphabetically

INSURANCE

HPMBC Clyde & Co is undoubtedly the best insurance firm in France. Before the merger in May 2002, *HPMBC* already enjoyed a leading position, being the result of the combination of two specialist firms, *Honig Buffat Mettetal* and *Duprey Preel Coulon*, while **Clyde & Co** was already involved in insurance via its shipping activity. With further offices in Nantes, London and New York, the firm is well placed on international insurance matters, with a particular focus on reinsurance. At the same time, the firm is involved in sectors such as aviation, shipping and transport, energy and natural resources, construction (industrial risks business) and acted in the main insolvency and corporate restructurings in the insurance industry over the last few years. The firm advises almost all the insurance and reinsurance companies (AXA, AGF, MMA, Royal & SunAlliance, and Scor to name a few) and also works for industrial companies (product liability) such as Alcatel and Airbus. Recently, TotalFinaElf (Toulouse AZF explosion) and Airbus (New York crash) have been advised. Well-known insurance specialists include Gérard Honig, Jean-Marie Preel and Denys Duprey (industrial risks specialists), Bernard Mettetal (reinsurance and insurance insolvency), and Xavier Perinne (regulatory).

New firm **Bouckaert Ormen Passemard Sportes** is the result of a split from **Norton Rose** in late 2003. Christian Bouckaert has a strong reputation through acting for many leading European and US insurers as well as commercial and industrial clients on a variety of contentious and non-contentious matters. He is also a well-known reinsurance specialist (arbitration). Pascal Omen, Rémi Passemard and Carole Sportes are the other partners active. In 2003, the firm represented the reinsurers involved in the Toulouse AZF explosion; a group of insurers in the context of collapsing mines in the Lorraine area; and was granted a reinsurance case related to the World Trade Center in New York.

Fernand Garnault is a firm specialising in air transport. Its expertise, as well as a relationship with **Beaumont and Son** in the UK, is extended to aviation insurance since the firm works for the national airline and its insurers.

At **Gide Loyrette Nouel**, Emmanuel Fontaine and Philippe Rames handle insurance issues linked to the firm's activities in shipping, aviation, construction, industrial risks and product liability. They have been advising on insurance products contracts, due diligence, insurance contract distribution, insurance company regulation (authorisation, merger) and various insurance and reinsurance disputes.

In the construction industry, Jean-Pierre Karila (**Karila & Associés**) is well known.

LeBoeuf, Lamb, Greene & Macrae L.L.P. is internationally renowned for its insurance practice. Jean Alisse handles the work in Paris.

Other firms are worth a mention: construction experts **Caston Cabouche Gabrielli Marquet**, **Neveu Sudaka & Associés** and **Naba et Associés**; shipping specialists **Bouloy Grellet & Godin**, **Ince & Co**, **Holman Fenwick & Willan** and **Rembauville-Nicolle & Bureau - Rbm2l**; insurance niche firms **Hascoët Trillat** and **Tétaud Lambard Jami & Associés**; **de Pardieu Brocas Maffei & Leygonie**; **Rambaud Martel**; **Lefèvre Pelletier & Associés**; and **Moquet Borde & Associés**.

INSURANCE

HPMBC CLYDE & CO ✪

BOUCKAERT ORMEN PASSEMARD SPORTES

Fernand Garnault
Gide Loyrette Nouel ✪
Karila & Associés
LeBoeuf, Lamb, Greene & Macrae L. L. P.

Bouloy Grellet & Godin
Caston Cabouche Gabrielli Marquet
De Pardieu Brocas Maffei & Leygonie ✪
Hascoët Trillat
Holman Fenwick & Willan ✪
Ince & Co ✪
Lefèvre Pelletier & Associés
Naba et Associés
Neveu Sudaka & Associés
Rambaud Martel ✪
Rembauville-Nicolle & Bureau - Rbm2l
Tétaud Lambard Jami & Associés

Bertagna - Berrymans
Clifford Chance
EY Law ✪
Herbert Smith ✪
Linklaters ✪
Lussan Brouillaud
Moquet Borde & Associés ✪
Raffin Raffin-Courbe Gofard

Firms are listed A-Z in tiers which are ranked in order of priority
✪ Indicates firm displays contact details at the end of this chapter.

INTELLECTUAL PROPERTY

At **Allen & Overy**, Pierre Lenoir arrived from **EY Law** and created the IP department. He works primarily in patents and trade marks. Within the patents area, the firm advises a number of important international pharmaceutical clients, while in trade marks, the client base is focused on retailers. Work is both contentious and non-contentious and benefits from the international network.

Grégoire Triet and Arnaud Michel head the IP department at **Gide Loyrette Nouel**, which also comprises nine associates. Patent litigation, trade marks and copyright are the focus of the practice. Longstanding clients include Levi-Strauss and Philip Morris.

Linklaters' IP specialist is Alain Monégier du Sorbier who is particularly known for his patent expertise. The team is developing internationally oriented advisory work, especially M&A-derived IP work, with a client portfolio which includes hi-tech and pharmaceutical companies. **Linklaters** has a strong European IP team, notably in Cologne and London.

At **Lovells**, the IP department is three-partners strong (Dominique Ménard, Milan Chromecek and Marie-Aimée de Dampierre), and 50 lawyers deal with IP in Europe. The practice can be divided into three areas: IP litigation, arbitration and other forms of dispute resolution; IP asset management, advisory, counselling and transactional work including a filing practice (other than patents); media and entertainment advisory, counselling and transactional work.

Patents (electronics, pharmaceuticals) and trade marks (fashion) account for the majority of the work at **Armengaud Guerlain**. Jacques Armengaud is vice-president of the Association of Intellectual Property Lawyers and Stéphane Guerlain of the Association des Praticiens du Droit des Marques et des Modèles (APRAM).

At **Courtois Lebel**, three partners, among them Arnaud Casalonga, cover patent, trade marks and author rights, IT litigation and advice.

Pierre Cousin, at **Cousin & Moatty**, sources a significant proportion of its turnover from patent work, particularly in the fields of pharmaceuticals, chemicals, mechanics and optics.

Intellectual property represents 50% of **Duclos Thorne Mollet-Viéville & Associés**' activity. Five dedicated lawyers handle about 100 cases per year covering patent litigation, trade marks and copyright issues.

INTELLECTUAL PROPERTY: BOUTIQUE FIRMS

ARMENGAUD GUERLAIN
COURTOIS LEBEL
COUSIN & MOATTY
DUCLOS THORNE MOLLET-VIÉVILLE & ASSOCIÉS
ESCANDE HAVARD-DUCLOS
GAULTIER LAKITS - JOSSE SZLEPER
GILBEY DE HAAS
GREFFE
PHILIPPE COMBEAU
VÉRON & ASSOCIÉS

Champagner Katz & Goldnadel
Cléry de la Myre Mory
Cousté & Cousté ✪
Hoffman
Hollier-Larousse
Jean-Louis Lagarde
Michel Huet
Nataf & Fajgenbaum

Firms are listed A-Z in tiers which are ranked in order of priority
✪ *Indicates firm displays contact details at the end of this chapter.*

INTELLECTUAL PROPERTY: FULL SERVICE FIRMS

ALLEN & OVERY ✪
GIDE LOYRETTE NOUEL ✪
LINKLATERS ✪
LOVELLS ✪

August & Debouzy ✪
Bird & Bird ✪
Freshfields Bruckhaus Deringer ✪
Lamy Ribeyre & Associés ✪
Latham & Watkins ✪
Rambaud Martel ✪
Salans

Baker & McKenzie ✪
Clifford Chance
De Gaulle Fleurance & Associés ✪
Deprez Dian Guignot ✪
NomoS ✪

BMH Avocats - Breitenstein Meillassoux Hauser Roth ✪
Bignon Lebray & Associés
CMS Bureau Francis Lefebvre ✪
Coblence & Associés
DS Avocats
Denton Wilde Sapte ✪
Dubarry Le Douarin Veil ✪
EY Law ✪
Herbert Smith ✪
Jones Day ✪
Moquet Borde & Associés ✪
Simmons & Simmons ✪
Sokolow Dunaud Carreras
Thieffry & Associés
UGGC & Associés ✪

Firms are listed A-Z in tiers which are ranked in order of priority
✪ *Indicates firm displays contact details at the end of this chapter.*

Escande Havard-Duclos is particularly known for its work in unfair competition, trade marks and is increasingly active in patent litigation. Michel-Paul Escande's clients include some big names in the automotive, luxury and food industries.

Geoffroy Gaultier heads **Gaultier Lakits - Josse Szleper** (formerly *Cabinet Mathély*), which comprises five lawyers. The firm handles substantial amounts of patent litigation.

Richard John Gilbey and Charles de Haas at **Gilbey de Haas** are recommended, while at **Greffe**, IP is the largest practice area and caters to a diverse client base boasting a number of names in the fashion (haute-couture and ready-to-wear) and industrial sectors.

Philippe Combeau and his two associates deal with around 30 patent litigation cases per year. The firm's client base is diverse and includes large pharmaceutical companies.

Pierre Véron of **Véron & Associés** is highly praised for his work in patent litigation. He created the department at the then *Lamy Véron Ribeyre & Associés* and maintains a close relationship with his former partners. Ten lawyers (also including Isabelle Romet and Thomas Bouvet) focus on patents, trade marks, designs and models, with cases such as Agilent Technologies/Waters, Air Liquide/Aga, Bayer CropScience/Monsanto, L'Oréal/Bourjois, and Schneider Electric/Siemens.

Other recommended specialists include: Isabelle Renard (**August & Debouzy**); Jean-François Bretonnière (**Baker & McKenzie**); Isabelle Leroux (**Bird & Bird**); Olivier de La Myre Mory and Alain Cléry (**Cléry de la Myre Mory**); Christian Lachèze (**Clifford Chance**); Marina Cousté (**Cousté & Cousté**); Louis de Gaulle (**De Gaulle Fleurance & Associés**); Pierre Deprez (**Deprez Dian Guignot**); Xavier Buffet-Delmas (**Freshfields Bruckhaus Deringer**); Serge Hoffman (**Hoffman**); Christian Hollier-Larousse (**Hollier-Larousse**); Yves Bizollon and Jean-Guillaume Monin (**Lamy Ribeyre & Associés**); Rein Jan Prins **Latham & Watkins**; Fabienne Fajgenbaum (**Nataf & Fajgenbaum**); Christophe Pecnard (**NomoS**); Pierre Lubet (**Rambaud Martel**); and Gérard Delile (**Salans**).

MARITIME AND TRANSPORT

Bouloy Grellet & Godin's Luc Grellet handles trade, industrial risk, charter party, international credit documentation, international sales and arbitration. He advised the shipowner in the *Erika* case. Philippe Godin is a specialist in transport and advises forwarding agents and insurance companies on the freight side.

UK-based **Holman Fenwick & Willan** currently comprises some 20 lawyers, with further offices in Rouen and Nantes. Best known partners are Jean-Jacques Ollu and Guillaume Brajeux, Olivier Purcell and Timothy Clemens-Jones. They have recognised experience in French and international litigation (contentious matters account for 90% of the firm's activity). Within its broad practice, the firm focuses on charter party, admiralty, insurance, international trade and customs law, industrial risks, ship finance, and international debt recovery. Recently, the firm was involved in many large shipping casualties (*Estonia*, *Levoli Sun*, etc.).

Constant & Constant no longer operates in Paris; all the lawyers of the office joined **Ince & Co** in January 2002. Twelve lawyers in Paris and Le Havre are involved in maritime law. Gilles Gautier handles shipping and marine insurance litigation. The other partners are Fred Vroom (for the finance aspects) and Andrew Charlier (general non-contentious matters). Jérôme de Sentenac is in charge of the Le Havre office, with Mathieu Croix specialising in shipping litigation. Clients include maritime transport companies and insurers.

Fellow UK firm **Richards Butler** fields ten lawyers in Paris, four of them partners, specialising in shipping matters. The practice is broad,

MARITIME AND TRANSPORT

BOULOY GRELLET & GODIN
HOLMAN FENWICK & WILLAN ✪
INCE & CO ✪
RICHARDS BUTLER
RICHEMONT & ASSOCIÉS
VILLENEAU ROHART SIMON & ASSOCIÉS

Gide Loyrette Nouel ✪
HPMBC Clyde & Co ✪
Le Berre Engelsen Witvoet
Norton Rose
Orrick
Pierre-Marie Rossignol
Rembauville-Nicolle & Bureau - Rbm2l

Courtois & Finkelstein
Dagorne - Huchet
Laroque & Associés
Lassez & Associés ✪
Penningtons
Schmill Lombrez
Tinayre & Associés

Firms are listed A-Z in tiers which are ranked in order of priority
✪ *Indicates firm displays contact details at the end of this chapter.*

covering transport litigation, incidents at sea, international sales, insurance, reinsurance and protective measures. The two partners in charge, Peter Iglikowski and Lars Lewis, are of British origin and possess the dual qualification of French *avocat* and English solicitor. The firm is involved in the *Erika* case, acting for the shipowners.

Richemont & Associés' Henri de Richemont is well regarded. Known as a P&I clubs and shipowners' lawyer, he and his five-lawyer team also act for charterers and other road and maritime transport operators. The firm was involved in maritime cases such as the *Tanio* and the *Erika* wrecks.

Villeneau Rohart Simon & Associés' eight-lawyer practice focuses on maritime law. Patrick Simon and Jean-Serge Rohart are particularly well known, the latter being president of the Association Française de Droit Maritime. The firm has forged a reputation for dealing with major accidents, such as *Amoco Cadiz* and *Estonia*. The majority of the work is international and clients include P&I clubs and shipowners.

At **Gide Loyrette Nouel**, Emmanuel Fontaine is a litigation specialist. He is regularly involved in major ship transactions as well as in maritime pollution. Philippe Rames is specialised in insurance and industrial risks. In particular, he has developed an expertise in matters relating to maritime and land transport accidents.

UK firm **Clyde & Co** merged with insurance specialist *HPMBC* to create **HPMBC Clyde & Co**. The combined firm has a strong maritime practice, headed by Gildas Rostain whose activity is mainly contentious, for international shipowners, P&I clubs and insurers.

Four-partner, three-associate **Le Berre Engelsen Witvoet** focuses on shipping, general transport law, insurance, international arbitration, product liability and commercial litigation cases. In maritime law, the firm is particularly active on the litigation side.

We also mention here two firms active in shipping finance: **Norton Rose** and **Orrick**.

Pierre-Marie Rossignol now works independently after spending many years at **Gide Loyrette Nouel**. His clients are mainly foreign and French insurers.

Rembauville-Nicolle & Bureau - Rbm2l has offices in Paris and Le Havre. Patrice Rembauville-Nicolle and Xavier Bureau act for shipowners, P&I clubs and shippers.

We also recommend the following niche firms: **Courtois & Finkelstein**; **Dagorne - Huchet**; **Laroque & Associés**; **Lassez & Associés**; **Penningtons**; **Schmill Lombrez**; and **Tinayre & Associés**.

MEDIA AND ENTERTAINMENT: FULL SERVICE FIRMS

Bignon Lebray & Associés' media team is led by Anne-Marie Pecoraro. Well known within the music industry (she advises artists and editors), the activities of her team also encompass TV, cinema, press and edition.

At **Bird & Bird**, Alexandre Vuchot is a specialist in media and sports law and has considerable experience in broadcasting rights acquisition. He represents domestic and international media companies on regulatory issues and transactional matters.

At **Cariddi Mee Rué/Hogan & Hartson LLP**, Winston Maxwell handles media and communications issues on transactional and regulatory aspects, notably in the TV and cable industries.

Clifford Chance is involved in TV rights matters and is active in sport law issues (Marc d'Haultfoeuille, Yves Wehrli).

MEDIA AND ENTERTAINMENT: FULL SERVICE FIRMS

Bignon Lebray & Associés
Bird & Bird ✪
Cariddi Mee Rué/Hogan & Hartson LLP ✪
Clifford Chance
Denton Wilde Sapte ✪
Gide Loyrette Nouel ✪
NomoS ✪
Salans
Sokolow Dunaud Carreras
Taylor Wessing ✪
Vatier & Associés ✪
Weil, Gotshal & Manges ✪

Firms are listed alphabetically
✪ *Indicates firm displays contact details at the end of this chapter.*

In 2002, Gilles Vercken joined **Denton Wilde Sapte** and has particular expertise in media and entertainment (television, music, film). A former head of legal of the Sacem-Sdrm and Saces and legal director of Ellipse Canal + Cable, he recently worked for clients such as TPS Group, Dreamcatcher and France Télévision Distribution.

Gide Loyrette Nouel's practice in the media field focuses on film and television with Olivier Cousi and Rémy Fekete.

NomoS has a media team with Eric Lauvaux, a specialist in the music industry. Héléna Delabarre is the other partner. They are developing in the audiovisual industry.

The media and audiovisual team at **Salans**' Paris office is significantly involved in the world of entertainment, music, television and audiovisual production activities.

Sokolow Dunaud Carreras is active in the TV industry through Jean-Michel Iscovici and Patrick Dunaud. The firms acts for TV channels, negotiates sport rights and is familiar with cable and satellite issues.

Taylor Wessing set up in France by taking a team of 30 lawyers from **Landwell & Associés / Partners**. Arnaud de Sénilhes and Christian Valsamidis focus on the media sector. Clients include Sony, NCR and BMG.

At **Vatier & Associés**, Ann Creelman, Olivier Saumon and Yves René Guillou are active.

Claude Serra, at **Weil, Gotshal & Manges**, is an expert of television issues, with clients in the cable industry for instance. He also advises producers and financial institutions.

MEDIA AND ENTERTAINMENT: BOOK PUBLISHING

The name partners of **Dartevelle Benazeraf Merlet** are exclusive legal advisers to the Gallimard Group, but also work for Flammarion and the National Publishers Association (Syndicat National de l'Edition).

Dominique de Leusse de Syon represents two of the largest book publishers in France as well as a number of smaller publishing houses.

At **Zylberstein & Halpern**, Jean-Claude Zylberstein is renowned for his practice in copyright in the publishing sector. He works for Plon and Robert Laffont, mainly on libel and plagiarism issues.

MEDIA AND ENTERTAINMENT: BOOK PUBLISHING

DARTEVELLE BENAZERAF MERLET
DOMINIQUE DE LEUSSE DE SYON
ZYLBERSTEIN & HALPERN

Firms are listed alphabetically

MEDIA AND ENTERTAINMENT: FILM
BITOUN & ASSOCIÉS
GIDE LOYRETTE NOUEL ✪
MICHEL LIBERMANN
WALKER, BOROWSKY & HAIDAR

Firms are listed alphabetically

✪ Indicates firm displays contact details at the end of this chapter.

MEDIA AND ENTERTAINMENT: FILM

The six lawyers of **Bitoun & Associés** enjoy close and longstanding links with the film industry, advising directors, scriptwriters, actors, producers and TV production companies.

In 2003, **Gide Loyrette Nouel** enhanced its practice in the movie industry, especially in the field of financing production and distribution. Olivier Cousi and Rémy Fekete provide a wide range of services including assistance to independent producers and to financing institutions, negotiation of all forms of national, international distribution and co-production agreements and also for assistance in litigation.

Michel Libermann is based in Paris and New York, where he advises major players in the European film industry on the American market and vice-versa. Areas covered in the US are contracts, co-production, multi-source financing and the acquisition and marketing of licensing rights.

Walker, Borowsky & Haidar offers a wide range of services covering all TV and film-related legal issues: project finance, loan guarantees, capital markets transactions, negotiations with actors and their agents, contracts, co-production agreements, distribution and dealing with public regulators and censors. Partner Daniel Walker's client base consists of TV stations, capital investors, banks, and French, US, British, German and Scandinavian actors agents.

MEDIA AND ENTERTAINMENT: MUSIC

The phonographic industry is dominated by four main players: EMI, Universal, Sony Music BMG, and Warner. A handful of French lawyers work regularly for the major companies and have become experts in this highly specialised area of law. Amongst them, Anne-Marie Pecoraro (**Bignon Lebray & Associés**), **Jean Ennochi**, Jean Castelain at **Granrut**, Eric Lauvaux at **NomoS** and Nicolas Boespflug of **Greffe** are all highly regarded.

MEDIA AND ENTERTAINMENT: MUSIC
BIGNON LEBRAY & ASSOCIÉS
GRANRUT
JEAN ENNOCHI
GREFFE
NOMOS ✪

Firms are listed alphabetically

✪ Indicates firm displays contact details at the end of this chapter.

MEDIA AND ENTERTAINMENT: NEWSPAPERS AND MAGAZINES
ADER AMIGUES & JOLIBOIS
BAUER BIGOT & HUGOT
BIZOT BOISMILON TEULIER
LUSSAN BROUILLAUD
LYSIAS

Firms are listed alphabetically

MEDIA AND ENTERTAINMENT: NEWSPAPERS AND MAGAZINES

Yves Baudelot (**Lysias**); Marc-Noël Louvet (**Ader Amigues & Jolibois**); Jean-Yves Dupeux (**Lussan Brouillaud**); Christophe Bigot (**Bauer Bigot & Hugot**); and Bruno Landry (**Bizot Boismilon Teulier**) are acknowledged as excellent *avocats* who represent their publishing clients in court as well as advising them on more traditional areas of press law, such as violations of privacy, defamation and image rights.

Christophe Bigot advises Hachette Filipacchi. Since January 2000, he has been a name partner of **Bauer Bigot & Hugot**, which specialises in communications law.

Yves Baudelot, a partner at **Lysias**, is active in media law, specialising in journalism and editorial matters. Clients include *Le Monde* and specialist financial and business papers.

Bruno Landry (**Bizot Boismilon Teulier**) also concentrates on the written word, working mainly for the Express Group and publishing house Hachette.

Lussan Brouillaud has three lawyers handling communications and media: Jean-Yves Dupeux, Thierry Massis and Alain Hazan. They regularly represent the interests of various French magazines, including those published by Prisma Presse.

MEDIA AND ENTERTAINMENT: TELEVISION/RADIO

Louis Bousquet, at **Bousquet**, has for many years acted as legal counsel to the Bouygues Group. The firm became active in media law during the privatisation of TF1. Its practice covers issues ranging from corporate transactions to regulatory matters. Partners Olivier Sprung and Philippe Moncorps also handle TV and radio work.

At **Carbonnier Lamaze Rasle & Associés**, around half of Michel Rasle's time is spent on TV-related work. Teamed with three associates, Rasle regularly undertakes both advisory and litigation work for broadcasters.

Televisual matters are also to the fore at **Deprez Dian Guignot**, where partner Philippe Dian is exclusive adviser to a national TV station. The firm handles all areas of law for this client, from commercial to press law.

Martine Coisne advises a private broadcaster and several medium-sized film and TV production companies.

At **Sokolow Dunaud Carreras**, Jean-Michel Iscovici and Patrick Dunaud work for distributors (Eurosport, TPS, TF1). They handle negotiations linked with sports law and are very active in the cable and satellite sectors (CNN, Time Warner).

Claude Serra at **Weil, Gotshal & Manges** is another acknowledged expert in broadcast media law. His clientele includes a number of cable companies, which he advises on infrastructure matters, as well as production companies and institutional investors.

MEDIA AND ENTERTAINMENT: TELEVISION/RADIO
BOUSQUET
CARBONNIER LAMAZE RASLE & ASSOCIÉS
DEPREZ DIAN GUIGNOT ✪
MARTINE COISNE
SOKOLOW DUNAUD CARRERAS
WEIL, GOTSHAL & MANGES ✪

Firms are listed alphabetically

✪ Indicates firm displays contact details at the end of this chapter.

MERGERS AND ACQUISITIONS

In 2003, the M&A market was dominated by LBOs, many transactions having been done by private equity funds. Therefore, the LBO ranking must be considered alongside the more traditional M&A firms when making a choice of adviser in the current climate.

Bredin Prat is involved in most of the major transactions. Its reputation in M&A rests particularly on the shoulders of Jean-François Prat (public offerings and stock market battles) and Didier Martin (privatisations). The firm also distinguishes itself by having three US partners (Maria Ruegg, Elena Baxter and Richard Schepard), and two English (Tim Portwood and Douglas Keane). The firm advised Orange France in the acquisition of a 14% stake by France Télécom; Pechiney in the merger with Alcan; Fiat (Italy) in the acquisition of Toro Assicurazioni by De Agostini; Kesa Electricals (UK) in the spin-off by Kingfisher's shareholders; Crédit Agricole SA in the merger with Crédit Lyonnais; and Vivendi Universal in the acquisition of 26% of Cegetel. In the US, **Bredin Prat** works with **Cravath, Swaine & Moore LLP** and **Davis Polk & Wardwell**, and in Europe with celebrated best friends **Slaughter and May** (UK), **Hengeler Mueller**

(Germany), **Bonelli Erede Pappalardo** (Italy), and **Uría & Menéndez** (Spain).

Cleary Gottlieb Steen & Hamilton is involved in public bids (Pierre-Yves Chabert), as well as in transnational transactions, and is well positioned for roles on privatisations. Other partners involved include Jean-Michel Tron. Last year, the firm represented Crédit Lyonnais in its €19.5bn acquisition by Crédit Agricole , the largest global banking deal in 2003, and Euronext and its subsidiary Clearnet in the merger of the latter and the London Clearing House.

Clifford Chance handles both classic M&A work and more complex transactions, such as public bids or LBOs. The firm has a broad client base, which includes numerous French and foreign investment funds, and is on good terms with a number of investment banks. **Clifford Chance**'s ten-partner team which includes Dominique Bompoint, Marcus Billam, Frédéric Peltier, Christophe Salamon, Thierry Schoen and Yves Wehrli, recently acted for the French Ministry of Economy and Finance in restructuring negotiations with Alstom; London Clearing House in its merger with Clearnet; Apax Partners on its LBO acquisition of Pareo Finance and Pareo Management, holding companies of the Frans Bonhomme group; Vivendi Universal in connection with the sale of part of its interest in UGC; and the French Treasury on the accelerated auction sale of its 11% shareholding in Crédit Lyonnais.

The four name partners at **Darrois Villey Maillot Brochier** are particularly active in M&A and Jean-Michel Darrois is particularly famous. Olivier Diaz also deserves a mention. The firm frequently handles public bids, (friendly or hostile with contentious aspects), as well as a number of more classic M&A transactions. In 2003, the firm advised Alcan in the Alcan/Pechiney deal; Caisses d'Epargne in the capital restructuring of Eulia and the acquisition of San Paolo; and Carlyle and Eurazeo in the Saint-Gobain Terreal LBO. The firm was also involved in the privatisations of Air France, Autoroutes du Sud de la France and Gaz de France. **Darrois Villey Maillot Brochier** works closely with New York M&A powerhouse **Wachtell, Lipton, Rosen & Katz**.

At **Freshfields Bruckhaus Deringer**, eight partners handle M&A, including Yves de Mahenge, Patrick Bonvarlet, Jean-Claude Cotoni, Isabelle MacElhone and Bertrand Pellet, a private equity partner who joined from **Norton Rose**. The firm handles both French M&A issues and those with an international dimension. Major recent transactions include advising a pool of banks (Crédit Agricole Indosuez, BNP Paribas, Société Générale) in connection with the restructuring of various credit facilities granted to Alstom and on its rescue plan; Westbrook Partners LLC in relation to the acquisition and the financing of two real estate portfolios (Simco and Gécina); Barilla on the acquisition of Harry's group from Artal; Kingfisher and Kesa Electricals on the demerger of Kesa Electricals; Groupe Norbert Dentressangle in relation to the acquisition of Stockalliance from Consortium de Réalisation via a privatisation process; and West LB in relation to the acquisition of a 15% stake in the acquisition vehicle of Fraikin.

The 15-partner M&A team at **Gide Loyrette Nouel** remains one of the most prominent with a special mention to Youssef Djehane, Antoine Bonnasse and Olivier Puech. Christophe Eck, Didier G Martin, Jean-Emmanuel Skovron and Serge Tatar are also well known. Recent highlights include advising Caisse des Dépôts et Consignations on the sale of CDC ixis to CNCE; France Télécom on the sale of Eutelsat to Eurazéo; JPMorgan (counsel of Pechiney) in the scope of the unsolicited takeover bid initiated by Alcan; Société Foncière Lyonnaise for the acquisition of Sophia (takeover bid); SNCF on the creation of a joint venture with Cegetel; and the French Government in the Air France/KLM merger. **Gide Loyrette Nouel** is very often appointed as legal adviser on the privatisation.

Three main areas merit mention at **Linklaters**: takeover bids (Thierry Vassogne, Marc Loy); private acquisitions and joint ventures (Patrick Laporte, Jean-Marc Lefèvre); and LBOs (Alain Garnier, Fabrice de la Morandière and Thierry Riguet – David Aknin having left for **Weil, Gotshal & Manges**). The firm was involved in deals such as the unsolicited tender offer for Pechiney by Alcan (advising Morgan Stanley); the acquisition by Origny-Naples of a 53.8% stake in Béghin-Say held by Edison (advising the purchaser); the LBO acquisition of Actaris from LBO France (advising Montagu Private Equity); the takeover bid by Air France on KLM's securities (advising the French airline); the acquisition by Vodafone of SBC's interests in Cegetel (advising the purchaser); and the sale by Schlumberger of Sema to Atos Origin. The firm is also very active in the insurance industry.

The M&A team at **Rambaud Martel** has established its reputation on the basis of its practice in major transactions involving listed companies. Jean-Pierre Martel is among the leading lawyers called in on the country's most important stock market battles. Other partners include Jean-Michel Leprêtre, Mathieu Rambaud, Luc Saucier and Stéphane Benouville. For example, the firm advised Pechiney in connection with the unsolicited tender offer from Alcan; Vinci in the acquisition of an interest in Autoroutes du Sud de la France following the opening of their capital; BNP Paribas in the acquisition of a participation of the French state in the capital of Crédit Lyonnais in connection with the public offer of Crédit Agricole on Crédit Lyonnais; the Ministry of Economy in the privatisation of Electricité de France; Sophia in the tender offer initiated by Société Foncière Lyonnaise; Rallye in a public offer of exchange; and Bull on its financial restructuring.

The five-partner M&A team at **Allen & Overy** handles both French and cross-border

MERGERS AND ACQUISITIONS

BREDIN PRAT ✪
CLEARY GOTTLIEB STEEN & HAMILTON ✪
CLIFFORD CHANCE
DARROIS VILLEY MAILLOT BROCHIER ✪
FRESHFIELDS BRUCKHAUS DERINGER ✪
GIDE LOYRETTE NOUEL ✪
LINKLATERS ✪
RAMBAUD MARTEL ✪

Allen & Overy ✪
Ashurst ✪
Brandford-Griffith Baverez Pasturel ✪
De Pardieu Brocas Maffei & Leygonie ✪
JeantetAssociés ✪
Jones Day ✪
Latham & Watkins ✪
Lovells ✪
Moquet Borde & Associés ✪
Shearman & Sterling LLP
Veil Jourde La Garanderie ✪
Willkie Farr & Gallagher LLP ✪

Baker & McKenzie ✪
Coudert Frères ✪
Herbert Smith ✪
Norton Rose
SJ Berwin ✪
Salans
Simmons & Simmons ✪
Skadden, Arps, Slate, Meagher & Flom LLP
Slaughter and May ✪
Sullivan & Cromwell LLP
White & Case LLP

August & Debouzy ✪
Bignon Lebray & Associés
CMS Bureau Francis Lefebvre ✪
Davis Polk & Wardwell
Denton Wilde Sapte ✪
Eversheds-Frere Cholmeley
EY Law ✪
Fidal
Franklin ✪
Fried, Frank, Harris, Shriver & Jacobson LLP ✪
Gibson, Dunn & Crutcher LLP
Ginestié Paley-Vincent & Associés ✪
Haarmann Hemmelrath ✪
Cariddi Mee Rué/Hogan & Hartson LLP ✪
Hughes Hubbard & Reed ✪
Kahn & Associés ✪
Landwell & Associés / Partners
LeBoeuf, Lamb, Greene & Macrae L. L. P.
Mayer, Brown, Rowe & Maw
NomoS ✪
Ratheaux ✪
Sokolow Dunaud Carreras
UGGC & Associés ✪
Vatier & Associés ✪
Viguié Schmidt
Weil, Gotshal & Manges ✪

Firms are listed A-Z in tiers which are ranked in order of priority
✪ Indicates firm displays contact details at the end of this chapter.

LEVERAGED BUY-OUTS

ASHURST ✪
WILLKIE FARR & GALLAGHER LLP ✪

LINKLATERS ✪

Cleary Gottlieb Steen & Hamilton ✪
Clifford Chance
Freshfields Bruckhaus Deringer ✪
Gide Loyrette Nouel ✪
SJ Berwin ✪
Weil, Gotshal & Manges ✪
White & Case LLP

Darrois Villey Maillot Brochier ✪
Jones Day ✪
Latham & Watkins ✪
Lovells ✪
NomoS ✪
P.D.G.B.
Rambaud Martel ✪
Salans
Veil Jourde La Garanderie ✪

Allen & Overy ✪
Baker & McKenzie ✪
Bredin Prat ✪
De Pardieu Brocas Maffei & Leygonie ✪
Deloitte & Touche Juridique et Fiscal ✪
Denton Wilde Sapte ✪
EY Law ✪
Ginestié Paley-Vincent & Associés ✪
JeantetAssociés ✪
Mayer, Brown, Rowe & Maw
Moquet Borde & Associés ✪
Norton Rose
Simmons & Simmons ✪
Sokolow Dunaud Carreras

Firms are listed A-Z in tiers which are ranked in order of priority
✪ Indicates firm displays contact details at the end of this chapter.

transactions, with a great deal of public transactions in the recent months. The team, led by Edouard Didier and with partners Jean-Claude Rivalland, Nicolas Bichot, Armelle Walters-Renaud and Frédéric Moreau, advised: Boursorama on the acquisition of Selftrade; BNP Paribas in connection with its acquisition of 90% of Facet; UBS Warburg, BNP Paribas and Lazard in the public listing of Kesa Electrical (demerger from Kingfisher); and Edison in the sale of Provimi to PAI/CVC.

Ashurst's practice focuses on LBOs, where the firm is top of the market on both the equity and the debt sides (its acquisition finance expertise is outstanding). The firm is also involved in straight acquisitions. The team is made of 35 lawyers, among which Thomas Forschbach is the best known, having been involved in all the major acquisitions carried out by financial companies recently (Legrand, TDF, VUP, Béghin-Say etc). Of note, **Ashurst** advised Bain Capital on the acquisition of SygmaKalon (TotalfinaElf) for €1bn; PPM Ventures on the acquisition of Preciozo; and Activa Capital in relation to the acquisition of Mont Blanc SA, sold by Nestlé France.

Brandford-Griffith Baverez Pasturel is widely dedicated to M&A work, its partners having been involved in such transactions in their former firms. Henri Brandford-Griffith has notably been active in mergers involving stock exchange battles, such as BNP/Paribas or TotalFina/Elf Aquitaine. Cross-border transactions, stock exchange litigation and public M&A are also dealt with. Recently, the partners advised Groupe Crédit Agricole in its tender offer and public offer of exchange with Crédit Lyonnais; Bull on the European sale of its European services to Groupe Stéria; and Séché Environnement in the context of its alternative tender offer for Tredi Environnement.

At **De Pardieu Brocas Maffei & Leygonie**, Thierry Brocas works with banks, investment funds and insurance companies. The team also includes Jean Leygonie, Anne Tolila, Marie-Chrystel Dang Tran and Guillaume Touttée. They all handle increasing volumes of international deals. The firm has recently been involved in numerous restructurings (workouts, insolvency, LBOs), notably in the real estate sector. The firm advised AGF and Société Générale in connection with the tender offer for Sophia by Société Foncière Lyonnaise (€1.5m); DCN (Direction des Constructions Navales) in the transfer to a subsidiary by the French state of €5bn of assets; a consortium in connection with the acquisition from US Group Holiday Retirement of Groupe Serience (33 retirement homes); Groupe Axa in the acquisition of real estate assets in joint venture with a Singapore investor; and US fund The Lightyear Fund, LP in the acquisition of a stake in broking house Julius Baer Brokerage, the first acquisition of an investment company by a fund in France.

M&A continues to be one of the areas in which **JeantetAssociés** excels, especially cross-border (Georges Terrier, Yvon Dréano) advising banks as well as industrials. Two lateral hires this year with Fabrice Maraux and Bruno Solle from **CMS Bureau Francis Lefebvre**. Recently, the firm advised: Areva in the Alstom case; the French state in the restructuring of Bull; Madison Dearborn Partners in the acquisition of the Jefferson Smurfit Group; and Kingfisher Group in the acquisition of Dubois Matériaux. **JeantetAssociés** also acted in the privatisation of Compagnie des Alpes. The firm traditionally advises Suez, LVMH and Areva.

At **Jones Day** Wesley Johnson handles major cross-border negotiated transactions, along with three other partners, and Olivier Edwards is a private equity and tech start-ups expert. The firm regularly advises Rhône-Poulenc, Rhodia, La Poste and Renault. Recent deals include advising a holding company, owned by a French bank, in its acquisition of a 20% stake in a US broker-dealer firm; Abbott France SAS in its divestiture of a

CORPORATE: FUNDS

SJ BERWIN ✪

✪ Indicates firm displays contact details at the end of this chapter.

pharmaceutical plant; Rhodia in the sale of its industrial and commercial activities in France related to basic chemicals to Bain Capital; and Groupe General Electric, through its subsidiary GE Real Estate Investissement France, on its takeover bid for Sophia.

Latham & Watkins is active in classic M&A as well as in private equity, acting for Axa Private Equity and ABN Amro Capital for example. Some ten partners, with a special mention to Dominique Basdevant, Patrick Beauvisage and Nicolas Bombrun, regularly handle M&A work. Recent highlights include acting for ABN Amro Capital in the MBO acquisition of Protection One; SITQ/Lucia in the €433m sale of Tour Adria in La Défense to DB Real Estate Investment; Goldman Sachs Group in the acquisition of 80% MCM Africa; and the Carlyle Group in the acquisition of French entities of Rexnord/Brook Hansen Group.

Lovells continues to work for large international clients (Barclays, Lloyds, SBC, Prudential, Xerox) whilst at the same time developing a quality French clientele: AXA, BNP Paribas, CDR, MAAF, Michelin, Rhodia, to name some. Ten partners are active and recent deal highlights include advising Alstom in connection with the sale of its transmission and distribution business to Areva; Lloyds TSB in connection with the sale of its private banking business to UBS Warburg; SBC Communication, in connection with the sale to Vodafone of its 15% shareholding in Cegetel; and AXA France and its subsidiaries on the sale of its video and audio surveillance business to a subsidiary of the BNP Paribas group

At **Moquet Borde & Associés**, some eight partners are involved in M&A. Transactions often have a stock exchange dimension (Dominique Borde, Aline Poncelet) and the firm is involved in privatisations, property deals for funds (Andrew Armfelt) and private equity (Olivier Deren). Another specialisation is Eastern Europe, with offices in Tallinn and Budapest. Major recent transactions include the spin-off of the consulting practice of Deloitte & Touche; the acquisition of Dubois Matériaux by the Point P subsidiary of Saint Gobain; and the sale of 50% of Groupe Citadines to Ascott of Singapour Group by Whitehall Street Real Estate Fund and Westmount Hospitality.

Four partners handle M&A at **Shearman & Sterling LLP**, including Jacques Epstein, frequently in deals with a cross-border element. The firm advised Danone and its subsidiary Danone Waters of North America Inc in a joint venture with Suntory Water Group Inc; Electricité de France/SAE and SCPA in the sale of their common subsidiary Sogema to Sea-Invest; Eon AG in the sale of a participation in Bouygues Télécom SA; and Eurazeo SA in a strategic alliance with Colony Capital LLC to set up a European real estate investment fund. **Shearman & Sterling LLP** has also been very active in privatisations in recent years, on the issuer side (Air France, Crédit Lyonnais, Aérospatial, Thomson and Wanadoo, for example).

Jean Veil of **Veil Jourde La Garanderie** has an M&A practice dealing with listed companies, public takeover bids and privatisation. Private acquisitions, LBOs and restructurings are dealt with by Guillaume Kuperfils, Ariel Harroch, Patrick Jaïs and Daniel Katz. The firm advises Vivendi Universal on a general basis and funds such as Atria, Apax, ABN Amro Capital and Eurazeo. Recently **Veil Jourde La Garanderie** acted for Suez in the sale of its stake in TPS; BNP Paribas in its sale of Banque Directe; Eurazeo in the acquisition of Fraikin from Iveco (Fiat); Exor in the sale of SCA Château Margaux to Soparexo; and Generali on the acquisition of a French insurance business.

Willkie Farr & Gallagher LLP handles both LBOs (where it is among the top Paris firms, with Michel Frieh and Daniel Payan), and M&A (Daniel Hurstel and Laurent Faugérolas for listed deals). Last year, the firm advised the sellers of Materis Participations (CVC Capital Partners, Carlyle, Advent International, Lafarge and various managers) to LBO France; PAI Partners for the launched but unsuccessful tender offer on GrandVision SA; Santé Luxembourg SA in the sale of approximately 38.5% of its shareholding in Générale de Santé SA; and the Minister of Finance and Privatisation of the Kingdom of Morocco in the sale of 80% of Régie des Tabacs to Altadis.

Baker & McKenzie's M&A practice consists of corporate group restructurings, transactional work, and stock exchange-related deals (with the arrival of Raphaële François-Poncet from *HSD Ernst & Young*). The firm is also increasingly involved in private equity, working for funds like One Equity Partners and Platinum Equity. Recently, the team that includes Eric Lasry, Laurent Epstein and Laurent Barbara, advised Italfarmaco and Liconsa in the public tender offer for the shares of Effik (pharmaceuticals); One Equity Partners in connection with its acquisition of the Mauser Group; MFN in connection with the sale of its French telecoms network services business to management; and Core Finance in connection with the sale of the electrotechnic business of Eurofarad to the Gespac Group.

Coudert Frères handles cross-border transactions and domestic M&A for its French and foreign clients. The firm is very active for industrial clients, especially in the food, automobile and healthcare industries. For the latter, Alain Decombe and his six-associate team was recruited from **EY Law** (ex-*Archibald Andersen*), after Jacques Buhart had departed for **Herbert Smith**. Geroge T Yates is also well known.

Herbert Smith is developing an M&A practice, with four partners (including Mike Kingston) and one of counsel involved on a permanent basis. Sylvie Dariosecq left for **Eversheds-Frere Cholmeley** while Jacques Buhart and a team was joining from **Coudert Frères**. Last year, the firm was active on behalf of PwC Consulting and the Consulting Partners on PwC's separation of its worldwide management consulting business, including the disposal to IBM; Securicor in relation to the sale of its French business interests; Monitor Clipper Equity Partners (US) on the disposal of Technal (France) to Norsk Hydro (Norway); Euronext in relation to the establishment of a joint venture with EuroMTS; and Electricité de France (EDF) on the acquisition of Louis Dreyfus' share capital in EDF Trading.

Norton Rose's M&A department in Paris had comprised two partners, including Eric Laplante (Bertrand Pellet left for **Freshfields Bruckhaus Deringer**). The team was boosted by the arrival, at the time of writing, of five corporate partners from **Sokolow Dunaud Carreras**, which should reinforce the M&A and private equity practices, notably in the communications, media, biotech and energy sectors. The client base, made up of banks, private equity investors and industrial clients, is 40% domestic, the rest being equally divided between the UK and the US. The firm has been appointed as the exclusive legal adviser to Nestlé SA for all M&A occurring in France.

SJ Berwin's Paris office was created in 2001 and its M&A practice is developing with a strong focus on LBOs. The private equity specialist has four partners dedicated to this area, two partners having joined the firm from **Clifford Chance** in May 2003. George Pinkham has been a specialist in funds establishment for years and the firm can cash in on their knowledge of funds to build up transactional activity. Recently, **SJ Berwin** advised Pierre & Vacances in connection with the acquisition of Center Parcs Europe; Banexi Capital Partenaires in connection with the acquisition of FTFM La Toulousaine; and Viventures Partners in its acquisition from Vivendi of a group of American investors.

Salans has an extensive M&A practice, covering company purchases, stock market operations, joint ventures and private equity. In that field, the team made up of four partners, including Paul Morel and John Flanigan, was reinforced by the arrival of Pascal Jardin from **Deloitte & Touche Juridique et Fiscal**. Some ten partners are active in M&A in general. The firm recently advised Bertelsmann on the acquisition of the direct mail division of Eurodirect Marketing; EADS on the constitution of Roxel, a joint venture between MBDA and SNPE Matériaux Energétiques; and Pfizer on the French aspects of the transfer of Adams (Pastilles de Vichy and Cachou Lajaunie) to Cadbury Schweppes.

Simmons & Simmons is developing its corporate practice with three partners dedicated to private (Stephen Walters, Jacques de Taisne) and public (Thierry Gontard) deals, and is willing to build up a private equity ability. The firm advised CDC Capital Partners in the acquisition by Généfitec (Société Générale) of a minority shareholding in a Ghanaian bank; Sagem SA in the acquisition of subsidiaries of Leica Geosystems; MACC in the public offering on MACC shares by the holding company; and Savvis Corp (US) in the global acquisition of remote storage business in various jurisdictions.

Skadden, Arps, Slate, Meagher & Flom LLP is active in both public and private M&A, with a few LBOs. The practice is diverse and goes with a strong corporate finance expertise. Partners involved are Pierre Servan-Schreiber, Christopher Baker and Eden Quainton. The firm advised Office Dépôt in the acquisition of Guibert from PPR; UK fund Doughty Hanson in the LBO acquisition of SAFT; Business Object in the public offer of exchange on Cristal Decision; Scor in connection with the subsidiarisation of its life insurance pole; and Barilla on various acquisitions.

Joint ventures and M&A make up about half of the business at **Slaughter and May**'s Paris office, with part of the work undertaken in Paris coming via the London office. Five partners are mostly dedicated to M&A work: Peter Kett, Antoine-Audoin Maggiar, Alexander Blackburn, Brigitte Leclerc and Eric Grangeon. The firm is well respected for its work in pharmaceuticals, property, defence and aeronautics, security, insurance, and financial services. **Slaughter and May** has a relationship locally with **Bredin Prat**. Examples of recent work include: advising Orange SA on the public exchange offer launched by France Télécom to purchase minority interests in Orange; Alcatel on the disposal of SAFT; and Estée Lauder in relation to the acquisition of the Darphin group.

Sullivan & Cromwell LLP is primarily involved in transactions with an international/US dimension. Richard Asthalter and Gérard Mazet handle significant deals, such as advising Alcan in the takeover bid for Péchiney; the financial advisers to France Télécom in the bid to buy remaining shares in Orange; and the financial advisers to Crédit Lyonnais in their acquisition by Crédit Agricole.

White & Case LLP has a good M&A practice, especially on the private equity side (partners involved are François Leloup and Vincent Morin). Other partners are Philippe Sarrailhé and Bernard Tézé. The following sectors remain active: the finance and insurance sector; work for Nordic region clients; hotels and real estate; North Africa; and industrial outsourcing transactions. Clients include: Carlyle on the €400m acquisition by Carlyle and Eurazeo of Terreal; Industri Kapital on the acquisition of Labeyrie, a listed company; residential care organisation Orpea in its agreement to acquire a 29.3% stake in Medidep, the private hospital company; and AT Plastics in its merger with Acetex.

PROJECTS AND ENERGY

Allen & Overy's projects practice is led by Tim Scales and Rod Cork, aided by the public law practice. They advise banks, sponsors and other institutions on various projects, including those involving multilateral institutions and export credit agencies. The firm is involved in various sectors, particularly energy and natural resources, infrastructure and telecoms, with a growing focus on North Africa and across the Central and Eastern Europe region. **Allen & Overy** advised Algerian Cement Company in relation to the project financing of a cement plant; a consortium bidding in relation to the A19 motorway project; the project company on the $1bn project financing for Nigeria LNG; Crédit Lyonnais on the refinancing of a co-generation project in the Czech Republic; and EDF in relation to a power project in Vietnam.

Clifford Chance retains an outstanding Paris office, where Michael Elland-Goldsmith and Anthony Giustini head up a projects practice principally advising banks and sponsors. Transport infrastructure projects in France (PPP) are particularly prominent at present. Other sectors where the firm has solid experience include power and leisure facilities. The firm is counsel to France and Spain with a view to entering into the concession agreement for the construction, financing and operation of a railway link between the two countries. **Clifford Chance** also advises GIE CDG Express (grouping the SNCF, RFF and Aéroports de Paris) for the completion of a rail link between Paris and Charles de Gaulle airport (€800m in works); SACE in connection with the co-financing of a South African telecoms company; the IFC and the EIB on a $150m cement plant project financing (first private sector project financing in Algeria); the African Development Bank and four ECAs in connection with the $1bn financing for an LNG plant in Nigeria.

Gide Loyrette Nouel's lawyers (John Crothers, Bruno de Cazalet, Rupert Reece and François Krotoff) are mainly present in countries with a strong French influence - Maghreb, Africa, Vietnam and China, and in Eastern European countries where the firm has offices. The firm increased its North African capacity with the opening of a new office in Casablanca in addition to the Tunis office opened in 2001. An office in Algiers is planned in early 2004. Areas of focus include infrastructure, water, electricity and telecommunications. The firm has been involved in the following projects: PSP Municipal Water and Wastewater (Banja Luka, Bosnia and Herzegovina), advising the World Bank on the legal framework for PSPs in the municipal water sector; Beijing and Nanjing Water projects (China), advising a consortium bidding for contracts to build, rehabilitate and operate waste treatment plants; the first independent power plant in France to operate a private transmission network, advising the sponsor; and an IFI for a review and analysis of concession laws in the 27 countries of Eastern and Central Europe and the CIS.

Herbert Smith is active on the sponsors' side in a wide range of sectors, including oil, gas, mining, water, electricity, telecoms and infrastructure (pipelines, refineries, power plants), but increasingly represents banking clients. Geographically, the firm acts mainly in Africa (60% of the work), but also in Europe and the Middle East. The group consists of 16 lawyers, including four partners, notably Neil Brimson and Stéphane Brabant. In 2003, the firm advised Electricité de France in connection with its EDF Trading joint venture with Louis Dreyfus; Eurotunnel in relation to various innovative transactions involving its £7bn debt and other matters, including a tender offer for the redemption of equity notes; Energy Africa on a $75m loan facility, arranged by BNP Paribas and ABN Amro, secured on petroleum assets in the Republic of Congo and Equatorial Guinea; Miferso on the optimisation of the Falemé iron mine in Senegal, including the financing of mining operations and rail and port facilities for iron ore transportation (equity, debt, project finance); and the Republic of Senegal in relation to a BOT for the construction of a new airport in Dakar.

Maybe less pre-eminent in volume but not in technical nature, **Linklaters** has been active in project finance for many years, advising for example the Eurotunnel banking syndicate on both French and English law. Bertrand Andriani is highly praised and the firm is increasingly active in France and well positioned on the emerging PPP market with a new public law team. **Linklaters** represented the borrower on the financing of the project costs and refinancing of bridge loan facilities of Shin Satellite Public Company Ltd; Citibank and EKF as guarantors to the EIB for the financing of the first private sector cement plant to be built in Algeria; a mining major in the financing of a nickel mining and metallurgical project in New Caledonia; and the sponsor of an underground line in Thessaloniki (Greece).

Ashurst is active mainly in Central and Eastern Europe, the Middle East and in West Africa. Michel Lequien deals with projects issues (BOT, concessions, public law, regulation etc), with Laurent Mabilat and Diane Sénéchal being in charge of the financing aspects. The team is also positioned on the growing PPP field in France and was chosen by Caisse des Dépôts et Consignations in connection with the A4-A86 motorway project. Mainly working for sponsors, the firm also advises international institutions such as SFI, the EBRD, and commercial banks. Recent projects include advising a French railway operator in connection with an international freight project; a major waste treatment operator on a innovative financing for several installations in the context of delegation of public services; and Vivendi Environnement (Aquiris) for a wastewater treatment plant in Brussels. **Ashurst** was also active in Gabon (telecoms) and Burkina Faso (electricity).

De Pardieu Brocas Maffei & Leygonie mainly advises banks, and has worked on credits guaranteed by Coface. The firm has experience in Asia, having advised a syndicate on the establishment of the TGV in Korea, and on Laïbin B in China. **De Pardieu Brocas Maffei & Leygonie** represented Crédit Lyonnais in the financing of a cellular phone project in Algeria; Crédit Agricole Indosuez in the financing for the upgrading and increase of capacity of an aluminium refinery operated by CVG Bauxilum, located in Venezuela; Crédit

PROJECTS AND ENERGY: PROJECT FINANCE

ALLEN & OVERY ✪
CLIFFORD CHANCE
GIDE LOYRETTE NOUEL ✪
HERBERT SMITH ✪
LINKLATERS ✪

Ashurst
De Pardieu Brocas Maffei & Leygonie ✪
Freshfields Bruckhaus Deringer ✪
Norton Rose
Simmons & Simmons ✪
Slaughter and May ✪
Sullivan & Cromwell LLP
White & Case LLP

Cleary Gottlieb Steen & Hamilton ✪
Curtis, Mallet-Prevost, Colt & Mosle ✪
Franklin ✪
Latham & Watkins ✪
Lovells ✪
Orrick

Firms are listed A-Z in tiers which are ranked in order of priority

✪ *Indicates firm displays contact details at the end of this chapter.*

PROJECTS AND ENERGY: ENERGY

Ashurst ✪
Cleary Gottlieb Steen & Hamilton ✪
Clifford Chance
Coudert Frères ✪
Denton Wilde Sapte ✪
Eversheds-Frere Cholmeley
Franklin ✪
Gide Loyrette Nouel ✪
Herbert Smith ✪
JeantetAssociés ✪
Salans

Firms are listed alphabetically

✪ *Indicates firm displays contact details at the end of this chapter.*

Agricole Indosuez, ABN Amro and ANZ Investment Bank in the financing for the construction of a power facility in Mexico; and BNP Paribas in the financing for repair, refurbishment, upgrade and management of the Manilla water supply system.

Freshfields Bruckhaus Deringer offers project management from the bid and setting up of the project to the financing. The major areas covered are water, power, oil and gas, mines, transport and telecommunications. Traditionally, **Freshfields Bruckhaus Deringer** advises sponsors or multilateral organisations, but also acts for banks and governments. Last year, Jean L'Homme advised Tanger-Méditerranée Special Agency (TMSA) in connection with the construction of the new international port of Tangier (Morocco); BNP Paribas in connection with the lease financing of two co-generation power plants respectively arranged for Rhodia and Suez; Bouygues TP and Dragados in relation to the preparation of their offer in the context of the construction of the high-speed train link between Perpignan and Figueras; and FL SMIDTH in relation to the construction of a cement plant in Nigeria.

Norton Rose mainly advises banks, but also sponsors, with Martin Gdanski and Nigel Ward as well known partners. Recent work concerned renewable energies, acting for a PPP fund for the funding of its first two windfarms in France. The firm is also involved in the oil and gas sectors, particularly in the offshore sector, advising leading French oil companies and banks on oil, gas projects and on trade/commodity transactions in Africa.

At **Simmons & Simmons**, Australia-born Christophe Asselineau is the partner in charge. The five-lawyer team mainly works for sponsors, with a strong focus on energy and mining. Recent deals include representing Black & Veatch Africa in the $405m Arzew power and desalination plant in Algeria; the consortium (Cobra/Codesa/ Sadyt/Aben sur) in connection with the Hamma desalination plant; America Mineral Field for two mining projects in Congo; Crédit du Nord in the €13.5m financing of a windfarm in France; and the French government's special advisory task force on all legal aspects of the Koniambo and mining projects in New Caledonia

Slaughter and May (Antoine-Audoin Maggiar, Alexander Blackburn, Andrew McClean) advises sponsors, companies and lenders on the structuring and financing of major projects (with a focus on gas and electricity) around the world. Examples of work include advising Elf Trading in connection with the French regulatory aspects of certain derivatives transactions; Entergy Koch in connection with the French regulatory aspects of electricity and gas trading; and Innogy Plc in respect of French energy supply contracts.

Sullivan & Cromwell LLP's project finance activity is headed by Richard Vilanova and was reinforced by the arrival of Nikolaos Andronikos from the New York office. The firm has advised European principals for many years on project finance matters, particularly in South America, Africa, and the Middle East, and is currently advising on several pending projects in the oil, mining and natural gas/petrochemicals sectors.

At **White & Case LLP**, Paule Biensan and Jacques Bouillon are in charge. The firm advises sponsors, governments and financial institutions on projects all over the world, notably in Africa in a variety of sectors, including power, infrastructure, mining and telecoms. For example, the projects team advised Orascom in connection with the $500m long-term debt financing of a GSM network in Algeria; Aluminium Pechiney on the $228m financing of the de-bottlenecking of Bauxite mining facilities owned by CVG Bauxilum CA in Venezuela; and Crédit Lyonnais and AFD in the €179m financing of a power plant in New Caledonia.

We also mention firms involved in the contractual, corporate and regulatory aspects of energy and infrastructure projects. In addition to specialists already mentioned here above, the following experts are recommended: Jean-Pierre Vignaud (**Cleary Gottlieb Steen & Hamilton**); Jean-Claude Petilon (**Coudert Frères**); Héctor Farina (**Denton Wilde Sapte**); Rodman Bundy (**Eversheds-Frere Cholmeley**); Jérôme Michel (**Franklin**); Thierry Lauriol (**JeantetAssociés**); and Jeffrey Hertzfeld (**Salans**).

REAL ESTATE

FRESHFIELDS BRUCKHAUS DERINGER ✪
GIDE LOYRETTE NOUEL ✪
LEFÈVRE PELLETIER & ASSOCIÉS

CLIFFORD CHANCE
DE PARDIEU BROCAS MAFFEI & LEYGONIE ✪

Jones Day ✪
Linklaters ✪
Mayer, Brown, Rowe & Maw
White & Case LLP

Ashurst ✪
Baker & McKenzie ✪
CMS Bureau Francis Lefebvre ✪
Caubet Chouchana Meyer
JeantetAssociés ✪
Moquet Borde & Associés ✪
Rambaud Martel ✪
UGGC & Associés ✪
Zurfluh Lebatteux

August & Debouzy ✪
Bignon Lebray & Associés
DS Avocats
EY Law ✪
Lacourte Balas & Associés
Lafarge Flécheux Campana Le Blevennec
Norton Rose
Salans
Vatier & Associés ✪

Firms are listed A-Z in tiers which are ranked in order of priority
✪ Indicates firm displays contact details at the end of this chapter.

REAL ESTATE

Working in very close collaboration with a firm of notaries, **Freshfields Bruckhaus Deringer** offers a broad spectrum of property services. The clientele comprises buyers, investment funds (US and German), banks, financial institutions and insurance companies. Recently, the firm has been active advising on property securitisations (national and offshore) and on the setting up of real estate funds. Three partners handle property work: Antoine Vignial, Benoît Marcilhacy, Pascal Schmitz. They advised CDC ixis Capital Markets on the first pan-European real estate sale and lease-back transaction of a portfolio of 15 European sites from Alstom; Coface in relation to the sale and lease-back of its 28,000 sq m headquarters in Paris La Défense; Hines in relation to the setting up of a joint venture with AXA for purposes of acquiring land in Meudon (40,000 sq m of offices); and Westbrook Partners LLC in relation to the acquisition and financing of two real estate portfolios from Simco and Gécina (€1.2bn).

Gide Loyrette Nouel has a strong international practice and has been active in property law since the 1970s, when it started advising UK investors in Paris. The team comprises six partners among which Gérard Tavernier, Frédéric Nouel and Jean-Jacques Raquin stand out. The scope of work is wide and includes advising on the restructuring of loan portfolios, the externalisation of the state's real estate assets, and property financing. Clients are mostly of German, US and Middle Eastern origin. Last year, **Gide Loyrette Nouel** was involved in the launch of the construction operation of 40,000 sq m CBX Tower in La Défense for Tishman Speyer (€150m); advised François Pinault Trust in the Ile Seguin redevelopment, the largest urban redevelopment in progress in Ile de France; negotiated a 12-year 50,000 sq m lease for Technip; and handled the Unibail's Coeur Défense refinancing and securitisation, the largest French real estate securitisation to date (over €800m).

The other top French firm is **Lefèvre Pelletier & Associés**, where real estate continues to account for 40% of the overall turnover. Philippe Lefèvre is an expert in property investment and fellow name partner Philippe Pelletier is expert in rent and co-ownership issues. Clients include property investors, banks, promoters, builders and insurance companies, among others. With nine partners and 20 associates, this is probably the largest team in Paris.

Clifford Chance founded its Paris practice on property back in the 1960s and since then, has participated in many of the biggest property transactions in Paris, acting for overseas investors (Ronald Austin deals with many German funds at the moment) as well as lessees. Henry Lazarski had to retire from the firm and now works for **Mayer, Brown, Rowe & Maw**, while François Roux also left and acts as a *notaire*. Counsel Jean-Louis Martin is very active. The firm is involved in property financing and boasts one of the best property tax teams in Paris. Recent experience includes advising Société Générale on the sale to Difa of the Centre d'Affaires Paris Trocadéro; AIG on the sale to Siemens Kapitalanlagegesellschaft.mbh of an office building located in Courbevoie; and CGI on the acquisition from Axa of an office building located in Montrouge.

Historically advising banks (BNP Paribas, Crédit Lyonnais, HypoVereinsbank) in connection with real estate loans, **De Pardieu Brocas Maffei & Leygonie** is also very active in corporate and financing aspects of commercial property, working for property developers like Cogedim, and widely involved in litigation related to insurance, buying and selling issues. Jacques Henrot heads the department; Paul Talbourdet, Constance de la Hosseraye and Emmanuel Fatome are also recommended. They advised Morgan Stanley Real Estate Investment Fund and Foncière des Régions SA on the acquisition of the second real estate portfolio sold by France Télécom; AXA group on the acquisition by entities linked to GIC of an interest in the vehicle holding the 6/8 Bd Haussmann Building; the seller on the sale of the Périsud property asset (Montrouge) to CGI (Commerz Grundbesitz); LVMH group within the context of a sale and lease-back transaction; and BNP Paribas on a financing for the benefit of property companies (*foncières*) managed by AXA Reim.

Jones Day is mainly recommended for its property financing expertise (François Bonteil, Philippe Billot) but the firm recently welcomed Emmanuel Chauve, a property tax expert who previously worked at **EY Law**, and also handles corporate aspects. Last year, the firm advised Morgan Stanley Real Estate Fund in connection with its sale to Foncière des Régions of its 80% interest in EDF and France Télécom real estate portfolios; Deutsche Bank in connection with the refinancing and the sale of entities holding real estate assets located in Meudon; Westbrook Real Estate Fund IV in connection with the acquisition and the lease-back of real property assets consisting of buildings from IBM and as borrower, in connection with the financing of this acquisition; and GE Real Estate in connection with the acquisition from Suez of several real property assets located in the golden triangle of Paris, the lease-back, the transfer of capital lease agreements and the setting up of a development agreement.

Linklaters' team, led by Françoise Maigrot, acts on complex deals, town planning as well as environment, construction and property financing/securitisation. The group works closely with strong corporate, banking and tax teams. The firm acted this year for Barclays in restructuring the financing of the Marriott-Champs Elysées Hotel; TIAA in refinancing the purchase of 25 floors in the Aréva Tower (La Défense); and The Ascott Group Limited in its joint venture with Whitehall in respect of the Citadines short-term residential housing group. **Linklaters** also has an ongoing relationship with AXA Reim, WP Carey and ProLogis Real Estate Fund.

Mayer, Brown, Rowe & Maw is growing in Paris and set up a real estate team in September 2003. Jean-Pierre Daniel arrived from **DS Avocats** and was soon joined by one of the big names of property law in France, Henry Lazarski, who had retired from **Clifford Chance**. They intend to cash in on the firm's international real estate reputation to build up a strong practice in France.

At **White & Case LLP**, Emmanuel Rosenfeld is well respected. He is a specialist in litigation and real estate, works for funds, very often American, and his activity has developed alongside the firm's financing practice. The arrival of Franck Peter from **Clifford Chance** has increased the capacity. Clients include Bass, Caisse des Dépôts & Consignations, CDC ixis Immo, Euralille, France Télécom, Hilton Hotels, Klépierre, Ségécé, Société Centrale Immobilière de la Caisse des Dépôts & Consignations, Unibail and Visteon.

The new team at **Ashurst** is also worth a mention. Dorothée Bontoux (an ex-notary who used to work at **Linklaters**), and Philippe None are the two partners in charge. They advise funds and investors in acquisitions, financing and tax issues related to property deals, town planning and commercial leases.

Baker & McKenzie's team expanded with the recruitment of **EY Law**'s Olivier Mesmin and a team of four associates (**EY Law** also lost Emmanuel Chauve to **Jones Day**).

CMS Bureau Francis Lefebvre (Jean-Luc Tixier) is mainly involved in real estate transactions, acting for Ville de Paris or for German and English investors. The firm is also widely involved in commercial leases (Philippe Riglet) and corporate aspects of property (Philippe Rosenpick).

Caubet Chouchana Meyer is also recommended. The firm advises investment and pensions funds as well as Anglo-Saxon businesses investing in France. Michel Meyer, Christian Lachaume and Robert Meilichzon are recommended.

JeantetAssociés' real estate expertise lies mainly in financing, with Philippe Dubois advising banks on a regular basis.

At **Moquet Borde & Associés**, Andrew Armfelt works for US funds, while **Rambaud Martel**'s practice focuses on commercial leases and property cases in general, both on the advisory and contentious sides. Catherine Saint-Geniest's team works closely with strong public and construction departments.

UGGC & Associés handles financial and commercial aspects of property projects, with a special focus on town planning (Bernard Lamorlette), while **Zurfluh Lebatteux** specialises in co-ownership.

REAL ESTATE: COMMERCIAL LEASES

We recommend **Bruno Boccara & Associés**, where Bruno Boccara and Danièle Lipman-Boccara are well known specialists. Other lawyers include Marie-Odile Vaissié (**Lefèvre Pelletier & Associés**); **Jehan Barbier**, **Philippe-Hubert Brault**, **Jean-Pierre Blatter**, André Guillemain and Marie-Laurence Sainturat (**Guillemain Banide & Sainturat**); André Jacquin (**Jacquin Maruani**); François Roux (**Clifford Chance**); Catherine Saint-Geniest (**Rambaud Martel**); and **Bousquet**.

TAX

CMS Bureau Francis Lefebvre is without doubt the pre-eminent tax practice in Paris and benefits from various expert teams (no less than 30 lawyers specialising in VAT for example). The firm and its 73 partners enjoy an excellent reputation, particularly Jean-Claude Bouchard, Henri Bardet and Jean Guilmoto on the domestic side. Pierre Sébastien Thill, Bruno Gouthière, Bruno Gibert, Edouard Milhac and Pierre-Jean Douvier are frequently mentioned for their international expertise. The latter was reinforced last year with the arrival of a three-partner team specialising in transactional and international tax from **EY Law**. The practice covers company tax law, restructurings and M&A, transfer pricing as well as assistance in *fiscal* control, in sectors such as real estate, banking and insurance, energy, telecoms, pharmaceuticals and the hotel industry. Its international reach has obviously been broadened through the alliance sealed with *CMS*, and the French firm is heavily involved in developing the tax practice of other members.

Cleary Gottlieb Steen & Hamilton boasts the most highly recommended tax practice among US firms; Gilles Entraygues in particular is widely praised. Three other partners also focus on tax matters within the firm's broad practice: Arnaud de Brosses, Pascal Coudin and Jean-Michel Tron, who also handles M&A.

The **Linklaters** team comprises seven lawyers, including two partners: Philippe Derouin (a well-known tax specialist) and Annick Lainé-Audouard. The tax work handled is very much linked to its corporate and finance practices, often with an international dimension. Major transactions include public and private M&A deals, corporate reorganisations and, on the finance side, CDO-CLO issues and structured financings, in the real estate field for instance.

TAX

CMS BUREAU FRANCIS LEFEBVRE ✪

CLEARY GOTTLIEB STEEN & HAMILTON ✪
LINKLATERS ✪

Bredin Prat ✪
Clifford Chance
Freshfields Bruckhaus Deringer ✪
Sullivan & Cromwell LLP

Allen & Overy ✪
Baker & McKenzie ✪
Brandford-Griffith Baverez Pasturel ✪
Gide Loyrette Nouel ✪
Jones Day ✪
Latham & Watkins ✪
Veil Jourde La Garanderie ✪
Willkie Farr & Gallagher LLP ✪

Ashurst ✪
De Pardieu Brocas Maffei & Leygonie ✪
JeantetAssociés ✪
Lefèvre Pelletier & Associés
Moquet Borde & Associés ✪
Rambaud Martel ✪
Shearman & Sterling LLP
Slaughter and May ✪
White & Case LLP

Alexen Avocats ✪
August & Debouzy ✪
Barsi Doumith & Associés
Bignon Lebray & Associés
Bird & Bird ✪
Caubet Chouchana Meyer
Denton Wilde Sapte ✪
Franklin ✪
Herbert Smith ✪
Kléber
LeBoeuf, Lamb, Greene & Macrae L. L. P.
Lovells ✪
Magellan
Moisand Boutin & Associés
NomoS ✪
Norton Rose
Orrick
SJ Berwin ✪
Salans
Simmons & Simmons ✪
Sokolow Dunaud Carreras
Thieffry & Associés
UGGC & Associés ✪
Weil, Gotshal & Manges ✪

Firms are listed A-Z in tiers which are ranked in order of priority

✪ Indicates firm displays contact details at the end of this chapter.

Some contentious work is also carried out. Recent deals include the merger of Air France and KLM, the sale of SchlumbergerSema to Atos Origin, and the acquisition by Origny-Naples of a stake in Beghin-Say.

The arrival in 2002 of two partners, including Renaud Streichenberger, and four associates at **Bredin Prat** boosted the firm's tax profile. **Bredin Prat** had previously worked with the team on M&A-related tax issues before they left **CMS Bureau Francis Lefebvre**. The new team dealt with the tax aspects of transactions such as Orange/France Télécom; Pechiney/Alcan; Kingfisher/Kesa; Grandvision/PAI Partners; and Fraikin/Eurazeo.

Clifford Chance's tax department continues to develop. The team now comprises 18 lawyers, including three partners - Eric Davoudet, Eric Zeller and Alexandre Lagarrigue. The tax practice is strongly linked to the real estate, structured finance and corporate practices, notably in the private equity sector. The group has developed particular expertise in structuring investment funds and employee share plans, and worked for clients such as STAM, Merrill Lynch and HVB, JPMorgan, Apax Partners and Goldman Sachs.

Freshfields Bruckhaus Deringer's team comprises three partners and ten associates. Antoine Colonna d'Istria, Eric Thomas and James Vaudoyer deal with M&A, financial tax and real estate matters. They were involved in the tax aspects of the demerger of Kingfisher; advised Westbrook in the acquisition of real estate assets from Gecina and Simco; and handled the tax aspects of a securitisation for Air France.

Sullivan & Cromwell LLP, with Jean-Pierre Le Gall, provides both US and French advice on the broad array of transactional capital markets and M&A matters. The team was reinforced in 2003 by the arrival of Gauthier Blanluet from **JeantetAssociés**.

Allen & Overy's team comprises seven lawyers, and the activity is split between corporate (Patrice Couturier) and finance (Siamak Mostafavi). Cross-border tax arbitrations and French/US tax-driven deals, tax aspects of securitisations (advising Merrill Lynch for a whole business securitisation for Xerox), asset finance (Qantas, on the first-ever French tax lease in Australasia), and employee stock option plans are areas of growth. The firm was also involved in the first Tier 1 financing (for Cofinoga) utilising an English limited partnership.

Baker & McKenzie's tax practice headed by Pierre-Yves Bourtourault was boosted by the arrival of Véronique Millischer and her team from *Archibald* in September 2002. The group now comprises 30 tax advisers, including six partners, specialising in international tax optimisation, contentious matters, and personal patrimonies, and is particularly visible in the industrial and property fields.

Brandford-Griffith Baverez Pasturel created a tax practice from scratch at the end of 2003 with the recruitment of Pierre Ullman from **Jones Day**. He is a leading tax lawyer in France and an expert on taxation aspects of corporate transactions and real estate deals.

At **Gide Loyrette Nouel**, Richard Beauvais, Olivier Dauchez and Gilbert Ladreyt are the tax partners. Their activity has a strong international dimension and is highly transaction-orientated. They work in conjunction with specialists from other departments in the firm: M&A, finance and real estate. The tax department also plays an active role in corporate, finance, employee benefits, tax ruling and litigation.

Jones Day's tax activities are diverse, with particular expertise in post-acquisition restructuring, real estate and finance. While head of department Pierre Ullmann left the firm for **Brandford-Griffith Baverez Pasturel**, Emmanuel Chauve, a real estate tax specialist, arrived from **EY Law**, Vincent Agulhon being the other partner in charge. The team advised Pfizer in a tax-efficient restructuring after the worldwide acquisitions of Warner-Lambert and Pharmacia; Morgan Stanley Real Estate Fund in connection with its sale to Foncière des Régions of its 80% interest in the EDF and France Télécom real estate portfolios; and Veolia Environnement and its American subsidiaries in connection with the syndicated financing of a $300m letter of credit facility.

Latham & Watkins' tax specialists are Olivier Delattre, Christian Nouel and Xavier Renard. The firm's tax team comprises some ten people and encompasses international tax, M&A and finance aspects of tax. In particular, the team is very active in restructurings and acquisitions and also handles contentious work. About half of the business is auto-generated.

At **Veil Jourde La Garanderie**, Alain Frenkel specialises in tax litigation and negotiation with the tax administration, whereas Ariel Harroch deals with corporate tax.

Willkie Farr & Gallagher LLP's tax practice comprises three partners (Allard de Waal, Marie-Hélène Raffin and Bernard Le Pezron), plus nine associates. Their activity is close to the general activity of the firm and therefore concerns M&A and LBOs in an international context. Financial tax, patrimonial tax and stock options are also dealt with, for clients including banks, funds, and companies in the entertainment, pharmaceuticals, automotive, steel, telecoms and audiovisual sectors.

We also recommend Catherine Charpentier and Christopher Potter (**Ashurst**); Patrice Lefèvre-Péaron (**De Pardieu Brocas Maffei & Leygonie**); Dominique Godet and Philippe Losappio (**JeantetAssociés**); Eric Ginter (**Lefèvre Pelletier & Associés**); Henri de Feydeau and Alain Jouan (**Moquet Borde & Associés**); Roland Poirier (**Rambaud Martel**); Isabelle Chauvet and Niels Dejean (**Shearman & Sterling LLP**); Pierre-Pascal Bruneau and Yves-Charles Zimmermann (**Slaughter and May**); Alexandre Ippolito and Norbert Majerholc (**White & Case LLP**).

TAX: THE BIG FOUR

EY LAW ✪

FIDAL

Landwell & Associés / Partners

Deloitte & Touche Juridique et Fiscal ✪

Firms are listed A-Z in tiers which are ranked in order of priority

✪ Indicates firm displays contact details at the end of this chapter.

TAX: THE BIG FOUR

The merger between *HSD Ernst & Young* and *Archibald* gave birth to a new heavyweight on the Paris tax scene. The scope of tax issues covered by **EY Law** is impressive, ranging from international taxation to tax aspects of acquisitions or restructurings, indirect taxation (VAT/customs duties), arbitration and tax litigation, as well as company taxation, supply chain, transfer pricing and tax management for wealthy individuals. Well-known tax specialists include Patrick Dibout (European tax law), Robert Tarika (international tax), Olivier Mesmin (property tax), Hervé Lehérissel, Antoine Glaize and Yann de Kergos. That said, the merged firm did suffer a number of defections to other practices.

Fidal's unsurpassed national reach determines its strength, working primarily for a client base made up of small and medium-sized businesses. The Paris office undertakes chunkier advisory roles, but also day-to-day tax declarations and executive tax matters. The tax practice is built on well-known names such as Pierre-Yves Demazière (asset tax), Eric Lecocq (litigation), Jean-Luc Menu (corporate), François Bon and Guillaume de Brondeau (international), Jean-Dominique Delannoy (asset, insurance, real estate) and finally Jean-Louis Dieudonné (VAT).

Apart from a focus on individual taxation (comprising executives and expatriates) led by Michael Jaffe and Georges Morisson-Couderc, **Landwell & Associés/Partners** also boasts a well-established company tax department. Robert Magnan (M&A) and Marc Cretté (real estate) both have good reputations. Arrivals from *Archibald* include Hervé-Antoine Couderc and David de Pariente (patrimony tax).

At **Deloitte & Touche Juridique et Fiscal**, Dominique Bera (worldwide consolidated profits), Bernard Boutemy (litigation), Gianmarco Monsellato (transfer price) and Antoine Morterol (transactions) are well-known.

WHITE-COLLAR CRIME

BREDIN PRAT ✪

DARROIS VILLEY MAILLOT BROCHIER ✪

FARTHOUAT ASSELINEAU & ASSOCIÉS

FRANCIS SZPINER

HERVÉ TÉMIME

JEAN-YVES LEBORGNE

LIÉNARD ARDAILLION-LIÉNARD LANDON

LOMBARD & ASSOCIÉS

METZNER ASSOCIÉS

PHILIPPE LEMAIRE

RAMBAUD MARTEL ✪

THIERRY HERZOG

THIERRY LÉVY, ORLY REZLAN ET ASSOCIÉS

VARAUT CARRÈRE VARAUT

Barsi Doumith & Associés

Christine Courrégé

Dartevelle Benazeraf Merlet

French Cornut-Gentille

Gide Loyrette Nouel ✪

Granrut

Jean-Paul Lévy

JeantetAssociés ✪

Kiejman & Marembert

Lysias

Michel Zaoui

Moquet Borde & Associés ✪

Olivier Schnerb

Salans

Soulez Larivière et Associés

Vatier & Associés ✪

Veil Jourde La Garanderie ✪

White & Case LLP

Cahen & Associés

Caubet Chouchana Meyer

Clifford Chance

Franklin ✪

Fischer Tandeau de Marsac Sur & Associés

Lafarge Flécheux Campana Le Blevennec

Lussan Brouillaud

Montbrial et Associés

Thieffry & Associés

Firms are listed A-Z in tiers which are ranked in order of priority

✪ Indicates firm displays contact details at the end of this chapter.

WHITE-COLLAR CRIME

The following lawyers are recommended for white-collar crime: Olivier Metzner (**Metzner Associés**); Jean-Marc Varaut (**Varaut Carrère Varaut**); **Jean-Yves Leborgne**; **Philippe Lemaire**; **Thierry Lévy, Orly Rezlan et Associés**; **Francis Szpiner**; Jean-Yves Liénard (**Liénard Ardaillion-liénard Landon** in Versailles); Paul Lombard and Olivier Baratelli (**Lombard & Associés**); Jean-René Farthouat (**Farthouat Asselineau & Associés**); Jean-Michel Darrois and Emmanuel Brochier (**Darrois Villey Maillot Brochier**); Jean-Denis Bredin, Jean-François Prat and Eric Dezeuze (**Bredin Prat**); and Jean-Pierre Martel, Thierry Dalmasso and Philippe Goosens (**Rambaud Martel**).

Our list also includes: Roger Doumith (**Barsi Doumith & Associés**); **Christine Courrégé**; Bernard Dartevelle (**Dartevelle Benazeraf Merlet**); Jean-Marie Burguburu and Kiril Bougartchev (**Gide Loyrette Nouel**); Pierre Cornut-Gentille (**French Cornut-Gentille**); Bernard du Granrut (**Granrut**); Bernard Vatier (**Vatier & Associés**); Yves Baudelot (**Lysias**); Bernard Gorny and Henri Hajdenberg (**JeantetAssociés**); Georges Kiejman (**Kiejman & Marembert**); **Jean-Paul Lévy**; Daniel Soulez Larivière (**Soulez Larivière et Associés**); **Olivier Schnerb**; **Michel Zaoui**; Michel Jéol and Sylvie-Claire d'Arvisenet (**Moquet Borde & Associés**); Bernard Cahen (**Cahen & Associés**); Jean-Pierre Chouchana (**Caubet Chouchana Meyer**); Xavier Flécheux and Grégoire Lafarge (**Lafarge Flécheux Campana Le Blevennec**); Philippe Pech de Laclause (**Salans**); Yann Colin (**Franklin**); Thibault de Montbrial (**Montbrial et Associés**); Jean Thieffry (**Thieffry & Associés**); Jean Veil and Georges Jourde (**Veil Jourde La Garanderie**); and Emmanuel Rosenfeld (**White & Case LLP**).

THE REGIONS

We mention here the leading law firms in the regions. This includes the Big Four. Some of these firms are also represented in Paris and, for that reason, can sometimes be direct competitors to Parisian firms.

Adamas has offices in Lyon, Paris and in Asia (Beijing, Shanghai, Taipei, Canton). The firm's activities revolve around four departments: public and environmental law, Asia and foreign investments in China, international business law (M&A, arbitration, IP), and general litigation.

THE REGIONS

ASA Avocats Associés *Strasbourg*

Adamas *Lyon* ✪

Alexandre Lévy Kahn *Strasbourg*

Bignon Lebray & Associés *Aix-en-Provence, Lille, Lyon*

CJA Beucher *Angers*

CMS Bureau Francis Lefebvre *Lyon*

Camille & Associés *Toulouse*

Cornet Vincent Ségurel *Nantes*

Decker & Associés *Toulouse*

Deloitte & Touche Juridique et Fiscal *six offices* ✪

Delsol & Associés *Lyon*

Duel *Lille*

Dutat Lefebvre & Associés *Lille*

EY Law *12 offices* ✪

Fidal *107 offices*

Lamy Lexel Avocats Associés *Lyon, Alps*

Lamy Ribeyre & Associés *Lyon*

Landwell & Associés / Partners *nine offices*

Lebas & Associés *Lille*

Legalis *Lille*

Moquet Borde & Associés *Lyon*

Morvilliers Sentenac *Toulouse*

Ratheaux *Lyon, Nice* ✪

Requet Chabanel *Lyon*

Soulier *Lyon*

Firms are listed alphabetically

✪ Indicates firm displays contact details at the end of this chapter.

Strasbourg-based **ASA Avocats Associés** is very highly regarded. A variety of areas are covered: company and commercial, banking and finance, commercial property, distribution and competition. The firm also has an office in Paris.

Also in Strasbourg, **Alexandre Lévy Kahn** is renowned throughout the region for its superb company and commercial work and the firm's four partners and nine associates also handle banking and distribution cases. The firm has a largely court-based practice.

Bignon Lebray & Associés is in Lyon, Lille, Aix-en-Provence, Paris and Madrid, with about 80 lawyers. It is the result of the splitting up of *Bignon, Lebray, Delsol & Associés* in 2003. The firm is active in general corporate and commercial law, M&A, banking, collective procedures, labour law, tax, public law, for French and international clients. The firm is part of the *Meritas* network.

CJA Beucher is considered a quality, full-service practice in the West region and enjoys a good reputation. Its practice is advisory as well as contentious and its core activity is corporate, tax and labour law. Patrick Beucher is particularly acknowledged for his expertise within the food industry.

CMS Bureau Francis Lefebvre Lyon in Lyon is the new name of *Boyer Clément Pégand* after the Paris tax and business law heavyweight increased its stake in the firm to 51% in 2003. Clients include mid-size businesses and subsidiaries of large manufacturing, retail and service corporations based in the Rhône-Alpes region. The firm is active in corporate, labour, public and tax law and litigation. Some 40 lawyers work in Lyon.

Camille & Associés is one of the oldest firms in Toulouse and also has an office in Barcelona. The firm is well regarded for its work in commercial, banking, labour and property law and has a varied clientele encompassing the industrial, retail and service industry sectors.

Cornet Vincent Ségurel is indisputably one of the major players in general company and commercial law in the western region of the country. Comprising some 30 lawyers in Nantes and Paris, it is the product of a successful merger between a firm of *avocats* and a firm of *conseils juridiques*. The firm is notably active in insolvency, distribution, new technologies, transport, property and public law.

Decker & Associés of Toulouse has six partners and is renowned for its commercial practice which is particularly strong in banking and aviation law. A large proportion of the client base consists of commercial banks and the firm has developed close and successful relationships within this sector, often being called upon to advise on the financing of M&A transactions. The firm also has a number of clients in the food sector.

Deloitte & Touche Juridique et Fiscal has offices in Marseille, Lyon, Bordeaux, Tours, Lille and Nantes. For example, in Lyon, **Deloitte & Touche Juridique et Fiscal** is home to three partners and more than 30 associates. The firm offers a full service, with a special focus on national and international M&A, commercial law, tax and labour law. The firm also has a strong litigation department.

Delsol & Associés is the result of the splitting-up of *Bignon, Lebray, Delsol & Associés* in 2003. It comprises nine partners (five in Lyon and four in Paris). The firm acts for a national and international clientele in business law – M&A, company law, tax, labour, litigation, public law – with some niche expertise in the tourism sector.

In Lille, **Duel** has 11 partners and 19 associates who handle company and employment law, commercial law, construction and insolvency. The firm has further offices throughout the region (Douai, Tourcoing, Béthune), as well as Paris. Clients include local companies, banks and insurance companies.

Dutat Lefebvre & Associés has offices in Lille, Valenciennes and Cambrai and its 22 partners are active in all areas of law, including tax, labour, insurance, construction, M&A and white-collar crime. They advise regional companies and handle litigation.

EY Law resulted from the merger between *HSD Ernst & Young* and *Archibald* and has offices in 12 cities (Bordeaux, Grenoble, Lille, Lyon, Marseille, Monaco, Montpellier, Nantes, Nice, Saint-Etienne, Strasbourg, Toulouse). The merger only affected Lyon and Strasbourg, the only cities where the previous member of the *Andersen Legal* network had offices. The Lyon office is especially strong. The firm's three main areas of activity are tax, labour law and corporate/M&A, but depending on the office, skills have been developed in various areas of law, such as banking and finance in Lyon for instance.

With a network of 107 offices in 21 regional centres, **Fidal** has offices all over France. The strength of the firm is in general corporate and commercial work, tax and labour law but it also increasingly handles contentious work.

Lamy Lexel Avocats Associés has a staff of 85 lawyers divided between Paris, Lyon, Annecy, Chambéry and Albertville. In Lyon, 40 lawyers act for medium and large companies. Apart from traditional activity in company and commercial law, the firm's expertise also encompasses distribution, tax and public law, sports law (with a ten-lawyer dedicated team), as well as litigation/arbitration and labour law, which has always been one of its strengths, especially in the Paris office.

Lamy Ribeyre & Associés is considered one of the major general commercial practices in Lyon. Its staff of about 90 avocats (including **Fromont Briens & Associés**) is organised into specialist teams. Though the firm has built up its reputation in a broad range of areas on the basis of its litigation expertise, it does not handle labour law, this being undertaken instead by **Fromont Briens & Associés**, with which **Lamy Ribeyre & Associés** has a partnership.

Landwell & Associés/Partners has nine offices outside Paris (Bordeaux, Grenoble, Lille, Lyon, Marseille, Montpellier, Nantes, Rennes, Strasbourg). The biggest one is Lyon, with some 40 lawyers specialising in tax law, but also in company law, contracts, restructurings and M&A. They also handle labour law and contentious work in fields such as banking and collective proceedings.

Based in Lille and with 20 lawyers, **Lebas & Associés** is particularly well regarded for the quality of its trial work, but has been developing an advisory practice which now comprises half of the firm's activity. The firm has a good reputation in company and commercial law. The client base includes national and regional institutions and mail order companies.

One of the important firms in the North-east region (based in Roubaix, near Lille) is **Legalis**, although this is more due to its good reputation and substantial client base than its size. The practice covers company and commercial law, competition and insolvency. The firm is particularly well regarded for the quality of its trial work. Clients are mainly small and medium-sized companies, although there are also several larger banking and industrial clients.

A Parisian firm, **Moquet Borde & Associés** has offices in Lyon, Brussels, Budapest and Tallinn. In Lyon, the firm is an all-rounder with a focus on M&A, finance and company law very often related with foreign investments.

Toulouse-based **Morvilliers Sentenac** enjoys a superb reputation locally. Ten lawyers represent a regional and national client base mainly in the medical and pharmaceutical sectors, including some major laboratories. Other strings to the firm's bow include IP, a solid reputation for tax, company law, insolvency and M&A, and banking and IT, as well as particular experience in international relations.

Ratheaux is home to 30 lawyers, 11 of them partners, with a solid reputation in business law (company law, tax, contracts) while developing know-how in other fields such as labour law, securities and regulation and economic law. The firm handles a lot of work for international companies wishing to establish themselves in France. Two further offices are located in Paris and Nice.

Requet Chabanel, in Lyon, is active in company law, tax, economic law and labour law. The firm has a partnership with two other firms to handle litigation and intellectual property. Eight partners and ten associates compose the team.

With offices in Paris and Lyon, **Soulier** has established a good name in national and international law. Handling labour law, intellectual property and international arbitration, the firm also has a wider practice in company and commercial law.

ADAMAS

55 BOULEVARD DES BROTTEAUX
69006 LYON

Telephone: +33 4 72 41 15 75
Fax: +33 4 72 41 15 70
E-mail: lyon@adamas-lawfirm.com
Website: www.adamas.com.cn

Languages
English, German, Mandarin, Spanish

Other offices
Beijing, Canton, Paris, Shanghai, Taipei

Number of lawyers 32
at this office 19

CATEGORIES OF WORK

Mergers and acquisitions, investments
Robert Guillaumond

International arbitration
Robert Guillaumond

Administrative law, public law
Alain Serge Mescheriakoff, Georges Xynopoulos

Environmental law
Yvan Razafindratandra

Social law, labour law
Jean-Michel Ghinsberg

Banking law,
Laurence Bremens

Taxation
Jean-Claude Chocque

China law, investments in China
Franck Desevedavy, Olivier Dubuis

Industrial property rights
Barbara Bertholet, Laurence Bremens

DUTEIL AVOCAT

7 PLACE ANTONIN PONCET
69002 LYON

Telephone: +33 4 78 37 24 24
Fax: +33 4 78 37 24 34
E-mail: online@duteil-avocat.com
Website: www.duteil-avocat.com

Languages
English, French

Number of lawyers 4

Contacts
François Duteil, Carole Dahan,
Delphine Descamps, Olivia Dubois

CATEGORIES OF WORK	
Mergers and acquisitions	**Capital investment**
Stock exchange engineering	**Venture capital**
Financial engineering	**Equity investment**
Banking, finance and securities	**Corporate law**

THE FIRM

Duteil Avocat was created in 1996 by François Duteil, who had previously been head of the legal department at a major bank in Lyon for ten years.

The firm is particularly competent in carrying out complex mergers and acquisitions transactions (which account for 40% of the annual turnover), notably in finalising cross-border sales amounting to more than €150m. In particular, the firm specialises in advising foreign clients on their external growth deals in France.

Duteil Avocat is particularly skilled in the field of stock exchange law and has many clients that are listed companies. Some of the most important capital investment and venture capital institutions in the south east of France trust Duteil Avocat to conceive and carry out their legal and financial transactions, including LBOs, shareholders' agreements and issue of complex securities.

Three major principles govern the legal services provided by the firm: personalisation of the relationship with the client; the search for an optimal reactivity; and concern about confidentiality.

A significant arrival at the firm in 2003 was that of Delphine Descamps, a bilingual lawyer who has recently spent six years in the US. Since the beginning of her career, she has mainly been involved in international transactions, and she will be dedicated to the development of such transactions at Duteil Avocat.

AREAS OF PRACTICE

Mergers and acquisitions: recent transactions include the acquisition of Soleri group (Euronext Paris – Second Market) by DaimlerChrysler (Germany); the acquisition of Façonnable group by Nordstrom (US); the minority sale of Teisseire (Euronext Paris – Second Market); and mergers for the LVL Medical Groupe (Euronext Paris – Second Market).

Stock exchange engineering: recent transactions include the IPOs (all Euronext Paris – Second Market) of April Group; Coletica; Maitre Fournil; Tessi; and the takeover bid on Petit Boy.

Financial engineering: recent transactions include the Mercura LMBO; and the LBO of Petit Boy.

Banking, finance and securities: the firm provides legal advice on all types of transactions for clients including CIC Banque de Vizille.

Other recent transactions include: capital investment work for clients including GPV (Garnier Ponsonnet-Vuillard); venture capital work for Spring Technologies; equity investments for Belvédère (Euronext Paris – New Market); and other corporate transactions.

LAMY RIBEYRE & ASSOCIÉS (GROUPE)

40 RUE DE BONNEL
69484 LYON CEDEX 03

Telephone: +33 4 78 62 14 00
Fax: +33 4 78 62 14 99
E-mail: info@lamy-ribeyre.com
Website: www.lamy-ribeyre.com

Languages
English, German, Italian, Spanish

Other offices
Paris

Number of lawyers 97
at this office 65

Member
TERRALEX

CATEGORIES OF WORK

International arbitration
Christoph Martin Radtke, Anne Covillard

Commercial and corporate disputes
Alain Ribeyre, Philippe Genin

Competition, distribution and consumption
Anne Covillard, Rémi Llinas

Insolvency and reorganisation
Alain Ribeyre, Annie David

Finance and banking law
Alain Ribeyre, Annie David

Tax law and dispute resolution
Gérard Legrand, Eric Baroin

Property disputes, technical and technological litigation
Yves Bizollon, Jean-Guillaume Monin

Criminal law for business
Alain Ribeyre, Philippe Genin

International law and European law
François Balsan, Christoph Martin Radtke

Industrial and intellectual property
Yves Bizollon, Jean-Guillaume Monin

Corporate
Bruno Lamy, Dominique Grivet

Mergers and acquisitions
François Balsan, Eric Baroin

Health
Bruno Lamy, Anne Bolland-Blanchard

Employment, pensions, social security
Gilles Briens, Catherine Millet-Ursin

Labour
Philippe Clement, Marilyn Favier

Labour litigation
Yves Fromont, Hugues Pelissier

RATHEAUX

40 RUE DE BONNEL
69484 LYON CÉDEX 03

Telephone: +33 4 72 61 75 75
Fax: +33 4 78 60 00 09
E-mail: ratheaux@ratheaux.fr
Website: www.ratheaux.fr

Languages
English, Italian, Spanish

Other offices
Nice, Paris

Number of lawyers 35

Member
EEIG Consulegis

CATEGORIES OF WORK

Corporate and company
Georges Morel, André Monet

Tax law and litigation
Serge Berrettoni, Christian Muller

Mergers and acquisitions
Michel Bottazzi, Gaëtan de la Bourdonnaye

Private equity, venture capital
Pierre Cote, Michel Belin

Labour, employment law
Marie-Claude Chautard

Commercial litigation
Sylvain Roussat

IP copyright, patents and trade marks
Bernard Ughetto

Contracts, competition, distribution
Henri Saint-Père

Bankruptcy, debt collection
Michel Bottazzi, Sylvain Roussat

LMBO, joint ventures
Henri Saint-Père, Michel Belin

International arbitration
Bernard Ughetto

Pensions, social security
Marie-Claude Chautard

EU, international and foreign investment
Henri Saint-Père

VAT, excise and customs
Serge Berrettoni, Christian Muller

Corporate restructuring, asset deals
Georges Morel, André Monet

Product liability, industrial risks
Sylvain Roussat, Bernard Ughetto

CMS BUREAU FRANCIS LEFEBVRE

1-3 VILLA ÉMILE BERGERAT
92522 NEUILLY-SUR-SEINE CEDEX

Telephone: +33 1 47 38 55 00
Fax: +33 1 47 38 55 55
E-mail: central@bfl-avocats.com
Website: www.bfl-avocats.com

Languages
English, German, Italian, Mandarin, Portuguese, Russian, Spanish

Other offices
Berlin, Brussels, Bucharest, Buenos Aires, Casablanca, Düsseldorf, Lyon, Madrid, Montevideo, Moscow, New York, São Paulo, Shanghai, Strasbourg

Number of lawyers 441
at this office 311

Contact
Robert Baconnier

Member
CMS Network

CATEGORIES OF WORK

Direct taxation	**Patrimonial law**
VAT	**Dispute and arbitration**
Registration fees – wealth tax	**Contracts and regulations**
Local taxes	**Banking and finance, insurance**
International taxation	**Real estate and public law**
Customs & Excise duties	**Intellectual property and information technology law**
Employment law	**Competition, distribution and customer law**
International law	**EU law and dispute**
Corporate law, M&A	
Insolvency law	

THE FIRM
With more than 75 years of experience, CMS Bureau Francis Lefebvre ranks among the foremost business and law firms in France.

It has, over the years, continuously expanded its scope of expertise ranging from structuring and negotiating complex transactions to representing clients in front of regulatory agencies, legislators and courts. Moreover, it offers to its clients the services of its 12 international offices reinforced by the CMS network, which is composed of the following firms:

CMS Adonnino Ascoli & Cavasola Scamoni (Italy), CMS Cameron McKenna (United Kingdom), CMS Derks Star Busmann (The Netherlands), CMS Lexcelis (Belgium), CMS Hasche Sigle (Germany), CMS Strommer Reich-Rohrwig Karasek Hainz (Austria) and CMS von Erlach Klainguti Stettler Wille (Switzerland).

Thus, CMS Bureau Francis Lefebvre together with these firms include more than 1,900 lawyers who cover 16 countries in Europe and nine countries across the other continents.

DELOITTE & TOUCHE JURIDIQUE ET FISCAL

181 AVENUE CHARLES DE GAULLE
92524 NEUILLY SUR SEINE CEDEX

Telephone: +33 1 40 88 22 50
Fax: +33 1 40 88 22 17

Languages
Arabic, Dutch, English, German, Greek, Italian, Japanese, Mandarin, Portuguese, Russian, Spanish

Other offices
Bordeaux, Lille, Lyon, Marseille, Nantes, Tours

Number of lawyers 340

Contact
Pascale Ponroy (communication manager)

Member
International Fiscal Association;
American Chamber of Commerce

CATEGORIES OF WORK

Banking and finance
Marie-France Vernay

Communications, media
Philippe Emiel, Antoine Morterol

Corporate tax
Antoine Morterol

Indirect tax, VAT and customs
Odile Courjon, Xavier Casal

Individual tax, international assignment services, immigration
Patrick Tyrrell, Anne Vaucher

Insolvency law, bankruptcy
Stéphanie Chatelon

International tax structuring
Antoine Morterol,
Sophie Blégent-Delapille

Joint ventures, corporate reorganisation, takeovers
Jean-Victor Prevost

Mergers and acquisitions
Philippe Emiel

Real estate tax
Alex Burri, Sylvie Magnen

Social law
Véronique Béal-Child

Tax audit and litigation
Bernard Boutemy

Transfer pricing
Gianmarco Monsellato

Worldwide tax consolidation
Dominique Béra

THE FIRM

Deloitte & Touche Juridique et Fiscal offers a comprehensive range of French and international law services across a variety of business areas to domestic and multinational clients around the world. The firm provides clients with the international expertise of business and tax lawyers and tax professionals.

With over 300 professionals, the firm is one of the leaders in the tax and business law areas in France. Clients benefit from the expertise of business lawyers in the Deloitte global legal network as well as the support of tax lawyers and tax specialists in the Deloitte network. This combines local expertise and experience with international transactions management skills, ensuring seamless, integrated and consistent quality services wherever the clients operate. Deloitte & Touche Juridique et Fiscal is the associated firm of Deloitte in France, the professional services firm.

All of the lawyers are members of the Hauts de Seine Bar and therefore authorised to appear before the French courts. Several of them are also members of the New York Bar.

AREAS OF PRACTICE

Specialising in a wide range of both domestic and international tax and legal work to multinational corporations, international financial institutions, and sovereign governments.

The office provides clients with legal and tax assistance and advice on mergers and acquisitions, joint ventures, reorganisation and structuring in France. Its lawyers also have cohesive experience of cross-border and multi-jurisdictional transactions.

The firm's mergers and acquisitions network of non-US offices is staffed by more than 500 lawyers, primarily members of the local Bar who are experienced in tax and legal mergers and acquisitions matters within their jurisdictions, as well as in US-style transactions.

The firm's bankruptcy and insolvency department represents institutional investors. It also acts regularly for unsecured creditors, and business debtors.

The banking and finance (financial products/structured finance) practice involves representation of major banks and capital providers in a broad spectrum of national and cross-border lending and structured finance transactions, defeasance structures and related transactions.

The firm also handles arbitration and litigation.

The firm is actively involved in corporate international tax planning, VAT and custom duty planning. The practice serves all the international tax planning and dispute-related needs of national and multinational clients including co-ordination of multi-country tax planning, transfer pricing etc, profit reparation, planning strategic tax consulting, value-added tax issues, custom duty planning.

Clients are advised on social law matters including employment contracts, landing redundancies and relations with trade unions, etc.

ALERION

5 RUE JEAN MERMOZ
75008 PARIS

Telephone: +33 1 58 56 97 00
Fax: +33 1 58 56 97 01
E-mail: paris@alerionavocats.com
Website: www.alerionavocats.com

Languages
French, English, Spanish, German, Korean, Chinese

Number of lawyers 25

CATEGORIES OF WORK

Banking and finance
Dominique Doise, Philippe Mathurin

Bankruptcy
Philippe Mathurin

Corporate and business law
Pierre-Olivier Brouard, Christophe Gerschel

M&A
Pierre-Olivier Brouard, Jacques Bouyssou

Private equity, capital markets
Jacques Bouyssou, Pierre-Olivier Brouard

Competition, distributorship, EC
Catherine Robin

Labour law
Jacques Perotto

International investment
Joong-Ho Kim

Tax law
Christophe Gerschel

Commercial property and real estate
Philippe Mathurin

Product liability and insurance
Philippe Mathurin, Patrick Lescop De Moÿ

Litigation, arbitration
Dominique Doise, Jacques Bouyssou

Public law
Philippe Mathurin

Sports and entertainment
Christophe Gerschel

Korean business law
Joong-Ho Kim

ALLEN & OVERY

EDOUARD VII
26 BOULEVARD DES CAPUCINES
75009 PARIS

Telephone: +33 1 40 06 54 00
Fax: +33 1 40 06 54 54
E-mail: information@allenovery.com
Website: www.allenovery.com

Languages
English, German, Spanish, Italian

Other offices
Amsterdam, Antwerp, Bangkok, Beijing, Bratislava, Brussels, Budapest, Dubai, Frankfurt, Hamburg, Hong Kong, London, Luxembourg, Madrid, Milan, Moscow, New York, Paris, Prague, Rome, Shanghai, Singapore, Tokyo, Turin, Warsaw

Number of lawyers 2,305
at this office 105

Contacts
Edouard Didier (senior partner)
Isabelle Epp (marketing contact)

CATEGORIES OF WORK

Banking/syndications

Acquisition finance/private equity

Securitisation/asset finance

Projects/telecoms finance

Corporate/commercial

Mergers and acquisitions

Restructuring

Intellectual property/ information technology

Real estate

EU and competition

Employment and incentives

Public, administrative and environmental

Debt and equity capital markets

Derivatives

Tax

Structured financings

Financial services

ALEXEN AVOCATS

47 RUE DE MONCEAU
75008 PARIS 35

Telephone: +33 1 56 69 50 00
Fax: +33 1 56 69 50 22
E-mail: avocats@alexen.com

Languages
English, German, Italian, Japanese, Polish, Russian, Spanish

Other offices
Lyon, London

Number of lawyers 77
at this office 35

CATEGORIES OF WORK

Banking, securities
Marie Alice Godot-Sorine, Patrick Gentil

Company law, corporate law
Rémi Turcon, Marie Alice Godot-Sorine

Trust and estate planning
Vincent Vervandier

National taxation
Jean-Claude Cavaillé, Vincent Vervandier

International taxation
Jean-Claude Cavaillé, Vincent Vervandier

Family law, estate planning
Michèle Gillet-Vinet, Vincent Vervandier

International transactions, foreign investment
Rémi Turcon

Distribution, franchising
Patrick Gentil, Laurent Vienot

Intellectual property law
Cyril Fabre, Patrick Gentil

Labour and social security law
Michèle Gillet-Vinet

Litigation
Michèle Gillet-Vinet, Anick Bénat

Product liability, industrial risks
Michèle Gillet-Vinet, Anick Bénat

Mergers and acquisitions
Rémi Turcon, Laurent Vienot

Restructuring
Jean-Claude Cavaillé, Vincent Vervandier

Real estate and commercial leases
Rémi Turcon, Laurent Vienot

THE FIRM

Formed in 1998, Alexen Avocats is the regrouping of the three French law firms: Office Juridique Français et International (OJFI), established in 1945 with offices in Paris and Lyon, CEJEF, established in 1978, and Degueldre & Gramblat, established in 1967. Several other law firms such as the labour law firm Chassany & Watrelot, and individual lawyers have joined Alexen Avocats since its creation.

Alexen Avocats comprises 28 partners, 77 lawyers and a total staff of 160 and has offices in Paris, Lyon and London.

AREAS OF PRACTICE

The firm specialises in a wide variety of both domestic and international commercial work for corporate clients, from private individuals to multinational companies, through the entire range of privately and publicly owned companies and commercial entities.

The firm is organised into practice groups which cover the entire spectrum of legal, judicial and tax specialities. The firm regularly advises foreign companies, more particularly European, North American and Japanese companies doing business in France as well as French companies and individuals doing business abroad. The firm is also closely connected with the consulting firm Yamada Consulting Ltd, advising primarily Japanese companies on their investment projects in Europe.

The commercial department of the firm handles real estate and general commercial and retail work, while about 50% of activity is of a corporate nature.

The private client department deals more particularly with complex international family structures, international estates and tax planning as well as all matters related to individuals and their estate and focusing on legal and tax issues both in France and abroad.

Another major area of work is the general litigation and arbitration practice. The firm has a full litigation practice in France and other areas of general commercial law, corporate law, mergers and acquisitions, administrative law, banking and securities laws, bankruptcy law, competition and European law, copyright law, entertainment law, labour law, insurance law, real estate law, taxation law, and trust and international estates.

The firm recently developed an information technology and electronic commerce department and specialises in particular in trade mark and copyright protection, computer, multimedia and Internet law, and electronic commerce transactions.

A brochure providing more details is available upon request.

AUGUST & DEBOUZY

6-8 AVENUE DE MESSINE
75008 PARIS

Telephone: +33 1 45 61 51 80
Fax: +33 1 45 61 51 99
E-mail: contact@augdeb.com
Website: www.august-debouzy.com

Languages
English, French, German, Hungarian, Italian, Persian, Portuguese, Russian, Serbo-Croatian, Spanish, Turkish

Other offices
Brussels

Number of lawyers 75

Contact
Fabienne Haas

CATEGORIES OF WORK

Corporate law, M&A
Gilles August, Ferenc Gonter

Securities, private equity
Gilles August,
Valéry Denoix de Saint Marc

Real estate and construction
Gilles August, Ferenc Gonter,
Valéry Denoix de Saint-Marc

Tax
Caroline Bertin Delacour

Bankruptcy, insolvency
Gilles August

White-collar crime
Valéry Denoix de Saint-Marc,
Pierre Charles Ranouil

Arbitration
Valéry Denoix de Saint-Marc

Labour and social security law
Emmanuelle Barbara, Fabienne Haas

Pensions
Nathalie Meynent

Commercial transactions
Isabelle Renard, Mahasti Razavi

Intellectual property
Isabelle Renard, Mahasti Razavi

IT, media and entertainment
Isabelle Renard

Public, environment and regulatory law
Olivier Debouzy, Jean-Dominique Bloch

Product and industrial liability
Olivier Debouzy, Brigitte Daille-Duclos

EU and competition law
Olivier Debouzy, Jean-Dominique Bloch

THE FIRM

Founded in 1995 by Gilles August and Olivier Debouzy, August & Debouzy is one of the leading French law firms. With a team of 75 lawyers (including 13 partners and 10 of counsel), A&D is a full-service law firm divided into four practice groups which cover all areas of the company's activities: corporate structure, regulatory environment, its commercial activities and human resources; each practice group including a team of litigators. Approximately half of the firm's clients are foreign, in particular US, UK and major EU countries, as well as foreign governments and state-owned enterprises. Cross-border and international matters include M&A, restructurings, securities, infrastructure projects, and regulatory issues. The firm has established working relationships with leading firms throughout the world in specific practice areas in major jurisdictions enabling it to form highly effective and competent international teams to work on multi-jurisdictional corporate, regulatory, securities, commercial and other matters.

AREAS OF PRACTICE

The firm advises clients in connection with cross-border investments, M&A, restructurings, joint ventures, shareholder agreements, infrastructure projects, takeovers and securities offerings, including transaction structuring and tax analysis. The firm represents a substantial number of CAC/40 companies on a regular basis as well as large international groups on major transactions.

The firm advises clients in all areas of labour law, with a specific emphasis on restructuring and collective dismissal in the context of M&A, joint ventures and bankruptcy, collective agreement and work duration. The firm also specialises in pensions and benefits, including healthcare and contingency schemes, retirement and savings plans. The firm also represents clients in the context of individual employment relationship and represents its clients before the relevant tribunals or government agencies in matters involving labour and social security.

New technologies have traditionally been a strong practice area within the firm. Clients include the major IT firms as well as the motion picture and television industries in the areas of licensing, IP protection and enforcement, and Internet-related issues.

The firm regularly advises French and multinational companies on a regular basis in commercial-related matters including litigation in the context of sales, services, agency, and more generally distribution agreements, taking into account French and European competition law, consumer protection, advertising or promotions regulations. A recognised leader in this area, the firm has special expertise in advising clients on administrative compliance, representation before public agencies, legislative and regulatory developments, including at EU level. With established local government contacts and strong relationships with leading firms in the US and Europe, the firm is uniquely qualified to advise on local and EU-wide matters.

The firm has a strong litigation and arbitration practice, including advising and representing foreign clients. It has special expertise in litigation involving international corporate and commercial matters, technology and media, as well as regulatory matters. The firm represents clients in ICC and ad hoc arbitrations and its attorneys often act as arbitrators in international arbitrations. The firm also advises corporations or individuals in the area of white-collar crime.

The firm has special expertise in the area of product liability, and through its litigation and regulatory knowledge and experience in this area is particularly well qualified to represent clients on product liability issues.

The firm represents major French and foreign groups in connection with large-scale real estate transactions and construction projects.

The firm represents individuals and corporations (claimants or defendants), in the context of financial and securities-related criminal matters, such as insider trading, misuse of corporate assets and embezzlement.

AYACHE SALAMA & ASSOCIÉS

47 AVENUE HOCHE
75008 PARIS

Telephone: + 33 1 58 05 38 05
Fax: +33 1 58 05 38 00
E-mail: b.ayache@ayache-salama.com

Languages
English, German, Spanish

Number of lawyers 29

Contacts
Denis Salama, Bernard Ayache

Member
Law Exchange International (LEI)

CATEGORIES OF WORK	
Mergers and acquisitions	**Competition law**
Private equity	**Distribution law**
Banking and finance	**Public economic law**
Corporate law	**Tax law**
Arbitration	**Intellectual property**
Litigation	**Real estate**

THE FIRM

The specialist commercial law firm Ayache Salama & Associés advises and represents French and foreign companies in a wide range of legal areas.

The firm's client base comprises mainly large companies, predominantly in the industrial sector, and also a large number of investment banks, financial institutions and investment funds.

AREAS OF PRACTICE

Although Ayache Salama & Associés' commercial law practice encompasses both non-contentious advice and litigation, today the firm mainly acts in an advisory capacity.

Ayache Salama & Associés advises on mergers and acquisitions transactions – an area that has seen considerable growth within the firm, in traditional industries, as well as in the new economy. The firm also handles financial markets work and regularly advises large industrial concerns and investment funds on their acquisition deals. It is also involved in LBO financing, eurobonds and derivative products. In addition, Ayache Salama & Associés has considerable expertise relating to legal disputes in the banking, stock market and financial sectors.

The firm provides contentious and non-contentious advice in the area of competition and distribution law. These practice areas constitute a significant part of the firm's overall practice, due to the large number of large distribution chains, both French and overseas, in its client base. This area of expertise is complemented by an excellent knowledge of the legal matters affecting the commercial property business, and, in particular, shopping centres.

Ayache Salama & Associés' intellectual property practice has expertise in brands, designs and models and patents.

Tax lawyers at the firm have solid experience in both domestic and international company and private tax law.

The firm is also involved in economic public law and local authority law, acting mainly on behalf of banks, local authorities, and public enterprises. The public law department is led by an attorney who is a professor of law (professeur agrégé des facultés de droit).

ASHURST

22 RUE DE MARIGNAN
75008 PARIS

Telephone: +33 1 53 53 53 53
Fax: +33 1 53 53 53 54
Website: www.ashurst.com

Languages
English, German, Hebrew, Russian, Spanish

Other offices
Brussels, Frankfurt, London, Madrid, Munich, Milan, New Delhi*, New York, Singapore, Tokyo

Number of lawyers 813
at this office 73

Contacts
Christopher Crosthwaite, Thomas Forschbach

CATEGORIES OF WORK

Commercial law (general)

Mergers and acquisitions

Companies, corporations

Banking, securities and finance

Competition, antitrust

Arbitration and litigation

Tax

Insurance

Bankruptcy, insolvency

Contract

BMH AVOCATS
BREITENSTEIN MEILLASSOUX HAUSER ROTH

29 RUE DU FAUBOURG `
SAINT-HONORÉ
75008 PARIS

Telephone: +33 1 42 66 63 19
Fax: +33 1 42 66 64 81
E-mail: bmh@bmhavocats.com
Website: www.bmhavocats.com

Languages
English, German, Russian, Spanish

Other offices
Brussels

Number of lawyers 25
at this office 24

Contacts
Dr Martin Hauser (Paris),
Prof Mathijsen (Brussels)

CATEGORIES OF WORK

E-commerce and information technology
André Meillassoux

Intellectual property
Martin Hauser

Mergers and acquisitions
Christian Roth, Catherine Nelken

Company law
Hans Messmer

Commercial litigation
Olivier Hoebanx, Anouk Darcet-Felgen

EC law (antitrust)
Stéphanie Ponsot, Pierre Mathijsen

International arbitration
Martin Hauser, Olivier Hoebanx

Labour and social law
Anne-Marie Senechal-L'Homme

BAKER & McKENZIE

32 AVENUE KLÉBER
BP 2112
75771 PARIS CEDEX 16

Telephone: +33 1 44 17 53 00
Fax: +33 1 44 17 45 75
E-mail: paris.info@bakernet.com
Website: www.bakernet.com

Languages
English, German, Italian, Japanese, Spanish

Other offices Almaty, Amsterdam, Antwerp, Bahrain, Baku, Bangkok, Barcelona, Beijing, Berlin, Bogotá, Bologna, Brasilia, Brussels, Budapest, Buenos Aires, Cairo, Calgary, Caracas, Chicago, Dallas, Düsseldorf, Frankfurt, Geneva, Guadalajara, Hanoi, Ho Chi Minh City, Hong Kong, Houston, Juarez, Kyiv, London, Madrid, Manila, Melbourne, Mexico City, Miami, Milan, Monterrey, Moscow, Munich, New York, Palo Alto, Porto Alegré, Prague, Rio de Janeiro, Riyadh, Rome, St Petersburg, San Diego, San Francisco, Santiago, São Paulo, Shanghai, Singapore, Stockholm, Sydney, Taipei, Tijuana, Tokyo, Toronto, Valencia, Vienna, Warsaw, Washington DC, Zürich

Number of lawyers 3,380
at this office 105

Contact Eric Lasry

CATEGORIES OF WORK

Corporate law
Marie-Francoise Bréchignac, Pierre Ray

Competition, distribution
Mireille Dany, Alex Dowding

Employment and immigration
Denise Broussal, Gilles Jolivet

Intellectual property
Jean-François Bretonniére

Information technology
Rémy Bricard

Litigation and arbitration
Jean-Dominique Touraille

Mergers and acquisitions
Laurent Barbara, Eric Lasry

Pharmaceutical and health industries
Laurent Epstein, Henry de Suremain

Public and environmental law
Arnaud Cabanes

Real estate
Eric Pomonti

Telecommunications
Emmanuel Guillaume

Tax
Pierre-Yves Bourtourault, Véronique Millischer

BARBÉ CARPENTIER THIBAULT GROENER & ASSOCIÉS

14 AVENUE GOURGAUD
75017 PARIS

Telephone: +33 1 44 15 61 00
Fax: +33 1 44 15 91 81

Languages
English, French, German, Portuguese, Spanish

Number of lawyers 24

Contact
Juan Carlos Groener

CATEGORIES OF WORK

Mergers and acquisitions
Marc Barbé, Séverin Kullmann

Banking and finance
Marc Barbé, Marie-Pierre Carpentier

Commercial and company law
Jean-Philippe Thibault, Juan Carlos Groener

EU and competition law
Jean-Philippe Thibault

Litigation
Juan Carlos Groener, Philippe Lebrut

Intellectual property law
Gaëlle Bloret, Hervé Bonnard

Labour and employment
Marc Barbé, Sabine de Paillerets

Insolvency
Juan Carlos Groener

Real estate
Marie-Pierre Carpentier, Philippe Lebrut

Energy
Marie-Pierre Carpentier, Catherine Dupuy

Construction
Marie-Pierre Carpentier, Diane Mouratoglou

Regulatory and government affairs
Marc Barbé, Catherine Dupuy

Tax
Marc Barbé

Public and environmental
Hervé Bonnard

Insurance
Diane Mouratoglou

Sports law
Jean-Philippe Thibault

BARTHÉLÉMY & ASSOCIÉS, member of ius laboris

RUE DE BERRI 24
75008 PARIS

Telephone: +33 1 44 95 48 00
Fax: +33 1 45 63 99 62
E-mail: bysauret@barthelemy-associes.fr
Website: www.barthelemy-associes.fr

Languages
English, Spanish

Other offices
Bordeaux, Clermont Ferrand, Lille, Lyon, Marseille, Montpellier, Nantes, Sophia Antipolis, Nîmes, Rennes, Saint Etienne, Strasbourg, Toulouse

Number of lawyers 200
at this office 60

Contacts
Alain Sauret, Pascal Lagoutte

Member
ius laboris, International Employment Law Pensions and Employee Benefits Alliance

CATEGORIES OF WORK

Labour and employment law	Working time
Compensation and benefits	Social security
Pensions	Sports law
Restructuring plans	Executive employment contracts
Collective labour law	Litigation and dispute resolution
Works council	Health and safety at work

THE FIRM

Established in 1964 by Jacques Barthélémy, the law partnership of Barthélémy and Associates is one of France's leading employment law practices with 200 lawyers.

The firm is located in Paris, but the partnership has 14 well-staffed branch offices in France's most important cities.

The firm is ISO 9001 certified.

AREAS OF PRACTICE

Barthélémy and Associates was one of the first firms in the country to specialise in labour law, social security, and pension law. The firm is able to provide assistance in all areas relating to the application of labour and employment law for companies with a view to preventing or resolving individual or collective employment disputes.

Barthélémy works closely with leading universities and academic centres in the field of professional training, research, and the development of legislative reform. Several of the partners collaborate actively with a variety of specialist legal publications.

BIRD & BIRD

CENTRE D'AFFAIRES EDOUARD VII
6 RUE DE CAUMARTIN
75009 PARIS

Telephone: +33 1 42 68 60 00
Fax: +33 1 42 68 60 11
E-mail: paris@twobirds.com
Website: www.twobirds.com

Languages
English, French, German

Other offices
Brussels, Düsseldorf, Hong Kong, London, Milan, Munich, Stockholm, The Hague

Number of lawyers 358
at this office 53

Contact
Frédérique Dupuis-Toubol

CATEGORIES OF WORK

Advertising	**Internet and e-commerce**
Broadcasting (national and EU)	**Intellectual property**
Communications	**Life sciences**
Competition and EU law	**Litigation and dispute resolution**
Corporate finance	**Media, film and entertainment**
Employment law	**Sport**
Information technology	**Tax**

BRANDFORD-GRIFFITH BAVEREZ PASTUREL

9 RUE DES PYRAMIDES
75001 PARIS

Telephone: +33 1 44 55 44 55
Fax: +33 1 44 55 44 00
E-mail: office@bgbp.com

Languages
English, French, Spanish, German

Number of lawyers 23

Contacts
Henri Brandford-Griffith, Nigel Hartridge

CATEGORIES OF WORK

Stock exchange
Henri Brandford-Griffith,
Vanina Paolaggi

Mergers and acquisitions
Henri Brandford-Griffith,
Nigel Partridge

Tax
Pierre Ullmann

Public and administrative law
Nicolas Baverez

Litigation and arbitration
Diane Pasturel,
Henri Brandford-Griffith

Capital markets
Laurent Sablé

Private equity
Jérôme Brosset

BREDIN PRAT

**130 RUE DU FAUBOURG
SAINT-HONORÉ
75008 PARIS**

Telephone: +33 1 44 35 35 35
Fax: +33 1 42 89 10 73
E-mail: bredinprat@bredinprat.com

Languages
English, German, Italian, Russian, Spanish

Other offices
Brussels

Number of lawyers 57
at this office 53

CATEGORIES OF WORK	
Mergers and acquisitions	**EC and French competition law**
Securities law	**Banking and finance**
Litigation and arbitration	**Company and commercial**
Tax	**Capital markets**

THE FIRM

Founded in the 1960s, Bredin Prat specialises in business law, in particular high-level mergers and acquisitions (including major French privatisations). It also undertakes work in finance and capital markets, competition law, tax law, commercial litigation and arbitration, and white-collar criminal law.

Approximately three-quarters of the firm's lawyers are French. Four American partners, one British partner and British and American associates make up the balance of the firm. Practice is conducted in both French and English.

Bredin Prat has chosen to remain independent from network organisations which would require the firm to work with designated firms or offices outside of France. The firm has instead chosen the route of developing strong working relationships with several firms in all the European capitals and in the United States (and to a more limited extent in Asia) that can be called upon to form the appropriate international team for specific transborder or multi-jurisdictional transactions.

In early 1999, a group of Brussels-based lawyers specialising in European Community law joined the firm to open Bredin Prat's Brussels office.

The Brussels office represents an integrated expansion of the European competition law group in Paris.

In November 2002, a high-evel tax team of lawyers joined the firm.

AREAS OF PRACTICE

Following the firm's tradition of specialisation in chosen practice areas or in specific types of transactions – as opposed to a broad-based corporate, commercial practice – the firm's transactional work today is concentrated on securities and public takeover law, significant (and often cross-border or multi-jurisdictional) mergers, acquisitions, divestitures, joint ventures, reorganisations, privatisation, tax, and corporate finance.

Similarly, a significant part of Bredin Prat's litigation practice – representing French and foreign clients before the French courts, French and European Community regulatory bodies and French and international arbitral tribunals – is today concentrated in the areas of finance, securities law, corporate law, tax law, competition and antitrust law, and white-collar criminal matters related to the foregoing. The firm's traditional civil and private international law practice in particularly significant matters continues to represent an important part of its litigation and arbitration practice.

The firm's Brussels office practices European Community law with a particular focus on competition law, mergers and state aids.

CARIDDI, MEE, RUÉ/HOGAN & HARTSON LLP

AVOCATS ASSOCÉS À LA COUR DE PARIS

12 RUE DE LA PAIX
75002 PARIS

Telephone: +33 1 42 61 57 71
Fax: +33 1 42 61 79 21
E-mail: afcariddi@hhlaw.com
Website: www.hhlaw.com

Languages
Dutch, English, German, Portuguese, Spanish, Vietnamese

Other offices
Baltimore, Beijing, Berlin, Boulder, Brussels, Budapest, Colorado Springs, Denver, London, Los Angeles, McLean, Miami, Moscow, Munich, New York, Prague, Tokyo, Warsaw, Washington DC

Number of lawyers 1,018
at this office 20

Contact
Alan Cariddi

CATEGORIES OF WORK

Mergers, acquisitions and divestitures	Banking
Joint ventures and strategic alliances	Labour and employment
Venture capital, private equity and strategic investments	Intellectual property
Commercial transactions	Technology transfer and licensing
Litigation and arbitration	Tax
Corporate and project finance	Telecommunications
	Internet and media

CLEARY GOTTLIEB STEEN & HAMILTON

41 AVENUE DE FRIEDLAND
75008 PARIS

Telephone: +33 1 40 74 68 00
Fax: +33 1 45 63 66 37
Website: www.clearygottlieb.com

Languages
Arabic, English, German, Italian, Spanish

Other offices
Brussels, Cologne, Frankfurt, London, Milan, Moscow, Rome

Number of lawyers 937
at this office 88

CATEGORIES OF WORK

Antitrust	Mergers and acquisitions
Arbitration and litigation	Privatisations
Banking and finance	Tax
Capital markets/securities	Technology, media and telecommunications
Joint ventures	

COTTY VIVANT MARCHISIO & LAUZERAL

91 RUE DU FAUBOURG
SAINT HONORE
75008 PARIS

Telephone: +33 1 55 73 20 20
Fax: +33 1 55 73 20 21
Website: www.cvml.com

Languages
English, German, Italian, Spanish

Number of lawyers 15

CATEGORIES OF WORK

Mergers and acquisitions, securities
Thierry Cotty, Fabrice Marchisio

Employment and labour law
Antoine Vivant

Commercial litigation and arbitration
Philippe Lauzeral, Fabrice Marchisio

THE FIRM

Cotty Vivant Marchisio & Lauzeral was founded in November 2003 by four attorneys who have worked in some of the most prestigious law firms in Paris: Gide Loyrette Nouel, Bredin Prat, Darrois Villey Maillot Brochier, Barthélémy and Eversheds.

Today, it is composed of 15 attorneys (four partners and 11 associates) who have attained the highest in academic standards (HEC, ESCP, Sciences-Po), who speak many languages and who share the same values: the pursuit of excellence and the quest for pragmatic and effective solutions.

The firm has a wide area network at its disposal both in France and in Europe, selected for the excellence of its services and put into use each time a case requires it.

The firm's specificity resides not only in the personalised services it renders to its clients, often leading to a long-term trusting relationship, but also in its dual practice of counsel and litigation.

AREAS OF PRACTICE

Cotty Vivant Marchisio & Lauzeral advises on all operations, both domestic and cross-border, relating to the financial strategy of public and private entities (mergers, acquisitions, joint ventures, takeover bids, public exchange offers, public buy-out offers, stock exchange listings and other equity transactions).

The firm has strong relationships with most of the leading players in the buy-out/private equity market place, whether deal leaders or providers of equity, mezzanine or debt finance.

The firm practises counselling and litigation in any area of employment and labour law. It claims a large expertise in the field of collective relationship, restructuring and redundancies programs, working time, collective bargaining agreement negotiation, remuneration policies (SOP, share option schemes), individual termination, welfare schemes. The firm also specialises in assisting in merger and acquisition operations under the employment and labour law perspective.

In every field of expertise, Cotty Vivant Marchisio & Lauzeral works to help its clients resolve disputes efficiently and effectively – whether through arbitration, litigation or other techniques – in a manner that promotes their business objectives.

COUDERT FRÈRES

52 AVE DES CHAMPS-ELYSÉES
BP 639
75367 PARIS CÉDEX 08

Telephone: +33 1 53 83 60 00
Fax: +33 1 53 83 60 60
E-mail: infoparis@coudert.com
Website: www.coudert.com

Languages
Arabic, Chinese, English, German, Hebrew, Italian, Russian, Spanish

Other offices
Almaty, Antwerp, Bangkok, Beijing, Berlin, Brussels, Budapest*, Frankfurt, Ghent, Hong Kong, Jakarta*, London, Los Angeles, Mexico City*, Milan, Moscow, New York, Palo Alto, Prague*, Rome, St Petersburg, San Francisco, Shanghai, Singapore, Stockholm, Sydney, Tokyo, Washington DC

Number of lawyers 650+
at this office 55

Contact
George T Yates (managing partner.)

CATEGORIES OF WORK

Mergers and acquisitions (international) and US law
George T Yates III, Joseph Aragonés

Arbitration
W Lawrence Craig, Michael Polkinghorne, Philip Dunham

African law, mining law and telecommunications
Jean-Claude Petilon

Healthcare law
Alain Decombe

Labour law
Monique Beguiachvili

Public law
Catherine Jeancolas

Corporate, mergers and acquisitions (French)
Joseph Aragonés, Pascale Gros

Litigation
Stephen Montravers, Xavier Nyssen

Banking law, media
Jonathan Wohl

Competition
Philippe Rincazaux, Dominique Brault

Capital markets
Alain Gauvin

Tax
Jacques Messeca

THE FIRM

Coudert Brothers was established in 1853 by French émigrés and was the first US law firm to set up an international legal practice. The firm now has more than 650 lawyers worldwide, operating as one single partnership with a common emphasis on client service of the highest quality.

The firm has extensive experience in international investment, trade and finance. Cross-border commercial transactions are a major focus, as is international arbitration and other complex dispute resolution. Coudert Brothers also provides domestic advice in countries where the firm has offices.Coudert Brothers has offices in 30 cities in 18 countries around the world. These offices are located in the major financial and business centres of Europe, the United States and Asia Pacific region. More than 300 Coudert Brothers professionals now practice in Europe, making it the largest region in the firm's worldwide network.

The Paris office clients also benefit from the expertise of its multidisciplinary teams, drawn from the specialist areas relevant to each project.

AREAS OF PRACTICE

Coudert Paris earned its strong reputation in commercial law through its work in the areas of mergers and acquisitions, international arbitration, litigation, competition law, mining and African law and financial law.

The mergers and acquisitions department assists clients, including many Fortune 500 companies and leading European and Japanese groups, in connection with French corporate reorganisations, mergers, takeovers of public companies and insolvencies, the supervision and the co-ordination of acquisitions, divestitures, reorganisation and joint ventures occurring throughout Europe, either as single or related transactions. This activity regularly involves contacts at all levels with governmental authorities.

Coudert Paris plays a major role in international arbitration. The firm acts in substantial arbitrations under the rules of the International Chamber of Commerce and under the auspices of the arbitration arm of the World Bank (ICSID). The types of disputes which the firm has handled are wide ranging and include governmental contracts, joint ventures, natural resource agreements, construction projects, insurance and reinsurance, trade, licensing, marine, aviation, energy, D&O, E&O, and other international commercial disputes. Coudert Brothers lawyers also act in numerous ad hoc proceedings as well as in mediation and conciliation proceedings.

COURNOT ASSOCIATION D'AVOCATS

24 RUE DE PRONY
75017 PARIS

Telephone: +33 1 44 29 33 70
Fax: +33 1 44 29 33 71
E-mail: sjcournot@24rueprony.fr

Languages
English, French, German, Italian

Number of lawyers 20

Contact
Stéphane Cournot

Member
Washington DC Bar; Paris Bar

CATEGORIES OF WORK

Arbitration (national and international)
Laurent Paris

Capital markets
Richard Dehé

Employment
Laurence Pinchou

Insolvency
Stéphane Cournot, Arnaud de Corbière

Mergers and acquisitions
Stéphane J Cournot, Richard Dehé, Arnaud de Corbière

Tax
Richard Dehé

Corporate and commercial
Stéphane Cournot, Arnaud de Corbière

Commercial litigation
Laurent Paris, Laurence Pinchou

IT, telecoms and Internet
Arnaud de Corbière

Intellectual property and trade marks
Laurence Pinchou

Project finance
Richard Dehé

White-collar crime
Laurent Paris

COUSTÉ & COUSTÉ

29 BLD RASPAIL
75007 PARIS

Telephone: +33 1 42 22 46 11
Fax: +33 1 45 44 97 04
E-mail: marina.couste@wanadoo.fr

Languages
English, German, Spanish

Number of lawyers 4

Contact
Marina Cousté

Member
INTA (International Trademark Association); LES France (Licensing Executive Society); AIPPI (International Association for Intellectual Property Protection); APRAM (Association des Practiciens du Droit des Marques et des Modèles); EPLA (European Patent Lawyers Association)

CATEGORIES OF WORK

Industrial and intellectual property:

Patents
Marina Cousté,
François Jonquères

Trade marks, copyright, designs
Marina Cousté,
Amaury de Saint-Amand,
Charlotte Portmann

Computer law and technology information
Marina Cousté, Charlotte Portmann

Advertising and competition
Marina Cousté, François Jonquéres

Biotechnologies
Marina Cousté,
François Jonquères

CURTIS, MALLET-PREVOST, COLT & MOSLE LLP

15 RUE D'ASTORG
75008 PARIS

Telephone: +33 1 42 66 39 10
Fax: +33 1 42 66 39 62
E-mail: info@cm-p.com
Website: www.cm-p.com

Languages
English

Other offices
Frankfurt, Houston, London, Mexico City, Milan, Muscat, New York, Newark, Stamford, Washington DC

Number of lawyers 178
at this office 6

Contacts
Yves E Lepage, Geoffroy Lyonnet, Peter M Wolrich

Member
American Society of International Law; French Arbitration Committee; International Chamber of Commerce; Institute of International Business Law and Practice; London Court of International Arbitration

CATEGORIES OF WORK

International transactions
Peter M Wolrich, Geoffroy Lyonnet

Mergers and acquisitions
Geoffroy Lyonnet, Yves E LePage

EU law

Contracts
Peter M Wolrich, Geoffroy Lyonnet

Litigation and arbitration
Peter M Wolrich

Structured finance
Yves E LePage

Antitrust

Infrastructure and project finance
Yves E LePage

Privatisation
Yves E LePage

Transnational joint ventures
Yves E LePage

Power generation
Yves E LePage

Petroleum and petrochemical contracts
Yves E LePage, Peter M Wolrich

Construction contracts
Yves E LePage, Peter M Wolrich

Equipment sale and leaseback
Yves E LePage

DEBEVOISE & PLIMPTON LLP

21 AVENUE GEORGE V
7008 PARIS

Telephone: +33 1 40 73 12 12
Fax: +33 1 47 20 50 82
E-mail: akirry@debevoise.com
Website: www.debevoise.com

Languages
Czech, Danish, English, Farsi, French, Spanish

Other offices
Hong Kong, Frankfurt, London, Moscow, New York, Shanghai, Washington DC

Number of lawyers 600+
at this office 30

CATEGORIES OF WORK

Mergers and acquisitions
Antoine Kirry, Marc Castagnede

Private equity
Antoine Kirry

Capital markets
Pierre Clermontel, Eryl Besse

Financing
Pierre Clermontel, Eryl Besse

International dispute resolution
Michael M Ostrove

DARROIS VILLEY MAILLOT BROCHIER

69 AVENUE VICTOR HUGO
75116 PARIS

Telephone: + 33 1 45 02 19 19
Fax: + 33 1 45 01 91 68
E-mail:
firstinitialsurname@darroisvilley.com

Languages
Dutch, English, German, Italian, Spanish

Number of lawyers 29

Contacts
Jean-Michel Darrois, Matthieu de Boisséson

CATEGORIES OF WORK

Mergers and acquisitions
Alain Maillot, Olivier Diaz

Complex corporate transactions
Philippe Villey

Stock exchange law
Marie-Noëlle Dompé

Governmental and privatisation matters
François Sureau

EU, regulatory matters
Didier Théophile

International arbitration
Matthieu de Boisséson

Criminal business law
Jean-Michel Darrois

Litigation
Emmanuel Brochier

International matters
Andrew Plump, David Scemla

Private equity
Alain Maillot, Oliver Diaz

THE FIRM

Darrois Villey Maillot Brochier is a highly specialised firm of 29 lawyers concentrating on, and limiting its practice to, two distinct but often related activities. The firm provides advisory services concerning complex corporate and financial operations including: mergers and acquisitions; tender offers and tender offer defences; company reorganisations; stock exchange and company law issues; and privatisations and related transactions with governmental bodies and administrations, including European Union regulatory advice and compliance services. The firm also renders services concerning litigation and arbitration matters, including particularly, international arbitration matters arising out of such corporate and financial operations, specialising in complex corporate and securities regulation issues. The firm's expertise in regard to these activities has evolved since its creation in 1982 as a result of its consistent involvement in major acquisitions and tender offers in France and in the resolution of highly visible business disputes.

The firm is frequently involved in friendly combinations and reorganisations of major multinational enterprises, and has handled many unusually complex combinations in regulated industries. The evolution of the firm's activities in cross-border and international matters enables the partners of the firm to act as advisers to multinational clients with respect to their investment strategies and to co-operate with leading independent firms in other jurisdictions, such as Wachtell, Lipton, Rosen & Katz in New York.

Over the years, the firm has maintained close client relationships with many major multinational enterprises, for which it has acted both as strategic adviser and transaction counsel, either alone or in co-operation with selected firms in other jurisdictions. The firm also maintains close and ongoing relationships with the major investment banks active in the key financial market places.

AREAS OF PRACTICE

Mergers and acquisitions: since the time of its formation, the firm has been involved in major acquisitions, securities regulation matters and corporate financial transactions. From its early landmark tender offer matters, the firm has consistently been involved in the major corporate events in its marketplace. The complex corporate and financial operations handled by the firm include privatisation and related transactions involving enterprises controlled by the state and governmental entities. The firm currently advises the French State and state entities on several significant matters.

Litigation and arbitration: throughout its history, the firm has been involved in high-profile litigation and arbitration matters. A significant number of such matters arise out of corporate and financial operations, particularly complex securities regulation issues. However, the range of the firm's litigation activity extends to both civil and criminal matters. The firm's partners include a recognised authority on international arbitration and the firm is generally involved in several such matters, both as counsel to parties in arbitration and through the appointment of partners as arbitrators.

Finance and capital markets: the firm often advises on the financial aspects and structures involved in the corporate transactions which it handles, including advice concerning the conception, documentation and implementation of securities issues in the capital markets in France as well as elsewhere in Europe and North America. The firm both advises its clients directly and acts in co-operation with other firms and investment banks in structuring and co-ordinating such securities issues.

Corporate and tax: in the course of its involvement with combinations and reorganisations of enterprises, the firm is often called upon to advise on French and international investment and tax structures and to co-ordinate the creation and implementation of such structures. The firm's clients for such advice also include investment funds from various countries and selected individual and family group investors.

DE GAULLE FLEURANCE & ASSOCIÉS

11 RUE PORTALIS
75008 PARIS

Telephone: +33 1 56 64 00 00
Fax: +33 1 56 64 00 01
E-mail: ecourville@dgfla.com

Languages
English, French, Spanish

Number of lawyers 24

Contacts
Louis de Gaulle, Henri-Nicolas Fleurance

CATEGORIES OF WORK

Commercial law and antitrust
Louis de Gaulle, Jean-Marie Job

Intellectual property, IT and sports
Louis de Gaulle, Julien Horn

Corporate and tax, M&A, finance and restructuring and labour
Henri Nicolas Fleurance,
Bénédicte Colin

THE FIRM

De Gaulle Fleurance & Associés is a business law firm. It aims to offer its clients a high-value added, prompt, customised and pragmatic service with an international approach. Through its flexible and effective organisation, the firm supports its clients both in the transactional and litigation areas.

The firm has centred its development on the complementary nature of its practice groups to co-ordinate any case by using transverse skills.

AREAS OF PRACTICE

The firm assists clients in devising and implementing their commercial, sourcing, protection and defence policy in connection with all aspects of commercial law and competition law in the context of the specific regulatory frameworks applicable. In this respect, the firm drafts, negotiates and conducts due diligences of contracts, and places the defence of the commercial interests of its clients at the core of its practice. The commercial and competition attorneys work in close teamwork with attorneys from the firm's other practice groups (IP/IT, corporate and tax).

For maximum effectiveness the firm has developed expert know-how focusing on transverse competences. In particular, the firm supports its clients in connection with acquisitions, disposals, restructuring, project financing or refinancing and the launch of international operations. Throughout such transactions, the firm provides services in relation to contract drafting, negotiation and analysis, legal and tax due diligence, preparation of research papers and opinions. During each engagement, the firm ensures that its counsels fully comply with its clients financial and operational restraints.

The firm provides advisory and litigation assistance and support to its clients in the development of their policy for the protection, exploitation and defence of their intellectual property assets. It is active in all areas pertaining to intellectual property, new technologies and related matters. The firm provides services to all types of industries such as information technology, e-commerce, cinema, television, entertainment, music, press, advertising and promotional events (including sports). The firm has developed specific expertise in the leisure sector, such as theme parks, gaming and hotel properties, both in France and throughout the world.

The firm also provides support to its clients in all areas related to health law in the context of national and EU regulations. More than many other industries, the health sector is nowadays highly internationalised. This is why the firm works with foreign correspondents, in particular in the US. The firm's activity in the health sector is conducted in close co-operation with the teams in charge of other practice areas (intellectual property and new technologies, corporate and tax law). The firm's client base comprises French and foreign pharmaceutical companies, enterprises manufacturing or distributing proprietary medicines, manufacturers of medical equipment and companies from the health services sector.

DE PARDIEU BROCAS MAFFEI & LEYGONIE

64-66 AVENUE D'IÉNA
BP 2004
75761 PARIS CEDEX 16

Telephone: +33 1 53 57 71 71
Fax: +33 1 53 57 71 70

Languages
Dutch, English, German, Russian, Spanish

Number of lawyers 75

Contact
Charles-Henri de Pardieu

CATEGORIES OF WORK

Banking and finance
CH de Pardieu, A Maffei, P Minor, O Hubert

Capital markets
A Maffei, P Minor

Bankruptcy, insolvency
J Henrot, P Talbourdet

Competition, EU law
T Brocas, D Lefort

Corporate law
T Brocas, G Touttée

Corporate finance
T Brocas, P Minor

Environment law
P Talbourdet, C de La Hosseraye

Insurance
CH de Pardieu, P Talbourdet

Labour and employment law
F Vergne

Litigation and arbitration
J Henrot, D Lefort, P Talbourdet

M&A, stock exchange law
T Brocas, G Touttée

Property law, property finance
J Henrot, E Fatôme

Privatisation
T Brocas, G Touttée

Telecommunications, hi-tech
F Guthfreund-Roland, M Georges

Administrative law
J Henrot, E Fatôme

White-collar crime
D Lefort

Tax
P Lefèvre-Péaron

THE FIRM

The firm initially gained its reputation, both in France and internationally, with its premier banking and finance practice. It has become a full-service firm which offers clients advice across a wide range of legal practice.

Partners of De Pardieu maintain regular contact with overseas law firms, among them some of the most renowned firms in the major international business and finance centres. Collaborating with these firms enables the members of the firm to bring together multi-disciplinary teams to work on cross-border transactions at any time, and to ensure the successful completion of these transactions in the relevant jurisdictions.

The firm's international activities extend mainly to Europe, the US and to Asia.

The firm represents banks, financial institutions, insurance companies, service companies and industry.

AREAS OF PRACTICE

De Pardieu Brocas Maffei & Leygonie operates teams which specialise in the key areas of commercial legal practice and is regularly called to assist clients with their international expansion.

Together with banking and finance, insurance, corporate, M&A, real estate and litigation practice, the firm has expanded its expertise in EU and competition, stock exchange and capital markets, tax, and employment law. At the same time, the firm has developed strong credentials in telecommunications, administrative law and environmental law.

DENTON WILDE SAPTE

43 RUE DU FAUBOURG ST-HONORÉ
75008 PARIS

Telephone: +33 1 53 05 1600
Fax: +33 1 53 05 9727
E-mail: paris@dentonwildesapte.com
Website: www.dentonwildesapte.com

Languages
English, French, German, Italian, Spanish

Other offices
Abu Dhabi, Almaty, Beijing, Cairo, Dubai, Gibraltar, Hong Kong, Istanbul, London, Milton Keynes, Moscow, Muscat, Singapore, Tashkent, Tokyo

Number of lawyers 876
at this office 60

Contact
Dominque Deveaux

CATEGORIES OF WORK

Administrative law

Aircraft financing and leasing

Arbitration and litigation

Asset finance

Banking and finance

Competition and distribution

Corporate and commercial

Environmental law

Insolvency

Intellectual property

International projects, energy and infrastructure

Labour law

Mergers and acquisitions

Private equity

Structured finance

Tax and customs

Technology, media and telecommunications

Real estate

DEPREZ DIAN GUIGNOT

21 RUE CLÉMENT MAROT
75008 PARIS

Telephone: +33 1 53 23 8000
Fax: +33 1 53 23 8001
Website: www.ddg.fr

Languages
English, German, Portuguese, Spanish

Number of lawyers 35

Member
INTA; International Fiscal Association

CATEGORIES OF WORK

International property, litigation
Pierre Deprez, Vincent Fauchoux

Information technology
Vincent Fauchoux

Trade marks
Jacques Beaumont

Media
Philippe Dian

EU and competition law
Pierre Deprez, Jean-Christophe André

Food and drugs
Jean-Christophe André

Arbitration and litigation
Emmanuel Bouttier

Mergers and acquisitions
Michel Guignot, Ana-Paula Reis Lopes

Labour law
Laurent Carrié

DUBARRY LE DOUARIN VEIL

6 PLACE DE NARVIK
75008 PARIS

Telephone: +33 1 44 30 25 00
Fax: +33 1 44 30 25 01
E-mail: dlvlaw@dlvlaw.com
Website: www.dlvlaw.com

Languages
English, German, Hebrew, Spanish, Italian

Number of lawyers 35

Contacts
Pierre-François Veil, Yann Le Douarin, Philippe Netto

Member
European Legal Alliance (England, Scotland, Ireland, Germany, Spain, France)

CATEGORIES OF WORK

Corporate, M&A, private equity
Philippe Netto, Claire de Bussy

Commercial contracts
Yann Le Douarin, Jean-Claude Dubarry

Information technology
Bruno Ducoulombier, Lucie Walker

Intellectual and industrial property, media
Bruno Ducoulombier, Lucie Walker

Distribution and product liability
Yann Le Douarin, Frédéric Dereux

Competition, antitrust law
Mario Celaya

Criminal business law
Pierre-François Veil

Financial market law
Pierre-François Veil

Banking, securities and finance
Jean-Claude Dubarry, Rémi Kleiman

Insolvency, restructuring
Yann Le Douarin, Philippe Glaser

Tax
Frédéric Dereux

Employment and labour law
Valérie Dubaile, Thierry Gillot

Litigation and arbitration
Jean-Claude Dubarry, Claire de Bussy

Real estate
Yann Le Douarin, Frédéric Dereux

Health care
Eric Gaftarnik

THE FIRM

Dubarry Le Douarin Veil is a longstanding and well-established law firm based in Paris. Founded in 1984, the firm specialises in business law, offering commercial clients a wide range of legal services.

The firm's activities cover both non-contentious advice and litigation for a domestic and international client base. The firm works closely with its clients to provide a quality service in all matters of their business activities.

The majority of the firm's lawyers have considerable experience of the full range of commercial legal practice and are able to offer specialist services against this general commercial background. Clients benefit from the firm's lawyers being able to offer legal solutions in a business environment.

Dubarry Le Douarin Veil has a total staff of more than 50, including 14 partners. The firm operates flexible and responsive teams of lawyers, drawn from different disciplines, to provide the optimum service to its clients.

In addition, as a founding member of the European Legal Alliance, Dubarry Le Douarin Veil offers pan-European expert advice on a wide range of practice areas. The European Legal Alliance brings together five commercial law firms under a single brand and is based in England, France, Germany Ireland and Scotland.

AREAS OF PRACTICE

Dubarry Le Douarin Veil has wide experience in assisting both French and foreign clients from all over the world, from different business and industry sectors, in commercial and corporate matters.

The firm has particular expertise in the field of corporate law, mergers and acquisitions, private equity, commercial and banking litigation, intellectual property and information technology law, tax, real estate, and employment law.

The firm offers clients complete assistance and advice from start-up and formation, throughout its operations, offering the client the full range of advice where necessary.

The firm's lawyers are experienced in acquisitions, sales, IPOs, mergers and takeovers. The firm has considerable expertise in advising foreign clients on establishing business operations in France.

The firm is able to offer contentious and court practice in all of the practice areas listed above.

EY LAW

TOUR ERNST & YOUNG
92037 PARIS-LA-DÉFENSE CEDEX

Telephone: +33 1 46 93 70 00
Fax: +33 1 58 47 70 12
Website: www.eylaw.avocat.fr

Languages
English, German, Italian, Malagasy, Spanish, Swedish

Other offices
Bordeaux, Grenoble, Lille, Lyon, Marseille, Montpellier, Nantes, Nice, Saint-Etienne, Strasbourg, Toulouse

Number of lawyers 800

Contact
Hervé Labaude

CATEGORIES OF WORK

International tax services

Corporate tax

VAT, customs and excise

Human capital

Corporate law/ mergers and acquisitions

Distribution and competition

Intellectual property and information technology law

Litigation and arbitration

Employment and labour law

Public law

Private wealth

Banking and insurance law

Not-for-profit organisations/ professional bodies

Insolvency and bankruptcy

FRANKLIN

26 AVENUE KLÉBER
75116 PARIS

Telephone: +33 1 45 02 79 00
Fax: +33 1 45 02 79 01
E-mail: info@franklin-paris.com
Website: www.franklin-paris.com

Languages
English, German, Italian, Russian, Spanish

Number of lawyers 25

CATEGORIES OF WORK

Mergers and acquisitions
Yam Atallah, Alexandre Marque

Administrative law, environment
Jérôme Michel, Jean-Pierre Delvigne

Project finance
Jérôme Michel, Emmanuelle Raoult

Company, commercial
Yam Atallah, Alexandre Marque

Information technology, telecommunications
Bradley Joslove, Andréi Krylov

Private equity (MBO/LBO, fund structuring, ventures
Mark Richardson, Yam Atallah

Tax
Jean-Christophe Bouchard, Olivier Roumélian

Intellectual property
Yann Colin, Xavier Carbasse

Arbitration and litigation
Yann Colin, Xavier Carbasse

Advertising, competition and distribution
Jérôme Michel, Xavier Carbasse

EU law
Jérôme Michel, Emmanuelle Raoult

Media and entertainment
Yann Colin, Xavier Carbasse

Labour
Yann Colin, Marie-Cécile de la Chapelle

FLICHY & ASSOCIÉS

7 RUE KEPLER
75116 PARIS

Telephone: +33 1 56 62 30 00
Fax: +33 1 56 62 30 01
E-mail: flichy@flichy-associes.com
Website: www.flichy-associes.com

Number of lawyers 27

Contacts
Hubert Flichy, Claire Toumieux

Member
EELA, GESICA

CATEGORIES OF WORK

Labour law

THE FIRM

Flichy & Associés is among France's leading employment law firms.

Founded in February 1999 by Hubert Flichy, in partnership with Isabelle Ayache-Revah and Philippe Montanier, the firm has since experienced continuous growth. Claire Toumieux, Philippe Langlois Christophe Ricour, and Arnaud Chaulet joined the partnership in May 2000, April 2001, January 2002 and January 2003 respectively.

The firm's sole practice area is employment law and social security law; it has become well known for its handling of redundancy schemes, issues relating to working hours, and the labour aspects of restructuring operations. The firm's clientele is essentially made up of French, British and American companies, in industry, banking and telecommunications.

PRACTICE AREAS

Flichy & Associés's practice is dedicated to employment law, and social security law. It has concentrated on negotiations, labour disputes, and issues arising from restructuring operations and from mergers and acquisitions. Another area of expertise involves the labour aspects of transnational operations, as well as mobility and expatriation.

Flichy & Associés also advises on all aspects of social security law (basic and complementary benefits), high-risk individual disputes and company savings plans, and on labour issues arising in publicly owned companies.

FRESHFIELDS BRUCKHAUS DERINGER

69 BOULEVARD HAUSSMANN
75008 PARIS

Telephone: +33 1 44 56 44 56
Fax: +33 1 44 56 44 00
E-mail: email@freshfields.com
Website: www.freshfields.com

Languages
Extensive language capabilities

Other offices
Amsterdam, Bangkok, Barcelona, Beijing, Berlin, Bratislava, Brussels, Budapest, Cologne, Düsseldorf, Frankfurt, Hamburg, Hanoi, Ho Chi Minh City, Hong Kong, London, Madrid, Milan, Moscow, Munich, New York, Rome, Shanghai, Singapore, Tokyo, Vienna, Washington

Number of lawyers 2,504
at this office 245

Contact
Jean-Luc Michaud

CATEGORIES OF WORK

Corporate

Finance

Employment, pensions and benefits

Antitrust, competition and trade

Dispute resolution (including environment, planning and regulatory)

Tax

Real estate

Intellectual property and IT

FRIED, FRANK, HARRIS, SHRIVER & JACOBSON LLP

5 BOULEVARD DE LA TOUR-MAUBOURG
75007 PARIS

Telephone: +33 140 62 22 00
Fax: +33 140 62 22 29
E-mail: info@ffhsj.com
Website: www.friedfrank.com

Languages
English, German, Italian, Spanish

Other offices
New York, Washington DC, Los Angeles, London

Number of lawyers 522
at this office 12

Contact
Eric Cafritz

A Delaware Limited Liability Partnership

CATEGORIES OF WORK

Cross-border mergers and acquisitions

Complex financings (M&A, mezzanine, project, leasing, REITS)

Industrial development in Europe

Securities law

Commercial litigation

Arbitration

GIDE LOYRETTE NOUEL

26 COURS ALBERT 1ER
75008 PARIS

Telephone: +33 1 40 75 60 00
Fax: +33 1 43 59 37 79
E-mail: info@gide.com
Website: www.gide.com

Languages
Arabic, Bulgarian, Chinese, Czech, English, German, Hungarian, Italian, Polish, Romanian, Russian, Spanish, Turkish, Vietnamese

Other offices
Algiers, Beijing, Brussels, Bucharest, Budapest, Casablanca, Hanoi, Istanbul, London, Moscow, New York, Prague, Riyadh, Shanghai, Tunis, Warsaw

Number of lawyers 480
(Number of partners 88)

Contacts
Gérard Tavernier (tavernier@gide.com),
Xavier de Kergenmeaux
(kerganmeaux@gide.com)

CATEGORIES OF WORK

Arbitration
Pierre Raoul-Duval,
Christian Camboulive

Bankruptcy, insolvency
Jean-Michel Lucheux, Olivier Puech

Economic law, EU
Joëlle Salzmann, Antoine Choffel

Finance, project finance
Emmanuel Fontaine, Kamel Ben Salah

Intellectual property
Arnaud Michel, Grégoire Triet

Internet, e-commerce
Bertrand Nouel, Grégoire Triet

Labour law
Joël Grangé, Philippe Desprès

Litigation
Gilles Duquet, Aurélien Boulanger

Media, information technology and telecommunications law
Bertrand Nouel, Olivier Cousi

M&A, corporate law
Youssef Djehane, Hugues Mathez

Public law, environmental law
Laurent Deruy, Michel Guénaire

Real estate, property law
Gérard Tavernier, Renaud Baguenault

Tax
Richard Beauvais, Olivier Dauchez

Transport, maritime and insurance
Emmanuel Fontaine, Philippe Rames

White-collar crime
Jean-Marie Burguburu,
Kiril Bougartchev

THE FIRM

Building from a premier position in France into a powerful independent international law firm, Gide Loyrette Nouel operates out of 17 offices around the world. With 88 partners and 400 associates drawn from over 30 nationalities, the firm offers some of the most respected specialists in each if the various sectors of national and international finance and business law.

For more than 80 years, Gide Loyrette Nouel has been offering legal advice and assistance to companies, public and private institutions, and governments. Constantly demanding the highest quality from its lawyers, the firm is able to assist clients in resolving all manner of legal issues, no matter how complex or diverse.

The firm has offices in Europe (Brussels, Bucharest, Budapest, Istanbul, London, Moscow, Paris, Prague and Warsaw), in the US (New York), in the Middle East (Riyadh), in North Africa (Algiers, Casablanca, and Tunis) and in Asia (Hanoi, Beijing and Shanghai).

AREAS OF PRACTICE

Lawyers at Gide Loyrette Nouel advise and represent clients in all aspects of commercial law. Over 60 lawyers at the firm work on mergers and acquisitions, takeover bids, public offers of exchange, stocks and bonds issues, stock exchange flotations, and privatisations, both in Paris and abroad.

Gide Loyrette Nouel's banking and finance team is one of the most prominent in the market, offering French, English and US banking and finance law capability: more than 110 lawyers, located both in Paris and London, deal with all aspects of banking and finance law, in particular all types of financing (including classic bank financing, structured finance, acquisition finance, project finance and securitisation), international debt and capital securities issues, accounting, and derivative and structured products.

The firm is also renowned for its real estate law practice. It acts on behalf of investors, property developers, or tenants at all stages of real estate transactions, in France and abroad. In addition, Gide Loyrette Nouel's lawyers have a well-established reputation in arbitration, litigation, tax law, labour law and public law. They have developed a high level of expertise in matters relating to patents, brands, information technology law, the Internet, e-commerce, media and telecommunications. Finally, by virtue of its presence in Brussels for more than 35 years, the firm has a proven track record in economic and EU law. In particular, it is regarded as a leader in the fields of competition, WTO and anti-dumping law.

In order to provide its clients with the best possible service in Paris and abroad, the firm operates through multinational and multi-disciplinary teams.

GINESTIÉ PALEY-VINCENT & ASSOCIÉS

10 PLACE DES ETATS-UNIS
75116 PARIS

Telephone: +33 1 53 23 40 00
Fax: +33 1 53 23 97 00
E-mail: gpva@ginestie.com
Website: www.ginestie.com

Languages
English, French, German, Italian, Spanish

Other offices
London

Number of lawyers 40
at this office 39

Contact
Francoise Ciaudo-Ginestié

Member
DLA Group (international partnership of independent law firms, Europe and South East Asia)

CATEGORIES OF WORK

Mergers and acquisitions
Philippe Ginestié

Corporate
Jean-Luc Blein

Private equity
Anne Dabezies

Stock exchange
Jean-Christophe Vidal

Information Technology
Isabelle Gavanon

IP, copyright and trade marks
Francoise Ciaudo-Ginestié

Tax
Brigitte Berdugo

Labour
Stéphane Laubeuf

Health and civil litigation
Catherine Paley-Vincent

Commercial litigation
Catherine Ottaway

Competition
Nathalie Englender

THE FIRM

Ginestié Paley-Vincent & Associés was created in 1973 by Philippe Ginestié. It brings together the expertise of lawyers specialising in various areas of practice, covering both advice on corporate law as well as business litigation.

Ginestié Paley-Vincent & Associés is committed to creating an individualised combination of legal, tax and financial expertise, searching for the most efficient way to draft agreements, developing expertise in negotiation, and reaching decisions while working closely with clients to meet their specific needs

The firm is comprised of 40 lawyers, including 10 partners, each specialising in different fields of expertise.

Ginestié Paley-Vincent & Associés has a well-established policy focused on improving the quality of its services and client relations. In recognition of this ongoing commitment, Ginestié, Paley-Vincent & Associés was awarded ISO 9001: 2000 certification on 15 January 2003 by BVQI.

Ginestié Paley-Vincent & Associés established its London office in 1998 to handle the increasing flow of Anglo-French business. The resident London team serves as an interface with the UK and the French legal environments for both French and English clients.

The firm is part of DLA Group – an exclusive alliance of international full-service law firms with a shared vision. Established in 1999, DLA Group now has over 2,200 lawyers across 21 countries, who deliver expert local know-how and international solutions.

DLA Group provides legal advice in 36 major cities across Europe, Singapore, Thailand, Hong Kong and the People's Republic of China.

AREAS OF PRACTICE

The firm is organised into the following departments: corporate (corporate finance, private equity, funds, IPO and listed companies regulation); IT (telecom, Internet); employment (litigation, redundancies and restructuring); tax (advice planning and litigation); intellectual property (copyright, trade marks); and litigation (commercial, arbitration, criminal and health regulation).

Over the years, Ginestié Paley-Vincent & Associés has acquired particular expertise in the creation of investment funds, M&A and venture capital.

The clients which the firm represents on an ongoing basis include a range of French and multinational companies in the banking and investment industry, luxury and distribution.

A brochure providing more details is available upon request.

HPMBC CLYDE & CO

SOCIÉTÉ D'AVOCATS

12 RUE MAGELLAN
75378 PARIS CEDEX 08

Telephone: +33 1 44 43 88 88
Fax: +33 1 44 43 88 77
Video conference: +33 1 44 43 88 99
E-mail: paris.office@clydeco.fr
Website: www.clydeco.com

Languages
English, German, Italian, Spanish

Other offices
Belgrade, Caracas, Cardiff, Dubai, Guildford, Hong Kong, London, Nantes, Piraeus, St Petersburg, Singapore

Number of lawyers 386
at this office 42

Contacts
Gildas Rostain, Gérard Honig, Bernard Mettetal

CATEGORIES OF WORK

Arbitration
Gérard Honig, Bernard Mettetal

Aviation
Gérard Honig

Construction contracts
Jean-Marie Preel

Environmental
Bernard Mettetal

Shipping
Gildas Rostain

Insolvency law
Bernard Mettetal

Insurance and reinsurance
Gérard Honig, Bernard Mettetal

Product liability – industrial risks
Jean-Marie Preel, Gérard Honig

Professional indemnity and directors' and officers' liability
Jean-Marie Preel, Bernard Mettetal

Life insurance and regulatory
Bernard Mettetal

HAARMANN HEMMELRATH

23, RUE BALZAC
75008 PARIS

Telephone: +33 1 53 53 02 80
Fax: +33 1 53 53 02 81
E-mail:
paris@haarmannhemmelrath.com
Website:
www.haarmannhemmelrath.com

Languages
Dutch, English, German, Italian, Japanese, Mandarin, Spanish

Other offices
Berlin, Bielefeld, Brussels, Bucharest, Budapest, Cologne, Dusseldorf, Frankfurt, Hamburg, Leipzig, London, Milan, Moscow, Munich, Prague, Rome, Shanghai, Singapore, Stuttgart, Tokyo, Vienna, Warsaw

Number of lawyers 281
at this office 17

CATEGORIES OF WORK

Company and commercial law
Anja Droege, Marc-Alexis Fauvet

Mergers and acquisitions
Anja Droege, Yann François

Corporate finance, securitisation
Dr Alfred Fink, Dr Bernd Sagasser

Banking and finance
Dr Alfred Fink, Dr Bernd Sagasser

Private equity, venture capital
Marc-Alexis Fauvet, Dr Bernd Sagassser

International tax law
Jacques Prats, Dr Bernd Sagasser

National tax law
Jacques Prats, Pascal Schultze

Real estate transactions
Yann François, Pascal Schultze

Litigation and arbitration
Marc-Alexis Fauvet, Nathalie Sinavong

Competition and EU law
Martina Maier, Nathalie Sinavong

State aids
Martina Maier, Dr Antje Luke

Public and regulatory law
Martina Maier, Bruno Lefébure

German law
Dr Bernd Sagasser, Dr Antje Luke

HERBERT SMITH

20 RUE QUENTIN BAUCHART
75008 PARIS

Telephone: +33 1 53 57 70 70
Fax: +33 1 53 57 70 80
E-mail: contactparis@herbertsmith.com
Website: www.herbertsmith.com

Languages
Arabic, Dutch, English, French, German, Greek, Hebrew, Italian, Russian, Spanish

Other offices
Bangkok, Beijing, Brussels, Hong Kong, London, Moscow, Shanghai, Singapore, Tokyo

Number of lawyers 1,108
at this office 80

CATEGORIES OF WORK

International finance and banking
Georges Dirani, Clotilde Dirnat

Corporate finance, mergers and acquisitions
Bruno Basuyaux, Jacques Buhart

Project finance
Neil Brimson, Stéphane Brabant

Employment
Sophie Brézin

Tax
Jean-Luc Calisti

Litigation and arbitration
Charles Kaplan, Denis Chemla

Competition
Jacques Buhart

HUGHES HUBBARD & REED

47 AVENUE GEORGES MANDEL
75116 PARIS

Telephone: +33 1 44 05 80 00
Fax: +33 1 45 53 15 04
E-mail: hall@hugheshubbard.com
Website: www.hugheshubbard.com

Languages
Arabic, English, German, Italian, Portuguese, Spanish

Other offices
New York, Washington DC, Los Angeles, Miami, Jersey City, Tokyo

Number of lawyers 27

Contact
Merrikay Hall

CATEGORIES OF WORK

Arbitartion, litigation
Axel Baum, José Rosell

Bankruptcy, insolvency
Thierry Brezillon

Labour, employment
Nadine Voisin, Thierry Brezillon

Real estate and construction
Claire Ayer

Corporate M&A and commercial
Merrikay Hall, Christopher Mesnooh

IP, technology, media and telecoms
Christopher Mesnooh

HOLMAN FENWICK & WILLAN

3 RUE LA BOETIE
75008 PARIS

Telephone: +33 1 44 94 40 50
Fax: +33 1 42 65 46 25
E-mail: holmans@hfw-france.com
Website: www.hfw.com

Languages
English, German, Italian, Russian, Spanish

Other offices
Rouen, Nantes, London, Piraeus, Hong Kong, Shanghai, Singapore

Number of lawyers 178
at this office 18

CATEGORIES OF WORK

Admiralty
Jean-Jacques Ollu, Oliver Purcell

Industrial risk
Guillaume Brajeux, Jean-Jacques Ollu

Shipping litigation and arbitration
Timothy Clemens-Jones, Guillaume Brajeux

European law
Timothy Clemens-Jones, Edouard Tay Pamart

International trade
Timothy Clemens-Jones, Jean-Jacques Ollu

Customs and excise
Guillaume Brajeux, Edouard Tay Pamart

Commercial litigation
Guillaume Brajeux, Stéphane Sélégny

Ship finance
Timothy Clemens-Jones, Edouard Tay Pamart

Insurance and reinsurance
Oliver Purcell, Jean-Jaques Ollu

Labour law
Stéphane Sélégny

Finance, company and commercial
Sybille Elleboode-Merlier, Janet Butterworth

THE FIRM

Holman Fenwick & Willan is an international law firm specialising in shipping and transport, trade and energy, insurance and reinsurance and commercial law. The firm has a reputation worldwide for excellence and innovation. It has one of the largest international arbitration and dispute resolution practices of its kind, with offices in Europe and Asia Pacific.

The firm's international practice is founded upon its principal offices in London, Paris, Piraeus, Hong Kong, Singapore and Shanghai and over 120 years' experience of working with other law firms in jurisdictions throughout the world.

The Paris office was opened in 1997. The firm has two further offices in France – Rouen (opened 1993) and Nantes (opened 1997) – with a total of 24 lawyers. There are five French, one Anglo-French and two English partners. Shipping and maritime litigation and arbitration, including Admiralty work, represents about 50% of the firm's activities in France. The firm has a growing insurance, reinsurance, customs and industrial risk practice, which together with general commercial and international litigation and arbitration represents another 30%.

The commercial practice also continues to grow. The firm's offices in France are involved in most aspects of corporate and commercial law, including labour law, project and asset finance, and mergers and acquisitions.

AREAS OF PRACTICE

All aspects of shipping including Admiralty, international trade, insurance and reinsurance, customs law, commercial litigation and arbitration, financial, company, commercial and labour law, all relevant aspects of European law, aviation, project and asset finance.

HUGLO LEPAGE & ASSOCIÉS CONSEIL

40 RUE DE MONCEAU
75008 PARIS

Telephone: +33 1 56 59 29 59
Fax: +33 1 56 59 29 39
E-mail: paris@huglo-lepage.com
Website: www.huglo-lepage.com

Languages
Dutch, English, German, Italian, Spanish

Other offices
Brussels

Number of lawyers 39

Member
GESICA

CATEGORIES OF WORK

Environmental law
C Huglo, C Lepage, M Wemaëre

Environmental audit
C Huglo, C Lepage

European law
C Lepage, M Wemaëre

Classified installations law
C Huglo

Healthcare
C Huglo, RP Drai

Medical law
RP Drai

Biotechnology
C Lepage, I Cassin

Consumer protection
C Lepage, I Cassin

Zoning and planning
I Cassin, E Bineteau

Urban planning
I Cassin, E Bineteau

Building law
RP Drai, E Bineteau

Public law
C Lepage, C Huglo

Local government law
E Bineteau, O Schmitt

Economic public law
MY Benjamin, O Schmitt

Public procurement
MY Benjamin, O Schmitt

JONES DAY

120 RUE DU FAUBOURG
SAINT-HONORE
75008 PARIS

Telephone: +33 1 56 59 39 39
Fax: +33 1 56 59 39 38
Website: www.jonesday.com

Languages
Chinese, English, German, Italian, Romanian, Russian, Spanish, Swedish, Vietnamese

Other offices
Atlanta, Beijing, Brussels, Chicago, Cleveland, Columbus, Dallas, Frankfurt, Hong Kong, Houston, Irvine, London, Los Angeles, Madrid, Menlo Park, Milan, Munich, Mumbai, New Delhi, New York, Pittsburgh, San Francisco, Shanghai, Singapore, Sydney, Taipei, Tokyo, Washington DC

Number of lawyers 2,200
at this office 77

CATEGORIES OF WORK

Banking and structured finance
Philippe Billot, Pierre-Nicolas Ferrand, Edward J Nalbantian

Securities and stock exchange regulation
Jean-Marc Franceschi, Edward J. Nalbantian

Mergers and acquisitions
Wesley R Johnson Jr, Gaël Saint Olive, Sophie Hagège, Arnaud Vanbremeersch

Venture capital, private equity
Olivier Edwards, Renaud Bonnet

Tax
Vincent Agulhon

Real estate tax
Emmanuel Chauve

Arbitration
John F Crawford, Michael Bühler

Competition law and distribution
Eric Morgan de Rivery, Lucie Carswell Parmentier

Corporate and commercial litigation
Laurent Martinet

Labour law
Anne Boileau

Real estate
François Bonteil

Intellectual property
Catherine Muyl

INCE & CO

164 RUE DU FAUBOURG
SAINT HONORÉ
75008 PARIS

Telephone: +33 1 53 76 9100
Fax: +33 1 5376 9126
E-mail: firstname.lastname@incelaw.com
Website: www.incelaw.com

Languages
English, Dutch, Spanish

Other offices
Hamburg, Hong Kong, Le Havre, London, Piraeus, Shanghai, Singapore

Number of lawyers at this office 12

CATEGORIES OF WORK

Shipping and transport
Gilles Gautier, Fred Vroom

International trade
Gilles Gautier, Fred Vroom

Insurance
Gilles Gautier, Jerome de Sentenac

Reinsurance
Gilles Gautier, Jerome de Sentenac

General corporate
Fred Vroom, Andrew Charlier

Trade finance
Fred Vroom, Andrew Charlier

Aviation and ship financing
Fred Vroom, Andrew Charlier

Employment
Fred Vroom, Jacques Le Vaillant

Banking
Fred Vroom, Andrew Charlier

Property
Andrew Charlier

Commercial litigation
Gilles Gautier, Jerome de Sentenac

International arbitration
Gilles Gautier, Jerome de Sentenac

Aircraft and ship (sale and purchase)
Fred Vroom, Andrew Charlier

THE FIRM

Ince & Co is an international law firm with a worldwide reputation as a leading practitioner in shipping, insurance and reinsurance, energy, aviation and international trade law. Founded in the City of London in 1870, the firm also has offices in Hamburg, Hong Kong, Le Havre, Paris, Piraeus, Shanghai and Singapore.

AREAS OF PRACTICE

Ince & Co's Paris and Le Havre offices opened in January 2002. The firm's links with the French shipping and insurance markets have existed for many years. Ince & Co has acted for major institutions in both industries. The Paris and Le Havre offices, which practise both French and English law, also provide a service to the firm's clients globally on French law in the areas of non-contentious shipping and insurance, banking (including project and asset-based structured finance), and commercial law. The firm conducts litigation before the French courts and arbitrations before the International Chamber of Commerce and the Chambre Arbitrale Maritime de Paris.

The contact details for the Le Havre office are: 136 Rue Victor Hugo, 76600 Le Havre. Telephone: +332 3522 1888. Fax: +332 3522 1880. E-mail: firstname.lastname@incelaw.com. For all matters please contact Mathieu Croix or Jerôme de Sentenac.

JEANTETASSOCIÉS

87 AVENUE KLÉBER
75116 PARIS

Telephone: +33 1 45 05 80 08
Fax: +33 1 47 04 20 41
E-mail: info@jeantet.fr
Website: www.jeantet.fr

Languages
English, German, Italian, Spanish

Other offices
New York

Number of lawyers 68

Contacts
Yvon Dréano, Philippe Portier,
Brigitte R. Gambini (New York)

CATEGORIES OF WORK	
Mergers and acquisitions	**Business criminal law**
Banking and finance	**Administrative law**
Antitrust, competition and distribution	**Bankruptcy, insolvency and restructuring**
International contracts and trade	**Real estate**
Tax	**Energy and natural resources**
Labour law	**Litigation and alternative dispute resolution**

THE FIRM

JeantetAssociés is one of France's premier independent law firms.

Founded in Paris in 1924, JeantetAssociés is a full-service firm with significant activity in long-term financing operations and litigation. The firm has 68 lawyers, of which 19 are partners (all members of the Paris Bar), and it is structured so as to be able to act as a single, multi-disciplinary legal and tax team.

The firm has had an international focus since it was founded and, more particularly, since the 1950s, when a large proportion of its foreign clients were from the US. During the last two decades, it has diversified its client base so that, while a third are still North American, a third are now large French industrial and financial groups and the remaining third are mostly European.

To further reinforce existing close relationships with its US-based clientele, the firm established an office in New York in 1991. This office has since grown its practice by attracting new US companies doing business in France, including American law firms, which need assistance with their clients' transatlantic matters. Moreover, the New York office provides support to French clients investing in the US by liaising, advising and co-ordinating on any pertinent legal matter with local American law firms.

On the other continents, JeantetAssociés maintains excellent connections with foreign independent law firms, particularly in Europe and the US.

AREAS OF PRACTICE

JeantetAssociés offers a wide but selected range of legal services to companies (banking, financial and industrial groups) and institutions – public or private, national or international – and government bodies.

JeantetAssociés' practice is focused on areas of law requiring high added value, particularly mergers and acquistions, corporate restructurings, banking and finance, tax, competition, labour law and administrative law.

KAHN & ASSOCIÉS

51 RUE DUMONT D'URVILLE
75116 PARIS

Telephone: +33 1 45 01 45 01
Fax: +33 1 45 01 45 00
E-mail: contact@kahnlaw.com
Website: www.kahnlaw.com

Languages
English, German, Spanish

Other offices
Sophia-Antipolis

Number of lawyers 40

Contacts
Daniel Kahn, Douglas Glucroft

CATEGORIES OF WORK

M&A
Douglas Glucroft, Olivia Lê Horovitz

Computer, telecoms and space law
Fabrice Perbost,
Marie-Laure de Cordovez

E-commerce and Internet
Fabrice Perbost,
Marie-Laure de Cordovez

Intellectual and industrial property
Marie-Laure de Cordovez,
Fabrice Perbost

Licence contracts
Marie-Laure de Cordovez,
Fabrice Perbost

Employment
Frédérique David, Sébastien Ducamp

Corporate
Daniel Kahn, Diane Hedary

Property and construction
Diane Hedary

Taxation
Régis Bernard

Litigation and arbitration
Jérôme Richardot,
Pascale Trager-Lewis

Commercial contracts
Marie-Laure de Cordovez,
Diane Hedary

Private equity
Pascale Trager-Lewis, Marie-Laure de Cordovez

THE FIRM

Kahn & Associés is an international business law firm based in Paris counting 40 lawyers, of whom ten are partners, and a total staff of 67. It is located in a building one block from the Arc de Triomphe, and has a branch office in the technology park of Sophia-Antipolis (Côte d'Azur).

Kahn & Associés works with its clients in all aspects of business law and at all stages in their development, both in France and abroad. While representing a significant number of clients in traditional industries, Kahn & Associés has become a leading and prestigious adviser to high-growth technology companies and investors.

AREAS OF PRACTICE

Among the clients of Kahn & Associés are: companies (public as well as privately held companies) in traditional industries, as well as in the fields of technology, telecommunications, media and life sciences (biotechnology, medical instruments, etc); emerging companies; and both French and foreign venture capital investors and intermediaries.

The clients in traditional sectors cut across a wide range of industries: aviation, chemicals, pharmaceuticals, industry, advertising, etc.

Kahn & Associés represents and advises numerous foreign clients, including many multinationals and their French subsidiaries. These clients are principally headquartered on the west coast of the United States, but also come from throughout Europe and Israel. They include a large number of industry leaders.

Technology, media and telecommunications clients have a broad and varied range of businesses, including in the following fields: computer hardware; software; multimedia; e-commerce; media; television; Internet and Internet access; semiconductors and microcomputers; computer services (including web and ASP services); and satellites.

For a number of years, Kahn & Associés has been working with the most prestigious investment funds that are focused on technology, media and telecom sectors, enabling them to benefit from the firm's knowledge and expertise in this area of business, both in investments and in managing their portfolios.

The firm has received a number of awards since its founding, including being named 'European Technology Law Firm' in 2000. Awarded in London, this award recognises the best business law firm in Europe active in the field of representation of hi-tech companies. In June 2002, the firm was quoted by the French magazine, *Décideurs Juridiques et Financiers*, as one of the four major actors in the area of private equity in France and venture capital in 2003.

LAMY LEXEL AVOCATS ASSOCIÉS

9 BLD MALESHERBES
75008 PARIS

Telephone: +33 1 55 27 24 00
Fax: +33 1 55 27 24 24
E-mail: paris@lamy-lexel.com
Website: www.lamy-lexel.com

Other offices
Lyon, Albertville, Chambery

Number of lawyers 74

Contacts
Jean-Pierre Gitenay, Jérôme Saleur

Member
Pannone Law Group

CATEGORIES OF WORK

Company law, mergers and acquisitions
Jean-Pierre Gitenay, Patrick Vergnole

Employment law and social security law
Jean-Pierre Duprilot,
Jean-Marc Lavallart

Development of contracts, new technology
Michel Masoero, Jérôme Saleur

EU law, international relations
Jean-Pierre Viennois

Public law
William Azan, Philippe Nugue

Litigation, arbitration
Florence Baudouin-Thierrée,
Édouard Bertrand

Tax law
Christian Caruelle, Christian Guichard

THE FIRM

Lamy Lexel Avocats Associés was formed in 1998 from the merger of two large law firms: Lamy Avocats Associés, a multi-disciplinary practice with over 100 years' experience, whose main area of expertise was labour law, and Lexel Conseil, a corporate and commercial law firm.

Today, Lamy Lexel Avocats Associés is one of the most important independent law firms in France, with offices in Paris, Lyon, Albertville and Chambery.

With a staff of 130, of whom 74 are lawyers, the company is a human-sized structure that favours real consulting relationships.

The lawyers have an understanding of the commercial and social factors affecting the firm's clients and the environment they operate in, and assist businesses in their development as they have integrated several legal dimensions beyond their specific expertises.

Lamy Lexel Avocats Associés, close to the company world's preoccupations, is characterised by a great operational implication close to its clients thanks to its pragmatical spirit that brings together creativity, reactivity, availability and results culture.

In response to the European and international development of its clients' business activities, the lawyers at Lamy Lexel Avocats Associés are proficient in several European languages and operate in overseas legal systems via long-term collaborative relationships with their partners within the Pannone Law Group (a 'GEIE' encompassing 550 lawyers in Europe, South America, the USA and Canada).

AREAS OF PRACTICE

Lamy Lexel Avocats Associés has developed particular expertise in labour law, tax law, mergers and acquisitions, company law and stock exchange law. The firm is also involved in the development of contracts, especially in the new technologies sector.

Additional areas of expertise are EU law and international relations, litigation and arbitration, joint legal actions, public law and know-how in socio-economic matters.

The firm has also expanded specific skills in several areas, which are intellectual property, information technology, advanced technologies, environment, sport law and transport. In recent months, Lamy Lexel Avocats Associés has seen the expansion of its advanced technologies, labour law, taxation and public law departments.

Breakdown of work: tax law and company law, mergers and acquisitions 33%; employment law and social security law 30%; contracts, commercial law, advanced technologies 20%; social economics, public law 8%; EU law, international relations 6%; and others 3%.

LASSEZ ET ASSOCIÉS

51 AVENUE MONTAIGNE
75008 PARIS

Telephone: +33 1 42 56 44 81
Fax: +33 1 45 51 91 12
E-mail: lassez@avocaweb.tm.fr

Languages
English, Italian

Number of lawyers 6

CATEGORIES OF WORK

Shipping and transportation	**Litigation**
International trade	**Insurance**
Arbitration	

LATHAM & WATKINS

53 QUAI D'ORSAY
75007 PARIS

Telephone: +33 1 40 62 20 00
Fax: +33 1 40 62 20 62
Website: www.lw.com

Languages
Dutch, English, German, Italian, Spanish, Russian

Other offices
Boston, Brussels, Chicago, Frankfurt, Hamburg, Hong Kong, London, Los Angeles, Milan, Moscow, New Jersey, New York, Northern Virginia, Orange County, San Diego, San Francisco, Silicon Valley, Singapore, Tokyo, Washington DC

Number of lawyers 1,500
at this office 95

CATEGORIES OF WORK

Mergers and acquisitions, capital markets and private equity	**EU and competition law**
Financing	**Labour law**
Tax	**Intellectual property and new technologies**
Real estate	**Litigation and arbitration**

LATOURNERIE WOLFROM & ASSOCIÉS

**164 RUE DU FAUBOURG
SAINT HONORÉ
75008 PARIS**

Telephone: +33 1 56 59 74 74
Fax: +33 1 56 59 74 75
E-mail:
contact@latournerie-wolfrom.com
Website: www.latournerie-wolfrom.com

Languages
English, German, Italian, Spanish

Number of lawyers 23

CATEGORIES OF WORK

Mergers and acquisitions
Christian Wolfrom

Corporate and company
Christian Wolfrom

Banking and finance
Christian Wolfrom

Capital markets and business start-ups
Christian Wolfrom

Copyright and intellectual property
Marie-Hélène Tonnellier

Information technology and computers
Marie-Hélène Tonnellier

Libel
Jean Latournerie, Nathalie Karpik

Distribution and competition
Nathalie Karpik,
Marie-Hélène Tonnellier

Telecoms, Internet and e-commerce
Marie-Hélène Tonnellier

Administrative and public law
Jean Latournerie

Environment
Jean Latournerie

Commercial law and commercial litigation
Nathalie Karpik,
Marie-Hélène Tonnellier

Unfair competition
Nathalie Karpik

Litigation and arbitration
Nathalie Karpik, Jean Latournerie

Media and broadcasting, entertainment
Marie-Hélène Tonnellier

Employment and labour law
Joëlle Hannelais

CABINET LIPWORTH

**18 AV FRANKLIN D ROOSEVELT
75008 PARIS**

Telephone: +33 1 53 75 41 41
Fax: +33 1 53 75 14 12
E-mail: office@cabinet-lipworth.com
Website: www.cabinet-lipworth.com

Languages
Cantonese, English, Mandarin

Number of lawyers 5

CATEGORIES OF WORK

Mergers and acquisitions
Frank Lipworth, Myriam Smith

Banking (financing, syndications)
Frank Lipworth, Iris Bellanger

Private equity
Frank Lipworth, Myriam Smith

Commercial leases
Myriam Smith

IT agreements
Iris Bellanger, Garance Grandchamp

Commercial litigation
Frank Lipworth, Myriam Smith

Music contracts
Frank Lipworth, Garance Grandchamp

Regulatory matters (financial services)
Frank Lipworth, Myriam Smith

Acquisitions of receivable portfolios
Frank Lipworth, Iris Bellanger

International joint ventures
Frank Lipworth, Iris Bellanger

LINKLATERS

25 RUE DE MARIGNAN
75008 PARIS

Telephone: +33 1 56 43 56 43
Fax: +33 1 43 59 41 96
Website: www.linklaters.com

Languages
All commercial and local languages in the countries where Linklaters operates

Other offices
Alicante, Amsterdam, Antwerp, Bangkok, Beijing, Berlin, Bratislava, Brussels, Bucharest, Budapest, Cologne, Frankfurt am Main, Hong Kong, Lisbon, London, Luxembourg, Madrid, Milan, Moscow, Munich, New York, Prague, Rome, São Paulo, Shanghai, Singapore, Stockholm, Tokyo, Warsaw

Number of lawyers 2,000 worldwide

Contacts
Jean-Marc Lefèvre, Thierry Vassogne

CATEGORIES OF WORK

Banking
Bertrand Andriani, Nathalie Hobbs

Capital markets
Gilles Endréo

Commercial law
Stéphanie Faber

Corporate/M&A
Jean-Marc Lefèvre, Thierry Vassogne

EU and competition
Olivier d'Ormesson

Employment
Jérome Cordier,
Florence Dupont-Fargeaud

Intellectual property
Denis Monégier du Sorbier

Litigation
Arnaud de La Cotardière

Projects
Bertrand Andriani

Public law/public-private partnerships
Bertrand Andriani, Paul Lignières

Real estate
Françoise Maigrot

Regulatory
Jean-Jacques Essombé

Tax
Philippe Derouin

THE FIRM

Linklaters advises the world's leading companies, financial institutions and governments on their most challenging transactions and assignments. With 2,000 lawyers, including 470 partners, and offices in major business and financial centres, its clients choose the firm for its distinctive combination of technical skill, commercial experience and outstanding service.

Linklaters has built a formidable global practice through organic growth and a series of mergers, joint ventures and co-operations with other respected law firms. In 2001, Linklaters merged with three of Europe's leading law firms to form Linklaters Oppenhoff & Rädler in Germany, Linklaters in Sweden, Linklaters De Bandt in Belgium and Linklaters Loesch in Luxembourg. In the same year, the firm formed a co-operation with Brazilian firm Goulart Penteado, Iervolino e Lefosse. This co-operation combines Linklaters' international capability with GPIL's extensive knowledge of the Brazilian market. In Singapore, the firm practises as Linklaters Allen & Gledhill, a joint venture with the premier Singapore practice of Allen & Gledhill, while in Italy, Linklaters has an exclusive relationship with Italian law firm Gianni, Origoni, Grippo & Partners.

LOVELLS

6 AVENUE KLÉBER
75116 PARIS

Telephone: +33 1 53 67 47 47
Fax: +33 1 53 67 47 48
E-mail: information@lovells.com
Website: www.lovells.com

Languages
English, German, Italian, Spanish

Other offices
Alicante, Amsterdam, Beijing, Berlin, Brussels, Budapest*, Chicago, Düsseldorf, Frankfurt, Hamburg, Ho Chi Minh City, Hong Kong, London, Milan, Moscow, Munich, New York, Prague, Rome, Shanghai, Singapore, Tokyo, Vienna*, Warsaw, Zagreb*

Number of lawyers 1,600
at this office 114

Contact
Robert Follie

CATEGORIES OF WORK

- Aviation
- Banking, project finance
- Bankruptcy
- Business restructuring
- Capital markets, structured finance
- Consumer and advertising law
- Competition and EU law
- Corporate law
- Distribution law
- Employment law
- E-commerce
- Insurance law
- IP, technology and media
- Litigation and arbitration
- Oil and gas
- Outsourcing
- Pharmaceutical and biosciences
- Private equity
- Property law
- Public law
- Public/private partnerships and economic public law
- Tax, including cross-border
- Telecommunications
- Venture capital and management buyouts

MEFFRE & GRALL

80 AVENUE MARCEAU
75008 PARIS

Telephone: +33 1 53 57 31 70
Fax: +33 1 47 20 90 40
E-mail: meffregrall@meffre-grall.avocat.fr
Website: www.meffre-grall.avocat.fr

Languages
English, French, German, Greek, Spanish

Number of lawyers 12

International groupings
LEXLINK

CATEGORIES OF WORK

French and EU competition law
JC Grall, JM Meffre, C Guet, N Kouchnir-Cargill, C Grass

Distribution law
JC Grall, T Lamy, C Guet, N Kouchnir-Cargill, C Grass

Media, entertainment and intellectual property
JC Grall, E Laur

Marketing law
JC Grall, S Coulaux, N Kouchnir-Cargill

Litigation
E Bordenave, S Coulaux, N Kouchnir-Cargill, E Le Morhedec

Information technology
S Coulaux, P Georganta

Employment
V Maricot, E Bordenave

Corporate immigration
S Coulaux, V Maricot

MEYRIER FAYOUT LACOSTE

74 AVENUE PAUL DOUMER
75116 PARIS

Telephone: +33 1 45 03 50 00
Fax: +33 1 45 03 01 38
E-mail: mfl@mflbar.net

Languages
English, French

Number of lawyers 4

Contacts
Francis Meyrier, Deborah Barbizet, Frederic Fayout, Thierry C Lacoste

CATEGORIES OF WORK

Company commercial law	**Information technology law**
Banking and finance law	**Intellectual and artistic property rights**
Entertainment law and audiovisual	**Media and publicity**
French and international litigation	
French and international arbitration	

MOQUET BORDE & ASSOCIÉS

30 AVENUE DE MESSINE
75008 PARIS

Telephone: +33 1 42 99 04 50
Fax: +33 1 45 63 91 49
E-mail: mb@moquet-borde.com
Website: www.moquet-borde.com

Languages
English, German, Italian, Czech

Other offices
Lyon, Brussels, Budapest, Tallinn

Number of lawyers 105

CATEGORIES OF WORK

Mergers and acquisitions, private equity	**Tax**
Privatisations	**Labour**
Capital markets	**IT and intellectual property**
Banking and finance	**Bankruptcy and insolvency**
Real estate	**Regulatory/public administrative law**
White-collar crime	**Insurance**
Dispute resolution and arbitration	
Competition/EU	

NOMOS

13 RUE ALPHONSE DE NEUVILLE
75017 PARIS

Telephone: +33 1 43 18 55 00
Fax: +33 1 43 18 55 55
E-mail: nomos@nomosparis.com
Website: www.nomosparis.com

Languages
English, German, Italian, Spanish

Number of lawyers 50

Contacts
Eric Lauvaux, Christophe Pecnard, Monique Sentilles-Dupont

Member
IBA, IAEL, AEC, AFDIT, ACEECA

CATEGORIES OF WORK

Media and entertainment
Eric Lauvaux,

Intellectual property, IT
Héléna Delabarre

Competition, distribution, advertising
Christophe Pecnard

Tax law
Jean-Claude Bignon, Anne-Marie Hatchondo

Mergers and acquisitions
Monique Sentilles-Dupont, Pierre Jouglard

Private equity
Jean-François Pourdieu, Monique Sentilles-Dupont

Company law
Claude Ravon

General litigation
Josette Arnold

Labour law
Anne Ciret

THE FIRM

Founded in 1998, NomoS is a young, modern practice which is highly specialised in developing industry sectors and nurtures a close working relationship with its clients. The firm's name did not belong to a founding partner but actually means 'custom having the force of law' in ancient Greek.

The firm was founded by seven partners from Thomas & Associés who were joined by two partners from Jeantet & Associés and August & Debouzy. After having made three associates partner, the firm consolidated its mergers and acquisitions and company law expertise by welcoming three new partners from the firm Orsay. Today, the firm employs 50 lawyers, 11 of whom are partners.

AREAS OF PRACTICE

NomoS is active both in an advisory capacity and in contentious matters. The firm acts as the legal partner of its French and international clients, which include large groups and dynamic small to medium-sized companies, assisting them in their day-to-day operations as well as in their more unusual transactions.

The firm is involved in the following areas of commercial law: mergers and acquisitions, company law, labour law, intellectual property and IT law, tax law, competition law, distribution law and consumer law.

The firm is particularly active within developing industry sectors, such as private equity, media/communications/entertainment, new technologies, distribution, food processing and advertising. NomoS advises its clients over the long term, enabling the firm's lawyers to build longstanding relationships with its clients.

Within the firm, legal work is undertaken by teams who combine an in-depth understanding of each client's marketplace with specialist legal knowledge.

The firm does not belong to a network or alliance, but has developed a 'web' of trusted correspondents within each of its main areas of activity.

PROSKAUER ROSE

68 RUE DU FAUBOURG SAINT-HONORÉ 75008 PARIS

Telephone: +33 1 53 05 60 00
Fax: +33 1 53 05 60 05
E-mail: jpberthet@proskauer.com
Website: www.proskauer.com

Languages
English, Spanish

Other offices
Boca Raton, Los Angeles, Newark, New York, Washington

Number of lawyers 628
at this office 18

Contact
Jean-Philippe Berthet

CATEGORIES OF WORK

Corporate and commercial
William Krisel, Bernard Husson

Private equity
William Krisel, Delia B Spitzer

Labour, employment
Yasmine Tarasewicz

Pharmaceutical law
Christophe Hénin

International transactions
Delia B Spitzer, Jean-Philippe Berthet

Competition and distribution
Christophe Hénin

Tax
Jean-Luc Cuadrado

SJ BERWIN

64 AVENUE KLÉBER 75116 PARIS

Telephone: +33 1 44 346 346
Fax: +33 1 44 346 347
E-mail: info-paris@sjberwin.com
Website: www.sjberwin.com

Languages
English, French, Portuguese, Spanish

Other offices
Berlin, Brussels, Frankfurt, London, Madrid, Munich

Number of lawyers 411
at this office 33

Contact
George Pinkhorn

CATEGORIES OF WORK

Private equity, fund structuring
George Pinkham, Sylvie Vansteenkiste

Tax law
Sylvie Vansteenkiste, Jean Goncalves

Private equity, corporate, MBO/LBO
Christophe Digoy, Maxance Bloch

Corporate finance, M&A
Laurence Pinot-Lacan, Pierre-Louis Périn

EU and competition
Marc Lévy

Venture capital
Pierre-Louis Périn

RAMBAUD MARTEL

25 BOULEVARD DE
L'AMIRAL BRUIX
75782 PARIS CEDEX 16

Telephone: +33 1 40 67 17 00
Fax: +33 1 40 67 28 80
E-mail: rm@rambaud-martel.com
Website: www.rambaud-martel.com

Number of lawyers 120

Contacts
Jean-Pierre Martel, Delphine Deschamps

CATEGORIES OF WORK

- Corporate, M&A, restructurings
- Stock exchange regulation
- Issuance of securities
- Private equity
- Joint ventures, strategic alliances
- Privatisation
- Banking and finance
- Insolvency
- Tax (corporate, structuring, optimisation of M&A, income/wealth, litigation)
- Business criminal law
- French competition law/antitrust
- International law
- Public and regulatory law
- Litigation, dispute resolution, arbitration and mediation
- Real estate and construction
- Contract law
- Insurance law
- Professional, product and industrial liability
- Bankruptcy law
- Labour and employment
- IP, technology, media and telecoms
- Pharmaceuticals and medical law
- Sports financing and investment

THE FIRM

Rambaud Martel is an established, leading French law firm based in Paris, which is highly regarded for the quality of advice it gives its clients and its representation of their specific interests.

The firm acts for many major French companies, financial institutions and government authorities, a large number of multinationals as well as smaller operations, advising on all aspects of their businesses. Rambaud Martel provides a full range of legal services to domestic and international companies in a variety of industries. Today there are 120 lawyers at Rambaud Martel.

AREAS OF PRACTICE

The firm's practice is equally balanced between transactional work and litigation or other forms of dispute resolution. The firm's partners have wide experience of general legal practice, with many also recognised as leading advisers in their particular fields of expertise.

The firm's practice in both transactional work and litigation enables each lawyer to represent clients during significant transactions or major legal disputes.

The firm's service is characterised by its lawyers' hands-on style and close working relationships with clients. Rambaud Martel can be distinguished from other firms by its offer to clients of practical and competitive alternatives, built on expertise and deep knowledge of the issues faced by its clients. The firm's lawyers are known for their strategic approach and total availability. They contribute a personalised service based on clients' real needs. Rambaud Martel further brings a creative and innovative approach to the services it offers.

The firm operates through highly responsive teams of lawyers, which are tailored to clients' specific needs. These specialised teams work in a flexible and co-operative way to ensure clients receive the best advice and representation during complex cases where the advice of lawyers well versed in different fields of expertise is a key factor.

SAVIN MARTINET ASSOCIÉS

**66 RUE DU FAUBOURG
SAINT-HONORÉ
75008 PARIS**

Telephone: +33 1 53 43 22 20
Fax: +33 1 53 43 22 21
E-mail: contact@smaparis.com
Website: www.smaparis.com

Languages
Dutch, English, German, Spanish

Number of lawyers 11

CATEGORIES OF WORK

Criminal, civil and administrative litigation, arbitration and mediation
Yvon Martinet, Arnaud Constant

Regulatory audits, risk audits, environmental and social reporting
Patricia Savin, Yvon Martinet

Corporate business law, retail and competition, customs
Yvon Martinet, Arnaud Constant

Health and safety law
Patricia Savin, Yvon Martinet

Food and consumer law
Yvon Martinet

Environmental law
Patricia Savin

Polluted sites, land law
Patricia Savin

Natural resources law
Patricia Savin, Yvon Martinet

SIMMONS & SIMMONS
SOLICITORS, AVOCATS À LA COUR, RECHTSANWALT

**5 BOULEVARD DE LA MADELEINE
75001 PARIS**

Telephone: +33 1 53 29 16 29
Fax: +33 1 53 29 16 30
E-mail: enquiries@simmons-simmons.com
Website: www.simmons-simmons.com

Languages
English, German

Other offices
London, Rotterdam, Lisbon, Milan, Rome, Düsseldorf, Frankfurt, Brussels, Madrid, Padua, Oporto, Madeira, Abu Dhabi, Qatar, Hong Kong, Shanghai, Tokyo, New York

Number of lawyers 754
at this office 53

Contact
Jacques de Taisne

CATEGORIES OF WORK

Corporate

Banking

Capital markets

Taxation

Projects, PFI

EU, competition

Dispute resolution

Intellectual property

Employment

Financial markets

Pharmaceutical and biotechnology

Energy and utilities

TMT

Aerospace and defence

Transport

Real estate and construction

Consumer goods

SLAUGHTER AND MAY

ENGLISH SOLICITORS AND AVOCATS À LA COUR

112 AVENUE KLÉBER
75784 PARIS CEDEX 16

Telephone: +33 1 44 05 60 00
Fax: +33 1 44 05 60 60
E-mail: paris@slaughterandmay.com
Website: www.slaughterandmay.com

Other offices
London, Brussels, Singapore, Hong Kong, New York

Number of lawyers 569
at this office 42

CATEGORIES OF WORK

General corporate and commercial
Antoine-Audoin Maggiar, Brigitte Leclerc

Mergers and acquisitions
Antoine-Audoin Maggiar, Brigitte Leclerc

Banking
Peter Deckers, Andrew McClean

Capital markets
Peter Deckers, Andrew McClean

Project finance
Peter Deckers, Alexander Blackburn

Tax
Pierre-Pascal Bruneau, Yves-Charles Zimmerman

Regulatory and administrative law
Antoine-Audoin Maggiar, Brigitte Leclerc

Intellectual property/Information technology
Brigitte Leclerc

Commercial property
Antoine-Audoin Maggiar

Litigation and arbitration
Antoine-Audoin Maggiar, Edouard Bertrand

Labour
Antoine-Audoin Maggiar, Eric Grangeon

Competition
Alexander Blackburn, Brigitte Leclerc

THE FIRM

Slaughter and May, a leading international law firm with a worldwide corporate, commercial and financing practice, established its office in Paris in 1974. Slaughter and May in Paris practises both French and English law. All of its lawyers, including the nine partners, are bilingual in French and English and most of the English lawyers are also qualified to practise French law.

Slaughter and May aims to provide a professional service of the highest calibre, combining technical excellence with commercial awareness and a practical, constructive approach. This is reinforced by its hands-on approach and the flexibility of its working method which enables it to provide the highest quality of advice and service across the world. Through the firm's other offices and close working relationships with lawyers from leading independent law firms around the world, Slaughter and May is able to provide its clients with a fully integrated and seamless international service of the highest quality.

The office's bicultural identity, developed through its French and English lawyers' working closely together, is of great value to the firm's international practice.

AREAS OF PRACTICE

Slaughter and May advises clients on the French and English legal and tax aspects of an extensive range of commercial, financial and banking transactions. The core practice areas are mergers and acquisitions (mostly international), financing (including complex asset finance and project finance) and corporate tax. The firm also has significant expertise in competition, intellectual property, labour law, litigation/arbitration and public law matters. Rather than develop single specialisms, lawyers in the core practice areas are encouraged to adopt a multi-disciplinary approach and the firm is well known for its innovative work. The approach is reflected by the firm not being divided into departments/specialist groups (save the tax department) but one team of 42 lawyers.

SONIER ET ASSOCIÉS

69 AVENUE VICTOR HUGO
75116 PARIS

Telephone: +33 1 45 02 17 17
Fax: +33 1 45 01 26 65
E-mail:
sonier-associes@sonier-associes.avocat.fr

Languages
English, German, Spanish

Number of lawyers 7

Member
INSOL International; INSOL Europe; Association des Praticiens des Procedures Collectives; Association Nationale des Juristes de Banque

CATEGORIES OF WORK

Insolvency and bankruptcy

Commercial law

Banking and finance

Construction and real estate

Company law

International business law

Distribution and competition

Criminal business law

Litigation

TAYLOR WESSING

42 AVENUE MONTAIGNE
75008 PARIS

Telephone: +33 1 72 74 03 33
Fax: +33 1 72 74 03 34
E-mail: paris@taylorwessing.com
Website: www.taylorwessing.com

Languages
English, French, German

Other offices
Alicante, Berlin, Brussels, Cambridge, Dubai*, Düsseldorf, Frankfurt, Hamburg, Munich, Shanghai

Number of lawyers 550
at this office 50

Member
Interlex

CATEGORIES OF WORK

Banking, finance
Arnaud de Senilhes,
Christophe Flaicher (tax)

Corporate – tax law
Arnaud de Senilhes, Claire Deleris

Public law
Olivier de Chazeaux

EU law, competition and regulatory
Olivier de Chazeaux

Mergers and acquisitions
Gilles Amsallem, Christophe Flaicher

Telecoms
Marc Shuler, Christophe Flaicher (tax)

Real estate
Olivier de Chazeaux

Media and entertainment
Christian Valsamidis, Frédéric Guy

Employment
Claudia Jonath

IP, IT, telecoms
Marc Schuler, Christophe Flaicher

TOUATI HENDERSON SELARL

15 RUE D'ASTORG
75008 PARIS

Telephone: +33 1 42 94 00 08
Fax: +33 1 42 94 08 84
E-mail: contact@touati-henderson.com
Website: www.touati-henderson.com

Languages
Danish, English, Portuguese, Spanish

Number of lawyers 6

Member
Franco-British Chamber of Commerce; EELA; ABA; IBA

CATEGORIES OF WORK

Employment and labour law	**Criminal law**
Employee benefits	**Social security law**

THE FIRM

The law firm was founded in 1998. Focusing on employment law, with an increasing emphasis on international practice and tailored services, the firm places its extensive litigation experience at the service of its advisory role. Jean-Jacques Touati was formerly a lecturer at the University of Law in Paris, and was a lawyer in labour law at several international law firms and is renowned for his articles and book on transfer of undertakings. He is the author of the two studies in dismissal for gross negligence and in serious cause, of the prestigious collection 'Juris-classeur Employment Law Encyclopedia', and also has an extensive practice in litigation. Ming Henderson-Vu Thi, partner, is a French-qualified lawyer of French and British background and has developed a practice of labour and employment law for global clients having their business in France.

AREAS OF PRACTICE

The team, accustomed to working for companies and international groups with a global view, provides advisory and litigation services in all areas of labour law, including restructuring and redundancy, employee representations, benefits and retirement, termination, social security and labour litigation, international mobility, executive packages.

UGGC & ASSOCIÉS

47 RUE DE MONCEAU
75008 PARIS

Telephone: +33 1 56 69 70 00
Fax: +33 1 56 69 70 71
E-mail: cabinet@uggcavocats.com
Website: www.uggcavocats.com

Languages
Arabic, Dutch, English, German, Italian, Portuguese, Spanish

Other offices
Brussels, Casablanca

Number of lawyers 90
at this office 80

CATEGORIES OF WORK

Corporate law, mergers and acquisitions
Jean-Jacques Uettwiller, Bernard Grelon

Tax law
Michel Turon, Jean-Jacques Uettwiller, Laurent Chambaz

Transport law
Michel Gout

Litigation and arbitration
Bernard Grelon, Michel Gout, Jean-François Canat

ADR/mediation
Jean-François Canat, Thierry Montéran

Real estate and urban planning
Bernard Lamorlette

Public law
Thierry Dal Farra, Bernard Lamorlette, Jean-Nicolas Clément

Environment
Jean-Nicolas Clément

Bankruptcy/insolvency
Thierry Montéran, Bernard Grelon

Labour law
Roseline Sauser, Pascal Bathmanabane, Sophie Uettwiller

EU competition law and intellectual property law
Elisabeth Logeais, Corinne Khayat, Michel Ponsard

Art law
Jean-François Canat

Trust law
Laurent Chambaz

VATIER & ASSOCIÉS

12 RUE D'ASTORG
75008 PARIS

Telephone: +33 1 53 43 15 55
Fax: +33 1 53 43 15 78
E-mail: acr@vatier-associes.com

Languages
English

Number of lawyers 31

CATEGORIES OF WORK

Arbitration
Bernard Vatier

Litigation (general commercial, enforcement and criminal)
Daniel Paquet, Bernard Vatier

Commercial (distribution – including direct sales, competition, commercial agreements)
Arnaud Moquin, Ann V Creelman

Corporate (including all aspects of company law, joint ventures, M&A, corporate restructuring)
Ann V Creelman, Bernard Vatier

Bankruptcy
Bernard Vatier, Olivier Saumon

Property (construction, promotion, financing, urban development and zoning)
Agnès Hunault, Daniel Paquet

Employment
Marie-Sylvie Vatier, Arnaud Moquin

Public service contracts
Yves-René Guillou

Health (malpractice for public and private institutions, distribution of regulated products and services)
Olivier Saumon, Martine Caillaud

Administrative law
Martine Caillaud, Yves-René Guillou

Intellectual property
Oliver Saumon

International
Ann V Creelman, Bernard Vatier

ADVOKATFIRMAN VINGE

21 RUE JEAN GOUJON
75008 PARIS

Telephone: +33 1 53 53 42 30
Fax: +33 1 53 53 42 31
Website: www.vinge.se

Languages
English, Swedish, German, Spanish

Other Offices
Brussels, Gothenburg, Helsingborg, Hong Kong, London, Malmö, Shanghai, Stockholm

Number of lawyers 262
at this office 4

Contact
Anders B Åberg

Member
Scandinavian Law Alliance with Kromann Reumert (Denmark) and Thommessen (Norway); Lex Mundi

CATEGORIES OF WORK	
Corporate finance	Telecoms
Mergers and acquisitions	Litigation
Corporate	Environmental
Capital markets	Real estate
EU and antitrust	Tax
Intellectual property	Insolvency and restructuring
IT	Insurance
Media	Employment
Marketing	Transport

THE FIRM

Established through a merger between leading Swedish firms in 1983, Vinge is today one of the largest firms in Scandinavia, with some 262 lawyers in nine Swedish and overseas offices. In 1991, the firm set up the Scandinavian Law Alliance together with the Danish law firm Kromann Reumert and the Norwegian firm Thommessen. Vinge is also a member of Lex Mundi.

AREAS OF PRACTICE

Vinge has a substantial international practice, with a strategic focus on M&A and corporate finance. The firm has acted in most of the major mergers and acquisitions in Sweden in recent years, and has consistently achieved top positions on *Merger Market*'s list of M&A advisers in the Nordic market. The firm regularly represents clients in connection with large international financing transactions, including project financing and structured finance arrangements. Vinge's competition law team is one of the most distinguished and experienced in the Nordic markets. A full-service firm, Vinge also advises domestic and international clients within a number of specialist areas such as employment, intellectual property, IT, media marketing, property, telecom, litigation and arbitration, insolvency, insurance, tax, and transport. In addition to four offices in Sweden, the firm has a presence in London, Paris, Brussels, Hong Kong and Shanghai.

VOGEL & VOGEL

30 AVENUE D'IÉNA
75116 PARIS

Telephone: +33 1 53 67 76 20
Fax: +33 1 53 67 76 25
E-mail: info@vogel-vogel.com
Website: www.vogel-vogel.com

Languages
English, German, Spanish

Other offices
Brussels, Frankfurt

Number of lawyers 36

Contact
Joseph Vogel

CATEGORIES OF WORK

European competition law
Louis Vogel, Joseph Vogel

French competition law
Louis Vogel, Joseph Vogel

Merger control
Louis Vogel, Joseph Vogel

State aid
Louis Vogel, Joseph Vogel

Unfair competition law
Charles Fahrner, Xavier Henry

Media and telecoms
Louis Vogel, Joseph Vogel

Product liability, defence to consumer actions
Charles S Fahrner

Distribution law (franchising, agency, selective distribution, termination of dealerships)
Joseph Vogel, Xavier Henry

Advertising
Charles S Fahrner

Litigation/arbitration
Louis Vogel, Joseph Vogel

Relations between France and Germany
Louis Vogel, Charles S Fahrner

Relations between France and the USA
Louis Vogel, Joseph Vogel

Automobile distribution
Joseph Vogel, Xavier Henry

THE FIRM

Louis and Joseph Vogel founded the firm of Vogel & Vogel in 1990. Since its creation the firm has grown steadily and now employs 22 attorneys (two partners and 20 associates) and 14 consultant lawyers. Vogel & Vogel, in recognition of the growing international nature of business, has always placed great importance on being able to offer its clients an international service. Accordingly, the firm has established offices in Paris, Frankfurt and Brussels. The firm has also established legal relations with other law firms around the world so as to ensure its clients a comprehensive service.

The success of Vogel & Vogel can be traced to its commitment to excellence and its promise to provide the highest quality service to its clients. Vogel & Vogel listens to its clients and seeks to become an effective tool in fulfilling their business objectives. The firm places great importance on developing longstanding relationships with its clients so as to allow the development of a true culture of understanding.

AREAS OF PRACTICE

The firm is particularly recognised for its expertise in the areas of EU and French competition law, distribution law matters, automobile law, product liability and generally all areas of international and French commercial law practice. The firm also specialises in the field of Franco-German and Franco-American legal relations. To this end both Louis and Joseph Vogel are qualified lawyers with the New York Bar.

When working with clients the firm seeks not only to advise them comprehensively as to the legal issues before them, but also endeavours to use the law as an instrument of their commercial policy. Consequently, the firm does not merely offer legal solutions, but rather seeks to apply the law in tandem with its client's business strategy. The firm is dedicated to offering a constructive, efficient and friendly service. Client contact is welcomed and partner participation is guaranteed.

VEIL JOURDE LA GARANDERIE

38 RUE DE LISBONNE
75008 PARIS

Telephone: +33 1 56 69 56 69
Fax: +33 1 53 53 94 94
E-mail: contact@veilpartners.com
Website: www.veilpartners.com

Languages
English, German, Spanish

Number of lawyers 36

CATEGORIES OF WORK

Mergers and acquisitions
Guillame Kuperfils, Patrick Jaïs

Stock exchange regulations (public transactions)
Jean Veil, Patrick Jaïs

Restructuring
Jean Veil, Guilhem Bremond

Tax
Ariel Harroch

Litigation and arbitration
Jean Veil, George Jourde

Public law
Pierre-Alain Jeanneney

Employment
Marie Alice Jourde,
Dominique de la Garanderie

Intellectual property
Nicolas Brault

WILLKIE FARR & GALLAGHER LLP

21-23 RUE DE LA VILLE L'EVÊQUE
75008 PARIS

Telephone: +33 1 53 43 45 00
Fax: +33 1 40 06 96 06
Website: www.willkie.com

Languages
English, French, German

Other offices
New York, Washington DC, London, Milan, Rome, Frankfurt, Brussels

Number of lawyers 560
at this office 65

Contact
Daniel Payan

CATEGORIES OF WORK

Telecoms, internet, media, and entertainment (TIME)
François Bloch

Mergers and acquisitions
Daniel Payan, Michel Frieh,
Laurent Faugérolas, Daniel Hurstel,
Annette Péron, Jeffrey Fouts

Securities and capital markets
Laurent Faugérolas, Daniel Hurstel,
Ines Le Gris

Business reorganisation and restructuring
Jean Dominique Daudier de Cassini,
Alexandra Bigot

Competition
Dominique Berlin

Tax
Allard de Waal, Bernard Le-Pezron,
Marie-Hélène Raffin, Philippe Grudé

Litigation
Dominique Mondoloni

WATSON, FARLEY & WILLIAMS

44 AVENUE DES CHAMPS-ELYSEES
75008 PARIS

Telephone: +33 1 56 88 21 21
Fax: +33 1 56 88 21 20
Website: www.wfw.com

Languages
Cantonese, Danish, English, German, Greek, Gujarati, Hebrew, Italian, Malay, Mandarin, Norwegian, Polish, Russian, Spanish, Swahili, Swedish, Thai

Other offices
Bangkok, London, New York, Piraeus, Rome, Singapore

Number of lawyers 175
at this office 10

CATEGORIES OF WORK

Banking and finance
Jean Thibaud

Corporate
Lucien Rapp

Cross-border leasing
Gilles Cervoni

Structured finance
Jean Thibaud, Gilles Cervoni

Project finance
Jean Thibaud

Shipping and ship finance
Nigel Moss, Andrew Wettern

Trade finance
Jean Thibaud

Tax
Gilles Cervoni

Public and administrative law
Lucien Rapp

Competition and antitrust
Lucien Rapp

THE FIRM

Watson, Farley & Williams, established in London in 1982, opened its Paris office in 1989.

The firm specialises in finance law, capital markets, corporate law and contract law. Its clientele comprises mainly of French and foreign banks, investment funds and major industrial groups, both French and international.

The firm has a reputation for excellence in shipping finance and is also involved in aircraft finance transactions. It specialises, in particular, in French and cross-border finance leasing and was the first law firm in France to implement American LILO and QTE and to adopt the new GIE tax regime. The firm is also involved in structured finance and derivatives as well as investment service regulation. In addition, the firm has been involved in complex debt programmes and corporate restructuring deals.

The firm acts for governments and companies, particularly power and telecoms utilities and banks involved in project finance and privatisations in French-speaking Africa. The firm's tax department deals with all the tax implications arising from the above transactions, both in France and internationally, and now benefits from a well-established reputation for providing tax advice in relation to structured finance transactions.

The Paris office also has a particular specialism in public and administrative law, competition and antitrust and EU law.

AREAS OF PRACTICE

A key feature is the firm's division into four international practice areas. These groups are not divided by location, but work together internationally for the firm's international clients.

International finance group: the firm's lawyers advise on general banking finance, structured finance, securities and capital markets, derivatives, trade finance, asset finance, project finance, cross-border tax leverage lending and leasing, and work outs and insolvencies. The firm's client base comes from a number of industry sectors heavily dependent on the financing of large capital assets.

International corporate group: clients receive a wide range of domestic and international expertise covering all aspects of international corporate law, including mergers and acquisitions, public offerings of securities, management buy-outs and buy-ins, business and asset sales, debt structuring, equity financings, corporate restructurings, privatisations, and a wide range of commercial agreements. The group also offers specialist advice on all aspects of European Union and competition law.

International litigation group: large-scale litigation, arbitration and dispute resolution matters are handled by the group on a worldwide basis. The firm represents clients in shipping; banking; international trade; aviation; marine pollution; marine insurance; enforcement of security over vessels; shipbuilding; charterparties; and offshore oil and gas contracting.

International tax group: the firm's lawyers advise on domestic and cross-border tax leasing, non-asset-based structured finance, tax planning, investigations and litigation, and indirect tax.

WEIL, GOTSHAL & MANGES

2 RUE DE LA BAUME
75008 PARIS

Telephone: +33 1 44 21 97 97
Fax: +33 1 42 89 57 90
Website: www.weil.com

Other offices
Austin, Boston, Brussels, Budapest, Dallas, Frankfurt, Houston, London, Miami, Munich, New York, Prague, Silicon Valley, Singapore, Warsaw, Washington DC

Number of lawyers 1,000
at this office 27

Contacts
Claude Serra, Joe Tortorici

CATEGORIES OF WORK

Mergers and acquisitions	Reorganisation and restructuring
Private equity	Competition
Taxation	Regulation
Corporate finance	Intellectual property
Litigation, arbitration and dispute resolution	

THE FIRM

Established in 1931 in New York, Weil, Gotshal & Manges combines lawyers worldwide to meet clients' needs in recognition of the benefits of broad industry and regional experience. The lawyers in the firm's practice groups work together to provide full-service legal advice to clients in sectors as diverse as energy, financial services and hi-tech.

The firm developed a network of offices across the US in the 1970s and 1980s to cater for its expanding client base, and was one of the first international law firms to establish a major presence in central Europe. The firm now has established offices in Brussels, Budapest, Frankfurt, London, Paris, Prague, Singapore and Warsaw.

The firm advises a broad and diverse group of clients, including many of the largest and most prominent corporations and government agencies around the globe, and leading financial institutions.

AREAS OF PRACTICE

The firm's US and European antitrust practice advises on international M&A regulatory notifications, antitrust distribution counselling, cartels, litigation and government and state competition policy. Expertise includes software and computer, healthcare, telecommunications and media, transportation, utilities, heavy industry, consumer goods, financial services and sports.

The corporate department is the firm's largest. The department advises international financial institutions and corporate clients in complex public and private M&As, private equity deals and strategic alliances.

The firm's corporate governance practice is recognised as one of the pre-eminent counsellors of corporate boards, management and institutional investors on the full range of governance issues, including board composition, structure and processes; executive and director compensation; director responsibilities; internal and governmental investigations of alleged accounting or other corporate misconduct; and shareholder initiatives. The firm has advised the World Bank, the OECD, the European Commission and various stock exchanges and regulatory bodies, and is a leader in providing director training programmes worldwide.

The firm advises on a wide range of financing activities and has particular expertise in acquisition finance, asset-based finance, debt restructuring and insolvency, debt and equity capital markets, derivatives, high-yield debt, securitisation, structured finance and telecoms and multimedia financing.

The firm has a leading IP and technology practice and advises some of the world's major technology, media and telecommunications companies. It also acts for investors in technology, media and communications entities. The practice handles patent infringements, outsourcing transactions, strategic alliances, cross-border mergers and acquisitions, investments and IPOs, and advises on the protection and exploitation of IP and on a wide range of e-commerce matters, including data protection. It has expertise in regulatory telecoms matters.

The litigation practice advises international clients on all major areas of the law and has extensive experience in all aspects of dispute resolution. It advises clients in jury trials and appeals, arbitration and alternative dispute forums.

The firm's real estate practice handles complex real estate transactions (including finance, securitisations, development, leasing, sales, acquisitions and debt restructurings) across the US and Europe. It also advises clients on real estate M&A transactions involving real estate investment trusts.

The firm has one of the largest bankruptcy and business reorganisation practices in the world. It includes attorneys in New York, Boston, Dallas, Frankfurt, Houston, London and Miami. The department has been involved in virtually all of the major chapter 11 reorganisation cases in the US and in major national and international out-of-court debt restructurings.

The tax department provides advice on international and domestic taxation, covering many different economic sectors. The department works with the firm's other departments to find innovative solutions to problems that present various and competing multi-disciplinary considerations.

GERMANY

Population	**82.5 million**
Number of lawyers	**More than 116,000**
Professional title	**Rechtsanwalt; Rechtsanwältin**
Currency	**Euro (€)**

Index

Germany is a federal state wedged between France, Benelux and Central and Eastern Europe. Its borders also stretch from the North and Baltic seas in the north to Austria in the south. Germany has 16 states each with its own parliament, judiciary and administration. In 2002 it adopted the euro (€).

The coalition of the Social Democratic Party (SPD) and the Greens (Bündnis90/Grüne), has been in power since 1998. The coalition won the general election in September 2002, although the SPD lost votes to the second major party, the conservative CDU/CSU.

Unlike states such as France and the UK, Germany's economy is less centralised. It has important trade and financial centres across the jurisdiction, though Frankfurt is considered the financial hub with many of the banks' headquarters located there as well as the Stock Exchange. Many foreign law firms established their first German offices in the city.

Berlin is now the administrative capital following the collapse of the Iron Curtain in 1990. Many companies have established headquarters in or near the city, but the region is far from prosperous in the economic sense.

Hamburg, in the north, is the country's second-largest city and is home to Europe's second-biggest port. The city is also a media centre, hosting a number of major publishing houses. Traditionally, family-owned businesses and trade companies are an important part of the regional economy. Several firms based there handle trade and shipping law issues.

The state of North Rhineland-Westphalia is a strong economic area. The majority of the largest German corporations are based here, along with the traditional coal, steel, machinery and chemical industries and the newer IT, biotechnology and genetic technology sectors. Cologne and Düsseldorf are widely considered to be important strategic cities for law firms to be located. Firms are also able to take advantage of the Federal Cartel Office being located in nearby Bonn and the Court of Appeal in Düsseldorf.

Stuttgart, and its surrounding Swabian area, is another economic hot spot. The area is dominated by some quarter of a million medium-sized (Mittelstand) companies, along with global giants such as DaimlerChrysler. South-west of Stuttgart is the Bavarian capital, Munich. The city, also known as 'Isar Valley', is home to about one-third of the biggest hi-tech companies in Germany, including Apple, Siemens and IBM, and the various private equity and venture capital outfits found in areas of hi-tech development.

BILLING

Charge-out rates for lawyers in Germany are generally significantly lower than in the UK and other core European jurisdictions. With the intense competition brought by the encroachment of UK and US firms, billing rates are under serious pressure and many clients have not surprisingly exploited the situation. Furthermore, with the economic slump and lack of notable instructions, many firms have felt it prudent to be more than aggressive on fees, so as to boost or create market share. According to clients, it is the English and Anglo-German firms who are the chief exponents. According to the German Lawyers' Fee Regulations (BRAGO), the fee charged by a lawyer should be based on 'dispute values', ie the value of the disputed case in question. These fees were supposed to be adjusted in 2002 but the proposed reform failed.

Hourly rates, generally unknown a few years ago, average between €250 and €300, but specialist lawyers often charge higher rates, which can easily exceed €350. Law firms in more rural areas or in the east of Germany often charge less than €150 per hour. Fixed rates, agreed on in advance, have gained popularity, due to the growing number of beauty parades.

MARKETING

Firms are more conservative in Germany than many other jurisdictions in western Europe. But with the revision of the official Code of Conduct for Lawyers (Berufsordnung) in 1997, more and more law firms are using marketing strategies to promote their services. Prior to this, marketing activities were strictly forbidden and only the publication of factual and objective information was permitted. Traditional advertising is still not allowed.

The mergers of German and Anglo-American law firms in 2000 ignited not only competition in the legal market, but also the marketing business. Now, almost every law firm has a brochure and an Internet site describing its services. Full-time marketing managers have become a regular institution in the major law firms, often working in teams of up to a dozen employees. Many of the smaller law firms continue to avoid any form of

The largest firms

1	Freshfields Bruckhaus Deringer	573
2	Clifford Chance	416
3	Linklaters Oppenhoff & Rädler	355
4	CMS Hasche Sigle	306
5	Lovells	226
6	Taylor Wessing	211
7	Luther Menold Rechtsanwaltsgesellschaft mbH	210
8	Beiten Burkhardt Rechtsanwaltsgesellschaft mbH	193
9	White & Case	191
10	Hengeler Mueller	189
11	Nörr Stiefenhofer Lutz	173
12	Heussen Rechtsanwaltsgesellschaft mbH	168
13	Gleiss Lutz	165
14	Baker & McKenzie	155
15	Haarmann Hemmelrath	140
16	Heuking Kühn Lüer Wojtek	138
17	Allen & Overy	122
18	Norton Rose Vieregge	115
	Shearman & Sterling LLP	115
20	Flick Gocke Schaumburg	107
21	Buse Heberer Fromm	105
22	Graf von Westphalen Bappert & Modest	104
23	Rödl & Partner GbR	101
24	ARCON Rechtsanwälte Schmidt-Sibeth Heisse Weisskopf Kursawe	92
25	Latham & Watkins LLP	85

These figures represent the total number of lawyers in this country only, and have been supplied by the firms themselves. The figures should be accurate as at 1 January 2004.

marketing. Still many firms are coy about revealing client names or the specific instructions that they have been involved in.

IN-HOUSE LAWYERS

In-house legal departments (Rechtsabteilungen) are a common feature in most German companies. BMW for instance has an immense in-house department and rarely looks to private practice for additional help. Nevertheless the advent of specialisation heightened by the presence of the Anglo-Saxon firms has increased the awareness of in-house lawyers that using private practice is prudent.

In-house lawyers deal with general civil law issues, with contracts and employment as well as internal company matters.

ECONOMIC CLIMATE

Germany has suffered one of the worst periods in its economic history over the last few years. Although the global economic slump explains much of it, Germany sustained a notably tougher period than its large economic contemporaries in western Europe. The country has suffered high unemployment and the rapidly ageing population is ranking high on the political agenda. The state pension system is seriously under pressure and the unemployment situation is not helping. The fall in government revenues and the significant rise in expenditures has brought the deficit close to the EU's 3% limit.

The abandonment of the Neuer Markt, the stock market for growth industries, was symptomatic of Germany's diving capital markets. The collapse of media giant Kirch Media highlighted the serious financial issues facing German companies. The government is trying to address the situation and has reduced corporate taxes. Tax and pension reforms are the key issues facing the current administration.

LEGAL MARKET

2003 proved to be a quiet year for Germany's legal market. Mergers between firms were not at a premium, but some elected to launch new offices.

Most notable was **Cleary Gottlieb Steen & Hamilton**'s decision to open a new office in Cologne by hiring leading antitrust specialist Dirk Schroeder and his protégé Romina Polley from **Linklaters Oppenhoff & Rädler** in November 2003. The firm followed it up with the hire of M&A specialist Klaus Riehmer from **Haarmann Hemmelrath** in December. **Cleary Gottlieb Steen & Hamilton** rarely makes lateral hires, particularly in Germany, and the latest high-profile recruits outline the firm's aggressive intention to gain market share in the jurisdiction.

UK firms **Bird & Bird** and **Simmons & Simmons** also elected to branch out of their Düsseldorf HQs and launched new offices in Munich and Frankfurt respectively. For **Bird & Bird**, the new office augments the firm's sectoral focus on media and technology companies. **Simmons & Simmons** is now able to service its impressive investment banking client base from Germany's financial centre. To assist this, **Simmons & Simmons** also recruited **Luther Menold Rechtsanwaltsgesellschaft mbH**'s head of banking and finance, Ingrid Kalisch. The firm also hired **Clifford Chance**'s media and corporate star, Donald Hess in 2003.

Luther Menold Rechtsanwaltsgesellschaft mbH's poor luck was made worse by losing one of its young M&A stars, Hans-Jürgen Lütt to **Latham & Watkins LLP**. Property partner Martin Meissner also switched allegiance to the US firm. **GÖRG Rechtsanwälte** also acquired **Luther Menold Rechtsanwaltsgesellschaft mbH** partners Klaus von Gierke, Volker Alvensleben and Frank Weberndorfer to launch its new Hamburg office.

True to its acquisitive nature, **White & Case** brought in further new names. The experienced project finance specialist Stephen Hodgson joined from **Baker & McKenzie**, and private equity lawyer Axel Pajunk transferred from **SJ Berwin Knopf Tulloch Steininger**.

Osborne Clarke's four partner Frankfurt practice elected to defect to **Taylor Wessing**, adding to the Anglo-German firm's corporate credibility in particular and bringing some welcome good news to the firm after several years of high-profile departures.

Dechert also launched a credible private equity practice by taking over **Coudert Brothers LLP**'s Munich office.

ANTITRUST

With one of the leading antitrust practices across Europe and most notably in Brussels, **Freshfields Bruckhaus Deringer** augments this with an outstanding team in Germany. Martin Klusmann leads the German team, which handles the full range of issues including merger control, state aid and public procurement, but most notably the German team has played a pivotal role in a number of cartel investigations. Gerhard Wiedemann, Cornelius Canenbly and Jochim Sedemund receive a plethora of plaudits.

Gleiss Lutz benefits from its association to strong antitrust firms **Herbert Smith** and **Stibbe**. But with Rainer Bechtold in Stuttgart, the firm boasts one of the leading practitioners in Germany. **Gleiss Lutz** has its own office in Brussels and has an impressive track record advising blue-chip multinationals and important domestic corporates.

Hengeler Mueller operates an integrated team with **Slaughter and May**, which boasts a leading practice in London and both firms have strong teams in Brussels. With such resources, **Hengeler Mueller** is able to offer a more than credible service to its flourishing domestic and

ANTITRUST

FRESHFIELDS BRUCKHAUS DERINGER ✪
GLEISS LUTZ ✪

HENGELER MUELLER ✪

CMS Hasche Sigle ✪
Cleary Gottlieb Steen & Hamilton ✪
Linklaters Oppenhoff & Rädler ✪
Shearman & Sterling LLP
Wilmer Cutler Pickering LLP ✪

Baker & McKenzie ✪
Clifford Chance
Lovells ✪

Allen & Overy ✪
Graf von Westphalen Bappert & Modest ✪
Haver & Mailänder
Heuking Kühn Lüer Wojtek ✪
Latham & Watkins LLP ✪
Nörr Stiefenhofer Lutz ✪
Schulte Rechtsanwälte
Taylor Wessing ✪
White & Case

Firms are listed A-Z in tiers which are ranked in order of priority
✪ Indicates firm displays contact details at the end of this chapter.

international client base. Jochen Burrichter is highly recommended and recently represented Allianz AG in proceedings before the German Federal Cartel Office against industrial insurers.

CMS Hasche Sigle is considered a strong outfit in merger control proceedings before the German Federal Cartel Office and the European Commission. The firm has solid expertise in most of its German offices as well as in Brussels. Partner Harald Kahlenberg is a key player.

Cleary Gottlieb Steen & Hamilton's hire of Dirk Schroeder and Romina Polley from **Linklaters Oppenhoff & Rädler** in November 2003 enabled it to claim the title of one of Europe's leading antitrust practices. Schroeder was instrumental in building a respected practice at **Linklaters Oppenhoff & Rädler** and with the two working from **Cleary Gottlieb Steen & Hamilton**'s new office in Cologne, the firm is within close proximity of the Court of Appeal in Düsseldorf and the Federal Cartel Office in Bonn.

Linklaters Oppenhoff & Rädler's lost one of the most established names and a rising stars in the German market in Dirk Schroeder and Romina Polley respectively. Both joined **Cleary Gottlieb Steen & Hamilton** in November 2003 and left a gap in **Linklaters Oppenhoff & Rädler**'s antitrust credibility. Daniela Seeliger is left to fly the flag in Cologne and link up with the immensely experienced Wolfgang Deselaers in Brussels.

Shearman & Sterling LLP is recommended for merger control cases, where it has immense experience. With its presence in Düsseldorf it boasts proximity to the Court of Appeal and the Federal Cartel Office in Bonn. Hans-Joachim Hellmann is highly recommended.

Wilmer Cutler Pickering LLP has credible expertise and experience in German and European antitrust work. Its standing was demonstrated by it representing Deutsche Telekom in an investigation by the European Commission concerning the operator's wholesale and retail charges for access to the local loop. The litigation eventually came before the European Court of First Instance. Ulrich Quack deserves high praise for creating a formidable practice.

Baker & McKenzie is another firm which benefits from its broad European resources, including an excellent team in Brussels. Thomas Lampert and Jörg-Martin Schultze receive consistent praise.

Merger control and state aid are notable strengths of **Clifford Chance**'s group. It too has a superb department in Brussels and Joachim Schütze heads the German group from Düsseldorf. Holger Wissel and Martin Wissmann are also commended.

As with **Lovells**' progress in the corporate and transactional market, so has its antitrust team come to the fore. Thomas Jestaedt provides the bridge with the Brussels office where he spends most of his time. The experienced Walter Klosterfelde in Hamburg and Düsseldorf's Martin Sura provide strength on the ground.

With Ellen Braun's election to the partnership in May 2003, **Allen & Overy**'s nascent practice now has credibility. The seasoned Wolfgang Witz also has considerable competition expertise. The team recently advised DS Smith on antitrust risks and the re-issue of its compliance programme.

Graf von Westphalen Bappert & Modest boasts a Brussels practice, working alongside the firm's UK 'best friend' **Wragge & Co**. The solid team in Germany, particularly in Hamburg, boasts chief protagonists Carsten Bittner and Lothar Harings. The seasoned Jürgen Gündisch continues to be a major name in the market, but his fee-earning time is gradually decreasing.

Stuttgart-based **Haver & Mailänder** is a firm with particular strength in media and telecoms-related antitrust work. A number of experienced partners, including Peter Mailänder are widely commended and have the added resource of a Brussels office.

Latham & Watkins LLP now offers a credible German antitrust team across its Frankfurt, Hamburg and Brussels offices. Brussels and Frankfurt partner Andreas Weitbrecht successfully represented Tetra Laval in an antitrust matter brought before the Court of First Instance to object to a Commission ban on the merger between Tetra and Sidel. Hamburg partner Marco Núñez Müller is also recommended.

Nörr Stiefenhofer Lutz is recommended for media and technology antitrust work, while **Schulte Rechtsanwälte** has built up an impressive record acting for banks in EU and competition matters.

Taylor Wessing hired Markus Wirtz as a partner from **Hengeler Mueller** in 2003, adding further strength to the firm's antitrust practice, historically known for its IP focus in this sector.

White & Case's antitrust practice has evolved into a position of strength, benefiting from its highly acclaimed presence in Brussels. Antje Mattfeld and Jörg Schmeding are solid practitioners.

BANKING AND FINANCE

Allen & Overy's banking and finance practice deserves its rapid ascendance up the rankings, thanks in no small part to the rocketing reputation of Neil Weiand. After the success of Weiand, the firm continued to hire experienced in-house counsel from the major banks and convert them into leading private practice lawyers; Peter Hoegen and Peter Stenz are other prime examples. Clients acknowledge the team's strength on syndicated loans and project finance. 'They make you understand that they know what they are doing. We feel comfortable with them,' one said. The team also boasts a large market share in acquisition finance. It has not rested on the firm's eminent banking name and has won mandates from some of Germany's more blue-chip corporates including E.on, Bertelsmann and Continental AG. Wolfgang Melzer is now the group's key asset finance specialist, since Peter Hein transferred to New York.

Clifford Chance has the broadest banking and finance expertise in the German market. 'The finance team is pretty strong and we use them on acquisition and leveraged finance,' one client said. Despite a string of departures and senior members such as Caroline Jury returning to London over the last few years, Riko Vanezis still heads a an excellent group. The firm has invested heavily into the still nascent project finance market with Nicholas Wong transferring from Washington DC in 2001 and Rodney Short splitting his time between London and Frankfurt. The firm took roles in the only two PPP deals so far, and represented the German government on the motorway-widening scheme. Hypovereinsbank, KFW and HSH Nordbank are key clients. The firm's asset finance practice continues to impress, particularly in the aircraft and real estate areas.

Linklaters Oppenhoff & Rädler's Carl-Peter Feick and Eva Reudelhuber are making significant progress on the acquisition finance front. HVB, JPMorganChase, Citibank and Barclays Capital are key clients. The firm acted for Barclays Capital as arranger of the €1.7bn senior and mezzanine facilities to finance the LBO of the Bertelsmann Springer business by Cinven and Candover through its earlier acquired Kluwer Academic Publishing business. Clients highlight the firm's strength on the syndicated loans and bonds side, particularly in EMTN programmes. 'The communication is good and the cost quotations are favourable,' one said. US and German qualified

BANKING AND FINANCE

ALLEN & OVERY ✪
CLIFFORD CHANCE
LINKLATERS OPPENHOFF & RÄDLER ✪

FRESHFIELDS BRUCKHAUS DERINGER ✪
HENGELER MUELLER ✪

BAKER & McKENZIE ✪
WHITE & CASE

Ashurst ✪
CMS Hasche Sigle ✪
Cleary Gottlieb Steen & Hamilton ✪
Debevoise & Plimpton LLP ✪
Gleiss Lutz ✪
Latham & Watkins LLP ✪
Lovells ✪
Mayer, Brown, Rowe & Maw LLP ✪
Norton Rose Vieregge

Coudert Brothers LLP ✪
Davis Polk & Wardwell
Haarmann Hemmelrath ✪
Luther Menold Rechtsanwaltsgesellschaft mbH ✪
Nörr Stiefenhofer Lutz ✪
Simmons & Simmons ✪
Weil, Gotshal & Manges LLP ✪

Bette – Brink ✪
Dewey Ballantine LLP ✪
Esche Schümann Commichau
GSK Gassner Stockmann & Kollegen ✪
Graf von Westphalen Bappert & Modest ✪
Heimann
Taylor Wessing ✪

Firms are listed A-Z in tiers which are ranked in order of priority
✪ *Indicates firm displays contact details at the end of this chapter.*

Christopher Arend adds trade finance and ECA facilities acumen into the mix. Berthold Kusserow leads the team and adds considerable strength, particularly on structured products.

Freshfields Bruckhaus Deringer is better known for its advice to corporates, but its investment banking connections are steadily improving. Syndicated loan work has increased substantially under the leadership of new practice head Dirk Schmalenbach. Andreas König has returned to full-time client work. Clients appreciate the firm's ability in German law, but acknowledge that some of its finest banking and finance practitioners have now retired. One of few firms to seriously target the project finance sector, Ulrike Daniel Reichert-Facilides now takes overall responsibility for the area. It has an established market position in asset finance and regulatory issues.

Like **Freshfields Bruckhaus Deringer**, **Hengeler Mueller** is traditionally a corporate adviser. Nevertheless the firm's excellent reputation has extended to investment banks, thanks largely to its impressive track record in structured finance. Clients acknowledge its pre-eminent position in ABS and synthetic transactions, thanks to Stefan Krauss. Thomas Cron is recommended for syndicated lending and regularly acts for Deutsche Bank, while Hendrig Haag is one of the most seasoned names in German banking and finance.

In Rainer Magold **Baker & McKenzie** boasts one of Germany's most experienced and respected acquisition finance specialists. The firm was one of the first to target the sector before the UK firms arrived en masse. Munich partner Michael Foundethakis is also recommended. Clients highlight the firm's acquisition and project finance expertise, but have noted the loss of project finance specialist Stephen Hodgson to **White & Case** in November 2003.

White & Case's recruitment of Stephen Hodgson from **Baker & McKenzie** brings gravitas to its project finance practice which until now was driven by the Düsseldorf office. The firm's excellent reputation in acquisition finance is much to the credit of Annica Lindegren. A well-known figure in the market, clients have expressed their willingness to transfer their business after her move from **Clifford Chance** in 2001. Julia Müller is another acquisition finance specialist, while Eberhard Meincke and Sebastian Kühl spearhead the respected asset finance team.

Ashurst's loss of Hans-Günther Nordhues to **Nörr Stiefenhofer Lutz** in May 2003 leaves the firm without one of Germany's most experienced and respected names in banking and finance. Under current head of finance, Andreas Zahn the firm has shifted its focus almost entirely onto structured and acquisition finance, particularly structured notes and asset-backed CDOs. The team recently advised Deutsche Bank on credit-linked notes and Morgan Stanley and ING on a tranche of CDOs. Stephan Kock leads the acquisition finance side of the practice.

CMS Hasche Sigle's Frankfurt office has considerable strength in mainstream banking and finance, but its Hamburg branch adds weight in ship and aircraft finance. It is also one of few firms to deliver a credible asset finance practice. The Stuttgart office completes the matrix with its record in acquisition finance and MBOs. Christoph Schücking has a fabulous reputation.

In line with its global standing, **Cleary Gottlieb Steen & Hamilton**'s Frankfurt office has an excellent regulatory practice for which Christof von Dryander receives numerous accolades. The firm took important roles in the restructuring of Bank Austria through its relationship with Hypovereinsbank. Other key clients include Morgan Stanley and Citigroup.

Debevoise & Plimpton LLP is noted for its debt work and corporate bond expertise. The firm's excellent know-how in investment management tallies with its superb global private equity practice.

Gleiss Lutz's Frankfurt finance team is led by Burkhard Jäkel and is making progress in acquisition finance and syndicated lending. With asset finance strength the team advised Angel Trains on the leasing of rolling stock as well as a significant aircraft finance transaction. Olaf Otting is strong on the regulatory side.

Latham & Watkins LLP continues to make progress after the arrival of Uwe Eyles from **Gleiss Lutz** in September 2002. Eyles is a recognised banking regulatory name and, with Philipp von Randow on the more structured side, the firm has the beginnings of a strong practice. Frankfurt managing partner John Watson does little fee-earning these days but has a background in leveraged finance and high-yield debt work.

Lovells is an acknowledged leader in media financing. Thomas Lindemann has garnered an excellent reputation.

Former **Clifford Chance** partner Manfred Heeman is making excellent progress at **Mayer, Brown, Rowe & Maw LLP**. Clients pick out his technical and commercial prowess in syndicated loans, and he has also impressed banks on the other side of transactions.

Norton Rose Vieregge has made remarkable progress since the launch of the practice in 2001. The firm has duplicated its reputable global asset finance practice in Germany with Ralf Springer to the fore on largely aircraft finance. Dirk Trautmann is an able support. Former investment funds specialist Frank Herring now concentrates on banking regulation. New partner Tom Beckerhoff and the seasoned Herbert Wiehe have made excellent headway in acquisition finance for clients such as Credit Lyonnais and RBS.

Coudert Brothers LLP, **Davis Polk & Wardwell** and **Haarmann Hemmelrath** all have capable banking and finance practice. **Luther Menold Rechtsanwaltsgesellschaft mbH** has a similar standing, but lost practice head Ingrid Kalisch to **Simmons & Simmons** in 2003.

Nörr Stiefenhofer Lutz launched a viable banking and finance practice in May 2003 by hiring the highly respected Hans-Günther Nordhues from **Ashurst**. The firm boasts six other fee-earners in the group.

Frankfurt and Düsseldorf-based **Simmons & Simmons** recruited head of banking and finance at **Luther Menold Rechtsanwaltsgesellschaft mbH**, Ingrid Kalisch, in October 2003. She links up with structured finance specialist Stephen Moller. Kalisch acted for the successful bidder for the Austrian Toll Road project and intends to focus on the development of PPP/PFI in Germany. The firm acts for Deutsche Bank in London and is beginning to make inroads in Germany. Mark Norris returned to London from Düsseldorf.

Weil, Gotshal & Manges LLP is extremely strong in the non-performing loan market. It acted for US investment firm Lone Star on its acquisition of a loan portfolio made up of largely non-performing loans, from Gontard & Metallbank AG.

Klaus Bette at **Bette – Brink** launched the firm in 1962 with a strong focus on banking and finance. The firm retains a solid profile in the market.

BANKING AND FINANCE: PROJECT FINANCE

ALLEN & OVERY ✪
CLIFFORD CHANCE

Freshfields Bruckhaus Deringer ✪

Baker & McKenzie ✪
Hengeler Mueller ✪
Lovells ✪

Gleiss Lutz ✪
Göhmann Wrede Haas Kappus & Hartmann
Heuking Kühn Lüer Wojtek ✪
Shearman & Sterling LLP
Simmons & Simmons ✪
Taylor Wessing ✪
Weil, Gotshal & Manges LLP ✪

Firms are listed A-Z in tiers which are ranked in order of priority
✪ Indicates firm displays contact details at the end of this chapter.

2003 proved to be a mixed year for **Dewey Ballantine LLP**. Having recruited Philipp von Ilberg from **Clifford Chance** in September 2003, the firm subsequently suffered the departure of practice head Geza Toth-Feher.

Esche Schümann Commichau has a number of domestic banks on its client portfolio.

GSK Gassner Stockmann & Kollegen's Markus Escher is a recommended banking regulation and asset finance expert. In the last two years the firm has advised on new licences for eight banks looking to create new services. HSH Nordbank is a major client. Frankfurt partner Andreas May is praised for real estate finance work, but Munich is the firm's strongest office for banking.

Graf von Westphalen Bappert & Modest's Michael Nicolaus and Frank Büchler are recognised banking specialists. Christian Wolf's work with a number of banks in relation to the Flowtex scandal is also noteworthy.

Hamburg-based **Heimann** has a strong profile in investment funds. Carl Graf Hardenberg is widely acknowledged as one the jurisdiction's leading lawyers in this area.

Taylor Wessing recruited Claus Goedecke from **Haarmann Hemmelrath** in September 2003 to add further credibility to the practice. Peter Seeman is developing the firm's market share in acquisition finance, security packages and financial restructurings.

CAPITAL MARKETS

FRESHFIELDS BRUCKHAUS DERINGER ✪
HENGELER MUELLER ✪

Allen & Overy ✪
Cleary Gottlieb Steen & Hamilton ✪
Clifford Chance
Linklaters Oppenhoff & Rädler ✪
Shearman & Sterling LLP

Baker & McKenzie ✪
CMS Hasche Sigle ✪
Gleiss Lutz ✪
Lovells ✪

Davis Polk & Wardwell
Haarmann Hemmelrath ✪
Mayer, Brown, Rowe & Maw LLP ✪
Norton Rose Vieregge
Sullivan & Cromwell LLP
White & Case

Firms are listed A-Z in tiers which are ranked in order of priority
✪ Indicates firm displays contact details at the end of this chapter.

CAPITAL MARKETS

Freshfields Bruckhaus Deringer's Andreas Fabritius heads the equity side of the practice which is considered by clients to be the most experienced in Germany. 'They're a notch better than most firms,' one said. Under US-qualified partner Mark Strauch the firm has a thriving high-yield bonds business. Munich-based partner Hans-Jörg Ziegenhain has also won respect from clients following leading roles in a string of high-profile transactions. Dirk Schmalenbach heads the debt group, but the firm's resources are more limited on this side of the practice.

Hengeler Mueller has a high-quality team and not surprisingly has enviable connections to German corporates. Hendrik Haag, Hannes Schneider and Torsten Busch deserve special mention in this respect. Younger partner Wolfgang Groß has also impressed clients. 'He can answer any question immediately and his draft documents have no mistakes,' one remarked.

With its eminent connections to the world's leading investment banks, **Allen & Overy** has built up a capital markets track record in Germany with some ease. Despite the quiet market conditions, the firm was mandated to advise Münchener Rückversicherung on its immense €3.8bn rights issue.

Cleary Gottlieb Steen & Hamilton has established connections with financial institutions such as Deutsche Bank, Commerzbank and Hypovereinsbank. The firm is well plugged into the key intermediaries in the German capital markets sector. Through Hypovereinsbank, the firm won a pivotal mandate on Bank Austria Creditanstalt AG's €1bn IPO in July 2003, involving a listing on the Vienna Stock Exchange and Rule 144A placement in the US. With three German and three US partners in the Frankfurt team, the firm claims the largest US/German combined practice in the jurisdiction. The firm has an even split between debt and equity issuances.

Clifford Chance boasts a similar profile, but surprisingly has yet to exploit its exemplary investment banking contacts and gain a leading market share in capital markets work. It is has a stronger brand for securitisation transactions. Nevertheless Markus Pfüller is a solid equity issuance specialist.

Linklaters Oppenhoff & Rädler is acknowledged by clients as a leader in bonds and of late in MTN and EMTN programmes. Berthold Kusserow is the firm's big name in this sector and is commended by clients for his debt expertise. Clients commend the firm's organisation and management of transactions.

Shearman & Sterling LLP deserves its promotion up the ranks this year due to its growing profile even in a quiet market. Clients acknowledge the partners' cerebral capacity, clear advice and transaction management, but point out that it is lacking in US capital markets expertise in Germany. Nevertheless, Stephan Hutter is US qualified and the firm is gaining a number of cross-departmental instructions with its rapidly improving finance practice. The firm retains a multitude of German industrial clients as well as investment banks, and has recently handled numerous privatisations in Austria.

Equity focused **Baker & McKenzie** is active in secondary offerings, with Düsseldorf partner Peter Veranneman and Manuel Lorenz in Frankfurt to the fore. Clients applaud Veranneman's experience, accessibility and attentive approach. The group forms part of the firm's corporate practice.

CMS Hasche Sigle is acknowledged as a solid issuers' counsel.

Gleiss Lutz's Hoimar von Ditfurth is the firm's most notable equity issuance specialist. In September 2003 the firm was appointed to the transactional panel of RBS. On the debt side the firm acts for both banks and borrowers.

Lovells is better known for more structured products, but did recently advise a leading investment bank on a dual listing in the US and Germany. Oliver Kessler has broad expertise in this sector.

Davis Polk & Wardwell advised a consortium of banks on the Bank Austria Creditanstalt AG €1bn IPO in July 2003. Patrick Kenadjian deserves much of the credit for the firm's excellent reputation.

Haarmann Hemmelrath's Mirko Sickinger and Andreas Lehmann are regular capital markets advisers. The firm has also completed a number of privatisations, many of which are generated by its excellent Berlin office. **Mayer, Brown, Rowe & Maw LLP** has a similar standing.

Norton Rose Vieregge's Rüdiger Litten has shored up connections with the leading investment banks on the debt side, while the equity team is gaining market share, most notably a considerable amount of Central and Eastern European listing work.

Sullivan & Cromwell LLP's global reputation and connections to leading investment banks has enabled it to gain considerable market share in Germany. The firm recently provided US counsel to Allianz AG on its €4.4bn capital increase consisting of a public rights offering in Germany and private placements in the US and other jurisdictions. The team is made of both US and German qualified lawyers.

White & Case advised on two of the first ten IPOs on the Neuer Markt and, with a strong ECM focus and additional resources on the securitisation and derivatives side, the firm is well placed to exploit capital markets activity when it returns. Markus Hauptmann is recommended.

CORPORATE AND COMMERCIAL

Andreas Fabritius now heads the corporate practice at **Freshfields Bruckhaus Deringer**, with Axel Epe stepping down after three years' service and returning to full-time client work. Clients acknowledge the firm's broad corporate expertise. 'It has the best and most experienced people on board,' said one. The team took its fair share of corporate restructurings and squeeze-outs in the last year. With a range of corporate clients and Mittelstand entities it has no shortage of instructions. Of the Anglo-German firms **Freshfields Bruckhaus Deringer** clearly has the broadest corporate business and superior resources.

Hengeler Mueller is the aristocrat of the German legal market. It has historical links to German industry and blue-chip corporates and boasts enviable connections to top-tier firms across Europe and in New York. It has gained a respectable international standing and clients acknowledge the high standards of academia amongst the partners. Bayer AG instructed the firm on the realignment of its corporate structure, corporate overhaul and de-merger of Bayer Vital. Andreas Austmann led the team.

With more than 400 lawyers in Germany, **Clifford Chance**'s international connections to investment banks is a major benefit to gaining valuable mandates. Nevertheless, its corporate relationships are blossoming and it now acts for 26 DAX companies in Germany. Under the auspices of corporate head Andreas Dietzel, the team has developed its industrial client base and won instructions from multinational heavyweights such as Coca-Cola.

Gleiss Lutz has strong ties to insurance companies, including Munich Re and the automotive industry. As one of Germany's leading independent firms (though it is allied to UK Magic Circle firm **Herbert Smith**) it gains a considerable amount of work on referral and this has added much to its impressive track record and experience in the most sought-after mandates. Clients acknowledge its leading strength in merger control, competition, cartel and tax issues.

Linklaters Oppenhoff & Rädler has gained a raft of accolades from clients for its all-round corporate expertise and 'hands on' approach. It is a tightly administered firm and many clients, particularly the investment banks, admire the firm's pragmatic and commercially focused advice as well as the way transactions are managed. Cologne partner Hans-Ulrich Wilsing is commended for his work in complex restructurings and advice to boardrooms of listed companies.

Shearman & Sterling LLP is the real success story of the last decade, particularly in transactions. But with the experience and credibility of its senior partners the firm is gaining further recognition in general corporate and commercial. Clients such as DaimlerChrysler and Deutsche Bank AG outline the firm's popularity amongst the blue-chip client sector.

Allen & Overy's rise in corporate profile was exemplified by its advice to Wella on its €5.5bn takeover by Procter & Gamble. The wide skills-set of the partners allows the team to advise on issues ranging from outsourcing to stock option plans and with clients such as Deutsche Telekom, SAP and Bilfinger Berger, **Allen & Overy** is rapidly becoming a first-choice corporate adviser to many blue-chip corporates operating in Germany. It also attracted new client Munich Re for which it provided German and US advice on its €4bn rights issue, the third largest ever by a German company.

Munich partner Walter Henle leads the corporate and private equity practice at **Baker & McKenzie**, with Matthias Jaletzke heading the M&A team. It is private equity where the firm wins more accolades with clients such as Apax, PPM and EQT on its client portfolio. The firm boasts a solid base of German industrial clients on its portfolio.

With its growing track record in complex and high-value M&A, **CMS Hasche Sigle** has an enviable client base of leading corporates and a vast array of Mittelstand companies. It makes full use of its broad proliferation across Germany. In Munich the firm's links with financially sound Bavarian business has served it well. Many of these mid-sized entities are internationally oriented and transaction intensive. The firm certainly dominates the Munich market (alongside **Nörr Stiefenhofer Lutz**). Oliver Thurn handles incoming transactions, while Thomas Meyding in Stuttgart is one of the firm's strongest corporate partners. Stefan-Ulrich Müller is head of private equity in Munich and links up well with Martin Kuhn.

The Mittelstand's choice firm, **Haarmann Hemmelrath** has long been linked to the TMT sector and completed a multitude of listings on the Neuer Markt before its demise. It has now shifted its sights onto the biotech and pharmaceutical sectors and the Berlin office has acquired several key banking clients. The firm's strong legal and tax advisory practice has enabled it to mark itself out as one of Germany's leading law firms and with its impressive proliferation of offices it is considered to be a solid one-stop-shop.

Lovells' stronghold in corporate and commercial lies in Frankfurt and Düsseldorf, the former profiting from the recruitment of corporate and transactional specialist Tim Brandi from **Gleiss Lutz** in December 2003. The firm's international client base is steadily growing, but it retains strong links to the Mittelstand.

CORPORATE AND COMMERCIAL

FRESHFIELDS BRUCKHAUS DERINGER ✪
HENGELER MUELLER ✪

CLIFFORD CHANCE
GLEISS LUTZ ✪
LINKLATERS OPPENHOFF & RÄDLER ✪
SHEARMAN & STERLING LLP

Allen & Overy ✪
Baker & McKenzie ✪
CMS Hasche Sigle ✪
Haarmann Hemmelrath ✪
Lovells ✪
Nörr Stiefenhofer Lutz ✪
White & Case

Buse Heberer Fromm ✪
GSK Gassner Stockmann & Kollegen ✪
Graf von Westphalen Bappert & Modest ✪
Heuking Kühn Lüer Wojtek ✪
Latham & Watkins LLP ✪
Norton Rose Vieregge
P+P Pöllath + Partners ✪
Simmons & Simmons ✪
Taylor Wessing ✪

Aderhold von Dalwigk Knüppel Rechstanwälte GmbH
ARCON Rechtsanwälte Schmidt-Sibeth Heisse Weisskopf Kursawe
Ashurst ✪
Beiten Burkhardt Rechtsanwaltsgesellschaft mbH ✪
Büsing, Müffelmann & Theye
Coudert Brothers LLP ✪
Göhmann Wrede Haas Kappus & Hartmann
GÖRG Rechtsanwälte ✪
Happ Recke Luther
Haver & Mailänder
Hölters & Elsing ✪
Jones Day
KSB INTAX
McDermott, Will & Emery ✪
PPR & Partner ✪
Rödl & Partner GbR
SJ Berwin Knopf Tulloch Steininger ✪
Wilmer Cutler Pickering LLP ✪

Firms are listed A-Z in tiers which are ranked in order of priority
✪ *Indicates firm displays contact details at the end of this chapter.*

Nörr Stiefenhofer Lutz's original office and current HQ is Munich where its client base emerged from the Bavarian Mittelstand. It now has a national client base and strong links with Central and Eastern Europe, with five offices in the region. The firm is best known for corporate work in the media sector, but it has diversified, bringing in a multitude of insurance and automotive clients. Tobias Bürgers concentrates on the automotive sector with Dieter Schenk recommended for his pharmaceutical industry knowledge. Thomas Schulz leads the corporate team and has recently concentrated on the firm's prosperous private equity business.

As one of the world's ubiquitous firms it is no surprise that **White & Case** acts for mainly internationally oriented clients. The firm has a strong Hamburg office and revenues are driven considerably by Central and Eastern European business. It is also building a brand in outsourcing in the banking sector, particularly back office operations thanks in no small part to the efforts of former bank in-house counsel Matthias Kasch.

Buse Heberer Fromm boasts a broad corporate and commercial practice with a solid domestic and international scope demonstrated by its recent advice to a US investor on its $600m acquisition of a German battery manufacturer. The Hamburg office boasts the largest corporate team and includes a China desk that the firm launched in 2001. As a consequence the firm recently advised a Chinese client on its acquisition of a German company in receivership. The firm is part of the *European Legal Alliance*, which includes UK firm **Field Fisher Waterhouse**.

Another **Beiten Burkhardt Rechtsanwaltsgesellschaft mbH** spin-off, **GSK Gassner Stockmann & Kollegen** has become a credible firm in its eight years of existence. The corporate and commercial side of the practice is driven largely by its thriving real estate work that accounts for 60-70% of the firm's revenues. In the latter half of 2003, the firm opened its seventh German office in Düsseldorf; impressive proliferation bearing in mind it has never merged with another firm. Instead it has made astute lateral hires of partners from respected firms such as **Freshfields Bruckhaus Deringer**, **Hengeler Mueller** and **Lovells**. Internationally the firm works with **Nabarro Nathanson** in the UK and France's **August & Debouzy**.

Graf von Westphalen Bappert & Modest merged with the Hamburg-based auditors *Busch & Partners* at the beginning of 2003, boosting the corporate and tax side of the firm. The firm now boasts 20 tax advisers and accountants in its bid for MDP credibility. After losing its Frankfurt office in 2001, the firm has rebuilt with a number of mergers including acquiring a pharmaceutical practice in Freiburg and a corporate finance boutique in Munich, *Kloyer Barthmes Klar*, both in 2002. Andreas Kloyer and Rupert Klar are now key members of the corporate team. At the beginning of 2003, the firm entered an association with UK national firm **Wragge & Co LLP**.

Heuking Kühn Lüer Wojtek's Hamburg and Düsseldorf offices generate the large proportion of corporate and commercial work for the firm. It boasts excellent links to the Mittelstand and wealthy business owners, particularly in the transportation, engineering and energy sectors. It has also developed a track record in squeeze-outs.

Since arriving in Germany in 2001, US-based **Latham & Watkins LLP** has continued its aggressive expansion. With major multinational clients such as Volvo, Sun Microsystems and VeriSign, the demand for resources on the ground means its determined growth is well founded.

Norton Rose Vieregge's Frankfurt office has become a hub for the firm's growing business in Central and Eastern Europe, thanks to the efforts of Campbell Steedman. The German team has also played a pivotal role in growing the firm's international business. Under Steedman, it led the pitch that ultimately won a place on Nestlé's panel of advisers.

P+P Pöllath + Partners has an excellent reputation in mid-cap private equity and venture capital, but the firm has an excellent M&A record and a reputation for advice to boardrooms and shareholders.

Simmons & Simmons is gaining ground in the media and Mittelstand markets. The hire of Wolgang Hess from **Clifford Chance** in October 2003 augments the media presence already provided by Stefan Weinheimer. Franz-Josef Schöne concentrates on international and domestic transactions.

After a number of partner losses in 2001, **Taylor Wessing** has rebuilt its practice and now boasts an impressive 56 corporate lawyers mainly based in the Hamburg, Munich and Düsseldorf offices. The firm also recently bolstered its team in Frankfurt with three corporate partners from **Osborne Clarke**. The Hamburg office boasts a multitude of shipyard clients, with the Düsseldorf branch advising a variety of classical industrial corporates. The Munich office is oriented towards technology and Mittelstand companies.

Aderhold von Dalwigk Knüppel Rechstanwälte GmbH is the legal arm of MDP RölfsPartner. The firm has developed quite a reputation in corporate restructuring. Reinhard von Dalwigk is the firm's chief protagonist in this sector and recently advised Mobilcom on its financial restructuring.

ARCON Rechtsanwälte Schmidt-Sibeth Heisse Weisskopf Kursawe's original and most populous office is in Munich, but it has seven offices across Germany, none of which were acquired by merging with another firm. Largely the firm acts for mid-sized corporates, but also some blue-chips in Munich. The firm completed 15 IPOs on the Neuer Markt, as well as the first IPO in 2003. The capital markets practice was significantly enhanced with the arrival of Alexander Honrath from WestLB in September 2003.

Ashurst's growing presence in M&A and private equity outlines it as a firm with a future in Germany. The small transactional oriented office has additional resources and support on the finance side.

Beiten Burkhardt Rechtsanwaltsgesellschaft mbH continues to boast considerable senior level expertise, despite a turbulent few years, involving its tie-up to KPMG and a flurry of spin-off firms reducing its famous resources. The firm still has strong ties to German industries and is a respected adviser to those in positions of management.

Büsing, Müffelmann & Theye is a medium-sized firm with the bulk of its resources in Bremen. A number of senior and experienced partners draw significant instructions from the region, while offices in Frankfurt and Berlin give clients further options and expertise.

In Munich, **Coudert Brothers LLP** lost a thriving private equity practice under Federico Pappalardo to **Dechert** in 2004. The Frankfurt office handles more generic corporate issues. The experienced duo of Markus Bauer and Bernhard Mielert gain praise for M&A work. Rainer Jacob deserves special mention for his telecoms industry expertise.

Göhmann Wrede Haas Kappus & Hartmann is recognised for general corporate and projects work, but with offices in Spain the firm handles an increasing flow of business between the two EU nations.

GÖRG Rechtsanwälte continued its steady growth in 2003, by recruiting three partners from **Luther Menold Rechtsanwaltsgesellschaft mbH** and launching a new Hamburg office. Though historically regarded as one of Germany's leading insolvency practices, the firm is quietly building an excellent name in corporate and related support practices, including employment.

Happ Recke Luther boasts a solid corporate practice led by Wilhelm Happ. The firm recently handled a major restructuring. **Haver & Mailänder** has a similar reputation.

Transactional-focused **Hölters & Elsing** has developed a broader corporate practice with major joint venture and restructuring mandates flooding into the small Düsseldorf-based firm, which also has offices in Berlin and Frankfurt. Recently Wolfgang Hölters advised on the restructuring of a major insurance group.

Jones Day launched a new IP and litigation driven office in Munich in January 2003, which augments its respected industrial client corporate practice in Frankfurt. As well as a strong mid-cap M&A business the firm has developed a strong restructuring enterprise, by focusing on distressed companies. The recruitment of restructuring specialist Volker Kammel from **Clifford Chance** in September 2003 further enhanced this area.

McDermott, Will & Emery has created a German practice of 27 lawyers in 18 months since its launch in 2001. In July 2003, the firm acquired a further partner, Hans-Joachim Schreiber from a Munich-based venture capitalist firm.

PPR & Partner is the legacy of *Clev + Pape Rechtsanwälte Wirtschaftsprüfer Steuerberater* after name partner and tax specialist Heinrich Clev departed on 1 July 2003. The firm still boasts a strong corporate and employment reputation.

SJ Berwin Knopf Tulloch Steininger has an established reputation for the tax aspects of private equity and the establishment of funds, but the firm is winning recognition in the M&A market. Uwe Steininger is the main practitioner.

Wilmer Cutler Pickering LLP has created a leading Berlin corporate base augmented by its strong name in the US. The Berlin branch is very much a reflection of the firm's strong global administrative law name.

DISPUTE RESOLUTION

Aderhold von Dalwigk Knüppel Rechstanwälte GmbH's Jürgen Witte is a former judge and attorney in the Court of Appeal. He handles a range of contentious issues including D&O cases, largely for insurance companies.

Allen & Overy continues to generate widespread acclaim particularly for its sturdy banking litigation practice. The firm acts for Deutsche Bank on a regular basis, demonstrating its excellent rapport with the financial sector, for which Carsten Salger deserves much of the credit. Wolfgang Witz is recommended for IP and commercial disputes. Other new clients of the practice include Oracle Germany and Imperial Tobacco. Cornelius Fischer-Zernin and Arndt Overlack are recommended for arbitration.

Baker & McKenzie's dedicated litigation and arbitration group has won further market recognition in a range of areas. Günther Pickrahn is an acknowledged leader in post-merger disputes and stock market issues. A range of partners including Stephan Spehl and Jörg Risse deals with construction and infrastructure cases.

With one of Germany's strongest forensic practices, **Beiten Burkhardt Rechtsanwalts-gesellschaft mbH** boasts a multitude of experienced partners with exceptional contentious skills. Hans-Jürgen Schroth is recommended for corporate disputes and international arbitrations. Matthias Stecher and Bernhard von Linstow are IP and technology disputes specialists.

CMS Hasche Sigle is recommended for shareholder disputes. Florian Bauer is the most senior litigator in Munich, while Peter Endres also wins accolades. Klaus Sachs is experienced in arbitration. Dorothee Ruckteschler (Stuttgart) and Helmut Borngräber (Düsseldorf) are also highly commended arbitration specialists.

The original German firm, *Pünder* had an established litigation practice long before **Clifford Chance LLP** came into the equation. Fabian von Schlabrendorff is a seasoned and respected name in the contentious arena and well liked by financial institutions. He is a regular arbitrator. Uwe Hornung wins accolades for his civil fraud work.

Danckelmann & Kerst's Hans Beeg is an experienced arbitration specialist and has appeared regularly before the ICC in Paris.

Esche Schümann Commichau and **FPS Fritze Paul Seelig** also have considerable contentious expertise within their ranks.

Freshfields Bruckhaus Deringer's Gunhild Schäfer is praised for her product liability and commercial litigation expertise. Wilhelm Danelzik and Thomas Kreifels are acknowledged for commercial litigation, and Bernd Kunth and Reinhard Densch for arbitration. Frankfurt-based Rolf Trittmann is widely considered to be one of the leading disputes specialists in Germany.

Gleiss Lutz recently created a distinct litigation and arbitration group, consisting of five partners and ten associates. It has made considerable headway in recent years, particularly after recruiting respected litigation specialist Stefan Rützel from **Freshfields Bruckhaus Deringer** in 2002. Stephan Wilske is a seasoned international arbitration and commercial litigation expert. The firm recently acted in the largest ever state liability case.

Graf von Westphalen Bappert & Modest does not have specialist litigators, but many of its partners have a contentious leaning. The firm is known for its regular appearance in major arbitrations. Friedrich Graf von Westphalen and Klaus Landry deserve a particular mention.

Gurland's Jens Bredow is a respected international arbitrator, while **Haver & Mailänder** is recommended for arbitration, much to the credit of the excellent Rolf Winkler. He acts as both counsel and arbitrator.

Hengeler Mueller's Peter Heckel is Germany's best-known litigator and has handled some of the country's most notable disputes, including high-profile defamation disputes. With commercial litigator Markus Meier having almost an equal standing, the firm clearly offers one of the leading teams in the jurisdiction.

Heuking Kühn Lüer Wojtek has a strong disputes practice in Hamburg, thanks largely to Frank Mitzkus and Thomas Wambach. Wolfgang Kühn acts as a chairman in UNICTRAL and ICC proceedings.

Hölters & Elsing partners Siegfried Elsing and the elder statesman Otto Sandrock are respected specialists in corporate disputes and arbitration.

Jones Day's reputation for having the largest global litigation practice is not let down by the German office. Thomas Mahlich handles international litigation, while Friedrich Klinkert stands out for contentious IP matters. Johannes Zindel is commended for unfair competition litigation and of-counsel Eckart Hild for white-collar crime.

At **Jordan Rechtsanwalts-GmbH**, name partner Helmuth Jordan advises on intellectual property disputes in Germany and Switerland.

Linklaters Oppenhoff & Rädler provides one of the largest teams of litigators in Germany and as a result one of the broadest bases of expertise, ranging from banking litigation to product liability disputes. Klaus Saffenreuther heads the litigation and arbitration group and specialises in German civil litigation and arbitration. The firm's contentious reputation has won recognition from well-known names such as former tennis professional Boris Becker, whose partner Laurenz Schmitt was represented in proceedings regarding the insolvent Sportsgate.

Gino Lörcher at **Lörcher & Lörcher** is another international arbitration specialist with substantial experience of ICC proceedings.

Lovells' main areas of strength are product liability, insolvency litigation and professional liability. The firm is generally involved in all the major claims against accountancy firms. In Volker Triebel, Alexander Loos and Thilo von Bodungen, the firm boasts a formidable arbitration team.

Ulrich Theune at **Luther Menold Rechtsanwaltsgesellschaft mbH** has a similar reputation, but the firm is also noted for its forensic expertise.

Nörr Stiefenhofer Lutz's Michael Molitoris is a product liability partner of exceptional calibre. He recently represented the tobacco giant Philip Morris in German litigation, as well as a premium German car manufacturer in a product liability case. His work led the firm to gain further corporate work from the latter.

Schwarz Kelwing Wicke Westpfahl's Walter Eberl is an arbitration and mediation specialist and regularly appears before the ICC.

Shearman & Sterling LLP's excellent domestic and international disputes practice offers the expertise of leading commercial litigators Jochem Reichert, Martin Winter and Thomas Liebscher. Richard Kreindler is involved in a number of trans-national disputes.

Simmons & Simmons' Hans-Hermann Aldenhoff is an experienced contentious practitioner particularly in relation to banking and employment disputes. **Taylor Wessing**'s Düsseldorf office holds the firm's core expertise in commercial litigation, where Dietrich Max is building a high profile. Frankfurt is to the fore in product liability cases, Munich is IP-focused, while Hamburg provides a formidable team of arbitration specialists.

Veltins & Wilkinson, Barker, Knauer, Leitermann's Michael Veltins is an experienced arbitrator in international ICC arbitrations.

White & Case is recommended for its broad expertise in litigation and arbitration. Hans-Jürgen Hüesker, Gerd Lembke and Christian Wirth are all experienced contentious practitioners.

Wilmer Cutler Pickering LLP represented Deutsche Lufthansa in a dispute concerning airport fees at Düsseldorf Airport.

EMPLOYMENT

CMS Hasche Sigle advised Deutsche Telekom AG on the group-wide restructuring of directors' service contracts. The 36-lawyer employment practice also advises blue-chip companies such as Bertelsmann and Hypovereinsbank, along with a solid German-wide Mittelstand client base. The Hamburg office is a key centre of activity, along with Stuttgart and Düsseldorf.

Freshfields Bruckhaus Deringer is recommended for complex, cross-border transactions and restructurings. The practice advised Hays on the sale of several businesses and represented ABN

EMPLOYMENT

CMS HASCHE SIGLE ✪
FRESHFIELDS BRUCKHAUS DERINGER ✪
GLEISS LUTZ ✪
KÜTTNER RECHTSANWÄLTE

Baker & McKenzie ✪
Cornelius Bartenbach Haesemann & Partner, member of ius laboris ✪
Linklaters Oppenhoff & Rädler ✪
Neef & Schrader
Schmitt-Rolfes, Faltermeier, Staudacher ✪

Beiten Burkhardt Rechtsanwaltsgesellschaft mbH ✪
Clifford Chance
Gravenhorst, Färber, Schumacher, Röhrborn, Simdorn, Kirchner ✪
Hengeler Mueller ✪
Kasper, Knacke, Wintterlin & Partner
Kliemt & Vollstädt
Lovells ✪
Luther Menold Rechtsanwaltsgesellschaft mbH ✪
Nörr Stiefenhofer Lutz ✪
Norton Rose Vieregge
Taylor Wessing ✪
Tschöpe, Schipp, Clemenz

Allen & Overy ✪
Coudert Brothers LLP ✪
Graf von Westphalen Bappert & Modest ✪
Heuking Kühn Lüer Wojtek ✪
KSB INTAX
Latham & Watkins LLP ✪
Loh Von Hülsen Michael Rechtsanwälte
McDermott, Will & Emery ✪
PPR & Partner ✪
Simmons & Simmons ✪
White & Case

Firms are listed A-Z in tiers which are ranked in order of priority
✪ *Indicates firm displays contact details at the end of this chapter.*

Amro on its reorganisation in Germany. Prof Dr Heinz Josef Willemsen in the firm's Düsseldorf office has an exceptional reputation.

Gleiss Lutz boasts wide-ranging expertise in employment matters, including terminations, company pension schemes, plant closures and negotiations with trade unions. Dr Jobst-Hubertus Bauer, based in Stuttgart, heads a team of 21 lawyers.

Cologne-based **Küttner Rechtsanwälte** is a highly respected niche employment practice, headed by name partner Klaus-Dietrich Küttner. Clients come from the automotive, financial, manufacturing and entertainment industries.

Baker & McKenzie advised Schott-Zwiesel on a restructuring project and represented a major nutritional products producer on a pan-European closure of plants. Günther Heckelmann and Gregor Dornbusch in Frankfurt head a practice of 22 lawyers, with additional expertise in Berlin, Munich and Düsseldorf.

Cornelius Bartenbach Haesemann & Partner, member of Ius Laboris, based in Cologne, represents blue-chip clients from the automotive, chemical and pharmaceutical sectors. Clients include Allianz, Tyco, SAS, the Schäfer Group, Saturn and DHL. Name partner Prof Dr Kurt Bartenbach is renowned for expertise in law concerning employee inventions.

Linklaters Oppenhoff & Rädler advises employers such as Dow Chemical and Pirelli on the full spectrum of employment law matters.

Neef & Schrader, based in Hanover, is a nine-lawyer firm with a focus on employment law. Clients include a major German car manufacturer. Former name partner Ulrich Tschöpe left the firm to establish **Tschöpe, Schipp, Clemenz**.

Schmitt-Rolfes, Faltermeier, Staudacher, based in Munich, advises clients such as Siemens, Bayer and IBM. On the employee side, the firm also acts for senior employees and managers. Name partner Peter Staudacher is recommended.

Beiten Burkhardt Rechtsanwaltsgesellschaft mbH's employment department includes a team of six partners in Munich, Cologne and Berlin which advises clients such as BMW, Merck and Grundig.

Clifford Chance's Frankfurt office advises on transactional employment issues for the firm's extensive international client base.

Six-partner, four-associate **Gravenhorst, Färber, Schumacher, Röhrborn, Simdorn, Kirchner**, located in Düsseldorf, acts for banking, media, IT, biotech as well as football sector clients. Litigation work is a forte of the practice. The firm represents several clients with Italian interests. Dr Meike Kirchner joined the firm from **CMS Hasche Sigle**.

Hengeler Mueller is especially recommended for experience in transactional matters. Clients include Deutsche Telekom AG.

Kasper, Knacke, Wintterlin & Partner is recommended for expertise in internal labour relations, including collective agreements, employee share options and pension plans. The eight-lawyer Stuttgart practice represents trading companies, auto makers and electronics clients. Dr Wolfgang Hesse is recommended.

11-lawyer **Kliemt & Vollstädt**, formed in 2002, acts for clients such as Xerox and CC-Bank AG. Other companies are drawn from the auto, insurance, chemical and insurance sectors. Name partners Dr Michael Kliemt and Dr Oliver Vollstädt formerly worked at **Clifford Chance**. The firm's head office in Düsseldorf is supported by a smaller Berlin office.

Lovells advised Deutsche Bahn on collective bargaining agreements with unions. Other transactions include acting for Akzo Nobel on closing a plant in Germany. Thomas Ubber heads a team of five partners and 26 associates located in Munich, Frankfurt, Hamburg, Düsseldorf and Berlin.

Luther Menold Rechtsanwaltsgesellschaft mbH is recommended for a broad geographical spread of employment expertise offered from its 12 German offices.

Nörr Stiefenhofer Lutz has broad-ranging expertise in restructuring, collective agreements and pensions matters. Clients include Philip Morris, Walt Disney Company, Swatch and Mobilcom. Munich-based partners Dr Stefan Tomicic and Dr Hans-Christoph Schimmelpfennig head a team of 21 lawyers across offices in Frankfurt, Berlin, Düsseldorf and Dresden.

Norton Rose Vieregge advised Canada Life Assurance on employment-related advice during the acquisition of a competitor. Matthis Kappus heads a team of 15 lawyers; the bulk of the department is centred in Cologne, with additional expertise based in Munich.

Taylor Wessing advised clients such as Suzuki and Dole Fresh Fruit Europe on collective labour agreements. Other clients come from the media, electronics and retail sectors. Hamburg-based partner Axel Filges heads a team of 20 lawyers based across all of the firm's German offices.

Niche firm **Tschöpe, Schipp, Clemenz** boasts an excellent reputation in name partner Ulrich Tschöpe, who formerly worked at **Neef & Schrader**.

Allen & Overy advised banks and major international corporates on a wide range of employment matters. Frankfurt-based partner Dr Anja Breitfeld is recommended. The firm works closely with its London and international network of offices.

Coudert Brothers LLP's Michael Magotsch in Frankfurt advises on company restructuring, mass redundancies and outsourcing.

Graf von Westphalen Bappert & Modest advised major German and Japanese companies on a wide range of employment issues. Dr Thomas Hennings and Dr Christoph Fingerle, based in Hamburg and Freiburg respectively, are prominent members of the five-partner, four-associate team.

Heuking Kühn Lüer Wojtek advises banks, consultancies and manufacturing companies. Kay Jacobsen and Andreas Walle, based in Hamburg, and Wilhelm Moll and Dirk Kolvenbach, based in the Cologne and Düsseldorf offices respectively, are recommended. The firm advises several major clients from the metal-working and transport industries.

Latham & Watkins LLP advises banks, breweries, pharmaceutical companies and airlines. Clients include Airbus Deutschland and Hamburg Airport. Peter Markl, Dr Stefan Lunk and Dr Mathias Preuss are well known.

At Berlin-based **Loh Von Hülsen Michael Rechtsanwälte**, Dr Ernesto Loh has particular expertise in advice to chief executives of companies on contracts with their employer. Other clients include Bombardier Transportation, Herlitz AG and several banks and media companies.

At **McDermott, Will & Emery**, Düsseldorf-based partner Volker Teigelkötter advises on a wide range of employment issues for employers as well as employees and executive staff. Munich partner Kristina Schweier is also recommended.

PPR & Partner in Düsseldorf undertook work for a US client on employee reductions and advised a German corporate on the relocation of 170 employees from Germany to the Netherlands. Clients include ATX Technologies and Ryder Deutschland. Dieter Pape is recommended.

Simmons & Simmons advised US, European and Japanese companies and financial institutions on employment issues. Highlights include representing Starbucks Coffee on obtaining work permits for foreign employees. Dr Hans-Hermann Aldenhoff heads a practice in Düsseldorf which works closely with the firm's international network of offices.

White & Case advised Mobilcom on personnel reduction and represented Jean Pascale AG on negotiation of a social compensation plan. Ingrid Deuchler heads a team of three partners and 17 associates based in Frankfurt and Hamburg.

IP: COPYRIGHT

CMS HASCHE SIGLE ✪
LÖFFLER WENZEL SEDELMEIER

Freshfields Bruckhaus Deringer ✪
Gleiss Lutz ✪
Harmsen Utescher ✪
Hertin Anwaltssozietät
Lovells ✪
Schwarz Kelwing Wicke Westpfahl ✪
Taylor Wessing ✪
Unverzagt – von Have

Baker & McKenzie ✪
Beiten Burkhardt Rechtsanwaltsgesellschaft mbH ✪
Boehmert & Boehmert
Graf von Westphalen Bappert & Modest ✪
Lausen Rechtsanwälte
Linklaters Oppenhoff & Rädler ✪
Norton Rose Vieregge
Rospatt Osten Pross ✪
Sasse & Partner
Schweizer, Kanzlei, Prof
Wilmer Cutler Pickering LLP ✪

Heuking Kühn Lüer Wojtek ✪
Kropp-Olbertz Schulte-Franzheim Seibert
Latham & Watkins LLP ✪
Lichte Rechtsanwälte

Firms are listed A-Z in tiers which are ranked in order of priority
✪ Indicates firm displays contact details at the end of this chapter.

IP: COPYRIGHT

CMS Hasche Sigle's Hamburg-based partner Friedrich Graf Luckner heads a practice which represents major publishing, media and sporting clients.

Niche firm **Löffler Wenzel Sedelmeier** based in Stuttgart, has an excellent reputation amongst IT, media and publishing clients.

Freshfields Bruckhaus Deringer advises blue-chip technology, biotech and publishing companies from its Germany-wide offices.

Gleiss Lutz acts for Internet, publishing and pharmaceutical clients from its offices in Stuttgart, Frankfurt and Berlin.

Harmsen Utescher, based in Hamburg, represents pop groups, artists and major German design companies.

Berlin-based **Hertin Anwaltssozietät** is a niche IP firm headed by renowned partner Prof Dr Paul W Hertin. The practice advises several major IT and software clients.

Lovells advises publishing houses, media companies, computer game companies and online providers. The Hamburg and Düsseldorf offices are particularly active.

Schwarz Kelwing Wicke Westpfahl advises film, television, IT and publishing clients from its Berlin as well as its Munich and Cologne offices.

Taylor Wessing advised TF1, the French television company, on film copyright advice surrounding its bid for the assets of Kirch Media Group. Munich-based Dr Sabine Rojahn heads a team of 25 partners across Germany.

Unverzagt – von Have, with offices in Hamburg and Berlin, advises media, music, recording and sporting clients. Dirk Feldmann has notable experience of advising photography clients.

Baker & McKenzie's Constanze Ulmer-Eilfort led a team which advised Hewlett-Packard in relation to copyright levies imposed on PCs and printers. Other clients include pharmaceutical, technology and media companies.

Beiten Burkhardt Rechtsanwaltsgesellschaft mbH advises a wide range of media, music and computer industry clients such as Magazinpresse Verlag and Vogel Media Group.

Boehmert & Boehmert represents artists, software developers, authors, musicians, orchestras and publishing houses. The practice reports an increase in work involving distribution of movies on the Internet, especially for US clients. Prof Dr Wilhelm Nordemann in the Postdam office has an excellent reputation.

Graf von Westphalen Bappert & Modest's Norbert Hebeis in the firm's Freiburg office advises several publishing and media clients.

Lausen Rechtsanwälte advises major media and entertainment clients from the film, television and publishing industries. Munich-based name partner Dr Matthias Lausen is recommended.

Linklaters Oppenhoff & Rädler acts for publishers, online service providers and film producers. Highlights include advising Rebecca Horn on copyright and licensing law and representing several German film production companies on copyright law involving film music.

Norton Rose Vieregge advised EMI Electrola in relation to copyright claims against an unauthorised CD rental agency. Other clients include Vodafone and the Rolling Stones. Cologne-based partner Dr Albrecht Piltz heads the team.

Ten-lawyer **Rospatt Osten Pross**, based in Düsseldorf and Mannheim, is highly recommended for design protection advice. The firm advises software, furniture, jewellery and handcraft clients.

Name partner Helge Sasse at **Sasse & Partner** heads a team of 12 lawyers based across offices in Munich, Cologne, Hamburg and Berlin. The practice advises film, music, entertainment and literary clients.

Kanzlei Prof Schweizer is recommended for advice to newspaper and electronic media clients. Name partner Prof Dr Robert Schweizer is well known.

Wilmer Cutler Pickering LLP advises technology, biotech and airline clients on licensing agreements.

Heuking Kühn Lüer Wojtek advises media, publishing and IT clients on copyright issues. Recommended partners include Michael Schmittmann (Düsseldorf), Dr Søren Pietzcker (Hamburg) and Rudolf du Mesnil (Frankfurt).

Cologne-based **Kropp-Olbertz Schulte-Franzheim Seibert** represents publishers, authors and artists.

Latham & Watkins LLP advises several major music companies. Highlights include acting for Warner Music on copyright issues. Hamburg-based partner Dr Ulrich Börger is recommended.

Lichte Rechtsanwälte, based in Hamburg, advises several clients from the music industry, including agencies, music producers and record companies. Name partner Walter Lichte is recommended.

IP: PATENTS/REGISTERED DESIGNS (DISPUTE RESOLUTION/ADVICE)

Ten-lawyer **Klaka Rechtsanwälte**, based in Munich, advises major European and Japanese clients from the pharmaceuticals, automotive, manufacturing and food industries. Dr Michael Nieder is well known. Olaf Giebe also continues to build an excellent name.

At **Lovells**' Düsseldorf office, Clemens Plassmann and Martin Chakraborty successfully represented Medinol, the medical products manufacturer, in German and Dutch cross-border proceedings against Boston Scientific. Andreas von Falck and Sandra Rinnert are also highly recommended.

Rospatt Osten Pross name partner Peter von Rospatt heads a team in Düsseldorf and Mannheim which advises a wide range of German clients, including several major biotech and genetics industry enterprises. The firm also acts for a range of blue-chip US and Asian corporates in relation to patent work.

Bardehle Pagenberg Dost Altenburg Geissler advised on major patent litigation cases

IP: PATENTS/REGISTERED DESIGNS (DISPUTE RESOLUTION/ADVICE)

KLAKA RECHTSANWÄLTE ✪
LOVELLS ✪
ROSPATT OSTEN PROSS ✪

Bardehle Pagenberg Dost Altenburg Geissler
Bird & Bird ✪
Clifford Chance
Lichtenstein, Körner & Partner

Gleiss Lutz ✪
Krieger, Gentz, Mes & Graf von der Groeben ✪
Lorenz Seidler Gossel
Preu, Bohlig & Partner
Wildanger Kehrwald & Graf v. Schwerin

Boehmert & Boehmert
Grünecker, Kinkeldey, Stockmair & Schwanhäusser
Harmsen Utescher ✪
Hoffmann.Eitle
Taylor Wessing ✪

CMS Hasche Sigle ✪
Freshfields Bruckhaus Deringer ✪
Patzina Rechtsanwälte
White & Case

Baker & McKenzie ✪
Latham & Watkins LLP ✪
Norton Rose Vieregge
Simmons & Simmons ✪

Firms are listed A-Z in tiers which are ranked in order of priority
✪ Indicates firm displays contact details at the end of this chapter.

IP: PATENTS/REGISTERED DESIGNS (REGISTRATIONS)

Boehmert & Boehmert
Eisenführ, Speiser & Partner
Grünecker, Kinkeldey, Stockmair & Schwanhäusser
Hoffmann.Eitle
Uexküll & Stolberg ✪

Bardehle Pagenberg Dost Altenburg Geissler
Harmsen Utescher ✪
Viering, Jentschura & Partner
Vossius & Partner

Firms are listed A-Z in tiers which are ranked in order of priority
✪ Indicates firm displays contact details at the end of this chapter.

for clients from the medical and semiconductor industries. Clients include GlaxoSmithKline, Bose and L'Oréal.

Bird & Bird advised DeLaval, the Swedish farming equipment manufacturer, on a patent infringement case against its Dutch competitor, Lely. Other clients include Bayer, Electrolux, Aventis and Valeo. Wolfgang von Meibom, based in Düsseldorf, has an excellent reputation. The firm opened a new office in Munich in October 2003.

Clifford Chance advised pharmaceutical, chemical and automotive industry clients on patent law and disputes.

Lichtenstein, Körner & Partner, based in Stuttgart, advises chemical, automotive, computer and manufacturing clients on both contentious and non-contentious work. Eberhard Körner has an outstanding reputation. The firm has a particularly strong US client base.

Gleiss Lutz, based in Stuttgart, advises major chemical and biotech clients. Dr Thomas Bopp represents several major pharmaceutical companies.

Krieger, Gentz, Mes & Graf von Der Groeben in Düsseldorf acts for a wide range of biochemistry, genetics, semiconductor technology, software, telecoms and pharmaceutical clients.

Lorenz Seidler Gossel, based in Munich, advises electronics, mechanical engineering and automotive companies on both contentious and non-contentious patent work.

Preu, Bohlig & Partner's Munich and Düsseldorf offices offer expertise in protected privilege cases.

Wildanger Kehrwald Graf v. Schwerin & Partners acts for clients from Germany, Japan and Korea in the technology, manufacturing and retail sectors. The firm is particularly known for its dispute resolution work in Düsseldorf. Name partner Günther Wildanger is well known.

Boehmert & Boehmert has an excellent reputation for advice to medical, biotechnology and life sciences clients. The practice's core focus is Munich, with support from the firm's other German offices. The firm advised on due diligence work in relation to several M&A transactions in the biotechnology sector.

Grünecker, Kinkeldey, Stockmair & Schwanhäusser advises a wide range of German and international engineering, software, chemistry and biotech clients from its Munich head office. The team includes several patent attorneys.

Hamburg-based **Harmsen Utescher** undertakes filing and litigation work for a wide range of multinational chemical, biotech, food and retail sector clients. Dr Michael Schaeffer is very well known.

Hoffmann.Eitle fields a team of experienced lawyers, patent attorneys and technical specialist advisers. The Munich practice works closely with its London office. The firm represents several major Japanese clients.

Taylor Wessing's Düsseldorf, Munich and Frankfurt offices advise major German and multinational clients from the technology, engineering and food industries. A team of five partners and three associates specialises in patent infringement litigation. The German practice works closely with its UK office.

CMS Hasche Sigle advises companies from the electronics, software and manufacturing sectors. Clients include Vobis Microcomputer AG and Novar plc.

Freshfields Bruckhaus Deringer advised blue-chip clients such as Aventis, Colgate Palmolive and Intel Corporation on patent infringement suits. The firm's Düsseldorf and Frankfurt offices are particularly active.

Patzina Rechtsanwälte advised Rothenberger AG on patent infringement cases. Frankfurt-based partner Dr Andreas Bock is recommended.

White & Case represented Max Bahr, the German DIY chain, on patent issues, and acted for Novartis in relation to a dispute over the patent for biotechnology products. Christian Rohnke has an excellent reputation.

Baker & McKenzie advises German, Swiss and US companies from the automotive, pharmaceutical and medical industries. Frankfurt-based partner Günther Pickrahn has a special focus on patent litigation work.

Latham & Watkins LLP's Hamburg office advised a major European electronics producer on a patent infringement case relating to projectors. The practice received a boost when Gerd Jaekel joined the Hamburg office as of-counsel from **Lovells**. The firm advises engineering, software, biotech and engineering clients, working closely with its European and US offices.

Norton Rose Vieregge's Dr Gordian Hasselblatt heads a seven-lawyer department which acted for Gerdes, the automotive supplier, on a €2.5m patent infringement case, and advised a well-known French producer of titanium glasses on several patent infringement cases. Other clients include toy companies and wine growers.

At **Simmons & Simmons**, Düsseldorf-based partner Peter Meyer advised Tarkett SA on a patent infringement case.

IP: TRADE MARKS

All of the firms listed combine know-how in registration and strategic matters with high-quality contentious capability.

Linklaters Oppenhoff & Rädler advises a wide range of international clients including Johnson & Johnson, Procter & Gamble and Reebok. Highlights include advising Universal Music and Ali G on a case involving trade mark piracy. Cologne-based Kay-Uwe Jonas heads a team of 18 lawyers. Monika Wenz is also well known.

Lovells is recommended for its broad national and international reach, acting for clients such as Deutsche Telekom and Anheuser-Busch. Highlights include representing Philips Electronics on protecting its three-headed shaver trade marks. The firm is particularly recommended for expertise in three-dimensional trade marks for clients such as Lego. The department boasts strong practices in Hamburg and Düsseldorf. Burkhart Goebel and Andreas Bothe are recommended. The team suffered a setback when experienced partner Dr

Henning Harte-Bavendamm joined **Allen & Overy** in 2003.

At **Baker & McKenzie**, Frankfurt-based partner Michael Fammler heads a practice which advises on complex trade mark disputes and re-branding-projects. Highlights include representing Christian Dior Parfums on a trade mark dispute.

Beiten Burkhardt Rechtsanwaltsgesellschaft mbH advises major German and US clients on trade mark issues.

Bird & Bird advised Deutsche Telekom AG on two colour trade marks and represented Deutscher Sparkassen- und Giroverband on a trade mark for a logo. Other clients include Diageo and Henkel. Wolfgang von Meibom has an outstanding reputation.

Boehmert & Boehmert is renowned for its patent law expertise, but also fields a respected trade mark department in the Munich and Bremen offices. Munich-based partner Michaela Huth-Dierig heads a team which advises clients from the film, entertainment and food industries.

CMS Hasche Sigle undertook trade mark work for AOL Germany, La Chemise Lacoste, Europcar, Intel and Deutsche Bahn.

Freshfields Bruckhaus Deringer advised clients such as Air Berlin, Bose and Colgate-Palmolive on trade mark issues. The practice is recommended for its depth of expertise and geographical spread, thanks to its extensive network of German offices.

Gleiss Lutz advises on filing and defence of trade marks for clients in the automotive, chemical, biochemical, pharmaceuticals and manufacturing sectors. The firm has particularly strong connections with clients in the Stuttgart area. Dr Stefan Völker is well known.

Harmsen Utescher, located in Hamburg, acts for major multinational clients from the pharmaceutical, electrical and retail sectors. Dr Michael Schaeffer heads a team of eight partners.

Lichtenstein, Körner & Partner in Stuttgart advises German and international companies from the automotive, technology and manufacturing sectors. The firm has a particularly strong US client base. Carmen Lichtenstein and Dr Thomas Sambuc are well known. Service is perceived as 'excellent, swift and very client oriented'.

Twelve-lawyer **Lorenz Seidler Gossel**, based in Munich, represents several technology clients.

Mayer, Brown, Rowe & Maw LLP's Frankfurt office works closely with its European and US network of offices in advising blue-chip clients on their trade mark portfolios.

Allen & Overy's practice received a boost when experienced partner Dr Henning Harte-Bavendamm joined the firm in 2003 from **Lovells**. The firm advised Levi-Strauss, Chanel and BMG Berlin Musik on trade mark issues.

Clifford Chance is especially strong in transactional matters, working together with its corporate department.

Niche IP firm **Eisenführ, Speiser & Partner** offers specialist trade mark filing and litigation expertise. Six lawyers and a large team of patent attorneys are based across four offices in in Bremen, Munich, Berlin and Hamburg.

Nörr Stiefenhofer Lutz advised Buena Vista International on a trade mark dispute surrounding the screening of a major US film in Germany. The practice also represented EM.TV Merchandising AG on acquiring the licence for FIFA trade marks in the 2006 World Cup. Other clients include Quiksilver, Miller Brewing Company and Walt Disney Company. Munich-based partner Georg Jahn heads a team of six lawyers and eight associates.

Taylor Wessing advised German and international companies from the manufacturing, automotive and retail sectors. Deutsche BP AG is a major client. The department is located in offices in Berlin, Düsseldorf, Frankfurt, Hamburg and Munich.

White & Case advised Barry Callebaut on its international trade mark portfolio and represented KWS AG on a colour trade mark. Other clients include American Express, Citicorp and Colgate-Palmolive. The department works closely with its network of continental and Eastern European offices. Hamburg-based partner Christian Rohnke heads a three-partner, 13-associate practice recommended by clients for timeliness and reasonably priced advice.

Bardehle Pagenberg Dost Altenburg Geissler's Munich head office acts for clients such as adidas, Bosch and L'Oréal on trade mark issues. The firm works closely with its Paris office.

FPS Fritze Paul Seelig has particular expertise in trade mark piracy cases. The practice also advises on registration and litigation.

Grünecker, Kinkeldey, Stockmair & Schwanhäusser advises on trade mark registration and litigation for a wide range of German and international clients. The firm has special expertise in the technology, chemistry, computer science and biotech sectors.

Hengeler Mueller advises blue-chip clients on piracy cases. The practice advised a perfume manufacturer on the sale of its global trade mark rights.

Heuking Kühn Lüer Wojtek advises on registration and protection of trade marks from its offices in Frankfurt, Cologne and Hamburg. The practice acts for several clients in the textile and food industries.

Hoffmann.Eitle acts for several US and Japanese clients. Munich-based partner Alexander Nette heads the team.

Niche firm **Klaka Rechtsanwälte**, based in Munich, advises major banking, automotive and pharmaceutical clients on trade mark cases.

Kleiner Rechtsanwälte advises chemical, IT and food companies. The firm has offices in Düsseldorf, Stuttgart and Mannheim.

Latham & Watkins LLP advises several medicine and biotechnology sector clients from its offices in Hamburg and Frankurt.

IP: TRADE MARKS

LINKLATERS OPPENHOFF & RÄDLER ✪
LOVELLS ✪

Baker & McKenzie ✪
Beiten Burkhardt Rechtsanwaltsgesellschaft mbH ✪
Bird & Bird ✪
Boehmert & Boehmert
CMS Hasche Sigle ✪
Freshfields Bruckhaus Deringer ✪
Gleiss Lutz ✪
Harmsen Utescher ✪
Lichtenstein, Körner & Partner
Lorenz Seidler Gossel
Mayer, Brown, Rowe & Maw LLP ✪

Allen & Overy ✪
Clifford Chance
Eisenführ, Speiser & Partner
Nörr Stiefenhofer Lutz ✪
Taylor Wessing ✪
White & Case

Bardehle Pagenberg Dost Altenburg Geissler
FPS Fritze Paul Seelig ✪
Grünecker, Kinkeldey, Stockmair & Schwanhäusser
Hengeler Mueller ✪
Heuking Kühn Lüer Wojtek ✪
Hoffmann.Eitle
Klaka Rechtsanwälte ✪
Kleiner Rechtsanwälte
Latham & Watkins LLP ✪
Meissner, Bolte & Partners
Patzina Rechtsanwälte
Schwarz Kelwing Wicke Westpfahl ✪

Ashurst ✪
Graf von Westphalen Bappert & Modest ✪
Heussen Rechtsanwaltsgesellschaft mbH ✪
Klinger & Kollegen
Jones Day
Luther Menold Rechtsanwaltsgesellschaft mbH ✪
Norton Rose Vieregge
PPR & Partner ✪
Spitz · Gaul · Golda
Rospatt Osten Pross ✪

Firms are listed A-Z in tiers which are ranked in order of priority
✪ Indicates firm displays contact details at the end of this chapter.

Meissner, Bolte & Partners' clients include Bernard Callebaut, the chocolate maker and Van Houten, the cocoa producer. Munich and Bremen are key centres of expertise in the firm's network of seven German offices.

Patzina Rechtsanwälte advises blue-chip clients such as Ferrari, Swatch and major Italian fashion labels. Dr Andreas Bock heads a team of three partners and five associates.

Schwarz Kelwing Wicke Westpfahl advises several media clients on trade mark issues.

Ashurst advised Jack Wolfskin on the transfer of international trade marks.

At **Graf von Westphalen Bappert & Modest** Freiburg-based partner Norbert Hebeis heads a team of seven lawyers which advises Wilkinson Sword on managing trade mark portfolios and acted for Swiss International Airlines in relation to the introduction of the new trade mark 'Swiss'.

Klinger & Kollegen advises clients from the auto, textile, food and media sectors on trade marks. Dr Alfred Klinger heads a team of four lawyers.

PPR & Partner in Düsseldorf provides ongoing advice to German and US clients on around 900 trade marks.

Spitz · Gaul · Golda, based in Munich, manages several thousand trade marks for fashion, sporting and technology clients such as adidas, Marco Polo and Konami, the Japanese computer game manufacturer. Dr Volker Spitz heads a team of nine lawyers.

At **Rospatt Osten Pross** Stephan von Petersdorff-Campen advised Erpo, the German furniture company, on trade mark issues. The firm also undertook work on registering slogans and colours.

INFORMATION TECHNOLOGY

Freshfields Bruckhaus Deringer's 42-partner TMT practice offers unrivalled breadth of expertise in regulatory, financing, competition, restructuring and antitrust matters. The practice acted for Amadeus on the acquisition of a travel marketing system from Lufthansa and advised Messe Berlin, Thomas Cook and O2 on outsourcing work.

SSW Schneider Schiffer Weihermüller, based in Munich, advises clients such as online banks, brokers and e-commerce and computer companies. Highlights include acting for a Singaporean client on a reverse takeover of a German fibre optics manufacturing company. Peter Waltl and Prof Dr Jochen Schneider are well known.

Baker & McKenzie successfully acted for a software manufacturer in litigation over software licence agreements and advised an airline manufacturer on setting up an Internet portal for aircraft in transit. Dr Matthias Scholz in Frankfurt and Dr Wolfgang Fritzemeyer, based in Frankfurt and Munich respectively, are respected practitioners.

Fifteen-lawyer **Bartsch und Partner GbR**, located in Karlsruhe, advises software companies, ISPs and multimedia companies. Name partner Prof Dr Michael Bartsch is recommended.

CMS Hasche Sigle advises on outsourcing projects and software development. The firm acted for Atos Origin on outsourcing projects and represented Vishay Intertechnology, the electronic components manufacturer, on the acquisition of BC Components Holdings BV.

Clifford Chance is recommended for complex, international outsourcing and consulting projects. The firm's Frankfurt office was particularly active in advising major banking clients on IT outsourcing projects. Other highlights include advice to a multinational confectionery manufacturer on its global IT system.

Linklaters Oppenhoff & Rädler's ten-lawyer department is headed by Michael Abels in Cologne, with additional expertise in the firm's Frankfurt and Munich offices. The practice advised on several major outsourcing, software distribution and licensing and e-commerce transactions. Highlights include advising BP on intra-group data transfer. The department also advises several major defence companies on IT matters.

Lovells advised Sparkassenverband Baden-Württemberg on insourcing the IT infrastructure of its savings banks, and represented a major satellite TV equipment company on licence and manufacturing agreements. Munich-based partner Wolfgang Büchner is well known.

Nörr Stiefenhofer Lutz advised eBay on installing software. Other clients include, Oracle and DataDirect Technologies. Dr Peter Bräutigam and Dr Andreas Leupold in Munich are recommended.

Willkie Farr & Gallagher LLP advises on outsourcing, systems integration and e-commerce matters. Thomas Heymann and Katharina Scheja are respected members of a team which acts for several prestigious US technology clients.

Beiten Burkhardt Rechtsanwaltsgesellschaft mbH advises software, media and Internet clients, including SV Medienservice and Tomorrow Focus Internet AG. Reinhard Gaertner is highly recommended.

Gleiss Lutz advises Internet, e-commerce and major European and US computer companies. The firm has a special focus on advice in relation to recognition of digital signatures.

Hengeler Mueller advises Internet and software companies such as freenet.de and Infineon Technologies.

Latham & Watkins LLP advised Airbus Industries on protecting cross-border personal data and represented Philip Morris on data privacy and IT matters. Other clients include Sun Microsystems and Mastercard. Partners Ulrich Wuermeling in Frankfurt and Ulrich Börger in Hamburg have excellent reputations.

SHS Schreiber Hahn Schmidt's Klaus Sommerlad has an excellent reputation for outsourcing advice.

Taylor Wessing is recommended for licensing and distribution, systems implementation and IT outsourcing advice. In 2002, the practice advised Buch.de, the Internet bookseller, on the acquisition of Bertelsmann-owned BOL shops in Germany, Austria and Switzerland. Hamburg partner Jörg Wimmers heads a team of 31 lawyers across Germany.

White & Case acted for Gontard & Metallbank AG on installation of an IT system, and represented Comparex on court proceedings in relation to the defective maintenance of a main server. Martin Munz and Norbert Wimmer have excellent reputations.

Niche firm **Witte** in Munich advises medium and small-sized IT clients on a wide range of IT contracts, outsourcing, e-commerce, data protection and computer law. Name partner Andreas Witte is recommended.

Allen & Overy advised Swisscom on the acquisition of WLAN AG, and represented Oracle on software licensing agreements in Germany.

Brehm & v. Moers advised Internet providers and suppliers on data protection and software issues, and acted for Internet radio stations, carriers and production companies on generating and transmitting mobile content. The practice also advised on cryptology and concept developments such as setting up satellite-connected content terminals. Practice head Benedikt Wemmer in the

INFORMATION TECHNOLOGY

FRESHFIELDS BRUCKHAUS DERINGER ✪
SSW SCHNEIDER SCHIFFER WEIHERMÜLLER

Baker & McKenzie ✪
Bartsch und Partner GbR
CMS Hasche Sigle ✪
Clifford Chance
Linklaters Oppenhoff & Rädler ✪
Lovells ✪
Nörr Stiefenhofer Lutz ✪
Willkie Farr & Gallagher LLP ✪

Beiten Burkhardt Rechtsanwaltsgesellschaft mbH ✪
Gleiss Lutz ✪
Hengeler Mueller ✪
Latham & Watkins LLP ✪
SHS Schreiber Hahn Schmidt
Taylor Wessing ✪
White & Case
Witte

Allen & Overy ✪
Brehm & v. Moers
Godefroid & Pielorz
Graf von Westphalen Bappert & Modest ✪
Haver & Mailänder
Heuking Kühn Lüer Wojtek ✪
Heussen Rechtsanwaltsgesellschaft mbH ✪
Jones Day
McDermott, Will & Emery ✪
Norton Rose Vieregge
Oppenländer Rechtsanwälte
PPR & Partner ✪
Rödl & Partner GbR
Schwarz Kelwing Wicke Westpfahl ✪
Schweizer, Kanzlei, Prof
Wilmer Cutler Pickering LLP ✪

Firms are listed A-Z in tiers which are ranked in order of priority
✪ Indicates firm displays contact details at the end of this chapter.

Berlin office, as well as Guido Hettinger in Frankfurt and Dirk Scheumann in Munich are recommended.

Godefroid & Pielorz in Düsseldorf is a small but respected firm which advises software companies and banks on IT matters.

Graf von Westphalen Bappert & Modest acted for GE Medical Systems Information Technologies in relation to distribution and service agreements for medical software and IT systems, and advised a consortium of leading drinks manufacturers on IT outsourcing. Klaus Brisch in Cologne and Werner Bachmann in Freiburg head a team of eight lawyers.

Haver & Mailänder's Stuttgart office offers specialist advice in e-banking, Internet law and B2B platforms.

Heuking Kühn Lüer Wojtek provides ongoing advice to a major online service provider. Ralf Wojtek and Dr Søren Pietzcker are recommended.

Jones Day's Dr Hans-Werner Moritz in Munich has an excellent reputation for IT advice; he previously worked in-house at IBM.

McDermott, Will & Emery advises equipment manufacturers, fibre optics providers and satellite owners from its offices in Düsseldorf and Munich.

Norton Rose Vieregge advised Deutsche Post Euro Express on structuring IT purchase agreements and represented Detecon, the consultancy firm, on software development. Joint heads of department Dr Alexander von Bossel and Dr Robert Strasser head a team of six partners and 20 associates.

Oppenländer Rechtsanwälte advises on licensing agreements, website design and domain issues. Dr. Markus Köhler is an authority on Internet law.

PPR & Partner advised webMethods, the US software producer, on licence agreements under German law. The firm also advises on data protection and technology transfer agreements.

Rödl & Partner GbR advises several e-commerce, Internet and multimedia companies.

Schwarz Kelwing Wicke Westpfahl advised on several domain name disputes for Internet clients. Infineon is a key client. The practice also advises several major US clients.

Kanzlei Prof Schweizer advises e-commerce, software and market research institute clients.

Wilmer Cutler Pickering LLP advises major Internet and software clients. The Berlin office works closely with the firm's Brussels and Washington DC offices.

INSOLVENCY

Hess Wienberg Wilhelm has an outstanding reputation for insolvency advice from its head office in Mainz, with excellent support from 16 offices across Germany. Name partner Dr Harald Hess is well known.

Kübler offers wide-ranging insolvency expertise, including advisory, receivership and insolvency issues. The Cologne head office works closely with a network of 14 German offices, in addition to an office in Wroclaw, Poland. Name partner Bruno Kübler is a respected practitioner.

At **Schultze & Braun**, Dr Eberhard Braun in the firm's Achern head office heads a team of 22 partners which works closely with its extensive offices across Germany. The multi-disciplinary team includes lawyers, tax advisers and auditors, and offers complementary expertise in employment and commercial law. Dr Edgar Grönda is also well known.

Wellensiek Grub & Partner's 14-lawyer office in Heidelberg offers expertise in insolvency and receivership, with support from a network of ten offices in Germany. Jobst Wellensiek and Volker Grub are recommended.

Forty-six-lawyer **Brinkmann & Partner** advises on a wide range of receivership work from its 12 offices across Germany. Name partner Berthold Brinkmann in the Hamburg office and Carlos Mack in Munich are recommended. The firm opened new offices in Leipzig and Suttgart, a move that boosted its profile across the geographical breadth of Germany. Highlights include advising on the insolvency of Behnke, the electronics company, as well as BkmU Bank AG, a major Berlin-based private bank. Manuel Sack in Hanover also advised on major insolvencies such as Kinopolis München GmbH.

Görg Rechtsanwälte advises on heavyweight insolvency restructurings and reorganisations from its Berlin, Cologne, Essen and Frankfurt offices. Name partner Dr Klaus Hubert Görg is well known. The firm has been part of the *DLA Group* internationally since 2001.

At **Hermann** a team of lawyers, tax accountants and auditors advises on a wide range of insolvency proceedings. The firm operates from five offices in Germany, including Frankfurt, Berlin and Leipzig. Name partner Ottmar Hermann is recommended.

Leonhardt & Partner, based in Berlin, advises on major insolvency proceedings and receivership work. Peter Leonhardt heads the practice.

Tiefenbacher's Thomas Kohl in Heidelberg heads a respected niche practice. In addition to its Heidelberg office, the firm operates out of Stuttgart, Munich, and the eastern German cities of Dresden, Chemnitz, Erfurt and Magdeburg.

White & Case advised Premiere Fernsehen on proceedings against the former Kirch Group. Other clients include major financial institutions, telecoms companies and media companies. Well-known, Hamburg-based partner Dr Klaus Pannen is respected for broad-ranging legal knowledge, combined with 'an appreciation of the overall economic aspects of transactions' and an approach which is 'down-to-earth' and 'not overly scientific'. Sven-Holger Undritz is also recommended.

Clifford Chance's Frankfurt and Berlin offices are particularly active. The firm works closely with its international network of offices.

INSOLVENCY

HESS WIENBERG WILHELM
KÜBLER
SCHULTZE & BRAUN ✪
WELLENSIEK GRUB & PARTNER

Brinkmann & Partner
GÖRG Rechtsanwälte ✪
Hermann
Leonhardt & Partner
Tiefenbacher
White & Case

Clifford Chance
Gleiss Lutz ✪
Heuking Kühn Lüer Wojtek ✪
Jaffé und Kollegen Rechtsanwälte/Insolvenzverwalter
Metzeler, van Betteray, Buchalik
Piepenburg & Gerling Rechtsanwälte
Weiland & Partner, Dr

Amend & Collegen
Andres (Dr) & Schneider
CMS Hasche Sigle ✪
Dithmar & Westhelle Assenmacher & Zwingmann
Feser & Spliedt
Freshfields Bruckhaus Deringer ✪
Hengeler Mueller ✪
Johlke, Niethammer & Partner
Kebekus & Zimmermann
Lieser, Rombach & Kollegen
Linklaters Oppenhoff & Rädler ✪
Lovells ✪
Nörr Stiefenhofer Lutz ✪
Rödl & Partner

Firms are listed A-Z in tiers which are ranked in order of priority
✪ Indicates firm displays contact details at the end of this chapter.

Gleiss Lutz advises banks and shareholders. The firm works closely with **Herbert Smith** internationally.

Heuking Kühn Lüer Wojtek advises on major recoveries and receiverships. Hans-Jochem Lüer, Peter Fissenewert and Achim Freiherr von Griessenbeck, based in Cologne, Berlin and Chemnitz respectively, are particularly active.

Jaffé und Kollegen Rechtsanwälte/Insolvenzverwalter is a highly respected niche insolvency practice. Name partner Michael Jaffé in the Munich head office overseas a team of 12 lawyers based across Germany in Frankfurt, Nürnberg, Erfurt and Münster. Four of the firm's lawyers are insolvency receivers. Highlights in the past year include ongoing advice in the Kirch Media insolvency.

Metzeler, van Betteray, Buchalik's Wolfgang van Betteray heads a practice which is well known for its expertise in heavyweight insolvencies, particularly in the media sector.

Piepenburg & Gerling Rechtsanwälte, based in Düsseldorf, is a highly respected five-lawyer insolvency practice. Horst Piepenburg and Klaus Gerling are well known.

At **Dr Weiland & Partner** Gerd Weiland is a well-known receiver. A team of around 120 lawyers, tax advisers and accountants are based in the Hamburg head office, Berlin and Paris.

Amend & Collegen's Angelika Amend advises on major insolvencies. In 2003, the firm advised on insolvencies of media, construction and fashion companies in the in Frankfurt area.

Dr Andres & Schneider is a niche firm based in Düsseldorf, with additional offices in Hagen, Jena, Leipzig and Halle. Name partner Winfred Andres is recommended.

CMS Hasche Sigle in Leipzig advises on small and medium-sized insolvencies.

Dithmar & Westhelle Assenmacher & Zwingmann advises on tax and business issues from its offices in Kassel and Erfurt.

Feser & Spliedt has expertise in insolvencies in the building, construction and social service sectors. Dr Jürgen Spliedt and Udo Feser are recommended.

Freshfields Bruckhaus Deringer's network of German offices advised several financial institutions and property companies in relation to insolvency proceedings. The practice works closely with its UK and US offices on international transactions.

Hengeler Mueller advises a wide range of corporate clients and shareholders on restructurings and acquisitions out of insolvencies. Highlights include advice to Alvarez & Marsal on reorganisation matters. Dr Reinhold Ernst in Düsseldorf is building a strong reputation.

Johlke, Niethammer & Partner is recommended for its experience in northern Germany. From its offices in Hamburg, Kiel and Schwerin, a team which includes well-known partner Horst Johlke is especially recommended for its role acting as receiver.

Niche firm **Kebekus & Zimmermann** advises on insolvencies from its Düsseldorf office. Name partner Frank Kebekus is recommended.

Lieser, Rombach & Kollegen's name partner Jens Lieser heads a practice with more than 35 years' experience. In addition to its main Koblenz office, the firm also has an office in Erfurt.

Nörr Stiefenhofer Lutz advises companies and creditors. Highlights include advising Herlitz-Consortial Banks on insolvency proceedings. Partners Dr Thomas Hoffmann in Berlin and Dr Christoph Schotte in Munich have strong practices.

Rödl & Partner is recommended for its expertise in complex insolvencies involving groups of companies. The firm has particular knowledge of tax law.

MARITIME AND SHIPPING

CMS Hasche Sigle is recommended for extensive experience of dry and wet shipping, as well as ship finance. Clients include shipping companies, shipyards, trading companies and financial institutions. The firm advised two shipowners in relation to the *Tricolor* casualty in the English Channel and acted for a Maltese shipbroker on a dispute in relation to a broker's commission. Hamburg-based practice head Dr Volker Looks and Dr Dieter Rabe are renowned practitioners.

Hamburg-based **Dabelstein & Passehl** advises a wide range of clients from the shipping industry, including transport companies, ship operators, ship building suppliers, banks and port authorities. Dr Dieter Schwampe, Dr Thomas Brüggemann and Dr Jan Dreyer are well known members of a team of seven lawyers. The firm has a particularly strong client base in Bremen.

Lebuhn & Puchta advises on marine insurance, hull claims, charter parties, collisions, salvage claims and ship financing. A team of eight shipping lawyers includes Dr Christian Breitzke, Dr Johannes Trost and Dr Ulrich Stahl; Dr Heinrich-Werner Goltz has complementary expertise in both corporate and shipping law.

Dr Schackow & Partner advises shipping, insurance and financial sector clients on shipping and transport law from its offices in Hamburg, Bremen and Rostock. Hamburg partner Dr Julius Drumm is recommended. Dr Hans-Georg Friedrichs, based in Bremen, has a good name for employment law advice to shipping clients.

At **Ahlers & Vogel**, a team of ten lawyers based in Hamburg and Bremen advises German and international shipyards, shipowners, charterers and banks on dry and wet shipping and shipping finance. Prof Dr Rolf Herber and Dr Ronald Wöhrn in Hamburg and Dr Wolfgang Dierks in Bremen are recommended.

Blaum Dettmers Rabstein is especially recommended for advice to cargo owners; other clients include several major German and British insurance companies. Dr Joachim Bartels and Claus Holzhüter in Bremen are recommended.

Ince & Co opened a Hamburg office in 2001, which works closely with the firm's renowned London office. Axel Salander and Dr Detlef Zschoche are recommended. Dr Jan Hungar was promoted to partner in 2003.

Remé Rechtsanwälte, located in Hamburg, advises ship companies, brokers and average adjusters. The practice has strong links in Scandinavia and the Baltic States. Name partner Thomas Remé and Hartmut von Brevern are recommended.

Segelken & Suchopar's Hans-Helmut Segelken heads a team of 11 lawyers in Hamburg which is well known for its dry shipping expertise. Clients include several major insurance companies.

Taylor Wessing is recommended for dry, wet and ship finance expertise. Highlights include advising Olympic Cruise Lines on a €150m arbitration and representing Blohm + Voss on purchasing fast cruising vessels. Department head Dr Christoph Hasche, Dr Klaus Kostka and of-counsel Dr Johannes Trapp are well known.

MARITIME AND SHIPPING

CMS HASCHE SIGLE ✪
DABELSTEIN & PASSEHL ✪
LEBUHN & PUCHTA
SCHACKOW & PARTNER, (DR)

Ahlers & Vogel
Blaum Dettmers Rabstein
Ince & Co ✪
Remé Rechtsanwälte
Segelken & Suchopar
Taylor Wessing ✪

Cyrus Makowski
Dirksen & Schwadtke
Ehlermann (Dr) & Jeschonnek
Esche Schümann Commichau
Heuking Kühn Lüer Wojtek ✪
Kretschmar von Teuffel Leverkus

Bollmann & Partner GbR ✪
Johansson Rechtsanwälte – Notare
Lauprecht Rechtsanwälte Notare

Firms are listed A-Z in tiers which are ranked in order of priority
✪ Indicates firm displays contact details at the end of this chapter.

At **Cyrus Makowski** a team of eight lawyers in Hamburg advises shipping and transportation clients. Name partner Dr Joachim Cyrus is recommended; Dr Arnt Vespermann is also well known.

Niche firm **Dirksen & Schwadtke**, based in Hamburg, is a well-regarded shipping specialist firm. Name partners Klaus Dirksen and Hans-Joachim Schwadtke are respected practitioners.

Tweleve-lawyer Hamburg firm **Dr Ehlermann & Jeschonnek**, headed by partners Dr Peter Ehlermann and Hans Jeschonnek, is a highly recommended shipping practice.

Esche Schümann Commichau, one of Hamburg's largest firms, employs lawyers, tax advisers and accountants. Dr Joachim Umlauf advises on commercial, insurance and ship finance transactions for clients in the shipping industry.

Heuking Kühn Lüer Wojtek advises insurance companies, shipping companies and container links on dry and wet shipping cases. Practice head Ulrich Wittkopp in Hamburg is recommended.

Kretschmar von Teuffel Leverkus advises on registration, shipbuilding contracts for international shipping companies, ship builders and dockyards. Name partner Dr Nikolai von Teuffel is an experienced practitioner.

Hamburg-based **Bollmann & Partner GbR** also has offices in Copenhagen and St Petersburg. The firm advises German, European and Chinese clients.

Johansson Rechtsanwälte – Notare, located in Kiel, advises clients from Germany, Scandinavia and the Baltic States on maritime law.

MEDIA, ENTERTAINMENT AND PRESS

Brehm & V. Moers advised on major M&A transactions for TV station and news agency clients. Other clients include film companies and Internet radio stations. Wolfgang Brehm and Dr Butz Peters in the Berlin office are recommended. The firm is also known for its film finance expertise; the practice received a boost when Dirk Poppendieck, previously an in-house lawyer at Constantin Film AG, joined the firm in 2003.

Nörr Stiefenhofer Lutz's 18-lawyer department advises a broad range of music, sports, radio and film clients. Highlights include conducting licence proceedings for sonnenklar TV. Other clients include Sony, Warner Brothers and Disney.

Schwarz Kelwing Wicke Westpfahl advises publishing, film, TV and new media clients. The firm's Munich office is particularly active; Prof Dr Mathias Schwarz is highly recommended.

MEDIA, ENTERTAINMENT AND PRESS

BREHM & V. MOERS
NÖRR STIEFENHOFER LUTZ ✪
SCHWARZ KELWING WICKE WESTPFAHL ✪

Hertin Anwaltssozietät
Kornmeier Kollegen Rechtsanwälte
Lichte Rechtsanwälte
Unverzagt – von Have

Clifford Chance
Freshfields Bruckhaus Deringer ✪
Hogan & Hartson Raue L.L.P. ✪
Latham & Watkins LLP ✪
Linklaters Oppenhoff & Rädler ✪
Norton Rose Vieregge

Beiten Burkhardt Rechtsanwaltsgesellschaft mbH ✪
Damm & Mann
Fromm · Maurer
Frömming & Partner
Gleiss Lutz ✪
GÖRG Rechtsanwälte ✪
Graf von Westphalen Bappert & Modest ✪
Heuking Kühn Lüer Wojtek ✪
Heussen Rechtsanwaltsgesellschaft mbH ✪
Kamin & Wilke
Lausen Rechtsanwälte
Lovells ✪
McDermott, Will & Emery ✪
Rittershaus ✪
Sasse & Partner
Scheuermann Westerhoff Strittmatter
Senfft, Kersten, Voss-Andreae & Schwenn
Taylor Wessing ✪
Thümmel, Schütze & Partner
White & Case

Firms are listed A-Z in tiers which are ranked in order of priority
✪ Indicates firm displays contact details at the end of this chapter.

At **Hertin Anwaltssozietät** Prof Dr Paul Hertin heads a niche practice which advises well-known artists, musicians, sporting personalities and politicians.

Kornmeier Kollegen Rechtsanwälte's seven-lawyer team in Berlin, Frankfurt and Cologne advises clients in the film, television, music and multimedia sectors. Name partner Dr Udo Kornmeier is recommended.

Lichte Rechtsanwälte name partner Walter Lichte in Hamburg advises major artists, musicians and producers on contracts for labels, concert tours, videos and films.

Unverzagt – von Have, based in Hamburg and Berlin, advises on media, entertainment and creative arts projects. Name partners Alexander Unverzagt and Harro von Have are respected practitioners.

Clifford Chance advises a wide range of media, film and TV clients, working closely with its network of international offices.

Freshfields Bruckhaus Deringer offers a wide range of regulatory, competition and financing expertise (including film financing). The practice advises media clients such as Bertelsmann, EM.TV & Merchandising, Gruner + Jahr, Sony Pictures Entertainment and WPP. Other clients come from the finance sector, such as Goldman Sachs Capital Partners and Permira. Transaction highlights include advice to Saban Capital Group on the acquisition of Europe's largest film library from the Kirch Group.

Hogan & Hartson Raue L.L.P. advised Saban Capital Group on the acquisition of a majority stake in ProSieben Sat.1 Media AG, and represented NewsCorp in relation to the sublicensing of UEFA Champion's League. Christoph Wagner is recommended.

Latham & Watkins LLP advised key client Stage Holding on theatre rights in relation to musicals such as *Lion King* and *Mamma Mia*.

Linklaters Oppenhoff & Rädler advises film studios, TV and music companies. Highlights include advice to several Hollywood film studios on film financing ventures. Viacom is a key client. Gert Dittert in Cologne is recommended.

Norton Rose Vieregge advises TV companies, publishing houses and media agencies. The firm advised on licence agreements for major TV game shows.

Niche Hamburg firm **Damm & Mann** represents TV, newspaper, publishing and media companies. Clients include one of the world's largest online service providers. Dr Roger Mann heads a team of four lawyers.

Graf von Westphalen Bappert & Modest advised RTL Television on 45 cases involving press law disputes in 2002. Other clients are film, television and publishing houses. Dr Wolfgang Schmid and Prof Dr Elmar Schuhmacher are recommended.

Heuking Kühn Lüer Wojtek advises CNN, Turner Broadcasting, AOL, Discovery Channel Group and major publishers. Rudolf du Mesnil in Frankfurt and Michael Schmittmann in Düsseldorf are recommended. Peter Fissenewert also acts for several high-profile celebrities on their dealings with the German press.

Lausen Rechtsanwälte's Dr Matthias Lausen heads a practice which advises German and US publishers, film production companies and broadcasting stations.

Lovells' Hamburg office advises a wide range of media clients. Heinrich Bauer Verlagsgruppe is a key client.

White & Case advises cable and TV clients from its Hamburg and Frankfurt offices. Martin Munz and Norbert Wimmer are recommended.

MERGERS AND ACQUISITIONS

Freshfields Bruckhaus Deringer battles it out for the top spot with **Hengeler Mueller**, but profits from its international coverage. Clients acknowledge the huge local and international resources of the firm as well as the array of experienced M&A partners. Christian Wilde, Axel Epe and Andreas Fabritius have taken the bulk of the plaudits in recent years, with a string of complex and high-value transactions. Despite the firm's international orientation, it boasts a large market share in Mittelstand transactions.

Hengeler Mueller continues to outpace its rivals on the domestic front with its position as Germany's leading independent firm, and clients consistently highlight the sheer intelligence of the partners. It advises on most of the high-profile and high-value transactions. With strong corporate practices in Frankfurt and Düsseldorf, the firm handles a multitude of international transactions as well as those driven by its industrial clients from the Ruhr. The firm also derives a multitude of cross-border deals through its strong connections to the leading firms in the world's largest economies, including the UK's **Slaughter and May** and New York firm **Davis Polk & Wardwell**. Michael Hoffmann-Becking and Max Schiessl are outstanding transactional lawyers. Oleg de Lousannoff advises a multitude of investment banks, dispensing the popular myth that the firm is only a corporate adviser.

With Georg Maier-Reimer's fabulous position in the M&A market, 'a real star of M&A' according to one client, **Linklaters Oppenhoff & Rädler** is able to sell its global transactional brand to good effect in Germany. The team is less experienced than its top-tier rivals, but its market share suggests it punches above its weight. Clients acknowledge its commercial style. 'You get a more efficient service and better transaction management,' one said. Michael Lappe and Ulrich Wolff are commended by banking clients. 'They're hands on, effective and are creative lawyers that can handle difficult situations,' according to one. Corporate clients also praise Stephan König.

With an excellent team, including Georg Thoma and Jochem Reichelt, **Shearman &**

Sterling LLP has made the best of its historic ties to Goldman Sachs and has subsequently created an outstanding reputation for M&A in Germany. The firm has increased its market share exponentially over the last ten years in high-value deals. Clients highlight the firm's documentation ability and willingness to 'get the deal done'.

Clifford Chance developed its M&A practice through its links to Europe's leading investment banks. Of late it has a developed a notable track record in pharmaceutical and hospital M&A. Arndt Stengel and Hans-Rolf Goebel continue to lead from the front and clients such as Interbrew, Coca-Cola and Deutsche Telekom outline the firm's strong brand.

Gleiss Lutz's growing reputation in M&A was evidenced by its mandate to advise Procter & Gamble on the €4.55bn acquisition of Wella. Stephanie Beinert, Gerhard Wirth and Michael Arnold were lead partners. The firm is also successful in the mid-cap market with eminent connections to traditional German industries. Clients acknowledge its ability on both 'mid-cap and elephant' transactions. 'They are very flexible,' one said. Gerhard Wegen is widely praised.

Allen & Overy has made rapid inroads into the German M&A market, through strong ties to financial and reinsurance institutions. According to the league tables, the firm is now consistently operating in the upper echelons of the German M&A rankings. Advice to Wella in its €4.55 acquisition by Procter & Gamble marks it out as the new major player on the market. Hartmut Krause has wide-ranging M&A experience, while Mark Hoenike is an acknowledged telecoms industry expert. Reinhard Hermes focuses on more traditional industries, such as car component manufacturers.

Baker & McKenzie is strong in chemical, pharmaceutical and electronics industry M&A. The firm relies on its corporate client base rather than investment banks for instructions. Clients include Degussa, mg Technologies and Clariant. Andreas Hoffmann has close connections with Siemens in Munich and advised it on its €50m takeover of Cycos. Matthias Jaletske juggles his equally strong M&A and private equity practice.

Haarmann Hemmelrath advised the three regional utilities Elektrizitätswerk Minden-Ravensberg, PESAG Aktiengesellschaft and Elektrizitätswerk Wesertal on their merger to form E.on Westfalen Weser outlining its regional and energy reputation. Heinrich Rodewig, Mirko Sickinger and Christoph Binge are highly recommended. The seasoned Detlef Olufs has excellent corporate contacts around Germany.

2003 was a year when **Lovells** made a significant impact in M&A. It advised regular client DZ Bank on its €447m acquisition of the consumer credit baking unit, Norisbank. Katrin Solmecke led the team. The firm has also developed its investment banking client portfolio and now receives transactional instructions from Morgan Stanley, NM Rothschild, JPMorganChase and CSFB. Oliver Felsenstein is gaining considerable market recognition.

Nörr Stiefenhofer Lutz boasts an acquisitive client base particularly in the Bavarian region, but its strong Central and Eastern European network provides a healthy flow of quality instructions and puts the firm in a solid position for EU expansion in 2004. Thomas Schulz is an excellent M&A lawyer.

White & Case has gained considerable experience of transactions within restructurings and insolvency proceedings of late. Andreas Stilken, Joerg Schmeding and Frank Evers are key partners. The firm outlined its German strength by advising Dräger Medical AG & Co on its €1.1bn joint venture with Siemens Medical Solutions.

Despite all the departures and having severed its links to KPMG, **Beiten Burkhardt Rechtsanwaltsgesellschaft mbH** still boasts rainmakers of real calibre in Gerhard Beiten (now of-counsel), Jürgen Burkhardt and Jack Schiffer, though all are well over 50. The firm needs to establish a younger generation of high-profile individuals to ensure its continued success.

CMS Hasche Sigle makes much of its excellent Mittelstand business, but the firm is no stranger to high-value and complex instructions. It advised Deutsche Shell on the €3bn disposal of its share in Ruhrgas to E.on. The firm also represented British Petroleum on a number of high-value transactions.

Cleary Gottlieb Steen & Hamilton has less of a profile in M&A than its excellent capital markets practice, but the arrival of the highly respected Klaus Riehmer from **Haarmann Hemmelrath** in December 2003 was a significant boost. Riehmer previously acted for Vodafone in its merger with Mannesmann. Stephan Barthelmess has a considerable track record in joint ventures and Thomas Buhl and Christof von Dryander are also gaining recognition for public M&A. The firm's emergence in this sector was evidenced in 2003 by advising Siemens on its €1.1bn acquisition of Alstom's industrial turbine unit.

Hölters & Elsing is a small firm with a massive reputation in cross-border M&A, particularly with the US. Siegfried Elsing is a member of the New York Bar and completed a stint as an attorney in New York. As a result the firm has excellent relations with mid-sized US law firms. Wolfgang Hölters is also a major name in M&A, while Wilhelm Nolting-Hauff is the young, up-and-coming star.

Jones Day has a credible M&A practice, most notably in the mid-cap market and fully deserves its climb up the rankings. Much credit goes to Jurgen Reemers who advised La Poste on a series of acquisitions that resulted in it gaining an 85% share in the German parcel service, Deutsche Paket Dienst. Karl Herold adds further gravitas to the team.

Latham & Watkins LLP continues to enhance its M&A practice with the hire of Hans-Jürgen Lütt from **Luther Menold Rechtsanwaltsgesellschaft mbH** in 2003. Before joining the firm, he led the team advising on the TeleColumbus acquisition by leveraged buy-out firm BC Partners. The Hamburg office has a strong corporate reputation and handles numerous transactions for industrial clients and Mittelstand companies. Hamburg partner Christoph von Teichman also has a fabulous reputation.

Norton Rose Vieregge is making excellent progress, particularly in the mid-cap market. Clients commend Erich Michel. 'He has expertise, he's well connected and experienced,' one acknowledged. His role as adviser to the government on Frankfurt

MERGERS AND ACQUISITIONS

FRESHFIELDS BRUCKHAUS DERINGER ✪
HENGELER MUELLER ✪
LINKLATERS OPPENHOFF & RÄDLER ✪
SHEARMAN & STERLING LLP

Clifford Chance
Gleiss Lutz ✪

Allen & Overy ✪
Baker & McKenzie ✪
Haarmann Hemmelrath ✪
Lovells ✪
Nörr Stiefenhofer Lutz ✪
White & Case

Beiten Burkhardt Rechtsanwaltsgesellschaft mbH ✪
CMS Hasche Sigle ✪
Cleary Gottlieb Steen & Hamilton ✪
Hölters & Elsing ✪
Jones Day
Latham & Watkins LLP ✪
Norton Rose Vieregge
P+P Pöllath + Partners ✪
Sullivan & Cromwell LLP
Taylor Wessing ✪
Weil, Gotshal & Manges LLP ✪

Bird & Bird ✪
Brödermann & Jahn
GSK Gassner Stockmann & Kollegen ✪
Gibson, Dunn & Crutcher LLP
Heuking Kühn Lüer Wojtek ✪
Hogan & Hartson Raue L.L.P. ✪
Huth Dietrich Hahn ✪
Löhde Leo Schmidt-Hollburg & Witte
Luther Menold Rechtsanwaltsgesellschaft mbH ✪
Mayer, Brown, Rowe & Maw LLP ✪
McDermott, Will & Emery ✪
Rittstieg Rechtsanwälte
SJ Berwin Knopf Tulloch Steininger ✪
Simmons & Simmons ✪
Velten Franz Jakoby
Wilmer Cutler Pickering LLP ✪

Firms are listed A-Z in tiers which are ranked in order of priority
✪ Indicates firm displays contact details at the end of this chapter.

Airport's IPO won him a lot of credibility and has earned him instructions in the M&A arena. Cologne partners Klaus Jäger, Ralph Drouven and Katharina Specht-Jonen are regular advisers of Mittelstand companies.

P+P Pöllath + Partners is a highly recommended M&A and private equity boutique. Reinhard Pöllath is a well-known adviser of senior executives and boardrooms.

Sullivan & Cromwell LLP's transactional record in Germany is more than impressive. Its sustained activity during the M&A slump outlines it as one of the leading US firms in Germany in this area. In January 2003, it represented the financial adviser to American Water Works on its $4.6bn acquisition by RWE Aktiengesellschaft AG.

Taylor Wessing handles a multitude of mid-cap M&A deals, but is no stranger to high-value transactions. The firm advised Aker Yards As on its acquisition of 85% of the shares owned by Kvaerner Warnow Werft GmbH in Rostock-Warnemünde. Bernhard Kloft, Gustav Lange, Peter Hellich and Friedhold Andreas have formidable reputations.

Weil, Gotshal & Manges LLP's small M&A practice punches far above its weight thanks largely to the high-profile Gerhard Schmidt. The firm's standing was exemplified by a key instruction from General Electric Company's consumer finance division on the acquisition of Allgemeine Privatkundenbank Aktiengesellschaft (Allbank) from Bankgesellschaft Berlin to form GE Bank.

Bird & Bird's Düsseldorf office boasts real M&A calibre thanks in no small part to the impressive Alexander Schroeder-Frerkes, who has handled a number of major transactions for Lufthansa in recent years.

Brödermann & Jahn is a young and reputable firm best known for energy and media M&A.

GSK Gassner Stockmann & Kollegen's transactional record is generated by its real estate and banking practice. Recently the firm was involved in the merger of two securities transactions. Andreas Bauer is a recommended transactional and private equity specialist.

Gibson, Dunn & Crutcher LLP's Munich office is an M&A boutique of some calibre. Benno Schwarz, Christoph Hoebbel and Christoph Kuhmann are widely regarded as intelligent and commercially aware lawyers.

Heuking Kühn Lüer Wojtek's kinship to many Mittelstand companies and German business owners enables it to gain roles in some of the nation's major transactions. It advised the family owner of Wella AG in its €6.5bn acquisition by Procter & Gamble. Andreas Urban led the team. It also advised the Royal Dutch Shell Group on the acquisition of RWE/DEA.

Hogan & Hartson Raue L.L.P. is recommended for energy and media M&A. The firm acted for Saban Capital Group in its acquisition of a majority share in ProSieben Sat.1 Media AG.

Hamburg-based firms **Huth Dietrich Hahn** and **Rittstieg Rechtsanwälte** are also active transactional M&A-focused firms.

Löhde Leo Schmidt-Hollburg & Witte is a small spin-off from *Luther & Partner* and has a notable record in both domestic and cross-border M&A.

2003 proved to be a landmark year for **Luther Menold Rechtsanwaltsgesellschaft mbH**. A number of partners left the firm including Klaus von Gierke to **GÖRG Rechtsanwälte**'s new Hamburg office and Hans-Jürgen Lütt to **Latham & Watkins LLP**. The firm's Stuttgart office also split as a result of German rules relating to auditor independence.

Mayer, Brown, Rowe & Maw LLP is another firm with a strong domestic base in Frankfurt and Cologne, alongside its excellent international name, driven largely by the US and London.

McDermott, Will & Emery's Martin Kock is an M&A specialist in the restructuring arena, while Ralf Eckert is well versed in the tax aspects of M&A. Christian von Sydow historically focused his time on venture capital, before concentrating more on capital markets work during the IPO boom and latterly more M&A. It's still early days for this nascent transactional oriented practice, but it has young, astute talent that deserves recognition.

SJ Berwin Knopf Tulloch Steininger has earned recognition beyond its private equity stronghold. Clients acknowledge its ability in mid-cap M&A. 'It provides an alternative to other firms and they do a good job,' one said.

Simmons & Simmons' key partners are MBO and privatisation specialist Franz-Josef Schöne and Stefan Weinheimer, recommended for public and private M&A and joint ventures. Germany managing partner Jane Newman also adds further gravitas.

Velten Franz Jakoby is also recommended for mid-cap M&A. Christian Franz is experienced in domestic and Franco-German transactions.

Wilmer Cutler Pickering LLP is recommended for domestic and US/German transactions.

PRIVATE EQUITY

Clifford Chance has the size and international resources in the private equity field, and Germany department head Christopher Kellet has an excellent reputation. With key international funds such as CVC, KKR and Blackstone in its client portfolio the firm is the choice adviser for the high-value and complex transactions.

Freshfields Bruckhaus Deringer is noted for its private equity expertise, particularly in Munich where the respected international practice co-head Peter Nussbaum is based. Private equity funds such as Apax Partners, Carlyle, Cinven and Soros instruct the firm, but the practice also has a strong track record in acting for vendors. The firm put its international knowledge base to good effect when it advised the consortium of Apax Partners, Providence Equity and Goldman Sachs PIA on its acquisition of six Deutsche Telekom regional cable television networks.

PRIVATE EQUITY

CLIFFORD CHANCE
FRESHFIELDS BRUCKHAUS DERINGER ✪

HENGELER MUELLER ✪
P+P PÖLLATH + PARTNERS ✪

Baker & McKenzie ✪
Linklaters Oppenhoff & Rädler ✪

Allen & Overy ✪
Ashurst ✪
CMS Hasche Sigle ✪
Debevoise & Plimpton LLP ✪
Dechert
Gleiss Lutz ✪
Haarmann Hemmelrath ✪
Latham & Watkins LLP ✪
Lovells ✪
Nörr Stiefenhofer Lutz ✪
SJ Berwin Knopf Tulloch Steininger ✪
Shearman & Sterling LLP
Taylor Wessing ✪
Weil, Gotshal & Manges LLP ✪
White & Case

Firms are listed A-Z in tiers which are ranked in order of priority
✪ Indicates firm displays contact details at the end of this chapter.

Hengeler Mueller is better known for its role on the vendor side, but wins many of the higher-value instructions from private equity funds such as Cinven and EQT. The excellent Max Schiessl is commended for his private equity acumen as well as M&A, while Reinhold Ernst also wins accolades.

P+P Pöllath + Partners has an excellent standing, most notably on the funds side, reflecting the firm's strong tax heritage. Andreas Rodin is a funds guru and Matthias Bruse wins many accolades for his transactional acumen.

Baker & McKenzie's Walter Henle and Matthias Jaletzke are first-rate transactional lawyers, with Christian Brodersen commended for fund structuring work. GE Capital, Barclays Private Equity and Allianz Venture Partners are key clients.

Linklaters Oppenhoff & Rädler's private equity team is based mainly in Frankfurt and Munich. It is making considerable headway under Graham White in London. Wolfgang Krauel heads the German practice from Munich, but Cologne partner Klaus Hoenig also deserves a particular mention. The firm has handled a number of transactions, including LBOs for Barclays Capital, but much of its work is on the financing side.

Allen & Overy's work for Soros Private Equity Partners on its €235m acquisition of the polymer latex business from Degussa and Bayer, marks it out as a serious player in this field. The firm has also handled transactions for Heidelberg Innovations Fonds, CIBC and Investcorp.

Markus Strelow is having considerable success in replicating **Ashurst**'s global private equity reputation in Germany. The firm has handled several transactions for Bain Capital, amongst other multinational funds. Jörg Kirchner is also recommended.

CMS Hasche Sigle's Stefan-Ulrich Müller, Udo Simmat and Martin Bell are recommended. The team boasts a good mix of small to large funds in its client portfolio including 3i, Deutsche Venture Capital and ECM Equity Capital.

Debevoise & Plimpton LLP continues its efforts in Germany, despite the fact that key private equity client Clayton, Dubilier & Rice has withdrawn from the market. Former **Nörr Stiefenhofer Lutz** partner Thomas Schürrle is the firm's most notable specialist.

Dechert has an established name in private equity having acquired **Coudert Brothers LLP**'s Munich office in January 2004. Federico Pappalardo regularly works for 3i.

Gleiss Lutz's transactional name has enabled it to get gain experience in the private equity field. It has struggled to attract the attention of many of the most active private equity funds in Germany, but in 2003 it was appointed by Blackstone Capital Partners on its bid to acquire the outstanding shares of Celanese AG. The potentially huge transaction outlines the firm's emergence in this sector.

Haarmann Hemmelrath has excellent tax expertise in this sector and has targeted the mid-cap market with some success. It acted for Hannover Finanz GmbH and BLB Equity Management GmbH on the LBO/MBO of Metall Technologie. Christoph von Einem and Mirko Sickinger are recommended.

With the private equity giant KKR on its books, **Latham & Watkins LLP** can't fail to feature regularly in the market. Thankfully it has the expertise to match the requirements of its esteemed client.

Lovells profits from its leading reputation in London and with key client Doughty Hanson being so acquisitive in Germany, the team has been kept busy of late. Its purchase of ATU Group was one of the most significant European deals of 2002. In 2003 the firm was involved in four of the seven largest completed private equity transactions. Other European fund clients include 3i and Apax and it also advises numerous smaller and domestic funds. Julie Bradshaw receives numerous commendations.

Nörr Stiefenhofer Lutz's private equity group is led by Thomas Schulz and Georg Schneider. Schulz handles the financing side with Schneider focusing on tax structuring. Since the end of 2000, the firm has made significant progress in this sector with a number of leading international and German private equity houses. On the seller side the firm profits from its connections to IT and media clients. The firm acted for the seller in ATU Group's sale to private equity giant Doughty Hanson (advised by **Lovells**). This was one of the largest European private equity transactions of 2002.

SJ Berwin Knopf Tulloch Steininger is recommended in particular for tax structuring in which it has an enviable record. Nonetheless it is showing the beginnings of a solid transactional practice.

Shearman & Sterling LLP's Thomas König and Harald Selzner are immensely experienced in the private equity field. The firm boasts a number of leading domestic and international private equity funds on its books including Investcorp, Goldman Sachs Capital Partners and IndustriKapital.

Taylor Wessing puts its longstanding Munich presence to good use in the private equity market. The firm has a notable transactional and funds formation practice. Stephan Heinemann is recommended.

Weil, Gotshal & Manges LLP is recommended for its strong European private equity practice, in which the Frankfurt office has played a key role. The firm recently advised Hicks, Muse, Tate & Furst on its bid for the broadband cable business of Deutsche Telekom. The launch of a new Munich office in January 2004 will allow it to exploit the Bavarian region.

White & Case's Frankfurt office is its centre of corporate excellence for the firm and has a solid private equity reputation. Markus Hauptmann and Andreas Stilcken are the key partners for private equity. The firm recently represented the German management of Fitness First and its subsidiary Fitness Company Freizeitanlagen GmbH on its €300m public takeover and MBO by Cinven.

PUBLIC SECTOR

This practice area combines different sectors of public law, environment, energy law and also planning/construction which are strongly interlinked. The latter topics are dealt with in a separate section (see **Real estate and construction**). As commercial law firms typically will have to cover several of these aspects in most cases, the firms' activities are not described separately. The additional tables for environment and energy list those firms with specific expertise.

Clifford Chance has broad-ranging expertise in public law, including environment, energy and planning matters. The practice advised Industriepark Hoechst on polluted sites and soil protection, and represented biogas power plants on waste law and extension of supply agreements. Other clients include major pharmaceutical companies. The firm's Düsseldorf office has a strong focus on energy transactions.

At Stuttgart firm **Dolde & Partner**, name partner Prof Dr Klaus-Peter Dolde heads a team of six lawyers which advises on planning, energy and public procurement, as well as environment and constitutional law. The firm has particular expertise in pollution and recycling matters.

PUBLIC SECTOR

CLIFFORD CHANCE
DOLDE & PARTNER
FRESHFIELDS BRUCKHAUS DERINGER ✪
GLEISS LUTZ ✪
REDEKER SELLNER DAHS & WIDMAIER

Gaßner, Groth, Siederer & Coll
Hengeler Mueller ✪
Lenz and Johlen
Lovells ✪
Nörr Stiefenhofer Lutz ✪
White & Case
Zenk Rechtsanwälte

Allen & Overy ✪
Baker & McKenzie ✪
Baumeister, Rechtsanwälte
CMS Hasche Sigle ✪
Eisenmann Wahle Birk
Hogan & Hartson Raue L.L.P. ✪
Linklaters Oppenhoff & Rädler ✪
Zuck & Quaas

ARCON Rechtsanwälte Schmidt-Sibeth Heisse Weisskopf Kursawe ✪
Ashurst ✪
Baumann Rechtsanwälte
Becker Büttner Held, Rechtsanwälte Wirtschaftsprüfer Steuerberater
Böckmann & Partner GbR, Dr
Bogsch, Jäger, Schwarzer
Caemmerer - Bender - Lenz
Cornelius Bartenbach Haesemann & Partner, member of ius laboris ✪
Graf von Westphalen Bappert & Modest ✪
Günther, Heidel, Wollenteit, Hack
Heuking Kühn Lüer Wojtek ✪
Köhler & Klett, Rechtsanwälte
Latham & Watkins LLP ✪
Loh Von Hülsen Michael Rechtsanwälte
Norton Rose Vieregge
Niedersberg Rechtsanwalt, Dr
Mannheimer Swartling ✪
Schulte-Wissermann (Dr), Kunz Müller und Kollegen
Seufert Rechtsanwälte
Taylor Wessing ✪
Wilmer Cutler Pickering LLP ✪

Firms are listed A-Z in tiers which are ranked in order of priority
✪ Indicates firm displays contact details at the end of this chapter.

Freshfields Bruckhaus Deringer advised the German Federal Ministry for Transport on a toll scheme for lorries, acted for a mining authority on environmental projects in Europe and represented a German city on a leveraged lease of its rail network. A team of 11 partners in Berlin, Düsseldorf, Cologne, Frankfurt and Hamburg have broad expertise in regulatory, environmental and energy issues.

PUBLIC SECTOR: ENERGY

BECKER BÜTTNER HELD, RECHTSANWÄLTE WIRTSCHAFTSPRÜFER STEUERBERATER
CLIFFORD CHANCE
FRESHFIELDS BRUCKHAUS DERINGER ⊙
GLEISS LUTZ ⊙

Allen & Overy ⊙
CMS Hasche Sigle ⊙
Dolde & Partner
Hogan & Hartson Raue L.L.P. ⊙
Linklaters Oppenhoff & Rädler ⊙
Nörr Stiefenhofer Lutz ⊙
White & Case

Baker & McKenzie ⊙
Baumann Rechtsanwälte
Böckmann & Partner GbR, Dr
Eisenmann Wahle Birk
Günther, Heidel, Wollenteit, Hack
Hengeler Mueller ⊙
Heuking Kühn Lüer Wojtek ⊙
Latham & Watkins LLP ⊙
Niedsersberg Rechtsanwalt, Dr
Mannheimer Swartling ⊙

Firms are listed A-Z in tiers which are ranked in order of priority
⊙ Indicates firm displays contact details at the end of this chapter.

PUBLIC SECTOR: ENVIRONMENT

DOLDE & PARTNER
FRESHFIELDS BRUCKHAUS DERINGER ⊙
GAßNER, GROTH, SIEDERER & COLL
GLEISS LUTZ ⊙
REDEKER SELLNER DAHS & WIDMAIER

Baker & McKenzie ⊙
Baumeister, Rechtsanwälte
Clifford Chance
Köhler & Klett, Rechtsanwälte
Lenz and Johlen
Linklaters Oppenhoff & Rädler ⊙
Zenk Rechtsanwälte

ARCON Rechtsanwälte Schmidt-Sibeth Heisse Weisskopf Kursawe ⊙
Bogsch, Jäger, Schwarzer
CMS Hasche Sigle ⊙
Eisenmann Wahle Birk
Graf von Westphalen Bappert & Modest ⊙
Günther, Heidel, Wollenteit, Hack
Hengeler Mueller ⊙
Heuking Kühn Lüer Wojtek ⊙
Norton Rose Vieregge
Taylor Wessing ⊙

Firms are listed A-Z in tiers which are ranked in order of priority
⊙ Indicates firm displays contact details at the end of this chapter.

Gleiss Lutz boasts broad-ranging expertise in environmental, construction, infrastructure and energy matters. Stuttgart-based Prof Dr Christoph Moench has expertise in advice to societies and works councils on energy, environmental and building law. Berlin partner Dr Ralf Thaeter has a focus on energy matters. Dr Olaf Otting in Frankfurt has great experience in PPP transactions. Clients include DaimlerChrysler and IBM.

Redeker Sellner Dahs & Widmaier advises on public procurement, privatisation and regulatory matters, including environmental law; the firm has a good name for pollution expertise. The firm works closely with its newly opened Brussels office.

Gaßner, Groth, Siederer & Coll, with offices in Berlin and Potsdam, advises on building, planning and environmental law. The practice has niche expertise in traffic law and power plants.

Hengeler Mueller is respected for advice both to public sector bodies and corporations. The firm has an exceptional reputation for regulatory advice in Germany and in Brussels. Clients include Hydro Energy Germany.

Cologne firm **Lenz and Johlen** advises on construction, waste disposal and environmental matters. Prof Dr Heribert Johlen heads a team of 13 lawyers.

Lovells offers expertise in energy, pollution, water, sewage and emission control matters to clients from both the public and private sectors.

Nörr Stiefenhofer Lutz advises on privatisation, environmental law, emission control and contamination. The practice advised the State of Berlin on reclaiming subventions from construction companies. Other clients include restaurants and fast food chains, which the firm advised on environmental and waste disposal law.

White & Case has an excellent reputation for advice to governments, financial institutions, airports and transport sector clients. The firm advised KfW on state aid cases and acted for Deutsche Bahn on a major rail project in Berlin. Berlin-based partners Henning Berger and Norbert Wimmer and Hamburg-based partner Kersten Wagner-Cardenal are highly recommended.

Zenk Rechtsanwälte advises on public and environmental law from its Hamburg head office, with additional expertise located in Berlin, Cologne and Brussels. The firm has a special focus on waste management issues.

Allen & Overy advised a client on a dispute in Brussels in relation to waste shipment, and represented a major pharmaceutical company on its waste emissions. Thomas Pschera has a special focus on water, waste and soil protection matters.

Baker & McKenzie is recommended for expertise in environmental and energy law. The practice has a strong reputation for advice on soil and water contamination cases. Highlights include advice to a US corporation in relation to the contamination of soil and ground water. The practice also advised the City of Hamburg on the privatisation of its hospitals and acted for CSC Ploentzke on its bid for the privatisation of Budeswehr IT. Joachim Scherer heads a team of five partners.

Baumeister, Rechtsanwälte is recommended for environmental, waste, water and pollution expertise. The 18-lawyer head office in Münster receives additional support from a smaller Leipzig office.

CMS Hasche Sigle advises on privatisation, reorganisation, planning, construction and environmental law from its Stuttgart and Hamburg offices. The practice advised the Association of Border Shops in Schleswig-Holstein on administrative law disputes, publicity work and lobbying.

Eisenmann Wahle Birk, based in Stuttgart, offers expertise in construction, planning and environmental law. Name partner Hans-Jörg Birk is well known. The firm has an additional office in Dresden.

Hogan & Hartson Raue L.L.P., based in Berlin, has an excellent name for energy-related work in partner Christian von Hammerstein.

Linklaters Oppenhoff & Rädler is recommended for privatisation, energy, planning, rail and roads expertise. The practice advised the State of North Rhine-Westphalia on the construction and operation of a magnetic suspension railway, and represented Bilfinger Berger on a road construction project for expanding existing federal highways. Dr Kai Uwe Pritzsche in Berlin has expertise in energy matters. The Cologne office is also active.

Niche Stuttgart firm **Zuck & Quaas** advises on public transport law, especially aviation matters. Prof Dr Michael Quaas and Dr Holger Zuck are recommended.

REAL ESTATE AND CONSTRUCTION: CONSTRUCTION

Heiermann Franke Knipp is highly experienced in construction work. From its offices in Frankfurt, Munich, Berlin, Essen and Vienna, the firm advises on heavyweight projects such as highways, railways and public infrastructure projects. Clients include architects, engineers and project consultants.

Kapellmann Und Partner is amongst the country's leading construction firms. A team of over 50 lawyers based in offices in Düsseldorf, Berlin, Frankfurt, Mönchengladbach and Munich advises on construction projects across Germany. The firm also has an excellent name for litigation and arbitration work. Prof Dr Klaus Kapellmann is well known.

At **Schilling Dr Marbach Niemöller Dr Griem & Partner**, a team of 20 lawyers comprises a Frankfurt-based niche practice which advises on property, construction and public procurement for a wide range of construction companies and financiers.

CMS Hasche Sigle advised Transrapid in relation to the Bavarian Transrapid project, and acted for TMW Property Funds AG on the creation of an investment fund for institutional investors to

REAL ESTATE AND CONSTRUCTION: CONSTRUCTION

HEIERMANN FRANKE KNIPP
KAPELLMANN UND PARTNER
SCHILLING DR MARBACH NIEMÖLLER DR GRIEM & PARTNER

CMS Hasche Sigle ✪
GSK Gassner Stockmann & Kollegen ✪
Leinemann & Partner
Lovells ✪

ARCON Rechtsanwälte Schmidt-Sibeth Heisse Weisskopf Kursawe ✪
Bornheim, v. Rosenthal & Kollegen
Clifford Chance
Gleiss Lutz ✪
Graf von Westphalen Bappert & Modest ✪
Hecker, Werner, Himmelreich & Nacken
Hölters & Elsing ✪
Koeble, Donus, Fuhrmann, Locher & Partner
Kupferschmid, Englert, Pichl, Grauvogl & Kollegen
Mock Rechtsanwälte
Nörr Stiefenhofer Lutz ✪
O & P Oberthür & Partner ✪
White & Case

Allen & Overy ✪
Hengeler Mueller ✪
Heussen Rechtsanwaltsgesellschaft mbH ✪
KSB INTAX
Latham & Watkins LLP ✪
PPR & Partner ✪
Wagensonner Luhmann Breitfeld Helm

Firms are listed A-Z in tiers which are ranked in order of priority
✪ Indicates firm displays contact details at the end of this chapter.

invest in Asian real estate. The firm's Stuttgart and Berlin offices are particularly well respected.

GSK Gassner Stockmann & Kollegen is building a formidable reputation for its real estate, construction and infrastructure work. The practice reports growth in real estate closed-end and mutual investment fund work. The Munich office is particularly active; the firm opened new offices in Stuttgart and Düsseldorf.

At niche firm **Leinemann & Partner** a team of 22 lawyers in Frankfurt and Berlin advised on the construction of a new Lufthansa HQ at Berlin airport. Other highlights include construction of a railway station and underground tube lines, and PPP projects for universities. Further afield, the firm advised on a motorway project in Romania. Name partner Dr Ralf Leinemann is recommended.

Lovells advised on a wide range of building, infrastructure and industrial plant projects. The firm advised BBI Partner Consortium on contract negotiations for construction of the Berlin-Brandenburg International Airport and represented the University of Dresden on construction of a new €100m university clinic. Dr Roland Bomhard in the Düsseldorf office is recommended. Construction lawyer Dr Olav Wagner was promoted to partner in Berlin.

ARCON Rechtsanwälte Schmidt-Sibeth Heisse Weisskopf Kursawe advised a construction company on the €1.6bn construction of a semiconductor manufacturing plant in Frankfurt. The firm is also experienced in airport, infrastructure and environmentally sensitive projects.

At **Bornheim, v. Rosenthal & Kollegen** a team of 35 lawyers in Berlin, Frankfurt and Düsseldorf offers engineering, development and architecture expertise. The firm has extensive experience in arena and technology park construction. Recent project highlights include representing German and Dutch clients in relation to football stadiums, ice rinks and shopping centres projects.

Clifford Chance is particularly recommended for complex financing advice, including real estate funds, PPP projects and securitisations. Notable transactions include advising Accor on the purchase of around 100 hotels from the Ebertz Group and representing ABN Amro and JPMorgan as arrangers of a €350m pan-European securitisation. Klaus Minuth heads a team of over 60 lawyers.

At **Gleiss Lutz** a team of around 20 lawyers advises on private and public construction projects including urban development, zoning matters and technical planning. The practice also provides advice in relation to unit trusts and investment trusts.

Graf von Westphalen Bappert & Modest acted for a US facility-construction company on a pipeline project in Germany and represented an investor on planning and construction of a commercial property in Hamburg's city centre. The department is also recommended for advice on joint venture constructions and structuring of special purpose vehicles; highlights include advising a UK project developer on a joint venture with a US investor for a logistics project in southern Germany. Ernst-Jürgen Mellin and Dr Peter Decker head a team of 16 lawyers. The firm often works closely with UK firm **Wragge & Co LLP**.

Hecker, Werner, Himmelreich & Nacken is recommended for a broad range of construction expertise, including development, financing, planning, construction and acquisitions. The practice represents two multinational plant constructors. Other clients include engineering and plant companies.

Hölters & Elsing is recommended for extensive experience in complicated transactions, as well as for its involvement in smaller grass-roots projects from its offices in Berlin, Düsseldorf and Frankfurt. The firm advised Deutsche Post World on the sale of the an office building in Frankfurt valued at over €100m, and advised investors on pollution advice in connection with industrial facilities.

REAL ESTATE AND CONSTRUCTION: REAL ESTATE

CLIFFORD CHANCE
FRESHFIELDS BRUCKHAUS DERINGER ✪

CMS Hasche Sigle ✪
White & Case

Baker & McKenzie ✪
Gleiss Lutz ✪
Graf von Westphalen Bappert & Modest ✪
Latham & Watkins LLP ✪
Linklaters Oppenhoff & Rädler ✪
Lovells ✪
Schäfer, Riedl, Viechtl, Weichler, Segbers

GSK Gassner Stockmann & Kollegen ✪
Hölters & Elsing ✪
Mayer, Brown, Rowe & Maw LLP ✪
Taylor Wessing ✪
Wagensonner Luhmann Breitfeld Helm

Allen & Overy ✪
Cornelius Bartenbach Haesemann & Partner, member of ius laboris ✪
Heussen Rechtsanwaltsgesellschaft mbH ✪
KSB INTAX
Norton Rose Vieregge
PPR & Partner ✪

Firms are listed A-Z in tiers which are ranked in order of priority
✪ Indicates firm displays contact details at the end of this chapter.

Reutlingen-based **Koeble, Donus, Fuhrmann, Locher & Partner** is a niche firm of eight lawyers specialising in engineering and architecture law. The firm acts for both public bodies and private investors from Germany, as well as the UK, France, Switzerland and Austria. Name partner Wolfgang Koeble is well known.

Kupferschmid, Englert, Pichl, Grauvogl & Kollegen is recommended for expertise in civil engineering and infrastructure projects such as railway projects. The firm also undertakes construction and property work.

Mock Rechtsanwälte, located in Berlin, boasts an impressive combination of experience in construction, administrative law, finance matters and arbitration. Klaus Mock heads an 11-partner, 11-associate department.

Nörr Stiefenhofer Lutz advised a major construction company on a €286m stadium in Munich and represented a multinational cigarette company on the reconstruction of a plant in Berlin. Other clients include a major US chain of fast food restaurants. A team of 50 lawyers in five German offices also works closely with the firm's network of offices in Eastern Europe.

O & P Oberthür & Partner is especially strong for projects in the northern German cities of Hamburg, Bremen and Kiel. Clients include shopping centres, supermarkets and railway industry clients.

White & Case advised Rezidor, the hospitality management company, on hotel projects in Frankfurt and Berlin, and represented Sireo, a joint venture between Deutsche Telekom, Morgan Stanley and Corpus, on a closed-end fund for institutional investors. Other clients include Bouygues, Nike and Jones Lang La Salle. Hamburg-based partner Jan-Peter Kecker and Berlin-based partner Endrik Lettau head an eight-partner, 18-associate department.

Allen & Overy is especially recommended for real estate finance work, including securitisations, in addition to a range of general real estate and construction advice. Highlights include advising Furukawa on a building scheme in a disused industrial site, advising KPNQwest on site development in Germany and representing Citigroup on a securitisation of Italian commercial and residential mortgage loans.

Baker & McKenzie advised AIG/Lincoln on the acquisition and development of land for use by IBM in Munich. Partner Peter Wessels, located in Berlin, heads a team of 16 fee-earners across the firm's offices in Germany.

Freshfields Bruckhaus Deringer is recommended for expertise in complex national and cross-border transactions, with excellent support from the firm's network of international offices. The firm advised Goldman Sachs on acquiring a €230m portfolio of properties from Deutsche Telekom and represented Degussa on the sale of its properties in Frankfurt. Dr Johannes Conradi, based in Hamburg, is highly recommended.

Gleiss Lutz advised on a wide range of real estate, construction and real estate finance transactions. Highlights include advice on a components factory for New Venture Gear (a joint venture of DaimlerChrysler and General Motors), and representing DG/DZ Bank on the sale of office buildings in Berlin. Berlin-based partner. Dr Johannes Niewerth heads a team of around 40 lawyers.

Latham & Watkins LLP provides advice on office and shopping centre developments. The firm is also active in advising institutional investors on open real estate funds. Notable transactions include advising HPE Group on construction of a major office building in Hamburg. Hamburg partner Jürgen Hübner is particularly active.

Linklaters Oppenhoff & Rädler advised Ciments du Sahel SA in relation to the construction of a new cement plant in Kirène/Senegal and the seizure of a loan by a German bank. The practice also acted for a major European building company on litigation relating to the development of an airport.

Norton Rose Vieregge advised Deka Immobilien Investment on acquiring property valued at €500m in central Frankfurt for a high-rise building development. The practice also acted for several banking clients on lease agreements. Hans-Dieter Schulz-Gebeltzig heads a team of four partners and seven associates.

PPR & Partner, based in Düsseldorf, advised a major US restaurant chain on lease agreements in Germany.

Wagensonner Luhmann Breitfeld Helm advised on multi-million-euro skyscraper projects in Frankfurt and Munich. Helmut Wagensonner in Munich is recommended.

STRUCTURED FINANCE AND SECURITISATION

Hengeler Mueller has a first-rate, asset-backed and synthetic transactions group, thanks in no small part to the market's leading individual, Stefan Krauss. 'The firm has a very good standing in the German market, because they advise from a German law perspective,' one client acknowledged. The firm's chief role in the True Sale Initiative (TSI) for KFW demonstrates its market leading credentials.

Clifford Chance has the leading asset securitisation practice in Germany; the firm is also playing a key role in the TSI Initiative. Michael Weller deserves credit in this respect, and the group is recommended as arrangers' counsel. Kirti Vasu and Peter Scherer are also recommended, with Leonard Cleland impressing many with his technical aptitude.

Linklaters Oppenhoff & Rädler took three leading roles in the True Sale Initiative for KFW. Kurt Dittrich deserves much of the credit and banks commend his ABS expertise. 'He's made it into the circle of advisers in connection with KFW and that is important,' one banker acknowledged. Peter Waltz is another strong securitisation player. The firm advised Commerzbank on a €1bn Mittelstands-ABS-Platform under the bank's Kaiserplatz Programme. Berthold Kusserow is an astute structured finance practitioner.

The loss of Bodo Schaar to **Orrick, Herrington & Sutcliffe**'s London office in 2003 was a blow to **Allen & Overy**, particularly with Ulf Kreppel also departing to **White & Case**. Nevertheless, the firm still boasts structured finance and structured finance expertise, with new partner Matthew Howard and banking partner Peter Stenz. The firm recently worked on two securitisations in the property sector and advised Lehman Brothers and Erste Bank as lead managers on the €220m securitisation of Austrian automobile lease receivables.

Freshfields Bruckhaus Deringer's Stuart Axford followed the development of structured finance and securitisation in the UK before transferring to Frankfurt in 2001. Banks applaud the capital markets and securitisation acumen of Andreas König and Bernhard Kaiser, but also the complement of Thomas Wiesenbart's tax capability in this sector.

Lovells is developing a noteworthy standing in German structured finance. The firm has completed a multitude of synthetic CDOs for Dresdner Kleinwort Benson. It also represented WestLB on a €2bn synthetic securitisation under JPMorgan's Bistro programme. Oliver Kessler is an acknowledged expert in this area and is supported by securitisation specialist Jens Rinze, a recent hire from **Hengeler Mueller**.

Ashurst's Andreas Zahn is emerging on the structured finance scene. The firm is best known for structured notes and asset-backed CDOs, as well as energy derivatives and securitisation.

Baker & McKenzie's Dietmar Helms is recommended, particularly in ABS and syndicated deals.

Cleary Gottlieb Steen & Hamilton acts for Standard & Poor's on all its structured finance transactions. The immensely respected Christof von Dryander and Werner Meier are the firm's most established names in this sector. In December 2002 it took the role as German originator's counsel to Deutsche Bank in the securitisation of bank loans.

Latham & Watkins LLP boasts an emerging structured finance practice under Philipp von Randow, while **Mayer, Brown, Rowe & Maw LLP** has also made headway in this sector, led by securitisation specialists Ralf Hesdahl and Jörg Wulfken.

Simmons & Simmons' Stephen Moller is a solid structured finance lawyer, particularly in the asset-backed arena. The firm boasts a solid influx of CDO work, but is beginning to generate more complex instructions after launching its Frankfurt finance practice in 2002.

White & Case's structured finance and securitisation practice was given a significant boost with the arrival of Ulf Kreppel from **Allen & Overy** in March 2003.

STRUCTURED FINANCE AND SECURITISATION

HENGELER MUELLER ✪

CLIFFORD CHANCE
LINKLATERS OPPENHOFF & RÄDLER ✪

Allen & Overy ✪
Freshfields Bruckhaus Deringer ✪
Lovells ✪

Ashurst ✪
Baker & McKenzie ✪
Cleary Gottlieb Steen & Hamilton ✪
Latham & Watkins LLP ✪
Mayer, Brown, Rowe & Maw LLP ✪
Simmons & Simmons ✪
White & Case

Firms are listed A-Z in tiers which are ranked in order of priority
✪ Indicates firm displays contact details at the end of this chapter.

TAX

With its role as tax advisers to Wella in its acquisition by Procter & Gamble, **Flick Gocke**

TAX

FLICK GOCKE SCHAUMBURG ✪
FRESHFIELDS BRUCKHAUS DERINGER ✪
HAARMANN HEMMELRATH ✪

LINKLATERS OPPENHOFF & RÄDLER ✪

Clifford Chance
Gleiss Lutz ✪
Peters, Schönberger & Partner ✪
Shearman & Sterling LLP

CMS Hasche Sigle ✪
Hengeler Mueller ✪
Lovells ✪
Nörr Stiefenhofer Lutz ✪
P+P Pöllath + Partners ✪
Raupach & Wollert-Elmendorff Rechtsanwaltsgesellschaft mbH
Rödl & Partner GbR

Baker & McKenzie ✪
Graf von Westphalen Bappert & Modest ✪
Streck Mack Schwedhelm
White & Case

Caemmerer – Bender – Lenz
Esche Schümann Commichau
Heuking Kühn Lüer Wojtek ✪
Jones Day
KSB INTAX
Kapp, Ebeling & Partner
McDermott, Will & Emery ✪
Müller-Horn, Püschel & Luther
PNHR Pelka Niemann Hollerbaum Rohde
PPR & Partner ✪
Simmons & Simmons ✪

Firms are listed A-Z in tiers which are ranked in order of priority
✪ *Indicates firm displays contact details at the end of this chapter.*

Schaumburg cemented its position as Germany's leading niche firm in this sector. Christoph Schulte led the team.

Freshfields Bruckhaus Deringer acquired considerable tax expertise through the *Deringer* merger and augmented this with the banking tax expertise brought into the fold by *Freshfields*. The firm advised the bondholders of Apollo Management and Pequot on the acquisition of shares involved in the restructuring of iesy Hessen GmbH & Co. Stephan Eilers co-heads the global practice.

Haarmann Hemmelrath boasts an excellent tax team with expertise in corporate transactions, private equity, restructurings and many other legal disciplines including white-collar crime proceedings. Wilhelm Haarmann personifies the broad strength of the team, but the loss of Eugen Bogenschütz to **Allen & Overy** in October 2002 did not boost the firm's historical prowess.

Linklaters Oppenhoff & Rädler is a well-deserved leading practice thanks in no small part to the reputation of the seasoned Albert Rädler. The firm boasts a significant market share owing to its historical strength long before the **Linklaters** merger. Karl Schäfer heads the group from the Munich office that wins a multitude of accolades for its tax work in the fields of structured finance and restructuring.

Clifford Chance's tax team has broad expertise, but is particularly noted for restructuring-related advice where Detlef Haritz and Manfred Benkert are widely applauded. Patrick Biagosch deserves credit for his tax work in the private equity funds arena.

Gleiss Lutz has an emerging practice with the immensely experienced Wolfgang Blumers and the younger Stefanie Beinert making an impression on the market. Aside from the usual corporate tax structuring expertise, the firm is commended for tax litigation and criminal tax disputes.

Munich-based **Peters, Schönberger & Partner** has a hotbed of tax talent. In Jürgen Peters and Christopher Schönberger, the firm has two of Germany's most experienced and commercially minded tax lawyers. A vast array of talent exists within the rest of the firm where most of the lawyers concentrate much of their time on tax work.

Shearman & Sterling LLP has made the best of its fabulous connections to some of the most active investment banks in Germany. It is in corporate transactions where the firm really adds significant value, with newly arrived partner Gottfried Breuninger and Hanno Berger taking the practice to new levels.

CMS Hasche Sigle launched a discrete tax practice mid-2002. Despite the firm's traditional transaction-based practice, it now delivers a greater proportion of succession structure, restructuring and international tax law advice.

With its immense record in German corporate transactions and its leading structured finance practice, **Hengeler Mueller** has delivered its tax lawyers a multitude of demanding mandates. Blue-chip clients such as Deutsche Bank and Deutsche Telekom are regular clients. Martin Klein, Friedhelm Jacob and Ernst-Thomas Kraft are regularly applauded.

Lovells and **Nörr Stiefenhofer Lutz** both have able tax departments to support their corporate departments. With both firms' growing their finance practices, the tax group is gaining further credibility.

P+P Pöllath + Partners has formidable tax expertise and it comes as no surprise that the firm excels in the private equity sector. Reinhard Pöllath's knowledge of the tax regime in this area is legendary, but the team's general corporate tax strength should not be overlooked.

Raupach & Wollert-Elmendorff Rechtsanwaltsgesellschaft mbH's strong contentious practice is led by the highly respected Arndt Raupach. The firm has taken roles in some of the most important tax cases of recent years.

Rödl & Partner GbR has a similarly strong practice with additional national and international resources.

Baker & McKenzie continues to make progress under the respected Christian Brodersen. With its European resources the firm has won instructions from blue-chip multinationals such as Vivendi and Ingersoll-Rand.

Graf von Westphalen Bappert & Modest merged with the Hamburg-based auditors Busch & Partners at the beginning of 2003, significantly enhancing its MDP oriented tax advisory approach.

Tax litigation and criminal tax disputes boutique **Streck Mack Schwedhelm** remains a serious force in the German market. Michael Streck is a formidable contentious practitioner.

In Gerhard Laule, Günther Kahlert and Andreas Knebel, **White & Case** boasts a number of experienced tax professionals. The team's work is largely transactional oriented.

Caemmerer – Bender – Lenz, **Kapp, Ebeling & Partner**, **Müller-Horn, Püschel & Luther** and **PNHR Pelka Niemann Hollerbaum Rohde** also deserve strong recommendations for tax advice, while Hanover-based **KSB INTAX** boasts considerable tax expertise thanks in no small part to the excellent Christian Knoke.

Esche Schümann Commichau and **PPR & Partner** also offer strong and broad tax practices, though the latter suffered the departure of name partner Heinrich Clev to launch his own practice, **Heinrich Clev Rechtsanwalt & Steuerberater** in July 2003.

Other law firms with significant tax practices include **Heuking Kühn Lüer Wojtek** where three specialist partners (Dieter Bohnert, Wolfram Meven, Gerd Kostrzewa) are recommended and regularly advise on international tax planning, double taxation treaties, domestic tax work and tax litigation; **Jones Day** where Joachim Borggräfe is a seasoned tax specialist with strong connections to Germany's Mittelstand; **McDermott, Will & Emery** where Ralf Eckert is a strong tax lawyer particularly in transactions; and **Simmons & Simmons** which launched its tax practice in January 2003 with the hire of tax partner Hans-Jörg Wittmann.

Others deserving of a mention are **Dr Böckmann & Partner GbR**; **Alpers & Stenger**; **Taylor Wessing**; **Beiten Burkhardt Rechtsanwaltsgesellschaft mbH**; the two Bavarian firms **Honert Funke Maute Neumayer** and **BTU Simon Schneider Göckel**; **Luther Menold Rechtsanwaltsgesellschaft mbH**

TELECOMS

Baker & McKenzie advised E-Plus Mobilfunk on UMTS infrastructure and represented the Federal Ministry of Economics on access to broadband communications networks. Joachim Scherer heads a 12-lawyer practice in Frankfurt recommended for in-depth and longstanding expertise in the telecoms industry, combined with excellent support from its international network of offices.

Freshfields Bruckhaus Deringer advises a broad range of telecoms clients such as ADC Telecommunications, Arcor, Cable & Wireless and France Télécom. Dr Michael Haidinger, Dr Thomas Tschentscher and Dr Raimond Schütz are well known members of a team of 42 partners across Germany. The practice combines regulatory, competition, financing and restructuring expertise.

Eleven-lawyer **Piepenbrock & Schuster** is a highly respected niche firm in Düsseldorf. Clients include Mobilcom, 01051 Telecom and Talkline. Dr Hermann-Josef Piepenbrock and Dr Martin Geppert are well known. The firm also employs an economist and an engineer specialised in telecom matters.

At **Redeker Sellner Dahs & Widmaier**'s Bonn office, Dr Thomas Mayen is renowned for broad-ranging regulatory and administrative expertise in relation to telecoms companies.

Allen & Overy advised Swisscom on a wide range of transactional and regulatory matters. Other clients include FLAG Telecom and KPN. Dr Mark Hoenike is 'hard working' and has 'detailed knowledge of a wide range of telecoms and infrastructure issues'. Dr Helge Schäfer is also recommended.

Clifford Chance advises on administrative and regulatory matters including billing procedures, licences and data protection. Key names include Martin Wissmann and Joachim Schütze in Düsseldorf and Bernd Meyer-Witting in Frankfurt.

Hengeler Mueller's Frankfurt, Düsseldorf and Berlin offices advice clients such as Deutsche Telekom and T-Online on regulatory, transactional and administrative matters. The firm enjoys a successful relationship with **Slaughter and May**. Berlin partner Dr Wolfgang Spoerr is building a strong reputation.

Hogan & Hartson Raue L.L.P. represented Telefonica/Quam on the build-up and roll-out of services in Germany, and advised O2 on telecommunications and regulatory matters. Christoph Wagner and Christian von Hammerstein, based in Berlin, are recommended.

Wilmer Cutler Pickering LLP's six-lawyer team advised Deutsche Telekom on merger control proceedings and represented T-Mobile on regulatory and competition issues.

CMS Hasche Sigle's Dr Jens Neitzel in Munich heads a practice that advised Colt Telecom on its regulatory framework.

Coudert Brothers LLP's Rainer Jacob in Frankfurt advises on regulatory and transactional matters.

Heuking Kühn Lüer Wojtek's Wolfgang von Reinersdorff and Michael Schmittmann, based in Hamburg and Düsseldorf respectively, advise clients such as the German Association of Private CATV Operators and the Deutsche Netzmarketing GmbH.

Roland Bornhofen at **Hölters & Elsing**'s Düsseldorf office advises on telecoms infrastructure, Internet start-ups and regulatory issues.

Linklaters Oppenhoff & Rädler advised a major European telecoms company on a network agreement. Major clients include BT and Alcatel. Dr Christian Hey is recommended.

Lovells' Wolfgang Büchner in Munich heads a practice which advises clients such as T-Online and Motorola on regulatory and transactional work.

McDermott, Will & Emery advised a major US carrier on interconnection arrangements in Europe and represented and international satellite operator on EU sanction matters. Dr Ralf Weisser is well known.

Norton Rose Vieregge's Dr Christian Scherer-Leydecker led a team which advised BerliKomm on a complaint with the European Commission regarding telecommunications fees.

White & Case advised Sonera on German aspects on the merger of Telia and Sonera, and represented O2 on litigation over a distribution contract. Martin Munz and Norbert Wimmer are well known names.

Velten Franz Jakoby advises on a wide range of regulatory, competition and contract law issues for telecoms industry clients including Telefónica Deutschland and TELE2. Peter Rädler is recommended.

Five-partner **Veltins & Wilkinson, Barker, Knauer, Leitermann** offers niche expertise in the regulatory aspects of telecoms law.

Willkie Farr & Gallagher LLP's Frankfurt office advises cable TV providers, fixed and mobile wireless carriers and telecoms equipment manufacturers. The practice works closely with the firm's Washington DC office on regulatory matters.

TELECOMS

BAKER & McKENZIE ✪
FRESHFIELDS BRUCKHAUS DERINGER ✪
PIEPENBROCK & SCHUSTER
REDEKER SELLNER DAHS & WIDMAIER

Allen & Overy ✪
Clifford Chance
Hengeler Mueller ✪
Hogan & Hartson Raue L.L.P. ✪
Wilmer Cutler Pickering LLP ✪

CMS Hasche Sigle ✪
Coudert Brothers LLP ✪
Gleiss Lutz ✪
Haarmann Hemmelrath ✪
Haver & Mailänder
Heuking Kühn Lüer Wojtek ✪
Hölters & Elsing ✪
Linklaters Oppenhoff & Rädler ✪
Lovells ✪
McDermott, Will & Emery ✪
Norton Rose Vieregge
Velten Franz Jakoby
Veltins & Wilkinson, Barker, Knauer, Leitermann
White & Case
Willkie Farr & Gallagher LLP ✪

Firms are listed A-Z in tiers which are ranked in order of priority
✪ Indicates firm displays contact details at the end of this chapter.

SCHULTZE & BRAUN

EISENBAHNSTR 19-23
77855 ACHERN

Telephone: +49 78 41 70 80
Fax: +49 78 41 70 83 01
E-mail: mail@schubra.de
Website: www.schubra.de

Languages
English, French, Italian, Russian

Other offices
Bremen, Chemnitz, Dortmund, Dresden, Erfurt, Essen, Frankfurt, Freiburg, Halle, Hanover, Hof, Karlsruhe, Konstanz, Leipzig, Magdeburg, Munich, Nürnberg, Offenburg, Oldenburg, Osnabrück, Saarbrücken

Number of lawyers 63
at this office 23

International groupings
AEPPC/EIPA; IBA Committee J

CATEGORIES OF WORK

Insolvency
Dr Eberhard Braun, Edgar Grönda

Banks and banking
Dr Ferdinand Kießner

Business law
Claudia Dietrich, Martina Dietrich

Commercial law
Dr Rainer Riggert, Bertram Wolf

Company law
Achim Frank, Harald Kroth

Construction law
Christian Forcher, Judith Franz

Corporate law
Dr Eberhard Braun, Harald Bußhardt

Criminal law
Theo Naendrup

Economic law
Martina Dietrich

Family law
Barbara Meider

International law
Dr Peter de Bra

Labour and employment
Bertram Wolf, Joachim Zobel

Corporate restructuring
Dr Eberhard Braun

Securities
Dr Rainer Riggert

THE FIRM

Schultze & Braun is a partnership of independent lawyers, auditors, tax consultants and sworn accountants. The services it offers covers the whole range of legal and tax counselling requirements for individuals, craftsmen, trade and industry. Schultze & Braun currently has a staff of about 350.

Fritz Beck's independent tax counselling practice was founded in 1949. 1969 saw the arrival of Wolfgang Schultze as tax consultant, thereby establishing the firm. The composite company of Schultze & Braun was formed in 1975, as tax consultants and lawyers. The insolvency department was reorganised in 1980, thereby extending the firm's activities. In 1987, Schultze & Braun included auditing as part of its service.

AREAS OF PRACTICE

Schultze & Braun offers in its partnership comprehensive counselling in all legal and tax matters – it is both a specialist and a generalist. A host of highly qualified specialists all within one organisation deal with each case according to its specific problems.

As one of the first composites, Schultze & Braun surmounted the division of the professions of the legal adviser and the tax consultant in 1975.

The advantages of this are still obvious today – countless legal points are bound up with tax matters, and almost every tax problem has a legal question in the background.

Even within the field of legal advice, no one person can master the full range of court work, civil and public law.

What is more, business matters are becoming increasingly important. This means that it is now part of the role of the auditor to determine the most opportune legal and commercial organisational arrangements. Thus, for example, it would be unthinkable to run a company without an operational report system.

Liquidity planning and profits planning by comparing desired and actual figures are important prerequisites for successful company management. Schultze & Braun also pays particular attention to these points.

Securities management and realisation through pools of trusts are features of the work of the business law department; the department works with this conceptually and operationally for banks and suppliers on problems where furnishing collateral, securities management and realisation are all involved, with or without liquidation proceedings.

Schultze & Braun deals with business problems, cost accounting, budget planning and supervision, advice on establishment, and investment and financial analysis, as well as drawing up annual reports and index and comparative accounts. Presentation of accounts and balance sheets for French and English as well as German companies is a further area of the firm's activity.

Schultze & Braun is also prepared to act in companies' boards of directors and as executors of wills.

ARCON RECHTSANWÄLTE

SCHMIDT-SIBETH HEISSE WEISSKOPF KURSAWE

KURFÜRSTENDAMM 217
10719 BERLIN

Telephone: +49 30 88 48 08 0
Fax: +49 30 88 48 08 84
E-mail: berlin@arcon-net.com
Website: www.arcon-net.com

Languages
Catalan, Dutch, English, Finnish, French, Greek, Italian, Portuguese, Russian, Spanish

Other offices
Brussels, Cologne, Düsseldorf, Erfurt, Frankfurt am Main, Hamburg, Munich

Number of lawyers 92
at this office 7

Contacts
Carsten Brüninghaus, Jörg Zeise

CATEGORIES OF WORK

- Corporate law, mergers and acquisitions, reorganisations
- IPO, capital markets
- Construction and real estate
- Labour law, employment
- EU law
- Commercial law (general)
- Trade marks, intellectual property, media law
- Competition, antitrust
- Litigation and arbitration
- Contract
- Tax
- Administrative and environment
- Probate and family law
- Estate planning
- Internet, IT and computer law

BEITEN BURKHARDT RECHTSANWALTSGESELLSCHAFT mbH

KURFÜRSTENSTRASSE 72-74
10787 BERLIN

Telephone: +49 30 26 471 0
Fax: +49 30 26 471 123
E-mail: bblaw-berlin@bblaw.de
Website: www.bblaw.de

Languages
Cantonese, Czech, English, French, Hungarian, Italian, Mandarin, Polish, Russian, Slovak, Spanish

Other offices
Beijing, Brussels, Budapest, Cologne, Dusseldorf, Frankfurt am Main, Hamburg, Hong Kong, Leipzig, Moscow, Munich, Nuremberg, St Petersburg, Shanghai, Warsaw

Number of lawyers 232
at this office 25

CATEGORIES OF WORK

- Company law
- Banking and finance
- European law and cartel law
- Industrial property rights
- Labour and employment law
- Procurement law
- Public law
- Media and telecommunications law, information technology
- Forensic services, corporate compliance
- Law of associations, societies and sports law
- Probate, company succession
- Litigation and arbitration
- Property law
- Insurance law

BAKER & McKENZIE

FRIEDRICHSTRASSE 79-80
10117 BERLIN

Telephone: +49 30 20 38 76 00
Fax: +49 30 20 38 76 99
Website: www.bakernet.com

Languages Dutch, English, French, Italian, Russian, Spanish

Other offices Almaty, Amsterdam, Antwerp, Bahrain, Baku, Bangkok, Barcelona, Beijing, Bogotá, Bologna, Brasilia, Brussels, Budapest, Buenos Aires, Cairo, Calgary, Caracas, Chicago, Dallas, Düsseldorf, Frankfurt, Geneva, Guadalajara, Hanoi, Ho Chi Minh City, Hong Kong, Houston, Juarez, Kyiv, London, Madrid, Manila, Melbourne, Mexico City, Miami, Milan, Monterrey, Moscow, Munich, New York, Palo Alto, Paris, Porto Alegré, Prague, Rio de Janeiro, Riyadh, Rome, St Petersburg, San Diego, San Francisco, Santiago, São Paulo, Shanghai, Singapore, Stockholm, Sydney, Taipei, Tijuana, Tokyo, Toronto, Valencia, Vienna, Warsaw, Washington DC, Zürich

Number of lawyers 3,380
at this office 16

CATEGORIES OF WORK

Administrative law
Frank-Rainer Töpfer

Banking and finance
Wilhelm Hebing

Company and commercial law
Ulrich Hennings, Peter Wessels

Environmental law
Ulrich Hennings, Frank-Rainer Töpfer

IT, media and computer law
Stefan Dittmer

Labour law
Andre Sayatz

Law of the former German Democratic Republic
Frank-Rainer Töpfer, Andre Sayatz

Litigation and arbitration
Stefan Dittmer, Frank-Rainer Töpfer

Mergers and acquisitions
Wilhelm Hebing, Ulrich Hennings

Privatisation
Wilhelm Hebing, Frank-Rainer Töpfer

Real estate
Frank-Rainer Töpfer, Peter Wessels

Tax
Christian Birkholz, Wilhelm Hebing

Venture capital
Peter Wessels

THE FIRM

Founded in Chicago in 1949, Baker & McKenzie is a global law firm with 66 offices in 36 countries. A multinational network of over 4,400 legal professionals offers clients resources and knowledge in every area of business law, in virtually every important financial and commercial centre in the world.

Baker & McKenzie has been established in Europe for over 40 years, having opened its first European offices in 1957. Since then, the European and Middle Eastern network has grown to 29 offices, giving it unparalleled geographical coverage.

The Frankfurt am Main office was formed in 1962; the office in Berlin was opened on 1 March 1990; the Munich office on 1 April 1997; and the Düsseldorf office on 1 April 1999.

Since their formation, the German offices of Baker & McKenzie have advised their clients on all questions of German, European and international industrial and commercial law with particular emphasis on cross-border and multinational transactions. At present, more than 170 attorneys-at-law (Rechtsanwälte), admitted in the Federal Republic of Germany including the new federal states, tax advisers, and varying numbers of foreign admitted lawyers work in the German offices of Baker & McKenzie.

All attorneys are at least bilingual; most of them have completed additional graduate legal studies at foreign law schools. Several attorneys are simultaneously admitted as CPAs, tax advisers, tax attorneys, attorneys for administrative law or attorneys for labour law.

AREAS OF PRACTICE

Baker & McKenzie co-ordinates its core practice areas on local, regional and global levels, giving most of its lawyers experience in more than one jurisdiction, as well as providing multinational teams of specialists.

Utilising a global practice group structure and ground-breaking technology coupled with a personal, detailed understanding of a client's specific business, Baker & McKenzie is able to organise its extensive resources to provide focused and strategic counsel to clients.

Baker & McKenzie advises multinational enterprises, large German companies, medium-sized enterprises, banks and insurance companies, as well as institutions and entities under public law in all questions of German, European, and international industrial and commercial law including company law, competition and cartel law, intellectual property, banking and finance, labour law, administrative law, and tax law. Furthermore, the firm handles litigation and arbitration matters. Several partners have expertise in specialised areas of law, such as European Community law, the law of cosmetics, food and drug law, trade marks, franchising, corporate finance, new financial products, government procurement, real estate transactions, and media telecommunications law.

BUSE HEBERER FROMM

KURFÜRSTENDAMM 217
10719 BERLIN

Telephone: +49 30 880 230
Fax: +49 30 882 1108
E-mail: berlin@buse.de
Website: www.buse.de

Languages
English, French, Italian, Spanish, Turkish

Other offices
Dusseldorf, Essen, Frankfurt am Main, Hamburg, Milan, Munich, Palma de Mallorca, Sydney, Zurich

Number of lawyers 120
at this office 24

Member
The European Legal Alliance (Beauchamps, Ireland; Dubarry Le Douarin Veil, France; Field Fisher Waterhouse, England; Harper Macleod, Scotland)

CATEGORIES OF WORK

Banking and finance

Antitrust and merger control

Commerce, transport, insurance

Commercial delinquency

Corporate/M&A

Industrial property and copyrights

Information technology and telecommunications

Labour and employment

Litigation and arbitration, national and international

Press and media

Property and construction

Public law

Tax

CMS HASCHE SIGLE

MARKGRAFENSTRASSE 36
CARREE AM GENDARMENMARKT
10117 BERLIN

Telephone: +49 30 203 600
Fax: +49 30 203 60 290
E-mail: berlin@cmslegal.de
Website: www.cmslegal.de

Languages
Dutch, English, French, Italian, Spanish

Other offices
Dusseldorf, Frankfurt, Hamburg, Leipzig, Munich, Stuttgart, Chemnitz, Dresden, Brussels, Belgrade, Moscow, Prague, Shanghai

Number of lawyers 306
at this office 25

Other CMS law firms
CMS Adonnino Ascoli & Cavasola Scamoni, Italy; CMS Bureau Francis Lefebvre, France; CMS Cameron McKenna, UK; CMS Derks Star Busmann, Netherlands; CMS von Erlach Klainguti Stettler Wille, Switzerland; CMS Lexcelis, Belgium; CMS Strommer Reich-Rohrwig Karasek Hainz, Austria

CATEGORIES OF WORK

Corporate and commercial

Mergers and acquisitions

Privatisation and restructuring

Banking, securities and finance

Unfair competition and antitrust

Tax

Labour law and service contracts

Bankruptcy and reorganisation

Intellectual property, IT, media

Real estate and construction

Environmental and administrative

Distribution, franchising

Maritime law

Arbitration and litigation

Utilities

FLICK GOCKE SCHAUMBURG

FRIEDRICHSTRASSE 69
10117 BERLIN

Telephone: +49 30 21 00 20 20
Fax: +49 30 21 00 20 99
E-mail: berlin@fgs.de
Website: www.fgs.de

Languages
English, French, Italian

Other offices
Bonn, Frankfurt

Number of lawyers 107
at this office 11

Contacts
Dr Lenhard Jesse, Dr Thomas Mueller-Thuns, Dr Martin Oltmanns

CATEGORIES OF WORK

German and international tax law	Transfer pricing
Corporate and business law	Estate planning
Mergers and acquisitions	Real estate transactions
Reorganisation of group structures	Tax litigation
IPOs	Customs law
Inbound investment	Due diligence and special audits

FRESHFIELDS BRUCKHAUS DERINGER

POTSDAMER PLATZ 1
10785 BERLIN

Telephone: +49 30 20 28 36
Fax: +49 30 20 28 37 66
E-mail: email@freshfields.com
Website: www.freshfields.com

Languages
Extensive language capabilities

Other offices
Amsterdam, Bangkok, Barcelona, Beijing, Bratislava, Brussels, Budapest, Cologne, Düsseldorf, Frankfurt, Hamburg, Hanoi, Ho Chi Minh City, Hong Kong, London, Madrid, Milan, Moscow, Munich, New York, Paris, Rome, Shanghai, Singapore, Tokyo, Vienna, Washington

Number of lawyers 2,504
at this office 62

Contact
Helmut Bergmann

CATEGORIES OF WORK

Corporate	Tax
Finance	Real estate
Intellectual property and IT	Dispute resolution (including environment, planning and regulatory)
Antitrust, competition and trade	Employment, pensions and benefits

GSK GASSNER STOCKMANN & KOLLEGEN

MOHRENSTRASSE 42
10117 BERLIN

Telephone: +49 30 203 907 0
Fax: +49 30 203 907 44
E-mail: berlin@gsk.de
Website: www.gsk.de

Languages
English, French, Italian, Russian

Other offices
Düsseldorf, Frankfurt, Hamburg, Heidelberg, Munich, Stuttgart

Number of lawyers 75
at this office 15

Contacts
Dr Christian R Schmidt (Berlin), Dr Andreas Bauer (Munich), Dr Andreas May (Frankfurt), Dr Philipp Jebens (Hamburg), Dr Peter Ladwig (Stuttgart), Holger Lampe (Düsseldorf), Wolfgang Böhm (Heidelberg)

CATEGORIES OF WORK

- Banking and finance, capital markets, project finance
- Corporate, M&A, venture capital, private equity
- Infrastructure, public sector
- Real estate, construction

GLEISS LUTZ
RECHTSANWÄLTE

FRIEDRICHSTADT-PASSAGEN
QUARTIER 206
FRIEDRICHSTRASSE 71
10117 BERLIN

Telephone: +49 30 20 94 64 00
Fax: +49 30 20 94 64 44
E-mail: info@gleisslutz.com
Website: www.gleisslutz.com

Languages
Dutch, English, French, Italian, Mandarin, Cantonese, Polish, Portuguese, Spanish, Russian, Czech, Slovak

Other offices
Frankfurt, Munich, Stuttgart, Brussels, Prague, Warsaw

Number of lawyers 200
at this office 40

Contact
Dr Ralf Thaeter LLM

CATEGORIES OF WORK

- German, EC and international law
- Insurance
- Banking, securities and finance
- Litigation and arbitration
- Commercial law (general)
- Mergers and acquisitions
- Companies, corporations
- Real estate
- Competition, antitrust
- Tax
- Electronic commerce, Internet law
- Telecommunications, media and broadcasting
- Employment, labour
- Trade marks, intellectual property
- Environment and pollution control

GÖRG
RECHTSANWÄLTE

TIERGARTEN DREIECK
KLINGELHÖFERSTRASSE 5
10785 BERLIN

Telephone: +49 30 884 50 30
Fax: +49 30 882 71 50
E-mail: berlin@goerg.de
Website: www.goerg.de

Languages
English, French, Italian, Russian, Spanish

Other offices
Amsterdam*, Antwerp*, Bangkok*, Barcelona*, Bergen*, Birmingham*, Bradford*, Brussels*, Cologne, Copenhagen*, Edinburgh*, Essen, Frankfurt/M, Glasgow*, Hamburg, Hong Kong*, Leeds*, Liverpool*, London*, Madrid*, Manchester*, Milan*, Oslo*, Paris*, Prague*, Rotterdam*, Salzburg*, Sarajevo*, Shanghai*, Sheffield*, Singapore*, Stockholm*, Vienna*, Zagreb*

Number of lawyers 83
at this office 26

Member
DLA Group

CATEGORIES OF WORK

Corporate law and antitrust	Unfair competition and trade marks
Mergers and acquisitions	IT and telecommunications
Finance and capital markets	Insurance law
Insolvency and reorganisation	Medical law
Employment	Pharmaceutical and drug law
Commercial and distribution	Transport
National and international tax	Product liability
Construction law	Private wealth
International transactions	Litigation and arbitration
Real estate	Notarial services
Media and entertainment	Administrative law

GRAF VON WESTPHALEN BAPPERT & MODEST

RAUCHSTRASSE 26
10787 BERLIN

Telephone: +49 30 726 1110
Fax: +49 30 726 111 123
E-mail: berlin@westphalen-law.com
Website: www.westphalen-law.com

Languages
English, French, Italian, Spanish

Other offices
Brussels, Cologne, Dresden, Freiburg, Hamburg, Munich, Vienna

Number of lawyers 110
at this office 12

In exclusive co-operation with
Wragge & Co, UK;
Kemmler Rapp Böhlke, Belgium

CATEGORIES OF WORK

Corporate, private equity	Public private partnership
Mergers and acquisitions, privatisation	Intellectual property, product piracy and unfair trading
Commercial	Administrative, planning and environmental
Real estate, construction and project development	Labour and employment
Corporate real estate	Information technology, media and entertainment
Distributor contracts	Tax
Arbitration and litigation	
EC law	

HAARMANN HEMMELRATH

MARKGRAFENSTRASSE 33
10117 BERLIN

Telephone: +49 30 2 64 73 0
Fax: +49 30 2 64 73 1 33
E-mail:
berlin@haarmannhemmelrath.com
Website:
www.haarmannhemmelrath.com

Languages
Bulgarian, Croatian, Czech, Dutch, English, French, Hungarian, Italian, Japanese, Mandarin, Norwegian, Polish, Portuguese, Romanian, Russian, Slovak, Spanish, Vietnamese

Other offices
Bielefeld, Brussels, Bucharest, Budapest, Cologne, Dusseldorf, Frankfurt, Hamburg, Leipzig, London, Milan, Moscow, Munich, Paris, Prague, Rome, Shanghai, Singapore, Stuttgart, Tokyo, Vienna, Warsaw

Number of lawyers 281
at this office 24

CATEGORIES OF WORK

M&A, reorganisations
Detlef Olufs, Dr Christoph Binge

Corporate finance, banking, leasing
Dr Stephan Busch, Dr Christoph Binge

Fund structuring
Detlef Olufs, Dr Hermann Meller

Corporate and business law, IPO
Dr Christoph Binge, Dr Hermann Meller

Privatisation
Dr Stephan Busch, Dr Thomas Winkemann

Real estate transactions
Thomas Santüns, Dr Jan Kreikenbohm

International tax law
Detlef Olufs, Dr Thomas Winkemann

Corporate, national tax, compliance
Dr Stephan Busch, Dr Thomas Winkemann

Labour law
Dr Peter Diedrich, Thomas Wahlig

Audit and accounting services
Dr Dirk Rabenhorst,
Benjamin Nockemann

Notarial services
Dr Peter Diedrich, Thomas Santüns

Media
Dr Anneke Flatow

Intellectual property law
Dr Anneke Flatow

Construction law
Johannes Dombrowski,
Dr Jan Kreikenbohm

Law of statutory insurance system
Johannes Dombrowski

Arbitration and mediation, litigation
Johannes Dombrowski

Structured finance
(after fund structuring)
Dr Hermann Meller

HENGELER MUELLER

CHARLOTTENSTRASSE 35/36
10117 BERLIN

Telephone: +49 30 20374 0
Fax: +49 30 20374 333
E-mail: hmbln@hengeler.com
Website: www.hengeler.com

Other offices
Düsseldorf, Frankfurt, Brussels, London, Budapest, Prague

Number of lawyers 195
at this office 29

Contact
Dr Julius Budde, Dr Ulrich Blech

CATEGORIES OF WORK

M&A/corporate

Private equity and venture capital

Banking, finance and capital markets

Insolvency and reorganisation

Litigation and arbitration

Regulatory and environment

Privatisation and public sector restructuring

Public procurement

Healthcare and life sciences

Telecommunications and media

Real estate

HEUKING KÜHN LÜER WOJTEK

FRIEDRICHSTRASSE 149
10117 BERLIN

Telephone: +49 30 88 00 97 0
Fax: +49 30 88 00 97 99
E-mail: berlin@heuking.de
Website: www.heuking.de

Languages
German, English, French

Other offices
Brussels, Chemnitz, Cologne, Düsseldorf, Frankfurt, Hamburg, Munich

Number of lawyers 16

Contact
Dr Peter Fissenewert

CATEGORIES OF WORK

Corporate law	**Administrative law**
Mergers and acquisitions	**Labour law**
Litigation	**Real estate and construction law**
Privatisations	**Insolvency and receiverships**
Public tenders and bids	**Tax law**

THE FIRM

Heuking Kühn Lüer Wojtek was founded in Düsseldorf, Germany, in 1971. Since then, the firm has spread geographically, and Heuking Kühn now has seven significant offices in Germany, as well as an office in Brussels.

The firm has an extensive international network of law firms, enabling it to provide its clients with seamless 'one-stop shopping', on international transactions and regulatory matters. Since its formation, Heuking Kühn Lüer Wojtek has specifically chosen to remain an independent law firm. It is Heuking Kühn Lüer Wojtek's philosophy that, to provide the best possible service to its clients, the firm must be able to co-operate with various other law firms which are at the top of the profession in their respective countries. This gives the firm the ability to make alternative counsel suggestions to its clients, giving the clients a choice of the best suitable law firm or lawyer in each country and for each matter. Over the last 30+ years, Heuking Kühn Lüer Wojtek has developed excellent relationships with the key firms in all of the major jurisdictions worldwide.

Heuking Kühn Lüer Wojtek is a name which is synonymous with legal competence. The firm is one of the largest commercial law firms in Germany, with more than 150 specialised lawyers and tax advisers, representing the interests of national and international clients. Included in the client list are large and medium-sized German and international companies in all areas of the manufacturing industry, as well as trade and service industries, associations, governmental and public sector organisations and private clients and trusts.

The firm prides itself on substantive legal competence and on the excellent education and continuing legal education of its lawyers. Moreover, virtually all of the lawyers are German-English bilingual.

Extensive specialisation and comprehensive knowledge of specific industry sectors provide the basis of all of Heuking Kühn Lüer Wojtek's legal counselling. Experienced partners and carefully selected associate lawyers develop innovative solutions to complex legal problems. The lawyers regularly work in their specific practice area groups and also in multi-group and multi-disciplinary teams with clients and outside consultants or advisers. Entrepreneurial thinking on behalf of firm clients, as well as efficient, quality, cost-effective and timely work and the highest personal dedication are key components of Heuking Kühn Lüer Wojtek's culture.

AREAS OF PRACTICE

Heuking Kühn Lüer Wojtek is a full-service commercial law firm. Cross-border and cross-sector knowledge in combination with a deep understanding of business reasoning enables service to clients with the broadest possible support in all their negotiations and business decisions. This applies equally to M&A transactions, to legal advice on company structure, business risk management, negotiations and negotiation tactics, training, crisis and insolvency counselling, corporate financial matters, and complex litigation and arbitration. Thanks to a variety of strong business clients, the firm has built long-term relationships with its clients and can assist them, beginning with the establishment of a business, followed by implementing business goals, including day-to-day legal work, reorganisations, acquisitions and divestitures.

Heuking Kühn Lüer Wojtek is actively involved with its clients in providing regulatory counselling in all areas of commercial law, as well as assisting them in organising and implementing their M&A transactions in Germany, throughout Europe, and internationally. Heuking Kühn Lüer Wojtek has particular expertise in German and EU company law; competition law, merger control and state aids; international investment, trade, and taxation matters; banking and finance; labour law; intellectual property rights; environmental, health, and safety regulation; product-specific regulation; real estate and construction law; telecoms, IT and media law; transport, postal services and shipping law; public procurement; family law; and private clients and family office matters.

HEUSSEN
RECHTSANWALTSGESELLSCHAFT MBH

LISE-MEITNER-STRASSE 1
10589 BERLIN

Telephone: +49 30 2636 4900
Fax: +49 30 2636 4989
E-mail: info@landwell.de
Website: www.landwell.de

Languages
Arabic, Dutch, English, French, Greek, Italian, Russian, Spanish, Swedish

Other offices
Cologne, Düsseldorf, Frankfurt, Hamburg, Munich, Stuttgart

Number of lawyers 100
at this office 7

Contact
Dr Benno Heussen

International groupings
Landwell, correspondent law firms of PricewaterhouseCoopers

CATEGORIES OF WORK

Commercial and competition
Dr Gunther Braun

Corporate structuring
Robert Dorr

Dispute resolution
Dr Reiner Ponschab

Technology, media and communications
Dr Axel Czarnetzki, Rafaela Wilde

Employment and human resources
Hans Stefan Korsch

Financial services
Dr Gunther Braun

Intellectual property
Dr Axel Czarnetzki

Mergers and acquisitions
Dr Karl Maria Walter, Michael Ketterl

Public law
Dr Michael W Mütze

Real estate
Dr Michael W Mütze

HOGAN & HARTSON RAUE LLP

POTSDAMER PLATZ 1
10785 BERLIN

Telephone: +49 30 726 115 0
Fax: +49 30 726 115 100
E-mail: gmeinel@hhlaw.com
Website: www.hhlaw.com

Languages
English, French, Hebrew, Spanish

Other offices
Baltimore, Beijing, Boulder, Brussels, Budapest, Colorado Springs, Denver, London, Los Angeles, McLean, Miami, Moscow, Munich, New York, Paris, Prague, Tokyo, Warsaw, Washington DC

Number of lawyers 1,018
at this office 39

Contact
Gernod Meinel

CATEGORIES OF WORK

Mergers and acquisitions
Corporate law
Tax and customs
Banking and capital markets
Project finance
Privatisation
Labour law
Litigation and arbitration
Insolvency law
Copyright, publishing and press law
Patents and trade marks
Environmental law
Infrastructure projects
Internet and e-commerce
Antitrust law
Public procurement law
Intellectual property
Media and telecommunications
Real estate
Construction
Utilities
Healthcare and biotechnology
Sports and entertainment

LOVELLS

SCHLÜTERSTRASSE 37
10629 BERLIN

Telephone: +49 308 89 19 0
Fax: +49 308 89 19 100
E-mail: reception.berlin@lovells.com
Website: www.lovells.de

Languages
English, French

Other offices
Alicante, Amsterdam, Beijing, Brussels, Budapest*, Chicago, Düsseldorf, Frankfurt, Hamburg, Ho Chi Minh City, Hong Kong, London, Milan, Moscow, Munich, New York, Paris, Prague, Rome, Shanghai, Singapore, Tokyo, Vienna*, Warsaw, Zagreb*

Number of lawyers 1,600
at this office 36

Contact
Volkmar Jesch

CATEGORIES OF WORK

Corporate/M&A, private equity	Intellectual property
Restructuring and insolvency	Property
Banking	Projects
Antitrust and unfair competition	Technology, media, telecommunications
Capital markets	Litigation, product liability
Project finance, public private partnerships	International arbitration
Tax	Food and drug regulations
Employment	Law of Eastern Europe

MANNHEIMER SWARTLING

RECHTSANWÄLTE UND SCHWEDISCHE ADVOKATEN

MAUERSTRASSE 83-84
10117 BERLIN

Telephone: +49 30 22 66 990
Fax: +49 30 22 66 9910
Website: www.mannheimerswartling.se

Languages
English, French, Swedish

Other offices
Brussels, Frankfurt, Gothenburg, Helsingborg, Malmö, New York, St Petersburg, Stockholm

Number of lawyers 330
at this office 10

Contact
Dr Thomas Kaiser-Stockmann

CATEGORIES OF WORK

Corporate	Construction and projects
M&A	Environment
Banking and insurance	Intellectual property
Securities	Employment
Real estate	Arbitration and litigation

NÖRR STIEFENHOFER LUTZ

CHARLOTTENSTRASSE 57
10117 BERLIN

Telephone: +49 30 20 94 20 00
Fax: +49 30 20 94 20 94
E-mail: nslbln@noerr.de
Website: www.noerr.de

Languages
English, Dutch, French, Italian, Polish, Spanish

Other offices
Bucharest, Budapest, Dresden, Düsseldorf, Frankfurt, Munich, Moscow, Prague, Warsaw

Number of lawyers 237
(+ 53 tax advisers, public accountants and tax assistants)
at this office 38
(+7 tax advisers and public accountants and tax assistants)

Contact
Dr Dirk Lentfer

CATEGORIES OF WORK

- Media and entertainment law
- Company and tax law
- Mergers and acquisitions
- Antitrust law
- Restitution claims and restoration of property in eastern Germany
- Reorganisation
- International and commercial law
- Trade, industry and labour law
- Real estate
- Planning and zoning
- Administrative law
- Banking law
- Audit and accounting services

P+P PÖLLATH + PARTNERS

POTSDAMER PLATZ
LINKSTRASSE 2
10785 BERLIN

Telephone: +49 30 253 530
Fax: +49 30 253 53 999
E-mail: ber@pplaw.com
Website: www.pplaw.com

Languages
English, French

Other offices
Frankfurt, Munich

Number of lawyers 45
at this office 17

Contacts
Andreas Rodin, Thomas Toeben

CATEGORIES OF WORK

- Private equity
- M&A
- Corporate finance
- Tax
- Real estate
- Restitution
- Family (high-net-worth, succession)
- Trusts, foundations, charities

SJ BERWIN KNOPF TULLOCH STEININGER

RECHTSANWÄLTE – STEUERBERATER – WIRTSCHAFTSPRÜFER

KURFÜRSTENDAMM 63
10707 BERLIN

Telephone: +49 30 88 71 71 10
Fax: +49 30 88 71 71 66
E-mail: berlin@sjberwin.com
Website: www.sjberwin.com

Languages
English, French, Spanish

Other offices
Brussels, Frankfurt, London, Madrid, Munich, Paris

Number of lawyers 411
at this office 12

Contact
Dr Frank Vogel

CATEGORIES OF WORK

Corporate law
Dr Frank Vogel, Dr Andreas Wuesthoff

Venture capital
Dr Frank Vogel, Dr Andreas Wuesthoff

M&A, joint ventures
Dr Frank Vogel, Dr Frank Ludwig

Intellectual property
Dr Jan Dirk Heerma

Alternative investments
Dr Till Flock

Private equity
Dr Frank Vogel, Dr Frank Ludwig

Fund structuring
Dr Jan Dirk Heerma, Dr Darius Salus

Tax
Dr Till Flock

Banking and financial services
Dr Till Flock

SCHWARZ KELWING WICKE WESTPFAHL

KURFÜRSTENDAMM 220
10719 BERLIN

Telephone: +49 30 88 59 27 0
Fax: +49 30 88 22 26 0
E-mail: berlin@skwlaw.de
Website: www.skwlaw.de

Languages
English, French, German, Spanish

Other offices
Cologne, Dresden, Frankfurt am Main, Munich

Number of lawyers 62
at this office 18

Member
Terralex; PLG

CATEGORIES OF WORK

Administrative
Matthias Druba, Dr Marc Gabriel

Banking and finance
Hellmut Sieglerschmidt

Commercial property, real estate
Helge Eimers, Ralph Nielebock

Construction
Dr Olaf Kreißl, Sebastian Büchner

Corporate and commercial
Hellmut Sieglerschmidt

Dispute resolution – litigation and arbitration
Monika Birnbaum, Helge Eimers

Employment
Monika Birnbaum, Alexandra Henkel

Environment
Ermbrecht Rindtorff, Dr Marc Gabriel

Fraud and white-collar crime
Sebastian Büchner

Insolvency law
Dr Olaf Kreißl

Trade marks, intellectual property, copyright
Dr Alexander Freys

Media and entertainment
Dr Alexander Freys

Privatisation and restitution (East Germany)
Matthias Druba

Public procurement, public services
Ermbrecht Rindtorff

TAYLOR WESSING

HAUS MENDELSSOHN
JÄGERSTR 51
10117 BERLIN

Telephone: +49 30 88 56 36 0
Fax: +49 30 88 56 36 46
E-mail: berlin@taylorwessing.com
Website: www.taylorwessing.com

Languages
English, Dutch, French, Italian, Mandarin, Spanish

Other offices
Alicante*, Brussels, Cambridge, Dubai*, Düsseldorf/Neuss, Frankfurt, Hamburg, London, Munich, Paris, Shanghai*

Number of lawyers 550
at this office 20

Member
World Law Group; Tech Law Group

CATEGORIES OF WORK

Banking and finance
Claus Goedecke, Peter Seemann

China desk
Florian Ranft

Commercial
Dr Christoph Hasche

Corporate/M&A
Bernhard Kloft

Employment and pensions
Axel C Filges

EU law/antitrust
Dr Marco Hartmann-Rüppel, Markus Wirtz

Intellectual property
Dr Sabine Rojahn

Life science
Dr Ulrich Steffen

Media and entertainment
Martin von Albrecht

Private client
Romana Traichel

Projects and finance
Dr Rüdiger von Hülst

Public commercial law
Dr Walter Potthast

Real estate and construction
Jan Wunschel

Regulatory affairs
Andreas Haak

Tax
Bernd Michel

Technology/IT/telecoms
Joerg Wimmers

WILMER CUTLER PICKERING LLP

FRIEDRICHSTRASSE 95
10117 BERLIN

Telephone: +49 30 20 22 64 00
Fax: +49 30 20 22 65 00
E-mail: berlinlaw@wilmer.com
Website: www.wilmer.com

Languages
German, English, French

Other offices
Baltimore, Brussels, London, New York, N Virginia, Washington DC

Number of lawyers 545
at this office 43

CATEGORIES OF WORK

International business
Dieter Lange, Matthias Wissmann

Corporate
Roland Steinmeyer, Alexander Kollmorgen

M&A
Frank Roitzsch, Martin Seyfarth

Real estate, notary
Roland Steinmeyer, Georg Graf zu Castell-Castell

Litigation
Klaus Schubert

International arbitration
Gary Born, Wolfgang Rosener

Deregulation, privatisation
Matthias Wissmann, Frank Roitzsch

IT/IP
Klaus Schubert

Tax
Oliver Bugge

Labour
Stefan Fischer, Joachim Littig

Competition, antitrust
Ulrich Quack, Karlheinz Quack

Aviation
Dieter Lange, Natalie Lübben

Telecommunications, media
Natalie Lübben, Paul von Hehn

Regulatory, public policy
Natalie Lübben, Martin Seyfarth

Public procurement
Rainer Velte, Natalie Lübben

HAARMANN HEMMELRATH

KÖNIGSBREEDE 1
33605 BIELEFELD

Telephone: + 49 521 16 45 0
Fax: + 49 521 16 45 133
E-mail:
bielefeld@haarmannhemmelrath.com
Website:
www.haarmannhemmelrath.com

Languages
Catalan, English, French, German, Italian, Portuguese, Spanish, Turkish

Other offices
Berlin, Brussels, Bucharest, Budapest, Cologne, Dusseldorf, Frankfurt, Hamburg, Leipzig, London, Milan, Moscow, Munich, Paris, Prague, Rome, Shanghai, Singapore, Stuttgart, Tokyo, Vienna, Warsaw

Number of lawyers 281
at this office 5

CATEGORIES OF WORK

Arbitration
Achim Heining

Banking and stock market law
Achim Heining

Company and commercial law
Henning Rolf, Claudia Leipelt

Company succession
Henning Rolf, Katrin Kaßmann

Contract law
Claudia Leipelt

Labour law
Claudia Leipelt

Litigation
Achim Heining

Mergers and acquisitions
Henning Rolf

Tax law
Katrin Kaßmann, Henning Rolf

ARNOLD BOESEN

KAISER-FRIEDRICH-STR. 3
53113 BONN

Telephone: +49 0228 215 290
Fax: +49 0228 215 491
E-mail: news@boesen.de
Website: www.boesen.de

Languages
English, French

Number of lawyers 12

CATEGORIES OF WORK

National public procurement
RA Arnold Boesen

European law
RA Arnold Boesen

European public procurement
RA Arnold Boesen

Competition law
RA Arnold Boesen

Construction law
RA Arnold Boesen

Privatisation
RA Arnold Boesen

THE FIRM

The firm was founded in 1996 and has promptly reached its current size of 12 highly-qualified lawyers and a total staff of 16. Its founder, Arnold Boesen, started his legal career as a judge at German administrative courts. He then worked as a counsellor in the office of international law at the German Ministry of Justice and later as a principal administrator at the European Commission with the Directorate General Internal Market. On the basis of the experience gained during the different stages of his career, Arnold Boesen set up the firm according to a new concept of legal counselling. In pursuing a policy of unconditional quality, the firm is dedicated to the principle of only accepting a few selected mandates. For every mandate a closely knit team of lawyers is formed to match the special requirements of the case. Thus the firm provides legal advice for clients with issues of great economic significance.

AREAS OF PRACTICE

The firm advises big international corporations, industrial federations as well as government contractors nationwide. It mainly serves its clients in the following areas: national and European public procurement law; construction law; European and competition law; and privatisation.

In the field of public procurement the firm has achieved a reputation as one of the leading German law firms. The firm acts on behalf of bidders as well as contracting authorities.

Major recent cases include: legal management of Germany's biggest ever awarding procedure for services and counselling a leading European environment service supplier in one of the most noticed procurement cases in 2003. The firm enabled numerous clients to come out on top of heavily contested bidding for renowned public contracts.

The firm's activities regarding construction law range from rendering expert opinion on various related legal issues to accompanying major building projects. The firm, for example, coordinates and manages most legal aspects of building the new headquarter for a German blue-chip corporation. It furthermore assists in real estate transactions for one of Germany's biggest real estate owners.

FLICK GOCKE SCHAUMBURG

JOHANNA-KINKEL-STRASSE 2-4
53175 BONN

Telephone: +49 228 95 940
Fax: +49 228 95 94 100
E-mail: bonn@fgs.de
Website: www.fgs.de

Languages
English, French, Italian

Other offices
Berlin, Frankfurt

Number of lawyers 107
at this office 82

Contacts
Klaus Kappe, Dr Jörg W Lüttge,
Dr Stephan Göckeler, Dr Reimar Pinkernell

CATEGORIES OF WORK

- German and international tax law
- Transfer pricing
- Corporate and business law
- Estate planning
- Mergers and acquisitions
- Real estate transactions
- Reorganisation of group structures
- Tax litigation
- IPOs
- Customs law
- Inbound investment
- Due diligence and special audits

CMS HASCHE SIGLE

HARTMANNSTRASSE 7
09111 CHEMNITZ

Telephone: +49 371 3 69 740
Fax: +49 371 3 69 74 21
E-mail: chemnitz@cmslegal.de
Website: www.cmslegal.de

Languages
English

Other offices
Berlin, Dusseldorf, Frankfurt, Hamburg, Leipzig, Munich, Stuttgart, Dresden, Brussels, Belgrade, Moscow, Prague, Shanghai

Number of lawyers 306
at this office 5

Other CMS law firms
CMS Adonnino Ascoli & Cavasola Scamoni, Italy; CMS Bureau Francis Lefebvre, France; CMS Cameron McKenna, UK; CMS Derks Star Busmann, Netherlands; CMS von Erlach Klainguti Stettler Wille, Switzerland; CMS Lexcelis, Belgium; CMS Strommer Reich-Rohrwig Karasek Hainz, Austria

CATEGORIES OF WORK

- Corporate and commercial
- Intellectual property, IT, media
- Mergers and acquisitions
- Real estate and construction
- Privatisation and restructuring
- Environmental and administrative
- Banking, securities and finance
- Distribution, franchising
- Unfair competition and antitrust
- Maritime law
- Tax
- Arbitration and litigation
- Labour law and service contracts
- Utilities
- Bankruptcy and reorganisation

HEUKING KÜHN LÜER WOJTEK

WESTSTRASSE 16
09112 CHEMNITZ

Telephone: +49 371 382 030
Fax: +49 371 382 03100
E-mail: chemnitz@heuking.de
Website: www.heuking.de

Languages
German, English, French

Other offices
Berlin, Brussels, Cologne, Düsseldorf, Frankfurt, Hamburg, Munich

Number of lawyers 9

Contact
Annemarie Rott

CATEGORIES OF WORK	
International corporate law	**Commercial law**
Mergers and acquisitions	**Tax law**
Joint ventures	**Labour law**
Customs and trade law	**Financial and banking law**
Property transactions	**Litigation and arbitration**
Construction law	**Energy law**

THE FIRM

Heuking Kühn Lüer Wojtek was founded in Düsseldorf, Germany, in 1971. Since then, the firm has spread geographically, and Heuking Kühn now has seven significant offices in Germany, as well as an office in Brussels.

The firm has an extensive international network of law firms, enabling it to provide its clients with seamless 'one-stop shopping', on international transactions and regulatory matters. Since its formation, Heuking Kühn Lüer Wojtek has specifically chosen to remain an independent law firm. It is Heuking Kühn Lüer Wojtek's philosophy that, to provide the best possible service to its clients, the firm must be able to co-operate with various other law firms which are at the top of the profession in their respective countries. This gives the firm the ability to make alternative counsel suggestions to its clients, giving the clients a choice of the best suitable law firm or lawyer in each country and for each matter. Over the last 30+ years, Heuking Kühn Lüer Wojtek has developed excellent relationships with the key firms in all of the major jurisdictions worldwide.

Heuking Kühn Lüer Wojtek is a name which is synonymous with legal competence. The firm is one of the largest commercial law firms in Germany, with more than 150 specialised lawyers and tax advisers, representing the interests of national and international clients. Included in the client list are large and medium-sized German and international companies in all areas of the manufacturing industry, as well as trade and service industries, associations, governmental and public sector organisations and private clients and trusts.

The firm prides itself on substantive legal competence and on the excellent education and continuing legal education of its lawyers. Moreover, virtually all of the lawyers are German-English bilingual.

Extensive specialisation and comprehensive knowledge of specific industry sectors provide the basis of all of Heuking Kühn Lüer Wojtek's legal counselling. Experienced partners and carefully selected associate lawyers develop innovative solutions to complex legal problems. The lawyers regularly work in their specific practice area groups and also in multi-group and multi-disciplinary teams with clients and outside consultants or advisers. Entrepreneurial thinking on behalf of firm clients, as well as efficient, quality, cost-effective and timely work and the highest personal dedication are key components of Heuking Kühn Lüer Wojtek's culture.

AREAS OF PRACTICE

Heuking Kühn Lüer Wojtek is a full-service commercial law firm. Cross-border and cross-sector knowledge in combination with a deep understanding of business reasoning enables service to clients with the broadest possible support in all their negotiations and business decisions. This applies equally to M&A transactions, to legal advice on company structure, business risk management, negotiations and negotiation tactics, training, crisis and insolvency counselling, corporate financial matters, and complex litigation and arbitration. Thanks to a variety of strong business clients, the firm has built long-term relationships with its clients and can assist them, beginning with the establishment of a business, followed by implementing business goals, including day-to-day legal work, reorganisations, acquisitions and divestitures.

Heuking Kühn Lüer Wojtek is actively involved with its clients in providing regulatory counselling in all areas of commercial law, as well as assisting them in organising and implementing their M&A transactions in Germany, throughout Europe, and internationally. Heuking Kühn Lüer Wojtek has particular expertise in German and EU company law; competition law, merger control and state aids; international investment, trade, and taxation matters; banking and finance; labour law; intellectual property rights; environmental, health, and safety regulation; product-specific regulation; real estate and construction law; telecoms, IT and media law; transport, postal services and shipping law; public procurement; family law; and private clients and family office matters.

ARCON RECHTSANWÄLTE

SCHMIDT-SIBETH HEISSE WEISSKOPF KURSAWE

SPICHERNSTRASSE 75-77
50672 KÖLN

Telephone: +49 221 39 07 10
Fax: +49 221 39 07 129
E-mail: cologne@arcon-net.com
Website: www.arcon-net.com

Languages
Catalan, Dutch, English, Finnish, French, Greek, Italian, Portuguese, Russian, Spanish

Other offices
Berlin, Brussels, Düsseldorf, Erfurt, Frankfurt am Main, Hamburg, Munich

Number of lawyers 92
at this office 18

Contact
Anja Bornemann

CATEGORIES OF WORK

- **Corporate law, mergers and acquisitions, reorganisations**
- **IPO, capital markets**
- **Tax**
- **Construction and real estate**
- **Estate planning**
- **Labour law, employment**
- **EU law**
- **Administrative, environment, energy, privatisations**
- **Commercial law (general), contract**
- **Trade marks, intellectual property, media law, entertainment, sports**
- **Competition, antitrust**
- **Litigation and arbitration**
- **Criminal law**
- **Public procurement law**
- **Internet, IT, telecommunications**
- **State and subsidy law**

CORNELIUS BARTENBACH HAESEMANN & PARTNER, member of ius laboris

BISMARCKSTRASSE 11-13
50672 COLOGNE

Telephone: +49 221 951 900
Fax: +49 221 951 90 90
E-mail: cbh@cbh.de
Website: www.cbh.de

Languages
Dutch, English, French, Hungarian, Italian, Russian, Spanish

Other offices
Berlin, Cottbus

Number of lawyers 60
at this office 55

Contacts
Werner M Mues, Ernst Eisenbeis, Dr Manfred Hecker

Member
ius laboris, International Employment Law, Pensions and Employee Benefits Alliance

CATEGORIES OF WORK

Employment
Werner M Mues, Ernst Eisenbeis

Intellectual property
Kurt Bartenbach, Dr Manfred Hecker

Construction, real estate
Manfred Haesemann, Joachim Strieder

Public private partnership
Manfred Haesemann, Stefan Hertwig

IT, media
Klaus Gennen

Corporate
Dr Manfred Hecker

M&A, company and commercial
Dieter Korten

Banking
Paul Assies

Public administration
Stefan Rappen

Litigation/arbitration
Dieter Korten

THE FIRM

C B H offers highly specialised legal services, from treating and solving individual legal issues to ongoing comprehensive support of companies and groups of companies in key areas of practice, including continuous consulting services in the preliminary stages of legal problems. C B H develops strategies and represents clients in dealings with government agencies and authorities, in litigation and in arbitration.

AREAS OF PRACTICE

In employment law, C B H focuses on continuous legal services for HR departments of companies, develops and implements restructuring programs and corporate changes, and handles disputes with individual employees. Services comprise negotiations with unions, staff, committees and work councils and litigation in labour courts throughout Germany. As the German member of ius laboris, the firm is able to provide international services in all sectors of employment law.

In intellectual property C B H works on employee inventions, patents, licences, unfair competition, trade marks and trade names.

Corporate and M&A work includes establishing and restructuring of companies, transactions and IPOs.

The property and construction team provides consulting services to investors, the construction industry and government institutions, in planning, acquisition and construction, financing and marketing of property.

A team of specialists for public administration law works on property-related issues and in the field of environmental care.

FRESHFIELDS BRUCKHAUS DERINGER

HEUMARKT 14
50667 COLOGNE

Telephone: +49 221 20 50 70
Fax: +49 221 20 50 790
E-mail: email@freshfields.com
Website: www.freshfields.com

Languages
Extensive language capabilities

Other offices
Amsterdam, Bangkok, Barcelona, Beijing, Berlin, Bratislava, Brussels, Budapest, Düsseldorf, Frankfurt, Hamburg, Hanoi, Ho Chi Minh City, Hong Kong, London, Madrid, Milan, Moscow, Munich, New York, Paris, Rome, Shanghai, Singapore, Tokyo, Vienna, Washington

Number of lawyers 2,504
at this office 86

Contact
Klaus Beucher

CATEGORIES OF WORK

Corporate	**Dispute resolution (including environment, planning and regulatory)**
Antitrust, competition and trade	**Tax**
Finance	**Employment, pensions and benefits**
Intellectual property and IT	**Real estate**

GÖRG
RECHTSANWÄLTE

SACHSENRING 81
50677 KÖLN

Telephone: +49 221 33 66 00
Fax: +49 221 33 66 080
E-mail: cologne@goerg.de
Website: www.goerg.de

Languages
Arabic, English, French, Italian, Spanish

Other Offices
Amsterdam*, Antwerp*, Bangkok*, Barcelona*, Bergen*, Berlin, Birmingham*, Bradford*, Brussels*, Copenhagen*, Edinburgh*, Essen, Frankfurt/M, Glasgow*, Hamburg, Hong Kong*, Leeds*, Liverpool*, London*, Madrid*, Manchester*, Milan*, Oslo*, Paris*, Prague*, Rotterdam*, Salzburg*, Sarajevo*, Shanghai*, Sheffield*, Singapore*, Stockholm*, Vienna*, Zagreb*

Number of lawyers 83
at this office 36

Member
DLA Group

CATEGORIES OF WORK

Corporate law and antitrust	**Unfair competition and trade marks**
Mergers and acquisitions	**IT and telecommunications**
Finance and capital markets	**Insurance law**
Insolvency and reorganisation	**Medical law**
Employment	**Pharmaceutical and drug law**
Commercial and distribution	**Transport**
National and international tax	**Products liability**
Construction law	**Private wealth**
International transactions	**Litigation and arbitration**
Real estate	**Notarial services**
Media and entertainment	**Administrative law**

GRAF VON WESTPHALEN BAPPERT & MODEST

SALIERRING 42
50677 COLOGNE

Telephone: +49 221 20 80 70
Fax: +49 221 23 92 55
E-mail: koeln@westphalen-law.com
Website: www.westphalen-law.com

Languages
English, French

Other offices
Berlin, Brussels, Dresden, Freiburg, Hamburg, Munich, Vienna

Number of lawyers 110
at this office 22

In exclusive co-operation with
Wragge & Co, UK;
Kemmler Rapp Böhlke, Belgium

CATEGORIES OF WORK

Trade law

Distributor contracts and leasing

Product liability and insurers' liability

Intellectual and industrial property, product piracy, unfair trading and competition

Information technology media and entertainment

E-commerce, IT-security and electronic signature

Banking, insolvency and project finance

Real estate, construction and project development

Contract law

Labour and employment

Corporate

Arbitration and litigation

Succession and property

EC law

HAARMANN HEMMELRATH

KÖLNTURM, IM MEDIAPARK 8
50670 COLOGNE

Telephone: +49 221 2 70 58-0
Fax: +49 221 2 70 58-133
E-mail:
cologne@haarmannhemmelrath.com
Website:
www.haarmannhemmelrath.com

Languages
English, French, Norwegian

Other offices
Berlin, Bielefeld, Brussels, Bucharest, Budapest, Dusseldorf, Frankfurt, Hamburg, Leipzig, London, Milan, Moscow, Munich, Paris, Prague, Rome, Shanghai, Singapore, Stuttgart, Tokyo, Vienna, Warsaw

Number of lawyers 281
at this office 11

CATEGORIES OF WORK

Corporate and business law
Dr Mirko Sickinger, Andreas Lehmann

Corporate restructuring
Andreas Lehmann, Thomas Windhöfel

Mergers and acquisitions
Dr Mirko Sickinger, Dr Jiri Jaeger

Asset-backed securities
Andreas Lehmann

Venture capital, stock options
Dr Mirko Sickinger, Andreas Lehmann

IPO
Thomas Bula, Dr Mirko Sickinger

Stock corporations
Dr Mirko Sickinger,
Dr Jörg aus der Fünten

Privatisation
Dr Mirko Sickinger

Intellectual property and unfair competition
Rolf Uecker

Media, IT and e-commerce
Dr Jörg aus der Fünten, Rolf Uecker

International tax
Thomas Bula, Ralf Lohmann

National tax law and compliance
Thomas Bula, Ralf Lohmann

Audit and accounting services
Thomas Bula, Ralf Lohmann

Agency and distribution
Rolf Uecker

Public procurement
Rolf Uecker

Insurance
Rolf Uecker

HEUKING KÜHN LÜER WOJTEK

MAGNUSSTRASSE 13
50672 COLOGNE

Telephone: +49 221 20 520
Fax: +49 221 20 521
E-mail: koeln@heuking.de
Website: www.heuking.de

Languages
German, English, Dutch, French

Other offices
Berlin, Brussels, Chemnitz, Düsseldorf, Frankfurt, Hamburg, Munich

Number of lawyers 26

Contact
Dr Hans-Jochem Lüer

CATEGORIES OF WORK

Corporate and partnership law, mergers and acquisitions

General commercial law

Competition, merger control

Insurance, reinsurance

Banking and finance

Insolvency and restructuring

Media, publishing, copyright

Industrial property

Food and drug law

Employment and labour law

THE FIRM

Heuking Kühn Lüer Wojtek was founded in Düsseldorf, Germany, in 1971. Since then, the firm has spread geographically, and Heuking Kühn now has seven significant offices in Germany, as well as an office in Brussels.

The firm has an extensive international network of law firms, enabling it to provide its clients with seamless 'one-stop shopping', on international transactions and regulatory matters. Since its formation, Heuking Kühn Lüer Wojtek has specifically chosen to remain an independent law firm. It is Heuking Kühn Lüer Wojtek's philosophy that, to provide the best possible service to its clients, the firm must be able to co-operate with various other law firms which are at the top of the profession in their respective countries. This gives the firm the ability to make alternative counsel suggestions to its clients, giving the clients a choice of the best suitable law firm or lawyer in each country and for each matter. Over the last 30+ years, Heuking Kühn Lüer Wojtek has developed excellent relationships with the key firms in all of the major jurisdictions worldwide.

Heuking Kühn Lüer Wojtek is a name which is synonymous with legal competence. The firm is one of the largest commercial law firms in Germany, with more than 150 specialised lawyers and tax advisers, representing the interests of national and international clients. Included in the client list are large and medium-sized German and international companies in all areas of the manufacturing industry, as well as trade and service industries, associations, governmental and public sector organisations and private clients and trusts.

The firm prides itself on substantive legal competence and on the excellent education and continuing legal education of its lawyers. Moreover, virtually all of the lawyers are German-English bilingual.

Extensive specialisation and comprehensive knowledge of specific industry sectors provide the basis of all of Heuking Kühn Lüer Wojtek's legal counselling. Experienced partners and carefully selected associate lawyers develop innovative solutions to complex legal problems. The lawyers regularly work in their specific practice area groups and also in multi-group and multi-disciplinary teams with clients and outside consultants or advisers. Entrepreneurial thinking on behalf of firm clients, as well as efficient, quality, cost-effective and timely work and the highest personal dedication are key components of Heuking Kühn Lüer Wojtek's culture.

AREAS OF PRACTICE

Heuking Kühn Lüer Wojtek is a full-service commercial law firm. Cross-border and cross-sector knowledge in combination with a deep understanding of business reasoning enables service to clients with the broadest possible support in all their negotiations and business decisions. This applies equally to M&A transactions, to legal advice on company structure, business risk management, negotiations and negotiation tactics, training, crisis and insolvency counselling, corporate financial matters, and complex litigation and arbitration. Thanks to a variety of strong business clients, the firm has built long-term relationships with its clients and can assist them, beginning with the establishment of a business, followed by implementing business goals, including day-to-day legal work, reorganisations, acquisitions and divestitures.

Heuking Kühn Lüer Wojtek is actively involved with its clients in providing regulatory counselling in all areas of commercial law, as well as assisting them in organising and implementing their M&A transactions in Germany, throughout Europe, and internationally. Heuking Kühn Lüer Wojtek has particular expertise in German and EU company law; competition law, merger control and state aids; international investment, trade, and taxation matters; banking and finance; labour law; intellectual property rights; environmental, health, and safety regulation; product-specific regulation; real estate and construction law; telecoms, IT and media law; transport, postal services and shipping law; public procurement; family law; and private clients and family office matters.

HEUSSEN
RECHTSANWALTSGESELLSCHAFT MBH

ERFTSTRASSE 19 A
50672 COLOGNE

Telephone: +49 221 50 00 35
Fax: +49 221 50 00 36 36
E-mail: info@landwell.de
Website: www.landwell.de

Languages
Arabic, Dutch, English, French, Greek, Italian, Russian, Spanish, Swedish

Other offices
Berlin, Düsseldorf, Frankfurt, Hamburg, Munich, Stuttgart

Number of lawyers 100
at this office 11

Contact
Rafaela Wilde

International groupings
Landwell, correspondent law firms of PricewaterhouseCoopers

CATEGORIES OF WORK

Commercial and competition
Dr Gunther Braun

Corporate structuring
Robert Dorr

Dispute resolution
Reiner Ponschab

Technology, media and communications
Dr Axel Czarnetzki, Rafaela Wilde

Employment and human resources
Hans Stefan Korsch

Financial services
Dr Gunther Braun

Intellectual property
Dr Axel Czarnetzki

Mergers and acquisitions
Dr Karl Maria Walter, Michael Ketterl

Public law
Dr Michael W Mütze

Real estate
Dr Michael W Mütze

LUTHER MENOLD RECHTSANWALTSGESELLSCHAFT

LUDWIGSTRASSE 8
50667 COLOGNE

Telephone: +49 221 277 95 00
Fax: +49 221 277 95 10
E-mail: contact@de.eylaw.com
Website: www.eylaw.com/de

Languages
Chinese, Dutch, English, French, Italian, Japanese, Portuguese, Spanish, Swedish

Other offices
Berlin, Dresden, Düsseldorf, Essen, Frankfurt, Hamburg, Hanover, Leipzig, Mannheim, Munich, Stuttgart

Number of lawyers 250
at this office 33

Member
EY Law

CATEGORIES OF WORK

Banking and finance
Dr Wolfgang Richter

Commercial, litigation and arbitration
Dr Ulrich Theune

Corporate, M&A
Dr Stefan Kraus

Employment
Axel Braun

Intellectual property, information technology
Dr Fritjof Börner

International trade and antitrust
Dr Thomas Kapp

Real estate
Stefan Sihler

ZACHER & PARTNER

RICHARD-WAGNER STRASSE 12
50678 KÖLN

Telephone: +49 221 94 38 90 0
Fax: +49 221 94 38 90 60
E-mail: info@zpanwaelte.de
Website: www.zpanwaelte.de

Languages
English, French, German

Number of lawyers 6

Contact
Prof Dr Thomas Zacher, MBA

CATEGORIES OF WORK

Capital markets, IPOs
Prof Dr Thomas Zacher,
Claudia Stöcker

Company law
Prof Dr Thomas Zacher,
Claudia Stöcker

Tax law
Prof Dr Thomas Zacher,
Claudia Stöcker

Banking and finance
Prof Dr Thomas Zacher,
Claudia Stöcker

Property and real estate
Monika Fink-Plücker,
Markus Pillok

Employment and labour law
Markus Pillok

Family and inheritance law
Monika Fink-Plücker

IT, media, intellectual property
Markus Pillok

CMS HASCHE SIGLE

AN DER DREIKÖNIGSKIRCHE 10
01097 DRESDEN

Telephone: +49 351 82 64 40
Fax: +49 351 8 26 47 16
E-mail: dresden@cmslegal.de
Website: www.cmslegal.de

Languages
English

Other offices
Berlin, Dusseldorf, Frankfurt, Hamburg, Leipzig, Munich, Stuttgart, Chemnitz, Brussels, Belgrade, Moscow, Prague, Shanghai

Number of lawyers 306
at this office 3

Other CMS law firms
CMS Adonnino Ascoli & Cavasola Scamoni, Italy; CMS Bureau Francis Lefebvre, France; CMS Cameron McKenna, UK; CMS Derks Star Busmann, Netherlands; CMS von Erlach Klainguti Stettler Wille, Switzerland; CMS Lexcelis, Belgium; CMS Strommer Reich-Rohrwig Karasek Hainz, Austria

CATEGORIES OF WORK

Corporate and commercial

Mergers and acquisitions

Privatisation and restructuring

Banking, securities and finance

Unfair competition and antitrust

Tax

Labour law and service contracts

Bankruptcy and reorganisation

Intellectual property, IT, media

Real estate and construction

Environmental and administrative

Distribution, franchising

Maritime law

Arbitration and litigation

Utilities

GRAF VON WESTPHALEN BAPPERT & MODEST

AN DER FRAUENKIRCHE 12
01067 DRESDEN

Telephone: +49 351 34 08 70
Fax: +49 351 34 08 718
E-mail: dresden@westphalen-law.com
Website: www.westphalen-law.com

Languages
English, French, Russian, Spanish

Other offices
Berlin, Brussels, Cologne, Freiburg, Hamburg, Munich, Vienna

Number of lawyers 110
at this office 5
(+1 tax adviser)

In exclusive co-operation with
Wragge & Co, UK;
Kemmler Rapp Böhlke, Belgium

CATEGORIES OF WORK

- Corporate, mergers and acquisitions
- Succession
- Banking and insolvency
- Real estate and construction
- Public procurement
- Labour and employment
- Product liability and insurance
- Environmental and planning
- Public health care
- Life sciences
- Energy law
- Tax law
- Arbitration and litigation

NÖRR STIEFENHOFER LUTZ

LOUIS-BRAILLE-STRASSE 5
01099 DRESDEN

Telephone: +49 351 81 66 00
Fax: +49 351 816 60 81
E-mail: nsldd@noerr.de
Website: www.noerr.de

Languages
English, French, Italian, Russian

Other offices
Berlin, Bucharest, Budapest, Düsseldorf, Frankfurt, Moscow, Munich, Prague, Warsaw

Number of lawyers 237
(+ 53 tax advisers, public accountants and tax assistants)
at this office 13
(+2 tax advisers, public accountants and tax assistants)

Contact
Otto Stolberg-Stolberg

CATEGORIES OF WORK

- Mergers and acquisitions
- Company and commercial law
- Property and real estate law
- Restitution claims and investment law
- Administrative and environmental law
- Banking law
- Greenfield investments
- Construction law
- Law relating to commercial leases
- Labour law and industrial relations
- Planning and construction law
- East German (formerly DDR) law, especially commercial law
- Tax law
- International private and contract law

ARCON RECHTSANWÄLTE

SCHMIDT-SIBETH HEISSE WEISSKOPF KURSAWE

STEINSTRASSE 1/KO
40212 DÜSSELDORF

Telephone: +49 211 82 89 59 0
Fax: +49 221 82 89 59 60
E-mail: dus@arcon-net.com
Website: www.arcon-net.com

Languages
Catalan, Dutch, English, Finnish, French, Greek, Italian, Portuguese, Russian, Spanish

Other offices
Berlin, Brussels, Cologne, Erfurt, Frankfurt am Main, Hamburg, Munich

Number of lawyers 92
at this office 10

Contact
Andreas Seidel

CATEGORIES OF WORK

Corporate law, mergers and acquisitions, reorganisations	Litigation and arbitration
IPO, capital markets	Contract
Construction and real estate	Tax
Labour law, employment	Administrative and environment
EU law	Probate and family law
Commercial law (general)	Estate planning
Trade marks, intellectual property, media law	Internet, IT and computer law
Competition, antitrust	

BIRD & BIRD

KARL-THEODOR-STRASSE 6
40213 DÜSSELDORF

Telephone: +49 211 20 05 60 00
Fax: +49 211 20 05 60 11
E-mail: duesseldorf@twobirds.com
Website: www.twobirds.com

Languages
English, French, German

Other offices
Brussels, Hong Kong, London, Milan, Munich, Paris, Stockholm, The Hague

Number of lawyers 358
at this office 33

Contacts
Wolfgang von Meibom (chairman),
Dr Alexander Schröder-Frerkes (vice-chairman)

CATEGORIES OF WORK

Arbitration	IT and e-commerce
Aviation	Litigation
Commercial	Media
Communication	Mergers and acquisitions
Corporate	Public procurement
Employment	Real estate
EU and competition	Regulatory
Intellectual property	Sport and sponsorship

BAKER & McKENZIE

NEUER ZOLLHOF 3
40221 DÜSSELDORF

Telephone: +49 211 31 11 60
Fax: +49 211 31 11 61 99
Website: www.bakernet.com

Languages
Dutch, English, French, Japanese, Spanish

Other offices Almaty, Amsterdam, Antwerp, Bahrain, Baku, Bangkok, Barcelona, Beijing, Berlin, Bogotá, Bologna, Brasilia, Brussels, Budapest, Buenos Aires, Cairo, Calgary, Caracas, Chicago, Dallas, Frankfurt, Geneva, Guadalajara, Hanoi, Ho Chi Minh City, Hong Kong, Houston, Juarez, Kyiv, London, Madrid, Manila, Melbourne, Mexico City, Miami, Milan, Monterrey, Moscow, Munich, New York, Palo Alto, Paris, Porto Alegré, Prague, Rio de Janeiro, Riyadh, Rome, St Petersburg, San Diego, San Francisco, Santiago, São Paulo, Shanghai, Singapore, Stockholm, Sydney, Taipei, Tijuana, Tokyo, Toronto, Valencia, Vienna, Warsaw, Washington DC, Zürich

Number of lawyers 3,380
at this office 22

CATEGORIES OF WORK

Commercial law
Jürgen Mark

Company law
Ernst-Markus Schuberth, Barbara Deilmann

Information technology, media and computer law
Heiko Plaßmeier

Labour law
Markus Kappenhagen

Mergers and acquisitions
Bernd Mayer, Joachim Drude

Litigation and arbitration
Jürgen Mark

Product liability
Jürgen Mark

Venture capital and capital markets
Peter Verannemann, Ernst-Markus Schuberth

THE FIRM

Founded in Chicago in 1949, Baker & McKenzie is a global law firm with 66 offices in 36 countries. A multinational network of over 4,400 legal professionals offers clients resources and knowledge in every area of business law, in virtually every important financial and commercial centre in the world.

Baker & McKenzie has been established in Europe for over 40 years, having opened its first European offices in 1957. Since then, the European and Middle Eastern network has grown to 29 offices, giving it unparalleled geographical coverage.

The Frankfurt am Main office was formed in 1962; the office in Berlin was opened on 1 March 1990; the Munich office on 1 April 1997; and the Düsseldorf office on 1 April 1999.

Since their formation, the German offices of Baker & McKenzie have advised its clients on all questions of German, European and international industrial and commercial law with particular emphasis on cross-border and multinational transactions. At present, more than 170 attorneys-at-law (Rechtsanwälte), admitted in the Federal Republic of Germany including the new federal states, tax advisers, and varying numbers of foreign admitted lawyers work in the German offices of Baker & McKenzie.

All attorneys are at least bilingual; most of them have completed additional graduate legal studies at foreign law schools. Several attorneys are simultaneously admitted as CPAs, tax advisers, tax attorneys, attorneys for administrative law or attorneys for labour law.

AREAS OF PRACTICE

Baker & McKenzie co-ordinates its core practice areas on local, regional and global levels, giving most of its lawyers experience in more than one jurisdiction, as well as providing multinational teams of specialists.

Utilising a global practice group structure and ground-breaking technology coupled with a personal, detailed understanding of a client's specific business, Baker & McKenzie is able to organise its extensive resources to provide focused and strategic counsel to clients.

Baker & McKenzie advises multinational enterprises, large German companies, medium-sized enterprises, banks and insurance companies, as well as institutions and entities under public law in all questions of German, European, and international industrial and commercial law including company law, competition and cartel law, intellectual property, banking and finance, labour law, administrative law, and tax law. Furthermore, the firm handles litigation and arbitration matters. Several partners have expertise in specialised areas of law, such as European Community law, the law of cosmetics, food and drug law, trade marks, franchising, corporate finance, new financial products, government procurement, real estate transactions, and media telecommunications law.

BUSE HEBERER FROMM

KÖNIGSALLEE 98A-100
40215 DÜSSELDORF

Telephone: +49 211 388 000
Fax: +49 211 373 678
E-mail: duesseldorf@buse.de
Website: www.buse.de

Languages
English, French, Italian, Spanish

Other offices
Berlin, Essen, Frankfurt am Main, Hamburg, Milan, Munich, Palma de Mallorca, Sydney, Zurich

Number of lawyers 120
at this office 13

Member
The European Legal Alliance (Beauchamps, Ireland; Dubarry Le Douarin Veil, France; Field Fisher Waterhouse, England; Harper Macleod, Scotland)

CATEGORIES OF WORK

- Banking and finance
- Antitrust and merger control
- Commerce, transport, insurance
- Commercial delinquency
- Corporate/M&A
- Industrial property and copyrights
- Information technology and telecommunications
- Labour and employment
- Litigation and arbitration, national and international
- Press and media
- Property and construction
- Public law
- Tax

CMS HASCHE SIGLE

BANKSTRASSE 1
40476 DÜSSELDORF

Telephone: +49 2 11 49 340
Fax: +49 2 11 49 20 097
E-mail: duesseldorf@cmslegal.de
Website: www.cmslegal.de

Languages
English, French, Spanish

Other offices
Berlin, Frankfurt, Hamburg, Leipzig, Munich, Stuttgart, Chemnitz, Dresden, Belgrade, Brussels, Moscow, Prague, Shanghai

Number of lawyers 310
at this office 27

Other CMS law firms
CMS Adonnino Ascoli & Cavasola Scamoni, Italy; CMS Bureau Francis Lefebvre, France; CMS Cameron McKenna, UK; CMS Derks Star Busmann, Netherlands; CMS von Erlach Klainguti Stettler Wille, Switzerland; CMS Lexcelis, Belgium; CMS Strommer Reich-Rohrwig Karasek Hainz, Austria

CATEGORIES OF WORK

- Corporate and commercial
- Mergers and acquisitions
- Privatisation and restructuring
- Banking, securities and finance
- Unfair competition and antitrust
- Tax
- Labour law and service contracts
- Bankruptcy and reorganisation
- Intellectual property, IT and media
- Real estate and construction
- Environmental and administration
- Distribution and agency
- Maritime law
- Arbitration and litigation
- Utilities

FRESHFIELDS BRUCKHAUS DERINGER

FREILIGRATHSTRASSE 1
40479 DÜSSELDORF

Telephone: +49 211 49 790
Fax: +49 211 49 79 103
E-mail: email@freshfields.com
Website: www.freshfields.com

Languages
Extensive language capabilities

Other offices
Amsterdam, Bangkok, Barcelona, Beijing, Berlin, Bratislava, Brussels, Budapest, Cologne, Frankfurt, Hamburg, Hanoi, Ho Chi Minh City, Hong Kong, London, Madrid, Milan, Moscow, Munich, New York, Paris, Rome, Shanghai, Singapore, Tokyo, Vienna, Washington

Number of lawyers 2,504
at this office 112

Contact
Thomas Kreifels

CATEGORIES OF WORK

Corporate

Finance

Antitrust, competition and trade

Intellectual property and IT

Tax

Real estate

Dispute resolution (including environment, planning and regulatory)

Employment, pensions and benefits

HAARMANN HEMMELRATH

MARTIN-LUTHER-PLATZ 26
40212 DUSSELDORF

Telephone: +49 211 83 99 0
Fax: +49 211 83 99 133
E-mail:
dusseldorf@haarmannhemmelrath.com
Website:
www.haarmannhemmelrath.com

Languages
Bulgarian, Croatian, Czech, Dutch, English, French, Hungarian, Italian, Japanese, Mandarin, Norwegian, Polish, Portuguese, Romanian, Russian, Slovak, Spanish, Vietnamese

Other offices
Berlin, Bielefeld, Brussels, Bucharest, Budapest, Cologne, Frankfurt, Hamburg, Leipzig, London, Milan, Moscow, Munich, Paris, Prague, Rome, Shanghai, Singapore, Stuttgart, Tokyo, Vienna, Warsaw

Number of lawyers 281
at this office 16

CATEGORIES OF WORK

Mergers and acquisitions
Andreas Dietl, Dr Ulf Hackenberg

Corporate finance
Thomas Bula, Joerg Schoberth

Venture capital, private equity
Harald Plewka, Dr Susanne Rückert

Fund structuring
Harald Plewka, Torsten Grob

Capital markets
Andreas Dietl, Dr Susanne Rückert

Banking, leasing
Dr Bernd Sagasser, Harald Plewka

Corporate and business law
Andreas Dietl, Dr Susanne Rückert

IP, IT, antitrust, EU law
Dr Waldemar Joschko, Heiko Tietz

Inheritance law
Harald Plewka, Dr Jürgen Schimmele

Public law and regulatory matters, environment and energy law, privatisation
Dr Matthias Lang, Dr Ulrich Mutschler

Labour
Dr Waldemar Joschko, Dr Monika Schmidt

Litigation, mediation, arbitration
Dr Waldemar Joschko, Dr Günter Fußbahn

Corporate recovery, insolvency
Hans-Jörg Hegerl

International tax law
Dr Bernd Sagasser, Harald Plewka

National tax law and compliance
Thomas Bula, Christine Vogel

Corporate taxation
Harald Plewka, Dr Jürgen Schimmele

Accounting
Joerg Schoberth, Susann Ihlau

GRAVENHORST, FÄRBER, SCHUMACHER, RÖHRBORN, SIMDORN, KIRCHNER

HEINZ-SCHMÖLE-STRASSE 12
POSTFACH 10 26 53
40227 DÜSSELDORF

Telephone: +49 211 72 06 70
Fax: +49 211 72 06 711
Website: www.kanzlei-arbeitsrecht.de

Languages
English, Italian, French

Number of lawyers 11

Contacts
Dr Wulf Gravenhorst, Dr Peter Färber, Dr Renate Schumacher, Dr Stefan Röhrborn, Uwe Simdorn, Dr Meike Kirchner

CATEGORIES OF WORK

- Employment and labour law
- Due diligence, M&As
- Unfair dismissals
- Mass dismissals
- Employment law for managing directors and members of the board
- Rationalisation projects
- Training in employment and labour law
- Social plans
- Company pension schemes
- Labour law and employment litigation
- Labour leasing
- In-house training for companies
- Collective bargaining agreements
- Sponsorship and labour law for professional sports

THE FIRM

The firm is regarded as one of the leading law firms in Germany regarding all aspects of labour law and employment. Initially the firm was established by Dr Wulf Gravenhorst in 1983 after 12 years of labour and employment law experience as an associate lawyer in German industry and as a partner at a well-known commercial law firm. In 1987, Dr Peter Färber joined the firm after several years' experience in labour law as an attorney and associate lawyer. In 1994, Dr Renate Schumacher joined the firm followed, in 1999, by Dr Stefan Röhrborn and Uwe Simdorn, and in 2003 Dr Meike Kirchner. The firm employs five further associate lawyers. Traditionally all partners of the firm and all associate lawyers have specialised in labour law and employment, representing both employers and employees.

AREAS OF PRACTICE

The only area of work for all lawyers of the firm is collective and individual labour law including litigation with respect to both domestic and international clients. The firm provides advice on unfair and mass dismissals, negotiating with works councils, and legal aspects of outsourcing. Services are provided by either an individual lawyer or as a team where necessary.

Dr Gravenhorst mainly represents managing directors, members of the board of directors and leading employees. He is also a leading expert in any kind of collective labour law. Dr Färber is a well-known expert in collective labour law, social plans, and the M&A business. His clients are well-known companies covering all sectors (banking and finance, insurance, automotive, IT, industry). Dr Schumacher has specialised upon representing managing directors, leading employees and sales representatives as well as privately owned companies. Dr Röhrborn has focused upon legal due diligence, outsourcing and rationalisation projects, labour leasing and labour law for professional sports. He represents companies involved in IT, fashion, and banking and finance as well as members of the board of directors, managing directors and leading employees. Mr Simdorn has specialised in collective labour law and social plans. His clients include private and public owned companies in all sectors. Dr Kirchner covers issues regarding unfair dismissal and company pension schemes.

All members of the firm provide services as in-house and institutional trainers for all labour law matters.

HENGELER MUELLER

BENRATHER STRASSE 18-20
40213 DÜSSELDORF

Telephone: +49 211 8304 0
Fax: +49 211 8304 170
E-mail: hmdus@hengeler.com
Website: www.hengeler.com

Other offices
Frankfurt, Berlin, Brussels, London, Budapest, Prague

Number of lawyers 195
at this office 64

Contact
Dr Gerd Krieger

CATEGORIES OF WORK

M&A

Private equity and venture capital

General corporate and corporate restructuring

Insolvency and reorganisation

Equity capital markets

Corporate finance

Competition

IP/IT

Regulatory and environment

Telecommunications and media

Real estate

Energy

Litigation and arbitration

HEUSSEN
RECHTSANWALTSGESELLSCHAFT MBH

WERDENER STRASSE 10
40227 DÜSSELDORF

Telephone: +49 211 981 8000
Fax: +49 211 981 8010
E-mail: info@landwell.de
Website: www.landwell.de

Languages
Arabic, Dutch, English, French, Greek, Italian, Russian, Spanish, Swedish

Other offices
Berlin, Cologne, Frankfurt, Hamburg, Munich, Stuttgart

Number of lawyers 100
at this office 16

Contact
Edith Rautenbach

International groupings
Landwell, correspondent law firms of PricewaterhouseCoopers

CATEGORIES OF WORK

Commercial and competition
Dr Gunther Braun

Corporate structuring
Robert Dorr

Dispute resolution
Dr Reiner Ponschab

Technology, media and communications
Dr Axel Czarnetzki, Rafaela Wilde

Employment and human resources
Hans Stefan Korsch

Financial services
Dr Gunther Braun

Intellectual property
Dr Axel Czarnetzki

Mergers and acquisitions
Dr Karl Maria Walter, Michael Ketterl

Public law
Dr Michael W Mütze

Real estate
Dr Michael W Mütze

HEUKING KÜHN LÜER WOJTEK

CECILIENALLEE 5
40474 DÜSSELDORF

Telephone: +49 211 600 55 00
Fax: +49 211 600 55 050
E-mail: duesseldorf@heuking.de
Website: www.heuking.de

Languages
German, English, French, Japanese

Other offices
Berlin, Brussels, Chemnitz, Cologne, Frankfurt, Hamburg, Munich

Number of lawyers 40

Contacts
Dr Wolfgang Kühn, Dirk Kolvenbach

CATEGORIES OF WORK

Corporate, partnerships, international mergers and acquisitions, general commercial law

German and international tax law

Private clients and family office

Competition, merger control, antitrust

Banking and finance

Insurance

Leasing and finance

Litigation, arbitration and mediation

Administrative law

Entertainment, media, publishing, copyright

Industrial property

Employment and labour law

Real estate transactions and construction law

Environmental law

Family law

Telecommunications law

THE FIRM

Heuking Kühn Lüer Wojtek was founded in Düsseldorf, Germany, in 1971. Since then, the firm has spread geographically, and Heuking Kühn now has seven significant offices in Germany, as well as an office in Brussels.

The firm has an extensive international network of law firms, enabling it to provide its clients with seamless 'one-stop shopping', on international transactions and regulatory matters. Since its formation, Heuking Kühn Lüer Wojtek has specifically chosen to remain an independent law firm. It is Heuking Kühn Lüer Wojtek's philosophy that, to provide the best possible service to its clients, the firm must be able to co-operate with various other law firms which are at the top of the profession in their respective countries. This gives the firm the ability to make alternative counsel suggestions to its clients, giving the clients a choice of the best suitable law firm or lawyer in each country and for each matter. Over the last 30+ years, Heuking Kühn Lüer Wojtek has developed excellent relationships with the key firms in all of the major jurisdictions worldwide.

Heuking Kühn Lüer Wojtek is a name which is synonymous with legal competence. The firm is one of the largest commercial law firms in Germany, with more than 150 specialised lawyers and tax advisers, representing the interests of national and international clients. Included in the client list are large and medium-sized German and international companies in all areas of the manufacturing industry, as well as trade and service industries, associations, governmental and public sector organisations and private clients and trusts.

The firm prides itself on substantive legal competence and on the excellent education and continuing legal education of its lawyers. Moreover, virtually all of the lawyers are German-English bilingual.

Extensive specialisation and comprehensive knowledge of specific industry sectors provide the basis of all of Heuking Kühn Lüer Wojtek's legal counselling. Experienced partners and carefully selected associate lawyers develop innovative solutions to complex legal problems. The lawyers regularly work in their specific practice area groups and also in multi-group and multi-disciplinary teams with clients and outside consultants or advisers. Entrepreneurial thinking on behalf of firm clients, as well as efficient, quality, cost-effective and timely work and the highest personal dedication are key components of Heuking Kühn Lüer Wojtek's culture.

AREAS OF PRACTICE

Heuking Kühn Lüer Wojtek is a full-service commercial law firm. Cross-border and cross-sector knowledge in combination with a deep understanding of business reasoning enables service to clients with the broadest possible support in all their negotiations and business decisions. This applies equally to M&A transactions, to legal advice on company structure, business risk management, negotiations and negotiation tactics, training, crisis and insolvency counselling, corporate financial matters, and complex litigation and arbitration. Thanks to a variety of strong business clients, the firm has built long-term relationships with its clients and can assist them, beginning with the establishment of a business, followed by implementing business goals, including day-to-day legal work, reorganisations, acquisitions and divestitures.

Heuking Kühn Lüer Wojtek is actively involved with its clients in providing regulatory counselling in all areas of commercial law, as well as assisting them in organising and implementing their M&A transactions in Germany, throughout Europe, and internationally. Heuking Kühn Lüer Wojtek has particular expertise in German and EU company law; competition law, merger control and state aids; international investment, trade, and taxation matters; banking and finance; labour law; intellectual property rights; environmental, health, and safety regulation; product-specific regulation; real estate and construction law; telecoms, IT and media law; transport, postal services and shipping law; public procurement; family law; and private clients and family office matters.

HÖLTERS & ELSING

IMMERMANNSTRASSE 40
40210 DÜSSELDORF

Telephone: +49 211 36 78 70
Fax: +49 211 35 39 28
E-mail: duesseldorf@hoelters-elsing.com
Website: www.hoelters-elsing.com

Languages
Dutch, English, French, German, Portuguese, Spanish, Swedish

Other offices
Berlin, Frankfurt

Number of lawyers 46
at this office 25

CATEGORIES OF WORK

Business organisations
Dr W Hölters, Dr SH Elsing

Business litigation and arbitration
Dr SH Elsing, Dr M Alberts

Employment and labour issues
Dr M Sondermann

Competition, intellectual property
TA Oerter

Administrative law
Dr P Zimmermann

Mergers and acquisitions
Dr W Hölters, Dr SH Elsing

Antitrust law
Dr M Alberts

Insurance law
Dr R Woltereck

Tax law
Dr W Hölters

Company law
Dr W Hölters, Dr SH Elsing

Real property law
Dr P Zimmerman, Dr M Alberts

Telecommunications law
R Bornhofen

KRIEGER GENTZ MES & GRAF VON DER GROEBEN

GEORG GLOCK STRASSE 3
40474 DÜSSELDORF

Telephone: +49 211 44 03 370
Fax: +49 211 43 70 707
E-mail: info@krieger-mes.de
Website: www.krieger-mes.de

Languages
Dutch, English, French, Italian

Number of lawyers 9

Member
AIPPI; IBA

CATEGORIES OF WORK

Patents, utility models including employee's inventions

Trade marks

Design patents

Copyright law

Unfair competition

Antitrust law

National and international litigation, including multinational litigation

Arbitration and mediation (national and international)

Licensing and franchising

Commercial contracts

LOVELLS

KENNEDYDAMM 17
40476 DÜSSELDORF

Telephone: +49 211 13 68 0
Fax: +49 211 13 68 100
E-mail: receptiondus@lovells.com
Website: www.lovells.de

Languages
Dutch, English, French, Italian, Portuguese, Russian, Spanish

Other offices
Alicante, Amsterdam, Beijing, Berlin, Brussels, Budapest*, Chicago, Frankfurt, Hamburg, Ho Chi Minh City, Hong Kong, London, Milan, Moscow, Munich, New York, Paris, Prague, Rome, Shanghai, Singapore, Tokyo, Vienna*, Warsaw, Zagreb*

Number of lawyers 1,600
at this office 58

Contact
Erhard Keller

CATEGORIES OF WORK

- Corporate/M&A, private equity
- Restructuring and insolvency
- Banking
- Antitrust and unfair competition
- Capital markets
- Project finance, public private partnerships
- Tax
- Employment
- Intellectual property
- Property
- Projects
- Technology, media, telecommunications
- Litigation, product liability
- International arbitration
- Food and drug regulations
- Law of Eastern Europe

MAIWALD PATENTANWALTS GMBH

NEUER ZOLLHOF 2
40221 DÜSSELDORF

Telephone: +49 211 669 698 40
Fax: +49 211 669 698 60
E-mail: mail@maiwald.de
Website: www.maiwald.de

Languages
English, French, German, Spanish

Other offices
Hamburg, Munich

Number of lawyers 14
at this office 2

Contacts
Dr Stefan Michalski, Lutz Kietzmann

CATEGORIES OF WORK

- Patents
- Trade marks
- Intellectual property – related copyrights
- Unfair competition
- Competition and software law
- Internet law
- Business and commercial law
- Licensing and litigation

McDERMOTT, WILL & EMERY

STADTTOR 1, 15TH FLOOR
40219 DÜSSELDORF

Telephone: +49 211 3003 400
Fax: +49 211 3003 444
Website: www.mwe.com

Languages
All main business languages

Other offices
Boston, Brussels, Chicago, London, Los Angeles, Miami, Milan, Munich, New York, Orange County, Rome, San Diego, Silicon Valley, Washington DC

Number of lawyers 1,000
at this office 9

CATEGORIES OF WORK

Antitrust and regulatory
Dr Thomas Hauss

Capital markets
Konstantin Günther

Corporate
Konstantin Günther,
Dr Alexander Hirsch

Intellectual property
Dr Thomas Hauss

Labour and employment
Volker Teigelkötter

Mergers and acquisitions
Konstantin Günther,
Dr Alexander Hirsch

Private equity, venture capital
Konstantin Günther,
Dr Alexander Hirsch

Taxation
Dr Richard Schmidt

THE FIRM

McDermott, Will & Emery is a premier international law firm with a diversified business practice. Numbering more than 1,000 lawyers, nearly 70 years of serving the broad scope of clients' interests has positioned its lawyers to handle the gamut of legal challenges. The firm understands the issues faced by corporate decision-makers and how the interplay of economic, social and political issues can affect the decision-making process.

The firm's presence in Germany is part of a robust international practice and delivery of high-end legal services to its clients in Germany, Europe and beyond. The German practice group, which includes lawyers primarily in its Düsseldorf, Munich and New York offices, concentrates on all aspects of cross-border transactions from corporate counselling to labour agreements. This cross-office, cross-cultural practice group is familiar with many different legal and cultural approaches in the global markket place. The German practice group is fully integrated with the international practice. Connected by cutting-edge technology, German lawyers collaborate with the firm's lawyers in its other offices worldwide.

AREAS OF PRACTICE

The German practice provides legal counsel to multinational enterprises and foreign clients with German and European interests, as well as to Germany's enterprises, including its 'Mittelstand'. The group handles various corporate and commercial matters, including cross-border mergers and acquisitions, joint ventures, cross-border financings and securities matters. In addition, the German practice group has substantial experience in the areas of antitrust and competition, capital markets, corporate, intellectual property, labour and employment, mergers and acquisitions, private equity/venture capital, taxation, and telecommunications, media and information technology.

NÖRR STIEFENHOFER LUTZ

VICTORIAPLATZ 2
40477 DÜSSELDORF

Telephone: +49 211 49 98 60
Fax: +49 211 49 98 61 00
E-mail: nsldus@noerr.de
Website: www.noerr.de

Languages
English, French, Italian, Russian, Spanish

Other offices
Berlin, Bucharest, Budapest, Dresden, Frankfurt, Moscow, Munich, Prague, Warsaw

Number of lawyers 237
(+ 53 tax advisers, public accountants and tax assistants)
at this office 15

Contact
Dr Stefan Tomicic

CATEGORIES OF WORK

Mergers and acquisitions

Company and tax law

International and commercial law

Litigation, civil law

Insolvency, reorganisation

Professional liability

Labour law

Real estate

Administrative and regulatory law

PPR & PARTNER

ATTORNEYS CERTIFIED PUBLIC ACCOUNTANT TAX ADVISORS

KÖNIGSALLEE 70
40212 DÜSSELDORF

Telephone: +49 211 828 929 0
Fax: +49 211 828 929 29
E-mail: kontakt@ppr-partner.de
Website: www.ppr-partner.de

Languages
English, French, Italian, Spanish

Number of lawyers 12

Contacts
Dieter G Pape, Dr Theo Rauh

Member
Lexwork

CATEGORIES OF WORK

Competition and antitrust law
Jörg Meyer, Anton Horn

Construction and real estate
Markus Melcher

Corporate law
Hans-Peter Palenberg, Dr Theo Rauh

Foodstuffs law
Jörg Meyer

Employment law
Dieter G Pape, Petra Wübbeke

Information technology
Anton Horn

International commercial law
Dr Theo Rauh, Anton Horn

Inheritance and inheritance tax law
Hans-Peter Palenberg, Gesa Vygen

Mergers and acquisitions
Hans-Peter Palenberg, Dr Theo Rauh

National and international tax law
Hans Peter Palenberg, Klaus T Stalpers

Public law
Markus Melcher

Sale and distribution law
Anton Horn

Trade mark, intellectual property
Jörg Meyer, Julia Jakubowski

ROSPATT OSTEN PROSS
RECHTSANWÄLTE

PO BOX 11 09 35
KAISER-FRIEDRICH-RING 56
40509 DÜSSELDORF

Telephone: +49 211 57 72 45 0
Fax: +49 211 57 72 45 55
E-mail: mail@rospatt.de
Website: www.rospatt.de

Languages
English, French

Other offices
Mannheim

Number of lawyers 10
at this office 9

CATEGORIES OF WORK

- **Patents, utility models**
- **Unfair competition**
- **Trade marks**
- **Product liability**
- **Design patents**
- **Litigation, arbitration, licensing**
- **Copyrights**

SIMMONS & SIMMONS

KÖNIGSALLEE 98A
40215 DÜSSELDORF

Telephone: +49 211 47 05 30
Fax: +49 211 43 12 88
E-mail: enquiries@simmons-simmons.com
Website: www.simmons-simmons.com

Languages
English, French, Dutch, Spanish

Other offices
London, Rotterdam, Paris, Lisbon, Milan, Rome, Frankfurt, Brussels, Madrid, Padua, Oporto, Madeira, Abu Dhabi, Qatar, Hong Kong, Shanghai, Tokyo, New York

Number of lawyers 754
at this office 19

Contact
Jane Newman

CATEGORIES OF WORK

- **Corporate**
- **Financial markets**
- **Banking**
- **Pharmaceutical and biotechnology**
- **Capital markets**
- **Energy and utilities**
- **Taxation**
- **TMT**
- **Projects, PFI**
- **Aerospace and defence**
- **EU, competition**
- **Transport**
- **Dispute resolution**
- **Real estate and construction**
- **Intellectual property**
- **Consumer goods**
- **Employment**

TAYLOR WESSING

KÖNIGSALLEE 92A
40212 DÜSSELDORF

Telephone: +49 211 83 87 0
Fax: +49 211 83 87 100
E-mail: duesseldorf@taylorwessing.com
Website: www.taylorwessing.com

Languages
Dutch, English, French, Italian, Mandarin, Spanish

Other offices
Alicante*, Berlin, Brussels, Cambridge, Dubai*, Frankfurt, Hamburg, London, Munich, Paris, Shanghai*

Number of lawyers 550
at this office 52

Member
World Law Group; Tech Law Group

CATEGORIES OF WORK

Banking and finance
Claus Goedecke, Peter Seemann

China desk
Florian Ranft

Commercial
Dr Christoph Hasche

Corporate/M&A
Bernhard Kloft

Employment and pensions
Axel C Filges

EU law/antitrust
Dr Marco Hartmann-Rüppel, Markus Wirtz

Intellectual property
Dr Sabine Rojahn

Life science
Dr Ulrich Steffen

Media and entertainment
Martin von Albrecht

Private client
Romana Traichel

Projects and finance
Dr Rüdiger von Hülst

Public commercial law
Dr Walter Potthast

Real estate and construction
Jan Wunschel

Regulatory affairs
Andreas Haak

Tax
Bernd Michel

Technology/IT/telecoms
Joerg Wimmers

WEBER & SAUBERSCHWARZ

KÖNIGSALLEE 1
40212 DUSSELDORF

Telephone: +49 211 440 3930
Fax: +49 211 440 39 399
E-mail: mail@weber-sauberschwarz.de
Website: www.weber-sauberschwarz.de

Languages
English, French, Greek

Number of lawyers 8

Member
AIPPI (International Association for the Protection of Intellectual Property)

CATEGORIES OF WORK

Unfair competition
Dr Werner Sauberschwarz, Hans Michael Prange

Antitrust
Dr Werner Sauberschwarz, Hans Michael Prange

Design protection
Dr Lambert Pechan

Trade mark
Dr Lambert Pechan, Stefanie Körber

Copyright
Barbara Bleifeld, Stefanie Körber

Labour law
Barbara Bleifeld, Dr Claudia Pappas

IT and Internet law
Hans Michael Prange, Dr Lambert Pechan

Communication law
Hans Michael Prange, Barbara Bleifeld

Commercial and corporate law
Dr Werner Sauberschwarz

THE FIRM

The firm was founded in 1963 by Dr Guenter Weber. Throughout Germany, the firm advises and represents major companies primarily engaged in trade, advertising, telecommunications, IT and the service sectors. It also represents the interests of clients in select issues of labour law, business law and business-related civil matters.

The firm's clients expect and can expect outstanding expertise and considerable experience. Such expectations measure the professional and personal competence of the partners and associates against high standards. With eight attorneys, the firm has attained the optimal size for meeting these requirements. All of the firm's attorneys are highly specialised and motivated in their areas of practice. In matters involving complex issues, the attorneys work closely together. Therefore they are able to advise clients and represent their interests with cumulative expertise throughout Germany. As a result, the firm holds an exceptional position among the firms practising in this area of the law.

AREAS OF PRACTICE

From its inception, it has been highly specialised in the areas of intellectual property, in particular competition and antitrust law, EU law, trade mark law, design protection law, communications law and copyright law.

The firm has brought about more than 100 leading decisions in the Federal Supreme Court for its clients. In this way, it has significantly contributed to developments in the law, particularly in the areas of competition and antitrust law.

ARCON RECHTSANWÄLTE
SCHMIDT-SIBETH HEISSE WEISSKOPF KURSAWE

BAHNHOFSTRASSE 46
99084 ERFURT

Telephone: +49 361 56 56 20
Fax: +49 361 56 56 236
E-mail: erfurt@arcon-net.com
Website: www.arcon-net.com

Languages
Catalan, Dutch, English, Finnish, French, Greek, Italian, Portuguese, Russian, Spanish

Other offices
Berlin, Brussels, Cologne, Düsseldorf, Frankfurt am Main, Hamburg, Munich

Number of lawyers 92
at this office 10

Contacts
Dr Wolfgang Weisskopf, Dr Kathrin Thiele

CATEGORIES OF WORK

Corporate law, mergers and acquisitions, reorganisations

IPO, capital markets

Construction and real estate

Labour law, employment

Public procurement law

EU law

Commercial law (general)

Trade marks, intellectual property, media law

Competition, antitrust

Litigation and arbitration

Contract

Tax

Administrative and environment

Probate and family law

Estate planning

Internet, IT and computer law

BETTE – BRINK

SEMMELWEISSTRASSE 12
99096 ERFURT

Telephone: +49 361 34 74 00
Fax: +49 361 34 74 099
E-mail: bette-brink@erfurt.juropartner.de
Website: www.bette-brink.de

Languages
English, French, Russian, Spanish

Other offices
Berlin, Mainz

Number of lawyers 11
at this office 3

Member
Juropartner (European Society for Economic Interests)

CATEGORIES OF WORK

Construction law
Birgit Anuschek, Christian Stückrad

Industrial relations law
Birgit Anuschek

Commercial law
Birgit Anuschek

Company law
Christian Ceranski

Banking law
Christian Ceranski

Leasing law
Christian Ceranski

Traffic accident law
Christian Stückrad

Law of the new Federal States
Birgit Anuschek

Computer law
Christian Ceranski

Law for the promotion of the fuel and electricity industries
Christian Ceranski

BUSE HEBERER FROMM

HUYSSENALLEE 86-88
45128 ESSEN

Telephone: +49 201 175 80
Fax: +49 201 175 84 00
E-mail: essen@buse.de
Website: www.buse.de

Languages
English, French, Italian, Spanish

Other offices
Berlin, Dusseldorf, Frankfurt am Main, Hamburg, Milan, Munich, Palma de Mallorca, Sydney, Zurich

Number of lawyers 120
at this office 14

Member
The European Legal Alliance (Beauchamps, Ireland; Dubarry Le Douarin Veil, France; Field Fisher Waterhouse, England; Harper Macleod, Scotland)

CATEGORIES OF WORK

- Banking and finance
- Antitrust and merger control
- Commerce, transport, insurance
- Commercial delinquency
- Corporate/M&A
- Industrial property and copyrights
- Information technology and telecommunications
- Labour and employment
- Litigation and arbitration, national and international
- Press and media
- Property and construction
- Public law
- Tax

GÖRG
RECHTSANWÄLTE

BREDENEYER TOR
EINIGKEITSTRASSE 9
45133 ESSEN

Telephone: +49 201 43 77 60
Fax: +49 201 43 77 620
E-mail: essen@goerg.de
Website: www.goerg.de

Languages
English, French, Italian, Russian, Spanish

Other offices
Amsterdam*, Antwerp*, Bangkok*, Barcelona*, Bergen*, Berlin, Birmingham*, Bradford*, Brussels*, Cologne, Copenhagen*, Edinburgh*, Frankfurt/M, Glasgow*, Hamburg, Hong Kong*, Leeds*, Liverpool*, London*, Madrid*, Manchester*, Milan*, Oslo*, Paris*, Prague*, Rotterdam*, Salzburg*, Sarajevo*, Shanghai*, Sheffield*, Singapore*, Stockholm*, Vienna*, Zagreb*

Number of lawyers 83
at this office 5

Member
DLA Group

CATEGORIES OF WORK

- General and international law practice
- Corporate and commercial
- Banking
- Bankruptcy and insolvency law
- Mergers and acquisitions
- Litigation and arbitration
- Labour and co-determination law
- Antitrust
- Unfair competition and intellectual property law
- Media and computer law
- Conflict of laws
- EU law
- Insurance and reinsurance
- Tax

ALLEN & OVERY

TAUNUSTOR 2
60311 FRANKFURT AM MAIN

Telephone: +49 69 2648 5000
Fax: +49 69 2648 5800
E-mail: information@allenovery.com
Website: www.allenovery.com

Languages
Dutch, English, French, Hungarian, Italian, Japanese, Polish, Spanish

Other offices
Amsterdam, Antwerp, Bangkok, Beijing, Bratislava, Brussels, Budapest, Dubai, Hamburg, Hong Kong, London, Luxembourg, Madrid, Milan, Moscow, New York, Paris, Prague, Rome, Shanghai, Singapore, Tokyo, Turin, Warsaw

Number of lawyers 2,305

Contacts
Dr Cornelius Fischer-Zernin, Dr Arndt Overlack

CATEGORIES OF WORK

- Asset financing/leasing
- Antitrust/competition law
- Arbitration
- Banking regulatory
- Bond issues
- Business restructurings
- Company law
- Derivatives
- Employment law
- Energy law
- Environmental law
- Equity capital markets
- Global loans
- IP/IT
- Joint ventures and takeovers
- Leveraged finance
- Litigation
- MBO and LBOs
- Mergers and acquisitions
- Private equity
- Project finance
- Public and administrative law
- Real estate and finance
- Securitisation
- Tax
- Telecommunications law

ARCON RECHTSANWÄLTE
SCHMIDT-SIBETH HEISSE WEISSKOPF KURSAWE

KAISERSTRASSE 5
60311 FRANKFURT AM MAIN

Telephone: +49 69 91 33 01 0
Fax: +49 69 91 33 01 19
E-mail: frankfurt@arcon-net.com
Website: www.arcon-net.com

Languages
Catalan, Dutch, English, Finnish, French, Greek, Italian, Portuguese, Russian, Spanish

Other offices
Berlin, Brussels, Cologne, Erfurt, Düsseldorf, Hamburg, Munich

Number of lawyers 92
at this office 8

Contacts
Dr Christian Berger, Jan Pater Voß

CATEGORIES OF WORK

- Banking and finance
- Commercial and contract
- Corporate, venture capital transactions, IPOs
- EC law
- Employment
- Estate planning, company succession
- Intellectual property, trade marks, competition
- IT, Internet
- Litigation and arbitration
- Mergers and acquisitions
- Real estate and construction
- Restructuring
- Telecommunications and media

ASHURST

OBERLINDAU 54-56
60323 FRANKFURT AM MAIN

Telephone: +49 69 97 11 26
Fax: +49 69 97 20 52 20
Website: www.ashurst.com

Languages
English, French, Swedish

Other offices
Brussels, London, Madrid, Milan, Munich, New Delhi*, New York, Paris, Singapore, Tokyo

Number of lawyers 813
at this office 46

Contact
Hermann Schlindwein

CATEGORIES OF WORK

Banking, securities and finance	Employment law
Competition	Intellectual property
Corporate and commercial law	Litigation
EC law	Mergers and acquisitions
Tax	Sport
Private equity	Venture capital

BEITEN BURKHARDT RECHTSANWALTSGESELLSCHAFT mbH

BOCKENHEIMER ANLAGE 15
MOZARTPLATZ
60322 FRANKFURT

Telephone: +49 69 75 60 95 0
Fax: +49 69 75 60 95 512
E-mail: bblaw-frankfurt@bblaw.de
Website: www.bblaw.de

Languages
Cantonese, Czech, English, French, Hungarian, Italian, Mandarin, Polish, Russian, Slovak, Spanish

Other offices
Beijing, Berlin, Brussels, Budapest, Cologne, Dusseldorf, Hamburg, Hong Kong, Leipzig, Moscow, Munich, Nuremberg, St Petersburg, Shanghai, Warsaw

Number of lawyers 232
at this office 35

CATEGORIES OF WORK

Company law	Forensic services, corporate compliance
Banking and finance	Law of associations, societies and sports law
European law and cartel law	Probate, company succession
Industrial property rights	Litigation and arbitration
Labour and employment law	Property law
Procurement law	Insurance law
Public law	
Media and telecommunications law, information technology	

BAKER & McKENZIE

BETHMANNSTRASSE 50-54
60311 FRANKFURT AM MAIN
Telephone: +49 69 29 90 80
Fax: +49 69 29 90 81 08
Website: www.bakernet.com

Languages
Arabic, Chinese, Dutch, English, French, Italian, Latvian, Polish, Portuguese, Russian, Spanish

Other offices
Almaty, Amsterdam, Antwerp, Bahrain, Baku, Bangkok, Barcelona, Beijing, Berlin, Bogotá, Bologna, Brasilia, Brussels, Budapest, Buenos Aires, Cairo,Calgary Caracas, Chicago, Dallas, Düsseldorf, Geneva, Guadalajara, Hanoi, Ho Chi Minh City, Hong Kong, Houston, Juarez, Kyiv, London, Madrid, Manila, Melbourne, Mexico City, Miami, Milan, Monterrey, Moscow, Munich, New York, Palo Alto, Paris, Porto Alegré, Prague, Rio de Janeiro, Riyadh, Rome, St Petersburg, San Diego, San Francisco, Santiago, São Paulo, Shanghai, Singapore, Stockholm, Sydney, Taipei, Tijuana, Tokyo, Toronto,Valencia, Vienna, Warsaw, Washington DC, Zürich

Number of lawyers 3,380
at this office 93

CATEGORIES OF WORK

Administrative and environmental law
Joachim Scherer, Ulrich Ellinghaus

Antitrust and competition law
Jörg-Martin Schultze

Banking and finance
Rainer Magold

Capital markets
Manuel Lorenz

Company and commercial
Ulf Wauschkuhn

Food and drugs
Thilo Räpple

Information technology, media and computer law
Matthias Scholz

Intellectual property, trade marks
Michael Fammler

Labour law
Günther Heckelmann, Gregor Dornbusch

Litigation and arbitration
Günter Pickrahn

Mergers and acquisitions
Matthias Jaletzke, Florian Kästle

Product liability
Axel Hamm

Real estate and construction
Karl-Ludwig Koenen

Tax
Christian Brodersen, Ulrich Ränsch

Telecommunications
Joachim Scherer, Ulrich Ellinghaus

Venture capital
Florian Kästle

THE FIRM

Founded in Chicago in 1949, Baker & McKenzie is a global law firm with 66 offices in 36 countries. A multinational network of over 4,400 legal professionals offers clients resources and knowledge in every area of business law, in virtually every important financial and commercial centre in the world.

Baker & McKenzie has been established in Europe for over 40 years, having opened its first European offices in 1957. Since then, the European and Middle Eastern network has grown to 29 offices, giving it unparalleled geographical coverage.

The Frankfurt am Main office was formed in 1962; the office in Berlin was opened on 1 March 1990, the Munich office on 1 April 1997 and the Düsseldorf office on 1 April 1999.

Since its formation, the German offices of Baker & McKenzie have advised their clients on all questions of German, European and international industrial and commercial law, with particular emphasis on cross-border and multinational transactions. At present, more than 170 attorneys-at-law (Rechtsanwälte), admitted in the Federal Republic of Germany including the new federal states, tax advisers, and varying numbers of foreign admitted lawyers work in the German offices of Baker & McKenzie.

All attorneys are at least bilingual; most of them have completed additional graduate legal studies at foreign law schools. Several attorneys are simultaneously admitted as CPAs, tax advisers, tax attorneys, attorneys for administrative law or attorneys for labour law.

AREAS OF PRACTICE

Baker & McKenzie co-ordinates its core practice areas on local, regional and global levels, giving most of its lawyers experience in more than one jurisdiction, as well as providing multinational teams of specialists.

Utilising a global practice group structure and ground-breaking technology coupled with a personal, detailed understanding of a client's specific business, Baker & McKenzie is able to organise its extensive resources to provide focused and strategic counsel to clients.

Baker & McKenzie advises multinational enterprises, large German companies, medium-sized enterprises, banks, and insurance companies, as well as institutions and entities under public law in all questions of German, European, and international industrial and commercial law including company law, competition and cartel law, intellectual property, banking and finance, labour law, administrative law, and tax law. Furthermore, the firm handles litigation and arbitration matters. Several partners have expertise in specialised areas of law, such as European Community law, the law of cosmetics, food and drug law, trade marks, franchising, corporate finance, new financial products, government procurement, real estate transactions, and media telecommunications law.

BUSE HEBERER FROMM

GROSSE GALLUSSTRASSE 1-7
60311 FRANKFURT AM MAIN

Telephone: +49 69 97 10 97 0
Fax: +49 69 97 10 97 10
E-mail: frankfurt@buse.de
Website: www.buse.de

Languages
English, French, Italian, Portuguese, Spanish

Other offices
Berlin, Dusseldorf, Essen, Hamburg, Milan, Munich, Palma de Mallorca, Sydney, Zurich

Number of lawyers 120
at this office 18

Member
The European Legal Alliance (Beauchamps, Ireland; Dubarry Le Douarin Veil, France; Field Fisher Waterhouse, England; Harper Macleod, Scotland)

CATEGORIES OF WORK

- **Banking and finance**
- **Antitrust and merger control**
- **Commerce, transport, insurance**
- **Commercial delinquency**
- **Corporate/M&A**
- **Industrial property and copyrights**
- **Information technology and telecommunications**
- **Labour and employment**
- **Litigation and arbitration, national and international**
- **Press and media**
- **Property and construction**
- **Public law**
- **Tax**

CMS HASCHE SIGLE

FRIEDRICH-EBERT-ANLAGE 44
60325 FRANKFURT/MAIN

Telephone: +49 69 71 70 10
Fax: +49 69 71 70 11 10
E-mail: frankfurt@cmslegal.de
Website: www.cmslegal.de

Languages
English, French, Spanish

Other offices
Berlin, Dusseldorf, Hamburg, Leipzig, Munich, Stuttgart, Chemnitz, Dresden, Brussels, Belgrade, Moscow, Prague, Shanghai

Number of lawyers 306
at this office 40

Other CMS law firms
CMS Adonnino Ascoli & Cavasola Scamoni, Italy; CMS Bureau Francis Lefebvre, France; CMS Cameron McKenna, UK; CMS Derks Star Busmann, Netherlands; CMS von Erlach Klainguti Stettler Wille, Switzerland; CMS Lexcelis, Belgium; CMS Strommer Reich-Rohrwig Karasek Hainz, Austria

CATEGORIES OF WORK

- **Corporate and commercial**
- **Mergers and acquisitions**
- **Privatisation and restructuring**
- **Banking, securities and finance**
- **Unfair competition and antitrust**
- **Tax**
- **Labour law and service contracts**
- **Bankruptcy and reorganisation**
- **Intellectual property, IT, media**
- **Real estate and construction**
- **Environmental and administrative**
- **Distribution, franchising**
- **Maritime law**
- **Arbitration and litigation**
- **Utilities**

CLEARY GOTTLIEB STEEN & HAMILTON

MAIN TOWER
NEUE MAINZER STRASSE 52
60311 FRANKFURT AM MAIN

Telephone: +49 69 9 71 03 0
Fax: +49 69 9 71 03 199
Website: www.clearygottlieb.com

Languages
English, French, Italian, Polish, Spanish

Other offices
Brussels, Cologne, London, Milan, Moscow, Paris, Rome

Number of lawyers 937
at this office 45

CATEGORIES OF WORK

Antitrust	Corporate
Banking and finance	Joint ventures
Capital markets/securities	Mergers and acquisitions
Commercial	Tax

CURTIS, MALLET-PREVOST, COLT & MOSLE LLP

STAUFENSTRASSE 42
60323 FRANKFURT AM MAIN

Telephone: +49 69 971 44 20
Fax: +49 69 17 33 99
E-mail: info@cm-p.com
Website: www.cm-p.com

Languages
English, French

Other offices
Houston, London, Mexico City, Milan, Muscat, New York, Newark, Paris, Stamford, Washington DC

Number of lawyers 178
at this office 2

Contacts
Marie-Thérèse Allen, Ute Tünnermann-Kasch

Member
International Bar Association; American Chamber of Commerce in Germany; Frankfurt Bar Association; Frankfurt Attorneys Union

CATEGORIES OF WORK

Mergers and acquisitions	Labour and employment
Joint ventures	Project finance
International contracts	Privatisation
Sales and distribution arrangements	Real estate
Litigation	Immigration
Intellectual property	International arbitration
Investment fund management	

COUDERT BROTHERS LLP

FRIEDRICH-EBERT-ANLAGE 2-14
CITY-HAUS
PLATZ DER REPUBLIK
60325 FRANKFURT AM MAIN

Telephone: +49 69 7549 0
Fax: +49 69 7549 290
E-mail: info-frankfurt@coudert.com
Website: www.coudert.com

Languages
English, French, Italian, Mandarin,

Other offices
Almaty, Antwerp, Bankok, Beijing, Berlin, Brussels, Budapest*, Ghent, Hong Kong, Jakarta*, London, Los Angeles, Mexico City*, Milan, Moscow, New York, Palo Alto, Paris, Prague*, Rome, St. Petersburg, San Francisco, Shanghai, Singapore, Stockholm, Sydney, Tokyo, Washington DC

Number of lawyers 650+
at this office 33

Contact
Hans-Peter Hansen (office managing partner)

CATEGORIES OF WORK

M&A
Dr Bernhard Mielert

Labour
Michael Magotsch

Telecommunications
Rainer Jacob

Intellectual property
B Christian Haager

Capital markets/IPO/venture capital
Martin Heinsius

Wills probate
Dr Jan Rohls

Banking
Wolfgang Althaus

Litigation
Dr Axel Hofmann

Real estate
Waltraud Langenbruch

French desk
Dr Christophe Jäger

Tax
Hans-Peter Hansen, Dr Gerald Beyer

THE FIRM

Coudert Brothers was established in 1853 by French émigrés and was the first US law firm to set up an international legal practice. The firm now has more than 650 lawyers worldwide, operating as one single partnership with a common emphasis on client service of the highest quality.

The firm has extensive experience in international investment, trade and finance. Cross-border commercial transactions are a major focus, as is international arbitration and other complex dispute resolution. Coudert Brothers also provides domestic advice in countries where the firm has offices.

Coudert Brothers has offices in 30 cities in 18 countries around the world. These offices are located in the major financial and business centres of Europe, the United States and Asia Pacific region. More than 300 Coudert Brothers professionals now practice in Europe, making it the largest region in the firm's worldwide network.

Local legal experts work side-by-side with experienced international lawyers to optimise the structure and execution of complex business transactions, very much in the spirit of the firm's goal to combine *Global Reach* with *Local Strengths*. This approach ensures that the best legal talent, wherever located, is directed to meet the clients' needs. From Almaty to Brussels, Beijing to Berlin, New York to Hong Kong or London to Tokyo, Coudert Brothers' lawyers work together as a team to ensure that their clients' business goals are met.

AREAS OF PRACTICE

Clients of the Frankfurt office include large multinational as well as family-owned companies in the manufacturing, chemicals, telecommunications, customer goods, banking and finance, engineering and real estate sectors, and the automotive supply industries. A significant number are foreign enterprises or German subsidiaries of foreign-based companies.

DEBEVOISE & PLIMPTON LLP

TAUBENSTRASSE 7-9
60313 FRANKFURT AM MAIN

Telephone: +49 69 20 97 50 00
Fax: +49 6 20 97 55 55
E-mail: dfhickok@debevoise.com
Website: www.debevoise.com

Languages
English, German

Other offices
Hong Kong, London, Moscow, New York, Paris, Shanghai, Washington DC

Number of lawyers 600+
at this office 16

CATEGORIES OF WORK

Mergers and acquisitions
Dr Thomas Schürrle, David Hickok

Private equity, investment management
Marcia MacHarg, Dr Friedrich Hey

Capital markets
David Hickok, Philipp von Holst

Financing
Hans Bertram-Nothnagel, Philipp von Holst

Restructuring
Dr Thomas Schürrle

Corporate tax
Dr Friedrich Hey

International dispute resolution
Dr Thomas Schürrle

DEWEY BALLANTINE LLP

FRANKFURTER WELLE
REUTERWEG 16
60323 FRANKFURT

Telephone: +49 69 36393 0
Fax: +49 69 36393 333
E-mail: pilberg@deweyballantine.com
Website: www.deweyballantine.com

Languages
English, German

Other offices
Austin, Budapest, East Palo Alto, Houston, London, Los Angeles, Milan, New York, Prague, Rome, Warsaw, Washington DC

Number of lawyers 606
at this office 5

Contact
Philipp von Ilberg

CATEGORIES OF WORK

Acquisition financing

Mergers and acquisitions

Capital markets

Private equity, venture capital

FPS FRITZE PAUL SEELIG

ESCHERSHEIMER LANDSTRASSE 27
60322 FRANKFURT AM MAIN

Telephone: +49 69 95 95 70
Fax: +49 69 95 95 71 66
E-mail: frankfurt@fps-law.de
Website: www.fps-law.de

Languages
English, French, Italian, Russian, Spanish

Other offices
Berlin, Erfurt, Hamburg, Munich

Number of lawyers 80
at this office 48

Contact
Dr Robin L Fritz

Member
Meritas

CATEGORIES OF WORK

Company, mergers and acquisitions	Energy and environmental
Commercial property and real estate	Banking and insolvency
Corporate	Product liability, insurers' liability
Capital markets	EC law
Trade and distributor contracts	Employment
Tax	New media, e-commerce, computer
Construction, leasing	IT, media and entertainment
Real estate	Insurance
Public private partnership (PPP)	Antitrust
Public procurement	Arbitration and litigation
Competition and EU	IP, product piracy, unfair trading
Mergers and acquisitions	

FLICK GOCKE SCHAUMBURG

PLATZ DER EINHEIT 1
60327 FRANKFURT AM MAIN

Telephone: +49 69 71 703 0
Fax: +49 69 71 703 100
E-mail: frankfurt@fgs.de
Website: www.fgs.de

Languages
English, French, Italian

Other offices
Berlin, Bonn

Number of lawyers 97
at this office 14

Contacts
Dr Klaus Sieker, Dr Christoph Schulte, Dr Marcus Mick

CATEGORIES OF WORK

German and international tax law	Transfer pricing
Corporate and business law	Estate planning
Mergers and acquisitions	Real estate transactions
Reorganisation of group structures	Tax litigation
IPOs	Customs law
Inbound investment	Due diligence and special audits

FRESHFIELDS BRUCKHAUS DERINGER

TAUNUSANLAGE 11
60329 FRANKFURT AM MAIN

Telephone: +49 69 27 30 80
Fax: +49 69 23 26 64
E-mail: email@freshfields.com
Website: www.freshfields.com

Languages
Extensive language capabilities

Other offices
Amsterdam, Bangkok, Barcelona, Beijing, Berlin, Bratislava, Brussels, Budapest, Cologne, Düsseldorf, Hamburg, Hanoi, Ho Chi Minh City, Hong Kong, London, Madrid, Milan, Moscow, Munich, New York, Paris, Rome, Shanghai, Singapore, Tokyo, Vienna, Washington

Number of lawyers 2,504
at this office 189

Contact
Klaus-Albert Bauer

CATEGORIES OF WORK

Finance

Corporate

Tax

Intellectual property and IT

Real estate

Dispute resolution (including environment, planning and regulatory)

Antitrust, competition and trade

Employment, pensions and benefits

GLEISS LUTZ
RECHTSANWÄLTE

MENDELSSOHNSTAßE 87
60325 FRANKFURT

Telephone: +49 69 95 51 4 0
Fax: +49 69 95 51 41 98
E-mail: info@gleisslutz.com
Website: www.gleisslutz.com

Languages
Dutch, English, French, Italian, Mandarin, Cantonese, Polish, Portuguese, Spanish, Russian, Czech, Slovak

Other offices
Berlin, Munich, Stuttgart, Brussels, Prague, Warsaw

Number of lawyers 200
at this office 40

Contact
Dr Hoimar von Ditfurth

CATEGORIES OF WORK

German, EC and international law

Banking, securities and finance

Commercial law (general)

Companies, corporations

Competition, antitrust

Electronic commerce, Internet law

Employment, labour

Environment and pollution control

Insurance

Litigation and arbitration

Mergers and acquisitions

Real estate

Tax

Telecommunications, media and broadcasting

Trade marks, intellectual property

GÖRG
RECHTSANWÄLTE

PLATZ DER EINHEIT 2
60327 FRANKFURT

Telephone: +49 69 17 00 00 17
Fax: +49 69 17 00 00 27
E-mail: frankfurt@goerg.de
Website: www.goerg.de

Languages
English, French, Italian, Spanish

Other Offices
Amsterdam*, Antwerp*, Bangkok*, Barcelona*, Bergen*, Berlin, Birmingham*, Bradford*, Brussels*, Cologne, Copenhagen*, Edinburgh*, Essen, Glasgow*, Hamburg, Hong Kong*, Leeds*, Liverpool*, London*, Madrid*, Manchester*, Milan*, Oslo*, Paris*, Prague*, Rotterdam*, Salzburg*, Sarajevo*, Shanghai*, Sheffield*, Singapore*, Stockholm*, Vienna*, Zagreb*

Number of lawyers 83
at this office 8

Member
DLA Group

CATEGORIES OF WORK

Corporate law and antitrust

Mergers and acquisitions

Finance and capital markets

Insolvency and reorganisation

Employment

Commercial and distribution

National and international tax

Construction law

International transactions

Real estate

Media and entertainment

Unfair competition and trade marks

IT and telecommunications

Insurance law

Medical law

Pharmaceutical and drug law

Transport

Products liability

Private wealth

Litigation and arbitration

Notarial services

Administrative law

HAARMANN HEMMELRATH

NEUE MAINZER STRASSE 75
60311 FRANKFURT AM MAIN

Telephone: +49 69 9 20 590
Fax: +49 69 9 20 59 133
E-mail:
frankfurt@haarmannhemmelrath.com
Website:
www.haarmannhemmelrath.com

Languages
Bulgarian, Croatian, Czech, Dutch, English, Finnish, French, Hungarian, Italian, Japanese, Mandarin, Norwegian, Polish, Portuguese, Romanian, Russian, Slovak, Spanish, Swedish, Vietnamese

Other offices
Berlin, Bielefeld, Brussels, Bucharest, Budapest, Cologne, Dusseldorf, Hamburg, Leipzig, London, Milan, Moscow, Munich, Paris, Prague, Rome, Shanghai, Singapore, Stuttgart, Tokyo, Vienna, Warsaw

Number of lawyers 281
at this office 37

CATEGORIES OF WORK

Mergers and acquisitions
Prof Dr W Haarmann, Dr Markus Wenserski

IPO
Dr Markus Wenserski, Dr Rainer Bommert

IP, antitrust, EU law
Dr Thomas Stögmüller, Thomas Fischer

Corporate and business law
Dr Klaus U Eyber, Dr Rainer Bommert

Telecommunications, IT and media law
Dr Thomas Stögmüller

Arbitration
Prof Dr W Haarmann

Banking law
W Michael Waldeck, Dr Chr Faßbender

Litigation, forensic services
Dr Klaus U Eyber, Dr Chr Faßbender

Real estate
Barbara Busch, Thomas Busching

International tax law
Prof Dr W Haarmann, Oliver Dörfler

National tax law, tax litigation
Prof Dr W Haarmann, Oliver Dörfler

Transfer pricing
Thomas Busching, Oliver Dörfler

Estate planning, family office
Barbara Busch, Thomas Busching

Corporate recovery, insolvency
Wolfgang Jamin, Michael Eifler

Venture capital, private equity
Dr Markus Wenserski, Barbara Busch

Privatisation
W Michael Waldeck, Michael Eifler

Reorganisation, structured finance
Dr Markus Wenserski, Wolfgang Jamin

Fund structuring
Barbara Busch, Dr Markus Wenserski

HENGELER MUELLER

BOCKENHEIMER LANDSTRASSE 51
60325 FRANKFURT

Telephone: +49 69 17095 0
Fax: +49 69 725773
E-mail: hmffm@hengeler.com
Website: www.hengeler.com

Other offices
Düsseldorf, Berlin, Brussels, London, Budapest, Prague

Number of lawyers 195
at this office 95

Contact
Dr Hendrik Haag

CATEGORIES OF WORK

Banking, finance and capital markets	**M&A/corporate**
Bank regulatory law	**Private equity and venture capital**
Asset management	**Tax**
Syndicated lending	**Insolvency and reorganisation**
Acquisition finance	**Competition**
Project finance	**Labour and employment**
Derivatives	**IP/IT**
Equity capital markets	**Real estate**
Debt capital markets	**Litigation and arbitration**
Asset-backed securities	

HEUKING KÜHN LÜER WOJTEK

LINDENSTRASSE 37
60325 FRANKFURT

Telephone: +49 69 9 75 610
Fax: +49 69 9 75 61 200
E-mail: frankfurt@heuking.de
Website: www.heuking.de

Languages
German, English, French

Other offices
Berlin, Brussels, Chemnitz, Cologne, Düsseldorf, Hamburg, Munich

Number of lawyers 8

Contact
Rudolf du Mesnil de Rochemont

CATEGORIES OF WORK

Corporate, partnerships, international mergers and acquisitions, general commercial law

Competition, merger control, antitrust

Banking and finance

Insurance

Litigation and arbitration

Administrative, public and constitutional law

Entertainment, media, publishing, copyright

Property and real estate law

Industrial property

Employment and labour law

Real estate transactions

THE FIRM

Heuking Kühn Lüer Wojtek was founded in Düsseldorf, Germany, in 1971. Since then, the firm has spread geographically, and Heuking Kühn now has seven significant offices in Germany, as well as an office in Brussels.

The firm has an extensive international network of law firms, enabling it to provide its clients with seamless 'one-stop shopping', on international transactions and regulatory matters. Since its formation, Heuking Kühn Lüer Wojtek has specifically chosen to remain an independent law firm. It is Heuking Kühn Lüer Wojtek's philosophy that, to provide the best possible service to its clients, the firm must be able to co-operate with various other law firms which are at the top of the profession in their respective countries. This gives the firm the ability to make alternative counsel suggestions to its clients, giving the clients a choice of the best suitable law firm or lawyer in each country and for each matter. Over the last 30+ years, Heuking Kühn Lüer Wojtek has developed excellent relationships with the key firms in all of the major jurisdictions worldwide.

Heuking Kühn Lüer Wojtek is a name which is synonymous with legal competence. The firm is one of the largest commercial law firms in Germany, with more than 150 specialised lawyers and tax advisers, representing the interests of national and international clients. Included in the client list are large and medium-sized German and international companies in all areas of the manufacturing industry, as well as trade and service industries, associations, governmental and public sector organisations and private clients and trusts.

The firm prides itself on substantive legal competence and on the excellent education and continuing legal education of its lawyers. Moreover, virtually all of the lawyers are German-English bilingual.

Extensive specialisation and comprehensive knowledge of specific industry sectors provide the basis of all of Heuking Kühn Lüer Wojtek's legal counselling. Experienced partners and carefully selected associate lawyers develop innovative solutions to complex legal problems. The lawyers regularly work in their specific practice area groups and also in multi-group and multi-disciplinary teams with clients and outside consultants or advisers. Entrepreneurial thinking on behalf of firm clients, as well as efficient, quality, cost-effective and timely work and the highest personal dedication are key components of Heuking Kühn Lüer Wojtek's culture.

AREAS OF PRACTICE

Heuking Kühn Lüer Wojtek is a full-service commercial law firm. Cross-border and cross-sector knowledge in combination with a deep understanding of business reasoning enables service to clients with the broadest possible support in all their negotiations and business decisions. This applies equally to M&A transactions, to legal advice on company structure, business risk management, negotiations and negotiation tactics, training, crisis and insolvency counselling, corporate financial matters, and complex litigation and arbitration. Thanks to a variety of strong business clients, the firm has built long-term relationships with its clients and can assist them, beginning with the establishment of a business, followed by implementing business goals, including day-to-day legal work, reorganisations, acquisitions and divestitures.

Heuking Kühn Lüer Wojtek is actively involved with its clients in providing regulatory counselling in all areas of commercial law, as well as assisting them in organising and implementing their M&A transactions in Germany, throughout Europe, and internationally. Heuking Kühn Lüer Wojtek has particular expertise in German and EU company law; competition law, merger control and state aids; international investment, trade, and taxation matters; banking and finance; labour law; intellectual property rights; environmental, health, and safety regulation; product-specific regulation; real estate and construction law; telecoms, IT and media law; transport, postal services and shipping law; public procurement; family law; and private clients and family office matters.

HEUSSEN
RECHTSANWALTSGESELLSCHAFT MBH

IM TRUTZ FRANKFURT 55
60322 FRANKFURT AM MAIN

Telephone: +49 69 15242 0
Fax: +49 69 15242 111
E-mail: info@landwell.de
Website: www.landwell.de

Languages
Arabic, Dutch, English, French, Greek, Italian, Russian, Spanish, Swedish

Other offices
Berlin, Cologne, Düsseldorf, Hamburg, Munich, Stuttgart

Number of lawyers 100
at this office 24

Contact
Dr Karl Maria Walter

International groupings
Landwell, correspondent law firms of PricewaterhouseCoopers

CATEGORIES OF WORK

Commercial and competition
Dr Gunther Braun

Corporate structuring
Robert Dorr

Dispute resolution
Reiner Ponschab

Technology, media and communications
Dr Axel Czarnetzki, Rafaela Wilde

Employment and human resources
Hans Stefan Korsch

Financial services
Dr Gunther Braun

Intellectual property
Dr Axel Czarnetzki

Mergers and acquisitions
Dr Karl Maria Walter, Michael Ketterl

Public law
Dr Michael W Mütze

Real estate
Dr Michael W Mütze

THE FIRM
Heussen Rechtsanwaltgesellschaft mbH is a member of Landwell. Landwell is one of the largest international law practices with 2,800 business and tax lawyers worldwide. Landwell provides a full range of legal services through specialists organised in global networks. Landwell's main focus is on cross-border M&A transactions and corporate transformation projects. Working closely with PricewaterhouseCoopers, Landwell is a market leader in the design and delivery of complex corporate change. This is achieved through a focus on strong local capabilities with a global outlook and by ensuring that its implementation skills match its legal ones.

AREAS OF PRACTICE
Landwell provides a full range of business law services, through specialist lawyers organised in global networks. In this way, consistent high standards of advice and service are guaranteed for both international and local clients. Landwell's international strengths include: legal consulting on mergers and acquisitions; corporate structuring; technology, media and communications; and employment law.

KAYE SCHOLER (GERMANY) LLP

BOCKENHEIMER LANDSTRASSE 61
60325 FRANKFURT

Telephone: +49 69 25 49 40
Fax: +49 69 25 49 44 44
E-mail: frankfurt@kayescholer.com
Website: www.kayescholer.com

Languages
English

Other offices
Chicago, Hong Kong, London, Los Angeles, New York, Shanghai, Washington DC, West Palm Beach

Number of lawyers 500
at this office 7

Contact
Dr Harald Rieger

Member
Am Cham (American Chamber of Commerce)

CATEGORIES OF WORK

M&A and private equity
Matthias Götz

Capital markets and finance
Dr Ami de Chapeaurouge, Herbert Rögner

Business reorganisation and bankruptcy
Till Hafner

Antitrust
Dr Harald Rieger

General corporate
Michael Mölling

Litigation
Dr Sebastian Jungermann

LATHAM & WATKINS LLP

FRANKFURTER WELLE
REUTERWEG 20
60323 FRANKFURT AM MAIN

Telephone: +49 69 60 62 60 00
Fax: +49 69 60 62 60 60
Website: www.lw.com

Languages
English, French, German, Greek

Other offices
Boston, Brussels, Chicago, Hamburg, Hong Kong, London, Los Angeles, Milan, Moscow, New Jersey, New York, Northern Virginia, Orange County, Paris, San Diego, San Francisco, Silicon Valley, Singapore, Tokyo, Washington DC

Number of lawyers 1,500
at this office 25

CATEGORIES OF WORK

Banking

Capital markets

Corporate finance

Commercial litigation

Company law

Leveraged finance

Insolvency

Competition/EU

Infrastructure/public finance

Intellectual property/information technology

Mergers and acquisitions, privatisations and joint ventures

Private equity/venture capital

Restructurings

Project development and finance

Real estate

LINKLATERS OPPENHOFF & RÄDLER

MAINZER LANDSTRASSE 16
60325 FRANKFURT AM MAIN

Telephone: +49 69 71 00 30
Fax: +49 69 71 00 33 33
Website: www.linklaters.com

Languages
All commercial and local languages in the countries where Linklaters operates

Other offices
Alicante, Amsterdam, Antwerp, Bangkok, Beijing, Berlin, Bratislava, Brussels, Bucharest, Budapest, Cologne, Hong Kong, Lisbon, London, Luxembourg, Madrid, Milan, Moscow, Munich, New York, Paris, Prague, Rome, São Paulo, Shanghai, Singapore, Stockholm, Tokyo, Warsaw

Number of lawyers 2,000 (worldwide)

Contacts
Rudolf Cölle, Markus Hartung

CATEGORIES OF WORK

M&A/corporate
Wolfgang Sturm (*Cologne*)

Banking and finance
Carl-Peter Feick (*Frankfurt*)

Tax
Karl Schäfer (*Munich*)

Real estate
Michael Steinbrecher (*Frankfurt*)

IP, trade marks and copyrights
Gert Dittert (*Cologne*)

EU and cartel law
Wolfgang Deselaers (*Cologne/Brussels*)

Litigation and arbitration
Klaus Saffenreuther (*Munich*)

Employment
Karl-Dietmar Cohnen (*Cologne*)

Public law, environmental law
Kornelius Kleinlein (*Berlin*)

I, T & C
Michael Abels (*Cologne*)

Regulated markets
Kai Pritzsche (*Berlin*)

Private equity
Wolfgang Krauel (*Munich*)

Insolvency and restructuring
Wolfgang Sturm (*Cologne*)

Media
Stefan Lütje (*Berlin*)

Healthcare
Peter Klappich (*Cologne*)

THE FIRM

Linklaters advises the world's leading companies, financial institutions and governments on their most challenging transactions and assignments. With 2,000 lawyers, including 470 partners, and offices in major business and financial centres, its clients choose the firm for its distinctive combination of technical skill, commercial experience and outstanding service.

Linklaters has built a formidable global practice through organic growth and a series of mergers, joint ventures and co-operations with other respected law firms. In 2001, Linklaters merged with three of Europe's leading law firms to form Linklaters Oppenhoff & Rädler in Germany, Linklaters in Sweden, Linklaters De Bandt in Belgium and Linklaters Loesch in Luxembourg. In the same year, the firm formed a co-operation with Brazilian firm Goulart Penteado, Iervolino e Lefosse. This co-operation combines Linklaters' international capability with GPIL's extensive knowledge of the Brazilian market. In Singapore, the firm practises as Linklaters Allen & Gledhill, a joint venture with the premier Singapore practice of Allen & Gledhill, while in Italy, Linklaters has an exclusive relationship with Italian law firm Gianni, Origoni, Grippo & Partners.

LOVELLS

DARMSTÄDTER LANDSTRASSE 125
60598 FRANKFURT AM MAIN

Telephone: +49 69 962 36 0
Fax: +49 69 962 36 100
E-mail: reception.frankfurt@lovells.com
Website: www.lovells.de

Languages
English, French, Italian, Polish, Russian, Spanish

Other offices
Alicante, Amsterdam, Beijing, Berlin, Brussels, Budapest*, Chicago, Düsseldorf, Hamburg, Ho Chi Minh City, Hong Kong, London, Milan, Moscow, Munich, New York, Paris, Prague, Rome, Shanghai, Singapore, Tokyo, Vienna*, Warsaw, Zagreb*

Number of lawyers 1,600
at this office 107

Contact
Ingo Winterstein

CATEGORIES OF WORK

- Corporate/M&A, private equity
- Restructuring and insolvency
- Banking
- Antitrust and unfair competition
- Capital markets
- Project finance, public private partnerships
- Tax
- Employment
- Intellectual property
- Property
- Projects
- Technology, media, telecommunications
- Litigation, product liability
- International arbitration
- Food and drug regulations
- Law of Eastern Europe

MANNHEIMER SWARTLING
RECHTSANWÄLTE UND SCHWEDISCHE ADVOKATEN

WILDUNGER STRASSE 9
60487 FRANKFURT AM MAIN

Telephone: +49 69 974 01 20
Fax: +49 69 741 01 43
Website: www.mannheimerswartling.se

Languages
English, French, Swedish

Other offices
Berlin, Brussels, Gothenburg, Helsingborg, Malmö, New York, St Petersburg, Stockholm

Number of lawyers 330
at this office 10

Contact
Alexander Foerster

CATEGORIES OF WORK

- Corporate finance
- M&A
- Banking and insurance
- Securities
- Real estate
- Construction and projects
- Environment
- Intellectual property
- Employment
- Arbitration and litigation

MAYER BROWN ROWE & MAW LLP

BOCKENHEIMER
LANDSTRASSE 98-100
60323 FRANKFURT/MAIN

Telephone: +49 69 79 41 0
Fax: +49 69 79 41 100
E-mail: germany@mayerbrownrowe.com
Website: www.mayerbrownrowe.com

Languages
English, French, Italian, Spanish

Other offices
Brussels, Charlotte, Chicago, Cologne, Houston, London, Los Angeles, Manchester, Mexico City (correspondence office), New York, Palo Alto, Paris, Beijing and Shanghai (partner offices), Washington DC

Number of lawyers 1,400
at this office 60

Contact
Reinhart Lange (managing partner)

CATEGORIES OF WORK	
Corporate	Tax
M&A	Insolvency
Private equity	Biotech
Banking and finance	Pharma
Securitisation	Life science
Intellectual property	Information technology
Antitrust and competition	Telecommunications
Real estate	Internet and media
Environment	Litigation
Employment and labour	Dispute resolution

THE FIRM

The German offices of Mayer, Brown, Rowe & Maw, located in Frankfurt/Main and Cologne, serve an integral role in one of the world's leading law firms. Originally established in 1881, the firm now has over 1,400 lawyers located in six European and seven US offices, and offers its clients sophisticated legal services on both sides of the Atlantic.

AREAS OF PRACTICE

Mayer, Brown, Rowe & Maw has grown over decades together with its clients. Over 70 lawyers in Frankfurt am Main and Cologne advise its German and international clients as to a wide range of complex legal issues. In doing so, the firm's lawyers draw upon their in-depth local knowledge of the German market and practices as well as the resources of a major international law firm.

Firmwide, Mayer, Brown, Rowe & Maw represents major multinational corporations, start-up ventures, financial institutions and insurance companies, public utilities, trade associations, governments, companies of every size and industry, and many non-profit organisations as well.

A thorough knowledge of the firm's client's operations is indispensable. To optimally meet the individual requirements of various branches and markets, the firm has built up branch-specific intelligence in numerous business fields over many years. They include: biotech, pharma and life science, chemicals, automotive, steel, metal processing, machine tool engineering, building construction, property development and management, planning, food and beverages, consumer goods, retail textiles, financial services and insurance, information technology, telecommunications, Internet and media, and sports marketing.

MORGAN LEWIS

GUIOLLETTSTRASSE 54
60325 FRANKFURT AM MAIN

Telephone: +49 69 714 00 07 10
Fax: +49 69 714 00 07 0
E-mail: info@morganlewis.com
Website: www.morganlewis.com

Other offices
Boston, Brussels, Chicago, Harrisburg, Irvine, London, Los Angeles, Miami, New York, Palo Alto, Philadelphia, Pittsburgh, Princeton, San Francisco, Tokyo, Washington DC

Number of lawyers 1,150+
at this office 22

CATEGORIES OF WORK

Antitrust
Dr Christian Zschocke, Dr Jürgen Beninca

Mergers and acquisitions
Adi Seffer, Nils Rahlf

Takeover law
Dr Christian Zschocke, Nils Rahlf

Technology, IP, life sciences
Adi Seffer, Marlee S Myers

Financial services
Dr Uwe Jahn, Stephen P Farrell

Corporate
Adi Seffer, Dr Uwe Jahn

THE FIRM

Opened in 1989, the Frankfurt office is a highly specialised office concentrating on corporate (in particular, M&A and corporate restructuring), securities services, and technology, as well as German and European antitrust law. Lawyers are qualified in German and other international jurisdictions (in particular in US-American law) and are able and accustomed to handling complex assignments, simultaneously, in German and English.

AREAS OF PRACTICE

Through the firm's Frankfurt office, clients in Germany are able to receive the excellent legal advice and the all-round support from the cumulative knowledge and experience of a law firm working around the globe, regardless of whether it be for activities in Germany or in the international arena, whereas the specialised knowledge and experience of the firm's highly qualified legal experts make the German market accessible for international clients. As is the case in every Morgan Lewis office, a modern communications and computer system is available in Frankfurt, which is supported by the Morgan Lewis network and by every resource of the entire law firm at any time. This includes online access to e-rooms, around-the-clock availability by e-mail and cellular telephone as well as video telephone. These facilities ensure a smooth co-operation with international clients, in particular those operating in different time zones.

NÖRR STIEFENHOFER LUTZ

FRIEDRICHSTRASSE 2-6
60323 FRANKFURT AM MAIN

Telephone: +49 69 97 14 77 0
Fax: +49 69 97 14 77 100
E-mail: nslfra@noerr.de
Website: www.noerr.de

Languages
Arabic, English, French, Italian, Russian, Spanish

Other offices
Berlin, Bucharest, Budapest, Dresden, Düsseldorf, Moscow, Munich, Prague, Warsaw

Number of lawyers 237
(+ 53 tax advisers, public accountants and tax assistants)
at this office 23

Contact
Dr Thomas Bergmann

CATEGORIES OF WORK

Mergers and acquisitions	Company
Banking and finance	Real estate and development
Capital markets	Litigation and arbitration
German and EC antitrust and cartel law	Unfair competition law
Commercial law	Labour law
Tax law	Private clients
Public and administrative law	

P+P PÖLLATH + PARTNERS

HAUPTWACHE
ZEIL 127
60313 FRANKFURT AM MAIN

Telephone: +49 69 247047 0
Fax: +49 69 247047 30
E-mail: fra@pplaw.com
Website: www.pplaw.com

Languages
English, French

Other offices
Berlin, Munich

Number of lawyers 45
at this office 6

Contacts
Ralph Wagner, Wolfgang Hohensee

CATEGORIES OF WORK

Private equity	Real estate
M&A	Restitution
Corporate finance	Family (high-net-worth, succession)
Tax	Trusts, foundations, charities

RITTERSHAUS

LAW OFFICES, NOTARY OFFICE, TAX CONSULTANTS, CHARTERED ACCOUNTANTS

MAINZER LANDSTRASSE 61
60329 FRANKFURT AM MAIN

Telephone: +49 69 27 40 400
Fax: +49 69 27 40 40 25
E-mail: info@rittershaus.net
Website: www.rittershaus.net

Languages
English, French, Italian, Russian, Spanish

Other offices
Mannheim

Number of lawyers 36
at this office 10

Contacts
Rainer Dietmann, Wendelin Frhr von Ketelhodt

CATEGORIES OF WORK

Companies, corporations
Rainer Dietmann, Andreas Nitsch

Mergers and acquisitions
Rainer Dietmann,
Andreas Nitsch

Competition, antitrust
Dr Wolf-Henrik Friedrich
Christoph Nagel

Inheritance law
Dr Wolf-Henrik Friedrich,
Wendelin Frhr von Ketelhodt

Banking, securities and finance
Wendelin Frhr von Ketelhodt,
Christoph Nagel

Contract
Jörg Döhrer, Mark Oliver Kühn

Real property and construction law
Wendelin Frhr von Ketelhodt,
Dr Wolf-Henrik Friedrich

Sports and entertainment
Rainer Dietmann

Tax
Rainer Dietmann

IT law, e-business
Mark Oliver Kühn

Employment, labour
Jörg Döhrer

Notary office
Wendelin Frhr von Ketelhodt

SJ BERWIN KNOPF TULLOCH STEININGER

RECHTSANWÄLTE – STEUERBERATER – WIRTSCHAFTSPRÜFER

POSEIDON-HAUS
HAMBURGER ALLEE 1
60486 FRANKFURT AM MAIN

Telephone: +49 69 50 50 32 500
Fax: +49 69 50 50 32 499
E-mail: frankfurt@sjberwin.de
Website: www.sjberwin.com

Languages
Danish, English, French, Greek

Other offices
Berlin, Brussels, London, Madrid, Munich, Paris

Number of lawyers 411
at this office 26

Contacts
Rüdiger Knopf, Anthony Tulloch

CATEGORIES OF WORK

Private equity MBOs, M&A
Rüdiger Knopf, Detlef Rüskamp

Venture capital funds
Anthony Tulloch, Dr Hansjörg Piehl

Estate planning
Dr Andreas Söffing

Corporate taxation
Gerald Thomas, Markus Hill

Financial due diligence
Dr Gunter Franzke

Commercial law
Stephan Schmidt,
Dr William Panagiotides

Corporate law/VC transactions/IPOs
Dr Michael Roos, Dr Tobias Lenz

Corporate finance, M&A
Sebastian Gronstedt,
Frank Breitenöder

Employment law
Dr Holger Thomas

SCHWARZ KELWING WICKE WESTPFAHL

MÖRFELDER LANDSTR 117
60598 FRANKFURT

Telephone: +49 69 63 00 01 0
Fax: +49 69 63 55 22
E-mail: info-ffm@skwlaw.de
Website: www.skwlaw.de

Languages
English, French, German

Other offices
Berlin, Cologne, Dresden, Munich

Number of lawyers 62
at this office 9

Contacts
Stefan Kridlo, Michael Wahl, Dr Tatjana Schroeder

Member
Terralex; PLG

CATEGORIES OF WORK

Corporate and commecial law
Dr Manfred Westpfahl, Dr Tatjana Schroeder

Real estate law, conveyancing, construction
Stefan Kridlo, Dr Manfred Westpfahl

Banking and finance
Wilfried Maas, Dr Jan Marwede

Arbitration and litigation
Martin Stück, Wilfried Maas

Unfair competition
Stefan Kridlo

Labour and employment law
Michael Wahl

Succession law
Dr Manfred Westpfahl

Copyright, trade marks, intellectual property
Martin Stück

Mergers and acquisitions
Stefan Kridlo, Dr Tatjana Schroeder

SIMMONS & SIMMONS

MESSETURM
FRIEDRICH-EBERT-ANLAGE 49
60308 FRANKFURT AM MAIN

Telephone: +49 69 90 74 540
Fax: +49 69 90 74 54 54
E-mail: enquiries@simmons-simmons.com
Website: www.simmons-simmons.com

Languages
Dutch, English, French, Spanish

Other offices
London, Rotterdam, Paris, Lisbon, Milan, Rome, Düsseldorf, Brussels, Madrid, Padua, Oporto, Madeira, Abu Dhabi, Qatar, Hong Kong, Shanghai, Tokyo, New York

Number of lawyers 754
at this office 11

Contact
Stephen Moller

CATEGORIES OF WORK

Corporate

Banking

Capital markets

Taxation

Projects, PFI

EU, competition

Dispute resolution

Intellectual property

Employment

Financial markets

Pharmaceutical and biotechnology

Energy and utilities

TMT

Aerospace and defence

Transport

Real estate and construction

Consumer goods

TAYLOR WESSING

SENCKENBERGANLAGE 20-22
60325 FRANKFURT AM MAIN

Telephone: +49 69 9 71 30 0
Fax: +49 69 9 71 30 100
E-mail: frankfurt@taylorwessing.com
Website: www.taylorwessing.com

Languages
English, Dutch, French, Italian, Mandarin, Spanish

Other offices
Alicante*, Berlin, Brussels, Cambridge, Dubai*, Düsseldorf/Neuss, Hamburg, London, Munich, Paris, Shanghai*

Number of lawyers 550
at this office 30

Member
World Law Group; Tech Law Group

CATEGORIES OF WORK

Banking and finance
Claus Goedecke, Peter Seemann

China desk
Florian Ranft

Commercial
Dr Christoph Hasche

Corporate/M&A
Bernhard Kloft

Employment and pensions
Axel C Filges

EU law/antitrust
Dr Marco Hartmann-Rüppel, Markus Wirtz

Intellectual property
Dr Sabine Rojahn

Life science
Dr Ulrich Steffen

Media and entertainment
Martin von Albrecht

Private client
Romana Traichel

Projects and finance
Dr Rüdiger von Hülst

Public commercial law
Dr Walter Potthast

Real estate and construction
Jan Wunschel

Regulatory affairs
Andreas Haak

Tax
Bernd Michel

Technology/IT/telecoms
Joerg Wimmers

WEIL, GOTSHAL & MANGES LLP

MAIN TOWER, 31ST FLOOR
NEUE MAINZER STRASSE 52-58
60311 FRANKFURT AM MAIN

Telephone: +49 69 21 65 96 00
Fax: +49 69 21 65 96 99
Website: www.weil.com

Other offices
Austin, Boston, Brussels, Budapest, Dallas, Houston, London, Miami, Munich, New York, Paris, Prague, Silicon Valley, Singapore, Warsaw, Washington DC

Number of lawyers 1,000
at this office 37

Contact
Gerhard Schmidt (managing partner)

CATEGORIES OF WORK

Capital markets	**Real estate**
Corporate law	**Restructuring**
Litigation	**Structured finance**
Mergers and acquisitions	**Taxation**
Private equity	

THE FIRM

Established in 1931 in New York, Weil, Gotshal & Manges combines lawyers worldwide to meet clients' needs in recognition of the benefits of broad industry and regional experience. The lawyers in the firm's practice groups work together to provide full-service legal advice to clients in sectors as diverse as energy, financial services and hi-tech.

The firm developed a network of offices across the US in the 1970s and 1980s to cater for its expanding client base, and was one of the first international law firms to establish a major presence in central Europe. The firm now has established offices in Brussels, Budapest, Frankfurt, London, Paris, Prague, Singapore and Warsaw.

The firm advises a broad and diverse group of clients, including many of the largest and most prominent corporations and government agencies around the globe, and leading financial institutions.

AREAS OF PRACTICE

The firm's US and European antitrust practice advises on international M&A regulatory notifications, antitrust distribution counselling, cartels, litigation and government and state competition policy. Expertise includes software and computer, healthcare, telecommunications and media, transportation, utilities, heavy industry, consumer goods, financial services and sports.

The corporate department is the firm's largest. The department advises international financial institutions and corporate clients in complex public and private M&As, private equity deals and strategic alliances.

The firm's corporate governance practice is recognised as one of the pre-eminent counsellors of corporate boards, management and institutional investors on the full range of governance issues, including board composition, structure and processes; executive and director compensation; director responsibilities; internal and governmental investigations of alleged accounting or other corporate misconduct; and shareholder initiatives. The firm has advised the World Bank, the OECD, the European Commission and various stock exchanges and regulatory bodies, and is a leader in providing director training programmes worldwide.

The firm advises on a wide range of financing activities and has particular expertise in acquisition finance, asset-based finance, debt restructuring and insolvency, debt and equity capital markets, derivatives, high-yield debt, securitisation, structured finance and telecoms and multimedia financing.

The firm has a leading IP and technology practice and advises some of the world's major technology, media and telecommunications companies. It also acts for investors in technology, media and communications entities. The practice handles patent infringements, outsourcing transactions, strategic alliances, cross-border mergers and acquisitions, investments and IPOs, and advises on the protection and exploitation of IP and on a wide range of e-commerce matters, including data protection. It has expertise in regulatory telecoms matters.

The litigation practice advises international clients on all major areas of the law and has extensive experience in all aspects of dispute resolution. It advises clients in jury trials and appeals, arbitration and alternative dispute forums.

The firm's real estate practice handles complex real estate transactions (including finance, securitisations, development, leasing, sales, acquisitions and debt restructurings) across the US and Europe. It also advises clients on real estate M&A transactions involving real estate investment trusts.

The firm has one of the largest bankruptcy and business reorganisation practices in the world. It includes attorneys in New York, Boston, Dallas, Frankfurt, Houston, London and Miami. The department has been involved in virtually all of the major chapter 11 reorganisation cases in the US and in major national and international out-of-court debt restructurings.

The tax department provides advice on international and domestic taxation, covering many different economic sectors. The department works with the firm's other departments to find innovative solutions to problems that present various and competing multi-disciplinary considerations.

WILLKIE FARR & GALLAGHER LLP

SENCKENBERGANLAGE 16
60325 FRANKFURT AM MAIN

Telephone: +49 69 79302 0
Fax: +49 69 79302 222
Website: www.willkie.com

Languages
English, French, Italian

Other offices
New York, Washington DC, Paris, London, Milan, Rome, Brussels

Number of lawyers 560
at this office 22

Contact
Thomas Heymann

CATEGORIES OF WORK

Telecoms, internet, media, and entertainment (TIME)
Sven-Erik Heun

Intellectual property
Dr Katharina Scheja

Corporate and financial services
Thomas Heymann,
Dr Bernhard von Braunschweig

Information technology
Thomas Heymann, Dr Katharina Scheja

Litigation
Dr Katharina Scheja

Mergers and acquisitions
Thomas Heymann

Private equity
Thomas Heymann

Restructuring
Thomas Heymann

Tax
Dr Bernhard von Braunschweig

Real estate
Dr Bernhard von Braunschweig

GRAF VON WESTPHALEN BAPPERT & MODEST

KAISER-JOSEPH-STRASSE 284
79098 FREIBURG

Telephone: +49 761 21 80 80
Fax: +49 761 21 808 500
E-mail: freiburg@westphalen-law.com
Website: www.westphalen-law.com

Languages
English, French, Greek, Italian, Russian, Spanish, Turkish

Other offices
Berlin, Brussels, Cologne, Dresden, Hamburg, Munich, Vienna

Number of lawyers 110
at this office 24
(+4 accountants and 4 tax advisers)

In exclusive co-operation with
Wragge & Co, UK;
Kemmler Rapp Böhlke, Belgium

CATEGORIES OF WORK

Corporate, mergers and acquisitions

Private equity and venture capital

International trade

Distribution

Intellectual property, media and entertainment

Arbitration and litigation

Administrative and environmental

Real estate and construction

Banking and insolvency

Labour and employment

IT and telecommunications

Life sciences

Product liability and insurance

Accounting

Tax

Corporate finance

ALLEN & OVERY

KEHRWIEDER 12
20457 HAMBURG

Telephone: +49 40 82 22 120
Fax: +49 40 82 22 12 200
E-mail: information@allenovery.com
Website: www.allenovery.com

Languages
Dutch, English, French, Hungarian, Italian, Japanese, Polish, Spanish

Other offices
Amsterdam, Antwerp, Bangkok, Beijing, Bratislava, Brussels, Budapest, Dubai, Frankfurt, Hong Kong, London, Luxembourg, Madrid, Milan, Moscow, New York, Paris, Prague, Rome, Shanghai, Singapore, Tokyo, Turin, Warsaw

Number of lawyers 2,305

Contacts
Dr Cornelius Fischer-Zernin, Dr Arndt Overlack

CATEGORIES OF WORK

- Asset financing/leasing
- Antitrust/competition law
- Arbitration
- Banking regulatory
- Bond issues
- Business restructurings
- Company law
- Derivatives
- Employment law
- Energy law
- Environmental law
- Equity capital markets
- Global loans
- IP/IT
- Joint ventures and takeovers
- Leveraged finance
- Litigation
- MBO and LBOs
- Mergers and acquisitions
- Private equity
- Project finance
- Public and administrative law
- Real estate and finance
- Securitisation
- Tax
- Telecommunications law

ARCON RECHTSANWÄLTE

SCHMIDT-SIBETH HEISSE WEISSKOPF KURSAWE

GROẞE BLEICHEN 16
20354 HAMBURG

Telephone: +49 40 35 08 12 40
Fax: +49 40 35 08 12 49
E-mail: hh@arcon-net.com
Website: www.arcon-net.com

Languages
Catalan, Dutch, English, Finnish, French, Greek, Italian, Portuguese, Russian, Spanish

Other offices
Berlin, Brussels, Cologne, Düsseldorf, Erfurt, Frankfurt am Main, Munich

Number of lawyers 92
at this office 2

Contacts
Lars Bollensen, Dr Ingo Seidner

CATEGORIES OF WORK

- Corporate law, mergers and acquisitions, reorganisations
- IPO, capital markets
- Construction and real estate
- Labour law, employment
- EU law
- Commercial law (general)
- Banking law
- Trade marks, intellectual property, media law
- Competition, antitrust
- Litigation and arbitration
- Contract
- Tax
- Administrative and environment
- Probate and family law
- Estate planning
- Internet, IT and computer law
- Public procurement law

BOLLMANN & PARTNER GbR

NEUER WALL 42
20354 HAMBURG

Telephone: +49 40 37 86 87 0
Fax: +49 40 37 86 87 20

Languages
English, French

Other offices
Copenhagen, St Petersburg

Number of lawyers 5

Contact
Dr Michael Boemke
(dr.boemke@bollmann-hh.de),
Dr Knut Suhr
(dr.suhr@bollmann-hh.de),
Alexander Schmidt
(a.schmidt@bollmann-hh.de),
Verena Zahn
(verena.zahn@web.de)

CATEGORIES OF WORK

Company law
Dr Michael Boemke, Dr Knut Suhr

International sales law
Dr Knut Suhr, Dr Michael Boemke

Agency
Dr Knut Suhr, Dr Michael Boemke

Arbitration
Dr Knut Suhr, Dr Michael Boemke

Litigation
Verena Zahn, Alexander Schmidt

Employment law
Verena Zahn

Labour law
Verena Zahn

Transport and maritime law
Dr Knut Suhr, Alexander Schmidt

Administrative law
Alexander Schmidt

Tax
Jobst-Günther Maeder

Family law
Verena Zahn

BUSE HEBERER FROMM

ABTEISTRASSE 57
20149 HAMBURG

Telephone: +49 40 419 990
Fax: +49 40 419 991 69
E-mail: hamburg@buse.de
Website: www.buse.de

Languages
Chinese, English, French, Italian, Portuguese, Spanish, Swedish

Other offices
Berlin, Dusseldorf, Essen, Frankfurt am Main, Milan, Munich, Palma de Mallorca, Sydney, Zurich

Number of lawyers 120
at this office 25

Member
The European Legal Alliance (Beauchamps, Ireland; Dubarry Le Douarin Veil, France; Field Fisher Waterhouse, England; Harper Macleod, Scotland)

CATEGORIES OF WORK

Banking and finance

Antitrust and merger control

Commerce, transport, insurance

Commercial delinquency

Corporate/M&A

Industrial property and copyrights

Information technology and telecommunications

Labour and employment

Litigation and arbitration, national and international

Press and media

Property and construction

Public law

Tax

CMS HASCHE SIGLE

STADTHAUSBRÜCKE 1-3
20355 HAMBURG

Telephone: +49 40 37 63 00
Fax: +49 40 37 63 03 00
E-mail: hamburg@cmslegal.de
Website: www.cmslegal.de

Languages
English, French, Italian, Spanish

Other offices
Berlin, Dusseldorf, Frankfurt, Leipzig, Munich, Stuttgart, Chemnitz, Dresden, Brussels, Belgrade, Moscow, Prague, Shanghai

Number of lawyers 306
at this office 62

Other CMS law firms
CMS Adonnino Ascoli & Cavasola Scamoni, Italy; CMS Bureau Francis Lefebvre, France; CMS Cameron McKenna, UK; CMS Derks Star Busmann, Netherlands; CMS von Erlach Klainguti Stettler Wille, Switzerland; CMS Lexcelis, Belgium; CMS Strommer Reich-Rohrwig Karasek Hainz, Austria

CATEGORIES OF WORK

Corporate and commercial

Intellectual property, IT, media

Mergers and acquisitions

Real estate and construction

Privatisation and restructuring

Environmental and administrative

Banking, securities and finance

Distribution, franchising

Unfair competition and antitrust

Maritime law

Tax

Arbitration and litigation

Labour law and service contracts

Utilities

Bankruptcy and reorganisation

DABELSTEIN & PASSEHL

GROSSE ELBSTRASSE 36
22767 HAMBURG

Telephone: +49 40 31 77 97 0
Fax: +49 40 31 77 97 77
E-mail: hamburg@da-pa.com
Website: www.da-pa.com

Languages
English, French

Other offices
Leer

Number of lawyers 9

CATEGORIES OF WORK

Carriage of goods/bill of lading
Dieter Schwampe, Rüdiger Warnke

Yachtbuilding and insurance
Joachim Rassau, Jan Dreyer

Ship finance
Thomas Brüggemann, Stefan Schrandt

Ship arrest
Thomas Brüggemann

Ship and plant construction
Jan Dreyer, Stefan Schrandt

German-English legal proceedings
Rüdiger Warnke, Esther Mallach

Land and air transport
Esther Mallach, Rüdiger Warnke

Charterparty disputes
Thomas Brüggemann, Dieter Schwampe

Insurance
Dieter Schwampe, Jan Dreyer

DÄNISCHE ADVOKATEN
FOCUS ADVOKATER LLP

AN DER ALSTER 71
20099 HAMBURG

Telephone: +49 40 24 91 92
Fax: +49 40 24 04 09
E-mail:hamburg@focus-advokater.dk
hamburg@daenische-advokaten.de
Website: www.focus-advokater.dk

Languages
English, French, Spanish, the Scandinavian languages

Other offices
Copenhagen, Odense

Number of lawyers 35
at this office 1

Contacts
Knud K Damsgaard, Uwe Teichert

The categories listed apply only to Focus Advokater, the firm's office in Denmark

CATEGORIES OF WORK

- Arbitration and litigation
- Banking, securities and finance
- Companies, commercial law (general)
- Construction
- EU and competition
- Environmental law
- Family law (wills and estates)
- Insolvency
- Intellectual property
- Mergers and acquisitions
- Ship and aircraft finance
- Sports and entertainment law
- Tax
- Transport

FRESHFIELDS BRUCKHAUS DERINGER

ALSTERARKADEN 27
20354 HAMBURG

Telephone: +49 40 36 90 60
Fax: +49 40 36 90 61 55
E-mail: email@freshfields.com
Website: www.freshfields.com

Languages
Extensive language capabilities

Other offices
Amsterdam, Bangkok, Barcelona, Beijing, Berlin, Bratislava, Brussels, Budapest, Cologne, Düsseldorf, Frankfurt, Hanoi, Ho Chi Minh City, Hong Kong, London, Madrid, Milan, Moscow, Munich, New York, Paris, Rome, Shanghai, Singapore, Tokyo, Vienna, Washington

Number of lawyers 2,504
at this office 62

Contact
Hans Jochen Waitz

CATEGORIES OF WORK

- Corporate
- Finance
- Antitrust, competition and trade
- Intellectual property and IT
- Tax
- Real estate
- Dispute resolution (including environment, planning and regulatory)
- Employment, pensions and benefits

GÖRG
RECHTSANWÄLTE

JUNGFERNSTIEG 7
20354 HAMBURG

Telephone: +49 40 18 88 80
Fax: +49 40 18 88 811
E-mail: hamburg@goerg.de
Website: www.goerg.de

Languages
English, French, Italian, Russian, Spanish

Other offices
Amsterdam*, Antwerp*, Bangkok*, Barcelona*, Berlin, Bergen*, Birmingham*, Bradford*, Brussels*, Cologne, Copenhagen*, Edinburgh*, Essen, Frankfurt/M, Glasgow*, Hong Kong*, Leeds*, Liverpool*, London*, Madrid*, Manchester*, Milan*, Oslo*, Paris*, Prague*, Rotterdam*, Salzburg*, Sarajevo*, Shanghai*, Sheffield*, Singapore*, Stockholm*, Vienna*, Zagreb*

Number of lawyers 83
at this office 8

Member
DLA Group

CATEGORIES OF WORK

General and international law practice

Corporate and commercial

Mergers and acquisitions

Labour and co-determination law

Litigation

Commercial law

Banking law

Seed law

Technology, communications and media law

GRAF VON WESTPHALEN BAPPERT & MODEST

GROSSE BLEICHEN 21
20354 HAMBURG

Telephone: +49 40 35 92 20
Fax: +49 40 35 92 21 23
E-mail: hamburg@westphalen-law.com
Website: www.westphalen-law.com

Languages
English, French, Hungarian, Spanish

Other offices
Berlin, Brussels, Cologne, Dresden, Freiburg, Leipzig, Munich, Vienna

Number of lawyers 110
at this office 34
(+5 accountants and 3 tax advisers)

In exclusive co-operation with
Wragge & Co, UK;
Kemmler Rapp Böhlke, Belgium

CATEGORIES OF WORK

Corporate, mergers and acquisitions

Commercial and international trade

Tax

Distributor contracts

Construction and leasing

Product liability and insurers' liability

Banking and insolvency

Intellectual property, product piracy and unfair trading

Administrative, planning and environmental

EC law

Consumer, food and drugs

Antitrust law

Labour and employment

Arbitration and litigation

Information technology, media and entertainment

Customs regulations

HAARMANN HEMMELRATH

JUNGFERNSTIEG 30
20354 HAMBURG

Telephone: +49 40 35 00 60
Fax: +49 40 35 00 61 33
E-mail:
hamburg@haarmannhemmelrath.com
Website:
www.haarmannhemmelrath.com

Languages
Bulgarian, Croatian, Czech, Dutch, English, French, Hungarian, Italian, Japanese, Mandarin, Norwegian, Polish, Portuguese, Romanian, Russian, Slovak, Spanish, Vietnamese

Other offices
Berlin, Bielefeld, Brussels, Bucharest, Budapest, Cologne, Dusseldorf, Frankfurt, Leipzig, London, Milan, Moscow, Munich, Paris, Prague, Rome, Shanghai, Singapore, Stuttgart, Tokyo, Vienna, Warsaw

Number of lawyers 281
at this office 10

CATEGORIES OF WORK

Corporate and business
Dr Udo Henkel,
Dr Sven Riemenschneider

Mergers and acquisitions
Dr Udo Henkel, Thilo Rohde

Privatisation
Dr Udo Henkel

Legal and tax reorganisations
Dr Sven Riemenschneider,
Dr Thomas Lübbehüsen

Capital markets
Jan Sudmeyer

Real estate development and construction
Dr Marc Biebelheimer

Banking law, leasing
Dr Stefan Kilgus

International tax
Dr Udo Henkel,
Dr Sven Riemenschneider

National tax
Dr Udo Henkel

Audit and accounting services
Holger Böge, Markus Schmal

Due diligence services
Dr Udo Henkel, Uwe Wolf

Corporate restructuring, insolvency
Stefan Ulrich Denkhaus

IP, antitrust, EU
Dr Christoph von Einem

Labour law
Dr Daniela Heise

HARMSEN UTESCHER

ALTER WALL 55
20457 HAMBURG

Telephone: +49 40 376 909 0
Fax: +49 40 376 909 99
E-mail: contact@harmsen.utescher.com
Website: www.harmsen.utescher.com

Languages
English, French, Italian, Portuguese, Spanish

Number of lawyers 15

CATEGORIES OF WORK

German and international trade mark law

Patent and utility-model law

Unfair competition law

IT and new media law

Copyright law, registered design law

Medical preparations law, medical products law

Food and cosmetics law

German and European antitrust law

Media law

Sports law

HEUKING KÜHN LÜER WOJTEK

BLEICHENBRÜCKE 9
20354 HAMBURG

Telephone: +49 40 35 52 800
Fax: +49 40 35 52 80 80
E-mail: hamburg@heuking.de
Website: www.heuking.de

Languages
German, English, French, Italian, Spanish

Other offices
Berlin, Brussels, Chemnitz, Cologne, Düsseldorf, Frankfurt, Munich

Number of lawyers 28

Contact
Dr Ralf Wojtek

CATEGORIES OF WORK

Corporate, partnerships, international mergers and acquisitions, general commercial law

Competition, merger control and state aids

Project finance

Insurance

Litigation and arbitration

Environmental and public law

Energy law

Entertainment, media, publishing, copyright

Intellectual property law

Property and real estate law

Employment and labour law

Maritime law

Transport law, postal services and logistics

IT, e-commerce and telecommunications

THE FIRM

Heuking Kühn Lüer Wojtek was founded in Düsseldorf, Germany, in 1971. Since then, the firm has spread geographically, and Heuking Kühn now has seven significant offices in Germany, as well as an office in Brussels.

The firm has an extensive international network of law firms, enabling it to provide its clients with seamless 'one-stop shopping', on international transactions and regulatory matters. Since its formation, Heuking Kühn Lüer Wojtek has specifically chosen to remain an independent law firm. It is Heuking Kühn Lüer Wojtek's philosophy that, to provide the best possible service to its clients, the firm must be able to co-operate with various other law firms which are at the top of the profession in their respective countries. This gives the firm the ability to make alternative counsel suggestions to its clients, giving the clients a choice of the best suitable law firm or lawyer in each country and for each matter. Over the last 30+ years, Heuking Kühn Lüer Wojtek has developed excellent relationships with the key firms in all of the major jurisdictions worldwide.

Heuking Kühn Lüer Wojtek is a name which is synonymous with legal competence. The firm is one of the largest commercial law firms in Germany, with more than 150 specialised lawyers and tax advisers, representing the interests of national and international clients. Included in the client list are large and medium-sized German and international companies in all areas of the manufacturing industry, as well as trade and service industries, associations, governmental and public sector organisations and private clients and trusts.

The firm prides itself on substantive legal competence and on the excellent education and continuing legal education of its lawyers. Moreover, virtually all of the lawyers are German-English bilingual.

Extensive specialisation and comprehensive knowledge of specific industry sectors provide the basis of all of Heuking Kühn Lüer Wojtek's legal counselling. Experienced partners and carefully selected associate lawyers develop innovative solutions to complex legal problems. The lawyers regularly work in their specific practice area groups and also in multi-group and multi-disciplinary teams with clients and outside consultants or advisers. Entrepreneurial thinking on behalf of firm clients, as well as efficient, quality, cost-effective and timely work and the highest personal dedication are key components of Heuking Kühn Lüer Wojtek's culture.

AREAS OF PRACTICE

Heuking Kühn Lüer Wojtek is a full-service commercial law firm. Cross-border and cross-sector knowledge in combination with a deep understanding of business reasoning enables service to clients with the broadest possible support in all their negotiations and business decisions. This applies equally to M&A transactions, to legal advice on company structure, business risk management, negotiations and negotiation tactics, training, crisis and insolvency counselling, corporate financial matters, and complex litigation and arbitration. Thanks to a variety of strong business clients, the firm has built long-term relationships with its clients and can assist them, beginning with the establishment of a business, followed by implementing business goals, including day-to-day legal work, reorganisations, acquisitions and divestitures.

Heuking Kühn Lüer Wojtek is actively involved with its clients in providing regulatory counselling in all areas of commercial law, as well as assisting them in organising and implementing their M&A transactions in Germany, throughout Europe, and internationally. Heuking Kühn Lüer Wojtek has particular expertise in German and EU company law; competition law, merger control and state aids; international investment, trade, and taxation matters; banking and finance; labour law; intellectual property rights; environmental, health, and safety regulation; product-specific regulation; real estate and construction law; telecoms, IT and media law; transport, postal services and shipping law; public procurement; family law; and private clients and family office matters.

HUTH DIETRICH HAHN

WARBURGSTRASSE 50
20354 HAMBURG

Telephone: +49 40 41 52 50
Fax: +49 40 41 52 51 11
E-mail: hdh@huthdietrichhahn.de
Website: www.hdh.net

Languages
English, French, Spanish

Number of lawyers 18

CATEGORIES OF WORK

Mergers and acquisitions, corporate finance
All partners

IPO
All partners

Corporate law
All partners

Private equity
All partners

Tax law
All partners

Venture capital
Dr Röttger

Real property law
Dr Stucken, Herr Strasburger

Antitrust law
Dr Aries

Public law
Herr Strasburger

Media law
Dr Aries

Succession planning, heritage law
Dr Wittuhn

THE FIRM

Huth Dietrich Hahn which was established in 1990, currently has 18 lawyers, 11 of whom are partners. The size of the firm has the advantage of being big enough to take on and deal effectively with considerably large matters, for example in the field of mergers and acquisitions, whilst also retaining a reputation of advising individual clients on smaller matters.

All of the partners of the firm have had considerable working experience in the legal profession in different jurisdictions, with some of the firm's partners having graduated with Masters Degrees in the United States.

As a result of such extensive international experience and expertise, the firm has been able to associate with, and establish a network with other firms of foreign lawyers. Such firms were selected by Huth Dietrich Hahn on the strength of the high-quality services which they provide to their clients and accordingly, the firm is able to offer its clients services not only within Germany and the rest of Europe, but in almost all countries worldwide.

AREAS OF PRACTICE

The firm specialises in the field of acquisitions and mergers, and is able to provide a broad range of advice on acquisitions, restructuring and corporate finance. The firm will advise the client throughout the transaction, from the letter of intent, during the due diligence process, through negotiation, whilst also advising on the tax implications of the transaction, restructuring and financing. The firm is also able to provide related services in the areas of antitrust and labour law.

Huth Dietrich Hahn's practice also covers matters of IPOs of companies, and further areas of the firm's expertise include real property, the laws of succession (in particular with respect to companies), tax law for both corporate bodies and individuals, antitrust law, European Community law and public law (especially in the areas of East German law).

INCE & CO

GROSSE ELBSTRASSE 47
22767 HAMBURG

Telephone: +49 40 38 0860
Fax: +49 40 38 086100
E-mail: firstname.lastname@incelaw.com
Website: www.incelaw.com

Languages
English, French, Sinhalese, Spanish

Other offices
Hong Kong, Le Havre, London, Paris, Piraeus, Shanghai, Singapore

Number of lawyers at this office 11

CATEGORIES OF WORK

Shipping
Axel Salander, Detlef Zschoche
David McInnes

Insurance/reinsurance
Detlef Zschoche, David McInnes

International trade
Axel Salander

Commercial litigation
Axel Salander, Detlef Zschoche,
David McInnes

Shipbuilding
Detlef Zschoche

Ship sale and purchase (including megayachts)
Jan Hungar, Detlef Zschoche

Arbitration (international)
Axel Salander, David McInnes

Ship finance
Detlef Zschoche, Jan Hungar

Corporate
Detlef Zschoche, Jan Hungar

Ship registration
Markus Eichhorst, Jan Hungar

EU law
Markus Eichhorst

ADR
Detlef Zschoche

Aviation
Robert Kempkens

THE FIRM

Ince & Co is an international law firm with a worldwide reputation as a leading practitioner in shipping, insurance and reinsurance, energy, aviation and international trade law. Founded in the City of London in 1870, the firm also has offices in Hamburg, Hong Kong, Le Havre, Paris, Piraeus, Shanghai and Singapore.

AREAS OF PRACTICE

Ince Hamburg opened in October 2001 to provide a wide range of legal services, with particular emphasis on insurance and reinsurance, shipping, international trade and energy, both contentious and non-contentious. For many years, the firm has enjoyed close contact with the German shipping and insurance markets, and has represented clients across both industries. Hamburg's logistical importance to the maritime, insurance and reinsurance industries makes it a logical base for the firm's German and northern European activities.

LATHAM & WATKINS LLP

WARBURGSTRASSE 50
20354 HAMBURG

Telephone: +49 40 41 40 30
Fax: +49 40 41 40 31 30
Website: www.lw.com

Languages
English, French, German, Italian, Portuguese, Russian, Spanish, Swedish

Other offices
Boston, Brussels, Chicago, Frankfurt, Hong Kong, London, Los Angeles, Milan, Moscow, New Jersey, New York, Northern Virginia, Orange County, Paris, San Diego, San Francisco, Silicon Valley, Singapore, Tokyo, Washington DC

Number of lawyers 1,500
at this office 60

CATEGORIES OF WORK

Antitrust law	Mergers and acquisitions, privatisations and joint ventures
Banking, investment funds, insurance and reinsurance	Patent law
Commercial litigation and arbitration	Product liability
Communications and media law	Private equity/venture capital
EU/competition	Public and administrative law
Labour law	Real estate
Insolvency	Tax
Intellectual property/ information technology	Transport and insurance
	Corporate finance

LOVELLS

WARBURGSTRASSE 50
20354 HAMBURG

Telephone: +49 40 419 93 0
Fax: +49 40 419 93 200
E-mail: reception.hamburg@lovells.com
Website: www.lovells.de

Languages
English, French, Italian, Russian, Spanish

Other offices
Alicante, Amsterdam, Beijing, Berlin, Brussels, Budapest*, Chicago, Düsseldorf, Frankfurt, Ho Chi Minh City, Hong Kong, London, Milan, Moscow, Munich, New York, Paris, Prague, Rome, Shanghai, Singapore, Tokyo, Vienna*, Warsaw, Zagreb*

Number of lawyers 1,600
at this office 59

Contact
Volker Meinberg

CATEGORIES OF WORK

Corporate/M&A, private equity	Intellectual property
Restructuring and insolvency	Property
Banking	Projects
Antitrust and unfair competition	Technology, media, telecommunications
Capital markets	Litigation, product liability
Project finance, public private partnerships	International arbitration
Tax	Food and drug regulations
Employment	Law of Eastern Europe

MAIWALD PATENTANWALTS GMBH

BALLINDAMM 37
20095 HAMBURG

Telephone: +49 40 555 89 50
Fax: +49 40 555 40 525
E-mail: mail@maiwald.de
Website: www.maiwald.de

Languages
English, French, German, Spanish

Other offices
Düsseldorf, Munich

Number of lawyers 14
at this office 2

Contacts
Volker Hamm, Dr Sigrid von Krosigk

CATEGORIES OF WORK

Patents

Trade marks

Intellectual property – related copyrights

Unfair competition

Competition and software law

Internet law

Business and commercial law

Licensing and litigation

O & P OBERTHÜR & PARTNER

ARNOLD-HEISE-STRASSE 10
20249 HAMBURG

Telephone: +49 40 35 50 57 0
Fax: +49 40 35 50 57 13
E-mail: info@oberthuer.de
Website: www.oberthuer.de

Languages
English, French, Spanish

Number of lawyers 7

Contact
Ms Andrea Bohl

CATEGORIES OF WORK

Public real estate law

Private real estate law (including consultancy, preparation of project management and other contracts)

Construction law

Architectural law

Legal consultancy (purchase and sale, valuation and commercialisation of properties, realisation of major building schemes during the course of approval procedure, etc)

Commercial and environmental law

Public duty and fee

Public contracts

Placing of public orders

Federal air pollution

Neighbourhood problems

Expropriation and eminent domain

Development costs

Development schemes

TAYLOR WESSING

NEUER WALL 44
20354 HAMBURG

Telephone: +49 40 3 68 03-0
Fax: +49 40 3 68 03 280
E-mail: hamburg@taylorwessing.com
Website: www.taylorwessing.com

Languages
Dutch, English, French, Italian, Mandarin, Spanish

Other offices
Alicante*, Berlin, Brussels, Cambridge, Dubai*, Düsseldorf/Neuss, Frankfurt, London, Munich, Paris, Shanghai*

Number of lawyers 550
at this office 53

Member
World Law Group; Tech Law Group

CATEGORIES OF WORK

Banking and finance
Claus Goedecke, Peter Seemann

China desk
Florian Ranft

Commercial
Dr Christoph Hasche

Corporate/M&A
Bernhard Kloft

Employment and pensions
Axel C Filges

EU law/antitrust
Dr Marco Hartmann-Rüppel, Markus Wirtz

Intellectual property
Dr Sabine Rojahn

Life science
Dr Ulrich Steffen

Media and entertainment
Martin von Albrecht

Private client
Romana Traichel

Projects and finance
Dr Rüdiger von Hülst

Public commercial law
Dr Walter Potthast

Real estate and construction
Jan Wunschel

Regulatory affairs
Andreas Haak

Tax
Bernd Michel

Technology/IT/telecoms
Joerg Wimmers

UEXKÜLL & STOLBERG

BESELERSTR 4
22607 HAMBURG

Telephone: +49 40 899 65 40
Fax: +49 40 899 654 88
E-mail: postmaster@uex.de
Website: www.uex.de

Languages
English, German

Other offices
Munich

Number of lawyers 19
at this office 17

CATEGORIES OF WORK

Patents and licensing – chemistry
Dr Allard von Kameke, Dr Peter Franck

Patents and licensing – biotechnology
Ingeborg Voelker

Patents and licensing – medical and electrical engineering
Jürgen Suchantke

Trade marks
Dr Frank Dettmann

Design registration
Jürgen Suchantke

Unfair competition
Dr Frank Dettmann

CMS HASCHE SIGLE

AUGUSTUSPLATZ 9
04109 LEIPZIG

Telephone: +49 341 2 16 720
Fax: +49 341 2 16 723 3
E-mail: leipzig@cmslegal.de
Website: www.cmslegal.de

Languages
English, French, Italian

Other offices
Berlin, Dusseldorf, Frankfurt, Hamburg, Munich, Stuttgart, Chemnitz, Dresden, Brussels, Belgrade, Moscow, Prague, Shanghai

Number of lawyers 306
at this office 17

Other CMS law firms
CMS Adonnino Ascoli & Cavasola Scamoni, Italy; CMS Bureau Francis Lefebvre, France; CMS Cameron McKenna, UK; CMS Derks Star Busmann, Netherlands; CMS von Erlach Klainguti Stettler Wille, Switzerland; CMS Lexcelis, Belgium; CMS Strommer Reich-Rohrwig Karasek Hainz, Austria

CATEGORIES OF WORK

Corporate and commercial

Mergers and acquisitions

Privatisation and restructuring

Banking, securities and finance

Unfair competition and antitrust

Tax

Labour law and service contracts

Bankruptcy and reorganisation

Intellectual property, IT, media

Real estate and construction

Environmental and administrative

Distribution, franchising

Maritime law

Arbitration and litigation

Utilities

HAARMANN HEMMELRATH

NEUMARKT 9A
04109 LEIPZIG

Telephone: +49 341 12 63 0
Fax: +49 341 12 63 133
E-mail:
leipzig@haarmannhemmelrath.com
Website:
www.haarmannhemmelrath.com

Languages
English, French, Russian

Other offices
Berlin, Bielefeld, Brussels, Bucharest, Budapest, Cologne, Dusseldorf, Frankfurt, Hamburg, London, Milan, Moscow, Munich, Paris, Prague, Rome, Shanghai, Singapore, Stuttgart, Tokyo, Vienna, Warsaw

Number of lawyers 281
at this office 6

CATEGORIES OF WORK

Corporate and business law
Bernd Brinkmann

Mergers and acquisitions
Bernd Brinkmann

Intellectual property, antitrust, EU law, media law, telecommunications
Bernd Brinkmann

Corporate recovery, insolvency
Niels Bahr

Public law
Dr Gabriel Glos

National tax law and compliance
Niels Bahr

Audit and accounting services
Niels Bahr

Construction law
Dr Gabriel Glos

Labour law
Dr Dagmer Unger

Litigation, mediation, arbitration
Bernd Brinkmann

BETTE – BRINK

GROSSE BLEICHE 60-62
55116 MAINZ

Telephone: +49 61 31 28 77 00
Fax: +49 61 31 28 77 099
E-mail: bette-brink@mainz.juropartner.de
Website: www.bette-brink.de

Languages
Czech, English, French, Spanish

Other offices
Berlin, Erfurt

Number of lawyers 11
at this office 7

Member
Juropartner (European Society for Economic Interests)

CATEGORIES OF WORK

Banking law
Dr Ulrich Brink

Company law
Dr Ulrich Brink, Almut Diederichsen

Fiscal law
Dr Ulrich Brink

Leasing law
Dr Ulrich Brink

Industrial relations law
Christian v der Lühe

Company environment law
Christian v der Lühe

European law
Almut Diederichsen

International private law
Almut Diederichsen

Law governing factoring and financing
Barbara Kohl, Dr Ulrich Brink

RITTERSHAUS

LAW OFFICES, TAX CONSULTANTS, CHARTERED ACCOUNTANTS

HARRLACHWEG 4
68163 MANNHEIM

Telephone: +49 621 42 56 0
Fax: +49 621 42 56 25 0
E-mail: info@rittershaus.net
Website: www.rittershaus.net

Languages
English, French, Italian, Russian, Spanish

Other offices
Frankfurt

Number of lawyers 36
at this office 26

Contacts
Prof Dr Gerald Rittershaus, Manfred Wissmann

CATEGORIES OF WORK

Companies, corporations
Manfred Wissmann,
Dr Christof Hettich

Mergers and acquisitions
Dr Vera Lieberwirth,
Dr Christof Hettich

Competition, antitrust
Dr Daniel Weisert, Dr Bernd M Zinow

Real property and construction law
Andreas Pauli, Britta Weichsel

Banking, securities and finance
Prof Dr Gerald Rittershaus,
Dr Vera Lieberwirth

Arbitration
Prof Dr Gerald Rittershaus,
Manfred Wissmann

Private clients, inheritance law
Dr Martin Bürmann,
Dr Patrick Certa

Employment, labour
Dr Andreas Notz, Annette Sättele

Sports and entertainment
Dr Daniel Weisert, Nico Rittershaus

Tax
Prof Dr Frank Grafmüller,
Dr Peter Gohlke

Insolvency law, restructuring
Andreas Schmidt LLM,
Dr Martin Bürmann

Private equity
Verena Eisenlohr LLM,
Dr Barbara von Horstig

ROSPATT OSTEN PROSS
RECHTSANWÄLTE

JANDERSTRASSE 8
68199 MANNHEIM

Telephone: +49 621 845 5375
Fax: +49 621 845 5376
E-mail: mail@rospatt.de
Website: www.rospatt.de

Languages
English, French

Other offices
Düsseldorf

Number of lawyers 10
at this office 1

CATEGORIES OF WORK

- Patents, utility models
- Trade marks
- Design patents
- Copyrights
- Unfair competition
- Product liability
- Litigation, arbitration, licensing

ARCON RECHTSANWÄLTE
SCHMIDT-SIBETH HEISSE WEISSKOPF KURSAWE

MAXIMILIANSPLATZ 5
80333 MÜNCHEN

Telephone: +49 89 54 56 50
Fax: +49 89 54 56 52 01
E-mail: munich@arcon-net.com
Website: www.arcon-net.com

Languages
Catalan, Dutch, English, Finnish, French, Greek, Italian, Portuguese, Russian, Spanish

Other offices
Berlin, Brussels, Cologne, Düsseldorf, Erfurt, Frankfurt am Main, Hamburg

Number of lawyers 92
at this office 37

Contacts
Dr Matthias Heisse, Dr Stefan Kursawe, Dr Georg Anders

CATEGORIES OF WORK

- Corporate law, reorganisations
- Corporate finance, capital markets
- Mergers and acquisitions
- Construction and engineering
- Real estate
- Labour law, employment
- EU law
- Commercial law (general)
- Banking
- Trade marks, intellectual property, media law
- Competition, antitrust
- Litigation and arbitration
- Tax
- Administrative and environment
- Probate and family law
- Estate planning
- Internet, IT and computer law

ASHURST

PRINZREGENSTRASSE 18
80539 MÜNCHEN

Telephone: +49 89 244 421 100
Fax: +49 89 244 421 101
Website: www.ashurst.com

Languages
English, German, Greek

Other offices
Brussels, Frankfurt, London, Madrid, Milan, New Delhi*, New York, Paris, Singapore, Tokyo

Number of lawyers 813
at this office 19

Contact
Hermann Schlindwein, Karl Wach

CATEGORIES OF WORK

Banking and finance

Competition

Complex litigation

Arbitration

Professional negligence

Corporate and commercial

Employment

Information technology/ intellectual property

Insolvency

White-collar crime

M&A

Private equity

Venture capital

Tax

BEITEN BURKHARDT RECHTSANWALTSGESELLSCHAFT mbH

GANGHOFERSTRASSE 33
80339 MUNICH

Telephone: +49 89 3 50 65 00
Fax: +49 89 3 50 65 123
E-mail: bblaw-muenchen@bblaw.de
Website: www.bblaw.de

Languages
Cantonese, Czech, English, French, Hungarian, Italian, Mandarin, Polish, Russian, Slovak, Spanish

Other offices
Beijing, Berlin, Brussels, Budapest, Cologne, Dusseldorf, Frankfurt am Main, Hamburg, Hong Kong, Leipzig, Moscow, Nuremberg, St Petersburg, Shanghai, Warsaw

Number of lawyers 232
at this office 64

CATEGORIES OF WORK

Company law

Banking and finance

European law and cartel law

Industrial property rights

Labour and employment law

Procurement law

Public law

Media and telecommunications law, information technology

Forensic services, corporate compliance

Law of associations, societies and sports law

Probate, company succession

Litigation and arbitration

Property law

Insurance law

BAKER & McKENZIE

THEATINERSTRASSE 23
80333 MÜNCHEN

Telephone: +49 89 55 23 80
Fax: +49 89 55 23 81 99
Website: www.bakernet.com

Languages
English, French, Italian, Polish, Spanish

Other offices
Almaty, Amsterdam, Antwerp, Bahrain, Baku, Bangkok, Barcelona, Beijing, Berlin, Bogotá, Bologna, Brasilia, Brussels, Budapest, Buenos Aires, Cairo, Calgary, Caracas, Chicago, Dallas, Düsseldorf, Frankfurt, Geneva, Guadalajara, Hanoi, Ho Chi Minh City, Hong Kong, Houston, Juarez, Kyiv, London, Madrid, Manila, Melbourne, Mexico City, Miami, Milan, Monterrey, Moscow, New York, Palo Alto, Paris, Porto Alegré, Prague, Rio de Janeiro, Riyadh, Rome, St Petersburg, San Diego, San Francisco, Santiago, São Paulo, Shanghai, Singapore, Stockholm, Sydney, Taipei, Tijuana, Tokyo, Toronto, Valencia, Vienna, Warsaw, Washington DC, Zürich

Number of lawyers 3,380
at this office 24

CATEGORIES OF WORK

Banking and finance
Michael Foundethakis

Capital markets
Walter Henle

Company and commercial law
Walter Henle

Information technology, media and computer law
Wolfgang Fritzemeyer, Truiken Heydn

Intellectual property
Stephan Spehl, Wolfgang Fritzemeyer

Labour law
Bernhard Trappehl

Litigation and arbitration
Stephan Spehl, Truiken Heydn

Mergers and acquisitions
Andreas Hoffmann, Lutz Zimmer

Venture capital
Walter Henle, Lutz Zimmer

Tax
Stefan Süß

THE FIRM

Founded in Chicago in 1949, Baker & McKenzie is a global law firm with 66 offices in 36 countries. A multinational network of over 4,400 legal professionals offers clients resources and knowledge in every area of business law, in virtually every important financial and commercial centre in the world.

Baker & McKenzie has been established in Europe for over 40 years, having opened its first European offices in 1957. Since then, the European and Middle Eastern network has grown to 29 offices, giving it unparalleled geographical coverage.

The Frankfurt am Main office was formed in 1962; the office in Berlin was opened on 1 March 1990; the Munich office on 1 April 1997; and the Düsseldorf office on 1 April 1999.

Since its formation, the German offices of Baker & McKenzie have advised their clients on all questions of German, European and international industrial and commercial law with particular emphasis on cross-border and multinational transactions. At present, more than 170 attorneys-at-law (Rechtsanwälte), admitted in the Federal Republic of Germany including the new federal states, tax advisers, and varying numbers of foreign admitted lawyers work in the German offices of Baker & McKenzie.

All attorneys are at least bilingual; most of them have completed additional graduate legal studies at foreign law schools. Several attorneys are simultaneously admitted as CPAs, tax advisers, tax attorneys, attorneys for administrative law or attorneys for labour law.

AREAS OF PRACTICE

Baker & McKenzie co-ordinates its core practice areas on local, regional and global levels, giving most of its lawyers experience in more than one jurisdiction, as well as providing multinational teams of specialists.

Utilising a global practice group structure and ground-breaking technology coupled with a personal, detailed understanding of a client's specific business, Baker & McKenzie is able to organise its extensive resources to provide focused and strategic counsel to clients.

Baker & McKenzie advises multinational enterprises, large German companies, medium-sized enterprises, banks and insurance companies, as well as institutions and entities under public law in all questions of German, European, and international industrial and commercial law including company law, competition and cartel law, intellectual property, banking and finance, labour law, administrative law, and tax law. Furthermore, the firm handles litigation and arbitration matters. Several partners have expertise in specialised areas of law, such as European Community law, the law of cosmetics, food and drug law, trade marks, franchising, corporate finance, new financial products, government procurement, real estate transactions, and media telecommunications law.

BIRD & BIRD

PACELLISTRASSE 14
80333 MUNICH

Telephone: +49 89 3581 6000
Fax: +49 89 3581 6011
E-mail: muenchen@twobirds.com
Website: www.twobirds.com

Languages
English, French, German

Other offices
Brussels, Düsseldorf, Hong Kong, London, Milan, Paris, Stockholm, The Hague

Number of lawyers 358
at this office 11

Contacts
Dr Ulrich Goebel, Dr Joseph Fesenmair, Dr Reinhard Gaertner

CATEGORIES OF WORK

Arbitration
Aviation
Commercial
Communication
Corporate
Employment
EU and competition
Intellectual property
IT and e-commerce
Litigation
Media
Mergers and acquisitions
Public procurement
Real estate
Regulatory
Sport and sponsorship

BUSE HEBERER FROMM

MAXIMILIANSPLATZ 18
80333 MUNICH

Telephone: +49 89 22 66 51
Fax: +49 89 22 44 68
E-mail: muenchen@buse.de
Website: www.buse.de

Languages
English, French, Italian, Spanish

Other offices
Berlin, Dusseldorf, Essen, Frankfurt am Main, Hamburg, Milan, Palma de Mallorca, Sydney, Zurich

Number of lawyers 120
at this office 4

Member
The European Legal Alliance (Beauchamps, Ireland; Dubarry Le Douarin Veil, France; Field Fisher Waterhouse, England; Harper Macleod, Scotland)

CATEGORIES OF WORK

Banking and finance
Antitrust and merger control
Commerce, transport, insurance
Commercial delinquency
Corporate/M&A
Industrial property and copyrights
Information technology and telecommunications
Labour and employment
Litigation and arbitration, national and international
Press and media
Property and construction
Public law
Tax

CMS HASCHE SIGLE

BRIENNER STRASSE 11/V
80333 MÜNCHEN

Telephone: +49 89 23 80 70
Fax: +49 89 23 80 71 10
E-mail: muenchen@cmslegal.de
Website: www.cmslegal.de

Languages
Dutch, English, French, Italian, Russian, Spanish

Other offices
Berlin, Dusseldorf, Frankfurt, Hamburg, Leipzig, Stuttgart, Chemnitz, Dresden, Brussels, Belgrade, Moscow, Prague, Shanghai

Number of lawyers 306
at this office 48

Other CMS law firms
CMS Adonnino Ascoli & Cavasola Scamoni, Italy; CMS Bureau Francis Lefebvre, France; CMS Cameron McKenna, UK; CMS Derks Star Busmann, Netherlands; CMS von Erlach Klainguti Stettler Wille, Switzerland; CMS Lexcelis, Belgium; CMS Strommer Reich-Rohrwig Karasek Hainz, Austria

CATEGORIES OF WORK

- Corporate and commercial
- Mergers and acquisitions
- Privatisation and restructuring
- Banking, securities and finance
- Unfair competition and antitrust
- Tax
- Labour law and service contracts
- Bankruptcy and reorganisation
- Intellectual property, IT, media
- Real estate and construction
- Environmental and administrative
- Distribution, franchising
- Maritime law
- Arbitration and litigation
- Utilities

FRESHFIELDS BRUCKHAUS DERINGER

PRANNERSTRASSE 10
80333 MUNICH

Telephone: +49 89 20 70 20
Fax: +49 89 20 70 21 00
E-mail: email@freshfields.com
Website: www.freshfields.com

Languages
Extensive language capabilities

Other offices
Amsterdam, Bangkok, Barcelona, Beijing, Berlin, Bratislava, Brussels, Budapest, Cologne, Düsseldorf, Frankfurt, Hamburg, Hanoi, Ho Chi Minh City, Hong Kong, London, Madrid, Milan, Moscow, New York, Paris, Rome, Shanghai, Singapore, Tokyo, Vienna, Washington

Number of lawyers 2,504
at this office 32

Contact
Bernhard Heiss

CATEGORIES OF WORK

- Corporate
- Finance
- Antitrust, competition and trade
- Intellectual property and IT
- Tax
- Real estate
- Employment, pensions and benefits
- Dispute resolution (including environmental, planning and regulatory)

FROHWITTER

POSSARTSTRASSE 20
81679 MÜNCHEN

Telephone: +49 89 99 80 90
Fax: +49 89 99 80 95 55
E-mail: info@frohwitter.com
Website: www.frohwitter.com

Languages
English, French, German, Italian, Romanian, Russian

Number of lawyers 12

CATEGORIES OF WORK

Patent and trade mark prosecution

Biotechnology, biochemical, pharmacy
Dr Christian Helbig, Dr Norman Klix

Mechanical engineering
Dr Thomas Leske

Electronics
Dr Edward Tomlinson

Computer and IT
Jan Gigerich

Telecommunications
Iouri Kobiako

Patent and trade mark litigation
Bernhard Frohwitter, Dr Tatjana Kowal-Wolk

Unfair competition
Dr Tatjana Kowal-Wolk, Dr Ludwig Vohland

International patent strategy, international property counselling, licensing hi-tech patent practice
Bernhard Frohwitter

GSK GASSNER STOCKMANN & KOLLEGEN

LUDWIGSTRASSE 10
80539 MÜNCHEN

Telephone: +49 89 288 174 0
Fax: +49 89 288 174 44
E-mail: muenchen@gsk.de
Website: www.gsk.de

Languages
English, French, Italian, Russian

Other offices
Berlin, Düsseldorf, Frankfurt, Hamburg, Heidelberg, Stuttgart

Number of lawyers 75
at this office 23

Contacts
Dr Andreas Bauer (Munich), Dr Christian R Schmidt (Berlin), Dr Andreas May (Frankfurt), Dr Philipp Jebens (Hamburg), Dr Peter Ladwig (Stuttgart), Holger Lampe (Düsseldorf), Wolfgang Böhm (Heidelberg)

CATEGORIES OF WORK

Banking and finance, capital markets, project finance

Infrastructure, public sector

Corporate, M&A, venture capital, private equity

Real estate, construction

GLEISS LUTZ
RECHTSANWÄLTE

PRINZREGENTENSTRASSE 50
80538 MUNICH

Telephone: +49 89 216 670
Fax: +49 89 216 67 111
E-mail: info@gleisslutz.com
Website: www.gleisslutz.com

Languages
Dutch, English, French, Italian, Mandarin, Cantonese, Polish, Portuguese, Spanish, Russian, Czech, Slovak

Other offices
Berlin, Frankfurt, Stuttgart, Brussels, Prague, Warsaw

Number of lawyers 200
at this office 15

Contact
Dr Ingo Brinker

CATEGORIES OF WORK

German, EC and international law	Employment, labour
Banking, securities and finance	Insurance
Commercial law (general)	Litigation and arbitration
Companies, corporations	Mergers and acquisitions
Competition, antitrust	Tax
Electronic commerce, Internet law	Trade marks, intellectual property

GRAF VON WESTPHALEN BAPPERT & MODEST

WIDENMAYERSTRASSE 15
80538 MUNICH

Telephone: +49 89 68 90 77-0
Fax: +49 89 68 90 77-77
E-mail: muenchen@westphalen-law.com
Website: www.westphalen-law.com

Languages
English, French, Italian

Other offices
Berlin, Brussels, Cologne, Dresden, Freiburg, Hamburg, Vienna

Number of lawyers 110
at this office 7
(+1 accountant and 1 tax adviser)

In exclusive co-operation with
Wragge & Co, UK;
Kemmler Rapp Böhlke, Belgium

CATEGORIES OF WORK

Corporate, mergers and acquisitions	Renewable energies
Corporate finance	Succession and property
Private equity and venture capital	Distributor contracts
Project finance	Construction and leasing
Tax	Antitrust law
Funds	Arbitration and litigation
Life sciences	

HAARMANN HEMMELRATH

MAXIMILIANSTRASSE 35
80539 MUNICH

Telephone: +49 89 21 63 60
Fax: +49 89 21 63 61 33
E-mail: munich@haarmannhemmelrath.com
Website: www.haarmannhemmelrath.com

Languages
Bulgarian, Croatian, Czech, Dutch, English, French, Hungarian, Italian, Japanese, Mandarin, Norwegian, Polish, Portuguese, Romanian, Russian, Slovak, Spanish, Vietnamese

Other offices
Berlin, Bielefeld, Brussels, Bucharest, Budapest, Cologne, Düsseldorf, Frankfurt, Hamburg, Leipzig, London, Milan, Moscow, Paris, Prague, Rome, Shanghai, Singapore, Stuttgart, Tokyo, Vienna, Warsaw

Number of lawyers 281
at this office 27

CATEGORIES OF WORK

Corporate and business law
Dr Andreas Oldenbourg
Dr Heinrich J Rodewig

Mergers and acquisitions
Dr Andreas Oldenbourg,
Dr Heinrich J Rodewig

Due diligence
Dr Simon Preisenberger,
Stefanie Schmid

Reorganisation, corporate recovery
Thomas Krempl, Stephan Abele

Audit and accounting services
Bodo Richardt, Hansjörg Zelger

Telecommunications and IT
Dr Christoph von Einem, Dr Uwe Bohnet

Real estate, environmental law
Ulrich Steffen, Dr Alexander Venus

Fund structuring, leasing
Prof Dr Alexander Hemmelrath,
Jürgen Fahrenberg

IP, antitrust, EU law, media law
Dr Christoph von Einem

Corporate finance, venture capital, private equity
Dr Christoph von Einem,
Dr Simon Preisenberger

Labour law
Thomas Krempl, Friederike Göbbels

International tax law
Prof Dr Alexander Hemmelrath,
Prof Dr Claus Schild

National tax law and compliance
Doris Pflieger-Steininger,
Stefan Heinrichshofen

HEUSSEN
RECHTSANWALTSGESELLSCHAFT MBH

BRIENNER STRASSE 9
AMIRAPLATZ
80333 MUNICH

Telephone: +49 89 29097 0
Fax: +49 89 29097 200
E-mail: info@landwell.de
Website: www.landwell.de

Languages:
Arabic, Dutch, English, French, Greek, Italian, Russian, Spanish, Swedish

Other offices
Berlin, Cologne, Düsseldorf, Frankfurt, Hamburg, Stuttgart

Number of lawyers 100
at this office 30

Contact
Dr Gunther Braun

International groupings
Landwell, correspondent law firms of PricewaterhouseCoopers

CATEGORIES OF WORK

Commercial and competition
Dr Gunther Braun

Corporate structuring
Robert Dorr

Dispute resolution
Dr Reiner Ponschab

Technology, media and communications
Dr Axel Czarnetzki, Rafaela Wilde

Employment and human resources
Hans Stefan Korsch

Financial services
Dr Gunther Braun

Intellectual property
Dr Axel Czarnetzki

Mergers and acquisitions
Dr Karl Maria Walter, Michael Ketterl

Public law
Dr Michael W Mütze

Real estate
Dr Michael W Mütze

HEUKING KÜHN LÜER WOJTEK

PRINZREGENTENSTRASSE 48
80538 MUNICH

Telephone: +49 89 540 31 0
Fax: +49 89 540 31 54 0
E-mail: muenchen@heuking.de
Website: www.heuking.de

Languages
German, English, French

Other offices
Berlin, Brussels, Chemnitz, Cologne, Düsseldorf, Frankfurt, Hamburg

Number of lawyers 11

Contact
Dr Ulrike Helkenberg

CATEGORIES OF WORK	
Corporate law	**Construction**
Mergers and acquisitions	**Real estate**
Commercial law	**Labour law**
Litigation	**Information technology**
Restructuring	**Intellectual property rights**

THE FIRM

Heuking Kühn Lüer Wojtek was founded in Düsseldorf, Germany, in 1971. Since then, the firm has spread geographically, and Heuking Kühn now has seven significant offices in Germany, as well as an office in Brussels.

The firm has an extensive international network of law firms, enabling it to provide its clients with seamless 'one-stop shopping', on international transactions and regulatory matters. Since its formation, Heuking Kühn Lüer Wojtek has specifically chosen to remain an independent law firm. It is Heuking Kühn Lüer Wojtek's philosophy that, to provide the best possible service to its clients, the firm must be able to co-operate with various other law firms which are at the top of the profession in their respective countries. This gives the firm the ability to make alternative counsel suggestions to its clients, giving the clients a choice of the best suitable law firm or lawyer in each country and for each matter. Over the last 30+ years, Heuking Kühn Lüer Wojtek has developed excellent relationships with the key firms in all of the major jurisdictions worldwide.

Heuking Kühn Lüer Wojtek is a name which is synonymous with legal competence. The firm is one of the largest commercial law firms in Germany, with more than 150 specialised lawyers and tax advisers, representing the interests of national and international clients. Included in the client list are large and medium-sized German and international companies in all areas of the manufacturing industry, as well as trade and service industries, associations, governmental and public sector organisations and private clients and trusts.

The firm prides itself on substantive legal competence and on the excellent education and continuing legal education of its lawyers. Moreover, virtually all of the lawyers are German-English bilingual.

Extensive specialisation and comprehensive knowledge of specific industry sectors provide the basis of all of Heuking Kühn Lüer Wojtek's legal counselling. Experienced partners and carefully selected associate lawyers develop innovative solutions to complex legal problems. The lawyers regularly work in their specific practice area groups and also in multi-group and multi-disciplinary teams with clients and outside consultants or advisers. Entrepreneurial thinking on behalf of firm clients, as well as efficient, quality, cost-effective and timely work and the highest personal dedication are key components of Heuking Kühn Lüer Wojtek's culture.

AREAS OF PRACTICE

Heuking Kühn Lüer Wojtek is a full-service commercial law firm. Cross-border and cross-sector knowledge in combination with a deep understanding of business reasoning enables service to clients with the broadest possible support in all their negotiations and business decisions. This applies equally to M&A transactions, to legal advice on company structure, business risk management, negotiations and negotiation tactics, training, crisis and insolvency counselling, corporate financial matters, and complex litigation and arbitration. Thanks to a variety of strong business clients, the firm has built long-term relationships with its clients and can assist them, beginning with the establishment of a business, followed by implementing business goals, including day-to-day legal work, reorganisations, acquisitions and divestitures.

Heuking Kühn Lüer Wojtek is actively involved with its clients in providing regulatory counselling in all areas of commercial law, as well as assisting them in organising and implementing their M&A transactions in Germany, throughout Europe, and internationally. Heuking Kühn Lüer Wojtek has particular expertise in German and EU company law; competition law, merger control and state aids; international investment, trade, and taxation matters; banking and finance; labour law; intellectual property rights; environmental, health, and safety regulation; product-specific regulation; real estate and construction law; telecoms, IT and media law; transport, postal services and shipping law; public procurement; family law; and private clients and family office matters.

HOGAN & HARTSON RAUE LLP

SCHACKSTRAßE 1
80539 MUNICH

Telephone: +49 89 2050 8880
Fax: +49 89 2050 888 10
E-mail: jhegemann@hhlaw.com
Website: www.hhlaw.com

Languages
English, French

Other offices
Baltimore, Beijing, Berlin, Boulder, Brussels, Budapest, Colorado Springs, Denver, London, Los Angeles, McLean, Miami, Moscow, New York, Paris, Prague, Tokyo, Warsaw, Washington DC

Number of lawyers 1,018
at this office 4

Contact
Jan Hegemann, Steven Ballew

CATEGORIES OF WORK

- **Entertainment**
- **Media**
- **Life science**
- **Corporate law**
- **Project finance**
- **Copyright**
- **Publishing and press law**
- **Internet and e-commerce**
- **Intellectual property**
- **Mergers and acquisitions**
- **Banking and capital markets**
- **Litigation and arbitration**
- **Public procurement law**
- **Telecommunications**
- **Private equity**
- **Venture capital**

KLAKA RECHTSANWÄLTE

DELPSTRASSE 4
81679 MÜNCHEN
(BOGENHAUSEN)

Telephone: +49 89 99 89 190
Fax: +49 89 98 00 36
E-mail: info@klaka.com
Website: www.klaka.com

Languages
English, Spanish

Number of lawyers 10

CATEGORIES OF WORK

Patent law, utility models, employee inventions
Michael Nieder, Olaf Giebe

Trade mark law, firm name
Andreas Schulz, Ralf Hackbarth

Copyright law, design patents
Wolfgang Götz, Ralf-Michael Burkhardt

Unfair competition law
Wolfgang Straub, Wolfgang Götz

Anti-trust law, public procurement
Wolfgang Straub, Michael Nieder

Food and drug law
Andreas Schulz, Michael Nieder

IT and Internet law
Ralf Hackbarth, Olaf Giebe

Press and media law
Ralf-Michael Burkhardt, Andreas Schulz

General commercial, banking law
Wolfgang Straub, Ralf-Michael Burkhardt

LOVELLS

KARL-SCHARNAGL-RING 5
80539 MÜNCHEN

Telephone: +49 89 290 12 0
Fax: +49 89 290 12 222
E-mail: reception.munich@lovells.com
Website: www.lovells.de

Languages
English, French, Italian, Polish, Russian

Other offices
Alicante, Amsterdam, Beijing, Berlin, Brussels, Budapest*, Chicago, Düsseldorf, Frankfurt, Hamburg, Ho Chi Minh City, Hong Kong, London, Milan, Moscow, New York, Paris, Prague, Rome, Shanghai, Singapore, Tokyo, Vienna*, Warsaw, Zagreb*

Number of lawyers 1,600
at this office 69

Contact
Christoph Hiltl

CATEGORIES OF WORK

Corporate/M&A, private equity

Restructuring and insolvency

Banking

Antitrust and unfair competition

Capital markets

Project finance, public private partnerships

Tax

Employment

Intellectual property

Property

Projects

Technology, media, telecommunications

Litigation, product liability

International arbitration

Food and drug regulations

Law of Eastern Europe

MAIWALD PATENTANWALTS GMBH

ELISENHOF
ELISENSTRASSE 3
80335 MÜNCHEN

Telephone: +49 89 74 72 66 0
Fax: +49 89 77 64 24
E-mail: info@maiwald.de
Website: www.maiwald.de

Languages
English, French, German, Spanish

Other offices
Hamburg, Düsseldorf

Number of lawyers 14
at this office 10

Contacts
Dr Walter Maiwald, Dr Regina Neuefeind, Udo Preuss, Stephan Schneller, Korbinian Kopf, Matthias Gottschalk

CATEGORIES OF WORK

Patents	**Competition and software law**
Trade marks	**Internet law**
Intellectual property – related copyrights	**Business and commercial law**
Unfair competition	**Licensing and litigation**

THE FIRM

Maiwald Patentanwalts GmbH was founded in 1995 on the basis of a predecessor firm in a different legal format, which had ben founded in 1991 by Dr Walter Maiwald. The firm has approximately 70 staff members presently, comprising 14 attorneys and about as many junior associates and trainees. The firm has offices in Munich, Hamburg, Düsseldorf and New York, and continues to establish further offices in major German cities. Maiwald Patentanwalts GmbH offers full legal services to its clients by closely co-operating with selected general law firms.

Maiwald Patentanwalts GmbH is a professional association of intellectual property attorneys with extensive experience in securing and defending the intellectual property of its clients. It is the oldest patent attorney GmbH in Germany.

AREAS OF PRACTICE

Maiwald Patentanwalts GmbH practises in patents, trade marks, intellectual property-related copyright, media, unfair competition, computer and software law, Internet law, business and commercial law, as well as licensing and litigation.

The firm advises and represents major domestic and international clients, covering all technical fields and all aspects of national and international law in the field of intellectual property.

McDERMOTT, WILL & EMERY

NYMPHENBURGER STRASSE 3
80355 MUNICH

Telephone: +49 89 12 71 20
Fax: +49 89 12 71 111
Website: www.mwe.com

Languages
All main business languages

Other offices
Boston, Brussels, Chicago, Düsseldorf, London, Los Angeles, Miami, Milan, New York, Orange County, Rome, San Diego, Silicon Valley, Washington DC

Number of lawyers 1,000
at this office 17

CATEGORIES OF WORK

Antitrust and regulatory
Dr Oliver Steffens

Capital markets
Christian von Sydow

Corporate
Dr Martin Kock, Dr Jörg Kretschmer

Intellectual property
Boris Uphoff

Labour and employment
Kristina Schweier

Mergers and acquisitions
Dr Ralf Eckert, Christian von Sydow

Private equity, venture capital
Dr Martin Kock,
Hans-Joachim Schreiber

Taxation
Dr Ralf Eckert

Telecoms, information technology and media
Dr Ralf Weisser,
Dr Wolfgang von Frentz

THE FIRM

McDermott, Will & Emery is a premier international law firm with a diversified business practice. Numbering more than 1,000 lawyers, nearly 70 years of serving the broad scope of clients' interests has positioned its lawyers to handle the gamut of legal challenges. The firm understands the issues faced by corporate decision-makers and how the interplay of economic, social and political issues can affect the decision-making process.

The firm's presence in Germany is part of a robust international practice and delivery of high-end legal services to its clients in Germany, Europe and beyond. The German practice group, which includes lawyers primarily in its Düsseldorf, Munich and New York offices, concentrates on all aspects of cross-border transactions from corporate counselling to labour agreements. This cross-office, cross-cultural practice group is familiar with many different legal and cultural approaches in the global markket place. The German practice group is fully integrated with the international practice. Connected by cutting-edge technology, German lawyers collaborate with the firm's lawyers in its other offices worldwide.

AREAS OF PRACTICE

The German practice provides legal counsel to multinational enterprises and foreign clients with German and European interests, as well as to Germany's enterprises, including its 'Mittelstand'. The group handles various corporate and commercial matters, including cross-border mergers and acquisitions, joint ventures, cross-border financings and securities matters. In addition, the German practice group has substantial experience in the areas of antitrust and competition, capital markets, corporate, intellectual property, labour and employment, mergers and acquisitions, private equity/venture capital, taxation, and telecommunications, media and information technology.

NÖRR STIEFENHOFER LUTZ

BRIENNER STRASSE 28
80333 MÜNCHEN

Telephone: +49 89 28 62 80
Fax: +49 89 28 01 10
E-mail: nslmuc@noerr.de
Website: www.noerr.de

Languages
Afrikaans, Czech, Dutch, English, French, Hungarian, Italian, Persian, Portuguese, Russian, Spanish, Swedish

Other offices
Berlin, Bucharest, Budapest, Dresden, Düsseldorf, Frankfurt, Moscow, Prague, Warsaw

Number of lawyers 237
(+ 53 tax advisers, public accountants and tax assistants)
at this office 84
(+21 tax advisers, public accountants and tax assistants)

Contact
Dr Dieter Schenk

CATEGORIES OF WORK

Corporate law (including corporate finance, venture capital, IPO)

Mergers and acquisitions, antitrust law

Banking, capital investment, project financing

Media law, computer law and new media

Industrial property and copyright law

Distribution law (including franchising, leasing, agency)

Reorganisation and insolvency

Privatisation

Labour law

Tax law (national and international)

Environmental and product liability

Zoning, construction and real estate

Aviation law

Litigation and arbitration

Law relating to tax offences

Audit and accounting services

THE FIRM

Nörr Stiefenhofer Lutz is among the highest profile law firms on the European legal market, at the same time one of the few independent German law firms dealing with major national and international transactions and projects. With a current strength of almost 300 professionals, the firm serves a stable base of medium-sized companies, international groups and wealthy private individuals.

Nörr Stiefenhofer Lutz stands for unrestricted full service. In contrast to many other large offices which have withdrawn from areas not immediately connected with acquisitions and mergers, Nörr Stiefenhofer Lutz continues to offer its services over the entire spectrum of commercial law, specifically drawing attention to its commitment to labour law, intellectual property law, litigation and arbitration.

The firm's multi-disciplinary approach follows logically from its full service philosophy. In major transactions and reconstructions in particular, financial and tax parameters play at least as important a part as the legal details. For this reason, approximately 20% of the firm's professionals are tax advisers and auditors, many of them with long experience in leading positions in industry and business.

AREAS OF PRACTICE

Nörr Stiefenhofer Lutz is strongly present internationally as well as nationally. Its five German offices are situated in the most important commercial centres. By concentrating expertise in particular offices – media law in Munich and Berlin, corporate finance in Frankfurt, cartel law in Berlin and IT business in Munich – the firm can respond to the particular requirements of its clients.

The chosen focus of the international offices is central and eastern Europe. Nörr Stiefenhofer Lutz identified the potential of this region at an early stage, and has guided investors on the ground in this market since the end of the 1980s in the planning and implementation of their projects. In the western European and Anglo-American legal world, as well as in other parts of the world, the firm can rely on a closely connected and long-established network of 'best friends'. Furthermore, Nörr Stiefenhofer Lutz is a member of Lex Mundi, the world's leading network of independent law firms.

Offices in Germany: Berlin, Düsseldorf, Dresden, Frankfurt am Main, Munich

Offices abroad: Bucharest, Budapest, Moscow, Prague, Warsaw

P+P PÖLLATH + PARTNERS

FÜNF HÖFE
KARDINAL-FAULHABER-STRASSE 10
80333 MUNICH

Telephone: +49 89 24 24 00
Fax: +49 89 24 24 09 99
E-mail: muc@pplaw.com
Website: www.pplaw.com

Languages
English, French

Other offices
Berlin, Frankfurt

Number of lawyers 45
at this office 22

Contacts
Andrea von Drygalski, Matthias Bruse

CATEGORIES OF WORK

Private equity

M&A

Corporate finance

Tax

Real estate

Restitution

Family (high-net-worth, succession)

Trusts, foundations, charities

PETERS, SCHÖNBERGER & PARTNER

SCHACKSTRASSE 2
80539 MÜNCHEN

Telephone: +49 89 38 17 20
Fax: +49 89 38 17 22 04
E-mail: psp@pspmuc.de
Website: www.pspmuc.de

Languages
English, French, Italian, Russian, Spanish

Number of lawyers 15
(+22 tax advisers and CPAs)

Member
DFK International; Eurolegal

CATEGORIES OF WORK

Company law/capital market
Dr K Höfner, Dr C Wallner

Family office, global custody
Ch Schönberger, B Winterstetter

Film production/taxation of artists
H Dörfler, Dr C Wallner

International tax
Dr J Peters, R W Graf

Real estate and building
Ch Schönberger, S Fritsche

Mergers and acquisitions
Dr K Höfner, S Fritsche

Management buy-out
S Fritsche, S Nowack

Determination of succession
Ch Schönberger, Dr K Höfner

Foundations/public charity
J Doppstadt, Dr K Maierhofer

Reorganisation tax
Dr K Höfner, H Dörfler

Shareholder moderation/mediation
B Winterstetter, S Neuenhahn

Corporate and commercial
Dr K Höfner, S Fritsche

IT
S Fritsche, Dr C Wallner

Stock options
S Fritsche, H Dörfler

Due diligence
B Winterstetter, Dr K Höfner

IAS/IFRS introduction projects
B Winterstetter, R P Scholz

Audit of financial statements and consolidated financial statements
B Winterstetter, H Dörfler

SJ BERWIN KNOPF TULLOCH STEININGER

RECHTSANWÄLTE – STEUERBERATER – WIRTSCHAFTSPRÜFER

MARIA-THERESIA-STRASSE 5
81675 MUNICH

Telephone: +49 89 89 08 10
Fax: +49 89 89 081 100
E-mail: munich@sjberwin.com
Website: www.sjberwin.com

Languages
English, French

Other offices
Berlin, Brussels, Frankfurt, London, Madrid, Paris

Number of lawyers 411
at this office 15

Contact
Dr Uwe Steininger

CATEGORIES OF WORK

Corporate law
Thomas P Pauls, Dr Justus F Binder

Tax law
Dr Michael Kreft, Dr André Gloede

Venture capital
Dr Axel Pajunk, Dr Justus F Binder

Private equity
Dr Uwe H Steininger, Thomas P Pauls

Fund structuring
Dr Uwe H Steininger, Dr André Gloede

EU and competition
Dr Alexander Rinne

Alternative investments
Achim Puetz, Dr Uwe H Steininger

M&A, joint ventures
Thomas P Pauls, Dr Michael Kreft

Banking and financial services
Achim Puetz

SCHMITT-ROLFES FALTERMEIER STAUDACHER

ANWALTSSOZIETÄT

DESTOUCHESSTRASSE 4
80803 MUNICH

Telephone: +49 89 38 38 40 0
Fax: +49 89 38 38 40 20
E-mail: info@sfs-law.de

Languages
English

Number of lawyers 5

CATEGORIES OF WORK

Employment and labour law

Collective employment law

Restructurings

Company and commercial law

SCHWARZ KELWING WICKE WESTPFAHL

WITTELSBACHERPLATZ 1
80333 MÜNCHEN

Telephone: +49 89 28 64 00
Fax: +49 89 280 94 32
E-mail: muenchen@skwlaw.de
Website: www.skwlaw.de

Languages
Czech, English, French, Italian, Spanish

Other offices
Berlin, Cologne, Dresden, Frankfurt am Main

Number of lawyers 62
at this office 32

Contacts
Prof Dr Mathias Schwarz, Dr Walter Eberl, Dr Michael Brauch, Thomas von Petersdorff-Campen

Member
Terralex; PLG

CATEGORIES OF WORK

Corporate and commercial law
Dr Armin Schwerdtfeger

Real estate law, conveyancing, construction
Dr J Zeller, W Schaller

Media and entertainment
Dr Ch Haesner, T v Petersdorff-Campen

Internet and e-commerce
Dr Andreas Peschel-Mehner

Trade marks, intellectual property
Dr Patrick Baronikians, Dr Dorothee Altenburg,

Arbitration and litigation
Dr Walter Eberl

Mergers and acquisitions
Dr S v Wallwitz, Dr M Brauch

Banking and finance
Dr Ulrich Muth

Unfair competition
Dr Ulrich Muth, Dr A Peschel-Mehner

Labour and employment law
Dr Bernd Joch

Probate, succession law
Dr Josef Zeller, Sigrid Koppenhöfer

Copyright
Prof Dr Mathias Schwarz

Administrative law
Dr Christoph Brandenburg

TAYLOR WESSING

ISARTORPLATZ 8
80331 MUNICH

Telephone: +49 89 2 10 38-0
Fax: +49 89 2 10 38 300
E-mail: muenchen@taylorwessing.com
Website: www.taylorwessing.com

Languages
English, Dutch, French, Italian, Mandarin, Spanish

Other offices
Alicante*, Berlin, Brussels, Cambridge, Dubai*, Düsseldorf/Neuss, Frankfurt, Hamburg, London, Paris, Shanghai*

Number of lawyers 550
at this office 56

Member
World Law Group; Tech Law Group

CATEGORIES OF WORK

Banking and finance
Claus Goedecke, Peter Seemann

China desk
Florian Ranft

Commercial
Dr Christoph Hasche

Corporate/M&A
Bernhard Kloft

Employment and pensions
Axel C Filges

EU law/antitrust
Dr Marco Hartmann-Rüppel, Markus Wirtz

Intellectual property
Dr Sabine Rojahn

Life science
Dr Ulrich Steffen

Media and entertainment
Martin von Albrecht

Private client
Romana Traichel

Projects and finance
Dr Rüdiger von Hülst

Public commercial law
Dr Walter Potthast

Real estate and construction
Jan Wunschel

Regulatory affairs
Andreas Haak

Tax
Bernd Michel

Technology/IT/telecoms
Joerg Wimmers

CMS HASCHE SIGLE

SCHÖTTLESTRASSE 8
70597 STUTTGART

Telephone: +49 711 976 40
Fax: +49 711 976 49 00
E-mail: stuttgart@cmslegal.de
Website: www.cmslegal.de

Languages
Dutch, English, French, Italian, Spanish

Other offices
Berlin, Dusseldorf, Frankfurt, Hamburg, Leipzig, Munich, Chemnitz, Dresden, Brussels, Belgrade, Moscow, Prague, Shanghai

Number of lawyers 306
at this office 79

Other CMS law firms
CMS Adonnino Ascoli & Cavasola Scamoni, Italy; CMS Bureau Francis Lefebvre, France; CMS Cameron McKenna, UK; CMS Derks Star Busmann, Netherlands; CMS von Erlach Klainguti Stettler Wille, Switzerland; CMS Lexcelis, Belgium; CMS Strommer Reich-Rohrwig Karasek Hainz, Austria

CATEGORIES OF WORK

Corporate and commercial	Intellectual property, IT, media
Mergers and acquisitions	Real estate and construction
Privatisation and restructuring	Environmental and administrative
Banking, securities and finance	Distribution, franchising
Unfair competition and antitrust	Maritime law
Tax	Arbitration and litigation
Labour law and service contracts	Utilities
Bankruptcy and reorganisation	

GLEISS LUTZ
RECHTSANWÄLTE

MAYBACHSTRASSE 6
70469 STUTTGART

Telephone: +49 711 89 97 0
Fax: +49 711 85 50 96
E-mail: info@gleisslutz.com
Website: www.gleisslutz.com

Languages
Dutch, English, French, Italian, Mandarin, Cantonese, Polish, Portuguese, Spanish, Russian, Czech, Slovak

Other offices
Berlin, Frankfurt, Munich, Brussels, Prague, Warsaw

Number of lawyers 200
at this office 70

Contact
Prof Dr Gerhard Wegen LLM

Stuttgart is the head office of this firm

CATEGORIES OF WORK

German, EC and international law	Insurance
Banking, securities and finance	Litigation and arbitration
Commercial law (general)	Mergers and acquisitions
Companies, corporations	Real estate
Competition, antitrust	Tax
Electronic commerce, Internet law	Telecommunications, media and broadcasting
Employment, labour	Trade marks, intellectual property
Environment and pollution control	

HAARMANN HEMMELRATH

ROTEBÜHLPLATZ 23
70178 STUTTGART

Telephone: +49 711 28 450 0
Fax: +49 711 28 450 133
E-mail: stuttgart@haarmannhemmelrath.com
Website: www.haarmannhemmelrath.com

Languages
Bulgarian, Croatian, Czech, Dutch, English, French, Hungarian, Italian, Japanese, Mandarin, Norwegian, Polish, Portuguese, Romanian, Russian, Serbian, Slovak, Spanish, Vietnamese

Other offices
Berlin, Bielefeld, Brussels, Bucharest, Budapest, Cologne, Dusseldorf, Frankfurt, Hamburg, Leipzig, London, Milan, Moscow, Munich, Paris, Prague, Rome, Shanghai, Singapore, Tokyo, Vienna, Warsaw

Number of lawyers 281
at this office 4

CATEGORIES OF WORK

M&A, reorganisations
Dr Matthias Schüppen

Corporate finance, financial due diligence
Georg Tominski

Corporate and business law
Dr Matthias Schüppen

Real estate
Verena Gahn

Construction law
Verena Gahn

Real estate transactions
Dr Heinrich Hübner, Verena Gahn

International tax law
Dr Matthias Schüppen

Corporate and national tax law
Dr Heinrich Hübner

Compliance
Dr Heinrich Hübner

Labour law
Dr Matthias Schüppen

Audit and accounting services
Georg Tominski

Entrepreneurial succession, inheritance, inheritance tax
Dr Heinrich Hübner

HENNERKES, KIRCHDÖRFER & LORZ

JAHNSTRASSE 43
70597 STUTTGART

Telephone: +49 711 725 79 0
Fax: +49 711 725 79 20
E-mail: info@hennerkes.de
Website: www.hennerkes.de

Languages
English, French

Number of lawyers 11

CATEGORIES OF WORK

Company
Prof Dr Brun-Hagen Hennerkes, Rainer Kirchdörfer

Mergers and acquisitions
Rainer Kirchdörfer, Dr Rainer Lorz

Tax
Rainer Kirchdörfer

Estate planning
Prof Dr Hennerkes, Dr Rainer Lorz

Initial public offerings
Prof Dr Hennerkes, Rainer Kirchdörfer

Corporate finance, capital markets
Rainer Kirchdörfer, Dr Rainer Lorz

Reorganisations
Rainer Kirchdörfer

Insolvency
Dr Andreas Wiedemann

Trusts and foundations
Dr Rainer Lorz, Dr Rainer Kögel

Commercial
Dr Andreas Wiedemann, Dr Rainer Kögel

International law
Dr Rainer Lorz, Dr Katia Voegele

Competition and antitrust
Dr Rainer Kögel

Employee stock ownership plans
Dr Andreas Wiedemann

Fiscal offences
Dr Andreas Wiedemann

HEUSSEN
RECHTSANWALTSGESELLSCHAFT MBH

FRIEDRICHSTRASSE 14
70174 STUTTGART

Telephone: +49 711 228400
Fax: +49 711 2284011
E-mail: info@landwell.de
Website: www.landwell.de

Languages
Arabic, Dutch, English, French, Greek, Italian, Russian, Spanish, Swedish

Other offices
Berlin, Cologne, Düsseldorf, Frankfurt, Hamburg, Munich

Number of lawyers 100
at this office 9

Contact
Ute Bilger-Jung

International groupings
Landwell, correspondent law firms of PricewaterhouseCoopers

CATEGORIES OF WORK

Commercial and competition
Dr Gunther Braun

Corporate structuring
Robert Dorr

Dispute resolution
Dr Reiner Ponschab

Technology, media and communications
Dr Axel Czarnetzki, Rafaela Wilde

Employment and human resources
Hans Stefan Korsch

Financial services
Dr Gunther Braun

Intellectual property
Dr Axel Czarnetzki

Mergers and acquisitions
Dr Karl Maria Walter, Michael Ketterl

Public law
Dr Michael W Mütze

Real estate
Dr Michael W Mütze

GIBRALTAR

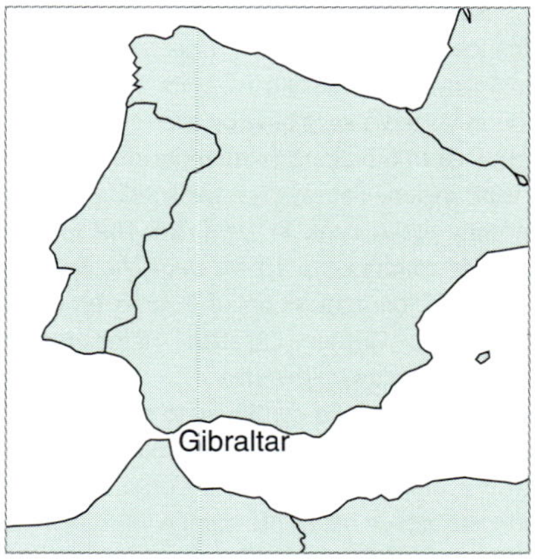

Population	28,520
Number of lawyers	131
Professional title	Solicitor; barrister
Currency	Gibraltar pound/pound sterling

Index

Gibraltar, 'the Rock', is a UK overseas territory located at the southern tip of Spain. The Strait of Gibraltar passes between the Rock and North Africa, linking the Mediterranean with the North Atlantic.

Gibraltar has been self-governing in all domestic matters since 1969, when it was granted a constitution establishing the unicameral House of Assembly. The UK, meanwhile, remains responsible for defence, foreign policy, and internal security.

Gibraltar's enviable position within the EU but outside the EU VAT area means it can offer tax-exempt company status.

BILLING

Lawyers charge almost exclusively by the hour in Gibraltar. Hourly rates range from €115 for an associate to €575 for a senior partner.

MARKETING

There are no major restrictions on solicitors and barristers promoting their practices.

IN-HOUSE LAWYERS

The employment of in-house counsel is uncommon in Gibraltar.

SOVEREIGNTY

Gibraltar's status has been a source of contention between the British and Spanish for centuries. Since the Rock was ceded to Britain by Spain in 1713, the Spanish have been unwavering in their quest to get it back. Gibraltarians regard themselves as unequivocally British and are fundamentally opposed to the idea of joint sovereignty. In two referendums, they voted overwhelmingly to remain a UK dependency. The sovereignty question continues to cause friction between the two countries, and has led to all kinds of problems such as border delays, restrictions on the use of Spanish airspace for flights to and from Gibraltar, and restrictions on telephone access between Spain and Gibraltar.

ECONOMIC CLIMATE

The local economy is driven by the financial sector, tourism, and shipping. The financial services sector is thriving, owing to Gibraltar's unique position as an offshore finance centre within the EU. The costs of establishing and operating a business through Gibraltar compare favourably with anywhere else in the world as a result of its preferential tax regulations. The financial services sector also benefits from having access to the EU's financial markets. Banks, insurance companies and investment services on the Rock can all operate in the EEA and the UK through special 'passporting rights' granted to Gibraltar.

LEGAL SYSTEM

Gibraltar's legal system is based on English common law and statutes. The 1962 English Law (Application) Ordinance outlined the extent to which English law is in force in Gibraltar, listing those English statutes which apply to the colony.

Lawyers are either solicitors or barristers, with no distinction made between the two in respect of rights of audience in court and direct contact with clients.

The profession's governing body is the General Council of the Bar, but disciplinary powers are vested in the Chief Justice.

The civil courts in Gibraltar are, in ascending order: the Court of First Instance, the Supreme Court, the Court of Appeal, and the Privy Council in London.

LEGAL MARKET

The legal market in Gibraltar is small but very active. A handful of firms dominate large-scale corporate and commercial work. The majority of firms consist of only one or two practitioners. Lateral hires are uncommon.

Hassans, established in the 1930s, is the largest firm in Gibraltar. **Isola & Isola** and **Triay and Triay** both share lengthy legal histories on the Rock, having been set up in 1892 and 1905 respectively. The most significant development in recent years was the creation of **Triay Stagnetto Neish**, following the merger of *Louis W Triay & Partners* and *Stagnetto & Co*, both of which had been present on the Rock since the 1950s. The new firm, formed in 2001, is now headed by Louis Triay QC and AV Stagnetto QC. **Denton Wilde Sapte** is the only international firm with a presence in Gibraltar. Formerly one of *Fox and Gibbons'* offices, **Denton Wilde Sapte** was set up in 2000 following the merger of *Denton Hall* and *Wilde Sapte*. **Marrache & Co** was the first law firm to open its own office in London in 1996 in addition to

The largest firms

1	Hassans	40
2	Marrache & Co	21
3	Isola & Isola	15
	Triay and Triay	15
5	Triay Stagnetto Neish	9
6	Attias & Levy	4
	Denton Wilde Sapte	4
8	Charles A Gomez, Barrister-at-Law	3
	Stephen Bullock & Company	3
10	Budhrani & Co	2
	Cruz & Co	2
	Massias & Partners	2
	Nuñez & Co	2

These figures represent the total number of lawyers in this country only, and have been supplied by the firms themselves. The figures should be accurate as at 1 January 2004.

representative offices in Lisbon and Marbella. The Gibraltar office was opened in 1984.

Most firms have in-house trust companies and company management arms.

BANKING AND FINANCE

Gibraltar is an attractive offshore finance centre. Heralded as an exemplary 'benchmark' finance centre, the Rock boasts one of the most stringent regimes for financial regulation in Europe. The independent Financial Services Commission provides investor protection to the financial services sector in general, and implements supervisory principles and standards equivalent to those in the EU and the UK.

At the same time, the Rock has succeeded in developing its profile as a home for insurance companies – the number of companies operating in Gibraltar has more than doubled in the past 18 months – and for securitisation SPVs.

With one of the leading banking and finance practices in the UK, **Denton Wilde Sapte**'s Gibraltar office benefits from a regular flow of work from London. It recently advised Morgan Stanley on the Gibraltar aspects of property securitisation work, and has been busy advising on a significant number of insurance licence applications in response to the booming insurance sector. Other work has seen the firm advising on custodian and sub-custodian duties in relation to a proposed new fund flotation on the Irish Stock Exchange.

Hassans partner Nigel Feetham has established a successful practice in repackaging and securitisation, and has acted for a host of international banks including Deutsche Bank, Goldman Sachs, and UBS Warburg. He has also been heavily involved in insurance repackaging. In the last 12 months, he acted in setting up ten insurance companies, including Advantage Insurance Company Limited and Saga Insurance Company Limited. Feetham is a recognised expert on implementing structures such as Protected Cell Companies (he advised the government on the implementation of PCC legislation), and SPVs for repackaging. Senior partner James Levy has a leading name for banking. He is currently involved in setting up a subsidiary of a major European bank, as well as the restructuring of a local bank.

Triay and Triay acts for many international banks on all aspects of banking law including compliance and other regulatory matters. Partners Javier Triay and Robert Vasquez are recognised for their expertise.

Isola & Isola advises international and local financial institutions on all aspects of Gibraltar company and banking law. Its finance arm continues to be kept busy by overseas investors attracted to Gibraltar's tax-friendly environment. Clients include Barclays, Nat West, RBS, and more recently Jyske Bank in Denmark. The finance practice continues to act for Deutsche Bank on the €2.525bn acquisition of a large group of companies. Partner Christian Hernandez is particularly active in this area.

Marrache & Co continues to advise clients including RBS, Banco Santander, Credit Suisse First Boston, and Anglo-Irish Bank Corporation. The firm also acts on behalf of a number of companies listed in London by offering tax advice to shareholders. Securitisation forms another large chunk of work. Any private investment work which cannot be dealt with in Gibraltar can be referred to the London office.

Massias & Partners is one of the leading small firms on the island, with a strong focus and recognised presence in international banking. The firm acts for a large number of international banks, including Citibank and Deutsche Bank.

Triay Stagnetto Neish acts for a wide range of international and local financial institutions.

Charles A Gomez, Barrister-at-Law advises on debt recovery matters, while **Nuñez & Co** offers advice to banks and financial institutions in Gibraltar on loan agreements in particular.

Stephen Bullock & Company handles banking and finance for various international clients.

BANKING AND FINANCE

DENTON WILDE SAPTE ✪
HASSANS ✪
TRIAY AND TRIAY ✪

Isola & Isola

Marrache & Co ✪
Massias & Partners
Triay Stagnetto Neish

Charles A Gomez, Barrister-at-Law
Nuñez & Co
Stephen Bullock & Company

Firms are listed A-Z in tiers which are ranked in order of priority
✪ Indicates firm displays contact details at the end of this chapter.

CORPORATE AND COMMERCIAL

Gibraltar's status as a major finance centre within the EU makes it a magnet for offshore corporate formations.

As the largest firm on the Rock, **Hassans** can provide specialisation on a range of practice areas that few can match. The bulk of the firm's corporate work involves major, multi-jurisdictional corporate formations. Highly recommended partner Michael Castiel is valued by clients for his ability to deal efficiently with complex transactions which can involve multiple restructurings, often at short notice. Most recently, Castiel advised French electrical company, the Wendel Consortium, in relation to all the Gibraltar aspects of the €3.63bn acquisition of the Legrand group. He also advised on the €420m leveraged management buyout of French manufacturing company the Actarius

CORPORATE AND COMMERCIAL

HASSANS ✪

ISOLA & ISOLA
TRIAY AND TRIAY ✪

Denton Wilde Sapte ✪
Marrache & Co ✪
Triay Stagnetto Neish

Attias & Levy
Charles A Gomez, Barrister-at-Law
Eric C Ellul & Co

Glaisyers
Massias & Partners
R A Triay & Co
Stephen Bullock & Company

Firms are listed A-Z in tiers which are ranked in order of priority
✪ Indicates firm displays contact details at the end of this chapter.

group. Like many firms across Europe, **Hassans** is increasingly dealing with IP matters for the bio-tech sector. The firm has M&A experience. Other clients of note include Shell Gibraltar.

Isola & Isola's successful corporate department laps up a sizeable chunk of international work. The firm has expertise in corporate and trust matters, particularly the formation of offshore companies and trusts within the jurisdiction and abroad. It works with firms such as **Clifford Chance LLP**, **Ashurst Morris Crisp** and **Allen & Overy**, mainly handling multi-jurisdictional transactions with a Gibraltar aspect. Transactions in the last six months include the multi-million pound acquisition of a group of companies by a major gaming group. Managing partner Peter A Isola is recognised as an excellent corporate practitioner. **Isola & Isola**'s affiliated company management business, Fiduciary Management Ltd, is the largest in Gibraltar.

Triay and Triay's corporate work is focused on M&A, insolvency, and company reconstructions. Partners Javier Triay and Robert Vasquez are both well regarded in Gibraltar for their work in these areas. Senior partner Joseph Emanuel Triay QC is also a leading commercial practitioner.

Denton Wilde Sapte is the only international law firm with an office in Gibraltar, and is able to call upon the resources of its international network as required. **Denton Wilde Sapte** has provided advice on all Gibraltar aspects of international corporate restructurings over the past 12 months. Clients include Morgan Stanley. Large oil companies including Gazprom and Lukoil also receive regular assistance from the firm. Insurance companies and gaming clients are part of a growing client base.

Marrache & Co has undergone some internal reorganisation in the last year. A sports management department is among others established by brothers Benjamin and Isaac Marrache. Significant corporate work of the past year has seen Isaac Marrache involved in the $300m acquisition of a mobile phone licence in Eastern Europe. The firm also acted on behalf of German clients in the purchase of three factories in Eastern Europe in a deal worth $103m. Restructuring work has kept the firm busy as well.

Joint senior partner Louis Triay QC and managing partner Louis B Triay of **Triay Stagnetto Neish** have developed a strong reputation for M&A, trusts and tax planning and are both well respected lawyers.

Private client work forms the backbone of **Attias & Levy**'s commercial services, whilst property matters, particularly in Spain, also contribute a large amount of work. Partner Levi Attias advises on offshore company formations and trusts, increasingly for businesses from the Middle East.

Charles A Gomez, Barrister-at-Law handles lower-value corporate work, whilst **Eric C Ellul & Co** has ability in offshore structuring and tax planning.

Glaisyers has experience in establishing companies and negotiating commercial contracts in Gibraltar. The firm also has offices in Birmingham and Manchester.

Massias & Partners deals in M&A, conveyancing, and securitisation work. Isaac Massias recently advised on the purchase of a large number of betting companies.

Raymond Triay of **R A Triay & Co** , formerly of **Triay and Triay**, set up his own firm in October 2001, working with two associates. The firm handled the acquisition of a Portuguese hotel by a well-known company in Gibraltar in a deal worth €7m, and was involved in the sale of a cosmetics brand to a UK plc. Mr Triay also advised a UK plc on the IP aspects of a £13m deal.

Stephen Bullock & Company provides tax advice to companies establishing a presence in Gibraltar.

CORPORATE TAX

Tax planning is the mainstay of legal practice in Gibraltar. Legislation abolishing corporate tax and the current legislation that differentiates between residents and non-residents was due to come into place in July 2003, making the Rock compliant with EU rules. This has been postponed until July 2004, when a package of measures is expected on tax reform.

The Gibraltar government instructed **Hassans** to draft legislation on the new package of measures, which are awaiting approval. Senior partner James Levy is an expert in international tax and trust law, and represents major international clients. James Levy, Javier Chincotta, Nigel Feetham and Peter Montegriffo are all recognised for their expertise in this area. The firm is very well known for its work in the management and control of assets and the development of large asset holding companies.

CORPORATE TAX

HASSANS ✪
ISOLA & ISOLA
TRIAY AND TRIAY ✪
TRIAY STAGNETTO NEISH

Denton Wilde Sapte ✪
Marrache & Co ✪

Charles A Gomez, Barrister-at-Law
Glaisyers

Firms are listed A-Z in tiers which are ranked in order of priority
✪ Indicates firm displays contact details at the end of this chapter.

At **Isola & Isola**, Peter A Isola has broad tax expertise, and is very much involved with private client work, offering tax advice and offshore trust matters.

Triay and Triay was jointly responsible for drafting the entire new system of tax legislation for the Government of Gibraltar two years ago, with Chris White of **Hassans**.

Triay Stagnetto Neish's Louis W Triay QC has specialist tax expertise. Both he and A V Stagnetto QC were instrumental in the establishment of Gibraltar as a finance centre. The firm attracts a wide client base.

The tax aspect of **Denton Wilde Sapte**'s practice has also increased with the demand from insurance and gaming clients moving to Gibraltar and requiring corporate tax and structuring advice. Peter Young, previously a corporate tax and commercial lawyer in London, has joined the Gibraltar office to support the corporate, corporate tax, commercial and banking practices.

The **Marrache & Co** brothers are both noted tax specialists, with experience in multi-jurisdictional tax planning.

Charles A Gomez, Barrister-at-Law, has a good reputation for tax litigation.

Glaisyers' practice also offers tax planning for both individuals and corporations.

DISPUTE RESOLUTION

Hassans has a dedicated and well-structured litigation department, boasting an experienced team of specialist lawyers headed by partner Lewis Baglietto. The department now has nine lawyers, two of whom have been recent lateral hires - Nicholas Howard from **Isola & Isola**, who specialises in general commercial litigation, and Gillian Guzman, who is very active in local work and heads the family, personal injury and clinical negligence section. Guzman was previously with **Attias & Levy**. David Dumas is one of Gibraltar's most experienced commercial litigators, dealing with international litigation, insolvency issues and corporate disputes. Lewis Baglietto deals mostly in civil and commercial litigation. He was part of the legal team claiming the UK government was in violation of ECHR rules regarding the Gibraltan electorate's right to vote in European elections. In recent years he has regularly

DISPUTE RESOLUTION

HASSANS ✪
ISOLA & ISOLA
TRIAY AND TRIAY ✪
TRIAY STAGNETTO NEISH

Attias & Levy
Budhrani & Co
Charles A Gomez, Barrister-at-Law
Cruz & Co
Denton Wilde Sapte ✪
Eric C Ellul & Co
Marrache & Co ✪
R A Triay & Co
Stephen Bullock & Company

Firms are listed A-Z in tiers which are ranked in order of priority
✪ Indicates firm displays contact details at the end of this chapter.

appeared in the Court of Appeal, as has Dumas. Other competent litigators are partner Gilbert Licudi, with specialist knowledge on employment law in Gibraltar, industrial tribunal, and trust litigation, and partner and accredited mediator John Restano, whose strengths are commercial litigation and shipping. Most of the litigation dealt with has a strong international element, and the firm has a very good network of contacts with law firms in the City of London.

The litigation department at **Isola & Isola** boasts the respected Peter J Isola, recognised as one of the best litigators in Gibraltar, and associate Daniel Feetham, who is highly active. Feetham recently acted for one of the largest companies in Gibraltar, Blands, in a case against the Attorney General, and the FSC in the leading case previously mentioned.

Triay and Triay senior partner Joseph E Triay, and AA Vasquez QC are the leading personalities for litigation at this firm, although all lawyers are involved in litigation work.

James Neish QC at **Triay Stagnetto Neish** is regarded as one of the jurisdiction's leading advocates, evidenced by resounding recent successes before the Court of Appeal. The firm has represented the government in various contentious matters, and most recently has been involved in a high-value trust dispute.

Attias & Levy conducts litigation in a broad range of areas, and took on three more lawyers to work in this area in 2003. The firm specialises in commercial litigation and admiralty matters.

Budhrani & Co is a two-lawyer litigation outfit led by Haresh Budhrani QC. Its main area of expertise is landlord and tenant disputes.

Charles A Gomez, Barrister-at-Law advises on a variety of contentious matters, including professional negligence and construction arbitration, while **Cruz & Co** specialises in personal injury and has been involved in employment disputes.

Denton Wilde Sapte is increasing its profile in this area. The firm currently has instructions from large oil clients and is also undertaking defence work for trusts and trustees. Lawyers are currently defending a trustee in a litigation matter in which criminal charges have been brought against one of the trust's beneficiaries. The London office is assisting.

Eric C Ellul and Mark Ellul, partners at **Eric C Ellul & Co**, are barristers with considerable litigation experience.

Litigation at **Marrache & Co** mostly centres around shipping, handled by Isaac Marrache.

Raymond Triay of **R A Triay & Co** appeared as counsel in the successful defence in the Court of Appeal of a substantial personal injuries claim against employers for an accident at work.

Trans-national litigation is a major area of work for **Stephen Bullock & Company**.

IT AND TELECOMS

Following liberalisation of the telecoms market, more firms have developed specialist expertise in the field.

Hassans is one of the leading practitioners in telecoms in Gibraltar. Managing partner Tony Provasoli, new chairman of the Bar Council, is one of the firm's specialists. He has advised the Gibraltar government extensively in relation to IT and telecoms matters, and has also advised several foreign governments on deregulation. The telecoms team also boasts knowledgeable senior partner Peter Montegriffo, the former Minister for Trade and Industry, who has been very involved in advising various online gaming operators, including Ladbrokes and the Cassava Group, which recently relocated to Gibraltar. Montegriffo has a close relationship with the regulatory, tax, employment and other authorities in Gibraltar.

Isola & Isola won a landmark case three years ago after advising the first ISP, Gibnet Ltd, to establish in Gibraltar. Associate Daniel Feetham has since successfully represented small companies struggling to apply for telecoms licences as a result of a state monopoly on communications. Feetham has also appeared in some of the leading judicial review cases in connection with the telecoms sector. More recently, he acted for the Financial Services Commission in a high-profile case on regulatory cooperation and the power of the Financial Services Commissioner in Gibraltar. This is going to the Court of Appeal. Peter A Isola is highly regarded in the online gaming sector, and acts for a number of businesses in Gibraltar.

Marrache & Co's IT and telecoms practice has been kept busy in the last year, acting for Global Switch on establishing an operation in Gibraltar, and also for a telecoms multinational looking at setting up cable operating systems in Eastern Europe. It is also acting on behalf of an international company currently in the process of purchasing a stake in the national telecoms carrier. Other work includes handling the $300m acquisition of a mobile phone licence in Eastern Europe.

Triay and Triay has acted for numerous local and international companies in relation to online securities and finance. Partner Robert Vasquez has experience in satellite work.

Attias & Levy acts for clients applying for a telecoms and gaming licences.

Denton Wilde Sapte advised Gibnynex following the break-up of the telecoms monopoly in early 2001. The firm has also been retained by a major IT company to provide advice on all aspects of Gibraltar law.

IT AND TELECOMS

HASSANS ✪
ISOLA & ISOLA
MARRACHE & CO ✪
TRIAY AND TRIAY ✪

Attias & Levy
Denton Wilde Sapte ✪

Firms are listed A-Z in tiers which are ranked in order of priority
✪ Indicates firm displays contact details at the end of this chapter.

PRIVATE CLIENT

Private client and trusts work is traditionally the mainstay of law firms in Gibraltar. It is too early to speculate on how tax reforms will affect Gibraltar's future as a tax haven.

Senior partner at **Hassans**, James Levy is involved in the establishment of trusts and personal tax planning. The firm advises on the management of assets, general wealth protection and enhancement.

Isola & Isola is home to the respected Peter A Isola who is able to provide excellent trust and tax planning advice.

Benjamin Marrache at **Marrache & Co** advises on multi-jurisdictional tax planning for a large number of high-net-worth individuals. He has extensive knowledge of trust matters.

Julian Triay and AA Vasquez QC of **Triay and Triay** cover the whole gambit of estate planning work, from relocations to conveyancing.

PRIVATE CLIENT

HASSANS ✪
ISOLA & ISOLA
MARRACHE & CO ✪
TRIAY AND TRIAY ✪

Denton Wilde Sapte ✪
Glaisyers
Triay Stagnetto Neish

Attias & Levy
Charles A Gomez, Barrister-at-Law
Massias & Partners

Firms are listed A-Z in tiers which are ranked in order of priority
✪ Indicates firm displays contact details at the end of this chapter.

Much of the private client work at **Denton Wilde Sapte** is generated through the activities of the firm's insurance and gaming clients. The firm also benefits from the office network for referral of high-net-worth-individuals.

Partner Michael Harvey heads **Glaisyers**' practice in Gibraltar. The majority of the firm's workload is private client-based, and includes the setting up of trusts and trust management.

Triay Stagnetto Neish offers a solid private client practice. Managing partner Louis B Triay has earned a considerable reputation in this area.

Lawyers at **Attias & Levy** offer advisory and managerial services to numerous private and corporate clients, with partner Levi Attias handling a lot of business with clients in the Middle East.

Name partner Charles Gomez at **Charles A Gomez, Barrister-at-Law** is recommended for trust work.

Trusts, tax planning and asset structuring for private clients is a growing area of work for partners Isaac Massias and Victoria Castiel at **Massias & Partners**.

REAL ESTATE AND CONSTRUCTION

Gibraltar is enjoying a burgeoning property market, with residential construction continuing to be the fastest growth area.

The property team at **Hassans** is headed by experienced practitioner, partner Dick Azopardi. The firm acts for many of the major local and international developers including Taylor Woodrow.

Isola & Isola boasts extensive experience in the field of property and construction in Gibraltar. Its client base includes the owner of the Rock's largest commercial development and the largest local group of residential property developers.

Marrache & Co 's property work is mainly concentrated in Spain and Portugal. A Spanish department has been established as part of the recent reorganisation of the firm. In Gibraltar, the firm is acting on behalf of joint owners Multiplex and Chelsfield of a £300m development comprising 1,600 apartments, two five-star hotels and a marina. In addition, the firm represents a number of sports personalities in the purchasing of property in Spain and Portugal. In September 2003, Benjamin Marrache represented David Beckham in relation to a property matter.

Charlie Lavarello is an established property lawyer at **Triay Stagnetto Neish**. The firm continues to act for some of Gibraltar's largest property developers, and has been involved in legal work for most of the major property developments over the last decade.

The highly recommended Abraham Saferty QC at **Triay and Triay** advises commercial and private clients on all areas of property law. This includes property financing, conveyancing, landlord and tenant matters, and the drafting of security documents. The firm is currently acting on behalf of the government in connection with a major development project on Gibraltar's East Side.

Denton Wilde Sapte is acting for the prestigious new commercial/retail property development in Gibraltar, Monaco Ocean Village, comprising a multi-million-pound complex of apartments, commercial properties and marinas, including handling all negotiations with the Government. The firm has also been retained for the first time in Gibraltar by a large UK listed bank to advise on all financing and security aspects of lending in Gibraltar. Since the passporting of financial services from Gibraltarhas been approved, **Denton Wilde Sapte** has been assisting large commercial private equity investment clients on all aspects of their property acquisitions.

Property development and conveyancing forms a large part of **Attias & Levy**'s legal services, and practitioners act for a number of estate agents, developers, landlords and individual buyers. The firm mainly deals with property matters in Spain, and offers advice and assistance to an international clientele interested in settling there. The past year has seen the expansion of the Spanish department with two qualified Spanish lawyers joining as full-time practitioners.

Eric C Ellul & Co has a close association with Spanish and Portuguese lawyers, and has advised clients at home on property transactions in the Costa del Sol and the Algarve.

Conveyancing forms the bulk of property work at **Massias & Partners**.

REAL ESTATE AND CONSTRUCTION

HASSANS ✪
ISOLA & ISOLA
MARRACHE & CO ✪
TRIAY STAGNETTO NEISH
TRIAY AND TRIAY ✪

Denton Wilde Sapte ✪

Attias & Levy
Charles A Gomez, Barrister-at-Law
Eric C Ellul & Co
Massias & Partners

Firms are listed A-Z in tiers which are ranked in order of priority
✪ Indicates firm displays contact details at the end of this chapter.

SHIPPING

Gibraltar sits on one of the world's busiest shipping lanes. As the second biggest bunkering port in Europe, it is not surprising that there are some excellent shipping practices.

Hassans has a specialist maritime department acting for a whole range of creditors. The department has particular experience in acting on behalf of mortgagee banks in relation to ship arrests, and is valued for its ability to act swiftly in turning around the arrest and sale of a vessel. It has strong links with major international shipping firms. Ship registration and ship finance are also dealt with. Partners John Restano and Lewis Baglietto, and Nicholas Howard, a recent lateral hire from Isola and Isola, are very knowledgeable on shipping law.

Triay and Triay is arguably the foremost shipping firm in Gibraltar, handling 90% of all admiralty work that arises on the Rock. J Triay Jr and James Ramagge are recognised experts.

Isola & Isola has a major shipping dispute practice, and receives instructions from major London shipping law firms including **Ince & Co**, **Clyde & Co**, and **Holman Fenwick & Willan**. The firm also acts for the union of crew members, the ITS, and major classification societies, Bureau Veritas and Detnorske Veritas.

Raymond Triay of **R A Triay & Co** was for 15 years a partner and head of the admiralty and shipping department of **Triay and Triay**, and has extensive experience as a maritime lawyer. He was involved in the Renaissance arrests acting for the concessionaires of the hotel, restaurants and bars on board the Renaissance Fleet. The firm has been involved in numerous ship finance and registration transactions, as well as several arrests and admiralty matters.

Both joint senior partnerGuy Stagnetto (Snr) QC and Guy Stagnetto at **Triay Stagnetto Neish** are recommended for their ability in both shipping and admiralty. The firm acts for international bunker suppliers and various P&I clubs.

Attias & Levy deals with ship and yacht registration, and ship arrests, as do **Charles A Gomez, Barrister-at-Law** and **Cruz & Co**.

Denton Wilde Sapte is advising clients on ship and yacht registration in Gibraltar.

Eric C Ellul & Co has acted in ship arrests involving luxury liners owned by Renaissance Cruise Lines. The firm also handles a large amount of yachting work in Gibraltar, such as charter applications, tax and insurance.

Marrache & Co advises on the registration of vehicles among other things.

SHIPPING

HASSANS ✪
TRIAY AND TRIAY ✪

ISOLA & ISOLA

R A TRIAY & CO
TRIAY STAGNETTO NEISH

Attias & Levy
Charles A Gomez, Barrister-at-Law
Cruz & Co
Denton Wilde Sapte ✪
Eric C Ellul & Co
Marrache & Co ✪

Firms are listed A-Z in tiers which are ranked in order of priority
✪ Indicates firm displays contact details at the end of this chapter.

DENTON WILDE SAPTE

REGAL HOUSE
QUEENSWAY
PO BOX 246
GIBRALTAR

Telephone: +350 77750
Fax: +350 77800
E-mail: mailgi@dentonwildesapte.com
Website: www.dentonwildesapte.com

Languages
English, Spanish

Other offices
Abu Dhabi, Almaty, Beijing, Cairo, Dubai, Hong Kong, Istanbul, London, Milton Keynes, Moscow, Muscat, Paris, Singapore, Tashkent, Tokyo

Number of lawyers 876
at this office 5

Contact
Nicholas Keeling

CATEGORIES OF WORK

Banking
Nicholas Keeling, Brendan Murphy

Commercial property
Brendan Murphy, Peter Young

Company, commercial
Nicholas Keeling, Brendan Murphy

E-commerce
Nicholas Keeling, Brendan Murphy

Financial services regulation and compliance
Nicholas Keeling, Brendan Murphy

Gaming
Brendan Murphy

Insurance
Nicholas Keeling, Brendan Murphy

Mutual funds
Brendan Murphy

Shipping
Peter Young, Nicholas Keeling

Tax
Nicholas Keeling, Peter Young

Trusts
Nicholas Keeling, Donna Del-Greco

Dispute resolution
Gabrielle O'Hagan

TRIAY AND TRIAY

PO BOX 15
28 IRISH TOWN
GIBRALTAR

Telephone: +350 72020
Fax: +350 72270
E-mail: triay@triay.com
Website: www.triay.com

Languages
English, French, Hebrew, Spanish

Number of lawyers 15

Contact
JE Triay Jnr

International groupings
Association of European Lawyers; International Lawyers Group; LEXLINK; ITPA

CATEGORIES OF WORK

Banking
FJ Triay

Company and commercial
AB Serfaty QC, FJ Triay

Employment
MW Isola, JR Triay

Family
C Simpson

Insurance
FJ Triay

Investment schemes and financial services
RM Vasquez

Litigation
AA Vasquez QC, JE Triay

Insolvency
AB Serfaty QC

Personal injuries
MW Isola, SP Triay

Property
AB Serfaty QC, JR Triay

Shipping and Admiralty
JE Triay, J Ramagge

Taxation
RM Vasquez

Telecommunications and e-commerce
RM Vasquez

Trusts
JE Triay, FJ Triay

Wills and probate
SP Triay, JR Triay

HASSANS

INTERNATIONAL LAW FIRM

57-63 LINE WALL ROAD
PO BOX 199
GIBRALTAR

Telephone: +350 79000
Fax: +350 71966
E-mail: info@hassans.gi
Website: www.gibraltarlaw.com

Languages
Chinese (Cantonese, Mandarin), English, French, Hebrew, Italian, Portuguese, Spanish

Number of lawyers 40

Contacts
James Levy (senior partner)
Michael Castiel

Member
TerraLex

CATEGORIES OF WORK

Corporate and commercial
Michael Castiel, Fabian Picardo

Banking
Tony Provasoli, Valerie Holliday

Litigation
David Dumas, Gilbert Licudi

Tax
James Levy, Michael Castiel

Private client
James Levy, Javier Chincotta

Telecommunications
Tony Provasoli

Employment
Gilbert Licudi

Pensions, trusts
Peter C Montegriffo

Company management
James Levy, Desmond Reoch

Admiralty, maritime
Lewis Baglietto, John Restano

Insurance
Nigel Feetham

Bankruptcy, insolvency
David Dumas

Property, real estate
Dick Azopardi

Corporate redomiciliation
Michael Castiel, Nigel Feetham

Securitisation
Nigel Feetham

Dispute resolution
David Dumas, Lewis Baglietto

Internet gaming
Peter C Montegriffo

THE FIRM

Hassans was founded in 1939, and is the largest law firm in Gibraltar. It was the first in Gibraltar to structure itself as a modern international law firm, with separate departments for different fields of specialisation. Its aim is to give a high-quality, personal and effective service to its clients of whatever size or nature. The firm has an international clientele, which it continues to develop. It has links with major London, continental and US law firms.

Three quarters of the firm's work is related to international clients. Many of them use Gibraltar companies and trusts to structure their fiscal, fiduciary or investment requirements and, over the years, strong links have been forged with major multinationals, financial institutions, banks, law and accountancy firms throughout the world. Gibraltar's status as part of the European Union is often a significant factor in attracting such institutions and businesses to it. The firm's international clients come above all from the US, the UK, Israel and continental Europe (in particular Luxembourg, the Netherlands, Spain and Portugal). They include major multinationals, banks and building societies.

AREAS OF PRACTICE

Corporate and commercial: The firm provides a full range of legal services for clients ranging from small businesses to major multinationals. It advises corporate clients working in or through Gibraltar on a wide variety of cross-border transactions and financing structures. Other matters handled include international corporate restructures, joint ventures, M&A, corporate franchising, tax and e-commerce.

Litigation: The department handles most aspects of litigation, with a niche focus on international commercial and trust litigation. The firm's litigators practise as both barristers and solicitors, and provide a full range of litigation services at all levels for both local and international clients.

International finance and banking: The firm has particular experience in banking and financial markets. Its lawyers also advise in banking regulation and licensing work, including the establishment of offshore operations and regulatory advice, as well as the implementation of various legal and tax structures including repackaging and securitisation. It is the only firm in Gibraltar to combine specialist expertise in derivatives regulation with a substantial banking, tax and securitisation practice.

Telecoms: The firm has advised on the privatisation of the government of Gibraltar's telephone services and advises one of the main carriers. The firm advises on all aspects of telecoms including broadcasting and wireless telegraphy, and was instructed by the International Telecommunications Union to report on the state of telecoms legislation in various territories in the Caribbean region.

Private client: The firm has specialist lawyers who regularly advise on all aspects of private client matters, including asset protection trusts, domiciliation and taxation.

Drafting: The firm advised the government on the transposition of EU Directives into Gibraltar law. Principally, this work has concerned legislation relating to financial services and telecoms. Contacts have also been established with a number of other governments requiring assistance in this area.

Trust and company administration: Through an associated company (Line Management Services Ltd) the firm provides administration services for both companies and trusts. Among the users of these services are international clients who the firm advises on the use of Gibraltar trusts and offshore companies.

Maritime: The firm has strong links with major English shipping firms and has been involved in a number of significant international admiralty cases. It also handles ship registration and finance.

Property: The firm acts for most of the major local and international developers and builders. It advises in matters concerned with secured lending, mortgages and charges for most banks and building societies in Gibraltar.

MARRACHE & CO

5 CANNON LANE
PO BOX 85
GIBRALTAR

Telephone: +350 79918
Fax: +350 73315
E-mail: mail@marrache.com
Website: www.marrache.com

Languages
English, French, Italian, Portuguese, Spanish

Other offices
Lisbon, London, Marbella, Milan

Number of lawyers 28
at this office 21

International groupings
Lex Mundi; WSG; STEP; ITPA; IBA

CATEGORIES OF WORK

Company/commercial
Isaac Marrache, Carol Haw

Property and construction
Leanne Turnbull

Private client
Benjamin Marrache, Doreen Durante

Spanish department
Gabriel Garcia Benavides

Litigation
Anthony Christodoulides

Restructurings and financial services
Jeevan Daswani

Admiralty and shipping
Penny Garcia

Sports management
D Suissi

THE FIRM

The Marrache family arrived in Gibraltar 300 years ago and, over the years, the firm of Marrache & Co has grown to its current size of over 25 lawyers and fee-earners making it one of the largest firms on the Rock of Gibraltar.

Marrache & Co has an established reputation as an international law firm in Gibraltar. With over 80% of its current workload being of an international nature this cross-border expertise is what differentiates the firm from other firms on the Rock. The fact that Marrache & Co is the only Gibraltarian law firm with offices in London, Lisbon and Marbella results in the firm being able to act as a one-stop point for clients requesting cross-border advice in the Iberian Peninsula.

The firm is divided into eight departments and the firm's corporate arm, Gibland Secretarial Services Ltd, manages over 3,500 companies.

Marrache & Co is reviser of the Martindale Hubbell directory and is the Gibraltar member of the World Service Group Association and member of the Bars of England and Wales, Portugal and Spain. The firm is also a member of the International Tax Planning Association, the International Bar Association, the American Bar Association, the Society of Trust and Estate Practitioners and the Pension Lawyers Association.

AREAS OF PRACTICE

Marrache & Co provides commercially focused legal services for a global client base comprising multinational business and private clients who are seeking advice on Gibraltar law.

The firm has always been at the forefront of innovation, and has accumulated a wealth of experience in client care due to its direct, hands-on approach. Consistently ranked in the top tier of directories in banking and finance, private client, litigation, insolvency and restructuring, the firm's in-depth knowledge of the use of offshore structures in tax planning has earned it a reputation as being consistent, professional and first class.

The firm is unique in the provision of sports management advice in Gibraltar, it has acted on behalf of many celebrities in the field of sport, including, this year, the renowned footballer David Beckham.

The Spanish department, comprising six qualified bilingual Spanish lawyers, has acted in most of the developments in the Spanish Costa del Sol and acts on behalf of The Royal Bank of Scotland (Gibraltar) Ltd in most of its lending for Spanish properties.

The private client department advises international clients on the use of Gibraltar trusts and is at the forefront of the industry in attracting high-net-worth individuals to Gibraltar to become residents within the meaning of the tax-advantageous residency programme.

The commercial and restructuring departments have been involved in several major corporate restructurings on behalf of well-renowned listed companies, including the largest commercial transaction in Gibraltar's history involving the merger of three multinational pharmaceutical companies.

The firm also advises in respect of listings in the London Stock Exchange and the Alternative Investment Market.

Finally, members of the litigation department have been involved in high-profile complex cases during the last year which have served to enhance their reputation as very effective litigators and highly regarded insolvency practitioners.

GREECE

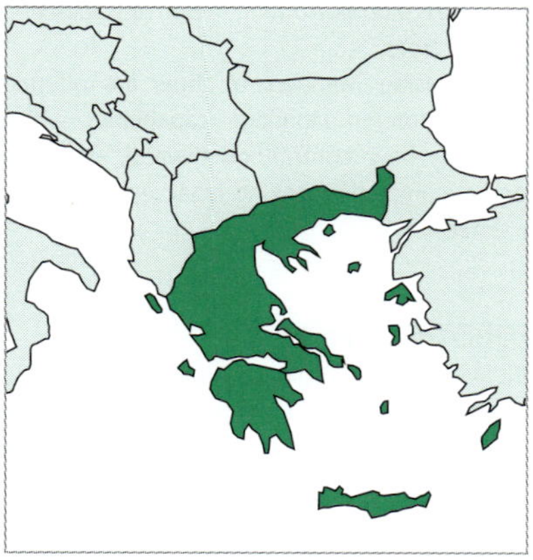

Population	**11.1 million**
Number of lawyers	**25,000**
Professional title	**Dikigoros**
Currency	**Euro (€)**

Index

Officially known as the Hellenic Republic, Greece is the southern-most country on the European mainland. In addition to the main land mass, which shares borders with Albania, the Former Yugoslav Republic of Macedonia (FYROM), Bulgaria and Turkey, the country has over 2,000 islands dotted around the eastern Mediterranean.

Greece's strategic geographical position affords it prime access to the sizeable and emerging markets of the Balkans, Black Sea, eastern European and eastern Mediterranean regions. The only EU country that is also a Balkans member, Greece is considered to be the point of political and economic stability in the region. At almost 4%, the country's GDP growth rate is far superior to the EU average, placing it among the best performing economies within the Eurozone.

The beginning of 2003 saw Greece take up its fourth presidency of the EU, and, as the EU prepares for enlargement to 25 member states on 1 May 2004, Greece has remained a vociferous advocate of an enlargement process that will ensure the integration of its more volatile neighbours and increase stability in the south-eastern Europe region as a whole.

BILLING

The vast majority of firms now charge an hourly rate, and in some cases, a percentage to cover up-front fees and disbursements. Rates vary from approximately €70 to €400 per hour, with more specialised work attracting slightly higher rates. Some firms operate a 'special rate' system whereby a set fee is agreed on a per client basis at the start of a transaction.

MARKETING

The advertising of services is not permitted, although firms run websites detailing practice sector coverage and speciality areas. Many individuals and firms actively publish material on various aspects of Greek legal practice. Referrals, via local contacts or international links, continue to play an important part in the promotion of legal services countrywide.

IN-HOUSE LAWYERS

Greek businesses tend to employ their own in-house legal staff; however, some retain the services of experienced private practitioners. As part of their day-to-day client support activities, a number of firms have reached more formal arrangements whereby their lawyers are based at clients' offices for an agreed number of hours per week.

ECONOMIC CLIMATE

Liberalisation and privatisation are, arguably, the twin drivers of Greece's economic success. The country has sought to enhance its strong economic performance by deepening structural reforms relating to products, as well as capital and labour markets in order to sharpen productivity and increase competitiveness.

The banking, telecommunications, energy and maritime sectors have all been transformed as a result of extensive market liberalisation. State privatisations continue unabated and have, to date, included: the Hellenic Telecommunications Organisation (OTE); Hellenic Industrial Development Bank (ETBA Bank); Postal Savings Bank; Football Prognostics Organisation (OPAP); Public Power Corporation; Public Gas Corporation (DEPA); Hellenic Petroleum; and Piraeus Port Authority. In 2002, proceeds from privatisation projects accounted for 2% of GDP.

In September 2003, the Hellenic state unveiled a 'Convergence Charter' – the blueprint for wealth creation in Greece. The Charter, which details steps to be taken during the period 2004-2008, proposes a reduction in higher-rate income tax from 40% to 35%, plus a gradual reduction in corporate tax by 5% down to 30% between 2005 and 2008. Special advisory and financial assistance packages will be made available to small and medium-sized business, and red-tape procedures associated with setting up, liquidating or reviving a company that has gone into liquidation will be significantly reduced. Further job creation measures designed to address the unemployment crisis were also announced.

Whether or not these plans come to fruition remains to be seen – in the run-up to the 2004 general elections and the Olympic Games, the Greek state has more pressing issues at hand including a ballooning public sector fiscal deficit that reached 5.5% of GDP during the first eight months of 2003, which is higher than the 3% of GDP limit set by the terms of the Maastricht Treaty, plus a rate of inflation which at 3.6% is, on average, 1.5% higher than the rest of the Eurozone.

Construction and infrastructure have received much attention and investment over the past

The largest firms

1	Kyriakides – Georgopoulos Law Firm	54
2	I.K. Rokas & Partners	45
3	Zepos & Yannopoulos	43
4	Kallimopoulos Loukopoulos & Chiotellis	40
	Sarantitis & Partners	40
6	Vgenopoulos & Partners	36
7	PI Partners	33
	Tsibanoulis & Partners Law Firm	33
9	M & P Bernitsas	30
10	Karatzas & Partners	25
	Norton Rose	25
12	Law Office TJ Koutalidis	24
13	Avramopoulos & Partners Law Firm	23
14	Daniolos, Issaias and Partners Law Offices	22
15	Calavros and Partners	21
16	Elias Sp. Paraskevas Attorneys at Law	20
	Nomos Thessaloniki Law Firm	20
	S. A. Felios & Associates	20
	Theo V Sioufas, Law Offices	20
	Voutyras Zannas & Associates	20
21	Bahas, Gramatidis & Partners	18
	Ziouvas & Partners	18
23	Fotis Kremmydas – Philippos Doris & Associates	17
24	Dontas Law Offices	15
	Dr Helen Papaconstantinou & Associates	15
	Dryllerakis & Associates	15
	Gr J Timagenis	15

These figures represent the total number of lawyers in this country only, and have been supplied by the firms themselves. The figures should be accurate as at 1 January 2004.

few years and the Games have provided added impetus to this process. €3.2bn has been invested in building new motorways, and three of the country's ports are being upgraded in order to enhance capacity. One of the biggest infrastructure projects to date in Greece is the state-of-the-art Athens International Airport which opened in 2001.

LEGAL MARKET

While small, family-run, traditional law firms continue to dominate the Greek legal map, there are clear signs that the picture is starting to change, albeit at a slow rate. Mid- to-large firms are ushering in an era of change, both in their method of working and in the way they structure their operations. Practice divisions based around specific business sectors and run by sector specialists are, increasingly, the norm in larger Greek firms as they continue to compete for an increasing share of international clients.

Some larger firms offer salaried positions as a means of encouraging stability and reducing staff turnover, particularly at junior level. Although external collaborations with key specialist individuals are firmly entrenched, moves are being made towards harnessing specialist skills in-house.

Exposure to risk is a concern and recruitment is down, particularly higher up the ranks. Law firms are demonstrating a preference for organic growth over lateral hires as a means of filling senior positions, with the vast majority of new hires taking place at assistant or associate level.

Cross-border network alliances continue to be a motor for international work. Potamitis Illiadou, now rebranded as **PI Partners** is aligned to **EY Law**, which in turn is associated with Ernst & Young. **Professor K. Kremalis & Partners, member of ius laboris** underlines its employment law slant through its membership of *ius laboris*, the international employment law pensions and employee benefits alliance. **Zepos & Yannopoulos** is a member of *Lex Mundi*, and **A Metaxopoulos Law Offices** belongs to the Brussels-based *TELFA*. **Moussas & Tsibris**, meanwhile, is part of London-based *Transatlantic Law International*, and **Stavropoulos, Tsiri & Papadopoulou** is a member of the *Euro-American Lawyers' Group*.

Other less formalised relationships exist, and in common with the majority of firms, **Dr Helen Papaconstantinou & Associates** calls on the services of specialist consultants for certain areas of work. The firm collaborates closely with 45 technical counsellors, the majority of whom have been involved in academic research.

Dominating the top-end of the Greek legal market across a range of practice areas is **Kyriakides - Georgopoulos Law Firm**, boasting the largest practice of 54 lawyers and dominance across corporate, banking, IT and telecoms matters. Other heavyweights are **Zepos & Yannopoulos**, with its strong tax specialisation, **Karatzas & Partners** backed by its impressive banking division, and **M & P Bernitsas**, another high performer in multiple fields of practice, plus **I.K. Rokas & Partners**, **Sarantitis & Partners** and **Vgenopoulos & Partners**.

A number of mid-sized firms are top performers in their fields. **Dr Helen Papaconstantinou & Associates** is a recognised expert in IP matters, while **Elias Sp. Paraskevas Attorneys at Law** continues to outperform in the privatisation and projects areas.

Increasing numbers of firms are offering multiple foreign language capabilities which some say have contributed towards attracting foreign companies seeking legal representation in Greece.

FOREIGN OFFICES

The wider Balkan region is providing increasing opportunities for Greek law firms.

PI Partners has set up affiliated law offices in Romania and Bulgaria which operate under the new PI trade name.

I.K. Rokas & Partners operates offices in Bulgaria, Romania and Yugoslavia with the addition of three more – in the Czech Republic, Albania and the Russian Federation – in 2003. The firm also has footholds in Australia and the US.

Ziouvas & Partners runs a small office in Germany staffed by a team of four lawyers.

FOREIGN FIRMS

Athens-based foreign firms offering cross-border capabilities through an international network include British firms **Norton Rose** and **Shadbolt & Associates**, and Italy-based **Pinci & Associates, PLLC**.

The vast majority of foreign firms are based or have an operational presence in the port city of Piraeus, home to the Greek shipping industry and an independent financial centre in its own right. Among those represented are **Clyde & Co**; **Constant & Constant**; **Hill Taylor Dickinson**; **Holman Fenwick & Willan International**; **Stephenson Harwood Consultants O.E.**; **Law Office Reece & Tomazos in association with Richards Butler**; **Watson, Farley & Williams**; and **Law Office Weiss, Elvey & Askins in association with Ince & Co**.

BANKING, FINANCE AND CAPITAL MARKETS

The banking and finance sectors have been marked by a wave of legislative changes in recent years. There is an increased emphasis on the transparency of information, and sweeping reforms have been launched in a bid to simplify transactions. In 2001, the Athens Stock Exchange (ASE) was upgraded to a mature stock market.

BANKING, FINANCE AND CAPITAL MARKETS

KARATZAS & PARTNERS
KYRIAKIDES - GEORGOPOULOS LAW FIRM ✪
M & P BERNITSAS ✪
TJ KOUTALIDIS, LAW OFFICE ✪
ZEPOS & YANNOPOULOS ✪

Calavros and Partners ✪
Dracopoulos & Vassalakis ✪
E Stratigis, Law Office
Elias Sp. Paraskevas Attorneys at Law ✪
Gr J Timagenis
I.K. Rokas & Partners
Moussas & Tsibris ✪
Norton Rose
PI Partners ✪
Sarantitis & Partners ✪
Theo V Sioufas, Law Offices
Tsibanoulis & Partners Law Firm ✪
Vgenopoulos & Partners ✪

Avramopoulos & Partners Law Firm ✪
Bahas, Gramatidis & Partners
Ballas, Pelecanos & Associates ✪
C Papacostopoulos and Associates
Chrysses Demetriades & Co Law Office
Daniolos, Issaias and Partners Law Offices
Drylerakis & Associates ✪
George Lazarimos & Sons
Markatos - Lamnides Athens Law Firm
Moratis - Passas
Roussos & Hatzidimitriou Law Offices ✪
S & A Papadimitriou & Co ✪
Stavropoulos, Tsiri & Papadopoulou ✪

Anagnostopoulos Bazinas Fifis ✪
Apostolos Georgiades & Associates ✪
Kallimopoulos Loukopoulos & Chiotellis
Reece & Tomazos in association with Richards Butler, Law Office

Firms are listed A-Z in tiers which are ranked in order of priority
✪ *Indicates firm displays contact details at the end of this chapter.*

Karatzas & Partners demonstrates extensive experience in banking transactions including financing and corporate tax law. In addition to representing its many banking institution clients, the firm advised Fourlis Holdings and its subsidiary, Housemarket, the Greek franchise of Ikea, on a bond loan valued at €95m.

Headed up by Konstantinos Vouterakos, **Kyriakides - Georgopoulos Law Firm**'s banking, finance and capital markets division delivers expertise across a raft of domestic and cross-border transactions.

Nikos Papachristopoulos and Athanassia Tsene lead a team of junior partners at **M & P Bernitsas** handling matters relating to banking, finance, bond issues and stock exchange transactions. Recent cases include advising JPMorganChase in relation to a $650m facility. Med Nautilus, Bank of Tokyo Mitsubishi and Piraeus Bank feature prominently on the firm's list of clients.

Law Office TJ Koutalidis has been involved in ongoing finance deals, handling some 14 subordinated floating rate issues – each issue ranging in value from €11.4m to €1.5bn. Alpha Bank, Deutsche Bank and UBS are among those represented.

Zepos & Yannopoulos acted for the Caisse Nationale de Crédit Agricole on the implementation of co-operation agreements with Ermis Mutual Fund Management Company and Investment Bank. The firm advised the National Bank of Greece on the update of its €1bn global term note programme. Other clients include American Express Funds, Dexia, UBS Warburg and BNP Paribas.

Calavros and Partners is known for its pharmaceutical expertise, which spans pharma product development, production and distribution, plus pricing and reimbursement by the state's national health insurance organisation.

Dracopoulos & Vassalakis advised on three issues by the Hellenic Republic of privatisation certificates that were exchangeable for shares in companies being privatised. The transactional value of each issue was €500m, €800m and €1.7bn.

A client roster of some 40 banks and financial institutions provides evidence of **Elias Sp. Paraskevas Attorneys at Law**'s continued strength in this area. The firm has acted for a prominent Greek bank on both its bancassurance and consumer credit operations, and has supported the establishment of a representative office of a German bank in Greece.

I.K. Rokas & Partners is active in banking and finance and, together with Bayerische Hypo- und Vereinsbank, recently completed a first lease finance-based windfarm project on behalf C Rokas ABEE Group, the largest windfarm construction and operation company. The firm is currently advising on four loan-based finance projects for windfarm projects and a major retailer.

Banking and finance is a particular strength of **Moussas & Tsibris**. Michael Tsibris is a securities expert and acts as legal counsel to the Bank of Greece's Hellenic Deposit Insurance Fund. Partner Nicholas Moussas has gained active experience of regulatory and banking matters. The firm advises a clutch of foreign and Greek banks and investment companies on complex financial transactions.

International banks, financial institutions and credit agencies feature strongly on **Norton Rose**'s client list. English as well as Greek law issues are handled in equal measure and the practice now offers capabilities in corporate loan handling. The firm has acted for the financial backers of the Titan Group on loan facility transactions valued at $30m to $65m each.

Under the joint expertise of Stathis Potamitis and George Bersis, **PI Partners**' finance group provides recognised expertise in capital markets issues. The team continues to advise Hellenic Petroleum on its €2bn merger with Petrola, and acted for Rosehill Investments, of the Abela Group, on the financial restructuring of the longstanding debt of its subsidiary Abela Hellas. Of the 12 public offerings which took place during 2003, the firm delivered advice in four instances.

Sarantitis & Partners is active in investment funds, having acted for a consortium of foreign and local entrepreneurs on the formation of a closed-end venture capital mutual fund valued at €24m. The firm's financial division handles all facets of two further mutual funds for the Hellenic Bank of Industrial Development and Natwest Bank.

Tsibanoulis & Partners Law Firm provides advice on a range of cross-border corporate finance transactions, and numbers BNP Paribas and Crédit Lyonnais among its clients. Mainstream retail banking and capital markets in particular have contributed to the growth of the practice. Managing Partner, Dr Dimitris Tsibanoulis, is the lead adviser to the government of Cyprus on capital markets legislation. The firm's merger with *Bailas & Partners* and the addition of respected Elena Bailas to its staff, complement the firm's international banking and finance capabilities.

Vgenopoulos & Partners regularly provides advice to international as well as local banks and represents a broad spectrum of clients, raising money in various markets. The firm is currently advising Marfin Bank on its acquisitions of other banks.

Avramopoulos & Partners Law Firm is active in banking and securities issues.

Greek and Italian banks are among those supported by **Bahas, Gramatidis & Partners**' banking and finance group. The practice has ongoing dealings with Ignatia Bank to which it provides day-to-day support. The firm handled a major due diligence exercise for Banca di Roma involving the purchase of a Fiat subsidiary.

TMT specialist **Ballas, Pelecanos & Associates** delivers a range of financial legal services.

Drylerakis & Associates continues to be active in the financial arena, servicing the needs of a predominantly ASE-listed client base. Armed with the specialist in-house skills of John Apsouris, the firm has recently been involved in new bond legislation.

Under the leadership of Ioannis Stavropoulos, **Stavropoulos, Tsiri & Papadopoulou**'s 12-strong team was granted tax consulting and representation assignments by prominent companies quoted on the Bourse de Paris.

Run by joint name partners George Bazinas and Ilias Anagnostopoulos, **Anagnostopoulos Bazinas Fifis** runs a banking and finance practice that covers capital adequacy, insolvency and bankruptcy. The firm advised Plena Group on the restructuring of its Greek subsidiary and the containment of bankruptcy-related risk. Partner George Bazinas is widely published on the Greek insolvency process and is also a member of the International Insolvency Institute.

CORPORATE AND COMMERCIAL

Cross-border M&A activities remain an area of strength for **Karatzas & Partners**. Led by Catherine Karatzas, the corporate team advised Global Finance on the acquisition of Galileo Hellas, the Greek distributor of Galileo's airline reservation system. The firm also acted as legal counsel to Aspis Bank, the country's leading retail bank, on its acquisition of Standard Chartered Grindlays Bank's network in Greece.

Heavyweight firm **Kyriakides - Georgopoulos Law Firm** boasts full-service corporate capability. The firm acted on behalf of Starbucks Coffee International on its joint venture with Marinopoulos Brothers. The deal has led to the establishment of a total of 12 Starbucks coffee shops in Greece to date. Headed up by newly promoted partner, Christos Tzavaras, the group has acted on an additional Starbucks joint venture involving the establishment of new outlets in Cyprus. The firm severed links with **Landwell** in November 2002.

M & P Bernitsas covers a range of areas with a particular emphasis on M&A. The firm's corporate practice is headed by Linda Vasaka who was also the lead partner advising Stet Hellas Telecommunications on the acquisition of 100% of the share capital of Telesoft Hellas. Other clients include Intel, Western Union and BMW.

A leading player in the corporate and commercial arena, **Sarantitis & Partners** boasts such clients as Deloitte & Touche, HSBC, Morgan Stanley, Telenor and Deutsche Telekom, and has played an active role in the establishment of offshore as well as Greek limited liability companies. The ten-strong corporate division, led by managing partner Yiannis Sarantitis, represented Gamesa in all areas of the Spanish company's business activities in Greece.

Headed up by Dr Tryfon Koutalidis, **Law Office TJ Koutalidis** boasts an extensive client roster comprising national and international clients.

The 40-strong team at **Vgenopoulos & Partners**, constitutes one of the largest law firms in the country. The firm has advised a Greek bank on its acquisition of a majority stake in a larger bank.

Building on its growing success, **Zepos & Yannopoulos** has continued to attract a solid base of international clients. The firm advised Cadbury Schweppes on the acquisition of Warner Lambert.

Bahas, Gramatidis & Partners services a healthy client list which includes a large number of banking institutions. The firm acted for armoured vehicle contractor Krauss-Maffei Wegman in a €2bn purchase by the Greek government of 172 military tanks.

I.K. Rokas & Partners provides advice to a network of international firms, both through its Greek offices and its network spread across south-eastern Europe. The firm increased its presence in early 2003 with the addition of three new operations in Albania, the Czech Republic and the Russian Federation.

Norton Rose advised ABN Amro on the sale of its minority stake in a Greek brokerage business to General Bank of Greece. Led by the skilled Elena Tsohou, the firm acted for Sofinco, a subsidiary of Crédit Agricole, on a joint venture with Emporiki Bank of Greece to form Emporiki Credicom Bank.

TMT and the automobile sectors remain areas of specialist focus for **Ballas, Pelecanos & Associates**.

Calavros and Partners runs a broad commercial practice handling M&A, joint ventures, privatisation, foreign investment and other corporate affairs. The firm is a regular adviser to Greek construction and engineering companies.

Under the skilled leadership of John Dryllerakis, **Dryllerakis & Associates** delivers a wealth of corporate legal services to a list of predominantly ongoing clients. The firm has advised on the establishment of more than 20 limited companies over the last 12-month period and acted as counsel to the Greek government on a number of M&A deals involving private entities and state corporations.

Elias Sp. Paraskevas Attorneys at Law's corporate team services a varied list of clients and covers M&A, joint ventures and company formation. The firm provides services to a global aerospace company in respect of a due diligence audit.

Law Offices Papaconstantinou acted as adviser to a large multinational in connection with the acquisition of the majority share capital of a same-sector Greek entity in a deal valued at more than €370m.

As the leading shipping firms in Greece, **Gr J Timagenis** and **Theo V Sioufas, Law Offices** provide support to clients in corporate matters relating to shipping. **Theo V Sioufas, Law Offices** continues to offer corporate and commercial capabilities as part of its Greek market offering.

Media and entertainment companies feature prominently in **A Metaxopoulos Law Offices** client list. The firm provides corporate and litigation services plus labour law expertise.

Under the leadership of name partner Vassilis Avramopoulos, **Avramopoulos & Partners Law Firm**'s corporate team undertakes a range of corporate housekeeping activities for clients. The team handles contracts for Aramark-Dasko SA, which was awarded the catering services and accommodation facilities contract for the 2004 Olympic Games.

C Papacostopoulos and Associates advises clients hailing from the banking and automotive sectors on a range of corporate activities including M&A transactions.

Dontas Law Offices delivers corporate advice to a range of clients. The 18-strong firm boasts a particularly active public procurement caseload as a result of Olympic Games contracts.

Markatos - Lamnides Athens Law Firm and **Massouridis Stavropoulos & Associates** deliver advice to a list of major companies.

CORPORATE AND COMMERCIAL

KARATZAS & PARTNERS
KYRIAKIDES - GEORGOPOULOS LAW FIRM ✪
M & P BERNITSAS ✪
SARANTITIS & PARTNERS ✪
TJ KOUTALIDIS, LAW OFFICE ✪
VGENOPOULOS & PARTNERS ✪
ZEPOS & YANNOPOULOS ✪

Bahas, Gramatidis & Partners
I.K. Rokas & Partners
Norton Rose

Ballas, Pelecanos & Associates ✪
Calavros and Partners ✪
Dryllerakis & Associates ✪
Elias Sp. Paraskevas Attorneys at Law ✪
Gr J Timagenis
Papaconstantinou, Law Offices ✪
Theo V Sioufas, Law Offices

A Metaxopoulos Law Offices ✪
Avramopoulos & Partners Law Firm ✪
Basil T Patkos, Law Offices of
C Papacostopoulos and Associates
Daniolos, Issaias and Partners Law Offices
Dontas Law Offices ✪
Kallimopoulos Loukopoulos & Chiotellis
Markatos - Lamnides Athens Law Firm
Massouridis Stavropoulos & Associates
Moratis - Passas
Moussas & Tsibris ✪
PI Partners ✪
Reece & Tomazos in association with Richards Butler, Law Office
Roussos & Hatzidimitriou Law Offices ✪
S. A. Felios & Associates ✪
Souriadakis, Frangakis & Associates
Tsibanoulis & Partners Law Firm ✪

A Voutsas Law Office
Anagnostopoulos Bazinas Fifis ✪
Chrysses Demetriades & Co Law Office
Cocalis & Psarras ✪
Dracopoulos & Vassalakis ✪
Fotis Kremmydas - Philippos Doris & Associates ✪
Nikitaides & Associates
Nomos Thessaloniki Law Firm
S & A Papadimitriou & Co ✪
Sotiropoulos Law Office, Dr P
Stavropoulos, Tsiri & Papadopoulou ✪
Thanos Masoulas & Partners, Law Firm
Theologidis Lascaratos Mitrakos Myrillos
Voutyras Zannas & Associates
Ziouvas & Partners

Firms are listed A-Z in tiers which are ranked in order of priority
✪ *Indicates firm displays contact details at the end of this chapter.*

Moratis - Passas provides corporate advice alongside its more established banking and finance expertise.

Moussas & Tsibris' team of 11 lawyers is led by partners Nicholas Moussas and Michael Tsibris. The practice advises companies quoted on the ASE, as well as handling transactions for companies based elsewhere in the Balkans.

Newly re-branded **PI Partners** (formerly *Potamitis Illiaduo*) has witnessed an expansion of its corporate and commercial activities. The practice is handling the largest merger in Greece following two years of ongoing negotiations and planning. Partner Xenophon Paparigopoulos has, since 1988, acted as legal consultant in the legislative preparation department of the Hellenic Parliament and was instrumental in the drafting of introductory notes governing renewable sources of energy.

Following the departure of Dorothea Tomazos, John Reece has taken up the reigns as branch head at **Law Office Reece & Tomazos in association with Richards Butler**. The firm has advised on the drawing up of contracts to both the private and state sectors. Calling on the skills of its UK and Greek lawyers, the firm handles a selection of commercial matters. Recent activities in the region comprise transactions in Bulgaria, Romania, FYROM and Yugoslavia.

Anagnostopoulos Bazinas Fifis acts on corporate restructuring matters related to insolvency.

Dracopoulos & Vassalakis is active in M&A and delivers advice to a mixture of national and international clients. In a landmark case, the firm acted for a Greek investment services entity on the acquisition of a UK asset management firm.

The vast majority of **Nomos Thessaloniki Law Firm**'s client work lies in the corporate and commercial area. Matters handled include M&A activities, share sale and repurchase, and debt recovery.

S & A Papadimitriou & Co is active in the corporate arena, while **Stavropoulos, Tsiri & Papadopoulou** represented a major mineral water company in a merger with a main player in the beverages market.

DISPUTE RESOLUTION

Highly regarded **A Metaxopoulos Law Offices** specialises in dispute resolution. Under the leadership of Kriton Metaxopoulos, the practice services an impressive range of multinational clients, and is particularly known for its employment expertise. Increasingly, the firm has acted as co-counsel in cross-border arbitration and foreign deals.

A leading practice in dispute resolution, **Anagnostopoulos Bazinas Fifis** acts for a varied list of high-profile clients. The firm represented Shell Hellas oil and energy group in a complex civil and criminal litigation case regarding product liability and professional negligence as a result of an incident at one of the company's facilities. A number of other prominent clients feature on its records.

Although no longer the firm's principal area of activity, **I.K. Rokas & Partners** continues to deliver advice on litigation matters and represent clients before the Greece courts.

PI Partners has represented the Sarantitis Group in disputes involving compensation claims relating to the termination of agency and distribution agreements. The firm works with a number of other clients within the banking, retail and power sectors.

Law Office TJ Koutalidis' litigation department represented Intralot in a €22m arbitration against the state-owned lottery organisation, OPAP.

Theo V Sioufas, Law Offices acts as legal counsel in international commercial arbitration on a variety of issues including sale and purchase of ships, admiralty matters and commodities trading.

Vgenopoulos & Partners delivers litigation expertise on a range of corporate and commercial matters.

Fully active in the field of dispute resolution, **Avramopoulos & Partners Law Firm**'s team is led by George MarazIones who joined the firm in 2002 with over 23 years' experience in civil, commercial and litigation activities.

Dryllerakis & Associates has enjoyed a particularly active year in litigation relating to corporate and commercial activities, with the number of cases handled in excess of 400. The firm is currently advising on a number of major arbitrations including a dispute between the shareholders of a technical company on the annulment of a dispute between the majority and local minority interests in the management of a major multinational.

Headed up by partners George Bairactaris and Nicholas Manoussakis, **G E Bairactaris & Partners**' litigation team handles commercial and maritime litigation. In 2003, the firm represented Nissho Iwai Corporation in a $36m shipbuilding contract dispute with Sasebo Heavy Industries and a Greek shipowner.

Kyriakides - Georgopoulos Law Firm remains highly active in disputes. The ten-strong team, led by Anthony Hadjioannou, successfully handled an arbitration case on behalf of Thessalian Steal Mills which was awarded €3.8m. The team is handling an arbitration for Pioneer before the International Chamber of Commerce in Paris.

M & P Bernitsas has built itself a name in commercial litigation and arbitration and numbers Siemens Medical Solutions Health Services Corporation and UPS among its clients.

Norton Rose's English and Greek dispute resolution practices have been in operation since 2001 and 1990 respectively. Under the leadership of Chris Hobbs, the eight-strong team advised clients of a Nasdaq-listed US company on claims arising following the termination of distribution agreements relating to software provision to major banks. HSBC was also represented in connection with trade name abuse by an individual Greek insurance agent.

Law Office Reece & Tomazos in association with Richards Butler's Piraeus office works closely with its other offices to deliver collision, salvage, cargo claims and marine insurance advice.

Sarantitis & Partners' eight-member litigation and arbitration team successfully represented Psichogios against Checkpoint Systems International in the first preliminary hearing of the €6m lawsuit. During the first half of 2003, the firm advised Sarmed in a lawsuit against Fiat Auto Hellas and TNT Logistics, resulting in the award of €1.2m in damages to the logistics provider.

°DISPUTE RESOLUTION

A Metaxopoulos Law Offices ✪
Anagnostopoulos Bazinas Fifis ✪
Bahas, Gramatidis & Partners
Ballas, Pelecanos & Associates ✪
Gr J Timagenis
I.K. Rokas & Partners
PI Partners ✪
TJ Koutalidis, Law Office ✪
Theo V Sioufas, Law Offices
Vgenopoulos & Partners ✪

A Voutsas Law Office
Apostolos Georgiades & Associates ✪
Avramopoulos & Partners Law Firm ✪
Calavros and Partners ✪
Chrysses Demetriades & Co Law Office
Daniolos, Issaias and Partners Law Offices
Dryllerakis & Associates ✪
Economou & Economou Law Office
Elias Sp. Paraskevas Attorneys at Law ✪
Flogaitis, Pamboukis, Siuoutis Tzavaras & Associates
G E Bairactaris & Partners ✪
Holman Fenwick & Willan International ✪
Karatzas & Partners
Kyriakides - Georgopoulos Law Firm ✪
M & P Bernitsas ✪
Moussas & Tsibris ✪
Norton Rose
Papaconstantinou, Law Offices ✪
Reece & Tomazos in association with Richards Butler, Law Office
S & A Papadimitriou & Co ✪
Sarantitis & Partners ✪
Souriadakis, Frangakis & Associates
Zepos & Yannopoulos ✪

Firms are listed A-Z in tiers which are ranked in order of priority
✪ Indicates firm displays contact details at the end of this chapter.

EU AND COMPETITION

Highly regarded in EU and competition matters, **M & P Bernitsas** boasts the skills of name partner Panayotis Bernitsas and a team of able specialists in antitrust and competition activities. A number of Greek clients are represented before the Competition Commission and Greek Courts. Other cases entail the submission of complaints to the European Commission for breaches of EU legislation.

EU AND COMPETITION

M & P BERNITSAS ✪

BALLAS, PELECANOS & ASSOCIATES ✪
CALAVROS AND PARTNERS ✪
DRYLLERAKIS & ASSOCIATES ✪
NORTON ROSE

Avramopoulos & Partners Law Firm ✪
Bahas, Gramatidis & Partners
Kyriakides - Georgopoulos Law Firm ✪
Papaconstantinou, Law Offices ✪
TJ Koutalidis, Law Office ✪
Zepos & Yannopoulos ✪

A Voutsas Law Office
Cocalis & Psarras ✪
Elias Sp. Paraskevas Attorneys at Law ✪
I.K. Rokas & Partners
PI Partners ✪
Sarantitis & Partners ✪
Scandamis C.S.
Souriadakis, Frangakis & Associates
Vgenopoulos & Partners ✪

Firms are listed A-Z in tiers which are ranked in order of priority
✪ Indicates firm displays contact details at the end of this chapter.

Demonstrably high levels of expertise, particularly with respect to the impact of EU and competition rules on the pharmaceutical sector, are the hallmarks of **Calavros and Partners**' practice.

Dryllerakis & Associates advised on a prominent antitrust case involving AEPI, the Organisation of the Collective Management of Intellectual Property Rights for composers and poets. A specialist in competition law, name partner John Dryllerakis was a member of the Competition Committee for six years and is currently a member of the Special Committee of Experts. In addition, the firm has published a vast collection of books, articles and other documents on competition law.

Bahas, Gramatidis & Partners is representing Regal Petroleum in the company's acquisition of a large oil production concern in northern Greece.

Zepos & Yannopoulos assisted Allied Domecq in the drafting of supply and distribution agreements for the Greek market in line with competition law provisions. The firm also advised an international supermarket chain on the compatibility of its parallel imports of technological equipment in relation to legal requirements.

Elias Sp. Paraskevas Attorneys at Law provides advice on EU matters, particularly regarding notifications in Greece and compliance with EU regulation and directives.

Scandamis C.S. delivers legal services to clients on a range of EU enforcement issues covering petroleum products, VAT, competition and antitrust activities. The firm provided antitrust advice to Intercar, the exclusive distributor of BMW Hellas in connection with block exemptions applicable to the automobile industry.

ENERGY

Karatzas & Partners
Kyriakides - Georgopoulos Law Firm ✪
M & P Bernitsas ✪
PI Partners ✪
Sarantitis & Partners ✪
Vgenopoulos & Partners ✪

Firms are listed alphabetically
✪ Indicates firm displays contact details at the end of this chapter.

ENERGY

In line with EU regulations, the Greek government has introduced legislation to deregulate the electricity market. A steady increase in the demand for energy is forecast for 2004 and beyond, with increased competition triggering the search for and development of new sources of energy.

Karatzas & Partners advised German energy company Eon Group on its proposed investments in the windpark energy sector and provided assistance in electricity grid tender procedures. The firm has also acted for Bayerishche Hypo-und Vereinsbank and Landesbank Schleswig-Holstein on the financing and construction activities of windparks.

Kyriakides - Georgopoulos Law Firm has advised the public and private sectors on all matters relating to the energy sector including wind and solar parks, co-generation and hybrid power plants. The practice is currently advising a German wind power company on the regulatory issues relating to wind power projects in Greece. Other clients include the Greek Ministry of Finance, Cinergy Global Trading and Trafigura, among others.

M & P Bernitsas is developing a significant presence in the energy market, while **PI Partners** has cemented its energy practice with high-profile cases in the petroleum sector. The firm currently advises on the regulatory framework and due diligence associated with the planned acquisition of a windpark. Other clients include Hellenic Petroleum, Enel Produzione and two divisions within the ENEL Group.

Sarantitis & Partners has ongoing dealings with Energy Developments, an affiliate of Australian Energy Developments Ltd regarding the Ano Liossia landfill site earmarked for the production of electric and thermal energy. The team provides advice on the general energy legislative framework governing the extraction and use of biogas in the region.

Vgenopoulos & Partners is developing its energy practice. The firm advises a private concern on its electricity provision strategies.

IT AND TELECOMS

AVRAMOPOULOS & PARTNERS LAW FIRM ✪
M & P BERNITSAS ✪
SARANTITIS & PARTNERS ✪
TJ KOUTALIDIS, LAW OFFICE ✪

Bahas, Gramatidis & Partners
I.K. Rokas & Partners
Kyriakides - Georgopoulos Law Firm ✪
Zepos & Yannopoulos ✪

Ballas, Pelecanos & Associates ✪
Calavros and Partners ✪
Chrysses Demetriades & Co Law Office
Cocalis & Psarras ✪
Dryllerakis & Associates ✪
Reece & Tomazos in association with Richards Butler, Law Office
Themistos Law Offices
Vgenopoulos & Partners ✪

Firms are listed A-Z in tiers which are ranked in order of priority
✪ Indicates firm displays contact details at the end of this chapter.

IT AND TELECOMS

Avramopoulos & Partners Law Firm advises a cluster of IT and telecoms companies on their business expansion strategies in Greece. Clients include EDS Corporation, AT Kearney and Nortel Networks for whom the firm manages GSM contracts.

A major area of **M & P Bernitsas**' practice is telecommunications regulation. The firm has advised Mediterranean Nautilus Greece on the provision of telecoms services and made the necessary submissions to the National Telecommunications and Postal Committee.

Sarantitis & Partners has advised a clutch of IT and telecoms providers, including First Business Bank, a newly-established Greek business, seeking to enter the e-banking market.

Law Office TJ Koutalidis advises Intracom, a longstanding client, on the company's national and international activities. The firm also provides ongoing support to Vodafone-Panafone

Bahas, Gramatidis & Partners is involved in an Olympic Games security project and the related tender by the Greek government for the installation of the Tetra security system, which is designed to instantly mobilise troops anywhere in the country in the event of an attack during the Games.

Both telecommunications law specialists, Alkitis Marina Christofilou and Virginia Murray at **I.K. Rokas & Partners** lead a team which advises clients on telecoms and related issues.

Zepos & Yannopoulos delivers multi-contract support to SchlumbergerSema on the provision of IT services to the telecoms industry.

Calavros and Partners is a noted specialist in telecoms regulatory issues.

Armed with the IT skills of Emmanuel Dryllerakis, **Dryllerakis & Associates** is increasingly delivering advice in this area.

Themistos Law Offices acts as legal adviser to a large printing and electronic information processing

INSURANCE

I.K. ROKAS & PARTNERS

Gr J Timagenis
Professor K. Kremalis & Partners, member of ius laboris ✪
Sarantitis & Partners ✪
Theo V Sioufas, Law Offices

Bahas, Gramatidis & Partners
C Papacostopoulos and Associates
Daniolos, Issaias and Partners Law Offices
M & P Bernitsas ✪
Souriadakis, Frangakis & Associates
Vgenopoulos & Partners ✪
Zepos & Yannopoulos ✪
Ziouvas & Partners

Firms are listed A-Z in tiers which are ranked in order of priority
✪ Indicates firm displays contact details at the end of this chapter.

INTELLECTUAL PROPERTY

A METAXOPOULOS LAW OFFICES ✪
DR HELEN PAPACONSTANTINOU & ASSOCIATES✪

A Voutsas Law Office
Ballas, Pelecanos & Associates ✪
Dontas Law Offices ✪
Kallimopoulos Loukopoulos & Chiotellis
Patrinos & Kilimiris
Sarantitis & Partners ✪

Bahas, Gramatidis & Partners
Cocalis & Psarras ✪
Daniolos, Issaias and Partners Law Offices
Drylلerakis & Associates ✪
I.K. Rokas & Partners
Kyriakides - Georgopoulos Law Firm ✪
Lambadarios Law Offices
M & P Bernitsas ✪
Souriadakis, Frangakis & Associates
Tavlaridis Tsimikalis & Kalonarou
Thanos Masoulas & Partners, Law Firm
Themistos Law Offices
Vgenopoulos & Partners ✪
Zepos & Yannopoulos ✪
Ziouvas & Partners

Firms are listed A-Z in tiers which are ranked in order of priority
✪ Indicates firm displays contact details at the end of this chapter.

PROJECTS AND PRIVATISATION

KARATZAS & PARTNERS

ELIAS SP. PARASKEVAS ATTORNEYS AT LAW ✪
KYRIAKIDES - GEORGOPOULOS LAW FIRM ✪
M & P BERNITSAS ✪
SARANTITIS & PARTNERS ✪
TJ KOUTALIDIS, LAW OFFICE ✪

Apostolos Georgiades & Associates ✪
Bahas, Gramatidis & Partners
Calavros and Partners ✪
Dracopoulos & Vassalakis ✪
Dryllerakis & Associates ✪
I.K. Rokas & Partners
Norton Rose
PI Partners ✪
S & A Papadimitriou & Co ✪
Vgenopoulos & Partners ✪
Zepos & Yannopoulos ✪

Firms are listed A-Z in tiers which are ranked in order of priority
✪ Indicates firm displays contact details at the end of this chapter.

company based in the Balkans. The firm additionally serves as adviser to Teleplan in its dealings with the Greek National Telecommunications and Post Commission regarding a nationwide management monitoring system.

Vgenopoulos & Partners continues to be active in ongoing IT cases.

INSURANCE

I.K. Rokas & Partners is active in insurance matters and regularly represents Lloyd's. The firm participated in the redrafting of insurance legislation in Bosnia-Herzegovina, and more recently, in a joint venture with PricewaterhouseCoopers, acted as legal adviser on the Moscow-based TACIS Project for the modernisation of the insurance sector in the Russian Federation. As a result, the firm has established a base in that jurisdiction.

Gr J Timagenis boasts a strong team of insurance specialists, while the four-partner practice of **Professor K. Kremalis & Partners, member of ius laboris** provides ongoing specialist advice to clients on a range of insurance issues. Areas covered include occupational pension funds, social security, compensation and employee benefits.

Daniolos, Issaias and Partners Law Offices and **Souriadakis, Frangakis & Associates** provide insurance advice to their clients.

Ziouvas & Partners delivers specialist insurance advice to companies in the shipping and insurance sectors.

INTELLECTUAL PROPERTY

A Metaxopoulos Law Offices has represented the interests of artists, particularly in the music business before the antitrust committee.

The largest and most recognised firm in its class, **Dr Helen Papaconstantinou & Associates** specialises in all aspects of intellectual property law, delivering advice on patents, trade marks, customs monitoring, industrial property and licence agreement matters to an international clientele in Greece and other Balkan jurisdictions. The firm has acted for L'Oréal and a number of other multinationals.

Best known as a full-service firm, **A Voutsas Law Office** offers good IP capabilities, while IP cases are also handled by **Ballas, Pelecanos & Associates**.

A surge in litigation means that 13 out of **Dontas Law Offices**' 18 lawyers service an IP caseload exclusively, with more staff hires in the pipeline. The team, led by senior partner Nicolas Dontas, has been particularly active in enforcement matters while running a full-service practice covering anti-piracy, counterfeit, parallel imports and trade mark misuse.

Kallimopoulos Loukopoulos & Chiotellis is recognised for its work in the IP field.

Sarantitis & Partners' full range of IP services such as copyright, patent, design, franchise and registration issues are delivered by a dedicated team of four IP specialists. The team represents Delan in its dispute with Telestet regarding the trade mark 'Be Free' in a claim valued at €7.5m.

Trade marks and computer software protection are two main areas of activity at **Cocalis & Psarras**, while **Vgenopoulos & Partners** offers general corporate IP experience.

PROJECTS AND PRIVATISATION

Privatisation has been given added impetus by the Greek government over the last few years, creating a flurry of activity for law firms throughout the country. A number of tender projects – including the Spata Airport Project, the Rio-Antirio Bridge, the Egnatia Highway and the PATHE Motorway – have been awarded, with others ongoing. Private sector involvement in large-scale projects has grown since Athens was named the venue of the 2004 Olympic games.

Karatzas & Partners' solid experience in state privatisations and banking puts it at the forefront of the field this year. The firm acted for EFG Eurobank Eragasias on the combined offering of shares on the ASE and global depository shares on the London Stock Exchange for Cosmote, the largest mobile telecoms operator in Greece. The firm also advised the Hellenic Petroleum Group on restructuring, privatisation and listing on the ASE.

Led by Dimitris E. Paraskevas, **Elias Sp. Paraskevas Attorneys at Law** demonstrates possession of an ongoing share of the privatisation market. The team acted in a national privatisation deal worth €1bn which involved the introduction of enabling legislation.

Kyriakides - Georgopoulos Law Firm is advising the state-owned gas company, DEPA on the second round of privatisations of the Greek network. The firm is also active on a number of project finance deals in the oil, transport, infrastructure and banking sectors.

M & P Bernitsas managing partners Panayotis Bernitsas and Dimitris Roussis lead the team covering all major privatisation projects in Greece. The team is acting on behalf of a consortium of foreign entities regarding the acquisition of a strategic stake in the Public Gas Corporation, and has represented international bidders in relation to motorway concession projects.

Sarantitis & Partners represented Attica, a leading Athens-based publisher in which Italian publishing group, Arnoldo Mondatori, acquired a stake; the transaction value was some €40m.

Under the direction of Nicolas Koritsas, **Law Office TJ Koutalidis**' privatisation team is working with a range of clients including Greek General Bank and Société Générale.

Bahas, Gramatidis & Partners acted for Kinross Gold Corp in a complex €300m transaction involving the sale of state-owned mines. The firm is also involved in aircraft leasing and the structuring of lease arrangements for Olympic Airways' fleet of aeroplanes.

Dryllerakis & Associates has represented clients in a spate of privatisation transactions. The firm acted as adviser to the Greek state on the privatisation of Piraeus and Thessaloniki ports prior to their listing on the ASE. Currently, the team is handling the privatisation of Hellenic General Bank and advising on the sale of the bank's shares to a strategic investor.

I.K. Rokas & Partners represents Greek interests throughout the Balkan region, and under the leadership of resident specialist Yiannis Kelemenis together with Alkistis Christofilou an external specialist, the firm acts as adviser to the government of FYROM on the regulations relating to the liberalisation of the energy sector.

Norton Rose advised a consortium bidding for the award of concessions to build, operate and finance motorways in Greece. The firm has also acted for the Hellenic Republic and Hellenic Exchanges in connection with the offering of shares in exchange for privatisation certificates.

During 2003, **PI Partners** delivered public works advice and conducted negotiations between its client, Roma Multiservi and Eretbo following the award to their joint venture of a €30m contract to develop the open spaces of the Olympic Village.

Investment advice is a strength of **S & A Papadimitriou & Co**; the firm has acted for Probank on a global management closed-end fund. The firm is active in venture capital investments.

Zepos & Yannopoulos has been active in projects relating to the Olympic Games and has gained work with clients such as Infostrada, Aggreko and Telcordia Technologies.

REAL ESTATE

Greece has undergone a surge in investments in real estate transactions and construction in recent years, and the outlook for business, tourism and related sectors remains strong.

Vgenopoulos & Partners witnessed an increase in real estate disputes handled, including some of the largest of the past year. The firm acted on a number of acquisitions, sales, re-sale and lease-back operations – including one valued at over €60m, on behalf of Carrefour Marinopoulos, the international retailer.

Zepos & Yannopoulos is particularly active in real estate transactions, and has worked on some of the largest and most complex projects to deliver tax-efficient advice in relation to real estate management. The firm is advising a major French bank regarding the acquisition of a €100m property portfolio. Further support is being provided to LaSalle concerning the acquisition of a shopping centre from Carrefour-Marinopoulos, valued at €19m.

Contracts relating to the construction of Greek hypermarkets and purchases for high-net-worth individuals are among the issues dealt with by the real estate team at **A Metaxopoulos Law Offices**.

In a joint venture transaction, **Bahas, Gramatidis & Partners** represents Chandris Group in the construction of a luxury five-star hotel complex in Thessaloniki. The firm is handling all matters relating to land purchase, negotiations, related contracts and management in the €30m deal.

Elias Sp. Paraskevas Attorneys at Law has represented a selection of private and statutory investors in property transactions.

Kyriakides - Georgopoulos Law Firm's real estate division is led by Claire Pavlou and advises on construction, development contracts and special leasehold arrangements for a prominent domestic and international clientele.

M & P Bernitsas provides support to a range of domestic and foreign investors, including Hellenic Land International, a subsidiary of SOROS Real Estate Partners.

Themistos Law Offices has worked on real estate transactions totalling some €3m, and **Ziouvas & Partners** delivers real estate advice to a sizeable corporate client roster.

REAL ESTATE

VGENOPOULOS & PARTNERS ✪
ZEPOS & YANNOPOULOS ✪

A Metaxopoulos Law Offices ✪
Apostolos Georgiades & Associates ✪
Bahas, Gramatidis & Partners
C Papacostopoulos and Associates
Daniolos, Issaias and Partners Law Offices
Elias Sp. Paraskevas Attorneys at Law ✪
Fotis Kremmydas - Philippos Doris & Associates ✪
Kyriakides - Georgopoulos Law Firm ✪
M & P Bernitsas ✪
Themistos Law Offices
Ziouvas & Partners

Firms are listed A-Z in tiers which are ranked in order of priority
✪ Indicates firm displays contact details at the end of this chapter.

SHIPPING AND MARITIME

GR J TIMAGENIS
THEO V SIOUFAS, LAW OFFICES

Sarantitis & Partners ✪
Vgenopoulos & Partners ✪

Norton Rose

Clyde & Co ✪
Constant & Constant
Daniolos, Issaias and Partners Law Offices
G E Bairactaris & Partners ✪
Hill Taylor Dickinson
Holman Fenwick & Willan International ✪
PI Partners ✪
Panos D Mavroyannis & Partners
Paul C Avrameas & Partners Law Office
Roussos & Hatzidimitriou Law Offices ✪
Scorinis Law Offices
Watson, Farley & Williams ✪
Weiss, Elvey & Askins in association with Ince & Co, Law Office ✪

Basil T Patkos, Law Offices of
Deucalion Rediadis & Sons
I.K. Rokas & Partners
Karatzas & Partners
Reece & Tomazos in association with Richards Butler, Law Office
S & A Papadimitriou & Co ✪
Stephenson Harwood Consultants O.E.
TJ Koutalidis, Law Office ✪
Theologidis Lascaratos Mitrakos Myrillos
Ziouvas & Partners

Antony Antapassis - George Albouras Law Office
Calavros and Partners ✪
Chrysses Demetriades & Co Law Office
Constantin Mattheos Law Offices
Lallis Voutsinos & Anagnostopoulos
Dr P Sotiropoulos Law Office
Savramis & Partners Law Offices
Souriadakis, Frangakis & Associates
Tsibanoulis & Partners Law Firm ✪

Firms are listed A-Z in tiers which are ranked in order of priority
✪ Indicates firm displays contact details at the end of this chapter.

SHIPPING AND MARITIME

Widely noted for its shipping expertise, **Gr J Timagenis** serves a mixed portfolio of shipowners and international clients across a broad range of shipping matters.

Another dominant player in the shipping market, **Theo V Sioufas, Law Offices** is recognised for its expertise in handling diverse admiralty and shipping matters.

Under the leadership of Despina Maroulis, **Sarantitis & Partners**' shipping practice advised Metrostar Management Group on the sale of its 21-vessel crude carrying fleet to New York-based General Maritime Corporation in a €450m transaction.

Noted for its skill in shipping matters, **Vgenopoulos & Partners**' team of shipping and transport lawyers provides advice on such areas as shipping finance, purchase and sale and the acquisition of shipping companies to clients nationally and internationally.

Increased activity has led to the expansion of **Norton Rose**'s shipping litigation and ship finance division. Under the direction of Dimitri Sofianopoulos, the practice advised on the financing of Stelmar Shipping's 2002/2003 $188m newbuild programme. Other prominent deals involving Citibank and Minoan Lines Shipping, among others, figure.

Martin Hall heads up **Clyde & Co**'s Piraeus office. The firm advises the maritime community on matters relating to salvage, general average, insurance, international trade disputes, charterparty disputes, and most other contentious and non-contentious issues. Russell Rawlings recently joined the Piraeus team from the firm's Guildford office, the aim being to develop the firm's wet practice.

Constant & Constant delivers advice on diverse shipping finance matters including lititgation.

G E Bairactaris & Partners deals with all aspects of dry and wet shipping, including ship finance. During 2003, the firm acted on behalf of Greek and foreign shipowners on the sale and purchase of 42 vessels.

Holman Fenwick & Willan International's nine-strong team of specialists covers a range of shipping-related matters including charterparty issues, claim and purchase, new building, negotiation of terms, and related commercial and financial activities. Banking institutions feature among the firm's clients.

Over the past 12 months, **PI Partners** has provided advice on ship sale, purchase and financial transactions for a growing number of shipping companies.

Panos D Mavroyannis & Partners is another player of note in the Greek shipping market.

Jointly run by partners Costas Roussos and Zafiris Hatzidimitriou, **Roussos & Hatzidimitriou Law Offices** handles admiralty and maritime matters on behalf of its diverse client base.

Led by Jeremy Watson, **Watson, Farley & Williams**' Piraeus office advises financing institutions and corporate borrowers on all aspects of shipping law.

The London-founded **Law Office Weiss, Elvey & Askins in association with Ince & Co** offers expertise predominantly in dry shipping, major marine-related casualties and disputes.

Law Office Reece & Tomazos in association with Richards Butler's Piraeus-based office has advised on a number of shipping-related matters including transhipment.

Calavros and Partners delivers arbitration expertise.

Opened during 2003, **Tsibanoulis & Partners Law Firm**'s shipping division covers contentious and non-contentious shipping matters. The group is led by Vasso Vouga.

TAX

Zepos & Yannopoulos' tax and accounting practice group provides a comprehensive service spanning national and international markets and covering the full range of tax issues including corporate income tax planning, VAT, and customs and excise duties. The firm advised Kleppiere on a complex real estate transaction and supported CDC Ixis Capital Markets in its acquisition of a €100m property portfolio.

Dryllerakis & Associates delivers advice on a raft of tax issues, particularly VAT, and has advised on two major cases – valued at €12m – in which clients' official accounts had been rejected by the authorities.

Stavropoulos, Tsiri & Papadopoulou is a recognised major player in the tax field.

Avramopoulos & Partners Law Firm delivers advice on tax issues related to corporate and commercial activities.

Following a change in legislation regarding the tax treatment of offshore real estate, **Bahas, Gramatidis & Partners** provides tax advice to a number of private corporations.

C Papacostopoulos and Associates advises banking clients on a number of tax issues.

Chrysses Demetriades & Co Law Office delivers tax expertise to a national and international client roster.

Dracopoulos & Vassalakis advises a clutch of international clients on tax planning issues. The majority of the firm's caseload in this area is derived from foreign banks seeking to finance Greek borrowers, and M&A transactions targeted at Greek companies and new business start-ups.

Under the leadership of Christos Theodorou, **I.K. Rokas & Partners** advises on tax efficiency issues relating to Greece and elsewhere in south-eastern Europe. Clients benefit from expertise in tax planning, and a range of other tax matters aligned to M&A, joint ventures, limited partnerships and project finance.

Constantine Kyriakides heads up **Kyriakides - Georgopoulos Law Firm**'s tax practice, which deals with a range of tax-related issues.

M & P Bernitsas delivers advice on tax-related issues alongside its general corporate practice to a clutch of multinational firms.

TAX

ZEPOS & YANNOPOULOS ✪

Dryllerakis & Associates ✪
Stavropoulos, Tsiri & Papadopoulou ✪

Avramopoulos & Partners Law Firm ✪
Bahas, Gramatidis & Partners
C Papacostopoulos and Associates
Chrysses Demetriades & Co Law Office
Dracopoulos & Vassalakis ✪
I.K. Rokas & Partners
Kaldis Law Offices
Karatzas & Partners
Kyriakides - Georgopoulos Law Firm ✪
M & P Bernitsas ✪
Massouridis Stavropoulos & Associates
Moratis - Passas
Norton Rose
Papaconstantinou, Law Offices ✪
Sarantitis & Partners ✪
Souriadakis, Frangakis & Associates
TJ Koutalidis, Law Office ✪
Theo V Sioufas, Law Offices
Vgenopoulos & Partners ✪

Firms are listed A-Z in tiers which are ranked in order of priority
✪ Indicates firm displays contact details at the end of this chapter.

A METAXOPOULOS
LAW OFFICES

79 VASILISSIS SOPHIAS AVENUE
115 21 ATHINAI

Telephone: +30 210 722 3862
Fax: +30 210 721 5330
E-mail:
metaxopoulos@metaxopouloslaw.gr
Website: www.metaxopouloslaw.gr

Languages
English, French, German, Italian, Spanish

Other offices
Brussels, Salonika*

Number of lawyers 12

Member
Trans-European Law Firms Association (TELFA)

CATEGORIES OF WORK

Intellectual property
K Vossos, K Metaxopoulos

Company law
A Metaxopoulos, K Metaxopoulos

Commercial law
I Daroussou, F Stathopoulou

Privatisation and projects
K Metaxopoulos, V Monso

Litigation and arbitration
K Metaxopoulos, I Zouliatis

EU and competition law
V Monso, I Daroussou

Labour law
N Kourentzi, I Zouliatis

Civil law
I Zouliatis, N Kourentzi

Industrial property
A Elianou, K Vossos

Mergers and acquisitions
A Metaxopoulos, V Monso

Real estate
R Spinassa, F Stathopoulou

Adminsitrative law
F Stathopoulou, R Spinassa

Tax, banking, finance
K Metaxopoulos, V Monso

Media, entertainment, telecoms
K Metaxopoulos, K Vossos

Stock exchange law
F Stathopoulou, E Tsakoumi

Public procurement
E Tsakoumi, V Monso

ANAGNOSTOPOULOS BAZINAS FIFIS

ODOS ALOPEKIS 11
106 75 ATHENS

Telephone: +30 210 725 4800
Fax: +30 210 725 4835
E-mail: info@abf.gr
Website: www.abf.gr

Languages
English, French, German

Number of lawyers 15

Contacts
IG Anagnostopoulos, GB Bazinas

CATEGORIES OF WORK

Litigation	Securities regulation
Corporate and commercial	Fraud and white-collar crime
Insolvency and corporate restructuring	Tax and customs offences
Banking and finance	Environment
Mergers and acquisitions	Extradition and mutual assistance
Media	Money laundering

THE FIRM

The firm was established in 1990 and assumed its present form in 1996 with the union of Anagnostopoulos & Fifis, Counsellors & Attorneys at Law with Law Offices GB Bazinas, with the aim of utilising the synergies of comprehensive representation in business matters of a contentious nature.

It pioneered the integration of top-level commercial law counsel with expert representation in relation to economic and corporate crime, and ranks among the country's premier providers of litigation and dispute management services. The firm today is recognised as a dynamic, niche legal service provider with a distinctive character and market position.

AREAS OF PRACTICE

The firm is active in a variety of work areas. Although litigation has traditionally formed the core of its work, today the firm offers a wide range of consultative services in matters of Greek, European and international law to a number of major international and domestic corporations from the energy, defence, banking and financial services, automobiles, pharmaceuticals, raw materials and media sectors, as well as domestic and foreign public and governmental organisations.

The firm ranks among the country's premier providers of dispute management services and among the clear leaders in the domain of economic and corporate crime. With one of the country's strongest litigation teams, the firm is able to offer across-the-board tactical options to a wide international and domestic corporate client base.

The firm has an extensive corporate and commercial law practice and is regularly instructed in relation to both mainstream international business transactions and highly innovative projects, such as combined IT and credit transactions, transfer of technology projects and spin-off companies. It regularly acts on such matters as corporate acquisitions, shareholder minority disputes, group structuring and implementation, EU-funded projects and directors' liability.

Noted for its experience with complex international litigation, cross-border insolvency and related proceedings, as well as voluntary and enforced corporate restructuring, the firm is regularly instructed to advise and represent creditors, debtors, turnaround professionals and foreign liquidators in matters of Greek and European insolvency law.

The firm performs a significant volume of mainstream banking and financial services law work, including secured and unsecured credit, documentary credit, revolving facilities and post-petition funding in the course of domestic or cross-border restructuring. It is regularly involved in the drafting and enforcement of security over a variety of assets, including vessels, aircraft, securities and real estate, either in conjunction with the drafting of lender or other documentation, or tracking master agreements governed by the laws of the major credit and paper markets.

After acquiring, in 2002, a specialist media law practice, the firm is now able to offer top-notch consulting and representation in all aspects of media and IT, including print media, free-to-air and subscriber television and radio, production, advertising and Internet law.

Regularly acting for several prime international and domestic financial institutions in contentious and non-contentious securities regulation matters, the firm enjoys a growing international reputation for both its consultative and its litigious work in this domain.

The firm also advises and represents some of the largest international and domestic corporations from the energy, defence, financial services, automobile and raw materials industries in relation to securities regulation, corporate criminal liability, tax and customs offences, extradition and mutual assistance, and environmental liability matters. Name partner Professor Ilias G Anagnostopoulos has served as lead counsel in many of the major economic and corporate crime cases over the past 15 years.

APOSTOLOS GEORGIADES & ASSOCIATES

35 OMIROU STREET
106 72 ATHENS

Telephone: +30 210 362 3338
Fax: +30 210 361 9130
E-mail: info@georgiades.com
Website: www.georgiades.com

Languages
English, French, German

Number of lawyers 13

Contacts
Dr Apostolos Georgiades,
Dr Stavros Georgiades

CATEGORIES OF WORK

Banking and finance
Prof A Georgiades, Dr Stavros Georgiades

Mergers and acquisitions
Dr Stavros Georgiades, A Mageirou

Securities and capital markets
Dr Stavros Georgiades, Antigoni Kourvissianou

Corporate finance
Dr Stavros Georgiades, A Kourvissianou

Commercial and company law
Dr Stavros Georgiades, G Iatrou

International arbitration
Prof A Georgiades, Angela Georgiades

Construction
A Georgiades, G Papacharalampous

Public works and procurement
Angela Georgiades, George Georgiades

Agency and distributorships
G Papacharalampous, E Labaki

Privatisations
Dr Stavros Georgiades, George Georgiades

EU and competition law
Angela Georgiades, Nikolaos Georgiades

Commercial and civil litigation
Dr Stavros Georgiades, A Mageirou

Franchising
Prof A Georgiades, A Kourvissianou

Property and real estate
Prof A Georgiades, E Labaki

Foreign investment consulting
Angela Georgiades, G Iatrou

International transactions
Dr Stavros Georgiades, G Iatrou

Industrial and intellectual property
Angela Georgiades, A Kourvissianou

Human rights
Prof A Georgiades, Angela Georgiades

THE FIRM

Apostolos Georgiades & Associates is a highly respected Greek law firm actively involved in both domestic and international transactions and disputes, with a long legal tradition and profound expertise in most areas of Greek business law.

Name partner Dr Apostolos Georgiades, professor at the University of Athens Law School and one of the most renowned Greek jurists, established the firm in 1969. In the past ten years the firm has grown and expanded steadily to become one of the leading corporate firms in the country. Currently the firm, being one of the few partnerships in Greece, consists of thirteen attorneys and advises a wide range of national and international corporate clientele on all areas of Greek business law. Furthermore, it has developed strong and long-lasting law firms in Europe and the US.

AREAS OF PRACTICE

The firm stands out for its leading expertise in banking, finance and securities law. It regularly advises underwriters, financial advisers and issuers with respect to initial share offerings, capital increase, private equity transactions and public offers for takeovers. In the past four years the firm has been involved in the listing of more than sixty companies on the ASE. Lately the firm has also been engaged in several corporate bond offerings and syndicated loans.

Furthermore, the firm is renowned for its international arbitration practice. The senior partners of the firm in particular have been serving as umpires, arbitrators, counsellors and experts for more than 30 years in some of the most important disputes in Greece and abroad. The firm has a strong reputation for international construction arbitration.

Another major area of work is public procurement, public contracts and privatisation. The firm has represented and advised domestic and foreign bidders in international tenders for infrastructure projects and for capital share in public-owned companies. It has also significant experience in contract management and administration in relation to infrastructure projects.

The firm is also active in the fields of implementation of foreign investments in Greece focusing on major real estate development projects and franchising agreements. The practice includes choice of corporate vehicle, formation of companies, joint venture agreements, conception and implementation of commercial deals, licensing, and so on.

In recent years, the team of lawyers that regularly attends to clients' corporate issues has also been engaged in a series of company acquisitions, takeovers and mergers, addressing, amongst others, issues of competition law as well as compliance with stock exchange and securities regulations.

The firm also undertakes civil and commercial litigation work. The litigation team of lawyers at the firm has discreetly handled some of the most weighty cases ever presented before the Greek and European Courts of Justice.

Other important areas of practic include intellectual property, agency and distributorships, trusts and estates, telecommunications and media law. Finally, members of the firm participate actively in the preparation of legislation and regulations, particularly in the area of financial transactions and real estate.

AVRAMOPOULOS & PARTNERS LAW FIRM

70 PANORMOU STREET
115 23 ATHENS

Telephone: +30 210 691 2200
Fax: +30 210 691 1211
E-mail: info@avralaw.gr
Website: www.avramopoulos.com

Languages
English, French, German, Greek, Italian

Other offices
Nicosia*

Number of lawyers 25

Contact
Vassilis D Avramopoulos

Member
The State Capital Law Firm Group

CATEGORIES OF WORK

Corporate, commercial and tax	Labour and social insurance
Mergers and acquisitions	Commercial property, real estate
Privatisation and investments	Media and entertainment
IT and telecommunications	Hotel and resort development
EU and competition law	Gaming and licensing
Banking, finance and securities	Aviation
Construction and public procurement	Intellectual property
Infrastructure and project finance	Government business, regulatory
Litigation and arbitration	Fraud and white-collar crime

THE FIRM
Avramopoulos & Partners provides a comprehensive business law service for its clients, both domestic and international. The key areas of its service are set out below.

AREAS OF PRACTICE
Commercial and corporate services: the commercial department acts for corporate business and banking clients, both Greek and international in a number of areas including joint ventures, mergers and acquisitions, management buy-outs, corporate reorganisations, franchising, distribution and agency agreements, asset financing and commercial lending.

The firm also regularly advises domestic and international clients regarding investments in Greece and is also active in the area of private finance initiatives both from the state and business client point of view.

IT and telecommunications: the firm is very well regarded and advises a large number of business clients in this rapidly expanding area. It advises and represents in Greece some of the world's leading companies in the area of information technology and telecommunications.

Labour and social insurance: the firm's substantial employment law department advises a large range of corporate clients in this area and has been involved in a number of significant cases.

Banking finance and securities: the firm is substantially involved in the sectors of banking, finance and capital markets, including legal services regarding the underwriting procedure for the listing of companies in the Athens stock market, consulting regarding the regulatory aspects for the listing/initial public offerings (IPO) of new stocks in the Athens stock market, agreements for the provision of investment services and especially discretionary portfolio management agreements, consulting regarding the sector of private banking, tax issues raised for the best management of clients' assets, term loan agreements, credit facilities, revolving credit facilities, loan note instruments, syndicated loans, and tax law consulting regarding the above matters.

Construction and public procurement: Avramopoulos & Partners has acted on behalf of some of the most well-known construction companies in Europe. The firm has been involved in major construction works and public procurement projects.

Detailed information is available upon request.

BALLAS, PELECANOS & ASSOCIATES

4 LYCABETTUS STREET
KOLONAKI
106 71 ATHINAI

Telephone: +30 210 362 5943
Fax: +30 210 364 7925
E-mail: balpel@otenet.gr

Languages
English, French, German, Italian

Number of lawyers 16

Contact
George A Ballas

Member
Counterforce Network; International Bar Association; European Patent Institute

Formerly Simitis Law Offices, established in 1930

CATEGORIES OF WORK

- Company and commercial
- Corporate law
- Foreign investments
- Privatisation and projects
- Mergers and acquisitions
- Corporate finance
- EU and competition (unfair and antitrust)
- Industrial and intellectual property
- Patents, trade marks, designs (including litigation)
- Copyright and allied rights (including litigation)
- Licences, franchising
- Contract
- Litigation and arbitration

CALAVROS AND PARTNERS

42 ASKLIPIOU STREET
114 71 ATHENS

Telephone: +30 210 369 8700
Fax: +30 210 369 8750
E-mail: calavros@calavros.com
Website: www.calavros.com

Languages
English, French, German

Number of lawyers 21

Member
International Association for Civil Procedure & International Arbitration; International Association for Comparative Law; International Federation for European Law; Comparitive Law Society

International groupings
In association with Habscheid–Thyssen (Dresden-Munich-Lausanne)

CATEGORIES OF WORK

- Commercial and corporate law
- EU and competition
- Mergers and acquisitions
- Spin-offs and privatisations
- Pharmaceutical law
- Telecommunications
- Intellectual property
- Contract law
- Capital markets, banking, investment
- Litigation and arbitration
- Administrative law
- Tax law
- Labour and social security law
- Private international law
- Environmental law
- Criminal law

COCALIS & PSARRAS

14 SOLONOS STREET
106 73 ATHENS

Telephone: +30 210 361 3661
Fax: +30 210 364 1258
E-mail: info@tclaw.gr
Website: www.tclaw.gr

Languages
English, French, German, Italian

Number of lawyers 11

Contact
Dimitri Cocalis

CATEGORIES OF WORK

Mergers and acquisitions
DN Cocalis, S Papadopoulou

Investment
DN Cocalis, L Ioannidou

Banking and finance
DN Cocalis, L Ioannidou

Competition
AC Psarras, DN Cocalis

Telecoms
AC Psarras, DN Cocalis

IT
AC Psarras, DN Cocalis

Intellectual property
AC Psarras, L Ioannidou

Media
AC Psarras, S Papadopoulou

Energy
DN Cocalis, AC Psarras

Aviation
AC Psarras, J Georgountzou

Selective distribution network
AC Psarras, P Gavrilis

Commercial
S Papadopoulou, L Ioannidou

Contract
DN Cocalis, AC Psarras

Corporate
N Raxi, L Ioannidou

Litigation
N Raxi, S Papadopoulou

Tax
DN Cocalis, P Gavrilis

Arbitration
DN Cocalis, AC Psarras

Advertising
AC Psarras, J Georgountzou

THE FIRM

Cocalis & Psarras (formerly Tsecouras & Cocalis) has concentrated since its early days on corporate clients and created a boutique policy, which has allowed it to offer specialised and personalised services of a high standard to Greek and foreign clients for nearly a century. Cocalis & Psarras is an incorporated partnership.

AREAS OF PRACTICE

The firm covers many areas of practice, with particular emphasis and expertise in M&A, investment, banking and finance, competition, telecommunications, IT, intellectual property, media, energy, aviation, and outsourcing and selective distribution networks. Apart from its core practice, the firm has developed significant activity in Eastern Europe, the Balkans, the Black Sea and the Mediterranean areas. Among other projects, thanks to its extensive experience in the energy sector, Cocalis & Psarras was retained for the negotiation and closing of the original contracts for the procurement of natural gas, between Greece and the then Soviet Union, and between Greece and Algeria. Due to its expertise in the banking and finance sector, the firm was involved in related projects in Bulgaria, FYROM and Albania, as well as significant telecoms projects, including turnkey construction projects in the Ukraine, Serbia, Armenia, Moldova, Lithuania and Jordan.

DONTAS LAW OFFICES

14 VOULIS STREET
ATHENS 10563

Telephone: +30 210 323 5525
Fax: +30 210 324 1761
E-mail: dontaslaw@otenet.gr

Languages
English, French, German

Number of lawyers 15

Contacts
Kyriacos Dontas, Nicholas Dontas, Sotiris Antoniou

CATEGORIES OF WORK

Anti-piracy	Litigation and arbitration
Antitrust	Media, entertainment, telecoms
Copyright	Patents and designs
Corporate	Public procurement
Information technology	Trademarks
Internet-related disputes	Unfair competition
Licensing, distribution, franchising	

DRACOPOULOS & VASSALAKIS

25A ALOPEKIS STREET
106 75 ATHENS

Telephone: + 30 210 729 9999
Fax: + 30 210 721 1560
E-mail: info@dvlaw.gr

Languages
English, French, Greek

Number of lawyers 8

CATEGORIES OF WORK

Capital markets	Project finance
M & A	Corporate taxation
Banking	Corporate finance
Energy	Privatisations

DRYLLERAKIS & ASSOCIATES

25 VOUKOURESTIOU STREET
106 71 ATHENS

Telephone: +30 210 362 8159
Fax: +30 210 364 4218
E-mail: lawoffice@dryllerakis.gr
Website: www.dryllerakis.gr

Languages
English, French, German, Italian, Russian, Spanish

Number of lawyers 15

Contact
JC Dryllerakis

Member
International Business Law Consortium (IBLC)

CATEGORIES OF WORK	
Company and commercial	**Securities and stock exchange**
Competition	**Gaming law**
Tax	**Privatisation and projects**
Mergers and acquisitions	**Finance**
Foreign investment	**Real estate**
Trade marks	**Arbitration and litigation**

THE FIRM

The formation of Dryllerakis & Associates as a firm of lawyers has been considered necessary in order to secure the best organisation and a better quality of service in the substantial and serious matters that the firm handles.

The firm has operated in Athens since 1970, and in its present form since 1978. In 1994, the firm's name changed from Theofanopoulos-Dryllerakis to its current name. The firm has five partners. It offers a full range of professional legal and administrative services. The senior partner and special adviser have experience that stems from positions as general counsel and general tax counsel in major multinationals, and also from participation in management teams and boards of directors of Greek and international companies.

AREAS OF PRACTICE

Dryllerakis & Associates is oriented towards providing consultation to international clients and businesses in general. The firm also has a long tradition in mergers and acquisitions work and has handled more than 40 cases so far, it also has special experience in tax law, environmental law and business contracts. The firm has also successfully handled important privatisation cases.

All the lawyers have extensive experience in court practice and arbitration. Senior lawyers frequently handle matters in the Supreme Courts and especially in the Conseil D'Etat and the Supreme Administrative Court.

All the lawyers are fluent in English and most of them have a working knowledge of French, while others speak a variety of languages including German, Spanish, Italian and Russian.

Allocation of cases is based on several criteria such as expertise and seniority, specialisation and availability.

The company operates from its head office (as above) as well as in a neighbouring building at 30 Voulourestiou Street. Both buildings are served by modern communication systems that allow inter-office communication, telephone conferencing, etc; as well as being fully equipped with a modern computer network system.

The senior partners participate in the board of directors and the management of several major companies including clients of the firm (such as Barilla's affiliate, Belersdorf, Hyatt, Shell, etc) and offers them significant experience in current managerial and business issues which develop the firm's legal knowledge and facilitate the provision of advice and solutions to clients' specific legal needs.

Owing to the participation of the senior partner, Mr JC Dryllerakis in the public administrative process, the firm has substantial experience in this field and concerning the way subjects are treated by the administration. Mr Dryllerakis was a regular member of the Independent Competition Committee for six years and a member of the board of directors of the Capital Markets Committee for two years, assisting in the regulation of the capital market. He has participated in the drafting committees of several pieces of legislation, the office having been assigned to the drafting of the law for liquidation of the Restructuring Organisation.

Representative clients include: Aegean Airlines, AEPI SA, Allatini SA, Barilla, Beiersdorf AG, Blue Palace Hotel, Danone Group, Delta Dairy Products SA, Grande Bretagne, IBM Hellas SA, ICC Inc, EFG Eurobank Ergasias SA, EFG Eurobank Properties, Eurocorp AEPEY, Exelixi Portfolio Investments SA, Exxon Corporation, Forthnet SA, Hyatt Regency Hotels & Tourism (Hellas) A.E., Klonatex Group, Leo Burnett, Lectra SA, LoyalWard Ltd, SCA Packaging A.E., Minoan Lines, Natalys SA, Nintendo, Paneuropean Oil & Ind. Hold.SA, Petrola Hellas AEBE, Pechiney (Aluminium de Grece), Raytheon Co, Shell SA, Sonae-Charagionis SA, Tate & Lylle/Amylum Group, Tesa SA, TVX Gold Inc.

ELIAS SP. PARASKEVAS ATTORNEYS AT LAW

7 ASKLEPIOU STREET
106 79 ATHENS

Telephone: +30 210 361 0333
Fax: +30 210 364 5329
E-mail: info@paraskevaslaw.com
Website: www.paraskevaslaw.com

Languages
English, French, German, Italian

Number of lawyers 20

Contact
Dimitris Paraskevas (managing partner)

CATEGORIES OF WORK

Mergers and acquisitions
Dimitris Paraskevas, Evangelos Spyridakis

Privatisation and projects
Dimitris Paraskevas, Evangelos Spyridakis

Banking, finance and capital markets
Dimitris Paraskevas, Spyros Valvis

Company and corporate governance
Irene Grammatopoulou

Real estate
Dr Vassilis Skouteris

EU and competition
Irene Grammatopoulou

IT and telecoms
Constantinos Ploubis

Litigation and dispute resolution
Dr Vassilis Skouteris

THE FIRM

Elias Sp. Paraskevas Attorneys at Law is one of the leading law firms in Greece. It was established in 1933 by Elias Sp. Paraskevas (1912-1991), who in the course of nearly 60 years of legal practice, came to be referred to as the 'Dean of Greek lawyers' and is cited throughout the casebooks.

The firm is a full corporate law service provider with particular expertise in the areas set out below.

AREAS OF PRACTICE

Mergers and acquisitions, privatisations and projects: The firm's clients include the Hellenic Republic, most of the leading international and domestic investment banks, overseas law firms, and local and foreign corporations. In the last three years, the firm has been involved in over 50 mergers and acquisitions projects, which have included almost all major privatisations in Greece.

Banking, finance and capital markets: Since 2000, the firm has advised more that 40 banks and financial institutions from 12 different countries, including most of the leading investment banks.

Company and corporate governance: The firm provides advice mainly to international companies carrying our business in Greece on a wide variety of matters including the participation in tenders, general corporate and commercial law, private equity and venture capital transactions. Since 2000, the firm has advised over 70 companies in this area and members of the firm have been called upon to sit on the boards of clients and companies that feel they benefit from their experience.

Real estate: In this area, the firm has represented domestic and international investors, including the USA in the acquisition of property for the US diplomatic mission in Greece.

EU and competition: The firm provides advice on EU law, particularly undertaking notifications in Greece and has advised on compliance with EU regulations and directives in the case of monopolies, anti-competitive practices, mergers and acquisitions, public procurement and state aid. Among the cases that the firm has been involved, is the strategic cooperation between Commercial Bank of Greece SA and Caisse Nationale de Credit Agricole and the sale of 100% of the share capital in Hellenic Shipyards SA to the consortium of German shipbuilding companies Howaldtswerke-Deutsche Werft AG (HDW) and Ferrostaal AG.

IT and telecoms: The firm has acted on behalf of leading international and domestic software and telecommunications companies, providers and carriers in corporate and transactional matters, intellectual property and litigation, as well as in licensing and regulatory issues.

Litigation and dispute resolution: The firm acts on behalf of Greek and overseas clients in the resolution of highly complex disputes, both through litigation and alternative dispute resolution methods, focusing on all aspects of commercial litigation and has a particular expertise in company restructuring and bankruptcy proceedings.

A brochure providing detailed information on the firm's lawyers' areas of expertise and the transactions in which the firm has been involved is available upon request. More information about the firm can be found by visiting its website: www.paraskevaslaw.com.

FOTIS KREMMYDAS-PHILIPPOS DORIS AND ASSOCIATES

37 ACADEMIAS AVE, 5TH FLOOR
ATHENS 10672

Telephone: +30 210 363 6084
Fax: +30 210 361 8841
E-mail: info@kremlaw.gr

Languages
English, French, German

Other offices
London

Number of lawyers 20
at this office 17

CATEGORIES OF WORK

Company law
Fotis Kremmydas, Efi Kyriazi

Business transactions
Fotis Kremmydas, Dimitris Boukis

Tax
Costis Mallios, Fanny Karayianni

Litigation
Roula Liossi, Fanny Karayianni

Arbitration
Fotis Kremmydas, Roula Liossi

Family and inheritance
Patricia Adamopoulou,
Fanny Karayianni

Property law
Efi Kyriazi, Froso Dimakou Kiaou

Labour law
Nicholaos Dounavis, Costis Mallios

Intellectual property
Dimitris Boukis, Patricia Adamopoulou

Banking and finance
Dimitris Boukis, Costis Mallios

GEORGE K STEFANAKIS & ASSOCIATES

18 AKADIMIAS STREET
106 71 ATHENS

Telephone: +30 210 361 8722
Fax: +30 210 363 9409
E-mail: info@stefanakislawfirm.gr

Languages
English, French, German, Italian

Number of lawyers 12

CATEGORIES OF WORK

Corporate and commercial
KP Papadiamantis, IG Stefanaki

Tax
A Chatjitjani

Labour
S Fanourgakis, IK Konstantinou

Civil law and litigation
GK Stefanakis, NG Deskas

Arbitration
GK Stefanakis, KP Papadiamantis

Insolvency
GK Stefanakis, NG Deskas

Insurance
NG Deskas

Economic criminal law
NG Deskas, IK Konstantinou

Intellectual and industrial property
GK Stefanakis, KP Papadiamantis

EU law, competition and agency
KP Papadiamantis, AA Kortesis

Foreign investments and project finance
KP Papadiamantis, IG Stefanaki

Mergers and acquisitions
KP Papadiamantis, IK Konstantinou

Real estate
NG Deskas, S Sideraki

Wills and estate planning
A Chatjitjani, S Sideraki

Administrative
GK Stefanakis, KP Papadiamantis

Public works and procurement
GK Stefanakis, KP Papadiamantis

Information technology
IG Stefanaki, AA Kortesis

DR HELEN PAPACONSTANTINOU & ASSOCIATES

LAW OFFICES

2 COUMBARI STREET
KOLONAKI
106 74 ATHENS

Telephone: +30 210 362 5757
Fax: +30 210 362 6742
E-mail: mail@hplaw.biz

Languages
Dutch, English, French, German, Italian, Spanish

Number of lawyers 14

Contact
Maria Athanassiadou

CATEGORIES OF WORK

Trade mark law
E Yazitzoglou, M Theodoridou

Patent law
Dr H Papaconstantinou, M Athanassiadou

Litigation in patents
Dr H Papaconstatinou, Th Goussios

Litigation in trade marks
E Lappa, A Chandanou

Competition law – copyright
Dr H Papaconstantinou, T Goussios

Community trade marks
K Delouka, A Roussou

International trade marks
E Yazitzoglou, M Theodoridou

Licensing
K Delouka, D Katsouli

Maintenance of trade marks
D Karatza

Searching – watching
D Karatza, I Louvis

European patents, SPCs
C Dimou, A Roussou

Customs monitoring procedures
F Kardiopoulis

Domain names
M Anestopoulou, E Lappa

Designs
M Athanassiadou

THE FIRM

The firm Dr P D Theodorides & Dr H G Papaconstantinou, which started as a solo practice, was founded by Panagiotis Theodorides in 1920 and is one of the oldest trade mark and patent firms in Greece. In order to better serve its clients and maintain a competitive practice which covers the broad spectrum of intellectual property law, the firm evolved into two distinct branches in 1996, one under the old firm name (Law Office Dr P D Theodorides – Dr H G Papaconstantinou) covering trade marks, domain names, copyright and related litigation, and the other under the name Dr Helen Papaconstantinou & Associates, covering patents, designs, utility models and related litigation. Dr Helen Papaconstantinou, who graduated from the University of Athens with a law degree and holds a Dr Juris degree from the Free University of Berlin, has headed the firm since 1986. In addition to being active in numerous other international organisations (INTA, ITMA, CIPA ao), Dr Helen Papaconstantinou is vice president of the AIPPI Group of Greece, member of the executive committee of FICPI, member of the board and former secretary general of the European Patent Institute and a council member of ECTA.

Over the past 80 years, the firm has grown steadily to become the largest firm of its kind in Greece. The firm's staff consists of 41 people, including 14 attorneys, most of whom possess postgraduate degrees from Greece and abroad, with considerable experience in intellectual property matters over many years of practice, five paralegals and four foreign secretaries. Three of the firm's attorneys are European patent attorneys, one is a UK barrister and one has extensive experience in international arbitration practice in the USA. Most of the firm's attorneys are members of various professional bodies.

The firm is able to serve foreign clients in English, French, German, Spanish, Italian and Dutch. The firm collaborates closely with 45 technical counsellors who have accredited degrees in sciences. The majority of them are or have been involved in academic research, are competent translators for English, French and German, and provide consulting services based on their technical expertise in patent matters.

AREAS OF PRACTICE

The firm specialises in intellectual property law, including patents, trade marks, copyright, designs, domain names, supplementary protection certificates for plant protection and medicinal products, unfair competition, customs monitoring procedures and all related litigation. It also offers expert consulting and quality advice in all areas of industrial and intellectual property law as well as on franchising distribution and license agreements and on advertising, marketing and consumer law.

The firm's client base covers a very broad spectrum. Its clients range from trade mark and patent departments of large and small international companies directly represented by the firm, through to multinational and small companies represented by the firm indirectly through trade mark and patent agents from all over the world.

In addition to its intellectual property activities in Greece, the firm maintains a close collaboration with law offices in Cyprus and all the Arabic countries, and has acquired experience in the handling of trade mark and patent matters in these countries for many years.

The firm of Dr Helen Papaconstantinou & Associates is both flexible and adaptable in its ability to serve multi-farious needs of clients. As a result, it has expanded its scope of representation to include intellectual property matters from all Balkan countries.

PROFESSOR K. KREMALIS & PARTNERS, member of ius laboris

35, KYRILLOU LOUKAREOS STR
114 75 ATHENS

Telephone: +30 210 643 1387
Fax: +30 210 646 0313
E-mail: info@kremalis.gr
Website: www.kremalis.gr

Languages
English, French, German, Italian, Spanish

Number of lawyers 11

Contacts
Konstantinos Kremalis (kkremalis@kremalis.gr),
Dani Praunseis (secr.athens@kremalis.gr)

Member
ius laboris, International Employment Law Pensions and Employee Benefits Alliance

CATEGORIES OF WORK

Labour and employment law (including mediation and arbitration, consulting, litigation, compensation and benefits, expatriation, drafting and negotiations for individual and collective agreements, restructuring, transfer and merger of undertakings)

International and European social law

International private law

Media and Internet law

Social security law (including retirement protection, pension funds, health and medical law, social policy research projects)

Administrative law

Tax law

Private insurance law (including life and group insurance, occupational schemes)

Finance and investment law

Corporate law

Intellectual property law

Competition and trade mark law

KYRIAKIDES - GEORGOPOULOS LAW FIRM

268 KIFISSIAS AVENUE (HALANDRI)
152 32 ATHENS

Telephone: +30 210 817 1500
Fax: +30 210 685 6657/8
E-mail: kg.law@kglawfirm.gr
Website: www.kglawfirm.gr

Languages
English, French, German

Other offices
Piraeus, Thessalonica

Number of lawyers 54
at this office 39

Contacts
Constantine Kyriakides,
Leonidas Georgopoulos

CATEGORIES OF WORK

Commercial and competition	**Financial services/banking**
Corporate structuring	**Intellectual property**
Dispute resolution	**Mergers and acquisitions**
Technology, media and communications	**Public law**
Employment and human resources	**Real estate**
Energy, mining, oil and gas	**Telecommunications**
Aviation	**Maritime**
Tax	

THE FIRM

Kyriakides – Georgopoulos was established by the late Kyriacos S Kyriakides in 1933. In 1999, the firm was incorporated as a professional partnership.

Throughout the years of its existence, Kyriakides – Georgopoulos has developed special expertise in corporate and business law matters.

Its dedication to the defence of its clients' interests, as well as its appreciation of the commercial environment in which its clients operate, means that they strive for legal excellence. Kyriakides – Georgopoulos' multi-disciplinary teams of lawyers have been trained and are capable of working closely with clients to find innovative and practical solutions to the most complex problems.

AREAS OF PRACTICE

Kyriakides – Georgopoulos Law Firm provides a full range of business law services, through specialist lawyers organised in groups, each supervised by a partner of the firm. In this way, consistent high standards of advice and service are guaranteed for both international and local clients. Its international strengths include: legal consulting on mergers and acquisitions; corporate structuring; financial services; technology, media and communications; and employment law.

M & P BERNITSAS

5 LYKAVITTOU STREET
106 72 ATHENS

Telephone: +30 210 361 5395
Fax: +30 210 364 0805
E-mail:
m&p.bernitsas@bernitsaslawoffices.gr
Website: www.bernitsaslawoffices.gr

Languages
English, French, German, Italian, Spanish

Number of lawyers 35

CATEGORIES OF WORK

Banking and finance
N Papachristopoulos, A Tsene

Project finance
D Georgacopoulos, I Kourniotis

Commercial and company law
L Vasaka, N Vouhiounis

Land development and property
N Vouhiounis, V Athanassoglou

Privatisations
P Bernitsas, D Roussis

Mergers and acquisitions
P Bernitsas, D Georgacopoulos

Public works and procurement
D Roussis, M Androulakakis

Tax and leasing
N Papachristopoulos, M Patiti

Aviation law
K Papantonopoulou

EU and competition
A Almyroudi, M Androulakakis

Telecommunications
A Almyroudi, E Gyparaki

Information technology
C Vlachtsis, L Belessis

Industrial and intellectual property
Y Chryssospathis, L Vasaka

Litigation, commercial arbitration and ADR
P Bernitsas, D Georgacopoulos

Human rights
D Mirasyesi

Labour law
C Vlachtsis, E Kitsou

MOUSSAS & TSIBRIS

34 ASKLIPIOU ST
106 80 ATHENS

Telephone: +30 210 339 20703
Fax: +30 210 339 0591
E-mail: info@moussastsibris.gr
Website: www.moussastsibris.gr

Languages
English, French, German, Italian

Number of lawyers 11

CATEGORIES OF WORK

Corporate
M Tsibris, N Moussas

Commercial
V Moussas, M Tsaoussi

Banking
N Moussas, M Tsibris

Insurance
N Moussas, V Moussas

Financial markets regulation
M Tsibris, G Plagou

Distributorships
V Moussas, K Tzamalouka

Franchising
N Moussas, K Tzamalouka

International trade
N Moussas, G Plagou

Commercial and civil litigation
V Moussas

Tax
L Papahatzi, A Tsibri

Real estate
V Moussas

Telecommunications, media
N Moussas, G Plagou

Sports law
N Moussas, V Moussas

S. A. FELIOS & ASSOCIATES

10 NEOFYTOU VAMVA STREET
KOLONAKI
106 74 ATHENS

Telephone: +30 210 729 9630
Fax: +30 210 729 9651
E-mail: contact@felioslawfirm.gr
Website: www.felioslawfirm.gr

Languages
Dutch, English, French, German, Italian, Spanish

Number of lawyers 20

Member
Libralex European Economic Interest Group

CATEGORIES OF WORK

Corporate and commercial Evangelia Vouza, Maria Skagou	**Banking and financial** Nikos Papanikolaou, Spyros Themelis
International investments Sotiris Felios, Maria Skagou	**Stock exchange law** Evangelia Vouza
Competition law Sotiris Felios, Maria Skagou	**Taxation** Fotini Apostolopoulou
Telecoms, IT and the Internet Maria Skagou, Fotini Apostolopoulou	**Real estate** Maria Nelly Pavlous
New technologies Fotini Apostolopoulou	**Aviation law** Violetta Vasilakou
Broadcasting and advertising law Maria Skagou, Evangelia Vouza	**Energy** Sotiris Felios, Evangelia Vouza
Sports law Fotini Apostolopoulou, Spyros Themelis	**EU law** Evangelia Vouza, Maria Skagou
Art law Sotiris Felios, Maria Skagou	**Administrative law** Evangelia Vouza
Intellectual property Mari Damaskopoulou	**Labour law** Mari Damaskopoulou, Maria Skagou

THE FIRM

Established as a law office in 1975 by Sotiris Felios and now operating as a law firm, S. A. Felios & Associates is recognised as one of the most prominent law firms in Greece. Two years ago, the firm moved to its new, dedicated offices in Neofytou Vamva Street, Kolonaki. The firm is equipped with the latest technology and now employs 20 attorneys at law, with the assistance of six paralegals and secretarial support.

AREAS OF PRACTICE

Corporate law and related matters: finance; commercial contracts (exclusive or non-exclusive agency, distribution, supply, franchising); industrial property; advising major companies on establishment, operation, M&A, privatisations and investments; commercial arbitration and international transaction agreements; acquisition of shares; joint ventures; participation in public procurement procedures; establishment and operation of companies and branch offices; management agreements and related subjects; and consumer protection policy issues.

Competition law: supporting companies before the Greek Competition Committee and the European authorities; matters of transfer of control over businesses; antitrust; consummation of transactions exceeding the thresholds of Law 703/77, as well as the degree of implementation of the Greek legislation with EU antitrust specifications.

Telecoms, IT, new technologies and broadcasting: acquisition of telecoms licences and company shareholding; provision of services, supply of equipment and network operation (including mobile telephone networks); call-centre operations and services (including licensing, privacy, data protection, and the legal aspects of conducting market surveys); the creation and operation of websites, e-commerce and other Internet services (including issues related to the security of e-commerce transactions, encrypted signatures, identification of data, and so on); protection of personal data.

Sports law: club ownership; transfer of players; employment contracts; financing and construction of sports stadiums; commercial agreements for the exploitation of sports rights, including TV rights, sponsorship and marketing agreements and representation, as well as organisation of the Olympic Games in 2004 (including the Cultural Olympiad).

Art law: artist-dealer relations; private sales; IP and copyright (including their application to works produced or distributed through new means and technologies); trade marks.

Banking and finance, stock exchange law and taxation: corporate and inter-bank lending; debt restructuring; financial counsellor services and agreements; due diligence; financing of activities (including major construction works); investments; restructuring or participation in projects financed by European funds and programmes; bank mergers and acquisitions; advice and representation before authorities with reference to stock exchange law (including listing, transfer of shares and compliance); advising clients on their present and potential tax liability.

Real estate: acquisition, sale and lease of real estate with a view to developing activities; expropriations; town planning; real estate investment funds.

Aviation law: activities ranging from tax- and finance-related issues to disputes between airlines and their customers.

Energy: analysing regulatory frameworks; advising on the operational aspects of restructuring; production of electricity from environmentally friendly sources; due diligence.

EU law: advice and representation before the European authorities, including the directorates of the European Commission, as well as the courts of the EU; advice on the implementation of EU directives in Greece.

Labour law: all aspects of employment relations, representing clients before the courts and public authorities or in negotiations with labour unions.

The firm also practices in administrative law and public procurement.

S. D. AFENDRAS & PARTNERS LAW OFFICES

38 SINA STREET
10672 ATHENS

Telephone: +30 210 364 6105
Fax: +30 210 364 3191
E-mail: afendras@afendras.gr
Website: www.afendras.gr

Languages
English, French, German, Italian

Number of lawyers 12

Contact
Stavros Afendras, Yota Psarogiorgou

CATEGORIES OF WORK

Mergers and acquisitions
S Afendras, E Kastrinaki

Commercial and civil
Ch Doukas, E Kastrinaki

Capital markets
S Afendras, Y Psarogiorgou

Taxation
S Afendras, N Zorbala

Banking and finance
S Afendras, S Panagiotopoulos

Corporate criminal
O Kapachtsi, A Konstas

Energy
Y Psarogiorgou, O Kapachtsi

European law
E Kastrinaki, S Korrao

Investment
S Afendras, N Zorbala

Sports
S Panagiotopoulos

Corporate
A Konstas, Y Psarogiorgou

Intellectual property
S Corrao, N Zorbala

Telecommunications
Ch Doukas

THE FIRM

The firm was formed initially by Stavros D Afendras in 1986. At the beginning, the firm provided services mainly in the fields of European and corporate law. Progressively, the firm grew, and in order to cover the needs of its clientele, expanded its services into other areas of law too.

The firm's offices are located at the heart of the Athens city centre and staffed with lawyers that are specialised and qualified to deal with the law matters the firm undertakes.

AREAS OF PRACTICE

Afendras & Partners Law Offices provide a full range of corporate and trade law services, from company establishment to advising on mergers and acquisitions. Other principal practice areas include banking and finance, capital markets, investment and securities, as well as tax and insolvency practitioning. In the field of industry and enterprises, the firm has extensive experience in energy, telecommunications and investment projects.

Afendras & Partners clientele consists of major local and international companies, as well as financial institutions and important investors in the field of industry.

Legal advice is also offered in relation to Greek civil law matters and sports law. Anticipating the demand for legal expertise in several practice law areas, the office established certain groups of specialised lawyers, in order to meet client requirements.

SARANTITIS & PARTNERS

9 ANAGNOSTOPOULOU STREET
106 73 ATHENS

Telephone: +30 210 367 0400
Fax: +30 210 362 1595
E-mail: athens@sarantitis.com
Website: www.sarantitis.com

Languages
English, French, German, Italian, Spanish

Other offices
Piraeus, Thessaloniki

Number of lawyers 40
at this office 22

Contacts
Mr Yiannis Sarantitis, Mr Dorotheos Samoladas

CATEGORIES OF WORK

Corporate and commercial	**EU law**
Banking and finance	**Taxation**
Foreign investments	**Telecommunications, IT and media**
Privatisations	**Maritime law**
Labour law	**Arbitration and litigation**

THE FIRM

Sarantitis & Partners serves its clients internationally from offices in all three major financial centres of Greece: Athens, Piraeus and Thessaloniki. Sarantitis & Partners is regarded as one of the leading law firms in Greece, being, at the same time, one of the largest in size. Established by its senior partner in 1965, today the firm represents an impressive list of companies, banks and enterprises within Greece and abroad. Sarantitis & Partners handles substantial transactions, while continuing to provide the personal services its clients value.

In order to provide broader and more effective legal services, S&P co-operates closely with other firms around the world in such cities as New York, London, Paris, Rome, Moscow, Oslo, Hong Kong, Brussels and Tokyo. The firm's local network of correspondents covers Greece, Cyprus and the Balkans, with the main emphasis on business centres and commercial ports.

AREAS OF PRACTICE

From its head office in Athens, Sarantitis & Partners offers a diverse corporate and commercial practice ranging from general corporate representation to important M&A activity, including privatisation projects in the Greek public sector as well as in other Balkan countries. The team specialising in stock exchange and security law has extensive experience on high-profile IPOs, as well as private equity transactions. The firm has, for the last thirty years, provided legal consultancy services to banks and other financial institutions dealing with a variety of financial products and other services. The firm's banking practice has been involved in various aspects of banking law, beginning with the establishment of foreign banks in Greece, their operation and expansion, takeovers/mergers, transfers of shares, purchase and sale of retail and commercial operations.

The team of lawyers specialising in IT, media and telecoms law has gained the trust and the responsibility to represent leading firms in the Balkans and across Europe. Sarantitis & Partners holds a leading position in providing expertise in drafting and successfully negotiating the full spectrum of IT and telecoms projects, having engaged in some of the major IT projects, Internet law cases and telecoms contracts that have marked the development of these markets in Greece.

The Piraeus office has an influential presence in one of Europe's largest shipping and trading centres, having significantly participated in the legal affairs of the Greek shipping sector for over 35 years. Due to its longstanding presence and active involvement in this particular field of law, the firm is not only known as the oldest, but also as one of the foremost national firms specialising in maritime law in the region.

Thessaloniki, which is an autonomous economic centre and major port in the north of Greece, serves as a gateway to the greater Balkan area, which enables Sarantitis & Partners to serve their clients in their business activities in Northern Greece and the Balkan region. Members of the Thessaloniki office practice corporate and commercial law and have been engaged in substantial legal cases in the areas of taxation, property development and real estate, major franchising as well as maritime law.

STAVROPOULOS, TSIRI & PAPADOPOULOU

18 VALAORITOU STREET
ATHENS 106 71

Telephone: +30 210 363 4262
Fax: +30 210 363 3204
E-mail: info@stplaw.com
Website: www.stplaw.com

Languages
English, French, German, Spanish

Number of lawyers 12

Contact
Ioannis Stavropoulos

Member
Euro-American Lawyers Group (EALG)

CATEGORIES OF WORK

Corporate and commercial law

Securities law

Taxation

Real estate and construction law

Mergers and acquisitions

Trade marks and patents law

Competition law

Administrative law

EU law

Litigation and arbitration

Finance and banking law

LAW OFFICE TJ KOUTALIDIS

4 VALAORITOU STREET
106 71 ATHENS

Telephone: +30 210 360 7811
Fax: +30 210 360 0069
E-mail: info@koutalidis.gr
Website: www.koutalidis.gr

Languages
English, French, German, Italian, Spanish

Number of lawyers 24

CATEGORIES OF WORK

Shipping and aviation
TJ Koutalidis, KJ Protopapa

Infrastructure
GP Logothetis, M Michalovits

Banking and finance
NC Koritsas, NV Salakas

Investment law
NE Pimblis, IE Deloucas

Construction
DC Hadjigrigoriadis, PE Koutalidis

Litigation and arbitration
A Mandakou, GP Logothetis

Corporate
TJ Koutalidis, NC Koritsas

Mergers and acquisitions
KJ Protopapa, KN Kyriakakii

European law
NP Fortsakis, P Tsatsa

Taxation
NC Koritsas, GD Naskaris

TSIBANOULIS & PARTNERS LAW FIRM

18 & 24 OMIROU STREET
106 72 ATHENS

Telephone: +30 210 367 5100
Fax: +30 210 367 5115
E-mail: info@tsibanoulis.gr

Languages
English, French, German, Spanish

Other office
Piraeus

Number of lawyers 33

Contacts
Dr D Tsibanoulis, Caroline Friedrich, Elena Bailas, Vasso Vouga

Member
European Financial Market Lawyers Group (EFMLG), German Greek Law Association, International Federation for European Law (FIDE), Greek Competition Law Society, Greek Commercial Law Society, International Bar Association (IBA), German Hellenic Chamber of Commerce

CATEGORIES OF WORK

Banking and finance
Dr D Tsibanoulis, E Bailas

Capital markets
Dr D Tsibanoulis, A Gabrielides

European financial markets
Dr D Tsibanoulis, Dr E Avgouleas

Private equity, venture capital
C Friedrich, A Petsinari

Structured finance and derivatives
Dr E Avgouleas, T Katsas

Project finance
E Bailas

E-commerce and Internet banking
Dr E Avgouleas, K Somou

Corporate and commercial
Dr D Tsibanoulis, C Friedrich

Mergers and acquisitions
Dr G Siganidis, C Friedrich

Real estate and commercial leasing
A Apostolaki

Antitrust
Dr G Siganidis

Intellectual property
M Perraki, S Anastasyadis

Privatisation
Dr G Siganidis, Dr E Avgouleas

Litigation
G Papastylos, Dr G Siganidis

Corporate taxation
E Bailas, G Frentzos

Shipping law and shipping finance
V Vouga, A Parr

THE FIRM

Tsibanoulis & Partners has established a reputation as one of Greece's leading law firms in the fields of banking law and financial services, capital market regulation and securities law, offering quality legal services to major Greek and international banking and financial institutions, blue-chip corporations and high-net-worth individuals. The firm has eight partners and 25 associates. Most are multi-lingual and hold qualifications from leading European and American universities. Many of the firm's lawyers are qualified in other European jurisdictions allowing the firm to offer clients both multi-jurisdictional experience and legal expertise in order to meet their changing needs in the international market effectively. Work is conducted in Greek, English, French, German and Spanish.

AREAS OF PRACTICE

The firm's reputation for transactional work, including international bond issues, syndicated loan facilities, structured finance, derivatives and securitisations, and general corporate work, is among the best in the field. Partners from the firm have acted in several cross-border acquisitions of banks and other financial institutions, major corporate mergers and acquisitions, banking and corporate restructurings, securities and project finance transactions. Since November 2000, managing partner Dr Dimitris Tsibanoulis has been lead adviser to the government of the Republic of Cyprus for the reform of its capital markets law. The firm's international banking and finance capability has recently been strengthened with its merger with Bailas & Partners (est 1972), and the firm's breadth of expertise continues to grow with the recent establishment of new offices in Piraeus serving the diverse needs of the domestic and international shipping industry. The Piraeus office offers considerable expertise and quality legal advice on all aspects of ship finance, acting for both lenders and borrowers. It also handles contentious and non-contentious shipping law matters and advises on international corporate law, including the establishment of corporate and private trust structures in a number of jurisdictions.

Standing out for its extensive experience in the areas of banking, finance and corporate law and the commercial awareness of its lawyers, the firm regularly acts for foreign governments, international and domestic financial institutions, large investment services firms, multinational corporations and companies listed in the Athens Stock Exchange together with major European and US law firms. The firm offers legal advice on a variety of corporate, finance and banking law matters including stock exchange and securities regulations, and on the structuring of finance facilities and highly complex and innovative products, and acts for them in the context of a large number of complex credit, finance and corporate transactions, including mergers and acquisitions, joint ventures and partnership agreements.

Responding to its clients' needs, Tsibanoulis & Partners also runs a sizeable general corporate and commercial practice, offering comprehensive advice and conducting commercial and labour law litigation and contentious work. The firm is frequently asked to act for its clients in a variety of commercial law agreements including franchise, licensing, agency and distribution, industrial and intellectual property contracts, and provides expert advice on corporate taxation, tax-driven structures and various aspects of EU law.

VGENOPOULOS & PARTNERS

LAW FIRM

15 FILIKIS ETERIAS SQUARE
106 73 ATHINAI

Telephone: +30 210 720 6900
Fax: +30 210 723 1462
E-mail: mail@vplaw.gr
Website: www.vplaw.gr

Languages
English, French, German, Italian, Russian

Other offices
Piraeus, Salonika*

Number of lawyers 40
at this office 35

Contacts
Loukas Roufos, Eliana Paschalides, John Papapetros

CATEGORIES OF WORK

Aviation
Dr Alexandros Kalantzis, Calliope Metaxotou

Banking and finance, securitisation
John Papapetros, Calliope Metaxotou

Capital markets
Loukas Roufos, Stephanos Karaiskakis

Real estate and construction
Eliana Paschalides, Nikos Damigos

EU law and competition
Dr Alexandros Kalantzis, Dr Ioanna Anastassopoulou

Corporate and commercial
Loukas Roufos, Sterios Anastassiadis

Dispute resolution
Eliana Paschalides

Litigation
Aris Anghelakos, George Iatridis

Energy and natural resources
Dr Alexandros Kalantzis, Dr Ioanna Anastassopoulou

Government business, regulatory
Stephanos Karaiskakis, Aris Anghelakos

Insurance
Dr Alexandros Kalantzis

Intellectual property
Laoura Liberopoulou

Mergers and acquisitions
Loukas Roufos, Stephanos Karaiskakis

Shipping and transport
John Papapetros, Milto Papangelis

Tax
Angelos Georgoussis

Telecommunications
Dr Alexandros Kalantzis

THE FIRM

Vgenopoulos & Partners is a Greek law firm that was established in 1983 in Piraeus by its current senior partners.

In the beginning, the firm's main area of practice was shipping law, covering all aspects of the law as it relates to shipping and shipping finance. Within a short period of time the firm expanded into other areas of practice, summarised in the list of categories of work above. Given the number of lawyers working for the Athens and Piraeus offices of the firm (40 lawyers in total), Vgenopoulos & Partners is one of the largest firms in Greece.

The firm's policy is to combine a personal approach with the highest professional standards and to provide clients with clear, comprehensive and business-orientated legal services and with rapid responses in changing business situations. The firm is highly sensitive to the importance of preserving the confidentiality of client information as well as to the need for effective cost management. Although the firm is continually expanding, it remains a young and enterprising practice.

Most of the firm's attorneys have studied at postgraduate level in foreign universities and have had experience and training in law offices in western Europe. Many of the firm's attorneys regularly participate in seminars, conferences and other continuing legal education programmes. All of the firm's offices are equipped with the latest technology, tailored to meet the needs of modern commercial clients.

AREAS OF PRACTICE

The firm is organised into several practice groups, each headed by a highly experienced partner and staffed by specialised and experienced lawyers.

Vgenopoulos & Partners' clients consist of local and international banks and financial institutions, multinational companies and joint ventures, local and foreign-based manufacturers, insurers and service companies, foreign law firms and shipping companies.

ZEPOS & YANNOPOULOS

75 KATEHAKI & KIFISSIAS AVE
115 25 ATHENS

Telephone: +30 210 775 4571
Fax: +30 210 770 2825
E-mail: info@zeya.com
Website: www.zeya.com

Languages
English, French, German, Italian

Other offices
Athens, Salonika

Number of lawyers 40
at this office 38

Contacts
Dimitrios Zepos, Yerassimos Yannopoulos

Member
Lex Mundi

CATEGORIES OF WORK

Banking and finance
V Digenopoulos, T Mitsidis

Capital markets
V Lazarakou, S Papastavrou

Commercial and tax litigation
V Digenopoulos, A Tsourouflis

Corporate and commercial law
D Zepos, C Sarantis

Energy
C Sarantis, M Kolia

EU and competition
E Mastromanolis, I Koimtzoglou

International taxation
M Akrividou, M Stavrinou

IT and e-commerce
P Kakouris, D Cozonis

Labour law
C Kabilafkas, R Papakonstantinou

Mergers and acquisitions
N Dessypris, M Allamani

Privatisations and projects
T Mitsidis, M Kolia

Real estate
C Kallideris, M Allamani

Taxation
Y Yannopoulos, V Moraitis

Telecommunications
S Papastavrou, A Skolarikou

VAT
I Mitroyanni, A Karopoulos

ARISTIDES ECONOMIDES & CO

LIVANOS BUILDING
47-49 AKTI MIAOULI
185 36 PIRAEUS

Telephone: +30 210 429 2590
Fax: +30 210 429 3036
E-mail: infopir@economidesco.gr
Website: www.economidesco.gr

Languages
English, French, German

Other offices
Athens

Number of lawyers 8

Contacts
John A Economides, Panagiotis A Tzioumas

CATEGORIES OF WORK

Criminal law

Litigation

Alternative dispute resolution

Civil law

Business law

Commercial

Banking and finance

Administrative law

Real estate

Transportation and tourism

EU and competition

Maritime law

CLYDE & CO

10 ATKI POSEIDONOS
185 31 PIRAEUS

Telephone: +30 210 417 0001
Fax: +30 210 417 0002
E-mail: info@clyde.gr
Website: www.clydeco.com

Languages
English, French, German, Greek

Other offices
Belgrade, Caracas, Cardiff, Dubai, Guildford, Hong Kong, London, Nantes, Paris, St Petersburg, Singapore

Number of lawyers 386
at this office 2

Contact
Martin Hall

CATEGORIES OF WORK

Marine (wet and dry)	Collision and insurance work
Contractual disputes	

G E BAIRACTARIS & PARTNERS

130 KOLOKOTRONI STREET
185 36 PIRAEUS

Telephone: +30 210 428 4608
Fax: +30 210 428 4626
E-mail: bairalaw@internet.gr
Website: www.bairactaris.com

Languages
English, French, German, Italian

Number of lawyers 14

Contacts
George E Bairactaris (managing partner), John S Vafiadis (shipping and finance), Vangelis G Bairactaris (corporate, shipping and finance), Nikolas Manoussakis (litigation), Christina Gennadopoulou (corporate and commercial)

Member
Geneva Group International

CATEGORIES OF WORK

Shipping	Commercial and civil litigation
Capital markets	Communications
Corporate and commercial	Competition
International trade and commodities	International arbitration
Banking and finance	Mergers and acquisitions
EU and competition law	Private client
E-commerce and IT	Aviation
Property and construction	Energy

HOLMAN FENWICK & WILLAN

INTERNATIONAL

6TH FLOOR
86 FILONOS STREET
185 36 PIRAEUS

Telephone: +30 210 429 3978
Fax: +30 210 429 3118
E-mail: holmans@hfw.com.gr
Website: www.hfw.com

Languages
English, French,German, Greek

Other offices
London, Paris, Nantes, Rouen, Hong Kong, Shanghai, Singapore

Number of lawyers 176
at this office 9

CATEGORIES OF WORK

Admiralty and marine insurance
Charles Lowe, Dimitri Vassos

Commodities
Gareth Williams

Marine litigation/arbitration
David Pitlarge, Gareth Williams

Shipping and project finance
Dan Tindall

Commercial litigation/arbitration, international trade
Gareth Williams, Dimitri Vassos

THE FIRM

Holman Fenwick & Willan is an international law firm specialising in shipping and transport, trade and energy, insurance and reinsurance and commercial law. The firm has a reputation worldwide for excellence and innovation. It has one of the largest international arbitration and dispute resolution practices of its kind, with offices in Europe and Asia Pacific.

The firm's international practice is founded upon its principal offices in London, Paris, Piraeus, Hong Kong, Singapore and Shanghai and over 120 years' experience of working with other law firms in jurisdictions throughout the world.

The Piraeus office was opened in 1993 to provide enhanced services to one of the shipping industry's most important strategic centres. The office provides services in relation to English law matters with the emphasis on commercial and shipping-related litigation and casualties. The office has particular expertise in marine and insurance matters, including hull and cargo claims, charterparty disputes, casualty investigation and collisions, salvage, oil pollution, wreck removal, constructive and actual total losses, sale and purchase and commodity-related and other commercial issues.

AREAS OF PRACTICE

Shipping litigation/Admiralty, commercial litigation, marine insurance and project finance.

ROUSSOS & HATZIDIMITRIOU LAW OFFICES

5-7 FILELLINON STREET
185 36 PIRAEUS

Telephone: +30 210 429 4200
Fax: +30 210 429 4625
E-mail: randhlaw@internet.gr

Languages
English, French, German, Spanish

Number of lawyers 11

Member
Eurolegal

CATEGORIES OF WORK

Litigation
Costas Roussos, Costas Cotsiyannis

Commercial
Zafiris Hatzidimitriou, Ioanna Dimopoulou

Corporate
Io Grekoussi, Costas Cotsiyannis

Admiralty and maritime
Costas Roussos, Zafiris Hatzidimitriou

Maritime insurance
Costas Roussos, Areti Arvaniti

Banking and investment
Zafiris Hatzidimitriou, John Christoforidis

Contracts
Costas Cotsiyannis, Areti Arvaniti

Real estate
Costas Cotsiyannis, Costas Roussos

Mergers and acquisitions
Zafiris Hatzidimitriou, John Christoforidis

Ship finance
Costas Roussos, Io Grekoussi

Privatisation
Costas Roussos, Zafiris Hatzidimitriou

Civil law
Costas Roussos, Costas Cotsiyannis

Industrial and intellectual property
Costas Cotsiyannis, Angeliki Antonopoulou

Employment
Costas Cotsiyannis, Maria Giakoumi

Telecommunications
Zafiris Hatzidimitriou, Angeliki Antonopoulou

WATSON, FARLEY & WILLIAMS

8TH FLOOR, IONIAN BUILDING
DEFTERAS MERARCHIAS 2
185 36 PIRAEUS

Telephone: +30 210 459 4000
Fax: +30 210 459 4004
Website: www.wfw.com

Languages
Cantonese, Danish, English, French, German, Gujarati, Hebrew, Italian, Malay, Mandarin, Norwegian, Polish, Russian, Spanish, Swahili, Swedish, Thai

Other offices
Bangkok, London, New York, Paris, Rome, Singapore

Number of lawyers 175
at this office 9

Contacts
Jeremy Watson, George Paleokrassas
John Krzywkowski

CATEGORIES OF WORK

Ship finance

Commercial shipping and corporate shipping

Shipping litigation and marine insurance

Tax and tax-based leasing

Property

Banking, international finance, trade finance, project finance

Capital markets - public and private equity and debt issues

Sale and purchase, new building contract sales and re-sales

EU law

THE FIRM

Watson, Farley & Williams was founded in the City of London in 1982 and has expanded rapidly into a successful international practice, able to advise on English, French, Russian, Thai, New York, and US Federal law.

The firm offers a comprehensive legal service to commercial clients while concentrating its expertise in the areas of shipping, energy, banking, corporate and commercial, EC and competition, taxation, litigation, and property.

AREAS OF PRACTICE

The firm is perhaps best known in the area of shipping, ship finance, and shipping and insurance litigation (both admiralty and commercial marine). Watson, Farley & Williams acts for lenders, shipowners, shipbuilders, ship operators, P&I clubs, salvors, charterers, brokers and others involved in international maritime transactions. The firm also advises on marine pollution risk and liability.

In addition, the Greek office advises on all aspects of banking law, including syndicated lending, project financing, and banking regulation as well as having considerable experience in insolvency and work-outs.

The firm's corporate expertise allows it to advise on corporate finance work including acquisitions, flotations, and restructurings in both shipping and non-shipping matters. The firm also gives advice on commercial agreements with specialists in intellectual property, employment and immigration.

In its other European offices, EC law is an important part of the practice and the firm has particular expertise in the area of competition law. The international litigation group handles commercial litigation and arbitration with an emphasis on the maritime, energy and commodities sectors. The firm's taxation specialists are experienced in financing, shipping and energy transactions as well as tax litigation and VAT. The property section deals with commercial property transactions including developments, environment law and secured lending. The central and eastern Europe team deals with privatisations, joint ventures, acquisitions and corporate transactions.

LAW OFFICE WEISS, ELVEY & ASKINS

IN ASSOCIATION WITH INCE & CO

7TH FLOOR
137 FILONOS STREET
185 36 PIRAEUS

Telephone: +30 210 429 2543
Fax: +30 210 429 3318
E-mail: firstname.lastname@incelaw.com
Website: www.incelaw.com

Languages
English

Other offices
Hamburg, Hong Kong, Le Havre, London, Paris, Shanghai, Singapore

Number of lawyers at this office 8

CATEGORIES OF WORK

Shipping
Jonathan Elvey, Stephen Askins

International trade
Jonathan Elvey, Stephen Askins

Insurance
Jonathan Elvey, Stephen Askins

International arbitration
Jonathan Elvey, Stephen Askins

Commercial litigation
Jonathan Elvey, Stephen Askins

Admiralty
Stephen Askins, Paul Billowen

THE FIRM

Ince & Co is an international law firm with a worldwide reputation as a leading practitioner in shipping, insurance and reinsurance, energy, aviation and international trade law. Founded in the City of London in 1870, the firm also has offices in Hamburg, Hong Kong, Le Havre, Paris, Piraeus, Shanghai and Singapore.

AREAS OF PRACTICE

The office in Piraeus opened in 1993 to provide a broad range of services on English law matters to the Greek maritime community, including dry marine, admiralty, commercial law, and insurance and reinsurance.

GUERNSEY

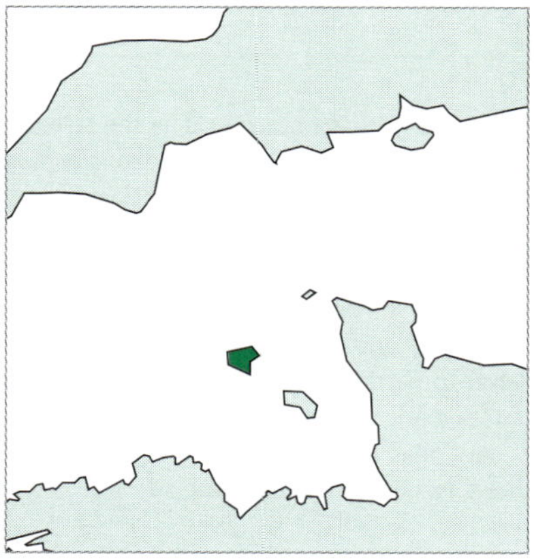

Population	**60,000**
Number of lawyers	**80**
Professional title	**Advocate**
Currency	**Pound sterling (£)**

Index

Guernsey and Jersey are both crown dependencies, part of the British Isles, but not part of the United Kingdom. Guernsey is the smaller of the two islands, although the Bailiwick of Guernsey also includes the islands of Alderney, Sark and Herm.

Matters relating to foreign relations and defence are looked after for the Channel Islands by the Crown through the UK government. The Channel Islands are neither full nor associate members of the EU (although they fall within the common customs area and therefore levy the common external tariff). Their relationship with the EU is determined by Protocol 3 to the UK's Treaty of Accession.

BILLING

Typically fees are charged on the basis of an hourly rate decided in advance by the parties. Scale fees exist for conevyancing work. However, fees may vary depending on the lawyer instructed and the job in hand. Clients can expect costs not dissimilar to those charged by City of London firms: around £160 for a newly qualified lawyer, rising to around £350 at partner level.

MARKETING

Law firms are free to advertise within the framework of the Rules of Professional Conduct.

THE LEGAL 500

Readers should note that the following is taken from the **Offshore Britain** section of the 2003 edition of *The Legal 500* (UK edition), available at www.legal500.com.

LEGAL MARKET

The Channel Islands' legal community changed shape when *Carey Langlois* made the dramatic move of securing a merger with Jersey-based *Olsens*. Announced in March 2003, the merger creates **Carey Olsen**, the largest Channel Islands firm. One of the most ambitious Jersey firms, *Olsens* already had a Guernsey presence. *Carey Langlois* has picked up valuable extra resources for both contentious and non-contentious commercial work.

As on Jersey, a more fluid market for lateral partner hires reflects intense competition between firms. The biggest move of 2002 was William Simpson's from **Ozannes** to **Ogier & Le Masurier**. As well as being a first-rate lawyer, Simpson had kept **Ozannes**' profile high and had injected a level of dynamism into the firm. Securing such a charismatic partner is a shrewd move by **Ogier & Le Masurier**.

But there are few firms remaining static, and **Ozannes** secured its own lateral coup when it took star litigator Jeremy Wessels from **Babbe Le Pelley Tostevin**. His move, and the fact that **Ogier & Le Masurier** still does no contentious work on Guernsey, means that Guernsey's strongest litigators are found exclusively in the top two firms.

Prior to its merger, *Olsens* was staking a strong claim to the status as Guernsey's 'third firm'. **Collas Day** and **Babbe Le Pelley Tostevin** now vie for this title, with both firms working on notable commercial transactions of late.

Note that **Babbe Le Pelley Tostevin** addressed the loss of Jeremy Wessels by recruiting litigation partner Iain Harris from **Collas Day** in June 2003.

Foreign firms **Turcan Connell**, **Wedlake Bell Guernsey** and **Conyers Dill & Pearman** have a presence on Guernsey.

COMMERCIAL AND BANKING

The **Carey Olsen** combination can call on partners like Graham Hall, Nigel Carey and Ben Morgan. The team has a reputation for high-quality work, and acts for numerous banks, corporates, and funds.

Collas Day's reputation is largely based on the commercial acumen and knowledge of Ian Kirk, who advises on company and business acquisitions, joint ventures and mergers, banking, insurance and general corporate and fiduciary matters. The sizeable commercial practice includes partner Chris Bound who specialises in advising financial institutions.

Ozannes is smaller than **Carey Olsen** but matches its rival in quality of work and lawyers.

COMMERCIAL AND BANKING

CAREY OLSEN
COLLAS DAY
OZANNES

Babbe Le Pelley Tostevin
Ogier & Le Masurier ✪

Firms are listed A-Z in tiers which are ranked in order of priority
✪ Indicates firm displays contact details at the end of this chapter.

The largest firms

1	Carey Olsen	54
2	Ozannes	27
3	Collas Day	20
4	Babbe Le Pelley Tostevin	16
5	Ogier & Le Masurier	11
6	Wedlake Bell Guernsey	3

These figures represent the total number of lawyers in this country only, and have been supplied by the firms themselves. The figures should be accurate as at 1 January 2004.

Younger partners like Gavin Farrell, made up in January 2003, are taking their place alongside established names like Peter Harwood - a strong contender for the title of Guernsey's best corporate lawyer - and the versatile David Moore. The firm advised on C&W's acquisition of Guernsey's telecoms company.

Babbe Le Pelley Tostevin has three excellent commercial partners in Richard Babbe, Simon Howitt, and Mark Helyar, who advised ABN Amro Private Equity in the MBO of Commodore Ferries, where it linked up with Jersey alliance partner **Bedell Cristin**. Peter Wilding is an IP and e-commerce expert.

Ogier & Le Masurier boosted its Guernsey profile by hiring William Simpson from **Ozannes** to combine with the formidable Roger Le Tissier. The firm's work for banks and investment funds is of the highest quality. As an example, the firm was able to handle the Guernsey end of the migration of Investec Bank (Jersey) to Guernsey in tandem with its Jersey lawyers.

COMMERCIAL LITIGATION

Guernsey's three best litigators are **Carey Olsen**'s John Greenfield, **Ozannes**' Peter Ferbrache, and Jeremy Wessels, who last year moved to **Ozannes** from **Babbe Le Pelley Tostevin**. Jeremy Wessels had helped make **Babbe Le Pelley Tostevin** a genuine alternative to the top two firms, reflecting both his technical qualities and his ability to bring in new instructions.

Indeed, **Carey Olsen** and **Ozannes** dominate contentious work on the island. **Carey Olsen** now has an even bigger litigation practice in Guernsey, drawing as it does on the combined resources of *Carey Langlois* and *Olsens*, whose litigators include Jason Morgan and rising star Alison Ozanne. Their arrival will help give John Greenfield the senior level support necessary to maintain the team's top-tier position. In *Ansol Ltd v Ashton*, John Greenfield successfully obtained *ex parte* the first anti-suit injunction in Guernsey.

Similarly, the standing of **Ozannes**' Peter Ferbrache should not overshadow the work of Gordon Dawes or Robert Shepherd. This strength in depth means the firm can work on the vast majority of Guernsey's heaviest cases. Hiring Jeremy Wessels has added to **Ozannes**' contentious insurance practice. The firm also handles asset tracing, professional negligence, and banking litigation, and acts for the States of Guernsey. It is advising a leading clearing bank in defence of a large constructive trust claim.

Although **Babbe Le Pelley Tostevin** lost top litigator Jeremy Wessels to **Ozannes**, it bolstered its practice with the hire of partner Iain Harris from **Collas Day** and by promoting advocate Mark Helyar to partner. We also recommend Andrew Laws and Andrew Ayres.

At **Collas Day**, Mark Ferbrache remains well known for contentious expertise.

COMMERCIAL LITIGATION

OZANNES
CAREY OLSEN

Babbe Le Pelley Tostevin

Collas Day

Firms are listed A-Z in tiers which are ranked in order of priority

INSURANCE

CAREY OLSEN
OZANNES

Babbe Le Pelley Tostevin
Collas Day

Ogier & Le Masurier ✪

Firms are listed A-Z in tiers which are ranked in order of priority
✪ Indicates firm displays contact details at the end of this chapter.

INSURANCE

The former *Carey Langlois*, now **Carey Olsen**, formed the first captive insurance company on Guernsey in 1922 and has been active ever since. John Langlois has over 30 years' experience. Graham Hall is recommended for advice on the formation of protected cell companies.

Ozannes has long handled London-sourced work. Chris Anderson, recruited from Australian firm **Clayton Utz** in 2002, has helped the firm win more local instructions. David Moore has a fantastic work-rate and this combines with his commercial approach to win over clients.

Babbe Le Pelley Tostevin's Richard Babbe is respected for his length of service and knowledge, and the firm won impressive new instructions in 2002. **Collas Day** partner Ian Kirk is very strong.

INVESTMENT FUNDS

Nigel Carey at **Carey Olsen** is one of Guernsey's leading investment funds lawyers, while Graham Hall is 'a safe pair of hands' for funds work, which is the commercial department's core activity. Ben Morgan, who arrives as part of the *Olsens* merger, is also recommended.

Hiring William Simpson from **Ozannes** to work alongside Roger Le Tissier has doubled **Ogier & Le Masurier**'s partner-level funds expertise in Guernsey. William Simpson has won significant instructions from local fund administrators and City law firms in his first year. Consequently, **Ogier & Le Masurier** earns a move into the top tier.

But **Ozannes** still advises a large number of listed Guernsey funds. Gavin Farrell is excellent

INVESTMENT FUNDS

CAREY OLSEN
OGIER & LE MASURIER ✪
OZANNES

Collas Day

Babbe Le Pelley Tostevin

Firms are listed A-Z in tiers which are ranked in order of priority
✪ Indicates firm displays contact details at the end of this chapter.

and has helped keep the firm in number one position in the *Fitzrovia International* table of legal advisers to Guernsey investment funds. **Ozannes** advised on the establishment of a £55m closed-ended umbrella investment company for Close.

Sean Cheong at **Collas Day** is involved in the establishment of collective investment schemes and has strong regulatory expertise.

Babbe Le Pelley Tostevin has seen significant growth in private equity and other funds work.

PERSONAL TAX, TRUSTS AND PENSIONS

Carey Olsen advises a large number of local fiduciary companies. It acts for trustees, settlors and beneficiaries on new and existing trust structures, and offers sophisticated training that many clients appreciate. Michael Eades is a charity law expert, while Paul Buckle is the island's leading pensions expert.

PERSONAL TAX, TRUSTS AND PENSIONS

CAREY OLSEN
COLLAS DAY
OZANNES

Babbe Le Pelley Tostevin
Ogier & Le Masurier ✪

Ashton Allen

Conyers Dill & Pearman
Turcan Connell
Wedlake Bell Guernsey

Firms are listed A-Z in tiers which are ranked in order of priority
✪ Indicates firm displays contact details at the end of this chapter.

Collas Day's senior partner Peter Atkinson is recommended, while Jason Green advises on wills, succession, estate administration, trusts, and family law.

Ozannes' Roger Perrot has significant property and trust experience and a strong arbitration practice. St John Robilliard, the successful applicant in the landmark case of *Stuart-Hutcheson v Spread Trustees Ltd (2002)*, is a brilliant tax and trusts litigator.

Ashton Allen is a new firm set up by Pauline Allen from **Collas Day** and tax expert Raymond Ashton from *Carey Langlois*. It has significant private client and trust expertise.

REAL ESTATE

BABBE LE PELLEY TOSTEVIN
CAREY OLSEN
COLLAS DAY
OZANNES

Wedlake Bell Guernsey

Firms are listed A-Z in tiers which are ranked in order of priority

REAL ESTATE

Piers Dereham continues to grow the commercial property practice at **Babbe Le Pelley Tostevin**.

Carey Olsen's Ian Beattie advised on Guernsey's largest ever property deal, putting together a large team at short notice and seconding staff to the Guernsey property registrar's office to help complete the transaction.

Collas Day's Richard Ogier has 20 years' experience of Guernsey property law, and deals with residential and commercial conveyancing, including property company acquisitions and disposals, development projects, commercial leases, and planning and housing law.

Ozannes was involved in a number of the largest property transactions in 2002, including the acquisition of one of Guernsey's most important development sites.

Wedlake Bell Guernsey's partner Quentin Spicer advises on real estate investment and development for offshore and non-UK residents, funds, corporate entities and private clients.

OGIER & LE MASURIER

COUTTS HOUSE
LE TRUCHOT
ST PETER PORT GY1 1WD

Telephone: +44 1481 721672
Fax: +44 1481 721575
E-mail: info@ogier.com
Website: www.ogier.com

Languages
English, French

Other offices
Cayman Islands (Ogier & Boxalls), Jersey, London

Number of lawyers 110
at this office 11

Member
Association of European Lawyers (AEL); STEP; Guernsey International Lawyers Association; EVCA; BVCA

CATEGORIES OF WORK

Banking
William Simpson, Roger Le Tissier

Securitisation and structured finance
William Simpson, Roger Le Tissier

Mergers and acquisitions
William Simpson, Roger Le Tissier

Investment funds
Roger Le Tissier, William Simpson

Corporate and commercial
William Simpson, Roger Le Tissier

Corporate finance
William Simpson, Roger Le Tissier

Trust and estate planning
William Simpson, Marcus Leese

Private client
William Simpson, Marcus Leese

Employment law
William Simpson, Marcus Leese

Regulatory
Roger Le Tissier, Lisa Fisher

THE FIRM

Ogier is one of the leading and largest offshore providers of legal and administration services with approximately 370 employees across offices in Jersey, Guernsey, London and the Cayman Islands following its merger this year with Boxalls, a Cayman Islands law firm.

Ogier comprises Ogier & Le Masurier in the Channel Islands, Ogier & Boxalls in the Cayman Islands, and Ogier Fiduciary Services, its administration business. Ogier & Le Masurier, Guernsey continues to develop its strength in depth as one of the leading commercial law firms in the Channel Islands, delivering practical commercial advice to clients.

Ogier has developed an extensive portfolio of international clients and intermediaries and provides legal and administration services to them through its dedicated teams.

Ogier & Le Masurier provides its international private clients with Channel Island structures to preserve and manage their wealth as well as trust companies providing trustee services.

All work undertaken is managed by a team of specialists, led by a partner specifically selected to achieve the commercial objectives of the client. A large proportion of the firm's qualified lawyers have worked in some of the world's leading financial centres outside the Channel Islands and bring exceptional experience and expertise sought by today's clients.

AREAS OF PRACTICE

Banking: Ogier & Le Masurier is widely regarded as a premier firm for banking and international finance. It specialises in advising on all areas of banking, security, structured finance, banking regulation and the establishment of banks.

Corporate and commercial: Ogier's highly experienced and extensive team covers mergers and acquisitions, employment and privacy laws, IT/IP and e-commerce.

Securitisation: Ogier has one of the leading and largest securitisation and capital markets teams, with particular expertise in asset-backed securities, CBOs, ABCP and structured notes.

Structured finance: The structured finance team covers structured equity, asset finance and tax neutral transactions.

Investment funds: Ogier's fund practice comprises one of the largest funds teams in Guernsey, Jersey and the Cayman Islands, and advises on the establishment and structuring of funds as well as on regulatory and compliance issues.

Trusts: The trust and estate planning group has one of the largest trusts teams exclusively dedicated to advising trust companies, intermediaries and individuals in matters of trust law.

Private client: Ogier continues to develop and grow its private client practice. The private client team can provide a full range of administration services to trusts, companies and limited partnerships established in the Channel Islands, as well as to entities established elsewhere.

Fiduciary services: Ogier Fiduciary Services provides professional administration and accounting services to trusts, companies and limited partnerships.

HUNGARY

Population	10.2 million
Number of lawyers	8,000
Professional title	Attorney
Currency	Hungarian Florint (Ft)

Index

Hungary is bordered by Austria, Slovakia, Ukraine, Romania, Serbia and Montenegro, Croatia and Slovenia. Formerly a part of the Soviet bloc, in April 2003 84% of the ten-million-strong population voted in favour of joining the European Union. Accession will take place in May 2004. Hungary joined Nato in 1999.

Economically Hungary is among the most mature markets in the region. The private sector accounts for over 80% of its €111bn GDP and it has garnered over €19bn of foreign investment since 1990. Hungarian sovereign debt is now the second highest rated among all Central European transition countries.

In 2003 the country progressed with its privatisation process. The emphasis is on restructuring and selling the golden cows of Hungarian industry as well as those businesses seen as most complicated or sensitive in the initial rounds of privatisation. The completion of the Postabank privatisation in 2003 was a landmark in this sense. The core industries of mining, construction, food-processing, textiles, chemicals and pharmaceuticals production and auto manufacturing remain strong. However, Hungary is increasingly recognised as a viable low-cost destination for European back office work and this is expected to be a major growth area in 2004. Several major outsourcing projects already happened in 2003. Capital markets remain flat. The BSE was one of the best performing bourses in the region until the Russian Financial Crisis. Private equity and funds investment has made a resurgence in 2003 and investment levels were at near-record levels in late-2003, according to the EBRD.

Former Communist leader Peter Medgyessy was elected Prime Minister in 2002, representing the Socialist Party. Head of State is President Ferenc Madl whose five-year term expires in 2005.

BILLING

The high level of competition among foreign-associated firms in Budapest has caused massive downward pressure on hourly fees. The effects are greatest on innovative matters in which firms are desperate for experience, such as new privatisation projects, or for highly commoditised work and repeat instructions.

On the face of it lower legal fees can only be a good thing. However, reports suggest deals done at fixed fee or capped rates are often victim to proportionally lower levels of care and senior-level attention. As such clients requiring quality rather than cost-effectiveness are recommended to use a top-tier firm which is not offering cut price rates.

Quoted prices remain averaged at €350 per hour for partners and €100 per hour for assistants at foreign-affiliated law firms. Reports suggest some partners will commonly work for €100 per hour. At domestic firms prices are already lower and have been equally affected by the bidding war.

MARKETING

Insofar as marketing activities of internationally-focused commercial law firms go, the draconian domestic Bar remains a toothless dog. Its regulations prohibiting advertising by law firms, including the production of brochures and placement of professional cards are largely only heeded by domestic litigators and sole practitioners.

IN-HOUSE LAWYERS

Most of the large corporate houses in Hungary employ teams of in-house lawyers that will handle all but the most complex or specialist areas of law. In-house lawyers are admitted to the Bar and may appear in Court.

LEGAL MARKET

A high-potential economy, aesthetically pleasing capital and relatively conducive legal system have conspired to attract foreign law firms to Hungary in droves, since liberalisation started in 1989. By 2003 the market had reached saturation point with far more highly trained, qualified and experienced lawyers and indeed law firms than work. For clients this is good news. Firms are literally fighting each other for instructions while the emphasis on delivering quality, value-added products is unprecedented.

Due to a Hungarian Bar Association regulation that all foreign firms must work in association with a local law firm, most of the entrepreneurial Hungarian law firms have been assimilated into foreign networks.

Among these **Martonyi és Kajtár Baker & McKenzie**, **Köves Clifford Chance** and **Réczicza Law Firm White & Case LLP** have the longest histories of consistent involvement in the cream of domestic and international business in Hungary. All have immaculate connections, high capacities and the know-how to complete the most challenging transactions. **Berecz & Andrékó Linklaters** came to

The largest firms

1	Dezsö Réti & Antall Landwell	47
2	Köves Clifford Chance	40
	Martonyi és Kajtár Baker & McKenzie	40
	Ormai és Társai CMS Cameron McKenna	40
5	Oppenheim és Társai Freshfields Bruckhaus Deringer	37
6	Berecz & Andrékó Linklaters	25
7	Nagy és Trócsányi	24
8	SBG & K Patent and Law Office	23
	Szabó Kövári Teresák & Partners	23
10	Gide Loyrette Nouel	22
11	Réczicza Law Firm White & Case LLP	20
12	Allen & Overy	18
	DLA Weiss-Tessbach	18
	Szecskay Law Firm - Moquet Borde & Associés	18
15	Squire, Sanders & Dempsey LLP Komáromi és Erös Üqyvédi Iroda	17
16	Réti Szegheö and Partners, Attorneys at Law	15
17	Bogsch & Partners	14
	Law Office of Gárdos, Füredi, Mosonyi, Tomori	14
19	Burai - Kovács & Partners	12
	Bán S Szabó & Partners	12
21	Bálintfy & Partners Law Office	11
	Cerha Hempel Spiegelfeld Hlawati	11
	Hayhurst Robinson	11
24	Nógrádi Law Office	10
	Nörr Stiefenhofer Lutz	10

These figures represent the total number of lawyers in this country only, and have been supplied by the firms themselves. The figures should be accurate as at 1 January 2004.

the market later than its rivals but has lost no time leveraging its premier global reputation to attain a top-tier standing in Hungary. **Allen & Overy** remains widely revered for its outstanding banking and finance work and **Ormai És Társai CMS Cameron McKenna** for projects. **Weil, Gotshal & Manges** is the firm to turn to for M&A.

Other notable foreign-affiliated law firms are **DLA Weiss-Tessbach** (Austria), **Squire, Sanders & Dempsey LLP Komáromi és Erös Üqyvédi Iroda** and **Nagy & Pintér Hogan & Hartson**, **Szecskay Law Firm – Moquet Borde & Associés** (France) and **Oppenheim és Társai Freshfields Bruckhaus Deringer**.

Among the independent local law firms **Nagy És Trócsányi** is the oldest, largest and best known. **Forgó, Varga and Partners** has risen swiftly through the ranks and can now be recommended as a safe pair of hands. **Nógrádi Law Office** is the local firm several foreign lawyers use for referrals in Budapest and as such is highly recommended. **Sándor, Szegedi, Szent-Ivány**, **Law Office of Gárdos, Füredi, Mosonyi, Tomori**, **SBG & K Patent and Law Office**, **Burai – Kovács & Partners** and **Bogsch & Partners** are all solid commercial firms.

BANKING AND FINANCE

ALLEN & OVERY ✪
BERECZ & ANDRÉKÓ LINKLATERS ✪
KÖVES CLIFFORD CHANCE
ORMAI ÉS TÁRSAI CMS CAMERON McKENNA

DLA Weiss-Tessbach ✪
Hayhurst Robinson in association with Mátrai Law Office ✪
Martonyi és Kajtár Baker & McKenzie ✪
Oppenheim és Társai Freshfields Bruckhaus Deringer ✪
Réczicza Law Firm White & Case LLP
Réti Szegheö and Partners, Attorneys at Law ✪
Squarra & Partos (in association with Lovells) ✪
Weil, Gotshal & Manges ✪

Bihary, Balassa & Partners Attorneys at Law ✪
Burai - Kovács & Partners
Dezsö Réti & Antall Landwell ✪
Gárdos, Füredi, Mosonyi, Tomori, Law Office of
Gide Loyrette Nouel ✪
Nagy & Pintér Hogan & Hartson ✪
Nagy és Trócsányi ✪
Nörr Stiefenhofer Lutz ✪
Sándor, Szegedi, Szent-Ivány ✪
Szecskay Law Firm - Moquet Borde & Associés ✪

Firms are listed A-Z in tiers which are ranked in order of priority
✪ *Indicates firm displays contact details at the end of this chapter.*

BANKING AND FINANCE

Allen & Overy's top-notch banking team had another good transactional year in 2003, advising CIB Bank and Raiffeisen Securities as arranger and dealer on a HUF40bn (€151m) MTN programme for ÁÉB Bank and subsequently the first HUF10bn (€38m) note issue under it. It also advised Concorde Securities and ÁPV on the public offering of shares in the FHB Land Credit and Mortgage Bank Plc and its BSE listing. Practice head and international partner Marcell Németh is highly recommended.

Berecz & Andrékó Linklaters gained involvement in a large proportion of the relatively scant large banking and finance deals to take place in Hungary in 2003. Lending work included a multi-type $850m loan regarding film rights transfers and securitisation work, also in the film sector. Managing partner Csaba Berecz and Csilla Andrékó advise several major domestic and international banks.

Köves Clifford Chance has a large team of banking lawyers with specialists in derivatives, structured finance and securitisation. The 'highly esteemed' Richard Lock is practice head. In 2003 clients included ING Bank, OTP, Sumitomo and DZ Bank. Notably it advised the banks on the finance of Earth Tech and prepared a feasibility study for the first-ever securitisation of receivables of a major Hungarian company.

Ormai És Társai CMS Cameron McKenna's finance experience reflects its excellent standing in both the real estate and infrastructure tables. In 2003 representative transactions include advice to Credit Lyonnais on its €98m loan for the retrofit of AES Tisza Power Plant and to Trigránit Finance on the provision of a HUF3bn (€11m) loan. Other clients include OTP Bank and Vivendi subsidiary Matel.

Hayhurst Robinson in association with Mátrai Law Office continues to advise Gresco on the €58m financing of the Four Seasons Gresham Palace Hotel project. It has significant experience with multilateral investment banks and regional investment projects.

Martonyi és Kajtár Baker & McKenzie has experience with all the major lenders and with borrowers in most sectors. In 2003 it advised core client MOL on EBRD and ING Bank senior revolving credit facilities and credit extensions exceeding €600m. It also advised the lead arrangers on a loan to BorshodChem. Practice head Konrád Siegler and associate Annie Williams have been recommended.

Oppenheim és Társai Freshfields Bruckhaus Deringer worked for the National Bank of Canada and the Bank of Nova Scotia on a syndicated facility and notably advised Credit Lyonnais on aspects of the first-ever securitisation deal involving a Hungarian Bank.

Réczicza Law Firm White & Case LLP considerably ramped up its banking and finance team in 2003 by hiring Klára Kecskeméti from **Oppenheim és Társai Freshfields Bruckhaus Deringer** and Victoria Westcott from **Freshfields**

Bruckhaus Deringer in Paris, alongside Károly Fóti, previously regional general counsel for Citibank Hungary and Zsolt Lájer, formerly general counsel of Commerzbank Hungary. The firm completed several mid-size deals with Hungarian banks in 2003 and is well placed for an increasingly prominent position in this table as it leverages more domestic work.

Réti Szegheö and Partners, Attorneys at Law's Mihály Barcza has advised Hungarian banks FHB and Erste Bank on commercial and privatisation matters, Deutsche Bank on a tender for a 25% stake in MOL, and handled IPOs and forex transactions.

Squarra & Partos (in association with Lovells) benefits from a highly ranked banking and finance team in London and elsewhere in Europe, including Central Europe. It advised OTP Bank in 2003 and worked on project finance in the real estate sector.

Weil, Gotshal & Manges has experience of mid-size lending and borrowing, mainly with Hungarian clients. In 2003 it notably advised Citibank on the Hungarian aspects of a $550m loan and advised the EBRD in Hungary.

CAPITAL MARKETS

Allen & Overy featured on several of the most complex capital markets-related deals in 2003, including advising the Hungarian State Debt Management Agency on aspects of its €1bn eurobond offering

Berecz & Andrékó Linklaters advised on key transactions in 2003 including the first international mortgage bond issue of a Hungarian mortgage bank and a €1bn eurobond issue by a state agency. Clients include several of the largest domestic and foreign investment banks active in Hungary and consumer loan companies. Name partner Csilla Andrékó is recommended.

Köves Clifford Chance in 2003 advised a Dutch conglomerate on its public offer for Prímagáz Hungary followed by a squeeze-out and de-listing. 'A well-run deal' by recommended expert Richard Lock. The firm is well placed locally and globally for any increase in capital markets work.

Martonyi és Kajtár Baker & McKenzie has been involved in arguably the widest range of debt and equity securitisation transactions of any firm in Hungary. In 2003 it furthered that experience with advice to a significant Hungarian investment services provider on a securitisation, handling a domestic public offering of shares of an SMF fund and advising an international investment bank on the proposed international offering of shares and GDRs of a Hungarian blue-chip company. The firm also acts as counsel in connection with ADRs and US listings.Konrad Siegler is 'perhaps the most highly respected capital markets lawyer in Hungary'.

Réczicza Law Firm White & Case LLP has best been known for its equities work. With the slowdown in that sector the firm has successfully diversified into other areas, in 2003 including work by long-revered partner Zsuzsanna Kovács, and Károly Fóti on the structuring and implementation of a repo programme with Hungarian companies by Nomura, advising Perrier Vittel on the squeeze-out of minority shareholders under Hungarian capital markets legislation and Citibank on a swaps programme.

Hayhurst Robinson in association with Mátrai Law Office acted for Csopak in its public offering for outstanding shares on the BSE and the subsequent take-private.

Oppenheim és Társai Freshfields Bruckhaus Deringer has notable experience of takeovers. In 2003 it completed several interesting transactions with VCP Capital partners subsidiaries and advised Interbrew company Borsodi Sörgyár on management and employee share purchase plans.

Ormai és Társai CMS Cameron McKenna advised privatisation agency ÁPV on the €70m privatisation and public listing of Forrás.

Réti Szegheö and Partners, Attorneys at Law partner Mihály Barcza has prior experience of capital markets work. He now sits as a permanent arbitrator on capital markets issues.

Squarra & Partos (in association with Lovells) advised Hungarocamion on the dematerialisation of its shares and a treasury stock purchase of shares through a voluntary purchase offer. It also advised on restructuring of listed companies.

Squire, Sanders & Dempsey LLP Komáromi és Erös Üqyvédi Iroda's Akos Mester has capital markets experience.

Weil, Gotshal & Manges' David Dederick is recommended for M&A transactions involving listed companies.

CAPITAL MARKETS

- ALLEN & OVERY ✪
- BERECZ & ANDRÉKÓ LINKLATERS ✪
- KÖVES CLIFFORD CHANCE
- MARTONYI ÉS KAJTÁR BAKER & MCKENZIE ✪
- RÉCZICZA LAW FIRM WHITE & CASE LLP

- Gárdos, Füredi, Mosonyi, Tomori, Law Office of
- Gide Loyrette Nouel ✪
- Hayhurst Robinson in association with Mátrai Law Office ✪
- Oppenheim és Társai Freshfields Bruckhaus Deringer ✪
- Ormai és Társai CMS Cameron McKenna
- Réti Szegheö and Partners, Attorneys at Law ✪
- Squarra & Partos (in association with Lovells) ✪
- Squire, Sanders & Dempsey LLP Komáromi és Erös Üqyvédi Iroda ✪
- Weil, Gotshal & Manges ✪

Firms are listed A-Z in tiers which are ranked in order of priority
✪ Indicates firm displays contact details at the end of this chapter.

COMPETITION

Martonyi és Kajtár Baker & McKenzie's longstanding position as a market leader for competition advice in Hungary was reflected in 2003 with instructions from a leading Hungarian mobile telephony company in connection with two competition office investigations and a film distributor involved in a cartel investigation. The firm continues to advise on EU accession and merger control, benefiting from an excellent Brussels office. Zoltán Hegymegi-Barakonyi is 'number one in Hungary for competition work'.

Réczicza Law Firm White & Case LLP handled competition aspects of many of the largest M&A transactions taking place in or involving Hungary in recent years, with merger control specialist Szabolcs Posta and unfair competition disputes specialist Ildiko Csák achieving the strongest reputations. In 2003 it advised AIG on its acquisition of Vivendi Telecom and provided ongoing advice to Colgate-Palmolive on its unfair competition disputes.

Berecz & Andrékó Linklaters' work remains almost exclusively limited to merger control, albeit with some of the largest companies in Hungary. It has also handled aspects of unfair competition, abuse of dominant position and cartel agreements. Balázs Máthé is the best known individual. Dániel Kaszás is 'prolific'. Further development of this practice area is expected in 2004.

Köves Clifford Chance acted for UCI/Palace Cinemas on its defence against price cartel allegations by the Hungarian Competition Office. It also advised on merger control aspects of an acquisition in Hungary by GE Power Systems and handled aspects of an outsourcing arrangement by VistEon.

Oppenheim és Társai Freshfields Bruckhaus Deringer advised on aspects of the Motorway cartel case, representing the companies belonging

COMPETITION

- MARTONYI ÉS KAJTÁR BAKER & MCKENZIE ✪
- RÉCZICZA LAW FIRM WHITE & CASE LLP

- Berecz & Andrékó Linklaters ✪
- Köves Clifford Chance
- Oppenheim és Társai Freshfields Bruckhaus Deringer ✪

- Allen & Overy ✪
- Dezsö Réti & Antall Landwell
- Gide Loyrette Nouel ✪
- Nagy & Pintér Hogan & Hartson ✪
- Nagy és Trócsányi ✪
- Réti Szegheö and Partners, Attorneys at Law ✪
- SBG & K Patent and Law Office ✪
- Sándor, Szegedi, Szent-Ivány✪
- Szecskay Law Firm - Moquet Borde & Associés ✪
- Weil, Gotshal & Manges

Firms are listed A-Z in tiers which are ranked in order of priority
✪ Indicates firm displays contact details at the end of this chapter.

to the Colas and Strabag groups. The case is the largest currently ongoing cartel investigation before the Hungarian Competition Office and covers aspects of collusive tendering, bid rigging, market sharing and customer allocation. Merger control work in 2003 including advising Eon and Ruhrgas.

Allen & Overy remains popular among telecoms clients, in 2003 advising Pannon GSM on a cartel case involving all the Hungarian mobile market, as well as advising PanTel on the acquisition of Novacom. The firm is also advising Novartis Group on the acquisition of LEK. Senior associate Tamás Riesz is the firm's leading specialist. Emese Szitási worked in Brussels in 2003.

Nagy & Pintér Hogan & Hartson advised the largest Hungarian pharmaceutical company GedEon Richter on horizontal and vertical issues, Hungarian and EU market and data exclusivity matters. It also advised the Hungarian subsidiary of Merck and Co on harmonisation with the EU Transparency Directive.

Nagy és Trócsányi represented Pannon GSM and Philip Morris in various litigious and administrative proceedings in 2003, including a case before the Competition Office. It has experience of merger control procedures.

Réti Szegheö and Partners, Attorneys at Law has experience of cartel work, mainly with clients in the advertising sector. It also handled preliminary aspects of merger control for a merger in the banking sector in 2003.

SBG & K Patent and Law Office partner Katalin Szamosi is president of the Hungarian Competition Association. The firm is advising the state on bringing Hungarian competition laws in line with EU regulations.

Sándor, Szegedi, Szent-Iványן has experience of merger clearance proceedings involving foreign companies. In 2003 it advised local parties to a merger in the food industry.

Weil, Gotshal & Manges advises on competition matters insofar as they arise from its work with private equity, media and general corporate and commercial clients. The firm has a leading reputation in Hungary for M&A and is highly experienced in all aspects of merger clearance at the Hungarian and European levels.

CORPORATE AND COMMERCIAL

BERECZ & ANDRÉKÓ LINKLATERS ✪
KÖVES CLIFFORD CHANCE
MARTONYI ÉS KAJTÁR BAKER & MCKENZIE ✪
RÉCZICZA LAW FIRM WHITE & CASE LLP

Allen & Overy ✪
DLA Weiss-Tessbach ✪
Forgó, Varga and Partners ✪
Nagy & Pintér Hogan & Hartson ✪
Nagy és Trócsányi ✪
Oppenheim és Társai Freshfields Bruckhaus Deringer ✪
Ormai és Társai CMS Cameron McKenna
Squire, Sanders & Dempsey LLP Komáromi és Erös Üqyvédi Iroda ✪
Weil, Gotshal & Manges ✪

Bihary, Balassa & Partners Attorneys at Law ✪
Bogsch & Partners
Burai - Kovács & Partners
Dewey Ballantine LLP ✪
Dezsö Réti & Antall Landwell ✪
Gárdos, Füredi, Mosonyi, Tomori, Law Office of
Gide Loyrette Nouel ✪
Hayhurst Robinson in association with Mátrai Law Office ✪
Nógrádi Law Office ✪
Nörr Stiefenhofer Lutz ✪
Réti Szegheö and Partners, Attorneys at Law ✪
SBG & K Patent and Law Office ✪
Sándor, Szegedi, Szent-Ivány ✪
Squarra & Partos (in association with Lovells) ✪
Szecskay Law Firm - Moquet Borde & Associés ✪

Bálintfy & Partners Law Office
Bán S Szabó & Partners
Bárd, Cseri & Partners
Beiten Burkhardt Déri & Lovrecz
Füsthy & Martony Law Office
Haarmann Hemmelrath ✪
Heinzelman és Társai
Kovacs Barborjak Kende Kendvai & Katona
Marai & Associates
Radványi & Partners
Simon, Bûrös & Partners

Firms are listed A-Z in tiers which are ranked in order of priority
✪ Indicates firm displays contact details at the end of this chapter.

CORPORATE AND COMMERCIAL

Berecz & Andrékó Linklaters' corporate and commercial practice was very active with privatisation and M&A transactions in 2003. In addition it worked with telecoms, media, financial services and energy clients including Pannon GSM, Winterthur and BP.

Köves Clifford Chance is clearly a corporate and commercial leader, with some of the broadest high-end experience of any firm in Hungary. In 2003, as well as advising on a Postabank bid, it advised Alcoa Inc, one of the largest investors in Hungary, on the restructuring of all its Hungarian operations, including corporate and tax aspects. It continues to advise household names such as Mastercard. Richard Lock is highly recommended for general advice, Péter Lakatos for TMT and Zoltán Faludi for energy.

Martonyi és Kajtár Baker & McKenzie has been lead counsel to multinationals including Ford, Suzuki, AT&T, Johnson Controls and Pioneer on their corporate and commercial activities in Hungary, for well over a decade. It is also general counsel to Pepsi-Cola. In 2003 it advised aviation electronics group Rockwell & Collins on distributor agreements and Hitachi on the localisation of software licences. Practice head Géza Kajtár is supported by 11 associates.

Réczicza Law Firm White & Case LLP is regular outside counsel to household names such as Colgate-Palmolive, advising on all matters including employment, leasing, advertising and contracts. The firm is best known for its outstanding transactional practice which in 2003 advised on complex deals including Nestlé's spin-off of its frozen vegetables subsidiary and Electricité de France's €95.5m sale of a stake in Északdunántúli Áramszolgáltató, the Hungarian electricity distribution company, to EON Hungária by mandatory public tender offer. Rob Irving is unreservedly recommended, as are Istvan Réczicza and Zsuzsanna Kovács.

Allen & Overy has not leveraged much work from its outstanding international network. Nonetheless it maintains a respectable client base in Hungary including three major mobile telecoms companies which it advises on regulatory, infrastructure and corporate issues. In 2003 the firm won a heavily contested tender process to advise state privatisation agency ÁPV on the privatisation of Postabank, the largest deal in Hungary in 2003. Éva Hegedus is the best known individual and only corporate partner.

Forgó, Varga and Partners is primarily recommended to mid-cap Hungarian companies and foreign investors with transactional requirements. The firm has a particular specialisation in corporate advice to TMT clients. It acts for big names including Hungarian ISP Elender/PSINet, and web portal index.hu.

Nagy & Pintér Hogan & Hartson has good mid-cap experience with Hungarian and US clients, with Kornelia Nagy-Koppany the best known individual. In 2003 it advised on the restructuring of multiplex operator InterCom and the purchase of a business quota for an Australian company. The firm has a strong London office.

Nagy És Trócsányi has a large core client base and handles frequent instructions from foreign firms without Budapest offices. In 2003 it won an instruction from Peugeot to handle all negotiations for the site selection of its Hungarian manufacturing plant.

Oppenheim és Társai Freshfields Bruckhaus Deringer worked with some household names in 2003, including counselling Elly Lilly on a 'media crisis', acting as an external counsel for Mars and advising GE Hungary on setting up a European Operation Services Division. Zsolt Zamostny is practice head.

Ormai És Társai CMS Cameron McKenna's corporate practice is almost exclusively pre-occupied with handling transactional matters, in 2003 including major privatisations in the banking sector and M&A matters. The firm also advises Hungarian airline Malév on its activities in 36 jurisdictions and handles corporate and commercial matters for several of **CMS Cameron McKenna**'s international clients.

Squire, Sanders & Dempsey LLP Komáromi és Erös Üqyvédi Iroda advises multinationals including GE, Audi and Tesco in Hungary. Notably in 2003 it advised Audi on the construction of an engine factory in western Hungary and represented global communications company Saatchi & Saatchi SRL throughout its negotiation and signing of a €1.3m contract with the European Commission and Romanian government.

Weil, Gotshal & Manges continues to work on general corporate and commercial matters but is best known for its top-tier M&A and private equity work. Clients include HBO, Pogo Producing Company, US Steel Kosice and UCB Hungary. Managing partner David Dederick is highly regarded in Budapest as a 'quality-driven practitioner'.

Bihary, Balassa & Partners Attorneys at Law is active across the board but specialises in corporate aspects of real estate and banking.

Bogsch & Partners is general counsel to some companies in Hungary but remains almost exclusively focused on intellectual property and to a lesser extent competition law.

Burai – Kovács & Partners was previously the *Andersen Legal* firm in Hungary. As such it has first-class experience of all commoditised corporate and commercial legal work. It also has some reputation for energy work, based around name partner János Burai–Kovacs.

Dewey Ballantine LLP maintains an office in Budapest primarily to service its major energy clients. Typical corporate and commercial instructions in 2003 include advice to ADM International on its investment in Hungary and handling M&A in the energy sector. Beáta Tátrai is managing partner.

Dezsö Réti & Antall Landwell is affiliated with Big Four accountant PricewaterhouseCoopers. It is broadly experienced in all aspects of company formation and administration as well as offshore company establishment and management. In 2003 a team of lawyers joined the firm from German rival MDP **Haarmann Hemmelrath** including managing partner Mark Madl.

Law Office of Gárdos, Füredi, Mosonyi, Tomori is a Hungarian corporate law-focused office.

Gide Loyrette Nouel works mainly with French investors and Hungarian companies with interests in Francophone regions.

Hayhurst Robinson in association with Mátrai Law Office has offices in Bucharest, Bulgaria and Belgrade, in addition to Budapest. The firm has leading experience with investors in the energy, financial services, real estate and manufacturing sectors. In Budapest Ferenc Matrai and Robert Hayhurst are well known individuals.

Nógrádi Law Office is recommended primarily to Israeli clients and all mid-cap companies with corporate, real estate, and litigious interests in Hungary. Name partner Péter Nógrádi is the best known individual.

Réti Szegheö and Partners, Attorneys at Law is recommended for small and mid-cap corporate work with Hungarian companies and advice on the regulatory environment for foreigners. Clients include JC Decaux, Erste Group, Skanska, WPP Group and several well-known German clients.

SBG & K Patent and Law Office is an intellectual property, patent and trade mark office with extensive contentious experience and some wider corporate and commercial capabilities. It represents several international clients mainly on competition, intellectual property and IT matters as well as advising small and mid-cap companies. Managing partner Katalin Szamosi is head of corporate.

Sándor, Szegedi, Szent-Ivány was until 2003 a part of the *Denton International* network. It continues its close association with the UK firm – **Denton Wilde Sapte** – and has excellent links with other mid-size law firms in the region. Clients include a major automotive manufacturer and other international companies with general corporate, M&A and real estate requirements, including negotiations with the privatisation agency ÁPV.

Squarra & Partos (in association with Lovells) in 2003 gained further experience of large restructuring projects, including advising Hungarian state shipping company Mahart on the pre-privatisation process, and Italian steel manufacturer Cogne on the restructuring and liquidation of its Hungarian subsidiary RAM.

Szecskay Law Firm – Moquet Borde & Associés has an international client base that includes Vivendi and Auchan.

DISPUTE RESOLUTION

The vast majority of contentious work in Hungary is handled by sole practitioners. Of the internationally recognised firms in Budapest several do nonetheless have dedicated disputes practices.

Köves Clifford Chance represented the Hungarian Government in a major investment protection dispute that progressed to arbitration in 2003. It also advised Deloitte & Touche on the $300m litigation initiated by the Hungarian State regarding the audit of Postabank. Name partner Peter Köves is 'one of the most highly respected disputes experts in Hungary'.

Nagy és Trócsányi name partner Peter Nagy is a heavyweight player in litigation in Hungary. In 2003 he advised the National Radio and Television Board in a dispute with a commercial radio station. He has also counselled clients on arbitration and works regularly with Philip Morris. Highly recommended.

Réczicza Law Firm White & Case LLP has litigation, arbitration and mediation experience with public and private sector clients including the Hungarian State before ICSID, energy group MVM in an environmental arbitration and pharmaceutical giants Bayer and Schering at the Hungarian and European levels. István Réczicza is acknowledged as a giant of Hungarian dispute resolution and corporate law.

DISPUTE RESOLUTION

Köves Clifford Chance
Nagy és Trócsányi ✪
Réczicza Law Firm White & Case LLP
Squire, Sanders & Dempsey LLP Komáromi és Erös Üqyvédi Iroda ✪
Szecskay Law Firm - Moquet Borde & Associés ✪

Bogsch & Partners
Burai - Kovács & Partners
Danubia
Forgó, Varga and Partners ✪
Martonyi és Kajtár Baker & McKenzie ✪
Nógrádi Law Office ✪
Oppenheim és Társai Freshfields Bruckhaus Deringer ✪
Weil, Gotshal & Manges ✪

Bálintfy & Partners Law Office
Dezsö Réti & Antall Landwell ✪
Gárdos, Füredi, Mosonyi, Tomori, Law Office of
Réti Szegheö and Partners, Attorneys at Law ✪
SBG & K Patent and Law Office ✪
Sándor, Szegedi, Szent-Ivány ✪

Firms are listed A-Z in tiers which are ranked in order of priority
✪ Indicates firm displays contact details at the end of this chapter.

Squire, Sanders & Dempsey LLP Komáromi és Erös Üqyvédi Iroda's Judit Kelemen was formerly a judge at the Central District Court. In 2003 she led the firm's advice to nuclear power plant company Paks in its dispute with Fromatome, and continued to advise Budapest Bank on contentious aspects of its portfolio. Peter Komaromi has international arbitration experience.

Szecskay Law Firm – Moquet Borde & Associés is well known for its arbitration work. US-educated of-counsel Laurent Niddam has been highlighted as 'highly capable'.

Bogsch & Partners and **Danubia** are both niche intellectual property firms and have extensive contentious experience.

Burai – Kovács & Partners name partner János Burai-Kovács is a highly experienced arbitrator and litigator. The firm is best known for its energy work and also handles tax litigation.

Forgó, Varga and Partners promoted the 'excellent' Gábor Damjanovic to partner in 2003, recognising the superb dispute settlement practice he has built up at the firm. Litigation experience includes advice to a US software distribution company on Hungarian aspects of a US case, a client with a dispute before the state debt collection agency, and Carte Blanche in an intellectual property infringement case. Arbitration work includes advice to ÁPV on a privatisation agreement dispute before the Austrian Chamber of Commerce.

Martonyi és Kajtár Baker & McKenzie's star international corporate partner Géza Kajtár has experience of litigation and arbitration cases involving international companies, although his practice is largely non-contentious. Former Hungarian foreign minister and founding partner of **Martonyi és Kajtár Baker & McKenzie**, János Martonyi is highly recommended for advice pertaining to international trade disputes and public international law as well as commercial litigation and arbitration.

Nógrádi Law Office invested in its disputes practice in 2003. It subsequently advised wholesaler Fotex on a contentious case and worked on labour law cases.

Oppenheim és Társai Freshfields Bruckhaus Deringer is recommended for litigation arising from competition, intellectual property and construction. Clients have included cement producer Holcim Hungária which challenged a merger control clearance and publishing company Sanoma Budapest Kiadói in its dispute with Axel Springer Kiadói.

Weil, Gotshal & Manges' disputes practice reflects the firm's strengths in securities, corporate and media. In 2003 it advised HBO Central Europe on a competition case against Canal+ in the Hungarian Supreme Court, two US Government enterprise funds and HJ Heinz on corporate and securities litigation and arbitration proceedings.

Dezsö Réti & Antall Landwell has tax litigation experience.

Réti Szegheö and Partners, Attorneys at Law has represented several state owned entities in contentious matters. It also handles litigation for Ernst Bank Hungary Investment Ltd. Tamás Éless has ADR experience and is a chartered mediator.

SBG & K Patent and Law Office is recommended for contentious intellectual property matters and competition law advice, including hearings before the Competition Commission.

ENERGY

Berecz & Andrékó Linklaters in 2003 advised regular client RWE/Mátrai power plant on power purchase agreements with MVM in the electricity sector and in negotiations with the Hungarian Energy Office. The firm also completed a major downstream transaction for prestigious global client BP involving the sale of 60 petrol stations.

Köves Clifford Chance partner Zoltan Faludi has one of the best reputations for energy-related work of any lawyer in Hungary. Praised for the 'breadth and exactitude' of his knowledge, in 2003 he demonstrated his awesome prowess with advice to ING in connection with the financing of the first Hungarian private waste water facility construction project for the national oil and gas company MOL.

Martonyi és Kajtár Baker & McKenzie has a long-standing arrangement with Hungarian oil major MOL. The firm has handled all aspects of privatisation, M&A, regulatory and finance matters with that company. Notably in 2003 it advised MOL on the sale of its oil drilling subsidiary by auction.

Réczicza Law Firm White & Case LLP has a dominant position in the provision of advice to MVM in no small part due to the outstanding respect with which István Réczicza is held by the public sector. In 2003 the firm advised MVM on the renegotiation of power purchase agreements in compliance with EU directives. It also advised on a major wind power project, completed a study for MAVIR (the independent operator of the Hungarian electricity grid) and advised Gaz de France, Electricité de France and PannonPower on transactional matters. Highly recommended Rob Irving and Zsuzsanna Kovacs also have significant experience in this area.

Allen & Overy is highly recommended for finance aspects of all energy projects, while **Burai – Kovács & Partners** managing partner János Burai-Kovacs continues to advise multinational oil-major Exxon and MOL on Hungarian corporate matters.

Dewey Ballantine LLP advised World Minerals Inc on the acquisition of a Hungarian mine in 2003. The firm has experience of PPAs and M&A transactions in the energy sector in Hungary and has an excellent global reputation for energy work.

Oppenheim és Társai Freshfields Bruckhaus Deringer has advised clients from German-speaking Europe including RWE and EON on aspects of their energy operations in Hungary. Experience includes advice on liberalisation, regulation, negotiations and M&A. Well-known individual and managing partner Ulrike Rein is practice head.

ENERGY

BERECZ & ANDRÉKÓ LINKLATERS ✪
KÖVES CLIFFORD CHANCE
MARTONYI ÉS KAJTÁR BAKER & MCKENZIE ✪
RÉCZICZA LAW FIRM WHITE & CASE LLP

Allen & Overy ✪
Burai - Kovács & Partners
Dewey Ballantine LLP ✪
Oppenheim és Társai Freshfields Bruckhaus Deringer ✪
Ormai és Társai CMS Cameron McKenna
Squire, Sanders & Dempsey LLP Komáromi és Erös Üqyvédi Iroda ✪
Weil, Gotshal & Manges ✪

Dezsö Réti & Antall Landwell ✪
Gide Loyrette Nouel ✪
Hayhurst Robinson in association with Mátrai Law Office ✪
Sándor, Szegedi, Szent-Ivány ✪
Szecskay Law Firm - Moquet Borde & Associés ✪

Firms are listed A-Z in tiers which are ranked in order of priority
✪ Indicates firm displays contact details at the end of this chapter.

Ormai és Társai CMS Cameron McKenna has a major strength in project finance work. As well as a leading finance practice the firm also advises PannonPower and Budapest Power Plant on construction and regulation for their facilities.

Squire, Sanders & Dempsey LLP Komáromi és Erös Üqyvédi Iroda represented Tyco Group company Earth Tech in the retrofit of the wastewater and incinerator facility of oil company MOL, including the negotiations for a 15-year operating lease.

Weil, Gotshal & Manges has advised TVK, El Paso Production Company, BP, and Pogo Producing Company on all aspects of corporate and commercial activities, finance, exploration and distribution agreements and regulatory changes.

Dezsö Réti & Antall Landwell partner György Antall has worked with the Hungarian energy regulator. In 2003 he advised foreign investors on entry to the Hungarian electricity and gas markets. New partner Mark Madl has niche experience of wind farm law.

Gide Loyrette Nouel is corporate counsel to several French companies in Hungary, including some in the energy sector.

INTELLECTUAL PROPERTY

Danubia and **SBG & K Patent And Law Office** remain the unredoubtable captains of intellectual property advice in Hungary. Both firms have specialised in intellectual property for over a decade and have extensive experience of all aspects of patents and trade marks, utility models, designs and copyright, as well as contentious advice. Both firms also offer wider corporate and commercial capabilities through **Bogsch & Partners** and in-house expertise respectively.

Berecz & Andrékó Linklaters' lateral hire of Andrea Simandí as senior associate from **Bogsch &**

INTELLECTUAL PROPERTY

DANUBIA
SBG & K PATENT AND LAW OFFICE ✪

BERECZ & ANDRÉKÓ LINKLATERS ✪

Oppenheim és Társai Freshfields Bruckhaus Deringer ✪
Szecskay Law Firm - Moquet Borde & Associés ✪

Bogsch & Partners
Dezsö Réti & Antall Landwell ✪
Köves Clifford Chance
Martonyi és Kajtár Baker & McKenzie ✪
Nagy és Trócsányi ✪
Nógrádi Law Office ✪
Réti Szegheö and Partners, Attorneys at Law ✪
Sándor, Szegedi, Szent-Ivány ✪

Firms are listed A-Z in tiers which are ranked in order of priority
✪ Indicates firm displays contact details at the end of this chapter.

Partners has in two years yielded an accomplished, if understated, largely transactional-focused intellectual property practice with solid experience advising top tier clients. It also boasts trade mark litigation, film rights, copyright and licensing experience and, in 2003 advised the Hungarian Patent Office on a multi-jurisdictional matter.

Oppenheim és Társai Freshfields Bruckhaus Deringer won new instructions from Mars and General Electric in 2003. This on top of already impressive instructions from Microsoft and publishing house Sanoma and experience of data protection, trade mark and domain name registration and contentious issues for clients in the software and media sectors ensures the firm moves up the table this year.

Szecskay Law Firm – Moquet Borde & Associés managing partner András Szecskay is an intellectual property expert, as is Judit Budai. The firm has a large French speaking client base.

Dezsö Réti & Antall Landwell advises media clients in intellectual property.

Köves Clifford Chance TMT expert Péter Lakatos handles intellectual property advice for some of the firm's larger clients.

Martonyi és Kajtár Baker & McKenzie has been recommended for intellectual property matters arising from its large IT practice.

Nógrádi Law Office name partner Péter Nógrádi advises several of his Israeli clients on intellectual property aspects of their Hungarian investments.

Réti Szegheö and Partners, Attorneys at Law has advised Caterpillar, Ford, Mazda and Scotch Whiskey on intellectual property enforcement actions in Hungary.

MERGERS AND ACQUISITIONS

ALLEN & OVERY ✪
BERECZ & ANDRÉKÓ LINKLATERS ✪
KÖVES CLIFFORD CHANCE
MARTONYI ÉS KAJTÁR BAKER & MCKENZIE ✪
RÉCZICZA LAW FIRM WHITE & CASE LLP
WEIL, GOTSHAL & MANGES ✪

Forgó, Varga and Partners ✪
Nagy és Trócsányi ✪
Oppenheim és Társai Freshfields Bruckhaus Deringer ✪
Ormai és Társai CMS Cameron McKenna
Squire, Sanders & Dempsey LLP Komáromi és Erös Üqyvédi Iroda ✪

DLA Weiss-Tessbach ✪
Dewey Ballantine LLP ✪
Dezsö Réti & Antall Landwell ✪
Gide Loyrette Nouel ✪
Hayhurst Robinson in association with Mátrai Law Office ✪
Nagy & Pintér Hogan & Hartson ✪
Nógrádi Law Office ✪
Réti Szegheö and Partners, Attorneys at Law ✪
Sándor, Szegedi, Szent-Ivány✪
Squarra & Partos (in association with Lovells) ✪
Szecskay Law Firm - Moquet Borde & Associés ✪

Bogsch & Partners
Burai - Kovács & Partners
Gárdos, Füredi, Mosonyi, Tomori, Law Office of
Nörr Stiefenhofer Lutz ✪
SBG & K Patent and Law Office ✪

Firms are listed A-Z in tiers which are ranked in order of priority
✪ Indicates firm displays contact details at the end of this chapter.

MERGERS AND ACQUISITIONS

Allen & Overy gained valuable experience with privatisation agency ÁPV, advising it and Concorde Securities on the high-profile privatisation of Postabank – one of the most sought after deals of 2003 and easily the largest of the year. Managing partner Éva Hegedus and senior associate Alex Cook were the two most senior individuals involved. Other transactions in 2003 included advice to PanTel on its acquisition of alternative telecoms provider Novacom.

Berecz & Andrékó Linklaters has an outstanding portfolio of M&A clients, in 2003 including BP, Vodafone and Ernst & Young. Notable deals included Balázs Máthé's advice to Telenor Mobile on the post-completion restructuring of its holding companies after the acquisition of outstanding shares in Pannon GSM, including a capital increase and liquidations. It also advised Telenor Business Solutions on the MBO of Nextra Hungary and OTP Bank in its bid for the privatisation of Postabank.

Köves Clifford Chance has quantifiable experience across a wide range of M&A scenarios. In 2003 it handled big-ticket work including a bid for the Postabank privatisation, the sale of a business by Lafarge, and working with Dutch conglomerate SHV on its public offer for Prímagáz Hungary including the subsequent squeeze-out and de-listing – a 'well run public to private' deal.

Martonyi és Kajtár Baker & McKenzie has excellent experience of M&A in Hungary. In 2003 alongside an active corporate and commercial portfolio, the firm advised Wallis, the largest Hungarian investment holding company, Tesco, Degussa, MOL, and MATÁV both domestically and regionally. Ines Radmilovic and Pál Takács have excellent experience in a wide range of industries.

Réczicza Law Firm White & Case LLP is a 'safe pair of hands' for all corporate and M&A work. In Rob Irving, István Reczicza and Zsuzsanna Kovács it fields one of the most senior teams on the market, reinforced by a superior regional and international network. In 2003 it notably advised AIG subsidiaries on the acquisition of Vivendi Telecoms. It also advised AIG-CET Capital Management and the EBRD on the $600m sale by TriGranit of assets in Budapest and Bratislava – the largest commercial real estate transaction in Central Europe to date.

Weil, Gotshal & Manges managing partner David Dederick is an 'expert' for innovative and complex M&A advice involving domestic and foreign companies at all levels. Building on a superb track record in 2003, the firm advised TriGranit throughout the above-mentioned MBO, the largest of its kind in Central European history. It also provided ongoing advice to El Paso Oil & Gas in its planned disposal of $3.4bn in non-core Central European assets, and continued to represent the Hungarian American Enterprise Fund on a number of sales and acquisitions. The firm also has an outstanding private equity practice.

Forgó, Varga and Partners has solid experience advising Hungarian and foreign M&A participants as well as acting as local counsel for major US and UK firms. In 2003 it handled an impressively diverse portfolio of transactions including acquisitions of listed pharmaceutical companies, the sale of a stake in a Hungarian commercial television channel and working with foreign and domestic private equity groups. Widely experienced managing partner Zoltán Forgó is the best known individual for this kind of work.

Nagy és Trócsányi has excellent M&A experience in the small to mid-cap range. It notably advised shareholders in Hungarian business magazine HVG on the negotiations and sale of a 75% stake. It has extensive experience acting as Hungarian counsel on international transactions.

Oppenheim és Társai Freshfields Bruckhaus Deringer advised new client Tengelmann on the transfer of Kaiser supermarkets to Soar and the acquisition of new assets. It also worked with logistics company UPS on Hungarian aspects of its multi-jurisdictional merger with Fritz/UNI-DATA, and counselled Sumitomo Corporation on the acquisition of a Hungarian automotive supplier.

Ormai és Társai CMS Cameron McKenna had an extremely successful 2003 on the corporate front, advising Erste Bank in its €400m acquisition of Postabank, and privatisation agency ÁPV on the €70m privatisation and public listing of Forrás. It also advised SanPaolo IMI International on its €40m public takeover of Inter Europa Bank and Austrian cement manufacturer Wopfinger on an acquisition from cement group Lafarge.

Squire, Sanders & Dempsey LLP Komáromi és Erös Üqyvédi Iroda represents major corporations including Audi, GE and Tesco on aspects of their Hungarian businesses, in 2003 including several M&A transactions.

Dewey Ballantine LLP remains most active with energy clients in Hungary, reflected in 2003 with instructions from US Steel Kosice on acquisitions in Serbia and Montenegro and NRG Energy in connection with the sale of its European operations, including the Csepel power plant in Hungary.

Dezsö Réti & Antall Landwell continues its assault on the transactional market in Hungary, in 2003 advising PricewaterhouseCoopers on a €1bn asset transaction, handling sales and acquisitions in the newspaper industry and advising a real estate fund manager on the acquisition of holding companies.

Gide Loyrette Nouel advises several French companies in Hungary.

Hayhurst Robinson in association with Mátrai Law Office Bucharest partner Todd Robinson has been recommended for his regional M&A and privatisation work, including in Hungary.

Nagy & Pintér Hogan & Hartson worked in conjunction with **Hogan & Hartson** London to advise MOL on aspects of its acquisition of a 1% stake in Croatian oil and gas company INA. It also advised Amcor on an acquisition and Fairchild Corporation on a sale. Kornelia Nagy-Koppany is recommended.

Nógrádi Law Office advised a large Dutch conglomerate on its purchase of a network of Hungarian companies for a value exceeding €500m, proving the firm's burgeoning transactional capacity. The firm has a large real estate practice and Peter Nógrádi is particularly recommended to Israeli clients.

Réti Szegheö and Partners, Attorneys at Law advised BNP Paribas in the preparatory stages of an acquisition in the banking sector in 2003. It has handled acquisitions in the food sector.

Squarra & Partos (in association with Lovells) boosted its M&A experience in 2003 with involvement in a multinational acquisition in the automotive sector. It also handled the sale of a toxicological research company to a Canadian investor and advised an ABB business on an acquisition.

PROJECT FINANCE

Berecz & Andrékó Linklaters was Hungarian counsel to several major global deals co-ordinated by other **Linklaters** offices in 2003. The firm advised Credit Suisse First Boston on its €769m financing to TotalFinaElf which included complex Hungarian regulatory issues. Name partner Csilla Andrékó is a widely respected project finance expert.

Köves Clifford Chance carries a sterling reputation for finance advice to project sponsors in Hungary. In 2003 the firm advised a consortium led by ING Bank on a €600m facility to MOL, Sumitomo on a €500m syndicated loan to the Republic of Hungary and ING Bank on the first private water infrastructure finance deal in Hungary. Banking expert Péter Köves and energy expert Zoltán Faludi are both leading lights and 'make a formidable team'.

Ormai és Társai CMS Cameron McKenna moves up the tables this year based on the consistent recommendations its energy, projects and construction team has garnered from peers and clients. It is a pre-eminent source of advice to borrowers, having an intimate knowledge of most forms of infrastructure and associated regulations in Hungary and Central Europe. PannonPower is a highly active client.

Allen & Overy is highly recommended to international and local banks involved in project finance in Hungary. It also has experience with borrowers. In 2003 it advised on property finance and several loans to the power industry. Notably it acted for K&H Bank in its late-2002 project finance agreement with PannonPower, and AES-Tiszai in relation to a €100m syndicated project finance loan. Marcell Németh is practice head.

DLA Weiss-Tessbach advises some German and Austrian lenders on their activities in Hungary.

Dewey Ballantine LLP continued to advise the Hungarian Ministry of Transport and Economy on its renegotiation of the M5 Motorway Concession Contract.

Hayhurst Robinson in association with Mátrai Law Office advises a Hungarian State Ministry on aspects of the BOT construction, financing and development of Hungary's new €110m national sports and entertainment arena.

Martonyi és Kajtár Baker & McKenzie has represented core client MOL on various credit raising ventures in 2003, including securing several EBRD credit facilities and euro-denominated revolving credit facilities. 'Massively experienced' banking partner Konrád Siegler also advised AÉB, CIT, OTP Bank and ING Bank as lead arrangers of an unsecured facility provided to BorschodChem and another consortium of domestic and international banks on the multi-million euro credit facility for the national motorway programme.

Nagy és Trócsányi advises Banca Commerciala Italiana subsidiaries CIB Bank and CIB Leasing on project finance deals. It has worked with venture capitalists and counselled US law firms on Hungarian law.

Oppenheim és Társai Freshfields Bruckhaus Deringer has advised lenders and borrowers in Hungary primarily on real estate and energy projects.

Réczicza Law Firm White & Case LLP in 2003 acted for Electricité de France as sponsor of the project financing of a combined cycle cogeneration gas plant. The firm has impressive experience of project finance and energy projects in Hungary and worldwide.

Squarra & Partos (in association with Lovells) has notable expertise of PPP in London which it is leveraging off in Hungary with advice to the Ministry of Economy and Transport on pilot PPP projects in Hungary. The firm is also working on project finance in the real estate sector, advising RBS and Kereskedelmi & Hitel Bank.

Weil, Gotshal & Manges' David Dederick has top-notch project finance experience. In 2003 the firm did well during a slack year, advising Synergy and another project company on the €10m non-recourse project financing of a water treatment facility in northern Hungary, and TVK Erömü on the €45m finance arrangement for a power plant construction.

PROJECT FINANCE

BERECZ & ANDRÉKÓ LINKLATERS ✪
KÖVES CLIFFORD CHANCE
ORMAI ÉS TÁRSAI CMS CAMERON McKENNA

Allen & Overy ✪
DLA Weiss-Tessbach ✪
Dewey Ballantine LLP ✪
Hayhurst Robinson in association with Mátrai Law Office ✪
Martonyi és Kajtár Baker & McKenzie ✪
Nagy és Trócsányi ✪
Oppenheim és Társai Freshfields Bruckhaus Deringer ✪
Réczicza Law Firm White & Case LLP
Squarra & Partos (in association with Lovells) ✪
Weil, Gotshal & Manges ✪

Firms are listed A-Z in tiers which are ranked in order of priority
✪ *Indicates firm displays contact details at the end of this chapter.*

REAL ESTATE

Ormai És Társai CMS Cameron McKenna's focused strategy in Hungary has in no sector realised more success than real estate. The firm is recognised by clients and competitors alike as pre-eminent for all aspects of construction and real estate advice. It has traditionally worked with major developers such as PannonPower but has increasingly significant experience with investment banks including Credit Lyonnais Bank. Real estate clients include GTC International and Dixons. 'Impressive and commercial' István Kövári heads the energy, projects and construction practice. Gabriella Ormai and Gábor Czike are 'strong'.

DLA Weiss-Tessbach advises a number of Austrian and German construction companies on their activities in Hungary.

Dezsö Réti & Antall Landwell advises several large German construction companies and investment funds on Hungarian real estate matters. Name partner Attila Dezsö and real estate/environment specialist Katalin Veszely are the best known individuals in this practice.

Köves Clifford Chance partner Richard Lock, and Zsolt Osi lead a dedicated real estate practice with structuring, development, finance and construction. The firm advised Pricoa on a regional commercial property investment in 2003. It also advised Emerson Electric in a matter before the Hungarian environmental authorities.

Martonyi és Kajtár Baker & McKenzie's international reputation for real estate work is reflected in Budapest with an ongoing mandate from Tesco for site acquisitions and high-volume leases in Hungary. In 2003 the firm also advised on a major greenfield investment by an Austrian company and prepared an environmental study of contaminated land regimes for Transelektro.

REAL ESTATE

ORMAI ÉS TÁRSAI CMS CAMERON McKENNA

- DLA Weiss-Tessbach ✪
- Dezsö Réti & Antall Landwell ✪
- Köves Clifford Chance
- Martonyi és Kajtár Baker & McKenzie ✪
- Nagy és Trócsányi ✪
- Nógrádi Law Office ✪
- Oppenheim és Társai Freshfields Bruckhaus Deringer ✪
- Réczicza Law Firm White & Case LLP
- Squire, Sanders & Dempsey LLP Komáromi és Erös Üqyvédi Iroda ✪
- Weil, Gotshal & Manges ✪

- Allen & Overy ✪
- Burai - Kovács & Partners
- Gide Loyrette Nouel ✪
- Haarmann Hemmelrath ✪
- Hayhurst Robinson in association with Mátrai Law Office ✪
- Nagy & Pintér Hogan & Hartson ✪
- Nörr Stiefenhofer Lutz ✪
- Réti Szegheö and Partners, Attorneys at Law ✪
- Sándor, Szegedi, Szent-Ivány ✪
- Squarra & Partos (in association with Lovells) ✪
- Szecskay Law Firm - Moquet Borde & Associés ✪

Firms are listed A-Z in tiers which are ranked in order of priority

✪ *Indicates firm displays contact details at the end of this chapter.*

Nagy és Trócsányi advised Toyota-Peugeot and Peugeot-Citroen on manufacturing plant investments in Hungary. It also represents outsourcing group Trammel Crow Wallis on real estate matters in Hungary and Lexmark, Volksbank and Samsung on industrial developments.

Nógrádi Law Office works with a large and impressive Israeli client base on all aspects of portfolio management, commercial, residential, and distribution centre development. It also advises banks on real estate finance for development and acquisition and members of the diplomatic corps on embassy buildings.

Oppenheim és Társai Freshfields Bruckhaus Deringer's real estate experience mostly involves handling mid-size sales, acquisitions and leases. In 2003 it notably advised cement company Holcim Beton on a €6.5m transaction. The firm has experience of greenfield projects, real estate finance and most construction matters. Eva Fried-Kallós is the best known individual.

Réczicza Law Firm White & Case LLP has a growing real estate practice in Hungary advising clients on equity investments and debt financings, real estate leases and shopping centre developments. In 2003 the firm also advised on major regional deals including for AIG-CET Capital Management and the EBRD on the sale by TriGranit of assets in Budapest and Bratislava. The firm has commercial leasing experience with Regus, Colgate-Palmolive and Honeywell.

Squire, Sanders & Dempsey LLP Komáromi és Erös Üqyvédi Iroda represents several multinationals in Hungary, including on real estate issues. In 2003 it counselled Audi on the construction of an engine factory in western Hungary, and Tyco Group on the retrofit of a wastewater facility, including significant environmental law aspects.

Weil, Gotshal & Manges is recommended for all commercial and residential real estate matters. It represents major player and long term client GTC Real Estate Development in all its Hungarian projects and in 2003 in Serbia. It also advises Pricoa on sales and negotiations and advised AIG-Lincoln on the sale of the M1 Business Park and Airport Business Park.

Allen & Overy remains focused on securities and corporate work in Hungary. Its has handled real estate matters in the context of infrastructure projects and project finance transactions.

Burai - Kovács & Partners has handled construction, leasing and real estate matters for several of its major energy and corporate clients.

Judit Gaal is head at **Gide Loyrette Nouel**'s standalone real estate practice, which has advised French-speaking clients on all aspects of construction and real estate, including finance and litigation.

Hayhurst Robinson in association with Mátrai Law Office is involved in the finance and construction of the Four Seasons Gresham Palace Hotel.

Nagy & Pintér Hogan & Hartson has advised Hungarian and US clients on real estate acquisitions in Budapest.

Réti Szegheö and Partners, Attorneys at Law acts for construction companies including Skanska and several prominent German groups. It has handled purchases of industrial facilities, mines and agricultural land, and advised a Dutch investment group on the construction, acquisition and sales of commercial space.

Sándor, Szegedi, Szent-Ivány is involved in ongoing aspects of a major airport construction project, advising on construction and real estate issues.

Squarra & Partos (in association with Lovells) advised banks on project finance in the real estate sector in 2003.

Szecskay Law Firm - Moquet Borde & Associés has acquisition experience in the real estate sector.

TMT

ALLEN & OVERY ✪
BERECZ & ANDRÉKÓ LINKLATERS ✪
KÖVES CLIFFORD CHANCE
RÉCZICZA LAW FIRM WHITE & CASE LLP

- Dewey Ballantine LLP ✪
- Dezsö Réti & Antall Landwell ✪
- Forgó, Varga and Partners ✪
- Martonyi és Kajtár Baker & McKenzie ✪
- Oppenheim és Társai Freshfields Bruckhaus Deringer ✪
- SBG & K Patent and Law Office ✪
- Weil, Gotshal & Manges ✪

- Bogsch & Partners
- DLA Weiss-Tessbach ✪
- Danubia
- Gide Loyrette Nouel ✪
- Haarmann Hemmelrath ✪
- Hayhurst Robinson in association with Mátrai Law Office ✪
- Nagy és Trócsányi ✪
- Ormai és Társai CMS Cameron McKenna
- Réti Szegheö and Partners, Attorneys at Law ✪
- Squarra & Partos (in association with Lovells) ✪
- Szecskay Law Firm - Moquet Borde & Associés ✪

Firms are listed A-Z in tiers which are ranked in order of priority

✪ *Indicates firm displays contact details at the end of this chapter.*

TMT

Allen & Overy has advised M-RTL Televizió and News Outdoor Hungary on various corporate and commercial matters. It also has regulatory experience with Modern Times Group member Viasat Broadcasting. Senior associate Tamás Riesz advises BT Hungary, KPN Telecom, Pantel and Pannon GSM on corporate and regulatory matters.

Berecz & Andrékó Linklaters excels in this area, advising some of the best-known names on the biggest transactions taking place in Hungary. In 2003 examples include advising MGM Studios on the transfer of film rights to its local subsidiary, providing regulatory and commercial guidance to Vodafone, Pannon GSM and Telenor, and transactional advice to large hi-tech companies. Versatile commercial practitioner Andrea Simándi is well known in each of these areas.

Köves Clifford Chance fields a particularly large, impressively experienced team of 11 led by big name Péter Lakatos. Clients in 2003 included Hungarotel, advised on a new interconnection agreement and Vivendi Telecom counselled on international aspects of the Vivendi Telecom sale. It handled two large outsourcing projects.

Réczicza Law Firm White & Case LLP has a dedicated TMT practice with regulatory, procurement, contracting, finance and intellectual property experience with a cross-section of clients including Malév, Graphisoft and IDOM. The firm also advises the Hungarian Ministry of IT and Communications on amendments necessary under EU law. On the telecoms side the firm notably advised the Hungarian Ministry of Telecommunications and Informatics in the drafting of a new telecoms act in line with EU directives and works with big names including

Deutsche Telekom. István Réczicza is highly recommended in this sector.

Dewey Ballantine LLP continues to represent some MCI WorldCom subsidiaries in connection with licensing and regulatory issues in Hungary.

Dezsö Réti & Antall Landwell is highly recommended for media law advice and commercial transactions involving media companies. It has several large German-speaking clients, including Ringier which in 2003 acquired a large printing plant in Hungary. It also advised the largest daily newspaper in Hungary on the acquisition of a new share package in 2003 and handled joint ventures, contentious matters and mergers in this sector.

Forgó, Varga and Partners has one of the largest TMT practices of any Hungarian law firm and experience of corporate, commercial and regulatory matters. In 2003 it advised EDS on an outsourcing project by MATÁV, UK-based multinational IT company Lofica on a procurement and Exact Hungary on intellectual property and commercial matters. Elender/PSINet, Hungary's second largest ISP, remains a core client.

Martonyi és Kajtár Baker & McKenzie has telecoms experience with Matáv, AT&T and Sun Microsystems, mainly handling commercial matters.

Oppenheim és Társai Freshfields Bruckhaus Deringer has print and electronic media clients which it advises on acquisitions, start-ups and general commercial matters. Alongside a clutch of smaller clients it also advised publishing house Sanoma on transaction and regulatory issues connected to its acquisitions and VIVA+ on its distribution negotiations with UPC and MATÁV. IT experience includes work with software, media and consulting firms, including General Electric's European Operations Services and Microsoft.

SBG & K Patent and Law Office represents a number of hi-tech clients on their contentious and non-contentious patent, trade mark and intellectual property matters. It has a dedicated anti-counterfeiting practice headed by László Bérczes. Kinga Kelemen has some media and entertainment clients.

Weil, Gotshal & Manges has a niche specialisation in laws and regulations pertaining to the satellite broadcasting industry. Clients include Telespazio, advised on the licensing of satellite uplinking services in Hungary. It also represents HBO, Sláger Rádió and its parent company Emmis Communications, Híd Rádió and DMX Music on a wide range of media matters. David Dederick is recommended.

TAX

Berecz & Andrékó Linklaters expanded its tax practice in 2003 with the transfer of regional tax partner Henk Goossen to Budapest as head of tax. Senior associate Pál Jalsovszky maintained a higher profile through 2003 advising several core clients on tax and BP, TriGránit and Metro-Goldwyn-Mayer on complex tax aspects of sales and distribution agreements. The firm also advised on a multi-million dollar restructuring of a corporate group in 2003, including tax aspects.

Dezsö Réti & Antall Landwell primarily handles legal matters for clients of Big Four accountant PricewaterhouseCoopers. On a stand-alone basis it also handles a large volume of offshore work. In 2003 the firm benefited from the addition of former **Haarmann Hemmelrath** Budapest managing partner Marc Madl and a small team.

Köves Clifford Chance has extensive experience of providing advice on tax implications and tax structuring of corporate, commercial and securities deals. In 2003 it advised Alcoa on its restructuring, KBC Bank on tax aspects of its local merger with ABN Amro, and JP Morgan Securities on various tax issues.

Martonyi és Kajtár Baker & McKenzie partner Géza Kajtár combines his role as head of corporate and commercial, dispute resolution, real estate, TMT and transport with his position as head of tax. Tax planning and offshore specialist Gergely Riszter has a higher profile, in 2003 advising several household name companies on aspects of audit, tax structuring and contracts and tax due diligence.

TAX

BEITEN BURKHARDT DÉRI & LOVRECZ
BERECZ & ANDRÉKÓ LINKLATERS ✪
DEZSÖ RÉTI & ANTALL LANDWELL ✪
KÖVES CLIFFORD CHANCE
MARTONYI ÉS KAJTÁR BAKER & MCKENZIE ✪
NÖRR STIEFENHOFER LUTZ ✪
OPPENHEIM ÉS TÁRSAI FRESHFIELDS BRUCKHAUS DERINGER ✪

Allen & Overy ✪
Burai - Kovács & Partners
Réczicza Law Firm White & Case LLP

Gide Loyrette Nouel ✪
Haarmann Hemmelrath ✪
Nógrádi Law Office ✪
Ormai és Társai CMS Cameron McKenna

Firms are listed A-Z in tiers which are ranked in order of priority
✪ Indicates firm displays contact details at the end of this chapter.

Oppenheim és Társai Freshfields Bruckhaus Deringer has established a successful niche for itself providing serious tax advisory and tax planning services, led by practice head and former KPMG auditor Peter Oszkó. In 2003 it advised Credit Lyonnais on the tax implications of the securitisation of trade debts in several sectors, DaimlerChrysler on the tax implications of leaseback transactions, GE on EU accession and Hewlett-Packard on tax planning.

Allen & Overy senior associate Szilvia Horváth is experienced on corporate finance matters, including tax-driven offshore structures and investments.

Burai – Kovács & Partners, formerly associated with Ernst & Young, has extensive experience of corporate matters.

Réczicza Law Firm White & Case LLP hired former **Gide Loyrette Nouel** head of tax György Molnár Biró in 2003. It advised on contentious and non-contentious tax matters including on tax law and structuring for investments, auditing, and disputes with customs authorities.

ALLEN & OVERY

MADÁCH TRADE CENTER
MADÁCH IMRE UTCA 13-14
1075 BUDAPEST

Telephone: +36 1 483 2200
Fax: +36 1 268 1515
E-mail: information@allenovery.com
Website: www.allenovery.com

Languages
English, French, German, Hungarian, Russian

Other Offices
Amsterdam, Antwerp, Bangkok, Beijing, Bratislava, Brussels, Dubai, Frankfurt, Hamburg, Hong Kong, London, Luxembourg, Madrid, Milan, Moscow, New York, Paris, Prague, Rome, Shanghai, Singapore, Tokyo, Turin, Warsaw

Number of lawyers 2,305
at this office 14

Contacts
Éva Hegedûs, Zoltàn Lengyel, Marcell Nèmeth, Alex Cook

CATEGORIES OF WORK

Banking/finance
Marcell Németh

International capital markets
Zoltán Lengyel

Corporate/commercial
Eva Hegedûs, Alex Cook

Derivatives
Zoltán Lengyel

Energy
Marcell Németh

Environment
Éva Hegedûs, Csaba Polgár

EU law
Tamás Riesz, Éva Hegedûs

Competition
Tamás Riesz

Intellectual property
Szilvia Horváth

PPP
Marcell Németh, Alex Cook

Mergers and acquisitions
Éva Hegedûs, Alex Cook

Privatisation
Éva Hegedûs, Alex Cook

Project finance and trade finance
Marcell Németh, Szilvia Horváth

Real estate
Éva Hegedûs, Tamás Riesz

Telecommunications/media
Tamás Riesz

Off shores
Szilvia Horváth, Ágnes Bejó

Tax
Szilvia Horváth

Private equity
Alex Cook

ANDREAS NEOCLEOUS & CO – TULLER & KLESICS

BALASSI BU 25
GROUND FL 5
1055 BUDAPEST

Telephone: +36 1 311 3135
Fax: +36 1 354 0677
E-mail: info@neocleous_bp.hu
Website: www.neocleous.com

Languages
English, German, Russian and local languages where Andreas Neocleous & Co operates

Other offices
Limassol, Paphos, Nicosia, Moscow, Kiev, Prague

Number of lawyers 60
at this office 7

CATEGORIES OF WORK

Company and commercial law

Tax law and international tax planning

Intellectual property

IBC services

Litigation and arbitration

Property and construction

Leasing

Internet, e-commerce and IT law

Banking and finance

Project finance

Real estate

EC law

BERECZ & ANDRÉKÓ LINKLATERS

AKADÉMIA BANK CENTER
SZÉCHENYI RAKPART 3
1054 BUDAPEST

Telephone: +36 1 428 4400
Fax: +36 1 428 4444
Website: www.linklaters.com

Languages
All commercial and local languages in the countries where Linklaters operates

Other offices
Alicante, Amsterdam, Antwerp, Bangkok, Beijing, Berlin, Bratislava, Brussels, Bucharest, Cologne, Frankfurt am Main, Hong Kong, Lisbon, London, Luxembourg, Madrid, Milan, Moscow, Munich, New York, Paris, Prague, Rome, São Paulo, Shanghai, Singapore, Stockholm, Tokyo, Warsaw

Number of lawyers 2,000 worldwide

Contact
Dr Csaba Berecz

CATEGORIES OF WORK

Corporate and commercial
Dr Balázs Máthé

Mergers and acquisitions
Dr Balázs Máthé

Banking
Dr Csilla Andrékó, Dr Csaba Berecz

Capital markets
Dr Csilla Andrékó

Project finance
Dr Csilla Andrékó, Dr Csaba Berecz

Intellectual property
Dr Andrea Simándi

Energy regulatory
Dr Andrea Miskolczi

Tax
Henk Goossen, Dr Pál Jalsovszky

EU/competition
Dr Balázs Máthé, Dr Dániel Kaszás

Telecommunications
Dr Andrea Simándi

Information technology, Internet and e-commerce
Dr Andrea Simándi

Media
Dr Andrea Simándi

Environmental
Dr Balázs Máthé

THE FIRM

Linklaters advises the world's leading companies, financial institutions and governments on their most challenging transactions and assignments. With 2,000 lawyers, including 470 partners, and offices in major business and financial centres, its clients choose the firm for its distinctive combination of technical skill, commercial experience and outstanding service.

Linklaters has built a formidable global practice through organic growth and a series of mergers, joint ventures and co-operations with other respected law firms. In 2001, Linklaters merged with three of Europe's leading law firms to form Linklaters Oppenhoff & Rädler in Germany, Linklaters in Sweden, Linklaters De Bandt in Belgium and Linklaters Loesch in Luxembourg. In the same year, the firm formed a co-operation with Brazilian firm Goulart Penteado, Iervolino e Lefosse. This co-operation combines Linklaters' international capability with GPIL's extensive knowledge of the Brazilian market. In Singapore, the firm practises as Linklaters Allen & Gledhill, a joint venture with the premier Singapore practice of Allen & Gledhill, while in Italy, Linklaters has an exclusive relationship with Italian law firm Gianni, Origoni, Grippo & Partners.

BIHARY, BALASSA & PARTNERS ATTORNEYS AT LAW

HARANGVIRÁG U.5
1026 BUDAPEST

Telephone: +36 1 391 44 91
Fax: +36 1 200 80 47
E-mail: office@biharybalassa.hu
Website: www.biharybalassa.hu

Languages
English, French, German

Number of lawyers 8

CATEGORIES OF WORK

- Banking and financial services
- Company law
- Competition law, unfair competition, antitrust law
- Construction law
- Dispute resolution and arbitration
- Foreign investment in Hungary
- Internet law
- Joint ventures
- Labour law
- Media law
- Mergers and acquisitions
- Privatisation
- Project finance
- Public procurement
- Real property law
- Technology transfer
- Telecommunications

CERHA HEMPEL SPIEGELFELD HLAWATI
PARTNERSCHAFT VON RECHTSANWÄLTEN

BUDAY LÁSZLÓ U 12
1024 BUDAPEST

Telephone: +36 1 345 45 35
Fax: +36 1 345 45 43
E-mail: office.chsh@szecsenyi.com
Website: www.chsh.at

Languages
English, German, Russian

Other offices
Brussels, Vienna, Zagreb

Number of lawyers 65
at this office 11

Contacts
László Szécsényi, Alfred Nemetschke, Walter Anderl

CATEGORIES OF WORK

- Banking, securities and finance
- Companies, corporations
- Mergers and acquisitions
- Arbitration and litigation
- Commercial law (contracts)
- Franchising and distribution
- Information technology
- Real estate, construction, building
- Competition, antitrust, intellectual property
- Privatisation, telecommunications
- Regulation, administrative, constitutional law
- International/comparative law

DLA WEISS-TESSBACH

ALKOTÁS U. 50.
1123 BUDAPEST

Telephone: +36 1 325 3020
Fax: +36 1 325 3021
E-mail: budapest@dla.com
Website: www.dla.com

Languages
Czech, English, French, German, Italian, Russian, Slovak

Other offices
Amsterdam, Antwerp, Bangkok, Bergen, Berlin, Birmingham, Bradford, Bratislava, Brussels, Cologne, Copenhagen, Edinburgh, Essen, Frankfurt, Glasgow, Hamburg, Hong Kong, Leeds, Liverpool, London, Madrid, Manchester, Milan, Moscow, Oslo, Paris, Prague, Rotterdam, Salzberg, Sarajevo, Shanghai, Sheffield, Singapore, Stockholm, Vienna, Zagreb

Number of lawyers 82
at this office 18

Contact
Moniká Horváth

Member
DLA Group

CATEGORIES OF WORK

Corporate	**Litigation**
Mergers and aquisitions	**Intellectual property**
Project finance, financing	**Real estate**
General commercial	**Banking**

THE FIRM

Weiss-Tessbach was established in 1878 and is one of the longest-established law firms in Austria. 15 years ago, the firm decided on an extremely dynamic development. Since 1990, the number of lawyers at the firm has increased more than four times from 15 to over 80, and the number of offices from one to seven. On October 1st 2003, Weiss-Tessbach was integrated with DLA on the basis of a shared vision to become a top five full-service European law firm. With its current offices in six central and eastern European countries, DLA Weiss-Tessbach will continue to expand into the region at a time of EU accession for many countries.

DLA Weiss-Tessbach is part of DLA Group. DLA Group is an exclusive alliance of international full-service law firms with a shared vision. Established in 1999, DLA Group now has over 2,200 lawyers across 21 countries, who deliver expert local know-how and international solutions. DLA Group provides legal advice in 37 major cities across Europe, Singapore, Thailand, Hong Kong and the People's Republic of China.

AREAS OF PRACTICE

The firm has strengthened its core areas of expertise (commercial and corporate, M&A, banking and finance, intellectual property, real estate), and has expanded into other areas of law (administrative, employment, telecoms, technology, venture capital). Today, the firm is able to assist its corporate clients in all aspects of their activities.

DLA Weiss-Tessbach has well-established relations with clients of various backgrounds. The firm advises small and medium-sized enterprises as well as leading (often publicly listed) international and domestic industrial groups, service providers, banks and other financial institutions and individuals.

DLA Weiss-Tessbach has established a particular reputation for its ability to handle cases in international cross-border contexts. It carefully views the ongoing developments in central Europe with the aim of combining the needs of the constantly changing international legal market and industry, whilst also upholding the high-standard services that the firm has always been able to offer to its clients.

DEZSÖ, RÉTI & ANTALL LANDWELL

DEZSÖ, RÉTI & ANTALL LAW FIRM
WESSELÉNYI U. 16/A
1077 BUDAPEST

Telephone: +36 1 461 9888
Fax: +36 1 461 9898
Website: www.landwellglobal.com/hu

Languages:
English, French, German, Russian

Number of lawyers 47

Contact
László Réti (managing partner)

International groupings
Landwell, correspondent law firms of PricewaterhouseCoopers

CATEGORIES OF WORK

Commercial and competition
Dr Ilona Csordás

Corporate structuring
Dr Dóra Horváth,
Dr Andrea Presser-Müller

Dispute resolution, tax litigation
Dr Attila Dezsö, Dr Zoltán Várszegi

Technology, media and communications
Dr László Réti

Employment and human resources
Dr László Szücs

Financial services
Dr Norbert Christ

Intellectual property
Dr László Réti

Mergers and acquisitions
Dr Marc-Tell Madl

Real estate
Dr Katalin Veszely

Energy
Dr György Antall

Telecoms
Dr Zsolt Szakály

Hungarian off-shore companies, company secretary services
Dr László Réti

THE FIRM

Dezsö, Réti & Antall is a member of Landwell.

Landwell is one of the largest international law practices with 2,800 business and tax lawyers worldwide. Landwell provides a full range of legal services through specialists organised in global networks. Landwell's main focus is on cross-border M&A transactions and corporate transformation projects. Working closely with PricewaterhouseCoopers, Landwell is a market leader in the design and delivery of complex corporate change. This is achieved through a focus on strong local capabilities with a global outlook and by ensuring that its implementation skills match its legal ones.

Dezsö, Réti & Antall is one of the largest law firms in Hungary. It employs a professional staff of more than 40 persons, with eight law firm members and ten senior lawyers.

AREAS OF PRACTICE

Landwell provides a full range of business law services, through specialist lawyers organised in global networks. In this way, consistent high standards of advice and service are guaranteed for both international and local clients. Landwell's international strengths include: legal consulting on mergers and acquisitions; corporate structuring; technology, media and communications; and employment law. Dezsö, Réti & Antall also has special expertise in energy law and real estate.

DEWEY BALLANTINE LLP

VÁCU U. 81
1056 BUDAPEST

Telephone: +36 1 327 0920
Fax: +36 1 327 0921
E-mail: btatrai@deweyballantine.com
Website: www.deweyballantine.com

Languages
English, French, Hungarian

Other offices
Austin, East Palo Alto, Frankfurt, Houston, London, Los Angeles, Milan, New York, Prague, Rome, Warsaw, Washington DC

Number of lawyers 606
at this office 3

Contact
Beáta Tátrai (btatrai@deweyballantine.com)

In association with
Beáta Tátrai Law Office

CATEGORIES OF WORK

- Mergers and acquisitions
- Privatisations
- Telecommunications
- Environmental law
- Banking and capital markets
- Real estate
- Intellectual property
- Competition
- Project finance
- Energy and natural resources
- General corporate law
- Joint ventures
- International trade
- Litigation
- Construction

EISELSBERG NATLACEN WALDERDORFF CANCOLA

PETŐFI SÁNDOR U 11/I/1
1052 BUDAPEST

Telephone: +36 1 327 0407
Fax: +36 1 327 0410
E-mail: budapest@enwc.com
Website: www.enwc.com

Languages
Czech, English, French, German, Italian

Other offices
Prague, Vienna

Number of lawyers 39
at this office 7

Contacts
Dr Raimund Cancola, Dr Roland Kölcsey-Rieden

CATEGORIES OF WORK

- Company and commercial
- Intellectual property
- Mergers and acquisitions
- International arbitration and litigation
- Banking and finance
- Insurance
- Labour and employment
- Real estate
- Construction and building
- EU law

FORGÓ, VARGA & PARTNERS

LAW FIRM

ALKOTÁS U 17-19 (DÉLI POINT)
III FLOOR
1123 BUDAPEST

Telephone: +36 1 214 0080
Fax: +36 1 214 0078
E-mail: office@forgovarga.com

Languages
English

Number of lawyers 9

Contacts
Zoltán Forgó, János Tamás Varga

CATEGORIES OF WORK

Company law	Telecommunications
Mergers and acquisitions	Media
Venture capital	Commercial law
Privatisation	Competition law
Internet	Labour law
E-commerce	Litigation
Information technology	Arbitration
Intellectual property rights	Pharmaceuticals

GIDE LOYRETTE NOUEL

EMKE BUILDING
RÁKÓCZI ÚT 42, BP 409
1072 BUDAPEST

Telephone: +36 1 411 74 00
Fax: +36 1 411 74 40
E-mail: gln.budapest@gide.com
Website: www.gide.com

Other offices
Algiers, Beijing, Brussels, Bucharest, Casablanca, Hanoi, Istanbul, London, Moscow, New York, Paris, Prague, Riyadh, Shanghai, Tunis, Warsaw

Number of lawyers 480
at this office 22

Contacts
Jacques de Servigny (servigny@gide.com),
Judit Gaál (gaal@gide.com),
István Molnár (molnarp@gide.com)

CATEGORIES OF WORK

Mergers and acquisitions	Media
Privatisation	E-commerce and the Internet
Company law	Competition
Real estate transactions and financing	Distribution
Project finance	Labour law
Banking and finance	Tax
Telecommunications	

HAARMANN HEMMELRATH

VÖRÖSMARTY TÉR 4
1051 BUDAPEST

Telephone: +36 1 4 84 04 84
Fax: +36 1 4 84 04 33
E-mail: budapest@haarmannhemmelrath.com
Website: www.haarmannhemmelrath.com

Languages
Bulgarian, Croatian, Czech, Dutch, English, Finnish, French, Italian, Japanese, Mandarin, Norwegian, Polish, Portuguese, Romanian, Russian, Slovak, Spanish, Vietnamese

Other offices
Berlin, Bielefeld, Brussels, Bucharest, Cologne, Dusseldorf, Frankfurt, Hamburg, Leipzig, London, Milan, Moscow, Munich, Paris, Prague, Rome, Shanghai, Singapore, Stuttgart, Tokyo, Vienna, Warsaw

Number of lawyers 281
at this office 6

CATEGORIES OF WORK

Mergers and acquisitions
Dr Jádi Németh Andrea

Corporate
Dr Jádi Németh Andrea

Labour
Dr Gömöri Krisztina

International tax
Stricca Lilla

National tax
Stricca Lilla

Arbitration and litigation
Dr Gömöri Krisztina, Dr Jádi Németh Andrea

Greenfield investments
Dr Jádi-Németh Andrea

Commercial real property
Dr Baracsi Zoltán

Construction
Dr Gömöri Krisztina

Joint ventures and investments in central and eastern Europe
Dr Jádi Németh Andrea

HAYHURST ROBINSON
MÁTRAI LAW OFFICE

46 TERÉZ KRT, 2ND FLOOR
1066 BUDAPEST

Telephone: +361 332 9980
Fax: +361 332 9981
E-mail: hrbudapest@hrintlaw.com
Website: www.hrintlaw.com

Languages
Bulgarian, English, French, Hungarian, Romanian, Russian, Serbian

Other offices
Belgrade, Bucharest, Sofia

Number of lawyers 40
at this office 11

Contact
Barbara Mendler (bmendler@hrintlaw.com)

International groupings
Interlex Group; IBA

CATEGORIES OF WORK

Foreign investment
Robert Hayhurst, Roland Jabronka

Privatisation
Robert Hayhurst, Ferenc Mátrai

Energy and natural resources
Robert Hayhurst, Ferenc Mátrai

Real estate
Robert Hayhurst, Ferenc Mátrai

Project and corporate finance
Robert Hayhurst, Neil Berlad

Banking
Neil Berlad, Ferenc Mátrai

Private equity
Robert Hayhurst, Neil Berlad

Mergers and acquisitions
Robert Hayhurst, Ferenc Mátrai

Telecoms
Todd Robinson, John Fitzpatrick

Pharmaceutical
David Butts, Zsofia Hermann

Licensing and hi-tech
Roland Jabronka, John Fitzpatrick

Insurance
David Butts, Neil Berlad

Municipal infrastructure
Robert Hayhurst

Shipping
Neil Berlad, Roland Jabronka

Transport infrastructure
Todd Robinson, Robert Hayhurst

General corporate
Ferenc Mátrai, Gábor Bebök

Corporate insolvency and bankruptcy
Ferenc Mátrai, Gábor Bebök

MARTONYI ÉS KAJTÁR BAKER & McKENZIE

ANDRÁSSY ÚT 102
1062 BUDAPEST

Telephone: +36 1 302 33 30
Fax: +36 1 302 33 31
E-mail: janos.martonyi@bakernet.com
Website: www.bakernet.com

Languages
Croatian, English, French, German, Spanish

Other offices
For a list of all offices and other information regarding the firm please consult Baker & McKenzie's London office entry

Number of lawyers 3,380
at this office 40

Contact
János Martonyi (managing partner)

Baker & McKenzie is a global law firm with 66 offices in 36 countries.

CATEGORIES OF WORK

Arbitration and litigation
Géza Kajtár, János Martonyi

Asset finance, securities
Konrád Siegler, Attila S Horváth

Banking and finance
Attila S Horváth, István Gere

Capital markets
Konrád Siegler, Gábor Szabó

Commercial property, real estate
Géza Kajtár, Gabriella Kicska

Competition, trade, EU law
János Martonyi, Zoltán H Barakonyi

Corporate and commercial
Géza Kajtár, Gabriella Kicska

Information technology
Kinga M Hetényi, Andrea Soós

Infrastructure and project finance
Attila S Horváth, Anne-Marie Fortier

Intellectual property
Zoltán H Barakonyi, Gabriella Kicska

Labour law
Pál P Takács, Ákos Fehérváry

Mergers and acquisitions
Ines K Radmilovic, Pál P Takács

Privatisations
János Martonyi, Pál P Takács

Tax
Gergely Riszter, Géza Kajtár

Telecommunications
Kinga M Hetényi, Péter Vörös,

Venture capital/private equity
Pál P Takács, László Nagy

NAGY & PINTÉR HOGAN & HARTSON
LAW OFFICE

BANK CENTER, GRANITE TOWER
BUDAPEST V, SZABADSÁG TÉR 7-9
1054 BUDAPEST

Telephone: +36 1 302 9050
Fax: +36 1 302 9060
E-mail: knagykoppany@hhlaw.com
Website: www.hhlaw.com

Languages
English, French, German, Russian, Spanish

Other offices
Baltimore, Beijing, Berlin, Boulder, Brussels, Colorado Springs, Denver, London, Los Angeles, McLean, Miami, Moscow, Munich, New York, Paris, Prague, Tokyo, Warsaw, Washington DC

Number of lawyers 1,018
at this office 7

Contact
Kornelia Nagy-Koppany

CATEGORIES OF WORK

Mergers, acquisitions and divestitures

Company formation and corporate counselling

Pharmaceutical and healthcare

Entertainment and gambling

Venture capital and private equity

Corporate finance

Bankruptcy, insolvency and corporate restructurings

Competition law

Labour and employment

Intellectual property

Technology transfer

Real estate

Telecommunications and e-commerce

NAGY ÉS TRÓCSÁNYI

UGOCSA U 4/B
1126 BUDAPEST

Telephone: +36 1 487 8700
Fax: +36 1 487 8701
E-mail: budapest_office@nagyestrocsanyi.hu
Website:www.nagyestrocsanyi.hu

Languages
English, French, German

Other offices
New York

Number of lawyers 25
at this office 24

CATEGORIES OF WORK

Antitrust and competition law	Energy law
Arbitration and litigation	Greenfield investments
Aviation law	Intellectual property
Banking and corporate finance	Joint ventures
Capital markets and securities	Media
Commercial law	Mergers and acquisitions
Commercial real property	Taxes
Company and trade law	Telecommunications
Construction	Trade marks

NÓGRÁDI LAW OFFICE

SZÉPVÖLGYI OFFICE PARK
3A MONTEVIDEO STREET
1037 BUDAPEST

Telephone: +36 1 240 63 54
Fax: +36 1 240 63 53
E-mail: nogradi@enternet.hu

Languages
English, Hebrew

Number of lawyers 10

Contact
Dr Péter Nógrádi

Member
International Bar Association

CATEGORIES OF WORK

Contracts	Privatisation
Corporate law	Company law
Mergers and acquisitions	Labour law
Family law	Arbitration
Civil litigation	Insolvency
Intellectual property	Banking
Taxation	Real estate

NÖRR STIEFENHOFER LUTZ

BATTHYÁNY U 49 IX/I
1015 BUDAPEST

Telephone: +36 1 224 0900
Fax: +36 1 224 0495
E-mail: nslbud@noerr.hu
Website: www.noerr.de

Languages
English, French, German, Italian, Russian

Other offices
Berlin, Bucharest, Dresden, Düsseldorf, Frankfurt, Moscow, Munich, Prague, Warsaw

Number of lawyers 237
(+ 53 tax advisers, public accountants and tax assistants)
at this office 10
(+ 4 tax advisers, public accountants and tax assistants)

Contacts
Zsolt K Radnóczy, László Mészáros

CATEGORIES OF WORK

- Company law
- Commercial law
- Real estate and investment law
- Labour law
- Banking and foreign exchange law
- Intellectual property and trade mark law
- Tax and customs law
- Law relating to commercial leases
- Competition and antitrust law
- Construction law

OPPENHEIM ÉS TÁRSAI FRESHFIELDS BRUCKHAUS DERINGER

KÁROLYI MIHÁLY U. 12.
1053 BUDAPEST

Telephone: +36 1 486 2200
Fax: +36 1 486 2201
E-mail: email@freshfields.com
Website: www.freshfields.com

Languages
Extensive language capabilities

Other offices
Amsterdam, Bangkok, Barcelona, Beijing, Berlin, Bratislava, Brussels, Cologne, Düsseldorf, Frankfurt, Hamburg, Hanoi, Ho Chi Minh City, Hong Kong, London, Madrid, Milan, Moscow, Munich, New York, Paris, Rome, Shanghai, Singapore, Tokyo, Vienna, Washington

Number of lawyers 2,504
at this office 37

Contact
Willibald Plesser (Vienna)

CATEGORIES OF WORK

- Corporate
- Finance
- Antitrust, competition and trade
- Intellectual property and IT
- Tax
- Real estate
- Dispute resolution (including environment, planning and regulatory)
- Employment, pensions and benefits

RÉTI SZEGHEÖ & PARTNERS

ATTORNEYS AT LAW

ZUGLIGETI ÚT 41
1121 BUDAPEST

Telephone: +36 1 275 2785
Fax: +36 1 275 2784
E-mail: ars@ars.hu
Website: www.ars.hu

Languages
English, French, German

Number of lawyers 14

Member
Balms Group International

CATEGORIES OF WORK

Corporate and commercial
Dr Olga Réti

Mergers and acquisitions
Dr András Réti

Banking and finance
Dr Mihály Barcza

Capital markets
Dr Mihály Barcza

Project finance
Dr Mihály Barcza

Real estate
Dr Attila Kovács

Intellectual property
Dr Tamás Éless

Competition law
Dr Tamás Éless

Information technology
Dr Zoltán Zárdai

Data protection
Dr László Majtényi

Labour and employment law
Dr Zoltán Zárdai

Insolvency law
Dr Attila Kovács

Arbitration, litigation, ADR
Dr Tamás Éless

SBG & K PATENT AND LAW OFFICE

ANDRÁSSY ÚT 113
1062 BUDAPEST

Telephone: +361 461 1000
Fax: +361 461 1099
E-mail: mailbox@sbgk.hu
Website: www.sbgk.hu

Languages
English, French, German

Number of lawyers 23

Member
AIJA; LES; AIPPI; ITMA; UNILAW; TAGLaw; LAWorld; Globalaw; AIA; ECU; INTA; IBA; FICPI; LIDC

CATEGORIES OF WORK

Corporate
Dr Katalin Szamosi, Dr Gábor Germus

Mergers and acquisitions
Dr István Bajkai, Dr Gábor Germus

Infrastructure, project financing
Dr István Bajkai, Dr Gábor Germus

Commercial property, real estate
Dr István Bajkai

Taxation
Dr Gábor Germus

Competition
Dr Katalin Szamosi, Dr Gábor Germus

Litigation, arbitration
Dr Katalin Szamosi, Dr Róbert Bérczes

Patents
Ádám Szentpéteri Jr, Dr Tamás Bokor

Trade marks
Dr Katalin Szamosi,
Dr Gabriella Sasvári

Anti-counterfeit
Dr Katalin Árva, Dr László Bérczes

Copyright
Dr Kinga Kelemen, Dr Enikö Karsay

Technology transfer
Dr István Bajkai

E-commerce
Dr Katalin Szamosi, Dr Enikö Karsay

Labour law
Dr Kinga Kelemen

Media and entertainment
Dr László Bérczes, Dr Kinga Kelemen

SÁNDOR, SZEGEDI, SZENT-IVÁNY

PASARETI ÚT 59
1026 BUDAPEST

Telephone: +36 1 394 3121
Fax: +36 1 392 4949
E-mail: office@sandor-advocat.hu
Website: www.sandor-advocat.hu

Languages
English, French, German, Russian

Number of lawyers 9

Contact
Dr Tamás Sándor

CATEGORIES OF WORK

- Corporate law
- Mergers and acquisitions, privatisation
- Commercial law
- Antitrust and cartel law
- Project finance
- Media law
- Real estate, construction law
- Labour law
- Energy and utilities
- Public procurement
- Telecommunications
- Administrative, environmental law
- Banking and financial services
- Litigation and arbitration
- Competition law

SQUARRA & PARTOS
IN ASSOCIATION WITH LOVELLS

ANDRÁSSY UT 2
1061 BUDAPEST

Telephone: +36 1 474 2080
Fax: +36 1 474 2081
E-mail: information@lovells.com
Website: www.lovells.com

Other offices
Alicante, Amsterdam, Beijing, Berlin, Brussels, Chicago, Düsseldorf, Frankfurt, Hamburg, Ho Chi Minh City, Hong Kong, London, Milan, Moscow, Munich, New York, Paris, Prague, Rome, Shanghai, Singapore, Tokyo, Vienna*, Warsaw, Zagreb*

Number of lawyers 1,600
at this office 8

Contact
Dr Thomas Squarra

CATEGORIES OF WORK

- Banking
- E-commerce
- Corporate/commercial including M&A
- Commercial property
- Intellectual property
- Venture capital, private equity
- Employment law
- Capital markets
- Litigation/arbitration
- Telecommunications

SQUIRE, SANDERS & DEMPSEY L.L.P. KOMÁROMI ÉS ERÖS ÜGYVÉDI IRODA

ANDRÁSSY ÚT 64.
1062 BUDAPEST

Telephone: +361 428 7111
Fax: +361 428 7100
E-mail: kconnor@ssd.com
Website: www.ssd.com

Languages
English, French, German, Italian, Romanian, Spanish

Other offices
Beijing, Bratislava, Brussels, Cincinnati, Cleveland, Columbus, Hong Kong, Houston, London, Los Angeles, Madrid, Miami, Milan, Moscow, New York, Palo Alto, Phoenix, Prague, Rio de Janeiro, San Francisco, Taipei, Tampa, Tokyo, Tysons Corner, Washington DC, Bucharest*, Dublin*, Kyiv*

Number of lawyers 710
at this office 17

Contact
Kevin Connor

Member
American Chamber of Commerce; Joint Venture Association, Hungary; Hungary-Japan Economic Club; Hungarian Chamber of Commerce

CATEGORIES OF WORK

Capital markets
Kevin Connor, Dr Akos Mester

Corporate finance, banking
Dr Ákos Erös, Kevin Connor

EU competition law
Dr Peter Komáromi, Dr Ákos Mester

Infrastructure, project asset finance
Kevin Connor, Dr Ákos Erös

Intellectual property
Dr Attila Lotz

International arbitration
Dr Iván Szász, Dr Péter Komáromi

International transactions
Dr Ákos Erös, Kevin Connor

Labour law
Dr Attila Lotz, Csaba Vari

Litigation
Dr Judit Kelemen, Dr Attila Lotz

Mergers and acquisitions
Bryan Jardine, Dr Ákos Erös

Power generation, energy
Dr Ákos Erös, Richard Eordogh

Privatisations
Dr Iván Szász, Dr Péter Komáromi

Real estate
Dr György Udvardi, Dr Ákos Mester

Securities
Dr Ákos Erös, Dr Attila Lotz

THE FIRM

Founded in 1890, Squire, Sanders & Dempsey is a multi-jurisdictional law firm with 710 lawyers practising in offices in Europe, the Americas and Asia. The firm's practice covers most substantive areas of the law, with an emphasis on business and finance matters.

The firm operates as a single global partnership, which ensures client accountability and the seamless delivery of uniformly high-quality legal services throughout the world. The firm's lawyers come from many countries and cultures, are licensed to practise in both common law and civil law jurisdictions, and communicate with clients in their native languages. Today, the firm remains committed to the fundamental principles ordained by its founders: to serve clients effectively and maintain the professional standards that distinguish both the firm and its people.

AREAS OF PRACTICE

The firm is organised around four major practice areas: advocacy, business, capital markets and regulated industries. Within these practice areas, the firm's work can be divided into numerous areas of specialisation, including banking, bankruptcy and restructuring, biotechnology and pharmaceuticals, communications, competition law, converging technologies, corporate, energy, environmental, healthcare, intellectual property, international dispute resolution, labour and employment, litigation, mergers and acquisitions, privatisations, project finance, real estate, securities and taxation.

Since its opening in 1991, Squire Sanders' Budapest office has served as an adviser to clients on key privatisation and investment opportunities, financing and securitisations, mergers and acquisitions, joint ventures, intellectual property, regulatory, communications, energy, real estate, labour and environmental issues. A multilingual staff of attorneys includes Western-trained foreign lawyers.

Considered one of the leading law firms in Hungary, the Budapest office provides counsel to Hungarian firms and foreign entities doing business in the region as well as governmental institutions.

Intellectual property rights, joint ventures and licensing arrangements are among the matters lawyers handle for clients. In addition, the Budapest office has represented a number of businesses in connection with cross-border litigation, arbitration and commercial transactions.

SZECSKAY LAW FIRM - MOQUET BORDE & ASSOCIÉS

KOSSUTH TÉR 16-17
1055 BUDAPEST

Telephone: +36 1 472 30 00
Fax: +36 1 472 30 01
E-mail: mba@szecskay.hu
Website: www.szecskay.hu

Number of lawyers 18

Languages
English, French, German, Romanian

Contacts
Dr András Szecskay, Dr Judit Budai, Laurent A Niddam

CATEGORIES OF WORK	
Mergers and acquisitions	Labour law
Company law	European law
Corporate finance	Competition law
Capital markets	Insolvency
Tax law and tax planning	Real estate
Media and entertainment law	Environmental law
Information technology	Procurement law
Intellectual property	Litigation and arbitration
Telecommunications	Banking law

WEIL, GOTSHAL & MANGES

BANK CENTER
GRANITE TOWER
SZABADSÁG TÉR 7
1054 BUDAPEST

Telephone: + 36 1 302 9100
Fax: + 36 1 302 9110
Website: www.weil.com

Other offices
Austin, Boston, Brussels, Dallas, Frankfurt, Houston, London, Miami, Munich, New York, Paris, Prague, Silicon Valley, Singapore, Warsaw, Washington DC

Number of lawyers 1,000
at this office 8

Contact
David Dedenck

CATEGORIES OF WORK

Banking and finance	**Competition**
Capital markets	**Dispute resolution**
Energy	**Labour and employment**
IP, technology and communications	**Private equity and venture capital**
Mergers and acquisitions	**Privatisation**
Project finance	**Real estate**
General corporate and commercial	**Telecoms and media**

THE FIRM

Established in 1931 in New York, Weil, Gotshal & Manges combines lawyers worldwide to meet clients' needs in recognition of the benefits of broad industry and regional experience. The lawyers in the firm's practice groups work together to provide full-service legal advice to clients in sectors as diverse as energy, financial services and hi-tech.

The firm developed a network of offices across the US in the 1970s and 1980s to cater for its expanding client base, and was one of the first international law firms to establish a major presence in central Europe. The firm now has established offices in Brussels, Budapest, Frankfurt, London, Paris, Prague, Singapore and Warsaw.

The firm advises a broad and diverse group of clients, including many of the largest and most prominent corporations and government agencies around the globe, and leading financial institutions.

AREAS OF PRACTICE

The firm's US and European antitrust practice advises on international M&A regulatory notifications, antitrust distribution counselling, cartels, litigation and government and state competition policy. Expertise includes software and computer, healthcare, telecommunications and media, transportation, utilities, heavy industry, consumer goods, financial services and sports.

The corporate department is the firm's largest. The department advises international financial institutions and corporate clients in complex public and private M&As, private equity deals and strategic alliances.

The firm's corporate governance practice is recognised as one of the pre-eminent counsellors of corporate boards, management and institutional investors on the full range of governance issues, including board composition, structure and processes; executive and director compensation; director responsibilities; internal and governmental investigations of alleged accounting or other corporate misconduct; and shareholder initiatives. The firm has advised the World Bank, the OECD, the European Commission and various stock exchanges and regulatory bodies, and is a leader in providing director training programmes worldwide.

The firm advises on a wide range of financing activities and has particular expertise in acquisition finance, asset-based finance, debt restructuring and insolvency, debt and equity capital markets, derivatives, high-yield debt, securitisation, structured finance and telecoms and multimedia financing.

The firm has a leading IP and technology practice and advises some of the world's major technology, media and telecommunications companies. It also acts for investors in technology, media and communications entities. The practice handles patent infringements, outsourcing transactions, strategic alliances, cross-border mergers and acquisitions, investments and IPOs, and advises on the protection and exploitation of IP and on a wide range of e-commerce matters, including data protection. It has expertise in regulatory telecoms matters.

The litigation practice advises international clients on all major areas of the law and has extensive experience in all aspects of dispute resolution. It advises clients in jury trials and appeals, arbitration and alternative dispute forums.

The firm's real estate practice handles complex real estate transactions (including finance, securitisations, development, leasing, sales, acquisitions and debt restructurings) across the US and Europe. It also advises clients on real estate M&A transactions involving real estate investment trusts.

The firm has one of the largest bankruptcy and business reorganisation practices in the world. It includes attorneys in New York, Boston, Dallas, Frankfurt, Houston, London and Miami. The department has been involved in virtually all of the major chapter 11 reorganisation cases in the US and in major national and international out-of-court debt restructurings.

The tax department provides advice on international and domestic taxation, covering many different economic sectors. The department works with the firm's other departments to find innovative solutions to problems that present various and competing multi-disciplinary considerations.

ICELAND

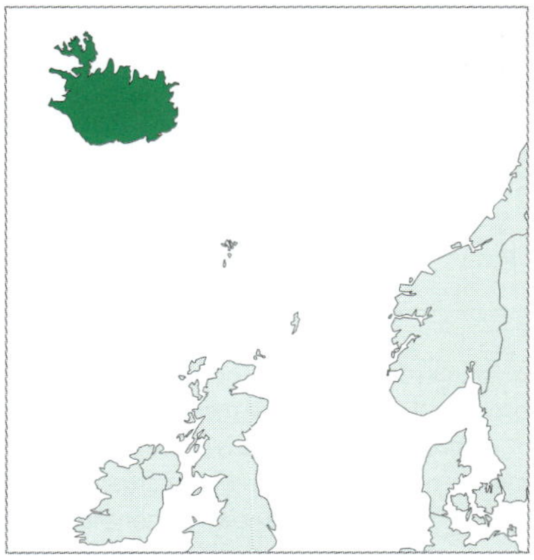

Population	**280,800**
Number of lawyers	**1,500**
Professional title	**Lawyer; advocate**
Currency	**Icelandic Króna (Isk)**

Index

Iceland has been an independent republic since 1944. It is a civil law jurisdiction, with a legal system based on Danish law.

A centre-right coalition currently holds power over a sparse, highly literate population, the vast majority of which speaks Icelandic, although English and Danish are widely understood. Nearly all of the major law firms are situated in the country's capital, Reykjavik, home to the country's Supreme Court. The Althing (Iceland's present-day parliament) was founded in 930, and is the world's oldest existing national assembly.

Of the country's 1,500 lawyers, around 650 are members of the Bar with rights of audience before the District Court, while 215 lawyers also have rights of audience before the Supreme Court.

BILLING

Law firms in Iceland generally bill by the hour. Billing rates are comparatively low by international standards, but are expected to move closer into line over the coming years. Partner rates at the larger firms currently fall between €175 and €250 per hour, with associates billed out at around three-quarters of those levels. Firms will normally charge international clients more than domestic entities.

MARKETING

The Icelandic Bar Association's Code of Conduct includes provisions regarding the marketing of commercial law firms. A firm advertising its legal services must give an honest indication of its expertise without inappropriate exaggeration. A number of leading firms use websites to publicise their practices, and the Code specifically regulates this form of advertising.

IN-HOUSE LAWYERS

Felag logfraedinga fjarmalafyrirtaekja, Iceland's Association of In-House Lawyers in Financial Institutions, represents the interests of 160 lawyers working in banks, insurance companies and securities houses. Almost half of these are members of the Icelandic Bar, and have partial rights of audience before the District Court.

ECONOMIC CLIMATE

Iceland's economy suffered a downturn following its strong upswing from 1996-2000. After a period of turmoil marked by a large deficit in the country's trade balance, a steadily weakening króna and growing inflation, there are now increasing indications that the economy is recovering and that new expansion is underway.

Iceland's trade is historically heavily dependent on the fisheries sector, while manufacturing exports, primarily aluminium, are rising and economic diversification continues; fast-growing sectors include the country's software and biotechnology industries, tourism and the export of fisheries know-how.

In an effort both to reduce the country's reliance on its fisheries and to regenerate its rural economy, the government is taking advantage of abundant supplies of hydroelectric and geothermal power and expanding Iceland's heavy industry, although the moves have met with widespread concern from environmentalists. Key projects include the construction of the Reyðarfjörður aluminium smelter and related hydroelectric plant in eastern Iceland, and Norðurál's planned expansion of its aluminium smelter in Grundartangi.

Iceland is not a member of the EU, but has been a member of European Free Trade Association (EFTA) since 1970 and of the European Economic Area (EEA) since 1994, entitling it to access to the EU internal market. Under the terms of the EEA Agreement, Iceland is subject to certain EU legislation, with the vital exception of agriculture and fisheries management. Iceland's long-standing Prime Minister, Davíð Oddson, has repeatedly expressed his reluctance to cede further ground to Europe. Under the terms of the coalition agreement struck between Mr Oddson's Independence Party and the Progressive Party following the 2003 general election, he will step down as Prime Minister in September 2004 in favour of the Progressive Party's Halldór Ásgrímsson, who is currently Minister of Foreign Affairs and known to be more pro-European.

The government's privatisation programme is now broadly complete, although Iceland Telecom remains in public hands following a failed attempt to sell in 2002.

LEGAL MARKET

After a static period matching the country's general economic slowdown, most firms are now reporting very healthy levels of activity. Iceland's legal market is small and still dominated by sole practitioners, and it is common for clients to

The largest firms

1	Logos – Legal Services	21
2	Lex Law Offices	15
3	AM Praxis	8
	Backman & Björgvinsson	8
	Lagastod – Sigurmar K Albertsson	8
6	Jonsson & Hall	7
	Landslog Law Offices	7
8	Attorneys at Hofdabakki	6
9	Lögborg	5
	Lögmenn Klapparstig	5
	Lögmenn Skolavordustig 6B	5
12	Fjeldsted, Blöndal & Fjeldsted	4
	LM Attorneys	4
	Landwell	4
	Law Office Solicitor Sudurlandsbraut 6	4
	Lögfrædipjónustan ehf	4
17	LAG – Atli Gislason, Law Office	3
	Law Office Solicitors Soleyjargotu 17	3
	Löggardur ehf	3
	Páll Arnór Pálsson hrl & Ragnar Baldursson hdl	3
	Solnes Law Office	3
22	Adalsteinsson & Partners	2
	JP Lögmenn	2
	Sigurjonsson & Thor	2
25	Faktor Patentbureau ehf	1
	Kjartan Ragnars Law Offices	1

These figures represent the total number of lawyers in this country only, and have been supplied by the firms themselves. The figures should be accurate as at 1 January 2004.

instruct different firms to advise on different aspects of their business. There are mixed views within the legal community whether the large firms necessarily offer the best quality of service. Nevertheless **Logos – Legal Services** and **Lex Law Offices**, with 12 partners each, continue to stand out for their size and the range of services that they offer. It appears unlikely that they can grow much larger without risking conflicting themselves out of significant new instructions, whilst there is obvious scope for consolidation amongst the numerous flourishing but less sizeable firms in the market. **Jonsson & Hall** remains particularly competitive in the corporate and banking sectors, while **Attorneys at Hofdabakki** and **JP Lögmenn** are among the few firms to have increased partner numbers in 2003. In a significant development at **Lex Law Offices**, highly-rated Bjarni Benediktsson was elected as a member of parliament for the Independence Party in the spring, together with a second partner in Sigurður Kristjánsson, who has left the firm to pursue a full-time political career. Benediktsson has stepped down as managing partner, and Heiðrun Jónsdóttir, former head of PR at Iceland Telecom, has joined the firm as managing director. Although Benediktsson is still a partner, it remains to be seen how much time he will be able to devote to legal practice and what impact the changes will have on the firm as a whole.

INTERNATIONAL ASSOCIATIONS

Jonsson & Hall is a member of the *State Capital Law Firm Group*.

Legalis Law Office is a member of the international network *Globalaw*.

Landwell is part of the Pricewaterhouse-Coopers-tied network of the same name.

Logos – Legal Services is a member of the international networks *Lex Mundi* and *TerraLex*.

BANKING AND FINANCE

Iceland's financial sector is well served by in-house lawyers and, as a result, external advice is sought relatively rarely.

Jonsson & Hall has advised the two largest domestic banks (Kaupþing Búnaðarbanki and Íslandsbanki) on a case-by-case basis, and has also advised an array of US banks and other foreign institutions. Ragnar H Hall at the firm is a recognised authority in the insolvency and corporate restructuring sector.

Lex Law Offices has an established record of advising international and domestic banks, as well as borrowers, with partners Ólafur Haraldsson and Aðalsteinn Jónasson specialising in the sector. Haraldsson led the firm's advice to the Royal Bank of Scotland, BNP Paribas SA and Fortis Bank on the $185m refinancing of the Norðurál aluminium smelter. **Lex Law Offices** also advised a syndicate of banks on the $53m term loan facility extended

BANKING AND FINANCE

JONSSON & HALL ✪
LEX LAW OFFICES ✪
LOGOS – LEGAL SERVICES ✪

AM Praxis ✪
LM Attorneys ✪
Landwell ✪
Lögmenn Skolavordustig 6B

Attorneys at Hofdabakki ✪
Fjeldsted, Blöndal & Fjeldsted
Landslog Law Offices
Reykjavik Law Office
Solnes Law Office

Firms are listed A-Z in tiers which are ranked in order of priority
✪ Indicates firm displays contact details at the end of this chapter.

to domestic telecoms operator Íslandssími following the Og Vodafone merger.

Logos – Legal Services is a recognised leader in terms of project finance work; partner Jakob R Möller is the firm's best-known personality in the field.

AM Praxis is historically known for its domestic banking advice, but has also advised a number of US banks regarding investment on the Icelandic stock market.

Kristján Thórbergsson at **LM Attorneys** is a specialist in domestic banking and finance work; his clients have included the Reykjavik Savings Bank.

Landwell, in addition to advising Kaupþing Búnaðarbanki on the financing of the Bakkavör and Huurre buyouts, recently advised Icelandic computer games producer CCP on a €1.1m bond issue.

Lögmenn Skolavordustig 6B has experience of providing corporate and regulatory advice to domestic banks. Its recent work in the sector includes advice to a group of bidders, backed by Búnaðarbanki Íslands hf, on a tender offer for the initial capital contribution shares in SPRON, Iceland's largest savings bank; the bid raised an array of banking regulatory issues.

Attorneys at Hofdabakki moves into the table on the back of its appointment of new partner Björn Lindál, with whom the firm is hoping to build its profile in the sector. Lindál's background includes 15 years with the National Bank of Iceland, as well as time spent as the Icelandic representative in the Nordic Department of the World Bank. The firm has recently assisted Irish bank DEPFA on its €16m refinancing of a privatised home for the elderly in Reykjavik, the first of its kind in Iceland.

Skuli Fjeldsted at **Fjeldsted, Blöndal & Fjeldsted** is active in the field of aircraft finance, as well as handling aircraft registration matters. Clients include foreign lessors and financial institutions.

Landslog Law Offices is known for its work for government agencies as well as for private sector companies; the firm has provided extensive advice to the State on its relationship with foreign investors.

CORPORATE AND COMMERCIAL

Jonsson & Hall has an impressive range of domestic and international clients. Gunnar Jónsson at the firm, who has been president of the Icelandic Bar Association since 2002, continues to advise global aluminium producer Alcoa Inc on its Icelandic operations. In June 2003, the company concluded a deal with the Icelandic government and local municipalities for the construction of the Reyðarfjörður aluminium smelter in eastern Iceland, which has a scheduled production capacity of 322,000 tonnes per year. With the smelter valued at approximately $1bn, the project represents the largest ever contract entered into by Alcoa and the largest ever foreign investment in Iceland. The national power company, Landsvirkjun, has signed up to power the smelter for the first 40 years, and is currently building a hydroelectric plant at Kárahnjúkar dedicated to the smelter, at an estimated cost of $1.2bn. Jónsson is commended for his 'hands-on, personable and knowledgeable' approach.

Lex Law Offices has been involved in an impressive array of corporate transactions, for clients including Shell, domestic insurer Sjóvá Almennar and Straumur Investment Company. Partner Aðalsteinn Jónasson advised Straumur on the disposal of its shareholding in Eimskip to an Eimskip subsidiary, partly in exchange for a sizeable shareholding in Icelandair; the deal, valued at around $74m, was part of a wider transaction resulting in substantial changes in the ownership of many of Iceland's largest companies. **Lex Law Offices** was also involved in the Reyðarfjörður project, advising the owners of the project company, Reyðarál, on the sale of their holdings to Alcoa, and providing construction and employment law advice to the principal contractor, Bechtel International Inc.

Logos – Legal Services' practice is focussed on corporate and commercial advice for the firm's extensive portfolio of domestic and international clients, including around 40% of the companies listed on Iceland's Stock Exchange. The firm's highest-profile corporate lawyers are managing partner Gunnar Sturluson and Pétur Guðmundarson.

AM Praxis, whose four partners include former Iceland Telecom CEO Thorarinn V Thorarinsson, advises an impressive roster of international clients. The firm has added Apple Computer Inc to established clients such as Nike, Japan Tobacco, Microsoft and Bristol-Myers Squibb.

Hreinn Loftsson at **Attorneys at Hofdabakki** is chairman of Iceland's largest retail company, the Baugur Group, and has longstanding links with the Icelandic government. He is now concentrating on private practice following ten years of service on the Privatisation Task Force, from which he resigned as chairman in 2002. His recent corporate work includes acting for the Icelandic Drilling Company on its acquisition of Björgun, a major domestic mining and land development company, for around Isk2.4bn (€27m). The firm has added two new partners to its numbers; Björn Lindál joined in May 2003 following a 15-year stint as deputy CEO and managing director at the National Bank of Iceland, while Einar Sigurjónsson is a former sole practitioner who merged his practice with **Attorneys at Hofdabakki** in April 2003. Sigurjónsson's work is focussed on insurance, investment and debt collection.

CORPORATE AND COMMERCIAL

JONSSON & HALL ✪
LEX LAW OFFICES ✪
LOGOS – LEGAL SERVICES ✪

AM Praxis ✪
Attorneys at Hofdabakki ✪
LM Attorneys ✪
Landslog Law Offices
Landwell ✪
Legalis Law Office
Lögmenn Skolavordustig 6B
Reykjavik Law Office

Fjeldsted, Blöndal & Fjeldsted
GAJ Law Firm ehf
JP Lögmenn
Páll Arnór Pálsson hrl & Ragnar Baldursson hdl
Tax.is Law Office

Firms are listed A-Z in tiers which are ranked in order of priority
✪ *Indicates firm displays contact details at the end of this chapter.*

LM Attorneys continues to advise a selection of hi-tech and IT clients, together with clients from more traditional sectors. It has taken a number of instructions from genetic research companies, including deCODE genetics, a leading population-based genomics operation headquartered in Reykjavik. Partners Kristján Thórbergsson and Jóhannes B Björnsson provide a broad range of legal advice to the Icelandic National Broadcasting Service.

Landslog Law Offices, which has offices in Reykjavik and Keflavik, is a domestically focussed firm. Jón Sveinsson and Garðar Garðasson have a proven record in corporate and related competition work; former associate Viðar Lúðvíksson has recently been made up to partner and also specialises in these areas.

Corporate and banking specialist **Landwell** is part of the PricewaterhouseCoopers-tied international network. It is a small firm and a relative newcomer to the market, having completed only two years of operation in the jurisdiction, but this year moves up to the second tier on the back of the impressive array of instructions which it continues to attract. The firm has advised Kaupþing Búnaðarbanki on the bank's €62.6m acquisition of a majority stake in Finnish investment company Novestia Ohj, the leveraged management buyout of the Bakkavör Group's seafood business for approximately €41m and the joint venture MBO of Finnish refrigerating company Huurre for €83m. Other clients include DHL and the French and Canadian Embassies in Iceland. The firm's two partners are Asgeir Ragnarsson and Baldvin Björn Haraldsson, and associate Einar Árnason is soon to be made up.

Legalis Law Office is a domestic-oriented business law practice. Its three partners provide corporate, commercial and related advice to a diverse range of clients including commercial banks, loan funds, import companies and a variety of public bodies.

Lögmenn Skolavordustig 6B's practice is focussed on contentious work, but the firm also has extensive experience in the corporate and commercial sector. Its recent work has included representing an individual and related corporations on their disposal of approximately Isk1bn (€11.2m) worth of shares in investment company Afl fjarfestingarfelag, a Landsbanki subsidiary. It has also advised two of the four sellers of a majority stake in a real estate company holding over 120,000 square metres of land in Reykjavik.

Reykjavik Law Office's seven partners advise a predominantly domestic clientele on a wide range of matters, including corporate, commercial and tax law.

Though specialising in business law advice, **Fjeldsted, Blöndal & Fjeldsted** is also known for its experience in trade mark and aviation work.

Tax.is Law Office, the only law firm in Iceland which specialises in tax law and tax-related issues, has strengthened its focus on tax and business law. It has been joined by a new partner in Vala Valtysdóttir, a former head of department of the Internal Revenue Directorate and attorney at KPMG and Ernst & Young in Iceland. Gardar Valdimarsson and his team provide tax and broader advice to a wide range of predominantly international clients, mainly corporations but also institutions, associations and individuals. The firm's clients include numerous US, Canadian and UK inward investors. Two of **Tax.is Law Office**'s more generalist partners Guðgón Ólafur Jónsson and Eyvindur Gunnarsson, left to join **JP Lögmenn** at the beginning of 2003; the firm now has four partners, and, together with its insolvency experience, offers a range of general commercial advice.

DISPUTE RESOLUTION

Jonsson & Hall's founding partner, Gestur Jónsson, sits on the panel of arbitrators for the Icelandic Chamber of Commerce and has a formidable reputation as a commercial litigator.

DISPUTE RESOLUTION

JONSSON & HALL ✪
LÖGMENN SKOLAVORDUSTIG 6B
LOGOS – LEGAL SERVICES ✪

Adalsteinsson & Partners
JP Lögmenn
Landslog Law Offices
Lex Law Offices ✪

AM Praxis ✪
Attorneys at Hofdabakki ✪

Firms are listed A-Z in tiers which are ranked in order of priority
✪ *Indicates firm displays contact details at the end of this chapter.*

Ragnar H Hall at the firm is also highly respected in the field.

Both partners at **Lögmenn Skolavordustig 6B**, Jón Steiner Gunnlaugsson and Karl Axelsson, are Supreme Court advocates. Gunnlaugsson is the more experienced of the two and enjoys a first-class reputation. Recently the firm successfully defended in two high-profile actions the interests of a group of minority shareholders in Icelandic Pharmaceuticals; Gunnlaugsson was praised not only for his technical prowess but also for the delicacy with which he handled the proceedings. The firm also advised Búnaðarbanki Íslands hf after the Icelandic Stock Exchange levied its first ever fine against it.

Logos – Legal Services' Hákon Árnason and Jakob R Möller are highly regarded for their contentious insurance work.

Ragnar Adalsteinsson at **Adalsteinsson & Partners** is widely admired for his advocacy skills and is an internationally renowned human rights lawyer. In September 2003, he attracted widespread media attention when he filed a lawsuit with Iceland's State Criminal Prosecutor on behalf of practitioners of the Falun Gong spiritual movement, charging Luo Gan with crimes of torture, genocide and crimes against humanity. Gan, a head of China's '6-10 Office', was on a two-day visit to Iceland. Sigríður Rut Júlíusdóttir, previously an associate at **Jonsson & Hall**, is Adalsteinsson's new partner at the firm. In one of the country's longest ever District Court cases, currently due for appeal before the Supreme Court, she successfully defended the owner of an art gallery charged with forgery (*The People v Pétur Þór Gunnarsson and Jónas Freydal Þorsteinsson*).

Jóhann H Nielsson at **JP Lögmenn** has a very strong reputation as an insolvency litigator, while Vilhjálmur H Vilhjálmsson at **Landslog Law Offices** is recommended for insurance and shipping-related litigation.

Lex Law Offices' key litigation client is domestic insurer Sjóvá Almennar, which uses the firm on an exclusive basis for advice in relation to a high volume and full range of claims work, including corporate, shipping and personal injury claims.

AM Praxis is recommended for securities litigation.

Attorneys at Hofdabakki has represented Landsvirkjun on a variety of cases, including the high-profile litigation relating to the environmental impact assessment of the Kárahnjúkar plant. The firm also represented the Baugur Group on the major investigation instigated by the Icelandic Police following allegations made about the Group's CEO by a former supplier, as well as on related litigation before the courts in Iceland and the US. The supplier, Nordica Inc, was represented by **Lögmenn Skolavordustig 6B**.

EU AND COMPETITION

Lögmenn Skolavordustig 6B's high reputation in the sector is due largely to the expertise of partners Heimir Örn Herbertsson and Karl Axelsson. The firm regularly advises the Icelandic Competition Authority, and is in the unique position of having been involved in every competition dispute to have come before the courts since Iceland's Competition Act was enacted in 1993. The firm has worked on two notable actions recently, one regarding the Authority's investigation into the Icelandic oil market and the other relating to fines levied against fruit and vegetable distributors for anti-competitive behaviour.

Logos – Legal Services' practice includes a significant quantity of EU and competition advice on the back of its corporate work, and the firm has recently represented a number of oil companies and insurance companies. Many partners at the firm have gained experience of EU matters during time spent abroad, and both Árni Vilhjálmsson and Helga Melkorka Óttarsdóttir have previously worked at the EFTA Surveillance Authority. Gunnar Sturluson is another highly rated competition law practitioner.

AM Praxis represents mainly foreign clients, including a number of pharmaceutical companies, on competition matters.

Jonsson & Hall continues to be very active in its competition work, in particular partner Hörður Felix Harðarson whose recent work has included representing clients such as Shell before the authorities.

LM Attorneys is another firm with EU and competition expertise, and has recently represented the Leifur Eiriksson Air Terminal at Iceland's international airport in two competition disputes.

Thórunn Guðmundsdóttir heads **Lex Law Offices**' competition practice; she has represented Sjóvá Almennar in relation to the authorities' long-running and ongoing investigation into Iceland's insurance market, as well as acting for one of the distributors involved in the landmark fruit and vegetables case. The firm also has extensive experience of acting on EU merger notifications.

EU AND COMPETITION

LÖGMENN SKOLAVORDUSTIG 6B
LOGOS – LEGAL SERVICES ✪

AM Praxis ✪
Jonsson & Hall ✪
LM Attorneys ✪
Lex Law Offices ✪
Lögmenn Klapparstig
Sudurlandsbraut 6, Law Office Solicitor

Attorneys at Hofdabakki ✪
Landslog Law Offices
Landwell ✪
Reykjavik Law Office

Firms are listed A-Z in tiers which are ranked in order of priority
✪ *Indicates firm displays contact details at the end of this chapter.*

Stefán Thórisson at **Lögmenn Klapparstig** was previously employed at the EFTA Surveillance Authority and is highly rated, with clients including a number of domestic banks.

Andri Árnason at **Law Office Solicitor Sudurlandsbraut 6** enjoys an exceptionally high reputation in the sector.

Attorneys at Hofdabakki has established a solid reputation for its competition advice on the back of its corporate practice; its recent case load has included advice to the Hagkaup supermarket chain.

Competition work represents a increasing part of **Landslog Law Offices**' practice, and the firm has this year been included in the third tier. Partner Jóhannes K Sveinnson and new partner Viðar Lúðvíksson (formerly an associate at the firm) have advised, in addition to a number of the firm's regular domestic clients, a major US pharmaceutical company on competition matters.

The other new inclusion in the tier is **Landwell**, where Baldvin Björn Haraldsson has represented computer and software distributor EJS and travel agency Terra Nova Sol in competition disputes.

EMPLOYMENT

Gestur Jónsson at **Jonsson & Hall** has extensive employment law experience, and is best known for his work with unions and employees. He has represented Iceland's largest union of government workers for around 20 years. Ragnar H Hall at the firm has also represented unions and is a recognised expert. The firm's recent employment work includes advice to Alcoa Inc in relation to the Reyðarfjörður project.

Atli Gislason at **LAG – Atli Gislason, Law Office** is recommended for his advice to trade unions and pension funds. His clients include Framsyn, one of Iceland's largest pension funds.

Logos – Legal Services' Jakob R Möller is known for his advice to employers, which is also the focus of **AM Praxis**' employment work.

EMPLOYMENT

JONSSON & HALL ✪
LAG – ATLI GISLASON, LAW OFFICE
LOGOS – LEGAL SERVICES ✪

AM Praxis ✪
Lex Law Offices ✪

Firms are listed A-Z in tiers which are ranked in order of priority
✪ *Indicates firm displays contact details at the end of this chapter.*

Thorarinn V Thorarinsson at **AM Praxis** advised Italian multinational Impregilo, the main contractor on the Kárahnjúkar hydroelectric plant, and on this basis the firm has been added to the second tier. The project involves the extensive import of foreign labour, and has accordingly raised a range of complex employment issues.

Lex Law Offices' employment work is generated mainly by its corporate clientele. The firm's most significant recent advice has been to construction multinational Bechtel International Inc in relation to the Reyðarfjörður project. Partner Hanna Lára Helgadóttir is an experienced practitioner.

IT AND TELECOMS

The most significant transaction in the sector has been the recent completion of a merger between three companies at the forefront of Iceland's telecommunications market, TAL, Íslandssími and Halló! Frjáls fjarskipti. The merged entity (branded as Og Vodafone) was launched in cooperation with the Vodafone Group in April 2003 and, with nearly a quarter share of the market, is the main competitor to state-owned Landssími (Iceland Telecom).

Founding partner Ragnar Adalsteinsson at **Adalsteinsson & Partners** is an extremely experienced telecoms practitioner. Having left **Logos – Legal Services** some years ago to work as a sole practitioner, he joined forces with partner Sigríður Rut Júlíusdóttir towards the end of 2002. Adalsteinsson advised TAL on the merger, which involved the sale of TAL for around Isk4.1bn (€46m), and he continues to advise Og Vodafone.

Ragnar Tómas Árnason at **Logos – Legal Services** is another recognised telecoms expert, while Andri Árnason at **Law Office Solicitor Sudurlandsbraut 6** is also a highly reputed specialist in the field; he has been advising Iceland Telecom for over 20 years.

Hlynur Halldórsson at **LM Attorneys** deserves a mention for his IT and data protection work; the firm advises a number of domestic IT companies including market-leader Skyrr and Tern Systems, an Air Traffic Control research and development firm.

Lex Law Offices has provided occasional advice to Iceland's telecoms regulator, and advised a syndicate of banks on the significant term loan facility extended to Íslandssími following the Og Vodafone merger.

IT AND TELECOMS

ADALSTEINSSON & PARTNERS
LOGOS – LEGAL SERVICES ✪
SUDURLANDSBRAUT 6, LAW OFFICE SOLICITOR

AM Praxis ✪
Jonsson & Hall ✪
LM Attorneys ✪
Lex Law Offices ✪
Reykjavik Law Office

Firms are listed A-Z in tiers which are ranked in order of priority
✪ *Indicates firm displays contact details at the end of this chapter.*

INTELLECTUAL PROPERTY

IP boutique **Faktor Patentbureau ehf** was founded by Jon Arnalds. Now semi-retired, he is an experienced lawyer and has completed a lengthy stint as a district court judge. His team, including two other partners, primarily handles patent work; it claims to deal with around 45% of all domestic patent filings of foreign origin. It is also active in trade mark and contentious IP work, including copyright and competition litigation. The mainstay of the firm is its overseas client base. It boasts some of the world's largest pharmaceutical companies in its portfolio.

Logos – Legal Services has part ownership, together with Danish firm **Plougmann, Vingtoff & Partners**, of the patent and trade mark agency A&P Árnason Intellectual Property Group. As an IP consultancy rather than a law firm, A&P is not licensed to represent its clients in court; it specialises in drafting and prosecuting patent and trade mark applications.

The other heavyweight in the field is **Sigurjonsson & Thor**. The firm enjoys a comparable client base and work spread, though with a slightly heavier emphasis on trade mark filings. Partners Valborg Kjartansdottir and Magnus H Magnusson are recommended for their contentious IP work.

Hróbjartur Jónatansson at **AM Praxis** remains active in his mainly contentious IP work, including trade mark litigation, piracy work, and general brand preservation.

Ragnar Adalsteinsson at **Adalsteinsson & Partners** is recommended for his copyright work; he has long acted as legal adviser to the Icelandic Association of Writers.

Jonsson & Hall has continued to provide IP advice to an impressive array of clients, including Iceland's largest music publisher and a number of software companies.

Erla S Árnadóttir at **Lex Law Offices** is a well-known and experienced IP practitioner, advising on contentious and non-contentious matters and lecturing part-time on the field. Ragnheiður M Olafsdóttir, who previously worked at the Icelandic Patent Office, leads the firm's growing registration practice, mainly advising domestic companies on the protection of trade marks abroad.

Both **GH Sigurgeirsson** and **Fjeldsted, Blöndal & Fjeldsted** are specialist trade mark firms with impressive overseas client bases; the latter also specialises in trade mark litigation.

Kjartan Ragnars Law Offices advises mainly foreign clients on patent and trade mark issues, as well as offering broader business law advice.

INTELLECTUAL PROPERTY

FAKTOR PATENTBUREAU EHF
LOGOS – LEGAL SERVICES ✪
SIGURJONSSON & THOR

AM Praxis ✪
Adalsteinsson & Partners
Jonsson & Hall ✪
Lex Law Offices ✪

Fjeldsted, Blöndal & Fjeldsted
GH Sigurgeirsson
Kjartan Ragnars Law Offices

Firms are listed A-Z in tiers which are ranked in order of priority
✪ *Indicates firm displays contact details at the end of this chapter.*

MARITIME AND TRANSPORT

Logos – Legal Services provides a wide range of shipping advice, including advice on cargo claims. Partner Einar Baldvin Axelsson enjoys a very high reputation in the sector, and is commended for his attentiveness and dedication. The firm's clients include Iceland's largest shipping company.

Gardar Briem at **Law Office Solicitors Soleyjargotu 17** is another very experienced practitioner and is particularly known for his insurance and cargo claims work, much of which is generated by US and UK P& I clubs.

MARITIME AND TRANSPORT

LOGOS – LEGAL SERVICES ✪
SOLEYJARGOTU 17, LAW OFFICE SOLICITORS

AM Praxis ✪
Jonsson & Hall ✪
LM Attorneys ✪
Landslog Law Offices
Lex Law Offices ✪
Lögmenn Skolavordustig 6B

Fjeldsted, Blöndal & Fjeldsted
Solnes Law Office

Firms are listed A-Z in tiers which are ranked in order of priority
✪ *Indicates firm displays contact details at the end of this chapter.*

Senior consultant Jónatan Sveinsson at **AM Praxis**, whose qualifications include a degree from the Icelandic Maritime School, has a proven record of advising fishing industry clients on transactions and transfer of quota.

Jonsson & Hall continues to advise Iceland's second-largest shipping line, Samskip, and two airlines, Iceland Express and Islandsflug. Hörður Felix Harðarson at the firm is currently representing the former, a low-budget airline, in its battle against market leader Icelandair before the competition authorities.

Jóhannes B Björnsson at **LM Attorneys** has longstanding links with the National Association of Fishing, and also acts for the Federation of Icelandic Fishing Vessel Owners.

Vilhjálmur H Vilhjálmsson at **Landslog Law Offices** is a similarly admired specialist. The firm's clients have included a range of insurers and shipping companies.

Lex Law Offices' clients include Samskip, which it advises on a range of issues including collision claims, and Sjóvá Almennar, which it represents on maritime-related claims work.

AM PRAXIS

SIGTÚN 42
IS 105
REYKJAVIK

Telephone: +354 533 3333
Fax: +354 533 2333
E-mail: amp@amp.is
Website: www.amp.is

Languages
English, the Scandinavian languages

Number of lawyers 8

Contact
Hrobjartur Jonatansson (hj@amp.is)

CATEGORIES OF WORK

Corporate and commercial	**Computer law**
Banking	**IT and communications**
Securities and finance	**Licensing**
Mergers and acquisitions	**Labour law**
Competition law	**Insurance**
Intellectual property	**Debt collection**

ATTORNEYS AT HOFDABAKKI

HOFDABAKKI 9
6TH FLOOR
110 REYKJAVIK

Telephone: +354 587 1286
Fax: +354 587 1247
E-mail: logmenn@justice.is
Website: www.justice.is

Languages
Danish, English

Number of lawyers 4

CATEGORIES OF WORK

Commercial and company law
Hreinn Loftsson, Thordur Bogason

Banking and finance
Björn Lindal

Competition law
Hreinn Loftsson, Thordur Bogason

Litigation
Thordur Bogason, Hreinn Loftsson

EU law and administrative law
Thordur Bogason, Björn Lindal

Energy, infrastructure and the environment
Thordur Bogason

Debt collecting and bankruptcy
Einar Sigurjönsson

Insurance
Hreinn Loftsson

JONSSON & HALL

MÖRKIN 1
108 REYKJAVÍK

Telephone: +354 581 21 22
Fax: +354 581 21 50
E-mail: law@law.is
Website: www.law.is

Languages
English, the Scandinavian languages

Number of lawyers 7

Member
State Capital Global Law Firm Group

CATEGORIES OF WORK

Arbitration

Banking and finance

Company and commercial

Commercial litigation

Competition

Insolvency

Insurance

IP law

Labour and employment

Media and entertainment

Mergers and acquisitions

International investments

Securities law

LM ATTORNEYS

SKOLAVÖRDUSTIG 12
3RD FLOOR
101 REYKJAVIK

Telephone: +354 562 1018
Fax: +354 562 9666
E-mail: hlh@lm.is
Website: www.lm.is

Languages
Danish, English

Number of lawyers 4

CATEGORIES OF WORK

Company and commercial
Kristjan Thorbergsson, Johannes Bjarni Bjornsson, Hlynur Halldorsson

Banking and finance
Kristjan Thorbergsson, Johannes Bjarni Bjornsson

Intellectual property
Kristjan Thorbergsson, Hlynur Halldorsson

Labour law
Johannes Bjarni Bjornsson, Kristjan Thorbergsson

IT and telecommunications
Hlynur Halldorsson

Maritime and transport
Johannes Bjarni Bjornsson, Hlynur Halldorsson

Litigation
Johannes Bjarni Bjornsson, Kristjan Thorbergsson

LANDWELL

SKOGARHLID 12
105 REYKJAVIK

Telephone: +354 550 0500
Fax: +354 550 0505
E-mail: landwell@is.landwellglobal.com
Website: www.landwellglobal.com/is

Languages
Danish, English, French

Number of lawyers 4

Contacts
Asgeir A Ragnarsson, Baldvin B Haraldsson

International groupings
Landwell, correspondent law firms of PricewaterhouseCoopers

CATEGORIES OF WORK

Commercial and competition
Asgeir A Ragnarsson,
Baldvin B Haraldsson

Corporate structuring
Katrin Hallgrimsdottir

Dispute resolution
Baldvin B Haraldsson

Technology, media and communications
Asgeir A Ragnarsson,
Baldvin B Haraldsson

Employment and human resources
Einar Baldvin Arnason,
Katrin Hallgrimsdottir

Financial services
Baldvin B Haraldsson

Intellectual property
Einar Baldvin Arnason

Mergers and acquisitions
Asgeir A Ragnarsson

Public law
Einar Baldvin Arnason

Real estate
Katrin Hallgrimsdottir

THE FIRM

Landwell is one of the largest international law practices with 2,000 business and tax lawyers worldwide. Landwell provides a full range of legal services through specialists organised in global networks. Landwell's main focus is on cross-border M&A transactions and corporate transformation projects. Working closely with PricewaterhouseCoopers, Landwell is a market leader in the design and delivery of complex corporate change. This is achieved through a focus on strong local capabilities with a global outlook and by ensuring that its implementation skills match its legal ones.

AREAS OF PRACTICE

Landwell provides a full range of business services, through specialist lawyers organised in global networks. In this way, consistent high standards of advice and service are guaranteed for both international and local clients. Landwell's international strengths include: legal consulting on mergers and acquisitions; corporate structuring; technology, media and communications; and employment law.

LEX LAW OFFICES

SUNDAGÖRDUM 2
PO BOX 8975
128 REYKJAVIK

Telephone: +354 590 2600
Fax: +354 590 2606
E-mail: lex@lex.is
Website: www.lex.is

Languages
English, German, the Scandinavian languages

Number of lawyers 18

Contact
Heidrún Jónsdóttir (managing director)

Lex Law Offices is in co-operation with KLegal International, with over 3,000 lawyers worldwide

CATEGORIES OF WORK

Banking, securities and finance
Ólafur Haraldsson, Adalsteinn Jónasson

Corporate and commercial law
Adalsteinn Jónasson, Jónas A Adalsteinsson

Mergers and acquisitions
Jónas A Adalsteinsson, Adalsteinn Jónasson

Foreign investments, international contracts
Hanna Lára Helgadóttir, Thórunn Gudmundsdóttir

Tax
Halldór Jónsson

Administrative law
Helgi Jóhannesson, Halldór Jónsson

Bankruptcy, insolvency
Helgi Jóhannesson, Halldór Jónsson

Maritime and transport law
Ólafur Haraldsson, Adalsteinn Jónasson

Trade marks
Thórunn Gudmundsdóttir, Lilja Jónasdóttir

Copyright, licensing, intellectual property
Erla S Árnadóttir, Lilja Jónasdóttir

EU
Thórunn Gudmundsdóttir

Labour law
Hanna Lára Helgadóttir

Energy and environmental law
Halldór Jónsson, Jónas A Adalsteinsson

Insurance, accident, injury claims
Lilja Jónasdóttir, Ólafur Haraldsson

Competition law
Thórunn Gudmundsdóttir

LOGOS – LEGAL SERVICES
SINCE 1907

EFSTALEITI 5
103 REYKJAVÍK

Telephone: +354 540 0300
Fax: +354 540 0301
E-mail: logos@logos.is
Website: www.logos.is

Languages
English, German, Spanish, the Scandinavian languages

Number of lawyers 24

Contact
Gunnar Sturluson (managing partner)

CATEGORIES OF WORK

Aviation
Othar Örn Petersen, Erlendur Gíslason

Banking, securities and finance
Pétur Gudmundarson, Jakob R Möller, Óttar Pálsson

Bankruptcy, insolvency
Erlendur Gíslason, Jakob R Möller

Companies, corporations
Pétur Gudmundarson, Gunnar Sturluson

Commercial law (general)
Pétur Gudmundarson, Óttar Pálsson, Ragnar T Árnason

Competition
Árni Vilhjálmsson, Óttar Palsson, Helga Melkorka Óttarsdóttir

Admiralty, maritime
Einar Baldvin Axelsson

Accident, injury claims, labour
Hákon Árnason, Jakob R Möller

Construction, building
Othar Örn Petersen, Erlendur Gíslason

EU and EEA law
Árni Vilhjálmsson, Helga Melkorka Óttarsdóttir

Insurance
Hákon Árnason

Litigation
Hákon Árnason, Othar Örn Petersen

Licensing
Gunnar Sturluson, Árni Vilhjálmsson

Tax
Erlendur Gíslason

Trade marks, intellectual property
Árni Vilhjálmsson, Ragnar T Árnason

IRAN

Population	**68.9 million**
Number of lawyers	**2,500**
Professional title	**Attorney**
Currency	**Rial**

The Islamic Republic of Iran shares borders with Iraq, Turkey, Armenia, Azerbaijan, Turkmenistan, Afghanistan and Pakistan. It has coastlines along the Persian Gulf, the Caspian Sea, and the Sea of Oman. The capital is Tehran.

Known as Persia until 1935, Iran became an Islamic republic in 1979 after the Iranian Revolution when the ruling shah was forced into exile. The US severed diplomatic ties after Iranian students seized 63 hostages at the US embassy. There followed a bloody, eight-year war with Iraq over disputed territory. In 1997 Mohammad Khatami was elected president, leading to a period of stability and gradual reform. In 2002 President Bush accused Iran of supporting terrorism and declared the country part of the 'axis of evil'. Relations with Western Europe are gradually improving, at the expense of the US, which continues to impose trade sanctions.

BILLING

Fees are commonly charged by the hour although fixed and contingency fees may also be agreed. Hourly rates range from around €80 ($100) to more than €200 ($250) an hour, depending on seniority.

MARKETING

There are no major restrictions on lawyers promoting their practices and leading firms have capitalised on the growing popularity of the Internet by establishing detailed websites. Direct mail, brochures and CD-roms are popular methods of promotion.

IN-HOUSE LAWYERS

The public sector is the largest employer of in-house lawyers for day-to-day legal work, particularly in the oil and gas sector. Many private practice lawyers are former in-house lawyers.

ECONOMIC CLIMATE

Iran's economy relies upon oil revenues which continue to be the main export, earning the country two-thirds of its hard currency.

Both its oil and gas industries require heavy investment and redevelopment. Some projects are being developed on a 'buy-back' basis, in which foreign oil majors such as TotalFinaElf and Shell act as contractors to the National Iranian Oil Company. Since 1997 deals with foreign oil companies valued at $15bn have been agreed

The economy is vulnerable to fluctuations in oil prices, whilst the state is a dominant force through ownership of the oil sector and other large enterprises. Reducing oil dependency and diversifying the economy is a necessity and the government, aided by organisations such as the United Nations Development Programme, has made the development of non-oil exports a priority.

So far progress has been limited; the country fails to provide a legal infrastructure conducive to foreign investment. Obstacles include the lack of a transparent and modern legal system and stringent labour, tax and foreign exchange laws. Iran's banks were nationalised in 1979. The largest commercial bank is Melli, followed by Sepah, Saderat, Refah Karegaran, Tejerat and Mellat. Privatisation of state-owned entities is being encouraged via listing on the Teheran Stock Exchange, which counts over 400 companies.

Foreign direct investment in Iran is possible only through partnership with Iranian nationals and with contribution in the share of existing or newly established companies. The maximum foreign contribution allowed in joint ventures is 49%. The Law Concerning the Attraction and Protection of Foreign Investment in Iran, passed in November 1995 outlines the official framework for foreign investment. The recent move to allow foreigners to purchase up to 10% of total shares on Iran's stock market is an example of initiatives to encourage inward investment.

In September 2003 Iran became a signatory to the Madrid Agreement Concerning the International Registration of Trade Marks, an agreement that grants each other's nationals patent and trade mark rights identical to those of their own nationals.

Despite trade sanctions imposed by the US, imports from the West have continued to increase. Major trading partners are Japan, Germany, France, Italy, the UK, United Arab Emirates and Belgium. The European Union has opposed US sanctions and several European oil companies have signed large deals with Iran. President Khatami, a liberal voted in for a second term by 77% of the population in 2001, and his reformists continue to cultivate the confidence of the international community by helping promote Iran as a stable and moderate country.

The largest firms

1	**Law Offices A A Atai & Associates**	5
2	**Foreign Legal Affairs Group**	3
	Torossian, Avanessian & Associates	3
4	**Studio Legale de Capoa e Associati**	2

These figures represent the total number of lawyers in this country only, and have been supplied by the firms themselves. The figures should be accurate as at 1 January 2004.

LEGAL MARKET

The majority of Iran's law firms are based in Tehran, the political, administrative and commercial capital. Many firms have less than five lawyers and there are only a few firms large enough to handle corporate work. Internal division into specialist departments is rare with most lawyers acting in more than one area.

Firms such as **Clyde & Co**, **Norton Rose** and **Denton Wilde Sapte** have a capability in the region through offices in Abu Dhabi, Oman, Dubai and Bahrain and advise on significant Iranian transactions.

The majority of international firms rely on working in a non-exclusive relationship with local counsel. Although in 1999 **Berrymans Lace Mawer** and **Towers & Hamlins** entered into talks with Iranian firms neither has a formal association.

One of the few foreign firms to have a presence on the ground is Italian firm **Studio Legale de Capoa e Associati**, which specialises in international commercial law and has other branches in Budapest, Bucharest, Warsaw, Bratislava and Belgrade. The firm's Tehran office opened in 2000 and is staffed by two Iranian lawyers and resident Italian lawyer Elisabetta Cavanna. **Studio Legale de Capoa e Associati** is a member of *IAG International*.

Other firms are unlikely to follow the Italian's lead until US sanctions are relaxed and multinational companies show an interest in the country, when significant fees may justify opening a local office.

Firms with experience of acting as local counsel are **Adib Law Firm**; **Atieh Associates**; **International Law Office Dr Parviz Savrai & Associates**; **Dr Shamsaei & Associates**; **Hami Legal Services**; **International Law Office Dr Behrooz Akhlagi and Associates**; **Law Offices Dr Ali Laghaee & Associates Inc International**; **Legal Iran International Services Bureau**; **Tavakoli & Shahabi**; and **Torossian, Avanessian & Associates**.

Dr Shamsaei & Associates is the Iranian member of the *Juritax* network, an international association of smaller and medium-sized firms. The ten-partner firm co-operates with several international law firms and has a particular association with **Murdochs Solicitors** based in the UK and **Abdullah Kh. Al-Ayoub & Associates**, a leading firm based in Kuwait.

Law Offices Dr Ali Laghaee & Associates Inc International has no formal relationships but works with **Al Tamimi & Co** in Dubai and **Abu-Ghazaleh Intellectual Property** across the Arab world.

International Law Office Dr Behrooz Akhlagi and Associates has an office in San Francisco, and works with a number of Western, Far Eastern and Indian law firms.

Law Offices A A Atai & Associates works with Italian, German and Japanese firms and has acted as local counsel for **Norton Rose** and **Towers & Hamlins**. In the US it is affiliated with **Mahmoud Katirai**, an Iranian firm based in Washington, DC.

Other firms with the capability required by international clients are **Pars Associates**, **International Law Offices of Dr Nader Sheybani & Associates** and **Tavakoli & Shahabi**.

Firms with well-recognised niches include **Raysan Patent & Trademark Agents**, **Law Offices of R Aghababian & Co** and **Abbas Mohajerian & Partners** which are general practice firms with a particular focus on IP matters – **Abbas Mohajerian & Partners** specialises in international patents. **Dr Alexander Aghayan & Associates Inc** is another primarily IP practice with offices in New York and Paris.

Iran's legal market has remained fairly static and quiet. One of the few changes was the merger between *Z A Afshari Law Firm* and *Law Offices M Ebadi & Associates*. The post-merged firm, operating as **M Ebadi & Associates** has a client base of over 300 international companies including Total SA and Wella AG.

J Nouraei & M Mostafavi Law Office, **Alavi & Associates** and **Law Offices of J Bokharai & Associates** are also active in the Iranian market.

CORPORATE AND COMMERCIAL

The majority of corporate work in Iran centres on agency and joint venture agreements between foreign companies and Iranian entities.

Law Offices A A Atai & Associates is one of the most internationally experienced of the local outfits. Examples of recent work include acting on the joint ventures between lamp manufacturers, Osram GmbH and an Iranian company, as well as Australian company, Macro Strategic Investment, and Qeshm Free Authority. It has also assisted Swiss mineral company, Glencore International in setting up a local branch. Banking work includes advising the local branch of Deutsche Bank. The arrival of Jalal Soltan Ahmadi further strengthens the firm's litigation capability. Volvo is the firm's biggest client, and others include Daewoo, the Swedish Embassy and Juki Corporation.

One of the largest local full service firms is **Adib Law Firm,** with 15 fee-earners. Highlights include representing two global companies on acquisitions, and acting as local counsel to UK-based firm **Stephenson Harwood** on a secured loan transaction involving an Iranian charter of two vessels. It regularly advises large domestic companies such as Iranian International Engineering Company on activities outside the Republic. Founder and name partner, Dr Adib is highly respected and under his leadership the firm has a reputation for diligence and the ability to meet tight deadlines. The firm has an impressive track record of advising international companies including Emirates Airlines and Gulf Air on a wide range of issues.

Dr Mohammad Shamsaei, an expert in international law and a former judge at the Iranian

CORPORATE AND COMMERCIAL

A Atai & Associates, Law Offices ✪
Adib Law Firm
Shamsaei, (Dr) & Associates

Alavi & Associates
Albert Bernardi & Associates, Law Offices of
Ali Laghaee, (Dr) & Associates Inc International, Law Offices
Atieh Associates
Behrooz Akhlagi, (Dr) and Associates, International Law Office
Hami Legal Services
J Bokharai & Associates, Law Offices of
Jamal Seifi, (Dr) & Associates
M Ebadi & Associates
Nader Sheybani, (Dr) & Associates, International Law Offices of
Pars Associates
Parviz Savrai, (Dr) & Associates, International Law Office
Tavakoli & Shahabi

Firms are listed A-Z in tiers which are ranked in order of priority
✪ *Indicates firm displays contact details at the end of this chapter.*

Ministry of Justice, is founder of the ten-partner firm, **Dr Shamsaei & Associates**. A mixture of domestic and international clients includes several technology companies.

Corporate and commercial is the cornerstone of **Alavi & Associates**' practice. The firm has an extensive track record of assisting foreign companies entering the Republic.

Three-fee-earner **Law Offices of Albert Bernardi & Associates** is one of Iran's oldest firms and provides general advice concentrating on international matters, corporate law and IP. Clients include SmithKlineBeecham Pharmaceuticals, Mitsubishi, Ferrari and Thomas Miller. The firm's founder, Dr Bernardi is regarded as an expert in maritime law and has represented P&I clubs in the UK, Belgium and Japan. He is also the official legal adviser to the Italian embassy in Iran.

IP matters comprise 90% of **Law Offices Dr Ali Laghaee & Associates Inc International**'s practice, and 99% of clients are foreign companies, including several global names. The firm's anti-counterfeit and litigation department recently established a dedicated team to investigate the extent of counterfeiting on behalf of a Japanese tobacco manufacturer. On the corporate side it tends to be transactional work for local businesses and advising foreign companies on registration of Iranian entities. The firm benefits from working with **Al Tamimi & Co** in Dubai and counts many Dubai companies active in Iran as clients.

Babak Namazi, a highly regarded international lawyer heads up four-strong **Atieh Associates**. The firm advised the managers, BNP and Commerzbank, on the first and second eurobond issues by the Government of Iran; and is currently advising a foreign telecoms company with regard to its bid for the second GSM licence in Iran. Among several significant oil and gas transactions, the firm advised the Italian project sponsors on the construction of Pareh Sar, the first independent power plant built under BOT structures. **Norton Rose** advised the project company.

Hami Legal Services is a well-established full service law firm headed up by two partners, Hassan and Mohammad Badamchi. The firm provides a broad range of corporate and commercial advice to clients including international names in the oil, stationery and photography sectors. It is perhaps best known for advising on IP matters.

Law Offices of J Bokharai & Associates, under the leadership of IP expert and name partner Jalal Bokharai advises across corporate, oil and gas, maritime, foreign investment, joint venture and technology transfer matters

Five-strong firm, **Dr Jamal Seifi & Associates** provides advice to local and international clients on all aspects of Iranian law. Examples of work in 2003 include providing advice on commercial and corporate matters to a French company with an interest in an Iranian engineering company, and advising an Iranian telecoms company on expansion issues. The firm also offers intellectual property capabilities. Name partner Dr Jamal Seifi is a highly regarded international arbitration lawyer who has acted in several major international cases.

M Ebadi & Associates is the result of the merger between intellectual property practice *Z A Afshari Law Firm* and *Law Offices of Ebadi & Associates*, a firm that has provided full services for the last 27 years including successful roles on several recent disputes.

International Law Offices of Dr Nader Sheybani & Associates' practice is mainly corporate law including international matters, foreign investment, joint ventures and oil and gas. Clients include Skoda, BMW and Hermes.

Pars Associates has two partners, Z Majdzadeh Ameli and MR Matine, and counts several international contracting companies, airlines, car manufacturers and engineering concerns among its clients.

Since establishment in 1995, **International Law Office Dr Parviz Savrai & Associates** has provided advice on corporate and commercial matters to clients from start-ups to multinationals. The eight fee-earners concentrate on international commercial transactions, oil and gas projects and intellectual property. Recently it advised a South Korean engineering and construction company on banking law and a Dutch subsidiary of a global leader in automation on competition matters. It also undertakes trade mark registration for a global soft drinks manufacturer and a Taiwanese baby product manufacturer.

Full service firm **Tavakoli & Shahabi** represents European, Australian, Canadian, Japanese, South American, Middle and Far Eastern companies in a wide range of areas, including sector expertise in oil and gas, and mining.

LAW OFFICES A. A. ATAI & ASSOCIATES, ATTORNEYS AT LAW

NO 8, 3RD FLOOR, 14TH STREET
ENTEFAZAH AVENUE
VOZARA
TEHRAN 15117

Telephone: +98 21 87 13 850
Fax: +98 21 87 15 252
E-mail: atai@ataiassociates.com
Website: www.ataiassociates.com

Languages
English, Farsi

Number of lawyers 5

Contact
Mr Ali Akbar Atai

CATEGORIES OF WORK

Company and commercial	**Banking and finance**
International business law	**Corporate and contract law**
Investment law	**Marine law**
Oil and gas	**Litigation**

THE FIRM

The law firm of A.A. Atai & Associates has offered a full range of legal services since 1975, and has developed an enviable reputation as one of Iran's leading international law firms, largely due to its ability to combine an understanding of international markets with dependable interpretation of relevant developments in Iran's legal system.

AREAS OF PRACTICE

Located in Tehran, the firm regularly advises European and Asian companies operating in Iran's oil, gas, transportation, telecoms and banking industries on a wide range of business matters, including setting up representative offices, investing in free trade and special economic zones, establishing joint ventures and participating in major government sponsored economic projects.

The firm is available to advise, draft, interpret and negotiate documents in English as well as Farsi.

IRELAND

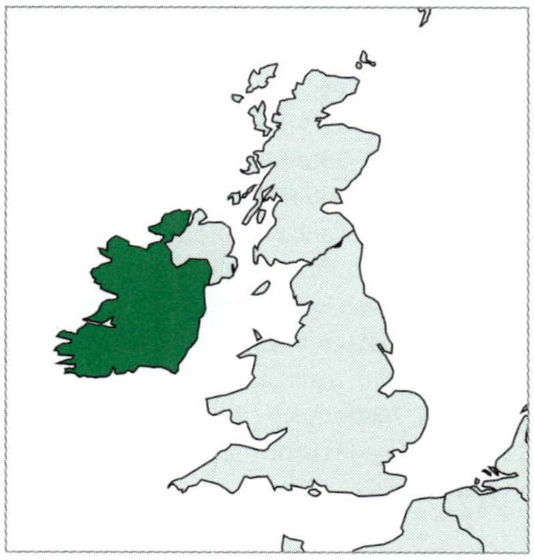

Population	**3.8 million**
Number of lawyers	**6,500 solicitors; 1,400 barristers**
Professional title	**Solicitor; barrister**
Currency	**Euro (€)**

Index

Ireland is a 26-county state, with a US-influenced written constitution and a legal system modelled on that of the UK. Full independence from the UK dates back to 1949, when the 26 counties partitioned from Northern Ireland under the Anglo-Irish Treaty of 1921, left the British Commonwealth and became the Republic of Ireland.

The country joined the EEC in 1973 and is now a full member of the EU. It adopted the euro as its currency in January 2002.

The Irish government established the International Financial Services Centre (IFSC) in Dublin's docklands in 1987 and succeeded in attracting a wide range of financially-oriented companies with the offer of a 10% tax regime and other fiscal advantages. The IFSC now ranks as one of the world's leading centres for international banking, investment funds, corporate treasury and insurance activities, although its tax regime gave way to the economy-wide corporation tax rate of 12.5% in January 2003.

BILLING

Partners' hourly rates range from €250 to €450. The market is highly competitive, and firms are increasingly charging on agreed fee, capped fee and other alternative bases.

MARKETING

The regime governing law firms' marketing practices was tightened by the Solicitors (Amendment) Act 2002. It specifies what information may be included in an advertisement, and introduces a ban on advertisements 'in an inappropriate location', for example hospitals and doctors' surgeries, and on certain advertisements which refer to damages claims for personal injuries. The Act specifically covers electronic communications, such as websites, and restates existing provisions prohibiting advertisements that are false or misleading or that reflect unfavourably on other solicitors.

IN-HOUSE LAWYERS

Around 600 of the Republic's 6,500 solicitors work in-house.

ECONOMIC CLIMATE

The Republic enjoyed extraordinary economic growth in the second half of the 1990s, helped by a series of national economic programmes designed to curb inflation, reduce government spending, increase labour force skills and promote foreign investment.

The so-called 'Celtic Tiger' era has given way to more moderate expansion since 2001, with real GDP growth forecast to be 1.8% in 2003, a significant decline from the 2002 figure of 6.9%. This is attributable in part to the appreciation of the euro, which has hit exports, and a decline in investment.

The current weak trend is forecast to give way to modest acceleration in 2004, with medium-term GDP growth forecast to fall between 4% and 5%.

LEGAL SYSTEM

Ireland is a common law jurisdiction, as modified by national legislation and by the country's 1937 written constitution. As a full member of the EU, it is bound by EU legislation and the decisions of the European Court of Justice; EU law, where applicable, takes precedence over national law. The 1937 constitution contains a Bill of Rights and established, amongst other institutions, the country's parliament (the Oireachtas). The Oireachtas is divided into two houses, the directly-elected Dáil and the indirectly-elected Seanad. The solicitors' profession is represented and regulated by the Law Society of Ireland.

LEGAL MARKET

Each of the Republic's Big Five firms, **A&L Goodbody**, **Arthur Cox**, **Matheson Ormsby Prentice**, **McCann FitzGerald** and **William Fry**, has a distinctive culture and reputation; of the five, **Arthur Cox** is probably the most widely admired, for reasons including its premium record on corporate work and the strength of its indigenous client base. Together, the five remain ahead of the rest of the field in terms of the quality of their clients and the range of their practice areas, as well as fee-earner numbers.

The market includes a number of excellent, smaller competitors, of which **Mason Hayes & Curran**, **LK Shields** and funds specialist **Dillon Eustace** in particular stand out, while other firms on the rise include **BCM Hanby Wallace** and **O'Donnell Sweeney**.

Lateral hires at partner level remain comparatively rare in the Republic. Banking specialist Orla Brennan joined **William Fry** from **Landwell**

The largest firms

1	McCann FitzGerald	233
2	A&L Goodbody	231
3	Matheson Ormsby Prentice	229
4	Arthur Cox	174
5	William Fry	161
6	Mason Hayes & Curran	87
7	BCM Hanby Wallace	60
8	Dillon Eustace	53
9	Beauchamps	50
10	Eugene F Collins	42
11	Ivor Fitzpatrick & Company	35
	Ronan Daly Jermyn	35
13	O'Donnell Sweeney	32
14	LK Shields	31
15	Whitney, Moore & Keller	29
16	Landwell Solicitors	26
17	Holmes O'Malley Sexton	21
18	Masons	18
	PJ O'Driscoll & Sons	18
20	Orpen Franks	17
21	O'Flynn Exhams & Partners	16
22	Binchys Solicitors	15
23	Conway Kelleher Tobin	14
	Noel Smyth & Partners	14
25	Kilroys	13
	Nolan Farrell & Goff	13
	Reddy Charlton McKnight	13

These figures represent the total number of lawyers in this country only, and have been supplied by the firms themselves. The figures should be accurate as at 1 January 2004.

Solicitors, while energy specialist John Gaffney left **William Fry** to join **O'Flynn Exhams & Partners** in Cork. Commercial property partner Kenneth Egan joined **Arthur Cox** from **Matheson Ormsby Prentice**, while **Landwell Solicitors** associate Fionán Breathnach joined **Mason Hayes & Curran** as partner to launch the firm's investment funds practice.

2003 saw the dissolution of *Gerrard, Scallan & O'Brien*; a number of staff, including three senior partners, joined **Arthur Cox**, while banking partner Anne McHale joined **Ivor Fitzpatrick & Company**. Meanwhile **Eugene F Collins** merged with niche property firm *George D Fottrell & Sons* in June 2003, and John Kehoe left **Mason Hayes & Curran** to establish corporate/M&A boutique **KLW**, which is the first new firm of its kind in Dublin for many years.

On the management side, Pádraig Ó Ríordián succeeded Eugene McCague as managing partner at **Arthur Cox** in November 2003, while tax heavyweight Liam Quirke took over as managing partner at **Matheson Ormsby Prentice** in January 2004, succeeding Donal Roche.

THE BIG FOUR

The Big Four accountancy firms, each of which has in-house counsel, remain a serious force in the market, particularly in relation to tax matters, on which they continue to receive a significant number of instructions from law firms. While some of the larger firms have recruited accountants, **Matheson Ormsby Prentice** is the only firm that currently presents a credible threat to their dominance in this area. **Landwell Solicitors**, with its links to PwC, is still the only accountancy-related law firm in the Republic, and this is likely to remain the case for the foreseeable future.

LINKS ABROAD

Four of the Big Five firms have offices in London. **A&L Goodbody**'s is now managed by corporate partner Julian Yarr, following Paul White's return to the Dublin office, and includes a strong media practice led by Geraldine East. **Matheson Ormsby Prentice** has an expanding London office, and in March 2003 appointed corporate partner Andrew Doyle as senior resident partner. **McCann FitzGerald**'s London practice was established in 1986, and is focused on corporate and financial services work. **Arthur Cox** has had a London office since 2001; it is headed by partner John Matson, who is also responsible for the firm's New York office.

On the US side, **Dillon Eustace** opened an office in Boston in August 2003, which focuses on financial services work. It is the sixth Irish law firm to establish an office across the Atlantic; **A&L Goodbody**, **Arthur Cox**, **McCann FitzGerald** and **Mason Hayes & Curran** each have an office in New York, while **Matheson Ormsby Prentice** has an office in Palo Alto and **A&L Goodbody** has a second US office in Boston.

Arthur Cox is the only Big Five firm with an office in Belfast, although three of the other four have cross-border links in place. **McCann FitzGerald** has been allied with **L'Estrange & Brett** since 1999 (the *North South Legal Alliance*), while **William Fry** is closely tied with **Tughans**. **Matheson Ormsby Prentice** established the *All Island Legal Alliance* with **Cleaver Fulton Rankin** in 2002. Other Dublin-Belfast alliances are **Eugene F Collins**' 'best friends' relationship with **C & H Jefferson**, in place since 2002, and **Mason Hayes & Curran**'s *i-law alliance* with **Carson McDowell**. **A&L Goodbody** broke off its alliance with **Elliott Duffy Garrett** in 2002 and runs all of its Northern Ireland work from Dublin. UK firm **Masons** has an office in Belfast, where a senior associate is now based full-time.

Dillon Eustace has had an office in Tokyo since 2001 and maintains its association with **Arendt & Medernach** in Luxembourg. **A&L Goodbody** and **McCann FitzGerald** each has an office in Brussels.

AGRICULTURE AND FOOD

Maree Gallagher heads **Arthur Cox**'s foods, pharmaceuticals and product safety group. The firm advises clients such as Masterfoods and Heinz on the regulatory side, along with authorities including the Food Safety Authority. Recent M&A work in the sector includes advising Kerry Group plc on its acquisition of Freshways, and acting for Great Spirits Company LLC on its acquisition of the Roaring Water Bay Spirits Group.

Raymond O'Rourke at **Mason Hayes & Curran** is a food law specialist, and lectures extensively on the field. He has advised numerous EU applicant countries on food law matters, while other clients include the Irish Food Board and German retail chain Lidl, which he advises on food safety matters.

A&L Goodbody has a strong M&A presence in the sector. Recent transactions include advising Irish Distillers on the disposal of BWG Group and advising BWG on a number of subsequent acquisitions. The firm also acts for Irish Food Processors, one of Europe's largest food processing companies.

Neil Keenan heads **Matheson Ormsby Prentice**'s agriculture and life sciences group, which has advised on matters such as food labelling and hygiene standards regulation, and is currently representing the Department of Agriculture on litigation relating to the destruction of a consignment of intervention beef in the early 1990s. Other clients include a range of creameries and a number of firms in the fish-farming and feed business.

McCann FitzGerald provides ongoing advice to a range of clients in the food and drinks sector, together with a number of agricultural co-operatives, on corporate and commercial

AGRICULTURE AND FOOD

ARTHUR COX ✪
MASON HAYES & CURRAN ✪

A&L Goodbody ✪
Matheson Ormsby Prentice ✪
McCann FitzGerald ✪
Ronan Daly Jermyn ✪
William Fry ✪

Anthony Carroll & Co
LK Shields ✪
MA Regan McEntee & Co
Maurice Power

Firms are listed A-Z in tiers which are ranked in order of priority
✪ *Indicates firm displays contact details at the end of this chapter.*

matters including food regulation. Clients include the Irish Food Board, Coca-Cola Bottlers Ireland, Diageo and Lakeland Dairies.

Ronan Daly Jermyn advises farmers on day-to-day issues and has a particular niche advising them on the disposal of land for development purposes.

William Fry, in addition to advising retail and distribution clients such as Tesco and Nature's Best, has a long-standing niche advising parties in the thoroughbred bloodstock industry. The firm's expertise includes dealing with the sale and purchase of racehorses and breeding stock, as well as advising on financing and syndication, dispute resolution and insurance matters.

BANKING AND FINANCE

A&L Goodbody's banking practice is led by the well-regarded Catherine Duffy. The firm advised Valentia/eircom on its recent financing, which included a €1.3bn senior-secured syndicated loan. It also acted for Anglo Irish Bank and syndicate banks on a €375m financing of Dundrum Shopping Centre, and for Bennett Construction on a €60m construction financing relating to the Ballymun Regeneration Project. The firm has a dedicated financial services regulation group, headed by Kevin Allen, which advises a host of domestic service providers as well as providing transactional support.

Arthur Cox added two new banking partners to its ranks in 2003, in Liam Carney and structured finance and securitisation specialist Cormac Kissane. The firm advised the banks (led by Deutsche Bank) on the refinancing of the Valentia/eircom debt. It also advised banks led by Bank of Ireland on facilities of £588m for Independent News and Media Group, while asset finance work included advising Aer Lingus on significant lease finance transactions. William Johnston and Grainne Hennessy are recommended.

William Prentice heads **Matheson Ormsby Prentice**'s banking and finance group, and is extremely highly regarded. Clients include many of the leading domestic banks and international financial institutions. The firm recently acted for Allied Irish Bank and a number of other lenders in relation to the €200m refinancing of the property portfolio of one of Ireland's leading property holding companies. The firm has strong asset finance experience; the growing team is led by Chris Quinn, and recently acted for a major international financial institution on the refinancing of nine aircraft operated by a European airline.

Banking and finance is historically **McCann FitzGerald**'s standout practice; the group is the Republic's largest (with 14 partners and more than 50 lawyers in total), and has real strength on the financing side, with Niall Powderley particularly highly thought of. The firm recently advised on the financing of the Arnotts, Riverdeep and Dunloe Ewart take privates, and acted for ABN Amro on the refinancing of the Minorco Lisheen mine, and for Anglo Irish Bank on the Ardagh demerger; it also advised Bord Gáis Éireann on a €500m revolving credit facility. Catherine Deane and Hilary Marren are market-leading aircraft finance experts; recent work includes advising BNP Paribas on the restructuring of Swissair Group subsidiary Flightlease's aircraft lease portfolio.

Dillon Eustace's excellent banking practice continues to grow on the secured lending side, with property partners Michael Barker and Paul Eustace advising a range of clients including Bank of Scotland and Irish Life & Permanent. Recent work includes advising a UK bank on secured lending to a start-up windfarm operation. The firm has strong asset finance expertise, and, on the financial services side, has recently acted on the establishment of a number of front office managers in Ireland, including MPS Asset Management Ireland Ltd's quantitative asset management operation.

William Fry's practice has been strengthened by the arrival of banking specialist Orla Brennan as partner from **Landwell Solicitors**. The firm has recently advised a leading Irish lender on its €30m loan portfolio to investors in the UK commercial property market, an international cosmetics company on a €400m multi-currency credit facility, and McInerney Holding plc on the refinancing of its UK credit facilities.

Eugene F Collins' banking specialists are Laura MacDermott, who advised Anglo Irish Bank on the financing of the Richard Nesbitt-led bid for Arnotts, and Eileen Grace, who advised the bank on a €410m syndicated loan facility. Corporate partner Gerard Coll and commercial partner Leonara Malone are also experienced.

LK Shields' two banking partners are Joe Gavin and David Williams; they advise a range of international investment banks, asset managers and multinationals on regulated and unregulated funding structures. The firm has recently added Citibank to its client list.

Mason Hayes & Curran's practice is headed by project finance specialist Kevin Hoy. His team's recent work includes advising AWG/Morrisons on the debt financing of residential development projects in the Dublin area, and ACC Bank on various tax-based financing projects in the leisure sector. The firm also represented the eircom ESOP in relation to the Valentia/eircom restructuring and refinancing.

BANKING AND FINANCE

A&L GOODBODY ✪
ARTHUR COX ✪
MATHESON ORMSBY PRENTICE ✪
McCANN FITZGERALD ✪

Dillon Eustace ✪
William Fry ✪

Eugene F Collins ✪
LK Shields ✪
Mason Hayes & Curran ✪

BCM Hanby Wallace ✪
Beauchamps ✪
Ivor Fitzpatrick & Company ✪
Kilroys ✪
O'Donnell Sweeney ✪
Robert Ryan & Associates ✪
Ronan Daly Jermyn ✪

Binchys Solicitors ✪
Dockrell Farrell
E P Fanning & Co, Solicitors
Landwell Solicitors ✪
PJ O'Driscoll & Sons
Reddy Charlton McKnight
Whitney, Moore & Keller

Firms are listed A-Z in tiers which are ranked in order of priority
✪ *Indicates firm displays contact details at the end of this chapter.*

BCM Hanby Wallace has a growing banking and property finance practice, which advises a range of clients on all aspects of lending transactions and structurings. Partners Paul McGennis and Ciara Gunning have particular experience in the area.

Ivor Fitzpatrick & Company is looking to make inroads into the sector with the addition of two new partners in Alfred Thornton, who previously ran Bank of Ireland's main banking division, and Anne McHale, who joined the firm from the now dissolved *Gerrard, Scallan & O'Brien*.

Boutique commercial firm **Kilroys** has extensive banking and finance expertise alongside its well-regarded investment funds practice; Eamon Jones is the head of the firm's lending practice.

Patricia Heffernan, who heads **O'Donnell Sweeney**'s banking and finance practice, has a good reputation, while **Robert Ryan & Associates** is a two-partner firm best known for its specialist banking work; the firm's clients include industry banking organisations, as well as a number of domestic and international institutions.

Ronan Daly Jermyn continues to attract the vast majority of banking work in the Munster area, and has added new clients IIB and ACC Bank to established clients such as Bank of Ireland, Bank of Scotland and Ulster Bank.

CAPITAL MARKETS

Whilst Ireland's debt capital markets were busy in 2003, most of the activity on the equity side took place in the context of companies being taken private and hence being de-listed from the Irish Stock Exchange.

A&L Goodbody's capital markets group, headed by John Olden, acted for Valencia/eircom on the €1.1bn high-yield bond issued as part of its recent financing, and for Icon plc on its IPO of 1.5 million ADSs. The firm also advised IIB Bank Ltd on the establishment of its €1.5bn MTN programme, as well as acting for a number of other Irish issuers in respect of existing note programmes.

Arthur Cox advised Deutsche Bank as arranger of the Valencia/eircom high-yield bond, and advised the initial purchasers regarding Kerry Group's $650,000,000 private placement of senior notes into the US. As well as advising on a range of major ongoing note programmes, the firm acted for DZ Bank Ireland on the establishment of its €10bn debt issuance programme and advised Morgan Stanley as arranger of Elan Capital Corporation's $460m convertible guaranteed bond issue.

Matheson Ormsby Prentice acted on a range of major structured finance transactions, including advising ABN Amro NV, Deutsche Bank AG London and iBond Securities plc on the establishment of a €20bn secured note programme and the structuring of the initial €1.5bn bond issue, and advising Helaba on the establishment of a €3bn hybrid multi-seller CP programme. On the equity side, the firm advised Independent News on a €107m rights issue and a NZ$225m fundraising. Tim Scanlon and Turlough Gavin are recommended.

McCann FitzGerald advised a range of clients, including Diageo Finance Ireland, EBS, First Active and UniCredito, in relation to MTN programmes. Roy Parker is particularly recommended.

William Fry has continued to advise Sachsen and Helaba on major MTN programmes. The firm also acted for Ardagh Glass on its €175m bond issue (having previously acted for Ardagh plc on the demerger of its glass business to the company), Axis Capital Holdings on its IPO and listing on the NYSE and the underwriters of the Independent News €107m rights issue.

Dillon Eustace's practice has, since 2001, included a listing department, which advises clients on listing issues and has been approved by the Irish Stock Exchange to act as a listing sponsor in relation to the listing of investment funds, unit trusts and other securities and instruments. The firm's clients include a range of collective investment schemes. The department is enjoying significant growth and is led by Tara O'Callaghan.

CAPITAL MARKETS

A&L GOODBODY ✪
ARTHUR COX ✪
MATHESON ORMSBY PRENTICE ✪
McCANN FITZGERALD ✪
WILLIAM FRY ✪

DILLON EUSTACE ✪

Eugene F Collins ✪
LK Shields ✪
Mason Hayes & Curran ✪

BCM Hanby Wallace ✪
Beauchamps ✪
Kilroys ✪
O'Donnell Sweeney ✪

Firms are listed A-Z in tiers which are ranked in order of priority
✪ Indicates firm displays contact details at the end of this chapter.

Partner Eileen Grace at **Eugene F Collins** has strong capital markets expertise. She recently advised Anglo Irish Bank on a £90m Tier One capital securities issue, and on its MTN Programme update and increase to €4bn, as well as on a prior €350m Tap issue under the programme.

LK Shields has a solid record of advising on IPOs and other offerings, domestic and overseas listings and compliance issues, while **Mason Hayes & Curran** has expertise on a similar range of matters. Partners Paul Egan and Niamh Callaghan at **Mason Hayes & Curran** have particularly strong profiles, and the firm has been appointed by the Irish government to advise on actual and proposed share offerings, as well as representing several quoted Irish issuers and their sponsors.

COMMERCIAL PROPERTY

John Walsh leads **Arthur Cox**'s market-leading, seven-partner commercial property team, which includes new partner Ken Egan, who joined the firm this year from **Matheson Ormsby Prentice**. On the development side, the firm is advising Spencer Dock Development Company Ltd on the Spencer Dock Scheme and Green Property on its sale of various investment properties in Dublin for a total of more than €250m, while other clients include Citywest Business Campus and Lagan Developments. The firm also represents a range of private and institutional investors, including Irish Life, Canada Life and Royal & SunAlliance.

A&L Goodbody's five-partner team is headed by Mairead Sherlock. The firm acted for Irish Pension Fund Property Unit Trust on the €80m sale to Tesco of the Wilton Shopping Centre in Cork and for Green Property on the sale of two shopping centres for a total of over €34m. Other significant instructions included advising Irish Life Asssurance plc on the sale of Harcourt Square, Dublin for more than €70m, and advising AIB on the sale of AIB International House.

COMMERCIAL PROPERTY

ARTHUR COX ✪

A&L GOODBODY ✪
MATHESON ORMSBY PRENTICE ✪
McCANN FITZGERALD ✪
WILLIAM FRY ✪

BCM Hanby Wallace ✪
Beauchamps ✪
Dillon Eustace ✪
Eugene F Collins ✪
LK Shields ✪
Mason Hayes & Curran ✪
O'Donnell Sweeney ✪
Ronan Daly Jermyn ✪
Whitney, Moore & Keller

Binchys Solicitors ✪
Dockrell Farrell
Ivor Fitzpatrick & Company ✪
Noel Smyth & Partners
Reddy Charlton McKnight

Conway Kelleher Tobin
Duncan Grehan & Partners
Kilroys ✪
McEvoy Partners ✪

Firms are listed A-Z in tiers which are ranked in order of priority
✪ Indicates firm displays contact details at the end of this chapter.

Matheson Ormsby Prentice advised the purchaser of a major telecoms headquarters in the centre of Dublin, and acted for the John Sisk/Park Developments joint venture on a significant residential development project in Dublin's docklands. The firm advises a range of retail clients and banks, and recently acted for a bank on a €54m property company refinancing. Andrew Muckian heads the team.

McCann FitzGerald advised the syndicate of private investors on the acquisition and related financing of AIB International House, and on a range of other impressive transactions for investment house and corporate clients. The firm continues to advise the Dublin Docklands Development Authority. Lonan McDowell and Colin Keane are recommended.

William Fry's team is led by Nora White and Edward Spain. It advised on the development and disposal of Trinity Hall, Dublin and acted for the buyers on the year's two major private investor acquisitions (Harcourt Square and Adelaide Road – both office developments), as well as advising Tesco on its purchase of Wilton Shopping Centre. Other retail clients include Zara, Next, Boots and First Choice.

BCM Hanby Wallace advised a consortium of developers on the acquisition of a site near Bray, County Wicklow and is now advising on its development; it is expected to be one of the largest mixed-use developments undertaken in the Republic. The firm continues to advise the developers on lettings for the Dundrum Town Centre, with headline work in 2003 including a 12,000 sq m letting to Marks & Spencer. Chairman Brian Wallace is a recognised expert in the field.

Beauchamps has a well-regarded commercial property practice. Notable partners include department head Aidan Marsh, managing partner Imelda Reynolds and Niall Coleman.

Dillon Eustace's property department is headed by Paul Eustace and Michael Barker, and acts for a range of banks and other financial institutions (including Bank of Scotland and Irish Life & Permanent), as well as for developers.

Eugene F Collins now boasts five partners and a consultant in its property practice, following its merger in June 2003 with *George D Fottrell & Sons*. The firm has recently acted on transactions for the likes of French Connection, Irish Distillers, Greenstar Recycling Holdings Ltd (formerly Celtic Waste Ltd) and Treasury Holdings, as well as a range of financial institutions.

Nicola Palmer is the sole partner in **LK Shields**' property department. Clients include a range of engineering, architecture and project management firms.

Maeve Hayes continues to develop **Mason Hayes & Curran**'s property team. The firm has experience in the retail market, and also advises on commercial and residential developments. Clients include Gresham Hotel Group and Specsavers.

O'Donnell Sweeney has a very strong commercial property department, with Rory O'Donnell and newly made-up partner Joe Stanley particularly recommended.

Ronan Daly Jermyn is acting for O'Callaghan Properties on its development of the €300m Mahon Point Project, which is Ireland's largest new-start retail project this year. The firm also acts for the Musgrave Super-Valu group on its property transactions and continues to advise the developers of the Liffey Valley Centre in Dublin.

Whitney, Moore & Keller's three-partner property department continues to receive a regular supply of work from institutional clients such as Irish Life, British Land and Green Property. Michael Doran and department head Michael Carney are well regarded.

Binchys Solicitors has solid experience on commercial and residential property development work, while at **Dockrell Farrell** partners Ernest Farrell and Brendon O'Donovan are both active on property and development matters.

Ivor Fitzpatrick & Company's property partners are Jennifer Blunden and Michael O'Connor. The department has acted on a range of development work and will benefit from the arrival of Alfred Thornton on the banking side.

Thomas Marren heads **Reddy Charlton McKnight**'s three-partner practice, which advises on a range of matters including commercial property, development and property taxation matters.

CONSTRUCTION

Highly-rated Dudley Solan heads **Masons**' practice, which distinguishes itself on the strength of the broad range of local, UK and overseas contractors for which it acts on high-profile contentious and non-contentious matters; clients include Pierse Contracting, P J Hegarty & Sons and Balfour Beatty. The firm, like **McCann FitzGerald**, has also represented a number of local authorities on procurement. Recent highlights include advising the international contractor consortia on the sub-sea pipeline and plant contracts relating to the Ringsend waste water treatment plant.

McCann FitzGerald's construction practice continues to lead the field. Led by Tim Bouchier-Hayes, it includes 15 lawyers who work exclusively on construction matters and advises across the full range of construction matters, covering dispute resolution (with an emphasis on mediation and conciliation) as well as advisory work. Key clients include Ballymun Regeneration, Coras Iompair Eireann, Jacobs International and Dublin Docks Development Authority, which the team advises on a range of projects forming part of the area's regeneration. Kevin Kelly and Michael O'Reilly, as well as Tim Bouchier-Hayes, are highly recommended.

A&L Goodbody has an expanding practice, led by projects specialist Kevin Feeney. The firm's recent work includes advising the AIB-led banking syndicate on the construction funding of the Dundrum Shopping Centre (capital value €450m), and developer Bennett Construction in relation to the Ballymun complex and the refurbishment of a large Victorian warehouse (Stack A, IFSC). Eamonn Gill is recommended.

Arthur Cox advises mainly project sponsors, but also acts for contractors and sub-contractors, consultants and financiers. Key work includes advising Spencer Dock Development Company on the first stage of its multi-tower commercial development, and advising Aer Rianta on the new terminal facility and associated works at Cork Airport (with a value of around €120m). Ted Williams heads the group.

Hussey Fraser is a two-partner niche construction practice, where Anthony Hussey is particularly recommended. The firm acts primarily for contractors and sub-contractors; clients include Ascon Ltd (Ireland's largest civil engineering contractor) and its sister company Rohcon Ltd, for both of which it acts on an exclusive basis. The firm is strong on the full range of construction advice, including arbitration and conciliation.

Matheson Ormsby Prentice recently advised Hutchison 3G Ireland in relation to the design and construction of its Irish network, and Bank of Scotland on the financing of the Beacon Court Office development. Mark Varian, recently appointed as partner, heads the department.

Major recent non-contentious transactions for **William Fry** include advising John Player & Sons on the development of its new cigarette manufacturing facility in Dublin, and Fingal County Council on a major infrastructure project at Balbriggan. The practice, led by Liam McCabe, has also seen an upturn in the volume of its contentious work.

BCM Hanby Wallace's construction practice is one of the firm's historic niches and remains active; the firm has a long track record of acting for residential and commercial property developers as well as advising on the financing side.

Dillon Eustace advises a number of financial institutions and developers on construction matters, on the back of its strong commercial property practice.

Eugene F Collins' commercial property practice has grown significantly following the firm's merger with *George D Fottrell & Sons*, and has experience of advising on construction matters; John Territt represents a number of developers, and also acted for Pierse Contracting on the joint development of a 108-apartment site at Clondalkin.

LK Shields' construction work is led by commercial property partner Nicola Palmer and litigator Edmund Butler. The firm has experience of advising a wide spectrum of clients on construction matters, including public and semi-state authorities, financial institutions as well as private contractors and developers.

Mason Hayes & Curran has an expanding construction practice, and has advised Newlyn Developments and AWG plc on the construction aspects of various residential developments. The firm also advises building contractor JJ Rhattigan & Company.

O'Donnell Sweeney is strong on the contentious side; Dermot McEvoy has extensive experience of litigating and mediating construction disputes.

CONSTRUCTION

MASONS
McCANN FITZGERALD ✪

A&L GOODBODY ✪
ARTHUR COX ✪
HUSSEY FRASER
MATHESON ORMSBY PRENTICE ✪
WILLIAM FRY ✪

BCM Hanby Wallace ✪
Beauchamps ✪
Dillon Eustace ✪
Eugene F Collins ✪
LK Shields ✪
Mason Hayes & Curran ✪
Noel Smyth & Partners
O'Donnell Sweeney ✪
Ronan Daly Jermyn ✪
Whitney, Moore & Keller

Firms are listed A-Z in tiers which are ranked in order of priority
✪ Indicates firm displays contact details at the end of this chapter.

Ronan Daly Jermyn, based in Cork, has advised a range of large construction companies in the south of the country, and recently acted on the development of student accommodation centres for local university, UCC.

CORPORATE AND COMMERCIAL

A&L Goodbody's headline corporate work, in addition to its role in the Alphyra and Arnotts buy-outs, included advising longstanding client Elan Corporation plc on its restructuring programme, which involved the disposal of up to €1.5bn of assets. Private equity work included advising ICC Venture Capital on its €11.3m investment into Bio-Medical Research Ltd. David Sanfey heads the firm's commercial department.

Arthur Cox advises on the full range of corporate and commercial matters, led by outstanding senior partner James O'Dwyer and other high-profile group heads Michael Meghen, Colm Duggan and Ciarán Bolger, while Pádraig Ó Ríordián and Brian O'Gorman are also recommended. The firm scooped a lead counsel role on the largest corporate deal of the year in Ireland, advising First Active on its €900m takeover by Royal Bank of Scotland.

Matheson Ormsby Prentice had a strong year on domestic and international M&A, including advising a number of Irish listed companies for the first time; Andrew Doyle, Tim Scanlon and Edward Miller are recommended. Highlights on the commercial side include advising Hewlett-Packard on Bank of Ireland's proposed outsourcing of its IT infrastructure services. Head of corporate and managing partner Donal Roche retired from the firm at the end of 2003.

McCann FitzGerald's corporate and public M&A practice is headed by Barry Devereux, while Paul Heffernan heads the firm's private M&A and commercial practice. The firm had a role in all of the year's main take-private transactions, including advising the financiers on the Riverdeep and Arnotts buy-outs. Other work included advising clients such as AOL and Marconi on corporate restructurings, as well as advising in relation to a number of joint ventures.

On the corporate side, **William Fry** has seen significant venture capital and restructuring work, in addition to the firm's M&A and capital markets activity; managing partner Owen O'Connell advised ACT Venture Capital on its €180m fundraising, and the firm also acted for Ardagh plc on the demerger of its glass interests to Ardagh Glass Ltd. The firm has recently advised clients such as Tesco, BP Castrol and Green Isle on commercial matters.

Paul Egan heads **Mason Hayes & Curran**'s corporate department and maintains an excellent reputation, while Anthony Burke and John Kettle are particularly recommended on the commercial side. The hub of the firm's commercial practice is its regulatory work, advising clients such as the Irish Energy Regulator, ComReg (Ireland's communications regulator) and state broadcaster RTÉ.

CORPORATE AND COMMERCIAL

A&L GOODBODY ✪
ARTHUR COX ✪
MATHESON ORMSBY PRENTICE ✪
McCANN FITZGERALD ✪
WILLIAM FRY ✪

MASON HAYES & CURRAN ✪

DILLON EUSTACE ✪
EUGENE F COLLINS ✪
LK SHIELDS ✪

BCM Hanby Wallace ✪
Beauchamps ✪
O'Donnell Sweeney ✪
Whitney, Moore & Keller

Binchys Solicitors ✪
Dockrell Farrell
Gore & Grimes ✪
Ivor Fitzpatrick & Company ✪
KLW
Kilroys ✪
Landwell Solicitors ✪
McEvoy Partners ✪
PJ O'Driscoll & Sons
Reddy Charlton McKnight
Ronan Daly Jermyn ✪

Brian O'Donnell & Partners
Conway Kelleher Tobin
Holmes O'Malley Sexton
Maurice Power
O'Flynn Exhams & Partners
Orpen Franks
Robert Ryan & Associates ✪
Sweeney McGann
Vincent & Beatty ✪

Firms are listed A-Z in tiers which are ranked in order of priority
✪ Indicates firm displays contact details at the end of this chapter.

Though best known for its investment funds and financial services work, **Dillon Eustace** has an expanding corporate and commercial practice. In addition to its recent M&A work, it has advised extensively on front office asset management issues, and has a dedicated compliance and regulatory department, focusing on corporate governance, auditing and accounting.

Eugene F Collins has a good range of predominantly domestic clients and a strong record on corporate and M&A work. Partners Gerard Coll, Anthony Collins and Eileen Grace are all recommended.

LK Shields advised on an impressive range of corporate, M&A and private equity transactions, besides playing a notable role in the year's take-private activity. As well as name partner Laurence Shields, corporate finance specialist Emmet Scully and M&A partners Gerard Halpenny and Justin McKenna are well regarded.

BCM Hanby Wallace has a strong reputation for its private equity and venture capital investment work. The firm recently acted for Smart Telecom on its €11m fundraising, and also advised Bio-Medical Research Ltd in relation to its fundraising with ICC Venture Capital. On the commercial side, the firm advises seven out of Ireland's nine health boards on a wide range of issues.

Beauchamps' department, headed by Shaun O'Shea, has a range of experience across corporate finance and general commercial matters.

David O'Beirne at **O'Donnell Sweeney** has particular experience acting on both the acquisition and the disposal of owner-managed businesses, while David Beattie acts for a number of listed companies, notably in the oil and gas sectors.

Whitney, Moore & Keller's corporate and commercial department is headed by Theresa Rochford, and has particular experience on venture capital investments and private M&A work. It also recently advised Glencar Mining plc on restructuring debt in excess of $40m.

Binchys Solicitors has extensive experience on corporate finance and commercial matters, while **Dockrell Farrell** has an active and wide-ranging commercial practice, headed by John Dockrell.

Gore & Grimes' corporate and commercial practice has a solid reputation, as does **Ivor Fitzpatrick & Company**'s commercial practice.

Newly established corporate/M&A boutique **KLW** has already received some impressive instructions, including representing Pfizer on its European restructuring following completion of its acquisition of Pharmacia. Founder John Kehoe was previously a corporate partner at **Mason Hayes & Curran**, and prior to that worked for Kvaerner Corporate Development in Hong Kong and for **Clifford Chance LLP** in London. With his track record and contacts, and new partner appointments planned, the firm looks set to become a significant market presence.

Niche practice **Kilroys** is well regarded for its corporate and commercial work, with five of its seven partners (including managing partner Kevin O'Brien) practising in the area. On the commercial side, the firm has particular expertise in the areas of insurance, IT and telecoms.

Edward Evans heads **Landwell Solicitors**' corporate practice, which is focused on international restructuring work, much of it sourced from and in conjunction with PwC. The firm has also recently advised on a number of M&A and private equity transactions.

McEvoy Partners is a four-partner boutique established in September 2002. It specialises in M&A and other corporate work, and clients include a range of AIM-listed companies including African Gold plc and African Diamonds plc. Recent work includes acting for Stafford Holdings on its acquisition of Clashfern Holdings/Campus Oil. Bernard McEvoy is recommended.

PJ O'Driscoll & Sons, which has offices in Cork and Dublin, has a good reputation, while Paul Keane and Fergal McKnight at **Reddy Charlton McKnight** are recommended.

Ronan Daly Jermyn, based in Cork and headed by John Dwyer, is the Republic's leading regional firm. It advised Thomas Crosbie Holdings on its €10m acquisition of *The Irish Post*.

DISPUTE RESOLUTION

Peter Law heads **A&L Goodbody**'s 45-fee-earner department. The firm's recent caseload includes acting for the Law Society of Ireland, the Irish Pension Fund Property Unit Trust, the Nightclub Industry Association and Irish Hotel Federation, and a group of Irish and European tobacco companies (on the group's successful challenge to domestic legislation that would have banned all tobacco advertising and retail display). The firm places a strong emphasis on advisory work and alternative dispute resolution, and partner Joe Kelly is a council member of the recently founded Irish Commercial Mediation Association. Caroline Preston carries an impressive reputation.

Arthur Cox's litigation department, headed by David O'Donohoe, continues to act on a number of significant cases. The firm is representing Gallaher/Benson & Hedges in ongoing litigation brought against it by smokers and former smokers. It is also acting for generics manufacturer Synthon BV on the Irish element of worldwide litigation brought by GlaxoSmithKline for alleged infringement of its patent for an anti-depressant. Key partners include Isabel Foley, Gregory Glynn and Conor McDonnell. Previous department head Paul McLaughlin stepped down as partner in2003 but remains a consultant to the firm.

Matheson Ormsby Prentice's litigation team, led by Stuart Margetson and Michael Tyrell, includes a range of specialist contentious lawyers and has advised the full gamut of clients across the private, financial services, and government and semi-state sectors. As well as acting for a multinational tobacco company in ongoing multi-plaintiff product liability litigation, the department's recent activity includes acting on the judicial review of procedures arising out of the Mini CTC signalling project inquiry and acting in alleged VAT carousel fraud proceedings brought by the Criminal Assets Bureau in relation to the mobile phone industry.

McCann FitzGerald's recent caseload covers a range of areas including judicial review, significant insurance claims, commercial disputes, property disputes and product liability. Clients include the Institute of Chartered Accountants, the Irish Blood Transfusion Service and the Medical Defence Union It continues to advise Imperial Tobacco on its defence of tobacco litigation claims.

Dillon Eustace has a wide-ranging practice, which includes expertise on maritime, aviation, personal injury, insurance and commercial litigation. The firm acts for many UK and European insurers (including Allianz and AXA) as well as a number of airline operators.

DISPUTE RESOLUTION

A&L GOODBODY ✪
ARTHUR COX ✪
MATHESON ORMSBY PRENTICE ✪
McCANN FITZGERALD ✪

DILLON EUSTACE ✪
EUGENE F COLLINS ✪
LK SHIELDS ✪
MASON HAYES & CURRAN ✪
WILLIAM FRY ✪

BCM HANBY WALLACE ✪
BEAUCHAMPS ✪
LANDWELL SOLICITORS ✪
O'DONNELL SWEENEY ✪
RONAN DALY JERMYN ✪
WHITNEY, MOORE & KELLER

Binchys Solicitors ✪
Conway Kelleher Tobin
Dockrell Farrell
Duncan Grehan & Partners
Ivor Fitzpatrick & Company ✪
Kilroys ✪
Maurice Power
McAleese & Co
Reddy Charlton McKnight
Robert Ryan & Associates ✪

Firms are listed A-Z in tiers which are ranked in order of priority
✪ Indicates firm displays contact details at the end of this chapter.

Terry Leggett at **Eugene F Collins** is highly recommended as a commercial litigator. His recent caseload includes defending a major international bank against a multi-jurisdictional tracing claim and representing a developer on a successful judicial review application of a county borough council's re-zoning decision. Managing partner David Cantrell also has considerable experience across a wide range of commercial litigation, while Ronan O'Neill has particular expertise in IP litigation and medical law.

LK Shields's practice has a very high reputation, particularly as regards its niche expertise in professional negligence defence, shareholder disputes and taxation litigation. The firm acted on behalf of the liquidator appointed to Macks Bakeries in the high-profile action he took against the company's former solicitors, and is also representing Sir Alex Ferguson against John Magnier in relation to the horse 'Rock of Gibraltar'. Edmund Butler is recommended.

Litigation is one of **Mason Hayes & Curran**'s key practice areas. Declan Black is highly regarded, while Maurice Curran, now a consultant, is particularly recommended for his arbitration work. The firm has a dedicated contentious and non-contentious public and administrative law group, and recently acted for the Commission for Communications Regulation in proceedings against eircom in relation to the unbundling of the local loop.

Though not known as one of the firm's focal practice areas, **William Fry**'s dispute resolution practice includes specialist employment, construction, media and commercial units, representing corporate clients and a number of high-net-worth individuals. Recent cases have included acting in a major shareholder dispute that has given rise to allegations of oppression, and defending the owners of one of Ireland's largest industrial plants against claims of industrial pollution and damage to animal and human health. The firm has a growing product liability defence practice.

The bedrock of **BCM Hanby Wallace**'s litigation practice, headed by Gerard Butler, is insurance company defence work, although it continues to expand into more general commercial litigation. Highly-rated employment specialist Gary Byrne is a fellow of the Chartered Institute of Arbitrators, while Pamela Cassidy has extensive experience on media and defamation matters.

Gabriel Daly heads **Beauchamps**' broad-based litigation practice, which includes commercial litigation specialist Claire Callanan and contentious employment expert Mark Heslin.

At **Landwell Solicitors**, employment specialist Jim Trueick and IP/IT specialists Carol Plunkett and Garrett Breen are all recommended for their contentious work. The firm acted for the Commission for Aviation Regulation in relation to the judicial review of a determination of the Commission regarding the maximum level of airport charges that could be imposed by Aer Rianta; it was one of the largest cases before the Irish courts in 2003. Aer Rianta was advised by **Arthur Cox**, while notice parties Aer Lingus and Ryanair were advised by **McCann FitzGerald** and**A&L Goodbody** respectively.

O'Donnell Sweeney specialises in complex commercial litigation, and has notable construction litigation and contentious employment experience. Dermot McEvoy and Norman Fitzgerald are recommended.

Ronan Daly Jermyn's commercial litigation department is headed by Richard Martin. The firm has recently acted in a number of leading judicial review cases.

Whitney, Moore & Keller has a broad-based commercial litigation practice, with particular expertise in contentious IP work. Clients include the Institute of Chartered Accountants. Gerry Carroll is recommended.

EU AND COMPETITION

Vincent Power is the head of **A&L Goodbody**'s five-fee-earner competition team, which includes two senior associates and a new partner in Alan McCarthy. In addition to providing competition, merger control and regulatory advice to a diverse range of clients, the firm has been advising Ryanair in respect of the European Commission's

EU AND COMPETITION

A&L GOODBODY ✪
ARTHUR COX ✪
MATHESON ORMSBY PRENTICE ✪
McCANN FITZGERALD ✪
WILLIAM FRY ✪

LK Shields ✪
Landwell Solicitors ✪
Mason Hayes & Curran ✪
Masons
Robert Ryan & Associates ✪

Beauchamps ✪
Conway Kelleher Tobin
Dillon Eustace ✪
Dockrell Farrell
Eugene F Collins ✪
Kilroys ✪
O'Donnell Sweeney ✪
Ronan Daly Jermyn ✪
Whitney, Moore & Keller

Firms are listed A-Z in tiers which are ranked in order of priority
✪ *Indicates firm displays contact details at the end of this chapter.*

high-profile and ongoing Charleroi investigation, and the Law Society of Ireland in respect of the Competition Authority's Study of the Professions.

Arthur Cox has been involved in a number of significant recent competition law investigations and cases, including advising eircom on litigation taken by ESAT/BT under the terms of the Competition Act 2002 and advising RTÉ on a complaint made to the Competition Authority by TV3. Recent merger control work includes advising First Active in relation to its acquisition by Royal Bank of Scotland, and advising Anglo American on its acquisition of the Lisheen Mine. Partners John Meade and Patrick O'Brien head the practice.

Helen Kelly heads **Matheson Ormsby Prentice**'s EC, competition and regulatory group, which includes three other fee-earners. The group has recently advised on a number of high-profile mergers, including acting for Ryanair on its acquisition of Buzz from KLM, and advising Stena on its proposed acquisition of a significant part of P&O's operations on the Irish Sea. The firm has represented a number of clients subject to Competition Authority cartel investigations, as well as advising a wide range of clients in the regulated sectors.

McCann FitzGerald's two competition partners are Gerald FitzGerald and Damian Collins, who is located full time in the firm's Brussels office. Gerald FitzGerald is a highly respected practitioner; he is the only solicitor appointed to the advisory panel of the Competition Authority, and was previously a member of the government-led Mergers Review Group. The firm has recently advised clients such as Aer Rianta, BMW and Eirgrid on competition matters.

John Handoll, who leads **William Fry**'s competition group, has a very strong reputation. The firm has a proven record advising a wide spectrum of clients on the full range of competition issues, including merger control, horizontal and vertical agreements, abuse of dominant position and the application of state aid rules. It also retains a strong presence in other areas of regulation, advising on sectors such as telecoms, broadcasting, energy and e-commerce, and boasts a growing practice in public procurement advice.

Marco Hickey at **LK Shields** has extensive experience of advising on contentious and non-contentious EU and Irish competition law issues.

Landwell Solicitors has strong regulatory experience; clients include the Commission for Aviation Regulation, which the firm has been representing in the long-running battle against Aer Rianta to defend a cap on airport charges. Garrett Breen at the firm recently acted for the Office of Utility Regulation in Guernsey in an appeal against a decision brought by Cable & Wireless Guernsey.

Anthony Burke and John Kettle at **Mason Hayes & Curran**, in addition to their merger control experience, specialise in advising on regulated industries; the firm's clients include RTÉ, ComReg and the Irish Energy Regulator, which it continues to advise on the liberalisation of the Irish electricity market.

Masons has considerable niche experience of advising on the EU aspects of public procurement, for which Barbara Linehan is recommended.

Robert Ryan & Associates has recently advised Irish banking industry organisations on the Competition Authority banking study.

EMPLOYMENT

All of the larger commercial firms have extensive experience of advising on the employment aspects of M&A and other corporate transactions, including advising on the implications of the EU Acquired Rights Directive.

Arthur Cox has an excellent three-partner employment practice. The group advises on all aspects of national and EU employment law and industrial relations. Clients include global and domestic companies, public sector bodies, and executives and senior managers. Consultant Dr Mary Redmond is one of Ireland's best-known employment law and industrial relations experts.

BCM Hanby Wallace's employment department has an excellent reputation, with partners Gary Byrne, Michael Kennedy and discrimination and equality specialist Michelle Ni Longain all recommended.

Ian Moore heads **A&L Goodbody**'s practice. The firm advises mainly on the employer side, with a client range including banks, airlines and blue-chip multinationals. The firm has extensive experience of advising on senior executives' contracts and terminations, and regularly defends companies and directors against prosecution by the Health & Safety Authority. Eoin MacNeil has recently advised the Football Association of Ireland on employment matters. Highly-rated partner Joanne Hyde left the firm in September 2003 to work in-house for Intel.

EMPLOYMENT

ARTHUR COX ✪
BCM HANBY WALLACE ✪

A&L GOODBODY ✪
MASON HAYES & CURRAN ✪
MATHESON ORMSBY PRENTICE ✪
McCANN FITZGERALD ✪
WILLIAM FRY ✪

LK Shields ✪
Ronan Daly Jermyn ✪

Beauchamps ✪
Conway Kelleher Tobin
Dillon Eustace ✪
Eugene F Collins ✪
Landwell Solicitors ✪
McAleese & Co
O'Donnell Sweeney ✪
Whitney, Moore & Keller

Firms are listed A-Z in tiers which are ranked in order of priority
✪ *Indicates firm displays contact details at the end of this chapter.*

Mason Hayes & Curran's employment unit is one of the firm's focal practices. Partners Emer Gilvarry and Peter McInnes are both litigators, and the unit has recently become increasingly involved in contentious matters involving management-level terminations, large-scale redundancy schemes and absenteeism issues.

Matheson Ormsby Prentice's employment and equality law group has advised companies in the technology, telecoms and energy sectors, amongst others. Practice head Paul Glenfield has provided extensive advice to Hewlett-Packard, in relation both to its merger with Compaq and to the outsourcing of Bank of Ireland's IT systems to the company.

McCann FitzGerald has a strong contentious and non-contentious practice, acting for clients such as Bank of Ireland, DePfa, Diageo and Motorola. The firm has recently advised on a number of business closures and rationalisation and downsizing plans. Terence McCrann has a very good reputation.

William Fry's employment group advises many of Ireland's leading companies, as well as FAS (the semi-state employment training body) and the Royal Dublin Society, and has also acted for a number of senior executives in negotiating severance terms. Maura Roe is a TUPE specialist, while department head Boyce Shubotham is a renowned litigator.

LK Shields advises on all aspects of the employer/employee relationship and on the employment law issues raised by M&A and inward investment transactions. The firm also has extensive contentious experience.

Ronan Daly Jermyn's team is headed by Fergus Long and Jennifer Cashman. New client gains in the area include the National Recruitment Federation of Ireland, the national umbrella group for Ireland's employment agencies.

ENERGY AND NATURAL RESOURCES

Arthur Cox's energy and natural resources practice has recently acted for Viridian Group plc on the development of a new 400MW IPP near Dublin, as well as advising BPB Group plc on the development of a gypsum mine in County Cavan, and advising the Chief State Solicitor and the Department of Communications, Marine & Natural Resources on the development of Ireland's first two proposed offshore windfarms (Arklow Banks and Codling Banks). Energy specialist Alex McClean is highly recommended, and the group has been reinforced by the addition of John Glackin and Bryan Strahan from *Gerrard, Scallan & O'Brien*, both of whom are experienced in the fields of mining and natural resources law.

Projects expert Kevin Feeney plays a key part in **A&L Goodbody**'s energy practice. The firm advised GE on the development of the Arklow Banks offshore windfarm, as well as acting on a number of onshore windfarm project financings, including advising Barclays Bank on the financing of the Snugborough windfarm in County Cavan. It is also acting for Tiru SA on its bid to procure and run the proposed Dublin waste-to-energy plant (valued at around €200m), and continues to advise Innogy on the purchase of gas from Ramco, which owns the Seven Heads gasfield.

Matheson Ormsby Prentice has advised on a range of significant project finance transactions in the sector, including acting for Bank of Scotland on the £71m financing of the development of the Seven Heads gasfield. It also acted for Bord Gáis Éireann on the procurement of a gas pipeline for Northwest Pipeline in Northern Ireland. Other clients include IIB Bank (also on the project financing side) and Saorgus Energy Ltd. Michael O'Connor heads the practice and is very highly regarded.

McCann FitzGerald's clients include the Irish National Grid, Edenberry Power, Ireland Power, and Coillte Teoranta, which the firm has recently advised on its involvement in windfarm projects. Patricia Lawless is recommended.

Mason Hayes & Curran, where Kevin Hoy is an expert in the wind energy sector, acted on the financing side of a number of windfarm projects, including the Ecopower windfarm in County Mayo, and is advising the Commission for Energy Regulation on its current competition for new generation capacity (with **Arthur Cox, Matheson Ormsby Prentice** and **William Fry** each involved on the bid side).

William Fry's team, led by corporate partner Aislinn O'Farrell, acts for a number of domestic and international clients in the energy sector. It advised PowerGen on the acquisition by its parent company of the Edenberry Power Station, and Aughinish Alumina on the construction of its combined heat and power plant at Askeaton. Partner John Gaffney left the firm in June 2003 to join **O'Flynn Exhams & Partners** in Cork.

BCM Hanby Wallace has solid project finance experience, which includes advising in relation to a number of windfarm and alternative energy projects, while **Beauchamps**' multi-disciplinary energy and natural resources unit has advised on a number of power station projects.

Dillon Eustace has recently advised in relation to a number of windfarm projects, including acting for the operator and developer of a 12MW windfarm in south-west Ireland.

Leonara Malone at **Eugene F Collins** has continued to act for Enterprise Energy in relation to the development of the Corrib Field, while David Beattie at **O'Donnell Sweeney** has attracted some impressive instructions in the sector.

O'Flynn Exhams & Partners has a strong energy and natural resources practice, strengthened by the arrival of John Gaffney from **William Fry**. Gaffney specialises in the competition and regulatory aspects of the field.

Ronan Daly Jermyn's clients include Enterprise Oil, while **Whitney, Moore & Keller** recently advised AIM-listed Petroceltic International plc on a variety of matters including its acquisition of an option over gas exploration blocks in the Celtic Sea, and also advised investors in the development of windfarms at Coillelea, County Mayo.

ENERGY AND NATURAL RESOURCES

ARTHUR COX ✪

A&L GOODBODY ✪
MATHESON ORMSBY PRENTICE ✪
McCANN FITZGERALD ✪

Mason Hayes & Curran ✪
William Fry ✪

BCM Hanby Wallace ✪
Beauchamps ✪
Dillon Eustace ✪
Eugene F Collins ✪
O'Donnell Sweeney ✪
O'Flynn Exhams & Partners
Ronan Daly Jermyn ✪
Whitney, Moore & Keller

Firms are listed A-Z in tiers which are ranked in order of priority
✪ Indicates firm displays contact details at the end of this chapter.

IT, TELECOMS AND E-COMMERCE

A&L Goodbody has advised on a number of significant IT outsourcing arrangements, including assisting BearingPoint on its successful conclusion of a contract with the Irish Department of Foreign Affairs as prime contractor to provide a new Irish passport system. Other clients that the group has advised include e-learning provider Intuition, the Football Association of Ireland, eircom and, in relation to e-commerce, the Department of Public Enterprise. The firm is also active in the biotechnology and healthcare sectors.

Arthur Cox's technology practice originally grew out of the firm's work for US technology multinationals, and the firm now also acts for many of the country's own established and emerging technology companies. It advises clients such as eBay, PayPal and AIB on e-commerce issues, and recently acted for Openet Telecom on a $20m, third-round venture capital funding and for OpenMIND Networks in relation to its €1.7m first-round funding. The group is headed by John Menton and benefits significantly from the consultancy of Professor Robert Clark.

Mason Hayes & Curran's practice, led by Anthony Burke, has a particularly strong reputation for its e-commerce work; it continues to advise Bank of Ireland on its e-banking facilities and has also advised Textus in relation to mobile phone/e-commerce solutions to companies in the aviation and travel industries. Other clients which the firm has advised on technology issues include RTÉ and Fujitsu Consulting.

Matheson Ormsby Prentice, as well as advising Hewlett-Packard on Bank of Ireland's outsourcing of its IT infrastructure, has advised Google on the establishment of its European operations in Dublin, and acts for Microsoft's European Operations Centre on all its operational and outsourcing contracts for the EMEA region. Don McAleese and Anne-Marie Bohan are both highly recommended.

IT, TELECOMS AND E-COMMERCE

A&L GOODBODY ✪
ARTHUR COX ✪
MASON HAYES & CURRAN ✪
MATHESON ORMSBY PRENTICE ✪
McCANN FITZGERALD ✪
WILLIAM FRY ✪

Eugene F Collins ✪
LK Shields ✪
Landwell Solicitors ✪
O'Donnell Sweeney ✪

BCM Hanby Wallace ✪
Beauchamps ✪
Dockrell Farrell
Kilroys ✪
Masons

Binchys Solicitors ✪
Conway Kelleher Tobin
Dillon Eustace ✪
McAleese & Co
Ronan Daly Jermyn ✪

Firms are listed A-Z in tiers which are ranked in order of priority
✪ Indicates firm displays contact details at the end of this chapter.

McCann FitzGerald's practice, led by William Earley, has recently advised telecoms clients such as ComReg, British Telecom, O2 and Esat BT. It also acts for a number of major banking and corporate clients (including AIB and Diageo) on e-commerce matters, for which Paul Lavery is particularly recommended.

William Fry's corporate team has maintained its reputation for technology M&A and fund-raisings, while the commercial team has been acting on a range of impressive instructions in the IT, e-commerce, telecoms and digital media areas; partner David Cullen has advised clients such as DoubleClick and Siemens, and Victor Timon is also recommended. The firm boasts an expanding practice advising in relation to new and emerging technologies, particularly in the biotechnology sector.

Eugene F Collins' IT practice is headed by partner David Hackett, who was previously in-house counsel at GSM Association. Corporate partner Anthony Collins advised Columbia Ventures Corporation on its €5.2m purchase of telecoms assets from 360Network's Irish subsidiaries; other recent work includes advising Promedia GCV on the supply of a new computer system to Golden Pages.

LK Shields advises a significant number of technology clients, both suppliers and purchasers, with a particular emphasis on the IP aspects of their contractual arrangements. The firm regularly acts for start-ups, and also advises clients on telecoms and e-commerce matters.

Carol Plunkett at **Landwell Solicitors** has a strong reputation for her IT work. On the transactional side the firm recently advised SITA on its acquisition of aviation software firm Eland Technologies.

Tony McGovern at **O'Donnell Sweeney** has good experience of advising growing technology and biotechnology companies, while managing partner Francis Hackett (former corporate counsel at eircom) has extensive knowledge on the regulatory side.

BCM Hanby Wallace has experience on a range of IT and emerging technology matters, although specialist partner Eileen Prendergast is now focusing more on banking and finance matters.

Commercial partners Shaun O'Shea and **Beauchamps** and Mark Pery-Knox-Gore both have experience on IT and telecoms matters, while John Dockrell at **Dockrell Farrell** has experience in the telecoms field, with clients including a significant mobile phone network.

Kilroys acts for a number of companies in the infrastructure and content provision areas. Clients include Telenor, which is Norway's largest telecoms company.

Masons' recently established Dublin IT team is led by John Salmon. It works closely with the firm's projects practice and is instructed by a number of indigenous IT businesses.

INSOLVENCY

Arthur Cox has played a key role in most of Ireland's major insolvencies and corporate recoveries in the last 15 to 20 years. Recent work includes acting for KPMG as receiver of three companies in the Cunningham Group, acting for the liquidator of Navan Carpets Ltd on its high-profile liquidation, and acting on the restructuring of a major Irish manufacturing company with over €100m in syndicated bank debt. William Day and Eugene McCague are widely recommended.

Barry O'Neill heads **Eugene F Collins**' renowned insolvency practice, in which litigator Terry Leggett also plays a key role. The firm recently acted for Navan Carpets Ltd in its liquidation and for the receiver of Murpet Fish Company Ltd. O'Neill is an insolvency consultant on the Law Society's Education Programme and has lectured extensively on the field.

Matheson Ormsby Prentice's recent work includes advising a Citibank-led banking syndicate and receivers in the KPNQwest receivership and sale of assets to Interoute, and advising various European subsidiaries of Peregrine Systems Overseas Ltd, which was in Chapter 11 in the US. Partners Rod Ensor and Tony O'Grady are both highly regarded in the field.

McCann FitzGerald recently advised Irish Fertiliser Industries on its high-profile liquidation, and the examiner in relation to the examinership of property company Lark Developments Ltd. Jane Marshall, a former president and current director of INSOL Europe, has an excellent reputation; she retired as partner in 2002 but remains active as a consultant, alongside partner Emma Crowley.

A&L Goodbody's insolvency unit is jointly headed by corporate partner Paul Dobbyn and litigator David Baxter. Recent work includes acting for the receiver in relation to 360networks (Ireland) and for the examiner (and subsequently the official liquidator) of Lissadell Towels Ltd. The firm also advised the board of Irish Fertilisers Industries pre-insolvency.

Litigator Declan Black heads **Mason Hayes & Curran**'s insolvency practice, which mainly advises domestic practitioners, but has also been instructed on a number of international insolvencies (notably in relation to the exit from Chapter 11 of Global Crossing and Flag Telecom). The firm is advising KPMG on the liquidation of certain USIT Group companies; the group was the second largest provider of student travel services in the world.

Whitney, Moore & Keller's practice, headed by the highly-regarded Paul Hayes, has strong experience in the field, advising insolvency practitioners, lending institutions and creditors.

William Fry's team is led by Michael Quinn, alongside Mark Traynor and Frank Sowman, who stepped down as partner in May 2003 but continues to work as a consultant. The firm has acted on a range of recent liquidations, including Irish Ispat Ltd (the formerly state-owned Irish Steel company) and Mitek Holdings Ltd (which had been one of Ireland's leading pharmaceutical manufacturers). The firm also advises the Investor Compensation Company Ltd, and in this capacity has been involved in issues arising from the administration of insolvent stockbroking firms.

LK Shields regularly acts on behalf of liquidators and advises companies and creditors with regard to solvency-related issues; litigator Ed Butler is recommended.

Norman Fitzgerald at **O'Donnell Sweeney** is an experienced adviser, and the firm has been instructed on liquidations and receiverships by all of the major accountancy practices.

Insolvency remains a growing area for Cork-based **Ronan Daly Jermyn**; Nicholas Comyn has acted on a number of recent liquidations and enjoys a fine and far-reaching reputation.

INSOLVENCY

ARTHUR COX ✪
EUGENE F COLLINS ✪
MATHESON ORMSBY PRENTICE ✪
McCANN FITZGERALD ✪

A&L GOODBODY ✪
MASON HAYES & CURRAN ✪
WHITNEY, MOORE & KELLER
WILLIAM FRY ✪

LK Shields ✪
O'Donnell Sweeney ✪
Ronan Daly Jermyn ✪

Beauchamps ✪
Ivor Fitzpatrick & Company ✪
Landwell Solicitors ✪
Lavelle Coleman Solicitors
Reddy Charlton McKnight

Firms are listed A-Z in tiers which are ranked in order of priority
✪ Indicates firm displays contact details at the end of this chapter.

INSURANCE

James Grennan at **A&L Goodbody** is one of Ireland's best-known insurance lawyers. The firm advised longstanding client Prudential on the sale of its German life assurance business to Canada Life, together with the scheme for court approval of the transfer of policy holders, and also advised on the Irish aspects of an MBO of certain of Chubb's international insurance operations. The firm has recently been nominated to a panel of advisers by the State Claims Agency and has been involved in advising on the establishment of the Personal Injuries Assessment Board.

Liam Flynn heads **Matheson Ormsby Prentice**'s corporate and regulatory insurance practice, which has recently advised Carphone Warehouse on the establishment of its EU mobile phone insurance subsidiary in Ireland, as well as acting for Employers Reinsurance Corporation, a division of GE, on the sale of its Irish captive insurance

INSURANCE

A&L GOODBODY ✪
MATHESON ORMSBY PRENTICE ✪
WILLIAM FRY ✪

Arthur Cox ✪
Dillon Eustace ✪
McCann FitzGerald ✪

Mason Hayes & Curran ✪

Beauchamps ✪
Dockrell Farrell
Kilroys ✪
LK Shields ✪
Landwell Solicitors ✪
O'Donnell Sweeney ✪
Ronan Daly Jermyn ✪
Whitney, Moore & Keller

BCM Hanby Wallace ✪
Binchys Solicitors ✪
Duncan Grehan & Partners
Eugene F Collins ✪
Good & Murray Smith & Company
Gore & Grimes ✪
Ivor Fitzpatrick & Company ✪

Firms are listed A-Z in tiers which are ranked in order of priority
✪ *Indicates firm displays contact details at the end of this chapter.*

and investment management business. Litigation partner Sharon Daly heads the contentious practice, and has an excellent reputation.

Significant corporate transactions for **William Fry** included advising Great-West Lifeco on its acquisition of Canada Life, and acting for Axis Capital Holdings on its IPO and listing on the NYSE. The firm also advised a range of international companies, including Pirelli and Tesco, on the establishment of captive operations in Ireland, as well as advising insurance clients such as Irish Life and Royal Bank of Canada Reinsurance.

Arthur Cox acted for Canada life on its acquisition of Prudential's German life business, as well as providing ongoing advice to clients such as Eagle Star and Allianz plc. On the contentious side, the firm successfully represented the plaintiffs in Analog *Devices BV and Others v Zurich Insurance Company and American Guarantee and Liability Company*, which related to the defendant insurers' refusal to indemnify losses of over $5m.

At **Dillon Eustace**, financial services specialist Andrew Bates is very highly rated for his regulatory work and acts for a large portfolio of cross-border life operations, including Grow Life (MPS Group) and Inora Life (SG Group). Kieran Cowhey is recommended for his defence litigation work.

McCann FitzGerald offers major insurance claims work as well as advice on regulatory issues, IFSC establishment and contract terms. Clients include Lloyd's Underwriters, Provident and Standard Life, together with a raft of IFSC-based insurers and reinsurers. On the corporate side, the firm advised Canadian insurer ManuLife on its failed bid for Canada Life.

Mason Hayes & Curran has a strong defence insurance practice; the firm handles road traffic and professional and medical negligence claims and has recently added a number of major international insurance companies to its client list. Lorcan Buckley heads the group, and Ailbhe Gilvarry is also recommended.

Beauchamps' insurance practice is focused on contentious work, and has acted for a range of well-established Irish, UK and European insurers.

Dockrell Farrell has a solid insurance defence practice, acting for domestic and international insurers as well as self-insured clients. Litigator Margaret Carey is recommended.

Kilroys' practice, headed by Anthony Layng and Eamon Jones, is focused on the field of non-life insurance regulation, and represents the Allianz group companies in Ireland. Jones has niche expertise in the field of credit insurance and has advised the Irish government on the state's export credit scheme.

LK Shields advises on all aspects of insurance contracts, with particular experience in professional negligence work, while **Landwell Solicitors**' insurance work is focused on regulatory compliance.

Dermot McEvoy at **O'Donnell Sweeney** has advised on a number of professional negligence claims, while Peter Fahy regularly advises clients on regulatory matters.

Ronan Daly Jermyn has the largest defence litigation practice outside of Dublin, and has been instructed by all of the major insurance companies as well as by a number of public bodies. The firm has recently been appointed as adviser to the Clinical Indemnity Board.

Whitney, Moore & Keller has a well-regarded defence practice, under litigation partner John Lynch.

Of the firms in the fifth tier, **Duncan Grehan & Partners** is notable for its niche advising insurers in Germany and Austria on risk.

INTELLECTUAL PROPERTY

A&L Goodbody's intellectual property group advises clients across a broad range of sectors, including media, pharmaceuticals and food and drink companies, and recently resumed its representation of Microsoft in its Irish anti-counterfeiting and channel piracy programme. The group, headed by partners from the firm's litigation and corporate/commercial departments, has been strengthened by the return to the firm of John Whelan as partner in October 2003. Whelan had spent five years working for **Freshfields Bruckhaus Deringer** in London and Asia, and has experience on contentious and non-contentious intellectual property and IT matters.

Patricia McGovern heads **LK Shields**' intellectual property team, which advises clients across a range of industries on the full range of contentious and non-contentious intellectual property matters. The firm continues to advise Celador (producers of *Who Wants to be a Millionaire?*) on its intellectual property matters in Ireland; other clients include News International and Northern & Shell/Express Newspapers. Michael Kavanagh has extensive experience on the contentious side.

McCann FitzGerald's group regularly advises high-profile clients including Diageo, Procter & Gamble and GlaxoSmithKline. It recently advised Miss World Ltd in a name dispute over the name 'Miss Ireland'. The group is led by the widely respected Grace Smith and includes partner Yvonne McNamara, who specialises in intellectual property in e-commerce matters.

Arthur Cox has developed a strong contentious practice, and is advising Synthon BV on the Irish element of the patent litigation brought by GlaxoSmithKline in relation to an anti-depressant, in what is likely be the first patent trial to come before the Irish courts in the last 20 years. Other clients that the firm has advised on intellectual property matters recently include Repak, Bacardi and the Irish Music Rights Organisation. Professor Robert Clark, who is head lecturer in intellectual property at University College Dublin, is a consultant to the firm.

Eugene F Collins' practice is headed by intellectual property and IT specialist David Hackett, who has recently been made partner and is particularly strong on the transactional side. Litigation partner Ronan O'Neill specialises in intellectual property matters, particularly trade mark and copyright infringement cases.

INTELLECTUAL PROPERTY

A&L GOODBODY ✪
LK SHIELDS ✪
McCANN FITZGERALD ✪

ARTHUR COX ✪
EUGENE F COLLINS ✪
MATHESON ORMSBY PRENTICE ✪
WILLIAM FRY ✪

Beauchamps ✪
Landwell Solicitors ✪
Mason Hayes & Curran ✪
Whitney, Moore & Keller

BCM Hanby Wallace ✪
Dillon Eustace ✪
Dockrell Farrell
Gleeson McGrath Baldwin
O'Donnell Sweeney ✪
McAleese & Co
Reddy Charlton McKnight
Ronan Daly Jermyn ✪

Firms are listed A-Z in tiers which are ranked in order of priority
✪ *Indicates firm displays contact details at the end of this chapter.*

Intellectual property partner Eugene Murphy retired towards the end of 2003.

Matheson Ormsby Prentice advises a range of major corporate clients on brand protection. Recent contentious work includes acting for IMRO and BSkyB on a campaign to reduce copyright infringement and advising a major pharmaceutical company on patent infringement issues and product launch, while the firm's non-contentious work includes supporting on securitisation transactions and advising copyright collection societies and on trade mark registrations. Department head Michael Tyrell is particularly recommended for his contentious expertise.

William Fry's intellectual property team, headed by David Cullen, advises clients across a diverse range of sectors beyond its traditional corporate and technology client base. Recent work includes advising a number of celebrities in relation to trade mark and copyright matters and personality rights, advising Special Olympics on event merchandising rights relating to the Special Olympic Games 2003, and advising an Irish environmental company on a technology transfer from a leading Irish university.

Commercial head Shaun O'Shea and litigator Gary Rice at **Beauchamps** have a range of experience on intellectual property matters, while Carol Plunkett and more recent partner Garrett Breen at **Landwell Solicitors** are both highly rated for their contentious and non-contentious intellectual property work.

Mason Hayes & Curran has an active contentious and non-contentious intellectual property practice, headed by litigation partner Richard Woulfe. The firm recently acted for HiberGen Ltd, a leading Irish biotechnology firm, on the negotiation and licensing of strategic patents from UCC.

Intellectual property specialist Ken Parkinson at **Whitney, Moore & Keller** maintains a strong reputation, in particular for his patent litigation work.

INVESTMENT FUNDS

As well as being involved in a range of high-calibre hedge funds work, **A&L Goodbody** notably advised Morgan Stanley Investment Management on the establishment in Dublin of an umbrella UCITS money market fund, and Deutsche Bank on the sale of its Irish fund administration and custody business to State Street. Paul Dobbyn and Brian McDermott at the firm are recognised experts in the industry, while mutual funds expert Barry McGrath, who was made up as partner in May 2003, is also recommended.

Dillon Eustace's exceptional funds practice continues to grow, expanding further in the hedge fund, property fund and private equity fund areas as well as advising in relation to an increasing number of retail products. Clients include SGAM, Ivy Asset Management and Ivesco on the hedge fund side, and Nmás1 and LGT on the private equity fund side. The firm continues to benefit from its alliance with **Arendt & Medernach** in Luxembourg, and has an expanding US client base; in August 2003 it established an office in Boston, one of the world's key centres for mutual funds. Andrew Bates and Lorcan Tiernan, who specialises in hedge funds and alternative investment products, have particularly strong reputations.

Arthur Cox's clients include Barclays Global Investment (which the firm advises on all its Irish hedge fund and alternative investment product work), Federated and Merrill Lynch. The firm has acted for 16 of the 18 exchange-traded funds established in Ireland, and, on the multi-manager funds side, has acted for Frank Russell since 1994.

Matheson Ormsby Prentice's practice is headed by Michael Jackson and James Scanlon and advises a number of major investment funds promoters. It recently acted for Goldman Sachs on the establishment of a hedge fund product structured as a unit trust for distribution in Japan, and for Royal London Asset Management and Henderson Global Investors in relation to liquidity products.

McCann FitzGerald's funds practice is headed by Ambrose Loughlin and has an excellent IFSC-related client base. The firm's clients include Flemings Private Fund Management, DePfa Investment Bank and JPMorganChase. Significant recent work includes advising Williams de Broë Assetmaster Fund plc in relation to Ireland's first UCITS III fund.

William Fry has a strong record of advising in relation to alternative investment products, money-market products and multi-manager funds. The firm recently established a fund of hedge funds for Geneva-based manager Reyl & Cie, launched a new euro-denominated fund for Bank of America, and advised Barclays Global Investors on the first corporate bond exchange-traded fund. On the M&A side, the firm acted for State Street on its acquisition of Deutsche Bank's administration and custody businesses.

LK Shields has an active practice, advising a number of property and private equity funds. The firm advises BNP Paribas on its prime brokerage activities and acts as co-ordinating Dublin counsel for new client Citibank.

Kilroys has a boutique investment funds practice, which advises both fund promoters and service providers. It is headed by Hilary Griffey, who joined the firm in 2000 having spent six years as head of investment funds at the Irish Stock Exchange.

Ex-**Landwell Solicitors** associate Fionán Breathnach has joined **Mason Hayes & Curran** as a partner to launch its investment funds practice; he advises on all aspects of investment fund law and regulation.

INVESTMENT FUNDS

A&L GOODBODY ✪
DILLON EUSTACE ✪

ARTHUR COX ✪
MATHESON ORMSBY PRENTICE ✪
McCANN FITZGERALD ✪
WILLIAM FRY ✪

LK Shields ✪

Kilroys ✪
Mason Hayes & Curran ✪

Firms are listed A-Z in tiers which are ranked in order of priority
✪ Indicates firm displays contact details at the end of this chapter.

MARITIME AND SHIPPING

Catherine Duffy at **A&L Goodbody** is recommended for her ship finance work, while Vincent Power is an expert on EU and competition law as it relates to the shipping sector. The firm's clients include two major European shipping companies, and it has recently advised on a number of syndicated ship financings.

Dillon Eustace has a strong reputation for its wet work, and is now focusing increasingly on the financing side. The firm advises most of the UK P&I clubs and all of the major ferry companies, including Stena.

Petria McDonnell heads **McCann FitzGerald**'s maritime practice, and is one of the country's leading experts in the field. Her team's work includes advising on vessel arrests and personal injury, salvage and pollution claims, and clients include a range of Irish, UK and Dutch P&I clubs. The firm recently advised on the significant salvage claim arising from the Spanish Armada wrecks off the west coast of Ireland, and on the claim arising from out of the MV Bluebird Collision at Dublin Port.

Arthur Cox's practice has been strengthened by the arrival of Bryan Strahan from *Gerrard, Scallan & O'Brien*. The firm has experience of advising on the full range of maritime matters, including claims work and ship finance, and recently acted for the Bank of Ireland-led syndicate financing the MV Atlantic Dawn, one of the largest fishing trawlers in Europe. Clients include Dublin Port Company and

MARITIME AND SHIPPING

A&L GOODBODY ✪
DILLON EUSTACE ✪
McCANN FITZGERALD ✪

ARTHUR COX ✪
MATHESON ORMSBY PRENTICE ✪

Conway Kelleher Tobin
Kennedy McGonagle Ballagh incorporating Bell Branigan O'Donnell & O'Brien
Ronan Daly Jermyn ✪
Vincent & Beatty ✪

Firms are listed A-Z in tiers which are ranked in order of priority
✪ Indicates firm displays contact details at the end of this chapter.

the Stafford Shipping line. Kathleen Garrett is widely recommended.

Matheson Ormsby Prentice has a strong multi-disciplinary transport practice, which includes shipping expertise. The firm is advising Stena on its proposed acquisition of a significant part of P&O's Irish Sea operations, and has also advised the Department of Agriculture on marine insurance policies. Michael Tyrell is recommended.

MEDIA AND ENTERTAINMENT

Matheson Ormsby Prentice has a full-service media and entertainment practice. Transactional specialist James Hickey heads the entertainment team, which also includes highly-regarded partner Ruth Hunter. It has acted in connection with the financing and production of a wide range of feature films, as well as advising on high-profile television and stage productions and acting for various copyright collection societies. The media team, meanwhile, is headed by Michael Tyrell; its work includes acting for publishers and broadcasters, including Newsgroup Newspapers and Lite FM, on pre-publication and defamation matters.

A&L Goodbody's entertainment practice is run largely out of the firm's London office; partners include Paul White (now back in Dublin) and Geraldine East, who is particularly highly regarded. As well as acting as production lawyers on various film and television projects, the firm has extensive experience on the financing side. Clients include the Irish Film Board, which the firm advised on investment in a range of feature films and in relation to the Company Development Initiative. Eoin MacNeill has a good niche in sports law, and recently advised Nissan on its sponsorship of the 2003 Irish Golf Open.

McAleese & Co is Ireland's leading specialist defamation practice. The firm handles all of Independent Newspapers' Ireland pre-publication, post-publication and litigation work and recently represented the client before the European Court of Human Rights (*Independent Newspapers v Ireland*). Other clients include Mirror Group Newspapers, Today FM, Random House and defamation insurers Markel. Managing partner Simon McAleese is widely recommended.

McCann FitzGerald's media and entertainment group advises on areas including film finance, electronic publications, entertainment contracts, sponsorship and defamation. The firm recently advised Alliance Atlantis International and MTV on co-production agreements and related security arrangements, and GlaxoSmithKline, ICC (now Bank of Scotland) and PGA European Tour Ltd on sports sponsorship deals. Other clients include Windmill Lane Productions and the National Gallery of Ireland. William Earley and Paul Lavery are recommended.

Ronan Daly Jermyn acts for the Thomas Crosbie Holdings media group, with Richard Martin advising the group's newspapers (including the *Irish Examiner* and *The Sunday Business Post*) on pre-publication and defamation matters. The firm also acts for a number of local radio stations.

William Fry has a multi-disciplinary team that includes corporate partner Ken Casey and defamation specialist Michael Kealey. Clients include a number of Irish and international celebrities and a range of publishing, radio, television and new media businesses, including Associated Newspapers, Scottish Radio Holdings and Chorus. The firm continues to advise the government in relation to the Digital Hub.

Arthur Cox's media group advises on a range of commercial media and regulatory issues, with clients including RTÉ, the Irish Music Rights Organisation and a number of independent production companies. On the M&A side, the firm's recent work includes acting for UTV plc on its acquisitions of Dublin's Lite FM and Limerick's 98 FM.

Partner Pamela Cassidy heads **BCM Hanby Wallace**'s media and defamation practice, which advises on a range of pre-litigation and litigation issues.

Litigator Gary Rice at **Beauchamps** has experience on contentious sport and media matters, while Claire Callanan's specialist areas include defamation work.

Paul Gill at **Dillon Eustace** is very well regarded for his media work, with current clients including the *Daily Star* and *Private Eye*. The firm's film finance practice continues to grow.

Litigator Eugene Murphy at **Eugene F Collins** has a good reputation for his defamation work, while **Gleeson McGrath Baldwin** has extensive experience across a broad range of media and entertainment matters.

MEDIA AND ENTERTAINMENT

MATHESON ORMSBY PRENTICE ✪

A&L GOODBODY ✪
McALEESE & CO
McCANN FITZGERALD ✪
RONAN DALY JERMYN ✪
WILLIAM FRY ✪

Arthur Cox ✪
BCM Hanby Wallace ✪
Beauchamps ✪
Dillon Eustace ✪
Eugene F Collins ✪
Gleeson McGrath Baldwin

Binchys Solicitors ✪
Dockrell Farrell
E P Fanning & Co, Solicitors
LK Shields ✪
Landwell Solicitors ✪
Lennon Heather & Company
Mason Hayes & Curran ✪
Whitney, Moore & Keller

Firms are listed A-Z in tiers which are ranked in order of priority
✪ *Indicates firm displays contact details at the end of this chapter.*

MERGERS AND ACQUISITIONS

In a year dominated on the domestic front by management buy-outs and public-to-private transactions, the standout M&A deal of the year was Royal Bank of Scotland's €900m takeover of First Active plc, on which **Arthur Cox** acted as sole adviser to First Active. The firm also advised Cadbury Schweppes on its acquisition of certain operations of Pfizer Inc (the transaction had a global value of $4.2bn), Canada Life on its €129m acquisition of Prudential's German life assurance business, and Electric Paper on the reverse takeover with RTG (now Third Force plc).

A&L Goodbody's take-private work included advising Ulster Bank and the Royal Bank of Scotland on the sale of NCB Group (one of Ireland's largest corporate finance houses) to management and certain other investors, advising the trustees of Arnotts Staff Pension Fund, a key strategic shareholder, in the sale to management of Arnotts plc and advising the directors of Alphyra Group plc on their €90m public-to-private takeover offer. The firm also advised Prudential on the sale to Canada Life, and acted as local lawyers to Royal Bank of Scotland on the First Active deal.

William Fry's take-private work included advising both Riverdeep plc and Arnotts plc on their takeovers (€350m and €257m respectively). The firm also advised Great-West Lifeco on its acquisition of Canada Life and acted on a series of other major M&A transactions for clients such as Jefferson Smurfit and State Street. Houghton Fry and Owen O'Connell have formidable reputations.

Matheson Ormsby Prentice advised Hertal Acquisitions plc and Nesbitt Acquisitions Ltd on the Riverdeep and Arnotts buy-outs respectively, and also acted for Galen Holdings plc on two major product acquisitions, from Ely Lilly and Pfizer. The firm's international M&A work included advising Peregrine Remedy Inc on a $350m business sale to BMC Software Inc.

McCann FitzGerald was involved in all of the year's major take-private deals, advising the buyer and Key Capital on the MBO/MBI of NCB Group, the MBO team and venture capitalists on the Alphyra buy-out, and acting for the financiers on the Riverdeep and Arnotts buy-outs.

LK Shields advised the NCB Group management on their MBO and merger with Key Capital, and acted for the MBO vehicle on the Conduit plc take-private. It also advised BCP Group on the sale of the BCP Stockbrokers' business to Dolmen Corporate Finance.

Mason Hayes & Curran saw significant take-private activity, including advising NCB Corporate Finance in relation to the Arnotts deal and the bidder in relation to its takeover offer for Sherry Fitzgerald Group plc (advised by **McCann FitzGerald**). The firm also advised Campbell Soup Company on its acquisition of Erin Foods. While the firm has been hit by the departure of John Kehoe in the spring of 2003, corporate head Paul Egan is

MERGERS AND ACQUISITIONS

A&L GOODBODY ✪
ARTHUR COX ✪
WILLIAM FRY ✪

MATHESON ORMSBY PRENTICE ✪
McCANN FITZGERALD ✪

LK Shields ✪
Mason Hayes & Curran ✪

BCM Hanby Wallace ✪
Dillon Eustace ✪
Eugene F Collins ✪
KLW
Landwell Solicitors ✪
O'Donnell Sweeney ✪
Ronan Daly Jermyn ✪
Whitney, Moore & Keller

Beauchamps ✪
Binchys Solicitors ✪
Dockrell Farrell
Gore & Grimes ✪
Ivor Fitzpatrick & Company ✪
Kilroys ✪
McEvoy Partners ✪
PJ O'Driscoll & Sons
Reddy Charlton McKnight
Robert Ryan & Associates ✪

Firms are listed A-Z in tiers which are ranked in order of priority
✪ *Indicates firm displays contact details at the end of this chapter.*

very widely respected, and partners Liam Brazil and David O'Donnell are also recommended.

BCM Hanby Wallace acted for Sita Belgium in its disposal of waste company Sita Environmental, and for CNG Hotels on its $25m acquisition of Tzell Travel & Tours Inc.

Dillon Eustace has an expanding M&A practice, and has recruited Abigail Kennedy from **Arthur Cox** to head the practice. The firm recently advised Bank of Ireland and J&E Davy Holdings Ltd on the acquisition of Focus Investments Ltd, and Lone Star on the Irish aspects of its acquisition of a controlling stake in Korea Exchange Bank.

Eugene F Collins advised Liam Carroll and his bid vehicle in relation to the €140m takeover offer for Dunloe Ewart plc, and acted for the *Leinster Leader* on its €20m acquisition of the *Limerick Leader*. Anthony Collins has a strong reputation.

KLW, recently set up by ex-**Mason Hayes & Curran** partner John Kehoe, looks set to become a strong presence in the market, with a particular focus on international work.

Landwell Solicitors, under Edward Evans, acted for SITA on its acquisition of aviation software firm Eland Technologies, and for the purchasers of the Microbio and Rehide businesses from Clashfern Holdings.

David Beattie at **O'Donnell Sweeney** recently acted for IFG on the sale of 50% of its mortgage business to GE Capital. The firm has a niche strength in advising in the area of owner-managed businesses; David O'Beirne has extensive experience acting both on the acquisition and disposal of such entities.

Ronan Daly Jermyn remains the only firm outside Dublin with a significant M&A presence, and recently acted for Thomas Crosbie Holdings on its €10m acquisition of *The Irish Post*.

Whitney, Moore & Keller has a solid M&A practice, with recent transactions including acting for the selling shareholders on a €10m sale of a company that owned and operated a multi-storey car park business, and representing a corporate purchaser on a €10m pharmacies acquisition.

PENSIONS AND EMPLOYEE BENEFITS

A&L Goodbody's employee benefits and share schemes unit advises on all types of employee share scheme; it is headed by Sheena Doggett, who is widely recommended along with Roddy Buckley, who heads the firm's three-partner pensions unit. Recent activity includes advising the Trustees of the Arnotts Staff Pension Fund on the Fund's shareholding in Arnotts plc during the sale of the company; the unit has also advised on the pensions aspects of various outsourcing projects and advised employers and life office clients on PRSAs.

Arthur Cox's pensions partners, Declan Drislane and Philip Smith, are both very highly regarded. The group has a proven record in transactional support, and has recently advised a leading financial institution on the significant rationalisation of its pensions arrangements. Pension scheme clients include Allianz, Gallaher Tobacco, IBM Ireland and RTÉ.

BCM Hanby Wallace's pensions and employee benefits work is handled by the firm's employment group, and Gary Byrne in particular is recommended.

Fiona Thornton heads **LK Shields**' pensions and employee benefits unit. The firm has extensive experience on contentious and non-contentious pensions matters and, on the benefits side, has advised on the design and roll-out of a number of share plans as well as on the Irish implications of overseas share offerings to Irish-based employees.

Brian Buggy heads **Matheson Ormsby Prentice**'s pensions and employee benefits practice. The group recently advised Hewlett-Packard on the pensions law aspects of its merger with Compaq Computer in Ireland, and acted for the Irish Department of Social and Family Affairs in drafting legislation to facilitate the introduction of PRSAs in Ireland. Buggy is Chairman of the Association of Pensions Lawyers in Ireland.

McCann FitzGerald's group is now led by Maureen Dolan, following Ultan Stephenson's departure from the firm in April 2003. The firm advises both private and public sector clients, and recent work includes advising Pfizer on the harmonisation of pension and share schemes following its merger with Warner Lambert and Pharmacia.

PENSIONS AND EMPLOYEE BENEFITS

A&L GOODBODY ✪

Arthur Cox ✪
BCM Hanby Wallace ✪
LK Shields ✪
Matheson Ormsby Prentice ✪
McCann FitzGerald ✪
O'Donnell Sweeney ✪
William Fry ✪

Beauchamps ✪
Landwell Solicitors ✪
Mason Hayes & Curran ✪
Whitney, Moore & Keller

Firms are listed A-Z in tiers which are ranked in order of priority
✪ *Indicates firm displays contact details at the end of this chapter.*

O'Donnell Sweeney has developed a significant niche ESOP practice, and acts for the founders and/or the ESOP of all of Ireland's major employee share schemes, including eircom ESOP and TSB ESOP. Peter Fahy is one of Ireland's leading pensions and trusts lawyers.

William Fry's pensions department, headed by Michael Wolfe, advised on the local pensions law aspects of a range of major corporate transactions, including State Street's acquisition of Deutsche Bank's global custody services. It also acted for the trustees of a large domestic company's pension scheme on a landmark Pension Board determination. Maura Roe heads the firm's employee share schemes group; recent work, as well as advising on the Arnotts plc, Riverdeep plc and Ardagh plc transactions, includes implementing an approved profit-sharing scheme for the Irish employees of Tullow Oil plc.

PLANNING AND ENVIRONMENT

Arthur Cox's planning and environment group is headed by Deborah Spence and benefits from the consultancy of Dr Yvonne Scannell, one of Ireland's leading authorities in the field. Recent projects include acting for a private waste operator in obtaining regulatory approval for the first engineered residual waste facility under the government's new regional waste management plans. The firm also represented a major pharmaceutical company in relation to waste disposal-related environmental claims, and advised on a number of waste-to-energy and windfarm projects.

Matheson Ormsby Prentice's group, led by Patrick Sweetman and environmental specialist Stuart Margetson, advises clients including government, semi-state and private entities. It recently advised the government on the sale of a Cork oil refinery and acted for Noble Waste on the sale of its waste management business. It also

PLANNING AND ENVIRONMENT

ARTHUR COX ✪
MATHESON ORMSBY PRENTICE ✪
McCANN FITZGERALD ✪

A&L Goodbody ✪
BCM Hanby Wallace ✪
Beauchamps ✪
William Fry ✪

Dillon Eustace ✪
O'Donnell Sweeney ✪
Ronan Daly Jermyn ✪

Eugene F Collins ✪
LK Shields ✪
Landwell Solicitors ✪
Mason Hayes & Curran ✪
Whitney, Moore & Keller

Firms are listed A-Z in tiers which are ranked in order of priority
✪ *Indicates firm displays contact details at the end of this chapter.*

advised a three-way consortium in relation to the proposed Kildare power plant.

McCann FitzGerald has an excellent record of advising on environmental and contentious and non-contentious planning matters. Compliance specialist Michael O'Reilly has recently advised clients such as Aer Rianta, Ballymun Regeneration, Esso and Kildare County Council.

A&L Goodbody advised A1 Waste, one of Ireland's largest waste disposal operations, on its application for a waste licence from the Environmental Protection Agency, and Rolls-Royce Power Ventures Ltd on its plans for a gas-to-electricity facility in Dungarvan. The firm continues to advise a range of IPC-licensed facilities on compliance issues. Alison Fanagan, the only partner in the team, is highly regarded.

BCM Hanby Wallace has strong experience on planning, development and environmental matters, with chairman Brian Wallace particularly recommended. Recent work includes advising the developers on planning matters relating to the Adamstown development in West Dublin.

Beauchamps' planning unit includes lawyers from the firm's commercial property and litigation departments, with associate Ainsley Hefferman specialising in the field.

William Fry's environmental planning and waste management practice is led by barrister Conor Linehan. Recent work includes representing a major international client on its successful opposition to a proposed waste incinerator in County Tipperary, and advising the Liquidator of Irish Ispat in relation to the former steel plant's remediation issues. Corporate partner Bryan Bourke has advised on a number of waste transactions, for clients including environmental consultancy RPS Group plc and Greenstar.

Paul Eustace at **Dillon Eustace** is recommended for his planning experience, while Rory O'Donnell and Sean Greene at **O'Donnell Sweeney** both have planning and environmental experience, in particular on the regulatory side.

Ronan Daly Jermyn has benefited from Cork being an important location for the pharmaceuticals industry, and advises clients including GlaxoSmithKline on planning and environmental matters.

PROJECT FINANCE AND PPP

On the PPP side, **A&L Goodbody** is advising the Southern Health Board on the procurement of Ireland's first healthcare project, and a consortium in relation to the Fermoy bypass project (currently at BAFO stage), as well as acting on a number of PFI projects in Northern Ireland. The firm has also had a strong year on the project finance side, in relation to windfarm projects such as Arklow Banks. Kevin Feeney has an outstanding reputation.

Masons' team is headed by the extremely highly-regarded Eamonn Conlon, and has real strength on PPP. The firm's recent work includes advising the EuroLink consortium on the financial close of the Kinnegad Motorway real toll project and the Railway Procurement Agency on phase 1 of the Dublin Metro project. It also acted for two bidding consortia in relation to the Dundalk and Waterford road projects and advised at sub-contractor level in relation to the National Maritime College, Cork project (on which **A&L Goodbody** advised the Department of Education and Science, and **McCann FitzGerald** advised Bovis Lend Lease/Focus Education).

McCann FitzGerald maintains its reputation in the field and continues to advise the National Roads Authority in relation to a series of road projects, including the Kinnegad Motorway, Waterford bypass and Limerick Southern Ring Road projects. The firm is also advising Campus & Stadium Ireland in relation to the development of the State aquatic and leisure centre. Partners Tim Bouchier-Hayes, Kevin Kelly and Eamonn O'Hanrahan are all recommended.

Arthur Cox, as well as having proven project finance expertise, recently advised Celtic Roads Group in respect of the Dundalk and Waterford projects, and Cork County Council on a waste disposal facility being procured on a PPP basis.

Matheson Ormsby Prentice's PPP work includes advising Cathró Consortium in relation to the Dublin Metro project and advising Leeway 20:20 Ltd on the Cork Waste Recycling project. Recent project finance work, in addition to extensive activity the energy sector, includes advising Bank of Scotland on the financing of the construction of a Dublin Hotel.

William Fry advised on a number of PPP projects, including acting for the lenders on the Kinnegad project and advising a consortium in relation to the Fermoy bypass, as well as advising Digitial Media Developments in relation to Dublin's Digital Hub project.

PROJECT FINANCE AND PPP

A&L GOODBODY ✪
MASONS
McCANN FITZGERALD ✪

ARTHUR COX ✪
MATHESON ORMSBY PRENTICE ✪
WILLIAM FRY ✪

BCM Hanby Wallace ✪
Beauchamps ✪
Dillon Eustace ✪
Eugene F Collins ✪
Kilroys ✪
LK Shields ✪
Mason Hayes & Curran ✪
O'Donnell Sweeney ✪
Ronan Daly Jermyn ✪
Whitney, Moore & Keller

Firms are listed A-Z in tiers which are ranked in order of priority
✪ *Indicates firm displays contact details at the end of this chapter.*

Of the firms in the third tier, Patrick Ryan at **Kilroys** has extensive experience in the area of public procurement, as has **LK Shields** which acts for one of the largest semi-state harbour authorities on the infrastructure and commercial development of port facilities. **O'Donnell Sweeney** has good projects and PPP experience, while **Ronan Daly Jermyn**'s team, led by Finola McCarthy, picks up high-quality work in the Cork area and has recently advised in relation to the new Dublin Waterworld centre.

SECURITISATION

A&L Goodbody's securitisation and repackaging unit is headed by Ciaran Rogers. As well as acting for two domestic originators on the structuring of their first securitisations into new asset classes, the firm acted as local counsel on a range of international programmes. Headline work included advising Air France, Credit Lyonnais and the issuing vehicle on a €425.6m aircraft securitisation, and advising in connection with the €1.025bn Toll Road Funding programme, one of the largest non-RMBS securitisations in Europe in 2003.

Arthur Cox's securitisation group, led by Cormac Kissane, advised EBS Building Society on its €750m residential mortgage securitisation in May 2003; at the time it was the largest ever securitisation for an Irish originator. The firm's international securitisation practice has continued to expand; highlights included advising Chalet Finance No.1 plc on a €2.2bn synthetic mortgage transaction for Credit Suisse, and advising Morgan Stanley in relation to the listing of ELOC No. 10, the first-ever *fonds commun de créances* listed on the Irish Stock Exchange.

Matheson Ormsby Prentice has an outstanding structured finance team led by Turlough

SECURITISATION

A&L GOODBODY ✪
ARTHUR COX ✪
MATHESON ORMSBY PRENTICE ✪
McCANN FITZGERALD ✪

DILLON EUSTACE ✪
LK SHIELDS ✪

William Fry ✪

Firms are listed A-Z in tiers which are ranked in order of priority
✪ *Indicates firm displays contact details at the end of this chapter.*

Gavin. The firm advised on a high volume of securitisations and repackaging transactions in the last year, including acting for Deutsche Bank and Caixa-Banco de Investimento in relation to the Galp Investment plc €210m oil receivables securitisation, which was the first term corporate securitisation to be implemented in Portugal.

McCann FitzGerald maintains its reputation in the field. The firm was instrumental in drafting the Asset Covered Securities Act 2002, which facilitated the introduction of the *Pfandbrief* securitisation product in Ireland, and has advised DePfa ACS Bank on three asset-covered securities issues under the legislation, the first of which raised €4bn. The firm has advised First Active plc on all eight of its Celtic home loan securitisations. Roy Parker is highly recommended.

Mark Thorne and David Dillon at **Dillon Eustace** specialise in securitisation, along with Conor Houlihan at the firm's Tokyo office, and the team has been particularly active in the Far East. Recent work includes advising on the Korean Airlines ticket receivables securitisation (with a value of more than $200m), and acting for the trustee on Friends First's car loan securitisation. Other current clients include Lehman Brothers, Citibank, ABN Amro and CSFB.

LK Shields' financial services unit, led by partners Joseph Gavin and David Williams, advises Nomura on its warehouse funding activities and has acted on a significant volume of repackaging work for another major international investment bank.

Banking partners Elaine Hanly, Daragh Bohan and Orla Brennan at **William Fry** all have experience in handling corporate securitisation work; Bohan has recently advised Fiat Auto on its pan-European programme.

TAX

MATHESON ORMSBY PRENTICE ✪

A&L GOODBODY ✪
WILLIAM FRY ✪

Arthur Cox ✪
McCann FitzGerald ✪

Landwell Solicitors ✪

Firms are listed A-Z in tiers which are ranked in order of priority
✪ *Indicates firm displays contact details at the end of this chapter.*

TAX

Matheson Ormsby Prentice boasts Ireland's standout tax practice, in terms of its size, the depth and diversity of its experience and the extent of the front-end service that it provides; less than half of its work can be classified as transactional support. It is the only law firm that currently presents a threat to the hegemony of the accountancy firms. Significant recent work, in addition to substantial structured finance and securitisation advice, includes advising Nesbitt Acquisition Ltd on the Arnotts takeover, in the largest acquisition of an Irish public company in which an Irish law firm has been entirely responsible for the tax advice. The firm also acted as Irish counsel on the first multi-lateral transfer pricing Competent Authority application in Ireland, and advised the International Aviation Transport Association in its suit against the Irish VAT Authority. Liam Quirke, who replaced Donal Roche as managing partner in January 2004, heads the group and is widely admired, and Anthony Walsh and John Gulliver are also recommended.

A&L Goodbody has an excellent record on transactional support, in particular in the areas of M&A and structured finance. As well as advising on a raft of securitisations and repackaging programmes, headline work included advising Valentia/eircom on the tax aspects of the refinancing of the group's acquisition debt and advising Ulster Bank on the tax issues relating to the sale of NCB Group to a management-led team. Peter Maher heads the team and is highly recommended, along with David Glynn. John McGlone arrived from KPMG in September 2002 as head of VAT.

William Fry's tax group is headed by Martin Phelan, who is another ex-accountant, and has recently provided significant advice in the areas of M&A, capital markets and PPP. Notable work for the firm includes acting as Irish tax advisers to Great-West Lifeco on its acquisition of Canada Life, and to Bermuda-based Axis Capital Holdings on its IPO and listing on the NYSE. It is also lead adviser on Ireland's largest personal tax litigation trial. Partners Greg Hollingsworth and Michael O'Connor are recommended.

The strength of **Arthur Cox**'s tax group, in which Caroline Devlin is recommended, lies in its record of supporting the firm's premium M&A practice; it has recently advised in relation to Greencore's disposal of non-core businesses, Cadbury Schweppes' acquisition of certain assets of Pfizer Inc and Sage's acquisition of GFK Technology. The group has also advised on a range of corporate restructurings and financial services transactions, including securitisations and bond issues. The firm has recently announced that Conor Hurley, senior tax partner at **Linklaters** in London and one of the UK's leading specialists, will be joining the firm in early 2004 as head of the tax department.

McCann FitzGerald has had a discrete tax group since 2000. It is headed by the highly-regarded Michael Ryan, formerly of KPMG, and focuses on tax-driven investment structures, securitisations and other structured finance activities as well as M&A, energy and PPP projects. It has recently advised Bord Gáis Éireann, Citibank, Dolmen Securities and Ireland Power.

BARRISTERS

Although mediation of commercial disputes is gaining increasing acceptance in Ireland, alternative dispute resolution remains a relatively undeveloped area in Ireland, and barristers are much in demand. Solicitor-advocates are rare in the High Court.

Dermot Gleeson, Paul Gallagher, Donal O'Donnell, Michael Collins, Richard Nesbitt and John Gordon are particularly well-thought-of senior counsel, and Paul Gardiner, Gerard Hogan, Paul Screenan, Eoin McGonigal and Michael Cush are also highly regarded. Gleeson, a former Attorney-General is most noteworthy and widely seen as Ireland's finest barrister.

Dan O'Keeffe, Ian Finlay, Lyndon McCann, Eoin McCullough and Bill Shipsey win strong praise from instructing solicitors. Among junior counsel, the same applies to Oisin Quinn, David Barniville and Eileen Barrington.

In specific practice areas, senior counsel Brian O'Moore, John Gordon and Richard Nesbitt are among Ireland's leading intellectual property barristers, and Dennis McDonald also has a first-rate reputation. Among junior counsel, Michael Howard and John Breslin stand out.

Thomas McCann is generally seen as Ireland's leading tax counsel, and John Farrell wins similar praise in property. For construction, Dermot Gleeson and Paul Gallagher are both high profile.

There are a plethora of top-quality employment barristers. These include Tom Mallon, Frank Callanan, Gerard Durcan, Ercus Stewart, Ian Finlay, John Rodgers, Roderick Horan and Mark Connaughton.

Durcan is also a leading EU expert, as are Anthony O'Connor, James O'Reilly and Richard Nesbitt.

In insurance, Paul Screenan, Michael Collins and Dennis McDonald are recommended, as are Colm Allen and Murray McGrath. David Barniville is particularly active in this area.

In shipping law, we recommend Brian McGovern and Denis McDonald, along with junior counsel Colm O'Hoisin.

RONAN DALY JERMYN

12 SOUTH MALL
CORK

Telephone: +353 21 480 2700
Fax: +353 21 480 2790
E-mail: info@rdj.ie
Website: www.rdj.ie

Languages
English, French, German

Number of lawyers 35

Contact
John Dwyer (managing partner)

CATEGORIES OF WORK

Corporate, M&A
Frank Daly, Garvan Corkery

Inward investment
John Dwyer, Garvan Corkery

IT and e-commerce
Garvan Corkery, Adrian Wall

EU and competition
Lynn Sheehan

Employment
Fergus Long, Jennifer Cashman

Insolvency and debt recovery
Nicholas Comyn, Fergal Dennehy

Banking and finance
Frank Daly, Thomas Fox

Media and defamation
Richard Martin, John Buckley

PPP/construction
Finola McCarthy, Margaret Ring

Commercial property
John Dwyer, Pat Ahern

Litigation/dispute resolution
Fergus Long, Richard Martin

Maritime
Richard Martin, James O'Sullivan

Private client
John Jermyn, Rosemary Horgan

Matrimonial and family law
Rosemary Horgan

A&L GOODBODY

INTERNATIONAL FINANCIAL SERVICES CENTRE
NORTH WALL QUAY
DUBLIN 1

Telephone: +353 1 649 2000
Fax: +353 1 649 2649
E-mail: law@algoodbody.ie
Website: www.algoodbody.ie

Languages
Cantonese, Dutch, French, German, Malay, Mandarin

Other offices
Brussels, Boston, London, New York

Number of lawyers 191
at this office 185

Member
TerraLex

CATEGORIES OF WORK

Banking and financial services
Catherine Duffy (department head)

Commercial
David Sanfey (department head)

Litigation and dispute resolution
Peter Law (department head)

Pensions
Roddy Buckley (department head)

Private client
Michael Gorman (department head)

Property
Mairead Sherlock (department head)

Tax
Peter Maher (department head)

Mergers and acquistions
John Given

Corporate finance
Eithne Fitzgerald

Venture capital
John Olden

Capital markets
John Olden

Inward investment
John Coman

Partnerships
John Olden

Projects and construction
Kevin Feeney, Eamonn Gill

Asset finance
Catherine Duffy

Securitisation
Ciaran Rogers

Outsourcing
Jack O'Farrell

Insurance
James Grennan

EU, regulatory and competition
Vincent Power

Compliance and corporate financial governance
Kevin Allen

Insolvency and corporate recovery
Paul Dobbyn

E-commerce/ telecoms and technology
Liam Kennedy, Mark Ward

Investment funds
Brian McDermott

ADR
Joe Kelly

Intellectual property
John Whelan, Alison Fanagan

Sports law
Eoin MacNeill

Leisure and licensing
Joe Kelly, Stephen O'Riordan

Life sciences and healthcare
David Widger, Cliona Hickey

Media and entertainment
Paul White

Environmental and planning
Alison Fanagan

Food and agriculture
John Coman

Employment
Ian Moore, Joanne Hyde

Pensions and employee incentives
Eamon Brady, Sheena Doggett

Debt recovery
Eileen Roberts

Product liability
Caroline Preston

A&L Goodbody Consulting
Peter Brennan

Corporate offences
Joe Kelly

ARTHUR COX

EARLSFORT CENTRE
EARLSFORT TERRACE
DUBLIN 2

Telephone: +353 1 618 0000
Fax: +353 1 618 0618
E-mail: mail@arthurcox.com
Website: www.arthurcox.com

Languages
English, French, German, Italian, Spanish

Other offices
Belfast, London, New York

Number of lawyers 198
at this office 174

CATEGORIES OF WORK

Mergers and acquisitions, corporate finance
James O'Dwyer, Colm Duggan

Capital markets
Ronan Walsh, Mark Saunders

Corporate and commercial
Michael Meghen, Ciarán Bolger

Tax-based financing, corporate and capital taxation
Caroline Devlin, Niamh Caffrey

Banking
William Johnston, Kathleen Garrett

Project and asset finance
Grainne Hennessy, Liam Carney

Inward investment
Declan Hayes, Declan Drislane

International financial services and funds
Carl O'Sullivan, Sarah Cunniff

Corporate restructuring and insolvency
Eugene McCague, William Day

Securitisation
Cormac Kissane, Grainne Hennessy

EU and competition law
John Meade, Patrick O'Brien

E-commerce and technology
John Menton, Pádraig Ó Ríordáin

Pensions
Declan Drislane, Philip Smith

Employee share schemes
Stephen Hegarty, Anne Corrigan

Commercial property
John Walsh, Mark Barr

Commercial litigation
Conor McDonnell, Andrew Lenny

Professional negligence
Donogh Crowley, Margaret Muldowney

Defamation
Donogh Crowley, Joseph Leyden

Insurance litigation
David O'Donohoe, Greg Glynn

Employment and industrial relations
John V O'Dwyer, Séamus Given

Energy and natural resources
Patrick McGovern, Alex McLean

Environment and planning
Deborah Spence, Yvonne Scannell

Telecommunications
Patrick McGovern

Intellectual property
David O'Donohoe, Louise Carey

Food law
Maree Gallagher

Construction/public private partnerships
Mark Barr, Ted Williams

Product liability
Isabel Foley, David O'Donohoe

BCM HANBY WALLACE

88 HARCOURT STREET
DUBLIN 2

Telephone: +353 1 418 6900
Fax: +353 1 418 6901
E-mail: info@bcmhanbywallace.com
Website: www.bcmhanbywallace.com

Languages
French

Other offices
Sutton

Number of lawyers 60
at this office 58

Contact
Gary Byrne (managing partner)

CATEGORIES OF WORK

Commercial property
Michael Walsh, Catherine Guy

Residential property
James Moran, Daniel Murphy

Construction
Breda Sweeney, Elizabeth Gaffney

Corporate and commercial
Colin Sainsbury

Employment
Gary Byrne, Michael Kennedy

Equality
Michelle Ni Longain

Health services
Sinéad Kearney

Corporate finance
Feargal Brennan, Sean Wallace

Corporate banking
Ciara Gunning, Eileen Prendergast

Commercial property finance
Paul McGennis

Litigation and dispute resolution
Gerard W Butler

Media law and defamation
Pamela Cassidy

Private client
Carolyn Wallace, Jane Matthews

Planning and environmental
Brian Wallace, Rebecca Waddington

BINCHYS
SOLICITORS

40 LOWER BAGGOT STREET
DUBLIN 2

Telephone: +353 1 667 9800
Fax: +353 1 676 0189
E-mail: mail@binchys.com
Website: www.binchys.com

Languages
French

Number of lawyers 12

Contact
Jennifer Caldwell (managing partner)

CATEGORIES OF WORK

Company and commercial

Corporate finance and banking

Intellectual property

Commercial property

EU law

Entertainment and media law

Mergers and acquisitions

Information technology and e-commerce

Litigation

International tax law

Private client

Employment and pensions law

BEAUCHAMPS

DOLLARD HOUSE
WELLINGTON QUAY
DUBLIN 2

Telephone: +353 1 418 0600
Fax: +353 1 418 0699
E-mail: securemail@beauchamps.ie
Website: www.beauchamps.ie

Languages
English, French, German, Italian

Number of lawyers 50

Contacts
Imelda Reynolds (managing partner),
Mark J Heslin (business development partner)

CATEGORIES OF WORK

Banking and finance
Aidan Marsh, Maitiu O'Donaill

Construction and property
Imelda Reynolds, Richard Liddy

Healthcare and life sciences
Gabriel Daly, Aisling Gannon

Hospitality and leisure
Richard Liddy, Pauric Heraghty

Private client
John Cunningham, Kate O'Connor

Retail and manufacturing
Niall Coleman, John White

Technology and communications
Shaun O'Shea, Daniel Cashman

Inward investment
Shaun O'Shea, John White

Environment and planning
Niall Coleman, Ainsley Hefferman

Mergers and acquisitions
Mark Pery-Knox-Gore, Shaun O'Shea

Entertainment and sports law
Gary Rice, Pauric Heraghty

Residential property
Joseph Bowe, Marianne Thynne

Construction
Aidan Marsh, Aisling Foley

Product liability
Mark Heslin, Philip Smith

Employment and industrial relations
Claire Callanan, Mark Heslin

Dispute resolution
Gabriel Daly, Claire Callanan

Insurance litigation
Berchmans Gannon, Philip Smith

EU and competition
Gary Rice, John White

Intellectual property and franchising
Imelda Reynolds, Gary Rice

Public procurement
Mark Pery-Knox-Gore, Ruth Geaney

Public private partnership
Niall Coleman, Ruth Geaney

Trusts and charities
John Cunningham

Corporate restructuring and insolvency
Claire Callanan, Gabriel Daly

Corporate and commercial
Shaun O'Shea, Mark Pery-Knox-Gore

Professional negligence
Berchmans Gannon, Mark Heslin

Project and asset finance
Aidan Marsh, Maitiu O'Donaill

Commercial litigation
Gabriel Daly, Philip Smith

DILLON EUSTACE

GRAND CANAL HOUSE
1 UPPER GRAND CANAL STREET
DUBLIN 4

Telephone: +353 1 667 0022
Fax: +353 1 667 0042
E-mail: info@dilloneustace.ie
Website: www.dilloneustace.ie

Languages
French, German, Italian

Other offices
Boston, Tokyo

Number of lawyers 56

CATEGORIES OF WORK

Banking and finance
David Dillon, Denise Kinsella

IFSC, financial services
Andrew Bates, Lorcan Tiernan

Aviation litigation
Kieran Cowhey, John Doyle

Insolvency and corporate recovery
Brian Kelliher, Lorcan Tiernan

Public issues, securitisation
David Dillon, Mark Thorne

Investment funds
Andrew Bates, Brian Kelliher

Litigation and arbitration
Kieran Cowhey, Paul Gill

Maritime
Paul Gill, Paul Breen

Listing (funds/ABS)
Tara O'Callaghan, Ian McLaughlin

Mergers and acquisitions, joint ventures
Catherine McKnight, Abigail Kennedy

Commercial property and construction
Paul Eustace, Michael Barker

Corporate and commercial
David Dillon, Catherine McKnight

Insurance (life/non-life)
Andrew Bates, Brian Dillon

Asset finance
David Dillon, Lorcan Tiernan

Defamation
Paul Gill, John Doyle

Employment
John Doyle, Lorna Kennedy

Regulatory/compliance
Paul Kelleher, Orla Beaton

THE FIRM

Dillon Eustace, with a staff of over 125 including 56 lawyers, is one of Ireland's most respected and fastest-growing law firms. Founded in 1992, the firm has developed an excellent reputation worldwide in a number of areas of expertise.

Dillon Eustace is structured into four main departments: financial services; corporate and commercial; property/real estate; and litigation. Within each department, the firm has developed a number of areas of particular expertise (see 'Areas of practice') which has enabled Dillon Eustace to establish itself as one of the leading practices in its chosen fields.

AREAS OF PRACTICE

Dillon Eustace has one of the largest dedicated groups of lawyers in Ireland working in the area of international financial services. Every partner in the financial services group has been involved with the development of the International Financial Services Centre (IFSC) since its introduction by the Irish government. The level of expertise offered by Dillon Eustace has been recognised worldwide and the firm has been engaged on a consultancy basis in assisting offshore centres in drafting their mutual funds laws.

The financial services department is active across a wide spectrum of banking and financial services, including asset management investment vehicles and acting for leading international bancassurers in the development of IFSC- and non-IFSC-based life operations. Securitisation, group treasury, structured finance, public offers and private placements are among the other active practice areas for which the department is highly regarded.

Since its establishment, Dillon Eustace has advised on the formation of more than 850 mutual funds and has once again been acknowledged as the leading Irish law firm in this field by the 2003/2004 Fitzrovia Dublin Report. It represents a broad range of fund promoters/service providers from all major financial centres in countries such as the US, the UK, Japan, South Africa, Australia, Italy, France, Korea, Switzerland and Germany. Dillon Eustace is a leader in the structuring of hedge funds and other alternative investment products for national and international promoters.

The Dillon Eustace corporate and commercial team has extensive experience and expertise in the principal corporate and commercial practice areas. Acting for domestic and international clients, recent work includes LBO and MBO work and credit institution disposals.

Dillon Eustace has a highly-regarded litigation and arbitration practice serving a variety of both national and international clientele, and advising on all major areas of liability insurance. The firm offers advice in a broad range of practice areas, but has acknowledged expertise in certain specific areas: commercial and insurance litigation; aviation litigation; maritime; product liability; EU; competition and defamation.

The firm has developed a strong marine and aviation expertise acting for most of the major P&I clubs and for shipowners, cargo interests, airlines and aircraft operators.

The firm also has well-recognised expertise in defamation matters, particularly defence work for newspapers and other publications.

The property department has been associated with a number of large property developments, shopping centres and domestic housing developments. It advises on issues arising on landlord and tenant law, planning law and environmental law, and advises banks and other financial institutions in connection with secured lending transactions, working with the members of the corporate and commercial team in such transactions. The department advises companies establishing in Ireland for the first time on property issues.

In 2000, Dillon Eustace and the Luxembourg firm Arendt & Medernach, entered into a strategic alliance in the area of investment funds; establishing the first cross-border legal co-operation between Ireland and Luxembourg. Dillon Eustace has offices in Boston and Tokyo focusing on financial services.

EUGENE F COLLINS

TEMPLE CHAMBERS
3 BURLINGTON ROAD
DUBLIN 4

Telephone: +353 1 202 6400
Fax: +353 1 667 5200
E-mail: lawyer@efc.ie
Website: www.efc.ie

Languages
French, German

Number of lawyers 42

Contact
David Cantrell (managing partner)

CATEGORIES OF WORK

Mergers and acquisitions
Anthony Collins, Gerard Coll

Banking, securities and finance
Laura MacDermott, Eileen Grace

Companies, corporations
Anthony Collins, Leonora Malone

Capital markets
Eileen Grace, Leonora Malone

Commercial litigation
Terry Leggett, Ronan O'Neill

Property, real estate
David Ensor, John Territt

Bankruptcy, insolvency
Barry O'Neill, Terry Leggett

Intellectual property
David Hackett

Information technology
David Hackett

Labour
Maura Connolly

Defamation
Terry Leggett

Directors advice
Eileen Grace

Arbitration
Michael Carrigan

Immigration
David Cantrell

Private client
John Costello

Energy
Leonora Malone

GORE & GRIMES

CAVENDISH HOUSE
SMITHFIELD
DUBLIN 7

Telephone: +353 1 872 9299
Fax: +353 1 872 9877
E-mail: solrs@goregrimes.ie
Website: www.goregrimes.ie

Languages
English, French

Number of lawyers 10

CATEGORIES OF WORK

Company and commercial
Anthony Gore-Grimes, Louis Healy

Commercial property
John Gore-Grimes, Louis Healy

Private client litigation
David Martin, Liam Collins

Intellectual property
Brian O'Neill

Arbitration
John Gore-Grimes

Commercial litigation
Louis Healy, David Martin

Family law
Mary Hayes, Helen Gore-Grimes

Property and development
John Gore-Grimes, Sian Harper

Probate and trusts
Karl Hayes

EU and competition
Anthony Gore-Grimes

Employment
Helen Gore-Grimes

IVOR FITZPATRICK & COMPANY

SOLICITORS

44-45 ST STEPHENS GREEN
DUBLIN 2

Telephone: +353 1 678 7000
Fax: +353 1 678 7004
E-mail: info@ivorfitzpatrick.ie
Website: www.ivorfitzpatrick.ie

Languages
French, German, Spanish

Number of lawyers 35

CATEGORIES OF WORK

Corporate and commercial, banking and finance
Alfred Thornton, Annette Hale

Mergers and acquisitions, project finance and PPP
John King, Annette Hale

Civil litigation
Susan R Stapleton

Insolvency, insurance
Deirdre Courtney, Margaret Scully

Debt management
Margaret Scully

Labour and employment
Mary Claire Markey

Intellectual property, IT, telecoms and commerce
John King

Media and entertainment
John King, Deirdre Courtney

Commercial property, construction
Michael J O'Connor, Jennifer Blunden

Product liability, medical negligence
Susan R Stapleton

Defamation and newspaper law, commercial litigation
Deirdre Courtney, Mary Claire Markey

Probate, wills and trusts
Susan R Stapleton

Asset finance, maritime and shipping
Ivor Fitzpatrick

Corporate tax, EU and competition
Cormac Gordon, John King

Dispute resolution
Deirdre Courtney

International banking
Cormac Gordon

THE FIRM

Established in 1981, Ivor Fitzpatrick & Company is one of Ireland's best-known and most respected law firms. Based in landmark premises in the heart of Dublin's business district, the partners and solicitors of Ivor Fitzpatrick & Company constitute one of Dublin's top legal teams, and are highly regarded, individually and collectively, for their legal acumen.

The firm's lawyers provide legal services of the highest levels in corporate, commercial, banking, property, medical and personal matters. Fee-earners total 43, and together with administrative and support personnel, the firm comprises over 90 staff.

The firm has enjoyed unprecedented growth in both international and domestic markets, and Ivor Fitzpatrick & Company has well-established links with international law firms in Europe and the USA.

AREAS OF PRACTICE

Ivor Fitzpatrick & Company has five main practice areas covering corporate law, civil litigation, commercial litigation, banking and finance, property law and debt recovery/insolvency.

The firm's active corporate law department specialises in mergers and acquisitions and IPOs/flotations, serving e-commerce and telecoms, as well as more traditional business sectors. Acting for domestic and overseas clients, the department's lawyers are highly knowledgeable on all aspects of corporate and commercial business law.

The firm's dynamic commercial litigation department serves both the corporate and private sectors and all aspects of banking corporate and commercial law. The department's performance history is renowned, with numerous landmark judgments and high-profile rulings attributed to its lawyers.

Ivor Fitzpatrick & Company's civil litigation department has specialist teams for mass tort and product liability actions, as well as clinical negligence, insurance defence work, personal injury litigation and family law. This department advises a wide range of clients, including insurance companies, corporate bodies, professional and voluntary organisations and individuals.

Experts in property law carry out a full range of property transactions, and Ivor Fitzpatrick & Company has represented clients in many of the recent key property developments in Ireland. Clients in this area range from property developers and property managers to semi-state bodies and major financial institutions.

The firm is a renowned specialist in debt recovery and insolvency, being one of the largest debt recovery firms in Ireland, servicing government bodies and institutional clients, as well as more traditional business sectors, such as banking and shipping.

KILROYS
SOLICITORS

69 LOWER LEESON STREET
DUBLIN 2

Telephone: +353 1 439 5600
Fax: +353 1 439 5602
E-mail: info@kilroys.ie
Website: www.kilroys.ie

Languages
French, Italian

Number of lawyers 13

International groupings
International Bar Association; Computer Law Association; Irish Internet Association; Institute of Taxation of Ireland; Alternative Investment Management Association

CATEGORIES OF WORK

Company and commercial law
Kevin O'Brien, Joanne Griffin

EU and competition law
Kevin O'Brien, Anthony Layng

Insurance law
Anthony Layng, Eamon Jones

Telecommunications
Kevin O'Brien, Patrick Ryan

Commercial dispute resolution
Eamon Jones, Thomas Simpson

Intellectual property
Anthony Layng, Patrick Ryan

E-commerce and IT
Kevin O'Brien, Patrick Ryan

Financial services
Kevin O'Brien, Hilary Griffey

Investment funds
Hilary Griffey

Employment law
Anthony Layng, Thomas Simpson

Property
Eamon Jones, Patrick Ryan

Public procurement
Patrick Ryan

Energy and natural resources
Patrick Ryan

LK SHIELDS
SOLICITORS

39-40 UPPER MOUNT STREET
DUBLIN 2

Telephone: +353 1 661 0866
Fax: +353 1 661 0883
E-mail: email@lkshields.ie
Website: www.lkshields.ie

Languages
English, French, German, Italian

Number of lawyers 30

CATEGORIES OF WORK

Corporate and commercial
Laurence K Shields, Justin McKenna

Banking and finance
Joe Gavin, David JH Williams

Corporate finance
Justin McKenna, Emmet Scully

Employment and employee benefits
Michael Kavanagh, Fiona Thornton

Public/private partnerships and public procurement
Philip Daly

Intellectual property and information technology
Patricia McGovern, Eoin Cunneen

Commercial property
Nicola Palmer, Orlaigh O'Dwyer

EU and competition
Marco Hickey, Derval O'Halloran

Commercial litigation and dispute resolution
Edmund Butler, Michael Kavanagh

Insolvency and bankruptcy
Hugh Garvey

Pensions
Fiona Thornton

LANDWELL

SOLICITORS

GARDNER HOUSE
WILTON PLACE
DUBLIN 2

Telephone: +353 1 662 6655
Fax: +353 1 662 6788
E-mail: info@ie.landwellglobal.com
Website: www.landwellglobal.com/ie

Languages
English, French, German

Number of lawyers 27

Contacts
Edward Evans, Gerry Bohan, Carol Plunkett, Jim Trueick, Garrett Breen

International groupings
Landwell, worldwide network of law firms

CATEGORIES OF WORK

Commercial and competition
Edward Evans, Gerry Bohan

Corporate structuring
Gerry Bohan

Dispute resolution
Carol Plunkett, Jim Trueick

Technology, media and communications
Carol Plunkett, Garrett Breen

Employment and human resources
Jim Trueick

Financial services
Edward Evans

Intellectual property
Carol Plunkett, Garrett Breen

Mergers and acquisitions
Gerry Bohan, Edward Evans

Public law
Carol Plunkett, Garrett Breen

Real estate
Gerry Bohan

MASON HAYES & CURRAN

6 FITZWILLIAM SQUARE
DUBLIN 2

Telephone: +353 1 614 5000
Fax: +353 1 614 5001
E-mail: mail@mhc.ie
Website: www.mhc.ie

Languages
Dutch, French, German, Spanish

Other offices
New York

Number of lawyers 85

Contact
Declan Moylan (managing partner)

CATEGORIES OF WORK

Corporate, mergers and acquisitions
David O'Donnell, Paul Egan

EU and competition law
Anthony Burke, John Kettle

Banking, securities and finance
Kevin Hoy

Inward investment
Declan Moylan, Liam Brazil

Information technology
Anthony Burke, John Kettle

Investment funds
Fionan Breathnach

Real property, conveyancing
Maeve Hayes, Declan Curran

Employment and labour law
Emer Gilvarry, Richard Woulfe

Insolvency
Declan Black, Maurice Phelan

Litigation and arbitration
Maurice Curran, Lorcan Buckley

Biotechnology and life sciences
Philip Nolan, Una Brien

THE FIRM

Mason Hayes & Curran is one of Ireland's leading firms and is the product of a series of mergers in the 1960s and 1970s. Growth has been rapid, both size and turnover having trebled over the past five years, and the firm is now one of the best known and most progressive in Dublin. The bulk of the firm's work is for corporate, institutional and government clients.

The firm has recently opened an office in New York headed by US lawyer Daniel Walsh. Its international practice continues to grow, and an increasing number of American companies choose Mason Hayes & Curran as Irish counsel.

i-law, the strategic alliance between Mason Hayes & Curran and Northern Ireland firm Carson McDowell, continues to serve clients with cross-border transactions and to represent the various all-island bodies established under the Belfast Agreement.

AREAS OF PRACTICE

The firm gives a comprehensive business law service to an extensive foreign and domestic client base. The commercial department acts for corporate, business and banking clients, both Irish and international, in the following areas: joint ventures, mergers and acquisitions, public issues, corporate reorganisations, franchising, distribution and agency agreements, intellectual property, commercial lending, and asset financing.

It deals with a significant volume of litigation work, undertaking all aspects of insurance, construction, commercial and employment litigation and arbitration. It has also handled major cases before the European Court of Justice and drafted and lodged complaints before the Commission with regard to tax, health regulations, and restrictions on trade. The firm has a growing insolvency practice, advising liquidators, receivers, and corporate clients in financial difficulties as well as secured and unsecured creditors seeking to protect their rights. The property department deals with every stage of development schemes, both large and small, and represents both local and overseas property investors in Ireland. The firm also undertakes agricultural work relating to land purchase and sale, agri-produce, livestock, bloodstock, and co-operatives. There is also a strong private client department which principally covers tax, wills, trusts, and probate.

Mason Hayes & Curran provides a dedicated elegal service to its clients specialising in Irish and European e-commerce regulations, website and portal design agreements, Internet agreements, consumer protection issues, intellectual property, technology start-ups and data protection.

MATHESON ORMSBY PRENTICE

30 HERBERT STREET
DUBLIN 2

Telephone: +353 1 619 9000
Fax: +353 1 619 9010
E-mail: mop@mop.ie
Website: www.mop.ie

Languages
Dutch, French, German, Italian, Spanish

Other offices
London, New York, Palo Alto (CA)

Number of lawyers 200

CATEGORIES OF WORK

Asset finance
Chris Quinn, Anthony Walsh

Banking
William Prentice, Patrick Molloy

Capital markets
Tim Scanlon, Michael Jackson

Commercial litigation and dispute resolution
Stuart Margetson, Michael Tyrrell

Commercial property/real estate
Andrew Muckian, Deirdre Morris

Construction
Andrew Muckian, Mark Varian

Corporate and commercial
Andrew Doyle, Patrick Spicer

Corporate restructuring and insolvency
Rod Ensor, Tony O'Grady

EC and competition
Helen Kelly, Karen Gibbons

Employment
Paul Glenfield, Stuart Margetson

Entertainment
James Hickey, Ruth Hunter

Energy and natural resources
Michael O'Connor, Kerri Crossen

Healthcare and biosciences
Tom Maher, Neil Keenan

Insurance regulation
Liam Flynn, Sharon Daly

Intellectual property
Michael Tyrrell, James Hickey

Investment services
Michael Jackson, James Scanlon

Inward investment
Liam Quirke, John Ryan

IT and e-commerce
Don McAleese, Anne-Marie Bohan

Media
Sharon Daly, Michael Tyrrell

Mergers and acquisitions
Robert Heron, Tim Scanlon

Outsourcing
Anne-Marie Bohan, Patrick Spicer

Pensions and employee benefits
Brian Buggy, Frank O'Neill

Planning and environmental
Patrick Sweetman, Stuart Margetson

Private client
Graham Richards, Paraic Madigan

Private equity
Edward Miller, Stanley Watson

Privatisations
Robert Heron, Michael O'Connor

Project finance/PPP
Michael O'Connor, Mark Varian

Retail and leisure
Lorraine Compton, Andrew Muckian

Structured finance, securitisation and repackaging
Turlough Galvin, Tara Doyle

Tax
Liam Quirke, John Ryan

Transport and shipping
Michael O'Connor, Bríd Munnelly

McCANN FITZGERALD

2 HARBOURMASTER PLACE
INTERNATIONAL FINANCIAL SERVICES CENTRE
DUBLIN 1

Telephone: +353 1 829 0000
Fax: +353 1 829 0010
E-mail: postmaster@mccannfitzgerald.ie
Website: www.mccannfitzgerald.ie

Languages
Afrikaans, Cantonese, French, German, Italian, Spanish

Other offices
Brussels, London, Belfast* (North South Legal Alliance with L'Estrange & Brett)

Number of lawyers 233

CATEGORIES OF WORK

Banking and financial services
Ronan Molony, Niall Powderly

Capital markets
Roy Parker, Richard Rice

Commercial property
Colin Keane, Lonan McDowell

Commercial disputes
David Clarke, Helen Collins

Corporate and commercial
William Earley, Paul Heffernan

Corporate finance, M&A
Barry Devereux, David Byers

Employment and pensions
Terence McCrann, Maureen Dolan

Energy
Patricia Lawless, Gerald FitzGerald

Insolvency and restructuring
Jane Marshall, Emma Crowley

Construction
Timothy Bouchier-Hayes, Max Abrahamson

EU and competition
Damian Collins (Brussels), Gerald FitzGerald

Intellectual property
Grace Smith, Yvonne McNamara

Inward investment
Michael Ryan, Guy French

Maritime and transport
Petria McDonnell, Mark Pearson

Private client
Susan O'Connell, Muriel Walls

Product liability
Roderick Bourke, Helen Collins

Public private partnership/PFI
Timothy Bouchier-Hayes, Eamonn O'Hanrahan

McEVOY PARTNERS

CANADA HOUSE
65-68 ST STEPHEN'S GREEN
DUBLIN 2

Telephone: +353 1 415 5900
Fax: +353 1 476 0551
E-mail: info@mcevoypartners.ie
Website: www.mcevoypartners.ie

Languages
English, French

Number of lawyers 7

Contact
Bernard McEvoy

CATEGORIES OF WORK

Mergers and acquisitions

Management buy-outs/buy-ins

IPOs/flotations

Commercial property

Equity/debt fundraising

Franchising distribution

Corporate restructuring

Entertainment

O'DONNELL SWEENEY
SOLICITORS

ONE EARLSFORT CENTRE
EARLSFORT TERRACE
DUBLIN 2

Telephone: +353 1 664 4200
Fax: +353 1 664 4300
E-mail: info@odonnellsweeney.ie
Website: www.odonnellsweeney.ie

Languages
French, German, Spanish

Number of lawyers 32

Member
TELFA; Law Europe

CATEGORIES OF WORK

Company and commercial
David Beattie, David O'Beirne

Mergers and acquisitions
Joseph R Sweeney, Seán Ryan

Banking securities and finance
Patricia Heffernan

Capital markets
David Beattie, Chelita Healy

Construction
Rory O'Donnell, Joseph Stanley

Commercial property
Patricia Heffernan, Alan Murphy

Contracts, real estate
Joseph Stanley, Laura Delaney

Intellectual property
Francis Hackett, Feilim O'Caoimh

Insolvency
Norman Fitzgerald, Niamh Herron

Government business/regulatory
Francis Hackett, Peter Fahy

Commercial litigation, arbitration
Dermot McEvoy, Norman Fitzgerald

Civil litigation
Norman Fitzgerald, Pamela O'Neill

EU, competition
Seán Ryan

Information technology
Tony McGovern, Ruth Murphy

Employment law
David Fagan

Employee benefit schemes
David Beattie, Peter Fahy

Landlord and tenant
Annette Crowley

Planning and environment
Sean Greene

ROBERT RYAN & ASSOCIATES

23 BALLSBRIDGE TERRACE
BALLSBRIDGE
DUBLIN 4

Telephone: +353 1 667 4255
Fax: +353 1 667 4050
E-mail: rryan@ryansolicitors.com
Website: www.ryansolicitors.com

Number of lawyers 4

CATEGORIES OF WORK

Corporate and commercial
Eimear Scully

Mergers and acquisitions
Robert Ryan, Eimear Scully

Banking and finance
Robert Ryan

Commercial property
Cora Doyle

EU and competition law
Robert Ryan, Eimear Scully

Litigation and arbitration
Cora Doyle

Capital markets
Robert Ryan

Intellectual property
Eimear Scully, Robert Ryan

Employment
Eimear Scully

Insolvency
Cora Doyle

VINCENT & BEATTY

67-68 FITZWILLIAM SQUARE
DUBLIN 2

Telephone: +353 1 634 0000
Fax: +353 1 634 0001
E-mail: postmaster@vblaw.ie

Languages
French, German

Other offices
Belfast

Number of lawyers 10

Contact
Walter Beatty (managing partner)

CATEGORIES OF WORK

Mergers, acquisitions and companies
Walter Beatty

Banking and finance
Caitriona McCabe

Commercial litigation and insolvency law
David Irwin

Admiralty, maritime, competition law
Cian Ó Cathain

Taxation
Miriam Delaney

Construction building and commercial property
Peter Maguire

Arbitration
Walter Beatty Sr

Private client and employment law
Alec Gabbett

Domestic conveyancing
Kathi Ó Riain

WILLIAM FRY

FITZWILTON HOUSE
WILTON PLACE
DUBLIN 2

Telephone: +353 1 639 5000
Fax: +353 1 639 5333
E-mail: info@williamfry.ie
Website: www.williamfry.ie

Languages
English, French, German, Italian, Spanish

Number of lawyers 160

Other offices
Belfast* (Tughans Solicitors)

CATEGORIES OF WORK

Arbitration and dispute resolution
Owen O'Sullivan, Michael Kealey

Asset management
Dan Morrissey, Tara O'Reilly

Banking and financial services
Neville O'Byrne, Elaine Hanly

Biotechnology and life sciences
Myra Garrett, David Cullen

Capital markets
Myra Garrett, Brendan Heneghan

Construction
Liam McCabe, Jeremy Curran

Corporate and commercial
Houghton Fry, Alvin Price

E-commerce
Victor Timon, David Cullen

Employment
Boyce Shubotham, Maura Roe

Energy and waste management
Aislinn O'Farrell, Bryan Bourke

EU/competition
John Handoll, Cormac Little

Insolvency and corporate recovery
Frank Sowman, Michael Quinn

Insurance
John Larkin, Daniel Morrissey

Intellectual property
Victor Timon, David Cullen

Investment funds
Daniel Morrissey, Patricia Taylor

Inward investment
Brendan Cahill, David Carthy

Litigation
Edmund Fry, Owen O'Sullivan

Media and broadcasting
Michael Kealey, Ken Casey

Mergers and acquisitions
Owen O'Connell, Brendan Cahill

Pensions/employee share schemes
Michael Wolfe, Maura Roe

Planning and environmental
Conor Linehan, Liam McCabe

Project finance (PPP)
Sonja Price, Liam McCabe

Property
Nora White, Edward Spain

Public procurement
Neville O'Byrne

Securitisation
Elaine Hanly, Daragh Bohan

Taxation
Martin Phelan, Greg Hollingsworth

Technology
Myra Garrett, Victor Timon

Telecommunications
John Handoll, Victor Timon

Trusts and estates
Edmund Fry

ISLE OF MAN

Population	60,000
Number of lawyers	192 (110 Manx advocates and 82 registered practitioners)
Professional title	Advoctae
Currency	Pound sterling (£)

The Isle of Man continues to build on its reputation as a well-regulated financial services centre. The insurance sector in particular goes from strength to strength.

While maintaining strong links with the UK mainland, the commercial success of the jurisdiction means that, like Jersey and Guernsey, dependence on the UK is waning as more institutional clients come from overseas – increasingly from the US, the Middle East (UAE) and South Africa.

The Manx Bar is a fused profession and Manx advocates enjoy rights of audience and also undertake the role played by solicitors on the mainland. In addition, it is straightforward for advocates to register as solicitors on the mainland. However, UK solicitors do not enjoy reciprocal rights. Foreign lawyers have, since 1986, only been able to practise as Registered Legal Practitioners – restricted from undertaking conveyancing, litigation or being probate practitioners. In May 1997, the Isle of Man Law Society reluctantly voted to relax the rules forbidding non-Manx lawyers from becoming members of the Bar. However, multinational partnerships between lawyers are still prohibited. The rules continue to restrict the areas of practice foreign lawyers may undertake.

BILLING

The Advocates' Scale Fees Act (1963) lays down four scale fees covering every aspect of legal services. However, fees may vary depending on the lawyer instructed and the job in hand. Clients can expect costs not dissimilar to those charged by City of London firms: around £160 for a newly qualified lawyer, rising to around £350 at partner level.

MARKETING

Advocates may advertise their services reasonably freely although there are regulations which demand that any publicity be accurate and in good taste.

THE LEGAL 500

Readers should note that the following is taken from the **Offshore Britain** section of the 2003 edition of *The Legal 500* (UK edition), available at www.legal500.com.

LEGAL MARKET

Cains Advocates Limited is a body corporate which employs six directors (partner-level equivalent) and 22 assistants and advocates, one-quarter of whom are not Manx-qualified. The firm focuses almost all its work on the commercial sector.

The island's other major law firm is **Dickinson, Cruickshank & Co**, which employs 15 partners. While the firm has a significant commercial client base, it retains a larger private client department than its major rival.

Simcocks quietly goes about advising both commercial and private clients, and is gaining a name as the island's firm of choice on commercial property matters.

Both **Mann & Partners** and **Mann Benham Ltd** were created by Tim Mann, who left the former to create the latter. Both have strong names in litigation and commercial, although at two directors apiece, they are somewhat smaller than the island's leaders.

Another small practice with a good mixture of work is **Quinn Kneale**. The firm has a steady flow of commercial instructions, which complement its lower-end criminal work.

Gough & Co retains a good name for litigation after its late 2002 merger with *Wright & Co*. Readers in need of criminal advice should refer to the island's leading criminal defence firm **Carter Jones McDonald**, where name partner Terry McDonald and Shirley McDonald both come highly recommended.

There are long-established links between the island and South Africa, whose nationals make up 2% of the island's population. **Maitland & Co** (part of the international South African practice **Webber Wentzel Bowens**) and **Stuart Smalley & Co LLC** have a presence to service their clients' offshore commercial requirements.

BANKING AND FINANCE

Banks with a presence on the island include the Royal Bank of Scotland International, National Australia Group (Northern Bank), Coutts and Merrill Lynch.

A six-strong team led by Andrew Corlett at **Cains Advocates Limited** handled Barclays' project Pyramid, the £14bn re-organisation of its offshore holdings. The firm is sole adviser to the Isle of Man Film Commission for which partner Andrew Fingret completed eight deals in 2002.

The largest firms

1	Dickinson, Cruickshank & Co	29
2	Cains Advocates Limited	26
3	Simcocks	14
4	Quinn Kneale	8
5	Maitland & Co	6
	Mann & Partners	6
	Stuart Smalley & Co LLC	6
8	Gough & Co	4
	Kelly Luft Stanley Ashton	4
10	Gelling Johnson Farrant	2
11	Hyde & Hanson	1
	Richard Penn	1

These figures represent the total number of lawyers in this country only, and have been supplied by the firms themselves. The figures should be accurate as at 1 January 2004.

BANKING AND FINANCE

CAINS ADVOCATES LIMITED

DICKINSON, CRUICKSHANK & CO

Mann & Partners
Simcocks ✪

Firms are listed A-Z in tiers which are ranked in order of priority
✪ Indicates firm displays contact details at the end of this chapter.

Richard Vanderplank continues to be a strong choice for clients, including the Bank of Ireland. The firm's depth of resources and deal profile sees it pull ahead of its major rivals. 'They are the best option' (on the island), claims one client.

Major departmental clients at **Dickinson, Cruickshank & Co** include Royal Bank of Scotland International, Standard Bank, HSBC and AIB. Joanne Kelly is building an aircraft leasing practice. Former head of commercial David Doyle left in 2003 to take up the judicial post of Her Majesty's Second Deemster.

Paul Branford handles the banking work at **Mann & Partners**. The firm ensures that new island-based products, such as current account mortgages, comply with local regulations.

Simcocks acts for a number of banking clients looking to restructure their offshore holdings; David Spencer is a specialist.

COLLECTIVE INVESTMENT FUNDS

The vast majority of new fund formation on the Isle of Man takes place through **Cains Advocates Limited**. Clients include Close Brothers Investment and BoE International Fund Managers. Director Richard Vanderplank and assistant Andrew Baker are the island's leaders in fund work.

Joanne Kelly, who joined **Dickinson, Cruickshank & Co** from the FSC, advises clients on regulatory matters.

Paul Branford of **Mann & Partners** had ten years' funds industry experience before qualifying as a lawyer.

Ita McArdle, head of commercial at **Simcocks**, handles the firm's funds work, along with associate Kay Henry. They established 15 funds in 2002. The firm receives instructions from Europe, South Africa and emerging markets.

COLLECTIVE INVESTMENT FUNDS

CAINS ADVOCATES LIMITED

Dickinson, Cruickshank & Co
Mann & Partners
Simcocks ✪

Firms are listed A-Z in tiers which are ranked in order of priority
✪ Indicates firm displays contact details at the end of this chapter.

COMMERCIAL

CAINS ADVOCATES LIMITED

DICKINSON, CRUICKSHANK & CO

Mann & Partners
Simcocks ✪

Gough & Co
Maitland & Co
Mann Benham Ltd
Quinn Kneale
Stuart Smalley & Co LLC

Firms are listed A-Z in tiers which are ranked in order of priority
✪ Indicates firm displays contact details at the end of this chapter.

COMMERCIAL

Cains Advocates Limited remains the island's leading firm in terms of commercial outlook, acumen, client base and quality of lawyer. The island's largest firm, it competes for work in other offshore international investment centres. The firm is handling an increasing level of shipping, film finance and banking work in addition to its innovative satellite sector work. Managing director Andrew Corlett, who is president of the island's law society, is viewed as a visionary leader.

Dickinson, Cruickshank & Co made up three partners in February 2002; Mark Humphrey and John Rimmer on the private client side, along with Nick Verardi on the commercial side. Simon Cain is recommended for shipping and is now co-head of the commercial practice, alongside Nick Verardi.

Commercial work at **Mann & Partners** is headed by Chris Murphy, who has a niche expertise in the gaming industry. The departure of Paul Beckett (now a consultant at **Carters**) has dented the firm's growth, although Paul Branford looks set to fill the gap.

Ita McArdle heads the commercial practice at **Simcocks**. The firm offers film finance advice, in addition to its strong funds and commercial property work. Former government advocate Andrew Corlett has advised clients on the implications of the Human Rights Act.

Gough & Co's commercial practice is headed by Paul Kerruish. The firm advises on matters including aviation, M&A, shipping and e-commerce.

South African firm **Maitland & Co** offers corporate, international tax planning and M&A advice to the island's large South African client base.

Six-fee-earner **Mann Benham Ltd**'s name partner Tim Mann (who also set up **Mann & Partners** some years ago) leads the firm's commercial practice.

Jeremy Callin heads the commercial practice at 14-fee-earner firm **Quinn Kneale**. The firm has a strong local authority client base.

Stuart Smalley & Co LLC represents banks, insurance companies, accountants, and high-net-worth individuals on international tax and commercial matters.

COMMERCIAL LITIGATION

CAINS ADVOCATES LIMITED
DICKINSON, CRUICKSHANK & CO

Mann & Partners
Gough & Co

Mann Benham Ltd
Quinn Kneale
Simcocks ✪

Firms are listed A-Z in tiers which are ranked in order of priority
✪ Indicates firm displays contact details at the end of this chapter.

COMMERCIAL LITIGATION

Manx advocates act as both barristers and solicitors. While only locally qualified solicitors have rights of audience at the Isle of Man courts, barristers from England and Wales are able to obtain licences to appear before the courts.

Seth Cain oversees the nine-strong, recently merged local and international litigation department at **Cains Advocates Limited**. Peter Clucas handled the contentious aspects of the $1bn restructuring of DDCC, while Seth Cain handled the innovative FSC action in *AML v Solly*. Giles Hill joined the firm in 2002 from **Morgan Cole**. The firm is advising the SEC on a case over the collapse of Nasdaq-listed Arenisoft.

Dickinson, Cruickshank & Co's litigation department has Manx- and English Bar-qualified contentious experts, and is headed by Paul Morris, widely viewed as one the island's leading litigators. Major recent work includes litigation arising from the downfall of Arenisoft. Robert Long handles the firm's asset-freezing and tracing work.

At **Mann & Partners**, John Aycock is heavily involved in director disqualification cases on behalf of the FSC of the Isle of Man ('His high success rate speaks for itself'). His practice also covers estate work, employment litigation, and clinical negligence work (on behalf of the island's DHSS). Advocate Andrew Bridson has good links with the island's corporate service providers. Keiron Murray joined the firm from **Cains Advocates Limited** in February 2003.

Gough & Co has grown through its merger with *Wright & Co*, bringing on board additional litigation experience in the form of John Wright. Alan Gough's asset tracing work is highly respected.

At **Mann Benham Ltd**, Miles Benham's profile is growing. Work handled included a major cross-border case for a petroleum company valued at £1.5bn, and a £175m trust assets fraud action. The firm also has a corporate service provider's licence enabling it to form and administer companies.

Quinn Kneale has a good commercial litigation practice in addition to its criminal defence work.

Chris Arrowsmith heads the litigation department at **Simcocks**, while Kevin O'Riordan has gained a good reputation for high-net-worth divorce cases.

INSURANCE

CAINS ADVOCATES LIMITED
SIMCOCKS ✪

Dickinson, Cruickshank & Co

Mann & Partners

Firms are listed A-Z in tiers which are ranked in order of priority
✪ Indicates firm displays contact details at the end of this chapter.

INSURANCE

A strong insurance industry on the Isle of Man is based in part on the reputation of the island's strong regulator, the Insurance and Pensions Authority (IPA).

Captive insurance work, though mainly handled by in-house departments, is a major source of work for leaders **Cains Advocates Limited** and **Simcocks**.

Cains Advocates Limited has handled a number of change-of-control applications to the IPA on behalf of several large UK Plcs. The firm's captive insurers work is handled by David Birmingham.

While **Simcocks** handles work for Aon, Ita McArdle sits on the board of numerous captives, including Transco, one of the largest in the world. David Spencer has been advising the island's regulator on insurance and captives legislation.

Dickinson, Cruickshank & Co's head of commercial David Doyle and Nick Verardi acted for Friends Provident on its acquisition of Royal & SunAlliance. Joanne Kelly acts for major insurance clients, while the firm has strong links with the IPA.

Mann & Partners acts for major insurance and life assurance companies, such as Direct Line (on litigation matters) and Royal Skandia (on commercial matters).

PERSONAL TAX, TRUSTS AND PROBATE

Senior partner Martin Moore at **Dickinson, Cruickshank & Co** oversees the island's leading private client practice. STEP member and associate John Rimmer had an exceptionally busy year, handling employee benefit trusts, pensions schemes, estate planning and trust litigation. Probate work for non-resident clients is handled by Jonathan Kewley, who also specialises in charitable and community trusts.

Cains Advocates Limited's practice, headed by Jeremy Walton , offers a broad spectrum of services to both domiciled and non-domiciled clients.

Simcocks chief executive Philip Games and head of commercial Ita McArdle are regularly involved in trusts work.

Stuart Smalley & Co LLC handles English legal advice and has a very good high-net-worth-individual client base.

PERSONAL TAX, TRUSTS AND PROBATE

DICKINSON, CRUICKSHANK & CO

Cains Advocates Limited
Simcocks ✪
Stuart Smalley & Co LLC

Gough & Co
Kelly Luft Stanley Ashton
Maitland & Co
Mann & Partners
Quinn Kneale

Firms are listed A-Z in tiers which are ranked in order of priority
✪ Indicates firm displays contact details at the end of this chapter.

REAL ESTATE

Cains Advocates Limited's property team acts for clients such as the Manx Electricity Board and Royal Skandia Life Assurance Ltd. Practice head Jeremy Walton and former **Lovells** solicitor, Mike Polson, are both recommended. In 2002, the firm acted for a range of funders, banks, lessees, and developers.

Dickinson, Cruickshank & Co's commercial property practice focuses on retail lease work, and is headed by Geoff Karran. The firm additionally handles major planning issues on government capital projects.

Led by associate Irini Newby, **Simcocks** has an excellent commercial property practice, which has advised clients on the Isle of Man's three largest-ever transactions.

Gough & Co and **Kelly Luft Stanley Ashton** have traditional property practices.

Mann & Partners' director Chris Murphy and experienced legal executive Carol Young handle work for major utilities and Prudential.

Mann Benham Ltd's legal executive Alex Mitchell handles the firm's retail, office and industrial estate leases (with rental values ranging from £1m to £10m).

Quinn Kneale's Ken Terry handles work for major local developers.

REAL ESTATE

CAINS ADVOCATES LIMITED
DICKINSON, CRUICKSHANK & CO
SIMCOCKS ✪

Gough & Co
Kelly Luft Stanley Ashton
Mann & Partners
Mann Benham Ltd
Quinn Kneale

Firms are listed A-Z in tiers which are ranked in order of priority
✪ Indicates firm displays contact details at the end of this chapter.

The largest firms

1	Herzog, Fox & Neeman	84
2	Balter, Guth, Aloni & Co	76
3	Yigal Arnon & Co	73
4	Naschitz, Brandes & Co	64
5	S. Horowitz & Co	62
6	Goldfarb, Levy, Eran & Co	60
7	I Gornitzky & Co	53
	M. Firon & Co Advocates and Notaries	53
9	Gross, Kleinhendler, Hodak, Halevy, Greenberg & Co	52
10	Yehuda Raveh & Co.	46
11	Fischer, Behar, Chen & Co	45
	S Friedman & Co, Advocates	45
13	Reinhold Cohn & Partners	40
	Shiboleth, Yisraeli, Roberts, Zisman & Co	40
15	Meitar, Liquornik, Geva & Leshem Brandwein	37
16	Eitan, Pearl, Latzer & Cohen-Zedek	36
17	Zellermayer, Pelossof & Co., Advocates	33
18	Aaronsohn, Aboulafia, Gal-On, Tzin, Amoday & Co	30
	Caspi & Co	30
	M Seligman & Co	30
	Yaacov Salomon, Lipschutz & Co	30
22	Danziger, Klagsbald, Rosen & Co	29
	Weksler, Bregman & Co	29
24	Haim Zadok & Co	28
25	Zysman, Aharoni, Gayer & Co	27

These figures represent the total number of lawyers in this country only, and have been supplied by the firms themselves. The figures should be accurate as at 1 January 2004.

intellectual property are among its key exports. Important areas of development are medical electronics, agro-chemicals, telecommunications, software and hardware for computers, food processing and solar energy.

Agriculture has developed to a high level, and despite the obstacles of water shortage and a lack of arable land the country produces over 90% of its own food. Imports of grain, seeds, meat, coffee and other commodities are required, and Israel also imports water from Turkey.

Israel's GDP is around $106bn, with a per capita average of around $17,000. Exports are valued at just under $40bn, with imports totalling over $43bn.

Trade is vital for Israel, which is why the global economic downturn has hit the country hard. Though economically the signs are more positive than in the last two years, the intifada has compounded the effects of the downturn. However, hi-tech industries are more insulated from security problems than other important industries such as tourism, which has suffered from the political unrest in the Middle East.

Hi-tech firms are more heavily impacted by the performance of Nasdaq, and the fact that there have been almost no Israeli IPOs on Nasdaq in the last two years shows how bad the economic situation has been. M&A activity has also been dramatically reduced compared to 2000.

LEGAL MARKET

There is a very high number of lawyers per capita in Israel compared to most countries. There are many highly skilled individual practitioners but these focus mainly on domestic work.

The market for international work is dominated by relatively few large firms, though some medium-sized firms and boutiques specialising in areas such as intellectual property also have foreign clients.

Large firms that operate in a wide range of practice areas include **Yigal Arnon & Co**; **Herzog, Fox & Neeman**; **Naschitz, Brandes & Co**; **S. Horowitz & Co**; and **Goldfarb, Levy, Eran & Co**, though many others such as **Meitar, Liquornik, Geva & Leshem Brandwein** or **Yehuda Raveh & Co.** are also highly respected.

As well as domestically trained lawyers, Israel also attracts many lawyers from abroad, mainly the US and the UK.

At some of the larger firms work may not always be partner-led, and depending on the size of a transaction it may be worthwhile for foreign clients to investigate medium-sized firms or specialist boutiques.

FOREIGN FIRMS

Only locally qualified lawyers can practise in Israel, and foreign lawyers are required to pass the Israel Bar Association exams, which are set in Hebrew. No official partnerships with foreign-qualified lawyers are allowed, though many firms have close ties with law firms in the US, UK and elsewhere.

INTERNATIONAL NETWORKS

Given the international nature of many large transactions in Israel, several firms are members of international legal networks, such as *TagLaw* and *Interlaw*. **Herzog, Fox & Neeman**, for instance, is a member of *World Law Group*.

Other firms have representation on international business networks such as the American-Israeli Chamber of Commerce or the Japan-Israeli Chamber of Commerce. Often these networks result in referrals of work from international clients.

BANKING AND FINANCE

The banking sector in Israel is dominated by a few large banks, which engage a number of firms in different capacities. Among the leading banking and finance lawyers is Alan Sacks of **Herzog, Fox & Neeman**, who has been involved in transactions such as the sale of a controlling interest in First International Bank of Israel (FIBI), the country's fifth-largest banking group. The firm has also been involved in a lot of refinancing activity in the last year, largely for Bank Leumi and Bank Hapoalim.

Dalia Tal of **Kantor Elhanani Tal & Co** is regarded as a leading banking lawyer in Israel, while Hugh Michael Kowarsky of **S. Horowitz & Co** is also highly thought of in this sector. The firm has recently been involved in the refinancing of a $500m loan for Tower Semiconductor. It has also acted in the financing of the launch and construction of the Amos II communications satellite, which is only Israel's second commercial satellite. Other transactions include major domestic and international syndicated financings in Israel.

Amit, Pollak, Matalon & Co retains an active banking and finance practice, while **Caspi & Co** is one of only a few firms in Israel that can handle work relating to derivatives products, thanks to partner Menachem Feder.

Efrati, Galili & Co has recently been involved in advising on a very large loan from Bank of Scotland to a hi-tech company in Israel. The firm also represents Mizrahi Bank, which ranks as the fourth-largest banking group in Israel, for which it handles corporate work as well as class actions. Among the firm's other clients are a number of the world's best-known investment banks.

Goldfarb, Levy, Eran & Co has well-established links with underwriters and investment bankers in New York, London, Tel Aviv, Zurich, Paris, Frankfurt and other international centres.

I Gornitzky & Co has represented a group of purchasers of one of the leading banks in Israel,

BANKING AND FINANCE

HERZOG, FOX & NEEMAN ✪
KANTOR ELHANANI TAL & CO
S. HOROWITZ & CO ✪

Amit, Pollak, Matalon & Co
Caspi & Co ✪
Efrati, Galili & Co ✪
Ephraim Abramson & Co
Goldfarb, Levy, Eran & Co
Gross, Kleinhendler, Hodak, Halevy, Greenberg & Co ✪
I Gornitzky & Co ✪
Meitar, Liquornik, Geva & Leshem Brandwein ✪
Shiboleth, Yisraeli, Roberts, Zisman & Co ✪
Weksler, Bregman & Co ✪
Yaacov Salomon, Lipschutz & Co ✪
Yehuda Raveh & Co. ✪
Yigal Arnon & Co ✪
Zellermayer, Pelossof & Co., Advocates ✪

Avniel, Salomon & Co
Bach, Arad, Scharf & Co Law Offices
Balter, Guth, Aloni & Co
Baratz, Bar-Nathan & Co, Attorneys-at-Law & Notaries
Dankner Lusky & Co
Danziger, Klagsbald, Rosen & Co ✪
ES Shimron, I Molho, Persky & Co ✪
Eitan, Pearl, Latzer & Cohen-Zedek
Erdinast, Ben Nathan & Co ✪
Fischer, Behar, Chen & Co ✪
Haim Samet, Steinmetz, Haring & Co
Haim Zadok & Co ✪
Hamburger, Evron, Raviv-Berson & Co ✪
Heskia-Hacmun Law Firm ✪
J Weinroth (Dr) & Co ✪
Joseph Levy & Co ✪
M Porath & Co
M Seligman & Co
Naschitz, Brandes & Co ✪
Shavit Bar-On Inbar, Law Offices ✪
Yuval Levy & Co ✪

Firms are listed A-Z in tiers which are ranked in order of priority
✪ Indicates firm displays contact details at the end of this chapter.

which is controlled by FIBI. Israeli and Australian investors bought controlling shares in FIBI in a deal worth over £100m. Pinhas Rubin handled the deal.

Meitar, Liquornik, Geva & Leshem Brandwein has a broad base of international banking expertise and its deals have included institutional lending and asset-based lending transactions, aircraft leveraged leases, operating and capital lease transactions and syndicated financings. The firm has advised on transactions based on ISDA documentation, including interest rate swaps, credit derivatives and credit-linked notes.

Shiboleth, Yisraeli, Roberts, Zisman & Co has acted for Israel's Bank Hapoalim, Bank Leumi, Union Bank, Maritime Bank and FIBI, as well as for foreign banks such as BNP Paribas and Sao Paolo Banqua of Italy. It also includes investment banks such as Charterhouse, Merrill Lynch, Salomon Brothers, and Prudential Securities among its clients. Richard M Roberts is its key attorney in this sector.

Weksler, Bregman & Co also provides services to many banking institutions in Israel, with its work including negotiations, legal opinions, litigation, the issuance of various types of governmental licences and other related services.

Yehuda Raveh & Co. renders legal services to banks on a daily basis and is a leading firm in this sector, while **Yigal Arnon & Co** has acted for clients such as Deutsche Bank, Bank of New York, Discount Bank, Union Bank, and Bank Hapoalim through its dedicated division, headed by Yigal Arnon and Amnon Lorch.

Zellermayer, Pelossof & Co., Advocates advises major international banks and financial institutions in their Israeli activities with respect to various financial services, from underwriting and project financing, to specialty products and retail. The firm is also involved in commercial bank loans and private placement transactions in which it advises domestic and foreign borrowers and issuers, banks, finance companies, insurance companies and other institutional investors. Recently it advised a large foreign corporation on a $270m debt restructuring, through various financing agreements and acquisition of high-yield bonds.

Bach, Arad, Scharf & Co Law Offices acts for seven Israeli financial institutions as well as for Rothschild Asset Management, one of the most active foreign banking groups in Israel.

Balter, Guth, Aloni & Co has worked for BNP Paribas, Natwest, as well as representing a number of Australian and US banks and financial services institutions.

At **Haim Zadok & Co** partner Nitza R Posner is head of the banking and finance department, which has represented Zeevi Group in negotiations with Israeli banks.

Amos Hacmun heads the transactional practice at **Heskia-Hacmun Law Firm**. The firm also handles finance-based disputes (Dor Heskia) including liquidation and insolvency proceedings.

Yuval Levy & Co has experience in this sector and Levy himself has served on the board of directors of Mercantile Discount Bank for 15 years, while Opher Levy serves as a director of an Israeli affiliate of an international credit analysis and credit ratings company. The firm is also legal counsel to Leumi Card, a subsidiary of Bank Leumi.

CAPITAL MARKETS AND SECURITIES

While in many countries practice areas are clearly defined, in Israel the distinctions are less clear, and **Capital markets and securities** is a good example. Securities law touches many corporate deals in Israel and firms sometimes include securities work in either their corporate and commercial or banking and finance departments.

Ashok Chandrasekhar, a partner skilled in securities law works at **Goldfarb, Levy, Eran & Co**. The firm has a strong reputation in taking Israeli companies to Nasdaq. Securities law remains one of the firm's core strengths, particularly in the hi-tech sector. The firm has also done some asset-backed financing, which is a relatively underdeveloped activity in Israel.

Gross, Kleinhendler, Hodak, Halevy, Greenberg & Co advises many Israeli companies on securities and investment both domestically

CAPITAL MARKETS AND SECURITIES

GOLDFARB, LEVY, ERAN & CO
GROSS, KLEINHENDLER, HODAK, HALEVY, GREENBERG & CO ✪
HERZOG, FOX & NEEMAN ✪
MEITAR, LIQUORNIK, GEVA & LESHEM BRANDWEIN ✪
NASCHITZ, BRANDES & CO ✪
YIGAL ARNON & CO ✪

Caspi & Co ✪
Efrati, Galili & Co ✪
Fischer, Behar, Chen & Co ✪
Haim Samet, Steinmetz, Haring & Co
I Gornitzky & Co ✪
S. Horowitz & Co ✪
Shiboleth, Yisraeli, Roberts, Zisman & Co ✪
Yaacov Salomon, Lipschutz & Co ✪
Zellermayer, Pelossof & Co., Advocates ✪

Balter, Guth, Aloni & Co
Barnea & Co ✪
Danziger, Klagsbald, Rosen & Co ✪
Doron Cohen – David Cohen Law Offices
Ephraim Abramson & Co
Kantor Elhanani Tal & Co
M Seligman & Co
S Friedman & Co, Advocates ✪
Tulchinsky-Stern & Co
Volovelsky, Dinstein, Sneh & Co
Weksler, Bregman & Co ✪
Zeev Holender (Dr) Law Offices

Baratz, Bar-Nathan & Co, | Attorneys-at-Law & Notaries
Cohen Lahat & Co ✪
Dankner Lusky & Co
Erdinast, Ben Nathan & Co ✪
J Weinroth (Dr) & Co ✪
Joseph Levy & Co ✪
M. Firon & Co Advocates and Notaries
M Porath & Co
Melcer & Co Law Offices
Zysman, Aharoni, Gayer & Co ✪

Firms are listed A-Z in tiers which are ranked in order of priority
✪ Indicates firm displays contact details at the end of this chapter.

and abroad, with Joseph Gross being a leading light of the firm. He often represents businesses trying to raise capital on the US markets, while Gene Kleinhendler and Amir Halevy are co-authors of the Israel section of a new book called 'ISR International Securities Regulation'. Partner David Hodak also specialises in securities law.

While the IPO market has been quiet, **Herzog, Fox & Neeman** is involved in one big listing that is to happen soon. Alan Sacks has good standing in the market.

Meitar, Liquornik, Geva & Leshem Brandwein specialises in US securities law and represents issuers, underwriters and stockholders in all stages of initial and secondary public offerings of equity, debt and hybrid securities in the US, Europe and Israel. The corporate and securities practice group represents companies and domestic and international venture capital funds as well as other sophisticated investors in private financing transactions.

Naschitz, Brandes & Co comes highly recommended, particularly if the client is doing a US IPO and due diligence needs to be done. The same can be said for **Yigal Arnon & Co**, which has extensive past experience of representing companies and underwriters in IPOs in New York, the European stock markets and Tel Aviv.

Caspi & Co has Menachem Feder, who is an expert on instruments such as equity-linked notes and exotic paper, while **Efrati, Galili & Co** has recently been involved in a multi-million dollar securitisation for a leading industrial company in Israel. The firm has previously handled dozens of Nasdaq listings, mainly in the hi-tech sector, though there is little of this activity at the moment. Partner David Efrati was the first to take an Israeli company to Nasdaq.

Fischer, Behar, Chen & Co has a corporate and securities department that advises clients in a variety of transactions and regularly counsels clients on Israeli securities laws and regulations. It also handles private and public offerings of debt and equity in Israel.

I Gornitzky & Co recently represented one of the largest Israeli groups of companies, Cardan Investors, which controls many construction operations. The company wanted its stocks to be listed not only on the Tel Aviv Stock Exchange (TASE) but also on Euronext. The firm dealt with TASE and the Israeli authorities, and was involved in the preparation of the IPO.

S. Horowitz & Co is among the firms that have been active in the relatively new area of securitisation, having helped the city of Tel Aviv securitise its car parks. This was the first time a municipality had been allowed to securitise a revenue stream, and as such was a major transaction.

Shiboleth, Yisraeli, Roberts, Zisman & Co has Itzhak Zisman, who is an expert in the securities field. The firm recently represented Pryor-Tech, a public company that operates several wholly and majority owned subsidiaries in the electronic packaging and related application systems industry, in its IPO listing.

Zellermayer, Pelossof & Co., Advocates has represented clients such as Warburg Dillon Read in floating Card Guard on the SWX New Market of the SWX Exchange, which was the first IPO of an Israeli company on the Swiss market. The firm has also been involved in many Nasdaq and TASE listings.

Balter, Guth, Aloni & Co is usually involved in IPOs for companies listing on US exchanges, although in the current climate, there is little of this work available.

COMPETITION

Competition law is another area that is often included in other practice areas in Israel. Many commercial and corporate transactions involve dealing with Israel's antitrust authority, and most firms will have some competency in antitrust law though some firms retain particular expertise.

Caspi & Co has David Tadmor, former director of the antitrust authority, while Avigdor Klagsbald at **Danziger, Klagsbald, Rosen & Co** is also known for his experience with criminal antitrust cases.

Fischer, Behar, Chen & Co has built up a well-known antitrust and regulatory practice group, which handles all aspects of antitrust and trade regulation from structuring compliance programmes for major industrial commercial and financial concerns, to complex antitrust litigation.

Zvi Agmon at **Zvi Agmon Law Offices** has a good reputation based on his considerable experience, while **Gross, Kleinhendler, Hodak, Halevy, Greenberg & Co** also handles regulatory aspects including antitrust regulations.

Herzog, Fox & Neeman maintains antitrust expertise as the discipline impinges upon its large transactions domestically and for foreign clients. The firm has recently taken on someone from the office of the government's Antitrust Director to add more expertise. Telecommunications, where three cable companies are merging into one entity, is the source of significant antitrust work for the firm at the moment.

Ron Gazit, Rotenberg & Co remains active in this area, assisting clients with clearing mergers, notifying and approving agreements in restraint of trade, and defending against monopolisation charges. The firm also has experience in private enforcement litigation involving high-profile competition law issues.

S. Horowitz & Co boasts Yehoshua Horesh and Asgad Stern among its leaders in this area. Stern handles a significant amount of litigation in the areas of securities law and antitrust and is currently involved in one very large ongoing case.

Weinstock-Zecler & Co has Niv Zecler, who comes highly recommended for telecoms-related competition law, and who was formerly legal adviser to the Antitrust Commission.

Yigal Arnon & Co, where Ronit Amir-Yaniv leads the practice, has represented clients such as Tevel, Tadiran, Telrad, Nike Israel, and General Motors-Daewoo.

Yuval Levy & Co has Opher Levy, who is an expert in competition law, while **Efrati, Galili & Co** advises on all aspects of antitrust and competition law for clients such as Degussa AG, a leading chemical producer, and the Dead Sea Bromide Group (DSBG). The firm acted in extensive anti-dumping proceedings brought by a subsidiary of Makteshim Chemical Plants Ltd, regarding the importing of Hydrogen Peroxide by DSBG from Degussa.

S Friedman & Co, Advocates recently represented Israeli shipping companies in a case involving handling charges and restrictive practices.

Shiboleth, Yisraeli, Roberts, Zisman & Co also claims a strong competency in this area, with antitrust and regulatory cases including the representation of TeleCom Italia in all its antitrust and regulatory issues in Israel, and Camtek Ltd, which the firm helped with its regulatory work in listing in the US and Israeli markets, as well as its subsequent de-listing in Israel.

COMPETITION

CASPI & CO ✪
DANZIGER, KLAGSBALD, ROSEN & CO ✪
FISCHER, BEHAR, CHEN & CO ✪
ZVI AGMON LAW OFFICES

Erdinast, Ben Nathan & Co ✪
Gross, Kleinhendler, Hodak, Halevy, Greenberg & Co ✪
Herzog, Fox & Neeman ✪
I Gornitzky & Co ✪
Joseph Levy & Co ✪
Ron Gazit, Rotenberg & Co
S. Horowitz & Co ✪
Weinstock-Zecler & Co ✪
Yigal Arnon & Co ✪
Yuval Levy & Co ✪

Amit, Pollak, Matalon & Co
Efrati, Galili & Co ✪
Haim Zadok & Co ✪
Kantor Elhanani Tal & Co
S Friedman & Co, Advocates ✪
Shavit Bar-On Inbar, Law Offices ✪
Shiboleth, Yisraeli, Roberts, Zisman & Co ✪
Weksler, Bregman & Co ✪
Yehuda Raveh & Co. ✪

Firms are listed A-Z in tiers which are ranked in order of priority
✪ Indicates firm displays contact details at the end of this chapter.

CORPORATE AND COMMERCIAL

Corporate and commercial accounts for a large proportion of the legal work done in Israel, and many firms are active in this area. However, much

CORPORATE AND COMMERCIAL

GOLDFARB, LEVY, ERAN & CO
HERZOG, FOX & NEEMAN ✪
S. HOROWITZ & CO ✪
YIGAL ARNON & CO ✪

EFRATI, GALILI & CO ✪
GROSS, KLEINHENDLER, HODAK, HALEVY, GREENBERG & CO ✪
I GORNITZKY & CO ✪
MEITAR, LIQUORNIK, GEVA & LESHEM BRANDWEIN ✪
NASCHITZ, BRANDES & CO ✪
ZELLERMAYER, PELOSSOF & CO., ADVOCATES ✪

Caspi & Co ✪
Danziger, Klagsbald, Rosen & Co ✪
Fischer, Behar, Chen & Co ✪
Kantor Elhanani Tal & Co
Shiboleth, Yisraeli, Roberts, Zisman & Co ✪
Yehuda Raveh & Co. ✪

Amit, Pollak, Matalon & Co
Bach, Arad, Scharf & Co Law Offices
Balter, Guth, Aloni & Co
Baratz, Bar-Nathan & Co, Attorneys-at-Law & Notaries
Barnea & Co ✪
Dankner Lusky & Co
Eitan, Pearl, Latzer & Cohen-Zedek
Ephraim Abramson & Co
Erdinast, Ben Nathan & Co ✪
Gilead Sher & Co Law Offices
Haim Zadok & Co ✪
M. Firon & Co Advocates and Notaries
M Seligman & Co
Ron Gazit, Rotenberg & Co
S Friedman & Co, Advocates ✪
Tulchinsky-Stern & Co
Weksler, Bregman & Co ✪
Y. Ben-Dror & Co Law Offices
Yaacov Salomon, Lipschutz & Co ✪
Yuval Levy & Co ✪
Zell, Goldberg & Co

continued

CORPORATE AND COMMERCIAL (continued)

Aaronsohn, Aboulafia, Gal-On, Tzin, Amoday & Co
Avital, Dromi & Co ✪
Avniel, Salomon & Co
Berkman Wechsler Sahar Bloom & Co
Cohen Lahat & Co ✪
ES Shimron, I Molho, Persky & Co ✪
Epstein, Chomsky & Co
Haim Samet, Steinmetz, Haring & Co
Hamburger, Evron, Raviv-Berson & Co ✪
Hermann, Makov & Co
Heskia-Hacmun Law Firm ✪
J Weinroth (Dr) & Co ✪
Joseph Levy & Co ✪
Lipa Meir & Co
M Porath & Co
Melcer & Co Law Offices
Miron, Bension & Prywes
Primes, Shiloh, Givon, Meir, Law Firm
Raved Magriso Benkel & Co ✪
S. Mizrahi, B. Arnon & G. Makov
Schuman, Livnat & Mayer
Shavit Bar-On Inbar, Law Offices ✪
Shinar, Shachor, Weissberger ✪
Shraga F Biran & Co
Volovelsky, Dinstein, Sneh & Co
Yossifoff, Cohen & Co Law Offices
Zysman, Aharoni, Gayer & Co ✪

Firms are listed A-Z in tiers which are ranked in order of priority
✪ Indicates firm displays contact details at the end of this chapter.

work for international clients is concentrated among the firms in the top tiers.

Many Israeli firms have separate practices such as M&A or international departments that come under the heading of corporate and commercial work. The relatively poor economic situation in Israel in recent years, and the ongoing effects of the intifada, has resulted in a lack of M&A activity, and has reduced the number of IPOs to virtually none.

Privatisation of state industries has been important in this area, though the number of completed deals has not matched the government's strong appetite. The recent finalisation of the privatisation of El Al Airlines, which has taken years to complete, has been one of the largest concerns for Israel's Ministry of Finance.

Israel is still dealing with the impact of changes to the Companies Law. The law was passed in 1999, but its effects are still filtering down, resulting in ongoing compliance advice.

Goldfarb, Levy, Eran & Co is among the firms with a good reputation for international work, and in the past has been involved in numerous listings on Nasdaq market. The lack of activity on Nasdaq has reduced this business, but the firm works with many US clients and is one of the few firms that reports activity in M&A in the last year. Though this market has been quiet in 2003 the firm has been involved in a number of large deals such as the acquisition of Midbar by Macrovision, and it acted for shareholders in Innowave when Alverion purchased it.

Herzog, Fox & Neeman is widely considered to be one of Israel's best international firms and handles a lot of international work. It attracts a large number of lawyers from the UK and handles work for numerous UK clients. It is active in bankruptcy, insolvency, corporate reorganisation, M&A and many other areas, with the technology sector being one of its main sources of work. Partners including Michael Fox, Alan Sacks and Isaac Herzog are very well known in Israel's legal community and among international clients.

S. Horowitz & Co has not been as active as in previous years, but has still seen some major deals, including an acquisition by concrete manufacturer, Readymix. The firm also represented Starbucks in the closure of its operations as the company exited the market in Israel. It also represents a number of cable companies in Israel and has acted for US entertainment companies Universal and Warner Brothers.

Yigal Arnon & Co is another highly respected firm that is active for both foreign and domestic clients. It has three offices in Tel Aviv and Jerusalem and is seen as having one of the leading M&A practices in Israel. Last year its clients included Veritas-Precise, HP-Compaq and IBM-PWC. Doron Tamir, Paul Baris and Shiri Shaham handle privatisation.

Efrati, Galili & Co has a senior partner in Alon Galili who has been involved in a lot of corporate and M&A work in Israel in recent years. Recent highlights include representing Teva, one of the world's leading generic pharmaceutical companies, in its purchase of Sicor in a transaction worth $2.5bn. The firm was also involved in the recently completed privatisation of El Al.

Gross, Kleinhendler, Hodak, Halevy, Greenberg & Co advises on all aspects of general corporate law and its department, headed by Joseph Gross, usually handles significant amounts of M&A. Gross has also acted for the Israeli government on matters relating to floating shares in two of Israel's leading banks – Bank Hapoalim and Bank Leumi. Partner David Hodak also specialises in M&A and international transactions.

A very important deal for **I Gornitzky & Co** was the merger of two of Israel's largest food companies – Elite, which specialises in sweets and chocolate, and Strauss, which is known for ice-cream, salads and milk. The head of the firm was selected to see this complicated merger through to completion.

Meitar, Liquornik, Geva & Leshem Brandwein was formed in 2003 by the merger of two well-known corporate law firms, and is widely believed to have benefited as a result. The firm now has several clients active in domestic and cross-border transactions, with experience in structuring, negotiating and drafting complex as well as more standard commercial transactions. M&A is an important practice area, and clients hail from industries such as pharmaceuticals, biotechnology, healthcare, software, semiconductors, computers, chemicals, agro-chemicals, oil and gas, and plastics, among others.

Naschitz, Brandes & Co represents small start-up companies in hi-tech and biotechnology, as well as large public companies and government-controlled industries. Among its clients are *Fortune 500* companies, leading IT businesses and software houses. The firm was recently involved in advising on a major foreign investment into an Israeli water company.

Zellermayer, Pelossof & Co., Advocates has a corporate department with over 15 advocates, and its activities range from providing general counsel for corporations, to arranging special ventures and partnerships. It has recently acted in M&A deals for companies such as Tadiran Communications, and Cable & Wireless for which it advised in a $643m sale of a stake in Bezeq. Much of its M&A activity has involved telecoms and IT companies.

One firm that is expected to grow rapidly in the coming years is **Fischer, Behar, Chen & Co**. The firm has been taking on more corporate work and has been recruiting more lawyers in the last year. The firm has been involved in purchases, sales and M&A, and regularly advises on complex corporate transactions.

Yaacov Yisraeli is the key attorney in the corporate and commercial department of **Shiboleth, Yisraeli, Roberts, Zisman & Co**, which represents clients such as Israeli duty free company, James Richardson, and US company, Prior-Tech Ltd. It also counts Wrigley Israel, the chewing gum manufacturer, and Israeli Military Industries (IMI) among its clients. Richard Roberts is also an expert in this field.

Yehuda Raveh & Co. holds its clients' names in strict confidence, but it has represented many entities in the banking sector, as well as companies involved in infrastructure projects in Israel. Lisa Tross heads its corporate and commercial team, with Chagai Ulman in charge of insolvency cases and Carmit Bar-On specialising in hotels and tourism. Yuval Raveh is considered an expert on corporate and commercial transactions, specialising in M&A, real estate and infrastructure. The firm is also heavily involved in privatisation.

A $1bn transaction for a pharmaceutical company is one of the highlights of 2003 for **Bach, Arad, Scharf & Co Law Offices**. The deal saw Sanofi merge with French company, Synthelabo to become Sanofi-Synthelabo Inc. The firm helped with the restructuring of the company's Israeli operations. The firm has also advised on the corporate restructuring for Roche Diagnostics and Eli Lilly in Israel.

Balter, Guth, Aloni & Co is one of the firms that has been involved in the growing number of privatisations in Israel. It has recently acted for a US company that acquired a government entity, and was also party to the EL Al deal, as well as acting for a number of banks.

Managing partner Benjamin Baratz practises commercial and civil law at **Baratz, Bar-Nathan & Co, Attorneys-at-Law & Notaries**. He has worked on public offerings – though there has been few in Israel this year – and is a court-appointed trustee in bankruptcy proceedings. Lori Almouli-Confino also has expertise in commercial law.

Barnea & Co, which was formerly *Shimonov, Barnea & Co*, advised Lockheed Martin on its recent acquisition of defence company, Titan in the US, both companies having Israeli assets. It also advised the world's second largest electrical manufacturer, another US company with many Israeli assets, in setting up subsidiaries. The firm has an increasingly international perspective.

Dankner Lusky & Co is seen as a firm that punches above its weight in corporate matters, while **Eitan, Pearl, Latzer & Cohen-Zedek** handles a significant amount of corporate work for clients in the hi-tech sector.

Ephraim Abramson & Co comes recommended for advice on Israeli and US securities, and is one of the many firms that has advised Israeli telecommunications monopoly, Bezeq in its domestic operations. Ephraim Abramson himself heads the corporate and securities department.

Meanwhile **Erdinast, Ben Nathan & Co** has seen its corporate and commercial practice grow significantly over recent years. Its diversification into other areas of corporate and commercial law have seen it represent a growing number of prominent Israeli corporations and institutions, including one of the purchasers of IDB holdings, one of Israel's most important companies, and Eden Springs, along with its controlling shareholders, in a merger and the creation of a joint venture with global food and beverage conglomerate, Danone.

Gilead Sher & Co Law Offices has a good track record for infrastructure projects, but also has a number of significant corporate clients. The four-partner corporate team is headed by Amir Kadari. The firm advises a number of commercial clients within the real estate sector, notably the Greek Orthodox Patriarch and the Patriarchate of Jerusalem.

Partner Ilan Shavi is the head of the Corporate Bankruptcy and Reorganisation department of **Haim Zadok & Co**, which has acted in a stay of proceedings against Feuchtwanger Industries Group and its sale to an outside investor for NIS700m (€124m). The firm also represented Sony Entertainment division, Columbia-Pictures – Tristar Int during the stay of proceedings against one of Israel's cable TV companies, and was also involved in the sale of assets of United Steel Mills Group – a transaction with a similar value. The firm also represents Accor Tourism Group in all its business activities.

M. Firon & Co Advocates and Notaries was formerly known as *Firon Karni Sarov & Firon – Renato Jarach*. Its corporate and commercial division includes well-known practitioners Eldad Firon, Zvi Firon and Rivi Firon-Irani.

Ron Gazit, Rotenberg & Co acts for both private and public companies, both Israeli and foreign, for which it prepares commercial agreements including distribution, licensing and franchising. It also handles corporate litigation and has helped with the formation of joint ventures between foreign and Israeli companies.

S Friedman & Co, Advocates has many clients within the shipping and transport industries, but also undertakes other commercial and corporate work. In the last year it was involved in a significant deal with a steel manufacturer in the north of Israel; the firm bought the company's steel mills in a very large deal on behalf of one of its clients.

Tulchinsky-Stern & Co is involved in a number of corporate and securities activities, including M&A, corporate consulting and the formation of start-up companies. Much of its corporate work is for clients in the technology industries. In the past it handled the largest merger in the history of Israel – the $5bn transaction that saw Chromatis Networks merge with Lucent Technologies. It has also served as Israeli counsel for deals involving Teva Pharmaceutical Industries. In addition it has a strong commercial litigation department.

Weksler, Bregman & Co represents a number of corporations, partnerships and branches of foreign companies in Israel, as well as joint ventures. The firm deals with government agencies and advises international clients establishing incentive-based investments in industry and tourism. As well as its cross-border work, the firm also deals with liquidation and receivership, and its lawyers often act as receivers on behalf of commercial banks. Senior partner Uri Bregman has been nominated as Special Administrator for the Trade Bank Ltd, which is in temporary liquidation.

Yaacov Salomon, Lipschutz & Co has a good reputation in this area, and **Y. Ben-Dror & Co Law Offices** is also usually active, being a corporate boutique firm headed by two partners. The firm has a strong client base within the media and IT sectors.

Yuval Levy & Co continues to build on its base of domestic and foreign clients, and last year represented investors in various Israeli and US entities. The firm is also legal counsel to Daimler-Chrysler Financial Services Ltd, which is a joint venture between the US carmaker and an Israeli automotive importer.

Zell, Goldberg & Co counts Galtronics, a Middle Eastern multinational electronics manufacturer, among its clients, and also advises Internet-related start-ups on matters relating to commercial law.

Aaronsohn, Aboulafia, Gal-On, Tzin, Amoday & Co has a department headed by David Aboulafia that advises on purchases, sales, M&A, private equity and debt offerings, loans and other forms of financing and banking matters for its commercial clients.

Avital, Dromi & Co is considered the leading telecoms firm in Israel, but is also active in international commercial deals, though mainly through its telecoms clients. However, the firm also led the way in the privatisation of agricultural communities, in which its members become share-holders. It maintains many kibbutzim as clients.

Dor Heskia heads the corporate practice at **Heskia-Hacmun Law Firm**. The firm represents a 50:50 domestic and international clientele.

DISPUTE RESOLUTION

Israel is a litigious society by any standard, perhaps almost as much as the US, and the economic downturn has seen significant growth in usually rare class actions. Though the tendency is for disputes to go through the courts, there is a growing trend towards arbitration and mediation, which are both relatively new features of the Israeli legal system.

DISPUTE RESOLUTION

J WEINROTH (DR) & CO ✪
S. HOROWITZ & CO ✪
YIGAL ARNON & CO ✪

BACH, ARAD, SCHARF & CO LAW OFFICES
CASPI & CO ✪
HERZOG, FOX & NEEMAN ✪
I GORNITZKY & CO ✪
M SELIGMAN & CO
YUVAL LEVY & CO✪

Amit, Pollak, Matalon & Co
Danziger, Klagsbald, Rosen & Co ✪
Erdinast, Ben Nathan & Co ✪
Fischer, Behar, Chen & Co ✪
Haim Zadok & Co ✪

J Segev (Dr) Law Offices
Naschitz, Brandes & Co ✪

Balter, Guth, Aloni & Co
Efrati, Galili & Co ✪
Gilead Sher & Co Law Offices
Goldfarb, Levy, Eran & Co
Gross, Kleinhendler, Hodak, Halevy, Greenberg & Co ✪
Heskia-Hacmun Law Firm ✪
Kantor Elhanani Tal & Co
Meitar, Liquornik, Geva & Leshem Brandwein ✪
S Friedman & Co, Advocates ✪
Shiboleth, Yisraeli, Roberts, Zisman & Co ✪
Tulchinsky-Stern & Co
Weksler, Bregman & Co ✪
Yehuda Raveh & Co. ✪
Zell, Goldberg & Co

Avniel, Salomon & Co
Baratz, Bar-Nathan & Co, Attorneys-at-Law & Notaries
Berkman Wechsler Sahar Bloom & Co
Eitan, Pearl, Latzer & Cohen-Zedek
Ephraim Abramson & Co
Hermann, Makov & Co
Joseph Levy & Co ✪
Luthi & Co ✪
M Porath & Co
Miron, Bension & Prywes
Raved Magriso Benkel & Co ✪
Ron Gazit, Rotenberg & Co
Seligsohn Gabrieli Levit & Co
Shavit Bar-On Inbar, Law Offices ✪
Shlomo Cohen (Dr) & Co Law Office
Yaacov Salomon, Lipschutz & Co ✪

Firms are listed A-Z in tiers which are ranked in order of priority
✪ Indicates firm displays contact details at the end of this chapter.

Jacob Weinroth of **Dr J Weinroth & Co** is a litigation specialist with a good reputation, while **S. Horowitz & Co** claims to have the largest litigation department in Israel. The firm has been involved in many of the major commercial disputes due to its experience in acting in every type of court and tribunal in areas such as banking and finance, insurance, IP and IT.

Yigal Arnon & Co has represented clients such as Tevel Cables, Yaacov Nimrodi, Yachin-Hakal, Dror Vigdor and Amnon Lorsch. The firm acts for domestic and international clients in cases including arbitration, commercial litigation and high-profile civil and criminal matters.

Bach, Arad, Scharf & Co Law Offices has performed litigation for clients such as Novartis and handles a lot of international work, while **Herzog, Fox & Neeman** saw its litigators become more active in 2003. The firm has recruited more litigators in the last year, including Joseph 'Yossi' Ashkenazi, who joined from **Dr J Weinroth & Co**, partly due to the increase in litigation derived from the poor economy.

I Gornitzky & Co maintains a strong litigation practice, while **Yuval Levy & Co** has seen its practice grow through the defence of class actions.

Erdinast, Ben Nathan & Co has been involved in some of Israel's biggest business disputes, and has represented large telecoms companies, such as DBS Satellite Ltd, as well as insurance groups and a number of banks.

Fischer, Behar, Chen & Co has a litigation department that handles all types of civil business litigation, representing both plaintiffs and defendants, while **Haim Zadok & Co** has partner Eyal Rosovsky heading a litigation department, which represents many kinds of clients. Partner Ehood Schneider heads the class actions department, while Advocate Dan Meridor, formerly Minister of Finance, Minister of Justice, Minister of Strategic Affairs, Secretary to the Cabinet and Chairman of the Foreign Affairs and Defence Committee in the Israeli parliament, joined the firm in July 2003.

Naschitz, Brandes & Co has a highly respected litigation practice that handles general commercial issues as well as product liability, banking, insurance, maritime, securities and intellectual property.

Dr Shaul Aloni of **Balter, Guth, Aloni & Co** spent many years as a judge in the District Courts and the Magistrates Court, and heads the firm's arbitration department.

Efrati, Galili & Co has seen the recession bring more litigation work, particularly class actions, of which the firm was involved in six in 2003.

Gilead Sher & Co Law Offices offers a three-partner disputes practice led by Deuel Peli. The firm recently successfully represented long-standing client Phone-Or Ltd in a $13m repurchase agreement dispute with shareholders.

Goldfarb, Levy, Eran & Co maintains a strong litigation practice again fed by more class actions, though it is seeing more activity in alternative dispute resolution.

The litigation department at **Gross, Kleinhendler, Hodak, Halevy, Greenberg & Co** deals with commercial and employment litigation, with respect to claims filed in Israel by or against multinational organisations and government agencies.

Dor Heskia at **Heskia-Hacmun Law Firm** has represented a well-known German telecoms company in a dispute with its Israeli partners, as well as acting for a singer who has won the Eurovision Song Contest in a lawsuit against Bezeq International, claiming that its TV and other commercials were infringing his client's rights.

Meitar, Liquornik, Geva & Leshem Brandwein has earned a solid reputation for effectively handling complex cases at the highest level in the fields of corporate, commercial, securities, tax, technology, real estate and labour law. Its clients include large local and international entities.

At **Shiboleth, Yisraeli, Roberts, Zisman & Co**, Hillel Ish-Shalom leads the litigation practice, which acts for clients such as Bezeq and Migdal Insurance, Israel's largest insurer.

Yehuda Raveh & Co. has Yuval Grayevsky in charge of litigation, which is one of the firm's core activities. The firm recently represented a large mortgage bank in a class action valued at $250m.

Zell, Goldberg & Co still handles disputes for an Israeli military equipment manufacturer and has generally seen rapid growth in litigation, especially complex cross-border cases.

ENERGY AND NATURAL RESOURCES

Energy, along with water is another crucial focus for infrastructure projects and the development of more power plants remains a priority. Israel is not as energy rich as its neighbours, and the recent discovery of natural gas off the Israeli coast is leading to major projects being put into development.

Herzog, Fox & Neeman is again a leading firm in this area, and Michael Fox, known mostly for his corporate work, has been noted for his legal contributions to the development of infrastructure, energy and natural resources in Israel. Members of the firm's energy and natural resources team, which include Yaacov Brandt and Mark Phillips, have advised international bidding groups on the Ashkelon and Ashdod desalination plants, the tender for the transport of potable water from Turkey to Israel, and projects for the construction of power plants such as the 450MW Mishor Rotem combined cycle gas turbine project.

I Gornitzky & Co has played a part in all tenders for the construction of gas and electric

ENERGY AND NATURAL RESOURCES

HERZOG, FOX & NEEMAN ⭘
I GORNITZKY & CO ⭘
S. HOROWITZ & CO ⭘

Balter, Guth, Aloni & Co
Caspi & Co ⭘
Dankner Lusky & Co
ES Shimron, I Molho, Persky & Co ⭘
Efrati, Galili & Co ⭘
Ephraim Abramson & Co
Haim Zadok & Co ⭘
M. Firon & Co Advocates and Notaries
Meitar, Liquornik, Geva & Leshem Brandwein ⭘
Ne'eman, Shafir, Ben-Artzi & Co. Advocates ⭘

Shiboleth, Yisraeli, Roberts, Zisman & Co ⭘
Yaacov Salomon, Lipschutz & Co ⭘
Zellermayer, Pelossof & Co., Advocates ⭘

Firms are listed A-Z in tiers which are ranked in order of priority
⭘ Indicates firm displays contact details at the end of this chapter.

power stations as well as a number of water desalination projects. It has represented the Israeli government in matters of deeds, papers and finance.

S. Horowitz & Co is an important player in this sector, partly due to its involvement with the construction of a gas pipeline across Israel, but also for its work in representing the interests of the state monopoly, Israel Electric Corporation.

Balter, Guth, Aloni & Co has, in Jacob Liraz, a partner who was formerly at the Energy Ministry, while it also handles water projects as part of its agricultural focus.

Dankner Lusky & Co has been involved in the purchase of land, development, establishment and management of power centres in Netania, Hod Hasharon, Bilu Junction and Nazareth, and the firm also acts for Dor Energy.

Efrati, Galili & Co has handled a tender for the Israel Natural Gas Project, while **M. Firon & Co Advocates and Notaries** handled the first waste-to-energy tender in Israel.

Shiboleth, Yisraeli, Roberts, Zisman & Co represented the Delek Group in the establishment of the power plant at a water desalination plant, and **Zellermayer, Pelossof & Co., Advocates** counts energy companies among its clients. The firm has recently represented a US corporation in its efforts to erect the first major independent power plant in Israel before the local electricity monopoly and all relevant government bodies, with project finance estimated at $300-$400m.

HI-TECH

Israel's higher education establishments offer many courses in sciences and serve as research institutions with international reputations, reflecting the country's high concentration of hi-tech industries. IT, biotechnology and life sciences are all well established in Israel, as scientific research and development are seen as ways to compensate for the country's lack of natural resources.

The country has seen significant amounts of venture capital invested in hi-tech start-ups in recent years, though in the last two years this funding has been reduced because of the downturn in the global economy, which has particularly affected the technology sector. However, hi-tech industries are less affected than others by the security situation as they deal in research, ideas and innovation rather than physical product.

Though the economic downturn has hit hard there are signs that venture capital funds are starting to raise more money to fund Israeli hi-tech companies and many people are predicting another boom in the sector.

Danziger, Klagsbald, Rosen & Co handles a significant amount of work from venture capital funds, including Pitango, which is among Israel's leading funds. Pitango has built a reputation for nurturing innovation and has invested widely in seed companies, as well as in expanding hi-tech companies in Israel, the UK and the US.

Efrati, Galili & Co is among those firms that predict a recovery in the hi-tech sector, with chairman David Efrati a leading voice. The firm handles a large amount of biotechnology work as well as representing a number of venture capital funds such as Genesis Partners and the Challenge Fund. The firm has a well-known technology group, which has clients in hardware, software, Internet development and information processing.

Goldfarb, Levy, Eran & Co is recommended for hi-tech work, and has previously been involved in taking many Israeli companies to Nasdaq. There have been fewer Nasdaq listings in the last year, but the firm retains its expertise in the sector. It has also been involved in deals such as the takeover of Algotec by Kodak, in which it acted for Algotec and its shareholders, as well as the acquisition of Midbar Tech by Macrovision. It has also continued to act for venture capital investors as it represents some of the larger funds that have sustained their activity.

Gross, Kleinhendler, Hodak, Halevy, Greenberg & Co has a dedicated department that advises hi-tech companies of all sizes, and has handled public and private offerings in Israel, the US and Europe. Gene Kleinhendler, formerly an attorney at the US Securities and Exchange Commission, now counsels mature technology companies in complex international transactions, securities law, and financing and corporate reorganisation. Amir Halevy also has extensive expertise in this sector.

Meitar, Liquornik, Geva & Leshem Brandwein has a technology group with extensive experience in structuring and negotiating IT transactions from development and licensing, to the procurement and distribution of IT products and services. The firm represents many media, Internet and e-commerce enterprises, and also advises both providers and customers of outsourcing transactions. Other clients include biotech start-ups and international pharmaceutical companies.

HI-TECH

DANZIGER, KLAGSBALD, ROSEN & CO ⭘
EFRATI, GALILI & CO ⭘
GOLDFARB, LEVY, ERAN & CO
GROSS, KLEINHENDLER, HODAK, HALEVY, GREENBERG & CO ⭘
MEITAR, LIQUORNIK, GEVA & LESHEM BRANDWEIN ⭘
YIGAL ARNON & CO ⭘

Berkman Wechsler Sahar Bloom & Co
Eitan, Pearl, Latzer & Cohen-Zedek
Fischer, Behar, Chen & Co ⭘
Herzog, Fox & Neeman ⭘
I Gornitzky & Co ⭘
Kantor Elhanani Tal & Co
Naschitz, Brandes & Co ⭘
S. Horowitz & Co ⭘
Shiboleth, Yisraeli, Roberts, Zisman & Co ⭘
Tulchinsky-Stern & Co
Zellermayer, Pelossof & Co., Advocates ⭘

Amit, Pollak, Matalon & Co
Barnea & Co ⭘
Doron Cohen – David Cohen Law Offices
Ephraim Abramson & Co
Erdinast, Ben Nathan & Co ⭘
Gilead Sher & Co Law Offices
Ron Gazit, Rotenberg & Co
Schuman, Livnat & Mayer
Volovelsky, Dinstein, Sneh & Co
Weinstock-Zecler & Co ⭘
Yehuda Raveh & Co. ⭘
Yossifoff, Cohen & Co Law Offices

Avital, Dromi & Co ⭘
Balter, Guth, Aloni & Co
Baratz, Bar-Nathan & Co, Attorneys-at-Law & Notaries
Caspi & Co ⭘
Cohen Lahat & Co ⭘
Eyal Khayat, Zolty & Co ⭘
Heskia-Hacmun Law Firm ⭘
M. Firon & Co Advocates and Notaries

Raved Magriso Benkel & Co ⭘
Y. Ben-Dror & Co Law Offices
Yuval Levy & Co ⭘
Zeev Holender (Dr) Law Offices
Zysman, Aharoni, Gayer & Co ⭘

Firms are listed A-Z in tiers which are ranked in order of priority
⭘ Indicates firm displays contact details at the end of this chapter.

Yigal Arnon & Co, as one of Israel's largest firms, puts much emphasis on the hi-tech sector, representing both large corporations and start-ups in varying stages of development. The firm also counsels many of the leading Israeli, US and European venture capitalists and investment funds. Its services come highly recommended within Israel's legal community.

Berkman Wechsler Sahar Bloom & Co has an active hi-tech practice, while **Eitan, Pearl, Latzer & Cohen-Zedek** has a software and electronics group that works with clients involved in the development, production and manufacture of semiconductor technology. This group advises clients on the patentability of inventions, patent prosecution and enforcement, as well as working closely with the firm's licensing, finance and tax groups on structuring licence agreements, joint ventures, M&A and taxation solutions. In addition, the firm has a life sciences group.

Fischer, Behar, Chen & Co provides advice for many hi-tech companies at various stages of development and also helps guide businesses with regard to government support for research and development. It also represents a number of investors, venture capital funds and technology incubators.

Herzog, Fox & Neeman represents venture capital firms and sees their interest in Israeli hi-tech companies growing. In fact, it sees many funds already waiting with money to invest, though they are choosing their targets more carefully than a few years ago. The firm also anticipates more M&A activity in hi-tech in the coming years, though at the moment much of its work for hi-tech clients is in the area of debt refinancing.

I Gornitzky & Co has successfully taken an important case to court recently in which it represented a Jewish billionaire in an attempt to release himself from a commitment to invest over $13m in an Israeli hi-tech company. It is also involved in advising many hi-tech clients in structuring their businesses and seeking funding.

Naschitz, Brandes & Co is a leading hi-tech firm, representing some 200 companies within the sector.

S. Horowitz & Co is very active in the biotechnology sector, and acts for the main incubator fund The Weissman Institute of Science. Partner, Yoav Ben-Dror has also been involved in a large amount of financing for many hi-tech firms through venture capital funds.

Shiboleth, Yisraeli, Roberts, Zisman & Co offers Lior Aviram, who is a key attorney in its hi-tech practice. The firm represents venture capital funds such as Walden Israel, which has a portfolio of $185m. Seabridge Israel, which makes access switches for ATM networks, is also a client.

Tulchinsky-Stern & Co is known for its corporate and investment activities in technology industries.

Zellermayer, Pelossof & Co., Advocates represents numerous venture capital funds that provide seed money and advance stage funding to start-up enterprises and then make special equity investments in established enterprises in areas such as telecoms, data transfer, healthcare, biotechnology and Internet development. Its VC fund clients include Giza, Benchmark, Shamrock, Columbine and RDC.

Barnea & Co is currently working for six hi-tech companies seeking to list in the UK, having already listed two companies on AIM. Mickey Barnea is seen as one of the leading technology lawyers in Israel. The firm recently did a deal in which a Finnish company bought a genetics company in Israel.

Some firms such as **Eyal Khayat, Zolty & Co** specialise in hi-tech, and given the importance of the hi-tech sector to Israel's economy many firms have hi-tech practice groups, though many have seen less activity in the last three years.

INSURANCE

The Israeli insurance industry now represents about 6% of GDP and is still growing steadily. The insurance market has undergone some consolidation with five insurance groups holding over 80% of the local market, and smaller companies making up the rest.

Throughout the legal industry in Israel **Levitan, Sharon & Co** is seen as the leading firm in insurance. It specialises in insurance and reinsurance law, including litigation, with specific expertise in complex international issues. The firm acts for Israeli and foreign insurers and reinsurers including Lloyd's, Swiss Re, Munich Re, Gerling, Zurich Re, and many others. It has established an international reputation.

Aaronsohn, Aboulafia, Gal-On, Tzin, Amoday & Co, which was formed by merger between *Aaronsohn, Aboulafia, Amoday*, a leader in insurance law, and *Gal-On, Tzin & Co*. Shmuel Aaronsohn leads its life insurance and medical malpractice division, and the firm represents many leading Israeli insurance companies.

Balter, Guth, Aloni & Co remains active in insurance for clients such as Marsh McLennan, one of the world's leading insurance brokers and risk advisers.

Naschitz, Brandes & Co also has a good reputation in Israel and regularly represents leading Israeli and international insurance and reinsurance companies, advising on commercial and regulatory issues, and acting in litigation and most subrogation matters. It also specialises in maritime insurance. The firm's senior partner, PG Naschitz is chairman of the Israel section of the International Association of Insurance law.

S. Horowitz & Co advises insurance and reinsurance companies in both contentious and non-contentious matters, while **I Gornitzky & Co** has dealt with large cases involving the likes of Israel Phoenix Assurance Company.

Meitar, Liquornik, Geva & Leshem Brandwein derives insurance expertise from Leshem Brandwein, and **Yehuda Raveh & Co.** numbers insurance companies among its clients.

INSURANCE

LEVITAN, SHARON & CO ✪

Aaronsohn, Aboulafia, Gal-On, Tzin, Amoday & Co
Balter, Guth, Aloni & Co
Ilan Orly & Co
M Seligman & Co
Naschitz, Brandes & Co ✪
S. Horowitz & Co ✪

Baratz, Bar-Nathan & Co, Attorneys-at-Law & Notaries
Efrati, Galili & Co ✪
Goldfarb, Levy, Eran & Co
Hermann, Makov & Co
I Gornitzky & Co ✪
M Porath & Co
Meitar, Liquornik, Geva & Leshem Brandwein ✪

Sahar, Stobiecki & Co
Shavit Bar-On Inbar, Law Offices ✪
Yaacov Salomon, Lipschutz & Co ✪
Yehuda Raveh & Co. ✪

Firms are listed A-Z in tiers which are ranked in order of priority
✪ Indicates firm displays contact details at the end of this chapter.

INTELLECTUAL PROPERTY

Intellectual property is an important area of practice in Israel due to the prevalence of hi-tech research and development in the country. As a result many firms that handle hi-tech work or are active in corporate and commercial transactions retain some IP expertise.

Boutiques for IP also sprang up during the hi-tech boom in the late 1990s, though some have suffered since. Few lawyers in Israel qualify with the necessary IP specialisation and scientific knowledge, and now that the technology sector is showing signs of recovery IP expertise may well be in great demand.

Eitan, Pearl, Latzer & Cohen-Zedek is a firm that is growing rapidly in its hi-tech and intellectual property activities, and has lawyers such as Shirley Gal Zaken, Dor Cohen-Zedek, Daniel Bustanai and Maty Barzam in its trade mark department. The firm leverages intellectual property rights and assets by structuring and negotiating technology transfers and licences, forming and formalising international joint ventures, and representing domestic and international clients in the sale and purchase of technology and technology-based assets.

Luthi & Co is recognised as an IP heavyweight, and continues to be involved in virtually all the major patent litigation cases in Israel. The firm handles international litigation

INTELLECTUAL PROPERTY

EITAN, PEARL, LATZER & COHEN-ZEDEK
LUTHI & CO ⊙
RON GAZIT, ROTENBERG & CO
S. HOROWITZ & CO ⊙
SELIGSOHN GABRIELI LEVIT & CO
SHLOMO COHEN (DR) & CO LAW OFFICE

Efrati, Galili & Co ⊙
Goldfarb, Levy, Eran & Co
Gross, Kleinhendler, Hodak, Halevy, Greenberg & Co ⊙
Herzog, Fox & Neeman ⊙
Yigal Arnon & Co ⊙

Amit, Pollak, Matalon & Co
Avital, Dromi & Co ⊙
Balter, Guth, Aloni & Co
Berkman Wechsler Sahar Bloom & Co
ES Shimron, I Molho, Persky & Co ⊙
Gilead Sher & Co Law Offices
Haim Samet, Steinmetz, Haring & Co
Jacob & Hana Calderon, Advocates
Jeremy M. Ben-David & Co. Ltd
Raved Magriso Benkel & Co ⊙
Shiboleth, Yisraeli, Roberts, Zisman & Co ⊙
Volovelsky, Dinstein, Sneh & Co
Zysman, Aharoni, Gayer & Co ⊙

Firms are listed A-Z in tiers which are ranked in order of priority
⊙ Indicates firm displays contact details at the end of this chapter.

management, validity and infringement assessment, protection and enforcement strategy, pharmaceutical regulatory affairs and due diligence enquiries, as well as trade mark and design registration. Clients include companies in the pharmaceuticals, biotechnology, agricultural and industrial chemicals, electronics, IT and communications sectors.

Ron Gazit, Rotenberg & Co provides IP services for users and suppliers of IT, having been involved in many of Israel's largest and most important IT deals. The firm regularly assists large international software companies in enforcing their copyrights and trade marks and in combating software piracy.

S. Horowitz & Co has Avi Ordo, who undertakes significant amounts of patent prosecution. IP has always been an active area for the firm.

Dr Shlomo Cohen & Co Law Office has a team of 16 lawyers and scientists and is the largest firm in Israel that deals exclusively in IP. Dr Cohen, President of the Israel Bar Association, is head of a firm that is very well regarded in the Israeli legal community, and which represents major multinational corporations, local companies and start-ups, most of which are hi-tech or science-based. Clients include Johnson & Johnson, Abbot Laboratories, Intel, Nokia, Aventis, Reebok, Nike. In the last year the firm has added four new IP specialists. Much new foreign work is seen coming from the pharmaceutical and chemical industries, as well as from telecoms.

Efrati, Galili & Co is building one of the leading technology practices in Israel and as such has expertise to advise clients at all stages of IP development. The firm recently represented an Israeli pharmaceutical company in a letter of rogatory proceeding for patent infringement instituted in Israel by a Canadian court.

Herzog, Fox & Neeman calls in its IP team when working on large acquisitions, while **Balter, Guth, Aloni & Co** merged this year with a small IP firm to give it greater expertise. Dr Sarah Presenti was added to the firm's Tel Aviv office, and brought four IP practitioners with her.

Jeremy M. Ben-David & Co. Ltd handles patent, trade mark and design registration as its stock-in-trade. A multinational team advises on a range of issues, including preparation and filing of applications, prosecution and renewals.

PROJECT FINANCE AND INFRASTRUCTURE

Infrastructure development is a priority for the Israeli government and many important projects have been tabled in recent years, however few have made it to completion and many projects suffer from delays.

BOT and PPP projects are schemes implemented by government to bring private money into infrastructure development. The government has issued tenders for the private operation of a prison, the building and maintenance of 1,000 school classrooms for municipalities and for the private construction of the Cross-Israel Highway.

Power plant projects are important, as are desalination plants to address the country's lack of water – a situation worsened by Israel's requirement to export water to Jordan as part of the countries' peace agreement, even though Israel imports water from Turkey for its own use. Of four planned desalination plants only one has so far been constructed – at Ashkelon – and progress on other projects such as the national highway has been slow.

Herzog, Fox & Neeman has been involved in all the major infrastructure projects either for the concessionaire or the lender. It has been working on the Cross-Israel Highway, which has now become active again, with construction completion due soon. The firm hopes that the next project to be kick started will be the Carmel Tunnel, a hitherto beleaguered project for a four-tunnel complex under Mount Carmel, connecting the north and south of Haifa. The firm also acts for the concessionaire on the Jerusalem Light Railway and has acted for four consortia that have pre-qualified for a tender to build the Tel Aviv Light Railway.

I Gornitzky & Co has acted for the government on the Cross-Israel Highway project and has a very strong reputation for project finance and infrastructure development. It has worked on the water desalination projects and is involved in two projects for the construction of underground railways, as well as having a hand in all power station projects. It is also active in the ongoing Tel Aviv Light Railway project.

PROJECT FINANCE AND INFRASTRUCTURE

HERZOG, FOX & NEEMAN ⊙
I GORNITZKY & CO ⊙
YEHUDA RAVEH & CO ⊙.

EFRATI, GALILI & CO ⊙
GILEAD SHER & CO LAW OFFICES
JOSEPH LEVY & CO ⊙
MELCER & CO LAW OFFICES
S. HOROWITZ & CO ⊙
YIGAL ARNON & CO ⊙
ZELLERMAYER, PELOSSOF & CO., ADVOCATES ⊙

Baratz, Bar-Nathan & Co, Attorneys-at-Law & Notaries
Caspi & Co ⊙
Dankner Lusky & Co
Erdinast, Ben Nathan & Co ⊙
Fischer, Behar, Chen & Co ⊙
Goldfarb, Levy, Eran & Co
Gross, Kleinhendler, Hodak, Halevy, Greenberg & Co ⊙
M. Firon & Co Advocates and Notaries
Yaacov Salomon, Lipschutz & Co ⊙

Firms are listed A-Z in tiers which are ranked in order of priority
⊙ Indicates firm displays contact details at the end of this chapter.

Yehuda Raveh & Co. has a number of experts in this field, including Yehuda Raveh and Yehuda Glatt, who handle BOT and PFI projects, while Yuval Grayevsky serves as legal counsel to many large construction projects. Project finance is one of the firm's leading departments, which works for both borrowers and lenders.

Efrati, Galili & Co handles infrastructure projects for a very rich private individual whose efforts are shrouded in secrecy.

Gilead Sher & Co Law Offices is involved in some notable projects, including advising the government on the Jerusalem and Tel Aviv Light Railways and acting for the municipality of Beer Sheva in the construction of its new stadium. Founding partner Gilead Sher comes highly recommended and department head Amir Kadari is one to watch.

Joseph Levy & Co has a good track record in infrastructure projects, while **Melcer & Co Law Offices** has been involved in the Carmel Tunnels project.

S. Horowitz & Co advises on project financings in various sectors, including electricity, roads, tunnels, construction, telecommunications and infrastructure. The firm has advised sponsors, construction companies, consortium members, and lenders on most of the major projects in Israel. It also handles significant amounts of work in relation to Israel Electric Corporation construction, and has been involved in the plans for a $400m gas pipeline between Haifa and Tel Aviv.

Yigal Arnon & Co has a number of experts in corporate finance including Barry Levenfeld, Paul Baris, Eran Ilan, David Schapiro and David Osborne. It has represented a number of major international consortia tendering for national infrastructure and complex project finance undertakings.

Zellermayer, Pelossof & Co., Advocates also represents numerous infrastructure consortia and companies in Israeli BOTs and BOOs, including a US/UK/French/Israeli consortium bidding for the Cross-Israel Highway project.

Goldfarb, Levy, Eran & Co handled the financing of the Ashkelon desalination plant in an unusual structure that saw a bank put together institutional lenders in a syndicated loan.

Gross, Kleinhendler, Hodak, Halevy, Greenberg & Co has a team specialising in BOT and BOO projects, municipal debentures and similar issues.

M. Firon & Co Advocates and Notaries is active in many civil projects and Raphael Melman and Tamar Firon-Smorodinsky are key partners.

REAL ESTATE

Construction is in the doldrums because of the economic downturn. There is a sense that Israel has reached saturation in some of its urban centres and many property developers are facing financial crisis. However, firms like **Shraga F Biran & Co** retain excellent reputations for specialist real estate advice.

Weksler, Bregman & Co also has considerable experience in commercial and industrial real estate development, and has been involved in a variety of projects ranging from commercial centres and shopping malls to hotels. The firm represents Africa Israel Investments Ltd, one of the leading investment companies in Israel, which engages in land development, construction, trade, and hotels and tourism.

Yehuda Raveh & Co. provides legal services to construction enterprises and represents developers of all sizes, as well as statutory authorities active in industrial, commercial and residential development. It also handles a number of municipal projects. Among its clients is the Mamilla Project, a $300,000 residential, commercial and hotel development.

Yigal Arnon & Co has a team that represents some of the leading property companies both in Israel and abroad.

Balter, Guth, Aloni & Co is also active for domestic and foreign businesses. It also acts for kibbutzim and moshavim in selling and developing land.

Dankner Lusky & Co represents some of the largest development and construction companies in Israel in their large-scale acquisitions and development of commercial, mixed-use, hotel, shopping mall and residential projects and offers expertise in the field of real estate tax planning and construction financing.

Efrati, Galili & Co has seen at least one big deal of late and remains counsel to a Spanish hotel chain that owns, among other properties, a hotel on the Dead Sea.

Herzog, Fox & Neeman has still seen activity despite the downturn in construction, and the same is true for many firms. Firms such as **M. Firon & Co Advocates and Notaries**, **Meitar, Liquornik, Geva & Leshem Brandwein** and **Naschitz, Brandes & Co** nevertheless retain considerable expertise.

REAL ESTATE

SHRAGA F BIRAN & CO
WEKSLER, BREGMAN & CO ✪

YEHUDA RAVEH & CO. ✪
YIGAL ARNON & CO ✪

Balter, Guth, Aloni & Co
Caspi & Co ✪
Dankner Lusky & Co
Efrati, Galili & Co ✪
Fischer, Behar, Chen & Co ✪
Herzog, Fox & Neeman ✪
I Gornitzky & Co ✪
Kantor Elhanani Tal & Co
M. Firon & Co Advocates and Notaries
Meitar, Liquornik, Geva & Leshem Brandwein ✪
Miron, Bension & Prywes
Naschitz, Brandes & Co ✪
S Friedman & Co, Advocates ✪
S. Horowitz & Co ✪
Yaacov Salomon, Lipschutz & Co ✪
Yossifoff, Cohen & Co Law Offices
Yuval Levy & Co ✪

Aaronsohn, Aboulafia, Gal-On, Tzin, Amoday & Co
Amit, Pollak, Matalon & Co
Bach, Arad, Scharf & Co Law Offices
Baratz, Bar-Nathan & Co, Attorneys-at-Law & Notaries
Berkman Wechsler Sahar Bloom & Co
Cohen Wilchek & Co
Gilead Sher & Co Law Offices
Goldfarb, Levy, Eran & Co
Gross, Kleinhendler, Hodak, Halevy, Greenberg & Co ✪
Haim Zadok & Co ✪
Hamburger, Evron, Raviv-Berson & Co ✪
Hermann, Makov & Co
J Weinroth (Dr) & Co ✪
Joseph Levy & Co ✪
M Porath & Co
Raved Magriso Benkel & Co ✪
Ron Gazit, Rotenberg & Co
Shavit Bar-On Inbar, Law Offices ✪
Volovelsky, Dinstein, Sneh & Co
Zysman, Aharoni, Gayer & Co ✪

Firms are listed A-Z in tiers which are ranked in order of priority
✪ Indicates firm displays contact details at the end of this chapter.

SHIPPING AND TRANSPORT

Shipping and transport are areas where many smaller firms have a presence. Though many large firms may number companies involved in these industries among their clients, they are mostly active in corporate and commercial matters rather than issues relating specifically to shipping or transport matters.

Shipping is still active, but there are few players in Israel because of the Arab boycott.

S Friedman & Co, Advocates represents many Israeli shipowners and P&I clubs, and it is from this area of work that the firm grew into a broader commercial practice. Last year it was involved in a dispute between the Israeli Shippers Council and the shipowners themselves over handling charges. The firm also handles aircraft financing and has foreign companies, including a Portuguese entity among its clients.

The firm regularly encounters **Naschitz, Brandes & Co**, which has a specialisation in maritime law as well as an active shipping insurance practice.

Hermann, Makov & Co specialises in aviation, while **Ilan Orly & Co** is focused on its maritime practice.

Caspi & Co represents transport clients of many kinds, from airlines to bus companies, while **Primes, Shiloh, Givon, Meir, Law Firm** centres its practice on maritime issues.

SHIPPING AND TRANSPORT

S FRIEDMAN & CO, ADVOCATES ✪

NASCHITZ, BRANDES & CO ✪

Hermann, Makov & Co
Ilan Orly & Co
Leshem-Kipperman, Law Offices & Notary ✪

Caspi & Co ✪
Primes, Shiloh, Givon, Meir, Law Firm
S. Horowitz & Co ✪
Zaslansky & Harris

Elkes, Stern, Ascher, Rom
Jacov Rubin
M Seligman & Co
Yaacov Salomon, Lipschutz & Co ✪

Firms are listed A-Z in tiers which are ranked in order of priority
✪ Indicates firm displays contact details at the end of this chapter.

S. Horowitz & Co has a number of airlines as clients, along with courier company Fedex.

Zaslansky & Harris has acted in many maritime law cases, including the disputed arrest and subsequent sale by judicial execution of a container vessel for $1,750,000. It also acted in a charterparty dispute in which it represented owners in a claim against charterers relating to losses and damages resulting in a vessel's grounding at one of the load Ports.

Sole practitioner **Jacov Rubin** also runs a shipping and aviation-led practice.

TAX

Tax is another practice area that often overlaps with other work, particularly corporate and commercial, though some firms maintain separate specialist departments. Over the year a lot of work for lawyers in this area has stemmed from radical revision of Israeli tax laws, which, along with other changes, introduced taxation for Israelis working abroad.

Large firms retain tax experts in-house, but there are also a number of specialist tax boutiques that come very highly recommended.

Among these boutiques is **Dr Avi Alter & Co Law Offices**. Dr Alter formerly served as deputy income tax commissioner in Israel and head legal counsel to the Tax Commission before establishing his firm in 1990, and still regularly serves on various commissions. He is chairman of the Israeli branch of the International Fiscal Association, and the chairman of the Israeli Bar Tax Committee. He recently participated in two committees appointed by the Israeli Minister of Finance to recommend reforms in the Israeli tax code, particularly relating to income and real estate taxation.

D Potchebutzky Law Offices has maintained a top tier tax practice following the death of Jacob Potchebutzky in 2002 and is now run by Dr Gideon Klugman. The firm has represented many clients before the tax authorities and has appeared in many of the leading tax cases in Israel's history. The firm represents major foreign investors in planning investments in Israel, and includes cellular and telephone manufacturers and operators in the telecommunications field, as well as clients from many other industries.

Herzog, Fox & Neeman has a tax department that operates in conjunction with many other teams within the firm, and considers itself very strong in this area. All cross-border deals have tax implications so it is important for a firm with an international clientele to have this expertise. The firm is now working, for instance, on sheltering overseas trusts from domestic tax.

I Gornitzky & Co handles the tax planning implications for all the deals it does in its other practice areas, as well as servicing high-net-worth individuals. Partner Pinhas Rubin is recognised for his tax expertise, and he and Joshua Rosensweig have sat on committees nominated by the Secretary of Finance examining reform in real estate tax and income tax.

Goldfarb, Levy, Eran & Co has two excellent tax partners in Oded Eran and Tal Atsmon, while **Gross, Kleinhendler, Hodak, Halevy, Greenberg & Co** has added Dr Samuel Borenstein to head its newly enlarged tax department.

S Friedman & Co, Advocates has added to its tax expertise in its offices in the north of Israel through hiring Doron Schweppe and two other lawyers in Haifa. The firm specialises in both international and domestic tax.

Yigal Arnon & Co is also respected in tax law and **Balter, Guth, Aloni & Co** has a well-known partner and CPA in Avi Gera, while **M. Firon & Co Advocates and Notaries** has Michael Firon and Zvi Firon who are active in this area.

TAX

AVI ALTER & CO (DR) LAW OFFICES ✪
D POTCHEBUTZKY LAW OFFICES
HERZOG, FOX & NEEMAN ✪
I GORNITZKY & CO ✪

Goldfarb, Levy, Eran & Co
Gross, Kleinhendler, Hodak, Halevy, Greenberg & Co ✪
S Friedman & Co, Advocates ✪
Tulchinsky-Stern & Co
Yigal Arnon & Co ✪
Zellermayer, Pelossof & Co., Advocates ✪

A Rafael & Co
Amit, Pollak, Matalon & Co
Bach, Arad, Scharf & Co Law Offices
Balter, Guth, Aloni & Co
Berkman Wechsler Sahar Bloom & Co
Eitan, Pearl, Latzer & Cohen-Zedek
M. Firon & Co Advocates and Notaries
M Seligman & Co
Naschitz, Brandes & Co ✪
S. Horowitz & Co ✪
Shaham Shefet
Shiboleth, Yisraeli, Roberts, Zisman & Co ✪
Weksler, Bregman & Co ✪
Yaacov Salomon, Lipschutz & Co ✪
Yossifoff, Cohen & Co Law Offices

Firms are listed A-Z in tiers which are ranked in order of priority
✪ Indicates firm displays contact details at the end of this chapter.

TELECOMS

Many firms in Israel act for the state telecoms company, Bezeq, which is now facing competition for many services from the cable companies, the lengthy merger of which has been the main transaction in the last year. The telecoms activities of the cable companies have already merged and the focus is now on combining their broadcasting activities.

Avital, Dromi & Co is the undisputed leader in this area, and partners Ori Rahat and Ariel Lauri act for the cable companies and cellular network operators. The firm also represents the ICP production company, which operates the movie channel and the family channel. It is also involved in a huge project with Orange and Panther Communications relating to the operation of a 3G network in Israel.

Erdinast, Ben Nathan & Co is currently representing DBS Satellite Services, the first and only operator of satellite telecasting in Israel in a High Court action.

Herzog, Fox & Neeman has a telecommunications and media practice that offers transactional and regulatory services focused primarily on cross-border transactions. It has represented many international telecoms companies in Israel, including satellite and cable TV, mobile phone networks and Internet service providers.

I Gornitzky & Co deals with telecoms as part of its commercial work, while **Ron Gazit, Rotenberg & Co** acts for several telecoms and broadcasting companies, usually in regard to obtaining licences.

S. Horowitz & Co has acted for the banks in relation to the cable companies' merger.

TELECOMS

AVITAL, DROMI & CO ✪

ERDINAST, BEN NATHAN & CO ✪
HERZOG, FOX & NEEMAN ✪
I GORNITZKY & CO ✪
RON GAZIT, ROTENBERG & CO
S. HOROWITZ & CO ✪
ZELLERMAYER, PELOSSOF & CO., ADVOCATES ✪

ES SHIMRON, I MOLHO, PERSKY & CO ✪
GOLDFARB, LEVY, ERAN & CO
MEITAR, LIQUORNIK, GEVA & LESHEM BRANDWEIN ✪
YIGAL ARNON & CO ✪

Amir Nechmad
Caspi & Co ✪
Eitan, Pearl, Latzer & Cohen-Zedek
Fischer, Behar, Chen & Co ✪
J Weinroth (Dr) & Co ✪
Shiboleth, Yisraeli, Roberts, Zisman & Co J

Gross, Kleinhendler, Hodak, Halevy, Greenberg & Co ✪
Joseph Levy & Co ✪
Kantor Elhanani Tal & Co
M Seligman & Co
Schuman, Livnat & Mayer
Yaacov Salomon, Lipschutz & Co ✪
Yehuda Raveh & Co. ✪
Zysman, Aharoni, Gayer & Co ✪

Firms are listed A-Z in tiers which are ranked in order of priority
✪ Indicates firm displays contact details at the end of this chapter.

Zellermayer, Pelossof & Co., Advocates advises telecoms and data service providers in their day-to-day affairs. Recent clients include a consortium in a government bid for a licence to operate a system using LMDS and WLL protocols.

ES Shimron, I Molho, Persky & Co has a good reputation, while **Yigal Arnon & Co** represents many international and domestic companies.

Eitan, Pearl, Latzer & Cohen-Zedek provides antitrust, communications and transactional advice to clients active in the telecommunications field, while **Fischer, Behar, Chen & Co** represents many of Israel's largest firms in the industry. **Shiboleth, Yisraeli, Roberts, Zisman & Co** has Lior Aviram and Helena Beilin in its department, which represented Bezeq in a multi-million dollar purchase of a software billing system from Amdocs.**Gross, Kleinhendler, Hodak, Halevy, Greenberg & Co** advises several high-profile clients including leaders in the cellular phone industry.

AVITAL, DROMI & CO

53 HASHALOM ROAD
(VERED TOWER)
GIVATAYIM 53454

Telephone: +972 3 573 3000
Fax: +972 3 573 4000
E-mail: adlaw@adlaw.co.il

Languages
English, Hebrew

Other offices
Granot

Number of lawyers 16
at this office 14

CATEGORIES OF WORK

Telecommunications and entertainment law
Ori Rahat, Esther Sternbach

International commercial transactions
Arie Lamay, Gideon Avital

Corporate and commercial
Arie Lamay, Liad Sider

Information technology and hi-tech
Arie Lamay, Ori Rahat

Intellectual property
David Blum, Arie Lamay

Litigation
Itzhak Fink

Communications licensing
Ori Rahat, Esther Sternbach

Antitrust law
Liad Sider, Esther Sternbach

Energy law
Liad Sider, Gideon Avital

Infrastructure projects
Liad Sider, Jacob Dromi

Agricultural sector and real estate
Liad Sider, Ram Tsiddon

Chapter 11 proceedings
Arie Lamay, Ram Tsiddon

THE FIRM

Avital, Dromi & Co was established in 1986 by Gideon Avital and Jacob Dromi. Since then, the firm has grown and become specialised in various fields of law, including telecommunications law, international law and commercial law.

The firm is one of the leading law firms in Israel in the field of telecommunications law as well as various related fields.

The telecommunications team at Avital, Dromi & Co consists of seasoned lawyers with vast experience and expertise in this field. Founder Gideon Avital, former adviser to the Israeli Minister of Communications, is the chairman of the Israeli Bar Association's Telecommunication Legislation Committee. Esther Sternbach, formerly chief legal adviser to Bezeq, the Israeli Telecommunications Corporation, is a lecturer on telecommunications law in the law faculty of the Hebrew University in Jerusalem.

The activities of the firm involve frequent, close contact with all relevant regulatory authorities and governmental bodies in Israel. In order to remain informed of regulatory and technological developments worldwide, Avital, Dromi & Co maintains intensive, ongoing, working relationships with several US and European law firms that specialise in similar fields of practice.

AREAS OF PRACTICE

Avital, Dromi & Co represents Israel's leading telecommunications and hi-tech companies. The firm also represents foreign companies that have activities, interests and operations in Israel's growing telecommunications sector and local companies engaged in telecommunications ventures worldwide (Europe, US, South America and Asia).

The firm regularly advises the Israeli cable operators on the broad legal, commercial and regulatory aspects of their activities. These include participation in negotiations, preparation of various agreements for the purchase of content from foreign and local publishers, programmers and producers, dealing with competitive issues arising from the activity of Israel's DBS operator, regulatory matters concerning the content of television programming and advice concerning the cable operators' entry into telecommunications service provision.

The firm also specialises in a broad range of transactions relating to transmission, infrastructure and content. The firm accompanies its clients through all stages of their transactions: representation in the commercial negotiation; solving problems that arise during negotiation; examining legal aspects; drafting contracts; and, whenever required, obtaining permits from the authorities.

Avital, Dromi & Co also provides legal services to foreign companies, cellular operators, Internet service providers, satellite telecommunication companies and added-value services licensees that operate on local telephony, cable and cellular infrastructure. The firm provides its clients with licensing, commercial, contractual advice and general legal support.

Among the firm's other prominent clients are private and public companies that are involved in worldwide activities, mainly in the hi-tech and telecommunications infrastructure sectors. The firm also specialises in licensing agreements for software and technology and provides its clients with legal and commercial services worldwide.

In recent years, the firm has become intensively involved in the privatisation of Israel's agricultural sector whilst representing many kibbutzes (unincorporated associations). Avital, Dromi & Co has also provided these kibbutzes with legal services in the process of entry of investors to their hi-tech industries. The firm's northern branch in Granot was established mainly to provide these services.

Avital, Dromi & Co has also accompanied large projects related to the opening of Israel's electricity market to competition and other infrastructure projects.

YAACOV SALOMON, LIPSCHUTZ & CO

64 HAMEGINIM AVENUE
HAIFA 33264

Telephone: +972 4 853 5231
Fax: +972 4 855 7038
E-mail: office-haifa@ysl-law.com

Languages
Arabic, English, French

Other offices
Ramat Gan

Number of lawyers 30
at this office 25

Contact
David Goldenblatt
(david-goldenblatt@ysl-law.com)

CATEGORIES OF WORK

General law practice	Licensing
Corporate and commercial	Litigation
Taxation	Real estate and construction
Securities and investments	Town planning
Banks and banking	Capital markets
Labour	Energy
Insurance	Patents and trade marks
Franchises and franchising	Shipping and Admiralty

BARNEA & CO

AMZUR HOUSE
8 HASADNAOT STREET
HERZLIYA PITUACH 46728

Telephone: +972 9 9600 700
Fax: +972 9 9516 002
E-mail: mbarnea@barlaw.co.il
Website: www.barlaw.co.il

Languages
English, Hebrew, French, Spanish

Number of lawyers 12

CATEGORIES OF WORK

Securities and capital markets
Michael Barnea

Corporate and commercial
Michael Barnea, Simon Jaffa

Mergers and acquisitions
Michael Barnea, Simon Jaffa

Technology law
Michael Barnea,

International transactions
Michael Barnea, Simon Jaffa

Real estate
Aya Lavi-Bezalel, Susan Caspi

Private equity
Michael Barnea, Simon Jaffa

Private client, trusts
Simon Jaffa, Arie Ramot

Litigation and arbitration
Michael Barnea

Banking
Arie Ramot

EYAL KHAYAT, ZOLTY & CO

ACKERSTEIN TOWERS
9 HAMENOFIM STREET
PO BOX 2136
HERZLIYA PITUACH 46120

Telephone: +972 9 957 71 71
Fax: +972 9 957 71 77

Languages
English, Hebrew

Number of lawyers 6

Contacts
Eyal Khayat (eyal@khayatlaw.com)
Amir Zolty (amir@khayatlaw.com)

CATEGORIES OF WORK

Mergers and acquisitions

Company and commercial

Corporate finance

Hi-tech

YEHUDA RAVEH & CO

26 USISHKIN STREET
PO BOX 7722
JERUSALEM 91077

Telephone: +972 2 563 5232
Fax: +972 2 561 7101
E-mail: lawfirm@yraveh.co.il
Website: www.yraveh.co.il

Languages
English, French, German, Hebrew

Other offices
Beer-sheva, Haifa, Tel Aviv

Number of lawyers 46
at this office 28

CATEGORIES OF WORK

Infrastructure projects
Yehuda Raveh, Yehuda Glatt

Building and development
Lisa Tross, Yuval Grayevsky

Mergers and acquisitions
Yehuda Glatt, Yehuda Raveh

Planning and building law
Tamar Raveh, Uri Yamin

Antitrust
Carmit Bar-On

Hi-tech companies and projects
Yehuda Glatt, Yehuda Raveh

International law and international transactions
Yehuda Raveh, Yehuda Glatt

Corporate
Yehuda Raveh, Lisa Tross

Intellectual property
Gabi Robenbach

Taxation
Professor Itzhac Hadari

Litigation
Yuval Grayevsky, Haim Stern

Bankruptcy and liquidation
Hagai Ulman

Environmental matters
Sara Shalom

Banking
Lisa Tross, Yehuda Raveh

Privatisation of government corporations
Yehuda Raveh

Hotels
Carmit Bar-On, Yehuda Raveh

THE FIRM

The firm was established in the 1940s by Gideon Hausner, and has grown to be one of Israel's largest law firms. Mr Hausner served as the Attorney-General of Israel and as a cabinet minister in the country's government.

Today the firm is led by Mr Yehuda Raveh, and has a staff of 71 lawyers, associates and administrative personnel. The firm has grown from two lawyers in 1979 to 46. The firm has offices throughout the country in Jerusalem, Tel Aviv, Haifa and Beer-sheva.

AREAS OF PRACTICE

All aspects of commercial and corporate law, including, among others, real estate development and infrastructure projects (BOT), hotels, banking and insurance, mergers and acquisitions, corporate and project finance, national and international capital markets, privatisation, international transactions, litigation, environmental projects, intellectual property, bankruptcy cases, licensing, distributorship, trust of all kinds and estate planning.

The firm possesses special expertise in rendering services to foreign residents and foreign investors, be they large conglomerates, medium or small size corporations, or individuals. The firm has developed a unique knowledge of Israel's Free Trade Agreements with the EU and with the US and Canada, and the potential benefits of the use of such FTA's to manufacturers and exporters aiming at the EU and the US market.

The firm's main fields of specialisation are BOT and infrastructure projects, public and private income generating projects such as the Cross-Israel Highway, railways and light trains, sewage and water projects, student dormitories and tourist accomodation, shopping centres, office buildings and parking facilities. Mr Raveh was chosen to serve as a member of the BOT expert group of The United Nations.

The firm has been involved in the establishment and legal representation of technological incubators in Israel. The firm represents one of the largest R&D companies in the country and advises several other hi-tech companies. Mr Raveh serves as the president of one of the largest hi-tech groups of investors in start-up companies. The group has invested seed money in many hi-tech companies and continues to do so successfully.

The firm represents major developers and constructors of both residential and commercial projects and industrial parks all over the country. The firm has expertise in hotel development and hotel management throughout Israel and represents numerous owners, developers and major national and international hotel companies.

The firm advises banking clients on a case-by-case basis, on different matters ranging from legal options on various banking matters, to negotiations of complicated project finance, conducting due diligence process for banks and other lending institutions and serving as receivers and liquidators in bankruptcy cases.

The firm has developed unique expertise in the telecommunications field, including television, cable TV and the Internet.

The firm handles extensive distributorship agreements, mergers and acquisitions (mainly for foreign investors), telecommunications transactions, bankruptcy and liquidation proceedings and intellectual property matters.

The firm's tax department accompanies all transactions handled by the firm, covering local and international corporate and individual tax aspects.

COHEN LAHAT & CO

GIBOR SPORT BUILDING
25TH FLOOR
7 MENACHEM BEGIN STREET
RAMAT GAN 52521

Telephone: +972 3 611 0611
Fax: +972 3 611 0600
E-mail: cld@cldlaw.co.il
Website: www.cldlaw.co.il

Languages
English, Hebrew, Spanish

Number of lawyers 18

Contact
Dan Lahat

CATEGORIES OF WORK

- Corporate and securities
- Foreign direct investment
- Corporate restructuring
- Mergers and acquisitions
- Dispute resolution, litigation and arbitration
- Media advertising and entertainment
- Real estate
- Intellectual property

THE FIRM

The firm was founded in August 1989 by two partners who had previously worked in a leading Israeli firm. The firm is young, yet well-experienced. It is located in the greater Tel Aviv area, in the centre of Israel. The partners have handled very large and complicated transactions and litigation cases in Israel, as well as in Europe, the USA and Latin America. The firm is on the rise (in the past year seven associates have joined the firm) and has earned wide professional recognition in its areas of practice. A wide variety of professional and efficient legal services are offered by the firm, including current legal counselling to various companies and corporations, especially in the areas of capital markets, information technology, corporate/commercial law, real estate and commercial property.

The firm has acquired unique experience in IPOs and private placements in various capital markets around the world. It also represents a wide variety of clients in various legal disputes and claims, including judicial and administrative proceedings and arbitration. The firm is currently involved with assisting start-up companies and with rendering services to capital ventures, investment banks, capital market brokers and commercial property investors.

AREAS OF PRACTICE

The firm's pillars of practice are capital markets, hi-tech and investment transactions (both domestic and foreign), real estate and litigation. On these pillars stands the firm's distinguished body of knowledge and experience in various complicated issues and subjects. The firm's activities in capital markets has included involvement in public offerings and private placements for Israeli and foreign companies on the NASDAQ, New York Stock Exchange, Alternative Investment Market (AIM), Neuer Markt and Tel-Aviv Stock Exchange. The firm has represented issuers and underwriters and has accumulated significant knowledge, experience and familiarity with the various laws pertaining to securities and exchanges worldwide.

The firm's vast experience in the field of commercial transactions includes the handling of the tax implications and tax planning aspects of such transactions. These transactions have included, among others, deals with foreign investors, transactions for the sale of companies or commercial operations, the setting-up of partnerships and joint ventures, in Israel, Europe, the USA and Latin America. The firm has vast experience in representing venture capitals (VC) and investors in various transactions.

The firm also renders ongoing and comprehensive consultation and representation services to a wide range of businesses, including leading food manufacturers and distributors, a major retail supermarket chain, leading advertising agencies, construction corporations and private business persons. These services include different areas of law, such as intellectual property, including the registration of trade marks, legal opinions and representation in regard to tax matters, employment and subcontracting, suppliers (inclusive of comprehensive system suppliers) and computerisation and software. The firm has developed special expertise in commercial agency and licensing agreements.

The firm's extensive contacts and expertise enable it to advise on the wider issues that may arise in the course of real estate transactions. The firm is involved in all aspects of construction and planning, including the acquisition, sale and lease of commercial properties, all related transactions and agreements, the representation of entrepreneurs in all planning institutions, and litigation in administrative courts and tribunals.

The firm has vast experience in various types of disputes conducted by arbitration or litigation in Israel's courts, including all commercial and administrative issues, appeals and related criminal proceedings. The firm renders litigation services to both domestic and foreign clientele. The firm is representing both claimants and defendants, at all instances of court and tribunals in Israel, including Israel's Supreme Court.

DANZIGER, KLAGSBALD, ROSEN & CO

GIBOR SPORT BUILDING
7 MENACHEM BEGIN ST
(28 BEZALEL STREET)
RAMAT GAN 52521

Telephone: +972 3 611 0700
Fax: +972 3 611 0707
E-mail: office@danklaw.co.il

Languages
Dutch, English, French, Hebrew

Number of lawyers 29

Contact
Dr Yoram Danziger

CATEGORIES OF WORK

Corporate law
Yoram Danziger

Litigation
Avigdor Klagsbald

Hi-tech
Ori Rosen

Real estate/liquidation and receiverships
Ronen Matry

THE FIRM

Danziger, Klagsbald, Rosen & Co is one of Israel's leading corporate firms. The firm is known for its experience, professionalism and expertise in two major areas: the first–corporate, venture capital and hi-tech legal advice and representation; and second–complex civil and commercial litigation.

The firm is an active international practice, representing Israeli companies operating internationally, and international corporations operating in Israel or seeking advice in Israel-relating matters.

The firm has represented major US and foreign venture capital firms in their investments in Israel and Israeli-related companies, and assisted US banking institutions in granting secured working capital loans to technology and venture-stage Israeli companies. In representing such clients, the firm provides advice on: formation of domestic and foreign venture capital limited partnerships; internal management, compensation and distribution arrangements; diligence reviews and propriety information audits, including preparation and negotiation of licence and other technology transfer agreements; and structures of venture capital 'portfolio company' investments, including bridge loans, convertible stock, common stock, warrants, notes, leveraged buy-outs and leasing transactions. Amongst others, the firm acts for issuers, underwriters, placement agents and investors in public and private placements, M&A and similar transactions. It is also involved in venture capital and hi-tech activity in Israel, representing local and foreign venture capital funds in their investments.

The firm represents a range of international clients in the manufacturing, software, telecommunication, shipping and transportation, banking and finance, and many other sectors.

AREAS OF PRACTICE

Corporate law: The firm serves as legal counsel to numerous private companies, as well as to publicly-held companies. The firm provides day-to-day legal advice on aspects of corporate operations, including directors' and officers' duties, indemnification and the business judgement rule. The firm regularly provides advice to corporate boards of directors and board committees on governance matters.

Advising on all aspects of M&A, the firm is adept at handling the acquisition and financing of public and private companies of any size. The firm also represents clients in a variety of commercial transactions, strategic alliances and other business relationships.

Hi-tech: The firm is recognised as a leader in the representation of venture capital funds, start-ups, and hi-tech companies, providing counsel to many of Israel's top venture capital and investment banking firms.

The firm provides numerous companies in emerging hi-tech markets such as software, hardware, semiconductors, communications, Internet and e-commerce, and life sciences, with counsel for addressing day-to-day business issues. The firm has participated in the formation and growth of numerous technology-related companies and works with clients through all phases of growth, helping to start venture capital investments, preparing and carrying out IPOs, and orchestrating major M & A deals and strategic partnering arrangements.

Litigation: The firm represents domestic and international clients before courts and arbitration panels, including the Israeli Supreme Court, lower courts and judicial and administrative tribunals, and have set several notable precedents in areas of company law, constitutional law, bids and tenders, antitrust, and white collar/economic crime. The firm has special expertise in: securities and corporate control litigation; antitrust and trade regulation; commercial arbitration; criminal defense; bankruptcy law; liquidations; and receiverships.

Real estate: Has extensive experience in development and entrepreneurship of properties and construction projects.

HAMBURGER, EVRON, RAVIV-BERSON & CO

PAZ TOWERS
31 BEZALEL STREET
RAMAT GAN 52521

Telephone: +972 3 751 7124
Fax: +972 3 751 7130
E-mail: evron@evronlaw.com

Languages
English, Hebrew, Russian, Spanish

Number of lawyers 30

CATEGORIES OF WORK

Banking and finance
Gabriel Moyal, Asal Englard

Bankruptcy and liquidation
Gabriel Moyal, Menachem Abramovich

Zoning, planning and construction
Amnon Evron, Haim Weintrob

Intellectual property
Oded Evron

Real estate
Haim Weintrob, Dor Shacham

Administrative and public
Amnon Evron, Haim Weintrob

International transactions
Shai Pines, Oded Evron

Tax law
Amnon Sorek

Commercial and company law
Amnon Sorek, Oded Evron

Arbitration
Amnon Evron

Corporate finance
Oded Evron

THE FIRM

Hamburger, Evron, Raviv-Berson & Co is one of Israel's longest-practising and most respected law firms. Founded in 1928 by the late Arie Hamburger, the firm has been headed by senior partner Amnon Evron since the mid-1970s. The firm has evolved over the passing decades into a highly diversified practice, involved in numerous high-profile trial cases and notable domestic transactions. The firm has recently merged with the law firm S Pines & Co, established in 1990, and now employs some 60 individuals.

AREAS OF PRACTICE

The merged firm is a full-service practice, and efficient in the following areas: international transactions; banking and financial services; bankruptcy and liquidation; commercial; property and real estate; development and taxation; zoning; planning and construction; corporate; communications; hi-tech, mergers and acquisitions; securities; intellectual property and technology transfer; local taxation; international tax planning; civil and administrative litigation; class actions; white-collar crime litigation; and labour.

MEITAR, LIQUORNIK, GEVA & LESHEM BRANDWEIN

16 ABBA HILLEL SILVER ROAD
RAMAT GAN 52506

Telephone: +972 3 610 3100
Fax: +972 3 610 3111
E-mail: meitar@meitar.co.il
Website: www.meitar.co.il

Languages
English, Hebrew

Other offices
Jerusalem

Number of lawyers 58

CATEGORIES OF WORK

Corporate
Dan Geva, Dror Brandwein

Litigation
Israel Leshem, Israel Pfeffer

Securities
Cliff Felig, Dan Shamgar

Venture capital and start-ups
Maya Liquornik, David Chertok

Mergers and acquisitions
Dan Geva, Dan Shamgar

Technology
Maya Liquornik, Bill Galkin

Labour and employment
Moti Arad

Antitrust and administrative
Moti Arad

White-collar criminal
Israel Leshem, Nadav Weisman

Commercial transactions
Yoram Movshovitz, Edo Likhovski

Telecoms
Daphna Nechmad, Ronen Bezalel

Life sciences
David Chertok, Raanan Lerner

Insurance
Dror Brandwein

Banking and derivatives
Cliff Felig, David Glatt

Real estate
Amos Goren

Taxation
Meir Akunis

THE FIRM

Meitar Liquornik Geva & Leshem Brandwein is a leading Israeli law firm with a reputation for excellence on domestic and international matters. MLG&LB provides clients with comprehensive expert counsel and representation in a variety of business contexts, from sophisticated transactions to complex litigation and beyond. The approach has always been to ensure that each client's matters are handled by the best professionals in the relevant area of expertise, with a view towards meeting their business objectives. Clients are represented from both the international and domestic Israeli business communities and professionals offer clients in-depth knowledge of, and expertise in, a number of disciplines and industries, hands-on international legal experience and innovative thinking.

Working closely with clients and with their non-Israeli counsel, the firm facilitates cross-border transactions, bridge international boundaries and assists clients by opening doors both in Israel and overseas. Through all stages of clients' growth, from seed financing, through private and public offerings, mergers and acquisitions and beyond, the firm brings distinct added value and among the finest international and domestic representation to clients to help them achieve their strategic goals. The firm regularly assists non-Israeli clients in understanding the local business culture and landscape, including its local players, as well as regulatory processes and the Israeli judiciary.

MLG&LB's clients include leading multinational and domestic corporations, private and publicly-traded companies in areas such as technology, communications, pharmaceutical and medical, media and publishing, energy, construction, banking, financial services and advertising, venture capital funds and investment companies, investment banks, holding companies and high-net-worth individuals.

MLG&LB was created by the merger of two leading Israeli law firms, Meitar, Liquornik, Geva & Co and Leshem, Brandwein & Co., each leaders in their respective fields.

AREAS OF PRACTICE

Corporate and securities: a major part of the firm's work consists of venture capital investments; public offerings; M&A; private placements; equity and debt offerings in Israel and abroad; banking and derivatives; and securitisations. The firm also specialises in corporate restructuring, including splits, spin-offs, share buy-backs, joint ventures and management buy-outs. The firm acts regularly in corporate, partnership and joint venture formation, establishment and implementation of stock option and compensation plans, and financing transactions.

Litigation: this department handles a wide range of commercial litigation, including contests for corporate control and class actions, labour law and insurance matters. Its attorneys appear in all Israeli courts, arbitration proceedings, and specialised courts and regulatory bodies.

Technology: the firm is intensively involved in structuring and negotiating the international transactions of its clients: OEM; licensing; distribution; VAR; joint development; outsourcing and similar agreements with expertise in complex software transactions. The firm handles all aspects of deals including: participation in negotiations on the commercial terms; drafting of agreements; setting up local entities; creating financial arrangements; ensuring protection of intellectual property rights; and co-operating with local counsel worldwide.

Telecoms: the firm acts for one of Israel's largest conglomerates involved in telecoms provision, represents one of Israel's three international operators, and has represented clients in tenders for cellular operations, as well as in many regulatory, telecoms and antitrust issues.

Taxation: the firm provides tax advice and planning in a range of areas: international taxation; corporate tax planning; employee compensation plans; real estate; trusts and estates; and personal tax planning.

General legal services: the firm also provides services in areas such as: real estate, banking and commercial papers; regulatory matters; labour-related issues; antitrust and other matters.

DR AVI ALTER & CO

LAW OFFICES

8 SHAUL HAMELECH BLVD
TEL AVIV 64733

Telephone: +972 3 696 66 33
Fax: +972 3 696 66 63
E-mail: avnat@altertax.co.il
Website: www.altertax.co.il

Languages
English, German, Hebrew

Number of lawyers 11

CATEGORIES OF WORK

International/national taxation
Anat Tenne, Udi Shostak

International/national tax planning
Dr Avi Alter, Ziv Sharon

Direct and indirect taxation
Udi Shostak, Nir Horenstein

Tax rulings in Israel and abroad
Amichai Pery, Anat Tenne

Taxation of mergers and acquisitions
Nir Horenstein, Helena Ben-Baruch

Taxation of public offerings, ESOPs and ESPPs
Amichai Pery, Shlomi Regev

Taxation of hi-tech companies and employees
Shlomi Regev, Ori Kalif

Tax litigation
Ronen Aroyo, Ziv Sharon

Arbitration
Helena Ben-Baruch, Sharon Bachar (Ben-David)

Israeli tax legislation – advisers and initiators
Dr Avi Alter, Ziv Sharon

THE FIRM

The firm was established in 1990 by Dr Avraham Alter Adv who, until that time, served as deputy income tax commissioner in Israel and head legal counsel to the Tax Commission.

Dr Alter has been practicing tax law for the past 20 years and has served on various commissions and organisations, such as the chairman of the Israeli branch of the International Fiscal Association, and the chairman of the Israeli Bar Tax Committee. He is today considered one of the top tax lawyers in the country.

Recently, Dr Alter has participated in two committees appointed by the Israeli Minister of Finance to recommend reforms in the Israeli tax code. The recommendations of these committees, regarding the real estate taxation, and the taxation of income, were accepted by the Knesset in 2002.

Dr Alter is also a lecturer in tax law at the law, accounting and business administration faculties at the Bar Ilan University, and co-ordinator of taxation subjects at the same faculties.

AREAS OF PRACTICE

Since the firm specialises only in tax law, it maintains direct and daily contact with the Israeli tax authorities. It can therefore advise its clients not only on the black letter law, but also on the different trends and opinions of the different Israeli tax authorities.

The firm also attains for the benefit of its clients tax rulings from the Israeli tax authorities, as well as from other tax jurisdictions.

The firm's client base includes famous international and national clients, including governments, governmental agencies, national and international banks, major conglomerates, computer software companies, space and military technologies, hi-tech corporations, political parties, real estate companies, investment funds and companies, and national and international organisations in other fields.

One of the firm's most active practices is the international taxation of public offerings, including buy-outs as well as employee stock option plans. The firm has achieved many successes in this area, including very unique tax rulings which grant the client not only a deferral on taxes, but also a reduction of taxes.

The firm also specialises in international tax planning, tax treaties and offshore jurisdictions. It establishes such corporate structures for its clients and continues to maintain a close relationship with the client throughout the project to avoid mistakes. The firm has excellent ties with the best tax advisers throughout the globe, and can therefore provide its clients with a full package deal for their international tax planning.

The VAT and betterment tax departments of the firm provide tax planning and consultation to corporate as well as individual clients, whether national or international. The firm, among other things, represents clients in their dealings with the various tax authorities, submits reports on their behalf, and gives detailed explanation to their accountants or other advisers, granting the clients a full package tax representation.

Moreover, as a matter of daily routine, the firm supplies written tax opinions in English and Hebrew, and provides any other legal assistance the client may wish in their dealings with the tax authorities. Since the firm only deals with tax aspects, it always maintains close ties with the client's other legal advisers, supplying them with current full and exact advice as to the tax aspects of the representation.

Other important practice areas include providing advice in connection with specific agreements and transactions as well as representing the clients in all tax litigations, and representing clients in the Israeli courts and on tax instances.

CASPI & CO

33 YAVETZ STREET
TEL AVIV 65258

Telephone: +972 3 796 1000
Fax: +972 3 796 1001
E-mail: office@caspilaw.co.il

Number of lawyers 30

Contact
Norman Menachem Feder

CATEGORIES OF WORK

Administrative and constitutional
Ram Caspi, Gad Ticho

Civil
Ram Caspi

Commercial and corporate (domestic)
Ram Caspi

Commercial and corporate (international)
Norman Menachem Feder

Competition
David Tadmor

Construction and housing
Assaph Caspi

Criminal
Navot Tel-Tzur

Energy
Ram Caspi

Finance (derivatives/securitisation/ structured)
Norman Menachem Feder

Finance (project)
Norman Menachem Feder

Litigation and arbitration
Gad Ticho, Navot Tel Zur

Real estate and conveyancing
Assaph Caspi , Guy Caspi

Securities
Ram Caspi, Ami Gilad

Telecommunications
Yossi Abadi

Transportation
Assaph Caspi, Orna Kedar

ES SHIMRON, I MOLHO, PERSKY & CO

PLATINUM TOWER
21 HA'ARBA'AH STREET
TEL AVIV 64739

Telephone: +972 3 685 3685
Fax: +972 3 685 3853
E-mail: officeta1@smplaw.co.il

Languages
English, French, German, Hebrew, Italian

Other offices
Jerusalem

Number of lawyers 22
at this office 9

Contact
Orrin Persky

CATEGORIES OF WORK

Corporate and commercial
Isaac Molho, David N Shimron

Mergers and acquisitions
Isaac Molho, Orrin Persky

Competition and antitrust law
Jakob Melcer, Dov Abramowitz

Telecoms and entertainment law
Isaac Molho, Dov Abramowitz

Charitable organisations
Isaac Molho, David N Shimron

Energy
David N Shimron, Dov Abramowitz

Labour
Michal Arlosoroff, Tel Ranel-Cohen

Liquidation, insolvency and bankruptcy
Isaac Molho, Jakob Melcer

Real estate development
Orrin Persky, David N Shimron

Intellectual property
Isaac Molho, Michal Shur-Ofry

Hi-tech
Isaac Molho, Orrin Persky

Banking and securities
David N Shimron, Michal Arlosoroff

Government authorities
David N Shimron, Shai Ganor

Civil and commercial litigation
Orrin Persky, Michael Rabello

Wills and trusts
Orrin Persky, Michal Arlosoroff

Venture capital
Isaac Molho, Shai Ganor

ERDINAST, BEN NATHAN & CO

25 NACHMANI STREET
TEL AVIV 65794

Telephone: +972 3 621 2500
Fax: +972 3 525 0896
E-mail: office@ebnlaw.co.il
Website: www.ebnlaw.co.il

Languages
English, French, Hebrew

Number of lawyers 22

CATEGORIES OF WORK

Corporate and commercial law	International transactions
Commercial litigation	Mergers and acquisitions
Telecoms and media	Energy and infrastructure
Venture capital	Project finance
Technology	Banking and finance
Intellectual property	Class actions
Antitrust	Constitutional law
Securities	Administrative law

THE FIRM

Erdinast, Ben Nathan & Co was established in 1988 by Giora Erdinast and Rami Ben-Nathan. The firm is located in the heart of Tel Aviv's business district and consists of 22 advocates (four partners and 18 associates) and several trainee advocates. Having played a major role in some of the most complex transactions and legal proceedings conducted in Israel in recent years, the firm is recognised as one of the leading commercial law firms in the country.

The firm represents some of the most prominent corporations and institutions in the Israeli economy, and has developed a wide ranging international network. The firm's client roster includes publicly traded corporations, multinational corporations, entrepreneurial companies, venture capital funds, insurance companies, banks, and financial institutions.

Most of the firm's attorneys graduated with honours, some are admitted to the New York State Bar, and others have served as assistant teachers and lecturers in various fields of law or on the editorial boards of their universities' legal publications.

The firm's multilingual legal team provides a profound knowledge and deep understanding of the markets, both local and overseas, in which the firm is involved. Work is undertaken with a commercial approach and in a highly professional manner.

AREAS OF PRACTICE

The firm specialises in civil and commercial law, with particular emphasis on corporate law, mergers and acquisitions, media and communications, antitrust law, capital markets, banking, project finance, class actions, and commercial litigation.

The firm acts as general counsel to businesses of all types, including some of the leading corporations in Israel, and serves as special counsel in a variety of matters. The firm routinely represents its clients in complex transactions, including multinational transactions, investment agreements, financing agreements, mergers and acquisitions, takeovers, public and private offerings, entrepreneurial agreements, BOT and PFI agreements, and various other commercial agreements. The firm also represents various corporate clients in a wide variety of commercial litigation with a special focus on mergers and acquisitions, class actions, antitrust law, banking law, communications and media law, and petitions to the High Court of Justice on fundamental issues of administrative law.

In order to maintain and enhance its position at the forefront of the Israeli legal community, the firm constantly expands and diversifies its legal competencies in response to changes in the economy and in the corporate world. The firm's growing reputation in the areas of communications and hi-tech in recent years and its focus on project finance and banking law are examples of this approach.

The firm is morally and professionally committed to the exercise of its professional capacity for the good of the public at large and is always prepared to consider pro-bono representation.

EFRATI, GALILI & CO

6 WISSOTSKY STREET
TEL AVIV 62338

Telephone: +972 3 545 2020
Fax: +972 3 604 0111
E-mail: office@eglaw.co.il
Website: www.efratigalili.com

Languages
English, French, Hebrew

Number of lawyers 20

Contact
Karin Mayer Rubinstein

CATEGORIES OF WORK

General corporate and commercial
Alon Galili, Hanan Feldmus

M&A, joint ventures
David Efrati, Alon Galili

Capital markets, finance, securities
David Efrati, Hanan Feldmus

Venture capital, private equity
David Efrati, Ian Rostowsky

Technology
David Efrati, Ian Rostowsky

Life sciences and pharmaceuticals
David Efrati, Karin Mayer Rubinstein

Privatisation
David Efrati, Hanan Feldmus

Infrastructure and project finance
David Efrati, Karin Mayer Rubinstein

Government and municipalities
David Efrati, Karin Mayer Rubinstein

Competition
Alon Galili, Tal Tsuk

Litigation, dispute resolution
Alon Galili, Merav Tabib

Class actions
Alon Galili, Merav Niv-Geva

Environment and energy
Alon Galili, Merav Niv-Geva

Wills, trusts and estates
David Efrati, Alon Galili

Insurance
Alon Galili, Hanan Feldmus

Labour law
Alon Galili, Merav Niv-Geva

Real estate and tourism
David Efrati, Alon Galili

FISCHER, BEHAR, CHEN & CO

3 DANIEL FRISCH ST
TEL AVIV 64731

Telephone: +972 3 694 4111
Fax: + 972 3 609 1116
E-mail: fbc@fbclawyers.com
Website: www.fbclawyers.com

Languages
Arabic, English, French, German, Hebrew, Hungarian, Serbo-Croatian, Spanish, Yiddish

Number of lawyers 50

CATEGORIES OF WORK

Litigation
Reuven Behar, Dr Gil Orion

Antitrust
Tal Eyal-Boger, Tamar Turjeman

Corporate
Avraham Well, Eran Yaniv

International
Avi Fischer, Ronald Lehmann

Telecommunications
Reuven Behar

Real estate
Amir Chen, Michal Faktor

Securities
Avraham Well, Nataly Mishan

Intellectual property
Reuven Behar, Karni Lotan

Administrative
Yoram Bonen

Technology
Avi Fischer, Atir Hardof-Jaffe

Trusts and estates
Isachar Fischer

Labour
Romina Rafe-Meyer

GROSS, KLEINHENDLER, HODAK, HALEVY, GREENBERG & CO

AZRIELI CENTER ONE
CIRCULAR BUILDING
TEL AVIV 67021

Telephone: +972 3 607 4444
Fax: +972 3 607 4422
E-mail: law@gkh-law.com
Website: www.gkh-law.com

Languages
English, Arabic, Dutch, French, German, Spanish, Hebrew

Number of lawyers 52

Contacts
Prof Joseph Gross (chairman),
Amir Halevy (managing partner)

CATEGORIES OF WORK

Commercial and corporate	**Taxation**
Securities and underwriting	**Commercial property**
Technology and venture capital	**Real estate**
Mergers and acquisitions	**Litigation**
Investments	**Antitrust and competition**
Intellectual property	**Labour and employment**
Cross-border transactions	

THE FIRM

In January 2001, Prof Joseph Gross, Hodak, Greenberg & Co (est 1979) merged with Kleinhendler and Halevy (est 1984) to form Gross, Kleinhendler, Hodak, Halevy, Greenberg & Co.

GKH is engaged in all aspects of corporate and commercial legal practice, representing a large number of publicly held corporations traded on US, Israeli and European stock exchanges. The firm also represents international investment banks, privately held corporations of all sizes, newly formed businesses, partnerships and joint ventures. Clients served comprise a broad range of industrial, commercial, energy, retail, transportation, financial, and service enterprises. The firm's expertise includes representation before government ministries, regulatory agencies and the Bank of Israel.

Several firm members are licensed to practise in the US and Europe, and much of the firm's work is conducted in English.

AREAS OF PRACTICE

GKH's attorneys advise on a wide range of corporate matters including corporate governance, dividend distributions, compensation, indemnification and insurance of officers and directors, and shareholder agreements.

Commercial transactions: GKH's work in this area encompasses all forms of domestic and international commercial transactions, including the perfection of security interests in tangible and intangible property, and franchising. The firm's attorneys draft commercial contracts including licensing, lease, distribution and manufacturer representation agreements, as well as agency and non-competition agreements.

GKH's restrictive trade department conducts ongoing reviews of issues relating to various transactions, handles local and international merger filings and exemption requests related to restrictive arrangements.

Public financing, securities and corporate finance: specialising in both US and Israeli securities law, GKH has represented hundreds of issuers in connection with domestic and international, equity and debt securities offerings. The firm also counsels major international underwriters and investment banks in connection with securities offerings of Israeli companies and other aspects of their activities in Israel. GKH's attorneys represent clients in private placements, bridge financing, mezzanine financing, credit agreements, project finance, securitisation and repurchase agreements.

GKH have long been advising clients on formation of start-ups through to public and private offerings, in Israel, the US and Europe. GKH also counsels venture capital funds on their structure, and handles financing rounds from seed through mezzanine financing. The firm's IP department provides services with regard to trade marks, licensing arrangements and real time consultation with international patent attorneys working in affiliation with GKH.

Renowned for its involvement in complex reorganisations, and in M&A activities of large Israeli and multinational organisations, GKH provides comprehensive coverage from structuring transactions, tax planning, negotiation, court submissions, and representation before regulatory bodies. The firm represents offerors and offerees in tender offers and takeovers, and acts as counsel in proxy contests.

Tax: GKH provides strategic tax planning to corporations on a variety of transactions and to individuals on complex tax issues. The department also prepares opinions relating to interpretation of tax laws.

GKH's rapidly expanding litigation department deals with all aspects of commercial litigation, including claims filed in Israel by or against multinational organisations and government agencies.

GKH provides advice on all aspects of employment law ranging from representation at tribunals to retirement benefits counselling senior officers.

Telecommunications: specialising in company restructuring, cross ownership and preparation of tender offers, the firm also provides advice and opinions to local regulatory authorities concerning the establishment and implementation of new laws and practices. GKH's ongoing observation of global developments in this field provide its internationally active clients with a full range of current advice.

GILAT, BAREKET & CO

5 HAR SINAI STREET
PO BOX 4480
TEL AVIV 61044

Telephone: +972 3 566 7999
Fax: +972 3 566 9030
E-mail: info@gilatadv.co.il
Website: www.rcip.co.il

Languages
Arabic, English, French, German, Hebrew, Portuguese

Number of lawyers 40
at this office 10

Contact
Daphna Gilat

CATEGORIES OF WORK

Intellectual property

Information technology

Hi tech, computers and software

Antitrust and trade regulations

Pharmaceuticals, biotechnology

Commercial and corporate

Technology transfer

Franchises

Litigation

Advertising and marketing

HAIM ZADOK & CO

RUBINSTEIN BUILDING
18TH FLOOR
20 LINCOLN STREET
TEL AVIV 67134

Telephone: +972 3 625 4000
Fax:+972 3 625 4040
E-mail: general@zadokco.co.il
Website: www.zadokco.co.il

Languages
Arabic, English, French, German, Hebrew, Hungarian, Italian

Number of lawyers 29

CATEGORIES OF WORK

Corporate and commercial
Ilan Shavit, Tzachi Feldman, Gideon Toledano

Banking and finance
Ilan Shavit, Nitza R Posner

Bankruptcy and reorganisation
Ilan Shavit, Nitza R Posner

Investment
Dan Meridor, Ilan Shavit, Gideon Toledano

International business
Dan Meridor, Ilan Shavit, Gideon Toledano

Arbitration and mediation
Dan Meridor, Eyal Rosovsky

Real estate
Avi Drexler, Tzachi Feldman

Litigation and dispute resolution
Eyal Rosovsky

Constitutional and administrative
Dan Meridor

Hi tech and securities law
Tzachi Feldman, Gideon Toledano

Liquidation and receivership
Ilan Shavit, Nitza R Posner

Environmental
Ehood Schneider

Competition
Gideon (Doni) Toledano

Infrastructure
Ehood Schneider

HERZOG, FOX & NEEMAN

ASIA HOUSE
4 WEIZMANN STREET
TEL AVIV 64239

Telephone: +972 3 692 2020
Fax: +972 3 696 6464
E-mail: hfn@hfn.co.il
Website: www.hfn.co.il

Languages
Hebrew, English, French, German

Number of lawyers 82

Contact
Michael Fox (senior partner)

Member
World Law Group; International Bar Association

CATEGORIES OF WORK

Corporate
Michael Fox, Alan Sacks

Mergers and acquisitions
Alan Sacks, Janet Levy Pahima

Capital markets and securities
Ehud Sol

Banking and finance
Alan Sacks, Eliot Sacks

Telecoms and media
Yaacov Sharvit

Venture capital and investment funds
Janet Levy Pahima, Eldar Ben-Ruby

Infrastructure development and project finance
Michael Fox, Adam Eytan

Commercial litigation and arbitration
Tuvia Erlich

Tax
Meir Linzen, Eldar Ben-Ruby

Real estate and construction
Yaakov Brandt

Labour and employment
Meir Linzen, Orly Gerbi

Energy and natural resources
Michael Fox, Adam Eytan

Commercial law
Amir Seraya

Intellectual property and IT
Neil Wilkof

Antitrust and competition
Ehud Sol

Internet and e-commerce
Meir Linzen

Administrative and public law
Meir Linzen

THE FIRM

Herzog, Fox & Neeman (HFN) is one of Israel's foremost corporate and commercial law offices representing leading companies worldwide. HFN was founded in 1972 by the late Chaim Herzog, later to become the sixth president of the State of Israel; Michael Fox, formerly a partner in a London law firm; and Dr Yaakov Neeman, author of numerous books and articles on tax law and one of Israel's foremost authorities on income tax. HFN has grown into Israel's largest (as rated by Dun and Bradstreet) and best-known international corporate law firms. Its legal staff comprises a significant number of native English speakers with experience in leading international firms in the US, the UK and Australia.

AREAS OF PRACTICE

The firm's principal practice areas are corporate; M&A; tax; banking and finance; infrastructure development and project finance; capital markets and securities; commercial litigation; IP/IT; telecoms; property and construction; energy and natural resources; the Internet and e-commerce; venture capital; employment; and antitrust and competition.

The corporate department at HFN is among the largest and most experienced in Israel, with much of its work internationally sourced. The lawyers in this department have a wealth of experience in a range of corporate work, including: share purchases/sales; joint ventures; mergers; corporate re-organisations; and asset purchases/sales. The firm continues to feature prominently in significant international transactions.

HFN's tax department is the largest of any Israeli law firm and covers all aspects of taxation relating to commercial activities in Israel. It's main focus is the provision of tax advice to Israeli and cross-border transactions.

HFN advises leading American and European international banks and has a strong following from local and investment banks. The banking department has been involved in virtually all the major PFI projects in Israel.

HFN is known internationally for its substantial experience in project finance and infrastructure, representing banks and concessionaries in high profile Israeli projects, involving telecoms, tunnels, natural gas extraction and pipelines, power projects, desalination, toll roads and transport.

HFN's securities and capital markets practice enjoys a leading reputation for its cross-border work and is well known for its work involving local and international underwritersand public offering of securities listed on the Tel Aviv Stock Exchange, the New York Stock Exchange, Nasdaq as well as European markets.

The IT/IP department works with the corporate group on technology transactions and also covers a variety of IT/IP activities, including licensing and technology transfer, trade mark prosecution, litigation, computer and cyberspace law and copyright matters.

The telecoms and media department has become a leader in its field representing a number of international telecoms corporations as well as bidders in all major telecoms in Israel.

The real estate, construction and property development department provides a complete service to foreign and domestic developers.

HFN's litigation department is one of the largest and best-resourced in Israel, able to deploy many lawyers for complex commercial actions both domestic and cross-border, and representing many multinationals conducting litigation in Israel.

HFN represents a large and ever-growing number of domestic and international venture capital funds and private investors, as well as the portfolio companies in which they invest, through the whole development process of incubation, start-up, emergence and maturity.

The energy and natural resources department has been at the forefront of recent growth in this sector including the exploitation of Israel's natural gas resources.

Further information can be found on the HFN website: www.hfn.co.il.

HESKIA-HACMUN LAW FIRM

AZRIELI CENTER
THE TRIANGULAR TOWER
TEL AVIV 67023

Telephone: +972 3 608 1122
Fax: +972 3 608 1123
E-mail: main@hh-law.co.il
Website: www.hh-law.co.il

Languages
English, German, Hebrew

Number of lawyers 5

Contact
Dor Heskia, Amos Hacmun

Member
German-Israeli Lawyers Association; Israeli-German Chamber of Commerce; American-Israeli Chamber of Commerce and Industry; British-Israeli Chamber of Commerce; Japan-Israeli Chamber of Commerce; Swiss-Israeli Chamber of Commerce

CATEGORIES OF WORK

Corporate and commercial

Dispute resolution, litigation and arbitration

Telecommunications

Intellectual property

Banking and finance

Insolvency, corporate restructuring

Media and entertainment

Mergers and acquisitions

Foreign direct investment

Information technology

DR J WEINROTH & CO

10 HUBERMAN STREET
TEL AVIV 64075

Telephone: +972 3 685 2778
Fax: +972 3 685 6210
E-mail: office@weinrothlaw.co.il

Languages
English, French, German

Number of lawyers 25

Contact
Avinoam Cohen

CATEGORIES OF WORK

Civil litigation
Dr Jacon Weinroth

Dispute resolution and arbitration
Dr Avraham Weinroth, Boaz Ben Zur

Fraud and white-collar crime
Dr Jacob Weinroth

Banking and finance
Yaron Fueredi, Dr Avraham Weinroth

Corporate and commercial
Dr Avraham Weinroth

Commercial litigation
Boaz Ben-Zur, Yaron Fueredi

Securities regulation
Yaron Fueredi

Government business/regulatory
Dr Avraham Weinroth

Insolvency/corporate restructuring
Dr Jacob Weinroth

Commercial property
Dr Avraham Weinroth

Insurance
Boaz Ben-Zur

Private client
Dr Jacob Weinroth,
Dr Avraham Weinroth

I GORNITZKY & CO

ROTHSCHILD AVE 45
TEL AVIV 65784

Telephone: +972 3 710 91 91
Fax: +972 3 560 65 55

Languages
English, French, German, Spanish

Other offices
Herzliya Pituach

Number of lawyers 53
at this office 50

Contacts
Pinhas Rubin, Moriel Matalon, Joshua Rosensweig, Ariel Zelichov, Zvi Ephrat

CATEGORIES OF WORK

Commercial

Corporate

Mergers and acquisitions

Antitrust

International business transactions

Agency, distribution and franchise agreements

Securities and public offerings

Taxation and international taxation

Trusts and estates

Financing

Banks and banking

Insurance

Real estate

Infrastructure projects and project finance

Litigation

Arbitration and mediation

White-collar crimes

Class actions

Liquidation, insolvency and bankruptcy

Hi-tech and venture capital

Telecommunications

Energy projects

THE FIRM

I Gornitzky & Co was founded in 1938 by the late Israel Gornitzky and has since grown to its current size of 53 attorneys and a total staff of 105, making it one of the leading firms in Israel. The partners in the firm are Pinchas Rubin (chairman), Moriel Matalon (managing partner), Dr Joshua Rosensweig, Ariel Zelichov, Zvi Ephrat, Jack Smith, Daphna Talgam, Dr Dalia Even-Lahav, Eyal Marom, Gur Y Savir, Revital Aviram, Ofer Tzur, Itay Geffen and Eyal Raz. Several of the firm's attorneys are native English and French speakers, qualified in various foreign jurisdictions.The firm's main offices are situated in the centre of Tel Aviv with a branch office in Herzlia.

In the past several years, I Gornitzky & Co has been classified as a leading firm in different legal fields by the editorial departments of the main international guides. Additionally, many of the firm's partners have attained positions of recognition as 'experts' in their fields of practice. For example, Adv Pinhas Rubin, the firm's chairman, was chosen by his colleagues in a 'Ma'ariv' poll as the best taxation lawyer and one of the five leading commercial lawyers in Israel, and by *The Marker* as one of the top 100 influential persons in the Israeli economy. He is also a member of two governmental committees on the Reform of Income Taxation and on the Reform of Real Estate Taxation. In the same 'Ma'ariv' poll, Dr Joshua Rosensweig was ranked as one of the top five taxation lawyers in Israel. Dr Rosenweig is also a member of the committees mentioned above and recently became chairman of the First International Bank, one of Israel's top five banks. Finally, the Israeli Bar Association awarded Dr Dalia Even-Lahav with the 'Legal Woman of the Year' award.

I Gornitzky & Co is committed to providing a professional 'one-stop-shop' service of the highest quality, combining legal knowledge and expertise with commercial and business understanding. The firm takes pride in its legal staff members, which have been chosen from the best academic institutions in Israel and abroad.

AREAS OF PRACTICE

I Gornitzky & Co's clientele includes the State of Israel, domestic and international clients, from multinational corporations through public and private companies to private individuals. It provides its clientele with legal consultation and services focusing primarily on the following areas:

Commercial, corporate, mergers and acquisitions, antitrust (including obtaining approvals from the Controller of Restrictive Trade Practices), international transactions and agency, distribution and franchise agreements (for local and foreign clients), securities and public offerings (on the Tel Aviv Stock Exchange and in foreign stock exchanges).

Taxation and international taxation (including the structuring of large transnational projects), trusts and estates, financing and investments, banks and banking (consultation to many of the major Israeli and foreign banks), insurance (commercial and corporate consultation to many major insurance companies in Israel).

Real estate, hotels and tourism (consultation to several international hotel chains and real estate conglomerates in domestic and international commercial, corporate, real estate and labour law issues), infrastructure projects and project finance (tenders, bids and consultation regarding desalination, power stations, toll highway and light rail projects).

Litigation (appearing in all Israeli courts in issues primarily relating to corporate, commercial and tax law), white-collar crimes (representation in hearings before the state and district attorneys and in the Israeli courts), class actions, arbitration and mediation (including serving as arbitrators), liquidation, bankruptcy and insolvency (consultation and representation of companies, liquidators and creditors, and serving as liquidators and creditors of large Israeli companies).

Hi-tech, and start-ups, venture capitals, communications and telecommunications, including representation of Israel's sole satellite licensee; representation of oil and gas, industrial and pharmaceutical companies and their shareholders.

JOSEPH LEVY & CO

4 KOIFMAN STREET
TEL AVIV 68012

Telephone: +972 3 510 2491
Fax: +972 3 510 2493
E-mail: main@ljlaw.co.il

Languages
Hebrew, English, Spanish

Number of lawyers 21

CATEGORIES OF WORK

Antitrust/competition law
Joseph Levy, Michal Schwartz

Government contracts and tenders
Joseph Levy, Noa Mei-Dan

Securities
Amir Nachlieli, Asher Bichoonski

Project finance
Joseph Levy, Noa Mei-Dan

Banking
Noa Mei-Dan, Brian Aron

Corporate
Amir Nachlieli, Oded Kahana

Trade
Joseph Levy, Tal Dagan

Litigation
Eyal Blizovsky, Livian Segal

Communications
Amir Nachlieli, Oded Kahana

Administrative law
Eyal Blizovsky, Yuli Rudin

Commercial
Joseph Levy, Noa Mei-Dan

Property law
Tal Dagan, Avital Dagan

THE FIRM

Joseph Levy & Co was established in 1992, and employs 21 lawyers. Based in Tel Aviv, the firm has an active domestic and international practice and serves as a regular outside counsel or as a project specialist to a number of major corporations, banks, investment groups, and trade associations. The firm's advice is also sought by national and municipal government entities such as the Ministry of Finance, Ministry of Transportation, the Ministry of National Infrastructures and the Ministry of the Environment.

AREAS OF PRACTICE

Joseph Levy & Co has extensive experience in tenders law. The firm's lawyers were actively involved in the process by which legislation of the Mandatory Tenders Law and its regulations were enacted in the Knesset – Israel's Parliament. The firm has been engaged in the preparation of tenders; is accompanying tender processes on behalf of various government ministries; and is representing local and overseas clients in various legal proceedings, in tenders established by the state, municipalities, government companies, public bodies, etc.

The firm has drawn up the tender and the concession agreement for the Carmel Tunnels Project and provides legal counsel to the Ministries of Finance and Transportation on this project. The Carmel Tunnels is a Build, Operate and Transfer (BOT) project for the privatisation of Haifa Metropolitan's major transportation infrastructure, granting a concession for collecting tolls. The firm represents a major highway developer for the Tel Aviv Metropolitan, and also acts as an adviser for the tender committee selecting the concessionaire for a Private Finance Initiative (PFI) toll highway between the cities of Modi'in and Tel Aviv.

Joseph Levy & Co has drawn up the tender documents and the concession agreement for the setting up of a seawater desalination project for 100 million cubic meters of water annually. This is also a BOT project and the firm acts as legal counsel to the Ministries of Finance, National Infrastructures and the Environment and the Water Commission on this project. In addition, Joseph Levy & Co has drawn up the tender documents and the concession agreement for seawater desalination facilities on a BOO basis. For this project, the firm also acts as legal counsel for the Ministries of Finance, National Infrastructures and the Environment and the Water Commission. The firm is an adviser to two of the largest banks in Israel in the bridge financing of a large-scale natural gas project.

Joseph Levy & Co participated in preparing the tender for the selection of the country's second cellular phone operator. This involvement was on behalf of Coopers & Lybrand, advisers to the government on preparing the tender. The firm also assisted the Ministry of Communications in the preparation of the tender for cable television's shopping channel. The firm is currently an adviser to one of the largest international telecommunication and Internet services provider companies in Israel.

The firm has developed extensive practical experience in the area of antitrust. The firm provides ongoing legal advice to various bodies on such topics as the application of programs for the internal enforcement of the Israeli Antitrust Law, and represents clients before the Antitrust Authority. In this respect, the firm represents a major food manufacturer and distributor, a leading international credit card company, a major pension fund and one of the country's largest mortgage banks.

Joseph Levy & Co assisted one of Israel's largest mortgage banks in establishing, formulating and structuring a secondary market for mortgages. The firm's work included conducting comprehensive comparative research on the topic, and compiling and submitting a position and opinion paper to the Ministers of Finance and Justice. This paper was also prepared for the sub-committee headed by the Comptroller General of the Ministry of Finance, which was set up to investigate the matter. The firm also formulated the protocol agreements to regulate the secondary mortgage market. In addition it has represented a leading worldwide software provider in the acquisition of several Israeli high-tech companies.

LESHEM-KIPPERMAN, LAW OFFICES & NOTARY

13 BALFOUR STREET
TEL AVIV 65211

Telephone: +972 3 629 0780
Fax: +972 3 629 0789
E-mail: lk@leshem-kipperman.co.il
Website: www.leshem-kipperman.com

Languages
English

Number of lawyers 3

Contacts
Moshe Leshem, Irit Leshem-Kipperman

CATEGORIES OF WORK

- Air transportation
- Aviation, commercial and regulatory matters
- Transportation cargo recoveries
- Aircraft purchase, lease and finance
- Admiralty, marine and shipping
- Litigation and arbitration
- Tort law, product liability
- Insurance

LEVITAN, SHARON & CO

57 YIGAL ALON STREET
TEL AVIV 67891

Telephone: +972 3 688 6768
Fax: +972 3 688 6769
E-mail: office@levitansharon.co.il

Languages
English, French, German, Hebrew, Russian

Number of lawyers 24

Contacts
Rachel Levitan, Peggy Sharon

Member
International Bar Association; Professional Liability Underwriting Society (PLUS); Federation of Defense and Corporate Counsel (FDCC); AIDA

CATEGORIES OF WORK

- Aviation
- Claims handling
- Crisis management
- Dispute resolution/ litigation and arbitration
- Financial lines insurance
- Insurance
- Insurance corporate/regulatory work
- International litigation
- Product liability
- Reinsurance

LUTHI & CO

AMERICA HOUSE
35 SHAUL HAMELECH BLVD
PO BOX 33113
TEL AVIV 64927

Telephone: +972 3 695 2268
Fax: +972 3 695 1120
E-mail: mail@luthi.co.il
Website: www.luthi.co.il

Languages
English

Number of lawyers 9

Contacts
Richard Luthi, Christopher Brice

CATEGORIES OF WORK

Patents

Confidential information

Data protection

Trade marks, service marks and brand protection

Copyright, designs; author's and moral rights

Pharmaceuticals and biotechnology

Food technology

Agricultural and industrial chemicals

Information and communications technology

Materials science

Aviation and space technology

Imaging and photography

Toys, games and sports equipment

NASCHITZ, BRANDES & CO

ADVOCATES AND NOTARIES

5 TUVAL STREET
TEL AVIV 67897

Telephone: +972 3 623 5000
Fax: +972 3 623 5005
Website: www.nblaw.com

Languages
English, French, German, Hebrew, Italian

Other offices
Haifa

Number of lawyers 64
at this office 53

Member
International Attorneys Club;
Mackrell International;
International Bar Association;
AIDA International Insurance Law Association;
Israel Maritime Law Association

CATEGORIES OF WORK

Technology
H Brandes, Y Razin

Insurance
PG Naschitz, A Rothman

Banking
EA Naschitz, P Broder

Corporate
G Brandes, Y Feuchtwanger

Taxation
S Amir, Y Dolan

Intellectual property
S Chertow, Y Horowitz

Funds and venture capital
S Amir

Marine
PG Naschitz, M Asulin

Subrogation
G Atar

Litigation
PG Naschitz

Investments
A Lampert, N Spira

Communications
O Motola

Aviation
PG Naschitz, T Kareth

Biotech
E Balan

Stock exchange and IPOs
H Brandes, A Lampert

Real estate
Z Feit, S Lechner

NE'EMAN, SHAFIR, BEN-ARTZI & CO ADVOCATES

TOP TOWER, 50 DIZENGOF ST
64332 TEL AVIV

Telephone: +972 3 525 4141
Fax: +972 3 525 3818
E-mail: mneeman@nsblaw.com

Languages
English, Hebrew

Number of lawyers 15

Contact
Moshe H Ne'eman

CATEGORIES OF WORK

Corporate and commercial

Securities and capital markets

Dispute resolution – litigation and arbitration

IT and telecommunications

Infrastructure

Commercial property/real estate

Emerging companies and venture capital

Mergers and acquisitions

Energy and natural resources

Privatisation

Bankruptcy and insolvency

Asset finance/securitisation

Competition and antitrust

E-commerce

Employment

Hi-tech

Regulatory

Non-profit

RAVED MAGRISO BENKEL & CO

37 SHAUL HAMELECH BLVD
PO BOX 21411
TEL AVIV 61213

Telephone: +972 3 606 0260
Fax: +972 3 606 0266
E-mail: rmb@rmblaw.co.il
Website: www.rmblaw.co.il

Languages
English, French, Russian

Number of lawyers 21

Contact
Yoram Raved

CATEGORIES OF WORK

Corporate
Yoram Raved, Inbal Tzion

Mergers and acquisitions
Yoram Raved

Corporate reorganisations
Yoram Raved, Joseph Benkel

Securities
Yoram Raved, Inbal Tzion

Banking and finance
David Magriso

Corporate finance
Yoram Raved, David Magriso

Foreign investments
Yoram Raved, Ofer Zuzovsky

International transactions
Yoram Raved, David Magriso

Hi-tech
Inbal Tzion

Litigation and arbitration
Joseph Benkel, Shmuel Galinka

Construction and real estate
David Magriso, Ofer Zuzovsky

Infrastructure and project finance
David Magriso, Ofer Zuzovsky

Energy and natural resources
David Magriso

Antitrust
Joseph Benkel, Yoram Raved

Town planning
Joseph Benkel

REINHOLD COHN & PARTNERS

21 AHAD HA'AM STREET
TEL AVIV 65151

Telephone: +972 3 710 9333
Fax: +972 3 560 6405
E-mail: info@rcip.co.il
Website: www.rcip.co.il

Languages
Arabic, English, French, German, Hebrew, Portuguese

Other offices
Jerusalem

Number of lawyers 40
at this office 30

Contact
Dr Bossmat Gonen

CATEGORIES OF WORK

Life sciences and chemistry
Ilan Cohn, Bossmat Gonen

Hi tech
Ehud Hausman, Jonathan J Topper

Technology
David de Vries, Ena Pugatsch

Trade marks
David Gilat, Ronit Barzik-Soffer

Litigation and commercial law
David Gilat, Eran Bareket

S FRIEDMAN & CO
ADVOCATES

25 HAMERED ST
TEL AVIV 68125

Telephone: +972 3 796 1500
Fax: +972 3 796 1501
E-mail: tel-aviv@friedman.co.il

Languages
English

Other offices
Haifa, Herzliya

Number of lawyers 25

CATEGORIES OF WORK

Admiralty and shipping
A Kesary, A Cohen-Dor

International joint ventures
D Malkoff, Y Mehulal

Aviation and general transport
A Safran, A Kesary

Securities, mergers and acquisitions
A Rabinowitz, Y Mehulal

Tax
Y Mehulal, Dr D Herman

Financing and international credits
A Safran, D Malkoff

Corporate
A Safran, I Anaby

Aircraft and shipping finance
A Safran, D Malkoff

Personal injury and insurance
M Safran, A Kesary

Litigation and arbitration
A Kesary, A Cohen-Dor

Technology and communications
CB Gottlieb, S Molcho

Real estate and construction
D Malkoff, K Betser

Labour and employment
A Kesary, T Enat Ben Arieh

Banking
A Kesary, I Anaby

Antitrust and restraint of trade
A Rabinowitz, A Kesary

Commercial
I Anaby, U Sudri

WEKSLER, BREGMAN & CO

SHALOM TOWER
9 ACHAD HA'AM STREET
TEL AVIV 65251

Telephone: +972 3 511 93 93
Fax: +972 3 511 93 94
E-mail: office@wblaw.co.il
Website: www.wblaw.co.il

Languages
English, French, Hebrew, Japanese

Number of lawyers 29

CATEGORIES OF WORK

Corporate
Adv Uri Bregman, Adv Irit Biran

Company
Adv Ofer Yancovich, Adv Dror Toren

Real estate and BOT projects
Adv Uri Bregman, Adv Avi Ben-Yaakov

Banking and finance
Adv Ora Dvir, Adv Ofer Yancovich

Commercial
Adv Uri Bregman, Adv Dror Toren

Securities and capital markets
Adv Ora Dvir, Adv Ofer Yancovich

Public offering
Adv Uri Bregman, Adv Ora Dvir

Planning and zoning
Adv Taly Salton-Yeshua

International commercial transactions
Adv Ron Salpeter, Adv Uri Bregman

Hi-tech investments
Adv Dror Toren, Adv Ron Salpeter

Litigation and arbitration
Adv Doron Dan, Adv Amit Pines

Liquidation and receivership
Adv Amit Pines, Adv Doron Dan

Employment and labour
Adv Irit Biran, Adv Yaron Rossman

Mergers and acquisitions
Adv Uri Bregman, Adv Dror Toren

Antitrust; tender law
Adv Amit Pines, Adv Ofer Yancovich

THE FIRM

Established in 1936, the firm of Weksler, Bregman & Co is one of the oldest corporate and commercial law firms in Israel. The firm with 29 attorneys, has a general, full-service business practice, with specialisation in real estate, securities, banking and commercial transactions. Weksler, Bregman & Co's clientele encompasses corporations and public bodies in these sectors.

AREAS OF PRACTICE

The firm services its corporate clients through the organisation of business structures. These include: the establishment and ongoing representation of corporations, partnerships, branches of foreign corporations in Israel and joint venture entities; negotiation, counselling and other services relating to asset purchase transactions, and mergers and acquisitions; the drafting of R&D and technology and licensing agreements, including stock option schemes, and a variety of other types of commercial agreements. The firm acts as legal counsel to the Israeli representatives of leading western European, North American and Japanese manufacturers and trading companies. The firm also offers special expertise in all aspects of the new Israeli Company Law, which came into effect in February 2000.

The firm has vast experience in commercial, residential, industrial, real estate development and infrastructure projects, ranging from the construction of commercial centres, large residential areas, shopping malls and hotels, and is intensively involved in all aspects of the Cross-Israeli Highway project. The firm represents a leading Israeli investment company engaged in land development, construction, insurance, trade, hotels and tourism, including the regional franchise for a major international hotel chain.

The firm offers broad expertise in the securities field and has extensive experience in public offerings and private placements, representing both issuers and underwriters. It has handled the public offerings of leading Israeli banks, investment and holding companies. The firm also provides corporate planning in the selection and design of business structures, and in the financing of corporate reorganisations and other transactions. The firm's work also includes the preparation of documentation, the conducting of due diligence reviews, and complex negotiations with regulatory and securities and exchange authorities.

The firm renders legal services to banking institutions in Israel. Work performed includes counselling, negotiations, legal opinions, issuance of various types of governmental licences and other related services.

The firm deals with governmental bodies and agencies and advises its clients on the establishment of incentive-based investments in industry and tourism. In serving its clientele in cross-border transactions, the firm also offers the services of an Israeli lawyer with extensive legal experience in Japan and South Korea.

The firm represents clients in commercial litigation, arbitration and labour disputes. The firm supervises foreign litigation on behalf of its Israeli clientele and represents foreign clients in Israeli courts.

The firm offers broad expertise in matters relating to liquidation and receivership procedures of corporations, and the firm's lawyers act as liquidators or receivers of companies, especially on behalf of banks.

WEINSTOCK-ZECLER & CO

1 AZRIELI CENTER
132 PETACH TIKVA ROAD
TEL AVIV 67021

Telephone: +972 3 696 8333
Fax: +972 3 696 4222
E-mail: law@w-z.co.il

Languages
English, French

Number of lawyers 8

CATEGORIES OF WORK

Competition and antitrust
Niv Zecler

Corporate law and financing
Gidon Weinstock, Ofer Argov

Dispute resolution/litigation and arbitration
Niv Zecler, Gidon Weinstock

Banking
Gidon Weinstock, Ofer Argov

YEHUDA RAVEH & CO

RUBINSTEIN HOUSE
20 LINCOLN STREET
TEL AVIV 67134

Telephone: +972 3 562 0303
Fax: +972 3 561 8558
E-mail: ravehtlv@ravehtlv.co.il
Website: www.yraveh.co.il

Languages
English, French, German, Hebrew

Other offices
Beersheva, Haifa, Jerusalem

Number of lawyers 46
at this office 15

CATEGORIES OF WORK

Infrastructure projects
Yehuda Raveh, Yehuda Glatt

Building and development
Lisa Tross, Yuval Grayevsky

Mergers and acquisitions
Yehuda Glatt, Yehuda Raveh

Planning and building
Tamar Raveh, Uri Yamin

Antitrust
Carmit Bar-On

Hi-tech companies and projects
Yehuda Glatt, Yehuda Raveh

International law and international transactions
Yehuda Raveh, Yehuda Glatt

Corporate law
Yehuda Raveh, Lisa Tross

Intellectual property
Gabi Robenbach

Taxation
Professor Itzhac Hadari

Litigation
Yuval Grayevsky, Haim Stern

Bankruptcy and liquidation
Hagai Ulman

Environmental matters
Sara Shalom

Banking
Lisa Tross, Yehuda Raveh

Privatisation of government corporations
Yehuda Raveh

Hotel industry
Yehuda Raveh, Carmit Bar-On

YIGAL ARNON & CO

ADVOCATES AND NOTARY

1 AZRIELI CENTER
PO BOX 33777
TEL AVIV 67021

Telephone: +972 3 608 7777
Fax: +972 3 608 7724
E-mail: info@arnon.co.il
Website: www.arnon.co.il

Languages
English, French, Hebrew

Other offices
Jerusalem

Number of lawyers 73
at this office 50

CATEGORIES OF WORK

Antitrust and competition
Ronit Amir Yaniv

Banking and financial services
Amnon Lorch, Shiri Shaham

Bankruptcy and creditors' rights
Dror Vigdor, Doron Tamir

Corporate finance
Paul Baris, Eran Ilan

Emerging growth companies
Barak Platt

IP and corporate partnering
Barry Levenfeld

Labour law, executive compensation and employment benefits
Hagai Shmueli

Life sciences
Barry Levenfeld, Barak Platt

Litigation
Yigal Arnon, Dror Vigdor

Mergers and acquisitions
Paul Baris, Barry Levenfeld

Project finance
David Schapiro, Shiri Shaham

Public tenders
Amnon Lorch, Doron Tamir

Real estate and development
Amalia Meshi, Rami Kook

Securities
David Schapiro, Shiri Shaham

Tax
Harry Kirsh

Telecommunications
Gil Oren, David Osborne

Venture capital
Barry Levenfeld, David Schapiro

THE FIRM

Yigal Arnon & Co. is one of Israel's largest and most dynamic law firms. It provides a full spectrum of legal services to a wide-ranging client base. Clients seek out Yigal Arnon & Co. when looking for professionalism, service and integrity to resolve complex and challenging problems.

Clients choose the firm for its good business judgment, a multi-disciplinary legal approach and a thorough understanding of the clients' objectives. A reputation for achieving timely and positive results has attracted high-profile clients, demanding cases and exceptional lawyers.

AREAS OF PRACTICE

Antitrust and competition: Provides antitrust counselling and litigation services encompassing monopolies, strategic alliances, exclusive commercial relationships and M&A.

Banking and finance: Represents Israeli and overseas commercial banks, investment banks and stock exchanges in: obtaining licences for local operations; banking and money laundering regulations; complex derivatives, securitisation; stock lending and hedging.

Bankruptcy and creditors' rights: Represents troubled companies and creditors, receivers and liquidators of major enterprises in connection with creation and enforcement of security interests, debt restructuring, loan syndications, reorganisations and liquidation proceedings.

Corporate finance: One of the largest corporate finance practices in Israel negotiates private placement, venture capital and debt financing; domestic and international strategic alliances, joint ventures and other corporate partnering arrangements; public offerings and M&A.

Emerging growth companies: Specialises in representation from before creation through and beyond their public offering or acquisition.

IP and corporate partnering: Has considerable experience in proprietary asset exploitation, strategic partnerships, technology transfer, manufacturing, distribution and marketing, with specific expertise in software, telecommunications, semiconductors and biotechnology.

Labour law: Provides tax and regulatory advice regarding private and public company employee option and stock purchase plans; also handles labour and employment matters, including executive employment.

Life sciences: Works with international and domestic companies including biotechnology, pharmaceutical, bioinformatics, medical devices and healthcare service companies; universities and academic centres.

Litigation: One of the foremost litigation practices in Israel represents clients in complex and high-profile litigation: commercial litigation, white collar crime, class action defence; unfair competition, environmental matters, employment issues; real estate, banking and insurance cases.

M&A: Has assisted domestic and overseas companies in many of the country's largest, most significant and most complex transactions.

Project finance and public tenders: Represents Israeli and overseas companies and financial institutions in infrastructure, electricity generation, semi-conductor manufacture, roads, railways, waterworks and waste management projects on BOT and more traditional bases.

Real estate and development: Assists major Israeli and international construction companies, financial institutions, real estate developers and individual entrepreneurs active in various projects: commercial, industrial, office, shopping centre, hotel, resort, residential and mixed-use real estate.

Securities: Assists clients in listings and in over 100 public offerings in the US and Europe for the issuer, underwriter or key selling shareholders.

Tax: Covers the Israeli tax aspects of financial instruments, transfer pricing for international groups, technology transfer, M&A, venture funds, employee stock options, and tax planning for high-net-worth individuals.

Telecoms: Clients includes cable television companies, Internet providers, global fibre infrastructure companies, telecom equipment manufacturers and Internet telephony companies; also assists in securing broadcast licences, establishing program distribution, determining rate regulations and preparing fixed line and wireless access permits.

Venture capital: Represents many prominent Israeli and overseas venture capital funds; deals in fund formation and has assisted funds in several hundred portfolio investments.

YUVAL LEVY & CO

YUVAL LEVY HOUSE
8 NESS ZIONA ST
TEL AVIV 63904

Telephone: +972 3 517 2303
Fax: +972 3 516 4185
E-mail: office@yuvalaw.co.il
WWW: www.yuvalaw.co.il

Languages
English, Hebrew

Number of lawyers 16

Member
Legal Network International (an association of independent law firms)

CATEGORIES OF WORK

Corporate
Prof Yuval Levy, Opher Levy

Commercial litigation
Prof Yuval Levy, Yechiel Kasher

Commercial
Tamar Krongrad, Ami Cohen

Intellectual property
Prof Yuval Levy, Opher Levy

International transactions
Opher Levy, Tamar Krongrad

Antitrust and unfair competition
Opher Levy, Yechiel Kasher

Mergers and acquisitions
Opher Levy, Ami Cohen

Environmental law
Prof Yuval Levy, Idit Reiter, Yigal Borochovsky

Criminal litigation
Prof Yuval Levy, Yechiel Kasher

Banking
Prof Yuval Levy, Benny Lerner

Securities
Opher Levy, Benny Lerner

Arbitration
Prof Yuval Levy, Yechiel Kasher

Reorganisation and insolvency
Opher Levy, Yechiel Kasher

Financing
Opher Levy, Tamar Krongrad

Real property
Galit Rosovsky, Yuval Bracha

THE FIRM

Prof Yuval Levy founded the firm of Yuval Levy & Co in 1973, having been a partner in one of Israel's top law firms specialising in commercial, maritime and international law. Since its establishment, the firm has expanded in size and fields of practice, and now comprises sixteen attorneys (four partners and twelve associates). The professional staff hold degrees from top-ranking Israeli and American universities, and many of the attorneys graduated with honours, hold graduate degrees, have served as teaching assistants, or have otherwise excelled, and are recognised, in their fields. Attorneys practise in both English and Hebrew, allowing the firm's overseas clients to receive an efficient and professional service.

The firm represents a myriad of domestic and international clients, and enjoys a strong reputation in antitrust and intellectual property litigation, commercial litigation, the credit card industry, environmental law, securities law, hi-tech, mergers and acquisitions, corporate and transactional law, and financing. As the sole Israeli member of the Legal Network International (an association of 40 independent law firms strategically located in more than 25 countries worldwide) Yuval Levy & Co provide worldwide representation to its clients in key geographic markets where and when needed, utilizing lawyers uniquely qualified and positioned to assist in all aspects of international and foreign law.

The firm's partners have been recognised consistently in the last few years by Dun & Bradstreet, and are regularly cited in Israeli media and professional publications regarding their fields of expertise.

AREAS OF PRACTICE

Commercial ltigation: The firm's litigation spans a wide variety of areas of law, particularly antitrust, environmental law, intellectual property, and commercial disputes. The firm's members appear in all Court and administrative forums in Israel, as well as arbitrational forums, and have represented inter alia, major Israeli financial institutions and worldwide corporate entities. Members of the firm have appeared before the Supreme Court of Israel on numerous claims. Particularly noteworthy is this firm's extensive representation of clients before the Commissioner.

Corporate law and financing: Yuval Levy & Co provides legal counsel to leading banking and financial institutions in Israel, and serves as general counsel to Leumi Card Ltd., the credit card subsidiary of Bank Leumi le Israel. The firm specialises in the re-organization of existing corporate entities, and in negotiations for mergers, purchases and sales of companies, partnerships and joint ventures of various types, and has advised both lenders and lendees on international financing projects from overseas.

Technology: As part of its ongoing representation of corporate entities, Yuval Levy & Co focuses on IP protection, licensing arrangements, and research and development projects. The firm's members have extensive experience in negotiating and drafting computer hardware and software agreements, as well as technology transfer agreements. Yuval Levy & Co provides ongoing services regarding marketing agreements of various types (distributorships, agencies and OEM Agreements).

Real estate: The firm has a thriving property practice, with its reputation steadily growing in 'start to finish' representation of property entrepreneurs in large projects throughout the country – the building of malls, hotels, and residential and commercial properties. The litigation aspect of the firm's property practice touches on contractual aspects (disputes between purchasers and sellers, as well as those between entrepreneurs and tenants) and criminal ones (regarding violations of urban planning laws). The firm has had significant 'wins' in the field of urban planning.

Bankruptcy and liquidation: Members of the firm have served, and continue to serve, as liquidators/receivers of private and public companies. The firm has waged legal battles on behalf of clients in connection with liquidation and bankruptcy proceedings and have handled numerous and extensive litigations dealing with companies in liquidation.

Additional information can be obtained from www.yuvalaw.co.il.

ZELLERMAYER, PELOSSOF & CO., ADVOCATES

THE RUBINSTEIN HOUSE
20 LINCOLN STREET
TEL AVIV 67134

Telephone: +972 3 625 5555
Fax: +972 3 625 5500
E-mail: general@zelpel.com
Website: www.zelpel.com

Languages
Hebrew, English, French, German, Spanish

Number of lawyers 35

Contacts
Michael Zellermayer, Avi D Pelossof, Eli Mei-Tal, Guy Tsafrir, Guy Even-Ezra, Itay Hacohen, Helit Ben-Israel, Dr Avraham Ortal, Mimi Zemah

CATEGORIES OF WORK

Corporate and commercial law
Mergers and acquisitions, joint ventures
Banking and corporate financing
Securities and capital markets
Tax law
Telecommunications
Energy and infrastructure
Licensing and technology transfer
Labour law
Litigation
Real estate and zoning
Environmental law
Bankruptcy and liquidation

THE FIRM

Zellermayer, Pelossof & Co. was founded in 1984 by Michael Zellermayer (chairman). By 1981, he was a leading partner at a New York firm. He handled more than 100 leveraged buy-outs in the 1980s, has extensive experience in M&As, and specialises in all forms of corporate finance. He has been deeply involved in the telecoms market, including representing the successful bidder for the second cellular licence, handling the country's two largest telecoms acquisitions, and representing several multinationals in their Israeli operations. Managing partner Avi D Pelossof joined the firm in 1986. He has extensive industry experience, having served as the CEO of Israel's largest food manufacturer (Elite), chairman of Haifa Chemicals and the Tel Aviv Stock Exchange, a director of Israel Aircraft Industries, and has advised the Industrialists Association. Most of the firm's lawyers have international experience, and most of the firm's clients and activities are international.

AREAS OF PRACTICE

The firm specialises in all spheres of business law, in particular corporate and securities, administrative, licensing, tax, real estate, labour, telecoms, and environmental laws; as well as in commercial litigation. Its broad expertise allows the firm's lawyers to provide full legal support in an array of advanced business activities, in Israel and worldwide. The firm's clients, being a multitude of nationalities, cover a broad range of industrial, finance, technology and energy businesses, governmental and private.

M&As: a full range of transactional experience covers all deal aspects from negotiations and tax planning, to handling antitrust and other regulatory matters, performing due diligence, covering securities issues, as well as IP, labour relations, and real estate. This enables the firm to be regularly involved in some of the largest transactions in the country, such as representation of: triumphant shareholders in the first proxy contest involving an Israeli company; the largest asset management company in Israel; and a consortium of banks and other financial sponsors in the leveraged acquisition of one of the world's largest BOPP manufacturers.

Telecoms: in addition to its presence in the M&A field, the firm advises and represents major telecoms/datacom service and equipment companies in their ongoing affairs, such as regulatory and government matters, infrastructure, real estate, financing, labour, and participates in legislative advisory committees.

Technology: represents several US VC funds in the establishment of their Israeli companies and represents numerous fast-growing hi-tech companies, thus forming a meeting point for entrepreneurs and institutional investors. The firm has advised on major technology privatisation projects, including the Ministry of Defence's Armament Development Authority (Rafael), Israel Aircraft Industries and the Government Biological Institute.

Banking and capital markets: advises major investment banks and financial institutions, from underwriting and project financing to speciality products and retail. The firm has advised on numerous public offerings of Israeli companies in the US and European equity markets such as the representation of Baran Group in its recent merger with o2wireless and its registration and listing on Nasdaq.

Project financing and government bids: experience includes representing consortia in bidding for government franchises in communications and BOT infrastructure projects. The firm was actively involved in negotiating and securing the projects' financing arrangements.

Gas and energy: experience includes representing several gas exploration, development and distribution ventures, including the owners of the current largest natural gas reserves in Israel, as well as the country's cement monopoly, and IPP projects.

Environmental: representation of Israeli and multinational companies in transactions related to environmental solutions, and the adjustment of the activities of senior Israeli organisations to the new environmental laws.

ZYSMAN, AHARONI, GAYER & CO
LAW OFFICES

52A HAYARKON STREET
TEL AVIV 63432

Telephone: +972 3 795 5555
Fax: +972 3 795 5550
E-mail: mail@zag-law.co.il
Website: www.zag-law.co.il

Languages
English, Hebrew

Other offices
Eilat, Haifa, New York, Rosh Pina

Number of lawyers 39
at this office 29

CATEGORIES OF WORK

Hi-tech	**Torts**
Corporate and commercial	**Commercial insolvency**
Communication and media	**Arbitration and mediation**
Real estate	**Intellectual property**
Sports	**Computers and software**
Litigation	**Mergers and acquisitions**

ITALY

Population	**57.9 million**
Number of lawyers	**70,000**
Professional title	**Avvocato**
Currency	**Euro (€)**

Index

The Italian Republic is shedding its reputation as the economic under performer of Europe. Although the country in no way dominates the known world as it did in the glory days of the Roman Empire nearly two thousand years ago, the current government has enacted numerous reforms aimed at improving competitiveness and long-term growth. Over the last decade Italy has benefited from lower interest and inflation rates, and now has a diversified industrial economy with approximately the same total and per capita output as France and the UK. Italy is now the world's fifth largest industrial economy. Its economic strength is in the processing and manufacturing of goods, primarily in small and medium-sized family-owned businesses specialising in products that require high-quality design and engineering. Italy's major industries are precision machinery, motor vehicles, chemicals, pharmaceuticals, electrical goods, textiles, clothing and footwear. Manufacturing accounts for about 25% of GDP and about 90% of total merchandise exports. GDP growth is expected to pick up from an estimated 0.4% in 2003 to about 1.5% in 2004 and 2% in 2005.

Problems, such as illegal immigration, corruption, high unemployment, organised crime and the disparity in income and technical standards between the southern regions and the prosperous north still persist. Italy's current Prime Minister, Silvio Berlusconi, is a figure constantly grabbing headlines for the wrong reasons. He was elected into his second term of office in the early summer of 2001, but given widening divisions within the government, some onlookers no longer expect the right of centre coalition to remain in power until the end of the legislative term in mid-2006. Berlusconi's first administration, in 1994, lasted only seven months before he was brought down by a combination of corruption charges, street protests, and rifts with political allies. In November 2003, the prime minister faced charges of bribery in the trial where the Forza Italia senator, Cesare Previti, also former lawyer to Berlusconi, was found guilty of corruption. Parliament however intervened with a law granting the top five state positions, including the prime minister, immunity from legal prosecution while in office. This, however, was later to be revoked by Italy's Constitutional Court.

The north-east of Italy is among the most vibrant regions in Europe. Padua is an especially important commercial centre with a strong hi-tech sector specialising in fibre optics, pharmaceuticals and chemicals. Vicenza and Verona are also extremely important areas in the Veneto region and have benefited from the development of the economy.

Further west, Milan remains Italy's premier centre for commercial activity. Most leading commercial law firms have a presence in the city. Still further west, Turin is also thriving and its rapidly expanding textiles and telecoms industries have made the city's over reliance on Fiat a thing of the past. The announcement that Turin will host the 2006 Winter Olympics has redoubled civic leaders' efforts to improve local infrastructure with high-speed rail links with Milan and Lyons.

Nearby, Genoa is the country's leading shipping and insurance market, and also has booming electronics and communications sectors. Florence and Bologna are the north's other major commercial centres, and are also flourishing.

Rome is the country's second commercial and legal centre, and home of the Supreme Court, the competition authorities and the focus of administrative law. As with Milan, most leading law firms have an office in Rome.

South of the capital, the disparity between the industrial north, dominated by private companies, and the agricultural south, plagued by unemployment becomes clear. In southern Italy agriculture and tourism remain the main sources of income. The EU has poured money into the region in, what has seemed to date, a vain attempt to bring parity in technology and telecoms with the north. Although Naples is an important shipping hub, it is falling further behind Genoa as Italy's main shipping centre. Along with reducing the budget deficit and reforming Italy's generous pension system (state pensions account for 15% of GDP), boosting commercial activity in the south remains a top priority for the government.

BILLING

Theoretically Italy's Civil Code allows for contractual liberty. In practice however, certain guidelines do need to be adhered to. The method for calculating charge-out rates depends on the area of practice involved. For commercial legal advice, a fee of between 0.5% and 3.0% of the transaction's value is usually charged. This figure will vary according to the firm instructed and the nature and complexity of the work. In light of recent market conditions, more predominantly international firms are willing to be flexible on fee

The largest firms

1	EY Law	275
2	Gianni, Origoni, Grippo & Partners	258
3	Allen & Overy	200
4	Bonelli Erede Pappalardo	185
5	Clifford Chance Studio Legale Associato	152
6	Pavia e Ansaldo	150
7	Freshfields Bruckhaus Deringer	141
8	Chiomenti Studio Legale	120
	NCTM – Studio Legale Associato	120
10	Baker & McKenzie	113
11	Studio Legale Tonucci	110
12	Macchi di Cellere Gangemi	108
13	Pirola Pennuto Zei & Associati	75
14	Hammonds Rossotto	73
15	McDermott, Will & Emery/Carnelutti	65
16	CMS Adonnino Ascoli & Cavasola Scamoni	62
17	Ughi e Nunziante	60
18	Studio Legale Sutti	57
19	Nunziante Magrone	56
20	Studio Associato Consulenza Legale e Tributaria Associato a KPMG International	55
21	Simmons & Simmons	54
22	Frau & Partners SLA	53
23	Di Tanno e Associati	50
	Vita Samory, Fabbrini e Associati	50
25	Piergrossi Villa Bianchini Riccardi	49

These figures represent the total number of lawyers in this country only, and have been supplied by the firms themselves. The figures should be accurate as at 1 January 2004.

structures. A capped fee is common for larger transactional work.

Since 1994, hourly rates have been allowed for contentious work. A senior partner usually bills at €500 per hour, while mid-level associates charge between €100 and €150 per hour. International firms charge substantially more than mid-sized corporate firms and, as with transactional work, costs increase even further for more complex work.

Traditionally, to avoid undercutting, Italian firms have agreed on minimum fees among themselves. To get in line with EC competition directives, however, the government has for some time been planning a consultation on the matter.

MARKETING

The code governing professional advertising was amended in 1999. Lawyers can now provide information regarding their firms, including areas of specialisation, through legal directories and brochures and the Internet. Following the Anglo-Saxon and American example, the use of professional marketing, particularly among the larger Italian firms is on the increase.

IN-HOUSE LAWYERS

It is not unusual for Italian lawyers to divide their time between private practice and a role in a company. Many of the most highly respected commercial lawyers sit on the boards of their own corporate clients.

LEGAL PROFESSION

The traditional model of Italian legal practice, the sole practitioner or family-based firm staffed by independent, generalist lawyers remains the country's norm.

However, times are changing. Increasingly, an elite of commercial law firms is expanding and shifting towards the Anglo-Saxon model. This band of law firms, members of which generally number upwards of 50 lawyers can offer clients faster, more efficient services, and their lawyers greater scope for specialisation.

In terms of specialisation, at the other end of the spectrum, there are also small firms set up by academics that hold professorial seats at Italy's universities and offer specialist advice, commercialising academic advice, often in banking and antitrust law.

The proliferation of Anglo-Saxon firms within the country has had a significant impact on domestic commercial law firms beyond encouraging specialisation as a way of improving efficiency. Particularly important is the reform of the partnership system. The traditional Italian model of a single equity holder has given the Italians the reputation of having among the wealthiest lawyers in the world. Largely due to the widespread dissatisfaction among younger partners, this system is losing favour. In its place firms are opting for more 'democratic' partnership systems, usually on a modified lockstep basis.

LEGAL MARKET

With the increasing presence of Anglo-Saxon firms in Italy, first through UK internationals and now by US legal giants, the market is in a state of perpetual motion. Some senior associates and partners are being lured by the lockstep systems of the international firms and others are refusing to be engulfed by the 'foreigners', preferring to set up their own practices in line with the traditional Italian model when their previously independent firms merge. In what must be the next logical step, there is even movement between the US and the UK firms as individual lawyers look for the management structure and style that suits them. The end result is that legal CVs are landing on interesting desks. Lateral hires have been abundant in the last year, and in some circumstances whole teams have dispersed.

The very real danger that recent defections by strong local partners becomes a mass migration is driving change. Even some of the seemingly traditional firms are welcoming new management systems. In addition, founding partners are increasingly considering the issue of succession and how to prepare the firms to become institutions after they retire.

US firms are increasing in number in Italy. It was announced in the autumn that American firm **McDermott, Will & Emery** had merged with *Carnelutti, Studio Legale Associato* to form a 19-partner practice based in Milan and Rome called **McDermott, Will & Emery/Carnelutti**. It wasn't just outsiders who were startled by the news. Among those that chose not to remain at the merged firm were Paolo Barozzi, who joined the partnership in the Milan-based corporate and financial services department of **Studio Legale Delfino e Associati, Willkie Farr & Gallagher LLP**, and Filippo Disetore who joined **NCTM – Studio Legale Associato**. **Clifford Chance Studio Legale Associato** took advantage of **McDermott, Will & Emery/Carnelutti**'s merger, taking on the whole team when *Carnelutti, Studio Legale Associato's* Padua office was left out in the cold. The firm has recently appointed three new partners and three new counsel.

Dewey Ballantine caused quite a stir in 2003. In October two offices were opened in Milan and Rome together with an Italian desk in London. The practice which currently consists of more than 20 fee-earners, including six partners is headed by former **Simmons & Simmons** M&A and private equity specialist Bruno Gattai. Along with three associates Gattai also took former **Simmons & Simmons** partners Nicola Brunetti, Giovanbattista Santangelo and Stefano Catenacci. Stefano

Speroni joined the American firm's partnership from **Gianni, Origoni, Grippo & Partners**, whilst Ugo Giordano had previously been employed by Merrill Lynch.

Although American advances into the Italian legal market include the new offices set up by **Shearman & Sterling LLP** in Rome in March 2002, expansion has not only been from west to east. **Chiomenti Studio Legale** opened an office in New York, despite its apparently harmonious alliance with **Skadden, Arps, Slate, Meagher & Flom LLP**. Growth continues to be a focus for the firm. In the last 12 months, seven partners were appointed internally, while an eighth, Manfredi Vianni Tolomei was welcomed from **Simmons & Simmons**.

Indeed, **Simmons & Simmons** has had a run of unfortunate losses. As well as the corporate defection en masse to **Dewey Ballantine** and the lateral hire of Manfredi Vianni Tolomei, in the Spring of 2003, the firm also lost partners Enrico Zattoni, Massimo Chiaia and Giovanni Bandera. New managing partner Richard Slater was seconded from London in September and hopes are high that he will be able to restore not only the quantity, but the quality of legal expertise in the firm's Italian offices.

Bonelli Erede Pappalardo has recently taken over **Allen & Overy**'s Italian desk in London. The firm has also launched a tax department under the guidance of Andrea Silvestre from Deloitte & Touche. **Allen & Overy** is however by no means losing its grip on the market. In January 2004 it announced the appointment of two new partners, Dr Andrea Manganelli and Francesco Parisi and Dr Quirino Imbimbo, of counsel, together with 15 new associates to its tax departments in Rome and Milan. **Gianni, Origoni, Grippo & Partners** is also following a programme of expansion. Its Bologna office was opened in 2002 and in 2003 a new branch was opened in Naples. The firm has appointed seven new partners. In 2004 Stefano Crosio will replace Tomaso Cenci as resident partner in New York.

Freshfields Bruckhaus Deringer has been joined by acclaimed administrative law professor Marcello Clarich. His former firm, the once impressive *Clarich, Libertini, Macaluso & Valli* has now splintered as other name partner Fabio Macaluso has accepted a position at Hutchison 3G. Former **Freshfields Bruckhaus Deringer** Rome-based lawyer Paolo Daviddi has joined **Norton Rose**'s partnership in Milan.

Other developments include the European spread of UK firm **DLA**. The firm's alliance with **De Berti Jacchia Franchini Forlani** was unceremoniously terminated, while the 37-fee-earner Milan office of **Coudert Brothers** has been welcomed into the UK firm, with the five partners rumoured to have come in at the top of the equity. A small practice in Rome is still associated with the American firm.

Bird & Bird has set up an office in Milan, headed by Massimiliano Mostardini. He and most of his team of 19 fee-earners have come from what was once *Andersen Legal*. **Orrick, Herrington & Sutcliffe LLP** has also announced its presence in Milan. In May 2003 the firm took on a group of 23 lawyers from the legal arm of what was *Studio Legale Tributario associated with Ernst & Young*, and is now **EY Law**. **Berwin Leighton Paisner** has entered into a formal alliance with **Studio Santa Maria**.

Studio Legale Sutti also set up a tax department during the year, headed by Dr Giampaolo Corabi. With the addition of 12 tax lawyers, the department now consists of 26 fee-earners.

BANKING, FINANCE AND CAPITAL MARKETS

Allen & Overy continues to lead the field in banking, finance and capital markets. Within the department Giancarlo Castorino is highly rated for his expertise in acquisition finance, and Franco Vigliano for project finance work. G Massimiliano Danusso provides exemplary advice on ICM and is spoken of highly by clients. The capital markets team includes two members of the New York Bar; senior partner Roberto Casati and international offerings specialist Max Aaron.

Two further banking partners were made up in 2003, Andrea Cristaudi and Andrea Arosio. One client commented that the team were always, 'available and efficient, offering a high quality service and, due to their skills and well-staffed teams, providing us with valuable advice even in complex and non standard transactions'.

Allen & Overy represented Merrill Lynch and UBSW in connection with the issue of a 30-year, $1bn SEC-registered bond for the Region of Lombardy, the first SEC-registered bond for an Italian region. The firm has gained considerable public finance expertise within its ICM practice. Recent work includes advising Merrill Lynch International in connection with the establishment of an EMTN programme for the Italian Region of Veneto, as well as in relation to the inaugral bond issue under the programme. Infrastructure and project finance is a strength; the firm advised Banca Intesa, UniCredit Banca Mobiliare, Sanpaolo IMI and Banca di Roma as mandated lead arrangers of a €908m guarantee facility to CAV.TO.MI in connection with the construction of the Milan-Turin high speed railway.

Chiomenti Studio Legale excels in capital markets and securitisation. The lawyers are hailed by clients as being 'efficient problem solvers' and the firm is instructed by most of the major Italian banks. The firm has recently acted on the Meta flotation, the Trevisan flotation and the Novuspharma and Cellthepeutics merger and subsequent quotation. The firm also advised on the tender offer for Interbanca by Banca Antonveneta. More general banking work includes advising on the acquisition financing of Fondiaria Sai and advising on the project Tiglio financing. Highly respected partner Francesco Ago leads the practice. Both he and Michele Carpinelli are highly sought after for their experience and expertise in the banking sector.

Under the dedicated management of partner Nicholas Wrigley, **Clifford Chance Studio Legale Associato**'s banking and finance department remains strong. Although the firm lost partner Luigi Chessa in 2003, numbers in the department have not faltered. Over the last year, two associates were welcomed into the partnership, two became counsel and Elizabeth Knox joined the firm as a securitisation partner. Clients have been impressed by the co-ordination with the firm's other international offices when dealing with cross-border issues.

Clifford Chance Studio Legale Associato advised the winning bidder, Permira Associati on the financing of the €5.5bn acquisition of SEAT Pagine Gialle and also advised the lead arrangers on the €2.3bn refinancing of Edipower. The firm

BANKING, FINANCE AND CAPITAL MARKETS

ALLEN & OVERY ✪
CHIOMENTI STUDIO LEGALE ✪
CLIFFORD CHANCE STUDIO LEGALE ASSOCIATO
GIANNI, ORIGONI, GRIPPO & PARTNERS ✪

BONELLI EREDE PAPPALARDO
FRESHFIELDS BRUCKHAUS DERINGER ✪

Ashurst ✪
Cleary Gottlieb Steen & Hamilton ✪
Giliberti Pappalettera Triscornia e Associati ✪
Grimaldi e Associati
Loiacono et Associati ✪
Macchi di Cellere Gangemi
McDermott, Will & Emery/Carnelutti ✪
NCTM – Studio Legale Associato ✪
Norton Rose
Pavia e Ansaldo
Simmons & Simmons ✪
White & Case, Varrenti e Associati

Baker & McKenzie ✪
Beltramo, Studio Legale
DLA ✪
Delfino e Associati, Willkie Farr & Gallagher LLP, Studio Legale ✪
Galgano ✪
Puopolo Sistilli Geffers & Luise ✪
Sutti, Studio Legale ✪
Tonucci, Studio Legale ✪
Ughi e Nunziante ✪
Vita Samory, Fabbrini e Associati ✪

Firms are listed A-Z in tiers which are ranked in order of priority
✪ Indicates firm displays contact details at the end of this chapter.

also advised BNP Paribas, Mediobanca and Lehman Brothers as mandated lead arrangers in relation to the €410m refinancing of the short-term acquisition debt, utilised for the financing of the public tender offer by De Agostini Invest SA for Lottomatica. Asset finance and securitisation work included advising the arrangers and lead managers in the fourth phase of the securitisation of the social security contributions of INPS.

Alberto Giampieri, who heads the three partner banking and finance department at **Gianni, Origoni, Grippo & Partners**, is extremely highly regarded by peers and clients alike. He specialises in structured acquisition and project finance as well as securitisation. Andrea Gianelli is also recommended, in particular for his expertise in derivatives, structured finance and securitsation. The firm acted for the mandated lead arrangers in connection with the €8.3bn structured facilities granted to support the Schemaventotto takeover of Autostrade SpA. This was the largest European acquisition financing deal in 2003. The firm also assisted on the Imser securitisation Srl, one of the first Italian private sector real estate securitisations. Project financing work over the last year includes advising Atel AG in connection with the financing for the construction of a 100 MW power plant in the north of Italy.

Bonelli Erede Pappalardo has, in particular, a strong private equity practice, and often represents Italian borrowers or foreign private equity sponsors. A new partner, from **Chiomenti Studio Legale** in Rome, joined the firm's structured finance team in January 2003. As well as the financing work that was involved in the representation of Autostrade SpA, the firm also advised on the possible refinancing of FL Selenia, with reference in particular to the existing contracts with the Fiat Group. It also advised Banca Intesa and other lending banks on restructuring the real and financial assets of Piaggio SpA. Another interesting instruction came from Argentinian Banco Hipotecario, in connection with the proposed restructuring of its outstanding debt obligations.

15 fee-earners make up **Freshfields Bruckhaus Deringer**'s dependable banking department. The firm is renowned for its capital markets practice, which was boosted by the arrival of Bruno Cas. The firm acted for Société Générale as sponsor, on Versicor Inc's listing on Nuovo Mercato. This listing was the first stock market listing in Italy of a US Nasdaq listed company. In debt capital markets, the firm advised Fortress Registered Investment Trust in connection with the rule 144A offer by Palazzo Finance Tre Srl of €776m backed by two portfolios of notes previously issued under the Italian securitisation law and a limited recourse loan.

The quality of the international finance department's work at **Ashurst** is on the up. Indeed the firm caused quite a stir when it appeared as adviser to the debt providers, BNP Paribas, Barclays Capital, CSFB and the Royal Bank of Scotland on the private equity consortium's agreed purchase of SEAT Pagine Gialle SpA from Telecom Italia SpA. Managing partner Ricardo Agostinelli and partner Leonardo Proni are thought of particularly highly.

Under the expert eye of partner Giuseppe Scassellati-Sforzolini, **Cleary Gottlieb Steen & Hamilton** has a very strong reputation for capital markets work. The firm represents six of the 11 Italian issuers listed on the NYSE, including Ducati Motor Holding SpA, Gucci Group NV and Enel SpA. The firm acted as counsel to the standby underwriters in an offering by Fiat SpA of €1.8bn in rights to subscribe for new Fiat ordinary shares.

Giliberti Pappalettera Triscornia e Associati has recently acted for Edipower and its sponsors (Atel, Aem MI, Aem TO, Edison) in the restructuring of its debt in relation to a pool of banks, and advised Impregilo SpA on financing a €414m waste-to-energy project in Naples. Managing partner Enrico Giliberti and head of project finance Mauro Maia have extremely strong reputations.

At **Grimaldi e Associati** name partner Vittorio Grimaldi and partner Francesco Novelli specialise in banking and finance. The firm advised Infrastructure SpA in connection with the High Speed Railway Funding Note Programme which aims to fund the financing of the design, development, construction and operation of the Turin-Milan-Naples section of the high-speed railway.

Loiacono e Associati though small, with only two partners, eight associates and one paralegal, has dealt with some interesting and high-value work. The firm advised the originator, Banco Popolare di Intra, in the €550m performing loans securitisation arranged by CSFB. Other clients include Citigroup, Credit Agricole Indosuez and Goldman Sachs.

Claudio Visco and Mario Padovan at **Macchi di Cellere Gangemi** are highly regarded by their peers. This independent firm focuses on capital markets, asset-backed securities and securitisation work. Clients include Credit Lyonnais and Morgan Stanley.

McDermott, Will & Emery/Carnelutti assists major financial groups with all aspects of banking and corporate finance. The department has valuable experience in assisting hedge funds and in setting up other innovative financial products. Recently the firm assisted Barclays Global investors in the authorisation and listing on the Italian stock exchange of four different mutual funds. Two of them are bond-related funds and will be the first 'bond ETF' listings in Italy.

NCTM – Studio Legale Associato provides specialist banking and finance advice to major Italian and international financial institutions. Alberto Toffoletto and Stefano Padovani are recommended, particularly for bank-related regulatory work. Recent clients include Banco Santander and Unicredito Italiano.

With only a three-year presence in Italy, **Norton Rose** has managed to make considerable headway into the energy and transport sectors in Italy and has advised on project finance internationally. Of note, the firm is advising Banca Intesa as lead arranger on a project to build the Milano-Brescia direct highway and is assisting Euromobiliare, as the financial adviser to the Municipal Authority of Palermo in relation to the privatisation of the Palermo Municipal Water Company.

Pavia e Ansaldo's banking and finance department is highly regarded, particularly for its contribution to structured finance transactions. Recently the firm worked on a €600m structured finance deal for ABN Amro, a €250m loan agreement in favour of Credifarma on behalf of Banca Nazionale del Lavoro, and advised CSFB on the acquisition of a minority stake in Safilo SpA.

Although the loss of finance expert Manfredi Vianini Tolomei was felt by **Simmons & Simmons**, the firm remains strong in private equity and securitisation. Significant private equity clients include 3i and Private Equity Partners. Recent work includes acting for Centrobanca and Banca Popolare di Cremona as dual originators in a mortgage loan securitisation.

In the past year three new partners have joined **White & Case, Varrenti e Associati**'s banking and finance team, including finance guru John Riggs, who relocated from the firm's Paris office. The firm continues to advise Banca di Roma on its worldwide group reorganisation project. Other banking clients include Deutsche Bank and Banca di Bologna. Andrea Ughi heads the capital markets group and is highly recommended. One client praised the securitisation team for its, 'timely and innovative advice.' The firm's project management skills were described as, 'outstanding'.

Alberto Fornari heads the banking finance and securities department at **Baker & McKenzie**'s Milan office. The firm advised Nexgen in the exchange of equity-linked notes for Italian listed shares. The value of the deal was €600m. The firm has also recently advised Dresdner Bank in relation to the project financing of a hospital. Partners Gianfranco Macconi and Alfredo Lucente are recommended.

Susanna Beltramo of **Studio Legale Beltramo** deals with all aspects of banking and finance work, but specialises in EMTN programmes. Clients describe the quality of service and efficiency provided as 'extremely high' and include the regions of Puglia and Marche, Finmeccanica and Banca Agrileasing SpA.

DLA's banking and finance group advises on cross-border finance structures, asset-backed securitisation transactions, syndicated financing and project financing. The firm also supports investment and merchant banks in the issuing, marketing and sale of shares, bonds, mutual funds and other securities and investment products.

Corporate and finance specialist **Studio Legale Delfino e Associati, Willkie Farr & Gallagher LLP** advised the lead investor EDV S.A in the financing for the development and construction of a windfarm. It also advised the deal structurer and arranger in the debt restructuring of Gruppo Coin SpA.

Clients consider **Galgano** to be 'proactive' and 'pragmatic'. Milan-based partner David Contini is praised for his contribution to the firm's banking and finance practice. He is working on the first Italian-US cross-border leasing transaction, advising US investor FleetBoston. Clients include UBS AG, Credit Agricole Indosuez, HSBC and Edison.

Independent firm **Puopolo Sistilli Geffers & Luise** has advised a number of international businesses on banking and finance issues. In particular the firm has assisted a US technology group with subsidiaries in Italy in negotiating refinancing agreements with Canadian and US banks.

Studio Legale Sutti, **Studio Legale Tonucci** and **Vita Samory, Fabbrini e Associati** specialise in other practice areas, but still have banking, finance and capital markets lawyers worthy of note.

Ughi e Nunziante's senior partner Marcello Gioscia has impressive capital markets and project finance expertise. The firm has been active in energy sector privatisations in recent years.

CORPORATE AND COMMERCIAL: MILAN AND ROME

Bonelli Erede Pappalardo's exceptional band of partners, including Roberto Cera, Umberto Nicodano, and Alberto Saravalle have maintained the standard of excellence set by the firm's name partners. Although nominally independent, the firm enjoys 'non-exclusive, 'best-friends' links', which focus primarily on M&A and capital markets, with **Bredin Prat** in France, **Slaughter and May** in the UK, **Uría & Menéndez** in Spain and **Hengeler Mueller** in Germany. As well as its domestic offices in Milan, Rome and Genoa, the firm also benefits from a five-partner office in Brussels and, since September 2003, a London office housing 16 fee-earners. In 2003 13 lawyers joined the firm's Rome and Milan offices.

Last year the firm advised Autostrade SpA in relation to the IPO of shares in Autostrade SpA, the reorganisation of the Autostrade Group and realisation of Project Mediterranean, and the merger of Autostrade into Newco 28 and its subsequent listing. Other recent work includes advising ACSM Como SpA on its proposed merger with another public utility, Bergamo Ambiente Servizi SpA. The value of the combined entity will be €270m.

Chiomenti Studio Legale has 23 partners split almost equally between its Milan and Rome offices. A further two partners head up London while two senior associates have, since September, manned a New York office. International referrals are still welcomed through the strategic alliance the firm has with **Skadden, Arps, Slate, Meagher & Flom LLP**.

CORPORATE AND COMMERCIAL: MILAN AND ROME

BONELLI EREDE PAPPALARDO
CHIOMENTI STUDIO LEGALE ✪
GIANNI, ORIGONI, GRIPPO & PARTNERS ✪

ALLEN & OVERY ✪
CLIFFORD CHANCE STUDIO LEGALE ASSOCIATO
GILIBERTI PAPPALETTERA TRISCORNIA E ASSOCIATI ✪
GRIMALDI E ASSOCIATI
PEDERSOLI E ASSOCIATI ✪

Baker & McKenzie ✪
Cleary Gottlieb Steen & Hamilton ✪
d'Urso, Studio Legale
Freshfields Bruckhaus Deringer ✪
Galgano ✪
Grande Stevens: Studio Legale Associazione Professionale
Macchi di Cellere Gangemi
Mazzoni E Associati – Verusio E Cosmelli Studi Legali Associati
McDermott, Will & Emery/Carnelutti ✪
NCTM – Studio Legale Associato ✪
Vita Samory, Fabbrini e Associati ✪

Ashurst ✪
Bernascone & Soci Squire Sanders & Dempsey L.L.P., Studio Legale ✪
Curtis, Mallet-Prevost, Colt & Mosle LLP in assoc con Gilioli, Alemani, Bocchiola, Tamburini e Partners ✪
DLA ✪
De Berti Jacchia Franchini Forlani ✪
Delfino e Associati, Willkie Farr & Gallagher LLP, Studio Legale ✪
Jones Day ✪
Lovells ✪
Orrick, Herrington & Sutcliffe LLP
Pavia e Ansaldo
Puopolo Sistilli Geffers & Luise ✪
Simmons & Simmons ✪
Sutti, Studio Legale ✪
Tonucci, Studio Legale ✪
Trevisan & Cuonzo ✪
Ughi e Nunziante ✪
White & Case, Varrenti e Associati

Firms are listed A-Z in tiers which are ranked in order of priority
✪ Indicates firm displays contact details at the end of this chapter.

Friendly and hostile acquisitions, leveraged and management buyouts, privatisations, joint ventures and corporate restructuring are all covered by the firm, as well as more general commercial and corporate matters. Wide-ranging expertise has ensured that not only the quality, but the quantity, of the work the firm has picked up over the last year. The firm was involved in the Telecom Italia SpA deal, and the Olivetti SpA deal – the largest Italian merger of the year. Other acquisitions that the firm has advised on include those by Unipol of Winthertur Assicurazioni and Ifil of participants in Fiat, San Paolo Bank, Juventus and Soiem. Partners Michele Carpinelli and Vittorio Tadei continue to be praised for their excellence in this field, whilst Francesco Tedeschini is hailed as a rising star.

With 265 lawyers, 46 of whom are partners, in seven offices worldwide, including a recently opened office in Naples, **Gianni, Origoni, Grippo & Partners** boasts the title of largest Italian firm. In this case, there is definitely strength in numbers. The firm, led by renowned managing partner Francesco Gianni, not only dominates the Italian M&A market but is a recognised force in Europe. It also benefits internationally from the exclusive relationship it enjoys with **Linklaters** with whom it is 'integrated professionally, if not economically'. Milan-based Cesare Vento and Rome-based Alessandro Giuliani are both highly recommended.

The firm represented Olivetti in the Telecom-Olivetti merger. Work included advising on a tender offer by Olivetti on Telecom shares funded through a €9bn funding structure, the listing of new Olivetti savings shares and a complex modification of the capital structure of the company surviving the merger. The firm also assisted Telecom Italia SpA on the demerger and subsequent sale to a private equity consortium of Seat Pagine Gialle SpA, the largest demerger completed in Italy and now the infamous 'yellow pages case'. The firm is also gaining valuable expertise in cross-border mergers having dealt with the only two such deals completed in Italy between a US listed company and an Italian listed company. In 2002 **Gianni, Origoni, Grippo & Partners** represented Versicor, Inc (now Vicuron, Inc) when it merged with Biosearch Italia, and last year acted on behalf of Cell Therapeutics, Inc on its merger with Novuspharma SpA.

The transition from *Brosio, Casati e Associati in associazione con Allen & Overy* to **Allen & Overy**, in 2002, was seemingly faultless. The firm, which has over 200 lawyers based in Milan, Rome and Turin, has embraced the international management structure that resulted from the merger. The firm's stellar banking department continues to provide strong support to its 15-partner corporate team on deals that are increasingly high value and high profile. Of particular note, the firm assisted British American Tobacco in the acquisition of the previously state-owned tobacco company Ente Tabacchi Italiani SpA (ETI). The firm also advised JP Morgan, Olivetti's financial advisers, in relation to the proposed public acquisition of Telecom Italia SpA. Also, the firm assisted Fiat SpA in the sale of Fiat Avio to the Carlyle Group and Finmeccania SpA. Milan-based partners Paolo Cerina and senior partner Roberto Casati are reputed to be two of Italy's finest M&A lawyers. The firm's expertise in the energy sector was aptly demonstrated when it advised Edipower SpA, on a multi-party, multi-fuel, multi-site tolling agreement for a 6,300 MW portfolio of six thermal power plants. Partner Paolo Esposito is recommended in the energy field.

Clifford Chance Studio Legale Associato now boasts 150 fee-earners, including 23 partners, spread across its three Italian offices. Although its corporate practice was depleted as a result of the firm's demerger with **Grimaldi e Associati**, particularly with the loss of Roberto Cappelli, the firm is certainly dealing with the same quantity of high-value deals as the market leaders. Expertise covers M&A, private equity/venture capital, corporate commercial, commercial property and real estate, privatisations, energy and natural resources, administrative and environmental, employment, litigation and intellectual property. Clients include Carrefour, Cisco Systems, ENEL, Fiat and Siemens, as well as private equity houses such as Dresdner Kleinwort Capital Advisory and investment banks such as UBS. Recently the firm advised Aviva Plc in connection with the exchange of shares with Fondazione CRT, a deal valued at €440m.

Enrico Giliberti, the managing partner of Milan-based **Giliberti Pappalettera Triscornia e Associati**, is singled out for praise by his contemporaries and clients. Of greatest significance, he led the team that advised the acquiring consortium on Telecom Italia's disposal of SEAT Pagine Gialle SpA. The six-partner boutique deals predominantly with complex corporate and financial transactions. Recently the firm has advised Leonardo Holdings SA in the €480m sale of a 44.7% interest in Aeroporti di Roma SpA to Macquarie Airport Group and Macquarie Bank. It has also advised Investitori Associati, BC Partners, CVC Capital Partners and Permira in the €5.65bn acquisition of a controlling equity participation in Seat SpA. The firm is currently advising the purchasers on the post- acquisition phase. One client describes both Enrico Giliberti and his colleague Carlo Pappalettera as, 'top class lawyers'.

Grimaldi e Associati has established itself as an Italian corporate legal force to be reckoned with. The combined experience of Vittorio Grimaldi, Francesco Novelli, Roberto Cappelli, Vallerio di Gravio and new partner Francesco Sciaudone, has ensured that the firm has been instructed by some of Italy's top corporate clients. The firm has 60 fee-earners, including 11 partners in offices based in Milan, Rome and Brussels. The firm advised the Italian Ministry of Economy and Finance on the sale of the state-owned ETI to the British American Tobacco Group, the purchase agreement for which was signed in July.

Pedersoli e Associati has over 50 lawyers working from offices in Milan and Rome. Although the firm was only established in 2001, when it splintered from *Studio Pedersoli Grande Stevens Lombardi e Associati*, it already has a reputation for excelling in M&A work. Partners Carlo Pedersoli and Giuseppe Lombardi are both highly recommended. The firm acted for Gruppo Intesa SpA when it agreed to merge its Argentinian subsidiary, Banco Sudameris Argentina SA with Banco Patagonia SA. It also acted for Intesa Bci Bank when IntesaBci Bank (Suisse) was acquired by Credit Agricole SA, a subsidiary of Credit Agricole Indosuez. The firm also acted for the Carlyle Group when, together with Finmeccanica SpA it agreed to acquire Avio Spa from Fiat SpA for €1.5bn.

Baker & McKenzie has 70 fee-earners in its Milan office and 30 fee-earners in its Rome office. The successful corporate and M&A department is a core practice area within the firm representing a variety of major multinationals. Most recent clients include Emerson Electric, Platinum Equity, Polaroid, American Standard, Mitsubishi and Cisco. Alberto Semeria and Gianfranco Macconi are highly recommended.

Although **Cleary Gottlieb Steen & Hamilton**'s greatest strength is in its EU, regulatory and competition work, it continues to win instructions from impressive blue-chip clients. The firm represented Enel in a €3.8bn sale by public auction of power generating company Interpower SpA. Other recent M&A work includes advising Groupe Canal+ SA and Canal+ BV in the €920m agreement to sell 100% of the capital stock of Italy's largest pay-TV company, Telepiù SpA to News Corporation. Resident partners William McGurn and Giuseppe Scassellati-Sforzolini provide excellent M&A advice.

Studio Legale d'Urso continues to focus successfully on M&A and capital markets. Carlo D'Urso, managing partner of the 14-partner firm, is one of Italy's highly respected corporate lawyers. Recent high-profile cases include assisting De Agostini SpA on the acquisition of Toro Assicurazioni SpA from the Fiat Group and acting for Immsi SpA on the acquisition of Paggio SpA from Morgan Grenfell.

Freshfields Bruckhaus Deringer has over 130 lawyers in Italy, 100 of whom are based in Milan. The firm's corporate department has been involved in a large number of major transactions, both domestic and cross-border. Of particular interest, the firm represented Hutchison 3G on an acquisition from rival operator Blu. It also advised Macquarie Airport Group on the acquisition of joint control over Aeroporti di Roma SpA. The firm was also active on the sale of TelefonicaDataCorp SA's stake in Atlanet SpA to the Fiat Group and the acquisition from Atlanet of a pro rata stake in Ipse.

Galgano has 'good friendships', although no strict alliances with a number of foreign firms including **Shearman & Sterling LLP**, **Macfarlanes** and **Taylor Wessing**. Over the last 12 months the firm's corporate department has been involved in transactions which, when valued in total, exceed €2bn. Guido Capelli and his team's clients include the Mariella Burani Fashion Group, Onama and Cedam. Bologna-based name partner Francesco Galgano is described by one competitor as 'a genius' and is highly recommended for his work in corporate litigation.

Name partner Franzo Grandes Stevens of **Grande Stevens: Studio Legale Associazione Professionale** established his reputation by advising the Agnelli family, the proprietors of Fiat.

Macchi di Cellere Gangemi is expanding. During the year the firm merged with Bologna-based *Borghesi Morara Venturoli* and consequently has over 100 fee-earners operating from six Italian cities and its office in Paris. By the end of 2003 the firm intends to have 17 partners working within its new UK-style modified lockstep compensation structure. This independent firm's clients tend to be multinational groups as it specialises in cross-border M&A deals. Name partner Luigi Macchi de Cellere concentrates on the telecoms and energy sectors. Managing partner Claudio Visco is recommended for his corporate finance work.

Successful 14-lawyer firm **Mazzoni E Associati – Verusio E Cosmelli Studi Legali Associati** has offices in Milan, Rome, Lucca, Lecce and Pisa. Name partner Alberto Mazzoni is recommended.

Studio Legale Carnelutti's surprise merger has left the firm, under its new guise of **McDermott, Will & Emery/Carnelutti**, with 19 partners in Milan and Rome. Market observers are interested to see what the future holds for this, the latest in international takeovers. The firm is regularly retained in negotiated transactions, including leveraged buy-outs, mergers, restructurings, spin-offs and joint ventures. In 2003 the firm advised Bierra Peroni on its sale of an initial 60% of the company to SABMiller. The value of the transaction was €625m.

23-partner independent **NCTM – Studio Legale Associato** was formed three years ago after the three-way merger between *Negri Clementi, Toffoletto* and *Studio Legale Cesaris*. Although the firm of 121 fee-earners is predominantly based in Milan, it also has offices in Rome, Vicenza and Verona. In 2003 partner Filippo Disertori joined the firm's corporate team. The department, and particularly managing partner Paolo Montironi has highly rated private equity expertise. Last year the firm represented De Agostini in the sale, valued at €2.4bn, of Toro Assicurazioni SpA from Fiat SpA to De Agostini SpA. Other recent clients include BS Private Equity and Santé Holdings.

Vita Samory, Fabbrini e Associati has ten partners and 30 other fee-earners in its Milan office. There is also a smaller office in Rome which houses four fee-earners and is headed by a solitary partner. The firm focuses on corporate, M&A and private equity work. The firm assisted in the acquisitions of Intercos Italia SpA and Radici Film SpA. It also dealt with a corporate bond issue by Campari. Name partner Luigi Vita Samory has a wealth of M&A experience and is also recommended for contentious matters.

Highly regarded managing partner, Daniele Raynaud leads the nine-partner Italian branch of **Ashurst** in Milan. The firm specialises in acquisition finance. In M&A the firm was instructed by Societa Assicuratrice Industriale SpA in connection with a €1bn acquisition of the majority shareholding of insurance company La Fondiaria Assicurazioni SpA.

Gabriele Bernascone, **Studio Legale Bernascone & Soci Squire Sanders & Dempsey L.L.P.**'s managing partner, is recommended for his corporate expertise. The firm is experienced in M&A, corporate finance, international distribution agreements and private equity deals. It specialises in cross-border transactions involving both Italian and foreign investors and lenders.

Curtis, Mallet-Prevost, Colt & Mosle LLP in assoc con Gilioli, Alemani, Bocchiola, Tamburini e Partners has a strong practice advising on M&A, joint ventures, and foreign direct investment. All the firm's lawyers are admitted both in Italy and the US. Managing partner Eric Gilioli is recommended for litigation. Finance partner Elena Berlucchi is also highly regarded.

As mentioned above, the five-partner Milan office, of **Coudert Brothers** has been taken over by **DLA**. When they find the right people, an office will be opened in Rome. The firm is marketing its new international network heavily, and claims to have a corporate team located across 16 jurisdictions. The 37 fee-earners' clients include major Italian and foreign corporate groups, local and foreign equity funds as well as medium-sized companies. Recently the corporate department has acted for a multinational steel manufacturer on a €50m deal and represented the vendors in the sale of four logistics companies for €78.5m.

It will be interesting to see what the future holds for **De Berti Jacchia Franchini Forlani** now that **DLA** has taken over the **Coudert Brothers** Milan office, and the firm has regained its independence. The firm appears optimistic. In the summer of 2003 it moved to larger premises that it says will support its growth over the next few years. Name partner Gianni Forlani is the firm's best known corporate lawyer. Among the department's clients are international corporations acting in Italy and medium and large sized Italian companies with international interests.

Managing partner Maurizio Delfino heads niche firm **Studio Legale Delfino e Associati, Willkie Farr & Gallagher LLP** and specialises in corporate and finance advice. The Milan office benefited from accepting ex-*Carnelutti, Studio Legale* lawyer Paolo Barozzi into the partnership in September 2003. Impressive recent work includes advising Citigroup Global Markets Ltd on the SEAT Pagine Gialle SpA deal. The firm also advised Lufthansa on the purchase of Air Dolomiti SpA for €29m and Avenance SA on its acquistion of Ristochef SpA for over €16m. Andrea Carreri and Emanuele Alemagna are also recommended for their corporate expertise.

Phillipe Billot is the senior partner of **Jones Day** in Milan. Work undertaken includes asset finance and securitisation, e-commerce, foreign direct investment, insolvency and corporate restructuring, and M&A. Clients include Vivendi Environment, Providence Equity, and Société Générale.

The Italian branch of **Lovells** continues to benefit from the firm's international network, receiving international referrals as well as instructions in its own right. Of note, the firm assisted SABMiller Italia Srl in its majority interest acquisition of Birra Peroni SpA. The firm also advised the Alstom Group in the sale of its Italian transmission and distribution business to MIT Monza Instrument Transformers Srl, part of the AEG group.

Orrick, Herrington & Sutcliffe LLP opened an office in Milan in May 2003 with 23 lawyers from the legal arm of *Studio Legale Tributario associated with Ernst & Young*, now **EY Law**. The firm covers corporate, restructuring and project finance transactions. Clients include Enel, Amplifon and FINSIEN. The firm advised one of the American Banks in the acquisition of SEAT Pagine Gialle SpA.

Pavia e Ansaldo has learned to concentrate on its core offices in Milan, Rome, Padua, Turin and Moscow. The firm has retreated from New York and is reviewing its presence in the Far East. Adriano Villa, of counsel returned from Tokyo in 2002. International connections are still important though and the firm has a good working relationship with, among others, **Herbert Smith**. Corporate and Commercial clients include Lufthansa Technik AG and European Closures Group.

Seven-partner firm **Puopolo Sistilli Geffers & Luise** has offices in Milan and Rome and is headed by name partner Gianfranco Puopolo. The firm concentrates on the insurance and energy sectors and is currently assisting NZMP, a New Zealand company of the Fonterra Group on an acquisition in Italy. Other international clients include WorldCom. Clients praise the firm for 'quality of service', 'professionalism' and 'pro-activity'.

Having lost some of its corporate stars to, among others, **Dewey Ballantine**, it remains to be seen how **Simmons & Simmons**' Italian offices will be affected. The firm's strengths reflect those of its head office in London and include private equity, M&A and corporate advisory work. Clients in Italy include Telecom Italia Mobile SpA, Primafin SpA and the Royal Dutch Shell group.

Studio Legale Sutti continues to expand in south-eastern Europe. The firm now has offices in Bergamo and Brescia, Genoa, Monza, Rome, Bulgaria, Serbia and Montenegro and Romania as well as Japan and the UK. The firm is known for its expertise in IP and disputes. The firm deals with the acquisitions of Italian private companies, representing foreign purchasers interested in the hi-tech sector, and has advised on the buy-out of Mivar, the largest Italian television manufacturer and assisted in the establishment of an Italian operation for the US mainframe software company Levy Ray and Shoup.

Studio Legale Tonucci operates from eight offices worldwide. Partner Agostino Clemente joined the firm in 2003 from **Studio Legale Delfino e Associati, Willkie Farr & Gallagher LLP**. The firm recently advised the Italian Treasury on the sale of the Ministry's remaining stake in Telecom Italia SpA. Other clients include Alitalia, Technitrol and Petronas. Marco Nicolini is the firm's foremost corporate partner. Riccardo Troiano is also recommended for his energy sector expertise.

Trevisan & Cuonzo is best known for its impressive work in IP, however, it continues to provide quality commercial and corporate advice. Under the leadership of name partner Gabriel Cuonzo, the corporate department has attracted clients such as Nintendo of Europe, Bayer AG and ABB Industria. The firm also continues to assist vehicle and motorcycle manufacturers such as DaimlerChrysler, Porsche, Harley-Davidson and Caterpillar. The firm has now opened an office in Parma.

Only ten partners remain at **Ughi e Nunziante** although Gianni Nunziante remains highly respected among the profession. The firm advised the Treasury on the sale of Enel SpA shares to Morgan Stanley and represented d'Amico di Navigazione SpA on the acquisition of Italia di Navigazione Spa and its subsequent sale to CP Ships Limited.

Since **White & Case, Varrenti e Associati** merged in 2001, the Italian branch of the US giant has focused on expanding its core practice areas of corporate/M&A, capital markets and finance. John Riggs joined the firm's Rome office from its Paris branch in 2003. The firm represented UniCredito Italiano SpA in the acquisition of a 50% interest in Koc Financial Services. The firm also advised Celestica on the €4m acquisition of Cisco's manufacturing facilities in Italy. Allessandro Varrenti is recommended for his experience and expertise in M&A work.

EU, REGULATORY AND COMPETITION: MILAN AND ROME

Bonelli Erede Pappalardo's five-partner EU law department has extremely strong foundations. Not only was Aurelio Pappalardo formerly an EC Director General for Competition, but the firm also boasts Professor Luca Radicati, a renowned competition expert, Massimo Merolais and Clausio Tesauro. The firm provides advice on all aspects of EU law, including antitrust, mergers and joint ventures, state aid, public procurement, financial services, tax and customs, IP, telecoms, trade law, energy, privatisation, public monopolies and public undertakings.

Acclaimed partner Mario Siragusa leads **Cleary Gottlieb Steen & Hamilton**'s highly reputed EU, regulatory and competition practice.

EU, REGULATORY AND COMPETITION: MILAN AND ROME

BONELLI EREDE PAPPALARDO
CLEARY GOTTLIEB STEEN & HAMILTON ✪

Allen & Overy ✪
Clifford Chance Studio Legale Associato
Freshfields Bruckhaus Deringer ✪
Gianni, Origoni, Grippo & Partners ✪

Baker & McKenzie ✪
Chiomenti Studio Legale ✪
De Berti Jacchia Franchini Forlani ✪
Guarino, Studio Legale
Mondini-Rusconi, Studio Legale ✪
NCTM – Studio Legale Associato ✪
Rossi, Studio
Rucellai & Raffaelli
Santilli Acernese Montesi – LEXJUS
Sutti, Studio Legale ✪
Ughi e Nunziante ✪

Firms are listed A-Z in tiers which are ranked in order of priority
✪ *Indicates firm displays contact details at the end of this chapter.*

As well as Italian expertise, the Rome office is able to rely on the considerable experience of its sister offices in Brussels and Frankfurt. In 2003 the firm advised four private equity funds in connection with the antitrust issues raised by their then contemplated indirect acquisition of minority shareholdings in SEAT Pagine Gialle SpA. The firm is also representing Alitalia SpA in connection with a voluntary notification to the Italian Antitrust Authority of a proposed code-sharing agreement with the Italian airline Volare.

Allen & Overy's antitrust and competition team is headed by experienced Rome-based partner Silvia D'Alberti. Although part of the corporate department, it does not exist solely in support of the firm's M&A deals. Out of the ten antitrust specialists at the firm, four are former judicial assistants at the ECJ and the CFI. Several of the team have first-hand experience of working for national antitrust authorities. Areas of focus include mergers and joint ventures, cartel and behavioural investigations, the communications, media and hi-tech sectors, and energy and utility regulations as well as general issues of EC law. Clients include Edison, Enel, Agip Petroli SpA, Fiat and Bulgari SpA.

Clifford Chance Studio Legale Associato's competition practice is headed by highly regarded partner Cristofor Osti. His team offers advice on merger control, regulatory issues and antitrust compliance policies. It prides itself on its expertise for both local and multi-jurisdictional merger filings. The firm has provided assistance to Carrefour by filing several transactions relating to the purchase of supermarkets in Italy with the Italian Competition Authority. Other prominent clients include Mediobanca, San Paolo Wealth Management, Colony Capital LLC and the BG Group.

Although the EU regulatory and competition law department of **Freshfields Bruckhaus Deringer** lost Salvatore Lamarca in the last 12 months, in July 2003 it welcomed administrative law expert Marcello Clarich, formerly of *Clarich, Libertini, Macaluso*. The firm advises clients in relation to merger control proceedings, horizontal and vertical agreements, unilateral abuses of market power and state aid regulation. The firm has advised Enel on its pricing strategy and on electricity import regulatory issues, and Hewlett-Packard on a number of outsourcing agreements with Telecom Italia, Banksiel, Finsiel, Ericsson and Procter & Gamble.

The competition group at **Gianni, Origoni, Grippo & Partners** is relatively young. In a short space of time however, the team has consolidated an enviable practice, due not only to the wealth of knowledge that the group's lawyers display, but also, the strength of the firm's M&A department. Senior partner Alberto Pera is famed for his expertise in antitrust law. Before joining three years ago, he was secretary general of the Italian Antitrust Authority. Specialist antitrust partners Piero Fattori and Denis Fosselard are also highly recommended. The firm deals with merger control issues as well as antitrust matters, both on a national and international level.

At one time Commissioner of the Italian Antitrust Authority, Professor Giorgio Bernini joined **Baker & McKenzie**'s competition and EU department in 2002. Together with the head of practice Andrea Cicala, partner Franco Macconi and six assistants , the firm advised IMX in an antitrust dispute against Poste Italiane, and assisted the Cabot Group in connection with the European Commission's investigation into the Carbon Black industry.

Professor of International law, Andrea Giardini, continues to serve as counsel from **Chiomenti Studio Legale**'s office in Rome. The firm has represented clients from a variety of sectors including construction, insurance, air transport and defence before the EU Commission, the ECJ and the Italian antitrust Authority.

With an office in Brussels, as well as Rome, Milan, Genoa and Moscow, **De Berti Jacchia Franchini Forlani** is well placed to advise clients on EU, regulatory and competition matters. Milan-based Roberto Jacchia is respected for his knowledge of competition law.

Name partner Giuseppe Guarino, who was once a minister of finance and trade and industry heads nine lawyer boutique firm **Studio Legale Guarino** He holds professorial seats in administrative law at various state universities. Andrea Guarino is also recommended.

Partners Giorgio Mondini and Giacomo Bonelli of **Studio Legale Mondini-Rusconi** are recommended for their competition practice. Last year, the firm advised a global leader in pay-for-performance search services on the Internet on regulatory matters, and in the past has assisted big name clients such as AOL TimeWarner on antitrust issues. One client recommends Giorgio Mondini for 'steering UK- and US-based clients through the often bewildering complexities of doing business in Italy'.

NCTM – Studio Legale Associato's partner Alberto Toffoletto continues to demand a great deal of respect for his antitrust work from his competitors.

Studio Rossi's consultant Guido Rossi was once president of the Italian Stock Exchange Commission (CONSOB) and is highly recommended for his experience of antitrust law.

Rucellai & Raffaelli's standing is largely due to Enrico Adriano Raffaelli's reputation for providing excellent EU, regulatory and competition advice.

Francesco Maria Samperi, from 22-partner firm **Santilli Acernese Montesi – LEXJUS**, formerly *Santilli Acernese & Montesi*, is recommended for his antitrust advice. Of particular note last year, the firm assisted Unilever Group on antitrust issues. The firm also advises on commercial and regulatory issues for its clients in the communications sector

Studio Legale Sutti intends to further strengthen its European presence by opening an office in Brussels in 2004. This will no doubt benefit its competition and antitrust practice which is currently lead by Livia Oglio. In line with the firm's focus on the IT and e-commerce sectors, it recently represented the International Alliance for Compatible Technology in a pending complaint against Microsoft for abuse of a dominant position, and advised Seleco Multimedia in a case concerning state aid to the Italian consumer electronic industry.

Rino Caiazzo, from **Ughi e Nunziante** is rated highly by his competitors for his knowledge of competition law. Recently he assisted on a case between Colt Telecom and Telecom Italia Spa on an alleged abuse of a dominant position by Telecom Italia SpA in the telecoms market.

REAL ESTATE

Real estate transactions are another speciality of **Bonelli Erede Pappalardo**. Over the last year activity has included the establishment of real estate funds, M&A, disposals and restructuring of portfolios or companies active in the real estate sector and capital markets deals concerning real estate companies. Of note, the firm assisted Manifattura Lane Gaetano Marzotto & Figli SpA on the setting up of a joint venture with Pirelli Real Estate SpA for the development and management of industrial properties. The deal was valued at approximately €195m. The firm also advised Lehman Brothers (PTG) Limited with the acquisition of a portfolio of real estate from Assitalia SpA through a SPV. That deal was valued at €319m. Another example of the work undertaken was the advice given to Risanamento

REAL ESTATE

BONELLI EREDE PAPPALARDO
CLIFFORD CHANCE STUDIO LEGALE ASSOCIATO
FRESHFIELDS BRUCKHAUS DERINGER ✪
GIANNI, ORIGONI, GRIPPO & PARTNERS ✪

Allen & Overy ✪
Ashurst ✪
Chiomenti Studio Legale ✪
DLA ✪
Jones Day ✪
McDermott, Will & Emery/Carnelutti ✪
Mondini-Rusconi, Studio Legale ✪
Norton Rose

Firms are listed A-Z in tiers which are ranked in order of priority
✪ *Indicates firm displays contact details at the end of this chapter.*

SpA on the public offer for the acquisition of the entire share capital of IPI SpA, following the acquisition by Risanamento SpA of 55.95% of the share capital of IPI.

Over the last year, an impressive amount of **Clifford Chance Studio Legale Associato**'s corporate work has been, or resulted from, commercial real estate deals. Highly recommended partners Gian Luca Rabitti and Paolo Rulli head up the commercial property practice and have been involved in a number of the year's biggest transactions. In March 2003 the firm advised the Carlyle Group on its acquisition of a 36-building portfolio from SCIP. The firm is also instructed by Carrefour/GS and advised them on the sale and lease-back of 38 supermarkets to Whitehall (Goldman Sachs). The value of the transaction was €30m. Managing partner Nicholas Wrigley and partner Alberta Figari advised the bidding consortium made up by Generali Properties, RAS, Progestim, Lamaro and Grupo Lar in relation to the acquisition and redevelopment of property currently owned by Ente Autonomo Fiera Internazionale di Milano and used for international fairs and exhibitions.

Freshfields Bruckhaus Deringer's expertise in this sector is largely based on advising international clients. Partner Marzio Longo is highly regarded for his knowledge and experience. Three partners and eight associates make up the team which deals with both domestic and cross-border transactions. Recently the firm acted for Whitehall (Goldman Sachs) on the purchase from GS SpA (the Carrefour Group) and lease back to GS SpA of a portfolio consisting of 38 supermarkets. The firm also represented Pirelli Real Estate on a joint venture for the ownership and management of two retail and entertainment centres, and ING Real Estate on setting up a franchising agency network and the provision of services through the network.

Gianni, Origoni, Grippo & Partners is a market leader in this sector. Recently, the firm acted on one of the first Italian private sector real estate securitisations.

Allen & Overy's real estate group is part of its corporate practice. Giovanni Marini heads up the group, with Giancarlo Castorino providing expertise on property financing. Of particular note, the firm recently assisted Intesa Bci (now Banca Intesa) and Capitalia, as arrangers, on the €2.6bn financing of a real estate portfolio for Telecom Italia, Pirelli and Seat Pagine Gialle, Buffetti, Olivetti and Pirelli Real Estate (Project Tiglio) managed by Morgan Stanley real estate fund and Pirelli Real Estate.

Ashurst recently advised a consortium of Deutsche Bank, General Electric and Zunino Group on the acquisition of the real estate assets of Banca Popolare di Verona and Banca Popolare di Novara.

Chiomenti Studio Legale has also taken advantage of the recent upsurge in real estate and commercial property work. Recently the firm advised on the acquisition of Fondiaria Sai's portfolio by Morgan Stanley and Pirelli Real Estate and the acquisition of Generali Properties real estate portfolio by Investire Immobiliare sgr. The firm also established a real estate fund for Morgan Stanley and Telecom Italia.

The total value of all the real estate deals that were closed by **DLA** in the last year exceeds €2.7bn. In terms of sheer volume of transactions, the firm has excelled in this sector. The firm generally represents investors in the acquisition of single real estate assets and portfolios or the acquisition of corporate vehicles owning real estate properties. The firm advised on the largest single asset deal. It closed in October 2003 and was worth €215m. The firm also represents lenders and borrowers in financing and refinancing real estate transactions.

Jones Day has three partners that deal with commercial property. Partner Ettore Scandale advised GE Real Estate in connection with the bid for a portfolio of real estate assets belonging to RAS Spa.

Partner in charge of the Italian branch of **McDermott, Will & Emery/Carnelutti**, Luca Arnaboldi and partner Pietro Cuomo advised Curzon Global Partners in its acquisition of commercial real estate assets from Aedes Immobiliare SpA. The value of the transaction was €153m. The firm also advised on the related loan and security agreements. On a separate transaction, partner Paolo Scarduelli advised the Royal Bank of Scotland, the lender, on the Dorchester Group's acquisition of Milan's Hotel Principe di Savoia. In particular, advice was sought on securing facilities under Italian law.

Studio Legale Mondini-Rusconi assisted a major investor in a real estate project for the development of a tourist resort on the Red Sea.

Roberto Cornetta and Richard Hill lead the property and construction department at **Norton Rose**. The firm recently advised Corio, a Dutch company on the acquisition of one of the largest commercial centres now under construction in Italy. The purchase was made for €150m. The firm advised on all corporate and financial issues relating to the purchase as well as property and zoning regulations. Partner Nicolo Juvara is recommended.

TMT

Bonelli Erede Pappalardo's Sergio Erede no longer sits on the board of Telecom Italia, but the experience the lawyers gained from working with the telecoms giant has undoubtedly contributed to their market-leading position in the TMT sector. Of particular note is the expertise of Sergio Erede, Umberto Nicodano, Luca Radicati and Fabio Cappelletti. Recent work includes advising Lottomatica SpA, the market leader for Italy's gaming sector, in relation to its acquisition of 100% of the share capital of Totobit Informatica Software e Sistemi SpA. The value of the transaction was €40m.

Allen & Overy's specialist group advises on all issues relating to IT, telecoms, satellite, outsourcing, IP, media and convergence, e-commerce (including e-procurement and e-government), and data protection. Milan-based

TMT

BONELLI EREDE PAPPALARDO

ALLEN & OVERY ✪
BAKER & MCKENZIE ✪
CHIOMENTI STUDIO LEGALE ✪
CLEARY GOTTLIEB STEEN & HAMILTON ✪
CLIFFORD CHANCE STUDIO LEGALE ASSOCIATO
FRESHFIELDS BRUCKHAUS DERINGER ✪
GALGANO ✪
GIANNI, ORIGONI, GRIPPO & PARTNERS ✪
LOVELLS ✪
MCDERMOTT, WILL & EMERY/CARNELUTTI ✪

Mondini-Rusconi, Studio Legale ✪
NCTM – Studio Legale Associato ✪
Pavia e Ansaldo
Santilli Acernese Montesi – LEXJUS
Sutti, Studio Legale ✪
Tonucci, Studio Legale ✪
Trevisan & Cuonzo ✪
Ughi e Nunziante ✪

Abbatescianni e Associati
Bird & Bird ✪
Dalla Vedova
Guarino, Studio Legale
Hammonds Rossotto
Puopolo Sistilli Geffers & Luise ✪

Firms are listed A-Z in tiers which are ranked in order of priority
✪ *Indicates firm displays contact details at the end of this chapter.*

partner David D'Angelo is highly recommended for his experience in telecoms privatisation. As well as advising JPMorgan, as financial adviser to Olivetti, in connection with the proposed public acquisition of Telecom Italia, the firm recently assisted France Télécom SA in the sale of its 26.6% share in telecoms company Wind SpA and Enel SpA. Head of the corporate department, Paolo Cerino is admired for his IT and e-commerce advice.

Lorenzo de Martinis heads the e-commerce, telecoms, IT media and entertainment department at **Baker & McKenzie**'s Milan office. Clients of the eight-fee-earner department include Cisco Systems, Peoplesoft and Hewlett-Packard. In Rome, Fabio Brembati and Raffaele Giarda lead an active telecoms team.

Chiomenti Studio Legale provides excellent corporate advice on major media-related deals. It also assists on IP protection and exploitation issues, film distribution and TV broadcasting agreements and provides legal expertise in relation to technological developments. Recently the firm has assisted Hutchison 3G with its IT contracts. Other clients of note include the Mediaset Group.

Cleary Gottlieb Steen & Hamilton had a considerable number of instructions in the last year from market leaders in the areas of voice and data communications, Internet services, pay-television and software products. The firm has ten lawyers based in Italy who have experience in dealing with telecoms and media law matters. Unsurprisingly the firm specialises in antitrust investigations before the Italian Antitrust Authority, regulatory proceedings and civil litigation and arbitration proceedings. Clients include Atena Servizi SpA, Telecom Italia SpA, Telepiu SpA and United International Pictures Srl.

Clifford Chance Studio Legale Associato's TMT practice has largely resulted from its corporate and capital markets clients. The firm advised Palladio Finanziaria in relation to its participation in France Télécom's holding in Eutelsat SA organised by Eurazeo SA (Lazard). Christoforo Osti is recommended for his telecoms regulatory advice. He and Alberta Figari assisted Mediobanca, acting as monitoring trustee in the context of the divestiture of the digital and analogue terrestrial broadcasting assets of Telepiù.

Highly recommended Tommasso Salonico leads **Freshfields Bruckhaus Deringer**'s four-partner telecoms department. One of the partners, Matteo Orsingher also heads up its IP and IT group. The firm advises on regulatory advice in the fixed and mobile telecoms sectors, and deals with interconnection agreements, roaming arrangements and agreements for the installation of telecoms networks and sites. The firm's relationship with Hutchison 3G SpA is of great significance. It advised it on agreements concerning the turn-key roll-out of its mobile network and on regulatory issues concerning GPRS roaming. Other key clients include Hewlett-Packard and Enel Distribuzione Spa. IP and IT clients include RaiSat, RAI and Radiotelevisione Italiana the Walt Disney Corporation and Microsoft.

Galgano's reputation in TMT can be attributed to the dynamism of partner Marco Consonni who heads the five-fee-earner team. Senior associate Stefania Lucchetti is a new arrival to the department. In 2003 the group assisted Rhode & Schwartz in the formation of a joint venture with Sirti SpA for the supply to Rai Way of a digital terrestrial television network infrastructure. The firm also advised the joint venture in its agreement with Rai Way.

As well as assisting on the Telecom-Olivetti merger, **Gianni, Origoni, Grippo & Partners** advised Enel Group on the acquisition of the remaining share capital of Wind Telecomunicazioni SpA, Italy's third mobile telephone operator. The firm clearly continues to provide complex corporate advice to leaders in the TMT field.

Although a relatively new player in the market, **Lovells** continues to impress in the IP and IT sectors. Partner Luigi Mansoni is highly recommended for his expertise. Clients include eBay Italia Srl, and Deutsche Telekom AG.

The media, entertainment and telecommunications department at **McDermott, Will & Emery/Carnelutti** is going from strength to strength. The firm deals with issues ranging from pay-per-view contracts to digital copyright matters and the convergence of media and network technologies. Recently the firm has advised Deluxe Global Media Services Ltd, a wholly owned subsidiary of the Rank Group Plc on its acquisition of the European operations of Distronics Holdings Ltd for over €34m. The firm also advised Morgan Stanley in the placement of the Treasury's residual 3.5% stake in Telecom Italia. Also of note, the firm advised Mentor Graphics Corporation on the purchase of its Italian distributor Mento Italia Srl via Mentor Graphics (France) SARL.

Studio Legale Mondini-Rusconi has five partners that deal with IP, media and entertainment, telecoms, IT and e-commerce. Giorgio Mondini and Anna Carabelli are recommended for IP. Recently the firm assisted a major Italian software company operating in the publishing sector. The firm has considerable experience in dealing with matters concerning the music industry. Recently the firm drafted outsourcing agreements for the logistics services of a recording company of a US publishing giant. It also advised on the sale of a US-based multinational group's music publishing company and assisted a recording subsidiary of a US entertainment company in the acquisition of the artistic performances of some of the most popular Italian pop singers.

NCTM – Studio Legale Associato continues to provide its clients with sterling telecoms advice. Alberto Toffoletto is recommended for telecoms-related regulatory advice. Recent high-profile TMT clients include British Telecom.

Rome-based partner Francesca Lodigiani, from **Pavia e Ansaldo** has considerable expertise in this sector. The firm has a reputation for its work in the electronic microchip sector.

Santilli Acernese Montesi – LEXJUS has been nominated as regulatory and antitrust adviser to the Italian Communications Authority on the introduction of new communications markets following the introduction of the 2002 EU directives. The firm has advised on takeover procedures of domestic and international communications operators and currently assists mobile UMTS operators on regulatory and commercial issues.

Studio Legale Sutti prides itself on its IP, IT and e-commerce practice. The firm co-ordinated licensing and enforcement of MP3 patents for SISVEL, assisted on obtaining PC operating system technology licences, advised Credito Italiano on online banking issues and Bticino on the establishment of satellite TV channels. In particular the firm specialises in DVD media and has been involved in DVD zoning. Recently the firm assisted in the acquisition of Sound & Vision, an Italian leader in the field.

Although Fabrizio Cugia di Santorsola has left **Studio Legale Tonucci**'s telecoms department in Rome, the firm has welcomed a new head of practice, Michele Carrelli Palombi, a former partner at *Klegal* now **Studio Associato Consulenza Legale e Tributaria Associato a KPMG**. The firm advised the Italian Treasury on the sale of its remaining stake in Telecom Italia SpA. The firm also represented the Italian satellite TV broadcaster Plus Media Trading in proceedings before the EC against the acquisition of the satellite TV broadcaster Telepiù by the Murdoch Group.

Trevisan & Cuonzo is a small but highly successful IP boutique. The firm has acted for the Business Software Alliance since 1994. The firm is instructed by clients from diverse sectors including the manufacturers of pharmaceuticals, cosmetics, the steel industry, household furnishings and design and the software industry. In particular, recent clients include Dyson Ltd, Nintendo of Europe GmbH and Philips Intellectual Property & Standards. Partner Simona Lavagnini has been lobbying for changes in Italian copyright legislation and the implementation of EU directives in the fields of copyright and telecommunications.

Ughi e Nunziante's Rino Caiazzo is considered to be one of Italy's leading telecoms-related regulatory experts. The firm assisted in the Albacom SpA/Italian Government case that went before the ECJ and the Telecom Italia Spa/Wind Telecommunications SpA case that was heard before the Administrative Regional Court of Puglia. Rino Caiazzo also advised on the alleged abuse of a dominant position by Telecom Italia in the telecommunications market put forward by Colt Telecom.

Abbatescianni e Associati has three offices in Milan, Rome and a recently opened one in Brescia. Of note, partner Riccardo Roversi sat on the Italian telecoms commission and was instrumental in establishing the first online arbitration body for Internet domain name disputes. Partner Federico M Ferrara's practice covers media and entertainment law. He specialises in music, representing one of the top five music companies in Italy.

The Italian branch of **Bird & Bird** opened in April 2003 in Milan. Respected IP, TMT and life sciences expert Massimiliano Mostardini is the new managing partner. The firm has a corporate and banking capability in partner Alberto Salvadé, but focuses on IP litigation. The firm advised on the first Italian case of direct comparative advertising. Clients include Tele 2, UPS, and Honeywell.

Dalla Vedova has 15 fee-earners in Rome and an associate office in Milan. The firm is headed by name partner Marco Dalla Vedova who provides strong corporate and banking expertise and has a reputation for telecoms advice.

Name partner Professor Giuseppe Guarino of **Studio Legale Guarino** and Andrea Guarino are recommended for their expertise in the telecoms sector. In recent years the firm advised Blu in relation to its role in Italy's high-profile Hutchison 3G licence.

Hammonds Rossotto is a media boutique firm. Rome-based IP partner Pierluigi de Palma is a member of the International Association of Entertainment Lawyers and is one of Italy's top media law experts. Name partner Riccardo Rosotto is recommended for his advertising sector expertise.

Puopolo Sistilli Geffers & Luise provides communications companies, banks, investment groups and foreign law firms with advice on Italian telecoms law. Recently the firm has assisted WorldCom in connection with its Italian subsidiaries.

TAX

For specialist tax advice international and domestic companies as well as many of the top Italian law firms, request the expertise of the 62 lawyers at **Di Tanno e Associati**'s offices in Rome and Milan. Tomasso Di Tanno is renowned for his knowledge and experience in complex, tax-related issues. Industry acknowledgement of his standing is demonstrated by the number of seats he has been appointed to in organisations that span the insurance, banking and telecommunications sectors. In 2003 the firm represented JPMorgan in the Olivetti/Telecom deal that was valued at €15.5bn. It also acted for Finmeccanica in the Fiat/Avio deal. Other recent clients include De Agostini and Immsi.

Maisto e Associati specialises in providing corporate and personal tax advice, but also has considerable tax litigation expertise. Guglielmo Maisto is given the strongest of recommendations by his competitors and has, in the past, represented the Italian Association of Industry on tax matters at the OECD in Paris. Andrea Manzitti is also acknowledged as a leader in this field.

TAX

DI TANNO E ASSOCIATI ✪
MAISTO E ASSOCIATI
VITALI ROMAGNOLI & PICCARDI

Biscozzi Nobili
Camozzi & Bonissoni
Chiomenti Studio Legale ✪
EY Law ✪
F Gallo e Associati, Studio Legale Tributario
Freshfields Bruckhaus Deringer ✪
Gianni, Origoni, Grippo & Partners ✪
Uckmar, Studio

Abbatescianni e Associati
Ashurst ✪
Bonelli Erede Pappalardo
CMS Adonnino Ascoli & Cavasola Scamoni ✪
Fiorentini, Studio Legale Tributario
Haarmann Hemmelrath ✪
Macchi di Cellere Gangemi
McDermott, Will & Emery/Carnelutti ✪
NCTM – Studio Legale Associato ✪
Tonucci, Studio Legale ✪

Firms are listed A-Z in tiers which are ranked in order of priority
✪ Indicates firm displays contact details at the end of this chapter.

Since 1994 **Vitali Romagnoli, Piccardi e Associati** has had a formal association with **Clifford Chance Studio Legale Associato**, advising it on all its clients' tax issues and providing support to the firm's capital markets group. All three name partners, Enrico Vitali, Dario Romagnoli and Lorenzo Piccardi excel in this sector, giving exemplary tax advice to high-profile clients such as Merrill Lynch, Canal Plus and Banca di Roma.

Biscozzi Nobili is a traditional, independent firm. Its name partner Luigi Biscozzi has a strong reputation based on his long and successful career. He is permanent adviser to Enichem.

Full service commercial law firm **Camozzi & Bonissoni** has an excellent tax department that is highly rated among its competitors. With offices in Milan and Rome, the firm provides advice on sophisticated, tax-related issues to international law firms such as **Slaughter and May** and **Loyens & Loeff**.

Chiomenti Studio Legale has advised on tax issues related to the Acea/Electrabel operation, the Olivetti/ Telecom Italia merger and on the Seat acquisition finance operation. Michele Carpinelli is highly recommended.

Needless to say the legal departments within the accounting giants such as Deloitte & Touche are also highly respected for their tax expertise. Of particular note is **EY Law**. Despite the departure of many lawyers to **Orrick, Herrington & Sutcliffe LLP** the firm obviously provides high-quality advice on all matters pertaining to Italian tax law.

Professor Franco Gallo heads tax boutique **Studio Legale Tributario F Gallo e Associati**. He specialises in providing large corporate organisations with tax opinions. Accountant and tax consultant Professor Livia Salvini is recommended.

Freshfields Bruckhaus Deringer's five-fee-earner tax team largely supports the firm's corporate team, assisting on M&A, structured finance transactions, asset management and hybrid financial instruments. The team does however also provide a standalone service. Ronato Paternollo, and his team advised Goldman Sachs/Whitehall on the tax issues related to the acquisition of a real estate company from GS SpA, and Credit Suisse First Boston on the €2bn acquisition financing for SEAT Pagine Gialle. Banking clients include BNP Paribas, Citibank, and Deutsche Bank.

Highly respected partner, Agostini Massimo leads the tax department at **Gianni, Origoni, Grippo & Partners** and is renowned for his M&A and structured finance work. With two partners and 13 associates, the department is almost a tax boutique within the firm. It specialises in the tax aspects of corporate and structured finance, securitisation, private equity and tax-driven financial products as well as tax aspects of corporate reorganisations. In particular, the tax department is recommended for cross-border transactional work. Clients include the lenders in connection with the structured non-recourse facilities granted to support the Schemaventotto takeover of Italy's Autostrade and Olivetti in connection with the tender offer over Telecom Italia SpA.

Studio Uckmar has offices in Rome, Milan, Genoa and Buenos Aires. Victor Uckmar is highly regarded for the tax and financial advice he gives his clients.

Of 44 assistants, 36 operate from **Abbatescianni e Associati**'s main office in Milan. The building also houses its acclaimed tax department. Partner Angelo C Colombo, a commercialista (similar to a chartered accountant), heads the team that advises clients on tax and fiscal matters.

Stefano Serbini heads the tax department at **Ashurst**. His tax planning skills are a major asset for the firm.

Bonelli Erede Pappalardo has set up its own tax department, headed by Andrea Silvestri. The department offers domestic and international advice, and focuses on the tax treatment of corporations and financial operations. Clients include organisations from the real estate and banking sectors.

At **CMS Adonnino Ascoli & Cavasola Scamoni** professor Pietro Adonnino is recommended for his knowledge of tax law. The firm provides domestic and international clients with excellent advice on both contentious and non-contentious tax matters.

Tax boutique **Studio Legale Tributario Fiorentini** boasts six partners and 11 assistants in two offices. Stefano Fiorentini heads the Rome office, while Enrico Cerea heads the Milan office. The firm provides advisory services on contentious and non-contentious tax matters. Clients include major banks such as Banca Popolare di Milano, pharmaceutical houses, and real estate owners.

Haarmann Hemmelrath continues to provide excellent tax advice through Andrea Manganlelli based in its Rome office and Italian qualified tax adviser Paolo Calmetta in the firm's Milan office.

Macchi di Cellere Gangemi's tax department is headed by name partner Bruno Gangemi. His wealth of experience over a long and successful career has ensured that his team is renowned for providing clients with outstanding tax advice.

McDermott, Will & Emery/Carnelutti offers a full tax service, specialising in Italian corporate tax, VAT, stamp duties, tax planning, Inland Revenue investigations, tax litigation, trusts and international tax law. Partner Andrea Rittatore Vonwiller is highly recommended. He is a tax professional as well as a chartered and professional accountant.

Last year, the arrival of four new partners strengthened **NCTM – Studio Legale Associato**'s already specialist tax capability. Together with the rest of the tax team, set up in 2002, Piermauro Carabellese, Michele Iavagnilio, Federico Trutalli and Barbara Aloisi devise and implement strategies to optimise M&A and private equity transactions.

Partner Lucio Olivieri **Studio Legale Tonucci** is highly recommended for his expertise in matters concerning restructuring, tax planning and international taxation.

OTHER LEADING FIRMS

Firms recommended here are either specialist boutique firms or smaller, full-service commercial practices. These firms, for the most part are situated in Milan and Rome.

Italy's best-known sports lawyer, Massimo Coccia, heads **Coccia DeAngelis & Associati Studio Legale E Tributario.** The firm specialises in sports law and, to a lesser extent, on natural resources. It advises the Italian National Olympic Committee (CONI) and various international and national sports federations regarding high-profile transfer cases.

Montanari & Associati is a corporate boutique. Major transactions for the firm in 2003 include advising on the Olivetti/Telecom Italia merger. Managing partner Alberto Montanari leads a team that also handles real estate, litigation and banking matters. Clients include Siemens, UBS and European and international investment banks.

OTHER LEADING FIRMS

- Coccia DeAngelis & Associati Studio Legale E Tributario
- Montanari & Associati
- Morano & Associati ✪
- Rosauer, Studio Legale
- Toffoletto e Soci, member of ius laboris ✪
- Zambelli Luzzati Meregalli e Associati

- Albertazzi & Associati Studio Legale
- Biolato Longo Ridola & Mori
- CBM & Partners
- Cajola & Associati ✪
- Capaccioli, Studio
- Casella, Minoli e Associati
- Coggiatti, Studio Legale
- de Meo & Associati, Studio Legale
- Dore & Associati
- Forlati – Minelli – Rizzi, Studio Legale
- Franceschelli, Studio Legale
- Franzosi Dal Negro Pensato Setti
- Frau & Partners SLA ✪
- Fusillo & Associati, Studio Legale
- Grieco e Associati ✪
- Jenny & Partners ✪
- Mastellone, Studio Legale
- Nodari, Saletti & Associati, Studio Legale
- Nunziante Magrone ✪
- Olivieri – Ciapetti & Partners, Studio Legale
- Padovan, Studio Legale
- Pellegrino & Dragotti
- Piergrossi Villa Bianchini Riccardi
- Pinci & Associates, PLLC
- Pojaghi, Studio Legale
- Portolano Colella Cavallo Prosperetti ✪
- Rapisardi, Studio Legale ✪
- Rubino-Sammartano e Associati ✪
- Sardo, Studio Legale
- Tosi & Bontempo

Firms are listed A-Z in tiers which are ranked in order of priority

✪ Indicates firm displays contact details at the end of this chapter.

With offices in Milan and Turin, **Morano & Associati** has grown considerably in the past year. It is an independent outfit advising major companies such as Alcatel Italia, Cisco Systems, and 3i Group on corporate and commercial, banking and finance, private equity, and real estate matters. The firm also has a new practice area of pharma and biotech. Noted for his enthusiasm and excellent English skills, partner Enrico Zattoni is recommended for industrial and corporate matters, while Alberto Morano is recognised for his expertise in banking and finance.

Studio Legale Rosauer was particularly involved in international arbitration transactions in 2003. Noted by clients for its international experience and commercial expertise, the firm advises a range of clients including Filtrona Italia SpA and Trelleborg Wheel Systems SpA.

Known as the leading employment boutique firm in Italy, **Toffoletto e Soci, member of ius laboris** has the advantage of having serious international commercial experience. The firm has seen lateral and organic growth with the addition of three new partners in 2002 and continues to build on its alliance with *ius laboris*. Senior partner Franco Toffoletto is highly respected by clients as 'one of the best employment lawyers in Italy'.

Zambelli Luzzati Meregalli e Associati provides a full corporate and commercial service. The firm is associated with **Studio Legale Beltramo** in Rome and **ACLAW – Ceccon & Associati**, forming an alliance comprising some 37 lawyers.

Albertazzi & Associati Studio Legale advises on corporate and commercial work but its main strength is in the energy sector. The 25-lawyer, Rome-based firm has advised on some major transactions over the year for key international clients. Partner Ivo Formigaro is recommended for energy, and name partner Roberto Albertazzi is recommended for M&A.

Biolato Longo Ridola & Mori advises on corporate and commercial, shipping and real estate matters. The small firm has grown with the addition of professor Giorgio Marasa. Clients include P&O and Meridien and Hilton hotel chains. Name partner Giuseppe Biolato heads the firm.

CBM & Partners was established in September 2002 as the result of a merger. The firm comprises four equity partners, two salaried partners and nine associates, and advises European as well as domestic clients on a range of corporate matters.

Milan-based **Cajola & Associati** advised and represented Panasonic Italia Spa regarding corporate, commercial and labour law in 2003. Other work includes IP advice for the Seiko Epson corporation and the representation of AOM Air Liberté (AIR LIB) following the bankruptcy of the Swissair Group. It is a member of the *INTERLEGAL* Network of International law firms.

Studio Capaccioli has offices in Rome, Florence, Ferrara and Milan. Its main practice areas are corporate and commercial, defence, aviation, and domestic and international tax practice.

Casella, Minoli e Associati was founded by Luca Minoli and Paolo Casella in 2001. The firm supports corporate and private clients.

Studio Legale Coggiatti is part of the three-way *EU-LEX* alliance formed in 2000 with **Studio Legale Mastellone** in Florence and **Studio Legale Sardo** of Milan. Having taken on two more lawyers in 2003 the firm has grown and specialises in corporate and commercial and tax law.

Studio Legale Mastellone provides legal support to both mid-sized Italian firms and foreign investors. Led by Carlo Mastellone, the firm advises on corporate and commercial, employment, transportation and real estate.

Studio Legale de Meo & Associati is led by name partner Michele de Meo, an expert in shipping and litigation, who was a former founding partner of **Ughi e Nunziante**. The firm provides support in all areas of commercial law and has offices in Rome, Milan, Naples and in the port of Rome, Civitavecchia. Clients include Mitsubishi Bank Switzerland Ltd, Marine Aviation and Banca di Roma.

Dore & Associati is a litigation boutique based in the Sardinian capital of Cagliari. Barrister Carlo Dore is the name partner and best-known personality at the firm. He leads a team of 13 lawyers, which is active across a range of areas including banking and insolvency, competition, tax, and labour law.

Venice-based **Studio Legale Forlati – Minelli – Rizzi** has a reputation for its litigation focus. Zeno Forlati heads the team of seven lawyers which handles a range of corporate and commercial and litigation matters. The firm is a member of the *Eurojuris* association.

Studio Legale Franceschelli is headed by name partner Professor Vincenzo Franceschelli. The firm is active in corporate, contracts, competition, patent and trade mark law.

Franzosi Dal Negro Pensato Setti is based in Milan where it is known for its IP expertise. The firm also offers advice in corporate and commercial matters.

Frau & Partners SLA works in corporate, commercial, banking and tax planning. The firm has offices in Milan, Rome and Verona.

Based in Rome, **Studio Legale Fusillo & Associati** is instructed on a number of corporate and commercial transactions. Alessandro Fusillo heads the firm and is known for his arbitration experience.

Established in January 2000, **Grieco e Associati** advises on corporate and commercial, litigation, banking and finance, and construction matters. Clients include major Italian construction companies. The Rome-based firm also has branches in Milan and Trieste.

At **Jenny & Partners** Christoph Jenny leads a team of 12 lawyers. It offers a full service to both domestic and international clients.

Paolo Nodari heads **Studio Legale Nodari, Saletti & Associati** which is instructed by an impressive client list on a variety of corporate and commercial transactions. The firm is also experienced in IP. Paolo Nodari and professor Saletti have a solid reputation.

Nunziante Magrone has increased in size since its merger with former leading firm *Ardito e Magrone*. Its practice areas include corporate and commercial, antitrust and regulated industries, and IP.

Florence-based **Studio Legale Olivieri – Ciapetti & Partners** advises on a range of corporate and commercial matters. Name partners Francesco Olivieri and Emilio Ciapetti are respected lawyers. The firm also has offices in Ancona, Florence, Modena and Reggio Emilia.

Founded in December 2002, **Studio Legale Padovan** has 15 lawyers in its Milan headquarters and a subsidiary office in Treviso. Founding partner Marco Padovan, recommended for banking and finance, is an ex- **Baker & McKenzie** lawyer and has a well-established reputation. Two-thirds of the firm's transactions are for international clients.

Pellegrino & Dragotti deals almost exclusively with IP law. The firm co-operates with other international firms such as **Bird & Bird** and **Linklaters** on some transactions.

Piergrossi Villa Bianchini Riccardi has worked in association with respected UK, national firm **Eversheds LLP** for the past two years. The firm is based in Milan but has been busy building up its Rome office, which has a stronger focus on real estate transactions. Main strengths are in corporate and commercial, arbitration, private equity and IP matters.

Pinci & Associates, PLLC is an international firm with offices in Rome, Milan, Florence, Genoa, Naples, New York and Athens. The firm represents US and European clients in corporate and commercial, IP, and TMT matters.

Alberto Pojaghi is the founding partner of **Studio Legale Pojaghi**. The firm offers legal advice on a range of corporate and commercial matters but is probably best known for its IP expertise.

Portolano Colella Cavallo Prosperetti of Rome was created from the former *Studio Prosperetti* in the first quarter of 2003. Due to lateral hiring, the firm, which concentrates on TMT, has grown. Partner Francesco Portolano, a former **Baker & McKenzie** partner, is the best-known personality at the firm and is widely recognised for his corporate and media expertise. According to clients, the firm possesses 'true talent and dedication that you very seldom find in lawyers'.

Studio Legale Rapisardi is an IP boutique firm. It has the reputation of being one of the first IP firms established in Italy and is known for its expertise in trade mark and patent law.

Rubino-Sammartano e Associati is a member of *LawFed* which comprises 12 Italian independent law firms and tax and accounting firms. Mauro Rubino-Sammartano heads the team and is known for his experience in contract and construction law.

Milan-based **Tosi & Bontempo** is a boutique specialising in IP, data protection, real estate and hi-tech litigation matters. Professor Emilio Tosi is particularly recommended for e-business data protection and IT law.

BOLOGNA

Bologna, the capital of the Emilia-Romagna region, is situated in north-central Italy. Few major international corporations are present with small to medium-sized companies providing the bulk of the commercial activity in the area. Car manufacturing and food production are the dominant industries. Clothing, footwear and engineering are also key features of the local economy.

BOLOGNA: LEADING FIRMS

Bernini associato a Baker & McKenzie, Studio Galgano ✪
Gianni, Origoni, Grippo & Partners

De Capoa & Associati, Studio Legale
Derra, Meyer & Partner
Macchi di Cellere Gangemi
Morresi, Studio Legale

Firms are listed A-Z in tiers which are ranked in order of priority
✪ *Indicates firm displays contact details at the end of this chapter.*

BOLOGNA: LEADING FIRMS

The legal market in Bologna is small and many firms here provide local support to small and medium-sized firms. Bologna is home to Europe's oldest university and still maintains its strong reputation as an academic centre. Many lawyers here double as university professors and are well known for their strong international connections.

Professor Giorgio Bernini, one of Italy's leading arbitration experts, heads **Studio Bernini associato a Baker & McKenzie**. The top international firm merged with Bernini's own practice in April 2002 and brings together international expertise with a highly respected local reputation. The six-lawyer team specialises in M&A, international commercial law, contracts, tax and arbitration. Bologna is **Baker & McKenzie**'s third Italian office.

Galgano is largely thought to be one to the best firms in Italy. **Galgano**, renowned for its strength in banking and finance, corporate, and particularly TMT, is praised by many of its rival law firms for the quality of its work. The 15-strong Bologna office is led by Francesco Galgano.

Leading Italian firm **Gianni, Origoni, Grippo & Partners** opened its seven-lawyer Bologna office in July 2002. Partners Cesare Vento and Renato Giallombardo are responsible for the Bologna office which is instructed by its existing client base from the Emilia-Romagna region. Clients include medium to large-sized companies such as Ferrari.

Studio Legale De Capoa & Associati specialises in international and EU law, and particularly emerging countries. The firm recently participated in EU projects in Slovakia, Poland and Russia. Other offices are located in Milan and Treviso as well as Eastern Europe.

German firm **Derra, Meyer & Partner** advises mainly on German and Italian commercial matters such as M&A from its Bologna office. The firm's subsidiary office in Milan strengthens **Derra, Meyer & Partner**'s presence in the Italian legal market.

The merger between the firm formerly known as *Studio Borghesi, Morara, Venturoli*, and **Macchi di**

Cellere Gangemi took place in 2003. The firm will continue to advise on a variety of corporate and commercial matters.

Studio Legale Morresi is also recommended.

GENOA

Genoa, the provincial capital of the Liguria region, is close to Turin in north-western Italy. Home to Italy's main commercial port, Genoa is characterised by its shipping and insurance sectors. The city is traditionally known for heavy industry such as steel works and ship building, but banking and finance sectors and more hi-tech industries are developing in the area. Alongside Lille, Genoa is the 2004 European City of Culture.

GENOA: LEADING FIRMS

Bonelli Erede Pappalardo, one of the best commercial firms in Italy, has an office in Genoa. Franco Bonelli, the best-known personality in the Genoa office, has a prestigious standing in both the local legal market and nationwide. The Genoa office is active primarily in corporate and commercial, banking and finance, and TMT. The firm is arguably the country's most prominent independent law firm.

Studio Uckmar is principally a tax specialist. The firm advises on a variety of tax issues and also has offices in Rome, Milan and Buenos Aires. Founding partner, Victor Uckmar, has a name for being a leader in this field.

Genoa-based **Studio Legale Afferni Crispo & C.** also has a representative office in Milan. The firm advises mainly on commercial and corporate law but also has experience in practice areas such as IP, competition and bankruptcy.

Partners Cristoforo Kielland and Riccardo Bressler front the small firm **Studio Legale Kielland Bressler**. A typical Genoan firm, it specialises in shipping and insurance. Cristoforo Kielland, a specialist in ship mortgages, is widely respected in the local legal market.

GENOA: LEADING FIRMS

Bonelli Erede Pappalardo
Uckmar, Studio

Afferni Crispo & C., Studio Legale
Kielland Bressler, Studio Legale
Piccinini & Associati
Pinci & Associates, PLLC
Sutti, Studio Legale

Acquarone, Studio
De Berti Jacchia Franchini Forlani
Ferrarini, Studio Legale
Riccomagno, Studio Legale

Firms are listed A-Z in tiers which are ranked in order of priority

Piccinini & Associati is a fairly small firm instructed by clients for insurance, shipping and commercial matters. Senior partner Michele Piccinini heads the team.

Pinci & Associates, PLLC has an office in Genoa which provides a variety of corporate and commercial services including advice on shipping and banking. The office has the support of its other Italian offices in Rome, Milan, and Florence. The firm also has sites in New York and Athens.

Studio Legale Sutti has an office of 11 lawyers, which was established in Genoa in 1948. The team has a solid shipping, Admiralty and maritime practice, operated under professor Guiliano Pennisi.

Studio Acquarone advises on corporate and commercial matters and is headed by Lorenzo Acquarone.

De Berti Jacchia Franchini Forlani opened its Genoa office in 2000. Work is mainly in corporate and commercial, and maritime law. The firm is based in Milan and also has offices in Rome, Brussels, and Moscow. The office works in conjunction with sole practitioner Khristian Kielland.

Headed by name partner Guido Ferrarini, **Studio Legale Ferrarini** works in the area of financial markets, company law and competition.

Studio Legale Riccomagno is also recommended.

NAPLES

Located in the Campania region, Naples is Italy's major industrial centre south of Rome. However, it is not as economically strong as the country's northern regions and does not share the commercial variety enjoyed by cities such as Milan. As a consequence few international law firms are located here. The EU has invested structural funds into the city and investors and bigger law firms are starting to show a renewed interest in the area. This can be seen with the recent opening of leading Italian law firm **Gianni, Origoni, Grippo & Partners**' office in Naples.

There is a strong presence of car and aeronautical industries and a major Fiat plant is positioned here. The significant commercial port at Naples is a major shipping and maritime centre and comes a close second to that of Genoa. Naples is also home to the most important international airport in the South of Italy.

Food production and tourism boost the local economy.

NAPLES: LEADING FIRMS

Although somewhat overshadowed by its Rome office, **Studio Legale de Meo & Associati** has a strong presence in Naples. The firm has expertise in maritime and shipping law and is overseen by the esteemed professor Michele de Meo who has an international reputation.

NAPLES: LEADING FIRMS

de Meo & Associati, Studio Legale
Michele Sandulli (Avv Prof) & Associati, Studio Legale

Carnelutti
Gianni, Origoni, Grippo & Partners
Puopolo Sistilli Geffers & Luise

EY Law
Lauro, Studio Legale
Militerni Nardone Ceceri & Associati
Morace, Studio Legale
Tesauro, Studio Legale

Firms are listed A-Z in tiers which are ranked in order of priority

Studio Legale Avv Prof Michele Sandulli & Associati has a good reputation in Naples and is held in high regard by competing firms. As well as international clients, in 2003 the firm advised Banco di Napoli Spa on a variety of banking and finance matters. Antonio Nardone heads the Naples head office. The firm has a similar sized office in Rome and a smaller office in Avellino.

Carnelutti's practice in Naples (not to be confused with the firm whose merger created **McDermott, Will & Emery/Carnelutti**) concentrates mainly on commercial maritime law and litigation. The 12-lawyer team is instructed by medium-sized local clients.

Gianni, Origoni, Grippo & Partners opened in Naples in September 2003 and currently comprises three lawyers. The Naples outfit benefits from the offices in Milan, Rome, Bologna, Padua, New York and London.

Puopolo Sistilli Geffers & Luise, although based in Rome, has an office which is a significant player in the Naples legal market. It is instructed by companies heading south and by international clients looking to invest in the area. The office is active in the corporate and commercial, banking and finance, insurance, and bankruptcy practice areas.

The Naples office of **EY Law** is led by the respected Ernesto Cesàro. It has a good reputation and attracts some top clients.

Studio Legale Lauro has its sole office in Naples. The five-lawyer team concentrates mainly on maritime, international and commercial law. The majority of clients are local small to medium-sized companies.

Militerni Nardone Ceceri & Associati advises on a range of M&A, contracts and dispute resolution. The firm has offices in Milan and Rome.

Studio Legale Morace advises on shipping and transport, corporate and finance, M&A, and litigation matters. Name partner Carlo Morace heads the office in Naples. The firm also has offices in Cagliari and Rome.

Managing partner Paolo Tesauro heads **Studio Legale Tesauro**, a small firm that deals with commercial transactions.

PADUA

The Padua legal market has been shaken up in the past year due to the departure of former leading firm *Carnelutti, Studio Legale Associato* from the area. Padua remains, however, a popular place for international firms to establish a regional presence. It is one of the wealthiest areas of north-eastern Italy. As the area is less dependent on finance than Milan, the legal market is less affected by economic changes.

Despite having a less industrial reputation than Turin, Padua has strong services, mechanical, optical and textile sectors. Many chemical and pharmaceutical companies are present.

PADUA: LEADING FIRMS

The Padua office of *Carnelutti, Studio Legale Associato* was not part of the merger deal with **McDermott, Will & Emery** that took place in September and the office will therefore cease to exist in 2004.

Oliviero Pessi, formerly the head partner *Carnelutti, Studio Legale Associato*'s office has been hired by **Clifford Chance Studio Legale Associato** along with four other ex-*Carnelutti, Studio Legale Associato* lawyers including head of litigation, Stefano Armellini.

Due to this lateral growth, **Clifford Chance Studio Legale Associato** has come to dominate the Padua legal market. Transactions for **Clifford Chance Studio Legale Associato** in 2003 included advising Pacifica Group Limited on the €37.5m acquisition of Automotive Products Group Ltd. Major Italian investment banks are also amongst its clients. The Padua office is led by Gianandrea Rizzieri.

Gianni, Origoni, Grippo & Partners' Padua office has been in operation since 2000. The key practice area is M&A but other important focuses for the office are in litigation, corporate, banking and labour. In 2003 the office advised on the sale of Speedline from US manufacturer Amcast.

35-lawyer **LCA Avvocati e Commercialisti D'Impresa**'s Padua office is described by clients as 'an ideal solution for legal support'. With strong local connections, clients include Volvo and financial leasing company Finagen Spa. Partners Francesco Camilotti and Claudio Giordano are the main personalities in the office.

Roberto Ceccon heads **ACLAW – Ceccon & Associati** which has its sole office in Padua. The small firm has a good local reputation for the quality of its work involving banking and finance, aviation, litigation and M&A. The firm has associated offices in Milan, Rome and Pordenone.

Pavia e Ansaldo provides advice on M&A, IP, sports law and civil litigation from its Padua office.

Simmons & Simmons has a combination of international, national and local clients. The ten-lawyer office is instructed across a number of commercial and corporate transactions in the region.

Carlo Scarpa heads the Padua office of **Studio Legale Tonucci**, which has a total of four partners and seven assistants. The firm has offices throughout Europe.

IP boutique **Cantaluppi & Partners** consists of four partners and 13 assistants. The firm specialises in patents, trade marks, copyright and domain names.

Pirola Pennuto Zei & Associati is also recommended.

PADUA: LEADING FIRMS

Clifford Chance Studio Legale Associato

Gianni, Origoni, Grippo & Partners
LCA Avvocati e Commercialisti D'Impresa ✪

ACLAW – Ceccon & Associati ✪
Pavia e Ansaldo
Simmons & Simmons ✪
Tonucci, Studio Legale

Cantaluppi & Partners
Pirola Pennuto Zei & Associati

Firms are listed A-Z in tiers which are ranked in order of priority
✪ Indicates firm displays contact details at the end of this chapter.

TURIN

Turin, situated in the north-west of Italy, plays host to a major part of the country's industry and manufacturing sites. The city, the capital of the Piedmont region, is the home of the Fiat (Fabrica Italiana Automobili Torino) headquarters. Fiat is the main industry in the city and has helped to establish Turin as a major area of hi-tech industry and manufacturing. Despite being affected by the general global economic slump, foreign investors such as Motorola and Michelin are still showing interest in the region.

Food companies are also prominent in the city, with major Italian coffee producers Ferrero and Lavazza present. Alongside the presence of many multinational corporations, Turin is also home to numerous small to medium-sized companies and manufacturers. Law firms present in Turin pride themselves on looking after clients of all shapes and sizes and developing local connections.

Turin will host the 2006 Winter Olympic Games which local lawyers feel will provide the city with a much needed economic boost with investors expected to move into the area.

Sport in general is a large part of the economy in Turin as the internationally renowned football club of Juventus is situated here.

Communications between Milan and Turin are becoming increasingly sophisticated. The high-speed rail link to Lyons and Milan is expected to open up business to the city.

TURIN: LEADING FIRMS

Allen & Overy ✪
Grande Stevens: Studio Legale Associazione Professionale

Buffa, Bortolotti & Mathis
Frignani e Associati Studio Legale
Hammonds Rossotto
Jacobacci & Associati, Studio Legale
Pavia e Ansaldo
Tosetto Weigmann e Associati

Gamna e Associati
Pirola Pennuto Zei & Associati

Firms are listed A-Z in tiers which are ranked in order of priority
✪ Indicates firm displays contact details at the end of this chapter.

TURIN: LEADING FIRMS

Allen & Overy's Turin office comprises 35 lawyers although rather than operating as a separate firm, the Milan, Rome and Turin sites liaise on many of the same transactions. The Turin office, however, also advises local medium-sized companies. Carlo Pavesio, managing partner in Turin, is renowned for his competition and EU law expertise.

Turin-based **Grande Stevens: Studio Legale Associazione Professionale** has a considerable reputation throughout Italy for the quality of its work and the clients that it attracts. Well-established relationships exist between the firm and leading Turin manufacturers such as Fiat. Franzo Grande Stevens is the best-known personality at the firm and is recommended for corporate law. Maria Ricci is recommended for bankruptcy issues. The firm also has offices in Milan and Rome.

Buffa, Bortolotti & Mathis is headed by Professor Fabio Bortolotti and Alberto Buffa. The firm is a member of the *European Law Group* and is linked to the association *LexJus* along with other firms across Italy. An 11-strong team advises on a variety of corporate and commercial matters.

Frignani e Associati Studio Legale specialises in competition and antitrust law, and, to a lesser extent, IP, consultation, litigation and international trade law. Professor Aldo Frignani who heads the firm is a venerable academic at the University of Turin. He is the firm's best-known personality and has a reputation for being a competition and European law expert.

Hammonds Rossotto is the result of a merger at the start of 2002 between UK firm **Hammonds** and *Rossotto e Associati*. It is instructed on a number of M&A, labour, IP, competition and antitrust transactions. It has a good reputation with Italian banks.

Studio Legale Jacobacci & Associati advises a number of top international and Italian clients including Gucci, Ferrari and Microsoft. A team of 21 lawyers works on corporate and commercial matters and in 2003 assisted the largest Italian motorway management company in a dispute with the Italian motorway and highway agency. The firm has special expertise in IP and trade mark matters, and also has offices in Milan and Rome.

Pavia e Ansaldo has a five-lawyer presence in Turin. The firm is well regarded for a variety of corporate and commercial work.

Tosetto Weigmann e Associati is an important player in the Turin legal market. It is active in corporate and commercial, M&A, IP and insurance and finance practice areas. Giovanni Gazzola is particularly recommended for commercial and corporate litigation.

Carlo Gamna heads **Gamna e Associati** which advises on corporate and commercial law. The firm opened its second office in Milan in 2002.

Pirola Pennuto Zei & Associati is a multi-disciplinary firm with a particular emphasis on tax law. Turin is a central part of the firm whose headquarters are in Milan.

GALGANO

VIA SANTO STEFANO, 11
40125 BOLOGNA

Telephone: +39 051 232622
Fax: +39 051 231238
E-mail: bologna@galgano.it
Website: www.galgano.it

Languages
English, French, German

Other offices
Milan

Number of lawyers 37
at this office 15

Contact
Federico Galgano

CATEGORIES OF WORK

Arbitration

Litigation

Banking and finance

Capital markets

Corporate

Mergers and acquisitions

Commercial

Antitrust

Information technology

Intellectual property

Employment

Contracts

ALLEN & OVERY

VIA MANZONI, 41/43
20121 MILAN

Telephone: +39 02 29 04 91
Fax: +39 02 29 04 93 33
E-mail: information@allenovery.com
Website: www.allenovery.com

Languages
English, French, German, Italian, Spanish

Other offices
Amsterdam, Antwerp, Bangkok, Beijing, Bratislava, Brussels, Budapest, Dubai, Frankfurt, Hamburg, Hong Kong, London, Luxembourg, Madrid, Moscow, New York, Paris, Prague, Rome, Shanghai, Singapore, Tokyo, Turin, Warsaw

Number of lawyers 2,305
at this office 100

Contacts
Roberto Casati (senior partner);
G Massimilano Danusso
(joint managing partner);
Stephen Denyer (joint managing partner);
Emanuele Borganti
(head of operations in Italy)

CATEGORIES OF WORK

Corporate
Paolo Cerina

Banking
Giancarlo Castorino

Tax
Andrea Manganelli

ICM
G Massimilliano Danusso

Litigation
Alberto Nanni

ASHURST

VIA SANT'ORSOLA 3
20123 MILAN

Telephone: +39 02 854 2301
Fax: +39 02 854 2344
Website: www.ashurst.com

Languages
English, French, Spanish

Other offices
Brussels, London, Madrid, Munich, New Delhi*, New York, Paris, Singapore, Tokyo

Number of lawyers 813
at this office 27

Contacts
Avv Daniele Raynaud, Avv Riccardo Agostinelli

CATEGORIES OF WORK

Mergers and acquisitions	**Real estate**
Private equity	**Antitrust**
Acquisition financing	**E-commerce**
Project financing	**Tax**

BAKER & McKENZIE

PIAZZA MEDA, 3
20121 MILANO

Telephone: +39 02 76 23 13 23
Fax: +39 02 76 23 16 23
E-mail: milan.info@bakernet.com
Website: www.bakernet.com

Languages
English, French, German, Spanish

Other offices
For a list of all offices and other information regarding the firm please consult Baker & McKenzie's London office entry

Number of lawyers 3,380
at this office 70

Contact
Gianfranco Di Garbo (managing partner)

Baker & McKenzie is a global law firm with 66 offices in 36 countries, including in Italy offices in Milan, Rome and Bologna.

CATEGORIES OF WORK

Antitrust and trade	**Information technology and communications**
Banking, financing and securities	**Litigation, arbitration**
Competition	**Major projects**
Employment	**Regulatory**
General corporate, mergers and acquisitions and commercial transactions	**Tax**
Intellectual property	

BIRD & BIRD

VIA MONTENAPOLEONE 10
20121 MILANO

Telephone: +30 02 30 35 60 00
Fax: +39 02 30 35 60 11
E-mail: milan@twobirds.com
Website: www.twobirds.com

Languages
English, French, Italian

Other offices
Brussels, Düsseldorf, Hong Kong, London, Munich, Paris, Stockholm, The Hague

Number of lawyers 358
at this office 21

Contact
Massimiliano Mostardini

CATEGORIES OF WORK

Advertising/media
Rita Tardiolo

Banking and finance
Raimondo Maggiore

Commercial
Alberto Salvadé

Communications
Claudia Ricciardi

Corporate
Alberto Salvadé

EC competition law
Charlotte De Panafieu

Employment
Caterina Rucci

Information technology
Debora Stella

Intellectual property
Massimiliano Mostardini, Giovanni Galimberti

Life sciences
Massimiliano Mostardini

Litigation
Giovanni Galimberti, Antonio Danile

BREVEGLIERI VERZINI E SOCI

VIA MONTE DI PIETA 24
20121 MILAN

Telephone: +39 02 881 284 1
Fax: +39 02 881 284 44
E-mail: bvs@bvs-taxlaw.com

Languages
English, French, Italian

Number of lawyers 14

CATEGORIES OF WORK

Corporate law

Mergers and acquisitions

Commercial agreements

Business law

Arbitration

Labour and employment

Intellectual property

Communications and media

Construction

Competition and antitrust regulation

Real estate

Family law

Bankruptcy

Litigation

Administrative law

Tax

Corporate criminal law

BUSE HEBERER FROMM

VIA DON GIOVANNI CALABRIA 20
20132 MILAN

Telephone: +39 02 259 37 99
Fax: +39 02 272 020 74
Email: mailand@buse.de
Website: www.buse.de

Languages
English, French, German, Spanish

Other offices
Berlin, Dusseldorf, Essen, Frankfurt am Main, Hamburg, Munich, Palma de Mallorca, Sydney, Zurich

Number of lawyers 120
at this office 2

Member
The European Legal Alliance (Beauchamps, Ireland; Dubarry Le Douarin Veil, France; Field Fisher Waterhouse, England; Harper Macleod, Scotland)

CATEGORIES OF WORK

- Banking and finance
- Antitrust and merger control
- Commerce, transport, insurance
- Commercial delinquency
- Corporate/M&A
- Industrial property and copyrights
- Information technology and telecommunications
- Labour and employment
- Litigation and arbitration, national and international
- Press and media
- Property and construction
- Public law
- Tax

CMS ADONNINO ASCOLI & CAVASOLA SCAMONI

VIA M. BUONARROTI, 39
20145 MILANO

Telephone: +39 02 4801 1171
Fax: +39 02 4801 2914
E-mail: aacs.milaw@aacs.it
Website: www.aacs.it

Languages
English, French, Swedish, Spanish, Bulgarian, Russian, Serbo-Croat

Other offices
Rome

Number of lawyers 62
at this office 20

Contact
Marco Frazzica

Other CMS law firms
CMS Francis Lefebvre, France; CMS Cameron McKenna, UK; CMS Derks Star Busmann, Netherlands; CMS von Erlach Klainguti Stettler Wille, Switzerland; CMS Hasche Sigle, Germany; CMS Lexcelis, Belgium; CMS Strommer Reich-Rohrwig Karasek Hainz, Austria

CATEGORIES OF WORK

- General civil practice
- Business and corporate law
- International contracts
- Foreign investment
- Banking
- Joint ventures
- EU law
- Intellectual property
- Foreign investment
- Mergers and acquisitions
- Labour law
- Administrative law
- Bankruptcy and credit recovery
- Property law
- Commercial litigation and arbitration

CAJOLA & ASSOCIATI

VIA G ROSSINI, 5
20122 MILANO

Telephone: +39 02 76 00 33 05
Fax: +39 02 78 01 77
E-mail: law@cajola.com
Website: www.cajola.com

Languages
English, French, Spanish

Number of lawyers 10

CATEGORIES OF WORK

Contracts

Joint ventures

Mergers and acquisitions

Corporate

Corporate finance

Commercial law

Banking law

Taxation

Intellectual property

Construction

Telecommunication and e-business

EU law

Employment law

Real estate

Litigation

Aviation law

CURTIS, MALLET-PREVOST, COLT & MOSLE LLP

IN ASSOCIAZIONE CON GILIOLI ALEMANI BOCCHIOLA TAMBURINI E PARTNERS

CORSO VENEZIA 5
20121 MILAN

Telephone: +39 02 76 23 20 01
Fax: +39 02 76 00 90 76
E-mail: info@cm-p.com
Website: www.cm-p.com

Languages
English, French, Spanish

Other offices
Frankfurt, Houston, London, Mexico City, Muscat, New York, Newark, Paris, Stamford, Washington DC

Number of lawyers 178
at this office 20

Contacts
Eric L Gilioli (Milan, New York), Michele Tamburini (Milan)

Member
American Chamber of Commerce in Italy; Union International des Avocats; Rotary International; Italian Chambers of Commerce in the United States and Mexico

CATEGORIES OF WORK

Mergers and acquisitions/ joint ventures
Eric L Gilioli, Elena A Berlucchi

Securities and finance
Maurizio Bocchiola, Elena A Berlucchi

Banking and broker-dealer
Giuseppe Alemani, Fabrizio Vismara

Commercial contracts
Daniel Gilioli, Michele Tamburini

International tax law
Fabrizio Vismara

European Union law
Michele Tamburini

Latin American trade and investment
Antonio M Prida

Investment management, private equity, venture capital
Carl A Ruggiero, Elena A Berlucchi

Infrastructure and public projects
Michele Tamburini

Arbitration
Maurizio Bocchiola, Enrico Gilioli

Litigation
Maurizio Bocchiola, Enrico Gilioli

Insolvency proceedings
Giuseppe Alemani, Maurizio Bocchiola

Employment law
Enrico Gilioli

Intellectual property
Michele Tamburini

Foundations
Giuseppe Alemani, Fabrizio Vismara

International trusts and estates
Daniel Gilioli

Private client
Giuseppe Alemani, Daniel Gilioli

CHIOMENTI STUDIO LEGALE

VIA ARRIGO BOITO 8
20121 MILAN

Telephone: +39 02 72 15 71
Fax: +39 02 72 15 72 24
E-mail: milano@chiomenti.net

Languages
English, French, German, Italian, Spanish

Other offices
Brussels, London, New York, Rome, Turin

Number of lawyers 140
at this office 60

Member
Lex Mundi

CATEGORIES OF WORK

Corporate and M&A	**IP, media and IT**
Banking and finance	**Litigation and arbitration**
Capital markets	**Insolvency and corporate restructuring**
Regulatory and financial services	**Employment and labour**
Tax	**Telecommunications**
European, competition and international law	**Energy**
Administrative and environmental law	**Real estate**

THE FIRM

Chiomenti Studio Legale continues the practice started by Pasquale Chiomenti in the late 1940s as one of the first Italian law firms with international capabilities, advising Italian and foreign clients in the progressive expansion of post-war economy.

Since then Chiomenti Studio Legale has steadily consolidated its initial position as one of Italy's leading law firms, meeting the challenge of increasing globalisation of business. Today the firm is composed of more than 150 lawyers and tax advisers and has offices in Rome, Milan, Turin, London, Brussels and – since September 2003 – New York.

Chiomenti has always been a leader in tailoring legal techniques developed in an international context for implementation in Italy and specifically in developing Italian legal techniques in order to accommodate the requirements of international business clients. This is of increasing importance today when the majority of business transactions in Europe have a cross-border dimension and a growing proportion of legal disputes have an international aspect.

In 2001, Chiomenti Studio Legale and Skadden, Arps, Slate, Meagher & Flom entered into a strategic alliance that combines their respective strengths in US, Italian and English law.

AREAS OF PRACTICE

Corporate and M&A: friendly and hostile takeovers, leveraged and management buy-outs, privatisations, joint ventures, company restructuring, general corporate and commercial transactions.

Banking and finance: debt and equity instruments, international and domestic loans, real estate loans, debt restructuring and rescheduling etc.

Capital markets: IPOs and other public offerings, equity offerings, financial products private and public placements.

Regulatory and financial services: rules and regulations applying to banks, financial intermediaries, investment funds and insurance companies. Representing clients before Bank of Italy, CONSOB and ISVAP, formations, mergers, spin-offs, purchases and sales.

Tax: corporate and individual taxation, mergers and acquisitions and corporate reorganisation, international and EU taxation.

European law, competition and international law: advice in connection with antitrust matters, public subsidies, telecoms, power, transportation, free circulation of goods and services, agriculture, concentration and consolidation of joint ventures and unfair competition.

Administrative law and environmental law: contracts and concessions of public works, service and supply contracts, legal assistance to administrative authorities and to private and public entities operating in the utilities sector.

IP, media and IT: copyrights, trade marks, trade secrets, patents, new communication and transmission systems and media and communications rules and regulations.

Litigation and arbitration: financial and commercial disputes before civil and administrative courts and administrative authorities and national supervisory authorities.

Insolvency and corporate restructuring: assistance in connection with bankruptcy procedures, pre-packaged bankruptcies, bankruptcy administration and liquidations.

Employment and labour: national, European and international employment and labour law.

Telecommunications and energy: regulatory issues, licensing, interconnection, telecoms securities offering and project financing.

Energy: regulatory issues, project finance, mergers and acquisitions, sales and joint venture.

Real estate: acquisition and sale, mergers and spin-offs, rentals, construction, bids, development, asset management services, leasing, credit over pledge securitisation, and credits from rentals.

DLA

VIA CORDUSIO 2
20123 MILAN

Telephone: +39 02 80 61 81
Fax: +39 02 80 61 82 02
E-mail: milinfo@dla.com
Website: www.dla.com

Languages
English, French, German, Italian

Other offices
Amsterdam, Antwerp, Bangkok, Bergen, Berlin, Birmingham, Bradford, Bratislava, Brussels, Budapest, Cologne, Copenhagen, Edinburgh, Essen, Frankfurt, Glasgow, Hamburg, Hong Kong, Leeds, Liverpool, London, Madrid, Manchester, Moscow, Oslo, Paris, Prague, Rotterdam, Salzberg, Sarajevo, Shanghai, Sheffield, Singapore, Stockholm, Vienna, Zagreb

Number of lawyers 35

Contact
Federico Sutti

Member
DLA Group

CATEGORIES OF WORK

M&A, PFI
Federico Sutti

Energy
Wolf Michael Kühne

Corporate
Giampaolo Salsi

Real Estate
Olaf Schmidt

Telecoms/IT
Stefano Modenesi

Banking
Elisabetta Poltronieri

Labour law
Franco Rindone

Technology
Stefano Modenesi

Tax
Nicola Zeni

Intellectual property
Giacomo Parmigiani

THE FIRM

DLA's Milan office provides a full-service, locally led law firm with over 10 years' experience and international capability across Europe and Asia. Lawyers specialise in all aspects of business law and regularly advise on cross-border transactions.

The firm provides a creative and business-like approach, which is practical yet flexible, to all companies, both local and international. The firm invests in its clients to understand what their needs really are and how value can be added to their business. Local lawyers work in teams to be able to really understand and empathise with clients' commercial needs, both locally and on a broader international level.

DLA is the founding member of DLA Group. DLA Group is an exclusive alliance of international full-service law firms with a shared vision. Established in 1999, DLA Group now has over 2,200 lawyers across 21 countries, who deliver expert local know-how and international solutions. DLA Group provides legal advice in 37 major cities across Europe, Singapore, Thailand, Hong Kong and the People's Republic of China.

AREAS OF PRACTICE

Further information, as well as a more detailed description of areas of practice, can be found on the firm's website: www.dla.com.

DE BERTI JACCHIA FRANCHINI FORLANI

VIA SAN PAOLO 7
20121 MILANO

Telephone: +39 02 725 541
Fax: +39 02 72 5546 00
E-mail: dejalex@dejalex.com

Languages
English, French, German, Russian, Spanish

Other offices
Brussels, Genoa, Moscow, Rome

Numbers of lawyers 55
at this office 38

Contact
Gianni Forlani (g.forlani@dejalex.com)

CATEGORIES OF WORK

- Administrative and regulatory law
- Antitrust and competition
- Banks and banking
- Corporate and commercial law, M&A
- Environmental law
- European Union law
- Finance and project finance
- Information technology
- Intellectual property
- Labour and employment
- Litigation and arbitration
- Planning law and real estate
- Russian and CIS law
- Taxation

STUDIO LEGALE DELFINO E ASSOCIATI WILLKIE FARR & GALLAGHER LLP

VIA MICHELE BAROZZI 2
20122 MILAN

Telephone: +39 02 76363 1
Fax: +39 02 76363 636
Website: www.willkie.com

Languages
English, French, German, Spanish

Other offices
New York, Washington DC, Paris, London, Rome, Frankfurt, Brussels

Number of lawyers 560
at this office 26

Contact
Maurizio Delfino

CATEGORIES OF WORK

- Mergers and acquisitions
- Private equity
- Capital markets
- Telecommunication
- Energy
- Tax
- Antitrust
- Litigation
- Arbitration

STUDIO LEGALE DEWEY BALLANTINE
IN ASSOCIAZIONE CON GATTAI, SPERONI, GIORDANO & PARTNERS

VIA MONTE DI PIETÀ 21
20121 MILAN

Telephone: +39 02 30 30 93 30
Fax: +39 02 30 30 93 40
Website: www.deweyballantine.com

Languages
English, French, German, Italian, Spanish

Other offices
Austin, Budapest, East Palo Alto, Frankfurt, Houston, London, Los Angeles, New York, Prague, Rome, Warsaw, Washington DC

Number of lawyers 606
at this office 11

Contacts
Bruno Gattai (bgattai@deweyballantine.com), Stefano Speroni (ssperoni@deweyballantine.com)

CATEGORIES OF WORK

Mergers and acquisitions

Private equity

Capital markets

Securitisation

Derivatives

Project finance/PPP

Privatisation

Real estate

Energy

Telecommunications

EY LAW

VIA CORNAGGIA 10
20123 MILANO

Telephone: +39 02 85141
Fax: +39 02 89010199
Website: www.eylaw.com

Languages
English, French, German, Spanish

Other offices
Ancona, Bari, Bologna, Florence, Naples, Padua, Rome, Turin, Treviso, Verona

Number of lawyers 270
at this office 80

Contact
Francesco Marotta

CATEGORIES OF WORK

General corporate
Francesco Marotta, Paolo Tanoni

Litigation
Francesco Aratari

Labour law
Prof Luciano Spagnuolo Vigorita

Real estate, property law
Raffaele Pendibene

Public law
Prof Fabrizio Cassella

Cross-border mergers and acquisitions
Raffaele Caldarone, Giuseppe Barreca

Banking and financial services
Corrado Verna

Intellectual property and information technology
Paolo Tanoni, Luigi Neirotti

Antitrust, regulatory
Eduardo Courir

Arbitration and Supreme Court
Prof Ernesto Cesaro, Prof Biagio Grasso

FRAU & PARTNERS SLA

VIA CARLO POERIO 15
20129 MILANO

Telephone: +39 02 76 42 71
Fax: +39 02 76 00 33 11
E-mail: info@fraupartners.org

Languages
English, French, German, Italian, Spanish

Other offices
Rome, Verona

Number of lawyers 55

Contacts
Avv Dr Maurizio Codurri
(managing partner, Milan)
Sen Prof Aventino Frau (Milan)

CATEGORIES OF WORK

Corporate	**Arts and leisure**
Banking, finance, capital	**Commercial arbitration**
TMT	**International law**
International taxation and investments	**International/foreign trusts**

FRESHFIELDS BRUCKHAUS DERINGER

VIA DEI GIARDINI 7
20121 MILAN

Telephone: +39 02 625 301
Fax: +39 02 625 30 800
E-mail: email@freshfields.com
Website: www.freshfields.com

Languages
Extensive language capabilities

Other offices
Amsterdam, Bangkok, Barcelona, Beijing, Berlin, Bratislava, Brussels, Budapest, Cologne, Düsseldorf, Frankfurt, Hamburg, Hanoi, Ho Chi Minh City, Hong Kong, London, Madrid, Moscow, Munich, New York, Paris, Rome, Shanghai, Singapore, Tokyo, Vienna, Washington

Number of lawyers 2,504
at this office 106

Contacts
Philip Richards, Mario Ortu

CATEGORIES OF WORK

Corporate	**Tax**
Dispute resolution (including environment, planning and regulatory)	**Intellectual property and IT**
	Antitrust, competition and trade
Finance	**Employment, pensions and benefits**
Real estate	

GALGANO

VIALE MAJNO 7
20122 MILAN

Telephone: +39 02 777 2141
Fax: +39 02 7639 7091
E-mail: milano@galgano.it
Website: www.galgano.it

Languages
English, French, German, Spanish

Other offices
Bologna

Number of lawyers 37
at this office 22

Contacts
Marco Consonni, Guido Capelli

CATEGORIES OF WORK

Corporate	**Telecoms**
Commercial	**E-commerce**
Banking and finance	**Data protection**
Capital markets	**Media and entertainment**
Securitisation	**Intellectual property**
Mergers and acquisitions	**Employment**
Project finance	**Arbitration**
Antitrust	**Litigation**
Information technology	

GILIBERTI PAPPALETTERA TRISCORNIA E ASSOCIATI

VIA VISCONTI DI MODRONE, 21
20122 MILAN

Telephone: +39 02 76 00 1585
Fax: +39 02 78 0858
E-mail: studio@giliberti-lex.net

Languages
English, French, German, Italian, Spanish

Number of lawyers 26

Contacts
Carlo Pappalettera, Alessandro Triscornia

CATEGORIES OF WORK

Mergers, acquisitions and corporate law	**Commercial property/real estate**
Joint ventures	**Corporate and commercial**
International contracts	**Infrastructure and project finance**
Banking and finance	**Insolvency/corporate restructuring**
Litigation and arbitration	**Privatisation**
Capital markets	**Private client**
Asset finance/securitisation	

HAARMANN HEMMELRATH

CORSO VENEZIA, 16
20121 MILAN

Telephone: +39 02 77 194 111
Fax: +39 02 77 194 133
E-mail: milan@haarmannhemmelrath.com
Website: www.haarmannhemmelrath.com

Languages
English, French, German, Polish, Portuguese, Russian, Spanish

Other offices
Berlin, Bielefeld, Brussels, Bucharest, Budapest, Cologne, Dusseldorf, Frankfurt, Hamburg, Leipzig, London, Moscow, Munich, Paris, Prague, Rome, Shanghai, Singapore, Stuttgart, Tokyo, Vienna, Warsaw

Number of lawyers 281
at this office 11

CATEGORIES OF WORK

Corporate law
Avv Paolo Francesco Calmetta, Avv Barnaba Ricci

Mergers and acquisitions
Avv Barnaba Ricci, Avv Paolo Francesco Calmetta

Litigation
Avv Barnaba Ricci

Real estate transactions
Avv Barnaba Ricci, Avv Paolo Francesco Calmetta

Civil law
Avv Barnaba Ricci, Avv Dietmar Zischg

Energy law
Avv Paolo Francesco Calmetta, Avv Dietmar Zischg

Environmental law
Avv Bruno Alberti, Avv Dietmar Zischg

JENNY & PARTNERS

VIA DURINI 27
20122 MILAN

Telephone: +39 02 77 8031
Fax: + 39 02 77 8032 33
E-mail: mail@jenny.it
Website: www.jenny.it

Languages
English, French, German, Spanish

Number of lawyers 12

Contact
Christoph Jenny

CATEGORIES OF WORK

Corporate finance, M&A and JVs
Christoph Jenny

Distributorships and commercial agencies
Simona Gallo

Intellectual property
Simona Gallo

Employment law
Maria Gabriella Polati

Commercial property, real estate and construction, environment
Marco Buraggi

Energy and utilities
Christoph Jenny, Simona Gallo

Banking and finance, insurance
Andrea Polizzi

Competition and EU
Paolo Venturini

Insolvency law
Marco Buraggi

Litigation and arbitration
Marco Buraggi

Corporate law
Marco Pasquino

Company law and commercial
Andrea Polizzi

Asset finance/securitisation, capital markets
Andrea Polizzi

JONES DAY

VIA TURATI 16-18
20121 MILANO

Telephone: +39 02 76 45 40 01
Fax: +39 02 76 45 44 00
Website: www.jonesday.com

Languages
English, French, German, Spanish

Other offices
Atlanta, Brussels, Chicago, Cleveland, Columbus, Dallas, Frankfurt, Hong Kong, Houston, Irvine, London, Los Angeles, Madrid, Menlo Park, Mumbai*, Munich, New Delhi*, New York, Paris, Pittsburgh, Shanghai, Singapore, Sydney, Taipei, Tokyo, Washington DC

Number of lawyers 2,100
at this office 21

*In association with Pathak & Associates

CATEGORIES OF WORK

Banking and structured finance
Philippe Billot, Ettore Scandale

Asset finance/securitisation
Philippe Billot, Ettore Scandale

Mergers and acquisitions
Philippe Billot,
Stefano Macchi di Cellere

Private client
Marco Lombardi

Tax
Marco Lombardi

Real estate tax
Marco Lombardi

Arbitration
David J Rosso

Competition law and distribution
Stefano Macchi di Cellere

Corporate and commercial litigation
Marco Lombardi,
Stefano Macchi di Cellere

Labour law
Fabrizio Faina, Sabrina Straneo

Real estate
Philippe Billot, Marco Lombardi

Infrastructure and project finance
David J Rosso, Ettore Scandale

LATHAM & WATKINS

VIA SAN MAURILIO, 20
20123 MILAN

Telephone: +39 02 85454 11
Fax: +39 02 85454 140
Website: www.lw.com

Languages
English, French, Italian

Other offices
Boston, Brussels, Chicago, Frankfurt, Hamburg, Hong Kong, London, Los Angeles, Moscow, New Jersey, New York, Northern Virginia, Orange County, Paris, San Diego, San Francisco, Silicon Valley, Singapore, Tokyo, Washington DC

Number of lawyers 1,500
at this office 3

CATEGORIES OF WORK

Corporate law

Debt and equity capital markets

EU/competition law

Mergers and acquisitions

Private equity

LOIACONO E ASSOCIATI

VIA MANZONI 31
20121 MILANO

Telephone: +39 02 63 61 12 11
Fax: +39 02 63 61 12 22
E-mail: info@loiacono.com
Website: www.loiacono.com

Languages
English, French, German, Spanish

Number of lawyers 10

Contact
Dario Loiacono

CATEGORIES OF WORK

Banking and financial services	**Asset management**
Capital markets	**Mergers and acquisitions**
Financial regulatory	**Financial litigation**

THE FIRM

Loiacono e Associati is a boutique law firm at the forefront of developments in banking and finance in Italy. The firm, formerly known as Studio Legale Loiacono, was founded in 1996 by two former investment bankers who, in addition to their local legal experience, worked for several years for two of Wall Street's leading law firms. The firm specialises in matters which require combined understanding of the legal, technical and commercial aspects of financial products and services. The firm is frequently called in to provide advice in crisis situations involving financial transactions, unexpected regulatory compliance and hostile situations in which the parties to a transaction or business venture have deal-breaking issues to resolve.

AREAS OF PRACTICE

The firm's practice covers international banking and financial services, capital markets, financial regulation and asset management. The firm also advises on mergers and acquisitions and joint ventures and assists clients in certain types of complex financial litigation. Clients include five of the six major US global investment banks; some of the largest European and US commercial banking and insurance groups; Italian and European Stock Exchanges, clearing houses and electronic communication networks; national and international centralised securities depositories; Italian and European asset management companies, hedge and private equity funds; and European equipment leasing companies and large industrial groups. In all areas of practice, the firm enjoys strong working relationships with the Bank of Italy, Consob, the Italian Economy Ministry, Italian and international financial industry associations and self-regulatory bodies. The firm also maintains close working relationships with specialised local and international law firms and financial and securities valuation consultants.

Banking and financial services: Loiacono e Associati has one of Italy's most interesting banking and finance practices, notwithstanding the fact that most of its competitors are significantly larger. The practice area extends over a wide range of financial products and business segments. The firm is particularly well-known for collaborating with clients in the development of innovative financial products and services for the Italian market.

Capital markets: the firm provides a full range of services for issuers and underwriters in initial public offerings and secondary offerings of various types of equity and debt instruments and in the structuring and execution of equity derivative products.

Financial regulation: Loiacono e Associati has one of the premier financial regulatory practices in Italy. This practice area strongly complements the others and provides an important base upon which to advise clients on the creation of new financial products and services and clients subject to ongoing financial market regulation and compliance requirements.

Asset management: clients include a wide range of funds, hedge fund selection organisations and prime brokers. The firm has been instrumental in establishing the securities lending and prime brokerage markets in Italy and in resolving certain cross-border collateral issues.

Mergers and acquisitions: the firm advises on both friendly and contested transactions, spin-offs, joint ventures, private equity transactions and other types of acquisitions or divestitures in financial and other business sectors. In addition, the firm frequently advises boards and major stakeholders in crisis situations.

Financial litigation: the firm advises on various aspects of disclosure, broker-dealer regulation, derivative and other financial product-related issues, and bankruptcy and insolvency law, which can present significant sources of potential liability. In special situations, usually involving complex financial instruments or services, the firm assists in the litigation of controversial issues.

LOVELLS

VIA FRATELLI GABBA 3
20121 MILAN

Telephone: +39 02 7202521
Fax: +39 02 72025252
E-mail: information@lovells.com
Website: www.lovells.com

Languages
English, French, German

Other offices
Alicante, Amsterdam, Beijing, Berlin, Brussels, Budapest*, Chicago, Düsseldorf, Frankfurt, Hamburg, Ho Chi Minh City, Hong Kong, London, Moscow, Munich, New York, Paris, Prague, Rome, Shanghai, Singapore, Tokyo, Vienna*, Warsaw, Zagreb*

Number of lawyers 1,600
at this office 26

Contact
Paolo Criscione

CATEGORIES OF WORK

Corporate (including M&A, private equity, privatisations)

Antitrust/competition

Tax

Financial services and investment funds

Banking

Capital markets

Project finance

Property and construction

Administrative and public law (including town planning, environment, energy)

Pharmaceutical

Insurance

Insolvency

Intellectual property, IT, e-commerce and media

Employment

Litigation and arbitration

Data protection

STUDIO LEGALE MONDINI-RUSCONI

VIA VISCONTI DI MODRONE 2
20122 MILANO

Telephone: +39 02 77 73 51
Fax: +39 02 77 73 53 33
E-mail: studiolegale@mondinirusconi.it
Website: www.mondinirusconi.it

Languages
English, French, German

Number of lawyers 21

CATEGORIES OF WORK

International and EC law
Giorgio Mondini, Anna Carabelli

Company law
Luca Tiberi, Giuseppe Rusconi

Copyright, trade marks and intellectual property
Giorgio Mondini, Anna Carabelli

Media law
Giorgio Mondini, Anna Carabelli

Contracts
Giorgio Mondini, Giuseppe Rusconi

Litigation
Giacomo Bonelli, Alessandro Fano

Telecommunications
Giorgio Mondini, Alessandro Fano

Labour
Giacomo Bonelli, Alessandro Fano

Tax
Giuseppe Rusconi

Construction law
Giuseppe Rusconi, Luca Tiberi

Commercial law – mergers and acquisitions
Giuseppe Rusconi, Luca Tiberi

MCDERMOTT WILL & EMERY/CARNELUTTI

STUDIO LEGALE ASSOCIATO

VIA PRINCIPE AMEDEO 3
20121 MILANO

Telephone: +39 02 655 851
Fax: +39 02 655 855 85
Website: www.mwe.com

Languages
All main business languages

Other offices
Boston, Brussels, Chicago, Düsseldorf, London, Los Angeles, Miami, Munich, New York, Orange County, Rome, San Diego, Silicon Valley, Washington DC

Number of lawyers 1,000
at this office 50

Contact
Luca Arnaboldi

CATEGORIES OF WORK

Mergers and acquisitions
Luca Arnaboldi, Marino Bastianini

Domestic and international taxation
Gilberto Comi,
Andrea Rittatore Vonwiller

Telecommunications, media and IT
Paolo Scarduelli, Nicolò Bastianini

Litigation and arbitration
Margherita Barié

Real estate
Guido Alberto Inzaghi

Labour and employment law
Olimpio Stucchi, Angelo Zambelli

Capital markets
Luca Arnaboldi

Corporate finance
Alberto Rittatore Vonwiller

Intellectual property
Margherita Barié

Energy
Rodolfo Radice, Alberto Croze

THE FIRM

McDermott, Will & Emery/Carnelutti is the combination of the practices of McDermott, Will & Emery and Carnelutti Studio Legale Associato. The firm is among the largest law firms in Italy. Its strength arises from vast international experience and organisation combined with an excellent knowledge of Italian legislation and market conditions. The firm has had a presence in Italy for over 100 years and has maintained a leading position by adequately responding to the fast-changing needs of its dynamic client base. As a result of its growth and development, the firm is able to offer a wide range of legal services in a variety of practice areas. The firm's services are tailored to the needs of individual clients and all of its lawyers are committed to longstanding traditions with the client. In addition, the structure and scale of the firm permits individual attorneys to develop depth in specialised fields, as well as to work in multi-disciplinary teams. Among the partners of the firm are tax advisers, providing the best advice from a legal and a tax perspective.

AREAS OF PRACTICE

The firm advises both Italian and international clients, and has a strong commitment to providing clients with international resources. The firm's core practice areas in Italy include M&A; general corporate; banking and corporate finance; tax; media, entertainment and telecoms; litigation and arbitration; real estate; labour; intellectual property and energy.

The firm advises on negotiated transactions, including leveraged buyouts, mergers, restructurings, spin-offs and joint ventures. The corporate lawyers advise on all aspects of general corporate law, including contract drafting, company formations, as well as the structuring, formation, funding and operations of business entities; conducting due diligence investigations; and advising on multi-party contracts. The lawyers assist financial groups particularly on matters concerning authorisations from the Italian Securities Commission (Consob) and the Bank of Italy to the distribution of quotas of mutual funds or shares of SICAV (UCITS). The firm offers a full range of Italian and international corporate/tax consulting and tax dispute resolution/litigation services, including Italian corporate tax, VAT, stamp duties; corporate and individual local/international tax planning; inland revenue investigations and tax litigation; trusts setting; and international tax law. The firm's media lawyers counsel clients on issues ranging from pay-per-view contracts to digital copyright matters and the convergence of media and network technologies, including licensing, regulatory matters, contractual advice, negotiations, outsoucing, equipment and software supply, and service provisions.

The firm's lawyers have particular experience in Italian and international arbitration acting both as counsel to either of the parties and as arbitrators, and the firm also provides assistance on alternative techniques of dispute resolution and in major Italian litigation. The firm's real estate practice advises Italian and foreign investors, users, owners, managers, developers and lenders in connection with their acquisition, financing, operation, leasing, construction and disposition of real estate projects. The firm assists industrial and financial groups in handling legal aspects of human resources management and employment issues. Services provided include the hiring of executives and employees; individual and collective dismissal procedures; collective bargaining with trade unions; reorganisation; pay and benefits; long-term incentive schemes; pensions; industrial relations; and employment litigation.

The firm's IP practice includes procurement and licensing in the patent, trade mark and copyright areas and client counselling and advice regarding trade secrets, unfair competition, advertising, entertainment and computer law. The firm also regularly advises energy producers and power plant contractors in Italy, Europe and the Middle East, including matters related to Italy's privatisation and liberalisation processes. The firm provides assistance in production sharing and supply agreements, energy field developments, construction projects and compliance and authorisation procedures.

MORANO & ASSOCIATI

CORSO MATTEOTTI 3
20121 MILAN

Telephone: + 39 02 76 011 939
Fax: + 39 02 760 11 940
E-mail: info-mi@morano-associati.com
Website: www.morano-associati.com

Languages
English, French, German, Italian, Spanish

Other offices
Turin

Number of lawyers 34
at this office 26

Contacts
Alberto Morano (senior partner)
Enrico Zattoni (managing partner)

CATEGORIES OF WORK

Mergers and aquisitions
Alberto Morano, Enrico Zattoni

LBOs
Alberto Morano,
Federico Cavazza Rossi

Structured finance
Alberto Morano

Pharmaceuticals and biotechnology
Enrico Zattoni

Employment
Roberto Rollero

Information technology
Enrico Zattoni, Gianpero Basso

Tax and financial services
Giovanni Bandena

Banking
Alberto Morano

Real estate
Federico Cavazza Rossi, Daniele Zanni

Commercial/general corporate
Gianpiero Basso, Enrico Zattoni

Regulatory
Giovanni Bandena, Massimo Chiaia

Asset finance and securitisation
Alberto Morano, Massimo Chiaia

Dispute resolution and litigation
Roberto Rollero, Daniele Zanni

Insurance
Massimo Chiaia

NCTM – STUDIO LEGALE ASSOCIATO

VIA AGNELLO 12
20121 MILAN

Telephone: +39 02 72 55 11
Fax: +39 02 72 55 15 01
E-mail: info@nctm.it
Website: www.nctm.it

Languages
English, French, German, Spanish

Other offices
Rome, Verona, Vicenza

Number of lawyers 120
at this office 91

Contacts
Filippo Cesaris, Paolo Montironi, Vittorio Noseda, Stefano Padovani, Alberto Toffoletto

CATEGORIES OF WORK

Mergers and acquisitions

Private equity

Capital markets

Banking and financing

Insolvency and debt restructuring

Antitrust and competition

Corporate and commercial

IT and telecommunications

Litigation and arbitration

Insurance

Real estate

Intellectual property

Tax

NUNZIANTE MAGRONE

FORO BUONAPARTE, 70
20121 MILANO

Telephone: +39 02 65 75 181
Fax: +39 02 65 70 013
E-mail: milano@nunziantemagrone.it
Website: www.nunziantemagrone.it

Languages
English, French, German, Spanish

Other offices
Bologna, Rome, Turin

Number of lawyers 56
at this office 18

CATEGORIES OF WORK

Corporate	Postal
Banking and finance	Aviation
Mergers and acquisitions	Environmental
Litigation and arbitration	Tax
Intellectual property	Real Estate
Administrative	White-collar crime
EU and competition	

PEDERSOLI E ASSOCIATI

VIA ANDEGARI 4/A
20121 MILANO

Telephone: +39 02 87 91 91
Fax: +39 02 87 91 93 33
E-mail: milano@pedersoli.it

Languages
English, French, German

Number of lawyers 30

Contact
Carlo Pedersoli

CATEGORIES OF WORK

Antitrust	Insolvency law
Banking	Litigation
Contracts	Mergers and acquisitions
Corporate and commercial law	Project finance
Debt restructuring	Securities law
Domestic and international arbitration	

STUDIO LEGALE RAPISARDI

VIA SERBELLONI 12
20122 MILAN

Telephone: +39 02 76 30 11
Fax: +39 02 76 30 13 00
E-mail: studio@rapisardi.it
Website: www.rapisardi.it

Languages
English, French, German

Number of lawyers 7

CATEGORIES OF WORK

- Trade mark, copyright, patent, utility and design model applications and registrations in Italy and abroad
- European patents and Euro-PCT patents
- Community trade marks, Madrid protocol registrations
- Domain name protection and website construction
- IP portfolio management (including infringement/ counterfeiting watching, patent and trade mark registrations maintenance, assignments, licensing and technology agreements)
- Intellectual property dispute resolution (administrative and judicial, including emergency remedies)
- Searches, watch searches

RINALDI E ASSOCIATI STUDIO LEGALE

VIA CONSERVATORIO 15
20122 MILAN

Telephone: +39 02 760 08860
Fax: +39 02 760 06944
E-mail: mailbox@rinaldilawf.com
Website: www.rinaldilawf.com

Languages
English, French, Portuguese, Spanish

Other offices
Rome

Number of lawyers 18
at this office 16

CATEGORIES OF WORK

- Antitrust and competition
- Banking and finance
- Commercial contracts
- Corporate law
- Employment, labour law
- Insolvency and bankruptcy law
- Intellectual property and information technology law
- Litigation
- Mergers and acquisitions
- Administrative and regulatory law
- Energy and natural resources law
- Environment
- International private law
- Non profit
- Real estate

STUDIO LEGALE RUBINI

CORSO MATTEOTTI 8
20121 MILANO

Telephone: +39 02 7631 9196
Fax: +39 02 7631 9180
E-mail: info@rubinilaw.it

Languages
English, French, Spanish

Other offices
Rome

Number of lawyers 10
at this office 8

Contacts
Elisabetta Rubini, Cristina Manasse

CATEGORIES OF WORK

Corporate and commercial law

Contracts

EU and competition law

Intellectual property and IT

Media law

Advertising and sponsorship

Internet

Art and cultural property

Charity and not-for-profit organisations

State-owned companies regulation

Inheritance and family law

Insolvency

White-collar crime

Litigation

RUBINO-SAMMARTANO E ASSOCIATI
LAWFED

VIALE CASSIODORO 3
20145 MILANO

Telephone: +39 02 481 90 41
Fax: +39 02 480 082 77
E-mail: rubinosammartano@lawfed.com
Website:www.lawfed.com

Languages
English, French

Other offices
London*, Paris*, Genoa, Rome, Turin

Number of lawyers 34
at this office 7

Contact
Mauro Rubino-Sammartano

Member
Law Fed, Federation of Law and Tax Law Firms

CATEGORIES OF WORK

Arbitration
Mauro Rubino-Sammartano, Massimo Curti

Construction
Mauro Rubino-Sammartano

Commercial law
Francesco Santi

International contracts
Mauro Rubino-Sammartano

Contract law
Francesco Santi, Massimo Curti

Litigation
Massimo Curti, Marco Vouch

Mergers and acquisitions
Mauro Rubino-Sammartano

Community law
Luisa Zanframundo

Joint ventures
Mauro Rubino-Sammartano, Marco Bellora

International private law
Luisa Zanframundo

Administrative law
Riccardo Villata

Employment
Riccardo Musatti, Marco Vouch

STUDIO SANTA MARIA

LARGO TOSCANINI 1
20122 MILAN

Telephone: +39 02 771 971
Fax: +39 02 771 97 260
E-mail: santamaria@santalex.com
Website: www.santalex.com

Languages
English, French, German, Portuguese, Spanish

Other offices
New York, Rome

Number of lawyers 40
at this office 34

Contact
Prof Alberto Santa Maria

International groupings
Kramer Levin Naftalis & Frankel (New York, Paris); Berwin Leighton Paisner (London, Brussels)

CATEGORIES OF WORK

Mergers and acquisitions	Banking and finance
EU and competition	Litigation
International law	Arbitration
International trade regulation	Bankruptcy
Corporate law	Tax

SIMMONS & SIMMONS

CORSO VITTORIO EMANUELE 1
20122 MILANO

Telephone: +39 02 72505 1
Fax: +39 02 72505 505
E-mail: enquiries@simmons-simmons.com
Website: www.simmons-simmons.com

Languages
English, German, French

Other offices
London, Rotterdam, Paris, Lisbon, Rome, Düsseldorf, Frankfurt, Brussels, Madrid, Padua, Oporto, Madeira, Abu Dhabi, Qatar, Hong Kong, Shanghai, Tokyo, New York

Number of lawyers 754
at this office 20

Contact
Richard Slater

CATEGORIES OF WORK

Corporate	Financial markets
Banking	Pharmaceutical and biotechnology
Capital markets	Energy and utilities
Taxation	TMT
Projects, PFI	Aerospace and defence
EU, competition	Transport
Dispute resolution	Real estate and construction
Intellectual property	Consumer goods
Employment	

SQUIRE, SANDERS & DEMPSEY L.L.P.
STUDIO LEGALE BERNASCONE & SOCI

PIAZZA SAN BABILA, 3
20122 MILAN

Telephone: +39 02 7772 1511
Fax: +39 02 7772 1515
E-mail: gbernascone@ssd.com
Website: www.ssd.com

Languages
English, French

Other offices
Beijing, Bratislava, Brussels, Budapest, Cincinnati, Cleveland, Columbus, Hong Kong, Houston, London, Los Angeles, Madrid, Miami, Moscow, New York, Palo Alto, Phoenix, Prague, Rio de Janeiro, San Francisco, Taipei, Tampa, Tokyo, Tysons Corner, Washington DC, Bucharest*, Dublin*, Kyiv*

Number of lawyers 710
at this office 8

Contact
Gabriele Bernascone

CATEGORIES OF WORK	
Corporate and commercial	Litigation, arbitration, labour
Corporate finance	Mergers and acquisitions
Data protection	Power generation, energy
Environment	Privatisation
EU competition	Project finance
Information technology	Reorganisation
Intellectual property	Securities
Joint ventures	Telecoms and IT
Life sciences/biotechnology	Venture capital

THE FIRM

Founded in 1890, Squire, Sanders & Dempsey is a multi-jurisdictional law firm with 710 lawyers in Europe, the Americas and Asia. The firm's practice covers most areas of law, with an emphasis on business and finance.

The firm operates as a single global partnership, which ensures client accountability and the seamless delivery of uniformly high-quality legal services throughout the world. The firm's lawyers come from many countries and cultures, are licensed to practise in both common law and civil law jurisdictions, and communicate with clients in their native languages. The firm remains committed to the fundamental principles ordained by its founders: to serve clients effectively and maintain the professional standards that distinguish the firm and its people.

AREAS OF PRACTICE

The firm is organised around four major practice areas: advocacy, business, capital markets and regulated industries. Within these practice areas, the firm's work can be divided into numerous areas of specialisation, including banking, bankruptcy and restructuring, biotechnology and pharmaceuticals, communications, competition law, converging technologies, corporate, energy, environmental, healthcare, intellectual property, international dispute resolution, labour and employment, litigation, mergers and acquisitions, privatisations, project finance, real estate, securities and taxation.

Originally an office of the former San Francisco-based Graham & James LLP, the Milan office combined practices with Squire Sanders in 2000 and has a long history representing international businesses in Milan. Lawyers provide counsel on a variety of issues involving energy, communications, corporate law, M&As, banking and financial services, e-business, dispute resolution, labour law, life science/biotech, IT, IP and data protection.

The lawyers assist both Italian companies and clients from Asia, Europe and the United States looking to do business in the Italian market. The firm is one of the only Italian firms that has a strong presence in Silicon Valley. The same range of services that Squire, Sanders regularly provides to the hi-tech community in the United States is also available in Milan.

The Milan lawyers' experience in energy matters includes mergers and acquisitions, project finance and development, privatisations and energy marketing as well as environmental law. Services range from the formation of corporations and consortiums to the drafting of shareholder agreements. Lawyers also conduct dispute resolution and regulation for large oil companies and regularly represent clients in both commercial and labour litigation, handling defence work particularly in product liability cases.

Milan lawyers provide counsel on domain rights and jurisdictional issues and have established joint ventures between domestic and foreign technology companies for licensing software. In fact, the office is recognised as a leading law firm in Italy for its representation of Japanese trading companies particularly with their licensing agreements with Italian primary fashion houses.

The corporate practice serves the transactional needs of public and private companies, emerging companies and financial institutions. Services include participation in complex business transactions including acquisitions and dispositions, joint ventures, commercial loans, asset- and mortgage-backed securitisations, public and private securities offerings, real estate activities, tax matters, secured transactions and creditors' rights.

Lawyers represent foreign investors in their acquisitions of Italian companies in such industries as textiles and fashion accessories, musical instruments, office equipment, home appliances, air conditioners, cars and motorbikes and food and beverages (including spirits).

The office is also active in the communications arena, advising on Italian and European legislation concerning antitrust, privatisation and liberalisation as it affects the hi-tech and telecoms industries.

Lawyers have significant experience in the life sciences/biotechnology arena. Over the years, Squire Sanders' lawyers have provided legal services to numerous clients including biotechnology/biomedical/medical devices companies. A team of Milan lawyers are also founders of SISB (The Italian Society for the Study of Biotechnology), an association involved in the research, study and analysis of the interactions between science, culture, ethics, economy, environmental impact and legislation.

STUDIO LEGALE SUTTI

VIA MONTENAPOLEONE 8
20121 MILANO

Telephone: +39 02 76 20 4
Fax: +39 02 76 20 48 05
E-mail: maildesk@sutti.com
Website: www.sutti.com

Languages
Bulgarian, Dutch, English, French, German, Italian, Japanese, Portuguese, Romanian, Serbian, Spanish

Other offices
Belgrade, Bucharest, Genoa, London, Rome, Sofia, Tokyo

Number of lawyers 130
at this office 40

Contact
Veruska De Prado

CATEGORIES OF WORK

Company, commercial law
Banking and finance
Mergers and acquisitions
Distribution, agency and franchising
Debt collection and insolvency
Commercial property law
Intellectual property
Patent and trade mark agency service
White-collar crime
EC, competition and antitrust law
IT and TLC law
Litigation and arbitration
Employment, labour law
Administrative law
Environmental law

STUDIO LEGALE TAGLIORETTI FARESE CICERCHIA

VIA VINCENZO MONTI, 15
20123 MILAN

Telephone: +39 02 480 21 811
Fax: + 39 02 481 93 877
E-mail: tfc.milano@taglioretti.com
Website: www.taglioretti.com

Languages
English, French, Spanish

Other offices
Rome

Number of lawyers 17
at this office 11

Contacts
Fortunato Taglioretti (Milan),
Paolo Farese (Rome)

Member
International Bar Association; AIPPI; FCIarb; Arbitration Chamber of Milan

CATEGORIES OF WORK

Antitrust
Arbitration
Bankruptcy
International licensing and distribution
Joint ventures
Corporate
Construction contracts
Intellectual property
Litigation
Labour and employment

TOFFOLETTO E SOCI, member of ius laboris
STUDIO LEGALE ASSOCIATO

VIA ROVELLO 12
20121 MILANO

Telephone: +39 02 721 441
Fax: +39 02 721 44500
E-mail: info@toffoletto.it
Website: www.toffoletto.it

Languages
English, French, German, Spanish

Other offices
Rome

Number of lawyers 44

Contact
Franco Toffoletto

Member
ius laboris, International Employment Law Pensions and Employee Benefits Alliance

CATEGORIES OF WORK

Labour and employment law	Collective labour relations
Social security	Collective dismissals
Pensions and human resources	European employment law
Contracts	Expatriates
Restructuring and transfer of undertakings	Stock options plans

STUDIO LEGALE TONUCCI

VIA DEI BOSSI 4
20121 MILAN

Telephone: +39 02 80 13 95
Fax: +39 02 86 04 68
E-mail: milano@tonucci.it
Website: www.tonucci.it

Languages
English, French, German, Spanish, Albanian, Romanian

Other offices
Rome, Padua, Prato, Paris, New York, Tirana, Bucharest

Number of lawyers 178
at this office 18

CATEGORIES OF WORK

Corporate	Environment
M&A and privatisation	Taxation
Commercial litigation	Information technology and media
Banking and finance, insurance	Intellectual property
Capital markets	Competition and anti-trust
Telecommunications	Criminal law
Energy and gas	Aviation
Administrative and real estate	East Europe and developing countries
Labour	

TREVISAN & CUONZO
AVVOCATI

VIA BRERA 6
20121 MILANO

Telephone: +39 02 86 46 33 13
Fax: +39 02 86 46 38 92
Email: info@trevisancuonzo.com
Website: www.trevisancuonzo.com

Languages
English, French, German, Spanish

Number of lawyers 35

CATEGORIES OF WORK

Anti-counterfeit and piracy	European Community
Commercial contracts	Insolvency
Commercial litigation	Intellectual property, patents, trade marks, copyright
Competition (EU and Italian)	Intellectual property litigation
Corporate	Internet and e-commerce
Debt collection	Mergers and acquisitions
Employment	Multimedia and communications
Information technology	Property
Franchising	Product liability

VITA SAMORY, FABBRINI E ASSOCIATI

CORSO G MATTEOTTI, 10
20121 MILANO

Telephone: +39 02 77 42 01
Fax: +39 02 76 39 43 61
E-mail: studio.milano@vita-fabbrini.com
Website: www.vita-fabbrini.com

Languages
English, French

Other offices
Rome

Number of lawyers 45
at this office 40

Contact
Guido Testa

CATEGORIES OF WORK

Antitrust law	Insurance law
Arbitration	International law
Banking and finance law	Investment and financial services
Bankruptcy/insolvency law	Labour law
Civil litigation	Mergers and acquisitions
Commercial law	Private equity
Contracts	Real estate
Corporate law	Software and IT law
Domestic and international taxation	Telecommunications
EU law	Venture capital

ACLAW – CECCON & ASSOCIATI

GALLERIA BORROMEO 4
35137 PADUA

Telephone: +39 049 877 4630
Fax: +39 049 875 0299
E-mail: lawfirm@aclaw.it
Website: www.aclaw.it

Languages
English, French, German, Spanish

Other offices
Milan*, Pordenone*, Rome*

Number of lawyers 40
at this office 10

Contact
Prof Avv Roberto Ceccon (senior partner)

CATEGORIES OF WORK

- General practice
- International and domestic practice
- Agency and distributorship
- Antitrust
- Arbitration and ADR
- Computers and software
- Communication and media
- Litigation
- Aviation
- Domestic and international trade law
- Labour and employment
- EU law
- Family law
- Finance
- Company criminal law
- Franchising
- Mergers and acquisitions
- Contracts
- Civil law
- Environmental law
- Bankruptcy
- Company law
- Tax law
- Privatisations
- Intellectual property and cyber law
- Wills, trusts and estate

LCA AVVOCATI E COMMERCIALISTI D'IMPRESA

GALLERIA BORROMEO, 3
35137 PADOVA

Telephone: +39 049 877 5811
Fax: +39 049 666 086
E-mail: padova@studio-lca.com
Website: www.studio-lca.com

Languages
Dutch, English, German, French, Portuguese, Spanish, Swedish

Other offices
London, Milan, Munich, Venice

Number of lawyers 33
at this office 23

Contacts
Francesco Camilotti, Cristiano Cerchiai, Claudio Giordano

CATEGORIES OF WORK

- Antitrust and EU law
- Arbitration
- Banking and finance
- Bankruptcy and insolvency
- Company and commercial law
- Corporate administrative service
- Corporate finance
- Debt recovery and insolvency
- Energy
- Family law
- Insurance law
- IT, intellectual and industrial property
- International and domestic trust and tax advice
- International chartered accountancy
- Labour, employment and immigration
- Litigation
- Mergers and acquisitions
- Private client matters
- Real estate
- Sports law
- Trade marks and copyright

SIMMONS & SIMMONS

LARGO EUROPA N1
35137 PADUA

Telephone: +39 049 875 0672
Fax: +39 049 875 3675
E-mail: enquiries@simmons-simmons.com
Website: www.simmons-simmons.com

Languages
English, French, German

Other offices
London, Rotterdam, Paris, Lisbon, Milan, Rome, Düsseldorf, Frankfurt, Brussels, Madrid, Oporto, Madeira, Abu Dhabi, Qatar, Hong Kong, Shanghai, Tokyo, New York

Number of lawyers 754
at this office 7

Contacts
Paolo Brugnera, Paolo Gnignati

CATEGORIES OF WORK

Corporate	**Financial markets**
Banking	**Pharmaceutical and biotechnology**
Capital markets	**Energy and utilities**
Taxation	**TMT**
Projects, PFI	**Aerospace and defence**
EU, competition	**Transport**
Dispute resolution	**Real estate and construction**
Intellectual property	**Consumer goods**
Employment	

ALLEN & OVERY

CORSO VITTORIO EMANUELE II, 284
00186 ROME

Telephone: +39 06 68 42 71
Fax: +39 06 68 42 73 33
E-mail: information@allenovery.com
Website: www.allenovery.com

Languages
English, French, German, Italian, Spanish

Other offices
Amsterdam, Antwerp, Bangkok, Beijing, Bratislava, Brussels, Budapest, Dubai, Frankfurt, Hamburg, Hong Kong, London, Luxembourg, Madrid, Milan, Moscow, New York, Paris, Prague, Shanghai, Singapore, Tokyo, Turin, Warsaw

Number of lawyers 2,305
at this office 55

Contacts
Roberto Casati (senior partner);
G Massimillano Danusso
(joint managing partner);
Stephen Denyer (joint managing partner);
Emanuele Borganti
(head of operations in Italy)

CATEGORIES OF WORK

Corporate Paolo Cerina	**ICM** G Massimilliano Danusso
Banking Giancarlo Castorino	**Litigation** Alberto Nanni
Tax Andrea Manganelli	

BAKER & McKENZIE

VIALE DI VILLA MASSIMO 57
00161 ROMA

Telephone: +39 06 44 06 31
Fax: +39 06 44 06 33 06
E-mail: rome.info@bakernet.com
Website: www.bakernet.com

Languages
English, French, Spanish

Other offices
For a list of all offices and other information regarding the firm please consult Baker & McKenzie's London office entry

Number of lawyers 3,380
at this office 30

Contact
Fabio M Brembati

Baker & McKenzie is a global law firm with 66 offices in 36 countries.

CATEGORIES OF WORK

Antitrust and trade
V Salce

Banking and finance
F Brembati

Corporate/mergers and acquisitions
A Giovannelli, F Brembati

Dispute resolution
G Brocchieri

E-commerce/data protection
M Russo

Employment
G Brocchieri

Energy
R Giarda

Intellectual property
F Brembati, R Giarda

International/commercial
M Riccio

IT/communications/media
F Brembati, R Giarda

Major projects/project finance
G Macconi, A Lucente

Pharmaceutical and health industry
A Giovannelli

Real estate, construction, environment and tourism
G Macconi, A Lucente

Tax
A Giovannelli

Venture capital
G Benedetti

BORGOGNONI VIMERCATI, BRANCADORO, ROMANO & WOOD

20 VIALE DI VILLA GRAZIOLI
00198 ROMA

Telephone: +39 06 853 7201
Fax: +39 06 855 3424
E-mail: avvocati@bvrlaw.it

Languages
English, French, Italian

Other offices
London, Milan

Number of lawyers 16
at this office 9

CATEGORIES OF WORK

Business and commercial law
Avv Gianbenso Borgognoni Vimercati

Contracts
Avv Gianbenso Borgognoni Vimercati

Intellectual property
Avv Gianbenso Borgognoni Vimercati

Trusts and estates
Avv Gianbenso Borgognoni Vimercati

EEC antitrust and trade regulations
Avv Gianluca Brancadoro

Banks and banking, company law
Avv Gianluca Brancadoro

Industrial property
Avv Gianluca Brancadoro

Mergers and acquisitions
Avv Giorgio Romano

Wills, probate
Avv Giorgio Romano

Civil law
Avv Giorgio Romano, Avv Federica D'Innocenzo

Franchises and franchising
Avv John G Wood

Internet law
Avv John G Wood

Trusts
Avv John G Wood

Civil law – insolvency
Avv Francesca Galli

Family law – litigation and torts
Avv Maria Grazia Licci

Administrative law
Avv Fabrizia De Nigris

Bankruptcy – company law
Avv Rosa Mercone

CMS ADONNINO ASCOLI & CAVASOLA SCAMONI

VIA AGOSTINO DEPRETIS 86
ROMA

Telephone: +39 06 478 151
Fax: +39 06 483 755
E-mail: info@aacs.it
Website: www.aacs.it

Languages
English, French, German, Spanish, Dutch

Other offices
Milan

Number of lawyers 62
at this office 42

Contact
Pietro Cavasola

Other CMS law firms
CMS Francis Lefebvre, France; CMS Cameron McKenna, UK; CMS Derks Star Busmann, Netherlands; CMS von Erlach Klainguti Stettler Wille, Switzerland; CMS Hasche Sigle, Germany; CMS Lexcelis, Belgium; CMS Strommer Reich-Rohrwig Karasek Hainz, Austria

CATEGORIES OF WORK

- General civil and tax practice
- Business and corporate law
- International contracts
- Joint ventures
- EU law
- Foreign investment
- Mergers and acquisitions
- Labour law
- Administrative law
- Commercial litigation and arbitration
- Italian and international taxation
- Business reorganisation, tax planning
- Transfer pricing policy
- Cost-sharing agreements
- Company evaluations

CLEARY GOTTLIEB STEEN & HAMILTON

PIAZZA DI SPAGNA 15
00817 ROME

Telephone: +39 06 695 22 1
Fax: +39 06 69 20 06 65
Website: www.clearygottlieb.com

Languages
English, French, German, Portuguese

Other offices
Brussels, Cologne, Frankfurt, London, Milan, Moscow, Paris

Number of lawyers 937
at this office 43

CATEGORIES OF WORK

- Capital markets/securities
- EU and competition law
- EU litigation
- Joint ventures
- Mergers and acquisitions
- Privatisations
- Regulatory issues
- Tax
- Telecommunications and energy

STUDIO LEGALE CARNELUTTI

VIA PARIGI, 11
00185 ROMA

Telephone: +39 06 47 39 01
Fax: +39 06 48 19 833
E-mail: postmaster@carnelutti.it
Website: www.carnelutti.it

Languages
English, French, German, Spanish

Other offices
Milan, Naples, Paris

Number of lawyers 52
at this office 31

Contacts
Franco L Incutti,
Ferdinando Carabba Tettamanti

Member
Terralex

CATEGORIES OF WORK

General civil practice	**Insurance law**
Conflict of laws and international civil procedure	**Administrative law, construction**
Company law, mergers and acquisitions	**International commercial law**
EC law	**Tax law, banking, economy, finance**
Trade marks, patents, copyrights	**Litigation**
Competition and antitrust	**Advertising, unfair competition**
International and domestic arbitration	**Real estate**
	Energy and natural resources

THE FIRM

Carnelutti was originally founded in Venice at the end of the 19th century by Professor Francesco Carnelutti, one of the greatest Italian jurists of all time, who was equally well-known for his practice in civil and commercial law, as well as for his practice in criminal law. As the fame of Professor Carnelutti gradually spread throughout Italy and abroad, the firm, through its offices in Rome and Milan, expanded its activities, particularly in civil/commercial matters with a special emphasis on corporate and contractual matters. In recent years, the structure of said offices underwent a series or reorganisations and innovations as a result of a will to expand and improve the services offered to clients. The long-established Carnelutti Rome office continues to carry on its professional activity at the historical address of Via Parigi, 11. Other offices are situated in Milan, Naples and Paris. Through these offices, Carnelutti is able to provide an effective service to commercial institutions of all types and sizes in the new global international economic scenario. The firm also has excellent contacts with lawyers practising in most other commercial centres throughout the world. At the beginning of 1999, Alexandre Carnelutti, professor of international business law in Paris, France, joined the Carnelutti law office in Rome as a partner. The son of the late Tito Carnelutti and grandson of Francesco Carnelutti, Alexandre Carnelutti practises in Paris and has acted in the past as counsel expert in EU law.

AREAS OF PRACTICE

The firm has a broad experience in assisting private clients and public and private corporations in the areas of civil, commercial and administrative law. The firm has particular expertise in the areas of mergers and acquisitions, joint ventures, banking, project finance, securities offering, privatisations, securitisations, litigation and arbitration, EC and antitrust, sports law, contracts, employment, telecommunications, media and entertainment, bankruptcy, real estate, family, insurance, intellectual property and in fiscal and tax planning matters.

CHIOMENTI STUDIO LEGALE

VIA XXIV MAGGIO 43
00187 ROME

Telephone: +39 06 466 221
Fax: +39 06 466 22 600
E-mail: roma@chiomenti.net

Languages
English, French, German, Italian, Spanish

Other offices
Brussels, London, Milan, New York, Turin

Number of lawyers 140
at this office 60

Member
Lex Mundi

CATEGORIES OF WORK

Corporate and M&A	**IP, media and IT**
Banking and finance	**Litigation and arbitration**
Capital markets	**Insolvency and corporate restructuring**
Regulatory and financial services	**Employment and labour**
Tax	**Telecommunications**
European, competition and international law	**Energy**
Administrative and environmental law	**Real estate**

THE FIRM

Chiomenti Studio Legale continues the practice started by Pasquale Chiomenti in the late 1940s as one of the first Italian law firms with international capabilities, advising Italian and foreign clients in the progressive expansion of post-war economy.

Since then Chiomenti Studio Legale has steadily consolidated its initial position as one of Italy's leading law firms, meeting the challenge of increasing globalisation of business. Today the firm is composed of more than 150 lawyers and tax advisers and has offices in Rome, Milan, Turin, London, Brussels and – since September 2003 – New York.

Chiomenti has always been a leader in tailoring legal techniques developed in an international context for implementation in Italy and specifically in developing Italian legal techniques in order to accommodate the requirements of international business clients. This is of increasing importance today when the majority of business transactions in Europe have a cross-border dimension and a growing proportion of legal disputes have an international aspect.

In 2001, Chiomenti Studio Legale and Skadden, Arps, Slate, Meagher & Flom entered into a strategic alliance that combines their respective strengths in US, Italian and English law.

AREAS OF PRACTICE

Corporate and M&A: friendly and hostile takeovers, leveraged and management buy-outs, privatisations, joint ventures, company restructuring, general corporate and commercial transactions.

Banking and finance: debt and equity instruments, international and domestic loans, real estate loans, debt restructuring and rescheduling etc.

Capital markets: IPOs and other public offerings, equity offerings, financial products private and public placements.

Regulatory and financial services: rules and regulations applying to banks, financial intermediaries, investment funds and insurance companies. Representing clients before Bank of Italy, CONSOB and ISVAP, formations, mergers, spin-offs, purchases and sales.

Tax: corporate and individual taxation, mergers and acquisitions and corporate reorganisation, international and EU taxation.

European law, competition and international law: advice in connection with antitrust matters, public subsidies, telecoms, power, transportation, free circulation of goods and services, agriculture, concentration and consolidation of joint ventures and unfair competition.

Administrative law and environmental law: contracts and concessions of public works, service and supply contracts, legal assistance to administrative authorities and to private and public entities operating in the utilities sector.

IP, media and IT: copyrights, trade marks, trade secrets, patents, new communication and transmission systems and media and communications rules and regulations.

Litigation and arbitration: financial and commercial disputes before civil and administrative courts and administrative authorities and national supervisory authorities.

Insolvency and corporate restructuring: assistance in connection with bankruptcy procedures, pre-packaged bankruptcies, bankruptcy administration and liquidations.

Employment and labour: national, European and international employment and labour law.

Telecommunications and energy: regulatory issues, licensing, interconnection, telecoms securities offering and project financing.

Energy: regulatory issues, project finance, mergers and acquisitions, sales and joint venture.

Real estate: acquisition and sale, mergers and spin-offs, rentals, construction, bids, development, asset management services, leasing, credit over pledge securitisation, and credits from rentals.

COCCIA DE ANGELIS & ASSOCIATI – STUDIO LEGALE E TRIBUTARIO

PIAZZA ADRIANA 15
00193 ROME

Telephone: +39 06 6880 3025
Fax: +39 06 6880 9416
Website: www.cdaa.it
E-mail: legal@cdaa.it

Languages
English, French, Italian, Spanish

Number of lawyers 10

Contact
Mr Massimo Coccia

CATEGORIES OF WORK

Arbitration and ADR
Massimo Coccia

Banking
Gabriele Bartolucci

Civil and commercial law
Riccardo La Cognata, Bruno Tassone

Competition and antitrust
Massimo Coccia, Bruno Tassone

Contracts
Francesca Troilo

Corporate and finance
Gabriele Bartolucci, Stefano De Angelis

Energy and oil
Frencesca Troilo

EU and international law
Massimo Coccia

Litigation
Riccardo la Cognata

Intellectual property
Bruno Tassone

Domestic taxation
Stefano de Angelis

International taxation
Gabriele Bartolucci

Sports law
Massimo Coccia, Riccardo la Cognata

STUDIO LEGALE DELFINO E ASSOCIATI WILLKIE FARR & GALLAGHER LLP

VIA DI RIPETTA 142
00186 ROME

Telephone: +39 06 68 63 61
Fax: +39 06 68 63 63 63
Website: www.willkie.com

Languages
English, French, German, Spanish

Other offices
New York, Washington DC, Paris, London, Milan, Frankfurt, Brussels

Number of lawyers 560
at this office 13

Contact
Maurizio Delfino

CATEGORIES OF WORK

Mergers and acquisitions

Private equity

Capital markets

Telecommunication

Energy

Tax

Antitrust

Litigation

Arbitration

DELLI SANTI & PARTNERS

VIA DI MONSERRATO 25
00186 ROME

Telephone: +39 06 681 0071
Fax: +39 06 6880 5488
E-mail: studio@dellisanti.it
Website: www.dellisanti.it

Languages
English, French, German, Italian, Spanish

Other offices
Bologna, Milan

Number of lawyers 30
at this office 20

Contact
Valentina Delli Santi

International groupings
Urban Land Institute (ULI)

CATEGORIES OF WORK

Real estate	Management of public services
Management of territory	Management of real estate assets

STUDIO LEGALE DEWEY BALLANTINE

IN ASSOCIAZIONE CON GATTAI, SPERONI, GIORDANO & PARTNERS

VIA PO 22
00198 ROME

Telephone: +39 06 45 20 62 20
Fax: +39 06 45 20 62 30
Website: www.deweyballantine.com

Languages
English, French, Italian

Other offices
Austin, Budapest, East Palo Alto, Frankfurt, Houston, London, Los Angeles, Milan, New York, Prague, Warsaw, Washington DC

Number of lawyers 606
at this office 4

Contacts
Stefano Speroni (ssperoni@deweyballantine.com); Giovan Battista Santangelo (gsantangelo@deweyballantine.com)

CATEGORIES OF WORK

Mergers and acquisitions	Project finance/PPP
Private equity	Privatisation
Capital markets	Real estate
Securitisation	Energy
Derivatives	Telecommunications

DI TANNO E ASSOCIATI

VIA PAISIELLO 33
00198 ROMA

Telephone: +39 06 84 56 61
Fax: +39 06 84 19 500
E-mail: ditannoeass@ditanno.it
Website: www.ditanno.it

Languages
English, French

Other offices
Milan, Treviso

Number of lawyers 50

Contacts
Tommaso Di Tanno, Stefano Petrecca

CATEGORIES OF WORK

Tax

Mergers and acquisitions

Tax litigation

Corporate finance

Commercial and company law

Banking and finance

Venture capital

EY LAW

VIA DEI VILLINI 13
00161 ROMA

Telephone: +39 06 67 48 91
Fax: +39 06 44 23 17 92
Website: www.eylaw.com

Languages
Danish, English, French, German, Spanish

Other offices
Ancona, Bari, Bologna, Florence, Milan, Naples, Padua, Turin, Treviso, Verona

Number of lawyers 270
at this office 70

Contact
Francesco Marotta (managing partner)

CATEGORIES OF WORK

General corporate
Francesco Marotta, Paolo Tanoni

Litigation
Francesco Aratari

Labour law
Prof Luciano Spagnuolo Vigorita

Real estate, property law
Raffaele Pendibene

Public law
Prof Fabrizio Cassella

Cross-border mergers and acquisitions
Raffaele Caldarone, Giuseppe Barreca

Banking and financial services
Corrado Verna

Intellectual property and information technology
Paolo Tanoni, Luigi Neirotti

Antitrust, regulatory
Eduardo Courir

Arbitration and Supreme Court
Prof Ernesto Cesaro,
Prof Biagio Grasso

FRESHFIELDS BRUCKHAUS DERINGER

PIAZZA DI MONTE CITORIO 115
00186 ROME

Telephone: +39 06 695 331
Fax: +39 06 695 33 800
E-mail: email@freshfields.com
Website: www.freshfields.com

Languages
Extensive language capabilities

Other offices
Amsterdam, Bangkok, Barcelona, Beijing, Berlin, Bratislava, Brussels, Budapest, Cologne, Düsseldorf, Frankfurt, Hamburg, Hanoi, Ho Chi Minh City, Hong Kong, London, Madrid, Milan, Moscow, Munich, New York, Paris, Shanghai, Singapore, Tokyo, Vienna, Washington DC

Number of lawyers 2,504
at this office 35

Contacts
Philip Richards, Mario Ortu

CATEGORIES OF WORK

Corporate

Finance

Tax

Antitrust, competition and trade

Intellectual property and IT

Dispute resolution (including environment, planning and regulatory)

Real estate

Employment, pensions and benefits

GIANNI, ORIGONI, GRIPPO & PARTNERS

IN ASSOCIATION WITH LINKLATERS

VIA DELLE QUATTRO FONTANE, 20
00184 ROMA

Telephone: +39 06 47 87 51
Fax: +39 06 48 71 101
Email: rome@gop.it
Website: www.gop.it

Languages
English, French, German, Spanish

Other offices
Bologna, London, Milan, Naples, New York, Padua

Number of lawyers 267
at this office 133

Contacts
Francesco Gianni, Giovanni Nardulli

CATEGORIES OF WORK

Mergers and acquisitions
Francesco Gianni, Alessandro Giuliani

Banking and finance
Alberto Giampieri, Giovanni Nardulli

Labour law
Matteo Fusillo, Alberto Maggi

Corporate law
Enzo Schiavello, Cesare Vento

Environmental
Andrea Mazziotti

Telecoms
Cesare Vento

Antitrust
Alberto Pera

Arbitration and litigation
Gian Battista Origoni Della Croce, Aulo Cossu

Tax
Massimo Agostini

Securities
Bruno Bartocci, Antonio Segni

EU law
Alberto Pera

Projects
Eugenio Grippo, Giovanni Nardulli

THE FIRM

Gianni, Origoni, Grippo & Partners is one of the largest Italian business law firms. Established in 1988, it has 267 professionals delivering first-class legal advice.

The firm combines domestic capability with global expertise. Through its offices in Rome, Milan, Padua, Bologna, Naples, London, and New York, and its association with Linklaters, the firm is well positioned in all major domestic and international business centres, and is widely regarded as a key player in international and domestic practice.

Gianni, Origoni, Grippo & Partners' clients range from large corporations to entrepreneurs in many diverse business sectors. The firm counts leading corporates, foreign multinationals, investment banks, and major financial institutions among its clients.

AREAS OF PRACTICE

Gianni, Origoni, Grippo & Partners provides a comprehensive range of legal services across all areas of practice: corporate and commercial, banking and finance, capital markets, antitrust and regulatory, real estate, labour, litigation and arbitration, tax and intellectual property.

The firm enjoys a formidable reputation for its expertise in M&A, topping all M&A league tables in Italy over the last three years. It is heavily involved in many of the most significant domestic M&A transactions and has regularly assisted international clients in several of the latest large cross-border acquisitions.

The firm has an extensive practice representing Italian and foreign clients in all their general corporate and commercial matters.

Gianni, Origoni, Grippo & Partners specialises in integrating its M&A capabilities with banking and finance know-how. The firm is recognised as a leader in this market, having worked on some of the most complex and high-profile banking and structured finance transactions.

In the last few years, the firm has built a remarkable team of lawyers dedicated to antitrust and regulatory matters, assisting clients in respect to mergers, abuses of dominant positions and restrictive agreements. The team is now regarded as one of the leaders in this legal market.

The firm has developed notable experience in the area of real estate transactions and construction law. It delivers a full array of legal services to the clients in this field, whether they are construction companies, real estate investors, developers or promoters. The clients are supported in all phases of their activity, through an interdisciplinary approach.

Gianni, Origoni, Grippo & Partners provides heavyweight expertise in the labour field. The firm's clients can count on one of the largest resources of labour professionals among Italian law firms. The labour attorneys work on behalf of industrial, commercial and financial groups, both domestic and foreign, as well as medium-sized businesses, and provide assistance in all the main fields of labour law, industrial relations and social security.

Areas of considerable strength are commercial litigation and arbitration. The firm's litigators represent the interest of clients in major legal disputes throughout Italy, including disputes before administrative, trial and appellate courts, as well as the Italian Supreme Court. The firm also represents clients before the European Court of Justice and through the association with Linklaters and a select number of correspondents in any country.

In the tax practice, the firm provides its clients with international tax advice and legal expertise integrated with their business transactions from one source. The tax department boasts prominent specialists in every area of domestic and international tax.

Gianni, Origoni, Grippo & Partners provides a broad range of expertise in the industrial law sector, with an emphasis on patents and trade marks, unfair competition, trade secrets and technology transfers.

GRIECO E ASSOCIATI

VIA PIEMONTE 39
00187 ROMA

Telephone: +39 06 42 03 881
Fax: +39 06 42 03 88 20
E-mail: a.grieco@griecoassociati.it
Website: www.info.martindale.com/griecoassociati.it

Languages
Italian, English, French

Other offices
Milan

Number of lawyers 16
at this office 12

Member
IBA; CILS (Congress of Fellows); Institute for International and Comparative Law (Dallas)

CATEGORIES OF WORK

Corporate law, M&A
Antonio Grieco, Chiara Mammoliti

Corporate litigation
Antonio Grieco, Francesco Grieco

Banking law
Francesco Grieco, Chiara Mammoliti

Product liability
Francesco Grieco

Securitisation of assets
Alessandro Cardia

Arbitration and international litigation
Antonio Grieco, Chiara Mammoliti

Public works
Cinzia Colaiacovo, Allessio Sambiagio

Public procurement
Allessio Sambiagio

Bankruptcy law
Francesco Grieco, Eugenio Krauss

THE FIRM

Established in January 2000 by a merger of the international, corporate, banking and administrative skills of its founding members, Grieco e Associati is an Italian law firm with a principal office in Rome and a branch office in Milan. In addition, the firm has excellent relationships with correspondent firms in most of the Italian cities, thus being able to provide clients with efficient and effective assistance throughout Italy.

While retaining its local expertise, the firm has developed an international background and is able to provide complete round-the-clock legal advice to domestic and international clients.

The firm's assistance and counsel is in fact carried out both in Italian and English and, apart from mainstream M&A, the corporate practice encompasses leading specialist practices and assistance in stock exchange and CONSOB regulatory requirements; company incorporation (including the drafting of the by-laws and of the other relevant deeds), loans and banking facility agreements; first-call guarantees and pledges; private banking and financial services.

The firm's clients vary from large Italian and foreign industrial multinational corporations and national banks, to individuals seeking advice on business and personal matters.

Among its main clients, the firm represents a number of public utility companies; car manufacturer and dealer companies as well as engineering and technology companies. The firm also provides legal assistance to banking and financial institutions.

Upon request the firm will be glad to provide a detailed list of its clients.

AREAS OF PRACTICE

The practice of the firm consists of counselling and litigation both in the domestic and in the international field.

As to the firm's major practice areas, Grieco e Associati is able to deliver faultless high-level legal services in the following fields: civil and corporate law, M&A, construction contracts, public utilities activities, particularly in the areas of water and electricity, public procurements, antitrust and competition practice, domestic tax practice, telecommunications, banking and finance, securities, industrial property, intellectual property, employment law, administrative law, EC law, litigation and arbitration.

As to the litigation and dispute resolution practice area, the firm helps its clients to resolve disputes efficiently and effectively – whether through arbitration, litigation or other dispute settlement methods – in a manner that promotes their business objectives. The firm also assists clients in the development of compliance programs and other techniques to minimise future litigation risks. The law suits in which the firm has expertise include corporate actions; director and/or auditor liability claims; challenges to corporate resolutions; product liability cases; and construction agreements.

The firm also offers solutions to companies experiencing all kinds of financial difficulties, as well as assistance in matters and transactions arising out of any bankruptcy proceedings.

The firm's diverse practice areas reflect the wide capabilities of its attorneys, drawn together in a common purpose – to achieve its clients' goals and provide them with the highest quality legal services.

HAARMANN HEMMELRATH

VIA GUGLIELMO SALICETO 7
00161 ROME

Telephone: + 39 06 44 065 111
Fax: + 39 06 44 065 133
E-mail: rome@haarmannhemmelrath.com
Website:
www.haarmannhemmelrath.com

Languages
English, French, Spanish

Other offices
Berlin, Bielefeld, Brussels, Bucharest, Budapest, Cologne, Dusseldorf, Frankfurt, Hamburg, Leipzig, London, Moscow, Munich, Milan, Paris, Prague, Shanghai, Singapore, Stuttgart, Tokyo, Vienna, Warsaw

Number of lawyers 281
at this office 3

CATEGORIES OF WORK

- **Corporate law, mergers and acquisitions**
- **Tax law**
- **Litigation**
- **Banking and financial law**
- **Real estate transactions**
- **Civil law**
- **Commercial law**

LOVELLS

VIA DEI DUE MACELLI 66
00187 ROME

Telephone: +39 06 6758231
Fax: +39 06 67582323
E-mail: information@lovells.com
Website: www.lovells.com

Languages
English, French, German

Other offices
Alicante, Amsterdam, Beijing, Berlin, Brussels, Budapest*, Chicago, Düsseldorf, Frankfurt, Hamburg, Ho Chi Minh City, Hong Kong, London, Milan, Moscow, Munich, New York, Paris, Prague, Shanghai, Singapore, Tokyo, Vienna*, Warsaw, Zagreb*

Number of lawyers 1,600
at this office 36

Contact
Fulvia Astolfi

CATEGORIES OF WORK

- **Corporate (including M&A, private equity, privatisations)**
- **Antitrust/competition**
- **Tax**
- **Financial services and investment funds**
- **Banking**
- **Capital markets**
- **Project finance**
- **Property and construction**
- **Administrative and public law (including town planning, environment, energy)**
- **Pharmaceutical**
- **Insurance**
- **Insolvency**
- **Intellectual property, IT, e-commerce and media**
- **Employment**
- **Litigation and arbitration**
- **Data protection**

MCDERMOTT, WILL & EMERY/CARNELUTTI

VIA PARIGI 11
00185 ROME

Telephone: +39 06 46 20 241
Fax: +39 06 48 90 6285
Website: www.mwe.com

Languages
All main business languages

Other offices
Boston, Brussels, Chicago, Düsseldorf, London, Los Angeles, Miami, Milan, Munich, New York, Orange County, San Diego, Silicon Valley, Washington DC

Number of lawyers 1,000
at this office 11

Contact
Massimo Trentino

CATEGORIES OF WORK

Corporate finance
Pietro Cuorno, Massimo Trentino

Litigation
Massimo Mellaro

Insurance
Pietro Cuomo

Mergers and acquisitions
Pietro Cuomo, Massimo Trentino

NUNZIANTE MAGRONE

PIAZZA DI PIETRA, 26
00186 ROMA

Telephone: +39 06 69 51 81
Fax: +39 06 69 51 83 33
E-mail: roma@nunziantemagrone.it
Website: www.nunziantemagrone.it

Languages
English, French, German, Spanish

Other offices
Bologna, Milan, Turin

Number of lawyers 56
at this office 29

CATEGORIES OF WORK

Corporate

Postal

Banking and finance

Aviation

Mergers and acquisitions

Environmental

Litigation and arbitration

Tax

Intellectual property

Real Estate

Administrative

White-collar crime

EU and competition

PORTOLANO COLELLA CAVALLO PROSPERETTI
STUDIO LEGALE

VIA CATONE, 3
00192 ROMA

Telephone: +39 06 39 74 54 37
Fax: +39 06 39 74 54 00
E-mail: info@pccp.it
Website: www.pccp.it

Languages
English, French, German, Spanish

Number of lawyers 10

Contact
Francesco Portolano

CATEGORIES OF WORK

M&A and venture capital
Francesco Portolano, Domenico Colella

Litigation and arbitration
Barbara Di Salvo

Corporate
Manuela Cavallo

Labour and employment
Barbara Di Salvo

Real estate
Domenico Colella

Information technology and e-commerce
Eugenio Prosperetti

Television, media and entertainment
Francesco Portolano, Eugenio Prosperetti

Sport
Barbara Di Salvo

Aviation
Domenico Colella

PUOPOLO SISTILLI GEFFERS & LUISE
STUDIO LEGALE

VIA LISBONA,11
00198 ROMA

Telephone: +39 06 884 1535
Fax: +39 06 884 2094
E-mail: info@psglaw.com
Website: www.psglaw.com

Languages
English, French, German, Spanish

Other offices
Milan

Number of lawyers 28
at this office 14

Contacts
Gianfranco Puopolo, Anthony Sistilli

Member
LG International

CATEGORIES OF WORK

Banking and finance

Company and commercial

Energy and environmental

Insurance

Pharmaceuticals and biotech

Information technology and communications

International transactions

SIMMONS & SIMMONS

VIA BARNABA ORIANI 85
00197 ROME

Telephone: +39 06 80 95 51
Fax: +39 06 80 95 59 55
E-mail: enquiries@simmons-simmons.com
Website: www.simmons-simmons.com

Languages
English, German, French

Other offices
London, Rotterdam, Paris, Lisbon, Milan, Düsseldorf, Frankfurt, Brussels, Madrid, Padua, Oporto, Madeira, Abu Dhabi, Qatar, Hong Kong, Shanghai, Tokyo, New York

Number of lawyers 754
at this office 27

Contact
Filippo Pingue

CATEGORIES OF WORK

Corporate	Financial markets
Banking	Pharmaceutical and biotechnology
Capital markets	Energy and utilities
Taxation	TMT
Projects, PFI	Aerospace and defence
EU, competition	Transport
Dispute resolution	Real estate and construction
Intellectual property	Consumer goods
Employment	

UGHI & NUNZIANTE

VIA VENTI SETTEMBRE, 1
00187 ROMA

Telephone: +39 06 47 48 31
Fax: +39 06 48 70 397
E-mail: ughi.e.nunziante@unlaw.it
Website: www.unlaw.it

Languages
English, French, German, Spanish

Other office
Milan

Number of lawyers 60
at this office 34

CATEGORIES OF WORK

Corporate and commercial	**EU and competition**
Banking and finance	**IT and telecommunications**
Securities	**Transport**
Insurance	**International commercial arbitration**
Litigation	**Taxation**
Labour and employment	**Media and entertainment**
Real estate	**Energy**
Bankruptcy	
Intellectual property	

THE FIRM

Ughi & Nunziante, whose origins go back to the 1950s, is one of the oldest law firms in Italy. The firm has 60 lawyers whose clients range from medium-sized corporations in their early stages of international expansion, to large multinationals, financial institutions, governments and non-profit organisations. Many of the firm's clients are non-Italian entities who turn to the firm for advice on legal issues connected with their existing Italian operations, on the establishment of new operations in Italy, or for assistance in international transactions which have an Italian element.

The contact details for the Milan offices of Ughi & Nunziante are: Via Sant' Andrea, 19,20121 Milano. Telephone: +39 02 76 21 71. Fax: +39 02 78 41 40. E-mail: ughi.nunziante@unlaw.it.

AREAS OF PRACTICE

As illustrated above, the firm offers clients the full range of corporate and commercial legal services.

The major areas of law practised by the firm include: corporate; banking; securities and insurance regulation; litigation; labour; real estate; bankruptcy; intellectual property; agency, franchise and distribution; computer and telecommunications; media and entertainment; environmental; energy; administrative law; EU law; antitrust; international and domestic arbitration; transport and insurance law; tax and international tax planning.

WATSON, FARLEY & WILLIAMS

VIA VITTORIO VENETO 96
00187 ROME

Telephone: +39 06 48 38 07
Fax: +39 06 42 01 17 89
Website: www.wfw.com

Languages
Cantonese, Danish, English, French, German, Greek, Gujarati, Hebrew, Italian, Malay, Mandarin, Norwegian, Polish, Russian, Spanish, Swahili, Swedish, Thai

Other offices
Bangkok, London, New York, Paris, Piraeus, Singapore

Number of lawyers 175
at this office 7

Contacts
Carlo Galdo, Eugenio Tranchino

CATEGORIES OF WORK

Project finance
Shipping, aviation and asset finance
Corporate finance
Banking and securities
Debt restructuring
Derivatives
Trade finance
Structuring finance and leasing
Securitisation
Insolvency matters
Mergers and acquisitions
Private equity
Projects
Joint ventures
Venture capital
Infrastructure and privatisations
Debt and corporate restructuring
Energy and natural resources
Commercial contracts
EU, competition and antitrust law
Intellectual property
General corporate advice
Commercial agreements
E-business and e-commerce
Real estate

ALLEN & OVERY

CORSO VITTORIO EMANUELE II, 68
10121 TURIN

Telephone: +39 011 511 21
Fax: +39 011 511 23 33
E-mail: information@allenovery.com
Website: www.allenovery.com

Languages
English, French, German, Italian, Spanish

Other offices
Amsterdam, Antwerp, Bangkok, Beijing, Bratislava, Brussels, Budapest, Dubai, Frankfurt, Hamburg, Hong Kong, London, Luxembourg, Madrid, Milan, Moscow, New York, Paris, Prague, Rome, Shanghai, Singapore, Tokyo, Warsaw

Number of lawyers 2,305
at this office 45

Contacts
Roberto Casati (senior partner);
G Massimillano Danusso
(joint managing partner);
Stephen Denyer (joint managing partner);
Emanuele Borganti
(head of operations in Italy)

CATEGORIES OF WORK

Corporate
Paolo Cerina

Banking
Giancarlo Castorino

Tax
Andrea Manganelli

ICM
G Massimilliano Danusso

Litigation
Alberto Nanni

JERSEY

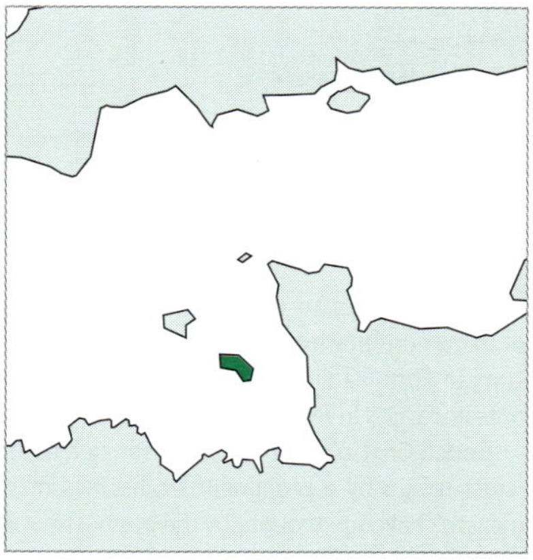

Population	85,150
Number of lawyers	182 members of The Jersey Law Society
Professional title	Advocate
Currency	Pound sterling (£)

Index

The Bailiwick of Jersey has the same relationship with the UK and Europe as that enjoyed by Guernsey (although there are in fact no formal links between the two Bailiwicks). As a Crown dependency and a member of the British Isles, though not the United Kingdom, some issues, namely foreign relations and defence, are administered for Jersey by the Crown through the UK government. Otherwise, the Jersey government (the States of Jersey) enjoys a great degree of autonomy. The island is also a member of the OECD (the Organisation for Economic Co-operation and Development).

Business on Jersey continues to boom as the island benefits from its growing reputation as a safe and well-regulated offshore jurisdiction. Its dependence on the UK as a source of business is declining, with more sophisticated forms of business replacing much of the traditional private client work. Jersey has also become a major centre for securitisation as the European industry has acknowledged the value of the island's special purpose vehicle (SPV) structures.

BILLING

Lawyers generally charge by the hour although scale fees still operate for conveyancing work. Fees may vary depending on the lawyer instructed and the job in hand. Clients can expect costs not dissimilar to those charged by City of London firms: around £160 for a newly qualified lawyer, rising to around £350 at partner level.

MARKETING

Jersey advocates may only advertise their services outside Jersey.

THE LEGAL 500

Readers should note that the following is taken from the **Offshore Britain** section of the 2003 edition of *The Legal 500* (UK edition), available at www.legal500.com.

LEGAL MARKET

The market for legal services in Jersey has enjoyed one of its most dynamic periods.

In January 2003, *Olsens* announced that it was hiring a group of six lawyers from **Crills**' financial services business group, including the respected Tony Hillman. Subsequently in March 2003 *Olsens* announced a cross-Channel Island tie-up with leading Guernsey firm *Carey Langlois* to create the largest Channel Islands firm, **Carey Olsen**. Although law firms cannot form single Jersey-Guernsey partnerships due to local regulatory restrictions, **Carey Olsen** will market itself and service clients as a single firm.

Some larger institutional clients have indicated that they appreciate getting both Jersey and Guernsey advice from one firm. This helps account for the ongoing success of **Ogier & Le Masurier**'s funds and general corporate practice. **Ogier & Le Masurier** opened a new office in London in April 2003, joining Jersey competitor **Mourant du Feu & Jeune** in the City. Then in February 2004, **Ogier & Le Masurier** announced its merger with Cayman Islands firm **Boxalls**, significantly expanding it coverage of the major offshore markets.

Meanwhile, there is lateral movement of senior assistants between Jersey firms and into Jersey by English solicitors and Australians, New Zealanders, and South Africans. Recruitment has allowed the larger firms to alter their gearing, with more assistants per partner helping to maintain profitability. However, some firms, notably **Bedell Cristin**, deliberately aim for a lower gearing on the grounds that clients prefer to work with partners.

The top four firms remain **Bedell Cristin**, **Carey Olsen**, **Mourant du Feu & Jeune**, and **Ogier & Le Masurier**. Of these, **Mourant du Feu & Jeune**, and **Ogier & Le Masurier** process the bulk of Jersey's top-tier legal work in major areas such as funds and structured finance. **Bedell Cristin** has excellent individual partners. And **Carey Olsen**, even before its groundbreaking merger, had a reputation as a fast-growing, young partnership that was successfully staffing up in key areas and poised to break its rivals' stranglehold in some areas, such as securitisation.

Bailhache Labesse is a top-tier property and litigation firm that is growing its commercial and finance practice, as is **Crill Canavan**.

BANKING

Bedell Cristin is historically a finance-led practice. The firm advised Lloyds TSB and Bank of Scotland in 2002. Partner Peter Byrne is recommended, and acted for Lloyds TSB on revolving credit and overdraft facilities to Gresham Property Partners LP.

The largest firms

1	Carey Olsen	63
2	Mourant du Feu & Jeune	58
3	Ogier & Le Masurier	57
4	Bedell Cristin	39
5	Bailhache Labesse	27
6	Crill Canavan	17
7	Viberts - Jersey Lawyers	15
8	Crills	14
	Voisin & Co.	14
10	Le Gallais & Luce	8
11	Backhurst Dorey & Crane	3
	Sinels	3

These figures represent the total number of lawyers in this country only, and have been supplied by the firms themselves. The figures should be accurate as at 1 January 2004.

BANKING

BEDELL CRISTIN ✪
CAREY OLSEN
MOURANT DU FEU & JEUNE ✪
OGIER & LE MASURIER ✪

Bailhache Labesse

Crills
VOISIN & CO.

Firms are listed A-Z in tiers which are ranked in order of priority
✪ Indicates firm displays contact details at the end of this chapter.

COMMERCIAL LITIGATION

BAILHACHE LABESSE
BEDELL CRISTIN ✪
CRILL CANAVAN
OGIER & LE MASURIER ✪
CAREY OLSEN

Mourant du Feu & Jeune ✪

Crills
Sinels
Viberts – Jersey Lawyers
Voisin & Co.

Firms are listed A-Z in tiers which are ranked in order of priority
✪ Indicates firm displays contact details at the end of this chapter.

Under Paul Sugden, **Carey Olsen** has set itself the task of advising financial institutions that are active in Jersey and Guernsey through its Channel Islands banking group. The firm has built up close relationships with a number of lenders, and advised on the merger in Jersey of Bank of Scotland Offshore and Halifax International.

Mourant du Feu & Jeune's banking team is headed by Edward Devenport. The firm advised on property finance transactions with a debt value of around £1bn in 2002. Its high-quality, international lender client base includes HSBC, Deutsche Bank, Bayerische Hypo- und Vereinsbank, and Eurohypo. Indeed, **Mourant du Feu & Jeune** is sufficiently respected for many international banks to instruct it directly rather than through London or other intermediaries.

At **Ogier & Le Masurier**, four partners regularly advise both local and international banks lending to Jersey structures. Chris Byrne and new team head Matthew Swan work well as part of the larger, cross-departmental teams that the firm can assemble. Marc Yates led a team advising Investec Bank (Jersey) on its migration to Guernsey – the first such move between the two islands.

An historical relationship with Barclays has kept **Bailhache Labesse**'s banking practice busy, and the firm advised on Jersey law in connection with the restructuring of Barclays offshore group.

Readers should also refer to the **Structured finance and securitisation** section.

COMMERCIAL LITIGATION

Only Jersey advocates have rights of audience in the Royal Court. We would single out three Jersey advocates – **Carey Olsen** senior partner Anthony Olsen, **Crill Canavan** partner Nuno Santos-Costa, and **Bailhache Labesse**'s Michael O'Connell – as lawyers whose advocacy skills mean that the Court will listen to them from the outset of a case.

Bailhache Labesse's litigation practice accounts for between 35% and 40% of the firm's workload. The team as a whole is capable of giving the opposition a real fight when necessary. The hugely experienced Michael O'Connell is backed up by the thorough Fraser Robertson and the solid Gillian Robinson. Fraser Robertson has been advising the German television and marketing company currently involved in litigation over the rights to Formula One, one of the most fiercely contested cases in Jersey.

Bedell Cristin's Anthony Robinson defended a trust set up by a prominent UK businessman against a challenge brought by the businessman's daughter-in-law in the Royal Court. The firm has a large litigation team, including contentious insolvency and asset tracing expert Anthony Dessain. Up-and-coming litigator David Cadin is a recent hire from **Mourant du Feu & Jeune**.

There are few top-line cases in Jersey that **Carey Olsen** does not have a role in. Senior partner Anthony Olsen scored a notable victory acting for HSBC against a local businessman who was successfully declared bankrupt. Advocate Nick Journeaux is also recommended and continues to act in *Re Esteem*, where he obtained a landmark decision in 2002 from the Royal Court that confirmed the law as to tracing remedies and fraudulent conveyances. **Carey Olsen** added to its strength in 2002 when it hired a young talent, Billy Grace from **Crills**.

At **Crill Canavan**, partner Nuno Santos-Costa heads a growing team which has recruited skilled advocates from larger local firms. The firm handles a large amount of trust and regulatory litigation as well as high-value personal injury work. Partner Jane Martin was second chair in the *Jersey Evening Post* case. The team's manpower and resources earns it promotion to the top tier.

Ogier & Le Masurier specialises in commercial litigation for its institutional clients. Advocate Matthew Thompson is recommended and has experience in the increasingly important area of contentious employment law. **Ogier & Le Masurier**'s litigation group also offers clients specialist compliance and regulatory training. Julian Clyde-Smith is recommended for trusts disputes. Timothy Le Cocq is another well-known advocate.

Mourant du Feu & Jeune lacks the profile of the other top firms, partly as a result of its strong connections with both banks and public authorities conflicting it out of some of Jersey's biggest multi-party disputes or compelling the firm to handle important but confidential regulatory investigations. But clients should be aware that the firm has a technically and commercially strong contentious practice, led by Beverley Lacey, Jonathan Speck, and David Wilson.

Crills' senior partner Richard Michel is recommended, and the firm has a dedicated personal injury department where Julian Gollup can be relied on not to drop the ball. Clients who definitely need a no-nonsense, tough litigator might consider instructing Philip Sinel of **Sinels**. **Voisin & Co.** also handles some important contentious work, as does **Viberts – Jersey Lawyers**.

CORPORATE AND COMMERCIAL

Bedell Cristin is known for its high level of partner attention and clear advice, particularly from Edward Bennett and Alan Dart. The firm advised Alliance & Leicester Plc on the disposal of its credit card business to MBNA – a large and complex deal.

Carey Olsen continues to add to the quality and quantity of its client base, in part by expanding its City referral network. The firm picked up Warner Estate Holdings Plc as a new client in 2002 and carried out significant restructuring work for it. It also acted for long-standing client Owl Technologies on a merger and AIM listing. Nicholas Crocker is recommended.

Mourant du Feu & Jeune advised Connex on its successful tender to provide bus services in Jersey – a good example of how the firm can field a team on a large, high-profile transaction. **Mourant du Feu & Jeune**'s company formation team had its most active year ever in 2002. Team head Tim Herbert is highly respected, while Wendy Malorey's employment law expertise – still something of a niche area in Jersey – is an asset.

Ogier & Le Masurier's Marc Yates confirmed his reputation for cutting edge work when he led a team that advised on the migration of Investec Bank (Jersey) into Guernsey under Jersey's amended companies law. The firm also advised on the merger of Le Riche Group and Ann Street. The firm acts for a number of London-listed Jersey companies. Along with **Mourant du Feu & Jeune**, it is the leading firm in the growth area of offshore property holding structures.

Bailhache Labesse has been building out from its historic strengths in property and litigation, with lateral hires into its commercial department. It increasingly features on deals with the big four – it advised on the Le Riche Group/Ann Street merger opposite **Ogier & Le Masurier**, for example. The firm has a longstanding relationship with Barclays. Mark Lewis identifies and delivers solutions to clients.

David Banks heads **Crill Canavan**'s commercial department, which handles the full range of commercial matters at sensible rates.

Crills' Peter Harris is still a name, although the firm lost a group of six lawyers from its financial services business group to **Carey Olsen** in 2002.

Voisin & Co. and **Viberts – Jersey Lawyers** also figure in the local commercial scene and have some international clients.

CORPORATE AND COMMERCIAL

BEDELL CRISTIN ✪
CAREY OLSEN
MOURANT DU FEU & JEUNE ✪
OGIER & LE MASURIER ✪

Bailhache Labesse

Crill Canavan

Voisin & Co.

Crills
Viberts – Jersey Lawyers

Firms are listed A-Z in tiers which are ranked in order of priority
✪ Indicates firm displays contact details at the end of this chapter.

INVESTMENT FUNDS

At **Bedell Cristin**, Simon Howard is a quality funds lawyer and consequently his team enjoys a strong reputation. In one noteworthy deal, the firm advised Deutsche Bank on the structure of a joint venture private equity fund with The Dubai Investment Office.

Historically, **Mourant du Feu & Jeune** advises a higher proportion of all the funds serviced in Jersey than any other law firm. But its practice is far from static and partners such as Tim Herbert and Edward Devenport have worked on innovative quasi-hedge fund structures for Deutsche Bank and Société Générale. Robert Hickling is also highly respected.

Clients are consistently comfortable using **Ogier & Le Masurier**'s funds team. They praise not only the quality of lead partner Nick Kershaw, but also the depth of expertise both at partner and assistant level. The team is solution-orientated and proactive in approaching the local regulators on clients' behalf, as is **Carey Olsen**.

Indeed, although still overshadowed in terms of volume of work processed by its three top-tier competitors, **Carey Olsen** offers strong advice on establishing funds and on regulatory and structural issues. Clients respond to Edward Quinn's approachable manner, while Eve Kosofsky's profile continues to rise. Lateral hires from **Crills** in 2002 included Sinead Meehan and heavyweight consultant Tony Hillman who moved to a consultancy position at **Carey Olsen**.

Bailhache Labesse has significantly added to its practice by hiring Adrian Odell from a firm in the British Virgin Islands. The firm already had a strong funds practice and was sole Jersey counsel on the incorporation of Threadneedle Jersey Funds Ltd, an OEIC feeder fund.

Voisin & Co. benefits from the excellent Ian Strang.

INVESTMENT FUNDS

BEDELL CRISTIN ✪
CAREY OLSEN
MOURANT DU FEU & JEUNE ✪
OGIER & LE MASURIER ✪

Bailhache Labesse
Voisin & Co.

Crills

Firms are listed A-Z in tiers which are ranked in order of priority
✪ Indicates firm displays contact details at the end of this chapter.

PERSONAL TAX, TRUSTS AND PROBATE

OGIER & LE MASURIER ✪

Bailhache Labesse
Bedell Cristin ✪
Carey Olsen
Mourant du Feu & Jeune ✪

Crill Canavan
Crills
Voisin & Co.

Backhurst Dorey & Crane
Le Gallais & Luce
Viberts – Jersey Lawyers

Firms are listed A-Z in tiers which are ranked in order of priority
✪ Indicates firm displays contact details at the end of this chapter.

PERSONAL TAX, TRUSTS AND PROBATE

At **Ogier & Le Masurier**, the esteemed triumvirate of Steven Meiklejohn, Julian Clyde-Smith, and Marc Yates keep their firm at the top of the table. Clients always receive service and attention of the highest calibre and as a result have huge regard for all three.

Bailhache Labesse's Andrew Pim is recommended. Guy Le Sueur at **Bedell Cristin** retains a strong reputation. **Carey Olsen** boasts a private wealth management expert in Anthony Olsen and one of the island's leading trusts and pensions specialists, Paul Matthams. **Mourant du Feu & Jeune** remains active.

REAL ESTATE

A brace of top-quality individual practitioners define the best commercial property practices on Jersey – John Bisson of **Bailhache Labesse** and Chris Renouf of **Ogier & Le Masurier**.

Bailhache Labesse decided to specialise in commercial property earlier and to a greater degree than any other firm. This has given John

REAL ESTATE

BAILHACHE LABESSE
OGIER & LE MASURIER ✪
Bedell Cristin ✪
Carey Olsen
Crill Canavan
Mourant du Feu & Jeune ✪
Crills
Voisin & Co.

Firms are listed A-Z in tiers which are ranked in order of priority
✪ *Indicates firm displays contact details at the end of this chapter.*

Bisson an admirable commercial understanding of the Jersey property scene, and this, combined with his intellectual rigour, makes him the leader of the pack. Although a substantial part of his time is spent advising leading developer, Dandara Group, his phenomenal work-rate and able support from partner Timothy Hart has led to work from other notable clients, including Waterfront Enterprise Board Ltd and Barclays Group.

The strongest competition comes from **Ogier & Le Masurier**'s similarly focused and well-resourced team. Head of department Chris Renouf's attention to detail is legendary, as is his grasp of issues which go beyond mere conveyancing matters. While Dandara instructs **Bailhache Labesse**, **Ogier & Le Masurier** acts for up-and-coming clients like Cool Waters Group, which instructed the firm on its £6m acquisition of the Sandringham and Les Arches hotels, and which continues to use the firm on the Waterfront development. The firm now joins **Bailhache Labesse** in the top tier in recognition of Chris Renouf's achievement in building a rounded property practice.

Outside of the top two, the most frequently recommended individual is Guy Le Sueur of **Bedell Cristin**. The firm has advised on purchases of property investment and mortgage portfolios.

Carey Olsen's growing team is led by John Kelleher, who is known for handling high-profile property disputes.

Crill Canavan's Geoffrey Crill has a niche strength in advising on retail leases.

Mourant du Feu & Jeune's Elizabeth Breen and Gio Pollano have grown and kept strong connections locally and among London-based clients and referrers that have provided an impressive deal flow.

Michael Voisin of **Voisin & Co.** also handles property work and is one of Jersey's leading planning lawyers.

STRUCTURED FINANCE AND SECURITISATION

A separate structured finance and securitisation table reflects the growing importance of these areas to Jersey firms.

Measured by resources and volume of work processed, for securitisation the two leading firms are **Mourant du Feu & Jeune** and **Ogier & Le Masurier**. The gap is less pronounced in other areas of structured finance work, with **Carey Olsen** also highly visible and **Bedell Cristin** active.

Mourant du Feu & Jeune boasts star names like Robert Hickling, Alastair Syvret, and Ian James. But bulking out the team and adding further quality are younger lawyers like partner Ben Robins and associate Jonathan Rigby. The team advises on a range of capital markets products including bond issues, derivatives and repackagings, Tier 1 capital raisings, and securitisations. The team as a whole is known to give commercial and pragmatic advice.

Ogier & Le Masurier has a similarly well-equipped practice that handles an equally eclectic range of work. Its securitisation team advises on a high proportion of all the listed securities issued

STRUCTURED FINANCE AND SECURITISATION

MOURANT DU FEU & JEUNE ✪
OGIER & LE MASURIER ✪
BEDELL CRISTIN ✪
CAREY OLSEN
Bailhache Labesse
Voisin & Co.

Firms are listed A-Z in tiers which are ranked in order of priority
✪ *Indicates firm displays contact details at the end of this chapter.*

by Jersey vehicles, and has acted on Japanese and New York-sourced securitisations. Chris Byrne and Michael Lombardi head its separate securitisation and structured finance teams. **Ogier & Le Masurier** has a comprehensive working knowledge of international capital markets products and uses this to give the most relevant possible Jersey law advice from deal to deal.

Bedell Cristin benefits from the presence of two experienced finance partners. Richard Gerwat is never less than solid, while Shane Hollywood's profile is growing. It has handled the Jersey end of various credit card receivables (where it is probably the most active Jersey firm) and utilities securitisations.

Until its audacious hire of consultant Tony Hillman from **Crills**, **Carey Olsen**'s reputation for structured finance work rested squarely on the shoulders of Alex Ohlsson, who in 2002 worked on various commercial mortgaged-backed deals. Alex Ohlsson is completely service-oriented, and Tony Hillman is a veteran securitisation lawyer whose experience stretches back to the early 1990s.

Bailhache Labesse has attempted to grow its structured finance market share recently.

BEDELL CRISTIN

PO BOX 75
26 NEW STREET
ST HELIER JE4 8PP

Telephone: +44 1534 814814
Fax: +44 1534 814815
E-mail: enquiries@bedellcristin.com
Website: www.bedellcristin.com

Languages
Afrikaans, English, French, German, Italian, Spanish, Thai

Number of lawyers 39

CATEGORIES OF WORK

Financial services group including: Capital markets and structured finance
Richard Gerwat, Shane Hollywood

Investment funds and private equity
Martin Paul, Michael Richardson

Banking and corporate
Peter Byrne, Martin Paul

Trust and private capital
Edward Bennett, Zillah Howard

Tax
Richard Gerwat, Michael Richardson

Insolvency and asset tracing
Anthony Dessain, Mark Taylor

Information services
Zillah Howard

Litigation group
Anthony Robinson, Mark Taylor

Private client and local business group, including: Private clients
Guy Le Sueur, Anita Regal

Commercial property
Guy Le Sueur

Local business clients
Guy Le Sueur

Fiduciary and company administration services
Alan Dart, Michael Richardson

THE FIRM

Bedell Cristin is a full-service law firm and a leading provider of legal services to the banking and finance industry. It has been involved in the establishment of a significant proportion of the banks, investment funds and structured finance vehicles carrying on business from Jersey. Consistently ranked one of the top firms in the Island, and highly rated for the professionalism and technical expertise of its lawyers, Bedell Cristin provides a partner-led, client-focused service tailored to the commercial needs of clients and intermediaries globally. The firm acts for banks, financial institutions and companies throughout the world on a variety of international transactions involving a Jersey element.

The firm was established in 1939 and was instrumental in the development of Jersey as a finance centre. The firm has excellent contacts with financial institutions and law firms in the world's major financial centres, counting many blue-chip entities amongst its extensive client base, including: ABN Amro, Bank of America, Bank of Nova Scotia, Bank of Scotland, Barclays, Bank of Ireland, Capital One, Chase, Citibank, CSFB, Deutsche Bank, Egg Banking, HSBC, ICI, MBNA, Merrill Lynch/Mercury, Prudential, Rabobank, Rothschild, Royal Bank of Canada, RBS and Schroders.

AREAS OF PRACTICE

Capital markets and structured finance: this group has a strong reputation in asset-backed finance, having acted as Jersey counsel in some of the most innovative transactions in the market. Together with Bedell Cristin Trust and Bedell SPV, the practice area provides a 'one-stop-shop' for establishing SPVs in Jersey.

Investment funds and private equity: this group focuses on the establishment and legal servicing of pooled investment structures qualifying as public collective investment funds or non-public collective investment schemes, private equity funds and pension schemes. Sponsorship and listing services in connection with the Channel Islands Stock Exchange are available through Bedell Channel Islands Limited, which is a category 1 sponsorship member of the Exchange.

Banking and corporate: advice is provided to many of the banks having a presence in Jersey and Jersey law advice and legal opinions are provided to banks and multinationals globally. This group also advises on Jersey elements of international M&A transactions, joint venture arrangements, shareholders' agreements/arrangements and acquisitions/disposals of Jersey companies.

Trust and private capital: this group is the largest of its kind on the island, and comprises 14 practitioners, including five partners, who provide specialist trust and related corporate law advice to individual and institutional clients based in Jersey and internationally. The areas on which the group provides specialist advice include wealth preservation and management, employee and executive share incentive schemes, bespoke trust drafting, the restructuring of assets held in trust and advice to fiduciaries.

Litigation: the firm's litigation group is one of the largest in Jersey. A full range of litigation and dispute resolution services is provided but particular growth has taken place in contentious trust and regulatory work. Other key work areas are banking, insolvency and asset tracing.

Private client and local business: the firm advises on a wide range of Jersey property matters and private client matters, including matrimonial matters, estate planning and probate. Advice is also provided to local business clients, the group having particular experience in IT and telecoms matters (acting for, amongst others, Jersey Telecom).

Bedell Cristin Trust Company, a wholly owned subsidiary of the law firm, and is one of the leading independent trust companies in Jersey, providing fiduciary and company administration services to institutional and high-net-worth private clients. It is regulated by the Jersey Financial Services Commission under the Financial Services (Jersey) Law 1998.

MOURANT DU FEU & JEUNE

PO BOX 87
22 GRENVILLE STREET
ST HELIER JE4 8PX

Telephone: +44 1534 609000
Fax: +44 1534 609333
E-mail: mdfj@mourant.com
Website: www.mourant.com

Languages
English, French, German, Italian, Portuguese, Spanish

Other offices
Guernsey, London, Luxembourg

Number of lawyers 61

Member
Lex Mundi; Uni Law

CATEGORIES OF WORK

Capital markets
Ian James, Robert Hickling

Structured finance
Ben Robins, Jonathan Rigby

Collective investment funds
Tim Herbert, Cyman Davies

Banking
Rob Hickling, David Wilson

Trusts
Cyman Davies, Edward Devenport

Corporate and business law
Tim Herbert, Wendy Malorey

Corporate finance
Jonathan Rigby, Ben Robins

Insurance
Simon Gould

Commercial litigation
Jonathan Speck, Beverley Lacey

Commercial property
Elizabeth Breen

Private wealth management
Alan Binnington, James Crill

Securitisation
Alastair Syvret, Jonathan Walker

Private funds
Jacqueline Richomme, Julia Chapman

Mergers and acquisitions
Wendy Malorey

Corporate structures administration
Rupert Walker

Corporate property structures
Rupert Walker

Share plan administration
Dominic Jones

THE FIRM

Mourant du Feu & Jeune is part of Mourant, the largest Channel Island-based legal and specialist administration services provider, with 26 partners heading 600 staff in offices in Jersey, Guernsey, the UK and Luxembourg.

It specialises in offshore legal services for international corporations and high-net-worth individuals. Areas of expertise include capital markets, structured finance, securitisation, funds, property holding and investment, private wealth management, Jersey commercial and corporate law and commercial litigation.

The firm acts for global financial institutions in international finance and advises City lawyers and investment banks on the Jersey aspects of securitisation and structured finance transactions. Work for collective investment funds includes advising the largest management buy-out of a private equity fund in Europe and several other major European funds.

Mourant's specialist administration teams work on complex international private funds, onshore and offshore financing and holding structures for property assets, and employee share plans. In the year to June 2003, Mourant acted for 71% of the FTSE100 companies and 50% of the top 100 companies in Business Week Global 1,000.

AREAS OF PRACTICE

International finance: the firm advises global financial institutions on the Jersey legal aspects of securitisation, capital markets transactions, structured and corporate finance and banking.

Funds: the firm has advised on almost 50% of Jersey-domiciled funds, and specialises in particular in private equity and venture capital funds.

Commercial: the commercial team specialises in advising businesses on Jersey commercial and corporate law, in particular banking and company law, collective investments, financial services regulation, M&A, employment and property law.

Commercial litigation: the practice focuses on banking and trust litigation, asset tracing and fraud.

Specialist administration services: Mourant also provides the following services:

Mourant Equity Compensation Solutions is a specialist administrator of complex global, UK domestic and offshore employee share plans. It acts for 42% of the UK FTSE100 index, while the largest of its 200+ global share plans has over 50,000 active participants.

Mourant Private Wealth Management provides lawyer-led independent wealth management for clients with the most exacting standards.

Mourant International Finance Administration offers highly skilled administration for complex international private funds. It administers some of the chief European private equity funds, with fund assets of over US$17bn under administration and can offer services in a choice of favourable jurisdictions.

Mourant International Finance Administration advises on the establishment and administration of onshore and offshore financing and holding structures for property assets. Its services include off-balance sheet financing arrangements, securitisation of property assets and joint venture structures for property co-ownership and property holding structures.

Mourant International Finance Administration has a strong reputation in the administration of capital markets and structured finance vehicles, repackaging programmes, specialist fiduciary products and bespoke corporate structures for large institutional and financial clients. Management of SPVs in a range of favourable jurisdictions is a particular strength. Jurisdictions offered include Ireland, Italy, UK, Luxembourg, Jersey, Guernsey, Switzerland, the Netherlands and the Cayman Islands.

OGIER & LE MASURIER

WHITELEY CHAMBERS
DON STREET
ST HELIER JE4 9WG

Telephone: +44 1534 504000
Fax: +44 1534 504444
E-mail: info@ogier.com
Website: www.ogier.com

Languages
French, German, Portuguese, Spanish

Other offices
Cayman Islands (Ogier & Boxalls), Guernsey, London

Number of lawyers 110
at this office 57

Member
Association of European Lawyers (AEL); STEP; EVCA; BVCA

CATEGORIES OF WORK

Banking
Matthew Swan, Christopher Byrne

Securitisation and structured finance
Christopher Byrne, Michael Lombardi

Capital markets
Christopher Byrne, Matthew Swan

Investment funds
Nick Kershaw, Clive Chaplin

Employee benefits and share plan administration
Clive Chaplin, Phil Norman

Real estate administration
Nick Kershaw, Michael Lombardi

Corporate and commercial
Marc Yates, Richard Thomas

Trust and estate planning
Steve Meiklejohn, Julian Clyde-Smith

Private client
Jonathan White, Steve Meiklejohn

Commercial and residential property
Christopher Renouf, Peter Bertram

Commercial litigation
Matthew Thompson, Kerry Lawrence

Employment law
Matthew Thompson

Regulatory
Matthew Thompson, Steve Meiklejohn

Fiduciary services
Simon Willing, Paul Willing

THE FIRM

Ogier is one of the leading and largest offshore providers of legal and administration services with approximately 370 employees across offices in Jersey, Guernsey, London and the Cayman Islands.

Ogier comprises Ogier & Le Masurier in the Channel Islands, Ogier & Boxalls in the Cayman Islands, and Ogier Fiduciary Services, its administration business. Ogier & Le Masurier continues to develop its strength in depth as one of the leading commercial law firms in the Channel Islands, delivering practical commercial advice to clients with the highest possible client service.

Ogier has developed an extensive portfolio of international clients and intermediaries and continues to provide legal and administration services to them through its dedicated teams.

All work undertaken is managed by a team of specialists, led by a partner specifically selected to achieve the commercial objectives of the client.

AREAS OF PRACTICE

Banking: Ogier & Le Masurier is widely regarded as a premier firm for banking and international finance. It specialises in advising on all areas of banking, security, structured finance, banking regulation and the establishment of banks.

Corporate and commercial: Ogier's highly experienced and extensive team covers mergers and acquisitions, employment and privacy laws, IT/IP and e-commerce.

Securitisation: Ogier has one of the leading and largest securitisation and capital markets teams, with particular expertise in asset-backed securities, CBOs, ABCP and structured notes.

Structured finance: The structured finance team covers structured equity, asset finance and tax neutral transactions.

Investment funds: Ogier's fund practice comprises one of the largest funds teams in Jersey, Guernsey and the Cayman Islands, and advises on the establishment and strucuturing of funds as well as on regulatory and compliance issues.

Real estate: Ogier Real Estate Services Ltd provides company secretarial, accounting and administration services to a wide range of real estate-related structures. Ogier's real estate team specialises in the establishment and administration of corporate structures in most European jurisdictions.

Employee benefits: The employee benefits team is committed to providing an innovative and flexible approach to assist clients to achieve employee or clients' employee incentive requirements, tailored administration services, comprehensive advice and a quality, efficient and cost-effective service.

Trusts: The trust and estate planning group has one of the largest teams of trust lawyers dedicated to advising trust companies, intermediaries and individuals in matters of trust law.

Private client: Ogier continues to develop and grow its private client practice. The private client team can provide a full range of administration services to trusts, companies and limited partnerships established in the Channel Islands, as well as to entities established elsewhere.

Commercial litigation: Ogier & Le Masurier has a specialist and highly regarded trust and commercial litigation group involved in the majority of the leading high-profile Jersey cases. The litigation group is the sole litigation practice in Jersey specialising exclusively in commercial litigation.

Commercial property: One of the leading, largest commercial and residential property law teams in Jersey with two dedicated property partners. Ogier & Le Masurier acts in most of Jersey's major property transactions for the buyer, seller or financier.

Fiduciary services: Ogier Fiduciary Services provides professional administration and accounting services to trusts, companies and limited partnerships.

JORDAN

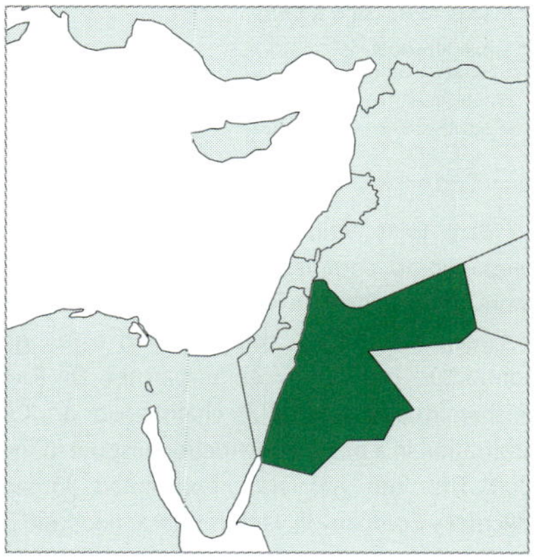

Population	5.5 million
Number of lawyers	8,000 approx
Professional title	Attorney
Currency	Dinar (JOD)
Index	
Corporate and commercial	714
Country index	5

Jordan is a young state, winning its independence from British rule in 1946, and occupies ancient land frequently associated with the Bible and ancient Middle Eastern civilisations. It is bordered by Syria to the north, Iraq to the east and by Saudi Arabia to the south. Jordan boasts 16 miles of coastline and is an arid country with extensive desert land, suffering frequent drought and periodic earthquakes.

Jordan, whose capital city is Amman, was for the most part since independence ruled by King Hussein who died in 1999. He successfully navigated pressures from a number of countries including the US, USSR, Arab states, Israel and internally from the Palestinian population (half the total population of Jordan) and led the country through wars and internal strife.

Some 98% of the population is Arab and, whilst the official language is Arabic, English is widely understood amongst the middle and upper ranks of society. The vast majority are Sunni Muslims, while Christians constitute most of the minority.

BILLING

Billing is usually in US dollars and hourly rates range from $85 to $300 for the most senior partner. Firms bill on the basis of the hours worked, the importance of the case and whether court action is required, with a minimum fee of 5% of the value of a claim, and a maximum of 25%.

POLITICAL CLIMATE

Jordan has a constitutional monarch who enjoys wide powers. The present sovereign, King Abdullah II, has taken on his father's mantle and followed through an aggressive programme of economic reforms which led to Jordan's accession to the WTO in January 2000, signing the free trade agreements with the US in 2000 and with the European Free Trade Association in 2001.

Jordan's most recent legislative instrument, the 1952 constitution, increased executive responsibility. Jordan's prime minister, currently Faisal al-Fayez, is appointed by the monarch and the cabinet is appointed by the prime minister in consultation with the monarch. The country has a parliamentary form of government but the sovereign remains the country's ultimate authority over the executive, legislature and judiciary.

Constitutionally, the Senate comprises 40 'notables', appointed by the king for four years, and 80 'deputies' in the House of Representatives for which elections are held at least every four years (although frequently suspended).

ECONOMIC CLIMATE

As a small state with inadequate supplies of natural resources (including water), Jordan suffers the perennial problem of debt and poverty, unemployment and related economic problems. Unemployment currently stands at 15%. These problems have progressively worsened since the mid-1990s. In 1997, for the third time an agreement was signed to write off the country's debt of more than $1bn to the US. The World Bank did the same, and also extended another loan to boost Jordan's flagging economy – Jordan's outstanding public debt (government and guaranteed) stood at JOD5,505m ($7.75bn) at the end of October 2003.

The 2003 Iraq war resulted in negative economic consequences for Jordan, which relied on Iraq for the supply of its oil at a discounted price. How Jordan will continue to finance energy is not yet clear. However, Jordan's economic performance generally exceeded expectations over the three years to 2002 under the extended arrangement with the IMF, with particularly strong results in 2001.

Jordan's government has set out a range of economic objectives that it aims to achieve through privatisation. And privatisation was part of the overall economic package that the government adopted as of the early '90s, namely the economic adjustment programme and self-reliance in the aftermath of the economic crisis that befell the country.

In March 1999 the Amman Financial Market split to create the Jordan Securities Commission (JSC), the Securities Depository Centre and the Amman Stock Exchange (ASE). In 2002, 158 companies were listed on the ASE and market capitalisation stood at JOD5bn ($7bn) – in both cases, a decrease over the preceding two years.

The ASE index rose by 30% to 2002, partly due to the ratification of the Free Trade Agreement (FTA) with the US and strong financial performance of the banking sector.

The Jordanian banking system is characterised by a variety of activities. It consists of 21 banks, two of which are Arab, three foreign and 16 Jordanian. There are 14 commercial banks, five investment and two working according to Islamic shari'a.

The largest firms

1	Abu-Ghazaleh Legal Services (ABLE)	16
2	International Business Legal Associates	15
3	Khalaf Masa'deh & Partners	11
4	Petra for Law and Intellectual Property	10
5	Middle Eastern Global Advocates & Legal Consultants	8
6	A Ghniem & Partners Law Firm	4

These figures represent the total number of lawyers in this country only, and have been supplied by the firms themselves. The figures should be accurate as at 1 January 2004.

LEGAL SYSTEM AND LEGAL MARKET

Jordan's legal market is presently recovering from the unstable political circumstances in the region and particularly the Iraqi situation. Consistently affected by a sluggish economy, there is currently insufficient work for many lawyers. In Jordan, there is very little specialisation with lawyers handling most types of work.

The judiciary is nominally independent and Jordan's court system is made up of two main divisions: civil and criminal. These comprise three categories: the regular courts including magistrates, courts of first instance, courts of appeal and cassation; religious courts, for example, an Islamic Court exercising jurisdiction over matters of personal status; and special courts which exercise jurisdiction over matters such as land, property and tax.

Under the Constitution, laws are proposed by the Council of Minister for parliament's approval and all laws have ultimately to be approved by the King.

Lawyers practising in Jordan must join the Jordanian Lawyers Association and are obliged to undergo a period of training before being permitted to plead cases in the courts.

PRIVATISATION

King Abdullah is progressing broad economic reforms to improve long-term living standards. Privatisation is also making headway and the country's accession to the WTO and similar measures have helped improve productivity and investment for Jordan.

Privatisation was part of the overall economic package that the government adopted in the early '90s in the aftermath of Jordan's economic crisis at that time. Its government has set out a range of economic objectives it aims to achieve through privatisation.

Privatisation Law No 25 of the year 2000 was promulgated the same year, setting explicit provisions to regulate the privatisation process. Privatisation of government institutions and corporations is already well on its way.

The reputable **Nabulsi & Associates** is legal counsel to the government of Jordan in relation to the telecommunications sector restructuring programme and drafting the telecommunications law. The firm also advises one of Jordan's two cellular operators. **Khalaf Masa'deh & Partners**' practice also offers services to the aviation and electricity sectors in relation to Jordan's privatisation programme.

CORPORATE AND COMMERCIAL

Commercial and construction work is abundant in Jordan at present, indicative of the increasing levels of expansion in the country. The principal corporate and commercial laws are found in the Civil Code law no 43 (1976); Companies law No 22 (1997); and Financial Papers law No 23 (1997).

CORPORATE AND COMMERCIAL

Hashem Law Office
International Business Legal Associates
Khalaf Masa'deh & Partners
Nabulsi & Associates

A Ghniem & Partners Law Firm
Abu-Ghazaleh Legal Services (ABLE) ✪
Bassam Al-Salfiti
Maran Al Hussein & Sons
Salah Hmoud

Firms are listed A-Z in tiers which are ranked in order of priority
✪ *Indicates firm displays contact details at the end of this chapter.*

In a joint action, **Hashem Law Office** is preparing to commence an arbitration worth more than $80m in a construction dispute between a Jordanian company and a foreign contractor. The firm's senior partner, Dr Fadi Hashem, recently acted as chairman of an ICC arbitration in a major construction dispute in the Gulf. The firm has also represented Jordan Electricity Company in various transactions and is retained by some of the biggest local and international contractors and consulting engineers.

International Business Legal Associates is a leading firm in Jordan, having a broad-based commercial and corporate practice serving a large portfolio of local and international clients in, for example, manufacturing, banking and insurance, transport and construction contracts. The firm routinely assists businesses in incorporating and restructuring under Jordan's Company Law and setting up international business schemes.

Khalaf Masa'deh & Partners' roster of international clients includes Deloitte & Touche, acting on behalf of the government of Jordan in its launching of an e-government initiative to improve government performance and boost e-commerce activities (amongst other objectives). The firm also acted for Jordan University of Science and Technology in relation to probably the largest-ever arbitration in Jordan's history involving a construction dispute. The firm also recently acted for a major US multinational corporation in a highly sensitive corporate and commercial matter.

A wide range of reputable Jordanian and international companies and institutions, including the World Bank are represented by **Nabulsi & Associates** which has longstanding relationships with several major law firms throughout the world. The firm is legal counsel to major international oil and gas companies and acted for a joint venture consisting of two leading construction companies in a project to construct one of the most important highways in Jordan. Other clients include Motorola Inc, McDonald's International, Shell International, the Bank of New York, Sony Corporation, and Benetton Group.

A Ghniem & Partners Law Firm acts for a number of national and international corporate clients which range from the Giangsu Geology and Engineering Ltd (Jordan's branch of a Chinese company) and Serck Controls (Global Solutions UK and Australia), to Amman Surgical Hospital.

Abu-Ghazaleh Legal Services (ABLE) is part of the *Talal Abu-Ghazaleh International (TAGI)* family of firms which, for over three decades, has offered the Arab world a complete range of high-quality, professional services ranging from accounting to management consulting and intellectual property protection. *TAGI* is the largest Middle East practice operating through its network of 33 offices in the Arab world. The firm's corporate and business law practice involves a variety of both adversarial and transactional work and clients include domestic and international companies ranging from start-up enterprises to leading companies. Chairman Mr Talal Abu-Ghazaleh, has been appointed as the new chair of ICC's Commission on Telecommunications and Information Technology. The firm has extensive experience in intellectual property work as well as in drafting laws and regulations for various governments including Bahrain, UAE, Tunisia, Egypt and the Gulf Cooperation Council.

Bassam Al-Salfiti represents numerous well-known Jordanian companies and acts for two of the largest clothes manufacturers in the Middle East – Sajeda and Jawharet al Quds.

With links with law firms worldwide, **Maran Al Hussein & Sons** represents corporations, non-profit organisations, individuals, and public sector agencies throughout Jordan, the Middle East and the rest of the word.

Salah Hmoud is a specialist in Jordan's Companies Act. The firm's experience is concentrated on commercial issues, including investment from Germany and Austria, as well as neighbouring Arab countries.

ABU-GHAZALEH LEGAL SERVICES (ABLE)

ASSOCIATED FIRM OF ABU-GHAZALEH INTELLECTUAL PROPERTY (AGIP)

TAGI HOUSE, QUEEN NOOR STREET
SHMEISANI, PO BOX 921100
AMMAN 11192

Telephone: +962 6 566 9603
Fax: +962 6 569 6284
E-mail: able@tagi.com
Website: www.able-law.com

Languages
Arabic, French, English

Other offices
Abu Dhabi, Ajman, Al-Khobar, Algiers, Ankara, Beirut, Cairo, Casablanca, Damascus, Doha, Dubai, Fujairah, Gaza City, Jebel Ali, Jeddah, Karachi, Khartoum, Manama, Muscat, Nablus, Riyadh, Safat, Salalah, Sana'a, Sharjah, Tripoli, Tunis

Number of lawyers 205
at this office 16

Contact
Mr Rami Olwan

Member
Talal Abu-Ghazaleh Organisation (TAGCO)

CATEGORIES OF WORK

Intellectual property protection services:

Enforcement of intellectual property rights

IP transfer

IP portfolio management

IP watch service

IP litigation

Online IP

Advice on IP laws and regulations

IP evaluation

Franchising

Corporate and business legal services:

Establishment of companies

Business litigation

E-commerce business legal issues

Dispute resolution

Arbitration

Tax

Real estate

Labour

WTO-related issues

Mergers and acquisitions

KUWAIT

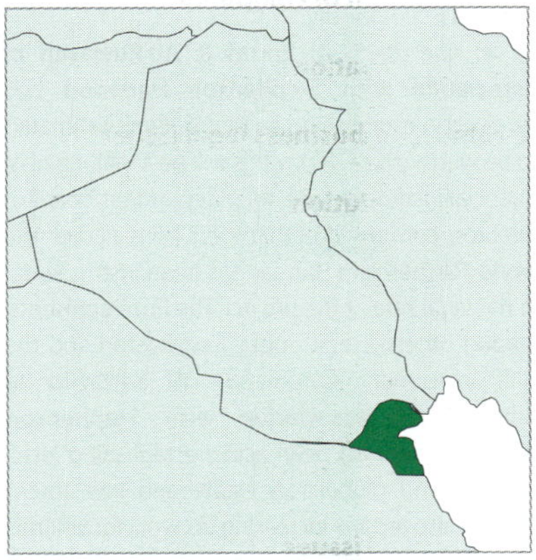

Population	**2.48 million (including 1.3 million non-nationals)**
Number of lawyers	**n/a**
Professional title	**Advocate**
Currency	**Kuwaiti Dinar (KD)**

Index

Kuwait is making good on promises to liberalise its society following the end of the second Iraq war, although there is some disquiet at the slow pace of reform in certain areas.

In a landmark ruling in July 2003, Emir Sheikh Jaber al-Ahmed al-Sabah separated the post of prime minister from the role of Crown Prince. Although the link between the two positions was never enshrined in law, it had been a tradition for many years that the Crown Prince would assume the responsibilities of prime minister.

The removal of Saddam Hussein took away a long-term threat to the very existence of Kuwait, demonstrated in 1991 when Iraq occupied the country. Yet continuing instability across the region makes for an unsettled scene and creates obstacles to economic diversification. Speculation over America's policy towards not just Iraqi oil reserves but towards the region as a whole will help shape the political and economic future of Kuwait.

In the meantime, the state-owned oil industry dominates, providing 75% of government income.

Kuwait may be small, but its international importance is immense, controlling as it does one-tenth of world crude oil reserves. Sitting at the north-western end of the Persian Gulf, Kuwait borders Iraq and Saudi Arabia. In line with other countries in the region, the official religion is Islam, although there is religious freedom and other religions are openly practised. The majority are Sunnis, though there is a strong Shia minority. This religious tolerance is welcomed by the diverse population that lives and works there, as well as by foreign multinationals with offices there.

The new situation in Iraq creates a whole new field of opportunity. Massive reconstruction projects are under way and leading Kuwaiti law firms are advising the Western companies involved. The new prime minister is said to favour privatisation and globalisation.

BILLING

Various billing methods are employed, including hourly rates, a percentage of transaction or dispute value (result-determined) and lump sums. The method is agreed in advance. Rates can top €400 per hour, according to the seniority of the lawyer.

MARKETING

Law firms in Kuwait put a great deal of work into their websites, yet word of mouth, client recommendation and personal contacts are the true currency here.

ECONOMIC CLIMATE

The war in Iraq put everything on hold from March to May 2003, but things picked up quickly thereafter. Real GDP was predicted to soar by 4.7% in 2003, slowing to 2.2% in 2004, although the predictions were made before the war. The picture is still too unstable to call accurately, but Kuwait's involvement in Iraqi reconstruction should prove an enormous boost to the economy and the nation's law firms.

The Kuwait Stock Exchange has been performing extremely well as inward investment continues to pour in. Multinationals such as Coca-Cola and Warner Brothers have been taking an increasing interest in Kuwait in recent months. The Gulf Co-operation Council (GCC), a kind of fast-track European Union, was formed in January 2003 and is making steady progress towards its stated aims of monetary union in 2005 and a single currency before 2010. This has encouraged greater trade between the six GCC states, but has also made it possible for its members to get involved with new projects such as developing oilfields. The GCC militates against the restrictions on trade involved in Kuwaiti state ownership of the oil industry, and some interesting joint projects are under way. **Al-Wagayan & Al-Awadhi & Al-Saif Law Firm** is involved in what it calls a ground-breaking private investment project in a new oil platform – clients Dubal (India) and Aminco (US) are part of a large private consortium including companies with the GCC and the EU.

In June 2003, SOMO, the state oil marketing company in Iraq awarded the first post-war crude oil tender to six different companies for ten million barrels of oil held in storage. The companies were Spanish refiners Repsol and Cepsa, Turkey's Tupras, Italy's ENI, Total of France and Chevron Texaco of the United States.

LEGAL MARKET

Foreign law firms usually work through a Kuwaiti partner firm, rather than establishing their own offices. This is due to the law in Kuwait restricting foreign ownership of any business. Although this is set to be reformed, an enforcement date continues to hang in abeyance.

The largest firms

1	Al Sarraf & Al Ruwayeh in association with Stephenson Harwood	43
2	M M Al-Ghazali & Partners	40
3	Law Office of Al-Essa, Al-Bader & Partners	21
4	Abdullah Kh. Al-Ayoub & Associates	17
5	Salman Duaij Al Sabah Law Office	11
6	Ali & Partners	9
7	Al Hekook, Advocates & Legal Consultants	8
	Mashora Advocates & Legal Consultants (in assoc with Bryan Cave LLP)	8
9	The Law Firm of Labeed Abdal	6

These figures represent the total number of lawyers in this country only, and have been supplied by the firms themselves. The figures should be accurate as at 1 January 2004.

Salman Duaij Al Sabah Law Office has an association with **Jones Day**; **Mashora Advocates & Legal Consultants (in assoc with Bryan Cave LLP)** is another US tie-up. **Al Sarraf & Al Ruwayeh** is associated with the UK's **Stephenson Harwood**.

In 2003 **M M Al-Ghazali & Partners** announced it was entering into an affiliation with **Squire, Sanders & Dempsey**.

Of the international firms without local associations, **Clifford Chance LLP** is perhaps the busiest. It advised the Kuwait Petroleum Corporation on issues arising from the 1991 Gulf War, as well as contractual disputes involving the Kuwait National Petroleum Company (owned by KPC).

Most of the larger Kuwaiti firms have international departments, with some, such as **Salman Duaij Al Sabah Law Office** or **Al-Wagayan & Al-Awadhi & Al-Saif Law Firm**, splitting their operation into two parts – domestic and international.

There is some concern over the small number of genuinely bilingual lawyers who can practise law in both English and Arabic.

The basic laws of Kuwait date back to Napoleonic Egypt and the system is less adversarial than in Anglo-Saxon countries. The shari'a has an influence, mainly confined to personal status areas.

BANKING AND FINANCE

Paradoxically, Kuwait is attracting major international interest in its securities market despite the insecurity in the region as a whole. This is partly because although the political problems are worsening, economic ties between Gulf states are becoming closer, through the GCC and because of the joint initiatives which led to its formation. It also helps that GCC members are usually members of the World Trade Organisation, a fact which tends to accelerate the process of liberalisation in financial markets.

BANKING AND FINANCE

AL-ESSA, AL-BADER & PARTNERS, LAW OFFICE OF
AL SARRAF & AL RUWAYEH IN ASSOCIATION WITH STEPHENSON HARWOOD ✪

Al-Saleh & Partners
Al-Wagayan & Al-Awadhi & Al-Saif Law Firm
M M Al-Ghazali & Partners
Mashora Advocates & Legal Consultants (in assoc with Bryan Cave LLP)

Abdullah Kh. Al-Ayoub & Associates
Al Hekook, Advocates & Legal Consultants
Ali & Partners
Anwar Al-Bisher & Partners

Firms are listed A-Z in tiers which are ranked in order of priority
✪ Indicates firm displays contact details at the end of this chapter.

Kevin Burke of **Law Office of Al-Essa, Al-Bader & Partners** handles almost all the firm's banking and finance work. He reports that another major eurobond deal was due to close before the end of 2003. The firm offers general capital markets advice and clients include the Bank of Kuwait & the Middle East. The firm worked on three previous eurobond issues and, along with **Al Sarraf & Al Ruwayeh in association with Stephenson Harwood**, takes care of around 85% of bond issues locally.

In late 2003, **Al Sarraf & Al Ruwayeh in association with Stephenson Harwood** was involved in establishing an Islamic Bank. Estimated to be worth over €100m, this will be a major global financial institution with an independent board of directors composed of members from all over the world. Partner Sam Habbas has been instrumental in the legal side of the project. The firm represents, among others, Credit Suisse First Boston and the Gulf Investment Corporation. **Al Sarraf & Al Ruwayeh in association with Stephenson Harwood** has also been active establishing local, regional and global real estate and investment funds. It also reports increasing tax work for all kinds of foreign companies. The firm is heavily involved in capital markets work, recently completing two bond issues, and is working on another three, all of which are worth between €50m and €100m. The work is carried out for managers or arrangers.

The burgeoning popularity of Islamic finance is creating increased workloads for the major finance practices. Eleven-strong **Al-Saleh & Partners** reports involvement in a bond issue for a global investment interest; an agreement for international investment through local placement agents and a bond issue for the National Bank of Kuwait.

Al-Wagayan & Al-Awadhi & Al-Saif Law Firm conducts local banking work and represents several Kuwaiti banks.

M M Al-Ghazali & Partners has represented the Global Investment House, through Asmaa Ahmed A Al-Mefleh. The firm represents banks and investment houses based both at home and abroad, usually in connection with bond issues and the sale of securities.

Mashora Advocates & Legal Consultans (in assoc with Bryan Cave LLP) advised a Kuwait bank over the launch of five investment funds.

Abdullah Kh. Al-Ayoub & Associates assisted in obtaining government authorisation for not only the registration but also for the marketing of an international investment fund in Kuwait, acting on behalf of a major European investment bank.

Ten-strong **Anwar Al-Bisher & Partners** helped a European company resolve tax issues with the Department of Income Tax going back over several years. The firm also advised an investment company on a new website for trading in US and Kuwaiti securities. **Anwar Al-Bisher & Partners** also acted on an unusual reverse takeover deal for a local corporate client. Mary Ann Sharp and Anwar Al-Bisher are both highly regarded.

CORPORATE AND COMMERCIAL

AL SARRAF & AL RUWAYEH IN ASSOCIATION WITH STEPHENSON HARWOOD ✪
MASHORA ADVOCATES & LEGAL CONSULTANTS (IN ASSOC WITH BRYAN CAVE LLP)

Abdullah Kh. Al-Ayoub & Associates
Al-Essa, Al-Bader & Partners, Law Office of
Al-Saleh & Partners
Al-Wagayan & Al-Awadhi & Al-Saif Law Firm
Anwar Al-Bisher & Partners
International Counsel Bureau
M M Al-Ghazali & Partners
Salman Duaij Al Sabah Law Office

Abdul Razzaq & Partners Law Firm
Al Hekook, Advocates & Legal Consultants
Ali & Partners
Labeed Abdal, The Law Firm of ✪

Firms are listed A-Z in tiers which are ranked in order of priority
✪ Indicates firm displays contact details at the end of this chapter.

CORPORATE AND COMMERCIAL

There is growing impatience at the Kuwait government's failure to enact a law allowing foreigners to own more than 49% of any Kuwaiti business. The old limit effectively remains in force despite the 2001 legislation. However, several joint ventures are in the planning stages and the effect of these will be to add to the pressure on the government to enact the law. A piece of Kuwaiti social legislation states that a proportion of any contract awarded to a foreign company must be reinvested in Kuwait, in areas such as education and training.

Al Sarraf & Al Ruwayeh in association with Stephenson Harwood has a long list of international clients, including Cisco Systems, General Electric, Nestlé and Shell. It benefits from referrals and works with international law firms including **Clifford Chance LLP** on corporate matters.

Mashora Advocates & Legal Consultants (in assoc with Bryan Cave LLP) assisted Kuwait-based Mobile Telecommunications Company KSC (MTC) in the €359m acquisition of 90% of Jordan Mobile Telephone Services Company (Fastlink) from Orascom Telecom Holding SAE. The firm benefits from a close connection with **Bryan Cave**, especially the London office. **Mashora Advocates & Legal Consultans (in assoc with Bryan Cave LLP)** recruited the able Stephen Rodd of **Bryan Cave**'s Abu Dhabi office.

Abdullah Kh. Al-Ayoub & Associates has acted for major foreign multinationals on agency agreements and has a list of clients which includes many world-renowned, household name companies. In 2003 the firm advised a client in the oil and gas sector on restructuring labour practices. It has a total of 18 fee-earners, including Abdullah Al-Ayoub. Its other leading lights are Mohammed Hassan Omar, Jasmin Kohina (head of the international division) and Mijibel Al-Rashdan. The firm advised a major US defence corporation on the legal implications of paying commissions or gratuities in government contracts.

Kevin Burke at **Law Office of Al-Essa, Al-Bader & Partners** is the firm's public face as far as international clients are concerned. The firm represents the Kuwait state oil company.

Al-Saleh & Partners represents a multinational client base which includes Novartis, Kuwait National Petroleum Company, Lucent Technologies, Kuwait Stock Exchange, Cegelc and Genpharm. It also counts Microsoft, Debenhams, Exxon Mobil and Principles Retail among its clients.

Al-Wagayan & Al-Awadhi & Al-Saif Law Firm has boosted its commercial and international practice with eight new lawyers, taking the firm's total number of lawyers to 34. The firm advised the Kuwait ruling family and the army on the investment of funds. The commercial practice is headed by managing partner Mamoun Hariri.

Anwar Al-Bisher & Partners advised a multinational client on setting up a local holding company, negotiating land lease, construction, and banking contracts, as well as franchise agreements and trade mark registrations. Other highlights include a listing on the Kuwait stock market.

Abdul Rahman Al-Haroun is a respected lawyer at the **International Counsel Bureau**; the firm has been busy with joint venture projects, shipping and many other areas.

M M Al-Ghazali & Partners's new affiliation with **Squire, Sanders & Dempsey** will boost its profile for inward investment work. Majed Y Amin was in-house lawyer for T-Mobile Austria from 2000 until 2003 and speaks Arabic, English and German.

Salman Duaij Al Sabah Law Office represents a very wide variety of Western corporate clients, providing advice on all legal aspects of doing business in Kuwait. It also advises on agency, tax, securities, and labour laws. Clients include three multinational automobile manufacturers, an American airfreight company, a large regional shipping company and the Middle East arm of a major soft drinks company.

Abdul Razzaq & Partners Law Firm, which has six lawyers and a paralegal department, has been involved in advising major contractors on the offset rules. The firm was formed in the summer of 2003 when the law firm of *Abdul Razzaq, Al-Saeed & Al-Oudah* split into three firms.

Al Hekook, Advocates & Legal Consultants' clients include Qatar Airways and Greek refrigeration company Frigorex. The firm has three partners: Meshaal A Al Nemesh; Ayyad H Al Adwani, who is a registered arbitrator; and Nedal Al Humaidan, who is legal adviser to the Kuwaiti minister of information.

Ali & Partners has affiliated offices across the Middle East and also an associate office in Washington DC. The firm offers a wide commercial service.

DISPUTE RESOLUTION

ABDULLAH KH. AL-AYOUB & ASSOCIATES
AL SARRAF & AL RUWAYEH IN ASSOCIATION WITH STEPHENSON HARWOOD ✪
MASHORA ADVOCATES & LEGAL CONSULTANTS (IN ASSOC WITH BRYAN CAVE LLP)
SALMAN DUAIJ AL SABAH LAW OFFICE

Al-Essa, Al-Bader & Partners, Law Office of
Al Hekook, Advocates & Legal Consultants
Al-Saleh & Partners
Al-Wagayan & Al-Awadhi & Al-Saif Law Firm
Ali & Partners
Anwar Al-Bisher & Partners
M M Al-Ghazali & Partners

Firms are listed A-Z in tiers which are ranked in order of priority
✪ Indicates firm displays contact details at the end of this chapter.

Six-lawyer commercial firm, **The Law Firm of Labeed Abdal** led by the eponymous senior partner, offers international investors expertise across the range of commercial and contentious disciplines.

DISPUTE RESOLUTION

Kuwaiti firms are happy to handle the bread-and-butter late payment and agency disputes into which international companies are occasionally drawn. Several of the firms are expert in alternative forms of dispute resolution, such as arbitration and commercial litigation expertise is widely available.

The war in Iraq has brought much litigation work for Kuwaiti firms, for example representing the British and American armies. Those Kuwaiti firms which have represented defendants accused of acts of terror, such as the attack on American soldiers in March 2003, report that this has not stood in their way of securing work from US or British companies.

Abdullah Kh. Al-Ayoub & Associates filed a claim for compensation at the London Court of International Arbitration against a UK insurance company, relating to the termination of an agency agreement.

Al Sarraf & Al Ruwayeh in association with Stephenson Harwood lists the UK Ministry of Defence as a client, while **Al Hekook, Advocates & Legal Consultants** works for Al-Jazeera and Qatar Airways.

Salman Duaij Al Sabah Law Office is representing politician Saud Al-Matawa in litigation relating to alleged irregularities during the 2003 elections.

Najib Al-Wagayan, partner with **Al-Wagayan & Al-Awadhi & Al-Saif Law Firm**, represented those particular defendants and their families but the firm also takes instructions for the US and British Army.

Anwar Al-Bisher & Partners has advised clients in litigation against the Kuwait Free Zone and the Kuwait government.

INTELLECTUAL PROPERTY

Al-Essa, Al-Bader & Partners, Law Office of
Al Hekook, Advocates & Legal Consultants
Al-Saleh & Partners
Al Sarraf & Al Ruwayeh in association with Stephenson Harwood ✪
M M Al-Ghazali & Partners
Salman Duaij Al Sabah Law Office

Abdullah Kh. Al-Ayoub & Associates
Ali & Partners
Al-Wagayan & Al-Awadhi & Al-Saif Law Firm
Labeed Abdal, The Law Firm of ✪
Mashora Advocates & Legal Consultants (in assoc with Bryan Cave LLP)

Firms are listed A-Z in tiers which are ranked in order of priority
✪ Indicates firm displays contact details at the end of this chapter.

INTELLECTUAL PROPERTY

Kuwait retains its poor reputation for trade mark piracy and has been criticised in the past by the International Intellectual Property Alliance for taking steps, which, while in the right direction, are often slow and cumbersome. Still, Kuwait is signed up to TRIPS and thanks to the GCC, there is growing understanding of the importance of IP in Kuwait. The concern internationally is over enforcement and penalties.

State raids on suspected trade mark pirates have become more regular. There are signs that firms will pick up more work in this area, although few firms have the expertise to deal with it as yet.

Law Office of Al-Essa, Al-Bader & Partners represented the Business Software Alliance and the US Embassy in IP cases in 2003 and is helping them to lobby for the enforcement of copyright law.

Al Hekook, Advocates & Legal Consultants was instructed by Vega Media and Rotana Video & Audio on enforcement matters.

Al-Saleh & Partners acted for Etienne Aigner, Microsoft, Debenhams, Exxon Mobil and Principles Retail in the IP arena in 2003. Of its 23 lawyers, four are in IP.

Al Sarraf & Al Ruwayeh in association with Stephenson Harwood reports an increasing volume of trade mark work and is currently representing a major US household name client whose goods were being counterfeited.

Salman Duaij Al Sabah Law Office is recommended. The firm is currently acting for a major film company in a video piracy case.

PRIVATISATION AND PROJECT FINANCE

Projects work was depressed by the war in Iraq, but privatisation continues to move forward. The Kuwait Investment Authority (KIA) has sold 80% of its stake in Alafco, the financing and leasing arm of Kuwait Airways Corporation (KAC). This is a stage towards the planned total privatisation of KAC, though progress has ebbed and flowed in line with the financial performance of KAC. Kuwait Oil Tanker Company (KOTC) and the Petrochemical Industries Company (PIC) are also privatisation targets, as are the telecommunications network, water and electricity utilities. The Kuwaiti government has sold its stake in nearly 24 companies since 1994, resulting in an income of about $3bn.

According to the Middle East Infrastructure Development Congress, a further $2.5bn of build, operate and transfer (BOT) power projects are planned. It says the first BOT waste water project at Sulaibiya will be followed by more projects of a similar nature. Plans for an Iraq-Kuwait pipeline are also said to be progressing on a BOT basis.

This sector is set to expand, thanks to opportunities in Iraq, oilfield developments and other projects, such as the part-privatisation of the airport in Kuwait City. Iraq's Provisional Coalition Authority has begun awarding tenders for infrastructure projects.

Law Office of Al-Essa, Al-Bader & Partners is highly regarded. The firm is representing clients involved in two new power stations and on two planned petrochemical plants.

Forty-one strong **Al Sarraf & Al Ruwayeh in association with Stephenson Harwood** acted in Kuwait Petroleum Corporation's calcinised coke privatisation project and has been involved with the Kuwait Northern Oilfields Development Project. KPC is a new client for the firm, as are Lockheed Martin and York International. The firm has also advised ExxonMobil on its Qatar-Kuwait pipeline project and has experience on BOTs.

Fifteen-strong **M M Al-Ghazali & Partners** lists the Equate Petrochemical Company as a client, as well as Boubyan Petrochemical Company, Exxon Exploration Company and Al-Khorayef Commercial Company, a large Saudi Arabian oil sector service and product provider. It also has experience in public sector procurement and represents clients tendering for oil and gas, utilities, defence, construction and transport contracts, as well as companies in dispute with the Kuwaiti government. Managing partner and founder, Mishari Al-Ghazali specialises in privatisation. He helped two Kuwaiti companies and Union Carbide to establish Equate and served as the company's legal consultant until the end of 2002.

PRIVATISATION AND PROJECT FINANCE

AL-ESSA, AL-BADER & PARTNERS, LAW OFFICE OF
AL SARRAF & AL RUWAYEH IN ASSOCIATION WITH STEPHENSON HARWOOD ✪
INTERNATIONAL COUNSEL BUREAU
M M AL-GHAZALI & PARTNERS

Abdul Razzaq & Partners Law Firm
Abdullah Kh. Al-Ayoub & Associates
Ali & Partners
Al-Wagayan & Al-Awadhi & Al-Saif Law Firm
Anwar Al-Bisher & Partners
Mashora Advocates & Legal Consultants (in assoc with Bryan Cave LLP)

Firms are listed A-Z in tiers which are ranked in order of priority
✪ Indicates firm displays contact details at the end of this chapter.

Abdul Razzaq, now leading a new firm **Abdul Razzaq & Partners Law Firm**, has also been active in this area for many years, especially in government procurements.

Abdullah Kh. Al-Ayoub & Associates handled a transaction relating to the sale and installation of radar systems to the Kuwait Coastguard. It also prepared agreements and organised the relationship between a major contractor and sub-contractors involved in infrastructure and reconstruction projects in Iraq since the latest war.

As well as the ground-breaking new oil platform mentioned above, **Al-Wagayan & Al-Awadhi & Al-Saif Law Firm** is also involved in the privatisation of a new part of the airport which will feature shops, entertainment and leisure facilities. Clients include local and US architects. Partners Nader Al-Awadhi, Najib Al-Wagayan and Emad Al-Saif are highly regarded by clients and peers.

Anwar Al-Bisher & Partners advised a major US defence contractor in a significant sale of aircraft to Kuwait. It also advised a Kuwait government entity on the sales of former embassy properties in Greece, Germany, Spain and Iran.

THE LAW FIRM OF LABEED ABDAL

**AL-MUBARAKIYA, ALI AL-SALIM ST
HAMAD COMMERCIAL CENTER
BESIDE COMMERCIAL BANK
(HEAD OFFICE)
FIRST FLOOR
PO BOX 29175 SAFAT
KUWAIT 13152**

Telephone: +965 24 07 020
Fax: +965 24 33 757
E-mail: lalaw@qualitynet.net

Languages
English

Other offices
Cairo*, Cyprus*, Dubai*, Geneva*, Greece*, Iraq, Lebanon*, London*, Paris*, Riyadh*, USA*

Number of lawyers 6

Contact
Mr Labeed Abdal

CATEGORIES OF WORK

- Admiralty and maritime
- Advertising and marketing
- Art and cultural property
- Banking, financial litigation
- Bankruptcy
- Civil and human rights
- Communications
- Constitutional law and administrative
- Construction
- Corporate and commercial
- Criminal law and traffic offences
- Environmental
- Estate and trust
- Franchising, agency and distribution
- Insurance
- Intellectual property
- International trading
- IT, e-commerce and Internet
- Litigation and arbitration
- Labour law
- Real estate
- Patents and trade marks
- Privatisation
- Space law
- Traffic
- White-collar crime

AL SARRAF & AL RUWAYEH

IN ASSOCIATION WITH STEPHENSON HARWOOD, LONDON

**SALHIYA COMPLEX
GATE 1, 3RD FLOOR
PO BOX 1448
SAFAT 13015**

Telephone: +965 240 0061
Fax: +965 240 0064
E-mail: asar@asarlegal.com
Website: www.asarlegal.com

Languages
Arabic, English, French

Associated offices
Bucharest, Guangzhou, Hong Kong, London, Paris, Piraeus, Singapore

Number of lawyers 42

Contact
Sam Habbas

CATEGORIES OF WORK

- Corporate and commercial
- Finance and capital markets
- Government contracts
- International arbitration
- Oil and gas industry
- Real estate
- Insurance
- Securities
- Intellectual property law
- General international trade law
- International banking
- Project finance
- Foreign investments
- Litigation and advocacy
- Agency and distributorships
- Property and shipping work
- Franchising
- Taxation
- Construction law
- Private client services

LATVIA

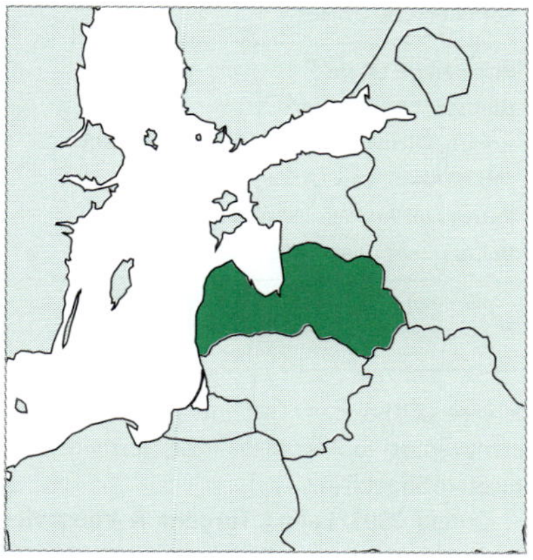

Population	2.4 million
Number of lawyers	600
Professional title	Advokat; advokàts
Currency	Latvian lat (LVL)

Index

Latvia is one of the three Baltic States located on the eastern coast of the Baltic Sea between Estonia and Lithuania. The country benefits from both geographical and economic links with Scandinavia.

In September 2003, Latvians voted in favour of EU membership and the country is poised to join in May 2004. After September's referendum, President Vaira Vike-Freiberga said she hoped EU accession would wipe out forever the divisions on the map of Europe that were put in place during the Second World War.

Up until the late 1980s, native Latvians formed just over half the population following the mass deportations to Siberia in 1949. In the wake of Mikhail Gorbachev's policies, Latvian dissidents started to become outspoken and the country finally gained independence from the Soviet Union in 1991. However, the last Soviet troops did not leave Latvia until 1994. Over time its identity has been largely restored, yet inhabitants of Latvian origin still only account for 58% of the population.

BILLING

Some firms charge up to €300 per hour, although rates typically range from between €150 and €250 per hour. Fixed fees are also often available for certain transactions, and capped fees can sometimes be negotiated for longstanding clients.

MARKETING

Marketing is restricted, but the rules are fairly flexible. Law firms are allowed to advertise as long as they do not promote themselves as market leaders. Most firms have websites providing an outline of their services and personnel.

IN-HOUSE LAWYERS

In most leading companies, in-house teams will comprise no more than one or two lawyers. In-house lawyers in Latvia are not required to be members of the Bar. The major Latvian banks tend to have larger in-house legal departments.

ECONOMIC CLIMATE

Following the Soviet era, Latvia was left with many polluted industrial areas and a dilapidated infrastructure. Immediately following independence the country suffered from negative growth, but its economy finally boomed after 1996. However, the Russian financial crisis resulted in another dip at the end of the '90s. The economy has since recovered, largely due to Latvia's increased trade links with the EU.

Currently about 80% of Latvia's exports are to EU member states. Analysts are predicting GDP growth for 2003 to be around 6.5%.

Despite the global economic slowdown, there has been development in all of Latvia's industries, in particular construction. The Latvian government believes the success stems from conservative macro-economic policies, strict monetary discipline, and a liberal currency exchange regime. Economic growth is expected for the future, aided by EU accession.

Latvia has a diverse manufacturing industry, which includes the manufacture of motor vehicles, synthetic fibres, agricultural machinery, pharmaceuticals, electrical equipment, textiles and electronics. Latvia has one of the highest mobile phone penetration rates in Central and Eastern Europe, and mobile phones comprise one of the fastest growing sub-sectors of the telecoms industry.

In 2003, very little was done on the privatisation front. Any law firms that handled work in this area were mostly finishing transactions that started some time ago. There are still a number of companies that are either fully or partially state owned, but overall the privatisation process is largely complete.

LINKS ABROAD

Baltmane & Bitans is a member of the global network **Landwell**, the correspondent legal practice of PwC.

Klavins & Slaidins benefits from associations with both *Lex Mundi* and the *World Services Group*.

Recently **Kronbergs Law Office** became a member of **EY Law**, a global network of legal services.

Law Office B2B maintains strong links with **Law Office Aivar Pilv** in Estonia.

Lejins, Torgans & Vonsovics is a member of *Meritas*, the law firm network that unites over 180 firms in 62 countries.

Liepa, Skopina/BORENIUS benefits from a strong association with one of Finland's oldest law firms, **Borenius & Kemppinen**.

Loze & Partners is a member of *TAGLaw* and is in the process of becoming a member of *Interlaw* and *AIJA*.

The largest firms

1	Loze & Partners	14
2	Klavins & Slaidins	12
	Sorainen Law Offices	12
4	Lejins, Torgans & Vonsovics	11
5	Liepa, Skopina/BORENIUS	10
6	Baltmane & Bitans	8
	Blueger & Plaude	8
	Kronbergs Law Office	8
	Skudra & Udris Law Offices	8
10	Law Offices of Valters Gencs	7
11	Spade un Mikelsons Law Office	6
12	Grunte & Cers	5
	Hough, Vilcins, Seppälä & Palubinskas SIA	5
14	E Rubenis & Partners	4
	Glimstedt & Partneri	4
16	Rödl & Partner	3
	Volksons & Petersons	3
18	Advokatu birojs Petrovs un Taukacs	2
	Rozenfelds & Partners	2
	Stanislavska, Lepik & Luhaäär	2

These figures represent the total number of lawyers in this country only, and have been supplied by the firms themselves. The figures should be accurate as at 1 January 2004.

Advokatu birojs Petrovs un Taukacs maintains a close working relationship with KPMG.

As well as being a member of the *German-Latvian Lawyers Association*, **Sorainen Law Offices** has links with firms in Copenhagen, Stockholm and Warsaw.

FOREIGN OFFICES

With offices in Estonia, Lithuania and Finland, **Sorainen Law Offices** is the largest pan-Baltic law firm.

Glimstedt & Partneri is the Latvian office of Swedish firm **Advokatfirman Glimstedt**, which also has a successful office in Lithuania, operating as **Law Firm Bernotas & Dominas Glimstedt**. Partner Frederic Forsman divides his time between the two offices.

Helena Stanislavska is the name partner in **Stanislavska, Lepik & Luhaäär**, which is the Latvian office of Estonia's highly respected **Law Office Lepik & Luhaäär**.

LEGAL MARKET

During 2003, Latvia saw a dramatic change in the make-up of its legal market. Citing a 'difference in management philosophy', regional heavyweight *Klavins, Slaidins & Loze* split to form a number of new firms, the largest of which are **Klavins & Slaidins** and **Loze & Partners**.

Law Office Laine Skopina was also founded at the beginning of 2003 due to the reorganisation of *Klavins, Slaidins & Loze*, where Laine Skopina was a partner. Then, in June, *Lauris Liepa* and *Law Office Laine Skopina* merged to form **Liepa, Skopina/BORENIUS**.

Klavins & Slaidins and **Lejins, Torgans & Vonsovics** both offer a full corporate service and consequently dominate the Latvian legal market. However, the smaller Latvian firms are more than capable of rivalling these big players, often through the reputation of just one partner. That said, some of the smaller firms may find it hard to remain independent if foreign law firms move into Latvia after EU accession.

Latvia's legal system is being adapted to meet EU requirements. However, the judiciary is still in need of reform and requires more funding and resources. The system comprises a number of general courts, with the Supreme Court the highest authority in all criminal and civil cases. It is independent from political influence, but is sometimes considered inefficient as it often suffers from long delays.

BANKING AND FINANCE

'Responsive and proactive' **Klavins & Slaidins** represented the EBRD on a number of investments and loans in Latvia. It was counsel on the original €9m secured infrastructure loan to Riga Water Company and is currently working on a €9m increase of the loan. The firm provides annual survey reports to JPMorgan Chase, Northern Trust and State Street Bank.

During 2003, **Lejins, Torgans & Vonsovics** provided legal opinion to the banking syndicate formed by Merita on a multi-million euro guarantee facility to the electricity company, Latvenergo. Some of its lawyers were also Latvian law expert witnesses in court proceedings brought, in Sweden, by the administrator of an insolvent Latvian bank.

Highly regarded in the field of litigation, **Blueger & Plaude** represented Rietumu Bank in a number of cases in the Supreme Court of the Republic of Latvia. These included a case against the State Revenue Department, and another against LLC Leopard Productions on the collection of losses amounting to $2.3m from the bank.

Grunte & Cers boasts an impressive track record in the finance and banking sector. Its lawyers advise banks and financial institutions on investment projects and derivatives transactions.

Kronbergs Law Office provided legal advice on the closed share emission of a leading Latvian bank. It also represented a number of institutional investors and fund managers.

Well-respected **Liepa, Skopina/BORENIUS** advised a major bank with regard to many of its loans and equity investments in Latvia. The firm also assisted NORD/LB in its share acquisition in First Latvian Commercial Bank.

At **Skudra & Udris Law Offices** name partner Ziedonis Udris is renowned for 'getting results'. The firm advised a consortium of international banks, led by Latvian Perex Bank on a syndicated loan facility for the state-owned electricity company Latvernergo.

Sorainen Law Offices advised on a multi-million euro loan refinancing transaction on behalf of a UK company. It also provided legal advice to the IFC on a guarantee facility agreement for the leading Latvian commercial banks.

BANKING AND FINANCE

KLAVINS & SLAIDINS ✪
LEJINS, TORGANS & VONSOVICS ✪

Blueger & Plaude
Grunte & Cers
Kronbergs Law Office ✪
Liepa, Skopina/BORENIUS ✪
Skudra & Udris Law Offices ✪
Sorainen Law Offices ✪

Baltmane & Bitans ✪
Glimstedt & Partneri ✪
Hough, Vilcins, Seppälä & Palubinskas SIA
"MERKANTS", Law Office
Petrovs un Taukacs, Advokatu birojs
Valters Gencs, Law Offices of ✪

Firms are listed A-Z in tiers which are ranked in order of priority
✪ Indicates firm displays contact details at the end of this chapter.

Baltmane & Bitans has an excellent reputation for banking and finance matters.

Praised for providing 'innovative solutions to business issues', **Glimstedt & Partneri** represented NEFCO on its loan facility projects in Latvia. It also advised the insurance company ERGO on financial law issues in Latvia.

Hough, Vilcins, Seppälä & Palubinskas SIA offers an extensive range of banking services.

Law Office "MERKANTS" provides clients with strong banking and finance advice.

Among other things, **Advokatu birojs Petrovs un Taukacs** advised Latvia Trade Bank and drew up agreements for Nordia Bank.

During 2003, **Law Offices of Valters Gencs** acted for investors in relation to tax issues and legal due diligence involved in acquiring a Latvian bank.

CORPORATE AND COMMERCIAL

Despite the recent split of *Klavins, Slaidins & Loze*, **Klavins & Slaidins** maintains an enviable reputation in the Latvian legal market. Across the board, clients praise the services rendered and are pleased with 'excellent quality of work'. Name partners Filip Klaivins and Raymond Slaidins are 'real professionals', but above all are 'pleasant and easy to work with'. Aside from its restructuring, it has been a busy year for the firm. **Klavins & Slaidins** was legal counsel for HEX Plc in its acquisition of the Riga Stock Exchange and the Latvian Central Depository. In addition, the firm assisted with various Latvian legal issues arising from HEX's merger with OM AB.

Lejins, Torgans & Vonsovics continues to provide clients with 'quality and value'. In 2003, two new associates joined the firm: Ms Klimovica, previously a legal consultant with the Finances and Capital Markets Commission of Latvia, and Ms Smilgaine who previously practised with KPMG. The firm performed due diligence on eight Latvian-registered companies in connection with Stora Enso Group's cross-border acquisition of Sylvester Group of companies.

'Highly focused' **Baltmane & Bitans** advised a client on the acquisition of shares in a subsidiary of an internationally known beverage company. In 2003, the firm assisted Norwegian sellers, Reitangruppen, in the sale of a chain of perfumery shops in Latvia.

Grunte & Cers continues to operate as one of the most respected law firms in Latvia. Renowned for its work in M&A, the firm boasts an extensive list of national and international clients. Name partner Gundars Cers is well known for his arbitration work.

At **Kronbergs Law Office**, name partner Valter Kronbergs is praised for his 'excellent strategic abilities' and 'knowledge of commercial issues'. The firm is currently involved in a six-company restructuring/merger project. Its client list includes a variety of household names.

Formerly with *Klavins, Slaidins & Loze*, 'extremely talented' Anita Tomberga stayed with Janis Loze following the split. The resulting **Loze & Partners** has retained longstanding clients who admire the firm's 'good value and excellence' and its 'quick response times'. Janis Loze has been the leading legal adviser for the two fuel traders, Neste and Statoil, for more than six years and has been providing assistance in drafting numerous business-related contracts. The firm also represents the Finnish pharmaceutical company Tamro.

With its connections across the Baltic States, clients are impressed with **Sorainen Law Offices** because of its 'quick assistance' and 'expertise in all fields of business law'. The firm was involved in the sale of several of Skanska's businesses in Latvia. It also assisted Coca-Cola Nordic in the legal aspects of marketing activities in the Baltic States.

Name partner Baiba Plaude of **Blueger & Plaude** has an excellent reputation for litigation. The firm continues to be involved in establishing new companies and re-registering others in accordance with the Commercial Code.

Peteris Dalderis and Erik Blumbergs at **Glimstedt & Partneri** are two highly regarded lawyers. Clients are 'very satisfied with the firm's level of expertise' and find it to be 'very responsive to urgent requests'. The firm advised Swedish construction company, PEAB, in its capacity as general contractor on a project for Finnish retail trade company, Stockmann, in Riga. It also represented General Electric in its acquisition of a major leasing company in Latvia.

Clients of newly merged **Liepa, Skopina/ BORENIUS** are 'absolutely satisfied' with services and commend the firm for 'treating every customer as someone special'. The firm assisted Group 4 Falck when it acquired cash- handling businesses of three major banks in Latvia. It also advised on the acquisition of Olympus Optical Co with its distributing company in Latvia.

Advokatu birojs Petrovs un Taukacs has very good relations with its clients, who agree the firm has 'exemplary standards of practice'. In 2003, the firm advised Stockmann on various commercial law issues with respect to starting its business in Latvia. It also advised ASVA and Latvian Trade Bank.

At **Skudra & Udris Law Offices**, name partner Ziedonis Udris is known for litigation. The firm advised Accenture and British Telecom on establishing their business operations in Latvia.

Clients of **Law Offices Of Valters Gencs** praise the 'quick and proactive' firm. Recent instructions have included the Baltic expansion of the French cosmetic company L'Oréal into Lithuania and Estonia.

During 2003, among other transactions, **Law Office B2B** was involved in the merger of two major Latvian grain producers.

Hough, Vilcins, Seppälä & Palubinskas SIA advises on corporate incorporation, foundation agreements and shareholder agreements.

Law Office "MERKANTS" advises the biggest ferry company in Latvia, Riga Sealine. Other clients include Eden Springs – a water cooler company, and a major juice production company

In 2003, **Rozenfelds & Partners** provided legal opinions for such enterprises as Lavijas Gaze and Tilts Communications in international arbitration proceedings against the Republic of Latvia.

'Always alert' Helen Stanislavska of **Stanislavska, Lepik & Luhaäär** is applauded by clients for 'ensuring things run as smoothly as possible' during the transition period to the EU. The firm assisted Lafarge Tekkin, Colgate-Palmolive and Pfizer with drafting contracts and numerous other services.

CORPORATE AND COMMERCIAL

KLAVINS & SLAIDINS ✪
LEJINS, TORGANS & VONSOVICS ✪

Baltmane & Bitans ✪
Grunte & Cers
Kronbergs Law Office ✪
Loze & Partners ✪
Sorainen Law Offices ✪

Blueger & Plaude
Glimstedt & Partneri ✪
Liepa, Skopina/BORENIUS ✪
Petrovs un Taukacs, Advokatu birojs
Skudra & Udris Law Offices ✪
Valters Gencs, Law Offices of ✪

B2B, Law Office
Hough, Vilcins, Seppälä & Palubinskas SIA
"MERKANTS", Law Office
Rozenfelds & Partners ✪
Stanislavska, Lepik & Luhaäär

Firms are listed A-Z in tiers which are ranked in order of priority
✪ *Indicates firm displays contact details at the end of this chapter.*

FOREIGN INVESTMENT

Klavins & Slaidins is counsel for Metsliitto Cooperative, one of Finland's largest forestry co-operatives and pulp producers, who established a joint venture with the Latvian government to perform all preparatory work and construct a $900m pulp plant in Latvia. Both Filip Klavins and Raymond Slaidins were born and bred in the US, where they are members of the Bar.

A recent highlight for **Lejins, Torgans & Vonsovics** was advising the Danish real estate investment fund, Baltic Property Trust. In addition, it provided advice to a group of investors in connection with the development of the territory in the centre of Riga for a multi-purpose hall (to be built for the 2006 Ice Hockey Championship in Riga).

Kronbergs Law Office assists numerous foreign companies establishing legal entities in Latvia. It works with a good mix of big local firms and foreign companies. The firm is well known for assisting Microsoft on its establishment in Latvia.

About 90% of **Sorainen Law Offices**' clients are international companies. The firm advised the European developer, TK Development, on matters

FOREIGN INVESTMENT

KLAVINS & SLAIDINS ⭘
LEJINS, TORGANS & VONSOVICS ⭘

Kronbergs Law Office ⭘
Sorainen Law Offices ⭘

Baltmane & Bitans ⭘
Blueger & Plaude
Glimstedt & Partneri ⭘
Grunte & Cers
Liepa, Skopina/BORENIUS ⭘
Loze & Partners ⭘
Petrovs un Taukacs, Advokatu birojs
Skudra & Udris Law Offices ⭘
Valters Gencs, Law Offices of ⭘

Hough, Vilcins, Seppälä & Palubinskas SIA
Rozenfelds & Partners ⭘
Stanislavska, Lepik & Luhaäär

Firms are listed A-Z in tiers which are ranked in order of priority
⭘ *Indicates firm displays contact details at the end of this chapter.*

regarding commercial property acquisitions and development issues. It also represented a Dutch investment company in the acquisition of an office building in Riga with the value exceeding €10m.

The majority of **Baltmane & Bitans**' clients are foreign investors. The firm maintains an excellent reputation.

In 2003, widely praised firm **Blueger & Plaude** took on numerous projects involving foreign investment.

A recent highlight for **Glimstedt & Partneri** was assisting one of the largest pharmaceutical companies in the world.

Although best known for serving domestic clients, **Grunte & Cers** also advises several foreign investors.

'Extremely knowledgeable' **Liepa, Skopina/ BORENIUS** assisted a Russian company with its investing needs.

Loze & Partners represents the business activities of TeliaSonera in the Republic of Latvia, including its shareholding in Lattelekom, the Latvian telecoms company, amounting to $600m.

With the assistance of **Advokatu birojs Petrovs un Taukacs**, one of the largest Swedish wood exporters adjusted its capital and corporate structure in 2003. It also assisted a UK-based company with the purchase of shares in the largest Latvian IT company.

Skudra & Udris Law Offices advised foreign investors on the acquisition of the Latvian shipping company Amberholding Latvia.

Law Offices of Valters Gencs mainly represents investors from the Nordic countries, France and the US. It is also involved in some projects with German and UK investors.

Hough, Vilcins, Seppälä & Palubinskas SIA continues to represent several companies in connection with investing in the Baltic region.

Rozenfelds & Partners provided services to Amber Venture Partners in relation to investing in Latvia.

Stanislavska, Lepik & Luhaäär has excellent relations with its foreign investor clients.

INTELLECTUAL PROPERTY

Law firms must be registered with the Latvian patent and trade mark office in order to carry out IP work in Latvia. No registration is needed for copyright work.

The office of attorney Ineta Krodere-Imsa was founded in co-operation with **Grunte & Cers**. She is known as one of the leading experts of IP law in Latvia. The firm offers a range of legal services with respect to copyright, patents and trade marks, and other issues relating to intellectual property rights.

At **Loze & Partners**, Ivea Judinskса has an excellent reputation for IP matters.

Rozenfelds & Partners successfully represented JSC Latvijas Balzams, the major producer of alcoholic beverages in Latvia, in trade mark disputes.

Founded in 1991, **Agency Tria Robit** offers a range of services in the field of intellectual property.

A recent highlight for **Baltmane & Bitans** was representing the largest recording company in Latvia. The firm also successfully represented a number of clients in patent, trade mark, and copyright protection.

Raymond Slaidins of **Klavins & Slaidins** is a registered trade mark agent. The firm has a regular and ongoing trade mark practice.

Kronbergs Law Office continues to act as legal counsel to Microsoft, and is involved in a multiplicity of licensing and other IT-related agreements.

Lejins, Torgans & Vonsovics provides advice on IP protection measures and the maintenance of registration for household names such as Gillette, Sunkist Growers, Velux and Hugo Boss. The firm has two qualified patent attorneys who advise on trade marks.

Liepa, Skopina/BORENIUS has enjoyed growth in its IP practice.

Law Office "MERKANTS" advises numerous local musicians on IP matters, while **Skudra & Udris Law Offices** boasts a senior lawyer, specialising in IP, who has recently been involved in high-profile litigation.

Sorainen Law Offices has an excellent reputation for trade marks. It recently represented Stockmann Oy, the major supermarket chain, in registering a great number of trade marks in Latvia.

At **Stanislavska, Lepik & Luhaäär** lawyers prepare contracts for local and national writers.

Law Offices of Valters Gencs provides services in the patent, trade mark, design and trade secret fields. It arranged a licensing agreement for a famous Latvian opera singer with a recording studio in the UK.

INTELLECTUAL PROPERTY

GRUNTE & CERS
LOZE & PARTNERS ⭘
ROZENFELDS & PARTNERS ⭘

Agency Tria Robit
Baltmane & Bitans ⭘
Klavins & Slaidins ⭘
Kronbergs Law Office ⭘
Lejins, Torgans & Vonsovics ⭘
Liepa, Skopina/BORENIUS ⭘
"MERKANTS", Law Office
Skudra & Udris Law Offices ⭘
Sorainen Law Offices ⭘
Stanislavska, Lepik & Luhaäär
Valters Gencs, Law Offices of ⭘

Firms are listed A-Z in tiers which are ranked in order of priority
⭘ *Indicates firm displays contact details at the end of this chapter.*

REAL ESTATE AND CONSTRUCTION

In 2003, **Blueger & Plaude** was involved in high-profile proceedings before both the Constitutional Court and the Supreme Court of the Republic of Latvia.

Klavins & Slaidins continues to advise Skanska on various property matters in Latvia, in particular on Riga's prestigious Valdemara Centre. The firm also prepared agreements and negotiated transactions on behalf of several foreign investor clients.

Lejins, Torgans & Vonsovics advises an extensive number of real estate companies and investment funds on a diverse range of issues.

Liepa, Skopina/BORENIUS represents buyers and sellers of major commercial property in Latvia. It assisted Mid-Baltic Realty in several building acquisitions in the heart of Riga. The firm's other clients include Spire Baltics.

Lawyers at **Baltmane & Bitans** counsel clients in relation to all real estate issues. The firm assisted a major Latvian alcoholic beverages company in the construction of new warehouses. It also advised the Latvian National Post in the construction of a mail sorting centre.

Glimstedt & Partneri represents a major real estate developer in its ongoing expansion in Latvia.

Grunte & Cers offers a number of services ranging from the purchase or leasing of real estate, to providing advice on construction activities.

Kronbergs Law Office regularly provides advice to large property investors, while **Loze & Partners** represents major real estate developers, including Norwegian companies Linstow Varner and ICA group.

In 2003, **Advokatu birojs Petrovs un Taukacs** assisted NCC Industry and its subsidiaries with land renting issues and the sale of a building and assets.

In addition to assisting HeidelbergCement Group, **Sorainen Law Offices** also advised a Dutch investment company with a Latvian property acquisition.

REAL ESTATE AND CONSTRUCTION

BLUEGER & PLAUDE
KLAVINS & SLAIDINS ✪
LEJINS, TORGANS & VONSOVICS ✪
LIEPA, SKOPINA/BORENIUS ✪

Baltmane & Bitans ✪
Glimstedt & Partneri ✪
Grunte & Cers
Kronbergs Law Office ✪
Loze & Partners ✪
Petrovs un Taukacs, Advokatu birojs
Sorainen Law Offices ✪
Valters Gencs, Law Offices of ✪

B2B, Law Office
Hough, Vilcins, Seppälä & Palubinskas SIA
"MERKANTS", Law Office
Rozenfelds & Partners ✪
Skudra & Udris Law Offices ✪

Firms are listed A-Z in tiers which are ranked in order of priority
✪ *Indicates firm displays contact details at the end of this chapter.*

SHIPPING AND TRANSPORT

SORAINEN LAW OFFICES ✪

Grunte & Cers
Kronbergs Law Office ✪
Liepa, Skopina/BORENIUS ✪
Rozenfelds & Partners ✪
Valters Gencs, Law Offices of ✪

Firms are listed A-Z in tiers which are ranked in order of priority
✪ *Indicates firm displays contact details at the end of this chapter.*

TAX

BALTMANE & BITANS ✪
KRONBERGS LAW OFFICE ✪
PETROVS UN TAUKACS, ADVOKATU BIROJS
VALTERS GENCS, LAW OFFICES OF ✪

Blueger & Plaude
Glimstedt & Partneri ✪
Klavins & Slaidins ✪
Loze & Partners ✪
Sorainen Law Offices ✪

Firms are listed A-Z in tiers which are ranked in order of priority
✪ *Indicates firm displays contact details at the end of this chapter.*

Law Offices of Valters Gencs provided legal services to a Croatian construction company in relation to a governmental contract worth $150m.

Law Office B2B was involved in the settlement of a major construction dispute.

Hough, Vilcins, Seppälä & Palubinskas SIA advises on numerous real estate related issues.

Irish and American companies use **Law Office "MERKANTS"** to organise the purchase and financing of real estate.

Rozenfelds & Partners continues to be active in the field of commercial property.

Skudra & Udris Law Offices has a number of foreign clients it assists with real estate activities.

SHIPPING AND TRANSPORT

At **Sorainen Law Offices** 'well-connected' and 'well-qualified' Gints Vilgerts has an unsurpassed reputation. The firm acted on behalf of a leading Nordic shipowners' defence club, in attempts to arrest ships in Latvia following a collision in a Latvian port. It was also involved in litigation on behalf of one of the world's largest container carriers against several local road carriers.

In the field of maritime law, **Grunte & Cers** has successfully represented a range of foreign clients.

Kronbergs Law Office provided advice in relation to one of the largest shipping companies in Eastern Europe.

Among other things, **Liepa, Skopina/ BORENIUS** advises on the developing of cargo routes.

Name partner Janis Rozenfelds at **Rozenfelds & Partners** is described as a 'real diamond'. His firm handled a case, connected with privatisation issues, over an insurance payment owed by a Latvian shipping company.

Law Offices of Valters Gencs acted for the Latvian State as counsel in arbitration in Denmark regarding a maritime claim from a Swedish company.

TAX

With its PwC connection **Baltmane & Bitans** boasts sound tax expertise and has been involved with various issues including corporate income tax, VAT, real estate tax, and other applicable taxes and dues. In 2003, the firm appealed against State Revenue Service decisions on behalf of several Latvian and international companies.

Kronbergs Law Office offers an extensive range of tax services. The firm provides advice on corporate restructuring to many different companies, including two major Latvian oil transit companies; an Icelandic owned timber company, and two Swedish-owned telecoms companies. It also provides tax advice on domestic and international trade transactions, including analysis of VAT and customs treatment.

Associated with KPMG's legal arm, **Advokatu birojs Petrovs un Taukacs** has an excellent reputation. It assisted with tax audit and planning for the largest Latvian brewery, and advised Siemens SIA in resolving an international trade planning issue.

Law Offices of Valters Gencs has an outstanding reputation for tax litigation. The firm also employs a tax adviser from Ernst & Young who advises on VAT, payroll and corporate income tax for companies.

Blueger & Plaude is involved in various tax matters, including litigation while **Glimstedt & Partneri** maintains a good reputation for tax. Clients include HRX, a Finnish transportation company.

For the 'business-minded' **Klavins & Slaidins** the development of its tax department is a priority.

Loze & Partners is well regarded for its comprehensive range of tax services.

Sorainen Law Offices advises clients on tax issues ranging from product distribution, to analysing VAT and corporate income tax implications.

BALTMANE & BITANS

19 KR VALDEMARA IELA
1010 RIGA

Telephone: +371 709 4430
Fax: +371 709 4431
E-mail:
advokati.attorneys@lv.landwellglobal.com
Website: www.landwellglobal.com

Languages
English, Latvian

Number of lawyers 8

Contact
Lita Knopkena

International groupings
Landwell, correspondent law firms of PricewaterhouseCoopers

CATEGORIES OF WORK

Administrative law and procedure Maris Vainovskis	**Employment** Ilze Baltmane, Dace Cirule
EU and competition Maris Vainovskis, Lelde Lavina	**Insolvency/corporate restructuring** Agris Bitans, Maris Vainovskis
Corporate and commercial Ilze Baltmane, Janis Plavins	**Intellectual property** Agris Bitans
Real estate, commercial property Zinta Jansons, Lelde Lavina	**Media and entertainment** Agris Bitans
Construction Ilze Baltmane, Agris Bitans	**Foreign direct investment** Zinta Jansons, Janis Plavins
Litigation and arbitration Agris Bitans	**Mergers and acquisitions** Ilze Baltmane, Kristine Stege
E-commerce, IT and telecoms Agris Bitans, Maris Vainovskis	**Tax** Ilze Baltmane, Zinta Jansons

THE FIRM

Baltmane & Bitans is a correspondent law firm of Landwell, one of the largest international law practices with 2,850 business and tax lawyers worldwide. Landwell provides a full range of legal services, through specialists organised in global networks. The firm's main focus is on cross-border M&A transactions and corporate transformation projects. The firm is a market leader in the design and delivery of complex corporate change. This is achieved through a focus on strong local capabilities allied with a global outlook and by ensuring that the firm's implementation skills match its legal ones.

AREAS OF PRACTICE

The firm's lawyers assist and counsel clients in relation to all real estate issues, including acquisition, mortgages and other interests in real estate, commercial leasing, construction contracts and subcontracts, and other property and construction-related issues.

Baltmane & Bitans provides representation in most aspects of commercial law and competition law, including the formation, operation and disposition of business entities such as private and public limited companies, partnerships and joint ventures. The office has provided services to a number of local and international companies in respect of different competition law issues in Latvia, including co-operation agreements, joint ventures, distribution, and franchise and licence agreements, as well as notification of agreements to the Latvian authorities. The firm's experts provide advice in connection with contesting and defending alleged unfair market practices, such as abuse of dominant market position and anti-competitive agreements.

The firm's attorneys have successfully represented a number of clients in patent, trade mark and copyright protection and other legal disputes over intellectual property issues, including representation of the largest recording company in Latvia.

Baltmane & Bitans has accumulated valuable expertise in various cases involving corporate income tax, VAT, real estate tax and other applicable taxes and duties. Recent work includes appealing on behalf of several Latvian and international companies against State Revenue Service decisions.

GLIMSTEDT & PARTNERS

JERUZALEMES 1
1010 RIGA

Telephone: +371 701 6700
Fax: +371 701 6701
E-mail: riga@glimstedt.lv
Website: www.glimstedt.se

Languages
English, French, German, Latvian, Lithuanian, Russian, Spanish, Swedish

Other offices
Vilnius

Number of lawyers 33
at this office 8

CATEGORIES OF WORK

- **Company and commercial**
- **Banking and finance**
- **Mergers and acquisitions**
- **Privatisation**
- **Competition law**
- **Insolvency and business restructuring**
- **Intellectual property**
- **Telecommunications and information technology law**
- **Advertising and media**
- **Insurance**
- **Litigation, arbitration, dispute resolution**
- **Real estate and construction**
- **International trade and transportation**
- **Labour law**

KLAVINS & SLAIDINS

KR VALDEMARA 21
1010 RIGA

Telephone: +371 703 5222
Fax: +371 703 5252
E-mail: advokati@klavinsslaidins.lv
Website: www.klavinsslaidins.lv

Languages
English, German, Latvian, Russian

Number of lawyers 12

Member
Lex Mundi; World Services Group;
International Bar Association;
International Association of Young Lawyers

CATEGORIES OF WORK

Foreign investment in Latvia
Filip Klavins, Raymond Slaidins

Mergers and acquisitions
Filip Klavins, Raymond Slaidins

Banking and finance
Egons Pikelis

Litigation and arbitration
Daiga Zivtina, Ilga Gudrenika-Krebs

Real property
Liene Ciguze

Corporate and commercial
Filip Klavins, Raymond Slaidins

Employment, labour
Sanda Lace

European Union
Inese Lazdupe, Mikus Buls

Competition
Liga Hartmane, Sanda Lace

Intellectual property
Ilga Gudrenika-Krebs

Securities
Egons Pikelis

Tax
Elina Girne-Berzina

THE FIRM

Klavins & Slaidins is one of the pre-eminent law firms in Latvia, with a reputation for personal contact and superior legal work that sets it apart from its competitors. Filip Klavins and Raymond Slaidins, both USA attorneys of Latvian descent, began practising law in Latvia in 1992. The firm now has 12 lawyers in all and is one of the largest law firms in Latvia. Each of the firm's lawyers is fluent in Latvian and English, and the firm also has fluent Russian and German language capabilities. Three of the lawyers add valuable foreign experience to the firm, having been born and raised, educated and trained in law in the USA (two lawyers) and England.

The firm's lawyers have been at the centre of many of the most important legal matters in Latvia, and the entire team prides itself on maintaining the highest quality in its work product and the strength of its well-established reputation.

The firm is listed in most important law directories, and has the responsibility for preparing and revising the *Martindale-Hubbell Law Directory*, the prominent internationally published digest of Latvian law.

Klavins & Slaidins is concerned about its social environment. The firm donates its time and services to law schools and other worthy non-legal causes. It strives to set a best-practices example in ethics. The firm will not represent a client if the client or the goal of the representation is not completely ethical in substance – form is not enough.

Some of the important areas of activity by members of the firm include: membership of the boards of directors of American and British Chambers of Commerce in Latvia; member of the board and work as arbitrators at the Latvian Chamber of Commerce arbitration tribunal; lecturing at the Riga Graduate School of Law, at the University of Latvia Law Faculty and at the training centre for judges.

Klavins and Slaidins is active in the International Bar Association and the Foreign Investors Council in Latvia.

AREAS OF PRACTICE

Klavins & Slaidins is a specialist in transactions, especially those that are sophisticated or which present unusual circumstances where the firm can use its long years of experience to craft innovative and practical solutions. Klavins & Slaidins is a trusted and reliable outside corporate counsel, helping to fine tune the daily life of businesses. The firm is a fierce advocate for its clients, whether in negotiations or when formal dispute settlement procedures cannot be avoided and the client is in court or arbitration. The firm is international, with lawyers having practised in, and admitted to, the bars in the US and the UK, adding an additional depth of vision when it provides legal advice about Latvia to clients far beyond Latvia's borders.

Klavins & Slaidins' international practice is enhanced by its membership of the network of leading law firms in jurisdictions all over the world, Lex Mundi.

Klavins & Slaidins' general area of practice is business/commercial law. The firm provides legal consultation and advice to international clients coming to Latvia from all over the world, as well as experienced guidance for local Latvian clients. Klavins & Slaidins specialises in work as outside general counsel for a great many clients, as well as transactional expertise in sophisticated areas of corporate and joint venture structuring, mergers and acquisitions, sale and lease of business and property, loan documentation, all manner of contracts, privatisation, banking and securities, labour law and tax.

KRONBERGS LAW OFFICE

11 NOVEMBRA KRASTMALA 23
1050 RIGA

Telephone: +371 7 043 801
Fax: +371 7 043 804
E-mail: advocate@lv.eylaw.com
Website: www.kronbergs.lv

Languages
English, Latvian, Russian

Number of lawyers 14

Contact
Valters Kronbergs

Member
EY Law

CATEGORIES OF WORK

General practice	Securities
Company law	Finance
Corporate law	Telecommunications law
Mergers and acquisitions	Energy law
Competition law	Environmental law
Real estate	Maritime law
Leases and leasing	Shipping
Business law	European Union law
Privatisation	Construction law
Foreign investment	Debt collection
International commercial law	Labour and employment
Intellectual property	Tax law
Banking law	Civil litigation law

LEJINS, TORGANS & VONSOVICS

20 KR VALDEMARA IELA
1010 RIGA

Telephone: +371 782 1525
Fax: +371 782 1524
E-mail: lt–v@lt–v.lv
Website: www.lt–v.lv

Languages
English, Polish, Russian

Number of lawyers 11

Member
Meritas

CATEGORIES OF WORK

Banking and finance
Andrejs Lielkalns

Commercial property, real estate
Guntars Zile

Competition
Dace Silava-Tomsone

Commercial
Girts Lejins

Corporate
Dace Silava-Tomsone

Dispute resolution, litigation and arbitration
Romualds Vonsovics

Foreign investments
Girts Lejins

Insolvency, corporate restructuring
Iveta Mikelsone

Labour
Toms Sulmanis

Mergers and acquisitions
Dace Silava-Tomsone

Privatisation
Girts Lejins

Intellectual property
Romualds Vonsovics

Securities
Andrejs Lielkalns

Tax
Ieva Smilgaine

LIEPA, SKOPINA/BORENIUS

BLAUMANA 5A
1011 RIGA

Telephone: +371 7 201 800
Fax: +371 7 201 801
E-mail: advokati@borenius.lv
Website: www.borenius.lv

Languages
English, Finnish, French, German, Russian, Swedish

Number of lawyers 10

International groupings
In association with Borenius & Kemppinen (Helsinki); Luiga, Mugu & Borenius (Tallinn)

CATEGORIES OF WORK

Banking and finance	Litigation, ADR and arbitration
Capital markets	Maritime, shipping and transport
Commercial property	Mergers and acquisitions
Company and commercial	Private equity and venture capital
EU	Privatisation
Electronic commerce	Real estate
Foreign investments	Securities
IP/IT, broadcasting and media law	Tax law
Labour	

LOZE & PARTNERS

BLAUMANA IELA 22
1011 RIGA

Telephone: +371 783 0000
Fax: +371 783 0001
E-mail: advokati@loze.lv
Website: www.loze.lv

Languages
English, Latvian, Russian

Number of lawyers 14

International groupings
IBA; AIJA; TAGlaw

CATEGORIES OF WORK

Structuring and implementation of business transactions	**EU and competition law**
Real estate	**Mergers and acquisitions**
Intellectual property	**Corporate recovery and restructuring**
Litigation and arbitration	**Tax and financial advice**
Telecommunications and energy	**Employment and immigration**

THE FIRM

Loze & Partners has been operating under its current name since 2003, although the office has existed and has been providing legal services to its clients for more than a decade. The firm comprises 14 lawyers in all, of which four are partners and ten are associate lawyers. Loze & Kokins, an associated tax consulting firm, provides tax services.

The objective of the firm's day-to-day activities is to prove that Loze & Partners sets the top quality standard for legal services in Latvia and abroad. By providing legal advice to clients operating in Latvia's booming economy, the firm has attained the highest professional level and has become one of the leaders in the Latvian legal community. In order to provide advice, act efficiently and gain the appreciation of its clients, the firm exhibits a degree of courage in accepting full responsibility for its actions and opinions, working with an open mind and be willing to pursue atypical courses of action. The firm's intention is to remain the best and most reliable adviser to its clients and collaboration partners.

AREAS OF PRACTICE

Loze & Partners' general area of practice is business/commercial law. The firm provides legal consultation and advice to international clients coming to Latvia from all over the world, as well as experienced guidance for local Latvian clients. The firm emphasises work as outside general counsel for many clients, as well as transactional expertise in sophisticated areas of corporate and joint venture structuring, mergers and acquisitions, sale and lease of business and property, loan documentation, contracts, privatisation, banking and securities, and labour law. The firm has individual experts who work in the areas of intellectual property, telecommunications law and energy law. The firm provides due diligence and legal advice to foreign banks lending in Latvia, as well as with respect to loans granted to Latvian banks by foreign financial institutions.

The firm handles the design and implementation of tax efficient structures, corporate and shareholding structuring, structuring of business transactions such as sales, purchases, leasing and rent, financing and borrowing, transactions with intangible assets, import and export, and repatriation of profits. The firm advises on compliance assurance, tax reviews and tax due diligence and on disputes with authorities, and also provides professional advice on financial accounting matters.

The firm's established domestic clients include IBM, Linstow Varner, Microsoft, Norddeutsche Landesbank, Continental, TeliaSonera, RMC Group, Nokia, Kodak and many more internationally prominent businesses. Loze & Partners has been actively working on behalf of Neste and Statoil on their ongoing major oil terminal project in the Riga Port through successive levels of administrative co-ordination, approval and planning.

The firm's lawyers are active members of a number of professional and non-governmental organisations. Some of the important areas of activity by Loze & Partners staff members include the Latvian international arbitration tribunal, the board of directors of WWF Latvia, the board of directors of the Soros Foundation-Latvia, and the board of directors of Junior Achievement Latvia. The firm's staff is united in its conviction to spend as much time as possible assisting Latvian causes on a pro bono basis.

ROZENFELDS & PARTNERS

BLAUMANA STREET 11/13, APT 8
1011 RIGA

Telephone: +371 782 1563
Fax: +371 724 2202
E-mail: law@rozenfelds.lv
Website: www.rozenfelds.lv

Languages
English, Russian

Number of lawyers 2

Contact
Janis Rozenfelds

CATEGORIES OF WORK

Intellectual property – trade marks, copyright
Janis Rozenfelds

Real estate
Janis Rozenfelds

Litigation and arbitration
Janis Rozenfelds

Competition law
Janis Rozenfelds

Corporate law
Inese Ciema

Claims of damages
Inese Ciema

Labour disputes
Inese Ciema

Maritime law
Inese Ciema

SKUDRA & UDRIS

MARIJAS IELA 13
1050 RIGA

Telephone: +371 7 812 078
Fax: +371 7 828 171
E-mail: attorneys@su.lv
Website: www.su.lv

Languages
English, German, Russian

Number of lawyers 8

Contact
Ziedonis Udris

CATEGORIES OF WORK

Banking and finance
A Skudra

Mergers and acquisitions
A Skudra

Corporate finance
A Skudra

Litigation
Z Udris

Arbitration
Z Udris

Real property
Z Udris, I Berzina

Commercial law
Z Udris, M Krumins

Corporate law
A Skudra, Z Udris

EU and competition law
Z Udris

Shipping and transport
Z Udris

Media and entertainment
M Krumins

Energy and infrastructure projects
Z Udris

Intellectual property
M Krumins

Employment law
A Skudra

SORAINEN LAW OFFICES

KR VALDEMARA IELA 21
1010 RIGA

Telephone: +371 7 365 000
Fax: +371 7 365 001
E-mail: sorainen@sorainen.lv
Website: www.sorainen.com

Languages
English, Estonian, Finnish, French, German, Lithuanian, Polish, Russian, Spanish, Swedish

Other offices
Helsinki, Tallinn, Vilnius

Number of lawyers 37
at this office 12

CATEGORIES OF WORK

Banking, finance and securities
Girts Ruda, Daimars Skutans

Property, construction and environmental law
Daimars Skutans, Arnis Salnajs

Mergers and acquisitions
Gints Vilgerts, Girts Ruda

International trade, distribution and services
Agris Repss, Eva Berlaus-Gulbe

Shipping, maritime and transport
Gints Vilgerts, Daimars Skutans

Debt collection and insolvency
Girts Ruda, Agris Repss

Litigation and arbitration
Agris Repss, Daimars Skutans

Immigration law
Ieva Bela, Ieva Lokastova

Intellectual property rights, IT and e-business law
Brigita Terauda

Company law
Eva Berlaus-Gulbe, Brigita Terauda

Employment law
Agris Repss

Insurance law
Gints Vilgerts

Competition and EU law
Eva Berlaus-Gulbe, Edgars Koskins

Energy and public procurement law
Eva Berlaus-Gulbe

Tax and administrative law
Edgars Koskins

LAW OFFICES OF VALTERS GENCS

3RD FLOOR
VALDEMARA CENTER
VALDEMARA STREET 21
1010 RIGA

Telephone: +371 724 00 90
Fax: +371 724 00 91
E-mail: valters.gencs@gencs.lv
Website: www.gencs.lv

Languages
English, German, Russian

Number of lawyers 7

Contact
Valters Gencs (advocate)

Member
International Bar Association; Latvian Bar Association; Licensing Executives Society; International Trade Mark Association

CATEGORIES OF WORK	
Business law	Art law
Tax	Corporate transactions
Litigation and arbitration	Immigration and labour
Finance and banking	Intellectual property
Insolvency	Due diligence
Entertainment law	Real property
Competition	Company law
Mergers and aquisitions	Government contracts

THE FIRM

The Law Offices of Valters Gencs is a full-service, general practice, international business law firm focused on tax, litigation, corporate, immigration, finance and intellectual property law. The firm was established in 2000 by founding partner Valters Gencs and was previously part of the Ernst & Young Law network of law firms.

The firm is an active member of the Latvian Bar Association and International Bar Association, as well as foreign chambers of commerce in Latvia and international intellectual property professional associations, which gives the firm access to a global knowledge base.

The firm's staff comprises of five lawyers and one tax adviser. The firm's lawyers have previous experience of working with the Enterprise Register of Latvia, as well as the Ministry of Finance, the Ministry of Foreign Affairs and the European Integration Bureau. Members of the firm have lectured on tax and commercial law issues with the Stockholm School of Economics in Riga.

The firm's representative clients include multinational companies, as well as medium-size companies and entrepreneurial growth companies. The firm has also represented the government of Latvia in an international arbitration case in Denmark and Sweden.

Publicly-disclosed representative clients include: Statoil ASA (Denmark); Nestlé SA (Switzerland); Alstom Power (Sweden); L'Oreal (France); Wyeth Pharmaceuticals (UK); Old Bushmills Distillery & Co (Ireland); Coca-Cola (USA); Oracle (USA); Mitsubishi Chemical Media (Japan).

AREAS OF PRACTICE

Tax: Tax planning and optimisation; international cross-border transactions; VAT; social security; corporate income tax; withholding taxes; personal taxation, including filling of annual tax returns for expatriates; representation before tax authorities; appeal of tax assessments; preparation of declarations; arranging residence certificates according to double taxation agreements; property tax; payroll taxes; VAT representations and registration; excise tax; packaging tax; natural resource tax; state dues; land transfer dues; individual clients; tax audits; accounting consulting.

Litigation and arbitration: Arbitrating before the Latvian Chamber of Commerce and Industry; representation of clients with all the courts in the Republic of Latvia, including the Supreme Court and arbitrations.

Business law: Registrations with a commercial register; company establishments and start-ups; company restructuring and reorganisation; liquidations; mergers and acquisitions; contracts; real estate; mortgages and pledges; security interests; work contracts; registered office services; EU law.

Immigration: Arranging visas and residence permits for expatriates in Latvia, arranging work permits for expatriates, appealing decisions of immigration authorities.

Insolvency: Representing creditors within company insolvency procedures; purchases of assets from insolvent companies; criminal proceedings against bad-faith debtors.

Insurance: EU funds; arranging credit facilities; representing borrowing and lending entities; finance, including corporate finance; management consults.

Investments: Securing for legal protections of foreign investment in Latvia; application of investment protection treaties to dispute regarding changing of investment climate; securing of financial investments; investments in energy sector and infrastructure.

Intellectual property: Registering patents, trade marks, designs and mask works with the Latvian Patent Office; patent and trade mark protection management within the Baltic States and the rest of the former USSR; licensing and franchising of IP; unfair competitors and protection of know-how and trade secrets; valuation of IP; royalties; technology transfer.

Due diligence: Tax due diligence before company acquisitions; legal due diligence; post-acquisitions due diligence.

For further information please visit the firm's website or contact directly.

LEBANON

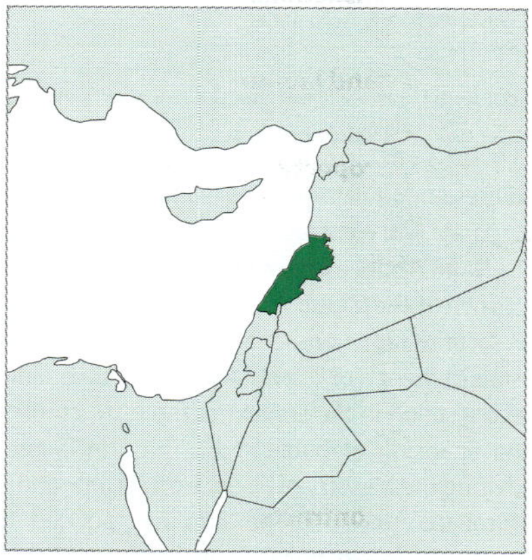

Population	**3.8 million**
Number of lawyers	**8,000**
Professional title	**Avocat à la cour**
Currency	**Lebanese pound (L£)**

Index

At the heart of the Middle East, Lebanon lies between Syria to the north and east, and Israel to the south. Beirut, the capital, is its major port, and has long been the convergence point of trade routes, the meeting place for a variety of people and the foundation of Lebanon's uniquely diverse and rich national culture.

Lebanon boasts free-market investment policies, a liberal economic environment and an entrepreneurial private sector, setting itself apart from its regional neighbours. Lebanon not only has one of the most advanced infrastructures in the Middle East (although the rail system was damaged by the civil war), it prizes itself on its most valuable asset: a highly educated, multi-lingual and highly skilled workforce, one of the best in the region. It has progressed, despite continuing recovery from a ravaging 16-year civil war, to become a regional and international hub for trade, finance, services, industry, culture and tourism.

However, since the re-opening of Beirut Stock Exchange (BSE) in 1995 the market has failed to match expectation and ambition. As at October 2003, just 14 companies were listed and there is a sense that business, both in foreign investment and for law firms, is stagnating. Lebanon's instability is compounded by wariness among foreign tourists to visit the Middle East and ongoing tensions among its neighbours.

Lebanon's social structure is distinctive for its religious composition: the population consists of a majority of Muslims and a large minority of Christians. Arabic is the official language with French and English widely spoken, marking its potential for foreign business.

BILLING

Certain legal services, including litigation, are commonly handled on a lump-sum basis. Lawyers are flexible in general and, depending on the client's needs and wishes, work on an hourly or fixed-fee basis. Billing is commonly in US dollars with hourly rates from $75 for an associate to a possible $350 for the most senior partner.

MARKETING

Restrictions by the Bar Association limit the ability of lawyers to market themselves. An increasing number of firms are setting up their own websites, which they say do not fall foul of the marketing regulations.

NETWORKS AND ASSOCIATIONS

Many law firms in Lebanon have formed links with international legal associations. **Badri and Salim El Meouchi Law Firm** is a member of the *Interleges* network; **Moghaizel Law Offices** is a member of the *Alliance of Arab Lawyers*, a network of independent law firms in the Arab world, and of *Lex Mundi*; and **Tyan & Associés** is a member of *TerraLex*.

POLITICAL CLIMATE

The head of government is billionaire prime minister Rafiq Hariri who has been in office since September 2000, the culmination of an impressive career in the Saudi construction industry. His ambition, to drive through a programme of economic reform, with deregulation and privatisation has only partially been successful. That said, the new telecoms law in Lebanon, expected to be enacted by parliament by the end of 2003, will reform the telecoms sector and create a separate regulatory body and telecoms operator (Liban Telecom).

President Emile Lahoud has been chief of state since 1998. Constitutionally, the president of Lebanon has a strong and influential position, appointing the Council of Ministers and designating one of them as prime minister. The president also has the authority to promulgate laws passed by the Nationality Assembly and issue supplementary regulations to ensure the execution of laws, and to negotiate and ratify treaties.

By a tradition dating back to 1943, the president was a Maronite Christian, the prime minister a Sunni Muslim and the speaker of the legislature a Shi'a Muslim. This custom aimed to ensure all religious groups were represented in government but in reality, tensions between the groups prevented the smooth running of government and the perceived sectarianism of the tradition contributed to the civil strife in Lebanon.

Recent events, however, have upset the delicate Muslim-Christian balance and resulted in a tendency for Christians and Muslims to group themselves for safety into distinct zones. All factions have called for further reform of the political system.

ECONOMIC CLIMATE

Lebanon prides itself on a liberal and open economy, particularly by Middle East standards. The country boasts a free foreign exchange market, full currency convertibility, complete

The largest firms

1	Badri and Salim El Meouchi Law Firm	27
2	Raphaël & Associés	26
3	Moghaizel Law Offices	21
4	Jamaleddine Law Firm	18
5	Abousleiman & Partners	17
6	Abouhamad, Merheb, Nohra, Chamoun, Chedid	15
7	Ibrahim Najjar Law Firm	13
8	Khattar Associates	12
	Lyan & Associés	12
10	Tyan & Associés	10
11	Ramzi Joreige and Partners	9
12	Berti Law Firm	7
	Nabil Abdel – Malek's Law Offices	7
14	Ghaleb S Mahmassani Law Firm	6
	Sami S Nahas Law Offices	6
16	Walid Nasser & Associates	5
17	Ferrell Schultz Carter & Fertel PA	1

These figures represent the total number of lawyers in this country only, and have been supplied by the firms themselves. The figures should be accurate as at 1 January 2004.

repatriation of capital and regulated banking secrecy. Lebanon offers an abundance of investment opportunities in all sectors, with a 15% corporate tax rate. Its laws are designed to encourage foreign investment with minimal administrative constraints.

LEGAL SYSTEM AND LEGAL MARKET

Lebanon's legal system is substantially based on French law and comprises a mixture of Ottoman law, canon law, Napoleonic code and civil law. There is no judicial review of legislative acts and it has yet to accept compulsory jurisdiction of the ICJ.

There are four Courts of Cassation (three for civil and commercial cases and one for criminal cases); a Constitutional Council (required under the Ta'if Accord's rules on constitutionality of laws); and the Supreme Council whose jurisdiction includes hearing any charges against the president or prime minister. Juries are not used in trials.

There are no offices of foreign firms in Lebanon – the tradition is for foreign firms to associate themselves contractually with, or to put work through, one local law firm.

Nabil Abdel – Malek's Law Offices works closely with a number of international law firms including **Allen & Overy**; **Linklaters**; **Denton Wilde Sapte**; **Freshfields Bruckhaus Deringer;** and **Baker & McKenzie**. **Badri and Salim El Meouchi Law Firm** works closely with **Clifford Chance LLP** in Dubai and London. **Moghaizel Law Offices**, has worked with the UK's **Richards Butler**, while **Abousleiman & Partners** regularly works alongside US firm **Dewey Ballantine**. Accountancy giant Ernst & Young has enjoyed a working presence in Lebanon since 1947 and associates with **Raphaël & Associés**. Florida-based **Ferrell Schultz Carter & Fertel PA** has a lawyer working with Beirut firm **Uthman Arakji & Associates**.

BANKING AND FINANCE

In spite of a sluggish economy, banking continues to be one of the most vibrant business sectors in Lebanon, keeping law firms busy. Recent years have seen a boom in the demand for securitisation.

Abousleiman & Partners has an excellent reputation. The firm has undertaken numerous capital markets transactions for clients including Banque de la Mediterannée SAL, and advised on the issue of a series of eurobonds and shares for leading Lebanese banks. The firm also handles project finance work.

Badri and Salim El Meouchi Law Firm advises numerous commercial banks. The firm acted for Fransabank SAL in its acquisition of three Lebanese banks; was counsel for Standard Chartered Bank in its acquisition of Metropolitan Bank; and advised a major Lebanese bank in the listing of its shares on the BSE. The firm also advises on regulatory issues within the financial, corporate and construction sectors.

BANKING AND FINANCE

ABOUSLEIMAN & PARTNERS
BADRI AND SALIM EL MEOUCHI LAW FIRM
NABIL ABDEL – MALEK'S LAW OFFICES

Ibrahim Najjar Law Firm ✪
Jamil Kanaan Law Office
Moghaizel Law Offices
Raphaël & Associés
Walid Nasser & Associates

Firms are listed A-Z in tiers which are ranked in order of priority
✪ Indicates firm displays contact details at the end of this chapter.

Nabil Abdel – Malek's Law Offices has been retained by the Ministry of Finance as legal adviser on securitisation transactions in Lebanon, and the establishment of Law No 430 governing securitisation in the context of the restructuring and financing of public debt. The firm is also advising the Ministry of Finance on securitisation of tobacco receipts. The firm has advised a number of international finance houses and is currently advising Standard Chartered Bank on its activities in Lebanon. It also has significant project finance experience. It was recently involved in the sale of ABN AmroBank NV Lebanon branch to Byblos Bank SAL.

Ibrahim Najjar, senior partner at **Ibrahim Najjar Law Firm**, and head of the Institute of Banking and Capital Markets at the Saint-Joseph University in Beirut, acts for Société Générale de Banque au Liban, in particular on debt collection.

Jamil Kanaan Law Office recently concluded a deal involving the sale by certain major shareholders in Ciments de Sibline SAL of 20% of the total shares to the Portuguese cement company, Cecil.

Moghaizel Law Offices advises on all aspects of banking and finance law, including bank security and loan syndications and other financings, debt restructuring and collection and derivatives. It has a good name for securitisation.

Raphaël & Associés acts as outside legal counsel to three leading Lebanese banks and as local counsel to three European banks.

Walid Nasser & Associates has recently been involved in drafting major stock purchase agreements for a Cayman Islands company to be listed on the UAE Stock Exchange; the firm also played a part in the Lebanese element of the internal restructuring of a major European Bank.

CORPORATE AND COMMERCIAL

Badri and Salim El Meouchi Law Firm boasts an impressive list of corporate and commercial clients, both local and international, including multinational corporations, local banks,

CORPORATE AND COMMERCIAL

BADRI AND SALIM EL MEOUCHI LAW FIRM
IBRAHIM NAJJAR LAW FIRM ✪
MOGHAIZEL LAW OFFICES
NABIL ABDEL – MALEK'S LAW OFFICES

Abousleiman & Partners
Albert and Ziad Najm Lawfirm
Jamil Kanaan Law Office
Khattar Associates
Nasri Antoine Diab Law Firm
Raphaël & Associés
Tyan & Associés
Uthman Arakji & Associates
Walid Nasser & Associates

Firms are listed A-Z in tiers which are ranked in order of priority
✪ *Indicates firm displays contact details at the end of this chapter.*

accountants plus clients in shipping, petroleum and luxury goods. The firm was counsel for Fransabank SAL in its acquisition of the Bank of Bekaa, and counsel for the Lebanese Ministry of Telecommunications on its renewal of agreements with existing operators, Libancell SAL and FTML SAL. The firm advised a group of hotel investors on the construction of a five-star hotel in Beirut and regularly advises financial organisations on mergers and acquisitions.

Ibrahim Najjar Law Firm has an impressive list of corporate clients including Renault, Samsung, KPMG and Louis Dreyfus. The firm has experience in domestic M&A and real estate.

Multi-lingual **Moghaizel Law Offices** is highly regarded and serves a domestic and international client base that includes governments and government-owned entities, Fortune 500 corporations, banks and financial institutions. International clients account for more than 60% of the firm's work, and include Citigroup, American Life Insurance Company, Microsoft Corporation, HSBC, Hewlett-Packard and Goldman Sachs. It acts as local counsel for the Lebanese branches of many multinational companies.

Nabil Abdel – Malek's Law Offices is renowned for its corporate and commercial practice, with a client list well balanced between international and local corporations. It advises on general corporate law, contracts and mergers and acquisitions. Recently, the firm advised an Emirates group on a franchise agreement in Lebanon.

Abousleiman & Partners has been involved in mergers and acquisitions, including the acquisition by the Heineken group of companies of Brasserie Amaza SAL, Lebanon's biggest brewery.

Albert and Ziad Najm Lawfirm has a strong reputation for commercial, insurance and shipping matters, where clients include Al Mashrek Insurance and Reinsurance and ACA Middle East Insurance. The firm is sole counsel to Lebanese footwear agent, BCL Trading.

The work of **Jamil Kanaan Law Office** centres on corporate and commercial advice. The firm displays experience in banking, construction and insurance matters. Clients including Sports Life SARL and Fransaland SAL turn to the firm for assistance.

Khattar Associates frequently advises major foreign corporations on Lebanese commercial matters. Clients include two major French fashion houses.

Nasri Antoine Diab Law Firm undertakes more general corporate and commercial work for its client base, including a major financial leasing company, and an oil industry port facility. It has also acted as counsel for a local bank during its $3.5m acquisition by a Jordanian bank. Sole principal, Nasri Diab, has just been appointed full professor of the Law School at the University of St Joseph in Beirut.

Raphaël & Associés is affiliated with Ernst & Young. The firm offers a full commercial service and has strength in both contentious and non-contentious practices and boasts experience of IPOs, M&A and structuring joint ventures, among other things. Name partner Moussa Raphael is very highly regarded. Clients include multinational corporations, telecoms and finance institutions.

In 2003, **Tyan & Associés** acted for Colgate-Palmolive in establishing a presence in Lebanon, and advised Danone in its distribution agreements in the country. It also advised on the preparation and negotiation of a joint venture between Maersk Sealand and its Lebanese partner and the establishment of the Maersk Lebanon SARL entity. High-profile clients also include McDonald's and Canon.

Uthman Arakji & Associates, which has a joint venture association with US firm **Ferrell Schultz Carter & Fertel PA**, has wide-ranging experience in corporate and commercial work, agency and distribution. International clients include Procter & Gamble and Barclays Bank, as well as leading corporations in Lebanon.

Walid Nasser & Associates advises a number of major international corporates including Motion Picture Association of America and Aventis.

DISPUTE RESOLUTION

Badri and Salim El Meouchi Law Firm advised the Lebanese Sugar Beet factory in a dispute with the government, and acted for the government in arbitration with various corporates. The firm was involved in a number of arbitrations between the Russian state and telecoms companies.

Ibrahim Najjar at **Ibrahim Najjar Law Firm** represented a major motor corporation in an important franchising dispute between a Korean Group and a Lebanese distributor. Ibrahim Najjar, senior partner at **Ibrahim Najjar Law Firm** has recently been recognised in the firm's role successfully advising the Lebanese government in an $80m tobacco industry arbitration, heard by the Cairo Centre for Commercial International Arbitration.

DISPUTE RESOLUTION

BADRI AND SALIM EL MEOUCHI LAW FIRM
IBRAHIM NAJJAR LAW FIRM ✪

Abousleiman & Partners
Albert and Ziad Najm Lawfirm
Antoine E Henoud Law Firm
Berti Law Firm
Khattar Associates
Moghaizel Law Offices
Nabil Abdel – Malek's Law Offices
Nasri Antoine Diab Law Firm
Raphaël & Associés

Firms are listed A-Z in tiers which are ranked in order of priority
✪ *Indicates firm displays contact details at the end of this chapter.*

The disputes portfolio of **Abousleiman & Partners** has expanded significantly with the inclusion of the Council of Development and Reconstruction in Lebanon among its clients.

Albert and Ziad Najm Lawfirm recently acted on behalf of **Clyde & Co** for the recovery of a major debt against a Lebanese company.

Antoine E Henoud Law Firm specialises in commercial disputes, and boasts a client base exclusively of large multinationals from the confectionery, chemical, pharmaceutical, cosmetics, sport and toy industries.

Both litigation and arbitration are a part of **Berti Law Firm**'s practice, typically representing foreign companies in disagreements over trade marks, copyright infringement or franchising disputes.

Michel Khattar, senior partner at **Khattar Associates** and former president of the Bar Association of Beirut has 50 years' experience in litigation.

Moghaizel Law Offices is experienced in alternative dispute resolution (mediation and conciliation). The firm boasts extensive experience in local and international arbitration, including ICC arbitration.

Nabil Abdel – Malek's Law Offices represents internationally known clients in litigation relating to commercial representation agreements, agency and licence agreements. Clients include United Biscuits; Nabisco; EMI Music International Services Limited; Standard Chartered Bank; and Tyco Electronics.

A major component of the practice of **Nasri Antoine Diab Law Firm** is international arbitration, having represented two foreign construction companies in a major dispute with the Lebanese authorities.

Raphaël & Associés has high-profile litigation and arbitration experience, including serving as counsel in complex UNCITRAL arbitration proceedings and negotiating various aspects of the dispute with the Lebanese Ministry of Telecommunications. The firm recently represented two cellular operators in disputes with the Lebanese government.

IP AND IT

In October 2003, the president of Lebanon's Professional Computer Association, told IT experts in Dubai: 'The Lebanese IT sector is witnessing rapid growth and transformation.' However, as far as intellectual property is concerned, Lebanon remains on the International Intellectual Property Alliance's Priority Watch List because of a severe piracy problem. In the four years since the passage of the Lebanese copyright law, key Lebanese government officials have taken virtually no action against piracy and infringement and enforcement needs drastic improvement.

Badri and Salim El Meouchi Law Firm advised a major Lebanese bank in litigation for its domain name pursuant to the ICANN procedure under the World Intellectual Property Organisation arbitration procedure. It also advised a major Lebanese bank in the financing of the Libanpost BOT project with the Ministry of Post and Telecommunications.

Berti Law Firm handles a variety of IP work including trade mark infringement, anti-counterfeiting, and franchising for an impressive roster of international clients including The Dow Chemical Company, Hard Rock Café and Canali SpA. Widely respected partner Kamal Berti has been general counsel for Saba & Co, the Middle East's largest trade mark attorney agency, for more than three decades.

Protection and enforcement are strengths of the IP practice at **Walid Nasser & Associates**. The firm won the first major criminal conviction against 42 cable pirates in Lebanon and has advised on amendments to the patent laws.

Antoine E Henoud Law Firm specialises in trade mark infringement matters. Sole principal, Antoine Henoud is one of the few local lawyers highly skilled in intellectual property and clients are exclusively large multinationals from the confectionery, chemical, pharmaceutical, cosmetics, sport and toy industries.

Ibrahim Najjar Law Firm undertakes general IP and franchising matters and advises on international distribution agreements.

Khattar Associates has expertise in obtaining patents and trade marks for local and international clients. The firm is active in a wide range of areas, and has been acting in a notable lawsuit to protect a major cable network from illegal cable operators.

Moghaizel Law Offices advises on patents and designs, trade mark and copyright issues and has advised foreign financial institutions on the provision of on-line financial services.

A multinational client base turns to **Nabil Abdel – Malek's Law Offices** for IP advice. The firm undertakes a significant amount of EMI's intellectual property work, both contentious and non-contentious, in Lebanon

Raphaël & Associés has trade mark, copyright, patent and licensing expertise, while **Uthman Arakji & Associates** has general experience in intellectual property.

IP AND IT

BADRI AND SALIM EL MEOUCHI LAW FIRM
BERTI LAW FIRM
WALID NASSER & ASSOCIATES

Antoine E Henoud Law Firm
Ibrahim Najjar Law Firm ✪
Khattar Associates
Moghaizel Law Offices
Nabil Abdel – Malek's Law Offices
Raphaël & Associés
Uthman Arakji & Associates

Firms are listed A-Z in tiers which are ranked in order of priority
✪ Indicates firm displays contact details at the end of this chapter.

PRIVATISATION

Experts see privatisation as the only answer to Lebanon's economic problems but privatisation laws have not yet been passed because of political issues still to be resolved. In a bid to push forward economic reforms, the Lebanese parliament has ratified a draft law for the privatisation of Electricité du Liban (EDL). A minimum 40% of the company's shares are to be sold to the private sector by 2005. Attempts by the government to privatise various sectors have resulted in a dispute involving cellular operators and the Government, the Ministry of Telecommunications and the Higher Council for Privatisation.

Badri and Salim El Meouchi Law Firm advised a major Lebanese bank on the financing of the privatisation of the post service, the Libanpost BOT project. The firm was also counsel for HSBC IB London, advising on the privatisation of the mobile sector and on issuance of twomobile licences and the grant of two management contracts. It also advised a major international lottery and gaming company in the tender for a licence for instant lottery, and advised on the regulatory aspects of privatisation for Transparency International – La Fassad in Lebanon.

Nabil Abdel – Malek's Law Offices advised Swedish telco, Billiant, on entering the Lebanese market and Ericsson on issues relating to the privatisation of the telecommunications sector in Lebanon.

Nasri Antoine Diab Law Firm assisted in the drafting of the Lebanese law on privatisation, and has advised a French bank on a bid for involvement in the proposed tobacco industry privatisation.

Abousleiman & Partners is very experienced and highly regarded. The firm has been extensively involved in the mobile telephone and electricity privatisations.

Raphaël & Associés has advised several telecommunications companies in their bids for GSM licences. The firm represented one of the two cellular operators in Lebanon in a dispute with the Lebanese government including negotiating aspects of the dispute with the Ministry of Telecommunications and with the High Council for Privatisation.

Tyan & Associés was recently counsel for France Télécom Mobiles Liban SAL on its BOT agreement. As adviser to the Higher Council for Privatisation, the firm has also been heavily involved in the privatisation of the mobile and electricity sectors.

Walid Nasser & Associates has been involved in drafting a large number of agreements concerning the licensing of sporting events and various television programmes; the firm has also provides preliminary advice to many major international companies considering tendering bids for privatisation contracts.

PRIVATISATION

BADRI AND SALIM EL MEOUCHI LAW FIRM
NABIL ABDEL – MALEK'S LAW OFFICES
NASRI ANTOINE DIAB LAW FIRM

Abousleiman & Partners
Raphaël & Associés
Tyan & Associés
Walid Nasser & Associates

Firms are listed A-Z in tiers which are ranked in order of priority

BAROUDI & ASSOCIATES

UCIC BUILDING
SAMI EL-SOLH STREET
PO BOX 11-7236
BEIRUT

Telephone: +961 1 388 745
Fax: +961 1 381 104
E-mail: jbaroudi@dm.net.lb

Languages
Arabic, English, French

Other offices
Basra, Dubai

Number of lawyers 25
at this office 20

CATEGORIES OF WORK

Banking
Samir Baroudi, Karim Kobeissi

Corporate
Jean Baroudi, Jamil Moubayed

Shipping and transport
Jean Baroudi, Jamil Moubayed

Construction
Jean Baroudi, Karim Kobeissi

Corporate restructuring
Jean Baroudi

Insurance
Richard Nader, Jean Baroudi

Capital markets
Karim Kobeissi

Intellectual property
Josiane Lahoud

Corporate finance
Samir Baroudi, Karim Kobeissi

Taxation
Karim Kobeissi, Jean Baroudi

Litigation
Richard Nader, Josiane Lahoud

Arbitration
Samir Baroudi, Jean Baroudi

Debt recovery
Josiane Lahoud

Commercial representation
Jean Baroudi, Josiane Lahoud

Privatisation
Samir Baroudi, Karim Kobeissi

Securitisation
Jean Baroudi, Karim Kobeissi

Project finance
Samir Baroudi

IBRAHIM NAJJAR
LAW FIRM

11 MADRASSAT EL-SALAM STREET
PO BOX 116/2270
BEIRUT

Telephone: +961 1 202 100
Fax: +961 1 201 974
E-mail: inajjar@dm.net.lb

Languages
Arabic, English, French, Spanish

Other offices
Paris

Number of lawyers 13

Contacts
Ibrahim Najjar, Nathalie Najjar

CATEGORIES OF WORK

International and domestic arbitration

International distribution agreements

Litigation

Family law

Intellectual property

Capital markets

Mergers and acquisitions

Real estate; acquisition of real estate by foreigners

Banking

Finance

Corporations

Franchise

JAMALEDDINE LAW FIRM

RAOUCHE AUSTRALIA STREET
EZZEDDINE BUILDING
PO BOX 13-5113
BEIRUT

Telephone: +961 1 809 999
Fax: +961 1 794 704
E-mail: fje@jamaleddinelawfirm.com
Website: www.jamaleddinelawfirm.com

Languages
Arabic, English, Finnish, French, German, Swedish

Number of lawyers 20

CATEGORIES OF WORK

Corporate law
Fady Jamaleddine, André Bouchaaya

Commercial law
Fady Jamaleddine, André Bouchaaya

Corporate finance
Fady Jamaleddine, André Bouchaaya

Banking law
Fady Jamaleddine, André Bouchaaya

Intellectual property
Fady Jamaleddine, André Bouchaaya

International trade
Jukka-Pekka Niemela, Fady Hassoun

Competition law
Jukka-Pekka Niemela, Fady Hassoun

Telecommunications
Fady Jamaleddine

Labour law
Yasser El-Hajj

Criminal law
Hussein Kazan, Fatima Hussein

Administrative law
Nada Baccar, Fatima Hussein

Real estate
Sana'a Daakour

Dispute resolution
Fady Jamaleddine

LIECHTENSTEIN

Population	33,525
Number of lawyers	103
Professional title	Rechtsanwalt; Rechtsanwältin
Currency	Swiss Franc (SFr)

The Principality of Liechtenstein is one of the world's smallest and wealthiest countries. Nestled in a beautiful valley, deep in the Swiss-Austrian Alps, the Principality has long been renowned for low tax rates and an 'ask no questions' banking system. Nevertheless, its appearance on a recent OECD blacklist of countries supporting money laundering has shocked the country into some hasty reforms of the financial sector. Though at least 75,000 companies continue to register nominal addresses in the Principality, it remains to be seen whether or not the reforms will affect future income.

A referendum in 2003 saw Liechtensteiners vote two-to-one in favour of increasing the constitutional power of their reigning monarch, Prince Hans Adam II. The Prince, a former banker, is Europe's only monarch with absolute authority to sack the government and to overrule parliament.

The current government was elected in 2001 and is based in the capital, Vaduz. Both the government and the monarchy support a modernising agenda that seeks to reaffirm the country's reputation as a legitimate hub for financial services.

Liechtensteiners speak German with a Swiss dialect.

BILLING

Complex billing laws are set out in the Liechtenstein Lawyer's Fee Act. The Act establishes a statutory tariff that permits a maximum charge of SFr1200 (€773) per hour depending on the nature of the work, and the value of the case. If the lawyer and client prefer, they may discard the tariff and agree to use task-based billing instead. Task-based billing is governed by the Autonomous Fee Guidelines of the Liechtenstein Bar, and ranges from SFr300 (€193) to SFr 1000 (€645) per hour. In practice, firms generally charge between SFr350 (€226) and SFr500 (€322) per hour for task-based billing.

For court work the tariff is used most frequently. Lawyers are not allowed to request a contingency fee, and only specific 'in-court' services may be charged. For all other 'out-of-court' services the lawyer may add a flat charge, the value of which must not exceed 40% or 50% of the total value of the in-court charge.

Requesting fees in advance, particularly when dealing with foreign clients or offshore companies, is a standard policy because Liechtenstein court awards cannot be enforced in foreign jurisdictions – the Principality is not a signatory to either the Lugano or Brussels conventions on the enforcement of foreign judgments.

MARKETING

A limited range of passive advertising, for example, a webpage or brochure describing practice areas, is permitted; anything else, including advertisements in the printed press, remain forbidden. It is illegal to refer to cases or clients in any advertisement.

IN-HOUSE LAWYERS

In-house lawyers are not admitted to the Liechtenstein Bar.

ECONOMIC CLIMATE

Economically, Liechtenstein is fully integrated with Switzerland, with which it maintains a monetary and customs union. Liechtenstein also entrusts Switzerland with the task of representing it on the international stage. As a member of the European Economic Area (EEA) Liechtenstein is afforded free trade rights with the EU, despite its union to a non-EU country.

Prime location, political stability, and EEA membership have all contributed to the dramatic post-war growth of Liechtenstein's economy. Once a rural backwater, the Principality is now highly industrialised, with almost half of the total workforce employed in manufacturing. Metal finishing is the largest manufacturing industry, but other notable sectors include textiles, ceramics, chemical and pharmaceutical, and electronics. The bulk of all manufactured goods are exported, primarily to the EU. Unemployment in the Principality is approximately nil.

However, it is the financial services sector that has done most to prosper the economy. As a low-tax haven, famed for banking discretion, the country attracts significant foreign investment, particularly in the areas of banking, trusts and insurance. Revenues from foreign companies account for 30% of the State's income.

LEGAL SYSTEM AND LEGAL MARKET

For civil and criminal cases, Liechtenstein operates a three-tier court system. Cases are initially heard in the District Court, and may progress to the

Superior Court and to the Supreme Court. For cases concerning government decisions and constitutional law there are two further courts, the Administrative Court and the Constitutional Court. Judges are typically part-time laymen. Traditionally, Swiss and Austrian judges may also sit.

The ruling monarch cannot be held legally responsible, having authority over parliament and the judiciary. Some 60% of Liechtenstein law is identical to Austrian law.

The legal market is small but very competitive. Firms doubt that changes in the constitution will have any adverse effect on the market. An influx of Austrian lawyers is making it increasingly difficult for many smaller firms to find new work.

The limited size of the market in Liechtenstein means that most firms offer a full service. Many firms were formed by, or have themselves formed, lucrative fiduciary companies and consequently much of their work involves advising on trusts. Owing to Liechtenstein's size, it is not unusual for lawyers to also hold positions in government, banks and business.

BANKING

There are currently 16 banking institutions in Liechtenstein, several of them Swiss- or Austrian-based. The three oldest banks, Liechtensteinische Landesbank (LLB), LGT Bank in Liechtenstein AG and Verwaltungs und Privat (VP) Bank AG, all belong to the Swiss Banking Association and are required to recognise most of the conventions of that Association. The leading banks all have large in-house legal teams and consequently only employ external law firms for court work. Large banks rarely employ one firm exclusively.

More than one-third of **Dr Batliner & Dr Gasser**'s work is dedicated to advising banking clients. The firm represents VP Bank as well as some of the largest public and private Swiss banks. A further third of the work derives from providing in-house counsel to leading trust services company, First Advisory Group. The firm also has experience of bank creation, and M&A, having founded Erste Sparkasse bank in 2001, which merged with Austrian bank Raiffeisen in 2003.

In addition to a host of smaller banking clients, **Batliner Wanger Batliner** represents one of the leading three banks and two other large Liechtenstein banks. Though the firm is young in its present form, semi-retired partner Dr Gerhard Batliner has more than fifty years' experience of advising leading banks. He is also a former board member of VP bank.

Law Office Holzhacker & Struth represents Credit Suisse in Liechtenstein and occasionally undertakes work for other foreign banks, including Deutsche Bank. The firm was previously known as *Meier & Holzhacker*, and was retained by Private Trust Bank until the departure of partner, and bank board member, Dr Guido Meier in late 2003.

BANKING

Batliner (Dr) & Dr Gasser
Batliner Wanger Batliner
Holzhacker & Struth, Law Office
Müller & Partner Rechtsanwälte
Walch & Schurti

Karlheinz Ritter (Dr iur), Lic iur Cornelia Ritter, Law Office
Marxer (Dr) & Partner, Advokaturbüro
Seeger, Frick & Partner
Sele Frommelt & Partner

Firms are listed A-Z in tiers which are ranked in order of priority

Based in Schaan, but with an office in Vaduz, **Müller & Partner Rechtsanwälte** represents LGT bank and its associated trust companies. The firm also represents another large bank domiciled in Austria. In 2001, the firm advised on a high-profile bank insolvency case.

Walch & Schurti estimates that more than half of its work is insurance and banking advice. The firm permanently represents the bank it created in 1992, in addition to other foreign and domestic banking clients. Of the eleven lawyers employed, both the partners and two of the associates are involved in advising banks.

Law Office Dr iur Karlheinz Ritter Lic iur Cornelia Ritter continues to advise the bank it created in 1999. Name partner Cornelia Ritter is able to draw on her experience as a board member of LLB bank.

Advokaturbüro Dr Marxer & Partner created a bank in 1992, and continues to represent it.

Partner Wolfgang Seeger of **Seeger, Frick & Partner** is chairman of New Century Bank, a private bank that the firm helped to found in 2001. The firm provides legal counsel to this, and to two other recently established banks.

Sele Frommelt & Partner continues to advise the private bank it created in 1998.

GENERAL COMMERCIAL

The profile of **Dr Batliner & Dr Gasser** rose in 2003 as the firm successfully defended the monarchy in the numerous proceedings brought about by the amendments to the constitution. Litigation now accounts for about one-third of the firm's work. The firm has also expanded, having taken on University of Vienna professor for criminal law, Dr Wolfgang Brandstetter as a seventh partner, and Italian jurist, Markus Schwingshackl, as an associate. To reflect these successes the firm appears in the top tier for the first time. Unburdened by any associated trust companies, the firm is committed to commercial, international, cross-border work, tailored to meet the needs of its clients. The firm includes lawyers from Austria and Italy, and is in partnership with **Simma Bechtold Gunz & Gasser** of Vorarlberg, Austria.

GENERAL COMMERCIAL

BATLINER (DR) & DR GASSER
BATLINER WANGER BATLINER
MARXER (DR) & PARTNER, ADVOKATURBÜRO
WALCH & SCHURTI

Batliner & Konrad
Gstoehl, Law Office
Holzhacker & Struth, Law Office
Karlheinz Ritter (Dr iur), Lic iur Cornelia Ritter, Law Office
Müller & Partner Rechtsanwälte
Sele Frommelt & Partner
Sprenger Kolzoff Ospelt & Partner, Advokatur
Wanger Advokaturbüro ✪

Norbert Seeger (Dr jur et lic oec), Advokaturbüro
Seeger, Frick & Partner

Firms are listed A-Z in tiers which are ranked in order of priority
✪ *Indicates firm displays contact details at the end of this chapter.*

The five lawyers at **Batliner Wanger Batliner** specialise in litigation and corporate law. All five undertake court work, although name partner and former head of the Liechtenstein government, Dr Gerard Batliner, is now semi-retired. The firm is not involved in the business of founding companies and trusts, and is consequently able to devote greater time to its banking and corporate clients.

Advokaturbüro Dr Marxer & Partner is the oldest and largest law firm. With nine partners, 15 associates, and one permanent consultant, the firm is able to offer a full service, as well as specialising in corporate, commercial, international law, banking and finance, trusts, estate planning and litigation. The firm is a member of *Lex Mundi* and is associated with trust company, Confida. Partner Dr Peter Marxer senior is a member of the International Academy of Estate and Trust Law.

There are eleven lawyers at **Walch & Schurti**, although only four are admitted in Liechtenstein. The others are admitted in Germany, the UK, and the US, from where many of the firm's clients originate. Both partners, Dr Ernst Walch and Dr Andreas Schurti, are admitted in Liechtenstein and the US, but much of their work is devoted to managing an associated trust company. Dr Walch is Liechtenstein's Minister for Foreign Affairs. A diverse commercial practice includes litigation, white-collar crime, insolvency, IP, tax, telecoms, banking and finance, capital markets, EU law, and corporate and commercial. The firm is a member of the *State Capital Global Law Firm Group* and maintains a number of non-exclusive links to noteworthy US firms.

Andreas Batliner and Karlheinz Konrad work alone at **Batliner & Konrad**, handling litigation and advising on white-collar crime issues for various trust companies, and national and international banks.

Law Office Gstoehl is known for the contentious work it undertakes for European clients, although it is focusing increasingly on administrative law. Name partner Harry Gstoehl is President of the Constitutional Court and advises on corporate and tax law. Second partner, Sabine Mohr-Egger, specialises in litigation, European law and, to a lesser degree, corporate and commercial. Two associates assist the two partners.

Following the departure of name partner Dr Guido Meier due to conflicts of interest, the well-established *Meier & Holzhacker* name has been superseded by **Law Office Holzhacker & Struth**. Owing primarily to Dr Gerhard Holzhacker's excellent reputation, particularly as a litigator on fraud and white-collar crime issues, the new team can expect to maintain many of the former firm's key clients. Clients such as the US Justice Department regard *Meier & Holzhacker* as being among 'the top tier of European law firms,' and Holzhacker as among the 'very best'. New partner Dr Thomas Struth was at **Advokaturbüro Dr Marxer & Partner** until 2002.

Established in the 1920s, **Law Office Dr iur Karlheinz Ritter Lic iur Cornelia Ritter** undertakes corporate, commercial, finance, tax, trusts and litigation work for international companies. Four lawyers assist partners Karlheinz Ritter and Cornelia Ritter.

Schaan-based firm **Müller & Partner Rechtsanwälte** is associated with two trust companies, Gassner Treuhand and Allgemeines Treuunternehmen. Litigation forms the bulk of the non-trust-related work undertaken by the five partners and one associate. Senior partner Dr Wolfgang Müller is a respected litigator. Leading clients include large Swiss companies. Junior partner Dr Robert Neudorfer advises two large insurance companies. Other practice strengths include corporate, insolvency, tort, and tax.

The four partners and five associates of **Sele Frommelt & Partner** are jointly employed by the trust company, Negele Sele Frommelt & Partner Trust Enterprise. Consequently, much of the firm's work is related to this trust business, and the only other practice areas offered are litigation and asset management advice. The firm permanently represents a number of established Swiss and Austrian trust and consultancy firms.

All six lawyers at **Advokatur Sprenger Kolzoff Ospelt & Partner** are admitted and the firm has particular experience in handling money-laundering litigation cases. However, the firm's main expertise is in trade marks and trust-related issues. The firm also manages an associated trust company and an associated bookkeeping company. Of the four partners at the firm, only Dr Robert Beck is devoted exclusively to legal work.

Wanger Advokaturbüro has undergone significant change in recent years as a rapid decline in the size of its associated trust companies led the firm to downsize. Of the three associates left, one is based in Austria and another in Switzerland. In 2003, sole partner Dr Markus Wanger handed over management of the law firm to young, incoming partner Markus Wille in order to pursue trust and other business interests. Markus Wille has been given the title of 'head of litigation' although the firm continues to offer a full and diverse commercial practice, with an increasing emphasis on IP work.

Advokaturbüro Dr jur et lic oec Norbert Seeger is a wing of trust company Arcomm. The firm is primarily known as a patent agency but also undertakes IP, administration and litigation work.

Seeger, Frick & Partner was created in 2002 when outgoing prime minister, Dr Mario Frick, joined small, commercial practice *Seeger and Seeger*. The firm is associated with a collection of trust companies and consequently much of the work of all three lawyers is business orientated. Other practice areas include IP and estate planning.

WANGER ®
ADVOKATURBÜRO

AEULESTRASSE 45
9490 VADUZ

Telephone: +423 237 52 52
Fax: +423 237 52 53
E-mail: wanger@wanger.net
Website: www.wanger.net

Languages
English, French, German

Other offices
Belgium, Switzerland, Austria*

Number of lawyers 5

Contact
Dr Markus H Wanger (senior partner),
lic iur Markus Wille (managing partner)

Member
WANGER GROUP represented in Austria, Belgium, Brazil, China, Czech Republic, Germany, Israel, Liechtenstein, Slovakia, Spain and Switzerland

CATEGORIES OF WORK

Arbitration
Dr Markus Wanger

Litigation
Dr Johannes Grabher,
Lic iur Markus Wille

EU, conflict of laws
Lic iur Markus Wille,
Dr Johannes Grabher

Banking, finance, capital markets
Dr Markus Wanger

Trusts, charities, non-profit organisations
Dr Markus Wanger

Estate and tax planning
Dr Markus Wanger,
lic iur Markus Wille

Company
Dr Markus Wanger,
lic iur Markus Wille

Commercial
Dr Markus Wanger, Lic iur Markus Wille

IP
Dr Markus Wanger, Lic iur Markus Wille

IT
Dr Markus Wanger

Art law, media, sport
Dr Markus Wanger

Employment
Dr Johannes Grabher
Lic iur Markus Wille

THE FIRM

Wanger® Advokaturbüro was founded in 1987 by Dr Markus Wanger. In 1995, Dr Wanger also established a patent law firm and trade mark agency, PATAG Patente & Lizenzen AG, as well as a trust and company secretarial auditing and bookkeeping services firm, AGENTIA Treuunternehmen, in 1991.

Both the law firm and patent law firm have, in due course, established offices in Switzerland and Austria. Following Liechtenstein's entry into the EEA, Wanger® Advokaturbüro also opened a representative office in Brussels, and is a member of Kangaroo Working Group as Tax Harmonisation. Recently Wanger® Advokatbüro opened a representative office in Beijing, China.

Wanger® Advokaturbüro is one of the largest commercial law firms in Liechtenstein, and the only one with offices abroad, comprising in the Wanger Group around 200 lawyers altogether.

AREAS OF PRACTICE

Wanger® Advokaturbüro specialises in the following areas: corporate and tax, banking and insurance, finance and capital markets, art and charities, media and sport, IP and IT.

Dr Wanger is the Liechtenstein member of the Counterfeiting Intelligence Force of the International Chamber of Commerce in Paris, and – being a fellow of the Chartered Institute of Arbitrators since 1994 – he became a member of the Court of Arbitration for Sports of the International Olympic Committee in Lausanne.

Wanger® Advokaturbüro acts as Liechtenstein counsel for international law firms, and most of its clients are corporate, including international financial institutions, self-regulatory organisations, banks, insurance companies, fund managers, information technology, telecommunications, pharmaceutical, and car industry. Wanger® Advokaturbüro is one of the founding members of ICQM, the Institute for Compliance and Quality Management, Liechtenstein.

LITHUANIA

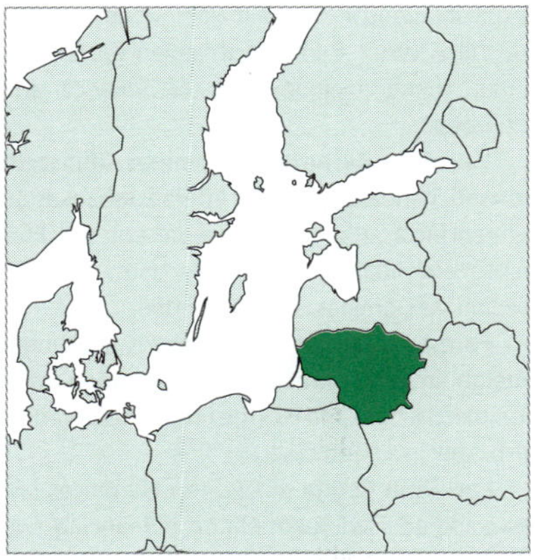

Population	3.5 million
Number of lawyers	1,081
Professional title	Advokat; jurist
Currency	Litas (LTS)

Index

Since its emergence as a nation in 1230, Lithuania has been pagan and Christian, democratic and communist, Polish and Soviet, imperial and subservient, not to mention torn between the geopolitics of East and West. Yet a strong sense of national identity has endured such vicissitudes, bolstered by long periods of self-rule and an intelligentsia bent on preserving traditional language and culture. Modern Lithuania embraces rich traditions and projects a strong sense of its own independent national character.

Lithuanian is one of the oldest languages in Europe. Today most Lithuanians can also speak Russian, a legacy of Soviet rule. Some 6.3% of the population are Russian, a contrast to Baltic counterparts Latvia and Estonia where as much as one-third of the population are Russian. English and German are widely spoken, especially in the business community, and Polish may be heard since 6.7% of citizens are of Polish origin.

Lithuania signed the EU Accession Treaty in April 2003, and 91% of Lithuanians voted in favour of EU membership in May 2003. Accession is set for May 2004, and the subject dominates political and economic agendas.

The largest and southernmost of the three Baltic States, Lithuania borders Latvia, Belarus, Poland and the isolated Russian outpost, Kaliningrad.

BILLING

Hourly rates range from €100 to €200 depending on the type of work and seniority of the lawyer.

MARKETING

The Lithuanian Bar prohibits law firms from advertising themselves as market leaders. They are allowed to provide an outline of their services and staff, and most law firms have a website.

IN-HOUSE LAWYERS

In-house lawyers do not have to be admitted to the Bar (non-Bar members are known as jurists). Conversely, advokats are not permitted to work in-house; officially they must work for a law firm. Larger companies have teams of up to ten in-house lawyers.

ECONOMIC CLIMATE

In the first quarter of 2003, Lithuania chalked up a 9.4% year-on-year growth rate. In 2002 the country took the title of fastest-growing economy in Europe, and the IMF predicts steady 6% growth for the Baltic state over the next two years. Such economic performance is all the more remarkable given that Lithuania was the neighbour hit hardest by Russia's financial collapse in 1998 and subsequently endured a shock-led recession.

Reliance on Russia has since decreased, though the country remains an important trading partner (alongside the UK, Latvia and Germany). Lithuania's imminent EU membership has significantly impacted the economy - the litas was pegged to the euro in 2002, the energy and banking sectors have been restructured, and in January 2003 the Bank of Lithuania announced its hope to join EMU by early 2007.

Yet despite earning the moniker of Baltic Tiger, per capita income hovers around 20% of the EU average and Lithuania has not managed to ditch its less prestigious branding as one of the poorest countries set to join the EU. Economy and infrastructure still suffer the legacy of Soviet centralisation, and the country's small size often dissuades foreign investors. Yet its reputation as one of the more advanced transitional economies is nonetheless deserved. Sweden, Finland and Denmark top FDI which grew by 6% in the first half of 2003. Forestry, electronics, engineering and IT are prominent industries.

LINKS ABROAD

Lithuanian firms are well connected. **AAA Legal Services** belongs to several US and European legal alliances, including the *International Association for the Protection of Intellectual Property*. The firm also has an office in Tallinn.

Baublys & Partners is a member of the *Russian European Business Club*, and opened a Moscow office at the beginning of 2003.

Law Firm Bernotas & Dominas Glimstedt belongs to the *European Association of Lawyers*, while **Hough, Gabartas, Sarzickas ir Partneri** belongs to a Baltic network of law firms.

Lideika, Petrauskas, Valiunas ir Partneriai has membership of several prestigious global alliances. **Law Firm Regija** is one of 20 'commercially orientated law firms' which form the *European Law Firm* network.

Sorainen Law Offices belongs to several international legal and business alliances. With offices in Tallinn, Riga and Helsinki, the firm considers its position as the largest pan-Baltic firm as its major strength.

The largest firms

1	Lideika, Petrauskas, Valiunas ir partneriai	29
2	Jurevicius, Balciunas & Partners EY Law	25
	Vilnius 2nd Law Firm	25
4	Law Firm Bernotas & Dominas Glimstedt	20
5	Zabiela, Zabielaite & Partners	18
6	Law Firm Regija	13
7	Sutkiene, Pilkauskas & Partners	12
8	AAA Legal Services	10
9	Sorainen Law Offices	9
10	Baublys & Partners	8
	Rödl & Partner	8
12	Foresta Business Law Group	6
	Norcous & Partners	6
	Vilnius 7th Law Firm	6
15	Budvytis Civilis And Partners, Law Firm	5
	Juridicon Law Office	5
	Praemissa Teises Firma Law Firm	5
18	Advokato Savinijaus Katausko Biuras	4
19	Hough, Gabartas, Sarzickas ir Partneri	3
	Law Firm Pukas and Partners	3
	Law Office of Vytas Ramanauskas	3
22	Law Office of Tadas Kilmas	2

These figures represent the total number of lawyers in this country only, and have been supplied by the firms themselves. The figures should be accurate as at 1 January 2004.

Sutkiene, Pilkauskas & Partners is an *IBA* and *Interlaw* member. Meanwhile, **Zabiela, Zabielaite & Partners** works in 'strong co-operation' with Finnish law firm **Borenius & Kemppinen**, which also has a Latvian office, and with the Estonian firm **Attorneys at law Luiga, Mugu & Borenius**.

Juridicon is owned by UK company Juridicon Services Limited.

In October 2003, **Law Office of Tadas Kilmas** opened an advisory office in Brussels.

Two firms are associated with the major accountancy practices. **Jurevicius, Balciunas & Partners** belongs to EY Law, the international network of 20 law firms associated with Ernst & Young.

Vilnius 7th Law Firm is PwC's first choice law firm in Lithuania.

FOREIGN FIRMS

Foreign firms are currently rare in Lithuania. **Law Firm Bernotas & Dominas Glimstedt** is an alliance partner of Swedish firm **Advokatfirman Glimstedt**, which also has a Latvian office.

LEGAL MARKET

Most Lithuanian law firms are in the capital, Vilnius. A number of smaller firms are situated in the second city, Kaunas. Maritime lawyers tend to be based in the principal port town, Klaipeda.

The legal landscape changed a little last year after well-reputed *Jaskuteli, Sutkiené & Maskiokas* split following partner disagreements. As a result, partner Eugenija Sutkiené took nine of the lawyers and formed new firm **Sutkiene, Pilkauskas & Partners.** The remaining ten lawyers joined **Law Firm Bernotas & Dominas Glimstedt**. Though Lithuania's largest firm **Lideika, Petrauskas, Valiunas ir Partneriai** still clearly leads the legal market, increased to 29 lawyers, **Law Firm Bernotas & Dominas Glimstedt** now rivals the leader in size.

A handful of firms join **Law Firm Bernotas & Dominas Glimstedt** in attempting to challenge **Lideika, Petrauskas, Valiunas ir Partneriai**'s dominance. They include **Sutkiene, Pilkauskas & Partners** and **Jurevicius, Balciunas & Partners**.

Several firms have increased their numbers this year, notably **Zabiela, Zabielaite & Partners** by five lawyers, **Law Firm Regija** by four, and **Sutkiene, Pilkauskas & Partners** by three.

The Lithuanian legal market is slowly developing, and competition is currently hotting-up for corporate and commercial work as foreign interest in the Baltics picks up. Some firms also report growth in telecoms following the liberalisation of the sector at the start of 2003.

The most significant legislative change in 2003 was to the Companies Law, which now meets EU requirements. In addition, the ongoing debate as to the extent of the role of jurists, lawyers who are not members of the Bar, was settled by the Lithuanian Parliament who ruled that jurists may not represent clients in court.

BANKING AND FINANCE

Lideika, Petrauskas, Valiunas ir Partneriai's banking and finance team has been exceptionally busy. It advised **Linklaters** on Lithuanian securities regulations, acted for the EBRD on a €10m loan, and advised a major investment bank on the issue of €400m Lithuanian eurobonds. Other clients include Bank of America and Citigroup.

Law Firm Bernotas & Dominas Glimstedt advised Standard Bank and AB Hansasbankas on refinancing a $28m loan, and represented NEFCO in several loan transactions. Name partner Gediminas Dominas is well-regarded.

Foresta Business Law Group is assisting a foreign investor with the incorporation of a commercial bank. In 2003 the firm represented an Irish bank in a fraud case.

Law Firm Regija moved to new offices last year, and advised Yukos Oil on refinancing two separate loans totalling $200m.

Sutkiene, Pilkauskas & Partners advised one of Lithuania's largest banks on a €20m acquisition and acted for Vilniaus Bank in a privatisation. Name partner Eugenija Sutkiené has worked in the US and for the Lithuanian government.

Zabiela, Zabielaite & Partners acted for the Lithuanian Ministry of Education and Science on extending a €29m EBRD loan, and did similar work for the Investment Fund for Central and Eastern Europe. The firm is growing steadily, and hired five new lawyers in 2003.

Juridicon provided refinancing advice to a Gazprom affiliate, while **Sorainen Law Offices** has advised several well-known banks and companies on loans and secured transactions.

Vilnius 7th Law Firm conducted due diligence for the real estate company of one of Lithuania's largest commercial banks.

BANKING AND FINANCE

LIDEIKA, PETRAUSKAS, VALIUNAS IR PARTNERIAI ✪

Bernotas & Dominas Glimstedt, Law Firm ✪
Foresta Business Law Group
Regija, Law Firm ✪
Sutkiene, Pilkauskas & Partners ✪
Zabiela, Zabielaite & Partners ✪

Baublys & Partners ✪
Juridicon ✪
Sorainen Law Offices
Vilnius 7th Law Firm ✪

Firms are listed A-Z in tiers which are ranked in order of priority
✪ Indicates firm displays contact details at the end of this chapter.

CORPORATE AND COMMERCIAL

Lideika, Petrauskas, Valiunas ir Partneriai has 29 lawyers at its main Vilnius office, and one lawyer based in the office at Klaipeda. The corporate and M&A team handled an impressive volume of work last year. It advised a Scandinavian telecoms company on a $117m acquisition, filed a merger for BP, and gave competition advice to an oil refinery. Other corporate clients include Nestlé Baltics, Vision Express and IBM.

Law Firm Bernotas & Dominas Glimstedt was significantly boosted by the incorporation of ten lawyers from the former *Jaskutelis, Sutkiene & Masiokas*. The arrival of new partner and well-known litigator Jonas Masiokas has strengthened the firm's litigation practice. The firm represented a number of well-known clients including Zurich on the liquidation of its Lithuanian operation, and advised on acquisitions.

Following the split of *Jaskutelis, Sutkiene & Masiokas*, name partner Eugenija Sutkiené took nine lawyers from the original firm to form **Sutkiene, Pilkauskas & Partners**. Three additional lawyers, including two former government advisers and an EU competition law specialist, were also hired. The firm provided acquisition advice to a large pharmaceutical wholesaler, and provides ongoing corporate advice to Philip Morris and Masterfoods. One client described the firm as 'outstanding'.

Baublys & Partners' corporate team has a good reputation for dispute resolution. The group advised a private client over voting rights in pledged shares, and represented a Lithuanian car manufacturer in an *ultra vires* action against the Lithuanian Armed Forces. The firm has seen an increase in Russian corporate clients following the opening of its two-lawyer office in Moscow in 2002.

Foresta Business Law Group advised a German crane company on incorporating a local subsidiary, and provides corporate advice to major international companies including those in the energy, manufacturing and insurance sectors. Partner Tomas Saulenas specialises in M&A work.

Jurevicius, Balciunas & Partners offers full corporate and commercial services. Partner Gintaras Balciunas lectures on commercial law at the Law University of Lithuania, and is the former Lithuanian Minister of Justice.

Juridicon advised a number of clients on acquisitions, including Gazprom on a $40m power plant acquisition. The firm continues to advise Gazprom on another energy project, and also represented Microlink on a transfer. The team specialises in drafting commercial agreements, and clients recommend it as being 'well-known and reputable, yet not too expensive'.

Law Firm Regija provided YIT Corporation with acquisition and competition advice. The firm also advised Yukos Oil on the sale and purchase of $85m worth of shares. Three new lawyers have joined the firm, including aviation and insurance specialists.

As well as providing general corporate and commercial advice, **Sorainen Law Offices** acted in

CORPORATE AND COMMERCIAL

LIDEIKA, PETRAUSKAS, VALIUNAS IR PARTNERIAI ✪

BERNOTAS & DOMINAS GLIMSTEDT, LAW FIRM ✪
SUTKIENE, PILKAUSKAS & PARTNERS ✪

Baublys & Partners ✪
Foresta Business Law Group
Jurevicius, Balciunas & Partners ✪
Juridicon ✪
Regija, Law Firm ✪
Sorainen Law Offices
Vilnius 7th Law Firm ✪
Zabiela, Zabielaite & Partners ✪

AAA Legal Services
Hough, Gabartas, Sarzickas ir Partneri
Sarka, Sabaliauskas, Jankauskas
Tadas Kilmas, Law Office of

Firms are listed A-Z in tiers which are ranked in order of priority
✪ Indicates firm displays contact details at the end of this chapter.

over 12 M&A transactions in 2003, representing foreign buyers in nearly all cases. The firm has grown steadily over the past five years and has worked with several top-tier international law firms.

It was a busy year for **Vilnius 7th Law Firm** which advised a pharmaceutical company on establishing a subsidiary, and a global food company on an acquisition. The firm provides ongoing advice to a large Scandinavian oil company.

Zabiela, Zabielaite & Partners is an experienced firm which handled a heavy workload during 2003. Among the deals advised on were the redistribution of capital in Chrysler Jeep Autocentras, the reorganisation of an advertising agency, several competition matters and the €1.73m acquisition of a kitchen company. The firm has advised BAT for the past three years, and was involved in the restructuring of Lithuania's energy sector.

IP specialist **AAA Legal Services** has expanded its practice to include general corporate and commercial work. The firm worked with **Lovells** to provide due diligence and M&A advice for Kappa Packaging, and established local companies for L'Oréal and Forever Living Products.

Hough, Gabartas, Sarzickas ir Partneri is a three-lawyer team, predominantly supplying medium and large sized companies with corporate and commercial advice. Several of their clients are US-based.

Sarka, Sabaliausksas, Jankauskas has established links with Germany. The eight-lawyer team advised a German gas provider on the €5.7m acquisition of shares in a Lithuanian heating company. It also assisted a German municipal utility company with a power plant acquisition, and aided a Liechtenstein holding company with the acquisition of a Lithuanian multimedia company. Partner Linas Sabaliauskas is valued by clients for his excellent contacts which augment the sound legal advice on offer.

Law Office of Tadas Kilmas is headed by Tadas Klimas, a member of the US Bar and dean at Vytautus Magnus University School of Law. The firm specialises in advising local affiliates of small and mid-sized foreign corporations on all legal matters. The firm is based in Kaunas, and recently opened a representative office in Brussels.

FOREIGN INVESTMENT

Lideika, Petrauskas, Valiunas ir Partneriai represents over half of Lithuania's 30 biggest foreign investors. The firm is currently advising SAS on the proposed privatisation of Lithuanian Airlines.

Law Firm Bernotas & Dominas Glimstedt's foreign investment clients include Stockholm-based Svenska Petroleum and Swedish-owned LNK, the largest TV channel in Lithuania.

Foresta Business Law Group advised a Russian alcohol company on an $8m investment, and is representing other clients on a number of ongoing deals.

Law Firm Regija provides investment advice to Yukos Oil.

Sorainen Law Offices has handled a considerable volume of foreign investment work over the year, with one deal valued at €40m. Clients include a Finnish mail-order business, a Latvian telecoms company and a Danish investment fund. Partner Kestutis Adamonis is 'exceedingly helpful' and fluent in English.

Vilnius 7th Law Firm continued to advise Gazprom on foreign investments.

Name partner Darius Zabiela at **Zabiela, Zabielaite & Partners** has specialised in FDI for the past five years. Recent projects include a €10m investment by polyester company Indorama, and an investment by a Danish wire company.

FOREIGN INVESTMENT

LIDEIKA, PETRAUSKAS, VALIUNAS IR PARTNERIAI ✪

BERNOTAS & DOMINAS GLIMSTEDT, LAW FIRM ✪

Foresta Business Law Group
Jurevicius, Balciunas & Partners ✪
Regija, Law Firm ✪
Sorainen Law Offices
Sutkiene, Pilkauskas & Partners ✪
Vilnius 7th Law Firm PricewaterhouseCoopers ✪
Zabiela, Zabielaite & Partners ✪

Sarka, Sabaliauskas, Jankauskas

Firms are listed A-Z in tiers which are ranked in order of priority
✪ Indicates firm displays contact details at the end of this chapter.

IT AND TELECOMS

AAA Legal Services
Bernotas & Dominas Glimstedt, Law Firm ✪
Foresta Business Law Group
Jurevicius, Balciunas & Partners ✪
Juridicon ✪
Lideika, Petrauskas, Valiunas ir Partneriai ✪
Regija, Law Firm ✪
Sorainen Law Offices
Sutkiene, Pilkauskas & Partners ✪
Tadas Kilmas, Law Office of
Vilnius 7th Law Firm ✪
Zabiela, Zabielaite & Partners ✪

Firms are listed alphabetically
✪ *Indicates firm displays contact details at the end of this chapter.*

INTELLECTUAL PROPERTY

AAA Legal Services
Foresta Business Law Group
Juridicon ✪
Lideika, Petrauskas, Valiunas ir Partneriai ✪
Regija, Law Firm ✪
Sorainen Law Offices
Sutkiene, Pilkauskas & Partners ✪
Tadas Kilmas, Law Office of
Vilnius 7th Law Firm ✪
Zabiela, Zabielaite & Partners ✪

Firms are listed alphabetically
✪ *Indicates firm displays contact details at the end of this chapter.*

MARITIME AND TRANSPORT

LIDEIKA, PETRAUSKAS, VALIUNAS IR PARTNERIAI ✪
VYTAS RAMANAUSKAS, LAW OFFICE OF

Hough, Gabartas, Sarzickas ir Partneri
Jurevicius, Balciunas & Partners ✪
Juridicon ✪
Regija, Law Firm ✪
Sarka, Sabaliauskas, Jankauskas
Sorainen Law Offices
Sutkiene, Pilkauskas & Partners ✪
Vilnius 7th Law Firm ✪
Zabiela, Zabielaite & Partners ✪

Firms are listed A-Z in tiers which are ranked in order of priority
✪ *Indicates firm displays contact details at the end of this chapter.*

With experience and knowledge of the German legal system as well as its home jurisdiction, **Sarka, Sabaliauskas, Jankauskas** is recommended for German clients. It has advised various foreign companies on investments in a range of sectors, including energy, textiles and automobiles.

IT AND TELECOMS

AAA Legal Services advised Scandinavian telecoms companies on the Lithuanian market and competition matters.

Law firm Bernotas & Dominas Glimstedt acts for Tele2, Lithuania's second largest telecoms operator, and is advising an IT company on expansion.

Foresta Business Law Group's IT work includes project implementation advice to one IT company, and assistance with telecoms regulation for another.

Juridicon is permanent legal adviser to IT company Microlink.

Lideika, Petrauskas, Valiunas ir Partneriai advises a number of telecoms companies including mobile operator Omnitel. The firm's experienced IT department is seeing an increase in work.

At **Law Firm Regija,** Mindaugas Civilka is recommended for IT and telecoms work. He lectures in e-commerce law at Lithuania's International School of Management.

An increase in IT and telecoms work following the liberalisation of the market led **Sorainen Law Offices** to hire Rita Svedaite, a lawyer with considerable experience in these fields. She previously worked at the Free Market Institute, a Vilnius-based think-tank, and now joins a four-strong IT and telecoms team. The firm boasts a couple of significant clients.

Following on from its role in the privatisation of the national telecoms company, **Sutkiene, Pilkauskas & Partners** continues to act for Lithuania Telecom, dealing mostly with competition matters. The firm is one of the first in Lithuania to have conducted Internet telecoms litigation.

Law Office of Tadas Kilmas principally acts for small to medium-sized foreign IT companies doing business in Lithuania, including a legal software company.

Vilnius 7th Law Firm assisted Ericsson in updating its stock option plan and conforming to Lithuanian laws. In IT, it advised Oracle on a public tender, and provided licensing advice to a large Lithuanian IT company.

Zabiela, Zabielaite & Partners has five lawyers dedicated to IT and telecoms who have advised a couple of significant clients on fixed-line and mobile matters.

INTELLECTUAL PROPERTY

AAA Legal Services is well-known for its expertise in trade mark and patent law. Aquafresh, Bic, Lego, Polaroid, adidas, Nike and Intel are among the slew of household names the firm has represented. Senior partner Marius Jason is a registered patent attorney in Lithuania and the US.

In 2003 **Foresta Business Law Group** provided an international hygiene company with packaging protection advice, and advised a German confectioner on trade mark rights.

Juridicon advises a postcard producer and an ISP on IP matters. Lawyer Andrzej Czajkowski has particular knowledge of trade secrets law, and contributed to the corresponding section of Lithuania's new Civil Code.

Law Firm Regija offers advice on e-commerce, including software copyright and Internet broadcasting.

At **Sorainen Law Offices**, partner Renata Berzankiene worked on three IP disputes last year which included protecting trade mark interests.

Sutkiene, Pilkauskas & Partners has seen an increase in IP work. It provides trade mark and patent advice to a US biotech company.

Vilnius 7th Law Firm advised the local subsidiary of Dupont on trade mark protection and gave IP advice to a leading hi-tech company.

Zabiela, Zabielaite & Partners' five-strong IP team advises a number of corporate and private clients. Recent work includes advice and litigation on patents, trade marks, name and image rights, and trade secrets.

MARITIME AND TRANSPORT

Lideika, Petrauskas, Valiunas ir Partneriai runs its comprehensive maritime practice out of the firm's Klaipeda office.

Law Office of Vytas Ramanauskas specialises in maritime law, and acted in several high-value shipping disputes last year.

Jurevicius, Balciunas & Partners assists a number of large Lithuanian transport companies on various carriage agreements, while **Juridicon** advises M&M International Holdings on transport law.

Law Firm Regija recently enhanced its transportation practice by hiring an aviation law specialist, Jurate Rusteikate.

At **Sarka, Sabaliauskas, Jankauskas**, partners Arunas Sarka and Laimutis Jankauskas have represented various companies in transport disputes. The firm has acted for several German companies across the transport spectrum.

In the privatisation of the Lithuanian Shipping Company, **Sutkiene, Pilkauskas & Partners** represented the buyer; **Sorainen Law Offices** advised other foreign private investors on the same deal.

Scandinavian transport company Scania consulted **Vilnius 7th Law Firm** on a number of legal issues last year.

Zabiela, Zabielaite & Partners prepared cession and purchase agreements for a local transport business and acted for a railroad freight company.

PRIVATISATION

Law Firm Bernotas & Dominas Glimstedt represented buyers in Lithuania's electricity, transport fleet and alcohol privatisations. The firm represents the government in the ongoing gas privatisation.

PRIVATISATION

BERNOTAS & DOMINAS GLIMSTEDT, LAW FIRM ✪
LIDEIKA, PETRAUSKAS, VALIUNAS IR PARTNERIAI ✪
SUTKIENE, PILKAUSKAS & PARTNERS ✪

Foresta Business Law Group
Sarka, Sabaliauskas, Jankauskas
Vilnius 7th Law Firm ✪
Zabiela, Zabielaite & Partners ✪

Firms are listed A-Z in tiers which are ranked in order of priority
✪ Indicates firm displays contact details at the end of this chapter.

Lideika, Petrauskas, Valiunas ir Partneriai is advising Scandinavian Airlines on the proposed privatisation of Lithuanian Airlines, and represents the government in the privatisation of four alcohol companies in deals totalling €69.5m.

Despite its split from the former *Jaskutelis, Sutkiene & Masiokas*, **Sutkiene, Pilkauskas & Partners** still commands a strong presence in the slowing privatisation market. The firm is representing the government in the privatisation of the electricity distribution sector, one of Lithuania's most sizeable deals. The firm is also advising the investors in all four of Lithuania's current alcohol privatisations, and representing a Scandinavian consortium in the national shipping company privatisation.

Foresta Business Law Group worked on two alcohol privatisations and three power privatisations in 2003.

Eight-lawyer **Sarka, Sabaliauskas, Jankauskas** advised potential investors in a power plant privatisation, and a municipal water privatisation.

Vilnius 7th Law Firm conducted due diligence on a Lithuanian gas company as part of the firm's ongoing privatisation advice to Gazprom. The firm is also advising an Italian wine producer on a proposed $30m alcohol privatisation.

Zabiela, Zabielaite & Partners advised a Danish company on the privatisation of industrial premises. The firm is well-versed in EU law.

REAL ESTATE AND CONSTRUCTION

LIDEIKA, PETRAUSKAS, VALIUNAS IR PARTNERIAI ✪

Bernotas & Dominas Glimstedt, Law Firm ✪
Sorainen Law Offices
Zabiela, Zabielaite & Partners ✪

AAA Legal Services
Baublys & Partners ✪
Foresta Business Law Group
Hough, Gabartas, Sarzickas ir Partneri
Jurevicius, Balciunas & Partners ✪
Regija, Law Firm ✪
Sarka, Sabaliauskas, Jankauskas
Sutkiene, Pilkauskas & Partners ✪
Vilnius 7th Law Firm ✪

Firms are listed A-Z in tiers which are ranked in order of priority
✪ Indicates firm displays contact details at the end of this chapter.

REAL ESTATE AND CONSTRUCTION

Lideika, Petrauskas, Valiunas ir Partneriai is advising on several commercial property deals, including the acquisition of 25 buildings by a transport company, and the purchase of Shell's service stations by an oil company. The firm is acting in a number of ongoing construction projects.

Law firm Bernotas & Dominas Glimstedt is assisting the biggest foreign real estate developer in Lithuania with expansion.

Sorainen Law Offices advised on a number of real estate projects in 2003. Work involved negotiating leases, structuring trading schemes and acquiring and developing real estate.

Zabiela, Zabielaite & Partners had another busy year. The firm advised a yarn company on lease agreements worth a projected €10m. It also drafted €2.6m contract works for a new auto-centre, and advised on other transactions totalling over €6m.

AAA Legal Services prepared sale, purchase and construction agreements for a Vilnius hotel and advised on a number of smaller construction projects.

Foresta Business Law Group advises an international real estate company.

Jurevicius, Balciunas & Partners assisted both local and international clients on various aspects of real estate and construction law in 2003.

Sarka, Sabaliauskas, Jankauskas advised a German developer on a €90m real estate project. The team employed knowledge of the energy sector in advising another German client on the construction of Lithuania's first wind power station. Name partner Linas Sabaiauskas is recommended.

Vilnius 7th Law Firm provided construction advice to the London-based Holocaust Educational Trust, and a global textiles business. It advised Finnish firm Teletekno on a real estate purchase, and provides ongoing legal services to successful construction company, Kaustas.

TAX

AAA Legal Services
Baublys & Partners ✪
Bernotas & Dominas Glimstedt, Law Firm ✪
Foresta Business Law Group
Hough, Gabartas, Sarzickas ir Partneri
Jurevicius, Balciunas & Partners ✪
Juridicon ✪
Lideika, Petrauskas, Valiunas ir Partneriai ✪
Regija, Law Firm ✪
Sorainen Law Offices
Tadas Kilmas, Law Office of
Vilnius 7th Law Firm ✪
Zabiela, Zabielaite & Partners ✪

Firms are listed alphabetically
✪ Indicates firm displays contact details at the end of this chapter.

TAX

Several US companies relied on **AAA Legal Services** for tax advice over the year, including Hewlett-Packard and Microsoft.

As part of its comprehensive range of legal tax services, **Baublys & Partners** has a busy tax litigation department. In 2003 it successfully represented a Lithuanian company before the Tax Dispute Commission, and obtained reduced taxes and penalties for a private client.

The arrival of tax specialist Arturas Baksys from *Jaskutelis, Sutkiene & Masiokas* at **Law firm Bernotas & Dominas Glimstedt** has expanded the firm's tax capacity, and added several US companies to its client list, including Mars.

Tax specialist Sigitas Groblys left KPMG to join **Foresta Business Law Group** in December 2002, bolstering the firm's tax practice, which serves 30 clients.

Jurevicius, Balciunas & Partners assists a number of leading Lithuanian companies with tax optimisation advice, and is experienced in tax litigation.

Tax law is the busiest practice area for **Juridicon** which provides Gazprom and Microlink Data with tax advice. The firm has links with several auditing firms and performs tax litigation.

Lideika, Petrauskas, Valiunas ir Partneriai's tax service benefited from the arrival of Gediminas Macys from PwC in Reading, UK.

Law Firm Regija still offers tax advice, but is no longer associated with KPMG.

In response to increased demand for tax advice, **Sorainen Law Offices** now has a lawyer fully dedicated to this area of law. Clients include a Russian oil company and a Scandinavian entertainment company.

Vilnius 7th Law Firm's tax practice benefits from its association with PwC.

Zabiela, Zabielaite & Partners provided advice on several tax disputes and represented Finnish embassy employees against the tax authorities. Tax lawyer Julius Bernatonis formerly worked at the Lithuanian Ministry of Finance.

BAUBLYS & PARTNERS

GOSTAUTO STREET 40
01112 VILNIUS

Telephone: +370 5 236 2708
Fax: +370 5 236 2709
E-mail: vilnius@baublys.net
Website: www.baublys.net

Languages
English, Russian

Other offices
Kaunas, Moscow

Number of lawyers 11
at this office 5

Contact
Kęstutis Švirinas

CATEGORIES OF WORK

Dispute resolution – litigation and arbitration
Gediminas Baublys, Kęstutis Švirinas

Insurance defense
Evaldas Rapolas, Mantas Arasmimavicius

Tax
Ligita Ramanauskaitė, Paulius Čerka

Company law
Ligita Ramanauskaitė, Aurimas Brazdeikis

Property (real estate) law
Kęstutis Švirinas, Ligita Ramanauskaitė

Securities and finance
Ligita Ramanauskaitė, Kęstutis Švirinas

BERNOTAS & DOMINAS GLIMSTEDT

JOGAILOS STR 4
2001 VILNIUS

Telephone: +370 5 269 0700
Fax: +370 5 269 0701
E-mail: glimstedt@glimstedt.lt
Website: www.glimstedt.lt

Languages
English, French, German, Latvian, Lithuanian, Russian, Swedish

Other offices
Riga

Number of lawyers 33
at this office 25

CATEGORIES OF WORK

Company and commercial

Banking and finance

Mergers and acquisitions

Privatisation

Competition law

Insolvency and business restructuring

Intellectual property

Telecommunications and information technology law

Advertising and media

Insurance

Litigation, arbitration, dispute resolution

Real estate and construction

International trade and transportation

Labour law

JUREVIČIUS, BALČIŪNAS & PARTNERS
EY LAW

SUBAČIAUS 7
01008 VILNIUS

Telephone: +370 5 274 2400
Fax: +370 5 274 2444
E-mail: advocate@lt.ey.com
Website: www.jbp.lt

Languages
English, German, Russian

Number of lawyers 49

Contacts
Raimundas Jurevičius, Gintaras Balčiūnas

Member
EY Law

CATEGORIES OF WORK

General practice
Company law
Corporate law
Mergers and acquisitions
Competition law
Real estate
Leases and leasing
Business law
Privatisation
Foreign investment
International commercial law
Intellectual property
Banking law
Securities
Finance
Telecommunications law
Energy law
Environmental law
Maritime law
Shipping
European Union law
Construction law
Debt collection
Labour and employment
Tax law
Civil litigation
Sports law

JURIDICON LAW OFFICE

TOTORIU STREET 5-7
01121 VILNIUS

Telephone: +370 5 269 1100
Fax: +370 5 269 1010
E-mail: office@juridicon.com
Website: www.juridicon.lt

Languages
English, German, Polish, Russian

Number of lawyers 5

Contact
Laimonas Marcinkevicius

CATEGORIES OF WORK

Company and corporate law
L Marcinkevicius, I Steponaviciene

Mergers and acquisitions
L Marcinkevicius, I Steponaviciene

Public tenders
I Steponaviciene, A Czajkowski

Energy law
A Czajkowski, I Steponaviciene

Commercial law
L Marcinkevicius, A Czajkowski

Securities
L Marcinkevicius, A Czajkowski

Banking and finance
L Marcinkevicius

Taxation
L Marcinkevicius

Competition, advertising law
A Czajkowski

Foreign investments and privatisation
L Marcinkevicius, A Czajkowski

Transport law (CMR Convention)
A Czajkowski

Copyrights
L Marcinkevicius, I Steponaviciene

Trade marks
L Marcinkevicius, A Czajkowski

Trade secrets
A Czajkowski

Employment and labour law
L Marcinkevicius, A Czajkowski

Civil and administrative litigation
L Marcinkevicius, A Czajkowski

Arbitration
L Marcinkevicius

LIDEIKA, PETRAUSKAS, VALIŪNAS IR PARTNERIAI

LABDARIŲ G 5
LT-01120 VILNIUS

Telephone: +370 5 268 1832
Fax: +370 5 212 5591
E-mail: lpvp@lpvp.lt
Website: www.lpvp.lt

Languages
English, French, German, Russian

Other offices
Klaipėda

Number of lawyers 28
at this office 27

Contact
Rolandas Valiūnas (managing partner)

CATEGORIES OF WORK

Banking and finance
G Stasevičius, G Rečiūnas

Communications
J Gumbis, L Skibarka

Competition
Š Keserauskas, M Juonys

Corporate and M&A
R Valiūnas, Ž Zinkevičius

Corporate restructuring, insolvency
M Kiškis, L Skibarka

Dispute resolution
V Vaitkutė Pavan, R Petravičius

Employment and social security
R Petravičius, A Augustinavičius

Energy and Natural Resources
J Gumbis, A Raziulytė

Environment
R Galvėnas, L Kasperūnaitė

Information technology
M Kiškis, M Juonys

Insurance
T Milašauskas, G Rečiūnas

Intellectual property
M Kiškis, G Pranevičius

Public private partnership
D Burgienė, G Stasevičius

Real estate and construction
R Galvėnas, T Milašauskas

Securities
G Stasevičius, G Rečiūnas

Tax
G Mačys, G Kveselaitienė

Trade
J Gumbis, M Juonys

Transport and maritime
V Vaitkutė Pavan, S Sudintas

THE FIRM

Lideika, Petrauskas, Valiūnas ir partneriai is one of the leading and largest law firms in Lithuania and the Baltic States. The firm renders services in all major fields of business and is distinguished by the excellence of services, extensive experience and leading specialists in Lithuania. The core principle of the firm's work is assisting the clients in achieving their business goals.

The firm's main office is situated in Vilnius and, since 1998, the branch has successfully operated in Klaipeda, a major Lithuanian port. Presently, Lideika, Petrauskas, Valiūnas ir partneriai has 28 lawyers, six assistant lawyers, two tax advisers and one adviser on competition matters. Most of the firm's lawyers have earned postgraduate degrees at US, UK, German and other Western universities. The firm takes an active part in the reform of the Lithuanian legal system, including drafting of the new legislation and other programs.

The firm's clients include multinational corporations, investment banks and international finance institutions as well as leading domestic companies. Cross-border transactions form a significant part of the firm's work and some 80% of the client base are international clients.

The firm has continuously sought specialisation of its lawyers and was probably the first law firm in Lithuania to have effectively introduced practice groups. The firm's lawyers now work in five practice groups – corporate and M&A; finance and tax; property and environment; trade and technologies; dispute resolution; labour; and transport.

Lideika, Petrauskas, Valiūnas ir partneriai is a member of leading international alliances. The firm's strong co-operative links with leading law firms in Latvia, Estonia and other countries allow it to ensure quality counselling to its clients in all Baltic States and other foreign countries.

AREAS OF PRACTICE

Lideika, Petrauskas, Valiūnas ir partneriai offers a full range of legal services. The firm has earned its reputation for being at the heart of the largest and most complex commercial and financial transactions in Lithuania.

The firm has vast experience in the corporate and M&A field gained through participation in major M&A and privatisation transactions, leveraged buy-outs, joint ventures, negotiating and implementing shareholders' agreements and other corporate matters. The firm has an outstanding reputation in privatisation matters – it has been successfully acting in either buyer-side or as adviser of the government (the State Property Fund) in virtually all major privatisation transactions in Lithuania.

The firm has a solid portfolio of international banking clients and regularly advises on debt, equity and derivatives offerings, subordinated and syndicated loans, commercial lending, investment and project financing as well as capital markets and securities.

The firm has a leading competition team practice which is characterised by diverse subject matter and a combination of legal and economic expertise. The firm assists clients in merger control, joint ventures, regulation of cartels and horizontal co-operation agreements, vertical restrictions, abuse of dominant position, state aid, and sector-specific regulation.

In communications and IT, the firm regularly advises major international and Lithuanian telecoms companies, representing them in regulatory matters and litigation with the regulator. The IT team has a strong IT client base including major multinationals and leading Lithuanian IT companies.

The firm's diverse IP practice includes registration of trade marks, drafting of licensing agreements, representing clients before the State Patent Bureau and the customs department, and representing in trade mark and other IP-related litigation.

The firm advises a number of leading real estate and construction companies and property investment funds on real estate acquisition and development, lease, planning, and construction as well as property insurance.

The firm has been recognised as one of the leading advisers to the shipping and transport industries, counselling on maritime issues (charterparties, bills of lading, ship registration, ship arrest) and other transport issues, and counts among its clients leading transport companies.

NORCOUS & PARTNERS

LAW OFFICES

GOŠTAUTO ST 12 A
01108 VILNIUS

Telephone: +370 5 268 3620
Fax: +370 5 268 3621
E-mail: office@norcous.lt
Website: www.norcous.lt

Languages
English, German, Russian, Lithuanian

Number of lawyers 6

CATEGORIES OF WORK

Mergers and acquisitions
Irmantas Norkus, Aušra Adomaitytė

Banking and finance
Irmantas Norkus, Saulius Milius

Commercial and company law
Aušra Adomaitytė, Lauras Butkevičius

Competition
Irmantas Norkus, Aušra Adomaitytė

Immigration and expatriates
Arūnas Šidlauskas

Litigation
Arūnas Šidlauskas, Mindaugas Žolynas

Privatisation
Irmantas Norkus, Arūnas Šidlauskas

EU law
Lauras Butkevičius

Real estate
Arūnas Šidlauskas, Mindaugas Žolynas

Securities
Irmantas Norkus, Aušra Adomaitytė

Tax law and tax disputes
Arūnas Šidlauskas

THE FIRM

Norcous & Partners was founded in 2001 by Dr Irmantas Norkus, a lawyer who had previously worked for a major Lithuanian law firm for six years. Since its foundation, Norcous & Partners has grown to be a medium-sized law firm in Lithuania, with six qualified lawyers and two legal assistants (two lawyers will join the firm in January 2004). A commitment to high-quality services and client satisfaction, as well as favourable conditions in the Lithuanian legal market, determined the fast growth of the firm. In 2003, the firm was offered membership by several international legal networks.

Since its formation, the firm's main areas of practice are mergers and acquisitions, privatisation law, corporate law, commercial and company law, and competition law. Teamwork and co-operation with other professional advisers enabled Norcous & Partners to take part in the large-scale projects in the field of M&A and privatisation, advising both local and international clients.

AREAS OF PRACTICE

Norcous & Partners is a commercial law office with a particular expertise in the field of mergers and acquisitions, privatisation law and competition law. In 2003, the firm acted for foreign investors in the privatisation of the key industries of Lithuania, such as shipping, power distribution and supply, and alcohol beverage manufacturing. Norcous & Partners represented both sellers and buyers in a number of private acquisition transactions, including the acquisition of a leading Lithuanian dairy.

The firm has a proven track record in advising and representing clients in competition law matters. In 2002 and 2003, the firm advised the dominant Lithuanian alcohol producer in relation to alleged infringements of competition law. In 2003, Norcous & Partners represented the National Association of Carriers, the leading Lithuanian wholesaler in oil products in the investigations carried out by the Lithuanian Competition Council. The firm represented the major Lithuanian breweries in obtaining an individual exemption for their agreement from the Lithuanian Competition Council.

REGIJA

J JASINKIO 16A
8TH FLOOR
2001 VILNIUS

Telephone: +370 5 264 9555
Fax: +370 5 260 8327
E-mail: regija@regija.lt
Website: www.regija.lt

Languages
English, German, Lithuanian, Russian

Number of lawyers 13

Member
European Law Firm

CATEGORIES OF WORK

Banking, finance and securities
Tomas Rymeikis, Ausra Mudenaite

Commercial law and company law
Dr Dalia Foigt, Tomas Rymeikis

Mergers and acquisitions
Dr Dalia Foigt, Mindaugas Civilka

EU and competition law
Dr Dalia Foigt, Mindaugas Civilka

Transportation law
Dr Dalia Foigt, Ausra Mudenaite

Media, IT and telecommunications
Dr Dalia Foigt, Mindaugas Civilka

Arbitration
Dr Dalia Foigt, Ausra Mudenaite

Intellectual property
Stasys Drazdauskas,
Skirmante Klumbyte

Real estate and construction
Ausra Mudenaite, Skirmante Klumbyte

Litigation
Ausra Mudenaite, Stasys Drazdaukas

Taxation
Mindaugas Civilka, Ausra Mudenaite

Privatisation
Dr Dalia Foigt, Tomas Rymeikis

Environment
Radvile Balcikoniene, Tomas Rymeikis

Labour law
Stasys Drazdauskas, Mindaugas Civilka

Corporate finance
Tomas Rymeikis, Ausra Mudenaite

SUTKIENE, PILKAUSKAS & PARTNERS

DIDZIOJI STREET 23
2600 VILNIUS

Telephone: +370 5 251 4444
Fax: +370 5 251 4455
E-mail: spp@spp.lt
Website: www.spp.lt

Languages
Dutch, English, Estonian, German, Lithuanian, Polish, Russian

Number of lawyers 12

Contacts
Eugenija Sutkiene (managing partner), Jonas Pilkauskas (managing partner)

Member
Interlaw

CATEGORIES OF WORK

Commercial law	**Insolvency**
Company law	**Litigation**
Competition law	**Intellectual property**
Labour law and immigration	**Media, communications and telecommunications**
Property (real estate) law	**M&A**
Energy and natural resources	
Securities and finance	

THE FIRM

Sutkiene, Pilkauskas & Partners (SPP) is a law firm of the highest standing. SPP was founded in spring 2003 following the reorganisation of the law firm Jaskutelis, Sutkiene & Masiokas. Founding members, Mrs Eugenija Sutkiene, who was instrumental in establishing the first multinational law firm to practice in Lithuania over a decade ago (McDermott, Will & Emery), and the highly-rated Mr Jonas Pilkauskas, both ensure high standards of service. Their reputation has been enhanced by teaming up qualified lawyers with diverse legal experience to provide sophisticated, quality advice to the leading national and multinational companies, financial institutions and government on their most challenging assignments and transactions in all areas of commercial law. A number of the SPP lawyers have already received, or are about to receive in the near future, academic degrees. Most of the firm's lawyers take an active part in drafting of the laws of the Republic of Lithuania.

AREAS OF PRACTICE

SPP focuses on privatisations and international trade and foreign investments, banking, bankruptcy, M&A, finance, securities, energy and natural resources, biotechnology, brewing and spirits production, real estate, telecommunications, tax, competition, employment and labour, and media law.

SPP offers legal services to international clients with interests in Lithuania and abroad. The firm's international experience covers most of its practice areas. It has gained expertise in handling a large number of cross-border commercial transactions and M&A. The firm often manages major transactions and processes, involving co-operation and alignment with other professionals.

The highlights of SPP services are set out below:

Company and commercial: One of the firm's core areas of practice is related to corporate matters. The firm assists on privatisations, M&A, incorporation, liquidation, reorganisation and restructuring of all types of enterprises; advises on company management, franchise, lease and other types of commercial agreements; represents clients in insolvency proceedings, managing bodies; and drafts all types of documents of a corporate and commercial nature.

Competition: SPP is expert in competition law. It advises clients on the exercise of the monopoly power, market concentration, prohibited agreements; prepares merger filings; drafts applications to grant individual exemption; submits complaints regarding the actions restricting the competition; and represents clients at the local competition authority as well as before the court.

Labour law and immigration: The firm provides legal services in all spheres of labour law, including consultations on senior executives' employment contracts, workplace issues, such as terminations, reductions in force, breaches of conduct, reimbursement, misappropriation of trade secrets and unfair competition. SPP also advises on immigration issues, including foreign employee recruitment.

Litigation: The firm has an extensive experience in preventing and resolving disputes. SPP represents the clients in civil, commercial, labour, tax, competition, and bankruptcy/administrative cases before the courts of all instances.

Telecommunications: The firm has gained exceptional professional expertise in all spheres of telecommunications. SPP lawyers have been providing ongoing legal representation of Lithuanian Telecom.

VILNIUS 7TH LAW FIRM

T SEVCENKOS 21
LT-03111 VILNIUS 9

Telephone: +370 5 239 2391
Fax: +370 5 239 2390
E-mail: law.firm@lt.pwc.com
Website: www.v7lf.lt

Languages
English, Russian

Number of lawyers 7

Contact
Jonas Saladzius (managing partner)

CATEGORIES OF WORK

Commercial and competition
Jonas Saladzius

Company law, corporate structuring
Jonas Saladzius

Dispute resolution
Jonas Saladzius, Rimtis Puisys

Technology, media and communications
Max Saveljev

Employment and human resources
Max Saveljev

Banking and finance
Jonas Saladzius

Intellectual property
Rimtis Puisys

Mergers and acquisitions
Jonas Saladzius

Public law
Ausrys Sliavas

Real estate
Jonas Saladzius

Privatisation
Jonas Saladzius

Energy and infrastructure projects
Ausrys Sliavas

THE FIRM

Vilnius 7th Law Firm, a correspondent law firm of Pricewaterhouse-Coopers, provides legal assistance to businesses and financiers, as well as governmental agencies in Lithuania. The firm's Lithuanian and international clients represent various industries such as wholesale and retail trade, energy, telecommunications, information technology, financial services, pharmaceuticals and light industry.

The firm's ability to draw upon the expertise of the world's largest professional services organisation, PricewaterhouseCoopers, uniquely positions Vilnius 7th Law Firm to deliver complete business solutions to clients.

The firm's expertise has been developed through years of extensive experience, which enables Vilnius 7th Law Firm to deliver high-quality services to all its clients.

AREAS OF PRACTICE

Vilnius 7th Law Firm focuses on all aspects of business law, including the areas of corporate and commercial law, financial services, banking, information technology, intellectual property, employment law and dispute resolution.

The firm is particularly well known for carrying out legal due diligence exercises, providing assistance with mergers and acquisitions, advising on corporate restructuring, drafting and reviewing the contracts, solving labour law issues, and advising on privatisation and other complex assignments.

The legal profession in Lithuania and the legal market are facing new challenges associated with EU integration. Vilnius 7th law Firm is prepared to advise clients on the legal implications of EU enlargement to their businesses.

A brochure providing more details is available on request.

ZABIELA, ZABIELAITE & PARTNERS

A JAKSTO STR 7
2600 VILNIUS

Telephone: +370 5 261 4033
Fax: +370 5 212 3430
E-mail: office@zabiela.lt
Website: www.zabiela.lt

Languages
English, French, German, Russian

Number of lawyers 18

CATEGORIES OF WORK

Corporate and commercial
Darius Zabiela, Saulius Zališauskas

Real estate and construction
Darius Zabiela, Albinas Raudonius

Energy and natural resources
Jūratė Zabielaitė, Darius Zabiela

Banking, securities and finance
Darius Zabiela, Jūratė Zabielaitė

Competition
Darius Zabiela

Tax
Darius Zabiela

Telecommunications
Jūratė Zabielaitė, Viktor Lavrinovič

Intellectual property
Jūratė Zabielaitė, Sabina Babravičienė

Employment
Jūratė Zabielaitė, Algis Krušna

Insurance
Darius Zabiela, Saulius Zališauskas

Admin law and public procurement
Jūratė Zabielaitė, Algis Krušna

Public law and regulatory
Jūratė Zabielaitė, Natalija Semionova

Media and entertainment
Jūratė Zabielaitė, Artūras Razgūnas

EC law
Darius Zabiela, Jūratė Zabielaitė

Criminal law
Vytautas Zabiela, Ričardas Suslavičius

Arbitration
Darius Zabiela, Algis Krušna

Litigation
Vytautas Zabiela, Algis Krušna

Project finance (EU structural funds)
Jūratė Zabielaitė, Natalija Semionova

LUXEMBOURG

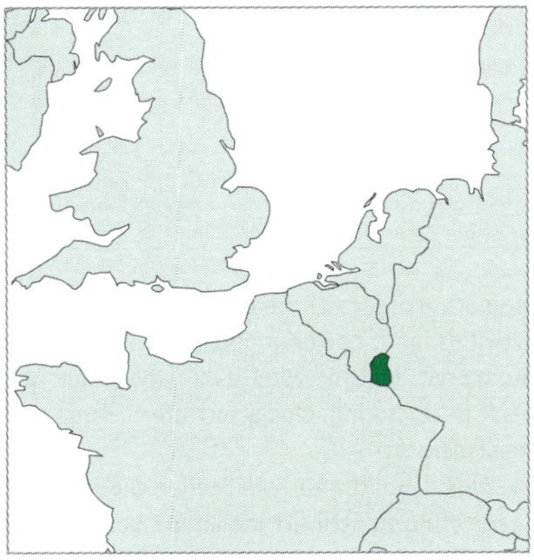

Population	451,000
Number of lawyers	850
Professional title	Avocat; Avocat à la Cour
Currency	Euro (€)

Index

The only Grand Duchy in the world, Luxembourg is a landlocked country, sharing borders with Belgium, France and Germany. It is the smallest member of the Euro-zone, but the most prosperous, boasting a per-capita GDP of $44,570 in 2002, the highest in the world. Stability, growth, low inflation and low unemployment prevail in spite of a global economic slump.

Luxembourg has progressed from an economy dominated by steel to one that boasts a robust service industry and a flourishing financial sector. Government-led diversification policies introduced in the 1970s encouraged the growth of non-heavy industries such as chemicals, plastics, rubber and mechanical equipment plus other sectors. The country's service industries account for 63% of GDP while banking and insurance contribute to 23.4 % of GDP.

A combination of favourable legal regimes have fuelled the growth of the financial services sector, with insurance, reinsurance and group treasury operations all benefiting. Foreign direct investment is encouraged and tax breaks, subsidised loans and other customised incentives have been drawn up with the aim of encouraging new ventures into the Grand Duchy, particularly in view of recent surges in the promotion of economic development activities in the US and Asia. The Luxembourg government has recently set up a satellite operation attached to the Ministry of Trade, tasked with promoting entrepreneurial activity.

One of the six founding members of the European Union, Luxembourg plays host to some ten European institutions, including the European Court of Justice, the European Court of Auditors and the European Court of First Instance. Its size enables it to quickly adopt EU law compared to its larger neighbours.

Luxembourg is a constitutional democracy, currently led by Prime Minister Jean-Claude Juncker's Christian Social Party and Democratic Party coalition government. The next general elections are due to take place in June 2004.

Languages spoken are French, German, Luxembourgish and English.

BILLING

Billing is usually by the hour, with junior associate rates pegged at around €125 to €200 per hour and senior/managing partners commanding rates of €300 to €500. Some firms are moving towards a fixed-rate billing structure, in which a set fee is agreed upfront with the client for an entire transaction. Other firms apply special account deals or fixed charge-out rates, particularly for cross-border deals.

MARKETING

Luxembourg's Bar Association rules prohibit marketing and advertising activities, although firms are allowed to run websites that provide details about their lawyers and practice area coverage.

IN-HOUSE LAWYERS

While some companies do have in-house lawyers, such in-house teams tend to be small.

ECONOMIC CLIMATE

Luxembourg's business environment has spawned a large concentration of banks and investment funds. Despite consolidation in recent years, Luxembourg remains a renowned international financial centre, boasting 188 banks. Investment funds are thought to be the next area of growth over the coming years, with some firms already witnessing a sustained strong performance in this area.

The Grand Duchy has been quick to implement EU directives relating to the financial services sector. Companies looking to take advantage of Luxembourg's protected climate have continued to fuel growth in M&A activity.

Over the next two-year period, the economic outlook is likely to undergo far-reaching changes as European harmonisation laws challenge the jurisdiction's banking secrecy laws and tax regime. A European ruling passed in June 2003 stating that Luxembourg must tax the savings of non-residents by 2005 could trigger a flight of capital out of the country.

LEGAL MARKET

Mergers between Luxembourg and international law firms have dominated the market headlines in recent years with a number of high-profile strategic alliances. Changes to the Luxembourg Bar rules, which came into effect during the first half of 2003, mean that the name of the Luxembourg firm

The largest firms

1	Arendt & Medernach	90
2	Bonn Schmitt Steichen	45
3	Linklaters Loesch	43
4	Elvinger, Hoss & Prussen	40
5	Allen & Overy Luxembourg	34
6	Kremer Associés & Clifford Chance	32
7	Wildgen & Partners	30
8	Noble & Scheidecker	26
9	Oostvogels & Pfister	25
10	Loyens & Loeff	24
11	Assa, Lutgen & Schaack	19
12	Molitor, Fisch & Associés	15
	Plottké, Brunel & Associates	15
	Schaeffer, Hengel & Associés	15
15	NCR Avocats, member of ius laboris	14
16	Le Goueff Avocats	10
17	Schiltz et Schiltz	9
18	Wagener, Rukavina & Kettenmeyer	8
19	Maitland & Co	7
	Michel – Schanen – Moyse	7
21	Adam & Bleser	6
	Dupong & Spielman	6
23	Dechert Luxembourg	5
	Felten & Associés	5
	Étude Wassenich	5

These figures represent the total number of lawyers in this country only, and have been supplied by the firms themselves. The figures should be accurate as at 1 January 2004.

need no longer appear alongside that of the foreign entity. Some practices have been quick to assume these changes, namely *Beghin & Feider en association avec Allen Overy* which has become **Allen & Overy Luxembourg**, and *Brucher & Seimetz in association with Dechert* is now known as **Dechert Luxembourg**.

Local firms are increasingly opting for membership of one or more international networks rather than taking the mega law firm merger route as a means of securing international referral work. In 2003 **Le Goueff Avocats** underwent an audit to gain admittance to the *Association of Commercial Lawyers*. **Bonn Schmitt Steichen** is a member of *Lex Mundi*, **Adam & Bleser** has long-standing links with *TAGLaw Group*, and **Assa, Lutgen & Schaack** is a member of the *International Lawyers Network*. **Michel Di Stefano Schanen & Moyse** has also discovered the benefits of global law networks. The firm is a member of both the *Association of European Lawyers* and the *Alpha International* network. That said, other firms such as **Plottké, Brunel & Associates** have declared their intention to remain independent.

While Luxembourg law firms are aware of the need to anticipate and address the needs of the market, many are treading carefully when taking on new staff. Recruitment is down on previous years, and generally organic growth – through the hire of newly qualified lawyers – is favoured. Lateral hiring is still taking place, albeit on a limited scale.

BANKING AND FINANCE

BANKING AND FINANCE

ARENDT & MEDERNACH
ELVINGER, HOSS & PRUSSEN
LINKLATERS LOESCH ✪

ALLEN & OVERY LUXEMBOURG ✪
BONN SCHMITT STEICHEN ✪
KREMER ASSOCIÉS & CLIFFORD CHANCE

Le Goueff Avocats
Oostvogels & Pfister ✪
Wildgen & Partners

Assa, Lutgen & Schaack

Firms are listed A-Z in tiers which are ranked in order of priority
✪ *Indicates firm displays contact details at the end of this chapter.*

Arendt & Medernach's financial services practice is jointly led by Paul Mousel and Philippe Dupont. The department delivers a raft of services to local and international banks, investment companies, and insurance and reinsurance companies. Capital markets experience includes IPOs, collaterisation and securitisation. In 2003, **Arendt & Medernach** was one of a team of global advisers on a large private placement worth $1bn.

Elvinger, Hoss & Prussen has a strong presence in banking and finance, due in part to the strong and acknowledged banking skills of partner Pit Reckinger.

Headed up by the highly rated Janine Biver, the team of nine banking and finance specialists at **Linklaters Loesch** focuses on capital markets and banking deals, including restructuring, domestic and cross-border investments and M&A. The firm's structured finance group also advises on Luxembourg special purpose vehicles (SPVs) investing in particular assets or unregulated fund schemes. The department has advised on capital markets issues for an Eastern European electricity operator.

Under the leadership of partner André Marc, **Allen & Overy Luxembourg**'s five-lawyer team's core activities include bank restructuring and mergers, corporate mergers, private banking activities and banking litigation. Among the prominent deals of 2003 were labour law and bank restructuring, plus a mixture of large and small mergers.

Alex Schmitt and Jean Steffen are the joint heads of **Bonn Schmitt Steichen**'s banking and finance department, covering regulatory issues, foreign direct investment, infrastructure and project finance. Private equity deals have flourished, leading the firm to set up a separate sub-division for this area.

Name partner Kristian Kremer runs **Kremer Associés & Clifford Chance**'s banking and finance practice. Over the last year, the firm has acted increasingly on complex financial transactions involving derivatives, bank lending, regulatory issues and securitisation.

Le Goueff Avocats has worked on two securitisations totalling €180m on behalf of a Canadian bank. Other deals include a number of M&A transactions for Luxembourg clients.

Cross-border transactions and deals involving UK-based finance houses dominate **Oostvogels & Pfister**'s workload.

Name partner André Lutgen along with two other **Assa, Lutgen & Schaack** lawyers advise on banking and financial issues, counting several banks among their clients.

CORPORATE AND COMMERCIAL

Arendt & Medernach's 30-strong team of corporate, tax and IP lawyers is headed up by partner Guy Harles. The firm advises on corporate and tax issues including M&A and company reorganisation. **Arendt & Medernach**, along with **Freshfields Bruckhaus Deringer**, advised on the merger of Compaq with Hewlett-Packard, in one of the Luxembourg firm's most prominent deals of 2002.

Guy Arendt leads **Bonn Schmitt Steichen**'s corporate and commercial team. Most of the work handled arises from transactions taking place in Luxembourg and encompasses M&A, tax-

CORPORATE AND COMMERCIAL

ARENDT & MEDERNACH
BONN SCHMITT STEICHEN ✪
ELVINGER, HOSS & PRUSSEN
LINKLATERS LOESCH ✪

ALLEN & OVERY LUXEMBOURG ✪
KREMER ASSOCIÉS & CLIFFORD CHANCE

Dupong & Spielman
Jim Penning & Associés
Le Goueff Avocats
Michel – Schanen – Moyse ✪
Molitor, Fisch & Associés ✪
Oostvogels & Pfister ✪
Plottké, Brunel & Associates ✪
Wagener, Rukavina & Kettenmeyer

Firms are listed A-Z in tiers which are ranked in order of priority
✪ Indicates firm displays contact details at the end of this chapter.

optimised group restructuring and private equity transactions.

The independent and non-affiliated **Elvinger, Hoss & Prussen** deals with corporate and general commercial matters. The team of ten, led by partner André Elvinger, was active in Luxembourg's largest securitisation and the $3bn merger of steel giants Aceralia, Arbed and Usinor. The same team is also advising a large Luxembourg bank on its demerger activities.

The corporate arm of **Linklaters Loesch** is active in private equity and LBOs. The team of 15 lawyers, managed by partner Tom Loesch, advised on the €4.9bn Legrand buyout of Schneider and the Bain Capital buyout of chemical group Rhodia, valued at €145m. The team also acted in the acquisition of Actaris Group by Montague Private Equity in a €425m transaction. Together, the deals generated most of the firm's work for that period.

Respected partners Marc Fieder and Pierre Schleimer are at the helm of **Allen & Overy Luxembourg**'s 14-strong corporate practice, covering corporate and taxation elements of restructurings.

Stéphan Le Goueff at **Le Goueff Avocats** specialises in corporate advice, including M&A. The firm has been involved in a number of mergers and acquisitions for banks and insurance companies in Luxembourg and further afield.

Michel – Schanen – Moyse's corporate division, headed by partner Mario Di Stefano is involved in M&A, company incorporations, corporate governance matters and advises on shareholder agreements. In 2002/2003, the firm advised a local company on the establishment of a tracker fund valued at €232m.

Molitor, Fisch & Associés delivers full-service company incorporation advice, encompassing company law, management, restructuring and, where necessary, liquidation to a roster of predominantly Dutch and US clients. A new partner, Dieter Eixler joined the department in October 2003. Formerly CEO of a prominent Luxembourg newspaper and book distributor, Mr Eixler brings business law and management expertise to the division.

Oostvogels & Pfister is active in corporate, with M&A being a particular strength. Two key hires in 2002 – a senior manager from **Ernst & Young** and a partner from Deloitte – have enabled the firm to bolster its restructuring practice.

Myriam Brunel at **Plottké, Brunel & Associates** is a respected corporate lawyer, known particularly for handling corporate disputes.

DISPUTE RESOLUTION

Allen & Overy Luxembourg deals with contentious matters, and boasts particular expertise in disputes arising out of administrative law.

Jean Medernach is a senior partner and head of **Arendt & Medernach**'s litigation practice. The department deals with a range of litigation matters including administrative, employment, civil and commercial disputes. Clients hail from a variety of sectors such as banking, insurance, aviation, construction, maritime, insolvency and real estate.

Bonn Schmitt Steichen's dispute resolution practice is headed by partner Fabio Trevisan. The firm acted on behalf of a client in a dispute resulting in the payout of a substantial dividend. Other clients are government departments, Internet bandwidth licensing companies and banks.

Elvinger, Hoss & Prussen's respected contentious practice is led by partner Marc Elvinger.

Kremer Associés & Clifford Chance seeks to grow its litigation department, its smallest division, through new hires and to this end two new appointments were made in 2003. The practice has witnessed growth in employment litigation, with a particular emphasis on commercial litigation.

Linklaters Loesch's team's recent matters include insolvency, corporate and financial fraud litigation.

Adam & Bleser manages an evenly split caseload of domestic and foreign commercial litigation cases. The firm is currently handling some US cases valued at around $100m, as well as an ongoing class action involving public sector employees.

Administrative, civil and contract disputes are handled by a number of lawyers at **Assa, Lutgen & Schaack**. The firm is currently advising on mobile phone mast issues.

The seizure of aircraft in Luxembourg has become a significant development, which, according to **Le Goueff Avocats**, has fuelled growth in this area of the firm's practice.

Michel – Schanen – Moyse's Luc Schanen provides civil and commercial litigation expertise, while François Moyse advises on public and administrative matters.

DISPUTE RESOLUTION

ALLEN & OVERY LUXEMBOURG ✪
ARENDT & MEDERNACH
BONN SCHMITT STEICHEN ✪
ELVINGER, HOSS & PRUSSEN
KREMER ASSOCIÉS & CLIFFORD CHANCE
LINKLATERS LOESCH ✪

Dechert Luxembourg
Molitor, Fisch & Associés ✪
Oostvogels & Pfister ✪

Adam & Bleser
Assa, Lutgen & Schaack
Dupong & Spielman
Jim Penning & Associés
Le Goueff Avocats
Michel – Schanen – Moyse ✪
Wagener, Rukavina & Kettenmeyer

Firms are listed A-Z in tiers which are ranked in order of priority
✪ Indicates firm displays contact details at the end of this chapter.

EMPLOYMENT

Employment law is a particular strength of the six-member team at **Adam & Bleser**. The firm boasts a strong local client base comprising mainly financial institutions

The highly respected Louis Berns heads up **Arendt & Medernach**'s employment practice, handling a wide range of industrial relations issues including employment agreements and contracts, stock options and collective dismissal matters. Clients include banks, insurance companies and other corporate bodies.

Anne Morel is head of the team at **Bonn Schmitt Steichen**. The firm is active in a number of ongoing deals from a cross-section of corporate, retail and IT clients.

EMPLOYMENT

ADAM & BLESER
ARENDT & MEDERNACH

Bonn Schmitt Steichen ✪
Elvinger, Hoss & Prussen
Linklaters Loesch ✪
Michel – Schanen – Moyse ✪
NCR Avocats, member of ius laboris ✪

Allen & Overy Luxembourg ✪
Dechert Luxembourg
Kremer Associés & Clifford Chance
Molitor, Fisch & Associés ✪

Firms are listed A-Z in tiers which are ranked in order of priority
✪ Indicates firm displays contact details at the end of this chapter.

Michel – Schanen – Moyse has a strong team offering both non-contentious and contentious services. Partners Roland Michel and Luc Schanen advise on social security and labour law matters related to M&A and restructuring.

Niche firm, **NCR Avocats, member of ius laboris** specialises in employment law and related matters. Guy Castegnaro, a member of the *European Employment Lawyers Association* and a specialist in employment law, pensions funds and employee benefits, heads up a dedicated team.

Allen & Overy Luxembourg's practice is run by André Marc and spans private banking employment issues across a number of sectors including food, textiles, insurance and IT. Disciplines covered include setting up, restructuring, mergers and outsourcing.

Dechert Luxembourg is active in labour law and has advised major Luxembourg banks and other clients on labour-related issues including directors' liability and employment aspects of procurement contracts.

Employment disputes and collective bargaining, pension schemes and regulatory are among the services offered by **Molitor, Fisch & Associés**.

IP AND IT

The law governing personal data protection, which came into full effect in August 2003, has produced a raft of liabilities, particularly with regard to banks. For example, employers are now obliged to prove that they have obtained prior authorisation before processing the personal data held on their workers; this has generated work for law firms.

Arendt & Medernach's IP practice, led by Sophie Chartier comes under the firm's corporate tax and IP umbrella. The firm offers the full range of IP and IT-related advice, including copyright, trade marks, domain name rights, unfair competition, e-commerce and data protection.

Respected name partners Nicolas Decker and Andrée Braun of **Decker, Bodry & Braun** head a team of six lawyers specialising in IP matters for a number of large and small foreign clients. The firm often works jointly with some of Luxembourg's heavyweight commercial firms.

IT, e-commerce and e-platforms are the areas in which **Le Goueff Avocats** first carved a niche for itself. Under Stéphan Le Goueff's leadership, the firm hopes to use its expertise of working with banking, IT, media and telecoms clients, to facilitate expansion into other specialities.

The IP practice of **Allen & Overy Luxembourg** advises on contentious and non-contentious IP matters. The firm also undertakes trade mark, copyright, e-commerce and data protection issues, and offers commercial law expertise covering unfair trade practices, arbitration and litigation. Contractual IT, patents and software issues are also handled.

Véronique Hoffeld has joined **Bonn Schmitt Steichen**'s IP and IT department, increasing the partner headcount to three. The group, led by practice head, Guy Arendt, advises on matters relating to e-commerce, entertainment, telecommunications and aviation.

Coverage of IP and IT issues is provided by a small team of three lawyers at **Elvinger, Hoss & Prussen**.

Assa, Lutgen & Schaack is active in IP and IT issues and has advised Microsoft on several matters; one case involved the use of illegal copies of software on several hundred company-owned computers. The firm has made one lateral hire from a Paris law firm: Nathalie Prüm-Carre, a specialist in administrative and IP litigation.

Michel – Schanen – Moyse provides trade mark and domain name registration services together with e-commerce and data protection advice.

IP AND IT

ARENDT & MEDERNACH
DECKER, BODRY & BRAUN
LE GOUEFF AVOCATS

Allen & Overy Luxembourg ✪
Bonn Schmitt Steichen ✪
Elvinger, Hoss & Prussen
Linklaters Loesch ✪

Assa, Lutgen & Schaack
Dechert Luxembourg
Michel – Schanen – Moyse ✪
Plottké, Brunel & Associates ✪

Firms are listed A-Z in tiers which are ranked in order of priority
✪ Indicates firm displays contact details at the end of this chapter.

INSURANCE

Allen & Overy Luxembourg's respected Pierre Schleimer, plus a team of five lawyers, has assisted major clients in setting up insurance and reinsurance companies. They have provided advice on insurance sector-related M&A and on the development of new life insurance products.

Arendt & Medernach's financial services team delivers advice to local and international insurance and reinsurance companies. The firm has also been active in M&A as well as the reorganisation of insurance and reinsurance companies.

Elvinger, Hoss & Prussen is active in insurance in the Luxembourg market.

Unit-linked insurance products and insurance are areas of strength for the **Linklaters Loesch** team. The practice is led by senior lawyer Marc Loesch who specialises in insurance law.

Insurance firms figure prominently among the clients of **Le Goueff Avocats**.

INSURANCE

Allen & Overy Luxembourg ✪
Arendt & Medernach
Elvinger, Hoss & Prussen
Kremer Associés & Clifford Chance
Linklaters Loesch ✪

Le Goueff Avocats
Schiltz et Schiltz
Wassenich, Étude

Firms are listed A-Z in tiers which are ranked in order of priority
✪ Indicates firm displays contact details at the end of this chapter.

INVESTMENT FUNDS

Luxembourg's investment funds sector responded favourably to the two 2001 EU directives that resulted in the implementation of Undertakings for Collective Investments in Transferable Securities (UCITS) by the Luxembourg parliament. The investment funds sector is currently valued at approximately $500m.

Arendt & Medernach's practice is co-headed by Claude Kremer and Claude Niedner. Both highly respected for their investment fund expertise, the practice heads are supported by 33 lawyers and act for major international financial institutions. Areas of particular emphasis are the structuring, taxation and registration of Luxembourg investment funds. In 2001, the team advised on a €214bn multi-jurisdictional portfolio of commercial real estate funds.

Elvinger, Hoss & Prussen's investment arm is led by Jacques Elvinger, supported by a six-strong team. It is very highly regarded.

Bonn Schmitt Steichen's investment funds activity has fuelled the development of its capital markets practice. The firm advises on more than 500 funds valued at around $80m.

Under Joëlle Hauser, **Kremer Associés & Clifford Chance** has become an active player in the funds arena. The firm advises on regulatory funds, private equity and the more complex funds linked to derivatives products.

Freddy Brausch leads a team of 15 lawyers at **Linklaters Loesch** whose particular strength lies

INVESTMENT FUNDS

ARENDT & MEDERNACH
ELVINGER, HOSS & PRUSSEN

Bonn Schmitt Steichen ✪
Kremer Associés & Clifford Chance
Linklaters Loesch ✪

Allen & Overy Luxembourg ✪
Dechert Luxembourg
Wildgen & Partners

Kill & Associates

Firms are listed A-Z in tiers which are ranked in order of priority
✪ Indicates firm displays contact details at the end of this chapter.

in investment and pension funds. The team worked with nine other **Linklaters** offices worldwide to co-ordinate the acquisition by State Street Bank of Deutsche Bank's $1.5bn worldwide global customer and investor services, which included the combined business services of Deutsche Bank and Bankers Trust. The Luxembourg office advised on Deustche Bank's Xavex SICAV standalone structured fund comprising 20 portfolios. The fund raised €2bn during the first 12 months of its launch.

Corinne Lamesch is senior investment fund counsel at **Allen & Overy Luxembourg**. Her team provides advice on the launch registration, listing, distribution and administration of collective investment schemes. In addition, the firm covers banking, corporate and e-commerce issues.

Under Marc Seimetz, whose specialist field is financial law and investment funds, **Dechert Luxembourg** acted for a large international concern on the incorporation of a hedge fund. In a separate deal, the firm advised on the liquidation of funds.

Jean-Paul Kill, partner at **Kill & Associates** specialises in funds and in particular UCITs.

TAX

The attractiveness and flexibility of Luxembourg's holding and financial structures – capital duty exemptions and flexible corporate law – have fuelled cross-border M&A activities. Ground-breaking tax reforms introduced in December 2001 heightened the attractiveness of corporate restructurings by opening up tax-neutral mergers and spin-offs, confirming the country's position as *the* jurisdiction for cost-efficient reorganisations. Consequently, there has been a surge in the number of M&A deals involving the use of Luxembourg structures over the past few years.

Existing banking and other financial clients are the major source of business for **Allen & Overy Luxembourg**'s team of six tax specialists. Corporate tax planning for companies and financial institutions are the group's strength. It handles a large number of structured finance deals, including hybrid entities and repurchase agreements applicable to Luxembourg and other jurisdictions. Exempt dividends, capital gains and flexible company law also provide high volumes of work for the firm.

Under the leadership of partners Alain Streichen, Jean Steffen and Alex Schmitt, **Bonn Schmitt Steichen**'s tax practice handles domestic taxation, tax planning and international taxation. The firm is involved in an ongoing international integration and restructuring deal in collaboration with law firms outside Luxembourg, valued at $74bn.

Arendt & Medernach's tax team, led by senior tax lawyer Eric Fort, advises on international corporate tax structures, joint ventures, mergers and acquisitions, company restructuring and recovery. Two new appointments: Philippe-Emanuel Partsch, former legal secretary of the European Court of Justice; and Simone Retter, who specialises in private wealth, will shore up plans to develop a financial law and corporate debt sub-division which will fall under the corporate and tax umbrella.

Due to its attractive tax structures, more companies are choosing to use Luxembourg for their M&A and corporate restructuring activities. **Kremer Associés & Clifford Chance** has benefited from an increase in activity in this area, adding to its client list.

Linklaters Loesch deals with an array of tax products, and provides international tax planning, asset-backed tax planning, tax structuring and structured finance advice.

Headed up by managing partner Jean Brucher, **Dechert Luxembourg** has undoubted strength in national and international corporate tax. The firm advises on regulatory issues and tax structures. Dechert Luxembourg has delivered corporate and tax advice in relation to the restructuring of a prominent European pharmaceutical group. New lateral hire, Pascale Bouvy concentrates on financial and corporate tax matters.

Teun Akkermann is head of **Loyens & Loeff**'s fiscal practice. The firm offers an array of tax services including general tax, M&A, restructuring and due diligence.

Michel – Schanen – Moyse delivers tax advice on M&A, corporate restructuring and individual tax matters.

TAX

ALLEN & OVERY LUXEMBOURG ✪
BONN SCHMITT STEICHEN ✪

Arendt & Medernach
Elvinger, Hoss & Prussen
Kremer Associés & Clifford Chance
Linklaters Loesch ✪

Dechert Luxembourg
Loyens & Loeff
Michel – Schanen – Moyse ✪
NCR Avocats, member of ius laboris ✪

Ernst & Young
NautaDutilh
Plottké, Brunel & Associates ✪
Schaeffer, Hengel & Associés

Firms are listed A-Z in tiers which are ranked in order of priority
✪ Indicates firm displays contact details at the end of this chapter.

NCR Avocats, member of ius laboris's Jean-Luc Schaus provides tax advice, specialising in social security and tax issues for individuals.

Naturally, there are a number of accountancy firms, such as **Ernst & Young**, who are prominent in the tax arena, offering valuable add-on services to clients such as audit and compliance.

NautaDutilh's Luxembourg practice provides tax advice on corporate finance, financial reorganisation, structured finance and M&A. The practice, which opened with one staff member – a tax specialist – in 2002 increased its headcount to three with the appointment to partner level of Frédéric Feyton, formerly of **Loyens & Loeff**, in April 2003.

Plottké, Brunel & Associates advises on tax optimisation and holding company matters. In the course of its international tax planning, the firm establishes entities in Luxembourg, the Netherlands, and in offshore jurisdictions. The firm is frequently engaged by private individuals whose assets are controlled through holding companies, but also advises foreign companies keen to benefit from Luxembourg's tax environment.

ALLEN & OVERY LUXEMBOURG

58 RUE CHARLES MARTEL
2134 LUXEMBOURG

Telephone: +352 44 44 551
Fax: +352 44 44 55 222
E-mail: information@allenovery.com
Website: www.allenovery.com

Languages
Dutch, English, French, German, Italian, Spanish

Other offices
Amsterdam, Antwerp, Bangkok, Beijing, Bratislava, Brussels, Budapest, Dubai, Frankfurt, Hamburg, Hong Kong, London, Madrid, Milan, Moscow, New York, Paris, Prague, Rome, Shanghai, Singapore, Tokyo, Turin, Warsaw

Number of lawyers 2,305
at this office 32

Contact
Marc Feider

CATEGORIES OF WORK

Banking
André Marc, Henri Wagner

Company (M&As, formations)
Marc Feider, Pierre Schleimer

Securities and capital markets
Henri Wagner

Contracts
Katia Manhaeve

Distribution
Katia Manhaeve

Labour law
André Marc

EC law
Paul Beghin

Offshore investments
Jean Schaffner

Public law
Paul Beghin

Taxation
Jean Schaffner

Telecoms
Pierre Schleimer

Investment funds
Corinne Lamesch

Intellectual property
Katia Manhaeve

Litigation and insurance
Pierre Schleimer

Real estate
André Marc

BONN SCHMITT STEICHEN

44 RUE DE LA VALLÉE
2661 LUXEMBOURG

Telephone: +352 45 58 58 1
Fax: +352 45 58 59
E-mail: mail@bsslaw.net
Website: www.bsslaw.net

Languages
Dutch, English, German, French, Italian, Spanish

Number of lawyers 45

Member
Lex Mundi

CATEGORIES OF WORK

Banking and finance
Alex Schmitt, Jean Steffen

Investment funds
Corinne Philippe, Luc Courtois

Private equity and venture capital
Alex Schmitt, Chantal Keereman

Labour and employment benefits
Guy Arendt, Anne Morel

Taxation and tax planning
Alain Steichen, Jean Steffen

Corporate and commercial law
Chantal Keereman, Jean Steffen

Mergers and acquisitions
Alex Schmitt, Alain Steichen

Intellectual property
Guy Arendt, Véronique Hoffeld

Capital markets
Laurent Lazard, Luc Courtois

Media, IT and e-commerce
Guy Arendt, Véronique Hoffeld

Securitisation and asset finance
Laurent Lazard, Jean Steffen

Litigation and arbitration
Fabio Trevisan, Guy Arendt

THE FIRM

Bonn Schmitt Steichen is one of Luxembourg's oldest, largest, and most prominent law firms. Bonn Schmitt Steichen is committed to providing personalised legal services to its clients by working closely with them to understand their business and legal needs. As members of a rapidly growing international and Luxembourg practice, Bonn Schmitt Steichen's attorneys are qualified to practise in Luxembourg, Belgium, France, Italy and New York, US. This unique combination of legal and linguistic experience allows Bonn Schmitt Steichen to deliver legal solutions and advice to clients doing business in one of Europe's leading financial centres.

AREAS OF PRACTICE

The firm's key practice areas include all aspects of banking, corporate, commercial, financial, labour, media, e-commerce and tax law. Bonn Schmitt Steichen is one of the few firms in Luxembourg that enjoys a truly global client base, assisting clients from North America and Asia as well as from Luxembourg and the European Union. The firm represents clients ranging form leading international banks, industrial corporations and national governments to financial service and media companies. The firm also regularly advises Luxembourg state and local authorities and regulatory authorities on a wide range of legal matters.

Bonn Schmitt Steichen is registered with the Luxembourg Bar, and is a member of several international legal organisations, including the International Bar Association and the Union Internationale des Advocats. Members of the firm have published articles in the *Journal of International Banking Law*, the *Stanford Journal of International Law*, *Butterworths' Journal of International Banking and Financial Law*, as well as numerous Belgian, Luxembourg and German journals. Each year, Bonn Schmitt Steichen writes the Luxembourg Law Digest for the *Martindale-Hubbell Directory*.

Bonn Schmitt Steichen's attorneys form a diverse and talented group. The firm's attorneys include law professors and lecturers at law schools around Europe. Over 50% of the firm's lawyers hold Master of Laws (LLM) degrees from law schools in the US and the UK. Bonn Schmitt Steichen also maintains close relationships with leading law firms around Europe, which strengthens the firm's ability to serve its clients in international matters. In addition, Bonn Schmitt Steichen sponsors visiting foreign lawyers and law students as interns in its Luxembourg office, reflecting the firm's global vision and its ongoing relationship with foreign law schools and law firms.

DI STEFANO AVOCATS

24 AVENUE MARIE-THÉRÈSE
BP 2648
1026 LUXEMBOURG

Telephone: +352 262 56 21
Fax: +352 262 56 22
E-mail: contact@mds-legal.com
Website: www.mds-legal.com

Languages
English, French, German, Italian, Luxembourgish, Portuguese, Dutch

Number of lawyers 4

Member
Alfa International; Association of European lawyers; Union Internationale des Avocats (UIA); Ausländischer Anwaltverein Deutschland e V (AAD)

CATEGORIES OF WORK

Company and corporate law
Mario Di Stefano, Joram Moyal

Contract law
Mario Di Stefano

Tax law
Mario Di Stefano

Antitrust and trade regulations
Mario Di Stefano

Mergers and acquisitions
Mario Di Stefano

European Union law
Mario Di Stefano, Joram Moyal

Business law
Mario Di Stefano

Litigation
Mario Di Stefano, Joram Moyal

Commercial law
Mario Di Stefano

Labour and employment
Mario Di Stefano

LAGA & PHILIPPE

AVENUE PRINCE HENRI 11
1724 LUXEMBOURG

Phone: +352 26 47 82 78
Fax: +352 26 47 82 79
E-mail: philipped@laga-philippe.com
Website: www.laga-philippe.com

Languages spoken
Dutch, English, French, German, Italian, Spanish, Russian, Slovak

Other offices
Brussels, Diegem, Ghent, Kortrijk

Number of lawyers 103
at this office 3

CATEGORIES OF WORK

Arbitration

Insolvency and reorganisation

Banking and finance

Insurance law

Commercial law

Intellectual property

Contract law

Medical and pharmaceutical law

Contractor law

Public law

Corporate, M&A

Real estate

Employment

Tax law

Estate planning

Torts and liabilities

European law

Trade practices

LINKLATERS LOESCH

4 RUE CARLO HEMMER
1734 LUXEMBOURG

Telephone: +352 2608 1
Fax: +352 2608 8888
Website: www.linklaters.com

Languages
All commercial and local languages in the countries where Linklaters operates

Other offices
Alicante, Amsterdam, Antwerp, Bangkok, Beijing, Berlin, Bratislava, Brussels, Bucharest, Budapest, Cologne, Frankfurt am Main, Hong Kong, Lisbon, London, Madrid, Milan, Moscow, Munich, New York, Paris, Prague, Rome, São Paulo, Shanghai, Singapore, Stockholm, Tokyo, Warsaw

Number of lawyers 2,000 worldwide

Contact
Freddy Brausch

CATEGORIES OF WORK

Mergers and acquisitions
Tom Loesch

Capital markets
Janine Biver

Banking
Janine Biver

Tax
Paul Tulcinsky

Real estate
René Diederich

Asset and structured finance
Tom Loesch

IT and communications
Emmanuelle Ragot

Employment, pensions and benefits
René Diederich

Public and administrative
Guy Loesch

Litigation and arbitration
Guy Loesch

Investment management
Freddy Brausch

THE FIRM

Linklaters advises the world's leading companies, financial institutions and governments on their most challenging transactions and assignments. With 2,000 lawyers, including 470 partners, and offices in major business and financial centres, its clients choose the firm for its distinctive combination of technical skill, commercial experience and outstanding service.

Linklaters has built a formidable global practice through organic growth and a series of mergers, joint ventures and co-operations with other respected law firms. In 2001, Linklaters merged with three of Europe's leading law firms to form Linklaters Oppenhoff & Rädler in Germany, Linklaters in Sweden, Linklaters De Bandt in Belgium and Linklaters Loesch in Luxembourg. In the same year, the firm formed a co-operation with Brazilian firm Goulart Penteado, Iervolino e Lefosse. This co-operation combines Linklaters' international capability with GPIL's extensive knowledge of the Brazilian market. In Singapore, the firm practises as Linklaters Allen & Gledhill, a joint venture with the premier Singapore practice of Allen & Gledhill, while in Italy, Linklaters has an exclusive relationship with Italian law firm Gianni, Origoni, Grippo & Partners.

MICHEL – SCHANEN – MOYSE

49 AVENUE DE LA GARE
1611 LUXEMBOURG

Telephone: +352 29 02 02 1
Fax: +352 29 02 02 2
E-mail: info@msmlaw.lu
Website: www.msmlaw.lu

Languages
English, French, German

Number of lawyers 7

Contacts
Luc Schanen, François Moyse

CATEGORIES OF WORK

Company and commercial
L Schanen

Finance and banking
F Moyse

Insolvency
L Schanen, R Michel

EU law
L Schanen

Competition law
F Moyse, L Schanen

Administrative and environment
F Moyse

Labour and employment
R Michel, L Schanen

Litigation and arbitration
R Michel, L Schanen

Offshore holdings and companies
R Michel, L Schanen

Criminal law
R Michel

Constitutional rights
F Moyse

Construction
L Schanen

E-commerce
F Moyse

International contracts
L Schanen, F Moyse

MOLITOR, FISCH & ASSOCIÉS

8 RUE SAINTE ZITHE
PO BOX 690
2016 LUXEMBOURG

Telephone: +352 297 2981
Fax: +352 297 299
E-mail: mfa@mfa.lu

Languages
English, French, German

Number of lawyers 15

CATEGORIES OF WORK

Arbitration and commercial litigation
Michel Molitor, Paulo Lopes Da Silva

Banking, finance and securities
Michel Molitor, Laurent Fisch

Corporate, mergers and acquisitions
Laurent Fisch,
Dieter Eixler

Industrial relations and employment
Michel Molitor, Paulo Lopes Da Silva

Information technology and telecoms
Laurent Fisch, Dorothée Ciolino

Real estate and construction
Paulo Lopes Da Silva, Dieter Eixler

NCR AVOCATS, member of ius laboris

AVENUE DU BOIS 99
1250 LUXEMBOURG

Telephone: +352 26 20 65 65
Fax: +352 26 20 05 55
E-mail: ncr@ncravocats.lu
Website: www.ncravocats.lu

Languages
English, French, German, Italian

Number of lawyers 14

Contacts
Guy Castegnaro (guy.castegnaro@ncravocats.lu), Roger Nothar, Anne Roth, Claude Werer

Member
ius laboris, International Employment Law, Pensions and Employee Benefits Alliance

CATEGORIES OF WORK

Labour law

Social security

Administrative law

Real estate

Construction law

Civil, criminal, public law

Supplementary pensions

Compensation and benefits

Company law

Corporate law

Intellectual property law

NOBLE & SCHEIDECKER

398 ROUTE D'ESCH
1471 LUXEMBOURG

Telephone: +352 26 48 42 1
Fax: +352 26 48 42 35 00
E-mail: name@mnks.com
Website: www.mnks.com

Languages
Dutch, English, French, German, Italian

Number of lawyers 26

Contacts
Marie-Béatrice Noble, Katia Scheidecker

CATEGORIES OF WORK

Corporate structuring
Marjorie Allo, Jean-François Findling

Dispute resolution
Katia Scheidecker

Technology, media and communications
Katia Scheidecker

Employment and human resources
Marie-Béatrice Noble, Marielle Stevenot

Financial services
Murielle Brouillet

Intellectual property
Katia Scheidecker, Sabine Zylberbogen

Mergers and acquisitions
Marie-Béatrice Noble

Real estate
Katia Scheidecker, Jean-François Findling

OOSTVOGELS & PFISTER

20 AVENUE MONTEREY
BP 603
2016 LUXEMBOURG

Telephone: +352 468 383
Fax: +352 468 484
E-mail: info@oostvogels.com
Website: www.oostvogels.com

Languages
English, French, Dutch, German, Italian, Spanish

Number of lawyers 25

CATEGORIES OF WORK

Corporate law and structures
Stef Oostvogels, François Pfister

Mergers, acquisitions and private equity
Stef Oostvogels, François Pfister

Banking, finance, investment funds
Stef Oostvogels, François Pfister

Contractual liabilities
Stef Oostvogels

International private law
François Pfister

Taxation
François Pfister, Stef Oostvogels

Audiovisual and new technologies
François Pfister, Stef Oostvogels

Commercial litigation and arbitration
Stef Oostvogels

PLOTTKÉ, BRUNEL & ASSOCIATES

54 RUE D'ANVERS
PO BOX 2038
1020 LUXEMBOURG

Telephone: +352 29 73 15
Fax: +352 29 73 16
E-mail: info@lawyerlux.lu
Website: www.lawyerlux.lu

Languages
English, French, German, Italian

Number of lawyers
12 (+ 3 related lawyers outsourced)

Contacts
Gilles Plottké (managing partner),
Myriam Brunel (litigation)

Member
Juris Network; LAWLINK

CATEGORIES OF WORK

European law

Company formation

Liability claims

Advice to administrators

Naval law

Firm taxation

Collective investment

Debt collection

Commercial contracts

Unfair competition

Lease and rent

Civil contracts

Divorces

Successions

Administrative law

Dismissals

Criminal law

Offences against goods and persons

Corporate and business law

Litigation and European law

MALTA

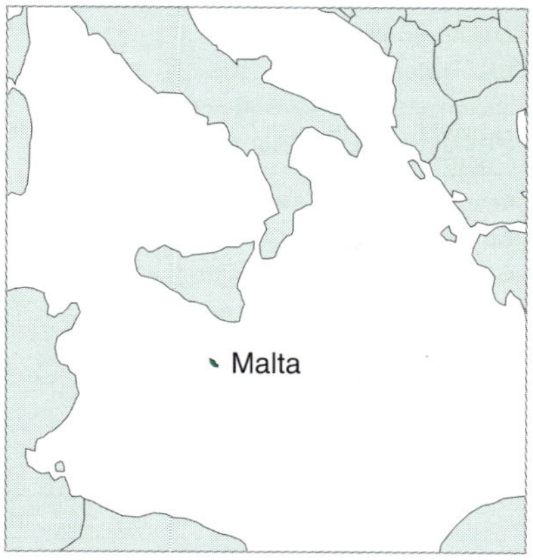

Population	**400,000**
Number of lawyers	**604**
Professional title	**Advocate; solicitor; legal procurator**
Currency	**Maltese Lira (LM)**

Index

Malta comprises a group of small islands in the Mediterranean Sea some 90km south of Sicily and 300km north of Africa. The three inhabited islands are home to a population of 400,000, making Malta one of the world's most densely populated countries.

EU membership has been Malta's main concern of late. In April 2003, a referendum approved EU membership and the general election saw the pro-Europe Nationalist Party remain in government.

There is much activity transposing EU legislation into national law in readiness for full membership on 1 May 2004. Maltese businesses' appetite for business in Europe means there is enthusiasm for the euro, though adopting it may take a further four years. Legislation imposed by the EU has affected many key industries in Malta, such as shipping, where stricter criteria for registration now apply.

BILLING

For general commercial work, hourly rates range from €60 for assistants to €150 for partners. In contentious matters, the rates litigators charge derive from a complex system of tariffs set by the courts, and depend on the nature of the work undertaken. Commercial property transactions may be charged *ad valorem*, with the fee a percentage of the deal value.

MARKETING

Until recently, the Code of Ethics prohibited law firms marketing directly to clients, but constraints were relaxed in 2003. Now firms can be identified as sponsors of events such as conferences and have greater freedom to be included in listings. More firms also have websites – allowed by the Maltese Chamber of Advocates. Confidentiality regarding names of clients remains obligatory.

IN-HOUSE LAWYERS

The trend toward foreign businesses in Malta hiring in-house lawyers is expected to continue after EU membership. In-house lawyers are concerned mostly with regulatory consultation and administration rather than the practice of law.

ECONOMIC CLIMATE

The Maltese economy is built on a number of key industries such as manufacturing, ship construction and repair, and tourism. Pressure on these has seen GDP drop in recent years. Tourism, for instance, which accounts for one-third of GDP, has been hard hit since 2001. The National Tourism Authority has, however, been granted a budget to revive the industry. Stimulating tourism revenue is now a priority, as evidenced by the construction of a new cruise line terminal.

LEGAL MARKET

Some 300 lawyers qualified in Malta in 2003 – more than in any single year before. However, they face an increased workload, fuelled largely by EU matters. Typically, advocates are versatile and practise in many areas, though specialists can be found in maritime law. Legal procurators, who are licensed to appear in lower courts, operate on a freelance basis, though are more frequently attached to particular firms.

EU law is the area expanding fastest, though IT, including data protection and e-commerce, is also growing quickly. There is also a nascent market for alternative dispute resolution (ADR).

FOREIGN FIRMS

Foreign firms are not permitted to open offices in Malta, though this will change with EU accession. However, being such a small legal market, which is well served by established local outfits, it is unlikely that the coming years will see any influx of foreign firms into the country.

BANKING AND FINANCE

Financial services are tightly regulated in Malta and recent changes have seen the reclassification of offshore regimes. Offshore companies are to be totally phased out by 2004, a move which has been seen to attract higher-quality clients to the island. Changes to legislation, such as the Special Funds (Regulation) Act, are intended to make financial services more competitive and to align Malta with commitments to the EU, WTO and OECD.

Late in 2003, **Camilleri Preziosi** advised an Austrian bank on setting up in Malta. Partner Louis Degabriele is seen as a leading practitioner in financial services and capital markets work. The firm acts for a number of local banks, including Bank of Valletta, for which it is principal outside counsel.

Fenech & Fenech Advocates has advised foreign banks setting up in Malta. The firm recently

The largest firms

1	Mamo TCV	20
2	Ganado & Associates	16
3	Fenech & Fenech Advocates	15
4	Grech Vella Tortell & Hyzler	11
5	Gatt Frendo Tufigno Advocates	9
	Muscat Azzopardi & Associates	9
7	Farrugia Schembri Orland Law Firm	8
	Ganado Sammut	8
	Hugh Peralta & Associates	8
10	Camilleri Preziosi	7
	Dingli & Dingli	7
	Emmanuel Mallia & Associates	7
	Farrugia Gatt & Falzon	7
	Thake Desira Advocates	7
15	AVMT Advocates	5
	CDF Advocates	5
	Cefai & Associates	5
	Guido de Marco & Associates	5
	Patrick J Galea & Associates	5
	R Frendo Randon & Associates	5
21	Zammit Pace & Co.	4
22	Bonello & Bonello	3
	Jos A Schembri & Associates	3
	Rutter Giappone & Associates	3
25	Busuttil & Busuttil	2

These figures represent the total number of lawyers in this country only, and have been supplied by the firms themselves. The figures should be accurate as at 1 January 2004.

assisted a foreign client with extensive international interests on applications for banking licences.

Ganado & Associates remains active in the licensing of banks and financial services companies, assisting its clients in obtaining the necessary approvals from the Maltese Financial Services Authority. The firm's tax practice is an acknowledged strength.

Andrew Muscat and Richard Camilleri at **Mamo TCV** are both highly regarded for their finance expertise. The firm advises a number of large Japanese banks as well as major domestic institutions. It has assisted one major client with all its syndicated finance in Malta for ten years, a recent example being advising Bank of Valletta on a €100m syndicated loan.

AVMT Advocates advised a leading international financial services company on a multi-million dollar project financing and gives the same client advice on Maltese tax and corporate law.

Cefai & Associates has strong finance capability with expertise in trusts work, while **Grech Vella Tortell & Hyzler**'s clients include the island's largest mobile telecoms provider and a local airline, which it has advised on privatisation matters and on securitisation. The firm has been involved in four of the six major privatisations that have taken place in the last two years.

CDF Advocates is largely involved on the regulatory side of banking and finance, particularly relating to new financial products and services brought to market by banks as well as government regulatory initiatives.

Galea Salomone & Associates recently advised Malta's listing authority, for which it helped to draw up listing rules along with the Maltese Stock Exchange. It also advises the Maltese Financial Services Authority, which it helped to draft the Financial Markets Act.

Financial services advice is a core activity at **Muscat Azzopardi & Associates.** Clients include a number of financial institutions, investment companies, fund managers and credit institutions. It has also advised regulatory bodies and governments on financial regulation issues, and has been prominent is setting up offshore banks in Malta.

R Frendo Randon & Associates has mainly concentrated on litigation work for banks and financial institutions.

Emmanuel Mallia & Associates deals with setting up and operating trusts, advising on foreign investment and the direction of local investment abroad. The firm advises banks on trade facilities and tax issues.

Farrugia Gatt & Falzon acts for a number of local banks, while **Gatt Frendo Tufigno Advocates** acts for some foreign banks and international trading companies, though its financial services work largely derives from its shipping practice.

Guido de Marco & Associates advises foreign companies on investments in Malta along with acting for a number of financial institutions

BANKING AND FINANCE

CAMILLERI PREZIOSI ✪
FENECH & FENECH ADVOCATES ✪
GANADO & ASSOCIATES ✪
MAMO TCV ✪

AVMT ADVOCATES
CEFAI & ASSOCIATES
GRECH VELLA TORTELL & HYZLER

CDF Advocates
Galea Salomone & Associates
Muscat Azzopardi & Associates
R Frendo Randon & Associates

Emmanuel Mallia & Associates
Farrugia Gatt & Falzon
Gatt Frendo Tufigno Advocates ✪
Guido de Marco & Associates
Hugh Peralta & Associates
Rutter Giappone & Associates
Zammit Pace & Co ✪

Firms are listed A-Z in tiers which are ranked in order of priority
✪ Indicates firm displays contact details at the end of this chapter.

and insurance companies. The practice is headed up by Dr Giannella Caruana Curran, while Dr Edward Saliba handles foreign direct investment and financial services.

Hugh Peralta & Associates acts mainly for foreign clients establishing offshore companies in Malta.

Rutter Giappone & Associates is also active on behalf of international clients, and **Zammit Pace & Co** has advised on a number of secured financing arrangements, credit instruments and bills of exchange, and comes recommended by a Maltese bank client.

CORPORATE AND COMMERCIAL

In 2003, a number of changes to commercial laws were introduced, including amendments to the Companies Act. Among many minor changes, more important amendments were introduced, such as provision for the re-domiciliation of companies, company recovery procedures and a provision stipulating the duties of directors. Changes resulting from EU membership still characterise this practice area.

With its London office, **AVMT Advocates** is the only Maltese firm to have a base outside Malta, reflecting its focus on international clients. As well as advising the government on EU matters relating to corporate and commercial law, it has also been involved in large privatisations, including that of Malta's international airport. Clients include consortia from South Africa and the Far East bidding for privatised entities.

At **Camilleri Preziosi** partner Louis Degabriele is highly thought of. The firm represents many large, local enterprises including the largest

CORPORATE AND COMMERCIAL

AVMT ADVOCATES
CAMILLERI PREZIOSI ✪
FENECH & FENECH ADVOCATES ✪
GANADO & ASSOCIATES ✪
GATT FRENDO TUFIGNO ADVOCATES ✪
GRECH VELLA TORTELL & HYZLER
MAMO TCV ✪

Buttigieg & Refalo Advocates
Galea Salomone & Associates
Ganado Sammut ✪
Guido de Marco & Associates
Hugh Peralta & Associates
Muscat Azzopardi & Associates
Sapiano & Associates

CDF Advocates
Camilleri Delia Randon & Associates
Cefai & Associates
Dingli & Dingli
Ellul Mifsud & Debono Advocates
Emmanuel Mallia & Associates
Farrugia Gatt & Falzon
Farrugia Schembri Orland Law Firm
Jos A Schembri & Associates
Patrick J Galea & Associates
R Frendo Randon & Associates
Rutter Giappone & Associates
Thake Desira Advocates

Firms are listed A-Z in tiers which are ranked in order of priority
✪ Indicates firm displays contact details at the end of this chapter.

commercial group on the island. It has also played a part in the privatisation of Malta's Freeport. The firm is expanding its international client base.

In the last year, **Fenech & Fenech Advocates** has been involved in a number of large transactions, including the $60m sale of a company that produces mineral resources. The firm is highly respected.

Ganado & Associates is widely seen as the leading law firm in Malta. The firm has advised the government in the run-up to EU accession. Its corporate department offers a full commercial service to local and foreign clients.

Gatt Frendo Tufigno Advocates continues to act for clients including local telecoms and insurance companies. Through its EuropAdvise subsidiary it has also taken a lead in helping local businesses prepare for EU membership.

Albert Grech heads up the corporate and commercial team at **Grech Vella Tortell & Hyzler**, where clients include Malta's largest mobile telecoms provider, a number of local insurance companies and property developers.

Mamo TCV has the most lawyers of any firm in Malta. Andrew Muscat and Richard Camilleri are well respected for corporate and commercial advice. The firm boasts international insurance companies, various European banks and travel consortia as clients. It has played a part in many of Malta's largest privatisations.

International companies are among the clients of **Buttigieg & Refalo Advocates**. The firm has experience in liquidations, restructurings, mergers and acquisitions, many of which have involved an international element.

Galea Salomone & Associates handles a good deal of M&A work, mainly for Maltese clients, though often with an international aspect and involving foreign shareholders.

Simon Busuttil leads the team at **Ganado Sammut**. The firm has real strength in EU law, having been part of the core team that negotiated Malta's EU membership. The firm is also active in privatisations, and was involved in those of the Maltese lottery and the Freeport.

Guido de Marco & Associates was set up by the current president of the Republic of Malta, who has a brilliant reputation in legal matters – one that is maintained by his children who are currently the leading partners in the firm. Mario de Marco heads the commercial practice, which represents numerous international companies across several industries, including tourism, aviation and telecoms. Dr de Marco is also part of a team negotiating Malta's entry into an international free-trade agreement with a state in North Africa.

A major European airline and an international bank are among clients who seek out the skills and experience of **Hugh Peralta & Associates**. A large proportion of its clients are international trading companies.

Muscat Azzopardi & Associates has a developed practice in competition law, offering advice in both EU and Maltese law. The firm also maintains an aviation practice which offers specialised legal and tax advice.

A relatively young firm by Maltese standards, **Sapiano & Associates** has grown rapidly and counts insurance companies and a European bank among its clients, as well as the largest retailer in Malta and a number of hotel operators.

CDF Advocates has been active in new projects over the year, such as the introduction of Internet banking, where it has dealt with contractual and corporate issues. Most of its corporate and commercial work is for local companies.

Camilleri Delia Randon & Associates has a long-established commercial practice.

Established since the mid-1970s, **Cefai & Associates** offers a full commercial service along with some property and private client work. International household names are advised on distribution matters within the country.

Dingli & Dingli is a highly respected firm, boasting a solid, all-round practice with strengths in maritime and financial services.

Ellul Mifsud & Debono Advocates' client base includes large Maltese companies in fields such as scientific research, consultancy and marketing, plus a UK company in the food industry. In August 2003, Tonio Ellul joined as a partner in this area.

Other firms which offer sound commercial services include **Emmanuel Mallia & Associates**, where partner Alexander Perici Calascione is recommended; **Farrugia Schembri Orland Law Firm**; and **Jos A Schembri & Associates**, whose clients include a number of insurance companies. **Patrick J Galea & Associates** advises on all areas of corporate and company law from formation and M&A to insolvency and dissolution.

R Frendo Randon & Associates acts for local banks as well as handling the registration of international companies in Malta, while **Rutter Giappone & Associates**, **Farrugia Gatt & Falzon** and **Thake Desira Advocates** are also active in corporate and commercial law.

DISPUTE RESOLUTION

Malta has traditionally been seen as a highly litigious society and remains so today. While there is a tendency to take most disputes through the courts, the length of the process has led to strong support for ADR methods. There are a number of initiatives on the island to popularise mediation and arbitration, and a significant number of advocates are now registering as mediators.

Fenech & Fenech Advocates is taking a lead in ADR and, with **Ganado Sammut**, has set up Malta Dispute Management, a joint venture initiative to offer ADR and mediation services.

Ganado & Associates has an extensive litigation practice and much of its activity in this area has an international dimension. The litigation department comprises two full-time advocates who have assisted numerous local and foreign clients in the Maltese courts. The firm is also actively promoting ADR methods, including arbitration, mediation and conciliation. Representatives of the firm have also played a part in developing Malta's legislation in these areas.

Guido de Marco & Associates' dispute resolution practice is headed by Giannella Caruana Curran and Mario de Marco, who act alongside Fiorella Camilleri and Ramon Rossignaud. It has a strong litigation department that specialises in areas including civil and commercial litigation, arbitration, industrial tribunal cases, family law, debt collection and insurance claims.

Also active in litigation, **Buttigieg & Refalo Advocates** is recommended, as is **Camilleri Preziosi**, which focuses on major litigation. The latter has been involved in three major disputes in the last year, one of which involved recouping interest on investments by a group of large banks. The case was handled by Louis Degabriele.

Ramona Frendo heads the team at **Emmanuel Mallia & Associates**, which handles most commercial and insurance claims. Clients are both local and international.

DISPUTE RESOLUTION

FENECH & FENECH ADVOCATES ✪
GANADO & ASSOCIATES ✪
GUIDO DE MARCO & ASSOCIATES

Buttigieg & Refalo Advocates
Camilleri Preziosi ✪
Emmanuel Mallia & Associates
Farrugia Gatt & Falzon
Ganado Sammut ✪
Gatt Frendo Tufigno Advocates ✪
Grech Vella Tortell & Hyzler
Jos A Schembri & Associates
Mamo TCV ✪
R Frendo Randon & Associates

Bonello & Bonello
CDF Advocates
Cefai & Associates
Ellul Mifsud & Debono Advocates
Farrugia Schembri Orland Law Firm
Galea Salomone & Associates
Hugh Peralta & Associates
Rutter Giappone & Associates
Thake Desira Advocates

Firms are listed A-Z in tiers which are ranked in order of priority
✪ Indicates firm displays contact details at the end of this chapter.

Ganado Sammut has become more active in dispute resolution and is active in the new joint venture Malta Dispute Management (see above). Interestingly, the firm is chaired by the well-known lateral thinker Edward de Bono. In addition to its developing ADR profile, the firm is increasingly active in debt collection.

Michael Frendo at **Gatt Frendo Tufigno Advocates** is among those who have registered as an arbitrator with the Malta Arbitration Centre. The firm has experience of arbitration and drafting arbitration clauses into commercial contracts.

Grech Vella Tortell & Hyzler has Joseph Zammit Maempel heading its litigation team. He is a highly respected litigator, having represented the prime minister of Malta along with a number of his cabinet colleagues. The team comprises four lawyers.

ADR is also offered by **Jos A Schembri & Associates** which boasts an established litigation team.

Mamo TCV has a litigation team of six lawyers, including Franco Vassallo, Joseph Borg Bartolo, Stephen Muscat and Neville Camilleri. This is one of the largest disputes teams of any firm on the island.

Bonello & Bonello has a busy litigation practice. The firm includes among its clients a Maltese bank for which it performs its debt collection.

Conversely, **CDF Advocates** does not maintain a large portfolio of litigation work, though it does act in large disputes. Recently it acted for a large Taiwanese company on a dispute in Malta that settled.

Cefai & Associates handles some local arbitration, while **Ellul Mifsud & Debono Advocates** has partner Tonio Ellul on the panel of arbitrators of the Malta Arbitration Centre. Currently, he is involved in a dispute between two prominent companies in Malta.

Farrugia Schembri Orland Law Firm is active in a number of cases in the Maltese courts, as is **Galea Salomone & Associates**. Debt collection is an important activity for **Hugh Peralta & Associates**, though it is also putting its weight behind the drive for mediation and arbitration.

We also recommend **Rutter Giappone & Associates** and **Thake Desira Advocates**, which continue to maintain acknowledged litigation departments.

INTELLECTUAL PROPERTY

Calls for improvements in intellectual property protection in Malta have been increasing in recent times. Driven to a large degree by the island's imminent accession to the EU, a growing number of businesses from outside Europe are also looking to register trade marks and copyright in Malta. In response, 2003 saw the introduction of the Intellectual Property Act, which seeks to offer better protection to owners of IPRs. In the last year, new cross-border controls against counterfeiting have been introduced and further amendments to the Patents Act, the Trademarks Act and the Copyright Act are also due to come into force during 2004.

Ganado & Associates is generally highly recommended and the firm is very active in the field, advising a wide range of clients on IP matters both domestically and internationally.

Grech Vella Tortell & Hyzler likewise comes with praise and the firm assists on IP matters for one of the largest and best-known international companies, one which has a wide range of household items in its product portfolio. The firm also handles patents for the largest mobile telecoms provider in Malta.

At **Mamo TCV**, Richard Camilleri, David Tonna and Antoine Camilleri act for clients including the world's largest software company, as well as international cigarette manufacturers and two of the world's best known sportswear brands.

Dingli & Dingli is recommended, while **Farrugia Gatt & Falzon** is also active across various IP disciplines.

In addition to filing and registration of trade marks and patents, **Ganado Sammut** acts for numerous clients in enforcement and, where necessary, litigation against infringers.

With a particular focus on soft IP, copyright and trade marks, **Patrick J Galea & Associates** also has extensive experience.

R Frendo Randon & Associates acts for foreign companies registering and monitoring trade marks in Malta. The firm represents clients from a diverse range of industries such as perfumery, footwear and fashion.

INTELLECTUAL PROPERTY

GANADO & ASSOCIATES ✪
GRECH VELLA TORTELL & HYZLER
MAMO TCV ✪

Dingli & Dingli
Farrugia Gatt & Falzon
Ganado Sammut ✪
Patrick J Galea & Associates
R Frendo Randon & Associates

Buttigieg & Refalo Advocates
CDF Advocates
Camilleri Preziosi ✪
Cefai & Associates
Fenech & Fenech Advocates ✪
Farrugia Schembri Orland Law Firm
Guido de Marco & Associates
Muscat Azzopardi & Associates

Camilleri Delia Randon & Associates
Ellul Mifsud & Debono Advocates
Emmanuel Mallia & Associates
Galea Salomone & Associates
Hugh Peralta & Associates
Rutter Giappone & Associates

Firms are listed A-Z in tiers which are ranked in order of priority
✪ Indicates firm displays contact details at the end of this chapter.

Buttigieg & Refalo Advocates remains active in IP, while **CDF Advocates** mainly handles matters that stem from its work with clients in its growing e-commerce practice. Like many others, the firm has seen an increase in demand for its IP advice arising out of developments in the IT sector. Along with EU accession, this is fuelling demand for IP services more than anything else.

Cefai & Associates has an active trade mark registration practice and also carries out copyright work for a number of international clients.

Fenech & Fenech Advocates is involved in some IP activity though it is not a major practice area.

The demand for trade mark registration from overseas clients has seen **Farrugia Schembri Orland Law Firm** acting for clients from the US and China as well as those closer to home in Europe.

Giannella Caruana Curran and Edward Saliba at **Guido de Marco & Associates** handle a wide range of IP services including trade marks, designs and patents, registration and litigation. The firm acts for a number of entertainment companies and clothing brands as well as the world's leading soft drinks company. As many of these clients are based in the US, the firm works closely with lawyers in that jurisdiction on IP protection and enforcement.

The IP practice at **Muscat Azzopardi & Associates** specialises in acting for clients from the film and entertainment business. The firm advises on registration and filing, enforcement, technology transfer, disputes and privacy matters.

Camilleri Delia Randon & Associates provides a solid service as does **Ellul Mifsud & Debono Advocates**, where Jeremy J Debono heads a practice that assists local and foreign clients in industries ranging from fashion to pharmaceuticals.

Matthew Brincat heads the IP department at **Emmanuel Mallia & Associates**, which frequently handles registration of trade marks and patents as well as dealing with copyright infringement.

Other firms we would recommend include: **Galea Salomone & Associates**; **Hugh Peralta & Associates**, which has acted for a number of US clients over the past year; and **Rutter Giappone & Associates**.

REAL ESTATE AND CONSTRUCTION

Given the size of the country, the scope for truly large-scale property developments and construction projects is somewhat limited. That said, however, there are a number of large, long-term projects in progress on the island that are intended to help reshape the future of key industries such as tourism.

Camilleri Preziosi is seen as very strong in construction, though the amount of new construction projects is limited. The firm acts for developer the Corinthia Group, handling all of its major overseas acquisitions as well as property issues in Malta.

Grech Vella Tortell & Hyzler acts for one of Malta's major hotel-owning groups which is currently very active.

Mamo TCV is involved in a number of the largest ongoing commercial property developments. The biggest of these is the Midi Project, which aims to turn Manoel Island and Tigné Point into prestigious residential and retail areas by 2012, and which includes the restoration of a number of historic buildings. The firm represents the consortium of developers and is also acting for a major player in a takeover bid for Malta International Airport. Richard Camilleri, Joseph Caruana Scicluna and Franco Vassallo are highly regarded.

Owners, developers, investors, contractors, banks and other financial institutions call on **Muscat Azzopardi & Associates** for assistance on property-related matters. It advises on commercial letting, development financing, institutional investment, joint ventures, redevelopments, corporate rescues and property litigation.

When **Patrick J Galea & Associates** was first formed, commercial property was a key area of expertise and remains so today. The firm advises on all types of property acquisition and disposal, and sees extensive activity in construction contracts.

Commercial property is also the most active practice area for **Buttigieg & Refalo Advocates**, where Professor Iain Refalo is the main advocate, while **Cefai & Associates** advises a number of clients, including the operator of a hotel chain that is about to open a new facility in Malta.

REAL ESTATE AND CONSTRUCTION

CAMILLERI PREZIOSI ✪
GRECH VELLA TORTELL & HYZLER
MAMO TCV ✪
MUSCAT AZZOPARDI & ASSOCIATES
PATRICK J GALEA & ASSOCIATES

Buttigieg & Refalo Advocates
Cefai & Associates
Emmanuel Mallia & Associates
Farrugia Schembri Orland Law Firm
Fenech & Fenech Advocates ✪
Ganado & Associates ✪
Ganado Sammut ✪
Guido de Marco & Associates
Sapiano & Associates

CDF Advocates
Farrugia Gatt & Falzon
Galea Salomone & Associates
Hugh Peralta & Associates
R Frendo Randon & Associates

Firms are listed A-Z in tiers which are ranked in order of priority
✪ Indicates firm displays contact details at the end of this chapter.

Emmanuel Mallia & Associates' property department has a broad, established client base. It advises both local and foreign investors and funding institutions on a wide range of commercial property matters. It also offers property management advice to operators in the telecommunications and entertainment sectors.

Farrugia Schembri Orland Law Firm represents large construction companies doing business in Malta and North Africa. It has advised foreign and local clients in acquiring commercial property in Malta, the UK, Croatia and Hungary.

Whilst the firm acts mainly for local clients, the active department at **Fenech & Fenech Advocates** is currently engaged in a transaction for a foreign client that is worth in the region of £50m sterling.

Ganado & Associates brings to property advice the strength in depth that it is able to offer across the board, while **Ganado Sammut** continues to be involved in a number of major projects including large-scale private developments and public sector works.

Guido de Marco & Associates, where Giannella Caruana Curran, Mario de Marco and Ramon Rossignaud run the team, is active in both commercial property and in construction. The firm acts for a number of hotel developers. Other current projects include advising on the construction of a power station, a large showroom and a multi-storey car park.

Sapiano & Associates considers commercial property a key area, having represented a foreign client involved in the construction of a new general hospital. It has also been engaged by the Maltese Roads Directorate to advise on the construction of the new road network. The firm acts for hotel operators in this area and played a part in the construction of a new shopping mall valued at around €30m.

CDF Advocates has recently dealt with a number of large transactions, including the sale of a hotel, while **Farrugia Gatt & Falzon** also remains active and has a good name.

Galea Salomone & Associates has seen an increase in commercial property activity during the last year; the firm acts for a major shareholder in the ongoing Midi Project. The firm also advises banks on financing property developments and acts on behalf of a number of commercial real estate agents in Malta.

Hugh Peralta & Associates has acted in deals worth LM4m (€8.8m) or more, while **R Frendo Randon & Associates** carries out a significant amount of conveyancing for both residential and commercial clients.

SHIPPING

Regulations that enable foreign companies to register ships under the Maltese flag through agents in Malta, along with revisions to the EU's Merchant Shipping Act, which tightened up matters of ship registration, ship inspection and maritime safety, are keeping lawyers busy. Recent accidents involving tankers under the Maltese flag have focused attention on the safety aspects of vessels registered under Maltese flag, but shipping nevertheless remains a key area of practice in

SHIPPING

DINGLI & DINGLI
FENECH & FENECH ADVOCATES ✪
GANADO & ASSOCIATES ✪
HUGH PERALTA & ASSOCIATES
MAMO TCV ✪

AVMT Advocates
Buttigieg & Refalo Advocates
Camilleri Preziosi ✪
Farrugia Schembri Orland Law Firm
Gatt Frendo Tufigno Advocates ✪

Cefai & Associates
Camilleri Delia Randon & Associates
Emmanuel Mallia & Associates
Farrugia Gatt & Falzon
Galea Salomone & Associates
Grech Vella Tortell & Hyzler
Guido de Marco & Associates
Muscat Azzopardi & Associates
R Frendo Randon & Associates
Rutter Giappone & Associates

Firms are listed A-Z in tiers which are ranked in order of priority
✪ Indicates firm displays contact details at the end of this chapter.

Malta. Amendments to ship registration legislation now permit the flagging of a vessel in Malta under the ownership of a foreign corporation.

There is a small number of firms in Malta that truly specialise in shipping, and among those **Dingli & Dingli** has a practice that is respected by both local and international clients, as well as by rival Maltese law firms.

In matters of maritime litigation, however, Ann Fenech of **Fenech & Fenech Advocates** is seen as the island's leading expert. She focuses exclusively on disputes work and has been involved in the majority of large marine litigation ranging from shipbuilding disputes and carriage of goods, to bunker contamination and tanker collisions. One Maltese advocate believes that 'There is no-one remotely close to her' on the island because of her 'vast international experience'. The firm also has one of the largest practices on the island for registration and ship finance.

Others in Malta, however, believe that **Ganado & Associates** has overall the top shipping law practice, and Max Ganado comes highly recommended by a number of other practitioners. The firm has long been active in ship finance, which is one of its key strengths, and has acted on behalf of numerous banks. Its ship finance department is home to four full-time lawyers. The firm is a leader in ship registration and ship arrests.

Hugh Peralta & Associates remains highly active in shipping and acts for a range of large clients including international banks and a shipping company from Eastern Europe.

Mamo TCV is also recommended. The firm acts for a number of German and Romanian banks, advising on financing, loans and mortgage registrations, along with a leading German cargo operator. The firm assists shipowners with all shipping and corporate matters.

Clients of **AVMT Advocates** include a company that provides services to military vessels in 56 countries. The firm remains firmly focused on clients outside Malta.

Buttigieg & Refalo Advocates is also recommended. Shipping remains a key activity for **Camilleri Preziosi**, though contentious matters dominate the firm's workload. The firm has a good reputation for its dispute resolution practice, acting largely for clubs and owners.

Farrugia Schembri Orland Law Firm is active in ship registration and services clients from Russia, Ukraine, Canada, UK, Poland, Turkey and Greece.

Gatt Frendo Tufigno Advocates handles much of the Maltese shipping work for a large bank in Greece and also acts for various international trading companies and banks in the area of ship finance.

Cefai & Associates continues to assist in the purchase and disposal of ships under the Maltese flag, while **Camilleri Delia Randon & Associates** remains focused on dry shipping work.

Emmanuel Mallia & Associates's Matthew Brincat heads a department which focuses on the registration of ships and shipping companies, but also advises on mortgages and charters.

Galea Salomone & Associates acts largely on instructions from UK law firms in relation to registrations, though it also advises banks on ship mortgages.

Grech Vella Tortell & Hyzler has chosen to focus its efforts on areas other than shipping in the last year, though it still handles financing and registration.

Guido de Marco & Associates provides legal advice to foreign shipowners and captains, and has been particularly active in the last year on issues such as fishing disputes in Maltese territorial waters.

Shipping advice is combined with aviation expertise at **Muscat Azzopardi & Associates**. The firm offers highly specialised services in legal and tax advice in both of these areas, as well as incorporating shipping companies and registering vessels under the Maltese flag.

R Frendo Randon & Associates retains its presence in the shipping sector. The firm offers registration and contentious services.

CAMILLERI PREZIOSI

ADVOCATES

LEVEL 2
VALLETTA BUILDINGS
SOUTH STREET
VALLETTA VLT 11

Telephone: +356 21 23 89 89
Fax: +356 21 22 30 48
Website: www.camilleripreziosi.com

Languages
English, French, Italian

Number of lawyers 7

CATEGORIES OF WORK

Banking and finance
Louis de Gabriele

Commercial property
Louis de Gabriele

Company law
Henri Mizzi, Louis de Gabriele

Investment services
Louis de Gabriele

Dispute resolution
Henri Mizzi

Capital markets
Louis de Gabriele

Commercial law
Henri Mizzi, Louis de Gabriele

Insurance
Henri Mizzi

Maritime
Henri Mizzi

Media and telecommunications
Henri Mizzi

EU
Louis de Gabriele

Competition law
Henri Mizzi

FENECH & FENECH ADVOCATES

198 OLD BAKERY STREET
VALLETTA VLT 09

Telephone: +356 21 241 232
Fax: +356 25 990 644
E-mail: f.f@fenlex.com
Website: www.fenechlaw.com

Languages
Arabic, English, French, Italian, German, Maltese

Number of lawyers 15

International groupings
World Services Group; Terralex

CATEGORIES OF WORK

Corporate finance
Dr Tonio Fenech

Mergers and acquisitions
Dr Tonio Fenech

International business transactions
Dr Tonio Fenech

Maritime and aviation
Dr Tonio Fenech

Estate planning
Dr Tonio Fenech

Trusts
Dr Tonio Fenech

Property administration
Dr Joseph Fenech

Conveyancing
Dr Joseph Fenech

Ship mortgage and registration
Dr Mark Fenech

Litigation
Dr Kenneth Grima

General civil law
Dr Edward Debono

Marine litigation
Dr Ann Fenech

Banking and financial services
Dr Rosanne Bonnici

Intellectual property
Dr Nicolai Vella Falzon

Trade mark and patent registration
Dr Nicolai Vella Falzon

Data protection and IT law
Dr Antonio Ghio

THE FIRM

Fenech & Fenech Advocates was established in 1897. It has grown to become one of the larger firms on the island and is well established in general legal practice, with a particular focus on commercial, shipping, corporate, transportation, mergers and acquisitions and finance law, and financial services together with a new area of practice, IT law. The largely international client base is serviced by 15 advocates and three legal procurators. A corporate services company specialising in back office administration and a licensed nominee service and trust company are amongst the firm's subsidiaries, as well as a company that provides alternative dispute resolution solutions with a special emphasis on mediation. The firm and its subsidiaries are served by 28 professional and paralegal staff.

AREAS OF PRACTICE

Fenech & Fenech has advised on various M&A transactions involving petrochemical, shipping, aviation and industrial projects, amongst others. The firm regularly acts for banks, particularly in the area of asset finance, and assists in tax-driven structuring of corporations, both locally and abroad. The firm's varied maritime and aviation practice is also a mainstay of its international work. The firm has also recently entered into the area of IT law, dealing mostly in data protection and e-commerce issues.

The firm's client base includes large supranational organisations, international banks, insurance firms, ship owners, charterers, protection and indemnity clubs, large companies and public organisations.

Maritime: the firm's maritime practice covers a wide spectrum of services ranging from ship registration, ship finance and related assistance to a cross-section of issues involving marine litigation and admiralty matters.

Banking and finance: the firm advises various banks on a range of issues including the setting up of branches on the island.

Foreign investment: the firm has assisted many international organisations in setting up production or service companies in Malta, guiding them through the various opportunities made available to foreign investors in terms of the Malta Business Promotion Act. Interest in this area has increased over the last year due to Malta's future membership of the European Union.

International tax planning: the firm advises on the Maltese tax system and its impact on international business operations. It also handles a substantial amount of investment-related work.

Trusts and estate planning: the firm advises on various aspects of trusts and estate planning, ranging from family wealth management planning to the more commercial field of trading trusts.

M&A: the firm has advised both European and US-based firms on varied cross-border arrangements including the acquisition of various Maltese and non-Maltese corporations.

Conveyancing: the firm has assisted a large number of individuals and companies in the purchase of residential and commercial properties both in Malta and overseas.

Corporate law: the firm has expertise covering all aspects of corporate and commercial law. Its practice in this field is one of the most established on the island.

Data protection and IT law: the firm has expertise in all aspects of data protection and assists corporate and commercial clients with the implementation of the necessary procedures for becoming data compliant, as well as providing data protection representative services. The firm has recently set up an IT and e-commerce department and is currently helping a number of international firms to develop strategies for their European e-commerce requirements.

GANADO & ASSOCIATES

171 OLD BAKERY STREET
VALLETTA VLT 09

Telephone: +356 2123 5408
Fax: +356 2122 5908
E-mail: lawfirm@jmganado.com
Website: www.jmganado.com

Languages
English, French, Italian

Number of lawyers 16

Contact
Dr Adrian Borg-Cardona

Member
Lex Mundi

CATEGORIES OF WORK

Shipping: registration, finance, mortgages, Admiralty, ship arrest and shipping companies

Banking: general, regulation, lending and security

Investment services: general, fund management, custody

Investment funds: retail funds, professional investor funds

Insurance: general, capital insurance

Capital markets: Malta Stock Exchange, alternative company listings

Employment and industrial law

Health and safety legislation

Corporate and trust services: Maltese corporate vehicles, limited partnerships, bankruptcy and insolvency, holding and trading companies, trusts, associations and foundations, nomineeships

Litigation

Intellectual property

Trade marks

Patents

Franchises

Taxation

Double taxtaion treaties

GANADO SAMMUT

35-36 ARCHBISHOP STREET
VALLETTA VLT 08

Telephone: +356 21 24 71 09
Fax: +356 21 24 71 70
E-mail: info@ganadosammut.com

Languages
English, French, German, Italian, Portuguese, Spanish

Number of lawyers 9

CATEGORIES OF WORK

Financial services
Dr Austin Sammut, Dr Hubert Dalli

Company law
Dr Hubert Dalli, Dr Sarah Galea

Maritime law
Dr Simon Galea Testaferrata,
Dr Sarah Galea

European affairs
Dr Simon Busuttil, Dr Hubert Dalli

Succession and estate management
Dr Peter Fenech,
Dr Simon Galea Testaferrata

Property and construction, insurance law
Dr Austin Sammut, Dr Peter Fenech

Intellectual property
Dr Mariosa Vella Cardona

Trusts and trust management
Dr Austin Sammut

Litigation and debt collecting
Dr Peter Fenech,
Dr Simon Galea Testaferrata

Joint ventures and investment
Dr Austin Sammut,
Dr Peter Fenech

Banking and finance
Dr Austin Sammut

Competition law
Dr Joanna Drake,
Dr Mariosa Vella Cardona

Telecommunications and media law
Dr Joanna Drake,
Dr Austin Sammut

GATT FRENDO TUFIGNO ADVOCATES

66 OLD BAKERY STREET
VALLETTA VLT 09

Telephone: +356 21 242 713
Fax: +356 21 242 714
E-mail: info@gftlex.com
Website: www.gftlex.com

Languages
English, French, Italian, Russian, Ukrainian

Number of lawyers 10

Contact
Dr Ivan Gatt

CATEGORIES OF WORK

Company law
Dr Robert Tufigno,
Dr Nikolai Muscat-Farrugia

Competition law
Dr Michael Frendo, Dr Gabriella Pace

Contract law
Dr Robert Tufigno, Dr Ivan Gatt

Employment
Dr Ivan Gatt, Dr Robert Tufigno

Food law
Dr Robert Tufigno

Financial services
Dr Robert Tufigno, Dr Ramona Piscopo

EU law
Dr Michael Frendo, Dr Gabriella Pace

Insurance
Dr Michael Frendo, Dr Ivan Gatt

Betting and gaming law
Dr Michael Frendo,
Dr Olga Caruana-Finkel

Property
Dr Ivan Gatt,
Dr Nikolai Muscat-Farrugia

Telecommunications and IT law
Dr Michael Frendo,
Dr Olga Caruana-Finkel

EU funding
Dr Gabriella Pace, Dr James Scicluna

Tourism and hoteliering
Dr Ivan Gatt, Dr Michael Frendo

IP including trade mark registration
Dr Ivan Gatt, Dr Michael Frendo

Registration of ships, ship mortgages and ship finance
Dr Robert Tufigno,
Dr Nikolai Muscat-Farrugia

MAMO TCV
(INCORPORATING JOHN MAMO & ASSOCIATES AND TONNA CAMILLERI VASSALLO & CO)

PALAZZO PIETRO STIGES
90 STRAIT STREET
VALLETTA VLT 05

Telephone: +356 21 232 271
Fax: +356 21 244 291
E-mail: info@mamotcv.com
Website: www.mamotcv.com

Languages
English, French, Italian

Number of lawyers 20

CATEGORIES OF WORK

Agency distribution and franchise
Dr Franco B Vassalo, Dr Richard Camilleri

Aviation
Dr David Tonna, Dr Ivan Vella

Banking, finance and investment
Dr David Tonna, Dr Andrew Muscat

Company law/corporate insolvency
Dr Richard Camilleri,
Dr Andrew Muscat

Commercial litigation, civil law practice and arbitration
Dr Joe Caruana Scicluna,
Dr Franco Vassallo

EU and competition law
Dr Andrew Muscat, Prof Peter Xuereb

Films and media
Dr David Tonna, Dr Anton Camillieri

Financial services and international trading companies
Dr Andrew Muscat, Dr Joseph Saliba

Hotel and touristic projects
Dr Joe Caruana Scicluna,
Dr Franco Vassallo

Joint ventures
Dr Richard Camilleri, Dr Andrew Muscat

Industrial/manufacturing companies
Dr Joe Borg Bartolo, Dr Franco Vassallo

Insurance
Dr Joe Borg Bartolo, Dr Richard Camilleri

Information law and technology
Dr Richard Camilleri, Dr Antoine Camilleri

Intellectual property law including trade mark and patent registration
Dr Richard Camilleri, Dr David Tonna

Maritime law, registration of ships and ship mortgages
Dr David Tonna, Dr Ivan Vella

Property and construction law
Dr Joe Borg Bartolo,
Dr Joe Caruana Scicluna

ZAMMIT PACE & CO.

SUITE 1
215 OLD BAKERY STREET
VALLETTA VLT 11

Telephone: +356 21 222 607
Fax: +356 21 226 087
E-mail: info@zammitpacelaw.com
Website: www.zammitpacelaw.com

Languages
English, French, Italian

Number of lawyers 4

Contacts
Roderick Zammit Pace,
Remigio Zammit Pace

CATEGORIES OF WORK

Banking and finance

Capital markets

Competition and EU

Corporate and commercial

Insolvency/corporate restructuring

Insurance

Mergers and acquisitions

Private client

Real estate/commercial property/ notarial

Regulatory

MONACO

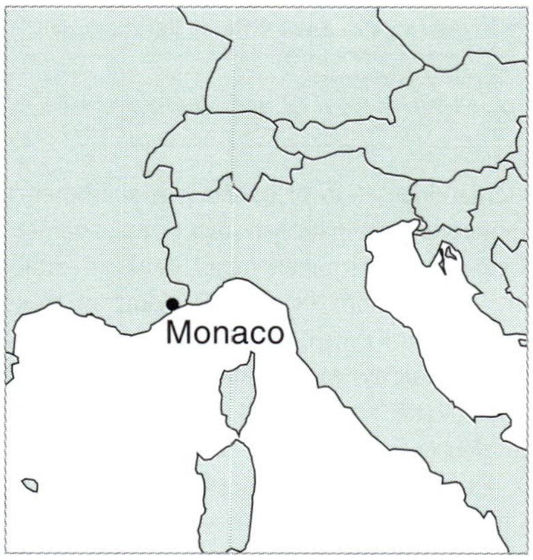

Population	**32,000**
Number of lawyers	**17 Avocats-défenseurs; 7 avocats**
Professional titles	**Avocat-défenseur; Avocat-stagiaire; conseiller juridique; notaire**
Currency	**Euro (€)**

Index

The Principality of Monaco covers an area of just two square kilometres on the Mediterranean Sea near the border of France and Italy. Monaco is home to approximately 32,000 people, almost half of whom are French citizens, 16% are native Monegasques, 15% Italians and the rest are citizens from other countries. French is the official language of the country but English, Italian and Monegasque are also widely spoken.

Many of the foreign inhabitants of Monaco are high-net-worth individuals, who are attracted by the country's tax regime. There is no income tax levied on individuals in the country, save for some French nationals who are charged tax under an agreement signed with France in 1963. Business tax is discussed below under **Economic climate**.

The Grimaldi family has ruled over the Principality since 1297, under the protection of several foreign powers including the Italians, Sardinians and the French. In 1911, the absolute monarchy was replaced by a constitutional monarchy, with the Prince retaining his position as head of state. Under the subsequent 1962 constitution, the Prince is assisted in his duties by a Minister of State (usually a senior French civil servant), an appointed Council of the Crown and an elected National Council, which must approve all laws proposed by the executive. However, the Prince retains the exclusive right of promulgation.

BILLING

Rates can vary greatly depending on the nature of the work being undertaken. Partners at leading firms can charge their international clients as much as €550 per hour, while more routine domestic transactions are likely to be charged out at around €350. Associates are charged at between €150 and €190 per hour.

Avocats-défenseurs charge the equivalent of €350-€400 per hour, plus expenses, but billing methods will vary. This is also the case with avocats who will charge approximately €200 per hour. There are additional court fees charged to foreigners.

Notaires must be employed for certain transactions and their fees, which are set by law, will be based on a percentage of the transaction value.

MARKETING

Avocats-défenseurs are prohibited by the Monaco Bar Association (Ordre des Avocats) from advertising their services. Instead they rely on reputation and the referral of work from law firms, accountants and other professionals. Legal advisers (conseillers juridiques) and international law firms are not restricted in their advertising, but, as much of the work they do is for private clients, discretion is usually preferred.

IN-HOUSE LAWYERS

Banks and major companies have their own in-house legal departments that deal with contracts and standard documentation. However, high-end advice to government, banks and corporations is generally provided by avocats-défenseurs and law firms.

ECONOMIC CLIMATE

Monaco is not a member of the European Union but is part of the single European market through its bilateral agreements with France. The agreements allow full integration of the monetary, customs and banking systems with France and ensure Monegasque goods and services have full access to the European market. The local currency is the euro.

Monaco has a diversified economy that produces a range of goods and services. However, the economy is still heavily reliant on tourism and much of the services and retail sector is geared to take account of high-net-worth individuals visiting the country.

Other important sectors of the economy include a small but burgeoning light industrial sector (producing mainly pharmaceuticals, chemicals and plastics), shipping, real estate and financial services. A recent boom in financial services has been brought about through the establishment of portfolio management companies and by the introduction of mutual funds. The sector now accounts for approximately 18% of annual turnover in Monaco and there are approximately 50 banks and financial institutions operating in the jurisdiction.

Real estate is also an important sector, not least because many wealthy individuals from around the world seek residence in the low tax environs. There are no regulatory restrictions on foreigners buying property but both France and Monaco must approve individuals before they can obtain residency status.

Generally, businesses in Monaco are taxed according to their activities and not their corporate form. Commercial or industrial companies that

The largest firms

1	Lawrence Graham	8
2	A.L.F.A. (Associated Legal & Fiscal Advisors)	4
3	Berg and Duffy, LLP	3
	Donald Manasse	3
	Groom Hill Law Offices	3
	Jean-Charles S Gardetto	3
	Somodeco SAM – Ernst & Young International	3
8	Christine Pasquier – Ciulla	2
	Evelyne Karczag-Mencarelli	2
	Georges Blot	2
	Maurizio Cohen	2
12	Billon Conseils & Services	1
	Cabinet Etienne Léandri	1
	Cabinet Rémy Brugnetti	1
	Jacques Sbarrato	1
	Jean-Pierre Licari	1
	Richard Mullot	1

These figures represent the total number of lawyers in this country only, and have been supplied by the firms themselves. The figures should be accurate as at 1 January 2004.

draw 75% or more of their income from the local market are exempt from paying tax on their profits (there is no tax on revenues at all). Pure holding companies are not allowed in Monaco and various regulatory hurdles must be overcome by businesses before they can start trading.

Value-added tax is applied to goods and services at the same rate as it is in France.

The recent abolition of inheritance tax in Italy, as well as the introduction of a more favourable tax regime in general for high-net-worth individuals, has resulted in a withdrawal of funds from the Principality. Italy has also taken steps to encourage luxury yachts to moor in its harbours in direct competition with other centres on the Riviera. It is not yet clear exactly what effect, if any, these measures will have on the economy of Monaco. However, there is unlikely to be any effect on the flow of money from the UK and other centres.

Monaco does not publish national income data. However, the unemployment rate in the country is thought to be approximately 3% and many companies actively recruit workers from outside the country, usually from neighbouring France.

LEGAL SYSTEM AND LEGAL MARKET

The courts and tribunals render justice in the name of the Prince yet they are completely independent of the executive branch and adhere to the principles of impartiality and fairness. Monegasque law has its roots in the Napoleonic Code and French law can be very persuasive.

Full rights of audience in Monaco's courts are reserved exclusively to avocats-défenseurs, who operate as sole practitioners. Some of them are, however, assisted by avocats or avocats-stagiaires, legal assistants or foreign lawyers. (See **Dispute resolution**.)

Conseillers juridiques (legal advisers) are licensed to operate by the government, but may not appear in court. These can be local practitioners who offer advice on Monegasque law to individuals, but also foreign firms offering international advice bound by the regulations of their home jurisdiction. As the conseillers juridiques cannot appear before the courts they will refer contentious matters to the avocats-défenseurs. In contrast, avocats-défenseurs or avocats are able to provide general legal advice and in this regard they are in competition with the law firms.

Notaires, of which there are three in Monaco, play a major role in property transactions, the conveyance of estates and the formation of general business corporations. Notaires are not lawyers nor do they appear in court.

BANKING AND FINANCE

During the past ten years, the banking sector in Monaco has grown significantly, due in part to the increasing diversification of products and the internationalisation of banking establishments. Numerous international asset management companies have joined major banks in establishing operations in Monaco. Some of these include Merrill Lynch, Julius, Baer, Deutsche Bank, UBS and Barclays. Monegasque portfolios are not subject to tax, nor are any duties levied on capital transfers or stock and share transactions.

BANKING AND FINANCE

- A.L.F.A. (Associated Legal & Fiscal Advisors)
- Berg and Duffy, LLP
- Christine Pasquier - Ciulla
- Donald Manasse
- Evelyne Karczag-Mencarelli
- Frank Michel
- Jean-Charles S Gardetto
- Lawrence Graham
- Somodeco SAM - Ernst & Young International

Firms are listed alphabetically

✪ Indicates firm displays contact details at the end of this chapter.

French banking law applies to all banking activities in the Principality, while Monaco's Financial Network Information Service (SICCFIN) is responsible for monitoring illegal transactions. Monaco has previously received criticism from the OECD and others who claim that the Principality has not done enough to deter money laundering. However, keen to allay this repute the government has since acted to tighten its controls and bolster its monitoring system.

The financial sector directly employs 1,500 people in Monaco and accounts for approximately 18% of the country's annual turnover.

Led by partners Mireille Chauvet and Jean-Pierre Campana, **A.L.F.A. (Associated Legal & Fiscal Advisors)** has a very strong banking and finance practice and receives solid referral work from large international firms in the UK and France. It is particularly recommended for its work advising banks on asset finance and securitisation and for its corporate and commercial work.

Berg and Duffy, LLP is the only US firm with an office in Monaco. The office, a member of the *Lex Mundi* and *TAGLaw* international networks, deals mainly with corporate and banking transactions, representing a large number of US companies with interests in the Principality and the south of France. James P Duffy III heads the firm and divides his time between Monaco and New York. While the focus for the firm is its international business client base, it also has a good private client practice, assisting individuals with residency, asset transfers and tax matters. Lucien R Le Lievre, the firm's senior attorney, also functions as the US Consular Agent due to the closing of the US Consulate in Nice.

Christine Pasquier - Ciulla is an avocat-défenseur who, along with her two collaborators is recommended for her work in the insurance, finance and construction sectors.

Donald Manasse is an American lawyer admitted to the Bars of Nice, Connecticut and New York. As a French avocat he has considerable litigation experience in the region but is not permitted to appear before Monegasque courts. Instead, **Donald Manasse** and his five collaborators offer excellent general practice advice, particularly on cross-border issues, and work with local avocats-défenseurs on matters before Monegasque courts.

Evelyne Karczag-Mencarelli is an avocat-défenseur with a very strong reputation in banking and finance work. She is assisted by avocat Alexis Marquet and French lawyers Cécile Peltier-Gauci and Stéphanie Guido. **Evelyne Karczag-Mencarelli** and her collaborators deal mainly with litigation but also provide out-of-court advice to clients, particularly on contentious issues.

Frank Michel has developed a strong reputation for his knowledge of commercial and banking law. As an avocat-défenseur he is also entitled to appear in court and regularly represents large banks and financial institutions.

Jean-Charles S Gardetto is an avocat-défenseur with extensive experience in banking litigation, representing institutions such as Merrill Lynch and Goldman Sachs and receiving regular referrals from large firms in Europe and the US. **Jean-Charles S Gardetto** and his two French collaborators, Valerie Zoccola and Guillaume Cardoen, also have a good general practice and are also recommended for advice on employment and shipping law.

London-based **Lawrence Graham** has opened its first overseas office after taking over control of **Eversheds LLP**'s Monaco practice. The eight-lawyer practice is the largest in the Principality and its numbers are further strengthened by its close links to UK-based specialists. William Easun, who has considerable experience practising in Monaco, continues to head the office under **Lawrence Graham**. He is joined by partner Peter Walford and six associates. The firm acts for several large international banks and finance houses in Monaco and counts a significant proportion of the Principality's private banks among its clients.

With six full-time lawyers, **Somodeco SAM - Ernst & Young International** is one of the larger firms in Monaco and deals mainly with banking and tax matters for a range of local and international clients. The firm receives steady referral work from law firms in the UK and through the Ernst & Young network. Tax specialist Francis Ferrari manages the firm, while Jean-Marie Canac heads up the solid banking and finance practice. **Somodeco SAM - Ernst & Young International** is closely linked to **Gordon S Blair Law Offices**, which handles private client matters.

CORPORATE AND COMMERCIAL

The highly regarded William Easun heads the **Lawrence Graham** office in Monaco. Easun is joined by partner Peter Walford and six associates, making it the largest law office in the country and one that is highly regarded for its corporate and commercial work. The office currently acts for an impressive list of UK and international clients with interests in the region. **Lawrence Graham** also specialises in the incorporation of companies in Monaco and other low tax regions. Christine Lloris heads the business law department, while Irene Luke is recommended for real estate matters.

The linked firms **Somodeco SAM - Ernst & Young International** and **Gordon S Blair Law Offices** are expert in delivering top quality legal advice to their clients, be they companies or individuals. This six-lawyer office specialises in tax and associated activities, such as the incorporation of companies, the establishment of trusts and the acquisition of real estate. Simon Huxford and Gareth Davies are both UK-qualified lawyers and are highly recommended.

Mireille Chauvet and Jean-Pierre Campana head the four-lawyer team at **A.L.F.A. (Associated Legal & Fiscal Advisors)**. The firm focuses mainly on its corporate and commercial work, including M&A and the incorporation of companies. The firm gets steady referrals from law firms based in the UK and France. Campana, who spent many years working for the government at the Directorate of Economic Expansion before joining the firm, is highly recommended for his corporate and commercial work.

Berg and Duffy, LLP has been operating from its Monaco office since 1986, dealing mainly with corporate, banking, securities and financial transactions. This New York-based firm has an impressive list of US and international clients with interests in Monaco and regional centres such as Nice. James P Duffy III is the resident senior partner who divides his time between Monaco and New York. Associate, Paola Rinaldi is also recommended on international and corporate law issues.

Donald Manasse is an American lawyer with offices in both Monaco and Nice. The five-lawyer team is recommended for corporate and commercial work, as well as advice on banking and finance transactions. **Donald Manasse** is particularly recommended for regional multi-jurisdiction transactions.

Groom Hill Law Offices is run by Simon Groom and James Hill and deals with a large amount of corporate and commercial work. However, clients tend to be individuals rather than large companies or banks given the firm's expertise in tax and estate planning.

Maurizio Cohen offers a broad commercial practice covering acquisitions, IP, sports issues and arbitration.

The following avocats-défenseurs are recommended for their advice on corporate and commercial transactions. They also have a good reputation for their dealings with the courts. **Evelyne Karczag-Mencarelli** is well versed in banking, real estate and construction matters; **Frank Michel** (avocat) has a very good commercial, banking and employment law practice; and **Jean-Charles S Gardetto** has a broad commercial practice, focusing on banking and company law.

CORPORATE AND COMMERCIAL

Lawrence Graham
Somodeco SAM - Ernst & Young International / Gordon S Blair Law Offices

---

A.L.F.A. (Associated Legal & Fiscal Advisors)
Berg and Duffy, LLP
Donald Manasse

Evelyne Karczag-Mencarelli
Frank Michel
Groom Hill Law Offices
Jean-Charles S Gardetto
Maurizio Cohen ✪

Firms are listed A-Z in tiers which are ranked in order of priority
✪ Indicates firm displays contact details at the end of this chapter.

PRIVATE CLIENT

Berg and Duffy, LLP
Donald Manasse
Gordon S Blair Law Offices
Groom Hill Law Offices
Lawrence Graham

Firms are listed alphabetically
✪ Indicates firm displays contact details at the end of this chapter.

PRIVATE CLIENT

Monaco does not levy an income or capital gains tax on individuals (with the exception of French nationals residing in the country) and as such it has become a popular destination for the rich and famous. High-net-worth individuals looking to invest in property or yachts, or simply wishing to take advantage of the Principality's tax arrangements, make up a lot of business for Monegasque law firms.

Berg and Duffy, LLP is known for its corporate and banking work but it also has a good private client practice, advising a number of wealthy US citizens who live along the French Riviera on all areas of tax and portfolio investments.

Donald Manasse is recommended for private client work, particularly tax matters and related real estate acquisitions in Monaco and the south of France.

Gordon S Blair Law Offices is closely linked with the Monegasque arm of Ernst & Young International, **Somodeco SAM - Ernst & Young International**. Both firms are managed by Francis Ferrari, although their client base and specialisms differ. **Gordon S Blair Law Offices** handles private client matters, dealing mainly with wills, trusts, asset planning and real estate. Francis Ferrari is highly recommended for his advice on tax matters, both for the private client and for commercial enterprises, Dominique Lucas is recommended for real estate transactions and Florence Pecheral is recommended for immigration and wills and trusts.

James Hill, previously with **Gordon S Blair Law Offices**, joined Simon Groom in 2000 to form **Groom Hill Law Offices**. The firm is expert in tax and estate planning and counts a large number of high-net-worth individuals amongst its clients. The firm acts mainly for local and UK-based individuals but is not connected with any international alliance or association, instead relying on an informal network for referrals. **Groom Hill Law Offices** is highly recommended for its work in estates planning, real estate acquisitions, trusts and immigration matters, as well as related local and international corporate and commercial work.

London-based **Lawrence Graham** has recently expanded its excellent tax and private capital practice by taking over the Monaco office of **Eversheds LLP**. Andrew Young leads the group from the London office, with William Easun, who has considerable experience practising in Monaco, heading the local team. The Monaco office receives a number of referrals through its international network but also recognises the importance of its local client base who would prefer to deal with local lawyers. William Easun and Peter Walford are highly recommended for their private capital work.

DISPUTE RESOLUTION

In order to become an avocat-défenseur, one must be a Monegasque national and member of the Monaco Bar, but must also have gained a French Maîtrise en Droit; there is no law school in Monaco. After obtaining a Maîtrise en Droit, the student aspiring to become an avocat-défenseur must undertake a three-year apprenticeship with a fully qualified avocat-défenseur. After that, he or she will be allowed to practise as an avocat, but will not be allowed to submit written pleadings. Only after independently practising for five years does the avocat gain the status of an avocat-défenseur. The supervisory body for avocats-défenseurs is the Ordre des Avocats. The following avocat-défenseurs are highly recommended:

Georges Blot has recently acted in high-profile cases, including for the defence in the Edmond Safra murder case.

Jean-Charles S Gardetto has a broad commercial practice, focusing on banking and company law. He also has a solid employment and family law practice which has handled some high-profile cases in recent years.

Evelyne Karczag-Mencarelli is a highly recommended avocat-défenseur, capable in all areas of Monegasque law. Karczag-Mencarelli is assisted by Alexis Marquet (avocat) who is recommended for employment and criminal matters, and by two French lawyers, Cécile Peltier-Gauci and Stéphanie Guido. The main practice areas for the office are banking and finance, real estate, construction and employment law.

Frank Michel has been at the Monaco Bar for 12 years and has developed a good reputation for his work in commercial, banking and employment law. He regularly appears in court acting for numerous large banks and financial institutions.

Richard Mullot is recommended for corporate and commercial, banking and finance matters, representing several high-profile individuals over the past year.

Christine Pasquier - Ciulla is recommended for her work for banks and insurance companies.

Yann Lajoux is an avocat highly recommended for his advice in a wide range of legal matters, including banking and finance, tax and private client.

Donald Manasse is not an avocat-défenseur but he is a member of the Nice Bar and has some capacity for litigation work. His continued involvement in the Edmond Safra case is a testament to his high-profile work.

AVOCATS-DÉFENSEURS

Michel Boeri, Cabinet
Georges Blot
Patrice Lorenzi
Jacques Sbarrato
Evelyne Karczag-Mencarelli
Etienne Léandri, Cabinet
Frédéric Sangiorgio, Cabinet
Rémy Brugnetti, Cabinet
Didier Escaut
Joëlle Pastor-Bensa
Christine Pasquier - Ciulla
Jean-Pierre Licari
Christiane Palmero
Jean-Charles S Gardetto
Frank Michel
Patricia Rey
Richard Mullot

Individuals are listed in order of accession to the Bar

AVOCATS

Géraldine Gazo
Christophe Sosso
Yann Lajoux
Sophie Lavagna-Bouhnik
Déborah Lorenzi
Alexis Marquet
Thomas Giaccardi

Individuals are listed in order of accession to the Bar

AVOCATS-STAGIAIRES

Arnaud Zabaldano

MAURIZIO COHEN

LES FLORALIES
3 AVENUE DE GRANDE BRETAGNE
98000 MONTE CARLO

Telephone: +377 93 25 75 10
Fax: +377 93 50 00 69
E-mail: group@interlawmonaco.com
Website: www.interlawmonaco.com

Languages
English, French, German, Italian

Number of lawyers 2

Member
IBA; ACB; STEP; ISL; ISLA; ABA (associate)

CATEGORIES OF WORK

International business law	International private law
Commercial law	Media law
Arbitration	Sports law
International contracts	International tax planning
Company acquisitions and sales	International estate planning
Banking law	Trusts
Financial law	Immigration law
Intellectual property	Property law

NETHERLANDS

Population	**16 million**
Number of lawyers	**11,200**
Professional title	**advocaat**
Currency	**Euro (€)**

Index

The Netherlands is a small country with a large economy that plays a central role in Europe. It is a hub for international business, in which nearly all deals have a cross-border element. However, the country's export-dependent economy means it has been hit harder than some of its European neighbours by subdued global growth and the stronger euro. In December 2003 provisional estimates by Dutch statisticians showed that the Netherlands was likely to breach EU guidelines by running a 3% budget deficit for the year, widening to 3.25% in 2004. This was an embarrassment to a country that has prided itself in being vocally pro-EU.

The Netherlands has also been affected by political instability. Following failed attempts at putting together a centre-left coalition, a new centre-right coalition government headed by Christian Democrat Appeal leader Jan Peter Balkenende took office in May 2003. The new government outlined a package of cuts aimed at reducing public spending by €11bn over the next four years and, while liberalisation of the electricity, gas and highly developed telecommunications markets is expected to continue, privatisation has virtually been put on hold, causing transactions in the energy sector to dry up.

However, the Netherlands is bound to benefit from the eurozone's tentative recovery. It has a very strong position in Europe, with a central location, advanced transport and telecoms infrastructure, and a very large workforce for its geographical size. Amsterdam is the financial centre, Rotterdam is the largest port in Europe and a key commercial centre, while The Hague is the administrative centre, home to the government, the major regulatory bodies and the Supreme Court. All three cities are very close geographically, in the urban conglomerate of the Ranstaad which would be viewed as a single city by the standards of many other countries. The location of the law firm which companies instruct has little importance in terms of travel arrangements.

BILLING

The rules relating to billing are fairly relaxed in the Netherlands: lawyers and their clients can come to their own arrangements and agree on a mutually acceptable price and method of billing. The average hourly billing rate for a corporate partner in Amsterdam is about €300, but some firms will charge closer to €400. At some international firms where the corporate work is of an international, cross-border nature, hourly fees can rocket to €750.

MARKETING

The absolute ban on advertising was lifted several years ago and attorneys are now allowed to advertise with the exception of cold calling. Dutch lawyers are generally very modest, and it is only the competition brought to the market by UK firms in recent years that has pushed local firms into showing the world what they are made of. Many law firms now have their own marketing departments and the increase in beauty parades means that firms are now trying to use their marketing teams to maximum effect. The stoic approach of Dutch firms continues to wane thanks to media-savvy international firms in Amsterdam.

IN-HOUSE LAWYERS

Unlike in some neighbouring countries, Dutch in-house lawyers are not treated as second-class citizens within the profession and have full rights of access to the Dutch Bar.

This membership of the Bar has meant that a growing number of organisations are employing lawyers, such as government departments, municipalities and large insurance companies, while other businesses have strengthened their legal departments with practising lawyers.

All of the major Dutch companies, such as Shell, and banks such as ABN Amro, ING and Rabobank, have extremely sophisticated in-house teams. Most of the leading law firms in this chapter are well versed in co-operating with in-house counsel.

CIVIL LAW NOTARIES

Notaries take on a much more important role in the Netherlands than in many other jurisdictions, and are particularly vital to M&A and commercial property work. Notarial deeds are compulsory in the conveyance of real estate, the creation of mortgages and the incorporation or alteration of a company's articles of association.

Most law firms in the Netherlands employ substantial numbers of notaries, and some of these have leading reputations within the legal profession. Although there is a long-running debate about potential conflicts caused by notaries' in-house role – notaries are appointed by

The largest firms

1	Loyens & Loeff	544
2	NautaDutilh	420
3	De Brauw Blackstone Westbroek	350
4	Houthoff Buruma	310
5	AKD Prinsen Van Wijmen	275
6	Dirkzwager advocaten en notarissen	240
7	CMS Derks Star Busmann	235
8	Allen & Overy	210
9	Holland van Gijzen	185
	Stibbe	185
	Van Doorne	185
12	Clifford Chance LLP	169
13	Boekel De Nerée	160
14	Baker & McKenzie	150
	Pels Rijcken & Droogleever Fortuijn	150
16	Landwell	130
17	Van Diepen Van der Kroef Advocaten	117
18	DLA SchutGrosheide	110
19	Nysingh Dykstra de Graaff	90
20	Kennedy Van Der Laan	85
21	Simmons & Simmons Trenité	81
22	Freshfields Bruckhaus Deringer	73
23	De Jonge Peters Remmelink	64
24	Van Benthem & Keulen	52
25	Ekelmans & Meijer Advocaten	47

These figures represent the total number of lawyers in this country only, and have been supplied by the firms themselves. The figures should be accurate as at 1 January 2004.

the Queen and supposedly independent – and a small minority of law firms refuse to employ them for this reason, it is generally recognised that integrated teams are the best way forward, particularly on property and shareholder transactions.

If instructing a firm for a real estate deal or a corporate transaction, clients should check the quota of notaries at the law firm. Having lawyers and notaries in-house is vital to the success of certain transactions, and some firms may try and bluff their notarial skills and say they work exclusively with a separate firm of notaries. This is rarely true and is no substitute for a co-ordinated service.

LIMITING LIABILITY

Negligence claims against law firms have risen globally and the Netherlands is no exception. As such law firms now have a certain level of professional indemnity insurance. Clients are advised to check the terms and conditions on their contracts and check out individual firm policies on their websites, as it is unclear at times when and how much insurers will pay.

LEGAL MARKET

The Netherlands is a relatively small jurisdiction, but it supports a number of large firms with more than 300 lawyers. Competition between them is fierce, and the standard of legal services is high. The largest firms bearing an international name – such as **Allen & Overy** and **Simmons & Simmons Trenité** – are the products of mergers with local firms, and are consequently deeply rooted into the local market, as is **Clifford Chance LLP**, which has grown organically over a period of 30 years.

However, the leading independent firms heaved a sigh of relief when the brakes were put on globalisation by the 2002 decision of the Netherlands' leading firm **De Brauw Blackstone Westbroek** not to merge with **Linklaters**. The other leading independent firms – **Loyens & Loeff**, **NautaDutilh** and **Stibbe** – felt that the pressure to find an international merger partner has lifted, though **Stibbe** has an ongoing and profitable exclusive alliance with UK-based **Herbert Smith**.

In 2003 US firm **Greenberg Traurig LLP** entered Europe by opening an office in Amsterdam which it intends to grow to full service, and US-based international IP boutique **Howrey Simon Arnold & White, LLP** also opened in Amsterdam. However it is generally felt that the Dutch legal market is too small to attract the top-tier US firms that have a presence in London and Frankfurt, and the top Dutch firms are not, so far, quaking in anticipation of an American invasion.

The wave of international activity has, nevertheless, created market unrest, and there are currently a high number of partners and their teams moving between the top ten firms due to differences of opinion over the direction these firms are taking. Some leading IP litigators, in particular, have felt unhappy with their firms' corporate focus and independent stance, and have left to found their own boutiques.

Also, the largest firms, both the independents and the Dutch offices of UK-based firms, have found their international growth hampered by a difficulty in recruiting internationally-qualified lawyers to work in the Netherlands.

The only recent international merger has been in the middle market. *SchutGrosheide* and UK-based **DLA** integrated their practices in January 2004 to form **DLA SchutGrosheide**. Also, one of the firms formerly tied to accountants has been snapped up by **Van Doorne** (see below).

ACCOUNTING FIRMS

The Netherlands had its own domestic version of Enron – the accounting scandal at Dutch food retailer Ahold, which shocked financial markets in February 2003 by revealing that it overstated earnings by more than €1bn in 2000-02.

Most of the Dutch law firms associated with accountants have been busy dissolving, with KPMG's *Steins Bisschop Meijburg & Co* going bankrupt in 2002, the Dutch *Andersen Legal* firm *Wouters Advocaten* merging with **AKD Prinsen Van Wijmen** and – the most recent development in the saga – PricewaterhouseCoopers' Dutch **Landwell** merging with **Van Doorne** in January 2004.

Holland van Gijzen is prevented by the Dutch ban on multi-disciplinary partnerships from using the name *EY Law*, but it does practise in association with Ernst & Young.

OFFICES ABROAD

International firms with a multitude of global offices dominate the top end of the Dutch market.

Leading independent firm **NautaDutilh** has closed its Madrid office as part of a move to focus on its core Benelux market, with support from New York and London offices. The firm opened a small Luxembourg office in 2003 to complete its trilogy of Benelux practices, and is intending to grow the office from a tax-focused to a general corporate practice.

De Brauw Blackstone Westbroek was the first Dutch firm to open in London and New York.

Stibbe has offices in London, Brussels and New York, as well as a close alliance with **Herbert Smith** and **Gleiss Lutz**, giving the firm access to a global network.

Both **Spigthoff** and **Van Doorne** have offices in Curaçao, and **Van Doorne** also has an Aruba and a London office.

Houthoff Buruma has a London and a Brussels office, and **Barents & Krans** also has an office in the Belgian capital.

Loyens & Loeff is part of a global tax firm which has offices in Tokyo, Aruba, Antwerp, Geneva, Berlin, Curaçao, Singapore, Luxembourg, Brussels, Paris, London, New York and Frankfurt.

ARBITRATION

The leading arbitration practice in the Netherlands is found at **De Brauw Blackstone Westbroek**, which has a significant number of high-profile arbitrators, including Bommel van der Bend, Piet Wackie Eysten and Wybe Taekema. The team has recently handled disputes for NEA – over joint ventures between electricity producers – and Railinfrabeheer – over the construction of the railway link between Rotterdam and Germany.

Freshfields Bruckhaus Deringer's large and impressive international arbitration team is led by US-qualified Brian King. Recent work includes representing NV Distrigas in an ICC arbitration arising out of a €40m dispute with a US shipping conglomerate.

NautaDutilh handles major national and international arbitrations for clients including Eureko, in its €1bn BIT arbitration against the Polish State. Practice group head Bart van Tongeren is handling this case.

Allen & Overy has been involved in some major corporate arbitrations recently, including representing a minority shareholder in an Italian sporting goods manufacturer in a €52m shareholder dispute.

Boekel De Nerée's Michel Deckers has recently acted in arbitrations concerning companies in the Middle East and the Netherlands Antilles.

CMS Derks Star Busmann is acting for some major construction companies accused of fraud.

Houthoff Buruma has a respected arbitration practice, where Freerk Falkena is recommended for general commercial work and Peter Hustinx for national and international utilities.

Stibbe has been acting for Edemol in an international arbitration against a German company over a production agreement. Tony van Hees and Jeroen Fleming are recommended.

Van Doorne has acted for Motivaction BV in several arbitrations related to the demerger after bankruptcy of EMIC NV.

ARBITRATION

DE BRAUW BLACKSTONE WESTBROEK ✪

FRESHFIELDS BRUCKHAUS DERINGER ✪
NAUTADUTILH ✪

Allen & Overy ✪
Boekel De Nerée ✪
CMS Derks Star Busmann ✪
Houthoff Buruma ✪
Pels Rijcken & Droogleever Fortuijn
Stibbe ✪
Van Doorne ✪

AKD Prinsen Van Wijmen ✪
Baker & McKenzie ✪
Barents & Krans ✪
DLA SchutGrosheide
Greenberg Traurig LLP
Norton Rose
Rozemond Van Ramshorst Smit

Firms are listed A-Z in tiers which are ranked in order of priority
✪ Indicates firm displays contact details at the end of this chapter.

ASSET FINANCE AND STRUCTURED FINANCE

The Netherlands is now the second largest market in Europe for securitisation, after the UK.

Allen & Overy has extensive experience in advising Dutch lessees on domestic transactions and on US cross-border leases. Bart Meesters is highly regarded for asset finance work. On the securitisation side, the firm advised issuer GMAC RFC and the Dutch subsidiary of General Motors, Acceptence Corporation in relation to the first Dutch residential mortgage-backed securitisation.

Clifford Chance LLP is particularly well known for its work for ratings agencies. The firm has also acted for Rabobank in relation to a €275m sugar sale and purchase facility for Cosum, and for Singapore Aircraft Leasing Enterprise/ Martinair in relation to a lease financing. Tineke Kothe is recommended.

De Brauw Blackstone Westbroek's group head, Berend Crans, is very highly regarded. His recent asset finance work includes acting as special Dutch counsel to the equity investors in two US lease financing transactions. On the structured finance side, he has acted for NIB Capital NV in relation to a $663m synthetic securitisation transaction.

NautaDutilh has longstanding experience in securitisation, having acted on the first ever deal in the Netherlands in 1996. The firm recently acted for ABN Amro in the €1bn securitisation of mortgage loans of Achmea Hypotheekbank. It is also strong on cross-border leasings (where Elizabeth van Schilfgaarde in the firm's New York office is recommended), and has acted on nearly all the major transactions involving Dutch assets.

Freshfields Bruckhaus Deringer has had a good year in structured finance work, particularly securitisation. Acting on the Vesteda real estate securitisation has allowed it to build up experience in real estate financing transactions. Jeroen Thijssen is recommended.

Clients speak extremely highly of the quality of the structured finance work done by Harm van Berkum at **Simmons & Simmons Trenité**. The firm advised on the first ever Czech securitisation and the first ever S&P-rated structured note issued by a Dutch multi-issuer. The firm also has a good track record in relation to ship and aircraft finance.

Stibbe's co-operation with **Herbert Smith** is giving a boost to its securitisation practice, which recently acted on the €350m securitisation of a portfolio originated by Interleasing Nederland BV.

ASSET FINANCE AND STRUCTURED FINANCE

ALLEN & OVERY ✪
CLIFFORD CHANCE LLP
DE BRAUW BLACKSTONE WESTBROEK ✪
NAUTADUTILH ✪

Freshfields Bruckhaus Deringer ✪
Simmons & Simmons Trenité ✪
Stibbe ✪

Baker & McKenzie ✪
Boekel De Nerée ✪
DLA SchutGrosheide
Houthoff Buruma ✪
Lovells ✪
Loyens & Loeff ✪
Norton Rose
Van Doorne ✪

Firms are listed A-Z in tiers which are ranked in order of priority
✪ Indicates firm displays contact details at the end of this chapter.

BANKING AND FINANCE

The market for bank finance work is currently economically difficult and competitive. There has been consolidation in the local banking industry, but none of the major players have sold off any core businesses.

BANKING AND FINANCE

ALLEN & OVERY ✪
CLIFFORD CHANCE LLP
DE BRAUW BLACKSTONE WESTBROEK ✪
NAUTADUTILH ✪

Freshfields Bruckhaus Deringer ✪
Loyens & Loeff ✪

Baker & McKenzie ✪
Houthoff Buruma ✪
Lovells ✪
Simmons & Simmons Trenité ✪
Stibbe ✪
Van Doorne ✪

AKD Prinsen Van Wijmen ✪
Barents & Krans ✪
Boekel De Nerée ✪
CMS Derks Star Busmann ✪
DLA SchutGrosheide

Firms are listed A-Z in tiers which are ranked in order of priority
✪ Indicates firm displays contact details at the end of this chapter.

The banking practice at **Allen & Overy** has an extremely global focus, and the firm has recently been expanding its UK law capability in the Netherlands. The firm fielded large teams to advise ABN Amro, ING, Goldman Sachs, JP Morgan and Rabobank on a rescue financing of €6bn for Royal Ahold. Victor de Serière, Julian Harris, Liesbeth Kooij and Ian Powell are market leaders.

As a global law firm, **Clifford Chance LLP** has a very high value-added practice in the Netherlands for banking regulatory work, bank finance and major restructurings. The Dutch office has been building up the amount of work it does for investment banks. A highlight of last year was acting for ABN Amro on the co-ordination of the restructuring of the debt of Geotronics. Frank Graaf, Mark Huddlestone, and its Jan ter Haar are the leading lawyers.

The banking practice at **De Brauw Blackstone Westbroek** has a strong transactional focus, and is driven by Jan Marten van Dijk, Francine Schlingmann and Jan Willem Hoevers. The firm's large corporate client base has meant that it has traditionally tended to act as borrower's counsel, but its practice base has recently broadened. The firm has acted for the Royal BAM Groep on the €610m bridge financing for an acquisition.

NautaDutilh has a very large and strong bank finance team, partly based in the firm's New York, Brussels and London offices, and is particularly well known for banking litigation. The firm has been representing a consortium of Dutch banks in the biggest ever refinancing in the Netherlands. The highlight of its work last year was, however, defending Dexia Bank against an unprecedented group action brought by several thousand customers for claims totalling more than €2bn. Pim Rank and Marc Blom are market leaders.

Freshfields Bruckhaus Deringer has acted for UBS Capital on the restructuring of its financing of the Minit Group, a very complex multi-jurisdictional transaction, and for Reed Elsevier on a $3bn credit facility. Jeroen Thijsen and Richard Norbruis are extremely highly recommended.

Loyens & Loeff advised ABN Amro on the €1.5bn financing of its acquisition of Krefima from KBC, and on the structure of its follow-up financing. Willem Jarigsma, Mariëtte van't Westeinde and Kitty Lieverse are highly recommended.

Baker & McKenzie is strong on the tax side of banking transactions, and major clients are NIB, Fortis and ING.

Houthoff Buruma advises several financial institutions on banking law issues in the Netherlands Antilles and Aruba, and has a particularly strong track record for debt-equity swap transactions. Matthieu van Sint Truiden is well regarded.

Lovells' transactional banking practice and its Dutch client base has been greatly strengthened by the arrival of Ken Breken from **Clifford Chance LLP**. He has recently advised Société Général, ING and Fortis Bank on the banking facilities for the multi-jurisdictional secondary buy-out of the Freshcom group. A highlight for the office was the autumn 2003 appointment to the global panel of ING.

Simmons & Simmons Trenité's banking clients include Mizuho Corporate Bank and HSH Nordbank AG, whom it recently advised in the refinancing of working capital worth €50m. Harm van Berkum is recommended.

Stibbe's banking department has been active in syndicated loan work, particularly on the borrowers' side. Through its co-operation with UK-based **Herbert Smith**, the firm is in the process of setting up an Anglo-Dutch finance desk in Amsterdam. Practice leaders are Jaap Willeumier and Allard Metzelaar, who have worked on a €581m term and revolving credit facility for the Athlon Group NV.

Van Doorne's banking clients include the Bank of Scotland, ING and CIBC World Markets, who it recently advised in connection with a refinancing.

AKD Prinsen Van Wijmen's banking and finance department has benefited from the firm's recent merger with *Wouters*. Partner Barend Post, who is particularly praised by clients, has expertise in the setting up of innovative funds.

CAPITAL MARKETS

Economically difficult times mean that convertible bonds have become an attractive source of finance for many Dutch companies concerned with their debt services. In the last year, the market has also seen a large amount of securitisation work concerned with tax-driven products, and a growth in collateralised debt obligations. The turn towards alternative rated forms of investment has been in response to prolonged bad conditions in the equity markets. **Allen & Overy** and **Clifford Chance LLP** have particularly strong experience in bond work.

CAPITAL MARKETS
ALLEN & OVERY ✪
CLIFFORD CHANCE LLP
DE BRAUW BLACKSTONE WESTBROEK ✪
Freshfields Bruckhaus Deringer ✪
NautaDutilh ✪
Stibbe ✪
CMS Derks Star Busmann ✪
Houthoff Buruma ✪
Lovells ✪
Loyens & Loeff ✪
Simmons & Simmons Trenité ✪
Van Doorne ✪

Firms are listed A-Z in tiers which are ranked in order of priority
✪ Indicates firm displays contact details at the end of this chapter.

Allen & Overy fielded an international team from its Amsterdam, New York and London offices to advise Dutch insurance group AEGON NV on the placement of 350 million ordinary shares, in a total offering of €3.5bn. The transaction also had a large corporate element, involving a restructuring, a large refinancing and corporate governance issues. Pim Horsten and Niels van de Vijver are recommended for capital markets work.

Clifford Chance LLP acts for nearly every major domestic and international financial institution with a presence in the Netherlands, and is a market leader for Dutch SPVs in CDOs. The firm recently acted as issuer and guarantor for EADS on the establishment on a €3bn EMTN programme, and on a debut €1bn note issue. Frank Graaf is one of the country's leading securities lawyers.

De Brauw Blackstone Westbroek is handling a large volume of debt deals, and is very active in the equity capital markets. It recently acted for Rabobank in its $1.75bn issue of non-cumulative guaranteed trust preferred securities in a specific transaction structure for the purpose of raising capital directed at US investors, the largest issue ever of Tier 1 capital in the US by a non-US banking institution. It also recently acted – jointly with **White & Case** – for Dutch issuer Royal Ahold on a €3bn rights issue.

Freshfields Bruckhaus Deringer has handled recent work for Rabobank, Essent and JP Morgan, advising the latter on a €1.25bn issue by Fortis.

NautaDutilh has been strengthening its ability to field transactional finance teams for work with sophisticated financial products. The firm is the ongoing legal counsel to Bank Nederlandse Germeenten, the largest issuer of notes in the Netherlands after the Dutch government. Highlight deals include acting for Impress in the first big high-yield offer of 2003, its issue of listed senior guaranteed notes worth €150m in the context of its refinancing. Kleis Broekhuizen is extremely highly recommended.

Stibbe has a longstanding reputation on capital markets transactions, particularly IPOs, with a focus on the equity capital markets. Recent work includes acting for ASM International NV on the €90m issuance of convertible subordinated notes. Heleen Kersten is recommended.

COMMERCIAL LITIGATION

Only specially appointed lawyers based in The Hague appear before the city's Supreme Court. The leading Supreme Court firms are **De Brauw Blackstone Westbroek**; **Houthoff Buruma** and **Pels Rijcken & Droogleever Fortuijn**, while locally based **Barents & Krans** is also strong. This section lists firms that are strong in major commercial disputes, rather than in practice areas dealt with elsewhere.

De Brauw Blackstone Westbroek's Ruud Hermans and Berto Winters have recently undertaken Supreme Court litigation for

COMMERCIAL LITIGATION

DE BRAUW BLACKSTONE WESTBROEK ✪
HOUTHOFF BURUMA ✪
PELS RIJCKEN & DROOGLEEVER FORTUIJN

Allen & Overy ✪
Barents & Krans ✪
DLA SchutGrosheide
Loyens & Loeff ✪
NautaDutilh ✪
Simmons & Simmons Trenité ✪
Spigthoff ✪
Stibbe ✪
Van Doorne ✪

AKD Prinsen Van Wijmen ✪
Baker & McKenzie ✪
Boekel De Nerée ✪
CMS Derks Star Busmann ✪
Clifford Chance LLP
Dirkzwager advocaten en notarissen
Freshfields Bruckhaus Deringer ✪
Höcker Rueb Doeleman Advocaten ✪
Lovells ✪
Nysingh Dykstra de Graaff
Oostwaard
Van Benthem & Keulen ✪
Van Diepen Van der Kroef Advocaten ✪

Firms are listed A-Z in tiers which are ranked in order of priority
✪ Indicates firm displays contact details at the end of this chapter.

Rodamco and for dredging company HBG, both of which cases led to landmark decisions in the area of corporate governance. Peter van Schilfgaarde, Maarten Schenck and Stef Wuisman are also highly recommended,

Houthoff Buruma also has a strong Supreme Court litigation capability, where Rob Meijer and Peter von Schmidt auf Altenstadt are recommended, and a strong reputation for real estate litigation, where it has acted for the companies involved in the hostile takeover bids of Rodamco and Versatel.

Hague-based **Pels Rijcken & Droogleever Fortuijn** has a very large litigation department and an outstanding Supreme Court practice. Many law firms refer work to it, or seek advice on their cases in the lower courts.

Allen & Overy is acting for AEGON in litigation commenced by Dexia to annul the sale of Bank Labouchere, in the largest case that was pending in the Dutch courts at the time of going to press.

Hague-based **Barents & Krans** has an excellent Supreme Court litigator in Eric Grabant. New partner Henk Waling has a strong specialism in international payments, particularly credit-secured products.

DLA SchutGrosheide has a strong practice, and Ellen Soerjatin has acted for shareholders of Laurus in relation to the company's takeover battle with Casino. Peter Kardoes is also recommended.

Loyens & Loeff has been acting for members of the supervising board of Laurus in an enquiry before the Enterprise Chamber, and for the supervisory directors of Amsterdam-listed trading house Ceteco. Hans de Savornin Lohman, Maarten Das and Winfried van den Muijsenbergh are recommended.

NautaDutilh has a major litigation group, lead by Bart Gerrten and Harmen de Mol van Otterloo. The firm is currently acting on cases involving an alleged conspiracy by public bodies to frustrate the enforcement of building contracts.

Simmons & Simmons Trenité's very experienced Hugo Smit has recently concluded a six-year case, winning €50m in damages from District Waterboards for investors and an engineering bureau for environmental technology.

Spigthoff is a corporate litigation specialist with a reputation for excellence and aggressiveness. Leo Spigt is recommended.

Stibbe acts for Laurus, ING and Fortis Bank. Toni van Hees, Marius Josephus Jitta and Fons Leijten are recommended.

Van Doorne's Dries Fransen van de Putte is recommended for product liability litigation, which has recently included acting for Imperial Tobacco. Walter Hendriksen is also recommended.

CONSTRUCTION

The major Dutch construction companies are currently being investigated by the government for fraud (see section on **Fraud and white-collar crime**).

Houthoff Buruma acts for all the major Dutch construction companies, including HBG and Ballast Nedam. Jan Mark Dingemans has recently been instructed by Royal Volker Wesssels Stevin in a large claim over rail maintenance. Jan Michiel Hebly is also highly recommended.

CONSTRUCTION

HOUTHOFF BURUMA ✪
NAUTADUTILH ✪
ROZEMOND VAN RAMSHORST SMIT
STIBBE ✪

Boekel De Nerée ✪
Pels Rijcken & Droogleever Fortuijn
Simmons & Simmons Trenité ✪

AKD Prinsen Van Wijmen ✪
CMS Derks Star Busmann ✪
Lexence
Loyens & Loeff ✪
Norton Rose
Van Doorne ✪

Firms are listed A-Z in tiers which are ranked in order of priority
✪ Indicates firm displays contact details at the end of this chapter.

At **NautaDutilh** a team led by the highly regarded Lieuwe de Boer advised the Municipality of Amsterdam on the structuring, procurement and contracting of the Amersterdam North/South underground project, one of the largest and most complex projects in the country. The firm also has an excellent track record in contentious work.

Rozemond Van Ramshorst Smit is a market-leading construction law boutique with a focus on disputes. It acts for all the large contractors in the Netherlands, and is currently involved in the following projects that are under construction: the HSL; the freight rail link between Rotterdam and Germany; the Amersterdam North/South underground project; and a major sky scraper construction project. Rob Bleeker is recommended.

Stibbe's Joop Jansen has a highly regarded practice. He has recently advised on the privately financed construction of two motorways, the A59 and the N31, and on the privately financed construction of cruise ship pier facilities on the island of St Martin.

Boekel De Nerée's Hans Nicaise has a particularly good reputation. He has recently worked on design and build contracts for the Prinsenhof project in The Hague.

Pels Rijcken & Droogleever Fortuijn is an extremely important firm in the construction field. Its experience in assisting the government in nearly all the construction cases in which the state is involved means that it has very important insights to offer the large number of private construction companies it also advises. Pieter Stuijt, René Kiers, Gert van't Hoff and Maarten van Rijn are recommended.

Simmons & Simmons Trenité has been acting on behalf of several major Dutch construction companies in relation to recovery claims by the Dutch government as a result of the fraud investigation which is rocking the Dutch building sector (see **Fraud and white-collar crime**). Sjoerd Rutten and Jos van de Vijver are well-recognised construction law experts.

CORPORATE AND COMMERCIAL

In the post-Ahold climate of the Netherlands, there have been significant developments in the field of corporate governance. The introduction of a new code of best practice is expected to generate a considerable amount of work leading up to shareholders' meetings in the spring of 2004. (Lawyers at **De Brauw Blackstone Westbroek** have been advising the government on the new code.)

De Brauw Blackstone Westbroek is the leading and most established corporate practice in the Netherlands, with a particularly strong focus on energy and telecoms. Almost half the Dutch major share issuers – such as Philips – are clients, and the firm has a significant international practice for longstanding clients such as Shell. The team, which includes key market players Bernard

CORPORATE AND COMMERCIAL

DE BRAUW BLACKSTONE WESTBROEK ✪

ALLEN & OVERY ✪
LOYENS & LOEFF ✪
NAUTADUTILH ✪
STIBBE ✪

Baker & McKenzie ✪
Bird & Bird ✪
Boekel De Nerée ✪
Clifford Chance LLP
DLA SchutGrosheide
Houthoff Buruma ✪
Lovells ✪
Norton Rose
Pels Rijcken & Droogleever Fortuijn
Simmons & Simmons Trenité ✪
Van Doorne ✪

Freshfields Bruckhaus Deringer ✪

AKD Prinsen Van Wijmen ✪
Barents & Krans ✪
CMS Derks Star Busmann ✪
Greenberg Traurig LLP
Höcker Rueb Doeleman Advocaten ✪
Hoegen Dijkhof Advocaten
Holland van Gijzen ✪
Kennedy Van Der Laan
Lexence
Russell Advocaten ✪
Spigthoff ✪

Adriaanse & Van der Weel
Buren van Velzen Guelen
De Jonge Peters Remmelink
Dirkzwager advocaten en notarissen
Hekkelman Terheggen & Rieter
Nysingh Dykstra de Graaff
Ploum Lodder Princen ✪
Rassers Advocaten en Notarissen
Schaap & Partners
Udink & De Jong
Van Diepen Van der Kroef Advocaten ✪
Van Dijk & Van Arnhem Advocaten Apeldoorn
Wieringa Advocaten

Firms are listed A-Z in tiers which are ranked in order of priority
✪ *Indicates firm displays contact details at the end of this chapter.*

Roelvink, Jan Willem de Boer and leading notary Martin van Olffen, has recently been strengthened by the recruitment of Professor Jaap Winter, formerly legal adviser to the managing board of Unilever.

Fellow members of what is increasingly considered to be a Dutch Magic Circle of firms are **Allen & Overy**, **Loyens & Loeff**, **NautaDutilh** and **Stibbe**.

Of these, **Allen & Overy** is arguably the strongest competitor to **De Brauw Blackstone Westbroek** in the corporate arena. The Netherlands office of the UK-based international firm, which fields market leaders Maarten Muller and Jan Luis Burggraaf, built up a strong local corporate practice when it was part of former Dutch giant *Loeff Claeys Verbeke*. The firm has recently formed a cross-departmental corporate governance team, been appointed to the global panel of the ING bank, and been advising ABN Amro on the establishment of a bancasssurance partnership with the Delta Lloyd Group.

The corporate practice at **Loyens & Loeff**, where Philip van Verschuer and notary Niek Zaman are highly regarded names, has particularly strong support on the tax aspects of transactions, as the firm combines its tax and legal practices in equal measures, with 50 of its 102 partners being tax partners. A recent highlight of the firm's work was advising Royal KPN on the €580m divestment of its directories business to 3i and Veronis Suhler Stevenson.

NautaDutilh has a strong financial client base, and handles significant corporate work for many major banks, including the Dexia merchant bank, for whom it recently acted in a major reorganisation. The firm also acts as lead counsel for ABN Amro, whom it also advised on its new corporate governance structure. Willem Calkoen is highly recommended.

Stibbe has a blue-chip reputation, and its flagship clients include Dutch and Belgian banking and insurance group Fortis, for whom it has recently been acting on the stapling of stock, various acquisitions, and the €170m sale of Theodoor Gilissen Bankiers to KBL. Paul van den Hoek and Marius Josephus Jitta are extremely well regarded.

Baker & McKenzie's corporate team has grown considerably over the last year, and has handled some major cross-border work for companies including Netherlands-based giant Kroymans. Edwin Liem advises on corporate governance.

The Dutch office of **Bird & Bird** is based in The Hague, close to the regulatory bodies that are important for a client base focused on telecoms, hi-tech and life sciences companies. The firm has just been appointed as the preferred international adviser of the US-listed credit information company Dun & Bradstreet, co-ordinating their legal work throughout Europe. Harry Rek is recommended.

Boekel De Nerée has 24 British Plcs on its client base and three UK-qualified corporate lawyers in its dedicated Anglo-American advisory group, jointly headed by Philip Paterson and Ferdnand Mason. The firm also has a strong US and German client base.

The long-established Dutch office of **Clifford Chance LLP** has historically focused on finance-related tax work, but its market share in corporate-orginated work has recently grown significantly. It also undertakes a significant amount of work in the public-to-private sector, for example for Vredestein NV. Clients appreciate the firm's strong multi-jurisdictional capacity, an example of which is its recent advice to Furgo NV in its €147.5m acquisition of the Thales Geosolutions Group. Hector de Beaufort is recommended.

DLA SchutGrosheide has a broad, mid-market corporate practice. Its corporate client base includes a major Dutch bank. Frans Stibbe is recommended.

Houthoff Buruma has a strong base of clients active in the fields of construction and real estate, such as Royal Voker Wessels Stevin, whom it recently advised on the successful public offer of its shares. Jan van der Horst and Michiel Wesseling are recommended.

The Dutch office of **Lovells** is strong in corporate finance. It has recently acted for PinkRoccade NV on the acquisition and outsourcing of the IT department of PCM Uitgevers. Notary Jan de Snaijer is particularly recommended.

The Dutch office of **Norton Rose** has an internationally focused group with particular strength in the communications, media and technology, financial institutions, energy and insurance industries, and expertise on corporate governance matters. It recently advised JPMorganChase on the financing and structuring of a €350m investment. Edo Groenewald is recommended.

Pels Rijcken & Droogleever Fortuijn is based in The Hague and is the major adviser on corporate and other issues to central and local government in the Netherlands, though it also acts for private sector clients.

The Dutch office of **Simmons & Simmons Trenité**, created through its merger with a Rotterdam-based firm, boasts a number of prestigious international clients; WorldCom, KPMG and US-listed Avaya, for whom it is the preferred law firm throughout Europe. However, it also has a strong client base in Rotterdam, where it acts for public bodies and a number of prestigious hi-tech clients. Leo Verhoeff is the corporate governance expert, while Willem de Nijs Bik, Jean-Pierre van Leeuwe, and notary Frank Roos are also highly recommended.

Van Doorne has a long-established German desk, and a corporate governance expert in Hugo Reumkens. The firm's corporate department was strengthened by its merger with **Landwell**'s Dutch practice, which added three partners to the department, including the well-regarded Ruolph Snethlage, who recently worked for Achmea on its purchase of the SNS Reaal insurance portfolio.

The Dutch office of **Freshfields Bruckhaus Deringer** has established a new employment, pensions and benefits group, which forms an integral part of the corporate transaction team. The firm has been advising Hewlett-Packard on the implementation of its merger with Compaq Computers. Jan Willem van der Staay and Richard Norbuis are recommended.

AKD Prinsen Van Wijmen is a firm that used to be provincially based but has grown through merger and consolidated into a national presence. Its corporate team is particularly strong in the hotel and leisure industry. The firm is a regular counsel to My Travel/Airtours in the Netherlands, and recently advised the company on its international restructuring.

Barents & Krans is based in The Hague. Its corporate practice has a tax focus, with particular expertise in deals that are being structured through the Netherlands for tax reasons. Recent work includes acting on the Dutch element of a transaction whereby Mexican factories purchased a Dutch holding for a US client.

CMS Derks Star Busmann is based in Utrecht, and has a significant number of foreign groups on its client base, including Lear Corporation, Armstrong World Industries and Cardinal Health. The firm has recently acted for Shamu BV in the sale of all shares of Nerema New Resource Management BV. Richard Montijn and Paulus van den Bos are recommended.

The inaugural European office of **Greenberg Traurig LLP**, which opened in Amsterdam in January 2003, is building a strong corporate team, led by Peter Roorda, formerly of **Stibbe**, and Jan Kees Brandse, formerly of **Baker & McKenzie** in the Netherlands. Hans Urlus, formerly of **Simmons & Simmons Trenité**, works on the competition aspects of transactions, and notary René Rieter is recommended. In its first year, the firm acted for Getronics in the €320m sale of its human resources division to NIB Capital, one of the largest divestments in the Netherlands. The firm also acted for Getronics in its subsequent restructuring transactions, and advised Royal Numico NV on the Dutch corporate aspects of multi-billion dollar divestments in the US.

Höcker Rueb Doeleman Advocaten is a mid-size, Amsterdam-based firm with a focus on the media industry. Its clients include the largest Dutch advertising agency, TBWA, whom it has recently advised on several acquisitions. Other clients include Paris-based advertising agency Euro RSCG.

Amsterdam-based **Hoegen Dijkhof Advocaten** is a boutique firm focusing on commercial work.

Holland van Gijzen has recently acted on some prominent retail transactions, for a Swiss listed company in the fashion retail business, Charles Vögele AG, and for Vendex KBB NV, a Dutch listed retailer.

Kennedy Van Der Laan provides corporate advice with a focus on restructuring and reintegration work to some prominent clients in the IT sector, including Microsoft, and Reed Business Information in its acquisition of Internet joint ventures. Its most significant recent deal was the €2.25bn acquisition by Saudi Basic Industries Corporation of the petrochemical division of DSM NV.

Lexence acts for many major companies in the construction industry, and for US and German investors in Dutch real estate. It has also recently acted cross-border for the selling shareholders Wijsmuller Group Holding BV in the €125m sale of its shares to Danish company Svitzer.

Russell Advocaten is a mid-sized firm, whose long-term client list includes a large number of foreign governments and airlines.

Spigthoff built up its name in commercial litigation, and its corporate practice has particular strength in contentious work.

Buren van Velzen Guelen acts for a significant number of Eastern European companies, with a focus on advice that allows them to structure transactions so as to take advantage of Dutch tax treaties.

Van Diepen Van der Kroef Advocaten acts for numerous German companies operating in the Netherlands. Corporate partner Axel Hagedorn is a native German speaker and dual qualified.

LEADING COMMERCIAL FIRMS: EINDHOVEN

Eindhoven is the 'capital' of the southern Netherlands, and the hi-tech centre of the country, the base of multinational Philips. The region is also known for its heavy industry.

The Eindhoven office of **AKD Prinsen Van Wijmen** is a local market leader in corporate law, with a strong focus on construction. It advises Philips on corporate employment matters, and recently acted for Voker Wessel Stevin, a major Dutch construction company, in relation to the redevelopment of a Philips site in Eindhoven, with a purchase contract worth €140m.

The Eindhoven office of **Holland van Gijzen** advises Rabobank on M&A matters and is also known for its corporate work in the construction industry.

Two other firms are also recommended for general corporate and commercial work in Eindhoven: **Boskamp & Willems**, which has notable strength in insolvency work; and **Keizers Poelman Advocaten**, useful for small M&A and insolvency work.

LEADING COMMERCIAL FIRMS: UTRECHT

Utrecht is the fourth-largest Dutch city. Its location in the centre of the Netherlands makes it a favourite enterprise location, and it is performing well economically in comparison to the rest of the country. The province of Utrecht is a leader in IT and the advanced sciences, particularly biotechnological R&D and manufacturing, and substantial building work is taking place there.

Utrecht-based national firm and international network member **CMS Derks Star Busmann** is by far the dominant legal player in the region. It has a strong, traditional corporate client base in its home city, with particular strength in the pharmaceutical and life sciences industries.

LEADING COMMERCIAL FIRMS: Eindhoven

AKD PRINSEN VAN WIJMEN
HOLLAND VAN GIJZEN

Boskamp & Willems
Keizers Poelman Advocaten

LEADING COMMERCIAL FIRMS: Utrecht

CMS DERKS STAR BUSMANN ✪

Wijn & Stael

Van Benthem & Keulen ✪
Van Riet & Associees Advocaten

AKD Prinsen Van Wijmen

Firms are listed A-Z in tiers which are ranked in order of priority
✪ *Indicates firm displays contact details at the end of this chapter.*

Wijn & Stael, **Van Benthem & Keulen** and **Van Riet & Associees Advocaten** are local firms with solid reputations in the corporate arena.

AKD Prinsen Van Wijmen has a 20-lawyer Utrecht office which acts for mid-market corporate clients, and whose commercial practice includes insolvency and employment advice.

EU AND COMPETITION

A major investigation into alleged price fixing by the dominant players in the Dutch construction industry is currently underway (see **Fraud and white-collar crime**). The Dutch Competition Authority is generally becoming much more active. First set up in 1998, it is now maturing into one of the largest and most effective groups in Europe, and starting to examine some hardcore cartel cases. Merger control legislation is expected in 2004. Among the Netherlands-based firms, **Stibbe**, **NautaDutilh**, **Houthoff Buruma** and **Barents & Krans** have Brussels offices.

Allen & Overy has a leading and long-established EU and regulatory practice, whose key clients are Heineken, KPN Mobile NV and UPS, for whom it has recently acted in cases against Deutsche Post for predatory pricing and excessive pricing.

Tom Ottervanger, who divides his time between the firm's Amsterdam and Brussels offices, is recommended.

De Brauw Blackstone Westbroek has a very large team, headed by the highly recommended Martijn Snoep, which has recently been representing Sky Radio before the Dutch courts in cases relating to the allocation of radio frequencies in the Netherlands.

Freshfields Bruckhaus Deringer is an extremely strong player in the competition field throughout Europe, and Amsterdam and Brussels-based Onno Brouwer is extremely highly

EU AND COMPETITION

ALLEN & OVERY ✪
DE BRAUW BLACKSTONE WESTBROEK ✪
FRESHFIELDS BRUCKHAUS DERINGER ✪
STIBBE ✪

Boekel De Nerée ✪
Clifford Chance LLP
Houthoff Buruma ✪
Loyens & Loeff ✪
NautaDutilh ✪
Pels Rijcken & Droogleever Fortuijn
Simmons & Simmons Trenité ✪

Baker & McKenzie ✪
Barents & Krans ✪
CMS Derks Star Busmann ✪

Firms are listed A-Z in tiers which are ranked in order of priority
✪ Indicates firm displays contact details at the end of this chapter.

recommended. Recent work includes representing Essent in numerous cases concerning tariff regulation in the electricity and gas markets.

Stibbe's Martijn van Empel has now retired from the partnership and is acting as a consultant, but the firm still fields a strong competition team that benefits on a European level from its association with **Herbert Smith**. The firm is acting for Heijmans in relation to the Dutch Competition Authority investigation into the construction industry. Christof Swaak is recommended.

Boekel De Nerée has been involved in the high-profile broadcasting matter, successfully representing Canal and Nederland BV before the Netherlands Competition Authority in relation to live broadcasting rights. Frederieke Leeflang is recommended.

The global practice of **Clifford Chance LLP** gives a high added value to its regulatory work out of the Netherlands. The firm has recently advised Reliant Energy on second-phase merger control procedures with the Dutch Competition Authority. Charles van Sasse van Ysselt has excellent experience in handling notifications of M&A transactions in the energy sector.

Houthoff Buruma's EU practice has been strengthened by the recruitment of Gerard van der Wal and his team from **Barents & Krans**. The practice has a strong focus on cartel work, where it has been involved in major investigations by the Dutch Competition Authority into the telecoms, petrol and building industries.

Loyens & Loeff often acts for ABN Amro in filings. It has also acted for REMU in its €1bn acquisition by Eneco.

NautaDutilh has lost Mark van der Woude, but its EU practice still benefits from a strong Brussels office and a strong market position in the energy and life sciences fields, where it acts for GlaxoSmithKline. Jaap Feenstra is recommended.

Pels Rijcken & Droogleever Fortuijn has built up stellar experience acting for the Dutch Competition Authority, while **Simmons & Simmons Trenité** has experience in trade issues involving the Dutch Antilles, and is developing a profile in cartel cases, including assisting a major construction group in ongoing dawn raids and cartel investigations by the Dutch Competition Authority. Marco Slotboom is recommended.

EMPLOYMENT

There are some powerful unions in the Netherlands, and the country's employment legislation has traditionally been strongly weighted in favour of the employee. This has slowly been changing, however incoming directives from Brussels are simultaneously introducing a raft of anti-discrimination laws.

AKD Prinsen Van Wijmen's Scipio van der Stoel is one of the Netherlands' leading employment practitioners. The firm's clients include Vendex KBB, Accentue, Philips, VNU Publitec and Essent. Recent work includes advising European Auto Trader on a full employment review, organisational changes and dismissals, including court proceedings.

The employment practice at **Allen & Overy**, headed by market leaders Ferdinand Grapperhaus and Leonard Verberg, is particularly strong on the employment aspects of cross-border transactions. Clients recently advised on major restructurings include Alcoa, ASML, KPN and DSM.

Baker & McKenzie has a strong team in Joseph van Vlijmen, Mirjam de Blécourt, Karin Bodewes and Anita de Jong. They have recently represented HP Compaq, Kodak, Levi-Strauss and Cisco on restucturings.

EMPLOYMENT

AKD PRINSEN VAN WIJMEN ✪
ALLEN & OVERY ✪
BAKER & MCKENZIE ✪
BOEKEL DE NERÉE ✪
DE BRAUW BLACKSTONE WESTBROEK ✪
LOYENS & LOEFF ✪
STIBBE ✪

Barents & Krans ✪
CMS Derks Star Busmann ✪
DLA SchutGrosheide
Holland van Gijzen ✪
Houthoff Buruma ✪
Kennedy Van Der Laan
NautaDutilh ✪
Simmons & Simmons Trenité ✪
Van Doorne ✪

Clifford Chance LLP
De Jonge Peters Remmelink
Dirkzwager advocaten en notarissen
Höcker Rueb Doeleman Advocaten ✪
Lovells ✪
Ploum Lodder Princen ✪
Van Diepen Van der Kroef Advocaten ✪

Firms are listed A-Z in tiers which are ranked in order of priority
✪ Indicates firm displays contact details at the end of this chapter.

Boekel De Nerée's clients include UPS, Dell Computers and De Nederlandsche Bank NV. The firm has been acting for the CEO of one of the largest Dutch insurance companies in a major dispute.

De Brauw Blackstone Westbroek's Rogier Duk is a leading employment practitioner who regularly brings cases before the Supreme Court. Clients include Ahold, Coca-Cola, ING and WorldCom.

Loyens & Loeff has a high-level practice with particular expertise in pensions.

The firm recently recruited Christian Willems from **Linklaters De Bandt** to head up the labour law practice in its Brussels office, thereby strengthening its corporate restructuring capabilities.

Stibbe's clients include KLM and Dutch bank Theodoor Gilissen, whom it has acted for in major restructurings. Jan Trap and Jaap van Slooten, the lead adviser to KLM, are recommended.

Max Keulaerds at **Barents & Krans** has been acting on some major reorganisations, **CMS Derks Star Busmann**'s Marco Meijer is well regarded, and the corporate side of **DLA SchutGrosheide**'s employment law team has been strengthened by the recruitment of Marnix Holtzer.

The large employment group at **Holland van Gijzen** has been handling large reorganisations and group lay-offs, while **Houthoff Buruma** has a strong pensions capability, spearheaded by market leader Louis Kuypers.

Kennedy Van Der Laan has a specialism in employment matters in the healthcare industry and a well regarded expert in Gerrard Boot. Clients praise the department as 'committed, results oriented and creative'.

NautaDutilh's labour law group has a solid reputation for advising on cross-border employment matters, while **Simmons & Simmons Trenité**'s employee benefits expertise was strengthened by the recruitment of Eunice Bruyninckx, and **Van Doorne** has been focusing on the healthcare sector.

ENERGY

The Kyoto Protocol is driving a push in the Netherlands towards the development of on- and offshore wind parks. A number of foreign companies are active here. Although liberalisation of the energy markets only began in 1999, it is developing ahead of France and Belgium, despite setbacks heralded by the change of government.

Allen & Overy's first-class energy team has particular expertise in the gas sector. Jan Erik Janssen and Henry Van Geen are recommended, as is Leigh Hancher for her experience on competition matters, which were an important component of the advice the firm recently gave to

Dutch energy company Nuon NV on the acquisition of Reliant Energy Europe BV.

De Brauw Blackstone Westbroek has been advising on the few major deals that have taken place recently in the energy market, such as the acquisition of TZH by TenneT. The firm has also advised Gasunie on the restructuring of the 'Gasgebouw' joint venture for the production of natural gas in the Netherlands, and has expertise in emissions trading. Jolling de Pree and Vincent-Paul Aarts are recommended.

NautaDutilh's Chris Fonteijn is widely regarded as the leading energy lawyer in the Netherlands. One client says: 'This firm is able to treat energy-related issues not in an isolated way but to integrate them with governance and broader regulatory issues.' The specialist, cross-departmental group works closely with the firm's New York and Brussels offices, and has been advising the Dutch State on the restructuring of the 'Gasgebouw' joint venture described above.

Clifford Chance LLP has been involved in two major recent transactions – advising ENECO Holdings NV in its winning €1bn bid for REMU and Reliant Resources Inc in the auction sale of its European operations. The firm has a large energy group and a broad client base which also includes Essent and Electrabel.

Loyens & Loeff has a leading practice headed by Max Oosterhuis, whose clients include Nuon, Remu and Eneco. The firm has been advising operators of North Sea cross-border gas fields on downstream activities.

Norton Rose has a market leader in Weero Koster, and a client base which includes Britned Development, Delta NV and RWE GAS AG. The firm has been doing significant specialist work on energy trading, including emissions trading.

Stibbe's primary focus is gas and oil. Major clients include AirLiquide, Norsk Hydro, Reliant, Electrabel and Aeon. Clients speak highly of the firm, and Martin In de Braekt is recommended.

ENERGY

ALLEN & OVERY ✪
DE BRAUW BLACKSTONE WESTBROEK ✪
NAUTADUTILH ✪

Clifford Chance LLP
Loyens & Loeff ✪
Norton Rose
Stibbe ✪

Baker & McKenzie ✪
Boekel De Nerée ✪
CMS Derks Star Busmann ✪
Freshfields Bruckhaus Deringer ✪
Houthoff Buruma ✪
Simmons & Simmons Trenité ✪

Firms are listed A-Z in tiers which are ranked in order of priority
✪ Indicates firm displays contact details at the end of this chapter.

ENVIRONMENT AND PLANNING

The Netherlands has very strict and complex environmental legislation, and environmental law is consequently a genuine specialism.

AKD Prinsen Van Wijmen fields an extremely large team, headed by Mary Lou Simons, who has particular expertise in environmental permits, soil pollution liability and the licensing of herbicides and pesticides. The firm is involved in the environmental aspects of major infrastructure projects, including the HSL and the Betuwe Route projects.

De Brauw Blackstone Westbroek has particular expertise in advising on emissions trading, thanks to expert Rutger de Witt Wijnen. The firm's industry clients include Akzo Nobel, Connexxion and Unilever, while on the government side it acts for the State of The Netherlands and the Rotterdam Port Authority.

Houthoff Buruma's Frank Thunnissen is advising on the zoning and planning aspects of Amsterdam's south axis development. Martin Gelpke, Bowine Meijer, Jaap Hoekstra and Robert Crince Le Roy, are also highly recommended. Other clients – for both advice and litigation – include BP, Corus Essent and numerous local authorities.

NautaDutilh's environmental team, which is particularly strong in the energy field, is currently representing E-Connection Project BV in a procedure regarding a wind farm in the North Sea. It also handles chemical waste and environmental issues for Stork Veco and the Municipality of Amsterdam. Ger Cartigny is the expert on emissions trading.

Pels Rijcken & Droogleever Fortuijn has a focus on environmental liability – where Willem Braams is recommended – particularly in connection with soil contamination. The firm acts primarily for central and local government, but also advises private companies on environmental and planning matters.

Stibbe has experience in advising on a raft of energy law issues. Niels Koeman, Robert Samkalden and Aaldert ten Veen are recommended.

Boekel De Nerée's Anne-Marie Klijn has been doing some high-profile work for AZ Vastgoed and Trammel Crow, while **Clifford Chance LLP**'s prestigious environmental work has recently included advising a US conglomerate on soil contamination and hazardous emissions.

CMS Derks Star Busmann's Frans Otten is an expert on environmental licences, noise pollution and waste. His colleague Bart van Meer has handled many large environmental liability cases.

DLA SchutGrosheide has recruited environmental specialist Lex de Kok from **Baker & McKenzie**. One client describes him as excellent, adding: 'Lex is a very accurate and detailed lawyer who is also very capable of finding practical solutions.'

Höcker Rueb Doeleman Advocaten has a good reputation for advising on building permits, while **Loyens & Loeff**'s excellent Henk Breeman leads a team that acts for large energy, chemical and offshore companies.

Van Diepen Van der Kroef Advocaten has particular expertise in waste, where Ron Laan and Bianca Liefting are recommended. Clients speak of very high standards and genuine specialism in the waste field.

ENVIRONMENT AND PLANNING

AKD PRINSEN VAN WIJMEN ✪
DE BRAUW BLACKSTONE WESTBROEK ✪
HOUTHOFF BURUMA ✪
NAUTADUTILH ✪
PELS RIJCKEN & DROOGLEEVER FORTUIJN
STIBBE ✪

Boekel De Nerée ✪
CMS Derks Star Busmann ✪
Clifford Chance LLP
DLA SchutGrosheide
Dirkzwager advocaten en notarissen
Höcker Rueb Doeleman Advocaten ✪
Lexence
Loyens & Loeff ✪
Simmons & Simmons Trenité ✪
Van Diepen Van der Kroef Advocaten ✪
Van Doorne ✪

Firms are listed A-Z in tiers which are ranked in order of priority
✪ Indicates firm displays contact details at the end of this chapter.

FRAUD AND WHITE-COLLAR CRIME

A wider range of offences are classified as criminal in the Netherlands than in Anglo-American jurisdictions; the alleged price fixing by the dominant construction companies in the Netherlands, which currently under parliamentary investigation, is one example.

CMS Derks Star Busmann has a strong practice in criminal tax law, EU fraud and environmental crimes. The expert Cees van Bavel and Ruud Verbunt represent companies accused of the construction fraud described above, and defendants in the VPV insider trading case.

NautaDutilh's Joost Italianer successfully acted for the former CEO of Philips, Cor Boonstra, in a high-profile insider trading case. He also advised ABN Amro on a $55m tax fraud scheme in which a former employee was one of the main suspects, with the result that no charges were filed against the bank.

Simmons & Simmons Trenité's Ed van Liere is currently representing the interests of a listed company in a large criminal investigation into fraudulent activities in the building industry.

Sjöcrona van Stigt is a specialist criminal defence boutique. The firm has advised a number of executive board members in relation to the construction fraud enquiry. The firm is also

FRAUD AND WHITE-COLLAR CRIME

CMS DERKS STAR BUSMANN ✪
NAUTADUTILH ✪
SIMMONS & SIMMONS TRENITÉ ✪
SJÖCRONA VAN STIGT
WLADIMIROFF & WALING ADVOCATEN

AKD Prinsen Van Wijmen ✪
Boekel De Nerée ✪
Hertoghs Tax Lawyers ✪

Allen & Overy ✪
DLA SchutGrosheide
De Brauw Blackstone Westbroek ✪
Höcker Rueb Doeleman Advocaten ✪
Loyens & Loeff ✪
Stibbe ✪

Firms are listed A-Z in tiers which are ranked in order of priority
✪ Indicates firm displays contact details at the end of this chapter.

recommended for insider trading cases, where the highly regarded Jan Sjöcrona has been acting in the VPV case.

Wladimiroff & Waling Advocaten is a specialist criminal law practice based in The Hague, with a focus on environmental criminal law and administrative sanctions. Mischa Wladimiroff is recommended.

AKD Prinsen Van Wijmen has dedicated tax litigators who handle tax fraud cases including, recently successfully defending two major banks in tax fraud cases against their Netherlands operations. Peter van Hagen is recommended.

Hertoghs Tax Lawyers is a boutique firm which also has significant tax litigation capabilities, while **Boekel De Nerée**'s Carel Raymakers has been assisting several prominent artists in traffic regulations.

INFORMATION TECHNOLOGY

The IT market in the Netherlands is not currently very strong, but a number of firms built up significant practices during the boom years, and these are now focusing on the demand for advice in the fields of piracy, e-commerce among traditional industries, and data protection, notably on a cross-border basis.

The ICT and e-commerce practice at **De Brauw Blackstone Westbroek** handles some major disputes, and does a large amount of work on the hot issues of piracy and data protection, where it advises Shell and Philips. The highly recommended Bart van Reeken acted for East-West e-Ticketing in relation to a new system for the Dutch public transport system, one of the major IT driven projects in the country at present. Lokke Moerel and Joris van Manen are also recommended.

Kennedy Van Der Laan has an outstanding reputation, and acts for Microsoft across the whole of Europe and Africa. Other major clients include Nike, Apple, Heinz and Euronext. The IT department has particular expertise on the new data protection legislation. Coen Drion is recommended for large IT projects.

At **Allen & Overy** the highly regarded Herald Jongen heads a large group with a focus on outsourcing, and clients speak in glowing terms about the firm's expertise in this sector. The firm advised EDS on a $1.3bn contract for the outsourcing of the global IT activities of ABN Amro's wholesale clients division, one of the largest and most complex outsourcing deals undertaken to date in the banking sector. Jongen also leads a strong e-commerce practice, where clients include Reed Elsevier.

Baker & McKenzie's IT clients include Peoplesoft, T-Mobile, Cisco, International Systems, Nedstat and NCR in the Netherlands. Serge Gijrath has a very good reputation in the market.

Bird & Bird's IT practice has a disputes focus, and clients include SSA and Toshiba. Outsourcing clients include Dun & Bradstreet, TNT Post, Orange and Tiscali.

Houthoff Buruma has strong experience in IT outsourcing and procurement. Margaret van Nauta Lemke has advised KPN Telecom on outsourcing.

NautaDutilh is strong in supporting clients on the IT aspects of corporate driven transactions. Ruprecht Herans has been advising Accenture on its tender for the e-ticketing system described above.

Stibbe focuses on providing advice on the IT aspects of major projects, and on IT-related litigation. Rineout Rinzema, who has an excellent reputation, acted for Translink Systems BV in relation to the e-ticketing system described above.

INFORMATION TECHNOLOGY

DE BRAUW BLACKSTONE WESTBROEK ✪
KENNEDY VAN DER LAAN

Allen & Overy ✪
Baker & McKenzie ✪
Bird & Bird ✪
Houthoff Buruma ✪
NautaDutilh ✪
Stibbe ✪

AKD Prinsen Van Wijmen ✪
Boekel De Nerée ✪
CMS Derks Star Busmann ✪
Clifford Chance LLP
Höcker Rueb Doeleman Advocaten ✪
Lovells ✪
Loyens & Loeff ✪
Oosterbaan & Van Eeghen
Van Doorne ✪

Firms are listed A-Z in tiers which are ranked in order of priority
✪ Indicates firm displays contact details at the end of this chapter.

INSURANCE

A new insurance code is expected to be introduced in 2005, as part of the complete overhaul of insurance law that is currently taking place.

Houthoff Buruma is widely regarded as the leading insurance firm in the Netherlands. It recently acted on the takeover of Zürich's Dutch branch by SNS Reaal, and in two multi-million-dollar class action suits from the US, one against Dutch giant Philips. Willem Hengeveld and Peter Drion are recommended.

NautaDutilh is involved in most major insurance cases in the Netherlands, including acting for the insurer of the party held liable for a fire at Schipol airport, in a claim worth around €10m, on which the highly regarded Eric van Neikerk is advising.

Van Doorne's high-level practice advises Deloitte & Touche as the chartered accountants of Vie d'Or life assurance. Dries Fransen van de Putte is recommended for advice on directors and officers' liability.

Boekel De Nerée has an excellent practice, with Jan ter Meer being particularly highly regarded for his expertise in marine insurance. The firm is advising a major US insurance company active in the Netherlands.

De Brauw Blackstone Westbroek's Marina de Kort-de Wolde has an excellent reputation.

Ekelmans & Meijer Advocaten is a specialist insurance law boutique whose clients include Nationale-Nederlanden and Aegon, the two largest insurers in the country.

Loyens & Loeff has specialist expertise in directors' and officers' liability, and has recently worked on claims against the supervisory directors of a major bankrupt company.

Pels Rijcken & Droogleever Fortuijn advises

INSURANCE

HOUTHOFF BURUMA ✪
NAUTADUTILH ✪
VAN DOORNE ✪

Boekel De Nerée ✪
De Brauw Blackstone Westbroek ✪
Ekelmans & Meijer Advocaten
Loyens & Loeff ✪
Pels Rijcken & Droogleever Fortuijn
Van Traa Advocaten ✪

AKD Prinsen Van Wijmen ✪
Allen & Overy ✪
DLA SchutGrosheide
Dirkzwager advocaten en notarissen
Dolk - Verburg - Diamand ✪
Kennedy Van Der Laan
Lovells ✪

Firms are listed A-Z in tiers which are ranked in order of priority
✪ Indicates firm displays contact details at the end of this chapter.

several government departments on insurance issues, and has a Supreme Court litigation focus.

Van Traa Advocaten, a high-powered transport boutique, acts on large industrial risks and for Lloyd's syndicate underwriters.

INTELLECTUAL PROPERTY

The Netherlands is an important jurisdiction for European-wide patents, and trade mark and copyright disputes in the country are increasingly becoming international in nature. The market for legal advice in the field is also in a state of flux, with top-level specialists increasingly uncertain whether they wish to remain with the largest full-service firms or to strike out on their own as boutique litigators. The decision by **De Brauw Blackstone Westbroek** not to merge with international giant **Linklaters** resulted in the departure of two prominent IP partners to found the Dutch office of US-based IP specialist **Howrey Simon Arnold & White, LLP** in 2003. And at the end of 2002 a handful of partners left leading firms to establish high-powered IP boutique **Klos Morel Vos & Schaap**.

The patent law side of the IP practice at **De Brauw Blackstone Westbroek** suffered a considerable blow with the departure of Willem Hoyng and Bart Van Den Broek to **Howrey Simon Arnold & White, LLP**. However, the firm still has a highly respected patent expert in Constant van Nispen, who acted for Alcatel in its cross-border patent dispute with CISCO. On the trade mark side, where Tobias Cohen and Joris van Manen are recommended, the firm acted for the Benelux Trademarks Bureau in the groundbreaking *Libertel* ECJ case in which it was decided that the colour orange could be registered as a trade mark, and in another ECJ case in which it was decided that the tune 'Für Elise' could be a trade mark.

Freshfields Bruckhaus Deringer has growing patent litigation capability, spearheaded by Peter Hendrick, notably in the electronics and pharmaceutical sectors. Clients here include Hoffan-La Roche. Hub Harmeling is recommended for trade mark matters.

Howrey Simon Arnold & White has a leading patent practice in the US, and its Amsterdam office has a focus on cross-border litigation. Willem Hoyng, who during his time at **De Brauw Blackstone Westbroek** chaired the wordwide IP practice group of **Linklaters**, has been acting for Philips in a trade mark case spanning six European jurisdictions. Other key clients include Dutch multinational Akzo Nobel.

Lovells has a very strong team whose leading lawyers are Marc Wallheimer, Klas Bisschop and Bert Oosting, who has been acting for Medinol Ltd in patent litigation.

NautaDutilh's IP department suffered a blow when two partners left to found **Klos Morel Vos & Schaap**, but still has a strong practice headed by Richard Ebbink (patents) and Charles Gielen (trade marks), and supported by a Brussels office. The patent group is acting for Sara Lee in its pan-European litigation.

Allen & Overy similarly suffered the loss of a partner to **Klos Morel Vos & Schaap**. The firm has, however, continued to use its international network of offices to carry out high-profile work, notably for Warner Bros and JK Rowling in relation to a successful action concerning copyright and trade mark infringements of the 'Harry Potter' books. Paul Reeskamp is a well known IP litigator, and Eric Keyzer has a transactional focus. One IP client described the firm as 'the best I have come across'.

Baker & McKenzie acts on brand issues for some high-profile clients, including US-based Liz Claiborne, and on counterfeiting issues for a major sports shoe manufacturer. The firm has developed a web-enabled tool to help clients stop counterfeits at the Dutch border. Alexander Odle is recommended.

Bird & Bird has a small but strong team which acts for Cartier against counterfeiters, and has been involved in some important disputes over coffee sachets.

INTELLECTUAL PROPERTY

DE BRAUW BLACKSTONE WESTBROEK ✪
FRESHFIELDS BRUCKHAUS DERINGER ✪
HOWREY SIMON ARNOLD & WHITE, LLP ✪
LOVELLS ✪
NAUTADUTILH ✪

Allen & Overy ✪
Baker & McKenzie ✪
Bird & Bird ✪
CMS Derks Star Busmann ✪
Kennedy Van Der Laan
Klos Morel Vos & Schaap
Simmons & Simmons Trenité ✪
Steinhauser Hoogenraad, Advocaten
Stibbe ✪

AKD Prinsen Van Wijmen ✪
Arnold + Siedsma, Attorneys at Law and Patent Attorneys ✪
Barents & Krans ✪
Boekel De Nerée ✪
Buren van Velzen Guelen
Clifford Chance LLP
De Jonge Peters Remmelink
Höcker Rueb Doeleman Advocaten ✪
Hoens & Souren Advocaten
Holland van Gijzen ✪
Houthoff Buruma ✪
Loyens & Loeff ✪
Ploum Lodder Princen ✪
Van Benthem & Keulen ✪
Van der Kroft Advocaten
Van Doorne ✪

Firms are listed A-Z in tiers which are ranked in order of priority
✪ Indicates firm displays contact details at the end of this chapter.

CMS Derks Star Busmann is strong in patent and trade mark cases involving the pharmaceutical industry.

Kennedy Van Der Laan's Alfred Meijboom is highly regarded by clients, as is his newly promoted partner Reina Weening, who has been advising a Switzerland-based company on the protection of its IP rights in the US.

Klos Morel Vos & Schaap is a five-partner IP litigation boutique. Sven Klos recently won a victory for Red Bull in the first application of the ECJ's decision in *Libertel*, described above. Gregor Vos has been acting for adidas in its 'three stripe' litigation, while Chantal Morel has a particularly strong reputation for her work in the pharmaceutical industry.

Simmons & Simmons Trenité has the extremely reputable Severin de Wit, who has been assisting ASML in co-ordinating worldwide patent litigation.

Steinhauser Hoogenraad, Advocaten is another specialist IP boutique with good experience in advertising, while **Stibbe** has some important clients in the publishing industry and the media. Dirk Visser acted for Libertel in the groundbreaking litigation described above, while Mark van Gardingen has been acting against adidas in the 'three stripe' litigation.

MEDIA AND ENTERTAINMENT

Allen & Overy's Eric Keyzer is a market leader who regularly advises on anti-piracy campaigns for major US clients. His team also has particular experience in film finance, including advising on the tax shelters available in the Netherlands for productions. Clients include EI, Time Warner and UPC, whom the firm is representing in a dispute with France-based Canal+.

Boekel De Nerée is advising Canal+ on a range of matters. Other key clients include *De Telegraaf*, the Netherlands' largest daily newspaper, and Columbia TriStar/Sony Pictures Entertainment. Pieter Ariëns Kappers is highly recommended, particularly for disputes concerning film production.

At **De Brauw Blackstone Westbroek**, Constant van Nispen has been litigating before the Supreme Court on behalf of the Dutch Football Association, while Mark Biesheuvel is a key player in litigation against the Dutch government relating to the distribution of radio frequencies.

NautaDutilh advises some of the leading players in the Netherlands' media industry on the development of a multi-media project centred around a new television programme.

At **Stibbe** Diana van Everdingen, who has an excellent reputation, has been acting for Radio 538 on a share swap.

Bird & Bird's media practice has a sports focus. The firm has been working for the CNN Cartoon Network, the Discovery Channel and Dutch broadcast organisations.

MEDIA AND ENTERTAINMENT

ALLEN & OVERY ✪
BOEKEL DE NERÉE ✪
DE BRAUW BLACKSTONE WESTBROEK ✪
NAUTADUTILH ✪
STIBBE ✪

Baker & McKenzie ✪
Bird & Bird ✪
CMS Derks Star Busmann ✪
Clifford Chance LLP
Höcker Rueb Doeleman Advocaten ✪
Houthoff Buruma ✪
Kalff Katz & Koedooder Media & Entertainment Lawyers
Kennedy Van Der Laan
Lovells ✪
Steinhauser Hoogenraad, Advocaten
Van Benthem & Keulen ✪
Van der Kroft Advocaten
Van Diepen Van der Kroef Advocaten ✪

Firms are listed A-Z in tiers which are ranked in order of priority
✪ *Indicates firm displays contact details at the end of this chapter.*

CMS Derks Star Busmann has been handling several important negotiations between television production companies and Endemol.

Höcker Rueb Doeleman Advocaten's clients include Sony Computer Entertainment and a world leading, US-based association of entertainment bodies. The firm is involved in a considerable amount of anti-piracy litigation. Gijsbert Brunt is recommended.

Kalff Katz & Koedooder Media & Entertainment Lawyers and **Steinhauser Hoogenraad, Advocaten** are both excellent specialist boutiques, as is **Van der Kroft Advocaten**, which acts for a number of high-profile Dutch pop groups, theatre companies, and events organisers.

Van Diepen Van der Kroef Advocaten has a strong media practice which is acting for US companies in relational to contract work in the Netherlands, and in film financing for Dutch production companies. Clients praise the firm for its useful contacts in the Dutch government.

MEDIATION

Mediation is becoming an important means of dispute resolution in the Netherlands, and legislation to regulate court-annexed mediation was, at the time of going to press, expected to be enacted in 2004.

De Brauw Blackstone Westbroek has handled some significant mediations in the energy and construction sectors. It has also worked on the mediation of *RAI v City of Amsterdam*, a dispute relating to the financial restructuring of an exhibition centre. Bommel van der Bend and Piet Wackie Eysten are recommended.

MEDIATION

DE BRAUW BLACKSTONE WESTBROEK ✪

Boekel De Nerée ✪
CMS Derks Star Busmann ✪
Van Diepen Van der Kroef Advocaten ✪

Firms are listed A-Z in tiers which are ranked in order of priority
✪ *Indicates firm displays contact details at the end of this chapter.*

Boekel De Nerée's Els Swaab is qualified as a mediator with the National Mediation Institute, and is a specialist in handling highly sensitive disputes.

CMS Derks Star Busmann has an experienced corporate mediator in John Bosnak, while **Van Diepen Van der Kroef Advocaten** has seven mediators on its staff, and has recently handled several mediations on shareholder issues, and mediations involving German companies. Fred Koller is recommended.

MERGERS AND ACQUISITIONS

The most significant Dutch deal of 2003 was the €784m cross-border merger between KLM Royal Dutch Airlines and Air France to create a leading European airline group. The transaction, which was particularly complicated due to considerations of air traffic rights and the interests of many stakeholders, was being considered by the competition authorities in Brussels and the US at the time of going to press, and was expected to close in April 2004. The merger was also the source of some conflict in the legal market, as KLM broke with longstanding legal advisers **De Brauw Blackstone Westbroek** to instruct **Allen & Overy** on the merger.

Generally, the market is still slightly depressed, with divestments being the primary M&A activity, and a dearth of national work. However, as most Dutch deals have an international element to them, M&A activity is benefiting from the global upturn.

Allen & Overy won the business of acting for KLM on its merger. The team, drawing on the firm's expertise in the financial and regulatory sectors, was led by head of corporate, Jan Louis Burggraaf. Another important deal for the firm was advising DSM NV on the €2.4bn acquisition of Roche's vitamins and fine chemicals division. Steven Schuit and Johan Kleyn are highly recommended.

De Brauw Blackstone Westbroek has an outstanding reputation as the corporate heavyweight in the Netherlands, and boasts market leaders in Bernard Roelvink, Jan Willem de Boer, Peter Wakkie, Ton Schutte and notary Martin van Olffen. It recently acted for the Dutch government in its €2.025bn sale of a 12% stake in Royal KPN, the former national telephone operator, to Citigroup. The firm combined its restructuring and transactional expertise when it advised Geotronics on a financial restructuring worth €850m and the public exchange offer on its outstanding convertible bonds.

MERGERS AND ACQUISITIONS

ALLEN & OVERY ✪
DE BRAUW BLACKSTONE WESTBROEK ✪
STIBBE ✪

FRESHFIELDS BRUCKHAUS DERINGER ✪
NAUTADUTILH ✪

Clifford Chance LLP
Loyens & Loeff ✪

Baker & McKenzie ✪
Bird & Bird
Boekel De Nerée ✪
DLA SchutGrosheide
Houthoff Buruma ✪
Lexence
Linklaters
Lovells ✪
Simmons & Simmons Trenité ✪
Van Doorne ✪

AKD Prinsen Van Wijmen ✪
Barents & Krans ✪
CMS Derks Star Busmann ✪
Holland van Gijzen ✪
Kennedy Van Der Laan
Ploum Lodder Princen ✪
Pels Rijcken & Droogleever Fortuijn

Firms are listed A-Z in tiers which are ranked in order of priority
✪ *Indicates firm displays contact details at the end of this chapter.*

Stibbe acted for the Dutch government, a major shareholder in KLM, in relation to the company's merger with Air France. The firm has also recently acted for Victor Rijssen in its €700m public offer for all the shares of Koninklijke Voker Wesslels. Marius Josephus Jitta, Paul van den Hoek, Fons Leijten, Joost van Lanschot and Charles Honée are the practice leaders.

M&A work has always been the driver for the worldwide business of **Freshfields Bruckhaus Deringer**. In the Netherlands, the firm recently acted for Invensys Plc in the high-profile and complex disposal, via a controlled auction process, of the Baan software business. The investment value of the transaction was €1.5bn. The firm has also been advising Pinault-Printemps-Redoute in its preparations for a public bid for Gucci.

NautaDutilh acted for Air France in its merger with KLM, and has also previously advised the Dutch government on British Airways' attempts to make a deal with KLM. Other recent high-profile work includes acting for Grupo Dragados on the €756m sale of Dutch construction company HBG to BAM NBM.

Clifford Chance LLP has been building its Dutch M&A practice, spearheaded by Tom de Waard and Thijs Alexander, and recently advised Pon in connection with its €300m successful public bid for Geveke NV, and ENECO in its winning €1bn bid for REMU.

Loyens & Loeff advised the French government on the merger between KLM and Air France. Another highlight was advising Paperlink, jointly with **Linklaters**, on the €746m acquisition of Paper Merchanting.

Linklaters, while remaining small in Amsterdam, has been involved in a number of other sizeable transactions.

Baker & McKenzie has advised Abbott Laboratories on the takeover of the coronary and peripheral-devices business of the bankrupt Jomed NV.

Bird & Bird's MVA clients include TNO, Menzies, Elbit, Kiadis, Aegis and NYSE-listed Dun & Bradstreet, for whom it co-ordinates legal work throughout Europe.

The M&A laywers at **Boekel De Nerée** have particular expertise in auction-based deals. The firm's Anglo-American advisory group acted for Euronext listed Royal Vopak in effecting a vendor's due diligence in respect of its €45m disposal of its European gas shipping business.

DLA SchutGrosheide does a large amount of work for informal investors and for asset management companies. Clients include Bridgepoint Capital.

One client described the performance of the M&A department at **Houthoff Buruma** as 'by far better than I have experienced anywhere else'. The firm is advising MerweOord and NPM Capital on the merger between Van Oord ACZ and Ballast Ham Dredging, creating the second largest dredging company in the world.

M&A clients at **Lexence** include training and consultancy operation the De Boertien Groep BV, and Liberty Media and Quote Media, for whom it sold the companies' interest in music channel The Box Holland BV. Michiel van Schooten and Luc Habets are recommended.

Lovells recently advised Ordina NV on all aspects of the acquisition of the entire share capital of Clockwork, and RAG Coal International AG and ThyssenKrupp Steel AG in the disposal of stakes in Rhinecontainer. Jan de Snaijer is recommended.

Clients speak highly of the expertise at **Simmons & Simmons Trenité** in relation to buy-outs, and consider it a good choice for medium-sized private transactions. The firm acted for CRH Nederland V in the €646m acquisition of a leading building materials group.

Van Doorne has recently advised Oshkosh Truck Corporation on the acquisition of the Geesink-Norba Group.

PRIVATE EQUITY

Private equity activity in the Netherlands has been picking up dramatically, fuelled by the upturn in the international markets, with a significant number of international private equity companies coming into the country seeking cheap buys. The middle market, in particular, is becoming very strong, and many domestic private equity houses are engaging in joint ventures.

PRIVATE EQUITY

ALLEN & OVERY ✪
CLIFFORD CHANCE LLP
LOYENS & LOEFF ✪

De Brauw Blackstone Westbroek ✪
Freshfields Bruckhaus Deringer ✪
NautaDutilh ✪
Simmons & Simmons Trenité ✪

Baker & McKenzie ✪
Bird & Bird ✪
Boekel De Nerée ✪
CMS Derks Star Busmann ✪
DLA SchutGrosheide
Houthoff Buruma ✪
Legal Capital
Lexence
Lovells ✪
Norton Rose
Stibbe ✪
Van Benthem & Keulen ✪
Van Doorne ✪

Firms are listed A-Z in tiers which are ranked in order of priority
✪ *Indicates firm displays contact details at the end of this chapter.*

Allen & Overy, with its outstandingly strong banking practice, is extremely prominent in the private equity arena. Department head Jan Louis Burggraaf is a well known specialist, as is his colleague Johan Kleyn. Their group has recently provided leveraged financing advice to the Carlyle Group, Providence Equity partners and GMT Communications in the €665m MBO of the Dutch cable television operator Casema from France Télécom.

Clifford Chance LLP advised the leading European buy-out specialists Cinven and Candover on a £600m buy-out of Kluwer Academic publishers, and also advised CVC and PAI in relation to the equity financing for their joint acquisition of a majority stake in Provimia SA, which is listed on Euronext Paris and based in the Netherlands. Thijs Alexander is recommended.

Loyens & Loeff has particular strength in domestic Dutch private equity deals, and uses its tax expertise to good effect in the setting up of private equity funds. The highly regarded Herman Kaemingk advised the management of Kluwer Academic publishers in the deal described above.

De Brauw Blackstone Westbroek has a cross-practice private equity group with strong links to the corporate and tax departments. Clients include Rabo Securities, Gilde Investments and Vodafone, whom it advised on the public offer for Libertel.

Freshfields Bruckhaus Deringer has represented most of the major Dutch private equity investors, and international players such as Warburg Pincus and UBS Capital. The firm recently acted for CVC Capital Partners and NIB Capital in a €1bn divestment. Jan Willem van der Staay is a well-known private equity specialist.

NautaDutilh's Jaap Jan Trommel headed a team which acted in an extremely tight time frame for Cerebus and General Atlantic in their acquisition of the Baan Group of Companies.

Simmons & Simmons Trenité has acted on the $665m buy-out of Casema, the Dutch cable TV operator, and on the secondary buy-out of the Refresco group for €240m. Clients praise the firm for its 'outstanding' ability to 'close gaps on the basis of business solutions'.

Houthoff Buruma has notable expertise in the LBO sector, where it has been advising the bidder on a successful public offer for all the shares in AXA Stenman.

PROJECT FINANCE

Public financing has always been strong in the Netherlands, and for smaller projects it is still cheaper than private finance. Usually only huge infrastructure projects are funded by a combination of public and private funds, although this is expected to become a more attractive option as the Dutch government falls short of funds. There are currently some important property projects taking place, and a key project is the €1.3bn high-speed rail link between Amsterdam and the Belgian border (the HSL project).

Allen & Overy has advised parties involved in all the first public private partnership (PPP) projects and in a variety of non-recourse financings in the Netherlands. The firm advised the winning consortium on the A59 road project, the first PFI and project financed road project in the Netherlands. Werner Runge is recommended.

Freshfields Bruckhaus Deringer has a premium infrastructure finance practice. The firm has continued to advise Infraspeed BV, the project company for the HSL project, on issues that have arisen during the construction phase. Other clients include Dexia Bank, Rabobank and the holding company for the D47 motorway in the Czech Republic. Jeroen Thijssen is recommended.

PROJECT FINANCE

ALLEN & OVERY ✪
FRESHFIELDS BRUCKHAUS DERINGER ✪

De Brauw Blackstone Westbroek ✪
Houthoff Buruma ✪
Pels Rijcken & Droogleever Fortuijn

Clifford Chance LLP
NautaDutilh ✪

Firms are listed A-Z in tiers which are ranked in order of priority
✪ *Indicates firm displays contact details at the end of this chapter.*

De Brauw Blackstone Westbroek's cross-departmental project finance industry group has acted for Shell in relation to the €250m Near Shore Windpark project, and for Fortis Bank in relation to the €250m Q7 offshore windpark project.

Houthoff Buruma has been a major player on almost all Dutch PPPs. Jaap Koster is extremely highly regarded. The firm recently acted as Dutch adviser to the arrangers of the €450m senior debt to Rijnmond Energie CV, the developer of a power plant in the Rotterdam area.

Pels Rijcken & Droogleever Fortuijn has developed its project expertise through advising the Dutch State. It has acted on the HSL-Zuid high-speed rail project, the Betuwe freightline and the Schipol Airport projects.

Clifford Chance LLP has acted for Rabobank in export project finance, for ABN Amro in a structured export financing transaction, and for Basell Orlen Polyolefins Sp in connection with a €530m project financing for the construction of plants in Poland.

NautaDutilh has a project finance team that works in tandem with construction, property, tax, banking and capital markets lawyers. The team worked on the first PFI project to include a contract relating to government housing, a deal for the refurbishment of the Dutch Ministry of Finance. It also advised UK-based sponsor InterGen on the €500m construction and financing of a power plant in north-western Europe.

REAL ESTATE

Dutch property is still a very attractive option for investors, particularly those from Germany. However, there is a considerable amount of vacant office space, and retail property is not performing well. One of the most prestigious developments (in Amsterdam's business district, the south axis), is the Mahler 4 project.

Dutch firms **Boekel De Nerée** and **Houthoff Buruma** are the market leaders. **Boekel De Nerée** acts for a very large percentage of the big Dutch property developers and boasts the five top brokers in the Netherlands as clients. The firm advises ING, G&S and Fortis on the Mahler 4 project. David Van Dijk has been advising flagship client Delta Lloyd on the 'De Omval' development project in Amsterdam. His colleague, Albert Flesseman is one of the most eminent real estate lawyers in the country, and notary Toon Schulte is also extremely well regarded.

One client described the real estate department at **Houthoff Buruma** – the largest in the Netherlands – as 'far better than elsewhere'. Its impressive client base includes investors ING and Rodamco and developers ABN Amro/Bouwfonds. Particularly recommended are partners Chris Goumans, Aart Barkey Wolf and Peter Habraken, and notaries Onno de Bruijn and Herman Lohman.

De Brauw Blackstone Westbroek's strong team, which includes notary Paul Kerckhoffs and lawyer Maarten Schepel, gives commercial property advice to the municipalities of The Hague, Utrecht and Heerlen, to the property investors ING, KFN, BPF and Rodamco, and to the developers Blauwhoed and Bouwfonds.

The commercial property department at **Lexence** is focused on acting for developers, and the firm is also strong in litigation on real estate matters, and on city centre developments. The firm is acting for a Netherlands-listed investment company in its multi-million-euro claim over damage to major buildings caused by the flooding of transport tunnels in the centre of The Hague.

At **Stibbe**, the highly regarded Joop Jansen has been working on the DBFO contracting of a large wastewater treatment plant worth €800m, and the proposed Maasvlakte development of the Rotterdam port area.

AKD Prinsen Van Wijmen's clients include Heijmans IBC, the third largest construction company in the Netherlands, who it is advising in negotiations with a local authority. Clients describe the lawyers as 'extremely skilled'.

CMS Derks Star Busmann has a large commercial property practice, which has been strengthened by the arrival of Peter van Mierlo, formerly the in-house counsel of AM, the largest development company in the Netherlands. Clients say they have had a 'very good experience' with the firm's real estate department.

Clifford Chance LLP has been advising a number of real estate funds, such as Lehman Brothers, in relation to real estate lending structures, and LaSalle in the structuring of various property investment funds.

Loyens & Loeff's ongoing real estate clients include Schipol Area Development Company NV. The team was strengthened by the recruitment in 2002 of Rotterdam-based Hamith Breedvald, who has extensive project development expertise, and acted for Rodamco in its acquisition of Batavia Stad, a huge factory outlet which is unprecedented in the Netherlands.

NautaDutilh has particular strength in property finance, lease and property management and compulsory purchase and compensation. Key clients include ING Real Estate. Hen Vrolijk, who advises ING, is recommended.

Simmons & Simmons Trenité has advised IMCA Vastgoed, one of the largest Dutch development companies, on the turn-key sale of one of the biggest office developments in the Netherlands this year, the Millennium Tower, to a German investor for €15m. Leading notary Geert Janssen is recommended.

REAL ESTATE

BOEKEL DE NERÉE ✪
HOUTHOFF BURUMA ✪

De Brauw Blackstone Westbroek ✪
Lexence
Stibbe ✪

AKD Prinsen Van Wijmen ✪
CMS Derks Star Busmann ✪
Clifford Chance LLP
Loyens & Loeff ✪
NautaDutilh ✪
Simmons & Simmons Trenité ✪

Allen & Overy ✪
Baker & McKenzie ✪
Barents & Krans ✪
DLA SchutGrosheide
Greenberg Traurig LLP
Kennedy Van Der Laan
Lovells ✪
Van Diepen Van der Kroef Advocaten ✪
Van Doorne ✪

Firms are listed A-Z in tiers which are ranked in order of priority
✪ Indicates firm displays contact details at the end of this chapter.

RESTRUCTURING AND INSOLVENCY

Due to the recent period of corporate sluggishness in the Dutch and worldwide economies, many law firms have been building up their insolvency practices, and there is a plethora of advice on the market at many different price ranges.

De Brauw Blackstone Westbroek has been involved in almost every major Dutch restructuring or insolvency. Its practice, headed by Sijmen de Rantiz, focuses on advising banks, including the ING Group, for whom it has recently been appointed as preferred counsel, and multinational companies including Ahold and Enron.

RESTRUCTURING AND INSOLVENCY

DE BRAUW BLACKSTONE WESTBROEK ✪
HOUTHOFF BURUMA ✪
SIMMONS & SIMMONS TRENITÉ ✪
STIBBE ✪

AKD Prinsen Van Wijmen ✪
Holland van Gijzen ✪
Loyens & Loeff ✪
NautaDutilh ✪
Pels Rijcken & Droogleever Fortuijn

Barents & Krans ✪
Boekel De Nerée ✪
Borsboom & Hamm Advocaten
CMS Derks Star Busmann ✪
Clifford Chance LLP
DLA SchutGrosheide
De Jonge Peters Remmelink
Höcker Rueb Doeleman Advocaten ✪
Ploum Lodder Princen ✪
Van Benthem & Keulen ✪
Van Doorne ✪

Firms are listed A-Z in tiers which are ranked in order of priority
✪ Indicates firm displays contact details at the end of this chapter.

Houthoff Buruma has recently acted on the restructurings of UPC, as creditors' counsel, and Enron, as liquidator to a large number of Dutch group-holding and financing companies.

Simmons & Simmons Trenité has a leading corporate recovery specialist in Gerhard Gispen. He is currently acting for Citibank, as agent to the lenders, in relation to the recovery of loans advanced under a €500m facilities arrangement.

The lawyers at **Stibbe**, in addition to advising companies, also act as court appointed administrators in insolvencies. The firm recently acted as administrator when VersaTel, the international telecommunications company, went into suspension of payment.

AKD Prinsen Van Wijmen fields a very large insolvency team, acting for banks and private investors and as court receivers. Jan Stadig is widely acknowledged as a market leader, and Ben Knüppe is also well regarded. The firm has acted as trustee on the bankruptcy of Fokker, the most high-profile and largest corporate failure ever in the Netherlands, and on the bankruptcy of KPN/Qwest Finance.

Holland van Gijzen has a track record in acting as receiver for listed companies. Louis Deterink is a well known receiver, and was recently appointed on a large refinancing operation for a Switzerland-based company.

Loyens & Loeff acts for the largest bondholders in the long-running insolvency of KPN/Qwest, on matters including litigation and bond restructuring. Hendrik van Druten has particular expertise in acting for bondholders.

NautaDutilh's Robert van Galen has been involved in a number of ground-breaking cases about insolvency issues, such as the legal proceedings regarding false tax claims worth €200m on behalf of Cargill Financial Markets, a creditor in the Fokker bankruptcies.

Pels Rijcken & Droogleever Fortuijn has some very strong insolvency practitioners, notably Dick Bouma and Jurjen Lemstra.

SHIPPING, AVIATION AND TRANSPORT

The shipping industry in the Netherlands is focused on the port of Rotterdam, where a wide selection of specialist shipping boutiques are based, in addition to some full-service firms with excellent transport practices. There is also some first-class transport law advice available in Amsterdam.

Rotterdam-based **AKD Prinsen Van Wijmen** has the largest traditional shipping practice. Headed by Vincent de Brauw, the team handles a considerable amount of arbitration. On the corporate side, the firm advised Progeco SARL – which is part of the largest shipping company in the world – in its recent acquisition of shares in ACC Beheer BV. Frans de Vries Lentsch, who is acting for one of the vessels that caused the sinking of the *Tricolor* in the English Channel, has an excellent reputation.

SHIPPING, AVIATION AND TRANSPORT

AKD PRINSEN VAN WIJMEN ✪
BOEKEL DE NERÉE ✪
VAN TRAA ADVOCATEN ✪

Boonk Van Leeuwen
De Brauw Blackstone Westbroek ✪
NautaDutilh ✪
Simmons & Simmons Trenité ✪

Allen & Overy ✪
Dolk – Verburg – Diamand ✪
Wiersma Mendel Prakke Advocaten

DLA SchutGrosheide
De Vries Advocaten
Houthoff Buruma ✪
Kernkamp Advocaten
Koster & Claassen
Smallegange, Van Dam & Van Der Stelt
Van Dunné Witholt Golterman
Van Gog Van Rijsbergen Advocaten
Van Harmelen Beijneveld Van Houten

Firms are listed A-Z in tiers which are ranked in order of priority
✪ Indicates firm displays contact details at the end of this chapter.

Boekel De Nerée has an excellent logistics and aviation team headed by Frans Vreede, which has acted in the aftermath of almost all major aviation accidents involving Dutch passengers or crew. Jan ter Meer is recommended for maritime work, while Joeri Cox focuses on road transport.

Van Traa Advocaten is the leading legal boutique offering full service to clients in the transport industry. Pieter den Haan, who is recommended for 'wet', or marine casualties work, is an expert in handling seizures of boats by the Dutch government following collisions, and is also advising a party with an interest in the cargo of the *Tricolor*. Bart Neervoort, who has recently been doing work relating to the explosion of the *Hanjin Oakland*, and air carrier defence work in the London market, is recommended for 'dry' work.

Boonk Van Leeuwen, another leading niche shipping firm, acts for numerous important shipowners.

De Brauw Blackstone Westbroek has a strong aviation practice headed by Berend Crans, which advises Schipol Airport and has acted for British Airways in litigation involving Dutch travel agents.

NautaDutilh advises the major ship financing banks in the Netherlands, including INB and Fortis. The well-regarded Erik Geerling recently acted for Commerzbank on its $22m cashflow financing to Smit International Transport and Installation NV.

Simmons & Simmons Trenité, the only international law firm whose Dutch base is in Rotterdam, has a well-respected practice in traditional shipping and aviation finance, and a leading customs practice. Jasper Helder is recommended.

Allen & Overy has a very strong aviation practice headed by Willem van Baren, while **Wiersma Mendel Prakke Advocaten**'s clients include shipowners Spliethoffs. The firm also acts for the American P&O Club and the owners of 'Vicky' in connection with the *Tricolor*, described above.

TAX

The Netherlands is widely regarded as a tax haven for non-EU companies, and many US and Asian corporates chose to set up their financing structures through the country. Thin capitalisation legislation is being introduced, to mitigate a drop in tax revenue, in response to a European Court of Justice ruling in the *Bosal* case in September 2003 that the deduction of costs relating to EU subsidiaries should be allowed.

Tax lawyers have a wider role in the Netherlands than in many other EU countries, and take a more important role in on the structuring of transactions. Tax advisers (*Belastingadvies*) are a separate profession, and some law firms employ both.

Loyens & Loeff is the leading tax law firm, with the highest volume of work and as many tax advisers as lawyers in the firm. It has particular strength in corporate tax advice, where major clients include KLM, Nuon NV and AGIP. The top tax practitioners are Guido Derckx, Hessel van der Kolk, Marco de Lignie, Tom van der Meer, Paul Simonis, Arnoud Viersen and Maarten van der Weijden.

Baker & McKenzie's outstanding tax team acted for Bosal Holding NV in the landmark case described above. The highly regarded Fred de Hosson led for Bosal. The firm is known for its restructuring tax planning practice, and recently advised Hewlett-Packard on the complicated restructuring following its acquisition of Compaq.

TAX

LOYENS & LOEFF ✪

Baker & McKenzie ✪

Allen & Overy ✪
Clifford Chance LLP
De Brauw Blackstone Westbroek ✪
Freshfields Bruckhaus Deringer ✪
NautaDutilh ✪
Stibbe ✪

AKD Prinsen Van Wijmen ✪
Boekel De Nerée ✪
CMS Derks Star Busmann ✪
Greenberg Traurig LLP
Houthoff Buruma ✪
Lovells ✪
Norton Rose
Simmons & Simmons Trenité ✪
Spigthoff ✪

Firms are listed A-Z in tiers which are ranked in order of priority
✪ Indicates firm displays contact details at the end of this chapter.

KLM is also a client of **Allen & Overy**, where the tax department works very closely with the firm's world-leading banking practice. The recent arrival of new department head Olaf Ernst van der Donk expanded its involvement in corporate transactions. This was particularly evident in the firm's recent advice to DSM on its €1,750m acquisition of the global vitamin business of Roche.

Frank de Vos, who heads the Amsterdam tax department of **Clifford Chance LLP**, is an expert in international tax, well known for his work on corporate restructurings. The practice, which has a financial focus, is a market leader in CDO transactions involving Dutch issuing vehicles. It recently advised Morgan Stanley & Co International Ltd and NIB Capital Bank NV on a €400m managed CLO transaction of senior and mezzanine leveraged loans.

De Brauw Blackstone Westbroek has expertise in tax litigation, structured finance and tax planning work, which is becoming increasingly important to US multinationals active in the Netherlands in the post Sarbanes-Oxley environment. The firm acted for Office Depot in an €800m acquisition of French Guilbert SA through a Dutch hybrid structure. Hans Bol and Peter Flipsen, who acted on this transaction, are recommended.

Freshfields Bruckhaus Deringer's international tax practice has a financial focus. It has acted recently on traditional debt issues, including a number of Spanish parties using EU issuing entities, and sophisticated structured finance (€7bn CSO for ABN Amro) and a number of high-profile securitisations for Société Generale, Rabobank and Goldman Sachs. Hans Galavazi is recommended.

The tax group at **NautaDutilh** has an emphasis on M&A, structured finance and project finance. The firm gave tax advice on the Air France/KLM merger, the acquisition by Cerberus and General Atlantic of the Baan Group of companies, and the issue of $350m 8.5% notes by JP Morgan Europe Ltd, Credit Suisse First Boston (Europe) Ltd and OJSC Kazkommertsbank. Roderick Bouwman and Nico Blom are recommended.

All the tax advisers at **Stibbe** are also required by the firm to be qualified as lawyers. Maarten In de Brakt, Stef van Weeghel and Michael Molenaars are recommended, particularly for their expertise on structured finance transactions. The firm provided tax advice to Burlington Resources in its $100m acquisition of shares of Clam Petroleum BV.

Spigthoff offers specialist tax litigation advice, as does **AKD Prinsen Van Wijmen**, whose dedicated tax litigators act in relation to large-scale investigation projects led by the Dutch Inland Revenue Service, and where Peter van Hagen is recommended.

TELECOMS

Since local telecoms provider KPN was privatised, foreign companies have rushed into the market, and there are now five licensed mobile operators in the Netherlands. The Dutch telecoms market is highly competitive, and though liberalisation is progressing, profitability still does not come easily. The Hague is the most important centre for telecoms – and for all the regulated sectors – as it is here that the competition authorities and the Dutch telecoms regulator, OPTA, are based.

Allen & Overy's Peter Eijsvoogel is a leading specialist. Recent work for flagship client KPN includes the initiation of proceedings against the other Dutch mobile operators in relation to mobile call termination charges.

Bird & Bird's Marjolein Geus is an absolute market leader in telecoms finance; her clients include Orange and KPN, the latter of whom she advises on the potential conflicts arising from its dominant position. She has also been advising the Dutch Minstry of Economic Affairs on underground cable infrastructure, and handling some major litigation.

Clifford Chance LLP is a market leader, but arguably just behind **Allen & Overy**. The firm has been instructed by new client Tele2 on 25 contentious regulatory matters against KPN. Geert van der Klis is recommended, as is Joachim Fleury, who is based primarily in the firm's London office.

The large telecommunications group at **De Brauw Blackstone Westbroek** boasts the excellent Martijn Snoep. He has been representing Vodafone in its public offer to acquire the contentious remaining outstanding shares in Vodafone Libertel.

TELECOMS

ALLEN & OVERY ✪
BIRD & BIRD ✪
CLIFFORD CHANCE LLP
DE BRAUW BLACKSTONE WESTBROEK ✪

Baker & McKenzie ✪
Houthoff Buruma ✪
Kennedy Van Der Laan
NautaDutilh ✪
Stibbe ✪

Boekel De Nerée ✪
CMS Derks Star Busmann ✪
Freshfields Bruckhaus Deringer ✪
Lovells ✪
Pels Rijcken & Droogleever Fortuijn
Van Doorne ✪

Firms are listed A-Z in tiers which are ranked in order of priority
✪ Indicates firm displays contact details at the end of this chapter.

Baker & McKenzie's notable Serge Gijrath has been advising a Dutch mobile operator on the shared roll-out of its radio access network.

Houthoff Buruma acted for T-Mobile in objection proceedings against the decision of the Dutch Competition Authority to fine it.

Kennedy Van Der Laan acts for Vodafone in relation to the company's operations in the Netherlands, on matters including disputes with the regulatory authorities and access fees. Patrick Wit is recommended.

NautaDutilh has assisted Orange Nederland NV on a joint venture with Vendex Group, and advised Deutsche Telekom on a purchase of infrastructure.

Stibbe's telecoms practice has a transactional focus. The firm acted for Vodafone Libertel in the €770m public offering by Vodafone, as the 77% shareholder in Vodafone Libertel, in the other 23%, listed on Euronext. Egbert Dommering is highly regarded.

AKD PRINSEN VAN WIJMEN

PO BOX 59280
1040 KG AMSTERDAM

Telephone: +31 20 582 5 100
Fax: +31 20 582 5 150
Website: www.akd.nl

Languages
Chinese, English, French, German, Italian

Other offices
Rotterdam, Utrecht, Eindhoven, Breda, Brussels, Milan

Number of lawyers 275
at this office 42

Contacts
Bert Heikens (bheikens@akd.nl),
Scipio van der Stoel (svanderstoel@akd.nl)

CATEGORIES OF WORK

Corporate and commercial law

Mergers and acquisitions

Shipping, transport and insurance law

Employment law

Administrative and environmental law

Commercial real estate law

European and competition law

Intellectual property and ICT law

Corporate recovery and insolvency law

Tax litigation

Family law

Health law

Criminal law

Civil law notaries

ALLEN & OVERY

APOLLOLAAN 15
PO BOX 75440
1070 AK AMSTERDAM

Telephone: +31 20 674 1000
Fax: +31 20 674 1111
E-mail: information@allenovery.com
Website: www.allenovery.com

Languages
English, French, German, Italian

Other offices
Antwerp, Bangkok, Beijing, Bratislava, Brussels, Budapest, Dubai, Frankfurt, Hamburg, Hong Kong, London, Luxembourg, Madrid, Milan, Moscow, New York, Paris, Prague, Rome, Shanghai, Singapore, Tokyo, Turin, Warsaw

Number of lawyers 2,305
at this office 210

CATEGORIES OF WORK

Corporate/M&A
Jan Louis Burggraaf

Corporate/notarial
Robert Jan Lijdsman, Gerbrand Visser

Private equity
Karine Kodde

Real estate law
Johan Bakker, Henry van Geen

Project finance
Bart Meesters, Werner Runge

Banking
Victor de Serière, Julian Harris

Tax
Olaf van der Donk

Competition
Tom Ottervanger, Paul Glazener

Regulatory, administrative
Hendrik Jan de Ru

International capital markets
Niels van de Vijver,
Annelies van der Pauw

Litigation
Willem van Baren,
Arnold Croiset van Uchelen

IP/media and entertainment
Paul Reeskamp, Eric Keyzer

Information technology
Herald Jongen

Restructuring/insolvency
Rob Abendroth, Ferdinand Grapperhaus

Employment
Leonard Verburg,
Ferdinand Grapperhaus

Telecommunications
Peter Eijsvoogel

Energy
Jan Erik Janssen

BAKER & McKENZIE

LEIDSEPLEIN 29
1017 PS AMSTERDAM
PO BOX 2720
1000 CS AMSTERDAM
Telephone: +31 20 551 75 55
Fax: +31 20 626 79 49
E-mail: amsterdam.info@bakernet.com
Website: www.bakernet.com

Languages
English, French, German, Italian, Spanish

Other offices
Almaty, Antwerp, Bahrain, Baku, Bangkok, Barcelona, Beijing, Berlin, Bogotá, Bologna, Brasilia, Brussels, Budapest, Buenos Aires, Cairo, Calgary, Caracas, Chicago, Dallas, Düsseldorf, Frankfurt, Geneva, Guadalajara, Hanoi, Ho Chi Minh City, Hong Kong, Houston, Juarez, Kyiv, London, Madrid, Manila, Melbourne, Mexico City, Miami, Milan, Monterrey, Moscow, Munich, New York, Palo Alto, Paris, Porto Alegré, Prague, Rio de Janeiro, Riyadh, Rome, St Petersburg, San Diego, San Francisco, Santiago, São Paulo, Shanghai, Singapore, Stockholm, Sydney, Taipei, Tijuana, Tokyo, Toronto, Valencia, Vienna, Warsaw, Washington DC, Zürich

Number of lawyers 3,380
at this office 150

Contact Maarten van der Lande

CATEGORIES OF WORK

Banking and securities law
Karin JT Smit, Piet LAM Schroeder

Commercial litigation practice
Eduard J Ferman, Frank Kroes

Corporate and commercial/M&A
Mike Jansen, Edwin TH Liem

Corporate contracts
Marco Wallart

Corporate notarial/ civil law notaries
Mark P Bongard, John CC Paans

Employment law
Jos F van Vlijmen, Karin WM Bodewes

EU and competition law
Jean-Paul PL van Marissing

ICT law/telecommunications law
Sergey H Gijrath

Intellectual property
Alexander RT Odle

Pharmaceuticals and healthcare law
Lenet T Leusink

Real estate
Mark P Bongard

Tax
Wouter A Paardekooper, Erik TH Scheer

THE FIRM

Baker & McKenzie Amsterdam was established in 1947. The Amsterdam office was the first in the Netherlands to form part of an international law firm. It now has almost 50 years' experience in international legal practice. Baker & McKenzie was also the first law firm in the Netherlands to set up a fully integrated civil law, tax and notarial practice. With 150 attorneys, tax consultants and civil-law notaries, the Dutch office has all the specialist expertise and experience required for a successful national and international legal practice.

Baker & McKenzie Amsterdam is one of the largest offices in the international Baker & McKenzie network which comprises 66 offices in 36 countries worldwide. With offices in every major business and financial centre, Baker & McKenzie offers an unrivalled international network. Baker & McKenzie has more than 620 partners and over 4,400 legal experts worldwide.

Baker & McKenzie focuses on providing legal services to clients in the business community. Baker & McKenzie Amsterdam has specialist expertise and experience in virtually every field of practice, but it offers more than expert legal knowledge alone. Its attorneys immerse themselves in their clients' companies, their needs and the branch of industry in which they operate in order to fully understand their clients' commercial, economic and social backgrounds. The client's interests are the focus of all services. In order to provide the required capacity for large-scale projects immediately, Baker & McKenzie can assign professionals at every level from its offices all over the world to work on specific long-term or short-term projects. Advanced technology, such as extranet, project management tools and intranet, guarantees efficient cross-border collaboration and a global exchange of expertise and know-how.

Baker & McKenzie makes great demands on its legal service professionals: enthusiasm combined with exceptional professional expertise; decisive action combined with a deep understanding of the client's industries and jurisdictions. The firm's dedicated professionals act as trusted advisers adept at offering solutions that are personalised and targeted to its clients priorities, strategies and goals.

The firm was founded on the concept of serving clients' needs across the globe. Baker & McKenzie continues to invest in its clients. Today and in the future. In the Netherlands and worldwide.

BOEKEL DE NERÉE

ATRIUM
STRAWINSKYLAAN 3037
PO BOX 2508
1000 CM AMSTERDAM

Telephone: +31 20 431 31 31
Fax: +31 20 431 31 43
E-mail: boekel.de.neree@bdn.nl
Website: www.boekeldeneree.nl

Languages
English, French, German, Italian, Spanish

Number of lawyers 160

Contacts
Philip Paterson (solicitor),
Ferdinand Mason (advocaat)

CATEGORIES OF WORK

Mergers and acquisitions
Philip H Paterson, Ferdinand Mason

Corporate and commercial law
Lisette Bieleveld, Pieter Ariëns Kappers

Real estate/commercial property
Paul Wanders, Albert Flesseman

Labour and industrial relations law
Johan Pel, Hester Uhlenbroek

Insurance law/maritime law
Jan ter Meer, Joeri Cox

Transport and aviation
Frans Vreede

Tax law
Joost Krebbers

Banking, securities and finance
Hans Sachse, Paul Jan Soest

EU and competition
Frederieke Leeflang

Environment law/government practice and administrative law
Anne-Marie Klijn

Information and communication technology
Lisette Bieleveld

Intellectual property
Annelies van Zoest

Insolvency law
Wouter Jongepier, Jacques Knol

Litigation
Michel Deckers, Wouter Jongepier

Media and entertainment
Pieter Ariëns Kappers,
Frederieke Leeflang

Personal injury and health law
Herman Bunjes, Hester Uhlenbroek

Notarial services
Willem Jan Poldermans, Hans Mannheim

THE FIRM

Boekel De Nerée is a leading independent Dutch commercial law firm based in Amsterdam. The firm's 160 lawyers, civil law notaries and tax advisers provide specialist tailor-made services to a wide range of domestic and international clients. The firm's core areas of business are corporate/M&A, real estate, employment and transport and insurance.

Through its in-house foreign lawyers, the firm has very close links with the United Kingdom, the United States and Germany. In addition, Boekel De Nerée has excellent ties with correspondent law firms throughout the world.

Boekel De Nerée has its offices in the Atrium Building Amsterdam, adjacent to the World Trade Center.

AREAS OF PRACTICE

Boekel De Nerée is a full service business law firm covering all areas of the law with the emphasis on corporate/M&A, real estate, employment, and transport and insurance.

One of the corporate department's main strengths is the Anglo-American Advisory Group. This group is specifically geared to serve the special needs of clients from English-speaking parts of the world (in particular the UK and North America) who are embarking on mergers, acquisitions and other corporate transactions in the Netherlands. The group is headed up by two British partners and features a highly experienced cross-border team with an international approach to problem-solving that takes into account global issues within the local market context.

The firm is renowned for having one of the largest and most respected real estate teams in the Netherlands, covering all aspects of real estate law.

The firm has one of the leading labour law practices in the Netherlands covering the entire spectrum of employment and industrial relations.

The firm's transport and insurance department is highly specialised and provides a full advisory and litigation service at national and international levels.

Each department of the firm deals with its own specific litigation as is customary in the Netherlands. Boekel De Nerée's litigation strength is epitomised by its ability to put together highly specialised cross-departmental litigation teams in complex proceedings.

Boekel De Nerée has a pronounced international character in the strategy and approach it adopts for solving client problems. Great importance is given in international transactions to advising clients from both a cross-cultural and cross-comparative legal perspective, hence the presence of the in-house foreign lawyers to give comfort and international guidance to foreign clients wishing to transact business in the Netherlands.

CMS DERKS STAR BUSMANN

MONDRIAAN TOWER
AMSTELPLEIN 8A
1096 BC AMSTERDAM

Telephone: +31 20 3016 301
Fax: +31 20 301 63 33
E-mail: amsterdam.office@cmsderks.nl
Website: www.cmsderks.nl

Languages
English, French, German, Hebrew, Italian, Russian, Spanish, Turkish

Other offices
Arnhem, Brussels, Hilversum, Utrecht

Number of lawyers 235
at this office 41

Contact
Roland Bos

Member
CMS Transnational Legal Services; World Law Group

CATEGORIES OF WORK

Banking and finance
Reinout Slot, Jelle Timmenga

Capital markets
Reinout Slot, Jelle Timmenga

Corporate law
Martika Jonk, Richard Montijn

Commercial
Christiaan Scholten van Aschat

Intellectual property, information technology and telecommunications
Marcoline van der Dussen

Mergers and acquisitions
Roman Tarlavski, Reinout Slot

Labour law
Marco Meijer

Pharmaceuticals
Jasper Bovenberg

Real estate
Roland Bos

Venture capital and private equity
Reinout Slot, Roman Tarlavski

Notarial law
Roland Bos

DOLK – VERBURG – DIAMAND

CRONENBURG 75
1081 GM AMSTERDAM

Telephone: +359 2 963 5007
Fax: +359 2 963 2792
E-mail: info@dolk-verburg-diamand.nl
Website: www.dolk-verburg-diamand.nl

Languages
Dutch, English, French, German

Number of lawyers 15

CATEGORIES OF WORK

Transport, maritime, air, road and insurance
AJ Dolk, H Posthumus Meyjes

Company law
H Hampe, BO Eschweiler

Real estate
H Hampe, PW Snoeker

IT law
RPM van Leeuwen, PW Snoeker

Injury
PMGW Bringmann

Procedural law
AJ Dolk, H Posthumus Meyjes

Agency and distribution agreements
H Hampe, BO Eschweiler

International contracts of sale
H Hampe, BO Eschweiler

Labour law
RM Dessaur, BO Eschweiler

Debt recovery
AJ Dolk, H Hampe

Cooperation agreements
BO Eschweiler, H Hampe

Arbitration
AJ Dolk

DE BRAUW BLACKSTONE WESTBROEK

TRIPOLIS 300
BURGERWEESHUISPAD 301
1076 HR AMSTERDAM

Telephone: +31 20 5771 771
Fax: +31 20 5771 775
E-mail: amsterdam@debrauw.com
Website: www.debrauw.com

Languages
Dutch, English, French, German, Italian, Spanish, Swedish

Other offices
London, New York, Rotterdam, The Hague

Number of lawyers 360
at this office 240

CATEGORIES OF WORK

Corporate, M&A
Bernard Roelvink, Lodewijk Hijmans van der Bergh

Corporate governance
Jaap Winter, Martin van Olffen

Corporate litigation
Ruud Hermans, Berto Winters

Banking and capital markets
Jan Marten van Dijk, Jan Willem Hoevers

Asset and structured finance
Berend Crans, Niek Biegman

Corporate restructuring and insolvency
Sijmen de Ranitz, Jako van Hees

Investment management
Paul Klemann, Kees Groffen

Tax
Bernard Roelvink

Employment and employee benefits
Evert Jan Henrichs, Liesbeth Sneek

Information technology
Bart van Reeken, Lokke Moerel

Intellectual property
Constant van Nispen, Joris van Manen

Real estate
Paul Kerckhoffs, Marja de Leeuw

Aviation
Berend Crans

Energy
Bernard Roelvink

Telecommunications
Bart van Reeken, Joris van Manen

THE FIRM

De Brauw Blackstone Westbroek is an independent business law firm. De Brauw specialises in providing legal advice in complex business transactions and commercial litigation. Ever since the firm was founded, in 1871, it has focused on providing top quality legal services and on developing outstanding lawyers. The firm continuously looks forward to breaking new ground, providing expertise and experience to its clients in their ever-changing markets – year after year. In some cases, for over a century.

Almost half of the top 100 companies in the Netherlands choose De Brauw Blackstone Westbroek as their lead law firm (KSU, Stand van de Advocatuur, 2003). Many of De Brauw's clients are large international companies or financial institutions and they regularly ask the firm to manage their cross-border corporate or financial transactions. Or they ask the firm to advise or litigate in international commercial disputes that involve a Dutch and/or Netherlands Antilles angle.

The full spectrum of corporate, M&A and finance activities is handled by a team of partners experienced in domestic and international transactions. They are supported by partners in specialist practices, such as EU/competition, tax and employment, who are also leaders in their field. De Brauw's lawyers understand the European and Anglo-American legal cultures and the demands of an international practice. Internationally, the firm maintains close working relationships with the leading firms in the major business jurisdictions.

AREAS OF PRACTICE

De Brauw Blackstone Westbroek offers a combination of a strong corporate and finance practice and a centre of excellence for litigation, believing it provides the ingredients for a unique service to its clients. It also helps the firm to develop innovative legal minds that bring commercial awareness and technical excellence to everything it does.

The firm's practice covers a broad range of Dutch, EU and Netherlands Antilles law. This includes corporate, mergers and acquisitions, private equity, banking, equity and debt capital markets, asset and structured finance, project finance, corporate recovery and insolvency, restructuring, investment management, tax, corporate and commercial litigation, arbitration and mediation, EU/competition, intellectual property, information technology and communication, public law, estate planning, real estate, employment and employee benefits. The firm has cross-practice groups for, among others, energy, pharmaceuticals, telecoms, financial institutions and public private partnerships, aviation, share plans.

FRESHFIELDS BRUCKHAUS DERINGER

APOLLOLAAN 151
1077 AR
AMSTERDAM

Telephone: +31 20 485 7000
Fax: +31 20 485 7001
E-mail: email@freshfields.com
Website: www.freshfields.com

Languages
Extensive language capabilities

Other offices
Bangkok, Barcelona, Beijing, Berlin, Bratislava, Brussels, Budapest, Cologne, Düsseldorf, Frankfurt, Hamburg, Hanoi, Ho Chi Minh City, Hong Kong, London, Madrid, Milan, Moscow, Munich, New York, Paris, Rome, Shanghai, Singapore, Tokyo, Vienna, Washington

Number of lawyers 2,504
at this office 73

Contact
Hans Galavazi

CATEGORIES OF WORK

Finance

Tax

Corporate

Employment, pensions and benefits

Intellectual property and IT

Dispute resolution (including environment, planning and regulatory)

Antitrust, competition and trade

Real estate

HÖCKER RUEB DOELEMAN ADVOCATEN

VAN EEGHENSTRAAT 98
1071 GL AMSTERDAM
PO BOX 74654
1070 BR AMSTERDAM

Telephone: +31 20 577 7700
Fax: +31 20 671 9710
E-mail: mail@hrd.nl
Website: www.hrd.nl

Languages
English, French, German, Italian, Russian

Number of lawyers 42

Contact
Leo Sapir (managing partner)

Member
Lexwork International; The Interlex Group

CATEGORIES OF WORK

Company/commercial law
Marc Wolters, Yvette Borrius

Insolvency law
Lucas van Eeghen, Kees van de Meent

Mergers and acquisitions
Antoine Endtz, Marc Wolters

Labour law
Jasper van Hulst, Inge Hofstee

Intellectual property law
Gijsbert Brunt, Eveline Schippers

ICT law
Gijsbert Brunt

Environmental law
Koos van den Berg

Entertainment law
Willem Roos

Family law
Anneke Karsten

Media law
Herman Doeleman, Willem Roos

Property law
Dolf Rueb

Mediation
Anneke Karsten, Herman Doeleman

HOUTHOFF BURUMA

PO BOX 75505
1070 AM AMSTERDAM

Telephone: +31 20 577 2000
Fax: +31 20 577 2700
E-mail: info@houthoff.com
Website: www.houthoff.com

Languages
English, French, German, Italian, Portuguese, Spanish

Other offices
Brussels, London, Rotterdam, The Hague

Number of lawyers 323
at this office 150

Contacts
Jan van der Horst, Robert Tieskens

CATEGORIES OF WORK

- **Administrative and government regulations**
- **Banking, finance, and securities**
- **Capital markets**
- **Construction and real estate**
- **Corporate and commercial**
- **Employment and pensions**
- **Energy and regulatory**
- **Information and communication technology**
- **Insolvency**
- **Insurance and reinsurance**
- **Intellectual property**
- **Liability**
- **Litigation and arbitration**
- **Media and entertainment**
- **Mergers and acquisitions**
- **Private equity**
- **Project finance**
- **Restructuring**
- **Tax**
- **Telecoms**

THE FIRM

Houthoff Buruma is one of the largest independent full service law firms in the Netherlands. Over 300 specialists provide tailor-made legal and tax services to businesses and organisations that strive for excellence. Houthoff Buruma provides legal and tax assistance to both domestic and international clients.

The firm is organised into practice groups in the traditional sense, but also has specialist industry groupings that combine professional industry experts from different legal disciplines.

In addition to its offices in Amsterdam, Rotterdam and The Hague, Houthoff Buruma also has offices in Brussels and London. The Brussels office provides legal services mainly on competition law and EU law. The London office provides Dutch legal services, primarily with respect to corporate law, banking and finance. A key objective of the London office is to co-ordinate projects and contacts for the firm's offices in the Netherlands, as well as to handle the firm's current international contacts in the legal, financial and commercial markets.

AREAS OF PRACTICE

Houthoff Buruma assists its clients in every area of law. The firm is a leading adviser in mergers and acquisitions, IPOs and financing. Complex transactions and projects are the day to day business of the firm. Other areas in which the firm has an excellent reputation are, among others, construction and real estate, employment and pensions, energy, insolvency and restructuring, insurance and reinsurance, litigation, project finance, and telecoms.

HOWREY SIMON ARNOLD & WHITE LLP

REMBRANDT TOWER, 31ST FLOOR
AMSTELPLEIN 1
1096 HA AMSTERDAM

Telephone: +31 20 592 44 11
Fax: +31 20 463 72 96
Website: www.howrey.com

Languages
Dutch, English, French, German, Spanish

Other offices
Brussels, Chicago, Houston, Irvine, London, Los Angeles, Menlo Park, San Francisco, Washington DC

Number of lawyers 543
at this office 8

Contacts
Willem Hoyng, Bart van den Broek

CATEGORIES OF WORK

Intellectual property litigation and counselling (patents, trade marks, copyright, trade secrets)
Willem Hoyng, Bart van den Broek

Information technology
Frank Eijsvogels

Competition law
Willem Hoyng

National and international litigation and arbitration
Willem Hoyng, Bart van den Broek

Patent and trade mark prosecution

LOVELLS

FREDERIKSPLEIN 42
1017 XN AMSTERDAM
POSTBUS 545
1000 AM AMSTERDAM

Telephone: +31 20 55 33 600
Fax: +31 20 55 33 777
E-mail: information@lovells.com
Website: www.lovells.com

Languages
English, French, Spanish

Other offices
Alicante, Beijing, Berlin, Brussels, Budapest*, Chicago, Düsseldorf, Frankfurt, Hamburg, Ho Chi Minh City, Hong Kong, London, Milan, Moscow, Munich, New York, Paris, Prague, Rome, Shanghai, Singapore, Tokyo, Vienna*, Warsaw, Zagreb*

Number of lawyers 1,600
at this office 61

CATEGORIES OF WORK

Corporate

Intellectual property and information technology

Property and regulatory

Banking and finance

Employment

LINKLATERS

3RD FLOOR
ATRIUM BUILDING
STRAWINSKYLAAN 3051
1077 ZX AMSTERDAM

Telephone: +31 20 799 6200
Fax: +31 20 799 6300
Website: www.linklaters.com

Languages
English

Other offices
Alicante, Antwerp, Bangkok, Beijing, Berlin, Brussels, Bratislava, Bucharest, Budapest, Cologne, Frankfurt am Main, Hong Kong, Lisbon, London, Luxembourg, Madrid, Milan, Moscow, Munich, New York, Paris, Prague, Rome, São Paulo, Shanghai, Singapore, Stockholm, Tokyo, Warsaw

Number of lawyers 2,000 worldwide

Contact
Richard Levy

CATEGORIES OF WORK

Banking and general finance

Corporate/M&A (including public and private takeovers, acquisitions and disposals, joint ventures and reorganisations)

Capital markets (including equity and debt transactions)

THE FIRM

Linklaters advises the world's leading companies, financial institutions and governments on their most challenging transactions and assignments. With 2,000 lawyers, including 470 partners, and offices in major business and financial centres, its clients choose the firm for its distinctive combination of technical skill, commercial experience and outstanding service.

Linklaters has built a formidable global practice through organic growth and a series of mergers, joint ventures and co-operations with other respected law firms. In 2001, Linklaters merged with three of Europe's leading law firms to form Linklaters Oppenhoff & Rädler in Germany, Linklaters in Sweden, Linklaters De Bandt in Belgium and Linklaters Loesch in Luxembourg. In the same year, the firm formed a co-operation with Brazilian firm Goulart Penteado, Iervolino e Lefosse. This co-operation combines Linklaters' international capability with GPIL's extensive knowledge of the Brazilian market. In Singapore, the firm practises as Linklaters Allen & Gledhill, a joint venture with the premier Singapore practice of Allen & Gledhill, while in Italy, Linklaters has an exclusive relationship with Italian law firm Gianni, Origoni, Grippo & Partners.

LOYENS & LOEFF

FORUM, FRED ROESKESTRAAT 100
1076 ED AMSTERDAM
PO BOX 71170
1008 BD AMSTERDAM

Telephone: +31 20 578 5785
Fax: +31 20 578 5888
E-mail: info@loyensloeff.com
Website: www.loyensloeff.com

Languages
English, French, German, Italian, Japanese, Russian, Spanish

Other offices
Arnhem, Eindhoven, Rotterdam, Antwerp, Aruba, Brussels, Curaçao, Frankfurt, Geneva, London, Luxembourg, New York, Paris, Singapore, Tokyo

The offices in Antwerp and Brussels practice under the name Loyens.

Number of lawyers 744
at this office 254

CATEGORIES OF WORK

Administrative, regulatory law

Banking and security, capital markets, project finance

Commercial law and litigation

Corporate law, mergers and acquisitions, joint ventures

Private equity

EU and competition

Real estate, construction law

Tax law

Corporate taxation international

Labour law, wage tax

Income tax

Indirect taxes

THE FIRM

Loyens & Loeff offers its clients integrated services in the legal, tax consultancy and notarial professions while retaining the dynamics of the various independent practice areas. In comparison to other domestic and international providers of legal services, the combination of attorneys, tax advisers and civil law notaries as equal components has placed the firm in a unique position. The Loyens & Loeff priority is to provide ingenious and efficient legal services at the highest level.

Loyens & Loeff clients can be assured of the firm's assistance anywhere in the world. Its offices have had extensive and long-standing international experience and are designed to provide clients with unique tax and advisory services, both at local and at international level. The foreign offices offer clients, in various countries, legal services by lawyers who are familiar with the country concerned and its national law. Loyens & Loeff also maintains excellent and long-standing relations with prominent law firms in Europe, the United States and elsewhere. This ensures that Loyens & Loeff has access to advice from foreign lawyers at the highest level at all times.

Loyens & Loeff is expanding its international network by developing a diversified 'best friends' concept, without committing to exclusive markets. This enables the firm on a case-by-case basis, for example in cross-border transactions, to set up teams of lawyers from different firms across Europe or in the US which can offer services of the highest quality in a seamless fashion. Certain teams are active on a more permanent basis focusing on particular industries and markets, whilst the purpose of other teams is to provide services to clients in specific cases. This approach gives the firm the competitive edge on globally operating one-stop shop firms.

AREAS OF PRACTICE

Loyens & Loeff is a full-service law firm which focuses mainly on large and medium-sized international corporations. It is recognised as being one of the leading firms in such areas of law as banking and securities, venture capital/IPO's, corporate law, M&A, joint ventures, privatisations, tax, real property, labour law, regulatory law, commercial law, litigation, environmental law and zoning, construction, transport, technology, media, telecommunications, energy, healthcare, intellectual property and EU and competition.

NAUTADUTILH

STRAWINSKYLAAN 1999
1077 ZZ AMSTERDAM

Telephone: +31 20 717 10 00
E-mail: info@nautadutilh.com
Website: www.nautadutilh.com

Languages
English, French, German, Italian, Japanese, Russian, Spanish

Other offices
Brussels, London, Luxembourg, New York, Rotterdam

Number of lawyers 503
at this office 207

CATEGORIES OF WORK

Capital markets
Petra Zjip

Construction/property
Cees Boodt

Commercial litigation/arbitration
Floris Bannier

Corporate litigation
Harmen de Mol van Otterloo

Employment
Warner Roeters van Lennep

EU, regulatory and competition
Erik Minderhoud

Finance litigation
Huib van Everdingen

Insurance and liability
Stijn Franken

Intellectual property and ICT
Charles Gielen

Loan finance
Marc Blom

Private equity
Erik Hammerstein

Projects/project finance
Thijs Lommen

Public M&A
Robert ten Have

Restructuring and insolvency
Robert van Galen

Structured finance and securitisation
Willem Ruys

Taxation
Nico Blom

Telecommunications and media
Piet Sippens Groenewegen

THE FIRM

NautaDutilh enjoys a strong reputation throughout the Benelux. With more than 500 attorneys, civil law notaries and tax advisers, and offices in Amsterdam and Rotterdam, NautaDutilh is one of the largest law firms in the Netherlands and its Brussels office has grown quickly to become a recognised player in the Belgian market. The firm's core businesses are corporate, banking, finance and tax law, but it has chosen to maintain a broader, market-focused practice than some of its peers.

The position established by the firm in its domestic market – and the interests of the clients it serves there – convinced it to resist the advances of global law firms and remain clearly and publicly independent. Nevertheless, it has invested in maintaining close but non-exclusive relationships with other market-leading (or specialist) law firms throughout the world, especially in the UK and the US. Today, over half of the firm's revenue comes from international business and it acts for many global corporations and (investment) banks. By nurturing its 'best friends' relationships, NautaDutilh has become the preferred Benelux referral firm for many leading overseas law firms, and it is convinced that it can offer each individual client a service tailor-made to their specific requirements. The firm's experience operating in the major financial centres of the world helps it to be even more effective in its domestic Benelux markets. Its offices in London and New York (which practise only Dutch and Belgian law) play an important role in supporting its corporate, banking and finance practice, and its Luxembourg office provides specialist support to its tax practice elsewhere.

AREAS OF PRACTICE

By listening carefully to its clients and studying the market place, NautaDutilh has recognised the need to focus its expertise in particular markets or business sectors. The firm has therefore organised itself in a range of market-driven practice groups, such as life sciences, energy and utilities, and shipping and logistics. Drawing their talents from throughout the firm, these groups offer clients a powerful concentration of legal and business skills tailored to their specific business needs and complement the firm's established areas of legal work.

Besides corporate, banking, finance and tax – NautaDutilh's core practices – the firm offers high-level advice on: construction/property; intellectual property and ICT; EU, regulatory and competition; employment; litigation; insurance and liability; and maritime law. The firm also offers its services to private clients.

RUSSELL ADVOCATEN

REIMERSBEEK 2
1082 AG AMSTERDAM

Telephone: +31 20 301 5555
Fax: +31 20 301 5678
E-mail: info@russell.nl
Website: www.russell.nl

Languages
Dutch, English, French, German, Spanish

Other offices
The Hague

Number of lawyers 20

CATEGORIES OF WORK

- Aviation, shipping and transport
- Arbitration and ADR
- Administrative/environmental law
- Art and law
- Corporate and commercial
- Corporate litigation
- Distribution, agency and franchise
- Family law
- Insurance and (professional) liability
- Insolvency law
- Intellectual property and information technology
- Labour law
- Mediation
- Property/real estate

SPIGTHOFF

DIJSSELHOFPLANTSOEN 14
PO BOX 75546
1070 AM AMSTERDAM

Telephone: +31 20 305 1600
Fax: +31 20 305 1699
E-mail: info@spigthoff.com
Website: www.spigthoff.com

Languages
Dutch, English, French, German

Other offices
Curaçao

Number of lawyers 36
at this office 26

CATEGORIES OF WORK

Corporate litigation Jacob Cornegoor	**Banking** Jerry Hoff
Corporate crime Martien Pelinck	**Tax** Charles Langereis
Securities Karel Frielink	**Insolvency** Leo Spigt

THE FIRM

Spigthoff was established on 1 January 2001 by well-known corporate attorneys Leo Spigt and Jerry Hoff. Other partners in the office are attorneys Karel Frielink, Jacob Cornegoor, tax advisers Arnold van der Smeede, Albert-Jan van Soelen, and attorneys/tax specialists Charles Langereis and Martien Pelinck. Partners at the Curaçao office are attorneys Kees Westermann and Martijn Welten, and tax adviser Xandra Kleine-van Dijk.

Spigthoff's office in Amsterdam employs 26 attorneys, and its Curaçao office has ten attorneys. The firm is also assisted by prominent emeritus attorneys and professors from external sources.

Spigthoff's return to a relatively small group of professionals sets a new trend in the legal profession, as it seldom has to refuse new cases because of conflicts of interest. The firm's offices are staffed by specialist attorneys and tax advisers, predominantly recruited from larger Dutch firms. They specialise in corporate litigation, corporate and securities law, mergers and acquisitions and in other large, complex matters, which often attract attention in the news.

From the outset, Spigthoff has been developed with a balance between attorneys and tax advisers, who work together as a co-ordinated team. Of the 11 partners, six are attorneys and five are tax specialists. The firm maintains a close, personal contact with its clients. It consists of creative deal-makers, noted for their toughness but, at the same time, aiming to solve problems and conflict situations amicably and expeditiously. Spigthoff works under the motto 'make the deal, settle peacefully if possible but go into battle if necessary'. Its lawyers are ready and able to enter into the fray and litigate thoroughly when necessary on their clients' behalf.

AREAS OF PRACTICE

Spigthoff specialises in corporate law, securities law and tax. It concentrates on (potential) conflict and critical situations. In transactions, its lawyers concentrate on making it happen. Their principal areas of practice are: litigation; restructuring, particularly in cases of insolvency; securities law; mergers, acquisitions and other complex transactions; financial law; and economic criminal law.

STIBBE

STRAWINSKYLAAN 2001
1077 ZZ AMSTERDAM

Telephone: +31 20 546 0606
Fax: +31 20 546 0123
E-mail: info@stibbe.nl
Website: www.stibbe.com

Languages
English, French, German, Italian, Mandarin, Norwegian, Russian, Spanish

Other offices
Brussels, London, New York

Number of lawyers 309
at this office 185

Contact
Joost van Lanschot

CATEGORIES OF WORK

Litigation and arbitration
Jeroem Fleming

Mergers and acquisitions
Joost van Lanschot

Equity capital markets
Heleen Kersten

Finance and banking
Jaap Willeumier

Telecoms and IT
Maarten Sanders

Employment
Jan Trap

Tax
Maarten de Bruin

Administrative and public, real estate
Niels Koeman

EU, competition and regulation
Christof Swaak

Intellectual property
Kurt Stöpetie

Notarial practice
Bart Kraak

VAN DIEPEN VAN DER KROEF ADVOCATEN

DIJSSELHOFPLANTSOEN 16-18
1077 BL AMSTERDAM
PO BOX 76729
1070 KA AMSTERDAM

Telephone: +31 20 5 74 74 74
Fax: +31 20 5 74 74 75
E-mail: amsterdam@vandiepen.com
Website: www.vandiepen.com

Languages
English, Dutch, French, German, Spanish, Russian

Other offices
Alkmaar, Bussum, Haarlem, Hoorn, The Hague, Utrecht

Number of lawyers 117
at this office 37

Contact
Dr Axel Hagedorn (a.hagedorn@vandiepen.com)

CATEGORIES OF WORK

Arbitration

Banking and finance

Commercial property

Competition law

Corporate and commercial

Environment/administrative law

German law

Information technology

Insolvency law/restructuring

Intellectual property

International/European law

Litigation

Media, telecoms and entertainment

Mediation

Mergers and acquisitions

Personal injury and health law

Private equity and venture capital

Transport and aviation

VAN DOORNE

JACHTHAVENWEG 121
1081 KM AMSTERDAM
PO BOX 75265
1070 AG AMSTERDAM

Telephone: +31 20 6789 123
Fax: +31 20 6789 589
E-mail: amsterdam@van-doorne.com
Website: www.vam-doorne.com

Languages
English, French, German, Italian

Other offices
Aruba*, Curaçao*, London

Number of lawyers 185

CATEGORIES OF WORK

Banking and finance
Roel Botter

Litigation and insurance
Walter Hendriksen

Competition
Sarah Beeston

Property
Michiel Faro, Saskia Laseur

Corporate
Onno Boerstra, Rudolph Snethlage

Tax
Thijs Clement

Employment
Paul Witteveen, Els de Wind

Insolvency
Paul Schaink

Intellectual property/information technology
Remco van Leeuwen, Kees Stuurman

Notarial practice
Saskia Laseur, Maaike van Meer

THE FIRM

Van Doorne is an independent Dutch law firm with its principal offices in Amsterdam. In addition, it provides Dutch law advice through its London offices and Dutch law and Netherlands Antilles law advice through its associated offices in Curaçao and Aruba. The professionals comprise lawyers, civil law notaries and tax advisers, who work fully integrated in the various practice groups. The spread of its practice groups enable Van Doorne to service its clients on all relevant areas of law. In its work, Van Doorne aims to apply the law as a tool for practical solutions. The firm is proud of its Dutch client base, which comprise large and medium-sized companies, banks, insurance companies, (quasi) governmental bodies and Dutch subsidiaries of foreign enterprises. Nonetheless, Van Doorne is well-know for its international practice. Historically, it serves a large number of international clients, particularly from the UK and the US. Moreover, the majority of transactional work carried out by the banking and corporate group (including tax) is cross-border. The independent status of Van Doorne provides its clients with a great opportunity to work with the best equipped law firms in other countries. For that purpose, it maintains for decennia close working relationships with leading law firms in all important jurisdictions. Van Doorne strongly believes in the advantage to be able to instruct in other jurisdictions, or to be instructed for Dutch law as the best possible firm required for the specific international transaction.

AREAS OF PRACTICE

Through eight practice groups and five business groups, Van Doorne provides a full range of services to its clients. Lawyers in the various practice groups co-operate in teams to ensure a high level of quality in all services rendered. Van Doorne is well-known in the areas of banking and finance, mergers and acquisitions, private equity, labour law, healthcare, property, PPI, intellectual property and information technology, competition, tax, litigation, professional liability and insurance.

HERTOGHS
TAX LAWYERS

PARKSTRAAT 8
PO BOX 4729
4803 ES BREDA

Telephone: +31 76 520 2266
Fax: +31 76 520 2288
E-mail: hertoghs@hertoghsadvocaten.nl
Website: www.hertoghsadvocaten.nl

Languages
English, French, German, Spanish

Number of lawyers 8

Contact
Hans Peek

CATEGORIES OF WORK

Tax litigation
Hans Hertoghs, Roel Kerckhoffs

Criminal tax law, business crime
Hans Peek, Guido de Bont

Unlawful government acts
Hans Hertoghs

Collection law (tax and customs)
Roel Kerckhoffs, Guido de Bont

Tax liability
Hans Peek, Roel Kerckhoffs

DE BRAUW BLACKSTONE WESTBROEK

BLAAK 34
3011 TA ROTTERDAM

Telephone: +31 10 240 65 00
Fax: +31 10 411 35 48
E-mail: rotterdam@debrauw.com
Website: www.debrauw.com

Languages
Dutch, English, French, German, Italian, Spanish, Swedish

Other offices
Amsterdam, London, New York, The Hague

Number of lawyers 360
at this office 10

CATEGORIES OF WORK

Corporate
Frederik Buijn, Cees de Monchy

Estate planning
Pieter van Onzenoort

THE FIRM

De Brauw Blackstone Westbroek is an independent business law firm. De Brauw specialises in providing legal advice in complex business transactions and commercial litigation. Ever since the firm was founded, in 1871, it has focused on providing top quality legal services and on developing outstanding lawyers. The firm continuously looks forward to breaking new ground, providing expertise and experience to its clients in their ever-changing markets – year after year. In some cases, for over a century.

Almost half of the top 100 companies in the Netherlands choose De Brauw Blackstone Westbroek as their lead law firm (KSU, Stand van de Advocatuur, 2003). Many of De Brauw's clients are large international companies or financial institutions and they regularly ask the firm to manage their cross-border corporate or financial transactions. Or they ask the firm to advise or litigate in international commercial disputes that involve a Dutch and/or Netherlands Antilles angle.

The full spectrum of corporate, M&A and finance activities is handled by a team of partners experienced in domestic and international transactions. They are supported by partners in specialist practices, such as EU/competition, tax and employment, who are also leaders in their field. De Brauw's lawyers understand the European and Anglo-American legal cultures and the demands of an international practice. Internationally, the firm maintains close working relationships with the leading firms in the major business jurisdictions.

AREAS OF PRACTICE

De Brauw Blackstone Westbroek offers a combination of a strong corporate and finance practice and a centre of excellence for litigation, believing it provides the ingredients for a unique service to its clients. It also helps the firm to develop innovative legal minds that bring commercial awareness and technical excellence to everything it does.

The firm's practice covers a broad range of Dutch, EU and Netherlands Antilles law. This includes corporate, mergers and acquisitions, private equity, banking, equity and debt capital markets, asset and structured finance, project finance, corporate recovery and insolvency, restructuring, investment management, tax, corporate and commercial litigation, arbitration and mediation, EU/competition, intellectual property, information technology and communication, public law, estate planning, real estate, employment and employee benefits. The firm has cross-practice groups for, among others, energy, pharmaceuticals, telecoms, financial institutions and public private partnerships, aviation, share plans.

HOLLAND VAN GIJZEN

ATTORNEYS AT LAW AND CIVIL LAW NOTARIES

GH BETZWEG 1
3068 AZ ROTTERDAM
PO BOX 488
3000 AL ROTTERDAM

Telephone: +31 10 406 5000
Fax: +31 10 406 5001
E-mail: gregor.bertens@hollandlaw.nl
Website: www.hollandlaw.nl

Languages
English, German, French, Italian, Russian, Spanish

Other offices
Amsterdam, Chicago, Eindhoven, The Hague, London, New York, Utrecht

Number of lawyers 200

Contact
Gregor Bertens

CATEGORIES OF WORK

Corporate and commercial
Jan Meijerman, Johan Westerhof

Mergers and acquisitions
Jan Meijerman, Dick Weiffenbach

Insolvency, corporate restructuring
Louis Deterink, Johan Westerhof

Competition and EU
Dirk Boselie, Dik Marijnen

Banking and finance
Alexander Filius

Employment law and human resources
Marc van Gelder, Hans van Gijzen

Commercial property and real estate
Bart Terhorst, Paul Liesker

Construction
Bart Terhorst, Paul Liesker

Intellectual property and IT
Lidia Ritzema

Media and entertainment
Lidia Ritzema

Dispute resolution – litigation and arbitration
Hugo Nieuwenhuizen, Frits van Hees

Energy and natural resources
Dick Weiffenbach

Administrative and public law
Huib van Olden

THE FIRM

Holland Van Gijzen is the result of a merger between several well-known firms of attorneys-at-law and civil law notaries. The firm has a strategic alliance with Ernst & Young Tax Advisers, which in turn forms an alliance with Ernst & Young Accountants. Together, these firms represent many years of experience.

By joining forces in this way and by its own distinctive working methods, Holland Van Gijzen has developed into a multi-disciplined firm with a nationwide and international reputation. With offices in Amsterdam, Eindhoven, The Hague, Rotterdam and Utrecht and legal desks in Chicago and New York, accommodating over 200 attorneys-at-law and civil law notaries, the firm is one of the larger-sized firms in The Netherlands. The firm offers the client a one-stop service.

Holland Van Gijzen is a participant in EY Law. EY Law is an international network of independent law practices associated with Ernst & Young. EY Law provides its clients with a co-ordinated and integrated approach towards legal services around the world. It aims to provide major international and national clients with innovative and commercial legal services that deliver real value and benefits. EY Law practices provide clients with a single point of contact through which they have ready access to experienced lawyers around the world.

AREAS OF PRACTICE

The firm's service concentrates on mergers and acquisitions; corporate restructuring and insolvency; antitrust and competition law; structured finance; banking and securities; employment; pensions and benefits; reorganisations and recovery; intellectual property, IT and entertainment; construction, property development and real estate; administrative and environmental law; litigation; private equity; and notarial services. In case of litigation, clients can rely on experienced, sophisticated and dedicated experts.

Holland Van Gijzen has numerous long-term contracts with clients and offers a broad-based, client-oriented service.

HOUTHOFF BURUMA

PO BOX 1507
3000 BM ROTTERDAM

Telephone: +31 10 217 20 00
Fax: +31 10 217 27 00
E-mail: info@houthoff.com
Website: www.houthoff.com

Languages
English, French, German, Italian, Portuguese, Spanish

Other offices
Amsterdam, Brussels, London, The Hague

Number of lawyers 323
at this office 100

Contacts
Michiel Wesseling, Herman Lohman

CATEGORIES OF WORK	
Construction and real estate	Litigation and arbitration
Corporate and commercial	Mergers and acquisitions
Corporate finance	Property finance
Employment and pensions	Private equity
Energy and regulatory	Project finance/PFI
Insolvency	Restructuring
Insurance and reinsurance	Transport and shipping
Liability	

THE FIRM

Houthoff Buruma is one of the largest independent full service law firms in the Netherlands. Over 300 specialists provide tailor-made legal and tax services to businesses and organisations that strive for excellence. Houthoff Buruma provides legal and tax assistance to both domestic and international clients.

The firm is organised into practice groups in the traditional sense, but also has specialist industry groupings that combine professional industry experts from different legal disciplines.

In addition to its offices in Amsterdam, Rotterdam and The Hague, Houthoff Buruma also has offices in Brussels and London. The Brussels office provides legal services mainly on competition law and EU law. The London office provides Dutch legal services, primarily with respect to corporate law, banking and finance. A key objective of the London office is to co-ordinate projects and contacts for the firm's offices in the Netherlands, as well as to handle the firm's current international contacts in the legal, financial and commercial markets.

AREAS OF PRACTICE

Houthoff Buruma assists its clients in every area of law. The firm is a leading adviser in mergers and acquisitions, IPOs and financing. Complex transactions and projects are the day to day business of the firm. Other areas in which the firm has an excellent reputation are, among others, construction and real estate, employment and pensions, energy, insolvency and restructuring, insurance and reinsurance, litigation, project finance, and telecoms.

KNEPPELHOUT & KORTHALS
ADVOCATEN

POSTBUS 546
3000 AM ROTTERDAM

Telephone: +31 10 400 51 00
Fax: +31 10 400 51 11
E-mail: mail@kneppelhout.nl
Website: www.kneppelhout.nl

Languages
English, French, German

Number of lawyers 26

Member
The Parlex Group of European Lawyers (associates in Barcelona/Madrid, Brussels, Copenhagen, Cyprus, Dublin, Edinburgh, Freiburg, Graz, Helsinki, Lisbon, London, Luxembourg, Oslo, Paris, Reykjavic, Stockholm, Thessaloniki, Turin/Milan, and Zurich)

CATEGORIES OF WORK

Commercial law
Hans Walhain

Construction law
Jan Willem Langeler

Corporate law, M&A
Jan Kneppelhout, Jan Willem Langeler

EU antitrust and competition law
Kees Capel, Jan Willem Langeler

Finance and securities
Jan Kneppelhout, Otto de Witt Wijnen

Franchising, agency and distribution
Jan Kneppelhout

Insolvency and bankruptcy
Hans Walhain, Otto de Witt Wijnen

Insurance and liability
Wibe Reddingius

Intellectual property
Kees Capel

International trade law
Jan Kneppelhout

Employment law
Wibe Reddingius, Arnold Birkhoff

Real estate and tenancy
Kees Capel

LOYENS & LOEFF

WEENA 690
3012 CN ROTTERDAM
PO BOX 2888
3000 CW ROTTERDAM

Telephone: +31 10 224 6224
Fax: +31 10 414 5839
E-mail: info@loyensloeff.com
Website: www.loyensloeff.com

Languages
English, French, German, Italian, Japanese, Russian, Spanish

Other offices
Arnhem, Eindhoven, Rotterdam, Antwerp, Aruba, Brussels, Curaçao, Frankfurt, Geneva, London, Luxembourg, New York, Paris, Singapore, Tokyo

The offices in Antwerp and Brussels practise under the name Loyens.

Number of lawyers 744
at this office 216

CATEGORIES OF WORK

Administrative, regulatory law

Banking and security, capital markets, project finance

Commercial law and litigation

Corporate law, mergers and acquisitions, joint ventures

Private equity

EU and competition

Real estate, construction law

Tax law

Corporate taxation international

Labour law, wage tax

Income tax

Indirect taxes

THE FIRM

Loyens & Loeff offers its clients integrated services in the legal, tax consultancy and notarial professions while retaining the dynamics of the various independent practice areas. In comparison to other domestic and international providers of legal services, the combination of attorneys, tax advisers and civil law notaries as equal components has placed the firm in a unique position. The Loyens & Loeff priority is to provide ingenious and efficient legal services at the highest level.

Loyens & Loeff clients can be assured of the firm's assistance anywhere in the world. Its offices have had extensive and long-standing international experience and are designed to provide clients with unique tax and advisory services, both at local and at international level. The foreign offices offer clients, in various countries, legal services by lawyers who are familiar with the country concerned and its national law. Loyens & Loeff also maintains excellent and long-standing relations with prominent law firms in Europe, the United States and elsewhere. This ensures that Loyens & Loeff has access to advice from foreign lawyers at the highest level at all times.

Loyens & Loeff is expanding its international network by developing a diversified 'best friends' concept, without committing to exclusive markets. This enables the firm on a case-by-case basis, for example in cross-border transactions, to set up teams of lawyers from different firms across Europe or in the US which can offer services of the highest quality, in a seamless fashion. Certain teams are active on a more permanent basis, focusing on particular industries and markets, whilst the purpose of other teams is to provide services to clients in specific cases. This approach gives the firm the competitive edge on globally operating one-stop shop firms.

AREAS OF PRACTICE

Loyens & Loeff is a full-service law firm which focuses mainly on large and medium-sized international corporations. It is recognised as being one of the leading firms in such areas of law as banking and securities, venture capital/IPOs, corporate law, M&A, joint ventures, privatisations, tax, real property, labour law, regulatory law, commercial law, litigation, environmental law and zoning, construction, transport, technology, media, telecommunications, energy, healthcare, intellectual property and EU and competition.

NAUTADUTILH

WEENA 750
3014 DA ROTTERDAM

Telephone: +31 10 224 00 00
Fax: +31 10 414 84 44
E-mail: info@nautadutilh.com
Website: www.nautadutilh.com

Languages
Arabic, English, French, German, Spanish, Swedish

Other offices
Amsterdam, Brussels, London, Luxembourg, New York

Number of lawyers 503
at this office 213

CATEGORIES OF WORK

Capital markets
Walter Schellekens

Construction/property
Lieuwe de Boer

Commercial litigation/arbitration
Bart van Tongeren

Corporate litigation
Bart Gerretsen

Restructuring and insolvency
Joost Vrancken Peeters

Employment
Jennifer Willemsen

Energy and utilities
Chris Fonteijn

Insurance and liability
Erik van Niekerk

Intellectual property and ICT
Richard van Oerle

Finance litigation
Walter Schellekens

Loan finance
Erik Vermeulen

Maritime
Arnold van Steenderen

Projects/project finance
Erik Geerling

Private equity
Roderik Bouwman

Public M&A
Willem Calkoen

EU, regulatory and competition
Norbert de Munnik

Taxation
Trudy Perié

THE FIRM

NautaDutilh enjoys a strong reputation throughout the Benelux. With more than 500 attorneys, civil law notaries and tax advisers, and offices in Amsterdam and Rotterdam, NautaDutilh is one of the largest law firms in the Netherlands and its Brussels office has grown quickly to become a recognised player in the Belgian market. The firm's core businesses are corporate, banking, finance and tax law, but it has chosen to maintain a broader, market-focused practice than some of its peers.

The position established by the firm in its domestic market – and the interests of the clients it serves there – convinced it to resist the advances of global law firms and remain clearly and publicly independent. Nevertheless, it has invested in maintaining close but non-exclusive relationships with other market-leading (or specialist) law firms throughout the world, especially in the UK and the US. Today, over half of the firm's revenue comes from international business and it acts for many global corporations and (investment) banks. By nurturing its 'best friends' relationships, NautaDutilh has become the preferred Benelux referral firm for many leading overseas law firms, and it is convinced that it can offer each individual client a service tailor-made to their specific requirements. The firm's experience operating in the major financial centres of the world helps it to be even more effective in its domestic Benelux markets. Its offices in London and New York (which practise only Dutch and Belgian law) play an important role in supporting its corporate, banking and finance practice, and its Luxembourg office provides specialist support to its tax practice elsewhere.

AREAS OF PRACTICE

By listening carefully to its clients and studying the market place, NautaDutilh has recognised the need to focus its expertise in particular markets or business sectors. The firm has therefore organised itself in a range of market-driven practice groups, such as life sciences, energy and utilities, and shipping and logistics. Drawing their talents from throughout the firm, these groups offer clients a powerful concentration of legal and business skills tailored to their specific business needs and complement the firm's established areas of legal work.

Besides corporate, banking, finance and tax – NautaDutilh's core practices – the firm offers high-level advice on: construction/property; intellectual property and ICT; EU, regulatory and competition; employment; litigation; insurance and liability; and maritime law. The firm also offers its services to private clients.

PLOUM LODDER PRINCEN

BLAAK 28
3011 TA ROTTERDAM
PO BOX 711
3000 AS ROTTERDAM

Telephone: +31 10 440 64 40
Fax: +31 10 436 44 00
E-mail: info@plp.nl
Website: www.plp.nl

Languages
English, French, German, Italian

Number of lawyers 45

Contact
Duco Lodder

Member
Osborne Clarke Alliance

CATEGORIES OF WORK

Asset finance
Stan Commissaris

Commercial contracts
Dorine ten Brink

Commercial litigation and arbitration
John van Baaren

Commercial property
John van Baaren

Competition and EU
Michel Jacobs

Corporate, M&A
Duco Lodder

Corporate recovery
Jeroen Princen, Carla Nijhuis

Employment
Rutger Ploum, Peter de Waal

Estate planning
Jolande van Loon

Full notarial services
Jolande van Loon, Stan Commissaris

Insolvency
Jeroen Princen, Carla Nijhuis

Intellectual property
Tom Ensink

IT and telecoms
Tom Ensink, Dorine ten Brink

Joint ventures
Duco Lodder

SIMMONS & SIMMONS TRENITÉ

WEENA 666
3012 CN ROTTERDAM

Telephone: +31 10 404 2111
Fax: +31 10 404 2333
E-mail: rotterdam@simmons-simmons.com
Website: www.simmons-simmons.com

Languages
Afrikaans, Arabic, Cantonese, Czech, Dutch, French, German, Greek, Hindi, Hungarian, Italian, Japanese, Latvian, Mandarin, Polish, Portuguese, Russian, Slovakian, Spanish, Swedish, Vietnamese

Other offices
London, Paris, Lisbon, Milan, Rome, Düsseldorf, Frankfurt, Brussels, Madrid, Padua, Oporto, Madeira, Abu Dhabi, Qatar, Hong Kong, Shanghai, Tokyo, New York

Number of lawyers 754
at this office 81

Contacts
Gerhard Gispen, Jan van Zuuren (managing partners)

CATEGORIES OF WORK

Corporate
Jean-Pierre van Leeuwe, Willem de Nijs Bik

Banking
Loet Venrooy

Capital markets
Harm van Berkum

Taxation
Peter de Brock

Commercial
Jan Willem Bitter

EU, competition
Marco Slotboom

Dispute resolution
Hugo Smit, Michael Gorsira

Intellectual property
Severin de Wit

Employment and benefits
Alexander Steensma, Vincent Disselkoen

Financial markets
Loet Venrooy, Harm van Berkum

Corporate restructuring
Gerhard Gispen

Energy and utilities
Jos Bos

TMT
Alan Steele Nicholson

Corporate criminal defence
Ed van Liere

Transport and customs
Jan Willem Bruidegom, Jasper Helder

Real estate and construction
Sjoerd Rutten, Geert Janssen

Projects, PFI
Jos Bos, Jos van de Vijver

Notarial services
Frank Roos, Jan Mathijs Hermans

VAN TRAA ADVOCATEN

MEENT 94
3011 JP ROTTERDAM

Telephone: +31 10 413 70 00
Fax: +31 10 414 57 19
E-mail: info@vantraa.nl
Website: www.vantraa.nl

Languages
English, French, German, Italian, Polish

Number of lawyers 21

Contacts
Robert de Haan, Benedict Janssen

CATEGORIES OF WORK

Maritime law (cargo claims, bill of lading and charterparty disputes, ship arrests)
Prof Maarten Claringbould, Robert de Haan

Hull and machinery (collision, salvage and shipbuilding contracts)
Pieter den Haan

Ship financing (mortgages, registry and auctions)
Pieter den Haan, Robert Pessers

Aviation (aircraft financing, passenger and cargo claims, accidents, insurance, licences and charters)
Marc van Maanen, Robert Pessers

Road transport (cargo claims, logistic contracts)
Jan Teunissen, Benedict Janssen

Insurance (general commercial liability, fire and construction)
Jan Teunissen, Bart Neervoort

Professional indemnity (lawyers, accountants, brokers and architects)
Bart Neervoort, Marc van Maanen

ARNOLD + SIEDSMA

ATTORNEYS AT LAW AND PATENT ATTORNEYS

SWEELINCKPLEIN 1
2517 GK THE HAGUE

Telephone: +31 70 365 4833
Fax: +31 70 361 5054
E-mail: admin@arnold-siedsma.nl
Website: www.arnold-siedsma.nl

Languages
Dutch, English, French, German, Italian, Spanish

Other offices
Amsterdam*, Breda*, Enschede*, Leeuwarden*, Nymegen*, Utrecht*, Zwolle*, Brussels*, Antwerp*, Munich*, Alicante*

CATEGORIES OF WORK

Trade mark law (Benelux, European)
Peter Verhaag, Marc van Wijngaarden

Utility model designs
Peter Verhaag, Marc van Wijngaarden

IP litigation
Dr Remco de Ranitz, Peter Verhaag

Patent prosecution
Bas 't Jong, Dr Hans W Prins

Patent law (Dutch, Belgian, European)
Dr Remco de Ranitz, Marc van Wijngaarden

Life sciences
Dr Remco de Ranitz, Marc van Wijngaarden

IT
Michel Rorai

BARENTS & KRANS
ADVOCATEN NOTARISSEN

PARKSTRAAT 107
POSTBUS 30457
2500 GL DEN HAAG

Telephone: +31 70 376 0606
Fax: +31 70 365 1856
E-mail: info@barentskrans.nl
Website: www.barentskrans.nl

Languages
English, French, German

Other offices
Brussels

Number of lawyers 55
at this office 54

CATEGORIES OF WORK

Corporate and commercial law
Henk Waling, Nick Surber

Mergers and acquisitions
Otto de Jong, Nick Surber

EU law
Pierre Bos, Laura Parret (Brussels)

Competition, antitrust
Harry Ferment, Laura Parret (Brussels)

Employment, labour
Peter Vas Nunes, Max Keulaerds

Trade marks, intellectual property
Harry Ferment, Marleen van den Horst

Banking and finance
William Schonewille

Commercial property, real estate
Joost Huijgen, Jacques Buiteman

Governmental and administrative law
Joost Huijgen

Distribution, agency and franchise
Harry Ferment

Insolvency
Alexander Beelaerts van Blokland, Dirk van den Berg

Insurance and liability
Herman Jansen

Supreme Court litigation
Eric Grabandt, Jan Paul Heering

Wills and estates
Frans van Rijckevorsel van Kessel, Marja Schimmel

BIRD & BIRD

PARKSTRAAT 31
2541 JD
2500 GH THE HAGUE

Telephone: +31 70 353 8800
Fax: +31 70 353 8811
E-mail: thehague@twobirds.com
Website: www.twobirds.com

Languages
English, Dutch, French, German

Other offices
Brussels, Düsseldorf, Hong Kong, London, Milan, Munich, Paris, Stockholm

Number of lawyers 358
at this office 37

Contacts
Marjolein Geus, Harry Rek

CATEGORIES OF WORK

Asia desk
Steven van der Waal

Communications
Marjolein Geus

Competition
Pauline Kuipers

Corporate
Harry Rek

Employment
Philip Hartman

Information technology
Jeroen van der Lee

Internet and e-commerce
Jeroen van der Lee

Intellectual property
Wouter Pors

Life sciences
Erik Limpens

Media
Marjolein Geus

Notarial practice
Steven van der Waal

Sport
Wouter Pors

Tax
Pieter Camps

DE BRAUW BLACKSTONE WESTBROEK

ZUID-HOLLANDLAAN 7
2596 AL DEN HAAG

Telephone: +31 70 328 5328
Fax: +31 70 328 5325
E-mail: thehague@debrauw.com
Website: www.debrauw.com

Languages
Dutch, English, French, German, Italian, Spanish, Swedish

Other offices
Amsterdam, London, New York, Rotterdam

Number of lawyers 360
at this office 100

CATEGORIES OF WORK

Litigation and arbitration
Maarten Schenck, Bommel van der Bend

EU, competition
Mark Biesheuvel, Martijn Snoep

Intellectual property
Koen Limperg, Tobias Cohen Jehoram

Public law
Godert van der Feltz, Vincent Aarts

Employment and employee benefits
Rogier Duk, Harro Knijff

Professional liability
Rob Polak, Marina de Kort-de Wolde

Energy
Vincent Aarts, Jolling de Pree

Pharmaceuticals
Constant van Nispen, Martijn Snoep

Telecommunications
Martijn Snoep

THE FIRM

De Brauw Blackstone Westbroek is an independent business law firm. De Brauw specialises in providing legal advice in complex business transactions and commercial litigation. Ever since the firm was founded, in 1871, it has focused on providing top quality legal services and on developing outstanding lawyers. The firm continuously looks forward to breaking new ground, providing expertise and experience to its clients in their ever-changing markets – year after year. In some cases, for over a century.

Almost half of the top 100 companies in the Netherlands choose De Brauw Blackstone Westbroek as their lead law firm (KSU, Stand van de Advocatuur, 2003). Many of De Brauw's clients are large international companies or financial institutions and they regularly ask the firm to manage their cross-border corporate or financial transactions. Or they ask the firm to advise or litigate in international commercial disputes that involve a Dutch and/or Netherlands Antilles angle.

The full spectrum of corporate, M&A and finance activities is handled by a team of partners experienced in domestic and international transactions. They are supported by partners in specialist practices, such as EU/competition, tax and employment, who are also leaders in their field. De Brauw's lawyers understand the European and Anglo-American legal cultures and the demands of an international practice. Internationally, the firm maintains close working relationships with the leading firms in the major business jurisdictions.

AREAS OF PRACTICE

De Brauw Blackstone Westbroek offers a combination of a strong corporate and finance practice and a centre of excellence for litigation, believing it provides the ingredients for a unique service to its clients. It also helps the firm to develop innovative legal minds that bring commercial awareness and technical excellence to everything it does.

The firm's practice covers a broad range of Dutch, EU and Netherlands Antilles law. This includes corporate, mergers and acquisitions, private equity, banking, equity and debt capital markets, asset and structured finance, project finance, corporate recovery and insolvency, restructuring, investment management, tax, corporate and commercial litigation, arbitration and mediation, EU/competition, intellectual property, information technology and communication, public law, estate planning, real estate, employment and employee benefits. The firm has cross-practice groups for, among others, energy, pharmaceuticals, telecoms, financial institutions and public private partnerships, aviation, share plans.

HOUTHOFF BURUMA

PO BOX 305
2501 CH DEN HAAG

Telephone: +31 70 35 29 500
Fax: +31 70 35 03 014
E-mail: info@houthoff.com
Website: www.houthoff.com

Languages
English, French, German, Italian, Portuguese, Spanish

Other offices
Amsterdam, Brussels, London, Rotterdam

Number of lawyers 323
at this office 60

CATEGORIES OF WORK

Administrative and government regulations	**Liability**
Competition and EU law	**Litigation and arbitration**
Construction and real estate	**Property transactions**
Employment and pensions	**Supreme Court litigation**
Environment	

THE FIRM

Houthoff Buruma is one of the largest independent full service law firms in the Netherlands. Over 300 specialists provide tailor-made legal and tax services to businesses and organisations that strive for excellence. Houthoff Buruma provides legal and tax assistance to both domestic and international clients.

The firm is organised into practice groups in the traditional sense, but also has specialist industry groupings that combine professional industry experts from different legal disciplines.

In addition to its offices in Amsterdam, Rotterdam and The Hague, Houthoff Buruma also has offices in Brussels and London. The Brussels office provides legal services mainly on competition law and EU law. The London office provides Dutch legal services, primarily with respect to corporate law, banking and finance. A key objective of the London office is to co-ordinate projects and contacts for the firm's offices in the Netherlands, as well as to handle the firm's current international contacts in the legal, financial and commercial markets.

AREAS OF PRACTICE

Houthoff Buruma assists its clients in every area of law. The firm is a leading adviser in mergers and acquisitions, IPOs and financing. Complex transactions and projects are the day to day business of the firm. Other areas in which the firm has an excellent reputation are, among others, construction and real estate, employment and pensions, energy, insolvency and restructuring, insurance and reinsurance, litigation, project finance, and telecoms.

CMS DERKS STAR BUSMANN

2 PYTHAGORASLAAN
PO BOX 85250
3508 AG UTRECHT

Telephone: +31 30 21 21 111
Fax: +31 30 21 21 333
E-mail: general@cmsderks.nl
Website: www.cmsderks.nl

Languages
English, French, German, Spanish

Other offices
Amsterdam, Arnhem, Brussels, Hilversum

Number of lawyers 235
at this office 128

Contact
Marek Guensberg

Member
CMS Transnational Legal Services;
World Law Group

CATEGORIES OF WORK

Corporate law
Dolf Segaar, Jan Willem Schenk

Corporate finance
Dennis Lange, Cees de Tombe

Mergers and acquisitions
Paulus van den Bos

Banking and finance
Reinoud Imhof, Marcel Groenewegen

Property, real estate and construction
Bob Bekker

Planning and zoning/environment
Frans Otten

EU and competition
Robert Bosman

Biotechnology/pharmaceuticals
Carla Schoonderbeek

Franchising
Patricia Hamelberg

Intellectual property, information technology and telecommunications
Willem Hoorneman, Hendrik Struik

Labour law
Jos Pothof

Tax law
Tom Feringa, Dennis Lange

Health law
Janneke van Craaikamp

Pharmaceuticals and life science law
Carla Schoonderbeek

THE FIRM

CMS Derks Star Busmann (CMS DSB) is one of the top ten firms of lawyers, civil law notaries and tax consultants in the Netherlands. It is the result of a number of mergers. These mergers welded together leading firms in Utrecht and Arnhem and combined these with equally high-quality firms in Amsterdam, Hilversum and Brussels .

With more than 550 staff, CMS DSB is among the largest providers of legal services in the Benelux. There are currently some 250 jurists (lawyers, civil law notaries and tax consultants) working in multi-disciplinary teams at all of the firm's offices.

CMS DSB offers legal services in the broadest sense of the word, and represents a diverse client portfolio in various legal fields and industry sectors. Its clientele comprises of national and multinational enterprises and organisations in the public and private sectors. CMS DSB is organised by means of specialised legal departments and industry sector groups, specialising not only in their respective fields of law, but also concentrating on the special requirements in various branches of industry.

Other CMS law firms: CMS Bureau Francis Lefebvre (France); CMS Cameron McKenna (UK); CMS von Erlach Klainguti Stettler Wille (Switzerland); CMS Hasche Sigle (Germany); CMS Lexcelis (Belgium); CMS Strommer Reich-Rohrwig Karasek Hainz (Austria); CMS Adonnino Ascoli & Cavasola Scamoni (Italy).

AREAS OF PRACTICE

The firm offers specialist advice and assistance in banking; biotechnology and pharmaceuticals; company law; corporate finance; corporate law; EU and competition; franchising; health law; IP, IT and telecommunications; insolvency; labour law; mergers and acquisitions; planning and zoning/environment; property, real estate and construction; private equity; venture capital; and tax law.

VAN BENTHEM & KEULEN

EUCLIDESLAAN 51
POSTBUS 85005
3508 AA UTRECHT

Telephone: +31 30 259 5959
Fax: +31 30 259 5500
E-mail: directie@vbk.nl
Website: www.vbk.nl

Languages
English, French, German, Italian, Russian, Spanish

Number of lawyers 52

CATEGORIES OF WORK

Corporate and commercial law
Tom Bax, Pim Schermer

Insolvency
Cees de Jong, Rinke Dulack

Labour
Arno van Beurden

Real estate, administrative
Marlies Muus-de Goede, Wim Vink

Intellectual property, media
Arjan Schuman

Health
John Kopp, Berend Keulen

Insurance
Berend Keulen

Contract law
Pim Schermer

Family
Anke Mulder

Environmental
Marlies Muus-de Goede

Venture capital
Tom Bax

Arbitration, alternative dispute resolution (ADR)
Martin Brink, John Kopp

Civil litigation and transport
Marcel Ruygvoorn

Corporate litigation, corporate governance
Martin Brink

THE FIRM

Van Benthem & Keulen is comprised of 50 lawyers in its (sole) office in Utrecht, the Netherlands. Utrecht is the fourth largest city in the Netherlands, situated in the centre of the country at a 30 minute drive from Amsterdam.

The firm was established in 1939. The firm has not merged with other law firms but grew steadily during the first decades and more rapidly during the 70s, 80s and early 90s to its present size.

The firm's clients are characterised by their diversity: publicly and privately held corporations, venture capital firms, municipalities and healthcare institutions form the backbone of the firm's client base.

One of the firm's top priorities is the recruitment of a qualified and diverse team of attorneys. This objective is ensured by maintaining close contacts with the leading Dutch law schools. Young lawyers are stimulated to specialise in areas of law which are important to the firm, and to publish articles in the leading law journals in the Netherlands. In addition, great attention is paid to improve the fluency of the attorneys in English, German, French, Italian and Russian.

AREAS OF PRACTICE

Van Benthem & Keulen has developed expertise in both the legal advice practice and litigation. The following is representative of the types of cases handled by the firm.

Corporate law: domestic and international mergers and acquisitions, joint ventures, venture capital transactions and reorganisations.

Commercial law: agency, distribution, licensing, computer contracts;

Insolvency law: reorganisations, suspension of payment and bankruptcy.

Health law: mergers and joint ventures between healthcare institutions, disputes between healthcare institutions and medical specialists, personal injury matters.

Competition law: public procurement law, merger control, trade restraints.

Intellectual property law: copyright, trade mark, entertainment and media.

Real estate law: environmental law, zoning and other governmental licensing, construction contracts, turnkey projects.

Labour law: collective labour agreements, collective dismissals, severance payments, workers council.

Family law: domestic and international divorces, estate planning, adoption, inheritance law, marital property law.

Arbitration and alternative dispute resolution: internal disputes within healthcare institution, contractual and corporate conflicts, family law matters.

Transport law: contracts of afreightment, warehousing, distribution and representation.

Litigation: litigation in all fields of law represented above.

NORWAY

Population	4.5 million
Number of lawyers	3,600
Professional title	Advokat
Currency	Norwegian krone (NOK)

Index

Norway approaches its centenary independence celebrations in 2005 enjoying one of the world's highest living standards. But a recent economic battering and global pressures have accelerated liberalisation of the 'welfare capitalism' which has successfully balanced state ownership and free markets since World War II. Privatisations and PPP initiatives are increasing and the Petroleum Fund, built up in good times as a buffer against oil exhaustion, may be raided to subsidise ailing pensions.

Norway's 'semi-detached' relationship with the EU inevitably remains on the agenda. The cost of Norway remaining in the European Economic Area (EEA), the wider free-trade area which allows trade, labour and capital access to the EU, increases five-fold from 2004. At an administrative level, over 500 EU directives have been adopted into Norwegian law. Euro-scepticism seems to be weakening and a further referendum on Norwegian EU membership by 2010 is predicted. Centenary year is also general election year. A precarious centre-right coalition government under Prime Minister Kjell Magne Bondevik emerged from the last election in 2001. At present, the 165 seats in the *Storting*, Norway's parliament, are divided among eight political parties, with Labour (43) and Conservatives (38) the largest.

BILLING

Billing rates have been under pressure. In private, lawyers admit that clients have been shopping around for quotations. For Oslo partners, the hourly charge ranges from €185 to €305, with some major firms as high as €375; for senior associates €175 to €245, and for junior associates €100 to €220. Rates in other centres are rather less. Insolvency rates are fixed by the Probate Court.

MARKETING

The drop in demand for legal services over the past three years has stimulated marketing efforts. One managing partner commented, 'A generation that's never seen troubled times now has to sell!'

Apart from the widespread shortening of firm names, 2003 also saw an increase in the number of in-house marketing specialists. **Advokatfirmaet Grette DA** and **Simonsen Føyen Advokatfirma DA** pushed the boundaries with imaginative advertising campaigns. Multilingual websites became the norm and direct promotional activities, such as newsletters and breakfast briefing seminars, increased.

Wiersholm, Mellbye & Bech, advokatfirma AS publishes a respected range of law titles and **Advokatfirmaet Steenstrup Stordrange DA** achieves a high level of press coverage with effective public relations work.

IN-HOUSE LAWYERS

Leading banks and major corporations have traditionally employed in-house counsel. However, the acquisition of many Norwegian businesses by foreign companies has brought a preference for the long-term secondment of in-house counsel from law firms. The movement of lawyers between industry and government and the profession continues. Many litigators start their careers as assistant judges and a high proportion of Supreme Court advocates are approved while government lawyers.

ECONOMIC CLIMATE

Norway, a tiny country in terms of population, is an energy giant. It is the fourth-largest oil producer in the world, as well as generating 99% of its own electricity needs. The North Sea is now a 'mature province' with perhaps another 40 years of production. Oil output should peak this decade with natural gas production taking over the lead. Smaller companies are moving in to 'licence trade' with the big players, which has given a fillip to energy law departments. 'Frontier areas' still exist further north, but the discovery rates are lower and exploiting such fields is more expensive, more technically demanding and environmentally challenging.

Merchant shipping still plays a significant part in the Norwegian economy. However, maritime law practices have declined as technology and containerisation have reduced the number of mishaps. But the sea is still a fruitful source of work. Fish farming is now Norway's second largest export and recent problems in the industry have kept refinancing experts busy.

As noted above, many core Norwegian businesses are now in foreign ownership. Equity markets have been very quiet although there were some listings in 2003. M&A activity also picked up. Regulatory and corporate governance matters replaced some of the transaction work lost to commercial departments.

Employment lawyers have been busy with downsizing problems and seem likely to find pensions issues next on the agenda. Privatisation

The largest firms

1	Advokatfirmaet Schjødt AS	142
2	Thommessen Krefting Greve Lund	141
3	Wikborg Rein	139
4	Wiersholm, Mellbye & Bech, advokatfirma AS	115
5	Bugge, Arentz-Hansen & Rasmussen	105
	Simonsen Føyen Advokatfirma DA	105
7	Advokatfirmaet PricewaterhouseCoopers DA	90
8	Ernst & Young Tax AS	87
9	Advokatfirma Selmer DA	83
10	Advokatfirmaet Haavind Vislie AS	82
11	Deloitte Advokatfirma DA	80
12	Advokatfirmaet Steenstrup Stordrange DA	77
13	DLA Nordic	74
14	Arntzen de Besche Advokatfirma AS	70
	Vogt & Wiig AS	70
16	Kluge Advokatfirma DA	64
17	Advokatfirmaet Hjort	51
18	KPMG Law Advokatfirma DA	50
19	Advokatfirmaet Grette DA	42
20	Brækhus Dege Advokatfirma ANS	32
21	Advokatfirma Ræder	29
22	Kvale & Co	27
23	Bull & Co ANS	26
24	Gram, Hambro & Garman	15
	Torkildsen, Tennøe & Co	15

These figures represent the total number of lawyers in this country only, and have been supplied by the firms themselves. The figures should be accurate as at 1 January 2004.

and PPP are also growth areas as the Norwegian state disengages from the economy.

LEGAL MARKET

A decline in quality legal instructions has created an oversupply of good lawyers. As elsewhere, the mid-tier firms are under pressure while larger firms and niche players weather the storm. The ongoing use of the lock-step model of profit sharing may prove a catalyst for change. While more traditional firms remain loyal to lock-step, many younger lawyers want profit share linked to performance and are willing to move firm to find it. No one was talking of mergers at the end of 2003 but some talented lawyers have transferred their loyalties.

The Norwegian legal market remains remarkably independent in global terms, although the majority of first- and second-tier firms have international connections. **Bugge, Arentz-Hansen & Rasmussen**, **Thommessen Krefting Greve Lund**, **Wiersholm, Mellbye & Bech, advokatfirma AS** and **Wikborg Rein** - which all grew rapidly in the '80s and '90s - are generally regarded as top tier. **Thommessen Krefting Greve Lund**, widely praised for its expertise, efficiency and excellent teams in all significant practice areas. **Wikborg Rein**, with a network of overseas offices in major maritime/finance centres and **Wiersholm, Mellbye & Bech, advokatfirma AS**, acknowledged by peers as 'advancing fairly aggressively', both offer strength across the board.

Simonsen Føyen Advokatfirma DA, enlarged by the absorption of the majority of PwC's commercial partners, and **Advokatfirmaet Schjødt AS**, sensibly restructured after what it acknowledges was an over-expansion, are of a similar size to the top tier and offer strong teams. Pan-Scandinavian *Lindh Stabell Horten* has joined the *DLA Group* and rebranded in March 2004 as **DLA Nordic**, thereby gaining access to wider European and Asian markets. **Advokatfirmaet Steenstrup Stordrange DA** added a Stavanger office to a comprehensive domestic network during 2003. **Advokatfirmaet Haavind Vislie AS** and **Arntzen de Besche Advokatfirma AS** are respected middle-market firms fielding excellent teams.

Advokatfirmaet Grette DA and **Advokatfirma Selmer DA** favour modern branding, while **Brækhus Dege Advokatfirma ANS** and **Vogt & Wiig AS** prefer a more traditional image. **Advokatfirmaet Hjort** boasts a high partner ratio of Supreme Court advocates; **Kvale & Co** is also a strong litigation practice. **Advokatfirma Ræder** is a solid commercial firm. **Deloitte Advokatfirma DA Ernst & Young Tax AS**, **KPMG Law Advokatfirma DA** and **Advokatfirmaet PricewaterhouseCoopers DA** all offer high levels of tax expertise backed by international networks.

Smaller players recommended include **Harboe, Eidem & Co AS**, **Aabø-Evensen & Co Advokatfirma**, **Rime & Co Advokatfirma DA**, **Ro Sommernes Advokatfirma DA**, **Rognlien & Djønne** and **Torkildsen, Tennøe & Co**.

BANKING AND FINANCE (INCLUDING SHIPPING FINANCE)

Bugge, Arentz-Hansen & Rasmussen's esteemed debt-capital practice is headed by Finn Myrhe and Terje Sommer. Rolf Johan Ringdal led for Statkraft on its recent $525m syndicated loan. **Bugge, Arentz-Hansen & Rasmussen** is also noted for ship finance expertise.

Advokatfirmaet Schjødt AS's banking group may have lost Jo Stokke to Nordea Bank last year, but with Einar Irgens in Oslo and Jarl Dybvik in Ålesund, the team remains among the leaders. Wilhelm Damm is rated for syndicated loans. Anne Gro Sundby, formerly of Arthur Andersen as well as her own practice, is known for loan and debt expertise, including maritime finance. **Advokatfirmaet Schjødt AS** advised on the NKr2.9bn (€337m) refinancing of Pan Fish during 2003.

Thommessen Krefting Greve Lund acted for both Nordea Bank and Den Norske Bank in the Pan Fish refinancing. Even Bratsberg and Hans Haugstad are particularly highly regarded. Infrastructure and project finance, including PPP, are handled by the finance and banking group.

Leif J Moltke-Hansen took over as head of **Wiersholm, Mellbye & Bech, advokatfirma AS'** banking and finance group from the highly regarded Erik Ramm during 2003. The top-ranked team, which regularly handles complex multi-track deals, includes Torkel Ernø and Erling Lind, as well as recent recruit Knut Bergo from **Wikborg Rein**. Recent clients include Gjensidige Nor and Fokus Bank.

Wikborg Rein's banking group was weakened by the defection of Knut Bergo to **Wiersholm, Mellbye & Bech, advokatfirma AS** and the transfer of Finn Bjørnstad to head the Singapore office. Nonetheless, the firm continues to act for blue-chip banks including Nordea Bank and DnB. During 2003 the team advised on a PPP-linked NKr1.4bn (€163m) loan facility and secured a €242m post-delivery ship financing for Color Group. Bernhard Haukali is recommended; rivals also rate Johan Rasmussen very highly.

Sven Iver Steen and Cecilie Ask of **Arntzen de Besche Advokatfirma AS** dealt with the conversion of mutual insurer KLP to a public company during 2003. The firm is retained as legal advisor by the Norwegian subsidiaries of several international blue-chip financial institutions. The vastly experienced Pål Sveinsson heads the well-connected group.

DLA Nordic advised on the listings of three savings banks on the Oslo Børs during 2003. In addition, it handled large recovery actions for, *inter*

BANKING AND FINANCE (INCLUDING SHIPPING FINANCE)

BUGGE, ARENTZ-HANSEN & RASMUSSEN
SCHJØDT AS, ADVOKATFIRMAET ✪
THOMMESSEN KREFTING GREVE LUND ✪
WIERSHOLM, MELLBYE & BECH, ADVOKATFIRMA AS ✪
WIKBORG REIN ✪

Arntzen de Besche Advokatfirma AS ✪
DLA Nordic ✪
Haavind Vislie AS, Advokatfirmaet ✪
Hjort, Advokatfirmaet ✪
Selmer DA, Advokatfirma ✪
Simonsen Føyen Advokatfirma DA ✪
Steenstrup Stordrange DA, Advokatfirmaet ✪

Brækhus Dege Advokatfirma ANS ✪
Kluge Advokatfirma DA ✪
Vogt & Wiig AS ✪

Firms are listed A-Z in tiers which are ranked in order of priority
✪ *Indicates firm displays contact details at the end of this chapter.*

alia, Handelsbanken AB, and high-value finance arrangements in all major sectors including shipping.

Advokatfirmaet Haavind Vislie AS' banking group has developed since the 2000 merger. With a solid core of bank clients, including Fortis and SEB, and excellent board-level contacts, the firm has attracted its share of the finance credit collapse work. Peter Brechan is noted for banking expertise and Halfdan Lowzow for complex aircraft finance.

Advokatfirmaet Hjort's Kristin Veierød advises Norfund and also negotiates numerous loan agreements with developing countries. Erik Keiserud, chair of the board of the Government Bank Investment Fund, has been at the cutting edge of change in Norwegian banking and finance.

Advokatfirma Selmer DA acts for Fokus Bank and Sparebanken Rogaland. Its banking team has wide international and domestic experience – Knut Endre, Lars Weyer-Larsen and Einar Grette are leading practitioners.

Simonsen Føyen Advokatfirma DA's considerable strengths in finance lie in shipping work and client debt renegotiation. Lead partner is the experienced Jørgen Stang Heffermehl.

Advokatfirmaet Steenstrup Stordrange DA's banking department is led by Ian Kenworthy, currently a member of the committee of the Oslo Børs. The team was involved in several of 2003's major deals including the complex Avantor bond issue. Odd Moe is expert in the savings bank sector.

Brækhus Dege Advokatfirma ANS reports an expanding practice. Expert partners Christen Mellbye Gjesdahl, acts for Fokus Bank, and Christian Solemslie handles copious amounts of work for SEB Finance.

Kluge Advokatfirma DA's Ola Bøe and Sverre Holm have wide experience of commercial finance in the shipping and airline sectors. Bank clients include Nordea Bank and Elcon Finans.

Vogt & Wiig AS' ship finance group has developed with the strong maritime law practice. Christine Rødsæther and Knut Erik Westad in Oslo are highly rated, as is Børge Knustad in Bergen. Key clients included Nordea Bank, Finansbanken and Fearnleys.

CORPORATE AND COMMERCIAL

Bugge, Arentz-Hansen & Rasmussen's M&A practice spans several sector groups. Equity markets leader Knut Brundtland led on Den norske Bank's $5.5bn merger with Gjensige Nor. Rolf Johan Ringdal advised Statoil on its $800m sale of Navion. Trond Sanfelt is also recommended.

Advokatfirmaet Schjødt AS' corporate team offers strength in all sectors. The firm has developed a strong presence in the private equity market, acting for Four Seasons Venture IV and partners in the NKr750m (€87m) acquisition of SND Invest. Erling Christiansen and Einar Caspersen are well known. Senior associate Jakob Villum is 'very technical, very clever'.

Thommessen Krefting Greve Lund is best known for capital markets transactions. A well-balanced group of 28 lawyers includes Kim Dobrowen, Hans Cappelen Arnesen, and Carl Erik Krefting. During 2003 the team acted for Gjensidige Nor both in connection with the IPO and on the merger with Den norske Bank.

The formidable group at **Wiersholm, Mellbye & Bech, advokatfirma AS** now comprises 18 lawyers. The team, under star dealmaker Erik Thyness, was joined by Knut Bergo and Jarle Kvam from **Wikborg Rein** during 2003. Andreas Mellbye advised the Ministry of Trade and Industry on the NKr7bn (€813m) divestment of part of Telenor, and Henrik Christensen handled the NKr450m (€52.3m) purchase of 50% of Capona by Choice Hotels Scandinavia and Home Invest.

Wikborg Rein's corporate department, headed by John Rein, handled some of 2003's major demergers and disposals including those of Tandberg Data and Bergesen. Arne Didrik Kjørnæs recently advised some major players on corporate governance. Haakon Blaauw, at the Bergen office, is recommended. Erik Rikheim, however, has now left the firm to take up a government role.

Several strong commercial lawyers provide breadth and depth at **Arntzen de Besche Advokatfirma AS**. Kåre I Moljord, who brings very practical tax expertise to deals, and Fred Gade, are highly rated commercial counsel. The firm advised Sucra on the purchase of the remaining 34% in Arcus-Gruppen during 2003, and was involved in the reorganisation and planned sale of the operating units of NOAH Holdings.

Business-focused **DLA Nordic** has begun to press the top-tier firms. A wide competence across the corporate field is strengthening with international referrals from the *DLA Group*. During 2003 the firm handled the Ensign-Bickford merger with Dyno Nobel and entered the expanding Russian sector when Norsk Hydro reached an agreement with RuAl, the aluminium producer.

Advokatfirmaet Haavind Vislie AS's widely respected corporate group acts for a blue-chip clientele and offers strength across the field. Tor Wilhelm Seim advised on the sale of Technoguide's software business to Schlumberger. The firm has also taken additional market share in the growing health sector. Harald Arnkværn and Johan Fredrik Remmen are recommended.

Advokatfirmaet Hjort's strong corporate team has sole or preferred counsel agreements with several leading companies including Borealis International and Alliance Unichem, the latter of which Terje Aakvaag recently assisted in a series of pharmacy acquisitions. Jørn Uggerud was adviser to Samlerhuset, which, with a Finnish partner, acquired the Royal Norwegian Mint.

Kluge Advokatfirma DA offers an integrated service through its three offices and is a well respected and popular choice for M&A, disposals and other transactional work. Recent blue-chip clients include Scana Industrier and Veidekke. Geir Even Asplin is recommended.

Advokatfirma Selmer DA offers a top-grade corporate group and a client-centred approach. Top-ranking partners include Thomas Michelet, Christian Selmer and Roy Slettvold. The firm is noted for its international work but also reports growth in domestic markets.

CORPORATE AND COMMERCIAL

BUGGE, ARENTZ-HANSEN & RASMUSSEN
SCHJØDT AS, ADVOKATFIRMAET ✪
THOMMESSEN KREFTING GREVE LUND ✪
WIERSHOLM, MELLBYE & BECH, ADVOKATFIRMA AS ✪
WIKBORG REIN ✪

Arntzen de Besche Advokatfirma AS ✪
DLA Nordic ✪
Haavind Vislie AS, Advokatfirmaet ✪
Hjort, Advokatfirmaet ✪
Kluge Advokatfirma DA ✪
Selmer DA, Advokatfirma ✪
Simonsen Føyen Advokatfirma DA ✪
Steenstrup Stordrange DA, Advokatfirmaet ✪
Vogt & Wiig AS ✪

Aabø-Evensen & Co Advokatfirma ✪
Brækhus Dege Advokatfirma ANS ✪
Bull & Co ANS ✪
Kvale & Co ✪
Ræder, Advokatfirma ✪
Rime & Co Advokatfirma DA ✪

Firms are listed A-Z in tiers which are ranked in order of priority
✪ *Indicates firm displays contact details at the end of this chapter.*

With offices in three major centres outside Oslo and sector-focused practice groups, **Simonsen Føyen Advokatfirma DA** tailors services to client needs. Claus R Flinder and Tor Birkeland handle a wide range of complex work and are recommended for corporate matters from due diligence to M&A.

Advokatfirmaet Steenstrup Stordrange DA continues to attract promising young lawyers from more traditional rivals. Robert Sveen heads the respected 17- partner group of 32 fee-earners, which offers expertise across the corporate law spectrum.

Vogt & Wiig AS offers a strong, reliable corporate team with a wide practice which includes clients such as AstraZeneca and Lufttransport. Tor Fredrik Kielland is recommended for M&A work.

M&A boutique **Aabø-Evensen & Co Advokatfirma** opened in 2002 when ex-**KPMG Law Advokatfirma DA** head of corporate services Ole Aabø-Evensen and two colleagues joined forces with former **Wiersholm, Mellbye & Bech, advokatfirma AS** associate Nils Olav Årseth. The hi-tech, entrepreneurial firm offers keen competition to M&A teams in larger corporate departments. Clients include Förenings-Sparbanken and Lindegaard.

Brækhus Dege Advokatfirma ANS provides commercial expertise with a bias towards its traditional real estate, construction and IT strengths.

Bjørn Blix heads the corporate group at **Bull & Co ANS**. The firm has a loyal following of blue-chip clients including Otis, Nord Stål and Eltel.

Kvale & Co offers a solid general practice commercial group which handles some interesting SME assignments.

John Sveinsvold, a leading authority on company law, became a partner in **Advokatfirma Ræder** during 2003. The firm's team, which includes Carl Garmann Clausen, is known for high standards and is strongly recommended for quality SME work.

Rime & Co Advokatfirma DA, the insolvency specialist, offers solid general commercial support to SMEs, particularly those involved in housing, building and construction.

DISPUTE RESOLUTION

Bugge, Arentz-Hansen & Rasmussen notes increasing demand for heavy litigation and has geared up accordingly. Øyvind Eriksen led for Aker Maritime in the $140m dispute over the company's sale of its deepwater business. Other recommended litigators include Helge Olav Bugge and Jan-Fredrik Rafen.

Advokatfirmaet Haavind Vislie AS' litigation and arbitration practice constitutes a high proportion of its work. With 16 Supreme Court advocates the firm can effectively handle the most difficult cases. Helge Jakob Kolrud and Ola Brekken are both first-rate, experienced advocates with specialisations in complex contractual matters and real estate respectively.

The finest concentrations of litigators in Oslo can probably be found at **Advokatfirmaet Hjort**. Erik Keiserud, who, with Harald Hjort, represented tobacco giant Tiedemanns in long-running law suits is a top all-rounder with a blue-chip client list. Else Bugge Fougner is lead counsel for auditor KPMG in connection with claims arising from the Finance Credit collapse. Frode Innjord is one of Norway's leading all-round lawyers. The firm's acknowledged expertise in matters of professional negligence extends to appointment by top-tier rivals. It is also handling an increasing number of international cases involving economic crime.

Advokatfirmaet Schjødt AS' litigators frequently appear in the Supreme Court and both Cato Schiøtz and Vidar Strømme, who recently represented ExxonMobil in what was reputed to be the largest by value litigation Norway has ever seen, are acknowledged heavyweights.

Advokatfirmaet Steenstrup Stordrange DA handles a high volume of litigation and with four elite Supreme Court advocates takes cases at the highest level. Morten Steenstrup is acknowledged to be a fine advocate by rivals, while Bjørn Stordrange is regarded as a very effective commercial litigator.

Thommessen Krefting Greve Lund's litigation team is now led by Pål Lorentzen. The firm offers top-grade advice and is firmly established in the first rank.

Wiersholm, Mellbye & Bech, advokatfirma AS is well known for the high quality of its litigation work. Anders Ryssdal is noted for competition and international arbitration matters, Magnus Hellesylt for arbitration. Jon Tenden is a skilled general advocate.

Wikborg Rein fields a strong team of Supreme Court litigators which had a successful 2003. Per Ristvedt won a difficult Sale of Property Act case in the Supreme Court. Jonas Myhre successfully argued a complex pharmaceutical trade mark issue before the EFTA Court on behalf of Paranova AS.

Arntzen de Besche Advokatfirma AS has a strong litigation team. Terje Granvang and Pål Sveinsson are recommended.

Brækhus Dege Advokatfirma ANS is a busy litigation practice and is commended for providing younger lawyers with opportunities to experience advocacy. Christen Gjesdahl, is a skilled arbitrator as well as a recommended litigator.

DLA Nordic fields some extremely able litigators and is recommended for insurance and construction disputes, particularly where cases have an international element. Bård Racin Meltvedt is a member of the International Council for Arbitration in Sport (ICAS).

Advokatfirmaet Grette DA's litigators are best known for IP work and since 1990 have pleaded nearly a third of the IP cases reaching the Supreme Court. However, the firm also takes general commercial cases which, in 2003, included handling fishing concessions for Domstein.

DISPUTE RESOLUTION

BUGGE, ARENTZ-HANSEN & RASMUSSEN
HAAVIND VISLIE AS, ADVOKATFIRMAET ✪
HJORT, ADVOKATFIRMAET ✪
SCHJØDT AS, ADVOKATFIRMAET ✪
STEENSTRUP STORDRANGE DA, ADVOKATFIRMAET ✪
THOMMESSEN KREFTING GREVE LUND ✪
WIERSHOLM, MELLBYE & BECH, ADVOKATFIRMA AS ✪
WIKBORG REIN ✪

Arntzen de Besche Advokatfirma AS ✪
Brækhus Dege Advokatfirma ANS ✪
DLA Nordic ✪
Grette DA, Advokatfirmaet ✪
Vogt & Wiig AS ✪

Bull & Co ANS ✪
Kluge Advokatfirma DA ✪
Selmer DA, Advokatfirma ✪
Simonsen Føyen Advokatfirma DA ✪

Firms are listed A-Z in tiers which are ranked in order of priority
✪ *Indicates firm displays contact details at the end of this chapter.*

Vogt & Wiig AS boasts some excellent litigators, including Frithjof Herlofsen, who is also qualified as a solicitor in England, Anders Færden and Morten Lund. The firm's core expertise lies in shipping-related law and Morten Lund frequently acts as arbitrator in high-profile maritime cases. The team is also recommended for injunction, catastrophic accident and personal injury work.

At **Bull & Co ANS** the arrival of Gøsta Thommesen from **Simonsen Føyen Advokatfirma DA** created the basis for a niche team specialising in alternative dispute resolution.

Kluge Advokatfirma DA has an excellent litigation practice whose advocates have argued 30 cases in the Supreme Court in the last five years.

Advokatfirma Selmer DA fields some strong litigators including Jon Vinje and Asbjørn Berg but frequently counsels negotiation and conciliation in dispute resolution.

Simonsen Føyen Advokatfirma DA's strength in offshore construction work carries through to litigation. Christian Steen Eriksen and Per Kyllingstad are both highly regarded.

EU AND COMPETITION

Bugge, Arentz-Hansen & Rasmussen's acclaimed Helge Stemshaug, formerly director of legal affairs at the Norwegian Competition Authority, and Beret Sundet head the EU/competition group, which is noted for cartel work.

Advokatfirmaet Schjødt AS' Trygve Olavson Laake and Jan Magne Langseth, who both worked for EFTA in Brussels before joining the firm, and

Ingvald Falch are the bright young lawyers who have grown **Advokatfirmaet Schjødt AS**' market share of EU and public procurement work. The firm's blue-chip clientele includes Coca-Cola and Amerada Hess.

Thommessen Krefting Greve Lund is acknowledged by many as the strongest domestic practice. Siri Teigum heads the excellent team. Eivind Vesterkjær is recommended for competition issues.

Wiersholm, Mellbye & Bech, advokatfirma AS' Anders Ryssdal, one of Norway's leading EU and competition lawyers, is highly respected. The top-rated team attracted more high-level government instructions during 2003, while also advising commercial clients such as Treade. However, the recommended Henrik Svane has now moved to **Kvale & Co**.

Wikborg Rein handles a wide portfolio of competition and EU work. During 2003 the firm defended Fjord Line against Color Line's hostile bid. Morten Goller, noted for expertise in public procurement, leads the group and Dag Mjaaland is also recommended. Jonas Myrhe, formerly at **Advokatfirmaet Hjort**'s Brussels office, has made a big contribution to the team.

DLA Nordic moves up the rankings for competition work. The team is particularly strong on industrial and service sector cartel and pricing issues, including those with a cross-border element, and also handles a good deal of distribution agreement work. Recent clients include Ceralia and Statoil Detalj. The EU and competition group is led by Jan Fjellestad.

Advokatfirmaet Haavind Vislie AS moves up a tier. The firm has seen growth in the EU/competition field with Ian Anders Tobiassen, the head of group, who recently appeared in several EU and EFTA cases, a leader in the field. Tor Wilhem Seim has attracted a following in public procurement work.

Advokatfirmaet Hjort's EU and competition practice is rebuilding after the personnel losses of recent years. Frode Elgeshem, with wide experience including several appearances before the European Court of Human Rights and the EFTA Court, has an excellent reputation.

Henrik Svane, noted for cartel expertise, joined **Kvale & Co** from **Wiersholm, Mellbye & Bech, advokatfirma AS** in January 2003, adding weight to the firm's EU and competition team. **Kvale & Co** advised Norsk Medisinaldepot during a major pharmaceutical pricing investigation by the Norwegian Competition Authorities (Konkurransetilsynet).

Advokatfirma Selmer DA's Harald Evensen is acknowledged as top tier by rivals and leads a strong team which effectively handles distribution agreements in a wide range of industries, competition issues in M&A negotiations, and price-fixing accusations.

Simonsen Føyen Advokatfirma DA deals with EU and competition work within its corporate group. Geir Sand is admired, as is Mona Søyland, who recently acted for Synnøve Finden in a complex series of cases.

Advokatfirmaet Steenstrup Stordrange DA handles numerous EU, EFTA and Norwegian Competition Authority cases. The firm has a broad-based practice with particular competence in acquaculture and telecoms.

Stein Ove Solberg at **Arntzen de Besche Advokatfirma AS** is recommended, particularly for cases involving environmental regulation. The firm has a solid practice with, perhaps, more strength in domestic than international matters.

Brækhus Dege Advokatfirma ANS' EU/competition presence is strengthening. Didier Rigault is recommended for international contractual matters while Christian Bendiksen is showing early promise.

Bull & Co ANS is recommended for competition work including price-fixing. The firm acted for Norges Taxi in the Oslo Airport taxi-market deregulation case.

Vogt & Wiig AS brings maritime expertise to EU and competition issues.

EU AND COMPETITION

BUGGE, ARENTZ-HANSEN & RASMUSSEN
SCHJØDT AS, ADVOKATFIRMAET ✪
THOMMESSEN KREFTING GREVE LUND ✪
WIERSHOLM, MELLBYE & BECH, ADVOKATFIRMA AS ✪
WIKBORG REIN ✪

DLA Nordic ✪
Haavind Vislie AS, Advokatfirmaet ✪
Hjort, Advokatfirmaet ✪
Kvale & Co ✪
Selmer DA, Advokatfirma ✪
Simonsen Føyen Advokatfirma DA ✪
Steenstrup Stordrange DA, Advokatfirmaet ✪

Arntzen de Besche Advokatfirma AS ✪
Brækhus Dege Advokatfirma ANS ✪
Bull & Co ANS ✪
Vogt & Wiig AS ✪

Firms are listed A-Z in tiers which are ranked in order of priority
✪ Indicates firm displays contact details at the end of this chapter

ELECTRICITY, NUCLEAR, RENEWABLES

Arntzen de Besche Advokatfirma AS deals with electricity distribution and production concerns within its outstanding energy practice.

Rune Svoren led **Bugge, Arentz-Hansen & Rasmussen**'s strategic move into the electricity sector and the firm has successfully attracted market share.

DLA Nordic has wide experience with the electricity industry including regulatory, licensing and distribution issues. Clients include Norsk Hydro and Mjøskraft AS.

ELECTRICITY, NUCLEAR AND RENEWABLES

Arntzen de Besche Advokatfirma AS ✪
Bugge, Arentz-Hansen & Rasmussen
DLA Nordic ✪
Haavind Vislie AS, Advokatfirmaet ✪
Hjort, Advokatfirmaet ✪
Simonsen Føyen Advokatfirma DA ✪
Thommessen Krefting Greve Lund ✪
Wiersholm, Mellbye & Bech, advokatfirma AS ✪
Wikborg Rein ✪

Firms are listed alphabetically
✪ Indicates firm displays contact details at the end of this chapter.

Advokatfirmaet Haavind Vislie AS' long experience in the sector has generated a blue-chip client following including Statkraft and Hydro Energi. Kristin Bjella is recommended for commercial matters and Johan Fredrik Remmen for disputes.

Advokatfirmaet Hjort has a strong presence in the electricity market, principally through representation of the municipalities which receive royalties for power plants located within their jurisdictions. This sector has recently produced a good deal of reorganisation work. Caroline Lund and Stein Erik Stinessen, joint leaders of the firm's energy group, receive peer recommendation.

Simonsen Føyen Advokatfirma DA's energy expertise extends to electricity with Peter Simonsen a leading authority in the sector.

Thommessen Krefting Greve Lund advises the Norwegian Electricity Industry Association and has developed an impressive legal competence based on in-depth experience of electricity generation, transmission, distribution and retailing. Gunnar Martinsen, now heading the energy group, has established his place at the top of the league.

Wiersholm, Mellbye & Bech, advokatfirma AS' electricity practice is most active where acquisition, divestment or investment is planned. The firm dealt with the sales of Hadeland Energi and Statnett SF during 2003.

Wikborg Rein represented TXU Europe Group in Norway's major power transaction of 2003, the sale of the Svartisen plant off-take rights to a Finnish consortium.

EMPLOYMENT

Arntzen de Besche Advokatfirma AS has an excellent employment practice which achieved a successful result for SAS in litigation following the Braathens takeover. Ingeborg Moen Borgerud and Lars Holo are also highly rated.

Brækhus Dege Advokatfirma ANS' Jan Dege, a prolific and esteemed author, is recommended. The firm's reputation in labour law litigation is second to none.

Advokatfirmaet Haavind Vislie AS' employment law department is one of the largest in Norway and provides a well-balanced team capable of handling everything from major corporate redundancies to international executive compensation. Liv Kjeldsberg brings tax expertise to employment matters. Erik Davidsen is first rate.

Wiersholm, Mellbye & Bech, advokatfirma AS attracted an interesting range of cases during 2003 including work on the Phillips-Conoco merger. Eli Aasheim is recommended.

Bugge, Arentz-Hansen & Rasmussen's employment practice has gained ground since Tarjei Thorkildsen moved from **Advokatfirmaet Schjødt AS** in 2002. The firm is recommended for large-scale, complex problems rather than individual cases. Senior lawyer Peter Hammerich, a pensions expert, is one to watch.

The well-balanced employment team at **DLA Nordic**, led by the energetic and determined Elizabeth Ege, maintains high levels of service through a very commercial approach. It has proved attractive to such clients as Enskilda Securities and Frans Maas Norge.

Else Bugge Fougner and Christian Bonnevie Hjort jointly head **Advokatfirmaet Hjort**'s highly rated labour and employment group. Recent cases have tended to involve corporate reconstruction and redundancy. Clients include Borealis and Norsk Lotteridrift.

Advokatfirmaet Schjødt AS' Trond Stang heads an excellent employment team with expertise in all areas of employment law.

Simonsen Føyen Advokatfirma DA has an experienced group of employment lawyers working within the corporate practice group.

Advokatfirmaet Steenstrup Stordrange DA's top-rated employment practitioners include Thomas Meinich, a very busy litigator who has recently handled some major redundancy programmes. The firm is recommended for its comprehensive approach to both key personnel disputes and expatriation.

Bull & Co ANS offers a solid labour law team which is recommended for SME work across the board.

Advokatfirmaet Grette DA's Johan Hveding, the star of the firm's respected, seven-strong employment group, successfully represented the employer in the record Norwegian 'golden parachute' case during 2003.

Kluge Advokatfirma DA has a reliable employment group, recommended equally to SME employers and aggrieved employees. Marco Lilli handles employment matters and Ingrid Skaanes Sørensen pensions problems.

Arne Seemann Berg at **Kvale & Co** is recommended for downsizing and executive package advice.

Advokatfirma Selmer DA's Pål Kvernaas is recommended. He leads an experienced team, which advises employers and workers on all aspects of collective bargaining and downsizing. Jeppe Normann is regarded as an effective negotiator.

EMPLOYMENT

ARNTZEN DE BESCHE ADVOKATFIRMA AS ✪
BRÆKHUS DEGE ADVOKATFIRMA ANS ✪
HAAVIND VISLIE AS, ADVOKATFIRMAET ✪
WIERSHOLM, MELLBYE & BECH, ADVOKATFIRMA AS ✪

Bugge, Arentz-Hansen & Rasmussen
DLA Nordic ✪
Hjort, Advokatfirmaet ✪
Schjødt AS, Advokatfirmaet ✪
Simonsen Føyen Advokatfirma DA ✪
Steenstrup Stordrange DA, Advokatfirmaet ✪

Bull & Co ANS ✪
Grette DA, Advokatfirmaet ✪
Kluge Advokatfirma DA ✪
Kvale & Co ✪
Selmer DA, Advokatfirma ✪
Storeng, Beck & Due Lund ANS, Advokatfirma
Thommessen Krefting Greve Lund ✪
Vogt & Wiig AS ✪
Wikborg Rein ✪

Firms are listed A-Z in tiers which are ranked in order of priority
✪ Indicates firm displays contact details at the end of this chapter

Advokatfirma Storeng, Beck & Due Lund ANS is recommended for excellent employment work.

Thommessen Krefting Greve Lund's developing employment team is effective, particularly in litigation.

Vogt & Wiig AS' employment practice has consolidated in recent years and is recommended to both employers and employees.

Wikborg Rein's employment team is usually to be found on the employer's side where redundancy is involved and offers effective support in acquisitions. Jan Backer leads.

INSOLVENCY AND CORPORATE RECOVERY

At **Ro Sommernes Advokatfirma DA**, Knut Ro, 'in a league of one', and long acknowledged as a superb litigator, has close relationships with banks and is always found where the numbers are big or the case complex. Ståle Sommernes is also recommended.

Wikborg Rein's Ketil Bøe, probably Oslo's busiest corporate finance practitioner, handled the $2.4bn debt restructuring of Petroleum Geoservices. Highly praised Leif Petter Madsen was appointed receiver of headline insolvency Finance Credit. Marius Gisvold is recommended for complex commercial restructuring.

Arntzen de Besche Advokatfirma AS acted as adviser to Petroleum Geo Services on the reorganisation of $2.5bn of debt following the company's landmark Chapter 11 filing, the first time a Norwegian company has petitioned for bankruptcy protection in the US. Aksel Hillestad is recommended.

INSOLVENCY AND CORPORATE RECOVERY

RO SOMMERNES ADVOKATFIRMA DA
WIKBORG REIN ✪

Arntzen de Besche Advokatfirma AS ✪
Brækhus Dege Advokatfirma ANS ✪
Kvale & Co ✪
Ræder, Advokatfirma ✪
Thommessen Krefting Greve Lund ✪
Wahlstrøm, Meltvedt, Thune
Wikborg Rein ✪

Bugge, Arentz-Hansen & Rasmussen
Bull & Co ANS ✪
DLA Nordic ✪
Grette DA, Advokatfirmaet ✪
Hjort, Advokatfirmaet ✪
Rime & Co Advokatfirma DA ✪
Schjødt AS, Advokatfirmaet ✪
Simonsen Føyen Advokatfirma DA ✪
Steenstrup Stordrange DA, Advokatfirmaet ✪
Wiersholm, Mellbye & Bech, advokatfirma AS ✪

Firms are listed A-Z in tiers which are ranked in order of priority
✪ Indicates firm displays contact details at the end of this chapter.

Brækhus Dege Advokatfirma ANS fields several insolvency heavyweights with an enviable reputation for cross-border and reconstruction work. The firm attracted several of the trustee appointments which emerged from the Finance Credit scandal. Trygve Tønnessen and Bjørn Køhler Thommessen are noted. Marte Voie Danielsen deserved her early partnership.

Kvale & Co is one of the most active players in the insolvency field. Tom Hugo Ottesen is handling the estate of Construction Management Nor, a major property development company and Espen Hamar is the trustee of KPNQwest, a large broadband company.

Advokatfirma Ræder's busy insolvency and reconstruction department expanded to 14 fee-earners during 2003. Erling Opdal and Leif Villars-Dahl are recommended.

Thommessen Krefting Greve Lund's insolvency and reconstruction team was strengthened by the arrival of experienced Jo Rodin from **Advokatfirmaet Schjødt AS** in September 2003.

Wahlstrøm, Meltvedt, Thune, created by a 2002 merger, has a sound reputation for reconstruction and insolvency work.

Bugge, Arentz-Hansen & Rasmussen's insolvency/corporate reconstruction team is drawn from several practice groups and brings considerable expertise to refinancing and rescue operations. Karstein Espelid, praised as a litigator, Geir Mikalsen, and Arne Tjaum are key partners.

The well-known Stein Inge Spurkland heads the **Bull & Co ANS** insolvency group which saw a busy 2003 advising on reconstructions and turnarounds.

DLA Nordic is handling an increasing amount of cross-border insolvency.

Advokatfirmaet Grette DA's recruitment of Jacob Bjønness-Jacobsen from **Arntzen de Besche Advokatfirma AS** considerably strengthened the insolvency and reconstruction team which now numbers ten, including the well-known Torgeir Myrstad. The firm is recommended for complex restructuring work.

Advokatfirmaet Hjort has been involved in significant rescue operations including the recapitalisation of Hurum Fabriker.

At **Rime & Co Advokatfirma DA**, the experienced Finn Rime has been joined by ex-**Advokatfirmaet PricewaterhouseCoopers DA** partner Siv Sandvik and a small team, adding strength to the cross-border capability of this insolvency boutique. With Johan Ratvik, who handled the Baltic Food Holdings insolvency and Morten Hauten specialising in building and construction companies, the firm deservedly takes a substantial share of complex, medium-size, debt and bankruptcy cases.

Advokatfirmaet Schjødt AS offers a solid, experienced, group which reports increasing business.

Simonsen Føyen Advokatfirma DA handles a large number of substantial reconstruction cases. The firm handled the NKr800m (€93m) fleet sale that formed part of the Actinor Shipping Group refinancing.

Advokatfirmaet Steenstrup Stordrange DA's Frode Finnøy advised in the restructuring of Geo Global Services during 2003. Overall, it was a year of growth for the 13-fee-earner department. Ole Martin Andreassen is recommended.

Wiersholm, Mellbye & Bech, advokatfirma AS handles reconstruction work within the banking group and dealt with Fjord Seafood, Norway's largest refinancing deal last year.

INTELLECTUAL PROPERTY

Bull & Co ANS offers broad expertise in commercial IP work with strengths in trade mark protection, anti-piracy and pharmaceutical patents. International clients include Gillette and Braun. Bente Holmvang heads a star team, which also includes Amund Grimstad, Gøsta Thommessen and Hans Skirstad. **Bull & Co ANS** is also one of Norway's top 'sports and showbiz' practices.

DLA Nordic offers an IP team with domestic and international expertise in pharmaceuticals, software, music, television, advertising and sport. Clients include Warner Chappell Music and Saatchi & Saatchi. Bård Racin Meltvedt is recommended.

Advokatfirmaet Grette DA's top-rank IP team attracts such global players as Anheuser-Busch, Novartis Biochemie and AstraZeneca. Gunnar Grette, Ragnar Vik and Svein Ruud Johansen are highly recommended for patent litigation, Astrid Lund for copyright law, and Felix Reimers, for trade mark infringement.

INTELLECTUAL PROPERTY

BULL & CO ANS ✪
DLA NORDIC ✪
GRETTE DA, ADVOKATFIRMAET ✪
SCHJØDT AS, ADVOKATFIRMAET ✪
THOMMESSEN KREFTING GREVE LUND ✪
WIERSHOLM, MELLBYE & BECH, ADVOKATFIRMA AS ✪

Haavind Vislie AS, Advokatfirmaet ✪
Selmer DA, Advokatfirma ✪
Simonsen Føyen Advokatfirma DA ✪
Steenstrup Stordrange DA, Advokatfirmaet ✪
Wikborg Rein ✪

Arntzen de Besche Advokatfirma AS ✪
Bugge, Arentz-Hansen & Rasmussen
Hjort, Advokatfirmaet ✪
Rognlien & Djønne

Firms are listed A-Z in tiers which are ranked in order of priority
✪ Indicates firm displays contact details at the end of this chapter.

Peter G Nitter at **Advokatfirmaet Schjødt AS** is known as both an excellent IP lawyer and fine litigator. He is backed by a team which includes Terje Svendsen whose portfolio includes sports law.

Thommessen Krefting Greve Lund's IP expert Arne Ringnes maintains his high profile in the patent and copyright field. Kristine Schei is recommended for IP litigation.

Wiersholm, Mellbye & Bech, advokatfirma AS' patent lawyers continue to impress and Nils Sejersted is strongly recommended. During 2003 the firm advised numerous clients, including Moorings Holdings on patent infringement. John Gulbrandsen is expert in copyright matters, particularly with regard to media and advertising.

Advokatfirmaet Haavind Vislie AS' Harald Bjelke chairs the Norwegian Anti-piracy Group and frequently litigates in the Supreme Court on IT matters. The firm has a particular strength in IT and software matters. Kjell Torkildsen is an experienced practitioner in media and entertainment.

Advokatfirma Selmer DA advises on IP issues including copyright, trade marks and publishing contracts. The firm is well known for its entertainment work.

Simonsen Føyen Advokatfirma DA is noted for its expert IT team. Much of the IP work attracted tends to be within the TMT field. Mention should be made of Arne Steen whose all-round expertise in the professional sports sector has drawn a star-studded following.

Advokatfirmaet Steenstrup Stordrange DA's Fredny Bade, who specialises in patents, trade marks and designs, heads a group which provides a broad, commercial approach to IT work. Søren Lous heads the media and entertainment group and handled the legal aspects of three feature film productions during 2003.

Gunnar Meyer heads **Wikborg Rein**'s experienced and effective IP team which offers skills across the board.

Jan Morten Evertsen at **Arntzen de Besche Advokatfirma AS** advises a range of clients on international and domestic IT issues including film, television and performing arts.

Bugge, Arentz-Hansen & Rasmussen's Aase Gundersen has handled some complex pharmaceutical patent litigation, with one case reaching the EFTA Court.

Advokatfirmaet Hjort has handled some complex patent and parallel import issues for Telenor. Kristin Veierød heads the IP group. As in most fields, **Advokatfirmaet Hjort** excels at IP litigation.

Eirik Djøenne offers 'the highest quality of copyright expertise' at boutique **Rognlien & Djønne**.

MARITIME AND OFFSHORE CONSTRUCTION (EXCLUDING FINANCE)

Vogt & Wiig AS is one of the two Norwegian firms still heavily involved across the board in maritime work. The firm handles both 'wet' and 'dry' cases and, increasingly, international insurance issues. Morten Lund is a maritime lawyer of the highest rank and integrity. **Vogt & Wiig AS** advised in most of the major shipping cases of 2003 and successfully argued for the insurers in the *MV Leros Strength* case before the Supreme Court.

Wikborg Rein, which added a five-lawyer Shanghai office to its Oslo, London, Singapore, and Købe network, is a respected member of the elite group of firms which now handle international 'wet' maritime work. Øystein Meland, in the Bergen office, is strongly recommended. London-based Morten Lund Mathisen is usually found close to major shipping disasters and currently acts for the owners in the $200m *Tricolor* car transporter wreck.

Bugge, Arentz-Hansen & Rasmussen fields a highly experienced maritime team, which mostly handles 'dry' and insurance work. Jan-Fredrik Rafen and Ole Lund are also recommended.

DLA Nordic is mainly known for 'dry' work and maritime insurance and reinsurance. With a 3:2 Supreme Court decision in favour of client Gjensidige Nor Forsikring on an insurance point and clients including Honda, Suzuki and Shell, the firm has made considerable progress in this market sector over the last year. Runar Hansen and Erik Blaker are recommended.

Simonsen Føyen Advokatfirma DA has a solid 'dry' practice, with Lars Musæus and Sindre Walderhaug both recommended. The firm is probably a little stronger in the offshore

MARITIME AND OFFSHORE (EXCLUDING FINANCE)

VOGT & WIIG AS ✪
WIKBORG REIN ✪

Bugge, Arentz-Hansen & Rasmussen
DLA Nordic ✪
Simonsen Føyen Advokatfirma DA ✪
Thommessen Krefting Greve Lund ✪
Wiersholm, Mellbye & Bech, advokatfirma AS ✪

Hjort, Advokatfirmaet ✪
Steenstrup Stordrange DA, Advokatfirmaet ✪

Firms are listed A-Z in tiers which are ranked in order of priority
✪ Indicates firm displays contact details at the end of this chapter.

construction industry where clients include Halliburton and Stena Drilling.

Stephen Knudtzon at **Thommessen Krefting Greve Lund** is recommended for his shipping expertise.

Wiersholm, Mellbye & Bech, advokatfirma AS is recommended for ship sale/purchase deals and maritime insurance.

Advokatfirmaet Hjort's Brussels-based Espen Fossum deals with maritime matters including insurance.

Advokatfirmaet Steenstrup Stordrange DA's Thor Ask Terkelsen formerly a partner in **Gram, Hambro & Garman**, has vast experience of maritime law, particularly ship and rig construction matters.

OIL AND GAS

One of the few legal teams acclaimed without dissent during our research was **Arntzen de Besche Advokatfirma AS**' oil and gas group. Years of experience and careful recruitment have created a world standard team capable of tackling all aspects of the industry. The firm has outsourcing agreements for legal services with several major firms and is also adviser to the Ministry of Petroleum and Energy. Christian Fr Michelet is outstanding and has dealt with such major projects as the part privatisation of Statoil and the creation of Gassco.

Bugge, Arentz-Hansen & Rasmussen remains at the forefront in energy, frequently advising on major acquisitions and disposals. The highly respected Anniken Høeg Rasmussen has left **Advokatfirmaet Schjødt AS** to take a partnership at **Bugge, Arentz-Hansen & Rasmussen** bringing a wealth of energy law experience with her.

Kvale & Co acted for Statoil and the other licensees in connection with a NKr2bn (€232m) insurance claim resulting from fractures in sub-sea flow lines at the Aasgard field. Anders Kvale is an acknowledged leader in energy law.

Advokatfirmaet Schjødt AS maintains a strong position in the sector with major clients including ExxonMobil and ConocoPhillips. The

OIL AND GAS

ARNTZEN DE BESCHE ADVOKATFIRMA AS ✪

BUGGE, ARENTZ-HANSEN & RASMUSSEN
KVALE & CO ✪
SCHJØDT AS, ADVOKATFIRMAET ✪
SIMONSEN FØYEN ADVOKATFIRMA DA ✪
THOMMESSEN KREFTING GREVE LUND ✪
WIKBORG REIN ✪

DLA Nordic ✪
Hjort, Advokatfirmaet ✪
Kluge Advokatfirma DA ✪
Selmer DA, Advokatfirma ✪
Steenstrup Stordrange DA, Advokatfirmaet ✪
Wiersholm, Mellbye & Bech, advokatfirma AS ✪

Firms are listed A-Z in tiers which are ranked in order of priority
✪ Indicates firm displays contact details at the end of this chapter.

firm anticipates growth in the Stavanger office as the NCS opens up to entrepreneurial independent operators.

Strengthened by a Stavanger presence, **Simonsen Føyen Advokatfirma DA** is currently advising several independent oil and gas industry clients in connection with fields within and outside Norwegian jurisdiction. The firm also advises foreign governments, including those of Mali and Mozambique. Bjorn-Erik Leerberg is an expert on trans-boundary fields. Rune Omdahl advises Gassco on the major restructuring of gas transportation from NCS to Scotland.

Thommessen Krefting Greve Lund brings all the weight of the corporate and tax teams to its energy work and frequently handles the super-deals which characterise the sector. Christian Bruusgaard's combination of tax and energy law knowledge is unique, and Jørgen Lund is recommended for contractual matters and litigation. **Thommessen Krefting Greve Lund** continues to advise the Ministry of Petroleum and Energy in connection with the part-sale of the state's interest in the Norwegian Continental Shelf and has also been appointed legal adviser to Gassco AS.

Jarle Erik Sandvik and Lars Olav Askheim are the stars of an experienced group at **Wikborg Rein**. Dong and BP were among major transaction clients in 2003. Jan Erik Clausen, at **Wikborg Rein**'s Bergen office is building a solid oil and gas niche within a corporate practice.

As in other practice sectors, **Advokatfirmaet Hjort**'s Erik Keiserud's prestigious position as legal counsel to Statoil militates against a deserved expansion in the oil and gas group due to conflicts of interest. However, the firm does act for Borealis on major gas feed stock contracts.

Kluge Advokatfirma DA gained a number of oil clients last year, including BP Norge. The firm, with its substantial Stavanger office, has long experience in the industry and also acts for Norsk Agip and Revus Energy. Clement Endresen is highly rated.

Anne Helene Osberg usefully combines energy and environmental law as a senior member of **Advokatfirma Selmer DA**'s experienced team

Advokatfirmaet Steenstrup Stordrange DA's new Stavanger office, headed by experienced Ulf-Einar Staalesen is well placed in the competition for new instructions as smaller operators take over NCS licences.

Wiersholm Mellbye & Bech, advocatfirma AS boasts long experience in the oil and gas sectors, particularly with construction and project contracts.

REAL ESTATE

Brækhus Dege Advokatfirma ANS is recommended for the breadth of expertise offered by practitioners, particularly to middle market developers, construction companies and investors. Stein Erik Hove is an effective all-rounder, while Ivar Barstad specialises in commercial matters and Embret Støeng in construction law.

Advokatfirmaet Haavind Vislie AS' group was strengthened by the arrival of real estate specialist Mikkel Vislie from **Advokatfirma Selmer DA**. The firm continues to act in the majority of major infrastructure projects in the Oslo area and has also moved into PPP work. With vast experience of onshore and offshore construction the team is eminently capable of tackling the most complex matters. Liv Aandal has enjoyed recent litigation success.

Advokatfirmaet Schjødt AS' respected property group led by experienced Geir Frøholm, was strengthened by the arrival of Geir Sand from **Simonsen Føyen Advokatfirma DA**. Einar Caspersen is considered a skilful lawyer. The firm acts for major contractors including Selmer Skanska and construction companies of all sizes.

Simonsen Føyen Advokatfirma DA's construction and property law group reports an increase in the PPP work handled, although commercial real estate transactions remain the mainstay. A new standard lease contract was recently developed for the Norwegian Alliance of Business Property Owners. Recent clients included the Oslo Harbour Authority and Avantor. Karl Marthinussen is highly regarded.

The property group at **Wikborg Rein** handles some substantial cases ranging from railways to syndicated developments and, increasingly, PPP projects. Leif Petter Madsen and Anne Sofie Bjørkholt are both recommended.

Arntzen de Besche Advokatfirma AS' property lawyers handle a good deal of offshore and onshore installation work and are also known for syndicated property advice, development finance and difficult arbitrations. Hans H Kværne heads a team of five.

At **Bugge, Arentz-Hansen & Rasmussen**, the commercial real estate department has gained a clear market presence since Stig Bech moved from **Wikborg Rein** in 2002, and handles an increasing number of large and syndicated transactions.

DLA Nordic continues to act for some major players including Dong Norge AS. The firm has lost some good property lawyers recently but is still a strong property and construction practice with a blue-chip client base which includes Selmer Skanska and Mestaand Peab AS. The team offers all-round expertise including in PPP contracts. Espen Moe and Are Hunskaar are recommended.

Frode A Innjord, **Advokatfirmaet Hjort**'s head of property, acted in connection with the transfer of the royal estate at Bygdøy to the Norwegian Museum of Cultural History whilst also dealing with a dispute over the ownership of a satellite base station on behalf of Telenor.

Kluge Advokatfirma DA has a reputation for seeing clients successfully through all stages of the construction cycle and for litigation. Odd Tvedt and Harald Kobbe are recommended.

Advokatfirma Ræder's property team members have wide experience of development and include Nordic construction giant NCC in a quality client list. Morten Optstad, Carl Christiansen and Terje Løyning are highly rated.

Advokatfirma Selmer DA's property group lost Mikkel Vislie to **Advokatfirmaet Haavind Vislie AS** but remains a strong team. Svein Sulland is recommended as a litigator and arbitrator.

Advokatfirmaet Sørlie Wilhelmsen is particularly recommended for offshore construction matters. Jan-Fredrik Wilhelmsen and Gunnar Sørlie started the boutique firm in 1996 and have built a seven-lawyer practice.

Advokatfirmaet Steenstrup Stordrange DA advises across the range on real estate and construction law. Søren Lous, head of department, is a strong practitioner and Dagfinn Strønstad is noted for construction litigation.

Thommessen Krefting Greve Lund's property and real estate group offers a solid all-round service, frequently providing expert input to the finance department on infrastructure and PPP issues.

Torkildsen, Tennøe & Co specialises in commercial real estate and is noted for successful long-term relationships with clients. Andreas Iversen is rated highly.

Vogt & Wiig AS' Bjørn Kise continues to advise the developers of Oslo's Bjørvika area and the firm also acts for Linstow and NSB.

Wiersholm, Mellbye & Bech, advokatfirma AS' construction and energy team is recommended for high-value commercial real estate work. Arne Engesæth heads the group. **Wiersholm, Mellbye & Bech, advokatfirma AS**' strength in property and construction litigation deserves particular mention.

Bull & Co ANS expanded its property department during 2003. The firm has a very strong following amongst real estate agencies, including Notar Eiendom and Spar Eiendom. Knut Bachke is recommended for transaction disputes and litigation.

REAL ESTATE

BRÆKHUS DEGE ADVOKATFIRMA ANS ✪
HAAVIND VISLIE AS, ADVOKATFIRMAET ✪
SCHJØDT AS, ADVOKATFIRMAET ✪
SIMONSEN FØYEN ADVOKATFIRMA DA ✪
WIKBORG REIN ✪

Arntzen de Besche Advokatfirma AS ✪
Bugge, Arentz-Hansen & Rasmussen
DLA Nordic ✪
Hjort, Advokatfirmaet ✪
Kluge Advokatfirma DA ✪
Ræder, Advokatfirma ✪
Selmer DA, Advokatfirma ✪
Sørlie Wilhelmsen, Advokatfirmaet
Steenstrup Stordrange DA, Advokatfirmaet ✪
Thommessen Krefting Greve Lund ✪
Torkildsen, Tennøe & Co
Vogt & Wiig AS ✪
Wiersholm, Mellbye & Bech, advokatfirma AS ✪

Bull & Co ANS ✪
Grette DA, Advokatfirmaet ✪

Firms are listed A-Z in tiers which are ranked in order of priority
✪ *Indicates firm displays contact details at the end of this chapter.*

The experienced Harald Fosse joined **Advokatfirmaet Grette DA** from *Lindh Stabell Horten* (now **DLA Nordic**) in 2003 to head the property and construction department. The impact of his appointment is beginning to show and the group is expected to expand over the short term.

TMT

Brækhus Dege Advokatfirma ANS' TMT expertise in major contract software procurement and licensing is recognised at the highest levels. In 2003 Per Bjørsen acted for the Central Bank and for the VAT authorities. Dag Stadheim is a well-known author and IT law guru.

Simonsen Føyen Advokatfirma DA has one of Norway's leading TMT teams, a comprehensive legal practice of 23 lawyers. *Inter alia*, the group has acted for NetCom, the major telecoms player, in several regulatory matters, and Itouch plc, the UK-listed company on a major acquisition. Arve Føyen is highly regarded. Also recommended are Herman Valen and Espen Tøndel.

Advokatfirmaet Steenstrup Stordrange DA's telecoms expertise is impressive. The firm also boasts a broad experience of IT issues. Anne Kirsti Brekke is widely respected. Blue-chip clients include Teletopia and Carnegie.

Thommessen Krefting Greve Lund's TMT work is admired and the firm has particular strength in M&A work in the sector. The respected Kai Thøgersen heads the team.

Arntzen de Besche Advokatfirma AS fields one of the leading teams in the TMT sector and offers a comprehensive service to new entrant SMEs and international players including Yahoo! and Microsoft. The firm has experience in most TMT fields including e-commerce and telecoms.

Svein Gerhard Simonnæs heads **Bugge, Arentz-Hansen & Rasmussen**'s TMT practice, which maintains a high profile.

DLA Nordic's excellent IP group also handles TMT and numbers Fujitsu-Siemens, Vikom and Visma among its clients. The team's expertise in IT, anti-piracy and broadband Internet issues, is impressive. Lars Jakob Blanck is recommended. Alf Marcus Wiegaard is an expert on data protection law.

Advokatfirmaet Grette DA's dedicated TMT group, headed by Amund Brede Svendsen, is very close to a top-tier listing. Clients include IT giant Ergo Group, pan-Nordic telecoms player Song Networks and CSC Solutions Norge AS. The firm offers wide-ranging expertise in fields as diverse as fibre-optic data streaming and financial software.

Advokatfirmaet Haavind Vislie AS' TMT department has wide experience in the IT and software sector. Dag Thorstensen has a strong track record in IT-purchase litigation.

Wiersholm, Mellbye & Bech, advokatfirma AS' top-grade media lawyers attract a large following including Eurosport, and Universal Music. The firm is gaining strength in the technology sector with IBM and Accenture on the client list. Per-Kaare Svendsen shows exceptional promise as a telecoms lawyer.

Wikborg Rein has wide experience of TMT and assists clients from start-ups to multinationals in such sectors as pharmaceuticals and IT. Torleif Dahl heads an impressive, 14-strong team.

TMT

BRÆKHUS DEGE ADVOKATFIRMA ANS ✪
SIMONSEN FØYEN ADVOKATFIRMA DA ✪
STEENSTRUP STORDRANGE DA, ADVOKATFIRMAET ✪
THOMMESSEN KREFTING GREVE LUND ✪

Arntzen de Besche Advokatfirma AS ✪
Bugge, Arentz-Hansen & Rasmussen
DLA Nordic ✪
Grette DA, Advokatfirmaet ✪
Haavind Vislie AS, Advokatfirmaet ✪
Wiersholm, Mellbye & Bech, advokatfirma AS ✪
Wikborg Rein ✪

Hjort, Advokatfirmaet ✪
Kvale & Co ✪
Ræder, Advokatfirma ✪
Schjødt AS, Advokatfirmaet ✪
Selmer DA, Advokatfirma ✪

Firms are listed A-Z in tiers which are ranked in order of priority
✪ *Indicates firm displays contact details at the end of this chapter.*

Advokatfirmaet Hjort has recently come to a preferred counsel agreement with Telenor which, by reason of conflict of interest, curtails client development in the telecoms sector. The firm is, however, active in IT, television and entertainment and is seeking to expand its TMT client base.

Kvale & Co provides in-house counsel and handles regulatory and licensing issues for Tele2 Norge AS, the principal competitor to Telenor.

Carl Garmann Clausen at **Advokatfirma Ræder**, who practised at the New York Bar for six years, has wide experience of international contracts, particularly in the IT sector.

Advokatfirmaet Schjødt AS' TMT team, includes Ola Toftegaard-Hox who is also licensed to practise in New York, and Kaare Risung, who joined in 2003 and was formerly senior regulatory lawyer at Telenor.

Selmer DA, Advokatfirma's expertise is linked closely to the firm's IP strengths and the convergence of 'new media' and entertainment law.

TAX

Deloitte Advokatfirma DA fields an excellent tax team from five offices across Norway backed by the global practice. With a business tax focus and in-depth experience of all sectors of the Norwegian economy the firm can handle the most complex transactions and planning assignments. Tore Paulus is recommended for M&A support and Petter Grüner for international matters.

Advokatfirmaet Haavind Vislie AS' Arne Haavind is a noted Supreme Court tax litigator, as is Hans Bang. The eight-strong tax team is frequently instructed by the government and is biased towards energy taxation. Ragnar Østensen is chair of the Oil and Gas Taxation Board.

Einar Harboe of **Harboe, Eidem & Co AS** is acknowledged to be one of the very best Norwegian tax lawyers.

Thommessen Krefting Greve Lund's excellent tax team works closely with other practice groups and has a reputation for effective transaction advice, particularly those with an international element. It is also noted for litigation. Sverre Koch, for general corporate tax, and Christian Bruusgaard, for petroleum taxes, are both highly respected.

Wiersholm, Mellbye & Bech, advokatfirma AS' tax group is particularly strong on international matters, corporate structuring and transaction tax planning. During 2003 **Wiersholm, Mellbye & Bech, advokatfirma AS** litigated the landmark 'Hegnar' Supreme Court case which overturned longstanding practice in the valuation of unquoted shares for inheritance tax. Terje Hoffmann heads the outstanding team. Arvid Aage Skaar and Nicolay Vold receive accolades.

Arntzen de Besche Advokatfirma AS' deserved reputation in the energy field tends to overshadow strength in other areas. In taxation the firm offers a substantial general practice. Jan Jansen is a recommended all-rounder with particular expertise in international partnerships and petroleum taxation.

TAX

DELOITTE ADVOKATFIRMA DA ✪
HAAVIND VISLIE AS, ADVOKATFIRMAET ✪
HARBOE, EIDEM & CO AS
THOMMESSEN KREFTING GREVE LUND ✪
WIERSHOLM, MELLBYE & BECH, ADVOKATFIRMA AS ✪

Arntzen de Besche Advokatfirma AS ✪
Bugge, Arentz-Hansen & Rasmussen
DLA Nordic ✪
KPMG Law Advokatfirma DA ✪
PricewaterhouseCoopers DA, Advokatfirmaet
Schjødt AS, Advokatfirmaet ✪
Simonsen Føyen Advokatfirma DA ✪
Steenstrup Stordrange DA, Advokatfirmaet ✪
Wikborg Rein ✪

Brækhus Dege Advokatfirma ANS ✪
Bull & Co ANS ✪
Ernst & Young Tax AS ✪
Hjort, Advokatfirmaet ✪
Kluge Advokatfirma DA ✪
Ræder, Advokatfirma ✪
Selmer DA, Advokatfirma ✪

Firms are listed A-Z in tiers which are ranked in order of priority
✪ Indicates firm displays contact details at the end of this chapter.

Bugge, Arentz-Hansen & Rasmussen's tax team lost Ernst Ravnass to **Advokatfirmaet Steenstrup Stordrange DA** and slips a tier but, with Trond Sanfelt, the former deputy director of the Ministry of Finance in charge, it remains a centre of expertise with particular strength in takeovers, acquisitions and mergers.

DLA Nordic's twelve-strong tax group was strengthened by the arrival of Sverre Hveding from **Thommessen Krefting Greve Lund**. One of the youngest tax teams in Norway, it offers energy and creativity with particular strengths in international and cross-border issues. The clientele includes Kverneland and Møller Gruppen. Rolf Bech-Sørensen is a fine tax litigator at the highest level.

KPMG Law Advokatfirma DA's team, now headed by top-rated tax author Anders Liland, offers comprehensive taxation support to national and global businesses, their owners and executives. The firm offers particular depth in M&A-related advice. For complex VAT issues, Per Ivar Skinstad is highly recommended.

Advokatfirmaet PricewaterhouseCoopers DA offers expert support in both transaction and tax planning with Morten Bech recommended for his outstanding expertise.

Advokatfirmaet Schjødt AS' Wenche Riiser and Trond Larsen are recommended. The **Advokatfirmaet Schjødt AS** tax team is smaller than some but offers first-rate expertise in petroleum taxes and VAT.

Simonsen Føyen Advokatfirma DA fields a large commercial tax team with an excellent reputation, particularly for international work. Trond-Erik Andersen, Petter Hartz-Hanssen, Frode Müller and Johan Henrik Vister are recommended.

Advokatfirmaet Steenstrup Stordrange DA's tax department, headed by VAT expert Eivind Bryne, gained Ernst Ravnass from **Bugge, Arentz-Hansen & Rasmussen**, adding breadth to an already impressive group. The firm is recommended for international issues and domestic strategic planning and compliance.

Wikborg Rein's tax group continues to handle the range of commercial tax work. The firm litigated for Orkla over tax issues arising from the reorganisation of investment activities. Marianne Iversen is highly rated.

Brækhus Dege Advokatfirma ANS' strong tax department is headed by Øystein Sverre, an experienced practitioner. The firm frequently litigates for the tax authorities and also acts as tax adviser to employers' organisations.

Bull & Co ANS' small but experienced tax department was strengthened by the arrival of Gunhild Buestad. The firm specialises in energy law and contentious matters, which are handled by Morten Wishman.

Per Oskar Tobiassen at **Ernst & Young Tax AS** receives praise for his VAT expertise.

Advokatfirmaet Hjort's tax group, headed by well-known Harald Nyhus, has particular expertise in the new property tax regime and in the tax aspects of company reorganisation. Caroline Lund and Stein Erik Stinessen are very strong tax litigators.

Kluge Advokatfirma DA is noted for a tax litigation team whose members frequently appear in the Supreme Court. Stig Tufte-Johnsen successfully represented Firda Seafarms in a property tax dispute. Eirik Jensen specialises in international and oil taxation and has acted for Norske Conoco Phillips in a number of tax appeals. Geir Even Asplin is recommended for SME tax work.

At **Advokatfirma Ræder**, Jens I Kobro, formerly a member of the Oil Taxation Committee, is recommended for energy taxation matters.

Advokatfirma Selmer DA's Einar Bakko and Jon Vinje are recommended for tax planning and transactional support particularly in M&A and reorganisations.

THOMMESSEN KREFTING GREVE LUND

STRANDGATEN 209
PO BOX 1970 NORDNES
5817 BERGEN

Telephone: +47 55 30 61 00
Fax: +47 55 30 61 01
E-mail: firmapost@thommessen.no
Website: www.thommessen.no

Languages
English, French, German, the Scandinavian languages

Other offices
Brussels, Hong Kong, London, Oslo, Paris, Moscow

Number of lawyers 142
at this office 20

Contact
Svein Aage Valen (managing partner)

Member
Lex Mundi; The Scandinavian Law Alliance

CATEGORIES OF WORK

Mergers and acquisitions
Bernt Jacob Pettersen

Banking and finance
Jan J Greve

Tax
Olav Haugland

IT/media
Svein Aage Valen, Pål W Lorentzen

Maritime and transport
Hans Olav Lindal, Jan J Greve

Litigation and arbitration
Pål W Lorentzen, Svein Aage Valen

Energy and natural resources
Vidar Havsgård

Real estate
Dagfinn Heradstveit, Endre Grande

Insurance
Vidar Havsgård

Fishery and marine farming
Bernt Jacob Pettersen

WIKBORG REIN

OLAV KYRRESGT. 11
PO BOX 1233 SENTRUM
5811 BERGEN

Telephone: +47 55 21 52 00
Fax: +47 55 21 52 01
E-mail: bergen@wr.no
Website: www.wr.no

Languages
Cantonese, English, French, German, Indonesian, Malay, Mandarin, Russian, the Scandinavian languages, Spanish, Taiwanese

Other offices
Kobe, London, Oslo, Shanghai, Singapore

Number of lawyers 156
at this office 26

Member
Den Norske Advokatforeningen

CATEGORIES OF WORK

Trade and industry
Dag Steinfeld, Peter Frølich

Corporate finance
Haakon Blaauw, Knud Lorentzen

Energy and natural resources
Jan Erik Clausen, Per Magne Standborg

Shipping and offshore
Øystein Meland, Jon Heimset

Banking and finance
Stein Pettersen, Christian Friis

Insolvency and restructuring
Peter Frølich, Knud Lorentzen

Company law
Haakon Blaauw, Peter Frølich

Labour legislation
Per Magne Standborg, Dag Steinfeld

Competition law (including EU and EEA law)
Haakon Blaauw, Øystein Meland

Litigation and dispute resolution
Dag Steinfeld

Stock exchange and securities legislation
Knud Lorentzen, Jan Erik Clausen

Real estate
Peter Frølich, Bjørn Frode Skaar

Energy and petroleum law
Jan Erik Clausen, Haakon Blaauw

Fisheries and fish farming law
Per Magne Standborg, Stein Pettersen

Insurance law
Knud Lorentzen, Jon Heimset

Contract and manufacturing
Bjørn Frode Skaar, Jon Heimset

Marine law/transport/marine insurance
Jon Heimset, Øystein Meland

VOGT & WIIG AS

FORTUNEN 1
BOKS 1213
5811 BERGEN

Telephone: +47 55 56 82 00
Fax: +47 55 56 82 01
E-mail: bergen@vogtwiig.no
Website: www.vogtwiig.no

Languages
English, French, German, the Scandinavian languages

Other offices
Oslo, Trondheim

Number of lawyers 70
at this office 20

Contacts
Børge Knustad, Arthur Duus

CATEGORIES OF WORK

Tax
Alf Nielsen, Rolf Husebø

Shipping and ship finance
Børge Knustad, Erik Solheim

Maritime and Admiralty
Bjarte Grønlien, Jan Vablum

Companies and corporate
Alf Nielsen, Arthur Duus

Commercial (general)
Gustav Wiig, Erik Solheim

Construction
Per Chr Eriksen, Bjarte Grønlien

Labour
Alf Nielsen, Per Chr Eriksen

Mergers and acquisitions
Alf Nielsen, Arthur Duus

Litigation and arbitration
Per Chr Eriksen, Alf Nielsen

Oil and energy
Gustav Wiig, Borge Knustad

International contracts and joint ventures
Arthur Duus, Børge Knustad

Administrative law
Bjarte Grønlien

Insolvency
Per Chr Eriksen, Rolf Huseby

EU and competition
Arthur Duus, Bjarte Grønlien

Securities
Børge Knustad, Jan Vablum

Fisheries and aquaculture
Arthur Duus, Jan Vablum

THE FIRM

Vogt & Wiig AS was established in 2001 when the renowned law firms Vogt & Co in Oslo and Wiig & Co in Bergen merged. Later the firm established an operation in Trondheim, and now has 70 lawyers in Norway's three largest cities. The units that today comprise Vogt & Wiig have more than 100 years of experience in attending to businesses' legal needs. Vogt & Wiig specialises in corporate law, and its maritime law expertise is considered to be among Norway's best.

The law firm offers legal advice to both domestic and international business clients.

The firm also offers legal advice to individuals, concentrating mainly on insurance/personal injury law, compensation claims and labour law.

AREAS OF PRACTICE

Vogt & Wiig's practice covers all legal needs of domestic and international corporations. The law firm is organised in departments and practice areas. Upon receiving an assignment, the most competent expertise from the most relevant practice areas is combined into a project team depending on the nature and scope of the assignment. The team is always led by a partner.

While the firm's most recognised area of practice is maritime law, its work in the corporate law field is widely recognised. The maritime law department comprises maritime and transportation law, shipping law, ship finance law, marine insurance law and fishery law.

The real estate practice is well recognised and is involved in major real estate developments In Norway and the former eastern Europe.

The financing practice assists clients in all matters pertaining to disputes and financial claims.

The IT, marketing and competition practice deals with competition law, EU law and intellectual property law within all business segments.

The contract, insolvency and labour practice assists clients in these specialist legal disciplines. The energy department has deep sector expertise within oil, natural gas, and energy. The group handling general business law includes all work within the corporate law discipline. Work undertaken includes the main areas of corporate law, in addition to tax, securities law, and banking and finance law.

The arbitration and litigation practice represents clients in complicated cases in court and outside.

AABØ-EVENSEN & CO ADVOKATFIRMA

GRENSEN 15
PO BOX 6944 ST OLAVS PL
0130 OSLO

Telephone: +47 2415 9000
Fax: +47 2415 9001
E-mail: law@aaboevensen.com
Website: www.aaboevensen.com

Languages
Danish, English, Norwegian, Swedish

Contacts
Nils Olav Årseth, Ole K Aabø-Evensen

CATEGORIES OF WORK	
Mergers and acquisitions	Private equity
Securities and corporations	Fishery and fish farming
Corporate finance	Property finance
Capital markets	Due diligence
Take private and MBOs	Labour and employment
Project finance	Dispute resolution

THE FIRM

Aabø-Evensen & Co was founded in 2002 by four ambitious and experienced commercial lawyers. It is a business law firm with wide knowledge and experience in business law both nationally and internationally. The firm aims to be leading with regard to expertise, personal service, client care and commitment.

The firm's business idea is to be a leading Norwegian business law firm with a focus on M&A and corporate transactions.

Aabø-Evensen & Co's mission statement is to help clients to find the best legal and commercial solutions and to secure their business transactions.

At Aabø-Evensen & Co, all partners and employees are committed to the following base values that shall pervade all their work: quality – the professional quality of the firm's work shall always be pre-eminent; engagement – to be dedicated and committed to clients' businesses; service – the firm will do its utmost to provide clients with swift and effective assistance and close follow-up and 'walk the extra mile' for clients; and creativity – to focus on solutions instead of problems.

The firm has focus and priority on acquiring, maintaining and sharing knowledge and experience. It is currently using some of the top-line software and technology solutions that are available in the market.

Aabø-Evensen & Co is an independent law firm that is not a member of any alliance or network. However, the firm has contacts with some of the best and most well regarded firms around the globe. Partners have extensive international experience and are proud of the firm's international approach. The firm is able to offer corporate clients the best foreign firm in each jurisdiction.

AREAS OF PRACTICE

Aabø-Evensen & Co specialises mainly in mergers and acquisitions, securities, corporate finance and private equity. The firm's partners have broad experience from some of Norway's largest transactions during the last decade.

The firm also has a strong practice in the Norwegian fishery and fishing industry.

The litigation practice has deployed the latest presentation and investigation technologies for the purpose of preparing and presenting clients' cases before the courts or arbitration tribunals. This enables the firm to take on the most complicated and challenging cases that any client wishes to pursue before a court or panel of arbitrators.

ARNTZEN DE BESCHE ADVOKATFIRMA AS

PO BOX 2734
SOLLI
0204 OSLO

Telephone: 47 23 89 40 00
Fax: 47 23 89 40 01
E-mail: mail@arntzendebesche.no
Website: www.arntzendebesche.no

Languages
English, French, German, Spanish, the Scandinavian languages

Other offices
Stavanger

Number of lawyers 70

CATEGORIES OF WORK

Litigation and arbitration
Fred Arne Gade, Terje Granvang

Oil, gas and energy
Christian Fredrik Michelet, Dag Erlend Henriksen

Banking and finance
Sven Iver Steen, Pål Sveinsson

Securities
Trond Vernegg, Cecilie Ask

M&A
Trond Vernegg, Jan B Jansen

Labour, employment
Lars Holo, Ingeborg Moen Borgerud

IT and telecommunications
Mimi K Berdal, Knut Glad

IP/media and entertainment
Jan Morten Evertsen, Hans-Henrik Kværne

Insurance
Rune Njøs Jacobsen, Sven Iver Steen

Tax
Jan B Jansen, Kåre I Moljord

Company and commercial
Fred Arne Gade, Kåre I Moljord

Real estate
Hans-Henrik Kværne, Erling Høyte

Construction
Christian Fredrik Michelet, Mimi K Berdal

Aviation
Jan B Jansen, Ståle Gjengset

Insolvency
Aksel O Hillestad, Henning E Asheim

EU and competition
Stein Ove Solberg

THE FIRM

Arntzen de Besche has 70 lawyers, including 23 partners. The firm offers legal services within the whole business area, and is a leading law firm in Norway within certain specific areas of practice (see below). A main objective of the firm is to render high-quality legal services in an efficient and problem-solving manner for its clients.

In order to meet the requirements of its clients, considerable resources are put into developing business insight and understanding. Several of the firm's partners have extensive working experience in the energy and finance sectors, as well as in the public area. The firm focuses on developing a modern, knowledge-based company in order to meet the requirements of clients for first-class legal advice and service.

The firm's lawyers have a long tradition of being the authors of legal textbooks and articles, including company and commercial law; oil, gas and energy; insurance; labour; finance; and telecoms. The firm has a strong international orientation, with broad experience in assisting in international transactions and foreign enterprises undertaking business activities in Norway.

The firm's visiting address in Oslo is Bygdøy Allé 2, 0257 Oslo. The firm also has an office in Stavanger, the postal address for which is: PO Box 711 Sentrum, 4003 Stavanger, Norway.

AREAS OF PRACTICE

The law firm Arntzen de Besche covers all core business-related areas, and has a leading position in banking/finance/securities and M&A, oil and energy, IT and telecoms, intellectual property rights, labour law, commercial real estate, and aviation. The firm also places emphasis on developing its already extensive litigation practice.

The experience from international projects – typically within finance, M&A and telecoms/e-business – also gives Arntzen de Besche a unique competence as partners in large transaction processes.

BRÆKHUS DEGE ADVOKATFIRMA ANS

HAAKON VII'S GT 5
PB 1369 VIKA
0114 OSLO

Telephone: +47 23 23 90 90
Fax: +47 22 83 60 60
E-mail: advokat@brakhusdege.no
Website: www.brakhusdege.no

Languages
English, French, German, Italian, the Scandinavian languages

Other offices
Angers (France), Sandvika (Norway)

Number of lawyers 32
at this office 27

CATEGORIES OF WORK

Commercial law (general)
Christen Mellbye Gjesdahl, Stein E Hove

Tax law
Øystein A Sverre, Pål Berg

Mergers and acquisitions
Øystein A Sverre, Pål Berg

VAT law
Petter Jørgen Pettersen

Labour law
Jan Tormod Dege, Espen Rønningen

Computer, communication and information law
Dag Kristen Stadheim, Per Bjørnsen

Banking and finance
Christian Solemslie, Christen Mellbye Gjesdahl

International contracts
Didier Rigault

Competition and EU law
Didier Rigault, Bjørn Køhler Thommessen

Bankruptcy and insolvency
Bjørn Køhler Thommessen, Trygve Tønnessen

Litigation and negotiations
Fredrik Agerup, Per Bjørnsen

Construction, building
Embret Støeng, Stein E Hove

Real estate
Ivar A Barstad, Embret Støeng

Torts and compensation
Jan Krohn

THE FIRM

Brækhus Dege ANS is a well-established firm founded early in the previous century.

The firm is specialised in national and international business law.

The partners of the firm have published several practical books for the business world related to international contract negotiations and drafting, export and taxation, IT, export and import, agents, licensing, European Community law, management of real estate and labour law.

The partners are frequently requested to speak at seminars in Norway and other countries. They are also requested to train professionals in European countries and overseas by multinational undertakings and international organisations.

AREAS OF PRACTICE

The firm's main areas of practice are: international corporate and national law; banking, securities and finance; international contracts (particularly joint venture, agency, distribution, licensing, contract manufacturing, sub-contracting, export/import), litigation and alternative dispute resolution in and outside Norway; tax and VAT law; labour law; computer, communication and information law; EU legislation; bankruptcy and insolvency; real estate and construction law; and personal injury.

The partners own three companies covering the following specialised fields: sale of real estate, management of real estates in Norway and value-added tax (Brækhus Dege Consult AS is the VAT representative in Norway of several foreign companies).

BULL & CO ANS

KIRKEGT 2
PB 552 SENTRUM
0105 OSLO

Telephone: +47 23 01 01 01
Fax: +47 23 01 01 11
E-mail: bull@bullco.no
Website: www.bullco.no

Languages
English, French, German,
the Scandinavian languages

Number of lawyers 26

Member
Association of European Lawyers;
Legal Network International

CATEGORIES OF WORK

Mergers and acquisitions
Bjørn Blix

Corporate and commercial
Bjørn Blix

Dispute resolution
Gøsta Thommesen

Trade marks
Bente Holmvang

IP and patents
Amund Grimstad

IT and telecoms
Amund Grimstad

Bankruptcy and insolvency
Stein Inge Spurkland

Contract
Haakon I Haraldsen

EU and competition
Hans E Skirstad

Real estate
Roger Vodal

Tax
Morten Wishman

Franchising
Hans E Skirstad

Labour and employment
Kåre Bjørlo

Electricity
Gunhild Buestad

Family law, wills
Knut Bachke

THE FIRM

Established in 1864, Bull & Co is a commercial law firm comprising 26 lawyers. From its office in Oslo, Bull & Co offers domestic and foreign companies a full range of legal services. The firm is a member of two international networks – the Association of European Lawyers (AEL) and Legal Network International (LNI). These networks provide cross-border legal services for clients.

Bull & Co is strong across a broad range of practice areas and, through the single partner assigned to their business, clients can draw upon a wealth of expertise and experience across the firm. The implementation of a modern, IT-based infrastructure at Bull & Co has resulted in the more cost-efficient management of projects, bringing the firm's services to a higher level of quality.

With the commercial concerns of clients in mind, Bull & Co continually strives to develop its business insight and understanding, and provide legal advice and services that will give clients the competitive edge that they require.

AREAS OF PRACTICE

Bull & Co covers all aspects of commercial law for corporate clients. The firm is particularly experienced in the fields of corporate and commercial, labour and employment, insolvency, marketing, EU and competition, tax, real estate and electricity law. Bull & Co has a strong position as one of the leading firms within the field of intellectual property. The firm's litigation practice is focused on IP, labour, insolvency, tax and real estate disputes, and the development of alternative dispute resolution.

The demand for legal expertise combined with commercial understanding has led to an internal structure focusing on the trends and development of the following business sectors: industry and trade; media and entertainment; IT and telecoms; real estate; and electricity.

Lawyers from Bull & Co serve as directors of several Norwegian and foreign entities, including entities owned by foreign shareholders.

The firm offers interactive legal services on its website. Users of the Internet may form limited liability companies or partnerships, register sole proprietorships and draw up stock options and employment agreements, as well as various documents relating to the lease and sale of real property. The firm has several dotcom clients and advises in the fields of e-commerce and IP on the Internet.

DLA NORDIC

HAAKON VII'S GATE 2
PO BOX 1364 VIKA
0114 OSLO

Telephone: +47 24 13 15 00
Fax: +47 24 13 15 01
E-mail: info@dlanordic.no
Website: www.dlanordic.com

Languages
English, French, German, the Scandinavian languages

Other offices
Bergen, Copenhagen, Stockholm and 33 offices across Europe and Asia

Number of lawyers 199
at this office 60

Contacts
Kai Gjesdal Henriksen, Erik Myhr Nilsen, Espen Moe, Nils-Roe Fjørtoft

Member
DLA Group

CATEGORIES OF WORK

Corporate
Bjørn Slaatta, Marius Lysell Andresen

Labour and employment
Elizabeth Ege, Per Benonisen

TIME
Bård R Meltvedt, Lars Jakob Blanck

Construction and real estate
Are Hunskaar, Espen Moe

Tax
Jan M Fjellestad, Ole Morten Huseby

Maritime, energy and transport
Runar Hansen, Tor Aasberg

Commercial and litigation
Mads Krohn, Morten Poulsson

Public law
Magne Revheim

THE FIRM

DLA Nordic is the only Nordic law firm, with offices in Copenhagen, Oslo, Bergen and Stockholm. The firm ranks among the leading law firms in its respective home markets in Denmark, Norway and Sweden. Each office provides a complete range of integrated legal services across borders, both in the local market and on a global basis.

DLA Nordic is is part of DLA Group. DLA Group is an exclusive alliance of international full-service law firms with a shared vision. Established in 1999, DLA Group now has over 2,200 lawyers across 21 countries, who deliver expert local know-how and international solutions. DLA Group provides legal advice in 37 major cities across Europe, Singapore, Thailand, Hong Kong and the People's Republic of China.

DLA Nordic's vision is to be the leading Nordic law firm, and is based on the observation that many clients hold operations in all three countries. DLA Nordic is a modern, growing practice with distinct client service focus; legal advice is based on a proactive approach and an understanding of the client's business. The firm offers a thorough and cost-effective mode of work, knowledge and insight in the local business environment, seamless Scandinavian and international legal services, and commercially based solutions.

Providing a full service in all major practice areas, the firm is organised into eight cross-border legal departments, concerning the practice areas. The departments work together making sure that legal expertise is exchanged and shared, utilising legal resources fully and providing optimal service to the client.

Clients include public and private companies in a variety of sectors: commerce; industry; manufacturing services; property; construction; finance; IT, telecoms, media and entertainment; transport; shipping; and oil, gas and electricity. The firm also serves a large number of international clients, including large corporations, banks, investment firms and venture capital funds.

AREAS OF PRACTICE

Commercial and company law: extensive experience in company reconstruction; flotations; shareholders/partnership agreements; liquidations and incorporations; and commercial contracts.

Mergers and acquisitions: advice in each phase of mergers and acquisitions; anti-takeover strategies; public and private financing; client due diligence; and competition law.

Banking and finance: represents lenders and borrowers in the financial market. Clients include Scandinavian and international banks, stockbroker firms and finance companies.

IT and media: specialising in law related to IT technology, telecoms, intellectual property, and media, marketing and entertainment. Represents IT companies of every kind.

Tax and public law: specialising in national and international tax law and assisting municipalities and other clients in a broad range of public law.

Litigation: a central part of the firm's practice, the integrated work method plays an important role, since litigation skills must often be combined with specialist knowledge.

Construction and property: an extensive construction and property law practice with clients which include several major real estate and construction companies in Scandinavia.

Employment: in-depth experience in labour and employment law and practical knowledge of a range of industries.

Oil and gas: specialises in international oil and gas law, electric legislation and experienced in offshore construction and legal contracts.

Maritime and shipping: experts assist insurance companies and ship-owners regarding claims, collisions and adjustment of averages.

DELOITTE ADVOKATFIRMA DA

PO BOX 347 SKØYEN
0213 OSLO

Telephone: +47 23 27 96 00
Fax: +47 23 27 96 01
Website: www.deloitte-legal.no

Languages
English, the Scandinavian languages

Other offices
Bergen, Trondheim, Stavanger, Haugesund, Kristiansand, Tønsberg

Number of lawyers 20,000
at this office 41

Contacts
National/Oslo:
Tore Paulshus (managing partner)
Bergen: Eivind OG Ottesen
Stavanger: Finn Eide
Trondheim: Kaare Lundeland
Kristiansand: Oddlief Olsen

Member
International network of Deloitte Tax & Legal

CATEGORIES OF WORK

Tax – international (international corporate tax, transfer pricing, expatriate (IAS))	**International transactions**
	EU/EEA and competition law
Tax – national (corporate tax, personal tax, succession planning)	**Sports, entertainment and culture**
VAT, custom	**E-business, TMT, trade marks, intellectual property**
Mergers and acquisitions	**Bankruptcy and insolvency**
Due diligence, tax and legal	**Labour and employment law**
Transaction support	**Commercial and company law**

THE FIRM

Deloitte Advokatfirma DA is one of the largest business law firms in Norway. The firm currently has 85 lawyers and tax advisers nationwide. Being a full-service law firm and being part of a multi-disciplinary environment gives the firm the ability to profoundly understand all the aspects of its clients' business. The firm's clients experience that this multi-disciplinary service not only resolves their legal problems, but gives added value to their business decisions.

Deloitte Advokatfirma DA has offices in all the major commercial centres in Norway: Oslo, Bergen, Trondheim, Stavanger, Kristiansand, Tønsberg and Haugesund.

Deloitte Advokatfirma DA is an active member of Deloitte Touche Tohmatsu, one of the world's leading multi-disciplinary professional services firms delivering services to more than 150 countries. This gives Deloitte Advokatfirma DA the unique ability to deliver seamless, consistent services wherever clients operate. The firm is ranked as the number one tax adviser globally by the 'International Tax Review 2003'.

AREAS OF PRACTICE

Deloitte Advokatfirma DA provides a full service in all of the legal problems that an international business client can meet. The firm's specialities are, in particular, tax, VAT, mergers and acquisitions, corporate law, EU/EEA and competition law, bankruptcy and debt negotiation, restructuring, TMT/IP/IT, and litigation and arbitration.

The firm has a large international client base. As a result of this the firm regularly assists in international transactions.

Deloitte Advokatfirma DA represents and assists both large and medium-sized companies within a variety of businesses such as e-commerce, finance, IT/hi-tech, telecom, media and entertainment, consumer, trade, industry, manufacturing, fish-farming and natural resources, services both public and institutional.

ERNST & YOUNG TAX AS

OSLO ATRIUM
CHRISTIAN FREDERIKS PLASS 6
PO BOX 20
0051 OSLO

Telephone: +47 24 00 24 00
Fax: +47 24 00 29 01
Website: www.ey.no

Languages
English, the Scandinavian languages

Other offices
Bergen, Stavanger, Trondheim

Number of lawyers 87
at this office 47

CATEGORIES OF WORK

Corporate tax
Hans Georg Wille, Bjørgun Jønsberg

International tax services
Øyvind Hovland, Martin Wikborg

Transfer pricing
Marius Leivestad, Terje Arntzen

VAT
Per Oskar Tobiassen, Christin Bøsterud

Global employment services
Johan Killengreen, Antonio Holstad

Corporate law
Hans Georg Wille, Einar Brask

Mergers and acquisitions
Hans Georg Wille, Øyvind Hovland

Accounting Act and related issues
Einar Brask, Hans Georg Wille

ADVOKATFIRMAET GRETTE DA

HIERONYMUS HEYERDAHLSGT 1
PO BOX 1397 VIKA
0114 OSLO

Telephone: +47 22 34 00 00
Fax: +47 22 34 00 01
E-mail: firmapost@grette.no
Website: www.grette.no

Languages
English, French, German, Italian, the Scandinavian languages

Number of lawyers 42

CATEGORIES OF WORK

Banking, finance and insurance
Carl R Heber

Commercial law
Rolf Andreassen

Construction and building
Torgeir Myrstad, Harald Fosse

Corporate/M&A
Carl R Heber, Johan Mohn

Energy and natural resources
Nils Gulnes

Environment
Ragnar Vik

EU; international law
Amund Brede Svendsen

Fisheries
Cato Myhre

IT, e-commerce, telecommunications
Ulf Alex Samer

IP (trade marks, patents and copyright)
Amund Brede Svendsen, Astri Lund

Labour law
Johan Hveding, Dag Horsberg Hansen

Litigation
Peter Chr Meyer

Real estate
Peter Chr Meyer, Kolbjørn Johnsen

Shipping
Ivar M Mathiassen

Tax law
Tore Karlsson, Jan Ola Hedblad

Transportation
Dag Horsberg Hansen

Bankruptcy and insolvency law
Jacob Bjønness-Jacobsen, Torgeir Myrstad

ADVOKATFIRMAET HAAVIND VISLIE AS

BYGDØY ALLÉ 2
POSTBOX 359 SENTRUM
0101 OSLO

Telephone: +47 22 43 30 00
Fax: +47 22 43 30 01
E-mail: post@haavind.no
Website: www.haavind.no

Languages
English, French, German, Italian, the Scandinavian languages

Number of lawyers 90

Contacts
Halfdan Lowzow, Tor Wilhelm Seim, Peter L Brechan

CATEGORIES OF WORK

Electricity
Johan Fr Remmen, Kristin Bjella

Banking and finance
Harald Arnkværn, Peter L Brechan

Corporate and commercial
Tor Wilhelm Seim, Peter L Brechan

Insolvency
Hans Otto Meyer

Tax
Ragnar Østensen, Arne Haavind

Distribution agreements
Håkon Bleken, Ian Anders Tobiassen

Oil, gas and mining
Helge J Kolrud, Wilfred Rohde Garder

Property and construction
Helge J Kolrud, Olav Bergsaker

IT and telecommunications
Wilfred Rohde Garder, Børge Krogsrud

Intellectual property
Geir Steinberg, Anne Marie Sejersted

EU and competition
Ian Anders Tobiassen, Trygve Norum

Labour and employment
Kjell Torkildsen, Arvid R Ødegård

Dispute resolution
Helge J Kolrud, Bjørg Ven

ADVOKATFIRMAET HJORT

AKERSGATEN 2
PO BOX 471
SENTRUM
0105 OSLO

Telephone: +47 22 47 18 00
Fax: +47 22 47 18 18
E-mail: advokatfirma@hjort.no
Website: www.hjort.no

Languages
English, French, German, Spanish, the Scandinavian languages

Other offices
Brussels

Number of lawyers 52
at this office 51

Member
Terralex; Norwegian Bar Association

CATEGORIES OF WORK

Company and commercial
Harald Hjort, Armund Fougner

Banking and finance
Erik Keiserud, Else Bugge Fougner

Tax
Harald G Nyhus, Caroline Lund

Insolvency
Harald G Nyhus, Terje Aakvaag

Intellectual property
Amund Fougner, Kristin Veierød

IT and telecommunications
Kristin Veierød, Jørn Uggerud

Labour and employment
Else Bugge Fougner, Christian B Hjort

Commercial property
Ola Mæland, Ulf Larsen

Public procurement
Frode A Innjord, Frode Elgesem

Energy and natural resources
Stein Erik Stinessen, Caroline Lund

Litigation and arbitration
Erik Keiserud, Frode A Innjord

Economic crime
Arne Gunnar Aas, Else Bugge Fougner

Oil and gas
Erik Keiserud, Arne Jørgensen

EU and competition
Frode Elgesem, Jan Petter Romsaas

Stock exchange and securities
Christian B Hjort, Else Bugge Fougner

Wills and probate
Elsbeth Bergsland, Annette J Musæus

Transactions
Sveinung O Flaaten, Terje Aakvaag

Maritime/insurance
Espen H Fossum

KPMG LAW ADVOKATFIRMA DA

SØRKEDALSVEIEN 6
POSTBOKS 7000 MAJORSTUEN
0306 OSLO

Telephone: +47 21 09 21 09
Fax: +47 21 09 29 45
E-mail: law@kpmg.no
Website: www.kpmg.no

Languages
English, the Scandinavian languages

Other offices
Bergen, Stavanger, Tromsø

Number of lawyers 50

Contacts
John Killengreen, Anders H Liland, Per Ivar Skinstad, Svein G Andresen, Tonje Christin Norrvall, Johannes Andersen

CATEGORIES OF WORK

National taxation

Companies and corporations

International taxation

EU law

VAT, customs and excise

Labour and employment

Mergers and acquisitions

Tax litigation

KLUGE ADVOKATFIRMA DA

FR. NANSENS PL 7
0117 OSLO

Telephone: +47 23 13 92 00
Fax: +47 23 13 92 01
Website: www.kluge.no

Languages
English, French, German, Italian, Nordic languages, Spanish

Other offices
Bergen, Stavanger

Number of lawyers 64
at this office 34

Contact
Ola Bøe

CATEGORIES OF WORK

Corporate and commercial
Clement Endresen, Geir Even Asplin

TMT
Torstein Arendt, Ingvild Mestad

Banking, finance and shipping
Ola Bøe, Sverre-André Holm

Labour and employment
Harald Kobbe, Marco Lilli

Property and construction
Odd Tvedt, Odd-Sverre Rage

Oil and gas
Clement Endresen, Preben Falck

Intellectual property
Torstein Arendt, Ingvild Mestad

Dispute resolution
Stig Tufte-Johnsen, Harald Kobbe

Tax
Stig Tufte-Johnsen, Eirik Jensen

KVALE & CO

FRIDTJOF NANSENS PLASS 4
PO BOX 1752 VIKA
0122 OSLO

Telephone: +47 22 47 97 00
Fax: +47 22 47 97 01
E-mail: post@kvaleco.no
Website: www.kvaleco.no

Languages
English, German, the Scandinavian languages

Number of lawyers 27

CATEGORIES OF WORK

General corporate and business practice
Gunnar Stake-Larsen

Company and commercial
Thomas S Farhang, Henrik Svane

Oil and energy
Anders Kvale, Jens Brede

Bankruptcy and insolvency
Tom Hugo Ottesen, Arne Seemann Berg

EU and competition
Per T Christoffersen, Henrik Svane

Litigation and arbitration
Anders Kvale, Jens Brede

Mergers and acquisitions
Gunnar Stake-Larsen, Thomas S Farhang

Labour law
Arne Seemann Berg, Laila Myksvoll

Contract
Jens Brede, Per T Christoffersen

Joint ventures, mergers and acquisitions
Gunnar Stake-Larsen

Employment
Arne Seemann Berg

Agency, distribution
Per T Christoffersen, Henrik Svane

Media
Arne Seemann Berg

Banking and finance
Jens Brede

Franchise
Per T Christoffersen

Telecommunications, media and IT
Anders Kvale, Laila Myksvoll

ADVOKATFIRMA RÆDER

VIKA ATRIUM
MUNKESDAMSVEIEN 45
PO BOX 1600 – VIKA
0119 OSLO

Telephone: +47 23 27 27 00
Fax: +47 23 27 27 00
E-mail: mail@raeder.no
Website: www.raeder.no

Languages
Scandinavian languages, English, French, German

Number of lawyers 30

Member
Eurojuris International

CATEGORIES OF WORK

Commercial property, real estate
Leif Villars-Dahl, Magnus Landmark

Corporate and commercial
Carl Garmann Clausen, John Sveinsvold

EU and competition
Carl A Christiansen, Karsten H Torkildsen

Agency and distribution
Chr Aasland, Ole Per Solum

Property and construction
Terje Løyning, Carl A Christiansen

Insolvency, corporate restructuring
Egil Hatling, Erling Opdal

Private clients
Lars Ole Evensen, Helge Rivedal

Tax
Jens I Kobro, Morten Opstad

Mergers and acquisitions
Carl Garmann Clausen, Joar Heide

Intellectual property
Leif Villars-Dahl, Carl A Christiansen

Insurance
Jan Tinus Larsen, Joar Heide

Employment
Karsten H Torkildsen, Ole Per Solum

Capital markets, securities
Morten Opstad, Carl Garmann Clausen

Dispute resolution
Lars Ole Evensen, Inge Grotli

Municipal and public law
Arve Lønnum, Knut Frigaard

Contracts
Rune Vikan, Chr Aasland

Arbitrators
Odd Wisløff, Jan Fredrik Ottesen

Trusts and estates
Finn O Eckbo, Morten Opstad

RIME & CO ADVOKATFIRMA DA

OVRE SLOTTSGATE 12B
0157 OSLO

Telephone: +47 23 00 34 00
Fax: +47 23 00 34 01
E-mail:lawfirm@rimeco.no
Website: www.rimeco.no

Languages
English, the Scandinavian languages

Number of lawyers 11

CATEGORIES OF WORK

Insolvency and restructuring
Morten Haugen, Siv Sandvik

Litigation and arbitration
Morten Haugen, Siv Sandvik

Corporate and commercial
Johan Ratvik, Siv Sandvik

Labour and employment
Johan Ratvik, Karen Margrethe Rime

Construction and building
Morten Haugen, Johan Ratvik

Family, estates and probate
Karen Margrethe Rime

Banking and finance
Morten Haugen, Siv Sandvik

Inheritance and succession
Karen Margrethe Rime

ADVOKATFIRMA SELAND, BLIKOM & CO DA

KLINGENBERGGT 7 B
PO BOX 1938 VIKA
0125 OSLO

Telephone: +47 24 13 43 40
Fax: +47 24 13 43 41
E-mail: post@sbc-law.no
Website: www.sbc-law.no

Languages
English, German, Scandinavian

Number of lawyers 11

Member
Lawspan International

CATEGORIES OF WORK

Company law
Johan S Seland, Einar Heiberg

Construction law
Johan S Seland

Tax law
Einar Heiberg, Audun Gjøstein

Litigation
Cato R Blikom, Einar Heiberg

Duty law
Johan S Seland

Arbitration
Einar Heiberg, Cato R Blikom

Contract law
Cato R Blikom, Espen Egseth

Compensation law
Terje Hensrud, Trude Ervik

Computer law
Audun Gjøstein, Anders Utne

Corporate and commercial
Einar Heiberg, Audun Gjøstein

Stock exchange law
Johan S Seland, Christian Fodstad

Securities law
Per Forsberg, Cato R Blikom

Real estate law
Johan S Seland, Anders Utne

Intellectual property
Odd Gunnar Hammernes, Terje Hensrud

Label law
Per Forsberg, Cato R Blikom

ADVOKATFIRMAET SCHJØDT AS

DRONNING MAUDS GT 11
POSTBOKS 2444 SOLLI
0201 OSLO

Telephone: +47 22 01 88 00
Fax: +47 22 83 17 12
E-mail: schjodt.osl@schjodt.no
Website: www.schjodt.no

Languages
English, French, German, the Scandinavian languages, Dutch, Spanish

Other offices
Bergen, Stavanger, Trondheim, Ålesund

Number of lawyers 140
at this office 96

Contact
Petter Chr Sogn

Member
The Club (European);
The World Law Group (Global)

CATEGORIES OF WORK

Capital markets
Erling Christiansen

Mergers and acquisitions
Erling Christiansen, Erling Veland

Oil, gas and energy
Peter A Hiorth, Cathrine Hambro

Tax
Wenche B Riiser, Cecilie Amdahl

Intellectual property
Peter G Nitter

Competition and EU
Trygve O Laake, Jan Magne Langseth

Banking and finance
Einar Irgens

Litigation and arbitration
Cato Schiøtz, Dagfinn Clemetsen

Venture capital
Morten Foros Krohnstad, Einar Caspersen

Construction and real estate
Nils-Henrik Pettersson, Geir Frøholm

Maritime, shipping
Per N Sperre, Øystein Horneland

International/ship finance, syndicated loans
Wilhelm Damm, Anne Gro Sundby

Aqua-culture/fisheries
Per N Sperre

Telecommunications
Kaare Risung

Information technology
Ola Toftegaard-Hox

Labour and employment
Trond Stang, Hans Dale

THE FIRM

Advokatfirmaet Schjødt is a leading commercial law firm in Norway. The firm, which traces its origins back to the beginning of the 20th century, has grown steadily over the years and now employs 140 lawyers. Headquartered in Oslo, it has offices in Bergen, Trondheim, Stavanger and Ålesund.

The firm has achieved its position by working hard to achieve success for its clients. Business acumen, creativity and perseverance are key elements in the value added legal services the firm provides.

A number of Advokatfirmaet Schjødt's lawyers have spent considerable time practising abroad and the firm regularly assists in international and multinational transactions.

AREAS OF PRACTICE

The firm is organised into departments covering either industries or legal practice areas, the most important of which are:

Capital markets: the firm is a leading law firm in this area in Norway. The clients range from domestic and international investment banks, merchant banks and stock brokerage firms, to listed companies and Norwegian and foreign companies seeking listing or other equity or debt financing.

Mergers and acquisitions: mergers and acquisitions represent a considerable part of the firm's transactional activities. The firm regularly assists foreign buyers in acquiring both public and privately held companies.

Oil, gas and energy: the firm has a very strong practice within the energy sector, and has worked with energy issues from the very start of the petroleum activities on the Norwegian continental shelf. It represents several international oil companies and companies in the electricity sector.

Intellectual property: the firm is at the forefront in the protection of investments in product developments and know-how. It advises on all aspects of commercialisation of intellectual property, including licensing and other intellectual property contracts.

Competition, EU and EEA law: the firm assists in all areas of competition and EU law, including litigation before the EFTA courts and notifications to competition authorities in Norway, in the EU and the EEA.

Banking and finance: the firm assists in all operative aspects of banks and financial institutions as well as organisational matters, including the legal framework for, and statutory regulations of, their establishment and activities.

Litigation: the firm has an important and highly reputable commercial litigation practice and litigates frequently before the Supreme Court. The practice spans all aspects relevant to the business community, such as corporate and securities law, contract disputes, intellectual property, media, competition, agency and distribution, employment disputes and regulatory affairs, including pollution matters.

Venture capital: the firm's venture capital group represents some of the leading investors in Norway as well as a number of exciting start-ups. It assists in setting up venture capital funds as well as their continued funding and investment activities.

Construction/real estate: the firm has one of Norway's premier construction law practices and normally represents contractors, but also receives instructions from developers. The firm advises in connection with contract negotiations and disputes, and litigates a large number of cases before arbitration courts and the ordinary courts.

Telecommunications: the firm has extensive experience in telecommunication projects, both domestic and international.

Employment: the firm assists employers in defining compensation schemes, including options, drafting and employment agreements, and advising non-competition issues and intellectual property. Schjødt's expertise includes collective agreements and individual issues such as reorganisations and termination of employees at all levels.

Media: The firm has amongst its clients a large number of prominent publishers, newspapers and other media.

ADVOKATFIRMAET SELMER DA

PO BOX 1324 VIKA
0112 OSLO

Telephone: +47 23 11 65 00
Fax: +47 23 11 65 01
E-mail: selmer@selmerlaw.com
Website: www.selmerlaw.com

Languages
English, Finnish, French, German, Italian, Polish, Russian, Spanish, the Scandinavian languages

Number of lawyers 95

Other offices
Trondheim

Contacts
Sverre S Tysland
(s.s.tysland@selmerlaw.com),
Thomas G Michelet
(t.michelet@selmerlaw.com)

CATEGORIES OF WORK

Mergers and acquisitions
Thomas G Michelet, Nils Bugge

Corporate
Andreas Rørvik, Roy M Slettvold

Energy and natural resources
Anne Helene Osberg, Sverre S Tysland

Banking, finance and insurance
Lars Weyer Larsen, Knut Endre

Litigation and arbitration
Jeppe Normann, Svein Sulland

Information, communications and technology (ICT)
Nils Kristian Einstabland

Family law, estates and probate
Anne Blanca Dahl

Taxes, duties and accounting
Einar Bakko, Jon Vinje

Securities/investment banking
Dag E Ramussen, Thomas G Michelet

EU/EAA/competition law
Harald Evensen, Asbjørn Berg

Intellectual property
Asbjørn Berg

Real estate and construction
Fredrik Astrup Borch, Svein Sulland

Shipping/offshore
Nils Bugge, Anders Rønningen

Marine industry
Christian Selmer, Mads Iversen

Media, entertainment, sports
Asbjørn Berg, Jeppe Normann

Strategic and financial advice
Frank Berg, Anders Rønningen

Insolvency
Jon Skjørshammer, Fredrik Borch

THE FIRM

Selmer is a modern and expanding human resources business. Selmer is one of Norway's leading law firms. The firm has more than 130 staff, of which approximately 80 are lawyers and 14 are financial advisers and state-certified accountants. Selmer works primarily with legal and strategic counselling towards the Norwegian and international business environment.

Selmer has a particularly strong expertise within banking and finance, energy (utilities and gas), public M&A (involving public offerings and IPOs) and private M&A (not involving securities issues), and real estate and construction. The firm has also experienced considerable growth within ICT and intellectual property, competition and antitrust, marine industry matters, tax and stratregic and financial advice.

Throughout the past decade, Selmer has developed a substantial strategic advice business based on its enhanced M&A/corporate and business development capabilities. Several senior partners and their teams have accomplished a variety of assignments related to restructuring of businesses, consolidations, integrations including mergers and divestitures of businesses, streamlining and development. Selmer has in 2002 announced the appointment of a certified accountant as a partner. Frank L Berg is in charge of the development of financial management consulting activity at Selmer.

In 2003, Selmer has substantially increased its focus on Russia/Eastern Europe. New recruitments include Louis Skyner (PhD) and Yevgeniy Tregubenko (PhD and admitted in both Russia and New York) who will work uniquely with investments and trade in Russia. The team is headed by Thomas Michelet. Selmer has also substantially strengthened its oil and gas practice. The firm has an extensive portfolio of legal, finance and strategy services. Five new lawyers and financial advisers have joined Selmer's team in 2003.

The firm is widely recognised for its top legal skills, friendly and informal atmosphere, personal and high-quality service. In addition to the firm's legal and strategic counselling, Selmer is often engaged as the project leader on large and complicated assignments.

Selmer's clients include Norwegian and foreign corporations, institutions, organisations, individuals as well as governmental bodies.

Insight into the industry in question, in combination with top-notch legal expertise, forms the backbone of Selmer's counselling. The firm has built up groups targeting specific market sectors focusing on industry developments and trends. The firm's strategy is to be the leading law firm in these sectors. Thanks to its in-depth expertise within various markets, Selmer has gained a strong position in business strategic and legal counselling.

Furthermore, Selmer has organised specialist groups that focus on jurisprudence to ensure that the firm maintains its state-of-the-art legal expertise. The firm's emphasis is on having a practical and goal-orientated approach.

SIMONSEN FØYEN ADVOKATFIRMA DA

PO BOX 6641, ST OLAVS PLASS
CJ HAMBROS PLASS 2D,
0129 OSLO

Telephone: +47 21 95 55 00
Fax: +47 21 95 55 01
E-mail: post@simonsenfoyen.no
Website: www.simonsenfoyen.no

Other offices
Kristiansand, Stavanger, Tromsø

Languages
English, French, German,
the Scandinavian languages

Number of lawyers 115

Contacts
Per Kyllingstad (chairman),
Marianne Smith Magelie (director of marketing and communication),
Terje Rognlien (managing director),
Stein Erikstad (Kristiansand),
Henning M Stephansen (Stavanger),
Kenneth Mikkelsen (Tromsø)

CATEGORIES OF WORK

Technology, telecoms and media
Espen Tøndel

Shipping and offshore
Per Seime

Construction and property
Heikki Giverholt

Corporate and tax law
Knut Boye, Tor G Birkeland

THE FIRM

Simonsen Føyen Advokatfirma DA is one of Norway's largest firms, with 115 lawyers and a total staff of 160, and is committed to providing clients with legal representation of the highest quality.

Simonsen Føyen is a market leader in IT law, and construction and property law. It is also strong in offshore construction, shipping and oil and gas, and corporate and tax law. All of the firm's lawyers work in one of the following practice groups: IT and media; construction and property; shipping and offshore; or corporate and tax.

A substantial amount of the firm's work is international. Through its network of co-operating law firms, Simonsen Føyen can also offer global services to its clients.

AREAS OF PRACTICE

IT and media: the IT, telecoms and media industries are converging into a common 'Infocom business', and industry players are faced with a constantly changing environment. Since the 1980s Simonsen Føyen has worked extensively with the IT, telecoms and media businesses, advising on contract negotiations, dispute resolutions, litigation, competition and regulatory issues, licence applications and acquisitions and mergers.

The firm's IT and media practice group now has 18 lawyers. There is close co-operation between it and the corporate and tax group, especially in connection with acquisitions and reorganisations.

Simonsen Føyen is considered a leading Norwegian firm within the field of IT and media law, being ranked number one in national and international rating publications, and has a well-established contact network of highly regarded law firms in Europe and the US, which is of great value to Norwegian clients needing assistance abroad.

Construction and property: Simonsen Føyen has extensive expertise in construction law, property law and development since 1969, when Føyen & Co was established on the basis of its particular knowledge of construction law. The construction and property group now has 17 lawyers, making it one of the largest in Norway. The firm represents some of the country's major builders, contractors and consultants and acts as legal adviser for local regional and national authorities.

Corporate and tax: the corporate and tax group deals with all legal problems related to trade and industry, including establishment and operation of companies, and serves a broad range of national and international clients. The corporate and tax group is the firm's largest, with 47 lawyers, and is divided into five main teams: corporate and corporate finance; tax and VAT; insolvency; securities law; and sports. The teams' lawyers have broad legal backgrounds in business law, as well as considerable international experience.

Petroleum/energy and shipping/ship financing: Simonsen Føyen's highly-regarded shipping practice was founded in 1948. Strong capabilities have since been established in petroleum and energy law, as well as in defence/aerospace and aquaculture/fishery matters. Petroleum/energy clients include national governments and UN agencies, major and independent oil/gas companies, petroleum industry suppliers, owners/operators of drilling rigs/ships, hydroelectric facilities and turbine suppliers. The firm has in-depth knowledge of the industries, with lawyers who have held senior positions in the Norwegian government and in oil majors. They maintain their strong position in offshore construction and services, with six to seven lawyers acting regularly on contract negotiation/drafting/administration and dispute resolution including litigation/arbitration of major claims. Simonsen Føyen continues to be acknowledged as a leading firm in the sector of shipping/ship financing, advising foreign and Norwegian clients on maritime law, financing/building/sale and purchase of ships, corporate law, taxation, marine insurance claims and disputes. The firm enjoys a particularly strong reputation in ship financing, as legal adviser and provider of documentation for the lender banks.

ADVOKATFIRMAET STEENSTRUP STORDRANGE DA

STORTINGSG 22
PO BOX 1829 VIKA
0123 OSLO

Telephone: +47 22 81 45 00
Fax: +47 22 81 45 01
E-mail: lawyers@steenstrup.no
Website: www.steenstrup.no

Languages
English, French, German, Russian, the Scandinavian languages

Other offices
Trondheim, Tromsø, Stavanger

Number of lawyers 77
at this office 59

Member
Interlex Group;
State Capital Law Firm Group

CATEGORIES OF WORK

Corporate and commercial Morten Steenstrup, Robert Sveen	**Tax** Ernst Ravnaas, Ove-Marthin Granlund
Banking and finance Ian W Kenworthy, Odd Moe	**VAT** Eivind Bryne, Knut-Morten Carlsen
Privatisation Ida Espolin Johnson, Stig Nordal	**EU and competition** Bjørn Stordrange, Trond Skogly
Mergers and acquisitions Robert Sveen, Håvard Bergli	**Litigation and arbitration** Ian W Kenworthy, Jane Veivåg Ulset
Maritime and shipping Thor Ask Terkelsen, F H Antonsen	**Consultations with government** Morten Steenstrup, Harald Ellefsen
Contracts Bjørn Stordrange, Hege B Ersdal	**Torts and compensation** Ola J Strømsmoen, Thomas Meinich
Commercial property/real estate Ola Nygard, Søren L Lous	**IT and telecommunications** Morten Steenstrup, Anne Kirsti Brække
Labour and employment Thomas Meinich, Magne Mjaaland	**Intellectual property** Søren L Lous, Fredny Bade
Bankruptcy and insolvency Odd Magne Gjerde, Frode Finnøy	**Construction** Ola J Strømsmoen, Ola Nygard

THE FIRM

Advokatfirmaet Steenstrup Stordrange DA is a modern, knowledge-based, expanding, full-service business law firm founded in 1989. The firm's goal is to give clients quick, effective, personal and professional assistance in all legal issues. Steenstrup Stordrange is a member of the State Capital Law Firm Group, an association of independent law firms located in all 50 US state capitals, and in business markets and financial centres around the world, that practice independently and not in a relationship for the joint practice of law. The firm is also a member of the Interlex Group, a worldwide association of leading law firms serving international clients.

AREAS OF PRACTICE

The firm's practice covers a full range of commercial work for both domestic and foreign clients. The lawyers act as advisers in all stages of commercial transactions, as well as representing clients in litigation and arbitration. In order to meet a client's legal requirements in any area, the firm has a staff of lawyers with expertise and experience within all legal jurisdictions. Of equal importance is the firm's unrivalled committment to quick, effective and available service at all times.

Mergers and acquisitions: the firm's transactions in this area include private acquisition and cross-border takeovers.

Corporate law: Steenstrup Stordrange advises on all aspects of general corporate law, including the drafting of contracts according to Norwegian law.

Stock exchange regulations: the firm handles matters on behalf of investment banks and for listed companies via the stock market and the Oslo Stock Exchange.

Telecommunications and computer law: the firm is very active in this sector. Steenstrup Stordrange advises on contracts, marketing law, intellectual property and employment matters, including CRM-related questions.

Litigation and arbitration: Steenstrup Stordrange deals with commercial litigation, national and international arbitration, and regularly handles cases before the City Courts, the Court of Appeal and the Supreme Court in Norway. The firm also represents international clients in criminal cases, specialising in white-collar crime.

Labour law: the firm handles all matters relating to Norwegian employment law.

The firm also has an extensive practice in the areas of EU law and competition law, both on the national and the EU/EFTA levels.

Strategic counselling: a milestone was reached this spring when the first non-legal partner joined the firm.

THOMMESSEN KREFTING GREVE LUND

HAAKON VII'S GATE 10
PO BOX 1484 VIKA
0116 OSLO

Telephone: +47 23 11 11 11
Fax: +47 23 11 10 10
E-mail: firmapost@thommessen.no
Website: www.thommessen.no

Languages
Dutch, English, French, German, the Scandinavian languages

Other offices
Bergen, Brussels, Hong Kong, London, Paris, Moscow

Number of lawyers 142
at this office 121

Contact
Jørgen Lund (managing partner)

Member
Lex Mundi; The Scandinavian Law Alliance

CATEGORIES OF WORK

Company and commercial
Anders Arnkværn, Kai Thøgersen

Mergers and acquisitions
Carl Erik Krefting, Sverre E Koch

Banking and finance
Kim Dobrowen, Hasse Arnesen

Tax
Henning Naas, Truls Leikvang

Insolvency
Gerhard Holm, Morten Fjermeros

EU and competition
Siri Teigum, Eivind Vesterkjær

Information technology
Arne Ringnes

Maritime and transport
Stephen Knudtzon, Jørgen Lund

Intellectual property
Kristine Schei, Arne Ringnes

Litigation and arbitration
Erik Samuelsen, Stephen Knudtzon

Oil and energy
Carsten Riekeles, Rune Solberg

Real estate
Gerhard Holm, Christian Müller

Insurance
Berit Stokke

THE FIRM

Thommessen Krefting Greve Lund AS is one of the largest law firms in Norway. The firm currently has approximately 230 total staff in Norway.

Of particular importance to the firm is the legal assistance of both Norwegian clients with foreign interests and foreign clients with interests in Norway. It has therefore entered into a corporate agreement with two of the biggest law firms in Denmark and Sweden, respectively Advokatfirmaet Kromann Reumert and Advokatfirman Vinge. The three firms together represent more than 350 lawyers and have foreign branch offices in London, Brussels, Paris, Moscow and Hong Kong. Thommessen Krefting Greve Lund is also a member of Lex Mundi, an international network facilitating co-operation between 158 law firms in 90 countries, which enables it to satisfy its clients' needs for legal services beyond Norway's borders.

The firm actively uses up-to-date information technology, both in daily work throughout the firm, and (subject to restraints arising due to the need for confidentiality) as a means of communication between its offices and with clients.

AREAS OF PRACTICE

The firm concentrates on the business community's legal problems, comprising in particular taxes, corporate law including company takeovers, mergers and split-ups, engineering contracts, contract law, property law, competition law, IT, telecommunications, media, intellectual property law, environmental law, labour law, banking and financing, Stock Exchange introduction, issues and securities trading, energy, oil and shipping, European Community law, bankruptcy and debt negotiation, litigation and arbitration.

In view of the increasing internationalisation of the business community, it is the objective of Thommessen Krefting Greve Lund to improve still further the possibilities of safeguarding the interests of its clients outside Norway.

One of the firm's partners is qualified both as a Norwegian advokat, and as a solicitor of the Supreme Court of England and Wales.

VOGT & WIIG AS

ROALD AMUNDSENS GATE 6
PO BOX 1503 VIKA
0117 OSLO

Telephone: +47 22 31 32 00
Fax: +47 22 31 32 01
E-mail: oslo@vogtwiig.no
Website: www.vogtwiig.no

Languages
English, German, the Scandinavian languages

Other offices
Bergen, Trondheim

Number of lawyers 70
at this office 35

CATEGORIES OF WORK

Maritime and transportation
Anders W Faerden, Frithjof Herlofsen

Ship finance
Christine Rodsaeter, Knut Erik Westad

Marine insurance
Morten Lund, Anders W Faerden

Real estate
Bjørn H Kise, Per Erik Bergsjø

Tort, personal injury and insurance
Per Erik Bergsjø, Stein Chr Hexeberg

Litigation
Bjørn Kjos, Per Erik Bergsjø

Tax
Arvid Dahm

Aviation
Frithjof Herlofsen, Bjørn H Kise

Securities
Morten Lund,
Christian Ditlev-Simonsen

Mergers and acquisitions
Tor Kielland,
Christian Ditlev-Simonsen

E-commerce
Anders W Faerden

Environmental law
Morten Lund, Frithjof Herlofsen

General and corporate business
Bjørn H Kise, Knut Erik Westad

Labour
Tor Kielland, Knut Erik Westad

THE FIRM

Vogt & Wiig AS was established in 2001 when the renowned law firms Vogt & Co in Oslo and Wiig & Co in Bergen merged. Later the firm established an operation in Trondheim, and now has 70 lawyers in Norway's three largest cities. The units that today comprise Vogt & Wiig have more than 100 years of experience in attending to businesses' legal needs. Vogt & Wiig specialises in corporate law, and its maritime law expertise is considered to be among Norway's best.

The law firm offers legal advice to both domestic and international business clients.

The firm also offers legal advice to individuals, concentrating mainly on insurance/personal injury law, compensation claims and labour law.

AREAS OF PRACTICE

Vogt & Wiig's practice covers all legal needs of domestic and international corporations. The law firm is organised in departments and practice areas. Upon receiving an assignment, the most competent expertise from the most relevant practice areas is combined into a project team depending on the nature and scope of the assignment. The team is always led by a partner.

While the firm's most recognised area of practice is maritime law, its work in the corporate law field is widely recognised. The maritime law department comprises maritime and transportation law, shipping law, ship finance law, marine insurance law and fishery law.

The real estate practice is well recognised and is involved in major real estate developments In Norway and the former eastern Europe.

The financing practice assists clients in all matters pertaining to disputes and financial claims.

The IT, marketing and competition practice deals with competition law, EU law and intellectual property law within all business segments.

The contract, insolvency and labour practice assists clients in these specialist legal disciplines. The energy department has deep sector expertise within oil, natural gas, and energy. The group handling general business law includes all work within the corporate law discipline. Work undertaken includes the main areas of corporate law, in addition to tax, securities law, and banking and finance law.

The arbitration and litigation practice represents clients in complicated cases in court and outside.

WIERSHOLM, MELLBYE & BECH, ADVOKATFIRMA AS

RUSELØKKVEIEN 26
PO BOX 1400 VIKA
0115 OSLO

Telephone: +47 21 02 10 00
Fax: +47 21 02 10 01
E-mail: mail@wiersholm.no
Website: www.wiersholm.no

Languages
English, French, German, Italian, Russian, the Scandinavian languages, Spanish

Number of lawyers 115

Contacts
Paul Bellamy (managing director/CEO), Harald Willumsen (chairman)

CATEGORIES OF WORK

General and corporate
Erling Lind, Harald Willumsen

Corporate finance/banking
Leif Moltke-Hansen, Erik Ramm

Mergers and acquisitions
Erik Thyness, Andreas Mellbye

Litigation
Stephen L Jervell, Magnus Hellesylt

Employment and pensions
Jan Fougner, Eli Aasheim

Tax
Arvid Aage Skaar, Terje Hoffmann

Intellectual property, copyright
John S Gulbrandsen, Nils J Sejersted

Insurance law/maritime insurance
Nic Brun-Lie, Trygve Hcnne

Securities and stock exchange
Knut Bergo, Tone Østensen

EU and competition law
Anders Ryssdal, Stephen L Jervell

TMT
John S Gulbrandsen, Magnus Hellesylt

Shipping and transportation
Nic Brun-Lie, Nils H Thommessen

Oil and gas
Andreas Mellbye, Per Raustøl

Electricity
Inge Ekker Bartnes, Jarle Kvam

Property and construction
Helge Morten Svarva, Arne Engesæth

THE FIRM

Wiersholm, Mellbye & Bech, advokatfirma AS is one of the leading law firms in Norway, founded in 1875. The firm presently has 115 lawyers, comprising 37 partners and 78 associates.

From the office site in Oslo, it serves a national and international client base, and frequently works with lawyers and clients overseas and within Europe.

The firm specialises in commercial practice. By combining its specialist areas, the firm offers its clients a full range of quality services on commercial and corporate transactions.

The firm has 10 foreign lawyers licensed in the US, UK and EU.

AREAS OF PRACTICE

Company and commercial law, including merger and acquisition; takeovers, disposals, equity offerings, flotations, corporate restructuring and management buy-outs; banking law,comprising of advising lenders and borrowers in relation to financial transactions, inter alia asset finance, project finance, lease finance and property finance, and international debt issues.

Additionally, the firm also has a number of specialised practice groups which brings together the skills, expertise and experience of the firm's lawyers. This enables Wiersholm, Mellbye & Bech to offer its clients quality advice in matters such as commercial property, construction, EC and competition law, energy law, corporate, taxation, intellectual property, copyright, media, information technology and telecoms, maritime and transportation law, insurance law, labour law as well as security and stock exchange.

Additionally, Wiersholm, Mellbye & Bech handles litigation and disputes in a wide range of commercial areas.

WIKBORG REIN

KRONPRINSESSE MÄRTHAS PLASS 1, PO BOX 1513 VIKA 0117 OSLO

Telephone: +47 22 82 75 00
Fax: +47 22 82 75 01
E-mail: oslo@wr.no
Website: www.wr.no

Languages
Cantonese, English, French, German, Indonesian, Malay, Mandarin, Russian, the Scandinavian languages, Spanish, Taiwanese

Other offices
Bergen, Kobe, London, Shanghai, Singapore

Number of lawyers 152
at this office 109

Member
Den Norske Advokatforeningen

CATEGORIES OF WORK

Corporate finance
John A Rein, Einar J Greve

Trade and industry
Morten Goller, Jan L Backer

Shipping/offshore
Trond Eilertsen, Øystein Meland

Energy/natural resources
Jarle Erik Sandvik, Per Magne Strandborg

Technology, media and telecoms
Torleif P Dahl

Labour legislation
Jan L Backer

Intellectual property law
Gunnar Meyer, Torleif P Dahl

Competition law (including EU and EEA law)
Morten Goller, Dag Mjaaland

Environmental law
Susanne Munch Thore, Trond Eilertsen

Accounting/tax/duties
Marianne Iversen, Olav E Klingenberg

Company law
Arne Didrik Kjørnæs, Susanne Munch Thore

Insolvency and restructuring
Leif Petter Madsen, Marius M Gisvold

Banking and finance
Bernhard Haukali, Stein Pettersen

Real estate
Anne Sofie Bjørkholt, Ola Haugen

Litigation and dispute resolution
Dag Steinfeld, Per Magne Ristvedt

Insolvency/restructuring
Leif Petter Madsen, Manüs M Gisvold

THE FIRM

Wikborg Rein is an international law firm based in Oslo with offices in Bergen, Kobe, London, Shanghai and Singapore.

The establishment of offices in Kobe in 1965, London in 1987, Singapore in 2000, and Shanghai in 2002 have contributed to the development of its international business. Today, with some 150 lawyers Wikborg Rein is one of the leading law firms in Norway.

The firm's traditions complement its modern approach to the management of its resources and the provision of advice and other legal services. As a leading firm in the area of information technology and management systems, the firm provides services of the highest quality in a cost-efficient manner.

Having a thorough understanding of the client's business, combined with the highest professional standards, the firm ensures that each client receives the best possible legal assistance.

AREAS OF PRACTICE

The firm's practice is broadly based, serving both international clients in Norway, and Norwegian clients domestically and abroad. Wikborg Rein's internal structure is organised for the specific purpose of serving clients in the following areas of business: trade and industry; banking and finance; energy and natural resources; technology, media and telecommunications; shipping, offshore and transport; corporate finance; real estate; litigation and dispute resolution.

The firm has extensive experience of the application of European law and advises on all aspects relevant to Norway's position as a member of the EEA but not the EU.

Within Norway the firm has pioneered links between business, academic research and the development of relevant legislation. This has enabled it to assist clients in negotiating with and lobbying government authorities and in developing legal practices in rapidly expanding areas of business.

OMAN

Population	2.8 million
Number of lawyers	n/a
Professional title	Lawyer
Currency	Omani rial (OR)
Index	

The Sultunate of Oman is the oldest independent state in the Arab world. It is in a strategically important location, at the mouth of the Arabian Gulf, bordered by the United Arab Emirates (UAE), Saudi Arabia and Yemen. It lies on important shipping routes for crude oil. The capital, Muscat, is on the Gulf of Oman coast.

Oman has been Islamic since the seventh century. Most people follow the Ibadi sect of Islam, created as a result of one of the first schisms in the religion.

The country has come under Portuguese, Persian and British influence, but has been controlled by the Al Bu Said dynasty since 1749. From 1932 to 1970, the country was led by Sultan Said bin Taimur. His unpopularity led to a revolt in Dhofar in 1965. In 1970, he was overthrown by his son Qaboos bin Said.

The Sultan is head of state and prime minister, as well as minister of foreign affairs, finance and defence. Educated in Britain, since coming to power the Sultan has initiated a wide-ranging modernisation programme. In 1981, he set up a consultative council, the Majlis al Dawla, to allow greater public participation in government. In October 2003, for the first time every citizen over the age of 21 was allowed to vote in elections to this council. For the last decade the council has had 80 members, who review social and economic legislation and help draft development plans.

In 1996, a 'basic law' was passed. It created an upper chamber called the Council of State. Along with the consultative council, this forms the Council of Oman, which spearheads the modernisation programme.

BILLING

Rates charged by law firms in Oman range from €150 an hour for an assistant to €300 an hour for a partner. Success or contingency fees for litigation are prohibited.

MARKETING

Advertising is permitted, and although there are no restrictions, it tends to be fairly conservative.

IN-HOUSE LAWYERS

In house lawyers are employed mainly by the financial, insurance and oil and gas sectors. They can appear in court for cases worth less than €5,000.

ECONOMIC CLIMATE

In common with other Gulf nations, Oman is heavily dependent on oil, which accounts for 40% of GDP and contributes 80% of export earnings. But only around 2% of the 2.8 million population is employed in this sector, with many still relying on agriculture and fishing for their livelihoods. Average incomes are modest compared with many neighbouring states.

Oman is a member of the World Trade Organisation but does not belong to OPEC, or the Organisation of Arab Petroleum Exporting Countries (OAPEC). Petroleum Development Oman LLC (PDO) holds 90% of all oil reserves, and is the second-largest employer after the government. It is a consortium 60% owned by the Omani government and 34% owned by Shell, with other oil companies holding small stakes.

Oman does not have the huge oil resources of some of its neighbours. The government is increasingly exploiting natural gas reserves as oil supplies become depleted. It hopes to reduce the oil sector's share of GDP to 9% by 2020.

Privatisation, as well as diversification away from dependence on oil revenues, is a priority of the sixth five-year plan, launched in 2000. Job creation for Omanis in the private sector and the development of the country's interior are being promoted. Petrochemical and fertiliser production are being encouraged. New generating plants are under construction to meet the rapidly rising demand for electric power, while the sector is being privatised. The service sector is playing an increasing role in the economy, and tourism is being developed in the Muscat area and at historic interior sites.

To encourage foreign investment, companies in certain industries may be eligible for five-year tax holidays. The government has been trying to attract foreign investors into tourism, light industry and electric power generation in particular. Japan, Britain and the UAE are key trading partners. In January 2003, Oman and five other nations in the Gulf Co-operation Council created a customs union. Full economic union is planned for 2005 and a common currency is scheduled for 2010.

LEGAL MARKET

The Oman legal market is small, but a few international law firms have offices there, and individuals in these firms have carved out good reputations. **Trowers & Hamlins** has operated in Oman for more than 20 years. In addition to offices in the region in Abu Dhabi, Dubai, Bahrain and Cairo, it

The largest firms

1	Al Alawi Mansoor Jamal & Co	17
2	Trowers & Hamlins	12
3	Denton Wilde Sapte	9
4	Adham & Associates	6
5	Curtis, Mallet-Prevost, Colt & Mosle LLP	2
	Rouhani & Partners	2
	Said Al-Shahry Law Office in association with Richards Butler	2

These figures represent the total number of lawyers in this country only, and have been supplied by the firms themselves. The figures should be accurate as at 1 January 2004.

has associations with firms in Yemen and Jordan. The firm also has informal correspondent relationships with law firms throughout the region. Partner Sean Angle is respected for his local knowledge and his contributions to British-Omani relations.

Denton Wilde Sapte has operated in Oman since 1998, when it acquired the business and client base of *Fox & Gibbons*, which had been in the country for 17 years. The firm is increasingly gaining a reputation for its commercial practice, where head of office Andrew Watson has made a mark. Clients are impressed by the firm's expertise in Arabic and shari'a law and its access to key players in the oil and gas sector.

The Dubai offices of a number of international firms take on work in Oman. They tend to leave the day-to-day commercial business to the firms with local offices, and concentrate instead on project finance and privatisation. **Allen & Overy**'s Bimal Desai is frequently in Muscat, as are lawyers from **Clifford Chance LLP**. **Clyde & Co** also advises on major Oman matters from Dubai. Operating from Abu Dhabi, **Simmons & Simmons** also attracts a steady stream of Omani business.

Curtis, Mallet-Prevost, Colt & Mosle LLP has a special role in Oman, acting for the government on a wide range of issues. Bruce Mullins runs the Muscat office and calls in specialist lawyers from New York on a project basis. The firm does not actively go out and look for other work, as this may lead to a conflict of interest with its role for the government.

Among local firms, one of the names that crops up most often is **Said Al-Shahry Law Office in association with Richards Butler**. It works closely with other leading international firms, among them **Linklaters**, **Allen & Overy**, **Norton Rose**, **Jones Day Gouldens** and **Shearman & Sterling LLP**. Said al Shahry is widely known for his legal ability as well as his unrivalled connections in Omani society. **Al Alawi Mansoor Jamal & Co** is another prominent local firm, where Mansoor Jamal himself is particularly well regarded.

Adham & Associates undertakes local work, including commercial and employment business. It is presently in the process of reorganising and changing its name. **Gulf Consultants** is a unique firm in Oman, focusing only on intellectual property law. It represents hundreds of clients in trade mark registrations, ranging from multinational corporations to individual entrepreneurs.

BANKING AND FINANCE

Oman's banking and finance business is largely left to locally-based firms. Here too, just a few firms dominate.

Denton Wilde Sapte represented Majan International Bank SAOC in relation to its merger with Bank Dhofar Al Omani Al Fransi. The firm has also advised a major Omani bank on its participation in a $50m syndicated facility to fund the acquisition of energy assets in the Gulf region. It advised Oman International Bank on its participation in $100m facility for Al Ahli Bank of Kuwait, and on financing Omani Government Development bonds.

Trowers & Hamlins advised Oman's largest bank, Bank Muscat, on a $455m unsecured bond issue in 2003. This was the first bond issue of this type carried out by the bank, and the bonds are now listed on the Muscat securities market. The firm also acted for the Bank Muscat in creating an investment fund to issue units to the public. Andrew Rae led the banking team acting for the National Bank of Oman in the private placement of debt, and in arranging a loan from the Oman Arab Bank and the Arab Bank plc to United Gulf Energy Resources, to finance a new drilling rig.

Al Alawi Mansoor Jamal & Co acts as the retained legal counsel for a number of leading banks, including Alliance Housing Bank, National Bank of Oman, Bank Muscat, Habib Bank Ltd and a number of other finance companies in Oman. **Al Alawi Mansoor Jamal & Co** advised a local bank on a $18m facility agreement and has organised a restructuring for indebtedness worth around $50m. The firm also acts in Oman for some large international banks, among them Citibank, Gulf International Bank, ANZ Grindlays, International Finance Corporation, HSBC and Commercial Bank of Dubai.

Curtis, Mallet-Prevost, Colt & Mosle LLP was appointed legal adviser to Oman's Ministry of Finance for 2000-02. It reviewed financing documents related to various projects with local and international banks. This included procurements for the Ministry of Defence.

The banking practice at **Said Al-Shahry Law Office in association with Richards Butler** has been expanding rapidly, guided by the highly respected Alastair Neale, who spent 12 years as counsel to the Arab Banking Corporation in Bahrain. The firm arranged a $150m syndicated facility agreement for Gulf International Bank and conducted due diligence for ABN Amro on a credit derivatives transaction. The firm is retained by the Bank Dhofar Al Omani Al Fransi, and assisted with the bank's merger with Majan International Bank in 2003.

From its Abu Dhabi office, **Simmons & Simmons** has during the year acted for banks across five jurisdictions, on an oilfield drilling deal worth up to $100m. The primary borrower is based

BANKING AND FINANCE

DENTON WILDE SAPTE ✪
TROWERS & HAMLINS

Al Alawi Mansoor Jamal & Co
Curtis, Mallet-Prevost, Colt & Mosle LLP ✪
Said Al-Shahry Law Office in association with Richards Butler

Firms are listed A-Z in tiers which are ranked in order of priority
✪ *Indicates firm displays contact details at the end of this chapter.*

in Oman. From Dubai, **Clyde & Co** has been advising on an OR21.4m (€47.3m) listing of a major ship repair company on the Omani stock exchange.

CORPORATE AND COMMERCIAL

After expanding rapidly in Oman in recent years, **Denton Wilde Sapte** has consolidated its reputation for corporate and commercial work in particular. Partner Andrew Watson and assistant Lara Shelton receive praise, with clients noting their ability to keep abreast of the rapid changes in commercial law in the Sultunate. One client described the duo's work in areas such as partnership agreements and registering companies as a 'star performance'. It is the retained law firm for Oman International Bank, advising on all aspects of corporate and commercial law. The firm represents a large number of Omani public companies including National Mineral Water Co, Oman Textile Mills Co and National Aluminium Products Co, advising on regulatory maters and Oman's new corporate governance regime. Among significant corporate deals this year, the firm acted for an oil major in negotiating a joint venture agreement with NPC of Iran. The deal related to a £1.5bn petrochemicals project. It also executed the first public-to-private conversions in Oman for Al Khuwair Development Services Co and Al Amal Industries Co.

Trowers & Hamlins has also been expanding its corporate practice, spearheaded by resident managing partner Sean Angle. The firm is well known locally for redrafting Oman's company law. Clients single out partner Andrew Rae and lawyer Adrian Jones for their corporate skills and for their flexibility in a highly bureaucratic environment. The firm acted in the sale of BP Group's stake in BP Oman, and has continued to act for the newly named Oman Oil Marketing Company (the former BP entity) in its change of name and rebranding throughout Oman. Other major corporate deals in 2003 included a public offering of 1.2 million shares (capitalised at approximately $3.7m) for Hotel Management Company International (HMCI), and its subsequent listing on Muscat Securities Market. HMCI owns a new landmark hotel in Oman, the Chedi Towers. The firm also assisted Travelex plc with its first business venture in the Middle East, establishing its money exchange business in Oman.

Al Alawi Mansoor Jamal & Co advises public joint stock companies on regulatory issues and is also used for shareholder-related matters.

Said Al-Shahry Law Office in association with Richards Butler is the largest wholly owned Omani law firm. Its corporate department, headed by Alastair Neale, attracts a substantial amount of work. In 2003, the firm acted for the Oman Oil Company in the acquisition of a 10% share in a Spanish Company, and for Matrah Cold Stores, forming a company to acquire six retail outlets. It also established a representative office for the Europa Aerospace Defence Company. Clients praise the firm for its 'one-stop-shop' approach to corporate work and its lawyers' ability to cut through red tape.

CORPORATE AND COMMERCIAL

DENTON WILDE SAPTE ✪
TROWERS & HAMLINS

Al Alawi Mansoor Jamal & Co
Said Al-Shahry Law Office in association with Richards Butler

---

Adham & Associates

Firms are listed A-Z in tiers which are ranked in order of priority
✪ Indicates firm displays contact details at the end of this chapter.

DISPUTE RESOLUTION

A new Civil and Commercial Procedure Law was introduced in 2002. This set up a Supreme Court and tightened up and extended the rules of civil procedure. Law firms have welcomed the increasingly sophisticated judiciary and court system, and some have taken on extra staff as a result.

Denton Wilde Sapte is advising Al Jizzi Electrical Contractors against KPMG for a claim of RO 6.6m (€14.6m) for compensation resulting from alleged professional negligence. The firm successfully acted for Jyoti Structures Ltd against International Construction Co LLC. It represented Hotels Management International Co in proceedings against its former deputy chairman, and Salalah Mills against Yayah Costain Co LLC in action relating to the construction of a flour mill.

Trowers & Hamlins is involved in a wide range of dispute resolution work. This is an expanding area of practice for the firm, because of a rising number of claims in Oman. Employment litigation is a particularly fast growing area of the practice. The firm handles employment disputes for several Omani oil companies, including Petroleum Development Oman LLC. It is also acting for a major Omani bank in international debt recovery actions, and has recently represented Volvo cars in a case involving a former distributor. Insurance is another busy area: the firm successfully defended Muscat Insurance Company at the Supreme Court in a case involving a $1m claim related to a factory fire. The firm also represents the London reinsurance market in Oman.

Al Alawi Mansoor Jamal & Co has one of the largest teams of litigators appearing before the Omani courts, handling disputes in the banking, maritime and other commercial sectors. The firm is currently defending a RO200m (€441m) claim for alleged unjustified termination of a longstanding agency, and defending actions for damages filed against an international auditing firm.

Said Al-Shahry Law Office in association with Richards Butler is prominent in dispute resolution and arbitration matters. Abbas al Siddig is carving out a reputation in litigation. In 2003, the firm worked on high-profile banking cases, and acted for Matrah Oil Stores against Sultan Shipping.

DISPUTE RESOLUTION

DENTON WILDE SAPTE ✪
TROWERS & HAMLINS

Al Alawi Mansoor Jamal & Co
Said Al-Shahry Law Office in association with Richards Butler

---

Firms are listed A-Z in tiers which are ranked in order of priority
✪ Indicates firm displays contact details at the end of this chapter.

PROJECT FINANCE AND PRIVATISATION

The international law firms operating from Dubai take a particular interest in project finance and privatisation work in Oman. There is plenty of work in the oil and gas sector, as well as the expansion of ports and the airport. Privatisation in the electricity and telecoms sectors is also attracting major firms.

From its Dubai office, **Clifford Chance LLP** has worked on the Sohar Refinery Project. The firm acted for the project company and its shareholders, including the Government of Oman, on the development and financing of a new $1.2bn greenfield refinery. Financing is to be provided by a syndicate of international banks. The firm has also advised on the operation of the Sohar Industrial Port complex. Another major deal was for Oman Polypropylene, where **Clifford Chance LLP** acted for the project company and its sponsors on the development of a $300m plant. The firm has been instructed by the Government of Oman and Omantel, on Omantel's proposed IPO. It is also helping introduce Private Finance Initiative (PFI) deals into Oman, based on the UK model. In 2003, it represented one of the shortlisted bidders to develop a military college structured on a PFI/PPP basis.

Denton Wilde Sapte is among Oman-based firms with high reputations in project finance. It is advising the government on the law relating to the privatisation of the country's electricity and related water sectors.

Trowers & Hamlins also has wide project finance experience. This area of its practice is led by Andrew Rae. It is active in the oil and gas sector as well as winning work from the government. As general counsel for the BP group, it completed the multi-million dollar sale of the oil giant's stake in BP Oman to the state-owned Oman Oil Company.

From its Dubai base, **Allen & Overy** is active in project finance in Oman. Recent deals have included acting for Oman LNG on its multi-billion dollar two-train LNG project at Qalhal, its $1.3bn

PROJECT FINANCE AND PRIVATISATION

CLIFFORD CHANCE LLP
DENTON WILDE SAPTE ✪
TROWERS & HAMLINS

Allen & Overy
Said Al-Shahry Law Office in association with Richards Butler
Shearman & Sterling LLP
Simmons & Simmons
White & Case LLP

Al Alawi Mansoor Jamal & Co
Curtis, Mallet-Prevost, Colt & Mosle LLP ✪

Firms are listed A-Z in tiers which are ranked in order of priority
✪ Indicates firm displays contact details at the end of this chapter.

refinancing of the 1997 project finance debt, and its current expansion project. The firm acted for the bidder on the Sharqiya Power Project and on the Salalah Power Project. **Allen & Overy** has also handled a number of privatisations. It advised the Oman Gas Company on the privatisation of the Omani gas system and the financing of certain new pipelines, and acted for Oman Aviation Services, helping to negotiate long-term concession agreements following the privatisation of Oman's airports. Along with **Clifford Chance LLP**, the firm is advising the government on the PFI concession for the proposed Joint Services Military Training College project.

Said Al-Shahry Law Office in association with Richards Butler's Said al Shahry and Alastair Neale have been active in project financing and privatisation deals. Recent work includes the $1bn Sohar Refinery Project financing and a $600m third-train LNG project financing for Oman LNG. The firm has acted for Dhofar Power Company on the privatisation of electricity generation and has worked on the privatisation of oil distribution networks.

Shearman & Sterling LLP has worked from London and regional offices including Abu Dhabi, on project finance and privatisations. The firm has advised on tenders for projects in the $500m to $750m range, using local firms to advise on specific legal issues. Since 2000, it has been retained for the Barka Power and Desalination Project, and it is currently working on the Salawa integrated power system privatisation.

Simmons & Simmons also works on project finance in Oman. From his Abu Dhabi office, partner Roger Clarke has been involved in advising the project sponsor on a large oil smelter project in Oman.

From Saudi Arabia and London, **White & Case LLP** represents many international banks in project finance deals. The firm acted for Société Générale as lead arranger on the $77.5m debt financing for constructing and equipping a container port facility for Salalah Port Services Company. This is a joint venture between the government of Oman, Sea-Land and Maersk. The firm also represented the arranger and lenders on a $30m financing for an extension of the facility.

Al Alawi Mansoor Jamal & Co is currently acting as local counsel to the government on setting up and financing the Sohar Oil Refinery Project and a polypropylene plant. It is also advising an international investor developing a methanol plant in Oman and a consortium of investors on the establishment of an aluminium smelter plant. Another project involves advising a consortium of investors on setting up a plant for the production of urea formaldehyde.

Curtis, Mallet-Prevost, Colt & Mosle LLP undertakes a substantial amount of project finance work for the Omani government. Since 1998, it has been advising on the Muscat Wastewater Project, which recently resulted in the formation of a government-owned project company. In 2003, the firm continued to advise on this project. It also advised on wastewater projects in the cities of Salalah and al Masarrat. Following the appointment of PricewaterhouseCoopers by the Oman Telecommunications Company (Omantel), the firm was appointed in June 1999 as legal adviser for the privatisation of payphone and calling card operations in Oman.

SHIPPING

Dubai-based **Clyde & Co** has a busy shipping and maritime practice in the region, acting for cargo insurers as well as carriers and P&I clubs. The firm recently represented insurers over an $80m claim in Oman, relating to the loss of military defence equipment when a vessel sank.

SHIPPING

CLYDE & CO
TROWERS & HAMLINS

Al Alawi Mansoor Jamal & Co
Curtis, Mallet-Prevost, Colt & Mosle LLP ✪
Denton Wilde Sapte ✪

Firms are listed A-Z in tiers which are ranked in order of priority
✪ Indicates firm displays contact details at the end of this chapter.

Trowers & Hamlins is retained counsel for Salalah Port Services Co. In 2003, the firm acted successfully for its client in litigation in the Omani courts over a sunken vessel and liabilities relating to the subsequent salvage operation. Very few maritime actions ever come before the courts in Oman, so it is significant that under a team led by Majid al Tokay, **Trowers & Hamlins** notched up success here. The firm also advises Salalah Port Services on financing, where the team is led by Andrew Rae.

Al Alawi Mansoor Jamal & Co acts primarily on litigation matters for Maersk and other shipping companies whose vessels come into Oman, while **Denton Wilde Sapte** also concentrates on marine litigation, although it does also undertake some marine insurance work.

Curtis, Mallet-Prevost, Colt & Mosle LLP is active in the shipping sector. In 2002, the firm was appointed legal adviser to the Ministry of Finance for the development of a national shipping company to acquire and operate a national fleet of LNG carriers. Work continued in 2003 for subsequent corporate development and financing. In 2002, the firm was also appointed by the Ministry of Finance for the acquisition of a 75% interest in Prestige Navigation & Shipping Company (now Oasis Navigation and Shipping), and for the joint ownership of a new LNG carrier with Mitsui OSK Lines and Mitsui & Co. The acquisition has been completed and work on the project continued in 2003.

CURTIS, MALLET-PREVOST, COLT & MOSLE LLP

SUITE 48, QURUM PLAZA
108 AL WALLAJ STREET
PO BOX 200 JEWEL BEACH
134 MUSCAT

Telephone: +968 564 495
Fax: +968 564 497
E-mail: info@cm-p.com
Website: www.cm-p.com

Languages
English

Other offices
Frankfurt, Houston, London, Mexico City, Milan, New York, Newark, Paris, Stamford, Washington DC

Number of lawyers 178
at this office 2

Contacts
Robert J Gruendel, Bruce Mullins

Member
Oman Chamber of Commerce; American Business Council of Oman; Maritime Law Association

CATEGORIES OF WORK

- Infrastructure and project finance
- Privatisation
- Shipping
- Port development and operation
- Transnational joint ventures
- Power generation
- Petroleum and petrochemical contracts
- Water resource concessions
- LNG sales
- Construction contracts
- Equipment sales and leaseback
- Public bidding
- Environmental waste concessions
- Aviation finance

DENTON WILDE SAPTE

FIRST FLOOR OFFICE SUITE 114
HATAT HOUSE
AL NAHDA STREET
PO BOX 3552 RUWI
112 MUSCAT

Telephone: +968 573 000
Fax: +968 573 097
E-mail: muscat@dentonwildesapte.com
Website: www.dentonwildesapte.com

Languages
Arabic, English, French, German

Other offices
Abu Dhabi, Almaty, Beijing, Cairo, Dubai, Gibraltar, Hong Kong, Istanbul, London, Milton Keynes, Moscow, Paris, Singapore, Tashkent, Tokyo

Number of lawyers 876
at this office 9

Contact
Andrew Watson

CATEGORIES OF WORK

- Banking and finance
- Commercial litigation and arbitration
- Corporate and commercial
- Energy
- IP and IT
- Infrastructure projects
- Insurance
- International projects
- Maritime regulatory

POLAND

Population	39 million
Number of lawyers	7,000
Professional title	Adwokat; Radca prawny
Currency	Polish zloty (PLN)

Index

Following an unexpectedly positive referendum result in June 2003 (59% turnout and 77% Yes vote), all eyes in Poland are now firmly fixed on accession to the European Union in May. All other economic and political worries have been put on hold until then.

Accounting for almost half the population and half the GDP of all ten acceding countries combined, Poland is by far the weightiest of the new entrants, a fact that has not gone unnoticed by the Polish people. Polish officials in Brussels, spurred on by a people demanding great things from the EU, are already carving out a reputation for being stubborn and difficult, particularly concerning farm subsidies and voting rights. The resulting antagonism between Poland and some member states, most significantly Germany, has not been helped by Poland's strong pro-Americanism (Poland, as a member of Nato, committed troops to Iraq).

Nevertheless, though Poland eagerly announces itself as champion of the East, the country has the least to boast about at home. A sluggish economy is presided over by a deeply unpopular government, crafted from an alliance of former communists. Beyond Warsaw, much of the country is impoverished and lacking infrastructure.

Many commentators also expect that Poland may be in for a shock in May, with accession bringing many more headaches than gains at first. If so, the government is unlikely to survive next year's general election. Progress in completing all the economic, administrative and legislative reforms required for EU membership is seriously delayed. Poland's desire to adopt the euro in 2007 would appear to be a dream, with a date somewhere in the next decade being touted as more realistic.

BILLING

Continued lack of demand, coupled with serious over-supply is proving ideal for clients. Though international firms may continue to post bold headline rates of between €300 and €400 per hour for partners, and between €200 and €300 per hour for associates, in reality firms may well work for less than half as much. Similarly, domestic firms quoting healthy hourly rates in the range €100 to €300 per hour will probably work for half or a third of those rates.

Increasingly, the market is witnessing very competitive capped fees and firms are vying to undercut each other. Whilst significant work remains scarce, major international firms are foregoing profits in an effort to attract clients. Work that may once have cost €100,000 in the late 1990s may now be purchased for one-fifth or one-sixth of that.

MARKETING

Advertising remains forbidden for both adwokats and radca prawny. However, the association of radca prawny is far less stringent in its reading of the rules than the Bar Association for adwokats, and indirect advertisements are permitted. Most firms have websites.

IN-HOUSE LAWYERS

There are no restrictions on in-house lawyers and they are free to join the Bar Association or association of radca prawny.

LEGAL MARKET

Another torrid year for law firms in Poland, with rumours abounding of office closures and the imminent withdrawal of big-name firms. For the most part though the rumours have failed to come to fruition and everyone now seems content to ride out the storm, in the hope that May 2004 will bring improved conditions.

The problem has not been so much a complete lack of work (there were some significant transactions in 2003 involving Netia, Elektrim, Lockheed Martin and Bank Austria Creditanstalt), but rather a market that is grossly over-saturated. The mass privatisations of the 1990s have long since passed and it is difficult to see where enough significant new work will come from, although the privatisation of the energy sector is often mentioned.

Though the market looked very much brighter at the close of 2003 than it did after the second quarter, many firms were said to have suffered considerable losses. Firms have reacted in different ways to the difficult conditions: **Allen & Overy** continued to downsize for the second year running; **Linklaters** was criticised for lowering its fees; and **White & Case – W. Danilowicz, W. Jurcewicz i Wspólnicy Kancelaria Prawna sp.K** adjusted downwards the salaries paid to associates.

Top-end domestic firms have also been hit. **Wardynski & Partners** is looking both to the east

The largest firms

1	Domanski Zakrzewski Palinka	92
2	Andrzej Tokaj Magnusson Wahlin Qvist Stanbrook i Wspólnicy Spólka Komandytowa	75
3	Soltysinski Kawecki & Szlezak Legal Advisors	64
4	Dewey Ballantine Grzesiak Limited Partnership	60
5	Linklaters	58
6	CMS Cameron McKenna	57
7	Baker & McKenzie	50
8	White & Case – W. Danilowicz, W. Jurcewicz i Wspólnicy Kancelaria Prawna sp.K	48
9	Wierzbowski i Wspólnicy	46
10	Weil, Gotshal & Manges	44
11	TGC Corporate Lawyers	39
	Wardynski & Partners	39
13	Clifford Chance	37
14	Gide Loyrette Nouel	36
15	Chadbourne & Parke Polska Sp. z o.o., Wujek, Radzikowski, Szubielska i Wspólnicy. Spólka Komandytowa	35
	Janusz Kasprzak & Partners	35
17	Salans	33
18	Brockhuis Schnell Jurczak Prusak Sp. k.	32
	Rödl, Korpalski Kancelaria Prawna sp.k.	32
20	Allen & Overy	30
	Drzewiecki, Tomaszek & Wspólnicy Spólka Jawna	30
	Miller, Canfield, W. Babicki i Wspólnicy Sp.k	30
23	Forystek Góralczyk Rychlicki Budzowska Fiutowski Jamorski Adwokaci i Radcowie Prawni	28
	Studnicki, Pleszka, Cwiakalski, Górski LLP	28
25	Beata Gessel & Partners	26

These figures represent the total number of lawyers in this country only, and have been supplied by the firms themselves. The figures should be accurate as at 1 January 2004.

and to the west for further work: strengthening ties with firms in Belarus, Lithuania and Ukraine; and opening a Brussels office in alliance with firms from Slovakia, the Czech Republic and Hungary. There have been a number of serious fractions among Polish firms, with senior partners departing from both **Wardynski & Partners** and **Beata Gessel & Partners**. Whether these experienced partners will set up independently remains to be seen, as does the future of the former *Altheimer & Gray* office in Warsaw which, in January 2004, announced that it had reached agreement with US firm **Chadbourne & Parke LLP** to become **Chadbourne & Parke Polska Sp. z o.o., Wujek, Radzikowski, Szubielska i Wspólnicy. Spólka Komandytowa**. At the time of writing it was not clear how the new partnership would fare but the office continues to retain some of the most prized talents in the market.

The troubles afflicting the legal wings of the global accountancy firms have also impacted on the Polish market. Both **Domanski Zakrzewski Palinka** and **Wierzbowski i Wspólnicy** are having to redefine former relationships with PwC and Ernst & Young respectively. German MDPs **Haarmann Hemmelrath** and **Rödl & Partner GbR** have also struggled, and, due to organisational changes, the latter now operates under two names in Poland: **Rödl, Bramorski Kancelaria Prawna sp.k.** in Wroclaw and **Rödl, Korpalski Kancelaria Prawna sp.k.** in Warsaw, Poznan and Cracow.

BANKING AND FINANCE

Although better than 2002, the continuing global slump has left firms short of banking and finance work. When work has materialised the competition has been fierce and the biggest international firms have tended to win, although domestic firms have won instructions to carry out standard regulatory work. A number of deals are on-going from 2002.

In terms of advising lenders **Allen & Overy** has had the most successful year of any firm in Poland. The firm has so seriously downsized its Warsaw office in recent years that a wealth of work advising lead banks on various multimillion euro syndicated loan facilities may have overshadowed other practice areas. Besides other deals the firm advised a syndicate of banks led by WestLB in relation to a €500m syndicated dual currency loan for PKN Orlen. Other clients include JPMorganChase and Unicredito Italiano Polonia. The highly-rated Arkadiusz Pedzich heads the department.

Few doubt the dominance of **Allen & Overy** and **Clifford Chance** in loan financing work. Even though **Clifford Chance** undertook very little finance work on the debt side in 2003, the global reputation of the firm is such that it is still seen as the leader in the field, particularly for insolvency and restructuring work. Head of the department

BANKING AND FINANCE

ALLEN & OVERY ✪
CLIFFORD CHANCE

Baker & McKenzie ✪
Dewey Ballantine Grzesiak Limited Partnership ✪
Linklaters ✪
Weil, Gotshal & Manges ✪
White & Case – W. Danilowicz, W. Jurcewicz i Wspólnicy Kancelaria Prawna sp.K

CMS Cameron McKenna ✪
Chadbourne & Parke Polska Sp. z o.o., Wujek, Radzikowski, Szubielska i Wspólnicy. Spólka Komandytowa
Gide Loyrette Nouel ✪
Hogan & Hartson M. Jamka, A. Galos, and Partners, LP ✪
Lovells ✪
Norton Rose, Piotr Strawa and Partners, Limited Partnership
Salans
Soltysinski Kawecki & Szlezak Legal Advisors ✪
Wardynski & Partners ✪

Domanski Zakrzewski Palinka ✪
Nörr Stiefenhofer Lutz ✪
Wierzbowski i Wspólnicy ✪

Beata Gessel & Partners ✪
Beiten Burkhardt K. Rastawicki Sp.K. ✪
Gleiss Lutz ✪
Miller, Canfield, W. Babicki i Wspólnicy Sp.k

Firms are listed A-Z in tiers which are ranked in order of priority
✪ Indicates firm displays contact details at the end of this chapter.

Grzegorz Namiotkiewicz is the finance lawyer most recommended by competitors. The firm advises Merrill Lynch and has advised BPH BPK on a number of acquisition facilities, including a €30m loan facility for an international corporate group.

Recent finance work at **Baker & McKenzie** has not been as high profile as might be expected from a firm with a fine reputation in this area. Nevertheless, Krzysztof Koreniewski's finance team has not been idle, advising LOT airlines on a €75m syndicated loan facility, advising GCH Manhattan on the raising of funds for Gdansk Shopping Mall, as well as advising various other international lenders.

Dewey Ballantine Grzesiak Limited Partnership advised more borrowers in high-profile finance deals than any other firm in 2003. On the sellers' side the firm represented Lockheed Martin on the largest investment ever made in Poland, the $3.5bn sale of military aircraft to the Polish government and its $6bn off-set contract. The firm also advised PKN Orlen on its arrangements for the €500m syndicated loan.

Acting for borrowers and lenders, **Linklaters**' banking and finance team is the largest in Poland. Major deals in which the firm acted, including advising TP SA as borrower in a €400m syndicated loan, demonstrate that it has now secured a leading position in the Polish market. Lenders for whom the firm acts include Bank Przemyslowo, ING Bank, Aareal Bank, and PKO Bank.

Weil, Gotshal & Manges advised Netia in the prominent $850m restructuring of that company's debt. The firm also advised private equity house Hicks, Muse, Furst and Tate in a €110m acquisition financing connected with the takeover of a group of cable companies.

Though **White & Case – W. Danilowicz, W. Jurcewicz i Wspólnicy Kancelaria Prawna sp.K** counts Bank of America, Dresdner Bank, HSBC Bank, Credit Agricole and other banks among its clients, the banking and finance team had a comparatively quiet 2003. The firm advised BPH PBK in its $24m credit agreements with a subsidiary of Advent. Practice head Jacek Czabanski is recommended.

The finance team at **CMS Cameron McKenna** has significant experience in advising lenders, particularly on project finance-related issues, such as BPH PBK in connection with a €180m secured loan facility for the acquisition of shopping galleries. The firm also advised Millennium Bank on the multi-million euro restructuring of Daewoo FSO, a high-risk deal because there was no investor backing the transaction.

Lacking the global resources of the largest firms, the banking and finance team at **Chadbourne & Parke Polska Sp. z o.o., Wujek, Radzikowski, Szubielska i Wspólnicy. Spólka Komandytowa** has traditionally struggled to compete in this area. Instead the firm has sought to operate a niche practice, advising on troublesome and complex issues. The firm advised Daewoo FSO during its restructuring, an instruction that required the firm to liaise between the Polish and Korean governments.

Gide Loyrette Nouel represents French lender Cetelem SA as it seeks to acquire both a Polish banking licence and a Polish bank. The firm is also acting as a counsel to Exide Technologies as it seeks to establish collateral in order to secure a €400m loan from an international consortium of banks.

Hogan & Hartson M. Jamka, A. Galos, and Partners, LP acts for lenders and borrowers. Smithfield Food is a major client and the firm is advising the US company on a number of issues including a PLN48m (€10.4m) revolving credit agreement with BPH PBK.

Clients of **Lovells** include the EBRD and Tel-Energo. The firm was recently involved in the establishment of a specialised Polish bank for a French car producer. The firm also advised a consortium of banks in relation to Polish security documents for a PLN400m (€84.8m) loan.

Grzegorz Dyczkowski, an associate at **Allen & Overy** left in 2003 to head the three-lawyer banking and finance team at **Norton Rose, Piotr Strawa and Partners, Limited Partnership**. The firm counts finance as one of its core focuses and recently advised ING Bank Slaski SA in its capacity as security agent for a €50m issue of euro notes in relation to the Netia debt restructure.

Banking and finance at **Salans** is often closely related to the firm's project finance work for clients such as French developer Apsys. Other clients include Raiffeisen Zentralbank AG and New York hedge funds.

Wardynski & Partners acts mainly for a domestic banking clientele, though it also receives referrals from firms in London and New York. Ewa Butkiewicz, former head of BRE Bank's legal department, is recommended for her experience of finance in Poland.

Domanski Zakrzewski Palinka acted for BRE Bank in the debt restructure of Impexmetal. Commerzbank is also a client.

Banking and finance work is a traditional strength for **Nörr Stiefenhofer Lutz** throughout CEE. Clients are predominantly German banks and include, Bankhaus Woelbern, HVB Group, and HSH Nordbank.

Wierzbowski i Wspólnicy has experience in bank finance restructuring work. The firm has also advised on the creation of e-banking systems.

CAPITAL MARKETS

Another slow year with some suggesting that the practice area has become something of a white-elephant, and others seeing growth in the last quarter as a positive sign for the future.

Allen & Overy advised the Ministry of Finance on a €5bn EMTN programme and worked for JPMorganChase on bonds issued under the Netia debt restructuring programme. Partner Jacek Jonak is highly recommended for his experience and reputation.

Also advising the Polish government on eurobond issues was **Clifford Chance** who otherwise had a slower 2003 for capital markets work. The firm advised Standard and Poor's and Citibank on the first CMBS transaction in Poland, a deal valued at €74m.

Dewey Ballantine Grzesiak Limited Partnership was probably without equal in the total value of capital markets transactions advised on in 2003. Guided by department head Jaroslaw Grzesiak's experience and partner Lejb Fogelman's deal-making skills, the firm advised PSE SA on a multi-billion-euro securitisation of loans, and PGNiG SA on a €1.4bn restructuring of bonds. **Dewey Ballantine Grzesiak Limited Partnership** also acted for Bank Austria Creditanstalt in its €1bn listing on the Warsaw Stock Exchange, the first ever dual listing of a foreign company in Poland.

Acting primarily for banks, **Linklaters** had a successful 2003 advising on prominent bond issues. Led by Patrick Bell the firm represented the arranger Morgan Stanley on a €1.5bn EMTN programme update for BRE Bank. The firm also represented BRE Bank on a number of issues including the PLN1bn (€213m) issue of bank securities. Marek Wierzbowski is recommended.

CAPITAL MARKETS

ALLEN & OVERY ✪
CLIFFORD CHANCE
DEWEY BALLANTINE GRZESIAK LIMITED PARTNERSHIP ✪
LINKLATERS ✪

Baker & McKenzie ✪
Domanski Zakrzewski Palinka ✪
Weil, Gotshal & Manges ✪
White & Case – W. Danilowicz, W. Jurcewicz i Wspólnicy Kancelaria Prawna sp.K

Gide Loyrette Nouel ✪
Norton Rose, Piotr Strawa and Partners, Limited Partnership
Salans
Soltysinski Kawecki & Szlezak Legal Advisors ✪
Wardynski & Partners ✪

Beata Gessel & Partners ✪
CMS Cameron McKenna ✪
Hogan & Hartson M. Jamka, A. Galos, and Partners, LP ✪
Lovells ✪
Wierzbowski i Wspólnicy ✪

Firms are listed A-Z in tiers which are ranked in order of priority
✪ Indicates firm displays contact details at the end of this chapter.

Baker & McKenzie continues to count capital markets as a focus. The firm represented a client in the first real estate securitisation transaction in Poland.

Frequently referred to as an expert capital markets adviser is name partner Grzegorz Domanski of **Domanski Zakrzewski Palinka**. Professor Domanski was formerly chairman of the Warsaw Stock Exchange. He counts a number of leading banks among his clients and advised on a number of bond issues in 2003.

Weil, Gotshal & Manges, as counsel to Netia, advised the company on its $850m debt restructuring. It also advises Elektrim in its ongoing €440m bond debt restructuring and 3M Viscoplast on its merger with 3M Poland, a deal that required the target to be de-listed. Partner Anna Frankowska is highly rated.

Led by practice heads Janusz Fiszer and Witold Jurcewicz, the **White & Case – W. Danilowicz, W. Jurcewicz i Wspólnicy Kancelaria Prawna sp.K** capital markets team reports a marked increase in the number of structured products that the practice is asked to advise upon. Clients include BIG Bank Gdanski, Nordea Bank and Inter Groclin Auto, which the firm represented in a new $18m share issue in 2003.

Gide Loyrette Nouel acted as a counsel to Whirlpool in the acquisition of a majority stake in a Polish household appliances company. The deal required the de-listing of the Polish company.

Led by Grzegorz Dyczkowski, the three banking and finance lawyers at **Norton Rose, Piotr Strawa and Partners, Limited Partnership** also advise on capital markets. Had the firm been able to close a transaction advising a foreign issuer on the first listing by a foreign company on the Warsaw stock exchange, then 2003 would have been successful. As it was, the 18-month project ended when the client terminated the deal.

Salans' Warsaw office no longer sees capital markets as a key focus, although the firm did represent PKP SA in connection with its PLN1bn (€212m) bond offering, one of the biggest bond issues in Poland.

Counsel to the bondholders in the Netia debt restructuring was **Wardynski & Partners**, working in conjunction with US firm **Cadwalader, Wickersham & Taft LLP**. Outgoing partner, Andrzej Wiercinski, and remaining partner, Pawel Ciecwierz, are impressive.

CORPORATE AND COMMERCIAL

Managing partner Marcin Gmaj has taken over corporate and commercial work at **Baker & McKenzie**, following the retirement due to family reasons of the highly rated Agnieska Duda. A rise to the top tier follows a successful year in all areas, with the firm acquiring two recommended partners from **CMS Cameron McKenna**, and maintaining major international clients in the pharmaceuticals, telecoms, banking and construction industries.

CMS Cameron McKenna's practice head Charles Waddell departed for London in 2003, leaving all corporate and commercial concerns in the hands of partners Dariusz Mioduski and Dariusz Greszta. Evidence suggests that the new managing team is faring well, having been appointed by the Polish government to draft the new PPP law, as well as advising over 30 other leading organisations in 2003 on corporate and commercial matters.

Managing partner Nick Fletcher continues to be in charge at **Clifford Chance**. In 2003 the firm advised Kimberley Clark on the acquisition of the Polish tissue manufacturer International Paper Klucze SA, and also advised Brazilian iron ore exporter CRD on the acquisition of a majority interest in the proposed Gdansk iron ore terminal. Other clients include Lafarge, Coca-Cola, Kraft foods and Bayer AG.

Boosted by the acquisition of the high-performing **Hunton & Williams** Warsaw office in 2002, **Dewey Ballantine Grzesiak Limited Partnership** continues to go from strength to strength. The firm is now a leading name in a great many practice areas and represents a number of the most active companies in Poland such as, TP SA, PSE SA and PKN Orlen.

The massive, 28-lawyer, corporate and commercial practice at **Linklaters** can no longer be ignored – corporate advice for major companies such as GE Capital, GTECH and PSE SA demands recognition and this is reflected by a first appearance in the top tier. Nevertheless, with the firm entering the market very much later than its competitors, successes have not been easily won. Competitors have been highly critical of the firm's aggressive pricing policies.

Soltysinski Kawecki & Szlezak Legal Advisors continues to rely on referrals from numerous international law firms, including **Skadden, Arps, Slate, Meagher & Flom LLP** and **Cleary Gottlieb Steen & Hamilton**.

Wardynski & Partners continues to be recommended for its corporate and commercial expertise, although the firm has witnessed a significant number of departures in the past year. The firm has numerous Polish clients particularly in the steel, telecoms and shipping industries and receives referrals from a number of New York and London-based firms, including **Slaughter and May** and **Freshfields Bruckhaus Deringer**.

The well-known Pawel Rymarz continues to head an unchanged **Weil, Gotshal & Manges** corporate and commercial team. PZU SA, Hortex SA and the Eastbridge Group are all clients, demonstrating that the firm maintains a strong foothold in the market. Insolvency and corporate restructuring is a key focus. The firm is retained as in-house counsel to Netia.

New clients garnered by the 22-lawyer **White & Case – W. Danilowicz, W. Jurcewicz i Wspólnicy Kancelaria Prawna sp.K** corporate practice in 2003 include Patria Vehicles Oy, Oto Melara, Grupo Celsa and Innova Capital. The firm is frequently cited by competitors for the impressive quality of its corporate work. Witold Danilowicz is a respected leader.

Allen & Overy, traditionally under the dual-management of Michael Davies and Andrzej Siemiatowski, is now managed solely by the latter, though both remain. Continuing a trend begun in 2002, the firm has continued to downsize cautiously and, with less than 30 lawyers, the office is now significantly smaller than those of its rivals. With fewer staff to fill the ranks the firm has had to reduce its capability in some practices in order to maintain its core banking and finance capability. Key corporate work includes advising Motorola on the implementation of a nationwide mobile communications system, and advising the EBRD on the Warsaw metro project and PPP.

Following the collapse of *Altheimer & Gray* in 2003, Gabriel Wujek's Warsaw office was courted by a number of US firms before opting to become **Chadbourne & Parke Polska Sp. z o.o., Wujek, Radzikowski, Szubielska i Wspólnicy. Spólka Komandytowa** in 2004. So far the 35-lawyer office retains all the significant personalities that were present under the previous regime, and is confident of maintaining its strong US and Polish client base. The firm is keen to expand its links in Russia and Ukraine.

CORPORATE AND COMMERCIAL

BAKER & McKENZIE ✪
CMS CAMERON MCKENNA ✪
CLIFFORD CHANCE
DEWEY BALLANTINE GRZESIAK LIMITED PARTNERSHIP ✪
LINKLATERS ✪
SOLTYSINSKI KAWECKI & SZLEZAK LEGAL ADVISORS ✪
WARDYNSKI & PARTNERS ✪
WEIL, GOTSHAL & MANGES ✪
WHITE & CASE – W. DANILOWICZ, W. JURCEWICZ I WSPÓLNICY KANCELARIA PRAWNA SP.K

Allen & Overy ✪
Chadbourne & Parke Polska Sp. z o.o., Wujek, Radzikowski, Szubielska i Wspólnicy. Spólka Komandytowa
Domanski Zakrzewski Palinka ✪
Gide Loyrette Nouel ✪
Gleiss Lutz ✪
Lovells ✪
Nörr Stiefenhofer Lutz ✪
Salans
Wierzbowski i Wspólnicy ✪

Beata Gessel & Partners ✪
Beiten Burkhardt K. Rastawicki Sp.K. ✪
Forystek Góralczyk Rychlicki Budzowska Fiutowski Jamorski Adwokaci i Radcowie Prawni
Haarmann Hemmelrath ✪
Hogan & Hartson M. Jamka, A. Galos, and Partners, LP ✪
Kochanski Brudkowski Olechowski i Wspólnicy sp.j.
Laszczuk Polimirski Korcz & Partners
Norton Rose, Piotr Strawa and Partners, Limited Partnership
Studnicki, Pleszka, Cwiakalski, Górski LLP
TGC Corporate Lawyers

Brockhuis Schnell Jurczak Prusak Sp. k.
Drzewiecki, Tomaszek & Wspólnicy Spólka Jawna
Joachim Hilla, Kancelaria
K Ziemski i Partnerzy spolka komandytowa, Kancelaria Prawna
Kunachowicz, Slusarek & Partners
M Lukowicz & Partners Attorneys at Law Limited Partnership
Miller, Canfield, W. Babicki i Wspólnicy Sp.k
Rödl, Korpalski Kancelaria Prawna sp.k.

Evico s.c., Kancelaria Prawnicza
Kuk, Suszynska, Lachowski & Matecki
Kalwas i Wspólnicy
Kaczor Klimczyk Pucher Wypiór – Advokaci Spólka Partnerska ✪
Peter Nielsen & Partners Law Office Sp z o.o.
Pociej, Dubois & Partners
Smoktunowicz & Falandysz

Firms are listed A-Z in tiers which are ranked in order of priority
✪ Indicates firm displays contact details at the end of this chapter.

With over 90 lawyers **Domanski Zakrzewski Palinka** is the largest law firm in Poland and a strong contender for the title of third most important Polish firm after **Soltysinski Kawecki & Szlezak Legal Advisors** and **Wardynski & Partners**. Approximately half of the firm's clients are non-Polish companies. Corporate work for pharmaceuticals companies is a key focus.

Lone representative of France-based international firms is **Gide Loyrette Nouel**. Once known for a solid French client base, the firm has successfully diversified in recent years and now boasts clients from all quarters of Europe and the US. Carlsberg, Peugeot, CASA and Whirlpool are examples. The firm sometimes works with **Soltysinski Kawecki & Szlezak Legal Advisors** on corporate matters.

Gleiss Lutz continues to benefit from its alliance with **Herbert Smith**, with partner Martina Asmar being based permanently in London. The firm has a German and international client base.

The global success of the **Lovells** brand has not yet been fully translated to the Polish market and the firm maintains a lower profile than other leading firms. A traditionally strong German client base has now been supplanted by a range of German, Polish and French clients. Partner Beata Balas-Noszczyk heads a specialist corporate insurance practice at the firm.

2003 witnessed a number of departures and arrivals at **Nörr Stiefenhofer Lutz**. Most significant was the arrival of local partner and head, Peter Urbanek, formerly of **Haarmann Hemmelrath**. With the firm as a whole expanding in CEE, it is keen to move away from a Germany-centred policy and establish itself more firmly in Poland and elsewhere. The firm benefits from strategic alliances with various Austrian and international firms, such as **Macfarlanes** and **O'Melveny & Myers LLP**.

Salans continue to cultivate a respectable and high-profile reputation for corporate work. The acquisition by **Salans** of so many of *Altheimer & Gray*'s European offices (albeit not the Warsaw office) can only strengthen the position of the firm in Poland. Vivendi, EDS and Tractebel are clients.

Landwell member **Wierzbowski i Wspólnicy** is undergoing a period of change as it redefines its relationship with PwC on a project-by-project basis. Nevertheless, many of the firm's key clients such as TP SA and Philips were won independently of the auditing company. A significant new client is PKN Orlen for whom the firm undertakes various contracts and corporate matters. Managing partner Krzysztof Wierzbowski is particularly well known for his telecoms work.

Beata Gessel & Partners (formerly *Beata Gessel, Andrzej Chajec & Partners*) has for many years been seen as the third leading Polish firm on the market. The firm was respected for its solid client list of Polish publicly listed companies However, the departure of half of the firm's four partners, including name partner Andrzej Chajec, is a serious blow.

The small, three-partner corporate practice of **Hogan & Hartson M. Jamka, A. Galos, and Partners, LP** found 2003 to be a slow year, lacking notable work.

Kochanski Brudkowski Olechowski i Wspólnicy sp.j. was founded in 1999 by former **Hogan & Hartson M. Jamka, A. Galos, and Partners, LP** managing partner Piotr Kochanski, who was also head of IP, litigation and arbitration at **White & Case – W. Danilowicz, W. Jurcewicz i Wspólnicy Kancelaria Prawna sp.K** for three years. An impressive client list includes Citibank Handlowy, US Pharmacia, Intel Corporation, Reckitt Benckiser and Axel Springer.

Laszczuk Polimirski Korcz & Partners is a medium-sized domestic firm with a broad commercial practice, with specific strengths in aviation, and advertising law. The firm represents Lufthansa, SAS and Avon cosmetics.

Norton Rose, Piotr Strawa and Partners, Limited Partnership entered the Polish market later than other international firms and has struggled to establish a foothold. Managing partner Piotr Strawa has previously been known as a 'star' corporate lawyer.

Leading Krakow firm **Studnicki, Pleszka, Cwiakalski, Górski LLP** was established in 1988. The firm maintains a strategic alliance with **Dewey Ballantine Grzesiak Limited Partnership**. Tomasz Studnicki is recommended by clients for joint venture finance, and all aspects of corporate and commercial law.

Formed in 1976 as the result of a merger, former London-based firm **TGC Corporate Lawyers** now consists of offices in Warsaw, Wroclaw and Prague. The 45-lawyer firm also maintains three business support subsidiaries (HR, admin, visa services) under separate management.

Although only four lawyers in size, **Kancelaria Joachim Hilla** is praised by clients for reliability and efficiency. Joachim Hilla was a partner at **Lovells** in Germany until 1998, when he founded his own office in Poland. The firm works closely with Frankfurt-based firm **ARCON Rechtsanwälte Schmidt-Sibeth Heisse Weisskopf Kursawe**. Corporate clients include UBS Warburg, SWL GmbH of Leipzig, and CBF of Warsaw

Virginia-based firm **Miller, Canfield, W. Babicki i Wspólnicy Sp.k** is best known as the firm representing Ford Motor Company from its offices in Warsaw, Katowice and Gdynia.

DISPUTE RESOLUTION

Owing to their cheaper rates, Polish firms can often win instructions to represent leading clients in high-profile disputes. A number of international firms recommend their clients not go to court, simply because of the great length of time many cases take.

DISPUTE RESOLUTION

WARDYNSKI & PARTNERS ✪
WEIL, GOTSHAL & MANGES ✪

Baker & McKenzie ✪
CMS Cameron McKenna ✪
Dewey Ballantine Grzesiak Limited Partnership ✪
Domanski Zakrzewski Palinka ✪
Drzewiecki, Tomaszek & Wspólnicy Spólka Jawna
Linklaters ✪
Soltysinski Kawecki & Szlezak Legal Advisors ✪
Wierzbowski i Wspólnicy ✪

Chadbourne & Parke Polska Sp. z o.o., Wujek, Radzikowski, Szubielska i Wspólnicy. Spólka Komandytowa
Clifford Chance
Gide Loyrette Nouel ✪
Hogan & Hartson M. Jamka, A. Galos, and Partners, LP ✪
Joachim Hilla, Kancelaria
Kochanski Brudkowski Olechowski i Wspólnicy sp.j.
Lovells ✪
Nörr Stiefenhofer Lutz ✪
Salans
Studnicki, Pleszka, Cwiakalski, Górski LLP
TGC Corporate Lawyers
White & Case – W. Danilowicz, W. Jurcewicz i Wspólnicy Kancelaria Prawna sp.K

Beata Gessel & Partners ✪
Beiten Burkhardt K. Rastawicki Sp.K. ✪
Laszczuk Polimirski Korcz & Partners
Miller, Canfield, W. Babicki i Wspólnicy Sp.k

Firms are listed A-Z in tiers which are ranked in order of priority
✪ Indicates firm displays contact details at the end of this chapter.

Wardynski & Partners retains its traditional top-spot for litigation and arbitration capability. Competitors and clients alike frequently cite the firm. Though not perceived to be as aggressive in style as nearest rival **Weil, Gotshal & Manges**, the firm is no less effective. It has an association with **Brick Court Chambers** in London to train its lawyers in litigation and EU law.

Weil, Gotshal & Manges is known for its aggressive style. Some clients would never consider any other firm for litigation and arbitration work.

Baker & McKenzie has nine lawyers and one of counsel to undertake major litigation and arbitration cases. Of counsel Andrzej Tynel is a member of both the Polish and American arbitration associations and president of the former. Respected of counsel Jerzy Skrzypowski left the firm in 2003.

There are four adwokats at **CMS Cameron McKenna** in what is a growing practice. The firm has litigation experience in the areas of IP, construction, product liability, and tobacco. White-collar crime is also an area of expertise, with the firm having advised companies in criminal proceedings against former board members.

Dewey Ballantine Grzesiak Limited Partnership has a strong, seven-lawyer dispute resolution team, with expertise in litigation and arbitration. Headline cases include the representation of LG Petrobank before the Polish judiciary in order to overturn an earlier decision issued by the Warsaw Arbitration Court.

As one of the biggest firms in Poland, **Domanski Zakrzewski Palinka**'s large body of legal advisers is able to manage a high volume of litigation work. Name partners Grzegorz Domanski and Krzysztof Zakrewski have also represented multinational corporations before the International Arbitration Court in Vienna, including acting for Deutsche Telekom in a $4bn dispute against Elektrim and BRE Bank.

Drzewiecki, Tomaszek & Wspólnicy Spólka Jawna is respected by competitors for its litigation capability. Partners Marcin Juszczyk and Andrzej Tomaszek are recommended.

Though the firm has long undertaken tax litigation, it was only in 2002 that **Linklaters** decided to form a separate litigation and arbitration practice. So far that decision has paid off, with the firm reporting ever increasing work. Successful litigation includes two separate proceedings representing toy manufacturer LEGO. Krystyna Szczepanowska-Kozlowska led (**Wardynski & Partners** represented LEGO).

Two partners and an unusually high number of associates are adwokats at **Wierzbowski i Wspólnicy**. Litigation experience includes representation of a major telecoms company before various regulatory bodies and courts, including two representations before the Supreme Court.

The litigation practice at **Chadbourne & Parke Polska Sp. z o.o., Wujek, Radzikowski, Szubielska i Wspólnicy. Spólka Komandytowa** was created primarily as a support for the firm's existing clients. Tax-related litigation is a particular strength and the firm successfully represented computer company Optimus SA in a highly publicised case against the state, after the company was charged with tax evasion.

Clifford Chance created a five-lawyer dispute resolution practice at the close of 2003. The team is under the day-to-day management of associate Bartosz Kruzewski and has expertise in real estate, construction and insurance litigation as well as bankruptcy and restructuring matters.

Gide Loyrette Nouel successfully represented Saint Luis Sucre in a €125m dispute against the State Treasury.

All four lawyers at **Kancelaria Joachim Hilla** are admitted in Poland. Name Partner Joachim Hilla is also admitted in Germany and clients value his Polish/German experience. He is highly-praised by clients.

Kochanski Brudkowski Olechowski i Wspólnicy sp.j. has an aggressive reputation, and focuses particularly on IP-related litigation.

In 2003 respected Krakow firm **Studnicki, Pleszka, Cwiakalski, Górski LLP** represented Polish railways in a dispute valued at €100m.

Beata Ordowska of **TGC Corporate Lawyers** has a leading reputation for disputes work. Also, partner Steven Wood, formerly of **Clifford Chance LLP**, recently settled a private client's claim against a large US multinational for seven figures.

INTELLECTUAL PROPERTY

Soltysinski Kawecki & Szlezak Legal Advisors continues to receive the highest recommendations for its IP work, primarily owing to the reputation of partner and senior statesman, Stanislaw Soltysinski. The firm has represented Business Software Alliance and other leading software companies for many years.

The already highly-rated **Baker & McKenzie** IP and IT team received a significant boost with the hire of **CMS Cameron McKenna**'s technology law expert Marek Rosinski, though the firm has also seen the departure of recommended of counsel Jerzy Skrzypowski. That the firm dedicates two partners to this area (and its wider media practice) demonstrates its commitment to invest in the practice, particularly in IT work. Clients the firm advises on IT-related issues include Hewlett-Packard and Accenture.

Seven lawyers form the dual IP and IT practice at **Dewey Ballantine Grzesiak Limited Partnership**. The firm is best known for IT work, such as advising on agreements regarding business support systems for BRE Bank, LUKAS Bank and TP SA. IP work includes advising Sony Music Polska, and Universal Music Polska on copyright and various other IP issues.

Hogan & Hartson M. Jamka, A. Galos, and Partners, LP houses a small but experienced IP and media practice. Impressively, the firm has represented Walt Disney Company, Warner Brothers, Universal Studios, Electronic Arts and Twentieth Century Fox in a wide range of contentious and non-contentious IP-related work. Partner Oskar Tulodziecki is recommended for his experience.

Three associates comprise the **Linklaters** IP team, with the well-respected Krystyna Szczepanowska-Kozlowska being the senior name. The firm reports an increase in EU trade mark work and in competition law. Clients include Danone, ECCO, Renault Polska, and 3M Deutschland.

The **Wardynski & Partners** IP team is often recommended for its experience. The work undertaken by the practice has increased in recent years particularly in the field of industrial property. The firm also advises various renowned sports companies and car producers on trade mark issues.

INTELLECTUAL PROPERTY

SOLTYSINSKI KAWECKI & SZLEZAK LEGAL ADVISORS ✪

BAKER & McKENZIE ✪
DEWEY BALLANTINE GRZESIAK LIMITED PARTNERSHIP ✪
HOGAN & HARTSON M. JAMKA, A. GALOS, AND PARTNERS, LP ✪
LINKLATERS ✪
WARDYNSKI & PARTNERS ✪
WIERZBOWSKI I WSPÓLNICY ✪

CMS Cameron McKenna ✪
Domanski Zakrzewski Palinka ✪
Gide Loyrette Nouel ✪
Kochanski Brudkowski Olechowski i Wspólnicy sp.j.
Laszczuk Polimirski Korcz & Partners

Allen & Overy ✪
Beata Gessel & Partners ✪
Beiten Burkhardt K. Rastawicki Sp.K. ✪
Chadbourne & Parke Polska Sp. z o.o., Wujek, Radzikowski, Szubielska i Wspólnicy. Spólka Komandytowa
Clifford Chance
Drzewiecki, Tomaszek & Wspólnicy Spólka Jawna
Gleiss Lutz ✪
Lovells ✪
Salans
Weil, Gotshal & Manges ✪
White & Case – W. Danilowicz, W. Jurcewicz i Wspólnicy Kancelaria Prawna sp.K

Firms are listed A-Z in tiers which are ranked in order of priority
✪ Indicates firm displays contact details at the end of this chapter.

Name partner Krzysztof Wierzbowski of **Wierzbowski i Wspólnicy** is recognised globally for his telecoms expertise and the IP/IT team that the firm has developed focuses primarily on issues related to telecoms and e-business.

CMS Cameron McKenna will look to patent attorney Bogdan Duda to maintain the inflow of IP work now that Marek Rosinski has departed. The firm recently advised GTC and a Polish credit agent on trade mark issues, and also represented a leading Polish newspaper publisher in a dispute over a title.

Domanski Zakrzewski Palinka represents a significant proportion of the prominent Polish pharmaceuticals market in advertising-related issues, including GlaxoSmithKline, Polpharma and Pfizer.

Gide Loyrette Nouel advises on trade marks and competition law for L'Oréal and other multinationals.

IP is a major focus at **Kochanski Brudkowski Olechowski i Wspólnicy sp.j.**. Tomasz Brudkowski has a good reputation for IP. The firm represents Axel Springer, Eurosport TV, radio and

TV companies. The firm's expertise includes media, technology and e-commerce.

Advertising law is a specialisation of **Laszczuk Polimirski Korcz & Partners** and clients include the Grey group, Ogilvy & Mather and several other international advertising agencies. IP litigation is also a strength and the firm represents trade mark holders in both state and private prosecutions. Partner Maciej Lazszcuk is known in this field.

IP, trade marks and IT are not core focuses for **Allen & Overy**, although the firm does advise a number of private clients and companies.

MERGERS AND ACQUISITIONS

There have been a host of visible small and medium-scale acquisitions but few major transactions. Competition between firms has been fierce and billing rates have been lowered in an attempt to win instructions.

Baker & McKenzie's sizeable M&A practice benefits from the leadership of former **Dewey Ballantine Grzesiak Limited Partnership** partners Marcin Gmaj and Tomasz Krzyzowski. The firm advised Hewlett-Packard Polska on its merger with Compaq Polska, and Abbott on the acquisition of JOMED Poland.

M&A is a traditional strength for Gabriel Wujek and the experienced corporate team at **Chadbourne & Parke Polska Sp. z o.o., Wujek, Radzikowski, Szubielska i Wspólnicy. Spólka Komandytowa**. The firm has particular experience advising major pharmaceuticals companies on their acquisitions in Poland. Pharmaceuticals clients include Baxter, Abbott and Pfizer.

Clifford Chance advised a major private equity fund on a leveraged buy-out of a Polish building products company, and advised a leading European retailer on a supermarket chain acquisition. The firm also won the tender to advise Netia in the acquisitions relating to that company's debt restructuring. Senior associate Bartosz Kruzewski is recommended for his impressive work with Netia.

Since its 2002 merger with the Warsaw office of **Hunton & Williams**, **Dewey Ballantine Grzesiak Limited Partnership** has been one of the strongest M&A firms on the market. This is due in no small part to the efforts of former **Hunton & Williams** Warsaw managing partner, Lejb Fogelman, whose reputation for deal-making is second to none. The firm shows no sign of noticing the poor market conditions, having advised PKN Orlen on the €101m acquisition of 494 BP gas stations, and Accor on the $100m sale of assets to Orbis, as well as continuing to advise on other significant acquisitions.

2003 was a year *par excellence* for **Gide Loyrette Nouel**'s M&A team, as it closed two massive transactions ongoing from 2002. As counsel to the sellers the firm represented Apsys Polska and DTC Casinos in the €220m sale of 13 shopping galleries to GE Capital. As counsel to buyers it represented Saint Louis Sucre in the complex €200m acquisition of 16 Polish sugar plants from the Polish State. Stanislas Dwernicki heads the practice.

Soltysinski Kawecki & Szlezak Legal Advisors is consistently rated highly for M&A work. Competitors praise its 'solid expertise' and international style. That expertise was gained whilst advising some of the largest banks and multinationals operating in Poland in prominent cross-border mergers and acquisitions. Krzysztof Pawlisz heads the department.

In a transaction ongoing from 2002, **Weil, Gotshal & Manges** assisted Bank of America in a buy-out of Polish food company Hortex Holding in 2003. Other buyers that the firm represented include Hicks, Muse, Tate and Furst on the acquisition of Aster City Cable, and NFI Hetman and CAIB on the acquisition of Wonlock IT. Sellers that the firm represents include Bolix Construction and BRE Bank.

Although reporting a slow year, **White & Case – W. Danilowicz, W. Jurcewicz i Wspólnicy Kancelaria Prawna sp.K** continued to attract significant work. Partner Janusz Fiszer led a team advising Nordea Bank on its two public tender offers relating to the acquisition of a $110m (€86.3m) majority shareholding in LG Petro Bank. Respected managing partner Witold Danilowicz led a team advising Grupo Celsa on the headline acquisition of Ostrowiec steelworks.

Mergers and acquisitions work for **Allen & Overy** include transactions begun with Sara Lee and Heidelberg Cement AG in 2002 were still ongoing into 2003. The firm represented Irish manufacturer of construction material, Kingspan Group, in the acquisition of Tarmont, a Polish manufacturer.

Dariusz Greszta led the **CMS Cameron Mckenna** M&A team advising the Enterprise Group on the PLN45m (€9.7m) leveraged buy-out of Poland's largest DIY retailer, Nomi, from the Kingfisher Group. The firm also advised lender Eurohypo on a consortium's financing of a €630m acquisition of 27 shopping malls from German multinational Metro.

Domanski Zakrzewski Palinka is well known as a frequent representative of Polish companies on the seller's side. However the firm has also represented Japanese clients, and a number of banks, in their acquisitions of Polish targets. Clients include Bolix Construction and PVC producer Ergis.

Four partners undertake M&A work at **Hogan & Hartson M. Jamka, A. Galos, and Partners, LP** with senior partner Maciej Jamka leading. **Hogan & Hartson M. Jamka, A. Galos, and Partners, LP** advised Budimex on the complex, simultaneous merger of five affiliated entities, designed to make Budimex Poland's largest construction company.

MERGERS AND ACQUISITIONS

BAKER & McKENZIE ✪
CHADBOURNE & PARKE POLSKA SP. Z O.O., WUJEK, RADZIKOWSKI, SZUBIELSKA I WSPÓLNICY. SPÓLKA KOMANDYTOWA
CLIFFORD CHANCE
DEWEY BALLANTINE GRZESIAK LIMITED PARTNERSHIP ✪
GIDE LOYRETTE NOUEL ✪
SOLTYSINSKI KAWECKI & SZLEZAK LEGAL ADVISORS ✪
WEIL, GOTSHAL & MANGES ✪
WHITE & CASE – W. DANILOWICZ, W. JURCEWICZ I WSPÓLNICY KANCELARIA PRAWNA SP.K

Allen & Overy ✪
CMS Cameron McKenna ✪
Domanski Zakrzewski Palinka ✪
Hogan & Hartson M. Jamka, A. Galos, and Partners, LP ✪
Linklaters ✪
Salans
Wardynski & Partners ✪
Wierzbowski i Wspólnicy ✪

Beata Gessel & Partners ✪
Gleiss Lutz ✪
Kochanski Brudkowski Olechowski i Wspólnicy sp.j.
Lovells ✪

Beiten Burkhardt K. Rastawicki Sp.K. ✪
Nörr Stiefenhofer Lutz ✪
M Lukowicz & Partners Attorneys at Law Limited Partnership
Norton Rose, Piotr Strawa and Partners, Limited Partnership
TGC Corporate Lawyers

Firms are listed A-Z in tiers which are ranked in order of priority
✪ Indicates firm displays contact details at the end of this chapter.

Partner Tadeusz Komosa and the **Linklaters** M&A team are pushing hard on the heels of the top tier. In terms of numbers of transactions undertaken **Linklaters** leads the second tier, having recently advised buyers, GE Capital, GTECH, ING Bank, PORR AG; and sellers, Capio Diagnostic, IDIP, and CSFB Polska.

Salans continues to advise Eiffage, Newell Rubbermaid and Vivendi.

Wardynski & Partners' reputation for M&A work will be seriously dented by the announcement that head of the M&A practice Andrzej Wiercinski is set to leave early in 2004. Clients describe Wiercinski's expertise as 'formidable' and it remains to be seen whether his departure will affect the firm's relationship with key M&A clients Makro and Costorama.

Regulatory work is a core specialisation at **Wierzbowski I Wspólnicy**, although the firm has experience in all aspects of M&A work. Senior associate Monika Smolarek advised on the merger of two Polish companies in the Nestlé group, as well representing B Brown Medical in the acquisition of several companies.

Former firm *Beata Gessel, Andrzej Chajec & Partners*, now **Beata Gessel & Partners**, was traditionally highly recommended for its M&A work but the departure of respected practice head Andrzej Chajec at the end of 2003 is a loss. Managing partner Beata Gessel will now head the department. Anti-monopoly concerns are an important source of work for the firm.

Kochanski Brudkowski Olechowski i Wspólnicy sp.j. recently undertook minor acquisition work for a multinational company with shares in a Polish optical business.

All three British partners and one of the two Polish partners at **TGC Corporate Lawyers** are involved in M&A when the market allows.

PRIVATISATION

Very few firms saw work in this area in 2003 and the only major privatisation currently on the horizon is the stalled €1bn sale of the G8 Group state energy companies. Still, there remains considerable latent expertise in this area and some positive hopes for post-May 2004.

Allen & Overy was a leader in the mass privatisations of the 1990s. However, since work dried up, the firm has downsized considerably, although it did recently advise Hungarian pharmaceuticals company, Gedeon Richter, in connection with the privatisation of Polfa holdings company in the small town of Grodzisk Mazowiecki.

Dariusz Mioduki led the team at **CMS Cameron McKenna** advising a Polish energy company in its bid for acquisition of the G8 Group.

Chadbourne & Parke Polska Sp. z o.o., Wujek, Radzikowski, Szubielska i Wspólnicy. Spólka Komandytowa represented Nafta Polska in a failed bid for the Gdansk refinery. The firm also has experience in the privatisation of the pharmaceuticals industry.

Clifford Chance is representing Vopak Oil Storage Company in the bid for Naftobazy fuel storage company. As in 2002 the firm is also advising leading energy company E.on in its G8 Group bid.

Opposite **Clifford Chance**, **Dewey Ballantine Grzesiak Limited Partnership** is representing Oiltanking GmbH in the bid for Naftobazy. The firm is also representing the US Steel Corporation and PKN Orlen in the planned privatisation of PHS SA and the Gdansk Refinery respectively.

Representing the State in the sale of the G8 Group is **Domanski Zakrzewski Palinka**. The firm also represents the government in the sale of Rybnik power plant.

Gide Loyrette Nouel represent EDF as it attempts to acquire a power plant from the Polish State. Saint Louis Sucre is also a significant client.

PRIVATISATION

ALLEN & OVERY ✪
BAKER & McKENZIE ✪
CMS CAMERON McKENNA ✪
CHADBOURNE & PARKE POLSKA SP. Z O.O., WUJEK, RADZIKOWSKI, SZUBIELSKA I WSPÓLNICY. SPÓLKA KOMANDYTOWA
CLIFFORD CHANCE
DEWEY BALLANTINE GRZESIAK LIMITED PARTNERSHIP ✪
DOMANSKI ZAKRZEWSKI PALINKA ✪
GIDE LOYRETTE NOUEL ✪
LINKLATERS ✪
SALANS
SOLTYSINSKI KAWECKI & SZLEZAK LEGAL ADVISORS ✪
WARDYNSKI & PARTNERS ✪
WEIL, GOTSHAL & MANGES ✪
WHITE & CASE – W. DANILOWICZ, W. JURCEWICZ I WSPÓLNICY KANCELARIA PRAWNA SP.K

Beata Gessel & Partners ✪
Beiten Burkhardt K. Rastawicki Sp.K. ✪
Gleiss Lutz ✪
Hogan & Hartson M. Jamka, A. Galos, and Partners, LP ✪
TGC Corporate Lawyers
Wierzbowski i Wspólnicy ✪

Firms are listed A-Z in tiers which are ranked in order of priority
✪ Indicates firm displays contact details at the end of this chapter.

Linklaters is advising the state-owned energy company Polskie Sieci Elektroenergetyczne (PSE) as it undergoes restructuring with a view to eventual privatisation.

Salans represents Tractebel, Electrabel and Elektrownia Polaniec in their G8 Group bid. The companies are also biding for other state-owned energy companies including Stoen, ZE Ostroleka and ZE PolnaOdra. Previously **Salans** represented Tractebel and Electrabel in the €270m acquisition of 100% of shares in Elektrownia Polaniec from the state treasury and company employees.

Weil, Gotshal & Manges represents the G8 Group in all aspects relating to its proposed privatisation.

Witold Danilowicz heads the privatisation team at **White & Case – W. Danilowicz, W. Jurcewicz i Wspólnicy Kancelaria Prawna sp.K**. The firm has experience on the seller's side, having represented the government during the mass privatisations of previous years. More recently the firm represented US company Pratt & Whitney in the complex acquisition of an 80% stake in state arms company WSK PZL Rzeszow.

In privatisation work domestic firms often win instructions from the Polish government. **Beata Gessel & Partners**, for example, has represented the State Treasury in a number of transactions.

TGC Corporate Lawyers advised a pharmaceutical company in the largest ever trade sales privatisation in Poland.

Wierzbowski i Wspólnicy is representing a client in a possible privatisation of a state coal mining company. Previous privatisations in which the firm has been involved include military, telecoms, beer and the edible oil industries.

PROJECT FINANCE

The global reputation of **Allen & Overy** in project finance is secure and whilst major financing work might currently be scarce in Poland, when it does return the investment banks will know where to turn.

CMS Cameron McKenna's excellent Warsaw energy and project finance team works closely with the firm's London office. The firm is leading the project financing of a major oil refinery, advising lender BPH in the financing of a CCGT plant, and advising Energetyka SP zoo on the project finance of a gas-fired turbine.

Dewey Ballantine Grzesiak Limited Partnership continues to advise PKN Orlen SA on the financing of the PKN Orlen SA/Basell joint venture polypropylene plant. The firm has also worked for Caterpillar Financial Services on the financing of a gas-fired co-generation system. Partners Jaroslaw Grzesiak and Stephen Horvath are recommended.

Wardynski & Partners is often cited for its project finance work. The likely wave of government-led infrastructure projects post-EU accession is bound to keep the firm busy. Areas currently being looked at are roads, railways, environment and sewage treatment.

Project finance at **Baker & McKenzie** is undertaken by Krzysztof Korzeniewski's six-lawyer banking and finance team. The firm continues to work for Polish Airports on the construction of a new terminal.

Six lawyers in the **Clifford Chance** corporate practice also advise on energy projects. Head Agnieszka Janicka-Sosna is well regarded by competitors.

Tomasz Dobrowolski at **Hogan & Hartson M. Jamka, A. Galos, and Partners, LP** is recommended for his knowledge of the energy sector. The firm has undertaken a significant amount of project finance-related work, including representing the EBRD as special counsel in regard to the €30m credit agreement between the bank and Dom Development SA.

Linklaters advised PKO BP as lender with regard to the financing of a restructured shipyard. The firm also has an active energy practice.

Salans instantly gained a reputation for project finance in 2002 when it hired the highly sought-after **Hunton & Williams** Warsaw project finance team, before the remainder of the firm went to **Dewey Ballantine Grzesiak Limited Partnership**.

PROJECT FINANCE

ALLEN & OVERY ✪
CMS CAMERON McKENNA ✪
DEWEY BALLANTINE GRZESIAK LIMITED PARTNERSHIP ✪
WARDYNSKI & PARTNERS ✪

Baker & McKenzie ✪
Clifford Chance
Hogan & Hartson M. Jamka, A. Galos, and Partners, LP ✪
Linklaters ✪
Salans
Soltysinski Kawecki & Szlezak Legal Advisors ✪
Weil, Gotshal & Manges ✪
White & Case – W. Danilowicz, W. Jurcewicz i Wspólnicy Kancelaria Prawna sp.K

Chadbourne & Parke Polska Sp. z o.o., Wujek, Radzikowski, Szubielska i Wspólnicy. Spólka Komandytowa
Gide Loyrette Nouel ✪
Gleiss Lutz ✪
Lovells ✪
Nörr Stiefenhofer Lutz ✪

Firms are listed A-Z in tiers which are ranked in order of priority
✪ *Indicates firm displays contact details at the end of this chapter.*

Weil, Gotshal & Manges is working in conjunction with **CMS Cameron McKenna** to provide the legal assistance and project financing for the stalled $1bn construction of the new Belchatow II power units. Roman Rewald remains in charge.

White & Case – W. Danilowicz, W. Jurcewicz i Wspólnicy Kancelaria Prawna sp.K is recommended for its occasional energy and project finance work, which builds on the firm's global expertise.

REAL ESTATE

CMS CAMERON McKENNA ✪
WEIL, GOTSHAL & MANGES ✪

Baker & McKenzie ✪
Chadbourne & Parke Polska Sp. z o.o., Wujek, Radzikowski, Szubielska i Wspólnicy. Spólka Komandytowa
Hogan & Hartson M. Jamka, A. Galos, and Partners, LP ✪
Linklaters ✪
Salans
Soltysinski Kawecki & Szlezak Legal Advisors ✪
Wardynski & Partners ✪

Allen & Overy ✪
Clifford Chance
Dewey Ballantine Grzesiak Limited Partnership ✪
Domanski Zakrzewski Palinka ✪
Gide Loyrette Nouel ✪
Laszczuk Polimirski Korcz & Partners
Lovells ✪
Miller, Canfield, W. Babicki i Wspólnicy Sp.k
TGC Corporate Lawyers
White & Case – W. Danilowicz, W. Jurcewicz i Wspólnicy Kancelaria Prawna sp.K
Wierzbowski i Wspólnicy ✪

Beata Gessel & Partners ✪
Gleiss Lutz ✪
Haarmann Hemmelrath ✪
Nörr Stiefenhofer Lutz ✪

Firms are listed A-Z in tiers which are ranked in order of priority
✪ *Indicates firm displays contact details at the end of this chapter.*

REAL ESTATE

CMS Cameron McKenna is traditionally seen as leader in this area and is still consistently recommended, though there were significant departures in 2003. The effects of the loss of department head Steven Shone to the Moscow office have been eased by the return of highly recommended Pawel Debowski, following a year in industry. The team advises various funds and developers on multi-million euro real estate investments.

Weil, Gotshal & Manges is experienced in all aspects of the finance, construction, selling and acquisition of real estate throughout Poland and CEE. Recently the firm represented ProLogis in the sale and development of a large scale warehouse distribution facility for Tesco. Eric Rosedale leads.

The three-partner team at **Baker & McKenzie** advised Caterpillar and Firestone on greenfield investment projects in 2003, as well as advising Autostrada Wielkopolska on the building of the A2 motorway project, one of the biggest infrastructure projects in Poland. The firm's commitment to this practice is evidenced by the hire of partner Malgorzata Pietrzak-Paciorek from **CMS Cameron McKenna**. Associate Tomasz Totomir is an expert on environmental law.

Real estate is a core focus at **Chadbourne & Parke Polska Sp. z o.o., Wujek, Radzikowski, Szubielska i Wspólnicy. Spólka Komandytowa**. The firm has particular expertise in real estate issues related to financial restructuring. Clients include various US developers and pensions funds, and Heitman Financial.

Hogan & Hartson M. Jamka, A. Galos, and Partners, LP is recommended for its large scale real estate finance work. Clients include Smithfield Foods, Hotel Atrium, Wolf Immobilien and Silver Screen.

Linklaters is confident that real estate work is set to increase in 2004 and this belief tallies well with the increase in work reported by the firm's real estate team in 2003. Key clients include Tesco Polska, Adgar Postepu and GE Capital Real Estate.

Salans continues to handle the acquisition of real estate sites, commercial real estate development and construction projects. The firm was boosted by the hire of real estate expert, Marek Grodek, who departed from **Clifford Chance** with major client Carrefour in tow.

The Polish Bar is traditionally very strong in real estate, one of the few areas of law that could be practised during the communist era. The leading Polish firms continue to command excellent reputations for real estate matters with the three-partner team at **Wardynski & Partners** chief among them, and **Soltysinski Kawecki & Szlezak Legal Advisors** close behind. **Soltysinski Kawecki & Szlezak Legal Advisors** has carried out large-scale greenfield projects for leading Japanese car manufacturers. **Wardynski & Partners** represents a number of domestic infrastructure companies, whilst continuing to expand its network of contacts in countries to the east of Poland, and also receiving referrals from its US and UK links.

Real estate is not a key focus at **Clifford Chance** although the firm continues to advise retail chains on minor real estate developments in Poland.

Dewey Ballantine Grzesiak Limited Partnership undertakes the loan and acquisition of real estate for major clients, such as BPH PBK, Caterpillar, and Microsoft. However it is noticeable that the firm is yet to replace former head of department Marcin Gmaj who departed for **Baker & McKenzie** in 2002.

Domanski Zakrzewski Palinka advises Saint Gobain construction company, one of the biggest French investors in Poland, on real estate matters. Other clients for whom the firm works include Media Markt, Hennes Mauritz, Skanska and TK Development.

In addition to shopping gallery acquisition work, **Gide Loyrette Nouel** has experience in urban planning law, the acquisition of plots, and all aspects of leasing and selling property. Clients for whom **Gide Loyrette Nouel** works include CASA, Daewoo Italy, Peugeot and Belgian company, Ghelamco.

Laszczuk Polimirski Korcz & Partners represented Danish group FORAS Holding A/S in connection with a €100m facility for the financing of shopping centre acquisitions. The firm has also advised the Starwood Hotel Group and Avon Cosmetics on construction projects throughout the country.

Lovells represented Commercial Union in a large-scale office lease transaction.

Miller, Canfield, W. Babicki i Wspólnicy Sp.k, a firm best known for its representation of Ford, views advising on real estate as its core discipline. Tesco Polska is also a client. Andrzej Chelchowski, head of the firm's Warsaw office, is recommended.

A majority of **TGC Corporate Lawyers**'s work is in the real estate sector. The firm represents American and European clients.

Whilst not having a standalone real estate practice **White & Case – W. Danilowicz, W. Jurcewicz i Wspólnicy Kancelaria Prawna sp.K** has nevertheless closed significant transactions in this area, including the acquisition of a major office tower in Warsaw

Wierzbowski i Wspólnicy advises on all aspects of real estate.

TAX

Owing to the fact that major transactions have a significant tax aspect to them, the leading firms all now maintain some degree of tax capability. However, for most firms, tax advice is seen as little more than a support service, though a few firms see more potential in a standalone practice.

When advising on tax issues **Baker & McKenzie** frequently calls on the support of its other European offices. The three-lawyer Warsaw practice has experience in all aspects of tax advice including tax assistance relating to the sale and recovery of bad debts, cross-border commissions, the IT sector, and stock options. The firm recently won a tender to advise France Télécom on tax issues.

The six-lawyer tax practice at **Chadbourne & Parke Polska Sp. z o.o., Wujek, Radzikowski, Szubielska i Wspólnicy. Spólka Komandytowa** has long been acknowledged as one of the finest in Poland. The vastly experienced Adam Wesolowski continues to advise on VAT and excise tax matters, and name partner Dorota Szubielska continues to advise on income tax and all other matters. Both lawyers also have excellent reputations for tax litigation cases.

Dewey Ballantine Grzesiak Limited Partnership's seven-lawyer team is one of the few standalone practices. The firm recently advised Orbis during a tax controversy. Partner Tomasz Kacymirow is frequently cited for his tax expertise.

Linklaters is keen to capitalise on the troubles facing MDP firms by expanding the expertise of its five-lawyer tax practice. Currently the firm only offers tax advice as a support service to its other practices. Tax litigation is a primary focus.

The well-established tax department at **Soltysinski Kawecki & Szlezak Legal Advisors** continues to demand respect. The department provides strategic advice to large companies as well as actively supporting the firm's corporate practice. Jaroslaw Bieronski leads.

Beiten Burkhardt K. Rastawicki Sp.K., formerly closely associated with KPMG, is increasingly undertaking tax work. The practice comprises two associates and three tax advisers.

Senior associate Arkadiusz Michaliszyn heads **CMS Cameron McKenna**'s four-lawyer tax team, undertaking tax structuring work for the firm's corporate clients.

The massive Auchan supermarkets asset deal that **Gide Loyrette Nouel** closed in 2003 had a significant tax component that was also handled by the firm. The firm has also previously carried out work with Ernst & Young on tax issues.

Kochanski Brudkowski Olechowski i Wspólnicy sp.j. began offering tax as a new specialism in 2003 in response to the needs of clients such as Philip Morris. The firm recruited the experienced Piotr Augustyniak from **White & Case – W. Danilowicz, W. Jurcewicz i Wspólnicy Kancelaria Prawna sp.K** to head the tax department.

Based in Krakow, the **Dewey Ballantine Grzesiak Limited Partnership** associated **Studnicki, Pleszka, Cwiakalski, Górski LLP** is often recommended for its tax capability.

TGC Corporate Lawyers has recently hired one tax adviser from PwC and another formerly at Arthur Andersen. The total number of permanent tax advisers at the firm is now three. This expansion reflects the firm's belief that its tax practice can be a market leader. Particular areas of expertise are employment tax and expatriate tax. The firm regularly carries out tax-related litigation and boasts that it has never lost a single tax appeal.

Weil, Gotshal & Manges' tax attorney Robert Krasnodebski has an excellent reputation, for advising the firm's corporate clients on tax issues.

Wierzbowski i Wspólnicy and **Domanski Zakrzewski Palinka** do not have their own tax capability, referring all such work to PwC and Ernst & Young respectively. German MDPs **Rödl, Korpalski Kancelaria Prawna sp.k.** and **Haarmann Hemmelrath** have associated tax and auditing businesses.

TAX

BAKER & McKENZIE ✪
CHADBOURNE & PARKE POLSKA SP. Z O.O., WUJEK, RADZIKOWSKI, SZUBIELSKA I WSPÓLNICY. SPÓLKA KOMANDYTOWA
DEWEY BALLANTINE GRZESIAK LIMITED PARTNERSHIP ✪
LINKLATERS ✪
SOLTYSINSKI KAWECKI & SZLEZAK LEGAL ADVISORS ✪

Beiten Burkhardt K. Rastawicki Sp.K. ✪
CMS Cameron McKenna ✪
Drzewiecki, Tomaszek & Wspólnicy Spólka Jawna
Gide Loyrette Nouel ✪
Kochanski Brudkowski Olechowski i Wspólnicy sp.j.
Studnicki, Pleszka, Cwiakalski, Górski LLP
TGC Corporate Lawyers
Wardynski & Partners ✪
Weil, Gotshal & Manges ✪
White & Case – W. Danilowicz, W. Jurcewicz i Wspólnicy Kancelaria Prawna sp.K

Allen & Overy ✪
Clifford Chance
Gleiss Lutz ✪
Hogan & Hartson M. Jamka, A. Galos, and Partners, LP ✪
Lovells ✪
Nörr Stiefenhofer Lutz ✪
Norton Rose, Piotr Strawa and Partners, Limited Partnership
Salans

Domanski Zakrzewski Palinka ✪
Haarmann Hemmelrath ✪
Rödl, Korpalski Kancelaria Prawna sp.k.
Wierzbowski i Wspólnicy ✪

Firms are listed A-Z in tiers which are ranked in order of priority
✪ Indicates firm displays contact details at the end of this chapter.

KACZOR KLIMCZYK PUCHER WYPIÓR
ADWOKACI SPÓLKA PARTNERSKA

UL. DIETLA 50/12
31-039 KRAKÓW

Telephone: +48 12 431 0599
Fax: +48 12 422 5296
E-mail: kancelaria@kkpw.pl
Website: www.kkpw.pl

Languages
Czech, English, French, German, Polish, Russian

Other offices
Warsaw

Number of lawyers 10
at this office 9

International groupings
International Chamber of Commerce, German-Polish Chamber of Industry and Commerce

CATEGORIES OF WORK

Real estate
Janusz Kaczor, Adam Klimczyk

Commercial property
Rafal Wypiór, Pawel Pucher

Construction
Rafal Wypiór, Pawel Pucher

Commercial law
Adam Klimczyk, Agata Kaczor

Dispute resolution
Agata Kaczor, Adam Klimczyk

Investments
Janusz Kaczor, Pawel Pucher

Intellectual property
Agata Kaczor, Rafal Wypiór

Mergers and acquisitions
Pawel Pucher, Janusz Kaczor

Employment
Adam Klimczyk, Pawel Pucher

Fraud and white-collar crime
Janusz Kaczor, Rafal Wypiór

ALLEN & OVERY

SIENNA CENTER
UL ZELAZNA 28/30
00-832 WARSAW

Telephone: +48 22 820 6100
Fax: +48 22 820 6199
E-mail: information@allenovery.com
Website: www.allenovery.com

Languages
English, French, German, Russian

Other offices
Amsterdam, Antwerp, Bangkok, Beijing, Bratislava, Brussels, Budapest, Dubai, Frankfurt, Hamburg, Hong Kong, London, Luxembourg, Madrid, Milan, Moscow, New York, Paris, Prague, Rome, Shanghai, Singapore, Tokyo, Turin

Number of lawyers 2,305
at this office 26

Contacts
Michael Davies, Andrzej Siemiatkowskí

CATEGORIES OF WORK

Arbitration/litigation
Andrzej Siemiatkowskí
Jaroslaw Iwanicki

Banking/finance
Arkadiusz Pedzich

Corporate/commercial
Andrzej Siemiatkowskí
Jaroslaw Iwanicki

Derivatives/securitisations
Arkadiusz Pedzich, Jacek Jonak

Energy
Michael Davies

Environment
Andrzej Siemiatkowskí

EU and competition
Andrzej Siemiatkowskí

Intellectual property
Andrzej Siemiatkowskí

International capital markets
Jacek Jonak, Arkadiusz Pedzich

Investments
Jaroslaw Iwanicki, Michael Davies

M&A
Andrzej Siemiatkowskí,
Jaroslaw Iwanicki

Privatisations
Michael Davies, Jaroslaw Iwanicki

Project finance
Michael Davies, Arkadiusz Pedzich

Real estate/construction
Andrzej Siemiatkowskí

Telecommunications
Jaroslaw Iwanicki

CMS CAMERON McKENNA

WARSAW FINANCIAL CENTRE
UL EMILII PLATER 53
18TH FLOOR
00-113 WARSAW

Telephone: +48 22 520 5555
Fax: +48 22 520 5556
E-mail: info@cmck.com
Website: www.law-now.com

Languages
English, French, German, Polish

Other offices
Aberdeen, Bristol, Brussels, Bucharest, Budapest, Hong Kong, London, Moscow, Prague, Toronto

Number of lawyers 776
at this office 60

Member
CMS Transnational Legal and Tax Services

CATEGORIES OF WORK

Banking
Jarosław Miller

Corporate and commercial
Dariusz Mioduski

Capital markets
Dariusz Greszta

Energy and projects
Andrew Kozlowski, Dariusz Mioduski

Environmental protection
Andrew Kozlowski, Stan Wajda

Insurance and reinsurance
Iain Batty

Dispute resolution
Andrzej Bednarek, Pawel Pietkiewicz

Real estate and construction
Paweł Dębowski, Piotr Szafarz

Competition
Andrew Kozlowski, Małgorzata Surdek

Tax
Arkadiusz Michaliszyn

Intellectual property
Dariusz Greszta, Bogdan Duda

IT and media
Dariusz Greszta, Bogdan Duda

THE FIRM

CMS Cameron McKenna is a full-service international commercial law partnership, advising businesses, financial institutions and governments. They are a top ten European firm in terms of size and, rank in the top ten City of London law firms. The firm is one of the largest UK law firms in central and eastern Europe, with offices in Warsaw, Budapest, Bucharest, Prague and Moscow. Their offices are staffed by both local and UK lawyers, and provide a full range of legal services to corporate clients and governments. The Warsaw office was established in 1993.

In 1999, the firm announced the launch of a transnational legal and tax services organisation, to form one of the largest legal groups in the world. The new organisation, named 'CMS', has a total staff of 3,500, including 1,700 lawyers. The founding firms have a long history of close association and already command a strong position in their home markets, as well as in the international market.

AREAS OF PRACTICE

CMS Cameron McKenna is the largest international law firm in Warsaw, and is therefore able to support clients in all areas of their business activities. The firm works with multinational companies and agencies, as well as large Polish businesses and organisations.

With the emphasis on quality and best international practice, the firm has attracted clients who have been involved in some of the most high-profile deals in the Polish market. CMS Cameron McKenna is particularly renowned for its work in the energy and real estate sectors. In both these sectors, the teams have historically undertaken groundbreaking work. Their credentials include advising in leading PPP assignments and infrastructure projects, as well as the creation of the first institutional investment lease.

The firm has also developed a strong reputation in other key practice areas. The corporate and commercial team have concentrated on building knowledge and expertise in several key sectors in order to offer clients a unique understanding of the issues involved. The team are also becoming known for the creation of innovative products in the private equity market. Integral to the work of the real estate, energy and corporate departments is the banking team. The banking team's work in project and real estate financing is widely recognised. Should clients come into dispute, CMS Cameron McKenna's significant litigation team has dedicated lawyers that can help. In addition to these core practice areas, the firm has niche competition, environment, insurance, employment, tax, IT and IP practices.

CMS Cameron McKenna runs a legal news service (which can be accessed at www.law-now.com), which provides regular updates on EU developments and other legal issues and how they affect the Polish market in three languages.

DEWEY BALLANTINE GRZESIAK LIMITED PARTNERSHIP

STOCK EXCHANGE BUILDING
UL KSIAZECA 4
00-498 WARSAW

Telephone: +48 22 690 61 00
Fax: +48 22 690 62 22
E-mail: woffice@deweyballantine.com
Website: www.deweyballantine.com

Languages
English, French, German, Polish, Russian

Other offices
Austin, Budapest, East Palo Alto, Frankfurt, Houston, London, Los Angeles, Milan, New York, Prague, Rome, Washington DC

Number of lawyers 606
at this office 60

Contacts
Lejb Fogelman, Jaroslaw Grzesiak

CATEGORIES OF WORK

Asset finance/securitisation
Jaroslaw Grzesiak, Zbignicw Mrowiec

Banking and finance
Jaroslaw Grzesiak, Jacek Michalski

Capital markets
Jaroslaw Grzesiak, Zbignicw Mrowiec

Competition
Jacek Michalski, Lukasz Redziniak

Corporate and commercial
Lejb Fogelman, Jaroslaw Grzesiak

Dispute resolution
Lukasz Redziniak

Energy and natural resources
Jaroslaw Grzesiak, Tomasz Kacymirow

Information technology
Lukasz Redziniak

Infrastructure and project finance
Jaroslaw Grzesiak, Tomasz Kacymirow

Intellectual property
Lukasz Redziniak

Insolvency/corporate restructuring
Jaroslaw Grzesiak, Tomasz Kacymirow

Mergers and acquisitions
Lejb Fogelman, Jacek Michalski

Privatisation
Lejb Fogelman, Jacek Michalski

Real estate
Jacek Michalski

Tax
Tomasz Kacymirow

Telecommunications
Tomasz Kacymirow

DOMAŃSKI ZAKRZEWSKI PALINKA

WARSAW FINANCIAL CENTRE
14TH FLOOR
UL EMILII PLATER 53
00-113 WARSAW

Telephone: +48 22 557 7600
Fax: +48 22 557 7601
E-mail: dzp@dzp.pl
Website: www.dzp.pl

Languages
English, French, German, Russian

Other offices
Poznan, Szczecin, Wroclaw

Number of lawyers 92

Contact
Krzysztof A Zakrzewski

CATEGORIES OF WORK

Corporate
Julita Zimoch-Tuchołka, Piotr Andrzejczak

Mergers and acquisitions
Krzysztof Zakrzewski, Marcin Krakowiak

Banking and finance
Józef Palinka, Andrzej Foltyn

Real estate and property development
Lech Żyżylewski

Regulatory
Grzegorz Domański, Wojciech Kozłowski

Energy
Paweł Grzejszczak

Arbitration/litigation
Grzegorz Domański, Józef Palinka

EU law
Janina Ligner

Intellectual property
Janina Ligner, Wojciech Kozłowski

Employment
Lech Żyżylewski, Józef Palinka

Antimonopoly law
Janina Ligner

THE FIRM

Established in 1993, Domański Zakrzewski Palinka is a full-service Polish law firm with 11 partners and 80 other lawyers, based in Warsaw, with local offices in Poznan, Wroclaw and Szczecin and providing services throughout Poland.

As a professional Polish legal firm, Domański Zakrzewski Palinka possesses knowledge of firms' methods of conducting business activities within Poland, which allows the firm to help foreign investors eliminate various obstacles that might be faced when dealing with Polish companies or with state or local government authorities.

AREAS OF PRACTICE

The firm offers legal advice regarding all aspects of law connected with business activity. The firm's clients include Polish companies with Polish capital, Polish companies with foreign capital, as well as foreign investors operating in various sectors of economy.

The firm's most developed team advises in the area of corporate issues and M&A. The firm's lawyers represent interests of clients participating in take-over transactions involving sale of businesses, company divisions and restructuring as well as privatisation transactions. Furthermore, the firm advises foreign clients who wish to establish business in Poland, including advice on formation of companies and relevant employment legislation. The firm's expertise also includes M&A transactions within the public securities market, advice to companies introducing their shares to the public market, and the establishment of investment funds and brokerage houses. To meet the challenge of dynamically developing e-commerce and IT sectors the firm employs a team of qualified lawyers specialising in these aspects of law. Moreover, the firm has been involved in work on antitrust and unfair competition issues, which includes representation of its clients in all types of financial transactions (advice to leading Polish and foreign banks). Other important work areas include advice on insurance activities and activities of other financial institutions (investment and pension funds) as well as advice on all aspects of telecommunications law and the media, real estate business and management, and intellectual property law.

A brochure providing more details is available upon request.

GIDE LOYRETTE NOUEL

STRATOS OFFICE CENTER
UL KS I SKORUPKI 5
00-546 WARSAW

Telephone: +48 22 583 67 01
Fax: +48 22 583 67 67
E-mail: gln.warsaw@gide.com
Website: www.gide.com

Other offices
Algiers, Beijing, Brussels, Bucharest, Budapest, Casablanca, Hanoi, Istanbul, London, Moscow, New York, Paris, Prague, Riyadh, Shanghai, Tunis

Number of lawyers 480
at this office 36

Contacts
Stanislas Dwernicki (dwernicki@gide.com),
Jean Rossi (rossi@gide.com),
Dariusz Tokarczuk (tokarczuk@gide.com)

CATEGORIES OF WORK

Mergers and acquisitions

Securities and capital markets

Banking and finance

Privatisation

Real estate transactions and financing

Construction

Major projects

Environment

Tax

Labour and employment

Intellectual property

GLEISS LUTZ

UL SIENNA 39
00 121 WARSAW

Telephone: +48 22 526 55 00
Fax: +48 22 526 55 55
E-mail: info@gleisslutz.com
Website: www.gleisslutz.com

Languages
German, English, French, Russian

Other offices
Berlin, Frankfurt, Munich, Stuttgart, Brussels, Prague

Number of lawyers 200
at this office 15

Contact
Dr Torsten Bogen

CATEGORIES OF WORK

Cross-border joint ventures

General corporate

Real estate, zoning

Trade marks

Antitrust, merger control

Labour law

General banking law, cross-border finance

Telecommunications

Environment and pollution control

HAARMANN HEMMELRATH

NORWAY HOUSE
UL LWOWSKA 19
00-660 WARSAW

Telephone: +48 22 82 00 800
Fax: +48 22 82 00 888
E-mail:
warsaw@haarmannhemmelrath.com
Website:
www.haarmannhemmelrath.com

Languages
Bulgarian, Croatian, Czech, Dutch, English, French, German, Hungarian, Italian, Japanese, Mandarin, Norwegian, Portuguese, Romanian, Russian, Serbian, Slovak, Spanish, Vietnamese

Other offices
Berlin, Bielefeld, Brussels, Bucharest, Budapest, Cologne, Dusseldorf, Frankfurt, Hamburg, Leipzig, London, Milan, Munich, Moscow, Paris, Rome, Prague, Shanghai, Singapore, Stuttgart, Tokyo, Vienna

Number of lawyers 281
at this office 9

CATEGORIES OF WORK

- Corporate and business law
- Mergers and acquisitions
- Leasing
- Competition law, antitrust
- Energy/environmental
- Stock exchange law
- Real estate transactions
- National and international tax law
- Privatisation
- Litigation/arbitration
- Audit and accounting services
- Telecommunications/media
- Banking and finance
- Labour law
- Administrative proceedings
- Construction/project

HOGAN & HARTSON M. JAMKA, A. GALOS AND PARTNERS LP

ATRIUM TOWER
AL JANA PAWLA II 25
00-854 WARSAW

Telephone: +48 22 653 4200
Fax: +48 22 653 4250
E-mail: agalos@hhlaw.com
Website: www.hoganhartson.pl

Languages
English, French, German, Italian, Russian, Spanish

Other offices
Baltimore, Beijing, Berlin, Boulder, Brussels, Budapest, Colorado Springs, Denver, London, Los Angeles, McLean, Miami, Moscow, Munich, New York, Paris, Prague, Tokyo, Washington DC

Number of lawyers 1,018
at this office 19

Contact
Aleksander Galos

CATEGORIES OF WORK

- Mergers, acquisitions and divestitures
- Company formation and corporate counselling
- Competition law
- Labour and employment
- Privatisations
- Intellectual property
- Litigation
- Municipal infrastructure projects
- Public/private partnerships
- Foreign investment
- Regulations and licensing
- Taxation and customs
- Capital markets
- Financial services (banking, insurance, investment and pension funds)
- Public and private procurement
- European Union law
- Telecommunications and new technology
- Real estate
- Healthcare and drug industry
- Agriculture and food industry
- Automotive industry

KAROL RUTKOWSKI LAW OFFICE SP. K.

AL. J. CH. SZUCHA 3/5
00-580 WARSZAWA

Telephone: +48 22 622 26 96
Fax: +48 22 622 26 97
E-mail: karolrutkowski@op.pl
Website: www.karolrutkowski.pl

Languages
English, German, Polish, Russian

Number of lawyers 5

Contact
Karol Rutkowski

CATEGORIES OF WORK

Banking, finance and capital markets	**Legislative reforms**
Compliance	**Litigation**
Corporate and commercial law	**Arbitration and ADR**
EU and competition law	**Real estate**

LINKLATERS

WARSAW TOWERS
UL SIENNA 39
00-121 WARSAW

Telephone: +48 22 526 50 00
Fax: +48 22 526 50 60
Website: www.linklaters.com

Languages
All commercial and local languages in the countries where Linklaters operates

Other offices
Alicante, Amsterdam, Antwerp, Bangkok, Beijing, Berlin, Bratislava, Brussels, Bucharest, Budapest, Cologne, Frankfurt am Main, Hong Kong, Lisbon, London, Luxembourg, Madrid, Milan, Moscow, Munich, New York, Paris, Prague, Rome, São Paulo, Shanghai, Singapore, Stockholm, Tokyo

Number of lawyers 2,000 worldwide

Contacts
Tadeusz Komosa

CATEGORIES OF WORK

Corporate/M&A Cezary Wiśniewski	**Labour law** Cezary Wiśniewski
Privatisation Tadeusz Komosa	**Tax** Mariusz Aleksandrowicz
Energy Krzysztof Golyński	**Real estate** Artur Kulawski
Intellectual property Krystyna Szczepanowska-Kozlowska	**Construction** Jonathan Gimblett
IT and communications Tadeusz Komosa	**Banking/finance** Patrick Bell
Litigation/arbitration Zbigniew Kruczkowski	**Capital markets** Patrick Bell
Competition/antitrust Jolanta Tropaczyńska	**EU law** Jolanta Tropaczyńska

THE FIRM

Linklaters advises the world's leading companies, financial institutions and governments on their most challenging transactions and assignments. With 2,000 lawyers, including 470 partners, and offices in major business and financial centres, its clients choose the firm for its distinctive combination of technical skill, commercial experience and outstanding service.

Linklaters has built a formidable global practice through organic growth and a series of mergers, joint ventures and co-operations with other respected law firms. In 2001, Linklaters merged with three of Europe's leading law firms to form Linklaters Oppenhoff & Rädler in Germany, Linklaters in Sweden, Linklaters De Bandt in Belgium and Linklaters Loesch in Luxembourg. In the same year, the firm formed a co-operation with Brazilian firm Goulart Penteado, Iervolino e Lefosse. This co-operation combines Linklaters' international capability with GPIL's extensive knowledge of the Brazilian market. In Singapore, the firm practises as Linklaters Allen & Gledhill, a joint venture with the premier Singapore practice of Allen & Gledhill, while in Italy, Linklaters has an exclusive relationship with Italian law firm Gianni, Origoni, Grippo & Partners.

LOVELLS

UL NOWOGRODZKA 50
00-695 WARSZAWA

Telephone: +48 22 529 2900
Fax: +48 22 529 2901
E-mail: information@lovells.com
Website: www.lovells.com

Languages
English, German

Other offices
Alicante, Amsterdam, Beijing, Berlin, Brussels, Budapest*, Chicago, Düsseldorf, Frankfurt, Hamburg, Ho Chi Minh City, Hong Kong, London, Milan, Moscow, Munich, New York, Paris, Prague, Rome, Shanghai, Singapore, Tokyo, Vienna*, Zagreb*

Number of lawyers 1,600
at this office 32

Contact
Christian Schmidt

CATEGORIES OF WORK

Mergers and acquisitions	Contract
Banking, securities and finance	Construction, building
Commercial law (general)	EC law
Competition, antitrust	Trade marks, intellectual property
Companies, corporations	Arbitration and litigation
Pensions	Telecommunications
Energy	Projects
Environment	Employment
Civil law	Commercial fraud
Insurance	

NÖRR STIEFENHOFER LUTZ

AL. ARMII LUDOWEJ 26
00-609 WARSZAWA

Telephone: +48 22 579 3060
Fax: +48 22 579 3070
E-mail: nslwaw@noerr.pl
Website: www.noerr.pl

Languages
English, German, Russian

Other offices
Berlin, Bucharest, Budapest, Dresden, Düsseldorf, Frankfurt, Moscow, Munich, Prague

Number of lawyers 237
(+ 53 tax advisers, public accountants and tax assistants)
at this office 8
(+ 3 tax advisers, public accountants and tax assistants)

Contact
Zsolt K Radnóczy, Peter Urbanek

CATEGORIES OF WORK

Company law	Banking and foreign exchange law
Commercial law	Tax and customs law
Real estate and investment law	Law relating to commercial leases
Labour law	Competition and antitrust law
Intellectual property and trade mark law	Privatisation

SOLTYSINSKI KAWECKI & SZLEZAK
LEGAL ADVISORS

UL WAWELSKA 15 B
02-034 WARSZAWA

Telephone: +48 22 608 70 00
Fax: +48 22 608 70 70
E-mail: office@skslegal.pl
Website: www.skslegal.pl

Languages
English, French, German, Russian

Other offices
Katowice, Poznan

Number of lawyers 64
at this office 54

Member
ius laboris, International Employment Law Pensions and Employee Benefits Alliance

CATEGORIES OF WORK

Administrative law	**Intellectual property law**
Antitrust and competition law	**Litigation**
Banking law	**Media and telecommunications law**
Commercial and commercial law	**Mergers and acquisitions**
Employment law	**Real estate and development**
Environmental law	**Securities law and capital markets law**
European Union law	**Tax, customs and foreign exchange law**
Foreign investments law	

THE FIRM

Soltysinski Kawecki & Szlezak (SK&S) is one of the leading law firms in Poland. Established in 1991, it relies on the unique background and experience of its founders. The firm has 14 partners and 64 associates of counsel, 12 full-time paralegals, and over 60 people in support staff.

The firm's main offices are in Warsaw, with smaller, branch offices operating in Poznan and Katowice. SK&S is unique among Polish law firms in at least one respect: many of its attorneys studied and/or practised law in Western countries, especially in the US and the UK. The firm has strong international links, particularly with EU countries. Many of the firm's foreign clients have been referred to it by several renowned law firms with which the firm has maintained excellent working relationships for years.

SK&S is one of the pre-eminent firms in Poland, with a strong reputation for professionalism in legal practice.

AREAS OF PRACTICE

The firm's practice covers most areas of commercial law, with particular emphasis on corporate and commercial law, securities and capital markets, banking and financing, intellectual property, as well as antitrust and unfair competition. The firm also provides legal services related to the acquisition of real estate and land development. It also advises in areas such as tax, customs and foreign exchange law, settlement of disputes, and employment law.

SK&S has represented the government and foreign investors in numerous successful privatisations of the Polish industry. The firm's extensive practice in the area of finance and banking includes local representation of several governmental, private and international financial organisations.

The firm's intellectual property department boasts an impressive practice, representing Business Software Alliance and leading software companies for many years in Poland.

The firm's litigation department has extensive experience in litigation before Polish courts, local and foreign arbitration tribunals, and the Polish Supreme Administrative Court.

SK&S has also been active in the area of securities law and capital market regulation. The firm provides regular advice in this area to several renowned, international investment banks.

The firm's tax lawyers provide strategic tax advice to many large companies and work closely with the firm's corporate attorneys in optimizing the tax aspects of all major transactions in which the firm is involved.

The department of antitrust and competition law provides Polish and foreign clients with comprehensive counselling in all areas of Polish antimonopoly laws, including merger and acquisition notification proceedings.

The employment law team provides comprehensive advice on individual and collective employment law, including, *inter alia*, collective bargaining, as well as employment and non-competition agreements for employees at managerial level.

WARDYNSKI & PARTNERS

AL UJAZDOWSKIE 10
00-478 WARSAW

Telephone: +48 22 437 82 00
Fax: +48 22 437 82 01
Website: www.wardynski.com.pl

Languages
English, French, German, Russian

Other offices
Brussels, Cracow*, Poznan

Number of lawyers 41
at this office 35

CATEGORIES OF WORK

- **Mergers and acquisitions**
- **Project financing**
- **Banking and securities law**
- **Real estate and property development**
- **Reprivatisation**
- **Restructuring of state enterprises**
- **Insolvency and settlement of debts**
- **Taxation**
- **Telecommunications and new technologies**
- **Corporate law**
- **Intellectual property**
- **Unfair competition, anti-monopoly law**
- **Litigation and arbitration**
- **Energy law**
- **Labour law**
- **Media**

WEIL, GOTSHAL & MANGES

WARSAW FINANCIAL CENTER
UL EMILII PLATER 53
00-113 WARSAW

Telephone: +48 22 520 4000
Fax: +48 22 520 4001
Website: www.weil.com

Other offices
Austin, Boston, Brussels, Budapest, Dallas, Frankfurt, Houston, London, Miami, Munich, New York, Paris, Prague, Silicon Valley, Singapore, Washington DC

Number of lawyers 1,000
at this office 44

Contacts
Pawel Rymarz, Anna Frankowska, Roman Rewald, Lech Gilicinski, Piotr Tomaszewski

CATEGORIES OF WORK	
Banking and finance	**Mergers and acquisitions**
Capital markets	**Private equity and venture capital**
Corporate	**Property**
Energy	**Reorganisation and restructuring**
Insurance	**Tax**
Intellectual property, e-commerce	**Telecoms**
Litigation and dispute resolution	

THE FIRM

Established in 1931 in New York, Weil, Gotshal & Manges combines lawyers worldwide to meet clients' needs in recognition of the benefits of broad industry and regional experience. The lawyers in the firm's practice groups work together to provide full-service legal advice to clients in sectors as diverse as energy, financial services and hi-tech.

The firm developed a network of offices across the US in the 1970s and 1980s to cater for its expanding client base, and was one of the first international law firms to establish a major presence in central Europe. The firm now has established offices in Brussels, Budapest, Frankfurt, London, Paris, Prague, Singapore and Warsaw.

The firm advises a broad and diverse group of clients, including many of the largest and most prominent corporations and government agencies around the globe, and leading financial institutions.

AREAS OF PRACTICE

The firm's US and European antitrust practice advises on international M&A regulatory notifications, antitrust distribution counselling, cartels, litigation and government and state competition policy. Expertise includes software and computer, healthcare, telecommunications and media, transportation, utilities, heavy industry, consumer goods, financial services and sports.

The corporate department is the firm's largest. The department advises international financial institutions and corporate clients in complex public and private M&As, private equity deals and strategic alliances.

The firm's corporate governance practice is recognised as one of the pre-eminent counsellors of corporate boards, management and institutional investors on the full range of governance issues, including board composition, structure and processes; executive and director compensation; director responsibilities; internal and governmental investigations of alleged accounting or other corporate misconduct; and shareholder initiatives. The firm has advised the World Bank, the OECD, the European Commission and various stock exchanges and regulatory bodies, and is a leader in providing director training programmes worldwide.

The firm advises on a wide range of financing activities and has particular expertise in acquisition finance, asset-based finance, debt restructuring and insolvency, debt and equity capital markets, derivatives, high-yield debt, securitisation, structured finance and telecoms and multimedia financing.

The firm has a leading IP and technology practice and advises some of the world's major technology, media and telecommunications companies. It also acts for investors in technology, media and communications entities. The practice handles patent infringements, outsourcing transactions, strategic alliances, cross-border mergers and acquisitions, investments and IPOs, and advises on the protection and exploitation of IP and on a wide range of e-commerce matters, including data protection. It has expertise in regulatory telecoms matters.

The litigation practice advises international clients on all major areas of the law and has extensive experience in all aspects of dispute resolution. It advises clients in jury trials and appeals, arbitration and alternative dispute forums.

The firm's real estate practice handles complex real estate transactions (including finance, securitisations, development, leasing, sales, acquisitions and debt restructurings) across the US and Europe. It also advises clients on real estate M&A transactions involving real estate investment trusts.

The firm has one of the largest bankruptcy and business reorganisation practices in the world. It includes attorneys in New York, Boston, Dallas, Frankfurt, Houston, London and Miami. The department has been involved in virtually all of the major chapter 11 reorganisation cases in the US and in major national and international out-of-court debt restructurings.

The tax department provides advice on international and domestic taxation, covering many different economic sectors. The department works with the firm's other departments to find innovative solutions to problems that present various and competing multi-disciplinary considerations.

WIERZBOWSKI I WSPÓLNICY

AL ARMII LUDOWEJ 14
00-638 WARSAW

Telephone: +48 22 523 4111
Fax: +48 22 523 4755
E-mail: kancelaria@wierzbowski.pl
Website: www.wierzbowski.pl

Languages
English, French, German, Italian, Russian, Spanish

Other offices
Wroclaw

Number of lawyers 45

Contact
Krzysztof Wierzbowski

International groupings
Close co-operation with Landwell, correspondent law firms of PricewaterhouseCoopers

CATEGORIES OF WORK

Commercial and competition
Bozena Ciosek, Henryk Romanczuk

Corporate structuring
Ewa Lachowska-Brol,
Magdalena Orzelska-Bratkowska

Dispute resolution
Henryk Romanczuk

Information technology
Magdalena Orzelska-Bratkowska

Employment and human resources
Ewa Lachowska-Brol

Financial services
Boguslaw Ptak

Intellectual property
Magdalena Orzelska-Bratkowska

Mergers and acquisitions
Monika Smolarek,
Krzysztof Wierzbowski

Pharmaceuticals
Bozena Ciosek

Real estate
Monika Smolarek

Personal data protection
Arwid Mednis

Telecommunications
Krzysztof Wierzbowski, Arwid Mednis

Mining and energy
Monika Smolarek

German desk
Zbgniew Gaj, Wojciech Andrzejczak

French desk
Arwid Mednis

THE FIRM

Wierzbowski i Wspólnicy provides a full range of business legal services. It is regulated by the National Bar Association and National Association of Legal Advisers. A team of experienced lawyers, headed by attorneys-at-law, is well qualified to offer an extensive scope of legal services to Polish and foreign commercial entities, including litigation. The professional expertise of the firm's lawyers, along with the immense technical resources of PricewaterhouseCoopers and Landwell, allow it to complete clients' large and complex projects. The firm has 45 lawyers, including four partners. Their professional expertise is supported by three of-counsel who are well-known Polish experts in the areas of competition, company and commercial law, privatisation and offset regulations.

The firm's offices are located in Warsaw and Wroclaw. The Wroclaw office was opened in 2000 to respond to the growing needs of existing clients, as well as an increasing number of new clients in the region.

AREAS OF PRACTICE

The firm's lawyers frequently work in integrated professional consulting teams to address clients' business issues. They are deal architects who structure and project manage transactions to their completion. They help clients to transform their business and increase its value.

The teams cover the following practice areas: banking and finance; competition; civil and commercial law; e-business; IT and telecommunications; personal data protection; employment; energy and mining; intellectual property; litigation; pharmaceutical law; privatisation; M&A; real estate; environmental protection; and EC law.

The firm has a leading market position in the areas of anti-monopoly, regulatory (telecommunications) and commercial litigation, mergers and acquisitions. It has particular expertise in the pharmaceutical industry, real estate and personal data protection.

Assistance in the areas of tax law, customs law and international trade is provided in co-operation with the specialised tax, customs law and international trade teams of PricewaterhouseCoopers, as well as lawyers from Landwell firms.

PORTUGAL

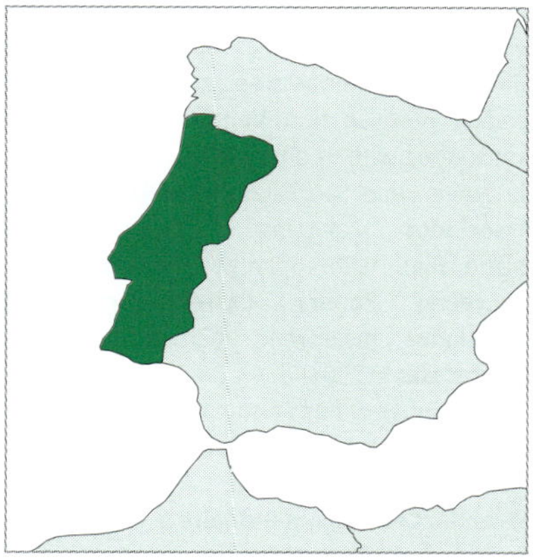

Population	10.2 million
Number of lawyers	17,400
Professional title	Advogado
Currency	Euro (€)

Index

Portugal is set on the Iberian peninsula, which it shares with Spain. The country joined the EU in 1986, and membership of the European Monetary Union (EMU) followed in 1999. Although Portugal has a strong commitment to Europe, it is by no means eurocentric. It displays a decidedly global outlook and is the focal point for some 200 million Portuguese speakers around the world.

The March 2002 elections brought a change of government. Following a seven-year rule by the Socialist Party, the present government is a coalition between the centre right Social Democratic Party (PSD), which holds a majority, and the conservative Popular Party (PP). PSD leader, Jose Manuel Durao Barroso, is the current Prime Minister, with the next elections scheduled for 2006.

Lisbon, located north of the river Tagus, is the financial and legal heart of the country. The second largest city, Oporto, is located in the industrial north and is home to the Futures and Options Exchange.

The archipelagos of Madeira and the Azores meanwhile are autonomous regions, complete with their own governments. Madeira operates its own offshore centre, and hosts the International Business Centre (IBC).

Portugal is due to host the Euro 2004 football championship, which is widely seen as an opportunity to boost the country's profile on the international stage.

BILLING

Portuguese legal fees are low, about 20% lower than neighbouring Spain. The Portuguese Bar Association adopts fixed rates for certain procedures such as standard intellectual property matters. Lawyers generally bill on an hourly basis according to international standards. Contingency fees are not permitted. Average hourly rates range between €80-€250 per associate, and €200-€400 for a partner.

MARKETING

Current Portuguese Bar Association rules, which date from 1984, prevent law firms from advertising their services or mentioning the names of clients. In practice, the Bar frequently closes its eyes to breaches of regulations and, following heavy lobbying by lawyers who feel at a distinct competitive disadvantage to their foreign colleagues, is currently in consultation with a view to relaxing the regulations.

IN-HOUSE LAWYERS

The recruitment of in-house lawyers is not common in Portugal. Corporates, such as banks and large construction and telecoms companies may, however retain in-house counsel for basic transactions. Those that are employed combine their corporate role with private practice.

ECONOMIC CLIMATE

Portugal's fortunes have been closely linked to the EU since joining in 1986; the country is a heavy recipient of EU funding, which can represent as much as 3% of GDP.

Although Portugal joined the European single currency in 1999, it has struggled with its balance of payments deficit for a number of years. In 2001 it became the first European country to have action taken against it by the European finance ministers for running an excessive deficit. The new coalition government has promised to keep the country's budget deficit within the 3% EU ceiling, with the ultimate aim of achieving a balanced budget by 2006. The main tools for achieving this have been spending cuts and a programme of privatisation, which to date has focused on the health and transport sectors.

Following a period of growth, the country has been hit by an economic slowdown since the end of 2002, in common with many of its European neighbours, and in 2003 it was expected to exceed the EU-agreed deficit limit again.

Although Portugal saw significant growth in foreign direct investment at the beginning of the decade, the trend has begun to reverse, and Portugal's competitiveness is currently ranked one of the lowest in the EU. To counter this, the government has introduced a raft of new measures, which have included reform of labour legislation to raise both productivity and competitiveness with neighbouring countries.

LEGAL MARKET

Portugal's legal market remains relatively traditional, with the majority of lawyers working as sole practitioners. Several sole practitioners will frequently set up in practice together, and share

The largest firms

1	PLMJ – AM Pereira, Sáragga Leal, Oliveira Martins, Júdice & Associados	115
2	Vieira de Almeida & Associados	71
3	Morais Leitão, J Galvão Teles & Associados	66
4	Gonçalves Pereira, Castelo Branco & Associados	64
5	Barrocas & Alves Pereira	58
6	Abreu, Cardigos & Associados Attorneys at Law	55
7	Simmons & Simmons	48
	Vasconcelos, F Sá Carneiro, Fontes & Associados	48
9	Ferreira Pinto, Olavo Cunha & Associados	43
10	F Castelo Branco & Associados Veiga Gomes, Marques da Cruz, Colmonero	42
11	Miranda, Correia, Amendoeira & Associados – Sociedade de Advogados	40
12	Carlos de Sousa e Brito & Associados	38
	Pena, Machete, Botelho Moniz, Nobre Guedes, Ruiz & Associados	38
14	Oliveira Martins Moura Esteves & Associados	37
15	Leónidas, Matos & Associados	35
16	Luis Brito Correia	34
17	Jardim, Sampaio, Caldas e Associados	31
18	Abreu & Marques, Vinhas e Associados	30
	Albuquerque & Associates	30
20	Barros, Sobral, G Gomes & Associados	28
21	Coelho Ribeiro e Associados	27
22	Franco Caiado Guerreiro & Associados	25
	Sérvulo Correia & Associados	25
24	Linklaters	23
	Teixera de Freitas, Rodrigues, Moura Costa e Associados	23

These figures represent the total number of lawyers in this country only, and have been supplied by the firms themselves. The figures should be accurate as at 1 January 2004.

the operating costs of doing so. Such ventures should not be confused with partnerships in the traditional sense; they are more of a cost-sharing than a profit-sharing exercise. Those firms that do operate as a partnership tend to be dominated by their founding partners.

Following a period of upheaval in 2001-02, which notably included the disintegration of *Grupo Legal Portugues*, 2003 was a somewhat quieter period on the domestic front, although **Barrocas & Alves Pereira** lost its name partner Alves Pereira during the year. The firm is understood to be changing its name imminently.

The relentless globalisation of legal services has, however, brought a new element to the market, with a number of international firms making their presence felt.

The notion of a single Iberian market still holds sway in Portugal, and a number of Spanish firms maintain a presence in the country through associations with local firms. Although some of these relationships have proved to be fruitful, others have been less so. Spanish firm, **Uría & Menéndez** has broken longstanding ties with **Morais Leitão, J Galvão Teles & Associados**, to set up its own smaller office. Conversely, **Gonçalves Pereira, Castelo Branco & Associados**, which has had an association with **Cuatrecasas** since 1996, merged fully with the firm in 2003, although it continues to operate under its own name in Lisbon.

UK firms are similarly starting to make their presence felt in the domestic market. **Simmons & Simmons** has a joint venture arrangement with M&A and energy specialist, Pedro Rebelo de Sousa at the helm. **Linklaters** meanwhile became the first Magic Circle firm to open an office in Lisbon in 2002, led by former **Morais Leitão, J Galvão Teles & Associados** partner, Jorge Bleck. While reaction was initially mixed, the firm, which consists of heavyweight Portuguese lawyers, has managed to make a mark for itself on the legal landscape. The other Magic Circle firms have watched **Linklaters**' entry into the Portuguese market with interest, but those that have an Iberian presence, such as **Clifford Chance SC**, remain content, for the time being at least, to oversee from Spain transactions with a Portuguese element.

Of the local firms, three remain in a league of their own. The largest of these, **PLMJ - AM Pereira, Sáragga Leal, Oliveira Martins, Júdice & Associados** boasts 125 lawyers, giving it a distinct competitive advantage over its nearest rivals **Vieira de Almeida & Associados** and **Morais Leitão, J Galvão Teles & Associados**. In the next category are a whole raft of firms, all of which are strong contenders for top-tier status, including **Gonçalves Pereira, Castelo Branco & Associados, Abreu, Cardigos & Associados Attorneys at Law**, and **Vasconcelos, F Sá Carneiro, Fontes & Associados. Miguel Galvão Teles, João Soares da Silva & Associados**, meanwhile, is held in high regard for its banking expertise.

FOREIGN OFFICES AND ASSOCIATIONS

Portuguese firms have traditionally eschewed formal links with specific foreign firms. However, membership of worldwide associations is common: **Morais Leitão, J Galvão Teles & Associados** is a member of *Lex Mundi*, while **Barrocas & Alves Pereira** has a longstanding involvement in international practice, and is a member of the *World Law Group*.

Some law firms have established closer links with Brazilian, as well as Spanish, law firms. **Simmons & Simmons** maintains strong links with leading Brazilian firm **Veirano e Advogados Associados**, with six offices in Brazil, including Rio de Janeiro and Sao Paulo. **Leónidas, Matos & Associados** maintains a good working relationship with Spanish firm **Garrigues**. **Gonçalves Pereira, Castelo Branco & Associados** meanwhile merged fully with **Cuatrecasas** in 2003.

A number of firms also have ties with Africa: **Gonçalves Pereira, Castelo Branco & Associados** has an office in Mozambique. **Miranda, Correia, Amendoeira & Associados - Sociedade de Advogados** also has an associated office in Mozambique, as well as in Sao Tome e Principe and Cape Verde.

BANKING AND FINANCE

Headed by Maria João Ricou, **Gonçalves Pereira, Castelo Branco & Associados** advises on both structured and asset finance. Clients include a number of national and international banks. The firm is currently involved in the national rail programme, as well as the Metro of Lisbon.

Led by the highly regarded António Soares, **Linklaters**' banking capability was boosted with the arrival of António Payan Martins, formerly legal counsel to the board of Banco Espírito Santo, SA. The firm advised Semapa and Seinpar on a €290m credit facility loan to be used to acquire 100% of the share capital of FLS Industries Ltd.

Miguel Galvão Teles, João Soares da Silva & Associados is held in high regard for its banking expertise. Clients include Banco Comercial Portugues (BCP). João Soares da Silva is recommended.

Morais Leitão, J Galvão Teles & Associados advised Zurich Financial Services Group on the acquisition of the Portuguese insurance assets of Deutsche Bank group. The firm's securitisation team is currently involved in the drafting of a new securitisation bill of tax and social security.

Led by Fernando Campos Ferreira, **PLMJ - AM Pereira, Sáragga Leal, Oliveira Martins, Júdice & Associados**' financial law group undertakes a mixture of structured and project finance. Highlights include representing a leading Spanish banking group on several restructuring operations in Portugal.

BANKING AND FINANCE

GONÇALVES PEREIRA, CASTELO BRANCO & ASSOCIADOS ✪
LINKLATERS ✪
MIGUEL GALVÃO TELES, JOÃO SOARES DA SILVA & ASSOCIADOS
MORAIS LEITÃO, J GALVÃO TELES & ASSOCIADOS ✪
PLMJ - AM PEREIRA, SÁRAGGA LEAL, OLIVEIRA MARTINS, JÚDICE & ASSOCIADOS ✪
SIMMONS & SIMMONS ✪
VASCONCELOS, F SÁ CARNEIRO, FONTES & ASSOCIADOS ✪
VIEIRA DE ALMEIDA & ASSOCIADOS

Abreu & Marques, Vinhas e Associados ✪
Abreu, Cardigos & Associados Attorneys at Law ✪
Albuquerque & Associates
Barrocas & Alves Pereira ✪
Barros, Sobral, G Gomes & Associados ✪
Franco Caiado Guerreiro & Associados ✪
Jardim, Sampaio, Caldas e Associados
Macedo Vitorino & Associados ✪
Marques Bom e Associados Sociedade de Advogados ✪
Miranda, Correia, Amendoeira & Associados - Sociedade de Advogados ✪
Sérvulo Correia & Associados ✪
Teixeira de Freitas, Rodrigues, Moura Costa e Associados ✪

Airão, Vieira de Castro, Silva Lopes, Pessanha ✪
Coelho Ribeiro e Associados
Ferreira Pinto, Olavo Cunha & Associados ✪
Lebre, Sá, Carvalho & Associados ✪
Leónidas, Matos & Associados ✪
Lopes Dias, Costa Basto, Fernandes e Associados
Lusojurist ✪
Neville de Rougemont & Associados
Serra Lopes, Cortes Martins & Associados ✪
Xavier, Bernardes, Bragança

Firms are listed A-Z in tiers which are ranked in order of priority
✪ Indicates firm displays contact details at the end of this chapter.

Simmons & Simmons advised on approximately 20 structured finance deals during the year for clients such as CSFB, Barclays, Merrill Lynch and Royal Bank of Scotland.

Vasconcelos, F Sá Carneiro, Fontes & Associados is held in high esteem by clients and competitors alike. Pedro Ferreira Malaquias is recommended.

Name partner, João Vieira de Almeida at **Vieira de Almeida & Associados** acts for a number of Portugal's largest banks. The firm is particularly active in securitisations.

Abreu & Marques, Vinhas e Associados advises a number of domestic banks and international banks on regulatory matters and bond issues.

Abreu, Cardigos & Associados Attorneys at Law undertakes a significant amount of derivatives, as well as asset finance and securitisation work for a number of European banks.

Albuquerque & Associates has assisted several European banks in establishing a presence in Portugal. Clients include both local and foreign banks, which the firm advises on all aspects of their work, often closely linked with the firm's privatisation and capital markets capability.

Barrocas & Alves Pereira is instructed by a number of local and international banks, such as Merrill Lynch, on loan transactions. The firm was also retained by a major US bank in a multinational restructuring of a consultancy services group which subsequently aborted.

Barros, Sobral, G Gomes & Associados has significant experience in the incorporation of financial institutions, as well as in drafting banking documentation relating to leasing, bank deposits and securities and loans.

Franco Caiado Guerreiro & Associados provides advice to a number of international banks in relation to the commercialisation of their investment funds in Portugal. The firm gained some significant new banking clients during the year.

Macedo Vitorino & Associados advises several international and local banks. During 2003 the firm acted in transactions amounting to €1.4m. Its derivatives and securitisation expertise is respected.

Miranda, Correia, Amendoeira & Associados - Sociedade de Advogados has made huge strides in the sector; the firm represented UBS AG on one of the largest issues of warrants on the Portuguese Stock Exchange. Daniel Salgado is recommended.

The arrival of Francisco Ferraz de Carvalho from **Morais Leitão, J Galvão Teles & Associados** did much to boost **Sérvulo Correia & Associados**' presence in the sector.

Teixeira de Freitas, Rodrigues, Moura Costa e Associados provides advice to a number of European banks on the Portuguese aspects of syndicated loans and other financing transactions. Recent deals include advising ING Bank and others on a multi-currency revolving facility granted to Numico/Nutricia group.

Ferreira Pinto, Olavo Cunha & Associados acts for a number of national and international banks.

Leónidas, Matos & Associados acted for a number of investment banks on structured finance deals.

Lusojurist regularly represents a Portuguese banking group on private equity agreements, as well on secured lending and mortgages.

Serra Lopes, Cortes Martins & Associados acts for a number of national and international banks on lending work. The firm is currently advising the lenders on a syndicated financing to a Portuguese group regarding a major privatisation.

Xavier, Bernardes, Bragança has advised a number of European banks on export finance and security documentation.

CAPITAL MARKETS

Portugal experienced a significant slowdown in capital markets activity in 2002/2003

Miguel Castro Pereira at **Abreu, Cardigos & Associados Attorneys at Law** is a leading player in the sphere.

Gonçalves Pereira, Castelo Branco & Associados acts on behalf of a number of funds, as well as on the public offering launched by a foreign company.

Linklaters benefits from one of the country's leading practices, led by the respected António Soares. The firm advised Vodafone Group Plc on negotiations relating to the takeover bid for the outstanding minority shares in its Portuguese listed subsidiary, Vodafone-Telecel, which formed part of a larger deal involving other subsidiaries in the Netherlands and Sweden. Rita Oliveira Pinto is renowned for her securities expertise.

Miguel Galvão Teles, João Soares da Silva & Associados has a strong presence in the

CAPITAL MARKETS

ABREU, CARDIGOS & ASSOCIADOS ATTORNEYS AT LAW ✪
GONÇALVES PEREIRA, CASTELO BRANCO & ASSOCIADOS ✪
LINKLATERS ✪
MIGUEL GALVÃO TELES, JOÃO SOARES DA SILVA & ASSOCIADOS
PLMJ - AM PEREIRA, SÁRAGGA LEAL, OLIVEIRA MARTINS, JÚDICE & ASSOCIADOS ✪
SIMMONS & SIMMONS ✪
TEIXEIRA DE FREITAS, RODRIGUES, MOURA COSTA E ASSOCIADOS ✪
VIEIRA DE ALMEIDA & ASSOCIADOS

Barrocas & Alves Pereira ✪
Franco Caiado Guerreiro & Associados ✪
Leónidas, Matos & Associados ✪
Macedo Vitorino & Associados ✪
Morais Leitão, J Galvão Teles & Associados ✪
Uría & Menéndez Abogados ✪
Vasconcelos, F Sá Carneiro, Fontes & Associados ✪

Albuquerque & Associates
Barros, Sobral, G Gomes & Associados ✪
Osório de Castro, Verde Pinho, Vieira Peres, Lobo Xavier e Associados - Sociedade de Advogados
Serra Lopes, Cortes Martins & Associados ✪
Sérvulo Correia & Associados ✪

Firms are listed A-Z in tiers which are ranked in order of priority
✪ Indicates firm displays contact details at the end of this chapter.

sector. Name partner, João Soares da Silva is recommended.

PLMJ - AM Pereira, Sáragga Leal, Oliveira Martins, Júdice & Associados' renowned capital markets group is led by Jorge Brito Pereira. Highlights include advising on the sale of Banco Nacional de Credito Imobiliario to Banco Popular Español, and on the takeover of INTERHOTEL.

Securitisation plays a key part in **Simmons & Simmons**' practice. The firm advised on 13 securitisation deals during the year, and is currently advising on a further five - notably receiving instructions from Caixa Geral de Depositos on its debut in the market. The firm also advised US investors on the private placement of senior notes in the US market, and CSFB on the establishment of a Portuguese securitisation fund management company.

Teixeira de Freitas, Rodrigues, Moura Costa e Associados has a thriving capital markets practice, which advises a number of European banks on transactions such as the issue of convertible bonds, the repackaging and offering of notes of Portuguese banks and companies in the international market, as well as on private and public offerings in Portugal. Clients include the London branch of Deutsche Bank and Dresdner Bank; the firm advised the former on the €100m issue of bonds exchangeable into shares of the Portuguese motorway company Brisa Auto-Estradas de Portugal SA.

Vieira de Almeida & Associados has vast experience of public offerings both in Portugal and in Spain.

Barrocas & Alves Pereira has advised on regulatory issues, notably for a major accountancy firm with regard to a listed Portuguese company.

Franco Caiado Guerreiro & Associados has advised several international companies in the financing and refinancing of their activities with international banks.

Leónidas, Matos & Associados has been involved in capital markets work on behalf of a leading Portuguese telecoms company.

Morais Leitão, J Galvão Teles & Associados carries out capital markets work in conjunction with its privatisation practice, but has lost Francisco Ferraz de Carvalho to **Sérvulo Correia & Associados**.

Uría & Menéndez, led by Carlos Costa Andrade, advised Commerzbank on the issue of warrants in Portugal, as well as representing the same bank on the first issue, public offer and listing of reverse convertobles in the country.

Albuquerque & Associates has a growing presence in the sector, and has been involved in stock market operations, including public offerings.

Barros, Sobral, G Gomes & Associados has experience of launching securities offerings, both initial and subsequent, in the Portuguese market.

Serra Lopes, Cortes Martins & Associados provides regulatory and compliance advice to a number of clients.

Francisco Ferraz de Carvalho's arrival from **Morais Leitão, J Galvão Teles & Associados** has boosted **Sérvulo Correia & Associados**' presence in the capital markets arena.

CORPORATE AND COMMERCIAL

PLMJ - AM Pereira, Sáragga Leal, Oliveira Martins, Júdice & Associados is by far the largest law firm in Portugal and boasts an impressive client base. The firm advised on 2003's largest M&A deal, which saw BNC (a private Portuguese bank) take a 5% stake in BPE. The firm was also involved in the takeover by Telecel of Vodafone. Jorge Brito Pereira has an excellent reputation.

Led by Juão Vieira de Almeida, **Vieira de Almeida & Associados** remains at the forefront of the market. The firm has a strong reputation in restructuring, telecoms and privatisation work.

Abreu & Marques, Vinhas e Associados has a significant number of multinational clients, which it advises on their Portuguese operations. Highlights include acting on the disposal of a large listed company, as well as representing the sellers of a consumer goods company.

Abreu, Cardigos & Associados Attorneys at Law acts for a raft of national and international corporates. 2003 saw the practice acting as counsel to the purchaser on a number of share acquisitions, as well as on the setting up of the Portuguese branch of a North American corporation.

Albuquerque & Associates has vast experience in M&A work, as well as acting on joint ventures and strategic alliances, most notably in the telecoms arena. Recent highlights include advising on the largest hostile takeover to take place in Portugal. The firm has considerable experience in public procurement and tenders, particularly in the defence industry. Advice is also regularly provided on distribution, agency and franchising law to clients in the soft drinks, pharmaceuticals and automotive industries.

Corporate and commercial work is a mainstay of **Barrocas & Alves Pereira**'s practice. Highlights included advising NYSE-listed Nordstrom on the acquisition of a major clothing retail group and assisting Norwegian-listed ORKLA Group in an acquisition in Portugal. The firm has also acted for the Portuguese government on the corporate structure for the implementation of the 7B-8B high-speed rail project. Manuel Barrocas is recommended.

Gonçalves Pereira, Castelo Branco & Associados has seen a substantial increase in activity, relating in particular to M&A and fund structures. The firm boasts strong client bases in the automotive and food industries.

Linklaters' practice has made huge strides during the year – Jorge Bleck and Teresa Anselmo Vaz are both highly regarded corporate lawyers. Highlights include advising the Portuguese state on the winding-up and privatisation of the state holding company IPE. The firm also represented

CORPORATE AND COMMERCIAL

PLMJ - AM PEREIRA, SÁRAGGA LEAL, OLIVEIRA MARTINS, JÚDICE & ASSOCIADOS ✪
VIEIRA DE ALMEIDA & ASSOCIADOS

ABREU & MARQUES, VINHAS E ASSOCIADOS ✪
ABREU, CARDIGOS & ASSOCIADOS ATTORNEYS AT LAW ✪
ALBUQUERQUE & ASSOCIATES
BARROCAS & ALVES PEREIRA ✪
GONÇALVES PEREIRA, CASTELO BRANCO & ASSOCIADOS ✪
LINKLATERS ✪
MORAIS LEITÃO, J GALVÃO TELES & ASSOCIADOS ✪
SIMMONS & SIMMONS ✪
VASCONCELOS, F SÁ CARNEIRO, FONTES & ASSOCIADOS ✪

Airão, Vieira de Castro, Silva Lopes, Pessanha Oporto ✪
Almeida Sampaio & Associados ✪
Azeredo Perdigao & Albuquerque da Fonseca ✪
Barros, Sobral, G Gomes & Associados ✪
Coelho Ribeiro e Associados
F Castelo Branco & Associados Veiga Gomes, Marques da Cruz, Colmonero ✪
Franco Caiado Guerreiro & Associados ✪
Henriques da Silva , Paes De Almeida, Corrêa De Sampaio & Associados, Sociedade de Advogados
Jardim, Sampaio, Caldas e Associados
Leónidas, Matos & Associados ✪
Lusojurist ✪
Macedo Vitorino & Associados ✪
Marques Bom e Associados Sociedade de Advogados ✪
Marques Mendes & Associados ✪
Miguel Galvão Teles, João Soares da Silva & Associados
Miranda, Correia, Amendoeira & Associados - Sociedade de Advogados ✪
Osório de Castro, Verde Pinho, Vieira Peres, Lobo Xavier e Associados - Sociedade de Advogados
Serra Lopes, Cortes Martins & Associados ✪
Sérvulo Correia & Associados ✪
Sousa Machado, Ferreira da Costa & Associados ✪
Teixeira de Freitas, Rodrigues, Moura Costa e Associados ✪

ANBM Advogados Azevedo Neves, Benjamin Mendes & Associados
Claudino Pereira Advogados
Ferreira Pinto, Olavo Cunha & Associados ✪
Jalles Advogados ✪
Lebre, Sá, Carvalho & Associados ✪
Lopes Dias, Costa Basto, Fernandes e Associados
Luis Brito Correia
Neville de Rougemont & Associados
Noronha Advogados
Uría & Menéndez ✪

Firms are listed A-Z in tiers which are ranked in order of priority
✪ Indicates firm displays contact details at the end of this chapter.

Scottish & Newcastle Plc, a client referred from the London office, on the acquisition of the remaining 51% holding in Sociedade Central de Cervejas (Portugal's second largest brewery).

Morais Leitão, J Galvão Teles & Associados maintains a strong presence in the market. Electricidade de Portugal, SA is a major client, which the firm has advised on the reorganisation of the natural gas sector in Portugal, as well as on the sale of its international assets in Chile and Morocco, and the reorganisation of its stake in CEM, the Macau utility company.

Led by the renowned Octàvio Castelo Paulo, **Simmons & Simmons** has a strong presence in the sector. The firm regularly acts for Portugal's largest soft drinks producer, Grupo Sumol, on general corporate and commercial matters, as well as corporate finance and capital markets work. It is currently advising the group on the renegotiation of the bottling contract for soft drink Guarana Antartica. Other clients include Associação Industrial Portuguesa (AIP), and its associated entities, and Empresa Pública de Urbanização de Lisboa. The firm also acts for a number of telecoms operators, including British Telecom and Portugal Telecom on corporate matters.

Vasconcelos, F Sá Carneiro, Fontes & Associados maintains a strong reputation, and is held in high regard by its peers.

Almeida Sampaio & Associados undertakes M&A work for Allied Domeq, Vivendi and Universal Music Portugal.

Azeredo Perdigao & Albuquerque da Fonseca has an established reputation in the sector, and advised on the sale of Cecime - Cimentos, SA.

Barros, Sobral, G Gomes & Associados provides corporate advice to both national and international companies operating in Portugal. E-commerce and IT expertise is also available. The firm's experience in the former encompasses advising financial institutions on the launch of cross-border on-line financial services as well as on on-line banking websites; in the latter, it includes the drafting of software licensing agreements.

F Castelo Branco & Associados Veiga Gomes, Marques da Cruz, Colmonero has an impressive client base, which includes the Portuguese Association of Travel Agencies. Highlights include advising on the Portuguese aspects of a high-profile merger of two large multinationals.

Franco Caiado Guerreiro & Associados has a very active practice, which during 2002/2003 saw particular growth in the healthcare and pharmaceutical sector. The firm regularly advises companies on raising share capital, as well as the compulsory acquisition of various minority shareholdings. The firm's partners, João Caiado Guerreiro and Tiago Caiado Guerreiro, regularly write opinion pieces for *Publico* and *Semanario Economico*. The firm is recommended by clients for the speed of its response and its problem-solving approach.

Henriques da Silva, Paes De Almeida, Corrêa De Sampaio & Associados, Sociedade de Advogados carries out M&A work for an international as well as domestic client base. The firm acted on the €7m acquisition of a Portuguese chain of soup shops by a Spanish company.

Leónidas, Matos & Associados has been involved in ongoing matters relating to IBM's acquisition of PwC Consulting, as well as in the restructuring of two IT groups, and a listed multimedia group. The firm is also able to offer expertise in sports law.

Lusojurist undertakes a mixture of corporate, banking and dispute resolution work. The firm's corporate department was recently involved in a number of restructurings.

Some 65% of **Macedo Vitorino & Associados**' client base encompasses English and American businesses. The firm is currently advising several clients on international M&A and competition matters. These include assisting a US Internet company in its acquisition of the Portuguese subsidiaries of a French e-commerce company, and advising a subsidiary of a German telecoms operator on its acquisition of a Portuguese portal. The firm also acts for several distribution companies involved in the food, luxury goods, entertainment and software sectors.

Led by Nuno Borges Alexandrino, **Marques Bom e Associados Sociedade de Advogados** represents a number of industrial and commercial companies - usually the Portuguese subsidiaries of international groups.

Marques Mendes & Associados advises a number of foreign companies on their activities in Portugal. Recent highlights include advising a US-based company in the acquisition of the Portuguese assets of a French company's subsidiary.

Miranda, Correia, Amendoeira & Associados - Sociedade de Advogados has a strong reputation acting for mining, as well as oil and gas, companies, from its Lisbon, as well as its African offices; the associated Angolan office represents many of the oil companies present in the country.

Osório de Castro, Verde Pinho, Vieira Peres, Lobo Xavier e Associados - Sociedade de Advogados has a strong reputation in corporate and M&A work; the firm regularly advises Sonae.

Serra Lopes, Cortes Martins & Associados has seen considerable growth in M&A work. The firm advised Compal on the acquisition of a renowned soft drinks label from the Portuguese division of Nestlé. Other highlights include representing the largest Portuguese media group on the acquisition of a media company, and advising on the sale of a Portuguese biscuit company to a UK-based multinational.

Sérvulo Correia & Associados acted on behalf of a French-based company on several M&A deals in the retail sector.

Teixeira de Freitas, Rodrigues, Moura Costa e Associados has been active in M&A, joint ventures and restructurings. Examples include the purchase of a minority stake by Deutsche Bank in Portuguese motorway company, Brisa Auto-Estradas de Portugal SA, for over €100m. The firm also boasts clients in the hotel, tobacco, food and beverage and pharmaceutical industries.

ANBM Advogados Azevedo Neves, Benjamin Mendes & Associados acts for clients in the automotive, tobacco and airline industries. The firm has a particular expertise in the latter; it acts for six European airlines.

Ferreira Pinto, Olavo Cunha & Associados acts for a number of car manufacturers as well as media clients.

Jalles Advogados has a diverse client base from North America and northern Europe, with a particular focus on German-speaking countries. The firm acts for a number of clients in the food industry.

Neville de Rougemont & Associados acts for a number of British and European clients with interests in Portugal.

DISPUTE RESOLUTION

The global slowdown has led to an increasing amount of work for many litigators. Although Portugal's court system is notoriously slow, a new Code of Procedure on Execution which came into effect in September 2003 is expected to free up some of their time. The intention of the Code is to streamline the current system for the execution of judgments, by taking the courts, who to date have played a huge part in the procedure, out of the equation.

Barrocas & Alves Pereira is particularly active in construction litigation; the firm is currently representing the contractors in the largest arbitration to date in Portugal involving the Alqueva dam. Other matters include advice to a client on a multi-million euro TMT dispute.

Rui Botica Santos at **Coelho Ribeiro e Associados** comes highly recommended.

Gonçalves Pereira, Castelo Branco & Associados' nine-fee-earner practice under Miguel Esperança Pina, has been involved in a number of arbitrations. The firm recently won an arbitration award on behalf of Swissair against Banco Epirito Santo.

Led by Miguel Pinto Cardoso, **Linklaters** has a strong presence in the sector, advising Parque Expo '98 on a claim brought by Climaespaço, as well as representing Sesil on a €200m dispute against Cimpor, involving seven different proceedings in Portugal, among them two injunctions. The firm also regularly advises Supergolf Amoreiras.

Morais Leitão, J Galvão Teles & Associados has a broad practice which encompasses expertise in arbitration and commercial and criminal litigation, including white-collar crime. The firm represented the Republic of Portugal in a lawsuit filed by Sonae in relation to the privatisation of Banco Português do Atlântico.

DISPUTE RESOLUTION

BARROCAS & ALVES PEREIRA ✪
COELHO RIBEIRO E ASSOCIADOS
GONÇALVES PEREIRA, CASTELO BRANCO & ASSOCIADOS ✪
LINKLATERS ✪
MORAIS LEITÃO, J GALVÃO TELES & ASSOCIADOS ✪
PLMJ - AM PEREIRA, SÁRAGGA LEAL, OLIVEIRA MARTINS, JÚDICE & ASSOCIADOS ✪
SERRA LOPES, CORTES MARTINS & ASSOCIADOS ✪

Abreu, Cardigos & Associados Attorneys at Law ✪
Albuquerque & Associates
Henriques da Silva , Paes De Almeida, Corrêa De Sampaio & Associados, Sociedade de Advogados
Jalles Advogados ✪
Jardim, Sampaio, Caldas e Associados
Luiz Gomes & Associados
Lusojurist ✪
Macedo Vitorino & Associados ✪
Marques Bom e Associados Sociedade de Advogados ✪
Miguel Galvão Teles, João Soares da Silva & Associados
Miranda, Correia, Amendoeira & Associados - Sociedade de Advogados ✪
Novais Leão Loureiro & Associados
Simmons & Simmons ✪
Sousa Machado, Ferreira da Costa & Associados ✪
Vasconcelos, F Sá Carneiro, Fontes & Associados ✪

Abreu & Marques, Vinhas e Associados ✪
Almeida Sampaio & Associados ✪
Azeredo Perdigao & Albuquerque da Fonseca ✪
Barros, Sobral, G Gomes & Associados ✪
F Castelo Branco & Associados Veiga Gomes, Marques da Cruz, Colmonero ✪
Ferreira Pinto, Olavo Cunha & Associados ✪
Franco Caiado Guerreiro & Associados ✪
SCA - Sociedade Civil de Advogados
Sérvulo Correia & Associados ✪
Vieira de Almeida & Associados

Firms are listed A-Z in tiers which are ranked in order of priority
✪ Indicates firm displays contact details at the end of this chapter.

Other clients include Radiotelevisao Portuguesa, SA, Schweppes Portugal and BP. Name partner, Joâo Morais Leitâo and José Manuel Galvâo Teles both come highly recommended.

PLMJ - AM Pereira, Sáragga Leal, Oliveira Martins, Júdice & Associados has a strong presence in litigation and arbitration work. The practice boasts a number of excellent litigators, including Nuno Libano Monteiro, Gabriela Rodrigues Martins and José Miguel Júdice.

Serra Lopes, Cortes Martins & Associados' litigation practice is held in high regard by its peers. The firm is currently involved in a number of construction and real estate disputes. Other highlights include advising the Portuguese branch of a Spanish transport company on a dispute over a distribution agreement. Name partner Maria de Jesus Serra Lopes is currently acting as arbitrator on an arbitration relating to the concession of the Hospital Amadora-Sintra.

Abreu, Cardigos & Associados Attorneys at Law represented a leading bank in relation to a dispute concerning a defaulting loan, and is currently involved in two arbitration proceedings on behalf of a leading telecoms company.

Albuquerque & Associates has a strong practice, with a particular expertise in insurance litigation. Ruy de Albuquerque has acted as arbitrator in relation to a number of banking disputes arising from privatisations.

Henriques da Silva, Paes De Almeida, Corrêa De Sampaio & Associados, Sociedade de Advogados acted on behalf of BIC in a recent dispute. The firm also acts for a number of financial institutions on debt collection matters.

Lusojurist undertakes a mixture of banking, property, IP and commercial litigation, as well acting on debt collection matters. Recent highlights include advising a group of shareholders in relation to an action before the Supreme Court, and successfully representing a client on the termination of an agency agreement without reasonable cause.

Macedo Vitorino & Associados' growing litigation group handles both major international matters as well as local disputes. The firm is currently involved in the restructuring of a Portuguese telecoms operator, and is acting on behalf of a minority shareholder against the controlling shareholders of a distribution company.

Miranda, Correia, Amendoeira & Associados - Sociedade de Advogados has an active arbitration practice; the firm is currently involved in a construction dispute relating to the oil industry.

Simmons & Simmons has a very active dispute resolution practice, acting on commercial disputes, as well as insolvency, insurance and debt recovery matters. The firm is currently advising a Brazilian entity on a professional liability claim worth around €100m, as well as assisting Interbanco and Ogilvy & Mather on debt recovery matters.

Almeida Sampaio & Associados boasts a thriving practice, which in 2003 was involved in the settlement of a distribution fees dispute on behalf of Universal Music Portugal.

Barros, Sobral, G Gomes & Associados has a wide-ranging practice which advises on disputes relating to commercial, employment, environment, fraud, insolvency, insurance, real estate and shipping matters.

Ferreira Pinto, Olavo Cunha & Associados acts on commercial litigation as well as debt collection matters.

Franco Caiado Guerreiro & Associados is currently representing an English bank and its lawyers in relation to a procedure against a Portuguese citizen. The firm also advises on fraud and white-collar crime.

Sérvulo Correia & Associados is legal counsel to a major private company on the complex 'Euroarea case' involving fraud and civil liability issues.

EU AND COMPETITION

Led by the highly regarded Isabel Jalles, **Jalles Advogados** has carved a leading reputation for EU expertise. The firm is currently involved in a huge arbitration with EU implications on behalf of a multinational company.

Marques Mendes & Associados has an established reputation, and is regularly involved in merger control and state aid cases. Recent highlights include advising a major Portuguese media group in two complaints against the incumbent telecoms operator for abuse of a dominant position, as well as representing a major player in the national energy market in proceedings before the European Commission. The firm also has vast litigation experience, acting on behalf of the Portuguese Republic in the first case concerning the involvement of a member state under article 21 of the Merger Control Regulations.

Led by Carlos Botelho Moniz, **Morais Leitão, J Galvão Teles & Associados** has a broad range of expertise in the area. Clients include Sociedade Independe de Comunicaçao, SA, which the firm represented before the CFI and the ECJ with regard to the annulment of the Commission's decision exempting European Broadcasting Union members from competition rules until the end of 2005.

PLMJ - AM Pereira, Sáragga Leal, Oliveira Martins, Júdice & Associados boasts a very active practice, which in 2003 provided ongoing advice to UEFA regarding Euro 2004. Other clients the firm represents on EC matters on a regular basis include Portucel, TAP Air Portugal, L'Oréal and Unilever. Jose Luis da Cruz Vilaca is a leader in the field.

Barrocas & Alves Pereira advises a range of clients on product liability and safety issues, as well as dealing with notifications to the competition authorities, and assisting on competition compliance. The practice is currently representing RAVE, the country's high-speed rail network, on EU issues.

Gonçalves Pereira, Castelo Branco & Associados carries out EU and competition work from its Lisbon and Brussels offices. The firm is frequently involved in notifications to the competition authorities, and recently acted for

EU AND COMPETITION

JALLES ADVOGADOS ✪
MARQUES MENDES & ASSOCIADOS ✪
MORAIS LEITÃO, J GALVÃO TELES & ASSOCIADOS ✪
PLMJ - AM PEREIRA, SÁRAGGA LEAL, OLIVEIRA MARTINS, JÚDICE & ASSOCIADOS ✪

Barrocas & Alves Pereira ✪
Gonçalves Pereira, Castelo Branco & Associados ✪
Jardim, Sampaio, Caldas e Associados
Linklaters ✪
Simmons & Simmons ✪

Abreu, Cardigos & Associados Attorneys at Law ✪
Albuquerque & Associates
Azeredo Perdigao & Albuquerque da Fonseca ✪
Franco Caiado Guerreiro & Associados ✪
Leónidas, Matos & Associados ✪
Miguel Galvão Teles, João Soares da Silva & Associados
Vieira de Almeida & Associados

Firms are listed A-Z in tiers which are ranked in order of priority
✪ *Indicates firm displays contact details at the end of this chapter.*

EMPLOYMENT

MORAIS LEITÃO, J GALVÃO TELES & ASSOCIADOS ✪
PLMJ - AM PEREIRA, SÁRAGGA LEAL, OLIVEIRA MARTINS, JÚDICE & ASSOCIADOS ✪
SARAIVA E SOUSA, GOMES DE ALMEIDA & ASSOCIADOS ✪
SIMMONS & SIMMONS ✪

ANBM Advogados Azevedo Neves, Benjamin Mendes & Associados
Abreu & Marques, Vinhas e Associados ✪
Abreu, Cardigos & Associados Attorneys at Law ✪
Albuquerque & Associates
Almeida Sampaio & Associados ✪
Azeredo Perdigao & Albuquerque da Fonseca ✪
Barrocas & Alves Pereira ✪
F Castelo Branco & Associados Veiga Gomes, Marques da Cruz, Colmonero ✪
Ferreira Pinto, Olavo Cunha & Associados ✪
Franco Caiado Guerreiro & Associados ✪
Gonçalves Pereira, Castelo Branco & Associados ✪
Henriques da Silva , Paes De Almeida, Corrêa De Sampaio & Associados, Sociedade de Advogados
Lebre, Sá, Carvalho & Associados ✪
Leónidas, Matos & Associados ✪
Lusojurist ✪
Marques Bom e Associados Sociedade de Advogados ✪
Miguel Galvão Teles, João Soares da Silva & Associados
Neville de Rougemont & Associados
Oscar Monteiro (Dr)
SCA - Sociedade Civil de Advogados
Sousa Machado, Ferreira da Costa & Associados ✪
Vasconcelos, F Sá Carneiro, Fontes & Associados ✪
Vieira de Almeida & Associados

Firms are listed A-Z in tiers which are ranked in order of priority
✪ *Indicates firm displays contact details at the end of this chapter.*

Somague against the Portuguese government regarding the award of a motorway project.

Carlos Pinto Correia at **Linklaters** has considerable expertise in dealing with the competition aspects of international transactions, particularly mergers and acquisitions.

Simmons & Simmons advised multinational healthcare company, Bbraun, on merger control issues relating to a Portuguese transaction. Other clients include BASF, CSFB and IMS Health, the leading international pharma-information company, which the firm assisted on its successful acquisition of Azyx Portugal, IMS' main local competitor.

Albuquerque & Associates is frequently involved in the notification of mergers and acquisitions before the national authorities, as well as in Brussels, on behalf of both Portuguese and international clients. Related to this is the firm's expertise in distribution, agency and franchise agreements.

Franco Caiado Guerreiro & Associados has had several dealings with the Portuguese Competition Authority on behalf of its corporate client base.

Leónidas, Matos & Associados has assisted in several filings under merger control regulations. The firm also provides assistance to out-sourcing operations in the banking and telecoms sectors. Other highlights include advising on negotiations for the termination of a distribution agreement with a major automative manufacturer.

EMPLOYMENT

Portuguese employment legislation was the subject of significant reform during 2003, resulting in the introduction of the Portuguese Labour Code, which came into effect on 1 December 2003. The main aims of the legislation are to unify and simplify current employment legislation and to increase flexibility in all aspects relating to employment matters, so as to increase international competitiveness. The labour law reforms have also led to changes in the social security regime.

Morais Leitão, J Galvão Teles & Associados has acted for a number of clients on reorgansiations, restructurings and demergers. These include PGA (Espírito Santo Group Airline Company), Schweppes and Grupo Pestana.

PLMJ - AM Pereira, Sáragga Leal, Oliveira Martins, Júdice & Associados focuses on all aspects of labour and employment law, and is regarded as a leader in the field. In common with many of its competitors, the firm has seen an increasing number of employment-related instructions from its outstanding corporate client base.

Saraiva e Sousa, Gomes de Almeida & Associados is held in high regard for its expertise in the sphere.

Simmons & Simmons has a growing presence in the sector; clients include AIG/ALICO, Publicis Group and FIAT Auto Portuguesa, which the firm advises on employment law, immigration and work permit issues. The firm's immigration practice has had some had some remarkable achievements during the year, notably for Nortel Networks.

ANBM Advogados Azevedo Neves, Benjamin Mendes & Associados' client base encompasses a number of embassies, which the firm assists on employment issues.

Abreu & Marques, Vinhas e Associados regularly provides transactional employment advice, while **Abreu, Cardigos & Associados Attorneys at Law** has been involved in a number of restructurings.

Albuquerque & Associates has vast experience in labour law, advising on the restructuring of personnel, the assignment of employment contracts, termination procedures and human resources management in general. Clients include companies in the shipping, food, chemical, software and telecoms industries.

Almeida Sampaio & Associados advised Universal Music on the restructuring of its operations in Portugal.

Azeredo Perdigao & Albuquerque da Fonseca has particular expertise in the aviation sector, and in 2003 was involved in labour litigation on behalf of Cateringpor.

Barrocas & Alves Pereira has been actively involved in a number of disputes, as well as on regulatory matters. The firm has advised on international employee offerings for the likes of Renault, BT and Aventis, alongside a number of foreign firms.

F Castelo Branco & Associados Veiga Gomes, Marques da Cruz, Colmonero provides transactional employment advice to its strong corporate client base.

Ferreira Pinto, Olavo Cunha & Associados advises on employment contracts as well as collective dismissals. The firm also has experience of labour litigation.

Franco Caiado Guerreiro & Associados has a very active practice which handles labour issues for a number of domestic and international clients. The firm is currently involved in a major labour restructuring.

Gonçalves Pereira, Castelo Branco & Associados has a growing practice in this sector. Clients include a major soft drinks manufacturer.

Henriques da Silva , Paes De Almeida, Corrêa De Sampaio & Associados, Sociedade de Advogados represented J Walter Thompson in relation to collective dismissals in Portugal. Other clients include BIC and Loja das Sopas.

Leónidas, Matos & Associados regularly acts for companies on restructurings and redundancies.

Lusojurist's two-fee-earner practice is also recommended.

Marques Bom e Associados Sociedade de Advogados has acted on a number of collective dismissals.

Neville de Rougemont & Associados carried out a collective dismissal for an IT company.

INTELLECTUAL PROPERTY

Cesar Bessa Monteira leads the team at **Abreu, Cardigos & Associados Attorneys at Law**. The firm advises numerous international clients on trade mark protection and litigation, and copyright and software protection, as well as domain name registration and protection. 2003 saw the firm representing a number of well-known international brands on counterfeiting matters.

Both **Albuquerque & Associates** and **PLMJ - AM Pereira, Sáragga Leal, Oliveira Martins, Júdice & Associados** are renowned for their intellectual property capability.

Led by Manuel Lopes Rocha, **Barrocas & Alves Pereira** provides ongoing IP advice to Microsoft, Warner Bros and the Gulbenkian Foundation.

F Castelo Branco & Associados Veiga Gomes, Marques da Cruz, Colmonero has a dedicated intellectual property practice. João Veiga Gomes is regarded as a leader in the field in Lisbon.

Franco Caiado Guerreiro & Associados advises its clients on trade marks, passing off, copyright, database rights, design rights and patents, and has recently been involved in a number of international branding issues. The firm also offers legal advice in connection with IT and e-commerce matters, most recently advising a client on a licence agreement for the distribution of software products. Media and entertainment expertise is also at hand.

Macedo Vitorino & Associados' clients include a telecoms subsidiary, as well as companies in the video gaming and luxury goods markets, which the firm advises on non-contentious matters such as trade mark registration. The firm also boasts an active IP litigation practice: recent cases include defending an author's royalties over a series of works and translations.

Morais Leitão regularly represents Hard Rock Café Lisbon on entertainment law and copyright issues. The firm also acts for Heinz on trade marks and any ensuing litigation.

INTELLECTUAL PROPERTY

- ABREU, CARDIGOS & ASSOCIADOS ATTORNEYS AT LAW ✪
- ALBUQUERQUE & ASSOCIATES
- BARROCAS & ALVES PEREIRA ✪
- PLMJ - AM PEREIRA, SÁRAGGA LEAL, OLIVEIRA MARTINS, JÚDICE & ASSOCIADOS ✪
- F Castelo Branco & Associados Veiga Gomes, Marques da Cruz, Colmonero ✪
- Franco Caiado Guerreiro & Associados ✪
- Macedo Vitorino & Associados ✪
- Morais Leitão, J Galvão Teles & Associados ✪
- Simmons & Simmons ✪

- Abreu & Marques, Vinhas e Associados ✪
- Almeida Sampaio & Associados ✪
- Barros, Sobral, G Gomes & Associados ✪
- Ferreira Pinto, Olavo Cunha & Associados ✪
- Gonçalves Pereira, Castelo Branco & Associados ✪
- Jalles Advogados ✪
- Lebre, Sá, Carvalho & Associados ✪
- Leónidas, Matos & Associados ✪
- Lopes Dias, Costa Basto, Fernandes e Associados
- Miranda, Correia, Amendoeira & Associados - Sociedade de Advogados ✪
- Neville de Rougemont & Associados
- Serra Lopes, Cortes Martins & Associados ✪
- Teixeira de Freitas, Rodrigues, Moura Costa e Associados ✪

Firms are listed A-Z in tiers which are ranked in order of priority
✪ Indicates firm displays contact details at the end of this chapter.

Led by Octàvio Castelo Paulo, **Simmons & Simmons** is currently advising Bacardi on a trade mark infringement case and PT on trade mark issues and domain name registrations.

Abreu & Marques, Vinhas e Associados provides advice on intellectual property and copyright issues affecting the record industry and theatre.

Almeida Sampaio & Associados handles IP work for a number of high-profile clients, including Universal Music Portugal and Intel. The firm is frequently also involved in IP disputes.

Ferreira Pinto, Olavo Cunha & Associados advises on e-commerce and media-related matters.

Maria da Glória Leitão leads the team at **Gonçalves Pereira, Castelo Branco & Associados**, which deals with the registration of trade marks and patents, as well as contentious matters.

Jalles Advogados has been active on infringement disputes on behalf of a number of international clients from the insurance, food and entertainment sectors.

Leónidas, Matos & Associados has a growing presence on Internet-related matters.

Led by João Luis Traça, **Miranda, Correia, Amendoeira & Associados - Sociedade de Advogados** regularly represents Aventis and BEA Systems.

Neville de Rougemont & Associados has a solid practice, acting for a number of US companies.

Serra Lopes, Cortes Martins & Associados has been advising companies in relation to sports sponsorship and merchandising rights.

Teixeira de Freitas, Rodrigues, Moura Costa e Associados has a thriving corporate client base for which it also carries out IP work. In 2003, the firm advised a leading Italian fashion group in establishing a trade mark licensing structure.

PRIVATISATION

Last year was quieter for privatisations in Portugal; one of the few that remained ongoing related to Portucel, the pulp and paper business.

Gonçalves Pereira, Castelo Branco & Associados acts for a range of national and international clients, which include a large paper company. Highlights included advising Iberdrola on the purchase of a stake in EDP.

Led by Segismundo Pinto Basto and Maria Antónia Menezes, **Morais Leitão, J Galvão Teles & Associados** has a leading presence in the sector, having been involved in the majority of sell-offs so far. It advised both Portucel and the Portuguese government on the second phase of its privatisation, as well as tourism group, Pestana, on its winning bid for the privatisation of 40

PRIVATISATION

- GONÇALVES PEREIRA, CASTELO BRANCO & ASSOCIADOS ✪
- MORAIS LEITÃO, J GALVÃO TELES & ASSOCIADOS ✪
- PLMJ - AM PEREIRA, SÁRAGGA LEAL, OLIVEIRA MARTINS, JÚDICE & ASSOCIADOS ✪
- SIMMONS & SIMMONS ✪
- VIEIRA DE ALMEIDA & ASSOCIADOS

- Abreu & Marques, Vinhas e Associados ✪
- Albuquerque & Associates
- Barrocas & Alves Pereira ✪
- Lebre, Sá, Carvalho & Associados ✪
- Leónidas, Matos & Associados ✪
- Linklaters ✪
- Neville de Rougemont & Associados
- Osório de Castro, Verde Pinho, Vieira Peres, Lobo Xavier e Associados - Sociedade de Advogados
- Serra Lopes, Cortes Martins & Associados ✪
- Sérvulo Correia & Associados ✪

Firms are listed A-Z in tiers which are ranked in order of priority
✪ Indicates firm displays contact details at the end of this chapter.

luxury hotels in historic castles in rural areas of outstanding interest.

PLMJ - AM Pereira, Sáragga Leal, Oliveira Martins, Júdice & Associados has been involved in almost all the privatisations that have taken place in Portugal. The firm has ongoing involvement in the privatisation of Portucel and TAP, as well as TAP's handling company, SPDH. The firm is also currently involved in the privatisation of ENATUR (the owner of Pousadas de Portugal).

Simmons & Simmons is currently advising the Portuguese government on the ongoing restructuring of the country's water system, with a view to full or partial privatisation.

Vieira de Almeida & Associados has acted on several of the country's privatisations, relating to motorways and the telecoms and electricity sectors.

Abreu & Marques, Vinhas e Associados has been representing one of the bidders in the partial privatisation of a major Portuguese company, while **Albuquerque & Associates** has also advised on numerous privatisations.

Barrocas & Alves Pereira advised a major Spanish operator on a privatisation in the water distribution sector.

Leónidas, Matos & Associados advised the underwriters in relation to the PT privatisation.

Linklaters advised the Portuguese state on the winding-up and privatisation of the its holding company, IPE.

Neville de Rougemont & Associados acts for a number of Spanish companies on small power stations.

Osório de Castro, Verde Pinho, Vieira Peres, Lobo Xavier e Associados - Sociedade de Advogados is currently representing Sonae, the leading private shareholder in Portucel, on the latter's privatisation.

Highlights at **Serra Lopes, Cortes Martins & Associados** have included advising on the sale, on a public tender basis, of a 51% publicly-owned stake in the largest Portuguese mining company.

PROJECT FINANCE

Albuquerque & Associates has been involved in numerous public tenders, in particular those relating to helicopters, military aircraft and tanks. The firm has acted on numerous power projects, and regularly advises a major oil exploiter.

Barrocas & Alves Pereira has a strong presence in the market; the firm is currently advising the government on the establishment of the PPP health programme, including the drafting of the relevant legislation, and has now been retained on the procurement and negotiation for all ten new hospitals. The firm is also currently acting as legal adviser to RAVE, the Portuguese high-speed rail network, which is also the country's biggest infrastructure project, including advice on the financial arrangements. Other highlights include advising on two port projects in Africa.

PROJECT FINANCE

ALBUQUERQUE & ASSOCIATES
BARROCAS & ALVES PEREIRA ✪
GONÇALVES PEREIRA, CASTELO BRANCO & ASSOCIADOS ✪
JARDIM, SAMPAIO, CALDAS E ASSOCIADOS
LINKLATERS ✪
MIGUEL GALVÃO TELES, JOÃO SOARES DA SILVA & ASSOCIADOS
MORAIS LEITÃO, J GALVÃO TELES & ASSOCIADOS ✪
PLMJ - AM PEREIRA, SÁRAGGA LEAL, OLIVEIRA MARTINS, JÚDICE & ASSOCIADOS ✪
SÉRVULO CORREIA & ASSOCIADOS ✪
VASCONCELOS, F SÁ CARNEIRO, FONTES & ASSOCIADOS ✪
VIEIRA DE ALMEIDA & ASSOCIADOS

ANBM Advogados Azevedo Neves, Benjamin Mendes & Associados
Abreu & Marques, Vinhas e Associados ✪
Abreu, Cardigos & Associados Attorneys at Law ✪
Almeida Sampaio & Associados ✪
Barros, Sobral, G Gomes & Associados ✪
Franco Caiado Guerreiro & Associados ✪
Macedo Vitorino & Associados ✪
Miranda, Correia, Amendoeira & Associados - Sociedade de Advogados ✪
Serra Lopes, Cortes Martins & Associados ✪
Simmons & Simmons ✪
Xavier, Bernardes, Bragança

Firms are listed A-Z in tiers which are ranked in order of priority
✪ Indicates firm displays contact details at the end of this chapter.

Gonçalves Pereira, Castelo Branco & Associados has longstanding involvement in the country's motorways programme, as well as in the hospitals PPP and the energy and water sectors. Clients include Iberdrola, which the firm is advising on a power plant.

Renewable energy forms a key part of **Linklaters**' activity. The firm advised BES Investimento as lender on a number of co-generation projects, as well as representing Enerpro as sponsor in a renewable energy project. The firm is also currently advising a consortium formed to bid for ten new hospitals, and is also in the process of advising the Republic of Portugal on setting up a PPP arrangement to implement an emergency telecoms system, the first such project to be carried out since the approval of new guidelines. Ongoing advice has also been provided to Metrosul do Tejo on the first BOT concession for a light railway system in Portugal, which closed during the course of the year. Pedro Siza Vieira and Jorge Goncalves are both renowned for their expertise in this sector.

Morais Leitão, J Galvão Teles & Associados maintains a leading presence in the sector, advising on a significant number of project financing deals. Highlights include advising the football club, Sporting Clube de Portugal, and a bank syndicate led by Banco Português de Investimento, on the finance for two new stadia for Euro 2004, the latter for Futebol Clube de Porto. The firm also represented a syndicate of banks led by Banco Espírito Santo on the Grande Porto shadow toll-road project in Oporto. Filipa Arantes Pedroso and Luis Branco are well-regarded.

PLMJ - AM Pereira, Sáragga Leal, Oliveira Martins, Júdice & Associados provides ongoing advice on a windfarm project, as well as on a motorway concession.

Sérvulo Correia & Associados has a strong presence in administrative law, government contracts and public procurement. It has acted on a number of tenders and contracts relating to the procurement of military equipment on behalf of the Ministry of Defence, which involved various complex financing arrangements. The firm is also currently involved in project finance schemes on behalf of the Portuguese government in relation to its ongoing public works concessions of several motorways.

Jardim, Sampaio, Caldas e Associados, **Miguel Galvão Teles, João Soares da Silva & Associados**; **Vasconcelos, F Sá Carneiro, Fontes & Associados** and **Vieira de Almeida & Associados** also come highly recommended, and have considerable experience in projects work.

ANBM Advogados Azevedo Neves, Benjamin Mendes & Associados acts for two municipalities on their administrative contracts.

Abreu, Cardigos & Associados Attorneys at Law has ongoing involvement in the construction of a mini-hydro power plant in Portugal.

Almeida Sampaio & Associados acted on the supply of submarines by a German consortium to the Portuguese government following a tender. The firm also advised the consortium led by Siemens AG which won the Tagus Southbank Light Rail Train tender.

Barros, Sobral, G Gomes & Associados has experience of advising financial institutions on project finance, including advising on the Portuguese and Brazilian implications of cross-border project finance ventures.

Franco Caiado Guerreiro & Associados is currently involved in a number of projects. These include finalising the project management contract for building a soccer stadium for Euro 2004. The firm has also been instructed on a number of hospital projects.

Macedo Vitorino & Associados has been very active in energy projects. The firm's clients include one of the largest EU windfarm developers. Other highlights include advising a syndicate of banks on security arrangements involving Portuguese contracts for the financing of the Nigerian LNG project.

Miranda, Correia, Amendoeira & Associados - Sociedade de Advogados is starting to make headway in this market on the back of its strong presence in the energy sector, as well as a growing presence in banking and finance work.

Serra Lopes, Cortes Martins & Associados is representing a Portuguese energy group on a €140m structured project finance deal in the renewable energy sector.

Simmons & Simmons is currently advising the Portuguese government on the ongoing restructuring of the country's water system, with a view to full or partial privatisation. The firm is also advising ABN Amro and Banco EFISA on their bid to supply financial services for the construction of the new airport in Ota (Portugal). Edison Mission Energy has instructed the firm on a windfarm project.

Xavier, Bernardes, Bragança has a strong presence in project finance and infrastructure work. The firm has been involved in the implementation of new PPP structures in the water, sewage and waste treatment sectors in eleven municipalities.

REAL ESTATE AND CONSTRUCTION

Barrocas & Alves Pereira advises most of Portugal's major construction companies. The firm is currently involved in a number of ongoing projects, such as Alqueva – the largest dam project in Iberia. The construction practice has also been retained by contractors involved on the construction of stations and extensions to the Lisbon Underground.

Gonçalves Pereira, Castelo Branco & Associados advises a number construction companies in Lisbon and Oporto on both contentious and non-contentious matters. The firm is currently involved in a number of residential and commercial developments.

Morais Leitão, J Galvão Teles & Associados has a strong practice, which is frequently involved in real estate, construction, urban development and public procurement projects. These include representing Sonae, as well as Lusotur, which the firm is currently advising in relation to a tourism project covering an area of 948,000 sq m. The firm is also representing Parque Expo in relation to project Cidade Administrativa regarding the urban regeneration and construction of public administration buildings.

PLMJ - AM Pereira, Sáragga Leal, Oliveira Martins, Júdice & Associados has a thriving practice which represents a number of investors in the Algarve.

Abreu & Marques, Vinhas e Associados boasts an active practice which was involved in the disposal of a large shopping centre.

Azeredo Perdigao & Albuquerque da Fonseca has a strong construction practice and regularly advises OPCA (Obras Publicas e Cimento Armado) on construction contracts.

F Castelo Branco & Associados Veiga Gomes, Marques da Cruz, Colmonero's practice is led by Vítor Marques da Cruz, and has acted on the acquisition of properties in southern Portugal on behalf of Spanish and Portuguese companies.

Ferreira Pinto, Olavo Cunha & Associados acts for a number of property companies and developers; the firm is currently representing two of the biggest investors in the Algarve.

Franco Caiado Guerreiro & Associados has advised a local developer on the acquisition of land near Lisbon for a commercial development.

With a growing focus in the sector, **Leónidas, Matos & Associados** represented the vendors on the sale of two luxury hotels and one golf course in the Algarve.

Linklaters advised five institutional investors on the purchase of 13 shopping centres in Portugal, forming part of a multi-jurisdictional deal involving the establishment of a fund through a joint venture with Sonae Imobiliaria Group and the purchase of five further shopping centres in Spain.

Marques Bom e Associados Sociedade de Advogados is involved in the construction of two power plants in Portugal. The firm also acts for a number of the companies involved in the construction of stadia for Euro 2004.

Sérvulo Correia & Associados advised a major private company on several urban planning and construction law issues in the centre and south of Portugal.

Simmons & Simmons regularly advises individual, as well as corporate clients, on the acquisition of real estate, as well as construction issues. The firm represented Associação Parque Junqueira (a joint venture between the Lisbon municipality and the Portuguese Industrial Association) on a development project in Lisbon worth €200m.

Teixeira de Freitas, Rodrigues, Moura Costa e Associados has been increasingly involved in town planning, as well as infrastructure and construction projects relating to residential and commercial sites. The firm is also involved in the management of shopping and business centres.

REAL ESTATE AND CONSTRUCTION

BARROCAS & ALVES PEREIRA ✪
GONÇALVES PEREIRA, CASTELO BRANCO & ASSOCIADOS ✪
MORAIS LEITÃO, J GALVÃO TELES & ASSOCIADOS ✪
PLMJ - AM PEREIRA, SÁRAGGA LEAL, OLIVEIRA MARTINS, JÚDICE & ASSOCIADOS ✪

Abreu & Marques, Vinhas e Associados ✪
Abreu, Cardigos & Associados Attorneys at Law ✪
Albuquerque & Associates
Azeredo Perdigao & Albuquerque da Fonseca ✪
Barros, Sobral, G Gomes & Associados ✪
F Castelo Branco & Associados Veiga Gomes, Marques da Cruz, Colmonero ✪
Ferreira Pinto, Olavo Cunha & Associados ✪
Franco Caiado Guerreiro & Associados ✪
Jardim, Sampaio, Caldas e Associados
Lebre, Sá, Carvalho & Associados ✪
Leónidas, Matos & Associados ✪
Linklaters ✪
Marques Bom e Associados Sociedade de Advogados ✪
Neville de Rougemont & Associados
Sérvulo Correia & Associados ✪
Simmons & Simmons ✪
Teixeira de Freitas, Rodrigues, Moura Costa e Associados ✪
Vieira de Almeida & Associados

Firms are listed A-Z in tiers which are ranked in order of priority
✪ Indicates firm displays contact details at the end of this chapter.

SHIPPING

Shipping in Portugal is dominated by boutique firms, such as: **Andrade Dias e Associados**; **Armando Henriques, Ana Cristina Pimentel & Associados - Sociedade de Advogados**; and **G Conceicao Silva Advogado**. A few of the larger firms, however, also have excellent shipping expertise. **Albuquerque & Associates** has a leading presence in the sector, particularly in ship finance, regularly acting for the country's major ship owners. The firm assists on international trade and charter contracts, as well as offering expertise in the field of ports and harbour administration in Portugal. The practice has participated in all the public tenders for the granting of port concessions that have taken place in Portugal in the last 15 years.

SHIPPING

ALBUQUERQUE & ASSOCIATES
ANDRADE DIAS E ASSOCIADOS
ARMANDO FELIX PEREIRA (DR)
ARMANDO HENRIQUES, ANA CRISTINA PIMENTEL & ASSOCIADOS - SOCIEDADE DE ADVOGADOS
BARROCAS & ALVES PEREIRA ✪
G CONCEICAO SILVA ADVOGADO
MEDEIROS COSMEFIND (DR)

Abreu, Cardigos & Associados Attorneys at Law ✪
Barros, Sobral, G Gomes & Associados ✪
Coelho Ribeiro e Associados
Morais Leitão, J Galvão Teles & Associados ✪
Neville de Rougemont & Associados
PLMJ - AM Pereira, Sáragga Leal, Oliveira Martins, Júdice & Associados ✪
Serra Lopes, Cortes Martins & Associados ✪
Simmons & Simmons ✪
Teixeira de Freitas, Rodrigues, Moura Costa e Associados ✪

Firms are listed A-Z in tiers which are ranked in order of priority
✪ Indicates firm displays contact details at the end of this chapter.

Barrocas & Alves Pereira has been particularly active in shipping litigation on behalf of P&I clubs, insurers and ship owners.

Abreu, Cardigos & Associados Attorneys at Law's shipping practice is led by Cesar Bessa Monteiro, while **Morais Leitão, J Galvão Teles & Associados** carries out shipping-related work from its Madeira office. The firm handles ship finance work as well as acting on the incorporation of shipping companies and ship registration.

Serra Lopes, Cortes Martins & Associados regularly acts for a major Portuguese shipyard.

Maria José Santana's arrival from **Oliveira Martins Moura Esteves & Associados**, boosted **Simmons & Simmons**' practice in the sector.

Teixeira de Freitas, Rodrigues, Moura Costa e Associados has been extensively involved in advising banks and ship owners on ship finance transactions.

TAX

Abreu & Marques, Vinhas e Associados advises on tax litigation as well as on international tax planning. The firm's tax team includes Manuel Faustino, a former deputy director of the Portuguese Tax Authority.

Abreu, Cardigos & Associados Attorneys at Law is a leader in the field. The firm undertakes a wide spectrum of transactional as well as litigious tax work, and provides advice to the European Venture Capital Association and the Portuguese Venture Capital Association, as well as representing the European Investment Fund. Miguel Teixeira de Abreu is recommended.

Azeredo Perdigao & Albuquerque da Fonseca is renowned for its tax expertise, and in particular its offshore investment advice relating to the Madeira Free Trade Zone. 2003 saw the firm undertake tax litigation on behalf of Spanish retailer, Zara.

Gonçalves Pereira, Castelo Branco & Associados' five-fee-earner team benefits from strong support in **Cuatrecasas**' tax team in Spain. The firm's client base encompasses investment banks, car manufacturers and construction companies, which the firm advises on transactional matters.

Morais Leitão, J Galvão Teles & Associados boasts a leading tax practice, which encompasses tax consultancy, restructuring and litigation. The client base in this sector is truly impressive, including Diageo Pernod Ricard, Akeler, Vivendi - Compagne Générale des Eaux du Portugal, SA, and Pestana Group. The litigation arm has scored some impressive wins over the last year, which included acting for Borealis on a successful challenge to a capital gains assessment following a reorganisation. Francisco Sousa da Câmara is renowned in the sector. The firm's Madeira office focuses on both International Business Centre clients as well as regional clients.

TAX

ABREU & MARQUES, VINHAS E ASSOCIADOS ✪
ABREU, CARDIGOS & ASSOCIADOS ATTORNEYS AT LAW ✪
AZEREDO PERDIGAO & ALBUQUERQUE DA FONSECA ✪
GONÇALVES PEREIRA, CASTELO BRANCO & ASSOCIADOS ✪
MORAIS LEITÃO, J GALVÃO TELES & ASSOCIADOS ✪
PLMJ - AM PEREIRA, SÁRAGGA LEAL, OLIVEIRA MARTINS, JÚDICE & ASSOCIADOS ✪
SÉRVULO CORREIA & ASSOCIADOS ✪
SIMMONS & SIMMONS ✪
TEIXEIRA DE FREITAS, RODRIGUES, MOURA COSTA E ASSOCIADOS ✪
XAVIER, BERNARDES, BRAGANÇA

Albuquerque & Associates
Barros, Sobral, G Gomes & Associados ✪
F Castelo Branco & Associados Veiga Gomes, Marques da Cruz, Colmonero ✪
Franco Caiado Guerreiro & Associados ✪
Henriques da Silva , Paes De Almeida, Corrêa De Sampaio & Associados, Sociedade de Advogados
Linklaters ✪

ANBM Advogados Azevedo Neves, Benjamin Mendes & Associados
Jalles Advogados ✪
Lebre, Sá, Carvalho & Associados ✪
Macedo Vitorino & Associados ✪
Marques Bom e Associados Sociedade de Advogados ✪
Neville de Rougemont & Associados
Osório de Castro, Verde Pinho, Vieira Peres, Lobo Xavier e Associados - Sociedade de Advogados
Vasconcelos, F Sá Carneiro, Fontes & Associados ✪

Firms are listed A-Z in tiers which are ranked in order of priority
✪ Indicates firm displays contact details at the end of this chapter.

Diogo Leite de Campoa at **PLMJ - AM Pereira, Sáragga Leal, Oliveira Martins, Júdice & Associados** comes highly recommended.

Led by Rogério M. Fernandes Ferreira, **Sérvulo Correia & Associados** acts as tax adviser to an important press and telecoms group, advising on both tax planning and tax litigation matters.

Simmons & Simmons maintains a leading tax practice, which is frequently assisting on banking and corporate transactions. Led by Vítor M Félix, the firm advised Cimpor on tax issues relating to the private placement of senior notes, and CSFB on the tax aspects of the 'Aqua Finance 2' securitisation for Finibanco.

Teixeira de Freitas, Rodrigues, Moura Costa e Associados advises its clients on both domestic and international tax issues. The firm has particular expertise in setting up complex international transactions through the International Business Centre of Madeira.

Xavier, Bernardes, Bragança has a strong presence in the market – Alberto Xavier comes highly recommended. In 2003 the firm advised on the reorganisation of assets of a hotel group, as well as on a share sale by a Brazilian company.

Albuquerque & Associates provides tax advice to both corporate entities and individuals.

Barros, Sobral, G Gomes & Associados advises on tax disputes and tax planning, in particular on international tax planning through the use of offshore structures. The firm has developed a leading role in the Free Trade Zone of Madeira, representing both corporations and financial institutions.

F Castelo Branco & Associados Veiga Gomes, Marques da Cruz, Colmonero's four-lawyer team is involved in tax planning and litigation, as well as advising on the tax aspects of corporate transactions.

Franco Caiado Guerreiro & Associados advises several international banks and construction companies on tax planning matters. The firm has been particularly active in VAT-related matters.

Henriques da Silva , Paes De Almeida, Corrêa De Sampaio & Associados, Sociedade de Advogados advises on both private client and corporate tax issues.

ANBM Advogados Azevedo Neves, Benjamin Mendes & Associados advises on both tax litigation, as well as tax planning, in particular in the use of international structures and offshore vehicles.

Jalles Advogados has been active in advising a number of offshore companies owning property in the Algarve.

TELECOMS

Macedo Vitorino & Associados acts for several multinational and local telecoms companies, representing about 20% of the operators registered and licensed in Portugal. Highlights include advising a Portuguese telecoms operator on the termination of vendor finance agreements for the development of a UMTS project.

Morais Leitão, J Galvão Teles & Associados' Filipa Arantes Pedroso and João Afonso have a very active practice. The firm is currently representing the Portuguese government on the sale of its basic telecoms network to PT Communicoes, SA, and is advising EDP on the transfer of the entire share capital of OTEP SGPS, SA, a telecoms holding company that indirectly holds a 25.49% stake in Optimus.

Simmons & Simmons has a leading telecoms, media and technology practice. The firm represents a number of telecoms operators

TELECOMS

MACEDO VITORINO & ASSOCIADOS ✪
MORAIS LEITÃO, J GALVÃO TELES & ASSOCIADOS ✪
SIMMONS & SIMMONS ✪
VIEIRA DE ALMEIDA & ASSOCIADOS

ABREU, CARDIGOS & ASSOCIADOS ATTORNEYS AT LAW ✪
ALBUQUERQUE & ASSOCIATES
BARROCAS & ALVES PEREIRA ✪
GONÇALVES PEREIRA, CASTELO BRANCO & ASSOCIADOS ✪
LEÓNIDAS, MATOS & ASSOCIADOS ✪
PLMJ - AM PEREIRA, SÁRAGGA LEAL, OLIVEIRA MARTINS, JÚDICE & ASSOCIADOS ✪

Coelho Ribeiro e Associados
Franco Caiado Guerreiro & Associados ✪
Jalles Advogados ✪
Jardim, Sampaio, Caldas e Associados
Marques Bom e Associados Sociedade de Advogados ✪
Serra Lopes, Cortes Martins & Associados ✪
Sérvulo Correia & Associados ✪
Sousa Machado, Ferreira da Costa & Associados ✪
Vasconcelos, F Sá Carneiro, Fontes & Associados ✪
Xavier, Bernardes, Bragança

Firms are listed A-Z in tiers which are ranked in order of priority
✪ Indicates firm displays contact details at the end of this chapter.

including Portugal Telecom on its multimedia business, as well as British Telecom. UK telecoms company, Inquam, and Radiomóvel are other regular clients; recent highlights include advising the latter on the interconnection process with other telecoms operators.

Abreu, Cardigos & Associados Attorneys at Law regularly advises PT, as well as its subsidiaries.

At **Barrocas & Alves Pereira**, Manuel Lopes Rocha heads the IT and e-commerce legislative committee of the Portuguese Bar. As well as regularly representing Cisco Systems, WorldCom/MCI and Nortel (the supplier of 3G UMTS equipment). The firm is currently advising the Portuguese government on draft legislation relating to the implementation of the country's e-government programme.

Gonçalves Pereira, Castelo Branco & Associados regularly acts for Jazztel, and was involved in the financing of PT. The firm's Mozambique office regularly acts for a leading mobile phone operator.

In addition to acting for PT, **Leónidas, Matos & Associados** represents a number of foreign telecoms operators with a presence in Portugal.

PT is also a regular client of **PLMJ - AM Pereira, Sáragga Leal, Oliveira Martins, Júdice & Associados**. The practice is highly recommended by clients and competitors alike.

Franco Caiado Guerreiro & Associados represents a number of telcoms companies, while **Jalles Advogados**' telecoms practice regularly advises on regulatory matters.

Marques Bom e Associados Sociedade de Advogados acts for a leading mobile phone company on their 3G activity in Portugal.

Serra Lopes, Cortes Martins & Associados represents a number of multimedia companies and ISPs.

Sérvulo Correia & Associados is legal counsel to a press and telecoms group listed on the Lisbon Stock Exchange.

Sousa Machado, Ferreira da Costa & Associados undertakes regulatory work for a major mobile phone operator.

Xavier, Bernardes, Bragança has a number of Brazilian telecoms clients which it advises on a regular basis; 2003 saw the firm advise a major PCS operator in the acquisition of a mobile operator. The firm has also had experience of advising on negotiations concerning the exploitation of telecoms infrastructure.

ABOGADOS AMYA

RUA VICTOR CÓRDON, 45 B, R/C
1200-483 LISBOA

Telephone: +351 21 343 1925
Fax: +351 21 343 2099
E-mail: alecky@mail.telepac.pt
Website: www.amya.es

Languages
English, French, German, Italian, Spanish

Other offices
Aachen*, Almancil (Quinta do Lago)*, Barcelona, Buenos Aires, Las Palmas, Madrid, Marbella, Miami, Panama, Paris, Piraeus, Rome, Valencia, Vigo

Number of lawyers 27
at this office 2

Contact
Alexandra von Böhm-Amolly

Member
IIDM

CATEGORIES OF WORK

Admiralty and shipping

Fisheries

Marine insurance

Transportation

Construction, real estate, property finance

Agriculture

Foreign and offshore investment, tax planning and Madeira free trade zone

Civil law

Corporate and commercial law

Litigation and arbitration

ABREU & MARQUES, VINHAS E ASSOCIADOS

RUA FILIPE FOLQUE 2-4º
1069-121 LISBOA

Telephone: +351 21 330 7100
Fax: +351 21 314 7491
E-mail: amva@amva.pt

Languages
English, French, Spanish, German

Other offices
Funchal, Luanda*, Maputo*, São Paulo*, Rio de Janeiro

Number of lawyers 30
at this office 25

CATEGORIES OF WORK

Administrative and environment law
Isabel Garcia, Sofia Amram

Arbitration and litigation
Jorge de Abreu, João Pedro Collares Pereira

Banking and finance, capital markets, investment funds
Afonso Barroso

Corporate and commercial law
Luis Vinhas, Afonso Barroso

EU and competition law
Luis Vinhas, Sofia Amram

Foreign investment
Jorge de Abreu, Luis Vinhas

Intellectual property
Jorge de Abreu

Labour law
Martim Anahory

Investment funds
Afonso Barroso

Madeira free-trade zone
Jorge de Abreu, Afonso Barroso

Mergers and acquisitions
Luís Vinhas, Martim Anahory

Privatisation
Jorge de Abreu, Luís Vinhas

Real estate, construction and tourism
Jorge de Abreu, Henrique Moser

Taxation
Isabel Garcia, Manuel Faustino

ABREU, CARDIGOS & ASSOCIADOS
ATTORNEYS AT LAW

AV. DAS FORÇAS ARMADAS 125
12TH FLOOR
1600-179 LISBOA

Telephone: +351 21 723 18 00
Fax: +351 21 723 18 99
E-mail: general@abreucardigos.com
Website: www.abreucardigos.com

Languages
English, French, German, Spanish

Number of lawyers 55

Contact
Miguel Teixeira de Abreu

Member
IBA; International Fiscal Association; AIJA; International Trade Mark Association; International Federation of Industrial Property Consultants; European Communities Trade Mark Association; EVCA; Multilaw Counsel Alliance; International Swaps and Derivatives Association (ISDA)

CATEGORIES OF WORK

M&A, MBOs, MBIs
Miguel Teixeira de Abreu

International taxation and tax planning
Miguel Teixeira de Abreu

EU, antitrust and competition law
Miguel de Avillez Pereira

Intellectual and industrial property
Cesar Bessa Monteiro

Environmental law
Manuel de Andrade Neves

Construction law and public works
Filipa Névoa

Foreign investment
Pedro Cardigos dos Reis

General civil and commercial practice, and labour law
Carmo Sousa Machado

Banking and financial services, swaps and derivatives
Pedro Cardigos dos Reis

Local taxation and tax litigation
Paulo Cordeiro de Sousa

Telecommunications law
Ana Fazendeiro

Capital markets
Miguel Castro Pereira

Sports and leisure law
Pedro Cardigos dos Reis

Civil and commercial litigation
Miguel Castro Pereira

THE FIRM

Abreu, Cardigos & Associados is a Portuguese law firm that acts, in particular, for corporate entities requiring specialist legal assistance and a range of complementary services. The firm's international experience was initially grounded on the founding partners' experience in major US and UK international law firms. The firm's client base includes some of the largest international companies operating in Portugal. Abreu, Cardigos & Associados is one of the largest law firms in Portugal and is the only one to have been certified by the IPQ, the Portuguese Institute for Quality, with the ISO 9001 norm. NP EN ISO 9001 (issued by SGS ICS International Certification Services) – (Certificate number 9311/35/55200/43201).

AREAS OF PRACTICE

M&A, MBOs, MBIs: the firm provides legal and tax assistance with regard to the purchase or disposal of Portuguese companies. It frequently conducts legal due diligence processes, as well as handling the acquisition and/or disposal structures of Portuguese businesses. It also acts in the execution of restructuring steps, including mergers, split-offs, flotations and asset divisions. Recently, the firm advised Portugal Telecom on the outsourcing of its information systems department.

Banking and financial services: the firm has been selected to advise the Republic of Portugal on operations connected with international financial instruments, including derivatives. The firm advises credit institutions in respect of the securitisation of receivables and mortgage-backed assets of their Portuguese clients.

Local and international taxation and tax planning: the firm provides specialist advice to resident and non-resident corporations, as well as to other law firms in Portugal and abroad. The firm has been involved in the establishment of tax structures regarding financial operations, acquisition of companies, corporate restructuring and international transactions for resident and non-resident corporations. The firm has also been retained in respect of the issuance of tax opinions in context with securitisations transactions in Portugal.

Capital markets: the firm regularly advises resident and non-resident investors on their duties before the Portuguese Capital Markets Regulatory Authorities. The firm has also been involved in the admission and listing of several Portuguese companies on the Lisbon Stock Exchange.

Industrial and intellectual property and IT law: the firm is able to provide prime assistance in the area of industrial and intellectual property law as well as in the field of IT law. Dr Cesar Bessa Monteiro is simultaneously a lawyer and an official industrial property agent. Dr Cesar Bessa Monteiro has been invited to be part of a government commission created to study and review the Portuguese Industrial Property Code. Currently the firm provides assistance to more than 300 international clients on all matters related to industrial and intellectual property law and IT law.

EU, antitrust and competition law: the firm regularly advises Portuguese companies on the implications of EU law. It has represented many multinational companies before the antitrust authorities in connection with mergers and other concentration operations.

Telecommunications: the firm advises resident and non-resident telecoms companies on their entry into the recently liberalised Portuguese telecoms market. The firm is also currently representing a Portuguese telecoms operator on a number of restructuring deals.

Environmental law: members of the firm founded Euronatura, an NGO dedicated to environmental law and policy, and the firm is regularly consulted by its clients on national and European environmental matters.

Labour law: the firm has been increasingly consulted on labour law matters, and represents some of the major international consultancy firms in this area. The firm is also involved in collective negotiation of labour agreements.

Civil and commercial litigaion: the firm has extensive experience before Portuguese courts and national and international arbitration.

ALMEIDA SAMPAIO & ASSOCIADOS

AV PRAIA DA VITÓRIA 71
EDIFÍCIO MONUMENTAL 5°B
1050-183 LISBON

Telephone: +351 21 353 69 25
Fax: +351 21 353 69 27
E-mail: as.law@asampaio-advogados.pt

Languages
English, French, German, Spanish

Number of lawyers 8
at this office 6

Contact
Mr Carlos de Almeida Sampaio

CATEGORIES OF WORK

Corporate law and contracts	Foreign investment
Taxation	Antitrust and trade regulation
Intellectual property	Mergers and acquisitions
Environmental law	Joint ventures and licensing

AZEREDO PERDIGÃO & ALBUQUERQUE DA FONSECA

LAW FIRM

RUA DE SÃO NICOLAU, 23 2º
1100-547 LISBOA

Telephone: +351 21 887 91 42
Fax: +351 21 886 06 33
E-mail:
miguelperdigao@azeredoperdigao.pt

Languages
English, French, Spanish

Other offices
Luanda (Angola)

Contact
Miguel de Azeredo Perdigão
(managing partner)

CATEGORIES OF WORK

Foreign investment and incorporation of companies	Arbitration, litigation and debt recovery
Corporate and commercial law	Agency and distribution agreements
Tax planning, offshore investment and Madeira Free Trade Zone	Telecommunications and energy
Banking, capital markets and finance	Intellectual property, trade marks and franchising
Tourism, property, construction and real estate	EC competition and antitrust law

BAIÃO DO NASCIMENTO, CASTRO NUNES, CASTRO E SOLLA & ASSOCIADOS

AVENIDA 5 DE OUTUBRO, 17, 9º
1050-047 LISBOA

Telephone: +351 21 319 0640
Fax: +351 21 319 0644
E-mail: bcslaw@bcs.pt

Languages
English, French, Italian, Spanish

Number of lawyers 15

CATEGORIES OF WORK

Commercial and financial transactions
Victor de Castro Nunes,
Felipe Baião do Nascimento

Corporate and tax
José Castro e Solla,
Élio Teixeira

Project finance
Victor de Castro Nunes,
Felipe Baião do Nascimento

Insolvency
Ana Paula Martins,
Cláudia de Meneses

Property and construction
Rui Gouveia

Litigation and arbitration
Ana Paula Martins,
Cláudia de Meneses

Banking and capital markets
Felipe Baião do Nascimento,
Maria José Campos

Mergers and acquisitions
Victor de Castro Nunes,
José Castro e Solla

BARROS, SOBRAL, G GOMES & ASSOCIADOS

RUA BRAAMCAMP, NO 40-8º ESQ
1269-013 LISBOA

Telephone: +351 21 387 57 02
Fax: +351 21 387 57 43
E-mail: law@bsgg.pt
Website: www.bsgg.pt

Languages
English, French, German, Italian, Spanish

Other offices
Madeira, Porto Alegre,
Rio de Janeiro, São Paulo, Washington DC

Number of lawyers 32
at this office 26

Member
Euro American Lawyers Group; European Labour Law Consulting; International Tax Planning Association; Brazilian Entrepreneur Association; several Chambers of Commerce

CATEGORIES OF WORK

Environmental
Paula Alcàntara Feliciano

Corporate and commercial
Rita Delgado, Susana Braz

Banking and finance
João Pedro Gomes,
Paulino Brilhante Santos

Capital markets
Susana Braz, Paula Alcàntara Feliciano

International tax planning
João Pedro Gomes,
Paulino Brilhante Santos

IT and telecoms
Rita Delgado, Paulo Sá Cunha

Project finance
Paulino Brilhante Santos, Susana Braz

Privatisation
João Pedro Gomes,
Sergio Sobral

Real estate
Rita Delgado, Susana Braz

Immigration/nationality
Susana Braz

Criminal law
Paulo Sá Cunha

Taxation
Paulino Brilhante Santos, Nuno Telleria

Mergers and acquisitions
Rita Delgado, Susana Braz

Labour and employment
Sónia de Magalhães Gonçalves,
Pedro Gonçalves Paes

Litigation
Sónia de Magalhães Gonçalves,
Bertha Parente Esteves

Maritime and shipping
Nuno Telleria, Gisela Xavier Martins

BARROCAS & ALVES PEREIRA

AMOREIRAS, TORRE 2
16TH FLOOR
1070-274 LISBON

Telephone: +351 21 384 3300
Fax: +351 21 387 0265
E-mail: info@bap.pt
Website: www.bap.pt

Languages
English, French, Italian, Portuguese, Spanish

Other offices
Porto, Luanda (Angola), Maputo (Mozambique)

Number of lawyers 73
at this office 58

Contacts
Manuel P Barrocas, Albano Sarmento,
Jorge Santiago Neves, Manuel Lopes Rocha

CATEGORIES OF WORK	
Corporate and M&A	**Project finance, PPP/PFI**
Shipping and transport	**Licensing and franchising**
Telecommunications	**Environment, planning and real estate**
Internet and information technology	**Intellectual property**
Energy, oil and gas	**Litigation and arbitration**
Pharmaceuticals and health	**Tax**
Criminal law	**Employment and labour**
Construction and public procurement	**EU and competition**

THE FIRM

Originally established in 1984, Barrocas & Alves Pereira is a highly effective and competitive organisation, offering a wide range of services, with a special emphasis on business law, and serving a primarily corporate clientele, including leading international corporations and organisations. The firm has handled a number of significant international transactions in the areas of telecommunications, energy, construction, utilities, banking, project finance, PPP/PFI, chemical, automotive industry, electronics, insurance, shipping, hotel operation and distribution. It has an extensive network of correspondent law firms worldwide and a client base that includes large multinational companies, public entities and governments.

AREAS OF PRACTICE

Corporate and M&A: the senior partners have over 30 years' experience in international M&A and advise international clients on the setting up of their businesses in Portugal in various sectors, as indicated above.

Shipping and transport: the firm is one of the few in Portugal with a consistent shipping and transport practice. The practice extends to all areas of work related to transportation, from accidents to sale and purchase, leasings and finance transactions.

Telecoms: the firm is actively involved in the UMTS contracts for the 3G mobile network. It advises major international suppliers.

Internet and IT: the firm advises large net operators, software and hi-tech companies, both national and international.

Energy, oil and gas: the firm advises governments of some African countries in the development and exploration of oil and natural gas resources, and has developed considerable expertise in this field.

Pharmaceuticals and health: advising major health institutions in Portugal, as well as the pharmaceutical regulatory authority.

Criminal law: an active department dealing with white-collar crimes led by one of the most prominent criminal lawyers in Portugal.

Construction and public procurement: advising some of the largest construction companies and international joint ventures in Portugal. The firm is currently dealing with the largest public works project under construction, and advises clients regularly on public procurement matters.

Project finance, PPP/PFI: the firm is at the forefront in new PPP/PFI programmes development in Portugal, and advises major clients in project finance concessions.

Licensing and franchising: dealing with all matters including selection of sites, rentals, real estate purchases, assistance to franchisers and franchisees and other related matters. The firm also has extensive experience in the fields of agency, distribution and license agreements.

Environment, planning and real estate: advising clients in the fields of real estate, planning, urbanisation, management and environment, both in tourism, where it has advised on some of the major developments in the south of Portugal, and in commercial property for office occupation.

Intellectual property: work includes copyright, trade mark, patent and related litigation. The firm provides regular legal assistance to major international clients in the software, film, video and audio industries.

Litigation and arbitration: in addition to an active commercial litigation department, including product liability, unfair competition, shareholders' rights, insurance and tort liability, the firm has a specific white-collar defence department, and is particularly active in arbitration and mediation proceedings.

Tax: providing specialist advice to companies in the fields of tax planning and tax litigation.

Employment and labour: the firm advises institutional clients in the fields of labour law, safety, social security and regulatory compliance. It has participated in collective employment issues and due diligences related to employment matters.

EU and competition: the firm provides antitrust, competition and related advice to companies operating in the Portuguese market.

CAETANO DE FREITAS & ASSOCIADOS

AVENIDA DA LIBERDADE
NO 180 A-9º ANDAR
1250-146 LISBOA

Telephone: +351 21 317 0620
Fax: +351 21 317 0629
E-mail: geral@caetanodefreitas.com

Languages
English, French, Italian, Spanish

Other offices
Funchal

Number of lawyers 15
at this office 10

Contact
Sofia Almeida Ribeiro
(sofia.ribeiro@caetanodefreitas.com)

Member
Interact Europe; EEIG

CATEGORIES OF WORK

Banking, capital markets and securities

Company and commercial law

Corporate and project finance

Employment, pensions and incentives

EU law, competition and antitrust

Insolvency and business reconstruction

Litigation and arbitration

Mergers, acquisitions and MBOs

Property, planning and environment

Tax law and tax planning

CARLOS AGUIAR, P. PINTO & ASSOCIADOS

AVENIDA DA LIBERDADE
200-4º ESQº
1250-147 LISBON

Telephone: +351 21 355 27 55
Fax: +351 21 355 27 56
E-mail: cappa@mail.telepac.pt
Website: www.cappa.pt

Languages
English, French, Spanish

Number of lawyers 15

Contact
Carlos Aguiar

Member
Ius Laboris; International Employment Law, Pensions and Employee Benefits Alliance

CATEGORIES OF WORK

Corporate
Carlos Aguiar, Pedro Pinto

M&A
Carlos Aguiar, Tiago Ferreira de Lima

Banking and finance
Manuel Costa Salema, Nuno Galinha

Capital markets
Manuel Costa Salema, Maria Valdez

Real estate/property finance
Pedro Pinto, Carlos Aguiar

Employment
Inês Reis, Bruno Barbosa

Litigation
Inês Reis, Sofia Sousinha

Tax law and planning
Tiago Mascarenhas

F CASTELO BRANCO & ASSOCIADOS VEIGA GOMES, MARQUES DA CRUZ, COLMONERO
SOCIEDADES DE ADVOGADOS

AVENIDA DA LIBERDADE 249-1
1250-143 LISBOA

Telephone: +351 21 358 75 00
Fax: +351 21 358 75 01
E-mail: fcbranco@fcb-legal.com
Website: www.fcb-legal.com

Languages
English, French, Spanish

Other offices
Oporto

Number of lawyers 49
at this office 45

Contact
Vitor Marques da Cruz (vmc@fcb-legal.com)

CATEGORIES OF WORK

Corporate/M&A

E-commerce and computer law

Employment

Litigation

Intellectual property

Banking and capital markets

Civil law

Taxation

Construction/real estate

PFI

Administrative and public

Environment

Tenders

Privatisations

Telecommunications

FERREIRA PINTO, OLAVO CUNHA & ASSOCIADOS

EDIFÍCIO MONUMENTAL
AV PRAIA DA VITÓRIA, °71A-7°E
1050-183 LISBOA

Telephone: +351 21 030 31 90
Fax: +351 21 030 31 99
E-mail: mail@lusolegal.pt

Languages
English, French, Italian, Spanish

Number of lawyers 43

CATEGORIES OF WORK

Arbitration and litigation
Carlos Costa, José Franqueira Dias

Banking
Fernando A Ferreira Pinto

Capital markets
Paulo Olavo Cunha

Corporate, M&A
Fernando A Ferreira Pinto

Corporate and commercial
Paulo Olavo Cunha, António Teles

E-commerce, telecommunications and media law
Pedro Dias

EU, antitrust and competition
Fernando Ribas Vieira

Energy
Sofia Carreiro

Intellectual property
José Franqueira Dias

Labour law
Pedro Furtado Martins

Real estate, construction and tourism
Paulo da Silva Almeida

Sports law
Paulo Olavo Cunha

Tax
Fernando Ribas Vieira

FRANCO CAIADO GUERREIRO & ASSOCIADOS
SOCIEDADE DE ADVOGADOS

RUA DUQUE DE PALMELA
Nº 25-5º
1250-097 LISBOA

Telephone: +351 21 359 3050
Fax: +351 21 359 3051
E-mail: law@fcguerreiro.com
Website: www.fcguerreiro.com

Languages
English, French, German, Spanish

Number of lawyers 25

Contact
João Caiado Guerreiro

Member
Globalaw;
ATTA (Transatlantic Association of lawyers)

CATEGORIES OF WORK

Banking and finance, M&A
João Caiado Guerreiro,
Diogo Coutinho de Gouveia

Tax
Tiago Caiado Guerreiro,
Maria Figueiredo

Competition
Diogo C Gouveia

Corporate and commercial
João Caiado Guerreiro,
Ricardo Costa Macedo

Commercial property, real estate
Ricardo Costa Macedo,
Angela Dias Coelho

Infrastructure and project finance
João Caiado Guerreiro

Capital markets
João Caiado Guerreiro,
Ricardo Rodrigues Lopes

Labour law
Ricardo Gameiro, Helena Isidoro Cabrita

Media and entertainment
Tiago Caiado Guerreiro

Telecommunications
Ricardo Costa Macedo

Administrative, environmental law
Ana Castro Gonçalves,
Mariana Gouveia de Oliveira

Pharmaceutical law
João Caiado Guerreiro,
Andreia Afonso Rodrigues

Foreign direct investment
João Caiado Guerreiro

Dispute resolution/litigation
Ricardo Gameiro, José Saramago

Civil law
Ricardo Gameiro

GONÇALVES PEREIRA, CASTELO BRANCO & ASSOCIADOS

PRAÇA MARQUÊS DE POMBAL 1-8º
1250-160 LISBOA

Telephone: +351 21 355 3800
Fax: +351 21 353 2362
E-mail: lisboa@gpcb.pt
Website: www.gpcb.pt

Languages
English, French, Portuguese, Spanish

Other offices
Oporto, Maputo (Mozambique), Alicante*, Barcelona*, Bilbao*, Brussels*, Gerona*, Llieda*, Madrid*, New York*, Santa Cruz de Tenerife*, Seville*, Valencia*, Zaragoza*

Number of lawyers 82
at this office 54

In association with Cuatrecasas Abogados

CATEGORIES OF WORK

Corporate and commercial law
Manuel Castelo Branco, José de Freitas

Joint ventures/mergers and acquisitions
Manuel Castelo Branco,
Diogo Perestrelo

Banking and insurance
Manuel Magalhães

Finance and capital markets
Maria João Ricou

Project finance
Manuel Castelo Branco,
Diogo Perestrelo

EU/competition
Frederico Pereira Coutinho

Intellectual property
Maria da Glória Leitão

Tax
Diogo Ortigão Ramos

Construction/real estate
Frederico Pereira Coutinho,
Diogo Perestrelo

Arbitration and litigation
Manuel Castelo Branco,
Miguel Esperança Pina

Administrative and environmental law
Tiago Amorim

Employment, benefits and pensions
Maria da Glória Leitão

Energy
Frederico Pereira Coutinho,
Luis Soares de Sousa

JALLES ADVOGADOS

AV ALVARES CABRAL 34
6TH FLOOR
1250-018 LISBON

Telephone: +351 21 388 4095
Fax: +351 21 388 1955
E-mail: jalles.law@mail.telepac.pt

Languages
Dutch, English, French, German, Italian, Russian, Spanish

Number of lawyers 10

Contact
Isabel Jalles

CATEGORIES OF WORK

Companies, mergers and acquisitions and taxation

Arbitration and litigation

EC, distribution and competition law

Aviation and transportation law

Telecommunications, media, intellectual property and entertainment

Banking, securities and finance

Privatisation law and administrative law

Family and inheritance

Real estate, construction and leasing law

Personal injury, product liability and food law

Environment law

LEBRE, SÁ, CARVALHO & ASSOCIADOS

SOCIEDADE DE ADVOCADOS

R JULIO DE ANDRADE 2
1150 LISBOA

Telephone: +351 21 885 23 31
Fax: +351 21 885 34 34
E-mail: lebre.assoc.adv@mail.telepac.pt

Languages
English, French, German, Italian, Spanish

Other offices
Aberdeen*, Ankara*, Arnhem*, Athens*, Barcelona*, Berlin*, Brussels*, Cairo*, Copenhagen*, Dublin*, Düsseldorf*, Edinburgh*, Geneva,* Halle*, Inverness*, Istanbul*, Izmir*, London,* Luanda*, Luxembourg*, Madrid*, Milan*, Nicosia*, Nijmegan*, Oslo*, Paris*, Rome*, Stockholm*, Vaduz*, Vienna*

Number of lawyers 12

Member
TELFA (Trans European Law Firms Association)

CATEGORIES OF WORK

Commercial, company and corporate law
José Lebre de Freitas, Rita Matias

Banking, securities and international finance
Ricardo Sá Fernandes, Alfaia de Carvalho

Administrative and planning
António Cordeiro

Arbitration and high-level litigation
José Lebre de Freitas

Industrial and intellectual property
António Cordeiro, Filipe Lebre de Freitas

Mergers and acquisitions
Ricardo Sá Fernandes, Rita Matias

Bankruptcy and insolvency
Ana Maria Peralta, João Redinha

Competition and antitrust
Ricardo Sá Fernandes, Alfaia de Carvalho

Commercial and labour litigation
João Redinha, Filipe Lebre de Freitas

Real estate, property
José Lebre de Freitas, Ana Maria Peralta

Environment
Alfaia de Carvalho, Filipe Lebre de Freitas

Contracts
José Lebre de Freitas, Rita Matias

Tax law
Ricardo Sá Fernandes

Construction
António Cordeiro, João Redinha

LEÓNIDAS, MATOS & ASSOCIADOS

RUA TIERNO GALVAN
AMOREIRAS TORRE 3-12º
1070-274 LISBON

Telephone: +351 21 382 1200
Fax: +351 21 382 1290

Languages
English, Spanish, French

Number of lawyers 35

Contacts
João Paulo Teixeira de Matos (jtm@lmalegal.pt),
Diogo Leónidas Rocha (dlr@lmalegal.pt)

In association with Garrigues Abogados Y Asesores Tributarios

CATEGORIES OF WORK

Commercial and corporate law
Diogo Leónidas Rocha, Mario Lino Dias

Mergers and acquisitions
João Paulo Teixeira de Matos, Mário Lino Dias

Banking, securities and finance
Diogo Leónidas Rocha

Labour law
João Paulo Teixeira de Matos, Rita Nogueira Neto

EU and competition law
João Paulo Teixeira de Matos

Telecommunications
Diogo Leónidas Rocha

Real estate law
Miguel Marques dos Santos

Industrial and intellectual property
Miguel Marques dos Santos

Environmental law
Miguel Azevedo

Insurance law
João Paulo Teixeira de Matos

E-business
Miguel Marques dos Santos, Diogo Leónidas Rocha

Arbitration and litigation
João Paulo Teixeira de Matos, João Duarte Sousa

LUSOJURIST

RUA ALMEIDA BRANDÃO 19
1200-602 LISBOA

Telephone: +351 21 397 51 80
Fax: +351 21 397 51 86
E-mail: info@lusojurist.pt
Website: www.lusojurist.pt

Languages
English, French

Number of lawyers 15

CATEGORIES OF WORK

Banking
João Freitas e Costa

Finance
João Freitas e Costa

Mergers and acquisitions
Luis de Gouveia Fernandes

Corporate and commercial
Luis de Gouveia Fernandes

Debt recovery
Ana Catarina Brilha, Pedro Carreira Albano

Labour and employment
Natália Garcia Alves

Real estate
Alexandre Oliveira Perdigão

Civil litigation
Pedro Branco, Ana Catarina Brilha

Retail banking litigation
Sandra Severino

LINKLATERS

AV FONTES PEREIRA DE MELO
14-15TH FLOOR
1050-121 LISBON

Telephone: +351 21 864 00 00
Fax: +351 21 864 00 01
Website: www.linklaters.com

Languages
All commercial and local languages in the countries where Linklaters operates

Other offices
Alicante, Amsterdam, Antwerp, Bankok, Beijing, Berlin, Bratislava, Brussels, Bucharest, Budapest, Cologne, Frankfurt am Main, Hong Kong, London, Luxembourg, Madrid, Milan, Moscow, Munich, New York, Paris, Prague, Rome, São Paulo, Shanghai, Singapore, Stockholm, Tokyo, Warsaw

Number of lawyers 2,000 worldwide

Contact
Jorge M Bleck

CATEGORIES OF WORK

Banking and Finance
António Soares

Debt Transactions
António Payan Martins

Capital Markets
António Soares

Corporate and Commercial
Teresa Anselmo Vaz

Mergers and acquisitions
Jorge M Bleck

Project/asset finance
Pedro Siza Vieira

Real Estate
Jorge Gonçalves

Labour
Nuno Lousa

IT and communications
Carlos Pinto Correia

Litigation
Miguel Pinto Cardoso

Private equity
António Soares

EU/Competition
Carlos Pinto Correia

Tax
Tânia de Almeida Ferreira

THE FIRM

Linklaters advises the world's leading companies, financial institutions and governments on their most challenging transactions and assignments. With 2,000 lawyers, including 470 partners, and offices in major business and financial centres, its clients choose the firm for its distinctive combination of technical skill, commercial experience and outstanding service.

Linklaters has built a formidable global practice through organic growth and a series of mergers, joint ventures and co-operations with other respected law firms. In 2001, Linklaters merged with three of Europe's leading law firms to form Linklaters Oppenhoff & Rädler in Germany, Linklaters in Sweden, Linklaters De Bandt in Belgium and Linklaters Loesch in Luxembourg. In the same year, the firm formed a co-operation with Brazilian firm Goulart Penteado, Iervolino e Lefosse. This co-operation combines Linklaters' international capability with GPIL's extensive knowledge of the Brazilian market. In Singapore, the firm practises as Linklaters Allen & Gledhill, a joint venture with the premier Singapore practice of Allen & Gledhill, while in Italy, Linklaters has an exclusive relationship with Italian law firm Gianni, Origoni, Grippo & Partners.

MACEDO VITORINO E ASSOCIADOS
SOCIEDADE DE ADVOGADOS

RUA GARRETT 12-2°
1200-204 LISBOA

Telephone: +351 21 324 19 00
Fax: +351 21 324 19 29
E-mail: mva@macedovitorino.com
Website: www.macedovitorino.com

Languages
English, French, German, Italian, Spanish

Number of lawyers 21

Contacts
João de Macedo Vitorino,
António de Macedo Vitorino

CATEGORIES OF WORK

- Banking, finance and derivatives
- Capital markets
- Construction and real estate
- Corporate and commercial
- Competition including EU competition law
- E-commerce
- Energy
- Foreign investment
- Inheritance and family law
- Intellectual property
- International private law
- Litigation and arbitration
- Mergers and acquisitions
- Privatisations
- Project finance
- Restructurings
- Securitisation
- Tax
- Technology, media and telecommunications

MARQUES BOM E ASSOCIADOS SOCIEDADE DE ADVOGADOS

AV DUQUE DE LOULÉ, 17°-6°
1050-085 LISBOA

Telephone: +351 21 350 45 10
Fax: +351 21 350 45 20
E-mail: geral@marquesbom.com

Languages
English, French, Spanish

Number of lawyers 12

Contacts
Francisco Marques Bom,
Nuno Borges Alexandrino

CATEGORIES OF WORK

- International contracts, mergers and acquisitions
- Foreign investment
- Banking and finance
- Corporate
- Labour
- Procurement
- Real estate, tourism, construction
- International transport and maritime law
- Tax and administrative law
- Litigation and arbitration

MARQUES MENDES & ASSOCIADOS

AV ENG DUARTE PACHECO, 19-12º
1070-100 LISBOA

Telephone: +351 21 382 63 00
Fax: +351 21 382 63 19
E-mail:
marquesmendes@marquesmendes.pt

Languages
English, French, Italian, Spanish

Number of lawyers 12

CATEGORIES OF WORK

Corporate, commercial, M&A
Mário Marques Mendes, Pedro Vilarinho Pires

Finance (including banking, insurance, securities and project financing)
Luís Morais, Pedro Vilarinho Pires

EU law, competition, antitrust
Mário Marques Mendes, Luís Morais

IT
Pedro Vilarinho Pires, Francisco Costa-Cabral

Telecommunications
Mário Marques Mendes, Pedro Vilarinho Pires

Energy
Mário Marques Mendes

Employment
Alexandra Aboim Inglez, Alexandra Dias Quitério

Entertainment and media
Mário Marques Mendes

Intellectual property
Mário Marques Mendes, Francisco Costa-Cabral

Litigation and arbitration
Mário Marques Mendes, Alexandra Aboim Inglez

MIRANDA, CORREIA, AMENDOEIRA & ASSOCIADOS
SOCIEDADE DE ADVOGADOS

THE STOCK EXCHANGE BUILDING
RUA SOEIRO P GOMES, 1-2 FL
1600-196 LISBOA

Telephone: +351 21 781 4800
Fax: +351 21 781 4802
E-mail: lisbon@mirandalawfirm.com
Website: www.mirandalawfirm.com

Languages
English, French, Italian, Spanish

Other offices
Luanda (Angola), Cabinda (Angola), Maputo (Mozambique), Cidade de São Tomé (São Tomé e Príncipe), Cidade da Praia (Cape Verde, ; Bissau (Guinea-Bissau)

Number of lawyers 55
at this office 40

CATEGORIES OF WORK

Oil and gas
Agostinho Pereira de Miranda

Energy
Rui Amendoeira

Tax
Rita Correia

Litigation
João Afonso Fialho

Commercial law
Diogo Xavier da Cunha

Mining
Catarina Távora

Banking and capital markets
Mafalda Oliveira Monteiro

IT and telecommunications
João Luis Traca

Competition
Rui Andrade

Project finance
Alberto Galhardo Simões

Employment
João Afonso Fialho

Real estate and construction
Rita Correia

Arbitration
Agostinho Pereira de Miranda

Intellectual property
João Luís Traça

MORAIS LEITÃO, J GALVÃO TELES & ASSOCIADOS
SOCIEDADE DE ADVOGADOS

RUA CASTILHO 75-1º
1250-068 LISBOA

Telephone: +351 21 381 7400
Fax: +351 21 381 7499
E-mail: mlgtlisboa@mlgt.pt
Website: www.mlgt.pt

Languages
English, French, Italian, Spanish

Other offices
Funchal, Oporto

Number of lawyers 66
at this office 58

Contact
Nuno Galvão Teles

Member
Lex Mundi

CATEGORIES OF WORK

Arbitration and litigation
José Manuel Galvão Teles,
António Pinto Leite

Banking and finance
Nuno Galvão Teles,
Pedro Gorjão Henriques

Capital markets
Nuno Galvão Teles, Rui Oliveira Neves

Real estate, construction and planning
Fernanda Matoso, João Pereira Reis

Corporate and commercial law
Filipa Arantes Pedroso,
Segismundo Pinto Basto

EU and competition law
Carlos Botelho Moniz

Energy and natural resources
Segismundo Pinto Basto

Environmental law
Teresa Morais Leitão

Intellectual property
Tomas Vaz Pinto

Mergers and acquisitions
Nuno Galvão Teles

Project finance
Filipa Arantes Pedroso

Administrative law and public procurement
João Serra, Margarida Cabral

Tax – international and domestic
Francisco Sousa da Câmara,

Telecommunications
Filipa Arantes Pedroso,
João Alfredo Afonso

Labour and employment
Luís Miguel Monteiro,
Joana Soares de Almeida

Tourism and entertainment
Teresa Morais Leitão, João Pereira Reis

MULLERAT

RUA RODRIGO DA FONSECA 149
1070 LISBON

Telephone: +351 21 381 26 20
Fax: +351 21 381 26 21
E-mail: mullerat.lisboa@mullerat.com
Website: www.mullerat.com

Languages
English, French, German, Italian, Portuguese

Other offices
Barcelona, Madrid, Palma de Mallorca,
San Sebastián

Number of lawyers 75
at this office 5

Contact
Leonor Chastre

CATEGORIES OF WORK

Banking, finance, securities

Litigation

Tax

EU, competition and consumer law

Distribution and franchising

Company law

Trade mark law

Labour law

Mergers and acquisitions

Patents and intellectual property

Criminal law

Real estate and zoning law

PLMJ - AM PEREIRA, SÁRAGGA LEAL, OLIVEIRA MARTINS JÚDICE & ASSOCIADOS

EDIFICIO EUROLEX
AV DA LIBERDADE 224
1250-148 LISBOA

Telephone: +351 21 319 73 00
Fax: +351 21 319 74 00
E-mail: plmjlaw@plmj.pt
Website: www.plmj.com

Languages
English, French, German, Spanish

Number of lawyers 115

Other offices
Porto, Algarve, Luanda (Angola)

Contacts
Dr Luís Sáragga Leal,
Dr Francisco Oliveira Martins,
Dr José Miguel Júdice

CATEGORIES OF WORK

Intellectual property
Dr António Maria Pereira,
Dr José Luis da Cruz Villaça

Labour law
Dr Abel Mesquita

Corporate finance
Dra Gabriela Rodrigues Martins

Energy and natural resources
Dr Manuel Santos Vitor

Tax
Prof Diogo Leite de Campos,

Media law
Dr Vasco Marques Correia

Zoning and town planning law
Dra Sofia Galvão

Capital markets
Dr Jorge Brito Pereira

EU and competition law
Dr José Luís da Cruz Vilaça

Finance law
Dr Fernando Campos Ferreira,
Dra Maria Castelos

Corporate, M&A
Dr Victor Réfega Fernandes,
Dra Dulce Franco
Dra Gabriela Rodrigues Martins

Real estate, construction and tourism
Dr Pedro Sáragga Leal,
Dra Maria José Verde

Litigation and arbitration
Dr Nuno L Monteiro, Dr Pedro Faria

Administrative law
Teresa Melo Ribeiro

Criminal law
Dr João Carlos Medeiros

Pharmaceutical law
Dr Abel Mesquita

THE FIRM

The foundation of PLMJ was laid down in the late sixties. The internationalisation and specialisation policies, pursued by the firm since its inception led to the continued growth of PLMJ over the following years and to its current position in the Portuguese legal market. PLMJ's sustained growth was achieved both in an organic manner and through an aggressive hiring policy of lawyers with an acknowledged academic background and professional experience in different areas of the law.

In the eighties, José Manuel Serra Formigal, Fernando Campos Ferreira, Victor Réfega Fernandes, Pedro Sáragga Leal and Dulce Franco became partners. In the nineties, José Luís da Cruz Vilaça, Nuno Líbano Monteiro, Gabriela Rodrigues Martins and Abel Mesquita were also made partners. Thereafter, Vasco Marques Correia, Manuel Santos Vitor, Luis Miguel Pais Antunes, Diogo Leite de Campos, Jorge de Brito Pereira, Ana Teresa Pulido, Pedro Faria, Maria José Verde, Teresa de Melo Ribeiro, Maria Castelos, Nuno Morais Sarmento, Sofia de Sequeira Galvão, Mônica Leite de Campos, José Filipe Abecasis, José Jácome and João Medeiros became partners as well.

PLMJ currently counts 30 senior partners and 32 junior partners in a total of more than 100 lawyers, and has, for many years, been one of the largest Portuguese law firms of acknowledged experience and reputation in all fields of law.

Professional quality, based on the continuous training as well as the academic and professional enhancement of its lawyers, an excellent work environment and human quality have always been fundamental values. Porto office: Av da Boavista, Edificio Passeio da Boavista N° 21214, 407, 4100-134 Porto, Tel: 351 22 607 47 00, Fax: 351 22 0747 50. Algarve office: Rua Pinheiro Chagas, 16-2° Dt°, 8000 Faro, Tel: 351 289 804 137, Fax: 351 289 803 588. Luanda office: Av de Portugal, 41 Entre Piso, Luanda, República de Angola, Tel: 351 21 319 7331, Fax: 351 21 319 7335.

AREAS OF PRACTICE

Structured and equipped to meet the growing challenges of modern times, PLMJ is internally organised in departments specially geared to the different fields of law, in particular: corporate, mergers and acquisitions; EU and competition; foreign investment and international contracts; privatisations; financial and capital markets; tax; labour; intellectual property; realty, construction and tourism; constitutional and administrative; public procurement; criminal; environment; maritime and transport; insurances; energy and natural resources; telecommunications; and pharmaceutical. PLMJ also has departments widely experienced in the various areas of litigation and arbitration.

The departments work under the co-ordination of senior partners who directly supervise the quality of the services provided. Whenever the volume or nature of the issues so justify, task forces composed of lawyers from various departments are set up and co-ordinated by one or more senior partners.

As a result of its wide experience, PLMJ has developed its own network of correspondents, both with domestic and foreign law firms, thus being prepared to provide unbounded legal assistance.

SARAIVA LIMA E ASSOCIADOS

AV ANTONIO AUGUSTO DE AGUIAR 19, 3º ESQ
1050-012 LISBOA

Telephone: +351 21 311 07 90
Fax: +351 21 353 29 63
E-mail: lisboa@slima-assoc.pt

Languages
English, French, German, Italian, Spanish

Other offices
Oporto

Number of lawyers 15
at this office 11

Contact
Paulo T Costa

Member
NOMOS

CATEGORIES OF WORK

Foreign investment and international contracts	EU and competition law
Corporate and commercial law	Transportation, shipping and maritime
Mergers and acquisitions	Labour law
Tax and administrative law	Real estate and tourism
Banking and insurance	General practice and litigation
Project finance and PFI-PPP	

SERRA LOPES, CORTES MARTINS & ASSOCIADOS

RUE GENERAL FIRMINO MIGUEL
TORRE 2, 12°
1600-100 LISBOA

Telephone: +351 21 723 4000
Fax: +351 21 723 4029
E-mail: slcm@slcm-advogados.pt
Website: www.slcm-advogados.pt

Languages
English, French, German, Italian, Spanish

Number of lawyers 12

CATEGORIES OF WORK

Corporate and commercial	Telecommunications and e-commerce
Mergers and acquisitions	Media and entertainment
Banking and finance	Energy and natural resources
Arbitration and dispute resolution	Public procurement and administrative law
Civil and commercial litigation	Shipping and maritime law
Capital markets	Sports law
Insurance	
EU and competition law	

SÉRVULO CORREIA & ASSOCIADOS

RUA ARTILHARIA UM 79-5
1250-038 LISBOA

Telephone: +351 21 383 6900
Fax: +351 21 383 6901
E-mail: lisboa@servulo.com
Website: www.servulo.com

Languages
English, French, German, Italian, Spanish

Number of lawyers 35
at this office 28

Other offices
Madrid

Contact
Bernardo Diniz de Ayala

Member
Legalink; Diro

CATEGORIES OF WORK

Administrative law
Sérvulo Correia, Bernardo Ayala

Antitrust and trade regulation
Rui Medeiros

Banking and finance
Sérvulo Correia,
Rogério M Fernandes Ferreira

Capital markets
Sérvulo Correia,
Rogério M Fernandes Ferreira

Company and commercial
Teresa Serra, Vasco A Marques

Constitutional law
Rui Medeiros

Criminal law and corporate liability
Teresa Serra

Due diligence
Vasco A Marques

Government contracts and public procurement
Sérvulo CorreiaJoão Amaral,
Bernardo Ayala

Litigation, arbitration and ADR
Sérvulo Correia, João Amaral

Mergers and acquisitions
Pedro M dos Santos

Project finance
João Amaral, Bernardo Ayala

Real estate
Teresa Serra, Vasco A Marques

Tax law
Rogério M Fernandes Ferreira

Urban planning and construction law
Rui Medeiros

Utilities
Pedro M dos Santos

SIMMONS & SIMMONS

RUA CASTILHO, 32-9º
1250-070 LISBON

Telephone: +351 21 313 1500
Fax: +351 21 313 1501
E-mail: enquiries@simmons-simmons.com
Website: www.simmons-simmons.com

Languages
English, French, German, Italian, Spanish

Other offices
London, Rotterdam, Paris, Milan, Rome, Düsseldorf, Madrid, Brussels, Frankfurt, Madeira, Abu Dhabi, Qatar, Hong Kong, Padua, Shanghai, Tokyo, New York

Number of lawyers 754
at this office 40

Contacts
Pedro Rebelo de Sousa, William Smithson

CATEGORIES OF WORK

Corporate

Banking

Capital markets

Taxation

Projects, PFI

EU, competition

Dispute resolution

Intellectual property

Employment

Financial markets

Pharmaceutical and biotechnology

Energy and utilities

TMT

Aerospace and defence

Transport

Real estate and construction

Consumer goods

SOUSA MACHADO, FERREIRA DA COSTA E ASSOCIADOS

RUA RODRIGO DA FONSECA
Nº 178, 6º/7º ESQ
1070 - 243 LISBOA

Telephone: +351 21 385 44 69
Fax: +351 21 385 48 15
E-mail: advoga@mail.telepac.pt

Languages
English, French, Italian, Spanish

Number of lawyers 18

Contacts
Manuel Ferreira da Costa,
Alexandre de Sousa Machado

CATEGORIES OF WORK

Corporate and commercial law
Manuel Ferreira da Costa,
Alexandre de Sousa Machado

Civil law
Alexandre de Sousa Machado,
Manuel Ferreira da Costa

Debt collection and insolvency
Manuel Ferreira da Costa

Insurance
Manuel Ferreira da Costa

EU and competition
Sergio Direito

Software and telecommunications
Alexandre de Sousa Machado,
Manuel Ferreira da Costa

Inheritance and family law
Alexandre de Sousa Machado

Labour law
Manuel Ferreira da Costa,
Jaime Dória Cortesão

Litigation
Manuel Ferreira da Costa,
Nuno Cardoso Ribeiro

Arbitration
Alexandre de Sousa Machado

Intellectual property
Alexandre de Sousa Machado

Administrative law
Manuel Ferreira da Costa,
Nuno Cardoso Ribeiro

Agency and distribution
Manuel Ferreira da Costa

TEIXEIRA DE FREITAS, RODRIGUES, MOURA COSTA E ASSOCIADOS

AVENIDA DA REPUBLICA
N32–4º ESQ
1050–193 LISBON

Telephone: +351 21 781 5660
Fax: +351 21 781 5679
E-mail: lawfirm@teixeiradefreitas.pt

Languages
English, French, Italian, Spanish

Other offices
Funchal (Madeira)

Number of lawyers 23
at this office 16

Contacts
Dr Luiz Augusto Teixeira de Freitas,
Dr Rosana Rodrigues,
Dr Mauricio de Moura Costa,
Dr Carlos Manuel Silva Gomes

Member
ITPA (International Tax Planning Association);
IFA (International Fiscal Association)

CATEGORIES OF WORK

Corporate

Tax

International tax planning

Commercial

Foreign investment

Shipping

Banking and securities

International contracts

Labour

Real estate

Litigation

Competition

Administrative law

URÍA & MENÉNDEZ
ADVOGADOS

EDIFICIO OMNI
AV.DUQUE D'AVILA, 141-6°
1050-081 LISBON

Telephone: +351 21 358 3000
Fax: +351 21 315 1962
E-mail: lisboa@uria.com
Website: www.uria.com

Languages
English, Spanish, French

Other offices
Barcelona, Bilbao, Brussels, Buenos Aires*, Lima*, London, Madrid, Mexico City*, New York, Santiago de Chile*, São Paulo*, Valencia

Number of lawyers 296
at this office 20

Contact
Duarte Garin (dmg@uria.com);
Coloma Armero (cam@uria.com)

International groupings
Marval, O'Farrell & Mairal (Buenos Aires); Philippi, Yrrarázaval, Pulido & Brunner (Santiago de Chile); Franck, Galicia y Robles, SC (Mexico City); Payet, Rey, Cauvi (Lima); Dias Carneiro Advogados (Sâo Paulo)

CATEGORIES OF WORK

Corporate and commercial

Mergers and acquisitions

Capital markets

Banking and finance

Project finance

Real estate

Litigation and arbitration

Labour

Tax

Telecom

Energy

Insurance

Competition and antitrust

VASCONCELOS, F SÁ CARNEIRO, FONTES & ASSOCIADOS

RUA CASTILHO 20
3º PISO
1250-069 LISBOA

Telephone: +351 21 030 8600
Fax: +351 21 030 8601
E-mail: lisboa@vscf.net

Languages
English, French, German, Italian, Spanish

Other offices
Oporto

Number of lawyers 48
at this office 41

CATEGORIES OF WORK

General corporate and commercial
Duarte Vasconcelos,
Ana Cristina Marques

Banking
Pedro Ferreira Malaquias,
Ana Rita Campos

Litigation and arbitration
Tito Arantes Fontes, João Santos

Mergers and acquisitions
Francisco Sá Carneiro,
Duarte Brito de Goes

Tax law
João Marques Pinto

Property and construction
Francisco Dória Nóbrega,
João Torroaes Valente

Capital markets
Pedro Ferreira Malaquias,
Sofia Leite Borges

EU, antitrust and competition law
Joaquim Caimoto Duarte

Projects and finance
Francisco Sá Carneiro,
Mónica Carneiro Pacheco

Telecommunications and media
Duarte Vasconcelos,
Maria Eduarda Godinho

Administrative/environmental law
Mónica Carneiro Pacheco,
Miguel Spinola

Energy
Monica Carneiro Pachelo,
Tiago Ferreira de Matos

Family and inheritance
João Santos, Alexandra Queiroz

Labour law
João Santos, Rui Pereira de Melo

Criminal law
Tito Arantes Fontes, Ana Clara Santos

Insolvency
Tito Arantes Fontes, João Santos

AIRÃO, VIEIRA DE CASTRO, SILVA LOPES, PESSANHA

LARGO DO ADRO 9
4050-016 PORTO

Telephone: +351 22 607 68 00
Fax: +351 22 609 46 88
E-mail: advogados@acrlex.com

Languages
English, French, German, Italian, Spanish

Number of lawyers 7

Member
The Interlex Group

CATEGORIES OF WORK

Civil and commercial law (general)
João Vieira de Castro

Company and corporate law
João Vieira de Castro

Mergers and acquisitions
Pedro Pessanha

Franchising, agency and distributorship
Pedro Pessanha

Banking
Vasco Airão

Securities and finance
Vasco Airão

Competition law
João Vieira de Castro

Intellectual property law
Vasco Airão

Administrative law
José Manuel da Silva Lopes

Labour and employment law
José Manuel da Silva Lopes

Litigation, arbitration and mediation
João Vieira de Castro, Vasco Airão

RUI PEIXOTO DUARTE & ASSOCIADOS – ADVOGADOS

203/205 RUA ANTÓNIO PATRÍCIO
4150-100 PORTO

Telephone: +351 22 606 79 08
Fax: +351 22 600 18 16
E-mail: info@rpda-law.com
Website: www.rpda-law.com

Languages
Portuguese, English, French, Italian, Spanish, Swedish, Finnish, Danish

Other offices
Lisbon

Number of lawyers 9

Contact
Dr Rui Peixoto Duarte

CATEGORIES OF WORK

Corporate and commercial
Rui Peixoto Duarte

Commercial property, real estate
José Carlos Vasconcelos

Dispute resolution – litigation and arbitration
Rui Peixoto Duarte

Foreign direct investment
Rui Peixoto Duarte

Intellectual property
Rui Peixoto Duarte

Labour law
Luís Freire de Andrade

Regulated activities
Nuno Barbosa

Mergers and acquisitions
Rui Peixoto Duarte,
José Carlos Vasconcelos

Banking and finance
Nuno Barbosa

Tax
Maria Dulce Soares

Contracts, distribution, commercial agency, franchising
Rui Peixoto Duarte

Sport and entertainment
Nuno Barbosa, Ricardo Costa

Inheritance, family law
Ricardo Costa

E-commerce
Siv Lindqvist

VASCONCELOS, F SÁ CARNEIRO, FONTES & ASSOCIADOS

RUA CAMPO ALEGRE
830 - SALA 11, 3º
4150-171 PORTO

Telephone: +351 220 308 600
Fax: +351 220 308 601
E-mail: porto@vscf.net

Languages
English, French, German, Spanish

Other offices
Lisbon

Number of lawyers 48
at this office 7

CATEGORIES OF WORK

General corporate and commercial law
João Anacoreta Correia, Mafalda Barreiros Pavia

Litigation and arbitration
João Anacoreta Correia, Paulo Ortigão de Oliveira

Labour law
Paulo Ortigão de Oliveira

Insolvency
João Anacoreta Correia, Paulo Ortigão de Oliveira

QATAR

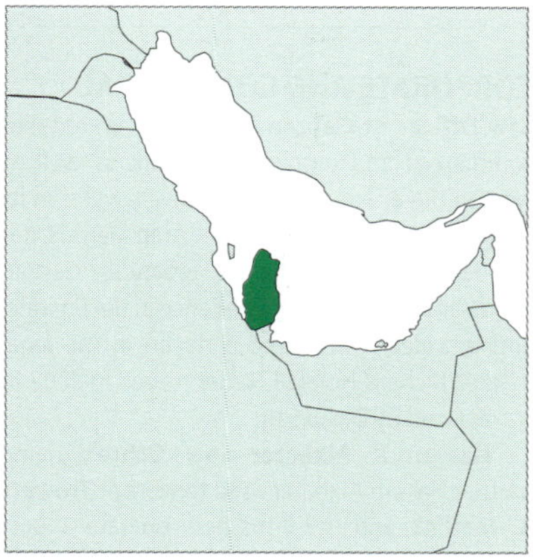

Population	817,000
Number of lawyers	n/a
Professional title	Lawyer
Currency	Qatari rial (QAR)

Index

A British protectorate until 1971, Qatar declined to join the United Arab Emirates and declared its independence. Despite vast oil and gas reserves, development lagged behind its neighbours until 1995 when Sheikh Khalifa was replaced by his son Emir Hamad Bin Khalifa al-Thani in a bloodless coup. Since then, the Qatar economy has been transformed. Western companies were invited to invest, more than €10bn was borrowed by the government, and massive gas reserves in the North Field opened up for investment. From no gas industry at all in 1996, Qatar now exports over ten million tonnes per year, which is expected to triple by 2007.

Behind the rhetoric of progress, Qatar remains a tribal autocracy. The Emir is assisted by a Council of Ministers headed by a prime minister, which recommends legislation for the Emir to approve. The Emir is very powerful, and as in Dubai the economic progress of the country largely depends on his personality. Unlike the UAE, Qatar shares some of the less commercially friendly qualities of Saudi Arabia, including strict Wahhabism. Like all its neighbours, Qatar also suffers from demographic problems. Native Qataris only make up 40% of the population, and a lack of skills, and experience of lavish state handouts, has engendered a less than positive work ethic which the government is trying to address through a policy of Qatarisation.

The government of Qatar is deeply conservative, but has not hesitated to plough its own furrow to further its national interests. It engages with Israel far more than many Arab neighbours, opposed sanctions against Iraq, and in the last two years has aligned itself strongly with the US. This relationship blossomed in 2002 when the US moved its Gulf HQ from Saudi Arabia to Qatar in the run-up to the second Gulf War.

ECONOMIC CLIMATE

Oil and gas account for more than half of Qatar's GDP. With proven oil reserves of 14.5 billion barrels it is well behind many other Middle Eastern countries, but its natural gas reserves exceed 17 trillion cubic metres, the third largest in the world after Russia and Iran. Profits from this lucrative industry are shared amongst a tiny population, and income and standards of living have reached European levels.

Recent development has focused on liquid natural gas exports, exploiting the North Field, the world's largest single gas reservoir. Opening the gas fields has caused a boom in huge projects. The Dolphin Project is potentially the largest cross-border deal in the history of the Middle East, transporting gas to the UAE, and perhaps eventually Oman as well. Other large projects include Shell's plans to build a $5bn gas-to-liquid plant, and ExxonMobil's proposed $8bn LNG plant. Qatargas and RasGas are both about to double the size of their LNG facilities. Major customers of gas include Japan, South Korea, India and Singapore.

In 2002 Qatar passed Law No 13 of 2000, allowing foreign investors greater economic freedom, including 100% ownership in certain circumstances, and easing of restrictions on setting up business, tax breaks and movement of capital.

Qatar is not trying to diversify to the extent that Dubai is, but is trying to develop a petrochemical industry, with ventures such as Qatar Vinyl Company and Qatar Chemical Company. Leading banks are Qatar National Bank, Commercial Bank of Qatar and Doha Bank, but compared to neighbouring Bahrain and the UAE its financial market is undeveloped. Since 1997 Qatar has had a stock exchange, which now includes 26 companies with a capitalisation of €6bn.

LEGAL SYSTEM

The constitution states that traditional Islamic law is the main source of legislation, but there is little influence of the shari'a outside family matters. Most other areas are classed as 'civil law,' and dealt with in the *adlia* court. Considering its history, there was little British influence on the early civil legal system, with French and other Arab presence more obvious.

Proceedings in all courts are conducted in Arabic, usually with written submissions. Appeals go to the Court of Appeal, which is the highest court. A committee headed by the Minister of Justice regulates admission to the legal profession.

LEGAL MARKET

During 2003 the Qatar legal market experienced huge changes. Having announced an association in 2002, **Hassan A Alkhater Law Office** and **Towers & Hamlins** downgraded their affiliation to a 'best friends' relationship only a year after it began. **Hassan A Alkhater Law Office** has also entered into a correspondent relationship with **Richards Butler**, which ceased its association with *Law Offices of Dr Najeeb Bin Mohammed Al-Nauimi* following Hugh Thompson's move in-house to

The largest firms

1	Al-Attiya Legal Consultant & Attorney	9
2	The International Office for Advocacy and Legal Consultation	8
3	Arab Law Bureau	6
	Rouhani & Partners	6
5	Law Office of Ali bin Nasser Al-Naimi	4
6	Simmons & Simmons	2

These figures represent the total number of lawyers in this country only, and have been supplied by the firms themselves. The figures should be accurate as at 1 January 2004.

Commercial Bank of Qatar. While it is without a formal presence at the moment, **Richards Butler** hopes to maintain a long-term commitment to Qatar.

In 2002 the Qatar government changed the law to allow foreign firms to open offices in Doha. Building on its presence in Abu Dhabi, **Simmons & Simmons** was the first to take advantage, bringing a strong record acting for the Qatar government and local clients as well as international clients in projects and construction. Washington, DC-based **Patton Boggs LLP** also opened an office in October 2003. The firm will focus on acting for the Qatar government, and government agencies, such as the Qatar Foundation for Education, Science and Community Development. Its new office will be headed by partner Susan Bastress.

Eversheds LLP has entered into a co-operation agreement with a small local firm to create **A Rahman Mohamed Al-Jufairi, Advocates & Legal Consultants in co-operation with Eversheds**, which advises on financial restructuring and banking litigation. In 2001 **Eversheds LLP** advised the Qatar government on its boundary dispute with Bahrain in the ICJ.

Latham & Watkins also undertakes a lot of work for the Qatar government. The firm was counsel to Ras Laffan Liquefied Natural Gas Company (RasGas) in the $2.5bn financing of an LNG project. Petrochemicals is also a strong sector: Q-Chem was advised on its joint ventures in the petrochemical plant in Masaieed; and Qatar Vinyl Company on the financing of a petrochemical plant. The firm has also acted for the US Exim Bank and SACE on the financing of the QatarGas II project.

Sullivan & Cromwell LLP acted for ExxonMobil on a gas pipeline from North Field to Kuwait, while **Skadden, Arps, Slate, Meagher & Flom LLP** handles a lot of banking in Doha.

From London, **White & Case** is representing the sponsors Qatar Petroleum and ExxonMobil Qatargas on the financing of the $6bn Qatargas II project, involving the construction of an LNG train in Qatar, and a receiving terminal in the UK.

In 2003, **Allen & Overy, Shook Lin & Bok Joint Law Venture** advised HSBC as lead manager on Qatar's $700m global Islamic sukuk issue, the world's largest such issue.

Clifford Chance LLP has offices in Saudi Arabia and Dubai, and a very strong presence in corporate and projects in the Middle East. The team has cleaned up on big regional projects: such as for Dolphin Energy on the $3.5bn Dolphin Project; and QP on the award-winning Ras Laffan IWPP. IPOs include representing QP/Qatar government on the reorganisation of downstream petrochemical and steel businesses and subsequent potential $2.3bn IPO.

There is very little intellectual property work, but if required readers could use trade mark agency **Abu-Setta & Partners**. In-house lawyers are quite common. Qatar Petroleum has about six, comparable in size to the largest firms.

CORPORATE AND COMMERCIAL

GEBRAN MAJDALANY, LAW OFFICES OF
HASSAN A ALKHATER LAW OFFICE

Ali bin Nasser Al-Naimi, Law Office of ✪
Arab Law Bureau
Simmons & Simmons ✪

Firms are listed A-Z in tiers which are ranked in order of priority
✪ Indicates firm displays contact details at the end of this chapter.

CORPORATE AND COMMERCIAL

Law Offices of Gebran Majdalany undertakes commercial and employment work as well as work in the energy sector. With five lawyers in its 'English' department, and eight Arab lawyers, it is the largest firm in Qatar. Lebanese Gebran Majdalany has 30 years' experience in the Emirate, and is widely considered a doyen in the legal market. Richard Horsfall Turner retired in 2002 to be replaced by David Salt.

Hassan A Alkhater Law Office's name partner Hassan Alkhater used to work at **Trowers & Hamlins**, and the firms now operate a 'best friends' relationship. The team includes five Arab lawyers and David Silver as a consultant, who has seven years' experience in Qatar. Apart from corporate work for oil majors like ExxonMobil and Occidental, and banks such as HSBC and Standard Chartered, the firm has a strong record on projects. Historically, it acted for LNG giant RasGas on its original plant trains one and two in 1996, and now also on trains three and four. The firm is now local counsel to Dolphin Energy, for which **Shearman & Sterling LLP** is international counsel. **Hassan A Alkhater Law Office** will also work closely in the future with **Richards Butler**, which has recently been acting for tenderers on the Dolphin Project, such as Bechtel.

Law Office of Ali bin Nasser Al-Naimi is a good local firm, with commercial links in Egypt, and a roster of clients such as Commercial Bank of Qatar, Gulf Air Company and Maersk Oil.

Arab Law Bureau has two partners and three assistants. Alaa Fathi Hamad is a former in-house lawyer at Arab Bank, and Mohammed Bin Rashid Al Khalifa is a former legal adviser to the Foreign Ministry. In 2003 the firm advised the developers of the West Bay Four Seasons complex on a $160m financing; and advised a major European contracting company on a €100m gas project. Banks make a up a significant portion of the client base, such as Standard Chartered, HSBC, Doha Bank; plus corporates like Q-Tel, Halliburton and Arab Insurance Company.

Simmons & Simmons opened in September 2003. Office managing partner Charles Pollock has experience in property and projects, and is aided by two assistants. They undertake a general practice for the Qatar government and commercial clients, with a focus on inward investment and employment.

LAW OFFICE OF ALI BIN NASSER AL-NAIMI

AL RAWABI STREET
ALMUNTAZA AREA
PO BOX 2457
DOHA

Telephone: +974 4432 959
Fax: +974 4432 595
E-mail: theqatarifirm@yahoo.com

Languages
Arabic, English

Number of lawyers 4

CATEGORIES OF WORK

Banking law/loans and Islamic banking
Dr Ahmed Osman

Maritime law
Dr Ahmed Osman

Building and construction law
Ali bin Nasser Al-Naimi

Exclusive distributorship and commercial agencies law
Dr Ahmed Osman

Taxation and Sharia law
Dr Ahmed Osman

Registration of lands and leasehold agreements
Ali bin Nasser Al-Naimi

Drafting of memoranda
Tajeldin Idris

Articles of association and registration of companies
Ali bin Nasser Al-Naimi

Labour law and employment contracts
Ali bin Nasser Al-Naimi

Oil law
Dr Ahmed Osman

Arbitration
Ali bin Nasser Al-Naimi

Aviation law
Tajeldin Idris

Intellectual property law
Tajeldin Idris

THE FIRM

The Law Office of Ali bin Nasser Al-Naimi was founded in 1981 by Mr Ali bin Nasser Al-Naimi, the ex-undersecretary of the Ministry of Justice in Qatar. The firm has grown into a reputable law office with a solid base of local clients and worldwide connections. In its relatively short, but prosperous, lifetime, the office has represented such reputable international corporations as BMW, Chrysler International and Maersk Oil Qatar. It is the policy of the firm to afford the highest level of assistance to its clients, which is fulfilled by highly qualified personnel. The office is a very active contributor to the G.C.C Arbitration Center's activities. It is a competitive all-round commercial and civil practice.

AREAS OF PRACTICE

In general, the firm specialises in civil and commercial law. A major area of work is that of exclusive distributorship and commercial agencies law.

The office has gained invaluable experience in maritime and aviation law, through its representation of Qatar navigation (a sole local player in maritime agencies) and Gulf Air.

A thorough knowledge of banking law (loans and Islamic banking transactions) is another of the firm's great assets, gained through its work advising and representing the Commercial Bank of Qatar and other banks.

The commercial department of the office handles real estate, investment and finance law, corporate law and general commercial work.

The office's practice in intellectual property law includes trade marks and copyright law.

Other important work areas include providing advice and handling litigation on taxation, Shari'a law, labour law and employment contract, oil law, building and construction law and leasehold agreements. As well as serving its local and international clients, the office operates as a local correspondent for several reputable international law firms.

SIMMONS & SIMMONS

8TH FLOOR
SALAM TOWER
AL CORNICHE STREET
PO BOX 23540
DOHA

Telephone: +974 483 9466
Fax: +974 483 9584
Website: www.simmons-simmons.com

Languages
Arabic, English

Other offices
London, Rotterdam, Paris, Lisbon, Milan, Rome, Düsseldorf, Frankfurt, Brussels, Madrid, Padua, Oporto, Madeira, Abu Dhabi, Hong Kong, Shanghai, Tokyo, New York

Number of lawyers 754
at this office 2

Contact
Charles Pollock

CATEGORIES OF WORK	
Corporate	Financial markets
Banking	Pharmaceutical and biotechnology
Capital markets	Energy and utilities
Taxation	TMT
Projects,PFI	Aerospace and defence
EU, competition	Transport
Dispute resolution	Real estate and construction
Intellectual property	Consumer goods
Employment	

ROMANIA

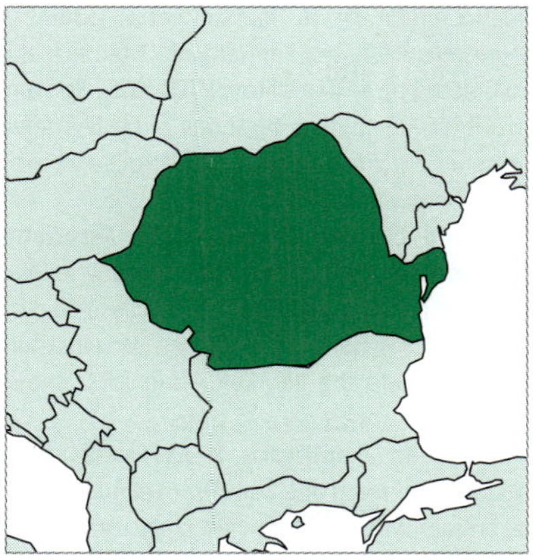

Population	21.6 million
Number of lawyers	12,562
Professional title	Advocate
Currency	Leu (lei)

Index

Romania is in the lower Danube basin, north of the Balkan Peninsula and adjoining the Black Sea. Bordered by Hungary, Moldova, Ukraine, Bulgaria and Yugoslavia, its capital city, Bucharest, is the centre of commercial and legal activity.

A 41-year stretch of communist rule ended in 1989 with the overthrow of Ceaucescu's despotic regime. President Ion Iliescu was elected in December 2000, having previously held office from 1990 to 1996. The SDP government has proposed that parliamentary and presidential elections be held on 12 December 2004. The forced resignation of three senior government ministers shows the government is serious about tackling high-level corruption, which has dogged the country for so long.

Romania signed its Nato membership accord in Brussels in March 2003 and is set to join in 2004. The country began negotiations for EU accession in 1999 and is making progress in meeting the political, economic, legislative and social accession targets required. The earliest joining date will be 2007.

Romania's key industries are steel, agriculture, manufacturing, shipping, aluminium, oil and gas, and automotive.

ECONOMIC CLIMATE

Romania has been dogged by resistance to structural reform from state bureaucracy and industry and unions, which has led to poor competitiveness of exports and large current account deficits.

Reform has been a necessity since Romania's application in 1999 to join the EU, and in the last year, structural and legislative reform has continued apace. The government is set to sign a new accord with the IMF by early 2004, which is likely to prioritise a cutback of arrears, strict control of state sector wages, and continued restructuring and privatisation of the energy sector.

The National Bank of Romania predicts that the country's external deficit is likely to reach 6.5% of GDP in 2003, triggered by an explosion of the commercial deficit in October, when imports outpaced exports by almost $1bn. Measures are expected to be introduced promptly to push the current account deficit down to 5% of GDP in 2004.

The government's objective to bring inflation down below 10% by the end of 2004 looks unlikely to be met, but should be achievable by the end of 2005.

Along with large companies, such as Renault and France Télécom already present in Romania, there are some small to mid-size companies which perceive opportunities in the country and continue to enter the market, especially in the agriculture and construction sectors. The deregulation of the market is also beginning to attract foreign capital for restructuring industry, public utilities and the financial sector in Romania which should help encourage sustained economic recovery.

BILLING

Minimum rates of billing are enforced by the Romanian Bar Association. Otherwise, all forms of billing familiar to Western business clients are considered. Capped and fixed fees are increasingly being demanded by some clients, with some firms acceding and believed by others to be winning work from those firms that continue to insist on hourly rates.

The hourly rate for a partner is generally between €300 and €600, and can be anything up to €750 for a senior partner. Where local lawyers work in foreign law firms their rates will tend to be lower than the rates of the foreign lawyers.

Standard rates of billing for junior lawyers are between €100 and €450 for expatriate lawyers and from as little as €60 up to €400 per hour for local lawyers.

MARKETING

Although the Romanian Bar ostensibly prohibits the advertising of legal services, marketing remains a grey area. Many foreign – and increasingly local – firms advertise in professional directories and the local press. Several have comprehensive websites and sponsorship of high-profile events represents a legitimate way of getting round the ban.

IN-HOUSE LAWYERS

Most major enterprises retain in-house lawyers who are increasingly turning to outside counsel for advice on projects of all sizes. In-house lawyers cannot belong to the Bar, and do not have rights of audience in Romanian courts.

LEGISLATIVE DEVELOPMENTS

Romania's bid to harmonise its legislation with the EU led to a host of new regulations which affected

The largest firms

1	Musat & Asociatii	70
2	Stefanica, Dutu & Partners	45
3	Nestor Nestor Diculescu Kingston Petersen	43
4	Linklaters Miculiti & Asociatii	26
5	Calin Zamfirescu & Associates	23
6	Studio Legale Sutti	20
7	Popovici & Asociatii	19
8	Deleanu Vasile – Lawyers	18
9	Georgescu, Nemoianu & Salcianu Law Firm	16
	Salans / Moore, Vartires & Associates SCPA	16
11	Hayhurst Robinson	15
	Racoti – Predoiu, Attorneys at Law	15
	Voicu & Filipescu	15
14	Danescu, Danescu & Associates	14
15	Stoica & Asociatii Attorneys at Law	13
16	Rubin Meyer Doru & Trandafir, Spca, in Association with Herzfeld & Rubin, P.C.	12
	Wood Lupascu Dumitrescu & Associates SCPA in association withHall, Dickler	12
17	Badea, Radu & Asociatii SCA	11
	CMS Cameron McKenna Cristina Brinzan Law Office	11
	IK Roka & C. Spiridon SCPA	11
20	David & Baias	10
	Gide Loyrette Nouel	10
	PI Partners	10
	Vilau & Mitel	10
24	Magda Volonciu Law Office Romania	9
25	Buzescu & Co	8
	Haarmann Hemmelrath	8
	Nörr Stiefenhofer Lutz	8
	Pachiu & Associates	8
	SCA Carnu, Dumitrache, Gherghina & Sebeni	8

These figures represent the total number of lawyers in this country only, and have been supplied by the firms themselves. The figures should be accurate as at 1 January 2004.

law firms and their clients.

The approval of a new constitution included provision for greater protection of human rights, the guarantee of private property and the development of mechanisms for judicial review.

The new Labour Code has been lauded by unions but caused a headache to employers who have had to amend employment contracts.

A new anti-corruption law aims to ensure transparency of public office and the business environment. The law also changed the security interests regime, and the legal provisions governing companies.

In a further bid to reduce bureaucracy and corruption, a new ordinance was adopted which provides that if a public authority does not respond to an application within the statutory term, the authorisation will be deemed to have been tacitly granted.

Amendments to the capital markets and securities laws pertaining to minority shareholder rights led to public takeover offers and high-profile litigation, while the new Fiscal Code to be adopted from 2004 is expected to give rise to tax structuring issues for many.

The opening up of the energy market led to a change in the legislative framework, while the liberalisation of the Romanian telecoms market led to much work in licensing procedures and establishing new businesses.

Rule changes also allowed for the creation of mortgage loan companies, while the ban on foreigners buying freeholds in Romania was lifted.

Legislative acts increased the priority of PPPs among local and central public authorities, particularly regarding the construction, development and renovation of the transportation network.

Competition law saw the introduction of new regulations on economic concentrations and exclusive agreements

BANKING, FINANCE AND CAPITAL MARKETS

Nestor Nestor Diculescu Kingston Petersen has a market-leading position for banking and finance, which continues despite the departure of partner Christine Moore. The firm acts for numerous international banks operating in Romania, including HSBC and Alpha Bank. It advised the European Commission on a €200m loan agreement to Romania, and advised Monifon Holdings BV in a bond issuance worth more than $200m on the Luxembourg Stock Exchange.

Badea, Radu & Asociatii SCA advised HVB Bank and JPMorgan on the $200m financing of Termoelectrica by fiduciary notes listed in Luxembourg. Alpha Bank, the EBRD, Deutsche Bank, Romgaz SA and ABN Amro are all clients.

Clients at **Linklaters Miculiti & Asociatii** include ABN Amro, Citibank and Deutsche Bank. Marian Dinu, the 'outstanding and shrewd' Ted Cominos, and Adrian Bulboac are recommended. Banking law relating to the energy and natural gas industries is a strong area.

The EBRD kept **Musat & Asociatii** busy with loan agreements. LBS Bayerische Landesbausparkasse and Citibank are also clients. The firm advised Bucharest Stock Exchange (BSE), and the National Securities Commission on regulatory issues.

Salans / Moore, Vartires & Associates SCPA's banking team advised HVB Bank on an export finance credit facility for Rompetrol ($30m). It represents Raiffeisen Zentralbank Osterreich and completed three mandatory PTOs to de-list from the RASDAQ market of three publicly traded cement companies controlled by HeidelbergCement.

Wood Lupascu Dumitrescu & Associates SCPA in association with Hall, Dickler advises on a range of banking and finance matters, including bond issues, syndicated loans and securitisation. Clients include the IFC, EBRD and ING, among others.

At **Calin Zamfirescu & Associates** Calin Andrei Zamfirescu and Stan Tirnoveanu are both recommended. The firm has particularly good expertise in bankruptcy law, banking litigation and competition law, as well as the regulatory aspects of Romanian banking products.

BANKING, FINANCE AND CAPITAL MARKETS

NESTOR NESTOR DICULESCU KINGSTON PETERSEN ✪

Badea, Radu & Asociatii SCA ✪
Linklaters Miculiti & Asociatii ✪
Musat & Asociatii ✪
Salans / Moore, Vartires & Associates SCPA
Wood Lupascu Dumitrescu & Associates SCPA in association with Hall, Dickler ✪

CMS Cameron McKenna Cristina Brinzan Law Office
Calin Zamfirescu & Associates ✪
David & Baias ✪
Despina Fruth Oprisan Law Offices
Georgescu, Nemoianu & Salcianu Law Firm ✪
Gide Loyrette Nouel ✪
Gruia Dufaut Law Office ✪
Haarmann Hemmelrath ✪
Nörr Stiefenhofer Lutz ✪
Mihaela Grama-Popovici, Law Office
Popovici & Asociatii ✪
Racoti – Predoiu, Attorneys at Law ✪
Rubin Meyer Doru & Trandafir, Spca, in Association with Herzfeld & Rubin, P.C.
Schönherr Rechtsanwälte OEG ✪
Stefanica, Dutu & Partners
Stoica & Asociatii Attorneys at Law ✪

Firms are listed A-Z in tiers which are ranked in order of priority
✪ Indicates firm displays contact details at the end of this chapter.

David & Baias advised BNR on a new inter-bank electronic payment system. The firm has niche strength in pioneering multi-million dollar factoring agreements for banking clients in London and Romania.

Georgescu, Nemoianu & Salcianu Law Firm is involved in securities advice. It advised shareholders of a medium-sized Romanian bank during the disposal of shares.

Gide Loyrette Nouel advised a banking consortium led by BRD – Groupe Société Générale SA, on the first syndicated credit facility agreement to be governed by Romanian law without the backing of a State guarantee.

Gruia Dufaut Law Office advised on insurance and bad debt collection. Dana Gruia Dufaut is team head.

Nörr Stiefenhofer Lutz's banking and finance team advises on credit facilities, securities, as well as leasing. Andreea Poenaru is well known for her advice to banks and leasing companies. Of late, the firm has advised a German/Austrian bank on the structuring and establishment of a multi-million euro bridging loan facility.

Popovici & Asociatii's banking clients include BNP Paribas, Banque Franco-Roumaine and RoBank. Florin Nitu is recommended for his capital markets work. Clients include Automobile Dacia (groupe Renault), Magnetto Wheels SpA and Amydex International Group.

Racoti – Predoiu, Attorneys at Law advised an international corporation on the takeover of a Romanian bank. Raiffeisen Commerzbank AG is a client.

Rubin Meyer Doru & Trandafir, Spca, in Association with Herzfeld & Rubin, P.C. advised Egnatia Bank in its acquisition of BNP/Dresdner's banking operations in Romania, and the National Bank of Greece in its proposed acquisition of Banca Romanesca. It is also advising a UK company with regard to its possible acquisition of Romania's largest private bank. The firm saw a fall in its capital markets work, although it is retained as first General Counsel of the Bucharest Stock Exchange.

Stefanica, Dutu & Partners acted for CFR Marfa on a eurobond issuance on the Luxembourg Stock Exchange and for Termoelectrica on a structured loan.

Stoica & Asociatii Attorneys at Law's clients include Société Générale, Credit Suisse First Boston, Deutsche Bank, Nordic Investment Bank and the EBRD.

CORPORATE AND COMMERCIAL

Still acknowledged as the top dog in Romanian legal circles is **Nestor Nestor Diculescu Kingston Petersen**. Led by the 'charming', 'vastly experienced' and 'outstanding' corporate partner, Ion Nestor, the department also houses Nestor's wife, the 'highly skilled, sophisticated, diligent, pragmatic and friendly' Manuela, who has a wealth of experience in the Romanian marketplace. The 'uniformly excellent' firm is respected not just by clients but also by peers: most rival firms said they would recommend **Nestor Nestor Diculescu Kingston Petersen** if they were conflicted out of a corporate transaction. However, having lost high-profile name partners, Andrew Kingston and Patricia Petersen, in 2001 when they returned to the US, **Nestor Nestor Diculescu Kingston Petersen** also lost heavyweight banking partner, Christine Moore, in 2003. The former ABN Amro lawyer left to set up her own practice. She took one major client (tobacco producer Michaillides), which she originally brought to the firm. The firm continues to flourish, however, and although no big-name partners have been recruited as replacements, the number of fee-earners has risen to 45 and the firm's international client list, including Philip Morris, Heineken, Hewlett-Packard, Kraft, Microsoft, and Trinity Industries, is the envy of competitors. The firm is particularly recommended for being 'able to resolve complex matters through insightful reasoning', for having a 'thorough understanding of business realities' and having the 'flexibility and patience' to advise clients on a wide range of legal matters.

Linklaters Miculiti & Asociatii continues to strengthen with office head, the 'extremely able and efficient' Michael Tétreault Schilling spending more time in Bucharest. The firm 'has the badge of a well-recognised international law firm and tends to be geared up for big ticket transactional work'. The firm brought in English lawyer, Sebastian Lawson-Foia from **Freshfields Bruckhaus Deringer** to head the tax, employee benefits and insurance departments. He has worked with the Romanian government on the new draft tax code. Marian Dinu (financial services, securities, M&A) is described as 'outstanding', while Lucian Mihai is recommended for IP. Deal highlights include advising GeCAD Software on the first acquisition by the Microsoft Corporation of proprietary technology developed by a Romanian company; advising OTE International Investments Ltd on the acquisition of RomTelecom, the national fixed line telecommunications operator; advising the Serbia Privatisation Agency on the €600m+ privatisation of Serbian tobacco companies, Duvanska industrija Niš and Duvanska industrija Vranje; and advising Bank Consolidation Company/JPMorgan on the sale of DSK Bank to OTP Bank of Hungary.

Clearly signing up to the big is beautiful ethos, **Musat & Asociatii**'s lawyer headcount now stands at around 70. **Musat & Asociatii** suffered a blow in January 2003 when four partners departed, taking with them several **Musat & Asociatii** assistants and some clients. The leavers were Ernest Popovici; Florian Nitu; Dragos Vilau; and Sorinel Mitel. In June 2003, **Musat & Asociatii** also lost senior IP associate, Cristian-Ionut Colan, to **Bostina & Associates**. **Musat & Asociatii** appears to have weathered the storm well though, promoting Mona Marian (Gheorghe Musat's daughter) and Cornel Popa to partner, and recruiting several lawyers from rival firms.

Notable joiners include Razvan Gheorghiu-

CORPORATE AND COMMERCIAL

NESTOR NESTOR DICULESCU KINGSTON PETERSEN ✪

LINKLATERS MICULITI & ASOCIATII ✪
MUSAT & ASOCIATII ✪

Buzescu & Co ✪
Georgescu, Nemoianu & Salcianu Law Firm ✪
Hayhurst Robinson ✪
Rubin Meyer Doru & Trandafir, Spca, in Association with Herzfeld & Rubin, P.C.
Salans / Moore, Vartires & Associates SCPA
Stephenson Har - Popescu & Associates
Voicu & Filipescu ✪

Badea, Radu & Asociatii SCA ✪
CMS Cameron McKenna Cristina Brinzan Law Office
Calin Zamfirescu & Associates ✪
David & Baias ✪
Gide Loyrette Nouel ✪
Gruia Dufaut Law Office ✪
Haarmann Hemmelrath ✪
Nörr Stiefenhofer Lutz ✪
PI Partners ✪
Popovici & Asociatii ✪
Racoti – Predoiu, Attorneys at Law ✪
SCA Carnu, Dumitrache, Ghergina & Sebeni
Stefanica, Dutu & Partners
Stoica & Asociatii Attorneys at Law ✪
Vilau & Mitel ✪
Wood Lupascu Dumitrescu & Associates SCPA in association with Hall, Dickler ✪

Babiuc, Sulica & Associates ✪
Bostina & Associates
Burchel & Partners
CMS Bureau Francis Lefebvre Catalina Marcu Law Office
Cobuz & Associates
Danescu, Danescu & Associates ✪
Deleanu Vasile – Lawyers ✪
Despina Fruth Oprisan Law Offices
Gutium si Asociatii SCA
IK Roka & C. Spiridon SCPA
Magda Volonciu Law Office Romania
Mihaela Grama-Popovici, Law Office
Norton Rose
Pachiu & Associates ✪
Schönherr Rechtsanwälte OEG ✪
Sutti, Studio Legale ✪
Tonucci, Studio Legale

Firms are listed A-Z in tiers which are ranked in order of priority
✪ Indicates firm displays contact details at the end of this chapter.

Testa, founder of *Testa, David & Associates*, now **PI Partners**; Gelu Maravela and Dominic Morega, previously respectively managing partner and partner with **Babiuc, Sulica & Associates**; Ioana Onica, previously president of the Fifth District Court; Delia Topoleanu, previously judge within the Fifth District Court; Marius Barladeanu, previously corporate associate with **CMS Cameron McKenna Cristina Brinzan Law Office**; Danut Bugnariu, former associate with **Calin Zamfirescu & Associates**; Silvana Ivan, previously associate with **Pachiu & Associates**; Iulia Raileanu, previously executive director of the Centre for Legal Resource; Mihaela Piticu, former associate with **Schönherr Rechtsanwälte OEG**; and commercial litigator, Ion Dragne. Apart from the high volume of work **Musat & Asociatii** provides to the government, corporate clients include Piraeus Bank Group, adidas, Gabriel Resources Ltd, Hoffman La Roche Ltd, Transfond SA, Balneoclimaterica, Orkla Foods and Chequepoint.

Buzescu & Co's acclaimed practice is headed by the 'personable and thorough' New York-qualified Peter Buzescu, who is praised for his knowledge of the practicalities of practising law in Romania and his 'rapid responses'. He is said to be 'good at thinking outside the box' and 'willing to put the work in out of hours'.

Deal highlights include acting for Goldman Sachs and Lazard Freres on the purchase of an aggregate of $225,000,000 principal amount of 12.50% Senior Notes due 2010 of Mobifon Holdings BV under a purchase agreement; acting for Grant on the liquidation of RBG Resources PLC, and its Romanian subsidiaries; and acting as counsel to Tomen Corporation, which is considering selling its stake in Mobil Rom to the majority shareholder, Orange. High-profile clients include Bell Helicopter, Bombardier, Coca-Cola, Procter & Gamble, Medochemie, Monsanto, Worldspan, The Timken Company and Martini & Rossi.

Georgescu, Nemoianu & Salcianu Law Firm works closely with KPMG in Romania and worldwide. The 'intelligent and creative' Nadia Georgescu draws respect from peers and clients for her professionalism and political independence. Her expertise includes investments and acquisitions, banking and finance, with a client list including Stork Fokker, Balli Group, Panfoods, Koenig Ludwig, Salco Grain, RoBank, Zone Vision, Swiss International Airlines, and EGL. Loredana Salcianu specialises in M&A and insurance and counts Skansa, Honeywell, Interbrew, Schosswender and Campina as clients, while Daniela Nemoianu specialises in banking, finance, investments and privatisations and has Halliburton, Mimel Insaat, Ministry of Public Finances, Hiproma, Tiriac Bank and TotalFinaElf in her stable.

Deal highlights include assisting Mimel Insaat v.e. Ticaret, in the implementation of a $150m PPP project with the Ministry of Transport, Construction and Tourism and assisting Dutch company Stork Fokker AESP BV entering into a joint venture with Aerostar SA.

Hayhurst Robinson's Romanian office is led by Canadian lawyer Todd Robinson, who is particularly recommended for private equity work, and Gabriel Sidere, the local Romanian partner, who specialises in equity and debt finance transactions. The firm lost last year's high-profile hiring – Nick Hammond, formerly of **Linklaters Miculiti & Asociatii** – who left to join **Gutium si Asociatii SCA**. However the firm has brought in the 'excellent' Cristian Lina, who is recommended for banking and energy matters.

Hayhurst Robinson has advised two multilateral financial institutions on a pre-privatisation equity investment in the largest Romanian commercial bank, and a foreign investor on the privatisation of and the investor's bid to acquire a majority interest in Petrom. The firm also advised RCS, a cable TV and Internet conglomerate on an equity investment and capital increase, and Atomic Energy of Canada Ltd on regulatory issues surrounding nuclear power facilities. Other highlights include acting for Kraft and Nestlé on negotiations with the Romanian government concerning EU harmonisation and drafting of relevant legislation.

At **Rubin Meyer Doru & Trandafir, Spca, in Association with Herzfeld & Rubin, P.C.** 'forthright and dynamic' partner Mark Meyer divides his time between Romania and the firm's affiliated New York office; he is chairman of the Romanian-American Chamber of Commerce and has good connections in Romanian political, diplomatic and business circles. Lia Trandafir, Herbert Rubin, Sergiu Doru and Corin Trandafir are other well-known names.

In 2003, the firm represented buyers of assets of banking institutions in Romania, automotive parts manufacturers, grain and milling operations, assistance in public tenders, assistance on international loans, as well as providing services in the restructuring of large corporate entities.

The big shock of 2003 was the announcement of *Altheimer & Gray*'s dissolution. Frantic negotiations eventually culminated in **Salans** taking on 57 ex-*Altheimer & Gray* lawyers and establishing five new offices – including **Salans / Moore, Vartires & Associates SCPA** in Bucharest.

The deal was only finalised in November 2003, thus taking up large chunks of the time of renowned partners Obie Moore and Dana Vartires, who remain to head a team of 17 lawyers. Although clearly subject to considerable disruption in 2003, Moore predicts that **Salans**' extensive worldwide network – including the former *Altheimer & Gray* offices in Bratislava, Istanbul and Prague – will lead to strong cross-practice synergies, making the firm more attractive to clients.

Although there are rumblings that the disruption has caused some clients to look elsewhere, the Bucharest practice retains key clients such as Gillette, Coca-Cola, Colgate Palmolive, SAB Miller, Commercial Union, Sara Lee, HeidelbergCement and Citibank. Obie Moore is 'an effective problem solver' and his extensive international experience complements the detailed local knowledge of Dana Vartires, meaning the firm 'is able to deal with complex and difficult situations and parties which takes into proper consideration the so-called Romania reality and the required behaviour of a western investor'. The firm is recommended for being 'open-minded, responsive, patient and flexible', and is highly rated for compliance and due diligence advice. Private equity and public-to-private deals are strengths of the firm and Tiberiu Csaki is described as a 'decent and excellent litigator'. It is also distinguished for high ethical standards and political independence.

Deal highlights include representing an affiliate of AIG Emerging Europe Infrastructure Fund on its acquisition of shares in Mobifon in Romania; advising European real estate developer Europolis in its acquisition of Europe House, one of the largest commercial office buildings in Bucharest in a $30m deal; and advising SABMiller, on its potential acquisition of a local brewery.

Stephenson Harwood – Popescu & Associatii's office works closely with the firm's other offices, particularly in London, Singapore, Paris and Piraeus. Romanian lawyer, Gheorghe Piperea, formerly of **Bostina & Associates** and a lecturer in company law and transport law at the Faculty of Law in Bucharest, joined the firm in December. He specialises in litigation, bankruptcy, company and transportation. David Stabb, Neil McGregor and Ligia Popescu are well known.

Deal highlights include advising Rothschild et Cie, Paris, on the disposal of its shareholdings in Terapia SA. This transaction was complicated by the change in Romanian securities legislation mid-transaction. The firm also advised on the acquisition by Unilever Bulgaria of the foods businesses of several Bulgarian companies.

Voicu & Filipescu is praised for it's 'high quality, reliable service' with name partner, Daniel Voicu, who handles corporate and M&A work, particularly praised for his 'seriousness and prompt responses' – he is also recommended for his private equity expertise and knowledge of the fund management industry.

The firm advised in the €164m sale of Brewery Holdings Limited (Advent International and Jupiter Asset Management) to Brau Union; represented Raiffeisen Zentralbank in the acquisition of a majority stake in the Romanian state-owned bank, Banca Agricola, and advised on the acquisition of mineral water company Dorna Apemin by Coca-Cola Hellenic Bottling Company/The Coca-Cola Company.

Badea, Radu & Asociatii SCA's 'dynamic and tenacious' name partner, Daniel Badea, brings extensive knowledge of banking and capital markets to bear on corporate advice, while the 'superb' Dragos Radu is recommended for his work in real estate and property. He acts for some of Romania's largest developers. Big name clients include Orange, Honeywell, Johnson Controls, Citibank, Deutsche Bank, JPMorgan, UBS, the EBRD, HVB Romania, CAID Securities, Sidex Trading and Credit Suisse First Boston.

CMS Cameron McKenna Cristina Brinzan Law Office partner Cristina Brinzan has a strong reputation for corporate matters. Clients include Advent, Citibank, ING, BRD/SocGen, Vinci, Eurobank, Banc Post, Terapia/Advent, Eurobank, FMO, Wintershall and Constanza. Stephen Forster a partner from London specialising in corporate and utilities/projects, who previously ran the Budapest office, now spends time in the office. The firm acted for Advent International on the acquisition of SC Terapia SA Cluj-Napoca.

Calin Zamfirescu & Associates is recommended for its 'clear and impressive' corporate advice relating to incorporation, commercial contracts and negotiation with administration and ministries, combined with a formidable reputation for litigation (especially in banking and bankruptcy). The firm also advises on competition and employment law. Name partner Calin Andrei Zamfirescu is president of the Romanian Bar Association and is admired by clients and rivals alike for his 'broad knowledge base' and 'fierce intellect'. Stan Tirnoveanu, who is recommended for banking, boasts clients such as Romanian Bank for Development, HVB Bank Romania, Bank Austria Creditanstalt AG and Finansbank.

David & Baias has a particular focus on corporate restructuring, securities, banking, privatisation, competition and tax law. The firm is praised for its 'extensive knowledge of legal matters'. Name partners, the 'genuine and knowledgeable' Sorin David and Flavius Baias head the team, with Dan Dascalu building up a good reputation for labour law issues, while Luiza Tomescu is recommended for IT work. Deal highlights include acting for the Romanian-American Enterprise Fund in negotiating the loan agreement and project agreements with the EBRD on financing an energy fund; assisting Pfizer in restructuring its Romanian operation; assisting South African Breweries in tax and commercial litigation matters; advising ING/Nederlanden in promissory notes litigation; and advising the National Bank of Romania on a new interbank electronic system.

Gide Loyrette Nouel works closely with its Paris office and its client list features several French blue-chips. Clients include Renault, Carrefour, BRD-Groupe Société Générale, Volvo Trucks, Michelin and Catinvest. The firm's heavyweights include office head, Bruno Leroy and the 'versatile' Jacques de Servigny.

The firm advised Renault on the mandatory public takeover offer of the remaining shares of Automobile Dacia – the first mandatory public takeover offer to have been successfully completed on the BSE market. It also advised Carrefour on the acquisition of land and the building of commercial centres in Romania.

Gruia Dufaut Law Office is headed by Dana Gruia Dufaut, a member of both the Paris and Bucharest bars. Renowned for her expertise in foreign investment in Romania, she spends some of her time working from the firm's office in Paris. The firm's clients include several blue-chip French clients from the agriculture, construction and retail sectors.

Practice head Gabriel Biris at **Haarmann Hemmelrath** is recommended for M&A and joint ventures. Deal highlights include advising shareholders in selling edible oil producer Muntenia to CEREOL in one of the largest deals in the food processing industry in Romania in 2003; advising Credisson – the biggest Romanian consumer credit company – in structuring its business; and advising Siemens in restructuring its operations in Romania.

Headed by Jörg K Menzer, **Nörr Stiefenhofer Lutz** is one of the few independent German law firms operating in Bucharest. The head office is in Munich; it also has a presence in Moscow, Prague and Warsaw. The firm brought in four additional lawyers in the last year to cope with the increasing number of international investors from Western Europe and now numbers 12 lawyers in Bucharest, of which seven make up the corporate team. Clients include INA Schaeffler KG, Kaufland Stiftung & Co. KG AG, Bank Austria Creditanstalt, Wien, Bombardier Transportation, HVB Romania SA, Holzindustrie Schweighofer GmbH, Vaillant GmbH and HVB Romania Leasing SRL. Beyond corporate work, the office also offers tax, property, IP, competition, employment and distribution capability.

PI Partners (formerly *Testa, David & Associates* acts for telecoms, petroleum and construction clients. The firm lost both respected corporate EU and competition lawyer, Razvan Gheorghiu-Testa, IP to **Musat & Asociatii** and banking and finance specialist, Anca Bocanici, in 2003. Daniela David (litigation), Iulian Patrascananu (employment, real estate) and managing partner, US lawyer Charles Vernon (M&A, corporate finance) remain. The firm has an association with Ernst & Young.

A notable addition to the market was spawned from two partners who left **Musat & Asociatii**. The 'well-respected and experienced' Ernest Popovici joined forces with Florian Nitu to form 19-lawyer **Popovici & Asociatii**. Nitu – 'an excellent communicator and a first class lawyer' and Popovici took 12 lawyers from **Musat & Asociatii** including the 'extremely competent' M&A lawyer, Irena Tudorie, the 'excellent litigator' Ilinca Stefanescu, banking senior, Cristina Alexe and Bogdan Stoica, a senior finance lawyer. The firm's client list includes Orange, Cora, Tenneco, Japan Tobacco International, Matra Nortel (Popovici) and Renault, Hewlett-Packard, Barrick Gold Corporation, Korn Ferry International, and CB Richard Ellis (Nitu). The firm looks set to be a big player.

At **Racoti – Predoiu, Attorneys at Law** name partner, Catalin Predoiu is recommended for his 'outstanding' work in privatisation and M&A. He heads the firm with Ioana Racoti. Many corporate transactions handled by the firm have a privatisation aspect. Clients include Rompetrol, Coca-Cola, Temereso, WS Atkins, Raiffeisen Commerzbank AG, Marco International and the Office of State Participations and Privatisation in Industry.

SCA Carnu, Dumitrache, Gherghina & Sebeni is recommended for M&A and real estate work, while **Stefanica, Dutu & Partners** has expanded rapidly to become one of the largest in Romania, with 36 lawyers. The firm's reputation in corporate matters is growing accordingly with managing partner, Daniel Stefanica, providing advice to Connex, Medicare, Cotecna, the IFC, Ministry of Sports, Ministry of Health, Termoelectrica and Halliburton. The client list of the 'dynamic and straight-talking' Patricia Osmani, a dual US and Romanian-qualified lawyer, includes Termoelectrica, CFR Marfa, Vacaresti Lake Project, Dracula Park, Compass Bank, Ministry of Transport and Halliburton, while Florin Dutu advises Romanian Post Office, Global Finance, Metal House and Sky Services.

Stoica & Asociatii Attorneys at Law, led by Cristiana Stoica, acts for a range of international clients in the petroleum, energy, pharmaceuticals, real estate and retail sectors. Litigation is a strong point. The firm was strengthened by the return of Valeriu Stoica from the Romanian Parliament. He is commended for 'outstanding' civil law work and IP.

Another firm created in 2003 by departures from **Musat & Asociatii** is ten-lawyer firm **Vilau & Mitel**. Headed by the 'quick-minded and responsive' Dragos Vilau – described as 'very professional and practical' – and Sorinel Mitel. The firm is described as a 'very pragmatic legal practice with a focus on getting the job done and is quite well attuned to the needs of Western clients' with Vilau in particular 'inspiring trust and confidence'. Vilau's client list includes GE Aircraft, GlaxoSmithKline, Intel Corporation, Lear Corporation, Unicredito Italiano, and Koninklijke Bunge BV, while Mitel has Eurocopter France/Eurocopter Romania, Suez Lyonnaise des Eaux, Romanian Radio Broadcasting Corporation, FCC Construccion SA, Axima Services SA and adidas.

Wood Lupascu Dumitrescu & Associates SCPA in association with Hall, Dickler is headed by Gilbert Wood. The firm was instrumental in establishing the Foreign Investors Council, a lobbying group with access to the Romanian government and legislature, representing approximately 80% of all foreign direct investment in Romania. Privatisation and foreign direct investment are major areas and it has additional expertise in telecommunications.

2003 saw the departure of high-profile corporate partner, Gelu Titus Maravela and M&A lawyer, Cornel Popa, from **Babiuc, Sulica & Associates**. Dan Sulica and Victor Babiuc are the remaining prominent partners with the latter being recommended for his expertise in trade law.

Bostina & Associates is headed by Doru Bostina. The firm's senior partner and litigation head is the 'excellent' Mircea Stroe. As well as bringing in Cristian-Ionut Colan from **Musat & Asociatii**, the firm also took on as a partner to head the capital markets department, Narcisa Galina Fatu, who was co-ordinator of the legal department of the BSE. Clients include Romanian Commodities Exchange, Electrica, Hidroelectrica, Termoelectrica, VA Tech Group, Siemens AG, BP Oil International Ltd, Air BP Ltd, and Energy Holding SRL.

CMS Bureau Francis Lefebvre Catalina Marcu Law Office name partner Catalina Marcu works closely with **CMS Bureau Francis Lefebvre** in Paris. The firm advises several French clients. The firm is based in the same offices as **CMS Cameron McKenna Cristina Brinzan Law Office** .

Danescu, Danescu & Associates has a 14-lawyer office and counts Coca-Cola HBC, ING Nederlanden Life Insurance, Romania SA, McDonald's Romania, Romanian-American Enterprise Fund and Scania Romania as clients.

Deleanu Vasile – Lawyers acted for the State Ownership Fund in high-profile litigation. Name partner Vasile Deleanu has particular expertise of real estate acquisitions and registration, as well as litigation arising out of such transactions. Clients include: Romanian State Television Company, Arbomedia SRL, Toyo Motor Center SRL (Toyota Importer), Kober SRL, Pitura SRL, Imsat Muntenia SA, Romprix SRL, Data Networks Associates Software, and Mag Krainer Consulting SRL.

Despina Fruth Oprisan Law Offices is a niche practice headed by Despina Fruth, a former judge who has a reputation for her broad knowledge of Romania's courtroom process and for advice on technical points of corporate and commercial law. Clients often instruct the firm on a specific matter while retaining a larger firm as their main adviser.

Gutium si Asociatii SCA was formed in August 2002 by former **Linklaters Miculiti & Asociatii** lawyer, Eugenia Gutium who heads the practice, and partner Romanita Alexandra Ivan. Both used to work in the legal department of the State Ownership Fund. The firm has a focus on real estate and energy and natural resources work and is active in the pharmaceutical sector. Deal highlights include advising Romanian government departments on the drafting of legislation, advising on privatisation strategies and acting for a major multilateral financing company on projects relating to the privatisation of water distribution in Romania.

IK Roka & C. Spiridon SCPA was established in 2002. Local partner, Cristina Spiridon heads the team which advises several Greek clients and institutions and has a head office in Athens and offices in Belgrade, Budapest, Piraeus, Skopia, Sofia, Thessaloniki, Zagreb, Sarajevo and Melbourne.

Law Office Mihaela Grama-Popovici is headed by name partner Mihaela Grama and is noted for corporate matters.

Norton Rose partner Campbell Steedman is based in Frankfurt but often works on Romanian transactions with local firms.

Pachiu & Associates managing partner Laurentiu Pachiu, is described as 'professional and well-informed'. Tax and IP law are a forte. Deal highlights include the acquisition and sale of a major Romanian print media enterprise; the acquisition of real estate and advice on project development for a large international consumer wholesale and retail operator and an office real estate project developer; the corporate and tax restructuring of a major medical operator; cross-border restructuring of international groups in the construction materials and energy sectors; and monitoring implementation of EU directives regarding consumer protection.

Schönherr Rechtsanwälte OEG is headed by M&A lawyer, Marcus Piuk who is 'devoted to his profession and hard working' and 'while young, is far more experienced and professional than most of his older colleagues'. Partner Christoph Lindinger divides his time between Bucharest and the firm's head office in Austria. He 'has an extremely wide international background and experience and is always willing and ready to go into detail'. Sebastian Gutiu is noted for his 'professional, high-quality service' while the firm draws praise for 'responding fast' to client demands, and is 'flexible and able to provide very creative solutions. Their personal involvement is excellent'. Clients include DaimlerChrysler, Pirelli, Oltchim, EVN and OMV.

Studio Legale Tonucci's clients range from large industrial multinationals and financial institutions to individuals seeking advice on business and personal matters. Silvia Magdalena Petrosel, Guiliano Marzi and Romanian lawyer Luminita Procopie are prominent lawyers.

DISPUTE RESOLUTION

Musat & Asociatii's impressive litigation department acted for the Romanian government on numerous matters, including on an important ICSID arbitration brought by CS Resita SA, on aggregate claims exceeding $300m. Other clients include: the Authority for Privatization, the Romanian Olympic Committee, Automobile Dacia, Electrica SA, and RomTelecom SA.

Nestor Nestor Diculescu Kingston Petersen advises on commercial, tax and real estate litigation and arbitration. The firm acted for several major banks in litigation regarding loan recovery, security and custody matters. Ana Diculescu is respected for litigation.

David & Baias partners Sorin David and Flavius Baias are both arbitrators of the Court of Arbitration of the Romanian Chamber of Commerce and Industry. The firm assisted Pfizer in employment litigation and South African Breweries in tax and commercial disputes. Dan Dascalu is recommended for labour law disputes.

Georgescu, Nemoianu & Salcianu Law Firm represents clients from the manufacturing and retail industry in commercial and employment litigation.

Linklaters Miculiti & Asociatii's Lucian Mihai has an excellent reputation for litigation and arbitration. Highlights included successfully acting for Interbrew Romania before the Supreme Court of Justice in a case involving fiscal issues. It also successfully represented Allied Domecq Spirits & Wine in a case involving breach of the trade mark 'Beefeater'.

Rubin Meyer Doru & Trandafir, Spca, in Association with Herzfeld & Rubin, P.C. is representing the three wealthiest families from pre-communist Romania on the multi-million dollar claims against the government under Romania's restitution laws in connection with property appropriated by the former communist government. Mark Meyer is a leading expert on restitution, having testified last July on the subject before the US Helsinki Commission in Washington DC.

Salans / Moore, Vartires & Associates SCPA partner Dana Vartires, a former judge, is a respected litigator. The firm represented Gillette in its successful litigation to halt trade mark infringement.

Calin Zamfirescu & Associates name partner Calin Andrei Zamfirescu enjoys a fearsome reputation for banking and bankruptcy litigation.

Deleanu Vasile – Lawyers is recommended for real estate, bankruptcy and debt recovery disputes, with name partner Vasile Deleanu cited as 'well-respected and a formidable opponent'. Clients include, Romanian Diplomatic Club, Romanian American Enterprise Fund, K-Tech Electronic SRL, Republica SA, Romanian International Bank (RIB),

DISPUTE RESOLUTION

MUSAT & ASOCIATII ✪
NESTOR NESTOR DICULESCU KINGSTON PETERSEN ✪

David & Baias ✪
Georgescu, Nemoianu & Salcianu Law Firm ✪
Linklaters Miculiti & Asociatii ✪
Rubin Meyer Doru & Trandafir, Spca, in Association with Herzfeld & Rubin, P.C.
Salans / Moore, Vartires & Associates SCPA

Calin Zamfirescu & Associates ✪
Deleanu Vasile – Lawyers ✪
Despina Fruth Oprisan Law Offices
Nörr Stiefenhofer Lutz ✪
Pachiu & Associates ✪
Popovici & Asociatii ✪
Stefanica, Dutu & Partners
Stoica & Asociatii Attorneys at Law ✪

Firms are listed A-Z in tiers which are ranked in order of priority
✪ Indicates firm displays contact details at the end of this chapter.

Vulcan SA, ICB Group, and Emcom SRL.

Despina Fruth Oprisan Law Offices name partner Despina Fruth is a former judge with extensive knowledge of the Romanian courts.

German firm **Nörr Stiefenhofer Lutz** offers a disputes practice, covering debt recovery, trade mark enforcement and consumer protection, among other areas. The firm recently acted for one of the world's largest trade agricultural products companies in an arbitration against a Romanian bank, before the arbitration court of Bucharest and the state courts.

Pachiu & Associates acts for several hi-tech and media companies from Germany.

Popovici & Asociatii acted for Orange, Lafarge – Romcim and Robert Bosch on a variety of litigation matters.

Stefanica, Dutu & Partners represented Mobifon SA in various litigation matters.

Cristiana Stoica from **Stoica & Asociatii Attorneys at Law** is recommended for litigation.

IT, TELECOMS AND MEDIA

Nestor Nestor Diculescu Kingston Petersen represented Microsoft in the acquisition of the IP assets of the Romanian anti-virus scanning technology maker, GeCAD Software. Ion Nestor is recommended.

Salans / Moore, Vartires & Associates SCPA remains a force in the telecoms sector. The firm acted for Telesystem International Wireless on $225m bond issuance by its subsidiary Mobifon Holdings BV, which holds 57.1% of Mobifon, Romania's leading mobile telecommunication services provider.

Linklaters Miculiti & Asociatii acted for OTE International Investments Ltd in acquiring a majority stake (54.1%) of RomTelecom, the national fixed line telecoms operator in Romania.

IT, TELECOMS AND MEDIA

NESTOR NESTOR DICULESCU KINGSTON PETERSEN ✪
SALANS / MOORE, VARTIRES & ASSOCIATES SCPA

Linklaters Miculiti & Asociatii ✪
Musat & Asociatii ✪

Buzescu & Co ✪
David & Baias ✪
Hayhurst Robinson ✪
Nörr Stiefenhofer Lutz ✪
Popovici & Asociatii ✪
Racoti – Predoiu, Attorneys at Law ✪
Rubin Meyer Doru & Trandafir, Spca, in Association with Herzfeld & Rubin, P.C.
Stefanica, Dutu & Partners

Firms are listed A-Z in tiers which are ranked in order of priority
✪ Indicates firm displays contact details at the end of this chapter.

Musat & Asociatii clients include RomTelecom, Atlas Telecom Holdings Inc, AT&T, Quintiles, First Data Corporation, Radio Contact Romania SA and Viasat Broadcasting UK.

Buzescu & Co acted for a major telecoms service provider on a $64m supplier credit facility for the digitalisation of the cellular telephone network; advised EBRD on participation to Emcom, a local Siemens joint venture for the manufacture of telephone equipment; and advised a Western consortium led by Motorola on a bid for a GSM licence.

David & Baias advised RomTelecom on real estate litigation, regulatory matters and debt-equity swaps.

At **Hayhurst Robinson**, Todd Robinson and John Fitzpatrick advise on telecoms, IT and hi-tech work.

Nörr Stiefenhofer Lutz benefits from its market-leading reputation for media work in Germany. The firm advises numerous foreign media and entertainment groups investing in Romania.

Popovici & Asociatii counts Orange Romania, Hewlett-Packard, Equant, Siveco Romania and Fujitsu Siemens Computers as clients.

Racoti – Predoiu, Attorneys at Law advised an investment bank on a consultancy agreement relating to the privatisation of RomTelecom.

Patricia Osmani is the principal expert at **Stefanica, Dutu & Partners**. Mobifon SA is an important client.

POWER, ENERGY AND NATURAL RESOURCES

Linklaters Miculiti & Asociatii has an excellent reputation with 'diligent and able' Adrian Bulboaca being highly recommended. The firm is advising on the privatisation of SNP Petrom SA and the privatisation of gas distribution companies, Distrigaz Sud SA and Distrigaz Nord SA.

Buzescu & Co acts for AB Electro-Invest, Amoco Corporation, Amromco Energy LLC, ARCO, Canadian Occidental, Chevron, Exxon Corporation, Glencore, International Water Ltd, Marathon, Mobil Corporation and Shell Aviation.

David & Baias raised its profile on the energy market when it acted for RAEF Energy Fund in a financing structure deal worth more than $11m.

Hayhurst Robinson acts for Atomic Energy of Canada on the maintenance of nuclear power facilities.

Nestor Nestor Diculescu Kingston Petersen acts for Electrica Banat, Electrica Dobregea, Electrica Moldova and Electrica Oltenia, and assisted Forest Oil International on concession agreements for Romanian petroleum fields.

Stephenson Harwood – Popescu & Associatii continues to obtain instructions in the electricity and water sectors.

POWER, ENERGY AND NATURAL RESOURCES

LINKLATERS MICULITI & ASOCIATII ✪

Buzescu & Co ✪
David & Baias ✪
Hayhurst Robinson ✪
Musat & Asociatii ✪
Nestor Nestor Diculescu Kingston Petersen ✪
Norton Rose
Rubin Meyer Doru & Trandafir, Spca, in Association with Herzfeld & Rubin, P.C.
Stephenson Harwood – Popescu & Associates

Firms are listed A-Z in tiers which are ranked in order of priority
✪ Indicates firm displays contact details at the end of this chapter.

PRIVATISATION

Most predict that the bulk of the heavyweight privatisation will be completed in Romania by the end of 2004. 2003 though saw much activity with the privatisation of the energy and utilities market high on everyone's agenda, as was the telecoms sector with RomTelecom's monopoly expiring.

Linklaters Miculiti & Asociatii is advising the consortium appointed to advise the Romanian government on the privatisation of Romania's national oil and gas company, SNP Petrom SA, and Romania's two national gas distributing companies – Distrigaz North and Distrigaz South. It is also advising OTE International Investments Ltd on the acquisition of the Romanian National Telecommunications Company RomTelecom SA.

Musat & Asociatii advised the Office for State Ownership and Privatisation in Industry (OPSPI), on the privatisation of shipyard Santierul Naval Mangalia, and the National Company Plafar, the largest Romanian producer of natural products of medicinal herbs. It also advised Enel Distribuzione SpA (Italy), on the privatisation of branches of Electrica SA (Romania's largest electricity distribution company); Occidental Oil and Gas Corporation (US), on the privatisation of the National Oil Company Petrom SA; and Landini Spa (Italy), on the acquisition of Tractorul SA Brasov (Romania's biggest tractor maker). Gabriel Zbarcea is recommended.

Nestor Nestor Diculescu Kingston Petersen was at the forefront of the action advising four electrical companies (Electrica Banat, Electrica Dobregea, Electrica Moldova and Electrica Oltenia) on pre-privatisation and privatisation matters, and advising the government on the privatisation of Romania's largest bank, Romanian Commercial Bank. Other privatisation projects included providing due diligence on ICMRS Galati, a large Romanian construction company, and on Avioane Craiova Galati, an airplane producer.

PRIVATISATION

LINKLATERS MICULITI & ASOCIATII ✪
MUSAT & ASOCIATII ✪
NESTOR NESTOR DICULESCU KINGSTON PETERSEN ✪

Gide Loyrette Nouel ✪
Racoti – Predoiu, Attorneys at Law ✪
Rubin Meyer Doru & Trandafir, Spca, in Association with Herzfeld & Rubin, P.C.
Salans / Moore, Vartires & Associates SCPA
Stephenson Harwood – Popescu & Associates
Wood Lupascu Dumitrescu & Associates SCPA in association with Hall, Dickler ✪

Babiuc, Sulica & Associates ✪
Badea, Radu & Asociatii SCA ✪
CMS Cameron McKenna Cristina Brinzan Law Office
Calin Zamfirescu & Associates ✪
Despina Fruth Oprisan Law Offices
Haarmann Hemmelrath ✪
Hayhurst Robinson ✪
Norton Rose
Popovici & Asociatii ✪
Schönherr Rechtsanwälte OEG ✪
Stoica & Asociatii Attorneys at Law ✪

Firms are listed A-Z in tiers which are ranked in order of priority
✪ *Indicates firm displays contact details at the end of this chapter.*

Gide Loyrette Nouel has been heavily involved in advising Renault on post-privatisation matters following the privatisation of Automobile Dacia. It also advised on the acquisition by Erdemir, a Turkish steel group of assets by auction from a Romanian state-owned company.

Racoti – Predoiu, Attorneys at Law was particularly busy in the privatisation field, working on due diligence and contracts involved in privatisations within the gas and oil, pipe works and optics sectors. The Rompetrol Group is a major client. Catalin Predoiu is 'highly regarded'.

Valentin Ionescu, who drafted some of Romania's laws dealing with privatisation, provides hands-on experience in his role as of-counsel to **Rubin Meyer Doru & Trandafir, Spca, in Association with Herzfeld & Rubin, P.C.**. The firm advised on the partial privatisation arrangements for a large Romanian power plant and is also counsel in the privatisation of water delivery systems in Transylvania.

Salans / Moore, Vartires & Associates SCPA represented SAB/Miller before Romanian post-privatisation authorities in relation to investment compliance related to acquisition of Vulturul and Pitber breweries.

Stephenson Harwood – Popescu & Associatii advised an Anglo-Dutch water company on its bid for a concession to operate the water and sewerage services in Constanta and advised on the privatisation of a power station.

Wood Lupascu Dumitrescu & Associates SCPA in association with Hall, Dickler has been focused on privatisation and FDI since the early '90s. The firm has had a strong showing on transactions to date, on both the buy and sell side.

Babiuc, Sulica & Associates was involved in the drafting of the Romanian legal framework under whose umbrella the privatisation process emerged. It advises the State Ownership Fund on privatisation matters including litigation related to significant privatisation deals.

Dragos Radu and Daniel Badea of **Badea, Radu & Asociatii SCA** are well known for their privatisation expertise. The firm advised LNM Holdings NV on the acquisition of Romanian steel company, Industria Saremi Campia Turzii; Sidex Trading on the acquisition of Admet; and a major US business on the acquisition of a large Romanian company from the aviation industry.

CMS Cameron McKenna Cristina Brinzan Law Office advised on a major water privatisation, acting for the County of Constanza .

Calin Zamfirescu & Associates was involved in the second step in the privatisation process of RomTelecom.

Haarmann Hemmelrath advises several German clients from the automotive and oil and gas industries. Gabriel Biris is respected.

Hayhurst Robinson is advising two multilateral financial institutions on a pre-privatisation equity investment in the largest Romanian commercial bank, and a foreign investor on the privatisation of and investor's bid to acquire a majority interest in Petrom.

Norton Rose's Frankfurt-based partner Campbell Steedman often works with local firms on a range of transactions.

Popovici & Asociatii acted for Société Générale on the proposed takeover of Chimopar SA and Victoria SA (Romanian chemical plants), and for a multinational consortium in the acquisition of Helitube Bucharest (Romanian steel pipe producer).

Schönherr Rechtsanwälte OEG advises German clients from the oil and gas industry.

Stoica & Asociatii Attorneys at Law advises the government and banking clients. Partner Cristiana Stoica has strong political connections

PROJECT FINANCE

LINKLATERS MICULITI & ASOCIATII ✪
NESTOR NESTOR DICULESCU KINGSTON PETERSEN ✪

Musat & Asociatii ✪

Buzescu & Co ✪
Georgescu, Nemoianu & Salcianu Law Firm ✪
Gide Loyrette Nouel ✪
Popovici & Asociatii ✪
Rubin Meyer Doru & Trandafir, Spca, in Association with Herzfeld & Rubin, P.C.
Stefanica, Dutu & Partners

Firms are listed A-Z in tiers which are ranked in order of priority
✪ *Indicates firm displays contact details at the end of this chapter.*

Linklaters Miculiti & Asociatii's solid projects practice boasts several telecoms and oil and gas clients. Recently the firm acted for Standard Bank London Ltd on the first private equity backed leverage buy-out in Romania, in a deal worth $40m.

Nestor Nestor Diculescu Kingston Petersen acted for Strabag AG on the development of a motorway between Bucharest and Ploiesti and has been retained by a consortium to advise on a motorway project between Predeal and Brasov. Raiffeisen Zentralbank and General Electric Canada are also clients.

Musat & Asociatii acted on highway and energy projects. It advised Enel Produzione SpA, on the PPP with Hidroelectrica SA.

Buzescu & Co acted as counsel for the EBRD with regard to several projects and to Standard Bank London Ltd on a project finance matter.

Georgescu, Nemoianu & Salcianu Law Firm advised Mimel Insaat ve Ticaret, in the implementation of a $150m PPP project with the Ministry of Transport, Construction and Tourism.

Gide Loyrette Nouel's Christian Mindru is well-regarded. The firm advised Apa Nova Bucuresti SA on a joint venture with the Municipality of Bucharest and the concessionaire of water supply service in Bucharest, in respect of a project financing for the Crivina Potable Water Treatment Plant.

Popovici & Asociatii advised Suez Lyonnaise des Eaux in two water-related projects and several international corporations on road building projects worth $300m.

Rubin Meyer Doru & Trandafir, Spca, in Association with Herzfeld & Rubin, P.C. advised the National Road Administration on a proposed €100m bond offering to be placed on the Luxembourg Stock Exchange.

Stefanica, Dutu & Partners advised on the $280m Vacaresti Lake project concession obtained by Royal Romanian Corp which is to be financed on a project basis and will encompass a golf course, five-star hotel, hippodrome, 200 villas and a shopping mall in Bucharest.

BABIUC, SULICA & ASSOCIATES

27 HENRI COANDA STREET
SECTOR 1
711192 BUCHAREST

Telephone: +40 21 315 1773
Fax: +40 21 315 1777
E-mail: office@btsa.ro
Website: www.btsa.ro

Languages
English, French, German, Romanian, Russian, Spanish

Number of lawyers 13

CATEGORIES OF WORK

Banking and finance
Adriana Puscas

Capital markets
Adriana Puscas

Commercial and company law
Radu Protopopescu

Intellectual property
Radu Protopopescu

Competition law
Veronica Gruzsniczki

Real estate
Dan Sulica, Nicolae Tanasoiu

Employment and pensions
Dan Sulica, Anca Puscasu

Tax
Adriana Puscas

International trade and foreign investments
Radu Protopopescu

Construction and engineering
Nicolae Tanasoiu

Litigation, arbitration, dispute resolution
Lucian Vonica

BADEA, RADU & ASOCIATII SCA

235 CALEA DOROBANTILOR
SECTOR 1
BUCHAREST

Telephone: +40 21 233 9216
Fax: +40 21 233 9217
E-mail: general@brg.ro
Website: www.badea-radu.ro

Languages
English, French

Number of lawyers 11

CATEGORIES OF WORK

Banking and finance
Daniel Badea

Securities and derivatives
Daniel Badea

Competition
Dragos Radu

Corporate and commercial
Dragos Radu

Employment and pensions
Dragos Radu

Energy and natural resources
Daniel Badea, Dragos Radu

IT and telecommunications
Daniel Badea

Mergers and acquisitions
Daniel Badea, Dragos Radu

Regulatory
Daniel Badea, Dragos Radu

Real estate and construction
Daniel Badea, Dragos Radu

Shipping
Daniel Badea

Securitisation and structured finance
Daniel Badea

Privatisation and foreign investments
Daniel Badea, Dragos Radu

BUZESCU & CO

22 EMANOIL PORUMBARU STREET
SECTOR 1
011421 BUCHAREST

Telephone: +40 21 222 4422
Fax: +40 21 222 2626
E-mail: pbuzescu@buzescu.com

Languages
English, French

Number of lawyers 8

Contact
Peter Buzescu

CATEGORIES OF WORK	
Foreign investments	**Taxation**
Joint ventures	**Energy and natural resources**
Project finance	**Intellectual property**
Privatisation	**Real estate**
Mergers and acquisitions	**Telecommunications**
Competition	**Corporate and commercial**

THE FIRM

Buzescu & Co was founded by Peter Buzescu in 1992 and now has a complement of eight lawyers.

Peter Buzescu was admitted to the Romanian Bar in 1978 and the New York Bar in 1985, after studying at Bucharest University School of Law and New York University School of Law.

Mr Buzescu is author of many publications including 'What to Expect from Joint Ventures in Moscow' (*The Wall Street Journal*, Europe edition, 6 January 1987); *Foreign Investment and Taxation of Foreign Enterprises and Individuals in Romania* (Library of Congress, ed 1986); 'Foreign Bank Operations in Switzerland: New Regulations and Some Practical Considerations' (The International Lawyer 897, 1985); 'Joint Ventures in Eastern Europe' (The American Journal of Comparative Law 407, 1984).

AREAS OF PRACTICE

The firm has been advising foreign investors on doing business in Romania since 1992. The practice has steadily expanded to become a successful firm offering professional services to a distinguished clientele, representing multinational companies operating or contemplating operations in Romania.

CĂLIN ZAMFIRESCU & ASSOCIATES

35 MIRCEA VODĂ BOULEVARD
BUILDING M27, 4TH FLOOR
SECTOR 3
BUCHAREST

Telephone: +40 21 323 7466
Fax: +40 21 323 7467
E-mail: office@cza.ro
Website: www.cza.ro

Languages
English, French

Number of lawyers 24

Contacts
Călin Andrei Zamfirescu, Stan Tîrnoveanu

CATEGORIES OF WORK

Banking and finance
Stan Tîrnoveanu

Mergers and acquisitions
Ioana Dulcă

Litigation
Călin Andrei Zamfirescu

Bankruptcy and liquidations
Stan Tîrnoveanu

Privatisation
Ioana Dulcă, Gabriel Udrea

Securities and negotiable instruments
Stan Tîrnoveanu, Daniela Gramaticescu

Arbitration
Călin Andrei Zamfirescu

Intellectual property
Ioana Dulcă

Capital markets
Stan Tîrnoveanu, Daniela Gramaticescu

Company and commercial
Tiberiu Savu, Daniela Gramaticescu

Fiscal and financial law
Tiberiu Savu

Competition law
Ioana Dulcă

Construction
Gabriel Udrea

Real estate
Gabriel Udrea

European law
Tiberiu Savu

THE FIRM

CZ&A was one of the first law offices to be founded in Romania, in accordance with the 1995 Act No 51/1995 governing the legal profession, and has been well known ever since for its advice and assistance to both corporate and private clients.

The firm's lawyers are trained to deal with a wide range of legal matters, working across several departments. CZ&A maintains close relationships with well-known foreign law offices, co-operating with them if required when offering legal assistance or representing clients during litigations. Its lawyers are fluent in English and French and are used to working in such commingled teams.

CZ&A provides legal assistance to Romanian and foreign companies, governmental institutions, professional and other associations, and foundations.

AREAS OF PRACTICE

The firm's activity is mainly focused on commercial law. Major work areas in which it is highly specialised include:

Banking and finance: CZ&A's expertise in this area extends to bank privatisation; banking regulations; drafting contracts and financial agreements; foreign and domestic credit agreements; current account operations; foreign exchange regulations; ordinary services offered by banks, including collateral and security interests; drafting internal rules of procedure; and co-ordinating such rules with domestic legal provisions. Mr Stan Tîrnoveanu is a leading specialist in this field, having been manager of the legal department at the Romanian Bank for Development – Groupe Société Générale for eight years.

Privatisation: services include legal due diligence and review for privatisation and investment, negotiation with the relevant authorities, and post-privatisation assistance.

Bankruptcy and liquidations: the firm assists, advises and represents clients at all stages of bankruptcy and liquidation proceedings.

Litigation and arbitration: CZ&A renders legal assistance and represents its clients during litigation before courts of law (including the Court of Appeal and the Supreme Court of Justice), the Court of Arbitrators, the Constitutional Court and the Court of International Commercial Arbitration attached to the Romanian Chamber of Commerce and Industry. Mr Călin Andrei Zamfirescu is a leading authority in this field, having been involved in over 8,000 civil, commercial, penal and administrative cases. He is also Arbitrator of the Romanian Court of International Commercial Arbitration.

Securities: the firm's services include legal assistance with compliance with the relevant securities legal provisions, legal opinion regarding the method of setting up and modifying the share capital of the open companies, and legal assistance with securities trading methods.

Competition law: services in this area include drafting exclusive or selective distribution contracts, drafting negotiations with regard to economic concentrations, legal opinions on monopolistic agreements, abuse of dominant position, economic concentrations and state aids, and legal opinions on unfair competition.

Intellectual property: CZ&A provides legal assistance before the State Office for Patents and Trademarks (OSIM), and services regarding the protection of trade marks and patents against infringements, including counterfeit and unfair competition,the concurrent application of the relevant domestic and international legal provisions, copyright and allied rights, the drafting of relevant agreements, and industrial property.

Energy and natural resources: the firm provides legal advice to energy companies on corporate restructuring, structured finance transactions, project financing and new IT solutions when the electricity grid is used to provide telecoms services, and all legal aspects of investing in energy companies.

A brochure providing more details is available upon request.

DANESCU, DANESCU & ASSOCIATES

35 ION LUCA CARAGIALE STREET
SECTOR 2
BUCHAREST

Telephone: +40 21 210 6555
Fax: +40 21 210 6566
E-mail: office@danescu.ro
Website: www.danescu.ro

Languages
English, French, Italian, Spanish

Number of lawyers 14

Contact
Mrs Alina Danescu

CATEGORIES OF WORK

Administrative law
Oana Nasta

Criminal law
Laurentiu Nae

Taxation
Oana Nasta

Labour law
Octavian Raclaru, Anda Dumitrescu

Antitrust and trade regulation
Cezar Dragomirescu

Real estate
Octavian Raclaru

Banks and banking
Alina Danescu

Intellectual property
Cezar Dragomirescu

Civil law
Corin Danescu, Valentin Constantinof

Commercial law
Alina Danescu, Oana Nasta

Company law
Alina Danescu

Competition law
Cezar Dragomirescu

Contracts
Corin Danescu, Alina Danescu

Copyrights and trade marks
Cezar Dragomirescu

Corporate law
Oana Nasta, Cezar Dragomirescu

Insurance law, securities
Alina Danescu, Octavian Raclaru

Litigation
Corin Danescu, Valentin Constantinof

Property law
Corin Danescu, Oana Nasta

DAVID & BAIAS

OPERA CENTER
1-5 COSTACHE NEGRI STREET
BUCHAREST 5

Telephone: +40 21 202 8770
Fax: +40 21 202 8771
E-mail: sorin.david@david-baias.ro
Website: www.pwcglobal.com/ro

Languages
English, French, German, Italian

Number of lawyers 17

Contacts
Sorin David (sorin.david@david-baias.ro)
Flavius Baias (flavius.baias@david-baias.ro)

International groupings
Landwell, correspondent law firms of PricewaterhouseCoopers

CATEGORIES OF WORK

Commercial and competition
Sorin David, Luiza Tomescu-Dinu

Corporate structuring
Sorin David, Laura Luputi

Dispute resolution
Flavius Baias, Dan Dascalu

Technology, media and communications
Luiza Tomescu-Dinu

Employment and human resources
Dan Dascalu, Anda Rojanschi

Financial services
Sorin David, Laura Luputi

Intellectual property
Luiza Tomescu-Dinu

Mergers and acquisitions
Sorin David, Flavius Baias

Public law
Camelia Nastase, Luiza Tomescu-Dinu

Real estate
Flavius Baias, Camella Nastase

Corporate services
Anda Rojanschi, Carmen Medar

Consumer protection
Sorin David, Laura Luputi

THE FIRM

David & Baias is a full-service Romanian law firm with particular emphasis in advising multinational companies and local businesses in a number of areas of the law, including banking, securities and financing, privatisation, mergers and acquisitions, legal audit, competition, trade practices and intellectual property. It has experience of handling complex cases in each of these areas.

David & Baias benefits from its close co-operation with PricewaterhouseCoopers, one of the world's largest professional services organisations, and from its association with Landwell, a worldwide network of law practices.

Lawyers at David & Baias form part of Landwell's global network of specialists. Landwell focuses primarily on cross-border M&A transactions and corporate transformation projects. Working closely with PricewaterhouseCoopers, David & Baias is a market leader in the design and delivery of complex corporate change. This is achieved through a focus on strong local capabilities allied with a global outlook, and ensuring that the firm's high-quality legal advice is matched by strong implementation skills.

AREAS OF PRACTICE

The firm's areas of practice include: commercial and competition; corporate structuring; dispute resolution; technology, media and communications; employment and human resources; financial services; intellectual property; mergers and acquisitions; public law; real estate; corporate services; and consumer protection.

DELEANU VASILE - LAWYERS

45 CAROL BOULEVARD
AP 5, SECTOR 2
BUCHAREST

Telephone: +40 21 312 45 36
Fax: +40 21 312 52 34
E-mail: office@deleanu.ro
Website: www.deleanu.ro

Languages
English, French, Italian, Spanish

Other offices
Brussels

Number of lawyers 17

CATEGORIES OF WORK	
Bankruptcy	Banking and finance
Debt recovery	Civil law
Corporate and commercial law	Tax law
Privatisation	Litigation
Intellectual property	

THE FIRM

Deleanu Vasile – Lawyers was established in June 1996, with a small staff, a lawyer and several assistants. In time, as the firm's activities, client base and success have increased, the firm has attracted new partners and lawyers.

Although the firm has a solid domestic client base, it has also been quick to recognise the increasing importance and influence of the European Union. In light of this, the firm opened its office in Brussels in early 2003.

Taking a flexible approach, the firm deals positively with the issues its clients face and enjoys being part of a client's business team - helping to overcome obstacles, accelerating progress and offering effective, economic solutions.

AREAS OF PRACTICE

The main areas of practice are those listed above, from which the emphasis is mainly on corporate and commercial law, and insolvency and debt recovery.

In time, the firm's field of activities has expanded, adapting to the market's and the clients' requests – trade companies with both state (public) and private investments, Romanian and/or foreign.

One major area of work involves consulting on EU-related issues. Given Romania's recent economic adaptation to the EU market, privatisation has been one of the firm's most important forms of activity.

In its extensive international practice, an important aspect is providing advice to foreign clients who wish to establish businesses in Romania, including the formation of companies and the relevant taxation legislation. Given its range of clients, the firm has represented several foreign companies in Romania in litigation as well as in arbitration proceedings.

Other important work areas include providing advice on tax regulations and on contractual negotiations.

A brochure providing more information is available on request.

GEORGESCU, NEMOIANU & SALCIANU LAW FIRM

CALEA SERBAN VODA NR 133
SECTOR 4
70517 BUCHAREST

Telephone: +40 21 336 2266
Fax: +40 21 336 1177
Website: www.kpmg.ro

Languages
English, French

Number of lawyers 16

CATEGORIES OF WORK

- Corporate and commercial
- Banking, finance and capital markets
- Mergers and acquisitions
- Privatisation and investment
- Infrastructure and project finance
- Insolvency and corporate restructuring
- Commercial property and real estate
- Dispute resolution
- Employment
- Energy and natural resources
- Intellectual property
- Regulatory
- Competition and EU
- Insurance
- Communications, technology and e-business

GIDE LOYRETTE NOUEL

10-12 STRADA MAIOR SONTU
SECTOR 1
BUCHAREST

Telephone: +40 21 223 03 10
Fax: +40 21 223 03 42
E-mail: gln.bucharest@gide.com
Website: www.gide.com

Other offices
Algiers, Beijing, Brussels, Budapest, Casablanca, Hanoi, Istanbul, London, Moscow, New York, Paris, Prague, Riyadh, Shanghai, Tunis, Warsaw

Number of lawyers 480
at this office 11

Contact
Bruno Leroy (leroyb@gide.com)

CATEGORIES OF WORK

- Mergers and acquisitions
- Privatisation
- Company law
- Competition and merger control
- State aid
- Distribution law
- Labour
- Real estate transactions and financing
- Banking law
- Project finance
- Concessions

GRUIA DUFAUT LAW OFFICE

**STRADA ALEXANDRU
DONICI NR 11
SECTOR 2
70 232 BUCHAREST**

Telephone: +40 21 211 01 41
Fax: +40 21 210 50 73
E-mail: bucarest@dgd-conseil.com

Languages
English, French, Italian, Romanian

Other offices
Paris

Number of lawyers 10
at this office 6

CATEGORIES OF WORK

Company and commercial	**Contracts**
Privatisation	**Real estate**
Mergers and acquisitions	**Tax and finance**
Competition law	**Intellectual property**
Labour and employment	**Litigation and arbitration**

THE FIRM

Gruia Defaut Law Office is a thriving French-based law firm with a strong reputation in its field, providing services to Romanian and foreign natural/legal entities, with significant expertise in Romanian law that has built up over more than 12 years.

The firm was founded by Dana Gruia Dufaut, a member of both the French and Romanian Bar, and it is one of the few local law firms providing Romanian and French assistance and advice.

From 1993 to 1996, Dana Gruia Dufaut was secretary of the International Lawyers Association for East European countries and since 1996, she has been adviser to the French Embassy in Romania. Since 1999, she has been Counsel of the Foreign Trade of France (Conseiller du Commerce Extérieur de la France).

The 10-lawyer team at Gruia Dufaut Law Office is supported by a dynamic and qualified staff of legal advisers, consultants, and accountants, fluent in French, English and Italian.

AREAS OF PRACTICE

Well known in Romania because of its ability to assist its clients in investing in Romania by setting up joint ventures, acquisition of Romanian companies and establishment of new Romanian legal entities, the firm's team provides a full range of legal advice and assistance to both Romanian and foreign companies.

Commercial and corporate: setting up of new companies; implementing joint ventures; drafting commercial contracts and all legal documentation; assistance in shares sale-purchase transactions; preparation of business plans and feasibility studies; mergers and acquisitions; other practical aspects of doing business in Romania; negotiations with business partners, local bodies and ministries involved; banking and insolvency proceedings.

Privatisation: carrying out due diligence assignments for acquisition and privatisation projects; negotiation with different governmental bodies or administrative authorities; bid preparation, negotiation and preparation of shares sale-purchase agreements; and closing, legal advice on post-control privatisation and so on.

Labour and employment: negotiation, drafting and registration of individual and collective employment agreements; assistance of employers in HR-related issues; negotiation with trade unions; assistance and representation in individual and collective labour conflicts; confidentiality and non-competition agreements.

Real estate: negotiation and drafting of option agreements and sale-purchase agreements; concessions; mortgages; registration with Land Register; obtaining relevant permits and authorisations; property vindication and nationalised property.

Tax and finance: advising on various issues on taxation, foreign exchange control and customs regulation; different forms of credit and financing; negotiation and drafting international commercial agreements, part of complex transactions of project finance.

Litigation and arbitration: representation before justice and arbitration courts in a wide range of matters pertaining to debt collection, property vindication and so on.

HAARMANN HEMMELRATH

28 HRISTO BOTEV STREET, SECT 3
030237 BUCHAREST

Telephone: +40 21 3 15 35 72
Fax: +40 21 3 15 35 77
E-mail: bucharest@haarmannhemmelrath.com
Website: www.haarmannhemmelrath.com

Languages
Bulgarian, Croatian, Czech, Dutch, English, French, Hungarian, Italian, Japanese, Mandarin, Norwegian, Polish, Portuguese, Russian, Slovak, Spanish, Vietnamese

Other offices
Berlin, Bielefeld, Brussels, Budapest, Cologne, Dusseldorf, Frankfurt, Hamburg, Leipzig, London, Milan, Moscow, Munich, Paris, Prague, Rome, Shanghai, Singapore, Stuttgart, Tokyo, Vienna, Warsaw

Number of lawyers 281
at this office 8

CATEGORIES OF WORK

Mergers and acquisitions
Catalin Grigorescu, Andrew M Costin

Antitrust and competition law
Catalin Grigorescu, Adriana Duncea

Banking and finance
Catalin Grigorescu, Anca Grigorescu

Corporate
Catalin Grigorescu, Anca Grigorescu

Finance, leasing
Gabriel Biris, Anca Grigorescua

Energy – oil and gas
Andrew M Costin

Private equity investment
Andreea Roventa

Privatisation
Andrew M Costin, Adriana Duncea

Public procurement
Adriana Duncea, Andreea Roventa

Labour law
Gabriel Biris, Anca Grigorescu

Litigation and arbitration
Adriana Duncea

Telecommunications
Anca Grigorescu

Real estate and commercial property
Andreea Roventa

Tax compliance and tax structuring
Gabriel Biris, Gabriel Sincu

Structuring of inward investments (foreign, domestic)
Gabriel Biris, Anca Grigorescu

Project finance
Gabriel Biris, Andrew M Costin

Auditing services
Bogdan Ion, Hubertus Eichler

Customs issues
Gabriel Biris

Financial and advisory services
Hubertus Eichler, Bogdan Jon

HAYHURST ROBINSON

24 PALEOLOGU STREET
030552 BUCHAREST

Telephone: +40 21 326 2096
Fax: +40 21 326 2097
E-mail: hrbucharest@hrintlaw.com
Website: www.hrintlaw.com

Languages
Bulgarian, English, French, Hungarian, Romanian, Russian, Serbian

Other offices
Belgrade, Budapest, Sofia

Number of lawyers 40
at this office 15

Contact
Barbara Mendler (bmendler@hrintlaw.com)

International groupings
Interlex Group; IBA

CATEGORIES OF WORK

Foreign investment
Todd Robinson, Gabriel Sidere

Privatisation
Dan Paulopol-Necula, Gabriel Sidere

Energy and natural resources
Robert Hayhurst, Gabriel Sidere

Real estate
Todd Robinson, Cristian Lina

Project and corporate finance
Robert Hayhurst, Gabriel Sidere

Banking
Cristian Lina

Private equity
Todd Robinson, Cristian Lina

Mergers and acquisitions
Todd Robinson, Gabriel Sidere

Telecoms
Todd Robinson, John Fitzpatrick

Pharmaceutical
David Butts, Csaba Kovacs

Licensing and hi-tech
David Butts, John Fitzpatrick

Insurance
Gabriel Sidere

Municipal infrastructure
Todd Robinson

Shipping
Gabriel Sidere

Transport infrastructure
Todd Robinson, Cristian Lina

General corporate
Cristian Lina, Gabriel Sidere

Corporate insolvency and bankruptcy
Cristian Lina, Gabriel Sidere

LINKLATERS MICULITI & ASOCIATII

8 NICOLAE IORGA
SECTOR 1
010434 BUCHAREST

Telephone: +40 21 307 1500
Fax: +40 21 307 1555
Website: www.linklaters.com

Languages
All commercial and local languages in the countries where Linklaters operates

Other offices
Alicante, Amsterdam, Antwerp, Bangkok, Beijing, Berlin, Bratislava, Brussels, Budapest, Cologne, Frankfurt am Main, Hong Kong, Lisbon, London, Luxembourg, Madrid, Milan, Moscow, Munich, New York, Paris, Prague, Rome, São Paulo, Shanghai, Singapore, Stockholm, Tokyo, Warsaw

Number of lawyers 2,000 worldwide

Contact
Michael Tétreault Schilling

CATEGORIES OF WORK

Corporate, M&A and capital markets
Marian Dinu

Banking and finance
Adrian-Catalin Bulboaca

Energy and natural resources
Simona Delia Pachiu

IT, telecommunications and media
Simona Delia Pachiu

Intellectual property
Dr Lucian Mihai

Litigation and arbitration
Dr Lucian Mihai

Real estate
Francisc Eduard Peli

Competition/antitrust
Francisc Eduard Peli

Tax, insurance and employee benefits
Sebastian Lawson-Foia

Balkan practice
K Todd Schollenbarger, Theodore Cominos

THE FIRM
Linklaters advises the world's leading companies, financial institutions and governments on their most challenging transactions and assignments. With 2,000 lawyers, including 470 partners, and offices in major business and financial centres, its clients choose the firm for its distinctive combination of technical skill, commercial experience and outstanding service.

Linklaters has built a formidable global practice through organic growth and a series of mergers, joint ventures and co-operations with other respected law firms. In 2001, Linklaters merged with three of Europe's leading law firms to form Linklaters Oppenhoff & Rädler in Germany, Linklaters in Sweden, Linklaters De Bandt in Belgium and Linklaters Loesch in Luxembourg. In the same year, the firm formed a co-operation with Brazilian firm Goulart Penteado, Iervolino e Lefosse. This co-operation combines Linklaters' international capability with GPIL's extensive knowledge of the Brazilian market. In Singapore, the firm practises as Linklaters Allen & Gledhill, a joint venture with the premier Singapore practice of Allen & Gledhill, while in Italy, Linklaters has an exclusive relationship with Italian law firm Gianni, Origoni, Grippo & Partners.

MUSAT & ASOCIATII

43 AVIATORILOR BOULEVARD
1ST DISTRICT
011853 BUCHAREST

Telephone: +40 21 223 3717
Fax: +40 21 223 3957
E-mail: general@musat.ro
Website: www.musat.ro

Languages
English, French, German, Italian, Spanish, Russian

Number of lawyers 70

Contacts
Gheorghe Musat (senior partner), Florentin Tuca (managing partner), Gabriel Zbarcea, Catalin Baiculescu, Stefan Damian, Mona Marian, Cornel Popa, Ion Dragne, Sorin Marius Vladescu, Andreea Ionescu, Dan Borbely

Member
Terralex

CATEGORIES OF WORK

Corporate and commercial
Gheorghe Musat, Florentin Tuca

M&A and privatisations
Gheorghe Musat, Gabriel Zbarcea

Banking and finance
Gheorghe Musat, Florentin Tuca

Energy and natural resources
Gabriel Zbarcea, Stefan Damian

IT and communications
Catalin Baiculescu, Stefan Damian

Competition
Stefan Damian

Property and construction
Gabriel Zbarcea, Cornel Popa

Intellectual property
Stefan Damian

Aviation and aerospace
Catalin Baiculescu

Shipping and transport
Gabriel Zbarcea, Stefan Damian

Insurance
Catalin Baiculescu

Employment and pensions
Stefan Damian

Capital markets and securities
Florentin Tuca, Stefan Damian

Taxation
Florentin Tuca

Litigation
Gheorghe Musat, Florentin Tuca

Regulatory legal services
Florentin Tuca, Catalin Baiculescu

Advertising
Gabriel Zbarcea, Mona Marian

Technical assistance
Gheorghe Musat, Gabriel Zbarcea

THE FIRM

Musat & Asociatii's name stands for high levels of expertise in business matters. The firm is highly reputed for its commercial approach to transactions and its profound understanding of the client's commercial goal. The firm currently has 70 lawyers, all fully admitted to the practice, as well as a further 34 non-legal staff. Over the years, Musat & Asociatii has represented international and domestic clients in all kinds of legal transactions and has gained its reputation by specialisation, efficiency and professional ethics. It is a member of the Romanian Bar Association and has close contacts and alliances with some of the most prestigious law firms in the EU and the US, enabling the provision of a fully global client service. The firm is the exclusive Romanian representative in Terralex, the worldwide network of independent law firms.

AREAS OF PRACTICE

The firm's practice covers the entire spectrum of business activities. Musat & Asociatii is an acknowledged market leader in the fields of: corporate and commercial; mergers, acquisitions and privatisation; banking and finance; energy and natural resources; communications and information technology; competition; intellectual property; property and construction; aviation and aerospace; shipping and transport; insurance; employment and pensions; capital markets and securities; taxation; litigation; regulatory legal services, advertising; technical assistance.

Over the years, Musat & Asociatii has acted for banks and other financial institutions, international businesses, venture capital funds, major Romanian public and private companies and governmental agencies. A large proportion of the firm's clients are European, North American, Japanese and other Asia Pacific-based companies.

Major clients and mandates in 2003 include: Enel Distribuzione SpA (Italy), in connection with the privatisation of two of the branches of Electrica SA (the largest electricity distribution company in Romania); Enel Produzione SpA (Italy) in connection with the public private partnership project with Hidroelectrica SA (the sole generator of hydroelectric power in Romania); Occidental Oil and Gas Corporation (US) in respect of the privatisation of the National Oil Company Petrom SA Ispat Co UK/LNM Holdings NV for the privatisation of Tepro SA (one of the largest Romanian steel pipes producers); Siderurgica SA Hunedoara and Petrotub SA Roman (the sole Roamanian producer of seamless steel pipes for the oil industry); EBRD in connection with the $50m loan agreement to BCR and a $20m loan agreement to Banc Post; EBRD on the loan agreement in a maximum amount of €20m to Billa Invest Construct SRL for the development of new Billa supermarkets, part of the international chain REWE Germany; EBRD, DEG - Deutsche Investitions-und Entwicklungsgesellschaft Mbh, FMO - Nederlanse Financierings-Maatschappij voor Ntwikkelingslanden NV and the Romanian bank Banca Trasilvania in respect of four loan agreements in total value of more than $20m granted to one of the largest Romanian CATV companies, Astral Telecom SA for the development of fixed lines telephony services; Gabriel Resources Ltd, the Canadian mining group in relation with operating the joint venture established with the Romanian state-owned company Minvest, for the purpose of exploration and exploitation of Rosia Montana, the biggest gold and silver mining site in Europe, with planned investments of $850m; Romtelecom in connection with the drafting of a new collective bargaining agreement and assisting the clients in the negotiation thereof with the trade unions; Romanian government in relation with a $300m ICSID arbitration regarding CS Resita SA commenced by a US investor under the Billateral Investment treaty between Romania and the USA; Thyssen Krupp in complex international litigation, claims exceeding $40m arising from sale and purchase of steel; Romanian government through the Ministry of Public Finances in a $10m UNCITRAL arbitration in the Permanent Arbitration Court in Hagues; Ispat Sidex SA, legal assistance in a commercial arbitration against Metal SA with claims exceeding $600m.

NESTOR NESTOR DICULESCU KINGSTON PETERSEN

NEOCITY TOWER, FLOORS 9-12
237B CALEA DOROBANTILOR
010566 BUCHAREST 1

Telephone: +40 21 20 11 200
Fax: +40 21 20 11 210
E-mail: ion.nestor@nnkp.ro
Website: www.nnkp.com

Languages
English, French

Number of lawyers 43

Member
The South East Europe Legal Group (SEE Legal); Lex Mundi; World Services Group (WSG)

CATEGORIES OF WORK

Privatisation, mergers and acquisitions
Ion Nestor, Alina Radu

Direct investment
Manuela Nestor, Adriana Gaspar

Project/corporate finance and banking
Manuela Nestor, Adina Chilim

Intellectual property
Alexandru Harsany, Radu Culic

Media, telecommunications and IT
Adina Chilim, Alexandru Harsany

Tax
Carmen Peli

Competition and regulatory
Carmen Peli, Cristina Filip

Energy and public utilities
Cristina Filip, Alina Radu

Labour and employment
Mihaela Rosca, Radu Culic

Securities and financial markets
Adriana Gaspar, Cristina Virtopeanu

Litigation
Ana Diculescu-Sova, Ion Nestor

THE FIRM

Established in 1990, Nestor Nestor Diculescu Kingston Petersen (NNDKP) now has four Romanian and two American partners and provides a full range of legal services in all aspects of commercial activity in Romania. The firm has 43 lawyers and four specialised consultants, and is acknowledged as an undisputed market leader.

In 2003, the firm restructured and enhanced its IP department as a response to steady growth in the market. Also, in September 2003, NNDKP co-founded The South East Europe Legal Group (SEE Legal), an organisation of leading independent local law firms from south eastern Europe.

AREAS OF PRACTICE

All projects listed below took place or were developed at the end of 2002 and during 2003.

Financing: Advised on significant private finance projects, including a bond issuance valued at more than $200m on the Luxembourg market. NNDKP also provided advice to various local and international companies regarding loan facilities valued in total at more than $600m.

Privatisation: The firm's extensive experience included advice to the national electrical company on pre-privatisation and privatisation matters related to four electrical distribution companies, and advising the Romanian government on the privatisation process of Romania's largest bank.

Mergers and acquisitions: NNDKP's substantial experience in diversified fields included representation as local counsel for Romania of international companies regarding various acquisitions made, or in progress, on the Romanian market in fields such as goods and oil and gas.

Intellectual property: NNDKP assisted a large software corporation in the acquisition of the IP assets of a Romanian software producer and assisted the leading mobile communications operator in Romania in evaluating its trade mark portfolio. NNDKP has assisted a number of international clients in IP prosecution and IP litigation.

Competition law: NNDKP has proved its strength in the competition area by assisting clients in obtaining the Romanian Competition Council's approval of economic concentrations, providing counseling under Romanian competition law governing pricing, distribution and consumer protection, as well as representing clients in litigation and investigation issues.

Real estate: NNDKP assisted several Romanian and international companies in acquiring various properties in Romania. Assistance ranged from legal advice concerning title to property and observance of all legal requirements to preparing draft sale-purchase or lease agreements and designing the most attractive tax structure of the transactions.

Tax: NNDKP advised on complex transactions implemented in the domestic market as well as on cross-border featured transactions. Also provided advice on new fiscal and currency legal framework developments.

Labour: Expertise covers analysis of employment relationships as well as assistance in negotiation and execution of collective and individual labour contracts, preparing draft internal regulations, confidentiality and non-competition agreements, and legal requirements in connection to collective dismissals.

Dispute resolution: Advised on commercial, tax and real estate litigation. Special attention was given to labour litigation, arbitration and IP matters.

IT and telecoms: NNDKP acted as local counsel to an international company in connection with the global IT infrastructure outsourcing agreement concluded with another international key player.

Energy: NNDKP assisted an international company in negotiations of concession agreements for several Romanian petroleum fields, as well as in negotiations with the National Agency for Mineral Resources.

Infrastructure: Acted as local council in connection with the development of two motorway projects. NNDKP also provided assistance in connection to projects related to the rehabilitation of an important national road.

NÖRR STIEFENHOFER LUTZ

**STR GENERAL CONSTANTIN
BUDISTEANU NR 28C, SECTOR 1
010775 BUCHAREST**

Telephone: +40 21 312 5888
Fax: +40 21 312 5889
E-mail: nslbuc@noerr.ro
Website: www.noerr.de

Languages
English, French, German, Italian

Other offices
Berlin, Budapest, Dresden, Düsseldorf, Frankfurt, Moscow, Munich, Prague, Warsaw

Number of lawyers 237
(+ 53 tax advisers, public accountants and tax assistants)
at this office 8
(+ 2 tax advisers)

Contacts
Zsolt K Radnóczy, Dr Jörg K Menze

CATEGORIES OF WORK

Corporate law

Mergers and acquisitions

Banking, capital investment, project financing

Media law

Tax law

Privatisation

Industrial property and copyright law

Labour law

Environmental and product liability

Zoning, construction and real estate

Distribution law

PI PARTNERS
EY LAW

**FORUM 2000 BUILDING
75, DR N STAICOVICI STREET,
4TH FLOOR, SECTOR 5
050557 BUCHAREST**

Telephone: +40 21 40 24 100
Fax: +40 21 41 06 987
E-mail: pi.partners@ro.eylaw.com
Website: www.eylaw.com/romania

Languages
Bulgarian, Dutch, English, French, German, Greek, Italian, Spanish

Other offices
Athens, Sofia, Thessaloniki

Number of lawyers 49
at this office 12

Contacts
Charles Vernon (charles.vernon@ro.eylaw.com)
Daniela David (daniela.david@ro.eylaw.com)

Member
EY Law

CATEGORIES OF WORK

Banking, finance and securities
Anca Bocanici, Anca Gherghin

M&A and privatisations
Charles Vernon

Commercial and corporate
Charles Vernon, Ioana Letca

Human capital services and labour
Iulian Patrascanu

Litigation and arbitration
Daniela David

Real estate
Iulian Patrascanu

PACHIU & ASSOCIATES

36 SPATARULUI STREET
SUITE NO 4
SECTOR 2
BUCHAREST

Telephone: +40 21 212 0023
Fax: +40 21 211 5636
E-mail: office@lp-legal.com
Website: www.lp-legal.com

Languages
English, French, German, Italian, Russian

Number of lawyers 8

CATEGORIES OF WORK

Asset finance
Cornel Tăbârţă, Claudia Oprea Popa

Banking and finance
Cornel Tăbârţă, Claudia Oprea Popa

Capital markets
Claudia Oprea Popa, Ioana Waszkiewicz

Commercial property/real estate
Cornel Tăbârţă, Marius Petroiu

Competition
Camelia Nicoară, Ioana Waszkiewicz

Corporate and commercial
Laurenţiu Pachiu, Marius Petroiu

Dispute resolution and litigation
Laurenţiu Pachiu, Claudia Oprea Popa

Energy and natural resources
Claudia Oprea Popa, Ioana Waszkiewicz

Government and regulatory
Camelia Nicoară, Cornel Tăbârţă

Information technology
Cornel Tăbârţă

Infrastructure and project finance
Cornel Tăbârţă

Insolvency/corporate restructuring
Camelia Nicoară, Ioana Waszkiewicz

Intellectual property
Cornel Tăbârţă, Marius Petroiu

Labour law
Camelia Nicoară, Ioana Waszkiewicz

Media and entertainment
Claudia Oprea Popa, Marius Petroiu

Mergers and acquisitions
Laurenţiu Pachiu, Cornel Tăbârţă

Tax
Laurenţiu Pachiu, Cornel Tăbârţă

Telecommunications
Claudia Oprea Popa, Marius Petroiu

THE FIRM

Pachiu & Associates was founded in 2002 by Laurenţiu Pachiu, and consists of experienced and motivated Romanian lawyers. All the firm's lawyers are graduates of leading universities in Romania or abroad, and the majority are senior members of the Bucharest Bar Association.

Since its formation, the firm has been involved in a number of major acquisition projects, project financing, real estate projects, asset finance and securitisation, and tax structures. It benefits from a professional network comprising public notaries and authorised experts and is therefore able to provide clients with an integrated package of services. The firm maintains a close relationship with some leading multinational law firms.

While the firm has enjoyed a constant and healthy growth in size since its formation, it concentrates on high-quality services rendered by experienced lawyers rather than promoting a significant increase in its staffing levels. Focus is set on clients' needs and provision of prompt services. Effective cost management and careful selection of attorneys and auxilliary staff is the foundation of the firm's policy in the fields of client management and recruitment.

AREAS OF PRACTICE

Since formation, the firm has been involved in major projects in various industries including: banking; media; white goods; energy; IT and telecoms; health and pharmaceuticals; defence; heavy industry; textile; construction and construction materials industry. The firm has been extensively involved in mergers and acquisitions in various fields of business and industry. It has assisted clients in the process of legal due diligence, public offerings, structuring of M&A transactions, related antitrust matters, and drafting of transaction deeds and contracts, as well as closing and post-closure follow-up. It provides due consideration of all relevant matters in the M&A field: corporate and corporate governance consolidation; competition approvals; most feasible tax structure; regulatory; labour relations; commercial registration; environmental compliance; and so on.

The firm has a proven professional approach to all types of corporate disputes including, amongst others, minority shareholders' rights and management-shareholder disputes.

The firm has an excellent relationship with local and foreign financial and tax advisers, which enables it to find the appropriate legal solutions for reducing tax burdens. The firm's global thinking gives it the strength to deal with complex and intricate matters, such as avoidance of double taxation, reporting of particular operations to local tax authorities and foreign currency regulations.

The firm is also actively involved in monitoring EC law and practice and its implementation in Romania in certain industries.

Another important area of the firm's work is advising investors on large real estate projects. The firm manages the complex relationship with both local and central authorities in obtaining the right approval and permits for particular industrial and office projects, and provides thorough legal due diligence prior to acquisition of a real estate asset. Its expertise involves thorough and competent research through all the records held with relevant authorities and issuing of a final report, which provides for the most appropriate solution.

Additional information is available on the firm's website.

POPOVICI & ASOCIATII

47 ALEXANDRU CONSTANTINESCU ST 1ST DISTRICT 011 472 BUCHAREST

Telephone: +40 21 224 79 19
Fax: +40 21 224 60 59
E-mail: office@popovici-partners.ro
Website: www.popovici-partners.ro

Languages
English, French, German, Italian, Spanish

Number of lawyers 19

CATEGORIES OF WORK

Corporate and commercial
Ernest Virgil Popovici, Florian Nitu

Employment
Sorin Alazaroaie, Vlad Neacsu

Insurance
Irena Tudorie, Cristina Alexe

Investments, infrastructure and real estate (including construction and utilities sub-group)
Ernest Virgil Popovici, Sorin Alazaroaie

Banking finance and capital markets
Florian Nitu, Bogdan Stoica

Mergers and acquisitions, privatisation
Ernest Virgil Popovici, Irena Tudorie

Litigation and arbitration
Ilinca Stefanescu, Ciprian Dontu

Telecommunications and IT
Ernest Virgil Popovici, Florian Nitu

THE FIRM

Popovici & Asociatii is one of the first incorporated professional partnerships in Romania. The firm's team brings together strong local capabilities, with exceptional credentials, outstanding records and distinguished careers in law, business and academia. With extensive experience in almost all major legal fields, the firm provides quality legal services backed up by a sincere relationship with its clients.

The firm has acted as outside counsel to a wide spectrum of legal entities, including key players in major industries, financial institutions, public authorities and investment funds. During the last decade, significant investment and acquisition projects on the Romanian market have been managed and carried out with the legal assistance of Popovici & Asociatii.

Through its local capabilities, Popovici & Asociatii covers a full range of legal services, ready to deliver the appropriate result under a complex business environment.

AREAS OF PRACTICE

Popovici & Asociatii is closely involved in the corporate and commercial field acting for multinationals and local companies, with work being broadly based and varied. Commercial advice also covers customs and taxation, competition and international trade topics.

The firm enjoys a reputation in employment, dealing with issues arising out of M&As, outsourcing projects and corporate restructuring. Mediation of labour disputes and negotiation of collective agreements represent a core area within the practice sub-group.

The infrastructure and real estate projects in Romania during the past ten years (most of them greenfield investments) have allowed team members to gain remarkable skills. This field is one of the firm's main areas of expertise. The team advises on a broad range of construction works, including industrial, residential, commercial and public. The firm covers various aspects of real estate construction and operation projects, especially designing contractual instruments and monitoring their implementation. The team has built a considerable body of practice and experience in the utilities field, particularly in road construction and rehabilitation projects, public/private partnerships and concession of utilities.

The firm has gained specific knowledge in the field of banking and finance, as well as in the Romanian insurance field. The firm's expertise in structuring trade finance schemes, as well as in international transactions involving factoring and forfeiting operations, is well regarded, with some team members being distinguished for their knowledge of debtor and creditor relationships.

Capital markets is one of the firm's foremost practices and is currently advising in all types of capital markets deals. Apart from the acquisitions implemented on the Rasdaq and Bucharest stock exchanges, listing and delisting and public offer projects for companies or investment funds, Popovici & Asociatii has been involved in the issuance of municipality bonds procedures and securitisation projects.

Team members have been involved in most of the major privatisation projects in Romania, allowing them to gain extensive knowledge in all types of legal assistance related to privatisation. The team has also handled key issues within significant M&A deals in Romania.

The firm has assisted and represented major private investments made in the telecoms and IT area, and has provided legal assistance for telecoms operators authorisation and licensing, on specific regulatory matters in drafting an negotiating service providers agreements, agreements for network building and operation, and other relevant advice.

The team has wide-ranging litigation and arbitration experience in most commercial litigation fields and civil proceedings. Litigation experts have experience in complex alternative dispute resolution cases.

RACOTI – PREDOIU, ATTORNEYS AT LAW

30 BATISTEI STREET, SUITE 2
SECTOR 2
701311 BUCHAREST

Telephone: +40 21 311 0517
Fax: +40 21 311 0519
E-mail: office@rps.ro
Website: www.rps.ro

Languages
English, French, Romanian

Number of lawyers 15

Member
International Bar Association;
INSOL Europe

CATEGORIES OF WORK

Commercial law
Dr Catalin Predoiu

Corporate law
Ioana Racoti

Capital markets
Ioana Racoti

Privatisation
Ioana Racoti, Raluca Dirjan

Civil law
Dr Marian Nicolae

Property law
Dr Marian Nicolae

Banking and finance
Dr Catalin Predoiu

Energy and natural resources
Bogdan Aldea

Labour and employment
Raluca Marian

Contracts
Bogdan Aldea

E-commerce
Anca Sandru, Serban Patriciu

Bankruptcy and insolvency
Radu Boanta

IP law
Daniel Lungu

Litigation and arbitration
Dr Catalin Predoiu

Competition law
Raluca Marian

Mergers and acquisitions
Raluca Marian

THE FIRM

Racoti – Predoiu, Attorneys at Law was founded in 1996 and has grown steadily to number 15 lawyers and a total staff of 21. The firm gained its place among the top providers of legal assistance on the Romanian market due to its distinctive approach to the legal profession: continuous professional specialisation, solid theoretical background and interdisciplinary collaboration.

The firm has initiated and maintained relations with reputable foreign law firms and has joined the International Bar Association, INSOL Europe and other regional and global professional bodies.

AREAS OF PRACTICE

Commercial and corporate: legal assistance in negotiating shareholders' agreements; drafting articles of incorporation; incorporating new companies; implementing joint ventures. The firm currently assists clients in corporate governance and compliance with the Romanian legal requirements pertaining to company secretarial.

Capital markets: services to both securities issuers and underwriters in cases of sale and purchase, public offerings, company listing and de-listing, and private placements. Having in-depth knowledge of Romania's National Securities Commission regulations, it offers overall legal assistance throughout, ensuring legal compliance of the transaction structure, and assisting with the drafting of documentation and presentation before the relevant authorities.

Privatisation: The firm has been involved in the privatisation of several major state-owned enterprises, providing legal due diligence and making preliminary enquiries, counselling throughout the tendering process, assisting during negotiations, and drafting share sale-purchase agreements and closing.

Civil and property law: the firm provides services and representation in a wide range of matters pertaining to concessions, expropriations, inheritance, mortgages, moveable and immovable property vindication, and nationalised property.

Banking and finance: the firm specialises in monetary and financial markets; currency and control regulations; financing methods and international reimbursement; financial and banking institutions and activities. It has advised on bank takeover procedures; facility arrangements; all forms of credit agreements and restructuring, and the provisions of the relevant Romanian legislation.

Energy and natural resources: significant experience in the procedures related to authorising and licensing in the field of natural gas distribution and in the energy sector.

Labour and employment: drafting of collective bargaining agreements; employment agreements; assisting employers in a wide variety of personnel matters, including discipline and severance agreements, development of policies, compliance with Romanian employment laws, unemployment compensation, trade union matters and social accompaniment protocols.

E-commerce: in-depth knowledge of the Romanian and European communication and IT fields, advising local and global clients in communications, e-commerce and the provision of Internet services.

IP law: assistance in matters pertaining to the legal protection of licences, patents, trade marks and copyrights, as well as providing representation before the relevant authorities and courts.

Bankruptcy and insolvency: the firm's professional liquidation and restructuring practitioners provide overall legal assistance, focusing on liquidation procedures, judicial and bankruptcy reorganisation procedures, and representation in secured and unsecured creditors' committees.

Litigation and arbitration: providing representation before courts of justice and various regulatory and supervisory bodies on the economic market, arbitration, and good offices for the amiable settlement of disputes.

SCHÖNHERR RECHTSANWÄLTE OEG

PIATA ROMANA 8
010375 BUCHAREST

Telephone: +40 21 212 05 80
Fax: +40 21 212 05 81
E-mail: office@schoenherr.ro
Website: www.schoenherr.at

Languages
English, French, German, Romanian

Other offices
Belgrade, Brussels, Vienna, Ljubljana, Zagreb

Number of lawyers 96
at this office 14

Contacts
Christoph Lindinger
(ch.lindinger@schoenherr.at),
Roxana Gologan, Sebastian Gutui, Matei Florea,
Mihai Radulescu

CATEGORIES OF WORK

International and Romanian practice

International contracts and foreign investment

Banking securities and finance

Project finance

M&A

Privatisations

Public private partnership

Real estate and commercial property

EU law

STOICA & ASOCIATII

OPERA CENTER II
STR DR N STAICOVICI NR 2, ETAJ 2
SECTOR 5
050558 BUCURESTI

Telephone: +40 21 40 20 930
Fax: +40 21 40 20 931
E-mail: sca@stoica-asociatii.ro
Website: www.stoica-asociatii.ro

Languages
English, French

Number of lawyers 13

CATEGORIES OF WORK

Corporate
Cristiana I Stoica

International contracts
Cristiana I Stoica, Valeriu Stoica

Privatisation
Cristiana I Stoica, Valeriu Stoica

International financing
Cristiana I Stoica, Valeriu Stoica

Foreign investments
Cristiana I Stoica, Valeriu Stoica

Tax
Cristiana I Stoica, Càtàlina Dicu

Mergers and acquisitions
Cristiana I Stoica, Valeriu Stoica

Administrative law
Valeriu Stoica

Competition
Valeriu Stoica

International public law
Cristiana I Stoica, Valeriu Stoica

Civil and commercial litigation
Cristiana I Stoica, Valeriu Stoica

Real estate
Càtàlina Dicu, Valeriu Stoica

Intellectual property
Valeriu Stoica, Càtàlina Dicu

Labour and social law
Cristiana I Stoica, Càtàlina Dicu

Capital markets
Cristiana I Stoica

Human rights
Cristiana I Stoica, Valeriu Stoica

Banking, financial and insurance
Valeriu Stoica

THE FIRM

STOICA & Asociatii was founded in 1995 by two lawyers and has grown steadily since then to its current size of 13, of which three are partners and the others are associates and assistants with a total staff of more than 23 persons.

The founding partners have extensive experience of legal practice, co-ordinating the firm's professional activity into two main departments: advising and litigation.

STOICA & Asociatii has developed important professional relationships with lawyers across the Romanian Bar, enabling the firm to practice not only in Bucharest, but also in other jurisdictions within Romania. In the course of time, strong international links have been maintained with law firms from USA, Canada, United Kingdom, France, Italy, Spain, Austria, Belgium, Hungary, Germany, Portugal and others.

AREAS OF PRACTICE

The firm offers a full range of legal services to clients, including international companies, governmental agencies, commercial and financial institutions and private individuals.

The principal areas of work are: business and corporate law, international contracts, privatisation, international banking and financing, foreign investment, taxation, mergers and acquisitions, administrative law, competition, international public law, civil and commercial litigation, real estate, intellectual property, labour and social law, financial and capital markets and human rights.

STOICA & Asociatii has experience with regard to the establishment and operation of companies, mergers, acquisitions, reorganisation and liquidation. The firm has specific expertise in taxation, advising on legal issues regarding the withholding tax and VAT, income tax and various tax-related procedures. Labour law, administrative proceedings and financial law are a permanent activity of the firm, dedicated to both international and Romanian clients.

Finally, STOICA & Asociatii advises on legal matters arising from intellectual property, involving trade mark and copyright law with regard to contracts and registration procedures, especially in the broadcasting, video, entertainment and pharmaceutical industries.

Most of the lawyers also have strong involvement in legal publishing, in Romania and abroad.

STUDIO LEGALE SUTTI

2, UNIRII BLVD, BL 8A, 5TH FLOOR
SUITE 25, SECTOR 4
BUCHAREST

Telephone: +40 21 337 0730
Fax: +40 21 337 3171
E-mail: maildesk@sutti.com
Website: www.sutti.com

Languages
Bulgarian, English, French, German, Italian, Japanese, Portuguese, Romanian, Serbian, Spanish

Other offices
Belgrade, Genoa, London, Milan, Rome, Sofia, Tokyo

Number of lawyers 130
at this office 20

CATEGORIES OF WORK

Company, commercial law

Banking and finance

Mergers and acquisitions

Distribution, agency and franchising

Debt collection and insolvency

Commercial property law

Intellectual property

Patent and trade mark agency service

White-collar crime

EC, competition and antitrust law

IT and TLC law

Litigation and arbitration

Employment, labour law

Administrative law

Environmental law

VILAU & MITEL

50 AV PETRE CRETU STREET
1ST DISTRICT
012052 BUCHAREST

Telephone: +40 21 224 0052
Fax: +40 21 224 0508
E-mail: office@vilaumitel.ro
Website: www.vilaumitel.ro

Languages
English, French, Italian

Number of lawyers 10

International groupings
INTA

CATEGORIES OF WORK

Aviation and aerospace
Dragos Vilau, Sorin Mitel

Banking and finance
Dragos Vilau, Alina Moldovan

Capital markets
Dragos Vilau, Sorin Mitel

Communication and IT
Iuliana Bobaru, Dragos Zaharia

Competition
Dragos Vilau, Gabriela Anton

Corporate and commercial
Dragos Vilau, Sorin Mitel

Dispute resolution and litigation
Sorin Mitel, Alina Moldovan

Employment and pensions
Sorin Mitel, Gabriela Anton

Energy, natural resources and utilities
Dragos Vilau, Iuliana Bobaru

Environment, planning and regulatory
Iuliana Bobaru, Dragos Zaharia

Intellectual property
Dragos Vilau, Madalina Paisa

Mergers and acquisitions
Dragos Vilau, Sorin Mitel

Public procurement, PPP and PFI
Sorin Mitel, Madalina Paisa

Real estate and construction
Alina Moldovan, Madalina Paisa

Taxation
Sorin Mitel, Gabriela Anton

VOICU & FILIPESCU

UNION INTERNATIONAL CENTER II
26-28 STIRBEI VODA STREET,
9TH FLOOR, SECTOR 1
010113 BUCHAREST 1

Telephone: +40 21 314 02 00
Fax: +40 21 314 02 90
E-mail: voicud@vf.ro
Website: www.voicufilipescu.ro

Languages
English, French, Spanish, Russian, Romanian

Number of lawyers 15

Contacts
Daniel Voicu (voicud@vf.ro),
Mugur Filipescu (filipescum@vf.ro)

CATEGORIES OF WORK

Corporate, mergers and acquisitions
Daniel Voicu, Mugur Filipescu

Competition
Daniel Voicu, Ancuta Leach

Energy
Mugur Filipescu, Daniel Costea

Telecommunications
Christian Enache, Daniel Voicu

Privatisation
Ileana Glodeanu, Marta Popa

Banking, finance
Mugur Filipescu, Daniel Voicu

Real estate, construction
Daniel Voicu, Claudiu Pop

Insurance
Mugur Filipescu, Ancuta Leach

Litigation
Christian Enache, Marta Popa

Intellectual property
Daniel Costea, Marilena Oprea

Employment
Daniel Voicu, Ileana Glodeanu

EU law
Daniel Voicu

THE FIRM

Voicu & Filipescu is a Romanian professional partnership established in 2001, following the acquisition of the Bucharest office of an international law firm. It has 15 lawyers and 12 non-legal staff, including a dedicated team of three certified English-Romanian translators.

AREAS OF PRACTICE

Voicu & Filipescu covers the whole spectrum of business law and advice to international and Romanian clients.

Corporate, M&A: the firm has advised foreign investors on all phases of mergers and acquisitions in the Romanian market, including due diligence of target companies, preparation of data rooms, drafting of transaction documents, negotiation of terms, and post-acquisition/merger integration matters. Transactions include the sale of Brewery Holdings Limited (Advent International and Jupiter Asset Management) to Brau Union, representation of Raiffeissen Zentralbank of Austria in the acquisition of a majority stake in Banca Agricola (the state-owned bank), and the acquisition of Dorna Apemin (the third mineral water company) by Coca-Cola Hellenic Bottling Company/The Coca-Cola.

Competition: the firm has advised more than twenty major investors on economic concentration and exclusive distribution issues and has represented clients on all issues related to the investigation procedures before the Romanian competition authorities.

Energy: the firm provides regulatory, transactional, project development, policy counselling, and legislative legal services to a range of clients in the electricity, oil and gas sectors. The firm recently advised US company Pelagas Ltd in the acquisition of the Romanian gas distributor VitalGaz from the EBRD. The firm drafts and revises legal documents and contracts relating to the energy field and has drafted opinions on conformity with domestic legislation, as well as advising on the harmonisation of Romanian energy law with EU legislation.

Telecoms: the firm has experience in advising clients on a diversity of telecommunications matters. Recent transactions include advising Antel Holdings Ltd in the acquisition of the regional data transmitter KPNQwest and Astral Telecom Ltd on the first interconnection agreement for fixed line telephony with a Romanian incumbent, Romtelecom. Specialised attorneys have lobbied for the improvement of existing domestic telecommunications legislation.

Real estate, construction: the firm has extensive experience in real estate issues including examination and appraisal of public or private domain sites, negotiating and drafting occupational and operational leases and construction contracts, preparation of an assortment of related documentation, and advising on the establishment of industrial parks, re-zoning issues and leasing and concession rights. The firm represented Belgian investors Liebrecht & Wood in acquiring over 65 hectares of land near Bucharest for development into commercial parks, and Regus UK on the restructuring of its Romanian operations.

Litigation: the firm represents clients before all Romanian courts and arbitration panels and advises on various litigation issues including taxation, customs, intellectual property, bankruptcy, commercial debt collection and procedural issues related to the enforcement of foreign judgments and arbitral decisions.

Intellectual property: the firm has a reputation for success in a variety of intellectual property issues, including trade mark, copyright and patents, licensing arrangements and related matters, and the enforcement of clients' IP rights before both the State Office of Patents and Trade Marks and the Romanian courts. The firm is currently involved in the upgrading of domestic IP and industrial property rights legislation.

WOOD LUPASCU DUMITRESCU & ASSOCIATES SCPA

IN ASSOCIATION WITH HALL, DICKLER

11-13 SOSEAUA KISELEFF
011342 BUCHAREST

Telephone: +40 21 222 8888
Fax: +40 21 223 4444
E-mail: gilbert.wood@wldlaw.ro
Website: www.wld.ro

Languages
English, French, German, Italian, Romanian, Spanish

Number of lawyers 12

Contact
Gilbert P Wood

Member
Global Advertising Lawyers Alliance (GALA)

CATEGORIES OF WORK

Banking and finance	Insurance and pensions
Telecommunications	Capital markets and securities
Mergers and acquisitions	Advertising and media law
Corporate and commercial	Energy and natural resources
Privatisation	Employment and human resources
Foreign investment	Intellectual property
Litigation and arbitration	Real estate

THE FIRM

Hall Dickler Kent Goldstein & Wood LLP (New York, NY) was the first Western law firm to open permanent offices in Romania. After being present in Romania as early as 1990, Hall, Dickler (Romania) SRL ('HDR') was established in 1992. During the past 14 years, HDR represented some of the most important multinational investors in Romania. Romania recently amended its legislation governing the practice of law by foreign persons in Romania. As a result, Wood Lupascu Dumitrescu & Associates SCPA ('WLD') was established in March 2002. Douglas J Wood, a named partner of WLD, is also co-executive partner of Hall Dickler Kent Goldstein & Wood LLP.

As a result of the firm's long history in Romania, its attorneys and business consultants are among Romania's leading commercial experts and are regularly entrusted to represent clients in high-value projects and corporate reorganisations.

Privatisations and foreign direct investments are major areas of the firm's practice. The firm has extensive expertise in the telecommunications sector, being a participant in all three major telecom deals, representing a combined FDI in excess of US$1bn. In particular, the firm has broad expertise in financial markets, especially banking and securities, having represented in excess of 30 major international financial institutions.

AREAS OF PRACTICE

Banking and finance: the firm is a leader in this category having been chosen as counsel for lenders in especially high-value deals such as (listed by size): 2002 State of Romania Bond Issue (€700m); 2001 State of Romania Bond Issue (€600m); International Finance Corporation (various US$330m); 2002 Termoelectrica Loan Facility (US$250m); Renel SA Loan Facility (US$150m); 2001 State of Romania Bond Issue (€150m). The department is headed by Florentina Dumitrescu.

Telecommunications: the firm is a leader in this category having been involved in three major projects in Romania, including (a) the equity side of GSM operator Connex from the pre-bid stage to establishing the corporation; shareholder general meeting preparation and oversight; capital increases; banking relations; government relations; and (b) the debt side of Mobil Rom (now Orange) with an IFC long-term loan of US$245m involving a series of complex pledges to provide the necessary security; and (c) the privatisation of Romtelecom, previous holder of the national landline monopoly.

Project finance: the firm represented Österreichische Volksbanken-Aktiengesellschaft ('OVAG') and Volksbank Romania SA regarding a loan to modernise the Coltea Clinic through a credit of US$90m. The firm co-ordinated efforts among the Central Finance and Contracts Unit ('CFCU') within the Ministry of Public Finance, USAID, and Booz Allen Hamilton regarding a non-reimbursable loan for treatment facilities for waste water.

Mergers and acquisitions: the firm acts as counsel to Holcim, the world's largest cement producer, regarding its domestic investments, including the purchase of majority shares in three large cement producing facilities. The firm recently completed one of Romania's largest corporate restructuring projects requiring extensive liaison with the Romanian authorities when five Holcim-owned companies merged.

Litigation and arbitration: the firm's department is headed by Nicu Lupascu, and has an extensive workout portfolio from a leading bank.

Insurance and pensions: the firm established both of the local corporations of the two top insurers in Romania, ING Nederlanden Asigurari de Viata SA and AIG Life Asigurari Romania SA.

Capital markets and securities: the firm assisted the establishment of RASDAQ.

Advertising and media law: the firm is the exclusive representative in Romania for the Global Advertising Lawyers Alliance (GALA).

RUSSIA AND THE CIS

Population	**143.2 million (Russia)**
Number of lawyers	**19,000**
Professional title	**Advocat**
Currency	**Rouble (Rbl)**

Index

The country impresses with its size and diversity. The largest on the globe, it spans ten time zones, and the part-European, part-Asian land mass covers over 17 million square kilometres. Its climate ranges from the Arctic north to the generally more temperate south. While Russians make up over 80% of its 143.2 million population and Orthodox Christianity is the main religion, there are many other ethnic and religious groups. Muslims, for example, are concentrated among the Volga Tatars, the Bashkirs, and in the North Caucasus.

Following the collapse of the Soviet Union in 1991, Russia has been forced to confront a number of serious challenges. Due to the prolonged period of Communist rule that started in 1917 the creation of a democratic political system and a fully functioning market economy has thus far proven elusive. After nearly ten years of crisis, peaking in August 1998 with the devaluation of the rouble, the Russian economy bounced back more quickly than many expected. However, it is heavily dependent on world oil prices. Under President Yeltsin, the privatisations in the 1990s provided Russian entrepreneurs with rich pickings. A small group – referred to by some as Yeltsin's 'family' and now commonly known as the oligarchs – acquired large interests in the energy and media sectors. Since coming to power at the end of 1999, President Putin has striven to assert his authority not only over the oligarchs, but also over separatist groups in Chechnya. Thousands have died since Russian troops were first sent in to put down a separatist rebellion in 1994 and guerrilla fighters continue to mount attacks.

ECONOMIC CLIMATE

Russia has always been an unpredictable place to do business. Throughout 2003, investment bankers flooded into Russia in ever-increasing numbers, unthinkable in the years that followed the government debt default of 1998 and ensuing financial crisis. For the first time since the 1917 Revolution that began Communist rule, some of Russia's corporate crown jewels were on offer for foreign investors.

In 2002, the total value of M&A was only $9.3bn. In just the first nine months of 2003, Russia leapt to fifth place in the European M&A league, with $35bn in deals. For much of 2003, talk focused optimistically on the country's two most powerful tycoons clinching the deal that would launch Russia's corporate history into a groundbreaking new era. Roman Abramovich's sale of shares in Sibneft to Mikhail Khodokovsky's Yukos was to mark the latest high point of a meteoric rise in Russian corporate activity.

Leading Russian aluminium group, Sual, had opened the way in January 2003 when it sold a 23% stake to the Fleming Family in the UK and agreed to hire a foreign chief executive. The following month, BP finally sealed its $16bn joint venture with TNK, giving it a 50% stake in one of Russia's largest oil groups. This deal had been on and off for years. Its completion was a watershed, engendering significant confidence on the part of the western investment community. When rating agency Moody's announced at the end of October that it was promoting the country to investment grade, Russia's remarkable rehabilitation appeared complete.

The arrest of the country's richest man, Yukos billionaire oil boss Mikhail Khodokovsky, changed all this and made the wild east tag, long associated with Russia, look more appropriate than ever. The midnight swoop at a bleak Siberian airport on 25 October that led to Khodokovsky's imprisonment caused Moscow's stock market to plummet. When state prosecutors froze 44% of Yukos shares, raising fears that it would be the first of many companies to be forcibly renationalised, as part of the authorities' assault on the oligarchs, panic deepened still further. Sibneft's eleventh-hour announcement that it was pulling out of the Yukos-Sibneft merger appeared to confirm that the Russian market had returned to its normal chaotic state.

RUSSIA: BILLING

Clients should expect to pay in the region of €400-€600 per hour for a partner, though the more experienced partners at some firms may charge as much as €750 per hour. Assistants charge €300-€350 per hour, though, in some instances, fees may be as low as €120 per hour or as high as €415 per hour. Fees at Russian firms are generally lower than those charged by international firms.

RUSSIA: MARKETING

There are no restrictions on the marketing of law firms in Russia. Most promote themselves through brochures, newsletters, directory listings and websites.

The largest firms

1	**Klishin & Partners**	**191**
2	**EY Law**	**80**
3	**Baker & McKenzie**	**51**
4	**Pepeliaev, Goltsblat & Partners**	**49**
5	**Laptev & Partners**	**48**
	Salans	**48**
7	**Iniurcolleguia, Attorneys at Law**	**45**
8	**Clifford Chance CIS Ltd**	**43**
9	**White & Case LLC**	**42**
10	**Egorov, Puginsky, Afanasiev & Partners LLC**	**40**
11	**Linklaters CIS**	**37**
12	**Freshfields Bruckhaus Deringer**	**33**
13	**Gorodissky & Partners**	**31**
14	**LeBoeuf, Lamb, Greene & MacRae**	**27**
15	**Padva & Partners**	**25**
16	**Reznik, Gagarin, Abushakhmin & Partners**	**24**
17	**CMS Bureau Francis Lefebvre**	**23**
	Coudert Brothers LLP	**23**
19	**Norton Rose**	**22**
20	**Herbert Smith CIS Legal Services**	**20**
	Nörr Stiefenhofer Lutz	**20**
22	**Beiten Burkhardt Rechtsanwälte (Attorneys-at-Law)**	**18**
23	**Alrud Law Firm**	**17**
24	**Akin Gump Strauss Hauer & Feld LLP**	**15**
	Allen & Overy	**15**
	Blishchenko & Partners	**15**
	Monastyrsky, Zyuba, Stepanov & Partners	**15**
	PricewaterhouseCoopers CIS Law Offices BV	**15**
	Russin & Vecchi LLC	**15**
	VISTA Foreign Business Support, JSC	**15**

These figures represent the total number of lawyers in this country only, and have been supplied by the firms themselves. The figures should be accurate as at 1 January 2004.

RUSSIA: IN-HOUSE LAWYERS

Many Russian companies do not appreciate the value of in-house legal advisers. It is a common experience for western lawyers advising international investment banks to be the only legal advisers on deals, even those involving some of the best-known Russian companies. The lawyers often find themselves, in effect, advising both sides. This is largely due to cost cutting considerations, as a result of which the number of in-house lawyers in Russia has decreased considerably in the last decade.

RUSSIA: THE LEGAL MARKET

The Russian legal market divides broadly along five lines. First, the international firms at the very top of the market. These have retained a relatively strong presence in Russia since the market for international legal services established itself in the early '90s (bearing in mind, of course, that few firms feel the need to have more than four partners on the ground in Russia at any one time). Firms such as **Freshfields Bruckhaus Deringer**, **Linklaters CIS** among the UK-based firms, and the likes of **LeBoeuf, Lamb, Greene & MacRae** and **White & Case LLC** of the Americans, are the foremost examples. Having weathered the storm of the 1998 crisis, they cashed in a wealth of experience to win instructions on the market-leading deals as the boom times returned in 2003, acting for Russia's top clients notably in the energy sector. In 2003, **White & Case LLC** consolidated its market-leading position after rapid expansion in recent years. The Moscow office now boasts five partners, having grown from one partner in 2000. Widely respected managing partner Hugh Verrier continues to drive the firm forward. The firm offers considerable expertise in a wide range of practice areas, receiving top slots for corporate and commercial/M&A, banking and finance, capital markets and energy.

The second group comprises the practices that have taken a hit along the way and are, to a greater or lesser extent, playing catch up. **Allen & Overy**, **Clifford Chance CIS Ltd** and **Herbert Smith CIS Legal Services** are prominent examples. All three have strong practices, winning hefty instructions, but have not achieved the blend of ingredients present among the first group.

Third, the international firms that play on their strong global reputations – due largely to the nature of the work these firms target (often capital markets and top-end M&A), they tend to retain a minimal partner presence in Moscow, drawing on proven high level expertise in London and/or New York, and flying in partners as necessary. This group includes **Cleary Gottlieb Steen & Hamilton LLC**, **Latham & Watkins LLP** and **Skadden, Arps, Slate, Meagher & Flom LLP**.

A fourth group, including **Baker & McKenzie**, **Beiten Burkhardt**, **Coudert Brothers LLP** and **Salans**, have an entirely different approach. These firms are unusual in having offices in the modern-day capital, Moscow, and the former capital, St Petersburg. Rather than competing for the very top-end corporate deals, these firms have carved a profitable niche targeting the middle ground. **Salans** has a remarkably strong presence in the region, boasting offices in Russia, Azerbaijan, Kazakhstan and Ukraine. The firm receives high rankings for corporate and commercial/M&A and dispute resolution.

The fifth group includes the local Russian firms. While in theory these firms compete in the same market as the international firms, the embryonic nature of Russia's commercial legal sector means that few, if any, are yet capable of competing for the top instructions. Nevertheless, one or two serious players are emerging – most notably **Pepeliaev, Goltsblat & Partners** – and they will be serious contenders in the near future.

BANKING AND FINANCE: RUSSIA

Financings in the oil and gas sectors continue to generate huge amounts of work for the leading finance practices in Russia. In particular, the Moscow offices of the leading UK firms thrive in this market.

Under the leadership of Moscow managing partner Peter Timchur, **Allen & Overy**'s banking and finance practice thrives despite the relocation of Calvin Walker to London. The firm leads the market in structured trade and pre-export financings and regularly advises ABN Amro, WestLB, BNP Paribas, and ING among other leading players in the Russian commercial bank lending market. In 2002-03, Edwin Tham advised Deutsche Bank on its \$300m unsecured loan to Gazprom. Timchur acted for Lukoil on its \$500m pre-export facility.

Regional managing partner Michael Cuthbert leads **Clifford Chance CIS Ltd**'s excellent 12-fee-earner banking and finance team. Partner Arthur Iliev provides strong support. The firm advised Société Générale as co-ordinating bank in a seven-bank syndicate on a \$1bn secured loan to Yukos – the largest Russian pre-export financing to date. The team also advised BNP Paribas on a \$300m, five-year syndicated loan to Tatneft.

Tobias Mueller-Deku leads **Freshfields Bruckhaus Deringer**'s banking and finance activities. The firm advised Raiffeisen Zentralbank Oesterreich on several loan facilities to Russian oil majors including a \$200m pre-export finance facility to TNK, a \$150m loan to Rosneft, and a \$130m loan to Transneft. The arrival in 2002 of two senior UK associates, Peter Schulze and Karen Young, who both specialise in banking and finance, significantly strengthened the practice. Other clients include Bayerische Hypo-und Vereinsbank, and Gazprombank.

Michael Bott, who became a partner in May 2003, heads **Linklaters CIS**' banking and finance practice. He is strongly supported by 'outstanding' Russian partner Dmitry Dobatkin. Throughout 2002-03 the team acted on some of the most complex and high-profile transactions in the market. The firm

BANKING AND FINANCE: RUSSIA

ALLEN & OVERY ✪
CLIFFORD CHANCE CIS LTD
FRESHFIELDS BRUCKHAUS DERINGER ✪
LINKLATERS CIS ✪
WHITE & CASE LLC

Akin Gump Strauss Hauer & Feld LLP ✪
Baker & McKenzie ✪
Coudert Brothers LLP ✪
Herbert Smith CIS Legal Services ✪
Latham & Watkins LLP ✪
LeBoeuf, Lamb, Greene & MacRae
Salans
Skadden, Arps, Slate, Meagher & Flom LLP

CMS Cameron McKenna
Cleary Gottlieb Steen & Hamilton LLC ✪
Nörr Stiefenhofer Lutz ✪
Norton Rose

Beiten Burkhardt Rechtsanwälte (Attorneys-at-Law) ✪
Blishchenko & Partners
Chadbourne & Parke LLP
Debevoise & Plimpton LLC
Denton Wilde Sapte ✪
Egorov, Puginsky, Afanasiev & Partners LLC ✪
Gide Loyrette Nouel ✪
Jurinflot, International Law Office ✪
Klishin & Partners
Laptev & Partners
Lovells ✪
Monastyrsky, Zyuba, Stepanov & Partners ✪
Vegas-Lex Law Firm ✪

Firms are listed A-Z in tiers which are ranked in order of priority
✪ Indicates firm displays contact details at the end of this chapter.

advised Société Générale on its $325m loan to Gazprom. It also acted for Citibank and Deutsche Bank on the $240m facility for Vneshtorgbank. This was the largest loan for a Russian bank since the 1998 crisis. Consultant Mark Kirsh is also recommended. Clients include Lukoil and SSSB.

White & Case LLC's Moscow managing partner Hugh Verrier heads the 'formidable' banking and finance team. It includes the extremely knowledgeable Marc Polonsky, and senior associate Maya Melnikas. Former Moscow partner Doug Peel provides strong support from London. Outstanding Russian partner Igor Ostapets advised Russian Aluminium group Rual Trade Ltd on financings totalling over $700m. Eric Michailov advised Aeroflot on a $300m financial lease of eight Airbus aircraft, the first financing of its kind to be supported by European export credit agencies (ECGD, Hermes and COFACE). The firm also has a particularly good reputation for representing lenders. Clients include ABN Amro, Citibank, and UBS Warburg

Akin Gump Strauss Hauer & Feld LLP has established an extremely strong finance practice. Recently, the firm advised Lukoil on its $350m convertible bond issue. It also advised VimpelCom on its $250m loan from JPMorgan.

Baker & McKenzie has established an extremely strong reputation in this area. Highly rated former Kiev managing partner David Scott heads the team. In 2002-03, it acted on one of the most successful recent eurobond issues, when it advised Alrosa Company on its $500m issue. Managing partner Max Gutbrod and Mitchell Gitin both have strong reputations for advising foreign banks. Clients include the EBRD and Gazprombank.

Coudert Brothers LLP has 'unparalleled experience' of finance matters relating to the Russian energy sector. The firm acted for the borrowers in the first project financings in the early '90s. In 2002-03, it advised TNK on two major financings supported by US Eximbank – a $334m financing involving the rehabilitation of the Samotlor oilfield, and a $231m financing involving the modernisation of TNK's refinery in Ryazan. Both restructurings closed in September 2003. Larisa Afanasyeva and St Petersburg managing partner Derek Bloom are recommended. Clients include Sakhalin Energy Investment Company.

John Balsdon's arrival at **Herbert Smith CIS Legal Services**'s Moscow office in September 2002 having departed **Clifford Chance CIS Ltd**, has put the firm's banking capability into a different league. Balsdon is one of the leading banking lawyers in Russia and brought with him an outstanding team including one senior and one junior assistant. Since joining, he has acted for ING on a $400m syndicated loan to TNK (the largest in Russia at the time). Key clients include ABN Amro, Credit Suisse First Boston, and Société Générale .

Latham & Watkins LLP is highly recommended for private equity matters.

Though **LeBoeuf, Lamb, Greene & MacRae** is primarily corporate focused, the firm nevertheless boasts considerable banking expertise. Brian Zimbler, who divides his time between London and Moscow, is particularly highly rated. Oleg Berger has 'a wealth of knowledge and local contacts'. Jonathan Hines is recommended for development financing in the energy and natural resources sector. Clients include Citibank and Rabobank

'Extremely knowledgeable' partner Mathieu Fabre-Magnan leads **Salans**' banking and finance activities. Between 1994 and 2003, the firm advised the EBRD on the $300m Russia Small Business Fund Programme. Its extensive work for the EBRD and experience in project and trade finance puts **Salans** among the leading firms in this area.

Skadden, Arps, Slate, Meagher & Flom LLP provides high-level advice on the full range of corporate finance and banking transactions. The firm recently acted for Salomon Brothers on the establishment of a GDR programme for bonds issued by the Russian ministry of finance. Other clients include Bank of America and Bank of Moscow.

Moscow managing partner David Griston oversees **CMS Cameron McKenna**'s activities in this area. He specialises in trade and project financings and has advised international and Russian banks on a range of investment projects throughout the region. A talented team of associates, notably Anna Proshina, who frequently leads financing matters and has built a significant following, supports him. The firm advised an Austrian bank on a $150m secured facility to a major Russian bank. It also advised Raiffeisen Zentralbank on a $33m unsecured loan to Ural Siberian Bank. Leonid Zubarev is also recommended.

While more focused on capital markets advice, **Cleary Gottlieb Steen & Hamilton LLC** has nevertheless developed a strong track record for banking matters. In November 2002, the firm advised OAO Gazprom on its $450m secured syndicated loan arranged by ABN Amro, Hypo- und Veriensbank, Dexia, and West LB.

Managing partner Peter Zier oversees **Nörr Stiefenhofer Lutz**'s banking and finance activities. In 2002-03, the firm advised Europe's largest manufacturer of agricultural machines on the financing of its greenfield investment in Krasnodar.

In a busy year, **Norton Rose**'s banking and finance practice has experienced exponential growth. The firm is particularly strong in the areas of commodities, trade financings, insolvency, and secured lending. The firm has been active advising international financial institutions such as the EBRD, western banks including Citibank and ABN Amro, as well as Russian borrowers, notably Lukoil.

Senior Russian lawyer Sergei Avramov, formerly of **Baker & McKenzie**, heads **Beiten Burkhardt**'s banking and finance team. He has been advising the Duma on derivatives legislation. The firm's managing partner Christian von Wistinghausen is also recommended.

Chadbourne & Parke LLP's managing partner Laura Brank is recommended for her extensive experience in corporate finance, project finance, and secured and unsecured lending. Patrick Seferovich is highly rated for his energy sector project and structured finance expertise. He represented Gazprom on energy-related projects, including the $2.3bn Blue Stream Pipeline project.

In December 2002, **Debevoise & Plimpton LLC** headed by Dmitri Nikiforov represented Aeroflot in the sale and leaseback of ten Boeing 737 aircraft from General Electric Capital Aviation Services (GECAS). The firm also has a reputation for advice on project financings in the oil and gas sector. Holly Nielsen is also recommended.

Denton Wilde Sapte's managing partner Doran Doeh has considerable experience and expertise in this area.

Vladimir Mednikov, managing partner at **Jurinflot, International Law Office**, has a reputation for ship finance advice.

Monastyrsky, Zyuba, Stepanov & Partners has a track record in this area having acted for clients such as JPMorganChase in insolvency litigation.

Albert Eganyan heads strong local four-partner firm **Vegas-Lex Law Firm**. Clients include American Express.

CAPITAL MARKETS: RUSSIA

Capital markets work is currently plentiful in Russia. Oil and gas-related bond and share offerings are commonplace and there is a large number of first-rate firms competing for market share.

Akin Gump Strauss Hauer & Feld LLP's handling of US and European capital markets financing of Russian companies is 'unsurpassed'. The firm advised VimpelCom on the first US SEC-registered IPO of a Russian issuer in the US. It also advised Lukoil on the first full listing by a Russian issuer of its ordinary shares on the London Stock Exchange. Recent highlights include advising Lukoil on its $350m convertible bond issue.

Irina Mashlenko heads **Allen & Overy**'s 'impressive' capital markets practice. She is strongly supported by Moscow managing partner Peter Timchur. In 2002-03, the firm acted on some of the first debt capital markets transactions since the 1998 crisis. Mashlenko advised ING Bank as manager of a $125m eurobond issue by Bank Zenit though a SPV in Luxembourg. Other clients of note include ABN Amro and Société Générale .

Cleary Gottlieb Steen & Hamilton LLC's Moscow practice is headed by highly-rated counsel Scott Senecal. In 2002-03, the firm advised on the largest Russian equity offering and the largest ever Russian corporate bond. In December 2002,it was counsel to the underwriter, Morgan Stanley, on the $775m offering by OAO Lukoil in the form of ADSs. In February 2003, the largest corporate bond offering saw the firm advise OAO Gazprom on its $1.75bn eurobond.

Michael Cuthbert and Arthur Iliev lead **Clifford Chance CIS Ltd**'s capital markets practice. The team advised MDM bank on the establishment of a $300m programme for the issuance of loan participation notes. It also advised Sibneft on the issue of $900m of loan participation notes. Other major clients include Alfa Bank, Citibank and Goldman Sachs.

Freshfields Bruckhaus Deringer's Tobias Mueller-Deku has 'firmly established his and the firm's position at the forefront of the market'. This is due in large part to the firm's role in Russia's first two domestic IPOs. It advised Aton Capital Group on the listing of the Internet company OAO RBC Information Systems. The firm also advised ING Bank as lead manager on the second domestic IPO in Russia by the Moscow Chemists chain 36.6.

Latham & Watkins LLP's managing partner Anya Goldin has established an 'outstanding reputation' for her work in this area. The firm has a particularly strong track record for advising on complex equity issues. In 2003, it advised Mobile TeleSystems, Russia's largest mobile phone company, on its NYSE listing.

Senior Russian partner Dmitry Dobatkin leads **Linklaters CIS**' 'extremely strong' capital markets practice. A remarkably successful year included acting for the sponsors, Morgan Stanley, on the listing of Lukoil on the London Stock Exchange, the first full listing of a Russian issuer in London. The firm also advised Dresdner Kleinwort Wasserstein and Morgan Stanley on Gazprom's $1.75bn debut bond issue, the largest ever by a Russian corporate. Managing partner Dominic Sanders is also highly recommended.

Skadden, Arps, Slate, Meagher & Flom LLP has an extremely strong reputation for advice on capital markets transactions, particularly top level equity deals. The firm advised the underwriters of the IPO, subsequent secondary listing and eurobond issue by, leading Russian mobile operator, VimpelCom. The IPO was the first SEC-registered offering by a Russian issuer since 1917. It also advised Yukos on its proposed equity and debt offerings.

Partner Alexandra Rutstein heads **White & Case LLC**'s capital markets practice and is universally lauded. She gains strong support from two 'outstanding' London partners, Francis Fitzherbert-Brockholes and Tim Jeveons. The firm has particular strength on the debt side. It advised TNK on a debut $400m eurobond, subsequently increased by a Regulation S $300m eurobond. **White & Case LLC** also advised UBS Warburg and Merrill Lynch as joint lead managers in a $175m Regulation S eurobond offering by Alfa Bank. Other notable clients include ABN Amro and Gazprombank.

Baker & McKenzie has established an extremely strong reputation in this area. Highly rated former Kiev managing partner David Scott, who heads the team, has significant capital markets experience. In 2002-03, it acted on one of the most successful recent eurobond issues, when it advised Alrosa Company on its $500m issue.

Coudert Brothers LLP partner Larisa Afanasyeva led the team that advised the Russian Federal Property Fund in its $775m public offering of shares in Lukoil on the London Stock Exchange. This was a groundbreaking transaction as it was the first Russian privatisation to take the form of sale of ADRs.

Debevoise & Plimpton LLC's team headed by Dmitri Nikiforov has experience in this area. Particularly for telecoms clients.

Herbert Smith CIS Legal Services is now able to field an impressive triumvirate of partners in this area. Managing partner Alan Hanen is particularly highly recommended. Banking specialist John Balsdon and Robin Wittering provide strong support.

Hogan & Hartson L.L.P.'s three-partner team is led by Michael Cheroutes who divides his time between London and Moscow. It also includes managing partner Peter Pettibone and Sergey Komolov.

Highly rated partners Brian Zimbler and Oleg Berger lead **LeBoeuf, Lamb, Greene & MacRae**'s activities in this area. On the equity side, the firm advised leading pharmacy chain 36.6 on the international offering of 20% its shares. On the debt side, it advised the lead manager on a $125m eurobond offering. Clients include Deutsche Bank and ABN Amro.

Partner Chris Viner leads **Norton Rose**'s capital markets practice. He gains strong support from Dimitry Gravin. The pair advised Bayerische Hypo-und Vereinsbank on derivatives arrangements with Russian counterparts. Other notable clients include HSBC and Rothschild Group.

Salans' partners Mathieu Fabre-Magnan and Robert Sexton have expertise in this area.

CAPITAL MARKETS: RUSSIA

- AKIN GUMP STRAUSS HAUER & FELD LLP ✪
- ALLEN & OVERY ✪
- CLEARY GOTTLIEB STEEN & HAMILTON LLC ✪
- CLIFFORD CHANCE CIS LTD
- FRESHFIELDS BRUCKHAUS DERINGER ✪
- LATHAM & WATKINS LLP ✪
- LINKLATERS CIS ✪
- SKADDEN, ARPS, SLATE, MEAGHER & FLOM LLP
- WHITE & CASE LLC

- Baker & McKenzie ✪
- Coudert Brothers LLP ✪
- Debevoise & Plimpton LLC
- Herbert Smith CIS Legal Services ✪
- Hogan & Hartson L.L.P. ✪
- LeBoeuf, Lamb, Greene & MacRae
- Norton Rose
- Salans

Firms are listed A-Z in tiers which are ranked in order of priority

✪ Indicates firm displays contact details at the end of this chapter.

CORPORATE AND COMMERCIAL/ M&A: MOSCOW

The Russian M&A market was remarkably buoyant in 2003, sustaining the corporate practices at a large number of firms. The energy and natural resources sector was most active. In what is a highly competitive market, clients are advised to shop around for the best value.

All change at **Coudert Brothers LLP** in 2002-03. Highly rated former managing partner Charles Keefe relocated to New York after five years in charge. Jonathan Cahn, previously managing partner of the Almaty office, succeeded him. Olga Anisimova also became a partner. The firm advised the Russian Federal Property Fund in its $775m public offering of shares in Lukoil on the London Stock Exchange. The firm also advised the Russian Federal Property Fund in its $1.85bn sale

CORPORATE AND COMMERCIAL/ M&A: MOSCOW

COUDERT BROTHERS LLP ⊙
FRESHFIELDS BRUCKHAUS DERINGER ⊙
LEBOEUF, LAMB, GREENE & MACRAE
LINKLATERS CIS ⊙
WHITE & CASE LLC

AKIN GUMP STRAUSS HAUER & FELD LLP ⊙
ALLEN & OVERY ⊙
BAKER & McKENZIE ⊙
CMS CAMERON MCKENNA
CLIFFORD CHANCE CIS LTD
HERBERT SMITH CIS LEGAL SERVICES ⊙
SALANS
SKADDEN, ARPS, SLATE, MEAGHER & FLOM LLP

CMS Bureau Francis Lefebvre ⊙
Chadbourne & Parke
Cleary Gottlieb Steen & Hamilton LLC ⊙
Debevoise & Plimpton LLC
Gide Loyrette Nouel ⊙
Hogan & Hartson L.L.P. ⊙
Latham & Watkins LLP ⊙
Nörr Stiefenhofer Lutz ⊙
Norton Rose

Beiten Burkhardt Rechtsanwälte (Attorneys-at-Law) ⊙
Jurinflot, International Law Office ⊙
Klishin & Partners
Lovells ⊙
Pepeliaev, Goltsblat & Partners ⊙
Russin & Vecchi LLC ⊙

Denton Wilde Sapte ⊙
Gorodissky & Partners
Laptev & Partners
Reznick, Gagarin & Partner

Haarmann Hemmelrath ⊙
Monastyrsky, Zyuba, Stepanov & Partners ⊙
PricewaterhouseCoopers CIS Law Offices BV
Squire, Sanders & Dempsey (Moscow) LLC ⊙

AR Consulting Law Firm ⊙
Alimirzoev & Trofimov
Alrud Law Firm ⊙
Blishchenko & Partners
Egorov, Puginsky, Afanasiev & Partners LLC ⊙
Smirnov, Davydov & Susskind Law Offices ⊙
Vegas-Lex Law Firm ⊙

Firms are listed A-Z in tiers which are ranked in order of priority
⊙ *Indicates firm displays contact details at the end of this chapter.*

of a 75% stake in Slavneft. Other notable clients include Telenor.

Jacky Baudon, the charming corporate generalist with a wealth of Russia experience, leads **Freshfields Bruckhaus Deringer**'s 'formidable' 35-lawyer Moscow presence. The team also boasts three of the strongest partners active in Russia: banking and capital markets-focused Tobias Müller-Deku; corporate and disputes partner Michael Schwartz; and energy-focused corporate partner Kirsten Floss. The firm has advised numerous oil majors on their joint ventures with local partners and on acquisitions of shares in Russian oil companies

LeBoeuf, Lamb, Greene & MacRae has been active in the Russian market for over 14 years. The wealth of experience displayed by the firm's four 'outstanding' partners – Oleg Berger, John Huhs, Brian Zimbler, and Jonathan Hines – paid major dividends in 2002-03. The firm provided corporate/M&A advice to energy sector clients on the market-leading deals. Most notably, Oleg Berger led the team that advised Yukos on its $35bn acquisition of Sibneft. The firm is heavily involved in the Sakhalin projects. It is also active throughout the CIS, and has offices in Moscow, Kazakhstan and Kyrgyzstan. Other clients include Exxon Mobil and Interbrew.

The 'impressive' Dominic Sanders heads **Linklaters CIS**' corporate team. The firm advised BP on its $20bn merger with TNK to create BP-TNK, the seventh largest oil company in the world. This deal also involved the largest investment in Russia to date. The firm advised PricewaterhouseCoopers on its $3.5bn sale of the consulting business to IBM Global. Another major deal saw **Linklaters CIS** advise Scottish & Newcastle on its $1.7bn acquisition of Harwell. Denis Uvarov, one of the firm's two outstanding Russian partners, is highly recommended for his experience in advising large Russian and multinational companies particularly in the energy sector.

Under the auspices of the 'universally respected' Hugh Verrier, **White & Case LLC** has successfully established a market-leading reputation. The corporate team also includes outstanding partners Eric Michailov, Igor Ostapets, Marc Polonsky and counsel Maya Melnikas. The firm is particularly active in the telecommunications, real estate and oil and gas industries. In 2003, Ostapets led the team that advised TNK and its shareholders Alfa/Access/Renova Group on its JV with BP. As part of the deal, BP purchased a 50% stake for $6.15bn from TNK's shareholders in the biggest foreign investment in Russia. Other notable clients include TeliaSonera and Marconi plc.

Richard Wilkie heads **Akin Gump Strauss Hauer & Feld LLP**'s Moscow practice. He is supported by Natalia Baratiants in Moscow, as well as Robert Langer (who divides his time between New York and Moscow), Melissa Schwartz (Washington DC and Moscow), and Daniel Walsh (London and Moscow). The team has a strong reputation for top-end corporate, capital markets and energy-related work. In 2002-03, highlights included advising Lukoil on its $350m bond issue. The firm also advised VimpelCom on its $250m loan from JPMorgan. Other notable clients include Alfa Group.

Allen & Overy's successful corporate team is headed by Edwin Tham. In 2002-03, he led the team that advised Transroup AS and Brunswick Capital on the establishment and funding of a new railcar leasing company. The 'highly personable' managing partner Peter Timchur led the team that advised a major international communications company on four acquisitions. Clients include Shell and Sibneft.

James Hitch heads **Baker & McKenzie**'s 'extremely strong', nine-partner corporate team. Peers regularly single out Paul Melling for recognition as one of the most experienced lawyers in Moscow. The firm is active across a wide range of sectors, including oil and gas, telecoms, pharmaceuticals, e-commerce and IT. In 2002-03, the firm advised Sibir Energy on the incorporation of the Moscow oil and gas company. Managing partner Max Gutbrod is also recommended. Other clients include Lukoil and Diageo.

David Griston became **CMS Cameron McKenna**'s Moscow office managing partner in October 2002, following John Hammond's relocation to Stuttgart. David Marshall has developed some of the more complex acquisitions and mergers in the market. Recently appointed partner Leonid Zubarev heads the firm's four-lawyer commercial group and is recognised as a leading pensions and insurance expert. He advised the Russian government on pension fund reform. The firm advised an international financial group on the acquisition of a Russian insurance company. Key clients include Aeroflot, Alcatel, and Hitachi Data Systems.

Clifford Chance CIS Ltd's Moscow practice underwent significant changes in 2002-03 precipitated in large part by the departure of partner John Balsdon to **Herbert Smith CIS Legal Services**. The firm appointed a managing partner and senior partner double act of Ivan Marisin and Michael Cuthbert, who also took on the role of regional managing partner for Central and Eastern Europe and the Russian Federation. Marc Bartholomy returned from Düsseldorf to head the Moscow corporate team. Under this new management regime, the firm is seeking increased penetration of the local Russian corporate sector in order to reduce dependence on international banks in an excessively competitive market. The firm advised Rusal on numerous transactions. Other notable clients include Deutsche Telekom and Nike.

Herbert Smith CIS Legal Services makes a meteoric ascent of our tables. This is due in no small part to the arrival in September 2002 of John Balsdon from **Clifford Chance CIS Ltd**. Balsdon is widely considered to be one of the leading banking lawyers in Russia. He brought with him an outstanding team including one senior and one junior assistant. Since joining, he has acted for ING on a $400m syndicated loan to TNK (the largest in Russia at the time). He also led the second largest corporate deal in Russia, advising Inpex on its $1.375bn acquisition of a 10% stake in the Azen-Chirag-Gunashi project.

The transfer from London of corporate partner Robin Wittering also considerably strengthened the firm's corporate capability.

Jane Tarassova heads **Salans**' Moscow office. The six-partner team also includes Sergei Marinich, Robert Sexton, Mathieu Fabre-Magnan, Anna McDonald, and Oleg Konnov. The 11-partner global Russian practice group drawing on expertise in London, Paris, and New York supports these partners, who are based in Moscow full time. In 2002-03, Robert Sexton returned from Paris to head the corporate/M&A team. The firm regularly advises major multinationals such as Gillette and Diageo on corporate matters.

Two factors paid significant dividends for **Skadden, Arps, Slate, Meagher & Flom LLP** in 2002-03. First, the firm's redoubtable global reputation, which proved attractive to Russia's super-rich energy sector oligarchs. Second the arrival of Andrey Dacourt, formerly a prominent member of the firm's Moscow team, as in-house counsel at Sibneft's holding company, Millhouse Capital. The combination of these factors saw the firm instructed on the headline deal of the year in Russia. A team led by 'formidable' London partner Bruce Buck advised Sibneft on the proposed $35bn merger with Yukos. Alexey Kiyashko heads the Moscow office.

Paris-based **CMS Bureau Francis Lefebvre** operates an 18-lawyer office in Moscow, is a member of the *CMS* network, and works closely with **CMS Cameron McKenna**.

Laura Brank is managing partner of **Chadbourne & Parke LLP**'s Moscow office. She has advised clients on their activities in the CIS for ten years and now divides her time between London and Moscow. Brank has extensive experience in corporate governance, corporate finance, project finance, and secured and unsecured lending. She recently advised Golden Telecom on its $100m acquisition of Sovintel. She also recently advised Gallaher Ltd, an English company, on its $390m acquisition of Liggett-Ducat, one of the largest acquisitions of a Russian company by a foreign company at the time.

Cleary Gottlieb Steen & Hamilton LLC's Moscow office, headed by highly regarded counsel Scott Senecal, has 12 resident lawyers. An additional 20 lawyers in the firm's other offices contribute to the Russian practice. The firm focuses mainly on three areas: capital markets where it is 'pre-eminent', banking and finance, and corporate. In 2002-03, it advised Yukos on its $100m JV with TNK to own and manage Rospan International.

Dmitri Nikiforov heads **Debevoise & Plimpton LLC**'s Moscow office. In December 2003, the firm acted for Aeroflot on the sale and leaseback of ten Boeing 737 aircraft from General Electric Capital Aviation Services (GECAS). Holly Nielsen also has considerable corporate and finance expertise.

Senior associate David Lasfargue heads **Gide Loyrette Nouel**'s Moscow presence. A strong 12-lawyer team supports him. The firm is active on M&A deals for European (particularly French) clients such as Lafarge.

Hogan & Hartson L.L.P.'s 'able' managing partner Peter Pettibone has considerable experience of providing M&A advice to clients in the Russian telecoms, oil and gas, and real estate sectors. In 2002-03 the firm advised a major international client on a $1bn sale of assets in the Russian oil industry.

Anya Goldin heads **Latham & Watkins LLP**'s Moscow office. She has an outstanding reputation, particularly for capital markets advice. The firm was also extremely active on corporate deals throughout 2002-03. It advised on seven large deals, including acting for the shareholders in the acquisition of a Ukrainian telecoms company.

Managing partner Peter Zier presided over a highly successful year for **Nörr Stiefenhofer Lutz**'s Moscow practice, which was established in1994. It grew extremely quickly in 2002-03, with the recruitment of 11 additional lawyers. This was largely as a response to the transfer of production lines from Western Europe. The firm is particularly active in the motor industry, where clients include Volkswagen and Audi, and the pharmaceutical sector where a major client is Fresenius. Nikolaj Piksin is recommended for litigation and solving problems arising between western investors and local companies. Ilja Rybalkin provides advice on local tax structures. Both provide strong support to the 13-lawyer corporate team. Other clients include Bombadier.

Valentina Gluhovskaya heads **Norton Rose**'s three-partner Moscow office. Since it became the first UK firm to open a Moscow office in 1991, the firm has built up a team of 18 associates, nicely balanced between UK and home grown Russian lawyers. Gluhovskaya and Chris Viner are recommended for corporate matters, particularly in the energy and real estate sectors. In 2002-03, the firm advised Rosneft on the takeover of Anglo Siberian.

Highly rated partner Christian von Wistinghausen heads **Beiten Burkhardt**'s 14-lawyer Russia team based in Moscow an St Petersburg. The firm acts mainly for European clients, two-thirds of which are from German-speaking countries. It is most active in the motor industry.

Vladimir Mednikov is managing partner of **Jurinflot, International Law Office**. The firm is largely focused on maritime matters, but is fast developing a strong reputation for corporate advice. Clients include Lukoil.

Alexei Klishin is managing partner of **Klishin & Partners**. The firm has established itself as one of the leading Russian firms with a large number of offices around Russia.

Chris Owen is managing partner of **Lovells**' two-partner Moscow office. Oxana Balayan is recommended for corporate matters. The firm advised Alstrom on the sale of its turbine business to Siemens.

Pepeliaev, Goltsblat & Partners is the most ambitious, and Western oriented, local firm in Russia. Its ambition includes growth from its current 45 lawyers to over 120 in the next three years. There is every reason to believe that, under the auspices of dynamic managing partners, Andrey Goltsblat who oversees the tax team, and Sergey Papeliev who heads the corporate and commercial team, this is eminently achievable. The firm boasts an impressive range of corporate clients including Mars and Pepsi.

Russin & Vecchi LLC's Moscow office is headed by name partner Jonathan Russin. The firm has three offices in Russia located in Moscow, Vladivostok and Yuzhno-Sakhalinsk. It was the first international firm to establish a presence in the Russian Far East. It has a reputation for advising oil and gas companies, and construction companies on general corporate matters. Major clients include Exxon Mobil, BP Amoco and Yukos. Partner Sergei Lazarev is also recommended.

Denton Wilde Sapte's five-lawyer Moscow office is headed by the widely respected Doran Doeh. The firm continues to perform at the top end of the market despite its small size and the loss of Patrick Seferovich to **Chadbourne & Parke LLP**. It is especially active in the energy sector, where Doeh is rated as one of the leading lawyers for upstream matters currently working in Russia.

Gorodissky & Partners is widely recognised as one of Russia's leading firms for IP advice. Managing partner Valery Medvedev heads the 11-partner firm with offices in Moscow, St Petersburg, Novi Novgorod, Krasnodar, Samara, Ekaterinburg, and Kiev. Clients include Du Pont, Unilever, and Motorola.

Laptev & Partners is recommended for advice to clients in the energy sector.

Nikolay Gagarin of **Reznick, Gagarin & Partner** is recommended for general corporate and commercial advice.

Firms in the sixth and seventh tiers are able to provide a reasonable standard of general corporate matters.

CORPORATE AND COMMERCIAL/ M&A: ST PETERSBURG

The shipping and automotive sectors generate a considerable amount of work for St Petersburg-based law firms.

Outstanding generalist Maxim Kalinin heads **Baker & McKenzie**'s St Petersburg office. He has 'significant expertise' in corporate as well as real estate and arbitration. The firm has a strong manufacturing sector client base with particular emphasis on the motor industry. It also acts for prominent telecoms and construction clients.

Highly experienced partner Derek Bloom heads **Coudert Brothers LLP**' St Petersburg presence. He has 'impressive knowledge', having advised Russia's Federal Commission for the Securities Market on its preparation of a corporate governance code. In 2002-03, the firm advised Russia's largest pulp and paper manufacturer Ilim Pulp Enterprise on its hostile takeover defence. Washington, DC partner Richard Dean also played

CORPORATE AND COMMERCIAL/ M&A: ST PETERSBURG

BAKER & McKENZIE ✪

Coudert Brothers LLP
Salans

Beiten Burkhardt Rechtsanwälte (Attorneys-at-Law)
Castrén & Snellman St Petersburg Ltd ✪
Clyde & Co ✪
Egorov, Puginsky, Afanasiev & Partners LLC
Hough, Kuraev & Co
JP Galmond & Co
Mannheimer Swartling ✪
Shcheglov & Partners

Firms are listed A-Z in tiers which are ranked in order of priority
✪ Indicates firm displays contact details at the end of this chapter.

a prominent role. Other clients include and Telenor.

Glenn Kolleeny heads **Salans**' 17-fee-earner St Petersburg office. He is recommended for M&A, capital markets, and structured finance matters. The firm has established a strong reputation advising multinational corporations on setting up operations in the region. In 2002-03, the firm advised the selling shareholders, including Barings Vostok and Creditanstalt Investment Bank, on the $300m sale of a controlling interest in Syktyvkar Forest Enterprise.

Beiten Burkhardt has established a strong reputation for advice to European and mainly German-speaking clients, particularly in the motor industry. Thomas Heidemann, who mans the firm's Russia desk in Düsseldorf, is also recommended.

Sergei Lee and Sergei Mamiev are the contacts for **Castrén & Snellman St Petersburg Ltd**. The firm founded its St Petersburg subsidiary in 1994. The St Petersburg office offers a comprehensive range of corporate and commercial matters to a variety of clients, most of whom are non-Russian. All matters are undertaken with supervision of the Helsinki office.

Trevor Barton heads **Clyde & Co**'s St Petersburg office. His main areas of practice are asset finance and he focuses on trade, insurance, shipping and ship finance, debt recovery and inward investment into Russia. The firm has a wealth of experience acting for western insurers and reinsurers on substantial claims in Russia.

Name partner Nikolai Egorov oversees **Egorov, Puginsky, Afanasiev & Partners LLC**'s St Petersburg practice. He is recommended for corporate and real estate matters. Ilya Nikiforov is recommended for IP and international arbitration.

William Hough, Vladimir Kuraev and Vadim Malashev at **Hough, Kuraev & Co** undertake a range of corporate and M&A advice for SMEs.

JP Galmond & Co has a reputaion for advice to clients in the telecoms sector.

Sven Lexner oversees **Mannheimer Swartling** St Petersburg office. It advises companies on start-ups, joint ventures, and acquisitions. The firm also represents companies and organisations in Eastern European-related arbitral proceedings, primarily in Moscow, Stockholm and Kiev.

DISPUTE RESOLUTION: RUSSIA

Lawyers who are not registered with the Russian Bar are forbidden from appearing before Russian courts.

Vladimir Haley heads **Baker & McKenzie**'s four-partner team. The firm advised a major energy sector client on two arbitrations in Stockholm relating to the development and construction of a new mining platform. The team also includes Paul Melling, Eugene Arievich and Evgeny Reyzman.

Clifford Chance CIS Ltd's 'redoubtable' Moscow managing partner Ivan Marisin leads the four-lawyer dispute resolution practice. The team acted for Moscow Narodny Bank in a dispute with Vneshtogbank.

Herbert Smith CIS Legal Services draws heavily on the 'impressive expertise' of London-based partner Simon Bushell. The firm wins praise throughout the Russian market for its work in international arbitrations. In 2002-03, the firm acted for CSFB on various issues relating to the supervisor-subordinate relationship.

Linklaters CIS' Alexei Dudko has attracted much praise from peers for his litigation expertise.

DISPUTE RESOLUTION: RUSSIA

BAKER & McKENZIE ✪
CLIFFORD CHANCE CIS LTD
HERBERT SMITH CIS LEGAL SERVICES ✪
LINKLATERS CIS ✪
MONASTYRSKY, ZYUBA, STEPANOV & PARTNERS ✪
SALANS
SIKAYLO, MATVEEV, GABBASOV & PARTNERS ✪

CMS Cameron McKenna
Chadbourne & Parke LLP
Coudert Brothers LLP ✪
Freshfields Bruckhaus Deringer ✪
Jurinflot, International Law Office ✪
Norton Rose
White & Case LLC

Akin Gump Strauss Hauer & Feld LLP ✪
Gowlings International Inc ✪
Haarmann Hemmelrath ✪
Intellect Ltd
Klishin & Partners
LeBoeuf, Lamb, Greene & MacRae
Nörr Stiefenhofer Lutz ✪
Russin & Vecchi LLC ✪
Vegas-Lex Law Firm ✪

Firms are listed A-Z in tiers which are ranked in order of priority
✪ Indicates firm displays contact details at the end of this chapter.

He gains strong support from London-based partner Tom Lidstrom, co-ordinator of the firm's injunction task force. The team acted for Pratt & Whitney in litigation by a minority shareholder to challenge the client's ownership of shares in Perm Motor Complex, a leading Russian aerospace group.

Monastyrsky, Zyuba, Stepanov & Partners' Yuri Monastyrsky has established a leading reputation for his litigation and arbitration expertise. Contentious matters account for at least half of the firm's practice. Tax-related disputes are another speciality.

Sergei Marinich leads **Salans**' dispute resolution team. The firm has been advising Diageo since 1995 on litigation relating to the Smirnoff trade mark. Robert Sexton and Georgy Azarov are also recommended.

Alexey Sikaylo is managing partner of six-partner **Sikaylo, Matveev, Gabbasov & Partners**. The focus of the 30-fee-earner firm is dispute resolution. The firm acted for commercial bank Aliba Alliance in its dispute with the Russian Federation in the European Court. Dimitry Matveev is also recommended.

CMS Cameron McKenna's dispute resolution team has recovered well from the loss of Yuri Efimov, who left the firm to set up his own practice. This recovery is thanks in large part to the firm's 'dynamic' litigators Vasily Zolotyuk (a former judge) and Sergey Yuriev.

Chadbourne & Parke LLP has a strong track record in debt recovery and debt restructuring-related disputes and has acted for the EBRD. It also acts for numerous manufacturing sector clients.

Highly respected partner Olga Anisimova heads **Coudert Brothers LLP**'s dispute resolution group. In 2002-03, the firm represented Royal Dutch/Shell's interests in a dispute between Salym Petroleum Development (SPD) and the Russian Ministry of Natural Resources regarding the fulfilment by SPD of its licence obligations. Larisa Afanasyeva is also recommended. The firm also advised Total on a tax dispute.

Highly rated partner Michael Schwartz leads **Freshfields Bruckhaus Deringer**'s disputes team. The firm advises on both domestic and international disputes before courts and arbitrators. It recently took a leading role in one of the most significant cases in Russia, acting for Petrochemical Holding AG, an Austrian creditor, in bankruptcy proceedings against AK Sibur, one of the largest local petrochemical holdings.

Jurinflot, International Law Office is highly recommended for disputes in the transport sector, particularly shipping-related matters. Managing partner Vladimir Mednikov and Vadim Ermolaev have strong reputations.

In 2002-03, **Norton Rose** experienced a considerable increase in the number of cross-jurisdictional claims in both international arbitrations and Russian civil courts. The firm continued to act for Archangel Diamond

Corporation in its dispute over the transfer of a mineral licence from a Russian company to a joint venture company. The firm represents a number of other natural resources companies, including Lukoil. Valentina Gluhovskaya and Dmitry Gravin are recommended.

In summer 2003, counsel William Spiegelberger joined **White & Case LLC**'s Moscow office from **Milbank, Tweed, Hadley & McCloy LLP** in New York to head the disputes practice His experience, including international commercial arbitration and multi-jurisdictional litigation in New York and Paris, makes him an ideal fit with the Moscow practice. David Miller also joined from **Hogan & Hartson L.L.P.**'s New York office in September 2003. They are strongly supported by Igor Ostapets. The team represented TNK in a successful application before the British Virgin Islands High Court to lift a freezing order on $383m of its Russian oil assets. Other notable clients include Nestlé Waters and Sidanco.

Marina Dumina at **Akin Gump Strauss Hauer & Feld LLP** has established a strong reputation for contentious matters. She has particular experience of employment and competition matters as well as advising oil industry clients on contract disputes before the International Commercial Arbitration Court.

Gowlings International Inc's Marina Drel has a leading reputation for contentious IP maters, while **Haarmann Hemmelrath** has a reputation for contentious matters and has international arbitration expertise.

Oleg Berger at **LeBoeuf, Lamb, Greene & MacRae** has considerable experience of international dispute resolution.

Nikolaj Piksin heads **Nörr Stiefenhofer Lutz**'s litigation group. The firm recently acted for a German engineering company against a municipal enterprise before the arbitration court of Krasnodar. It frequently acts for major car manufacturing clients in a wide variety of disputes.

Russin & Vecchi LLC is recommended for its international arbitration work. The firm advises telecoms and energy sector clients on contentious matters.

Vegas-Lex Law Firm has a reputation for arbitration and work in the Commercial Court.

EMPLOYMENT: RUSSIA

Evgeny Reyzman heads **Baker & McKenzie**'s excellent ten-fee-earner team. Julia Borozdna has a good reputation for disputes. The firm advised ZAO Ligget Ducat on a successful collective bargaining with a federal trade union.

Linklaters CIS' Henry Rutstein rates among the leading employment lawyers in Moscow. The practice wins accolades for 'consistently providing high-level advice' on some of the most complex matters in the market. One example was the BP-TNK JV. Other clients include Dell, Glaxo-SmithKline, and Nokia.

EMPLOYMENT: RUSSIA

BAKER & McKENZIE ✪
LINKLATERS CIS ✪

Akin Gump Strauss Hauer & Feld LLP ✪
Nörr Stiefenhofer Lutz ✪

Firms are listed A-Z in tiers which are ranked in order of priority
✪ Indicates firm displays contact details at the end of this chapter.

Akin Gump Strauss Hauer & Feld LLP's Marina Dumina has a good reputation for advice on labour disputes

Nörr Stiefenhofer Lutz provides advice to major clients such as Volkswagen on various aspects of employment of Russian and foreign nationals by international clients as an integral part of its full service approach. The firm also has a strong track record for contentious matters.

ENERGY AND NATURAL RESOURCES: RUSSIA

The market for energy and natural resources-related legal services is thriving. Russia is home to a host of leading oil and gas companies, which regularly generate massive M&A deals and project financings.

Akin Gump Strauss Hauer & Feld LLP retained its leading position in the increasingly competitive market for energy sector advice despite the departures of Jonathan Socolow and Alexander Abasov. In 2002-03, the firm advised Lukoil on its $1.4bn sale of a 10% stake in the Azeri-Chirag-Guneshi oilfield in Azerbaijan to Inpex Corporation. It also advised the Alfa Group and Access Industries on their $380m slaw of a 15% stake in Sidanco to BP.

Freshfields Bruckhaus Deringer has established an outstanding reputation in this area. The firm advises leading commercial companies, host states, monopoly utility companies and top international financiers. In 2002-03 it advised Russia's largest oil company Yukos on an acquisition of local energy targets Geoilbent and Tomskneftegas. It also advised RAO UES, the national power monopoly, on the acquisition of electricity generation, distribution and transmission facilities in Georgia. Jacky Baudon and Kirsten Floss are both recommended.

LeBoeuf, Lamb, Greene & MacRae's Jonathan Hines is widely regarded as the 'most knowledgeable energy lawyer active in Russia' and the CIS. He leads the firm's extensive advice on cutting-edge production and pipeline projects throughout Russia, Kazakhstan, Azerbaijan and Uzbekistan. The team recently advised the Caspian Pipeline Consortium of three governments – Russia, Kazakhstan, and Oman – and eight major oil producers on a $2.6bn pipeline. Other notable clients in the sector include CNP, Yukos, and Exxon Mobil.

Linklaters CIS' two 'outstanding' Russian partners, Denis Uvarov and Dmitry Dobatkin, lead the highly successful energy practice. The firm has consistently taken a leading role on some of the most significant deals in the sector. It advised BP on the $20bn JV with TNK. The firm is also heavily involved, with a leading role advising the project company, on the $10bn Sakhalin project. Other clients include Lukoil and Morgan Stanley.

Marc Polonsky heads **White & Case LLC**'s energy and natural resources practice. Senior Russian partner Igor Ostapets and managing partner Hugh Verrier also have strong reputations for their work in this sector. In 2003, the firm continued its heavy involvement in the Sakhalin projects, involving the largest project financing in Russia – Phase II alone is valued at $10bn. It also advised Yukos on its JV with TotalFinaElf for the development of the Shatsky Ridge oil and gas field in the Black Sea. Clients include Chevron Texaco and Exxon Mobil.

Allen & Overy's Peter Timchur and Edwin Tham provide significant advice in the sector. The firm continued to advise Shell on the development of the Salym oilfield. It also advised JSC Rosneft on issues arising from the Sakhalin Project. Other notable clients include Lukoil.

Baker & McKenzie is recommended for advice on licensing issues relating to mineral mining. It has also advised some of Russia's leading oil companies including Lukoil. The firm advised Harvest on the sale of its 34% interest in Russian oil company, Geoilbent, to Yukos. Managing partner Max

ENERGY AND NATURAL RESOURCES: RUSSIA

AKIN GUMP STRAUSS HAUER & FELD LLP ✪
FRESHFIELDS BRUCKHAUS DERINGER ✪
LEBOEUF, LAMB, GREENE & MACRAE
LINKLATERS CIS ✪
WHITE & CASE LLC

ALLEN & OVERY ✪
BAKER & McKENZIE ✪
CMS CAMERON MCKENNA
CHADBOURNE & PARKE LLP
COUDERT BROTHERS LLP ✪
DENTON WILDE SAPTE ✪
HERBERT SMITH CIS LEGAL SERVICES ✪
SALANS
VINSON & ELKINS L.L.P. ✪

Clifford Chance CIS Ltd
Lovells ✪
Norton Rose
Russin & Vecchi LLC ✪

Laptev & Partners
Macleod Dixon LLP
Nörr Stiefenhofer Lutz ✪

Firms are listed A-Z in tiers which are ranked in order of priority
✪ Indicates firm displays contact details at the end of this chapter.

Gutbrod is particularly active in the sector. Other clients include Slavneft.

Moscow managing partner David Griston and Natalia Kozyrenko are the leading lights of **CMS Cameron McKenna**'s energy practice. Griston has advised on oil and gas transactions in Central Asia and Russia for the past ten years. Kozyrenko has an outstanding reputation. She led the team that advised Russia's monopoly electricity provider, RAO UES, on the creation of a competitive market. Head of the firm's Energy practice in London, Mark Moseley provided support. The firm has also accrued considerable expertise in both offshore and onshore upstream oil and gas projects in Russia. Notable clients include BP, which the firm advises on upstream matters, and Shell, to which the firm provides corporate advice.

Chadbourne & Parke LLP's capability in this area was considerably strengthened by the arrival of **Denton Wilde Sapte**'s former Moscow managing partner Patrick Seferovich in 2002. He has more than 20 years' experience of oil and gas exploration, production and transportation, and acquisitions and disposals of oil and gas properties. He has acted for Gazprom on numerous energy-related projects, including the $2.3bn Blue Stream Pipeline project.

Coudert Brothers LLP' reputation in this area is thanks largely to Charles Keefe who is recommended for his 'down-to-earth, pragmatic and business-oriented approach'. Though Keefe recently relocated to New York he will continue to focus on Russia-related matters. Along with John Sheedy and Olga Sirodoeva he advised TNK on two major financings supported by US Eximbank – a $334m financing involving the rehabilitation of the Samotlor oilfield, and a $231m financing involving the modernisation of TNK's refinery in Ryazan. Both restructurings closed in September 2003. Clients include Total, Royal Dutch/Shell, and Exxon Mobil.

Denton Wilde Sapte's small, five-lawyer Moscow office punches above its weight in the oil and gas sector. Managing partner Doran Doeh is particularly highly recommended. He has more that ten years' experience advising in the Russian energy sector. Peers universally regard him as one of the leading experts on upstream matters. Clients include Gazprom and Rosneft-Shell.

Sergei Baranchenkov leads **Herbert Smith CIS Legal Services**' activities in this area. The team is currently advising on two major deals in the sector. The firm has also undertaken impressive energy-related banking and corporate matters. The 'talented and experienced' John Balsdon advised ING on a $400m syndicated loan to TNK (the largest in Russia at the time). He also led the second largest corporate deal in Russia, advising Inpex on its $1.375bn acquisition of a 10% stake in the Azen-Chirag-Gunashi project. The transfer from London of corporate partner Robin Wittering has also strengthened the team.

Managing partner of **Salans**' Moscow office, Jane Tarassova has an outstanding reputation for energy-related M&A advice. St Petersburg-based partner Glenn Kolleeny is among the most experienced partners advising on the mineral and metal extraction industries. The firm acts for numerous Russian and international oil companies on a wide variety of matters.

As a firm, **Vinson & Elkins L.L.P.** has a superb global reputation for energy-related advice. The Russia practice is no exception. Douglas Glass heads the strong three-partner team. In 2002-03, the team advised Fortnum and Lukoil as sponsors of a $200m project finance transaction to develop the South Shapkinskoye oilfield. Natalya Morozova and Joel Lambert are also recommended.

Clifford Chance CIS Ltd advises a number of major clients in the sector. The firm advised Rusal on numerous transactions. It also acts for Sibneft and Norilsk Nickel. Moscow managing partner Ivan Marisin is recommended.

In 2002-03, **Lovells**' Oxana Balayan acted for Metal One on structuring a JV for supply of coated pipes in relation to development of oilfields in Sakhalin II.

Chris Viner and Valentina Gluhovskaya at **Norton Rose** both have strong reputations. The firm advised De Beers on a range of commercial and regulatory matters in the diamond sector as well as negotiations with Russian diamond monopoly, Alrosa. Other clients include Rosneft, which the firm advised on the takeover of Anglo Siberian, and Lukoil.

Russin & Vecchi LLC wins promotion in our rankings as a result of the firm's commitment to the sector. It is the first foreign firm to establish offices in Russia's far east and is heavily involved in the Sakhalin projects as a result. The firm's impressive client list includes ExxonMobil, BP, and Yukos. Jonathan Russin and Sergei Lazarev are recommended.

Laptev & Partners' oil and gas and mineral resources practice has established a strong reputation. The firm advises oil majors on their investments in oilfields in Russia and the CIS.

Macleod Dixon LLP boasts mining law specialist Ivan Trifonov. The firm regularly advises clients on mining and mineral exploration projects across Russia and the CIS.

In 2002-03, **Nörr Stiefenhofer Lutz** advised a major Norwegian ship building company on customs, tax and public law exemptions relating to a tender to ship oil from Sakhalin II.

INTELLECTUAL PROPERTY: RUSSIA

Highly experienced partner Evgeny Arievich heads **Baker & McKenzie**'s 11-lawyer IP team. In 2002-03 the firm successfully acted for Diageo in a dispute relating to the infringement of the Smirnoff trade mark in a number of countries, including Latvia, Lithuania, Estonia, Moldova and Ukraine. Other clients include British-American Tobacco.

INTELLECTUAL PROPERTY: RUSSIA

BAKER & McKENZIE ✪
GORODISSKY & PARTNERS
GOWLINGS INTERNATIONAL INC ✪

Lovells ✪
Nörr Stiefenhofer Lutz ✪
Salans

ARS-Patent
Beiten Burkhardt Rechtsanwälte (Attorneys-at-Law) ✪
Blishchenko & Partners
CMS Cameron McKenna
Freshfields Bruckhaus Deringer ✪
Hogan & Hartson L.L.P. ✪
Intellect Ltd
Klishin & Partners
Latham & Watkins LLP ✪
LeBoeuf, Lamb, Greene & MacRae
Linklaters CIS ✪
Norton Rose
Pepeliaev, Goltsblat & Partners ✪
PricewaterhouseCoopers CIS Law Offices BV

Firms are listed A-Z in tiers which are ranked in order of priority
✪ Indicates firm displays contact details at the end of this chapter.

Gorodissky & Partners is widely recognised as one of Russia's leading firms for IP advice. Managing partner Valery Medvedev heads the 11-partner firm with offices in Moscow, St Petersburg, Novi Novgorod, Krasnodar, Samara, Ekaterinburg, and Kiev. Clients include Du Pont, Unilever, and Motorola.

Magdelena Sekula heads the Moscow office of Canadian-based **Gowlings International Inc**. The team includes Marina Drel who is recommended for contentious matters; Vladamir Dementiev is recommended for patents advice.

As a firm, **Lovells** has an outstanding reputation for advice on IP matters. The Moscow practice is no exception. Trade mark protection and technology transfer, as well as patent advice are strengths.

Highly rated partner Julianna Tabastajewa heads **Nörr Stiefenhofer Lutz**'s strong IP/IT department. The vast majority of the firm's activities concern trade marks (protection of trade marks as well as licensing and franchising agreements). The firm also has an outstanding reputation for e-commerce advice, and has established a large Internet sector client base. It also has a good reputation in the media and entertainment sector, regularly advising German media conglomerates on IP issues relating to their interests in Russia.

Rated partner Sergei Marinich heads **Salans**' IP group. Robert Sexton and Denis Voevidin are also recommended.

Seven-lawyer St Petersburg-based firm **ARS-Patent** is particularly recommended for its advice on patent issues.

Beiten Burkhardt has a good reputation for advice on copyright issues and trade mark infringement. Managing partner Christian von Wistinghausen has developed something of a specialism advising on encryption matters.

CMS Cameron McKenna provides a range of clients with high-level advice on copyright and trade mark issues.

Latham & Watkins LLP has three lawyers focusing on anti-piracy full-time. The firm undertakes all such matters for Microsoft in Russia. Lev Simkin and Igor Sosnovsky are both recommended. Simkin has a strong reputation for contentious matters, particularly domain disputes.

LeBoeuf, Lamb, Greene & MacRae associate Veronika Fridman focuses on IP matters. The firm has advised a range of television, publishing and film clients. Brian Zimbler is also recommended for IT-related IP matters.

Alexei Dudko heads **Linklaters CIS**' ITC and IP team. He advises Russian and international companies on complex corporate, banking, and commercial matters, as well as providing IP advice. Highly rated associate Anna Shashina focuses on IP and particularly trade mark protection. In 2002-03, the firm successfully attracted some impressive new clients, including GlaxoSmithKline, JPMorgan, and Johnson & Johnson.

Dimitry Gravin at **Norton Rose** is recommended for advice on IP matters. The majority of the firm's work relates to IP infringement cases. Clients include well-known vodka brand Stolichnaya and Telecom Italia.

Pepeliaev, Goltsblat & Partners name partner Andrey Goltsblat is recommended for IP matters.

REAL ESTATE: RUSSIA

Newly made up partner Andrei Soukhomlinov heads **Baker & McKenzie**'s three-partner team. The team suffered the relocation of highly rated partner Adrian Moore to the Geneva office, though he remains heavily involved in Russia-related matters. St Petersburg managing partner Maxim Kalinin is also recommended.

Norton Rose wins a large proportion of Moscow's high-profile real estate projects. Managing partner Valentina Gluhovskaya is recognised as one of the leading specialists in Russia. The firm is kept busy by one of Russia's most acquisitive real estate developers, Capital Group. In 2002-03, the firm advised it on negotiations with the Moscow City Government on a mixed usage complex as part of the Moscow City project. Other clients include CSFB and HSBC

Real estate forms a major part of 'up-and-coming' local firm **Pepeliaev, Goltsblat & Partners**'s fast expanding practice. The firm has recently advised numerous multinational companies, particularly in the construction and food sectors, on the acquisition of substantial industrial land plots in the Moscow region.

REAL ESTATE: RUSSIA

BAKER & McKENZIE ✪
NORTON ROSE
PEPELIAEV, GOLTSBLAT & PARTNERS ✪

Clifford Chance CIS Ltd
Linklaters CIS ✪
Nörr Stiefenhofer Lutz ✪
Salans
White & Case LLC

Beiten Burkhardt Rechtsanwälte (Attorneys-at-Law) ✪
CMS Cameron McKenna
Freshfields Bruckhaus Deringer ✪
Gide Loyrette Nouel ✪
Hogan & Hartson L.L.P. ✪
LeBoeuf, Lamb, Greene & MacRae

Firms are listed A-Z in tiers which are ranked in order of priority
✪ Indicates firm displays contact details at the end of this chapter.

Clifford Chance CIS Ltd's Marc Bartholomy has established a strong reputation for advising on real estate matters.

Consultant Konstantine Kouzine heads **Linklaters CIS**' strong real estate department. Experienced partner Xavier Hunter returned to Moscow in January 2003. He has a wealth of experience in international real estate matters including funds work. Clients include OAO Novinsky Boulvard 31 and Brunswick UBS Warburg.

Nörr Stiefenhofer Lutz regularly advises its corporate clients on real estate matters.

Salans' expanding real estate practice is headed by Anna McDonald. The group has been particularly active in St Petersburg. It advised RBI Holdings in its $100m development of a shopping and entertainment centre. James Mandel and Bob Sexton are also recommended.

Eric Michailov heads **White & Case LLC**'s excellent two-partner, seven-associate team. In 2003, the team advised local Russian developer DecMos in the reconstruction and redevelopment of the Moskva Hotel in the centre of Moscow. The firm also advised on the Turkish Trade Centre development and the Hilton hotel overlooking Red Square.

Both Roman Koloa and Florien Schneider at **Beiten Burkhardt** have strong reputations in this area.

CMS Cameron McKenna has targeted this as an important growth area. In September 2003, highly rated former Warsaw managing partner Steven Shone arrived to drive the practice forward. He specialises in real estate investment and finance, acting for international real estate investors, lenders and corporate users.

While this is not a priority area for the firm, **Freshfields Bruckhaus Deringer**'s highly capable corporate generalist Kirsten Floss has significant experience. The firm advised a major industrial group on the establishment of the first Russian company investing in the real estate market.

Gide Loyrette Nouel acts for a significant number of large European clients in the construction sector.

Hogan & Hartson L.L.P.'s Olga Oozier is widely regarded as a leading authority on real estate law. Since 1992, Oozier has been heavily involved in the drafting of government regulations.

Special counsel, Dmitri Kountze, heads **LeBoeuf, Lamb, Greene & MacRae**'s real estate group. The team is active on behalf of numerous clients, advising on the acquisition and sale of buildings and land as far afield as Kaliningrad to the west, and Sakhalin to the east. Clients include major hotel chain Sheraton.

SHIPPING AND TRANSPORT: RUSSIA

JURINFLOT, INTERNATIONAL LAW OFFICE ✪
NORTON ROSE

Linklaters CIS ✪
Salans
Vegas-Lex Law Firm ✪

Firms are listed A-Z in tiers which are ranked in order of priority
✪ Indicates firm displays contact details at the end of this chapter.

SHIPPING AND TRANSPORT: RUSSIA

Established in 1927, **Jurinflot, International Law Office** has long been recognised as Russia's leading shipping firm. Managing partner Vladimir Mednikov heads a highly able team. He undertakes ship finance advice, while Vadim Emulate is best known for admiralty. The firm acted for Newaygo BV, Rotterdam in its dispute with Conversant, Moscow. Other clients include the Sakhalin Shipping Company.

Norton Rose partner Dmitry Gravin has developed a considerable profile in this area. The firm was most active in 2002-03 in the aviation sector. Clients include Debits Air finance, for which the firm undertook due diligence of an airline, and Forties.

Linklaters CIS' managing partner Dominic Sanders oversees the firm's transport-related work. He advised the City of St Petersburg on its establishment of a model public-private partnership to overhaul municipal bus transport. Consultant Mark Kirsch is also recommended.

Salans' managing partner Jane Tarassova has a particularly strong reputation for advice in the aviation sector. In 2002-03, the firm advised leading French jet engine manufacturer, SNECMA, on its negotiations with a major Russian engine manufacturer.

Vegas-Lex Law Firm is active in the shipping and aerospace sectors.

TAX: RUSSIA

Alex Chmelev heads **Baker & McKenzie**'s strong, two-partner tax department. He is supported by Alexander Bychkov. The firm provides extensive tax structuring advice to various US and Canadian contractors in the oil and gas industry. In 2003/3, the team advised on the tax aspects of Alrosa's $500m eurobond offering. It also advised Harvest Natural Resources on the aspects its sale of a 34% interest in Russian oil company, Geoilbent, to Yukos.

Haarmann Hemmelrath's Stephan Busch has a strong reputation for providing tax advice on M&A transactions, while **Linklaters CIS** Victor Matchekhin has extensive experience in advising international investment and commercial banks on tax issues. The firm advised Sakhalin Energy on various aspects of Russian taxation, including tax litigation issues. Other notable clients include Lukoil, BP, and Mitsui.

Nörr Stiefenhofer Lutz focuses on tax planning of major construction projects and cross-border transactions, including distribution schemes, leasing, and project finance. It is also one of the few foreign firms offering clients customs planning services. It advised the Russian subsidiary of a major player in the German health and beauty industry on all tax issues relating to its complicated financing and leasing scheme. **Nörr Stiefenhofer Lutz** is highly regarded for its tax litigation work. Ilja Rybalkin provides advice on local tax structures.

Dynamic and fast-expanding local firm **Pepeliaev, Goltsblat & Partners** is extremely strong in this area. The firm was formed in January 2002 as a result of a merger between *Legal Practice LLC* and a team of tax lawyers from auditing firm, FBK. Joint managing partner Sergey Papeliaev is one of the leading tax lawyers in Moscow and is highly recommended.

Oleg Konnov heads **Salans**' tax group. The firm advises multinational companies such as Gillette and Colgate.

Beiten Burkhardt regularly advises its many Europe-wide corporate client base on tax issues.

TAX: RUSSIA

BAKER & McKENZIE ✪

Haarmann Hemmelrath ✪
Linklaters CIS ✪
Nörr Stiefenhofer Lutz ✪
Pepeliaev, Goltsblat & Partners ✪
Salans

Beiten Burkhardt Rechtsanwälte (Attorneys-at-Law) ✪
Clifford Chance CIS Ltd
Jurinflot, International Law Office ✪
Vegas-Lex Law Firm ✪

Firms are listed A-Z in tiers which are ranked in order of priority
✪ *Indicates firm displays contact details at the end of this chapter.*

Irina Dmitrieva heads **Clifford Chance CIS Ltd**'s tax practice. In 2002-03, the firm advised Deutsche Telekom AG on tax issues relating to disposal of shares in OAO MTS. Other clients include Siemens and Bayer.

Jurinflot, International Law Office's up-and-coming partner Alexander Mednikov, formerly with **Gide Loyrette Nouel**, has a good reputation for tax advice.

Anna Hudanova at **Vegas-Lex Law Firm** is recommended for tax matters.

AZERBAIJAN

Daniel Matthews heads **Baker & McKenzie**'s Baku office, which was established in 1998 and was among the first international law offices to be licensed by the Azerbaijani Ministry of Justice. The firm has been active recently advising on major projects in the region. It advised Consolidated Contractors International on the construction of the Baku-Tbilisi-Ceyhan oil pipeline and acted for major contractors, including McDermott, on development of the Azeri-Chirag-Guneshli offshore oilfield. Other significant clients include Vitol SA

Scottish-based firm **Ledingham Chalmers** has been active in the region since 1992, and was the first foreign law firm to open an office in Baku, and has established a longstanding reputation in this sector. The Baku office regularly acts for leading oil and gas companies and is highly regarded for its banking and finance expertise. Clients include international financial institutions such as the EBRD and the IFC. Resident lawyers Benjamin Paine, Ismail Askerov and Elchin Mammadov are recommended.

Alum Bati heads **Salans**' Baku team. The firm is, of course, heavily involved in the oil and gas sector. Darren Knoll is also recommended for advice in the sector.

In October 2003, highly rated counsel Christine Ferguson – who relocated to London – handed over the reins at **Baker Botts, L.L.P.**'s Azerbaijan office to Mark Rowley. Three other lawyers and a tax adviser support him. The firm acted as lead counsel on the $3bn Baku-Tbilisi-Ceyhan crude oil pipeline. Other notable energy-sector clients include Exxon, BP and Statoil.

AZERBAIJAN

BAKER & McKENZIE ✪
LEDINGHAM CHALMERS
SALANS

Baker Botts, L.L.P.

Firms are listed A-Z in tiers which are ranked in order of priority
✪ *Indicates firm displays contact details at the end of this chapter.*

BELARUS

BOROVTSOV & SALEI
VLASOVA & PARTNERS

Firms are listed alphabetically

BELARUS

Vassili Salei heads **Borovtsov & Salei**'s three-partner Minsk office. The firm provides general corporate and commercial advice to leading multinationals such as Coca-Cola, Ikea and Lufthansa. It is particularly active in advising on the establishment of subsidiaries in Belarus as well as regularly advising leading Russian companies on their interests in the region. The firm acted for Western banks on a $25m loan to a local telecoms company. Alexander Borovtsov is also recommended.

Name partner Lilya Vlasova heads leading Belarus firm **Vlasova & Partners**. The three-partner, ten-associate team receives referrals from leading international firms such as **Linklaters CIS** and **White & Case LLC**. The firm is also a member of *TerraLex*. It has established a strong reputation for advice on general commercial and contentious matters, with specialities including privatisation, foreign investment and tax. Clients include Commerzbank and Hitachi. Svetlana Dashuk and Tatyana Emelianova are also recommended.

KAZAKHSTAN

Baker & McKenzie's Almaty office is headed by experienced partner Curtis Masters. The firm suffered the loss of Mark Lockwood who left the Almaty office in October 2003. The firm has considerable experience advising clients particularly in the energy and natural resources sector. It has also developed a strong track record advising financial institutions such as the EBRD and the IFC on the funding of various projects in the region. Other clients include HSBC and ABN Amro.

Tom O'Brien is the sole resident partner in **Coudert Brothers**' Almaty office, following former

KAZAKHSTAN

Baker & McKenzie ✪
Coudert Brothers ✪
Denton Wilde Sapte ✪
Grata Law Firm
LeBoeuf, Lamb, Greene & MacRae
Macleod Dixon LLP
Michael Wilson & Partners ✪
Salans
White & Case LLP

Firms are listed alphabetically
✪ *Indicates firm displays contact details at the end of this chapter.*

The largest firms

Azerbaijan		
1	BM Law Firm	6
2	Baker & McKenzie	5
	Ledingham Chalmers	5
	Salans	5
5	Baker Botts, L.L.P.	4
6	Michael Wilson & Partners	2
7	Grata Law Firm	1
Belarus		
1	Vlasova & Partners	8
2	Borovtsov & Salei	5
Kazakhstan		
1	Grata Law Firm	55
2	Denton Wilde Sapte	16
3	Michael Wilson & Partners	14
4	Bracewell & Patterson, L.L.P.	12
	Salans	12
6	Coudert Brothers	11
7	Baker & McKenzie	10
8	LeBoeuf, Lamb, Greene & MacRae	7
9	McGuireWoods Kazakhstan LLP	5
	White & Case LLP	5
11	Macleod Dixon LLP	4
	The Zanger Law Firm	4
Kyrgystan		
1	LeBoeuf, Lamb, Greene & MacRae	2
2	Grata Law Firm	1
Moldova		
1	Advocate, LLP	5
	Ernst & Young SRL	5
	Levintsa & Associates	5
4	Buruiana & Partners	3

These figures represent the total number of lawyers in this country only, and have been supplied by the firms themselves. The figures should be accurate as at 1 January 2004.

KYRGYSTAN

LEBOEUF, LAMB, GREENE & MACRAE

Firms are listed alphabetically

MOLDOVA

BURUIANA & PARTNERS
LEVINTSA & ASSOCIATES

Firms are listed alphabetically

managing partner Jonathan Cahn's departure to head the firm's Moscow office. The Almaty office focuses largely on advising on oil and gas exploration and production, field operations, pipelines, refineries and privatisations. The firm's lawyers – US, Canadian, Kazakh and Uzbek – have many years of experience working in the region. Deep knowledge of Kazakhstan's legal system was established by assisting in the drafting of its commercial laws and handling the first privatisations of key entities in the natural resource sector.

Marla Valdez heads **Denton Wilde Sapte**'s Almaty office. Valdez has considerable expertise in the oil and gas and mining sectors, including the negotiation of host government hydrocarbon and mineral contracts, exploration and production licences, JV agreements, and privatisations. She advises on operations in Kazakhstan and Uzbekistan and gains support from a team including four strong senior associates. Kuanysh Kanlybayev is recommended for banking and corporate finance advice.

Grata Law Firm's Kazakhstan team is headed by three managing partners: Tlek Baigabulov, Aidar Saymsakov, and Akhmetzhan Abdullev. It is based in Almaty and boasts a presence throughout Kazakhstan: Atyrau, Aktau, Aksai, and Aktobe. It also has offices in other regional centres – Baku and Bishkek – as well as a London presence and has referral relationships with other firms in the region. The firm offers a broad commercial practice for an impressive list of domestic and international companies, particularly in the oil and gas sectors.

John Huhs oversees **LeBoeuf, Lamb, Greene & MacRae**'s market-leading presence in Central Asia. The Almaty office is the firm's main base in the region where it undertakes a wide variety of investment, financial, and privatisation matters, though the emphasis is predominantly on the energy sector. **LeBoeuf, Lamb, Greene & MacRae** also has a bureau in the country's oil centre, Atyrau. The firm advised the Caspian Pipeline Consortium of three governments – Russia, Kazakhstan, and Oman – and eight major oil producers on a \$2.6bn pipeline carrying crude oil from Tengiz in Kazakhstan to the Black Sea. It has also advised numerous companies on eurobond issues. Other clients include KazTransGaz.

Macleod Dixon LLP is regularly instructed by oil and gas sector clients on general commercial matters.

Former **Baker & McKenzie** lawyer Michael Wilson heads two-partner firm **Michael Wilson & Partners**. Headquartered in Almaty, it also has a presence in Baku. The firm was strengthened considerably in 2002 by the arrival of former **Richards Butler** partner John Emmot. Wilson has a strong reputation for work in the oil and gas sector. Emmot has added strong contentious capability. The firm advises an impressive range of big name clients, including British Airways and BP.

Aigoul Kenjebayeva manages **Salans**' Kazakhstan office. He gains strong support from two 'visiting' partners – James Hogan (Paris-based) and Glenn Kolleeny (St Petersburg-based). The office is heavily focused on the energy sector. It has been particularly active in advising clients such as PetroKazakhstan and British Gas. The firm has a strong reputation for advising foreign companies on the tax implications of opening up branches in the region.

Yuriy Maltsev heads **White & Case LLP**'s Almaty office. Senior associate Peter Sztyck provides strong support. The office has a strong reputation for advice on eurobond issues, and, in 2002-03, advised JPMorgan and CSFB on the \$350m issue and \$150m tap by Kazkommerts Finance. The firm also acted for Yukos on its acquisition of a Kazakhstan company. Other clients include Deutsche Bank and ABN Amro.

KYRGYSTAN

LeBoeuf, Lamb, Greene & MacRae's Bishkek office is staffed by two senior lawyers – one Kyrgyz and one American. The office focuses mainly on mining, telecoms, corporate, privatisation, and privatisation matters. It has a track record advising energy sector clients on establishing operations in the region.

MOLDOVA

Buruiana & Partners is highly rated for advice to its largely Romanian and German client base on cross-border transactions. It has strong IP, telecoms and media experience. Clients include France Télécom and Siemens.

Levintsa & Associates is also active in the telecoms sector, particularly in relation to privatisation.

UKRAINE

As the first foreign law firm to open an office in Kiev in 1992, **Baker & McKenzie** has a wealth of experience to draw upon. Extremely able partner James Hitch took over as **Baker & McKenzie**'s Kiev head following the departure of David Scott

The largest firms

Ukraine		
1	Grischenko & Partners	25
	Shevchenko Didkovskiy & Partners	25
3	Konnov & Sozanovsky	22
	Vasil Kisil & Partner	22
5	Magister & Partners	21
	Proxen	21
7	Baker & McKenzie	19
8	BC Toms & Co	14
9	EY Law	10
	Ilyashev & Partners	10
	Salans	10
12	Chadbourne & Parke	9
13	Ukrainian Legal Group, L.L.C.	8
14	Frishberg & Partners	6
15	Andreas Neocleous & Co	5
	Vykhrystenko & Partners	5
17	Gorodissky & Partners	4
	Jaanti DeBeck & Partners	4
	The Silecky Firm	4
20	Aitken Irvin Berlin & Vrooman, LLP	1
	Logush, Borshuk, Bronfman & Kalishevych	1
	Sikaylo, Matveev, Gabbasov & Partners	1
	Smith Lyons LLP	1

Uzbekistan		
1	Denton Wilde Sapte	3
2	Chadbourne & Parke LLP	2

These figures represent the total number of lawyers in this country only, and have been supplied by the firms themselves. The figures should be accurate as at 1 January 2004.

UKRAINE

BAKER & McKENZIE ✪
WHITE & CASE LLC

BC TOMS & CO ✪
SALANS
SQUIRE, SANDERS & DEMPSEY (MOSCOW) LLC

Frishberg & Partners
Magister & Partners ✪

Shevchenko Didkovskiy & Partners
Vasil Kisil & Partner

Andreas Neocleous & Co
Grischenko & Partners ✪
Ilyashev & Partners ✪
Konnov & Sozanovsky ✪
Lawrence Graham
Proxen
Smith Lyons LLP

Firms are listed A-Z in tiers which are ranked in order of priority
✪ Indicates firm displays contact details at the end of this chapter.

to the firm's Moscow office in July 2002. Hitch specialises in international investment, corporate and M&A. He is strongly supported by Serhig Chorny who specialises in banking and finance, and dispute resolution. The firm has been particularly busy recently advising on major EBRD-funded projects. Clients include Gastransit, Interbrew, ING Barings, and the Ukrainian Ministry of Finance.

Ian Clark heads **White & Case LLC**'s four-partner Kiev team. He is recommended for energy sector advice. In June 2003, the firm advised the Ministry of Finance on a highly successful $800m eurobond. John Williams led the team that acted for the Ministry of Foreign Affairs on the accidental destruction of the Sibir Airline passenger plane over the Black Sea in 2001. Margaret Cole is recommended for contentious matters and has also advised the Ukrainian government. Other clients include Natogaz.

BC Toms & Co provides advice on a wide range of areas. The experienced Bate Toms is recommended. The firm is most active on telecoms, construction, project finance, and oil and gas-related matters. The firm recently acted on an oil and gas sector JV between a UK company and a leading Ukrainian state enterprise. The firm is also recommended for its work in contentious matters.

Oleg Batyuk heads **Salans**' 12-fee-earner office. The firm has a wealth of experience in the telecoms, real estate and energy sectors. It is recommended for advice on privatisation, banking and currency laws and import and export restrictions. Andrew Bej is also recommended for corporate matters.

Helen Kryshtalowych heads **Squire, Sanders & Dempsey**'s Kiev office. In September 2003, the formed an affiliation with **The Silecky Firm** an independent law firm to complement and strengthen the Ukraine, CIS and international practices of both firms. The firms are particularly active in the telecoms and energy sectors. Clients include Alfa Telecom and OMV Aktiengesellschaft.

Frishberg & Partners is recommended for advice to international clients on investing in Ukraine.

Magister & Partners is highly regarded for advice on international trade. The firm also has expertise in intellectual property, tax and finance. It frequently receives referrals from foreign firms relating to international arbitrations. Clients include Diageo and Honeywell.

Shevchenko Didkovskiy & Partners is highly regarded for transactional advice largely to Dutch and Norwegian companies. Clients include Austrian Airlines and Telenor Mobile.

Vasil Kisil at **Vasil Kisil & Partner** is recommended for contentious matters. Cypriot firm **Andreas Neocleous & Co** undertakes general commercial, banking and dispute resolution matters.

Dmitry Grischenko at **Grischenko & Partners** undertakes general commercial matters.

Ilyashev & Partners is rated for tax advice, while **Konnov & Sozanovsky** and **Proxen** are recommended for general commercial and contentious matters.

Lawrence Graham's Mariupol practice is recommended for shipping, corporate and international trade advice. The firm has a reputation for handling contentious matters.

UZBEKISTAN

Associate Jamol Askarov oversees **Chadbourne & Parke LLP**'s Tashkent presence. The firm has a strong reputation for corporate, investment and transactional advice.

Igor Sidelnikov heads **Denton Wilde Sapte**'s Tashkent office. All of the office's five lawyers have a very wide range of expertise, regularly advising clients on corporate, property, banking and privatisation issues. The office frequently works in conjunction with the firm's first-rate Kazakhstan practice.

UZBEKISTAN

CHADBOURNE & PARKE LLP
DENTON WILDE SAPTE ✪

Firms are listed alphabetically
✪ Indicates firm displays contact details at the end of this chapter.

BM LAW FIRM

HYATT INTERNATIONAL CENTER
HYATT TOWER 3
1033 IZMIR STREET
370065 BAKU

Telephone: +994 12 971 914
Fax: +994 12 971 913
E-mail: bmlaw@azevt.com
Website: www.bmlawaz.com

Languages
Azeri, English, French, Russian, Turkish

Other offices
London, Oregon

Number of lawyers 15
at this office 10

Contact
Farhad Mirzayev (fmirzayev@bmlawaz.com)

International groupings
Correspondent law firm of Chadbourne & Parke LLP, Denton Wilde Sapte and Ashurst

CATEGORIES OF WORK	
Oil and gas	Environmental law
Privatisation	International private law
Banking and finance	Intellectual property
Security	Corporate finance
Aviation	M&A
Tax law	Real estate
Litigation	Mortgage
Labour law	Insolvency and bankruptcy
Commercial and company law	Family law
IT and telecommunications	Health law

THE FIRM

BM Law Firm was founded in 1993 in Baku in Azerbaijan by the well-known and experienced national lawyer, Jamal Baghirov, and subsequent growth has been in response to the needs of its clients. BM Law Firm has a strong practice born of expertise and service in business and commercial law. In Azerbaijan, as well as abroad, BM Law Firm has become known for providing legal advice on a highly professional level.

BM Law Firm is a leading national firm providing services to national and foreign clients. BM Law Firm represents companies of all sizes, and its client list includes more than 30 companies. The firm provides legal advice in more than 20 areas of practice to industries and business leaders in the Azerbaijan Republic, as well as around the world. The firm is proud of its ability to combine the talents of lawyers across different disciplines to meet its clients' needs. BM Law Firm has a longstanding reputation for being a provider of efficient legal services, using focused teams of lawyers and paralegals in a cost-effective manner. The diverse practice and depth of experience in this leading national law firm ensures stability, confidence and prosperity in business activity.

BM Law Firm's lawyers are experienced and provide high-quality legal services. They are recruited from the top law schools in the nation and are recognised as authorities in their disciplines. These lawyers have been involved in the process of development of a favourable legal framework for direct investments in Azerbaijan.

The firm's main aim is to act as business partner with its clients, combining legal experience to help them prosper, and its main goal is to ensure economic prosperity of the Republic, by assisting foreign and national investors and international organisations to realise their projects in Azerbaijan.

AREAS OF PRACTICE:

BM Law Firm offers a range of legal services to its clients in various spheres of law. The areas of law in which the firm's lawyers practice all have significance and importance for Azerbaijan in the current period of transfer for its market economy.

The firm has strong practice and unrivalled experience in the areas mentioned above.

BAKER & McKENZIE

THE LANDMARK BUILDING
96 NIZAMI STREET
BAKU AZ1000

Telephone: +994 12 97 18 01
Fax: +994 12 97 18 05
E-mail: baku.info@bakernet.com
Website: www.bakernet.com

Languages
Azerbaijani, English, Russian

Other offices:
For a list of all offices please consult Baker & McKenzie's Moscow office entry.

Number of lawyers 3,380
at this office 5

Contact
Daniel Matthews

Baker & McKenzie is a global law firm with 66 offices in 36 countries.

CATEGORIES OF WORK

- Banking and finance
- Corporate and commercial
- Dispute resolution
- E-commerce/telecoms
- Energy and natural resources
- Environment
- Insurance
- Intellectual property
- Labour law
- Mergers and acquisitions
- Privatisation
- Real estate and construction
- Tax

MICHAEL WILSON & PARTNERS

APARTMENT 16
44-46 RUZBEKH STREET
370002 BAKU

Telephone: +994 12 47 39 49
Fax: +994 12 47 39 49
E-mail: mwp@nursat.kz
Website: www.mwp.kz

Languages
English, Russian, Azerbaijani

Other offices
Almaty

Number of lawyers 2

CATEGORIES OF WORK

- Foreign investments and joint ventures
- Corporate, corporate finance and securities
- Intellectual property
- Arbitration, litigation and dispute resolution
- Banking, finance and project finance
- Tax and customs
- Real estate
- Mining and natural resources
- Engineering and construction
- Privatisation
- Power industry (generation, transmission and distribution) and utilities
- Labour, employment and work permit matters
- Telecommunications
- Transportation, shipping and aviation

BAKER & McKENZIE

SAMAL TOWERS, 14TH FLOOR
SAMAL-2
ZHOLDASBEKOV STREET
ALMATY 480099

Telephone: +7 3272 50 99 45
Fax: +7 3272 50 95 79
E-mail: almaty.info@bakernet.com
Website: www.bakernet.com

Languages
Arabic, Azeri, English, French, Georgian, German, Kyrgyz, Russian, Turkish, Ukrainian, Uzbek

Other offices
For a list of all offices please consult Baker & McKenzie's Moscow office entry.

Number of lawyers 3,380
at this office 10

Contact
Curtis B Masters

Baker & McKenzie is a global law firm with 66 offices in 36 countries.

CATEGORIES OF WORK

Banking and finance
Curtis Masters

Capital markets
Curtis Masters

Corporate and commercial
Curtis Masters

Dispute resolution, litigation and arbitration
Igor Novikov

E-commerce
Alexander Korchagin

Energy and natural resources
Azamat Kuatbekov

Environment
Alexander Korchagin

Information technology/telecoms
Alexander Korchagin

Insurance
Mariya Gekko

Intellectual property
Leila Tashenova

Labour law
Igor Novikov

Mergers and acquisitions
Curtis Masters

Real estate, construction
Igor Novikov

Tax
Sholpan Isakova

DENTON WILDE SAPTE

273 FURMANOVA 3RD FLOOR
ALMATY 480099

Telephone: +7 3272 581 950
Fax: +7 3272 581 905
E-mail: almaty@dentonwildesapte.com
Website: www.dentonwildesapte.com

Languages
English, Kazakh, Russian, Turkish

Other offices
Abu Dhabi, Beijing, Cairo, Dubai, Gibraltar, Hong Kong, Istanbul, London, Milton Keynes, Moscow, Muscat, Paris, Singapore, Tashkent, Tokyo

Number of lawyers 876
at this office 16

Contact
Marla Valdez

CATEGORIES OF WORK

Aviation

Banking, finance, securities and capital markets

Corporate law, joint ventures

Dispute resolution

Energy and natural resources

Investment and commercial law

Labour law

Mergers and acquisitions, privatisation

Property and infrastructure development

Telecommunications

COUDERT BROTHERS

96 BAITURSYNOV STR
ALMATY 480072

Telephone: +7 3272 58 18 28
Fax: +7 3272 58 18 80
E-mail: almaty@coudert.com
Website: www.coudert.com

Languages
Chinese, English, French, German, Kazakh, Russian, Spanish, Ukrainian, Uzbek

Other offices
Antwerp, Bangkok, Beijing, Berlin, Brussels, Budapest*, Denver, Frankfurt, Ghent, Hong, Kong, Jakarta*, London, Los Angeles, Mexico City*, Milan, Montreal, New York, Palo Alto, Paris, Prague*, St Petersburg, San Francisco, San Jose, Shanghai, Singapore, Stockholm, Sydney, Tokyo, Washington DC

Number of lawyers 650+
at this office 14

CATEGORIES OF WORK

- **Oil and gas**
- **Power and infrastructure**
- **Mining and metals**
- **Telecommunications**
- **Banking, finance and capital markets**
- **Real estate**
- **Consumer and intellectual property products**
- **Commodities trading**
- **Corporate planning and business formation**
- **Dispute resolution**
- **Legal reform and government advisory**

THE FIRM

Coudert Brothers was established in 1853 by French émigrés and was the first US law firm to set up an international legal practice. The firm now has more than 650 lawyers worldwide, operating as one single partnership with a common emphasis on client service of the highest quality.

The firm has extensive experience in international investment, trade and finance. Cross-border commercial transactions are a major focus, as is international arbitration and other complex dispute resolution. Coudert Brothers also provides domestic advice in countries where the firm has offices.

Coudert Brothers has offices in 30 cities in 18 countries around the world. These offices are located in the major financial and business centres of Europe, the United States and Asia Pacific region. More than 300 Coudert Brothers professionals now practice in Europe, making it the largest region in the firm's worldwide network.

Coudert was the first foreign law firm to open an office in Moscow in 1988. The firm's integrated Russia and CIS practice group has over 50 attorneys in offices in Moscow, St Petersburg, Almaty and bureaus in Atyrau, Western Kazakhstan, and Tashkent, Uzbekistan.

Coudert Brothers has 14 attorneys resident in Central Asia, including two expatriates and 12 nationals. All nationals are fluent in English, Russian and other languages, and most hold advanced degrees in law from US, UK and European universities.

Coudert's lawyers have advised on most of the largest oil and gas projects in Central Asia and the Caspian dating back to the time of privatisation. The firm's lawyers have advised on over 55 oil and gas investment projects in the Central Asia and Caspian region. No firm in the former Soviet Union has been involved in as many large projects in the oil and gas sector as Coudert Brothers.

AREAS OF PRACTICE

Coudert Brothers advises clients on matters involving oil and gas exploration and production, field operations, pipelines and refineries, power generation and infrastructure, mining and metals, telecommunications, banking, finance and capital markets, real estate, consumer products, commodities trading, intellectual property, corporate planning and business formation, and dispute resolution. Coudert Brothers is recognised as a leader in international energy and natural resources projects. In the most recent Energy Finance Awards published by Petroleum Economist, Coudert Brothers shared the distinction of being selected as the law firm with the best knowledge of energy law in the former Soviet Union. *The 2004 Guide to the World's Leading Financial Law Firms* published by International Finance Law also recommends Coudert as the best firm in Almaty for project finance and mergers and acquisitions advice, as well as a leading firm for banking and capital markets.

Information on the Almaty office and the practice of Coudert Brothers in Russia and the CIS is available on request, or at Coudert Brothers' website www.coudert.com.

MICHAEL WILSON & PARTNERS

5TH FLOOR
36 SAMAL-1
480099 ALMATY

Telephone: +7 32 72 58 48 90
Fax: +7 32 72 50 15 75
E-mail: mwp@nursat.kz
Website: www.mwp.kz

Languages
Czech, English, French, German, Kazakh, Polish, Russian, Spanish, Ukrainian

Other offices
Baku

Number of lawyers 12

Contacts
Michael E Wilson, John F Emmott

CATEGORIES OF WORK

Foreign investments and joint ventures

Corporate, corporate finance and securities

Intellectual property

Arbitration, litigation and dispute resolution

Banking, finance and project finance

Tax and customs

Real estate

Mining and natural resources

Engineering and construction

Privatisation

Power industry (generation, transmission and distribution) and utilities

Labour, employment and work permit matters

Telecommunications

Transportation, shipping and aviation

THE FIRM

Michael Wilson & Partners Ltd (MWP) is a full-service law firm in Almaty covering Kazakhstan, the central Asian region and the Caucasus. MWP's founding partner was previously the regional founding partner of a major international law firm with offices in Almaty, Bishkek, Baku, Astana and Tashkent.

As a fully independent law firm, MWP has the ability that international law firms do not have to meet clients' real legal and business needs when approaching and dealing with the most important business opportunities that exist in Kazakhstan and throughout the whole of central Asia.

As of January 2002, John F Emmott joined MWP as a partner, director and shareholder after eight years as an associate and 15 years as a partner in Richards Butler in London.

MWP is not just a law firm, but takes pride in partnering with its clients in relation to their business opportunities, challenges and threats and, in doing so, providing creative, timely and practical solutions specifically tailored to meet its clients' requirements, deadlines and budgets.

AREAS OF PRACTICE

MWP is a unique Kazakhstani firm in today's market, having some of the most experienced lawyers in their chosen fields on staff and can boast over 90 combined years of legal experience within its team. Most of MWP's people are bilingual, and are most sensitive and understanding to the business and cultural needs of the region and its industries.

Operating as a fully autonomous law firm, MWP's focus is on Kazakhstan and the other central Asian Republics of the former Soviet Union including Kyrgyzstan, Uzbekistan, Turkmenistan, Tajikstan, Azerbaijan, Georgia and Armenia. MWP offers a full range of commercial transactional services in the categories detailed above with a strong emphasis on the corporate sector, with a wide range and depth of both international and domestic clients.

The firm is considered one of the regional leaders in the mining and natural resources sector, utilities, and all aspects of foreign investment, joint ventures, financing, privatisations, restructuring, transportation, litigation, intellectual property and general commercial law. Full information on Michael Wilson & Partners Ltd, its staff, and major completed and ongoing projects can be viewed on its website at: www.mwp.kz.

AR CONSULTING LAW FIRM

9 GRANATNY PER, OFFICE 54
123001 MOSCOW

Telephone: +7 095 290 41 34
Fax: +7 095 234 38 89
E-mail: info@arconsulting.ru
Website: www.arconsulting.ru

Languages
English

Number of lawyers 8

Contact
Alexander Roubtsov

CATEGORIES OF WORK

- Corporate and commercial
- Mergers and acquisitions
- Corporate restructuring
- Privatisation
- Securities
- Foreign direct investment and joint ventures
- Company registration and accreditation services
- Taxation and tax planning
- Litigation and arbitration

AKIN GUMP STRAUSS HAUER & FELD LLP

DUCAT PLACE II
7 GASHEKA STREET
123056 MOSCOW

Telephone: +7 095 783 7700
Fax: +7 095 783 7701
Website: www.akingump.com

Languages
English, French, German, Russian

Other offices
Albany, Austin, Brussels, Chicago, Dallas, Houston, London, Los Angeles, New York, Northern Virginia, Philadelphia, Riverside, San Antonio, San Francisco, Washington DC, Riyadh (affiliate office)

Number of lawyers 950
at this office 15

Contacts
Natalia R Baratiants, Richard J Wilkie

CATEGORIES OF WORK

- Securities and capital markets
- Energy and infrastructure development
- Foreign investment
- Minerals
- Arbitration
- Telecommunications
- Banking and finance
- Private equity funds
- Corporate governance
- Intellectual property
- Construction and real estate
- Litigation

ALLEN & OVERY LEGAL SERVICES

DMITROVSKY PEREULOK 9
107031 MOSCOW

Telephone: +7 501 725 7900
Fax: +7 501 725 7949
E-mail: information@allenovery.com
Website: www.allenovery.com

Languages
English, French, Russian, Mandarin

Other offices
Amsterdam, Antwerp, Bangkok, Beijing, Bratislava, Brussels, Budapest, Dubai, Frankfurt, Hamburg, Hong Kong, London, Luxembourg, Madrid, Milan, New York, Paris, Prague, Rome, Shanghai, Singapore, Tokyo, Turin, Warsaw

Number of lawyers 2,305
at this office 17

Contact
Peter Timchur

CATEGORIES OF WORK

Banking/finance
Peter Timchur, Irina Mashlenko

International capital markets
Peter Timchur, Irina Mashlenko

Corporate/commercial
Peter Timchur, Edwin Tham

Energy
Peter Timchur, Irina Mashlenko

Investments
Peter Timchur, Irina Mashlenko

Mergers and acquisitions
Peter Timchur, Edwin Tham

Litigation and arbitration
Peter Timchur, Irina Mashlenko

Privatisations
Peter Timchur, Edwin Tham

Project finance
Peter Timchur, Edwin Tham

Trade finance
Edwin Tham, Dmitry Shiryaev

ALRUD LAW FIRM

6TH FLOOR
17 SKAKOVAYA STREET
125040 MOSCOW

Telephone: +7 095 234 9692
Fax: +7 095 956 3718
E-mail: info@alrud.ru
Website: www.alrud.ru

Languages
English, French, German, Russian, Spanish

Number of lawyers 17

Member
IAG International (Integrated Advisory Group)

CATEGORIES OF WORK

International trade
Dmitry Yeremin, Irina Anyukhina

Corporate law
Vassili Rudomino, Irina Anyukhina

Multi-level marketing
Vassili Rudomino, Dimitry Yeremin

Mass media law
Vassili Rudomino

Arbitration, international arbitration
Dmitry Yeremin, Aleksey Malovatsky

Mergers and acquisitions
Vassili Rudomino, Oksana Vishnyakova

Intellectual property
Vera Melusova, Irina Anyukhina

Real estate
Dmitry Yeremin, Konstantin Lapshin

Tax law
Vassili Rudomino, Vladimir Fokin

Commercial law
Irina Anyukhina, Aleksey Malovatsky

Due diligence
Vassili Rudomino, Aleksey Malovatsky

Investments in Russia
Vassili Rudomino, Irina Anyukhina

Competition law, antitrust
Oksana Vishnyakova, Irina Monina

Company registration
Oksana Vishnyakova, Irina Monina

Shareholders disputes
Oksana Vishnyakova, Irina Monina

Currency regulation
Dimitri Yeremin

Labour law
Konstantin Lapshin

Aviation and space law
Irina Anyukhina

ANDREAS NEOCLEOUS & CO

MALIY KOZIHINSKI PER 16/3
APT 2
MOSCOW

Telephone: +7 095 933 8703
Fax: +7 095 510 6421
E-mail: inforu@neocleous.com
Website: www.neocleous.com

Languages
English, Greek, Russian

Other offices
Limassol, Nicosia, Paphos, Budapest, Kiev, Prague

Number of lawyers 60
at this office 4

Contacts
Natalia Tarlo, Andrey Yermakov, Alexey Tokovinin, Aris Savvides, Olga Mikhailova (visiting associate), Andreas Neocleous (visiting partner), Elias Neocleous (visiting partner), Panayiotis Neocleous (visiting partner)

CATEGORIES OF WORK

Company and commercial law

Mergers and acquisitions

Banking and finance

Tax law and international tax planning

PPP and project finance

Competition law

European Union law

Intellectual property

Information technology

Real estate

Admiralty and shipping

BAKER BOTTS

7TH FLOOR
3 SMOLENSKAYA SQUARE
SMOLENSKY PASSAGE
MOSCOW 121099

Telephone: +7 095 937 8336
Fax: +7 095 510 5088
E-mail:
samantha.hampshire@bakerbotts.com
Website: www.bakerbotts.com

Languages
English, French, Russian

Other offices
Austin, Baku, Dallas, Houston, London, New York, Riyadh, Washington

Number of lawyers 676
at this office 3

Contact
Samantha Hampshire

Member
Lex Mundi

In association with
Afridi & Angell

CATEGORIES OF WORK

Corporate

Dispute resolution

Environment

Finance

Infrastructure

Intellectual property

Oil and gas

Other natural resources

Real estate

Power

Privatisations and restructurings

Telecoms, media and technology (TMT)

BAKER & McKENZIE

**SADOVAYA PLAZA, 11TH FLOOR
7 DOLGORUKOVSKAYA STREET
103006 MOSCOW**

Telephone: +7 095 787 2700
Fax: +7 095 787 2701
E-mail: moscow.office@bakernet.com
Website: www.bakernet.com

Languages
Belarussian, English, Flemish, French, German, Italian, Polish, Portuguese, Spanish, Swedish, Ukrainian

Other offices
Almaty, Amsterdam, Antwerp, Bahrain, Baku, Bangkok, Barcelona, Beijing, Berlin, Bogotá, Bologna, Brasilia, Brussels, Budapest, Buenos Aires, Cairo, Calgary Caracas, Chicago, Dallas, Düsseldorf, Frankfurt, Geneva, Guadalajara, Hanoi, Hong Kong, Ho Chi Minh City, Houston, Juarez, Kyiv, London, Madrid, Manila, Melbourne, Mexico City, Miami, Milan, Monterrey, Munich, New York, Palo Alto, Paris, Porto Alegré, Prague, Rio de Janeiro, Riyadh, Rome, St Petersburg, San Diego, San Francisco, Santiago, São Paulo, Shanghai, Singapore, Stockholm, Sydney, Taipei, Tijuana, Tokyo, Toronto, Valencia, Vienna, Warsaw, Washington DC, Zürich

Number of lawyers 3,380
at this office 44

CATEGORIES OF WORK

Arbitration and litigation
Vladimir Khvalei

Banking and finance
Vladimir Dragunov, David Scott

Corporate and commercial
Paul Melling

E-commerce/telecoms
Max Gutbrod, Paul Melling

Energy and natural resources
Max Gutbrod

Environment
Adrian Moore, Andrei Soukhomlinov

Pharmaceuticals
Paul Melling

Insurance
Max Gutbrod, Paul Melling

Intellectual property
Eugene Arievich

Labour and employment
Evgeny Reyzman

Mergers and acquisitions
Paul Melling, Sergei Voitishkin

Real estate, construction
Adrian Moore, Andrei Soukhomlinov

Tax
Alexander Chmelev, Alexander Bychkov

Venture capital
Max Gutbrod

THE FIRM

Founded in Chicago in 1949, Baker & McKenzie is a leading international law firm with 66 offices in 36 countries. The firm's multinational network of over 4,400 legal professionals offers clients resources and knowledge in every area of business law in virtually every important financial and commercial centre in the world.

Baker & McKenzie has been established in Europe for over 45 years, having opened its first European offices in 1957. Since then, the European and Middle Eastern network has grown to 29 offices, offering the firm unparalleled geographical coverage.

AREAS OF PRACTICE

Baker & McKenzie has long been recognised for its unique ability to combine international expertise with local knowledge. This is true of the firm's experience in the former Soviet Union, where its lawyers have been representing clients for over 30 years. Initially, the bulk of this representation was advice on East/West trade from the Chicago and London offices, but in the last decade Baker & McKenzie has developed both its CIS presence and practice, now offering local and expatriate staffed offices throughout the CIS, able to advise on all manner of legal issues.

The result of this history and commitment to expansion throughout the CIS region is that Baker & McKenzie has been at the forefront of doing business in Russia for many years, and therefore its knowledge and experience cannot be matched. Baker & McKenzie was the first Western law firm to establish an accredited office in Russia, with the founding of its Moscow office in 1989, and followed closely by St Petersburg in 1992. Both offices are uniquely qualified to assist companies in navigating through the dynamic, often complex, Russian business environment. From the most complicated securities issues to a straightforward corporate registration, the firm offers clients the benefit of experienced attorneys who are skilled in almost every aspect of corporate Russian and international law, thus ensuring that clients receive the highest level of service and advice.

Baker & McKenzie's CIS network, with offices in Kyiv (1992), Almaty (1995) and Baku (1998), further bolsters the level of local knowledge the firm can offer to clients. In addition to specialising in the Russian, Ukrainian, Kazakh and Azeri law local to those offices, Baker and McKenzie employs lawyers focusing on Uzbek, Belarusian and Kyrgyz law who are licensed to practise in those jurisdictions. With more than 70 lawyers supported by a highly competent staff of paralegals and translators, Baker & McKenzie's CIS practice offers clients the proven combination of international expertise with regional and local knowledge.

BECH-BRUUN DRAGSTED

BOLSHOY GNEZDNIKOVSKY PER 1
BUILDING 2
125009 MOSCOW

Telephone: +7 501 799 5684
Fax: +7 501 799 5687
E-mail: info.moscow@bechbruundragsted.com
Website: www.bechbruundragsted.com

Languages
Danish, English, French, German, Norwegian, Russian, Spanish, Swedish

Other offices
Aarhus, Brussels, Copenhagen

Number of lawyers 261
at this office 8

Contact
Lone Høgholt
(lone.hoegholt@bechbruunddragsted.com)

CATEGORIES OF WORK

- Registration of representative offices (including establishment and structuring of sales organisations)
- Real property tax law (including rights in respect of land, leases and tenancies)
- Mergers and acquisitions
- Employment law
- Competition law
- Intellectual property and telecoms
- Insurance
- Transport
- Construction projects (including financing and protection of investors rights, registration, approvals, licensing and environmental)

BEITEN BURKHARDT RECHTSANWÄLTE (ATTORNEYS-AT-LAW)

ULANSKY PER. 13/1
101000 MOSCOW

Telephone: +7 095 232 9635
Fax: +7 095 232 9633
E-mail: bblaw-moskau@bblaw.de
Website: www.bblaw.de

Languages
Cantonese, Czech, English, French, German, Hungarian, Italian, Mandarin, Polish, Slovak, Spanish

Other offices
Beijing, Berlin, Brussels, Budapest, Cologne, Dusseldorf, Frankfurt am Main, Hamburg, Hong Kong, Leipzig, Munich, Nuremberg, St Petersburg, Shanghai, Warsaw

Number of lawyers 232
at this office 11

Contacts
Dr Thomas Heidemann,
Dr Christian von Wistinghausen

CATEGORIES OF WORK

- Mergers and acquisitions
- Corporate law
- Corporate finance
- Information technology and intellectual property
- Telecoms
- Infrastructure investments
- Labour
- Competition
- Insolvency
- Real estate
- Litigation and arbitration

CMS BUREAU FRANCIS LEFEBVRE

10 USPENSKY PEREOULOK
103006 MOSCOW

Telephone: +7 502 221 49 03
Fax: +7 095 299 30 25
E-mail: bflrus@co.ru
Website: www.bfl-avocats.com

Languages
English, French, Russian

Other offices
Berlin, Brussels, Bucharest, Buenos Aires, Casablanca, Düsseldorf, Lyon, Madrid, Montevideo, New York, Neuilly-sur-Seine, São Paulo, Shanghai, Strasbourg

Number of lawyers 441
at this office 23

Contact
Jean-Luc Pipon

Member
CMS Network

CATEGORIES OF WORK

- Investments in the CIS countries
- Intellectual property
- Joint ventures
- Competition law
- Mergers and acquisitions
- Employment law
- Business law
- Customs and excise duties
- National and international taxation
- Arbitration law
- Contracts

CLEARY GOTTLIEB STEEN & HAMILTON LLC

PAVELELETSKAYA SQUARE 2/3
115054 MOSCOW

Telephone: + 7 501 258 5006
Fax: + 7 501 258 5011
Website: www.clearygottlieb.com

Languages
English, French, German, Mandarin, Spanish

Other offices
Brussels, Cologne, Frankfurt, London, Milan, Paris, Rome

Number of lawyers 937
at this office 9

CATEGORIES OF WORK

- Banking and finance
- Joint ventures
- Capital markets/securities
- Mergers and acquisitions

COUDERT BROTHERS LLP

ULITSA GASHEKA 7
123056 MOSCOW

Telephone: +7 095 258 5454
Fax: +7 095 258 5455
E-mail: info@mos.coudert.com
Website: www.coudert.com

Languages
English, French, German, Italian, Russian, Spanish, Ukrainian

Other offices
Almaty, Antwerp, Bangkok, Beijing, Berlin, Brussels, Budapest*, Frankfurt, Ghent, Hong Kong, Jakarta*, London, Los Angeles, Mexico City*, Milan, New York, Palo Alto, Paris, Prague*, Rome, St Petersburg, San Francisco, Shanghai, Singapore, Stockholm, Sydney, Tokyo, Washington DC

Number of lawyers 650+
at this office 19

CATEGORIES OF WORK

Banking and finance
Derek A Bloom, Jonathan D Cahn

Commercial property/real estate
Maria V Sandakova, Sergei M Areshev

Corporate and commercial
Larisa A Afanasyeva, Jonathan D Cahn

Energy and natural resources
Jonathan D Cahn, Pavel L Bakoulev

Dispute resolution – litigation and arbitration
Olga N Anisimova, Larisa A Afanasyeva

Intellectual property
Alexey V Barnashov, Ludmila A Yegorova

Mergers and acquisitions
Larisa A Afanasyeva, Jonathan D Cahn

Privatisation
Larisa A Afanasyeva, Jonathan D Cahn

Telecommunications
Larisa A Afanasyeva, Derek A Bloom

THE FIRM

Coudert Brothers was established in 1853 by French émigrés and was the first US law firm to set up an international legal practice. The firm now has more than 650 lawyers worldwide, operating as one single partnership with a common emphasis on client service of the highest quality.

The firm has extensive experience in international investment, trade and finance. Cross-border commercial transactions are a major focus, as is international arbitration and other complex dispute resolution. Coudert Brothers also provides domestic advice in countries where the firm has offices.

Coudert Brothers has offices in 30 cities in 18 countries around the world. These offices are located in the major financial and business centres of Europe, the United States and Asia Pacific region. More than 300 Coudert Brothers professionals now practice in Europe, making it the largest region in the firm's worldwide network.

Coudert Brothers has been at the forefront of legal development in serving its clients in Russia. From the first joint venture projects in the late 1980s, to the first offshore oil and gas projects in the early 1990s, to the defence of a major Russian company against a hostile takeover attempt at the turn of the millennium, Coudert continues to provide effective legal services to its clients.

AREAS OF PRACTICE

The Moscow and St Petersburg offices advise on a full range of corporate, finance and other commercial transactions in Russia in various sectors, including oil and gas, infrastructure, infrastructure finance, telecommunications, pharmaceuticals, timber, banking, real estate, intellectual property, transportation and power generation. Coudert attorneys also provide regulatory advice and litigation and arbitration services to clients in these and other businesses in Russia.

DENTON WILDE SAPTE

BOLSHAYA DMITROVKA 7/5
BUILDING 2
103009 MOSCOW

Telephone: +70 95 255 7900
Fax: +70 95 255 7901
E-mail: info@dentonwildesapte.ru
Website: www.dentonwildesapte.com

Languages
English, French, German, Russian, Spanish, Ukranian

Other offices
Abu Dhabi, Almaty, Beijing, Cairo, Dubai, Gibraltar, Hong Kong, Istanbul, London, Milton Keynes, Muscat, Paris, Singapore, Tashkent, Tokyo

Number of lawyers 876
at this office 10

Contact
Doran Doeh

CATEGORIES OF WORK

- Banking and finance
- Commercial
- Corporate
- Electricity
- Infrastructure development
- Intellectual property
- Litigation
- Mergers and acquisitions
- Oil and gas
- Privatisation
- Tax
- Telecommunications

FRESHFIELDS BRUCKHAUS DERINGER

KADASHEVSKAYA NAB 14/2
119017 MOSCOW

Telephone: +7 501 785 3000
Fax: +7 501 785 3001
E-mail: email@freshfields.com
Website: www.freshfields.com

Languages
Extensive language capabilities

Other offices
Amsterdam, Bangkok, Barcelona, Beijing, Berlin, Bratislava, Brussels, Budapest, Cologne, Düsseldorf, Frankfurt, Hamburg, Hanoi, Ho Chi Minh City, Hong Kong, London, Madrid, Milan, Munich, New York, Paris, Rome, Shanghai, Singapore, Tokyo, Vienna, Washington

Number of lawyers 2,504
at this office 33

Contact
Jacky Baudon

CATEGORIES OF WORK

- Corporate
- Finance
- Intellectual property and IT
- Real estate
- Antitrust, competition and trade
- Employment, pensions and benefits
- Dispute resolution (including environment, planning and regulatory)
- Tax

EY LAW

HEAD OFFICE
SADOVNICHESKAYA NAB 77, BLD 1
MOSCOW 115035

Telephone: +7 095 783 2500
Fax: +7 095 783 2501
Website: www.eylaw.com/cis

Languages
English, French, German, Georgian, Russian, Ukrainian

Other offices
Kyiv, St Petersburg, Tbilisi, Yuzhno-Sakhalinsk

Number of lawyers 2,000
at this office 45

Contacts
Lisa Gialdini (lisa.a.gialdini@ru.eylaw.com), Constantine Lusignan-Rizhinashvili (constantine.lusignan-rizhinashvili@ru.eylaw.com)

Member
EY Law Network

CATEGORIES OF WORK

Mergers and acquisitions
Constantine Lusignan-Rizhinashvili, James Mandel

Corporate and commercial
Constantine Lusignan-Rizhinashvili, Dmitry Tetiouchev

Banking and finance
Delphine Nougayrède

Tax law
Lisa Gialdini, Scott Antel

Labour law
Ekaterina Petrova

Real estate and construction
Sergey Koltchin

Intellectual property and information technology
Victor Naumov

Litigation and dispute resolution
Sergei Nosov, Olga Litvinova

Energy, utilities and infrastructure
Constantine Lusignan-Rizhinashvili

THE FIRM

EY Law in Russia and the CIS is a full-service legal practice with law offices in Moscow, St Petersburg, Yuzhno-Sakhalinsk, Tbilisi and Kyiv. Staffed by over 90 practising attorneys, it forms one of the largest legal service providers in the CIS marketplace. Core competences include: mergers and acquisitions; corporate and commercial law; real estate and construction; labour law; intellectual property and information technology; banking and finance; energy, infrastructure and utilities; litigation and dispute resolution; and tax law. Through its affiliation with Ernst & Young, it has access to professionals in multiple jurisdictions and across business disciplines, including tax, transaction advisory and financial services.

EY Law in Russia and the CIS is a participant in the EY Law international network of independently practising law practices associated with Ernst & Young. With 2,000 lawyers in 30 countries, EY Law ranks as one of the world's largest legal practices by headcount and geographical coverage. EY Law provides its clients with a co-ordinated and integrated approach towards legal services around the world. It aims to provide major international and national clients with innovative and commercial legal services that deliver real value and benefits.

AREAS OF PRACTICE

Corporate, mergers and acquisitions make up the core of the firm's CIS practice. It has advised on major international energy and other project investments, handling some of the largest foreign direct investment and cross-border transactions in the Caspian for both industry clients and financial institutions. In Mergermarket's guide to European M&A, EY Law's work in Russia placed it among the top ten legal advisers for energy, mining and utilities according to the value of transactions handled. Key offerings include integrated legal, tax and financial due diligence, deal structuring advice and full transaction and multi-jurisdictional implementation support.

The firm's multi-disciplinary focus and offices across the CIS equip it uniquely to advise on the complex web of legal, tax and transactional issues that arise in the region. It has advised on a wide variety of green and brown field projects as well as on all aspects of joint venture formation, equity and quasi-equity investments, and other forms of FDI, and acts for the full range of project participants, including lenders, sponsors, project joint ventures, insurers, contractors, government agencies and multi-lateral institutions. Its commercial advice encompasses the full range of employment, intellectual property, real estate and finance-related issues.

The firm has an impressive track record of success representing clients in tax-related disputes – with a near 90% success rate and a cumulative total of over US$120m of savings to clients, the firm is widely recognised as one of Russia's premier tax litigation firms. It also advises domestic and foreign investment banks, commercial banks, insurance firms, international financial institutions and regulatory agencies on the regulatory, corporate and transactional matters relevant to the Russian and CIS banking and financial services sectors.

The real estate and construction group has negotiated and documented complex domestic construction and urban development projects such as hotels, diplomatic missions, shopping centres, pipelines and industrial facilities, advising on infrastructure, utilities, mechanical and electrical systems, construction finance, construction insolvencies and construction insurance arrangements.

EGOROV, PUGINSKY, AFANASIEV & PARTNERS LLC

6 KRASNOPRESNENSKAYA NAB
11TH FLOOR
123100 MOSCOW

Telephone: +7 095 935 8010
Fax: +7 095 935 8011
E-mail: mow_office@epam.ru
Website: www.epam.ru

Languages
English, French, Spanish

Other offices
Philadelphia, St Petersburg

Number of lawyers 43
at this office 20

Member
Russian-American Business Council; American Chamber of Commerce in Russia; US-Russia Business Council; Canadian Business Association in Russia; Finnish-Russian Chamber of Commerce; American Bar Association; International Bar Association

CATEGORIES OF WORK

Commercial litigation and arbitration

Corporate transactions: M&A, takeovers, due diligence

Government relations

Securities regulation

Bankruptcy

International trade regulation

Tax and foreign exchange

Real estate and construction

Intellectual property

Maritime and shipping

Certification and standardisation

Insurance

Employment law

THE FIRM

Founded in 1993, Egorov, Puginsky, Afanasiev & Partners is a national law firm specialising in commercial law in Russia and internationally. The firm combines extensive local experience with international professional and ethical standards. It regularly represents foreign companies doing business in Russia and Russian companies internationally. The firm often serves as local counsel to various Western law firms.

The firm's partners have distinguished backgrounds in government and academia, and they lecture and publish extensively on Russian commercial law. Many of the firm's lawyers have received additional training in Europe and the US. They enjoy the status of advocates under Russian law, which provides important client protections not available to regular jurists.

AREAS OF PRACTICE

Commercial litigation and arbitration: the firm has handled high-profile commercial cases at all levels of the Russian court system, as well as international commercial arbitration matters in Russia and major Western capitals. It has represented clients in some of the largest hostile takeover defences in recent years.

Corporate transactions: the firm regularly represents Russian and foreign clients in acquisitions of shares in Russian and foreign companies, structuring complex corporate transactions, as well as providing ongoing corporate services and due diligence. The firm has extensive expertise in inbound investment regulation in Russia.

Government relations: the firm has developed a sophisticated government relations practice geared toward practical solutions based on an in-depth understanding of client issues and a search for alignment of interests in public policy. Due to the diplomatic experience of the firm's partners, it has advised clients on matters in the US, France, Colombia and certain African countries.

Securities regulation: the firm has represented clients in fund management, broker-dealing, securities placement and investment advisory. It drafted some of the Russian securities regulations in the 1990s.

Bankruptcy: the firm has represented debtors and creditors in major corporate bankruptcies, including some hotly contested cases.

International trade regulation: the firm has represented Russian producers in WTO and market access matters in the US.

Tax and foreign exchange: the firm has provided tax planning and litigation advice to foreign and Russian corporate clients and employs licensed auditors.

Real estate and construction: experience includes a major subway reconstruction, a Western hotel development, a dispute between a European bank and a Russian government borrower, a first Western-owned office space in St. Petersburg and the largest office tower in Eastern Europe.

Intellectual property: recent work includes designing general IP strategy for production clients, fighting counterfeit products, IP ownership disputes and litigation involving asset stripping through licensing contracts.

Maritime and shipping: the firm has represented maritime creditors and debtors in vessels seizures and other disputes in over 20 countries, as well as in St Petersburg and the Russian Far East.

Certification and standardisation: the firm has organised compliance with local safety, standardisation and hygienic requirements for several consumer products companies and supervised certification procedures.

Insurance: the firm has represented local insurance companies in corporate reorganisations and satellite launch reinsurance, and also advised the largest international insurance broker on product structuring.

Employment law: the firm has advised clients on labour contracts, restrictive covenants, confidentiality agreements and non-compete covenants, and has also represented Russian seafarers' unions against shipowners worldwide.

GIDE LOYRETTE NOUEL

STOLESHNIKOV PEREULOK, 14
107031 MOSCOW

Telephone: +7 095 258 31 00
Fax: +7 095 258 31 01
E-mail: gln.moscow@gide.com
Website: www.gide.com

Other offices
Algiers, Beijing, Brussels, Bucharest, Budapest, Casablanca, Hanoi, Istanbul, London, New York, Paris, Prague, Riyadh, Shanghai, Tunis, Warsaw

Number of lawyers 480
at this office 10

Contact
David Lasfargue (lasfargue@gide.com)

CATEGORIES OF WORK

Corporate, M&A

Joint ventures

Commercial contracts

Exchange control

Competition and antitrust

Distribution

Intellectual property

Customs law

Litigation

Labour law

Taxation

Banking and finance, pre-financing exports of raw materials

Real estate transactions and financing

GOWLINGS INTERNATIONAL INC

PRECHISTENSKY PEREULOK 14
BUILDING 1, 4TH FLOOR
119034 MOSCOW

Telephone: +7 095 787 2070
Fax: +7 095 787 2071
E-mail: kathryn.szymczyk@gowlings.com
Website: www.gowlings.com

Other offices
Montréal, Ottawa, Toronto, Hamilton, Kitchener, Calgary, Vancouver

Number of lawyers 12

Contacts
Magdalena MV Sekula (Head of the Moscow Representative Office), Viacheslav Klikukin

CATEGORIES OF WORK

Corporate and commercial
Michael Malloy

Litigation
Marina I Drel

Intellectual property
Vladimir N Dementiev, Magdalena MV Sekula

HAARMANN HEMMELRATH

UL. OSTOSCHENKA 23
119034 MOSCOW

Telephone: +7 095 797 90 70
Fax: +7 095 797 90 80
E-mail: moscow@haarmannhemmelrath.com
Website: www.haarmannhemmelrath.com

Languages
Bulgarian, Croatian, Czech, Dutch, English, French, German, Hungarian, Italian, Japanese, Mandarin, Norwegian, Polish, Portuguese, Romanian, Slovak, Spanish, Vietnamese

Other offices
Berlin, Bielefeld, Brussels, Bucharest, Budapest, Cologne, Dusseldorf, Frankfurt, Hamburg, Leipzig, London, Milan, Munich, Paris, Prague, Rome, Shanghai, Singapore, Stuttgart, Tokyo, Vienna, Warsaw

Number of lawyers 281
at this office 12

CATEGORIES OF WORK

Mergers and acquisitions
Dr Gerd Lenga, Roman Daschko

Company law
Roman Daschko, Falk Tischendorf

Capital markets
Roman Daschko, Anna Lessowa

Business and trade law
Irene Engel, Jekaterina Bogomolowa

Real estate and construction law
Natalie Iwanow, Jekaterina Bogomolowa

Lease and finance
Anna Lessowa, Olga Boltenko

Competition, merger control, antitrust law
Dr Gerd Lenga, Maria Blagowolina

Intellectual property and IT
Falk Tischendorf, Swetlana Turbanowa

Labour law
Irene Engel, Jekaterina Bogomolowa

Corporate finance
Marco Koschier, Olga Boltenko

National and international tax
Marco Koschier, Anna Lessowa

Audit and accounting services
Walentina Lewkowitsch, Jelena Chatjetowskaja

Energy, natural resources
Dr Gerd Lenga, Stanislaw Arbenin

Insolvency, litigation, and arbitration
Swetlana Turbanowa, Stanislaw Arbenin

Privatisation
Irene Engel, Maria Blagowolina

HERBERT SMITH CIS LEGAL SERVICES

4TH FLOOR
KOROBEINIKOV 24
119034 MOSCOW

Telephone: +7 095 363 6500
Fax: +7 095 363 6501
E-mail: contact@herbertsmith.com
Website: www.herbertsmith.com

Languages
English, Russian

Other offices
Bangkok, Beijing, Brussels, Hong Kong, London, Paris, Shanghai, Singapore, Tokyo

Number of lawyers 1,108
at this office 20

CATEGORIES OF WORK

Energy and natural resources
Alan Jowett

Inward investment
John Balsdon, Andrew Calderwood

Litigation
Simon Bushell, Dmitry Kurochkin

Arbitration
Simon Bushell, Dmitry Kurochkin

Mergers and acquisitions
Sergei Baranchenkov, Allen Hanen

Securities
Sergei Baranchenkov, John Balsdon

Capital markets
Andrew Calderwood, Clive Barnard

HOGAN & HARTSON LLP

AMBASSADOR BUILDING
14, PRECHISTENSKIY PEREULOK
119034 MOSCOW

Telephone: +7 095 797 9900
Fax: +7 095 797 9961
E-mail: pjpettibone@hhlaw.com
Website: www.hhlaw.com

Languages
English, French, Russian, Spanish

Other offices
Baltimore, Beijing, Berlin, Boulder, Brussels, Budapest, Colorado Springs, Denver, London, Los Angeles, McLean, Miami, Munich, New York, Paris, Prague, Tokyo, Warsaw, Washington DC

Number of lawyers 1,018
at this office 12

Contacts
Peter Pettibone, Todd Schafer, Sergey Komolov

CATEGORIES OF WORK

International joint ventures

Private equity

Capital markets

Privatisation

Technology transfers

Mergers and acquisitions

Finance

Energy

Telecommunications

Intellectual property

International trade

Technical service contracts

Regulatory compliance

International litigation

Project finance

Pharmaceuticals

Food and agriculture

Aviation and space

JURINFLOT, INTERNATIONAL LAW OFFICE

PO BOX 60
109147 MOSKVA

Telephone: +7 095 792 5701
Fax: +7 095 792 5700
E-mail: jurin@jurinflot.ru
Website: www.jurinflot.ru

Languages
Belorussian, English, French, German, Norwegian, Spanish, Ukrainian

Number of lawyers 12

Member
International Maritime Law Association; International Bar Associaton; Guild of Russian Advocates; Terralex; Juris Consult Alliance

CATEGORIES OF WORK

Company law
SP Kondrashin, VV Mandriouc

Commercial contracts
SP Kondrashin, VV Mandriouc

Transport and trading
VG Ermolaev, TT Mischenko

Maritime matters
VG Ermolaev, VA Mednikov

Insurance
BV Pavlov

Asset and project financing
VA Mednikov

Lending and security
VA Mednikov

Foreign investment
AV Mednikov, VV Mandriouc

Commercial litigation and arbitration
VG Ermolaev, KG Ryndin

Taxation
AV Mednikov

LINKLATERS CIS

PAVELETSKAYA SQUARE 2, BLD 2
115054 MOSCOW

Telephone: +7 095 797 9797
Fax: +7 095 797 9798
Website: www.linklaters.com

Languages
All commercial and local languages in the countries where Linklaters operates

Other offices
Alicante, Amsterdam, Antwerp, Bangkok, Beijing, Berlin, Bratislava, Brussels, Bucharest, Budapest, Cologne, Frankfurt am Main, Hong Kong, Lisbon, London, Luxembourg, Madrid, Milan, Munich, New York, Paris, Prague, Rome, São Paulo, Shanghai, Singapore, Stockholm, Tokyo, Warsaw

Number of lawyers 2,000 worldwide

Contact
Dominic Sanders

CATEGORIES OF WORK

Corporate/M&A
Dominic Sanders, Denis Uvarov

Capital markets
Dmitry Dobatkin, Dominic Sanders

Banking and finance
Michael Bott, Dmitry Dobatkin

Energy
Denis Uvarov

Competition
Denis Uvarov

Real estate
Xavier Hunter, Konstantine Kouzine

Employment
Henry Rutstein

Litigation
Alexei Dudko

Tax
Victor Matcheknin

Intellectual property
Denis Uvarov, Anna Shashina

THE FIRM
Linklaters advises the world's leading companies, financial institutions and governments on their most challenging transactions and assignments. With 2,000 lawyers, including 470 partners, and offices in major business and financial centres, its clients choose the firm for its distinctive combination of technical skill, commercial experience and outstanding service.

Linklaters has built a formidable global practice through organic growth and a series of mergers, joint ventures and co-operations with other respected law firms. In 2001, Linklaters merged with three of Europe's leading law firms to form Linklaters Oppenhoff & Rädler in Germany, Linklaters in Sweden, Linklaters De Bandt in Belgium and Linklaters Loesch in Luxembourg. In the same year, the firm formed a co-operation with Brazilian firm Goulart Penteado, Iervolino e Lefosse. This cooperation combines Linklaters' international capability with GPIL's extensive knowledge of the Brazilian market. In Singapore, the firm practises as Linklaters Allen & Gledhill, a joint venture with the premier Singapore practice of Allen & Gledhill, while in Italy, Linklaters has a preferred relationship with the law firm Gianni, Origoni, Grippo & Partners.

LATHAM & WATKINS LLP

ULITSA GASHEKA 7
DUCAT PLACE II, 9TH FLOOR
SUITE 900
123056 MOSCOW

Telephone: +7 095 785 12 34
Fax: +7 095 785 12 35
Website: www.lw.com

Languages
English, German, Russian

Other offices
Boston, Brussels, Chicago, Frankfurt, Hamburg, Hong Kong, London, Los Angeles, Milan, New Jersey, New York, Northern Virginia, Orange County, Paris, San Diego, San Francisco, Silicon Valley, Singapore, Tokyo, Washington DC

Number of lawyers 1,500
at this office 9

CATEGORIES OF WORK

- Capital markets
- Corporate finance
- Intellectual property
- Mergers and acquisitions, privatisations and joint ventures
- Project finance
- Venture and technology
- Telecoms and media
- Restructuring
- Real estate

LOVELLS

5TH FLOOR, USADBA CENTRE
22 VOZNESENSKY
PEREULOK
125009 MOSCOW

Telephone: +7 095 933 3000
Fax: +7 095 933 3001
E-mail: information@lovells.com
Website: www.lovells.com

Languages
Arabic, English, French, German, Italian, Mandarin, Polish, Russian, Spanish, Swedish, Ukrainian, Vietnamese

Other offices
Alicante, Amsterdam, Beijing, Berlin, Brussels, Budapest*, Chicago, Düsseldorf, Frankfurt, Hamburg, Ho Chi Minh City, Hong Kong, London, Milan, Munich, New York, Paris, Prague, Rome, Shanghai, Singapore, Tokyo, Vienna*, Warsaw, Zagreb*

Number of lawyers 1,600
at this office 16

Contacts
Chris Oiven, Oxana Balayan

CATEGORIES OF WORK

- Arbitration and litigation
- Banking and finance
- Corporate finance
- Energy
- Capital markets
- Corporate and commercial
- Information technology
- Intellectual property

MONASTYRSKY, ZYUBA, STEPANOV & PARTNERS

3/1 NOVINSKY BOULEVARD
MOSCOW 121099

Telephone: +7 095 231 4222
Fax: +7 095 231 4223
E-mail: moscow@mzs.ru
Website: www.mzs.ru

Languages
English, French, German, Swedish, Ukrainian

Number of lawyers 16

CATEGORIES OF WORK

Corporate law	Criminal law
Mergers and acquisitions	Personal services
Investments	Insolvency
Securities	Antitrust
Intellectual property	Land law
Taxation	Transportation
Banking regulation	Currency
Real estate	Foreign trade regulation
Insurance law	Mass media
Litigation	Labour law
Arbitration	Family and succession
Oil and gas	Customs regulation
Telecommunications	

THE FIRM

Monastyrsky, Zyuba, Stepanov & Partners was established in 1991 in Moscow, under the original name of MICE & Co. The firm has two offices located in the historical part of Moscow, within view of the Kremlin.

Monastyrsky, Zyuba, Stepanov & Partners very quickly established itself in the legal services market, becoming a major player in the field of large international transactions.

The firm specialises in legal services to a select number of large foreign investors and major domestic companies, providing highly personalised services tailored to the individual needs of the client, thus being able to meet the highest service standards.

AREAS OF PRACTICE

Monastyrsky, Zyuba, Stepanov & Partners' professional activities are many and varied, covering over 20 areas of specialisation.

The firm's financial stability and profitable status puts it in a position to undertake benevolent as well as research activities.

NÖRR STIEFENHOFER LUTZ

TSVETNOY BOULEVARD, 25
BUILDING 3
BUSINESS CENTRE, MOSENKA 2
127051 MOSKVA

Telephone: +7 095 799 56 96
Fax: +7 095 799 5697
E-mail: nslmos@dol.ru
Website: www.noerr.ru

Languages
English, French, German, Spanish

Other offices
Berlin, Bucharest, Budapest, Dresden, Düsseldorf, Frankfurt, Munich, Prague, Warsaw

Number of lawyers 237
(+ 53 tax advisers, public accountants and tax assistants)
at this office 20

Contacts
Dr Hans-Peter Zier, Ilja Rybalkin

CATEGORIES OF WORK

- **Antitrust law**
- **Arbitration and litigation**
- **Banking law and currency regulation**
- **Civil and contract law**
- **Company law and restructuring**
- **Customs regulation**
- **Insurance law**
- **Foreign exchange and trade law**
- **Intellectual property**
- **Labour law**
- **Distribution and leasing law**
- **Property and real estate law**
- **Tax law**
- **Internet and new media law**

PEPELIAEV, GOLTSBLAT & PARTNERS

7 DOLGORUKOVSKAYA
SADOVAYA PLAZA
127006 MOSCOW

Telephone: +7 095 258 5040
Fax: +7 095 258 5041
E-mail: info@pgplaw.ru
Website: www.pgplaw.ru

Languages
English

Other offices
St Petersburg

Number of lawyers 49

Contacts
Sergei Pepeliaev (managing partner),
Andrey Goltsblat (managing partner),
Svetlana Kleimenicheva(general director)

Member
Interlaw; International Trademark Association (INTA); American Chamber of Commerce; European Business Club

CATEGORIES OF WORK

Corporate law	Anti-monopoly legislation
Tax law, litigation and audit	Advertising legislation
Intellectual property	Consumer law
Real estate and construction	International private law
Customs law	Currency transactions
Labour law	Investment projects
Natural resources and environment	Commercial litigation
Securities	

THE FIRM

Pepeliaev, Goltsblat & Partners was established in January 2002 as a result of the merger between Legal Practice LLC, a full-service Russian law firm, and a team of lawyers from the tax and law department of the leading Russian auditing firm FBK. The firm offers a wide spectrum of legal services with particular emphasis on providing tax, legal and IP advice, and representing clients in courts of all levels.

The clientele of the firm ranges from major Russian companies to well-known multinational corporations from a wide range of industries including FMCG manufacturers, key players in car manufacturing, oil and gas industry, energy and natural resources, transport, food and agriculture, utilities, telecommunications, engineering, printing industry, real estate, construction, financial services, service sector, advertising and many other sectors.

AREAS OF PRACTICE

One of the basic principles of Pepeliaev, Goltsblat & Partners is to offer a wide scope of legal services to each client. In addition to its core focus of tax, legal and IP services, there is also an active practice in the areas of corporate law, real estate and construction, customs law, labour law, natural resources and environment, securities, anti-monopoly legislation, advertising legislation, consumer law, international private law, currency transactions, investment projects, commercial projects and litigation. Dealing with the most acute problems facing business entities in today's Russia each practice group has accumulated great practical experience.

Members of the corporate law team are primarily retained by foreign investors operating in Russia for corporate restructuring, mergers and acquisitions, charter capital operations, and incorporation of legal entities, branches and representative offices.

The real estate and construction practice group deals with due diligence, including title examination, legal support for land and real estate transactions, formalisation of rights to land plots for commercial use and acquisition of rights to existing manufacturing facilities for setting up production, and mortgages as security for obligations under commercial contracts. Being one of the first in Russia to perform land transactions, the firm's lawyers now possess experience-proven practical techniques based on a deep understanding of all the nuances of legal realities in Russia.

The intellectual property protection practice group's primary activities are IP advice; identification of protectable IP assets; transfer of a PCT application into the national phase in Russia; assistance in the registration of trade marks and patenting of utility models, industrial designs and inventions both in Russia and abroad; preparation and filing with the Chamber of Appeals and the High Patent Chamber objections to refusals to register trade marks and to issue patents for inventions, utility models and industrial designs; IP protection in court.

The firm lays particular stress on providing advice on complicated tax issues, its approach being tailored to specific business objectives, mindful of any future developments in the Russian tax regime. The provided services span a wide range of tax issues, including tax optimisation; legal examinations of official actions; tax audit and corporate planning; advice on tax incentives available to investors at the federal, regional and local levels,; preliminary assessment of tax implications of contracts and prevention of negative tax consequences.

The company is well known for its exceptionally positive tax litigation experience, the percentage of win cases being 98%. The lawyers of the company assist major taxpayers in resolving various disputes in court, acting as opponents to both other companies and the authorities. The court decisions rendered in these cases are of importance not only to the one company represented in court, but have a much wider relevance.

More detailed information is available on request or on the firm's website: www.pgplaw.ru.

RUSSIN & VECCHI LLC

ULITSA BOLSHAYA ORDYNKA 60/2
119017 MOSCOW

Telephone: +7 095 959 1288
Fax: +7 095 959 1290
E-mail: lawyers@russinvecchi.ru
Website: www.russinvecchi.com

Languages
Arabic, English, French, Spanish, Tatar

Other offices
Bangkok, Hanoi, Ho Chi Minh City, New York, Puerto Plata, Santo Domingo, Taipei, Vladivostok, Washington DC, Yangon, Yuzhno-Sakhalinsk

Number of lawyers 118
at this office 8

Contacts
Jonathan Russin, Sergei Lazarev

Member
Meritas (formerly Commercial Law affiliates)

CATEGORIES OF WORK

Corporate law
Jonathan Russin, Alexander Podolsky

Commercial law/ transaction structuring
Jonathan Russin, Rinat Zakirov-Ziev

Labour
Sergei Lazarev, Rinat Zakirov-Ziev

Mergers and acquisitions
Sergei Lazarev, Alexander Podolsky

Energy and natural resources
Vladislav Talantsev, Irina Paliashvili

Environment
Vladislav Talantsev, Thomas Mansbach

Agencies and distributorships
Jonathan Russin, Rinat Zakirov-Ziev

Government business/regulatory
Sergei Lazarev, William White

Asset finance/security
Alexander Podolsky, Rinat Zakirov-Ziev

Foreign direct investment
Jonathan Russin, Sergei Lazarev

Shipping and transport
Rinat Zakirov-Ziev, Vladislav Talantsev

Insolvency
Alexander Podolsky, Rinat Zakirov-Ziev

Media and entertainment
Sergei Lazarev, Vladislav Talantsev

Civil litigation and arbitration
Sergei Lazarev, Rinat Zakirov-Ziev

Trade marks
Sergei Lazarev, Vladislav Talantsev

Tax
Alexander Podolsky, Rinat Zakirov-Ziev

THE FIRM

Russin & Vecchi LLC is an international law firm with 12 independent, but affiliated offices spanning the globe. The firm was founded in 1969 in Bangkok, Saigon, Santo Domingo and Washington DC to create an international practice serving the developing commercial environments of Asia and Latin America. The Russian Practice Group, consisting of the Moscow, Vladivostok, Yuznho-Sakhalinsk and Washington offices, was formed in 1991 to carry on the firm's tradition of making legal services available in emerging economies.

AREAS OF PRACTICE

The Moscow office concentrates and specialises in the domestic law of Russia and the CIS countries in order to address the full spectrum of legal issues that confront multinational enterprises today. The Russian Practice Group's Moscow office advises on all areas of commercial activity including: oil and gas law; production sharing agreements (PSAs); natural resources law; corporate formation; licensing; franchising and foreign investments; registration and accreditation of foreign legal entities; shareholder agreements; mergers and acquisitions; bankruptcy and corporate reorganisation; arbitration and litigation; intellectual property; international trade and anti-dumping; administrative law; labour law; tax law and banking law.

Russin & Vecchi LLC was the first international law firm to open offices in Vladivostok and Yuzhno-Sakhalinsk and to maintain a permanent presence in the Russian Far East. Russin & Vecchi LLC is the only law firm with American and local lawyers permanently stationed on Sakhalin. The Vladivostok office opened in 1995 and specialises in admiralty and maritime law, tax and labour law, and litigation and arbitration. In 2001, Russin & Vecchi LLC opened an office in Yuzhno-Sakhalinsk to assist clients in the expanding oil and gas industry on Sakhalin Island. In addition to oil and gas law, the Yuznho-Sakhalinsk office advises on PSAs and Russian content, Sakhalin I and II tender bidders in creating joint ventures, operating with Russian and/or foreign partners and repatriating dividends, registering legal entities and accrediting branch offices, employer-employee relationships and labour law, and navigating customs regulations. In addition, Russin & Vecchi LLC conducts company due diligence on prospective investment targets and business partners, and provides continuing assistance to employers and expatriate personnel working in Russia and the Commonwealth of Independent States.

Russin & Vecchi LLC's commercial clients are involved in a variety of foreign investment and foreign trade transactions, including: minerals exploration and extraction ventures; oil and gas exploitation under production sharing agreements; export and import sales; installation of manufacturing plants and production facilities; corporate transactions with and without Russian participants; purchase of Russian stocks and government bonds; ship registration and secured maritime financing; hotel and tourism related enterprises and production of beer.

SIKAYLO, MATVEEV, GABBASOV & PARTNERS

ATTORNEYS AT LAW

OFFICE 2
M BRONNAYA STREET 32
MOSKVA 123001

Telephone: +7 095 202 0431
Fax: +7 095 202 0255
E-mail: attorneys@mtu-net.ru

Languages
English, French, Spanish

Number of lawyers 14

CATEGORIES OF WORK

Foreign investment and joint ventures
Alexey Sikaylo, Svetlana Romakhova

Natural resources
Marat Gabbasov, Svetlana Romakhova

Taxation
Dmitry Matveev, Natalia Shcherbakova

Banking and finance
Dmitry Matveev, Natalia Shcherbakova

Real estate
Marat Gabbasov, Oksana Zhdanovskaya

Corporate law
Alexey Sikaylo, Svetlana Romakhova

Litigation and arbitration
Alexey Sikaylo, Dmitry Matveev

Land law
Marat Gabbasov, Oksana Zhdanovskaya

Construction
Marat Gabbasov

Commercial property
Dmitry Matveev, Alexey Sikaylo

THE FIRM

Sikaylo, Matveev, Gabbasov & Partners (Attorneys at Law) was established in 1999, although the majority of the firm's lawyers have worked together since 1990.

The firm specialises in providing complex legal assistance to companies from the Russian Federation and the CIS, as well as companies overseas.

Sikaylo, Matveev, Gabbasov & Partners has solid experience of work not only in the various parts and regions of Russia, but also abroad. The firm's main specialisation is arbitration and litigation. The firm aims to provide client companies with advice and assistance in all litigation and arbitration matters.

In addition to its traditional advisory and litigation services, the firm provides advice based on the realities of today's market. During recent years, the firm has been associated with a number of large arbitration disputes (including the bankruptcy and corporate restructuring of some of the largest enterprises in Russia) which has had a wide resonance in the present Russian society.

In 2001, the lawyers of the firm acted as the founders of the International Bulgarian-Russian Legal Club intended to assist the development of the experience exchange between the lawyers from different countries. In the course of the last few years, the International Bulgarian-Russian Legal Club has conducted a number of international conferences with the participation of the president of Bulgaria, the juridical faculty of Sofia University, the representatives of the Supreme Court of the Russian Federation and the Superior Arbitration Court of the Russian Federation

The office of the firm is situated in the old historical part of Moscow. All attorneys speak at least two languages.

AREAS OF PRACTICE

Sikaylo, Matveev, Gabbasov & Partners holds consultations on various issues concerning the application of Russian legislation and international law. It prepares legal opinions with respect to contracts, letters, claims and other legal documents as well as preparation of drafts.

The firm participates in negotiations with clients and also the registration and reorganisation of companies. In addition Sikaylo, Matveev, Gabbasov & Partners represents clients with regard to arbitration and state authorities in both the Russian Federation and abroad, whilst also providing other general legal assistance.

SQUIRE, SANDERS & DEMPSEY (MOSCOW) LLC

2/2 PAVELETSKAYA SQUARE
115054, MOSCOW

Telephone: +7 095 258 5250
Fax: +7 095 258 5251
E-mail: itrifonov@ssd.com
Website: www.ssd.com

Languages
English, French, Portuguese, Spanish

Other offices
Beijing, Bratislava, Brussels, Budapest, Cincinnati, Cleveland, Columbus, Hong Kong, Houston, London, Los Angeles, Madrid, Miami, Milan, New York, Palo Alto, Phoenix, Prague, Rio de Janeiro, San Francisco, Taipei, Tampa, Tokyo, Tysons Corner, Washington DC, Bucharest*, Dublin*, Kyiv*

Number of lawyers 710
at this office 9

Contact
Ivan Trifonov

Member
American Chamber of Commerce; Russo-British Chamber of Commerce; US Russian Business Counsel

CATEGORIES OF WORK

Competition law
David Wack

Corporate finance, banking, capital markets
David Wack, Sergey Treshchev

Environmental
Ivan Trifonov

Infrastructure, project asset finance
David Wack

Intellectual property
David Wack, Anna Grozovskaya

International transactions
Sarah Carey

Litigation and arbitration
Sergey Treshchev

Mergers and acquisitions
David Wack

Oil and gas
Ivan Trifonov

Power generation, energy
David Wack, Ivan Trifonov

Real estate
Ivan Trifonov

Securities
Sergey Treshchev, David Wack

Telecoms
David Wack

THE FIRM

Founded in 1890, Squire, Sanders & Dempsey is a multi-jurisdictional law firm with 710 lawyers practising in offices in Europe, the Americas and Asia. The firm's practice covers most substantive areas of the law, with an emphasis on business and finance matters.

The firm operates as a single global partnership, which ensures client accountability and the seamless delivery of uniformly high-quality legal services throughout the world. The firm's lawyers come from many countries and cultures, are licensed to practise in both common law and civil law jurisdictions, and communicate with clients in their native languages. Today, the firm remains committed to the fundamental principles ordained by its founders: to serve clients effectively and maintain the professional standards that distinguish both the firm and its people.

AREAS OF PRACTICE

The firm is organised around four major practice areas: advocacy, business, capital markets and regulated industries. Within these practice areas, the firm's work can be divided into numerous areas of specialisation, including banking, bankruptcy and restructuring, biotechnology and pharmaceuticals, communications, competition law, converging technologies, corporate, energy, environmental, healthcare, intellectual property, international dispute resolution, labour and employment, litigation, mergers and acquisitions, privatisations, project finance, real estate, securities and taxation.

Established in 1992, the Moscow office advises both Russian clients and those doing business in the region on questions arising under corporate, intellectual property, environmental, labour, real property, securities, banking, tax, privatisation, antitrust and currency control laws. The Moscow office is part of Squire Sanders' CIS trade and investment practice.

Lawyers in the Moscow office are actively involved in all phases of the region's growing private sector – from assisting Russian and other CIS policy-makers in the transition to a market economy to structuring new business forms and creating a broad range of new private companies. In November 2001, the office was certified by the Russian Ministry of Justice's State Registration Chamber to register Russian and Western companies establishing operations in Russia.

The Moscow lawyers represent clients in dispute resolution proceedings, including local litigation, international arbitration, insolvency and workout proceedings.

Lawyers provide counsel to industries including aerospace, automotive, commercial and investment banking, energy (including oil, gas and power, as well as providers of equipment and services), engineering, equipment manufacturing, food processing and distribution, pharmaceuticals, mining, radio and television broadcasting, real estate, retail, software development, telecoms and transportation.

The Russia team, including in particular the members resident in Washington DC and London, have participated in the representation of US and other government agencies and international organisations in connection with their activities in Russia.

SMIRNOV, DAVYDOV & SUSSKIND
LAW OFFICES

FILIPPOVSKIJ PER 16
SUITE 2
119019 MOSKVA

Telephone: +7 095 913 35 48
Fax: +7 095 202 20 82
E-mail: sds@asvt.ru
Website: www.tamga.ru

Languages
English, Portuguese, Spanish

Number of lawyers 5

Contact
Dr Mikhail Smirnov

CATEGORIES OF WORK

- Customs law
- Banking law
- Import and export law
- VAT and excises
- Contracts
- Business immigration
- Agency and distribution
- Corporate law
- Foreign investments and joint ventures in Russia and abroad
- Russian law

VINSON & ELKINS LLP

NOVINSKY BULVAR 31
6TH FLOOR
MOSCOW

Telephone: +7 095 956 1995
Fax: +7 095 956 1996
Website: www.velaw.com

Languages
English

Other offices
Austin, Beijing, Dallas, Dubai, Houston, London, New York, Singapore, Washington DC

Number of lawyers 775

Contacts
Douglas Glass, Natalya Morozova, Alexey Condratchick, Joel Lambert

Member
International Bar Association; International Law Section of the American Bar Association; International Lawyers Group, Moscow

CATEGORIES OF WORK

- Banking and finance
- Infrastructure and project finance
- Capital markets
- Labour law
- Commercial property/real estate
- Media and entertainment
- Competition
- Mergers and acquisitions
- Corporate and commercial
- Privatisation
- Energy and natural resources
- Telecommunications
- Foreign direct investment

VEGAS-LEX LAW FIRM

22/25 BLDG 1
BOLSHOY STROCHENOVSKY
PEREULOK
115054 MOSCOW

Telephone: +7 095 933 0800
Fax: +7 095 933 0802
E-mail: vegaslex@vegaslex.ru
Website: www.vegaslex.ru

Languages
English, French, German, Italian, Spanish, Ukranian

Other offices
Krasnodar, London, Volgograd, Ulyanovsk

Number of lawyers 50
at this office 21

Member
Anglo-Russian Law Association (ARLA); International Bar Association (France); Chartered Institute of Arbitrators (UK)

CATEGORIES OF WORK

Project finance
Albert Eganyan

Mergers and acquisitions
Michael Safarov, Juri Borisenko

Corporate and commercial
Dmitry Orakhelashvili, Michael Safarov

Bankruptcy and corporate recovery
Juris Borisenko

Investment
Albert Eganyan, Constantine Saranchouk

Litigation
Anna Khudanova

Arbitration
Constantine Saranchouk

Tax, customs and excise
Anna Khudanova

International trade, anti-dumping
Alexandra Vasiukhnova

Transport and shipping
Constantine Saranchouk

THE FIRM

Vegas-Lex was founded in 1995 as a result of a young Russian lawyer's initiative to establish a legal consulting entity of international excellence in Russia. The lawyers of the firm graduated from leading universities across Russia, the UK and the US, and have gained experience with some of the world's largest consulting and law firms such as PricewaterhouseCoopers and White & Case.

Once set, the highest professional standard and strict business rules are scrupulously observed. Vegas-Lex was the first, and is still the only, law firm in Russia to offer its clients the InGosStrakh insurance policy, protecting them against any mistakes made by professional lawyers.

Over the years, the firm has expanded dramatically, and has now become a centre of legal advice for multinational, regional and local companies. Dedicated to a practical approach, Vegas-Lex has opened offices in a number of industrial regions in order to be even more flexible to the clients' needs and more efficient in dispute resolution.

Vegas-Lex has associated with Kennedys Law Firm (UK) and has a London office. In addition to traditional business ethics, the firm has developed the distinctive method of securing confidentiality, which is especially important in dealing with property cases.

The State Duma (Russian Parliament) has chosen Vegas-Lex as its official expert. Cooperation of this kind is constantly explored between the firm and a number of state agencies that have a direct impact upon the strategic planning of major Russian corporations. These include the Ministry of Economic Development and Trade, the Ministry of Finance, the Ministry for State Property, the Ministry for Taxes and Duties, the Ministry of Justice, and the State Customs Committee.

Today, Vegas-Lex is regarded as an elite Russian law firm, and services clients from almost every sector of the economy. Recent projects have related to natural resources, agriculture, the chemical and processing industries, banking, aerospace, transport, travel and communications. A number of multinationals refer a wide range of legal issues to Vegas-Lex, including American Express, Ernst & Young, Conoco, and several major Russian enterprises such as Sibur, Novorossiysk Shipyard, Magnitogorsk Mettalugical Complex.

AREAS OF PRACTICE

Recent surveys confirm the sound reputation of the firm. Surveys in the *Expert* analytical magazine (Russia) consistently rank Vegas-Lex either first or second in Russia, and particularly highlight the firm's outstanding experience and efficiency in the field of corporate and commercial legal consulting. In August 2003, a survey in *Izvestia* newspaper ranked Vegas-Lex second to none among the Russian legal consulting firms.

The firm's managing partner Albert Eganyan is one of the most reputable legal advisers to corporate clients and the expert for reference for the Russian legal profession. Being very efficient in establishing business links between European and Russian communities, he has made an impressive commitment to the on-going Russian Legal Reform. The firm's lawyers have extensive experience in litigation across Russia, and in arbitration, as well as an enforcement of foreign arbitration awards in Russia.

CLYDE & CO
(IN ASSOCIATION WITH MUSIN & PARTNERS)

APT 2, 23 ROENTGENA STREET
197101 ST PETERSBURG

Telephone: +7 812 327 5871
Fax: +7 812 327 5873
E-mail: russia@clyde.co.uk
Website: www.clydeco.com

Languages
English, Russian

Other offices
Belgrade, Caracas, Cardiff, Dubai, Guildford, Hong Kong, London, Nantes, Paris, Piraeus, Singapore

Contact
Trevor Barton (London)

CATEGORIES OF WORK

Inward investment

Shipping (wet and dry)

Property development

Road and rail carriage

Joint ventures

Trading

MANNHEIMER SWARTLING

DOM SHVETSII
MALAYA KONYUSHENNAYA 1/3A
191186 ST PETERSBURG

Telephone: +7 812 329 2505
Fax: +7 812 329 2507
Website: www.mannheimerswartling.se

Languages
English, German, Russian, Swedish

Other offices
Berlin, Brussels, Frankfurt, Gothenburg, Helsingborg, Malmö, New York, Stockholm

Number of lawyers 330
at this office 4

Contact
Sven Lexner

CATEGORIES OF WORK

All aspects of Russian commercial law

RUSSIN & VECCHI LLC

SUKHANOVA STREET, 3-A
VLADIVOSTOK 690091

Telephone: +7 4232 43 3015
Fax: +7 4232 43 2465
E-mail: russin@vladivostok.ru
Website: www.russinvecchi.com

Languages
English

Other offices
Bangkok, Hanoi, Ho Chi Minh City, Moscow, New York, Puerto Plata, Santo Domingo, Taipei, Washington DC, Yangon, Yuzhno-Sakhalinsk

Number of lawyers 118
at this office 2

Contacts
Nataliya Prisekina, Zhanna Radmaeva

Member
Meritas (formerly Commercial Law affiliates)

CATEGORIES OF WORK

Maritime and Admiralty
Nataliya Prisekina

Corporate formation and licensing
Nataliya Prisekina

Bankruptcy and corporate reorganisation
Zhanna Radmaeva

Arbitration and litigation
Nataliya Prisekina

Labour
Zhanna Radmaeva

Tax
Nataliya Prisekina

Banking
Nataliya Prisekina

RUSSIN & VECCHI LLC

SAKHINCENTER, SUITE 610
32 KOMMUNISTICHESKY PROSPECT
YUZHNO-SAKHALINSK 693000

Telephone: +7 4242 726 786
Fax: +7 4242 726 758
E-mail: russinvecchi@snc.ru
Website: www.russinvecchi.com

Languages
English

Other offices
Bangkok, Hanoi, Ho Chi Minh City, Moscow, New York, Puerto Plata, Santo Domingo, Taipei, Vladivostok, Washington DC, Yangon

Number of lawyers 118
at this office 5

Contacts
Rita Hoffmann, Denis Marchenko

Member
Meritas (formerly Commercial Law affiliates)

CATEGORIES OF WORK

Oil and gas
Denis Marchenko, Rita Hoffmann

Production sharing agreements
Denis Marchenko, William Ruddy

Joint venture creation
Denis Marchenko, Evgeny Kuzmenko

Corporate law
Denis Marchenko, Rita Hoffmann

Commercial transactions
Denis Marchenko, Rita Hoffmann

Labour
Denis Marchenko, Evgeny Kuzmenko

Environmental law
Rita Hoffmann, Evgeny Kuzmenko

Litigation and arbitration
Denis Marchenko

Maritime and admiralty
Denis Marchenko, William Ruddy

Tax law
Valery Bespalov

DR ARZINGER & PARTNER

VUL STARONAVODNITSKA 4A
APT 5
01015 KIEV

Telephone: +380 44 490 96 97
Fax: +380 44 490 96 98
E-mail: mail@arzinger.com.ua
Website: www.arzinger.com.ua

Languages
English, French, German, Russian, Ukrainian

Other offices
Berlin, Bratislava, Budapest, Moskow, Novosibirsk, Prague

Number of lawyers 53
at this office 14

Member
Interleges; EBA; German-Ukrainian Legal Association

CATEGORIES OF WORK

International and domestic litigation
Timur Bondarev

Securities
Wolfram Rehbock

Commercial law
Timur Bondarev, Sergei Schklyar

Foreign investments
Wolfram Rehbock

Joint ventures
Timur Bondarev

Banking and finance
Wolfram Rehbock

Mergers and acquisitions
Wolfram Rehbock, Timur Bondarev

Antitrust and competition law
Timur Bondarev, Sergei Schklyar

Privatisation
Sergei Schklyar

Taxation
Wolfram Rehbock, Timur Bondarev

Bankruptcy
Sergei Schklyar

Intellectual property
Wolfram Rehbock

Real estate
Timur Bondarev

BAKER & McKENZIE

BUSINESS CENTRE 'MILLENNIUM'
5TH FLOOR
12A VOLODYMYRSKA STREET
KYIV 01025

Telephone: +380 44 490 7070
Fax: +380 44 490 6787
E-mail: kyiv_info@bakernet.com
Website: www.bakernet.com

Languages
English, French, Italian, Polish, Russian, Ukrainian

Other offices
For a list of all offices and other information regarding the firm please consult Baker & McKenzie's Moscow office entry.

Number of lawyers 3,380
at this office 19

Contact
James T Hitch III

Baker & McKenzie is a global law firm with 66 offices in 36 countries.

CATEGORIES OF WORK

Arbitration and litigation
Serhiy Chorny

Banking and finance
Serhiy Chorny

Corporate and commercial
Olexander Martinenko, James T Hitch

E-commerce/telecoms
Olexander Martinenko

Energy and natural resources
Serhiy Piontkovsky

Environment
Serhiy Piontkovsky

Insurance
Serhiy Piontkovsky

Intellectual property
James T Hitch

Labour law
Serhiy Chorny, Vadym Vasko

Mergers and acquisitions
James T Hitch

Privatisation
Serhiy Piontovsky

Real estate and construction
Serhiy Piontkovsky

Tax
Serhiy Piontkovsky

B C TOMS & CO

18 PRORIZNA STREET, APT 1
KYIV 01034

Telephone: +380 44 228 1000
Fax: +380 44 228 6508
E-mail: bt@bctoms.com

Languages
English, French, German, Polish, Russian, Ukrainian

Other offices
London, Odessa

Number of lawyers 17
at this office 14

CATEGORIES OF WORK

Acquisition and privatisation
B Toms, V Sayenko

Banking
B Toms, V Sayenko

Company law
S Kheda, T Krivonogikh

Commercial law
S Kheda, O Prokopovych

Commercial property
D Serdyuk, S Kheda

Construction
O Kutsevol, D Serdyuk

Electricity
B Toms, T Krivonogikh

Insolvency
O Kutsevol, T Krivonogikh

Intellectual property
T Dumych, O Prokopovych

Litigation and arbitration
D Korbut, V Sayenko

Oil and gas
B Toms, D Serdyuk

Project finance
B Toms, V Sayenko

Securities
B Toms, O Prokopovych

Tax and customs
I Posypayko, Z Mylovanova

Telecommunications
T Dumych, S Kheda

THE FIRM
B C Toms & Co is a law firm of western and Ukrainian lawyers specialising in Ukrainian law. The firm was the first from the west to establish a Ukrainian law practice following Ukrainian independence in 1991. Presently it is among the largest law firms in the Ukraine.

In the last three years alone, the firm has acted for clients in transactions representing in value over $2bn of investments and loans into Ukraine. For example, the firm has handled the legal work for most of the oil and gas and electricity generation projects in Ukraine for western firms and joint ventures with western investment, many of the significant western investments in real estate development, many of the largest international loans to Ukraine, telecommunications projects, greenfield factory developments and many acquisitions of Ukrainian businesses (including through privatisation of state assets).

B C Toms & Co was founded by BC Toms, who was previously a partner in a multinational law firm and has substantial experience practising in the US, and Western as well as Eastern Europe. Toms studied Soviet Studies at university and law at Magdalene College, Cambridge and Yale Law School (where he was an editor of the *Yale Law Journal*).

For the past 14 years, the firm has recruited and trained its Ukrainian lawyers from among the highest ranked students at Ukraine's leading law schools, most of whom have also studied at US and UK law schools. Based on the firm's practical experience, it has written numerous articles on Ukrainian law, including the legal section of the ICC's book, *Doing Business in Ukraine*.

AREAS OF PRACTICE
As one of the largest law firm's in Ukraine, B C Toms & Co has a general practice. The principal practice areas include project finance and construction, real estate, oil and gas and electricity regulation law, investment and acquisition, securities and corporate law, mining, privatisation, franchising, distribution, telecommunications, trade, banking, labour, bankruptcy and administrative law, as well as lobbying on behalf of clients. In addition, the firm has an active litigation and arbitration practice. The firm also regularly advises on Ukrainian tax law including from a multinational tax planning perspective.

B C Toms & Co has prepared a wide variety of documentation for clients including joint venture agreements, construction contracts, project financing documentation, production sharing and oil and gas sales agreements, private placement agreements, loan agreements, leases, corporate acquisition, agency, distribution, franchises and licensing contracts. It can also provide practical commercial advice on how to establish and develop a Ukrainian business.

CHADBOURNE & PARKE LLP

11 MYKHAILIVSKA STREET
01001 KIEV

Telephone: +380 44 230 2534
Fax: +380 44 230 2535
E-mail: jzjohnson@chadbourne.com
Website: www.chadbourne.com

Languages
English, French, Polish, Russian, Ukrainian

Other offices
Beijing, Houston, London, Los Angeles, Moscow, New York, Tashkent, Warsaw, Washington DC

Number of lawyers 431
at this office 9

Contact
Jaroslawa Zelinsky Johnson

International groupings
American Chamber of Commerce in Ukraine; European Business Association

CATEGORIES OF WORK

Banking and finance
Jaroslawa Johnson, Adam Mycyk

Joint ventures
Volodymyr Baibarza

Mergers, acquisitions and privatisation
Jaroslawa Johnson, Volodymyr Baibarza

Securities, capital markets
Adam Mycyk, Olexiy Soshenko

Real estate
Jaroslawa Johnson, Sergiy Onishchenko

Dispute resolution
Volodymyr Baibarza, Valery Fedichin

Government relations
Jaroslawa Johnson, Volodymyr Baibarza

GRISCHENKO & PARTNERS

3RD FLOOR
20 MECHNIKOVA STREET
KIEV

Telephone: +380 44 290 09 73
Fax: +380 44 290 95 29
E-mail: adm@gp.ua
Website: www.gp.ua

Languages
English, Russian, Ukrainian

Number of lawyers 21

CATEGORIES OF WORK

Foreign investments

Joint ventures

Corporate finance, banking

Business, commercial and company law

Litigation/arbitration

Taxation and customs

Natural resources, oil and gas

Telecommunications

Real estate

Labour and employment

Due diligence

ILYASHEV & PARTNERS

4 CHAPAEVA STREET
01030 KYIV

Telephone: +380 44 246 5690
Fax: +380 44 246 5691
E-mail: office@attorneys.com.ua
Website: www.attorneys.com.ua

Languages
English, Russian, Ukrainian

Other offices
Kharkiv

Number of lawyers 11
at this office 10

CATEGORIES OF WORK

Litigation
Mikhail Ilyashev, Galina Lefor

Taxation
Mikhail Ilyashev

Arbitration
Mikhail Ilyashev, Roman Marchenko

Corporate law
Roman Molodetskiy, Evgen Solovyov

International arbitration
Mikhail Ilyashev, Roman Marchenko

Insolvency
Roman Marchenko, Evgen Solovyov

Real estate, construction
Maksim Kopeichikov

Project finance
Roman Marchenko

Anti-counterfeiting
Mikhail Ilyashev, Evgen Solovyov

Commercial property
Mikhail Ilyashev, Maksim Kopeichikov

Debt collection
Roman Marchenko, Svetlana Kienko

KONNOV & SOZANOVSKY

SUITE 5
23 SHOTA RUSTAVELI STREET
01023 KYIV

Telephone: +380 44 490 5400
Fax: +380 44 490 5490
E-mail: info@konnov.com
Website: www.konnov.com

Languages
English, French, German, Russian

Other offices
Chernovtsy, Moscow

Number of lawyers 28
at this office 16

CATEGORIES OF WORK

Antitrust
Helen Popko

Media law
Sergei Sozanovsky

Commercial law
Alexei Zolotov, Natalia Moskalenko

Real estate
Ilona Melnichuk

Copyright
Victor Mirsky

Securities
Galina Zagorodnyuk

Corporate law
Sergei Konnov

Tax
Yevgenia Derbal

Litigation
Natalia Subota, Maria Apollonova

Trade marks
Tatiana Glouhovskaya

MAGISTER & PARTNERS

10 MUZEYNY PROVULOK
01601 KYIV

Telephone: +380 44 255 5680
Fax: +380 44 255 5687
E-mail: info@magisters.com
Website: www.magisters.com

Languages
English, German, Russian, Ukrainian

Number of lawyers 21

Contacts
Oleg Riabokon (trade and commerce),
Eugene Korniychuk (finance, oil and gas),
Oleg Marchenko (tax and corporate)

CATEGORIES OF WORK

Arbitration and litigation	**International trade law**
Banking and finance	**Mergers and acquisitions**
Commercial transactions	**Oil and gas**
Corporate matters	**Securities regulation**
Foreign investment	**Taxation**

THE FIRM

Magister & Partners is a well-established, reputable and dynamic firm offering a wide range of services, a wealth of international experience and a qualified legal team. Since 1997, its lawyers have represented foreign companies conducting business in Ukraine, the CIS region, Western Europe and the Americas, as well as domestic blue-chip companies, seven of which lead the list of the 'Top 100 Best Companies in Ukraine'. Most of the firm's associates hold law degrees from the US, Canada or Western European universities, and have worked with leading attorneys in these jurisdictions.

The firm's excellence in the fields of Ukrainian and international law has been widely recognised by the business community and independent research publications. The national ranking, *Legal Olympus of Ukraine 2002*, named Magister & Partners 'the best Ukrainian law firm, which developed the most dynamically in the Ukrainian and foreign market of legal services through the year 2002'. *Yuridicheskaya Praktika*, Ukraine's law newspaper, ranked Magister & Partners one of the 'Top 20 Ukrainian law firms with the largest staff'. The *International Who's Who of Trade and Customs Lawyers 2003* listed Oleg V Riabokon, managing partner, as one of the 'foremost legal practitioners in the trade and customs field internationally'.

AREAS OF PRACTICE

Magister & Partners provides a wide range of legal services to corporate clients, as well as Ukrainian state bodies.

Its trade and commercial law practice, headed by managing partner Oleg Riabokon, specialises in all aspects of trade law, including intellectual property and maritime law. This department regularly engages in anti-dumping, countervailing and safeguard proceedings, general defence strategies in trade investigations, representation of clients during administrative hearings, negotiation of settlements and undertakings, and foreign market monitoring systems. The firm's lawyers also offer support for a wide range of international commercial transactions, such as drafting contracts and negotiating on behalf of clients.

The firm's finance practice, led by partner Eugene Korniychuk, offers a full range of products and transactional work, and regularly represents clients in public offerings, private placements, structured finance, foreign securities transactions, bankruptcy and debt restructurings, and fund and investment management. The firm represented and advised the Ministry of Finance of Ukraine on the issue of US$800m notes of external state borrowing in 2003 and of US$200m tap issue.

Magister & Partners' arbitration and litigation practice is experienced in representing clients in institutional and ad hoc arbitrations in Ukraine, Europe and the CIS.

The oil and gas practice focuses on a wide range of issues related to the energy, oil and gas sectors, and serves as legal adviser to the state joint stock company Naftogaz Ukrainy, the largest oil and gas industry player in Ukraine.

Led by partner Oleg Marchenko, Magister & Partners' tax practice specialises in tax-efficient structuring of complex cross-border and domestic commercial and investment transactions, including corporate mergers and acquisitions.

The firm's team of corporate law practitioners provides a wide range of corporate law services to clients in various industries, ranging from grain trading to steel manufacturing, and is experienced in handling matters such as corporate formation, establishment of joint ventures, M&A, compliance with anti-monopoly legislation, and so on. The firm assisted one of the world's largest international trading companies in the development and implementation of a relevant corporate scheme in connection with acquisitions and investments in Ukraine (the amount of planned investments exceeds US$100m).

PRICEWATERHOUSECOOPERS UKRAINE

38 TURGENEVSKA STREET
4TH-5TH FLOORS
KYIV 01054

Telephone: +380 44 490 6777
Fax: +380 44 244 4966
E-mail: elena.voloshina@ua.pwc.com
Website: www.pwc.com/ua

Languages
English, French, German, Russian, Spanish, Ukrainian

Number of lawyers 12

Contacts
Jorge E Intriago, Andrew Mac

CATEGORIES OF WORK

EU and competition
Jorge E Intriago, Natalia Burnosova

Bankruptcy
Dmitry Martynenko

Corporate
Boris Schwarzer, Konstantin Emelyanenko

Investment
Jorge E Intriago

Litigation and arbitration
Vyacheslav Petrashenko, Boris Schwarzer

Media
Andrew Mac, Konstantin Emelyanenko

M&A
Jorge E Intriago, Andrew Mac

Energy
Jorge E Intriago

Labour
Natalia Burnosova, Boris Schwarzer

Privatisation
Dmitry Martynenko

Securities
Andrew Mac, Konstantin Emelyanenko

Tax
Vladimir Didenko, Vyacheslav Petrashenko

THE FIRM

PricewaterhouseCoopers has been operating in Ukraine since 1993 and is now the leading professional services organisation in the country. Headquartered in Kiev, PricewaterhouseCoopers has a diverse team of professionals able to deliver premium service quickly and effectively. The firm's clients have the benefit of working with both Ukrainian experts skilled in the local legal and business environment and expatriate attorneys who bring legal knowledge and experience from PricewaterhouseCoopers' offices worldwide. Furthermore, the firm's global presence allows its legal teams to work together across borders, thus ensuring that clients have the leading specialists from around the world working to meet their specific needs.

AREAS OF PRACTICE

The firm's Ukrainian legal practice has broad experience in numerous areas such as corporate law (in particular relating to cross-border transactions), commercial law, competition law and labour law. The firm's lawyers work closely with a multi-disciplinary tax team in Ukraine, which consists of international and local experts specialising in tax structuring and planning, and corporate and individual taxation as well as value-added tax and customs law. This allows the firm to provide its clients with a complete range of services during any local or international business transaction.

Cross-border transactions involving the acquisition of Ukrainian enterprises by multinational investors are a major area of the firm's work. Currently, the firm is working on multiple US$100m acquisitions and it has also been engaged to provide counsel relating to significant green-field investments in Ukraine. The firm is staffed with international and local M&A attorneys who have broad transaction experience in Ukraine, the European Union and the US. The firm has also developed international methodologies to assist in global M&A projects. This includes unique software developed exclusively to enable the firm's lawyers to work effectively on cross-border transactions with its regional and global colleagues. The firm's M&A attorneys regularly undergo training and networking meetings abroad with their M&A colleagues (mainly EU) to analyse M&A problems and solutions.

In addition to the above, PricewaterhouseCoopers Ukraine has sophisticated tax, competition, corporate and labour law practices. It advises clients on a wide range of tax-related matters, including issues pertaining to corporate profit tax, interpretation of relevant tax regulations, personal income tax, transfer pricing and VAT. The firm's competition law attorneys advise top-tier multinationals regarding relevant aspects of Ukrainian anti-monopoly legislation, and the firm has filed numerous requests for regulatory approvals of large transactions. The firm's corporate and labour law practices counsel on general corporate and employment matters. A significant portion of their practice is devoted to advising foreign clients who wish to establish a commercial presence in Ukraine.

More information is available upon request.

DENTON WILDE SAPTE

90 ACAD VOSIT VOKHIDOV STREET
YAKKASARAYSKIY DISTRICT
700031 TASHKENT

Telephone: +998 71 120 6949
Fax: +998 71 120 6185
E-mail: tashkent@dentonwildesapte.uz
Website: www.dentonwildesapte.com

Languages
English, French, Russian, Tajik, Uzbek

Other offices
Abu Dhabi, Almaty, Beijing, Cairo, Dubai, Gibraltar, Hong Kong, Istanbul, London, Milton Keynes, Moscow, Muscat, Paris, Singapore, Tokyo

Number of lawyers 876
at this office 3

Contacts
Marla Valdez, Mouborak Kambarova

CATEGORIES OF WORK

Aviation

Banking and finance

Corporate law, joint ventures

Dispute resolution

Energy and natural resources

Investment and commercial law

Labour law

Mergers and acquisitions, privatisation

Property and infrastructure development

Securities and capital markets

Telecommunications

SAUDI ARABIA

Population	**22 million**
Number of lawyers	**N/A**
Professional title	**Advocate**
Currency	**Saudi Riyal (SR)**

Index

Founded in 1932 by King Abdul Aziz-Al-Saud, the modern Kingdom of Saudi Arabia has been ruled by the Al-Saud family ever since. The Kingdom's vast natural oil reserves and its position as the spiritual home of Islam have made it one of the most influential countries in the Middle East. Its strategic importance has left its rulers in an uneasy position, balancing the energy demands of the West, especially the US, and the religious mores of its Muslim population.

Since September 11 the strain has started to show. A series of bloody terrorist attacks on foreigners in 2003 has had an understandably negative impact on business coming into the Kingdom, and many westerners living in Riyadh have since moved out. The government has started to crack down on the more extremist elements of Saudi society, but much work is needed before the West's confidence in the Kingdom returns.

BILLING

Law firm fees vary, depending on the job at hand. As a rule, they charge between €100 and €300 for associates and between €300 and €600 for partners. Success fees remain common practice for litigation matters, and law firms regularly charge for added time costs.

MARKETING

There are presently no advertising restrictions on Saudi law firms, and most major firms have their own websites. Nevertheless, the majority of domestic firms rely more on personal connections, long term clients and word-of-mouth recommendations for their business, rather than through direct marketing.

IN-HOUSE LAWYERS

Most of the Kingdom's largest corporations and banks have in-house lawyers who are experts in their respective fields. Saudi Aramco's in-house department is held in particularly high regard, and is larger than most domestic law firms.

ECONOMIC CLIMATE

Despite possessing the world's largest oil reserves, Saudi Arabia has recognised that it cannot rely purely on an industry prone to major price fluctuations. Economic diversity is crucial, and, in 2000 the government implemented some of the most progressive legal and economic changes in the Kingdom's history. Reforms include the increased Saudiisation of the workforce, the expansion of the private sector and new foreign investment laws designed to make it easier for foreign investors to set up in the Kingdom. New changes to the foreign investment laws allow foreign companies 100% ownership, when they previously had to go into a partnership with a local business, as well as a reduction of corporation tax from 45% to 30%. This has certainly given impetus to the private sector, which is vital for the ever-growing Saudi workforce that cannot be supported by oil alone. The Kingdom is also motivated by its desire to join the WTO, and to do so it must adapt its trade policies to match global standards. Its membership of the Gulf Co-operation Council (GCC), which also comprises Bahrain, Kuwait, Oman, Qatar and the UAE, is evidence that it is moving in the right direction, and Saudi Arabia is now bound to reduce import duties on non-essential goods to 5%. A GCC-based customs union is also scheduled for a 2005 start.

Combined with its ongoing, yet admittedly slow, privatisation process, the Kingdom is taking steps in the right direction, yet there remains a long way to go. The pace of change is frustrating for some and the collapse of the original Natural Gas Initiatives is testament to the problems that can arise. Though these have been reborn in albeit a much more scaled down version, with the international oil majors now just doing upstream work on Saudi Arabia's vast gas reserves.

LEGAL MARKET

Saudi Arabia is not an easy legal market for Western firms to work in. Foreign law firms choosing to open an office in the Kingdom need an affiliation with a local firm and a licence from the Ministry of Commerce. Each office must also have a majority Saudi interest. Its legal system differs greatly from the West's in that it is governed by Islamic Shari'a law as well as the rulings of its leading scholars and Mullahs. For disputes, each case is decided on its own merits and the rule of precedent does not apply. Additionally, only lawyers who have been admitted in Saudi Arabia can appear before the court.

Security fears have also prompted several leading lawyers to leave the Kingdom, and a question mark hangs over the future of some offices, which might well relocate to the UAE or Bahrain. Nevertheless, in spite of these difficulties, as

The largest firms

1	The Law Firm of Salah Al-Hejailan	22
2	Bin Mahfouz International Law Firm	15
3	Al-Jadaan Law Firm in co-operation with Clifford Chance LLP	14
	The Alliance of Abbas F. Ghazzawi & Co. and Hammad & Al-Mehdar	14
5	The Alliance	12
6	Legal Advisers in association with Baker & McKenzie	10
7	Dr Audhali Law Firm	9
8	Nader Law & Translation Offices	8
	United Law Firm	8
10	Law Offices of Dr Mujahid M. Al-Sawwaf	7
11	Kadasah Law Firm (in assoc with Bryan Cave LLP)	5
	Law Office of Abdulaziz H. Fahad (in assoc with Akin Gump Strauss Hauer & Feld)	5
	Law Office of Hassan Mahassni (in assoc with White & Case LLP)	5
14	Saud M.A. Shawwaf Law Office in affiliation with LeBoeuf, Lamb, Greene & MacRae	3
	The Law Firm of Mohammed Al-Sharif in association with Johnson & Pump	3
16	Gide Loyrette Nouel	2
	Law Office of Mohanned bin Saud Al-Rasheed in association with Baker Botts L.L.P.	2
18	The International Law Firm	1

These figures represent the total number of lawyers in this country only, and have been supplied by the firms themselves. The figures should be accurate as at 1 January 2004.

the region's largest economy, Saudi Arabia still remains very attractive to western law firms. **Squire, Sanders & Dempsey L.L.P.**'s affiliation, in October 2003, with a local firm to create **Squire, Sanders & Dempsey L.L.P in associaton with the law firm of Abdul Aziz Al-Assaf** is indicative of the continuing appetite for work in the Kingdom.

Most of the western firms operating in Saudi Arabia are from the US, which historically has had closer ties with the Kingdom, as opposed to UK firms that are mostly found in the UAE. The majority of firms have two or three lawyers based on the ground, or seconded to their local affiliates, while extra partners and associates are flown in for the large instructions.

Law Firm of Yousef and Mohammed Al-Jadaan in co-operation with Clifford Chance LLP is the only UK firm practising in the Kingdom, and it has established itself an excellent reputation in the Saudi legal market, particularly for banking and finance, projects and privatisation. Of the US firms, **Legal Advisers in association with Baker & McKenzie** is the undisputed leader of the pack. The firm boasts superb corporate and banking practices, and with partners George Sayen and David Xefos it has two of the Kingdom's best known lawyers. Based in Jeddah and Riyadh, **Law Office of Hassan Mahassni (in assoc with White & Case LLP)** has a strong reputation for projects and energy-related work, though the departure of Robert Nicholls in 2003 will undoubtedly be felt.

Amongst the other US firms that have established themselves, **Law Office of Abdulaziz H. Fahad (in assoc with Akin Gump Strauss Hauer & Feld)** comes recommended. Local name partner Abdulaziz Fahad attracts plenty of respect from his peers, though other lawyers are not as visible. **Law Office of Mohanned bin Saud Al-Rasheed in association with Baker Botts L.L.P.** has a solid, six-fee earner practice based in Riyadh, which benefits from the litigation expertise of name partner Mohanned Al-Rasheed. Working closely with its offices in Kuwait, Abu Dhabi and Dubai, **Kadasah Law Firm (in assoc with Bryan Cave LLP)** also has a small presence in the Kingdom, as does **Saud M.A. Shawwaf Law Office in affiliation with LeBoeuf, Lamb, Greene & MacRae**. French firm **Gide Loyrette Nouel** is the only other western firm in Saudi Arabia, representing several French and European-based clients, particularly from the luxury goods sector.

Despite the obvious benefits that come with instructing major western firms, businesses seeking legal advice in the Kingdom should not be blinded by the famous US and UK names on offer. Some of the best legal advice in Saudi Arabia can come from local firms, which have successfully taken the independent route. International firms that do not have a toehold in the Kingdom are not afraid of referring work to them. There are a number of clear advantages for choosing such firms: most have long-term experience of working in Saudi Arabia, and benefit from impressive connections with the government and general business community. Clients can also be guaranteed that these firms will remain in the Kingdom even if the security situation deteriorates. Amongst the top local firms, it is **Law Offices of Dr Mujahid M. Al-Sawwaf** that leads the pack. It boasts healthy experience across the entire legal spectrum and has several top-end western lawyers who have practised in the region for over a quarter of a century. The firm's name partner Dr Mujahid Al-Sawwaf is also one of the Saudi Arabia's leading litigators. Not far behind, **The Alliance of Abbas F. Ghazzawi & Co. and Hammad & Al-Mehdar** is garnering a very good reputation as a full-service corporate firm, and comes highly recommended for its projects, banking, shipping and insurance work. **The Law Firm of Salah Al-Hejailan** is arguably the best known of the local Saudi firms, though for general commercial work its star has waned of late. Nevertheless, name partner Salah Al-Hejailan remains one of the Kingdom's most high-profile litigators.

BANKING AND FINANCE

Saudi Arabia's banking and finance sector is a complex affair, due to the fact that *riba* (usury) is forbidden by the Koran, which is interpreted as a prohibition of interest. As a result Islamic, or Shari'a-compliant finance has started to take off, with such financial transactions increasing in size and complexity. The majority of leading firms have strong expertise in this field.

Legal Advisers in association with Baker & McKenzie's top-tier banking and finance practice is headed by US partner John Xefos, who has an enviable reputation within the Saudi legal community. The firm is experienced in all aspects of finance work, from securitisations, through private placements, to Islamic finance. The firm has been heavily involved in project finance and recently advised lenders on a $1bn-plus power station project for Aluminium Bahrain (ALBA). Regular clients have included Arab National Bank, Gulf International Bank and Saudi American Bank.

Law Firm of Yousef and Mohammed Al-Jadaan in co-operation with Clifford Chance LLP's highly rated banking and finance practice is headed by Yousef Al-Jadaan. The practice will miss well-regarded **Clifford Chance LLP** associate Paul Mercer who left in December 2003, though associates Robert Kavanagh and Robert Manson remain. The firm has an extremely good command of project finance, recently acting for lenders on the successful $280m financing of Saudi Polypropylene Company (SPC)'s polypropylene plant in Jubail. It also advised lenders in connection with a $650m general corporate facility for SADAF.

Banking and finance is one of the key practice areas for **The Alliance of Abbas F. Ghazzawi & Co. and Hammad & Al-Mehdar**. The firm represents a host of impressive clients including

BANKING AND FINANCE

LEGAL ADVISERS IN ASSOCIATION WITH BAKER & McKENZIE ✪
YOUSEF AND MOHAMMED AL-JADAAN IN CO-OPERATION WITH CLIFFORD CHANCE LLP, LAW FIRM OF

Abbas F. Ghazzawi & Co. and Hammad & Al-Mehdar, The Alliance of ✪
Hassan Mahassni (in assoc with White & Case LLP), Law Office of
Kadasah Law Firm (in assoc with Bryan Cave LLP)
Mujahid M. Al-Sawwaf (Dr), Law Offices of
Salah Al-Hejailan, The Law Firm of ✪
The International Law Firm

Abdulaziz H. Fahad (in assoc with Akin Gump Strauss Hauer & Feld), Law Office of
Mohanned Bin Saud Al-Rasheed in association with Baker Botts L.L.P., Law Office of ✪
Saud M.A. Shawwaf Law Office in affiliation with LeBoeuf, Lamb, Greene & MacRae

---

Firms are listed A-Z in tiers which are ranked in order of priority
✪ Indicates firm displays contact details at the end of this chapter.

Bank of America, Credit Suisse First Boston, Citibank, Saudi American Bank and Abbey National. The finance practice has a strong projects bent, and advised lenders, alongside **Allen & Overy**, on the first IPP in Saudi Arabia, for Jubail Energy, which will provide power and steam to SADAF on a BOOT basis. Name partner Adli Hammad comes highly recommended for his expertise in Islamic finance.

Law Office of Hassan Mahassni (in assoc with White & Case LLP) continues to offer a fine banking practice, with a strong line in project finance and Islamic finance work. The firm regularly acts for the Saudi American Bank, and recently advised it on the restructuring of a $90m loan to a Saudi contractor. It also advised Banque Saudi Fransi on a $45m debt refinancing. Major clients include Dresdner Kleinwort Wasserstein, National Commercial Bank and Citibank. Name partner Hassan Mahassni is the firm's main practitioner.

Kadasah Law Firm (in assoc with Bryan Cave LLP) acts for several leading international investment banks, and has strong experience with Islamic finance. The firm works closely with its London office advising Saudi-based investors on Shari'a-compliant mortgages and investments in the UK.

Law Offices of Dr Mujahid M. Al-Sawwaf has an impressive banking and finance practice, which is experienced in loan restructurings and general project finance work. The firm has also developed a strong interest in aviation finance. Partner David Wells is highly recommended.

Islamic finance is a key focus for **The Law Firm of Salah Al-Hejailan**, which offers its international and domestic clients an extensive banking and finance service.

The International Law Firm has an active banking and finance practice and represents various high-profile banks. Partner Vernon Cassin is recommended.

Law Office of Abdulaziz H. Fahad (in assoc with Akin Gump Strauss Hauer & Feld) has a solid reputation for banking and finance, and regularly advises Saudi American Bank on its private placements.

Law Office of Mohanned bin Saud Al-Rasheed in association with Baker Botts L.L.P. advises banks on regulatory and corporate matters, as well as on regular finance work. It is currently advising lenders on the financing of the Equestrian Club, a major hotel and leisure complex in Jeddah.

Saud M.A. Shawwaf Law Office in affiliation with LeBoeuf, Lamb, Greene & MacRae is experienced in all areas of banking and finance law. Major clients include Al Rahji Bank, Saudi American Bank and Merrill Lynch.

CORPORATE AND COMMERCIAL

Few Saudi lawyers will deny **Legal Advisers in association with Baker & McKenzie**'s dominance of the legal market. US partner George Sayen heads its expanding corporate practice, which offers advice in all areas, including joint ventures, restructurings and acquisitions to several Fortune 500 clients, as well as major Saudi business houses. Highlights include advising the Saudi Telecommunications Company (STC) on its recent IPO. Major clients that it acts for on a regular basis include Cisco, Oracle, Surebeam Corporation and Microsoft.

The 'excellent' **Law Firm of Yousef and Mohammed Al-Jadaan in co-operation with Clifford Chance LLP** is praised by clients for its professional, responsive and business oriented services, and proactive approach. The firm offers a wholesale corporate service and is experienced in restructurings and acquisitions. In the past year the corporate team has been busy providing corporate support on the firm's various projects. The 'dedicated, hard working and client-focused' name partner Mohammed Al-Jadaan heads the practice.

With offices in Jeddah and Riyadh, **The Alliance of Abbas F. Ghazzawi & Co. and Hammad & Al-Mehdar** is one of the Kingdom's top independent firms. It is a regular referral favourite of major UK and US firms. The firm offers a comprehensive corporate service, and has recently been acting for several leading insurers, regarding their operations under the country's new insurance regulations. In 2003 it advised a Saudi financial institution on its 50% purchase of a $280m chain of pharmacies. It is also highly recommended for projects, finance and shipping work. Partners Ali Abedi and Majid Ghazzawi are both praised for their 'excellent connections with the local authorities'.

CORPORATE AND COMMERCIAL

LEGAL ADVISERS IN ASSOCIATION WITH BAKER & McKENZIE ✪
YOUSEF AND MOHAMMED AL-JADAAN IN CO-OPERATION WITH CLIFFORD CHANCE LLP, LAW FIRM OF

ABBAS F. GHAZZAWI & CO. AND HAMMAD & AL-MEHDAR, THE ALLIANCE OF ✪
HASSAN MAHASSNI (IN ASSOC WITH WHITE & CASE LLP), LAW OFFICE OF
MUJAHID M. AL-SAWWAF (DR), LAW OFFICES OF

Abdulaziz H. Fahad (in assoc with Akin Gump Strauss Hauer & Feld), Law Office of
Gide Loyrette Nouel ✪
Kadasah Law Firm (in assoc with Bryan Cave LLP)
Mohanned Bin Saud Al-Rasheed in association with Baker Botts L.L.P., Law Office of ✪
Salah Al-Hejailan, The Law Firm of ✪
Saud M.A. Shawwaf Law Office in affiliation with LeBoeuf, Lamb, Greene & MacRae
The International Law Firm

Dr Audhali Law Firm
Bin Mahfouz International Law Firm
Mohammed Al-Sharif in association with Johnson & Pump, The Law Firm of
Nader Law & Translation Offices

Firms are listed A-Z in tiers which are ranked in order of priority
✪ Indicates firm displays contact details at the end of this chapter.

The 'first-rate' **Law Office of Hassan Mahassni (in assoc with White & Case LLP)** is praised for its 'excellent service' and reliable and practical advice. The departure of two prominent fee-earners in 2003: partner Robert Nicholls and associate Julian Johanssen, is undoubtedly a loss, though senior associates Richard Hays and Basil Barrakhat swiftly replaced them. The practice continues to act for Saudi Aramco, which has instructed **White & Case LLP** since the early 1950s. Other major clients include Tetra Pak, Kimberly Clark and the Dabbagh Group, one of the Kingdom's largest business houses. Name partner Hassan Mahassni is a very experienced operator, while the 'very approachable' senior associate Tareq Hassan is also recommended. The firm has offices in both Riyadh and Jeddah.

Law Offices of Dr Mujahid M. Al-Sawwaf remains one of Saudi Arabia's leading independent law firms. Based in Jeddah, it boasts the experience of several top-rate western lawyers, including David Wells, who has practised in the Kingdom for 25 years, as well as Richard Tyner who is situated in Riyadh. The firm is recommended for all areas of corporate law and is often referred work by the major international law firms. It has also developed a strong niche in aviation law advising on joint ventures and restructurings. Name partner Dr Mujahid Al-Sawwaf is one of the Kingdom's top commercial litigators.

Name partner Abdulaziz Fahad of **Law Office of Abdulaziz H. Fahad (in assoc with Akin Gump Strauss Hauer & Feld)** enjoys a very strong reputation within Saudi Arabia's legal community. The five-fee-earner practice benefits greatly from Fahad's excellent connections with the Saudi government and business community. The firm advises several major Saudi companies.

Charles-Henri Arminjon heads **Gide Loyrette Nouel**'s five-strong office, which comprises two French and three Arab lawyers. Open since 1978, the practice mainly advises foreign investors on restructuring for the Saudi market as well as more general corporate issues. It acts for a range of major clients in the luxury goods market including Givenchy, LVMH Group and the Richmond Group. Recent additions to the firm's client list include engineering giants Alstom and Technip.

Kadasah Law Firm (in assoc with Bryan Cave LLP) forms an integral part of **Bryan Cave LLP**'s Middle East presence, which also includes offices in Dubai, Abu Dhabi and Kuwait, which is overseen by US-based partner John Lonsberg. The firm represents a host of international clients across a range of industries.

Law Office of Mohanned bin Saud Al-Rasheed in association with Baker Botts L.L.P. is headed by partners Mohanned Al-Rasheed and Stephen Matthews. The practice has six fee-earners, including three from **Baker Botts, L.L.P.**. Much of the firm's work is connected with the oil and gas industry, but lately it has also advised banking clients on a range of corporate matters. Recently it acted for Saudi American Bank on the expiration of a technical management agreement with Citibank, which is a 20% shareholder. Traditionally the firm has also advised a number of US defence contractors, though since the US military's departure from the Kingdom, this work has diminished.

The Law Firm of Salah Al-Hejailan is one of Saudi Arabia's largest and oldest law firms. Salah Al-Hejailan is one of the Kingdom's best-known lawyers, and his firm represents numerous high-profile clients. The firm's standing in the corporate sector is not as grand as it used to be, but its name still carries plenty of weight in the Saudi legal market. Based in Riyadh, it has an office in Jeddah headed by David Ball.

Managing partner Khaled Al-Thebity heads **Saud M.A. Shawwaf Law Office in affiliation with LeBoeuf, Lamb, Greene & MacRae**'s Riyadh-based practice. The firm enjoys close links with the Saudi government and represents several clients in the energy sector.

Based in Riyadh and Jeddah **The International Law Firm** is popular with both domestic and international clients. Partner Vernon Cassin is one of the firm's top practitioners and is widely admired by his peers.

Dr Audhali Law Firm practices from the east coast city of Al-Khobar, and is instructed by a number of major international clients requiring local representation. Clients include AT&T, McDonald Douglas, Babcock and Siemens. The firm also has an authorised translation office.

Founded in 1992, **Bin Mahfouz International Law Firm** has offices in Jeddah, Riyadh, Cairo and Khartoum. Dr Abdullah Bin Mahfouz heads the practice, which is experienced in all corporate matters including joint ventures and regulations pertaining to the new investment laws.

Name partners Ronald Pump and Mohammed Al-Sharif of **The Law Firm of Mohammed Al-Sharif in association with Johnson & Pump** are both experienced commercial lawyers. The firm advises a number of well-known clients, including Lockheed Martin, General Dynamics and Petrocon.

Jeddah-based law firm **Nader Law & Translation Offices** also advises on corporate matters.

DISPUTE RESOLUTION

Partners Mohammed Al-Mehdar and Majid Ghazzawi head **The Alliance of Abbas F. Ghazzawi & Co. and Hammad & Al-Mehdar**'s highly rated disputes practice. One of the firm's largest instructions is from a Saudi Arabian investment house called before the United States District Court for the District of Columbia, in a September 11-related action. The firm is particularly experienced in insurance and shipping disputes, and is also recommended for banking and corporate litigation and government claims.

Law Office of Abdulaziz H. Fahad (in assoc with Akin Gump Strauss Hauer & Feld)'s 'very bright' name partner Abdulaziz Fahad is an experienced and well-known litigator, who 'consistently delivers good work'. His practice comes highly recommended for complex commercial disputes.

Dr Mujahid Al-Sawwaf of **Law Offices of Dr Mujahid M. Al-Sawwaf** is widely considered to be one of the Kingdom's foremost experts in Shari'a law. Added to this his firm is experienced in all manner of commercial disputes.

Name partner Salah Al-Hejailan of **The Law Firm of Salah Al-Hejailan** has an extremely good name for litigation. The firm's disputes practice is popular with clients and it also has a strong arbitration experience. On top of its top-notch commercial disputes lawyers, the firm is also famous for its role in defending the five Britons accused of a series of bomb attacks in Riyadh. Attracting a lot of international controversy, this was the Kingdom's most high-profile criminal case. All five captives were eventually released in 2003.

DISPUTE RESOLUTION

ABBAS F. GHAZZAWI & CO. AND HAMMAD & AL-MEHDAR, THE ALLIANCE OF ✪
ABDULAZIZ H. FAHAD (IN ASSOC WITH AKIN GUMP STRAUSS HAUER & FELD), LAW OFFICE OF
MUJAHID M. AL-SAWWAF (DR), LAW OFFICES OF
SALAH AL-HEJAILAN, THE LAW FIRM OF ✪

Gide Loyrette Nouel ✪
Hassan Mahassni (in assoc with White & Case LLP), Law Office of
Kadasah Law Firm (in assoc with Bryan Cave LLP)
Mohanned Bin Saud Al-Rasheed in association with Baker Botts L.L.P., Law Office of ✪
Saud M.A. Shawwaf Law Office in affiliation with LeBoeuf, Lamb, Greene & MacRae
The International Law Firm
United Law Firm
Yousef and Mohammed Al-Jadaan in co-operation with Clifford Chance LLP, Law Firm of

---

Dr Audhali Law Firm
Bin Mahfouz International Law Firm
Legal Advisers in association with Baker & McKenzie ✪
Nader Law & Translation Offices

Firms are listed A-Z in tiers which are ranked in order of priority
✪ Indicates firm displays contact details at the end of this chapter.

Gide Loyrette Nouel has an active dispute resolution practice. It continues to represent AXA in a pending arbitration, and has also been instructed by Alcatel and Alstom. Shafik and Abdullah Othman are the firm's leading litigators.

Name partner Hassan Mahassni of **Law Office of Hassan Mahassni (in assoc with White & Case LLP)** is one of the Kingdom's leading litigators, boasting a number of major clients including Siemens AB, Sumitomo Corporation and Skanska International. A major highlight was successfully representing Ed Zublin AG in three contract claims worth $60m filed against a public sector utility. The practice is experienced in all manner of commercial disputes.

Kadasah Law Firm (in assoc with Bryan Cave LLP) has a good reputation for commercial dispute resolution, and name partner Nasser Kadasah is considered to be a highly skilled and perceptive litigator.

Law Office of Mohanned bin Saud Al-Rasheed in association with Baker Botts L.L.P. has a solid dispute resolution practice, which is particularly experienced in construction disputes. Name partner Mohanned Al Rasheed is the firm's main litigator.

Saud M.A. Shawwaf Law Office in affiliation with LeBoeuf, Lamb, Greene & MacRae, and **The International Law Firm** also have experienced litigation practices.

The 'personable and courteous' name partners Yousef Al-Jadaan and Mohammed Al-Jadaan, are the main points of contact for dispute work at **Law Firm of Yousef and Mohammed Al-Jadaan in co-operation with Clifford Chance LLP**. The firm is experienced in banking disputes, which go before the SAMA Committee, and has also advised on a number of construction and trade mark disputes. A recent highlight was defending a major international company against a $16m competition claim brought against it.

Dispute resolution is a key area for **Bin Mahfouz International Law Firm**, which also has experience in arbitration. **Dr Audhali Law Firm** and **Nader Law & Translation Offices**, also regularly handle commercial disputes.

Legal Advisers in association with Baker & McKenzie has no specialised litigation service, though it regularly refers disputes to local advocates, while also acting as a case manager.

EMPLOYMENT

In Riyadh-based partner Richard Tyner, **Law Offices of Dr Mujahid M. Al-Sawwaf** has one of the few Saudi-based lawyers with a specific focus in employment law. Major clients include Philips and Colgate-Palmolive.

Gide Loyrette Nouel advises existing clients on all employment-related matters. Recently the firm acted for Indian software company, ITTL on related issues, and it also advised Alcatel on a labour dispute.

Law Office of Hassan Mahassni (in assoc with White & Case LLP) offers its clients a fully-fledged employment practice. It acted for Kamal Osman Jamjoom Establishment on the transfer of employees from Saudi Arabia to another GCC jurisdiction. It has also advised Raytheon Middle East Systems and Oerlikon Contraves AG on ongoing labour issues.

Kadasah Law Firm (in assoc with Bryan Cave LLP) has a solid employment practice and advises existing clients on contentious and non-contentious labour issues.

Law Firm of Yousef and Mohammed Al-Jadaan in co-operation with Clifford Chance LLP regularly advises clients in the IT and leisure industries on labour risk management and Saudi Arabian employment contracts.

Legal Advisers in association with Baker & McKenzie, **The International Law Firm** and **The Law Firm of Salah Al-Hejailan** are also active in this area, advising clients in conjunction with their corporate and commercial needs, as and when they arise.

EMPLOYMENT

MUJAHID M. AL-SAWWAF (DR), LAW OFFICES OF

Gide Loyrette Nouel ✪
Hassan Mahassni (in assoc with White & Case LLP), Law Office of
Kadasah Law Firm (in assoc with Bryan Cave LLP)
Legal Advisers in association with Baker & McKenzie ✪
Mohanned Bin Saud Al-Rasheed in association with Baker Botts L.L.P., Law Office of ✪
Salah Al-Hejailan, The Law Firm of ✪
The International Law Firm
Yousef and Mohammed Al-Jadaan in co-operation with Clifford Chance LLP, Law Firm of

Firms are listed A-Z in tiers which are ranked in order of priority
✪ Indicates firm displays contact details at the end of this chapter.

INTELLECTUAL PROPERTY

The majority of firms do offer IP advice in conjunction with their general commercial practices. As Saudi Arabia strives to enter the WTO, the protection of IP rights is creeping up the agenda, and law firms are giving the sector more attention. Furthermore, as home to the GCC's patent office, Riyadh has become an important centre for IP in the Middle East, and patents issued from there apply to all GCC states.

Kadasah Law Firm (in assoc with Bryan Cave LLP) has an expanding and well-regarded IP practice, which advises domestic and international clients on patent, copyright and trade mark law. It is also experienced in anti-piracy actions and trade mark infringement matters.

Through its strong links with the Abu-Setta Trade Mark Agency, **Saud M.A. Shawwaf Law Office in affiliation with LeBoeuf, Lamb, Greene & MacRae** has a firm toehold at the top end of Saudi Arabia's IP legal market.

The International Law Firm is also well known for its top-tier IP practice, which is active in both litigation and licensing.

The luxury goods sector provides **Gide Loyrette Nouel** with a rich vein of IP work, where it offers strong advice on matters ranging from counterfeit goods to trade mark protection. Clients include Luis Vuitton, Givenchy and Bic.

Name partner Hassan Mahassni and senior associate Tareq Hassan of **Law Office of Hassan Mahassni (in assoc with White & Case LLP)**, are both experienced in contentious and non-contentious IP matters. Recently the firm represented a well-known US media group on an offshore joint venture with a Saudi company to promote the licensing of IP rights in the Middle East.

Legal Advisers in association with Baker & McKenzie has seen an increasing amount of IP work coming its way, mainly from banks regarding their proprietary software and systems.

The Alliance of Abbas F. Ghazzawi & Co. and Hammad & Al-Mehdar; **Law Office of Abdulaziz H. Fahad (in assoc with Akin Gump Strauss Hauer & Feld)**; **Law Office of Mohanned bin Saud Al-Rasheed in association with Baker Botts L.L.P.**; and **The Law Firm of Salah Al-Hejailan** all offer IP services to their regular clients.

INTELLECTUAL PROPERTY

KADASAH LAW FIRM (IN ASSOC WITH BRYAN CAVE LLP)
SAUD M.A. SHAWWAF LAW OFFICE IN AFFILIATION WITH LEBOEUF, LAMB, GREENE & MACRAE
THE INTERNATIONAL LAW FIRM

Abbas F. Ghazzawi & Co. and Hammad & Al-Mehdar, The Alliance of ✪
Abdulaziz H. Fahad (in assoc with Akin Gump Strauss Hauer & Feld), Law Office of
Gide Loyrette Nouel ✪
Hassan Mahassni (in assoc with White & Case LLP), Law Office of
Legal Advisers in association with Baker & McKenzie ✪
Mohanned Bin Saud Al-Rasheed in association with Baker Botts L.L.P., Law Office of ✪
Salah Al-Hejailan, The Law Firm of ✪

Firms are listed A-Z in tiers which are ranked in order of priority
✪ Indicates firm displays contact details at the end of this chapter.

MARITIME AND SHIPPING

For maritime and shipping in Saudi Arabia, **The Alliance of Abbas F. Ghazzawi & Co. and Hammad & Al-Mehdar** should undoubtedly be the first port of call. Partner Andreas Haberbeck heads the Jeddah-based practice, and is considered to be one of the region's shipping doyens. Haberbeck recently provided expert advice on Saudi Arabian law to the successful claimant in the London litigation, *Ali Reza-Delta Transport Co Ltd v United Arab Shipping Co*. The firm has very strong expertise in ship finance, and continues to rule the roost in insurance, advising numerous major insurers and P&I clubs. It is also regularly referred work from leading London-based shipping firms, including **Ince & Co**, **Richards Butler** and **Holman Fenwick & Willan**.

Law Office of Hassan Mahassni (in assoc with White & Case LLP) advised on the financing of two chemical tankers, as well as their registration under the Saudi Arabian flag. Shipping isn't a key focus for the firm but it is experienced in ship finance. It has worked with **Norton Rose** and advised Bakri Navigation Co and Saudi Arabian Oil Company on related matters.

The Law Firm of Salah Al-Hejailan often acts for clients in the shipping industry against personal injury and damaged property claims. The firm also has experience in shipping acquisitions and finance.

MARITIME AND SHIPPING

ABBAS F. GHAZZAWI & CO. AND HAMMAD & AL-MEHDAR, THE ALLIANCE OF ✪

Hassan Mahassni (in assoc with White & Case LLP), Law Office of
Salah Al-Hejailan, The Law Firm of ✪
Yousef and Mohammed Al-Jadaan in co-operation with Clifford Chance LLP, Law Firm of

Firms are listed A-Z in tiers which are ranked in order of priority
✪ Indicates firm displays contact details at the end of this chapter.

Law Firm of Yousef and Mohammed Al-Jadaan in co-operation with Clifford Chance LLP is active in shipping finance, and works closely with its **Clifford Chance LLP** office in Dubai. The Saudi practice is also making a concerted move toward more regulatory work.

PRIVATISATION

Slowly but surely Saudi Arabia is privatising its national industries. Patience, however, is key and sectors scheduled for privatisation might not enter the public domain for some years yet. Nonetheless, the privatisation of 30% of STC in 2003 was certainly an encouraging start, with two-thirds being publicly listed and the remainder going to the General Organisation for Social Insurance, a state-owned pension fund. Saudi Arabian Airlines and the Kingdom's water and electricity sectors are also pencilled in for privatisation at some point in the future.

Law Firm of Yousef and Mohammed Al-Jadaan in co-operation with Clifford Chance LLP enjoys a top-notch reputation for privatisation work. It continues to advise Saudi Arabian Airlines on its privatisation, it is also acting for the government on the proposed privatisation of the Kingdom's water and power sectors.

PRIVATISATION

YOUSEF AND MOHAMMED AL-JADAAN IN CO-OPERATION WITH CLIFFORD CHANCE LLP, LAW FIRM OF

Abbas F. Ghazzawi & Co. and Hammad & Al-Mehdar, The Alliance of ✪
Legal Advisers in association with Baker & McKenzie ✪

Hassan Mahassni (in assoc with White & Case LLP), Law Office of
Mujahid M. Al-Sawwaf (Dr), Law Offices of
Salah Al-Hejailan, The Law Firm of ✪
The International Law Firm

Firms are listed A-Z in tiers which are ranked in order of priority
✪ Indicates firm displays contact details at the end of this chapter.

Together with **McCarthy Tétrault LLP**, **The Alliance of Abbas F. Ghazzawi & Co. and Hammad & Al-Mehdar** advised the Saudi Communication Commission on the preparation and finalisation of the new telecommunications laws, following the sector's partial privatisation.

Legal Advisers in association with Baker & McKenzie is highly experienced in privatisation work, benefiting from a strong relationship with the Saudi government. The obvious highlight of 2003 was advising the STC on its groundbreaking IPO.

Law Office of Hassan Mahassni (in assoc with White & Case LLP) had a quiet year on the privatisation front. Nevertheless it has had plenty of experience in this area, and in the past has been involved in the privatisation of the Saudi telecoms and electricity sectors.

Law Offices of Dr Mujahid M. Al-Sawwaf; **The Law Firm of Salah Al-Hejailan**; and **The International Law Firm** are also experienced in privatisation work.

PROJECTS

Legal Advisers in association with Baker & McKenzie offers top-notch projects capabilities. The combined expertise of partners George Sayen and John Xefos and the rest of the team is hard to beat. The firm is equally comfortable advising lenders as it is acting for sponsors and developers. One of its largest instructions is from Shell and Total on the renewed gas initiatives in what was the old core venture three. It is also acting for the sponsors on the development of Chevron Phillips' petrochemical plant in Jubail.

Working closely with **Clifford Chance LLP**'s regional headquarters in Dubai, **Law Firm of Yousef and Mohammed Al-Jadaan in co-operation with Clifford Chance LLP** boasts superb projects capabilities, and has recently advised a host of lenders and developers on a variety of projects. Major highlights include advising the relevant Saudi Arabian government agencies on four independent power and water projects in the Kingdom. The firm is experienced in BOOT IPPs and continues to advise SABIC on the $1.5bn financing of a petrochemical complex.

The Alliance of Abbas F. Ghazzawi & Co. and Hammad & Al-Mehdar's heavy workload is testament to its fine projects practice. It regularly acts for lenders, sponsors and developers, as well as US and UK firms including **Shearman & Sterling LLP** and **Ashurst Morris Crisp**. It is acting for sponsors on the Kingdom's first independent water project, to be done on a BOOT basis for Saudi Aramco in Rabigh. Added to this was the finance advice it provided with **Allen & Overy** to lenders on Saudi Arabia's first-ever IPP.

Law Office of Hassan Mahassni (in assoc with White & Case LLP) has a strong reputation for projects work, and name partner Hassan Mahassni

PROJECTS

LEGAL ADVISERS IN ASSOCIATION WITH BAKER & McKENZIE ✪
YOUSEF AND MOHAMMED AL-JADAAN IN CO-OPERATION WITH CLIFFORD CHANCE LLP, LAW FIRM OF

Abbas F. Ghazzawi & Co. and Hammad & Al-Mehdar, The Alliance of ✪
Hassan Mahassni (in assoc with White & Case LLP), Law Office of
Mohanned Bin Saud Al-Rasheed in association with Baker Botts L.L.P., Law Office of ✪
Mujahid M. Al-Sawwaf (Dr), Law Offices of

Abdulaziz H. Fahad (in assoc with Akin Gump Strauss Hauer & Feld), Law Office of
Kadasah Law Firm (in assoc with Bryan Cave LLP)
Salah Al-Hejailan, The Law Firm of ✪
Saud M.A. Shawwaf Law Office in affiliation with LeBoeuf, Lamb, Greene & MacRae

Firms are listed A-Z in tiers which are ranked in order of priority
✪ Indicates firm displays contact details at the end of this chapter.

regularly acts for both developers and financiers. One of the firm's largest transactions of 2003 was for the Al Azizia Steel Company on the construction of a steel plant. Other clients have included Kindasa Water Services and Saudi Cable Company.

Baker Botts, L.L.P.'s US partner Stephen Matthews is the main point of contact for projects work at **Law Office of Mohanned bin Saud Al-Rasheed in association with Baker Botts L.L.P.**. The firm is well versed in oil and gas related projects, and is currently advising two oil majors on the renewed gas initiatives in the old core venture areas one and two. It also continues to act for Nokia Group on the implementation of its GSM infrastructure projects in the Kingdom.

Law Offices of Dr Mujahid M. Al-Sawwaf has an extremely well-regarded projects practice, which has strong experience in BOT projects. The firm is regularly referred work by UK firms including **Linklaters** and **Herbert Smith**.

Law Office of Abdulaziz H. Fahad (in assoc with Akin Gump Strauss Hauer & Feld) has a solid projects and energy practice, which is regularly supported on the larger instructions by partners from its London office. In 2003 it advised a number of unsuccessful bidders on major projects in the Kingdom.

Kadasah Law Firm (in assoc with Bryan Cave LLP) regularly advises international clients on projects within the Kingdom.

The Law Firm of Salah Al-Hejailan regularly acts for SABIC on its projects in the Kingdom. It also represents several US and European defence contractors on their Middle Eastern projects.

Saud M.A. Shawwaf Law Office in affiliation with LeBoeuf, Lamb, Greene & MacRae is also experienced in projects work.

THE ALLIANCE OF ABBAS F GHAZZAWI & CO AND HAMMAD & AL-MEHDAR

POST OFFICE BOX 6387
JEDDAH 21442

Telephone: +966 2 650 4475
Fax: +966 2 657 2007
Website: www.saudilaw.de

Languages
English, German

Other offices
Riyadh

Number of lawyers 14
at this office 12

Contacts
Ali Abedi, Mohammed Al-Mehdar, Majid Ghazzawi, Andreas Haberbeck, Adli Hammad

CATEGORIES OF WORK

Administrative law

Admiralty and maritime

Banking and finance

Bankruptcy

Commercial

Construction

Corporate

Environmental

Government contracts

Insurance

Intellectual property

International trade

Litigation

Project finance

LEGAL ADVISERS IN ASSOCIATION WITH

BAKER AND McKENZIE

PO BOX 4288
RIYADH 11491

Telephone: +966 1 291 5561
Fax: +966 1 291 5571
Website: www.bakernet.com

Languages
Arabic, English, French

Other offices
For a list of all offices and other information regarding the firm please consult Baker & McKenzie's London office entry

Number of lawyers 3,380
at this office 10

Contact
John Xefos (managing partner)

Baker & McKenzie is a global law firm with 66 offices in 36 countries.

CATEGORIES OF WORK

Aviation, ship and asset finance
Ian Siddell

Bank lending and other extensions of credit
Ian Siddell, John Xefos

Corporate and partnership law
George Sayen, John Xefos

Corporate financing (public and private)
John Xefos

Franchising, government contracting
George Sayen, John Xefos

Labour and employment law
George Sayen, Karim Nassar

Mergers and acquisitions
George Sayen, John Xefos

Project finance
Ian Siddell, John Xefos

Public contracts and utilities
George Sayen, Karim Nassar

Trade (Saudi Arabia, GCC)
Nasser Alfaraj, George Sayen

GIDE LOYRETTE NOUEL

PO BOX 4615
RIYADH 11412

Telephone: +966 1 476 60 39
Fax: +966 1 476 18 96
E-mail: gln.riyadh@gide.com
Website: www.gide.com

Other offices
Algiers, Beijing, Brussels, Bucharest, Budapest, Casablanca, Hanoi, Istanbul, London, Moscow, New York, Paris, Prague, Shanghai, Tunis, Warsaw

Number of lawyers 480
at this office 2

Contact
Charles-Henri Arminjon

CATEGORIES OF WORK

- Foreign investment
- Company law
- Joint ventures
- Public and administrative law
- Government liaison
- Public procurement
- Taxation
- Commercial litigation (agency, distribution and franchise matters)
- Arbitration
- Intellectual property
- Banking and finance
- Labour
- Litigation

LAW OFFICE OF MOHANNED BIN SAUD AL-RASHEED IN ASSOCIATION WITH BAKER BOTTS L.L.P.

PO BOX 62982
RIYADH 11595

Telephone: +966 1 464 3139
Fax: +966 1 464 9264
E-mail:
stephen.matthews@bakerbotts.com
Website: www.bakerbotts.com

Languages
Arabic, English, Farsi, Hindi, Spanish, Urdu

Other offices
Austin, Baku, Dallas, Houston, London, Moscow New York, Washington DC

Number of lawyers 676
at this office 2

Contact
Stephen Matthews

Member
Lex Mundi

In association with
Afridi & Angell

CATEGORIES OF WORK

- Arbitration and dispute resolution
- Banking
- Corporate – general
- Corporate – M&A
- E-commerce
- Energy (power) projects
- Maritime – commercial shipping
- Oil and gas projects
- Project finance
- Pipeline projects
- Privatisation
- Regulatory
- Telecommunications projects

THE LAW FIRM OF SALAH AL-HEJAILAN

PO BOX 1454
11431 RIYADH

Telephone: +966 1 479 2200
Fax: +966 1 479 1717
E-mail: lfshriyadh@hejailanlaw.com
Website: www.hejailannet.com

Languages
Dutch, English, French, German, Italian, Spanish

Other offices
Jeddah

Number of lawyers 22
at this office 15

CATEGORIES OF WORK

International and domestic arbitration
Salah Al-Hejailan, Jean-Benoît Zegers

Shari'a law
Said Yehya, Maher Seddawy

Commercial litigation
Yahya Samaan, Amal el-Fazairy

Agency and franchise disputes
David Ball, Robert Thoms

Government and ministry affairs
Hussam Al-Hejailan, Mohamed Mutairi

Foreign investment law
Yahya Samaan, Ebaish Zebar

Contract review and interpretation
Robert Thoms, Jean-Benoît Zegers

Maritime law
Said Yehya, Motamed Ghani

Corporate law
Robert Thoms, Michael O'Kane

Collection
Mohamed Mutairi, Fahad Suleiman

Banking and financial services
Motamed Ghani, Fares Al-Hejailan

Intellectual property
David Ball, Michael O'Kane

Internet law
Sultan Al-Hejailan

Labour
Anwar Bakhurji, Fahad Suleiman

Construction and engineering
Maher Seddawy, Sultan Al-Hejailan

SERBIA AND MONTENEGRO

Population	**10.7 million**
Number of lawyers	**6,000**
Professional title	**Advokat**
Currency	**New Yugoslav dinar (YUM)**

Index

Five independent republics were created following the collapse of the former Yugoslavia. These were Bosnia, Croatia, the Republic of Macedonia, Slovenia and what is now known as Serbia and Montenegro. The two republics of Serbia and Montenegro declared a new Federal Republic of Yugoslavia in 1992 but became known as Serbia and Montenegro in 2003 after a constitutional charter for the union was approved.

The ousting of the authoritarian leader, president Slobodan Milosevic, and the election of Vojislav Kostunica in 2000 marked the start of a more politically stable period. However, in the November 2003 elections, Serbia failed, for the third time in 14 months, to elect a president due to low voter turn out.

The government is conducting a national campaign to prepare for EU accession with a strong emphasis on privatisation.

The UN protectorate of Kosovo remains an autonomous province.

BILLING

Clients are charged per hour in Serbia and Montenegro but capped fees are common for larger projects such as privatisation. Most firms bill clients at a rate of between €90 and €200 per hour. International clients are charged at a higher hourly rate of between €300 and €400.

MARKETING

Law firms are permitted to advertise and many law firms maintain English-language websites.

IN-HOUSE LAWYERS

Many companies employ teams of in-house lawyers to aid in the process of due diligence and other matters. These in-house teams, however, tend to have little commercial experience compared to private practice lawyers.

ECONOMIC CLIMATE

The economy of Serbia and Montenegro is in transition. A process of consolidation and restructuring is well underway. Developments to encourage foreign investors and a government drive for the privatisation of the telecoms, electricity and oil industries have had a positive effect on the economy. In 2002, privatisation revenue reached €350m from the sale of 300 companies, exceeding expectations. Despite greater political stability in Serbia and Montenegro, the fairly uncertain political situation between the two republics and Kosovo has tended to discourage foreign investors.

The smaller republic of the union, Montenegro, separated its economy from that of Serbia during the Milosevic era. Montenegro continues to manage its own budget and uses the euro instead of the New Yugoslav dinar.

LEGAL MARKET

Competition is increasing in the legal market and new firms have established themselves in Belgrade. Clients have found however that securing a lawyer who has solid legal knowledge as well as commercial experience has proved difficult. This has led to a 'sellers market' where fees for international clients can be up to two-thirds the price of fees charged in western Europe.

New legislation designed to encourage privatisation of public services and increase foreign investment has brought new clients to Serbia and Montenegro. Privatisation and reconstruction provided the bulk of commercial legal work in 2003, however banking and finance are expected to be the major areas of growth in the market during 2004/2005.

Lawyers are not officially permitted to form firms, but in reality many practitioners get around this by forming contractual partnerships with other lawyers. Legal reform in this respect has been fairly slow. In order to practise local law, lawyers must be nationals of Serbia and Montenegro. Many international firms hire and train local lawyers.

CORPORATE AND COMMERCIAL

Branislav Manic heads **Branislav Manic Law Office & Patent Bureau**. He is recommended by clients for having 'a commercial mind to spot opportunities'. The firm has acted for SONY Music Entertainment, Virgin and EMI regarding intellectual property matters. Other major transactions include advising a Spanish investment bank on privatisation matters.

CMS Strommer Hasche Sigle d.o.o. is recommended for its experience of privatisation work. A major transaction for the firm was advising Henkel CEE on the €65m acquisition of a leading Serbian chemical producer. Clients describe it as 'a good and fair firm' and praised the lawyers' 'strong communication skills'.

BRANISLAV MANIC LAW OFFICE & PATENT BUREAU

PO BOX 84
NO 4, APT 1
FRANC ROZMAN STREET
1101 BELGRADE

Telephone: +381 11 244 2338
Fax: +381 11 304 5430
E-mail: branislav.manic@bmpatlaw.co.yu
Website: www.bmplatlaw.co.yu

Languages
English, Serbian

Number of lawyers 5

Contact
Branislav Manic

CATEGORIES OF WORK

Intellectual property
Branislav Manic

Privatisation, M&A, corporate
Branislav Manic

Banking
Branislav Manic

Litigation
Branislav Manic

Real estate
Aleksandra Spanovic

Labour law
Danijela Ilic

Environmental law
Aleksandra Spanovic

CMS STROMMER HASCHE SIGLE D.O.O.

KNEZ MIHAILOVA 33
11000 BELGRADE

Telephone: +381 11 30 30 136
Fax: +381 11 30 30 137
E-mail: office@cmslegal.co.yu
Website: www.cmslegal.co.yu

Languages
Croatian English, French, German, Serbian, Russian

Other offices
Berlin, Brussels, Chemnitz, Dresden, Düsseldorf, Frankfurt am Main, Hamburg, Leipzig, Munich, Prague, Stuttgart, Vienna, Zagreb

Number of lawyers 405
at this office 10

Contact
Radivoje Petrikic

Member
CMS Transnational Legal and Tax Services; World Law Group

CATEGORIES OF WORK

Antitrust and competition

Arbitration and litigation

Banking, capital markets, securities and finance

Construction and real estate

Corporate, M&A, restructuring

Employment, industrial relations, employee benefits and pensions

Government business, regulatory/public procurement

Intellectual property and trade marks

Privatisation

Tax

Telecommunications

CLYDE D.O.O. BELGRADE

GENEX APARTMENTS, APT A305
CG APARTMENTS
VLADIMIRA POPOVICA 6
11070 BELGRADE

Telephone: +381 11 31 14 620
Fax: +381 11 31 15 297
E-mail: clyde@clyde.co.yu
Website: www.clydeco.com

Languages
English, French, Japanese, Russian, Serbian

Other offices
Caracas, Cardiff, Dubai, Guildford, Hong Kong, London, Nantes, Paris, Piraeus, St Petersburg, Singapore

Number of lawyers 386
at this office 4

Contacts
John Whittaker, Radoje Stefanovic, Miodrag Trajkovic

Member
AmCham Yugoslavia (American Chamber of Commerce)

CATEGORIES OF WORK

Privatisation and joint ventures	**Employment, labour law**
Foreign investments	**Shipping**
International trade	**Property**
Banking and financial	**Insurance**
Corporate and commercial	**Litigation and arbitration**
Tax	**Environment**

HAYHURST ROBINSON

65 NJEGOŠEVA, 3RD FLOOR
11000 BELGRADE

Telephone: +381 11 308 6140
Fax: +381 11 308 6637
E-mail: hrbelgrade@hrintlaw.com
Website: www.hrintlaw.com

Languages
Bulgarian, English, French, Hungarian, Romanian, Russian, Serbian

Other offices
Bucharest, Budapest, Sofia

Number of lawyers 40
at this office 5

Contact
Barbara Mendler (bmendler@hrintlaw.com)

International groupings
Interlex Group; IBA

CATEGORIES OF WORK

Foreign investment
Todd Robinson, Nikola Jekic

Privatisation
Todd Robinson, Nikola Jekic

Energy and natural resources
Robert Hayhurst

Real estate
Robert Hayhurst

Project and corporate finance
Robert Hayhurst, Todd Robinson

Banking
Todd Robinson, Nikola Jekic

Private equity
Todd Robinson, Neil Berlad

Mergers and acquisitions
Robert Hayhurst, John Fitzpatrick

Telecoms
John Fitzpatrick

Pharmaceutical/biotech
David Butts, Miodrag Markovic

Licensing and hi-tech
David Butts, John Fitzpatrick

Transport infrastructure
Todd Robinson

General corporate
Miodrag Markovic

Corporate insolvency and bankruptcy
Miodrag Markovic

Intellectual property
Miodrag Markovic

SCHÖNHERR RECHTSANWÄLTE OEG

UZUN MIRKOVA 3
11000 BELGRADE

Telephone: +381 11 3283 153
Fax: + 381 11 3283 783
E-mail: office@schonherr.co.yu
Website: www.schonherr.at

Languages
English, French, German, Serbian

Other offices
Brussels, Bucharest, Ljubljana, Vienna, Zagreb

Number of lawyers 96
at this office 3

Contact
Christopher Lindinger
(ch.lindinger@schoenherr.at)

CATEGORIES OF WORK

- International and Serbian practice
- International contracts and foreign investments
- Banking securities and finance
- Project finance
- M&A
- Privatisations
- Public private partnership
- Real estate and commercial property
- EU law

STUDIO LEGALE SUTTI

6 DJURE SALAJA STREET
1100 BELGRADE

Telephone: +381 11 33 45 195
Fax: +381 11 33 45 182
E-mail: maildesk@sutti.com
Website: www.sutti.com

Languages
Bulgarian, Dutch, English, French, German, Italian, Japanese, Portuguese, Romanian, Serbian, Spanish

Other offices
Bucharest, Genoa, London, Milan, Rome, Sofia, Tokyo

Number of lawyers 130
at this office 15

Contact
Dubravka Kosic

CATEGORIES OF WORK

- Company, commercial law
- Banking and finance
- Mergers and acquisitions
- Distribution, agency and franchising
- Debt collection and insolvency
- Commercial property law
- Intellectual property
- Patent and trade mark agency service
- White-collar crime
- EC, competition and antitrust law
- IT and TLC law
- Litigation and arbitration
- Employment, labour law
- Administrative law
- Environmental law

TRIFUNOVIC, TOMIC, STEVIC DULIC & CVETKOVIC

BALKANSKA 47
11000 BELGRADE

Telephone: +38 1 11 3611 589
Fax: +38 1 11 3613 947
E-mail: office@ttsd.co.yu
Website: www.ttsd.co.yu

Languages
English, French, German

Number of lawyers 5

Contacts
Goran Cvetkovic, Jasna Trifunovic, Ljubica Tomic

Member
Serbian Bar Association

CATEGORIES OF WORK

Commercial and company law	Antitrust and trade
EU law	Intellectual property
International arbitration	Environment
Banking and finance	Privatisation
Business law and investments	Venture capital and private equity
Mergers and acquisitions	Tax law
Major projects and project finance	Employment, pensions and benefits
Corporate restructuring	Litigation
Public law	Construction and real estate
Customs and trade regulations	

WOLF THEISS

RAJICEVA 27-29
11 000 BELGRADE

Telephone: +381 11 34 04 050
Fax: +381 11 34 04 030
E-mail: beograd@wolftheiss.com
Website: www.wolftheiss.com

Languages
Bosnian, Croatian, English, German, Serbian

Other offices
Bratislava, Vienna, Prague, Ljubljana, Zagreb

Number of lawyers 98
at this office 8

Contacts
Horst Ebhardt, Markus Heidinger, Christian Hoenig, Dieter Spranz

CATEGORIES OF WORK

M&A and privatisations (due diligence, tenders, tax and corporate structuring, acquisition finance)

Banking and finance (regulatory, loan facilities, securities)

Arbitration

Real estate (commercial real estate, acquisitions, permits, commercial real estate development, construction contracts, planning, leases)

Regulatory and infrastructure (electricity and gas, telecoms, Internet)

THE FIRM

Wolf Theiss, founded in 1957, stands among the leading law firms in Central Europe, with a concentration on Austrian, European and international business law, and additional expertise in the legal regimes of Central and Eastern Europe.

At its six locations, in Vienna, Prague, Belgrade, Bratislava, Ljubljana and Zagreb, a total of 200 people, including 98 lawyers (42 of whom are partners), work for Austrian and international client companies in industry, trade and services, as well as banking and insurance. At the point of contact between law and business, Wolf Theiss develops innovative solutions on the basis of legal, tax and business know-how.

SLOVAKIA

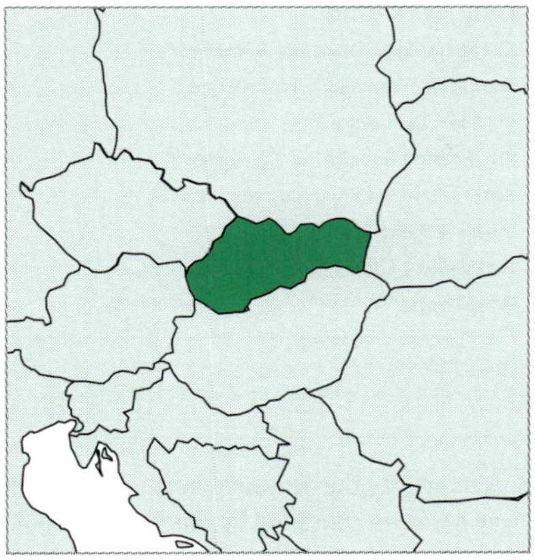

Population	5.4 million
Number of lawyers	1,400
Professional title	Advokát
Currency	Slovak Crown (SKK)

In 1918 the Slovaks joined the closely related Czechs to form Czechoslovakia. Following the Second World War, the country became a Communist nation within Soviet-ruled Eastern Europe. Soviet influence lasted until 1989 and Czechoslovakia existed until 1993 when the Slovaks and the Czechs agreed to separate peacefully, the so-called Velvet Divorce. Historical, political, and geographic factors have since caused the country to experience more difficulty in developing a modern market economy than some of its Central European neighbours. Trade between the two republics remains strong and the Czech Republic is Slovakia's main foreign trading partner after Germany.

Slovakia is located at the geographic centre of Europe. It is bordered by the Czech Republic to the west, Poland to the north, Ukraine to the east, Hungary to the south and Austria to the south-west.

BILLING

Hourly rates are most commonly used although fixed and contingency fees may also be agreed. Predictably there is a substantial difference between billing rates at international firms and the rates charged by local firms. International firms typically charge an hourly rate between €45 to €70 for a junior associate, rising to between €300 and €500 for a partner. Hourly rates at small, local firms will be much lower; most partners charge in the region of €100 to €200.

MARKETING

Marketing is presently restricted to foreign legal directories and magazines and the Internet. Rules are among the most restrictive in Europe, and allow firms to publicise only very basic details about themselves, such as addresses and names of lawyers. The majority of Slovak commercial law firms now possess well-produced, informative websites.

IN-HOUSE LAWYERS

The vast majority of qualified lawyers choose to work in private practice. Working in-house remains an unusual career choice although it is becoming increasingly common amongst the banks, financial institutions and the largest companies. In-house lawyers are not required to be members of the Bar and teams are invariably small and will typically instruct outside counsel for major matters

ECONOMIC CLIMATE

The elections of 1998 brought to power the reform-minded Mikulás Dzurinda. Since then, the centre-right coalition government has focused on the reintroduction of a market economy and forging closer links with the international economic and financial community.

Under Dzurinda, who won a second term in elections in September 2002, Slovakia completed its negotiations with the EU and Nato and is invited to join both organisations in May 2004. Foreign direct investment (FDI) is key to the country's economic recovery and the government has introduced a number of incentives to attract foreign companies. The rigid labour code has been overhauled to provide flexibility, which, along with a cheap, well-educated workforce, should make Slovakia a good source of labour. The country has one of the highest rates of unemployment in Europe with an average of 14% but as high as 30% in some areas.

Reforms to the tax regime include the introduction of a flat 19% income tax rate for companies and individuals. A fundamental part of the conversion to a market economy is the return of state-controlled enterprises to private ownership. The first wave of privatisations took place between 1991 and 1993 and the sale of Slovak Telecom to Deutsche Telekom in 2000 signalled the start of the second wave. Today, the banking sector is almost completely in foreign hands.

The success of privatisation and an improved perception of the economic and political climate have led to a rise in FDI which has grown from \$2bn to \$10bn since 1999. German companies are the largest foreign investors. Volkswagen, which arrived in 1990, produces 30,000 cars per year, employs over 7,000 and accounts for 16% of Slovakia's total exports. Other major foreign investors are Whirlpool, Siemens, Tesco, Philips, IBM and Kimberly-Clark. Meanwhile Peugeot's decision to invest \$750m in a facility has only served to increase the attraction of Slovakia to suppliers to the automotive industry.

LEGAL MARKET

The legal market has opened up as a result of the privatisation process and the approach of EU accession. Whilst a contingent of international firms has offices in Bratislava, many continue to operate from Prague or Vienna, both of which are in close proximity.

The largest firms

1	Linklaters	24
2	Valko & Partners	21
3	Law Firm Detvai Ludik Maly Udvaros	19
4	Law Office Ruzicka	16
5	Advokátskakanceléria	15
	Blaha, Erben & Partneri	15
	Csekes, Világi, Drgonec & Partners	15
	Dedak & Partners	15
	Freshfields Bruckhaus Deringer	15
10	Cechová Rakovsky	13
	Peterka & Partners v.o.s	13
	Weinhold Legal, v.o.s.	13
13	Allen & Overy	12
	Squire Sanders s.r.o.	12
15	Cernejová & Hrbek	11
	Havlát & Partners Law Office	11
17	White & Case	10
18	CMS Carnogursky	9
19	Rödl & Partner S.R.O.	7
20	DLA Weiss-Tessbach/Law Office Milan Cervenka	6
	Salans	6
22	Wolf Theiss	3
23	A.L.A. Spol. s r.o.	2
24	Rott, Ruzicka & Guttmann	1

These figures represent the total number of lawyers in this country only, and have been supplied by the firms themselves. The figures should be accurate as at 1 January 2004.

US firms **Squire, Sanders & Dempsey L.L.P.** and **White & Case** were the first foreign firms to arrive in Bratislava and originally dominated the market. In 2000 the raft of privatisations resulted in greater competition when the likes of **Allen & Overy** and **Linklaters** set up offices. Of the three trailblazers, only **White & Case** has been able to maintain its leading position. *Altheimer & Gray* was absorbed during 2003 by international law firm **Salans**. The year's other merger saw **DLA** enter Slovakia for the first time following its merger with one of Austria's most prominent firms **DLA Weiss-Tessbach**. **DLA Weiss-Tessbach**'s five fee-earners based in Bratislava will work closely with the **DLA** network of offices across Europe and Asia.

The other Austrian/Austrian-link-up firms with a strong presence in Bratislava, **Wolf Theiss** and **Freshfields Bruckhaus Deringer** tend to run big deals out of their Vienna offices.

Law Office Ruzicka operates a 16-lawyer office and replaces **CMS Carnogursky** as a member of the **CMS** network although **CMS Carnogursky** will continue to use the **CMS** name. A team of French-speaking lawyers has joined **CMS Carnogursky** which, amongst the Slovak law firms, boasts a strong French client base. The firm's clients include Ondeo France, Soletanche Bachy France and Mecanet France. **Peterka & Partners v.o.s.** also has a reputation for representing French clients and the majority of its fee-earners speak French as well as English.

International firms are seeking to transfer their experience outside Slovakia. Three years after absorbing the *Burns Schwartz* office in Brastislava, **Linklaters** is not only well established but now also working in Slovenia and Serbia. Meanwhile Hugh Owen, senior associate in **Allen & Overy**'s Bratislava office has become responsible for co-ordinating the firm's activities in Romania and Bulgaria where the privatisation process is just beginning. The move comes in response to client needs and in order to transfer skills learnt from privatisation in Slovakia.

Firms that have been extremely active in privatisation, are now looking for alternative sources of work. Slovakia's accession to the EU provides opportunities to advise on EU and competition law. Most local law firms continue to be happy to work through association with Western European law firms. However one local firm, **Cechová Rakovsky** has opened an office in Brussels shared with Czech firm **Kocián Solc Balastík** and Polish firm **Wardynski & Partners** for joint marketing and promotion purposes.

BANKING, FINANCE AND CAPITAL MARKETS

BANKING, FINANCE AND CAPITAL MARKETS

ALLEN & OVERY ✪
LINKLATERS ✪
WHITE & CASE

Blaha, Erben & Partneri
CMS Carnogursky ✪
Cechová Rakovsky ✪
Cernejová & Hrbek
Csekes, Világi, Drgonec & Partners ✪
DLA Weiss-Tessbach/Law Office Milan Cervenka ✪
Freshfields Bruckhaus Deringer ✪
Squire, Sanders & Dempsey L.L.P. ✪
Valko & Partners
Weinhold Legal, v.o.s.
Wolf Theiss ✪

Firms are listed A-Z in tiers which are ranked in order of priority
✪ Indicates firm displays contact details at the end of this chapter.

Allen & Overy's finance practice has a close relationship with all the major local banks, reflected in its latest appointment as preferred counsel to one of the largest banks. Igor Pálka is highly recommended. In a quiet year for capital markets activity, the derivatives team led by Hugh Owen has been consulted by almost every single bank active in the Slovak derivatives market. Hugh Owen and Patricia Oslovska are recommended. **Allen & Overy** has played an important role drafting the new Slovak security legislation and is currently advising the Slovak government on the redrafting of Slovakia's insolvency legislation (**Weinhold Legal, v.o.s.** is advising on the second phase of the insolvency legislation). The steadily increasing flow of foreign investors looking to take advantage of the impending freer market when Slovakia joins the EU is expected to lead to dynamic growth in real estate. Vojtech Pálinká is the powerhouse behind **Allen & Overy**'s team which has advised on a number of transactions.

Linklaters enhanced its capacity in both capital markets and structured finance matters with the transfer of specialist John McIlwaine from the Budapest office. McIlwaine, with Daniel Torsher, advised CSFB as lead manager on the issuance of €500m floating rate notes due in 2005. The notes were registered on the Luxembourg Stock Exchange and the proceeds were used for the repayment of existing debt of the Slovak Republic. The whole process took less than one month from announcement to receipt of funds despite being the largest such issue in the country in 2003. (The Slovak Republic was represented by **White & Case**'s finance team which has been strengthened by the arrival of Petr Maleček, following Ivan Cestr's move to an in-house position with gas company RWE. Associate Peter Viglasky, an ex-Citibank laywer, is another asset of the Bratislava-based team.) **Linklaters** has also established itself as a strong telecoms outfit advising a number of clients in this sector including Slovenské Telekomunikácie. In addition, the firm was the first to offer tax advice in-house and has stolen a march on its rivals, advising on several significant tax-driven transactions.

White & Case drew on its close links with its London banking team to represent Malzenice Power, a special purpose vehicle formed by Advanced Power AG and Siemens Project Ventures GmbH, in connection with the development of a combined-cycle gas-fired 380MW project in Malzenice, Slovakia. It represents one of the few project financings to take place in Slovakia. Ivo Barta advised with London-based Peter Finlay and senior associate Marek Staron. **White & Case** represented Skanska in connection with its joint venture with Japanese company Taisei, for the purpose of building Motorway D2 Lamačská cesta-Staré Grunty in Bratislava. Senior associate Roman Hamala was singled out for recommendation.

In a move to build up tax capability, **White & Case** recruited two former Ernst & Young tax advisers, Miroslav Tain and Miriam Galandova, during the last year.

Blaha, Erben & Partneri advised the purchaser of a $1m share in a large automobile company. Clients include Electrolux and Siemens but are predominantly local.

South Korean electronics giant Samsung was advised by **CMS Carnogursky** on its €13m investment in a manufacturing plant in Galanta. The firm also advised Slovenská konsolidačná, Devín banka and AG Banka on debt collection issues.

Cechová Rakovsky has solid banking and finance expertise. The firm is advising an independent company on the establishment and operation of a credit register for Slovak banks.

DLA Weiss-Tessbach represented an Austrian commercial bank in several forfeiting/export refinancing transactions relating to the provision of technical equipment to the government authorities.

Freshfields Bruckhaus Deringer's Slovakia practice has grown from two fee-earners in 1998 to 15 in 2003. Whilst its reputation is still largely based on its corporate expertise, the banking team is increasingly picking up big deals, such as the €64m facility agreement for Bank Austria Creditanstalt. Under Paul Luiki's direction out of Vienna, the firm strives to be at the forefront, bringing expertise to new areas for Slovakia such as aircraft leasing and PPP/project finance.

Squire, Sanders & Dempsey L.L.P.'s department boasts experience in syndicated loans, bond issues and liquidations. In co-operation with the Brussels office, the firm is handling a major state aid question for Slovak Savings Bank. In one of the biggest deals of the year the firm represented PSA Peugeot Citroen on all aspects of construction of a new assembly plant in Trnava, which, with a value of €700m, is the single largest investment in the Slovak Republic. **Squire, Sanders & Dempsey L.L.P.** also provided advice to Tesco on the opening of hypermarkets and acts as the retailer's exclusive counsel in Slovakia, a relationship that has grown with Tesco's large-scale expansion in the Republic during the last nine years. Recently, representation has expanded to include antitrust and regulatory work.

Valko & Partners enjoys good relations with various international firms. The partners have experience of advising on bank lending, bankruptcy and securities.

Weinhold Legal, v.o.s. is developing a speciality in outsourcing. The firm advised Accenture on the preparation and implementation of a complex (and the world's most advanced) customer care and billing system for Slovak Telecom. Additional advice related to advising Accenture on a massive outsourcing project of accounting services for a major Slovak petrochemical company. The firm has also begun to carve out a solid employment practice. Senior Slovak lawyer Miroslava Benediková is a key individual.

CORPORATE AND COMMERCIAL

In a challenging market **Allen & Overy** has managed to maintain its size, quality and client base with a steady stream of corporate activity under the highly regarded Igor Pálka. In the first matter of its kind in Slovakia, the firm advised leading life insurer AEGON in connection with obtaining its licence to carry out activities in the republic and the setting up of its branch in Slovakia. The 12-lawyer Bratislava office has had a role to play in nearly all the large privatisations to date, most recently advising HSBC Investment Bank plc, adviser to the Slovak government on the privatisation of Stredoslovenska Energeticka in a deal worth €158m. CME, AIG and Trident are amongst the firm's corporate clients.

Recommended local firm **Cechová Rakovsky** gained its seventh partner with the promotion of competition and antitrust specialist Tomás Maretta. He advised VS&A Communication Partners III on acquisition and merger control clearance on the purchase of telephone directory publisher, Mediatel. The firm regularly works on international mergers and acquisitions, such as advice to Czech construction company, Skanska CZ on the acquisition and merger clearance of the acquisition of Bankse stavby. Alexander Rakovský is recommended for his expertise in litigation.

Cernejová & Hrbek partner Alena Ernejova is respected for corporate work. The firm has become well established with corporate clients since setting up in the Republic in 1992.

M&A and competition work are two of **Csekes, Világi, Drgonec & Partners**' specialities. The firm represented Hungarian refinery MOL in its cross-border acquisition of additional shares in the Slovak refinery Slovnaft to bring its ownership to 67.8%. The transaction, valued at $360m is a follow-up to MOL's capital entry in Slovnaft in 2000. **Csekes, Világi, Drgonec & Partners** advised on both phases, with Erika Csekes singled out for recommendation. (Slovintegra and Slovbena were advised by **Allen & Overy**.)

Freshfields Bruckhaus Deringer acted for a consortium of Gaz de France, Ruhrgas and Gazprom, on the purchase of a 49% share in national gas distribution company, SPP. The deal represented the largest privatisation in the country's history, the price equalling 13% of GDP, and the largest single foreign investment in the history of the country. A good illustration of the international capabilities of **Freshfields Bruckhaus Deringer** was its role on the global merger of Hewlett-Packard and Compaq which involved 26 of the firm's offices, including Bratislava. The Bratislava office works very closely with Vienna. A typical recent deal involved advice to a London office client, Warburg Pincus on the cross-border acquisition of shares in Slovakofarma via an Austrian holding company. (**Linklaters** advised Slovakofarma.) Senior international lawyer Peter Hoffmann and advocate Miroslav Trenčan were singled out for their 'fantastic work'.

The largest firm in Slovakia (with 25 lawyers), **Linklaters** dwarves many of its rivals. Major clients include Samsung General Chemicals Co, Johnson Controls, Invensys, Slovakofarma, Slovenské Telekomunikácie and Unilever, among others. One recent highlight saw the firm advise CSFB and the Slovak government on a $2.7bn deal to privatise SPP. Daniel Torsher and Jason Mogg did 'an excellent job' supporting CSFB.

Squire, Sanders & Dempsey L.L.P. has been in Bratislava since the early 1990s. The office, part of a strong regional network, offers a full

CORPORATE AND COMMERCIAL

ALLEN & OVERY ✪
CECHOVÁ RAKOVSKY ✪
CERNEJOVÁ & HRBEK
CSEKES, VILÁGI, DRGONEC & PARTNERS ✪
FRESHFIELDS BRUCKHAUS DERINGER ✪
LINKLATERS ✪
SQUIRE, SANDERS & DEMPSEY L.L.P. ✪
WHITE & CASE

DLA Weiss-Tessbach/Law Office Milan Cervenka ✪
Detvai Ludik Maly Udvaros, Law Firm
Law Office Ruzicka ✪
Weinhold Legal, v.o.s.

Blaha, Erben & Partneri
CMS Carnogursky ✪
Peterka, & Partners v.o.s. ✪
Salans
Valko & Partners
Wolf Theiss ✪

Firms are listed A-Z in tiers which are ranked in order of priority
✪ *Indicates firm displays contact details at the end of this chapter.*

commercial service to a multinational client base, boasting strength in M&A, restructuring and privatisation. Partner Kevin Connor, who splits his practice between Bratislava and Budapest, is well known. **Squire, Sanders & Dempsey L.L.P.** led the privatisation and sale of the Eastern Slovak Electricity Distribution Company for the government. The firm worked in co-operation with BNP Paribas on the sale of the company to RWE. The two-partner Bratislava office counts Slovak Electric among its clients. Over the past seven years, the firm has represented the electricity company in more than $1bn of financing from foreign and domestic sources, and advised on a number of matters including regulatory, corporate and state aid issues.

White & Case's Ivo Barta and his team had a busy year acting for the National Property Fund of the Slovak Republic on a number of privatisations, the latest being on the privatisation of its interest in Banka Slovakia. (The bank, advised by **DLA Weiss-Tessbach** was sold to German-based Meinl Bank AG for SKK360m ($11m)). The firm also acted for the Government of the Slovak Republic in connection with a €700m investment by Peugeot Citroen Automobiles for its new car manufacturing plant in Trnava. **White & Case** has participated in nearly every significant acquisition in the country, including those involving strategic industrial companies, such as Transpetrol, Slovak Telecom, the Slovak banks and the insurance sector. Clients include Abbot Laboratories, Allianz, Banka Slovakia, Electricité de France, Orange Slovakia, Pfizer, and RWE Gas.

DLA Weiss-Tessbach has extensive experience of conducting due diligence for Austrian and German companies entering the Slovak market through joint venture or acquisition. It is working on behalf of a Dutch investor in the acquisition of a number of Slovak lime producers.

One of the largest Slovak firms, **Law Firm Detvai Ludik Maly Udvaros** has a broad base of clients across Europe, North America and Asia, and receives regular referrals from international law firms. The four name partners boast experience of corporate, finance and contentious practice.

Law Office Ruzicka's client base includes Siemens, Exxon Esso, Winterthur Life, Porsche and Skoda. The firm represented SPP in one of the year's biggest disputes.

Weinhold Legal, v.o.s. was formed in the Czech Republic in 1996 and opened an office in Bratislava in 1998, since when the practice has grown steadily to 13 fee-earners. Today the focus is on inward investment, real estate and banking and finance. On the corporate side, it advised SwiftAir, the Spanish airline, on the comprehensive restructuring of SkyEurope Airlines, a low-cost airline, in connection with a new financial investor. Robert Kovacik managed the deal. **Squire, Sanders & Dempsey L.L.P.** advised the other side and **Cechová Rakovsky** advised the financier.

At **Weinhold Legal, v.o.s.**, real estate specialist Kenneth Johnson has moved into the slot left vacant when Anelia Dinova moved to **EYLaw**. The firm, which is also a member of the Ernst & Young legal network, advised ING Real Estate on a joint venture for the purchase and development of a large mixed-use development in Bratislava with a total investment of approximately €50m.

Blaha, Erben & Partneri offers a range of commercial and corporate legal services. Name partners Anton Blaha and Pavol Erben have experience in employment, property and corporate, and in establishing the various investment vehicles available to foreign investors.

CMS Carnogursky, under the leadership of energy sector expert Jan Carnogursky, advised the Slovak Government on the privatisation of state-owned electricity company Zapadoslovenska energetika.

Czech firm **Peterka & Partners v.o.s.** has an office in Bratislava. The firm is the Slovakian member of the *Terralex* law firm network, and boasts clients in the automotive industry, supermarkets, financial institutions and software companies. Real estate is a growth area and the firm advised on a €20m greenfield investment for the construction of supermarkets on sites in several cities.

Valko & Partners was formed in the early 1990s. The firm offers a full commercial service to a multinational clientele, including advice on investment, plus related expertise in employment, property and IP. Name partner Ernest Valko has a strong contentious background and is an experienced arbitrator.

Wolf Theiss works for international clients and draws much of its expertise from its Prague and Vienna offices. The firm has represented the bidders on a number of privatisations, including advising ESTAG, a subsidiary of Electricité de France (EDF) on the privatisation of three Slovak power supply companies.

ALLEN & OVERY

CARLTON SAVOY BUILDING
MOSTOVÁ 2, 5TH FLOOR
81102 BRATISLAVA

Telephone: +421 2 5920 2400
Fax: +421 2 5920 2424
E-mail: information@allenovery.com
Website: www.allenovery.com

Languages
Slovak, English, Czech, German, French, Hungarian, Russian

Other offices
Amsterdam, Antwerp, Bangkok, Beijing, Brussels, Budapest, Dubai, Frankfurt, Hamburg, Hong Kong, London, Luxembourg, Madrid, Milan, Moscow, New York, Paris, Prague, Rome, Shanghai, Singapore, Tokyo, Turin, Warsaw

Number of lawyers 2,305
at this office 12

Contacts
Igor Pálka, Hugh Owen

CATEGORIES OF WORK

Acquisition and asset finance
Igor Pálka

Antitrust/competition law
Igor Pálka, Renátus Kollár

Arbitration/litigation
Martin Magál

Banking and finance
Igor Pálka, Hugh Owen

Bond and equity issues
Igor Pálka

Capital markets
Igor Pálka, Hugh Owen

Corporate/commercial
Igor Pálka, Martin Magál

Corporate and project finance
Igor Pálka

Employment
L'udmila Borloková

Derivatives and structured financial products
Hugh Owen, Patricia Olšovská

Mergers and acquisitions, syndicated lending
Igor Pálka, Hugh Owen

PFI/PPP
Igor Pálka, David Kennedy

Private equity
Hugh Owen, David Kennedy

Privatisations
Igor Pálka, Hugh Owen

Real estate
Vojtech Pálinkás, Martin Magál

Telecommunications
Hugh Owen, Igor Pálka

Utilities/energy
Igor Pálka, Hugh Owen

CMS ČARNOGURSKÝ

JELENIA 4
81499 BRATISLAVA

Telephone: +421 2 5720 17 17
Fax: +421 2 5720 17 77
E-mail: office@cmslegal.sk
Website: www.cmslegal.sk

Languages
Czech, English, French, German, Italian, Russian

Number of lawyers 9

Contact
Jan Čarnogurský

CATEGORIES OF WORK

Antitrust and competition
Martin Javorček, Viliam Karas

Arbitration and litigation
Ján Čarnogurský, Silvia Viskupičová

Banking, capital markets, securities and finance
Ján Čarnogurský, Martin Javorček

Central and Eastern Europe
Ján Čarnogurský, Viliam Karas

Construction and real estate
Ján Čarnogurský, Juraj Eliáš

Corporate, M&A, restructuring
Ján Čarnogurský, Martin Javorček

Employment, industrial relations, employee benefits and pensions
Peter Bartolčič

Energy law
Peter Bartolčič, Silvia Poláková

Government business regulatory/public procurement
Viliam Karas, Branislav Kapala

Insolvency
Martin Javorček, Juraj Eliáš

Intellectual property and trade marks
Silvia Poláková, Boris Šváby

Tax
Ján Čarnogurský, Martin Javorček

Telecommunications
Silvia Poláková, Viliam Karas

White-collar crime
Martin Javorček

CECHOVÁ RAKOVSKÝ

HURBANOVO NÁM 5
81103 BRATISLAVA

Telephone: +421 2 5441 4441
Fax: +421 2 5443 4598
E-mail: cechrak@cechrak.sk
Website: www.cechrak.sk

Languages
Czech, English, French, German, Italian, Russian

Other offices
Brussels

Number of lawyers 13

Contacts
Katarina Cechova, Tomas Maretta

Member
Lex Mundi; World Services Group

CATEGORIES OF WORK

Competition
Tomas Maretta, Tomas Zarecky

Antitrust
Tomas Maretta, Tomas Zarecky

Banking
Katarina Cechova, Zuzana Petrasova

Bankruptcy and insolvency
Katarina Cechova, Michaela Jurkova

Civil law
Alexander Rakovsky, Boris Bohunsky

Commercial litigation
Alexander Rakovsky, Boris Bohunsky

Corporate and company
Katarina Cechova, Zuzana Petrasova

Employment and labour
Boris Bohunsky, Tomas Rybar

Energy
Katarina Cechova, Michaela Jurkova

Foreign investment
Densia Kubinyiova, Zuzana Petrasova

Mergers and acquisitions
Katarina Cechova, Tomas Maretta

Privatisation
Katarina Cechova, Zuzana Petrasova

Project financing
Katarina Cechova, Zuzana Petrasova

Real estate
Boris Bohunsky, Tomas Zarecky

Telecommunications
Tomas Rybar

Trade marks
Denisa Kubinyiova

CSEKES, VILÁGI, DRGONEC & PARTNERS

SASINKOVA 12
81108 BRATISLAVA

Telephone: +421 2 529 66 330
Fax: +421 2 529 32 461
E-mail: office-ba@csekes-vilagi.sk
Website: www.csekes-vilagi.sk

Languages
Czech, English, French, German, Hungarian

Other offices
Dunajská Streda

Number of lawyers 15
at this office 12

Contact
Erika Csekes

Member
Law Firm Network

CATEGORIES OF WORK

Corporate and commercial law
Veronika Orvosová, Adriana Jančiarová

Mergers and acquisitions
Erika Csekes, Marko Polakovič

Privatisation
Oszkár Világi, Erika Csekes

Real estate
Ingrid Gyökeresová, Silvia Bernáthová

Securities
Erika Csekes, Petra Starková

Civil and commercial litigation
Ingrid Gyökeresová, Silvia Bernáthová

Corporate finance
Erika Csekes, Adriana Jančiarová

Intellectual property
Erika Csekes, Vladimír Gontkovič

Foreign investments
Erika Csekes, Marko Polakovič

Competition law
Erika Csekes, Adrián Tokár

Labour law
Beáta Kartíková

Bankruptcy
Oszkár Világi, Ingrid Gyökeresová

Telecommunications
Erika Csekes, Petra Starková

DLA WEISS-TESSBACH/LAW OFFICE MILAN CERVENKA

PANSKA 31
81101 BRATISLAVA

Telephone: +421 2 59 20 21 23
Fax: +421 2 54 43 45 85
E-mail: bratislava@dla.com
Website: www.dla.com

Languages
Czech, English, French, German, Hungarian, Italian, Russian

Other offices
Amsterdam, Antwerp, Bangkok, Bergen, Berlin, Birmingham, Bradford, Brussels, Budapest, Cologne, Copenhagen, Edinburgh, Essen, Frankfurt, Glasgow, Hamburg, Hong Kong, Leeds, Liverpool, London, Madrid, Manchester, Milan, Moscow, Oslo, Paris, Prague, Rotterdam, Salzberg, Sarajevo, Shanghai, Sheffield, Singapore, Stockholm, Vienna, Zagreb

Number of lawyers 82
at this office 6

Contacts
Peter Solt (Vienna)

Member
DLA Group

CATEGORIES OF WORK

General corporate	**Banking and finance**
General commercial	**Real estate**
Intellectual property	**EU integration**
Litigation	**Insurance**
Arbitration	**Mergers and aquisitions**

THE FIRM

Weiss-Tessbach was established in 1878 and is one of the longest-established law firms in Austria. 15 years ago, the firm decided on an extremely dynamic development. Since 1990, the number of lawyers at the firm has increased more than four times from 15 to over 80, and the number of offices from one to seven. On October 1st 2003, Weiss-Tessbach was integrated with DLA on the basis of a shared vision to become a top five full-service European law firm. With its current offices in six central and eastern European countries, DLA Weiss-Tessbach will continue to expand into the region at a time of EU accession for many countries.

DLA Weiss-Tessbach is part of DLA Group. DLA Group is an exclusive alliance of international full-service law firms with a shared vision. Established in 1999, DLA Group now has over 2,200 lawyers across 21 countries, who deliver expert local know-how and international solutions. DLA Group provides legal advice in 37 major cities across Europe, Singapore, Thailand, Hong Kong and the People's Republic of China.

Services in Slovakia: legal services in Slovakia are provided on the basis of a permanent co-operation agreement with the law office of Milan Cervenka.

AREAS OF PRACTICE

The firm has strengthened its core areas of expertise (commercial and corporate, M&A, banking and finance, intellectual property, real estate), and has expanded into other areas of law (administrative, employment, telecoms, technology, venture capital). Today, the firm is able to assist its corporate clients in all aspects of their activities.

DLA Weiss-Tessbach has well-established relations with clients of various backgrounds. The firm advises small and medium-sized enterprises as well as leading (often publicly listed) international and domestic industrial groups, service providers, banks and other financial institutions and individuals.

DLA Weiss-Tessbach has established a particular reputation for its ability to handle cases in international cross-border contexts. It carefully views the ongoing developments in central Europe with the aim of combining the needs of the constantly changing international legal market and industry, whilst also upholding the high-standard services that the firm has always been able to offer to its clients.

FRESHFIELDS BRUCKHAUS DERINGER

LAURINSKÁ 12
81101 BRATISLAVA

Telephone: +42 12 54 131 121
Fax: +42 12 54 131 123
E-mail: email@freshfields.com
Website: www.freshfields.com

Languages
Extensive language capabilities

Other offices
Amsterdam, Bangkok, Barcelona, Beijing, Berlin, Brussels, Budapest, Cologne, Düsseldorf, Frankfurt, Hamburg, Hanoi, Ho Chi Minh City, Hong Kong, London, Madrid, Milan, Moscow, Munich, New York, Paris, Rome, Shanghai, Singapore, Tokyo, Vienna, Washington

Number of lawyers 2,504
at this office 15

Contact
Willibald Plesser (Vienna)

CATEGORIES OF WORK

Corporate

Finance

Antitrust, competition and trade

Intellectual property and IT

Tax

Real estate

Dispute resolution (including environment, planning and regulatory)

Employment, pensions and benefits

LINKLATERS

HLAVNÉ NÁMESTIE 5
81101 BRATISLAVA

Telephone: +421 2 5929 1111
Fax: +421 2 5929 1210
Website: www.linklaters.com

Languages
All commercial and local languages in the countries where Linklaters operates

Other offices
Alicante, Amsterdam, Antwerp, Bangkok, Beijing, Berlin, Brussels, Bucharest, Budapest, Cologne, Frankfurt am Main, Hong Kong, Lisbon, London, Luxembourg, Madrid, Milan, Moscow, Munich, New York, Paris, Prague, Rome, São Paulo, Shanghai, Singapore, Stockholm, Tokyo, Warsaw

Number of lawyers 2,000 worldwide

Contact
Jason Mogg

CATEGORIES OF WORK

Antitrust
Monika Szabóová

Banking and finance
Daniel Torsher

Company and commercial
Jason Mogg, Miroslav Németh

Mergers and acquisitions
Jason Mogg, Patrik Bolf

Corporate finance
Jason Mogg, Daniel Torsher

Capital markets
Daniel Torsher

Private equity
Jason Mogg, Daniel Torsher

Privatisations
Jason Mogg, Daniel Torsher

Project finance
Jason Mogg, Daniel Torsher

Real estate/development
Patrik Bolf, Peter Hoffman

Telecoms
Patrik Bolf

Tax
Adam Hodonv

THE FIRM

Linklaters advises the world's leading companies, financial institutions and governments on their most challenging transactions and assignments. With 2,000 lawyers, including 470 partners, and offices in major business and financial centres, its clients choose the firm for its distinctive combination of technical skill, commercial experience and outstanding service.

Linklaters has built a formidable global practice through organic growth and a series of mergers, joint ventures and co-operations with other respected law firms. In 2001, Linklaters merged with three of Europe's leading law firms to form Linklaters Oppenhoff & Rädler in Germany, Linklaters in Sweden, Linklaters De Bandt in Belgium and Linklaters Loesch in Luxembourg. In the same year, the firm formed a co-operation with Brazilian firm Goulart Penteado, Iervolino e Lefosse. This co-operation combines Linklaters' international capability with GPIL's extensive knowledge of the Brazilian market. In Singapore, the firm practises as Linklaters Allen & Gledhill, a joint venture with the premier Singapore practice of Allen & Gledhill, while in Italy, Linklaters has an exclusive relationship with Italian law firm Gianni, Origoni, Grippo & Partners.

PETERKA & PARTNERS v.o.s

KAPITULSKÁ 18/A
81101 BRATISLAVA

Telephone: +421 2 544 18 700
Fax: +421 2 544 18 701
E-mail: office@cabinet.sk
Website: www.cabinet.sk

Languages
Czech, English, French, German, Hungarian, Russian, Slovak

Other offices
Prague

Number of lawyers 40
at this office 13

Contacts
Přemysl Marek, Ondřej Dušek

Member
TerraLex®; International Lawyers Network (ILN)

CATEGORIES OF WORK

Company and commercial

Mergers and acquisitions

Real estate development and construction

Litigation

Competition law

Intellectual property

Labour law

International law

Finance

LAW OFFICE RUZICKA

KAPITULSKÁ 15
81101 BRATISLAVA

Telephone: +42 12 544 33 490
Fax: +42 12 544 35 906
E-mail: ruzicka@ccsconsulting.sk

Languages
Croatian, Czech, English, German, Hungarian, Russian, Slovak

Other offices
Prague, Zagreb

Number of lawyers 28
at this office 16

International groupings
In association with CMS Cameron McKenna v.o.s; CMS Hasche Sigle; CMS Strommer Reich-Rohrwig Karasek Hainz

CATEGORIES OF WORK

Banking and finance
Mgr L Krechňák, Dr D Nemčíková

Mergers and acquisitions
Ian Parker, Dr D Nemčíková

Securities
Mgr L Krechňák, Dr D Nemčíková

Property finance
Dr J Ružička, Mgr L Krechňák

Capital markets
Mgr L Krechňák, Dr D Nemčíková

Litigation
Dr J Ružička, Mgr K Kováčová

Commercial and company law
Mgr Szabó, Dr D Nemčíková

Real estate and construction
Dr J Ružička, Mgr T Hozlár

Trade marks
Mgr S Szabó

Employment law
Mgr S Szabó, Mgr T Hozlár

Competition law
Ian Parker, Mgr L Krechňák

Energy (heating, gas, mining)
Dr D Nemčíková, Mgr S Szabó

Privatisation
Mgr L Krechňák, Ian Parker

SQUIRE SANDERS S.R.O.

ZOCHOVA 5
811 03 BRATISLAVA

Telephone: +421 2 5930 3411
Fax: +421 2 5930 3415
E-mail: kconnor@ssd.com
Website: www.ssd.com

Languages
Czech, English, French, German, Hungarian, Russian, Slovak, Spanish

Other offices
Beijing, Brussels, Budapest, Cincinnati, Cleveland, Columbus, Hong Kong, Houston, London, Los Angeles, Madrid, Miami, Milan, Moscow, New York, Palo Alto, Phoenix, Prague, Rio de Janeiro, San Francisco, Taipei, Tampa, Tokyo, Tysons Corner, Washington DC, Bucharest*, Dublin*, Kyiv*

Number of lawyers 710
at this office 12

Contacts
Kevin Connor, Julian Juhasz

Member
American Chamber of Commerce

CATEGORIES OF WORK

Capital markets
Ronald Surbey, Michal Luknár

Computer technology, multimedia services
Jana Pagáčová

Corporate finance, banking
Julian Juhasz, Jana Pagáčová

Environmental
Ronald Surbey, Nataša Nikitinová

EU competition law
Tatiana Lulkovicová, Jana Pagáčová

Infrastructure, project asset finance
Ronald Surbey, Tatiana Lulkovičová

Intellectual property
Jana Pagáčová, Tatiana Lulkovičová

International transactions, foreign and direct investment
Kevin Connor, Julian Juhasz

Joint ventures
Kevin Connor, Julian Juhasz

Mergers and acquisitions
Ronald Surbey, Julian Juhasz

Privatisations
Kevin Connor, Julian Juhasz

Power generation, energy
Kevin Connor, Julian Juhasz

Real estate
Julian Juhasz, Tatiana Lulkovičová

Securities
Julian Juhasz, Jana Pagáčová

Telecoms
Peter Šuba

THE FIRM

Founded in 1890, Squire, Sanders & Dempsey is a multi-jurisdictional law firm with 710 lawyers practising in offices in Europe, the Americas and Asia. The firm's practice covers most substantive areas of the law, with an emphasis on business and finance matters.

The firm operates as a single global partnership, which ensures client accountability and the seamless delivery of uniformly high-quality legal services throughout the world. The firm's lawyers come from many countries and cultures, are licensed to practise in both common law and civil law jurisdictions, and communicate with clients in their native languages. Today, the firm remains committed to the fundamental principles ordained by its founders: to serve clients effectively and maintain the professional standards that distinguish both the firm and its people.

AREAS OF PRACTICE

The firm is organised around four major practice areas: advocacy, business, capital markets and regulated industries. Within these practice areas, the firm's work can be divided into numerous areas of specialisation, including banking, bankruptcy and restructuring, biotechnology and pharmaceuticals, communications, competition law, converging technologies, corporate, energy, environmental, healthcare, intellectual property, international dispute resolution, labour and employment, litigation, mergers and acquisitions, privatisations, project finance, real estate, securities and taxation.

Established in 1991, Squire Sanders became the first foreign firm to establish a Bratislava office and has since been at the forefront of the market economy in the Slovak Republic. The Bratislava lawyers advise a broad range of established and emerging international and domestic clients on a variety of corporate matters including company formation and registration, investment and financing, labour and employment, corporate governance, real estate, environmental and EU competition law. In addition, the lawyers handle a significant number of mergers and acquisitions.

The Bratislava lawyers offer clients a strong combination of international transactional experience and familiarity with the legal infrastructure of Central and Eastern Europe. This combination enables the Bratislava lawyers to advise Slovak and foreign companies on privatisations of state enterprises in the region and in related joint venture, investment, restructuring and financing transactions.

The Bratislava lawyers have significant experience in communications and advise clients on a variety of related matters, including interconnection agreements for the national telecoms company and corporate work for Internet and e-commerce startups.

The Bratislava-based finance practice is expansive, handling some of the largest corporate finance transactions in the country.

WOLF THEISS

LAURINSKÁ 3
81101 BRATISLAVA

Telephone: +421 2 592 040 40
Fax: +421 2 592 040 49
E-mail: bratislava@wolftheiss.com
Website: www.wolftheiss.com

Languages
Czech, English, German, Slovak

Other offices
Vienna, Prague, Belgrade, Ljubljana, Zagreb

Number of lawyers 98
at this office 3

Contacts
Paul Sestak, Erik Steger

CATEGORIES OF WORK	
Mergers and acquisitions	**Banking and finance**
Privatisations	**Reorganisation and restructuring**
Real estate	**Corporate counsel**

THE FIRM

Wolf Theiss, founded in 1957, stands among the leading law firms in Central Europe, with a concentration on Austrian, European and international business law, and additional expertise in the legal regimes of Central and Eastern Europe.

At its six locations, in Vienna, Prague, Belgrade, Bratislava, Ljubljana and Zagreb, a total of 200 people, including 98 lawyers (42 of whom are partners), work for Austrian and international client companies in industry, trade and services, as well as banking and insurance. At the point of contact between law and business, Wolf Theiss develops innovative solutions on the basis of legal, tax and business know-how.

SLOVENIA

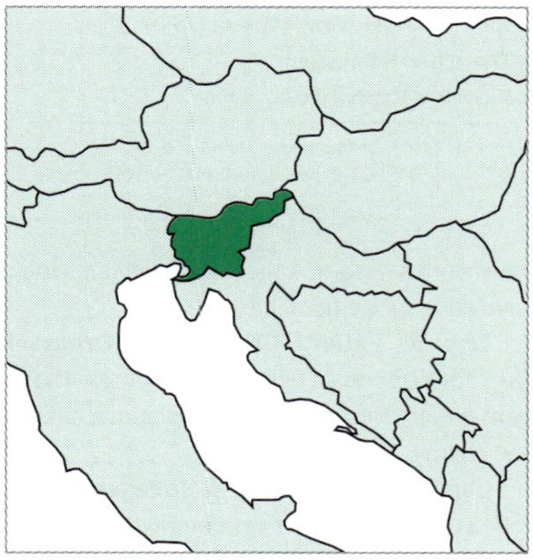

Population	2 million
Number of lawyers	947
Professional title	Odvjetnik
Currency	Tolar (SIT)

Index

Slovenia is located in south-eastern Europe and has strong historical ties with both western and eastern Europe. It was a country of the former Yugoslavia, but declared its independence in June 1991. Since then, Slovenia has consistently been the most prosperous of all the former Yugoslav republics, and unlike the others it has seen very little bloodshed.

In March 2003, Slovenes voted overwhelmingly in favour of EU membership and also voted to join Nato. Slovenia is the only country of the former Yugoslavia to be among the first group of candidates for membership of the EU in 2004 because of its political and economic stability.

BILLING

For the most part Slovenian lawyers bill on an hourly basis, with rates typically ranging between €140 and €250. Exceptionally a capped fee may be agreed, but usually only with longstanding clients. For litigation there is an official tariff, based on the value of the case; the tariff is set by the Slovenian Bar and approved by the government.

MARKETING

The Bar Association of Slovenia strictly prohibits advertising by law firms, but this looks likely to change after EU accession in May 2004.

POLITICAL AND ECONOMIC CLIMATE

The country has benefited from a stable coalition government since independence. Janez Drnovsek was elected president on 1 December 2002 and he leads the centre-left Liberal Democrats. Slovenia has contributed greatly to the stabilisation and unity of the Balkan region.

Compared with other EU candidate countries, Slovenia has good economic growth rates and low unemployment. Much of Slovenia's GDP comes from its manufacturing industry, which includes electronics, textiles, chemicals, and processed foods. However, the European Commission has warned Slovenia that it needs to speed up reforms of its economy. In particular, it has been told that it needs to be more open to outside investment, but public opinion is still not inclined towards it.

The privatisation process has been slowed due to the global downturn. The state still fully owns Slovenia's second largest bank, for example. The state also has a majority stake in its largest insurance company and in Telekom Slovenia.

LEGAL MARKET

All the major law firms are concentrated in Slovenia's capital, Ljubljiana. Two local firms **Jadek & Pensa** and **Colja, Rojs & Partnerji op dno** dominate the commercial market and have the highest number of foreign clients. In addition, there is a collection of local firms focused mostly on domestic corporate clients and regional investors. Following EU accession it is expected that due to the increased complexity of legal advice local firms will be required to grow. At present, sole practitioners account for around 90% of members of the Slovenian Bar.

Foreign law firms are still somewhat scarce in Slovenia. However, in anticipation of EU accession, Austrian firm **Wolf Theiss** opened a Ljubljiana office in 2003. **DLA Weiss-Tessbach** continues to represent the interests of Austrian clients in Slovenia from its Vienna office.

Slovenia has a good record of incorporating EU law into its own legislation in the run up to EU accession, and most of the necessary laws have already been adopted. A new draft of the Takeover Act was recently implemented, and in January 2003 new property laws were passed, making changes to land registration and lease agreements.

CORPORATE AND COMMERCIAL

Jadek & Pensa's name partners Srečo Jadek and Pavle Pensa are two of the best known lawyers in Slovenia. Clients applaud the 'highly efficient' and 'extremely good' services provided by the firm. Mr Jadek enjoys a reputation for forging 'excellent relationships' with clients. The firm boasts expertise in privatisation, mergers and acquisitions, corporate, commercial litigation, and arbitration. In 2003, the firm acted for local subsidiaries of Novartis, Schenker, and Hella KG Hueck & Co in squeeze-out procedures following successful takeovers. It also represented a former Slovenian oil company in international arbitration against a Croat oil pipeline. Other clients include Interbrew and Wrigley.

According to many lawyers in Slovenia, **Colja, Rojs & Partnerji op dno** is now a serious rival to **Jadek & Pensa**. Name partners Colja Marjan and Aleš Rojs are highly respected. They are described

The largest firms

1	Colja, Rojs & Partnerji op dno	14
2	Jadek & Pensa	10
3	Schönherr Rechtsanwälte OEG	8
4	Selih, Selih, Janezic & Jarkovic	7
5	Law Office Janko Pucnik	5
6	Kuhelj Law Office	3
	Wolf Theiss	3

These figures represent the total number of lawyers in this country only, and have been supplied by the firms themselves. The figures should be accurate as at 1 January 2004.

by clients as 'a force to be reckoned with' and 'always dedicated to the project'. **Colja, Rojs & Partnerji op dno** advises on sizeable transactions in Slovenia, which include direct investments, takeovers, and portfolio investments. In 2003, it opened an office in Belgrade, the first Slovenian law firm to do so.

The arrival of Aleš Lunder, a former partner of *Thorn & Lunder*, (now known as **Dr Thorn & Kollegen**) was a boost for Austrian firm **Schönherr Rechtsanwälte OEG**. In Slovenia its mergers and acquisitions team acted as local counsel in several cross-border transactions, generally advising the foreign investors. In 2003, along with many other projects, the firm advised Henley & Partners in its acquisition of Bavaria Wolltex.

Highly regarded **Selih, Selih, Janezic & Jarkovic** advises foreign and domestic clients, which include companies, banks, and financial institutions. It works with a number of major law firms, including many large London and New York-based law firms.

Praised by clients for 'rendering excellent services' **Wolf Theiss** advised Bank Austria on its bid in the privatisation of the second-largest Slovenian bank. The firm also advised a major international retail chain on corporate matters regarding the Slovenian market, and advised JPMorgan Securities on activities in Slovenia.

At **Law Office Janko Pucnik**, Janko Pucnik maintains a good reputation for intellectual property expertise. Clients praise the firm's trade mark work, saying 'no other Slovenian firm would have done such a good job'.

Law & Patent Office Nina Drnovsek has advised on a number of international transactions within the field of pharmaceuticals and energy.

German firm **Dr Thorn & Kollegen** advises various German clients on commercial matters in Slovenia. Dr Michael Thorn and Beatrice von Wallenberg Pachaly also advise Slovenian clients on business and commercial law in Germany.

Previously a sole practitioner, Barbara Kristof-Lucovnik has joined **Vidovic & Partnerji o.p. - d.n.o.**. The firm is recommended in the field of taxation.

CORPORATE AND COMMERCIAL

JADEK & PENSA

COLJA, ROJS & PARTNERJI OP DNO

Schönherr Rechtsanwälte OEG ✪
Selih, Selih, Janezic & Jarkovic
Wolf Theiss ✪

Janko Pucnik, Law Office
Nina Drnovsek, Law & Patent Office
Thorn (Dr) & Kollegen
Vidovic & Partnerji o.p. - d.n.o.

Firms are listed A-Z in tiers which are ranked in order of priority
✪ *Indicates firm displays contact details at the end of this chapter.*

KUHELJ LAW OFFICE

DALMATINOVA 10
1000 LJUBLJANA

Telephone: +386 1 232 7410
Fax: +386 1 230 1621
E-mail: mirjan.kuhelj@volja.net

Languages
English, German, Italian, Serbo-Croat

Number of lawyers 3

Contact
Mirjan Kuhelj

CATEGORIES OF WORK

General civil law

Commercial law

Collecting debts

SCHÖNHERR RECHTSANWÄLTE OEG

TOMŠICEVA 3
1000 LJUBLJANA

Telephone: +386 1 2000 980
Fax: +386 1 4260 711
E-mail: office@schoenherr.si
Website: www.schoenherr.at

Languages
Croatian, English, French, German, Serbian, Slovenian

Number of lawyers 96
at this office 8

Other offices
Belgrade, Brussels, Bucharest, Vienna, Zagreb

Contacts
Michael Lagler (m.lagler@schoenherr.at),
Aleš Lunder (a.lunder@schoenherr.at),
Florian Kirchhof (f.kirchhof@schoenherr.at)

CATEGORIES OF WORK

International and Slovenian practice

International contracts and foreign investment

Banking securities and finance

Project finance

M&A

Privatisations

Public private partnership

Real estate and commercial property

EU Law

WOLF THEISS

TIVOLSKA 30
1000 LJUBLJANA

Telephone: +386 1 425 0000
Fax: +386 1 425 0000
E-mail: ljubljana@wolftheiss.com
Website: www.wolftheiss.com

Languages
English, German, Slovenian

Other offices
Belgrade, Bratislava, Prague, Vienna, Zagreb

Number of lawyers 98
at this office 3

Contacts
Markus Bruckmüller, Ralf Peschek

CATEGORIES OF WORK

Mergers and acquisitions	**Banking and finance**
Corporate law	**Labour law**
Real estate	**Restitution**

THE FIRM

Wolf Theiss, founded in 1957, stands among the leading law firms in Central Europe, with a concentration on Austrian, European and international business law, and additional expertise in the legal regimes of Central and Eastern Europe.

At its six locations, in Vienna, Prague, Belgrade, Bratislava, Ljubljana and Zagreb, a total of 200 people, including 98 lawyers (42 of whom are partners), work for Austrian and international client companies in industry, trade and services, as well as banking and insurance. At the point of contact between law and business, Wolf Theiss develops innovative solutions on the basis of legal, tax and business know-how.

SPAIN

Population	42.7 million
Number of lawyers	104,000
Professional title	Abogados
Currency	Euro (€)

Index

Spain is the second-largest country in the EU and occupies four-fifths of the Iberian peninsula, which it shares with Portugal. The Spanish territory also includes the Balearic and Canary Islands, as well as the enclaves of Ceuta and Melilla in north Africa. Spain believes the return of Gibraltar, which it ceded to Britain in 1713, is long overdue. Gibraltarians do not agree. The country is divided into 17 regions with their own directly elected authorities. Tensions in the northern Basque region, which wants independence from Spain, have long plagued the country. Spain's system of government is a parliamentary monarchy, with the King as head of state. The centre-right Popular Party (PP) is a strong favourite to win the elections in 2004. Prime Minister Jose Maria Aznar will step down as leader before then.

ECONOMIC CLIMATE

Spain's economy grew at 2.4% in 2003, the highest growth rate among the large EU economies. The services sector dominates the economy, with retail, tourism, banking and telecoms all making significant contributions. The real estate sector continues to thrive, accounting for a higher proportion of GDP than in most other European countries. This is due to strong demand for tourism-related buildings and second homes, high levels of investment in infrastructure (reflecting the size of the country), and a shortage in quality housing. Vehicle production is the most prominent manufacturing industry. The biggest rise in spending in 2003 was in public investment. The Aznar administration continues to advocate liberalisation, privatisation and deregulation of the economy. Unemployment, though falling, remains high at 11.7%.

BILLING

Legal fees in Spain are among the lowest in Europe. Hourly rates are the most common form of billing and range between €300 and €400 for partners, and €180 and €250 for associates.

MARKETING

Spain was traditionally a jurisdiction with suffocating marketing rules. The Spanish Bar has done much to relax them, and law firms can now market them-selves freely. Whilst larger firms have developed powerful marketing machines, smaller, more traditional practices remain hesitant to promote themselves.

IN-HOUSE LAWYERS

The banking and telecoms sectors have the largest in-house legal teams. Whilst both of the biggest operators within these sectors have large resources of their own, they still turn to private practices for complex matters.

LEGAL MARKET

The legal market in Spain is fiercely competitive. At the top end of the market are the Big Four domestic giants, **Garrigues**, **Uría & Menéndez**, **Cuatrecasas** and **Gómez-Acebo & Pombo, Abogados**, plus a growing number of the UK powerhouses. The more established of these are **Clifford Chance SC**, **Freshfields Bruckhaus Deringer**, **Linklaters** and **Allen & Overy**. The influx of UK firms has led to domestic firms becoming stronger, either by means of diversifying or, in the case of mid-sized firms, creating alliances to respond to their clients' needs. Those which have diversified have been better placed to survive not only the intense competition, but also the global turndown.

FOREIGN OFFICES

Spanish firms can be found in many of the world's financial centres, and Spain's historical and corporate ties with South America have led many firms to develop on-the-ground presence there.

Uría & Menéndez has its own offices in London, Brussels, Lisbon and New York. It also has associations with firms in São Paulo (Brazil), Argentina, Chile, Mexico and Peru.

Cuatrecasas has offices in Lisbon and Porto, Brussels, New York and São Paulo. It is associated with leading Portuguese firm **Gonçalves Pereira, Castelo Branco & Associados**, Brazilian firm **Machado, Meyer, Sendacz e Opice - Advogados** and Argentina'a **Perez Alati, Grondona, Benites, Arntsen & Martinez De Hoz, Jr.** In all, the firm has 25 offices and 1,000 lawyers on three continents.

Garrigues is a member of the *World Services Group International Network*. It has offices in New York and Brussels, and has a close association with 36-lawyer, full-service Portuguese outfit **Leónidas, Matos & Associados**.

The largest firms

1	Garrigues	1304
2	Cuatrecasas	541
3	Taylor Wessing	488
4	Landwell, Abogados y Asesores Fiscales	445
5	KPMG Abogados	300
6	Uría & Menéndez	245
7	Gómez-Acebo & Pombo, Abogados	167
8	Ernst & Young Abogados, SL	152
9	Baker & McKenzie	147
10	Clifford Chance SC	145
11	Roca Junyent Abogados	137
12	Legalia Abogados	106
13	Deloitte	90
14	Adarve Corporación Jurídica	81
15	Despacho Albiñana & Suárez de Lezo	80
16	Mullerat	75
17	Freshfields Bruckhaus Deringer	71
18	Pintó Ruiz & Del Valle	65
19	Jausas	60
20	Linklaters	54
21	Brosa	53
22	Cremades & Calvo-Sotelo	50
23	Ramón & Cajal	42
	Sagardoy Abogados, member of ius laboris	42
25	Pérez-Llorca	41

These figures represent the total number of lawyers in this country only, and have been supplied by the firms themselves. The figures should be accurate as at 1 January 2004.

Gómez-Acebo & Pombo, Abogados has strategic alliances with firms in Latin America and Portugal, including **Pinheiro Neto Advogados** in Brazil, for example, and **Vieira de Almeida & Associados** in Portugal. The firm has its own office in Brussels.

With 66 offices in 36 countries, **Baker & McKenzie** has the largest network of lawyers in the world. It has a long-established presence in South America; after starting life in Chicago, the firm opened its second office in Venezuela.

Mullerat is an expanding, medium-sized firm with an office in Lisbon. **Roca Junyent Abogados** has offices in Buenos Aires and Moscow, whilst **B Cremades & Asociados** and **Brosa** are both present in Brussels.

FOREIGN FIRMS

Few dispute that of all the foreign firms in Spain **Clifford Chance SC** is top dog. Key to its success was building a strong reputation from the outset by recruiting outstanding lawyers in different specialist areas and competing with the Big Four Spanish firms.

Freshfields Bruckhaus Deringer offers a crucial combination of local know-how with cross-border expertise and resources of an international firm. Its strategy of focusing on top-end, complex work has ensured the firm's presence in some of the significant deals of the year. The firm, now comprising 81 lawyers, continues to attract large Spanish institutions.

Unlike some foreign firms, rapid expansion has not been **Allen & Overy**'s number one priority. It has adopted a more measured strategy for growth, whilst focusing on quality work. Although smaller than many of its foreign counterparts with 30 lawyers, the firm still attracts complex instructions and has been present in some cutting-edge transactions.

Baker & McKenzie started life in Spain in 1965, and since then has been evolving as a Spanish law firm in all but name. With an all-Spanish management board, the firm is becoming ever richer through its strategic plan of growing through mergers with and/or acquisitions from local boutique firms.

As a relative late comer to the Spanish market, **Linklaters** has achieved a lot in a short space of time. It may not be the leader of the pack, but it is a full service firm boasting an impressive client base and some excellent lawyers (recruited from leading firms in the market). 2003 saw consolidation in a number of practice areas and the further forging of client relationships. The firm's strong international network stands it in good stead.

Ashurst was another latecomer to the market. The firm followed in the footsteps of those before it and wasted no time in recruiting well-known local stars. More Spanish specialists joined the firm in 2003, bringing with them the necessary expertise and clients to gain a recognised presence in the market. The recruitment of Jesús Almoguera and his team from former local firm **Ariño & Associates**, and former head of legal at BT in Spain, Gonzalez Jiménez-Blanco, were key moves in the drive to become one of Spain's leading foreign firms.

SJ Berwin has really made its mark in the market as a forward-thinking and dynamic firm. Carlos Pazos is the driving force behind the firm's successes. His unconventional, can-do approach is what gives the firm its clout. It continues to attract major instructions.

Simmons & Simmons may not have expanded at the same pace as its UK counterparts, but the quality of work undertaken and calibre of lawyers is undisputed. Managing partner Luis Felipe Castresana, former general secretary and chief counsel of Spanish state holding company SEPI, leads a dedicated team. The firm offers a full Spanish legal service, and benefits from its international network of offices.

Jones Day and **Squire, Sanders & Dempsey** are the only US firms in Spain. The latter offers full-service capability under managing partner Juan Picón, whilst **Jones Day**, which opened in January 2000, is steadily building up its profile.

Lovells has a European trade mark office in Alicante but it does not service Spanish clients.

BANKING AND FINANCE

After a big dip in the balance sheets in 2002 following disastrous investment in South America, banks reported a better situation in 2003. Barclays' purchase of Banco Zaragozano, making it the sixth-largest financial institution in Spain, and the sale of Banco Atlantico has, however, alerted Spanish banks that some of their European counterparts, and domestic savings banks may take a stronger position in the country.

Clifford Chance SC's undisputed expertise in this sector and its position at the top of the table is fully endorsed by competitors. In the last year, the firm was once again at the forefront of most of the significant deals in Spain, advising major international and domestic financial players, including Citibank, Goldman Sachs, and Banco Popular. As evidence of this, partner Alberto Manzanares, formerly managing partner at *A Manzanares*, advised a group of 11 banks headed by HSBC and BBVA on the €1.35bn syndicated loan financing for the integration of Via Digital into Sogecable and the launch of Digital +.

Freshfields Bruckhaus Deringer handles the full range of banking and finance transactions, both locally and internationally. Its involvement in the securitisation market has continued to grow, and the firm has advised a number of leading financial institutions on the securitisation of Spanish assets. Work in syndicated financings has also increased; one example is the €6.33bn acquisition financing of Gas Natural in its aborted

BANKING AND FINANCE

CLIFFORD CHANCE SC
FRESHFIELDS BRUCKHAUS DERINGER ✪
URÍA & MENÉNDEZ ✪

Allen & Overy ✪
Cuatrecasas ✪
Garrigues ✪
Gómez-Acebo & Pombo, Abogados ✪
Linklaters ✪

Adarve Corporación Jurídica ✪
Albiñana & Suárez de Lezo, Despacho ✪
Ashurst ✪
Baker & McKenzie ✪
Castro, Sueiro & Varela Abogados ✪
M Vega Penichet, Bufete
Mullerat ✪
Ramón & Cajal ✪
Roca Junyent Abogados ✪
SJ Berwin ✪
Squire, Sanders & Dempsey ✪

Araoz & Rueda
B Cremades & Asociados
Broseta Abogados ✪
Deloitte ✪
Ernst & Young Abogados, SL ✪
KPMG Abogados ✪
Landwell, Abogados y Asesores Fiscales ✪
Legalia Abogados ✪
Lupicinio Eversheds ✪
Pérez-Llorca ✪
Ventura Garcés & López-Ibor, Abogados ✪

Firms are listed A-Z in tiers which are ranked in order of priority
✪ Indicates firm displays contact details at the end of this chapter.

bid for Iberdrola. Highly-rated duo Fernando Bautista and Javier Gómez-Acebo, assisted by office managing partner John Byrne, lead a strong team.

Uría & Menéndez has a long history of providing expert advice in the banking and securities market. The firm boasts some star finance lawyers including securities expert Ramiro Rivera and insolvency expert Rafael Sebastián, among many others. Work has included advising on the financing of the new Bilbao Exhibition Centres, arranging an Equity Line Agreement between Jazztel and Santander Central Hispano Investment, and the granting of a $21m loan facility by the IDB (Inter-American Development Bank) to support the construction of a new river port facility in western Uruguay.

Allen & Overy enjoys a pre-eminent position in banking and finance. It is home to two of Spain's leading finance lawyers; Iñigo Gómez-Jordana and Fernando Torrente. The firm advises on asset finance, leverage finance, restructuring and project finance, and has particular expertise in global loans and asset finance. The firm acted in the most important syndicated loans deals of 2003; Sogecable (€1.35bn), Uralita (€525m), and Iberdrola (€1,750m).

Cuatrecasas is very active in securitisations and has particular expertise in e-banking. The firm advised Credit Suisse First Boston on the largest synthetic securitisation deal in Spain to date at a value of €13.4bn. Other work included advising UBS Warburg on the issue of warrants and certificates to be traded on the Spanish Stock Exchange, and advising national and international financial institutions on the issue of mortgage- and asset-backed securitisation notes, as well as refinancing and restructuring matters.

Garrigues' banking practice has excellent capability in all types of structured finance. Partner Rafael González Gallaraza is a specialist in this area. The firm acted for banks including BSCH and BBVA in a prominent €1.6bn leveraged finance transaction for the acquisition by SACYR of national highways company ENA following its privatisation by the state.

Gómez-Acebo & Pombo, Abogados has the capacity to handle a range of finance work including syndicated loans, project finance and asset finance, in which the main focus is ship and aircraft finance. The firm advises a number of leading German and domestic banks on some of the biggest projects being undertaken in Spain.

Linklaters' banking and finance practice has become one of the strongest at the firm. It has the capacity to handle complex transactions and boasts highly regarded individuals like Iñigo Berrícano and Alejandro Ortiz (laterals from **Uría & Menéndez** and **Garrigues** respectively). A highlight of the year was acting for Endesa in the €1.5bn syndicated facility to Endesa. The firm advises on regulatory matters for HSBC and Merrill Lynch.

Adarve Corporación Jurídica handles a range of finance work including corporate and project finance, securities and derivatives, capital markets, debt recovery, and new financial products. Juan José García leads the department.

Despacho Albiñana & Suárez de Lezo has excellent capability in banking and finance matters. Carlos Peña is recommended for asset finance and securitisation, whilst Gracia Sainz is turned to for project finance. The firm acted for Eurohypo Bank in a transaction involving the construction of a large office building near Madrid.

Acquisition and structured finance were the mainstays of **Ashurst**'s finance practice in 2003. Former head of legal at BT España, Gonzalo Jiménez-Blanco heads the team. The firm acts for lenders and borrowers on a wide variety of banking and securities-related matters and advises international financial institutions on complex structural issues. Significant deals include acting for Lehman Brothers International (Europe) on the Spanish aspects of the €2.8bn acquisition financing of Legrand.

Baker & McKenzie's banking practice has well-known specialists working in structuring, derivatives and the regulatory aspects of banking. The firm has unrivalled cross-border capability, and in 2003 represented Banco Zaragozano in connection with the joint venture purchase of a commercial real estate property in Washington, DC, valued at $86m. Société Générale, Dresdner Bank and Gartmore are just a few of the firm's clients.

All three name partners at **Castro, Sueiro & Varela Abogados**, Juan Carlos Castro, José Ramón Varela and Miguel Sueiro are experts in banking, finance and securities. Particular strengths are project finance, asset finance, and contentious matters. The firm represented Chile in a dispute with the Madrid Stock Exchange over the Stock Exchange's alleged refusal to comply with the terms of a deal relating to its purchase of a Chilean company. It also advised on the financing of six windfarms in Galicia, at a value of €238m.

Mullerat is active in all finance matters, including asset finance and securitisation, single and syndicated loans, and the supervision of investments. The firm advised the Marriott Group in securitisation matters relating to the resorts of Marbella and Majorca, and is advising the European Investment Bank on the financing for trains for the Barcelona subway.

Ramón & Cajal specialises in banking and finance, and lists financial institutions, securities firms and investment fund managers as part of its client base. Large Spanish banks BBVA, SCH and ING, are also clients. The firm employs 45 lawyers. Sebastián Albella and Francisco Palá are experts in securities.

Partner Carlos Pazos at **SJ Berwin** focuses on high, value-added commodities work. A major aspect of the practice is instructions from banking institutions to handle the fund engineering for new financial products. The practice is currently working for a bank on a major new product to be sold over the counter, details of which remain confidential. Clients include ABN Amro Bank, Banco Comercial Portugués (BCP), and Citibank. Alejandro Hurtado heads the team.

Squire, Sanders & Dempsey's finance team advised Société Générale on the structuring and implementation of an equity line for Service Point Solutions. The firm advises Commerzbank in relation to all its corporate and capital market transactions in Spain.

Araoz & Rueda has a growing finance practice which complements its core area of work. The firm is attracting world-class clients, and recently represented the IFC in Spanish-sponsored lending transactions for project financings in Columbia and Mexico.

CAPITAL MARKETS

The Spanish capital markets showed some sign of recovery in 2003, though only one major flotation has been announced; that of Antena 3 Television. The debt markets have seen a little more activity.

CAPITAL MARKETS

CLIFFORD CHANCE SC
FRESHFIELDS BRUCKHAUS DERINGER ✪
URÍA & MENÉNDEZ ✪

Allen & Overy ✪
Cuatrecasas ✪
Garrigues ✪
Gómez-Acebo & Pombo, Abogados ✪
Linklaters ✪
Ramón & Cajal ✪

Albiñana & Suárez de Lezo, Despacho ✪
Ashurst ✪
B Cremades & Asociados
Baker & McKenzie
M Vega Penichet, Bufete
Mullerat ✪
Pérez-Llorca ✪
Roca Junyent Abogados ✪
SJ Berwin ✪
Squire, Sanders & Dempsey ✪

Firms are listed A-Z in tiers which are ranked in order of priority
✪ *Indicates firm displays contact details at the end of this chapter.*

Clifford Chance SC's expertise within the banking and finance sector extends to the firm's capital markets practice, headed by managing partner Jaime de San Roman. Particular expertise lies in securities transactions and other products sold into the capital markets. The highlight of the year was acting for the lead managers, JPMorganChase, Dresdner Kleinwort Wassertein and CSFB, on an issue of €300m preferred securities for Banco Popular. This was the first issue pursuant to a new Spanish law permitting issuances through Spanish SPVs. Manuel Sanchez de Movellán was the lawyer involved.

Freshfields Bruckhaus Deringer was again at the forefront of most relevant equity deals of the year. The highlight was acting as both Spanish and international counsel for the joint lead managers in the only successful Spanish offering of the year; the sale by Spain's four biggest utility companies of 28% of the share capital in Red Eléctrica. The firm also performed well in debt securities work and syndicated loans.

Uría & Menéndez has a sterling practice and is a clear leader in the capital markets domain. Partner Luis de Carlos led a team acting for selling shareholders Endesa, Iberdrola, Unión Fenosa and Hidroeléctrica del Cantábrico in the secondary offering of 28% of Red Eléctrica's issued share capital, the most important secondary offering in Spain of the year. He also represented Bami in the issue of €150m convertible bonds to finance the takeover bid of 10% of the shares of Metrovacesa.

Allen & Overy's leading capital markets practice comprises a group of experienced lawyers capable of advising on the full spectrum of debt and equity related capital markets work. The team is particularly strong in securitisations and IPOs. Fernando Torrente, who joined **Allen & Overy** from **Cuatrecasas** in 2002, is referred to in the market as 'Mr IPO'. The firm has been associated with some of the most difficult transactions in the securitisation arena, as well as highly complex derivatives. Recent work included advising HSBC on the issue by cigarette maker Altadis, of its €1.2bn EMTN programme.

Cuatrecasas has extensive experience in all types of transactions in the securities market. The firm was recently involved in the formation of the world's largest steel manufacturer, carried out by means of three simultaneous tender offers in Luxembourg and Belgium, France, and Spain. Clients include major domestic and European companies including Jazztel, SCHI, and Uralita.

Garrigues experienced a busy year and was involved in many of the most important transactions. The firm acted for Antena 3 and Telefónica in the listing of Antena 3 on the Spanish Stock Exchange and simultaneous distribution of 30% of its share capital to Telefónica shareholders. The size of the deal was €1.4bn. The firm also advised Red Electrica on the first issue of EMTNs under the €800m programme and an application for listing the EMTNs on the Luxembourg Stock Exchange.

Gómez-Acebo & Pombo, Abogados has a significant presence in the securitisation market in Spain, acting for AyT, the main issuer of securitisation bonds in Spain. The firm advised AyT Cedulas Cajas IV on the largest covered bond issue in the European market last year, for €3.8bn. The team also advises on the issue of bonds and preferred stock. Clients include Bloomberg, Alliance Capital, and Prudential International.

Linklaters has consolidated its capital markets practice in the last year, as evidenced by its involvement in some of the few relevant deals in the securities field. These include advising Goldman Sachs on the €2bn offering by Repsol YPF, SA of 102,988,486 ordinary shares of Gas Natural, and advising CSFB, SCH Investment and Banesto Bolsa on the offering by BSCH of rights to subscribe for new shares of Banco Español de Crédito.

Ramón & Cajal provides regular advice to several major companies in the area of capital markets, including Spanish and international banks.

Despacho Albiñana & Suárez de Lezo has excellent capability in the capital markets arena. Carlos Peña, Luis Miguel de Dios and partner César Albiñana are all experienced. The firm advised on the suspension of payment of the listed company Avanzit, one of the most relevant receiverships in Spain in recent years.

Ashurst acted for an important international bank and major Spanish savings bank in the €1.4bn financing of a public offer for shares in a listed Spanish company, and for Corporación Financiera Alba in relation to its public offering to its shareholders of shares in Vodafone Group, plc.

Squire, Sanders & Dempsey has advised a number of power distribution companies on privatisation, including Hidrocantábrico and Unión Fenosa Internacional. It also has capability in securitisation and asset finance.

CORPORATE AND COMMERCIAL

Despite a flat year for M&A, **Clifford Chance SC** notched up some substantial transactions. Head of corporate Ignacio Ojanguren advised Barclays Bank SA on its successful offer to acquire the entire issued capital of Banco Zaragozano, representing a total consideration of €1.143bn. Partner José María Fernández-Daza was ranked by *Thomson Financial* as among the top M&A lawyers in Europe. Iberdrola, Red Eléctrica and Iberia are among the firm's key clients in this area.

Cuatrecasas lost its lead in the corporate market in 2003 according to *Thomson Financial*. Whilst the firm topped the Spanish M&A tables for the first three quarters of 2002, it dropped to fourth place for completed deals for the same period this year. Nonetheless, the firm has been active in the deregulated gas and electricity sector. It was involved in the €1.87bn acquisition of Spanish power producer Grupo Viesgo from Endesa by ENEL.

Gómez-Acebo & Pombo, Abogados has seen a 10% increase in business in the corporate sector in the last three years. The firm has also increased activity in other areas, including joint ventures, divestitures (particularly for large German companies), corporate restructurings, and handling corporate governance contracts. It maintains its strong energy practice, advising big names in this sector including Union Fenosa on the sale of 50% of Union Fenosa Gas SA to ENI SPA. Francisco Peña is respected in the market and leads a large team comprising nine partners. Clients value the firm's service delivery culture, and corporate partner Rick Silberstein's familiarity with the US and Anglo-Saxon approach to law. The firm has clear ability to compete at the highest level, and its top-tier ranking this year reflects that.

Uría & Menéndez has once again maintained an impressive deal flow despite another quiet year for M&A. Competitors readily refer to the firm as a class act in the market. The corporate department comprises general corporate, finance, and M&A and capital markets practices, and is home to a number of respected lawyers. Highlights of 2003 include acting for the purchaser Infrastructuras de Alta Tensión in the acquisition of the electricity transmission grid of Iberdrola in a ground-breaking deal which triggered the acquisition of two other large transmission grids and led to changes in the law.

Freshfields Bruckhaus Deringer continued to pick up some major deals last year. Its involvement in almost all significant public M&A transactions such as Gas Natural's bid for Iberdrola, Barclays' offer for Banco Zaragozano and

CORPORATE AND COMMERCIAL

CLIFFORD CHANCE SC
CUATRECASAS ✪
GÓMEZ-ACEBO & POMBO, ABOGADOS ✪
URÍA & MENÉNDEZ ✪

FRESHFIELDS BRUCKHAUS DERINGER ✪
GARRIGUES ✪

LINKLATERS ✪

Albiñana & Suárez de Lezo, Despacho ✪
Allen & Overy ✪
Araoz & Rueda
Ashurst ✪
Baker & McKenzie ✪
SJ Berwin ✪

Adarve Corporación Jurídica ✪
Castro, Sueiro & Varela Abogados ✪
DLA ✪
Jones Day ✪
Landwell, Abogados y Asesores Fiscales ✪
Legalia Abogados ✪
Mullerat ✪
Pérez-Llorca ✪
Pintó Ruiz & Del Valle ✪
Roca Junyent Abogados ✪
Squire, Sanders & Dempsey ✪
Barrilero & Asociados, Bufete

Brosa
Deloitte ✪
Ernst & Young Abogados, SL ✪
Giménez Torres, Bufete
Jausas ✪
KPMG Abogados ✪
Lupicinio Eversheds ✪
M Vega Penichet, Bufete
Ramón & Cajal ✪
Simmons & Simmons ✪

Abogados y Economistas Asociados
Alexander Pitts, Bufete
Alza Abogados ✪
B Cremades & Asociados
Belzuz Abogados
Bufete Bertrán & Associats
Broseta Abogados ✪
CMS Bureau Francis Lefebvre
Davies Arnold Cooper ✪
De Haan & Mulder SCP Abogados - Advocaten
De Lorenzo Abogados ✪
Diaz-Bastien & Truan ✪
Echecopar Abogados
Ecija Abogados ✪
Olivencia-Ballester Abogados ✪
Roig Aran, Bufete
Ventura Garcés & López-Ibor, Abogados ✪

Firms are listed A-Z in tiers which are ranked in order of priority
✪ *Indicates firm displays contact details at the end of this chapter.*

Telefonica's offer for Terra Lycos are indicative of the type of top-quality corporate work being done. The firm acted for La Caixa in the biggest private equity deal of the year, and advised Total in relation to its dispute with SCH concerning shareholders' agreements in CEPSA. The firm has the capacity to attract major domestic and international players from all industry sectors.

Garrigues remains the firm of choice for many high-profile clients, as evidenced by its involvement in some significant transactions in 2003. These include the merger between listed company Vallehermoso and Grupo Sacyr in which the firm advised absorbing company Vallehermoso. **Garrigues** also advised Banco Zaragozano in the bank's acquisition by Barclays Bank. The corporate practice benefits from the firm's sterling tax department.

Linklaters' corporate practice now boasts top-quality lawyers and a strong client base of national and international clients including British American Tobacco, Centrica, and Spanish listed company Amadeus. Partners Antonio Sánchez-Pedreño and Alvaro Saínz lead a 13-strong team. The firm has mostly been involved in private and public acquisition deals and advised on the private offer by leading Spanish construction company FCC to acquire Grupo Cespa from Aguas de Barcelona and Suez. The corporate group also has expertise in private equity deals.

Despacho Albiñana & Suárez de Lezo is an excellent mid-sized firm with the resources to work on large transactions. The firm represented the Caltagirone Group in one of the largest hostile takeover bids in Spain for Metrovacesa (opposite **Uría & Menéndez**). It also represented Iberdrola in another very large takeover bid by Gas Natural. Joint managing partners César Albiñana and Rafael Suárez de Lezo are both respected M&A lawyers.

Allen & Overy's head of corporate and M&A Graham Donnell has significant experience in cross-border mergers and acquisitions, as well as in the energy sector. He has been busy advising on acquisitions and disposals, particularly in the renewables sector. Private equity is another strong area of work. Recently the firm advised South African media group Ster Cines on the disposal of its cinemas in Spain, and GE Capital on the disposal of its Spanish IT business. The firm was also involved in the high-profile Sogecable/Via Digital merger. Fernando Torrente and Iñigo Gómez-Jordana both have first-class reputations for corporate finance.

Araoz & Rueda is a well-respected, medium-sized corporate boutique reputed for top quality work. Its core business is M&A, but private equity work, project finance and international arbitration have been developed as a means of offsetting the slowdown in M&A. The firm boasts a host of international clients attracted by the quality service and dedicated team of lawyers. Clients include UK investment fund 3i and Finnish telecoms company Sonera. The firm represented the shareholders of Movilisto in the €65m sale of their participation to the British quoted company iTouch plc.

Ashurst is well placed in the market owing to the good reputation of corporate partner Jesús Almoguera. Previously name partner at **Ariño & Associates**, he has wide-ranging M&A and company experience. Deals of the year include advising Conserve Italia on its acquisition of Juver from Héro with the assistance of the Italian office, and advising ATB on its acquisition of Babcock Borsig.

Baker & McKenzie's Spanish offices continue to go from strength to strength. The acquisition of two-partner public law boutique *Garcia-Trevijano* in 2002 brought one of the most renowned public law practices in the country to the firm. New partner Francisco Escat has experience in privatisations and private capital transactions. The firm has strong local and cross-border M&A experience. Recent work includes acting for Ferrovial in its €514.5m acquisition of waste treatment group CESPA, and acting for Omega Capital in the €125m acquisition of the Hotel Ritz in Madrid.

SJ Berwin benefits from the dynamic leadership of Carlos Pazos. He scored a major coup back in 2001 when he represented EdP in its hugely successful bid for Hidroeléctrica de Cantábrico. That the firm flexed some muscle then has led to some major instructions since. The Madrid office has been instructed by US client Golden Gate Capital/Melita International to lead and manage the European aspects of the acquisition and restructuring of a major worldwide software group. It is the first time such an important and complex transaction has been managed from the Madrid office. The firm is a market leader for private equity transactions.

Adarve Corporación Jurídica is the only Spanish member firm of *TELFA*, and is member of *Integra Legal International*, an alliance of independent law firms in Europe. The firm is instructed by national and international clients, including Renault España and Citibank. Daniel Villar Valero heads the practice.

Castro, Sueiro & Varela Abogados has corporate and commercial capability, though it is best known for its finance expertise. The firm advised numerous Spanish clients on sales and acquisitions last year.

DLA acquired the Madrid practice of **Stephenson Harwood** in October 2002. Headed by Kenneth Bonavia, who has more than 20 years' corporate experience, the practice handles M&A and private equity work for international clients. The firm advised the Virgin Group in relation to a joint venture, and the Multi Development Corporation in the acquisition of land for three mixed retail and leisure centres and one office park in different parts of Spain. Tiscali is another client.

Private equity work was the mainstay of **Jones Day**'s corporate practice in 2003, but the firm was also involved in M&A transactions. The firm represented Lafarge Asland in the sale of all its cement production assets in Andaulucía to Cimpor. ABN Amro Ventures and CVC Capital Partners are also clients. The firm offers Spanish and US law capability under partner-in-charge, Juan Tena, who specialises in M&A and private equity work.

Legalia Abogados is a growing, full-service, medium-sized law firm with good national coverage. It was formed in 2002 after the merger of national firm *Legalia Compañia de Servicios Juridicos* and Barcelona tax boutique *Dominguez & Gros*. It has the ability to handle large, complex transactions and is heavily involved in the health sector, acting for one of the most important groups of hospitals, Ibérica de Diagnóstico y Cirugía. The firm is advising CVC Capital Partners on the private equity investment in Grupo El Arbol Distribucion y Supermercados. Talde is another client.

Mullerat is a much-respected domestic firm with full-service capacity and a solid international client base. It remains independent despite interest from US firms keen to enter the Spanish market. Miguel Torres heads the corporate department, which includes six partners. Alberto Echarri in the Madrid office is well known for his M&A experience. The firm handles a lot of work in the aviation industry. It has an office in Lisbon.

Name partner Pedro Perez-Llorca at **Pérez-Llorca** is a leading M&A lawyer and is very well respected in the market. The practice focuses on global and Spanish M&A deals, private equity, corporate governance and group restructurings. Despite a lack of M&A activity in 2003, the firm advised on a number of leading public and private deals, particularly in the communications and industrial sectors. These included advising Cadbury Schweppes plc on the Spanish aspects of the $4.2bn acquisition from Pfizer of the Adams global confectionery business. Johnson's and Chubb are other clients.

Pintó Ruiz & Del Valle was formed in 1999 following the merger of two of the oldest law firms in Spain; *Bufete Pinto Ruiz* and *Del Valle Abogados*. The firm is renowned for its sports law department, one of the best in Spain. It also advises on mainstream corporate matters.

Roca Junyent Abogados is a full-service firm with offices in Madrid, Barcelona, Gerona and Lleida.

US firm **Squire, Sanders & Dempsey** advises Spanish and international companies on their investments in Spain and overseas. The team, now comprising six partners, handles corporate restructuring operations including mergers, spin-offs and joint ventures. The firm advised Duke Street Capital on the incorporation in Spain of its first private equity fund abroad, worth €120m.

Firms in the remaining tiers have experience in cross-border work.

Jausas is an expanding, general practice law firm, well known for its specialised pharmaceutical and health law department which advises many of the leading national and international companies in this sector. The firm has opened two new offices in Italy.

Name partner Alexander Pitts at **Bufete Alexander Pitts** was a founding partner of **Clifford Chance SC** in Spain. The firm advises large multinationals and foreign investment funds.

Belzuz Abogados has grown to 25 lawyers. Enrique Belzuz founded the *International Grouping of Lawyers* (IGL) in 1979.

One of the leading firms in Valencia, **Broseta Abogados** enjoys a good reputation in the local community and east part of Spain. The firm has 25 lawyers and traditionally focuses on corporate and commercial law, advising on M&A, buy-outs, private equity deals and foreign investments. It has also developed other areas of expertise, including sports law. Baring Private Equity Partners and Ford España are clients.

CMS Bureau Francis Lefebvre is a member of the *CMS* network and offers dual French and Spanish law capability.

Davies Arnold Cooper's corporate group continues to grow and acts for a number of UK and European companies, although its clear area of expertise is insurance.

De Lorenzo Abogados is a medium-sized firm focused on medical law. It has 14 lawyers and advises a broad range of clients including hospitals, scientific societies, and insurance companies.

Bufete Roig Aran has offices in Madrid and Barcelona and acts for major Spanish companies including Luseo Spain. The firm is active in project finance and real estate.

Olivencia-Ballester Abogados is a respected Andalucian firm and advises a wide range of leading Spanish companies. Founding partner Francisco Ballester Almadana is a recognised expert in acquisitions and company restructurings.

DISPUTE RESOLUTION

Cuatrecasas is exceptionally strong in litigation, boasting a number of respected litigators, including practice head Antonio Hierro. The firm has experienced a significant increase in arbitration work, under the leadership of international arbitration specialist Iñigo Quintana. The firm is defending two companies accused of being responsible for nuclear incidents, (in one case compensation of €2.4bn is being sought), and also representing the owner of properties in the Olympic Village in Barcelona in proceedings for defective construction.

Garrigues was one of the first corporate firms to have a dedicated litigation practice. It was set up by now managing partner José María Alonso, and boasts 150 lawyers. The international arbitration practice has a South American focus. The team regularly conducts arbitration before the ICC, and recently did so for French, Argentinean and Spanish companies in the energy sector, to settle a $500m dispute over the purchase and sale of an Argentinean company.

Name partner Ramon Hermosilla Martin at boutique litigation practice **Bufete Ramon Hermosilla** has a high profile for contentious

DISPUTE RESOLUTION

CUATRECASAS ✪
GARRIGUES ✪
RAMON HERMOSILLA, BUFETE ✪

B Cremades & Asociados
Baker & McKenzie ✪
Clifford Chance SC
Gómez-Acebo & Pombo, Abogados ✪
Mullerat ✪
Pintó Ruiz & Del Valle ✪
Uría & Menéndez ✪

Albiñana & Suárez de Lezo, Despacho ✪
Araoz & Rueda
DLA ✪
Ernst & Young Abogados, SL ✪
Freshfields Bruckhaus Deringer ✪
Jones Day ✪
Pérez-Llorca ✪
Roca Junyent Abogados ✪

Allen & Overy ✪
Brosa
Castro, Sueiro & Varela Abogados ✪
Davies Arnold Cooper ✪
Deloitte ✪
Diaz-Bastien & Truan ✪
Ecija Abogados ✪
Fernando Scornik Gerstein ✪
Ignacio de Ros
Ramos & Arroyo
Ventura Garcés & López-Ibor, Abogados ✪

Adarve Corporación Jurídica ✪
Broseta Abogados ✪
Cabezuela & Gonzalez. Circulo Legal.
Hammonds
Linklaters ✪
Martínez Lage & Asociados ✪
Olivencia-Ballester Abogados ✪

Firms are listed A-Z in tiers which are ranked in order of priority
✪ Indicates firm displays contact details at the end of this chapter.

work. The firm is recognised for its successes in the courtroom.

B Cremades & Asociados has strength in dispute resolution and an excellent reputation in arbitration. The firm has been involved in a substantial number of international arbitrations, representing domestic and foreign clients including FCC, Endesa and Hypovereinsbank.

Baker & McKenzie's 18-strong litigation team is headed by leading veteran lawyers Jésus de Alfonso and Miguel Pintos, and has advised major Spanish and foreign companies in complex litigation cases. Most recently the firm obtained a landmark judgment for Ben Sherman in respect of trade mark rights.

With 20 lawyers in the litigation department including three partners, **Clifford Chance SC** has the capacity to serve its clients well. The firm focuses on big claims and sophisticated clients such as Tyco Electronics, new to the firm last year. Tyco was advised in three separate legal proceedings following its purchase of several Spanish manufacturing companies. Other work saw the team involved in insolvency proceedings relating to Lambdanet España.

Gómez-Acebo & Pombo, Abogados boasts a very strong practice in litigation and arbitration. It was the second practice area the firm developed after real estate. The department has been involved in complex business litigation matters and a high percentage of arbitration cases in Europe and South America. Fernando Pombo, president of the firm, is an active practitioner, and is currently acting in several arbitrations.

Mullerat has a well-established dispute resolution practice, handling all kinds of litigation. Partner Ramon Mullerat handles arbitration at international level.

Pintó Ruiz & Del Valle has a well-known reputation in litigation, and wide experience in arbitration. The firm represents Spanish and foreign clients, and is recognised for its work in bankruptcy.

Uría & Menéndez is the firm of choice for many high-profile Spanish companies when it comes to litigation. Banco Santander, Banesto, and Endesa are a few examples of the firm's growing client list. Jesús Remón Peñalver is a leading litigator, whilst Jose Miguel Fatás is a specialist in administrative law.

Despacho Albiñana & Suárez de Lezo has a quality dispute resolution team with long-established expertise in bankruptcy law.

Araoz & Rueda's litigation practice continues to be active. Arbitration is an area of growth.

The dispute resolution team at **Freshfields Bruckhaus Deringer** has been involved in high-quality, high-profile cases in the tobacco, pharmaceutical and food industries. The firm won a significant case regarding shareholders' disputes in connection with the reorganisation of the Spanish sugar sector.

Jones Day handles litigation and arbitration in a wide variety of areas. It advises almost all the big Spanish construction companies including Ferrovial, ACS, FCC, and Nesco, in arbitration matters. The Madrid office is currently advising a consortium of Spanish and German companies on procedural issues against public entity ETMVA in relation to the construction of the Medellin Metro in Columbia. Maria Mercedes Fernandez has a good reputation.

EU AND COMPETITION

As the competition market evolves, the larger firms are playing a more active role in competition law, mainly due to their networks and presence in Brussels. The situation may change, however, now that regional competition authorities can handle competition cases.

EU AND COMPETITION

MARTÍNEZ LAGE & ASOCIADOS ✪
URÍA & MENÉNDEZ ✪

Cuatrecasas ✪
Freshfields Bruckhaus Deringer ✪
Garrigues ✪
Gómez-Acebo & Pombo, Abogados ✪
SJ Berwin ✪

Albiñana & Suárez de Lezo, Despacho ✪
Allen & Overy ✪
Araoz & Rueda
Baker & McKenzie ✪
Clifford Chance SC
Ernst & Young Abogados, SL ✪
Linklaters ✪
Squire, Sanders & Dempsey ✪

Ashurst ✪
B Cremades & Asociados
Brosa
DLA ✪
Jones Day ✪
M Vega Penichet, Bufete
Pérez-Llorca ✪
Pintó Ruiz & Del Valle ✪
Roca Junyent Abogados ✪
Ruiz & Veiga Abogados ✪
Ventura Garcés & López-Ibor, Abogados ✪

Firms are listed A-Z in tiers which are ranked in order of priority
✪ *Indicates firm displays contact details at the end of this chapter.*

Martínez Lage & Asociados is a dedicated EU/competition boutique based in Madrid, where four partners concentrate solely on competition law. The firm was once again involved in the largest cases of the last year. These include clearance by the Spanish antitrust authorities following the acquisition by Sogecable of Via Digital, and representing GlaxoSmithKline in parallel trading proceedings before the Spanish antitrust authorities and the European Court of First Instance.

Uría & Menéndez's Jaime Folguera Crespo and Brussels-based Edurne Navarro are the two partners leading the firm's EU and competition department. The firm has more than fifteen years' experience in competition law, and provides advice on all areas, including unfair competition, trade law and antitrust. It is a market leader in merger control. Work in the last year has included notifying the European Commission on the purchase of Iberdrola's electricity transportation network on behalf of the purchaser.

Cuatrecasas suffered the loss of respected competition lawyer Antonio Creus last year, but gained partner Miguel Bravo-Ferrer, who is in charge of regulated markets, in particular telecoms. Apart from the notification of several merger transactions at EU and national level, the firm represented TotalFinaElf against Meroil in a case before the Spanish Supreme Court regarding service station contracts, and Christian Dior against Makro in a case regarding selective distribution. It continues to represent the Spanish bottlers of Coca-Cola in the PepsiCo/Schweppes dispute.

Freshfields Bruckhaus Deringer has a strong competition practice in Spain and Brussels. The Madrid office is headed by Francisco Cantos, who focuses solely on competition and EU work. New Spanish clients including Ferrovial, Endesa and La Caixa, instructed the firm on high-quality antitrust assignments in 2003. The competition team advised Ferrovial, the largest Spanish construction group, on the EU merger clearance relating to the takeover bid of Amey plc. Six Spanish associates are based in the firm's leading Brussels office.

Garrigues' practice focuses on both the advisory aspects of competition law and competition litigation. The Barcelona practice has been increasingly active in the last three years. The team handled the merger of retailers Leroy Merlin and Brico after the case was referred to the Spanish competition authorities from the European Commission. With excellent coverage in Spain, the firm is well placed to provide competition advice to regional clients. Marcos Araujo heads the practice.

Gómez-Acebo & Pombo, Abogados has been handling the competition aspects of big merger control deals for increasingly larger clients, particularly in the energy sector. These include advising Iberdrola in the takeover bid launched by Gas Natural, and advising Vivendi Universal in the acquisition of joint control over Via Digital by Sogecable. The firm receives regular instructions on antitrust matters.

SJ Berwin lost competition expert Julio Veloso last year, but the firm remained active in competition law. The team advised Universal Music on the competition aspects of a jointly developed Internet portal, among other clients. The firm produced a best practice report on Spanish competition law for the EC.

Despacho Albiñana & Suárez de Lezo's competition practice is one of the firm's strongest. The arrival of partner José Giménez in 2003, an expert in public and administrative law, was a big plus to the practice's eight-strong team, already home to leading law professor and competition expert Jesús Alfaro. The firm advised Heineken España in its defence of allegations of dominance and abusive business practices in Spain.

Allen & Overy was involved in some high-profile deals in 2003. It has capability in various market sectors including aviation, energy, technology, telecoms and media. The firm advised Twentieth Century Fox on compliance with the Spanish competition authorities regarding output deal agreements with Sogecable. Pedro Callol specialises in Spanish and EU antitrust and regulatory aspects of mergers, acquisitions and joint ventures.

Baker & McKenzie acted for Ferrovial before the Spanish, Portuguese and EU competition authorities over its acquisition of Cespa, and assisted a number of other Spanish firms on the competition aspects of corporate transactions.

Clifford Chance SC has improved its position in this area of the market. Miguel Odriozola and his five-strong team obtained EU competition clearance for Barclays' acquisition of Banco Zaragozano, EU and Spanish Government competition clearance for Red Eléctrica's acquisition of the electricity transmission assets of Iberdrola, and advised Iberdrola SA in the blocking of the hostile takeover bid by Gas Natural. The team is particularly focused on the telecoms and energy sector.

Silvia Pérez-Navarro, head of the EU and Spanish competition law department at **Linklaters** is one of the leading competition lawyers in Spain. The firm has an office in Brussels, where a Spanish lawyer focuses exclusively on Spanish matters. The firm's international network is also valued by clients.

Squire, Sanders & Dempsey provided merger notification to the EU Commission of the joint acquisition of Naturcorp by Hidrocantábrico and EVE.

DLA gained Gerard Perez Olmo, now head of competition, from **SJ Berwin** in 2003. The department handles merger control issues and advises clients on Spanish competition procedures, as well as notification to Spanish and EU authorities.

Jones Day boasts a strong competition and antitrust practice, which attracts high-profile clients. The firm provides ongoing competition advice to Renault Spain, Burger King Spain, and Colt Telecom. The firm represented five cable services providers in the merger review of Sogecable/Via Digital. Juan Jiménez-Laiglesia and Jose María Jiménez-Laiglesia are recommended.

Since being established in 2000, the small team at **Pérez-Llorca** has been very active and has quickly developed an impressive client base including Schweppes, Ence, Vestas and Camper. The team twice represented Cadbury-Schweppes in relation to competition law; once in a complaint against Coca-Cola Spain for alleged abuse of its position in the market, and again over Cadbury-Schweppes' acquisition of Pfizer's confectionery business.

EMPLOYMENT

Advsing on redundancy was the most active area of work in employment law in 2003, which was characterised by widespread restructuring.

Cuatrecasas has an outstanding employment law practice led by Pilar Cavero. The firm recently established a close association with Portuguese law firm **Gonçalves Pereira, Castelo Branco & Associados** and now has the second-largest employment team in Spain with 60 lawyers. The team advises on all aspects of labour law including social security matters, collective bargaining, mobbing, and e-labour. The firm handled the restructuring negotiations that involved the closure of a mining and metallurgical company affecting 896 workers. Clients include Coca-Cola Spain, Nestlé, and Cisco Systems.

Garrigues has a large employment department headed by Frederico Durán. The practice handles complex restructurings, and has been particularly active in the last year. A highlight was its involvement in the collective dismissal of 1,800 employees in retail company Grupo el Arbol. The firm was also involved in the design of a new labour model for the biggest mail distribution company in Spain, Correos, with 60,000 employees.

Sagardoy Abogados, member of ius laboris is a highly regarded employment and labour boutique, boasting a number of specialist divisions within its practice. These include employee benefits and pensions, international employment contracts, executive employment contracts, restructuring plans and collective labour law. The firm is a member of the prestigious *ius laboris*, an alliance of firms specialised in employment and labour law. Name partner Juan Antonio Sagardoy is well respected.

EMPLOYMENT

CUATRECASAS ✪
GARRIGUES ✪
SAGARDOY ABOGADOS, MEMBER OF IUS LABORIS ✪
URÍA & MENÉNDEZ ✪

Antras, Bufete
Baker & McKenzie ✪
Clifford Chance SC
Ernst & Young Abogados, SL ✪
Gómez-Acebo & Pombo, Abogados ✪

Cremades & Calvo-Sotelo ✪
Freshfields Bruckhaus Deringer ✪
Linklaters ✪
SJ Berwin ✪
Squire, Sanders & Dempsey ✪

Adarve Corporación Jurídica ✪
Bufete Bertrán & Associats
Brosa
Broseta Abogados ✪
Deloitte ✪
Echecopar Abogados
Fernando Scornik Gerstein ✪
KPMG Abogados ✪
Legalia Abogados ✪
Mullerat ✪
Pérez-Llorca ✪
Ventura Garcés & López-Ibor, Abogados ✪

Firms are listed A-Z in tiers which are ranked in order of priority
✪ Indicates firm displays contact details at the end of this chapter.

Uría & Menéndez's 25-strong team advises on all aspects relating to labour and employment law, from negotiations relating to downsizing, to labour litigation, collective dismissals and day-to-day advice to companies. An impressive client base includes Nokia, Zara, and Citibank. The team advised Jazztel and Nortel Networks on the downsizing of their operations in Spain.

Barcelona-based **Bufete Antras** is a five-lawyer outfit led by name partner Jose Maria Antras, a leading labour lawyer in Spain.

Baker & McKenzie's practice in Barcelona merged with traditional labour law firm boutique *Suarez Abogados*, resulting in a team of 23 lawyers, one of the largest in the country. It focuses on sophisticated employment work such as major labour litigation cases, corporate reorganisations, and redundancies. The firm assisted Pfizer in Spain in connection with labour and employment issues of its acquisition of Pharmacia Upjohn, the largest labour restructuring in this sector in Spain in the last few years.

Much of the work of the last year at **Clifford Chance SC** has been centred on the labour aspects of business restructurings or the closing of operations, specifically for Cooper-Standard Automotive, Bull España, TXU Europe and Air India. Juan Calvente, who heads the team, also advised a leading UK bank on the dismissal of its two top executives in Spain. The firm also deals with employment law aspects of major cross-border transactions.

Gómez-Acebo & Pombo, Abogados has expertise in all areas of labour law including corporate transactions, restructurings and contentious matters. It advises a cross-section of both international and Spanish clients including Sun Microsystems, Hermès, and the British Embassy.

Freshfields Bruckhaus Deringer advises on all aspects of employment law, including employment aspects of mergers and acquisitions, executive remuneration, and defence against individual claims from employees. Ongoing advice is given to Warner Bros, Turner Broadcasting Systems Spain SL, and the Mills Corporation.

Linklaters has an established employment and social security department headed by Luis Peinado, previously head of Ernst & Young's employment law practice in Barcelona. Advice is given to national and international companies in all aspects of labour law, and has been extended to international matters and outsourcing. The firm won new clients in 2003 including AXA, Temenos and Allied Domecq.

SJ Berwin's employment team advised on the takeover bid of a listed health company, a litigation process regarding disciplinary dismissals on unfair competition, and was involved in an appeal in relation to the dismissal of top executives. Universal Music International Ltd is a regular client.

Broseta Abogados regularly advises public institutions and companies in Valencia in respect of employment law, as well as international companies including Grupo Hoyos.

The employment practice at **Legalia Abogados**, headed by partner Angel García Moreno, was one of the fastest growing in 2003. The firm advises on a range of labour matters including corporate restructuring, collective bargaining and the termination of employment contracts with senior executives. The firm provides labour advice to Iberica de Diagnóstico.

Mullerat has an active employment practice, advising clients on a range of labour issues, particularly restructuring in the last year.

Pérez-Llorca recently hired well-regarded expert in employment law, Luis Fernandez Pallares from KPMG. He provides advice on all areas of employment relations, working closely with the corporate team on company restructuring. He represents clients before employment tribunals, on labour regulations, and on the transfer of employees following mergers and acquisitions.

ENVIRONMENT

ENVIRONMENT

GARRIGUES ✪
URÍA & MENÉNDEZ ✪

Baker & McKenzie ✪
Clifford Chance SC
Cuatrecasas ✪
Gómez-Acebo & Pombo, Abogados ✪
Linklaters ✪
Schiller Abogados
Squire, Sanders & Dempsey ✪

Broseta Abogados ✪
Davies Arnold Cooper ✪
Ernst & Young Abogados, SL ✪
Mullerat ✪
Rodrigo de Larrucea, Estudio Jurídico

Firms are listed A-Z in tiers which are ranked in order of priority
✪ *Indicates firm displays contact details at the end of this chapter.*

The energy sector has been the most important in the Spanish economy in recent years as a result of the liberalisation of the power and gas sectors and the rise of alternative energy sources such as windfarms and co-generation projects.

Garrigues' environment practice boasts strength in Antonio Baena and Santiago Garrido. The firm handled the environmental due diligence procedure in the sales of both Unión Fenosa Energías Especiales and Hidroeléctrica de Navarra. It also works regularly with the Ministry of the Environment in matters relating to environmental damage, and is working with businesses and organisations on the negotiation of the National Plan for Assignment of CO2 Rights.

Uría & Menéndez's environment practice has been growing steadily since 1995. It forms part of the real estate and urban planning department. Headed by leading environmental lawyer Carlos de Miguel, the team of five provides ongoing advice on environmental issues involving civil, criminal and administrative matters. The practice has experience in the biotech, pharmaceutical and food industries. It works closely with the local authorities.

Baker & McKenzie has a dedicated environmental and public law practice headed by internationally recognised environmental lawyer Javier Junquera, and leading experts in public law, partners José and Ernesto García-Trevijano. The firm has been assisting C02 Spain in the creation of the Carbon Spanish Fund to comply with the Kyoto Protocol requirements, and was recently instructed by a major company in relation to the oil spill from the *Prestige* tanker off the Galician coast.

Clifford Chance SC handles the environmental issues of M&A deals and is also advising clients on the post-Kyoto emissions energy trading regime. Partner María José Menéndez is an expert in environmental law.

Cuatrecasas is currently advising Belgian company Electrabel in relation to various energy-related matters, in particular the acquisition of two planned combined cycle natural gas stations in Tereul and Madrid. The firm is also advising Medgaz in its joint venture for the construction of an international gas duct connecting Algeria, Spain and France.

Gómez-Acebo & Pombo, Abogados has provided environmental advice on the construction of power stations and property developments in the last year, and acted for some leading manufacturers in relation to environmental compliance. The firm's dispute resolution team has advised on several high-profile environmental cases over the years.

The scope of advice offered by the **Linklaters** environmental team has broadened with the arrival of environmental law specialists Miguel Riaño and Ignacio Paz from **Garrigues** in late 2002. The Madrid office advised the Galician Regional Government on regulatory issues relating to the *Prestige* disaster, acted for Repsol on new environmental projects, and FCC on the acquisition of Grupo Cespa from Aguas de Barcelona and Suez.

Madrid-based **Schiller Abogados** is highly rated for environmental law and has been active in many contentious issues in this area.

Squire, Sanders & Dempsey has advised SCH and other banks on the environmental due diligences for licences, permits and project agreements related to biomass plants and wind parks.

Davies Arnold Cooper continues to be involved in some of the largest environmental losses in Spain and South America. The firm was recently involved in an oil spillage in Mexico, and advised Hewlett-Packard on its programme for the treatment of dangerous and non-dangerous waste.

IT AND TELECOMS

IT AND TELECOMS

CLIFFORD CHANCE SC
CREMADES & CALVO-SOTELO ✪
ECIJA ABOGADOS ✪
GÓMEZ-ACEBO & POMBO, ABOGADOS ✪
SÁNCHEZ PINTADO & NÚÑEZ
SQUIRE, SANDERS & DEMPSEY ✪
URÍA & MENÉNDEZ ✪

Ashurst ✪
Baker & McKenzie ✪
Cuatrecasas ✪
Freshfields Bruckhaus Deringer ✪
Garrigues ✪
SJ Berwin ✪

Albiñana & Suárez de Lezo, Despacho ✪
Allen & Overy ✪
Broseta Abogados ✪
Castro, Sueiro & Varela Abogados ✪
DLA ✪
Deloitte ✪
KPMG Abogados ✪
Legalia Abogados ✪
Linklaters ✪
Martínez Lage & Asociados ✪
Mullerat ✪
Pintó Ruiz & Del Valle ✪
Roca Junyent Abogados ✪
Villar Arregui

Firms are listed A-Z in tiers which are ranked in order of priority
✪ *Indicates firm displays contact details at the end of this chapter.*

Former incumbent Telefónica is by far the biggest operator in Spain, retaining 87% of the fixed telephony market despite its liberalisation. Competitors are now joining forces to increase their chances of access to the Internet network, which Telefónica also dominates. Terra Lycos is Spain's largest Internet company.

Clifford Chance SC has a number of top specialists in this field. José Ignacio Jiménez-Blanco, Pablo Mayor and José María Fernández-Daza provide corporate and ongoing commercial advice to a number of domestic and international players. Clients include Telefónica, which was advised in its cash bid to acquire the shares it did not already own in the Internet portal Terra Lycos.

Cremades & Calvo-Sotelo is a boutique firm specialising in telecoms, IT and Internet law. With ten partners and 50 lawyers, it has unrivalled resources in the sector, and a star quality client base. José Maria Molero Hernández is a former state attorney to the Ministry of Science and Technology.

Ecija Abogados was one of the first Spanish firms to advise companies on IT and telecoms matters. It is involved in some major projects to study legal problems created by the Internet, and offers a wealth of experience in this area. The firm is involved in the Euro61X project to support the introduction of a new Internet protocol. It acts for some of the largest telecoms multinationals in Spain.

Gómez-Acebo & Pombo, Abogados has a very strong telecoms team which advises big clients from the media, telecoms, e-commerce and IT sectors. In the last year, the firm advised Vodafone on the reorganisation of its distribution network in Spain, Terra Networks on the reorganisation of its business, and Vivendi Universal on regulatory matters. Partner Almudena Arpón de Mendívil heads the team.

Sánchez Pintado & Núñez boasts breadth and depth of expertise in telecoms, media and technology. Leading lawyers Emilio Sanchez Pintado and Ignacio Núñez Luque are both respected for their telecoms expertise.

Squire, Sanders & Dempsey has substantial capability in the areas of telecoms, e-commerce and technology. The firm is regulatory counsel to Spanish Telecommunications Ltd, Teleglobe and Ola Internet, along with other confidential clients in the field of technology. Managing partner Juan Picón and Josep Maria Julià are the main telecoms contacts.

Uría & Menéndez advises on all matters relating to telecommunications, from fixed telephony issues, to the financing of new mobile networks, amendment of licence terms, and conflicts between network operators and virtual operators. The firm advises many clients in the TV industry.

Ashurst's telecoms team now boasts former head of legal of BT España, Gonzalo Jiménez-Blanco. His wealth of experience in finance and telecoms has attracted star clients such as Jazztel, BT in Spain, and Carphone Warehouse's European subsidiaries. Banks have also been advised by the firm on issues relating to telecoms.

Baker & McKenzie boasts experienced practitioners in its IT and telecoms practice in Maite Diez and Jésus de Alfonso. Cristina Sanz is a well-known IT specialist responsible for the IT practice within the department. The firm acts for Telecom Italia and Cable & Wireless among other clients.

Cuatrecasas' e-commerce practice offers comprehensive advice to a range of clients. It has represented various financial institutions in negotiating agreements for the outsourcing of call centres, well-known trade mark holders on cyber-squatting cases before WIPO, and was involved in establishing a financial institution to distribute mortgages via the Internet for a Spanish bank. The firm also boasts a strong telecoms practice.

Garrigues advised Telefónica on the sale of Antena 3 TV, and has been involved in other matters involving radio and television which remain confidential. José María Anguiano is lead partner for e-business.

SJ Berwin advises on national and EU-related regulatory matters within the telecoms, e-commerce and media sectors. It recently advised Oniway in the sale of certain telecoms assets. Clients include Orbitel Telecomucations and Iber-X.

Despacho Albiñana & Suárez de Lezo was involved in some high-profile cases in 2003. The firm represented ONO before the Spanish Supreme Court challenging the authorisation of the acquisition of Via Digital by Sogecable.

The IT and new technologies department at **Broseta Abogados** has particular expertise in data protection legislation, and advises the Valencian Stock Exchange and Grupo Natra among other Valencian companies.

DLA has a rapidly expanding TMC department headed by Jason Flint. The telecoms practice covers regulatory and non-regulatory work and recently advised several international operators on spectrum trading. In technology, work includes Internet services, e-banking, software licensing and outsourcing. The firm has a growing international data protection practice. Clients Include Shields Environmental and Western Union.

The IT team at **Legalia Abogados** handles e-business-related issues and domain name disputes. The firm recently obtained the public contract for SESPA (the health service of the public administration for Asturias, the regional autonomy), and advises one of Spain's leading telecoms companies, Amena.

Javier Fernández-Samaniego has been building a specialist practice in IT, communications and data protection law at **Linklaters** for the last three years. The group of five lawyers provides advice to online brokers and e-banks. Its client base consists of AON Direct Group and MTV Networks Europe.

INSURANCE

DAVIES ARNOLD COOPER ✪

Cuatrecasas ✪
Sánchez-Calero, Estudio Juridico

Albors Galiano & Co Abogados ✪
Castro, Sueiro & Varela Abogados ✪
Clifford Chance SC
DLA ✪
Deloitte ✪
Freshfields Bruckhaus Deringer ✪
Garrigues ✪
Gómez-Acebo & Pombo, Abogados ✪
Uría & Menéndez ✪
Velasco & Co Abogados

Adarve Corporación Jurídica ✪
B Cremades & Asociados
Fernando Scornik Gerstein ✪
Mullerat ✪

Firms are listed A-Z in tiers which are ranked in order of priority
✪ Indicates firm displays contact details at the end of this chapter.

INSURANCE

Davies Arnold Cooper tops the table again this year for its combination of resources, experience, specialisation, and a first-class client base. The Madrid office, headed by Pablo Wesolowski (general representative of Lloyd's of London in Spain), boasts six partners and 23 associates, handling all types of insurance work, contentious and non-contentious. The firm continues to act for most of the major insurance and reinsurance companies, Lloyd's syndicates, brokers and other domestic and international players.

Litigator Iñigo Quitana heads a substantial insurance practice at **Cuatrecasas**, offering expertise in both contentious insurance claims and non-contentious matters. The firm advises clients including Dexia Life & Pensions, Sogecap and Rabobank, on the distribution of insurance products, and was involved in the €120m acquisition by Liberty Mutual of Genesis insurance company from MetLife Iberia.

Estudio Juridico Sánchez-Calero is a medium-sized firm firmly focused on insurance law. A leading competitor in the market, the firm boasts an enviable client list of some of the biggest insurers in Spain and Europe, London reinsurance companies and international brokers. Many of its lawyers are professors or lecturers. Managing partner Professor Fernando Sánchez-Calero is a leading authority on insurance law.

Albors Galiano & Co Abogados has an active insurance and reinsurance group, advising on both maritime and non-maritime matters. The firm advises in large claims to international and Spanish major insurers such as Zurich, Allianz, Estrella and Helvetia. Jose Ramos, former director of non-marine insurance at Repsol Ypf, has joined the department.

Clifford Chance SC's dedicated insurance practice is home to recognised specialists, including María José Menéndez, José Antonio Caínzos and Juan Calvente. Clients include Swiss Life, GE Insurance Holdings Ltd, and Standard Life Insurance. Recently, José Antonio Caínzos advised the reinsurers of Musini in a successful insurance litigation in connection with a butane gas explosion in a restaurant in Almería ten years ago.

DLA's insurance practice advises on a range of areas including maritime issues, public liability, medical malpractice, professional indemnity and property and building risk.

Freshfields Bruckhaus Deringer has a small but highly specialised insurance department, providing Spanish and international clients with high quality advice in relation to regulation, particularly solvency, derivatives and M&A. The department also advises on reinsurance matters.

Garrigues' insurance team is part of the banking and securities division, and is headed by Luis Gerreiro.

Gómez-Acebo & Pombo, Abogados has advised a number of insurers including Allianz AG, AXA, Cigna, and SOS International Group in the last year.

Uría & Menéndez's insurance practice is headed by Jose Maria Segova who advises national and large international insurance companies on regulatory matters and the insurance aspects of M&A transactions. The firm recently advised US life insurance company Metropolitan Life on a complex transaction involving the closure of its activities in Spain and transfer to another insurance company.

INTELLECTUAL PROPERTY

Gómez-Acebo & Pombo, Abogados is home to the highly praised Gonzalo de Ulloa, who heads the IP department. The firm offers the full range of IP advice to a string of high-profile clients including Nike, Toshiba, and Microsoft. Recently, the team advised Novartis on patent and trade mark matters, Aventis on patent litigation, Remington in an unfair competition case against Philips, and advised the huge US pharmaceutical company Schwarz Pharma on know-how licence agreements. The firm is advising Valencia's 2007 Consortium on the legal aspects of the America's Cup Challenge.

Baker & McKenzie's IP practice has been very active in the last two years, and was boosted in 2003 with the recruitment of José María Méndez, former IP partner in media and entertainment at **Squire, Sanders & Dempsey**. The firm provides a wide range of services in litigation, representing clients such as Calvin Klein and Ben Sherman, and has a recognised practice in trade marks. Jesús de Alfonso, partner in the Barcelona office, acted on behalf of Levi-Strauss and succeeded in banning the illegal import and sale of the client's products.

Clifford Chance SC's Barcelona office is where the bulk of the firm's IP capability is based. The firm specialises in trade mark, copyright and patent litigation. Recent successes include representing San Carlo Food Group España in its successful court action against Snack Ventures SA (PepsiCo group) for unfair competition, and securing Pfizer's successful action against Laboratorios Alter for infringements of patent rights related to the drug Amlodipine. Miguel Montañá was the lawyer involved.

Uría & Menéndez has a very successful IP practice which offers advice in a wide range of areas. These include patents, industrial design, trade mark, copyright, unfair competition among others. The firm represents clients from all sectors.

INTELLECTUAL PROPERTY

GÓMEZ-ACEBO & POMBO, ABOGADOS ✪

Baker & McKenzie ✪
Clifford Chance SC
Uría & Menéndez ✪

Abril Abogados, S.L. ✪
Albiñana & Suárez de Lezo, Despacho ✪
Cuatrecasas ✪
Ecija Abogados ✪
Elzaburu
Freshfields Bruckhaus Deringer ✪
Garrigues ✪
Herrero & Asociados ✪
Mullerat ✪
Pintó Ruiz & Del Valle ✪
Ruiz & Veiga Abogados ✪
SJ Berwin ✪
Squire, Sanders & Dempsey ✪

Adarve Corporación Jurídica ✪
Batalla Abogados ✪
Broseta Abogados ✪
Cremades & Calvo-Sotelo ✪
Deloitte ✪
Grau, Baylos & Angulo ✪
Linklaters ✪
Lupicinio Eversheds ✪
M Vega Penichet, Bufete
Santiago Mediano Abogados ✪
Ventura Garcés & López-Ibor, Abogados ✪
Villar Arregui

Firms are listed A-Z in tiers which are ranked in order of priority
✪ *Indicates firm displays contact details at the end of this chapter.*

Most recently, the firm advised Pfizer and US pharmaceutical company Abbott on patent litigation, Endemol for commercial copyright, and Microsoft on commercial IP in relation to software agreements. Jose Massageur leads the department.

Abril Abogados, S.L. is a relatively new firm specialising in IP law. The firm recently opened a new office in Barcelona headed by Carlos Moliner, to complement Madrid. Significant work includes representing Camper in a case involving domain names, and the Mexican Nobel Prize novelist, Octavio Paz in a copyright conflict. The international department has also initiated several police raids in Asian countries against the manufacture of counterfeit goods.

Despacho Albiñana & Suárez de Lezo's successful IP, media and new technologies practice was further consolidated with the arrival of both José Giménez as partner, and Mariano Yzquierdo, a qualified expert on IP matters. Vicente Arias heads the team.

Cuatrecasas has a strong contentious practice and has represented various companies in relation to trade mark violation. These include Andros Food (Group Uniq) against a fast food multinational. The firm also advises in the field of new technologies including the registration and recovery of different domain names, and has been involved in several appeals relating to the granting or denial of IP rights.

Ecija Abogados is well known for its IP expertise. It acts for large corporations from numerous sectors, especially in the field of film and TV production. The firm also acts for major Spanish Internet portals in copyright matters, and has one of the largest media litigation departments in Spain.

Elzaburu specialises in providing advice in industrial property, IP, licensing, unfair competition, and domain names. The firm boasts a number of highly specialised litigators who operate in courts at all levels and in all jurisdictions, including international arbitration boards and tribunals. The firm's Alicante office specialises in trade mark and design matters.

Freshfields Bruckhaus Deringer's IP group is linked with the firm's IT practice, and is active in media and advertising related matters. Examples of work include advising Mattel Inc in relation to copyright, industrial designs and unfair competition issues, and Nintendo of Europe on e-commerce and data protection advice.

Garrigues has a large industrial and intellectual property group headed by Miguel Moscardo. It advises on trade mark, anti-piracy, copyright and patents, both contentious and non-contentious.

Herrero & Asociados is a respected IP firm with a large litigation department. The firm represents a cross-section of high-profile international clients including Bayer, GlaxoSmithKline, Air Europa and Unilever. Founding partner Jose Antonio Hernández and partner Patricia Koch are both excellent litigators.

Mullerat does a lot of work in IP. The firm's high-profile clients include Burberry, Levi-Strauss, and adidas, in connection with brand protection matters in litigation.

Pintó Ruiz & Del Valle also has an excellent IP practice. Salvador Ferrandis and Antonio Selas are both recommended for their expertise in this area. The firm is a member of numerous intellectual property associations, and advises on copyright, technology transfer, know-how, and patent and trade mark enforcement among others.

Partners Carina Ruiz and Eduardo Veiga at **Ruiz & Veiga Abogados** are both considered specialists in IP and competition. The office specialises in all aspects of IP, including trade marks, patents, models, copyright, and is instructed by a number of multinational companies.

SJ Berwin advises on all aspects related to IP, with a strong focus on software licence creation and exploitation agreements, trade marks, e-commerce, Internet and data protection. Clients include Espasa-Calpe, Quiter and Melita International Software. The firm also attracts a lot of instructions from film producers.

Squire, Sanders & Dempsey's media practice suffered the loss of partner José María Méndez to **Baker & McKenzie** in 2003. It continues to advise television and film production companies on IP matters.

PROJECT FINANCE

Projects in the real estate, energy and infrastructure sectors are providing a regular source of work for law firms. In 2003, the New Concession Act was passed allowing private investors greater access to leveraged finance to boost investment in public infrastructure projects. The Act represents a major change in the legal framework relating to project finance.

Clifford Chance SC handles complex transactions in the energy and infrastructure sectors, building on the expertise it has developed over the years. The firm also benefits from the strong support of its securities practice. In 2003, advice was given to BBVA in the financing of the construction of Madrid's R4 toll highway comprising a €196m credit facility and a €360m guarantee facility. The work also covered the syndication process.

Cuatrecasas advised on a wide variety of projects last year. These included advising the Catalan Regional Government in the design and implementation of the financing of Line 9 of the Barcelona Underground for €3.35bn, advising the European Investment Bank on the structure of the financing of the Madrid shadow toll highway, plus advising on a number of development projects in Africa and South America.

Uría & Menéndez's Juan Ignacio González has been advising the Electricity Supply Board of Ireland (ESB) on the construction and start-up of a combined cycle power plant of 755MW in the Basque town of Amorebieta, the first of its kind in Spain. He also advised project company Bahía de Bizkaia Gas on the first limited recourse financing of €200m for the construction and operation of an LNG terminal in Spain.

Allen & Overy continues to attract significant instructions in the area of project finance. The highlight of 2003 was the firm's lead role in the €665m Cartagena IPP, one of only two such projects in Spain recently, and the largest-ever independent CCGT plant financed in Spain to date. Partners Graham Donnell and Eduardo Sebastián de Erice between them have notable experience in IPP financings, renewable energy and LNG projects, and the infrastructure sector.

Garrigues acted in half of the major projects of 2003. It has a well-resourced department comprising 18 lawyers and three partners. The firm has expertise in infrastructure finance. It acted for the sponsors in the €668m financing of two twin toll highways projects and the sponsors of the €192m financing of the Santiago-Ourense toll highway. Other interesting projects include the financing of mines in Huelva and Badajoz and a windfarms project in Galicia.

PROJECT FINANCE

CLIFFORD CHANCE SC
CUATRECASAS ✪
URÍA & MENÉNDEZ ✪

Allen & Overy ✪
Garrigues ✪
Gómez-Acebo & Pombo, Abogados ✪

Ashurst ✪
Baker & McKenzie ✪
Broseta Abogados ✪
Castro, Sueiro & Varela Abogados ✪
Freshfields Bruckhaus Deringer ✪
Legalia Abogados ✪
Linklaters ✪
SJ Berwin ✪
Squire, Sanders & Dempsey ✪

Firms are listed A-Z in tiers which are ranked in order of priority
✪ Indicates firm displays contact details at the end of this chapter.

Gómez-Acebo & Pombo, Abogados boasts a strong project finance team, often seen playing a leading role in many major projects. In 2003, the firm advised lead arrangers Caja Madrid, ICO and ING in the €686m financing of a toll highway, the largest financing of infrastructure last year. The firm's excellent track record includes advising on the Energías Eólicas Especiales windfarm, the largest windfarm financing in the world.

Ashurst enters the table this year. The firm acted for Dragados Construcciones and Bouygues on their €714m joint project to construct the international section between Figueras and Pergignan of the high-speed rail link Madrid-Barcelona-Montpellier, which did not complete. It also acted for Energy Finance on the construction and financing of a methane gas extraction project for clean energy production.

At **Baker & McKenzie**, Iñigo Fernandez de Córdova and Jose María Sanchez both have substantial experience of advising financial entities and borrowers in projects related to telecoms, energy and real estate. They recently advised Hines Interests Espana SL and Grupo Montisa as borrowers in negotiating a €84.2m credit facility for the construction of a seven-storey office building in Madrid.

Broseta Abogados has strong project finance practice, and advised two of the largest constrcution companies in Spain, FCC and LUBASA, on the finance aspects for the construction of the new international airport of Castellón.

Castro, Sueiro & Varela Abogados specialises in project finance. The firm advised on the construction of the first private international airport in Spain at a value of €200m.

Freshfields Bruckhaus Deringer is particularly active in energy-related and real estate projects. The firm handles complex and sophisticated cross-border transactions. It is currently advising Cintra (part of Ferrovial) on the refinancing of a motorway toll road in Portgual. It acted for the FSA in connection with the Perpignan high-speed rail link as part of a fresh round of bids, and Gaz de France in the €480m financing of its AES power generation project in Cartagena.

Legalia Abogados has a focused project finance department. The firm advises promoters, shareholders and financial bodies. It has considerable experience in the financing of wind projects, advising two very strong companies in this sector, Preneal SA Group and Energy 2. More recently, the firm advised Caja Espana de Inversiones and Caja de Ahorres y Monte de Piedad in a number of co-generation plants across the Iberian peninsula.

Linklaters has enjoyed a busy year, especially in the gas and electricity sectors. The firm has acted for sponsors and lending banks, and has worked extensively with the Ministry of the Environment and regional government of Galicia on several projects. The deal of the year was probably acting for RBS on a landmark power project in Amorebieta, Spain, the first internationally financed IPP in the country. Ignacio Paz and Miguel Riaño who joined the firm from **Garrigues** at the end of 2002, both have expertise in finance, regulatory and environmental issues.

Javier Santos heads a substantial infrastructure and project finance practice at **Squire, Sanders & Dempsey**. The firm advised SCH on both the €65m structured financing for the MBO of Binter Canarias, a regional airline in the Canary Islands, and for the financing of two wind parks in Spain.

REAL ESTATE

The construction industry is thriving with hotels, office buildings and shopping and leisure complexes being developed all over the country. Last year saw an increasing amount of investment from Spanish funds.

Gómez-Acebo & Pombo, Abogados started life as a real estate law firm before expanding into other areas. The first-class department now encompasses property, environment and urban development teams, and is headed by dedicated trio Victoria Llavero, Philippe Espósito, and Luis Jiménez-Díaz. The firm was a leader in the field in 2003. It played a lead role in the management of the Valdebebas urban development, the largest in Spain with a surface area of 11sq m, among other large-scale projects. The firm is advising Valencia's 2007 Consortium on the legal aspects of the America's Cup Challenge.

Uría & Menéndez has been involved in dozens of real estate projects in the last year. The large department is headed by Charles Coward. His practice has advised Multidevelopment

REAL ESTATE

GÓMEZ-ACEBO & POMBO, ABOGADOS ✪
URÍA & MENÉNDEZ ✪

CLIFFORD CHANCE SC
CUATRECASAS ✪
DLA ✪
FRESHFIELDS BRUCKHAUS DERINGER ✪
GARRIGUES ✪

Baker & McKenzie ✪
Deloitte ✪
Diaz-Bastien & Truan ✪
KPMG Abogados ✪
Linklaters ✪
Lupicinio Eversheds ✪
Pérez-Llorca ✪

Adarve Corporación Jurídica ✪
Ashurst ✪
Broseta Abogados ✪
Fernando Scornik Gerstein ✪
Mullerat ✪
Roca Junyent Abogados ✪

Firms are listed A-Z in tiers which are ranked in order of priority
✪ *Indicates firm displays contact details at the end of this chapter.*

Corporacion España on the development of a 90,000sq m shopping centre in Madrid, and is advising ING real estate on the acquisition and joint venture of the 44,000sq m GLA 'Vasco de Gama' shopping centre in Lisbon.

Clifford Chance SC's excellent reputation and expertise of handling big-volume transactions in this area has earned it a wide-ranging and impressive client list. The practice is one of the largest at the firm with 20 lawyers, and is led by well-known partners Carlos Portocarrero, Alfonso Benavides and Juan Antequera. During 2003, Antequera advised Rodamco in its €40m acquisition of the second phase of the Bonaire shopping complex in Valencia, and Portocarrero advised Endesa in the sale and lease back of 12 of its buildings in central Madrid, valued at €400m.

Cuatrecasas has a star real estate practice, boasting a solid track record in large transactions. Last year the firm was involved in the €125m purchase of the Hotel Ritz in Madrid, advised ING Real Estate on the sale and lease back of nine hypermarkets at a cost of €150m, and advised the Mills Corporation on the development of the Xanadu shopping and leisure centre on the outskirts of Madrid. It is also very active in litigation and arbitration in construction.

DLA is very active in the property world. The firm acts for leading German banks including AHBR, Aareal Bank as well as RBS on property financing. Fernando Rodriguez and Javier Ibanez are lead property partners in the Madrid office. The team recently advised Peel Holdings on a mixed commercial centre project in the south of Spain.

Freshfields Bruckhaus Deringer has been active in a significant number of major Spanish real estate transactions, acting for some notable UK, US and German institutional investors and investment trusts on the acquisition of large-scale office developments, shopping precincts and hotels. Leading property lawyer Juan Goméz-Acebo heads the practice.

Garrigues' real estate practice has had a very busy year and played a lead role in a number of transactions. These include acting for DB Real Estate Investment in the €137m acquisition of a shopping centre in Castellón, advising Carrefour in the sale of several shopping galleries to Klepierre, and advising the vendor Grubarges (FCC) on the sale of six hotels for €120m.

Baker & McKenzie's real estate department benefits from the firm's excellent tax lawyers. Zavier Junquera takes over from retired Avaro Espinos as head of practice in Barcelona. The firm advised private real estate company Ponte Gadea in the acquisition of four major buildings in Madrid, and Hines on its first real estate project in Madrid valued at more than €80m.

Linklaters attracted some big real estate clients in 2003 including GE Capital, Lend Lease and RBS. The recruitment of Jésus Varela, a top real estate lawyer at **Clifford Chance SC** was a boost for the firm, which has advised on some of the biggest real estate transactions in Spain and Portugal. These include acting for TIAA-CREF in the establishment of a €1.1bn real estate fund as a joint venture to purchase 18 shopping centres in Spain and Portugal. Rafael Molina heads the department.

Ashurst has had a presence in this area since the arrival of Cristina Calvo from **Baker & McKenzie**. Bigger transactions include acting for RBS on the acquisition financing of land plots for the construction of a shopping and leisure centre, and acting for the Hines Group on the sale of the €78m Torre Diagonal Mar office project.

SHIPPING

Although large firms handle shipping matters, the majority of maritime law is undertaken by smaller, more specialist firms.

Albors Galiano & Co Abogados, based in Madrid and Bilbao, is home to some of Spain's leading maritime practitioners - Eduardo Albors, Javier Galiano, and Javier Portales. In May 2003, the firm entered an association with London shipping firm **Thomas Cooper & Stibbard**, bringing it greater international exposure. The team acts on behalf of shipowners, carriers, insurers, shipyards and marine terminals, and has been involved in some significant casualties in Spanish waters, including the *Spabunker* IV sinking in Algeciras Bay, and the *Vistamar* collision in Ibiza.

Uría & Menéndez recently merged with boutique firm *Figuera Asociados*, enhancing an already strong shipping department. It boasts particular strengths in ship construction and finance. The firm is advising Spain in the co-ordination of legal actions to be taken abroad in relation to the cause of the oil slick disaster involving the *Prestige*. Other work has included advising the Fast Ship Group on the construction of a new generation of high-speed ships.

Abogados AMYA is an excellent maritime practice and José Maria Alcántara is a highly experienced lawyer. However, since splitting with partner Luis San Simon in 2000, which led to the departure of other lawyers, the firm does not field the same strength it once did. The firm offers comprehensive maritime law advice, and has associated offices in Lisbon, Paris, Panama, Buenos Aires, Rome and Piraeus.

DLA's shipping practice is one of the strongest at the firm. The team, headed by Carles Perez, advises on admiralty, ship finance, shipping litigation and structured finance transactions. The firm represents AP Möller (Maersk Group), the largest shipping line in the world, in various court proceedings throughout Spain.

Fernando Meana Green & Co Abogados consists of ten experienced lawyers working in Madrid and Bilbao. The firm has been active in

SHIPPING

ALBORS GALIANO & CO ABOGADOS ✪
URÍA & MENÉNDEZ ✪

AMYA, Abogados ✪
DLA ✪
Fernando Meana Green & Co Abogados ✪
Garrigues ✪
Goñi & Co Abogados
Lebrero & Co ✪
Ruiz Soroa & Zabaleta

Actio XXI Abogados
Castro, Sueiro & Varela Abogados ✪
Cuatrecasas ✪
Freshfields Bruckhaus Deringer ✪
Gómez-Acebo & Pombo, Abogados ✪
Ignacio de Ros
Ruiz Galvez & Asociados
San Simón Duch & Co
Velasco & Co Abogados

BBCA Law Firm
Bufete Bertrán & Associats
Maritimo Abogados, Estudio
Fernando Scornik Gerstein ✪
Francisco Sánchez Jurado
Ibarra & Lopez
Ramos & Arroyo
Rodrigo de Larrucea, Estudio Jurídico

Firms are listed A-Z in tiers which are ranked in order of priority
✪ *Indicates firm displays contact details at the end of this chapter.*

numerous pollution cases, collisions, salvage, cargo claims and personal injury matters over the year. The Bilbao office is receiving a greater number of instructions from a wide variety of clients, including P&I clubs and foreign law firms.

Garrigues' maritime department has excellent coverage in Spain, boasting offices in all the main ports. The 15-strong practice is headed by well-known maritime practitioner Manuel González, an expert in wet and dry cases. The firm advises on the sale of vessels, ship construction and financing, marine claims and casualties, as well as international arbitration. **Garrigues** is representing the Basque government in the proceedings arising from the *Prestige*.

Goñi & Co Abogados has considerable experience in maritime law and boasts a number of international clients.

Lebrero & Co's core activity is shipping, admiralty and aviation. The firm boasts a substantial international client base which includes ship financiers Deutsche Verkehrsbank and UK shipping firms **Ince & Co** and **Hill Taylor Dickinson**. The firm is involved in some significant cases including the collision between the *Millennium* and the *Auriga E*, and the sinking of the *Prestige*. The firm opened an office in Biarritz in September 2003.

Ruiz & Veiga Abogados is another well-respected shipping firm, boasting experts Jose Ruiz Soroa and Santiago Zabaleta. The firm is involved in the Prestige case.

Castro, Sueiro & Varela Abogados has substantial capability in ship finance. It also represents shipyards in litigation matters. The firm acted on behalf of Pymar, a group of Spanish shipyards, in a claim against Credit Suisse, and represented a Scottish shipyard against classification society Bureau Veritas.

Cuatrecasas receives instructions from the shipping sector although it does not have a separate shipping department in its own right. The firm handles ship arrests, has acted for insurers and owners of goods in cases related to damage insurance and civil liability, and assisted Norwegian shipyards in relation to arbitration proceedings regarding design licences for ship construction.

Freshfields Bruckhaus Deringer has been very active in ship finance transactions in Spain, and acts for many banks including HSBC and JPMorgan in this area.

Gómez-Acebo & Pombo, Abogados has a substantial ship finance practice which acts for banks, financial institutions and arrangers on the financing of major tankers and other vessels. It advised lead arrangers Neptune Lines in the financing of the construction of a vessel which constituted the first tonnage tax structure established in Spain.

Ignacio de Ros is a well-respected maritime lawyer with 30 years' experience. He works on behalf of P&I clubs, insurance companies and non-Spanish law firms. He specialises in ship arrests.

Velasco & Co Abogados has a dedicated shipping practice and represents many multinational companies.

TAX

The tax practice at **Cuatrecasas** is second to none, boasting180 lawyers and many specialists including Alejandro Escoda for international tax planning, Eduardo Ramirez for banking and insurance taxation, and Antonio Gil in real estate. Family business taxation and tax litigation are also specialist areas. The firm handles cross-border transactions with an international component, highly valued by Spanish companies expanding their international presence.

Since separating from *Andersen Legal* in March 2002, **Garrigues** has grown by 10%, only losing three partners since the split. Joint managing partner José María Alonso points to a loyal clientele, an increase in referrals from US firms that no longer see **Garrigues** as a competitor, and expertise inherited from *Andersen*, as positive factors. Competitors, however, are still speculating on the firm's future. Nonetheless, it has incomparable tax resources and coverage across Spain. Dragados, Banco Zaragozano and Endesa were all advised on the tax matters in relation to mergers and acquisitions.

Baker & McKenzie has a first-class tax department boasting leading lawyers in the field. Name partner Luis Briones specialises in international law, whilst Felipe Alonso is recommended for domestic tax and tax litigation. The practice is the second biggest at the firm with 40 lawyers, and covers all aspects of tax law from general corporate tax advice to global tax planning and personal wealth. The firm represents more than 80 wealthy family groups, three of whom are listed in the Forbes list of World Billionaires.

The Big Four-linked firms **Deloitte**, **Ernst & Young Abogados, SL**, **KPMG Abogados** and **Landwell, Abogados y Asesores Fiscales** all have substantial capability in tax planning and auditing, and advise companies across Spain on a range of tax-related matters.

Partner Santiago Diez is the main tax contact at **Despacho Albiñana & Suárez de Lezo**. The firm offers advice on all aspects of tax.

Bufete Barrilero & Asociados has a quality tax department led by well-known name partner Eduardo Barrilero. The firm advises on both corporate and personal taxation issues.

Clifford Chance SC's José Ignacio Jiménez-Blanco has recognised expertise in tax law. He advised Barclays Bank on the tax implications of the acquisition of Banco Zaragozano, and Red Eléctrica on the tax issues related to the acquisition of the electricity transmission assets of Iberdrola, Unión Fenosa and Endesa.

Freshfields Bruckhaus Deringer boasts a team of 14 tax structuring specialists in its independent practice. The team advises on complex, sophisticated deals such as structuring products for banks, and the tax aspects of complex finance deals. Headed by leading tax lawyer Miguel Klingenberg, the practice also initiates its own work.

Gómez-Acebo & Pombo, Abogados' tax department, led by partner Pablo Alarcón, advises domestic and international clients on restructuring and tax incentives. Most recently, the department has been working with the finance team on a new regulatory framework for structured tax leases in the field of ship construction.

Linklaters' tax department is led by Nicolas Martin, formerly a partner at KPMG, who advises on a wide range of tax issues. The department focuses on M&A and finance transactions. The firm's links with its international network allows it to work on cross-border deals involving other jurisdictions, particularly in South America, due to the increasing tax capablities of the **Linklaters** Brazil office. The team advised on

TAX

CUATRECASAS ✪
GARRIGUES ✪

Baker & McKenzie ✪
Deloitte ✪
Ernst & Young Abogados, SL ✪
KPMG Abogados ✪
Landwell, Abogados y Asesores Fiscales ✪

Albiñana & Suárez de Lezo, Despacho ✪
Barrilero & Asociados, Bufete
Clifford Chance SC
Freshfields Bruckhaus Deringer ✪
Gómez-Acebo & Pombo, Abogados ✪
Linklaters ✪
Squire, Sanders & Dempsey ✪
Uría & Menéndez ✪

Allen & Overy ✪
Araoz & Rueda
Ashurst ✪
Legalia Abogados ✪
M Vega Penichet, Bufete
Pérez-Llorca ✪
Pintó Ruiz & Del Valle ✪
Roca Junyent Abogados ✪
SJ Berwin ✪

Adarve Corporación Jurídica ✪
B Cremades & Asociados
Brosa
Broseta Abogados ✪
Castro, Sueiro & Varela Abogados ✪
Echecopar Abogados
Mullerat ✪
Ventura Garcés & López-Ibor, Abogados ✪

Firms are listed A-Z in tiers which are ranked in order of priority
✪ *Indicates firm displays contact details at the end of this chapter.*

tax issues related to the €690m power project in Amorebieta.

Squire, Sanders & Dempsey boasts international tax expertise in Carlos Rodriguez, who heads the practice. Tax advice is provided to businesses relating to their international restructuring and development.

Although **Uría & Menéndez** handles day-to-day compliance work within its tax practice, its focus is advising on more complex corporate transactions. Tax advice is provided on securities, corporate finance, insurance, M&A, project finance and restructuring. The practice, headed by Jesús López-Tello, works closely with the litigation department.

Allen & Overy created a new tax department in 2001 when Carlos Albiñana, previously with **Clifford Chance SC**, joined the firm as a partner. He now heads the tax department and specialises in M&A, corporate restructuring, and international tax planning. The department works closely with the firm's global tax practice, offering quality cross-border international tax advice.

Ashurst makes it into the table this year after gaining a former partner from the tax department at **Garrigues** in 2003. Eduardo Gracia is a specialist in Spanish, EU and international taxation of companies, and deals in cross-border company tax planning.

Legalia Abogados boasts 20 specialist tax lawyers led by highly-experienced Jordi Esparza. The team advises on a range of issues including private banking, tax planning, and tax appeals, but it mainly focuses on M&A and tax planning for companies and financial institutions including La Caixa and Caja España.

The tax department at **Pérez-Llorca** has been involved in many sizeable corporate/M&A global projects. Tax advice was provided on the Spanish aspects of the acquisitions by Cadbury-Schweppes plc of the Adams confectionery business and by Johnson Wax of the Baygon insecticide and pesticide business. Advice is also given in private equity projects and group restructurings.

LOVELLS

BILBAO 1
5º PISO
03001 ALICANTE

Telephone: +34 96 514 4105
Fax: +34 96 514 4303
E-mail: information@lovells.com
Website: www.lovells.com

Languages
English, German

Other offices
Amsterdam, Beijing, Berlin, Brussels, Budapest*, Chicago, Düsseldorf, Frankfurt, Hamburg, Ho Chi Minh City, Hong Kong, London, Milan, Moscow, Munich, New York, Paris, Prague, Rome, Shanghai, Singapore, Tokyo, Vienna*, Warsaw, Zagreb*

Number of lawyers 1,600
at this office 14

Contact
Dr Verena von Bomhard

CATEGORIES OF WORK

Intellectual property law (representation before the European Trade Mark Office – OHIM)

BAKER & McKENZIE

AVENIDA DIAGONAL, 652, EDIF D
8TH FLOOR
08034 BARCELONA

Telephone: +34 93 206 08 20
Fax: +34 93 205 49 59
E-mail: info.barcelona@bakernet.com
Website: www.bakernet.com

Languages
Catalan, English, French, German, Italian

Other offices
For a list of all offices and other information regarding the firm please consult Baker & McKenzie's London office entry

Number of lawyers 3,380
at this office 46

Contact
Rafael Jimenez-Gusi
(rafael.jimenez-gusi@bakernet.com)

Baker & McKenzie is a global law firm with 66 offices in 36 countries.

CATEGORIES OF WORK

Aviation

Banking and finance

Capital markets

Corporate/commercial/M&A

E-commerce

EU Law and competition

Environmental law

Energy and natural resources

General administrative/regulatory law

Information technologies

Insurance

Intellectual property, patents, trade marks, and unfair competition

Labour law and employment

Litigation/dispute resolution/arbitration

Media and entertainment

Real estate and zoning law

Tax

Telecommunications law

CUATRECASAS

PASEO DE GRACIA 111
08008 BARCELONA

Telephone: +34 93 290 5500
Fax: +34 93 290 5567
E-mail: info@cuatrecasas.com
Website: www.cuatrecasas.com

Languages
Dutch, English, French, German, Italian, Japanese, Portuguese

Other offices
Alicante, Bilbao, Brussels, Girona, Lisbon, Lleida, Madrid, New York, Oporto, Palma de Mallorca, San Sebastian, Sao Paulo, Tarragona, Valencia, Zaragoza

Number of lawyers 632
at this office 219

In association with
Machado, Meyer, Sendacz e Opice (Brazil); Perez Alati, Grondona, Benites, Artnsen & Martinez de Hoz (Argentina); merged with Gonçalves Pereira, Castelo Branco (Portugal)

CATEGORIES OF WORK

Banking and insurance
Adolfo Rovira

Finance
Enric Picanyol

Corporate and commercial
Raimon Segura

Employment
Jordi Puigbó, Salvador del Rey

Energy and environment
Alberto Raventós, Yolanda Guerra

EU and competition
Cani Fernández, Irene Moreno

Insolvency
Javier Castrodeza

Administrative law
Alberto Raventós

Mergers and acquisitions
José Luis Blanco

Capital markets
Emilio Coco

Arbitration and litigation
Jorge Badía

International tax
Alex Escoda

Intellectual property
Jorge Llevat

New technologies
Salvador del Rey

Real estate and construction
Gerard Hernández

Telecoms
Alberto Raventós, Juan C Hernanz

FRESHFIELDS BRUCKHAUS DERINGER

MESTRE NICOLAU 19
08021 BARCELONA

Telephone: +34 93 363 7400
Fax: +34 93 419 7799
E-mail: email@freshfields.com
Website: www.freshfields.com

Languages
Extensive language capabilities

Other offices
Amsterdam, Bangkok, Beijing, Berlin, Bratislava, Brussels, Budapest, Cologne, Düsseldorf, Frankfurt, Hamburg, Hanoi, Ho Chi Minh City, Hong Kong, London, Madrid, Milan, Moscow, Munich, New York, Paris, Rome, Shanghai, Singapore, Tokyo, Vienna, Washington

Number of lawyers 2,504
at this office 11

Contact
John Byrne

CATEGORIES OF WORK

Corporate

Antitrust, competition and trade

Finance

Tax

Intellectual property and IT

Employment, pensions and benefits

Real estate

Dispute resolution (including environment, planning and regulatory)

GRAU, BAYLOS & ANGULO

AVDA PAU CASALS 4, 6-2
08021 BARCELONA

Telephone: +34 93 202 34 56
Fax: +34 93 240 53 83
E-mail:
info@grau-baylos-angulo.com
Website: www.grau-baylos-angulo.com

Languages
Catalan, English, French, Italian, Spanish

Other offices
Madrid

Number of lawyers 12
at this office 7

CATEGORIES OF WORK

Intellectual property (including patent, trade mark, designs and copyright litigation; licensing and unfair competition)

JAUSÀS

AV DIAGONAL 407 BIS
10TH FLOOR
08008 BARCELONA

Telephone: +34 93 415 00 88
Fax: +34 93 415 20 51
E-mail: law@jnv.com
Website: www.jnv.com

Languages
Catalan, Dutch, English, French, German, Italian, Spanish

Other offices
Madrid

Number of lawyers 60
at this office 40

Member
Conférence Bleue; GESICA; Meritas; World IT Lawyers

CATEGORIES OF WORK

Agency and distributorships
Héctor Jausàs, Laura Gorri

Commercial property, real estate
Joan Vidal de Llobatera

Construction
Mercedes Caral, Dolores Alemany

Corporate and commercial
Gabriel Nadal, Maria Luisa de Alarcón

Company law
Nuria Clemente

Litigation and arbitration
Mercedes Caral, Joan Vidal de Llobatera

EU and competition law
Héctor Jausàs

E-commerce
Gabriel Nadal, José Manuel Pérez

Enviromental law
Rafael Muñoz de la Espada

Foreign direct investment, tax law
Maria Luisa de Alarcón

Healthcare, pharmaceutical law
Héctor Jausàs, Margot Subirats

IT and data protection, e-commerce
José Manuel Pérez, Margot Subirats

Infrastructure and project finance
Maria Luisa de Alarcón, Piet Holtrop

Insolvency, corporate restructuring
Gabriel Nadal, Agustí Bou

Intellectual property
Rafael Vignoly

Labour law
August Torá, Rafael Muñoz de la Espada

Mergers and acquisitions
Gabriel Nadal, Agustí Bou

Private client
Mercedes Caral, Yolanda Lobao

LUPICINIO EVERSHEDS

PASEO DE GRACIA 85
08008 BARCELONA

Telephone: +34 93 488 28 02
Fax: +34 93 488 27 33
E-mail: mail.ba@lupicinioeversheds.com
Website: www.lupicinioeversheds.com

Languages
English, French, German

Number of lawyers 37

Contact
Ángel Valdés

CATEGORIES OF WORK

Finance	Energy
Commercial and corporate	Litigation
Intellectual and industrial property	Public law
Labour law	Competition law
Telecommunications	Data protection
Tax	

MULLERAT

AVENIDA DIAGONAL 640
4TH FLOOR
08017 BARCELONA

Telephone: +34 93 405 93 00
Fax: +34 93 405 91 76
E-mail: mullerat.barcelona@mullerat.com
Website: www.mullerat.com

Languages
English, French, German, Italian, Portuguese

Other offices
Madrid, Palma de Mallorca, San Sebastián, Lisbon

Number of lawyers 75
at this office 40

Contact
Ramon Mullerat OBE

CATEGORIES OF WORK

Banking, finance, securities
Miguel Torres, Jorge Adell

Mergers and acquisitions
Jorge Adell, Fernando de la Mata

Litigation
Carles Prat, Isabel Mateu

Patents and intellectual property
Carles Prat, Cristina Duch

Tax
Pere M Pons

International commercial arbitration
Ramon Mullerat

EU, competition and consumer law
Carles Prat, Sonia Cortés

Criminal law, white-collar crime
Luis Batlló

Distribution and franchising
Sonia Cortés

Environment
Bernat Mullerat

Company law
Ramon Mullerat, Felipe Pineda

Real estate and zoning law
Jorge Adell, Joaquim Sallarès

Trade mark law
Carles Prat, Cristina Duch

Information technology
Sergio Giménez

Labour law
Sonia Cortés, Alfonso Pedrajas

Civil and human rights
Ramon Mullerat

PINTÓ RUIZ & DEL VALLE

BEETHOVEN 13-7º
08021 BARCELONA

Telephone: +34 93 241 30 20
Fax: +34 93 414 38 85
E-mail: bcn@pintoruizdelvalle.com
Website: www.pintoruizdelvalle.com

Languages
English, French, German, Italian

Other offices
Alicante, Granollers, Madrid

Number of lawyers 65
at this office 48

Contact
José Juan Pintó Sala

Member
Pannone Law Group EEIG; International Sport Law Association; Associazione Internazinale Giuristi di Lingua Italiana; International Wine Law Association; Spanish Group of the International Association for the Protection of Industrial Property; French Association of Practitioners of Trade Mark Law; Pharmaceutical Trade Mark Group; European Community Trademark Association International Trademark Association; National Association for the Defence of Trademarks

CATEGORIES OF WORK

Arbitration
José Juan Pintó Ruiz, David Muñoz

Banking/finance
Joaquín Malvesí,
Julieta López-Chicheri

Commercial/litigation
Sigrid Martens, Cristina Paloma

Intellectual property
Salvador Ferrandis, Antonio Selas

Labour
Manuel Cantueso,
Miguel Angel Gallardo

Tax
Francisco Bellavista,
Ramón María Parcerisa

Competition
María José Rodríguez, Antonio Selas

Sport law
José Juan Pintó Sala,
María del Mar Martín

Construction/real estate
Jorge Sánchez, David Peña

Franchising know-how
Fernando Rodríguez, Joan Vidal

Corporate
Rafael Abadía, Enrique Martínez

Internet
Camil Raich, Abel López

Mergers/acquisitions
Jorge López, José María Farré

Investments and finance
Javier del Valle Petersfeld, Javier Obispo

Criminal law
Alberto Bosch, Oscar Farré

IP/litigation
Victoria Ruiz de Velasco, Eva M Ochoa

Bankruptcy
Juan Carlos Noguera,
Lourdes Company

ROCA JUNYENT ABOGADOS

ARIBAU 198
08036 BARCELONA

Telephone: +34 93 241 92 00
Fax: + 34 93 414 50 30
E-mail: bcn@rocajunyent.com
Website: www.rocajunyent.com

Languages
English, French, German, Italian, Russian, Catalan, Euskera

Other offices
Buenos Aires, Girona, Lleida, Madrid, Moscow, Palma de Mallorca

Number of lawyers 140

Contact
Miquel Roca Junyent

CATEGORIES OF WORK

Administrative

Advertising and sponsorship

Arbitration

Audiovisual rights

Banking

City planning

Civil

Commercial contracts

Competition

Consumer rights

Corporate product

Court proceedings

E-commerce and electronic signatures

Energy

Environmental

Foundations and sponsorship

General advice to trading companies

Insolvency

Intellectual and industrial property

Investment

Labour and social security

Property and construction

Tax

Telecommunications

The stock market

VENTURA GARCÉS & LÓPEZ-IBOR
ABOGADOS

FREIXA 26-28
08021 BARCELONA

Telephone: +34 93 241 97 40
Fax: +34 93 209 83 91
E-mail:
ventura.garces@ventura-garces.com
Website: www.ventura-garces.com

Languages
English, French, German, Italian, Spanish

Other offices
Madrid

Number of lawyers 24
at this office 15

Contacts
Claudi Garcés, Ricard Gené

CATEGORIES OF WORK

Companies

Competition

Mergers and acquisitions

Arbitration, litigation

Tax

Intellectual property

Construction

Insolvency

Franchising

Telecommunications

Employment

Aviation

Banking

ABOGADOS AMYA

PRINCESA 61 5º
28008 MADRID

Telephone: +34 91 548 83 28
Fax: +34 91 559 45 85
E-mail: amya@amya.es
Website: www.amya.es

Languages
English, French, German, Greek, Italian, Portuguese

Other offices
Barcelona, Buenos Aires*, Las Palmas*, Lisbon, Marbella*, Miami, Panama, Paris*, Piraeus*, Rome*, Valencia, Vigo

Number of lawyers 27
at this office 7

Contact
José M Alcántara

Member
Spanish MLA; CMI; ICC; IBA; IMMTA; IIDM

CATEGORIES OF WORK

Shipping and Admiralty
José M Alcántara, Bárbara Berreteaga

Finance
Esther Zarza, José M Alcántara

Aviation law and road transportation
Esther Zarza

EC law
Macarena Alcántara, Bárbara Berreteaga

Commercial law
José M Alcántara, Javier Arias-Camisón

Environment law
José M Alcántara

Arbitration and litigation
José M Alcántara, Bárbara Berreteaga

Corporate law
Macarena Alcántara

Foreign investment
Esther Zarza, Javier Arias-Camisón

Competition and administrative law
Macarena Alcántara

Insurance
Javier Linaza, Javier Arias-Camisón

ABRIL ABOGADOS

CALLE COVARRUBIAS 9 2° D
MADRID 28010

Telephone: +34 91 702 0331
Fax: +34 91 308 3705
E-mail: abril@abrilabogados.com
Website: www.abrilabogados.com

Languages
English, French, German, Spanish

Other offices
Barcelona, Bilbao, Murcia, Valencia, Vigo

Number of lawyers 18
at this office 10

Member
INTA; ASIPI; AIPPI; LES; IBA

CATEGORIES OF WORK

Trade mark law
Pedro Manuel Del Castillo

Patent and biotechnology
Carlos Gonzalez

Unfair competition
Ignacio Temiño

Data protection
Alvaro Ramos

International IP law
Emma Barraclough

Distribution and franchising
Ignacio Temiño

Copyright and e-commerce
Clara Bordoy

Cross-border litigation
Amparo Del Rio

Software and Internet
Clara Bordoy, Alvaro Ramos

Licensing
Salvador Diaz, Ignacio Temiño

ADARVE CORPORACIÓN JURÍDICA

C/ FRANCISCO DE ROJAS 2
28010 MADRID

Telephone: +34 91 591 30 60
Fax: +34 91 591 30 61
E-mail: info@adarve.com
Website: www.adarve.com

Languages
Catalan, English, French, German, Italian

Other offices
Barcelona, Las Palmas de Gran Canaria, Palma de Mallorca, Santiago de Compostela, Seville, Valencia

Number of lawyers 81
at this office 60

Member
TELFA (Trans European Law Firm Alliance)

CATEGORIES OF WORK

Litigation
Juan Jose Garcia Garcia

Business and corporate law
Daniel Villar Valero

IT and IP
Daniel Villar Valero

Labour law
Cesar Castro

Tax law
Fernando Virseda

Real estate and construction
Ines Masedo

Family and inheritance
Luis Gutierrez

Banking and finance
Juan Jose Garcia Garcia

Environmental law
Mercedes Requena

Insurance law
Daniel Villar Valero

DESPACHO ALBIÑANA & SUÁREZ DE LEZO

C/ JOSÉ ABASCAL 58
28003 MADRID

Telephone: +34 91 451 93 00
Fax: +34 91 442 60 45
E-mail: dasl@dasl.es
Website: www.dasl.es

Languages
Arabic, English, French, German, Portuguese

Other offices
Seville, Marbella

Number of lawyers 80
at this office 70

CATEGORIES OF WORK

Corporate law
Cesar Albiñana, Rafael Suárez de Lezo

Mergers and acquisitions
Rafael Suárez de Lezo, Antonio Pino

Securities market
Carlos Peña, Luis Miguel de Díos

Banking and finance
Gracia Sainz, José Antonio Rodriguez

EU, antitrust and competition
Diego Crespo, Jesús Alfaro

Litigation and arbitration
Carlos Aguilar, Juan J Gonzalez

Insolvency, bankruptcy
Juan Ignacio Fernández-Aguado

Taxation
Santiago Diez, Ana Jiménez

Labour law
Diana Rodriguez

Administrative law
Javier Torrre de Silva, José Gimenez

Telecommunications
Cesar Albiñana, José Gimenez

Distribution, agency, franchise
Mariano Bautista, José R Meléndez

Criminal law
Carlos Aguilar, Nuria Serrano

Real estate
José Miguel Martin-Zamorano

Intellectual property
Vicente Arias

Media and information technology
Vicente Arias

ALBORS GALIANO & CO

VELÁZQUEZ 53
28001 MADRID

Telephone: +34 91 435 66 17
Fax: +34 91 576 74 23
E-mail: madrid@alborsgaliano.com
Website: www.alborsgaliano.com

Languages
Catalan, English, French, German

Other offices
Bilbao

Number of lawyers 22
at this office 19

Contacts
Eduardo Albors, Javier Galiano, Javier Portales

Member
SEAIDA (International Association for Insurance Law); Spanish Maritime Law Association; International Bar Association; International Maritime Committee

CATEGORIES OF WORK

Shipping

Admiralty

Transportation

Insurance and reinsurance

Aviation

International trade

Litigation and arbitration

Personal injury

Professional liability

Company and commercial

ALLEN & OVERY

PEDRO DE VALDIVIA 10
28006 MADRID

Telephone: +34 91 782 9800
Fax: +34 91 782 9899
E-mail: information@allenovery.com
Website: www.allenovery.com

Languages
English, French, German, Portuguese, Dutch

Other offices
Amsterdam, Antwerp, Bangkok, Beijing, Bratislava, Brussels, Budapest, Dubai, Frankfurt, Hamburg, Hong Kong, London, Luxembourg, Milan, Moscow, New York, Paris, Prague, Rome, Shanghai, Singapore, Tokyo, Turin, Warsaw

Number of lawyers 2,305
at this office 35

Contacts
Graham Donnell, Iñigo Gómez-Jordana

CATEGORIES OF WORK

Mergers and acquisitions
Fernando Torrente,
Graham Donnell,

General corporate
Fernando Torrente

Private equity
Iñigo Gómez-Jordana,
Fernando Torrente

International capital markets
Iñigo Gómez-Jordana,
Fernando Torrente

Banking and asset finance
Iñigo Gómez-Jordana,
Eduardo Sebastián de Erice

Project finance, infrastructure and energy
Graham Donnell,
Eduardo Sebastián de Erice

Tax
Carlos Albiñana

ALZA ABOGADOS

CALLE CONDE DE PEÑAVEL 86
28006 MADRID

Telephone: +34 91 402 74 74
Fax: +34 91 402 24 25
E-mail: alza@alza-sa.com
Website: www.alza-sa.com

Languages
English, French, German

Number of lawyers 30

Contacts
Juan Alonso Zamorano (president),
Luis Ortego Castaneda
(partner, and general manager),
Alfonso Suengas Goenechea
(executive manager)

CATEGORIES OF WORK

Corporate and commercial law

Mergers and acquisitions

Patent trade marks and copyright

Unfair competition

Distribution, agency, franchise

Minority shareholders

Bankruptcy, insolvency/ corporate restructuring

Dispute resolution, litigation and arbitration

Civil law

Family, probate, wills and succession

Consumer goods

Litigation

Criminal law

Banking and finance

Tax

Labour and social security law

Public law

Licensing

Real estate and construction

Intellectual property

New technologies

ALZAGA, CARO, G PALENCIA, SÁNCHEZ-TERÁN Y ASOCIADOS

MARQUES DE CUBAS 6
28014 MADRID

Telephone: +34 91 360 51 83
Fax: +34 91 521 54 26
E-mail: madrid@iberforo.net
Website: www.iberforo.net

Languages
English, French, German, Italian

Number of lawyers 32

Member
LG International

CATEGORIES OF WORK

Administrative law
Miguel Angel Sánchez-Terán

Arbitration and litigation
Oscar Alzaga, Miguel López

Civil law
Oscar Alzaga, Miguel López

Commercial and corporate
Carlos González-Bueno

EU and competition
Rafael García-Palencia

Distribution, agency and franchise
Rafael García-Palencia

Energy
Rafael García-Palencia

Insurance
Miguel López

Intellectual property
Carlos González-Bueno

IT, e-commerce and data protection
Carlos González-Bueno

Labour law
Carlos González-Bueno

Mergers and acquisitions
Rafael García-Palencia

Real estate
Miguel Angel Sánchez-Terán

Tax law
Aníbal Caro

Telecommunications
Rafael García-Palencia

ASHURST

ALCALÁ 44
28014 MADRID

Telephone: +34 91 364 9800
Fax: +34 91 364 9801
Website: www.ashurst.com

Languages
English, French, German, Italian, Portuguese

Other offices
Frankfurt, London, Milan, Munich, New Delhi*, New York, Paris, Singapore, Tokyo

Number of lawyers 813
at this office22

Contacts
Steven Fox, Jesús Almoguera

CATEGORIES OF WORK

Mergers and acquisitions

Private equity

Insolvency

TMT

Tax

Joint ventures

Corporate finance

Litigation

Real estate

BAKER & McKENZIE

PASEO DE LA CASTELLANA, 33
EDIFICIO FENIX, 6TH FLOOR
28046 MADRID

Telephone: +34 91 230 45 00
Fax: +34 91 391 51 45
E-mail: madrid.reception@bakernet.com
Website: www.bakernet.com

Languages
English, French, German, Italian

Other offices
For a list of all offices and other information regarding the firm please consult Baker & McKenzie's London office entry

Number of lawyers 3,380
at this office 101

Contacts
Maite Diez, Felipe Alonso

Baker & McKenzie is a global law firm with 66 offices in 36 countries.

CATEGORIES OF WORK

Aviation

Banking and finance

Capital markets

Corporate/commercial/M&A

E-commerce

EU law and competition

Environmental law

Energy and natural resources

General administrative/ regulatory law

Information technologies

Insurance

Intellectual property, patents, trade marks, and unfair competition

Labour law and employment

Litigation/dispute resolution/ arbitration

Media and entertainment

Real estate and zoning law

Tax

Telecommunications law

BATALLA ABOGADOS

GOYA 67, 6TH FLOOR
28001 MADRID

Telephone: +34 91 781 1626
Fax: +34 91 575 1494
E-mail:
enrique.batalla@lawoffice-batalla.com

Languages
English

Number of lawyers 10

Member
CLA; INTA; IT LAW; WIPO; LES; IBA; ECTA; IPBA; AIPPI; CILS

CATEGORIES OF WORK

IP and e-commerce law
Emilio Alonso Langle

Patent, trade mark and copyright litigation
Emilio Alonso Langle

Anticounterfeiting activities
Enrique J Batalla

Information technology
Enrique J Batalla

Unfair competition
Emilio Alonso Langle

Software and telecoms law
Enrique J Batalla

Transfer of technology contracts
Enrique J Batalla

General commercial practice and litigation
Berta Ramos

Licensing
Emilio Alonso Langle

Technology due diligence
Enrique J Batalla

Intellectual property arbitration
Francisco Gonzalez

Real estate law
Berta Ramos

Labour law
Iziar Mingo

International trade
Berta Ramos

Chapter XI
Francisco Gonzalez

Administrative law
Ana M Gomez-Tejedor

Acquisition
Maria Jesus Sanmartin

CASTRO, SUEIRO & VARELA
ABOGADOS

ALCALÁ 75, 1º
28009 MADRID

Telephone: +34 91 577 50 20
Fax: +34 91 431 59 31
E-mail: csv@csvabogados.com

Languages
English, French, Italian

Number of lawyers 15

Contacts
Juan Carlos Castro, Miguel Sueiro, José Ramón Varela

Member
Insurolaw; Globalaw

CATEGORIES OF WORK

- Commercial and corporate
- Banking, securities and capital markets
- Project finance
- Insurance
- Mergers and acquisitions
- Aviation and shipping
- Litigation and arbitration
- Real estate
- Taxation
- Administrative
- Internet
- Employment
- Competition law
- Information technology

COLL-NAVARRO-SANZ-VILLAR
ABOGADOS

ALFONSO XII 32-6º
28014 MADRID

Telephone: +34 91 420 21 08
Fax: +34 91 420 22 35
E-mail: cnsv@cnsvabogados.es

Languages
English, French

Number of lawyers 9

Contact
David Navarro de Palencia

Member
InterAct Europe EEIG (Amsterdam, Antwerp, Hamburg, Copenhagen, Lisbon, London, Madrid, Munich, Oslo, Paris, Reading, Stockholm)

CATEGORIES OF WORK

- Commercial law
- Corporate law
- Mergers and acquisitions
- Litigation
- Insurance law
- Real estate and construction law
- Labour law, social security
- Insolvency
- Tax
- Competition law

CREMADES & CALVO-SOTELO

SERRANO 27
28001 MADRID

Telephone: +34 91 426 40 50
Fax: +34 91 426 40 52
E-mail: info@cremadescalvosotelo.com
Website: www.cremadescalvosotelo.com

Languages
English, French, German, Italian, Portuguese

Number of lawyers 50

Member
International Telecommunications Advisory Group; Advoc

CATEGORIES OF WORK

Company and commercial law
Santiago Calvo-Sotelo

Copyright and intellectual property
Javier Cremades

Taxation law
Silvia Gerbolés

Labour law
Isabel Conde

Foreign investments law
Silvia del Rosario

Banking and finance law
Santiago Calvo-Sotelo

Litigation and arbitration
Rafel de Mendizábal

Competition and antitrust law
Alejandro Dominguez

Licensing
Javier Cremades

Public and administrative law
Jaime Rodriguez Arana

Patents and trade marks
Javier Cremades

Telecommunications, media and entertainment
Javier Cremades

E-commerce and Internet law
Javier Cremades

Mergers and acquisitions
Santiago Calvo-Sotelo

CUATRECASAS

VELÁZQUEZ 63
28001 MADRID

Telephone: +34 91 524 7100
Fax: +34 91 524 7124
E-mail: info@cuatrecasas.com
Website: www.cuatrecasas.com

Languages
Dutch, English, French, German, Italian, Japanese, Portuguese

Other offices
Alicante, Barcelona, Bilbao, Brussels, Girona, Lisbon, Lleida, New York, Oporto, Palma de Mallorca, San Sebastian, Sao Paulo, Tarragona, Valencia, Zaragoza

Number of lawyers 632
at this office 206

In association with
Machado, Meyer, Sendacz e Opice (Brazil); Perez Alati, Grondona, Benites, Artnsen & Martinez de Hoz (Argentina); merged with Gonçalves Pereira, Castelo Branco (Portugal)

CATEGORIES OF WORK

Banking and insurance
Eduardo Ramírez

Finance
Rafael Mínguez

Corporate and commercial
Julián García Rubí

Employment
Pilar Cavero

Energy and environment
Nicolás González-Deleito, Yolanda Guerra

EU and competition
Cani Fernández, Natalia Lacalle

Insolvency
Alejo López-Mellado

Administrative law
Nicolás G Deleito, Javier Barnés

Mergers and acquisitions
José Mª Balañá

Capital markets
Pere Kirchner

Arbitration and litigation
Antonio Hierro

International tax
Andrés Sánchez

Intellectual property
Enrique Sánchez-Quiñones

New technologies
Javier Aparicio

Real estate and construction
Ricardo Echevarría

Telecoms
Miguel Bravo-Ferrer, Nicolás G Deleito

DLA

PASEO DE LA CASTELLANA 35
28046 MADRID

Telephone: +34 91 319 1212
Fax: +34 91 319 1940
E-mail: kenneth.bonavia@dla.com
Website: www.dla.com

Languages
Catalan, English, French, German, Italian, Spanish

Other offices
Amsterdam, Bangkok, Bratislava, Brussels, Budapest, Copenhagen, Hong Kong, London, Milan, Oslo, Paris, Prague, Rotterdam, Salzberg, Sarajevo, Shanghai, Singapore, Stockholm, Vienna, Zagreb

Number of lawyers 30

Contact
Kenneth Bonavia (regional managing partner)

Member
DLA Group

CATEGORIES OF WORK

Banking and financial services
Juan E Díaz Hidalgo

Commercial and projects
Kenneth Bonavia, Juan E Diaz Hidalgo

EU and competition law
Gerard Pérez Olmo

Corporate finance and commercial
Kenneth Bonavia, José María Dutilh

Employment/human resources
Luis Peinado, Natalia Villabrille

Insurance and reinsurance
Carlos Pérez, Ángel Vallejo Chamorro

Litigation and arbitration
Ana Martínez Obradors

Real estate
Fernando Rodríguez Marín, Javier Ibáñez Gabernet

Shipping, aviation and transport
Carlos Pérez, Alfredo Cabellos

Tax
Antonio Cuéllar Prats

Technology, media, communications and data protection
Jason Flint

THE FIRM

Currently 30 lawyers strong, DLA's office in Madrid offers a full-service, locally led law firm with international capability across Europe and Asia. Lawyers specialise in all aspects of business law and regularly advise on cross-border transactions.

DLA is the founding member of DLA Group. DLA Group is an exclusive alliance of international full-service law firms with a shared vision. Established in 1999, DLA Group now has over 2,200 lawyers across 21 countries, who deliver expert local know-how and international solutions. DLA Group provides legal advice in 36 major cities across Europe, Singapore, Thailand, Hong Kong and the People's Republic of China.

AREAS OF PRACTICE

Banking and finance: the banking and financial services practice advises on a full range of international and Spanish finance investment activities. The office offers full financial support to a range of clients, from lenders developing financing techniques to borrowers identifying the most beneficial financing arrangements.

Commercial and projects: lawyers help Spanish and international clients in both the private and public sectors, with a range of infrastructure financing, structured joint ventures and contractual arrangements designed to minimise risk.

Litigation: where litigation arises, DLA Madrid provides high-level legal representation and dispute resolution services.

EU and competition: the competition and European Community practice applies antitrust regulatory know-how in order to minimise the risk of sanctions enforced upon companies by both national and European Community authorities.

Corporate finance and commercial: DLA Madrid's corporate finance and commercial team advise on all corporate matters including mergers and acquisitions, joint ventures, shareholders' agreements, restructurings, mergers and hive-downs, shareholders' disputes, director's liability, share issues, transfers and asset deals.

Employment: employment law experts advise on such highly specific areas as due diligence, collective and individual dismissals, employee benefits, compensation and senior executive contracts, pensions and social security.

Insurance: insurance and reinsurance clients are provided with a comprehensive service in every aspect of the industry, both regulatory and private.

Real estate: the team provides cross-border advice to national and international investors, developers, retailers and funders wishing to implement strategies in the Spanish market.

Shipping, aviation and transport: DLA Madrid's shipping, aviation and transport practice is unique in Spain, offering a fully comprehensive service of Admiralty, aviation, transport, litigation and finance advice to domestic and international clients.

Tax: the practice is focused on advising on local and international tax planning and on incentives and the available alternatives offered by the applicable tax legislation.

Technology, media, communications and data protection: broad experience of the legal and technical issues, combined with understanding of the Spanish market enables DLA Madrid's lawyers to advise national and international clients on constantly evolving technology, media and communications issues.

DAVID MÜLCHI & ASOCIADOS

C/VELÁZQUEZ 18, 1° DCHA
28001 MADRID

Telephone: +34 91 781 01 97
Fax: +34 91 577 84 62
E-mail: dmulchi.asociados@dmulchi.com
Website: www.dmulchi.com

Languages
English, French, German, Italian, Russian, Spanish

Other offices
Lugano

Number of lawyers 10

Member
Spanish Export Companies Club; AEDAF (Spanish Tax Advisors Association); IFA (International Fiscal Association); Italian Chamber of Commerce; REAF (Association of Economists and Tax Advisors Registrar)

CATEGORIES OF WORK

International taxation
David Mülchi, Adolfo Martin

International business law
David Mülchi, Natalie Halla

International corporate and commercial law
Jorge V Miera

Expatriates
Fernando Moreno de Barreda, David Mülchi

International arbitration
David Mülchi

Sportsmen and artists
David Mülchi, Jorge V Miera

THE FIRM

David Mülchi & Asociados was founded as a result of the experience accumulated by its founding partner in Switzerland. The firm stays in close contact with its clients, as well as with the Spanish administration, and has has an extensive worldwide network of top-quality and efficient correspondents.

The services provided by David Mülchi & Asociados are principally directed towards professionals in the legal and tax sectors, entrepreneurs, small and medium-sized companies and family-run businesses, either resident in Spain or overseas. As a result of the internationalisation of companies currently being experienced in Spain, quality and specialised advice is essential. In its overseas expansion process, Spain has not only become an investment exporter, but has also been able to understand and strengthen international investment.

The main distinguishing features of the firm are: specialisation instead of multi-disciplinary and multi-sectorial services; personalised advice; extensive network of external correspondents and advisers; perfect balance between planning and development.

AREAS OF PRACTICE

David Mülchi & Asociados offers international legal tax advisory services on a constant basis to private individuals as well as companies and professional law firms. The firm performs comprehensive audits designed to eliminate or reduce tax risk. The firm offers solutions to problems arising in relation to Spanish investments overseas, and foreign investments in Spain, especially: legal and tax issues involving European and non-European states; relations between companies belonging to groups subject to different jurisdictions; dividend, interest and royalty transfers; international double taxation issues, foreign trade in general; changes in personal residency; succession and donations involving foreign capital; arbitration; e-commerce.

David Mülchi & Asociados is able to undertake mandates for the appointing and co-ordination of foreign professionals. Due to the incorporation of new partners, the firm boasts an experienced and qualified team capable of successfully fulfilling the needs of professionals and their clients.

Both standard and special holding company systems in Spain are among the most attractive in Europe, even when compared to Luxembourg and the Netherlands. Since 1996 the firm has gained substantial practical experience in implementing holding companies. Under certain conditions, profits obtained from permanent establishments overseas or those distributed by foreign subsidiaries are exempt in Spain.

Spain has been authorised by the EU to adopt advantageous tax systems that may be used to optimise several business activities, from the provision of services to the creation of consortiums for public works or overseas supply contracts, international trade, and investment fund management. The firm provides advisory and support services for all types of investment and trade in Spain to both non-resident private individuals and companies.

David Mülchi & Asociados has the capability of providing services to entrepreneurs, executives, artists and sports people wishing to set up residency or offices in Spain. Particular emphasis is given to the analysis of legal and tax issues, enabling better planning to becoming established in Spain.

The firm is able to undertake mandates for the selection and co-ordination of Spanish or foreign professionals required for analysis, planning and implementing investments in or through Spain at highly competitive rates. David Mülchi boasts a highly qualified team of experts capable of successfully providing solutions to professionals and their clients in order for them to carry out investment projects and business activities in Spain or elsewhere.

DAVIES ARNOLD COOPER

ABOGADOS

PASEO DE LA CASTELLANA 20
2A PLANTA
28046 MADRID

Telephone: +34 91 781 6300
Fax: +34 91 576 8669
E-mail: dacmadrid@dacspain.com
Website: www.dacspain.com

Languages
Catalan, English, French, German

Other offices
London, Manchester, Mexico City

Number of lawyers 148
at this office 31

Contacts
Pablo Weslowski, Paulino Fajardo, Ignacio Figuerol, Javier de Dios, Mercedes Pallarés, Ricardo Garrido

CATEGORIES OF WORK

Insurance	Contingency risks
Reinsurance	Property insurance
D&O	Digital risks
Professional indemnity	Energy
Environmental liability	Arbitration and litigation
Fidelity bonds	Corporate
Product liability	Property and construction
Medical malpractice	Insurance regulatory

THE FIRM

Davies Arnold Cooper started operating back in 1989, headed by Pablo Weslowski, current managing partner of the Madrid office. Initially, DAC was in close association with the prestigious local law firm Ruiz Gallardón & Muñiz, whose lawyers more recently fully integrated with Davies Arnold Cooper.

In line with the main areas of practice of Davies Arnold Cooper, the Madrid operation has always focused on the insurance sector and other liability carriers' needs. Benefiting from the reputation and support of Davies Arnold Cooper in the international insurance markets, Davies Arnold Cooper Abogados is involved in the development of the insurance industry in Spain, mainly by providing legal services to local and international insurance and reinsurance companies, brokers, Lloyd's syndicates and other liability carriers. Where appropriate, DAC Madrid works closely with DAC London in order to provide a unique seamless service in international insurance and reinsurance matters.

The expertise acquired by being involved in major underwriting projects and developing products within the Spanish market has allowed DAC Madrid to be considered unanimously by Spanish business press as the only leading insurance law firm in Spain.

Currently, DAC Madrid comprises a team of 31 lawyers who speak fluent business English.

AREAS OF PRACTICE

DAC Madrid benefits from a notable expertise in insurance law and legal liability matters. From the incorporation of insurance companies in Spain, policy drafting and wording adaptation in accordance with Spanish legislation, to administration of Spanish claims for London and international reinsurers, handling local claims, arbitration and litigation. In this regard, DAC Madrid is involved in some of the largest claims in Spain and probably in Europe.

DAC Madrid protects insurers' interests both in the civil and criminal courts, as in Spain claimants may bring actions directly against insurers.

Professional liability: DAC Madrid has a leading reputation in directors' and officers' liability and all types of professional liability. These insurance areas developed rapidly in Spain in the early '90s and DAC Madrid having grown simultaneously with the expansion of the local marketplace. DAC Madrid therefore has an incomparable specialist knowledge and expertise in this sector of the insurance business.

Insurance/reinsurance: DAC Madrid is experienced in environmental liability, product liability, property insurance, bankers blanket bond, kidnap and ransom, reinsurance and ART. DAC Madrid's experience in these fields is wide and probably unique.

Corporate/regulatory: DAC Madrid has acted in the setting up of the Spanish branches of a number of foreign insurance companies, the firm being experienced in corporate processes (including due diligence procedures, mergers and acquisitions, liquidations, etc). DAC Madrid regularly advises on all the related employment and regulatory aspects. This department continues to grow and currently comprises seven lawyers.

Property and construction: DAC Madrid's expertise extends to all aspects of commercial property, property finance and development. Clients include domestic and international investors and construction companies.

DE LORENZO ABOGADOS

VELÁZQUEZ 124
28006 MADRID

Telephone: +34 91 561 17 12
Fax: +34 91 411 41 07
E-mail: firm@delorenzoabogados.es
Website: www.delorenzoabogados.es

Languages
English, French

Other offices
Córdoba, Valencia

Number of lawyers 14

Contacts
Ricardo De Lorenzo (senior partner),
Alfonso Cavalle (managing partner)

CATEGORIES OF WORK

Medical
Ricardo De Lorenzo, Isabel Burón

Healthcare and pharmaceutical
Ricardo De Lorenzo

Food and drug law
Carlos Fornes

Professional and product liability, litigation and dispute resolution
Isabel Burón, Miguel Roig

Family and matrimonial
Maria Diaz Aldao

Civil
Carlos Fornes, Salud Rodriguez

Labour
Ricardo De Lorenzo, Alfonso Cavallé

Administrative law
Ricardo de Lorenzo, Santiago Rincon

Tax and finance
Juan Angel Lopez-Romero

Medical writing unit and biomedical journals
Estrella Blanco

Data protection, new technologies and science, computers
Alfonso Cavallé, Laura Garcia

Insurance and reinsurance law
Miguel Roig, Ofelia De Lorenzo

THE FIRM

De Lorenzo Abogados is a medium-sized law firm founded in 1955, consisting of three offices in Spain – autonomous regions of Madrid, Valencia and Andalucía, set in Madrid, Valencia and Cordoba – with 14 lawyers and approximately 20 in the staff. The firm was set up in the field of medical law, being one of the first firms in Spain focused on this area. Since then, De Lorenzo Abogados has specialised in covering medical, dental, pharmaceutical, and nursing sectors.

The firms' serious commitment to the medical practice has enabled De Lorenzo Abogados to diversify into legal services in all areas relating to medical law. Nowadays, the firm is able to provide assistance in litigation and legal advice to a broad range of clients including, among others, small and large hospitals, health centres, national institutions, foundations, scientific societies, professional associations, insurance companies and pharmaceutical companies.

De Lorenzo Abogados' prestige is based on a thorough knowledge of the health sector, and also on the wide experience and legal training of its members.

AREAS OF PRACTICE

De Lorenzo Abogados' experience allows the firm to represent clients in a variety of complex matters to the healthcare field. The firm's services include: medical law; healthcare and pharmaceutical law; food and drug law; professional and product liability; litigation and dispute resolution; family and matrimonial law; civil law; labour law; administrative law; tax and finance; data protection; new technologies; electronic signature, medical writing unit; and biomedical journals; insurance and reinsurance law.

DELOITTE

RAIMUNDO FERNÁNDEZ VILLAVERDE 65
EDIFICIO WINDSOR PLANTAS 11, 12
28003 MADRID

Telephone: +34 91 582 09 00
Fax: +34 91 556 62 00
E-mail: contact@deloittelegal.com
Website: www.deloittelegal.com

Languages
Dutch, English, French, German, Italian, Japanese

Other offices
Barcelona, Bilbao, Las Palmas, Logroño, Malaga, Seville, Valencia, Vigo, Zaragoza

Number of lawyers 250
at this office 120

Member
Madrid and Barcelona Bar Associations

CATEGORIES OF WORK

Indirect tax
David Gómez Aragón

International assignment services
Victoria De Cas Heras

Transfer pricing
Victoria Alonso

Private clients
Javier Sánchez Moreno

M&A and due diligence
Pablo Moncada, Manuel de la Puerta

Commercial law
Manuel Verdera

Labour law
Guillermo Rujas

Public law
Carlos Pardo

Litigation
Fernando González de Zulueta

Real estate
Carlos Pardo

E-business
Ricardo Garcia Camacho

Global financial services industry
Javier Sánchez Moreno

Corporate tax
Enrique López, Rafa Sánchez

International tax
Luis Crespo, Javier Pelegay

DIAZ-BASTIEN & TRUAN

TORRE PICASSO, PLANTA 35
PLAZA PABLO RUIZ PICASSO, 1
28020 MADRID

Telephone: +34 91 577 36 60
Fax: +34 91 575 54 68
E-mail: dbtmadrid@dbtlex.com
Website: www.dbtlex.com

Languages
English, French, German, Italian

Other offices
London, Marbella

Number of lawyers 32
at this office 16

CATEGORIES OF WORK

Litigation/arbitration
Ernesto Diaz-Bastien, Frank Schoneveld

Company and commercial
Rafael Truan, Luis Juega

Real estate law
Hector Diaz-Bastien, Daniel Rueda

Hotel, leisure and travel
Hector Diaz-Bastien, Rafael Truan

Agency and distribution
Rafael Truan

EU and competition law
Frank Schoneveld

Intellectual property
Carlos Rogel

Tax
Jose Maria de la Cruz

Insolvency and corporate restructuring
Jose Maria de la Cruz, Rafael Truan

Fraud and white-collar crime
Ernesto Diaz-Bastien

Government business/regulatory
Jose Antonio Magdalena

M&A
Rafael Truan, Luis Juega

Shipping
Marco Coloma

Transport (rail)
Jose Antonio Magdalena

Private client
Conrado Truan

DIKEI ABOGADOS

JENNER 6
28010 MADRID

Telephone: +34 91 308 60 60
Fax: +34 91 308 0910
E-mail: abogados@dikei.com
Website: www.dikei.com

Languages
Spanish, English, French, Russian, Portuguese

Number of lawyers 20

CATEGORIES OF WORK

Administrative law, transport
Manuel Dapena, Pablo Galán

Civil law
Rocio Fernandez, Carmen Ramallo

Corporate and commercial
Paloma Perez de Leon, Cristina Martin

Communications and media
Gerardo Viada, Luis Ruiz-Rivas

Criminal law, extradition
Francisco Lozano, Leticia Fenoy

Employment law
Antonio Bernal, Cristina Rincón

Data protection
Cristina Martin

Business law/M&A
Miguel Angel Albaladejo, Maria Angeles Barrena

Family law, inheritance
Antonio Bernal, Rocio Fernandez

Intellectual property
Antonio Bernal, Luis Ruiz-Rivas

Litigation, arbitration
Gerardo Viada, Javier Moreno

Real estate
Paloma Pérez de Leon

Taxation
Pedro Lozano, Juan Antonio Falero

ECIJA ABOGADOS

JORGE JUAN 9
28001 MADRID

Telephone: +34 91 781 61 60
Fax: +34 91 578 38 79
E-mail: buzon@ecija.com
Website: www.ecija.com

Languages
Catalan, English, French, German, Italian, Portuguese

Number of lawyers 33

CATEGORIES OF WORK

Banking and finance
Javier González Espadas

Competition
Juan Salmeron Artero

Corporate and commercial
Alvaro Ecija

Dispute resolution
David Garcia Asenjo

Labour law
Javier Garcia de Gabiola

IT and telecommuncations
Carlos Alberto Saíz Peña

Intellectual property
Hugo Ecija

Media law and entertainment
Hugo Ecija, Pilar Sanchez Bleda Garcia

Mergers and acquisitions
Alvaro Ecija

Tax and insolvency
Josè M Nuñez Garcia

Real estate, inheritance and private client
Juan Salmeron Artero

Sports
Hugo Ecija

ERNST & YOUNG
ABOGADOS

TORRE PICASSO
PLAZA PABLO RUIZ PICASSO, 1
MADRID 28020

Telephone: +34 91 572 73 70
Fax: +34 91 572 72 38
Website: www.ey.com/es

Languages
English, French, German, Italian, Portuguese

Other offices
Barcelona, Bilbao, Las Palmas de Gran Canaria, Malaga, Palma de Mallorca, Pamplona, Santa Cruz de Tenerife, Seville, Valencia, Valladolid, Vigo, Zaragoza

Number of lawyers 450

Contact
Jaime López-Chicheri
(country managing partner)

Member
Ernst & Young Law Alliance

CATEGORIES OF WORK

Administrative law
Sabiniano Medrano

Antitrust, trade regulation and competition
Santiago Nadal

Corporate law
Miguel Angel Rodríguez-Sahagún, Nieves Briz

International law
Borja Otero

Real estate
Jaime Beltran, Juan Arencibia

Banking and finance
Sabiniano Medrano

Litigation and arbitration
Javier Díaz-Gálvez, Santiago Nadal

Insurance
Enrique López

International tax
Juan José Terraza, Victor Hernán

Labour law and employment
Miguel Angel Alcaraz

Mergers and acquisitions
Miguel Angel Rodriguez-Sahagún, Mabel Álvarez

Private clients
Javier Estella Lana, José María Durán

Tax
Enrique López

Communications and e-commerce
Ignacio Fernández García

Intellectual property
Santiago Nadal,
Ignacio Fernández García

THE FIRM

Ernst & Young Abogados was founded in Madrid more than 20 years ago by three lawyers and has grown since to its current size. Its Spanish network comprises 13 offices, 37 partners, 400 professionals, more than 150 staff, Spanish lawyers posted abroad (London, New York, Lisbon, Saõ Paolo) and lawyers within the Latin American Business Center. Ernst & Young Abogados is a full-service law firm, offering a full range of legal expertise. Its professionals are specialists in all areas of company law and private clients and are familiar with advancements in new technologies. It is a global firm providing professional services, respected for giving its clients value for money.

It is policy at Ernst & Young Abogados to be efficient and flexible towards clients' needs. The firm works on a global basis, acting locally to meet specific client demands.

AREAS OF PRACTICE

Ernst & Young Abogados' specialisations cover all sectors of the economy and of company law with a worldwide connection through Intranet. Its areas of practice include general tax, corporate tax, global financial services, litigation strategy, international taxation, human capital (global employment solutions), labour law, indirect tax, IT law, telecoms, transaction advisory services (due diligence: tax, law, labour, human resources, financial), private wealth, administrative law and proceedings, real estate, due diligence and e-commerce. The principal areas of work are listed above with details concerning the contact partners.

FERNANDO MEANA GREEN & CO

VELAZQUEZ 92-2 DCHA
28006 MADRID

Telephone: +34 91 432 38 75
Fax: +34 91 432 3876
E-mail: fmeanagreen@meanagreen.com

Languages
Spanish, English, French, German, Basque

Other office
Bilbao

Number of lawyers 11
at this office 7

Member
Commercial Arbitration Tribunal of Bilbao; Spanish Maritime Association; ENCR (Euro Arbitration)

CATEGORIES OF WORK

Maritime law (civil, criminal and administrative)

Carriage of goods by sea

Admiralty

Oil pollution

Marine Insurance

Administrative law

Transport (air, road, rail)

Aviation

Fisheries

Personal injury and labour law

EC law

International trade

ADR, litigation and arbitration

Insolvency

Commerce

Company and corporate law

FERNANDO SCORNIK GERSTEIN

ABOGADOS

CALLE ALBERTO ALCOCER Nº 7
3 IZQUIERDA
28036 MADRID

Telephone: +34 91 350 72 62
Fax: +34 91 350 73 06
E-mail: madrid@scornik-gerstein.com
Website: www.scornik-gerstein.com

Languages
English, French, German, Spanish

Other offices
Gran Canaria (2), Tenerife, London, Barcelona

Number of lawyers 41
at this office 10

Member
IAG; IBA; APIL; Association of European Lawyers; UIA; IPBA

CATEGORIES OF WORK

Litigation
Ignacio Casteleiro Cullen, Tamara Wegmann Lecue

Company and commercial
Isabel Lindemann, Saturia Ortega Félix

Immigration and nationality
Mariano Zunino, Georgina Scornik Centurión

Taxation
Fernando Scornik Gerstein, Roberto Igolnikow

Insurance
Ignacio Casteleiro Cullen, Isabel Lindemann

Foreign investment
Fernando Scornik Gerstein, Tamara Wegmann

Telecommunications
Fernando Scornik Gerstein, Georgina Scornik Centurion

Criminal law
Mariano Zunino, Ignacio Casteleiro Cullen

Personal injury
Ignacio Casteleiro Cullén, Alberto Perez Cedillo

Intellectual and industrial property
Georgina Scornik Centurion

Maritime law
Fernando Scornik Gerstein, Saturia Ortega Félix

Family law
Alberto Perez Cedillo, Matalda Soto

Inheritance law, probate
Alberto Perez Cedillo, Jose Maria Baños

Conveyancing
Mariano Zunino, Saturia Ortega Félix

Energy law
Isabel Lindemann, Silvia Ontañón

FRESHFIELDS BRUCKHAUS DERINGER

FORTUNY 6
28010 MADRID

Telephone: +34 91 319 10 24
Fax: +34 91 308 46 36
E-mail: email@freshfields.com
Website: www.freshfields.com

Languages
Extensive language capabilities

Other offices
Amsterdam, Bangkok, Barcelona, Beijing, Berlin, Bratislava, Brussels, Budapest, Cologne, Düsseldorf, Frankfurt, Hamburg, Hanoi, Ho Chi Minh City, Hong Kong, London, Milan, Moscow, Munich, New York, Paris, Rome, Shanghai, Singapore, Tokyo, Vienna, Washington

Number of lawyers 2,504
at this office 60

Contact
John Byrne

CATEGORIES OF WORK

- **Corporate**
- **Finance**
- **Antitrust, competition and trade**
- **Tax**
- **Intellectual property and IT**
- **Employment, pensions and benefits**
- **Real estate**
- **Dispute resolution (including environment, planning and regulatory)**

FRORIEP RENGGLI
SWISS LAWYERS

ANTONIO MAURA 10
28014 MADRID

Telephone: +34 91 523 77 90
Fax: +34 91 531 36 62
E-mail: madrid@froriep.es
Website: www.froriep.com

Languages
English, French, German, Spanish

Other offices
Geneva, London, Zug, Zurich

Number of lawyers 48
at this office 1

Contact
Jean-Marie Vulliemin

CATEGORIES OF WORK

- **Company and commercial**
- **Art**
- **Banking**
- **Sport**
- **Litigation, arbitration**
- **White-collar crime**
- **Wealth management/estate planning**
- **Tax**

GARRIGUES
ABOGADOS Y ASESORES TRIBUTARIOS

JOSÉ ABASCAL 45
28003 MADRID

Telephone: +34 91 514 52 00
Fax: +34 91 399 24 08
Website: www.garrigues.com

Languages
Catalonian, English, French, German, Italian, Japanese

Other offices
A Coruña, Alicante, Barcelona, Bilbao, Brussels, Burgos, Castellón, Cáceres, Granada, Las Palmas de Gran Canaria, León, Málaga, Murcia, New York, Oviedo, Palma de Mallorca, Pamplona, San Sebastián, Santa Cruz de Tenerife, Seville, Valencia, Valladolid, Vigo, Vitoria, Zaragoza

Number of lawyers 1,259

Contacts
José María Alonso, Miguel Gordillo (managing partners)

CATEGORIES OF WORK

Commercial and corporate law
Daniel García-Pita, José Ramón Martínez

Taxation
Ernesto Jiménez, Ricardo Gómez, Enrique Fonseca

Mergers and acquisitions
Ignacio Urbistondo, Ramón Bustillo

Banking, securities and insurance
Carlos Loring, Fernando Vives, Luis Guerreiro

Labour law
Federico Durán, Juan José Yago

Litigation and arbitration
José María Alonso, Miguel Moscardó

International tax
José Palacios

Administrative law
Pedro García Capdepón

Real estate law
Felipe Yannone

Energy and telecoms (utilities)
Javier Pérez-Ardá

Intellectual property
Miguel Moscardó, Carolina Pina

EU general and competition law
Marcos Araujo, Luis Ortiz

Environmental law
Antonio Baena, Santiago Garrido

New technologies
José Maria Angulano, Rafael Echegoyen

Insolvency
José María Alonso, Antonio Fernández

Sports and entertainment
Julio Senn, Javier Ferrero

GOMEZ-ACEBO & POMBO

CASTELLANA 216
28046 MADRID

Telephone: +34 91 582 91 00
Fax: +34 91 582 91 14
E-mail:
abogados@gomezacebo-pombo.com
Website: www.gomezacebo-pombo.com

Languages
Basque, Catalan, English, French, German, Italian, Japanese, Portuguese, Spanish

Other offices
Barcelona, Bilbao, Brussels, Las Palmas de Gran Canaria, Málaga, Seville, Valencia, Vigo

Number of lawyers 171

Contacts
Fernando Pombo (president), Ignacio Gómez-Acebo (honorary president), Manuel Martín (managing partner)

CATEGORIES OF WORK

M&A
Francisco Peña, Jose María Beneyto

Private equity, restructuring and insolvency
José María Álvarez

Corporate finance
Fernando de las Cuevas

Financial services
Fernando Igartua, Ángel Varela

Corporate and commercial
Francisco Peña, Manuel Martín

Shipping
Carlos Rueda

Intellectual property and technology
Gonzalo de Ulloa, Jesús Muñoz-Delgado

Labour
Ignacio Campos

Real estate, planning and environmental
Victoria Llavero, Philippe Espósito

Litigation and arbitration
Joaquín García-Romanillos, Miguel Ángel Fernández-Ballesteros

Criminal law
Javier Béjar

Communications, media and entertainment
Almudena Arpón de Mendívil, Richard A Silberstein

Administrative law, regulation, competition and EC law
Emiliano Garayar, Iñigo Igartua

Oil and gas
Luis Sancho

Tax
Pablo Alarcón

HERRERO & ASOCIADOS

C/ALCALÁ 35
28014 MADRID

Telephone: + 34 91 522 74 20
Fax: + 34 91 522 62 49
E-mail: info@herreroasociados.es
Website: www.herreroasociados.es

Languages
English, German, French, Italian

Other offices
Bilbao, Sevilla, Barcelona, Valencia

Number of lawyers 9

Contact
José Antonio Hernández

Member
INTA; AIPPI; AIPLA; ECTA; FICPI; APPA; EPI; Marques; Agesorpi; ITMA; ASIPI

CATEGORIES OF WORK

Intellectual property (prosecution and litigation)
Patricia Koch, Jose Miguel Lissen, José Antonio Hernández

Unfair competition
Patricia Koch, Juan Casulá

Information technology
Paz Martin, Jorge Sánchez

Internet
Paz Martin

E-commerce
Paz Martin

Copyright
Alvaro Cabeza, Fernando Ortega

Data protection
Paz Martin

JONES DAY

VELÁZQUEZ 51
28001 MADRID

Telephone: +34 91 520 3939
Fax: +34 91 520 3938
Website: www.jonesday.com

Languages
English, French, German, Portuguese, Spanish

Other offices
Atlanta, Beijing, Brussels, Chicago, Cleveland, Columbus, Dallas, Frankfurt, Hong Kong, Houston, Irvine, London, Los Angeles, Menlo Park, Milan, Mumbai*, Munich, New Delhi*, New York, Paris, Pittsburgh, San Francisco, Shanghai, Singapore, Sydney, Taipei, Tokyo, Washington DC

Number of lawyers 2,100
at this office 26

Contact
Juan Tena

*In association with Pathak & Associates

CATEGORIES OF WORK

Banking and structured finance
Luis Muñoz, Richard Puttré

Corporate transactions, M&A
Juan Tena, Federico Merino

Arbitration and litigation
Mercedes Fernández, Juan Gómez-Valcárcel

Real estate
Luis Muñoz, Federico Merino

Labour law
Nicolás Martín

Competition and trade; telecoms and new technologies
Juan Jiménez-Laiglesia, José María Jiménez-Laiglesia

Securities and stock exchange regulation
Luis Riesgo, Manuel Vara

Private equity
Federico Merino

Tax law
Pablo Baschwitz

KPMG
ABOGADOS

EDIFICIO TORRE EUROPA
PASEO DE LA CASTELLANA 95
28046 MADRID

Telephone: +34 91 456 34 00
Fax: +34 91 555 01 32
E-mail: kpmglegal@kpmg.es
Website: www.kpmg.es/abogados

Languages
Catalan, English, French, German, Japanese, Portuguese

Other offices
A Coruña, Alicante, Barcelona, Bilbao, Girona, Las Palmas de Gran Canaria, Malaga, Oviedo, Pamplona, Seville, Valencia, Vigo, Zaragoza

Number of lawyers 300
at this office 125

Contacts
María José Aguiló, Vicente Muñoz

CATEGORIES OF WORK

Banking and finance
Víctor Mendoza

Commercial and corporate
Ramón Pallarés

Competition
José Manuel Cajigas, Xavier Miravalls

Dispute resolution – litigation and arbitration
María Echevarría

E-commerce and new technologies
Juan Carlos Alfonso

Fraud
Vicente Muñoz

Government and regulatory
Juan Carlos Alfonso

Labour
Francisco Sierra

Mergers and acquisitions
Ramón Pallarés, Alain Casanovas

Taxation
María José Aguiló, Celso García Granda

EU law
Xavier Miravalls

International tax
Juan Rivero, Javier Sabau

LANDWELL
LANDWELL, ABOGADOS Y ASESORES FISCALES

PASEO DE LA CASTELLANA 53
28046 MADRID

Telephone: +34 91 568 4400
Fax: +34 91 568 4672
E-mail:
landwellmarketing@es.landwellglobal.com
Website: www.landwellglobal.com/es

Languages
English, French, German, Italian, Swedish, Catalan, Portuguese

Other offices
Alicante, Barcelona, Bilbao, La Coruña, Las Palmas de Gran Canaria, Logroño, Malaga, Oviedo, Palma de Mallorca, Pamplona, San Sebastian, Santa Cruz de Tenerife, Santander, Sevilla, Valencia, Vigo, Vitoria, Zaragoza

Number of lawyers 483

Contacts
Siro A Arias, Antonio Luis Bañón, José Luis Beotas

International groupings
Landwell, law firm associated with PricewaterhouseCoopers

CATEGORIES OF WORK

Competition law
Luis Comas

Corporate structuring/services
Antonio Cañadas

Dispute resolution
Paulino Borrallo

Employment and human resources
Marta Alamán

Energy
José Luis Beotas

EU law
Luis Comas

Financial services
Javier Maceira

E-business
Javier Ribas

Family company
José Luis Martin-Ballestero

Intellectual property
Luis Corno

Mergers and acquisitions/ due diligence
Javier Diaz de Bustamante

Public law
José Luis Beotas

Real estate
Javier García Camacho

Sports law
Miguel Trías

Tax
Siro A Arias, Miguel Cruz

Technology, media and communications
Enrique Sanz

LARRAURI & LOPEZ ANTE ABOGADOS

HERMOSILLA 30
28001 MADRID

Telephone: +34 91 431 1073
Fax: +34 91 577 0763
E-mail: info@larraurilopezante.com
Website: www.larraurilopezante.com

Languages
English, French, German, Italian, Portuguese, Spanish

Other offices
Bilbao

Number of lawyers 22
at this office 11

Member
ALLIURIS; INTA; LES; ECTA; AIPPI; IPBA; IBA

CATEGORIES OF WORK

Intellectual property	Corporate law and legal assistance
IP and e-commerce law	General commercial practice
Patent trade marks and copyright	Commercial litigation
Anti-counterfeiting activities	Tax law
Information technology	Real estate law
Unfair competition	Labour law and social security
Software and telecoms law	International trade
Transfer of technology contracts	Chapter XI
Licensing	Bankruptcy
Audits and diagnosis	Administrative
Technology due diligences	Acquisitions
Technology appraisals	Minority shareholders
IP arbitration	Competition law

LEBRERO & CO

VALENZUELA 8
28014 MADRID

Telephone: +34 915 313 605
Fax: +34 915 314 194
E-mail: general@lebreroandco.com
Website: www.lebreroandco.com

Languages
English, French, German, Italian, Portuguese

Other offices
Barcelona*, Bayonne*, Buenos Aires*, Malaga*, Palma de Majorca*, Las Palmas*, Vigo*

Number of lawyers 14

CATEGORIES OF WORK

Shipping and Admiralty
Rodolfo A Gonzalez-Lebrero, Monica Hervera

Aviation
Rodolfo A Gonzalez-Lebrero, Barbara del Campo

Mediation and arbitration
Rodolfo A Gonzalez-Lebrero, Maria del A De Miranda

Maritime and aviation finance
Rodolfo A Gonzalez-Lebrero, Barbara del Campo

Competition law
Maria del A De Miranda, Carmen Aznar

Administrative law
Maria Angeles Zamprogna, Manuel Urraca

Commercial and corporate law
Rodolfo A Gonzalez-Lebrero, Manuel Larrotcha

EU law
Maria del A De Miranda

Mergers and acquisitions
Barbara del Campo, Manuel Larrotcha

LEGALIA ABOGADOS

PASEO DE LA CASTELLANA 23-1º
28046 MADRID

Telephone: +34 913 912 066
Fax: +34 913 102 222
E-mail: legalia@legalia.com
Website: www.legalia.com

Languages
Catalan, English, French, German, Italian

Other offices
Barcelona, Lérida, Oviedo, Valladolid

Number of lawyers 106
at this office 41

International groupings
Law Firms of America (LFA)

CATEGORIES OF WORK

Banking and finance
Amalio Miralles

Corporate and commercial
José Luis Gros

Mergers and acquisitions
Xavier Vales

Project finance
Manuel Alvarez-Cienfuegos

Corporate tax
Jorge Carlos Esparza, Daniel Riopérez

Family business
Francisco Vinaches,
Inmaculada Navarrete

International
Rafael Monteio, Romá Bosch

Private equity
Celso Gonzalez

Civil law
Jose Manuel Delgado, Roberto Arias

Public law
Luis Castro

Employment and labour
Angel García Moreno

New technologies
Fernando Ramos

Criminal law
Rafael Muriedas

Real estate, urban planning
Pablo Artiñano

LOPEZ ACOSTA, RIVERO & GUSTAFSON ABOGADOS

CALLE SIL 21
28002 MADRID

Telephone: +34 91 561 51 01
Fax: +34 91 561 50 66
E-mail: l_acosta@lopez-acosta.com

Languages
English, French

Number of lawyers 8

Contact
Ignacio López Acosta

Member
Jurismundi Law Association

CATEGORIES OF WORK

Civil, corporate and commercial

Mergers and acquisitions

Litigation and arbitration

Real estate

Licensing, distribution and agency

Labour

Tax

Pharmaceuticals

Information technology

LINKLATERS

CALLE ZURBARÁN, 28
28010 MADRID

Telephone: +34 91 399 60 00
Fax: +34 91 399 60 01
Website: www.linklaters.com

Languages
All commercial and local languages in the countries where Linklaters operates

Other offices
Alicante, Amsterdam, Antwerp, Bangkok, Beijing, Berlin, Bratislava, Brussels, Bucharest, Budapest, Cologne, Frankfurt am Main, Hong Kong, Lisbon, London, Luxembourg, Milan, Moscow, Munich, New York, Paris, Prague, Rome, São Paulo, Shanghai, Singapore, Stockholm, Tokyo, Warsaw

Number of lawyers 2,000 (worldwide)

Contact
Miles Curley

CATEGORIES OF WORK

Banking and Finance
Alejandro Ortiz

Debt transactions
Pedro de Rojas

Equity/equity-linked transactions
Iñigo Berrícano

Capital markets
Iñigo Berrícano

Corporate and Commercial
Alvaro Sáinz

Labour
Naiara Rodríguez-Escudero

International finance
Conrado Tenaglia

Mergers and acquisitions
Alvaro Sáinz

Project/asset finance
Miguel Riaño

Real estate
Rafael Molina

Regulatory
Iñigo Berrícano

IT and communications
Javier Fernández-Samaniego

Litigation
Ignacio Díez-Picazo

Private equity
Alejandro Ortiz,
Antonio Sánchez-Pedreño

EU/competition
Silvia Pérez-Navarro

Tax
Nicolás Martín

Utilities and public sector law
Miguel Riaño

THE FIRM

Linklaters advises the world's leading companies, financial institutions and governments on their most challenging transactions and assignments. With 2,000 lawyers, including 470 partners, and offices in major business and financial centres, its clients choose the firm for its distinctive combination of technical skill, commercial experience and outstanding service.

Linklaters has built a formidable global practice through organic growth and a series of mergers, joint ventures and co-operations with other respected law firms. In 2001, Linklaters merged with three of Europe's leading law firms to form Linklaters Oppenhoff & Rädler in Germany, Linklaters in Sweden, Linklaters De Bandt in Belgium and Linklaters Loesch in Luxembourg. In the same year, the firm formed a co-operation with Brazilian firm Goulart Penteado, Iervolino e Lefosse. This co-operation combines Linklaters' international capability with GPIL's extensive knowledge of the Brazilian market. In Singapore, the firm practises as Linklaters Allen & Gledhill, a joint venture with the premier Singapore practice of Allen & Gledhill, while in Italy, Linklaters has an exclusive relationship with Italian law firm Gianni, Origoni, Grippo & Partners.

LUPICINIO EVERSHEDS
MEMBER OF EVERSHEDS INTERNATIONAL

VILLANUEVA 29
28001 MADRID

Telephone: +34 91 436 00 90
Fax: +34 91 435 30 49
E-mail: arf@lupicinioeversheds.com
Website: www.lupicinioeversheds.com

Languages
English, French, German

Number of lawyers 37

Contact
Lupicinio Rodríguez

CATEGORIES OF WORK

Finance
Hermenegildo Altozano

Tax
León Barriola

Commercial and corporate
Luis Manuel Garcia, León Barriola

Energy
Hermenegildo Altozano

Intellectual and industrial property
Kiko Carrión, José Ignacio Martinez

Litigation
Kiko Carrión

Labour law
José Maria Aguilera

Public law
Coral Yañez

Telecommunications
Luis Manuel Garcia, Ignasi Guardans

Competition law
Lupicinio Rodríguez, Ángel Valdés

Real estate
Angel Lavin

Data protection
Manuel Crómez Vaz

MARTÍNEZ LAGE & ASOCIADOS
ABOGADOS

CLAUDIO COELLO 37
28001 MADRID

Telephone: +34 91 426 44 70
Fax: +34 91 577 37 74
E-mail: abogados@m-lage.es

Languages
English, French, German

Other offices
Brussels*

Number of lawyers 15

CATEGORIES OF WORK

EU law

Mergers and acquisitions

EU and national competition law

Dumping

Unfair competition law

Utilities

Telecommunications law

Pharmaceutical law

Media law

Administrative law

Entertainment law

Company law

Intellectual property law

Arbitration and litigation

MICHAEL SOUL & ASOCIADOS

ABOGADOS

JOSÉ ORTEGA Y GASSET 34-1° B
28006 MADRID

Telephone: +34 91 435 12 69
Fax: +34 91 577 86 07
E-mail: mailbox@spanishlawyers.eu.com
Website: www.spanishlawyers.co.uk

Languages
English

Other offices
London, Marbella, Barcelona*, Palma de Mallorca*, Valencia*

Number of lawyers 12
at this office 3

CATEGORIES OF WORK

Company and commercial

Mergers, acquisitions and joint ventures

Foreign investment in Spain

Arbitration and litigation

Enforcement of foreign judgments

MONEREO, MEYER & MARINEL-LO

BÁRBARA DE BRAGANZA 11
2ND FLOOR
28004 MADRID

Telephone: +34 91 319 96 86
Fax: +34 91 308 53 68
E-mail: mad@mmmm.es
Website: www.mmmm.es

Languages
English, French, German, Italian

Other offices
Barcelona, Palma de Mallorca

Number of lawyers 27
at this office 14

Contacts
Andrés Monereo Velasco, Stefan Meyer, Calvin A Hamilton, Sonia Gumpert Melgosa (Madrid); Enrique Marinel-lo (Barcelona), Carlos Anglada Bartholmai (Palma de Mallorca)

Member
IBA; AIJA; AIPPI; CLA; DSJV; JCI; NYSBA; ABA; Advoselect; BSLA; IFA

CATEGORIES OF WORK

Real estate
Stefan Meyer, Carlos Anglada

Mortgage law
Stefan Meyer, Philipp Kirchheim

Commercial property
Andrés Monereo, Carlos Anglada

Urban renewal
Antonio Jimenez, Ana Sacristán

Corporate
Enrique Marinel-lo, Andrés Monereo

Mergers and acquisitions
Enrique Marinel-lo, Andrés Monereo

Commercial law
Enrique Marinel-lo, Michael Fries

Tax
Andrés Monereo, Carlos Enrech

E-commerce and IT
Sönke Lund, Belén Arribas

Environment, energy and natural resources
Sönke Lund, Calvin A Hamilton

Foreign direct investment and international transactions
Calvin A Hamilton

IP, media and entertainment
Sönke Lund

Distribution and licensing law
Stefan Meyer, Philipp Kirchheim

Common law
Michael Fries, Philipp Kirchheim

Litigation
Alex Ensesa, Sonia Gumpert

Arbitration and litigation
Calvin A Hamilton, Eva Vazquez

Employment law
Ana Gómez, Sabina Llauger

MULLERAT

TORRE PICASSO
PZA PABLO RUIZ PICASSO, 1
28020 MADRID

Telephone: +34 91 399 51 89
Fax: +34 91 399 49 13
E-mail: mullerat.madrid@mullerat.com
Website: www.mullerat.com

Languages
English, French, German, Italian, Portuguese

Other offices
Barcelona, Palma de Mallorca, San Sebastián, Lisbon

Number of lawyers 75
at this office 30

Contact
Alberto Echarri

CATEGORIES OF WORK

Banking, finance, securities
Alberto Echarri, Angel Pendas

Litigation
Pilar Brindle, Antonio Bravo

Tax
Juan Alberto Urrengoechea, Pablo Otero

EU, competition and consumer law
Alberto Echarri, Antonio Bravo

Distribution and franchising
Alberto Echarri, César Vázquez

Company law
Carmen Esteban, Ana de Quintana

Patents and intellectual property
María Dolores Garayalde

Labour law
Angel Pendás, Diego Navarro

Mergers and acquisitions
Angel Pendás, César Vázquez

International commercial arbitration
Alberto Echarri, Carmen Esteban

Criminal law, white-collar crime
Pilar Brindle, Vicente Roldan

Civil rights
Ruth Pérez, María Sanchez

BUFETE PÉREZ DE LA CRUZ

VELÁZQUEZ 51-5°
28001 MADRID

Telephone: +34 915 777 112
Fax: +34 915 773 766
E-mail: bufete@perezdelacruz.com
Website: www.perezdelacruz.com

Languages
English, French, German, Italian

Other offices
Málaga

Number of lawyers 9
at this office 7

CATEGORIES OF WORK

Administrative law

Arbitration

Banking and finance

Capital markets

Commercial distribution, franchising

Competition

Construction

Corporate and commercial

Foreign investments

Insolvency and corporate restructuring

Intellectual property

Litigation

Mergers and acquisitions

Real estate

Tax

PÉREZ-LLORCA

VELAZQUEZ 29
28001 MADRID

Telephone: +34 91 436 04 20
Fax: +34 91 436 04 30
E-mail: central@perezllorca.com
Website: www.perezllorca.com

Languages
Catalan, English, French, German, Italian, Spanish

Other offices
Barcelona

Number of lawyers 46
at this office 42

Contacts
Pedro Pérez-Llorca (Madrid), Gerard Serra (Barcelona)

CATEGORIES OF WORK

Corporate and financial
Pedro Pérez-Llorca

Competition and IP
Oriol Armengol

Litigation and arbitration
David Arias

Real estate
Luis Zurera, Gerard Serra

Tax
Javier Fernández Cuenca

Labour
Luis Enrique Fernández

PINTÓ RUIZ & DEL VALLE

VELÁZQUEZ, 146
28002 MADRID

Telephone: +34 91 563 86 78
Fax: +34 91 563 32 29
E-mail: ma@pintoruizdelvalle.com
Website: www.pintoruizdelvalle.com

Languages
English, French, German, Italian

Other offices
Alicante, Barcelona, Granollers

Number of lawyers 65
at this office 17

Contact
Salvador Ferrandis

Member
Pannone Law Group EEIG; International Sport Law Association; Associazione Internazinale Giuristi di Lingua Italiana; International Wine Law Association; Spanish Group of the International Association for the Protection of Industrial Property; French Association of Practitioners of Trade Mark Law; Pharmaceutical Trade Mark Group; European Community Trademark Association International Trademark Association; National Association for the Defence of Trademarks

CATEGORIES OF WORK

Arbitration
José Juan Pintó Ruiz, David Muñoz

Banking/finance
Joaquín Malvesí, Julieta López-Chicheri

Commercial/litigation
Sigrid Martens, Cristina Paloma

Intellectual property
Salvador Ferrandis, Javier del Valle

Labour
Manuel Cantueso, Miguel Angel Gallardo

Tax
Francisco Bellavista, Ramón María Parcerisa

Competition
Meritxell Ramon, Cristina Antequera

Construction/real estate
Jorge Sánchez, David Peña

Franchising know-how
Fernando Rodríguez, Eva M Ochoa

Corporate
Luis De La Torre, Rafael Abadía

Internet
Abel López, Camil Raich

Mergers/acquisitions
José Juan Pintó Sala, Jorge López

Investments and finance
Javier del Valle Petersfeld, Javier Obispo

Criminal law
Alberto Bosch, Oscar Farré

IP/litigation
Victoria Ruiz de Velasco, Ana Padial

RAMÓN & CAJAL

PASEO DE LA CASTELLANA 4, 3°
28046 MADRID

Telephone: +34 91 576 19 00
Fax: +34 91 575 86 78
E-mail: ramoncajal@ramoncajal.com
Website: www.ramoncajal.com

Languages
English, French, German

Number of lawyers 47

Contact
Sebastián Albella

CATEGORIES OF WORK

Capital markets and banking
Sebastián Albella

Corporate and commercial
Pedro Ortiz de Zúñiga

Corporate finance
Javier Menchén

Tax
José Luis Prada

Public and regulatory
Francisco Palá

Litigation
José Manuel Soriano

Property
Fernando Marín

RUIZ & VEIGA
ABOGADOS

C/RECOLETOS, 14, 1° A
28001 MADRID

Telephone: +34 91 435 28 80
Fax: +34 91 431 88 40
E-mail: ruiz&veiga@acttec.com
Website: www.acttec.com/ruiz&veiga

Languages
English, French

Number of lawyers 2

Contact
Carina Ruiz

Member
Spanish Group of the International Association for the Protection of Intellectual Property; Association Française des Practiciens du Droit des Marques et des Modèles.

CATEGORIES OF WORK

Industrial property

Intellectual property, copyright

Competition

Antitrust law

Licensing, franchising, distribution

Litigation and arbitration

Commercial law

Consumers law

BUFETE RAMÓN HERMOSILLA

CALLE CLAUDIO COELLO 32 1°
28001 MADRID

Telephone: +34 91 431 4816
Fax: +34 91 435 6366
E-mail:
r.hermosilla.abogados@mad.servicom.es

Languages
English, French, German, Italian

Other offices
Barcelona

Number of lawyers 23
at this office 21

CATEGORIES OF WORK

Companies and corporations
Ramón Hermosilla Gimeno, M Jésús Dehesa

Commercial law
Ramón Hermosilla Gimeno, Carmen Fernández Vadillo

Civil law
Ramón Hermosilla Martín, César Gil de Biedma

Banking law
Ramón Hermosilla Gimeno, M Jésús Dehesa

Litigation
Ramón Hermosilla Gimeno, Javier de Andrés

Mergers and acquisitions
Ramón Hermosilla Gimeno, M Jésús Dehesa

Administrative law
Pedro Rubio Escobar

Criminal law
Eduardo Junco, Juan Casanueva

Business crime
Ramón Hermosilla Gimeno, Eduardo Junco

Family, matrimonial
Elena García Ecenarro

Labour law
César Gil de Biedma, Javier de Andrés

Arbitration
Ramón Hermosilla Gimeno, José A Salgado

Environment law
M Jésús Dehesa, Pedro Rubio Escobar

THE FIRM

Bufete Ramón Hermosilla Abogados is a medium-sized law firm located in Madrid, which was founded in 1959 by Ramón Hermosilla Martin. The firm currently has 23 lawyers, seven of whom are partners, and a support staff of approximately 12 employees. Due to its expertise in commercial law, it has attracted a growing number of well-known national and international clients, including some of Spain's major corporations in such sectors as banking, publishing, construction, etc.

The partners of the firm are Ramón Hermosilla Martin, Ramón Hermosilla Gimeno, José Antonio Salgado Gonzalez, Eduardo Junco Otaegui, Juan Casanueva Pérez-Llantada, María Jesús Dehesa Pérez and César Gil de Biedma.

AREAS OF PRACTICE

The firm provides efficient legal advice and services on a wide range of practice areas for both national and international clients.

The firm is well known, and highly regarded, for its civil law and economic-related criminal law work. This base has allowed the firm to steadily increase its work in the following areas: general corporate law; commercial and company practice (eg banking law, mergers and acquisitions, commercial agreements – such as franchising and product distribution); general civil law (eg inheritance, family law, contracts and other obligation sources); insolvency and bankruptcy; arbitration; administrative; and labour law.

SJ BERWIN

C/CLAUDIO COELLO 37
1A PLANTA
28001 MADRID

Telephone: +34 91 426 00 50
Fax: +34 91 426 00 66
E-mail: madrid@sjberwin.com
Website: www.sjberwin.com

Languages
Arabic, Catalan, English, French, Galician, German, Italian, Portuguese

Other offices
Berlin, Brussels, Frankfurt, London, Munich, Paris

Number of lawyers 411
at this office 17

Contacts
Carlos Pazos, Javier Morera, Ramon Garcia Gallardo

CATEGORIES OF WORK

Corporate
Carlos Pazos

Banking and finance

Mergers and acquisitions
Carlos Pazos

E-commerce, media and telecommunications
Carlos Pazos

EU/competition
Ramon Garcia Gallardo

Private equity, MBOs, venture capital
Carlos Pazos

Tax
Javier Morera

SÉRVULO CORREIA ABOGADOS

C/SERRANO 76-5-I
28006 MADRID

Telephone: +34 91 781 5040
Fax: +34 91 781 5041
E-mail: madrid@servulo.com
Website: www.servulo.com

Languages
English, French, German, Portuguese

Other offices
Lisbon

Number of lawyers 35
at this office 7

Contact
Pedro Moreira dos Santos

Member
IBA; Legalink; Diro; TLC

CATEGORIES OF WORK

Company and commercial

Mergers and acquisitions

Public procurement

Banking, securities and financial services

Administrative law

Arbitration and ADR

Project finance

Real estate

Tax

Antitrust and competition law

Labour law

Telecommunications

Transportation, shipping and maritime

Zoning and environmental law

SAGARDOY ABOGADOS, member of ius laboris

TUTOR 27
28008 MADRID

Telephone: +34 91 542 90 40
Fax: +34 91 542 26 57
E-mail: abogados@sagardoy.com
Website: www.sagardoy.com

Languages
English, French

Other offices
Barcelona, Valencia, Pamplona, Oviedo

Number of lawyers 43
at this office 29

Member
ius laboris, International Employment Law
Pensions and Employee Benefits Alliance

CATEGORIES OF WORK

Labour and employment law
Juan Antonio Sagardoy,
José Manuel Martín

Employee benefits and pensions
Iñigo Sagardoy, Martin Godino

International employment contracts
Iñigo Sagardoy

Executive employment contracts
Ana Godino, Julia Alonso

Restructuring plans and collective labour law
Antonio Gómez de Enterria,
Manuel Codoni

Sports law
Jose Luis Fraile

Immigration
Montserrat Alonso

THE FIRM

The firm was founded in 1980 as a specialist in the field of labour and employment law for companies. Since then, Sagardoy Abogados has developed a wide range of legal services in Spain.

Juan Antonio Sagardoy is the managing partner of the law office of Sagardoy Abogados. He holds a doctorate in law and is Professor of Labour and Employment Law at the Complutense University of Madrid. Together with four other partners, they lead a team of over 40 lawyers across Spain (Madrid, Barcelona, Valencia, Pamplona and Oviedo).

Professor Sagardoy has led important litigious cases in Spain relating mainly to works councils, pension funds, collective bargaining agreements and salary matters. Furthermore, the firm has prepared strategic corporate restructuring plans and followed them through, including corporate labour audits, especially in connection with mergers and takeovers. Sagardoy Abogados also specialises in providing advice on labour law to foreign companies established in Spain.

Sagardoy Abogados is a founding member of *ius laboris*, an alliance set up in 2000, which has brought together prestigious law offices specialising in employment and social security law in 21 countries, worldwide. In addition, the firm has collaboration agreements with other law firms which also specialise in labour law.

Finally, Sagardoy Abogados has its own publication service for employment and labour law with contributions from leading figures specialising in the human resources area. It provides clients with current information on Spanish and European labour legislation. Sagardoy Abogados also organises national and international meetings in order to promote the knowledge of comparative law within this specialised area.

AREAS OF PRACTICE

The firm is able to provide assistance in all areas relating to the application of labour and employment law for companies, with a view to preventing individual or collective employment disputes.

It also provides legal assistance before the courts of law, the employment conciliation and arbitration authorities, in matters involving employment contracts, legal regulation of wages, working hours, subcontracting, senior executive contracts, collective employment disputes, strikes and lock-outs.

Furthermore, the firm provides counsel and physical presence at the negotiating table in mergers, takeovers and acquisitions, restructuring plans, collective bargaining agreements, as well as labour audits.

A complete range of legal services is offered through preferential contacts with other leading Spanish law firms in the commercial, administrative, civil and taxation fields.

Sagardoy Abogados has set up an advisory council composed of professors and permanent lecturers of employment law and social security from a number of Spanish universities. This body means that the firm has top-level support that can be consulted on particularly high-profile legal issues, and for anything relating to publications and seminars. Independent of this body, other high-profile figures in the employment field work with Sagardoy Abogados on training assignments.

There is also a consultative council within the firm, comprising mainly human resources directors of the most representative companies in Spain in various sectors. This body advises on the most relevant and topical issues affecting the work of the firm that arise in this field. Through it, Sagardoy Abogados tries to seek new objectives in the legal framework of human resources, and, fundamental to its work, blueprints are drawn up that aim to contribute to improving the configuration of labour relations.

SANTIAGO MEDIANO ABOGADOS

CAMPOAMOR 18 - 4º
28004 MADRID

Telephone: +34 91 310 6363
Fax: +34 91 310 6368
E-mail: info@santiagomediano.com
Website: www.santiagomediano.com

Languages
English, French, German, Italian, Russian, Spanish

Number of lawyers 21

Contact
Javier Berrocal

CATEGORIES OF WORK

Intellectual property, entertainment and media
Santiago Mediano

Trade marks and patents
Silvia Hernández

Information technology
Javier Berrocal

Dispute resolution and litigation
Arturo Fernández

International operations
Chris Cooke

Corporate and commercial
Maria José Verardini

Employment
Sandra Morales

Tax
Amalia Saavedra

Public law
Belén Piñeyro

THE FIRM

Santiago Mediano Abogados has a reputation of being one of the Spanish leading firms in intellectual property, entertainment and media and information technology. The lawyers of Santiago Mediano Abogados are aware that clients need a high-quality service not only in operations where large amounts of money or assets of great value are at risk, but also when it is about day-to-day work and in relatively smaller matters. Therefore, the goal of the firm is to serve its clients in all matters they may have while doing business in Spain, providing them with the same advice and services of any large firm, but offering the advantages and flexibility of the smaller practices. The firm has succeeded in combining the experience of its senior of counsel lawyers, both of them with more than 30 years' experience, with the capabilities, specialised skills and work capacity of younger practitioners, most of them with international experience. Santiago Mediano is internationally acknowledged as one of Spain's leading IP legal experts.

International experience: Santiago Mediano Abogados lawyers are familiarised in advising international clients in M&A, franchising, licensing and other commercial transactions, as well as protecting their intangible assets in Spain. The firm also handles international litigation.

International clients and operations: the firm's international client base includes major companies like US Hollywood Studios, as well as cable TV operators, Internet portals, record production and music publishing companies, various trade mark associations of the entertainment and IT industries, pharmaceutical companies and several press and book publishers.

AREAS OF PRACTICE

Intellectual property – entertainment and media: the firm has a very strong reputation in these areas of practice through the experience gained by Santiago Mediano and his team over the years. The firm advises on all traditional areas of intellectual property, such as trade marks, patents and copyrights. Santiago Mediano Abogados' IP and E&M lawyers regularly advise a large number of companies operating in all markets where intangible assets are the core of the business. This includes software producers, audiovisual studios, record and music publishers, military equipment and other hi-tech companies, broadcasters, press and book publishers, among others. The firm has also a trade mark and patent prosecution area of practice.

Information technology: the firm also specialises in IT, advising on personal data protection, content provision, mobile value-added services, e-commerce and other computer and telecommunications-related matters. US and European transnational clients, and local companies are the client base of this area of practice.

Dispute resolution and litigation: the firm's litigation practice is frequently involved in cross-border litigation related to the protection of intangible assets and advises a large number of domestic and international companies on their conflicts in Spain. The firm is co-founder and leader of an anti-piracy lawyers alliance (ACP) involving 23 firms and more than 100 lawyers in Spain, in association with the Antipiracy Federation. Arbitration in commercial disputes, national and international, before the CEMA and the ICC (Barcelona and Paris).

Company law: the firm provides a wide range of services in these areas, embracing the incorporation of new companies in Spain, the compliance with foreign investments regulations and the optimisation of international taxation structures among other matters. Santiago Mediano Abogados' lawyers advise the firm's clients in all kinds of commercial agreements, including distribution and agency agreements, mergers and acquisitions, corporate restructuring, due diligence reviews, employment and tax. The firm also provides its clients with corporate secretarial services and represents them before any public authorities.

SIMMONS & SIMMONS

MARQUES DE VILLAMAGNA
NO 3 QUINTA PLANTA
28001 MADRID

Telephone: +34 91 42 62 640
Fax: +34 91 57 82 157
E-mail: enquiries@simmons-simmons.com
Website: www.simmons-simmons.com

Languages
English, French, Italian

Other offices
London, Rotterdam, Paris, Lisbon, Milan, Rome, Düsseldorf, Frankfurt, Brussels, Padua, Oporto, Madeira, Abu Dhabi, Qatar, Hong Kong, Shanghai, Tokyo, New York

Number of lawyers 754
at this office 13

Contact
Luis Felipe Castresana

CATEGORIES OF WORK

Corporate	**Financial markets**
Banking	**Pharmaceutical and biotechnology**
Capital markets	**Energy and utilities**
Taxation	**TMT**
Projects, PFI	**Aerospace and defence**
EU, competition	**Transport**
Dispute resolution	**Real estate and construction**
Intellectual property	**Consumer goods**
Employment	

SQUIRE, SANDERS & DEMPSEY

CALLE VELÁZQUEZ 108-110
28006 MADRID

Telephone: +34 91 590 2420
Fax: +34 91 590 2421
E-mail: jpicon@ssd.com
Website: www.ssd.com

Languages
Catalan, English, French, German, Italian

Other offices
Beijing, Bratislava, Brussels, Budapest, Cincinnati, Cleveland, Columbus, Hong Kong, Houston, London, Los Angeles, Miami, Milan, Moscow, New York, Palo Alto, Phoenix, Prague, Rio de Janeiro, San Francisco, Taipei, Tampa, Tokyo, Tysons Corner, Washington DC, Bucharest*, Dublin*, Kyiv*

Number of lawyers 710
at this office 20

Contact
Juan Picón

Member
American Chamber of Commerce

CATEGORIES OF WORK

Capital markets
José de Bonilla Pella

Computer technology
Diego Ramos, Juan Picón

Corporate finance, banking
Javier Santos, José de Bonilla Pella

Employment law
Pilar Menor

Environmental and real estate
Gonzalo Aranzábal

EU competition law
Josep Julia

Infrastructure, project asset finance
Javier Santos, Manuel Mingot

International contract law
Eduardo Sebastian de Erice, Fernando Gomez Pomar

Joint ventures
Gonzalo Aranzábal, Joaquín Echanove

Media and intellectual property
Diego Ramos

Mergers and acquisitions
Juan Picón, Javier Santos

Power generation, energy
Javier Santos, Maria Pilar Garcia

Privatisations
Juan Picón, Javier Santos

Securities
José de Bonilla Pella

Tax
Carlos Rodriguez

Telecoms
Josep Julia, Juan Picón

THE FIRM

Founded in 1890, Squire, Sanders & Dempsey is a multi-jurisdictional law firm with 710 lawyers practising in offices in Europe, the Americas and Asia. The firm's practice covers most substantive areas of the law, with an emphasis on business and finance matters.

The firm operates as a single global partnership, which ensures client accountability and the seamless delivery of uniformly high-quality legal services throughout the world. The firm's lawyers come from many countries and cultures, are licensed to practise in both common law and civil law jurisdictions, and communicate with clients in their native languages. Today, the firm remains committed to the fundamental principles ordained by its founders: to serve clients effectively and maintain the professional standards that distinguish both the firm and its people.

AREAS OF PRACTICE

The firm is organised around four major practice areas: advocacy, business, capital markets and regulated industries. Within these practice areas, the firm's work can be divided into numerous areas of specialisation, including banking, bankruptcy and restructuring, biotechnology and pharmaceuticals, communications, competition law, converging technologies, corporate, energy, environmental, healthcare, intellectual property, international dispute resolution, labour and employment, litigation, mergers and acquisitions, privatisations, project finance, real estate, securities and taxation.

Established in 1997, the firm's Madrid office, counsels clients located or doing business in Spain on a variety of legal matters including company law, project finance, finance, banking, securities, communications, intellectual property, media law, energy, environmental, real estate, mergers and acquisitions, private equity, joint ventures, European Community law, antitrust issues, labour and employment, taxation, litigation and arbitration.

The corporate and commercial lawyers provide counsel to Spanish and international companies on their investments in Spain and overseas. Lawyers handle corporate restructuring operations by means of mergers, spin-offs and contribution of branches and joint ventures and strategic alliances.

The telecom group provides advice on licences and permits, public calls for tender, regulatory procedures before the Telecommunications Market Commission and Ministry for Science and Technology, interconnection and service contracts, project finance, litigation and the corporate aspects of alliances and consortiums, incorporation of companies and corporate monitoring of operators in the Spanish market.

In the project finance sector, experience extends from performing due diligence on licences and permits and revising project agreements to structuring guarantees and negotiating contractual documentation between borrowers and lenders.

The media and intellectual property practice represents clients ranging from television operators to producers and distributors of themed channels, audiovisual products and video games in a wide variety of specialised legal matters, from dispute resolution and strategic planning to the protection and exploitation of intellectual property rights.

In the energy sector, attorneys represent lenders and borrowers in project finance and structured finance transactions. They also handle mergers and acquisitions and privatisations.

URÍA & MENÉNDEZ
ABOGADOS

JORGE JUAN 6
28001 MADRID

Telephone: +34 91 586 04 00
Fax: +34 91 586 04 03
E-mail: madrid@uria.com
Website: www.uria.com

Languages
Catalan, English, Finnish, French, German, Italian, Polish, Portuguese, Russian

Other offices
Barcelona, Bilbao, Brussels, Buenos Aires*, Lima*, Lisbon, London, Mexico City*, New York, Santiago de Chile*, São Paulo*, Valencia

Number of lawyers 296
at this office 180

In association with
Marval, O'Farrell & Mairal (Buenos Aires); Philippi, Yrrázaval, Pulido & Brunner (Santiago de Chile); Franck, Galicia y Robles, SC (Mexico City); Payet, Rey, Cauvi (Lima); Dias Carneiro Advogados (Sâo Paulo)

CATEGORIES OF WORK

Administrative
Jose Miguel Fatas

Arbitration and litigation
Jesús Remón, Eduardo Trigo

Banking and securities
Salvador Sánchez-Terán, Luis de Carlos

Bankruptcy
Alberto Núnez-Lagos, Rafael Sebastián

Commercial and corporate
Ramiro Rivera, Salvador Sánchez-Terán

Competition
Jaime Folguera, Edurne Navarro

Energy
Luis Pastor, Juan Ignacio González

Environmental
Carlos de Miguel

Intellectual property and copyright
José Massaguer, Agustín González

Labour
Ignacio García-Perrote, Lourdes Martín

Maritime, transport and logistics
Luis Figaredo, Tomás Fernández-Quirós

Mergers and acquisitions
Christian Hoedl, Salvador Sánchez-Terán

Project finance
Carlos de Cárdenas

Real estate
Charles Coward, Ignacio Albiñana

Tax
Jesús López Tello, Juan Antonio Fernández-Velilla

Telecommunications
José Pérez Santos
Teresa Paz-Ares

VENTURA GARCÉS & LÓPEZ-IBOR
ABOGADOS

ALFONSO XII, 22
28014 MADRID

Telephone: +34 91 521 78 18
Fax: +34 91 524 00 93
E-mail: ventura.garces.mad@ventura-garces.com
Website: www.ventura-garces.com

Languages
English, French, German, Spanish

Other offices
Barcelona

Number of lawyers 24
at this office 9

Contacts
Alfonso López-Ibor, Marta Gil de Biedma

CATEGORIES OF WORK

Companies

Mergers and acquisitions

Tax

Construction

Franchising

Employment

Banking

Competition

Arbitration, litigation

Insolvency

Telecommunications

Aviation

BUSE HEBERER FROMM

CONSTITUCIÓ 1, 3A
ESQ PASSEIG DES BORN
07001 PALMA DE MALLORCA

Telephone: +34 971 425 740
Fax: +34 971 727 056
E-mail: palma@buse.de
Website: www.buse.de

Languages
English, French, German, Italian

Other offices
Berlin, Dusseldorf, Essen, Frankfurt am Main, Hamburg, Milan, Munich, Sydney, Zurich

Number of lawyers 120
at this office 3

Member
The European Legal Alliance (Beauchamps, Ireland; Dubarry Le Douarin Veil, France; Field Fisher Waterhouse, England; Harper Macleod, Scotland)

CATEGORIES OF WORK

Banking and finance

Antitrust and merger control

Commerce, transport, insurance

Commercial delinquency

Corporate/M&A

Industrial property and copyrights

Information technology and telecommunications

Labour and employment

Litigation and arbitration, national and international

Press and media

Property and construction

Public law

Tax

DE COTTA MCKENNA & SANTAFÉ

CENTRO COMMERCIAL
VALDEPINOS 1 Y 3A
URB CALYPSO
MIJAS COSTA, 29649 MALAGA

Telephone: +34 952 931 781
Fax: +34 952 933 547
E-mail: cottalaw@cybonline.com
Website: www.decottalaw.com

Languages
Dutch, English, French, German, Spanish

Other offices
Nerja

Number of lawyers 7
at this office 4

CATEGORIES OF WORK

Property and conveyancing
Antonio Diaz, Gisele Van Meer

Timeshare
Sandra Wrightson, Alex Radford

Commercial
Alex Radford, Sanda Wrightson

Family
Sandra Wrightson, Reyes Gomez Llorente

Litigation
Alex Radford, Reyes Gomez Llorente

Personal injury
Lydia Sanchez

Private client
Sandra Wrightson

Probate
Antonio Diaz

Regulatory
Jaime Santafé

ABOGADOS ASOCIADOS DE FORTUNY SL

AV RICARDO SORIANO N°12, 1°
OFFICE 4
26900 MARBELLA

Telephone: +34 952 82 15 35
Fax: +34 952 77 15 81

Languages
English, French, German

Other offices
Madrid, Sotogrande (Cadiz)

Number of lawyers 11
at this office 7

CATEGORIES OF WORK

Real estate law
Alejandro de Fortuny, Antonio de Fortuny

Purchase and sales transactions
Elena Jimenez Serrano

Company law
Antonio de Fortuny, Elena Larrañaga

Creation, running and legal advice of national and foreign companies
Alejandro de Fortuny, Elena Jimenez

Civil law (inheritance, procedure)
Juan Jose Mañanos

Litigation
Elena Larrañaga, Beatriz Romero

Private contracts
Alejandro de Fortuny, Diego Villegas

Tax advice
Elena Jimenez, Maria Hernandez

OLIVENCIA-BALLESTER ABOGADOS

C/FERNÁNDEZ Y GONZALEZ
Nº2 TERCERA PLANTA
41001 SEVILLA

Telephone: +34 954 50 14 14
Fax: +34 954 21 21 81
E-mail: informacion@olivencia-ballester.com
Website: www.olivencia-ballester.com

Languages
English, French, German, Italian

Other offices
Madrid

Number of lawyers 19
at this office 17

Contact
Luis M Olivencia-Brugger

CATEGORIES OF WORK

Corporate and commercial

Mergers and acquisitions

Privatisation and corporate restructing

Arbitration

Litigation

Insolvency

Environmental, fraud and criminal

Competition and EU law

Intellectual property

Tax

BROSETA ABOGADOS
ESTUDIO JURÍDICO Y TRIBUTARIO

PLAZA TETUAN 8 – 2º
46003 VALENCIA

Telephone: +34 96 392 10 06
Fax: +34 96 392 10 88
E-mail: info@broseta.com
Website: www.broseta.com

Languages
English, French, Greek, Italian

Number of lawyers 34

CATEGORIES OF WORK

Company law
Manuel Broseta, Alejandra Llorca

Commercial law
Manuel Broseta, Juan Perez

Securities, banking and finance
Antonio Navarro, Alejandro Rios

Bankruptcy, litigation and arbitration
Antonia Magdaleno, Patricia Gualde

Taxation
Leopoldo Gimeno

Mergers and acquisitions
Manuel Broseta, Juan Perez

Urban planning
Amparo Baixauli, Mariano Ayuso

Foreign investment
Antonio Navarro, Juan Pérez

Real estate and public law
Mariano Ayuso, Ana Falomir

Telecoms, Internet law, IP and IT
Juan Carlos Plaza

EU and competition
Fernando Martinez Sanz

Employment and labour law
Isabel Merenciano

IT and e-commerce
Antonio Navarro, Juan Carlos Plaza

Antitrust and trade regulations
Fernando Martinez Sanz

State aids and government subsidies
Migel Angel Ortega

Sports law
Beatriz Montes

LACASA ABOGADOS, PALACIOS & DIEZ AMORETTI

PLAZA DE LOS SITIOS 12 2°
50001 ZARAGOZA

Telephone: +34 976 468 358
Fax: +34 976 302 984
Website: www.abogados-lacasa.com

Languages
English, French, German, Italian

Number of lawyers 16

CATEGORIES OF WORK

Administrative
Pablo Solá Marti,
Daniel Serna Bardavio

Asset finance, securitisation
Juan Palacios Rubio, Francisco Amoretti

Banking and finance
FD Amoretti, José Ramon Bonilla Moreno

International trade
JIP Rubio, Raquel Altolaguirre Abril

Commercial property, real estate
Christina Seanz Beperet,
Elena Pastor Salarrullana

Construction
Fernando Lacasa Echeverria, CS Beperet

Corporate and commercial
F Lacassa Echeverria, JIP Rubio

Dispute resolution, litigation and arbitration
PS Marti, Miguel Ángel Palazón Esteban

Environment
Elena Pastor Salarrullana,
Beatriz de Felipe Sanmartin

Employment
Sergio Royo Garcia

Fraud and white-collar crime
PS Marti, MÁ Palazón Esteban

E-commerce
DS Bardavio, Raquel Altolaguirre Abril

Insolvency, corporate restructuring
MÁP Esteban, B de Felipe Sanmartin

Mergers and acquisitions
F Lacassa Echeverria, JRB Moreno

Tax
FD Amoretti, Jorge Aguilella Mediano

Infrastructure and project finance
Fernando Lacasa Echeverria,
Jorge Aguilella Mediano

SWEDEN

Population	8.9 million
Number of lawyers	3,800
Professional title	Advokat
Currency	Swedish krona (SEK)

Index

Sweden's rejection of the European single currency in September 2003 does not appear to have been the disastrous event that some would have thought. The krona was arguably a stronger currency than the struggling euro at the time of the referendum, and analysts believe that staying out of the single currency may even benefit the nation's economy in the short term. Since major trading partners are the UK, US and Germany, the immediate trading benefits of the euro are not huge, and there was concern at how adoption of the single currency and associated tax structures would affect the country's lavish welfare state. However, the long-term future of Sweden is the euro, with the belief that within four-to-ten years, there will be a new monetary system in place, probably without recourse to referendum this time, and the emergence of a 'two-speed' Europe has been mooted, with Sweden and the UK in the slow lane to full integration. The vast majority of no votes came from rural areas, while the more isolated industrial centres came out strongly in favour, and pro-euro prime minister Göran Persson's position is unthreatened despite the collapse of his major project, due to the lack of credible political opposition.

Sweden's IT and telecoms industries are strong, having eclipsed the traditional major industries of timber, pulp, paper, and copper and iron ore. Telia and Ericsson are leading the way, and the country is one of the most advanced nations in Europe in the IT/telecoms sector. Volvo, IKEA, Saab and Electrolux are also flagship companies. The capital, Stockholm is a thriving financial and commercial centre, with Gothenburg and Malmö also significant business areas. Sweden is joined to mainland Europe via the Oresund bridge, linking Copenhagen and Malmö. Links to the rest of the Nordic states remain stronger than with the rest of Europe as a result of language, culture and history.

ECONOMIC CLIMATE

Sweden has traditionally been an attractive port of investment for foreign countries, with key trade partners in the US, UK and Germany. Although growth is predicted to fall to 1.5% for 2004 (rising to 2.1% a year later), and unemployment to rise to 5%, these figures are still markedly better than the European average and are considered to be attributable to Sweden being out of the slumping Eurozone. Demands have been made that the government make economic concessions to Swedish industries to compensate for the effects of not joining, and to stimulate growth. The Swedish government is maintaining interest rates at 2.75%, and city analysts have predicted that the krona will weaken against the euro initially, but regain ground later in 2004, as interest rates rise. Sweden is also advocating itself as an attractive territory for the establishment of holding companies of overseas businesses, although the tax reforms which have made this possible are recent, and law firms report that they have not as yet been overwhelmed with instructions in this area.

LEGAL MARKET

Sweden is perhaps most reputed for its popularity as an international arbitration centre, for reasons of the number of multi-lingual lawyers, and Sweden's recent history as a neutral territory. The Arbitration Institute at the Stockholm Chamber of Commerce (SCC) is particularly active. Most, if not all, of the country's litigators are heavily involved in arbitration as counsel and arbitrator. Although the process is expensive, it is still a preferred method to going through the notoriously slow court system. The SCC also introduced a Mediation Institute as an alternative, which is commonly regarded as dormant, and also Expiditary Arbitration rules, limiting fees and timescales in certain arbitrations. The major problem for the larger commercial firms is reconciling strong corporate and banking practices with arbitration without breaching conflicts of interest regulations, and some lawyers are under review in the region for possible transgressions. However, since the accepted rule is that disputes arise in lean times when transactions drop, the firms can generally tailor their multi-skilled practices accordingly.

Although the level of specialisation amongst Swedish lawyers has increased as the firms focus departments in specific areas, the vast majority still practise in more than one field. This is unlikely to change much more as it is generally believed that the nature of instruction in Sweden requires competence in more than one area, and the market cannot support the costs of instructing numerous lawyers for tasks which are currently performed by one or two. The larger firms are the only ones whose numbers permit them to completely departmentalise without compromising the strength and breadth of their practice areas. However, sector focus

The largest firms

1	Mannheimer Swartling	295
2	Vinge	246
3	Linklaters	130
4	Advokatfirman Lindahl	111
5	Setterwalls	105
6	Advokatfirman Delphi & Co	92
7	Advokatfirman Glimstedt	89
8	Wistrand	85
9	Magnusson Wahlin Qvist Stanbrook	75
10	Hamilton & Co Advokatbyrå	72
11	Lindhs DLA Nordic	63
12	Gernandt & Danielsson Advokatbyrå	52
13	Gärde Wesslau Advokatbyrå	51
14	Advokatfirman Cederquist	47
15	Baker & McKenzie	45
	Hammarskiöld & Co	45
17	Advokatfirman Fylgia KB	44
18	White & Case Advokat AB	38
19	Bird & Bird	31
20	Hellström & Partners Advokatbyrå KB	26
21	RydinCarlsten Advokatbyrå AB	25
22	Advokatfirman Södermark	24
	Holm Advokatbyrå	24
24	Rosengrens Advokatbyrå	23
25	Advokatfirman Foyen & Co	21

These figures represent the total number of lawyers in this country only, and have been supplied by the firms themselves. The figures should be accurate as at 1 January 2004.

is creeping into the industry, with **Bird & Bird** taking a revolutionary approach to structuring itself by industry and client requirements rather than practice area. To that end, **Wistrand** has created a specialist transport area, and **Mannheimer Swartling** has reorganised its private equity practice to provide a full service to clients in that area from within one team.

The greater resources of certain firms, and the consequent ability to handle several demanding instructions at once, specifically in the core areas of corporate, M&A and dispute resolution, is often the only difference between the larger and mid-sized firms. It is generally appreciated that the likes of **Advokatfirman Cederquist**, **Hammarskiöld & Co** and **Gernandt & Danielsson Advokatbyrå** do not lag behind **Vinge**, **Linklaters** and **Mannheimer Swartling** in terms of legal expertise.

Linklaters' streamlining continued as the firm jettisoned its Malmö and Gothenberg offices, the latter being absorbed by **Setterwalls**.

Wistrand has recently merged with *Advokatfirman Andersson & Ekberg* of Malmö, enhancing the firm's strength in that region.

Johan Norman has taken his environment practice from **Baker & McKenzie** to **Advokatfirman Delphi & Co** in order to better access the domestic market.

Hellström & Partners Advokatbyrå KB has merged with *Michelson & Werner*, enhancing its environmental and litigation practices and boosting the practice to 34 lawyers.

Well-respected IP lawyer Kerstin Calissendorff has left **Advokatfirman Cederquist** to take a position as Justice of the Supreme Court of Sweden.

BILLING

There is overall acceptance that the presence of international firms has pushed hourly billing rates up, particularly amongst the mid-sized firms, and the submission of tenders is more common now. However, in reality the market is struggling to function at this elevated level, and firms are resorting to creative billing and sometimes artificially low tenders to secure clients. Variations in complexity of work, size of transaction and projected duration also have a bearing on hourly rates which hover around the SEK2,000 (€218) mark for associates and between SEK2,600 (€284) and SEK3,000 (€327) for senior associates and junior partners. Rates for senior partners range between SEK3,000 (€327) and SEK3,800 (€415). Smaller niche firms tend to pitch their services 20% lower, but even this figure can be negotiated.

MARKETING

Swedish law firms are still wary of Bar Association rules concerning advertising, despite the fact that they were relaxed substantially ten years ago. Some firms erroneously believe that they are still unable to describe their lawyers as specialists. **Advokatfirman Lindahl** has taken out a campaign of full page adverts in business media, though this has been toned down in the past twelve months. Many firms are following **Linklaters**' example in marketing by conducting roadshows and seminars, though these tend to be exclusive. **Vinge** is also credited with spreading awareness of the value of marketing with its own activities. Cold-calling and aggressive price-pitching is not unheard of.

IN-HOUSE LAWYERS

There is substantial movement of lawyers from in-house positions to private practice and *vice versa*, in particular within the telecoms and finance sectors. The collapse of Ernst & Young's legal practice in Sweden has seen a number of high-profile lawyers return to the legal market from the world of finance, blending expertise from both fields. Firms are keen to push the advantages of former in-house lawyers with first-hand knowledge and experience of the markets gleaned from their commercial backgrounds.

INTERNATIONAL LINKS

Expansion abroad is a possibility which is being explored with interest by some firms. Several already have long-standing relationships within the Nordic territories.

Magnusson Wahlin Qvist Stanbrook has offices in Estonia, Denmark, Poland, as well as the three in Sweden, and is actively seeking partnership in Finland. The Baltic States are also of interest, and the firm is observing the emergence of these states post-EU membership very closely. Whereas interaction between the proximate regions was mainly limited to acts of war 300 years ago, these days relations are hoped to be a great deal more productive as Sweden seeks to exploit its strategic position as the gateway to the Baltics.

Formerly a member of the now-defunct *Denton International* legal network, **Wistrand** has not sought membership of an alternative scheme, citing the economic downturn as a reason to stay independent while maintaining various 'good friends' relationships around Europe.

Setterwalls is a member of *Globalex* and *World Law Group*, and retains 'best friends' relationships with firms in Denmark and Norway. **Advokatfirman Södermark** is part of the *Terralex* network.

Lindh Stabell Horten, rebranded **Lindhs DLA Nordic** in March 2004, is the product of a three-way merger of firms based in Stockholm, Copenhagen, and Oslo and Bergen, and is the first and only pan-Scandinavian firm. The firm is also a member of UK firm DLA's international network.

Vinge is part of the *Scandinavian Law Alliance* and has offices in London, Paris, Brussels, Shanghai and Hong Kong.

Advokatfirman af Petersens AB is a member of the international legal network *Meritas*.

Gernandt & Danielsson Advokatbyrå is active in China and is seeking to establish the firm's name in that territory.

Hamilton & Co Advokatbyrå became a member of the global network *Interlaw* in 2003.

FOREIGN FIRMS

UK and US firms have a presence in Sweden, and there is debate over which is the more profitable, to be part of an international 'brand-name' network with the capability to seamlessly manage international deals across borders, or to rely on a larger circle of 'good friends' in other countries, avoiding potential conflicts of interest. The two largest firms by personnel, **Vinge** and **Mannheimer Swartling**, both remain independent and have no plans to integrate themselves into a global brand. By contrast, similarly-sized *Lagerlöf & Leman*, the merged product of two of the oldest firms in Sweden, is now **Linklaters**. UK Magic Circle firms are thought to be looking closely at moving into the market, although the jury is out on whether another major firm can be successful, and the **Linklaters** situation is being monitored.

White & Case Advokat AB has been in Sweden since 1983, but has maintained a highly regarded mid-sized practice with multi-tasking lawyers in the Swedish mould rather than attempt to unseat the Big Three with rapid expansion and acute specialisation. **Baker & McKenzie**, **Bird & Bird** and **Coudert Brothers Advokatbyrå AB** are relatively new arrivals, having absorbed local firms.

Although international firms take instructions from domestic clients, and vice versa, the general feeling amongst the mid-sized firms is that international and domestic firms can successfully co-exist advising international and local clients respectively. This client split was evidenced in the move of **Baker & McKenzie**'s environmental team, orientated around largely domestic matters, to **Advokatfirman Delphi & Co**. The largest proportion of overseas instruction to domestic firms is in arbitration.

BANKING AND FINANCE

Gernandt & Danielsson Advokatbyrå's recognised expertise in transactional work lends the comparatively small firm clout in the banking field, advising Song Networks in connection with a financial restructuring agreement with creditors and new equity investors, also comprising a debt-for-equity-swap with a face value in excess of €500m. The firm's work had a truly Scandinavian flavour, including advice to the purchaser on a €270m financed acquisition of certain properties from the Nordea real estate portfolio located in Norway, Sweden and Finland, and to the Danish bank Morso Sparekasse on financing issues of an indirect acquisition of real estate in Gothenberg. Hedge fund groups are frequent clients. Stefan de Geer, Karl-Erik Danielsson and particularly Dick Lundqvist stand out.

BANKING AND FINANCE

GERNANDT & DANIELSSON ADVOKATBYRÅ ✪
MANNHEIMER SWARTLING ✪
VINGE ✪

CEDERQUIST, ADVOKATFIRMAN ✪
HAMMARSKIÖLD & CO ✪
LINKLATERS ✪
WHITE & CASE ADVOKAT AB

Baker & McKenzie ✪
Delphi & Co, Advokatfirman ✪
Lindahl, Advokatfirman ✪
RydinCarlsten Advokatbyrå AB ✪
Setterwalls ✪
Wistrand ✪

Bird & Bird ✪
Carler KB, Advokatfirman ✪
Gärde Wesslau Advokatbyrå ✪
Hellström & Partners Advokatbyrå KB ✪
Hökerberg & Söderqvist Advokatbyrå KB ✪
Kilpatrick Stockton Advokat KB ✪
Lindhs DLA Nordic ✪
Magnusson Wahlin Qvist Stanbrook
Morssing & Nycander, Advokatfirman

Firms are listed A-Z in tiers which are ranked in order of priority
✪ Indicates firm displays contact details at the end of this chapter.

Mannheimer Swartling is involved in PPP work abroad, including waste and public water utilities in the Middle East. However, the firm's work at home is also extremely impressive, with advice in connection with a $600m refinancing of the Stena Group by a high-profile bank syndicate. The firm acted for Assa Abloy in establishing a $1bn Global Commercial Paper Programme, successfully raising short-term funding on the European and US commercial paper markets, and has been instructed as counsel to ABB New Finance AB in a $97.8m loan facility, and in two syndicated cash flow-based financings of real estate portfolios worth nearly $600m. The firm acts frequently as Swedish counsel to international clients, and is endorsed as 'extremely efficient and responsive' and 'superior to most of their competitors'.

For years, the banking and finance team at **Vinge** was seen to be the flagship of the firm, and the reputation of excellence has not been diluted by the emergence and nurturing of other departments. Stefan de Hevesy has a strong presence in real estate finance. Bo Adrianzon is highly regarded. Hans Wibom tends to specialise in purely banking and finance work. The firm is particularly active in aviation and aircraft finance, having advised Skandinaviska Enskilda Banken AB on a $97.8m senior secured term loan facility. The same client was also advised on a $200m term facility loan. Syndicated financing of real estate portfolios was also a notable activity over the year. The firm is frequently involved in the largest international banking and finance deals in the region, invariably acting for Scandinavian clients.

The 'experienced and amicable' Svante Hultqvist continues to hold a high profile for **Advokatfirman Cederquist** in the Swedish market, advising foreign banks in connection with financing structures. The firm advised Tele2 on the financing of the 3G joint venture between Tele2 and TeliaSonera, a deal valued at approximately SEK11bn (€1.2bn), and was involved in several high-profile buy-outs in Sweden. The arrival of Martin Rosell from **Vinge** has further strengthened the practice, especially in financial energy trading and risk management.

Bengt Kärde and Per Gustaf Ekbom are the leading lights in a highly regarded department at **Hammarskiöld & Co**, showing financial aptitude across the board. The department has been active as adviser to the Swedish National Bank, as well as its traditional focus on the areas of international finance projects and asset financing work, advising both foreign and domestic financial institutions. Clients refer to them as 'excellent people to work with in terms of attitude'. Per Gustaf Ekbom is prominent in aircraft financing.

Linklaters continue to innovate both within the practice, with the sub-division of the department into two groups specialising in asset and structured finance, and acquisition finance, and in terms of quality of advice. Many credit the firm as a catalyst in the rapid modernisation of Swedish banking law. Cross-border deals involving **Linklaters** offices in different territories are a speciality, in particular last year acting for Bank of America in a $428,750,000 secured syndicated credit agreement to Avnet Inc. The firm has expanded into debt capital markets. Clients included Citigroup Global markets Ltd in a credit facility as borrower, and Credit Suisse First Boston (International) in establishing a dual listed debt insurance programme of unlimited size. Department head Lena Hasselgren has been appointed as a specialist on a government committee on covered bonds in discussions over proposed new legislation.

White & Case Advokat AB has been active in financing aspects of cross-border transactions, an aspect of the firm's core practice areas of acquisition finance, asset finance and structured products, in particular working alongside the New York and London offices. Clients included Madison Dearborn Partners in the €2.5bn financing of the acquisition of the Jefferson Smurfit Group, and Merrill Lynch & Co, Salomon Smith Barney and Credit Suisse First Boston as the managers in a large financing transaction by Nordea.

Leif Gustaffson's banking team at **Baker & McKenzie** acted as lead counsel to Eurohypo AG in connection with a loan facility conceived to partially finance the biggest standalone real estate deal in Sweden during 2003, a SEK3.8bn (€418m) acquisition. The firm also acted primarily fr a number of international banks in a major debt refinancing involving real estate and industrial companies based in Sweden, and for an international group of companies on a €400m refinancing.

Advokatfirman Delphi & Co has been involved in leasing and financing transactions of production machinery. Cheddi Liljeström is active in aircraft financing.

Advokatfirman Lindahl's banking and finance team is now under the stewardship of Petra Hedengran. The firm's traditional shipping department has bequeathed interests in aviation finance. To that end, the firm has been involved in a SEK1.5bn (€164m) leasing transaction, and acted for the seller in an aircraft lease and loan portfolio worth $200m. The firm also advises mainly foreign banks involved in acquisition financing of real property in Sweden. Experienced bankruptcy receiver Felix Korling will join the department as of January 2004.

RydinCarlsten Advokatbyrå AB advises various clients in the finance sector, often in relation to investment and share capital issues.

Setterwalls advised on the securing of financing for a wastewater treatment plant in St Petersburg. The PPP required funds from four separate lenders. The firm also works frequently for the Swedish government offices, SIDA, the National Labour Market Board, Stockholm County Council and the Seventh Swedish Pension Fund on various assignments, including the drafting and negotiating of a number of loan and funding agreements, and is heavily involved in public procurement related matters. Richard Åkerman's aptitude in complex corporate matters is known, while Mats Waering and Maria Chambers are establishing a presence in aviation finance.

Wistrand advised Kista Galleria KB when the company raised an interim facility of SEK1.7bn (€186m).

Bird & Bird is active in aviation and shipping finance. The firm also represented an Israeli shipping company in the financing of a major Polish shipyard. Debt refinancing and venture capital work are other aspects of the practice.

Name partners Lars Soderqvist at **Hökerberg & Söderqvist Advokatbyrå AB** and Hans Wesslau at **Gärde Wesslau Advokatbyrå** are noted for work with local banks.

Lindhs DLA Nordic has acted as Swedish counsel for GMAC Commercial Finance, on instruction from **DLA** in London, on the funding of the Daisytek-ISA office and computer products distribution business in Europe, and in relation to the subsequent disposal of parts of the European group. The firm also advised on a public procurement deal in Croatia.

Dan M Öwerström's team at **Magnusson Wahlin Qvist Stanbrook** was occupied with a series of leasing and sale and lease-back transactions, advising the financing division of a leading global IT equipment supplier. Anders Ericsson is another recognised partner.

CAPITAL MARKETS

The recent emergence and rapid growth of this area has demanded that firms quickly get up to speed on the associated legal issues. IPOs in particular surged, with the top corporate firms making a play for the inevitably lucrative instructions, but whereas there were 21 IPOs on the Stockholm Stock Exchange in 2000, there was one in 2003.

The highly respected **Gernandt & Danielsson Advokatbyrå** advised on the only IPO of the year, involving Dometic International. Dick Lundqvist is the most recognised personality in the department, advising Swedish and international banks on the full range of securities issues.

Vinge was instructed on the acquisition of shares in Nordic Capital by Coller Capital Limited. Johan Cederlund, Jan Lombach and Pontus Enqvist are all prominent names in this area.

Advokatfirman Cederquist acted for Adera AB on its public offer to the shareholders of Mogul AB, and on the listing process following its application for re-listing on the O-list of the Stockholm Stock Exchange.

Name partner Peder Hammarskiöld and his respected team at **Hammarskiöld & Co** are invariably involved with the bigger deals in the market each year. Recent highlights were the divestiture of Electricité de France's shareholding in Graninge AB for €525m and Fischer Scientific International Inc's takeover of all shares in Perbio Science AB, Sweden's largest public takeover in 2003 at €641m.

Linklaters boasts the talents of Jörgen S Axelsson, who advised MTG on the spin-off and listing of Metro International and has a history of IPO work including Rule 144A placements in the US, a feature of **Linklaters**' international expertise. Peter Högström, a known capital markets specialist, is another heavyweight in the market.

Tom Hård and Göran Nyström at **Mannheimer Swartling** are recognised by peers as experts in what is one of the largest capital markets teams in the country, if not Scandinavia. The firm advised Lehman Brothers Real Estate Partners on the public offer for Fastighets AB Tornet in conjunction with Ratos, valued at SEK4.9bn (€538m).

White & Case Advokat AB acted as transaction counsel in Telia's merger with Sonera, a transaction which required requisite clearances from the Finnish FSA, the Helsinki Exchange, the US SEC and Nasdaq, in light of the fact that TeliaSonera's shares are listed on both the Helsinki Exchange and the Nasdaq National Market. The firm also advised on the financial restructuring of Nordico Invest AB, and the associated share issue of Nordic Shoes & Accessories AB, and continues to assist the Irish-based Jefferson Smurfit Group in its acquisition of Munskjö AB. Department head Clas Romander retains an excellent reputation and frequent presence in international transactions, while the reputation of Sven Krogius continues to grow.

Baker & McKenzie is involved in several share issues and acts as counsel to numerous global custodians with respect to securities depository functions. Leif Gustafsson and Cecilia Bjelle are particularly active.

Bird & Bird has advised Swedish companies on new share issues. While not specialising in this area, the firm advises clients in other sectors such as IT, media and life sciences on related matters.

Wistrand has assisted Stena AB on the Swedish element of the issue of $175m senior secured notes on the US market.

CAPITAL MARKETS

GERNANDT & DANIELSSON ADVOKATBYRÅ ✪
VINGE ✪

CEDERQUIST, ADVOKATFIRMAN ✪
HAMMARSKIÖLD & CO ✪
LINKLATERS ✪
MANNHEIMER SWARTLING ✪
WHITE & CASE ADVOKAT AB

Baker & McKenzie ✪
Bird & Bird ✪
Delphi & Co, Advokatfirman ✪
Hökerberg & Söderqvist Advokatbyrå KB ✪
Lindahl, Advokatfirman ✪
Lindhs DLA Nordic ✪
RydinCarlsten Advokatbyrå AB ✪
Setterwalls ✪
Södermark, Advokatfirman ✪
Wistrand ✪

Firms are listed A-Z in tiers which are ranked in order of priority
✪ Indicates firm displays contact details at the end of this chapter.

CONSTRUCTION

Mannheimer Swartling's name is typically mentioned in conjunction with every major construction project in Sweden. The firm is advising the employer Botniabanan AB on the SEK11bn (€1.2bn) Botnia Rail Link, the largest ongoing construction project in Sweden, including taking part in the closing of associated tunnel and bridge construction contracts. Operations abroad include two large BOT projects in Jordan, enhancing both the firm's reputation and its influence overseas. Jan Kansmark, Johan Granehult and Tore Wiwen-Nilsson are all highly regarded. The versatility of the department extends to construction-related disputes, sales of construction businesses and related antitrust proceedings.

Andersson & Gustafsson Advokatbyrå KB has a focus on construction clients, offering advice on contentious and non-contentious matters and insurance-related issues, with Rolf Andersson noted as an expert.

Advokatfirman Foyen & Co was founded by construction lawyers and unsurprisingly remains a top firm in this field, prominent in construction-related dispute resolution, and more recently involved in drafting construction agreements.

CONSTRUCTION

MANNHEIMER SWARTLING ✪

ANDERSSON & GUSTAFSSON ADVOKATBYRÅ KB
FOYEN & CO, ADVOKATFIRMAN
WHITE & CASE ADVOKAT AB

Baker & McKenzie ✪
Kilpatrick Stockton Advokat KB ✪
Magnusson Wahlin Qvist Stanbrook

Celsus Advokatbyrå
Delphi & Co, Advokatfirman ✪
Gärde Wesslau Advokatbyrå ✪
Hans Pedersen, Advokatfirman
Hellström & Partners Advokatbyrå KB ✪
Liman & Partners, Advokaterna
Lindskog Malmström Advokatbyrå
Linklaters ✪
Vinge ✪

Firms are listed A-Z in tiers which are ranked in order of priority
✪ Indicates firm displays contact details at the end of this chapter.

White & Case Advokat AB carries its celebrated disputes practice over to construction-related litigation and arbitration matters. The well-regarded Claes Zettermarck heads a team which has been involved in some of the most sensitive construction disputes in the region in recent years.

Kilpatrick Stockton Advokat KB's practice has been boosted by the recruitment of Nicklas Björkland from **Linklaters**. Thomas Rajala heads one of the specialist construction departments acting for property owners and developers, supporting the real estate practice and acting in disputes.

CORPORATE AND COMMERCIAL

Linklaters is probably the first, and certainly the largest international firm to bring its own influence to bear on the Swedish market, rather than tailoring its practice to suit the domestic surroundings. This has been pursued against a background of numerous departures at partner level, some of which were fallout of the original merger between Swedish firms *Lagerlöf* and *Leman*, with which **Linklaters** merged in 2001. Peter Högström and UK partner Keith Johnson are the best-known personalities in the department.

Mannheimer Swartling has restructured its private equity group into a multi-discipline, self-contained department headed by Peter Alhanko. The group focuses exclusively on private equity clients and their disparate requirements in an effort to get a strong hold on a new and rapidly expanding market in Sweden. The restructuring is accompanied by the departure of two Stockholm partners to set up an independent practice. Bo Söderberg is known for his prestigious clients.

The cream of **Vinge**'s corporate work over 2003 came from the acquisition and sale of Swedish real estate. As with most firms in Sweden, the firm is focused on transactional work, but Investor, Gambro, Accenture and Poolia are all heavyweight listed corporate clients in Stockholm, while the Malmö office advises HeidelbergCement among others. Hans Wibom, Ulf Salnäs and Jan Widlund are prominent in this field.

Advokatfirman Cederquist acted for DaimlerChrysler in Sweden in several matters, *inter alia*, the divestment of two retail facilities in western Sweden to one of DaimlerChrysler's retailers. The firm also served as secretary to the independent panel appointed to examine the relationship between the life insurance company Skandia Liv and its parent company Skandia.

Gernandt & Danielsson Advokatbyrå is a tight, lean operation, with experience, savvy and good business sense embedded in this transaction-weighted practice. Name partners Johan Gernandt and Karl-Erik Danielsson are top-level M&A practitioners and litigators.

Hammarskiöld & Co showed strongly in the market with advice to EQT Partners in the divesture of TAC Holding AB to Schneider Electric Industries for around €450m, the largest private equity transaction in 2003 in Sweden. Dynamic name partner Peder Hammarskiöld is the focal point of the practice.

White & Case Advokat AB retains a solid reputation for both technical expertise and prestigious clients. In 2003, instructions came from DnB in a SEK800m (€87m) credit facility, and from Unisys in respect of two major and complex outsourcing projects. Clas Romander and Göran Åseborn are known and respected figures.

Baker & McKenzie advised Scandinavian Airline Systems (SAS) in a number of aircraft sales and procurement assignments. The firm also has strong connections with IT outsourcing, advising SAS sister carriers, SAS Cargo and Snowflake on related matters. The newly established **Baker & McKenzie** European General Commercial Practice has been established as a means to source overseas clients and manage cross-border transactions between international offices in the network.

Bird & Bird advises clients in core industry areas on corporate and commercial matters. High-profile work is therefore often in the media, IT and life sciences sectors, including the establishment of two new independent music ventures, an area in which Staffan Boström retains a heavyweight client list. More generally, Michael Frie and Dick Poppelman are well thought of for investment and financial advice.

In the wake of the Enron and WorldCom scandals, **Setterwalls** has established a corporate governance group, with the aim of guiding clients through the new, stricter regulations on company management; the new group is headed by managing partner Richard Åkerman. Otto Rydbeck is currently investigating the insurance group Skandia with regard to recent allegations of fraud.

Advokatfirman Delphi & Co has recruited Anders Fernlund from *EY Law*, a recognised specialist in franchising.

Advokatfirman Lindahl has advised on several investment and private equity matters recently.

Mango Kask heads the team specialising in franchising and distribution agreements at **Magnusson Wahlin Qvist Stanbrook**, a source of considerable instructions over the year. In addition, the firm has been involved in various cross-border transactions, utilising its connections throughout Scandinavia and the Baltics. The firm also has a dedicated energy team, focused on all aspects of related transactions, including contract drafting, tariffs and offering advice regarding the implications of the deregulation of energy markets.

CORPORATE AND COMMERCIAL

LINKLATERS ✪
MANNHEIMER SWARTLING ✪
VINGE ✪

CEDERQUIST, ADVOKATFIRMAN ✪
GERNANDT & DANIELSSON ADVOKATBYRÅ ✪
HAMMARSKIÖLD & CO ✪
WHITE & CASE ADVOKAT AB

Baker & McKenzie ✪
Bird & Bird ✪
Setterwalls ✪

Delphi & Co, Advokatfirman ✪
Lindahl, Advokatfirman ✪
Magnusson Wahlin Qvist Stanbrook
RydinCarlsten Advokatbyrå AB ✪
Wistrand ✪

Coudert Brothers Advokatbyrå AB ✪
Foyen & Co, Advokatfirman
Fylgia KB, Advokatfirman
Gärde Wesslau Advokatbyrå ✪
Glimstedt, Advokatfirman ✪
Grünberger Advokatbyrå
Hamilton & Co Advokatbyrå
Hellström & Partners Advokatbyrå KB ✪
Hökerberg & Söderqvist Advokatbyrå KB ✪
Holm Advokatbyrå
Karlerö & Co Advokatbyra HB ✪
Kilpatrick Stockton Advokat KB ✪
Lindhs DLA Nordic ✪
Morssing & Nycander, Advokatfirman

Boman & Hessle HB, Advokatfirman
Hans Pedersen, Advokatfirman
Rosengrens Advokatbyrå
Södermark, Advokatfirman ✪
Wingqvist AB, Advokatfirman

Firms are listed A-Z in tiers which are ranked in order of priority
✪ Indicates firm displays contact details at the end of this chapter.

RydinCarlsten Advokatbyrå AB is strong in regulatory work, specifically rules governing corporate entities and stock market regulations, and advises on overseas investment in Sweden.

Although **Wistrand**'s core areas are insurance, transport and environment, the firm maintains a reputation for good corporate advice.

Kilpatrick Stockton Advokat KB retains a fairly strong mid-range corporate client base, with particular emphasis on structuring international real estate funds. Clients hail from the US, Russia as well as Sweden.

DISPUTE RESOLUTION

Sweden is a major centre for international arbitration, attracting substantial disputes from the Far East, China, the former Soviet Bloc, and elsewhere. Arbitrations involving no Swedish representation outside of the panel and counsel are almost as common as those featuring domestic interests, for reasons that Sweden has an international reputation for neutrality, and offers lawyers well-equipped to handle complex disputes in English. Although concerns have been raised as to the expense of arbitration, it is still cheaper than going to the courts, and the Stockholm Chamber of Commerce has recently introduced rules for Expeditary Arbitration, limiting time frames and costs. Mediation rules have also been drafted to offer an alternative, but clients are unwilling to enter into another costly procedure which could end up in arbitration regardless if not resolved. Litigation is not something that lawyers advocate as the courts are often slow, capricious and ungenerous in compensation. Dispute resolution practices in Sweden are invariably strong, and there is very little to choose between the top firms.

DISPUTE RESOLUTION

MANNHEIMER SWARTLING ✪
SÖDERMARK, ADVOKATFIRMAN ✪

VINGE ✪

CEDERQUIST, ADVOKATFIRMAN ✪
GERNANDT & DANIELSSON ADVOKATBYRÅ ✪
WHITE & CASE ADVOKAT AB
WISTRAND ✪

Baker & McKenzie ✪
Bird & Bird ✪
Hammarskiöld & Co ✪
RydinCarlsten Advokatbyrå AB ✪
Setterwalls ✪

Coudert Brothers Advokatbyrå AB ✪
Delphi & Co, Advokatfirman ✪
Dhunér Järvengren Advokatbyrå
Hellström & Partners Advokatbyrå KB ✪
Kilpatrick Stockton Advokat KB ✪
Lindahl, Advokatfirman ✪
Lindhs DLA Nordic ✪
Linklaters ✪
Magnusson Wahlin Qvist Stanbrook

Gärde Wesslau Advokatbyrå ✪
Hökerberg & Söderqvist Advokatbyrå KB ✪
Holm Advokatbyrå
Morssing & Nycander, Advokatfirman

Firms are listed A-Z in tiers which are ranked in order of priority
✪ *Indicates firm displays contact details at the end of this chapter.*

Claes Lundblad at **Mannheimer Swartling** is considered an outstanding practitioner, and regularly referred to as one of the top three in Sweden. Thorsten Leijonheilm, Stefan Brocker and Kaj Hobér are also well respected in a practice which is very much weighted towards arbitration. The firm is praised for its 'hands-on approach to solving problems' and features a number of up-and-coming lawyers in the department.

Advokatfirman Södermark is highly focused on dispute resolution. Despite the retirement of the venerable Bertil Södermark from partner to a new position of consultant, the firm has broadened its base of skilled lawyers with the canny recruitment of Christer Brantheim, Mats Larsson and Magnus Björck from the former Ernst & Young legal practice in Sweden. Torgny Wetterberg is habitually referred to as one of the top ten litigators in Sweden. Ohrlings PricewaterhouseCoopers has instructed the firm in a SEK 1.4bn (€153m) suit by the Banka Baltija bankruptcy estate.

Vinge has focused on bringing the disputes practice up to the level of its more prominent areas over the last five years. The team is relatively small for the size of the firm, but is well regarded. Christer Söderlund, Olle Flygt and Hans Bagner have all carved out good reputations. The firm was involved as counsel in the largest-ever court proceedings in Stockholm, regarding the challenge of an arbitral award. The firm is also counsel to the liquidator of the largest bank in the Baltic region, and various other high-profile domestic and international matters.

Advokatfirman Cederquist acts for four audit companies in several ongoing proceedings regarding auditor liability. The firm also acted for Tele2 in a dispute against former incumbent Telia for a claim regarding the recovery of interconnection charges, a dispute valued at over $100m.

Gernandt & Danielsson Advokatbyrå maintains a strong disputes practice alongside its extensive commercial client base – among the best for a mid-size, full-service firm. Name partners Johan Gernandt and Karl-Erik Danielsson are litigators of good standing, and Dick Lundqvist is also well regarded. The firm is consistently involved in prestigious international and domestic arbitration proceedings, and is also representing Vodafone Sverige before the Stockholm Administrative Court in a significant market power case.

Claes Zettermarck of **White & Case Advokat AB** is 'almost a brand name in himself', such is his stellar reputation in disputes work. He has recently advised the Swedish state through Socialstyrelsen in litigation. Olof Rågmark and Bengt Åke Johnsson are also recommended in a universally strong department.

Wistrand boasts two leading lights within its disputes practice – Harry Bergman is acting on behalf of the international gambling company Unibet.com against the Swedish government in a cross-border gambling dispute. Stefan Lindskog is also highly respected among fellow practitioners.

Jonas Benedictsson and Stefan Bessman are at the forefront of **Baker & McKenzie**'s disputes team, one of the few completely departmentalised disputes practices in Sweden. All contentious matters are handled by the team except tax and employment disputes which are handled by their respective departments. The firm has represented a Swedish corporation on a competition issue, a Canadian company on IP rights and various other disputes in the past twelve months, and is heavily involved in international arbitrations in Sweden and in other jurisdictions. The department also handles a higher than average level of litigation, in a territory where arbitration is the preferred means of dispute resolution.

Bird & Bird handles media-related litigation including a ground-breaking Internet-related trade mark infringement dispute on behalf of Sony Sverige. The firm is also is representing Hi3G Access AB in a trade mark dispute. Michael Frie is frequently involved in top-level telecoms regulatory disputes.

Hammarskiöld & Co's litigation practice is well regarded, though not as active as the non-contentious areas of the firm. Per Sundin is involved in insurance and reinsurance litigation. The firm is also active in the fledgling class-action arena, and in arbitration.

RydinCarlsten Advokatbyrå AB is held in high regard by fellow litigators, especially in IP disputes, where the firm has a solid all-round practice.

Setterwalls' focus on corporate and financial matters requires careful balancing of arbitration work to avoid conflicts of interest, but the firm maintains an effective and active disputes practice.

Advokatfirman Delphi & Co is involved in the oil cartel litigation, representing a well-known oil company. The well-reputed Dan Engström joined the firm in 2003 from the former Ernst & Young legal practice in Sweden.

Name partner Karl Johan Dhunér of **Dhunér Järvengren Advokatbyrå** is frequently appointed by the Arbitration Institute of the Stockholm Chamber of Commerce, and is also active in the ICC Commission on Arbitration.

Each department at **Kilpatrick Stockton Advokat KB** handles its own related disputes as they arise. The firm has been involved in arbitrations involving western companies and parties from the Baltic States and former Soviet Bloc. The firm has also advised on two challenges to Swedish arbitration awards, a rare issue since challenges can only be made on formal grounds and courts are loath to grant them.

Linklaters' commitment to banking and corporate clients has come at the cost of maintaining a strong arbitration practice through conflict of interest problems, and several heavyweight partners have moved elsewhere in search of high-profile arbitration work. The firm maintains a specialised litigation team headed by the respected Henrik Bielenstein.

Magnusson Wahlin Qvist Stanbrook name partner Per Magnusson's team was instructed on an arbitration by a world-leading petrochemical corporation in a construction contract dispute.

EU AND COMPETITION

The major talking points of the year were the investigations into alleged oil and asphalt cartels. Firms are looking to the outcome of these enquiries as indicators of the future direction of the area. Other predicted fertile areas are the expanding telecoms and life sciences sectors.

The renowned Kent Karlsson is head of the EU and competition department at **Linklaters**. His ten-year stint in Brussels combined with his practice history in Sweden gives him an unusually incisive view on all associated matters. The firm is still active in the notorious and long-running asphalt cartel case, acting for the Swedish National Road Association, and is also active in several antitrust cases in parallel with the M&A department. Erik Söderlind is another recognised figure for his contentious work, and is active in cases involving abuse of dominant position.

EU AND COMPETITION

LINKLATERS ✪
MANNHEIMER SWARTLING ✪
VINGE ✪

GERNANDT & DANIELSSON ADVOKATBYRÅ ✪

Baker & McKenzie ✪
Bird & Bird ✪
Cederquist, Advokatfirman ✪
Dhunér Järvengren Advokatbyrå
Hammarskiöld & Co ✪
Lindhs DLA Nordic ✪
Södermark, Advokatfirman ✪
White & Case Advokat AB

Delphi & Co, Advokatfirman ✪
Grundén & Gozzo Advokater
Hellström & Partners Advokatbyrå KB ✪
Magnusson Wahlin Qvist Stanbrook
Lindahl, Advokatfirman J
Setterwalls ✪
Wistrand ✪

Firms are listed A-Z in tiers which are ranked in order of priority
✪ *Indicates firm displays contact details at the end of this chapter.*

Mannheimer Swartling is acting for Svenska in the alleged asphalt cartel case. Former head of department Johan Coyet will replace Johan Carle as the managing partner of the Brussels office, with the latter returning to the firm's EU department in Sweden. Tommy Pettersson is the new head of the group.

The Brussels office of **Vinge** has been reorganised into a team of four headed by Olle Risland. The firm has advised on EQT's acquisition of Swedish cable-television operator Com Hem, the merger of radio operators Bonnier AB and SBS Broadcasting SA, and HeidelbergCement's acquisition of NCC's concrete business in the Baltic States, Poland and Russia. Johan Karlsson and Carl Wetter continue to be involved in most of the firm's work in this area.

Gernandt & Danielsson Advokatbyrå has a small but prodigious competition department, headed by sole partner Kenny Carlsson, who is widely recognised by his peers as a top notch lawyer, and has vast experience in the field following six years as the head of the legal secretariat at the Swedish Competition Authority.

Baker & McKenzie has been involved in various actions in relation to complaints brought before the Swedish Competition Authority. The firm regularly advises Flextronics International Sweden and Flextronics Network Services on matters arising from acquisitions and mergers. Wyeth Pharmaceuticals and Hewlett-Packard are also clients. Carl Bokwall is the lawyer with the most exposure in the department.

Bird & Bird has strengthened its competition practice with the recruitment of Henrik Nilsson from the Swedish Competition Authority. The firm continues to advise Nissan on the revised block exemption regulation for the motor vehicle sector, and has recently extended its representation in the asphalt cartel matter to 18 municipalities.

Advokatfirman Cederquist has advised on the merger control aspects of several substantial M&A transactions. The firm has also been involved in several joint ventures and administrative proceedings within the telecoms sector.

Competition activity at **Hammarskiöld & Co** has included advising Telia in the joint venture with Tele2 regarding the 3G telecoms enterprise Svenska-UMTS-nät, and the Swedish Alcohol Monopoly in its application to the Swedish Competition Authority for negative clearance regarding its standard form contracts. The department, headed by Claes Langenius, also advised TietoEnator on competition law matters. **Hammarskiöld & Co** and **Linklaters** have been jointly appointed as experts to review the new Competition Law in Sweden on behalf of the Swedish Bar Association.

Lindhs DLA Nordic maintains close links with the Brussels outpost of the *DLA Group*. Recent recruit Ola Wiklund is a European law academic.

Well-regarded Eric Ericsson of **Advokatfirman Södermark** is advising Preem Petroleum AB in one of the largest cartel cases ever in Sweden. He also represents NCC AB in the asphalt cartel case and YIT Building Systems AB in the ventilation cartel case.

White & Case Advokat AB offers expertise in a broad range of competition related matters, including merger filings and EU regulatory matters, and contentious and non-contentious work. The department, headed by Pontus Lindfelt, has also been instructed recently on private equity-related matters.

Former **Linklaters** lawyer Anna Ulfsdotter Forsell advises on public procurement matters at **Advokatfirman Delphi & Co.**

Magnusson Wahlin Qvist Stanbrook represented the Swedish Association of Parallel Importers before the ECJ in a case involving the increasingly important area of parallel imports of pharmaceuticals to Sweden.

EMPLOYMENT

Due to the recession, employment law instructions have recently revolved around redundancies, salary structure revisions and discrimination in the workplace, although there is a continuing requirement for such expertise in connection with M&A transactions. However, opinion is that genuinely specialised and focused employment teams are uncommon in Sweden.

Advokatfirman Cederquist has a renowned labour law practice. Jens Tillqvist handles disputes in this area, especially as adviser to companies facing redundancies, and his colleague Tom Johansson focuses on contentious labour issues arising from all matters corporate, including union issues and expatriate questions.

EMPLOYMENT

CEDERQUIST, ADVOKATFIRMAN ✪
LINKLATERS ✪
VINGE ✪

Baker & McKenzie ✪
Elmzell Advokatbyrå HB, member of ius laboris ✪
Lindhs DLA Nordic ✪
SJU Advokater

Axel Wahlberg, Advokatfirman
Hellström & Partners Advokatbyrå KB ✪
Mannheimer Swartling ✪
Setterwalls ✪

Delphi & Co, Advokatfirman ✪
Gernandt & Danielsson Advokatbyrå ✪
Hans Pedersen, Advokatfirman
Kilpatrick Stockton Advokat KB ✪
Lindahl, Advokatfirman ✪
White & Case Advokat AB
Wistrand ✪

Firms are listed A-Z in tiers which are ranked in order of priority
✪ *Indicates firm displays contact details at the end of this chapter.*

Employment is an area in which **Linklaters** is still active in contentious matters. The main focus of the practice is restructuring, and it is a partner to the M&A practice. While the majority of the firm's time was taken up with downsizing, the end of the year saw a rise in transaction work, requiring employment due diligence, and deal structures relating to pensions and contracts. Sten-Åke Zethraeus successfully defended the Swedish state on an ethnic discrimination charge, and Anders Nordström was involved with Microsoft's acquisition of Navision.

The 18-strong employment department at **Vinge** is spread between the Swedish offices in Stockholm, Gothenberg, Malmö and Helsingborg, and is active in complex M&A deals as well as as a standalone practice. In light of the recent economic downturn, the firm has been involved in several large-scale redundancy-related instructions in Sweden and Finland, but also in the employment issues of a joint venture agreement between two daily newspapers (resulting in the creation of Gota Media AB), and transfer of undertakings. Björn Lindskog heads the department.

Well-regarded Sten Bauer heads **Baker & McKenzie**'s team which advised on several large-scale redundancies at Swedish companies in the past year.

Elmzell Advokatbyrå HB, member of ius laboris exclusively advises employees, and is a member of the *ius laboris* alliance.

Lindhs DLA Nordic's employment practice was strengthened by the firm's merger with *Hägglund Ramm-Ericsson*. The firm has acted in various landmark cases, and frequently advises employees and trade unions in labour-related disputes on matters such as discrimination and working environments. Claes-Göran Westerberg heads the department.

SJU Advokater is a respected niche employment practice in Stockholm.

Hellström & Partners Advokatbyrå KB is active in drafting employment contracts and assists clients in lay-offs and workforce restructuring.

Mannheimer Swartling's employment practice revolves around assistance on M&A and outsourcing transactions.

Kilpatrick Stockton Advokat KB is emerging in this field with the recruitment of Cecilia Herm, former head of labour law and litigation at Svensk Handel AB, the Swedish Federation of Trade, Employers Association.

The employment department at **White & Case Advokat AB** is growing in stature, offering advice in employment disputes to various companies.

ENVIRONMENT

The introduction of the Environmental Code is predicted to have a positive knock-on effect on firms active in this area. The new legislation is generally accepted as being more complex and more demanding, for example in the requirement of permits prior to the commencement of construction and development projects, and therefore more reliant on specialists. Some firms are finding it necessary to maintain an environment team purely as a support function to other departments, and who do not, as such, have their own clients. Firms that offer themselves as specialists in this area, however, will have departments who perform both functions, and most will offer limited advice on environmental matters in isolation.

Advokatfirman Åberg & Co AB is a specialist environmental firm, with wide experience in waste management, and is heavily involved in the clean-up of polluted areas following the enactment of the Environmental Code. The firm also provides advice on environmental matters in major infrastructure projects such as harbours, railways and airports, including the Hallandsåsen railroad, and assists the Central Governmental Department of the Environment. Clemens Fredholm, Bo Nilsson and Marten Bengtsson are all regarded as experts in this field, the latter serving on an official committee reviewing the Environmental Code. Nils Ryrberg is also recommended.

Environmental law is a core practice at **Alrutz' Advokatbyrå AB**, where Thomas Carlberg and Louis Vasseur are recognised experts.

Mannheimer Swartling is aware of the changing face of environmental law in Sweden with the introduction of the Code, and is actively refocusing its team on a younger, fresher approach, for example preparing for extensive activity in emissions trading around Europe. Per Molander and Rolf Stromberg are the older heads of a young team which features rising star Mikael Hägglöff.

Advokatfirman Delphi & Co has annexed Johan Norman's environmental practice at **Baker & McKenzie**, a move which has expanded the department to eight lawyers. The firm advises on all aspects of environmental law, and assists major Swedish national and multinational industries. The recruitment of Norman has brought greater expertise in advising international corporations on chemical products and biotechnical organisms to the department.

The environmental team at **Vinge** is based in Gothenberg, and advised HeidelbergCement Northern Europe AB on the after-treatment of an industrial refuse dump and an industrial estate. The department has been involved in various permit applications for existing industrial clients to allow increased production in line with the new regulations.

Former head of the **Linklaters** team, Johan Lindberg has joined **Kilpatrick Stockton Advokat KB** as the firm attempts to establish itself in the environmental market in Sweden. This is a new focus for the expanding practice, in line with the firm's plans to build up to full service capability.

Linklaters' environmental practice is largely a support mechanism with no partners, but is reckoned to have good up-and-coming practitioners.

The Gothenberg-based environmental team at **Wistrand**, led by Rudolf Laurin, has advised Goteberg Energi AB on the establishment of a gas power plant and an offshore windmill park.

ENVIRONMENT

ÅBERG & CO AB, ADVOKATFIRMAN
ALRUTZ' ADVOKATBYRÅ AB
MANNHEIMER SWARTLING ✪

Delphi & Co, Advokatfirman ✪
Vinge ✪

Fylgia KB, Advokatfirman
Hellström & Partners Advokatbyrå KB ✪
Kilpatrick Stockton Advokat KB ✪
Lindahl, Advokatfirman ✪
Linklaters ✪
Magnusson Wahlin Qvist Stanbrook
Wistrand ✪

Lindskog Malmström Advokatbyrå
Morssing & Nycander, Advokatfirman

Firms are listed A-Z in tiers which are ranked in order of priority
✪ Indicates firm displays contact details at the end of this chapter.

IT AND TELECOMS

Sweden is one of the most advanced countries as far as telecommunications and technology are concerned, and most legal advice will centre around the telecoms networks and service providers, as well as hardware developers and producers. The expensive and problematic roll-out of the 3G network has involved most of the leading firms in one way or another. IT outsourcing is also huge, and growing.

Advokatfirman Cederquist lists Intel and Microsoft among its clients. The firm is involved in several finance projects within the sector and is one of two accredited suppliers of legal services to the Swedish Agency for Public Management, advising on IT matters.

Gernandt & Danielsson Advokatbyrå advised Vodafone on its application for a 3G licence and in the subsequent litigation, following the appeal of an unsuccessful applicant for a review.

Mannheimer Swartling advises local telecoms behemoth Telia as well as several other clients in the telecoms and broadcasting industries. One high-profile deal was the outsourcing of Ericsson's IT infrastructure to Hewlett-Packard. The department works closely with the M&A team, and is also involved in regulatory work and advice to suppliers.

Vinge is in the midst of negotiating major outsourcing IT contracts for international companies, and the separation issues in connection with the sale of a company division or subsidiary in several M&A transactions. Telecoms regulatory instructions came in from Tele2 and Hi3G. The firm

IT AND TELECOMS

CEDERQUIST, ADVOKATFIRMAN ✪
GERNANDT & DANIELSSON ADVOKATBYRÅ ✪
MANNHEIMER SWARTLING ✪
VINGE ✪

BIRD & BIRD ✪
LINKLATERS ✪
WHITE & CASE ADVOKAT AB

Baker & McKenzie ✪
Danowsky & Partners Advokatbyrå ✪
Delphi & Co, Advokatfirman ✪
Hammarskiöld & Co ✪
Lindahl, Advokatfirman ✪
Lindhs DLA Nordic ✪
Setterwalls ✪

Foyen & Co, Advokatfirman
Heidenstam & Nicander Advokatbyrå
Södermark, Advokatfirman ✪
Wistrand ✪

Firms are listed A-Z in tiers which are ranked in order of priority
✪ Indicates firm displays contact details at the end of this chapter.

also acted on the procurement of a common broadband network connecting the cities and villages in the Province of Skåne. Carl Johan af Petersens is almost ubiquitous in this field.

At **Bird & Bird**, Michael Frie handles telecoms regulatory work, and Johan Tyden has a top-drawer reputation and client list to match. The firm is at the cutting edge of technology law, including advising digital music provider Jambarine on legal issues surrounding the development of a mobile content platform and digital download platform.

Linklaters operates a joint ITC and IP practice, advising software houses, telecoms manufacturers and operators. Jörgen Axelsson has advised the Swedish government on the procurement of a nationwide communications network for a large proportion of the security services. Stefan Bernhard and Peter Nordbeck are referred to as 'thorough, yet quick on their feet'. The firm has been involved in assisting Hi3G Access AB in relation to the 3G network roll-out.

White & Case Advokat AB has an impressive track record in M&A in the communications sector, including acting as transaction counsel in the single largest M&A transaction in the Nordic market between Telia and Sonera, worth €6.6bn. The deal encompassed complex securities and competition law. The firm's long-standing involvement in satellite company transactions continued with financing advice to Swed-Dish Satellite Systems and the US Exim Bank with regard to the iPSTAR project in Asia. The global communications practice runs through the international network of **White & Case Advokat AB** offices, in which Rolf Olofsson and Mats Lindgren are key players. The firm has also advised Unisys AB as supplier in the TeliaSonera SEK1bn (€110m) outsourcing of its mainframe computer system, Cisco systems in investments and IP issues, and Scala Business Solutions on general licensing matters. Tony Ryden joined the firm last year from an in-house position at IT-company, Adera AB.

The IT team at **Baker & McKenzie** advised SAS Cargo and the low cost carrier, Snowflake in connection with negotiating ASP hosted services agreements. Other significant instructions came from Tiscali/World Online and software developer, Frango AB on general matters. Stefan Brandt is known for being able to handle the full range of IT agreements.

Advokatfirman Delphi & Co has advised Swedish companies in multi-billion krona outsourcing transactions.

The telecoms department at **Hammarskiöld & Co** lists Telia, Colt, Telenor and Cable & Wireless, among others, as clients. The department is led by Jacob Melander who has a transactions focus. IT-focused Thomas Lindqvist has advised numerous Scandinavian companies, as well as America Online.

Advokatfirman Lindahl's Erik Bergenstråhle and Anders Christner are the leading lights of a department with long-standing expertise in this field.

Lindhs DLA Nordic is regularly instructed on outsourcing of IT functions, and is also active in IT-related litigation matters. The firm also advised a Swedish telecoms operator on its application for a 3G licence.

Setterwalls assists several Swedish authorities in implementing the legal framework for electronic identification and electronic signatures. Magnus Dahlen is at the head of this project. The in-house team at Sony Ericsson works closely with the Malmö office.

Advokatfirman Södermark is instructed by telecoms company ABB.

INSOLVENCY

Insolvency work has been unfortunately prevalent in Sweden in the shadow of the Internet crash, where lawyers have been picking through the wreckage of ill-conceived Internet businesses for three years.

Setterwalls announced its ambition in this field with the capture of Rolf Åbjörnsson and Odd Swarting last year, who, along with fellow new recruit Marie Holmberg-Lüning, have formed the firm's new insolvency and restructuring group. The group aims to advise clients in avoiding financial difficulties before they arise, as well as dealing with the fallout of insolvency. The firm also handles cross-border insolvency matters, a more complex discipline than domestic cases.

Although no-frills insolvency work is not pursued by **Linklaters**, **Vinge** and **Mannheimer Swartling**, we include **Vinge** for maintaining an active interest in restructuring from the Stockholm office, and for two more expansive teams in Malmö and Gothenberg. Robert Wikholm has been appointed to restructure Bedminster AB, and is acting for international bank syndicates in connection with other bankruptcies.

INSOLVENCY

SETTERWALLS ✪
VINGE ✪
WISTRAND ✪

Fylgia KB, Advokatfirman
Gärde Wesslau Advokatbyrå ✪
Hamilton & Co Advokatbyrå
Hökerberg & Söderqvist Advokatbyrå KB ✪
Lindberg & Saxon, Advokatfirman
Lindhs DLA Nordic ✪

Coudert Brothers Advokatbyrå AB ✪
Delphi & Co, Advokatfirman ✪
Glimstedt, Advokatfirman ✪
Hellström & Partners Advokatbyrå KB ✪
Lindahl, Advokatfirman ✪
Lindskog Malmström Advokatbyrå
Magnusson Wahlin Qvist Stanbrook

Firms are listed A-Z in tiers which are ranked in order of priority
✪ Indicates firm displays contact details at the end of this chapter.

Margareta Andersson at **Wistrand** has been appointed administrator in the company reorganisation of a Swedish retail business group, and Leif Ljungholm at the same firm was the bankruptcy receiver for a hi-tech medical research company based in Helsingborg.

Advokatfirman Fylgia KB is noted for its experience and strength in insolvency work, with one of the largest dedicated departments in the country.

Hamilton & Co Advokatbyrå is involved in all aspects of this area, from advising corporate entities involved in buying or selling companies on protection against ensuing bankruptcies, to final dissolutions, but with emphasis on restructuring.

Hökerberg & Söderqvist Advokatbyrå AB combines expertise in banking and finance with insolvency, and positions itself to advise in these areas in particular.

Coudert Brothers Advokatbyrå AB reports a lot of instruction from companies who have made little preparation for the possibility of bankruptcy and require extensive advice in negotiating the legal issues.

Advokatfirman Delphi & Co's insolvency practice has dovetailed with IT and telecoms in the wake of the recent financial problems in those industries.

Magnusson Wahlin Qvist Stanbrook advises banks and financing companies on credit issues and securities. Specialists from the firm are often appointed as trustees in bankruptcies and reorganisations.

INSURANCE

Baker & McKenzie's reputable insurance practice boasts Steffan Bessman's aptitude in contentious matters of insolvency in relation to insurance and reinsurance, and Jonas Benedictsson's all-round litigious expertise. The firm continues to advise more than 50 reinsurers against the estate of the bankrupt credit insurer, Svenska Kredit, and various European and overseas insurers and reinsurers in bankruptcy claims against Folksam International Insurance Co and the bankruptcy estate of International Credit Insurance Co.

Christer A Holm leads a rapidly expanding insurance practice at **Advokatfirman Delphi & Co**. The firm assists domestic and international insurance companies, both in the preparation of new products for the local and international market as well as litigation and claim investigations.

Hammarskiöld & Co's insurance department works closely with the banking and finance department to find practical legal solutions for clients from the continually converging banking and insurance sectors. The firm has acted for Prudential Company of America, Zürich, Länsförsäkringar, and the Folksam Group among others. Demutualisation, acquisitions and transfers of insurance companies and/or portfolio restructuring and financing of insurance operations are all areas of the firm's practice, headed by Erik Swartling.

Vinge's insurance team acts for a number of major insurance companies with activities in Sweden, and has worked with the finance practice on behalf of Swedish banks in the process of establishing a secured $200m loan facility to the parent company of a Swedish insurance group. The department continues to act for the US insurance group White Mountains in finalising the acquisition of part of the bankrupt Folksam International.

INSURANCE

BAKER & McKENZIE ✪
DELPHI & CO, ADVOKATFIRMAN ✪
HAMMARSKIÖLD & CO ✪
LINKLATERS ✪
MANNHEIMER SWARTLING ✪
MORSSING & NYCANDER, ADVOKATFIRMAN
VINGE ✪
WISTRAND ✪

Kilpatrick Stockton Advokat KB ✪
Setterwalls ✪
White & Case Advokat AB

Gärde Wesslau Advokatbyrå ✪
Gernandt & Danielsson Advokatbyrå ✪
Lindskog Malmström Advokatbyrå
Magnusson Wahlin Qvist Stanbrook

Firms are listed A-Z in tiers which are ranked in order of priority
✪ Indicates firm displays contact details at the end of this chapter.

Jörgen Eklund heads the **Kilpatrick Stockton Advokat KB** insurance practice, acting for a significant number of international and domestic insurance companies.

White & Case Advokat AB is active in insurance and reinsurance matters, with associated involvement in litigation and arbitration, and is regularly appointed as liquidators by insurance companies. Bengt Åke Johnsson and Olof Rågmark are at the forefront of all activity in this field.

Dan M Öwerström of **Magnusson Wahlin Qvist Stanbrook** has field experience from his time as general counsel at Swedish insurance company Trygg-Hansa. He advises domestic and foreign clients on transactional and general matters.

INTELLECTUAL PROPERTY AND MEDIA

As there is very little contentious work in Swedish media law, most legal advice is based around IP rights relating to advertising, publishing, copyright, broadcasting licences and frequency auctions, and there is often a crossover into telecoms. Life sciences is growing exponentially, and instructions from pharmaceutical companies are becoming more and more common. As with all growing sectors, the issues of competition law must also be considered in these areas.

Bird & Bird is traditionally strong in all media-related and IP matters. Staffan Boström is particularly active in the music sector, with clients including the prestigious production houses Maratone AB and the Murlyn Group, and advised on the establishment of two independent music industry ventures set up by former leading lights at Universal Music Sweden and BMG Music UK. Heavyweight media specialist Hubert Best has transferred to the Stockholm office from the UK, but is currently occupied in IP issues surrounding the 2004 Olympics in Athens and has yet to impose himself on the Swedish market. Another high-profile recruit is Walo von Greyerz from Ericsson, specialising in all IP areas. The firm also advises the Swedish FA, and represented the Swedish Motorcycle Sports Association in a potential dispute. The international Life Sciences group is well placed to make a strong presence for itself in the burgeoning global pharmaceuticals industry.

Advokatfirman Cederquist has a strong reputation for advising on all aspects of intellectual property with regard to publishing, broadcasting and advertising. Kerstin Calissendorff, formerly head of the department, has recently left the firm to become a Justice of the Supreme Court, and has been replaced by Per Ugge, but the firm maintains a high-profile client list including the Bonnier Group, Warner Music, Sony Music and Microsoft.

Danowsky & Partners Advokatbyrå advises several Swedish newspapers on publishing and advertising issues, as well as whatever contentious matters arise in the area. The firm also advises various lotteries, and name partner Peter Danowsky is very well thought of in IP law.

INTELLECTUAL PROPERTY AND MEDIA

BIRD & BIRD ✪
CEDERQUIST, ADVOKATFIRMAN ✪
DANOWSKY & PARTNERS ADVOKATBYRÅ ✪
SÖDERMARK, ADVOKATFIRMAN ✪

DELPHI & CO, ADVOKATFIRMAN ✪
HAMMARSKIÖLD & CO ✪
LINDAHL, ADVOKATFIRMAN ✪
LINKLATERS ✪
RYDINCARLSTEN ADVOKATBYRÅ AB ✪

Baker & McKenzie ✪
Heidenstam & Nicander Advokatbyrå
Setterwalls ✪

Björkman AB, Advokatfirman
Boman & Hessle HB, Advokatfirman
Coudert Brothers Advokatbyrå AB ✪
Gärde Wesslau Advokatbyrå ✪
Gernandt & Danielsson Advokatbyrå ✪
Hellström & Partners Advokatbyrå KB ✪
Holm Advokatbyrå
Kilpatrick Stockton Advokat KB ✪
Lindhs DLA Nordic ✪
Luterkort, Advokatfirman
Magnusson Wahlin Qvist Stanbrook
Mannheimer Swartling ✪
Petersens AB, Advokatfirman af
Vinge ✪
Wistrand ✪

Firms are listed A-Z in tiers which are ranked in order of priority
✪ Indicates firm displays contact details at the end of this chapter.

Advokatfirman Södermark has strengthened its media practice with the recruitment of Mats Larsson and Christer Brantheim. Anders Beck-Friis is respected for all aspects of media law, including sports advice to the Djurgården football club, and other music and film clients.

Former **Linklaters** practitioner Agne Lindberg heads the department at **Advokatfirman Delphi & Co** which has a strong reputation in IP matters. The firm recently launched a Life Science (Biotech) Group in the university town of Uppsala, headed by Per Gröningsson.

Thomas Lindqvist and Claus Langenius at **Hammarskiöld & Co** advise on trade mark, copyright and marketing law matters. Clients who have been successfully represented include Netscape, McDonald's, Universal and the state owned Swedish Alcohol Retail Monopoly. The department also advises UPI, Universal and EMI on corporate matters.

Advokatfirman Lindahl has always placed emphasis on the media practice within the firm. Staffan Eklow stands out in a department which advised Hewlett-Packard in connection with the outsourcing of Ericsson's IT department.

Linklaters has advised on several trade mark protection issues for pharmaceutical companies as a result of parallel imports, noted by the firm as a growing trend. Trade marks are the speciality as the firm uses a joint trade mark filing system IPPO, where more than 16,000 trade marks are registered. The firm liases with offices in London and Germany on IP matters, which include licensing, software issues and patents, and recent clients include Hutchison Whampoa (Hi3G Access AB) and Microsoft.

Baker & McKenzie has advised on the restructuring of advertising business Publicis, and the entry of Thörn & Täckenström into the JWT network.

Gernandt & Danielsson Advokatbyrå advised Sweden's largest daily newspaper *Aftonbladet* on the acquisition of the e-commerce site blocket.se.

Kilpatrick Stockton Advokat KB has advised some legendary music industry figures on intellectual property and licensing matters, as well as maintaining involvement in advertising, Internet matters and lotteries.

Lindhs DLA Nordic has represented clients in contract negotiations with American and European film studios, as well as in television production, advised on films and sports rights on Pay Per View services and television distribution rights.

Magnusson Wahlin Qvist Stanbrook advises on IP matters, mainly copyright and counterfeit issues, and is also gaining expertise year-on-year in media, entertainment and sport with local sports clubs and Anschutz Entertainment among its clients.

Mannheimer Swartling's Karin Cederlund provides expertise in advertising and intellectual property law, with particular regard to copyright and trade marks. Annika Ryberg has left the firm for an in-house position.

Advokatfirman af Petersens AB is active in life sciences and pharmaceutical law.

MERGERS AND ACQUISITIONS

Gernandt & Danielsson Advokatbyrå has managed to remain active in a slightly depressed M&A market, advising ABN Amro on its financed acquisition of Global Garden Products for SEK5bn (€546m), Nordea on its disposal of Nordisk Renting to the Royal Bank of Scotland, and Kuwait Finance House on its refinancing and acquisition of real estate company Malon. Stefan de Geer and Anders Lundin are the stand-out practitioners.

Most of **Hammarskiöld & Co**'s flagship instructions comprise M&A, corporate and financing elements, and the firm has a heavyweight reputation in this field after years of work at the top end of the market. Name partner Peder Hammarskiöld and Jacob Melander have a hand in most M&A transactions, which of late have included Fischer Scientific's public bid for Perbio AB and the divestiture of the Swedish Greninge Power Plant by Electricité de France. Peder Hammarskiöld has been noted as a leading expert in M&A by more than one trade publication.

MERGERS AND ACQUISITIONS

GERNANDT & DANIELSSON ADVOKATBYRÅ ✪
HAMMARSKIÖLD & CO ✪
LINKLATERS ✪
MANNHEIMER SWARTLING ✪
VINGE ✪

CEDERQUIST, ADVOKATFIRMAN ✪
WHITE & CASE ADVOKAT AB

Baker & McKenzie ✪
Delphi & Co, Advokatfirman ✪
Kilpatrick Stockton Advokat KB ✪
Magnusson Wahlin Qvist Stanbrook
RydinCarlsten Advokatbyrå AB ✪
Setterwalls ✪
Wistrand ✪

Bird & Bird ✪
Coudert Brothers Advokatbyrå AB ✪
Hellström & Partners Advokatbyrå KB ✪
Lindahl, Advokatfirman ✪
Lindhs DLA Nordic ✪
Södermark, Advokatfirman ✪

Gärde Wesslau Advokatbyrå ✪
Grünberger Advokatbyrå
Hökerberg & Söderqvist Advokatbyrå KB ✪
Holm Advokatbyrå
Karlerö & Co Advokatbyra HB ✪
Landahl Advokatbyrå ✪
Morssing & Nycander, Advokatfirman

Firms are listed A-Z in tiers which are ranked in order of priority
✪ Indicates firm displays contact details at the end of this chapter.

Linklaters' commitment to specialisation is evident in its M&A work, where the department is split between corporate and real estate. Flagship deals included the merger of Pfizer with Pharmacia Corp, a 'US-style' merger in a Swedish jurisdiction. The Royal Bank of Scotland's acquisition of Nordisk Renting AB, which involved due diligence in five jurisdictions co-ordinated from Stockholm, Siemens' acquisition of the industrial turbine business of Alstom SA, and the public offer by Vodafone for Europolitan all attracted attention. The firm also advised the Novo Group plc on WM Data's €1.1bn public offer. Martin Börresen has taken over as department head from Peter Högström, who has left to head up the investment banking team. Other leading practitioners include UK lawyer Keith Johnson and Krister Hanson. New partner Fredrik Lindqvist has become very visible in the past year with involvement in some prestigious deals.

Mannheimer Swartling was involved in transactions including advising UBS Capital on the sale of Global Garden Products to ABN Amro Capital, Alstom on the sale of its industrial turbines business to Siemens, and various telecoms matters. Carl Gustaf De Geer and Göran Nystrom, as well as department head Axel Calissendorff, are widely regarded as M&A heavyweights.

Despite the economic slump causing a downturn in M&A work, **Vinge** has obtained instructions for EQT on the acquisition of cable operator Com Hem and sale of packaging company Stenqvist Holding AB, as well as advising on the merger of the Finnish Stock Exchange (Hex) with its Swedish counterpart, OM. The M&A team is strong, with Johan Cederlund, Fredrik von Baumgarten and Fredrik Wilkens enjoying healthy reputations. The firm has advised on 48 mergers throughout Sweden in the past twelve months.

Surprisingly, **Advokatfirman Cederquist**'s prominent recent work in this field has been mostly outside the media sector, but the well-regarded department has advised on the sale of a Nordic pharmaceutical company, a merger within the furniture industry and the acquisition of Emerging Technologies ET AB by Bonnierhuset AB, among others.

Slow market conditions have contributed to a lot of contemplated acquisitions which were never closed, but required advice from **White & Case Advokat AB** to some high-profile clients. One deal which did go through was the €230m acquisition of Cardo Rail AB by Vestar Capital Partners, which involved lawyers based in most of the commercial centres of the world. Claes Zettermarck, Göran Åseborn and Clas Romander are all afforded respect in the market.

Baker & McKenzie's Stockholm and London offices worked together to advise Advent on its bid for the cable TV company Com Hem, and the general commercial nous of Leif Gustafsson and Sten Bauer was evident in cross-border acquisitions. The firm also acted for Cardiac Science in the squeeze-out of Artema shareholders following last year's public takeover.

Advokatfirman Delphi & Co's M&A practice is housed within the firm's corporate finance department. Per Berglöf heads a team which specialises in advising Swedish companies in M&A transactions.

The presence of several former **Linklaters** practitioners at **Kilpatrick Stockton Advokat KB** has lent the American firm weight and experience in M&A work. Clients from traditional industries and emerging technologies have instructed the firm on matters with a combined transaction value of SEK15bn (€1.6bn).

Magnusson Wahlin Qvist Stanbrook works closely with UK-based **Pinsents** in cross-border transactions, notably jointly advising a consortium consisting of European Digital Partners and Cap Man in a cross-border transaction whereby Ericsson's opto-electronic business was acquired, and advising on Wagon plc's technology sharing transaction with Accra Teknik AB.

Bird & Bird advised on the sale by Dun & Bradstreet of its Nordic business, and on the establishment of a joint venture between

BrainheartCapital and Ericsson, amongst other deals. Despite its reputation for media-based work, the firm also remains active in M&A outside this sector.

Hellström & Partners Advokatbyrå KB represented Kuwait Petroleum Svenska AB in its merger with OK ekonomoisk förening, and Finnair Plc in the acquisition of Nordic Airlink Group, as well as some subsidiary divestments in Sweden. Hans Liljeblad leads an increasingly active department.

Lindhs DLA Nordic advised RaySearch Laboratories AB on an inverted acquisition of another SSE-quoted company, a transaction bearing the characteristics of an IPO. The firm also acted as counsel to Amadeus in its purchase of SMART AB from Scandinavian Airline Systems.

REAL ESTATE

There is a history of German investment in Swedish real estate, and a recent surge in Swedish investment in Poland and the Baltic States has kept the market healthy.

Linklaters' real estate practice is a core area for the firm in Sweden, and one which has benefited from long-term commitment. The firm is focused on the larger portfolio transactions and investments, and the property elements of M&A transactions. Recent deals include Royal Bank of Scotland's acquisition of Nordisk Renting AB, one of the largest property transactions ever seen in Sweden, at a total book value of SEK16.4bn (€1.8bn). The firm also advised Drott AB on the sale of two commercial properties in Stockholm to Deutsche Bank Real Estate at a value of SEK1.46bn (€159m). Magnus Lidman and Klas Falkenborn are recognised for their expertise. Jorgen Durban has moved to London as part of a move to integrate the London and Stockholm offices.

Mannheimer Swartling continued its association with Whitehall, a property investment vehicle of Goldman Sachs, with advice on the SEK5bn (€546m) acquisition of real estate from Drott. The same client was advised on a SEK1.7bn (€186m) real estate acquisition earlier in the year, and the firm has also advised on several large-scale property portfolio transactions in Stockholm, Gothenberg and Finland. Klas Wennström is considered a leader in his field.

Vinge advises on the sale and acquisition of commercial properties by international investment companies, and the real estate elements of M&A deals. Stefan de Hervesy retains a strong presence and reputation in this field.

Baker & McKenzie has advised long-term client, Flextronics in various matters, including the sale of industrial property, and the Swedish subsidiary of CLS Holdings plc in several lease negotiations and development of Solna Business Park.

Advokatfirman Cederquist advised Kungsleden on the acquisition of the largest player in private retirement homes in Sweden, and the lenders in one of the country's largest property transactions of the year.

Pontus Kågerman of **Kilpatrick Stockton Advokat KB** is universally recommended in the industry. Much of the firm's other work is tied in with the real estate practice, including tax, litigation and environmental instructions. The firm is involved in the heavy German investment in Swedish real estate. Nicklas Björkland has added to the construction expertise of the department following his arrival from **Linklaters**.

Magnusson Wahlin Qvist Stanbrook acted on the purchase by GE Real Estate and London Regional Properties of 14 distribution centres in Sweden from the ICA Group, a deal worth approximately SEK2.5bn (€273m). Patric Olofsson led the real estate element of the transaction.

White & Case Advokat AB has advised GE Real Estate on several separate matters, including sale and acquisition of property portfolios. The firm's liaison with the German office is important with regard to the heavy German investment in the Swedish real estate market.

REAL ESTATE

LINKLATERS ✪
MANNHEIMER SWARTLING ✪
VINGE ✪

Åberg & Co AB, Advokatfirman
Archibald Advokatbyrå
Baker & McKenzie ✪
Bird & Bird ✪
Cederquist, Advokatfirman ✪
Gärde Wesslau Advokatbyrå ✪
Gernandt & Danielsson Advokatbyrå ✪
Glimstedt, Advokatfirman ✪
Hammarskiöld & Co ✪
Kilpatrick Stockton Advokat KB ✪
Lindhs DLA Nordic ✪
Magnusson Wahlin Qvist Stanbrook
Setterwalls ✪
White & Case Advokat AB
Wistrand ✪

Firms are listed A-Z in tiers which are ranked in order of priority
✪ Indicates firm displays contact details at the end of this chapter.

SHIPPING AND TRANSPORT

Shipping is not a growing field and firms with a history of expertise are unlikely to be challenged from their positions as market leaders any time soon. However, senior lawyers have expressed concern that recruitment into shipping law has not been as popular as in other departments in recent years.

Jan Melander at **Advokatfirman Morssing & Nycander** is invariably the first name mentioned by other practitioners when asked to recommend shipping lawyers.

SHIPPING AND TRANSPORT

MORSSING & NYCANDER, ADVOKATFIRMAN
SETTERWALLS ✪
WHITE & CASE ADVOKAT AB

Delphi & Co, Advokatfirman ✪
Dhunér Järvengren Advokatbyrå
Lindahl, Advokatfirman ✪
Mannheimer Swartling ✪
Vinge ✪
Wistrand ✪

Baker & McKenzie ✪
Gärde Wesslau Advokatbyrå ✪
Hellström & Partners Advokatbyrå KB ✪
Linklaters ✪
Södermark, Advokatfirman ✪

Firms are listed A-Z in tiers which are ranked in order of priority
✪ Indicates firm displays contact details at the end of this chapter.

Setterwalls built an extensive multi-practice firm on a platform of specialisation in shipping, and maintains a strong presence in the market. As an offshoot, the firm advises on aviation finance through partners Mats Waering and Maria Chambers.

White & Case Advokat AB has advised several parties on contentious and non-contentious matters including refinancing, insurance, and has been involved in litigation and arbitration in this field. Instructions came from SCA on a ship refinancing matter, and from Stockholm Chartering AB with regard to the financing of two chemical tankers. Aircraft finance is a particular strength. Bengt Åke Johnsson and Olof Rågmark are well regarded amongst clients and fellow lawyers.

Advokatfirman Delphi & Co has a relatively strong presence in aviation through former SAS in-house counsel Cheddi Liljeström.

Two-partner **Dhunér Järvengren Advokatbyrå** is particularly active in all shipping matters. Lennart Jarvengren is former chief in-house lawyer in the formerly state-owned Swedish Yard Group, while Karl Johan Dhunér is a frequent arbitrator in *ad hoc* proceedings in shipping and transport matters.

Advokatfirman Lindahl advised on a €50m refinancing of three ro-ro vessels, negotiations for a ship-building contract, ongoing construction matters and several registrations.

Vinge is strong in aircraft finance and handles shipping instructions out of the Gothenberg office through Torsten Jacobsson and Per-Olov Skiöld.

Wistrand has created a new group in its Gothenberg office specifically aimed at serving the transport industry on all areas of law required. It comprises specialists in shipping and transport, banking, finance and insurance.

TAX

Mannheimer Swartling has the largest tax department among the law firms in Sweden, allowing the firm to offer advice in all areas of corporate tax matters, and also maintain a healthy tax litigation practice. Instructions include restructurings, M&A issues, structured finance, employee incentive schemes and VAT, with an emphasis on international matters. Britta Muck-Persson heads a 13-strong team and is well regarded both domestically and abroad.

All tax-related litigation is handled by the tax department at **Baker & McKenzie**. More straightforward instructions came from ABBOT in relation to its acquisition of Jomed.

Niche firm **Advokatfirman Bill Andréasson** has a tax practice of high repute, and is invariably mentioned by tax specialists as a market leader.

In 2003, Peter Sjögren joined **Advokatfirman Delphi & Co**, and heads a team of seven practitioners who are often involved in restructurings and incentive schemes, as well as advising on M&A matters.

The tax practice at **Kilpatrick Stockton Advokat KB** advises clients in areas of restructuring, general corporate taxation and VAT, as a part of the M&A department. The firm is also involved in a high-profile real estate tax case in the Swedish Supreme Administrative Court. Nils Skiöld heads the department.

Linklaters' three-partner team, headed by Mats Anderson is a solid complement in M&A, finance, real estate and incentive schemes. The department is also part of the firm's global tax group, and works closely with the offices in London and New York.

The defection of Sören Brekell and Pontus Bergman from Ernst & Young to **Setterwalls** raised eyebrows as the first of what may be substantial numbers of top-notch tax lawyers leaving accountancy firms for law firms. The recruitment puts **Setterwalls** in a strong position to join the market leaders in the near future.

The tax department at **Vinge** assists the other departments in company formation and restructuring matters, and also employee-related issues such as stock option programmes and relocations abroad. Lennart Larsson is recommended for tax aspects of private equity.

Wistrand's tax practice has been strengthened by the merger with Malmö firm Advokatfirman *Andersson & Ekberg*.

The department at **Advokatfirman af Petersens AB** specialises in company taxation issues.

TAX

MANNHEIMER SWARTLING ✪

BAKER & McKENZIE ✪
BILL ANDRÉASSON, ADVOKATFIRMAN

Cederquist, Advokatfirman ✪
Delphi & Co, Advokatfirman ✪
Kilpatrick Stockton Advokat KB ✪
Lindahl, Advokatfirman ✪
Lindhs DLA Nordic ✪
Linklaters ✪
Setterwalls ✪
Vinge ✪
Wistrand ✪

Archibald Advokatbyrå
Gärde Wesslau Advokatbyrå ✪
Hamilton & Co Advokatbyrå
Magnusson Wahlin Qvist Stanbrook
Nova, Advokatfirman
Petersens AB, Advokatfirman af
Wingqvist AB, Advokatfirman

Firms are listed A-Z in tiers which are ranked in order of priority
✪ *Indicates firm displays contact details at the end of this chapter.*

ADVOKATFIRMAN DELPHI & CO

ÖSTRA HAMNGATAN 29
411 10 GÖTEBORG

Telephone: +46 31 10 72 00
Fax: +46 31 13 94 69
E-mail: goteborg@delphilaw.com
Website: www.delphilaw.com

Languages
English, French, German, Japanese, Spanish

Number of lawyers 101
at this office 14

Other offices
Linköping, Malmö, Norrköping, Stockholm, Uppsala

Contacts
Rolf Karlsson, Hans L Bergqvist

CATEGORIES OF WORK

Corporate, M&A, capital markets
Anders Strid, Håkan Hedström

Commercial law (general)
Nanna Töcksberg, Patric Lundin

Litigation, arbitration
Rolf Karlsson, Nanna Töcksberg

EU and competition
Christer A Holm, Susanna Feinberg

Environment
Hans L Bergqvist, Leif Ramberg

Technology transfer
Anders Strid, Håkan Hedström

TIME (telecoms, IT, media, entertainment)
Catrine Bertheau

Insolvency, bankruptcy, reconstructuring
Hans L Bergqvist, Håkan Hedström

Employment labour
Leif Ramberg, Nanna Töcksberg

Commercial property
Per Håkansson

THE FIRM

Advokatfirman Delphi & Co is a national law firm with offices in four major business centres, Stockholm, Gothenburg, Malmö and Linköping. Delphi & Co is a full service commercial law firm focusing in particular on banking and finance, corporate including M&A, IT and telecommunications, EU, competition law, tax and environmental law.

The firm represents foreign multinational and global corporations in their activities in Sweden, including cross-border transactions. The firm's clients include a wide range of both publicly-traded and privately-held Swedish, US and European corporations, as well as banks, financial institutions and corporations conducting cross-border business. Many of Delphi & Co's clients are Fortune 500 companies.

AREAS OF PRACTICE

The firm handles all types of financial transactions, such as drafting consortium agreements, loan documentation and performing due diligence processes. In its M&A work, the firm works cross-departmentally, drawing on competition, corporate finance, environment, tax and employment. Recent acquisitions handled by the firm have ranged in value up to €1.5bn.

The firm has one of the largest IT practice groups in Sweden. In this area, the firm's activities include IT contracts and digital intellectual property rights, as well as e-commerce, IT-outsourcing and -contracts as well as telecommunications permits.

Working closely with corporations whose trademarks are well known and respected throughout the world, the firm specialises in patents, copyrights, trade marks, infringements and other issues. The firm's litigators represent enterprises in court proceedings, in arbitration and in mediation, both in Sweden and abroad. Several of its lawyers also serve as arbitrators in domestic and international arbitrations.

The firm handles on an ongoing basis notifications and filings with DG C in Brussels and the Swedish Competition Authority in Stockholm. Delphi & Co is one of the major law firms which are regularly used to review proposed new EU legislation.

MANNHEIMER SWARTLING

PO BOX 2235
40314 GÖTEBORG

Telephone: +46 31 35 51 600
Fax: +46 31 35 51 601
Website: www.mannheimerswartling.se

Languages
English, French, German, Polish, Russian, the Scandinavian languages

Other offices
Berlin, Brussels, Frankfurt, Helsingborg, Malmö, New York, St Petersburg, Stockholm

Number of lawyers 330
at this office 52

CATEGORIES OF WORK

Banking and insurance
Anders Wikström

Constitutional and administrative law
Claes Beyer

Corporate finance
Anders Wikström

Construction and projects
Torbjörn Molander

Corporate taxation
Robert Starck

Employment
Kristina Leffler

EU and competition
Clas Nyberg

Environment
Torbjörn Molander

Insolvency
Kristina Leffler

Intellectual property
Göran Kraft

Litigation and arbitration
Stefan Brocker

Maritime and transport
Jerker Sellén

Mergers and acquisitions
Hans-Elof Olsson

Private equity
Jan Holmberg

Real estate
Torbjörn Molander

Securities
Claes Beyer

Sport and entertainment
Torbjörn Molander

Telecoms, media and technology
Göran Kraft

SETTERWALLS

KUNGSTORGET 2
PO BOX 11235
404 25 GÖTEBORG

Telephone: +46 31 701 17 00
Fax: +46 31 701 17 01
E-mail:
first name.surname@setterwalls.se
Website: www.setterwalls.se

Languages
English, French, Finnish, German, Spanish

Other offices
Stockholm, Malmö

Number of lawyers 105
at this office 25

Member
World Law Group; Globalex

CATEGORIES OF WORK

Commercial and corporate law
Torsten Leman

IT and telecommunications law
Magnus Dahlén, Per Furberg

Sports, media and entertainment
Richard Hammarvid

Insolvency
Tomas Setterberg

EU and competition law
Dag Fredlund

Banking and finance and securities law
Johan Wilkens

Real estate and construction law
Anders I Bengtsson

Labour law
Dan Bullarbo

Intellectual property
Johan Karlbom

Mergers and acquisitions and corporate finance
Magnus Örtorp

Maritime and transportation law
Max Slotte

Tax law
Björn Ohde, Lars Wessman

Litigation and arbitration
Johan Wilkens

THE FIRM

Setterwalls was founded in Stockholm in 1878 and is one of Sweden's oldest law firms. Its experience and expertise extends to most areas of Swedish and international commercial law.

Setterwalls is a firm possessing significant resources with more than 100 lawyers located at offices in Stockholm, Gothenburg and Malmö working in co-operation with an international network of lawyers.

AREAS OF PRACTICE

IT and telecommunications: Provides legal services to all operators within the IT and telecom sectors such as telephone operators, Internet suppliers, e-commerce companies, manufacturers of hardware and computer software development companies. Setterwalls also regularly assists clients in other IT-related matters such as procurement of systems solutions, IT services, etc.

Sports, media and entertainment: The department offers legal services to a number of media enterprises, sports associations, event organisers, athletes and artists.

Pharmaceuticals and biotech: Provides advice to established and newly-started pharmaceuticals and biotech companies, as well as assistance in matters concerning financing, research and development, patents, licenses and royalties.

Insolvency and restructuring: The group provides clients with advice concerning financial difficulties and the preventing of them. The group consists of specialist lawyers with extensive experience of restructuring and insolvency matters with local as well as international dimensions.

EU and competition: Provides legal assistance in matters concerning Swedish and European competition law and other matters in connection with the EU. The firm assists in connection with the filing of various notifications with the Swedish Competition Authority and the European Commission, investigation of competition law aspects in agreements and business concentrations, and assistance in connection with compliance programmes. Setterwalls also represents clients before the Court of Justice of the European Communities and the Market Court.

Banking and finance and securities: Has substantial experience in providing legal assistance in matters regarding banking and finance. Work includes matters related to initial public offerings, procurement of capital and new issues of shares, loans and other financing, as well as securities law.

Real estate and construction: Assists clients in relation to the purchase, sale and development of real estate and in the procurement of construction contracts. Expertise includes applications for building permits to financing and final leasing or sale, as well as environmental law matters related to real estate. The firm has participated in some of the largest infrastructure projects in Sweden.

Labour law: Assists clients in all kinds of labour law matters.

Intellectual property: Regularly assists clients in matters relating to trade mark protection, copyright, patents and other intellectual property rights.

Mergers and acquisitions and corporate finance: Assists clients in domestic and cross-border business transactions, often in co-operation with banks and investors. Work usually comprises business transfers, investments, mergers, joint venture issues and other matters regarding corporate financing and procurement of capital.

Maritime and transportation law: Offers a full range of legal assistance in all areas of maritime and transportation law, including ship financing and transport matters.

Tax law: Offers tax law advice to Swedish and international companies, ranging from personal tax advice to cross-border business acquisitions.

Arbitration and litigation: The litigation department represents clients in national and international litigation and arbitration. Several lawyers are regularly appointed as arbitrators.

ADVOKATFIRMAN VINGE

NILS ERICSONSGATAN 17
BOX 11025
404 21 GÖTEBORG

Telephone: +46 31 722 35 00
Fax: +46 31 722 37 00
Website: www.vinge.se

Languages
English, French, German, Italian, Norwegian, Portuguese, Spanish

Other offices
Brussels, Helsingborg, Hong Kong, London, Malmö, Paris, Shanghai, Stockholm

Number of lawyers 262
at this office 61

Contact
Olof Jisland

Member
Scandinavian Law Alliance with Kromann Reumert (Denmark) and Thommessen (Norway); Lex Mundi

CATEGORIES OF WORK

Corporate finance
Fredrik Vinge, Michael Sterner

Mergers and acquisitions
Ulf Ohrling, Olof Jisland

Corporate
Torbjörn Sköld, Paulo Fohlin

Capital markets
Göran Petersson, Torbjörn Sköld

EU and antitrust
Björn Nicolai, Olle Lindén

Intellectual property
Torsten Jacobsson, Olof Jisland

IT
Ulf Ohrling, Lars Jonson

Media
Björn Aschan, Michael Sterner

Marketing
Olof Jisland, Torsten Jacobsson

Litigation
Paulo Fohlin, Lars Jonson

Environmental
Morgan Hallén, Hans-Erik Åhman

Real estate
Morgan Hallén, Olof Jisland

Tax
Raoul Svensson, Lennart O Larsson

Insolvency, restructuring
Fredrik Tengström, Morgan Hallén

Insurance
Johan Wetter, Robert Romlöv

Employment
Olle Lindén, Lars Jonson

Transport
Per-Olov Sköld, Torsten Jacobsson

THE FIRM

Established through a merger between leading Swedish firms in 1983, Vinge is today one of the largest firms in Scandinavia, with some 262 lawyers in nine Swedish and overseas offices. In 1991, the firm set up the Scandinavian Law Alliance together with the Danish law firm Kromann Reumert and the Norwegian firm Thommessen. Vinge is also a member of Lex Mundi.

AREAS OF PRACTICE

Vinge has a substantial international practice, with a strategic focus on M&A and corporate finance. The firm has acted in most of the major mergers and acquisitions in Sweden in recent years, and has consistently achieved top positions on *Merger Market's* list of M&A advisers in the Nordic market. The firm regularly represents clients in connection with large international financing transactions, including project financing and structured finance arrangements. Vinge's competition law team is one of the most distinguished and experienced in the Nordic markets. A full-service firm, Vinge also advises domestic and international clients within a number of specialist areas such as employment, intellectual property, IT, media marketing, property, telecom, litigation and arbitration, insolvency, insurance, tax, and transport. In addition to four offices in Sweden, the firm has a presence in London, Paris, Brussels, Hong Kong and Shanghai.

WISTRAND

LILLA BOMMEN 1
411 04 GÖTEBORG

Telephone: +46 31 771 21 00
Fax: +46 31 771 21 50
E-mail: gbg@wistrand.se
Website: www.wistrand.se

Languages
Czech, English, Finnish, French, German

Other offices
Malmö, Stockholm

Number of lawyers 85
at this office 29

CATEGORIES OF WORK	
Antitrust and EU	Intellectual property
Banking and finance	IT and telecoms
Commercial and corporate law	Labour and employment
Capital markets	Litigation and arbitration
Entertainment and sports law	Media and market law
Environmental	Mergers and acquisitions
Insolvency	Shipping and transport
Insurance	Tax law

MANNHEIMER SWARTLING

PO BOX 1384
251 13 HELSINGBORG

Telephone: +46 42 48 92 200
Fax: +46 42 48 92 201
Website: www.mannheimerswartling.se

Languages
English, French, German, Polish, Russian, the Scandinavian languages

Other offices
Berlin, Brussels, Frankfurt, Gothenburg, Malmö, New York, St Petersburg, Stockholm

Number of lawyers 330
at this office 16

CATEGORIES OF WORK

Banking and insurance
Göran Miörner

Construction and projects
Tore Wiwen-Nilsson

Corporate finance
Claes Albinsson

Corporate taxation
Göran Miörner

Employment
Madeleine Rydberger

EU and competition
Michael Karlsson

Environment
Mikael Wärnsby

Insolvency
Peter Idsäter

Intellectual property
Pär Andersson

Litigation and arbitration
Pär Andersson

Maritime and transport
Pär Andersson

Mergers and acquisitions
Michael Karlsson

Real estate
Lars Kongstad

Telecoms, media and technology
Peter Idsäter

ADVOKATFIRMAN VINGE

STALLGATAN 4
BOX 1064
251 10 HELSINGBORG

Telephone: +46 42 24 80 80
Fax: +46 42 24 80 85
Website: www.vinge.se

Languages
English, French, German, Italian

Other offices
Brussels, Gothenburg, Hong Kong, London, Malmö, Paris, Shanghai, Stockholm

Number of lawyers 262
at this office 11

Contact
Claes Enhörning

Member
Scandinavian Law Alliance with Kromann Reumert (Denmark) and Thommessen (Norway); Lex Mundi

CATEGORIES OF WORK

Corporate finance
Sven A Olsson

IT
Krister Azelius, Henrik Borna

Mergers and acquisitions
Sven A Olsson, Peter Abrahamsson

Litigation
Krister Azelius, Nils Petersen

Corporate
Sara Nilsson

Insolvency, restructuring
Claes Enhörning

Intellectual property
Krister Azelius

Employment
Nils Petersen

THE FIRM

Established through a merger between leading Swedish firms in 1983, Vinge is today one of the largest firms in Scandinavia, with some 262 lawyers in nine Swedish and overseas offices. In 1991, the firm set up the Scandinavian Law Alliance together with the Danish law firm Kromann Reumert and the Norwegian firm Thommessen. Vinge is also a member of Lex Mundi.

AREAS OF PRACTICE

Vinge has a substantial international practice, with a strategic focus on M&A and corporate finance. The firm has acted in most of the major mergers and acquisitions in Sweden in recent years, and has consistently achieved top positions on *Merger Market*'s list of M&A advisers in the Nordic market. The firm regularly represents clients in connection with large international financing transactions, including project financing and structured finance arrangements. Vinge's competition law team is one of the most distinguished and experienced in the Nordic markets. A full-service firm, Vinge also advises domestic and international clients within a number of specialist areas such as employment, intellectual property, IT, media marketing, property, telecom, litigation and arbitration, insolvency, insurance, tax, and transport. In addition to four offices in Sweden, the firm has a presence in London, Paris, Brussels, Hong Kong and Shanghai.

ADVOKATFIRMAN DELPHI & CO

DJURGARDSGATAN 1
PO BOX 465
581 05 LINKÖPING

Telephone: +46 13 35 62 00
Fax: +46 13 35 62 01
E-mail: linkoping@delphilaw.com
Website: www.delphilaw.com

Languages
English, French, German, Japanese, Spanish

Number of lawyers 101
at this office 13

Other offices
Gothenburg, Malmö, Norrköping, Stockholm, Uppsala

Contacts
Göran M Karlsson

CATEGORIES OF WORK

Corporate, M&A, capital markets
Göran M Karlsson, Bengt Ehrenborg

Commercial law (general)
Torbjörn Ivarsson, Ulrika Grenerfors

Litigation, arbitration
Anders Lindberg, Pernilla Glans

EU and competition
Torbkörn Ivarsson, Susanna Feinberg (*Stockholm*)

Environment
Hans L Bergqvist (*Gothenburg*)

Technology transfer
Christopher Bona, Göran M Karlsson

TIME (telecoms, IT, media, entertainment)
Christopher Bona, Per Magnusson

Insolvency, bankruptcy, reconstructuring
Erik Fock, Magnus Nedstrand

Employment labour
Erik Fock

Commercial property
Bengt Ehrenborg, Anders Lindberg

Tax
Stefan Lindh

THE FIRM

Advokatfirman Delphi & Co is a national law firm with offices in four major business centres, Stockholm, Gothenburg, Malmö and Linköping. Delphi & Co is a full service commercial law firm focusing in particular on banking and finance, corporate including M&A, IT and telecommunications, EU, competition law, tax and environmental law.

The firm represents foreign multinational and global corporations in their activities in Sweden, including cross-border transactions. The firm's clients include a wide range of both publicly traded and privately held Swedish, US and European corporations, as well as banks, financial institutions and corporations conducting cross-border business. Many of Delphi & Co's clients are Fortune 500 companies.

AREAS OF PRACTICE

The firm handles all types of financial transactions, such as drafting consortium agreements, loan documentation and performing due diligence processes. In its M&A work, the firm works cross-departmentally, drawing on competition, corporate finance, environment, tax and employment. Recent acquisitions handled by the firm have ranged in value up to €1.5bn.

The firm has one of the largest IT practice groups in Sweden. In this area, the firm's activities include IT contracts and digital intellectual property rights, as well as e-commerce, IT-outsourcing and -contracts as well as telecommunications permits.

Working closely with corporations whose trademarks are well known and respected throughout the world, the firm specialises in patents, copyrights, trademarks, infringements and other issues. The firm's litigators represent enterprises in court proceedings, in arbitration and in mediation, both in Sweden and abroad. Several of its lawyers also serve as arbitrators in domestic and international arbitrations.

The firm handles on an ongoing basis notifications and filings with DG C in Brussels and the Swedish Competition Authority in Stockholm. Delphi & Co is one of the major law firms which regularly are used to review proposed new EU legislation.

ADVOKATFIRMAN DELPHI & CO

STADT HAMBURGSGATAN 9 B
211 38 MALMÖ

Telephone: +46 40 660 79 00
Fax: +46 40 660 79 09
E-mail: malmoe@delphilaw.com
Website: www.delphilaw.com

Languages
English, French, German

Number of lawyers 101
at this office 14

Other offices
Gothenburg, Linköping, Norrköping, Stockholm, Uppsala

Contacts
Per-Ivar Svensson, Hanne Mannheimer

CATEGORIES OF WORK

Corporate, M&A, capital markets
Per-Ivar Svensson, Kent Sangmyr

Commercial law (general)
Per-Ivar Svensson, Hanne Mannheimer

Litigation, arbitration
Tomas Eliasson, Mats Engstrand

EU and competition
Tomas Eliasson, Anders Jemail

Environment
Hans L Bergqvist (*Gothenburg*)

Technology transfer
Per-Ivar Svensson, Kent Sangmyr

TIME (telecom, IT, media, entertainment)
Agne Lindberg, Ange Lindberg (*Stockholm*)

Insolvency, bankruptcy, reconstructuring
Erik Fock

Employment labour
Hanne Mannheimer, Anders Reutler

Commercial property
Mats Engstrand

Tax
Thomas Håkansson, Pär Abrahamsson

THE FIRM

Advokatfirman Delphi & Co is a national law firm with offices in four major business centres, Stockholm, Gothenburg, Malmö and Linköping. Delphi & Co is a full service commercial law firm focusing in particular on banking and finance, corporate including M&A, IT and telecommunications, EU, competition law, tax and environmental law.

The firm represents foreign multinational and global corporations in their activities in Sweden, including cross-border transactions. The firm's clients include a wide range of both publicly traded and privately held Swedish, US and European corporations, as well as banks, financial institutions and corporations conducting cross-border business. Many of Delphi & Co's clients are Fortune 500 companies.

AREAS OF PRACTICE

The firm handles all types of financial transactions, such as drafting consortium agreements, loan documentation and performing due diligence processes. In its M&A work, the firm works cross-departmentally, drawing on competition, corporate finance, environment, tax and employment. Recent acquisitions handled by the firm have ranged in value up to €1.5bn.

The firm has one of the largest IT practice groups in Sweden. In this area, the firm's activities include IT contracts and digital intellectual property rights, as well as e-commerce, IT-outsourcing and -contracts as well as telecommunications permits.

Working closely with corporations whose trademarks are well known and respected throughout the world, the firm specialises in patents, copyrights, trademarks, infringements and other issues. The firm's litigators represent enterprises in court proceedings, in arbitration and in mediation, both in Sweden and abroad. Several of its lawyers also serve as arbitrators in domestic and international arbitrations.

The firm handles on an ongoing basis notifications and filings with DG C in Brussels and the Swedish Competition Authority in Stockholm. Delphi & Co is one of the major law firms which regularly are used to review proposed new EU legislation.

MANNHEIMER SWARTLING

PO BOX 4291
203 14 MALMÖ

Telephone: +46 40 69 85 800
Fax: +46 40 69 85 801
Website: www.mannheimerswartling.se

Languages
English, French, German, Polish, Russian, the Scandinavian languages

Other offices
Berlin, Brussels, Frankfurt, Gothenburg, Helsingborg, New York, St Petersburg, Stockholm

Number of lawyers 330
at this office 42

CATEGORIES OF WORK

Banking and insurance
Göran Miörner

Construction and projects
Tore Wiwen-Nilsson

Corporate finance
Claes Albinsson

Corporate taxation
Göran Miörner

Employment
Madeleine Rydberger

EU and competition
Michael Karlsson

Environment
Mikael Wärnsby

Insolvency
Peter Idsäter

Intellectual property
Pär Andersson

Litigation and arbitration
Michael Karlsson

Maritime and transport
Pär Andersson

Mergers and acquisitions
Michael Karlsson

Private equity
Göran Miörner

Real estate
Jan Kansmark

Securities
Claes Albinsson

Sport and entertainment
Michael Karlsson

Telecoms, media and technology
Peter Idsäter

SETTERWALLS

STORTORGET 23
211 34 MALMÖ

Telephone: +46 40 690 04 00
Fax: +46 40 690 04 70
E-mail:
first name.surname@setterwalls.se
Website: www.setterwalls.se

Languages
English, French, German, Italian

Other offices
Stockholm, Gothenburg

Number of lawyers 105
at this office 30

Member
World Law Group; Globalex

CATEGORIES OF WORK

Commercial and corporate law
Kristian Lundlus, Magnus Berlin

IT and telecommunications law
Marc Tullgren, Jonas Frii

Sports, media and entertainment
Marc Tullgren, Sören Brekell

Pharmaceuticals and biotech
Lennart Arvidson, Hugo Wernbro

Construction
Lennart Iwar, Magnus Berlin

Banking and finance and securities law
Lennart Iwar

Real estate
Kristian Lundius

Labour law
Jörgen Rexö

Intellectual property
Hugo Wernbro, Lennart Arvidson

Mergers and acquisitions and corporate finance
Lennart Arvidson, Lennart Iwar

Environmental law
Erica Erkinheimo

Litigation and arbitration
Magnus Berlin, Gösta Westman

EU and competition law
Karl Olsson

Tax law
Sören Brekell, Pontus Bergman

Insolvency and restructuring
Jörgen Rexö

Insurance and tort
Gösta Westman

THE FIRM

Setterwalls was founded in Stockholm in 1878 and is one of Sweden's oldest law firms. Its experience and expertise extends to most areas of Swedish and international commercial law.

Setterwalls is a firm possessing significant resources with more than 100 lawyers located at offices in Stockholm, Gothenburg and Malmö working in co-operation with an international network of lawyers.

AREAS OF PRACTICE

IT and telecommunications: Provides legal services to all operators within the IT and telecoms sectors such as telephone operators, Internet suppliers, e-commerce companies, manufacturers of hardware and computer software development companies. Setterwalls also regularly assists clients in other IT-related matters such as procurement of systems solutions, IT services, etc.

Sports, media and entertainment: The department offers legal services to a number of media enterprises, sports associations, event organisers, athletes and artists.

Pharmaceuticals and biotech: Provides advice to established and newly-started pharmaceuticals and biotech companies, as well as assistance in matters concerning financing, research and development, patents, licenses and royalties.

Banking and finance and securities: Has substantial experience in providing legal assistance in matters regarding banking and finance. Work includes matters related to initial public offerings, procurement of capital and new issues of shares, loans and other financing, as well as securities law.

Real estate and construction: Assists clients in relation to the purchase, sale and development of real estate and in the procurement of construction contracts. Expertise includes applications for building permits to financing and final leasing or sale, as well as environmental law matters related to real estate. Setterwalls has participated in some of the largest infrastructure projects in Sweden.

Labour law: Assists clients in all kinds of labour law matters.

Intellectual property: Regularly assists clients in matters relating to trade mark protection, copyright, patents and other intellectual property rights.

Mergers and acquisitions and corporate finance: Assists clients in domestic and cross-border business transactions, often in co-operation with banks and investors. Work usually comprises business transfers, investments, mergers, joint venture issues and other matters regarding corporate financing and procurement of capital.

Environmental law: Assists clients in all kinds of matters related to environmental law, as well as applications for permits for water operations or environmentally hazardous activities, matters concerning polluted land and environmental damages.

Arbitration and litigation: The litigation department represents clients in national and international litigation and arbitration. Several lawyers are regularly appointed as arbitrators.

EU and competition: Provides legal assistance in matters concerning Swedish and European competition law and other matters in connection with the EU, as well as in connection with the filing of various notifications with the Swedish Competition Authority and the European Commission, investigation of competition law aspects in agreements and business concentrations, and assistance in connection with compliance programmes. Setterwalls also represents clients before the Court of Justice of the European Communities and the Market Court.

Tax law: Offers tax law advice to Swedish and international companies, ranging from personal tax advice to cross-border business acquisitions.

Insolvency and restructuring: The group provides clients with advice concerning financial difficulties and the preventing of them. The group consists of specialist lawyers with extensive experience of restructuring and insolvency matters with local as well as international dimensions.

ADVOKATFIRMAN VINGE

ÖSTERGATAN 30
BOX 4255
203 13 MALMÖ

Telephone: +46 40 664 55 00
Fax: +46 40 664 55 01
Website: www.vinge.se

Languages
English, German, French

Other offices
Brussels, Gothenburg, Helsingborg, Hong Kong, London, Paris, Stockholm, Shanghai

Number of lawyers 262
at this office 40

Contact
Peter Oscarsson

Member
Scandinavian Law Alliance with Kromann Reumert (Denmark) and Thommessen (Norway, Lex Mundi

CATEGORIES OF WORK

Corporate finance
Peter Linderoth, Anders Forkman

Mergers and acquisitions
Lars Gildéus, Peter Linderoth

Corporate
Tommy Hed, Peter Oscarsson

Capital markets
Erik Gabrielson, Peter Oscarsson

EU and antitrust
Rikard Azelius, Björn Mullaart

Intellectual property
Arne Källén

IT
Erik Gabrielson, Jesper Ottergren

Media
Lars Gildéus

Marketing
Fredrik Fors, Erik Sjöman

Litigation
Finn Madsen, Arne Källén

Environmental
Ingela Malmborg

Real estate
Peter Bengtsson

Tax
Patrik Gustafsson

Insolvency and restructuring
Lennart Atteryd

Employment
Ingela Malmborg

THE FIRM

Established through a merger between leading Swedish firms in 1983, Vinge is today one of the largest firms in Scandinavia, with some 262 lawyers in nine Swedish and overseas offices. In 1991, the firm set up the Scandinavian Law Alliance together with the Danish law firm Kromann Reumert and the Norwegian firm Thommessen. Vinge is also a member of Lex Mundi.

AREAS OF PRACTICE

Vinge has a substantial international practice, with a strategic focus on M&A and corporate finance. The firm has acted in most of the major mergers and acquisitions in Sweden in recent years, and has consistently achieved top positions on *Merger Market*'s list of M&A advisers in the Nordic market. The firm regularly represents clients in connection with large international financing transactions, including project financing and structured finance arrangements. Vinge's competition law team is one of the most distinguished and experienced in the Nordic markets. A full-service firm, Vinge also advises domestic and international clients within a number of specialist areas such as employment, intellectual property, IT, media marketing, property, telecom, litigation and arbitration, insolvency, insurance, tax, and transport. In addition to four offices in Sweden, the firm has a presence in London, Paris, Brussels, Hong Kong and Shanghai.

WISTRAND

BALTZAR CITY, SÖDERGATAN 22
20312 MALMÖ
PO BOX 4149

Telephone: +46 40 669 7100
Fax: +46 40 669 7101
E-mail: malmo@wistrand.se
Website: www.wistrand.se

Languages
Czech, English, Finnish, French, German

Other offices
Gothenburg, Stockholm

Number of lawyers 85
at this office 16

CATEGORIES OF WORK	
Antitrust and EU	Intellectual property
Banking and finance	IT and telecoms
Commercial and corporate law	Labour and employment
Capital markets	Litigation and arbitration
Entertainment and sports law	Media and market law
Environmental	Mergers and acquisitions
Insolvency	Shipping and transport
Insurance	Tax law

BAKER & McKENZIE

LINNÉGATAN 18
PO BOX 5719
114 87 STOCKHOLM

Telephone: +46 8 566 177 00
Fax: +46 8 566 177 99
E-mail: stockholm@bakernet.com
Website: www.bakernet.com

Languages
English, French, German, the Scandinavian languages

Other offices
Almaty, Amsterdam, Antwerp, Bahrain, Baku, Bangkok, Barcelona, Beijing, Berlin, Bogotá, Bologna, Brasilia, Brussels, Budapest, Buenos Aires, Cairo, Calgary, Caracas, Chicago, Dallas, Düsseldorf, Frankfurt, Geneva, Guadalajara, Hanoi, Ho Chi Minh City, Hong Kong, Houston, Juarez, Kyiv, London, Madrid, Manila, Melbourne, Mexico City, Miami, Milan, Monterrey, Moscow, Munich, New York, Palo Alto, Paris, Porto Alegré, Prague, Rio de Janeiro, Riyadh, Rome, St Petersburg, San Diego, San Francisco, Santiago, São Paulo, Shanghai, Singapore, Sydney, Taipei, Tijuana, Tokyo, Toronto, Valencia, Vienna, Warsaw, Washington DC, Zürich

Number of lawyers 3,380
at this office 45

Contact
Robert Fröman

Baker & McKenzie is a global law firm with 66 offices in 36 countries.

CATEGORIES OF WORK

Banking and finance
Leif Gustafsson, Tord Svensson

Corporate
Carl Svernlöv, Ingrid Björck

Corporate governance
Mauritz Silfverstolpe

Employment
Sten Bauer

Environment
Johan Norman

EU and competition
Leif Gustafsson, Carl Bökwall

Financial services
Leif Gustafsson, Cecilia Bjelle

Information technology
Stefan Brandt

Insurance
Stefan Bessman

Intellectual property
Stefan Brandt

Litigation, arbitration and insolvency
Jonas Benedictsson, Stefan Bessman

Media and entertainment
Mattias Hedwall

Mergers and acquisitions
Sten Bauer, Carl Svernlöv

Real estate and construction
Mauritz Silfverstolpe, Jan Alexanderson

Securities
Leif Gustafsson, Cecilia Bjelle

Tax
Bo Lindqvist, Erik Björkeson

Telecommunications
Stefan Brandt

Venture capital/private equity
Cecilia Bjelle, Anders Fast

BIRD & BIRD

NORRLANDSGATAN 15
BOX 7714
103 95 STOCKHOLM

Telephone: +46 8 506 320 00
Fax: +46 8 506 320 90
E-mail: stockholm@twobirds.com
Website: www.twobirds.com

Languages
English, German, Italian

Other offices
Brussels, Düsseldorf, Hong Kong, London, Milan, Munich, Paris, The Hague

Number of lawyers 373
at this office 31

Contact
Michael Frie

CATEGORIES OF WORK

Arbitration

Banking and finance

Communications

Commercial

Corporate

Employment

Information technology

Intellectual property

Life sciences

Litigation

Media and entertainment

Sport

ADVOKATFIRMAN CARLER KB

NORRLANDSGATAN 11
PO BOX 7557
10393 STOCKHOLM

Telephone: +46 8 545 184 50
Fax: +46 8 545 184 55
E-mail: carler@carler.se
Website: www.carler.se

Languages
English, French, German, the Scandinavian languages

Other offices
Linköping, Paris

Number of lawyers 20
at this office 10

Contact
Wim Dejonghe

Member
AIJA; AEDBF; CLA (Commercial Law Affiliates); Euro Franchise Lawyers; IBA; ICC; UIA

CATEGORIES OF WORK

Corporate and commercial
Mats Emthén, Jan Holmquist

Mergers and acquisitions
Mats Olofson, Mats Emthén

Intellectual property
Richard Wessman

Distribution, agency and licensing
Mats Olofson

Contract
Mats Olofson

Banking and financial
Mats Olofson

Financial reconstruction
Mats Emthén, Jan Holmquist

Bankruptcy
Mats Emthén, Jan Holmquist

Property and real estate
Jan Holmquist, Sören Birkeland

Arbitration and litigation
Mats Olofson, Mats Emthén

COUDERT BROTHERS ADVOKATBYRÅ AB

KUNGSGATAN 28
PO BOX 7418
103 91 STOCKHOLM

Telephone: +46 8 614 49 00
Fax: +46 8 611 04 04
E-mail: info-stockholm@coudert.com
Website: www.coudert.com

Languages
English, French, German, Spanish

Other offices
Almaty, Antwerp, Bangkok, Beijing, Brussels, Budapest*, Frankfurt, Ghent, Hong Kong, Jakarta*, London, Los Angeles, Mexico City*, Milan, Moscow, New York, Palo Alto, Paris, Prague*, Rome, St Petersburg, San Francisco, Shanghai, Singapore, Stockholm, Sydney, Tokyo, Washington DC

Number of lawyers 650+
at this office 18

Contact
Roland Sundqvist

CATEGORIES OF WORK

Antitrust, competition
Sascha Schaeferdiek

Construction
Lars Edlund, Roland Sundqvist

Employment and employee benefits
Mats Jansson

Financial restructuring and insolvency
Roland Sundqvist

Litigation and arbitration
Einar Wanhainen, Lars Edlund

Real estate, property
Roland Sundqvist

Media, entertainment
Mats Jansson

Tax
Anders Hedman

Banking and project finance
Alf-Peter Svensson

Corporate and commercial
Lars Wiking, Mats Jansson

Environmental
Roland Sundqvist

Intellectual property
Einar Wanhainen

Mergers and acquisitions
Lars Wiking, Anders Hedman

Securities
Alf-Peter Svensson

Telecoms
Lars Wiking

THE FIRM

Coudert Brothers was established in 1853 by French émigrés and was the first US law firm to set up an international legal practice. The firm now has more than 650 lawyers worldwide, operating as one single partnership with a common emphasis on client service of the highest quality.

The firm has extensive experience in international investment, trade and finance. Cross-border commercial transactions are a major focus, as is international arbitration and other complex dispute resolution. Coudert Brothers also provides domestic advice in countries where the firm has offices.

Coudert Brothers has offices in 30 cities in 18 countries around the world. These offices are located in the major financial and business centres of Europe, the United States and Asia Pacific region. More than 300 Coudert Brothers professionals now practice in Europe, making it the largest region in the firm's worldwide network.

The Stockholm office traces its roots to G Grönberg Advokatbyrå, a Swedish law firm that was formed in 1928, and merged with a German law firm, Schürmann & Partner, in 1998. That new firm joined Coudert Brothers in March 2000. The firm operated under the name of Coudert Brothers Schürmann & Grönberg until October 2002 when the name was changed to Coudert Brothers.

AREAS OF PRACTICE

Coudert Brothers in Stockholm serves a broad range of clients, including large multinational corporations as well as Swedish companies, in commercial litigation, general corporate law and a number of speciality areas such as antitrust and competition, mergers and acquisitions, and the TMT sector, among others.

Serving as the hub of Coudert Brothers' practice in the Scandinavian and Nordic countries, the Stockholm office has well-established ties with other eminent law firms in those countries and frequently co-ordinates matters relating to all countries in the region.

ADVOKATFIRMAN CEDERQUIST

NYBROKAJEN 15
PO BOX 1670
111 96 STOCKHOLM

Telephone: +46 8 463 65 00
Fax: +46 8 678 01 70
Website: www.cederquist.se

Languages
English, French, German

Number of lawyers 47

Contact
Ola Hansson

CATEGORIES OF WORK

Capital markets and securities
Wilhelm Lüning

Mergers and acquisitions
Olle Jansson

Banking and finance
Svante Hultqvist

Dispute resolution
Per Nordenson

Intellectual property
Per Ugge

Media and entertainment
Lennart Kanter

Corporate and commercial
Peter Wirell

Telecommunications
Per Nordenson

Information technology
Lars Perhard

Employment/labour law
Jens Tillqvist

EU and competition
Lars Johansson

Tax
Olle Stenman

Real estate
Erika Åslund

DANOWSKY & PARTNERS
ADVOKATBYRÅ

HOVSLAGARGATAN 5
PO BOX 16097
103 22 STOCKHOLM

Telephone: + 46 8 614 64 00
Fax: + 46 8 678 09 25
E-mail: lawfirm@danowsky.se
Website: www.danowsky.se

Languages
English

Number of lawyers 11

CATEGORIES OF WORK

Media and entertainment
Peter Danowsky, Ulf Isaksson

Commercial and company law
Johan Lidbeck, Mårten Lundmark

Litigation and arbitration
Peter Danowsky

Intellectual property
Peter Danowsky, Ulf Isaksson

Labour law
Mårten Lundmark

Mergers and acquisitions
Johan Lidbeck, Mårten Lundmark

Patents
Niclas Carlsson

ADVOKATFIRMAN DELPHI & CO

PO BOX 1432
111 84 STOCKHOLM

Telephone: +46 8 677 54 00
Fax: +46 8 20 18 84
E-mail: stockholm@delphilaw.com
Website: www.delphilaw.com

Languages
English, French, German, Japanese, Spanish

Number of lawyers 92
at this office 51

Other offices
Gothenburg, Linköping, Malmö

Contacts
Per Berglö,
Peter Utterström (managing partner)

CATEGORIES OF WORK

Corporate, M&A, capital markets
Per Berglöf, Örian Odenbro

Commercial law (general)
Anders Fernlund,
Carl-Fredrik Hedenström

Litigation, arbitration
Peter Skoglund, Dan Engström

EU and competition
Christer A Holm, Susanna Feinberg

Environment
Hans L Bergqvist, Leif Ramberg

Technology transfer
Bo Hjalmarsson, Per Granström

TIME (telecom, IT, media, entertainment)
Agne Lindberg, Sofia Geilert

Insolvency, bankruptcy, reconstruction
Erik Fock, Agneta Bern

Employment law
Martin Lundqvist, Anna Gustafsson

Commercial property
Cheddi Liljeström, Ulf Hårdeman

Tax
Peter Utterström, Anna Gustafsson

THE FIRM

Advokatfirman Delphi & Co is a national law firm with offices in four major business centres: Stockholm, Gothenburg, Malmö and Linköping. Delphi & Co is a full-service commercial law firm focussing in particular on banking and finance, corporate including M&A, IT and telecommunications, EU, competition law, tax and environmental law.

The firm represents foreign multinational and global corporations in their activities in Sweden, including cross-border transactions. The firm's clients include a wide range of both publicly traded and privately held Swedish, US and European corporations, as well as banks, financial institutions and corporations conducting cross-border business. Many of Delphi & Co's clients are Fortune 500 companies.

AREAS OF PRACTICE

The firm handles all types of financial transactions, such as drafting consortium agreements, loan documentation and performing due diligence processes. In its M&A work, the firm works cross-departmentally, drawing on competition, corporate finance, environment, tax and employment. Recent acquisitions handled by the firm have ranged in value from €10m to €1.5bn.

The firm has one of the largest IT practice groups in Sweden. In this area, the firm's activities include IT contracts and digital intellectual property rights, as well as e-commerce, IT outsourcing and contracts as well as telecommunications permits.

Working closely with corporations whose trade marks are well known and respected throughout the world, the firm specialises in patents, copyrights, trade marks, infringements and other issues. The firm's litigators represent enterprises in court proceedings, in arbitration and in mediation, both in Sweden and abroad. Several of its lawyers also serve as arbitrators in domestic and international arbitrations.

The firm handles on an ongoing basis notifications and filings with DG C in Brussels and the Swedish Competition Authority in Stockholm. Delphi & Co is one of the major law firms that are regularly used to review proposed new EU legislation.

ELMZELL ADVOKATBYRÅ HB, member of ius laboris

GAMLA BROGATAN 32
111 20 STOCKHOLM

Telephone: +46 8 21 16 04
Fax: +46 8 21 00 03
E-mail: advokat@elmzell.se
Website: www.elmzell.se

Languages
English, French, German

Number of lawyers 6

Contacts
Anders Elmér (anders.elmer@elmzell.se), Lars Hartzell (lars.hartzell@elmzell.se)

Member
ius laboris, International Employment Law Pensions and Employee Benefits Alliance

CATEGORIES OF WORK

- **Labour law (including traditional labour law, collective labour relations, European labour law, criminal aspects of labour law, restructuring and transfer of undertakings, work environment, expatriation, litigation, arbitration, mediation)**
- **Social security (including pensions)**

GÄRDE WESSLAU ADVOKATBYRÅ

NYBROGATAN 34
BOX 5208
102 45 STOCKHOLM

Telephone: +46 8 58 72 40 00
Fax: +46 8 58 72 40 01
E-mail: info@garde.se
Website: www.garde.se

Languages
English, French, German

Other offices
Borås, Gothenburg, Jönköping

Number of lawyers 51
at this office 25

CATEGORIES OF WORK

- **Companies, corporations**
- **Competition, antitrust**
- **Mergers and acquisitions**
- **Trade marks, intellectual property**
- **Arbitration and litigation**
- **Maritime and transportation law**
- **Insurance**
- **Insolvency law**
- **Banking, securities and finance**
- **Construction law**

GERNANDT & DANIELSSON
ADVOKATBYRÅ

HAMNGATAN 2
BOX 5747
114 87 STOCKHOLM

Telephone: +46 8 670 6600
Fax: +46 8 662 6101
E-mail: info@gda.se
Website: www.gda.se

Languages
English, French, German

Number of lawyers 52

Contact
Christer Danielsson (managing partner)

CATEGORIES OF WORK

Arbitration and litigation
Johan Gernandt, Karl-Erik Danielsson

Banking
Karl-Erik Danielsson, Dick Lundqvist

Corporate finance
Anders Wallén, Dick Lundqvist

Project finance
Stefan De Geer, Mats Hugoson

Commercial law (general)
Maths Heuman, Jonas Eklund

Companies, corporations
Anders Wallén, Maths Heuman

Mergers and acquisitions
Anders Lundin, Bob Johanson

IT and telecommunications
Stefan De Geer, Mats Hugoson

Competition and antitrust
Kenny Carlsson

Public procurement
Björn Tude

Employment law
Manfred Löfvenhaft

THE FIRM

Gernandt & Danielsson, established in 1992, is one of the leading law firms in Sweden. Many of the firm's partners had previously worked closely together for many years. Gernandt & Danielsson has been one of the fastest growing firms in recent years. The firm has doubled in size in the last five years, today employing 52 lawyers. G&D has well-established contacts with many leading firms in Europe and the US, but is not a member of any alliance or other grouping. Many of the firm's partners and senior associates have been on long term secondments to UK and US firms.

AREAS OF PRACTICE

Mergers and acquisitions: the firm advises public and private companies on all types of mergers and acquisitions, including negotiated and non-negotiated transactions, public and private sales, public offers and management buy-outs.

Banking and finance: the firm assists Swedish and international banks and financial companies in several areas, and is particularly experienced in planning and conducting large financial transactions and market flotations.

Corporate: the firm regularly handles shareholder and joint venture agreements and acts as adviser in the restructuring of companies and business groups. The firm frequently advises clients on issues concerning board responsibility, changes in capital structure, incentive programmes for employees and annual general meetings of shareholders.

Competition law/antitrust: the firm provides advice on all aspects of competition law, including merger clearances and cartel cases. The firm's competition group is headed by Kenny Carlsson who until late 1999 was head of the legal services at the Swedish Competition Authority. Jörgen Holgersson, former director general of the Competition Authority, is senior adviser to the firm, and Mats Bergman, former chief economist with the Competition Authority, is the firm's economic adviser.

Public procurement: the firm has advised and counselled authorities and suppliers in a range of matters in this area.

Litigation and arbitration: the firm assists in both international and Swedish arbitral proceedings, including under the Stockholm rules of arbitration, and in litigation proceedings. Several of the firm's lawyers are frequently appointed as arbitrators in Swedish and international arbitration matters.

Telecommunications: the firm's activities range from concessions and competition law matters to interconnect, supply, and customer agreements.

Labour law: the firm handles all matters relating to Swedish employment law.

ADVOKATFIRMAN GLIMSTEDT

BOX 16108
103 22 STOCKHOLM

Telephone: +46 8 566 119 00
Fax: +46 8 566 119 49
E-mail: stockholm@glimstedt.se
Website: www.glimstedt.se

Languages
Danish, English, French, Latvian, Lithuanian, Polish, Russian, Swedish

Other offices
Alingsås, Falun, Gothenburg, Helsingborg, Jönköping, Kalmar, Karlskoga, Lund, Nörrkoping, Örebro, Riga, Vilnius

Number of lawyers 119
at this office 13

Member
The Association of European Lawyers (AEL)

CATEGORIES OF WORK

Mergers and acquisitions
Jan Litborn, John Nordlund

Commercial property/transaction
Jan Litborn, Gunnar Tengroth

Stock exchange and corporate law
Jan Litborn, Jonas Gombrii

Banking and finance
Gunnar Tengroth, Jan Litborn

Telecommunications and IT
Mats Rydh

EU and competition law
Eva Oscarsson

Tenancy rights
Dan Sandahl

ADVOKATFIRMAN HAMMARSKIÖLD & CO AB

SKEPPSBRON 42
PO BOX 2278
103 17 STOCKHOLM

Telephone: +46 8 578 450 00
Fax: +46 8 578 450 99
E-mail: info@hammarskiold.se
Website: www.hammarskiold.se

Languages
English, French, German, Russian, Finnish

Number of lawyers 45

CATEGORIES OF WORK

Mergers and acquisitions
Peder Hammarskiöld, Jacob Melander

Banking and finance
Bengt Kärde, Per Gustaf Ekbom

Insurance and reinsurance
Erik Swartling

Intellectual property
Thomas Lindqvist, Claes Langenius

Telecommunications and computer law
Jacob Melander, Thomas Lindqvist

Marketing law
Ylva Lindquist

Litigation and arbitration
Per Sundin, Lars Ulrichs

European Community and competition law
Claes Langenius

General corporate law
Jacob Melander, Lars Ulrichs

Employment
Thomas Lindqvist

Securities and financial markets
Peder Hammarskiöld, Erik Swartling

THE FIRM

Hammarskiöld & Co is one of the leading law firms in Sweden.

Hammarskiöld & Co focuses mainly on the following areas: mergers and acquisitions, banking and finance, insurance and reinsurance, litigation and arbitration, and IT and intellectual property. The firm places special emphasis on client service and even though it has formed a number of specialist groups, the lawyers work in teams that are client centred.

Hammarskiöld & Co has extensive contacts with leading law firms around the world. However, Hammarskiöld & Co remains an independent law firm and is not a member of any alliance or network. Therefore, the firm can link its corporate clients with the very best foreign law firm in each jurisdiction for particular areas of work. All of the firm's lawyers have experience in other jurisdictions and the firm is proud of its international approach. This makes Hammarskiöld & Co a truly Swedish firm.

AREAS OF PRACTICE

Mergers and acquisitions: the firm has participated in several of the most significant M&A transactions in Sweden in recent years. The transactions have ranged from small private acquisitions to very large cross-border takeovers of listed companies.

Banking and finance: the firm represents a wide range of national and international clients, particularly within the banking and finance industries. The practice covers all of the traditional and recently developed areas of banking and finance.

Insurance and reinsurance: important areas of the firm's insurance practice include demutualising and restructuring treaties, and handling insurance and reinsurance litigation.

Intellectual property: the firm is experienced in all fields of IP law. Trade marks, patents, copyrights, licensing and franchising are just some of the areas of IP-related expertise.

Telecommunications and computer law: the firm's telecommunications and computer group can advise on all aspects of telecommunications and computer industries.

Marketing law: the firm's lawyers have substantial experience in connection with marketing guidelines and in handling consumer disputes before the Swedish Marketing Court. The marketing law group also deals with regulatory work and product liability questions.

Litigation and arbitration: the lawyers within the litigation group have vast experience in commercial litigation, national and international arbitration, and alternative dispute resolution (ADR).

European Community and competition law: the firm's competition lawyers have substantial experience in handling antitrust matters and other competition and marketing-related problems that companies face in the Swedish market.

Energy and public utilities: since the deregulation of the Swedish energy sector, this area of law has developed quickly. The firm is at the forefront of such developments.

General corporate practice: the firm advises on all aspects of general corporate law. The corporate practice includes drafting and advising on all types of commercial contracts, both international and Swedish.

Employment law: the firm advises on all aspects of Swedish employment law and provides services that range from the employment consequences of corporate acquisitions to employee terminations.

Securities and financial markets: the firm frequently advises on the Swedish legal environment relating to funds, securities and derivatives. The firm is also experienced in assisting investment firms in structuring their business and applying for the necessary licences and other approvals.

HELLSTRÖM & PARTNERS

KUNGSGATAN 33, XV
PO BOX 7305
103 90 STOCKHOLM

Telephone: +46 8 22 09 00
Fax: +46 8 20 40 90
E-mail: info@hpa.se
Website: www.hpa.se

Languages
English, Estonian, French, German, Polish

Number of lawyers 34

Contacts
Mats Hellström, Björn Ulvgården, Hans Liljeblad, Staffan Michelson, Thomas Ekenberg

CATEGORIES OF WORK

Banking and finance
Anders Lundberg, Bengt Olovsson

Commercial and contract law
Björn Ulvgården, Per Winnberg

Competition
Bengt Olovsson, Lennart Melchior

Corporate law
Björn Ulvgården, Thomas Ekenberg

Dispute resolution
Staffan Michelson, Kim Lindgren

Insolvency and restructuring
Guy Lofalk, Staffan Michelson

Technology, media and telecoms
Mats Hellström

Employment and human resources
Mats Hellström, Thomas Ekenberg

Intellectual property
Mats Hellström, Staffan Michelson

Mergers and acquisitions
Hans Liljeblad, Per Winnberg

Real estate
Lennart Melchior, Kim Lindgren

Environment
Staffan Michelson, Kim Lindgren

THE FIRM

Hellström & Partners was established in 1991 and offers a wide range of services in Swedish and international business and commercial law. Hellström & Partners represents both national and international clients and has been one of the fastest-growing law firms in recent years, with 34 lawyers and a total staff of 45.

In January 2004, Hellström & Partners merged with Michelson & Werner in Stockholm, a niche firm founded in 1921 and well reputed within the environmental, intellectual property and litigation fields. The merger with Michelson & Werner will strengthen Hellström & Partners even more, especially within insolvency, litigation, intellectual property and environmental law.

The firm's resources are carefully organised to meet its clients' requirements for quality, reliability and efficiency. Lawyers work in client-centred teams and the firm emphasises direct partner involvement and believes that a productive client-attorney relationship is often furthered by each client having contact with more than one partner. The firm has an explicit aim to be one of the best law firms in the country in each of its areas of practice. It has extensive experience in organising project groups in order to meet efficiently its clients' needs in larger transactions. At least one partner is involved in each transaction and the capacity exists for large parts of the firm to be engaged in a single transaction. The firm's working methods have proved very successful and its services are increasingly sought after.

AREAS OF PRACTICE

Hellström & Partners' practice is mainly focused on banking and finance; mergers and acquisitions; corporate and commercial law; litigation; EC law; competition law/antitrust; intellectual property law; insolvency and restructuring; employment; real estate; and environmental law. The firm's clients consist mainly of major and medium-sized Swedish and international companies, banks and financial institutions.

Hellström & Partners provides a full range of business law services through specialist lawyers organised in global networks. In this way, consistently high standards of advice and service are guaranteed for both international and local clients.

HÖKERBERG & SÖDERQVIST
ADVOKATBYRÅ KB

KUNGSGATAN 36
PO BOX 7836
103 98 STOCKHOLM

Telephone: +46 8 407 8800
Fax: +46 8 407 8801
E-mail: mail@hsa.se
Website: www.hsa.se

Languages
English, French, German,
the Scandinavian languages

Number of lawyers 17

Contact
Lars Söderqvist

CATEGORIES OF WORK

Banking, securities and finance

Bankruptcy, insolvency

Arbitration and litigation

Commercial law (general) and contract

Companies, corporations

Insurance law, tort, product liability

Mergers and acquisitions

Intellectual property

KARLERÖ & CO
ADVOKATBYRÅ HB

KUNGSGATAN 26
PO BOX 7330
103 90 STOCKHOLM

Telephone: + 46 8 20 06 10
Fax: + 46 8 20 06 04
E-mail: info@karlero.se
Website: www.karlero.se

Languages
English, German, the Scandinavian languages

Number of lawyers 10

Member
ADVOC

CATEGORIES OF WORK

Corporate and commercial
Lars-Gunnar Karlerö

Employment and benefits
Anne-Marie Thörn-Eriksson

Intellectual property
Karl Ole Möller

Corporate finance, M&A and JVs
Conny Tranberg

Life sciences
Lars-Gunnar Karlerö

Healthcare
Karl Ole Möller

Technology
Karl Ole Möller

Media and entertainment
Karl Ole Möller

Real estate and construction
Anne Liverud

Litigation and arbitration
Anders E Bengtsson

Restructuring and insolvency
Anders E Bengtsson

KILPATRICK STOCKTON ADVOKAT KB

PO BOX 5421
114 84 STOCKHOLM

Telephone: +46 8 505 646 00
Fax: +46 8 505 646 99
E-mail: info@kilpatrickstockton.com
Website: www.kilpatrickstockton.com

Languages
English, the Scandinavian languages

Other offices
Atlanta, Augusta, Charlotte, London, Raleigh, Washington DC, Winston-Salem

Number of lawyers 475
at this office 14

CATEGORIES OF WORK

Banking and finance
Pontus Kågerman

Information technology
Fredrik Ahlqvist

Corporate and commercial
Pontus Kågerman, Torbjörn Hultsberg

Construction
Thomas Rajala, Nicklas Björklund

Employment
Cecilia Herm

Environment
Johan Lindberg

Insurance
Jörgen Eklund

Intellectual property
Fredrik Ahlqvist

Dispute resolution
Jörgen Eklund

Mergers and acquisitions
Pontus Kågerman, Torbjörn Hultsberg

Private equity
Torbjörn Hultsberg, Jörgen Eklund

Real estate
Thomas Rajala, Pontus Kågerman

Tax
Nils Sköld

Media, entertainment and sport
Torbjörn Hultsberg, Fredrik Ahlqvist

KRISTRÖM ADVOKATBYRÅ AB

BIRGER JARLSGATAN 14
BOX 5717
114 87 STOCKHOLM

Telephone: +46 8 545 030 70
Fax: +46 8 545 030 80
E-mail: info@advokatbvra.com
Website: www.advokatbyra.com

Languages
English, German, French, Icelandic

Number of lawyers 12

International groupings
Cyrus Ross

CATEGORIES OF WORK

Banking and finance	Information technology
Construction	Insurance
Corporate and commercial	Intellectual property
Dispute resolution	Mergers and acquisitions
Litigation and arbitration	Media, entertainment and sport
Employment	Telecoms
Environment	White-collar crime

THE FIRM

Kriström Advokatbyrå is one of the oldest law firms still active in Stockholm. The firm was founded in the 1930s by the late lawyer Arne Kriström. The office is situated in the centre of Stockholm.

The firm has a solid domestic client base, basically corporate companies and organisations active on the Swedish market. The firm has also several international clients all over Europe, especially in the north of Europe (Denmark, Finland, Iceland and Norway), for example companies in the fields of construction, banking and finance and telecommunications. In consideration of the importance of the European Union, the firm is a member of the European law association Cyrus Ross International.

The mission for Kriström Advokatbyrå is to develop a long-term relationship with the client, to obtain and secure knowledge about the clients and their needs which make it possible to deliver legal service of high quality to the client through effective and flexible actions.

AREAS OF PRACTICE

The firm specialises in business law, especially in the areas of construction, real estate, telecommunications, employment, litigation and arbitration to corporate clients, mainly larger and smaller companies in the Swedish and the international market. However, the firm also represents private individuals. Besides these areas, the firm also provides a full-service in the fields of intellectual property, information technology and corporate and commercial law.

ADVOKATFIRMAN LINDAHL

LAW OFFICES

SERGELS TORG 12
BOX 14240
104 40 STOCKHOLM

Telephone: +46 8 670 58 00
Fax: +46 8 667 73 80
E-mail: reception.stockholm@lindahl.se
Website: www.lindahl.se

Languages
English, French, German

Other offices
Gothenburg, Helsingborg, Malmö, Örebro, Uppsala

Number of lawyers 114
at this office 55

Contact
Staffan Eklöw

CATEGORIES OF WORK

Arbitration and litigation	**Media and entertainment**
Banking and finance	**Mergers and acquisitions**
Capital markets	**Property law and environmental law**
Commercial law	**Shipping**
EC law, competition and antitrust	**Sports and major events**
Insolvency	**Trade marks and intellectual property**
IT and telecommunications	**Taxation**
Labour law	

THE FIRM

Lindahl is one of the leading Swedish law firms with approximately 110 lawyers and with offices in the main commercial centres in Sweden. Dating back to 1918, Lindahl has a longstanding tradition of business law practice. The firm advises Swedish and foreign clients in all areas of Swedish business law.

The clients include major and medium-sized Swedish and foreign companies as well as banks and other financial institutions. An increasingly important part of Lindahl's practice consists of advising other advisers, such as foreign law firms, investment banks, accounting firms and management consultants. Over the years, Lindahl has established a network of leading law firms worldwide with whom Lindahl liaises closely in order to be able to serve its clients on an international basis.

Lindahl has met the increasing demand for high-quality professional legal assistance by emphasising the need for specialisation and by organising groups within different areas of practice. At the same time, Lindahl expects all lawyers to maintain a good general knowldge of the entire legal field and to handle a wide range of work. Thereby Lindahl can offer not only a depth of expertise but also a breadth of commercial experience.

AREAS OF PRACTICE

Apart from corporate finance and IT, telecoms and new media, the practice groups include such areas as arbitration and litigation, insolvency, labour law, maritime law and taxation. Lindahl has also formed or reinforced groups in areas such as competition law, insurance, intellectual property, media and sports and major events.

LINDHS DLA NORDIC

KUNGSGATAN 9
PO BOX 7315
10390 STOCKHOLM

Telephone: +46 8 701 78 00
Fax: +46 8 701 78 99
E-mail: info@dlanordic.se
Website: www.dlanordic.com

Languages
English, French, German, Spanish, the Scandinavian languages

Other offices
Bergen, Copenhagen, Oslo and 33 offices across Europe and Asia

Number of lawyers 199
at this office 62

Contacts
Per Rönström, Ingrid Eliasson, Kent Hägglund, Gunnar Johansson

Member
DLA Group

CATEGORIES OF WORK

Corporate
Stefan Kamlin, Sven Rasmusson

TIME
Jan Råssjö, Jan Bryme

Tax
Thomas Pousette, Ronald Adolfsson

Commercial and litigation
Erika Abrahamsson, Stefan Sandén

Employment
Claes-Göran Westerberg, Sven Erfors

Construction and real estate
Henrik Wollsén, Peter Kindblom

Energy and transport
Gunnar Johansson, Arthur Csatho

Public, competition and EU law
Ola Wiklund, Peter Orander

Insolvency law
Ulf Mårtensson

THE FIRM

DLA Nordic is the only Nordic law firm, with offices in Copenhagen, Oslo, Bergen and Stockholm. The firm ranks among the leading law firms in its respective home markets in Denmark, Norway and Sweden. Each office provides a complete range of integrated legal services across borders, both in the local market and on a global basis.

DLA Nordic is part of DLA Group. DLA Group is an exclusive alliance of international full-service law firms with a shared vision. Established in 1999, DLA Group now has over 2,200 lawyers across 21 countries, who deliver expert local know-how and international solutions. DLA Group provides legal advice in 37 major cities across Europe, Singapore, Thailand, Hong Kong and the People's Republic of China.

DLA Nordic's vision is to be the leading Nordic law firm, and is based on the observation that many clients hold operations in all three countries. DLA Nordic is a modern, growing practice with distinct client service focus; legal advice is based on a proactive approach and an understanding of the client's business. The firm offers a thorough and cost-effective mode of work, knowledge and insight in the local business environment, seamless Scandinavian and international legal services, and commercially based solutions.

Providing a full service in all major practice areas, the firm is organised into eight cross-border legal departments, concerning the practice areas. The departments work together making sure that legal expertise is exchanged and shared, utilising legal resources fully and providing optimal service to the client.

Clients include public and private companies in a variety of sectors: commerce; industry; manufacturing services; property; construction; finance; IT, telecoms, media and entertainment; transport; shipping; and oil, gas and electricity. The firm also serves a large number of international clients, including large corporations, banks, investment firms and venture capital funds.

AREAS OF PRACTICE

Commercial and company law: extensive experience in company reconstruction; flotations; shareholders/partnership agreements; liquidations and incorporations; and commercial contracts.

Mergers and acquisitions: advice in each phase of mergers and acquisitions; anti-takeover strategies; public and private financing; client due diligence; and competition law.

Banking and finance: DLA Nordic regularly represents lenders, borrowers and other parties in the financial markets – both Scandinavian and international.

TIME: the firm has specialists in law related to IT, telecoms, intellectual property and media, and marketing and entertainment.

Tax: the firm has specialists in both national and international tax law.

Public competition and EU law: DLA Nordic assists in a wide range of questions concerning public law, some of its clients coming from within the municipal authorities.

Litigation: constitutes a central part of DLA Nordic's practice. The firm's integrated work method plays an important role, since litigation skills must often be combined with specialist knowledge.

Construction and property: DLA Nordic has an extensive construction and property law practice. Clients include several major real estate and construction companies in Scandinavia.

Employment: DLA Nordic has years of in-depth experience in labour and employment law and practical industry knowledge.

Oil and gas: specialising in international oil and gas law and electric legislation with experience of offshore construction and service contracts.

Maritime and shipping: DLA Nordic has experts assisting insurance companies and shipowners, regarding claims, collisions and adjustment of averages.

Insolvency: DLA Nordic gives advice on insolvency matters to creditors, as well as companies with financial problems.

LINKLATERS

REGERINGSGATAN 67
BOX 7833
103 98 STOCKHOLM

Telephone: +46 8 665 66 00
Fax: +46 8 667 68 83
Website: www.linklaters.com

Languages
All commercial and local languages in the countries where Linklaters operates

Other offices
Alicante, Amsterdam, Antwerp, Bangkok, Beijing, Berlin, Bratislava, Brussels, Bucharest, Budapest, Cologne, Frankfurt am Main, Hong Kong, Lisbon, London, Luxembourg, Madrid, Milan, Moscow, Munich, New York, Paris, Prague, Rome, São Paulo, Shanghai, Singapore, Tokyo, Warsaw

Number of lawyers 2,000 worldwide

Contact
Rolf Johansson

CATEGORIES OF WORK

M&A, corporate
Martin Börresen

Banking and finance
Lena Hasselgren

Tax
Mats Anderson

M&A, real estate
Rolf Johansson

ITC and IP
Jörgen Axelsson

EU and competition
Kent Karlsson

Employment and labour law
Anders Nordström

Litigation and arbitration
Henrik Bielenstein

THE FIRM

Linklaters advises the world's leading companies, financial institutions and governments on their most challenging transactions and assignments. With 2,000 lawyers, including 470 partners, and offices in major business and financial centres, its clients choose the firm for its distinctive combination of technical skill, commercial experience and outstanding service.

Linklaters has built a formidable global practice through organic growth and a series of mergers, joint ventures and co-operations with other respected law firms. In 2001, Linklaters merged with three of Europe's leading law firms to form Linklaters Oppenhoff & Rädler in Germany, Linklaters in Sweden, Linklaters De Bandt in Belgium and Linklaters Loesch in Luxembourg. In the same year, the firm formed a co-operation with Brazilian firm Goulart Penteado, Iervolino e Lefosse. This co-operation combines Linklaters' international capability with GPIL's extensive knowledge of the Brazilian market. In Singapore, the firm practises as Linklaters Allen & Gledhill, a joint venture with the premier Singapore practice of Allen & Gledhill, while in Italy, Linklaters has an exclusive relationship with Italian law firm Gianni, Origoni, Grippo & Partners.

MANNHEIMER SWARTLING

PO BOX 1711
111 87 STOCKHOLM

Telephone: +46 8 505 76 500
Fax: +46 8 505 76 501
Website: www.mannheimerswartling.se

Languages
English, Finnish, French, German, Polish, Russian, the Scandinavian languages

Other offices
Berlin, Brussels, Frankfurt, Gothenburg, Helsingborg, Malmö, New York, St Petersburg

Number of lawyers 330
at this office 189

CATEGORIES OF WORK

Banking and insurance
André Andersson, Helena Rempler

Constitutional and administrative law
Sven Unger

Corporate finance
Tom Hård

Construction and projects
Kaj Hobér

Corporate taxation
Brita Munck-Persson

Employment
Magnus Wallander

EU and competition
Tommy Pettersson

Environment
Per Molander

Insolvency
Biörn Riese

Insurance
Helena Rempler

Intellectual property
Karin Cederlund

Litigation and arbitration
Claes Lundblad

Maritime and transport
Sven Unger

Mergers and acquisitions
Axel Calissendorff

Private equity
Peter Alhanko

Real estate
Klas Wennström

Securities
Göran Nyström

Sport and entertainment
Johan Winnerblad

Telecoms, media and technology
Biörn Riese

SETTERWALLS

ARSENALSGATAN 6
111 47 STOCKHOLM

Telephone: +46 8 598 890 00
Fax: +46 8 598 890 90
E-mail:
first name.surname@setterwalls.se
Website: www.setterwalls.se

Languages
English, French, German, Italian, Finnish

Other offices
Gothenburg, Malmö

Number of lawyers 105
at this office 50

Member
World Law Group; Globalex

CATEGORIES OF WORK

Commercial and corporate law
Richard Akerman, Anders Månsson

IT and telecommunications law
Håkan Fohlin

Sports, media and entertainment
Owe Hjelmqvist

Pharmaceuticals and biotechnics
Maria Chambers

EU and competition law
Ulf Djurberg

Banking and finance and securities law
Åke J Fors

Real estate and construction law
Karl-Gustav Gripenvik

Labour law
Anders Lindow

Intellectual property
Owe Hjelmqvist

Mergers and acquisitions and corporate finance
Otto Rydbeck

Maritime and transportation law
Jörgen Almelöv

Aircraft financing and aviation law
Mats Waering

Tax law
Lars Samuelson

Litigation and arbitration
Claes Broman

Insolvency and restructuring
Odd Swarting

THE FIRM

Setterwalls was founded in Stockholm in 1878 and is one of Sweden's oldest law firms. Its experience and expertise extends to most areas of Swedish and international commercial law.

Setterwalls is a firm possessing significant resources with more than 100 lawyers located at offices in Stockholm, Gothenburg and Malmö working in co-operation with an international network of lawyers.

AREAS OF PRACTICE

IT and telecommunications: Provides legal services to all operators within the IT and telecom sectors such as telephone operators, Internet suppliers, e-commerce companies, manufacturers of hardware and computer software development companies. Setterwalls also regularly assists clients in other IT-related matters such as procurement of systems solutions, IT services, etc.

Sports, media and entertainment: The department offers legal services to a number of media enterprises, sports associations, event organisers, athletes and artists.

Pharmaceuticals and biotech: Provides advice to established and newly-started pharmaceuticals and biotech companies, as well as assistance in matters concerning financing, research and development, patents, licenses and royalties.

EU and competition: Provides legal assistance in matters concerning Swedish and European competition law and other matters in connection with the EU. The firm assists in connection with the filing of various notifications with the Swedish Competition Authority and the European Commission, investigation of competition law aspects in agreements and business concentrations, and assistance in connection with compliance programmes. Setterwalls also represents clients before the Court of Justice of the European Communities and the Market Court.

Banking and finance and securities: Has substantial experience in providing legal assistance in matters regarding banking and finance. Work includes matters related to initial public offerings, procurement of capital and new issues of shares, loans and other financing, as well as securities law.

Real estate and construction: Assists clients in relation to the purchase, sale and development of real estate and in the procurement of construction contracts. Expertise includes applications for building permits to financing and final leasing or sale, as well as environmental law matters related to real estate. Setterwalls has participated in some of the largest infrastructure projects in Sweden.

Labour law: Assists clients in all kinds of labour law matters.

Intellectual property: Regularly assists clients in matters relating to trade mark protection, copyright, patents and other intellectual property rights.

Mergers and acquisitions and corporate finance: Assists clients in domestic and cross-border business transactions, often in co-operation with banks and investors. Work usually comprises business transfers, investments, mergers, joint venture issues and other matters regarding corporate financing and procurement of capital.

Aircraft financing and aviation law: Provides assistance in all matters regarding the purchase, sale, leasing and other forms of financing of aircraft and railway vehicles, as well as all other legal matters related to the operation of airlines and railways.

Tax law: Offers tax law advice to Swedish and international companies, ranging from personal tax advice to cross-border business acquisitions.

Insolvency and restructuring: The group provides clients with advice concerning financial difficulties and the preventing of them. The group consists of specialist lawyers with extensive experience of restructuring and insolvency matters with local as well as international dimensions. The group also works within other areas of commercial law.

Arbitration and litigation: The litigation department represents clients in national and international litigation and arbitrations. Several lawyers are regularly appointed as arbitrators.

RYDINCARLSTEN ADVOKATBYRÅ AB

NORRMALMSTORG 14
PO BOX 1766
111 87 STOCKHOLM

Telephone: +46 8 463 39 00
Fax: +46 8 611 48 50
E-mail: info@rydincarlsten.se
Website: www.rydincarlsten.se

Languages
English, French, German, Russian

Number of lawyers 25

CATEGORIES OF WORK

Arbitration and litigation

Banking, securities, finance

Corporate and commercial law

Competition, antitrust

Contract law (international projects, sales and distribution)

Intellectual property, patent litigation

IT law

Marketing law

Mergers and acquisitions, joint ventures

Pharmaceutical law

ADVOKATFIRMAN SÖDERMARK

STRANDVÄGEN 1
PO BOX 14055
104 40 STOCKHOLM

Telephone: +46 8 670 57 50
Fax: +46 8 663 67 20
E-mail: mail@sodermark.se
Website: www.sodermark.se

Languages
English, French, German

Number of lawyers 22

CATEGORIES OF WORK

Litigation (domestic and international)
Bertil Södermark, Torgny Wetterberg

Maritime and transportation
Peter J Lindskog

General commercial law
Peter Bolmstedt
Christer Brantheim

Corporate law
Ulf Jonsson, Lars Sandberg

Real estate
Magnus Björk

Mergers and acquisitions
Lars Göthlin, Bertil Brinck

Insurance
Peter J Lindskog, Peter Haglund

Intellectual property, trade marks, copyright
Anders Beck-Friis

EU and competition
Eric Ericsson

Sports and entertainment
Mats Larsson

ADVOKATFIRMAN VINGE

SMÅLANDSGATAN 20
BOX 1703
111 87 STOCKHOLM

Telephone: +46 8 614 30 00
Fax: +46 8 614 31 90
Website: www.vinge.se

Languages
English, French, German, Italian, Russian, Spanish

Other offices
Brussels, Gothenburg, Helsingborg, Hong Kong, London, Malmö, Paris, Shanghai

Number of lawyers 262
at this office 143

Contact
Michael Wigge

Member
Scandinavian Law Alliance with Kromann Reumert (Denmark) and Thommessen (Norway); Lex Mundi

CATEGORIES OF WORK

Corporate finance
Bo Adrianzon, Stefan de Hevesy

Mergers and acquisitions
Bertil Villard, Fredrik von Baumgarten

Corporate
Hans Wibom, Christoffer Saidac

Capital markets
Johan Cederlund, Jan Lombach

EU and antitrust
Carl Wetter, Johan Karlsson

Intellectual property
Per Eric Alvsing, Stefan Widmark

IT
Karin Grauers, Björn Gustavsson

Media
Per Erik Alvsing, Stefan Widmark

Marketing
Per Erik Alvsing, Stefan Widmark

Telecoms
Carl Johan af Petersens

Litigation
Hans Bagner, Olle Flygt

Environmental
Thomas Sjöberg

Real estate
Stefan de Hevesy, Robert Wikholm

Tax
Lennart Larsson, Maria Schulzberg

Insolvency and restructuring
Leif Bæcklund, Robert Wikholm

Insurance
Peter Morawetz, Per Johan Eckerberg

Employment
Björn Lindskog, Fredrik Dahl

THE FIRM

Established through a merger between leading Swedish firms in 1983, Vinge is today one of the largest firms in Scandinavia, with some 262 lawyers in nine Swedish and overseas offices. In 1991, the firm set up the Scandinavian Law Alliance together with the Danish law firm Kromann Reumert and the Norwegian firm Thommessen. Vinge is also a member of Lex Mundi.

AREAS OF PRACTICE

Vinge has a substantial international practice, with a strategic focus on M&A and corporate finance. The firm has acted in most of the major mergers and acquisitions in Sweden in recent years, and has consistently achieved top positions on *Merger Market's* list of M&A advisers in the Nordic market. The firm regularly represents clients in connection with large international financing transactions, including project financing and structured finance arrangements. Vinge's competition law team is one of the most distinguished and experienced in the Nordic markets. A full-service firm, Vinge also advises domestic and international clients within a number of specialist areas such as employment, intellectual property, IT, media marketing, property, telecom, litigation and arbitration, insolvency, insurance, tax, and transport. In addition to four offices in Sweden, the firm has a presence in London, Paris, Brussels, Hong Kong and Shanghai.

WISTRAND

KLARABERGSVIADUKTEN 70, D:6
PO BOX 70393
107 24 STOCKHOLM

Telephone: +46 8 50 72 00 00
Fax: +46 8 50 73 00 00
E-mail: sthlm@wistrand.se
Website: www.wistrand.se

Languages
Czech, English, Finnish, French, German

Other offices
Malmö, Gothenburg

Number of lawyers 85
at this office 40

CATEGORIES OF WORK

Antitrust and EU	Intellectual property
Banking and finance	IT and telecoms
Commercial and corporate law	Labour and employment
Capital markets	Litigation and arbitration
Entertainment and sports law	Media and market law
Environmental	Mergers and acquisitions
Insolvency	Shipping and transport
Insurance	Tax law

SWITZERLAND

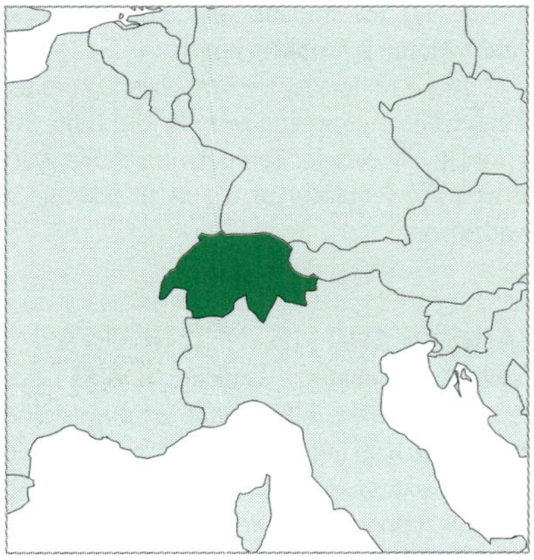

Population	7.3 million
Number of lawyers	6,200
Professional title	Rechtsanwalt: advokat fürsprech; fürsprecher; avocat; avvocato
Currency	Swiss Franc (SFr)

Index

Switzerland is bordered by France, Germany, Austria, Liechtenstein and Italy. Politically Switzerland is a European anomaly. It remains independent of the European Union, only joined the United Nations in 2002 and is not a member of Nato. Its wealth has long been predicated on an introverted approach of asset accumulation and the promotion of stability rather than territorial expansion or natural resource exploitation.

Switzerland's 7.3 million population lives in 26 autonomous cantons and is predominantly German, French and Italian speaking. Within these cantons there are four key centres.

Zurich is the commercial heart of the country. It is home to globally renowned banks such as UBS and Credit Suisse Group, as well as the headquarters for many of the largest Swiss corporate entities, including a large number of major international insurance companies. As such, it is also host to the largest number of lawyers and law firms in Switzerland.

Geneva is the commercial centre of French-speaking Switzerland. Internationally it is best known for the many international organisations that are headquartered there, but also features a large private banking industry and an impressive number of prestigious Swiss companies.

Bern is the federal and administrative capital of Switzerland. It features less prominently than either Geneva or Zurich on the international stage but is commercially important in Switzerland in its own right.

Basle is dominated by a massive chemical and pharmaceutical industry that includes many internationally renowned laboratories and companies.

Other important centres are Zug, which has attracted many foreign subsidiaries with attractive tax break policies, Lugano and Lausanne.

BILLING

Switzerland has not been immune from the price hikes that have affected all markets worldwide. Costs per hour for associates now range from €160 to €220, and for a partner anything between €250 to €350, although for larger international transactions prices exceeding €400 are apparently not unheard of. Considerable variation does exist between firms and cost-conscious clients are recommended to shop around.

MARKETING

Firms tend to limit their marketing activities to low-key activities such as publishing articles, speaking at conferences, advertising new partnership appointments in local newspapers and advertising in legal directories. This conservatism when compared to the branding activities of some other European law firms is a choice rather than obligation of Swiss firms. The Swiss Bar Association makes no provisions regarding advertising.

IN-HOUSE LAWYERS

Most of the major multinational and manufacturing companies in Switzerland field large in-house legal departments capable of handling commoditised company law matters. Although in-house lawyers can fulfil all the functions of a private practice lawyer, it is uncommon for them to appear in court or handle niche areas of law.

ECONOMIC CLIMATE

'It's not time to sell the Ferrari, you just don't take it out so often these days,' said one partner at a Zurich firm. In business terms that conservatism translates into a significantly calmer transactional environment in 2003 than that which typified the deal-heavy last four years.

Switzerland was largely isolated from the resurgence in private equity that started to affect the rest of Europe in late 2003. Likewise, its capital markets remained flat throughout the year. Cross-border mergers and acquisitions were almost non-existent, although several medium-size domestic deals did complete either independently or as part of ongoing restructurings, thus providing a steady work flow for most firms. Corporate and commercial work remains the mainstay for all law firms and ensures a steady bottom line. However, many transactional lawyers have been laid off and, with the exception of tax lawyers which are in huge demand Europe-wide, few were recruited in 2003.

LEGAL MARKET

The Swiss legal market has long been dominated by four market-leading incumbent firms: **Bär & Karrer**; **Homburger**; **Lenz & Staehelin**; and **Pestalozzi Lachenal Patry**. Their grip on the high-end market has been secured through a combination of professional excellence, strength in numbers and depth, and longstanding relationships with the

The largest firms

1	Lenz & Staehelin	130
2	Pestalozzi Lachenal Patry	108
3	Schellenberg Wittmer	95
4	Bär & Karrer	88
5	Baker & McKenzie	77
6	Python Schifferli Peter & Partners	76
7	Homburger	70
8	VISCHER	68
9	Niederer Kraft & Frey	65
10	KPMG Legal	60
11	EY Law AG	56
12	Walder Wyss & Partners	54
13	Wenger Plattner	50
14	Froriep Renggli	40
15	Meyer Lustenberger	38
16	Prager Dreifuss	37
17	Wenger Vieli Belser	35
18	CMS von Erlach Klainguti Stettler Wille	32
19	Staiger, Schwald & Partners	30
20	Borel & Barbey	28
21	Bratschi Emch & Partner	27
	Poncet Turrettini Amaudruz Neyroud & Partners	27
23	Suter & Partners Attorneys at Law	24
24	Badertscher Dörig Poledna	22
	De Pfyffer & Partners	22
	Novagraaf International SA	22
	RWB Avocats	22

These figures represent the total number of lawyers in this country only, and have been supplied by the firms themselves. The figures should be accurate as at 1 January 2004.

giants of Swiss business. These firms have also been the most obvious choices for foreign firms seeking Swiss counsel.

Although these firms remain undisputed leaders, their premiership standing is no longer exclusive. For the first time they are joined by one other law firm: **Baker & McKenzie**. Clients, lawyers and commentators all agree that the Zurich office of this international firm is without doubt of the highest calibre. In 2003, this was evidenced with successive involvement in some of the most interesting and complex deals in Switzerland to date. In no small part, it is also due to the fabulous reputation of managing partner and corporate guru Urs Schenker, a lawyer whose name was on everyone's lips in 2003, and the overall strength of the Geneva office.

While the integrity of the top tier remains safe for the meantime, its future is in no way assured. In the second tier of our corporate and commercial tables are a handful of highly dynamic, young and aggressive firms snapping at the heels of the incumbents. **Froriep Renggli**, **Schellenberg Wittmer**, **VISCHER**, **Walder Wyss & Partners**, **Wenger Vieli Belser** in Zurich, and **Bär & Karrer**, **Borel & Barbey**, **Gillioz Dorsaz & Associés** and **Tavernier Tschanz** in Geneva, have all won involvement in many of the deals that would have traditionally fallen to the top-tier firms, as well as instructions from large and medium-size UK and international law firms.

Clients preferring niche advice to one-stop-shop service are also well catered for in Switzerland. *The European Legal 500* recommends in the top tier **Wenger Plattner** for insolvency and restructuring; **Schumacher Baur Hürlimann** for real estate and construction; **ThomannFischer** for intellectual property; **Wiederkehr Forster** for TMT; **Benz Attorneys** for shipping and transport; and **Winston & Strawn LLP** for international dispute resolution.

FOREIGN OFFICES

London is the most popular locale for Swiss firms. **Bär & Karrer**, **Secretan Troyanov** and **Froriep Renggli** all have offices there, mainly for liaison purposes with large FTSE-listed Swiss companies. Reflecting the growing importance of the EU in Swiss affairs, **Pestalozzi Lachenal Patry** and **Python Schifferli Peter & Partners** have representative offices in Brussels. Further afield, **Wenger Vieli Belser** has an office in Beijing; **Python Schifferli Peter & Partners** in Tokyo; **Secretan Troyanov** in Moscow; **Froriep Renggli** in Madrid, also serving Latin America; **Umbricht Rechtsanwälte** in Johannesburg; and **Gloor & Sieger** in San José, Costa Rica.

FOREIGN FIRMS

There are no prohibitions on foreign law firms setting up advisory practices anywhere in Switzerland, but non-Swiss-trained lawyers may not represent their clients in court. Few international firms have taken advantage of this fact, preferring instead to focus on consolidating their expansion in more high-profile European cities and establishing informal referral relationships with Swiss firms.

Exceptions are US-based firms **Baker & McKenzie** in Zurich and Geneva, **Winston & Strawn LLP** which uses Geneva as the administrative centre of its international dispute settlement practice, and niche insurance specialists **Sedgwick, Detert, Moran & Arnold** in Zurich.

Under a bilateral agreement covering professional services between Switzerland and the EU, it is relatively easy for European-trained lawyers to pass the requisite Bar exams to practise in Switzerland.

BANKING AND FINANCE: GENEVA

Lenz & Staehelin's banking and finance department offers a full range of private and commercial banking services to clients including Deutsche Bank, JP MorganChase, Credit Suisse and UBS, supported by a very high-profile Zurich office. Recommended by clients and competitors alike are Jean-Paul Aeschimann and Shelby R du Pasquier.

Baker & McKenzie has worked with major international banks on finance transactions in the real estate and hotel industry in 2003, as well as maintaining its leading role in the area of public sector financing, project finance and commodity trade finance. Managing partner Martin Anderson is very well known in Geneva for his work on derivatives and acquisition finance-related matters.

Froriep Renggli is acting for the Cantonal Bank of Geneva in an ongoing €1.92bn case against Big Four accountant Ernst & Young. The firm advises from Geneva and Zurich on all aspects of banking and finance, including private equity and asset finance.

Pestalozzi Lachenal Patry's Jean Patry and Bernard Lachenal are both eminent personalities in Swiss banking circles. Banking specialist Charles-Jean Roguet is also well known. The firm advises a large number of major financial institutions and consortiums involved in major transactions.

Poncet Turrettini Amaudruz Neyroud & Partners partners Carla Lombardini, Philippe Neyroud and Michael Amaudruz have been recommended for banking and finance advice, as well as corporate advice to financial institutions, including on mergers and money laundering.

Schellenberg Wittmer banking specialists Lionel Aeschlimann and Bernard Haissley advise on all aspects of private banking as well as corporate finance, private equity and fund management.

Tavernier Tschanz eponymous partner Edmond Tavernier is a very highly regarded banking and finance expert advising several major banks and sitting on the board of others. The firm regularly advises on all aspects of licensing,

BANKING AND FINANCE: GENEVA

LENZ & STAEHELIN ✪

Baker & McKenzie ✪
Froriep Renggli ✪
Pestalozzi Lachenal Patry ✪
Poncet Turrettini Amaudruz Neyroud & Partners
Schellenberg Wittmer ✪
Tavernier Tschanz

ALTENBURGER
Bär & Karrer
Borel & Barbey ✪
Gillioz Dorsaz & Associés ✪
Lalive & Partners
Python Schifferli Peter & Partners ✪

Firms are listed A-Z in tiers which are ranked in order of priority
✪ *Indicates firm displays contact details at the end of this chapter.*

regulations, and matters before the federal banking commission, as well as providing advice to banks on compliance with risk management structuring and to investment funds.

ALTENBURGER is a Zurich firm with a large public and private banking client base. The firm's Geneva office opened in 2003 headed by Massimo Calderan.

Bär & Karrer has had some success breaking into the Geneva banking and finance market based on its established relationship with several major Zurich-based financial institutions.

Borel & Barbey works on the establishment and day-to-day operations of sector specific funds, banking regulations and other aspects of banking law, including contentious matters. Clients include international and Swiss banks. Oliver Dunnant and US-qualified Nicolas Killen are the best-known individuals.

Gillioz Dorsaz & Associés partners Christian Vallentini and Pierre Gillioz work with Swiss and foreign bank subsidiaries on aspects of day-to-day and regulatory matters, as well as bond issues and finance structuring. Also recommended to investment funds and borrowers.

Lalive & Partners handles compliance, debt collection, money laundering and financial crime, while **Python Schifferli Peter & Partners**' Geneva offices count several prominent banks among its clients. The firm is best known for its work with private banks and asset managers.

BANKING AND FINANCE: ZÜRICH

Bär & Karrer's banking and finance practice headed by Eric Stupp was involved in several highly contentious cases over non-performing portfolios in 2003, as well as advising longstanding clients on regulatory matters and outsourcing projects. The firm also increased its experience of convertible bonds work in 2003. Clients include foreign and domestic banks such as UBS and the Goldman Sachs-affiliated Sachs Bank.

Homburger is a key partner to many of the largest and most active banks in Switzerland. The firm's work on all kinds of finance and day-to-day banking operations has been widely recommended, with Peter Widmer, Daniel Daeniker and René Bösch highlighted as 'particularly capable' individuals. In 2003, the firm notably advised major client Zurich Financial Services on the sale of its private banking arm Rüed, Blass & Cie AG Bankgeschäft to Deutsche Bank (Switzerland) Ltd.

Lenz & Staehelin is particularly active in structured finance work as well as leasing transactions. In French-speaking Switzerland, the firm is considered pre-eminent. Longstanding clients include Deutsche Bank, JP MorganChase, Credit Suisse and UBS. In 2003, it also worked with RBS and HSBC on the Swiss aspects of their acquisition finance and derivatives businesses, and continued to advise on the ongoing negotiations concerning the bankrupted Swissair's credit facility. Stefan Breitenstein has been recommended for hedge fund structuring. A respected team which includes Patrick Hunerweld and Matthias Oertle, who are both well-known banking and finance experts, pushes the firm up a tier this year.

Niederer Kraft & Frey partner Andreas Casutt has been highly recommended for his work in this sector. Other extremely prominent figures at the firm include regulatory specialist and academic Peter Forstmoser, as well as François M Bianchi and Urs Pulver. In 2003, the firm worked on various asset management, corporate finance and lending activities. Clients include RBS.

Baker & McKenzie's finance work in 2003 included advice to WTF Holdings and Lehman Brothers on a commercial mortgage-backed securitisation project. The firm also advised Von Roll on a debt-to-equity swap and Züblin on a convertible bond issue. Urs Schenker is the most prominent partner at the firm for banking as well as corporate advice. Martin Furrer and Marcel Giger are joint heads of banking and finance, and together have forged a growing reputation for the practice in this area.

Pestalozzi Lachenal Patry handles day-to-day banking matters for household names including Royal Bank of Canada and JP MorganChase. In 2003, it was particularly involved on structuring finance products such as equity-linked derivatives with Credit Suisse. It also advised Credit Suisse in connection with two private placements of foreign fund notes aggregating over €900m, and represented an international banking consortium in connection with a large Swiss investment group in financial distress. Banking head Gerard Niggli is highly regarded as is Robert Furter. Silvan Hutter has also been recommended in this area.

VISCHER counts several major Swiss and foreign lenders among its clients, as well as private banks in Basle where the firm has a large office. Felix Häusler is well known for his work on sale and leaseback transactions and structured finance for major public infrastructure. Markus Guggenbühl also has significant banking experience.

Walder Wyss & Partners' banking team, led by Markus Kroll and benefiting from the tax expertise of former KPMG partner Martin Busenhardt and recommended partner Enrico Friz, is going from strength to strength. In 2003, the firm continued its work on structured finance and alternative risk transfer structures. It also advised on some notably complex matters, including the set-up and structuring of Allianz Suisse's personal financial services line, acting as Swiss counsel in the €208m refinancing of Swiss Life's loan facility and as Swiss transaction counsel in a $2.4bn fully-funded synthetic CLO referenced to a portfolio of residential mortgage loans held by Credit Suisse.

Bratschi Emch & Partner has advised public and private clients on basic financial matters including money laundering, taxation, misguided investments and international judicial assistance. Urs Emch is known for banking advice.

CMS von Erlach Klainguti Stettler Wille worked on several transactions and regulatory matters involving local subsidiaries of foreign

BANKING AND FINANCE: ZURICH

BÄR & KARRER ✪
HOMBURGER ✪
LENZ & STAEHELIN ✪
NIEDERER KRAFT & FREY ✪

Baker & McKenzie ✪
Pestalozzi Lachenal Patry ✪
VISCHER ✪
Walder Wyss & Partners ✪

Bratschi Emch & Partner ✪
CMS von Erlach Klainguti Stettler Wille ✪
De Capitani Kronauer Buis ✪
Froriep Renggli ✪
Henrici, Wicki & Guggisberg ✪
Schellenberg Wittmer ✪
Staiger, Schwald & Partners ✪
Wenger Vieli Belser ✪

ALTENBURGER
Hess Dallafior Attorneys at Law ✪
Meyer Lustenberger ✪
Nobel & Hug
Rinderknecht Klein & Stadelhofer ✪
Suter & Partners Attorneys at Law
Umbricht Rechtsanwälte ✪
von Meiss Blum & Partners ✪
Wenger Plattner ✪

Firms are listed A-Z in tiers which are ranked in order of priority
✪ *Indicates firm displays contact details at the end of this chapter.*

banks and domestic banks in 2003. The firm also has a small private banking practice. Name partner Ernest Klainguti and Kaspar E Landholt are both experienced practitioners.

De Capitani Kronauer Buis is best known for its advice to banks on commercial, employment, contentious and regulatory matters.

Froriep Renggli has advised big names including BNP Paribas, Citibank, Bank of Tokyo-Mitsubishi and UBS on asset finance and securitisation and general banking matters. In 2003, the firm was particularly active restructuring financial products for the real estate market.

Henrici, Wicki & Guggisberg advises banks and bank officers on regulatory issues and is experienced before the Swiss Federal Banking Commission. In 2003, Jürg Guggisberg was co-counsel in a mortgage securitisation transaction.

Schellenberg Wittmer continues to advise major banks on financial instruments including credit-linked notes, derivatives, investment funds, syndicated loans and bond issues for both private and public investors. Martin Lanz and Philippe Borens are the best-known individuals for advice to banks.

Staiger, Schwald & Partners represents some non-Swiss banks as well as private financial institutions. The firm has advised on structured finance and leasing transactions.

Wenger Vieli Belser partner Peter Altorfer advises banks and asset managers on various contentious and non-contentious matters including regulatory and funds work.

ALTENBURGER has clients in most of the major financial services sectors which it advises on a raft of operational and regulatory matters. In 2003, the firm opened an office in Geneva headed by Massimo Calderan to further serve its French-speaking client base in the banking sector.

Hess Dallafior Attorneys at Law partner Markus Hess advises on leasing transactions and compliance issues. He is very experienced in money laundering matters. Werner Schubinger handles investment fund structuring.

Nobel & Hug has some financial clients which it advises on day-to-day operations and regulatory matters. The firm opened in Zug in 2003.

Rinderknecht Klein & Stadelhofer is corporate counsel to several Swiss and international banks, while **Suter & Partners Attorneys at Law** handles some funds registration work and corporate finance matters.

Umbricht Rechtsanwälte concluded a multi-million dollar transaction for the foreign client of a large Swiss bank in 2003. Partner Gerhard Umbricht also advises foreign banks involved in real estate finance.

von Meiss Blum & Partners is best known for its work with private banks and individuals.

Wenger Plattner has a banking and finance practice with experience of bank contracts, securities law and compliance matters. It has advised investment funds on regulatory matters.

CAPITAL MARKETS

Bär & Karrer's banking, finance and capital markets practice is highly recommended for all aspects of public tender offers. In 2003, the firm notably advised Cablecom on the recapitalisation, debt-to-equity swap and purchase of a majority stake in NTL. The firm counts several well-known names in the capital markets arena in its partnership, including Christian Steinmann, Peter Kienast, Rolf Watter, Eric Stupp, Urs Bertschinger and Urs Brügger.

Homburger advised major client Zurich Financial Services on its 2003 €2.37bn share offering. Corporate partners Heinz Schärer, Claude Lambert and Hansjürg Appenzeller all have 'undoubted capital markets experience'.

Niederer Kraft & Frey's Hans Niederer is recommended for bonds work, and corporate partner François M Bianchi for derivatives and stock options.

Baker & McKenzie's Geneva managing partner Martin Anderson has extensive professional and academic knowledge and experience of the SWX. In 2003, he advised 4M Holdings on its restructuring and recapitalisation. The firm also advised REWE on aspects of the public tender offer for Bon Appétit, and continued its work with a host of private equity and investment funds seeking advice on derivative and equity-linked products.

Lenz & Staehelin's Patrick Scleiffer completed a convertible bond issue as part of the firm's work on the Centrepulse Orthopaedics deal in 2003. The firm regularly advises on aspects of the derivatives and funds business, as well as regulatory matters and corporate governance.

Pestalozzi Lachenal Patry's banking and financial services group also handles capital markets matters. In 2003, the firm was largely preoccupied with straight banking matters. It advised Credit Suisse on the issue of structured equity-linked derivatives. Robert Furter and Gerard Niggli have both advised on a whole gamut of transactions involving public listed companies, including IPOs.

Staiger, Schwald & Partners is recommended to publicly listed companies for all aspects of advice including capital increases. The firm has particular experience of share repurchases.

VISCHER has ongoing involvement advising boards on the restructuring of their public companies, an area mostly covered by Markus Guggenbühl. In 2003, the firm also advised Private Equity Holding AG on the refinancing of multi-million euro outstanding loans, and the Basle office advised a consortium of foreign banks on an infrastructure financing in the Canton of Zurich. The firm is well positioned for any future capital markets rebound with 'excellent experience of global and domestic bond offerings and IPOs'.

Walder Wyss & Partners partner Enrico Friz has capital markets experience with the London offices of several major Swiss and international banks and has succeeded in building a strong reputation.

CAPITAL MARKETS

BÄR & KARRER ✪
HOMBURGER ✪
NIEDERER KRAFT & FREY ✪

Baker & McKenzie ✪
Lenz & Staehelin ✪
Pestalozzi Lachenal Patry ✪
Staiger, Schwald & Partners ✪
VISCHER ✪
Walder Wyss & Partners ✪

CMS von Erlach Klainguti Stettler Wille ✪
Froriep Renggli ✪
Henrici, Wicki & Guggisberg ✪
Hess Dallafior Attorneys at Law ✪
Meyer Lustenberger ✪
Python Schifferli Peter & Partners ✪
Schellenberg Wittmer ✪
Tavernier Tschanz

Firms are listed A-Z in tiers which are ranked in order of priority
✪ *Indicates firm displays contact details at the end of this chapter.*

CMS von Erlach Klainguti Stettler Wille's banking and finance practice has advised GE on ongoing bond issues.

Froriep Renggli has capital markets, private equity and securities experience.

Henrici, Wicki & Guggisberg has advised on the acquisition and corporate restructuring of publicly traded investment companies.

Hess Dallafior Attorneys at Law partner Werner Schubinger has some capital markets experience. Jürg Guggisberg has significant transactional experience, while **Meyer Lustenberger** partners Thomas Lustenburger and Christoph Heiz have been recommended for capital markets work.

Python Schifferli Peter & Partners acts for several public companies in the west of Switzerland. Notably, the firm has an office in Tokyo.

Schellenberg Wittmer's Zurich office handles SWX matters and provides advice to some financial institutions, while **Tavernier Tschanz** name partner Edmond Tavernier provides business-oriented advice on all aspects of public and private corporate matters.

CORPORATE AND COMMERCIAL: BASLE

VISCHER's premiership standing and dominant size in Basle is reflected in its commendable cross-section of specialist expertise in that office. For advice to the biotech and pharmaceutical industries, Matthias Staehelin has been particularly recommended. In 2003, Sebastian Burckhardt and David Jenny also advised on two major transactions in the chemical and biotech fields. The firm maintains teams of capital markets, banking and finance lawyers in both Basle and Zurich. It

CORPORATE AND COMMERCIAL: BASLE

VISCHER ✪
WENGER PLATTNER ✪

Böckli Bodmer & Partner
Christen Rickli Partner
Dürr + Partner/SwissLegal ✪
Mathys Schmid Partner ✪
ThomannFischer ✪

Eulau Kaufmann Giavarini & Recher
Holliger, Simonius & Partners ✪
Joerin Hopf
Lenz · Caemmerer · Bender

Firms are listed A-Z in tiers which are ranked in order of priority
✪ *Indicates firm displays contact details at the end of this chapter.*

also has a large tax practice and Christoph Löw has been recommended for real estate work with construction companies. The firm counts a clutch of multinationals among its clients.

Wenger Plattner fields its largest and strongest office in Basle with 20 lawyers and extensive experience advising on cross-border aspects of corporate and commercial matters. The firm also works with various domestic SMEs. It is best known for the life sciences and biotech law advice of Gerhard Schmid and Alexander Gutmans. It counts several global pharmaceutical, chemical and healthcare companies among its client base. Peter Mosimann has also been recommended for intellectual property and media law advice.

Böckli Bodmer & Partner is a six-partner firm offering experience and expertise in all aspects of corporate and commercial law, as well as corporate finance, capital markets, litigation and arbitration and tax. Name partner Peter Böckli is the best-known individual at the firm.

Christen Rickli Partner handles corporate, commercial, real estate and dispute resolution instructions for a large number of Basle-based companies.

Dürr + Partner/SwissLegal focuses on construction, notary services, transport, banking and finance. The firm also has an office in Zug that handles tax and employment matters for multinational corporations.

Mathys Schmid Partner acts mainly for small and medium-size local Basle companies including some with cross-border and finance issues. It counts pharmaceutical, transport and cosmetic companies among its clients. Name partner Peter Mathys was involved in aspects of the Swissair insolvency and restructuring.

ThomannFischer is best known for the established intellectual property practice of Felix H Thomann which advises domestic and multinational clients in the Basle region and is highly rated. The firm also handles corporate and commercial transactions including M&A and tax structuring.

Eulau Kaufmann Giavarini & Recher advises several banks, insurance and pharmaceutical companies on their operations in Basle and Switzerland. It has an established real estate practice.

Holliger, Simonius & Partners, **Joerin Hopf** and **Lenz · Caemmerer · Bender** offer full-service corporate and commercial advice, including tax and dispute resolution, to domestic and international clients.

CORPORATE AND COMMERCIAL: GENEVA

Lenz & Staehelin's Geneva office is led by highly respected corporate and commercial partner Andreas von Planta. The office has extensive experience of both working on national transactions with the firm's offices elsewhere and of representing a large and longstanding client base in western Switzerland. It counts various major banks and financial institutions, pharmaceutical companies and industrial players among its clients.

Python Schifferli Peter & Partners is the firm with far and away the greatest capacity to serve the needs of French-speaking clients in western Switzerland. The 25-partner firm headquartered in Geneva has branch offices in Lausanne, Bern, Lausanne-Polly and Brussels, as well as an active office in Tokyo. Broadly experienced in all aspects of company and commercial law with public and private companies of all sizes, it offers partners specialising in intellectual property, tax, dispute resolution, banking and finance. The firm also has a very well-regarded private banking practice.

Schellenberg Wittmer's Geneva office is larger than that in Zurich, a fact reflected in a slightly higher profile in this city. Corporate and commercial lawyers Roy Ryan, Bernard Vischer and Lionel Aeschlimann, aided by several specialists in corporate support practice areas, have won the firm an outstanding reputation. Notably in 2003, it acted as the Swiss counsel to the joint global co-ordinators of the €2.36bn capital increase of Zurich Financial Services Group, as well as working more locally on various cross-border private equity and corporate transactions and local mergers and acquisitions.

Baker & McKenzie expanded and consolidated its presence in Geneva with the addition of seven new lawyers in 2002 and 2003. The office is active in all aspects of corporate and commercial, tax, finance, litigation and real estate law. In 2003, it advised on the restructuring of 4M Technologies, a major real estate financing and various acquisitions. Managing partner Martin Anderson is well known in Geneva, as is Denis Berdoz.

Bär & Karrer's Geneva branch office worked on numerous major corporate and commercial transactions in 2003 including tender offers, debt-equity swaps and acquisitions. It benefits from having been organically grown within the firm rather than merging into it. The firm represented Centrepulse Orthopaedics throughout its contested takeover.

CORPORATE AND COMMERCIAL: GENEVA

LENZ & STAEHELIN ✪
PYTHON SCHIFFERLI PETER & PARTNERS ✪
SCHELLENBERG WITTMER ✪

Baker & McKenzie ✪
Bär & Karrer
Borel & Barbey ✪
Froriep Renggli ✪
Gillioz Dorsaz & Associés ✪
Pestalozzi Lachenal Patry ✪
Tavernier Tschanz

Lalive & Partners
Poncet Turrettini Amaudruz Neyroud & Partners
Secretan Troyanov

Firms are listed A-Z in tiers which are ranked in order of priority
✪ *Indicates firm displays contact details at the end of this chapter.*

Borel & Barbey is a Geneva-based firm with a large and longstanding corporate client base as well as several prestigious private clients. In 2003, aside from regular corporate advice, the firm advised on a number of smaller M&A deals, including some with US aspects, as well as deals in the biotech, industrial, pharmaceutical and financial sectors. Nicholas Killon, Luc Hafner and Nicholas Pierard are recommended for corporate advice.

Froriep Renggli in Geneva and Zurich advised on major transactions including divestments and acquisitions, as well as litigation in 2003. The Geneva office is headed by Jean-Luc Herbez.

Gillioz Dorsaz & Associés maintains an excellent reputation in Geneva and internationally. Corporate and commercial lawyers Pierre Gillioz and Christian Valentini are supported by commercial litigation and arbitration specialist Bernard Doser and a recently acquired tax practice. The firm counts several Swiss, European and multinational companies among its clients.

Pestalozzi Lachenal Patry continues to work with many of the largest commercial and financial institutions in the Geneva canton. In 2003, it gained involvement in some of the most interesting restructurings to take place including that of the Cantonal Bank of Geneva.

Tavernier Tschanz's 18-lawyer single office specialises in advice to foreign and multinational clients, a service for which it has been very highly recommended. The firm offers partner-led specialisation in dispute resolution, finance and competition. Banking and corporate specialist Edmond Tavernier and well-known arbitrator Pierre Yves Tschanz are both highly recommended, as are Jacques Bonvin for biotech and hi-tech work and Silvio Venturi for competition.

Lalive & Partners is active on international and domestic transactions as well as being counsel to many Geneva-based companies. It has been recommended for its trade law expertise.

Poncet Turrettini Amaudruz Neyroud & Partners is recommended for mid-size corporate work and banking, finance, litigation and arbitration advice.

Secretan Troyanov is a referral favourite of many Zurich firms without their own Geneva offices. The firm also has offices in London and Moscow.

CORPORATE AND COMMERCIAL: ZURICH

Baker & McKenzie moves up to the first tier this year in recognition of the leading work of the corporate practice, especially that of widely admired partner Urs Schenker, practice head Kilian Perroulaz and Martin Frey. In 2003, the firm advised on a number of headline transactions including the restructurings of Alscom and Von Roll. It remains popular among corporate clients as one of the few firms offering 'genuine strength and depth' across all practice areas supported by a strong Geneva office and the ubiquitous **Baker & McKenzie** international network.

Bär & Karrer stands out for its consistent involvement with the movers and shakers of Swiss business. The corporate and commercial practice, led by highly regarded partner Felix Ehrat was predominantly involved in major M&A transactions in 2003. Notably the firm advised Centrepulse throughout its contested takeover. With offices in London, Zug, Lugano and Geneva, the firm also counts a large proportion of Swiss corporate heavy hitters and large and medium-size companies among its client base.

Homburger's established relationship as corporate counsel to many of the largest and most prestigious companies in Switzerland ensures it remains at the forefront of corporate deal making. Fielding 72 lawyers across the board with top-tier rankings in almost all practice areas, instructions from major-league clients including Roche, Nestlé, Siemens and others is unsurprising. Recommended corporate heads Daniel Daeniker and Heinz Schärer lead the recently expanded corporate practice.

Lenz & Staehelin's selection as adviser to Incentive Capital on the Centrepulse deal (work led by Rudolf Tschani) proved that the largest firm in Switzerland also remains among the best. In 2003, Patrick Hunerwadle and Christof Reinhardt continued to build on the firm's recognised strength in advising financiers on the deal structure for leasing transactions, notably advising on aspects of the $400m Zurich Airport car park sale and leaseback project. The firm retains its large domestic and international client base and is first choice for many foreign firms with referrals, on account of its size and resources.

Niederer Kraft & Frey is a strong corporate and commercial-based firm. It counts several well-known practitioners among its partnership, including Peter Isler and Gaudenz Zindel who act as corporate counsel to several household names in Switzerland.

Pestalozzi Lachenal Patry in 2003 advised Zimmer on its successful €2.65bn bid for Centerpulse Orthopedics – the second-ever counterbid to a public offer in Swiss history and far and away one of the most talked about and innovative transactions of the last 12 months or more. The work was led by corporate stars Jacob Herme and Christian Rouse. The firm retains its impressive Swiss, European, Japanese and American client base of top-ranking enterprises in sectors such as pharmaceuticals, automotive products, tobacco and publishing. Corporate partner and founding director of *Lex Mundi* Hans Bolman has been particularly recommended.

CMS von Erlach Klainguti Stettler Wille acts for a fairly equal proportion of foreign and domestic clients. It advises on issues ranging from day-to-day matters to complex restructuring, acquisition and divestment transactions. The firm is notable for its membership of the international *CMS* network: it provides the firm with a superior European connection that goes beyond mere branding. Hans Wille is head of the corporate and commercial practice. Rudolf von Erlach has been recommended for his work with multinational clients.

Froriep Renggli is recommended for all corporate and commercial matters. The firm has quantifiable strength across the full range of practice areas, as well as significant experience working as Swiss counsel on some of the largest international transactions in recent years. In 2003, the firm handled Swiss law aspects of several major M&A transactions and continued to work with its longstanding clients including airlines, hotel companies, financial institutions and manufacturers.

Schellenberg Wittmer in late 2002 acted as joint global coordinators for Zurich Financial Services Group on its €2.36bn capital increase, the largest such transaction in Swiss corporate history. The firm has extensive experience advising on all aspects of corporate and commercial law as well as private equity, corporate governance and contentious matters.

VISCHER's portfolio includes work on various multi-million euro corporate and private equity deals for clients in an impressively diverse cross-section of industries including energy, healthcare, real estate, and financial institutions. At the firm's Basle office, partners Matthias Staehelin, David Liene and Ernst Staehelin have gained particular reputations among pharmaceutical and biotech clients.

Walder Wyss & Partners' corporate practice really came of age in 2003, advising a party to the Centrepulse Orthopaedics hostile takeover. On the non-transactional side, the firm acts for a large and impressive number of companies, handling full corporate and commercial services for many of them. The firm's investment in its tax practice has paid off with positive comments from many clients.

CORPORATE AND COMMERCIAL: ZURICH

BAKER & McKENZIE ✪
BÄR & KARRER ✪
HOMBURGER ✪
LENZ & STAEHELIN ✪
NIEDERER KRAFT & FREY ✪
PESTALOZZI LACHENAL PATRY ✪

CMS von Erlach Klainguti Stettler Wille ✪
Froriep Renggli ✪
Schellenberg Wittmer ✪
VISCHER ✪
Walder Wyss & Partners ✪
Wenger Vieli Belser ✪

Badertscher Dörig Poledna ✪
Bratschi Emch & Partner ✪
Meyer Lustenberger ✪
Nobel & Hug
Prager Dreifuss
Staiger, Schwald & Partners ✪
Wenger Plattner ✪

Bill, Isenegger & Ackermann ✪
Henrici, Wicki & Guggisberg ✪
Hess Dallafior Attorneys at Law ✪
Rinderknecht Klein & Stadelhofer ✪
Suter & Partners Attorneys at Law
Umbricht Rechtsanwälte ✪

ALTENBURGER
Blatterpartners
Bürgi Nägeli ✪
Choquard Attorneys
Haymann & Baldi ✪
Rohner Rechtsanwälte ✪
Sedgwick, Detert, Moran & Arnold
Thouvenin Rechtsanwälte ✪
von Meiss Blum & Partners ✪

Firms are listed A-Z in tiers which are ranked in order of priority
✪ Indicates firm displays contact details at the end of this chapter.

Wenger Vieli Belser's large corporate and commercial client base includes multinational corporations and several listed companies. Christoph Schmidt heads the practice and also handles M&A and restructuring matters. The firm has placed particular emphasis on media matters. Notably among Swiss firms, it has an office in Beijing, headed by corporate partner, generalist, media law expert and Asia hand Paul Thaler.

Badertscher Dörig Poledna has been recommended for corporate, restructuring, privatisation, insurance, engineering, energy, TMT and leasing work. It has offices in Zurich and Lugano.

Bratschi Emch & Partner, with large offices in Bern and Zurich, is known for its corporate and commercial work with domestic and international clients, but also for a large amount of public law expertise, debt enforcement and bankruptcy. In 2003, the firm advised on several large transactions in the pharmaceutical sector, on private contracting projects of the Swiss Federal Railway and other governmental bodies, and other matters in the hi-tech, services and financial sectors.

Nobel & Hug is a small firm with a long-standing corporate and commercial and capital markets focus. Widely experienced in all aspects of day-to-day company operations, including joint ventures, mergers and acquisitions, litigation and finance, the firm opened an office in Zug in 2003 to further expand its client base there. Name partner Peter Nobel is known for his academic and commercial standing.

Prager Dreifuss is a 37-lawyer firm with a focus on corporate work for Swiss small and mid-cap companies. It has experience in the telecoms, entertainment and industrial sectors with both private and public companies. The firm's Bern office handles notary matters.

Staiger, Schwald & Partners' corporate practice, led by eponymous partner Hans Peter Schwald works in the main with small and mid-cap Swiss companies as well as with banks and some telecoms companies.

Wenger Plattner has established a strong and still growing practice in commercial transactions. Jürg Plattner and new partner Marc S Nater have advised a number of companies on corporate matters, including in 2003 the refinancing of a multinational technology company.

Bill, Isenegger & Ackermann is recommended for advice on corporate, commercial, restructuring and regulatory matters. Clients include domestic and international companies and institutions.

Henrici, Wicki & Guggisberg's five Zurich-based partners advise on a range of contentious and non-contentious matters. In 2003, the firm handled a number of restructurings involving public and private companies, and André Wicki advised on a nationally important board-level dispute over corporate governance.

Hess Dallafior Attorneys at Law is a young firm with a fresh approach to the practice of law. It has achieved notable prominence in the intellectual property, information technology and competition sectors, and offers general corporate and financial services advice.

Rinderknecht Klein & Stadelhofer is experienced in contentious and non-contentious cross-border corporate and corporate finance matters, as well as energy and natural resources laws and regulations.

Suter & Partners Attorneys at Law maintains a close affiliation with the PricewaterhouseCoopers legal network **Landwell**. Its main focus is on corporate and commercial work and contractual matters, including joint ventures, M&A and some financial services work. It has offices in Geneva, Bern, Lausanne and St Gallen as well as Zurich. Urs Suter is the firm's best known corporate practitioner.

Umbricht Rechtsanwälte is a 12-lawyer firm focused on providing corporate and commercial advice to small and mid-size companies and advising on public, administrative and constitutional law. The firm has an office in Johannesburg headed by Swiss lawyer Thomas Hepple.

ALTENBURGER's corporate and commercial expertise has been steadily expanding in recent years as the firm's reputation grows among public and private industrial companies, banks, insurance companies and smaller manufacturing clients. In 2003, the firm opened an office in Geneva to boost its already strong Zurich-based French-speaking capability.

Blatterpartners has offices in Zurich, Geneva, Bern and Lugano. It is recommended for advice on all aspects of domestic company and commercial law, as well as for foreign and private clients.

Bürgi Nägeli is best known for its restructuring and insolvency work. It also offers general corporate and commercial services through Zurich and Bern offices.

Choquard Attorneys' sole practitioner and California-qualified lawyer Maurice Choquard is a former in-house lawyer at a major shipping and transport company and established Swiss counsel to various foreign industrial, manufacturing, pharmaceutical and banking clients.

Haymann & Baldi's litigation practice is highly ranked. It also advises domestic, European and US clients on their day-to-day activities in Switzerland.

Rohner Rechtsanwälte is a small firm attempting to make the transition from traditional private client-based services to corporate and commercial services. It counts some industrial companies among its clients.

Sedgwick, Detert, Moran & Arnold in Zurich is an office of a US firm with a presence in London, Paris and San Francisco. Focused entirely on contentious and non-contentious insurance and reinsurance work, the firm counts a number of Swiss, French, UK and US clients among its portfolio. In 2003, office head Erik Sternberg acted for the European Reinsurance Company of Zurich in a contentious matter against Associated Electric and Gas before the Privy Council.

Thouvenin Rechtsanwälte name partners André Thouvenin and Hansjörg Stutzer both handle arbitration and corporate instructions.

von Meiss Blum & Partners is best known for its private client work. It also represents some Swiss industrial and commercial clients.

DISPUTE RESOLUTION

Bär & Karrer's substantial contentious practice has been a consistent feature of many of the largest, most complex and controversial disputes in recent years. The firm fields an excellent team, with particular notables including for arbitration Mark Blessing and Robert Karrer; for banking litigation Andreas Länzlinger; and for general litigation and disputes under sports law Michele Bernasconi.

Homburger has advised many of its prestigious corporate and financial services clients on disputes. Arbitrator Thomas Wirth and litigator Thomas Müller are the best-known practitioners alongside generalists Felix Dasser and Balz Gross. John Scriven left the firm in 2003 to go in-house at ABB.

Lenz & Staehelin is recognised nationwide as being in the dispute resolution master class. The expertise of litigators Peter Hafter and Martin Burkhardt in Zurich; Benoît Chappuis and Daniel Tunik in Geneva; and arbitrators Rudolf Tschäni in Zurich and Robert Briner, Eugène Ibig and Paolo Michele Patocchi in Geneva, is frequently highly commended.

Pestalozzi Lachenal Patry partner Pierre Karrer is a former president of the Swiss Arbitration Association and currently co-chairman of the Zurich Chamber of Commerce Arbitration Court. He is highly recommended for arbitration counselling. For litigation, Peter Straub is also well regarded. In 2003, he advised Motorola in its $4.3bn case versus several members of, and companies owned by, the

DISPUTE RESOLUTION

BÄR & KARRER ✪
HOMBURGER ✪
LENZ & STAEHELIN ✪
PESTALOZZI LACHENAL PATRY ✪
SCHELLENBERG WITTMER ✪
WINSTON & STRAWN LLP ✪

Lalive & Partners
Prager Dreifuss
Python Schifferli Peter & Partners ✪
VISCHER ✪
Wenger Plattner ✪

Baker & McKenzie ✪
CMS von Erlach Klainguti Stettler Wille ✪
Froriep Renggli ✪
Gloor & Sieger
Meyer Lustenberger ✪
Niederer Kraft & Frey ✪
Staiger, Schwald & Partners ✪
Tavernier Tschanz
Walder Wyss & Partners ✪

Böckli Bodmer & Partner
Borel & Barbey ✪
Gillioz Dorsaz & Associés ✪
Haymann & Baldi ✪
Henrici, Wicki & Guggisberg ✪
Hess Dallafior Attorneys at Law ✪

ALTENBURGER
Bratschi Emch & Partner ✪
Berger Recordon & de Saugy
Bürgi Nägeli ✪
Hartmann Müller Partners ✪
Stiffler & Nater ✪
Thouvenin Rechtsanwälte ✪
Wenger Vieli Belser ✪

Firms are listed A-Z in tiers which are ranked in order of priority
✪ *Indicates firm displays contact details at the end of this chapter.*

Turkish Uzan family. Bernard Lachenal in Geneva has also been recommended.

Schellenberg Wittmer's Gabrielle Kaufmann-Kohler sits on the ICC and American Arbitration Association panels and specialises in sports, arbitration. General arbitration counselling is provided by Georg von Segesser and Marc Ronca, litigation advice by Martin Bernt and Nathalie Voser. Corinna Klaus-Rüesch is an experienced mediator.

Winston & Strawn LLP is a major US firm that uses Geneva as the headquarters for its international arbitration practice. In 2003, the firm was involved in 12 major arbitration cases including before all the major trade and investment panels in Geneva. The office has also supervised international litigation in matters involving multi-jurisdictional product liability, M&A, antitrust and bankruptcy issues. Notably, it acted as counsel to the Eurotrain Consortium in an ICC arbitration against the Taiwan High Speed Rail Corporation, for Alstom Group in several cases, including before the Zurich Chamber of Commerce, and continued to act as international litigation co-ordinator for the Philip Morris Company in connection with product liability cases. Charles Adams is the Geneva managing partner and best-known individual alongside Marc Palay, Nicolas Ulmer and Michael Stepek.

Lalive & Partners partner Michael Schneider has been recommended for construction arbitration and Pierre Lalive for sports arbitration. The firm is also particularly involved in aspects of international trade law and dispute settlement in conjunction with several major Geneva-based international organisations.

Prager Dreifuss' dispute resolution practice includes litigators Gaudenz Domenig and André Lebrecht and of-counsel arbitrator Eric Dreifuss.

Python Schifferli Peter & Partners has a very large and experienced litigation and arbitration practice. For arbitration, Wolfgang Peter remains extremely active, advising dozens of parties to construction, commercial and financial dispute proceedings. Pierre-Yves Gunter and Dominique Henchoz are also active in arbitration. For litigation, Daniel Richard has experience of commodities and trade law cases and Thomas Legler of domain name and intellectual property litigation. Notably, Jacques Python is representing the State of Pakistan in its ongoing penal case in Geneva against its former Prime Minister, Benazir Bhutto.

VISCHER name partner Frank Vischer is well known as an arbitrator and Christoph Pestalozzi has burgeoning experience in this area. For litigation, Christian Brückber has a good reputation as does Andreas Meier.

Wenger Plattner name partner Werner Wenger acts as chairman in arbitration panels and appointed arbitrator in international and domestic proceedings under the rules of the ICC and other domestic chambers of commerce. Stephan Netzle is recommended for international sports arbitration especially before the Tribunal Arbitral de Sport. Dieter Gränicher and academic Gerhard Schmid in Basle also have arbitration experience.

Baker & McKenzie acts for multinational and domestic clients in all areas of dispute resolution. In 2003, the firm handled several arbitration proceedings concerning joint ventures and cross-border service and purchase agreements. It also acted before state courts and was involved in contentious aspects of insolvency and restructuring proceedings.

CMS von Erlach Klainguti Stettler Wille places a great deal of weight on investment in its large dispute resolution practice led by arbitrator Beat von Rechenberg and contentious specialist Damiano Brusa.

Froriep Renggli is acting for the Cantonal Bank of Geneva in its ongoing €1.92bn action against Ernst & Young. Claudia Kälin-Nauer is a well-known arbitrator closely affiliated with the Zurich Chamber of Commerce. Peter Merz handles banking litigation and Jean-Marie Vulliemin all aspects of international arbitration and litigation.

Gloor & Sieger partner Daniel Wehrli is a member of the Swiss Arbitration Association and has handled domestic and international proceedings. Beat Gino Keonig also has arbitration experience.

Niederer Kraft & Frey includes academic and arbitration expert Peter Forstmoser among its partners. The firm also advises on matters before Swiss courts, including sectoral tribunals.

Staiger, Schwald & Partners is experienced in banking and intellectual property-related litigation and contentious matters arising from insolvency proceedings. Partners Philip Känzig and Marc Bernheim have been recommended.

Tavernier Tschanz continued to grow its already highly regarded arbitration practice in 2003. The firm's prowess in this area is largely due to the presence of the massively experienced Pierre-Yves Tschanz, who has led the firm in an impressive number of large and complex cases.

Walder Wyss & Partners partners Daniel Wyss, Dieter Hoffman and Philipp Habegger all have extensive arbitration experience. In 2003, the firm advised on disputes exceeding €170m in value including acting as counsel to charitable organisations, German and Dutch subcontractors, a US resident involved in an embezzlement case and in the case of a Swiss bank involved in a fraud case with two insurance companies.

Böckli Bodmer & Partner handles both litigation and arbitration matters. The firm places considerable importance on dispute resolution. Of the six partners three – international arbitration expert Peter Böckli, Bernard Bodmer and Jan Bangert – handle arbitration and litigation instructions.

Borel & Barbey has an ongoing role advising several creditors involved in the Swissair insolvency. In 2003, the firm hired a mutual assistance and criminal specialist. Its litigation practice is headed up by former District Court of Geneva judge Patrick Blaser.

Gillioz Dorsaz & Associés partner Bernard Doser handles litigation and arbitration instructions. In 2003, the firm advised a client on a case concerning the activities of a major Swiss bank, an ICC arbitration and civil cases in Geneva.

Haymann & Baldi is a boutique Geneva-based dispute settlement firm. Name partner Michel Haymann is well known.

Henrici, Wicki & Guggisberg was involved in a number of commercial litigation and arbitration proceedings at the national and international level in 2003. All the firm's partners have experience of dispute resolution.

Hess Dallafior Attorneys at Law's dispute settlement practice handles a lot of work with the firm's financial services practice. In 2003, it advised on a number of leasing, investment and consumer goods-related cases, including acting for a major Swiss financial services provider. Roberto Dallafior is a known arbitrator especially in the sports sector. Florian Baumann specialises in criminal legal assistance and disputes with Swiss banks.

ALTENBURGER has a niche specialisation advising community and foundation clients on contentious matters arising under art law. It also advises on corporate and commercial and finance-related disputes.

Bratschi Emch & Partner handles a wide range of commercial litigation and arbitration. The firm includes contentious specialists in its banking, commercial and corporate practices.

Berger Recordon & de Saugy partner Pierre-Alain Recordon, **Hartmann Müller Partners**' forensic and ICC specialist Jürgen Hartmann, **Stiffler & Nater** and **Thouvenin Rechtsanwälte**'s André Thouvenin and Hansjörg Stutzer are all dispute resolution experts.

Wenger Vieli Belser's dispute resolution expertise is led by litigator Daniel Girsberger and arbitrator Marco Cereghetti.

EU AND COMPETITION

Baker & McKenzie is among the foremost competition law firms in Europe, and in Switzerland the firm's status is upheld by Peter Reinert and Philippe Reich. Among a multitude of other matters, the firm handled merger clearance for 3i Group-owned Vianel Acquisition AG in its acquisition of SR Technics Group; CapVis Ltd for the acquisition of SWX-listed business division Zellweger Uster; and REWE for its acquisition of a majority stake in Bon Appétit. In Geneva, the firm is more active on trade law matters and has gained a significant reputation for its WTO-related work.

Bär & Karrer works closely with a number of big names in Swiss business to manage competition matters. In 2003, the firm advised on a number of acquisitions with Swiss and multinational clearance aspects. Well known for his arbitration work, Mark Blessing also handles antitrust disputes and administrative hearings before the Swiss Competition Commission. Ronny Reinhardt advises

EU AND COMPETITION

BAKER & McKENZIE ✪
BÄR & KARRER ✪
HOMBURGER ✪
PESTALOZZI LACHENAL PATRY ✪

CMS von Erlach Klainguti Stettler Wille ✪
Hess Dallafior Attorneys at Law ✪
Lenz & Staehelin ✪
Meyer Lustenberger ✪
Prager Dreifuss
Python Schifferli Peter & Partners ✪
Schellenberg Wittmer ✪
Staiger, Schwald & Partners ✪
Tavernier Tschanz

Firms are listed A-Z in tiers which are ranked in order of priority
✪ *Indicates firm displays contact details at the end of this chapter.*

on merger control and competition law as well as European law.

Homburger partners Franz Hoffet and Georg Rauber are highly regarded by the market for their work on merger control. The firm has been Swiss counsel on some of the biggest global mergers to take place in recent years. However, 2003 saw its work restricted to several of the largest Swiss transactions, including Marcel Dietrich's work for US/Swiss pharmaceutical company Synthes-Stratec Inc on its €96m acquisition of a Mathys Medical Inc division.

Pestalozzi Lachenal Patry's Jürg Borer is recommended consistently by peers and major clients. In 2003, he advised Telekurs and Publicitas on antitrust matters and the Swiss Book Traders Association throughout its representation before the Swiss Federal Supreme Court regarding resale price maintenance. The practice is also experienced in European law and WTO matters and benefits from a permanent Brussels office run by Christoph Rapin.

CMS von Erlach Klainguti Stettler Wille benefits from significant *CMS* network-wide resources on all aspects of EU and competition law, including a large network office in Brussels. Patrick Sommer is recommended for Swiss competition issues, merger control and antitrust, as well as advice on changes arising from the forthcoming Swiss cartel laws. Alain Raemy has advised on EU and competition aspects of corporate transactions in the banking, telecoms and trade sectors.

Hess Dallafior Attorneys at Law advises a major media client on competition matters.

Lenz & Staehelin's Marcel Meinhardt is frequently highlighted as one of the premier competition lawyers in Switzerland. The firm handles Swiss merger control matters for several multinationals as well as for larger domestic corporate clients.

Prager Dreifuss partner Philipp Zurkinden has been highly recommended for the quality of his competition work.

Python Schifferli Peter & Partners maintains an office in Brussels headed up part-time by Lausanne office resident and EU and competition specialist Philippe Kenel.

Staiger, Schwald & Partners is recommended for competition advice in the electricity and oil sectors.

Tavernier Tschanz partner Silvio Venturi was among the first francophone lawyers to specialise in competition law. He has handled competition aspects of several major corporate transactions and is experienced before the Swiss Competition Commission.

INSOLVENCY AND CORPORATE RECOVERY

Baker & McKenzie advised both Swiss Dairy Foods and Systor on their restructurings. Lukas Glanzmann, Richard Gassman and Marcel Giger have all co-led restructuring transactions, while Daniel Peregrina in Geneva also advised 4M Technologies Holding in its 2003 turnaround, which included capital markets, general corporate and restructuring aspects.

Froriep Renggli is advising Unilever and Lusso Foods in Swiss Dairy Food's debt moratorium. Ronald Kaufmann has advised on a gamut of insolvency and restructuring-related issues.

Homburger was the main counsel to Swissair throughout its insolvency proceedings, handling all divestitures and related matters. The firm is also broadly experienced in debt restructuring. Ueli Huber and Thomas Müller have become two of the most experienced insolvency practitioners in the country.

Schellenberg Wittmer partners Thomas Bolliger in Zurich and Vincent Jeanneret in Geneva lead the firm's work on insolvency and restructurings in a very wide range of industries in German- and French-speaking Switzerland respectively. The firm is well known for its high-calibre work on some of the largest recent cases. It has also advised on contentious aspects arising from insolvency and restructurings.

Wenger Plattner's Karl Wüthrich and Fritz Rotenbühler acted as liquidators for Swissair and Swiss Dairy Products respectively, reflecting the firm's premier standing in this sector. The firm is frequently instructed by all parties to major restructuring and insolvency proceedings.

Bürgi Nägeli counts restructuring as one of its principal specialisations, alongside an active corporate and commercial practice. The firm advised on the Energis case as well as on significant aspects of the Swissair and OMD Productions bankruptcies.

Staiger, Schwald & Partners handles all aspects of insolvency and restructurings, including acting as receiver, handling contentious matters arising from insolvencies. It worked on the Swissair case. Philip Känzig and Mark Bernheim are both recommended.

INSOLVENCY AND CORPORATE RECOVERY

BAKER & McKENZIE ✪
FRORIEP RENGGLI ✪
HOMBURGER ✪
SCHELLENBERG WITTMER ✪
WENGER PLATTNER ✪

Bürgi Nägeli ✪
Staiger, Schwald & Partners ✪
VISCHER ✪

Bratschi Emch & Partner ✪
Hartmann Müller Partners ✪
Henrici, Wicki & Guggisberg ✪
Lenz & Staehelin ✪
Niederer Kraft & Frey ✪
Python Schifferli Peter & Partners ✪
Tavernier Tschanz

Firms are listed A-Z in tiers which are ranked in order of priority
✪ *Indicates firm displays contact details at the end of this chapter.*

VISCHER's Markus Guggenbühl advises boards of directors and public companies on all aspects of restructuring. The firm represented Crossair AG (now Swiss International Airlines) in its complex and successful restructuring.

Bratschi Emch & Partner partner Jürgen Brönnimann is a university lecturer in debt enforcement and bankruptcy work as well as civil procedure law. He advises several clients in those fields as well as sitting on expert panels drafting a new federal civil procedure law.

Hartmann Müller Partners has a dedicated insolvency practice led by Niklaus Müller and Rudolf Schaub.

Henrici, Wicki & Guggisberg advised two well-known companies on aspects of a major insolvency case in Switzerland. Capital markets and insolvency expert Jürg Guggisberg was also involved in the acquisition and corporate restructuring of publicly traded companies in 2003.

Lenz & Staehelin advised Micron Holdings on its restructuring in 2003.

Python Schifferli Peter & Partners has handled restructuring and insolvency matters for its French-speaking clients. Beat Mummenthaler is the best known individual at the firm for both this kind of work and for asset tracing.

Tavernier Tschanz advised on a major restructuring in 2003 including contentious aspects.

INTELLECTUAL PROPERTY

Homburger has a stand-alone intellectual property practice headed by recommended patent litigation expert Werner Stieger and Georg Rauber. As well as advising on all the firm's major transactional cases, which in 2003 included the €96m acquisition by Synthes-Stratec of a Mathys Medical division

INTELLECTUAL PROPERTY

HOMBURGER
LENZ & STAEHELIN
THOMANNFISCHER
TROLLER HITZ TROLLER & PARTNERS
WALDER WYSS & PARTNERS

Baker & McKenzie
Bär & Karrer
Froriep Renggli
Hess Dallafior Attorneys at Law
Junod Guyet Muhlstein & Levy
Meyer Lustenberger
Schellenberg Wittmer
Pestalozzi Lachenal Patry
VISCHER

CMS von Erlach Klainguti Stettler Wille
Python Schifferli Peter & Partners
Staiger, Schwald & Partners
Wenger Plattner

Firms are listed A-Z in tiers which are ranked in order of priority
Indicates firm displays contact details at the end of this chapter.

and prior to that the Swissair insolvency, the practice also handles intellectual property matters for several of its own exclusive clients.

Lenz & Staehelin is known for its contentious capability in this area, as well as for transactional intellectual property advice and trade mark work. Martin J Lutz and Thierry Calame are co-practice heads.

Thomannfischer in Basle remains best known for its niche intellectual property work. The practice is lead by eponymous partner Felix H Thomann. Clients include IT, e-commerce, chemical industry and pharmaceutical leaders as well as multinational businesses in Switzerland.

Troller Hitz Troller & Partners partner Patrick Troller has been highly recommended, while **Walder Wyss & Partners** counts intellectual property among its core practice areas and as such has made considerable investment in it. Among the 15-strong team, Didier Sangiorgio and Mark A Reutter have been singled out for particular praise. Also of note are Internet and e-commerce experts Markus Frick and Magda Streuli-Youseff.

Baker & McKenzie regularly acts on high-end trade mark, domain name and copyright litigation. The firm also has significant experience of managing intellectual property portfolios in the context of corporate and financial restructuring and has a niche speciality in Community Trade Mark law. Clients include Swiss, EU and US multinational and mid-sized companies in the cosmetics, food, tobacco, computer and pharmaceutical industries.

Bär & Karrer continues to manage intellectual property aspects arising from major corporate transactions and is expanding the practice to include some stand-alone elements. Markus Wang is the best-known practitioner.

Froriep Renggli competition expert Alessandro Celli has handled patent pooling, joint venture agreements and technology transfers.

Hess Dallafior Attorneys at Law represents various authors, artists and IT companies on trade mark, patent and general intellectual property-related matters. Reto Hilty is a prominent academic and Mathis Berger edits the Swiss Review of Intellectual Property.

Junod Guyet Muhlstein & Levy is a niche intellectual property firm with an impressive track record of advising big names including Gucci and Chanel in Switzerland. For contentious and non-contentious work alike, Michael Muhlstein is recommended.

Schellenberg Wittmer's intellectual property practice in 2003 advised Levi-Strauss on the largest trade mark counterfeiting case ever discovered in Switzerland. Andrea Mondini in Zurich and Yves Jeanrenaud in Geneva regularly advise on technology transfers, licensing, trade marks and domain name disputes. Andrea Mondini is a panellist in domain name disputes for the WIPO Arbitration and Mediation Center.

Pestalozzi Lachenal Patry seats intellectual property within its new technologies team reflecting the emphasis the firm has placed on working with hi-tech and Internet-based clients. In 2003, the firm handled a landmark biotechnology procedure before a Swiss agency relating to the field trials of genetically modified organisms. Name partner Peter Pestalozzi advises Pfizer and others on intellectual property. Robert Briner has been recommended for TMT-related advice.

VISCHER is recommended for intellectual property matters arising from transactions, and TMT and trade mark advice. Rolf Auf der Maur is a well-known and respected practitioner.

CMS von Erlach Klainguti Stettler Wille has handled intellectual property aspects of corporate and commercial transactions.

Python Schifferli Peter & Partners advises on intellectual property insofar as it arises in the day-to-day activities of its large French-speaking client base.

Staiger, Schwald & Partners regularly handles general intellectual property matters, including litigation.

Wenger Plattner's intellectual property team is led from Basle by construction and architecture specialist Peter Mosimann. It advises international companies on copyright, design and trade marks and has a focus on arts and entertainment matters.

MERGERS AND ACQUISITIONS

Baker & McKenzie moves into the top-tier M&A table for the first time based on the consistent involvement by the Geneva and Zurich offices in very high-end deals. In 2003, deals representative of the firm's capability and capacity included advice to REWE in its €192m acquisition of Bon Appétit, and to the Mathys family on the €96m divestment of Mathys Medical Ltd to Synthes-Stratec Inc. The firm also has significant experience in global transactions. In 2003, Markus Berni was lead Swiss adviser to Abbott during its global acquisition of Jomed. Corporate guru Urs Schenker and M&A practice head Kilian Perroulaz in Zurich are both highly prominent figures, as are Martin Anderson and Denis Berdoz in Geneva.

Bär & Karrer's M&A team led by Rolf Watter had an outstanding year considering the dearth of major cross-border transactions in Switzerland. In pole position is the firm's advice to Centrepulse Orthopaedics throughout its contested takeover by Zimmer and Smith & Nephew Group – only the second contested takeover in Swiss history and certainly the most innovative transaction of the year. The firm also acted as counsel to Mövenpick on the sale of its ice cream division to Nestlé, Bon Appétit on its acquisition by REWE, and to a Swiss consortium on the recapitalisation, debt-to-equity swap and purchase of majority participation in broadband company NTL.

Homburger acted as counsel to Nestlé in the above mentioned acquisition of Mövenpick's ice cream division. Longstanding client healthcare group Roché had an active year of acquisitions, calling on the firm for advice on acquisitions exceeding €83m and on the divestment of its vitamins and fine chemicals division to Dutch life science company DSM. In the finance sector, the firm advised Zurich Financial Services on the sale of its private banking division to Deutsche Bank (Switzerland) Ltd. Heinz Schärer and Daniel Daeniker are the best-known individuals for this work, supported by highly ranked competition, tax and IP practices.

Lenz & Staehelin is a favourite choice as Swiss counsel on global M&A transactions due to its considerable, quality resources. In 2003, the firm maintained its standing with large Swiss clientele notably advising Incentive Capital throughout the contested takeover of Centrepulse Orthopaedics in which Incentive was a majority shareholder. Rudolf Tschäni in Zurich and Andreas von Planta in Geneva are both very highly regarded for their corporate and M&A knowledge and experience.

Pestalozzi Lachenal Patry in Geneva and Zurich fields two of the largest, most highly accomplished and widely acclaimed M&A teams in Switzerland. In terms of individuals, practice heads Jakob Höhn and Hans Bollmann, Silvan Hutter and Jean Patry, can be selected as 'most prominent of a very prominent team'. In 2003, the firm advised Zimmer on its €2.62bn competing bid for Centrepulse Orthopaedics; Rührgas Industries on the share and asset deal for the acquisition of the 25-jurisdiction metering business of ABB; and The Coca-Cola Company on the acquisition of Valser Wasser from the Hess Group. It also acted as Swiss counsel on globally arranged deals including the acquisition by Texas Pacific Group of Gate Gourmet from Swissair Companies and of Novartis company Wander by Associated British Foods.

MERGERS AND ACQUISITIONS

BAKER & McKENZIE ✪
BÄR & KARRER ✪
HOMBURGER ✪
LENZ & STAEHELIN ✪
PESTALOZZI LACHENAL PATRY ✪

Froriep Renggli ✪
Niederer Kraft & Frey ✪
Schellenberg Wittmer ✪
VISCHER ✪
Walder Wyss & Partners ✪

CMS von Erlach Klainguti Stettler Wille ✪
Python Schifferli Peter & Partners ✪
Rinderknecht Klein & Stadelhofer ✪
Staiger, Schwald & Partners ✪
Tavernier Tschanz
Wenger Plattner ✪
Wenger Vieli Belser ✪

Badertscher Dörig Poledna ✪
Borel & Barbey ✪
Bratschi Emch & Partner ✪
Henrici, Wicki & Guggisberg ✪
Hess Dallafior Attorneys at Law ✪
Meyer Lustenberger ✪
Suter & Partners Attorneys at Law

Firms are listed A-Z in tiers which are ranked in order of priority
✪ Indicates firm displays contact details at the end of this chapter.

Froriep Renggli's corporate and M&A practice, led by specialist Eric Haymann, advised Imperial Tobacco on Swiss aspects of its purchase of Davidoff. (**Allen & Overy** was global arranger). It also advised ABB on aspects of its sale to GE. The firm has highly ranked competition, IP and tax practices and offices in London and Madrid.

Niederer Kraft & Frey has previously advised on sales arising from restructurings in the banking, food and manufacturing sectors.

Schellenberg Wittmer has very strong M&A practices in Zurich and Geneva. Notably in 2003, the firm won an instruction to act as joint global co-ordinator in the €2.37bn capital increase in Zurich Financial Services Group, the largest in Swiss corporate history. Martin Weber, Andrea Grimm, Roy Ryan and managing partner Bernard Vischer are the best-known lawyers for M&A, cross-border private equity investment and capital increases.

VISCHER has been ramping up its capability to work on cross-border M&A deals in recent years, largely on the purchaser side. Instructions from several leading UK firms on Swiss aspects of multi-million euro deals, representation of a Swiss-listed company in the sale of a large group of companies including foreign subsidiaries, and increasingly significant experience of large real estate portfolio transactions are all indicative of its maturity. Jürg Luginbühl is head of corporate and M&A.

Walder Wyss & Partners has outstanding experience with multinational, Swiss-listed and private companies. In 2003, it advised a leading Swiss insurance company on various demergers, a US-listed company on its acquisition of a Swiss company, a listed Swiss media group in the acquisition of the leading Swiss newspaper for commuters, and a German company on an acquisition in the hi-tech sector. Markus Vischer, Christoph Stäubli and Luc Defferrard have all been recommended.

CMS von Erlach Klainguti Stettler Wille advised on several domestic acquisitions in 2003. The firm has been active on several large restructurings and continues to advise Rabobank on its ongoing takeover of Bank Sarasin.

Python Schifferli Peter & Partners has advised various clients in western Switzerland on mergers and acquisitions as part of their day-to-day activities.

Rinderknecht Klein & Stadelhofer has handled several acquisitions in the energy sector as well as in media and biotech.

Staiger, Schwald & Partners is focused on general corporate and commercial, litigation, and insolvency work. Its advice to Swiss public and private companies has included aspects of M&A, including merger control advice.

Tavernier Tschanz has a track record that includes large and prestigious domestic M&A and restructurings. The firm is a referral favourite of several Zurich firms without Geneva offices as well as of foreign firms. Jacques Bonvin is the best-known individual for this work.

Wenger Plattner has advised on several international and domestic M&A deals and other cross-border deals. It primarily advises foreign vendors and domestic acquirers of privately held companies.

Wenger Vieli Belser is firm of first choice for many of Switzerland's more traditional industries. It has advised numerous non-market-listed companies on M&A work, as well as restructuring and buy-outs, particularly in the life sciences and technology industries. Christoph Schmidt has the highest profile for M&A advice. The firm also has an office in Beijing headed by Paul Thaler.

Badertscher Dörig Poledna is advising on the ongoing Swiss rail privatisation project, counselling the Swiss Federal Railway.

Borel & Barbey in Geneva has advised Swiss and US clients in the biotech, industrial and pharmaceutical sectors on M&A.

Bratschi Emch & Partner has a large mid-size client base. It has advised on M&A deals in industries including transportation, pharmaceuticals and hi-tech, sports clubs and publishing in 2003.

Henrici, Wicki & Guggisberg has an established corporate advisory practice that includes significant restructuring and insolvency experience. In 2003, the firm advised on the acquisition and restructuring of publicly-traded investment companies.

Hess Dallafior Attorneys at Law has domestic experience of M&A transactions.

Suter & Partners Attorneys at Law is experienced with foreign investors making acquisitions in Switzerland.

PRIVATE BANKING

Baker & McKenzie in Geneva and Zurich regularly acts for several of the largest and most important private banks, family offices and individual families. Recent assignments have included substantial strategic reviews for major Asian banks seeking to identify opportunities in the private banking field, a restructuring of $1bn in assets for a Swiss-based family office, as well as the development of compliance tools, training programmes and development strategies. In 2003, the firm gained unique experience of voluntary disclosure undertakings in several jurisdictions. Partners Philip Marcovici, Thomas O'Donnell and Richard Gassmann in Zurich and Stephanie Jarrett in Geneva are all highly recommended in this field.

Bär & Karrer handles private banking issues for several prominent individuals and institutions. It also has an established private client practice making it somewhat unique among other major firms in this sector. Thomas Bär, Nedim Peter Vogt and Christian Steinmann all advise private clients.

Niederer Kraft & Frey counts several property and inheritance management companies among its clients. Markus A Frey and Edgar H Paltzer also handle private banking and asset management matters for private banks and prominent individuals.

Pestalozzi Lachenal Patry in Zurich handles private banking work from within its corporate banking practice. The Geneva office headed by Jean Patry is better known for private client work with a raft of prominent individuals and institutions.

Borel & Barbey is one of the oldest firms in Geneva and includes among its clients a number of longstanding extremely eminent industrial and private high-net-worth clients. The firm also advises on private client matters such as estate planning and trust funds.

Lenz & Staehelin partners Jean-Paul Aeschimann, Dominique F Rochat, Guy Vermeil and Shelby R du Pasquier have all been recommended for private banking and private client advice, while **Poncet Turrettini Amaudruz Neyroud & Partners**' banking and finance team also advise some private banks and asset managers.

Python Schifferli Peter & Partners capitalises on its prominent position in Geneva to attract a large number of private banks and private clients. Most notably in 2003, Thomas Steiman handled the restructuring of royalty flows for a number of household name artists and athletes. Nicolas de Gottrau and Jacques Python are well known for their advice to banks and high-net-worth asset managers.

PRIVATE BANKING

BAKER & McKENZIE ✪
BÄR & KARRER ✪
NIEDERER KRAFT & FREY ✪
PESTALOZZI LACHENAL PATRY ✪

Borel & Barbey ✪
Lenz & Staehelin ✪
Poncet Turrettini Amaudruz Neyroud & Partners
Python Schifferli Peter & Partners ✪
Schellenberg Wittmer ✪
Tavernier Tschanz
von Meiss Blum & Partners ✪

ALTENBURGER
CMS von Erlach Klainguti Stettler Wille ✪
Lalive & Partners
Staiger, Schwald & Partners ✪
Wenger Plattner ✪

Firms are listed A-Z in tiers which are ranked in order of priority
✪ Indicates firm displays contact details at the end of this chapter.

Schellenberg Wittmer in Geneva has a longstanding private banking practice headed by Jacques Wittmer.

Tavernier Tschanz has some institutional clients in the private banking sector and handles trust and estate matters for several private clients. Edmond Tavernier is the most senior partner involved.

von Meiss Blum & Partners' Walter Boss has been recommended from a source very knowledgeable of the high-end private banking market.

ALTENBURGER counts diplomats, industrialists and royals with net worths ranging from millions to billions among its prestigious private client base. The firm advises on all aspects of financial structuring supported by a very strong tax practice headed by name partner Peter Altenburger.

CMS von Erlach Klainguti Stettler Wille's banking and finance practice counts a small number of private banks among its clients.

Lalive & Partners advises domestic and foreign subsidiary private banks on compliance and regulatory matters.

Staiger, Schwald & Partners counts several private banking institutions among its most important clients. The firm advises the asset management subsidiaries of some foreign banks on all financial and commercial activities and has experience in all aspects of wealth management.

Wenger Plattner in Zurich advises foreign and domestic high-net-worth individuals on asset management and risk strategies.

REAL ESTATE AND CONSTRUCTION

BAKER & McKENZIE ✪
SCHUMACHER BAUR HÜRLIMANN

CMS von Erlach Klainguti Stettler Wille ✪
Lalive & Partners
Python Schifferli Peter & Partners ✪
Wenger Plattner ✪

Lenz & Staehelin ✪
Pestalozzi Lachenal Patry ✪
Schellenberg Wittmer ✪

Firms are listed A-Z in tiers which are ranked in order of priority
✪ Indicates firm displays contact details at the end of this chapter.

Baker & McKenzie in Geneva now offers far and away the most formidable international real estate practice in Switzerland. Former Moscow partner Adrian Moore is resident in the office co-ordinating the transnational European real estate practice for the firm and advising on large real estate purchase and lease transactions. Administrative law specialist Daniel Peregrina has a local real estate practice experienced in all aspects of planning, environment, construction and lease arrangements.

Schumacher Baur Hürlimann remains recognised by peers, clients and commentators as the 'premier firm' for advice on Swiss real estate transactions and to construction companies throughout Switzerland. The firm's work has increased exponentially as other firms in Switzerland have cast off basic real estate work in favour of more complex commercial matters. Name partners Rainer Schumacher and Roland Hürlimann are firm mainstays.

CMS von Erlach Klainguti Stettler Wille has an active real estate practice that advises a number of significant institutional investors. Stefan Gerster and Dietrich K Settler also advise private clients on real estate assets in Zurich.

Lalive & Partners is recommended for construction related advice. Notably Michael E Schneider specialises in construction arbitration.

Python Schifferli Peter & Partners' Bernard Cron is well known for his work on construction and real estate issues in western Switzerland. The firm regularly acts for several well-known construction companies, developers and investors.

Wenger Plattner in 2003 expanded its broad construction and real estate practice with the addition of Thomas Wetzel, a specialist in real estate and construction management issues for public and private companies. The firm counts globally active institutional investors and private individuals among its clients and works with several real estate management and consulting companies. In Basle, Peter Mosimann has been particularly recommended for his work with architectural firms involved in international projects.

Lenz & Staehelin's real estate experience is limited to advice on large real estate finance deals and does not offer the broader range of services available at the other firms.

Pestalozzi Lachenal Patry has a longstanding US client with major real estate interests in Switzerland. Max Walter advises on all aspects of planning, zoning and environmental law.

Schellenberg Wittmer's real estate practice is headed by Yves Jeanrenaud.

TMT

Baker & Mckenzie has a widely recognised IP/IT/telecoms expert in Zurich in the shape of Markus Berni. Daniel Peregrina in Geneva advises several large telecoms groups on regulatory and contractual matters and, in 2003, on restructuring and M&A transactions. The firm also benefits from the of-counsel expertise of former International Telecoms Union head of legal Alfons Noll.

Bär & Karrer handles TMT matters through its telecoms, IT, media, entertainment and sport department, led by Michele Bernasconi. In 2003, the firm advised Cablecom on the recapitalisation, debt-to-equity swap and purchase of majority participation in NTL. The deal involved some complex telecoms issues.

Homburger has a stand-alone IP/IT practice, which also handles regulatory matters for Swisscom and other large corporate assignments. Intellectual property partner Georg Rauber is well known in the IT community.

Python Schifferli Peter & Partners partner Thomas Legler handles telecoms, IT and other hi-tech matters from the firm's Geneva office. Thomas Steinmann works with some artists and well-known personalities, and Pierre-Yves Gunter on data protection.

Walder Wyss & Partners has outstanding experience of a wide range of corporate and regulatory matters in this area. In 2003, the firm advised on an acquisition in the IT sector by a German company and leading private equity and venture capital funds on direct investments in software, biotech and hi-tech companies in Switzerland. The firm also acts for telecoms companies, an international sports association and several Swiss public relations companies. Reto Jacobs and Didier Sangiorgio are both highly recommended.

Wiederkehr Forster is popular among telecoms clients. Rolf Weber regularly counsels Sunrise on its activities in Switzerland.

ALTENBURGER in Zurich has a dedicated media practice with particular experience of contentious and non-contentious matters arising from arts and entertainment. The firm has a burgeoning specialty in art law, especially on the contentious side, working with various community and foundation clients.

Bratschi Emch & Partner advises IT and telecoms clients, especially web design and publishing companies. It is particularly recommended for insolvency work in these sectors. Clients also include print and electronic media firms, and large international sports and entertainment corporations. In 2003, it advised on the acquisition

TMT

BAKER & McKENZIE ✪
BÄR & KARRER ✪
HOMBURGER ✪
PYTHON SCHIFFERLI PETER & PARTNERS ✪
WALDER WYSS & PARTNERS ✪
WIEDERKEHR FORSTER

ALTENBURGER
Bratschi Emch & Partner ✪
CMS von Erlach Klainguti Stettler Wille ✪
Hess Dallafior Attorneys at Law ✪
Lenz & Staehelin ✪
Pestalozzi Lachenal Patry ✪
Prager Dreifuss
Tavernier Tschanz
VISCHER ✪
Wenger Plattner ✪

Badertscher Dörig Poledna ✪
Bill, Isenegger & Ackermann ✪
Meyer Lustenberger ✪
Niederer Kraft & Frey ✪
Schellenberg Wittmer ✪
Stiffler & Nater ✪

Firms are listed A-Z in tiers which are ranked in order of priority
✪ Indicates firm displays contact details at the end of this chapter.

of sports clubs, the establishment of a sports stadium and several ice hockey-related matters.

CMS Von Erlach Klainguti Stettler Wille advised telecoms giant Orange on the substantial regulatory aspects surrounding its investments in Switzerland in previous years. It continues to advise Orange on its day-to-day commercial activities. Alain Raemy and Oliver Blum also advise on aspects of e-commerce and outsourcing.

Hess Dallafior Attorneys at Law is highly recommended to IT, software and hi-tech clients, including start-ups. The firm counts several large software developers among its clients, which it advises on licensing, franchise agreements and commercial matters. It also advises a large Swiss media player on media law and competition.

Lenz & Staehelin is recommended for IT consulting and outsourcing. It has advised big names including Deloitte & Touche, Infonet, EDS, IBM and PricewaterhouseCoopers. The firm also has significant experience of corporate transactions in the telecoms sector.

Pestalozzi Lachenal Patry partner Robert G Briner assisted by Stefan Kohler in 2003 advised the Federal Institute of Technology on a landmark case before the Swiss Agency for Environment, Forests and Landscapes concerning field trials of genetically modified organisms. The firm is recommended for media, telecoms and IT contentious and non-contentious work.

Prager Dreifuss has a leading reputation for advice to media and entertainment clients as well as sports sponsorship companies. The firm is experienced in all aspects of television distribution and licensing agreements and has some Internet and e-commerce experience.

Tavernier Tschanz advises several start-ups, biotech and software companies in Geneva and French-speaking Switzerland. Jacques Bonvin leads the firm's work. He has been recommended as business-oriented and solution-driven.

VISCHER is active in IT outsourcing, transactions involving TMT companies and content-related issues in the telecoms sector. The firm also advises several foreign and domestic television channels, including Viva Media of Germany.

Wenger Plattner in Basle advises on global IT supply and procurement projects, e-commerce and Internet-related transactions. Partner Bernard Hausler also acts for leading Swiss football team FC Basle. Roland Mathys has been recommended. In Zurich, Stephan Netzle provides sports law advice to several international companies and sports organisations with a notable focus on sponsorship agreements. In 2003, he advised a large multinational on all their sponsorship activities for the 2004 Olympic Games.

Badertscher Dörig Poledna has IT and telecoms experience. **Bill, Isenegger & Ackermann** specialises in technology transfers. **Niederer Kraft & Frey** has handled outsourcing and contractual IT matters. **Schellenberg Wittmer** Zurich partner Corinna Klaus-Rüesch advises on IT-related matters. **Stiffler & Nater** has regulatory experience in the telecoms sector.

TAX

BAKER & McKENZIE ✪
HOMBURGER ✪
LENZ & STAEHELIN ✪
PESTALOZZI LACHENAL PATRY ✪

ALTENBURGER
Bär & Karrer ✪
Oberson & Partners
Python Schifferli Peter & Partners ✪
Schellenberg Wittmer ✪
VISCHER ✪
Walder Wyss & Partners ✪

Borel & Barbey ✪
Bratschi Emch & Partner ✪
CMS von Erlach Klainguti Stettler Wille ✪
Gillioz Dorsaz & Associés ✪
Meyer Lustenberger ✪
Niederer Kraft & Frey ✪
Staiger, Schwald & Partners ✪

Firms are listed A-Z in tiers which are ranked in order of priority
✪ Indicates firm displays contact details at the end of this chapter.

Baker & McKenzie provides Swiss and US law advice to various Swiss and non-Swiss multinationals on tax-efficient M&A structures, post-acquisition restructuring, and investment matters. The firm also advises on taxation aspects of debt and equity offerings, including on the application of international tax treaties and multi-jurisdictional transfer pricing analysis and advises a very large number of private clients on international tax planning. Philip Marcovici, Thomas O'Donnell and Hans Koch in Zurich are all specialist tax attorneys. Denis Berdoz in Geneva is one of the most experienced local practitioners. VAT expert Per Prod'hom joined the Geneva office as partner in 2003.

Homburger tax partner Eveline Saupper played a significant role in the firm's work on the €96m acquisition of Mathys Medical Inc, advising the purchaser. Peter Riedweg and Harold Grüninger are also experienced advisers on transaction-related tax matters, as well as offering standalone tax advice to the firm's significant commercial client base.

Lenz & Staehelin has one of the largest tax practices of all law firms in Zurich. It works with a large number of multinationals headquartered in Switzerland on tax structuring and planning. Substantial transactional experience in 2003 includes advising on the tax aspects of the Micron restructuring. The tax practice also works with a number of major private banks and private clients. Henri Torrione and Jean-Blaise Eckert in Zurich and Henri Ruedisuehli in Geneva are the firm's best-known tax experts.

Pestalozzi Lachenal Patry bolstered an already outstanding tax practice with the addition of former Andersen tax partner Maja Bauer-Balmelli in 2003. The practice includes academically and professionally-accomplished individuals including international taxation expert and practice head Silvia Zimmerman, and former president of the Swiss Tax Association, Marcus Desax. University of Zurich professor Markus Reich is a consultant and Philippe Cottier advises on taxation from Geneva. The firm has been recommended for all aspects of domestic and international tax planning and contentious matters.

ALTENBURGER managing partner Peter Altenburger is a well-known and highly regarded tax attorney. The firm advises several domestic and foreign industrial, financial and private clients on all aspects of taxation law arising from corporate and personal matters.

Bär & Karrer handles tax aspects insofar as they arise from the transactional nature of the firm's work. Peter Reinhardt and Daniel Lehman have also provided standalone tax advice. The firm has a high ranking in capital markets, restructuring and mergers and acquisitions, and has handled tax aspects arising from transactions in each of those practice areas.

Oberson & Partners in Geneva has been recommended for its work with private banks and high-net-worth individuals. Name partner Xavier Oberson commands considerable respect among his peers.

Python Schifferli Peter & Partners has continued with a programme of organic growth and lateral hires to build one of the largest tax practices in Geneva. The firm also has resident tax experts at its offices in Lausanne and Lausanne-Polly. Etienne von Streng is the firm's best-known individual in this area.

Schellenberg Wittmer recruited Michael Nordin in 2003 to boost the firm's tax practice in Zurich to complement its already significant practice in Geneva. The firm advises on all tax law matters.

VISCHER has strong tax practices in the Basle and Zurich offices which it recently expanded with lateral hires from Big Four accountant Ernst & Young. It continues to grow this practice reflecting the high emphasis its core clients place on tax structuring and planning and tax efficient transactional advice.

Walder Wyss & Partners' significant investment in its tax practice paid dividends in heaps in 2003. The firm's banking and corporate teams had a very active year, working on several major domestic and cross-border transactions, including restructuring on bonds and loans, requiring major input from the tax department. The renowned Thomas Meister is far and away the best-known tax attorney at the firm.

Borel & Barbey in Geneva offers full corporate and commercial services to several of its clients, including tax structuring, and also boasts a longstanding private client and private banking client base. Carl Heggli heads the four-strong tax practice.

Bratschi Emch & Partner has recently built a tax practice headed by former Andersen partner Reto Kuster and including tax expert Bruno Rieder. It advises corporations and private clients on national and international tax law.

CMS von Erlach Klainguti Stettler Wille handles tax aspects arising from its transactional corporate and banking practices. In July 2003, the firm hired certified tax expert and notary public (Canton of Zug) Philipp Andermatt.

Gillioz Dorsaz & Associés is a relatively small Geneva-based firm that places a significant emphasis on tax matters. Of its six lawyers, two, Pierre Gillioz and Myriam Nicolazzi, are tax experts. The firm has a distinguished client base of domestic and international companies several of which it advises on tax planning and structuring, including work arising from complex restructuring cases.

Staiger, Schwald & Partners counts former head of the Swiss Federal Tax Office Dieter Metzger among its partners, allowing it to provide its mid-size domestic client base with solid tax advice.

TRANSPORT

Benz Attorneys is the best-known firm for all aspects of road, rail, air, sea and mutli-modal transportation advice in Switzerland. Led by name partner Christian Benz, the firm works with major logistics companies as well as marine liability insurance companies.

Bratschi Emch & Partner is regularly instructed by one of the largest Swiss road transportation and logistics companies and has two partners specialising in aviation who represent a major foreign airline.

Neupert & Partners partner Dieter Neupert is chairman of the European Business Aviation Association, as well as a member of the Swiss Aviation Arbitration Court. The firm is recommended for contentious and non-contentious advice under aviation law.

Schellenberg Wittmer has some experience of shipping matters. Alexander von Ziegler in Zurich and Bernard Vischer both handle transportation and international trade instructions.

Schiller Denzler Dubs Rechtsanwälte has advised the aviation industry on regulatory matters and handled some major cases relating to aircraft accidents. Regula Dettling-Ott is an academic aviation law expert.

VISCHER partners Christoph Pestallozi and Ernst Staehlin are both aviation law experts. The firm counts a major foreign air carrier among its clients, as well as large transportation and logistics companies. It also works with P&I clubs.

TRANSPORT

BENZ ATTORNEYS

Bratschi Emch & Partner ✪
Neupert & Partners ✪
Schellenberg Wittmer ✪
Schiller Denzler Dubs Rechtsanwälte
VISCHER ✪

Firms are listed A-Z in tiers which are ranked in order of priority
✪ Indicates firm displays contact details at the end of this chapter.

DÜRR + PARTNER / SWISSLEGAL

CENTRALBAHNSTRASSE 7
4010 BASEL

Telephone: +41 61 205 93 93
Fax: +41 61 205 93 99
E-mail: info@swisslegal.ch
Website: www.swisslegal.ch

Languages
English, French, German, Italian,

Other offices
Zug, Zürich

Number of lawyers 9
at this office 6

CATEGORIES OF WORK

Arbitration
Prof Dr David Dürr, Dr Paul Rüst

Banking
Prof Dr David Dürr, Thomas Kaufmann

Commercial
Dr Balthasar Settelen, Thomas Kaufmann

Competition
Dr Balthasar Settelen, Dr Paul Rüst

Corporate
Christine Goetschy, Prof Dr David Dürr

Construction
Dr Paul Rüst, Christine Goetschy

Estate planning, trusts
Dr Balthasar Settelen, Sybille Plouda

Insolvency, bankruptcy
Christine Goetschy, Thomas Kaufmann

Intellectual property
Dr Balthasar Settelen, Dr Paul Rüst

Mergers and acquisitions
Prof Dr David Dürr, Thomas Kaufmann

Notarial
Dr Paul Rüst, Christine Goetschy

Real estate
Prof Dr David Dürr, Christine Goetschy

Tax
Dr Balthasar Settelen, Thomas Kaufmann

Labour
Dr Balthasar Settelen, Sybille Plouda

Litigation
Dr Balthasar Settelen, Thomas Kaufmann

Transportation
Dr Balthasar Settelen, Sybille Plouda

HOLLIGER, SIMONIUS & PARTNERS

AESCHENVORSTADT 67
4010 BASEL

Telephone: +41 61 206 45 45
Fax: +41 61 206 45 46
E-mail: holligersimonius@advokaten.ch
Website: www.advokaten.ch

Languages
English, French, German, Italian, Portuguese, Spanish

Other offices
Zurich

Number of lawyers 14

Contact
Dr Thomas Burckhardt

Member
DIRO

CATEGORIES OF WORK

Arbitration
Prof Pascal Simonius, Dr Thomas Burckhardt

Banking
Prof Pascal Simonius, Emanuel Wiemken

Commercial and contract law
Dr Heiner Schärrer, Dr Erik Johner

Corporate
Dr Thomas Burckhardt, Bernhard Simonetti

Criminal law
Dr Urs Beat Pfrommer, Susanna Marti

Estate planning and trusts
Bernhard Simonetti, David Levin

IT and e-commerce, labour
Dr Erik Johner, Susanna Marti

Insolvency and bankruptcy
Emanuel Wiemken, Philipp Simonius

Insurance
Dr Urs Beat Pfrommer, Dr Heiner Schärrer

Litigation
Prof Pascal Simonius, Emanuel Wiemken

Mediation
Dr Urs Beat Pfrommer, Susanna Marti

Notarial services
Dr Paul Holliger, Bernhard Simonetti

Real estate
Dr Paul Holliger, Prof Pascal Simonius

Social security
Dr Urs Beat Pfrommer, Dr Annemarie Imhof

Taxation
David Levin

Transport, shipping and aviation
Dr Thomas Burckhardt

MATHYS SCHMID PARTNER

DUFOURSTRASSE 5
4052 BASLE

Telephone: +41 61 270 99 00
Fax: +41 61 270 99 05

Languages
English, French, German, Italian, Portuguese

Number of lawyers 7

CATEGORIES OF WORK

Arbitration, ADR
Dr Roland Rasi

Administrative law and regulatory matters
Dr Donald Stückelberger, Dr Barbara Graham

Asset and estate planning
Dr Peter Mathys, Stefan Schmid

Commercial and contract law
Stefan Schmid, Dr Peter Mathys

Corporate, M&A, MBO
Dr Peter Mathys, Martin Wepfer

Competition
Dr Donald Stückelberger

IP and trade mark
Stefan Schmid, Dr Daniel Abt

Insolvency, bankruptcy
Dr Peter Mathys, Martin Wepfer

Litigation
Dr Peter Mathys, Dr Donald Stückelberger

Notarial services
Stefan Schmid, Dr Peter Mathys

Tax law, tax litigation
Dr Peter Mathys

THOMANNFISCHER

ELISABETHENSTRASSE 30
PO BOX 632
4010 BASEL

Telephone: +41 61 226 24 24
Fax: +41 61 226 24 25
E-mail: info@thomannfischer.ch
Website: www.thomannfischer.ch

Languages
English, French, German, Italian, Spanish

Number of lawyers 8

Contact
Felix H Thomann (senior partner)

CATEGORIES OF WORK

Corporate
Patrick Wamister, Benno Bucher

Intellectual property and IT
Felix H Thomann, Benno Bucher

Mergers and acquisitions
Benno Bucher, Patrick Wamister

Estate planning and wealth management
Alex Fischer, Philip Baumann

Real estate and construction
Markus W Stadlin

Litigation
Felix H Thomann, Markus W Stadlin

Taxes and fiscal
Benno Bucher, Markus W Stadlin

Banking
Philip Baumann

Notaries
Alex Fischer, Patrick Wamister

THE FIRM

ThomannFischer was founded in 1999 when partners of two well-renowned firms joined forces. All the partners have a long history of professional experience and comprehensive knowledge in their areas of practice. Furthermore, they have extensive international experience, which they gained not only through international client assignments from all continents but also by working on overseas secondments. The firm offers services in all areas of business law, be it legal advice, transactional work or litigation. It also provides full notarial services. ThomannFischer is perfectly able to handle cross-border assignments and to understand the needs and the 'language' of international clients. Foreign clients account for a considerable share in the firm's daily work.

AREAS OF PRACTICE

The firm focuses on business law, both domestic and international, for corporate clients and enterpreneurs. It advises multinationals as well as small and medium-sized companies in all aspects of commercial and corporate law, which are relevant for their undertakings. It gives support to domestic clients on outbound transactions and international clients on inbound projects. Felix H Thomann has excellent and longstanding expertise in intellectual property, competition, computer, software and online law. He is also sought as a litigator, particularly in patent, trade mark and unfair competition cases with special emphasis on pharmaceuticals. Patrick Wamister is also a notary public and authorised to notarise the transfer of German companies, where he was involved in major transactions for listed and unlisted companies, not only as a notary but also as an M&A adviser. Benno Bucher, a former general counsel of a chemicals multinational, has broad experience in industrial property, antitrust and competition law and as negotiator in complex merger and acquisition transactions. Markus W Stadlin specialises in real estate and construction law. He is also a notary public, and has prepared numerous demanding real property transfers for Swiss and foreign investors. Alex Fischer focuses on wealth and estate planning for Swiss and international private clients. Philip Baumann, a former general counsel of a major Swiss private bank, offers his long-standing expertise in banking law and estate planning. The firm is particularly strong in incorporating and restructuring companies, mergers and acquisitions, contract and banking law. The firm has advised clients on initial public offerings and financial institutions on regulatory affairs and cross-border takeovers.

VISCHER

AESCHENVORSTADT 4
4010 BASLE

Telephone: +41 61 279 33 00
Fax: +41 61 279 33 10
E-mail: lawyers@vischer.com
Website: www.vischer.com

Languages
English, French, German, Italian, Spanish

Number of lawyers 68
at this office 43

Contact
Dr David Jenny

CATEGORIES OF WORK

Arbitration, ADR
Prof Dr Frank Vischer, Dr Peter Gloor

Banking
Prof Dr Christian Brückner,
Thomas Ziegler

Competition
Dr Sebastian Burckhardt,
Dr Thomas Gelzer

Corporate
Dr Christoph Löw, Dr Michael Pfeifer

Employment law
Ursula Hubschmid

Environment
Dr Beatrice Wagner Pfeifer

Estate planning
Dr Bernhard Christ, Dr Niklaus E Schiess

Corporate finance
Dr Matthias Staehelin

Insolvency, bankruptcy
Dr David Jenny, Dr Roland Müller

Intellectual property
Dr Thomas Gelzer, Dr Ernst Staehelin

Litigation
Dr Christian Brückner,
Dr Ernst Staehelin

Mergers and acquisitions
Dr Sebastian Burckhardt,
Dr David Jenny

Notarial
Dr Roland Müller,
Dr Michael Pfeifer

Project finance
Felix Heusler, Dr Christoph Löw

Tax
Dr Hubertus Ludwig,
Dr Michael Pfeifer

WENGER PLATTNER

AESCHENVORSTADT 55
4010 BASLE

Telephone: +41 61 279 70 00
Fax: +41 61 279 70 01
E-mail: basel@wenger-plattner.ch
Website: www.wenger-plattner.ch

Languages
English, French, German, Italian, Portuguese

Other offices
Zurich, Bern

Number of lawyers 50
at this office 21

CATEGORIES OF WORK

Contract and commercial law
Dr Markus Metz, Dr Bernhard Heusler

Corporate, mergers and acquisitions
Dr Dieter Gränicher,
Dr Peter Mosimann

Arbitration
Dr Werner Wenger, Dr Dieter Gränicher

Commercial litigation
Dr Peter Mosimann,
Dr Dieter Gränicher

Civil law notary services
Stephan Cueni, Dr Alexander Gutmans

Constitutional and administrative law
Prof Dr Gerhard Schmid,
Dr Felix Uhlmann

Intellectual property
Dr Peter Mosimann,
Dr Dieter Gränicher

Telecoms, media, IT, sports and entertainment law
Dr Peter Mosimann,
Dr Bernhard Heusler

Social security and labour
Dr Peter Mosimann, Dr Markus Metz

Real estate and construction
Dr Markus Metz, Stephan Cueni

Competition law
Dr Dieter Gränicher,
Prof Dr Gerhard Schmid

Transportation and shipping
Stephan Cueni

Drug and biotechnology law
Prof Dr Gerhard Schmid,
Dr Alexander Gutmans

Trusts and estate planning
Dr Werner Wenger

BRATSCHI EMCH & PARTNER

BOLLWERK 15
POSTFACH 5576
3001 BERN

Telephone: +41 31 310 19 19
Fax: +41 31 310 19 20
E-mail: berneoffice@bep.ch
Website: www.bep.ch

Languages
English, French,German, Spanish

Other offices
Zürich

Number of lawyers 27
at this office 15

CATEGORIES OF WORK

Contract and commercial law
Dr P Bratschi, Lukas Wyss

Corporate and mergers and acquisitions
Dr P Bratschi, Mark Ineichen

Commercial litigation and arbitration
Dr P Bratschi, Prof Dr J Brönnimann

Banking and finance
Dr U Emch, Dr P Bratschi

Media and communication
Dr P Bratschi, Mark Ineichen

Taxation
Dr Reto Kuster, Bruno Rieder

Health and drug law
Dr P Bratschi

Environmental and construction law
Ulrich Keusen

Insolvency law
Prof Dr J Brönnimann, Dr U Emch

Competition
Prof Dr J Brönnimann, Mark Ineichen

International successions
Dr U Emch, Prof Dr J Brönnimann

Administrative law
Dr U Emch, Ulrich Keusen

NOTTER MÉGEVAND & PARTNERS

WALDEGGSTRASSE 72
3097 BERNE-LIEBEFELD

Telephone: +41 31 979 79 79
Fax: +41 31 979 79 80
E-mail: bern@nomea.ch

Languages
English, French, German

Other offices
Geneva, Fribourg

Number of lawyers 16
at this office 8

CATEGORIES OF WORK

Commercial

Corporate

Banking and finance

Bankruptcy and insolvency

Tax

Civil law

Administration and public law

International law

Litigation and arbitration

Family office

STAIGER, SCHWALD & PARTNERS

THUNSTRASSE 7
PO BOX 281
3000 BERN 6

Telephone: +41 31 356 48 48
Fax: +41 31 356 48 49
E-mail: ssplaw@ssplaw.ch
Website: www.ssplaw.ch

Languages
English, French, German, Italian

Other offices
Zurich

Number of lawyers 28
at this office 4

Contact
Dr Urs Leu

CATEGORIES OF WORK

Arbitration and litigation

Banking, securities, finance

Company and commercial law

Insolvency

Immigration

Competition, antitrust, trade marks and copyright

EU law and private international law

Mergers and acquisitions

Tax

Wills, trusts and estate planning

Media and entertainment

Energy market law

WENGER PLATTNER

JUNGFRAUSTRASSE 1
3000 BERN 6

Telephone: +41 31 357 00 00
Fax: +41 31 357 00 01
E-mail: bern@wenger-plattner.ch
Website: www.wenger-plattner.ch

Languages
English, French, German, Italian

Other offices
Basle, Zurich

Number of lawyers 50
at this office 6

CATEGORIES OF WORK

Civil, contract and commercial law
Dr Jürg Rieben, Dr Fritz Rothenbühler

Banking law
Dr Fritz Rothenbühler

Corporate, mergers and acquisitions
Dr Jürg Rieben

Arbitration
Dr Christoph Müller

Commercial litigation
Dr Jürg Rieben, Dr Fritz Rothenbühler

Bankruptcy and insolvency
Dr Fritz Rothenbühler

Competition law
Dr Jürg Rieben, Dr Fritz Rothenbühler

Constitutional and administrative law
Andreas Maeschi, Dr Jürg Rieben

Construction and planning
Andreas Maeschi

Family law
Andreas Maeschi

Inheritance law
Andreas Maeschi

Intellectual property and trade mark law
Dr Fritz Rothenbühler

International law
Dr Fritz Rothenbühler

Liability law
Dr Fritz Rothenbühler, Dr Christoph Müller

Medical law
Dr Jürg Rieben, Dr Christoph Müller

BAKER & McKENZIE

CHEMIN DES VERGERS 4
1208 GENÈVE

Telephone: +41 22 707 98 00
Fax: +41 22 707 98 01
E-mail: geneva.info@bakernet.com
Website: www.bakernet.com

Languages
English, French, German, Italian, Russian, Spanish, Swedish

Other offices
For a list of all offices and other information regarding the firm please consult Baker & McKenzie's London office entry

Number of lawyers 3,380
at this office 24

Contact
Martin Anderson (managing partner)

Baker & McKenzie is a global law firm with 66 offices in 36 countries.

CATEGORIES OF WORK

Arbitration and litigation
Philippe Preti, Daniel Peregrina

Banking and finance
Martin Anderson, Frédéric Bétrisey

Capital markets
Martin Anderson, Rashid Bahar

Competition, WTO
Serge Pannatier

Corporate and commercial law (general)
Frédéric Helbling

Insolvency, restructuring
Philippe Preti, Daniel Peregrina

Intellectual property
Nathalie Sierro

Labour law and immigration
Alain Stehlé

Mergers and acquisitions
Martin Anderson, Denis Berdoz,

Private clients, trusts and estates
Stephanie Jarrett

Public law, environmental law
Daniel Peregrina

Real estate, property finance
Adrian Moore, Daniel Peregrina

Tax
Denis Berdoz, Per Prod'hom

Telecoms
Daniel Peregrina, Alfons Noll

BOREL & BARBEY

2 RUE DE JARGONNANT
PO BOX 6045
1211 GENÈVE 6

Telephone: +41 22 707 18 00
Fax: +41 22 707 18 11
E-mail: mail@borel-barbey.ch
Website: www.borel-barbey.ch

Languages
English, French, German, Italian, Norwegian, Spanish

Number of lawyers 28

Contacts
Olivier Dunant, Nicolas Piérard

Other information
Established in 1907

CATEGORIES OF WORK

Commercial law (general) and contracts

Banking, securities and corporate finance

Competition, antitrust

Copyright, industrial property and media law

Mergers and acquisitions, corporate restructuring

Project finance

Tax

Distribution, agency, licensing

International arbitration, banking and commercial litigation

International legal assistance

Bankruptcy, creditors' rights

Wills, trusts and estate planning

Work and residence permits

CROISIER GILLIOZ & ASSOCIÉS

61 RUE DE RHÔNE
1211 GENÈVE 11

Telephone: +41 22 319 09 09
Fax: +41 22 319 09 11
E-mail: mail@cglaw.ch
Website: www.cglaw.ch

Languages
English, French, German, Italian, Spanish

Other offices
Zug, Zurich

Number of lawyers 35
at this office 5

CATEGORIES OF WORK

Corporate and commercial law
J P Croisier, A Gillioz

Litigation civil and commercial
P Prost, N Didisheim

Arbitration
P Prost, N Didisheim

Banking and finance
N Didisheim, A Gillioz

Trust
N Didisheim, J P Croisier

Tax
A Gillioz, J P Croisier

Contracts
A Gillioz, P Prost

Art law
J P Croisier, P Prost

Money laundering regulations
N Didisheim, J P Croisier

Estate planning
J P Croisier, N Didisheim

FRORIEP RENGGLI
SWISS LAWYERS

4 RUE CHARLES-BONNET
1211 GENÈVE 12

Telephone: +41 22 839 63 00
Fax: +41 22 347 71 59
E-mail: geneva@froriep.ch
Website: www.froriep.com

Languages
Arabic, English, French, German, Italian, Portuguese, Spanish

Other offices
London, Madrid, Zug, Zurich

Number of lawyers 48
at this office 15

Contact
Jean-Luc Herbez

CATEGORIES OF WORK

Company and commercial
Jean-Luc Herbez,
Jérôme de Montmollin

Mergers and acquisitions
Alain Gros, Nicolas Junod

Banking and securities
Jean-Luc Herbez

Private banking
Nicolas Junod

Sports
Jean-Marie Vulliemin,
Roland Kaufmann

Litigation
Jérôme de Montmollin, Alain Gros

Arbitration
Jean-Marie Vulliemin

International judicial assistance
Roland Kaufmann

Insolvency
Roland Kaufmann

Trusts and estates
Nicolas Junod

Employment
Roland Kaufmann

Art
Jean-Marie Vulliemin

GILLIOZ DORSAZ & ASSOCIÉS

11 RUE DU GÉNÉRAL-DUFOUR
1204 GENÈVE

Telephone: +41 22 702 19 00
Fax: +41 22 702 19 10
E-mail: gdvn@gdlaw.ch
Website: www.gdlaw.ch

Languages
English, French, German, Italian

Number of lawyers 6

CATEGORIES OF WORK

Commercial and company law

Banking and finance

Taxation

Litigation and arbitration

LENZ & STAEHELIN

GRAND'RUE 25
1204 GENEVA

Telephone: +41 22 318 70 00
Fax: +41 22 318 70 01
E-mail: email@lenzstaehelin.com
Website: www.lenzstaehelin.com

Languages
English, French, German, Italian, Portuguese, Romanian, Spanish

Other offices
Fribourg, Lausanne, Zurich

Number of lawyers 130
at this office 60

Contact
Andreas von Planta

CATEGORIES OF WORK

Swiss and international taxation
Henri Torrione, Jean Blaise Eckert

Banking, capital markets
Shelby du Pasquier, Olivier Stahler

Corporate finance
Andreas Rötheli, François Rayroux

Investment trusts, mutual funds
Shelby du Pasquier, Olivier Stahler

International commercial arbitration
Paolo Michele Patocchi,
Xavier Favre-Bulle

Commercial and contract law
Dominique Rochat, Guy Vermeil

Company law, mergers, acquisitions
Andreas von Planta, Andreas Rötheli

International organistations, institutional arbitration
Henri Torrione, Mark Barmes

Residence, work permits, real estate
Olivier Mach

Civil, criminal and administrative litigations, debt and bankruptcy
Benoît Chappuis, Daniel Tunik

Estate planning, trusts
Richard Pease, Caroline Delétra

International private investments
Shelby du Pasquier, Mark Barmes

Copyright, industrial property, unfair competition, media
Mark Barmes, Benoît Merkt

EEC law and antitrust
Olivier Mach

International legal assistance
Benoît Chappuis, Guy Vermeil

Pensions and retirement funds
Olivier Mach, Anne Troillet-Maxwell

MONFRINI CRETTOL & ASSOCIÉS

3 PLACE DU MOLARD
1204 GENÈVE

Telephone: +41 22 310 22 66
Fax: +41 22 310 24 86
E-mail: mail@mcswisslaw.com

Languages
English, French, German, Italian, Portuguese, Spanish, Swedish

Other offices
Crans-Montana

Number of lawyers 8

Contact
Enrico Monfrini, Gilles Crettol

CATEGORIES OF WORK

- Antitrust and unfair competition
- Arbitration
- Banking and finance
- Bankruptcy and debt collection
- Civil and commercial litigation
- Corporate and company
- Family office services
- Immigration and labour
- Intellectual property
- International art and auction
- International business law
- International complex litigation
- International contracts
- International tax and estate planning
- Media, television and entertainment
- Mergers and acquisitions
- Mutual assistance in penal matters, white-collar crime and tracing of assets
- Real estate
- Transportation

THE FIRM

Monfrini Crettol & Associés was founded in 1945 at Place du Molard, Geneva, by the late Alexandre Hauchmann as a general practice, although internationally oriented since its inception. In 1978, Alexandre Hauchmann was joined by Enrico Monfrini, who brought to the firm his knowledge and experience in complex litigation and arbitration, as well as international tax, banking and finance law.

In 2004, the firm was joined by Gilles Crettol, who will strengthen the areas of contract and corporate law, banking law and arbitration, as well as family office services.

Monfrini Crettol & Associés is now composed of eight lawyers (two partners, four associates and two junior lawyers), most of whom have previously worked in other prestigious law firms and have gained experience outside Switzerland and/or followed advanced studies in international law.

Although principally oriented toward international business law, Monfrini Crettol & Associés is determined to continually provide its clients with as wide a range of legal services as possible, and have therefore maintained a general practice.

Monfrini Crettol & Associés have decided to maintain the firm to a size that allows it to provide such services on a personal basis and has resisted the tendency to merger as observed in Switzerland and abroad. This middle size (for Swiss standards) and the complementary background of its lawyers, allows the firm to be cost-effective, efficient, rapid and flexible in order to best suit its clients' needs.

AREAS OF PRACTICE

The firm's clientele is principally composed of wealthy individuals residing in Switzerland and abroad, as well as of the companies they own. Monfrini Crettol & Associés typically provides legal counsel and representation to these persons and corporations in Switzerland, and co-ordinates the work with its network of foreign lawyers. Family office services are also provided.

Monfrini Crettol & Associés also represents corporations, such as banks, financial and portfolio management companies, media, commodities trading companies, insurance companies, multinational corporations, non-profit corporations, foreign governments and state-owned companies.

Monfrini Crettol & Associés has gained a strong reputation in assisting and representing individual claimants, companies and banks, as well as foreign governments in white-collar crime and mutual assistance proceedings. The firm assists foreign governments to recover the proceeds of crimes committed by former heads of state or other civil servants. In that context, Monfrini Crettol & Associés is conducting the largest international recovery proceedings ever on behalf of a government and one of the largest litigation cases in history that involves claims totaling more than $2bn in ten jurisdictions.

NOTTER MÉGEVAND & PARTNERS

PLACE CLAPAREDE 3
1205 GENEVA

Telephone: +41 22 703 47 50
Fax: +41 22 703 47 51
E-mail: geneve@nomea.ch

Languages
English, French, German

Other offices
Bern, Fribourg

Number of lawyers 16
at this office 8

CATEGORIES OF WORK

Commercial

Corporate

Banking and finance

Bankruptcy and insolvency

Tax

Civil law

Administration and public law

International law

Litigation and arbitration

Family office

PESTALOZZI LACHENAL PATRY

65 RUE DU RHÔNE
1204 GENÈVE

Telephone: +41 22 737 10 00
Fax: +41 22 737 10 01
E-mail: gva@plplaw.ch
Website: www.plplaw.ch

Languages
English, French, German, Italian, Spanish

Other offices
Brussels, Zurich

Number of lawyers 111
at this office 31

Contacts
Jean Patry, Claude Brechbuhl

Member
Lex Mundi

CATEGORIES OF WORK

Commercial law (general)
Jean Patry, Claude Brechbuhl

Companies, corporations
Alain Le Fort, Jean-Charles Roguet

Contract
Claude Brechbuhl, Christophe Emonet

Mergers and acquisitions
Bernard Lachenal, Alain Le Fort

Arbitration and litigation
Guy-Philippe Rubeli, Bernard Lachenal

Construction and environmental law
François Dugast, Philippe Cottier

Sports
Jean-Charles Roguet

Tax
Philippe Cottier

Trade marks, intellectual property
Christophe Rapin

Banking, securities and finance
Jean Patry, Alain Le Fort

Immigration
Guy-Philippe Rubeli

Competition, antitrust
Christophe Rapin

Inheritance, estate planning
François Dugast, Frédéric Cottier

PYTHON SCHIFFERLI PETER & ASSOCIÉS

9 RUE MASSOT
1206 GENÈVE

Telephone: +41 22 702 15 15
Fax: +41 22 702 14 14
E-mail: mail@psplaw.ch
Website: www.psplaw.ch

Languages
Dutch, English, French, German, Gujarati, Hebrew, Italian, Japanese, Persian, Portuguese, Spanish, Vietnamese

Other offices
Bern, Brussels, Lausanne, Pully–Lausanne, Sion, Tokyo

Number of lawyers 72
at this office 52

CATEGORIES OF WORK

Banking and finance

Commercial contracts

Corporate, capital markets and M&A

Venture capital

Arbitration and litigation

Insolvency and restructuring

Intellectual property, IT

Telecom and data protection

Tax

EU and competition

International legal assistance

Construction and real estate

Maritime and transport

Insurance

Private clients

SCHELLENBERG WITTMER

15 BIS RUE DES ALPES
PO BOX 2088
1211 GENÈVE 1

Telephone: +41 22 707 80 00
Fax: +41 22 707 80 01
E-mail: geneva@swlegal.ch
Website: www.swlegal.ch

Languages
English, French, German, Italian, Spanish

Other offices
Zurich

Number of lawyers 95
at this office 48

Contact
Bernard Vischer

CATEGORIES OF WORK

General commercial law and contracts

Litigation
Laurent Lévy, Christian Girod

Arbitration
Gabrielle Kaufmann-Kohler, Laurent Lévy

Corporations, mergers and acquisitions, corporate restructuring
Bernard Vischer, Roy Ryan

Banking and finance
Lionel Aeschlimann, Bernard Haissly

Intellectual property and information technology, e-business
Yves Jeanrenaud

Trusts/estate planning
Jacques Wittmer, Bernard Haissly

Taxation
Pietro Sansonetti, Joëlle Zumoffen

Real estate and construction
Yves Jeanrenaud

Transport and international trade
Bernard Vischer

Insolvency, bankruptcy
Vincent Jeanneret

International legal assistance
Vincent Jeanneret, Paul Gully-Hart

Employment and immigration
Raphael Biaggi

WINSTON & STRAWN LLP

43 RUE DU RHONE
1204 GENEVA

Telephone: +41 22 317 75 75
Fax: +41 22 317 75 00
E-mail: postmaster@winston.com
Website: www.winston.com

Languages
English, French, German, Italian, Spanish

Other offices
Chicago, London, Los Angeles, New York, Paris, San Francisco, Washington DC

Number of lawyers 850
at this office 12

CATEGORIES OF WORK

International arbitration
Charles C Adams, Nicolas C Ulmer

International judicial assistance
Michael J Stepek, Ricardo Ugarte

Product liability
Marc S Palay, David E Mollon

Commercial contracts
Nicolas C Ulmer, Franz X Stirnimann

International maritime and admiralty
Charles C Adams, Michael J Stepek

Mergers and acquisitions
Nicolas C Ulmer, Vanessa Liborio

International construction law
Charles C Adams, Marc S Palay

International property law
Marc S Palay, David E Mollon

Trusts and estates
Nicolas C Ulmer, Franz X Stirnimann

Banking and insurance
Ricardo Ugarte, Franz X Stirnimann

BADERTSCHER DÖRIG POLEDNA

VIA LODOVICO ARIOSTO 6
PO BOX 5162
6901 LUGANO

Telephone: +41 91 911 80 00
Fax: +41 91 911 80 08
E-mail: bdplaw@bdp.ch
Website: www.bdp.ch

Languages
Czech, English, French, German, Italian, Spanish, Slovak

Other offices
Zurich

Number of lawyers 22
at this office 2

Contact
Dr Markus Dörig

Member
MSI MacIntyre Sträter International Ltd; IBA; ALFA International

CATEGORIES OF WORK

Administration and public law
Beat Badertscher, Tomas Poledna

Arbitration, litigation
Markus Dörig, Beat Badertscher

Banking
Beat Badertscher

Company law
Markus Dörig, Beat Badertscher

Commercial law
Beat Badertscher, Markus Dörig

Capital markets
Beat Badertscher, Markus Dörig

Employment
Markus Dörig

Energy
Beat Badertscher

Intellectual property
Stefano Codoni

Information technology
Stefano Codoni

Healthcare
Tomas Poledna

Mergers and acquisitions
Markus Dörig, Jasmin Ghandchi

Privatisations
Tomas Poledna, Stefano Codoni

Telecommunications
Stefano Codoni, Lorenzo Marazzotta

E-commerce
Jasmin Ghandchi, Stefano Codoni

SPIESS BRUNONI PEDRAZZINI MOLINO

LAW OFFICE

VIA PIODA 14
PO BOX 6481
6901 LUGANO

Telephone: +41 91 911 74 11
Fax: +41 91 923 94 68
E-mail: info@legalnotarile.ch
Website: www.legalnotarile.ch

Languages
English, French, German, Italian

Other offices
Locarno

Number of lawyers 16

Contacts
Massimo Pedrazzini (mpedrazzini@legalnotarile.ch), Andrea Molino (amolino@legalnotarile.ch)

CATEGORIES OF WORK

- Administrative
- Commercial property, real estate
- Dispute resolution – litigation and arbitration
- Foreign direct investment
- Infrastructure and project finance
- Insurance
- Mergers and acquisitions
- Tax
- Banking and finance
- Corporate and commercial
- Employment
- Fraud and white-collar crime
- Insolvency, corporate restructuring
- Intellectual property
- Private client
- Notarial services
- Sports law
- Gambling and gaming

FRORIEP RENGGLI

SWISS LAWYERS

BAARERSTRASSE 37
6304 ZUG

Telephone: +41 41 710 60 00
Fax: +41 41 710 60 01
E-mail: zug@froriep.ch
Website: www.froriep.com

Languages
English, French, German, Swedish

Other offices
Geneva, London, Madrid, Zurich

Number of lawyers 48
at this office 4

Contact
Hans Stuber

CATEGORIES OF WORK

- Notarial services
- Tax
- Company and commercial
- Commercial litigation, arbitration
- Estate planning

REICHLIN & HESS

HOFSTRASSE 1A
6300 ZUG

Telephone: +41 41 729 10 70
Fax: +41 41 729 10 80
E-mail: law@reichlin-hess.ch
Website: www.reichlin-hess.ch

Languages
English, French, German

Number of lawyers 10

CATEGORIES OF WORK

Corporate

Banking and capital markets

Contracts

Estates

Litigation and arbitration

Real estate, construction and environmental matters

Intellectual property

Telecoms and media

Human resources

Foreigners

Public notarisation and legalisation

Fiscal matters

BADERTSCHER DÖRIG POLEDNA

MÜHLEBACHSTRASSE 32
PO BOX 769
8024 ZÜRICH

Telephone: +41 1 266 20 66
Fax: +41 1 266 20 70
E-mail: bdplaw@bdp.ch
Website: www.bdp.ch

Languages
Czech, English, French, German, Italian, Slovak, Spanish

Other offices
Lugano

Number of lawyers 22
at this office 20

Contact
Dr Markus Dörig

Member
MSI MacIntyre Sträter International Ltd; IBA; ALFA International

CATEGORIES OF WORK

Administration and public law
Beat Badertscher, Tomas Poledna

Arbitration, litigation
Markus Dörig, Beat Badertscher

Banking
Beat Badertscher, Markus Dörig

Company law
Markus Dörig, Beat Badertscher

Commercial law
Beat Badertscher, Markus Dörig

Capital markets
Beat Badertscher, Markus Dörig

Employment
Markus Dörig

Energy
Beat Badertscher, Allen Fuchs

Intellectual property
Martin Kurer, Stefano Codoni

Information technology
Stefano Codoni, Jasmin Ghandchi

Healthcare
Tomas Poledna

Mergers and acquisitions
Martin Kurer, Jasmin Ghandchi

Privatisations
Allen Fuchs, Tomas Poledna

Telecommunications
Allen Fuchs, Lorenzo Marazzotta

E-commerce
Jasmin Ghandchi, Stefano Codoni

BAKER & McKENZIE

ZOLLIKERSTRASSE 225
PO BOX
8034 ZÜRICH

Telephone: +41 1 384 14 14
Fax: +41 1 384 12 84
E-mail: zurich.info@bakernet.com
Website: www.bakernet.com

Languages
English, French, German, Italian, Romanian, Spanish, Swedish

Other offices
For a list of all offices and other information regarding the firm please consult Baker & McKenzie's London office entry

Number of lawyers 3,380
at this office 53

Contact
M Treis

Baker & McKenzie is a global law firm with 66 offices in 36 countries.

CATEGORIES OF WORK

Aircraft financing
J Frick

Arbitration and litigation
F Schenker, U Zenhäusern

Banking and finance
U Schenker, M Affentranger

Commercial law (general), contract law
F Schenker, M Berni

Companies, corporations
M Frey, M Berni

EC law
P Reich, P Reinert

Immigration
P Reinert

Information technology
M Berni, M Treis

Insurance
M Affentranger, J Frick

Intellectual property
M Treis, U Zenhäusern

Labour law
P Reinert

Mergers and acquisitions
U Schenker, M Frey

Tax
H Koch, P Marcovici

Trusts and estates
P Marcovici, R Gassmann

BÄR & KARRER

BRANDSCHENKESTRASSE 90
8023 ZÜRICH

Telephone: +41 58 261 50 00
Fax: +41 58 261 50 01
E-mail: zuerich@baerkarrer.ch
Website: www.baerkarrer.ch

Languages
English, French, German, Italian

Other offices
Geneva, London, Lugano, Zug

Number of lawyers 90

CATEGORIES OF WORK

Banking and finance
Eric Stupp, Urs Brügger

Transactions
Prof Rolf Watter, Eric Stupp

Listed companies and securities law
Urs Brügger, Ralph Malacrida

Arbitration
Marc Blessing, Michelle Sindler

Litigation
Daniel Hochstrasser, Andreas Länzlinger

Private clients, trusts and estates
Nedim Peter Vogt, Christian Steinmann

Commercial law (general) and international contracts
Felix Ehrat (senior partner), Peter Kienast

Tax
Peter Reinarz, Daniel Lehmann

Intellectual and industrial property and copyright, competition law and cartels, trade marks
Markus Wang, Marc Blessing

IT and telecoms law
Michele Bernasconi

Administrative law and real estate
Peter J Kienast, Daniel Hochstrasser

Construction, insurance, EC law
Marc Blessing

Notarial services
Markus Schnurrenberger (Zug office)

BILL, ISENEGGER & ACKERMANN

WITIKONERSTRASSE 61
POSTFACH
8030 ZÜRICH

Telephone: +41 1 386 88 88
Fax: +41 1 386 88 99
E-mail: admin@bialaw.ch
Website: www.bialaw.ch

Languages
English, French, German, Italian, Spanish

Number of lawyers 14

Contacts
Dr Urs Isenegger (ui@bialaw.ch),
Peter R Ackermann (pa@bialaw.ch)

CATEGORIES OF WORK

Contracts

Torts

Corporate law

Mergers and acquisitions

Communications law (including e-commerce, telecoms, Internet)

Intellectual property (including technology transfer and exploitation concepts) and competition law

Tax law, insolvency

Banking and securities

Aviation law

Inheritance law (including asset and estate planning)

Litigation and arbitration

Immigration

International private law

BRATSCHI EMCH & PARTNER

BAHNHOFSTRASSE 106
POSTFACH 7689
8023 ZÜRICH

Telephone: +41 1 211 16 64
Fax: +41 1 211 16 69
E-mail: zurichoffice@bep.ch
Website: www.bep.ch

Languages
English, French,German, Italian, Spanish

Other offices
Bern

Number of lawyers 27
at this office 12

CATEGORIES OF WORK

Contract and commercial
Dr C Schmid, F Szolansky

Corporate and M&A
Dr D Glasl, Dr R Arpagaus

Commercial litigation/arbitration
Dr C Schmid, Dr D Glasl

Competition
Dr C Schmid, Dr D Glasl

Banking and finance
Dr R Arpagaus, Dr C Schmid

Media and communication
F Szolansky

Intellectual property
Dr R Arpagaus

Estate and inheritance law
Dr C Schmid, Dr D Glasl

Administrative law
Dr I Häner

Construction and environmental
Dr I Häner

Sports law
F Szolansky, Dr R Arpagaus

Debt enforcement and bankruptcy
F Szolansky, Dr D Glasl

BÜRGI NÄGELI LAWYERS

GROSSMÜNSTERPLATZ 9
8001 ZURICH

Telephone: +41 1 268 40 00
Fax: +41 1 268 40 05
E-mail: info@bnlawyers.ch
Website: www.bnlawyers.ch

Languages
English, French, German, Italian, Spanish

Other offices
Bern, Schlieren

Number of lawyers 15
at this office 13

CATEGORIES OF WORK

- **Company and commercial**
- **Contracts**
- **Real estate and construction**
- **Insolvency and creditors' rights, debt collection**
- **Inheritance law, trusts, financial and estate planning**
- **Banking and finance**
- **Tax**
- **Intellectual property**
- **Communications**
- **Matters of public law**
- **Arbitration**
- **Litigation**

THE FIRM

Bürgi Nägeli Lawyers was founded by Urs Bürgi and Dr Catarina Nägeli in 1994; since its inception it has grown steadily. Today the law firm consists of six partners, each of whom has developed specific areas of expertise. The firm counts 15 attorneys in total, who – in co-operation with certified accountants, economists, architects, banking experts – offer a one-stop shop for the firm's clients. The firm places great importance on flexible, efficient, pragmatic and timely solutions, tailored to its clients' individual needs, and therefore generating added value for them. To speed up the implementation of such overall advice, Bürgi Nägeli Lawyers also use products of third parties via existing networks.

The offices are located in the heart of Zurich, directly facing the Grossmünster. The firm also maintains offices in Bern and Schlierein, in order to cater for the specific needs of its clients.

AREAS OF PRACTICE

Bürgi Nägeli Lawyers do not focus exclusively on legal foundations and their interpretation in theory and jurisdiction. Business and economic considerations accompany the legal advice.

Individuals, corporations, authorities and communities avail themselves of the services of Bürgi Nägeli Lawyers.

The business-oriented law office is active supra-regionally and internationally in an advisory and forensic capacity; Bürgi Nägeli Lawyers apply national, European and international law.

The firm's advisory activity focuses on prevention (compliance), risk management, risk assessment and out-of-court conflict settlement (mediation activity).

Bürgi Nägeli Lawyers regularly advise on: real estate and construction law – building and planning law, contract law in co-operative planning procedures, environmental law/legacies; estate planning, wills and trusts and inheritance law; company law – formation of companies, especially incorporation of companies and advice to foreign companies in matters of opening branch offices in Switzerland and to Swiss companies abroad, location consulting; commercial law; insolvency and creditors rights – debt collection and bankruptcy, company reorganisation, probate proceedings (as counsel for the debtor or as administrator/liquidator, private commissioner in bankruptcy); matters of public law; telecommunications, electronic media, Internet; arbitration; probate law, provisions, succession planning, life-cycle-consultancy; banking and securities; and notary support.

Bürgi Nägeli Lawyers also take on external legal services in an in-house and/or external relationship (outsourcing).

BUSE HEBERER FROMM

BAHNHOFSTRASSE 58
8001 ZURICH

Telephone: +41 1 253 2565
Fax: +41 1 253 2566
Email: zuerich@buse.de
Website: www.buse.de

Languages
English, French, Italian, Spanish

Other offices
Berlin, Dusseldorf, Essen, Frankfurt am Main, Hamburg, Milan, Munich, Palma de Mallorca, Sydney

Number of lawyers 120
at this office 1

Member
The European Legal Alliance (Beauchamps, Ireland; Dubarry Le Douarin Veil, France; Field Fisher Waterhouse, England; Harper Macleod, Scotland)

CATEGORIES OF WORK

Banking and finance

Antitrust and merger control

Commerce, transport, insurance

Commercial delinquency

Corporate/M&A

Industrial property and copyrights

Information technology and telecommunications

Labour and employment

Litigation and arbitration, national and international

Press and media

Property and construction

Public law

Tax

CMS VON ERLACH KLAINGUTI STETTLER WILLE
ATTORNEYS AT LAW

DREIKÖNIGSTRASSE 7
PO BOX 4088
8022 ZÜRICH

Telephone: +41 1 285 11 11
Fax: +41 1 285 11 22
E-mail: office@cmslegal.ch
Website: www.cmslegal.ch

Languages
English, French, German, Italian, Spanish

Number of lawyers 32

Member
CMS Transnational Legal Services

CATEGORIES OF WORK

Commercial law (general and international)
Hans Wille, Max Albers

Mergers and acquisitions, corporate restructuring
Hans Wille, Max Albers

Banking, securities and finance, capital markets
Ernest Klainguti, Kaspar Landolt

Competition, antitrust, and intellectual property
Patrick Sommer, Alain Raemy

Healthcare, drug and biotechnology
Rudolf von Erlach

Information technology, telecommunications
Alain Raemy, Oliver Blum

Tax (Swiss and international)
Hans Wille

Product liability, torts
Beat von Rechenberg, Damiano Brusa

Employment, work and residence permits
Rudolf von Erlach, Stefan Gerster

Wills, trusts and estate planning
Dieter Stettler, Rudolf von Erlach

Distribution, agency, licensing
Hans Wille

Civil, criminal and administrative litigations
Beat von Rechenberg, Damiano Brusa

Arbitration, international legal assistance
Beat von Rechenberg, Damiano Brusa

EC law, private international law
Patrick Sommer, Oliver Blum

Real estate
Dieter Stettler, Stefan Gerster

DE CAPITANI, KRONAUER, BUIS

LIMMATQUAI 3
8001 ZÜRICH

Telephone: +41 1 262 46 79
Fax: +41 1 252 98 04
E-mail: mail@decapitani.ch
Website: www.decapitani.ch

Languages
English, French, German, Italian

Number of lawyers 6

Contacts
Dr M Kronauer, Dr E Buis

CATEGORIES OF WORK

Commercial and banking litigation

Commercial and banking law

FRORIEP RENGGLI
SWISS LAWYERS

BELLERIVESTRASSE 201
8034 ZÜRICH

Telephone: +41 1 386 60 00
Fax: +41 1 383 60 50
E-mail: zurich@froriep.ch
Website: www.froriep.com

Languages
Dutch, English, French, German, Hebrew, Italian, Portuguese, Spanish, Turkish

Other offices
Geneva, London, Madrid, Zug

Number of lawyers 48
at this office 25

Contact
Felix M Mathis

CATEGORIES OF WORK

Company and commercial
Felix M Mathis, Eric Haymann

Mergers and acquisitions
Peter J Merz, Beat M Barthold

Capital markets
Eric Haymann, Beat M Barthold

Banking and finance
Peter J Merz, Beat M Barthold

Telecommunications
Alessandro L Celli

International judicial assistance
Peter J Merz, Marcel C Steinegger

White-collar crime
Marcel C Steinegger

Employment
Marcel C Steinegger

Intellectual property
Alessandro L Celli

Arbitration
Claudia Kälin

Litigation
Marcel C Steinegger, Peter J Merz

Trusts and estate
Eric Haymann

Competition
Alessandro L Celli

Insolvency
Felix M Mathis, Beat M Barthold

Aviation
Felix M Mathis

Corporate finance
Beat M Barthold

HARTMANN MÜLLER PARTNERS

ZÜRICHBERGSTRASSE 66
8044 ZÜRICH

Telephone: +41 43 268 83 00
Fax: +41 43 268 83 01
E-mail: contact@hmp.ch
Website: www.hmp.ch

Languages
English, French, German

Other offices
Zug

Number of lawyers 10
at this office 8

Member
MULTILAW

CATEGORIES OF WORK

Arbitration
Jürg Hartmann, Niklaus Müller

Banking and finance
Rudolph Schaub, Jürg Burger

Competition law
Jürg Hartmann, Beat Spörri

Contracts
Rudolph Schaub, Marco Barbatti

Corporate law
Jürg Hartmann, Beat Spörri

E-commerce
Marc Barbatti

Inheritance
Christoph Martig, Marc Barbatti

Insolvency and restructuring
Niklaus Müller, Rudolph Schaub

Intellectual property
Jürg Burger

Litigation
Niklaus Müller

Mergers and acquisitions
Jürg Hartmann, Rudolph Schaub

Transportation law
Christoph Martig

Work permits and immigration
Beat Spörri

HAYMANN & BALDI

ZELTWEG 44
POSTFACH 1622
8032 ZÜRICH

Telephone: +41 1 250 25 25
Fax: +41 1 250 25 00
E-mail: lawyers@hblaw.ch
Website: www.hblaw.ch

Languages
English, French, German, Italian, Portuguese, Spanish

Number of lawyers 9

Contacts
Michel Haymann, Peter Baldi

CATEGORIES OF WORK

Corporate and commercial, mergers and acquisitions

Banking, finance and securities

Initial public offerings and stock exchange law

Corporate taxation and international tax planning

International commercial litigation

International arbitration

Intellectual property

EU law

Estate planning and trusts

Judicial assistance in criminal matters

Antitrust and competition

Labour, employment

Eastern European and CIS privatisations

Project finance in the CIS

HENRICI, WICKI & GUGGISBERG
ATTORNEYS-AT-LAW

HOTTINGERSTRASSE 21
PO BOX 526
8024 ZÜRICH

Telephone: +41 1 266 65 00
Fax: +41 1 266 65 01
E-mail: mail@hwg.ch
Website: www.hwg.ch

Languages
English, French, German, Italian, Spanish

Number of lawyers 12

Contacts
Dr André Aloys Wicki, Jürg Guggisberg, Dr Hans-Peter Schaad, Dr Jodok Wicki, Bernhard Lötscher

CATEGORIES OF WORK

- Arbitration and litigation
- Banking (private and regulatory)
- Bankruptcy and insolvency law
- Business law
- Civil (general civil) practice
- Commercial law
- Commodities law
- Contract law
- Corporate law
- Estate planning
- Finance law
- Immigration and nationality or naturalisation law
- International business law
- International legal assistance
- Mergers and acquisitions
- Tort law

HESS DALLAFIOR ATTORNEYS AT LAW

RÄMISTRASSE 5
PO BOX
8024 ZÜRICH

Telephone: +41 1 250 49 49
Fax: +41 1 250 49 00
E-mail: info@hdlegal.ch
Website: www.hdlegal.ch

Languages
English, French, German, Italian

Number of lawyers 10

Contacts
Dr Roberto Dallafior, Dr Mathis Berger

CATEGORIES OF WORK

Commercial law
Dr Daniel Alder, Peter Schatz

Corporate law, mergers and acquisitions
Peter Schatz, Dr Mathis Berger

Banking and financial services
Werner A Schubiger, Dr Markus Hess

Intellectual property, information technology
Dr Daniel Alder, Dr Mathis Berger

Competition law
Dr Roberto Dallafior, Dr Mathis Berger

Labour law
Dr Daniel Alder

Litigation and arbitration
Dr Roberto Dallafior, Dr Florian Baumann

Insolvency
Dr Markus Hess, Peter Schatz

International legal assistance
Dr Florian Baumann

Private clients
Dr Markus Hess

HOMBURGER

WEINBERGSTRASSE 56-58
8006 ZÜRICH
PO BOX 338
8035 ZÜRICH

Telephone: +41 43 222 10 00
Fax: +41 43 222 15 00
E-mail: lawyers@homburger.ch
Website: www.homburger.ch

Languages
English, French, German, Italian

Number of lawyers 70

CATEGORIES OF WORK

Arbitration
M Wirth, F Dasser

Banking and finance
R Bösch, P Widmer

Capital markets
D Daeniker, B Maurenbrecher

Company and commercial law
C Lambert, H Appenzeller

Competition and antitrust
F Hoffet, M Dietrich

EU law
M Dietrich, F Hoffet

Information technology
G Rauber, G Bühler

Insolvency
U Huber

Intellectual property
W Stieger, G Rauber

Litigation
T Müller, B Gross

Mergers and acquisitions
H Schärer, F Romerio

Tax
E Saupper, P Riedweg

Trusts and estates
H Grüninger

LENZ & STAEHELIN

BLEICHERWEG 58
8002 ZÜRICH

Telephone: +41 1 204 12 12
Fax: +41 1 204 12 00
E-mail: email@lenzstaehelin.com
Website: www.lenzstaehelin.com

Languages
Czech, English, French, German, Italian, Russian, Spanish

Other offices
Fribourg, Geneva, Lausanne

Number of lawyers 130
at this office 64

Contact
Matthias Oertle

CATEGORIES OF WORK

Arbitration
Rudolf Tschäni, Martin Burkhardt

Banking and capital markets
Stefan Breitenstein, Patrick Schleiffer

Competition
Marcel Meinhardt

Corporate finance
Christoph Reinhardt, Patrick Hünerwadel

Employment and compensation
Urs L Baumgartner

Information technology
Lukas Morscher

Intellectual property and copyright law
Martin Lutz, Thierry Calame

Litigation
Martin Burkhardt, Peter Hafner

Mergers and acquisitions
Rudolf Tschäni, Marcel Meinhardt

Tax
Heini Rüdisühli

Trusts and estates
Peter Max Gutzwiller

MEYER LUSTENBERGER

FORCHSTRASSE 452
PO BOX 832
8029 ZÜRICH

Telephone: +41 1 396 91 91
Fax: +41 1 396 91 92
E-mail: zurich@ml-law.ch
Website: www.meyerlustenberger.ch

Languages
English, French, German, Italian, Norwegian, Portuguese, Spanish

Other offices
Geneva, Zug

Number of lawyers 33

Contact
Thomas Lustenberger

CATEGORIES OF WORK

Mergers and acquisitions
Thomas Lustenberger

Banking, capital markets and e-banking
Christoph Heiz

Company, securities, commercial and e-commerce
Alexander Vogel

Tax
Urs Behnisch

Intellectual property
Michael Ritscher

Competition and antitrust, public procurement
Martin Ammann

Media, IT and telecoms
Armin Zucker

Arbitration and litigation, forensic services
Marcel Lustenberger

MEYER MÜLLER ECKERT PARTNERS – ATTORNEYS AT LAW

KREUZSTRASSE 42
8008 ZÜRICH

Telephone: +41 1 254 99 66
Fax: +41 1 254 99 60
E-mail: office@mme-law.ch
Website: www.mme-law.ch

Languages
English, French, German

Number of lawyers 13

CATEGORIES OF WORK

International contracts
BF Meyer-Hauser, L Müller-Studer

Intellectual property
MK Eckert, BF Meyer-Hauser

Agency and distribution
L Müller-Studer, MK Eckert

Internet and multimedia
MK Eckert, L Müller-Studer

Telecommunications
MK Eckert, L Müller-Studer

Joint ventures
BF Meyer-Hauser, MK Eckert

Insurance and finance
M Kuhn, MK Eckert

Banking and stock exchange
M Kuhn, MK Eckert

Compliance law
L Müller-Studer, M Kuhn

Unfair competition
BF Meyer-Hauser, L Müller-Studer

Labour law
M Kuhn, L Müller-Studer

Mergers and acquisitions
BF Meyer-Hauser, MK Eckert

Arbitration and mediation
BF Meyer-Hauser, L Müller-Studer

International litigation
L Müller-Studer, BF Meyer-Hauser

Electronic public offerings
L Müller-Studer, MK Eckert

NEUPERT & PARTNERS

DUFOURSTRASSE 58
8702 ZOLLIKON-ZÜRICH

Telephone: +41 1 396 80 80
Fax: +41 1 396 80 88
E-mail: neupert@nplaw.ch

Languages
English, French, German, Hebrew, Hungarian, Italian, Russian, Spanish

Other offices
Geneva, Lugano, Zug

Number of lawyers 15
at this office 7

Contact
Dr Dieter W Neupert

Other information
Established 1851

CATEGORIES OF WORK

- Business law
- Corporate finance
- Banking
- Taxation
- Creditors' rights
- Real estate
- Employment
- Aviation
- Litigation
- Notarial services

NIEDERER KRAFT & FREY
RECHTSANWÄLTE

BAHNHOFSTRASSE 13
8001 ZÜRICH

Telephone: +41 58 800 8000
Fax: +41 58 800 8080
E-mail: nkf@nkf.ch
Website: www.nkf.ch

Languages
Dutch, English, French, German, Italian, Spanish

Number of lawyers 65

CATEGORIES OF WORK

- Banking, securities and finance
- Company and commercial
- Mergers and acquisitions
- Competition and antitrust
- Tax
- EU law
- IT and telecommunications
- Arbitration, litigation and judicial assistance
- Insolvency and restructuring
- Insurance
- Intellectual property
- Project finance (including aircraft finance)
- Wills, trusts and estate planning
- Environmental and healthcare law
- Sports law

PESTALOZZI LACHENAL PATRY

LÖWENSTRASSE 1
8001 ZÜRICH

Telephone: +41 1 217 9111
Fax: +41 1 217 9217
E-mail: zrh@plplaw.ch
Website: www.plplaw.ch

Languages
Dutch, English, French, German, Italian, Spanish, Swedish, Thai

Other offices
Brussels, Geneva

Number of lawyers 111
at this office 58

Contacts
Dr Robert Furter

Member
Lex Mundi

CATEGORIES OF WORK

Commercial law (general)
Christoph R Ramstein

Companies, corporations
Dr Jakob Höhn, Dr Hans Bollmann

Contract
Dr Jakob Höhn, Dr Peter Straub

Mergers and acquisitions
Dr Hans Bollmann, Dr Jakob Höhn

Arbitration and litigation
Dr Peter Straub, Dr Pierre A Karrer

Tax
Dr Silvia Zimmermann,
Dr Marcus Desax

Trade marks, intellectual property
Dr Peter Pestalozzi, Dr Robert G Briner

Banking, securities and finance
Gerhard Niggli, Dr Robert Furter

Immigration
Christian Roos, Dr Peter Straub

Competition, antitrust
Dr Jürg Borer, Christian Roos

Liability
Dr Marcus Desax, Dr Urs Jordi

Employment
Christian Roos, Dr Peter Straub

Insolvency
Dr Karl Arnold, Dr Max Walter

Telecommunications
Dr Robert Briner

Inheritance law, estate planning
Dr Urs Jordi, Dr Max Walter

RINDERKNECHT KLEIN & STADELHOFER

BEETHOVENSTRASSE 7
PO BOX 2755
8022 ZÜRICH

Telephone: + 41 1 287 24 24
Fax: + 41 1 287 24 00
E-mail: rks@rks.ch
Website: www.rks.ch

Languages
English, French, German, Italian, Portuguese, Russian, Spanish

Number of lawyers 9

Contact
Gerrit Straub

CATEGORIES OF WORK

Litigation, arbitration, international disputes, international legal assistance
Thomas Klein, Gerrit Straub

Banking and finance law, investment funds
Carl Stadelhofer, Thomas Klein

M&A and IPOs
Dr Thomas Rinderknecht,
Carl Stadelhofer

Oil, gas, energy and metals contracts and structures
Carl Stadelhofer, Gerrit Straub

International holding and tax structures
Dr Thomas Rinderknecht,
Carl Stadelhofer

Estates and wills
Dr Thomas Rinderknecht,
Petra-Nicole Marbach

Pharmaceuticals and life sciences law
Dr Thomas Rinderknecht,
Dr Jeannette Wibmer

Publishing and media law
Dr Thomas Rinderknecht,
Petra-Nicole Marbach

Information technology and e-commerce
Dr Jeannette Wibmer, Mario Ermini

Intellectual property rights, advertising and marketing
Dr Jeannette Wibmer, Mario Ermini

ROHNER RECHTSANWÄLTE

SEESTRASSE 131
8027 ZÜRICH

Telephone: +41 1 281 10 00
Fax: +41 1 281 00 00
E-mail: mail@rohnerlaw.ch
Website: www.rohnerlaw.ch

Languages
English, French, German, Italian, Spanish

Number of lawyers 3

Contact
Dr Louis Rohner

Member
Interleges

CATEGORIES OF WORK

Business and commercial law	**Product liability, torts**
Contract law, Internet, contracts	**Competition law**
Corporate law, joint ventures	**Tax law**
Banking, stock exchange and finance	**Employment law**
Securities law	**Rents and leases**
Real property transactions	**Immigration law**
Intellectual property	**Insolvency law**
Matrimonial and inheritance law	**Litigation and arbitration**
Estate planning, trust and foundations	

SCHELLENBERG WITTMER

LÖWENSTRASSE 19
PO BOX 6333
8023 ZÜRICH

Telephone: +41 1 215 52 52
Fax: +41 1 215 52 00
E-mail: zurich@swlegal.ch
Website: www.swlegal.ch

Languages
English, French, German, Italian

Other offices
Geneva

Number of lawyers 95
at this office 47

Contact
Dr Martin Lanz, Dr Oliver Triebold

CATEGORIES OF WORK

General commercial law and contracts

Litigation
Martin Bernet, Alexander Jolles

Arbitration
Georg von Segesser, Marc Ronca

Corporations, mergers and acquisitions, corporate restructuring
Martin Weber, Andrea Grimm

Banking and finance
Martin Lanz, Philippe Borens

Capital markets
Martin Lanz, Lorenzo Olgiati

Intellectual property and competition
Andrea Mondini, Martin Weber

IT, telecommunication, e-business
Corinna Klaus-Rüesch

Trusts/estate planning
Georg von Segesser

Taxation
Michael Nordin

Transport and international trade
Alexander von Ziegler

Insolvency, bankruptcy
Thomas Bolliger

International legal assistance
Martin Bernet, Nathalie Voser

Employment and immigration
Thomas Bolliger,
Christine Beusch-Liggenstorfer

Art law
Georg von Segesser, Alexander Jolles

STAIGER, SCHWALD & PARTNERS

GENFERSTRASSE 24
PO BOX 677
8027 ZÜRICH

Telephone: +41 1 283 86 86
Fax: +41 1 283 87 87
E-mail: ssplaw@ssplaw.ch
Website: www.ssplaw.ch

Languages
English, French, German, Italian

Other offices
Bern

Number of lawyers 28
at this office 24

Contacts
Dr Hans-Rudolf Staiger,
Lic iur HSG Hans-Peter Schwald,
Dr Marc Bernheim

CATEGORIES OF WORK

Arbitration and litigation

Banking, securities, finance

Company and commercial law

Insolvency

Immigration

Competition, antitrust, trade marks and copyright

EU law and private international law

Mergers and acquisitions

Tax

Wills, trusts and estate planning

Media and entertainment

Energy market law

STIFFLER & NATER
RECHTSANWÄLTE

DUFOURSTRASSE 101
8034 ZÜRICH

Telephone: +41 1 388 48 48
Fax: +41 1 388 48 00
E-mail: info@stn.ch
Website: www.stn.ch

Languages
English, French, German, Italian, Norwegian, Portuguese, Spanish

Number of lawyers 13

Member
Lexwork International, an association of mid-sized independent law firms in Europe

CATEGORIES OF WORK

Corporate and business law
Hans Nater, Eric R Scherrer

Commercial litigation
Laurent Killias, Paola Wullschleger

Mergers and acquisitions
Hans Nater, Heinz Klarer

Telecommunications
Hans Nater, Albert Schmid

Banking
Heinz Klarer, Eric R Scherrer

Wills
Mirko Roš, Regula Rhiner

Civil liability, medical malpractice
Heinz Klarer, Philipp Diederichs

Administrative law
Albert Schmid

Arbitration
Laurent Killias, Hans Nater

Intellectual property
Albert Schmid, Regula Bergsma

Sports law
Hans Nater

White-collar crime
Mirko Roš, Michael Aepli

Bankruptcy
Heinz Klarer

Energy law
Albert Schmid

Tax
Ruedi Bossi, Hans Sulser

THOUVENIN RECHTSANWÄLTE

KLAUSSTRASSE 33
8034 ZURICH

Telephone: +41 1 421 45 45
Fax: +41 1 421 45 00
E-mail: info@thouvenin.com
Website: www.thouvenin.com

Languages
English, French, German, Italian

Number of lawyers 18

Contact
David Känzig

CATEGORIES OF WORK

Arbitration
André Thouvenin, Hansjörg Stutzer

Litigation
Daniel Stoll, Hansjörg Stutzer

Banking and securities
Daniel Stoll, David Känzig

Competition law
Michael Kneller

Corporate
Hansjörg Stutzer, Michael Kneller

Distribution law
André Thouvenin, Michael Kneller

Employment law
Ulrich Mayer, André Thouvenin

Private clients
Michael Kneller

Insolvency law
David Känzig, André Thouvenin

Intellectual property
Thomas Loher, Marc Wenger

Mergers and acquisitions
David Känzig, Michael Kneller

Railways and transportation law
Ulrich Mayer

Real estate, lease and construction law
Ulrich Mayer

Telecommunications and new technologies
David Känzig, Hansjörg Stutzer

Turnaround management
Hansjörg Stutzer

Contracts
André Thouvenin, Hansjörg Stutzer

UMBRICHT
RECHTSANWÄLTE

BAHNHOFSTRASSE 22
8022 ZÜRICH

Telephone: +41 1 213 6363
Fax: +41 1 213 6399
E-mail: attorneys@umbricht.ch
Website: www.umbricht.ch

Languages
English, French, German, Italian

Number of lawyers 12

Contact
Dr Robert Umbricht

CATEGORIES OF WORK

Commercial law

Banking, securities and finance

Insolvency law

Mergers and acquisitions

Wills, trusts and estate planning

Tax

Companies and corporation

Arbitration and litigation

Constitutional and administrative law

International judicial assistance

WTO law

VISCHER

SCHÜTZENGASSE 1
8023 ZÜRICH

Telephone: +41 1 254 34 00
Fax: +41 1 254 34 10
E-mail: lawyers@vischer.com
Website: www.vischer.com

Languages
English, French, German, Italian, Spanish

Number of lawyers 68
at this office 25

Contact
Dr Christoph M Pestalozzi

CATEGORIES OF WORK

Commercial law, contract law
Dr Christoph M Pestalozzi, Urs Haegi

Banking and finance
Dr Markus Guggenbühl

Capital markets
Dr Markus Guggenbühl, Dr Jürg Luginbühl

Commercial litigation
Dr Marc Russenberger, Felix C Meier-Dieterle

Arbitration, ADR
Dr Christoph M Pestalozzi

Labour, employment
Urs Haegi

Corporate
Dr Jürg Luginbühl, Dr Markus Guggenbühl

Mergers and acquisitions
Dr Jürg Luginbühl, Dr Markus Guggenbühl

Estate planning
Dr Christoph M Pestalozzi

Insolvency, bankruptcy
Dr Marc Russenberger, Felix C Meier-Dieterle

E-commerce
Dr Rolf Auf der Maur

IT, IP
Dr Rolf Auf der Maur, Dr Leonz Meyer

Tax
Erwin R Griesshammer

Aviation
Dr Christoph M Pestalozzi

Media, entertainment
Dr Rolf Auf der Maur

VON MEISS BLUM & PARTNERS

USTERISTRASSE 14
8021 ZÜRICH

Telephone: +41 1 227 66 66
Fax: +41 1 227 66 77
E-mail: mail@mbp.ch
Website: www.mbp.ch

Languages
Dutch, English, French, German, Italian, Portuguese, Spanish

Number of lawyers 20

Contact
Dr Albrecht Langhart

Member
Association of Commercial Lawyers (ACL)

CATEGORIES OF WORK

Banking, securities and finance
Florian von Meiss, Albrecht Langhart

Companies, corporations
Rolf Schmid, Walter H Boss

Commercial, labour and civil
Albrecht Langhart, Rolf Schmid

Immigration, work and residence permits
Rolf Schmid, Stefan Wehrenberg

Mergers and acquisitions
Walter H Boss, Rolf Schmid

Tax, international tax planning
Walter H Boss, Claude Blum

Wills, trusts and estate planning
Claude Blum, Oliver Arter

Swiss, European and international public and administrative law
Stefan Wehrenberg, Andreas Ziegler

Arbitration
Albrecht Langhart, Florian Jörg

Litigation
Albrecht Langhart, Christian Sutter

International transactions
André Wahrenberger, Rolf Schmid

Intellectual property and copyright
André Wahrenberger, Christian Sutter

Swiss and European competition law
Albrecht Langhart, André Wahrenberger

E-commerce and IT
Florian Jörg, Oliver Arter

Sports and entertainment
André Wahrenberger, Adrian Hirzel

International and European trade and investment law
Stefan Wehrenberg, Andreas Ziegler

WALDER WYSS & PARTNERS

MÜNSTERGASSE 2
PO BOX 2990
8022 ZÜRICH

Telephone: +41 1 265 75 11
Fax: +41 1 265 75 50
E-mail: reception@wwp.ch
Website: www.wwp.ch

Languages
English, French, German, Italian, Spanish

Number of lawyers 54

Contacts
Didier Sangiorgio, Markus Pfenninger, Markus Vischer, Daniel Wyss, Martin Busenhart

Member
Techlaw

CATEGORIES OF WORK

Banking
Enrico Friz, Markus Pfenninger

Capital markets
Enrico Friz, Markus Pfenninger

Structured financial products
Markus J Kroll, Evan M Spangler

Insurance
Markus Pfenninger, Evan M Spangler

M&A, business reorganisation
Markus Vischer, Christoph Stäubli

Corporate and commercial
Markus Vischer, Christoph Stäubli

EU, competition, environment, energy and utilities
Reto Jacobs, Markus Vischer

Healthcare, life sciences
Reto Jacobs, Christoph Felder

IT, multimedia and telecommunications
Didier Sangiorgio, Reto Jacobs

Arts, sports and entertainment
Christoph Stäubli, Mark A Reutter

Intellectual property, copyright and advertising
Magda Streuli-Youssef, Markus Frick

Litigation, international legal assistance
Daniel Wyss, Dieter Hofmann

International arbitration
Daniel Wyss, Philipp Habegger

Venture capital and private equity
Luc Defferrard, Markus Pfenninger

Insolvency and restructuring
Christoph Stäubli, Jörg Witmer

Tax
Martin Busenhart, Thomas Meister

WENGER PLATTNER

SEESTRASSE 39
GOLDBACH-CENTER
8700 KÜSNACHT-ZÜRICH

Telephone: +4143 222 38 00
Fax: +41 43 222 38 01
E-mail: zuerich@wenger-plattner.ch
Website: www.wenger-plattner.ch

Languages
English, French, German, Italian

Other offices
Basle, Bern

Number of lawyers 50
at this office 23

CATEGORIES OF WORK

Contract and commercial law
Dr Jürg Plattner, Filippo Th Beck

Company law
Yves P Meili, Karl Wüthrich

Tax law
Dr Jürg Plattner, Yves P Meili

Arbitration
Dr Jürg Plattner, Dr Stephan Netzle

Litigation
Karl Wüthrich, Yves P Meili

Mergers and acquisitions
Yves P Meili, Dr Marc Nater

Real estate and construction
Peter Sahli, Dr Thomas Wetzel

Bankruptcy and insolvency
Karl Wüthrich, Peter Sahli

Banking and financial markets
Dr Jürg Plattner, Filippo Th Beck

Trusts and estates
Dr Jürg Plattner, Filippo Th Beck

Telecommunications, media, IT
Yves P Meili, Dr Stephan Netzle

Immigration and employment
Filippo Th Beck

Sports law
Dr Stephan Netzle, Dr Marc Nater

Legal assistance in civil and criminal matters
Filippo Th Beck, Dr Marc Nater

WENGER VIELI BELSER

DUFOURSTRASSE 56
MÜHLEBACHSTRASSE 38
8034 ZÜRICH

Telephone: +41 1 563 33 33
Fax: +41 1 563 33 66
E-mail: mail@wengerlaw.ch
Website: www.wengerlaw.ch

Languages
English, French, German, Italian, Mandarin, Spanish, Croatian

Other offices
Zug, Beijing

Number of lawyers 35

Contacts
Dr Christian Wenger, Dr Christoph Schmid

Member
Swiss Bar Association; Meritas

CATEGORIES OF WORK

Corporate, commercial and contract law

Corporate finance

Structured finance and venture law

Regulatory and general banking law

Banking litigation

Litigation

Arbitration

Mergers and acquisitions

Media law

Bankruptcy and insolvency

Employment law and work residence permits

Joint ventures

Life sciences law, antitrust and competition law

IT law

Intellectual property law

International judicial assistance

Estate planning and probate law

Expert opinions

Stock exchange and capital market law

Population	70.3 million
Number of lawyers	35,000
Professional title	Attorney
Currency	Turkish lira (TL)

Index

Turkey's future is dominated by its longstanding desire to join the European Union, which although likely will demand significant political and economic changes. A timeframe for full accession is expected by the end of 2004 but despite recent economic and legislative reforms, claims of political oppression, human rights abuses and censorship are all seen as significant obstacles to membership.

The terrorist attacks carried out in Turkey in late 2003 came at the end of a difficult year for the Justice and Development Party's Recep Tayip Erdogan who was installed as prime minister in March 2003 after his sweeping victory at the 2002 elections.

His delayed election to the parliament came after an amendment to the constitution having been barred from office by a constitutional court over a jail term served in 1999.

Erdogan is committed to continuing democratic reform in Turkey with moves to allow more political and press freedom high on his agenda. He is also keen to resolve the Cyprus issue, another possible stumbling block to EU membership, and abiding by IMF restrictions aimed at fostering economic recovery. The war in Iraq threatened to further hinder the long-awaited economic recovery from the country's worst recession in 50 years.

BILLING

Billing is either on an hourly basis or by retainer, although increasingly clients are focusing on total fees for work rather than hourly rates, with caps being imposed in many cases.

Hourly fees range from €100 for junior members handling local work up to €450 or more for partners.

MARKETING

Law firms and individuals are not allowed to advertise, with business being generated through coverage in the legal press, presentations at conferences and increasingly via the Internet. The Turkish bar associations have recently imposed restrictions on the information firms are allowed to include on websites.

IN-HOUSE LAWYERS

The privatisation of many significant corporations in Turkey in recent years has led to many companies, particularly in the banking and telecoms sectors, developing their own in-house teams.

ECONOMIC CLIMATE

The terrorist attacks carried out in Istanbul in late 2003 raised serious concerns about the effect on Turkey's recovering economy. It will be some time before the full impact is known but most commentators believe they will only have a limited effect on the growth seen recently after two years of deep recession.

A funding package of $13.5bn approved by the World Bank, the US and the IMF in November 2003 came as a welcome boost and will underpin improvements to infrastructure.

Although committed to a privatisation programme, many of Turkey's basic industries and 30% of the banking sector are still state owned. New legislation to encourage more foreign investment, under which investors no longer need to apply for permission to make investments in Turkey, is seen as paving the way for a dramatic increase in inward investment.

Exports have risen sharply on the back of the devaluation of the Turkish lira. Germany, the US and Italy are the three largest destination markets. Turkish industry is dominated by manufacturing, particularly clothing and textiles, consumer electronics and motor vehicles. Both construction and agriculture have seen their contribution to GDP continue to fall in recent years. Tourism, mainly based in the south and west of the country, recovered well from the war on Iraq in 2003 but it may have more long term effects.

LEGAL MARKET

The severe recession led to difficult times for the Turkish legal sector and a continuation of a trend which has seen small generalist firms and individual practitioners increasingly being replaced by larger and more specialist partnerships.

In 2001 changes to the law governing the legal system officially recognised partnerships, but their restrictive nature means they are not shared liability partnerships as seen in the West.

Turkish firms are barred from opening multiple offices in different cities, although there are ways of circumventing the restriction.

There were a number of new firms established in Turkey in 2003. The highly regarded Esin Taboglu

The largest firms

1	Hergüner Bilgen Özeke	40
2	White & Case LLP Müsavirlik Ltd. Sti.	38
3	M Fethi Pekin & Sefika Pekin	31
4	Derman Ortak Avukat Bürosu	27
	Çaga & Çaga Law Office	27
6	Pekin & Pekin	25
7	Yarsuvat Law Firm	24
8	Yamaner & Yamaner Law Offices	21
9	Birsel Law Offices	18
	D & D Law Firm	18
	Postacioglu Law Office	18
	Somay Hukuk Bürosu	18
13	Denton Wilde Sapte & Güner	16
	Gayret Consultant Services	16
	Hidayetoglu & Co	16
	Law Offices of M Fadlullah Cerrahoglu	16
17	CLO - Coskun Law Office	15
	Güner Law Office	15
	Ilhan Imik Law Office	15
20	Gürcan Law Offices	14
	Turunç & Savasçin	14
22	Ergenç Law Group	13
	Çakmak Ortak Avukat Bürosu	13
24	Mehmet Gün & Co	12
	Paksoy & Co	12
	Yarsuvat & Yarsuvat Law Offices	12

These figures represent the total number of lawyers in this country only, and have been supplied by the firms themselves. The figures should be accurate as at 1 January 2004.

established her own firm, **Taboglu Law Office** specialising in privatisation, M&A and banking matters, after leaving **Paksoy & Co**. The longstanding *Gur & Inal* partnership was dissolved during the year, apparently after differences between partners over the future direction of the firm. The former partners, Tevfik Gur and Seyma Inal, are now in their own practices: **Gur Law Firm** and **Inal Law Office** respectively.

Kitapçi & Aksakoglu changed its name to **Neyyir Kitapçi - Attorneys at Law**, after partner Evren Aksakoglu left.

FOREIGN FIRMS

Although foreign practices can register as firms, only Turkish lawyers can practise Turkish law or have rights of audience. Foreign firms can only advise on international legal matters, with the result that US and European firms provide a mixture of consultancy services, employ Turkish lawyers or enter into associations with Turkish firms.

International law firm **Salans** took on all the partners and staff from Chicago-based *Altheimer & Gray's* Istanbul office following the US firm's dissolution during 2003. The Istanbul office, which continues to operate in association with **Özel & Özel** was one of four European offices **Salans** acquired, along with Bratislava, Bucharest and Prague.

The Istanbul office of **Gide Loyrette Nouel**, established as a Turkish advice bureau under the name GLN Müsavirlik, is the only French firm currently providing services in Turkey.

White & Case Müsavirlik Ltd. Sti. continues to work with **Derman Ortak Avukat Bürosu** in Istanbul, and with **Çakmak Ortak Avukat Bürosu** in Ankara.

Ledingham Chalmers became the first UK law firm to open an office in Turkey when it established a small commercial practice in Istanbul in 1995, now headed by Jonathan Blythe. The move was to capitalise on its work advising part of a consortium developing oil and gas fields in the Caspian Sea.

BANKING, FINANCE AND CAPITAL MARKETS

Banking law in Turkey underwent a number of changes during 2003, aimed at protecting investors following a series of high-profile cases which added to the sector's reputation for instability.

High interest rates, inflation and instability of its currency has held growth in the banking sector back but positive responses next year to its EU aims will give the sector a platform. Although the state still controls a third of the banking system (compared to 10% across the EU), accession would lead to accelerated privatisation and merger programmes which will benefit lawyers specialising in the area.

BANKING, FINANCE AND CAPITAL MARKETS

BIRSEL LAW OFFICES
DENTON WILDE SAPTE & GÜNER ✪
DERMAN ORTAK AVUKAT BÜROSU
PAKSOY & CO ✪
PEKIN & PEKIN ✪
WHITE & CASE MÜSAVIRLIK LTD. STI.

Hergüner Bilgen Özeke ✪
Ledingham Chalmers
M Fadlullah Cerrahoglu, Law Offices of ✪
M Fethi Pekin & Sefika Pekin ✪
Neyyir Kitapçi - Attorneys at Law ✪
Reisoglu-Ensari-Budak
Tekinalp

CLO - Coskun Law Office ✪
Çakmak Ortak Avukat Bürosu
Dogru Law Office
Erdem & Erdem Law Office ✪
Ersoy & Bilgehan Lawyers & Consultants ✪
Gide Loyrette Nouel ✪
Gürcan Law Offices ✪
Ilhan Imik Law Office ✪
Salans
Somay Hukuk Bürosu
Turunç & Savasçin ✪
Yamaner & Yamaner Law Offices

Firms are listed A-Z in tiers which are ranked in order of priority
✪ Indicates firm displays contact details at the end of this chapter.

Capital markets work has been thin on the ground with no major non-privatisation IPOs during 2003, although a number of companies are expected to announce plans in 2004.

Birsel Law Offices' senior partner Mahmut Birsel leads a strong banking, securities and capital markets team, well-known for advising banks on investments in energy projects.

Denton Wilde Sapte & Güner has seen a significant increase in banking and capital markets work in recent years. Its transactions have included acting for the Bank of Tokyo Mitsubishi on a syndicated loan to Turkeximbank and for WestLB on its syndicated loan to Kocbank. It also acts for the World Bank and American Express Bank.

Derman Ortak Avukat Bürosu's 18-strong team, led by partners Mine Taygun and Aydın Duren, is representing Bank Bahrain in a $12m sovereign financing to the government for the construction of the Bursa Motorway Project. It also represented Société Générale in providing loans to Coca-Cola Içecek and Coca-Cola Degitim worth a total of $70m. With **White & Case Müsavirlik Ltd. Sti.**, the firm has worked on most of the significant international capital markets transactions in Turkey since 1985, and is assisting Alternatifbank with respect to financing and general banking law advice.

Paksoy & Co advised FMO, the Netherlands Development Finance Company, in connection with a proposed loan to a Turkish manufacturing company. It also advised JPMorgan in relation to a loan for an Italian company.

Pekin & Pekin's senior partner Ahmed Pekin, regarded by many as the leading banking lawyer in Turkey, leads a strong team which has represented more than two-thirds of the international banks in the *Fortune Global 500*. In 2003 it handled a number of major securitisation deals including a $325m cross-border transaction between a German and a Turkish bank.

Hergüner Bilgen Özeke acted for a financial corporation on more than 50 equity investments and lending transactions involving Turkish companies. The work included the first loan agreement involving a private university in Turkey. It also acted for a French bank over a potential acquisition in Turkey.

M Fethi Pekin & Sefika Pekin is acting for a foreign bidder in the sale of $360m of non-performing loans by the Turkish banking authorities.

Neyyir Kitapçi - Attorneys at Law is well-known for its experience in banking fraud and money laundering cases.

Reisoglu-Ensari-Budak's low-profile Professor Sezi Reisoglu was highly ranked by competitors for work with local and international banking clients.

CLO - Coskun Law Office advises Turkey's largest private bank, Akbank, on execution and collection procedures. The firm also worked on a project with a global investment bank relating to the set up of an asset management company.

Çakmak Ortak Avukat Bürosu's nine strong team, which acts for banking clients including HSBC and the World Bank, represented Agilent on the restructuring of securities for the acquisition of its Turkish subsidiary.

Erdem & Erdem Law Office's Dr Ercüment Erdem leads a small but well-thought-of banking and finance team which acted for a Turkish company on a loan agreement with a German bank, and represented a foreign shareholder in the sale of Turkcell by international public offering.

Ersoy & Bilgehan Lawyers & Consultants advised a number of international financial institutions over banking law issues following an overnight loan transaction affected by a devaluation of the Turkish currency in 2001.

Gide Loyrette Nouel acts for financial groups including Société Générale.

Ilhan Imik Law Office has a strong banking team including former in-house financial services lawyer Ugur Capkin.

Working with local firm **Özel & Özel**, **Salans** represented a major telecoms group on financing arranged with two major international institutions. The firms also acted for a foreign bank on the financing of two ferries.

Somay Hukuk Bürosu has advised two of the largest sports teams in Turkey on their public offerings.

Turunç & Savaşçin advises clients on banking and financial issues including legislation in the aftermath of the financial crisis in February 2001. The firm represents some 20 foreign banks, that have interests but no official presence in Turkey. The firm has been involved in asset-backed international securitisation covering almost all jurisdictions in Europe.

Yamaner & Yamaner Law Offices has a strong reputation among international clients. It advised two German companies in stock purchase transactions on the Istanbul Stock Exchange.

COMPETITION

Significant changes are being implemented in Turkey's antitrust legislation aimed at harmonising it with EU legislation. During 2003 the Competition Board also began an investigation into allegations of abuse of market dominance by two major telecoms groups.

Çakmak Ortak Avukat Bürosu is representing Lafarge Beton AS in an investigation initiated by the Competition Board. Together with **Derman Ortak Avukat Bürosu**, which it works closely with on competition matters, it advised on an investigation against Philip Morris on price fixing allegations. The Competition Board terminated the investigation without imposing any penalties, one of the few cases where the board has not imposed a fine after completing an investigation. **Derman Ortak Avukat Bürosu** also acts for clients including Hewlett-Packard, ExxonMobil and Kraft Food International.

ESC Consulting, an 11-strong niche practice headed by the highly regarded Professor Arif Esin, specialises in competition and anti-dumping proceedings. During 2003 it worked on the Turkish part of the Deutsche Post/DHL transaction and the RWE/Thames Water merger deal.

Law Offices of M Fadlullah Cerrahoglu has a strong competition department fed mainly by its M&A practice. It has recently acted for Alcan, Pfizer and BP.

Aybay & Aybay advised Hawaiian Tropic Enterprises on competition law related to a cosmetics distribution deal.

Denton Wilde Sapte & Güner acted for P&O Nedloyd on competition issues arising from its joint venture with Anadolu Group.

Ersoy & Bilgehan Lawyers & Consultants advised a leading UK bank on competition issues in the management buyout of a Turkish corporation.

Gide Loyrette Nouel regularly acts for clients before the Turkish authorities in anti-dumping procedures. It recently represented the Chinese government on a case involving the import of pencils and fountain pens.

Gürcan Law Offices regularly represents its M&A clients before the competition authorities and defending against allegations of market abuse.

COMPETITION

ÇAKMAK ORTAK AVUKAT BÜROSU
DERMAN ORTAK AVUKAT BÜROSU
ESC CONSULTING
M FADLULLAH CERRAHOGLU, LAW OFFICES OF ✪

Aybay & Aybay ✪
Denton Wilde Sapte & Güner ✪
Ersoy & Bilgehan Lawyers & Consultants ✪
Gide Loyrette Nouel ✪
Gürcan Law Offices ✪
Hergüne Bilgen Özeke ✪
Mehmet Gün & Co ✪
Paksoy & Co ✪
Pekin & Pekin ✪
Poroy and Özülkü Attorneys At Law
Tekinalp
Turunç & Savaşçin ✪
Yamaner & Yamaner Law Offices

Firms are listed A-Z in tiers which are ranked in order of priority
✪ Indicates firm displays contact details at the end of this chapter.

Paksoy & Co advised the Dow Chemical Company on its acquisition of Celanese AG's Acrylates business and worked for IBM on its purchase of Rational Software Corporation.

Pekin & Pekin has an active competition law practice handling issues including anti-dumping matters, while **Yamaner & Yamaner Law Offices** has advised a Japanese company in obtaining clearance from the Turkish competition authority for a cross border M&A deal.

Poroy and Özülkü Attorneys At Law, **Tekinalp** and **Turunç & Savaşçin** are also well regarded in competition matters.

CORPORATE AND COMMERCIAL

Mergers and acquisitions work saw a significant downturn in 2003 against the backdrop of a worsening global economy and the war in Iraq. However, there is optimism that major changes to the rules governing foreign investment coming into force this year which place fewer restrictions on investors will kick-start deal activity.

The relaxation moves are timely as figures last year showed foreign investment in Turkey had dropped to its lowest level since 1988.

Derman Ortak Avukat Bürosu's 23-strong corporate team, led by respected senior partner Emre Derman is regarded as a leading player in Turkey's M&A market and has been involved in every significant bank transaction during 2002 and 2003. It recently acted for Soros Investment Capital on its acquisition of Unikom Gida Sanayi ve Tic. It also acted for Kraft Foods International on its acquisition of Turkish crisp manufacturer Kar Gida, and represented Nestlé Waters on the acquisition of a stake in Turkish bottled water company Sansu. Clients described the work as

CORPORATE AND COMMERCIAL

DERMAN ORTAK AVUKAT BÜROSU
HERGÜNER BILGEN ÖZEKE ✪
M FADLULLAH CERRAHOGLU, LAW OFFICES OF ✪
WHITE & CASE MÜSAVIRLIK LTD. STI.

BIRSEL LAW OFFICES
MEHMET GÜN & CO ✪
PEKIN & PEKIN ✪

Denton Wilde Sapte & Güner ✪
Gide Loyrette Nouel ✪
M Fethi Pekin & Sefika Pekin ✪
Paksoy & Co ✪
Poroy and Özülkü Attorneys At Law
Salans
Tekinalp
Turunç & Savasçin ✪
Yamaner & Yamaner Law Offices
Yarsuvat Law Firm

Aksu & Savas & Çaliskan
Aybay & Aybay ✪
Bircanoglu & Bircanoglu ✪
CLO - Coskun Law Office ✪
Çaga & Çaga Law Office
Çakmak Ortak Avukat Bürosu
D & D Law Firm ✪
Duygun Yarsuvat & Ömür Yarsuvat Law Offices
Ersoy & Bilgehan Lawyers & Consultants ✪
Gökkiliç Law Office
Gürcan Law Offices ✪
Karaca & Associates ✪
Ledingham Chalmers
Neyyir Kitapçi - Attorneys at Law ✪
Okur and Okur
Postacioglu Law Office ✪
Sakmar & Partners Law Office
Serap Zuvin Law Offices
Somay Hukuk Bürosu

Firms are listed A-Z in tiers which are ranked in order of priority
✪ Indicates firm displays contact details at the end of this chapter.

first-class. Big-ticket work is carried out closely with **White & Case Müsavirlik Ltd. Sti.**, where partner Asli Basgoz is well rated by clients and other lawyers. In 2003 the firm represented Exxon Mobil in the divestiture of two major European joint ventures with Turkish partners.

Hergüner Bilgen Özeke's heavyweight corporate team moves into the top tier this year. The recruitment of several new commercial lawyers to take total fee-earners to 37 bolstered its position as Turkey's largest law firm and it is highly regarded by both clients and rivals. As well as acting as retained adviser to a number of leading Turkish companies, it also represents international companies with significant Turkish interests. Its recent work has included acting for a professional network over merging its operations in Turkey and for a major British retailer over acquiring a stake in a Turkish listed company.

Law Offices of M Fadlullah Cerrahoglu has worked on the Pfizer/Pharmacia merger and the Alcan/Hydro Aluminium acquisition. Its corporate team is headed by Prof Dr Fadlullah Cerrahoglu, named by many rivals as one of the most respected figures in the sector, and Dr Bekir Aroma who runs the foreign investment department.

Better known on the finance side, **Birsel Law Offices**' Mahmut Birsel leads a team with a strong reputation acting for foreign firms involved in Turkish M&A. During 2003 it acted for a German company in its merger with a Turkish machinery manufacturer.

Mehmet Gün & Co is known particularly for its M&A work and also for acting for foreign firms on regulatory issues on Turkish investments.

Pekin & Pekin has had a leading commercial practice for more than 30 years and is particularly respected by local and international banking clients.

Denton Wilde Sapte & Güner, whose corporate team includes rated partner Paul Sheridan, acted for Aviva/Commercial Union in relation to the setting up of pension funds to comply with new legislation. It also acted for Solutia in the sale of shares in its Turkish subsidiary.

Gide Loyrette Nouel's partner Guillaume Rougier-Brierre works for a number of French companies on corporate transactions and general advice in Turkey including Société Générale, L'Oréal, and Air France. Deals handled during the year include the sale of Lafarge's Northern Cyprus operations to Holcim Lebanon, and acting for Antalis in the acquisition of a majority stake in a distribution company.

M Fethi Pekin & Sefika Pekin has a particular reputation in white-collar crime, and is currently acting in a major case of alleged fraudulent exports against employees of a number of Turkish companies

Paksoy & Co assisted IKEA in the setting up of joint venture and franchise operations in Turkey during 2003. It also advised chemicals group Rutgers in connection with the purchase of shares in a Turkish chemicals company.

Poroy and Özülkü Attorneys At Law's Ümit Özülkü, former chief legal adviser to the Tekfen Group, has a strong reputation in commercial matters.

Salans, which co-operates closely with local firm **Özel & Özel**, almost exclusively represents multinational companies investing or carrying out transactions in Turkey and Turkish companies doing business abroad. It acted for a Spanish company on the acquisition of mining rights in Turkey and also represented a company in the acquisition of a minority stake in an agricultural business in Turkey.

Turunç & Savasçin advises in all areas of corporate and commercial law including foreign direct investment, mergers and acquisitions and joint ventures. More than 60% of the firm's client base is international.

Yamaner & Yamaner Law Offices is well-known for its cross-border corporate work and on litigation-based commercial work. Recent transactions have included advising an Israeli company on a joint venture project in Turkey and representing a leading German company in an M&A transaction in the chemicals sector.

Hüseyin Yarsuvat, who heads **Yarsuvat Law Firm** which was founded by his late father Ihsan in the 1940s, advises a number of major Turkish and international clients on employment and tax legislation where he is seen as a leading expert.

Aksu & Savas & Çaliskan is a new entrant to this year's table. Although only founded in 2001 by former in-house lawyers Murat Aksu, Mahmut Savas and Zeki Çaliskan, the practice has an eight-strong corporate team, which has a growing reputation.

Ali Kartal, well-regarded for corporate and commercial work, joined **Aybay & Aybay** as senior partner following the deaths of founding partner Gündüz Aybay and senior partner Atilla Aybay, who both passed away during 2003. Kartal, a member of the Aybay family, previously working for IBM Turkey in-house and ran his own private practice. The firm acted for Telenor, the Norwegian telecoms company, on its bid for a Turkish GSM licence.

Bircanoglu & Bircanoglu advised a company on a possible public offering on London's AIM market.

CLO – Coskun Law Office advised Thomas Cook AG on a joint venture liquidation and on the collection of loans from a Turkish partner company.

Corporate work is seen as **Çaga & Çaga Law Office**'s main strength and since being involved in Turkey's first merger it has been party to many of the largest M&A transactions. It also has a strong name in the fields of tax and employment legislation under the direction of partner Barbaros Çaga.

Çakmak Ortak Avukat Bürosu's nine-strong corporate and commercial department, led by respected partner Zeynep Cakmak, advised Rio Tinto on the setting up of a mining project company in Turkey and continues to advise the company on other matters. It also acted for Edison Mission Energy on a project to develop a gas fired co-generation plant in Esenyurt on a BOT basis.

D & D Law Firm's commercial team, led by Yaoyz Ali Dadli and Berna Akkor, acts for clients including ABN Amro, India Alloys and Turkish holding company Tezman.

Around 75% of **Duygun Yarsuvat & Ömür Yarsuvat Law Offices**' work is for multinational clients carrying out business in Turkey. Projects include stock and asset acquisitions, joint ventures and start-ups.

Ersoy & Bilgehan Lawyers & Consultants, although one the newest entrants to the Turkish legal market being founded in 1999, has established a strong reputation for corporate work. Its international clients include Mitsubishi,

LG and Volvo. It recently handled the asset sale of a Turkish company on behalf of Ford Motor Company, and is currently working on drafting of agreements on the restructuring of a major metals company. It is also advising Far Eastern companies interested in the acquisition of a number of power plants in Turkey being sold by public tender.

Gökkiliç Law Office (formerly *KLegal*), whose corporate team is led by Ekin Gökkilic, acted for S&T System Integration & Technology Distribution over its purchase of Turkish IT company Protek. It also represents clients including Singapore Airlines and Solectron Corporation.

Gürcan Law Offices' 16-strong commercial team is seen as a solid player in banking and M&A work and works with a number of leading international clients.

Karaca & Associates, a member of the *Mackrell International* network, has a good reputation in commercial work.

Ledingham Chalmers opened a Turkish office after it began operating in the Caspian Region in 1992 on oil and gas work, and now offers consultancy services supported by the practice's UK commercial team.

Okur and Okur's Dr Yigit Tahsin Okur is a leading figure in corporate law particularly in transactions involving joint stock companies.

Postacioglu Law Office acted for a Turkish transport company in its merger with a UK business.

The niche commercial practice of **Serap Zuvin Law Offices** has an eight-strong team specialising in foreign investment and export incentives.

Somay Hukuk Bürosu was involved in several M&A deals in 2003, including the acquisition of a minority interest in a $1bn energy company.

DISPUTE RESOLUTION

Relatively low levels of corporate work in recent years have led firms to look increasingly to their litigation departments for revenue. Dispute resolution work has grown significantly in recent years fuelled by the collapse of many joint venture and infrastructure projects.

Aybay & Aybay advised Tetra Pak Turkey on a civil litigation case and Nevio Scala, the Italian football coach, in litigation against a major Turkish football team.

Hergüner Bilgen Özeke is acting for a water project company over the settlement of a dispute by arbitration and for an Italian textile group in recovering money owed.

Mehmet Gün & Co has a strong reputation for dispute resolution work, particularly with regard to shareholder disputes and cases related to its intellectual property.

Yarsuvat Law Firm continues to enjoy a good name as a professional litigation practice.

Bircanoglu & Bircanoglu is a new entrant to this year's table on the back of involvement in a number of significant cases during the year when it acted for clients in claims totalling $50m.

Birsel Law Offices' litigation team, headed by senior partner Dr Mahmut Birsel, has a good name for dispute resolution in the banking sector.

Çaga & Çaga Law Office is another new entrant to this year's table. With 2,800 cases currently before the Turkish courts it represents both local and international companies in disputes including copyright infringement and employment disputes.

Çakmak Ortak Avukat Bürosu is working on a case that will set a precedent for actions over unfinished power projects in Turkey. It is acting for PSEG Global Inc, which has filed a claim against the government over a project.

Denton Wilde Sapte & Güner acted for Mark Warner and Tektronix in a number of claims and for two major insurance groups in litigation cases.

Derman Ortak Avukat Bürosu acquired the three-strong litigation practice headed by Mutlu Simayh during 2003 to bring in-house capability to the firm which previously used external lawyers to handle cases. The firm is representing the IFC in pursuing repayment of loans made to various Turkish borrowers. It is also acting for Universal Music International on litigation against minority shareholders of four of its subsidiaries in Turkey.

Duygun Yarsuvat & Ömür Yarsuvat Law Offices has a good reputation both as legal counsel and arbitrator in alternative dispute resolution, particularly in relation to cross-border transactions.

Erdem & Erdem Law Office is another new entry into this year's table for its work on a number of significant cases during 2003 including a $15m settlement in a suit over mortgage rights related to a retail development.

Gide Loyrette Nouel's Nazan Candaner Elver is an increasingly well-regarded figure in arbitration and is the youngest lawyer on the shortlist of recommended arbitrators compiled by the Istanbul Chamber of Commerce.

Gökkiliç Law Office recently acted for RMK Marine, one of the largest ship construction companies in Turkey, in securing a settlement in a dispute with the government.

Cuneyd Gürcan leads a strong litigation team at **Gürcan Law Offices** which benefits from work generated through its banking and corporate clients. At the end of 2003 the firm had claims totalling $60m before the Turkish courts.

Ilhan Imik Law Office has a strong litigation team including Ugur Capkin and Yalcin Unal with particular specialism in financial disputes.

Law Offices of M Fadlullah Cerrahoglu is involved in some of Turkey's most high-profile disputes, acting as the Turkish lawyers in the Motorola claim against the Uzan family, for example. It is also acting for Italian contractor Astaldi Bayindir Insaat in the Bolu Tunnel conflict.

Neyyir Kitapçi - Attorneys at Law has extensive litigation experience particularly in the areas of tax, real estate, IT and Internet-related matters.

Paksoy & Co represented the Turkish government in connection with a multi-million dollar claim before the International Centre for Settlement of Investment Disputes. The firm also acted for Austrian construction company Voest Alpine Industrieanlagenbau GmbH in a major claim in the Turkish courts.

Postacioglu Law Office acted for a Turkish company in an $80m arbitration case against the government.

Turunç & Savasçin acted for a *Fortune 500* company in successfully defending a product liability claim. It has also been instructed in two other disputes with a total value of $82m.

Yamaner & Yamaner Law Offices has focused increasingly on arbitration over the past decade and acts for a number of Turkish and international companies with particular expertise in energy and construction matters.

IT AND TELECOMS

During 2003 the Turkish Telecommunications Authority introduced new regulations aimed at increasing competition in the market and the use

DISPUTE RESOLUTION

AYBAY & AYBAY ✪
HERGÜNER BILGEN ÖZEKE ✪
MEHMET GÜN & CO ✪
YARSUVAT LAW FIRM

Bircanoglu & Bircanoglu ✪
Birsel Law Offices
Çaga & Çaga Law Office
Çakmak Ortak Avukat Bürosu
Denton Wilde Sapte & Güner ✪
Derman Ortak Avukat Bürosu
Duygun Yarsuvat & Ömür Yarsuvat Law Offices
Erdem & Erdem Law Office ✪
Gide Loyrette Nouel ✪
Gökkiliç Law Office
Gürcan Law Offices ✪
Ilhan Imik Law Office ✪
M Fadlullah Cerrahoglu, Law Offices of ✪
Neyyir Kitapçi - Attorneys at Law ✪
Okur and Okur
Paksoy & Co ✪
Postacioglu Law Office ✪
Sakmar & Partners Law Office
Tekeli Law Office
Tekinalp
Turunç & Savasçin ✪
Yamaner & Yamaner Law Offices

Firms are listed A-Z in tiers which are ranked in order of priority
✪ Indicates firm displays contact details at the end of this chapter.

of telecoms services and infrastructure capacity. The year also saw the first legislation to deal directly with online transactions, a move as part of efforts towards harmonising Turkish legislation with EU law.

Birsel Law Offices retains a number of corporate clients in the IT and communications sector.

Denton Wilde Sapte & Güner acts for Nokia and a UK telecoms group on issues in Turkey.

Derman Ortak Avukat Bürosu represents a number of key players in the sector, and during 2003 advised on the merger deal in respect of Cukurova Holdings' acquisition of Superonline and Digitürk, the leading ISP and digital platform operator in Turkey.

Hergüner Bilgen Özeke advised an international telecoms group on the setting up of a subsidiary in Turkey and on applying for licences to operate services.

Paksoy & Co has continued to develop a strong telecoms and IT practice since closing the $2bn Turkcell IPO in 2000.

Pekin & Pekin advises a number of international telecoms operators on participation in tender offers, negotiation of concession agreements and other licensing and regulatory issues in the Republic of Turkey.

White & Case Müsavirlik Ltd. Sti. represented Sonera in joint venture deals for the provision of cellular and other telecoms services.

Zyia Cailliau of **Gide Loyrette Nouel** is highly regarded for IT and telecoms work particularly in the area of market access regulations and acts for clients including Debitel AG, the German subsidiary of SwissTelecom.

Gökkiliç Law Office has a strong reputation in telecoms and is currently acting for a major international shareholder of one of Turkey's largest telecoms operators.

Mehmet Gün & Co has particular expertise in computer and software law and wins a significant amount of work in the sector on the back of its intellectual property strength.

IT AND TELECOMS

Birsel Law Offices
Denton Wilde Sapte & Güner ✪
Derman Ortak Avukat Bürosu
Hergüner Bilgen Özeke ✪
Paksoy & Co ✪
Pekin & Pekin ✪
Salans
White & Case Müsavirlik Ltd. Sti.

Gide Loyrette Nouel ✪
Gökkiliç Law Office
Mehmet Gün & Co ✪
Postacioglu Law Office ✪
Tekinalp

Firms are listed A-Z in tiers which are ranked in order of priority
✪ Indicates firm displays contact details at the end of this chapter.

Tekinalp is a new entrant in this year's table. Its fast growing telecoms team acts for clients including Turkcell.

INTELLECTUAL PROPERTY

Under international pressure to tackle the problem of piracy in Turkey (an estimated 60% of music CDs are illegal), the government has pledged more effort to clamp down. Moves to bring Turkey into line with EU IP legislation has also led to significant growth in the sector, with several firms developing their own niche divisions.

Mehmet Gün & Co retains its reputation as Turkey's leading IP specialist, described by one client as 'by far the best in the field', and has seen continued growth in its investigation department, launched in 2002. The department monitors breaches of IP in the main cities of Istanbul, Bursa, Izmir and Ankara and also in tourist areas during the peak season.

Established 40 years ago to specialise in intellectual property, **Arihan & Arihan** represents a number of leading European, Asian, African and American companies.

Çaga & Çaga Law Office is a new entrant to this year's table. The firm specialises in copyright and licence contracts and trade mark protection, with more than 200 applications for registration filed for clients in 2003.

Denton Wilde Sapte & Güner acted for an international telecoms company and a British retailer on IP matters in Turkey.

Derman Ortak Avukat Bürosu advised Philip Morris International with the registration of a number of industrial designs and the ITE Group in connection with a major trade mark application. The firm works closely with **White & Case Müsavirlik Ltd. Sti.**, which acts for a number of Turkish and multinational pharmaceutical and consumer product clients in licensing and distribution agreements, including Colgate Palmolive, Abdi Ibrahim Ilac and Hasbro.

INTELLECTUAL PROPERTY

MEHMET GÜN & CO ✪

Arihan & Arihan
Çaga & Çaga Law Office
Denton Wilde Sapte & Güner ✪
Derman Ortak Avukat Bürosu
Esref Alacayir Law Office
Gide Loyrette Nouel ✪
Gulay Karan Law Office
Hergüner Bilgen Özeke ✪
M Fadlullah Cerrahoglu, Law Offices of ✪
M Fethi Pekin & Sefika Pekin ✪
Paksoy & Co ✪
Pekin & Pekin ✪
Poroy and Özülkü Attorneys At Law
Postacioglu Law Office ✪
Tekinalp
White & Case Müsavirlik Ltd. Sti.
Yamaner & Yamaner Law Offices

Firms are listed A-Z in tiers which are ranked in order of priority
✪ Indicates firm displays contact details at the end of this chapter.

Esref Alacayir Law Office is one of a number of small firms specialising in IP and is known for its work on trade mark enforcement, anti-counterfeiting and patent advice.

Gide Loyrette Nouel acted for Philips in a major litigation case against Turkish counterfeiters producing television set top boxes. It also represents a number of French luxury goods manufacturers including L'Oréal and LMVH on patent and trade mark issues.

Gulay Karan Law Office's fast growing reputation in the field merits its inclusion as a new entrant this year. Affiliated with **Birsel Law Offices**, it acts for a major international tobacco company in ongoing counterfeiting investigations and brand protection in Turkey. In 2003 it also obtained the first civil court judgment given in Turkey for the destruction of counterfeit goods in transit.

Hergüner Bilgen Özeke is acting for a US retail company over alleged trade mark infringement by a Turkish firm.

Law Offices of M Fadlullah Cerrahoglu's Selale Kartal advises a number of corporate clients in IP matters.

Paksoy & Co acted for the Dow Chemical Company in a number of disputes over patent and trade mark infringement in Turkey during 2003. The firm also represented Schneider Electric of France in an intellectual property case.

Pekin & Pekin acted for a French hypermarket company in the registration of trade marks and filing of lawsuits to protect them. It also represented a British salt company in legal action over trade mark infringement.

Postacioglu Law Office has a specialist sister firm, IPP, dealing with intellectual property law.

Yamaner & Yamaner Law Offices acted for a German company in a dispute over the nullification of a trade mark, which arose during a merger transaction.

MARITIME, AVIATION AND TRANSPORT

Bounded by four seas (the Black Sea, the Sea of Marmara, the Aegean and the Mediterranean), and home to some of the most important strategic and commercial waterways in the world, shipping and maritime law are of central importance in Turkey.

Atamer & Karaman Law Firm's growing aviation department was instructed on behalf of London reinsurers in 2003 over the Turkish Airlines crash at Diyarbakir. It was also instructed in the case of the hijacked Turkish Airlines aircraft.

Gündüz Aybay, founding partner of **Aybay & Aybay** and regarded as the leading Turkish shipping lawyer, passed away in 2003 but the

MARITIME, AVIATION AND TRANSPORT

ATAMER & KARAMAN LAW FIRM
AYBAY & AYBAY ✪
ERSOY & BILGEHAN LAWYERS & CONSULTANTS ✪
HATEM LAW OFFICE
TAM & ERTAN LAW OFFICE
YAMANER & YAMANER LAW OFFICES

Çaga & Çaga Law Office
Denton Wilde Sapte & Güner ✪
Gur Law Firm ✪
Inal Law Office ✪
Postacioglu Law Office ✪
Teoman Law Firm
Turunç & Savasçin ✪
Yasar Öztürk Law Firm

Firms are listed A-Z in tiers which are ranked in order of priority
✪ *Indicates firm displays contact details at the end of this chapter.*

firm's strong reputation in the field continues under Mrs Sevin Kartal who worked with Gündüz Aybay for more than 20 years. In addition to ship finance and disputes, the firm also offers capability in aviation issues, including insurance.

Ersoy & Bilgehan Lawyers & Consultants, whose team includes partner and trained master mariner Ergun Ersoy, is highly regarded for its maritime work and has handled the majority of collision cases in Turkish waters in recent years. It handled several collision cases in Turkish waters during 2003 acting for shipowners and P&I clubs on pollution liability, wreck removal orders and other issues.

Hatem Law Office's Izzet Hatem enjoys a reputation as a leading authority on both wet and dry shipping matters.

Tam & Ertan Law Office specialises in maritime law and during 2003 was instructed by the P&I club of MV Yasar Kaptan in a dispute with cargo insurers. It has also acted for the owners of MV Edo in a dispute with time charterers.

Yamaner & Yamaner Law Offices has been one of Turkey's leading maritime practices since it was founded in 1920. It acts for shipowners, management companies, P&I clubs, insurers and financial institutions. Transactions have included advising a UK insurance company in a dispute with a Turkish shipowner and acting for a Russian shipowner in a cargo claim.

Çaga & Çaga Law Office is regarded as a leading player in aviation law, representing a number of international airlines.

Denton Wilde Sapte & Güner acted for Tibbett & Britten on a joint venture deal with Arakanli. It also represents P&O Nedloyd and Barsan Lojistiks.

Gur Law Firm, formed from the dissolution of *Gur & Inal*, acts for shipyards, owners and banks on contract construction for vessels and also specialises in advice to charter operators.

MEDIA AND ENTERTAINMENT

Çaga & Çaga Law Office
Denton Wilde Sapte & Güner ✪
Pekin & Pekin ✪
Yarsuvat Law Firm

Firms are listed alphabetically
✪ *Indicates firm displays contact details at the end of this chapter.*

Inal Law Office, headed by Seyma Inal who was formerly with *Gur & Inal* and one of Turkey's most respected maritime lawyers, has handled a number of significant shipping transactions recently including representing UK insurer West of England in long-running litigation over a collision in the Istanbul straits. It also represents Deutsche Schiffbank, Vereins Und-Westbank, Finansbank and Denizbank in ship finance matters.

Turunç & Savasçin has recently established a new maritime department headed by Dr Oya Ozciyr.

Yasar Öztürk Law Firm has a strong reputation in transport law and air/maritime finance with clients including Volvo Aero Services.

MEDIA AND ENTERTAINMENT

Turkey's victory in the 2003 Eurovision Song Contest focused attention on a music industry which has grown significantly in the past decade to cater for what is Europe's largest population of under-25s. Turkey's unusual demographics have also fuelled the dramatic rise of satellite TV, radio, and increasingly the Internet.

Çaga & Çaga Law Office, whose large media division is headed by Barbaros Çaga, represents one of Turkey's biggest media and entertainment groups which has now outsourced all of its legal issues to the firm. The firm also specialises in assisting companies to comply with regulations governing advertising.

Denton Wilde Sapte & Güner provided advice on regulatory issues to Fox Kids and to the Discovery Channel during 2003.

Yarsuvat Law Firm has significant experience in media law under managing partner Huseyin Yarsuvat and acts for several major media groups in Turkey.

PRIVATISATION

HERGÜNER BILGEN ÖZEKE ✪
PAKSOY & CO ✪
WHITE & CASE MÜSAVIRLIK LTD. STI.

Derman Ortak Avukat Bürosu
M Fethi Pekin & Sefika Pekin ✪
Pekin & Pekin ✪
Salans
Taboglu Law Office

Firms are listed alphabetically
✪ *Indicates firm displays contact details at the end of this chapter.*

2003 proved to be a busy year for privatisation lawyers in Turkey with three major companies – petrochemicals group PETKIM, Tupras and tobacco group Tekel all beginning the process. The 2004 programme is also likely to see significant work for privatisation specialists with state entities including the National Lottery, Turk Telekom and a number of energy companies expected to be privatised.

Hergüner Bilgen Özeke is well regarded on both the buy and sell side of privatisations. It acted for the global co-ordinator of the privatisation of a major Turkish oil company in an offering over three tranches.

Paksoy & Co represented the Korean Tobacco and Ginseng Corporation in connection with the privatisation of Turkish tobacco group Tekel in 2003. It also represented POAS, the largest petroleum distribution company in Turkey, on its offering of shares.

White & Case Müsavirlik Ltd. Sti. partner Asli Basgoz is representing Royal Caribbean Cruises International in the privatisation of the long-term operation rights of the Kusadasi and Bodrum cruise ship ports and marina. It works with **Derman Ortak Avukat Bürosu** which is representing Philip Morris International in the privatisation of the cigarette business of Tekel and Schroder Salomon Smith Barney in the strategic sale of shares in oil group Tupras.

M Fethi Pekin & Sefika Pekin acted for BP Group over the privatisation of the Petkim Petroleum Group and an international bidder in another privatisation. The practice also has a separate consultancy company, Pekin & Bayar, which provides advice on state tenders and privatisation. Senior partner Ugur Bayar served as the chairman of the Turkish Privatisation Administration from 1997 until 2002.

Salans, which works with **Özel & Özel** is a new entrant to this year's table. Among a number of significant privatisation transactions it handled during 2003, it represented a European tobacco group over the privatisation of a Turkish company.

Another new entrant to this year's table is **Taboglu Law Office**, established by Esin Taboglu after leaving her partnership role at **Paksoy & Co**. The firm acted as counsel to the Turkish Privatisation Administration over the privatisation of tobacco group Tekel. On the buyers side it acted for potential bidders for fertiliser group IGSAS and petrochemical firm IGSAS.

PROJECT FINANCE

Most firms reported a very quiet 2003 in project finance work as many infrastructure projects continue to be abandoned by the Turkish government. Difficulties over many existing or planned projects have led to significant dispute resolution work.

Birsel Law Offices acts for a number of international sponsors of projects in Turkey, particularly in the energy side.

Ankara-based **Çakmak Ortak Avukat Bürosu**'s project finance team, led by partners Mesut Cakmak, Zeynep Cakmak and Mehtap Yildirim-Ozturk, advised as local counsel to the Siemens/STEAG consortium in connection with the development and financing of a $1.45bn coal fired power plant in Iskenderun, Turkey's largest project finance deal. It also advised El Paso on natural gas exploration and development projects in the Mediterranean. The firm works closely with **White & Case Müsavirlik Ltd. Sti.**, which has a strong reputation in the field particularly for work on real estate, tourism projects and major power and infrastructure projects. In 2003 the firm represented Turkish real estate development company Necip Akar Holdings in the development of a hotel in Istanbul and assisted a foreign firm over financing and building of a water treatment works.

Hergüner Bilgen Özeke acted for a Belgian energy and infrastructure services group over the acquisition of a power plant project in Turkey. The firm is also acting for an international consortium on a project to build a major electricity generation project.

Bircanoglu & Bircanoglu has increasingly focused on work in Eastern European markets. It advised on project finance work for a PPP project in Romania, acting for a group of Turkish and British investors in the $200m transaction. It was the first project in Romania under the new BOT legislation there. It also advised a major IT company on a public authority transport management project in Istanbul.

Denton Wilde Sapte & Güner acted for Vivendi on a number of water projects and Nortel Networks on a series of telecoms projects.

Derman Ortak Avukat Bürosu which is well known particularly for its hotel project work, represented the Turkish Pension Fund in the $100m financing for the renovation of six hotels.

Banking lawyer Serdar Paksoy of **Paksoy & Co** has acted for a number of international banks on finance for projects in Turkey.

Pekin & Pekin has been involved in many of the ground-breaking project financings that have served as precedents for subsequent projects in Turkey, including the first BOT project to reach completion in Turkey.

Reisoglu-Ensari-Budak has a strong reputation for banking and acts for several major Turkish and international clients.

PROJECT FINANCE

BIRSEL LAW OFFICES
ÇAKMAK ORTAK AVUKAT BÜROSU
HERGÜNER BILGEN ÖZEKE ✪
WHITE & CASE MÜSAVIRLIK LTD. STI.

Bircanoglu & Bircanoglu ✪
Denton Wilde Sapte & Güner ✪
Derman Ortak Avukat Bürosu
Paksoy & Co ✪
Pekin & Pekin ✪
Reisoglu-Ensari-Budak
Salans

Firms are listed A-Z in tiers which are ranked in order of priority
✪ *Indicates firm displays contact details at the end of this chapter.*

AYBAY & AYBAY

SIRASELVILER CAD 87–8
TAKSIM
34433 ISTANBUL

Telephone: + 90 212 293 6744
Fax: + 90 212 245 3949
E-mail: aybay@aybaylaw.com

Languages
English

Number of lawyers 8

Contacts
Ali Kartal, Baris Aybay, Sevin Ozaydin Kartal

CATEGORIES OF WORK

- **Shipping**
- **Oil and gas**
- **Corporate and commercial**
- **Agencies and distributorships**
- **Competition**
- **Dispute resolution and litigation**
- **Intellectual property**
- **Insurance**
- **Aviation and air transport**
- **Finance and leasing**
- **Information technology**
- **Defense procurement**
- **Criminal law**

BIRCANOGLU & BIRCANOGLU

INONU CAD 69-71, D4
GUMUSSUYU
80090 ISTANBUL

Telephone: +90 212 292 0952
Fax: +90 212 292 1180
E-mail: counsel@bircanoglu.com
Website: www.bircanoglu.com

Languages
English, French, German, Greek, Russian

Number of lawyers 6

Member
International Law Firms (ILF)

CATEGORIES OF WORK

Banking and capital markets
M Erol Bircanoglu Jr

Real estate
Halit Karabul

Intellectual property
M Erol Bircanoglu Jr

Taxation
Sedat Ozkanli

Project finance
M Erol Bircanoglu Jr

Energy law
M Erol Bircanoglu Jr

Corporate law
F Erol Bircanoglu

Foreign investments
M Erol Bircanoglu Jr

Mergers and acquisitions
F Erol Bircanoglu

Competition law
M Erol Bircanoglu Jr

Information technology
M Erol Bircanoglu Jr

Litigation and arbitration
F Erol Bircanoglu

Bankruptcy and reorganisation
F Erol Bircanoglu

CLO – COSKUN LAW OFFICE

HARMANCI GIZ PLAZA
21ST FLOOR
LEVENT 80640
ISTANBUL

Telephone: +90 212 280 8661
Fax: +90 212 280 8840
E-mail: mail@clolaw.net
Website: www.clolaw.net

Languages
Turkish, English

Number of lawyers 15

Member
Geneva Group International

CATEGORIES OF WORK

Administrative
Eyup Yazici

Banking and finance
Ihsan Coskun, Sengul Kuruca

Capital markets
Mustafa Tokdemir, Erdal Kilbasoglu

Commercial property, real estate
Mustafa Tokdemir

Competition and EU
A Oktay Ugurlu, Erdal Kilbasoglu

Construction
Ihsan Coskun, Polat Dilli

Corporate and commercial
Sengul Kuruca

Dispute resolution - litigation and arbitration
A Oktay Ugurlu, Erdal Kilbasoglu

Employment
Erdal Kilbasoglu

Fraud and white-collar crime
Adem Erol, Hakim Demir

Insolvency, corporate restructuring
Polat Dilli, Osman Erusta

Intellectual property
Erdem Kapluhan

Media and entertainment
Ihsan Coskun

Shipping and transport
Sengul Kuruca

Tax
A Oktay Ugurlu

COSAR ORTAK AVUKAT BÜROSU

INÖNÜ CAD NO 26/2
GUMUSSUYU
34427 ISTANBUL

Telephone: +90 212 334 6000
Fax: +90 212 334 6090
E-mail: cosar@cosarlaw.com

Languages
English, German, Turkish

Other offices
Adana, Ankara

Number of lawyers 20

Contacts
E Arzu Cosar, M Utku Cosar

CATEGORIES OF WORK	
Commercial law	Labour law
Mergers and acquisitions	Intellectual property
Joint ventures	Arbitration
Foreign investment	Civil and administrative litigation
Competition law	Insolvency and bankruptcy
Banking and financial law	Privatisation law
Capital markets	Project finance
Consumer law	Energy law
Insurance law	Administrative law

THE FIRM

Established in 1969 by Aydin Cosar, Cosar Ortak Avukat Bürosu acts as legal counsel to a wide range of national and international clients and governmental agencies. The firm provides professional and high-quality legal services in almost all aspects of Turkish law. Having more than 30 years of experience, Cosar acts as counsel to some of the largest holding companies in Turkey, financial institutions, governmental agencies and numerous other Turkish and international companies operating in various sectors such as banking and investment, energy, retail, telecoms, information technology, steel and aluminium, construction, food and beverages, media and entertainment, textile, education and insurance.

AREAS OF PRACTICE

Corporate law: Cosar Ortak Avukat Bürosu provides legal assistance to its clients operating in a diverse range of sectors on general corporate matters, as well as on drafting and negotiating commercial transactions, including mergers and acquisitions and joint venture arrangements.

The firm's recent corporate work includes acting as counsel for a holding company for the transfer of its shares in a textile company to a multinational company, and providing legal advice to a major Turkish company in a complex transaction involving a hostile takeover, and the establishment of joint ventures in the retail and telecoms sectors. The firm also represented a respected company in the acquisition of shares of a telecommunication company, and acted as counsel for sellers of shares of one of the biggest transportation companies in Turkey.

Arbitration and civil and administrative litigation: Cosar has substantial experience in civil and administrative litigation. Its area of expertise in litigation includes debt restructuring, execution, bankruptcy proceedings, the collection of receivables, and alternative dispute resolution.

The firm's attorneys currently represent a public entity before the ICC in connection with two separate disputes regarding the transfer of operating rights of two plants. They also represent a leading LPG company in major administrative litigation proceedings involving environmental regulatory compliance issues. Its attorneys recently represented a securities trading company in various administrative proceedings concerning the continuation of its business activities, and also represented one of the shareholders of a major Internet provider in a lawsuit related to the exercise of pre-emption rights.

Privatisation and energy law: the firm currently acts as counsel to the Turkish Privatisation Administration in the privatisation of Turkey's largest petroleum refining company. Cosar also provides legal assistance in relation to various transactions in the energy sector involving sales, supply, purchase and transmission agreements. The firm advises a public entity in relation to a number of major BOT and BO projects, and acted as counsel for a public company concerning its natural gas contracts.

Intellectual property: Cosar provides legal advice on patents, trade marks, industrial designs and copyrights. The firm has extensive experience in negotiating and drafting agreements, particularly in the area of licensing. Its attorneys represent clients in IP litigation, including unfair competition and breach of contracts. The firm also has experience in design and copyright litigation.

Competition law: the firm provides legal assistance to a wide range of national and international companies in relation to Turkish competition law, particularly that relating to M&A and distributorship agreements. Its attorneys also have experience in competition litigation. Cosar represents companies operating in different sectors before the Turkish Competition Authority with regard to notification of M&A, and competition investigations. Cosar represented clients in numerous agreements regarding exclusive purchasing and distribution, joint venture, franchise and distribution, and servicing agreements. Cosar's experience in this area includes representing major multinational aluminium companies before the Turkish Competition Authority in a merger.

D & D LAW FIRM

CUMHURIYET CAD NO 18/9
ELMADAG
TAKSIM
ISTANBUL

Telephone: +90 212 291 0710
Fax: +90 212 291 0713
E-mail: bakkor@dved.net
Website: www.dved.net

Languages
English, French, Turkish

Other offices
Ankara, Izmir

Number of lawyers 18
at this office 10

Contact
Berna Akkor

Member
World Jurist Association; International Bar Association; UNCITRAL; European Network of Correspondent Law Firms; ICC (Paris)

CATEGORIES OF WORK

Corporate law, mergers and acquisitions

Joint ventures

Banking law

Litigation

Foreign investment

Intellectual property law

Criminal law

Arbitration

Labour law

Tax law

Licensing and franchising

Contract law

Energy and telecommunications

Maritime and aviation law

Competition law

Insolvency and bankruptcy law

BO and BOT projects

Commercial dispute resolution

DENTON WILDE SAPTE & GÜNER

SÜMBÜL SOKAK
11 ARALIK NO:99 DAIRE 1
LEVENT
34330 ISTANBUL

Telephone: +90 212 284 6091
Fax: +90 212 284 6096
E-mail: info@dwsgistanbul.com
Website: www.dentonwildesapte.com

Languages
English, French, German, Turkish

Other offices
Abu Dhabi, Almaty, Beijing, Cairo, Dubai, Gibraltar, Hong Kong, London, Milton Keynes, Moscow, Muscat, Paris, Singapore, Tashkent, Tokyo

Number of lawyers 876
at this office 16

Contact
Paul Sheridan

CATEGORIES OF WORK

Banking and finance
Paul Sheridan

Capital markets
John Dovey, Mustafa Akbilen

Commercial
Paul Sheridan

Competitio
Mustafa Akbilen, Kerim Pelister

Corporate
John Dovey

Dispute resolution
Paul Sheridan

Energy
John Dovey, Mustafa Akbile

Employment
Kerim Pelister

Intellectual property
Kerim Pelister

Media/technology
John Dovey

Mergers, acquisitions and joint ventures
Paul Sheridan, Mustafa Akbilen

Mining
Mustafa Akbilen

Projects
Paul Sheridan, Mustafa Akbilen

Telecommunications
Paul Sheridan

ERSOY BILGEHAN LAWYERS & CONSULTANTS

METE CADDESI 36
ESPLANAD APT D10
34437 TAKSIM
ISTANBUL

Telephone: +90 212 292 7272
Fax: +90 212 292 9296
E-mail: ersoybilgehan@superonline.com
Website: www.ersoybilgehan.com

Languages
English, French, German, Italian

Number of lawyers 9

Contacts
Ergun Ersoy, Zihni Bilgehan

CATEGORIES OF WORK

Company and commercial
Ozge Karaer

Banking and finance
Gulistan Baltaci

Capital markets
Ozge Karaer

Mergers and acquisitions
Ozge Karaer

Insurance/reinsurance
Ilknur Peksen

Energy
Ozge Karaer

Maritime
Ergun Ersoy, Zihni Bilgehan

Ship finance
Gulistan Baltaci, Zihni Bilgehan

Arbitration
Ergun Ersoy

Litigation
Ergun Ersoy

Telecommunications
Ozge Karaer

GIDE LOYRETTE NOUEL

BÜYÜKDERE CAD.
YAPI KREDI PLAZA
C BLOK KAT 3, LEVENT 34330
ISTANBUL

Telephone: +90 212 325 3581
Fax: +90 212 325 3587
E-mail: gln.istanbul@gide.com
Website: www.gide.com

Other offices
Algiers, Beijing, Brussels, Bucharest, Budapest, Casablanca, Hanoi, London, Moscow, New York, Paris, Prague, Riyadh, Shanghai, Tunis, Warsaw

Number of lawyers 480
at this office 10

Contact
Guillaume Rougier-Brierre (rougier@gide.com)

CATEGORIES OF WORK

Corporate law, mergers and acquisitions

Privatisation

Joint ventures

Banking and finance and project finance

Tax

Media, IT and telecommunications

Real estate transactions and financing

Litigation and arbitration

Intellectual property

Labour

Competition

State aid

Customs and exchange controls

Public procurement

Insurance

GÜNER LAW OFFICE

SÜMBÜL SOKAK
11 ARALIK NO:99 DAIRE 2
LEVENT
34330 ISTANBUL

Telephone: +90 212 282 4385
Fax: +90 212 282 4305
E-mail: gunerlaw@gunerlaw.com

Languages
English, French, German, Turkish

Number of lawyers 15

Contact
Ece Güner

CATEGORIES OF WORK

- Banking and finance
- Capital markets
- Commercial
- Competition
- Corporate
- Dispute resolution
- Energy
- Employment
- Intellectual property
- Media technology
- Mergers, acquisitions and joint ventures
- Mining
- Projects
- Telecommunications

GÜRCAN LAW OFFICES

MAÇKA CADDESI
NO 23/1, KAT: 4, DAIRE: 5
80200 MAÇKA
ISTANBUL

Telephone: +90 212 231 2115
Fax: +90 212 241 3490
E-mail: gurcan@gurcanlaw.com
Website: www.gurcanlaw.com

Languages
English, French

Other offices
Izmir

Number of lawyers 14
at this office 11

Member
The International Project Finance Association

CATEGORIES OF WORK

- Banking and finance
- Project finance
- Ship finance
- Privatisation
- Corporate law
- Mergers and acquisitions
- Capital markets
- Securities
- Commercial law
- Intellectual property law
- Arbitration and litigation
- Energy
- E-commerce

GUR LAW FIRM

HACI ADIL SOKAK NO 44
LEVENT
80620 ISTANBUL

Telephone: +90 212 325 9020
Fax: +90 212 325 9023
E-mail: info@gurlaw.com
Website: www.gurlaw.com

Languages
English, French, Greek, Italian, Turkish

Number of lawyers 10

Contact
Tevfik Gur

CATEGORIES OF WORK

Corporate	**Arbitration/enforcement of foreign judgments and arbitration awards**
Commercial	**Banking/debt recovery**
Maritime	**Real property**
Mergers and acquisitions	**Energy**
Employment law/contracts	**Finance**
Personal injury/death	

THE FIRM

The firm was originally established by Tevfik Gür in Mersin in 1984 where he dealt with a range of cases and achieved considerable success. He has been pursuing his career in Istanbul since 1993. Being one of the leading Turkish law firms, Gur Law Firm has an outstanding reputation with broad expertise and experience in many areas of law. The firm is well known for its substantial international practice. Gur Law Firm's lawyers are distinguished by their ability to combine imagination with perspectives.

AREAS OF PRACTICE

Gur Law Firm offers a full range of legal services as listed below.

Corporate: Gur Law Firm has an established corporate practice advising on a complete range of corporate and equity-based transactions, share purchase, partnership and joint venture agreements. The firm advises clients on structuring their corporate investments in Turkey.

Commercial: Gur Law Firm represents many commercial clients in sectors ranging from the fast moving world of IT to the more traditional commercial areas such as debt collection and contract enforcement. It handles all forms of commercial work in the contentious and non-contentious fields. The firm aims to achieve dispute resolution for its clients whether it be through arbitration, litigation or other means, but always consistent with the client's commercial objectives.

Maritime: the firm's maritime practice includes providing advice to shipyards, shipowners and banks in preparing, negotiating and drafting contracts for the construction, purchase and sale of vessels, and in contracts to finance such operations. The firm provides advice on charter contracts, maritime insurance, P&I, and all types of maritime proceedings and litigation. The firm is also an established collision handler.

Mergers and acquisitions: Gur Law Firm provides assistance to its clients in transactional structures, mergers and demergers, restructuring of companies, due diligence and acquisition funding. The firm provides assistance in the establishment and registration of legal entities, drafts articles of associations, charters, foundation and shareholders' agreements. The firm also drafts joint venture and consortium and pre-bid agreements.

Employment law/contracts: Gur Law Firm has the necessary experience in labour law/business law and the legal regulations in this area. The firm frequently engages in the preparation of business contracts for mutual clients as well as the settlement of disputes.

Personal injury/death: the firm represents its clients in cases of personal injury and death, and conducts negotiations with the opposition and also finalises the necessary legal procedures.

Arbitration/enforcement of foreign judgments and arbitration awards: the arbitration practice includes advising on the drafting of arbitration clauses, representing domestic and international clients as claimants and respondents in institutional and ad hoc arbitral proceedings, and conducting litigation to enforce arbitration awards.

Banking/debt recovery: the firm has the experience necessary for examining and preparing all contracts relating to loans and securities granted by foreign and domestic banks.

Energy, oil and gas: the firm provides its clients with specialised service and advice in designing the legal framework, and drafting contracts for foreign and Turkish joint ventures, consortiums and companies.

Real property: Gur Law Firm provides services and advice to clients in the acquisition of properties, negotiating construction agreements, conducting transactions regarding the development of properties, planning and structuring ownership rights.

Finance: Gur Law Firm advises on domestic and cross-border transactions on asset finance, project finance, capital markets, derivatives, convertible bonds, bond issues, debt trading, global loans, leveraged finance, real estate finance, restructuring, mergers and acquisitions, securitisation, telecoms, energy and infrastructure finance.

HERGÜNER BILGEN ÖZEKE

SÜLEYMAN SEBA CAD
SIRAEVLER 55
AKARETLER
343570 BESIKTAS
ISTANBUL

Telephone: +90 212 310 1800
Fax: +90 212 310 1899
E-mail: info@hbo-law.com.tr

Languages
English, French, German, Italian

Number of lawyers 40

Member
International Attorneys Club

CATEGORIES OF WORK

Oil and gas
Ümit Hergüner, Cüneyt Yüksel

Energy
Ender Özeke, Kemal Mamak

Project finance
Ümit Hergüner, Ender Özeke

Foreign investment and commercial
Ayse Bilgen, Meltem Azbazdar

Joint ventures, mergers and acquisitions
Ümit Hergüner, Itır Sevim Giftai

Competition
Tolga Danisman, Itır Sevim Giftai

Telecommunications
Ümit Hergüner, Ender Özeke

Banking, finance and capital markets
Ümit Hergüner, Gökhan Eraksoy

Privatisation
Ender Özeke, Gökhan Eraksoy

Government procurement
Ayse Bilgen, Gökhan Eraksoy

Litigation
Ayse Bilgen, Tolga Danisman

Arbitration
Ender Özeke, Cüneyt Yüksel

Intellectual property
Tolga Danisman, Cüneyt Yüksel

Licensing and franchising
Itır Sevim Giftai, Senem İsmen

THE FIRM

A leading Turkish law firm, Hergüner Bilgen Özeke is located in Istanbul. Founded in 1988, the firm now has seven partners, 33 associates, one paralegal and over 30 support staff.

AREAS OF PRACTICE

Hergüner Bilgen Özeke is one of the largest law firms in Turkey, representing international and Turkish firms, financial institutions and agencies. Practice areas include: foreign investment; litigation; commercial arbitration; contracts; joint ventures; M&A; corporate law; competition law; telecommunications; real estate; oil and gas; energy; project finance; banking, securities, capital markets; privatisation and government procurement; IP; employment law.

The firm offers legal advice on asset management for non-performing loans, securitisation issues, Turkey's nascent mortgage market and employee stock offering plans, project financings and M&A transactions. The firm represents a multilateral development bank in its equity and/or lending projects. Currently, the firm is advising a leading international investment bank in relation to a global bond offering of a Turkish company. In 2003, the firm advised a UK-based multinational retail company on the acquisition of a Turkish hypermarket chain. It has also advised a Japanese tobacco company regarding the privatisation of Turkey's state-owned monopoly in the tobacco sector and legal consultancy services to a consortium bidding for Turkey's largest oil refinery. The firm has advised a Turkish risk capital company in its participation in a leading Turkish IT firm. In 2003 the firm extended its experience in IP and real estate, and increased its number of partners and associates. The firm's legal advice has expanded beyond Turkey, as the firm currently advises clients on business transactions in Moldova, the Ukraine, Cyprus, Kazakhstan and Bulgaria.

The firm has acted as local legal counsel in the global merger of two major computer companies. It is currently advising a venture capital/private equity investment company several investment transactions in the IT sector.

The firm provides legal assistance to the oil companies in the multibillion dollar Baku-Ceyhan-Tblisi pipeline project and is acting as local legal counsel to the sponsors. It has been involved in several infrastructure projects in the transportation sector, and also turnkey projects and project financings.

Hergüner Bilgen Özeke has handled every phase of power plant development, and advised a development company consortium owned by major oil and engineering firms, with a leading Turkish construction company as the sponsor. Legal advice was given to a Belgian multinational energy and infrastructure services company in the construction of a gas-fired power plant in Ankara. It is well known for its expertise in energy law and advises BOT, BO and TOR companies regarding financing, and the new Electricity Market Law.

Hergüner Bilgen Özeke provides litigation services for its retainer clients, especially collection of receivables, debt restructuring, real estate and execution procedures. Following Turkey's economic crisis in 2001, the firm has shown significant success in international management and co-ordination.

One partner has been an arbitrator on a UNCITRAL-sponsored arbitration, and the firm is involved in several international dispute settlement efforts. The firm's attorneys are involved in energy-related contractual disputes. They represent a French-based multinational water network operations company in an arbitration over a development project sponsored by the World Bank.

The firm has acted as counsel to the Turkish Privatisation Administration in the privatisation of Türk Telekom and advised an investment bank and international underwriter on the privatisation of 31.5% of the shares of Turkey's largest refinery, which raised $1.3bn. The firm also contributed to new legislation and regulations for the telecoms sector to facilitate reform.

The firm has extensive experience in the pharmaceutical sector. In 2003, it rendered legal advice to three large pharmaceutical companies known worldwide. Currently, the firm is advising a major Turkish bank in its proposed restructuring of non-banking business participants. It is also involved in transactions concerning banks taken over by the state and in the consolidation efforts in the banking sector.

HIDAYETOĞLU & CO

POLARIS PLAZA K 4
80670 ISTANBUL

Telephone: +90 212 346 0225
Fax: +90 212 345 0232
E-mail: hq@hidayetoglulaw.com

Languages
Dutch, English, French, German, Italian, Turkish

Other offices
Ankara

Number of lawyers 16
at this office 14

Member
HB Consultancy Group

CATEGORIES OF WORK

Banking law
Volkan Hidayetoğlu, Murat Isci

International trade law
Volkan Hidayetoğlu, Baris Erdem

Intellectual property
Volkan Hidayetoğlu, Baris Erdem

EU law
Volkan Hidayetoğlu, Murat Isci

Labour law
Yalcin Hidayetoğlu, Okan Alp

International commercial arbitration
Volkan Hidayetoğlu, Baris Erdem

Competition law
Volkan Hidayetoğlu, Dr Nermin Berki

Energy law
Dr Nermin Berki, Volkan Hidayetoğlu

Energy and infrastructure projects
Dr Nermin Berki, Volkan Hidayetoğlu

Privatisation
Dr Nermin Berki, Volkan Hidayetoğlu

Joint ventures, M&A
Dr Nermin Berki, Volkan Hidayetoğlu

Banking and capital markets
Volkan Hidayetoğlu, Dr Nermin Berki

General advisory
Yalcin Hidayetoğlu, Volkan Hidayetoğlu

Commercial and civil litigation
Yalcin Hidayetoğlu, Ali Zafer Erdemli

THE FIRM

Hidayetoğlu & Co was established to meet the need for legal advisory services of an international standard and for the global business community that plans to invest in Turkey. The firm advises a high-level clientele of local and foreign corporations on a wide range of areas.

The firm has an office in Ankara headed by Dr Nermin Berki, who has an excellent public service background. Hidayetoğlu & Co has close connections with leading law firms in London, New York, Paris, Berlin and Baku that equip the firm with a distinct advantage in providing solutions to problems involving multi-jurisdictional aspects.

The partners of Hidayetoğlu & Co merge their previous experience of working as in-house counsel for large international corporations and as senior lawyers in leading law firms, as well as high-level bureaucrats. This enables the firm to understand the needs of corporations better and provide them with business-orientated legal advice in Istanbul and Ankara. The firm also acts in association with the leading US firm Sidley, Austin, Brown & Wood in public offerings and privatisation projects. Hidayetoğlu & Co was highly recommended in the areas of banking and capital markets, project finance, litigation and arbitration, corporate and commercial and construction in the 2001 edition of *The European Legal 500* and the June 2001 issue of *European Legal Business.*

AREAS OF PRACTICE

Energy and infrastructure projects: The firm has extensive experience in energy (oil and gas) and infrastructure projects, and also advises project companies and lenders on a continuous basis following the completion of the project. Work includes: Kangal and Syeitömer TOR model power projects; Tufanbeyli BOT model power project; Yamula BOT model power project; Izmit Bay crossing project; Emka-InterGen build/operate model energy projects; Xenel-Aliağa thermal power project; Çamlihemsin hydroelectric power project; Unimar capacity increase model; several autoproduction projects; and Enron global restructuring. The firm has provided advice to Zinerji (Koç Holding Energy Group), Doğan Holding, Enak Energy, Güneygaz, Enerjisa, Turkse Perenco, Türkuaz Petrol, Birlesik Petrol, Enron Power Holdings BV, DEG, KfW, ABN Amro Bank and Akbank.

Privatisation: The firm has considerable experience in privatisation projects in Turkey, including Petkim, Turkish Telecom and the third GSM licence.

Joint ventures, M&A: The firm has represented buyers and sellers in most of the material joint ventures and mergers and acquisitions that were finalised in Turkey including Akçimento-CBR, DEG-Penguen Gida, CarrefourSA, DanoneSA, YazakiSA, Olmuksa-International Paper and HoecSA projects. The firm acted in all phases of these projects including the drafting and negotiation of agreements and establishment of the legal structures for transactions. Current clients include a UK-based textiles company, Akçansa, DEG, Tepum Technologies and Borusan Technology.

International commercial arbitration: Partners have considerable experience in drafting and negotiation of arbitration clauses and agreements, and representing Turkish parties in arbitral procedures.

Banking and finance: Clients include Akbank, ABN Amro Bank, West LB, Ak Securities, Yapr Kredi Investment, Raymond James Securities, KfW, DEG, Garanti Investment and Finansinvest. The firm represented shareholders and undertakers in several global offerings of Turkish companies. The firm is external counsel to Akbank and ABN Amro Bank.

General advisory: The firm advises a wide range of foreign and local corporations and financial institutions on general coporate issues. Clients include Akbank, Ak Investment, Yap, Akçansa and Tepum Technologies.

Litigation: The firm has extensive experience in commercial and civil litigation, recognition and enforcement of foreign court judgments and arbitral awards, and execution and bankruptcy procedures. Partners have previously represented Polly Peck International Administrators, Citibank, Lloyd's Underwriters, Petrol Transport and Cyprus Eurobank.

ILHAN IMIK LAW OFFICE

KEMERALTI CAD
46/3 TOPHANE
ISTANBUL

Telephone: +90 212 251 2191
Fax: +90 212 251 1903
E-mail: iimik@superonline.com

Languages
English, German

Number of lawyers 15

Contact
Baris Oner

CATEGORIES OF WORK

Developing strategies on media and public relations
I Imik, B Oner

Competition law
I Imik, B Oner

Commercial law
I Imik, B Oner

Political counselling
I Imik, B Oner

Litigation and arbitration
I Imik, O Saglam

Debt collection and insolvency
F Esen, A Gokmen

Business law
O Akinci, N Boz

Real property law
I Imik, U Capkin

Establishment of foreign investments
I Imik, B Oner

Contracts
I Imik, B Oner

Licensing for foreign investments
B Oner, Y Unal

Maritime law
O Akinci, B Oner

Banking law
F Esen, U Capkin

Financial disputes
I Imik, N Boz

INAL LAW OFFICE

BUYUKDERE CADDESI
EREN TALU BINASI KAT:7
LEVENT 80620
ISTANBUL

Telephone: +90 212 339 0797
Fax: +90 212 339 0790
E-mail: office@inal-law.com
Website: www.inal-law.com

Languages
Turkish, English, Portuguese

Number of lawyers 6

Member
British Chamber of Commerce in Turkey (BCCT); Turkish American Businessmen's Association (TABA)

CATEGORIES OF WORK

Asset finance/securitisation
Seyma Inal

Banking, finance
Seyma Inal, Russell Welsh

Capital markets, privatisation
Ozlem Odabas Tavares

Corporate and commercial
Seyma Inal, O O Tavares

Competition, EC
Russell Welsh, Ebru Akbudak Sozer

Construction, project finance
Seyma Inal, O O Tavares

Dispute resolution, litigation
Seyma Inal, O O Tavares

Employment
Ebru Akbudak Sozer

Energy, natural resources
Ozlem Odabas Tavares

Foreign direct investment
Ebru Akbudak Sozer, O O Tavares

Information technology
Ebru Akbudak Sozer, Russell Welsh

Insurance, reinsurance
Seyma Inal

Intellectual property
Ebru Akbudak Sozer

Mergers and acquisitions
O O Tavares, Ebru Akbudak Sozer

Shipping, ship finance
Seyma Inal, Russell Welsh

Telecommunications
Ebru Akbudak Sozer, O O Tavares

Death, personal injury
Seyma Inal

Real estate
Ebru Akbudak Sozer, Seyma Inal

KARACA & ASSOCIATES

KORESHITLERI CAD NO 1
YONCA APT A-BLOK
KAT 2, D 8
34394 ESENTEPE
ISTANBUL

Telephone: +90 212 347 1031
Fax: +90 212 347 2095
E-mail: info@karacalaw.com
Website: www.karacalaw.com

Languages
English, Russian, Turkish

Number of lawyers 7

Member
Mackrell International

CATEGORIES OF WORK

Corporate and company law

Contract law and commercial disputes

Competition and European law

Labour law

Foreign investment law

Maritime and transportation law

Property law

Administrative and financial services law

Privatisation and government tenders

Project finance

International trade law

Litigation and commercial arbitration

Mergers and acquisitions

LAW OFFICES OF M FADLULLAH CERRAHOGLU

GÜLLÜ SOK. NO 1
3 LEVENT
80630 ISTANBUL

Telephone: +90 212 270 7014
Fax: +90 212 269 8910
E-mail: cerrahoglu@cerrahoglulaw.com

Languages
English, French, German

Other offices
Ankara

Number of lawyers 19
at this office 16

Contacts
M Fadlullah Cerrahoglu (managing partner), Bekir Aroma, Aysegül Yalçinmani

CATEGORIES OF WORK

Foreign investment
Bekir Aroma, Nural Bozkir

Business and commercial law
M Fadlullah Cerrahoglu, Aysegül Yalçinmani

Banking
M Fadlullah Cerrahoglu, Nural Bozkir

Execution and bankruptcy
M Fadlullah Cerrahoglu, Begüm Sibay

Labour
Eyüp Batal, Melis Biskin

Construction
M Fadlullah Cerrahoglu, Begüm Sibay

Mergers and acquisitions
Aysegül Yalçinmani, Nural Bozkir

Financial leasing
Bekir Aroma, Onur Gülsaran

Competition law
Secil Abali, Melis Biskin

Public offering (international and domestic)
Nural Bozkir, Selen Gür'es

Intellectual property
Melis Biskin, Selen Gür'es

Project finance
Nural Bozkir, Selen Gür'es

Litigation
M Fadlullah Cerrahoglu, Selale Kartal

M FETHI PEKIN & SEFIKA PEKIN

BEYBI GIZ PLAZA
MEYDAN SOK, NO 28 KAT 14
MASLAK
80670 ISTANBUL

Telephone: +90 212 290 2363
Fax: +90 22 290 2377
E-mail: pekin@pekin.com.tr
Website: www.pekinpekin.com

Languages
English, French, German

Other offices
Adana, Ankara, Izmir

Number of lawyers 31
at this office 22

CATEGORIES OF WORK

Banking and finance
Selin Bayar

Contracts, corporations, commercial
Sila Yavuz, Elif Tezcan

Mergers and acquisitions, IPOs
Selin Bayar, Sila Yavuz

Foreign/domestic investment, international trade
Sefika Pekin, Sila Yavuz

Government contracts, privatisations
Selin Bayar, Muharrem Kücük

Energy
Sefika Pekin, Muharrem Kücük

Property and real estate, leases, leasing, planning, land use
Can Oguzer, Hasan Caglayan

Construction
Deniz Altinay Sorguc

Intellectual property, trade marks, patents, copyrights, competition
Can Oguzer, Sila Muratoglu

European law
Sila Muratoglu, Muharrem Kücük

Communications, media, entertainment and art
Muharrem Kücük

Criminal law and litigation
Can Oguzer, Hasan Caglayan

Insurance
Deniz Altinay Sorguc

Environmental and natural resources
Sefika Pekin

Family, trust and estates, wills
Can Oguzer, Hasan Caglayan

Maritime and civil aviation
Deniz Altinay Sorguc

MEHMET GÜN & CO

KORESEHITLERÌ CAD
Nº 32 ZINCIRLIKUYU
ISTANBUL 80300

Telephone: +90 212 275 9003
Fax: +90 212 274 2095
E-mail: gun@mehmetgun.com.tr
Website: www.mehmetgun.com.tr

Languages
English, French, German

Other offices
Ankara, Izmir
(and correspondents in each EU country)

Number of lawyers 17
at this office 12

Contacts
Mehmet Gün, Selma Toplu Ûnlû

Member
TELFA (Trans European Law Firms Alliance); IBA; INTA; PTMG; ECTA

CATEGORIES OF WORK	
Banking	E-commerce
Commercial law	Employment
Commercial property	Energy law
Company law	Foreign investments
Competition law	Intellectual property
Computer law	Insurance
Contracts	Litigation
Copyright law	Privatisation law

THE FIRM

Mehmet Gün & Co was established in 1986 by name partner Mehmet Gün to provide full legal services to corporate clients. Since then, the firm has gained a reputation for professionalism and has become one of the leading law firms in Turkey. The firm's philosophy is to provide quality legal services while keeping the commercial objectives of the client at the forefront.

Mehmet Gün & Co is based in the financial centre of Istanbul, and has other offices in Ankara and Izmir. In addition, the firm has correspondent lawyers in Adana, Antalya, Bursa and Trabzon covering approximately 70% of Turkey.

AREAS OF PRACTICE

The firm has an outstanding reputation in intellectual property, unfair competition, corporate and commercial practice and litigation, and is unique for its full range of intellectual property services from copyrights, trade marks and patents to industrial designs prosecution and protection. The firm has established an investigation department to provide intelligence to the intellectual property practice.

Mehmet Gün & Co operates an extensive in-house training scheme for new graduates, sharing the expertise and experience of its lawyers in order to develop its future associates and partners. Most of the firm's lawyers have degrees from European legal institutions, and all of them are required to be familiar with other European cultures. Thus, the firm is often called upon to liaise between foreign clients and their local counterparts.

In addition to its correspondents in countries across Europe, the firm co-operates and works closely with major UK and US law firms, and has contacts with law firms all over the world.

The firm's clientele is a blend of foreign and local small, medium and large corporations from all over the world. The majority of clients, many of which were referred by satisfied clients, are from the UK, the US, and from European and Far Eastern countries.

Mehmet Gün & Co aims to provide a highly personal service to its clients in the most cost-efficient manner possible. The firm places great importance on the contributions it can make to clients' businesses. It provides detailed billing accounts, and always respects clients' queries.

Mehmet Gün & Co is fully committed to professionalism and to the professional rules of the Istanbul Bar Association and the Union of Turkish Bar Associations.

NEYYIR KITAPÇI ATTORNEYS-AT-LAW

ABIDE-I HÜRRIYET CAD
SOYAY APT. 226/5
34381 SISLI ISTANBUL

Telephone: +90 212 246 5428
Fax: +90 212 234 0669
E-mail: khlegal@khlegal.net

Languages
English, French

Number of lawyers 7

Member
International Lawyers Network (ILN); IBA

CATEGORIES OF WORK

Commercial and corporate
Neyyir Kitapçi

Litigation
Neyyir Kitapçi, Hüseyin Öz

Energy and infrastructure
Neyyir Kitapçi

Construction
Neyyir Kitapçi

Foreign investment
Tugba Basaran

Banking and finance
Neyyir Kitapçi

Mergers and acquisitions
Neyyir Kitapçi, Tugba Basaran

Consumer protection
Ufuk Yildirim

Intellectual property
Tugba Basaran

Execution and bankruptcy
Hüseyin Öz

Administrative litigation
Neyyir Kitapçi, Hüseyin Öz

Competition
Tugba Basaran

IT, Internet, telecoms
Tugba Basaran

Employment
Hüseyin Öz, Ufuk Yildirim

Maritime law
Hüseyin Öz, Tugba Basaran

THE FIRM

The firm, having been established by Neyyir Kitapçi in 1994, advises a high level of clientele of foreign and local corporations on a wide range of areas.

As a result of co-operation with outstanding law firms and participation in numerous projects, the firm has close connections with the leading law firms in a number of major cities worldwide. These contacts provide the firm with with a distinct advantage in providing solutions to problems involving multijurisdictional aspects. In addition to that, the firm is the exclusive Turkish member of the International Lawyers Network (ILN), a leading network of law firms with 80 members and 4,200 lawyers worldwide, spread along 61 countries in six continents.

AREAS OF PRACTICE

Neyyir Kitapçi Attorneys-at-Law is a full service law firm, specialising in a wide range of domestic and international work for corporate clients including foreign and domestic banks, holding companies, investment banks and foreign companies involved in a range of industries.

The firm has a strong banking litigation practice, with a high level of experience built on banking fraud and anti-money laundering cases.

The firm is also involved in a vast number of electricity and gas transactions and energy-related litigation in combination with administrative litigation.

Neyyir Kitapçi Attorneys-at-Law also represent several foreign and local corporations through its litigation department with an extensive experience in commercial, administrative and civil litigation, execution and bankruptcy procedures. Tax litigation, real estate litigation, IT litigation and Internet-related litigation is among the foremost areas of practice.

Consumer liability matters and IP, as well as IT/Internet issues, represent a significant share of the firm's work.

PAKSOY & CO

BEYBI GIZ PLAZA
MEYDAN SK NO 28 KAT 10,
MASLAK
34398 ISTANBUL

Telephone: +90 212 290 2350
Fax: +90 212 290 2355
E-mail: admin@paksoy-law.com
Website: www.paksoy-law.com

Languages
English, French

Number of lawyers 12

CATEGORIES OF WORK

International equity offerings	Licensing, distributing and franchising
Litigation	Capital markets and securities transactions
Project finance	IP
Privatisations	Competition law
Mergers and acquisitions	Telecommunications and IT
Corporate and joint ventures	Employment
Restructurings	Property, real estate
Banking and finance	Government procurement
Foreign investment	

THE FIRM

Paksoy & Co is a full-service law firm, based in Istanbul. The firm provides a comprehensive service to domestic and international corporations, government and institutional clients. The firm has two partners, ten associates and eight support staff.

AREAS OF PRACTICE

Paksoy & Co offers a full range of legal services to domestic and international business, and financial organisations. The firm advises its clients on corporate, commercial and financial matters, complex international transactions, restructurings, capital markets law covering international debt and equity issues, government procurement matters, privatisations, mergers and acquisitions, competition law, employment law issues, intellectual property, and litigation.

Paksoy & Co is highly regarded for its work in the areas of banking and finance, mergers and acquisitions, antitrust law, litigation and arbitration. Paksoy & Co advised the largest Turkish IPO to date with a mobile phone operator's flotation on the New York and Istanbul Stock Exchanges. The deal raised a total of $1.9bn. Currently, the firm is advising international and domestic underwriters in relation to a securities offering of a Turkish bottling company.

Paksoy & Co advised the Turkish Banking Regulatory and Supervisory Authority in connection with the sale of shares by the state in Demir Bank to HSBC International under the rehabilitation programme of the Turkish banking sector. Paksoy & Co is active in other banking law transactions including bank mergers and restructurings. One major project in 2003 has included advising on the purchase of a significant stake in Turkish energy companies by a US energy developer.

Paksoy & Co has been involved in many privatisation deals including strategic sales and public offerings of shares in state entities and has advised the Turkish Privatisation Administration on major deals.

The firm has considerable experience in international project financing. It acts for developers, lenders and borrowers in different areas of infrastructure projects including private power. The private power practice covers a broad range of IPPs on the BOT and BOO structure. Paksoy & Co has been involved in the BOT power projects completed in Turkey since the start of Turkey's IPP programme.

Paksoy & Co's telecommunications practice is also very strong. The firm has significant experience of advising telecommunications operators and service providers in all matters from commercial contract to mergers and acquisitions and financings.

The firm undertakes all aspects of intellectual property work both contentious and non-contentious, and assists companies in cases involving the WTO Agreement on Trade-Related Aspects of Intellectual Property Rights. Paksoy & Co advises domestic and international clients on major international licensing, franchising and distribution contracts. Paksoy & Co is representing a major software company in its anti-piracy proceedings in Turkey.

Paksoy & Co has a strong litigation practice, and has conducted arbitrations and handled numerous ICC commercial arbitrations in proceedings, through hearings and enforcement under the New York Convention. The firm has experience advising on disputes concerning complex contracts, international trade and construction projects. Currently, Paksoy & Co is acting for the Republic of Turkey on a major case involving the World Bank's ICSID arbitration in Washington DC against a US energy developer.

PEKIN & PEKIN

LAMARTINE CADDESI 10
TAKSIM
34437 ISTANBUL

Telephone: +90 212 313 3500
Fax: +90 212 313 3535
E-mail: postmaster@pekin-pekin.com
Website: www.pekin-pekin.com

Languages
English, French

Number of lawyers 25

Contacts
Ahmed Pekin (senior partner),
Fethi Pekin (managing partner)

Member
Lex Mundi; Terralex; The Association of European Lawyers; The Futures and Options Association (FOA); International Swaps & Derivatives Association (ISDA)

CATEGORIES OF WORK

Banking and finance
Securities law
Tax law
Commercial law
Capital markets law
Competition law
Mergers and acquisitions
Communications and media
Intellectual property (trade mark, patent, know-how)
Business law
Construction
Consumer law
Environmental law
European Community law
Project finance
Foreign investment law
Privatisation law
Information technology
Telecommunications
Labour law
Litigation
Insolvency and bankruptcy law
Financial leasing law
Foreign exchange
Real estate law

THE FIRM

Established in 1971, Pekin & Pekin is one of the largest law firms in Turkey. Pekin & Pekin has an outstanding reputation for its high-quality services to mainly English and French-speaking clients in Europe, Asia, the Middle East, and North America, as well as within Turkey. The firm employs 25 attorneys and a legal support staff of 25. The main office is based in Taksim, in the centre of Istanbul.

AREAS OF PRACTICE

The firm is well experienced in the fields of: anti-dumping; banking; finance; business law; capital markets law; commercial law; communications and media; competition law; construction; consumer law; environmental law; European Community law; financial leasing law; foreign exchange; foreign investment law; insolvency and bankruptcy law; information technology; intellectual property; labour law; litigation; mergers and acquisitions; privatisation law; real estate law; securities law; tax law; telecommunications.

Clients are represented both on retainer and case-by-case basis. The firm has represented numerous 'Fortune Global 500' companies, which include approximately 70% of the international banks listed, as well as several American 'Fortune 500' corporations and other smaller companies; major European companies and others; and major Japanese corporations. Additionally, the firm is counsel to a diverse group of major Turkish corporations and joint venture companies organised under the laws of the Republic of Türkiye.

POSTACIOĞLU LAW OFFICE

ABDI IPEKÇI CADDESI NO 65
NAZEM APT KAT 2 NO 2
MAÇKA ISTANBUL

Telephone: +90 212 232 22 02
Fax: +90 212 232 27 30
E-mail: contactist@postacioglu.com
Website: www.postacioglu.com

Languages
English, French, Italian

Other offices
Izmir, Paris

Number of lawyers 20
at this office 10

Member
International Business Law Consortium (IBLC)

CATEGORIES OF WORK

Domestic litigation	International joint ventures
International litigation	Mergers and acquisitions
International arbitration	Patents and trade marks
Labour law	Media law
Tax law	Entertainment law
Banking and finance	Law of execution and bankruptcy
Company law	Transportation law
Contract law	

THE FIRM

Postacioğlu Law Office was founded in 1907 by Ibrahim Etem Postacioğlu, and administrated by him until 1958. It was then headed by his eldest son, Sukru Postacioğlu, a professor in commercial law, until 1988. Since 1980, the grandson of the firm's founder, Etem Postacioğlu, has increased the dimensions of the offices in Izmir and Istanbul to an international level. In addition to the offices in Turkey, the firm is now represented in Paris.

The firm's lawyers' philosophy is to think simultaneously as lawyers and businessmen.

AREAS OF PRACTICE

The firm's main areas of practice can be divided up as follows:

Domestic and international litigation and arbitration: Postacioğlu Law Office has an intensive litigation and arbitration practice covering all aspects of civil law, property law, maritime law, private international law, international commercial law and law of contracts. The department works with clients to resolve disputes in a timely and effective manner through prompt assistance and sound legal advice. The firm has the capability to handle complex and urgent litigation thanks to its experience in a wide variety of claims and disputes.

Labour law: the firm offers a comprehensive service to its regular clients regarding labour law. Postacioğlu Law Office advises and represents companies on individual and collective labour claims of employees, for example on terms of employment, working rules and conditions, obligations under social security systems and so on. Services provided for clients include: drafting and negotiation of employment contracts; litigation in matters of dismissal and termination of employment contracts; work-related accidents and illness; interpretation and application of the laws and regulations regarding health and security in the workplace.

Tax law: the firm has significant experience in advising and assisting clients with regard to taxes on business activities. Its service includes submissions of enquiries to take authorities and advocacy to the courts concerning tax-related disputes.

Banking and finance: Postacioğlu Law Office advises and acts on behalf of borrowers and lenders in this field. Among its clients are local and international banks, and local and foreign companies and investors. The department concentrates on various aspects of banking law, loans, and finance of international trade (including letters of credit, counter-guarantees, accredits, etc).

Commercial law: Postacioğlu Law Office offers its clients extensive experience in various aspects of commercial law. The firm assists and represents a wide range of corporations and partnerships, as well as individuals, on regular business affairs and/or specific projects and undertakings. Advice to corporations covers matters such as: incorporations of companies in Turkey and abroad; shareholder agreements and corporate governance; capital-raising transactions; takeovers, mergers and acquisitions; and the establishment and dissolution of joint ventures, partnerships and limited-liability companies.

Intellectual property law: IPP is a company established within the organisational structure of Postacioğlu Law Office. IPP deals with all aspects of intellectual property law, for example: patent and trade mark protection; design registration; copyright and licensing of technology and related agreements on the transfer of such rights, etc. The firm's specialist intellectual property lawyers assist its clients on every single detail, and give worldwide service from consultation and registration steps through to acting in the courts in such cases as unfair competition, piracy and so on.

TURUNÇ & SAVASÇIN

MAÇKA CADDESİ 32/2
TESVİKİYE
80200 ISTANBUL

Telephone: +90 212 259 4536
Fax: +90 212 259 4538
E-mail: ts-info@turunc-savascin.com.tr
Website: www.turunc-savascin.com.tr

Languages
English, French

Other offices
Izmir, Ankara

Number of lawyers 14
at this office 5

Contact
Noyan Turunç

CATEGORIES OF WORK

Banking and finance
Noyan Turunç, Demir Savasçin

Capital markets and securities
Simhan Savasçin, Dr Esin Taylan

EU and competition law
Noyan Turunç, Dr Esin Taylan

Insolvency, bankruptcy
Demir Savasçin, Selen Egeli

Construction
Buket Önelge, Pinar Culha

Labour
Demet Cengiz

Litigation
Demir Savasçin, Yücel Ezberci

Foreign investment, commercial and corporate
Lerzan Nalbantoğlu, Selen Egeli

Mergers and acquisitions, joint ventures
Simhan Savasçin, Lerzan Nalbantoğlu

Intellectual property
Lerzan Nalbantoğlu

Oil and gas, energy
Noyan Turunç, Simhan Savasçin

Tax and customs
Buket Önelge, Selen Egeli

Insurance
Adnan Töre

Arbitration
Noyan Turunç, Dr Esin Taylan

Maritime
Dr Oya Özçayır

THE FIRM

Turunç & Savasçin was established in 1990 under the name of B&L Consultants, and changed its name in 1993. It has three offices in Istanbul, Izmir and Ankara. The firm has three counsels who are professors at different law schools, two banker advisers, three tax advisers, one customs adviser and one business adviser.

AREAS OF PRACTICE

In accordance with the practice in Turkey, Turunç & Savascin provides a comprehensive range of legal services in different areas of law by addressing the requirements of its international and local clientele in the Turkish market.

Banking and finance: the firm advises clients on banking and financial issues including legislation concerning Turkish currency, particularly considering the new enactments and amendments following the financial crisis in February. The firm represents some 20 foreign banks that have interests, but no presence, in Turkey. It has been involved in asset-backed international securitisation that covers almost all jurisdictions in Europe.

Competition: while advising on, reviewing and drafting contracts by considering the competition rules, on the investigation side examples of work include: (i) the Competition Board (corresponding to the Commission in the EU) at the preliminary stage of an investigation decided not to take any further actions against a multinational company (Fortune Top 50) because of preventive services by the firm; (ii) the firm prepared points of defences in an investigation by the Competition Board against another multinational (Fortune Top 100); and (iii) the firm prepared points of defence in an investigation by the Competition Board against a third multinational company (Fortune Top 50). One of the members of the firm has her doctorate degree in competition law, while another one has an LLM degree.

Corporate and commercial: the firm advises in all areas of corporate and commercial law, including direct foreign investment, mergers and acquisitions, and joint ventures. The firm represents many clients including multinationals in corporate and commercial matters. The client base is well balanced: 40% domestic, 60% international representing British, European, Australian, Japanese and US firms.

Direct foreign investment: similar to corporate law, the firm largely advises on foreign direct investment and in implementing local registrations of a foreign entity. The firm has represented German and US companies on direct investment in Turkey.

Mergers and acquisitions: the firm has been involved in mergers and acquisitions, from the early days of its establishment. It has been representing Australian, British, Dutch, German, Japanese and US companies who acquired varying shareholdings, including 100% acquisitions in local companies.

Intellectual property: a trade mark and patent attorney works in intellectual property issues, including litigation. The firm registers foreign trade marks in Turkey, works on registration of Turkish trade marks in some 50 jurisdictions, and reviews and drafts contracts regarding intellectual property and industrial matters.

Labour law: the firm advises on labour matters, including employment and unions, and negotiates collective labour agreements. The firm was involved in a transfer of services from a multinational company to another that was a part of a pan-European transaction. The task included substantial labour law work to cover all aspects of labour law.

Insolvency/corporate restructuring: the firm has been representing some 25 foreign entities in three bankruptcy proceedings in Turkey.

Dispute resolution; litigation and arbitration: the firm has been heavily involved in dispute resolution. The number of the cases in litigation reached a number in excess of 330 at civil courts, 853 at tax courts and 1,952 at administrative courts, regarding customs disputes. The firm has been working on a $4m international arbitration.

ERDEM & ERDEM LAW OFFICE

SEHIT NEVRES BULVARI NO. 10/7
35210 MONTRÖ IZMIR

Telephone: +90 232 441 6100
Fax: +90 232 466 2121
E-mail: izmir@erdem-erdem.com
Website: www.erdem-erdem.com

Languages
English, French, German, Turkish

Other offices
Istanbul

Contacts
Prof Dr H Ercüment Erdem, Piraye Erdem

CATEGORIES OF WORK

Administrative law	Environmental law
Agency and distributorships	Execution and bankruptcy law
ADR and international arbitration	Foreign investment law
Antitrust and trade regulation	Franchising and leasing
Aviation law	Insurance law
Banking and finance law	Intellectual property
Business and commercial law	International contracts
Capital markets	Joint ventures
Civil law	Litigation
Competition law	Maritime and transportation law
Construction law	Mergers and acquisitions
Corporate law	Privatisation and project finance
Energy and mining law	Tax law

THE FIRM

Founded in 1955, Erdem & Erdem Law Office is a dynamic general practice staffed by dedicated attorneys devoted to providing expert legal services in various areas of the law. The firm emphasises creative, aggressive and efficient business problem-solving founded on an extremely thorough knowledge of the law. The firm combines an energetic approach with a longstanding reputation as a provider of efficient legal services, using a focused team of attorneys and legal assistants in a cost-effective manner. The firm has distinguished itself in the fields of academic research and publications, particularly in the area of international commercial law, and continuously strives to keep abreast of all changes and developments in current legislation. Erdem & Erdem is primed to utilise its knowledge to the best potential of its clients' business and legal affairs.

The firm's lawyers are accustomed to working international hours and are fluent in Turkish, English, French and German relevant to international business.

AREAS OF PRACTICE

Having been involved in numerous projects over the course of more than 45 years of practice, Erdem & Erdem is experienced in a broad range of legal services. These areas include the following:

International arbitration: the firm has represented many national and international firms in arbitration before ICC, GAFTA, FOSFA, LCIA, IGPA, Waren-Verein Der Hamburger Börse e.V. and Liverpool Cotton Association as counsel. Prof Dr Erdem has also attended many ICC arbitrations as arbitrator.

Banking and finance law: Erdem & Erdem has dealt with many financing projects including: a financial lease agreement for Turkish Airlines and Onur Airlines; representing foreign banks such as BNP, Crédit Agricole, Indosuez, Hypo Vereinsbank and UBS; and representing national and foreign banks on their credit and loan agreements.

International contracts: Prof Dr Erdem has participated as a working committee member in the preparation of the *INCOTERMS 2000* and ICC models contracts such as Occasional Intermediary Contract (Non-Circumvention and Non-Disclosure Contracts), Distribution contract, Commercial Agency Contract, Selective Distribution Contract and International Mergers and Acquisitions Contract. Prof Dr Edrem is also a member of the ICC Incoterms Experts Panel and the ICC Institute of World Business Law.

Competition law: Erdem & Erdem has provided counsel regarding Turkish and European regulations relating to concentrations, dominant positions, discrimination and other restrictive trade practices to some of the world's largest multinational companies in a number of major industries. These industries include cement, consumer electronics, household products, management-consultancy services and water supply services in relation to the investigation of the Competition Authority.

Foreign investment law: Erdem & Erdem provided legal counseling to national and international firms concerning establishment of foreign investment companies in Turkey and abroad.

Capital markets: partners have been involved in the issuance of USD Notes by the Republic of Turkey, as well as the overseas issue realised by Türkiye Halk Bankasi AS, Osmanli Bankasi AS, Garanti Bankasi AS and Yapi Kredi Bankasi AS. Representative projects in this area include several IPOs concerning Turkcell, Altinyag, Batiçim and Bati Söke (West Anatolian Cement Company), Welcome plc.

Mergers and acquisitions: recent acquisitions projects illustrate the wide range of transactions that the firm is capable of undertaking. These include: acting for Batiçim (West Anatolian Cement Company) on its acquisition from Cement Francais; acting for Bayindir Construction Inc on acquisition of shares in Antalya International Airport Management Company by Flughafen Frankfurt/Main AG; and for Metesan Electrical Equipment Industry Co on acquisition of its shares by Lexel A/S.

UNITED ARAB EMIRATES

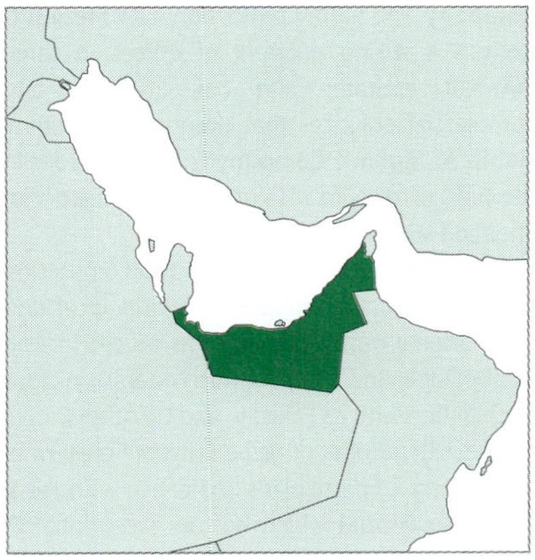

Population	2.5 million (foreigners 76%)
Number of lawyers	135 local lawyers
Professional title	Advocate
Currency	UAE Dirham (AED)

Index

Situated on the East Coast of the Arabian Peninsula, the United Arab Emirates (UAE) shares borders with Saudi Arabia and Oman. It is home to many regional-based international firms and in the past year has attracted new international players into the market.

Comprised of seven emirates, the UAE can be considered the most important legal market in the Middle East.

Abu Dhabi and Dubai are the two principal centres, and Sharjah, Ras al-Khaimah, Umm al-Qawain, Ajman and Fujairah are smaller sheikdoms.

The political powerhouse and federal capital of the country, Abu Dhabi, is the wealthiest of the seven emirates. Its ruler, Sheikh Zayid Bin Sultan Al Nuhayyan, has been president of the UAE federal government since 1971.

Dubai, the second biggest emirate, does not have wealth comparable to that of Abu Dhabi. This has cultivated a more enterprising and western business culture in Dubai, which relies more heavily on commercial business and tourism. Dubai's Sheikh, Maktum Bin-Rashid Al Maktum is prime minister and vice-president of the country.

The war in Iraq in 2003 had a significant effect on investor confidence and was directly responsible for the shaken tourism industry in Dubai. The war also caused a dip in the number of M&A transactions for law firms. This has proved to be a short-term blip, as, since the end of the war the country has seen a return to much better prospects in the region and optimism is strong amongst lawyers.

BILLING

Although rates vary depending on the complexity of the work, one could generally expect an hourly rate of up to €400 for a senior partner and €200 and above for an associate or junior partner.

Capped fees and fixed arrangements are more common for bigger transactions - mainly those in the project finance area. Top-end government work may be billed at a slightly higher rate.

MARKETING

The UAE imposes no restrictions on the marketing of law firms. Client confidentiality in some cases will be the only reason preventing lawyers from disclosing the names of clients or projects.

The reputation of lawyers, and connections within the market, often holds as much sway as marketing campaigns.

IN-HOUSE LAWYERS

As legal work in the UAE becomes more complex, in-house lawyers are increasingly common. Leading banks and oil and petrochemical companies, such as Enoc and Adnoc, often have a reasonably sized team of in-house lawyers to represent the companies' interests. Etisalat and Emirates Airlines also have good lawyers.

ECONOMIC CLIMATE

The UAE has 10% of the world's proven oil reserves and is home to the world's fourth-largest reserves of natural gas. Since it began exporting nearly 40 years ago the UAE has extracted an estimated $300bn worth of oil. As a consequence, the country has witnessed massive change over the past 30 years.

The free trade zones are an area of continued interest as they provide a haven for foreign investors. Companies establishing themselves in the free zones can be 100% foreign-owned and benefit from having no obligation for any local involvement. There are ten free zones at different stages of development. Jebel Ali Free Zone is the first and largest of them all. More interesting perhaps is the Dubai Technology, Electronic Commerce and Media Free Zone (TECOM) which includes Dubai Internet City (DIC) and Dubai Media City (DMC). DIC has attracted more than 200 companies to date and is increasingly popular with multinationals such as Microsoft, Oracle and IBM. This led **Denton Wilde Sapte** to open an additional office in DIC in 2003 and **Clyde & Co** to open an office in DMC.

The UAE is able to capitalise on its convenient location as it is situated in the middle of the UAE coast. The geography of the UAE means that it is an ideal base for businesses to bridge the gap between the Middle Eastern and Asian markets. 2003 also saw the introduction of a new airline – Etihad. The UAE continues to be a major defence purchaser with an ongoing $10bn procurement programme. It is also well placed to take an interest in the opportunities arising from the reconstruction of Iraq.

The Palm Island project in Dubai is still in the process of being built but has drawn a lot of interest so far. The two islands in the shape of a palm are an initiative to attract tourists and have increased the UAE's beachfront by 166%.

Dubai is managing to manoeuvre itself into a premier economic position in the Gulf, aided by

The largest firms

1	Al Tamimi & Co	42
2	Clifford Chance LLP	30
3	Clyde & Co	26
4	Denton Wilde Sapte	20
5	Afridi & Angell	18
6	Allen & Overy	17
	Habib Al Mulla & Company	17
8	Al Sharif Advocates & Legal Consultants	12
9	Trowers & Hamlins	11
10	Key & Dixon	8
	Rouse & Co. International	8
	Simmons & Simmons	8
13	Al-Sayegh Richards Butler	6
	Al-Suwaidi & Company	6
	Shearman & Sterling LLP	6
16	Al-Mehairi Legal Consultants – Bryan Cave LLP	5
	Norton Rose	5
18	Hill Taylor Dickinson	4
	James Berry & Associates Legal Consultants	4
	Trench & Associates	4
21	Berrymans Lace Mawer	3
	Donald H. Bunker & Associates	3
	Krauss Amereller Henkenborg & Khasawneh	3
	Vinson & Elkins L.L.P.	3

These figures represent the total number of lawyers in this country only, and have been supplied by the firms themselves. The figures should be accurate as at 1 January 2004.

the depleting oil reserves in Bahrain. In 2003 Dubai hosted the 2003 World Bank and IMF meeting.

Qatar continues to be a major source of work for firms. Projects in 2003 continue to develop such as the $10bn Dolphin pipeline project, which will carry gas from Qatar's offshore North Dome field through the UAE to Oman. A certain amount of privatisation is still being conducted.

The Gulf Co-operation Council has the ultimate goal of creating a more integrated regional economy in the Middle East with standard customs duty and even the idea of creating a single currency by 2010.

LEGAL MARKET

The increasing importance of the UAE legal market is evident in the number of firms setting up offices in the country. In 2003 international player **Norton Rose**, which already tops the tables with its practice in Bahrain, established itself in Dubai. American-based **Vinson & Elkins L.L.P.** also opened a five-lawyer office in Dubai. **Simmons & Simmons** sealed its commitment to the Gulf in 2003 by opening an extra office in nearby Qatar. Furthermore, firms already established in the UAE have opened additional offices around the country. This, together with the departure of firms such as **Clifford Chance LLP** and **White & Case LLP** from Bahrain, furthers the UAE's status as the region's leading legal market. This has had the added advantage for clients of raising the standards and quality of legal work in the country.

The differences between the two cities of the federal capital Abu Dhabi and commercially oriented Dubai make for two very different legal environments.

Much of the work in the federal capital, Abu Dhabi involves the energy sector and governmental work. Whereas with only 10% of its economy oil-related, Dubai sees much more inward investment and general commercial work. Dubai also has a wider variety of clients and needs rather than just the big-ticket work of Abu Dhabi.

Firms such as **Towers & Hamlins** and **Denton Wilde Sapte** have offices in both Abu Dhabi and Dubai for historic reasons. Both firms are encouraging co-operation between their two sites by increasingly using both offices to work on the same transactions.

Dubai, home to the fast growing DIC, is providing firms with an increasing number of IP, IT and hi-tech clients benefiting from the TECOM free zone. With this in mind both **Denton Wilde Sapte** and **Clyde & Co** have set up offices within TECOM.

Major international players **Allen & Overy** and **Clifford Chance LLP** have both been operating in the Emirates for more than two decades. They both use Dubai as a base for a wider regional practice and often work on transactions in neighbouring Oman, Saudi Arabia and Kuwait.

Clyde & Co has an established presence and reputation in the region. The firm is building an all-service practice in the UAE. In the past five years, the size of the firm has more than trebled and is now the biggest in the country advising blue-chip clients and increasing the reputation of its growing IP and IT practices.

The two local firms notably competing with international outfits for top-end commercial work are **Al Tamimi & Co** and **Habib Al Mulla & Company**. The highly professional **Al Tamimi & Co** has a strong network of offices in three different emirates and has litigation and commercial practices that deserve recognition. **Habib Al Mulla & Company** is a clear leader in the field of dispute resolution with a history of litigation successes.

Afridi & Angell which has a good reputation in several practice areas is a hybrid local and international outfit. The firm has offices in Abu Dhabi, Dubai and Sharjah, which operate in close conjunction with its Pakistan and US offices.

A small number of niche firms are present in the country. Of particular significance is **Rouse & Co. International** which has an exceptional IP practice. Also a specialist practitioner, **Donald H. Bunker & Associates** is the only aviation boutique in the Middle East. **Hill Taylor Dickinson** is particularly noted for its work in the maritime and shipping arena.

BANKING AND FINANCE

2003 witnessed an increase in the number of Islamic finance transactions in the UAE. Interesting new products, such as property-backed structures, are becoming available and lawyers are more frequently required to work on deals which demand a mixture of conventional and Islamic finance initiatives. A lot of the regulatory framework for the Dubai International Finance Centre (DIFC) has now been drafted. However, the centre is still waiting for a federal decree to give it the go-ahead. Dubai now poses a real threat to Bahrain, possibly knocking it from its position as the banking headquarters of the Middle East.

Allen & Overy has been instructed for around three-quarters of the DIFC's legal work. The Dubai office advised the centre on contracts, security, property, real estate, and employment law. Top-notch deals which stand out in 2003 include advising Standard Chartered Bank as arranger on a $150m term loan facility for Iran Foreign Investment Company; advising the borrower, National Central Cooling Company, in relation to the AED120m (€26m) Islamic financing of two central cooling plants in Abu Dhabi; and advising the arrangers, HSBC Bank, NBAD, SCB, NBD, EBI, in relation to the fixed rate AED1.5bn (€330m) bond by the government of Dubai. The banking and finance team is headed by Bimal Desai, valued by clients for his 'creative solutions'. Also recommended is the multilingual Luma Saqqaf.

BANKING AND FINANCE

ALLEN & OVERY ✪
CLIFFORD CHANCE LLP
SIMMONS & SIMMONS ✪

DENTON WILDE SAPTE ✪
NORTON ROSE
SHEARMAN & STERLING LLP

Donald H. Bunker & Associates
Key & Dixon

Afridi & Angell
Al Tamimi & Co
Al-Sayegh Richards Butler
Clyde & Co ✪
Habib Al Mulla & Company
Hadef Al Dhahiri & associates
Trowers & Hamlins
Vinson & Elkins L.L.P. ✪

Firms are listed A-Z in tiers which are ranked in order of priority
✪ *Indicates firm displays contact details at the end of this chapter.*

Working often in conjunction with its projects department, **Clifford Chance LLP** has an impressive banking and finance arm in Dubai which is well versed in capital markets, asset and structured finance and Islamic finance. Fronting the team is managing partner Tim Soutar, a notable leader in his field. In the past 12 months the firm advised the government of Dubai in connection with the $410m five-year fixed-rate note to be listed on the Dubai Financial Market. The firm acts for a host of lead arrangers in relation to the syndicated financing of banks and other large corporations in the Middle East. Clients include Abu Dhabi Islamic Bank and Emirates Airlines.

Simmons & Simmons has been responsible for drafting all laws and regulations relating to Islamic financial institutions and Islamic financing products for the DIFC. In the past 12 months the banking and finance department also acted on behalf of a syndicate of banks including Bank Muscat in Oman and the Gulf International Bank of Bahrain in the financing of a $50m acquisition of the energy division of a large corporation. Another major undertaking in 2003 was advising on a loan to finance the $245m development of a hotel, office and shop development in Abu Dhabi.

Denton Wilde Sapte has a robust banking and finance practice comprising four full-time banking partners and seven assistants. Neil Cuthbert, managing partner of the Dubai office, has a wealth of experience and under his guidance the firm acted for the Government of Brunei on its first eurocurrency general syndicated loan of $360m. Other highlight deals of the year include advising on numerous bilateral and syndicated Islamic financings and cross-border lease financings for clients such as HSBC, Dubai Islamic Bank, Standard Chartered Bank and a member of the UAE ruling family.

One of the key skills that **Norton Rose** brings to its new Dubai office is banking and finance expertise. With an excellent international reputation in Islamic banking deals, the firm looks set to continue its high calibre work in the UAE. **Norton Rose** will service its existing client base of major international banks, corporate players and governments.

Shearman & Sterling LLP has increased the size of its Abu Dhabi office over the past three years and is best known for its accomplished banking and finance, and project finance practices. It acted for the UAE Offsets group in the sale of a 25% interest in Project Dolphin and Dolphin Energy Limited to Occidental Petroleum Corporation. Recently the firm advised the International Petroleum Investment Company (IPIC) in the $450m financial restructuring of South Korea's Hyundai Oil Refining Company.

Donald H. Bunker & Associates is an aviation boutique and is the only specialist aviation firm in the Middle East. A small team advises the Dubai government on aviation matters and advises carriers on insurance claims. The Dubai office is used as a base for work in the Middle East and Asia.

Key & Dixon has experience iin public offerings, Islamic finance, debt restructuring and insolvency. The firm handles syndicated loan agreements for a mixture of local and international banks.

Around one-third of the legal work at **Afridi & Angell** lies in the banking and finance area. The firm advises big name international clients such as Lloyd's, Standard Chartered and Citibank and local banks like Emirates Bank International regarding credit facilities, syndications, work-outs, product development and regulatory matters. Ali Alfridi is well known for his aptitude for Islamic banking.

Local firm **Al Tamimi & Co** was instructed by the lead managers to the listing of the Emirates Airline $200m bond. Other deals include advising United Arab Bank in relation to syndicated loan of AED72m (€16m) to Citadel Properties. This firm has a reputation for its knowledge of Islamic financing.

Although stronger in the area of corporate and commercial work, **Al-Sayegh Richards Butler** has sound banking and finance experience. Under the leadership of the widely recognised Peter Michelmore, the firm advised on Boeing 777 financings for Emirates Airlines in 2003.

Jonathan Silver takes care of the banking and financing side of **Clyde & Co**'s practice in Dubai. Finance isn't the firm's main focus but it has a proven ability in this area. Its lawyers advised a Bahrain-based investment bank on the establishment of the first-ever shari'a compliant investment fund and developed a shari'a compliant cross-border structure for the fund. In addition, the firm advised on a UAE-based $50m Islamic venture capital fund.

Habib Al Mulla & Company also has experience of banking and finance transactions. Its clients are mainly locally based.

In 2003 **Hadef Al Dhahiri & associates** was involved in a number of restructuring, privatisation and other transactional banking matters. The firm advises both borrowers and lenders including local Islamic banks on various structured finance transactions. The government and the UAE Central Bank are among its clients.

Both the Abu Dhabi and Dubai offices of **Trowers & Hamlins** are responsible for handling banking and finance matters. In 2003 the firm acted for a leading regional bank and advised a major local business on a syndicated loan.

Vinson & Elkins L.L.P. plans to use its new Dubai base to build on its presence in the Middle East. It supports clients on a range of banking and Islamic finance matters.

CORPORATE AND COMMERCIAL

Despite a slight slump in corporate and commercial work due to the war in Iraq, the UAE has been recovering quickly since September 2003.

Allen & Overy maintains its position as one of the major leaders in corporate and commercial work in the UAE. Building on its strong regional reputation, the Dubai office has been active on a number of top deals in the Gulf in 2003 such as advising HSBC Private Equity Middle East on the $9m acquisition of Bahrain-based Havelock AHI. The corporate and commercial team also advised Standard Chartered Grindlays Bank on the integration of its businesses in UAE, Bangladesh, Sri Lanka, India, Pakistan and Jordan, and, under partner Duncan Macnab, advised on the restructuring of the Qatar power sector. Managing partner, and head of the Dubai office, Simon Roderick, ranks high in the region and has impressive commercial experience especially in M&A. Khalid Garousha is also recommended for his knowledge of both English and Arab legal systems.

Clifford Chance LLP has increased its presence in the UAE growing to two partners and 32 associates, including secondees in Riyadh, Bahrain, and Abu Dhabi. Clients claim that with 'a mixture of tact and leadership', the office continues to demonstrate that it can provide a full regional service out of Dubai without relying extensively on other **Clifford Chance LLP** offices. 2003 saw **Clifford Chance LLP** instructed by MTC Vodafone in Bahrain, advising on the successful bid for the second GSM mobile licence to be awarded in Bahrain. The office also advised on the legal and regulatory framework for the Dubai International Financial Centre (DIFC), and advised on negotiations for a number of major hotel developers around the region. The corporate team is spearheaded by partner Ewan Cameron, who has a wealth of experience in this area, and who also continues to handle a number of major privatisation deals in Saudi Arabia and Oman. Other noteworthy individuals are Scott Campbell

CORPORATE AND COMMERCIAL

ALLEN & OVERY ✪
CLIFFORD CHANCE LLP
CLYDE & CO ✪

AL-SAYEGH RICHARDS BUTLER
SIMMONS & SIMMONS ✪
TROWERS & HAMLINS

Afridi & Angell
Al Tamimi & Co ✪
Denton Wilde Sapte ✪
Habib Al Mulla & Company
Key & Dixon
Norton Rose
Vinson & Elkins L.L.P. ✪

Al-Mehairi Legal Consultants - Bryan Cave LLP
Al Sharif Advocates & Legal Consultants
Greenwald & Van De Kraats
Hadef Al Dhahiri & associates
James Berry & Associates Legal Consultants
Trench & Associates

Firms are listed A-Z in tiers which are ranked in order of priority
✪ *Indicates firm displays contact details at the end of this chapter.*

(for privatisation) and Paul Davies (for capital markets).

Clyde & Co is the biggest of the international firms in the UAE with five partners and 30 associates. The corporate and commercial department has seen lateral growth and in the past twelve months six new solicitors have joined the practice. The highly esteemed Jonathan Silver heads the corporate team and Anthony Garrod handles the commercial side. The DMC office undertakes mainly IP-related work but is increasingly focusing on commercial matters. **Clyde & Co**'s corporate and commercial track record in 2003 includes advising on the $3.5bn expansion programme for an international airport and advising a major international company on the domestic laws of Egypt, Qatar, Iran, Bahrain, Jordan , Lebanon, Syria, Kuwait, Oman and the UAE. Other highlights for the office during the year include acting for a large US company on the $13m acquisition of a specialist oil field equipment and services company with operations across the Middle East, and advising major European players on the reconstruction of commercial operations in the region. Clients praise the firm for being 'commercially aware'.

Abu Dhabi-based **Al-Sayegh Richards Butler** works on mid-ticket corporate and commercial deals. This six-lawyer outfit has corporate and commercial as its main strength, and as a consequence boasts an impressive list of international and domestic clients. According to clients, managing partner Peter Michelmore 'balances sound legal advice with common sense' and his work is widely acknowledged throughout the UAE. Anthony Trew, although retired, remains a consultant at the firm. Transactions of note include advising General Electric Power Systems on establishing a presence in Algeria, Morocco and Tunisia, and being instructed by Babcock Borsig Power regarding a joint venture in Qatar. The firm continues to advise Electricité de France and the UAE Ministry of Electricity and Water.

Simmons & Simmons has a seven-lawyer office in Abu Dhabi managed by partner Ibrahim Mubaydeen. Roger Clarke, a former banking partner from **Trowers & Hamlins**' Bahrain office, joined the firm at the end of 2002. In 2003 the corporate and commercial team advised the Bin Jabr Group on the $60m multi-jurisdictional acquisition of a drilling rig business. Another highlight of the year involved advising on a desalination plant in Abu Dhabi. The office is also instructed by the Abu Dhabi government on a number of deals. The firm expanded its presence in the Middle East in 2003 by opening an office in Qatar.

Towers & Hamlins has a corporate and commercial team which clients describe as 'responsive'. The firm is acting for a significant trading enterprise in its multi-million dollar acquisition of a number of overseas companies active in the oil and gas sector. In the past 12 months both the Abu Dhabi and Dubai offices have been involved in a number of significant cross-border M&A deals and have advised on commercial terms and conditions for a government defence contract. The firm also acted for the founder shareholders of a new UAE/South Africa joint venture company that was established in 2003. The Dubai office advised the British University in Dubai on its establishment and local operations.

Afridi & Angell has more of an international presence than other local firms. Its corporate and commercial work encompasses M&A, venture capital and private equity work. The Abu Dhabi office handles government work, while the Dubai office is more orientated towards mid-sized commercial transactions.

The well-connected local firm **Al Tamimi & Co** has a range of offices in the UAE including sites in Dubai, Dubai Internet City, Abu Dhabi, and Sharjah. Essam Al Tamimi is a well-known personality in the UAE legal market and the firm is considered by clients and rival firms as one of the best local practices in the country. Handling a mixture of large domestic and international clients, the firm has significant experience in the area of property development, restructuring and construction. Clients recommend 'supportive and responsive' Lisa Dale in this field.

Denton Wilde Sapte has, for historic reasons, offices in both Abu Dhabi and Dubai. Both offices worked together whilst acting for a new Abu Dhabi airline. The corporate practice is led by 'enthusiastic' managing partner Niall O'Toole in Abu Dhabi and the 'practical and dedicated' Jonathan Dawe in Dubai. In corporate and commercial the firm is instructed by a range of multinational companies as well as local and regional clients. In 2003, the corporate team advised Occidental Petroleum Corporation in the $340m acquisition of a stake in Dolphin Energy Limited. The firm opened an additional office in the Dubai Internet City in September 2003.

Habib Al Mulla & Company is renowned for its litigation expertise which makes up 50% of its workload. However, the local firm also has a strong corporate and commercial arm. The 17-lawyer firm is situated in Abu Dhabi and Dubai and is experienced in acting for major national and international companies on international joint ventures, M&A and franchising. All lawyers at the firm speak English and Arabic and some speak French.

Key & Dixon has experience of joint ventures, offshore formations, M&A and supports companies wishing to establish themselves within the UAE. Former *Fox & Gibbons* partner Christopher Dixon is well established in the region. In 2002 the firm formed an association with **Taylor Wessing**.

Norton Rose opened the doors of its UAE office in October 2003. Situated in the DIFC, it is well placed to capitalise on new commercial opportunities in the area. With a wealth of corporate and commercial experience already built up in the Middle East from its Bahrain office, the firm continues to serve existing corporate clients such as HSBC from Dubai and expects to take on more private equity and property funds, M&A and joint venture work throughout 2004. The five-lawyer office is fronted by the fine corporate and commercial lawyer, partner Graeme Muir, who was instrumental in the re-establishment of the firm's Hong Kong office in 2002.

The new Dubai office of **Vinson & Elkins L.L.P.** opened in October 2003. It currently has a team of two partners and three associates but this is expected to grow to five associates in 2004. The firm is using Dubai as a base for its work throughout the Middle East and North Africa. A large proportion of its corporate and commercial work is in the energy sector. Partner Jeffrey Eldredge has corporate and commercial experience particularly on cross-border and privatisation transactions.

Al-Mehairi Legal Consultants - Bryan Cave LLP has a series of offices in the Gulf but the UAE contingent of this network does not enjoy the same prestige as its association in Kuwait. The corporate and commercial practice is fronted from the US by John Lonsberg. Clients are mainly US companies but in 2003 the firm also advised a GCC manufacturing and industrial conglomerate on restructuring its operations in the Middle East.

Local firm **Al Sharif Advocates & Legal Consultants** is best known for its fairly comprehensive litigation and advocacy skills but it also covers corporate international transactions and commercial work for international and domestic clients. The 16-lawyer firm is proficient in contract and employment law.

Dubai-based **Greenwald & Van De Kraats** advises clients on the establishment and restructuring of companies in the UAE. The six-lawyer firm advises on corporate and contractual structures and arrangements in five jurisdictions. Managing partner, Daniel Jack Greenwald III, has particular experience in contracts law.

Hadef Al Dhahiri & associates has its main office in Abu Dhabi and a smaller office in Dubai. The corporate and commercial arm handles a range of transactions in this area and is allied with **Clifford Chance LLP** in Dubai. The team is spearheaded by managing partner Khaled Sifri and has a broad mix of Emerati and international lawyers.

James Berry & Associates Legal Consultants has a commercial practice which handles a range of transactions such as joint ventures in the Middle East, local licences and registrations. There is a growing involvement in finance work. Managing partner James Berry speaks English, Arabic and Swahili.

Managing partner Cynthia Trench heads the corporate and commercial practice at **Trench & Associates** which clients say provides 'high quality work for reasonable fees'. Recent work includes establishing the UAE Franchise Association with the Dubai Development & Investment Authority. The firm continues to develop its work in the area of IP, handling copyright cases.

DISPUTE RESOLUTION

Only Emirati nationals are permitted to appear in court, so local litigators must be employed for court work. Some international firms have Emirati advocates who can provide this service but many choose to employ local lawyers or small local firms when necessary. Litigation can be slow and time consuming as all documents must be translated into Arabic. Many large international firms with bases in the UAE choose to avoid this, working mainly in an arbitration and mediation capacity.

Habib Al Mulla & Company is led by Habib Al Mulla, who is held in high esteem by other lawyers in the UAE and is arguably the country's best local litigator. The 17-strong local firm is best known for its outstanding litigation practice which accounts for half of all the firm's work.

Al Tamimi & Co acts for a range of top companies from the international business community as well as on a national level. Its local knowledge is a distinct advantage in the dispute resolution arena. Clients include Ford, Microsoft, IBM, AIG and General Electric. The firm also has a good track record for dealing with construction disputes.

With an immense portfolio of arbitration experience, Simon Roderick spearheads the dispute resolution practice at **Allen & Overy**. A notable case in the past year was resolving a conflict regarding a $3bn military healthcare contract for the UAE armed forces. Other 2003 highlights include advising a major regional investment bank in an $400m ICC arbitration with regard to the acquisition of banks throughout the Middle East and Africa; advising the Government of Dubai in an ICSID arbitration in relation to an alleged misappropriation of an investor's assets; and advising a German and Swiss Bank in relation to a claim of breach of mandate before the courts in Dubai and Abu Dhabi.

DISPUTE RESOLUTION

HABIB AL MULLA & COMPANY

AL TAMIMI & CO ✪
ALLEN & OVERY ✪
CLIFFORD CHANCE LLP
CLYDE & CO ✪

Al-Mehairi Legal Consultants - Bryan Cave LLP
Al Sharif Advocates & Legal Consultants
Berrymans Lace Mawer
Hill Taylor Dickinson
Towers & Hamlins

Afridi & Angell
Hilal & Associates
Key & Dixon
Lutfi Al Bahar & Co.

Firms are listed A-Z in tiers which are ranked in order of priority
✪ Indicates firm displays contact details at the end of this chapter.

Terence Witzmann heads the litigation and dispute resolution team at **Clifford Chance LLP**. In 2003 the team advised Daimler Chrysler, Philip Morris and Coca-Cola regarding dispute resolution matters. The team includes a UAE-qualified lawyer who is able to appear in the courts.

Clyde & Co is credited with having a heavy litigation focus within its UAE practice. Alec Emmerson, known for his litigation and arbitration expertise, leads the dispute resolution contingent of the office, which has welcomed two additional lawyers in the past 12 months. Much of the firm's work in this area is for contractors and on agency disputes.

Al-Mehairi Legal Consultants - Bryan Cave LLP provides dispute resolution services for all types of commercial clients from its Dubai office.

Local firm **Al Sharif Advocates & Legal Consultants** is licensed by the UAE Ministry of Justice and has rights of audience before all UAE Courts, both local and federal. The firm's lawyers have experience as both prosecutors and defence counsellors. Particularly recommended for its experience in shari'a law, the team has been instructed in cross-border litigation cases involving international business law.

Berrymans Lace Mawer has taken on a number of international construction-related arbitrations in the past 12 months. Significant deals have been entered into of late regarding arbitration work for government departments. A major client is the consultants in a big Abu Dhabi-based sewerage pipeline dispute.

The dispute resolution practice at **Hill Taylor Dickinson** mainly relates to maritime transactions. However, general insurance and some commercial litigation is handled by the firm, which has experience of contract disputes and bank fraud.

Towers & Hamlins' dispute resolution practice is headed from the Dubai office by the respected Nick White. It is acting in a multinational ICC arbitration in relation to an agency dispute for a Middle Eastern claimant against a Japanese company; acting for a multinational insurance company on a claim brought against it in the Dubai courts; and is acting for an offshore bank.

Afridi & Angell supports clients with litigation and arbitration issues. In addition, the firm handles multi-jurisdictional dispute resolution and arbitration proceedings.

Local firm **Hilal & Associates** undertakes general commercial litigation work and also assists **Hill Taylor Dickinson** in shipping disputes.

Key & Dixon is involved in international litigation disputes. Some private client and agency work is also undertaken.

INFORMATION TECHNOLOGY

Dubai Internet City and Dubai Media City have promoted IT work in the UAE, thus increasing its status as a major communications hub in the Gulf. The major telecoms client in the country is Etisalat with a capitalisation of nearly $10bn.

Clyde & Co outstrips rival firms when it comes to IT work in the UAE. With a strong set of lawyers, the team advises on a wide variety of issues including website development and database agreements, software licences, digital content agreements and systems development agreements. Examples of its work in 2003 are advising a Gulf-based international airline on all aspects of its IT, including software licences, outsourcing agreements, systems development and website development agreements. The firm has also been instructed by several national and

INFORMATION TECHNOLOGY

CLYDE & CO ✪

Al Tamimi & Co ✪
Allen & Overy ✪
Al-Mehairi Legal Consultants - Bryan Cave LLP
Clifford Chance LLP
Denton Wilde Sapte ✪
Towers & Hamlins

Firms are listed A-Z in tiers which are ranked in order of priority
✪ Indicates firm displays contact details at the end of this chapter.

international Internet companies regarding data protection matters and design contracts.

With an office in Dubai Internet City, **Al Tamimi & Co** has developed its IT practice over the past year. The firm has attracted a range of new IT and media and entertainment clients due to its growing expertise. The firm has a particular aptitude for data protection, domain name registration and software protection.

Allen & Overy continues to service its one major IT client, Tejari.com, a regional B2B portal of the Dubai Ports Authority which it advises on a host of regional IT matters.

Al-Mehairi Legal Consultants - Bryan Cave LLP advises on a range of IT and telecoms issues. Clients include national and international companies.

Clifford Chance LLP offers a certain ability in IT work, although, as with IP, this is not the firm's main focus. It has experience in technology licensing arrangements relating to its project finance work.

Having established an additional office in Dubai Internet City, **Denton Wilde Sapte** is new to the list this year as it has made a commitment to developing its growing IT practice. Bringing a TMT specialist from London to man the office, the firm advised, among others, the Emirates Bank on its electronic banking contracts and customer terms and conditions for electronic banking.

The Abu Dhabi office of **Trowers & Hamlins** has IT capabilities. In 2003 it advised a government agency on the tendering, negotiation and conclusion of a series of IT contracts.

INSURANCE

Insurance is an important aspect of legal work in the UAE. A large proportion of insurance and reinsurance matters relate to the sizeable shipping industry. The sector is expected to develop further as leading insurance companies move into the DIFC.

Partners Alec Emmerson and Chris Mills head up **Clyde & Co**'s insurance practice. In 2003 the firm acted for insurers Property & Marine Open Cover in relation to the $85m non-petrochemical fire claim, the largest ever of its type in the Middle East. Of particular note is the firm's fine reinsurance specialist lawyer, Wayne Jones. Half of its insurance work is non-shipping related.

INSURANCE

CLYDE & CO ✪
HILL TAYLOR DICKINSON

Afridi & Angell
Berrymans Lace Mawer
Clifford Chance LLP

Firms are listed A-Z in tiers which are ranked in order of priority
✪ Indicates firm displays contact details at the end of this chapter.

Hill Taylor Dickinson has a strong reputation in the UAE for insurance work. The three partners and their four associates cover shipping insurance, broader commercial matters and litigation matters. The firm has experience of reinsurance.

Afridi & Angell handles insurance matters for the likes of foreign insurance company Eagle Star. The firm also represents clients in insurance disputes.

In the insurance field, **Berrymans Lace Mawer** acts for a range of employers, professionals and contractors. In 2003 it was instructed on several insurance-related disputes. The firm has a good track record for professional indemnity work within the construction industry.

Clifford Chance LLP liaises with its insurance groups in London on cases in the UAE. The Dubai office has experience in the insurance sector and shipping-related matters. Clients include the Bahrain government and Oman Insurance Co.

INTELLECTUAL PROPERTY

IP practice in the UAE has been changing due to additional legislation. New laws have been brought in to better protect trade marks and the introduction of royalties for copyright. However, the enforcement of these laws is not always as stringent as it could be. Counterfeiting is still fairly widespread although the extent of the problem has been decreasing over the past few years and the UAE was removed from the United States' section 301 watch list in 2002. The UAE was supposed to have reached TRIPS standards by 2000 but has been granted an extension. Due to a lack of staff who can grant patents in the UAE, there is a lot of outsourcing work to Austria which slows the process.

Two new lawyers joined the prestigious IP department at **Al Tamimi & Co** in 2003 which reinforced its position as the top local IP practice. Hoda Barakat is one of the finest IP lawyers in the country, and is described by clients as 'highly quaified and experienced'. Much of the firm's work in this area is litigation and enforcement. In the past 12 months the firm successfully won a high-profile piracy case for one of the world's largest IT companies. With a range of multinational clients, the firm also represents DaimlerChrysler regarding trade mark infringements and counterfeit goods.

Specialist practitioners **Rouse & Co. International** is also at the forefront in IP. The energetic and highly regarded Edward Hardcastle heads a 22-strong team. Key to their success is a dedicated investigation department within the office. The firm boasts a rich portfolio of enforcement, trade mark, patent filing and commercial work for clients such as Toshiba, Philips, GlaxoSmithKline, Japan Tobacco inc, Berkeley IP Services and L'Oréal.

Clyde & Co advises clients throughout the region on a range of IP matters including registration, protection and enforcement of trade marks, patents and copyright and database rights. Led by Anthony Garrod, a noteworthy transaction was the undertaking of anti-counterfeiting work for a US drug company and a multinational sportswear company relating to one of its core brands in several Middle Eastern jurisdictions. IP lawyer Rob Deans joined the team in 2003 from **Bird & Bird** in Hong Kong. The firm, which has an additional office in the Dubai Media City, is noted for advising clients on media, advertising and marketing matters.

INTELLECTUAL PROPERTY

AL TAMIMI & CO ✪
ROUSE & CO. INTERNATIONAL

Clyde & Co ✪

Clifford Chance LLP
Denton Wilde Sapte ✪
James Berry & Associates Legal Consultants
The Rights Lawyers

Firms are listed A-Z in tiers which are ranked in order of priority
✪ Indicates firm displays contact details at the end of this chapter.

IP is not a main focus of **Clifford Chance LLP**'s practice but it does undertake a limited amount of anti-counterfeiting work.

Denton Wilde Sapte operates a contentious and non-contentious IP practice. The non-contentious arm has a well-established trade mark registration practice which manages the UAE and regional trade mark portfolios for clients such as Reckitt Benckiser, Bausch & Lomb, Singapore Airlines and Mitsubishi. The contentious side mainly concentrates on copyright and trade mark infringement cases.

James Berry & Associates Legal Consultants advises on trade mark protection and registration, industrial designs and patents. The bulk of its IP work is within the technology sector.

Former **Clyde & Co** partner Mark Hill established **The Rights Lawyers** in September 2003. Operating out of Dubai Media City, the firm is a specialist IP, media and technology practice, acting for a range of clients across the TV, music and film production industries, among others.

MARITIME AND SHIPPING

Dubai remains a leading regional centre for maritime law and is helped by its enviable position in the middle of the Gulf. Major marine insurers, such as Norwich Union have offices in the UAE. Jebel Ali is the largest container port in the Middle East. Dubai Drydocks is one of the most important ship repair yards in the world.

Clyde & Co is the clear leader in maritime and shipping law in the Middle East. The firm acts for both cargo insurers and carriers and offers a comprehensive service. Disputes surrounding contracts and repairs are also handled.

MARITIME AND SHIPPING

CLYDE & CO ✪

Hill Taylor Dickinson

Afridi & Angell
Al Tamimi & Co ✪
Clifford Chance LLP

Firms are listed A-Z in tiers which are ranked in order of priority
✪ Indicates firm displays contact details at the end of this chapter.

Hill Taylor Dickinson's Dubai practice has a heavy bias on maritime and shipping matters. Partner Edward Newitt leads the other two partners and four assistants across a broad spectrum of work in this area. The team handles work for underwriters, owners, as well as charterparty disputes, collisions, pollution, ownership disputes and salvage.

Afridi & Angell advises on a range of wet and dry shipping matters. Mr Chakradaran is considered by clients to be an able shipping lawyer. The firm represents and advises ship owners and operators, P&I clubs, underwriters and ship repair yards.

Al Tamimi & Co has a good shipping lawyer in Richard Briggs. 2003 was busy again in all areas of shipping work.

Clifford Chance LLP has wet and dry shipping experience and advises mainly on maritime dispute resolution.

PROJECT FINANCE

The UAE has a burgeoning project finance market which is increasingly demanding higher quality legal work. The thriving construction industry provides a lot of opportunity in this area, particularly projects such as the Palm Island developments. The Dolphin Project and similar initiatives in the energy sector are also providing a lot of interesting work. Most of the projects work is centred around the more commercial Dubai rather than Abu Dhabi, which tends to have more government-sponsored schemes.

Market-leading **Allen & Overy** has impressive range and scope in its 'excellent' project finance department which is headed by Duncan Macnab, who has special expertise in privatisation. Top of the pile in its work in the past 12 months is advising the arrangers on the financing of a $80m waste water system in the Emirate of Ajman. On the other side, the firm advised the borrower, National Central Cooling Company, regarding the AED120m (€26m) Islamic financing of two central cooling plants in Abu Dhabi. The team has also been busy outside the UAE in Iran, Yemen, Lebanon and advising the arrangers, Kreditanstalt für Wierderaufbau on the financing of an urea and amonia fertiliser plant in Sohar, Oman.

PROJECT FINANCE

ALLEN & OVERY ✪
CLIFFORD CHANCE LLP
SHEARMAN & STERLING LLP

Denton Wilde Sapte ✪
Norton Rose
Simmons & Simmons ✪
Towers & Hamlins

Afridi & Angell
Key & Dixon
Vinson & Elkins L.L.P. ✪

Firms are listed A-Z in tiers which are ranked in order of priority
✪ Indicates firm displays contact details at the end of this chapter.

Second to none, **Clifford Chance LLP** has a heavy focus on big-ticket project finance work. The projects team has seen lateral growth with the addition of two more lawyers. Deals span the Middle East as a comprehensive regional service is carried out from Dubai. Noteworthy projects in 2003 were representing the Oman Oil Company and the Oman Government in the development of a $1.5bn refinery in Oman, and advising the Saudi International Petrochemical Company (SIPC) on the development and financing of a petrochemical plant in Jubail, Saudi Arabia. The firm continues to advise the Saudi Oger-led consortium on its bid in relation to the $750m Disi Water Pipeline project in Jordan.

Shearman & Sterling LLP is a big bidder for the top project deals in the UAE and the Middle East in general. The very able managing partner Philip Dundas is particularly recommended for his oil and gas expertise. The team is supported on projects work from the London office. The firm now has an augmented role in Kuwait, having recently represented Kuwait's Public Warehousing Company (PWC) in its joint venture with Bahrain Airport Services to create a new company named National Aviation Services Company to handle the management of all ground handling, traffic, cargo and other logistical operations at the airport.

The project finance team at **Denton Wilde Sapte** is based in the Dubai office and a lot of effort has been put into developing this practice. A landmark transaction for the team in 2003 was acting for sponsors Black & Veatch and Thames Water on the Ajman wastewater project which was the first limited recourse BOT project in the Middle East. Neil Cuthbert came from London in 2001 to lead the team. Another interesting transaction was advising on MB Petroleum's innovative Islamic/conventional financing for the Block 5 oil field in Oman. The firm has also been instructed on a significant number of government projects both in the UAE and elsewhere in the Gulf.

There will be a big focus on projects work for the new **Norton Rose** UAE office. Building on its reputation for major undertakings in this field in Bahrain and elsewhere in the Gulf, the firm is expected to develop a top practice in this area. The Dubai office will add clout to its already established project finance capabilities in the region.

Simmons & Simmons was responsible for advising on a range of large deals in project finance in the past 12 months. One of its major clients is the Abu Dhabi Water and Electricity Authority, for whom it provided advice regarding a desalination plant in Abu Dhabi; an aluminium smelter and an associated power plant in Oman; and on the $2.3bn Umm Al Nar independent water and power project. According to clients, partner Ibrahim Mubaydeen has 'first-class technical and commercial abilities'. In addition, the firm advised a range of banks such as HSBC, Barclays Bank Plc and Abu Dhabi Islamic Bank on the financing of the Fujairah Power Plant.

Project finance at **Towers & Hamlins** is handled out of the Abu Dhabi office but often relies on support from London. The team advised a group of multinational companies on the Umm Al Nar independent power and water project and has been instructed by an oil industry client in Oman. The firm continues to advise the developers of the Iran-Kuwait water pipeline project.

Afridi & Angell has a heavy projects focus. The firm advises on a range of matters including risk allocation, financing techniques, direct foreign investment, and export and import lending programmes. It represents lenders and developers for projects in the oil and gas, hotel, industrial and ship-building industries.

Key & Dixon is also recommended for its work on projects mainly involving the oil and gas industries. The firm is instructed by clients such as BP.

Vinson & Elkins L.L.P. has abilities in the project finance area particularly regarding energy projects. Work includes the Q-Chem II petrochemicals project in Qatar and the firm has played a role in the Dolphin Project, representing the Occidental Petroleum Corporation. Partner Lewis Jones heads this practice.

DENTON WILDE SAPTE

SUITE 1204
AL GHAITH TOWER
HAMDAN STREET
PO BOX 47656
ABU DHABI

Telephone: +971 2 6266 180
Fax: +971 2 6266 175
E-mail: abudhabi@dentonwildesapte.com
Website: www.dentonwildesapte.com

Languages
Arabic, Bengali, English, French, German, Urdu

Other offices
Almaty, Beijing, Cairo, Dubai, Gibraltar, Hong Kong, Istanbul, London, Milton Keynes, Moscow, Muscat, Paris, Singapore, Tashkent, Tokyo

Number of lawyers 876
at this office 6

Contact
Niall O'Toole

CATEGORIES OF WORK

Arbitration	Environment
Aviation	Hotels and leisure
Banking and finance	Intellectual property
Corporate and commercial	Islamic finance
Commercial litigation	Mergers and acquisitions
Construction	Project finance
Corporate finance	Telecoms
Energy and utilities	

SIMMONS & SIMMONS

PO BOX 5931
THE ADNIC BUILDING
KHALIFA STREET
ABU DHABI

Telephone: +971 26 27 55 68
Fax: +971 26 27 52 23
E-mail: enquiries@simmons-simmons.com
Website: www.simmons-simmons.com

Languages
Arabic, English, French

Other offices
London, Rotterdam, Paris, Lisbon, Milan, Rome, Düsseldorf, Frankfurt, Brussels, Madrid, Padua, Oporto, Madeira, Qatar, Hong Kong, Shanghai, Tokyo, New York

Number of lawyers 754
at this office 8

Contacts
Ibrahim Mubaydeen, Roger Clarke

CATEGORIES OF WORK

Corporate	Financial markets
Banking	Pharmaceutical and biotechnology
Capital markets	Energy and utilities
Taxation	TMT
Projects, PFI	Aerospace and defence
EU, competition	Transport
Dispute resolution	Real estate and construction
Intellectual property	Consumer goods
Employment	

AL TAMIMI & CO

DUBAI WORLD TRADE CENTRE
29TH FLOOR
PO BOX 9275
DUBAI

Telephone: +971 4 331 7090
Fax: +971 4 331 3177
Website: www.tamimi.com

Other offices
Abu Dhabi, Dubai Internet City, Sharjah

Number of lawyers 42

Contact
Essam Al Tamimi (managing partner)

CATEGORIES OF WORK	
Corporate	**Construction**
Commercial	**Property**
Banking and finance	**Litigation and dispute resolution**
Islamic banking	**Intellectual property and IT**
Maritime, trade and insurance	

THE FIRM

Al Tamimi & Co is one of the largest independent law firms in the Gulf region, comprising 45 lawyers and in excess of 100 total staff. Al Tamimi & Co has offices in Abu Dhabi, Dubai, Sharjah and Dubai Internet City, and a marketing office in London. More than half of the personnel are based in the Dubai head office.

Al Tamimi & Co is rich in local and international experience, qualifications and cultural diversity. The firm comprises experienced lawyers with qualifications from a range of jurisdictions, including the US, Canada, UK, UAE, other Arab countries and Iraq. Each lawyer contributes his or her specific skills and experience to the range of legal services offered.

The UAE is a regional hub from which Middle East business is conducted and co-ordinated by many companies. The UAE is also a recognised logistics and service base for the region. The firm acts for corporate clients, large and small, regional and international. Al Tamimi & Company works closely with lawyers and advisers from around the world on a range of business opportunities and challenges. Clients rely on Al Tamimi lawyers' proficiency in local and regional laws. Within the UAE, they enjoy long-established contacts within the public sector, and regularly confer with government departments and ministries, with respect to new legislation and regulations. Such local contacts and regional knowledge greatly assist the private sector clients, and the international corporations that represent the majority of the client base.

AREAS OF PRACTICE

The firm generally acts in all areas of business law, and provides specialised legal services in the fields of maritime, trade and insurance, construction, property, commercial and Islamic banking, project finance, intellectual property, information technology, arbitration, and local and foreign litigation matters.

ALLEN & OVERY

1603 API WORLD TOWER
SHEIKH ZAYED ROAD
PO BOX 3251
DUBAI

Telephone: + 971 4 332 3190
Fax: +971 4 332 3192
E-mail: information@allenovery.com
Website: www.allenovery.com

Languages
English, Urdu, Arabic, French, German, Spanish, Korean, Japanese

Other offices
Amsterdam, Antwerp, Bangkok, Beijing, Bratislava, Brussels, Budapest, Frankfurt, Hamburg, Hong Kong, London, Luxembourg, Madrid, Milan, Moscow, New York, Paris, Prague, Rome, Shanghai, Singapore, Tokyo, Turin, Warsaw

Number of lawyers 2,305
at this office 15

Contacts
Bimal Desai, Duncan Macnab, Simon Roderick

CATEGORIES OF WORK

Banking and finance
Bimal Desai, Luma Saqqaf

Project finance
Duncan Macnab, Bimal Desai

M&A
Khalid Garousha, Simon Roderick

Capital markets
Bimal Desai, Luma Saqqaf

Corporate
Simon Roderick, Khalid Garousha

Commercial
Simon Roderick, Khalid Garousha

Construction
Duncan Macnab, Judith Kim

Aviation
Simon Roderick, Duncan Macnab

Litigation and arbitration
Simon Roderick, Paul Stothard

IP/IT
Miranda Cudmore

Employment
Miranda Cudmore

Local establishment and licensing
Sahia Al Muhaisen

CLYDE & CO

PO BOX 7001
CITY TOWER 2
SHEIKH ZAYED ROAD
DUBAI

Telephone: +971 4 331 1102
Fax: +971 4 331 9920
E-mail: mero@clydeco.ae
Website: www.clydeco.com

Languages
Afrikaans, Arabic, English, French, German, Italian, Japanese, Latvian, Polish, Punjabi, Russian, Spanish, Urdu

Other offices
Belgrade, Caracas, Cardiff, Dubai Media City, Guildford, Hong Kong, London, Nantes, Paris, Piraeus, St Petersburg, Singapore

Number of lawyers 386
at this office 26

Contacts
Anthony Garrod, Alec Emmerson, Jonathan Silver

CATEGORIES OF WORK

Inward investment
Jane Clayton, Anthony Garrod

Corporate
Jonathan Silver, Simon Adams

Commercial, agency and distribution, franchising
Simon Adams, Anthony Garrod

Banking and financial services
Jonathan Silver, Muneer Khan

Establishment, government liaison
Mary Jabbour, Victoria Golden

Employment
Simon Adams, Philip O'Riordan

Oil, gas and energy
Jonathan Silver, Simon Adams

Construction and engineering
Jonathan Silver, Michael Grose

International trade
Alec Emmerson, Caleb Raywood

Shipping and transport
Christopher Mills, Caleb Raywood

Insurance and reinsurance
Alec Emmerson, Wayne Jones

Dispute resolution
Alec Emmerson, Christopher Mills

Debt recovery and insolvency
Alec Emmerson, Christopher Mills

E-commerce, IT and telecoms
Anthony Garrod, Robert Swade

IP and trade marks
Rob Deans

Media, advertising and sport
Robert Swade, Rob Deans

DENTON WILDE SAPTE

26TH FLOOR, API WORLD TOWER
SHEIKH ZAYED ROAD
PO BOX 1756
DUBAI

Telephone: +971 4 331 0220
Fax: +971 4 331 0201
E-mail: dubai@dentonwildesapte.com
Website: www.dentonwildesapte.com

Languages
Afrikaans, Arabic, Bulgarian, Dutch, English, French, Gujerati, Hindi, Serbo-Croat, Spanish, Urdu

Other offices
Abu Dhabi, Almaty, Beijing, Cairo, Dubai Internet City, Gibraltar, Hong Kong, Istanbul, London, Milton Keynes, Moscow, Muscat, Paris, Singapore, Tashkent, Tokyo

Number of lawyers 876
at this office 14

Contacts
Neil Cuthbert, Jonathan Dawe, Jayshree Gupta, Mathew Kidwell, Rahail Ali

CATEGORIES OF WORK

Banking and finance
Neil Cuthbert, Rahail Ali

Company, commercial
Jonathan Dawe, Jayshree Gupta

Construction
Nigel Truscott, Simon Theodore

Employment and labour
Ibrahim Elsadig, Rita Al Semaani

Energy
Neil Cuthbert, Mathew Kidwell

IT, media
Kate O'Leary, Jayshree Gupta

Infrastructure projects
Neil Cuthbert, Mathew Kidwell

Intellectual property
Jayshree Gupta, Ibrahim Elsadig

Islamic finance
Rahail Ali, Rustum Shah

Litigation and arbitration
Ibrahim Elsadig, Nigel Truscott

Mergers and acquisitions
Jonathan Dawe, Jayshree Gupta

VINSON & ELKINS LLP

11TH FLOOR
EMIRATES TOWERS OFFICE
SHEIKH ZAYED ROAD
DUBAI

Telephone: +971 4 330 1800
Fax: +971 4 330 1300
Website: www.velaw.com

Languages
Arabic, English, French

Other offices
Austin, Beijing, Dallas, Houston, London, Moscow, New York, Singapore, Washington DC

Number of lawyers 775
at this office 3

Member
International Bar Association; Union International des Avocats; Arab International Forum; American Business Council of Dubai and the Northern Emirates; Business Law, Corporate Counsel and International Law Sections, State Bar of Texas

CATEGORIES OF WORK

Mergers and acquisitions

Business law

Corporate law

Corporate finance

Privatisation transactions

Project finance and development

Telecommunications

Energy

Construction law

UNITED KINGDOM: ENGLAND AND WALES

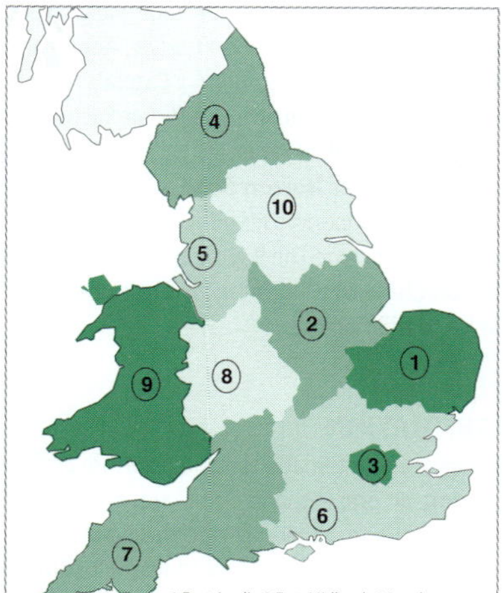

1 East Anglia 2 East Midlands 3 London
4 North 5 North West 6 South East
7 South West 8 West Midlands 9 Wales
10 Yorkshire and the Humber

Population	**52.5 million**
Number of lawyers	**solicitors 116,110** **barristers 13,985**
Professional title	**Solicitor, barrister**
Currency	**Pound sterling (£)**

Index

The last year has not been particularly kind to lawyers. UK firms across the board reported that corporate work, particularly M&A and capital markets, was slow. For many firms, however, litigation, restructurings, regulatory and employment remained relatively busy.

For a more detailed view of the UK legal market see *The Legal 500* – 2003 edition at www.legal500.com.

BILLING

Solicitors' charges dropped in 2003 by as much as 20%-25% at the top end of the market. Hourly rates for partners in a large City firm range from £250 to £375 for commercial property work; £250 to £425 for corporate/finance; and £250 to £400 for litigation work. Partners in large regional firms typically charge an hourly rate of between £195 and £240 depending on the geographical region rather than the type of work. Assistant solicitors' rates are approximately 50%-60% of partners' fees.

MARKETING

Law firms and barristers' chambers can freely advertise both in print and online as the UK marketing regulations are among the most relaxed in the world. Details of specific deals can be disclosed as long as the client's permission is granted beforehand.

THE PROFESSION

In the UK the profession is split into solicitors and barristers. The solicitor is usually a client's first port of call while barristers concentrate on in-court advocacy. There have been developments in recent years designed to improve the efficiency of the litigation process.

IN-HOUSE LAWYERS

There are over 10,000 legal professionals working in business in the UK. In recent years there has been an increase in lawyers choosing an in-house career due to the salary increases and general buoyancy in the in-house market.

LEGAL MARKET

Recent times have seen a number of mergers, most notably the merger of *Theodore Goddard* with *Addleshaw Booth & Co*, to create **Addleshaw Goddard**. The biggest surprise, however, was the merger that initially created *Jones Day Gouldens*. In December 2003 the firm renamed as **Jones Day** after the US powerhouse. *Gouldens* was one of the UK's most profitable corporate finance boutiques and most observers would have thought the firm could have thrived as an independent. Still, the merger gives *Gouldens* access to **Jones Day**'s enormous corporate client base across the globe.

Altheimer & Gray dissolved in August 2003 with a fair amount of its 50+ London-based lawyers moving to **Kilpatrick Stockton LLP**.

However, several top American firms have expanded the breadth of their UK practices and appear in high tiers of our tables. This trend looks set to continue. A number of US firms in London are proving serious competitors to the UK firms.

We cover specialist boutiques as well as providing details of the major commercial firms outside London.

ACQUISITION FINANCE

Allen & Overy and **Clifford Chance LLP** are universally recognised as the leading firms in acquisition finance.

Allen & Overy remains firmly ensconced at the top of the market. Key deals last year included the buy-out of Jefferson Smurfit and advising Barclays Capital on the Ontex buy-out. Partners Stephen Gillespie, Tony Keal and David Lines are all recommended.

Clifford Chance LLP, unlike **Allen & Overy**, has a practice that is evenly split between borrowers and banks. A total of 18 partners specialise in acquisition finance in London, among them Mark Stewart, James Johnson and Alan Inglis are all highly regarded by clients. The key deal last year was advising Permira on its £740m buy-out of Travelodge and Little Chef.

The **Ashurst** team led by Nigel Ward worked on 33 deals with a total financing requirement of €13.3bn in 2002. Highlights included advising CSFB, Lehman Brothers and The Royal Bank of Scotland on the financing for the €3.7bn acquisition of Legrand from Schneider, and acting for ING Bank, Bank of Scotland and Goldman Sachs on the £1.09bn acquisition by Apax of Focus Wickes Group.

Linklaters had an impressive year. Partners Nick Syson and Gideon Moore have led a charge which has brought in regular work from the likes of CSFB, ABN Amro, CIBC and Barclays Capital.

The largest firms

1	Eversheds LLP	1870
2	Linklaters	1205
3	DLA	1174
4	Allen & Overy	1068
5	Clifford Chance LLP	951
6	Freshfields Bruckhaus Deringer	913
7	Herbert Smith	833
8	Addleshaw Goddard	724
9	Hammonds	722
10	Denton Wilde Sapte	627
11	Norton Rose	605
12	Beachcroft Wansbroughs	589
13	Ashurst	573
14	CMS Cameron McKenna	554
15	Pinsents	551
16	Lovells	540
17	Slaughter and May	481
18	Nabarro Nathanson	466
19	Berwin Leighton Paisner	414
	Wragge & Co LLP	414
21	Dickinson Dees	411
22	Walker Morris	362
23	Baker & McKenzie	358
24	Simmons & Simmons	356
25	Barlow Lyde & Gilbert	328

These figures represent the total number of lawyers in this country only, and have been supplied by the firms themselves. The figures should be accurate as at 1 January 2004.

ACQUISITION FINANCE

ALLEN & OVERY ✪
CLIFFORD CHANCE LLP

ASHURST ✪

LINKLATERS ✪
LOVELLS ✪
SHEARMAN & STERLING (LONDON) LLP
WHITE & CASE ✪

CMS Cameron McKenna
DLA ✪
Denton Wilde Sapte ✪
Latham & Watkins ✪
Norton Rose ✪

Baker & McKenzie ✪
Freshfields Bruckhaus Deringer ✪
Macfarlanes ✪
Slaughter and May ✪
Travers Smith Braithwaite
Weil, Gotshal & Manges ✪

Dickson Minto WS
Hammonds
Osborne Clarke
Simmons & Simmons ✪
Simpson Thacher & Bartlett LLP
SJ Berwin ✪

Firms are listed A-Z in tiers which are ranked in order of priority
✪ Indicates firm displays contact details at the end of this chapter.

Aggregate deal value for Matthew Cottis and his team at **Lovells** for the year 2002 was £2.9bn, with one of the biggest deals being advice to CIBC World Markets on the £270m buy-out of BWG Group from Pernod Ricard.

Shearman & Sterling (London) LLP's London leveraged finance team benefits from the strength of the firm's German and French practices. A team led by the 'excellent' Anthony Ward also includes Clifford Atkins and Iain Goalen; clients include JP Morgan Chase, CIBC, Merrill Lynch and Morgan Stanley.

White & Case continues to build a strong pan-European acquisition finance practice, led in London by the highly regarded Maurice Allen. Clients include Barclays Capital, BNP Paribas, CIBC World Markets, Deutsche Bank and Morgan Stanley. The represented BNP Paribas and Citibank on the €1.34bn acquisition of Télédiffusion de France's towers and infrastructure business by Charterhouse and CDC Equity.

CMS Cameron McKenna's Will Meredith and John Naccarato acted for Enterprise Inns on its £1.28bn facilities to bid for Unique, Voyager and Laurel Pub estates. Key clients are ABN Amro, Royal Bank of Scotland and Lloyds TSB Bank.

DLA is praised by rivals for its increasingly strong profile in acquisition finance. Clients of the practice include Bank of Scotland, Royal Bank of Scotland and Barclays. Partner John Cutler is highly recommended.

Denton Wilde Sapte's head of acquisition finance Chris Fanner is praised by clients as 'a good operator who thinks outside the box'. Last year the team worked on 40 financings with an aggregate exceeding £11bn.

Latham & Watkins partners James Chesterman and Christopher Hall are building a senior debt practice that hopes to emulate the firm's incredible strength in high-yield work. Private equity clients include Carlyle, Apollo and Charterhouse Development Capital; banks include CSFB, Bear Stearns, Goldman Sachs, UBS Warburg and Bank of America.

The group at **Norton Rose** was boosted by the return of ex-partner Philip Whale. Clients continue to include The Royal Bank of Scotland, JP Morgan Chase, Mizuho Financial Group, Deutsche Bank and NIB Capital.

ARBITRATION

Domestic and international arbitration are both in upswing at present, and firms are investing in resources and training accordingly. It is increasingly rare for solicitors to instruct counsel in arbitration; the less formalised procedures involved are ideal for solicitor advocates to make their mark.

Clifford Chance LLP's superb practice is headed by 'formidable' John Beechey; high-profile partners Audley Sheppard, Rob Lambert and Nicholas Fletcher all lend considerable depth to the London practice. The firm conducted large-scale arbitrations for NEC (Japan) and the Republic of Latvia during the year. Partner Jason Fry is particularly recommended in the Paris office.

Allen & Overy has a very high-profile – and high-quality – arbitration team. Practice head Judith Gill regularly travels the globe on behalf of her prestigious client base and Stephen Jagusch has made his mark on the arbitration circuit.

Freshfields Bruckhaus Deringer's arbitration practice is spread across Paris, London, Amsterdam and Frankfurt – with the former being the brightest star in the constellation. London-based Nigel Rawding, Philip Croall, Gillian Eastwood, Jane Jenkins and Simon Stebbings are recommended as is Geoff Nicholas, who has assumed the role of London Group head from Rawding.

Herbert Smith has dedicated significant resources to arbitration with four star partners working exclusively in the field. Practice head Dr Julian Lew QC has an outstanding reputation and many years' experience; David Brynmor Thomas, Laurence Shore and Robert Volterra are all highly recommended. The firm has strong industry expertise in oil and gas, construction and engineering.

Lovells' London team benefits greatly from the firm's international presence and works closely with the French and German offices.

ARBITRATION

CLIFFORD CHANCE LLP

ALLEN & OVERY ✪
FRESHFIELDS BRUCKHAUS DERINGER ✪
HERBERT SMITH ✪
LOVELLS ✪

Linklaters ✪
Wilmer Cutler Pickering LLP ✪

Ashurst ✪
Baker & McKenzie ✪
CMS Cameron McKenna
Masons
Norton Rose ✪
Shearman & Sterling (London) LLP
Simmons & Simmons ✪
White & Case ✪

Debevoise & Plimpton LLP ✪
Eversheds LLP
Slaughter and May ✪

Clyde & Co ✪
Davies Arnold Cooper
Denton Wilde Sapte ✪
Hammonds
Holman Fenwick & Willan ✪
Mayer, Brown, Rowe & Maw LLP
Richards Butler

Ince & Co
Kennedys
Osborne Clarke
SJ Berwin ✪
Shadbolt & Co
Stephenson Harwood
Taylor Wessing ✪
Vinson & Elkins R.L.L.P. ✪
Watson, Farley & Williams

Firms are listed A-Z in tiers which are ranked in order of priority
✪ Indicates firm displays contact details at the end of this chapter.

Clients compliment the team's 'top-notch analysis, advice and responsiveness'. Highly esteemed Andrew Foyle heads the practice.

Linklaters' successful team acted on major arbitrations for the French Coal Board and the Republic of Poland during the year. Practice head Greg Reid devotes himself full-time to arbitration work and clients comment that he is 'extremely responsive, a pleasure to deal with, and good at knowing all the myriad details of a case.'

Wilmer Cutler Pickering LLP's high-quality practice is built upon the outstanding expertise of 'charismatic' Gary Born, who regularly acts as both advocate and arbitrator. Born is supported by a team of 12 assistants. The firm also has capability in Berlin, Brussels, New York and Washington.

At **Ashurst**, practice head Ronnie King is praised as a 'great strategic thinker'. 'Shrewd, commercial, and fun to work with' Christopher Vigrass is recommended for construction and engineering, while Tim Reid is an expert in energy disputes.

Baker & McKenzie has a strong track record in arbitrations held in central and eastern Europe, and central Asia. Gerald Cooke, Christopher Newmark and Jeremy Winter are all recommended.

CMS Cameron McKenna was instructed on a long list of arbitration matters during the year; department head Neil Aitken handles a full range of heavyweight domestic and international work.

Masons is receiving regular instructions advising on joint venture and consortium arrangements, as well as disputes relating to technology and commodities. Stars of the department include Tony Bunch, Mark Roe, Ray Werbicki and Peter Cassidy.

Norton Rose has an impressive reputation for arbitrations in the shipping, energy, commodities, construction engineering, investment and insurance sectors. Practice head Juliet Blanch succeeded in attracting some major client wins during the year.

Shearman & Sterling (London) LLP boasts a fantastic global arbitration practice, and its London presence goes from strength to strength. Well-regarded partner Christopher Colbridge leads a team of seven associates. Emmanuel Gaillard of the Paris office is internationally renowned for his arbitration skills.

At **Simmons & Simmons**, Karyl Nairn's team receives plaudits for its 'knowledge, efficiency and professionalism'; the firm was asked to draft custom-made arbitration laws for the Dubai International Financial Centre.

White & Case advised on some very significant matters during the year, under the leadership of John Bellhouse, an expert in construction arbitration. Also recommended are Richard Bamforth and Margaret R Cole.

At **Debevoise & Plimpton LLP**, Arthur Marriott QC is an established leader in international arbitration, with over 30 years' experience. Partner David Rivkin is now dividing his time between London and New York. The firm represented investor CME in a $500m dispute with the Czech Republic.

Strong on large-scale arbitrations, **Eversheds LLP** frequently appears before the ICC and LCIA. 'Capable' Nicholas Valner heads the practice; Alan Jenkins is also recommended.

Slaughter and May's litigation team is often involved in arbitrations for its prestigious corporate client base. Highlights of the year include representing a Swedish bank in a multi-million pound Stockholm Chamber of Commerce arbitration.

ASSET FINANCE AND LEASING

Allen & Overy has a top-tier asset finance practice, headed by Graham Smith, which spans aviation, rail and shipping. Instructions are becoming increasingly cross-border and in response the firm promoted Wolfgang Melzer to partner to lead the German practice, with Peter Hein relocating to New York to increase cross-border capabilities. Highlights include advising European Investment Bank (EIB) on $215m EIB-backed Japanese operating leases for two Airbus A340-300s.

Geoffrey White leads the seven-partner team at **Clifford Chance LLP**, which has a strong bias towards financiers and the aviation sector. Recent highlights include advising GE in relation to its acquisition of ABB's structured finance practice and advising commercial and lending syndicates in relation to the repossession and refinancing of aircraft leased to Sabena.

With a superb tax practice and excellent international coverage, **Freshfields Bruckhaus Deringer** has a top-tier asset finance practice across the board, although it is particularly well-known for its aviation expertise. Led by Tim Lintott, the practice advises lessors, lenders, lessees, borrowers and manufacturers. Recent highlights include advising Iberia Lineas Aereas de and advising Airbus in relation to easyJet's purchase of 120 A320 aircraft.

Norton Rose has one of the largest and broadest asset finance practices in the City. As well as having expertise across the aviation, rail and shipping sectors, the firm also boasts a strong PFI and PPP practice. Clients include Stena, easyJet, P&O, Lloyds TSB, HSBC Rail, HBOS and RBS.

Ron Gibbs at **Linklaters** has succeeded in building a top-tier practice in rail and real estate, where the firm's clients include Network Rail and SRA. The firm also has a credible asset finance practice in the US, which gives it an edge on its rivals. It advised the Emirates on its fleet acquisition programme.

Slaughter and May has a small but well-regarded team which advises a number of high-profile clients. Partners Tom Kinnersley and Peter Jolliffe are consistently described as two of the best lawyers in the market. Clients include British Airways, Boeing and Abbey National.

Denton Wilde Sapte has an excellent team that includes Nick Chandler, Greg Kahn, Nigel Weiss and Tony Rice who are well known. The firm continues to advise on leasing contracts, particularly in the shipping and aviation industries. Clients include Lombard Corporate Finance, Barclays Asset Finance, Lloyds TSB Leasing, HBOS and Sovereign.

CMS Cameron McKenna's team, which is led by Paul Richardson, has a strong presence in the aviation sector, where it acts for GATX Financial Corporation on leases to a vast number of airlines. The department has also been busy on the rail side, advising Metronet on the procurement of new rolling stock for the London Underground.

Lovells' asset finance team, which is headed by Robin Hallam, was kept busy advising Tube Lines on the PPP arrangements for London Underground. The group also moved into the area of vendor financing where it advised on deals for Barclays Asset Finance, Xerox and Alstom.

ASSET FINANCE AND LEASING

ALLEN & OVERY ✪
CLIFFORD CHANCE LLP
FRESHFIELDS BRUCKHAUS DERINGER ✪
NORTON ROSE ✪

LINKLATERS ✪
SLAUGHTER AND MAY ✪

DENTON WILDE SAPTE ✪

CMS Cameron McKenna
Lovells ✪
Simmons & Simmons ✪
Watson, Farley & Williams
White & Case ✪

Addleshaw Goddard
Berwin Leighton Paisner
Clyde & Co ✪
Herbert Smith ✪
Stephenson Harwood

Bryan Cave
Clark Ricketts
Osborne Clarke
Richards Butler
Travers Smith Braithwaite
Wragge & Co LLP ✪

Field Fisher Waterhouse
Harbottle & Lewis LLP
Hill Taylor Dickinson
LeBoeuf, Lamb, Greene & MacRae
Salans

Firms are listed A-Z in tiers which are ranked in order of priority
✪ *Indicates firm displays contact details at the end of this chapter.*

Simmons & Simmons' team led by Kim Walkling has been particularly active in the procurement of military assets. The Ministry of Defence is a major client and instructions include advising on the latest phase of the Future Strategic Tanker Aircraft project, the Advance Jet Training programme and the Strategic Sealift project.

In London, **Watson, Farley & Williams** specialises in shipping and has industry expertise in the offshore oil and gas industry and the LNG sector. The department is led by Michael Vernell.

At **White & Case** the current focus is aviation but the firm is also developing its international tax leasing expertise. Highlights include advising a syndicate of lenders in a $195m aircraft warehousing loan facility and forward sale agreement with. Mark Western is recommended.

Addleshaw Goddard has a broad asset finance group, which spans aviation, rail, property, general equipment and PFI. Led by James Ballingall and Rory MacCarthy, the team advises both lessees and lessors. Clients include Channel Express, Aviation Capital Group and GB Railways.

Berwin Leighton Paisner's asset finance practice, led by Nicola Davies, focuses on shipping, energy and project finance. Partner Robert Goss brings PFI and health expertise. Key transactions include advising A.W.S.R Shipping which has contracted with the Ministry of Defence for the supply of worldwide strategic transport services worth £950m.

Clyde & Co focuses on aviation and shipping. Leading names are Austen Hall and Trevor Barton. Highlights include advising MK Airlines and TotalFinaElf.

Herbert Smith's focus is on rail and water. It also has a strong PFI and project finance team. Heather Gething, David Moore and Nicholas Tott are all well known. Highlights include advising Eurotunnel on its acquisition of Abbey National March Leasing from Abbey National Treasury Services.

Stephenson Harwood's merger with *Sinclair Roche & Temperley* doubled the number of asset finance partners. The team, which is led by Mark Russell, specialises in shipping, where it focuses on the UK tax leasing market. Despite losing its Spanish office to **DLA**, it also has a strong Spanish practice where it acts for non-Spanish companies entering into Spanish tax leases.

AVIATION: AIRLINES, AIRPORTS AND REGULATORY

Aviation work is a highly specialised area covering commercial, international and UK regulatory advice for airlines and airports. The field is highly competitive. Expertise tends to lie in individual lawyers.

Lane & Partners advised on a state aid case involving the collapse of Sabena in Brussels and represented Ryanair in a case before the CAA. Richard Venables and William Morton are well regarded. Clients include KLM UK and Bristow Helicopters.

Wilmer Cutler Pickering LLP is recommended for complex contractual and competition issues. Highlights include acting for the 12 airlines comprising the Star Alliance and advising Lufthansa on acquisitions and strategic partnerships. The firm is also recommended for the close integration of its London, Brussels, Berlin and Washington DC offices. Practice head Michael Holter, Dieter Lange, Paul von Hehn and Stephen Doyle are recommended.

Denton Wilde Sapte's Hugh O'Donovan is an experienced force in the aviation industry. Strengths include UK and EU regulatory expertise, licensing, franchising and slots. Clients include easyJet.

DLA advised on the establishment of three new British airlines: Global Supply Systems; Jet2 and Now. The firm also acted on a major slot deal for an international carrier. Mark Franklin heads the practice.

Norton Rose's Patrick Farrell heads a team which advises airports, governments and carriers such as Continental Airlines. The practice is recommended for the broad expertise of its London and Brussels offices for competition and regulatory issues. John Cook led a team which represented bmi British Midland and United Airlines on securing clearance from the UK OFT and the EC on their transatlantic airline alliance.

Rory MacCarthy at **Addleshaw Goddard** is recommended by clients. He advised Airport Co-ordination Ltd on slot allocation, and acted for a major East European flag carrier on revenue sharing agreements.

Barlow Lyde & Gilbert advises on state aid and EU law issues. The practice also advised Lithuanian Airways on a slot exchange transaction. Richard Gimblett has a 'good grasp of the regulatory process'. Giles Kavanagh, Nicholas Hughes and Simon Phippard are also recommended.

Beaumont and Son's John Balfour is an expert on franchising and slot issues. The team works closely with the firm's aviation insurance lawyers.

Field Fisher Waterhouse advises airlines on transport route licence applications. Simon Chamberlain heads a practice that represents airlines, aviation service companies and trade associations.

Harbottle & Lewis LLP's Dermot Scully and Douglas Lochhead act for clients such as TNT and bmi British Midland.

Freshfields Bruckhaus Deringer's John Davies heads a practice which advised Continental Airlines on competition aspects of its US and European alliances. The firm also advised on slots and distribution agreements of airline reservation systems. The practice works closely with its Brussels office.

Michael Offer at **Lawrence Jones** advised on EU noise directive cases and acted for owners of executive jets on VAT issues of importation into the EU. The firm also undertakes work for several Middle Eastern clients.

Linklaters has worked on international airports and air-traffic projects, including privatisations, upgrades and financings. The practice, led by Ron Gibbs, has a focus on work in Asia and the Middle East.

Kim Walkling at **Simmons & Simmons** heads a team which advises high-net-worth individuals on fractional aircraft ownership. Clients include Marquis Jets and several European state airlines.

Slaughter and May is particularly recommended for competition and regulatory expertise. Malcolm Nicholson heads a team that advised British Airways on an economic review of London airports. Other clients include the Department for Transport.

Baker & McKenzie's Mark Henrick advises on alliance agreements and has acted for clients on regulatory and contract issues in conjunction with the firm's Brussels office. Clients include LOT Polish Airlines and Virgin Express.

Clark Ricketts' Ian Clark and Robert Ricketts advise airlines and helicopter companies.

AVIATION: AIRLINES, AIRPORTS AND REGULATORY

LANE & PARTNERS
WILMER CUTLER PICKERING LLP ✪

DENTON WILDE SAPTE ✪

DLA ✪
NORTON ROSE ✪

Addleshaw Goddard
Barlow Lyde & Gilbert
Beaumont and Son
Field Fisher Waterhouse
Harbottle & Lewis LLP

Freshfields Bruckhaus Deringer ✪
Lawrence Jones
Linklaters ✪
Simmons & Simmons ✪
Slaughter and May ✪

Baker & McKenzie ✪
Clark Ricketts
Ince & Co
Masons
Wragge & Co LLP ✪

Herbert Smith ✪
Howard Kennedy
Shadbolt & Co
Thomas Cooper & Stibbard

Bryan Cave
Clyde & Co ✪
Eversheds LLP
Fladgate Fielder
Hammonds
Hogan & Hartson ✪
Latham & Watkins ✪
LeBoeuf, Lamb, Greene & MacRae
Travers Smith Braithwaite

Firms are listed A-Z in tiers which are ranked in order of priority
✪ Indicates firm displays contact details at the end of this chapter.

Ince & Co's Anthony Fitzsimmons represents airlines and airports.

Masons is recommended for its UK and international expertise in PPP and privatisation and has advised on airport projects in Cyprus and Peru. Steven Mason heads the practice.

Wragge & Co LLP's broad-ranging practice is recommended for its regulatory, competition and property expertise. The firm advised major client British Airways on aircraft noise disputes and a new extranet service. Jane Pittaway heads a practice that also acts for a growing number of clients from the aerospace sector.

BANK LENDING

Allen & Overy offers clients a multitude of top-quality partners. David Morley, now the firm's managing partner, signed off in style when he led a team advising JPMorgan Chase and Citigroup on a $850m facility for the buyers of Burger King. He remains an important contact point for various banks. His successor, Jonathan Brayne, is one of London's most experienced banking lawyers and can be called on to address any number of complex problems on different deals. Stephen Gillespie remains awesomely successful. Other recommended partners include Christopher Rushton, who co-manages the department; Tony Keal, Michael Duncan, Peter Schulz, Timothy Arnheim and Trevor Borthwick. Jon Bevan, Richard De Basto and Mark O'Neill have successfully targeted property finance work.

Clifford Chance LLP's banking practice fields a range of quality partners that include Mark Campbell, Malcolm Sweeting, and Alan Inglis. James Johnson continues to delight clients with his non-stop enthusiasm. He advised the six lead arrangers on the €6.5bn financing for Imperial Tobacco's acquisition of Reemtsma. This is the kind of multi-country, resource-intensive deal that only the top banking firms can handle. **Clifford Chance LLP** 'is always businesslike,' according to one approving client. Also recommended are Michael Bates, Stephen Lucas, Geeta Khehar, Despina Pantelia (who knows how to staff and run deals to maximum effect) and Robert Smith. Internationally, **Clifford Chance LLP** has a large presence in both Germany and the US.

Linklaters has gone from strength to strength in the banking field in the last five years. Under John Tucker, the group has developed relationships with Citigroup, Barclays, HSBC and numerous others. Clients applaud the technical skills of the likes of Giles White, Gideon Moore, Jeremy Stokeld and Haydn Puleston Jones, and comment that the firm has 'a very good product offering overall.' In 2002 the firm closed six LBOs in six weeks. Four were for lenders, including RBS, mezzanine fund Hutton Collins & Co, ABN Amro and Commerzbank. The lender deals included Germany's largest LBO of the year and France's third-largest LBO ever.

Freshfields Bruckhaus Deringer boasts excellent partners in David Ereira; Jonathan Shann; Simon Hall; Sean Pierce on the leveraged side; Edward Evans for general lending; David Winfield; Bob Charlton, who has strong rail finance expertise; Nick Gamble; and Brian Gray. The firm has achieved a high level of integration within its European network, which international banks appreciate. **Freshfields Bruckhaus Deringer** has a very strong tax team, which gives it an edge on complex, cross-border structured products.

Shearman & Sterling (London) LLP maintains high-quality US/UK leveraged and structured finance skills, strong German and French practices, and longstanding ties to US banks active in Europe. For project and acquisition finance it boasts excellent partners such as Kenneth MacRitchie and Nicholas Buckworth (projects) and Anthony Ward, Clifford Atkins, Iain Goalen and Caroline Leeds Ruby (acquisition and

BANK LENDING

ALLEN & OVERY ✪
CLIFFORD CHANCE LLP

LINKLATERS ✪

FRESHFIELDS BRUCKHAUS DERINGER ✪
SHEARMAN & STERLING (LONDON) LLP

ASHURST ✪
HERBERT SMITH ✪
LOVELLS ✪
NORTON ROSE ✪
SLAUGHTER AND MAY ✪
WHITE & CASE ✪

Baker & McKenzie ✪
CMS Cameron McKenna
DLA ✪
Denton Wilde Sapte ✪
Latham & Watkins ✪

Berwin Leighton Paisner
SJ Berwin ✪
Simmons & Simmons ✪
Taylor Wessing ✪
Travers Smith Braithwaite
Weil, Gotshal & Manges ✪

Barlow Lyde & Gilbert
Jones Day ✪
Macfarlanes ✪
Richards Butler

Addleshaw Goddard
Bird & Bird ✪
Cadwalader, Wickersham & Taft LLP
Dechert
Field Fisher Waterhouse
Hammonds
Mayer, Brown, Rowe & Maw LLP
McDermott, Will & Emery ✪
Middleton Potts
Olswang
Osborne Clarke
Pinsents ✪
Skadden, Arps, Slate, Meagher & Flom LLP
Simpson Thacher & Bartlett LLP
Watson, Farley & Williams

Burness
Dundas & Wilson
Eversheds LLP
Howard Kennedy
Kirkland & Ellis International LLP ✪
Lawrence Graham
LeBoeuf, Lamb, Greene & MacRae
Maclay Murray & Spens
McGrigors
Nabarro Nathanson
RadcliffesLeBrasseur
Reed Smith
Stephenson Harwood
Withers LLP

Firms are listed A-Z in tiers which are ranked in order of priority
✪ Indicates firm displays contact details at the end of this chapter.

structured finance). The firm's banking relationships include Morgan Stanley Dean Witter, Merrill Lynch and UBS Warburg.

Ashurst's success in competing directly with the Magic Circle firms in its chosen areas justifies its high year-on-year ranking. This is primarily due to the quality of partners like international finance head Nigel Ward, Helen Burton, and less well-known names like Paul Gadd and Stephen Clark. The firm's strength in Paris, where Jonathan Nabarro is a star banking lawyer, helped it win instructions from the senior joint lead arrangers on Europe's largest private equity-funded LBO.

Herbert Smith has further strengthened lender relationships with Barclays, for whom Peter Long continues to impress, and BNP Paribas, which are both relatively new clients. Recommended partners include team head Clive Barnard; David Wyles; and Jason Fox (particularly for energy and project finance). Ewen Fergusson advised on an interesting deal that saw the DTI provide £1bn of financing to Royal Mail Group.

Lovells' international finance practice, managed by David Harris is going great guns; London banking group billings were up nearly 40% from 2001. Global head of banking Andrew Gamble is recommended for trade finance work. For acquisition finance, Matthew Cottis remains popular for his ability and coolness under pressure. New panel appointments include Société Générale, amongst others.

Norton Rose's Michael Ings deals with acquisition finance alongside his telecoms finance and restructuring. We would also recommend Stephen Parish for general banking; Harry Theochari, untouchable for ship finance; and Jeffery Barratt's projects and PFI team.

Slaughter and May may not have the breadth of ties to banks that its rivals enjoy, but it boasts partners of the highest quality. These include Andrew Balfour, Richard Slater, Ruth Fox, Simon Hall and George Seligman, who advised Nordea Bank on an $800m syndicated revolving multi-currency loan.

White & Case now has a real profile for London-sourced bank lending work. Maurice Allen leads a team which, with its strong presence in France and Germany, competes with the top UK firms for instructions on structured products from a core group of banks. American partner Mike Goetz impresses everyone he meets in London and provides valuable input on US structuring techniques.

Christopher Hogan heads the team at **Baker & McKenzie**, which acts for numerous banks. Bernard Sharp advised borrower EQT on the €1.2bn senior and mezzanine facilities for the 32-country LBO of Haarmann & Reimer Group and Dragoco Gerberding Group.

CMS Cameron McKenna's banking department engaged in more than £1bn worth of financings for client Lloyds TSB and its name appears regularly on syndicated loan documentation. Team head John White is known for his common sense advice.

Of the national firms with London offices, **DLA** remains way out in front for bank lending work thanks to the presence of John Cutler and Philip Butler. Having built contacts with lenders like Bank of Scotland and Barclays on mid-market work, the firm made the move into top-drawer financing transactions. Simon Woolley in Manchester is highly regarded.

Denton Wilde Sapte has remained extraordinarily resilient over the years despite haemorrhaging talent to the Magic Circle and other firms. **Denton Wilde Sapte** remains London's pre-eminent trade finance firm and is strong on the bank debt side of restructurings through Graham Paine, housing association finance through Ian Roberts, and has other reputable partners like Howard Barrie and Anthony Bonsor.

As one of the two best high-yield firms in the world, **Latham & Watkins** was always going to make an impact in London, and the firm has successfully teamed up with UK firms to advise on high-yield aspects of large financings (it worked alongside **Ashurst** on the Schneider/Legrand deal, for example). James Chesterman has impressive senior debt contacts and expertise.

Berwin Leighton Paisner has a top-tier property finance practice under Mark Waghorn and an impressive PFI practice. The firm advised on several cross-border structured financings last year. Jennifer Mackerras, Marc Palley and Mark Daley are all recommended.

SJ Berwin partners Paul Diss and Geoff Woolf's longstanding relationships with lenders have combined with an ability to leverage off the firm's property and private equity practices (where David Ryland and Steven Davis handle work for debt providers) to grow the practice spectacularly. The firm has acted for RBS-NatWest on a range of transactions and regulatory issues.

Simmons & Simmons' Nicholas Fisher is respected. The firm is on Barclays' general advisory panel and advised the bank on its acquisition of Charles Schwab Europe.

Taylor Wessing continues to increase its international growth in this area. The firm's Anglo-German capabilities, coupled with its enthusiasm for expanding its banking relationships, suggest that new clients can expect to receive a first-rate service. Rodney Dukes, Dominic Ross and Simon Dayes are all highly regarded. The firm advises on general banking, property finance, project finance, restructurings, acquisition and structured finance and a range of lending.

Clients of **Travers Smith Braithwaite** can call on the respected and popular Neil Murray. The firm's banking team was heavily involved in the epic NTL debt restructuring.

Weil, Gotshal & Manges' partners Chris Harrison and Richard Ginsberg and senior associate Phil Slater are excellent. They are bringing in their own contacts and targeting **Weil, Gotshal & Manges**' bank clients in the US, in addition to working with the firm's thriving private equity and restructuring practices.

Barlow Lyde & Gilbert partners Graham Wedlake and Neil James have actively grown their lender client base. The firm picked up more work from Barclays Leveraged Finance and continues to work with the bank on new bancassurance products. A highlight in spring 2003 was advising Bank of America Business Credit Europe as agent and arranger on the UK's first syndicated pan-European asset-based loan.

The merger of *Gouldens* into **Jones Day**, although primarily driven by both firms' corporate practices, brings two excellent banking partners into the same team, namely Tom Budd and the versatile Martin Bartlam. Tom Budd now has an international platform on which to exercise his Magic Circle-quality skills.

Macfarlanes remains more visible acting for borrowers. However, Julian Howard has built a banking team with key strength in niche buy-out markets.

Richards Butler's Gordon Stewart and Nola Beirne have good lender relationships. The firm has advised Lloyds TSB, Fortis Bank and Barclays. The team has niche expertise in lending to the transport and leisure sectors, and Nola Beirne acted for the Civil Aviation Authority on the protracted Nats PPP.

Addleshaw Goddard's City banking practice hit its stride last year when partner Karl Woolley picked up his first instructions from Bank of Scotland's London-based structured finance team, advising on the £30m acquisition of motorhome distributor Brownhills.

A firm with a strong technology and telecoms brand, **Bird & Bird** is a good choice for electronic banking and regulatory advice. But the firm also handles a good volume of conventional bank lending work.

For a team that was only created in March 2002, **Cadwalader, Wickersham & Taft LLP** has picked up impressive lender clients and is sensibly playing to its strengths in its domestic market, such as CMBS-related work. Stephen Mostyn-Williams and Christopher Kandel are well regarded.

Dechert remains focused on making the most of its cross-border presence and acting on big-ticket international deals and has grown both its commercial and investment bank client base in London. Much of the credit goes to Trevor Beadle.

For a smaller firm, **Field Fisher Waterhouse** punches above its weight in the banking arena. Team head Jon Fife advises on a wide range of banking and finance transactions. A nine-partner team acts for more than 50 banks and financial institutions around the world, including Citigroup, Bank of Scotland, Arab Bank and Standard Bank.

Hammonds has a broadly based national banking practice that includes lawyers in London.

Partner Douglas Colliver specialises in leveraged acquisition finance.

Mayer, Brown, Rowe & Maw LLP's Ian Coles is a versatile and experienced finance lawyer.

McDermott, Will & Emery's small but high-quality team includes project finance partner Andrew Watson and Chris Forrest. Team head Graham Rowbotham is highly recommended.

Middleton Potts is best known for its impressive Italian banking client base. The firm has acted on a number of syndicated loans and secured lending transactions, including a €100m syndicated loan for an Italian regional bank

At **Olswang**, Moni Mannings has been building a specialist banking practice that supports the firm's borrower clients and is now acting for certain banks in mid-market property and acquisition finance.

Osborne Clarke has a strong presence in the Bristol market and has undertaken good work lately for London lenders.

Pinsents' Judith O'Shea joins a strong London team that includes Rhodri Davies, a regular recipient of repeat business from volume lenders, and Susan Paton.

Mark Darley is building an impressive practice at **Skadden, Arps, Slate, Meagher & Flom LLP**.

In 2003, **Simpson Thacher & Bartlett LLP** recruited the highly regarded Euan Gorrie from **Allen & Overy** and Stephen Short from **Ashurst** to launch an English law practice in London

Watson, Farley & Williams has advised numerous household-name lenders and arrangers on asset financings and restructurings. Simon Kavanagh and Michael Kenny are experienced and highly regarded.

CONSTRUCTION

Despite increasingly stiff competition, **Masons** remains alone in the top tier. The practice is famous for representing contractors, and leads the way for contentious work. One of its largest clients is the Government of Lebanon, which it represented in arbitration against contractors working on Beirut International Airport. Although the firm is better known for dispute resolution, it also focuses heavily on legal risk management and procurement work. Partners Chris Dering, Andrew Hibbert and Martin Roberts are all highly regarded as is Michael Battye.

CMS Cameron McKenna continues to offer a top-class service. Partner John Uwins heads the contentious side of the practice, which accounts for 60% of the department's work, while Marc Hanson helms the procurement side. A highlight for the litigation team was successfully acting for members of the Unex Group in relation to the Unex/Panatown disputes. The firm advised the Chelsfield subsidiary, White City (Shepherd Bush) General Partner Ltd, on the massive £750m redevelopment of White City in West London.

At **Clifford Chance LLP**, partners Tim Steadman and John Beechey head the non-contentious and contentious departments respectively. It is one of the few firms with the breadth, size and experience to handle the largest international projects. The contentious team is active on international disputes and represented AB Geonafta, the privatised Lithuanian State Oil Company, in a major arbitration against Svenska Petroleum Exploration. Non-contentious partner David Metzger is highly regarded.

Fenwick Elliott remains one of the UK's finest construction firms. Senior partner Simon Tolson heads the practice, which grew following the arrival of partner Jon Miller from **Masons**. About 60% of the work is contentious and the firm is becoming increasingly involved in PFI and PPP.

Sally Roe heads **Freshfields Bruckhaus Deringer**'s highly respected construction practice. The department benefits from the firm's considerable corporate and international clout, and acts primarily on larger projects and disputes. Major clients include Honda Motor Company, London Transport and Dartford Borough Council.

Hammonds offers a consistently high-quality, UK-wide service. David Jones heads a team at the firm's highly rated London office, which boosted its PFI/PPP capabilities with the arrival of projects partner William Abraham from **Baker & McKenzie**. The practice is seeing growth in international projects and disputes work, and is acting for Amec on a substantial ICC arbitration in Jordan. London Underground is a major client and is instructing the firm on the £400m extension to King's Cross station.

Michael Davis's team at **Herbert Smith** enjoys a top-notch reputation. The firm is especially well regarded for its dispute work, and represented Kellogg Brown & Root in a major international arbitration. On the projects front it is advising Land Securities Trillium on the White City redevelopment as part of its property outsourcing deal with the BBC.

Linklaters' construction team is capable of handling a staggeringly large amount of domestic and international instructions, particularly on the development side. One of the firm's most high-profile jobs has been for Swiss Re on the construction of its headquarters on the site of the former Baltic Exchange. Clients include Petrobras, the Brazilian state oil company, in a $460m litigation. Partner Ann Minogue is recommended.

Lovells' construction practice is held in high regard, as is department head Phillip Capper. The contentious side is increasingly busy and has acted on a number of major disputes. The firm is advising Barclays Bank on the construction aspects of its Canary Wharf relocation. The department retains a strong presence in Europe and the Far East.

Mayer, Brown, Rowe & Maw LLP offers some of the best expertise in the industry for dispute resolution. Department head Michael Regan and partner Sally Davies both have excellent knowledge

CONSTRUCTION

MASONS

CMS CAMERON McKENNA
CLIFFORD CHANCE LLP
FENWICK ELLIOTT
FRESHFIELDS BRUCKHAUS DERINGER ✪
HAMMONDS
HERBERT SMITH ✪
LINKLATERS ✪
LOVELLS ✪
MAYER, BROWN, ROWE & MAW LLP
SHADBOLT & CO

Berwin Leighton Paisner
Denton Wilde Sapte ✪
Macfarlanes ✪
Nicholson Graham & Jones
Norton Rose ✪
Taylor Wessing ✪
Trowers & Hamlins ✪

Allen & Overy ✪
Ashurst ✪
Baker & McKenzie ✪
Corbett & Co
Davies Arnold Cooper
Glovers
Nabarro Nathanson
Simmons & Simmons ✪
Speechly Bircham
White & Case ✪
Winward Fearon
Wragge & Co LLP ✪

Addleshaw Goddard
Beale and Company
Berrymans Lace Mawer
Campbell Hooper
Eversheds LLP
Field Fisher Waterhouse
Kennedys
Lawrence Graham
Lewis Silkin ✪
Manches
Reynolds Porter Chamberlain
Wedlake Bell

Barlow Lyde & Gilbert
Clyde & Co ✪
DLA ✪
Dechert
Finers Stephens Innocent
Howard Kennedy
Kingsley Napley
Reed Smith
Richards Butler
SJ Berwin ✪
Slaughter and May ✪
Stephenson Harwood
Travers Smith Braithwaite

Firms are listed A-Z in tiers which are ranked in order of priority
✪ Indicates firm displays contact details at the end of this chapter.

of their practice area. The firm's US connections have led to an increase in international work, while at home the firm represented Hewden Cranes and its insurers in proceedings arising from a Canary Wharf crane collapse.

Under the guidance of Dick Shadbolt, one of the sector's undisputed heavyweights, **Shadbolt & Co** has carved itself an excellent reputation. The firm has a strong international reach, with offices in Paris, Athens and Dar es Salaam. It is increasingly involved in PFI work, particularly on the disputes side. Highlights include advising the BBC on the construction aspects of its move from Pebble Mill to the Mailbox in Birmingham. Partner Dominic Helps comes highly recommended.

Berwin Leighton Paisner's construction practice straddles all the major sectors in the industry, for both contentious and non-contentious work, and is particularly experienced in the oil, gas, power and utility sectors. Department head Julian Holloway comes highly recommended as do partners Caroline Pope, John Hughes-D'Aeth and Terry de Souza.

Denton Wilde Sapte's highly rated department recently advised on over 25 major domestic and international construction projects. Highlights include advising the Highways Agency on the £260m A1 DBFO scheme. It is also acting for Parkview International on the redevelopment of Battersea Power Station. Julian Pope heads the team.

The four-partner team at **Macfarlanes** is headed by Tony Blackler, and is well experienced in both projects and dispute work. The firm advised the Greater London Authority on its recently completed City Hall, while on the contentious side the firm acts for contractors and developers on all types of dispute resolution.

Nicholson Graham & Jones offers a broad and well-balanced practice. David Race heads the department, which boasts an array of highly regarded practitioners, including James Hudson and Linda Kent on the contentious side, and Kevin Greene and Christopher Causer for development work. Highlights include advising West African Portland Cement Company on the construction of a 3,000-tonne-per-day Nigerian cement works.

Headed by Chris Hill, the construction department at **Norton Rose** has six partners and 33 assistants. The firm is particularly well regarded for dispute resolution, which represents 60% of the practice, as well as PFI work. It is advising an English engineering company on two major arbitrations, worth £200m. Major clients include ABB Offshore, Ballast and Bechtel.

Clients praise the six-partner practice at **Taylor Wessing** for its expertise and personable approach. Helen Garthwaite and department head Christopher Bourgeois are both recommended. A recent instruction is from Mitsubishi Heavy Industries on prolonged loss and expense claims connected with a power plant.

Trowers & Hamlins boasts one of the UK's strongest non-contentious teams, particularly for public sector work. Major clients include BAE Systems, The Berkeley Group and Sheffield City Council. David Mosey heads the group.

The department at **Allen & Overy** is 'of the highest international calibre'. Shell Global Solutions is one of the team's largest clients. Recommendations include the 'very able' Nigel Pritchard and experienced associate Steven Blanch.

Christopher Vigrass heads the department at **Ashurst**, which has an excellent reputation in PFI/PPP, as well as being strong in pure construction work. The firm's contentious team is well experienced in mediation and arbitration, while the non-contentious side remains busy with a mix of international and domestic work.

Baker & McKenzie's global reach ensures a steady stream of major international projects, particularly in Asia and the Middle East. Department head Jeremy Winter is a solicitor advocate, and is highly experienced in international arbitrations.

Corbett & Co is a boutique firm, led by Edward Corbett, which focuses on domestic and international disputes. Highlights include a settlement for Hyundai, in a £31m High Court action against Prince Jefri of Brunei, regarding a marina designed for the Prince's luxury yacht and its attendant speedboats.

Daniel Gowan heads **Davies Arnold Cooper**'s impressive practice. Traditionally known for its insurer work, the firm is successfully expanding its mainstream client-base. The department is particularly strong for dispute work, acting for a range of clients, such as Jacobs Gibb, Alfred McAlpine and BP Chemicals.

David Miles heads team at **Glovers**, which, despite its small size, boasts a wealth of experience. The firm focuses primarily on contentious work, representing a wide range of clients in adjudications and international arbitrations. Major clients include Sir Robert McAlpine and Datum Contracts International.

Nabarro Nathanson's Roger Wakefield heads a team with a good reputation for non-contentious work. Major clients include Jarvis, Siemens, Mitsubishi Estates and HOK International.

The 'impressive' Robert Bryan heads the team at **Simmons & Simmons**. The practice has strong infrastructure and project capabilities and is advising the Strategic Rail Authority on its £500m station modernisation programme. The firm has a 100% success record in adjudications.

Speechly Bircham's respected contentious team led by partner Tim Raper has been busy. It acted for clients including Jacobs Engineering, The Co-operative Insurance Society and Cable & Wireless. The non-contentious side is advising Southpoint General Partnership on a proposed 400,000 sq ft central London office development.

For international projects and dispute work, **White & Case** has an enviable reputation. The firm represented the Lesotho Highlands Development Authority in an ICC arbitration hearing, and in the successful court challenge to the award. Department head Ellis Baker and executive partner John Bellhouse are well known for their work.

Winward Fearon is highly recommended by clients. The majority of the firm's work is contentious, though it has also developed a strong niche in surety bonds. Department head Max Wieliczko and senior partner David Cornes both offer 'service of the highest quality'.

Simon Baylis leads the much-admired department at Birmingham-based **Wragge & Co LLP**. The firm is involved in an increasing amount of dispute work, for both contractors and developers, and acted for Amec on claims arising from marine construction works at Dover harbour.

CORPORATE TAX

Clifford Chance LLP has been the main beneficiary of a shift in clients' needs to structured finance, securitisations, and property finance. In particular the firm has a reputation for innovation in structured finance products. The firm is also growing its private equity side. Michael Wistow's advice on two securitisations for Canary Wharf builds on the firm's brilliant reputation in this area. Douglas French, David Harkness, Jonathan Elman, Stephen Shea and Marian Thomas form a creative and technically sound team.

Freshfields Bruckhaus Deringer's tax department remains in a strong position. Department head David Taylor consistently wins plaudits for his project management and negotiation skills. Francis Sandison, Sarah Falk, Jonathan Cooklin, Tim Ling and Robert Kent are all praised as a pre-eminent team for big-ticket M&A. Colin Hargreaves is recommended for structured and project finance work. Stephen Hoyle is an excellent choice for insurance tax advice.

Linklaters enjoys a strong reputation for private equity work – a section of the corporate market that has borne up better than public M&A. That said, it would be hard for any area to eclipse the firm's record on the very largest acquisitions and sales, where Guy Brannan, Conor Hurley, Ian Bowler and Neal Todd form a 'dream team' for any £1bn-plus transaction. Yash Rupal, Martin Lynchehan, Andrew Beverley and Stephen Taylor are all highly skilled. Charles Hellier is recommended for investment funds work.

Slaughter and May's clients appreciate the firm's winning combination of 'technical excellence', 'commercial awareness' and 'imagination'. Though the team is chiefly known for its work on the very largest M&A deals, the team's partners have been equally at home working on financings, major restructuring projects, Tier 1 capital work, and tax litigation.

At **Allen & Overy**, partners Brenda Coleman, Patrick Mears, David Lewis, David Hughes Miles

CORPORATE TAX

CLIFFORD CHANCE LLP
FRESHFIELDS BRUCKHAUS DERINGER ✪
LINKLATERS ✪
SLAUGHTER AND MAY ✪

ALLEN & OVERY ✪

ASHURST ✪
CMS CAMERON McKENNA
HERBERT SMITH ✪
LOVELLS ✪
MACFARLANES ✪
NORTON ROSE ✪
SIMMONS & SIMMONS ✪

ADDLESHAW GODDARD
FIELD FISHER WATERHOUSE
JONES DAY ✪
McDERMOTT, WILL & EMERY ✪
OLSWANG
SJ BERWIN ✪
SIDLEY AUSTIN BROWN & WOOD
TRAVERS SMITH BRAITHWAITE

Baker & McKenzie ✪
Berwin Leighton Paisner
Dechert
Denton Wilde Sapte ✪
Eversheds LLP
Milbank, Tweed, Hadley & McCloy
Nabarro Nathanson
Stephenson Harwood
Taylor Wessing ✪
Watson, Farley & Williams
Weil, Gotshal & Manges ✪

Beachcroft Wansbroughs
Bird & Bird ✪
Bristows
Charles Russell
Cleary Gottlieb Steen & Hamilton ✪
Clyde & Co ✪
Dewey Ballantine
Dorsey & Whitney
Hammonds
Lawrence Graham
Mayer, Brown, Rowe & Maw LLP
McGrigors
Richards Butler
Shearman & Sterling (London) LLP
Skadden, Arps, Slate, Meagher & Flom LLP
Speechly Bircham

Firms are listed A-Z in tiers which are ranked in order of priority
✪ Indicates firm displays contact details at the end of this chapter.

Walton and Mark Brailsford are the leading names in a department with a genuine breadth of work and depth of expertise. Coleman and Mears in particular have had a good year on acquisitions and major debt restructuring work.

Praised as 'intelligent, efficient and well-connected', each partner at **Ashurst** advises on the full range of the department's work. Department head John Watson has a well-earned reputation for excellence among private equity clients; Sue Crawford's property work is the equal of any lawyer in the City; and Ian Johnson is an excellent choice for debt and derivatives work.

In addition to a solid M&A capability, Mark Nichols' team at **CMS Cameron McKenna** receives plaudits for the quality of its work on major projects. Keith Gregory and Simon Meredith offer 'clear and commercial' solutions on complex acquisitions. Richard Croker has an excellent track record on major restructurings.

At **Herbert Smith**, Heather Gething has a loyal client following – a 'calm and collected' head of department whose juniors are well supervised with excellent partner support. Gething and partner Ross Fraser are praised as particularly exceptional, combining a high degree of technical skill with a problem-solving approach to advice.

Though **Lovells** may not have the M&A throughput enjoyed by some firms, a loyal client base that values the 'efficient, intelligent and no-nonsense advice' of Daniel Friel and Karen Hughes delivers a flow of high-value acquisitions and disposals work to the firm. Kevin Ashman has a good reputation for contentious work. The firm also benefits from a premier property practice.

Macfarlanes' Nigel Doran heads a department respected as 'knowledgeable, commercial' and 'much in demand'. Mark Baldwin is one of the very best transactional lawyers in the City. Ashley Greenbank is also highly rated for solid, commercially oriented advice.

At **Norton Rose** Isla Smith, John Challoner, Christopher Norfolk, Christopher Bates and Dominic Stuttaford all inspire 'deep confidence without exception'.

Clients praise **Simmons & Simmons**' 'excellent turnaround times on unreasonable requests'. Edward Troup has a good technical grasp over a broad range of taxation issues, but is singled out for his insight into the mindset of the Revenue.

Addleshaw Goddard's clients can now call on one of the best practices of any mid-size City firm. Department head Peter Sayer and Paddy Grafton Green are good team players with a stand-alone practice that punches well above the firm's weight.

Clients recognise **Field Fisher Waterhouse**'s head of department Nicholas Noble as 'one of the City's best tax minds' for any financial services work. Other stars at the department include Graeme Nuttall for M&A, and Michael Stirling for transfer pricing work.

At **Jones Day**, Blaise Marin-Curtoud has an excellent reputation as a tax all-rounder, and the firm has a good trusts capability. Partners Keith Featherstone, Robert Gaut and Martin Rowley deserve credit for building an excellent practice.

McDermott, Will & Emery's 'personable, commercial and sharp' head of tax, Peter Nias serves both US and domestic blue-chip companies for high-value transfer pricing, structured finance and cross-border M&A deals.

Olswang's core clients – investment funds and media companies – praise the 'consistency', 'technical excellence' and industry knowledge of the tax team. Department head Kay Butler is recommended for joint venture and structured finance work.

SJ Berwin has made an excellent name for itself in complex and innovative structuring work – including work for private equity funds, property funds, corporate restructurings and M&A deals. Dominic Adams leads one of the very best private equity practices in the City, whilst Heather Corben has a premier reputation for complex property work

At **Sidley Austin Brown & Wood** Drew Scott wins plaudits for his advice on securitisations and structured credit work – 'expertise and an analytical nature guarantee high-quality services, which have proven to be very valuable'.

Alasdair Douglas and Richard Stratton at **Travers Smith Braithwaite** have impressed with their work on private equity deals, tax planning advice, corporate finance and property tax planning. Kathleen Russ has a growing reputation.

DISPUTE RESOLUTION

Herbert Smith's brand name remains unrivalled in UK High Court litigation. Given the one-off nature of major litigation, this fact alone is sufficient to haul in big instructions that pass other firms by. Achieving the impossible remains something of a forte: witness John Ogilvie's win for client Somatra against *Sinclair Roche & Temperly* which involved a 'trial within a trial'. On big litigation before the UK courts, **Herbert Smith** tends to feature prominently. Highlights include acting for AIG against FirstRand Bank in a $200m gold derivative trading joint venture dispute; a last-minute re-shuffle also brought the firm a major role in the $1bn Fruit Shippers litigation. The firm's top-level partners are comfortably among the leaders in their field. In this bracket are department head David Gold and partners Charles Plant, Christa Band, Ted Greeno, Richard Fleck and Sonya Leydecker.

Clifford Chance LLP offers true strength in depth across all contentious areas of practice. It is also closer to achieving a global litigation brand than its peers. Philip Hill and Philip Rocher concluded the Barings trials in 2003; Matthew Newick continues to act in the Sumitomo Copper affair; and Simon Davies acted for Kantupan Holdings. Partners with leading reputations not mentioned above include Iain Roxborough, Roger Leese, and Roger Best.

Freshfields Bruckhaus Deringer takes a single-department approach to litigation, with all specialists undertaking substantial volumes of general commercial litigation. Jo Rickard heads a department of prodigiously talented and

DISPUTE RESOLUTION

HERBERT SMITH ✪

CLIFFORD CHANCE LLP
FRESHFIELDS BRUCKHAUS DERINGER ✪
LOVELLS ✪

ALLEN & OVERY ✪

ASHURST ✪
LINKLATERS ✪
NORTON ROSE ✪
RICHARDS BUTLER
SIMMONS & SIMMONS ✪

SLAUGHTER AND MAY ✪

BAKER & McKENZIE ✪
BARLOW LYDE & GILBERT
CMS CAMERON McKENNA
CLYDE & CO ✪
SJ BERWIN ✪

Denton Wilde Sapte ✪
Eversheds LLP
Mayer, Brown, Rowe & Maw LLP
Nicholson Graham & Jones
Stephenson Harwood
Watson, Farley & Williams

Cadwalader, Wickersham & Taft LLP
Charles Russell
Coudert Brothers ✪
DLA ✪
Holman Fenwick & Willan ✪
Ince & Co
Jones Day ✪
Kendall Freeman
Olswang
Taylor Wessing ✪
Travers Smith Braithwaite
Weil, Gotshal & Manges ✪
White & Case ✪

Addleshaw Goddard
Berwin Leighton Paisner
Hammonds
Lawrence Graham
Lewis Silkin ✪
Macfarlanes ✪
Manches
McDermott, Will & Emery ✪
Nabarro Nathanson
Reynolds Porter Chamberlain
Shook, Hardy & Bacon International LLP
Speechly Bircham

continued

DISPUTE RESOLUTION (continued)

Bird & Bird ✪
Byrne & Partners
Davies Arnold Cooper
Field Fisher Waterhouse
Finers Stephens Innocent
Harbottle & Lewis LLP
Howard Kennedy
Irwin Mitchell
Kingsley Napley
LeBoeuf, Lamb, Greene & MacRae
Masons
Mishcon de Reya
Morgan Lewis ✪
Pinsents ✪
Reid Minty
Withers LLP

Firms are listed A-Z in tiers which are ranked in order of priority
✪ *Indicates firm displays contact details at the end of this chapter.*

intellectually able partners. Among them, Paul Bowden, Jon Lawrence, Raj Parker, Chris Pugh and Ian Taylor are rightly considered leaders in their field. Recent instructions included advising JT International on smoking-related issues; BNFL on the shipment of nuclear material across a number of European jurisdictions and defending Hoffman-La Roche in vitamin cartel litigation across Europe.

Lovells is arguably the largest general commercial litigation outfit in the City in terms of both personnel and turnover. Among the ranks of heavyweights are Christopher Grierson, currently engaged in litigation for the creditors of BCCI; Patrick Sherrington, head of department since 2001, is leading a team defending BAT against smoking-related claims. Russell Sleigh acted for ING in proceedings following the collapse of Barings.

Allen & Overy is arguably the fastest growing of the leading litigation practices, generating a 75% increase in fee income over the last three years. The practice has consistency in quality that few others can match. The firm demonstrated its acumen in 2002 acting for FirstRand Bank in defence of a $200m claim brought by AIG over a gold derivative trading joint venture. Among a substantial department, those with stellar reputations include head of department David Mackie QC; litigation managing partner Peter Watson, and head of banking Tim House.

Partners at **Ashurst** are immensely well regarded within and outside the profession. The team, though smaller than some in its peer group, is high quality, with attentive, hands-on partners. The strength of the team is reflected in the quality of instructions the firm has achieved over a prolonged period. The firm represented the claimants in two of the largest pieces of litigation before the commercial court: partner Ben Tidswell led a team in Barings and Chris Vigrass led in the Sumitomo Copper litigation. New instructions included acting for Tenaga, the Malaysian state electricity company in a $100m derivatives action. Head of department, Edward Sparrow is the relationship partner for Imperial Tobacco.

Although **Linklaters**' practice remains relatively small it is able to count some of London's leading practitioners among its number. Diana Good, currently suing vitamin cartelists across Europe, is prodigiously determined and experienced; Mark Humphries is among a handful that show solicitor advocacy is not just viable, but desirable; Christopher Style is vastly experienced and universally admired; John Turnbull now department head, likewise, demonstrates expertise in all aspects of commercial litigation.

Norton Rose lacks the corporate client base that underpins many of its competitors' practices. The success of the litigation unit is therefore all the more creditable. Careful departmental management by a succession of partners and continued by Peter Rees has put **Norton Rose** among a select few litigation practices. The results speak for themselves: the department acts for over 70 international retail and investment banks; numerous insurance clients, including AIG, and a host of shipping lines and multinational corporates.

Richards Butler continues to impress in general commercial litigation. The partners are experienced and knowledgeable with 'fine judgement.' Outstanding partners include Charles Hewetson, head of department, David Warne, Michael Skrein and the formidable Lista Cannon. Gautam Bhattacharyya is also developing a fine reputation in arbitration. The firm scooped some colossal instructions across a diverse range of areas.

The stature of **Simmons & Simmons**' litigation department continues to grow as it attracts further instructions from new clients. Its strength lies in the breadth of areas on which it advises, the expertise of the partners and an integrated European office network. Jonathan Kelly is safely among a handful of the City's leading banking and financial services litigators. Philip Vaughan, head of department, is a formidable operator with a high profile in energy-related disputes.

Slaughter and May's practice fields a versatile, if somewhat small, team of all-rounders. For all its lack of size, the department continues to scoop some choice instructions. Deborah Finkler enjoys a leading reputation for complex financial services litigation. Nick Archer and Efstathios Michael are recommended and department head Richard Grandison is a tough negotiator especially prominent in construction claims.

Baker & McKenzie remains an impressive if modestly proportioned litigation outfit. The firm's longstanding global network has involved it in the type of cross-border litigation that the Magic Circle firms have only recently begun to exploit. Among its star individuals are department head Nick Pearson, who continues to manage the Grupo Torras fraud claims as well as advising Railtrack directors on issues following the administration order. Andrew Keltie a number of major wins, including at the Court of Appeal for Compaq Computer in a complex multi-jurisdictional claim.

Barlow Lyde & Gilbert's connections with underwriters fuel a stunning catalogue of instructions. It is worth noting though that just 15 of the 52 London-based partners work exclusively on insurance issues. Clare Canning advised Ernst & Young on the Equitable Life case; Julian Randall concluded the Barings litigation in 2003, acting for Coopers & Lybrand; Richard Harrison won at the House of Lords in *Dubai Aluminium v Salaam;* and Richard Spafford advised ntl on a major claim against Vodafone.

CMS Cameron McKenna remains a formidable force in commercial litigation. Top-ranking partners Tim Hardy, Neil Aitken, Stephen Hallam and Tony Marks enjoy sterling reputations within and beyond the profession. Partners Robert Hickmott and Robert Phillips acted for the Department for Transport on the administration of Railtrack. Ongoing matters include representing Aventis Pasteur MSD in claims concerning the MMR vaccine.

Clyde & Co, while best known for insurance and shipping litigation, deserves credit for a formidable general commercial litigation practice. The firm is perhaps the dominant user of the commercial court. It is also prominent in mediations, with mediators of the calibre of Jane Andrewartha among its ranks. In addition to advising on disasters on land, sea and in the air, the firm has a hand in much of the finance-related litigation, including Enron, Wickes, MyTravel, Marconi and Split Capital Investments.

SJ Berwin retains some exceptionally talented and determined partners who add value to the litigation process through taking a genuine hands-on approach. Head of department Tim Taylor is 'seriously shrewd' and a fine operator. Richard Slowe, the first ever solicitor advocate, remains as tenacious as ever. Hilton Mervis, a successful solicitor advocate, is lauded for his 'doggedness' and ability to think laterally. Craig Pollack has also established an enviable reputation.

Mark Gill and Elizabeth Tout jointly head **Denton Wilde Sapte**'s dispute resolution unit. Focused along industry lines, the department combines genuine heavyweight commercial litigation capability with a pragmatic and commercial approach. The firm is also one of few to run a recognised advocacy unit, led by former barrister and now partner Rory McAlpine. Major recent matters include acting for Newline Underwriters, the liability insurers of Jarvis Plc and Jarvis Rail.

Eversheds LLP, with the most comprehensive national office network of any firm, necessarily undertakes a vast amount of London High Court litigation. In addition to a substantial and well-regarded team in London, the firm has first-class expertise around the country. In 2002, the firm advised Defra on foot and mouth claims, and seized a major role in the film finance litigation.

Mayer, Brown, Rowe & Maw LLP's practice is already reaping the benefits of merger. David Allen continues to lead a team defending Bank of America in multi-billion dollar proceedings brought by the liquidators of BCCI. Andrew Briggs and Stephen Brown are leading teams defending alleged vitamin cartelists Lonza and BASF AG. Chris Langford and Ian MacDonald are also highly rated litigators.

Nicholson Graham & Jones is an impressive outfit. Clients admire the experience and judgement of the partners, notably head of department John Magnin and partners Robert Hadley and Anne McCarthy. The firm acted for Ryder Cup Ltd on the consequences of postponing the 2001 Ryder Cup following the September 11 atrocities. The firm also brought a group action on behalf of the Association of British Travel Agents and around 400 travel agents concerning unpaid commission.

Stephenson Harwood retains an impressive litigation client base and advises on a broad range of matters. Leading individuals include John Fordham, department head, who is acting to recover damages following *Westminster City Council v Dame Shirley Porter*. Richard Gwynne has also made a mark in banking litigation acting in several reported cases. John Higham QC conducted a skilful cross-examination to recover $10m for a syndicate of banks in *Standard Bank London Ltd v Canara Bank*.

Under department head David Kavanagh **Watson, Farley & Williams**' litigation department is one of few to be genuinely moving forward at pace. Acting for a Vivendi joint venture partner, Kavanagh successfully concluded one of Europe's largest arbitrations. The firm is also increasing its share of instructions for the major banks, acting on some impressive derivative disputes in addition to a broad range of other matters.

Cadwalader, Wickersham & Taft LLP has fast acquired a name for aggressive litigation on behalf of minority bondholders, and has certainly ruffled feathers in the City. Michelle Duncan and James Douglas also defended Alvaro Noboa in the Fruit Shippers litigation, a $1bn family squabble before the Chancery Division.

Charles Russell's connections in media and technology served its expanding general commercial litigation department well. An impressive platform of heavyweight commercial litigation has been crowned with a number of headline-grabbing cases. Department head John Sykes and Dinah Spence acted for Gary Kemp in relation to a number of Spandau Ballet-related copyright actions.

Coudert Brothers' Maria Frangeskides and Simon Cockshutt are both well-regarded litigators and are the two best-known personalities at the London end of an 80-lawyer worldwide litigation practice. Imortant instructions included acting for the Bank of China in a case with major implications for freezing orders. The practice handles a broad range of litigation worldwide.

DLA is steadily increasing its profile in the City. The department's key strengths are in technology and financial services, and the firm is targeting further work with government bodies, local authorities, universities, manufacturers, chemicals and defence companies. Leading partners include Neil Micklethwaite, Julian Stait, Richard McGrane and Matthew Saunders.

Holman Fenwick & Willan remains best known for its shipping, insurance/re-insurance practice and international trade. But the firm's main business is commercial litigation. An immense number of partners focus on specialist areas. The firm acted for Ericsson in a major $235m business interruption case and for GNER against Fortis, the insurers of Gary Hart, the driver who fell asleep at the wheel causing the Selby rail crash, plus a substantial volume of confidential multi-million pound disputes. Leading partners include Simon Blows, Noel Campbell, Simon Congdon.

Ince & Co is best recognised for its insurance, reinsurance and shipping practice, but has a host of experienced general commercial litigators. Particular initiatives over the last few years have concerned keeping disputes out of the courts. Nick Shepherd heads the group that includes well-known names such as Peter Rogan, Ben Horn and Steven Fox.

The teaming of *Gouldens*' well-regarded litigation practice with that of **Jones Day**, probably the largest litigation firm in the world, is an exciting prospect. The jury is out on whether a full-scale American invasion is on the cards, but the prospect is making Magic Circle firms nervous.

Kendall Freeman emerged from the ashes of *DJ Freeman* as a primarily contentious practice. The core commercial dispute resolution practice retains such big hitters as managing partner Laurence Harris, head of litigation Kevin Perry, and high-calibre litigators Colin Joseph and Marcus Rutherford. The firm has retained its profile on the public international front acting for the Nigerian Government on various matters.

Olswang's litigation department continues to move forward under David Stewart's leadership. A six-partner team covers a broad spread of work, which included acting for American Airlines in the Deep Vein Thrombosis litigation. The practice also retains a good grip on contentious telecoms, media and sport matters.

Taylor Wessing is regularly instructed on complex high-value litigation by a range of clients. Richard Marsh, David Greig and department head Nick Burkill enjoy excellent reputations for sound judgement and personally overseeing cases.

Travers Smith Braithwaite has a highly experienced mid-size practice and a strong reputation in the City. John Kingston, head of department, and Jonathan Leslie are particularly well regarded. The firm is representing a group of former members of Equitable Life in mis-selling claims.

The charismatic Michael Jones is pioneering a new hybrid solicitor/barrister model of litigation department at **Weil, Gotshal & Manges.** Ongoing matters include asset recovery for Enron against multiple counterparties under power purchase agreements and financial swap agreements.

White & Case, under Alistair Graham's stewardship, made an impressive showing in 2002. Growth has come largely from more efficient exploitation of the firm's office network, alongside a developing domestic client base. The firm advised UPC on the vulture fund litigation concerning its €5.2bn recapitalisation. Recent clients include BA, Dresdner Bank, Lloyds TSB Bank (New York) and Sonera.

EU AND COMPETITION

Freshfields Bruckhaus Deringer is for many clients the 'definitive European competition firm', with a superb practice across jurisdictions. From a worldwide group of 54 partners, many stand out, but particularly Deirdre Trapp, David Aitman, Nicholas Spearing, Paul Lomas, Jon Lawrence and Rod Carlton. The impressive list of clients includes P&O Princess and Hoffman-La Roche.

With a fantastic track record in bold victories, **Herbert Smith**'s competition team is known for its pluck backed up by 'quality that is never compromised'. In Jonathan Scott, Craig Pouncey, Elizabeth McKnight and Stephen Kinsella, the department has some of the best practitioners around. In 2002, the firm advised the Carnival Corporation throughout the competition quagmire that was crucial to its successful hostile bid for P&O Princess.

Slaughter and May can, and often does, wipe the floor with competitors. Not least when the 'legendary' Malcolm Nicholson masterminded the historic victory by Airtours (now MyTravel) against the European Commission in the Court of First Instance over the Commission's decision to block Airtours' proposed merger with First Choice in 1998. Laura Carstensen, Philippe Chappatte, Bertrand Louveaux and William Sibree are all recognised as exceptional competition practitioners.

Allen & Overy has a strong international reputation for antitrust work, and maintains a balanced practice, handling not only merger control work for clients but also vital behavioural matters such as state aid investigations. In London, John Wotton, Mark Friend and Alistair Lindsay are singled out as market leaders.

Ashurst represents clients in some high-profile behavioural work, notably acting for Michelin in Article 82, as well as a number of cartel cases. On the merger control side, for which it is best known, the firm acted in the high-profile Tetra Laval/Sidel case against the Commission, for Tetra Pak. Nigel Parr and Roger Finbow are singled out as leaders in their field.

Baker & McKenzie's real strength lies in cartel work, but this wonderfully talented and accessible team, driven by star partners Lynda Martin Alegi, Samantha Mobley and Robbie Downing, can turn its hand to the full range of competition work. Clients include Shell, Freeserve and Sony Corp.

The strength of **Clifford Chance LLP**'s superb practice is not just in the quality of respected senior partners Alex Nourry and Simon Baxter, but also the stellar reputations of two young partners Elizabeth Morony and Oliver Bretz. The firm's key clients include EMI and BPB plc.

Linklaters has a 'very able' antitrust practice, and in Bill Allan it has one of the best respected competition lawyers in the UK. Partners Michael Cutting and Gavin Robert are also singled out for praise by clients.

Simon Polito at **Lovells** is named 'the best competition lawyer in London' by one client. The firm undoubtedly has excellent strength in depth, with John Pheasant, Lesley Ainsworth and Susan Bright all rated at the top of their games. Clients include Masterfoods, Granada and Telia.

SJ Berwin does not rely on a corporate practice to feed its competition team, which stands out as one of the truly exceptional practices of the firm. Clients find star partners Stephen Kon, Simon Holmes, Ralph Cohen and the 'first-class' Elaine Gibson-Bolton to be among the best in the City. Those clients include electrical retailer Dixons and Procter & Gamble.

Simmons & Simmons' department has quality lawyers in Tony Woodgate, Martin Smith, Clare Potter, Charles Bankes and Jenny Block. Described by clients as 'pleasant to work with and good on regulatory matters', the team excels at behavioural and regulatory advice but can also turn its hand to complex merger control matters when required.

Polly Weitzman has a fantastic reputation at **Denton Wilde Sapte**, ably assisted by the well-respected partner Suyong Kim. The team advised Hasbro in its high-profile avoidance of fines from the OFT in connection with resale price maintenance in the UK toy industry.

Norton Rose continues to run a strong competition practice through experienced partners Martin Coleman and John Cook. Major clients include HSBC in relation to OFT investigations, and has a number of key regulatory clients, including Norsk Hydro and TXU.

Shearman & Sterling (London) LLP is ranked highly thanks to the experience and reputation of Chris Bright. The team needs expansion, but Bright has been involved in some high-profile work, not least his role as a consultant to Carnival, giving a second opinion on competition advice on its bid for P&O Princess.

Macfarlanes' Jane Whittaker and Jane Tyler have a strong, stand-alone and rounded competition practice, regularly advising clients such as Itochu.

Frances Murphy is **Mayer, Brown, Rowe & Maw LLP**'s leading light in London. Such is the standard of work produced that it has won key instructions for clients such as BASF and Lonza from higher-profile rivals.

Olswang's practice has a focus that extends beyond the firm's traditional TMT remit, advising clients such as Ofgem, which appointed the firm to its panel in 2002. Howard Cartlidge and Alasdair Bell have excellent reputations.

Richards Butler excels at competition through specialists Katherine Holmes and Stephen Sayer. The firm provides consistent regulatory and competition advice to major clients such as the BBC and the Portman Group.

Our fifth tier includes firms that have one or two recommended competition, trade or regulatory specialists. **Addleshaw Goddard**'s Guy Leigh is a respected elder statesman of the UK competition law scene.

Arnold & Porter (UK) LLP's Tim Frazer represents major clients on competition matters, such as Philip Morris International and General Electric.

Bird & Bird's Richard Eccles arrived from the Brussels office of **CMS Cameron McKenna** in the summer of 2002. He brought clients such as Neste

EU AND COMPETITION

FRESHFIELDS BRUCKHAUS DERINGER ✪
HERBERT SMITH ✪
SLAUGHTER AND MAY ✪

ALLEN & OVERY ✪
ASHURST ✪
BAKER & McKENZIE ✪
CLIFFORD CHANCE LLP
LINKLATERS ✪
LOVELLS ✪
SJ BERWIN ✪
SIMMONS & SIMMONS ✪

Denton Wilde Sapte ✪
Norton Rose ✪
Shearman & Sterling (London) LLP

Macfarlanes ✪
Mayer, Brown, Rowe & Maw LLP
Olswang
Richards Butler

Addleshaw Goddard
Arnold & Porter (UK) LLP ✪
Bird & Bird ✪
Burges Salmon *Bristol*
CMS Cameron McKenna
Dechert
Eversheds LLP
Hammonds
Latham & Watkins ✪
Lawrence Graham
Nabarro Nathanson
Nicholson Graham & Jones
Taylor Wessing ✪

Firms are listed A-Z in tiers which are ranked in order of priority
✪ Indicates firm displays contact details at the end of this chapter.

Marketing Ltd with him to his new firm, whilst providing a service to existing **Bird & Bird** clients such as lastminute.com.

Burges Salmon is based in Bristol but is recommended because of the national reputation of stellar partner Laura Claydon, who is widely considered the finest competition lawyer outside the City.

CMS Cameron McKenna has notable strength on the regulatory side, particularly in rail, oil and gas and post. Sue Hankey and Richard Taylor are particularly recommended.

Eddie Kling and Peter Crockford at **Dechert** are highly rated competition experts. Kling is a swashbuckling litigator, with recent experience in ICC arbitration.

Eversheds LLP's Ros Kellaway has a strong track record in this area, acting for clients such as Dow Chemical Company and Volkswagen Group (UK) Ltd.

Hammonds has advised companies such as Water UK on competition issues and the firm has a strong and respected trade practice in Brussels. Partner Stephen Tupper is praised by clients for his high-quality service.

Latham & Watkins has a strong US and Brussels-based antitrust practice, and in London it can boast the talents of John Kallaugher and of-counsel John Colahan.

Lawrence Graham's sole competition partner, Anthony Woolich is described as 'very good in his field'. He has a strong portfolio of clients, including Sony Computer Entertainment, Scottish & Newcastle and the Football League.

Cyrus Mehta at **Nabarro Nathanson** has a strong overall practice, and recent experience includes representing the DTI in an action in the European Court of First Instance concerning allegations of discriminatory coal prices.

Nicholson Graham & Jones hired Neil Baylis from **Osborne Clarke** to head up its competition department, which has moved quickly to build up a strong client base that includes Maranello (Ferrari UK) and Britvic.

Martin Baker and Peter Willis at **Taylor Wessing** are long established competition experts, with an impressive client base that includes Eli Lily and Macmillan Publishers.

EMPLOYMENT

With its young group of partners, **Allen & Overy** has certainly one of the most energetic and proactive practices around. Mark Mansell deserves the credit for steering the firm to its leading position, while Karen Seward is surely London's most popular employment lawyer. Younger partners Julie Quinn and executive bonus specialist Stefan Martin are no less impressive.

Baker & McKenzie has not relied on clients of the corporate department to grow its portfolio. Its ability to win clients as a distinct unit is virtually unrivalled; the firm won a pitch against two Magic Circle firms to advise Deutsche Bank, adding another name to its impressive investment bank portfolio. Christine O'Brien leads the team that includes Ellen Temperton. John Evason and Sarah Gregory also garner praise, while Monica Kurnatowska is one of the City's finest associates.

Simmons & Simmons has a quality employment team that includes experienced partners William Dawson and Simon Watson. One banking client highlights Dawson's 'professionalism' on transactions, while his contentious ability can be daunting for opponents. New banking clients including UBS Warburg and ABN Amro demonstrate the high regard with which the practice is held in the City.

EMPLOYMENT

ALLEN & OVERY ✪
BAKER & McKENZIE ✪
SIMMONS & SIMMONS ✪

EVERSHEDS LLP
HERBERT SMITH ✪
LEWIS SILKIN, MEMBER OF IUS LABORIS ✪
LOVELLS ✪
MAYER, BROWN, ROWE & MAW LLP
McDERMOTT, WILL & EMERY ✪

Beachcroft Wansbroughs
CMS Cameron McKenna
Charles Russell
Clifford Chance LLP
DLA ✪
Denton Wilde Sapte ✪
Fox Williams
Linklaters ✪
Olswang
Taylor Wessing ✪

Barlow Lyde & Gilbert
Berwin Leighton Paisner
Bird & Bird ✪
Dechert
Farrer & Co
Freshfields Bruckhaus Deringer ✪
Macfarlanes ✪
Norton Rose ✪
Osborne Clarke
Pinsents ✪
SJ Berwin ✪
Slaughter and May ✪
Stephenson Harwood
Travers Smith Braithwaite

Ashurst ✪
Boodle Hatfield
Field Fisher Waterhouse
Hammonds
Jones Day ✪
Manches
Nabarro Nathanson
Richards Butler
Speechly Bircham

continued

Eversheds LLP is known for its immense turnover of contentious instructions. London head Elaine Aarons is highlighted. With a respected national practice headed by Viv Du-Feu in Cardiff, the group is considered to be one of the more forward-thinking and innovative in the country. The firm boasts an impressive European client base.

Herbert Smith continues to enhance its fabulous reputation, where the mixed skills of its partners are an obvious advantage. It is best known for its contentious expertise where Peter Frost is one of the City's finest employment litigators. For team poaching disputes, John Farr is highly recommended, while younger partner Andrew Brown earned his spurs after leading the demanding employment advice to PwC Consulting on its sale to IBM, involving the transformation of thousands of PwC partners into IBM employees.

Lewis Silkin, member of ius laboris boasts one of the largest and broadest practices in the City. Its appointment to the highly respected *ius laboris* global labour law alliance is a boon. Frontline partner Michael Burd is a fine litigator. A dynamic duo is completed with co-head James Davies, a fine advisory lawyer, acknowledged for his TUPE acumen. A multitude of other law firms instruct **Lewis Silkin** on employment issues, demonstrating its excellent reputation.

Lovells is regularly recommended for cross-jurisdictional transaction-related work and outsourcings, but with five partners the firm boasts a much broader skill set. Clients commend department head, David Harper for his solid contentious ability, while Elizabeth Slattery and Naomi Feinstein are also astute performers. Estée Lauder is a new client to the practice.

Mayer, Brown, Rowe & Maw LLP packs a considerable punch thanks in no small part to the hugely popular and client-friendly Nicholas Robertson and experienced department head Julian Roskill. The team's contentious ability is highlighted in particular, but on the advisory side it is praised for commercial and issue-focused advice.

McDermott, Will & Emery now has a four-partner team following the election of the client-friendly Rebecca Harding-Hill. Head of the team, Fraser Younson has a magnificent reputation and regularly works on major transnational projects. David Dalgarno is another client favourite, with immense experience in the finance sector. Though less visible on the contentious side, the firm boasts a fabulous client base including Oracle, United Airlines and Sainsbury's.

Beachcroft Wansbroughs' four experienced partners have excellent reputations and are led by Rachel Dineley in London, with Elizabeth Adams heading the extensive national practice. Though historically known for its work in the health sector, the employment team has an immense stand-alone portfolio of private sector clients. Partners Stephen Gummer and Charles Newman are widely commended.

EMPLOYMENT (continued)

Addleshaw Goddard
Bates, Wells & Braithwaite
Bevan Ashford
Campbell Hooper
Capsticks
Clyde & Co ✪
Davenport Lyons
Finers Stephens Innocent
Harbottle & Lewis LLP
Kingsley Napley
Lawrence Graham
Masons
McGrigors
Morrison & Foerster MNP ✪
Pritchard Englefield
Reed Smith
Reynolds Porter Chamberlain
Salans
Trowers & Hamlins ✪
Withers LLP

Firms are listed A-Z in tiers which are ranked in order of priority
✪ Indicates firm displays contact details at the end of this chapter.

Anthony Fincham and Simon Jeffreys spearhead **CMS Cameron McKenna**'s employment practice. The team has an impressive track record in project- and PPP-related advice and is one of few to have worked on the Retention of Employment Model.

Three partners, led by the hugely experienced and forward-thinking David Green, spearhead **Charles Russell**'s well-liked employment practice. The firm has built up an impressive track record in high-profile and landmark cases. It is also one of the more innovative teams in London. The group has built a name for itself in the sports sector, while the pharmaceutical, leisure and publishing industries remain lucrative.

Clifford Chance LLP's team is headed by Chris Goodwill and with Robert Davies' election to the partnership, the team is not short of senior-level practitioners. Pensions and employment specialist Imogen Clark continues to impress.

With six partners and 17 assistants, **DLA** boasts one of the larger employment practices in London, with a number of seasoned professionals in the ranks. The firm has concentrated on developing its training products over the past year with some success, while its HR exclusive online product allows clients to access their files and billings. The firm is particularly strong in professional services, hotel and leisure, and the financial sector.

Denton Wilde Sapte boasts a four-partner strong employment practice, led by the astute Stephanie Dale, praised for her industrial relations and trade unions acumen. The firm has strong connections with City institutions as well as airlines; it has advised British Airways for a number of years.

Fox Williams acts for more individuals than most and its partners are known for their pugnacious approach, personified by senior partner Ronnie Fox, a veteran of senior-executive level negotiations and lateral moves. The professional Jane Mann heads the fine employment department and advised City bond trader Kerim Derhalli on his record £10m claim against Lehman Brothers (an out-of-court settlement was reached in March 2003). With fewer corporate advisory clients than firms in the uppermost tiers, it has slipped down a tier. Nevertheless, the firm boasts some of the most astute and experienced employment specialists and for senior executive issues it remains a leader. New partner Anne Nicholson is commended for being 'commercially sound' and 'accessible'.

The immensely experienced Raymond Jeffers heads the practice at **Linklaters** and clients commend his fantastic leadership skills. Though recommended for corporate and transactional connected advice, the team boasts an employment litigation unit under solicitor advocate Mark Humphries.

Olswang has an extremely popular team, with a broad range of employment aptitude. The excellent Catherine Taylor leads a group of partners including the experienced Sarah Keeble, Julia Palca and Daniel Aherne. Taylor handled several High Court cases on behalf of Cantor Fitzgerald.

Taylor Wessing's Andrew Granger is an able department head and a respected adviser of directors and senior executives. Clients commend the firm for its knowledge of their businesses and attention to detail.

Led by the highly respected Gary Freer, **Barlow Lyde & Gilbert** ably warrants a position in the fourth tier. Clients commend the team's advisory style and have expressed their complete trust in the department. Robert Hill and Matthew Howse have superb reputations.

Robert Eldridge heads the three-partner and 11-assistant employment group at **Berwin Leighton Paisner**. It is known for its connections to the retail, hotel and catering, and finance sectors. Paul Mander is a restrictive covenant specialist, while Alexandra Davidson handles the full range of instructions for her impressive portfolio of catering and hotel clients.

Bird & Bird's Ian Hunter (non-contentious) and Corinne Aldridge (contentious) are immensely popular with clients and form an excellent duo at the head of the team, while the growth of the practice in Europe has added another dimension. Helen Parker is another young and dynamic partner.

Charles Wynn-Evans and Jason Butwick continue to drive **Dechert**'s employment practice forward. The former handles more non-contentious work, while Butwick has built up an impressive contentious track record. The firm has a solid insurance and financial services client base.

Farrer & Co's David Smellie has a friendly, common sense style that has won a multitude of admirers, including numerous law firms which refer conflict work. The practice is well supported by senior lawyers. Geoffrey Richards adds further gravitas and has vast experience garnered from 20 years as an employment specialist.

Having worked hard on its contentious profile, under the efforts of Caroline Stroud, **Freshfields Bruckhaus Deringer** is beginning to reap the rewards. A number of challenging instructions have come from financial institutions and investment banks. Practice head Nicholas Squire is widely recognised as an erudite and practical lawyer.

Macfarlanes' investment in employment law was highlighted by the election of Dan Lavender to the partnership. Tony Thompson has an excellent reputation for advice to high-net-worth individuals and senior executives.

Though **Norton Rose**'s Tim Russell continues to receive superb reports from clients, the team has suffered recently from a number of departures. The remaining team, which includes the experienced partner Peter Talibart, is strong. Russell's excellent reputation should ensure that **Norton Rose** continues to be a force.

Osborne Clarke's popular David Cubitt heads the team with Victoria Parry joining the partnership in 2003. With its focus on City companies the firm has won Credit Agricole Indosuez as well as United Airlines as new clients. Media is another area of strength.

Pinsents has a diverse portfolio of clients, including those from the finance and professional services sectors. The firm boasts an array of expertise and skills. It acted for a number of senior executives exiting from major Plcs as well as a multitude of claims brought against major financial institutions. Robert Mecrate-Butcher is also singled out for praise and is part of a team led nationally by the immensely respected John McMullen, based in Leeds.

SJ Berwin's employment practice continues to rake in admirers, many of which commend its down-to-earth approach and ability to work alongside their own legal teams. Hilary O'Connor is commended for her 'real world' style and technical expertise. Department head Nicola Kerr has an excellent reputation.

Roland Doughty heads the employment practice at **Slaughter and May**. Clients highlight the firm's ability in relation to senior executive and director issues.

The shock departure of Tom Flanagan to **Pinsents** was a major set-back for **Stephenson Harwood**. The firm is left with Kate Brearley alone at the helm. Her reputation for employment work, in particular restrictive covenant instructions, should keep the practice healthy.

Despite its City-focused orientation, **Travers Smith Braithwaite**'s quality team headed by Andrew Lilley handles the range of employment issues and clients are not found wanting. Dorothy Henderson is applauded for 'recommending a course of action and putting the issues on the table'.

Ashurst's team is led by the hugely experienced Caroline Carter. The team is acknowledged for its expertise on transaction support issues. James Cox is an experienced member of the team, a key member of the Employment Lawyers' Association (ELA) management. The team is commended for its expertise in the private equity sector.

Boodle Hatfield has won a number of City institutions as new clients, including some of the top investment banks. Its strong brand of contentious expertise and a growing reputation for day-to-day advice sees it as one of the most popular practices in London of its size. Russell Brimelow and Warren Wayne deserve credit for the group's extraordinary success.

Field Fisher Waterhouse's array of retail, consulting and public sector clients give the firm high praise: 'We were running 90 tribunals a year and now it's down to eight,' one says. Richard Kenyon's public sector experience was rewarded by a general advisory role to Transport for London. Margaret Davis is a tough litigator.

With national head Sue Nickson transferring from Manchester to London in 2002, **Hammonds** boasts another leading individual to work alongside City client favourite David Whincup and Caroline Noblet, a specialist on executive recruitment and severance. Nickson now intends to oversee the firm's growing European employment practice from London.

Jones Day boasts a large corporate client base with an immense institutional portfolio. Head of the practice Martin Piers handles numerous executive-level terminations. Richard Martin is applauded for his close attention to detail.

With Alasdair Simpson's retirement in 2003, **Manches** loses a director and boardroom adviser of immense experience and calibre. Department head Jane Amphlett is now charged with the task of taking on Simpson's lucrative practice. However, the department has still managed to broaden its focus onto the corporate side in recent years. WHSmith instructs the firm on the full range of employment issues.

The experienced and respected Sue Ashtiany leads the team at **Nabarro Nathanson**, alongside Valmai Adams. The department's growing reputation has attracted the patronage of a number of new clients across a variety of industry sectors.

The young and immensely impressive Robin Jeffcott leads the team at **Richards Butler** which now includes former **Osborne Clarke** partner Pattie Walsh. The firm's reputation on the advisory side has won new clients, including a top investment bank and leading insurer.

The seasoned Alan Julyan leads the group at **Speechly Bircham**, which includes the solutions-oriented Trevor Bettany. The team boasts an array of financial services clients, demonstrating its sophisticated advisory approach.

ENVIRONMENT

The 'business-oriented' team at **Allen & Overy** maintains a leading position in the market. The firm has long been highly rated for its non-contentious practice, thanks to the expertise of experienced department head Owen Lomas and the 'thorough' Ross Fairley. Among the transactional highlights were advising Intertek Testing Services on due diligence relating to its IPO, and Pechiney on its proposed acquisition of the aluminium assets of Corus.

Freshfields Bruckhaus Deringer has enviable breadth across transactional and litigation work. Paul Watchman is 'simply superb on both technicalities and fronting the negotiation' and is ably assisted by the 'precise' John Bowman. On the litigation side, Jonathan Isted is 'succinct, concise and capable'. Group head Paul Bowden is among the leading defence practitioners in the country. Malcolm Forster is the firm's international expert, responsible for co-ordinating the practice across the EU.

Helen Loose leads a 'prompt and efficient' three-partner team at **Ashurst**. Litigators John Evans and Mark Elvy are recommended. The firm acted for Union Railways Property on a waste issue concerning the Channel Tunnel Rail Link, and BNFL on an independent review of remediation planning.

Paul Sheridan's team at **CMS Cameron McKenna** is a force to be reckoned with. Sheridan is praised for his considerable litigation skills. The team advised Metronet on its bid for the London Underground PPP. Risk assessment, licensing, and compliance are also areas of strength.

The depth of resource of **Clifford Chance LLP**'s two-partner team earns it a place in the second tier. Brian Hall is one of London's leading environment lawyers, as is Michael Redman. The group is backed up by John Pickston, who is a prominent litigator, while David Cohen is recommended for his insurance work. The firm advised Acordis on contaminated land issues at sites across Europe.

Niche claimant firm **Leigh, Day & Co** is one of the top two firms for litigation. Name partner Martyn Day heads the product liability environment team, which acted for childhood leukaemia victims in claims against BNFL and the electricity industry. Richard Meeran has expertise in contaminated land, chemicals and asbestos cases.

Linklaters has an impressive track record for both advisory and contentious work. Vanessa Havard-Williams leads the team; David Watkins has a 'good body of knowledge', even though his major speciality is planning. Alison Smith is also recommended. The firm acted for Sakhalin Energy in its $10bn project financing of two offshore platforms, a pipeline and a processing plant.

Kathy Mylrea of **Simmons & Simmons** has a profile to match any of her rivals. The firm acted for the Ministry of Defence on the PPP of QinetiQ and advised Vivendi on its acquisition of Southern Water. It is equally well respected for contentious work; Nilema Bhakta is extremely well thought of.

Slaughter and May has a smaller team but, in Ed Keeble, a 'clear-minded and commercial' team leader. Dermot Rice is popular with clients, too. The firm acted for Croda International on the disposal of a distillation and solvent recovery business and for George Wimpey on the conditional acquisition of Laing Homes.

Baker & McKenzie's practitioners are high quality, in particular group head Christopher Norton and barrister James Cameron. The firm acted for Great Lakes Chemical Corporation on waste legislation, regulatory permitting and IPPC.

Andrew Waite at **Berwin Leighton Paisner** is praised for his advice. The firm's outstanding planning practice is also a major benefit. The firm advised English Partnerships on the environmental aspects of the sale of the Millennium Dome.

ENVIRONMENT

ALLEN & OVERY ✪
FRESHFIELDS BRUCKHAUS DERINGER ✪

ASHURST ✪
CMS CAMERON McKENNA
CLIFFORD CHANCE LLP
LEIGH, DAY & CO
LINKLATERS ✪
SIMMONS & SIMMONS ✪
SLAUGHTER AND MAY ✪

Baker & McKenzie ✪
Berwin Leighton Paisner
Denton Wilde Sapte ✪
Herbert Smith ✪
Jones Day ✪
Lovells ✪
Mayer, Brown, Rowe & Maw LLP
Nabarro Nathanson

Barlow Lyde & Gilbert
Bristows
Davies Arnold Cooper
Lawrence Graham
Masons
Nicholson Graham & Jones
Norton Rose ✪
SJ Berwin ✪

Addleshaw Goddard
Berrymans Lace Mawer
Field Fisher Waterhouse
Hammonds
Macfarlanes ✪
Manches
Richard Buxton Cambridge
Stephenson Harwood
Taylor Wessing ✪
Towers & Hamlins ✪

Firms are listed A-Z in tiers which are ranked in order of priority
✪ Indicates firm displays contact details at the end of this chapter.

Environmental impact assessments are a major area of strength.

Jacqui O'Keeffe, who heads the team at **Denton Wilde Sapte**, has expertise in both contentious and non-contentious work. Stephen Shergold is also recommended. The firm advised English Partnerships on its land stabilisation programme.

Clients praise Tony Dempster, litigation partner at **Herbert Smith**: he's 'proactive', 'impressive' and 'understands our needs brilliantly'. Amanda Willmott supports him and is also popular in the market. On the non-contentious side, Martin Dawbney heads the team, with strong assistance from Maria Cull. Trevor Turtle has a good knowledge of water law.

Linda Fletcher heads the team at **Jones Day** and is particularly active in advising manufacturing and chemical sector clients, notably acting for Johnson Wax Professional in its acquisition of Unilever's industrial cleaning business. Martin Bartlam and Stephen McNab are also recommended.

At **Lovells**, Louise Moore is 'competent' and a 'skilled negotiator'. David Moss is the firm's other major figure for transactional work, and the two advised a major energy client on the UK Emissions Trading Schemes. Moore also advised Tube Lines consortium on the acquisition of Infraco JNP from London Underground.

Mayer, Brown, Rowe & Maw LLP has five environment partners and strength in both advisory and contentious work. Cate Sharp heads the team, in which Michael Hutchinson is a key figure, while Chris Langford is a solid litigator. The firm advised ICI on its sale of Synetix to Johnson Matthey for £260m. On the litigation side, the firm was involved in two waste sector disputes involving regulatory and title issues.

Nabarro Nathanson clearly merits a place in the second tier for non-contentious work; the 'commercial' Anna Marshall's 'knowledge of the law is impressive'. Highlights include advising Quintain on securing the redevelopment of the Greenwich Peninsula including the Millennium Dome.

For environmental insurance and reinsurance, **Barlow Lyde & Gilbert** is unrivalled. Department head Valerie Fogleman advised Zurich London on its range of policies. The firm acted for XL Environmental in claims under environmental insurance policies.

We recommend **Bristows** primarily for environmental liability and regulation, as well as for its pan-European practice. Alexandra Lethbridge heads the team and is supported by Richard Burnett-Hall.

Davies Arnold Cooper has a strong reputation for litigation, with Fiona Gill particularly well thought of. The firm has a strong track record in advising on contaminated, derelict and problem sites including hospitals and airfields.

The two-partner team at **Lawrence Graham** includes Stephen Turnbull and Catherine Percy. Turnbull's strengths are predominantly on corporate support and stand-alone advice, while Percy's are on disputes and shipping-related work. Paul Rice heads the joint environment and health and safety team. The firm advised Antler Property on its purchase of a £32m industrial property.

Masons' Karen Cooksley is well thought of and Dr Collette McCormack is a renowned environmental law expert. The team works closely with the firm's water and energy groups, and has a niche in waste and PFI projects.

At **Nicholson Graham & Jones**, John Garbutt is the leading environment expert. The firm boasts a strong practice; it advised animal rendering companies on defending BSE and foot-and-mouth disease issues.

Brian Greenwood, who heads **Norton Rose**'s team, has a strong reputation, and is praised by clients for his ability to predict which strategies the opposition will employ. The firm acted for BMW on the environmental issues arising from the sales of Rover and Land Rover.

Mark Brumwell heads **SJ Berwin**'s environment group, with assistance from planning head Patricia Thomas OBE. It is acting for the Environment Agency on promoting new flood defence schemes across the country and for RBS on contaminated land issues.

IP: CONTENTIOUS

Bird & Bird partners Jane Mutimear and Peter Brownlow have exceptional 'soft' IP practices, advising a superb roster of clients that includes Nestlé and the Football Association.

Partners Paul Walsh and David Wilkinson at **Bristows** are undisputed leaders for trade mark and copyright litigation. Clients of the firm include Gillette and the BBC. Copyright clients include Sony Entertainment Europe.

Denton Wilde Sapte has a rounded and popular IP practice, with notable strength in trade mark and copyright work for clients such as easyGroup, Marks & Spencer and Sony.

Clients praise the 'exemplary service' of **Field Fisher Waterhouse**'s contentious IP practice. This is a firm where IP is a key practice and as such clients are guaranteed full commitment. Partners Nick Rose (on trade marks) and Sarah Whalley Coombes (on copyright) have had some notable successes recently. Highlights include taking easyJet to court in late 2003 over copyright in reservation booking systems for client Navitaire.

Olswang is the definitive soft IP firm, with an outstanding track record in both copyright, design and trade mark disputes. Partners Andrew Inglis and Paul Stevens are particularly praised by clients. Clients include Channel 4, AXA PPP and Dyson.

Simmons & Simmons' strength lies in the reputation of its practitioners, in particular the 'outstanding' department head Helen Newman for trade marks, and copyright expert Jeremy Morton. Major clients include Hugo Boss, Procter & Gamble and Barcardi-Martini.

Taylor Wessing has a first-rate squad of some of the best IP lawyers in the country, including

IP: CONTENTIOUS

- BIRD & BIRD ✪
- BRISTOWS
- DENTON WILDE SAPTE ✪
- FIELD FISHER WATERHOUSE
- OLSWANG
- SIMMONS & SIMMONS ✪
- TAYLOR WESSING ✪
- WILLOUGHBY & PARTNERS

- Addleshaw Goddard
- Ashurst ✪
- Baker & McKenzie ✪
- Blair & Co
- Davenport Lyons
- Harbottle & Lewis LLP
- Herbert Smith ✪
- Jones Day ✪
- Laytons
- Richards Butler
- SJ Berwin ✪
- White & Case ✪
- Wragge & Co LLP ✪

- Allen & Overy ✪
- Briffa
- Clifford Chance LLP
- DLA ✪
- Freshfields Bruckhaus Deringer ✪
- Howrey Simon Arnold & White ✪
- Linklaters ✪
- Lovells ✪
- Macfarlanes ✪
- Mayer, Brown, Rowe & Maw LLP
- McDermott, Will & Emery ✪
- McGrigors
- Nicholson Graham & Jones
- Norton Rose ✪
- Slaughter and May ✪
- Withers LLP

- Arnold & Porter (UK) LLP ✪
- Berwin Leighton Paisner
- CMS Cameron McKenna
- Charles Russell
- Collyer-Bristow
- Dechert
- Dorsey & Whitney
- Finers Stephens Innocent
- Hammonds
- Lewis Silkin ✪
- Manches
- Nabarro Nathanson
- Shook, Hardy & Bacon International LLP
- Stephenson Harwood

Firms are listed A-Z in tiers which are ranked in order of priority

✪ Indicates firm displays contact details at the end of this chapter.

Charles Lloyd, John Linneker and Niri Shanmuganathan for all soft-IP concerns. Experience includes acting for new client Sun Microsystems in trade mark registry oppositions and appeals.

Tony Willoughby, name partner at **Willoughby & Partners**, is widely regarded as the godfather of UK trade mark law and the first choice for many clients in high-profile litigation. Clients include Getty Images, Orange, Guinness UDV and GlaxoSmithKline.

The merger of *Addleshaw Booth & Co* and *Theodore Goddard* to create **Addleshaw Goddard** brings together a top trade mark practice with a leading copyright and designs firm. It acts for major clients such as the British Horseracing Board, Pentland (owners of key brands such as Ellesse, Speedo, Kickers and Mitre) and Bentley Motors.

Ashurst is a leading corporate and commercial firm, but has dedicated contentious IP ability through respected partner Ian Starr. His recent high-profile work includes High Court proceedings for Ritz Hotel Ltd over the use of the Ritz trade mark for gaming purposes.

Baker & McKenzie has a global reputation for IP excellence, and the London office is no exception. In Harry Small, Paul Rawlinson and Michael Hart the firm has an excellent team, acting for clients L'Oréal and Levi Strauss & Co.

Blair & Co is the low-key legal arm of leading trade mark and patents attorneys **Marks & Clerk**. The practice stands alone, but is housed in the same offices and shares some of **Marks & Clerk**'s stellar client base. Mark Blair receives some superb instructions from major global clients such as the Czech brewer Budejovicky Budvar and Lucas Film.

Davenport Lyons is a media firm with a dedicated and highly skilled copyright, designs and trade mark practice, led by Stuart Lockyear. The firm regularly advises FCUK on the full range of contentious IP work and has a strong portfolio of fashion clients.

Harbottle & Lewis LLP has a similar focus towards clients in the media and entertainment sector, acting for clients such as the Virgin Group, News International and a host of sports, arts and entertainment personalities on contentious IP issues.

Herbert Smith's Nick Gardner and Mark Shillito are two IP litigators at the top of their game in a department where team members can turn their hands to most types of case. Recent highlights include acting for Vodafone and the Fox Group.

Jones Day has run a strong contentious IP practice for some time under the control of respected head Charters Macdonald-Brown. GlaxoSmithKline and Eidos remain prized clients for trade mark work.

Laytons' acquisition of highly respected IP boutique *Lochners* has bolstered its standing in the market due largely to the reputation of leading partner Ludi Lochner in Guildford. Clients include Remington, BA and Nokia.

Richards Butler's Graham Simkin is singled out as a leading contentious IP practitioner. Clients include the BBC, Direct Line and new client Channel 4.

SJ Berwin's contentious practice is led by the aggressive Ray Black, an experienced contentious IP partner, along with equally respected David Rose. The firm counts as clients Guinness, the World Wrestling Federation and William Hill.

White & Case has a strong track record in IP litigation, born largely from the reputation of highly respected figurehead David Llewelyn. This team counts John Lewis and The Discovery Channel as key clients.

Birmingham's **Wragge & Co LLP** remains one of the few alternatives outside the City for heavyweight IP litigation. Clients, which include the likes of Microsoft and McDonald's Restaurants, particularly rate partners Gordon Harris and Patrick Duxbury.

Allen & Overy has a broad mix of contentious IP clients such as adidas and Philips, which the firm unsuccessfully represented in a European trade mark dispute with Remington. Catriona Smith is recommended.

Margaret Briffa, eponymous partner of **Briffa**, is well known and respected by peers for practical, client-friendly advice. The firm has a leading reputation for soft IP, particularly acting for 'David' clients against 'Goliath'-like major multinationals.

Clifford Chance LLP has a strong portfolio of trade mark clients, including Mars, Reuters and Rolex. Vanessa Marsland and Peter Taylor stand out as strong litigators.

The appointment of Jeremy Dickerson from **Hammonds** raises **DLA**'s contentious IP profile. He brings with him IP work for the Harrods Group, and had a starring role in the much publicised 'Vienetta' shape trade mark dispute. Another key IP client of the firm is Puma.

Freshfields Bruckhaus Deringer New York-based partner Dinah Nissen is a respected trade mark litigator. The team has advised major clients such as Microsoft and British Nuclear Fuels. The firm's focus is transactional IP and patent litigation.

Clients would do well to watch **Howrey Simon Arnold & White**'s London IP practice. New recruit Isabel Davies is a formidable litigator. She is joined by James Irvine, the respected former partner of City IP boutique *Arnander Irvine & Zeitman* which merged with the London office of **Shook, Hardy & Bacon International LLP**.

Linklaters' IP practice has suffered following high-profile departures in 2003. However, talented partners Roland Mallinson, Robert Swift, Ian Karet and Benedict Bird remain.

Lovells' soft IP practice is somewhat overshadowed by its strong patents practice, but Michael Golding leads a strong team which is advising Prudential in a global trade mark dispute with its US namesake, as well as Royal Mail in key trade mark disputes.

Macfarlanes' Geoff Steward has fashioned an impressive IP practice, acting for Anheuser-Busch in its ongoing fight with Czech brewer Budejovicky Budvar over the trade mark 'Bud'.

New partner Mary Bagnall has a strong reputation for contentious work at **Mayer, Brown, Rowe & Maw LLP**, where Ian Wood is regarded as a soft IP expert. The firm acted for The French Ministry of Agriculture in a significant dispute with Bernard Matthews against its registration of the 'Label Rouge' mark.

Most IP practitioners in the City consider **McDermott, Will & Emery**'s Larry Cohen as a force to be reckoned with. Recent instructions include acting for Jonathan Ball in a high-profile claim against the trustees of The Eden Project.

McGrigors' contentious IP capability was made clear through its work for Tesco in its highly public spat with Levi Strauss & Co over the parallel import of cut-price jeans. Catrin Turner and Eddie Powell are particularly recommended.

Nicholson Graham & Jones' Dominic Bray has a dedicated contentious IP practice and a highly impressive roster of clients that includes AOL Time Warner and the British Film Institute.

Chris Ryan at **Norton Rose** has over 30 years' experience of contentious IP and leads a team that has advised clients such as easyJet and BMW on soft IP litigation.

Slaughter and May's Susie Middlemiss and her strong team of assistants handle high-profile matters, such as acting for Reed Executive in a trade mark infringement action against Reed Business Information.

Withers LLP's John d'Auvergne Maycock is a highly respected elder statesman of the UK IP scene. His team has represented clients such as Eskandar, Moschino and Laboratoires Göemar on a range of contentious IP issues.

IP: NON-CONTENTIOUS

Allen & Overy has in Colleen Keck one of the leading transactional IP lawyers in the country. Dedicated work of the department includes a number of licensing and collaborative agreements on behalf of Celltech and News International.

Ashurst undertakes interesting non-contentious IP work that includes advising Omega Logic in its negotiations with one-2-one (now T-Mobile), and negotiated agreements for PRG Schultz International.

Fitting for a firm that has devoted itself to IP, **Bird & Bird**'s non-contentious IP capability is on a par with its litigious capability for which it is better known. Clients choose **Bird & Bird** for its understanding of IP in all areas of business and how to exploit those rights as much as possible. Key partners in the group have advised clients such as BT and Mastercard.

Bonella Ramsay at **Denton Wilde Sapte** has a well-established pedigree for non-contentious

IP: NON-CONTENTIOUS

ALLEN & OVERY ⭘
ASHURST ⭘
BIRD & BIRD ⭘
DENTON WILDE SAPTE ⭘
FRESHFIELDS BRUCKHAUS DERINGER ⭘
HERBERT SMITH ⭘
SIMMONS & SIMMONS ⭘
SLAUGHTER AND MAY ⭘
TAYLOR WESSING ⭘

Arnold & Porter (UK) LLP ⭘
Baker & McKenzie ⭘
Bristows
Clifford Chance LLP
Field Fisher Waterhouse
Harbottle & Lewis LLP
Jones Day ⭘
Linklaters ⭘
Macfarlanes ⭘
SJ Berwin ⭘
Stephenson Harwood
Wragge & Co LLP ⭘

Berwin Leighton Paisner
CMS Cameron McKenna
Campbell Hooper
Davenport Lyons
Dorsey & Whitney
Mayer, Brown, Rowe & Maw LLP
McGrigors
Nicholson Graham & Jones
Nabarro Nathanson
Olswang
Richards Butler

Firms are listed A-Z in tiers which are ranked in order of priority
⭘ Indicates firm displays contact details at the end of this chapter.

work in a firm that can boast strong corporate and commercial lawyers and where IP is of paramount importance. Major headline work includes acting for EH Shepard Estate in the sale of IP rights in Winnie the Pooh to Disney and the purchasers of the Millennium Dome in connection with the acquisition of IP rights.

Freshfields Bruckhaus Deringer has a strong non-contentious IP practice, led by the 'outstanding' Avril Martindale. Recent highlights include advising on Deloitte & Touche's acquisition of IP-heavy technology from Andersen in the UK.

Herbert Smith's excellent capability in non-contentious IP is evidenced by its work for NTT DoCoMo in licensing arrangements relating to its i-mode brand. All of the team's IP experts handle complex non-contentious work.

Simmons & Simmons' IP reputation and strong life sciences practice generates a lot of stand-alone IP work. Major instructions include advising the International Cricket Council and handling IP-heavy agreements with sponsors and broadcasters on major cricket events.

Nigel Swycher and Cathy Connolly are respected commercial partners at **Slaughter and May** who specialise in IT- and IP-heavy clients. A main stand-alone client of the department is Emap, which the firm has advised on a range of complex licensing agreements for titles including 'FHM' and 'Car'.

Taylor Wessing's non-contentious IP ability is also first-rate. Recent experience includes advising Molex Inc on a global licence agreement for electronics technology, and advising Metris Therapeutics.

IP: PATENT LITIGATION

Bird & Bird is one of a group of firms that have dominated the UK patents market for a number years. Mention high-profile patent litigation and the names Morag Macdonald and Trevor Cook trip off the tongue quickly. Latest conquests in a long and lustrous list of appearances include acting for Intel in its mammoth case against Via Technologies and Elitegroup Computer Systems. The firm also acted for Synthon BV, Allergan and Celltech in major disputes.

Bristows had more patent disputes scheduled for trial in the UK Patents Court for the period January 2003 to April 2004 than any other firm, and this has been the case for many years. In David Brown, Edward Nodder and Sally Field it has a patents dream team. It is advising Via Technologies on the other side of the Intel dispute.

Simmons & Simmons' major instructions include a whole raft of major injunctions and appeals for GlaxoSmithKline, and Korean electronics giant LG Electronics. Rowan Freeland has an outstanding reputation and is universally respected, as are partners Kevin Mooney, Jeremy Morton and Gerry Kamstra.

Taylor Wessing is renowned for its exemplary patent work and partners Richard Price, Simon Cohen and Mark Hodgson are regarded 'magnificent' by clients and peers. The firm is acting for Amgen in an ongoing, and high-profile, fight against **Bird & Bird**'s client Transkaryotic Therapies.

Andrew Rich and Bill Moodie are particularly recommended at **Herbert Smith**. The team continues to advise Roche in connection with the erythropoietin spat, although the client withdrew from proceedings early on. Other key clients include Vodafone, Nokia and BASF.

Lovells has a leading reputation for patent litigation, particularly for key client Merck. Other clients include Reuters and Daesang Corporation. Partners Robert Anderson and Nicholas Macfarlane have excellent reputations.

Stephen Jones at **Baker & McKenzie** has forged a strong patent capability within the department, advising clients such as Pfizer, Sony and Lloyds TSB on major patent disputes.

Clifford Chance LLP's John Hornby is a distinguished solicitor-advocate who has led on some extremely high-profile patent cases. These include acting for Coflexip in its litigation with Stolt Offshore and for Ajinomoto against Daesang.

IP: PATENT LITIGATION

BIRD & BIRD ⭘
BRISTOWS
SIMMONS & SIMMONS ⭘
TAYLOR WESSING ⭘

HERBERT SMITH ⭘
LOVELLS ⭘

Baker & McKenzie ⭘
Clifford Chance LLP
SJ Berwin ⭘
Wragge & Co LLP ⭘

Allen & Overy ⭘
Ashurst ⭘
Field Fisher Waterhouse
Freshfields Bruckhaus Deringer ⭘
Linklaters ⭘
McDermott, Will & Emery ⭘
Olswang
White & Case ⭘

Arnold & Porter (UK) LLP ⭘
Briffa
CMS Cameron McKenna
Denton Wilde Sapte ⭘
Eversheds LLP
Jones Day ⭘
Roiter Zucker
Stringer Saul
Willoughby & Partners

Firms are listed A-Z in tiers which are ranked in order of priority
⭘ Indicates firm displays contact details at the end of this chapter.

SJ Berwin has been a frequent visitor to the Patents Court recently, representing clients such as Cairnstores, Arrow Generics and Generics UK. The firm, particularly respected partner David Rose, has been largely successful in getting patents revoked for clients.

Wragge & Co LLP's Gregor Grant is a highly respected old hand of the UK patent scene, while Adam Cooke is also recommended. The team handled two cases concerning generic drugs for Delta.

Allen & Overy's Catriona Smith handles significant patent litigation, including acting for Celltech in defending a patent infringement suit brought by Amgen.

Ashurst has acted for Glycomed Science in High Court proceedings on the patentability and ownership of clinical trial results for an anti-cancer drug. Other clients include Motorola and Ark Therapeutics.

Field Fisher Waterhouse's Jonathan Radcliffe has rapidly developed a strong patent practice to challenge some of the established incumbents. In a bid to raise its patent profile, the firm also launched *Isoceles* in 2003, a joint venture with patent agents **Mathys & Squire** to provide clients with a cost-effective, one-stop-shop for patent filing, opposition and litigation.

Freshfields Bruckhaus Deringer significantly boosted its contentious patents practice with the appointment of Justin Watts, an expert in electronics and technology, adding to the practice of Chris Forsyth. The firm is handling patent litigation for both Sony Computer Entertainment and Bio-Medical Research.

Linklaters' Nigel Jones returned to London to bolster a depleted IP group, following the departure of Robin Whaite.

McDermott, Will & Emery's Larry Cohen is a revered all-rounder with an extremely tough reputation and patents experience comparable to most in the City. Recent work includes acting for Hitachi in successfully defending two patents in computer storage systems.

Olswang's experience in the Patents Court stems largely from ongoing instructions from key client Dyson. Other clients include Johnson Matthey and Enercon GmbH. The team also benefits from the skills of registered patent attorney Stephen Carter.

John Runeckles at **White & Case** has a strong patents practice. Recent highlights include acting for Princo GmbH in its ongoing dispute with Philips over recordable CD technology.

IP: TRADE MARK FILING AND OPPOSITION

Quality, not quantity, is the key to a leading filing and opposition practice within a law firm, and **Field Fisher Waterhouse** achieves both with considerable aplomb. Clients such as Warner Bros, Kettle Foods and Apple Computers praise the firm and particularly lead partner John Olsen. The firm leads this section because it is committed to making this service a profitable, thriving part of its business.

Baker & McKenzie handles the trade mark portfolios of BAT, Oracle and Tommy Hilfiger. Its strength in both opposition work and anti-counterfeiting strategy make it a popular choice for luxury brand clients.

Clifford Chance LLP has a superb pedigree in providing a holistic brands service to clients such as Gap, Mars and Whitbread.

Dechert's Paul Kavanagh is praised for commercial nous and approachability, providing cost-effective advice on all aspects of managing a trade mark portfolio. Clients include JMC and Oasis.

IP: TRADE MARK FILING AND OPPOSITION

FIELD FISHER WATERHOUSE

BAKER & McKENZIE ✪
CLIFFORD CHANCE LLP
DECHERT

Berwin Leighton Paisner
Bristows
Linklaters ✪
Manches
Nabarro Nathanson
Olswang
Pinsents *Leeds*
SJ Berwin ✪
Simmons & Simmons ✪

Firms are listed A-Z in tiers which are ranked in order of priority
✪ Indicates firm displays contact details at the end of this chapter.

INFORMATION TECHNOLOGY

Partner Laurence Jacobs at **Allen & Overy** heads an impressive practice that covers the range of advice required by most clients. Big-ticket outsourcing deals for customers such as Barclays and suppliers including EDS feature heavily in the firm's successful year. Partner Sasha Haines is recommended for IT litigation, while international communications, media and technology group head Ian Ferguson is recommended for corporate matters.

Baker & McKenzie has one of the leading technology practices in London. The integrated team acts for a broad range of IT suppliers and customers and also handles heavyweight contentious matters. Last year these included first-time instructions from ICL (now Fujitsu Services) on its high-profile dispute with CWS. Rated partners include IP and IT heavyweight Harry Small, regulatory specialist Robbie Downing, and global ITC practice head Michael Hart. The firm continued to advise 3G on its roll-out, and Bank of Bermuda on two parallel outsourcing deals.

Bird & Bird has an excellent reputation for IT outsourcing transactions; clients include Lloyds TSB, Mastercard, AXA, and BT. Partners Hamish Sandison and Roger Bickerstaff are recommended for major projects, while Graham Smith is well regarded for litigation.

Clifford Chance LLP maintains a 'rock-solid' focus on IT with a team headed by one of the City's most-respected, if understated, IT lawyers, David Griffiths. Highlights include advising ABN Amro on its €1.3bn IT agreement with EDS. Partner Iain Roxborough is recommended for IT litigation.

Barlow Lyde & Gilbert's IT team continues to grow in depth and visibility. The arrival of former **Shaw Pittman LLP** outsourcing expert Chris Holder confirms the firm's fast progress. Group head David Strang, Kit Burden, and Simon Shooter are all well regarded. PwC, Cap Gemini Ernst & Young, and 3 are key clients.

'A phoenix from the ashes' is how one client described **DLA**'s IT team. The firm enjoyed instructions from Transport for London on its £230m deal with Capita for London's congestion charging scheme. Non-contentious head Danelle Dinsdale is 'extremely able', while well-known TMT group head and contentious specialist Julian Stait is highly thought of.

Denton Wilde Sapte maintained its success in the public sector with its work on major projects for the Ministry of Defence. The firm has

INFORMATION TECHNOLOGY

ALLEN & OVERY ✪
BAKER & McKENZIE ✪
BIRD & BIRD ✪
CLIFFORD CHANCE LLP

BARLOW LYDE & GILBERT
DLA ✪
DENTON WILDE SAPTE ✪
FIELD FISHER WATERHOUSE
HERBERT SMITH ✪
KEMP LITTLE LLP
LINKLATERS ✪
LOVELLS ✪
MASONS

Ashurst ✪
Berwin Leighton Paisner
Bristows
Freshfields Bruckhaus Deringer ✪
Mayer, Brown, Rowe & Maw LLP
Nabarro Nathanson
Norton Rose ✪
Olswang
Osborne Clarke
Shaw Pittman LLP
Simmons & Simmons ✪
Taylor Wessing ✪
Wragge & Co LLP ✪

Addleshaw Goddard
CMS Cameron McKenna
Charles Russell
Clyde & Co ✪
Eversheds LLP
Harbottle & Lewis LLP
Nicholson Graham & Jones
Slaughter and May ✪
Stephenson Harwood
Tarlo Lyons
Weil, Gotshal & Manges ✪

Faegre Benson Hobson Audley LLP
Kirkland & Ellis International LLP ✪
McGrigors
Pinsents ✪
Richards Butler
SJ Berwin ✪
Steptoe & Johnson
Tite & Lewis
Withers LLP

Firms are listed A-Z in tiers which are ranked in order of priority
✪ Indicates firm displays contact details at the end of this chapter.

also made inroads into the supplier market, with instructions from EDS and Microsoft. Partner Catherine Bingham is best known for public sector work, while John Worthy has an excellent reputation for non-contentious technology issues. Partner Dan Burge is also highly rated.

Outsourcing in all its forms is a growth area for **Field Fisher Waterhouse**, notwithstanding the general downturn in IT. Key supplier client Accenture continues to instruct the firm on major matters. User clients include HM Treasury, the London Borough of Brent, and Transport for London. Commercial partners Michael Chissick, Nigel Wildish and Paul Barton are recommended for all IT matters.

Herbert Smith has an excellent reputation for both contentious (Nick Gardner) and non-contentious (Christopher Rees and Mark Turner) IT. Highlights include advising IMS on a worldwide data privacy audit; and Vodafone on a £100m dispute with ntl.

TMT boutique **Kemp Little LLP**'s name partner Richard Kemp's quality and the firm's industry focus helped win work from Deloitte & Touche, ICI Business Legal Services, and Toshiba Information Systems, while continuing to handle work for EDS.

Linklaters continues to win major instructions in the outsourcing sector and big-ticket matters generally. The team, led by IT partner John Crozier and 'all-rounder' Graeme Maguire, advised Unilever on the €1bn, seven-year contract for BT to manage and develop its entire global communications infrastructure.

Lovells has an understated strength to its IT team that clients appreciate. Low-key stars include IT all-rounders Quentin Archer, Conor Ward and the reputed data protection specialist Heather Rowe. Recent highlights include advising OM Grupen on its equity derivatives exchange and Loyalty Management UK on the launch of the Nectar loyalty card.

Masons' decision to focus on public sector projects brought it roles in six projects totalling £6.5bn capital value within the first three months of 2003. The firm has a leading reputation for contentious IT matters, with partners Clive Seddon and Robert McCallough both highly regarded. Highlights included advising Boots on a major IT outsourcing. Shelagh Gaskill is particularly recommended for data protection.

Ashurst's team is primarily recommended for non-contentious matters, although it has been involved in IT litigation for clients including IBM and Smith & Nephew. Partner Mark Lubbock heads the team.

Berwin Leighton Paisner has in Amanda Lewis a partner steeped in IT. She advises Tesco on its IT projects. The team also advised the FT and FT.com on a major new knowledge-management system. Partner Adam Rose heads the firm's tech-media group.

Some two-thirds of **Bristows**' lawyers have technology or engineering backgrounds. Primarily an IP-focused outfit with a reputation for litigation, the team features renowned patent litigator Philip Westmacott. The firm acted for Fujitsu and VIA Technologies.

M&A dominates the IT practice at **Freshfields Bruckhaus Deringer**, which advised HP on its merger with Compaq. However, this experience led to first-time global outsourcing instructions from HP. The solid team features the 'personable' Avril Martindale, and Richard Lister.

Mayer, Brown, Rowe & Maw LLP partner Mark Prinsley has a reputation for 'considered advice' in transactional IT. The growth area of offshore outsourcing provided one of his team's key deals, with Prinsley advising AMP on the outsourcing of applications development and maintenance services to Tata Consulting Services in India. Partner Andrew Scott is one to watch.

Nabarro Nathanson successfully advised the London Borough of Greenwich on its major IT outsourcing project, raising the team's profile in public sector maters. Practice head Paul Golding and outsourcing specialist partner Andrew Smith are both well known.

Norton Rose TMT head Mike Rebeiro continues to propel his supplier-focused team forward, winning significant big-ticket outsourcing projects in particular for market leaders such as Siemens, Capita, Xchanging and TXU.

Olswang saw its technology team boosted by the arrival of a Thames Valley team from the collapsed *Garretts*, and former TMT head Tony Leifer and IT partner Clive Davies join from the ashes of *D J Freeman*. The team advised BBC Technology on its arrangements for the launch of Freeview and Whitbread on its IT outsourcing to CSC.

The team at **Osborne Clarke**, headed by the highly regarded Simon Rendell, advises clients such as Microsoft, Adobe, and Vodafone as well as customers such as MFI, Bass and Citibank.

Shaw Pittman LLP is reputed to be one of London's premier customer-focused outsourcing outfits. The loss of Chris Holder, Andrew Moyle and Jenifer Mattingly dented that position in 2003. TMT expert and current London managing partner Alistair Maughan continues to be recommended for complex and global IT transactions.

Simmons & Simmons is predominantly involved in large IT projects for users, especially but not exclusively in the public sector. Global head of TMT, David Barrett's team was considerably strengthened by the arrival of outsourcing specialist Michael Sinclair. Highlights include advising the Office of the e-Envoy on several IT projects.

Taylor Wessing, which is distinguished by its longstanding IP expertise and US connections is particularly recommended for e-commerce, outsourcings, and major systems procurement. UK partners Glyn Morgan and Kiran Sandford are the firm's best-known IT specialists. Deal highlights include a hat-trick of major projects for software house AVT, and a major outsourcing for NCR.

Wragge & Co LLP, though primarily Birmingham-based, regularly competes for and wins major London instructions.

INSOLVENCY AND CORPORATE RECOVERY

Allen & Overy has lost high-profile insolvency partner Nick Segal to **Davis Polk & Wardwell** in New York. His departure leaves just Gordon Stewart from the trio recruited from *Cameron Markby Hewitt*, which propelled the firm to the top in this market. However, the firm's relationships with top investment banks ensure that it continues to be a main player in restructuring. Key transactions include advising on the restructurings of Marconi, SAirGroup, Telewest and TXU.

Clifford Chance LLP has had a strong year acting on a number of key deals. Relationships with the investment banks play a large part in the firm's success. The team is led by Mark Hyde, but Nicholas Frome is also highly recommended by clients. Highlights include acting for Deloitte & Touche on ITV Digital.

Denton Wilde Sapte has a large team that works across a broad range of sectors. Mark Andrews is widely praised by clients for his 'brilliance' while Graham Paine and Mark Gill are also recommended. The firm advised a UK-based finance house and the provisional liquidators on the insolvency and restructuring of Cenargo Group.

Linklaters has developed a first-class team in the last three years and is currently involved in a number of high-profile matters. Led by Robert Elliot, the 14-partner team advises a mixture of insolvency practitioners, lenders and corporates.

Freshfields Bruckhaus Deringer group head Peter Bloxham leads a four-partner team in the UK which has particular expertise in the aircraft, telecoms, power and insurance markets. Recent work includes advising Telewest Communications and Global Crossing International.

Herbert Smith has a high-profile team led by Stephen Gale, which has been involved in a number of key cases. Examples include advising TXU on its European restructuring, advising Arthur Andersen following the collapse of Enron and advising BSkyB on the administration and subsequent liquidation of ITV Digital.

The **Lovells** team's experience spans a broad section of industries but it is particularly well known for its insurance practice. It is also renowned for its work in relation to contentious matters. Key instructions include advising TXU Europe on its restructuring and acting for the UK liquidators of Swissair.

CMS Cameron McKenna's team is led by Duncan Aldred and fellow partner Rita Lowe is also highly regarded. The firm is acting for the Department for Transport on the administration of Railtrack and advising Ernst & Young as the administrators of TXU.

INSOLVENCY AND CORPORATE RECOVERY

ALLEN & OVERY ✪
CLIFFORD CHANCE LLP
DENTON WILDE SAPTE ✪
LINKLATERS ✪

FRESHFIELDS BRUCKHAUS DERINGER ✪
HERBERT SMITH ✪
LOVELLS ✪

CMS CAMERON McKENNA

BINGHAM McCUTCHEN LLP
CADWALADER, WICKERSHAM & TAFT LLP

Sidley Austin Brown & Wood
Slaughter and May ✪
Weil, Gotshal & Manges ✪

Ashurst ✪
DLA ✪
Norton Rose ✪

Baker & McKenzie ✪
Berwin Leighton Paisner
Debevoise & Plimpton LLP ✪
Jones Day ✪
Kirkland & Ellis International LLP ✪
Latham & Watkins ✪
Lawrence Graham
Mayer, Brown, Rowe & Maw LLP
Nabarro Nathanson
Orrick, Herrington & Sutcliffe
Richards Butler
SJ Berwin ✪
Shearman & Sterling (London) LLP
Simmons & Simmons ✪
Stephenson Harwood
Travers Smith Braithwaite
White & Case ✪

continued

INSOLVENCY AND CORPORATE RECOVERY (continued)

Addleshaw Goddard
Bird & Bird ✪
Bryan Cave
Clyde & Co ✪
Eversheds LLP
Field Fisher Waterhouse
Halliwell Landau
Hammonds
Holman Fenwick & Willan ✪
Kennedys
Moon Beever
Olswang
Taylor Wessing ✪

Beachcroft Wansbroughs
Charles Russell
Davenport Lyons
Davies Arnold Cooper
Dechert
Field Fisher Waterhouse
Fladgate Fielder
Manches
Nicholson Graham & Jones
RadcliffesLeBrasseur
Reynolds Porter Chamberlain
Withers LLP

Firms are listed A-Z in tiers which are ranked in order of priority
✪ *Indicates firm displays contact details at the end of this chapter.*

The 'excellent' duo of James Roome and Barry Russell at **Bingham McCutchen LLP** represent bondholders and noteholders in public and private restructurings. Examples include SwissAir Finance, Elektrim, Texon, Energis and Albert Fisher Group.

Cadwalader, Wickersham & Taft LLP's Andrew Wilkinson leads a team with a niche in bondholder restructuring. The firm has been involved at bondholder level with many of the major restructurings including NTL, Brunner Mond and Polestar. Wilkinson is widely acknowledged for his aggressive approach.

Last year **Sidley Austin Brown & Wood** took on partner Patrick Corr from **Pinsents**, where he was head of the corporate recovery team. With fellow partner Robin Parsons, the team has been involved in some cutting-edge restructuring work, including acting for Federal-Mogul Corporation and subsidiaries on Chapter 11 proceedings.

Despite lacking a dedicated insolvency team, **Slaughter and May** is involved in a number of major cases on the back of its corporate relationships. Led by Jonathan Rushworth the team is currently advising Ernst & Young as administrators of Railtrack. On the contentious side it is advising COLT in connection with a dispute with Highberry Limited.

Weil, Gotshal & Manges has taken on Chris Mallon from **Freshfields Bruckhaus Deringer** to set up an insolvency practice. The focus to date has been co-ordinating all non-US elements of restructuring for clients Enron, WorldCom and Global Crossing.

Ashurst's insolvency team is led by Nick Angel, who relocated from the Frankfurt office last year. The team combines corporate, litigation, banking and property lawyers and a large proportion of the work is derived from the firm's corporate client base. Highlights include advising KPMG as the administrative receivers of The Albert Fisher Group.

DLA has lost its head of insolvency Peter Cranston to **Gordons** in Leeds. The London team is now headed by Simon Neilson-Clark, who has strong relationships with the mid-tier insolvency practitioners.

Norton Rose has a diverse team, led by Richard Calnan, specialising in financial services, property, technology and insurance. The firm advised TXU on the restructuring and administration of TXU Europe. Hamish Anderson is highly recommended.

Baker & McKenzie's insolvency team, led by the 'capable' Jeremy Goldring, has a focus on corporate-driven restructurings, particularly in the TMT sector. It also has a steady flow of instructions from UK insolvency practitioners. Highlights last year include advising Genuity Inc and Metromedia Fiber and acting for Home Shopping Networks on its restructuring.

Berwin Leighton Paisner has a successful practice, led by David Leibowitz, advising mid-tier accountancy firms. It also has good relationships with Royal Bank of Scotland and Lloyds TSB. Highlights include advising Ford Credit and RBS on the receivership of the Quartic Motor Group.

Debevoise & Plimpton LLP advises on global restructurings. Highlights include advising Carrier 1 International on its pan-European restructuring.

Jones Day's team, which is headed by Barry Donnelly, advises on a mixture of contentious and non-contentious matters. Highlights include advising the administrative receivers and investors in the investigation of the collapse of the Finelist group. The firm has been involved in a number of restructurings including advising United Airlines on its Chapter 11 consequences and advising the equity holders of Callahan NRW on the insolvency of its German holding company.

Kirkland & Ellis recruited Lyndon Norley from **Cadwalader, Wickersham & Taft LLP** to set up an insolvency practice. The firm has been involved in a number of restructurings for debtors including advising the equity holders of Callahan NRW on the insolvency of its German holding company.

Latham & Watkins has poached John Houghton from **Simmons & Simmons** to set up an insolvency practice.

Lawrence Graham's head of insolvency, John Verrill, has a good name among insolvency practitioners. The firm has acted for the directors of WorldCom's European subsidiaries following the parent company's placement in Chapter 11.

Mayer, Brown, Rowe & Maw LLP's insolvency and corporate recovery department is led by David Allen and Ian Coles. The team advises a range of creditors, accountants and corporate and individual clients across a broad section of industries. It advised group companies and shareholders on the restructuring of Interoute.

Nabarro Nathanson's insolvency team spans tactical, preventative and transaction-planning advice to turnarounds and formal insolvencies. The team is led by Patricia Godfrey, who has considerable European experience and also heads the German practice. Recent successes include advising the Dutch trustee in the bankruptcy of SwissAir Finance.

Orrick, Herrington & Sutcliffe's Adrian Harris heads the firm's European insolvency and restructuring practice. He has been joined in London by Tony Pinci, formerly a New York partner and co-chair of the firm's bankruptcy and restructuring practice. The group focuses on bondholder and secured lender work.

Richards Butler's three-partner team, which is led by Jonathan Yorke, advises both corporates and individuals but has particular expertise in the insurance sector. New recruit Celia Gardiner advises both banks and borrowers, particularly in the area of debt restructuring.

SJ Berwin has a good corporate and venture capitalist client base. Insolvency practitioners describe department head Stephen Maffey as excellent.

Shearman & Sterling (London) LLP has been active in debt restructuring, particularly in the field of European telecoms. Led by Pamela Gibson, the team has advised on the $1.7bn restructuring of Versatel.

Simmons & Simmons' Peter Manning has a strong reputation in the market; the firm advised Ofgem in relation to Enron, British Energy and TXU. It also advised long-term corporate client Railtrack on its administration.

Stephenson Harwood has a 14-partner team, led by Paul Gordon-Saker, which advises on everything from major restructuring and insolvencies to small bankruptcies and voluntary arrangements. Key cases include acting for Ernst & Young as joint administrators of Daewoo Cars.

Travers Smith Braithwaite's restructuring practice is headed by Keith Bordell. It advises banks, corporates and investors, and clients include The Royal Bank of Scotland and Bridgepoint.

White & Case recruited Dan Hamilton from **CMS Cameron McKenna** to head up a restructuring and insolvency team. The firm has a particular focus on the utilities sector and its London and New York teams are advising UPC in relation to its worldwide restructuring.

INSURANCE: CORPORATE AND REGULATORY

Clifford Chance LLP boasts a large team of specialists giving it 'an ability to put sheer numbers of bodies with insurance expertise on to a transaction quickly'. Top names include corporate lawyer Katherine Coates, and Nicholas Munday, an expert in Lloyd's regulatory issues. The past year saw the firm advise on an impressive list of international deals, such as the complex 'insurance wrapping' of Hong Kong Mortgage Corporation's mortgage securitisation. Corporate experience also includes capital raisings for insurers (eg Standard Life's £500m and €750m subordinated bond issues).

Lovells continues to advise on groundbreaking deals such as CAN Re's sale to Tawa, the largest and most complex sale of a company in run-off. John Young is the single most highly rated lawyer in this practice area, combining experience and intellect with 'an ability to allow his team to play to their own particular strengths'. John Davidson is recommended for Lloyd's market work, while Charles Rix has a good reputation in life assurance. Clients include ACE, Equitable Life and Prudential.

Freshfields Bruckhaus Deringer services a mix of life and non-life insurers such as Swiss Re, Prudential, Irish Life and Allianz with two full-time

INSURANCE: CORPORATE AND REGULATORY

CLIFFORD CHANCE LLP
LOVELLS ✪

FRESHFIELDS BRUCKHAUS DERINGER ✪
HERBERT SMITH ✪
NORTON ROSE ✪

Allen & Overy ✪
Ashurst ✪
Linklaters ✪
Slaughter and May ✪

Barlow Lyde & Gilbert
Clyde & Co ✪
Dechert
Ince & Co
Kendall Freeman
Pinsents ✪

Charles Russell
Elborne Mitchell
Eversheds LLP
Holman Fenwick & Willan ✪
LeBoeuf, Lamb, Greene & MacRae
Speechly Bircham

Firms are listed A-Z in tiers which are ranked in order of priority
✪ Indicates firm displays contact details at the end of this chapter.

insurance partners, assisted by able corporate lawyers such as India expert Pratap Amin. There has been a recent increase in outsourcing and distribution work for the team, including Prudential's profits bonds distribution agreement with Abbey National.

While **Herbert Smith** has historically been known for its life insurance practice, the firm is now advising a client base split 50:50 between life and non-life. The team gained new client Global Aerospace. Recent work includes Swiss Life's SFr1.1bn capital raising. Geoffrey Maddock is recommended for life insurance and Adam Levitt for non-life.

A practice that has 'come into the limelight relatively recently,' **Norton Rose** is praised by clients as a 'balanced group that's good at transactions but also strong on operational day-to-day matters'. The team, headed by James Bateson, is particularly recommended for Lloyd's market work. Cheryl Ronaldson scooped the lead adviser role on Beazley's £150m IPO – the first Lloyd's IPO since 1998. Maria Ross is building a reputation for outsourcing work; she advised National Australia Insurance on its £317m arrangement with Junction Outsourcing.

Allen & Overy has built a substantial practice which wins praise for its 'excellent client handling' and is particularly recommended for portfolio transfer work. The team advised Aegon, one of the largest life insurance groups in the world, on its €3.5bn global share offering – the largest such offering in Europe at the time.

Lloyd's expert Jeremy Hill, a 'shrewd, level-headed and upbeat lawyer', is the force behind **Ashurst**'s practice. His team also includes Vivienne de Chermont. The pan-European practice advises several Bermuda-based insurers such as Goshawk Re, and has attracted new clients including Munich Re, GE Insurance Holdings and the BMA.

Alan Barker's practice at **Linklaters** is best known for insurance M&A and has been involved in several private deals over the year, such as Irish Life's £100m disposal of its industrial assurance business and RSA's €90m sale of German subsidiaries. The reputation of corporate insurance partner Duncan Barber is growing.

Slaughter and May's transaction-focused practice has enjoyed a busy year, advising among others, Legal & General and Canada Life on M&A. The department's reputation is largely down to Glen James, who has 'unsurpassed coal-face knowledge and experience in the application of insurance law'. Charles Randell is an M&A generalist who wins praise from insurer clients.

Barlow Lyde & Gilbert's contentious practice, for which it is best known, is thriving. Clients include Chubb, PWS International and Sterling Insurance Group.

The contentious practice at insurance/reinsurance specialist **Clyde & Co** also dominates, though the firm's excellent reputation for Lloyd's work has led to some sizeable non-contentious instructions. Examples include Lloyd's syndicate Marketform's acquisition of an interest in Marketform Holdings from UnionAmerica. Andrew Holderness has 'good commercial sense'.

Historically a niche Lloyd's practice, **Dechert** is expanding into non-Lloyd's insurance. Transactions in the past year included Primary Investment Group's acquisition of third-party schemes from UK Insurance and Dukes Place's acquisition of NWRe Group.

At **Ince & Co**, David Coupe 's practice handled the group reorganisations of two independent Lloyd's brokers, two business transfers worth over $20m each and the development of several new insurance products during the year.

Kendall Freeman has restructured itself as an insurance practice following the departure of much of its property and media departments to **Olswang**. Team head Richard Spiller 's transaction list includes the flotation of PRI Group. At £130m, this was the largest ever AIM flotation. On the regulatory side, Ambereen Salamat and other partners advised on ART transactions worth around $400m. Active clients included Mitsui Sumitomo, Deutsche Bank and Partner Re.

Pinsents is 'well-attuned to clients' in non-life insurance and reinsurance. While the firm's international M&A practice cannot compete with those of the top-tier players, it provides a sound alternative for regulatory advice and medium-sized deals. The team was boosted in 2002 by the arrival as head of department of Tim Burton, former general counsel at Benfield Group. Martin Membery also stands out.

INSURANCE/REINSURANCE LITIGATION

Barlow Lyde & Gilbert's dedicated insurance team is highly praised by clients for its 'practical and friendly' approach. Highlights of the year include representing brokers in the reactivated Minet/Kennecott mining case. Partners Roger Doulton, John Hanson and Sheila Simison all have a high degree of expertise. Yvonne Jefferies is also recommended. Reinsurance is a key strength of the firm; partner Colin Croly has an excellent knowledge of the insurance market. Michael Mendelowitz, Tim Hardy and Clive O'Connell are highly effective reinsurance litigators.

CMS Cameron McKenna's solid practice gained some big client wins from US insurers during the year. The team performs a good deal of construction- and film finance-related work. Partners Belinda Schofield, Mark Elborne, Stephen Tester, Anthony Hobkinson, Liam O'Connell and Maxine Cupitt all receive high praise from clients.

Insurance-focused **Clyde & Co** boasts considerable presence in the worldwide insurance market. The strong team has many talented insurance experts, including Michael Payton, Peter Farthing, Rod Smith, Jane Andrewartha and Nigel Chapman. Nigel Brook is particularly recommended for reinsurance. Active clients include Riverstone Management, ACE and Faraday.

Ince & Co's booming practice includes experienced experts Anthony Fitzsimmons, Chris Jefferis and Alan Weir, all of whom are proficient in both insurance and reinsurance matters. Key clients include ACE USA and White & Williams.

Terry O'Neill heads the well-resourced practice at **Clifford Chance LLP**, supported by leading names Nicholas Munday, Stephen Lewis, Philip Rocher and Leon Boshoff. Clients include AXA, Manulife and Sun Life of Canada.

Highly experienced partner David Reston heads the team at **Herbert Smith**. The practice specialises in complex, high-value cases, which often involve an international element. Partners Martin Bakes and Tony Dempster are recommended, while Terry Mehigan is described by clients as 'very commercial and straightforward'.

Norton Rose attracts an increasing amount of very high-value litigation. New reinsurance clients include Swiss Re, Northwestern National Insurance Co and ING Re. Practice head Francis Mackie is praised for his 'proactive attitude'.

At **Allen & Overy**, partners Joanna Page and Maurice Kenton form a formidable team. The pair are 'outstanding advocates'. Partner David Mackie QC is also recommended.

Berwin Leighton Paisner features in the table as a result of its thriving reinsurance practice, which achieved a 60% increase in turnover during the year. Jonathan Sacher, Anthony Lennox and Andrew Rose are all recommended.

Elborne Mitchell's practice head Tim Akeroyd is recommended for insurance, reinsurance and professional indemnity work, while Jolyon Patten heads the reinsurance side. Partner Rosalind Jones specialises in Names litigation at Lloyd's.

INSURANCE/REINSURANCE LITIGATION

BARLOW LYDE & GILBERT
CMS CAMERON McKENNA
CLYDE & CO ✪
INCE & CO

CLIFFORD CHANCE LLP
HERBERT SMITH ✪
NORTON ROSE ✪

Allen & Overy ✪
Berwin Leighton Paisner
Elborne Mitchell
Eversheds LLP
Freshfields Bruckhaus Deringer ✪
Holman Fenwick & Willan ✪
Kendall Freeman
Kennedys
Lovells ✪
Mayer, Brown, Rowe & Maw LLP
Reynolds Porter Chamberlain
Richards Butler
Slaughter and May ✪

Ashurst ✪
Baker & McKenzie ✪
Beachcroft Wansbroughs
Berrymans Lace Mawer
Bryan Cave
Charles Russell
Davies Arnold Cooper
Davies Lavery
Denton Wilde Sapte ✪
Fishburns
Hill Taylor Dickinson
Lawrence Graham
LeBoeuf, Lamb, Greene & MacRae
Middleton Potts
Mills & Reeve
Pinsents ✪
Simmons & Simmons ✪
Stephenson Harwood
Taylor Wessing ✪

Firms are listed A-Z in tiers which are ranked in order of priority
✪ Indicates firm displays contact details at the end of this chapter.

Eversheds LLP's active insurance practice was appointed by Center Parcs in a £74m claim against insurers, and advised a major market aviation broker on an EC cartel investigation. Anton Eisdell, David Webster and Simon Brooks are all recommended for insurance work, while David Murphy is an established expert in reinsurance.

Freshfields Bruckhaus Deringer is involved in some large-scale litigation for clients such as Sony Pictures Entertainment, Lloyd's and Aon Risk Services. Raj Parker heads the group. Roger Enock and Geoffrey Nicholas are also recommended.

Holman Fenwick & Willan's active department advises on a broad range of matters, from oil spillages to the Hatfield rail crash. Practice head John Duff has an excellent reputation, while Andrew Bandurka is highly recommended for reinsurance.

Kendall Freeman retains a strong insurance practice, acting for clients such as St Paul, TIG, Kemper and Chubb Atlantic. Practice head David Kendall is described as 'insightful and responsive'.

Under the leadership of senior partner Nick Thomas, niche practice **Kennedys** offers an excellent service for high-volume claims work. Steve Cantle is also recommended. The firm acts for clients including AIG and Royal & SunAlliance.

Lovells has a strong practice focused on corporate insureds; work includes acting for KPMG on the collapse of Australian insurers HIH. Practice head John F Powell is praised by clients while John Trotter is also highly esteemed.

Mayer, Brown, Rowe & Maw LLP performs an increasing amount of multi-jurisdictional work, including advice to reinsurers on the PA LMX spiral, and advice on the collapse of HIH in Australia. Karen Abbott heads the reinsurance group. On the insurance side, the firm has been instructed by several leading insurers in relation to asbestos claims.

Niche practice **Reynolds Porter Chamberlain** receives some extremely high-quality instructions; one highlight of the year involved advising reinsurers of the Brazilian state on a fire at a steel-processing plant which caused £85m of damage. Client-friendly Tim House heads the practice, backed up by highly knowledgeable partners Simon Greenley and Simon Kilgour.

Richards Butler has been particularly active in film finance-related work over the year, acting for clients such as Asset Backed Capital Ltd. It also acted for Stirling Cooke Brown in a personal accident excess of loss case. Mark Connoley heads the department, which includes highly regarded Margaret Campbell and Kyri Evagora.

Slaughter and May's results-driven practice acts for prestigious clients such as Marsh & McLennan, Cox Insurance, Colonial and Willis Group. Practice head Richard Clark and Richard Swallow are highly thought of. Partners Sarah Lee and Efstathios Michael are also highly esteemed.

INTERNATIONAL CAPITAL MARKETS: DEBT AND EQUITY

This section recommends UK law firms with strong UK debt and equity practices and US law firms with dual capability. The firms in the top tier have strong ties to investment banks and receive regular instructions and referrals on both the debt and the equity deals. Firms have also been ranked according to their US capability, which is vital for European and Asian issuers keen to tap the US capital markets.

Allen & Overy has a leading international capital markets team on both the debt and equity sides. The 40-partner group, led by Boyan

Wells, offers high-quality advice for the full range of financings, with the infrastructure to back it up. Quality is consistent across the board, though clients praise in particular Roger Wedderburn-Day and David Wootton for equity, Matthew Hartley for debt and Angus Duncan for structured finance.

In the last few years **Linklaters** has developed a debt practice that matches the strength of its equity practice. Despite the declining markets, the firm has been active in equity-linked and regulatory capital work. Highlights include issues for Burberry, Investec, SAB Miller and Xstrata on the equity side, and a high-yield debt offering for Bluewater Finance. Nick Eastwell, who is widely praised for his brilliance, is global head of capital markets. Clients also recommend Keith Thomson, Nigel Pridmore and Carson Welsh on the equity-linked side.

With capital markets expertise in virtually every jurisdiction, **Clifford Chance LLP** offers a truly global service. Despite the sluggish equity markets, the firm advised the underwriters on the William Hill IPO. However the bulk of its activity is on the debt side where it saw a strong flow across the board including European commercial paper, MTN programmes and Eurobond issues. Daniel Bushner is renowned for work on SEC-registered offerings. David Dunnigan and Stewart Dunlop are both recommended.

While **Freshfields Bruckhaus Deringer** has eschewed developing a straight debt practice, it is undoubtedly a top-tier practice on the equity side. The firm acted on issues by Burberry, Detica, HMV, Intertek Testing Services and William Hill. The firm was also active in the convertible and exchangeable markets where it advised on key transactions for ABB, Deutsche, Lufthansa and Fortis. Don Guiney, Ken Martin and Sarah Murphy have considerable experience in SEC-registered deals. Head of department Tim Jones is recommended.

Herbert Smith is recommended by clients as a top-tier practice for domestic equity work, although it is becoming increasingly active on global issues. Partners James Palmer and Henry Raine are singled out for their expertise. Key transactions include acting on rights issues for Swiss Life, easyJet and Enodis. Highlights include advising HBOS on the reorganisation of the group's regulatory capital structure.

Norton Rose consolidated its international strength, gaining a presence in Holland and integrating the German practice to take full advantage of cross referrals. The firm is stronger in the equity and equity-linked markets, where Mark Bankes and US-qualified partner Tom Vita, who is an expert in SEC-registered deals, are held in high esteem by the banks. Cheryl Ronaldson led a team advising Lloyd's syndicate Beazley Group on its £167m IPO.

Shearman & Sterling (London) LLP has a leading global capital markets practice specialising in SEC-registered offerings, Rule 144a and other placements of equity and equity-linked stock. Highlights include the $1.7bn Versatel restructuring, the $10.6bn restructuring for NTL and the IPO and subsequent €575m refinancing for Alfa Laval.

Slaughter and May has a very strong issuer practice on the equity side, led by George Goulding. The firm was involved in a number of the market's most high-profile transactions, including Punch Taverns, ASM Brescia and China Telecom's IPO. On the debt side, a team led by Sanjev Warna-kula-suriya advised Abbey National on two Tier 1 capital securities.

Baker & McKenzie has a burgeoning CIS capital markets practice and is particularly active in Russia. The firm has a weaker presence in the domestic market, but a bias towards the TMT sector means it advised on London listings for Taiwanese computer company Acer and optical components company Asia Optical.

INTERNATIONAL CAPITAL MARKETS: DEBT AND EQUITY

ALLEN & OVERY ✪
LINKLATERS ✪

CLIFFORD CHANCE LLP
FRESHFIELDS BRUCKHAUS DERINGER ✪

HERBERT SMITH ✪
NORTON ROSE ✪
SHEARMAN & STERLING (LONDON) LLP
SLAUGHTER AND MAY ✪

Baker & McKenzie ✪
Cleary Gottlieb Steen & Hamilton ✪
Latham & Watkins ✪
Simmons & Simmons ✪
White & Case ✪

Ashurst ✪
Lovells ✪
Milbank, Tweed, Hadley & McCloy
Sidley Austin Brown & Wood
Skadden, Arps, Slate, Meagher & Flom LLP
Weil, Gotshal & Manges ✪

Cadwalader, Wickersham & Taft LLP
Debevoise & Plimpton LLP ✪
Dewey Ballantine
Fried, Frank, Harris, Shriver & Jacobson (London) LLP ✪
LeBoeuf, Lamb, Greene & MacRae
Mayer, Brown, Rowe & Maw LLP
McDermott, Will & Emery ✪

CMS Cameron McKenna
Denton Wilde Sapte ✪
Travers Smith Braithwaite
Watson, Farley & Williams

Firms are listed A-Z in tiers which are ranked in order of priority
✪ Indicates firm displays contact details at the end of this chapter.

Cleary Gottlieb Steen & Hamilton has dual capability in London, a strong presence in France, Germany and Brussels and a good relationship with the investment banks. Highlights include advising the underwriters on a $775m offering by the Government of the Russian Federation of 50 million shares of AOA LUKOIL.

Latham & Watkins has a global reputation for its high-yield expertise and private placement work. However, it is also building a significant practice on the equity side. It advised Ericsson on a $3.25bn SEC-registered rights issue. Christopher McFadzean and Bryant Edwards are well known in the market.

Simmons & Simmons' team, led by Jeremy Hoyland, has a strong niche in repackagings. The firm advised on 19 structured note programmes and documented nearly 400 transactions for clients including Deutsche Bank, Lehman Brothers and UBS Warburg. Tony Smith and Helen Hancock are recommended.

White & Case is developing a pre-eminent position in capital markets in the CIS and Eastern Europe, particularly Turkey, Poland, The Czech Republic, Kazakhstan and Russia. The firm advised on the debut Eurobond offerings by Russia's largest bank, Alfa Bank. It is also a main player in the European high-yield bond market and advised Deutsche Bank on the Klöckner deal. The team is led by Rachel Hatfield and Francis Fitzherbert-Brockholes.

Ashurst focuses on equity capital markets and structured finance. The firm advised Imperial Tobacco Group on a rights issue and high-yield bond offer to fund the company's €5.8bn acquisition of tobacco company Reemtsma Cigarettenfabriken.

David Hudd at **Lovells** leads the team which advises on a mixture of debt and equity work. Highlights include advising Barclays Bank as the issuer of $1.4bn Tier 1 Capital and acting for Wellington Underwriting on a £74m equity capital raising.

Milbank, Tweed, Hadley & McCloy's team led by Tom Siebens focuses on structured finance and high-yield debt. Structured finance partner Andrew Brodie joined from **Allen & Overy**, adding strength. The firm advised the lead managers on the $260m high-yield bond for Bluewater Group.

Sidley Austin Brown & Wood has a strong name in capital markets and Hugh Frome and Mark Walsh hold sway with clients despite the loss of four partners.

Skadden, Arps, Slate, Meagher & Flom LLP advises on a mixture of debt and equity securities. Highlights for the team, led by James Healy, include representing the underwriters on a high-yield note issue by The Big Food Group and acting for the privatisation of Telkom SA.

Weil, Gotshal & Manges' capital markets practice, led by Mike Francis, is equity-based. Key deals include acting for Imperial Tobacco Group on its £1bn rights issues to fund its €5.8bn acquisition of Reemtsma Cigarettenfabriken.

MERGERS AND ACQUISITIONS

There are several points that clients highlight when asked to assess **Freshfields Bruckhaus Deringer**'s M&A practice: strength in depth at partner and associate level, international reach and a commercial approach to doing deals. Barry O'Brien remains the principal contact partner for client Tesco and led the team that advised the supermarket giant on its interest in Safeway, while Claire Wills is increasingly shouldering a greater deal volume for the company. David Higgins also stands out for his role alongside lead partner Mark Rawlinson on P&O Princess' merger with Carnival. Add experienced dealmakers Will Lawes, Edward Braham, James Davis and Simon Marchant, and the quality shines through.

The key to the success of **Linklaters**' M&A practice has been a blue-chip corporate client base, coupled with close ties to the investment banks. In recent years **Linklaters** has assiduously strengthened its links with key investment bank contacts. The firm topped the European and worldwide rankings with £84bn and £142bn worth of deals, respectively.

There are few firms worldwide with as strong an M&A brand as **Slaughter and May**. The firm may have eschewed the high-growth, global strategy of its top-tier rivals but in a sense the firm's very strength can be attributed to its tight hold on the partnership reins, ensuring an M&A team of unrivalled quality. Stephen Cooke continues to head the M&A side and maintains links with key clients such as British Airways and Diageo. Nigel Boardman, the head of corporate and one of the city's most respected M&A specialists, led the team that advised Shell on its £3.5bn acquisition of Enterprise Oil.

Allen & Overy reorganised its global corporate practice along sector and product group lines, encompassing industrials and services; financial institutions; communications, media and technology; environment and administration; private equity and equity capital markets. The firm has proved to be particularly adept at picking up new clients, adding the likes of RWE, Petro Canada, Imperial Tobacco and Sungard to its corporate base. Richard Cranfield is the global corporate head alongside Roberto Casati in Milan and Amsterdam-based Sietze Hepkema. In London, key partners in the practice include Mark Dighero, Mark Gearing, Susan Howard, Alan Paul, Jeremy Thomas, Mark Wippell and David Wootton.

Clifford Chance LLP's global head of M&A David Childs and up-and-coming partner Sarah Jones picked up the reins for Philip Morris (now Altria Group) on the disposal of Miller Brewing to South African Breweries. General Electric also turned to **Clifford Chance LLP** on its $2.3bn acquisition of the structured finance business of ABB. London managing partner of corporate David Pearson and partner Adam Signy are most often singled out for their dealmaking nous.

MERGERS AND ACQUISITIONS

FRESHFIELDS BRUCKHAUS DERINGER ✪
LINKLATERS ✪
SLAUGHTER AND MAY ✪

ALLEN & OVERY ✪
CLIFFORD CHANCE LLP
HERBERT SMITH ✪

ASHURST ✪

LOVELLS ✪
NORTON ROSE ✪

MACFARLANES ✪

CMS Cameron McKenna
Simmons & Simmons ✪
Travers Smith Braithwaite

Baker & McKenzie ✪
Denton Wilde Sapte ✪
Jones Day ✪
Mayer, Brown, Rowe & Maw LLP
SJ Berwin ✪
Weil, Gotshal & Manges ✪

Cleary Gottlieb Steen & Hamilton ✪
Latham & Watkins ✪
Shearman & Sterling (London) LLP
Skadden, Arps, Slate, Meagher & Flom LLP
Taylor Wessing ✪
White & Case ✪

Barlow Lyde & Gilbert
Berwin Leighton Paisner
DLA ✪
Dechert
Eversheds LLP
Hammonds
Olswang
Pinsents ✪
Richards Butler
Wragge & Co LLP *Birmingham* ✪

Bird & Bird ✪
Gibson, Dunn & Crutcher LLP
McDermott, Will & Emery ✪
Nabarro Nathanson
Osborne Clarke
Stephenson Harwood
Tite & Lewis
Watson, Farley & Williams

Firms are listed A-Z in tiers which are ranked in order of priority
✪ *Indicates firm displays contact details at the end of this chapter.*

Herbert Smith has continued to bolster its corporate client base. The firm picked up new instructions from Bank of Ireland, lastminute.com and Micromuse. The practice was also to the fore on the restructuring of TXU Europe that included the £1.37bn disposal of TXU's UK gas and power supply businesses to E.ON subsidiary Powergen. The firm has not neglected the investment banking community, winning appointments to Merrill Lynch's panel and CSFB's global panel. Caroline Goodall heads the practice.

Few firms are as steeped in deal making as **Ashurst**. In the face of the downturn in M&A the practice has grown its market share, snaring a number of roles on some recent prime deals – National Grid's merger with Lattice and the disposal of Railtrack to Network Rail both stand out – while maintaining the firm's staple diet of mid-market deals with a heavy private equity slant. Charlie Geffen heads the M&A team and remains arguably the city's most recognisable private equity specialist. On the public side, heavy-weight expertise can be found with corporate head Chris Ashworth. Further corporate specialists include Paul Gadd, David Kershaw, Nigel Stacey and Graeme Ward.

Lovells' had some of the choicest instructions in the market including South African Breweries' $5.6bn acquisition of Miller Brewing, with lead partner John Davidson and his team widely applauded by the market. The firm followed this by picking up the mandate to advise Granada on its merger with Carlton. Head of department Hugh Nineham is leading the team. In the 23-partner corporate team Frances Le Grys, Nigel Read, Richard Ufland and corporate insurance specialist John Young all draw praise for their deal-making skills.

Norton Rose is one of the City's corporate finance stalwarts. The firm has proved to be a leading adviser on M&A in the financial institutions sector and was once again in the limelight, advising key client HSBC on its $15bn takeover of Household Industries. Martin Scott led the team on the deal with partner Nick Adams. The immensely experienced Simon Sackman and London corporate finance head Barbara Stephenson remain the firm's best-known M&A specialists.

Although not as large as many firms in the upper echelons of our table, **Macfarlanes** is widely recognised for the strength of its corporate practice. Recent instructions have come from the likes of Pernod Ricard, Vivendi Universal and Virgin. Clients appreciate the deal-making gravitas of senior partner Robert Sutton. We would also highlight Charles Martin, Simon Martin and Tim Lewis.

CMS Cameron McKenna's role advising National Grid on its merger with Lattice – Europe's largest deal at the time – was an obvious highlight and a clear example of the M&A team's ability to manage long-term relationships. The firm has cemented its links with BP – it acted on the disposal of the upstream business of Veba and the $1.3bn disposal of the Forties field to Apache. Andrew Sheach has been instrumental in expanding this relationship alongside the firm's top-tier oil and gas team. Richard Price is one of the team's leading M&A specialists.

With 75% of its practice based outside of the UK, **Simmons & Simmons**' M&A group has a distinctly international flavour to it. The firm advised KPMG Consulting on the $284m acquisition of Andersen Worldwide's business consulting units, which involved 11 of **Simmons & Simmons**' international offices. On the domestic front, London head of corporate Jerry Walter led the team that acted for Railtrack Plc on its disposal by Railtrack Group to Network Rail.

Travers Smith Braithwaite is widely recognised as a quality corporate outfit. Private equity is a prominent feature of the practice but from public M&A to securities work the firm receives glowing praise. The firm acted for CREST on its immensely complex merger with Euroclear to create the largest pan-European securities settlement system. Experienced figures include Chris Hale, recently ensconced as head of corporate, senior partner Christopher Bell, Oliver Barnes, Charles Barter and Mark Soundy.

Baker & McKenzie's M&A practice operates in three teams covering TMT, public companies and energy, manufacturing and chemicals. This kind of specialisation has enabled the firm to strengthen its relationships with key clients such as Pacific Century, Aquila, BP and Clariant. Highlights include acting for Right Management Consultants on its £74m acquisition of Coutts Consulting Group from 3i. Global head of the practice Tim Gee is based in London, while Hugh Stewart offers further M&A expertise.

The key sector strengths of **Denton Wilde Sapte**'s M&A practice lie in TMT, energy, banking, insurance and manufacturing. A team led by Anthony Alexander advised LE Group on its £1.39bn acquisition of Seeboard. On the TMT side the firm acted for Microsoft in its acquisition of Rare for $375m. Many of the firm's key corporate partners have spent time in the overseas offices.

The merger between *Jones Day/Gouldens* now renamed **Jones Day** brought together one of the longest-established US firms in London and one of the City's most respected mid-market M&A firms. The merged firm brings together the M&A talents of Simon Allport, Russell Carmedy, Peter Faber and Max Thorneycroft.

There is compelling evidence that **Mayer, Brown, Rowe & Maw LLP**'s London M&A team has reaped considerable benefit from the merger of *Mayer Brown & Platt* and *Rowe & Maw*. Historically the latter's strength was always its relationship with a number of key corporates and through the merger these have been strengthened. The firm has integrated an international network of 13 international offices, lending credible cross-border capability. Among the corporate team of 30 partners we would highlight the deal-making contributions of Andrew Copley, Peter Dickinson, senior partner Paul Maher, and Mark Uhrynuk.

A key to the success of **SJ Berwin**'s M&A group is the diversity of its corporate offering. The firm's leading brand in private equity ensures its dealmakers are sated with a consistent dealflow and they continue to demonstrate expertise across a range of sectors including media, technology, property, leisure and retail. The firm advised Musgrave Group, the Irish grocery and food distributor, on its £315.3m offer for Budgens. A further highlight came advising Nice Systems on its cross-border $55m acquisition of Thales Contact Solutions. Partner Steven Davis led on the Nice deal and is one of the firm's principal deal-doers along with Peter Anderson, Robert Burrow and Jonathan Djanogly.

For English-law M&A advice, **Weil, Gotshal & Manges** is a leading player among the US firms in London. Underpinning much of its corporate strength is the private equity practice but in recent times the M&A team has also benefited from the firm's bountiful restructuring workload. In the 11-partner corporate team Mike Francies earns plaudits from clients and competitors alike. Paul Claydon commands a loyal client following particularly in the biotech and healthcare sectors, and new partner Will Rosen is one to watch.

M&A: ALSO RECOMMENDED

Addleshaw Goddard offers M&A expertise across its offices in London, Leeds and Manchester, with a track record for upper mid-level transactions. Sean Lippell leads the corporate group.

Charles Russell, led by Michael Scott and Glafkos Tombolis, acted for Reichold on the cross-border sale of its swift adhesives business for $210m. Partners Simon Gilbert and Mark Moncreiffe are also experienced.

Debevoise & Plimpton LLP has extensive experience in all major M&A areas, including cross-border deals, private equity transactions, and contested takeovers. English partner Colin Bogie is highly regarded, as are US partners James Kiernan and Andrew Sommer.

Dewey Ballantine has seven London partners in its M&A group, including energy specialist Mark Saunders. US partner Stephen Horvath joined from the London office of **Hunton & Williams**. US partner Douglas Getter is the firm's European M&A head.

Fox Williams name partner Tina Williams is an accomplished and sophisticated corporate practitioner. She worked on the acquisition of the Whistles retail chain for Karen Millen Holdings. Paul Osborne is also highly regarded for his corporate finance acumen, particularly in the hi-tech sector.

Hale and Dorr partners Richard Eaton and Struan Penwarden have extensive experience. The firm advises on technology mergers and acquisitions in Europe with an aggregate value of more than $1bn.

Kirkland & Ellis International LLP is best known for its private equity expertise for clients like Madison Dearborn and Bain Capital. Lateral

M&A: ALSO RECOMMENDED

- Addleshaw Goddard
- Charles Russell
- Debevoise & Plimpton LLP ✪
- Dewey Ballantine
- Fox Williams
- Hale and Dorr
- Kirkland & Ellis International LLP ✪
- Lawrence Graham
- LeBoeuf, Lamb, Greene & MacRae
- Lewis Silkin ✪
- Nicholson Graham & Jones
- Reed Smith
- Speechly Bircham

- Collyer-Bristow
- Covington & Burling ✪
- Dorsey & Whitney
- Dundas & Wilson
- Faegre Benson Hobson Audley LLP
- Field Fisher Waterhouse
- Finers Stephens Innocent
- Landwell
- Manches
- McGrigors
- Middleton Potts
- Reynolds Porter Chamberlain
- Wilmer Cutler Pickering LLP ✪

- Arnold & Porter (UK) LLP ✪
- Baker Botts ✪
- Bates, Wells & Braithwaite
- Bircham Dyson Bell
- Boodle Hatfield
- Bristows
- Campbell Hooper
- Clyde & Co ✪
- Coudert Brothers ✪
- Davenport Lyons
- Dawsons
- Dickson Minto WS
- Fladgate Fielder
- Goodman Derrick
- Halliwell Landau
- Harbottle & Lewis LLP
- Howard Kennedy
- Hunton & Williams
- Kemp Little LLP
- Kendall Freeman
- Marriott Harrison
- Masons
- Maclay Murray & Spens
- Mishcon de Reya
- Pritchard Englefield
- RadcliffesLeBrasseur
- Rosenblatt
- Shaw Pittman LLP
- The Simkins Partnership
- Trowers & Hamlins ✪
- Vinson & Elkins R.L.L.P. ✪
- Wallace & Partners

Firms are listed A-Z in tiers which are ranked in order of priority
✪ Indicates firm displays contact details at the end of this chapter.

partner hires include Nigel Dunmore from **DLA**. US partner Stuart Mills is an exceptional talent.

Lawrence Graham partner Jeffrey Elway advised Regent Inns plc in its disposal of 50 pubs for £40m. Michael Storar is the partner responsible for the Millfield Group. The team was bolstered with the arrival of Jonathan Sellors, formerly head of corporate at **The Simkins Partnership**, and Lance Feaver from *Garretts*.

LeBoeuf, Lamb, Greene & MacRae partner Tony Richmond led the team that advised Oberthur on its $35m acquisition of De La Rue's smartcard business.

At **Lewis Silkin**, Roger Alexander is the best known corporate finance/M&A partner. Partners Nigel Edwards and Jo Evans led on a number of major transactions. Industry specialities include marketing, advertising, restaurants, and dental companies.

Nicholson Graham & Jones advised on £250m of pure corporate deals. Partners Owen Waft and John Elgar are praised for 'their quality of service and exemplary project management skills'. The firm also recruited Jeremy Landau to head its private equity group.

Reed Smith advised McDonald's on the disposal of its Aroma cafe subsidiary in a sale to Caffe Nero, which involved 30 outlets around the UK. Leading partners include Peter Borrowdale and Tim Foster.

Speechly Bircham managing partner Michael Lingens is the joint head of the corporate department with Nick Janmohamed. Stephen Armstrong is also experienced. The firm acted as English legal counsel to Solutia Inc on the sale of its speciality resins, additives, and adhesives business to UCB Group of Belgium for £320m.

Collyer-Bristow partners John Bailey and Paul Sillis are good choices for clients who want hands-on partner attention. Clients include Fullers and building distribution company SAS Group.

Covington & Burling bolstered its M&A expertise with the hire of Simon Goodworth from *Theodore Goddard*. The office has extensive experience in both public and private M&A transactions.

Dorsey & Whitney has impressive UK and US strength in corporate finance and cross-border M&A. Key players include UK partners John Byrne and Andrew Rimmington.

The London office of **Dundas & Wilson** acted for Scottish and Southern Energy in the £130m acquisition of Dynegy Hornsea Limited from Dynegy Inc and in its unsuccessful £1bn bid for TXU UK. Colin Fergusson joined as a partner from *KLegal*, where he was head of corporate.

Faegre Benson Hobson Audley LLP is a small office with loads of talent. Partner Max Audley is highly regarded by clients and peers.

At **Field Fisher Waterhouse**, clients of corporate head Tim Davies include HM Treasury, the DTI and Thomas Cook. Andrew Blankfield focuses on the media, IT, and telecoms industries. Nicholas Thompsell has particular expertise in rail, financial services, and publishing.

Finers Stephens Innocent partners Paul Millett and Ashley Reeback have considerable experience on transactions in the £5m+ range. The firm advised Tragus Holdings on its £25m acquisition of the Café Rouge and Bella Pasta restaurant chains from Whitbread Group.

Landwell has nine partners in its M&A and restructuring group, including recent recruit Mark Satterly from **Herbert Smith**. Clients range from multinationals and large UK companies to management teams and private equity houses.

At **Manches** the amount of work for clients with interests abroad is steadily increasing. Melvin Pedro and Christopher Owen are leading individuals.

McGrigors partners Ian Binnie and Moray MacPherson are experienced M&A practitioners.

Middleton Potts has an impressive client base of foreign companies and state-owned institutions, with particularly strong ties to Italian banks. We recommend David Godfrey, David Rabagliati, Stephen Morrall, and Lindsey Hemingway.

At **Reynolds Porter Chamberlain**, partner Tim Anderson acted for Northcliffe, the subsidiary of Daily Mail and General Trust, on its £200m bid for the entire share capital of the publishing arm of SMG.

Wilmer Cutler Pickering LLP US partner Gerry Cater has experience in M&A, private equity, and international joint ventures; UK partner James Greig joined the London office in 2002. The London office advised the Carlyle Group on its $39m transaction with Lloyds TSB and Easymoney and represented Accucard in the disposal of its UK credit card business.

PENSIONS

FRESHFIELDS BRUCKHAUS DERINGER ✪
LINKLATERS ✪
MAYER, BROWN, ROWE & MAW LLP
SACKER & PARTNERS, MEMBER OF IUS LABORIS ✪

ALLEN & OVERY ✪
BAKER & McKENZIE ✪
CMS CAMERON McKENNA
LOVELLS ✪
PINSENTS ✪
SLAUGHTER AND MAY ✪
TRAVERS SMITH BRAITHWAITE

Clifford Chance LLP
Eversheds LLP
Hammonds
Herbert Smith ✪
Macfarlanes ✪
Nabarro Nathanson
Simmons & Simmons ✪

DLA ✪
Denton Wilde Sapte ✪
Norton Rose ✪
Richards Butler
Taylor Wessing ✪

Ashurst ✪
Berwin Leighton Paisner
Field Fisher Waterhouse
Jones Day ✪
Lawrence Graham
Stephenson Harwood
Wragge & Co LLP ✪ *Birmingham*

Firms are listed A-Z in tiers which are ranked in order of priority
✪ *Indicates firm displays contact details at the end of this chapter.*

PENSIONS

Freshfields Bruckhaus Deringer's three partners lead a large and balanced team within an integrated employment, pensions and benefits (EPB) practice. Group head Ken Dierden, David Pollard and Daniel Schaffer all enjoy excellent reputations in the industry. The firm has been advising the Railway Pension Scheme on funding issues and the consolidation of over 80 different scheme sections.

Linklaters boasts one of the largest teams of full-time pension lawyers in the country. It includes five 'A'-list partners, led by Ruth Goldman, who is 'always prepared to give advice', while Tim Cox remains the name on everyone's lips for technical expertise. In evidence of the calibre practice, **Linklaters** advises more blue-chip pension schemes than any other firm, including the BAT Pension Fund. It also acts for The Royal Bank of Scotland Group Pension Fund.

Mayer, Brown, Rowe & Maw LLP boasts an enviable client list, the product of the firm's long-established reputation in this field. TotalFinaElf, Prudential and Express Newspapers instruct the firm. Andrew White is the practice head, backed by seven specialist pensions law partners.

Completing our top tier is **Sacker & Partners, member of ius laboris**, the UK's only niche pensions specialists. The firm's depth of resources, focus and innovative work earns it top status. The firm is a UK member of the respected *ius laboris* network of international employment and pensions advisers, bringing a European dimension to the practice. Senior partner Mark Greenlees, Jonathan Seres and Ian Pittaway are among several well-known practitioners.

Allen & Overy rises in our table this year, the result of demonstrative premier advisory work. For example, it is acting for the trustees of a major UK blue-chip scheme, and a significant public sector fund, on serious funding issues. The Prudential, ExxonMobil, and The Royal Mail are among a long list of original standalone pensions clients.

Robert West at **Baker & McKenzie** is widely respected in the industry. Clients highlight the tailored advice that is delivered 'in a logical and understandable manner'. The firm handles ongoing advisory work for the likes of JP Morgan, the Co-operative Insurance Society and the Merchant Navy Officers Pension Fund.

CMS Cameron McKenna has long provided solid pensions advice and the practice is rising in status. Partner Mark Grant led the advice to the Iron and Steel Trades Confederation (ISTC) which successfully pressurised Caparo into reopening its final salary scheme. The firm is also advising the trustees of the Iceland Group Pensions Scheme on its controversial conversion to a money purchase scheme.

Lovells' stellar client list demonstrates a quality pensions team. Barclays, Centrica and the Royal Mail Group are all long-standing clients. Russell Strachan heads the practice while Jane Samsworth is a major player.

The heavyweight and 'extremely competent team' at **Pinsents** fields six full-time pensions partners and a new head of strategy in the well-known Robin Ellison. The firm is acting for employees of Ernst & Young following its controversial and high-profile decision to close its final salary scheme.

The cultivation of fresh blood at partner level is paying dividends for **Slaughter and May**'s pension practice, which can list a client base of 70 pension funds with assets in excess of £27bn in aggregate. Roland Doughty was promoted to partner and joins four other partners who divide their time advising on employment law and share schemes, as well as pensions.

Travers Smith Braithwaite, and in particular, department head Paul Stannard, continues to receive plaudits from both clients and competitors. While the team is leaner than others in this tier, it has a track record of advising trustees of FSTE 100 pension schemes, such as a leading UK bank's staff retirement fund. AXA, Trinity Mirror and ntl are clients.

Nick Sherwin took over the helm of the practice at **Clifford Chance LLP** in 2003, following the retirement of the respected Helen Cox. The firm has substantial pensions capability and a long list of pension scheme clients including Whitbread and British Energy.

Eversheds LLP's recognised national strength in employment law is balanced with equally impressive pensions ability. In evidence of this, the firm won the competitive tender to advise the trustees of the British Airways scheme. The firm has four full-time pension partners in London.

Fellow national firm **Hammonds** stakes claim to the largest pensions practice in the country. In London, Andrew Powell leads the team while the well-known Jane Marshall heads up the firm's international benefits practice. The firm notably advised the Thorn EMI Pensioners Association (TEPA) on a pro bono basis, successfully opposing a modification on the use of surplus.

Ian Gault runs an impressive practice at **Herbert Smith** that enjoyed significant income growth in the past year, defying its two-partner size. The firm has been advising Iceland/The Big Food Group on its well-publicised changes to its final salary scheme. Gault himself is 'possibly one of the smartest guys in the business', says one competitor.

Macfarlanes regularly rubs shoulders with top-tier firms, both at beauty parades and across the deal and disputes tables. While five partners advise full-time on pensions (two are litigators), Hugh Arthur is undoubtedly the draw card for clients such as the ex-Andersen (now Deloitte & Touche) pension schemes.

The pensions team at **Nabarro Nathanson** lost well-known industry figure John Quarrell last year. The lesser-known but experienced Geoffrey Preston succeeds him. The firm continues to act for major schemes, such as IBM, Invensys and Hoover.

Simmons & Simmons punches above its weight, advising a premium client base on heavyweight matters; such as the Ministry of Defence on the complex employees' transfer from a civil service scheme to a private plan. Clients include Interbrew, GlaxoSmithKline and Gallaher.

DLA's Michael Cowley, Jonathan Fenton and Michael Forkin make up a 'formidable team' in London, while the firm has 20 pensions specialists nationally.

Denton Wilde Sapte has a quality and well-resourced practice. It advises two of the largest schemes in the UK, the J Sainsbury pension scheme and the Royal Bank of Scotland fund. Alan Jarvis leads the team.

Peter Ford and Leslie Browning continue to build a potential top-quality practice at **Norton Rose**, shifting the former focus of corporate support to a credible advisory practice. The firm is advising Siemens in relation to the Mannesmann UK pension schemes, including a dispute concerning contracted-out benefits.

Richards Butler has long-enjoyed a reputation for quality pensions work, largely due to former partner Keith Wallace. Wallace remains at the firm on a full-time consultancy basis, leaving leadership to the 'very capable' Simon Hartley. The firm has been advising the Civil Aviation Authority pension scheme and received instructions from a major plc on funding issues.

Taylor Wessing continues to excel in contentious matters, but equally has considerable expertise in advisory and corporate work. As a result, the firm can count Crédit Lyonnais pension scheme trustees and Lehman Brothers scheme trustees among its clients. Partners Carolyn Saunders and Neil Smith, are 'excellent pensions lawyers' says a client.

PRIVATE EQUITY

'Private equity: debt' has been renamed **Acquisition finance** and is now at the beginning of this chapter.

At **Ashurst**, partners Charlie Geffen, Bruce Hanton and Simon Beddow are 'very young, very enthusiastic and very high-energy'. The team acted recently on 64 private equity transactions worth a total value of £17bn. Key clients remain Cinven, Electra Partners Europe, Legal & General Ventures and ABN Amro Private Equity. Partner Graeme Ward is also recommended.

Clifford Chance LLP has 12 full-time partners in the practice area in London, with stars Adam Signy and Matthew Layton praised by clients. In all, the team recently completed more than 70 deals with a total value of some £24bn. The extensive client base expanded to include The Carlyle Group, PPM Ventures and Sun Capital

PRIVATE EQUITY

ASHURST ✪
CLIFFORD CHANCE LLP

MACFARLANES ✪
TRAVERS SMITH BRAITHWAITE

ALLEN & OVERY ✪
FRESHFIELDS BRUCKHAUS DERINGER ✪
LOVELLS ✪

CMS CAMERON McKENNA
DICKSON MINTO WS
LINKLATERS ✪
SJ BERWIN ✪
SLAUGHTER AND MAY ✪
WEIL, GOTSHAL & MANGES ✪

Addleshaw Goddard
DLA ✪
Eversheds LLP
Jones Day ✪
Latham & Watkins ✪
Olswang
Pinsents ✪
Taylor Wessing ✪
Wragge & Co LLP ✪

Baker & McKenzie ✪
Berwin Leighton Paisner
Bird & Bird ✪
Cleary Gottlieb Steen & Hamilton ✪
Debevoise & Plimpton LLP ✪
Denton Wilde Sapte ✪
Dorsey & Whitney
Gibson, Dunn & Crutcher LLP
Hale and Dorr
Hammonds
Herbert Smith ✪
Kirkland & Ellis International LLP ✪
Mayer, Brown, Rowe & Maw LLP
McDermott, Will & Emery ✪
Norton Rose ✪
Osborne Clarke
Simmons & Simmons ✪
Skadden, Arps, Slate, Meagher & Flom LLP
Speechly Bircham
Wilmer Cutler Pickering LLP ✪

Firms are listed A-Z in tiers which are ranked in order of priority
✪ Indicates firm displays contact details at the end of this chapter.

Partners. Partners David Walker and David Pearson are also recommended.

At **Macfarlanes**, Charles Martin is 'a first-class performer', while his partners Charles Meek, who heads the group, Nicola Richards, and Ian Martin are also highly rated by clients. Regular clients include 3i, Alchemy, Candover and Botts & Company. New additions to the client base include Royal London Private Equity, West Private Equity, Kleinwort Capital and PPM Ventures. A strong funds practice is led by Bridget Barker.

Travers Smith Braithwaite's team worked on 56 transactions last year with a total value of £4.3bn. Partners Chris Hale, Charles Barter and Mark Soundy are popular with clients. The firm acted for management on the £820m buyout of NCP last year, while institutional clients include 3i, Apax Partners & Co, Bridgepoint Capital and Candover Investments.

Allen & Overy continues to develop a focus on private equity and consistently transacts a number of big deals. Partners Alan Paul, Jeremy Hunt, and Alison Beardsley are well liked. The firm advised Kohlberg Kravis Roberts & Co on its acquisition of Siemens' businesses worth €1.69bn, while other clients include DB Capital Partners and Morgan Grenfell Private Equity.

Freshfields Bruckhaus Deringer handles a small number of high-value private equity deals. New clients for the group, led by Chris Bown, include Apax and Carlyle Group and US fund Fox Paine. Longstanding clients include Cinven and Warburg Pincus. The firm's strength across Europe sets it apart from many of its rivals.

Last year **Lovells** worked on 66 completed deals (including those where it acted for banks) with an aggregate value of £7bn. It advised LW Investments on its £750m purchase of Littlewoods; other clients include 3i, HgCapital and Advent International. Marco Compagnoni is the group head.

CMS Cameron McKenna's key clients include ABN Amro Capital, Bridgepoint Capital and Lloyds TSB Development Capital, while the practice's largest deal was advising Enterprise Inns on its equity investment alongside Cinven to acquire the Unique Pub Company and Voyager Pub Group for more than £2bn. Partner Andrew Sheach is recommended.

Dickson Minto WS's clients include Charterhouse Development Capital, BC Partners and HgCapital, but big deals were thin on the ground as the firm was forced to turn down instructions because partners were acting for other players. Managing partner Alastair Dickson retains a strong profile in the market, while partners Martin McNair and Peter Uri are also recommended.

At **Linklaters**, 'outstanding' partner Graham White is beginning to make an impact. Key deals for the firm in 2002 included advising CVC Capital Partners on the £330m buyout of Kwik-fit, and, through the Paris office, advising KKR and Wendel on the €4.9bn leveraged buyout of Legrand. Other clients include JP Morgan Partners and Apax Partners.

SJ Berwin's most active clients remain Apax Partners and Graphite Capital, though the list extends to include Bridgepoint Capital, Permira, Hermes Private Equity and Cabot Square. In total, the firm has nine partners in London focusing on buy-out work, as well as a pre-eminent fund formation team led by Jonathan Blake. On the deals side, Steven Davis, Martin Bowen and Andrew Harris are recommended.

Slaughter and May is capitalising on the strong private equity practices of its 'best friend' firms across Europe – namely **Uría & Menéndez** and **Hengeler Mueller**. The firm advised CVC Capital Partners in 2002 on its €577m LBO of an electricity network from Iberdrola, alongside **Uría & Menéndez**. Other clients include Palamon Capital Partners and Advent International. Group head is Christopher Saul. Clients like partner Jeff Twentyman.

Weil, Gotshal & Manges has broadened its client base dramatically and now does work for the likes of CSFB Private Equity, Lehman Brothers, GE Equity and Dresdner Kleinwort Capital on top of flagship client Hicks Muse Tate & Furst. Partner Mike Francies is consistently highly rated, while Paul Claydon and Will Rosen are both recommended.

Addleshaw Goddard's team, led by partner Darryl Cooke, is praised for its client-focused approach, and acts for clients like 3i, ECI Ventures and Gresham Trust increasingly in London. Cooke is described by clients as 'refreshingly commercial'.

DLA's Peter Wayte leads a City practice that remains popular with clients. The nationwide practice continues to act for the likes of Bank of Scotland Integrated Finance, HSBC Private Equity, Gresham Trust and Bridgepoint Capital.

Eversheds LLP's partner Mark Spinner came back from a period at an Internet start-up and will head the London effort, alongside partner Ian Richardson and Manchester head Peter Halpin. Clients include Barclays Private Equity, HSBC Private Equity and Aberdeen Murray Johnstone.

Jones Day, formed by the merger of **Jones Day** and *Gouldens*, brings together two teams of private equity lawyers each with their own reputations in the City. **Jones Day**'s team, led by partner Daljit Singh, has historically done larger buy-out work for clients that include Electra, Alchemy and Star, while *Gouldens*', headed by Adam Greaves, has done smaller deals for clients like BancBoston Capital, Botts & Co and Sagitta.

Latham & Watkins won the instruction from Charterhouse Development Capital on its £860m purchase of Coral Eurobet, one of the largest deals in the market in recent years. Other work included advising The Carlyle Group on its £106m offer for Firth Rixson.

At **Olswang**, partner Fabrizio Carpanini continues to enjoy the affections of clients including Graphite Capital, ISIS Equity Partners, Gresham Trust, HgCapital and Barclays Private Equity. The firm is growing its mid-market profile; clients include Scottish Equity Partners, Sand Aire Private Equity and Sagitta Private Equity.

One client praises **Pinsents** for providing a 'commercial, cost-effective service', saying the practice is 'always attentive to our requirements'. The team acted for management on the £860m sale of Coral Eurobet to Charterhouse Development Capital.

Taylor Wessing's private equity team has grown its institutional client base dramatically in the last few years, and now boasts clients including Amadeus Capital Partners, Cazenove Private Equity and Granville Baird Capital Partners. Partner Martin Winter is popular with clients.

Wragge & Co LLP has boosted its London presence by relocating highly rated partners Maurice Dwyer and Andy Stylianou to the City from Birmingham. Both are liked by clients that include 3i, Aberdeen Murray Johnstone, Barclays Private Equity and Bridgepoint Capital.

PROJECT FINANCE

Few firms can match the project finance muscle at **Allen & Overy**. Graham Vinter's London team boasts a raft of heavyweight partners including Timothy Arnheim, Anne Baldock, Alan Rae Smith, Calvin Walker and Nick Williams. Highlights include a $1.6bn Nigeria LNG plant, acting for Wembley National Stadium and the Piacenza energy-from-waste project.

Clifford Chance LLP partners, including Tony Bankes-Jones, London group boss Peter Blake, Margaret Gossling, Geraint Hughes and Paul Simpson, win praise from clients in the manufacturing, petrochemicals, power and telecoms sectors. The firm advised sponsor Intergen on the $778m Spalding and the $608m Rijnmond power projects.

Alan Black's **Linklaters** team has a superb global reputation for advising sponsors, lenders and public bodies. The firm is acting for the Strategic Rail Authority and Network Rail on the UK rail refinancing, where Fiona Hobbs, David Weber and Bruce White were singled out for their 'excellence'.

Freshfields Bruckhaus Deringer continues to build on its reputation for quality, particularly in energy and infrastructure. The team's coverage for sponsors, public bodies and certain key lenders extends from Europe to the Middle East, Africa, Asia and South America. Leading team members include Nicholas Bliss, Roger McCormick, Perry Noble, and Kent Rowey.

Norton Rose has a fine reputation for power financing, oil and gas, infrastructure and transport projects. Tom Day and David Crane are praised for their work advising the lead arrangers for Tube Lines' London Underground bid and John Ellis was recommended for advising the consortium developing the new Home Office HQ.

PROJECT FINANCE

ALLEN & OVERY ✪
CLIFFORD CHANCE LLP
LINKLATERS ✪

FRESHFIELDS BRUCKHAUS DERINGER ✪
NORTON ROSE ✪
SHEARMAN & STERLING (LONDON) LLP
WHITE & CASE ✪

Baker & McKenzie ✪
CMS Cameron McKenna
Denton Wilde Sapte ✪
Lovells ✪
Milbank, Tweed, Hadley & McCloy
Slaughter and May ✪

Ashurst ✪
Dewey Ballantine
Herbert Smith ✪
Trowers & Hamlins ✪
Vinson & Elkins R.L.L.P. ✪

Coudert Brothers ✪
Latham & Watkins ✪
LeBoeuf, Lamb, Greene & MacRae
Masons
McCarthy Tétrault
Simmons & Simmons ✪
Taylor Wessing ✪

Berwin Leighton Paisner
Bryan Cave
Cadwalader, Wickersham & Taft LLP
Chadbourne & Parke
Debevoise & Plimpton LLP ✪
Fenwick Elliott
Hogan & Hartson ✪
Mayer, Brown, Rowe & Maw LLP
McDermott, Will & Emery ✪
Morrison & Foerster MNP ✪
Orrick, Herrington & Sutcliffe
Richards Butler
Skadden, Arps, Slate, Meagher & Flom LLP
Sullivan & Cromwell LLP

Firms are listed A-Z in tiers which are ranked in order of priority
✪ Indicates firm displays contact details at the end of this chapter.

Shearman & Sterling (London) LLP powered forward last year. The group targets flagship schemes. Notable projects include its 'admirable and excellent' work advising WestLB on the complex Wembley Stadium deal and acting for lead arrangers BNP Paribas and SocGen on the giant Rijnmond Energy Project. Key partners are Nicholas Buckworth, Kenneth MacRitchie, Stephen Peppiatt and Nigel Thompson.

White & Case had a stellar year, including acting for Advanced Power/Siemens Power on the Slovakian Malzenice Power Project and for Gold Fields on Australian mining asset acquisitions. The team which includes Peter Finlay, much-praised oil and gas partner Jason Kerr, emerging markets expert Doug Peel and energy project guru Philip Stopford, was joined by Neil Upton.

The London heads of **Baker & McKenzie**'s team, Michael Webster and Annie Williams, along with key partners such as Neil Donoghue, draw on the firm's global capabilities. The firm advised on polypropylene plants in Saudi Arabia and Oman and on mining and rail schemes in the Middle East.

CMS Cameron McKenna's Andrew Ivison led the team advising Metronet on the London Underground PPP. Richard Price advised John Laing/M40 Trains on the Chiltern Line extension while Jonathan Beckitt was praised for his work for the government on the restructuring of the Channel Tunnel Rail Link. The team advised on a slew of power deals across central and Eastern Europe. Recommended specialists include Ian Bendell, Trevor Butcher, Robert Phillips and Richard Temple.

Denton Wilde Sapte has global strength in the oil and gas sector as well as experience in infrastructure and transport projects. Ian Hodgson's team, which includes Howard Barrie and Stan Gniadkowski, works on projects and PFI/PPPs.

Led by the 'able and affable' Gavin McQuater, **Lovells**' practice also includes the 'consistently excellent' Shibeer Ahmed and Catherine Allinson. The firm has received plaudits for its 'impressive' work on the London Underground Project; its work on Europe's largest water project, in Croatia; and on the Malta International Airport proposal.

Milbank, Tweed, Hadley & McCloy's London office leads activity throughout Europe, the Caspian and Middle East, Africa and India. Phillip Fletcher, John Dewar, and Patrick Holmes spearhead a broad sponsor and lender practice. Its market-leading power experts advised on the final part of the Italian privatisation programme as well as on the Shoreham, Jawa and Uch power restructurings.

Slaughter and May's ten-partner projects practice is led by Christopher Saunders and includes Ian Goldie and Steven Galbraith. The team has a healthy balance advising lenders (such as Barclays, Crédit Agricole and EIB) and sponsors (including AES, Bombardier, DTI, MTR and Shell). Highlights include the $1.15bn Egyptian LNG project.

Mark Elsey 's team at **Ashurst**, which includes Alan Kitchin, Philip Hurst and Judith Sharrock, was active in Africa, Asia and Europe. Work included advising Kuwait Petroleum Corporation on a Qatar gas pipeline and on major petrochemical schemes. The firm also acted for Standard Bank in a South African gold mine financing.

James Simpson, Mark Saunders, and Adam Dann at **Dewey Ballantine** are recommended for their projects expertise. Recent work includes acting for NRG on the sale of power assets in the Czech Republic and Hungary.

Herbert Smith's combined projects, energy and PFI team, under the 'admirable leadership' of Nicholas Tott, includes recommended Adrian Clough, Alan Jowett and Andrew Preece. It has an excellent reputation in the electricity, oil and gas, water and rail sectors. It advised Centrica on tolling agreements at the Spalding Power Station, and acted for Oesterota on a Portuguese road scheme.

Towers & Hamlins' London office, led by Martin Amison, works with the firm's extensive Middle East office network. Innovative projects include advising Gulf Utilities on a massive Iran-Kuwait water transfer scheme and acting for the Jordanian government on its gas transportation project. Highly rated London partners include Adrian Creed and Nick Edmondes.

Power and oil and gas heavyweight **Vinson & Elkins R.L.L.P.** uses its London office to spearhead work across Europe, Africa and the Middle East. An experienced team includes Christopher Clement-Davies and Peter Gaines. The firm is advising on the renegotiations of project contracts for the Teesside power plant as well as on the ongoing Project Dolphin in the Middle East.

Coudert Brothers' team has a good reputation for electricity and power projects across Europe and Africa. Recent highlights include a major Kenyan power project and road schemes in Croatia. Alexander James has a particularly good name.

The outstanding Joseph Blum, along with energy expert Dennis Nordstrom and David Miles, are key players in **Latham & Watkins**' excellent global projects team.

Bruce Johnston and Keith Hughes spearhead the **LeBoeuf, Lamb, Greene & MacRae** team. The firm continues to represent various US electricity outfits in Europe. It advised Suez Lyonnaise des Eaux and Saur on water programmes and NIB on UK leisure and school projects.

Brian Kelsall at Canadian heavyweight **McCarthy Tétrault** is building a strong reputation for advising multilateral lenders throughout Europe and Africa. The expanding team advised the EBRD on infrastructure projects in Uzbekistan and Estonia.

Steven Bond manages a capital projects division at **Masons** that includes Annie Kilvington and Geoffrey Roberts. The firm is increasingly active in international PPP schemes and advises several banks as well as public bodies. Recent work includes advising the government on the South African Gautrain Rail Scheme.

Simmons & Simmons is active across the globe, particularly in defence and telecoms projects. One standout deal saw the firm advise the banks and the Abu Dhabi authorities, respectively, on the Fujairah and Shuweihat power and desalination projects. Edwin Godfrey heads the team.

Rodney Dukes and Declan Tarpey and the rest of the full-service projects team at **Taylor Wessing** advise on all sides of the projects table across Europe, the Middle East and Africa.

REAL ESTATE

Clients looking for a first-class, all-round real estate service can be sure that **Berwin Leighton**

REAL ESTATE

BERWIN LEIGHTON PAISNER
CLIFFORD CHANCE LLP
LOVELLS ✪

FRESHFIELDS BRUCKHAUS DERINGER ✪
HERBERT SMITH ✪
LINKLATERS ✪
NABARRO NATHANSON
SJ BERWIN ✪

Ashurst ✪
Dechert
Denton Wilde Sapte ✪
Jones Day ✪
Lawrence Graham

Addleshaw Goddard
Allen & Overy ✪
CMS Cameron McKenna
DLA ✪
Eversheds LLP
Macfarlanes ✪
Norton Rose ✪
Simmons & Simmons ✪
Taylor Wessing ✪
Wragge & Co LLP ✪

Field Fisher Waterhouse
Forsters
Hammonds
Mayer, Brown, Rowe & Maw LLP
Mishcon de Reya
Nicholson Graham & Jones
Olswang
Osborne Clarke
Pinsents ✪
Richards Butler
Slaughter and May ✪
Stephenson Harwood
Travers Smith Braithwaite

Boodle Hatfield
Campbell Hooper
Clyde & Co ✪
Fladgate Fielder
Gibson, Dunn & Crutcher LLP
Howard Kennedy
Lewis Silkin ✪
Manches
Maples Teesdale
Masons
Maxwell Batley
Penningtons
RadcliffesLeBrasseur
Speechly Bircham
Trowers & Hamlins ✪

continued

Paisner, will more than live up to its top-tier status. Highlights include the forward purchase by Legal & General of CB Hillier Parker's new central London HQ at Paternoster Square, as well as acting for RBS on the acquisition of the NCP car parks portfolio. The leisure and hospitality practice, led by David Levy, has seen notable growth: the firm was appointed by Six Continents to act on ongoing matters following the purchase of the Posthouse Chain by Compass, as well as by Jarvis Hotels, Belgo Group and Le Meridien. Simon Kenley is held in high regard by clients and peers.

Clifford Chance LLP's real estate strength is supported by a leading property finance practice, in addition to commendable support from environment, planning and property litigation. Highlights include advising Burford on the sale of Lazards' European headquarters at Mayfair Place, London to Ropemaker Properties. The developer practice acted for Spitalfields Development on the largest ever pre-letting in the City. Other clients include Safeway Stores and Canary Wharf Group. On the leisure front the firm advised Sun Capital Partners on the sale and leaseback of four holiday villages. Jonathan Solomon, Mark Rees-Jones, Iain Morpeth and Robert MacGregor are all highly recommended.

In an increasingly cost-conscious market, **Lovells**' team, led by Robert Kidby, has remained ahead of the game through its innovative Mexican Wave, under which the firm decides whether to handle the work itself, or to place it with a selected lower-cost firm. **Lovells** acts for investors such as Greycoat, Shaftesbury and Coal Pension Properties, for the latter on the sale of a portfolio of six shopping centres to a joint venture between Catalyst Capital and HBOS. Regeneration and development work is a growing strength. The firm has a leading reputation in corporate outsourcing, as well as a growing expertise in corporate headquarter moves. Jane Rigler and Michael Stancombe are recommended.

Freshfields Bruckhaus Deringer's nine-partner practice remains at the cutting edge of real estate deals through its involvement on outsourcing work for clients such as Land Securities Trillium. Scottish Widows is a key investor client; the team acted on the £72.9m sale to ND Properties of a 50% interest in three central London office buildings. Clients praise John Fordham for his ability to unlock complex real estate structures, while David Lewis is described as 'impressive'.

Led by James Barnes, **Herbert Smith**'s substantial presence in the sector is not to be underestimated. The practice has a particularly strong foothold in the investor market, as well as in development work, the latter backed up by a first-rate planning group. Significant client gains during the year included CIT and J.E. Roberts. Other clients include Hermes, Standard Life, Hammerson, Tischman Speyer and Selfridges.

Linklaters' large team, led by new department head Patrick Plant, maintains a strong investment practice, where clients include DIFA, BP Pension Fund and Aberdeen Property Investors. The firm offers outstanding back-up from planning and property litigation, and has a growing profile in the developer market. The firm

REAL ESTATE (continued)

Baker & McKenzie ✪
Beachcroft Wansbroughs
Beauchamps
Bevan Ashford
Bircham Dyson Bell
Charles Russell
Collyer-Bristow
Davenport Lyons
Davies Arnold Cooper
Dundas & Wilson
Finers Stephens Innocent
Halliwell Landau
Kidd Rapinet
McGrigors
Morgan Cole
Paul, Hastings, Janofsky & Walker LLP
Payne Hicks Beach
Reynolds Porter Chamberlain
Wedlake Bell
Weil, Gotshal & Manges ✪

Bates, Wells & Braithwaite
Bristows
Coudert Brothers ✪
Dawsons
Faegre Benson Hobson Audley LLP
Farrer & Co
Glovers
Hamlins
Hempsons
KSB Law
Kingsley Napley
Laytons
Maclay Murray & Spens
Memery Crystal
Middleton Potts
Pemberton Greenish
Reed Smith
Rosling King
Russell-Cooke
Steptoe & Johnson
Tarlo Lyons
Thomas Eggar
Tite & Lewis

Barlow Lyde & Gilbert
Bird & Bird ✪
Bowling & Co
Dorsey & Whitney
Goodman Derrick
Harbottle & Lewis LLP
Lee & Pembertons
Park Nelson
Pritchard Englefield
Rooks Rider
Rosenblatt
Russell Jones & Walker
Stepien Lake Gilbert & Paling
Wallace & Partners
Withers LLP

Firms are listed A-Z in tiers which are ranked in order of priority
✪ *Indicates firm displays contact details at the end of this chapter.*

remains involved in innovative deals, acting on outsourcing deals such as Bradford & Bingley's £39m sale and leaseback of operational space across the UK. Partner Martin Elliott is recommended for his commercial advice.

Nabarro Nathanson remains a force to be reckoned with. The client base is the envy of many and includes major property companies such as Land Securities, Great Portland Estates and Capital Shopping Centres, as well as GE Capital and Morley Fund Management. One of many highlights was acting on behalf of Morley Fund Management in the establishment and growth of The Mall Limited Partnership with Capital & Regional. The firm's development and growing urban regeneration practice is also not to be underestimated; it acted on behalf of Capital Shopping Centres in the £275m Norwich retail development.

SJ Berwin's boasts a formidable client base which encompasses the likes of MWB, British Land and Crown Estate. Led by the outstanding David Ryland, the group was instructed by Matrix Securities in connection with the establishment of the Matrix Portfolio No.1 Partnership Fund, a joint venture with the Bank of Scotland, valued at £350m. The hotels practice is outstanding, acting for Hilton on the sale and leaseback of ten hotels for £335m. Leisure work is carried out for both MWB and First Leisure, while on the retail front Sainsbury's and Marks & Spencer instruct the firm.

Ashurst's strength lies in the development, regeneration and corporate occupier spheres; it advised Chelsfield on its White City Shopping Centre; Hutchison Whampoa on its proposed redevelopment of South Kensington tube station and Silvertown Quays on its regeneneration proposals at London's Docklands. On the private equity front, the firm advised on the acquisition by Cinven of NCP for around £800m, and on the subsequent restructuring with RBS. Retailers who instruct the firm are Skechers, Tesco and H&M Hennes.

At **Dechert** new instructions came from an ING Real Estate and Starwood Capital joint venture for the purchase of West Riding House, Leeds, for £58m. Top-notch retail expertise is readily at hand for the likes of Arcadia and Dixons. Developer clients include Richardson Developments and Banner Homes. Mark Packer, Ciaran Carvalho and Steven Fogel are all highly recommended.

Led by Martin Quicke, **Denton Wilde Sapte** boasts a strong, all-round practice which made some notable client gains during the year. On the investment side these included London & Regional and Commercial Union Funds through Morley Fund Management, as well as Equitable Life and Canada Life. The firm's development group saw particular activity in urban regeneration work, notably acting for Complex Development Projects. Dixons Stores instructed the firm on development work. Indeed, the firm boasts a leading retail presence, which represents the Sainsbury's group and Marks & Spencer.

The ten-partner group at **Jones Day** is a force to be reckoned with and acts for some of the UK's leading property companies, including Pillar Property, Arlington Securities and Ashtenne Holdings. David Roberts, Clare Deanesly, Christopher Berry and Mark Emerson stand out for particular praise. Strong environmental and planning expertise is readily at hand.

The **Lawrence Graham** client base, which encompasses the likes of Legal & General, P&O Property Holdings, Allied Dunbar, AXA Sun Life and Sainsbury's, speaks volumes about the quality and depth of the firm's real estate expertise. Highlights include advising Legal & General on the sale of three shopping centres to The Performance Shopping Centre Limited for £211m. Robert Field, Andrew Wade, and Paul Walker are praised for their high standards.

Led by Paul Howell **Addleshaw Goddard** has become a strong player in the sector. Development expertise is offered to the likes of Fairview New Homes and Bridehall Developments; on the leisure front, Pizza Hut is a major client. The firm has an outstanding client base, which also includes Sainsbury's, Kvaerner and Threadneedle Property Investments and Green Property

Allen & Overy's practice saw some significant client gains recently, notably Land Securities Trillium; the firm was appointed to the company's panel dealing with major portfolio transactions. Other new clients include Nomura and Royal & SunAlliance. A market-leading property finance practice is a key strength of the group. Daniel McKimm is praised by clients.

CMS Cameron McKenna's real estate group includes seven partners dealing with commercial property issues. Clients include Britannic Asset Management, The Berkeley Group and Sainsbury's. Mark Heighton is described by clients as being very helpful, and providing a first-class service. The practice also benefits from a leading cross-departmental hotels group. Richard Price, Louise Wallace and Charles Romney stand out for particular praise.

DLA has a strong national presence in the sector, led by Philip Rooney. Key highlights included advising on the acquisition of 120 Moorgate, London EC2 through a limited partnership between GMAC and the Property Merchant Group, with a value of around £39m. Other clients include Akeler, UCI Cinemas, Arcadia, Boots The Chemist and Dixons Stores.

Eversheds LLP's relatively small London presence is backed up by a phenomenal national practice. Highlights in London include work on the Arsenal Stadium relocation project. London clients include Jarvis Plc and Catalyst Capital. Nationally, the firm acts for a number of leading housebuilders. Urban regeneration is another key focus at the national practice. Clients praise John Butler for providing an excellent service.

Macfarlanes acted on Kingfisher's headquarters' relocation to PaddingtonCentral, as well as on Kingfisher's disposal of Chartwell Land's retail parks and development sites for in excess of £500m. Development is another core strength; it is currently acting on behalf of P&O Developments in the redevelopment of the Regent Quarter Estate close to King's Cross station. High-profile investment work is carried out for the likes of Starwood Capital and Canada Life. Retail, hotels and leisure expertise is offered to Allders, Comet, David Lloyd Leisure and InnSpired Taverns.

Norton Rose's client base encompasses developers, investors, funders, public sector and regeneration bodies, as well as corporates. Key clients include Workspace Group, Persimmon Homes and CGI.

Simmons & Simmons boasts a significant investor client base; the firm acted for ING Barings and ING Real Estate Investment Management on the establishment of a Guernsey limited partnership, and the subsequent acquisition of a portfolio of investment properties for £120m. Other clients are Henderson Global Investors, Deka Immobilien Investment Gmbh and Abu Dhabi Investment Authority. The group also advises several government departments, notably the Ministry of Defence, on PFI and PPP transactions. Alan Butler and Stephen Elvidge are recommended.

Taylor Wessing acts for Marylebone Warwick Balfour and Canada Life, as well as Stannifer and London & Regional; a recent instruction was for Stannifer on the £150m redevelopment of High Wycombe town centre. The practice benefits from strong support in property finance.

Wragge & Co LLP received instructions from Pearson, Mapeley on the management of its STEPS portfolio, and Schroeder Exempt Property Unit Trust on its industrial portfolio. Investor clients include Carisbrooke and Royal London Asset Management. **Wragge & Co LLP** has an impressive leisure and hotels practice, which regularly acts for existing clients such as Allied Leisure and First Leisure. Property litigation is a key strength of the practice.

Field Fisher Waterhouse's group provides high-quality and reliable advice, and acted for Deutsche Asset Management. The firm has a leading leisure, as well as a growing hotels, practice; it acted for Marriott and Manhattan Loft Corporation on the redevelopment of the Grade I listed former Midland Hotel at St. Pancras station. Paul Houston is 'particularly strong on lease negotiations', while John Pedder is praised for his high-quality and reliable advice.

Forsters maintains a strong presence on the back of a broad-ranging practice which acts for a mixture of investor and developer clients. The development arm maintains a significant presence. Local authority/city centre redevelopment is a particular speciality; the group is acting for Chester City Council on the redevelopment of the city centre. The firm also maintains a strong leisure practice, acting for the likes of McDonald's Restaurants and Warner Village Cinemas.

Hammonds counts Allied London, Compass,

HBOS, John Lewis, Laura Ashley, Aldi, English Partnerships and the London Development Authority amongst its clients. Key deals included acting for Morley Fund Management on various disposals and acquisitions.

The group at **Mayer, Brown, Rowe & Maw LLP** is led by Jeremy Clay. Key Property Investments used the firm on the acquisition and leaseback of a portfolio of 19 properties and Teachers Fund instructed the firm on its joint venture with Scottish Widows. Retail clients include HMV and Waterstones.

Mishcon de Reya has a truly broad-ranging practice. On the investment side, the firm is instructed by Topland Group, Helical Bar and Morley Fund Management. Development work is carried out for Rialto and Frogmore. Retail and, in particular, leisure is a key area: instructions are regularly received from Mango, Holmes Place and Tootsies. Philip Freedman and Ronald Hooberman are singled out for praise.

Nicholson Graham & Jones provides a partner-led service, with particular expertise in acting for funds. Highlights include the £122m acquisition by Henderson UK Retail Warehouse Fund of a portfolio of four retail warehouse parks from Grantchester Properties. The firm offers strong support from property finance. Other regular clients include AXA Sun Life and Heron.

Olswang was appointed to the Land Securities Trillium legal panel and was instructed by UBS Global Asset Management (UK) on the restructuring of its UK property fund and the creation of an offshore property investment vehicle. Clients include Allied London, Benchmark and Capital & Regional.

Osborne Clarke boasts a well-resourced team. On the investment side the firm acts for the likes of British Airways Pensions and Close Brothers. The firm's development expertise continues to grow in stature; advising Innogy on the development of surplus land holdings and advising Welbeck Land on a number of development projects around the country. Retail expertise is offered to the likes of Somerfield, Marks & Spencer and Argos.

Pinsents' small London team is boosted by a significant presence in Birmingham, Manchester and Leeds. The firm acted for Birmingham City Council on the Masshouse Circus element of the Eastside redevelopment.

Richards Butler's practice acts for developers and investors, as well as leisure, hotel and retail operators. The firm advised Cantor Development on the redevelopment of Hackney Town Centre as a retail and residential site. The firm maintains a leading presence in the leisure sphere, where it acts for Rank, Warner and Grosvenor Casinos. Retail and hotels work is carried out for Rymans, La Senza and Orient-Express Hotels.

Slaughter and May has a broad-ranging practice. Clients include Grosvenor and George Wimpey. On the leisure, hotels and retail front, work is carried out for Whitbread, Sun Resorts, Tod's UK and Heal's.

Stephenson Harwood's practice encompasses developers, investors, banks, as well as hotel and leisure clients. Clients include Macdonald Hotels, Six Continents Hotels, London Development Agency and London & Regional Properties. The practice also acts on regeneration, education sector and PFI projects, as well as benefiting from a commendable planning and property finance practice.

Led by Robert Harman, **Travers Smith Braithwaite** punches above its weight, with a strong focus on investment, and, in particular, development work, backed up by a highly-regarded property finance practice. Lend Lease Europe, London Underground and Lothbury Property Unit Trust all instruct the firm.

SHIPPING: DRY

'Dry' shipping encompasses advice on charterparties, bills of lading and cargo claims.

Clyde & Co advised on headline matters including acting for the charterers in the *Prestige* sinking off the coast of Spain. Derek Hodgson heads the owners/charterers team. Tony Thomas heads the cargo team. Brian Nash and Irvine Marr are also recommended. Clients include major oil and gas companies.

Holman Fenwick & Willan handled several cases involving the carriage of dangerous cargo. Major cases include the *Hanjin Pennsylvania*. Leading practitioners include Marcus Bowman, Hugh Livingstone and Richard Crump. Vivienne Petroff advised on several cases on the law of arbitration.

Ince & Co advised the owners and P&I club on pollution aspects of the *Prestige*. *CMA Djakarta* and *Northern Pioneer* were other important cases. Practice head Bob Deering and Patrick Shaw are well known. Graham Crane continues to build the firm's reputation since joining the firm in 2002. Paul Herring provides 'precise and commercial pre-litigation advice'. Ian Chetwood is recommended for heavyweight, intellectual cases.

Richards Butler's Lindsay East heads a team of 13 partners and 23 solicitors. Charles Brown led teams that advised on high-profile cases including *Eurasian Dream*. The practice works closely with its international network offices, particularly Hong Kong and Paris. John Reece joined as managing partner of the Piraeus office. Andrew Taylor is also well known.

Stephenson Harwood's Paolo Ghirardani heads a team of 11 partners handling dry work, including Angus Johnson, Mark O'Neil, and Sean Gibbons. Major cases include advising Ocean Rig, the Norwegian oil company, on major arbitration and litigation. The firm works closely with its overseas offices in Hong Kong, Singapore, Shanghai and Piraeus.

Hill Taylor Dickinson advises owners, charterers, P&I clubs and insurance companies. The firm is perceived in the market to have special strength in hull insurance. Andrew Johnson and John Evans are recommended.

Clifford Chance LLP advises P&I clubs, shipping and oil companies and financial institutions. Major cases include *Silversea* and *Navigator Gas*. Mark Morrison, Alex Panayides and associate Sarra Kay provide 'immediacy of advice' and a 'one-stop shop service'. The firm is also recommended for working closely with its extensive network of overseas offices.

Norton Rose's broad-ranging shipping and transport practice works closely with several firm-wide international shipping, trade, offshore and energy clients. Highlights include advising P&O Princess on complex charter and sale transactions. Other clients include Mobil Oil Nigeria. The firm is also recommended for major arbitrations. Betty Pedrini, Neil Q Miller and Piraeus-based Chris Hobbs are recommended.

Barlow Lyde & Gilbert's Nigel Wagland heads a team which is recommended for heavyweight,

SHIPPING: DRY

CLYDE & CO ✪
HOLMAN FENWICK & WILLAN ✪
INCE & CO

RICHARDS BUTLER
STEPHENSON HARWOOD

HILL TAYLOR DICKINSON

Clifford Chance LLP
Norton Rose ✪

Barlow Lyde & Gilbert
Bentleys, Stokes & Lowless
Lawrence Graham
More Fisher Brown
Shaw and Croft
Thomas Cooper & Stibbard
Watson, Farley & Williams

Curtis Davis Garrard
Davies Arnold Cooper
Elborne Mitchell
Holmes Hardingham
Jackson Parton
Middleton Potts
Waterson Hicks

Bryan Cave
Constant & Constant
DLA ✪
Davis & Co
Lawrence Jones
Ross & Co
Taylor Wessing ✪
Waltons & Morse

Firms are listed A-Z in tiers which are ranked in order of priority
✪ Indicates firm displays contact details at the end of this chapter.

multi-jurisdictional litigation. The practice received a boost with the hire of Richard Black from niche shipping firm *RC Black & Co*.

Bentleys, Stokes & Lowless is rated by peers and clients as a solid, honest and experienced practice which is 'user-friendly, easy to work with' and reasonable in its fees. P&I clubs are an important part of the practice's client base. Senior partner Andrew Bardot, Paul Griffiths and Vernon Sewell are recommended.

Lawrence Graham's team is headed by Michael Lax and Imogen Rumbold. Major cases include *Stocznia Gdanska v Latreefers*. The firm advised on insurance issues arising out of the terrorist attack on the *Limburg*. The practice also undertook work on a number of confidential arbitrations.

More Fisher Brown is a firm of 20 lawyers, maintaining a strong reputation for its cost-effective work for several P&I clubs. Adrian Moylan, Edward Gray and Peter Jago stand out.

Shaw and Croft advises a wide range of insurers, brokers, insureds, foreign state-owned shipping companies, luxury yacht charterers and commodity traders. Richard Coles, Ben Browne and Michael Moon are recommended.

Tim Kelleher at **Thomas Cooper & Stibbard** heads a practice, which undertakes a wide range of cargo claims and charterparty disputes. We also recommend Paul Barfield and Darryl Kennard in the Singapore office, Douglas Bateson in Athens and Mark Sachs in Vancouver.

Highlights at **Watson, Farley & Williams** include advising SANA on High Court litigation involving the loss of a rig off Brazil, and acting for Pacific Trawlers on High Court litigation over a fleet of 11 supertrawlers. David Kavanagh, Charles Buss, and Charles Smallwood are recommended as is Tony Rooth. The firm works closely with its Singapore, Piraeus, New York and Bangkok offices.

Heathrow-based **Curtis Davis Garrard** has an excellent reputation for shipbuilding disputes. The firm also reports an increase in LNG work and litigation involving heavyweight marine construction. Simon Curtis and Ian Garrard are the best-known partners.

Davies Arnold Cooper acted for shipowners in major arbitration over asbestos injury. The practice is also recommended for shipping regulatory expertise on consortia agreements.

Elborne Mitchell's Peter Tribe, Roger Miles and David McKie head a team that advises charterers, owners and P&I clubs. Headline cases include *The Atrice*.

Holmes Hardingham was involved in major ongoing cases such as *Starsin* and *Happy Ranger*. Glenn Winter is noted.

Jackson Parton is a niche shipping firm recommended for excellent client care, providing good value for money and being 'pleasant, not stuffy and easygoing to deal with'.

Middleton Potts' shipping lawyers have excellent complementary expertise in commodities work. Senior partner David Lucas and Faye Doherty are well known. Andrew Ridings is also recommended.

Waterson Hicks continues to build a strong reputation for shipping, commodities and related insurance work. Clients include P&I clubs and major oil companies and oil traders. John Hicks and Martin Wisdom are well known for providing direct, commercial and no-nonsense advice.

SHIPPING: WET

'Wet' or admiralty lawyers act on cases arising out of collision, salvages, total loss and pollution.

Clyde & Co was involved in major casualty cases such as *Tricolor*, *Prestige*, *Hual Europe* and *Gaz Poem*. Simon Fletcher and Stephen Pink continue to build strong reputations.

Holman Fenwick & Willan's James Gosling and Hugh Brown were involved in a run of high-profile cases, including *Tricolor* (acting for the owners), *Prestige*, *Hanjin Pennsylvania* and *Limburg*.

Ince & Co secured instructions from the key parties on the *Prestige* (owners and P&I club) with a team led by master mariner and partner Faz Peermohamed. The practice also includes three admiralty managers. Partners James Wilson and Chris Beesley are recommended. Colin de la Rue is known for pollution law expertise.

Hill Taylor Dickinson's Andrew Johnson heads a practice renowned for its casualty expertise. The team also boasts three master mariners, including Michael Mallin. London works closely with the offices in Greece and Dubai.

Richards Butler was involved in major cases including acting for salvors on the *Hanjin Pennsylvania* and *Limburg*. The team includes two marine managers. We recommend Richard Harvey, Andrew Taylor, Piraeus-based John Reece and Hong Kong-based Paul Apostolis. The firm is recommended for its use of cutting-edge technology at critical times.

Shaw and Croft advises on collisions, salvage and towage matters. Ben Browne, Roland Jackson and Hamish Edgar are recommended.

Major cases at **Stephenson Harwood** include *Kodima*, a grounding on the Devon coast. Joe Atkinson is recommended. The practice also includes two master mariners. The firm also has offices in Greece and Hong Kong.

Bentleys, Stokes & Lowless is recommended for extensive and longstanding involvement in wet work. Joe Quain and Paul Griffiths, recommended for serious and complicated wet cases, are well known. The firm boasts five master mariners, four of whom are also qualified solicitors.

Clifford Chance LLP is recommended for multi-jurisdictional cases, working closely with its international offices. Major cases include *Aconcagua* and *Silversea*. Mark Morrison, Alex Panayides and associate Judith Prior are recommended.

Holmes Hardingham's Mike Ellis heads a team which advised on the salvage of the *Jody F Millennium*, New Zealand's biggest ever marine casualty and *Doric Chariot*, a vessel grounded in the sensitive waters of the Barrier Reef.

More Fisher Brown's Michael Mitchell is a respected authority on collisions and salvage work.

Norton Rose's Paul Williams heads a practice renowned for cruise work, multi-party disaster litigation and personal injuries arising out of casualties. Neil Q Miller is also well known. The team includes five legally qualified mariners.

Barlow Lyde & Gilbert's Simon Chumas heads a practice which advised on a major $50m arbitration over an oil spill in the USA.

Mike Allen at **Curtis Davis Garrard** is a chartered engineer who acts for several tug and salvage clients.

DLA's Mike Pollen is a well-known wet shipping personality.

Jackson Parton's Brian Roberts, David Hughes, Nicholas Parton, John Watling and assistant Jonathan Clyne are recommended for broad-ranging expertise in wet work.

Lawrence Graham acted for a slot charterer on a fire on the *Hanjin Pennsylvania*.

Middleton Potts advised on salvage and collision cases in Africa and Asia. Andrew Ridings is recommended.

Waltons & Morse's Michael Buckley undertakes salvage and collision cases.

SHIPPING: WET

CLYDE & CO ✪
HOLMAN FENWICK & WILLAN ✪
INCE & CO

HILL TAYLOR DICKINSON

Richards Butler
Shaw and Croft
Stephenson Harwood

Bentleys, Stokes & Lowless
Clifford Chance LLP
Holmes Hardingham
More Fisher Brown
Norton Rose ✪

Barlow Lyde & Gilbert
Curtis Davis Garrard
DLA ✪
Jackson Parton
Lawrence Graham
Middleton Potts
Waltons & Morse

Bryan Cave
Constant & Constant
Davies Arnold Cooper
Elborne Mitchell
Thomas Cooper & Stibbard
Waterson Hicks

Firms are listed A-Z in tiers which are ranked in order of priority
✪ Indicates firm displays contact details at the end of this chapter.

TELECOMS

Bird & Bird, best known for its market-leading regulatory practice, continued to handle significant corporate telecoms matters via the dismantling of BT's joint venture with AT&T, Concert. Partner David Ayers led the team advising BT, while in other matters Dominic Cook advised mmO2 on commercial arrangements relating to Genie. Chief executive and joint group head David Kerr continues to be among the best-known names in the telecoms market.

Clifford Chance LLP's Tim Schwarz is widely regarded as one of the leading advisers to emerging market governments on PTT privatisations, while fellow partner Elizabeth Hiester has an excellent reputation for regulatory advice. Internationally the firm has been most active in central and eastern Europe and the Middle East, where clients include the governments of Latvia and Lebanon. International practice head Joachim Fleury is recommended for private equity matters.

Allen & Overy's broad practice is built on the firm's traditional finance strengths but also encompasses regulatory, commercial and corporate expertise. Competition specialist Chris Watson advised T-Mobile in the high-profile calls to mobile inquiry. The firm is among the leaders for satellite projects.

Baker & McKenzie's telecoms team, headed by Peter Strivens, continued to advise 3 on the launch of its third-generation mobile service in 2003. A team led by regulatory specialist Robbie Downing advised Freeserve on the first appeal of an Oftel decision to the Competition Commission, concerning the roll-out of broadband by BT.

Regulatory has long been a strength of **Field Fisher Waterhouse**'s telecoms practice. Its track record was confirmed by partner Tony Ballard's advice to Orange on the Competition Commission's calls to mobile inquiry. The team also won Hutchison's 3 as a new client to advise on network-related property issues.

Freshfields Bruckhaus Deringer's highly regarded antitrust and regulatory practice, headed by Rachel Brandenburger, acted for mmO2 on the Competition Commission inquiry into call termination rates, and for WorldCom on a variety of EU and national matters. David Aitman is recommended for regulatory matters.

'Responsive' corporate partner Peter Dickinson heads **Mayer, Brown, Rowe & Maw LLP**'s transaction-focused telecoms practice. The firm, which counts Cable & Wireless as an anchor client, is particularly recommended for restructuring and insolvency matters as well as a broad range of commercial, competition and regulatory advice.

Ashurst's broad practice is particularly well regarded for satellite matters, with group head Clive Tucker leading the team advising the Riyadh-based ARABSAT on the acquisition of an in-orbit satellite from Lockheed Martin and Intersputnik. Regulatory specialist Caroline Easter is also highly regarded.

TELECOMS

BIRD & BIRD ✪
CLIFFORD CHANCE LLP

ALLEN & OVERY ✪
BAKER & McKENZIE ✪
FIELD FISHER WATERHOUSE
FRESHFIELDS BRUCKHAUS DERINGER ✪
MAYER, BROWN, ROWE & MAW LLP

ASHURST ✪
DENTON WILDE SAPTE ✪
LINKLATERS ✪
LOVELLS ✪
OLSWANG
SIMMONS & SIMMONS ✪

Addleshaw Goddard
Arnold & Porter (UK) LLP ✪
Charles Russell
DLA ✪
Slaughter and May ✪
Taylor Wessing ✪
Weil, Gotshal & Manges ✪
White & Case ✪
Wilmer Cutler Pickering LLP ✪

Eversheds LLP
Herbert Smith ✪
Kemp Little LLP
Norton Rose ✪
Osborne Clarke
Richards Butler
Shearman & Sterling (London) LLP
Travers Smith Braithwaite

CMS Cameron McKenna
Cadwalader, Wickersham & Taft LLP
Covington & Burling ✪
Latham & Watkins ✪
Lawrence Graham
LeBoeuf, Lamb, Greene & MacRae
McCarthy Tétrault
McGrigors
Nabarro Nathanson
SJ Berwin ✪
Steptoe & Johnson
Tite & Lewis
Watson, Farley & Williams

Firms are listed A-Z in tiers which are ranked in order of priority
✪ Indicates firm displays contact details at the end of this chapter.

Denton Wilde Sapte's international reach is of significant benefit to its telecoms practice, evidenced by its leading roles in the \$500m privatisation of the Bahamas Telecommunications Company. The large team, headed by partner Nicholas Higham, has expertise in mobile (Nokia and Virgin Mobile are key clients), regulatory issues, and satellite.

Linklaters has a stellar telecoms client list that includes Vodafone, BT and Telenor, as well as many of the leading banks active in the sector. The core banking and corporate expertise was displayed in advice to the Royal Bank of Scotland on the restructuring of Energis. The firm's commercial and regulatory team advised BT on a £1bn global telecoms agreement with Unilever.

Lovells is most active in international telecoms matters, highlighted by its competition advice to Telia on its merger with Sonera and its success in China. The team has a track record in advising major corporates on telecoms supply agreements for virtual private network services, and is also recommended for insolvency-related work.

Olswang's telecoms practice counts Cable & Wireless, WorldCom, and O2 among its clients. The team is particularly focused on corporate and regulatory matters. Partner Colin Long is known for his longstanding telecoms expertise, while fellow partner Kim Nicholson is best known for corporate finance advice to TMT clients. Former in-house lawyer Natasha Hobday is also well regarded for commercial matters.

Simmons & Simmons' major telecoms clients include WorldCom, COLT, and Cable & Wireless. Partner Tom Wheadon 'understands regulatory through and through', while partner Rhys Williams' profile continues to grow. The firm advised clients on the use of GSM Gateways, a method of bypassing the monopoly position of mobile network operators, and continues to advise Telewest on a wide range of matters.

Former Oftel in-house lawyer and competition expert Edward Pitt, is **Addleshaw Goddard**'s best-known telecoms specialist. As with many practices, the team has advised on a series of restructurings. Oftel, COLT, and Alpha Telecom are major clients.

Arnold & Porter (UK) LLP's Michael Ryan, a regulatory specialist, heads the London team that offers commercial and regulatory advice to a wide range of international telecoms clients including SBC.

Charles Russell has weathered the downturn well and grown its international telecoms practice. Transactional partner Mark Moncreiffe heads the group, which also features the regulatory-focused partners Sue Cozens and Trevor Smale, and contentious specialist John Sykes.

DLA's regulatory strength is apparent by its position on Oftel's panel and in its work for clients such as COLT and Cable & Wireless. The team, headed by contentious specialist Julian Stait, also counts Kingston Communications, Energis and MCI among its core clients.

Corporate and finance advice underpins **Slaughter and May**'s telecoms practice. Corporate partner William Underhill, TMT group head, counts COLT among his clients. The team also advises telecoms-related technology companies such as Symbian and Cambridge Silicon Radio.

Taylor Wessing regulatory heavyweight Ted Mercer continues to head a well-regarded team that has recently majored on insolvency-related matters for clients including Dolphin Telecommunications, Isle of Wight Cable and Telecomunications and Omne Communications.

Weil, Gotshal & Manges boasts one of the world's leading restructuring practices, with key roles for WorldCom, Telewest and the Polish Netia. Partner Graham Defries heads the London team, which also advises clients (including WorldCom EMEA) on commercial and regulatory issues.

White & Case has an excellent track record in international telecoms projects, particularly on private equity deals. On the contentious side, the firm advised UPC in vulture fund litigation relating to its €5.2m recapitalisation. London-based co-head of global telecoms David Eisenberg is recommended.

Wilmer Cutler Pickering LLP's London team, which works closely with its Brussels team on regulatory matters, counts Orange and T-Mobile as key clients in the mobile sector. Group head Paul von Hehn is well regarded for UMTS infrastructure sharing and national roaming agreements. The team was bolstered in June 2003 with the recruitment of Stephanie Liston from **McDermott, Will & Emery**. Liston is a well-known figure in the market and was re-elected to the board of ECTA in 2002 (the only lawyer on the board).

Eversheds LLP, the preferred adviser to O2 for the full range of legal matters, is carving out a substantial niche in broadband-related local and public authority work. Partners Neil Brown and Graeme Gordon are recommended for commercial and regulatory matters, respectively.

Herbert Smith's internationally focused and energised team won new clients during the year including Swisscom and Telekom Malaysia. The practice continues to impress with its broad-based approach, covering corporate, regulatory and litigation. Key clients include Vodafone, Nokia, and NTT DoCoMo.

Kemp Little LLP's name partner Richard Kemp continues to be among the most respected players in the TMT market. The team regularly advises Microsoft on telecoms-related issues.

Norton Rose's telecoms practice is finance-based, although partner Michael Grenfell is a 'first-class' regulatory expert. Telecoms clients include France Télécom and Batelco.

Group head Simon Rendell at **Osborne Clarke** is a well-regarded commercial specialist with a particular expertise in mobile work, while former BT in-house counsel Angus Finnegan is also well thought of. Highlights include advising Vodafone on commercial arrangements and United Business Media on its global voice and data service acquisition.

Richards Butler is recommended for its international corporate finance practice in the telecoms sector. The team, led by partner Philip Allford, advised JITCO on the IPO of Jordan Telecommunications, and also counts OTE and Korea Telecoms as clients.

Restructuring work dominated **Shearman & Sterling (London) LLP**'s year, advising France Télécom on the restructuring of ntl and on the MobilCom restructuring. London office managing partner Kenneth MacRitchie is the best-known name, with Chris Bright, who handles competition and regulatory matters.

Travers Smith Braithwaite advised ntl on its $12bn bond restructuring, the largest-ever and among the most complex in Europe. Corporate partner Spencer Summerfield is well thought of.

FOREIGN LAW FIRMS IN LONDON – OVERVIEW

As the top American law firms in London seek to plug holes in practices such as tax and competition and build UK practices that mirror their strengths in the States, the market for lateral partner hires remains buoyant. UK corporate lawyers are in high demand. For the first time, **Simpson Thacher & Bartlett LLP** recruited two UK finance partners in London. (See **Banking and finance** below.) **Milbank, Tweed, Hadley & McCloy** and **Shearman & Sterling (London) LLP** also bolstered their already-strong practices with prominent UK corporate partner hires (See **Corporate** below).

Mergers continue apace, with *Jones Day Gouldens* (now **Jones Day**) giving the US giant over 200 lawyers in London, with top-quality M&A, litigation, tax, property and IP expertise. However, **Ashurst** and **Fried, Frank, Harris, Shriver & Jacobson (London) LLP** broke off their merger talks in May 2003.

Another significant development of the year was the dissolution *of Brobeck Phleger & Harrison* in the US. Joint venture partner **Hale & Dorr LLP** took over the offices of the former *Brobeck Hale and Dorr* in London, Oxford, and Munich, though the former London head Tom Kellerman moved to the London office of **Morgan Lewis**.

Altheimer & Gray also announced plans to dissolve in 2003. Many partners ended up at **Kirkpatrick Stockton LLP**.

In early 2003, **Buchanan Ingersoll** lost its last two partners from its three-year-old London office, which at one point had 13 partners. The firm intends to maintain the office as an outpost, with no resident lawyers.

NEW OFFICE OPENINGS

London continues to attract American law firms as their clients aim to expand in Europe. In 2002, five new firms appeared on the landscape. **King & Spalding International LLP** moved a number of partners to its newly opened premises: John Cogan focuses on energy project development; John Keffer and Mark Thompson are M&A lawyers, Michael McMillen leads the Islamic finance practice, and managing partner George Branch intends to build an arbitration practice.

In June 2003, Boston IP and technology specialist **Mintz, Levin, Cohn, Ferris, Glovsky and Popeo, P.C.** announced its London opening.

Schulte Roth & Zabel International LLP established an office in London to capitalise on the growth of the hedge fund industry in Europe. The London office is led by Daniel Shapiro, a senior US tax partner who is a leading hedge fund lawyer in the US, and UK fund lawyer Christopher Hilditch, who was formerly with **Maples and Calder Europe** and **Simmons & Simmons**.

Troutman Sanders LLP specialises in energy trading work, led by partner John Varholy. The office is managed by real estate partner James Keaten.

In late May 2003, **Winston & Strawn LLP** opened in London with the recruitment from **Morgan Lewis** of partners Thomas Benz and Zoe Ashcroft. Both are experienced in corporate finance.

TRANSATLANTIC MERGERS

The transatlantic merger that created **Mayer, Brown, Rowe & Maw LLP** in early 2002 set the stage for further US-UK mergers to come. The biggest surprise was **Jones Day**'s, announcement in February 2003. Given that *Gouldens* was known in the market as one of the more profitable, focused firms, the announcement sent shivers down the spines of less healthy firms.

Two smaller London firms recently hooked up with regional US law firms. In early 2003 City corporate boutique *Hobson Audley* announced its merger with Minneapolis-based **Faegre & Benson LLP**, creating **Faegre Benson Hobson Audley LLP**. The combined firm offers corporate finance, dispute resolution, technology, employment and property law expertise.

US litigation firm **Shook, Hardy & Bacon International LLP** merged with London litigation specialist *Arnander Irvine & Zietman* in summer 2002 to form a transatlantic contentious practice with 17 partners and 35 other fee-earners. In London **Shook, Hardy & Bacon International LLP** was previously focused on product liability work; the merger expands the London capability to IP, fraud, and commercial litigation.

Note that the seven US firms that have merged with UK firms in the past three years – **Dechert**, **Faegre Benson Hobson Audley LLP**, **Jones Day**, **Mayer, Brown, Rowe & Maw LLP**, **Reed Smith**, **Shook, Hardy & Bacon International LLP**, and **Steptoe & Johnson** - are ranked alongside the UK law firms in the London chapters of *The Legal 500* because the mergers created substantial UK law practices. US firms with strong UK capability in various practice areas, where appropriate will also be ranked alongside UK firms in the London chapters.

US PRACTICES

The firms in this table practise US rather than UK law, although they may have dual-qualified

US PRACTICES

CRAVATH, SWAINE & MOORE LLP
DAVIS POLK & WARDWELL

FRIED, FRANK, HARRIS, SHRIVER & JACOBSON (LONDON) LLP ✪

Cahill Gordon & Reindel
Willkie Farr & Gallagher LLP ✪

Brown Rudnick Berlack Israels LLP
Curtis, Mallet-Prevost, Colt & Mosle LLP ✪
Fulbright & Jaworski LLP
Paul, Weiss, Rifkind, Wharton & Garrison LLP
Steel Hector & Davis International

Firms are listed A-Z in tiers which are ranked in order of priority
✪ Indicates firm displays contact details at the end of this chapter.

lawyers. These firms do not appear in the other tables in this chapter.

Top New York firm **Cravath, Swaine & Moore LLP** is known for its expertise in M&A, corporate finance, banking, and securities, but has no stated plans to break into the UK legal market. We recommend William Rogers and Phillip Boeckman.

Davis Polk & Wardwell specialises in M&A and finance work for insurance companies and other financial institutions. Partners Julia Coles, Keith Kearney, Paul Kumleben, Jeffrey Oakes, and David Wells are highly regarded by London investment bankers.

Fried, Frank, Harris, Shriver & Jacobson (London) LLP spent much of 2002 in discussions with **Ashurst**. These talks failed to materialise in a merger. The firm is now on the prowl for UK lawyers. Among the partners at **Fried, Frank, Harris, Shriver & Jacobson (London) LLP** are Robert Mollen and Sanford Krieger on the M&A side and Tim Peterson and Daniel Bursky finance experts. The London office is particularly strong in M&A and high yield offerings.

Cahill Gordon & Reindel partner Jim Robinson is highly regarded for capital markets work.

New York's **Willkie Farr & Gallagher LLP** has a small, two-lawyer satellite office in London.

Brown Rudnick Berlack Israels LLP has ten US lawyers who do primarily corporate work.

Curtis, Mallet-Prevost, Colt & Mosle LLP has three partners in London who focus on international corporate and energy work.

Fulbright & Jaworski LLP specialises in transactional work for the energy sector.

Paul, Weiss, Rifkind, Wharton & Garrison LLP opened in late 2002. The office is staffed by US lawyers with expertise in capital markets, private equity, and M&A. Mark Bergman and David Lakhdir are the partners in charge.

We rank the firms in our tables below primarily on the strength of their UK capability, though we take into account the quality of the US practice as well.

US: BANKING AND FINANCE

LATHAM & WATKINS ✪
MILBANK, TWEED, HADLEY & McCLOY
SHEARMAN & STERLING (LONDON) LLP
WHITE & CASE ✪

CLEARY GOTTLIEB STEEN & HAMILTON ✪
SIDLEY AUSTIN BROWN & WOOD
SIMPSON THACHER & BARTLETT LLP
SKADDEN, ARPS, SLATE, MEAGHER & FLOM LLP
SULLIVAN & CROMWELL LLP
WEIL, GOTSHAL & MANGES ✪

Cadwalader, Wickersham & Taft LLP
Debevoise & Plimpton LLP ✪
Dewey Ballantine
Kirkland & Ellis International LLP ✪
LeBoeuf, Lamb, Greene & MacRae

Akin Gump Strauss Hauer & Feld
Arnold & Porter (UK) LLP ✪
Gibson, Dunn & Crutcher LLP
McDermott, Will & Emery ✪
Squire, Sanders & Dempsey ✪
Vinson & Elkins R.L.L.P. ✪

Baker Botts ✪
Bingham McCutchen LLP
Bryan Cave
Coudert Brothers ✪
Morrison & Foerster MNP ✪
Orrick, Herrington & Sutcliffe
Paul, Hastings, Janofsky & Walker LLP

Firms are listed A-Z in tiers which are ranked in order of priority
✪ Indicates firm displays contact details at the end of this chapter.

US: BANKING AND FINANCE

Latham & Watkins is a world leader in high-yield debt and boasts a raft of investment banking clients. One banker calls Bryant Edwards 'good all round and calm in a crisis.' UK banking partner James Chesterman is highly regarded in the marketplace. The firm bolstered its insolvency practice with the hire of John Houghton from **Simmons & Simmons** and also nabbed capital markets partner Christopher McFadzean from **Linklaters**.

Milbank, Tweed, Hadley & McCloy has in-depth experience in acquisition finance, including senior bank loans, mezzanine, and high-yield tranches, as well as capital markets, securitisation, and structured finance. The firm has strong ties to investment banks and has worked on billion-pound financings opposite the likes of **Allen & Overy** and **Clifford Chance LLP**. Clients recommend Tom Siebens, Kevin Muzilla, and Patrick Holmes for acquisition finance and John Walker for structured finance.

Shearman & Sterling (London) LLP's London-based banking partners compete head-to-head with the Magic Circle firms for banking instructions. Clients praise the 'first-class service and style' of London managing partner Kenneth MacRitchie, who advised senior lender WestLB on the financing of the new Wembley stadium. Other top finance partners are Clifford Atkins, Iain Goalen and Anthony Ward. The firm also boasts one of the leading capital markets practices in Europe. One client calls David Beveridge 'the best high-yield lawyer in Europe. He always has solutions and a better technical knowledge than anyone else I have worked with'.

White & Case provides a superb cross-border finance, transaction and advisory service to a broad range of bank finance clients. The team includes such leading lights as Mike Goetz, Maurice Allen, Kate Allchurch and Emma Webster. Rich Reilly is head of structured products. One client describes capital markets partner Francis Fitzherbert-Brockholes as 'a truly wonderful, spirited and intelligent lawyer.'

Cleary Gottlieb Steen & Hamilton is best known for its US capital markets expertise. Leading partners include Daniel Braverman, Glen Scarcliffe and Ashar Qureshi.

The London office of **Sidley Austin Brown & Wood** is well known for its securitisation, property finance, and derivatives practices, which come under the umbrella of the international finance group led by Graham Penn and Howard Waterman. One client says of the team: 'I think the quality of partners is unparalleled: superb technical/legal knowledge backed by huge amounts of real-life deal experience They offer excellent, timely service and innovative, out-of-the-box thinking'. In January 2003, the firm recruited leading property finance partners Debbie Carslaw and Mark Menhennet from **Denton Wilde Sapte**. However, observers were surprised when **Sidley Austin Brown & Wood**'s highly regarded four-partner corporate securities group, led by US partner Christopher Mead, departed to set up the new London office of the Paris-based **Gide Loyrette Nouel**.

After a long search, the London office of **Simpson Thacher & Bartlett LLP** hired its first UK partner in early 2003; Euan Gorrie from **Allen & Overy**, who specialises in acquisition finance. Subsequently the firm recruited Stephen Short from **Ashurst**, who is also a finance partner.

In the London office of **Skadden, Arps, Slate, Meagher & Flom LLP**, managing partner Bruce Buck has impressive experience in cross-border financings, including equity, high-yield and other debt offerings, and strong ties to underwriters. UK partner James Healy is recommended for his capital markets expertise. In April 2002 the firm recruited Mark Darley, formerly a senior banking partner at **Lovells**.

Sullivan & Cromwell LLP is better known for its corporate expertise, but the firm has formidable relationships with most important investment banks.

Weil, Gotshal & Manges has extensive

experience in multi-jurisdictional secured financings, acquisition finance, bridge and mezzanine financings, capital markets, and securitisation. Clients include Credit Suisse First Boston, Dresdner Kleinwort Capital, Lehman Brothers, and WestLB. Key partners include Chris Harrison and Richard Ginsburg.

In 2002, **Cadwalader, Wickersham & Taft LLP** bolstered its banking practice with the recruitment of Stephen Mostyn-Williams and Christopher Kandel. The firm also hired first-rate project finance partner, Bill Rubin, who joined from **Weil, Gotshal & Manges**. Capital markets partner James Croke is universally praised by clients; one says he is 'of the highest quality and very professional – he dominates his field.'

In 2002 **Debevoise & Plimpton LLP** recruited Marwan Al-Turki from the London office of **Baker & McKenzie**. He is a leading fund formation and financial services lawyer.

At **Dewey Ballantine**, partner Camille Abousleiman heads the international capital markets group. One client praises his 'thorough knowledge of the law and ability to succinctly get to the point and resolve issues in the most efficient way possible'.

Kirkland & Ellis International LLP's dual-qualified partner Bronwen Jones offers secured lending expertise on acquisition and leveraged financing transactions. Lyndon Norley is praised by a client as 'one of the best' insolvency lawyers.

The London office of **LeBoeuf, Lamb, Greene & MacRae** enjoys a strong project finance practice led by Bruce Johnston, which complements the firm's global energy practice. Partner Joseph Ferraro is described as 'accommodating and well versed in capital markets', while Brian Zimbler is noted for his knowledge of the intricacies of the international capital markets and his first-rate financial acumen.

At **Akin Gump Strauss Hauer & Feld**, partner David Billings represents private investment funds and their sponsors and has extensive experience in fund formation and investment management.

The London office of **Arnold & Porter (UK) LLP** advised the Republic of Moldova on a Eurobond restructuring, and acted for the EBRD on several transactions in Russia.

A team at **Gibson, Dunn & Crutcher LLP** specialises in acquisition finance, investment funds and Islamic finance. Andrew Thomas heads the group.

At **McDermott, Will & Emery**, Graham Rowbotham leads the banking department, which has a speciality in energy and weather derivatives.

Squire, Sanders & Dempsey offers capital markets and project finance expertise primarily for media and telecommunications clients. We recommend Mara Babin, Mark Cusick, and Richard Sterling Surrey.

A strong energy-sector client base has bolstered the finance practice at **Vinson & Elkins R.L.L.P.** Partner Peter Gaines has advised an array of international banks and financial institutions on project, acquisition, and structured finance transactions.

Baker Botts recruited its first dedicated finance partner in London when it hired partner John White from **Pillsbury Winthrop**.

At **Bingham McCutchen LLP**, the 'intelligent, efficient and trustworthy' James Roome enjoys a strong client base of distressed hedge funds and investment banks with distressed debt, such as the bondholders in the Marconi restructuring. The firm also works for institutional investors in private placements. A highlight in 2003 was the recruitment of Sarah Coucher, head of leveraged finance at **Denton Wilde Sapte**, to lead its bank finance department.

Bryan Cave strengthened its London finance practice with the recruitment of Paul Flood from **Tite & Lewis**. He brings asset and project finance experience, particularly in the aerospace and defence sectors. Partner Richard Stewart has worked on projects in Europe, India, Pakistan, Bangladesh, the Far East and the Middle East and specialises in Islamic finance. The firm also has a strong investment funds practice, which was bolstered in 2003 with the hire of John Langan, who joined from *KLegal*.

At **Coudert Brothers**, Alexander Janes and Peter O'Driscoll are specialists in banking, finance and securities.

At **Morrison & Foerster MNP**, partner Brian Bates has a strong debt practice acting primarily for issuers. One client calls him 'technically superb and commercially focused'.

Orrick, Herrington & Sutcliffe partner Martin Stewart-Smith has a corporate and project finance practice, while Adrian Harris's focus is insolvency and restructuring.

At **Paul, Hastings, Janofsky & Walker LLP**, partners Joel Simon and Keith Ott are corporate finance specialists. On the UK side, the firm is best known for its property expertise.

US: CORPORATE

The firms in our top tier expanded quickly into mainstream UK practices and have built up bigger teams than their rivals. We rank them primarily on the quality and depth of their UK practices, but also consider their reputation and client base in the US, Asia and Europe.

The private equity team at **Latham & Watkins** enjoyed a watershed year in 2002. The firm hired widely admired private equity specialist Charles Fuller from **Simmons & Simmons** and picked up a key deal for Charterhouse Development Capital – the £860m purchase of Coral Eurobet. We recommend Michael Bond, Gay Bronson and Nigel Campion-Smith.

Shearman & Sterling (London) LLP nailed its third UK partner when it recruited M&A star Peter King from **Linklaters**. The firm advised on a number of debt restructurings, including Versatel's $1.7bn debt restructuring and advising France Télécom on the $10.6bn restructuring of ntl. The corporate practice is enhanced by a first-rate antitrust group led by Christopher Bright.

Known globally as an M&A powerhouse, **Skadden, Arps, Slate, Meagher & Flom LLP** boasts well-known UK partner Michael Hatchard, while Allan Murray-Jones, also an English lawyer, specialises in private equity transactions.

Weil, Gotshal & Manges has reputable M&A and private equity expertise in partners Mike Francies and Paul Claydon.

In a slow year for M&A, the corporate department at **White & Case**, led by Peter Finlay,

US: CORPORATE

LATHAM & WATKINS ✪
SHEARMAN & STERLING (LONDON) LLP
SKADDEN, ARPS, SLATE, MEAGHER & FLOM LLP
WEIL, GOTSHAL & MANGES ✪
WHITE & CASE ✪

CLEARY GOTTLIEB STEEN & HAMILTON ✪
DEBEVOISE & PLIMPTON LLP ✪
DEWEY BALLANTINE
GIBSON, DUNN & CRUTCHER LLP
KIRKLAND & ELLIS INTERNATIONAL LLP ✪
MILBANK, TWEED, HADLEY & McCLOY
SIDLEY AUSTIN BROWN & WOOD
SIMPSON THACHER & BARTLETT LLP
SULLIVAN & CROMWELL LLP

Cadwalader, Wickersham & Taft LLP
LeBoeuf, Lamb, Greene & MacRae
McDermott, Will & Emery ✪

Akin Gump Strauss Hauer & Feld
Arnold & Porter (UK) LLP ✪
Baker Botts ✪
Bryan Cave
Chadbourne & Parke
Coudert Brothers ✪
Covington & Burling ✪
Dorsey & Whitney
Hale and Dorr
Hogan & Hartson ✪
Holme Roberts & Owen
Kilpatrick Stockton LLP ✪
Morgan Lewis ✪
Shaw Pittman LLP
Squire, Sanders & Dempsey ✪
Wilmer Cutler Pickering LLP ✪

Cozen O'Connor
Hunton & Williams
Kaye Scholer LLP
Morrison & Foerster MNP ✪
Paul, Hastings, Janofsky & Walker LLP
Vinson & Elkins R.L.L.P. ✪

Firms are listed A-Z in tiers which are ranked in order of priority
✪ Indicates firm displays contact details at the end of this chapter.

had an impressive deal flow. The firm also bolstered its corporate recovery practice with the recruitment of Dan Hamilton from **CMS Cameron McKenna**.

At **Cleary Gottlieb Steen & Hamilton**, UK M&A partners Andrew Curran and Simon Jay carry out M&A work in tandem with the firm's European practices.

Debevoise & Plimpton LLP UK partner Colin Bogie heads the firm's UK M&A practice, while Katherine Ashton is dual qualified. Bogie has been involved in major cross-border restructurings and insolvencies. Private equity clients praise the firm's 'thoughtful, responsive, and commercial' service.

Dewey Ballantine partner Mark Saunders 'consistently provides top-notch, thorough representation' on M&A matters. Partner Adam Dann is praised for 'his commercial outlook and his first-class, proactive advice on a timely and cost-effective basis.' The M&A group is led by Douglas Getter. One happy client says:'The team at **Dewey Ballantine** has the edge. I would not look anywhere else for corporate advice.'

Sixty percent of the work in the London office of **Gibson, Dunn & Crutcher LLP** is corporate, which complements the firm's strong M&A practice in the US. Contact partners in London are Mark Pinder and Judith Shepherd.

Kirkland & Ellis International LLP expanded its English practice with the recruitment from **Cadwalader, Wickersham & Taft LLP** of partner Lyndon Norley, who will head the firm's English insolvency practice. The firm is best known for its private equity practice for clients such as Jefferson Smurfit and Bain Capital. Among the most active lawyers are US partners James Learner and Stuart Mills, and UK partner Nigel Dunmore.

Amid much media excitement, the London office of **Milbank, Tweed, Hadley & McCloy** hired, in early 2003, corporate partner Tim Emmerson from **Freshfields Bruckhaus Deringer**. He joins an M&A and private equity team led by the eminent Michael Goroff.

In May 2002, Andrew Parnell moved to the corporate group at **Sidley Austin Brown & Wood** from the London office of **Wilmer Cutler Pickering LLP**. **Sidley Austin Brown & Wood** now has four partners and 12 assistants in the highly regarded London corporate group.

The London office of **Simpson Thacher & Bartlett LLP** fields a team of first-rate US qualified lawyers with corporate finance and M&A expertise. Investment bankers praise the skills of Greg Conway and also rate younger partners Michael Wolfson and Ryerson Symons. The office is managed by Walter Looney, who is also highly regarded.

A 'sharp and professional' team of M&A and corporate finance partners inhabit the London office of **Sullivan & Cromwell LLP**. Clients frequently mention William Plapinger, Richard Morrissey, Robert Osgood and George Sampas. The firm has top-quality US capability in competition, real estate, and tax law.

Cadwalader, Wickersham & Taft LLP's corporate partners Andrew Wilkinson, Richard Nevins and Richard Gregorian specialise in financial restructurings.

At **LeBoeuf, Lamb, Greene & MacRae**, the best-known corporate transactional partners are Joseph Ferraro, Mitri Najjar, Tony Richmond and Brian Zimbler.

At **McDermott, Will & Emery**, the corporate group grew with the addition of Richard Britain from **Linklaters** and Nicholas Azis from **Skadden, Arps, Slate, Meagher & Flom LLP**, both of whom joined as partners. One client praises William Charnley for 'robust and pragmatic advice in an efficient fashion'.

Akin Gump Strauss Hauer & Feld has a strong energy practice, with clients such as Lukoil. Fred Heller is the partner in charge of London and concentrates on cross-border M&A. H Rey Stroube III moved to London in 2002. He chairs the firm's financial restructuring practice group.

Led by Jeremy Willcocks, the corporate team at **Arnold & Porter (UK) LLP** has developed a leading biotech private equity practice. The group has also completed significant M&A transactions for AOL and McArthur/Glen.

Baker Botts specialises in M&A work primarily in the energy and media sectors.

The lead partner of the London office of **Bryan Cave**, Charles Atlee, has an M&A and finance practice with an emphasis on financial services, investment funds and technology.

At **Chadbourne & Parke**, corporate finance partners William Greason and Claude Serfilippi handle primarily US securities and M&A work.

The best known partner at **Coudert Brothers** is Dean Poster. In late 2002, the firm hired Martin Byatt from **Clyde & Co**, who specialises in corporate finance for the oil and gas and mining sectors.

Covington & Burling specialises in corporate work for pharmaceutical and technology companies. One client praises the firm for its 'outstanding project management skills and high quality of work'.

Dorsey & Whitney is known for its venture capital expertise in the technology sector. Clients include Intel, The Carlyle Group, Doughty Hanson, Orange Ventures and Warburg Pincus. Recommended partners are Jeffrey Hurlburt and Michael McFall.

Hale and Dorr has eight partners based in London and Oxford who specialise in M&A work for technology companies. Chris Grew is a hands-on adviser to companies and investors in private equity deals.

Hogan & Hartson has considerable experience in international business transactions, particularly in the energy and communications industries.

Holme Roberts & Owen has worked on a number of joint ventures and acquisitions of UK and international telecoms businesses.

Among the six UK partners in the London office of **Kilpatrick Stockton LLP** are corporate partners Kenneth Boehner, Scott Nelson and Tim Mann.

At **Morgan Lewis**, we recommend US partner Peter Wallace. However, the firm lost corporate finance partners Tom Benz and Zoe Ashcroft to the new London office of **Winston & Strawn LLP** in May 2003.

The corporate team at **Shaw Pittman LLP** has built a high-quality practice for the firm's technology clients. Charles Severs and Robert Bishop, who specialise in M&A, private equity and capital markets, are praised by clients for their commercial acumen and technical expertise. However, the firm lost partnerAndrew Moyle to **Latham & Watkins** in May 2003.

Squire, Sanders & Dempsey is best known for its corporate and regulatory expertise in the telecommunications arena. Corporate partners include Mark Cusick, Paul Lewis, and Martin Walsh.

Wilmer Cutler Pickering LLP has a financial services and investment funds practice led by Simon Firth, James Greig, and David Capps. Partner Gerry Cater represents a number of venture capital and private equity funds in investments in private and public companies.

Cozen O'Connor has corporate expertise in its London office through partner Jonathan Lass.

The London office of **Hunton & Williams** appears in our **Corporate** table for the first time following its recruitment in 2002 of Peter Kavanagh from **Addleshaw Goddard** to work with Charles Ashton. One client says: 'Peter Kavanagh has a particular skill with restructurings, and we are happy to use him at **Hunton & Williams**.'

Guilherme Brafman manages the London office of **Kaye Scholer LLP**. Formerly at **CMS Cameron McKenna**, he has expertise in M&A, private equity, and joint ventures.

The London office of **Morrison & Foerster MNP** is best known for technology-related deals. Kristian Wiggert specialises in cross-border transactions.

At **Paul, Hastings, Janofsky & Walker LLP** US partner Joel Simon and dual-qualified partner Keith Ott are corporate finance specialists.

Vinson & Elkins R.L.L.P. has undertaken a number of acquisitions and divestitures for energy companies. Among the firm's four M&A partners in London are US partners John Lamaster and Jeff Eldredge and UK partner Christopher Prior.

US: DISPUTE RESOLUTION

Cadwalader, Wickersham & Taft LLP partner Michelle Duncan, alongside Lord Grabiner QC, led the successful defence of client Alvaro Naboa in the high-profile billion-dollar family dispute.

US: DISPUTE RESOLUTION

CADWALADER, WICKERSHAM & TAFT LLP
DEBEVOISE & PLIMPTON LLP ✪
HOWREY SIMON ARNOLD & WHITE ✪
McDERMOTT, WILL & EMERY ✪
MORGAN LEWIS ✪
SHEARMAN & STERLING (LONDON) LLP
SKADDEN, ARPS, SLATE, MEAGHER & FLOM LLP
WHITE & CASE ✪
WILMER CUTLER PICKERING LLP ✪
Arnold & Porter (UK) LLP ✪
Bryan Cave
Chadbourne & Parke
Coudert Brothers ✪
Covington & Burling ✪
Hunton & Williams
Latham & Watkins ✪
LeBoeuf, Lamb, Greene & MacRae
Baker Botts ✪
Kilpatrick Stockton LLP ✪
Milbank, Tweed, Hadley & McCloy
Morrison & Foerster MNP ✪
Vinson & Elkins R.L.L.P. ✪

Firms are listed A-Z in tiers which are ranked in order of priority
✪ *Indicates firm displays contact details at the end of this chapter.*

Debevoise & Plimpton LLP partner Arthur Marriott QC has a formidable reputation for international arbitration expertise. The firm's name was further strengthened by the transfer to London of US lawyer Mark Friedman. In addition, David Rivkin, one of the world's top arbitration lawyers, is now splitting his time between New York and London.

Howrey Simon Arnold & White welcomed Peter Fitzpatrick in October 2002, who joined from *Theodore Goddard* along with six assistants. Also joining were a group of IP and commercial litigation lawyers from **Shook, Hardy & Bacon International LLP**, including partners James Irvine, Geoffrey Gaucci and Charles Pugh. The firm is best known for its patent and trade mark litigation expertise, though Fitzpatrick brings a broader practice, including work for the Medical Defence Union.

McDermott, Will & Emery, led by John Reynolds, has acted on a number of important disputes, including litigation arising out of the Formula One World Championship. The firm has 13 lawyers in its London trade mark litigation practice led by Larry Cohen.

Four partners in the London office of **Morgan Lewis** have excellent reputations for their dispute resolution expertise in serious fraud, insurance, and commercial litigation and arbitration. In 2002, the group, led by Robert Goldspink, recruited Trevor Asserson, who was formerly head of global litigation at **Bird & Bird**.

In the London office of **Shearman & Sterling (London) LLP**, Christopher Colbridge heads the international commercial arbitration group.

At **Skadden, Arps, Slate, Meagher & Flom LLP**, international arbitration specialist Paul Mitchard has a stellar reputation.

The London office of **White & Case** bolstered its litigation department with the hire of Alistair Graham from **Travers Smith Braithwaite**. He becomes head of the 20-strong litigation team.

Partner Gary Born at **Wilmer Cutler Pickering LLP** is a force in the international arbitration community. He is considered one of the foremost arbitration practitioners in London.

The intellectual property litigation group at **Arnold & Porter (UK) LLP** led by Ian Kirby enjoys a strong reputation for copyright, design, patent, and trade mark litigation in the pharmaceutical and publishing sectors. The pharma litigation team won a major victory in the High Court in 2002 for its clients Schering Healthcare and Wyeth.

At **Bryan Cave**, Rod Cowper has extensive experience of commercial dispute resolution, including arbitration. Steven Blair joined the firm in June 2002 from **Buchanan Ingersoll** to set up a dedicated insurance and reinsurance department.

Chadbourne & Parke has three product liability partners in London who specialise in tobacco defence work.

Well known for its international arbitration practice, **Coudert Brothers** handles a broad range of commercial litigation, and boasts a reputable international arbitration practice. London partner Maria Frangeskides is well known.

Covington & Burling partner Charles Lister leads a team that has handled arbitrations for such prominent clients as Eli Lilly, Bacardi, and Benetton.

The London office of **Hunton & Williams** appears in our table for the first time following the recruitment of John Miles and Marie Kidwell in December 2002 from **Mayer, Brown, Rowe & Maw LLP**. Both are skilled in litigation and arbitration and popular with clients. Says one: 'I found John Miles very knowledgeable as well as very experienced and efficient in case management.'

Latham & Watkins announced in May 2003 the recruitment of international arbitration and litigation lawyer Philip Clifford, who joined the London office. He was previously at **Clifford Chance LLP**.

LeBoeuf, Lamb, Greene & MacRae partner David Waldron represented the claimant in the *Fruit Shippers* litigation and was also retained by the Government of Ghana in its dispute with American aluminum company Valco. The five-partner group includes new partner Nick Greenwood.

Baker Botts partner Jennifer Smith has expertise in litigation and arbitration.

At **Kilpatrick Stockton LLP**, partner Per Runeland has considerable experience in arbitration.

Milbank, Tweed, Hadley & McCloy branched into intellectual property litigation with the hire of David Perkins from **Clifford Chance LLP**.

We recommend the London office of **Morrison & Foerster MNP** for IP litigation.

Stephen York at **Vinson & Elkins R.L.L.P.** has a highly regarded arbitration practice.

US: IP/IT

Arnold & Porter (UK) LLP has one of the strongest IP and IT practices of all the US law firms in London. The firm handles corporate, regulatory, and IP work for telecoms, media and pharmaceuticals companies. The best known individuals are pharmaceutical and product liability expert Ian Dodds-Smith, biotechnology partner Julian Thurston, and IP partner Sarah Kirk.

The London office of **Shaw Pittman LLP** has a first-rate reputation in the IT marketplace. Instructions from clients like GlaxoSmithKline, Lloyds TSB, Deutsche Bank, and Royal & SunAlliance continue to keep the firm's technology lawyers busy. The London practice, led by Alistair Maughan, has made outstanding contributions to clients doing outsourcings and other complex technology transactions. Despite the general market malaise, the firm completed some of the largest technology and telecommunications transactions undertaken in 2002, for a total deal value of more than £12bn. However, the firm will have to rebuild its London practice following the departure of Andrew Moyle to **Latham & Watkins** and Jennifer Mattingly to **Pillsbury Winthrop**.

The London office of **Covington & Burling** specialises in regulatory and transactional advice

US: IP/IT

ARNOLD & PORTER (UK) LLP ✪
SHAW PITTMAN LLP
COVINGTON & BURLING ✪
HALE AND DORR
HOWREY SIMON ARNOLD & WHITE ✪
LATHAM & WATKINS ✪
McDERMOTT, WILL & EMERY ✪
MORRISON & FOERSTER MNP ✪
WEIL, GOTSHAL & MANGES ✪
WHITE & CASE ✪
Bryan Cave
Dorsey & Whitney
Kilpatrick Stockton LLP ✪
Kirkland & Ellis International LLP ✪
Milbank, Tweed, Hadley & McCloy
Pillsbury Winthrop
Shook, Hardy & Bacon International LLP
Squire, Sanders & Dempsey ✪
Wilmer Cutler Pickering LLP ✪

Firms are listed A-Z in tiers which are ranked in order of priority
✪ *Indicates firm displays contact details at the end of this chapter.*

to life sciences and technology companies. Leading individuals include Richard Kingham, Simon Goodworth and Simon Currie.

At **Hale and Dorr** the IP/IT team is led by Mark Haftke, formerly an IP partner at **Bird & Bird** and *KLegal*. The firm represents a number of biotechnology and life sciences companies. Despite the loss of corporate partner Tom Kellerman, the firm has several top-quality partners who undertake a range of financings and corporate work for technology companies.

Howrey Simon Arnold & White made two strong IP partner recruits in 2002-03. The firm hired former **Eversheds LLP** trade mark litigator Isabel Davies and James Irvine, a respected former partner of City IP boutique *Arnander Irvine & Zeitman*.

Latham & Watkins launched a technology practice with the high-profile recruitment of highly regarded partner Andrew Moyle from **Shaw Pittman LLP**.

McDermott, Will & Emery has a strong IP group led by Larry Cohen. However, the firm lost telecoms partner Stephanie Liston to **Wilmer Cutler Pickering LLP** in 2003.

The technology transactions practice of the London office of **Morrison & Foerster MNP** is led by David Naylor. Says one client: 'I find the quality of work to be impeccable – they are responsive, efficient, effective, and fair in their billing practices.' The firm also has a strong data protection group.

At **Weil, Gotshal & Manges**, Graham Defries and Barry Fishley are skilled in IT and IP advice. The group worked on a complex system integration deal for Churchill Insurance.

In the London office of **White & Case**, the venerable David Llewelyn heads the European IP practice. His clients include L'Oréal, Coca-Cola, John Lewis, and Bristol-Myers Squibb. Jon Lang specialises in IP litigation. Global TMT co-head David Eisenberg handles regulatory and transactional work in this sector.

Bryan Cave bolstered its London technology group with the recruitment of highly skilled IP lawyer Fiona Crawley from **Covington & Burling**.

Dorsey & Whitney has a wide range of TMT clients. John Byrne advises clients on the corporate side, while Victoria Lockley focuses on IP, media and entertainment.

Kilpatrick Stockton LLP has two UK IP partners, Rajita Sharma and Virginia Taylor.

Pierre-Andre Dubois launched an IP/IT practice at **Kirkland & Ellis International LLP** in July 2002 after he was recruited from **Hale and Dorr**. One client praises him for his 'solid guidance, attention to detail, swift feedback and turnaround and the fact that he treats us with utmost respect.'

Milbank, Tweed, Hadley & McCloy recently hired IP litigation partner David Perkins from **Clifford Chance LLP**.

Pillsbury Winthrop hired two IP/IT partners in 2003: Ashley Winton from **Osborne Clarke** and Jennifer Mattingly from **Shaw Pittman LLP**.

At **Shook, Hardy & Bacon International LLP**, Gerard Cronin and Conrad Arnander are highly regarded. Clients include Hoover, AstraZeneca and Canal+.

Squire, Sanders & Dempsey is recognised as a leader in IT and telecommunications. Anthony Corel is well known for his commercial and regulatory expertise. We also recommend James Nimmo.

Wilmer Cutler Pickering LLP counsel David Tudor specialises in transactions in the media sector. The London office strengthened its telecoms expertise with the hire of Stephanie Liston from **McDermott, Will & Emery**.

US: PROJECT FINANCE AND ENERGY

At **Dewey Ballantine**, Mark Saunders and Adam Dann are experts in the oil and gas industry. Clients praise the two partners for their excellent understanding of the industry and pragmatic approach. 'They are good communicators and will present us with a range of well-developed options at any stage of the project,' says one. The firm rises a tier in our table following of its recruitment in 2002 of Jonathan Simpson from **Allen & Overy** and Stephen Horvath from **Hunton & Williams**. Clients also praise partner James Simpson, who heads the projects group.

Milbank, Tweed, Hadley & McCloy has exceptional worldwide project finance expertise. The London team includes leading project finance partners Phillip Fletcher, who manages the office, and John Dewar. The office represents both lenders and sponsors across industrial sectors.

The global project finance practice at **Shearman & Sterling (London) LLP** is headed by the highly respected Nicholas Buckworth. The firm is a recognised leader in the energy sector, and works on projects around the globe. Partner Kenneth MacRitchie won the 2003 *Legal Business* award leading the Project finance team of the year.

White & Case has a top-quality projects and energy practice, with instructions from around the globe. The group is led by Philip Stopford, with strong support from Peter Finlay, Jason Kerr, Doug Peel, and Craig Nethercott.

At **Latham & Watkins**, Joseph Blum, Dennis Nordstrom, and David Miles are highly regarded for project finance and energy work.

LeBoeuf, Lamb, Greene & MacRae partner Brian Zimbler recently led a team acting for Russian oil major Yukos on its merger with the Siberian Oil Company. UK partner Bruce Johnston, formerly with **Weil, Gotshal & Manges**, has considerable experience in the development and financing of projects. Energy finance specialists include US partners Keith Hughes and Joseph Ferraro and UK partner Anthony Richmond. One client praises the firm's 'good understanding and grasp of sometimes complex legal issues'.

Skadden, Arps, Slate, Meagher & Flom LLP offers project finance expertise led by partner Douglas Nordlinger, who has represented developers on electric power projects and natural gas pipeline projects around the world. US partner Bruce Buck led the team that acted for the Siberian Oil Company in its sale of shares to Yukos in 2003.

Sullivan & Cromwell LLP has long represented European sponsors, lenders, and financial advisers involved in major projects around the world. We recommend UK partner Jamie Logie and US partner Stewart Robertson.

Vinson & Elkins R.L.L.P. is known globally for its leading energy practice. In the London office, Christopher Clement-Davies is the best known of the four partners in the practice, supported on the finance side by Peter Gaines.

Akin Gump Strauss Hauer & Feld has a leading energy practice in Russia.

Baker Botts has 21 fee-earners, among them seven partners, who act primarily for clients in the energy industry. We recommend partner Antony Higginson for upstream oil and gas work. The firm has a strong sponsor-led project finance practice, particularly in central and eastern Europe. Samantha Hampshire does regulatory work in the power and gas sectors.

Cadwalader, Wickersham & Taft LLP recruited Bill Rubin from **Weil, Gotshal & Manges** in 2002. Rubin, whose clients include the EBRD, will work alongside projects partner Paul Biggs.

Chadbourne & Parke partners Nabil Khodadad and Denis Petkovic are the best known of the five partners in the London project finance practice. One client says Khodadad is 'quick to spot issues and propose solutions'.

Coudert Brothers' Alexander Janes has a strong practice advising lenders. London banking

US: PROJECT FINANCE AND ENERGY

DEWEY BALLANTINE
MILBANK, TWEED, HADLEY & McCLOY
SHEARMAN & STERLING (LONDON) LLP
WHITE & CASE ✪

LATHAM & WATKINS ✪
LEBOEUF, LAMB, GREENE & MACRAE
SKADDEN, ARPS, SLATE, MEAGHER & FLOM LLP
SULLIVAN & CROMWELL LLP
VINSON & ELKINS R.L.L.P. ✪

Akin Gump Strauss Hauer & Feld
Baker Botts ✪
Cadwalader, Wickersham & Taft LLP
Chadbourne & Parke
Coudert Brothers ✪
Hogan & Hartson ✪
Hunton & Williams
McDermott, Will & Emery ✪
Orrick, Herrington & Sutcliffe

Firms are listed A-Z in tiers which are ranked in order of priority
✪ Indicates firm displays contact details at the end of this chapter.

clients range from the EBRD and the IFC to Barclays and Deutsche Bank.

In 2002, the London office of **Hogan & Hartson** recruited Garry Pegg and Hywel Jones from **LeBoeuf, Lamb, Greene & MacRae**, where they had led the oil and gas team. Clients include MOL and Occidental Petroleum.

The London office of **Hunton & Williams** has project finance expertise in partners Jane Templeton-Knight and Mark Frewin, both formerly with **Milbank, Tweed, Hadley & McCloy**. Clients praise their 'high level of service, quick response times, and very good client handling skills.' They will work with partner Drew Murphy.

The London project finance group at **McDermott, Will & Emery**, led by Andrew Watson, advised lenders on a number of significant UK and European projects in 2002.

At **Orrick, Herrington & Sutcliffe**, projects partner Martin Stewart-Smith is highly regarded for his commercial nous.

US: TAX

CLEARY GOTTLIEB STEEN & HAMILTON ✪
DEWEY BALLANTINE
MILBANK, TWEED, HADLEY & McCLOY
SHEARMAN & STERLING (LONDON) LLP
SIDLEY AUSTIN BROWN & WOOD
SKADDEN, ARPS, SLATE, MEAGHER & FLOM LLP
WEIL, GOTSHAL & MANGES ✪
WHITE & CASE ✪

Bryan Cave
Covington & Burling ✪
Fulbright & Jaworski LLP
Gibson, Dunn & Crutcher LLP

Hale and Dorr
Hogan & Hartson ✪
McDermott, Will & Emery ✪
Morgan Lewis ✪

Firms are listed A-Z in tiers which are ranked in order of priority
✪ *Indicates firm displays contact details at the end of this chapter.*

US: TAX

Partner Nikhil Mehta joined **Cleary Gottlieb Steen & Hamilton** in July 2002 as the first UK tax partner. He had been a partner at **Linklaters** since 1989 and now works with US partner James Duncan, the senior resident US tax partner at **Cleary Gottlieb Steen & Hamilton**. Duncan is praised by one client as 'an exceptionally clever adviser whose judgement I actively seek when addressing difficult issues.'

Dewey Ballantine's London managing partner Fred Gander heads the structured finance/tax group. The group has provided US and international tax planning advice on numerous cross-border financings; however the firm does not offer UK tax advice at present.

UK partner Russell Jacobs at **Milbank, Tweed, Hadley & McCloy** is a prominent tax practitioner who enhances the firm's strong finance and corporate practices.

Shearman & Sterling (London) LLP's international tax practice plays an important role in the firm's cross-border practice. Partner Michael McGowan, who leads the group, joined from **Allen & Overy** in 2002. He advised on the UK tax aspects of the financing of the new national stadium at Wembley.

The London office of **Sidley Austin Brown & Wood** advises on the UK tax aspects of domestic and international transactions, with a specialty in structured finance. Drew Scott heads the group.

Skadden, Arps, Slate, Meagher & Flom LLP partner Tim Sanders has a well-regarded corporate tax practice.

Weil, Gotshal & Manges provides integrated US and UK tax advice to corporates, banks, and private equity houses. Andrew Norwood has an excellent reputation.

At **White & Case**, Neil Woodgate specialises in UK and international corporate taxation.

At **Bryan Cave**, Richard Cassell writes extensively on US international tax issues, while Dyke Davies has designed international corporate and financial structures for families with a significant US tax exposure.

Covington & Burling recruited UK tax partner David Hinds from **SJ Berwin** in 2002. He specialises in structural tax issues surrounding the formation of funds.

At **Fulbright & Jaworski LLP**, Stephen Vogel focuses on US international tax planning and in-bound investments.

The tax practice at **Gibson, Dunn & Crutcher LLP** is led by Nicholas Aleksander.

Simon Court is head of corporate tax at **Hale and Dorr**.

McDermott, Will & Emery has a reputable tax practice headed by Peter Nias, although the firm lost Jonathan Ivinson to **Hogan & Hartson** in June 2003.

Morgan Lewis US partner Charles Lubar and UK partner Michael Cashman offer tax advice to wealthy individuals.

FRENCH, GERMAN, ITALIAN AND SPANISH FIRMS

Alexen Avocats *France*
Castaldi Mourre Sprague *France*
Chiomenti Studio Legale ✪ *Italy*
DS London *France*
Dabelstein & Passehl *Germany*
Diaz-Bastien & Truan *Spain*
Fernando Scornik Gerstein *Spain*
Gide Loyrette Nouel ✪ *France*
Ginestié Paley-Vincent & Associés *France*
Haarmann Hemmelrath ✪ *Germany*
Hartwig *Germany*
Hector Diaz & Co *Spain*
Hoffmann.Eitle *Germany*
JP Karsenty & Associés *France*
La Giraudière Larroze & Associés *France*
Michael Soul & Asociados - Abogados *Spain*
Redeker Sellner Dahs & Widmaier *Germany*
Sutti, Studio Legale ✪ *Italy*
Triplet & Associés *France*
Uría & Menéndez *Spain*

Firms are listed alphabetically
✪ *Indicates firm displays contact details at the end of this chapter.*

FRENCH, GERMAN, ITALIAN AND SPANISH FIRMS

France: The major development in 2003 was the announcement in May by French heavyweight **Gide Loyrette Nouel** of the opening of a London office. An impressive team of four US/UK-qualified partners from **Sidley Austin Brown & Wood** comprises New York-qualified lawyers Christopher Mead and Scott Cameron, and UK solicitors Colin Mercer and Michael Doran, as well as French partner, Arnaud Duhamel, an avocat at the Paris Bar. The team provides **Gide Loyrette Nouel** with significant expertise in finance, and in particular securitisation, structured finance and capital markets.

Paris-based **Alexen Avocats** specialises in a wide variety of both domestic and international commercial work for corporate clients, from private individuals to multinational companies, through the entire range of privately and publicly owned companies and commercial entities.

Castaldi Mourre Sprague was established in Paris 1996, bringing together a group of lawyers from different nationality of firm. Offices in London and Milan followed. The six-lawyer London office is led by Steven Sprague and offers UK and French law advice. The firm undertakes both commercial work and energy/utility related work.

DS London opened in London in 1998 and shares offices with its preferred UK associate firm, **Browne Jacobson**. London is one of the firm's network of nine offices across Europe and the Far East.

Similarly, Paris-based **Ginestié Paley-Vincent & Associés** has been in London since 1999 and works out of **DLA**'s London office. The firm is a member of **DLA**'s European network *D&P*, and acts as an interface for French clients active in the UK and for British companies in their dealings with France. It offers corporate and commercial advice under both French and English Law, including employment, banking, M&A and securities matters.

JP Karsenty & Associés offers its clients French law advice and has special links with **Beachcroft Wansbroughs**, while **La Giraudière Larroze & Associés** has a London presence through its association with UK firm **Hextalls**.

Lille-based **Triplet & Associés** is a member of

TagLaw and has a London office which offers French law advice from two part-time partners, Philip Jenkinson and Didier Lebon. The practice handles M&A, corporate and IP, company and commercial, employment, banking and commercial and residential property matters.

Germany: Hamburg-based **Dabelstein & Passehl** specialises in shipping and maritime, insurance and transport law and is experienced in dealing with shipping-related employment issues. Its three lawyers are admitted in Germany as well as in the UK. Clients include P&I clubs, ship- and cargo-owners. The firm, which has been in London since 1989, also offers advice on corporate matters.

Hans Hartwig's team at **Hartwig** concentrates on banking and property advice, with Manfred Kuhn leading the firm's considerable IP practice. The firm also undertakes a great deal of notarial work, from which much of its other work stems. Between them, the four lawyers are admitted in Germany, England, New York and Spain, and offer services in English, German, Spanish and Italian. In the UK, the firm is well known for its international commercial debt recovery practice, acting for banks and multinational companies. The firm, praised for its 'one-stop international reach' by one client, has its main markets in the UK, France, Germany and Italy.

Leading German MDP **Haarmann Hemmelrath** has grown rapidly since opening in London three years ago, and now boasts a six-partner team, which combines German and English lawyers, tax advisers and accountants. The office offers advice on M&A, tax and corporate law, as well as private equity and venture capital related matters. Clients include German and other foreign companies as well as UK law firms. Managing partner Philip Newhouse and senior partner Wilhelm Haarmann head the office.

Hoffmann.Eitle, one of the leading patent firms in Europe, is the only German patent law firm in London. Three patent lawyers handle German and British patent cases for companies like Gillette and Exxon Mobile. The vast majority of its clients are based in the US and Japan.

In Germany, **Redeker Sellner Dahs & Widmaier** is best known for its experience in privatisation and other public law matters. In London, the firm has concentrated on corporate and commercial matters since 1991. Clients are mainly UK and US companies doing business in Germany, such as pharmaceuticals and textiles companies. Two lawyers and one counsel offer additional advice in German trade mark, competition and employment law.

Italy: Chiomenti Studio Legale has three partners who spend time in its London office, including senior partner Luigi Bendi. The office specialises in banking and structured finance, for clients including Citigroup, JP Morgan Chase and BNP Paribas.

Acting exclusively for law firms, in-house counsel, patent and trade mark agents, **Studio Legale Sutti**'s London office is managed by Livia Oglio. The London team offers specialist IP advice, and is the Italian representative of the International Chamber of Commerce's 'Counterforce', an IP and anti-counterfeiting network.

Spain: Five Spanish firms currently have offices in London. **Diaz-Bastien & Truan** focuses purely on Spanish law advice, with the one-partner London office handling predominantly commercial law, advising existing UK clients on investment in Spain. The London office also works with the firm's other offices in Madrid and Marbella, in relation to cross-border litigation.

Fernando Scornik Gerstein has the largest Spanish team in London. The firm is strong in litigation, insolvency, commercial, and personal injury matters. The team provides Spanish, English, and Argentinian law advice to UK firms and an expanding group of insurance companies, and benefits from a strong network in Spain and Latin America.

The majority of **Hector Diaz & Co**'s work is property-related. Named partner Hector Diaz also undertakes a significant volume of general commercial and banking advice, and has acted as an expert witness in several property cases. Through its association with **KSB Law** the firm is able to provide motor industry clients with English law advice.

Michael Soul & Asociados - Abogados comprises a team of Anglo-Spanish lawyers established by senior partner Michael Soul, who is dual qualified as an English solicitor and Spanish abogado. The firm deals exclusively with cases involving Spain and Spanish law. Areas of focus include company law, property, insolvency and litigation, among others.

Uría & Menéndez first opened in London in 1990 and currently fields a three-lawyer office headed by aeronautical law expert Juan Francisco Falcón, with Juan Carlos Manchuga and Agustín Redondo. Former London managing partner Rafael Molina moved to **Linklaters**' Madrid office in November last year to build a real estate practice. **Uría & Menéndez**'s London office provides advice on Spanish law to UK-based clients with interests in Spain or who wish to establish a business presence, issue securities, make acquisitions or engage in trade within Spain, including tax advice.

BENELUX FIRMS

De Brauw Blackstone Westbroek was the first Dutch firm to open in the City. The office, which opened in 1990, now fields a two-partner team comprising Pierre Nijnens and Niek Biegman. The firm advises clients on both Dutch and international transactions with a focus on M&A, banking and securities issues. Additionally, the firm offers considerable tax expertise.

BENELUX FIRMS

De Brauw Blackstone Westbroek *Netherlands*
Houthoff Buruma ✪ *Netherlands*
Loyens & Loeff ✪ *Netherlands*
NautaDutilh ✪ *Netherlands*
Stibbe ✪ *Belgium/Netherlands*
Van Doorne *Netherlands*

Firms are listed alphabetically
✪ *Indicates firm displays contact details at the end of this chapter.*

Houthoff Buruma officially opened in London in May 2002. Corporate partner Albert Dreese relocated from Rotterdam to head up the office along with senior associate, Jessica Terpstra, and associate Erich Scherer. The London office provides Dutch law advice only and focuses on corporate and banking and finance.

Loyens & Loeff boasts an impressive global network of offices which focus almost exclusively on international tax work, for which the firm is undoubtedly pre-eminent internationally. International tax partner Marc Klerks heads the office, with corporate partner Bas Vetter. Vetter's arrival in London is testament to the firm's growing reputation in M&A and private equity transactions across Europe.

Leading Dutch independent, **NautaDutilh** opened in London in 1996 and provides Dutch law advice to international law firms, investment banks and other groups. The London practice focuses on corporate and banking, project finance, asset-backed finance and public and private equity and debt transactions, including listings of both Netherlands and foreign securities on Euronext Amsterdam N.V. and abroad. A strong team on the ground includes former Amsterdam securitisation head Joanne Kellermann, who moved to London in September 2001; corporate finance specialist Dirk Blaisse ; and Gijs Gerretsen, who specialises in M&A and corporate.

In addition to establishing its alliance with UK Magic Circle firm **Herbert Smith** and leading German outfit **Gleiss Lutz** in January 2002, premier Benelux corporate firm, **Stibbe** runs its own London office headed by sole partner Michael Molenaars. Molenaars specialises in international taxation with a focus on M&A, corporate reorganisations, innovative financial transactions and financial instruments.

Van Doorne's London office was established in 1996 and is currently headed by banking and finance partner Stefan van Rossum, who focuses on acquisition finance, financial restructuring, capital markets and regulatory matters.

SCANDINAVIAN FIRMS

Five Scandinavian firms maintain presences in London. Three of these firms, **Kromann Reumert** of Denmark, Norway's **Thommessen Krefting**

SCANDINAVIAN FIRMS

Hamilton & Co Advokatbyrå *Sweden*
Kromann Reumert ✪ *Denmark*
Thommessen Krefting Greve Lund *Norway*
Vinge ✪ *Sweden*
Wikborg Rein ✪ *Norway*

Firms are listed alphabetically
✪ *Indicates firm displays contact details at the end of this chapter.*

Greve Lund and Swedish giant **Vinge** share an office in the City and operate as the *Scandinavian Law Alliance*. The alliance was established by the three firms in 1990, and now brings together over 500 lawyers across Scandinavia in addition to joint offices in London and Brussels. (Each of the firms is also a member of *Lex Mundi*.)

Sweden's **Vinge** has operated out of London since the early 1980s. Corporate finance/M&A partner Maria-Pia Midenbäck-Hope now heads a team of two associates, following the return to Stockholm of the former London resident partners Karin Ulberstad and Hans Bagner. The team handles mainly corporate and transactional work, along with banking and finance. Clients include UK companies wishing to invest in Sweden and conversely Swedish corporates seeking investments in the UK.

Associate Thomas Kaas heads the London practice of Denmark's **Kromann Reumert**, while Sverre Tyrhaug is **Thommessen Krefting Greve Lund**'s representative in the City. The **Thommessen Krefting Greve Lund** team concentrates on finance and cross-border M&A work.

Swedish firm **Hamilton & Co Advokatbyrå** has had an office in London since 1984. The office is staffed by two partners, Dag Di Meo and Christoffer Hamilton, and focuses on assisting Scandinavian clients in London and UK clients with business interests in Sweden.

Leading Norwegian firm **Wikborg Rein** fields a four-lawyer office in London, headed by sole partner and well-known shipping specialist Morten Lund Mathisen. Given Mathisen's expertise, the office naturally has a focus on shipping, ship finance, and sale and purchase of vessels, but also advises on company and securities law and M&A.

SWISS, PORTUGUESE, RUSSIAN AND URAINIAN FIRMS

London is home to the offices of three Swiss firms. **Bär & Karrer**, a leading corporate commercial firm in Switzerland, has one resident partner, Gianpaolo Arrigoni, who focuses on corporate, M&A, banking, finance and capital markets. Christope Durrer is now also based in London and offers corporate, restructuring and insolvency expertise.

Froriep Renggli fields the largest team among the Swiss firms in London. The firm opened in London more than 15 years ago and it is currently led by the well-regarded Bruno Boesch. Areas of expertise include general corporate and banking work for Swiss clients, as well as the structuring and transfer of assets for wealthy individuals. Dunja Koch offers aviation expertise.

Secretan Troyanov opened in London in 1987. The office is currently led by Eva Stormann, who has been the resident partner in London since 1998. The office focuses on providing Swiss law advice on a range of matters, including finance, capital markets, investment funds, contract law and international arbitration. The office also serves as an interface between the firm's London-based clients and its Geneva and Moscow offices. Clients range from multinational to mid-sized companies and high-net-worth individuals.

BC Toms & Co combines western and Ukrainian lawyers and is one of the largest firms in Ukraine. In recent years, the firm has advised clients on investment and transactions into Ukraine, with an aggregate value in excess of $2bn, including oil and gas and electricity generation projects in Ukraine for western firms and joint ventures with western investment, many of the significant western investments in real estate development, several of the largest international loans to Ukraine, telecommunications projects, greenfield factory developments and numerous acquisitions of Ukrainian businesses (including through privatisation of state assets).

Russian firm **Laptev & Partners** is best known for its energy and natural resources practice. Its head office is in Tyumen, although it also has offices in Moscow and Novosibirsk, and European offices in London and Madrid, which it deems invaluable in referring inbound work to the firm's lawyers in the Russian Federation. The firm can advise foreign investors on all aspects of their investments in Russia and the CIS including those into oil and gas.

Portuguese firm **Neville de Rougemont & Associados, Sociedade de Advogados** fields a team of 16 lawyers (including four UK-qualified solicitors) across two offices – Lisbon and Maidenhead in the UK. The UK practice is headed by Rosemary de Rougemont.

SWISS, PORTUGUESE, RUSSIAN AND UKRAINIAN FIRMS

BC Toms & Co *CIS/Ukraine*
Bär & Karrer *Switzerland*
Froriep Renggli ✪ *Switzerland*
Laptev & Partners *Russia*
Neville de Rougemont & Associados, Sociedade de Advogados *Portugal*
Secretan Troyanov *Switzerland*

Firms are listed alphabetically
✪ *Indicates firm displays contact details at the end of this chapter.*

IRISH FIRMS

A&L Goodbody ✪
Arthur Cox ✪
Matheson Ormsby Prentice
McCann FitzGerald

Firms are listed alphabetically
✪ *Indicates firm displays contact details at the end of this chapter.*

IRISH FIRMS

Julian Yarr now heads **A&L Goodbody**'s London office; Paul White has moved back to Dublin. The main focus of the office is financial services and corporate work, including private company M&A and private equity transactions. The office remains strong in entertainment work – partner Geraldine East spends roughly 75% of her time in London, concentrating on high-profile film production and financing matters. Of note, Paul White has been advising the European Bioscience Fund I.

Arthur Cox opened a London office in February 2001. Partner John Matson heads the office which focuses on advising Irish and UK-based clients and international law firms on Irish corporate, financial and commercial law.

In summer 2003, Andrew Doyle replaced Emer Hunt as head of **Matheson Ormsby Prentice**'s London office. Doyle brings significant corporate weight to the London office and this will sit well with Michael Jackson's expertise in investment funds, structured finance and general banking and finance issues. A third partner, Patrick Spicer divides his time between London and Dublin.

McCann FitzGerald's London office has an outstanding banking and finance practice. The experienced Barbara Judge specialises in asset finance work. Backed by a team of five assistants, the office concentrates principally on debt work, structured finance and cross-border leasing and securitisation.

OFFSHORE FIRMS

Carey Olsen is the largest (120 lawyers) law firm based in the Channel Islands, formed out of the merger in March 2003 between *Carey Langlois* and *Olsens*. Corporate partner Fiona Fleming is head of the London office

Jersey-based **Ogier & Le Masurier** set up in London in 2003. The main contacts in London are Heather Tibbo and Aaron DeLacey. In early 2004, the firm announced its merger with **Boxalls** in the Cayman Islands, operating there as **Ogier & Boxalls**.

In April 2003, **Mourant du Feu & Jeune**'s Jonathan Walker, an expert in commercial, banking and capital markets, returned to the Jersey office and has been replaced in London by Jonathan Rigby.

Two leading Cayman Islands firms have a presence in London; **Maples and Calder Europe**, which opened back in 1997, and more recent arrival **Walkers**, which arrived in London in March

OFFSHORE FIRMS

Appleby, Spurling & Kempe *Bermuda*
Arias, Fábrega & Fábrega *Panama*
Carey Olsen *Guernsey*
Conyers Dill & Pearman *Bermuda*
Harney Westwood & Riegels LLP ✪ *British Virgin Islands*
Lennox Paton *Bahamas*
Maples and Calder Europe ✪ *Cayman Islands*
Mourant du Feu & Jeune *Jersey*
Ogier & Le Masurier ✪ *Jersey*
Patton, Moreno & Asvat *Panama*
Quijano & Associates *Panama*
Vallarino, Vallarino y Rivera *Panama*
Walkers *Cayman Islands*

Firms are listed alphabetically
✪ *Indicates firm displays contact details at the end of this chapter.*

2001. The latter firm is staffed by three partners, Ann Nealon, Susan Harper and David Whittome. The **Maples and Calder Europe** office continues to be headed by Anthony Travers, although he did relocate back to Cayman in spring 2003.

Bermuda-based **Conyers Dill & Pearman** fields a five-lawyer office in London, headed by Martin Lane, while **Appleby, Spurling & Kempe** retains a three-parter London presence. In early 2004, the firm announced its merger with **Hunter & Hunter** in the Cayman Islands.

Bahamas-based **Lennox Paton** also retains a London office, headed by Charles Crowe. The firm focuses on financial services and estate planning and trusts, as well as banking and finance, funds, hotel and resort development and disputes.

Also in London is British Virgin Islands-based **Harney Westwood & Riegels LLP**. The firm opened in London in August last year, relocating Peter Tarn to head the office. He was replaced in London in August by Leonard Birmingham, head of the firm's corporate and commercial practice.

All of the Caribbean offshore firms advise on corporate/commercial and private client matters.

MIDDLE EASTERN FIRMS

There are three Middle East-based firms with presences in London.

Abdullah Kh. Al-Ayoub & Associates is a leading firm based in Kuwait, led by managing partner, Abdullah Kh. Al-Ayoub, a well-known practitioner in Kuwaiti circles. The associated office in London serves a client base of predominantly Gulf companies, as well as western law firms. The office provides advice on all aspects of Kuwaiti law including international trade, international arbitration, energy, foreign investment, IP, tax, employment and shipping. Particular strengths include real estate and Islamic financing.

Two Iranian law firms operate out of London. **Dr A K Anvari & Associates** has been established

MIDDLE EASTERN FIRMS

Dr A K Anvari & Associates *Iran*
Abdullah Kh. Al-Ayoub & Associates *Kuwait*
Sabi and Associates *Iran*

Firms are listed alphabetically

in London since 1980, and has further offices in Tehran and Isfahan. The firm advises on international trade, finance, energy, foreign investment and shipping, and has experience of arbitration, and Islamic law. Dr A K Anvari heads the practice.

Sabi and Associates advises on Iranian law in matters of international dispute resolution, claims and litigation, primarily pursued against Iranian government agencies. Led by Hamid Sabi, the team of three fee-earners has a successful record, in representing a European, Middle Eastern and US client base, which includes household names such as Shell, BP and AT&T.

AUSTRALIAN FIRMS

Three of Australia's leading law firms retain offices in London. **Mallesons Stephen Jaques**, considered by many as 'the' premier firm in Australia, has been present in the City for many years and focuses on corporate and finance transactions, though it has been building tax capability in London. Corporate partner Tim Blue heads the team and was joined in London in late 2002 by finance and stamp duty expert Ken Astridge. The eight-fee-earner team is majority dual-qualified and advises on UK and Australian investment in both directions. Major clients include Telstra, Mellon Global Investments, Barclays Bank and Granada.

Minter Ellison was the first Antipodean firm to set up in London. The office boasts two partners, one of whom is seconded from Australia on a rotating basis, supported by five assistants. Michael Whalley has practised in London for more than 25 years and his broad expertise includes corporate, employee share schemes, international licensing and trade, telecoms and IT.

Blake Dawson Waldron enjoys a strong reputation for corporate work at home. Key lawyers in London include partners Geoff Hone, a corporate lawyer, tax specialist Sandra Lanigan, and senior associate Michael Beaumont, who focuses on fundraising and M&A; and Ron Harmer. The London office provides UK and European clients with advice on transactions affected by

AUSTRALIAN FIRMS

Mallesons Stephen Jaques
Minter Ellison

Blake Dawson Waldron

Firms are listed A-Z in tiers which are ranked in order of priority

SOUTH AFRICAN FIRMS

Bowman Gilfillan
Maitland & Co

Firms are listed alphabetically

Australian law, including IPOs, M&A, restructurings, insolvency, privatisation, foreign investment, securities regulation and fund management.

SOUTH AFRICAN FIRMS

Leading South African firm **Bowman Gilfillan** has been in London for over ten years and enjoys a good reputation for handling high-level UK/Africa corporate and finance transactions. Heather Duffey is the only resident partner in the London office. Duffey is a highly regarded corporate lawyers and advises a range of major international corporations and financial institutions. The firm is a member of *Lex Mundi*.

Maitland & Co is the European, multi-disciplinary network created by **Webber Wentzel Bowens**, one of South Africa's largest law firms. It offers legal and consulting services to major corporations as well as to families and individuals with holdings in multinational companies. The firm has five partners and eight associates in London, led by senior principal Eric Pfaff. **Maitland & Co** has further European offices in Dublin, Geneva, the Isle of Man, Luxembourg and Paris.

CANADIAN FIRMS

Blake, Cassels & Graydon LLP has a small London office with two partners – managing partner David Glennie and Bob Wooder, and one associate. The firm focuses on international M&A and finance, and has particular expertise in the natural resources sector, where clients include Lukoil and Lonmin plc. Of note, the London office advised William Grant & Sons Limited, the makers of Glenfiddich, in its purchase of the Gibson's Finest Canadian whisky business from Diageo. The London office was also involved in advising Great-West Lifeco, the successful bidder for Canada Life.

Fasken Martineau DuMoulin LLP's London practice is headed by John Elias, who has been in London for six years. Elias deals with a broad range

CANADIAN FIRMS

Blake, Cassels & Graydon LLP
Fasken Martineau DuMoulin LLP
McCarthy Tétrault
Ogilvy Renault
Stikeman Elliott LLP

Firms are listed alphabetically

of Canadian-related financing and M&A work, especially acquisition and mining finance. He acts for a number of banks including, Allied Irish Bank, Barclays, Citibank, Lloyds TSB, Standard Bank and UBS on financings. The London office advises on the Canadian tranches of global equity and debt offerings, and on the implementation, in Canada of equity-related employee incentive schemes (Allied Domecq, BA, Exxon Mobile are some clients in this area).

McCarthy Tétrault has built a strong local flavour, with most of the lawyers being dual qualified. The main areas of focus are mining, telecoms, project finance, oil and gas, and power. Managing partner Glen Ireland has been based in London for eight years and focuses on the mining sector and M&A work for clients such as Angloamerican, BHP Billiton and Gold Fields. Tanneke Heersche handles oil and gas and mining transactions within the growing practice and advises companies such as PanOcean and PetroCanada. Brian Kelsall focuses on project finance and telecoms work for clients such as the EBRD, the IFC and the Nordic Investment Bank (NIB).

Stikeman Elliott LLP is the longest-established of the Canadian firms, having opened in the City in 1969. Managing partner Shawna Miller heads the five-partner practice, which comprises ten lawyers, including recent lateral hire Derek Linfield who moved back to **Stikeman Elliott LLP** this summer, having previously been a resident partner in **Fasken Martineau DuMoulin LLP**'s London office. Linfield's return is a significant boost to **Stikeman Elliott LLP**'s capabilities. The firm represents a large number of banks, merchant banks and multinationals in corporate finance and international business transactions, with particular strength in eurobonds.

In London since 1989, **Ogilvy Renault** provides Canadian legal advice to European-based businesses and law firms on a variety of cross-border transactions. The two-partner London office (Francois Dupuis and Peter Noble) has particular expertise in banking and financial products, capital markets, M&A and general corporate/commercial law. **Ogilvy Renault** routinely acts as Canadian counsel on acquisitions in Canada by European businesses, and in connection with global securities offerings by European issuers. In conjunction with local firms, the office has acted for Canadian clients on M&A transactions in Europe, including asset sales by Nortel Networks and acquisitions by the Quebecor group of companies, Bombardier and Royal Bank of Canada.

INDIAN FIRMS

ALMT Legal was set up as an Indian firm in the UK in 2000. The London office now numbers five lawyers, including two partners – Shalini Agarwal and Sameer Tapia. Clients include UK and other European companies, as well as European subsidiaries of US corporates and Indian companies, spanning the blue-chip, SME and start-up sectors. The firm offers advice across corporate, M&A, disputes, infrastructure, media/entertainment and transport, in conjunction with its network of associated offices across India.

INDIAN FIRMS

ALMT Legal
Lexindia
Singhania & Co

Firms are listed alphabetically

Lexindia's office in London is headed by Tony Khindria and includes seven other fee-earners. The firm has other offices in New Delhi and Paris. In London the firm offers Indian legal and tax services for a mixed client base of start-ups and multinationals across a range of sectors including the automotive, banking, construction materials, defence, pharmaceuticals, power and telecoms industries, among others.

Singhania & Co was the first Indian firm to open an office in London – in 1990. In the City, the team currently comprises one partner, Vijay Goel, and five other lawyers. The London office offers expertise on corporate issues related to UK companies' investments in India, including IP matters and disputes, as well as advising Indian corporates with interests in the UK. The London office works closely with the firm's network of seven offices across India, as well as its second overseas office in New York. The firm advises a range of clients including several in the aviation, infrastructure and financial services sectors.

OUTSIDE LONDON: THE REGIONS

The main legal centre for the UK is London but there are a good number of firms with strong commercial practices in the regions. International clients could find that one of the leading regional firms perfectly fits their requirements; generally at a much lower cost.

EAST ANGLIA

Although Internet and software companies have found it difficult to find financing in a quiet economy, biotechnology and medical research companies in Cambridge, Ipswich and Norwich have proven robust. Meanwhile, property, agriculture and public sector work ensures a steady stream of business for law firms in East Anglia.

CORPORATE AND COMMERCIAL: CAMBRIDGE

Eversheds LLP boasts some of the most talented corporate lawyers in East Anglia. Anthony McGurk and Adrian Seagers are highly regarded for the depth of their experience and responsiveness. The team advised the University of Manchester and UMIST on their £430m merger. Other clients include Archant and the Jardine Motor Group.

Mills & Reeve's corporate finance and banking specialist Claire Clarke heads a team that acts on a wide range of high-profile transactions locally and nationally. Clarke led the team that acted for Bank of Scotland on the £17m debt for equity restructuring of the Pelcombe Group. The team also acted for Eastern Contracting Group on its £13m sale to Alfred McAlpine.

Hewitsons is a prominent and active founder member of the Cambridge Network. The Cambridge team, led by partner John Dix, was involved in 60 deals, with a total deal value of £160m. Dix advised Plastic Logic on raising £8m from investors. Other clients include Ranier and health and safety software company CamAxys.

Taylor Vinters' team, headed by John Short, is renowned for its pragmatic and no-nonsense approach. As well as heading the firm's innovative new food team Short specialises in advising start-up technology companies. Clients also praise corporate finance lawyer James Allen. Rising star Quentin Golder focuses on M&A. The team advised

CORPORATE AND COMMERCIAL CAMBRIDGE

EVERSHEDS LLP
MILLS & REEVE

Hewitsons
Taylor Vinters
Taylor Wessing

Firms are listed A-Z in tiers which are ranked in order of priority

CORPORATE AND COMMERCIAL IPSWICH

BIRKETTS
PRETTYS

Ashton Graham
Gotelee & Goldsmith

CORPORATE AND COMMERCIAL NORWICH

EVERSHEDS LLP
MILLS & REEVE

---

steeles (law) llp

Howes Percival

Greenland Houchen
Leathes Prior

Cozens-Hardy & Jewson
Hansells
Overbury Steward Eaton & Woolsey
Rogers and Norton

Firms are listed A-Z in tiers which are ranked in order of priority

French multinational Egide SA on its acquisition of Suffolk-based Europlus Technologies.

Outstanding corporate partner Simon Walker heads the Cambridge office of **Taylor Wessing**. Walker gains strong support from corporate finance specialist David Mardle who is 'commercial, responsive and an extremely nice guy to deal with.' The team advised First Cambridge Gateway Fund on all its investments. The firm provides corporate finance advice to IP-rich industries.

IPSWICH

Birketts fields top-echelon partners in Annette Whybrow, James Austin and Douglas Cotton. Many clients and peers regard Whybrow as the region's pre-eminent corporate partner.

Ian Waine heads **Prettys**' four-lawyer corporate team. The firm has undertaken numerous transport and technology-related M&A and MBO transactions.

NORWICH

Eversheds LLP's east of England team is headed by Terry Gould who is 'without doubt the best corporate lawyer in the region.' Gould also heads the firm's Norwich office, which continues to win top instructions in Norfolk. Clients note Andrew Croome's responsiveness and efforts to understand their businesses. The team acted for Archant on a major group reorganisation and re-branding exercise. Other clients include Norwich City Football Club and Porter and Haylett.

The presence of outstanding partners Nick

CORPORATE AND COMMERCIAL PETERBOROUGH

GREENWOODS

BUCKLES

Hegarty & Co
Hunt & Coombs

CORPORATE AND COMMERCIAL ELSEWHERE IN EAST ANGLIA

Greene & Greene *Bury St Edmunds*
Leeds Day *Huntingdon*

Ashton Graham *Bury St Edmunds*
Cunningham John *Thetford*
Gross & Co *Bury St Edmunds*
Nicholsons *Lowestoft*
Rustons & Lloyd *Newmarket*

Firms are listed A-Z in tiers which are ranked in order of priority

Fischl and Bryony Falkus ensures that **Mills & Reeve** remains one of the two firms of choice in Norwich. The team advised the principal shareholders of Highway Emergency Services on its sale to South Staffordshire Group for over £27m.

Nigel Lubbock heads **steeles (law) llp**'s corporate and commercial team. The firm recently acted on 11 deals with a total value of £64m. Partner Richard Bailey provides strong support. Key clients include Pi Group and East Lindsay District Council.

Howes Percival's corporate and commercial team was strengthened by the arrival of Jon Baskerville from **Herbert Smith**. He took over as head of the team in May 2003 and the four-partner team saw a marked increase in the volume and quality of instructions. Robert Halpin and Andrew Wood are regarded by clients as 'highly conscientious, fastidious, and good to work with.'

PETERBROUGH

Greenwoods boasts two of the region's leading corporate and commercial partners: managing partner Shelagh Smith and David Woods. The firm continues to advise major publishing company Emap and won Norfolk County Council as a new client.

The team at **Buckles**, headed by the intelligent and efficient Martin Lewis, has been transformed by the arrival of corporate finance specialist Nigel Moore, repeatedly recognised as one of the region's leading individuals. The firm was involved in 17 M&A deals ranging in value from £600,000 to £4.3m.

The two other firms in Peterborough with a track record for reliable advice on significant corporate and commercial transactions are **Hegarty & Co** and **Hunt & Coombs**.

COMMERCIAL LITIGATION CAMBRIDGE

MILLS & REEVE

Eversheds LLP
Hewitsons
Taylor Vinters

Barr Ellison
Few & Kester

Firms are listed A-Z in tiers which are ranked in order of priority

ELSEWHERE IN EAST ANGLIA

Greene & Greene and **Leeds Day** are recommended for MBOs and mergers.

COMMERCIAL LITIGATION: CAMBRIDGE

Mills & Reeve's Graeme Menzies heads the team. Clients note his 'flexibility of approach and willingness to understand the business'. The team acted for the defendant and counter-claimant in a multi-million-pound dispute involving an offshore installation.

Jane Lichtenstein heads **Eversheds LLP**'s creative and responsive team. It has particular strength in IP/IT disputes. Simon Oats is recommended for construction-related disputes. Highlights include the settlement of a shareholder dispute to enable a £30m share sale to proceed under extreme time pressure.

Dominic Hopkins heads **Hewitsons**' dispute resolution group. The team acted for a technology company in a £20m High Court claim. The group was boosted by the arrival of IP/IT specialist Mark Elmslie.

Edward Perrot heads **Taylor Vinters**' outstanding team. The group is particularly highly skilled in complex technology disputes. It acted for the major biotech company Genzyme on a complex competition case brought by the OFT.

IPSWICH

The highly respected Bob Wright heads the group at **Birketts**, which acts for regional clients, such as manufacturers and brewers, on contract claims and IP disputes. Angela Sydenham and Nigel

COMMERCIAL LITIGATION IPSWICH

BIRKETTS

PRETTYS

Gotelee & Goldsmith

Firms are listed A-Z in tiers which are ranked in order of priority

COMMERCIAL LITIGATION NORWICH

EVERSHEDS LLP **MILLS & REEVE**
Howes Percival **steeles (law) llp**
Fosters **Leathes Prior**
Cozens-Hardy & Jewson **Greenland Houchen** **Hansells** **Rogers and Norton**

Firms are listed A-Z in tiers which are ranked in order of priority

Farthing are highly recommended for rights of way disputes.

Peter Blake heads **Prettys**' two-partner litigation team. He gains strong support from partner Roland Sharp. The team receives abundant instructions, notably from the construction and transport sectors.

Gotelee & Goldsmith's Jonathan Ripman has an outstanding reputation.

NORWICH

Max Roessler heads **Eversheds LLP**'s Norwich team, while Paul Matthews and Charles Holloway are also highly recommended. The firm acted for John Tate, Treasury Solicitor, on the Bloody Sunday Inquiry. Other clients include Frans Maas (UK) and Eurotek Engineering.

Rachel Higgs heads **Mills & Reeve**'s Norwich commercial dispute resolution team. She is a specialist in contract and breach of warranty claims and partnership and shareholder disputes.

Andrew Barnes heads **Howes Percival**'s excellent four-partner team. Barnes has been particularly busy with a series of partnership disputes, mainly in the agriculture sector.

steeles (law) llp' three-lawyer commercial litigation team is headed by chartered arbitrator Chris Gilbert. It wins promotion in our table this year as a result of an increasingly diverse range of instructions. The firm acted for Bowater Windows on a complex search and seizure.

ELSEWHERE IN EAST ANGLIA

The highly rated James Maxey, former head of **Greenwoods**' commercial disputes team, joined **Buckles** in March 2003. He has experience of advising on a wide range of matters, including professional negligence and company and shareholder disputes. He has been appointed as a mediator by regional law firms.

Matthew Sidebottom heads **Hegarty & Co**'s team, which recently undertook 20 cases involving values over £15,000.

COMMERCIAL LITIGATION ELSEWHERE IN EAST ANGLIA

BUCKLES *Peterborough* **GREENWOODS** *Peterborough*
Hegarty & Co *Peterborough* **Hunt & Coombs** *Peterborough*
Cunningham John *Thetford* **Kenneth Bush** *King's Lynn* **Leeds Day** *Huntingdon* **Nicholsons** *Lowestoft* **Ward Gethin** *King's Lynn*

Firms are listed A-Z in tiers which are ranked in order of priority

Hunt & Coombs' head of civil and commercial litigation team, Julie McQuoid, is also recommended.

EAST MIDLANDS

The East Midlands comprises Derbyshire, Leicestershire, Lincolnshire, Northamptonshire and Nottinghamshire. Together these form the geographical heart of the UK. Greenfield and brownfield opportunities have attracted international companies to the region.

CORPORATE AND COMMERCIAL: NOTTINGHAM AND DERBY

Eversheds LLP's ability to service listed clients is unmatched in the region. Practice head Stephen Kitts is described by clients as 'first class'. The firm advises clients across the country and maintains a strong regional client base, acting for Udate.com on its $150m sale of USA Interactive, and advising Rolls-Royce on the sale of its nuclear engineering unit to Mitsui Babcock.

Browne Jacobson acted on over 70 deals in 2002. As expected, the local giant had a hand in all the key East Midlands deals, such as advising the management of Robinson Healthcare on its £22m secondary buyout. Practice head Rob Metcalfe has an impressive reputation. Gavin Cummings and Nigel Blackwell are recommended for their private equity expertise.

Edwards Geldard's three-partner team is headed by 'forward-thinking' partner Andrew Borkowski, a well-known corporate player. The firm advised the management on the £5m MBO of United Fillings. Partner Roman Surma specialises in utilities work.

Freethcartwright LLP's ambitious corporate team acted on 48 deals in the year, with an aggregate total of £285m. Practice head Karl Jansen receives particular praise for his succinct advice.

Shoosmiths' Peter Andrews focuses full time on merger control support and cartel work.

CORPORATE AND COMMERCIAL NOTTINGHAM AND DERBY

EVERSHEDS LLP *Nottingham*
BROWNE JACOBSON *Nottingham*
EDWARDS GELDARD *Nottingham, Derby* **FREETHCARTWRIGHT LLP** *Nottingham, Derby*
SHOOSMITHS *Nottingham*
Gateley Wareing *Nottingham*
Actons *Nottingham* **Nelsons** *Nottingham*
Berryman Shacklock *Nottingham* **Flint Bishop & Barnett** *Derby*

Firms are listed A-Z in tiers which are ranked in order of priority

Corporate head Oliver Brookshaw is praised by clients for his 'thorough and refreshing' style. The firm advised on large deals for Abbey National and Summit Financial Holdings.

Gateley Wareing's growing Nottingham practice is headed by the 'dynamic' Austin Moore; the firm has a good institutional client base.

Actons' SME-focused practice has had an active year. Practice head Adrian Forster is praised for his commercial nous, and the department has attracted a good number of instructions from abroad following the recruitment of French lawyer Sabrina Toscani.

Nelsons' corporate practice acts primarily for owner-managed businesses and advised on a number of MBOs in the year. Practice head Duncan Taylor has a good reputation.

Berryman Shacklock advised on 40 deals in the year, with a total value of around £120m. Managing partner Patrick Billyeald heads the practice, which acts for local clients such as PAT Print, Hy-Viz and The Willoughby Group.

In Derby, **Flint Bishop & Barnett** is expanding its commercial client base, acting on 27 deals in the year with a total value of £15m.

ELSEWHERE IN THE EAST MIDLANDS

Howes Percival is a strong corporate player. The Northampton office has developed solid outsourcing expertise, acting for clients such as Phoenix IT Services and Eurofleet. In Leicester, highlights include an acquisition for Ricardo plc and a joint venture for Shanks Group. Gerald Couldrake in Northampton and Jit Singh in Leicester are both highly recommended.

Gateley Wareing's strong corporate practice maintains excellent links with institutional referrers. Client-friendly Gareth John is highly recommended.

The largest law firm in Leicester, **Harvey Ingram Owston**'s four-partner practice has seen a very successful year, with a 25% increase in fee

CORPORATE AND COMMERCIAL ELSEWHERE IN EAST MIDLANDS

HOWES PERCIVAL *Northampton, Leicester*

Gateley Wareing *Leicester*
Harvey Ingram Owston *Leicester*
Hewitsons *Northampton*

Freethcartwright LLP *Leicester*
Shoosmiths *Northampton*

Spearing Waite *Leicester*
Wilkin Chapman *Grimsby*

Firms are listed A-Z in tiers which are ranked in order of priority

income. Partner Roy Botterill heads the department, which acts for local clients such as Weetabix and WR Group Holdings.

Hewitsons' three-partner Northampton practice is headed by the 'commercially impressive' Richard Ingram. Clients also recommend David Browne and Kevin Fletcher. The team advised on 46 deals during the year, with a combined value of over £160m.

Freethcartwright LLP's team, run by partner Robert Rowley, acts for a good range of Leicestershire clients. The firm advised Stardust Bingo Clubs on its reorganisation and buyback of shares.

Kit O'Grady heads **Shoosmiths**' Northampton team. Clients include Northampton Saints and Barclaycard. O'Grady is praised by clients for his straightforward approach.

Spearing Waite's growing corporate practice received a boost with the recruitment of an assistant from **Clifford Chance LLP**. Partner Nick Bridle heads the team.

Grimsby-based **Wilkin Chapman** has a strong local client base, and advised on £39m of transactions in the year. Practice head Richard Robinson is recommended.

COMMERCIAL LITIGATION: NOTTINGHAM AND DERBY

Browne Jacobson's clients include Express Dairies, Triumph Motorcycles and Parceline. Partner Peter Ellis is praised for his practical approach, while partner Paul Southby receives plaudits for his 'client-friendly manner'.

Eversheds LLP's won new clients such as Guildford Europe and Centrica from local rivals. Practice head Ian Gray is praised by clients for his first-rate litigation skills.

Freethcartwright LLP's large practice has achieved some impressive results for clients such as The Polestar Group. Philippa Dempster and Graham Greenfield in Nottingham are recommended.

Actons' litigation practice has advised on a wide variety of matters, including a £500,000 claim for deferred consideration under a share sale agreement. Partner Giles Gunstone heads the practice.

COMMERCIAL LITIGATION NOTTINGHAM AND DERBY

BROWNE JACOBSON *Nottingham*
EVERSHEDS LLP *Nottingham*
FREETHCARTWRIGHT LLP *Nottingham, Derby*

Actons *Nottingham*
Berryman Shacklock *Nottingham*
Edwards Geldard *Nottingham, Derby*
Flint Bishop & Barnett *Derby*
Nelsons *Nottingham, Derby*

Firms are listed A-Z in tiers which are ranked in order of priority

Practice head Richard Brackenbury is recommended at **Berryman Shacklock**, acting for clients such as Britcon (Scunthorpe) and Gibbon Ink & Coatings.

At **Edwards Geldard**, Nino Simone successfully represented a client in a £1m arbitration and also qualified as a mediator. Clients include Bowmer & Kirkland, Balfour Beatty Rail and Midlands Electricity.

Flint Bishop & Barnett's Andrew Cochrane has acted on some large landlord and tenant disputes during the year.

Nelsons' Nottingham litigation team has a strong client base in the local bicycle industry. Partner Chris Adams is recommended.

ELSEWHERE IN THE EAST MIDLANDS

Harvey Ingram Owston boasts the largest East Midlands litigation practice outside Nottingham, with six partners working full time in the field. As well as extensive employment litigation, the firm advised on a £1.5m fraudulent misrepresentation claim involving share sale warranties. Practice head John Simon is highly popular with clients.

Shoosmiths' excellent litigation practice is run by 'creative' partner John Hill, with five partners at the Northampton office. The firm focuses on financial institutions and won Nationwide Building Society as a client.

COMMERCIAL LITIGATION ELSEWHERE IN THE EAST MIDLANDS

HARVEY INGRAM OWSTON *Leicester*
SHOOSMITHS *Northampton*

Freethcartwright LLP *Leicester*
Hewitsons *Northampton*
Howes Percival *Leicester*

Chattertons *Boston*
EMW Law *Northampton*

Langleys *Lincoln*
Wilkin Chapman *Grimsby*

Firms are listed A-Z in tiers which are ranked in order of priority

At **Freethcartwright LLP**, national dispute resolution head Charles Powell, who specialises in product liability, is described as 'outstanding'. Partner Julian Middleton is also recommended.

Hewitsons' three-partner team has been highly active. Highlights include achieving the successful recovery of substantial funds for a South African investment company. Partner Dominic Hopkins is recommended.

At **Howes Percival**, heavyweight insolvency litigator Ashwin Mody moved from Leicester to Northampton, leading to rising star Geraint Davies' promotion to partner in Leicester.

THE NORTH

Newcastle is the largest legal and business centre north of Leeds and dominates the North. The region also includes Cleveland, Cumbria, Durham, Northumberland and Tyne & Wear.

CORPORATE AND COMMERCIAL: NEWCASTLE

Dickinson Dees remains Newcastle's corporate firm *par excellence*, due to its range of high-quality practitioners and breadth of practice. The firm's leading experts include M&A experts John Flynn, Jamie Pass and the 'outstanding' Nigel Williams, as well as department head Nigel Bellis; private equity specialist Chris Harker; and Jonathan Hewitt, who specialises in listings work. It advised Grainger Trust plc on its £477m joint bid for BPT Plc with Deutsche Bank. On the commercial side, new clients include Uniqema, Synextix and Huntsman.

Ward Hadaway is now the closest regional rival to **Dickinson Dees**. Noteworthy individuals include department head Colin Hewitt, M&A specialist Robert Thompson, Martin Hulls, who specialises in private equity, and Philip Jordan. Headline work includes advising The Sage Group on its £6m sponsorship agreement with the North Music Trust.

The departure of senior partner and high-profile rainmaker Michael Spriggs was a blow to **Eversheds LLP**'s corporate practice, although with Michael Spetch and Andrew Davison the department is in capable hands. Davison wins client praise as 'easily the best corporate lawyer I've come across'. Commercial head Ruth Connorton is also popular with clients. Spriggs, now managing director of UK Land Estates, remains a major client. Other clients include Newcastle International Airport and Reg Vardy.

A smaller firm that punches well above its weight, **Robert Muckle** boasts a number of highly rated individuals. Robert Phillips heads the department, while managing partner Hugh Welch

CORPORATE AND COMMERCIAL NEWCASTLE

DICKINSON DEES

WARD HADAWAY

EVERSHEDS LLP
ROBERT MUCKLE
WATSON BURTON

Hay & Kilner

Mincoffs

Sintons

CORPORATE AND COMMERCIAL CUMBRIA

BAINES WILSON *Carlisle*
BURNETTS *Carlisle*

Cartmell Shepherd *Carlisle*

Firms are listed A-Z in tiers which are ranked in order of priority

CORPORATE AND COMMERCIAL ELSEWHERE IN THE NORTH

Archers *Stockton on Tees*
Jacksons Commercial & Private Law LLP *Stockton on Tees*

Blackett Hart & Pratt *Durham*
Latimer Hinks *Darlington*
The Endeavour Partnership LLP *Teesdale*
Tilly Bailey & Irvine *Hartlepool*

Doberman Horsman *Middlesbrough*
Merritt & Co *Yarm*
Punch Robson *Middlesbrough*
Smith & Graham *Hartlepool*

Firms are listed A-Z in tiers which are ranked in order of priority

COMMERCIAL LITIGATION NEWCASTLE

DICKINSON DEES
EVERSHEDS LLP
WARD HADAWAY

Watson Burton

Crutes Law Firm
Hay & Kilner
Robert Muckle
Short Richardson & Forth
Sintons

Mincoffs

Firms are listed A-Z in tiers which are ranked in order of priority

and senior partner Ian Gilthorpe all have major profiles in the market. The firm acted in the MBO of Fathom Technologies, and advised the North Music Trust on a £6m sponsorship arrangement with The Sage Group.

Gillian Hall heads the 'exceptional' five-partner team at **Watson Burton** and wins client praise for her efficiency and her intellectual ability. The firm acted for management in the £7.5m MBO of Lionweld Kennedy. Senior partner Andrew Hoyle has a strong reputation.

Hay & Kilner is very popular with clients. Department head Nick James has a good reputation for client care and legal acumen. The firm acts primarily for owner-managed businesses. It advised on the transfer of Nick Swales' team of investment managers from Merrill Lynch to Laing & Cruickshank.

Paul Hughes and John Nicholson handle most of **Mincoffs**' corporate work. Senior partner Howard Gold wins praise from property clients. The firm advised Blacks Leisure on its takeover by JD Sports. **Mincoffs** also gives insurance advice to its commercial clients.

Karen Simms heads the two-partner team at **Sintons**, and is building an increasingly strong reputation. The firm handled 30 deals with a total deal value of £55m, almost double its previous total. Partnership advice is a niche area.

CUMBRIA

Senior partner John Wilson of **Baines Wilson** has a high profile and his firm, although smaller, specialises in commercial work to a greater extent than its rivals. Employment partner Rayner Jones is also respected. The majority of clients are local owner-managed businesses, particularly in the technology industry.

Burnetts remains a leading player, with Vaughan Jones and John Noctor highly regarded across the region.

Cartmell Shepherd's five offices across the region give it a broad spread of owner-managed clients.

ELSEWHERE IN THE NORTH

Partner John Richardson heads the excellent team at **Archers**. The firm has expertise in M&A, partnerships and commercial contracts, and top contacts with the owner-managed sector.

One of the region's largest firms, **Jacksons Commercial & Private Law LLP**' department head is senior partner Kevin Fletcher. The firm advises on M&A, flotations, start-ups and restructurings, and has a good track record for inward investment.

Gary Copeland and Neil Hilton are the major corporate specialists at **Blackett Hart & Pratt**, which has a number of offices worthy of recommendation in the region.

Latimer Hinks has seven commercial partners, many focused on property work, but it has, in Nick Poole, a high-quality corporate specialist.

Toby Tilly heads the team at **The Endeavour Partnership LLP**. The firm focuses on small-to-medium owner-managed businesses but maintains a number of high-profile clients, including Middlesbrough FC.

Tilly Bailey & Irvine has four offices, with its Hartlepool office dominant in the local market.

COMMERCIAL LITIGATION: NEWCASTLE

Guy Harvey leads **Dickinson Dees**' six-partner team together with the highly rated John Marshall. Harvey concentrates on London-centric disputes, and has substantial experience in trust litigation and professional negligence. Marshall is responsible for the firm's local work, with emphasis on contractual claims, breach of warranty and shareholder disputes.

Eversheds LLP benefits from its national and European experience and resources. Susan Howe is popular with clients. Firm litigation head Lex Dowie also has a strong reputation. The office continues to be involved in the Bloody Sunday Inquiry.

Ian Collinson heads the 11-fee-earner team at **Ward Hadaway**, where Bob Elliott is also highly regarded. Property litigator Margaret Lawson was joined in April 2003 by Alan Herbert, formerly national head of **Pinsents**' property litigation team.

Richard Pickersgill joined **Watson Burton** and strengthened its reputation for real estate litigation. He joins renowned construction expert Robert Langley. The firm's contentious capability stretches far beyond real estate, though, with Allan Henderson and Julian Gill high-profile practitioners.

The highly regarded Helen Ager heads **Crutes Law Firm**'s litigation department, which is building up insurance to match its strengths in public sector and mediation. Tim Wallis is the outgoing president of the Forum of Insurance Lawyers.

High-profile individuals at **Hay & Kilner** include senior partner Martin Soloman, insurance expert Ros Sparrow, and Neil Dwyer. The firm has a strong track record in ADR.

At **Robert Muckle**, highly regarded Paul Jonson heads the unit, while clients call Mary Anne Macharg 'absolutely fantastic.' Jonson handles a high number of injunctions, while Macharg specialises on commercial disputes involving technology or IP clients.

David Forth leads the litigation team at **Short Richardson & Forth**, which is developing a solid mediation practice.

Sintons hired ex-**Robert Muckle** partner Catherine Wood, to head its growing team jointly with David Dobbin.

COMMERCIAL LITIGATION ELSEWHERE IN THE NORTH

Burnetts *Carlisle*
Crutes Mounseys *Carlisle*
Jacksons Commercial & Private Law LLP *Stockton on Tees*

Cartmell Shepherd *Carlisle*
Hayton Winkley Kendal *Kendal*
Latimer Hinks *Darlington*
Tilly Bailey & Irvine *Hartlepool*

Firms are listed A-Z in tiers which are ranked in order of priority

ELSEWHERE IN THE NORTH

Commercial litigation is one of **Burnetts**' major strengths, with two prominent partners – Patricia Hall and Michael Cousins.

Partner Paul Forster is **Crutes Mounseys**' litigation specialist in Carlisle and a trained mediator.

Jacksons Commercial & Private Law LLP has an increasingly strong team, including arbitration experience. Clients range from plcs and statutory bodies to sole traders.

At **Latimer Hinks**, Ken Wiper and Mark Gardner handle commercial disputes.

NORTH WEST

North West covers law firms in Greater Manchester, Merseyside, Lancashire and Cheshire. The main centres are Manchester and Liverpool but reliable commercial advice is readily available in the satellite towns of Blackburn, Bolton, Chester, and Preston.

CORPORATE AND COMMERCIAL: MANCHESTER

Addleshaw Goddard boasts a host of Manchester's leading rainmakers in its corporate department. Clients and market commentators consistently identify Darryl Cooke, Paul Devitt and Richard Lee among the cream of the region's corporate lawyers. Keith Johnston and Geoff Yates also win plaudits. Clients include 3i, Time Retail Finance and JJB Sports.

DLA retains a top-notch reputation in transactional corporate work. Partners Jonathan Procter and Stephen Devlin are 'as good as they get,' clients say.

Eversheds LLP fields a first-class corporate team with a solid track record. The firm acted on a number of deals valued at over £200m. Led by the irrepressible Danny Hall, notable players include Edward Pysden; Geoff Blower; and Helen Ridge. The 'impressive' Alison Brearey is advising Vertex Data Science on a ten-year £450m strategic partnership deal with Westminster City Council.

Halliwell Landau is corporate counsel to 25% of AIM-listed companies that instruct North West law firms, and has strong links with private equity houses. Partner Sue Molloy is considered 'commercial and focused'; Rebecca Grisewood has demonstrated 'commercial sense and empathy with the client' on innovative transactions. John Whatnall, head of department, is consistently identified among the region's leading commercial lawyers. Clients include Aberdeen Murray Johnstone Private Equity and Lloyds Development Capital.

CORPORATE AND COMMERCIAL MANCHESTER

ADDLESHAW GODDARD
DLA
EVERSHEDS LLP

HALLIWELL LANDAU
HAMMONDS

Brabners Chaffe Street
Pinsents

Cobbetts
DWF

Laytons
Pannone & Partners

Kuit Steinart Levy
Wacks Caller

Hill Dickinson
Mace & Jones Solicitors
Nexus Solicitors
Turner Parkinson

Berg & Co
George Davies Solicitors

Firms are listed A-Z in tiers which are ranked in order of priority

Hammonds has continued to act on many of the region's largest deals, supported by a solid core of £5m to £25m transactions. Head of department Stephen Levy is 'shrewd, commercial and pragmatic'. William Downs is national head of **Hammonds**' utilities practice. Northern head of private equity, Jonathan Jones, bolsters one of the region's leading practices.

Brabners Chaffe Street name partner Robert Street is highly respected and has 20 years' experience negotiating deals. Partners Tom Burton, Mark Brandwood and Tony Harper bring a level of experience few firms can rival. Clients include European Leasing Plc, The Design Company and Flowcrete Plc.

As new kids in town, **Pinsents**' five-partner corporate department remains something of an unknown quantity. Institutional clients however speak highly of initial encounters, and some corporates report being 'eager to work with them'. Mike McGrath and Simon Masters held up the M&A side of the practice. Clients include Granville Baird Capital Partners, Speedy Hire Plc and Latium Group.

On the corporate side of **Cobbetts**, head of department Nicholas Fielden is rated for his 'commercial understanding of private equity'. Matthew Baker runs the team on the commercial side. Clients include Aberdeen Murray Johnstone Private Equity, Matalan Retail Ltd and Advanstar Communications Inc.

Partner Andrew Needham heads **DWF**'s nine-partner combined Manchester-Liverpool corporate practice. Private equity clients find **DWF** 'reasonably priced' and 'commercial'. Partners Jeremy Swift and Jim Davies are recommended.

David Sefton leads **Laytons**' corporate finance department. The department merits a mention here for its sustained high-quality service to commercial clients. The team has continued to build and strengthen its reputation, acting on some substantial and complex transactions. Clients include Compel Group Plc, Enterprise Plc and Enterprise Ventures.

Pannone & Partners' smaller listed and owner-managed client base has provided a reasonable flow of transactional work complemented by corporate restructuring and reorganisation. Søren Tattam heads a ten-partner team. Clients include British Tourist Board, Cotton Traders, Texaco and Urban Splash.

Robert Levy of **Kuit Steinart Levy** has a good reputation for shrewd and pragmatic negotiation as head of the firm's corporate practice. Clients include Wisdom Toothbrushes, Karrimor International and Stirling Group. The firm acted for Thomson's Group Plc in the acquisition of Harrogate-based IFA Investorcare Ltd.

Wacks Caller's six-partner team is led by Kevin Philbin and includes name partner Martin Caller. The firm has been busy working on transactions in the £1m to £5m value range. Commercial work included acting for Sirocom Ltd on a multi-million pound networking contract with STA Travel.

LIVERPOOL

DLA's corporate team has strong links with local businesses and remains the market leader. Michael Prince heads a team that includes the well-reputed David Cadwallader. Clients also rate Paul Jefferson, 'a tough negotiator' who 'fiercely protects' his clients' interests at all times.

Denise Walker heads **Brabners Chaffe Street**'s Liverpool corporate department. The department has continued to grow in a slow market. Clients include Rage Plc, Mersey Docks and Harbour Board, and Nationwide Autocentres.

Mark O'Connor heads **DWF**'s corporate department in Liverpool. The practice has a solid reputation among the local owner-managed sector, and works closely with partners in Manchester. Clients include Westbury Asset Management and Edward Billington & Sons.

CORPORATE AND COMMERCIAL LIVERPOOL
DLA
BRABNERS CHAFFE STREET
DWF
Cuff Roberts
Hill Dickinson
Lees Lloyd Whitley
Mace & Jones Solicitors
Weightman Vizards

Firms are listed A-Z in tiers which are ranked in order of priority

Partner Sue Russell heads **Cuff Roberts**' corporate department which is well regarded in the Liverpool market. The firm is strong in the owner-managed sector and acted on a number of £1m to £5m deals in 2002.

Hill Dickinson boasts a strong national corporate team with a hefty Liverpool bias. Key partners include Glyn Dale-Jones, Richard Paton, a recent recruit from **DLA**, Ian Vicary and Richard Martindale. The firm is instructed on a number of major transactions and enjoys a steady diet of commercial contracting work.

Lees Lloyd Whitley merits a ranking this year on the strength of its transactional practice. Clients rate department head Tim Polding as 'experienced and pragmatic'. The firm enjoys strong relationships with local businesses.

Mace & Jones Solicitors' Ian Hodgkinson heads the Liverpool corporate department. The firm continues to develop its share of the owner-managed sector. Deal highlights include acting for the management in the £17.5m MBO of FW Technologies.

Ex-*Addleshaw Booth & Co* head of corporate finance, Jonathan Shorrock is a big name in the region and he joined **Weightman Vizards** as head of corporate and tax in October 2002. The department is ably supported by a further 11 lawyers and has complementary teams of tax, property, employment and environmental specialists.

ELSEWHERE IN THE NORTH WEST

Aaron & Partners' company/commercial team, led by partner Ben Quirk, further bolstered its resources with the recruitment of partner Elizabeth Delgado, who brings asset finance and banking expertise to the team. The firm acts on a good volume of £1m to £5m transactions.

Partner John Boydell is **Brabners Chaffe Street**'s primary point of contact for corporate work in Preston. The department's profile is growing alongside that of the town.

Tim Dennis heads **Gorvins**' well-regarded company/commercial department, based in Stockport.

CORPORATE AND COMMERCIAL ELSEWHERE IN THE NORTH WEST
Aaron & Partners *Chester*
Brabners Chaffe Street *Preston*
Gorvins *Stockport*
Hill Dickinson *Chester*
Keoghs *Bolton*

Firms are listed A-Z in tiers which are ranked in order of priority

Hill Dickinson's three-partner team, comprising Robin Jones, Andrew Bogle and Peter Davenport, is among the strongest teams in the region outside Manchester and Liverpool.

Keoghs' head of corporate, Alan Robins is one of Bolton's leading deal-makers. In 2002 the firm completed 22 deals worth £130m.

COMMERCIAL LITIGATION: MANCHESTER

Addleshaw Goddard's John Gatenby takes a lead role in many of the firm's £1m+ cases and has a growing reputation for mediation and arbitrations under ICC rules. John Gosling impresses on commercial cases for blue-chip clients. Mark Amsden is recommended for IT outsourcing disputes.

DLA's forte is mid-to-high-value banking and finance litigation. Stewart Plant has an excellent reputation in Manchester's financial services sector.

Eversheds LLP boasts the most internationally focused practice of the Manchester firms. Clients recommend Michael Clavell-Bate, Jonathon Crook, Antony Gold and Mark Mattison for a consistent and talented team that has led high-value international arbitrations and substantial cases for plcs.

DWF's department includes a number of impressive niche areas not regularly handled by other firms, including Peter Moore's administrative and public law practice. Moore is also noted for fraud-related litigation.

Halliwell Landau's client base is particularly strong in the retail and construction sectors. Ian Austin is praised for the professionalism he brings to high-value commercial disputes. Karen Spencer has an excellent reputation for bond claims work.

Hammonds' Lucci Dammone leads a practice with a national standing for high-value health and safety-related litigation and product liability advice. The firm is also active on finance and building works cases. Partner Jan Levinson has joined **Beachcroft Wansbroughs**.

At **Pannone & Partners**, Richard Glithero, Vincent O'Farrell, William Lister, Graeme Smith and Alex Megaw bring strong courtroom skills to any case. Vincent O'Farrell, in particular, is a capable choice for high-value arbitrations. Sponsorship disputes are a firm speciality. Clients include banks and government bodies. William Lister handles defamation cases.

COMMERCIAL LITIGATION MANCHESTER
ADDLESHAW GODDARD
DLA
EVERSHEDS LLP
DWF
HALLIWELL LANDAU
HAMMONDS
PANNONE & PARTNERS
Cobbetts
Pinsents
Berg & Co
Berrymans Lace Mawer
Brabners Chaffe Street
Davies Arnold Cooper
Kuit Steinart Levy
Rowe Cohen

Firms are listed A-Z in tiers which are ranked in order of priority

Cobbetts' head of department Mark Whittell is recommended for insolvency and banking-related litigation.

Lee Dunnill's team at **Pinsents** has established a good reputation acting on £1m to £35m search and seizure orders.

Charles Khan at **Berg & Co** is recommended for both shareholder and contract disputes, while **Berrymans Lace Mawer**'s Mark Benson is recommended for product liability claims.

Paul Morton at **Brabners Chaffe Street** has a good reputation for injunctions.

Davies Arnold Cooper's managing partner Stephen Gorman is recommended for cases where insurance is a key element. Gareth Williams is recommended for agency and distribution and commercial contract disputes.

At **Kuit Steinart Levy** we recommend Damian Bailey and Jeff Lewis.

Mace & Jones Solicitors' senior partner Graeme Jump is recommended for insolvency-related disputes. Philip Farrelly and Richard Corran are recommended for property litigation.

Rowe Cohen has a niche specialism in legal expenses. Partner Anthony Dennison's High Court win for client The Accident Group determined that conditional fee agreements do not breach regulations.

LIVERPOOL

At **DLA** practice head Mark Goodwin has built an excellent department, highly rated for non-financial services litigation. In addition to mainstream litigation, the firm is respected for its judicial review, mediation and arbitration work. Keith Lewin wins plaudits in the expanding field of

COMMERCIAL LITIGATION LIVERPOOL

DLA

Brabners Chaffe Street
DWF
Weightman Vizards

Hill Dickinson

Bermans
Cuff Roberts
Lees Lloyd Whitley
Mace & Jones Solicitors

Firms are listed A-Z in tiers which are ranked in order of priority

IT disputes. Partner Colin Gibbons is also recommended.

At **Brabners Chaffe Street** department head Mark Manley has an excellent reputation for media disputes and a good track record on mediations.

DWF's Ian Titchmarsh heads an impressively broad, firm-wide department handling insurer-driven litigation.

Denis Hannon at **Weightman Vizards** acted for Hoover in its settled dispute with Dyson. Police work is a niche capability.

Hill Dickinson department head Noel Fagan receives plaudits for the team's ADR work. The firm's loyal client base includes high street banks, insurer St Paul (for major litigation) and Scottish Power. Jonathan Berkson is also recommended.

Bermans has established a distinctive practice, focused on serving the brewing industry and debt-recovery clients.

At **Cuff Roberts** David Rawlinson and David Hewitt are recommended for mediations, shareholder disputes and defamation. **Lees Lloyd Whitley**'s department head Manisha Kumar has considerable experience of arbitrations and adjudications.

ELSEWHERE IN THE NORTH WEST

In addition to handling general dispute resolution, Simon Carter's department at **Aaron & Partners** is recommended for the defence of cases involving the environment, road transport, health and safety, and trading standards.

Alexander Harris' David Harris is recommended for claimant work for multi-party actions and product liability cases.

Brabners Chaffe Street's Amanda Webster has an excellent reputation for cases with an environmental element. Clients include the Highways Agency, local authorities and contractors.

Name partner Martin Kippax at **Kippax Beaumont Lewis** is praised as an 'effective commercial litigator'. The firm gets things done and achieves results,' comments one client.

COMMERCIAL LITIGATION ELSEWHERE IN THE NORTH WEST

Aaron & Partners *Chester*
Alexander Harris *Altrincham*
Brabners Chaffe Street *Preston*
Kippax Beaumont Lewis *Bolton*
Maxwell Gillott *Lancaster*
Taylors *Blackburn*
Walker Smith Way *Chester*

Firms are listed alphabetically

Elaine Maxwell of **Maxwell Gillott** has established a national reputation acting for individuals in education cases.

Taylors and **Walker Smith Way** are also recommended.

SOUTH EAST

Forming a ring around London, the South East is the most diverse regional legal market. Its proximity to the capital makes it attractive to City lawyers and clients.

We divide the South East into five areas: Thames Valley; Berks, Oxon M4/M40; Kent, Surrey, Sussex; Hampshire; Beds, Bucks, Herts; and Essex.

CORPORATE AND COMMERCIAL: THAMES VALLEY, BERKS, OXON, M4/M40

Manches has forged an outstanding reputation in Oxford. Clients eulogise lead partner Peter Angel, who is described as 'a superb negotiator'.

Nabarro Nathanson is deservedly popular with clients, who pick out Glyn Taylor and Barry Maytum as the cream of this very slick group. Clients include Oracle, Schlumberger Sema and GE Capital.

Osborne Clarke dominates the M4 Corridor, offering superb corporate and commercial services from Bristol to London. Reading partners Hugh Jones and Greg Leyshon are singled out for praise by local companies, accountants and bankers. The firm has notable strength in private equity and acts regularly for 3i.

Pitmans has an excellent standing in the local market. Longstanding commercial clients of the firm include De Beers and Porsche Cars GB Ltd. One client observes that leading partner John Hutchinson 'appears to be well supported by salaried partners and qualified staff who are able to step into the partners' shoes when required'.

Morgan Cole remains a significant national player with a strong client base. It acts on a range of MBOs and other corporate acquisitions, and won a place on RAC's legal services panel in the summer of 2002. Duncan Macintosh and Guy Constant are praised by clients for work of a 'very high quality'.

Olswang's highly experienced and approachable Marshall Leopold leads the team, which has advised clients such as Thames Water and Svenska Handelsbanken on a range of M&A, restructuring and private equity work.

CORPORATE AND COMMERCIAL THAMES VALLEY, BERKS, OXON, M4/M40

MANCHES *Oxford*
NABARRO NATHANSON *Reading*
OSBORNE CLARKE *Reading*
PITMANS *Reading*

MORGAN COLE *Oxford, Reading*
OLSWANG *Reading*
SHOOSMITHS *Reading*

Blake Lapthorn Linnell *Oxford*
Boyes Turner *Reading*
Clarks *Reading*
Penningtons *Newbury*

Barlow Lyde & Gilbert *Oxford*
Blandy & Blandy *Reading*
Brookstreet Des Roches *Witney*
Charles Lucas & Marshall *Newbury*
Clifton Ingram *Wokingham*
Hale and Dorr *Oxford*
Henmans *Oxford*

Firms are listed A-Z in tiers which are ranked in order of priority

The extensive coverage of **Shoosmiths** in the South East and Midlands means the firm can call on resources beyond its Reading office. That said, Nigel Thorne and Dean Drew are both praised by local clients, with one commenting: 'Dean is extremely efficient in his conduct of transactions, and particularly in relation to documentation management and control.'

Blake Lapthorn Linnell has a strong all-round practice and is popular with owner-managed businesses. The team excels in advising education clients, particularly the University of Oxford.

The 'excellent' Bill Gornall-King and Roy Butler at **Boyes Turner** are appreciated by clients for the consistency and quality of their commercial advice. Clients include Onyx Environmental Group and PinkRoccade UK.

At **Clarks**, Richard Lee is well respected. The firm acted for major new client Carillion, which instructs its excellent employment and environment departments.

Penningtons has significant regional strength in its Newbury office, led by former **Denton Wilde Sapte** lawyer John Riddick. The team's major commercial clients include Exelcare Holdings and the Bewley Homes Group.

KENT, SURREY, SUSSEX

Cripps Harries Hall has long boasted a 'strong and experienced' corporate and commercial department, run by Trevor Carney, Christopher Langridge and US-qualified Lawrence Leporte.

CORPORATE AND COMMERCIAL
KENT, SURREY, SUSSEX

CRIPPS HARRIES HALL *Tunbridge Wells*
STEVENS & BOLTON *Guildford*

ASB Law *Crawley, Croydon*
Clyde & Co *Guildford*
DMH *Brighton*
Mundays *Cobham*
Shadbolt & Co *Reigate*

Charles Russell *Guildford*
Davies Lavery *Maidstone*
Furley Page *Canterbury*
Paul Davidson Taylor *Horsham*
Penningtons *Godalming*
Rawlison Butler *Crawley*
Thomas Eggar *Chichester, Horsham, Reigate, Worthing*

Barlows *Guildford*
Batchelors *Canterbury*
Hart Brown *Guildford*
Laytons*Guildford*
Mackrell Turner Garrett *Woking*
Robbins Olivey *Woking*
Thomson Snell & Passmore *Tunbridge Wells*

Firms are listed A-Z in tiers which are ranked in order of priority

The firm has wide-ranging experience, stretching from commercial advice to local owner-managed businesses to Yellow-Book work for major plcs, such as Hidden Hearing and South East Water. Partner Peter Garry is one of the UK's leading experts on partnership law.

Stevens & Bolton is described by one client as 'having the skills and resources to provide a London-quality service locally'. Jonathan Porteous recently joined to add to an array of talent that includes Richard Baxter, Keith Syson and commercial partner Beverley Whittaker. The firm has maintained longstanding relationships with clients such as Hays Plc and BOC, while gaining new panel appointments such as Gallaher.

ASB Law provides a holistic commercial service to clients throughout its seven-office empire in Kent, Surrey and Sussex. The team regularly deals with high-value procurement contracts, has a very strong reputation in the public sector, and has won a number of new local authority contracts. Partner Russell Bell and consultant Don Burstow are singled out by clients for praise.

City firm **Clyde & Co** has offered a Guildford annexe to its London practice since 1969. The quality of instructions is very impressive. The corporate team was established in 1997 by partners Andrew Holderness and Tim Matthews, who are noted by clients for their professionalism.

DMH is a Sussex heavyweight, commended for its 'excellent ability to work to tight deadlines and value for money'. Partners Vincent O'Brien, Alex Chester, Barbara Hurwood and the 'worldly' Ian Wilson come highly rated.

Mundays services owner-managed businesses as well as major corporates. The firm specialises in the healthcare, with clients such as Alliance UniChem, aviation and logistics sectors. Partners Peter Munday and David Irving combine tactical savvy with approachability, while Nicola Broadhurst is one of only a few true franchising specialists in the region.

Andrew Trotter leads a five-partner corporate team at **Shadbolt & Co** that won Securicor as a new client and advised Trans4m on the London Underground privatisation. The team is a serious market player, with an enviable reputation.

Geoffrey Sparks at **Charles Russell** leads a rapidly expanding corporate practice. The team is building up a loyal following of public sector and mid-range corporate clients.

In 2003 **Davies Lavery** hired the much-praised Stuart Butler-Gallie and his impressive commercial team from **Brachers**. One client says: 'Stuart has the energy and drive that makes us feel he's giving 110% at all times.'

Furley Page's commercial advice is described as 'very sound, very straightforward, very focused'. Head of department Christopher Wacher has a strong reputation.

Praised by clients and peers, **Paul Davidson Taylor** is noted for no-frills corporate and commercial advice. Partner Noel Ruddy has a strong factoring practice.

Penningtons' Godalming office has a reputable disposals practice, acting on the sale of local and national businesses. The office was boosted by the hire of Sarah Scarlett from **Hart Brown**.

Rawlison Butler has strong corporate and commercial capability, evident in the skills of experienced, widely praised partners James Chatfield and Tim Sadka.

At **Thomas Eggar**, Tony Edwards, Neil Hart and Nick Rutter are first-rate. Says one client: 'I see little reason to pay City prices when we receive such a high level of service from a provincial firm.'

HAMPSHIRE

Blake Lapthorn Linnell is a Hampshire heavy-hitter, and its corporate practice competes with national players. Sean Wright is 'much in demand and considered to be the best corporate lawyer on the South Coast'. The firm has niches in aviation, transport and charities work.

For corporate and commercial work throughout the South of England, **Bond Pearce** is a major force; in Hampshire it blows most of the competition away. One client says, 'We've never found **Bond Pearce** wanting.' Clients, including Safeway and B&Q, describe partner Stephen Pierce as 'very client-focused, commercial and accessible'. Nick Page is also very popular.

CORPORATE AND COMMERCIAL
HAMPSHIRE

BLAKE LAPTHORN LINNELL *Southampton*
BOND PEARCE *Southampton*

Coffin Mew & Clover *Fareham*
Paris Smith & Randall *Southampton*
Shoosmiths *Fareham*

Moore & Blatch *Southampton*
Penningtons *Basingstoke*

Clarke Willmott *Southampton*
Dutton Gregory *Winchester*
Lamport Bassitt *Southampton*
Trethowans *Southampton*
White & Bowker *Winchester*

Firms are listed A-Z in tiers which are ranked in order of priority

Amanda Brockwell at **Coffin Mew & Clover** is a popular corporate practitioner. She specialises in funding work for the likes of Halifax Bank of Scotland, and advised on the acquisition of Ashford Colour Press.

Paris Smith & Randall is noted for its no-nonsense, traditional approach. Partner Andrew Heathcock is a popular choice among corporates and banks. Highlights include the IPO of Rose Bowl Plc, the home of Hampshire CCC.

Shoosmiths' Solent Business Park team is led by 'safe pair of hands' Louise Finlayson. The firm acted in Abbey National's Coavista JV with Stiell.

Peter Jeffery and Roger Bailey at **Moore & Blatch** run a small but respected practice, acting for small to mid-sized corporates on a range of MBOs and MBIs as well as on AIM and OFEX listings.

Penningtons' managing partner Franco Bosi and partner Charles Brooks lead a strong team, acting for owner-managed businesses and the selling shareholders of larger groups.

BEDS, BUCKS, HERTS

Renowned for its transaction capabilities, **EMW Law** is one of three Milton Keynes-based firms that dominate the M1 Corridor between London and Birmingham. Ian Zant-Boer and Ian Morris head a small but extremely corporate-focused team.

Clients universally praise Brandon Ransley, managing partner of the Milton Keynes office of **Howes Percival**. He is described as 'primarily interested in getting the best result for us, not with getting the highest number of hours on the clock'. Ransley heads a team along with the 'dynamic and proactive' Andrew Harris.

Kimbells LLP's clients appreciate lead partner Jonathan Hambleton. The firm has a specialist niche in the leisure and brewing industry, advising some of the top brewers in the UK.

Watford's **Matthew Arnold & Baldwin** remains a powerful force in the local market.

CORPORATE AND COMMERCIAL BEDS, BUCKS, HERTS

EMW LAW *Milton Keynes*
HOWES PERCIVAL *Milton Keynes*
KIMBELLS LLP *Milton Keynes*

Matthew Arnold & Baldwin *Watford*
Shoosmiths *Milton Keynes*
Taylor Walton *Luton*

B P Collins *Gerrards Cross*
Fennemores *Uxbridge*
Iliffes Booth Bennett (IBB) *Uxbridge*
Moorcrofts Corporate Law *Milton Keynes*

Harold Benjamin *Harrow*
Machins *Luton*
Pictons *St Albans*
Stanley Tee *Bishops Stortford*
Turbervilles with Nelson Cuff *Uxbridge*

Firms are listed A-Z in tiers which are ranked in order of priority

Experienced and highly respected partner Chris Green takes the helm on general commercial work, while the young and affable Richard Phillips is a corporate dynamo.

Shoosmiths' Milton Keynes office continues its rise up the table, winning major instructions from The Open University and Northants Police. We recommend Keith Lewington.

Taylor Walton's strong Luton-based practice rides high on the strength of partner Moira Myers, celebrated in the local market. The firm's appointment to Bank of Scotland's corporate banking panel is a coup.

At **B P Collins**, David Stanning is a noted commercial practitioner, while David Jackson at **Iliffes Booth Bennett (IBB)** advises local banks and entertainment and leisure companies and is decribed as 'pragmatic, not dogmatic' by clients.

Despite its relatively small size, **Fennemores**' corporate and commercial practice punches above its weight. Chris Robinson excels in corporate finance, particularly on MBO/MBIs.

Moorcrofts Corporate Law's clients continue to be highly impressed by both 'its ability to tackle complex briefs quickly and effectively and by the professionalism of all its staff'. Founding partners Adrian Phillips and Andrew Katz have experience and standing in the market.

ESSEX

Wollastons stands head and shoulders above the rest of the Essex market for corporate and commercial work. Richard Wollaston, Nicholas Burnett, Richard Payne and Rafael Ruiz are all 'very highly rated' by clients.

Birkett Long is a premier firm. Partners Wanda Domhof and Stephen Williams have been busy with disposals and acquisitions for local owner-managed businesses. The firm has notable strength in advice to public health companies, charities and schools.

Tolhurst Fisher is a two-office, strong all-rounder. Philip Tolhurst and Robin Bain are prominent local players, acting for a number of household names.

Wortley Byers, led by Michael Lightowler, has a proven track record in providing cost-effective advice to smaller commercial clients.

Ellisons' Max Harden is a standout commercial partner at this thriving local firm.

Thompson Smith & Puxon is a high-street firm with a popular mix of private and commercial client work. Partner Mary Anne Fedeyko handles property and commercial work.

CORPORATE AND COMMERCIAL ESSEX

WOLLASTONS

Birkett Long
Tolhurst Fisher
Wortley Byers

Ellisons
Thompson Smith & Puxon

Firms are listed A-Z in tiers which are ranked in order of priority

COMMERCIAL LITIGATION: THAMES VALLEY, BERKS, OXON, M4/M40:

Clarks' three-partner team is led by Antony Morris, who is experienced in ADR and in obtaining search and seizure and freezing injunctions. Acting for a waste management company, **Clarks** successfully settled a multi-million-pound dispute in 2002.

Morgan Cole has solid litigation expertise in its Oxford and Reading offices, headed by Stephanie Walls and Philip Jones respectively.

Under the highly regarded Peter Sheppard, **Nabarro Nathanson**'s commercial litigation department is branching outside of its traditionally IT-focused remit. Contractual disputes, shareholder disputes, and trade finance issues are three sources of work; financial institutions are increasingly important clients.

Led by Tim Clark, **Olswang**'s litigation practice is flourishing. It is winning blue-chip clients and facing City law firms in key commercial disputes, often with a hi-tech bias.

Blake Lapthorn Linnell partner Jonathan Lloyd-Jones is experienced in ADR, while partner Richard Humphreys has a track record of litigating for finance companies. Abbey National Business Services is a client.

At **Boyes Turner**, department head Mike Robinson advised a former shareholder on a £14m breach of trust claim following a company sale.

Manches possesses an 'excellent' three-partner litigation team led by Julie Bond, which handles commercial and IP disputes; partner Steven Maier is 'pragmatic and commercial'.

Pitmans' robust commercial litigation practice is led by department head Sue O'Brien, who focuses on fraud and international commerce.

Under the 'brisk and efficient' Claire Rowe, **Shoosmiths** handles numerous high-value commercial contract disputes.

COMMERCIAL LITIGATION THAMES VALLEY, BERKS, OXON, M4/M40

CLARKS *Reading*
MORGAN COLE *Oxford, Reading*
NABARRO NATHANSON *Reading*
OLSWANG *Reading*

Blake Lapthorn Linnell *Oxford*
Boyes Turner *Reading*
Manches *Oxford*
Pitmans *Reading*
Shoosmiths *Reading*

Brookstreet Des Roches *Witney*
Owen White *Slough*

Firms are listed A-Z in tiers which are ranked in order of priority

KENT, SURREY, SUSSEX

Clyde & Co's Guildford office has 11 partners who undertake high-value and multi-jurisdictional litigation, often with a maritime or insurance focus. The Export Credits Guarantee Department is a longstanding client of practice head Jonathan Wood.

Charles Russell is increasingly involved in cross-border disputes. Guildford managing partner Duncan Elson, viewed as 'logical and articulate' by clients, has considerable High Court experience.

Peter Ashford heads **Cripps Harries Hall**'s dispute resolution team. Ed Weeks specialises in major contractual disputes, recently advising a geographical data-licensing company on claims exceeding £20m.

DMH's 'pragmatic' managing partner, Tim Aspinall, is noted for complex high-tech litigation, whilst dispute resolution head Simon Elcock is recommended for directors' and shareholders' liability.

Under Kate Matthews, **Shadbolt & Co**'s commercial litigation practice is emerging from the shadow of the firm's acclaimed construction practice.

Stevens & Bolton's 'user-friendly' practice is headed by Richard King, who is 'practical and down-to-earth, with an eye for the commercial'. Partner Michael Frisby successfully acted for the claimant in *Globalink v Wilmbury Ltd and ors*, a reported case involving directors' disposal of assets.

Brachers represented Eurotunnel in the *BAA v Eurotunnel* litigation; it has also advised the

COMMERCIAL LITIGATION KENT, SURREY, SUSSEX
CLYDE & CO *Guildford*
Charles Russell *Guildford*
Cripps Harries Hall *Tunbridge Wells*
DMH *Brighton*
Shadbolt & Co *Reigate*
Stevens & Bolton *Guildford*
Brachers *Maidstone*
Laytons *Guildford*
Rawlison Butler *Crawley*
ASB Law *Crawley*
Barlows *Guildford*
Furley Page *Canterbury*
Mundays *Cobham*
Paul Davidson Taylor *Horsham*
Thomas Eggar *Chichester, Horsham, Reigate, Worthing*
Thomson Snell & Passmore *Tunbridge Wells*

Firms are listed A-Z in tiers which are ranked in order of priority

company on complicated judicial review cases.

Laytons has handled numerous matters for Samsung.

Clive Lee, head of **Rawlison Butler**'s department, represented a major plc in a $40m ICC arbitration over a joint venture.

HAMPSHIRE

Blake Lapthorn Linnell's experienced partner Stephen Murfitt represented Alcatel in an LCIA case involving multiple European defendants and claims totalling circa £25m.

Gavin Matthews heads **Bond Pearce**'s dedicated retail litigation team, which recently acted in *Brighton & Hove District Council v Woolworths plc*. Michael Gunn is valued for his experience in minority shareholder disputes and advising directors in breach of fiduciary duty cases.

Philip Tebbatt, a specialist in disciplinary and regulatory disputes in the financial services sector, moved from Bristol to head **Clarke Willmott**'s Southampton dispute resolution team. As well as financial clients, the firm acts for plcs and private companies, and, drawing on its sports expertise, has acted for various football clubs.

Peter Byfield of **Coffin Mew & Clover** is acclaimed as 'highly efficient, and very professional, with good contacts and a sense of humour.'

Payne Marsh Stillwell recruited Hugh Storry Deans, formerly of **Berrymans Lace Mawer**, who brings his insurance and professional negligence capabilities to the team.

Shoosmiths' department head Richard Cook acted in *Johnson v Gore Wood & Co*, a successful House of Lords appeal involving abuse of process and recovery of damages by shareholders, which is set to be referred to the Court of Appeal.

COMMERCIAL LITIGATION HAMPSHIRE
BLAKE LAPTHORN LINNELL *Fareham*
BOND PEARCE *Southampton*
Clarke Willmott *Southampton*
Coffin Mew & Clover *Southampton*
Payne Marsh Stillwell *Southampton*
Shoosmiths *Fareham*
Lamport Bassitt *Southampton*
Moore & Blatch *Southampton*
Paris Smith & Randall *Southampton*
Penningtons *Basingstoke*
Trethowans *Southampton*
White & Bowker *Chandler's Ford*

Firms are listed A-Z in tiers which are ranked in order of priority

BEDS, BUCKS, HERTS

Denton Wilde Sapte's team, headed by James Fairbairn, recently handled a £46m dispute over alleged breaches of a joint venture agreement. The firm is retained on Bank of Scotland's commercial banking litigation panel.

Steven Mills, litigation head at **Matthew Arnold & Baldwin**, 'doesn't miss a trick', say clients. The firm has three partners dedicated to commercial disputes; it continues to handle all of Playboy TV's contentious work.

The arrival of Robert Johnson gives **Taylor Walton** a three-partner litigation practice. He recently defended a £15m fraud claim in the High Court.

COMMERCIAL LITIGATION BEDS, BUCKS, HERTS
DENTON WILDE SAPTE *Milton Keynes*
MATTHEW ARNOLD & BALDWIN *Watford*
TAYLOR WALTON *Luton*
EMW Law *Milton Keynes*
Fennemores *Milton Keynes*
Howes Percival *Milton Keynes*
Iliffes Booth Bennett (IBB) *Uxbridge, Chesham*
Kimbells LLP *Milton Keynes*
Pictons *St Albans*
Stanley Tee *Bishop's Stortford*
Turbervilles with Nelson Cuff *Uxbridge*
B P Collins *Gerrards Cross*
Harold Benjamin *Harrow*
Hawkins Russell Jones *Hitchin*
Machins *Luton*

Firms are listed A-Z in tiers which are ranked in order of priority

COMMERCIAL LITIGATION ESSEX
WOLLASTONS *Chelmsford*
Birkett Long *Colchester*
Ellisons *Colchester*
Thompson Smith & Puxon *Colchester*
Tolhurst Fisher *Southend on Sea*

Firms are listed A-Z in tiers which are ranked in order of priority

Fennemores' busy two-partner litigation team is led by Guy Brooks, who has expertise in e-commerce issues.

At **Howes Percival**, department head and solicitor advocate Andrew Myers divides his time between property and commercial litigation.

Iliffes Booth Bennett (IBB)'s team expanded with the hire of three new solicitors, including Lawrence Rodkin, who has niche outdoor advertising expertise. Renault is an important client for the Uxbridge office.

Under the 'very accomplished' Richard Brown, **Kimbells LLP**'s contentious practice draws on its brewing sector expertise; it has handled trading tie enforcement work for half a dozen major pub companies.

Pictons' Robert Ryall specialises in pension disputes.

EMW Law, **Stanley Tee**, and **Turbervilles with Nelson Cuff** are also recommended.

ESSEX

Wollastons' contentious capabilities are unparalleled within the county. Department head Bruce Bowler and partner Michael Callaghan, both CEDR-accredited mediators, were involved in a £1.25m-plus commercial dispute on behalf of flooring manufacturers Armorex, which settled.

Birkett Long's Adrian Livesley is a seasoned mediator with experience in contractual, engineering and construction disputes.

SOUTH WEST

Though essentially a small-firm economy, the South West is growing: its economic performance since 2000 has outstripped the national average. The thriving city of Bristol is home to most of the South West's leading law firms and the headquarters of several major companies. Exeter also boasts a high concentration of strong commercial firms.

CORPORATE AND COMMERCIAL: BRISTOL

Burges Salmon has a stronger focus on pure commercial work than rival **Osborne Clarke**, which has stood it in good stead during the

CORPORATE AND COMMERCIAL BRISTOL

BURGES SALMON

OSBORNE CLARKE

TLT Solicitors

Bevan Ashford
Bond Pearce
Lyons Davidson
Veale Wasbrough Lawyers

Clarke Willmott
Laytons

Beachcroft Wansbroughs

Firms are listed A-Z in tiers which are ranked in order of priority

CORPORATE AND COMMERCIAL DORSET AND SOUTH WILTSHIRE

LESTER ALDRIDGE *Bournemouth*

STEELE RAYMOND *Bournemouth*

Coles Miller *Poole*
Parker Bullen *Salisbury*

Firms are listed A-Z in tiers which are ranked in order of priority

CORPORATE AND COMMERCIAL M4 CORRIDOR AND GLOUCESTERSHIRE

CHARLES RUSSELL *Cheltenham*
CLARK HOLT *Swindon*

BPE *Cheltenham*

Rickerbys Solicitors *Cheltenham*
Thring Townsend *Bath, Swindon*
Wiggin & Co *Cheltenham*

Davies and Partners *Gloucester*
Willans *Cheltenham*
Withy King *Bath, Swindon*

Firms are listed A-Z in tiers which are ranked in order of priority

downturn. Chris Godfrey's corporate finance practice is also performing well thanks to a wide spread of clients, of which some 70% are based outside the region. Large deals included Centaur Grain's £58.1m merger with Aylsham Grain. The firm also won its first instructions from Tyco UK, which it advised on deals worth around £35m.

As a firm heavily reliant on transactional work and tech-focused clients, **Osborne Clarke** found itself over-resourced in a difficult corporate market. The firm advised on deals totalling over £720m in 2002, including Compact Power Holdings' flotation and Brunel Holdings' combined demerger and merger.

Snapping at the heels of the top-tier players is **TLT Solicitors**. Its seven-partner team has not suffered from the downturn, thanks to a steady flow of commercial work plus a string of deals for acquisitive companies like Hanson and Alfred McAlpine. The latter's £12.7m purchase of Ryan Utility Services was a highlight. 'Unflappable' managing partner David Pester is popular with clients.

While Exeter is the hub of **Bevan Ashford**'s corporate and commercial practice, Bristol corporate partner John Townsend is 'particularly effective at negotiating on financing'. Highlights of the year include long-standing client Invicta Leisure's £50m re-financing and £140m MBO.

Bond Pearce plays to its strengths in sectors such as renewable energy and retail/pubs/leisure, and the four-partner corporate team in Bristol has seen an increase in M&A work in these sectors as a result. Corporate finance head Simon Hewes' instruction on the £67m sale of Morrells to Greene King and transactional work for National Wind Power were important deals for the firm.

Roger Acock, one of six lawyers in **Lyons Davidson**'s commercial department, has an excellent transaction record. The firm advised on Grafton's £88.6m acquisition of Jackson Building Centres.

Veale Wasbrough Lawyers' strong focus on the local market has resulted in instructions on some of the region's largest transactions. Examples include the acquisition by Mole Valley Farmers (a local farmer-owned agricultural co-operative) of 19 SCATS Countrystores, and Duke Street Capital's £55m leveraged buy-out of Bristol-based Thornbury Nursing Services. Derek Bellew is recommended for partnership work.

Clarke Willmott is concentrating on particular markets as a means of attracting work: property, food and drink, sport, personal injury and private client. Paul Hardman has over 15 years' experience of the local market.

Laytons enjoyed a healthy volume of transactions for South West businesses such as Inchbrook Printers, national clients such as First National Group and international companies such as Aldes Aerolique. Richard Brown's team is also providing increasing levels of commercial support to major client Somerfield.

Beachcroft Wansbroughs handles commercial work for clients in the healthcare, IT and insurance industries.

DORSET AND SOUTH WILTSHIRE

David Ashplant's team at **Lester Aldridge** provides a good-quality service to a client base drawn from a broad spread of sectors and geographic regions. Clients include Biffa, Newday Group and Bath Travel. The firm recently advised a UK power-boat manufacturer on its sale to a German buyer.

Paul Longland's practice at **Steele Raymond** has an excellent reputation amongst mainly local clients. However, a highlight of the past year was the management buy-in of one of Jersey's largest construction groups, demonstrating an expanding reach.

In Salisbury, the region's second-largest commercial centre, **Parker Bullen** is the dominant commercial firm, while in Poole, **Coles Miller** is recommended.

M4 CORRIDOR AND GLOUCESTERSHIRE

Charles Russell's City-trained lawyers handle an impressive range of corporate finance work, from MBOs to complex, multi-jurisdictional acquisitions. Richard Norton advised Matcon Group on its joint venture with Nisshin Corporation in Japan while Francis Rundall acted on Montpelier's £14m acquisition of assets from Union Ltd.

Niche commercial firm **Clark Holt** gains a substantial percentage of its instructions from other professionals along the M4 Corridor and London, including other law firms. Its deal list illustrates the depth of expertise of its mainly City-trained lawyers. Richard Clark's team advised Full Circle LLP on its acquisition by Parkman Group and Health for Industry on its sale to Primary Group. Fortisbank is another client.

Most of **BPE**'s instructions come from outside the region. It is particularly recommended for AIM/OFEX work, having advised on seven AIM transactions in the past year including Dawmed Systems' transfer from OFEX to AIM. John Workman's three-partner team advised on the £33m funding of the Golden Tulip hotel chain's expansion in the UK.

In Cheltenham, **Rickerbys Solicitors**' 'calm and pragmatic' Richard Knight and Anne Compton are experienced commercial lawyers, advising clients such as Malvern Tyres and Blanchworth Care Group.

Thring Townsend's team acts for clients such as Statmatics and Richtec. Julian George is lead lawyer for the Milk Development Council.

Wiggin & Co is renowned for its media and IT focus; most corporate and commercial work is in these sectors. Examples include Tecnograv Group's MBO, the sale of Telewest's TV Travel Shop to USA networks and a rights issue for Ifonline Group.

Willans and **Withy King** focus on advice to owner-managed businesses and private company M&As. **Withy King**'s two-partner corporate finance team averages at least one £1m+ transaction per month.

THE WEST COUNTRY

Bevan Ashford's Exeter office is its corporate powerhouse, with a three-partner department

CORPORATE AND COMMERCIAL THE WEST COUNTRY

BEVAN ASHFORD *Exeter*

BOND PEARCE *Exeter, Plymouth*

Foot Anstey Sargent *Exeter, Plymouth*
Michelmores *Exeter*
Stephens & Scown *Exeter, Truro*

Clarke Willmott *Taunton*

Stones *Exeter*
The Stokes Partnership *Crewkerne*

Firms are listed A-Z in tiers which are ranked in order of priority

acting for clients such as English Heritage and Schlumberger Technologies. The energetic Simon Rous heads the team. Highlights include advising Actaris UK on the £2.9m sale of its Sangamo Electric Time Switch business.

Bond Pearce, Exeter has had its share of the firm-wide increase in deals while continuing to provide commercial services to local corporates such as DML and St Merryn Meat. Tim Jackman's team was boosted by technology specialist Richard Cobb's arrival. Cobb's expertise helped the office win instructions from Chicago-based communications company Andrew Corporation on its acquisitions in the region.

Foot Anstey Sargent handles a range of commercial work for local clients. Richard Coombs' team advised on Plymouth Marine Laboratory's transfer of assets from the NERC, while Mark Lewis acted on a major deal involving a network of over 250 independent financial advisers.

Malcolm Dickinson's team at **Michelmores** provides 'good value for money'. It has handled a large number of deals in the £1m+ range including WJ Watkin & Son's acquisitions of two egg production businesses. Other clients include the University of Exeter and Bank of Scotland.

Stephens & Scown's deal volume increased dramatically in 2002. Guy Curry advised Finance Cornwall on the establishment of investment funds worth £20m. The Truro office acted for Imerys Group on its multi-million-pound series of share sales.

Nigel Lindsay in **Clarke Willmott**'s Taunton office is 'down to earth', 'authoritative' and has 'wide-ranging knowledge beyond narrow specialisms'.

COMMERCIAL LITIGATION: BRISTOL

Bevan Ashford's Bristol team includes several solicitor advocates and Robin Neill, a specialist in international arbitration. Ongoing work includes advising a Middle Eastern government on a multi-million-pound, multi-party fraud case and defending a Friendly Society against a defamation claim.

COMMERCIAL LITIGATION BRISTOL

BEVAN ASHFORD
BURGES SALMON
OSBORNE CLARKE

CLARKE WILLMOTT
VEALE WASBROUGH LAWYERS

Beachcroft Wansbroughs
Laytons
TLT Solicitors

Bond Pearce
Lyons Davidson

Firms are listed A-Z in tiers which are ranked in order of priority

For general contractual disputes, **Burges Salmon**'s Adrian Llewelyn-Evans, an experienced arbitrator and mediator, is recommended. The rail team's two solicitor advocates act on liability disputes and inquiries resulting from train disasters. Banking litigator Paul Haggett is handling Enron-related claims for a major investment bank.

Osborne Clarke's 'bright, thorough and user-friendly' Peter Clough and able department head Clare Robinson handle cases up to the highest level. The firm acted in the Court of Appeal case *Bristol & West v Bartlett* on limitation periods and several financial services-related disputes. TMT clients are also providing an increasing volume of disputes work.

At **Clarke Willmott** in Bristol, William Whiteley has a good reputation for judicial reviews and work for local authorities. Michael Clarke specialises in international arbitration and recently defended a complex $150m dispute.

Simon Heald at **Veale Wasbrough Lawyers** handles a range of commercial disputes. The bulk of the firm's clients are local businesses such as software company Command-Alkon and local authorities; it also handles a portfolio of cases for London Electricity.

At **Beachcroft Wansbroughs**, Stephen Metcalfe advises a broad commercial client base including Marks & Spencer, Lucent Technologies, Standard Life, Imperial Tobacco and Railtrack.

Laytons handles a range of contractual cases (including a complex dispute between a contractor and utility). Bill Brydon is a CEDR-registered mediator.

Chris Owen's solid team at **TLT Solicitors** handles major disputes, including cross-border cases for its commercial client base. Notable successes included a win in the High Court for Hanson in a dispute against SIAC. It also advises Barclays, Lloyds TSB and Triodos Bank.

The Exeter office is **Bond Pearce**'s litigation hub and this supports the much smaller Bristol team. The Bristol team includes Stephen Lister, a pensions associate and retail specialist Tony Askham, who works out of Southampton and Bristol. Lister advised the trustees of both the MAN Truck & Bus and Redrow's pension schemes.

Lyons Davidson's Martin Bastow is recommended.

COMMERCIAL LITIGATION DORSET AND SOUTH WILTSHIRE

LESTER ALDRIDGE *Bournemouth*

STEELE RAYMOND *Bournemouth*

Wilsons *Salisbury*

Firms are listed A-Z in tiers which are ranked in order of priority

DORSET AND SOUTH WILTSHIRE

Lester Aldridge's heavyweight practice handles cases ranging from a waste management company's disputes with local authorities to a high-value conspiracy case involving the USA, Europe and the Middle East. Michael Giddins is recommended for his expertise in multi-jurisdictional actions.

Steele Raymond's Peter Rolph is a leading practitioner in contentious construction, who is currently advising on two multi-million pound disputes in the shipbuilding and pharmaceutical industries. Head of department Simon Outten is a commercial litigator with substantial employment expertise.

Wilsons is recommended for property and agricultural disputes. Michael Parker advised on the reported case of *Smith v Brudenell* on vehicular rights of way over private land.

M4 CORRIDOR AND GLOUCESTERSHIRE

Arbitrator Peter Scandrett's team at **Charles Russell** can call on the firm's London resources for help with large, complex cases. We recommend the firm for fraud, contentious construction and estates-related work. Rupert Croft recovered $150,000 for clients in a Nigerian fraud case, following a worldwide freezing injunction. He is also responsible for Eagle Star's mortgage work.

COMMERCIAL LITIGATION M4 CORRIDOR AND GLOUCESTERSHIRE

CHARLES RUSSELL *Cheltenham*

BPE *Cheltenham*
RICKERBYS SOLICITORS *Cheltenham*

Stone King *Bath*
Thring Townsend *Bath, Swindon*
Wiggin & Co *Cheltenham*

Firms are listed A-Z in tiers which are ranked in order of priority

BPE's two litigation partners are qualified mediators. As well as construction litigation, in which Theresa Adamson is an expert, the firm is establishing niche specialisms in asset finance and consumer credit litigation. Clients include mail order suppliers Scotts of Stow and Wolseley.

Rickerbys Solicitors' Derek Jones is a mediator and licensed insolvency practitioner. Examples of work handled in the past year include a farm partnership dispute, varying a freezing order for an established client, and a debt action for timber importers.

Stone King's Nick Watson is a highly experienced litigator, while Simon Holdsworth's team at **Thring Townsend** has specialist expertise in agricultural disputes, fraud and property litigation.

Wiggin & Co's media and high-tech clients call Simon Baggs a 'safe pair of hands'. He represented the UK record industry in a high-profile copyright case against a chain of cybercafes.

THE WEST COUNTRY

Ian Daniells at **Bevan Ashford** acts as an independent assessor between Equitable Life and its policy holders. His expanding team helps clients in the public and private sector and handles some international work.

Bond Pearce's general commercial litigation practice is centred in Exeter. Property and pensions litigation is handled out of Bristol, while shipping, IP and construction are resourced out of Plymouth. Firm-wide litigation head Andrew Tobey handles a wide range of cases ranging, in 2002, from a disciplinary inquiry for a mental health trust to a counterfeiting case for a large retailer.

Chris Taylor's team at **Clarke Willmott** handles an impressive number of high-level cases. These included a landmark Court of Appeal human rights case and the 'Parma Ham' case at the European Court of Justice.

COMMERCIAL LITIGATION THE WEST COUNTRY

BEVAN ASHFORD *Exeter*
BOND PEARCE *Exeter, Plymouth*

CLARKE WILLMOTT *Taunton*
FOOT ANSTEY SARGENT *Exeter, Plymouth*

Michelmores *Exeter*
Stephens & Scown *Exeter, Truro*

Nash & Co *Plymouth*
Stones *Exeter*
The Stokes Partnership *Crewkerne*

Firms are listed A-Z in tiers which are ranked in order of priority

Foot Anstey Sargent has an excellent reputation for banking litigation. The 'highly practical' Robin Brown's team has conducted some fairly complex trials. Angus McNicol wins praise for his efficient case handling.

WEST MIDLANDS

The West Midlands comprises Birmingham and the surrounding counties of Hereford and Worcester, Warwickshire, Shropshire and Staffordshire.

CORPORATE AND COMMERCIAL: BIRMINGHAM

Wragge & Co LLP has established one of the leading corporate practices outside of the City of London. Practice head Jeremy Millington leads a group of 22 partners which includes heavy-weights Ian Metcalfe and Richard Haywood. On the private equity side Maurice Dwyer and Andy Stylianou are focusing more of their dealmaking energies on London, leaving Andrew Lawton Smith and Peter McLintock as the leading specialists in Birmingham.

Leading corporate clients continue to warm to **Eversheds LLP**'s corporate team. The firm has recently picked up work from Centrica and from Druck Holdings. The £229m disposal of the latter to GE Measurement & Sensing Technologies Holdings was the first piece of corporate work the firm had handled for Druck. Sue Lewis, Peter McHugh, Guy Green and Mike Seabrook are as impressive a deal-making team as clients will find in the Birmingham market.

Pinsents' corporate team made great strides with the takeover of *Garretts*. The team augmented the practice with new clients and deals. Partners Gary Laitner and Paul Finlan are dealmakers with a proven track record. They join a team headed by Andrew Eastgate. On the transaction side, the firm enjoyed a number of notable highlights, including acting for Rare on its $375m disposal to Microsoft.

In a quiet corporate market **DLA** recently picked up two of the largest deals to be handled out of Birmingham. Working alongside the London office, the Birmingham corporate group advised Dignity Funerals Limited on its £220m MBO from Service Corporation International. Following this, Chris Rawstron picked up the reins for T&S Stores on its £530m acquisition by Tesco. Russell Orme heads the practice and, together with Rawstron, figures as **DLA**'s leading corporate partner. On the private equity side, Jim Lavery is a respected dealmaker.

While **Gateley Wareing**'s corporate group may not compare in size to the other leading players in Birmingham, it is more than a match in terms of quality. Senior partner Michael Ward and partners Paul Hayward and Andrew Madden are leading figures in Birmingham's corporate finance market. The focus of the practice remains on owner-managed businesses. However, the firm hired partners Paul Cliff and Katie Silvester, who have track records of advising Plcs.

CORPORATE AND COMMERCIAL BIRMINGHAM

WRAGGE & CO LLP ✪

EVERSHEDS LLP
PINSENTS

DLA

Gateley Wareing
Hammonds

Martineau Johnson

Cobbetts Lee Crowder
Heatons
The Wilkes Partnership

Cartwright & Lewis
Putsman.wlc
Shakespeares

Firms are listed A-Z in tiers which are ranked in order of priority
✪ Indicates firm displays contact details at the end of this chapter.

Hammonds hired Patrick Somers from an in-house position at Lattice. Among a range of deals, **Hammonds** continued to advise US electronics giant Jabil Circuit on M&A work around the world and acted for PwC on the £441m public-to-private of Britax. Clients praise practice head David Hull and partner Amanda Allen as leading transactional lawyers, with Hull singled out for his outstanding project management skills.

Martineau Johnson remains a leading player for M&A deals up to £50m for larger corporates and is increasingly targeting corporate work for smaller cap listed companies. On the private equity side, it has carved out a niche establishing venture capital trusts of up to £50m and smaller, publicly-funded private equity funds. Roger Blears heads the practice.

Cobbetts Lee Crowder's corporate group remains active in the mid-market sector. Among a range of deals, the firm acted for BMS Laboratories on its £12m disposal to Dr Reddy's, an Indian pharmaceutical company. Major clients of the practice include Royal Bank of Scotland, Longslow Food Group and Securicor Omega Holdings. Graham Muth heads the team.

Heatons has a growing reputation for corporate finance work in the West Midlands market. Partner Paul Wakefield is a considerable boon to the practice and in the £1m-10m deal bracket there are few more popular advisers in the market.

At **The Wilkes Partnership**, head of corporate Gareth O'Hara combines with partner Kate

CORPORATE AND COMMERCIAL ELSEWHERE IN THE WEST MIDLANDS

GEORGE GREEN SOLICITORS *Cradley Heath*
KENT JONES AND DONE *Stoke on Trent*
KNIGHT & SONS *Newcastle under Lyme*
WRIGHT HASSALL *Leamington Spa*

Alsters Kelley *Coventry*
Foster Baxter Cooksey *Wolverhampton*
Grindeys *Stoke on Trent*
Higgs & Sons *Brierley Hill*
Keelys *Lichfield*
Manby & Steward *Bridgnorth*
Martin Kaye Solicitors *Telford*
Reed Smith *Coventry*
Varley Hibbs *Coventry*

Blythe Liggins *Leamington Spa*
Brindley Twist Tafft & James *Coventry*
Goodger Auden *Burton-upon-Trent*
Hacking Ashton *Newcastle under Lyme*
Hadens *Walsall*
Lanyon Bowdler *Shrewsbury*

Firms are listed A-Z in tiers which are ranked in order of priority

Hackett and former 3i in-house lawyer Janet Humphries. The practice handles a broad range of corporate work and counts Avis, McCann Erickson and British Seafoods as leading clients.

ELSEWHERE IN THE WEST MIDLANDS

George Green Solicitors has a leading profile acting for SMEs and owner-managed businesses. The firm acted for Westley Group on the acquisition of the share capital of Birkett. Partners Richard Cliff and Paul Bennett both feature as dealmakers of note.

Kent Jones and Done advises banking, manufacturing and agricultural clients. Highlights include advising on the sale of Steelite International Plc. Department head Anthony Reeves and partner Peter Ellis are well known.

Knight & Sons advised on the acquisition by Abnormal Load Engineering Limited of the worldwide heavy lifting operations of Brambles S.A. The firm also represents a broad range of clients including newspaper publishers, universities and football clubs. Derek Miller heads the practice.

Wright Hassall continues to advise on a broad spread of work with a growing profile in cross-border deals. Robert Lee, for example, led a team that acted in the £6m cross-border MBO of Zebco Sports Europe. Mark Lewis has developed strong referral links with a number of US practices.

COMMERCIAL LITIGATION: BIRMINGHAM

Pinsents' Greg Lowson is recommended for being flexible enough to handle both small and large litigation cases, such as, last year, a $188m claim for breach of joint venture. Jonathan Fortnam provides 'efficient and commercially-driven advice'. Carl Garvie is also well known. The department grew dramatically with the arrival of Raymond Joyce and seven assistants from the former *Garretts* Birmingham office.

COMMERCIAL LITIGATION BIRMINGHAM

PINSENTS
WRAGGE & CO LLP ✪

EVERSHEDS LLP

DLA
HAMMONDS
MARTINEAU JOHNSON

Anthony Collins Solicitors
Cobbetts Lee Crowder
Gateley Wareing
Putsman.wlc
The Wilkes Partnership

Challinors Lyon Clark
Ferdinand Kelly
Irwin Mitchell
Shakespeares

Firms are listed A-Z in tiers which are ranked in order of priority
✪ Indicates firm displays contact details at the end of this chapter.

Wragge & Co LLP's team is led by Paul Howard and Andrew Manning Cox. Other well-known partners include: James Gordon, Ann Benzimra, Richard Ellison and Nicola Mumford. The firm is 'prompt, efficient, good at building relationships' and recommended for a flexible approach to billing and for state-of-the-art IT and Internet services which keep clients informed about ongoing cases. Highlights include a £153m claim for misrepresentation and acting for Land Rover on an injunction.

Eversheds LLP's practice is headed by Stephen Barker. The firm handles disputes valued between £10m and £100m range. The practice has also advised automotive, IT and retail sector clients.

DLA's Jim Sharkey has advised on a wide range of high-profile outsourcing, asbestos and regulatory cases. New clients include Carillion Plc.

Hammonds has a focus on ADR, advocacy and computer cases. Sarah Watson, Digby Rose and Jayne Willetts, who has a special focus on pensions work, are recommended. The firm advised on some ten international cases, including claims involving a US software company and a Spanish football club. The firm was also involved in several search and seizure cases.

Martineau Johnson has a focus on education, energy, professional negligence and regulatory cases. Department head Andrew Spooner is a Deputy District Judge and an accredited mediator and arbitrator.

Anthony Collins Solicitors has advised hotel and brewery clients as well as several housing associations. Andrew Lancaster is recommended.

Cobbetts Lee Crowder has a strong practice acting for motor industry clients and also reports a growth in financial services work. Richard Whittingham, who has particular knowledge of mediation, is head of a four-partner department.

Gateley Wareing has acted for gas and manufacturing clients on contractual and insurance disputes. Stephen Goodrham heads a team of six assistants.

Putsman.wlc was involved in a major motor-sports industry product liability claim in the High Court and also advised on a shareholder dispute of around £2m. Peter Adkins heads the practice.

The Wilkes Partnership advised on a US$50m product liability case. Senior partner Nigel Wood is recommended.

ELSEWHERE IN THE WEST MIDLANDS

Graham Neyt at **Kent Jones and Done** heads a four-partner team which advised two multinational companies on coal mining-related litigation.

Reed Smith has a first-rate litigation practice that is the equal of most of the leading Birmingham practices. Jonathan Hofstetter heads a core team of seven fee-earners. Among an impressive array of cases, the firm has been acting for a large oil service company in an ICC arbitration.

Wright Hassall has one of the West Midlands' largest litigation teams outside Birmingham. Richard Lane heads the five-partner team. The firm has handled a number of disciplinary hearings for the British Showjumping Association (BSJA) and the British Equestrian Federation (BEF).

George Green Solicitors' commercial

COMMERCIAL LITIGATION ELSEWHERE IN THE WEST MIDLANDS

KENT JONES AND DONE *Stoke on Trent*
REED SMITH *Coventry*
WRIGHT HASSALL *Leamington Spa*

George Green Solicitors *Cradley Heath*
Grindeys *Stoke on Trent*
Harrison Clark *Worcester*
Knight & Sons *Newcastle under Lyme*
Manby & Steward *Wolverhampton, Bridgnorth, Telford*
Martin Kaye Solicitors *Telford*
Morton Fisher *Halesowen*
Oldham Rust Jobson *Stafford*
Sullivan & Co *Malvern*

Foster Baxter Cooksey *Wolverhampton*
Hadens *Walsall*
Thursfields *Kidderminster*
Tinsdills *Stoke on Trent*

Firms are listed A-Z in tiers which are ranked in order of priority

litigation practice was dealt a blow when Neil Cutler moved to **Morton Fisher**. However, the firm hired Neil Williams from **Pinsents**, who has a focus on franchise litigation work.

Knight & Sons' two-partner practice is headed by Andrew Davidson. The firm has advised several chemical clients.

Manby & Steward is recommended for insurance cases. Peter Taylor deals with matters 'effectively, with sound, pragmatic advice'.

Morton Fisher scored a coup with the hire in early 2003 of commercial litigation guru Neil Cutler from highly rated **George Green Solicitors**.

Sullivan & Co has an outstanding reputation for insolvency litigation thanks to name partner John Sullivan.

YORKSHIRE AND THE HUMBER

Leeds remains a highly competitive legal market, second only to London in terms of fees generated and numbers of lawyers. With *Addleshaw Booth & Co's* recent merger with City firm *Theodore Goddard* to form **Addleshaw Goddard**, the newly created firm now boasts a strong London office to challenge its historic Leeds competitors **DLA**; **Eversheds LLP**; **Hammonds** and **Pinsents**.

CORPORATE AND COMMERCIAL: LEEDS, WEST YORKSHIRE

The M&A market has been tough in recent years with deal value down. Firms below the Big Six have benefited as clients seek the same service at a lower cost. In turn, top-end work has become more competitive.

With eight partners, a national client base, and regular instructions over £100m, **Addleshaw Goddard** is the market leader for corporate and commercial work. National head Sean Lippell is a first-class lawyer. Ian McIntosh is highly regarded for his technical ability and hands-on approach, while Yunus Seedat is a rising star in the private equity market.

DLA has six corporate partners and a strong national client base for which it regularly acts on high-value transactions. Clients commend Andrew Darwin, Alastair Da Costa and Wendy Harrison.

Eversheds LLP' six-partner team, led by Peter Halpin, advised on the largest number of deals in Yorkshire last year, though deal size has tended to be below £80m. Robin Johnson and Keith Froud are recommended for 'practical results and delivering on strategy'. The firm's focus on commercial services, headed by Jonathan Guest, has paid dividends: panel appointments include Granada, Centrica and Provident Financial.

Walker Morris's five-partner team is headed by the firm's chairman Peter Smart. He and fellow partner Paul Emmett are recommended for their expertise and the team advises on transactions up to and over £100m.

CORPORATE AND COMMERCIAL LEEDS, WEST YORKSHIRE

ADDLESHAW GODDARD *Leeds*

DLA *Leeds*

EVERSHEDS LLP *Leeds*
WALKER MORRIS *Leeds*

HAMMONDS *Leeds*
PINSENTS *Leeds*

Brooke North *Leeds*
Cobbetts *Leeds*
Ford & Warren *Leeds*
Gordons *Leeds*
Irwin Mitchell *Leeds*
Lupton Fawcett *Leeds*
McCormicks *Leeds*
Nelson & Co *Leeds*

Fox Hayes *Leeds*
Keeble Hawson *Leeds*
Last Cawthra Feather *Bradford, Shipley, Ilkley*
Lee & Priestley*Leeds*

Firms are listed A-Z in tiers which are ranked in order of priority

Hammonds has had a solid year in private equity, where Jonathan Jones is carving out a name for himself. Head of corporate Ian Greenfield and head of international operations David Armitage are first-class M&A lawyers.

Martin Shaw, who leads **Pinsents**' six-partner corporate team, is described by clients as an 'experienced negotiator'. The firm's commercial practice is led by Vincent King, who is applauded for his attention to detail and competence.

Brooke North has a three-partner team led by Hugh Middlemass. It tends to act for owner-managed businesses in transactions up to £40m.

Cobbetts has a four-partner corporate team led by Guy Jackson. The office has had a good year, drawing on resources from Manchester to increase its profile and reputation.

Ford & Warren boasts a two-partner team in Leeds, led by Peter Reeve. Its aggregate deal value in 2002 was £286m.

John Holden leads **Gordons**' four-partner team. Last year Peter Barton joined from **DLA**, bringing corporate finance and commercial expertise.

Irwin Mitchell has merged its Leeds and Sheffield practices to form a single corporate group, though Leeds is the mainstay of the practice. The 'very professional' team headed by Kevin Cunningham has a good reputation in the market. The firm provides an excellent service on smaller deals.

The 'commercial' Bob Harrap leads **Lupton Fawcett**'s five-partner team. The firm works for SMEs and has public company experience. Michele Phillips is also recommended.

McCormicks has a five-partner practice with strength in sport and media. Senior partner Peter McCormick is well known and has a strong relationship with the FA Premier League. Clients also recommend Clive Lawrence as 'exceedingly bright' and Richard Moran as 'outstanding'.

Nelson & Co has a small but highly regarded corporate practice. Tax partner Neil Masters joined from **Hammonds** last year. The firm's clients include local companies and young technology businesses. Clients call head of department Andrew Jordan 'proactive' and 'accommodating'.

At **Fox Hayes** a team led by Philip Drazen focuses on NASDAQ stock market flotation work, regulatory defence work and French legal matters.

Keeble Hawson's corporate head Andrew Coombe is based in Sheffield. Sharon Needle joined from the London office of **Coudert Brothers**, bringing expertise in Islamic finance-structured transactions.

Susan Clark, who heads the team at Bradford-based **Last Cawthra Feather**, acts for owner-managed businesses. IT specialist John Barker is also recommended.

Lee & Priestley's Morgan Williams is commended for his commercial approach and efficiency.

SHEFFIELD, SOUTH YORKSHIRE

DLA has the largest and most experienced corporate practice in Sheffield. Catherine Simister is recommended for M&A and private equity.

Nabarro Nathanson's two-partner department is headed by Clive Lightburn. The firm offers a solid service with expertise in transport, IT and life sciences. Clients include Siemens, Triumph Motorcycles, Sarnia Aircraft Leasing, British Waterways and Transdev.

HLW focuses on SMEs. Andrew Hartley and Roger Dyson are making headway in the local market with increasing mandates from local corporates.

Irwin Mitchell has three partners based in Sheffield although the department is run as a

CORPORATE AND COMMERCIAL SHEFFIELD, SOUTH YORKSHIRE

DLA *Sheffield*

Nabarro Nathanson *Sheffield*

HLW *Sheffield*
Irwin Mitchell *Sheffield*
Keeble Hawson *Sheffield*
Wake Smith *Sheffield*

AMS Law *Sheffield*

Richmonds *Doncaster*
Taylor & Emmet *Sheffield*

Firms are listed A-Z in tiers which are ranked in order of priority

CORPORATE AND COMMERCIAL EAST YORKSHIRE AND THE HUMBER
Gosschalks *Hull*
Rollits *Hull*
Andrew M Jackson *Hull*
Stamp Jackson & Procter *Hull*

Firms are listed A-Z in tiers which are ranked in order of priority

single office across South and West Yorkshire. While historically Sheffield has been stronger in corporate, the majority of the work is now led out of Leeds where head of department Kevin Cunningham is based. Michael Jelly is also highly regarded, described as 'very practical and very commercial'.

Head of **Keeble Hawson**'s department Andrew Coombe is based in Sheffield. He specialises in M&A, corporate governance and venture capital fund formation. Coombe is commended for being 'very switched on and easy to work with'.

Wake Smith has a four-partner team headed by the firm's senior partner John Hunt. The department, which includes finance and IT, boasted an aggregate deal value of nearly £1bn.

AMS Law has a two-partner team led by John Clowes. The department specialises in liquor licensing, education, IP and competition.

EAST YORKSHIRE AND THE HUMBER

Gosschalks' four-partner team is headed by Simon Lunt. Deal values last year ranged from £2m to £10m. Lunt is described as 'very commercial' while Nigel Beckwith is said to be 'technically excellent'.

Rollits has the largest department in Hull with an eight-partner team led by Richard Field. It advises on acquisitions and disposals, joint ventures, MBOs and MBIs. Last year Ralph Coyle joined from an in-house position, bringing expertise in media law, e-commerce and data protection.

Andrew M Jackson's team, headed by Mark Warburton, is smaller than **Rollits**' but has a strong reputation.

COMMERCIAL LITIGATION: LEEDS, WEST YORKSHIRE

Addleshaw Goddard's department head Simon Kamstra boasts a fine reputation and is supported by the astute Susan Garrett. The firm also has expertise in financial services, and recently acted for HBOS in its £7m appeal against decisions made by the Commissioners of Customs and Excise. For IP disputes, there's no finer practitioner in Yorkshire than Richard Kempner.

At **DLA**, department head Damian Crosse is a renowned specialist in IT, sport and media. The firm's defamation work is widely applauded, demonstrated by Cardinal Cormac Murphy O'Connor's decision to retain the firm in relation to alleged media smears. Andrew Dawson is known for his regulatory aptitude. Paul Stone saw off judicial review challenges to the Mayor's plans for congestion charging in central London. Hugh Evans is also held in high regard: 'He's the best litigator I've come across and I've used all the big firms,' a client applauds.

COMMERCIAL LITIGATION LEEDS, WEST YORKSHIRE
ADDLESHAW GODDARD *Leeds*
DLA *Leeds*
EVERSHEDS LLP *Leeds*
HAMMONDS *Leeds*
PINSENTS *Leeds*
WALKER MORRIS *Leeds*
Brooke North *Leeds*
Irwin Mitchell *Leeds*
Keeble Hawson *Leeds*
Lupton Fawcett *Leeds*
McCormicks *Leeds*
Cobbetts *Leeds*
Denison Till *Leeds*
Ford & Warren *Leeds*
Gordons *Leeds*
Nelson & Co *Leeds*

Firms are listed A-Z in tiers which are ranked in order of priority

Eversheds LLP Leeds head Jonathan Sinclair is a leading litigator, praised for his project management skills. National group head John Heaps also receives praise. The team is commended for its broad expertise and niche strength in product liability. Richard Matthews is applauded, while the amiable Gary Pellow is another erudite performer.

Hammonds' national head Peter Crossley is widely admired. For litigation requiring an aggressive approach, the firm is recommended by clients locally and nationally. David Williams' market recognition extends across the country. The Leeds team is well known for its ADR acumen; CEDR has showered it with awards.

Stuart Chapman heads **Pinsents**' Leeds practice and is acknowledged for his expertise in IT and media as well as commercial litigation. The innovative department recruits forensic accountants to assist on case analysis and strategy. Product liability specialist and Leeds senior partner Nigel Kissack still finds time for some fee-earning, while Stephanie Burras is one of few dual-qualified lawyers in Yorkshire (she is German qualified). The firm is particularly strong in IT disputes.

Walker Morris department head Gwendoline Davies boasts a fearsome reputation as a litigator. Her skill set extends from an impressive track record in commercial disputes, from banking to environment litigation. The group has built up an impressive track record in injunctive work. Malcolm Simpson is regarded as a thorough lawyer, while Nick Bates is a strong all-round litigator.

Richard Stockdale and Nigel Middlemass combine to create a formidable team at **Brooke North**. Both have impressive track records and noteworthy successes in Leeds and London courts. Middlemass handled a £25m fraud case and achieved a favourable result against one of the City's strongest firms.

Irwin Mitchell's contentious strength ensures that the firm is well equipped with litigators. Though most operate in the insurance arena, consultant Peter Bell heads a small team of commercial disputes practitioners.

Keeble Hawson's quality practice has a strong ADR vein. Consultant Anthony Glaister is regularly appointed as an adjudicator in the construction sector and as a mediator. The firm boasts a commercial litigation partner of real calibre in Charles Rothwell.

Lupton Fawcett boasts a nationally renowned litigation practice, known for its sharp ADR acumen. Paul Houghton receives accolades for his 'straight talking'. In the last three years, he has handled over 70 mediations.

Richard Cramer departed **McCormicks**' practice in 2002 to set up **Cramers Solicitors**. The firm replaced him with **Hammonds** senior associate Simon Young, who became a partner at **McCormicks**. Young has already impressed his new clients. 'He's very thorough and has built an impressive track record,' praises one.

Ford & Warren's Peter McWilliams and Christopher Charlesworth have fine reputations. The firm acts for the foodstuffs distributor Arla and its vehicle depots. Christopher Charlesworth receives accolades from clients. The team's work in the transport sector deserves special mention.

Regulatory expert Rupert Nevin's arrival at **Gordons** was a major boon to the firm's litigation practice. The firm recently advised a client on a major insider-dealing investigation. Property and commercial expert John Singleton enhances this solid team.

Former **Hammonds** associate Richard Nolan heads the practice at **Nelson & Co.** In 2002, the firm acted for the purchaser of a pig-breeding company on warranty and indemnity claims.

SHEFFIELD, SOUTH YORKSHIRE

The 'commercial' Ashley Mott at **DLA** has an excellent reputation in the Sheffield market and is backed up by a quality team. Cable & Wireless and COLT Telecommunications regularly instruct the Sheffield office. The firm has acquired some important instructions from the Coal Authority.

With Peter Bellamy at the helm, the Sheffield

COMMERCIAL LITIGATION SHEFFIELD, SOUTH YORKSHIRE
DLA *Sheffield*
Irwin Mitchell *Sheffield*
Nabarro Nathanson *Sheffield*
AMS Law *Sheffield*
HLW *Sheffield*
Keeble Hawson *Sheffield*
Taylor & Emmet *Sheffield*
Wake Smith *Sheffield*
Firms are listed A-Z in tiers which are ranked in order of priority

office of **Irwin Mitchell** boasts a lawyer with a track record of high-value and complex disputes, especially in the retail sector. The firm is not short of instructions; recently it acted for Esso Petroleum on some 100 claims from former retailers arising from promotional schemes.

For **Nabarro Nathanson**, the recruitment of Gerard Khoshnaw from **DLA** has turned out to be a savvy move. Clients that followed him – such as Kellogg Company, ICI, Persimmon and Dyson – enabled the group to grow its turnover by £1m. The firm also boasts trained mediators. Partner Roger Williams has high-calibre product liability and administrative law expertise.

HLW continues to forge an impressive reputation amongst local SMEs. The 'bright' Ron Whitlam is the firm's best-known litigator.

Partner Stuart Ward at **Keeble Hawson** is also commended. Ward regularly appears before the Lands Tribunal on non-domestic rating appeals.

Mark Serby heads the practice at **Wake Smith**. The firm has developed its mediation skills in recent years.

EAST YORKSHIRE AND THE HUMBER

Rollits' practice is led by the hugely experienced George Coyle. His impressive client base includes manufacturers and many car dealerships. He is also a regulatory specialist with a skill set that extends to product liability, consumer protection, trading standards and food safety. Michael Scanlan is another well-tuned litigator, particularly in the construction sector.

COMMERCIAL LITIGATION EAST YORKSHIRE AND THE HUMBER
Rollits *Hull*
Andrew M Jackson *Hull*
Gosschalks *Hull*
Langleys *York*
Stamp Jackson & Procter *Hull*
Firms are listed A-Z in tiers which are ranked in order of priority

Andrew M Jackson handles a range of disputes, but lead partner Hugh Smith is best known for his expertise in professional negligence and food law. The team is also commended for insolvency and construction disputes.

Commercial litigation at **Gosschalks** is handled by Christine Blakey, Ian Brown, Matthew Fletcher and Stephen Dillon.

Langleys' Jonathan Mortimer is praised by clients: 'He tells you what you will or will not achieve. He's on the ball,' says one.

WALES

Wales is a nation of diversity. The south-east and north are densely populated financial and manufacturing hubs and enjoy a relatively vibrant economy. The showpiece is Cardiff, one of the fastest growing cities in Europe.

CORPORATE AND COMMERCIAL: CARDIFF AND SOUTH WALES

Eversheds LLP, perhaps more expensive than its closest rivals, is a credible alternative for top-value deals ordinarily shipped out to London or Bristol firms. A large proportion of work undertaken is national and even international. For corporate work, dual US-qualified partner Michelle Thomas continues to raise her profile. The expanding commercial team is led by the 'very able' Bridgette Wilcox and attracted Orange as a client.

The ability of corporate boutique **M and A Solicitors** to endure the current M&A drought is testimony to an excellent and entrepreneurial practice. Senior partner Alan Whiteley continues to be the name on everyone's lips, but managing partner Stephen Berry is commended for his 'speed of work, highly desirable in a commercial negotiation'. The recruitment of Roy Thomas, former legal director of the WDA, was a significant coup for the firm.

CORPORATE AND COMMERCIAL CARDIFF AND SOUTH WALES
EVERSHEDS LLP *Cardiff*
M AND A SOLICITORS *Cardiff*
MORGAN COLE *Cardiff*
Berry Smith *Cardiff*
Edwards Geldard *Cardiff*
MLM *Cardiff*
Dolmans Solicitors *Cardiff*
Hugh James *Cardiff*
Palser Grossman *Cardiff*
Harding Evans *Newport*
Leo Abse & Cohen *Cardiff*
Robertsons *Cardiff*
Firms are listed A-Z in tiers which are ranked in order of priority

Morgan Cole boasts significant talent, even with rainmaker Duncan Macintosh focusing on the Thames Valley region. He paves the way for the younger Robert Cherry, based in Swansea and rising in stature, and Cardiff's Christopher Williams. For commercial work, Emryr Lewis is widely admired by clients. His practice is fortified by strong leadership in Bill Witter and the European law expertise of Rosa D'Sa.

Berry Smith's expanding corporate department, led by the ever-popular Andrew Bound, is the jewel in the firm's crown. It notched up an impressive number of deals in a difficult year, largely for local SMEs and increasingly, from outside of Wales. Partner Nigel Greenaway stands out, say clients, for being 'down to earth'.

Edwards Geldard remains a 'top-quality commercial outfit', say clients. There is a wealth of experience at the firm: Andrew Morris continues to impress, while Elin Morris and Jeff Pearson provide 'heavyweight ammunition'. Dual-qualified New Zealand lawyer Anita Waters joined from **Norton Rose** in 2003. The firm was appointed to the Finance Wales panel in 2002.

MLM has enjoyed another successful year. Managing partner and corporate head Jon Fernandez has 'probably undertaken more equity deal structurings than any other lawyer in Wales', says one client. His small but experienced team advises big-name and impressively loyal clients, such as Celtic House Venture Partners and S4C.

Cementing its position as a commercial player, **Dolmans Solicitors** joined the Finance Wales panel in 2002, and advised L'Oréal on the financing and development of its Welsh business. The firm continues to carve its niche in the SME market, a strategy that is paying dividends. Jonathan Rees receives widespread praise from clients.

Part of its cohesive Business Services Division, **Hugh James**' expanding team, led by Bill Snowdon, handled a number of local transactions, demonstrating a shift towards more corporate work. On the commercial side, the firm represents the Environment Agency and Welsh Water, two plum clients in the region.

Rebecca Mansfield, 'intuitive and quick, yet detailed and thorough', now heads up the corporate practice at **Palser Grossman**. Commercial clients are largely local SMEs, but also include Associated British Ports.

Newport's **Harding Evans** is the only firm in Gwent with a specialist corporate and commercial department, staffed by experienced practitioners, formerly of Cardiff's leading firms. They include Mike Jenkins and Stephen Dance.

Leo Abse & Cohen continues to build its practice via lateral hires. While its strength lies in contentious matters, it handles everyday commercial matters for local SMEs.

Robertsons boasts a respectable team handling local matters.

CORPORATE AND COMMERCIAL SWANSEA

MORGAN COLE

John Collins & Partners

Douglas-Jones Mercer
Morgan LaRoche

Firms are listed A-Z in tiers which are ranked in order of priority

CORPORATE AND COMMERCIAL NORTH AND MID WALES

Gabb and Co *Abergavenny, Crickhowell*
Gamlins *Rhyl, Holywell*

Gabbs *Hereford*
Clement Jones *Holywell*

Firms are listed A-Z in tiers which are ranked in order of priority

COMMERCIAL LITIGATION

EDWARDS GELDARD *Cardiff*
EVERSHEDS LLP *Cardiff*
HUGH JAMES *Cardiff*
MORGAN COLE *Cardiff, Swansea*

Palser Grossman *Cardiff*

Dolmans Solicitors *Cardiff*
Douglas-Jones Mercer *Swansea*
John Collins & Partners *Swansea*

Berry Smith *Cardiff*
Gamlins *Rhyl, Holywell*
Harding Evans *Newport*
Leo Abse & Cohen *Cardiff*
Loosemores *Cardiff*
MLM *Cardiff*

Firms are listed A-Z in tiers which are ranked in order of priority

SWANSEA

Morgan Cole has long been a leading force in Swansea. The 'experience' of Peter Jones and 'energy' of Robert Cherry keep the firm ahead of the field, evidenced by an unrivalled client base that includes BP and the WDA.

John Collins & Partners continues to grow in stature as a serious commercial player in the region. Its heavyweight and expanding commercial services division, led by Stephen Penny, provides clients with a one-stop-shop for business needs.

Another excellent option for local and national businesses is **Douglas-Jones Mercer**. Department head Ken Morgan 'gets straight to the core and cuts through the crap'. The practice has gained panel membership for various well-known pension providers.

Morgan LaRoche, better known for its property expertise, has quality corporate and commercial capability in William Barletta. He is advising on the purchase of Swansea Airport.

NORTH AND MID WALES

The former 15-partner *Gabb & Co* de-merged at the start of 2003, with the remaining Abergavenny and Crickhowell offices becoming **Gabb and Co** and the three Herefordshire offices taking the name **Gabbs**. Both firms offer substantial business services, but **Gabb and Co** has greater strength in depth, particularly in senior partner David Vaughan and fellow partner Sophie Williams.

Easily the largest firm in North Wales is **Gamlins**. Based in Rhyl, it has over 40 fee-earners, including five partners and a further five consultants. Senior partner Robert Salisbury leads the practice that handles all forms of business services, from business start-ups to M&A and partnership disputes.

Clement Jones' Holywell-based consultant Peter Richards is experienced in a broad range of business services.

COMMERCIAL LITIGATION

Paul Hopkins at **Edwards Geldard** is widely respected in the market. His expanding team advises a growing, high-profile client base: Citibank, the WDA and Western Power Distribution are all clients. The firm won a competitive tender to provide civil and commercial litigation services to the Environment Agency, Wales.

Eversheds LLP's team, led by national group head, Peter Watkin, is handling the first-ever inquiry commissioned by the Children's Commissioner for Wales. The practice has specialist litigators handling IT, inquiries and investigations, and commodities services.

With strength across the board for dispute work, **Hugh James** has a prestigious business litigation division, led by Gareth Williams. Pure commercial disputes include defending a £32m claim by a medical supplies company, represented by City firm **Lovells**. Of note is the firm's 'excellent' ADR team, led by barrister Paul Newman. Welsh Water and the Environment Agency are clients.

Morgan Cole continues to impress with considerable muscle in both Cardiff and Swansea. The array of talent includes Phillip Howell-Richardson, a Court of Appeal mediator and chairman of ADR Net; Amanda Wooding, an 'extremely effective' litigator with expertise in contractual disputes and commercial fraud; and Allan Wilson, singled out by clients as a 'litigation star'.

Palser Grossman's department head Chris Nott receives numerous plaudits from clients. The overall practice is described as 'excellent, professional and very proactive', while Nott himself 'doesn't entertain time-wasting'.

Dolmans Solicitors' 'highly experienced' duo, John Wilkins, head of business services, and senior partner Jeffrey MacWilkinson, provide the firm with 'first-rate' litigation capability. The bulk of the work is for SMEs.

In Swansea, **Douglas-Jones Mercer** continues to benefit from the talents of practice head, Hugh Hitchcock. It handles litigation for the National Children's Home as well as Swansea's two largest employers, Travel City Ltd and Alberto-Culver (UK).

Local rival **John Collins & Partners** has strength in numbers and ability, boasting four partners led by recently elected managing partner Paul Newman. The firm handles a broad range of commercial disputes.

The firms in the remaining tier all have quality contentious practices to support their commercial clients.

WRAGGE & CO LLP

55 COLMORE ROW
BIRMINGHAM B3 2AS

Telephone: +44 870 903 1000
Fax: +44 870 904 1099
E-mail: mail@wragge.com
Website: www.wragge.com

Languages
Afrikaans, Cantonese, Danish, Dutch, Farsi, French, German, Hindi, Hokkien, Italian, Japanese, Malay, Mandarin, Marathi, Punjabi, Russian, Singhalese, Spanish, Swahili, Urdu

Other offices
London, Brussels

Number of lawyers 414

Member
Individual partners are members of the International Bar Association and various committees of the International Chamber of Commerce. World Bank accredited.

CATEGORIES OF WORK

Banking and insolvency
Julian Pallett

Competition, public and regulatory
Guy Lougher, Bernardine Adkins

Construction
Simon Baylis

Corporate and private equity
Jeremy Millington, Maurice Dwyer

Dispute resolution
Eddie Breen

E-commerce and advertising
Rafi Azim-Khan

Employment, pensions
Martin Chitty, Glyn Ryland

Energy
Derek Goodban

Franchising
Michael Luckman

Intellectual property
Gregor Grant, Gordon Harris

Outsourcing
David Hamlett

PFI
Stephen Kenny

Property litigation
Suzanne Lloyd Holt

Public sector
Peter Keith Lucas

Real estate
Gerald Bland, Adrian Bland

Tax
Kevin Poole

Information technology
Bill Jones

Transport
Michael Whitehouse

THE FIRM

Wragge & Co is a major UK law firm providing a full range of legal services to businesses worldwide. The client base includes over 30 FTSE 100 companies such as BP, BT, GlaxoSmithKline, Marks & Spencer, HSBC, Lloyds TSB Group, 3i (panel), Smiths Group and some of the world's largest and most successful organisations including HJ Heinz, RMC Group (panel), British Airways, Cap Gemini Ernst & Young, Powergen, McDonald's, Enterprise Inns, BUPA, William Hill, RHM Foodservice, Castlemore Securities and ProLogis Developments. Around 25% of the firm's work is international and it has a formal association with leading independent German law firm Graf von Westphalen Bappert & Modest.

As one of the UK's largest firms with a main base outside London, Wragge & Co operates on a lower cost base than almost any other corporate firm with equivalent strengths and resources. With 1,013 people, including 115 partners, the firm has the resources to handle the largest transactions. Many Wragge & Co teams are acknowledged to be among the best in the UK, including for example: intellectual property; EU and competition; e-marketing; outsourcing; pensions; private equity; and construction. Many of the firm's lawyers have earned excellent reputations in their specialist areas and appear in the lists of the UK's leading legal experts.

Wragge & Co is renowned for its outstanding quality and client service, its people culture and its leading-edge technology. The firm is one of the largest to have achieved quality standard ISO 9001:2000, and provides commercial advice tailored and relevant to clients' needs while the approach to service delivery is client-focused and relationship-based.

The firm has used technology to achieve a 'genuine shift in working culture' according to one legal magazine, with 'unparalleled financial transparency and an exceptionally broad range of extranet facilities'. It also won the award for Best Use of IT by a National Law Firm and IT Team of The Year. The Financial Times placed the firm 13th in its list of the 50 best workplaces in the UK and the 100 best in the EU, whilst The Sunday Times ranked it 34 out of 100 in their list of the best companies for which to work.

Wragge & Co is proud of its pro-bono and community activity which is based on support in five areas: free legal advice; homelessness; education and mentoring; inner city projects; and charity support.

AREAS OF PRACTICE

Wragge & Co is a full-service firm with core work areas of corporate, real estate, human resources, dispute resolution and litigation, and finance projects and technology.

The firm has 15 specialist and dedicated sector teams, which range from aerospace and automotive to food and drink, healthcare, retail and public sector.

A&L GOODBODY

AUGUSTINE HOUSE
AUSTIN FRIARS
LONDON EC2N 2HA

Telephone: +44 20 7382 0800
Fax: +44 20 7382 0810
E-mail: info@algoodbody.com
Website: www.algoodbody.ie

Languages
Cantonese, Dutch, French, German, Malay, Mandarin

Other offices
Boston, Brussels, Dublin, New York

Number of lawyers 191
at this office 5

CATEGORIES OF WORK

Inward investment
John Coman, Michael Greene

General corporate and commercial
Julian Yarr, David Sanfey

Mergers and acquisitions
Julian Yarr, John Given

EU and competition
Vincent Power

Capital markets
John Olden, Jack O'Farrell

Banking and finance
Julian Yarr, Catherine Duffy

Funds
Paul Dobbyn, Brian McDermott

Insurance
James Grennan, Eithne Fitzgerald

Intellectual property
John Whelan, Alison Fanagan

Entertainment law
Paul White, Geraldine East

Litigation and dispute resolution
Peter Law, Marcus Beresford

Private finance
Kevin Feeney

Technology law, e-commerce
Liam Kennedy, Mark Ward

Corporate tax
Peter Maher

Commercial property
Mairead Sherlock

ALLEN & OVERY

ONE NEW CHANGE
LONDON EC4M 9QQ

Telephone: +44 20 7330 3000
Fax: +44 20 7330 9999
E-mail: information@allenovery.com
Website: www.allenovery.com

Languages
Arabic, Bengali, Cantonese, Czech, Danish, Dutch, Finnish, French, German, Greek, Hebrew, Hindi, Hungarian, Italian, Japanese, Korean, Malay, Mandarin, Persian, Polish, Portuguese, Punjabi, Russian, Spanish, Swedish, Urdu

Other offices
Amsterdam, Antwerp, Bangkok, Beijing, Bratislava, Brussels, Budapest, Dubai, Frankfurt, Hamburg, Hong Kong, Luxembourg, Madrid, Milan, Moscow, New York, Paris, Prague, Rome, Shanghai, Singapore, Tokyo, Turin, Warsaw

Number of lawyers 2,305
at this office 1,091

CATEGORIES OF WORK

Company and commercial law and equity capital markets
Richard Cranfield

Mergers, acquisitions and MBOs
Richard Cranfield, Alan Paul

EU and competition
Michael Reynolds

Corporate tax (including VAT)
Patrick Mears

Real estate
Adam Cleal

Banking
Jonathan Brayne

Projects/PPP
Graham Vinter, Anne Baldock

Insolvency and business reconstruction
Gordon Stewart

International capital markets
Boyan Wells

Commercial litigation
David Mackie, Peter Watson

Employment, pensions and incentives
Derek Sloan, Mark Mansell

Private client
Clare Maurice

Information technology, intellectual property
Ian Ferguson, Colleen Keck

Environmental
Owen Lomas

Energy
Ian Elder, Stuart Harray

THE FIRM

Allen & Overy is one of the UK's leading international law firms. Founded in 1930, it has over 4,800 staff, including some 440 partners, working in 26 major centres worldwide serving businesses, financiers and governments wherever there is a need for decisive legal advice on complex transactions.

Through its network of offices and close contacts with local law firms around the globe, the firm is well placed to respond quickly and effectively on a co-ordinated, worldwide basis.

AREAS OF PRACTICE

The main areas of work in which the firm is involved are: company and commercial law including takeovers, mergers and acquisitions, disposals, flotations, international equity offerings, joint ventures and strategic alliances, corporate restructurings and management buyouts; banking law covering all types of financing transactions both in the UK and overseas, including projects and project finance, real estate finance, trade finance, asset finance and lease finance, insolvency and reconstruction; international capital markets law covering international debt and equity issues including funding through derivatives and securitisation; litigation handling all forms of commercial dispute, including alternative dispute resolution, and national and international arbitration; and, uniquely amongst City law firms, the firm has a private client department advising wealthy individuals, trustees, families, museums, universities, charities and national and international partnerships. In addition, the firm has a number of specialist practice groups, which bring together the skills and experience of lawyers from different departments to advise clients on building societies, communications, construction, corporate and indirect taxation, derivative products, EU and competition law, employment, pensions and incentives, energy law, environmental law, financial services, housing associations, information technology, insurance law, intellectual property, media and entertainment, pharmaceuticals and medical products, the Public Private Partnerships, Private Finance Initiative (PFI), projects, privatisations, and real estate.

ARNOLD & PORTER (UK) LLP

TOWER 42
25 OLD BROAD STREET
LONDON EC2N 1HQ

Telephone: +44 20 7786 6100
Fax: +44 20 7786 6299
Website: www.arnoldporter.com

Languages
Arabic, Bengali, Chinese, Ebrou, Estonian, Farsi, Filipino, French, German, Greek, Hebrew, Hindustani/Punjabi/Urdu, Hungarian, Italian, Japanese, Konkani (Indian), Latin, Marathi, Portuguese, Russian, Sesotho, Spanish, Turkish, Vietnamese

Other offices
Brussels, Century City, Denver, Los Angeles, McLean (Virginia), New York, Washington DC

Number of lawyers 711
at this office 29

Member
The World Law Group

CATEGORIES OF WORK

Antitrust, competition and trade regulation
Tim Frazer (London), Bill Baer (DC)

Bankruptcy
Daniel Lewis (DC)

Corporate and commercial
Jeremy Willcocks (London), Steve Kaplan (DC)

Environmental
Thomas Milch (DC)

EU regulatory
Ian Dodds-Smith (London)

Financial institutions
Patrick Doyle (DC)

Food, drug and medical devices
John Bentivoglio (DC)

Intellectual property and technology
Joel Freed (DC), David Apatoff (DC)

International arbitration
Jean Kalicki (DC)

International trade
Larry Schneider (DC)

Life sciences, biotech
Richard Johnson (DC), Julian Thurston (London)

Litigation
Robert Weiner (DC)

Product liability
Ian Dodds-Smith (London)

Tax
Dick Hubbard (DC)

Telecoms/media and Internet
Michael Ryan (London), Patrick J Grant (DC)

Real estate
George Covucci (DC), Lee Narrow (London)

ARTHUR COX

MONTFICHET HOUSE
29 LUDGATE HILL
LONDON EC4M 7JE

Telephone: +44 20 7213 0450
Fax: +44 20 7213 0455
E-mail: london@arthurcox.com
Website: www.arthurcox.com

Languages
French, German, Italian, Spanish

Other offices
Belfast, Dublin, New York

Number of lawyers 198
at this office 3

CATEGORIES OF WORK

Corporate and commercial
John Matson, Michael Meghen

Inward investment
John Matson, Declan Drislane

EU and competition
John Meade, Patrick O'Brien

Mergers and acquisitions
James O'Dwyer, John Matson

Banking and finance
William Johnston, Kathleen Garrett

Capital markets
Mark Saunders, Brian O'Gorman

Structured finance
Grainne Hennessy, Cormac Kissane

Funds
Carl O'Sullivan, Sarah Cunniff

Litigation
Conor McDonnell, Isabel Foley

Project finance
Grainne Hennessy, Colin Byrne

Property
John Walsh, Mark Barr

E-commerce and technology
John Menton, Pádraig Ó Riordáin

Energy
Patrick McGovern, Alex McLean

Entertainment law
Colin Kavanagh

ASHURST

BROADWALK HOUSE
5 APPOLD STREET
LONDON EC2A 2HA

Telephone: +44 20 7638 1111
Fax: +44 20 7638 1112
E-mail: enquiries@ashurst.com
Website: www.ashurst.com

Languages
Dutch, French, German, Greek, Italian, Japanese, Portuguese, Russian, Serbo-Croat, Spanish, Swedish, Turkish

Other offices
Brussels, Frankfurt, Madrid, Milan, Munich, New Delhi*, New York, Paris, Singapore, Tokyo

Number of lawyers 813
at this office 576

CATEGORIES OF WORK

International finance
Nigel Ward

Buy-outs
Charlie Geffen

Company/commercial
Chris Ashworth

Competition law
Nigel Parr

Investment banking
Adrian Clark

EC
Julian Ellison

Employment
Caroline Carter

Energy, transport and infrastructure
Michael Johns

Financial institutions, products and services
Jeremy Hill

Intellectual property
Ian Starr

Litigation
Michael Madden

Real estate
Simon Cookson

Tax
John Watson

THE FIRM

Ashurst is an international law firm with offices in Brussels, Frankfurt, London, Madrid, Milan, Munich, New York, Paris, Tokyo and Singapore, as well as a liaison office in New Delhi. The firm has developed a top-class international M&A, corporate and structured finance practice, principally in Europe, but also on a wider international stage where its skills and expertise can benefit clients and the market.

Litigation, real estate, competition and antitrust, TMT, energy, transport and infrastructure are combined with the core businesses in M&A, corporate and structured finance, on a discrete or integrated basis, to support clients.

AREAS OF PRACTICE

The firm provides a comprehensive range of services in the following areas: buy-outs/private equity; commercial litigation; commercial real estate; construction and engineering; e-commerce; employment, incentives and pensions; energy, transport and infrastructure; environmental risk management; EU and competition; film; information technology; insurance and reinsurance; intellectual property; international arbitration and dispute resolution; international finance; investment banking; investment funds; life sciences; media; product liability; property litigation and licensing; public international law; reconstruction and insolvency; sports; tax; telecommunications; world trade.

BAKER & McKENZIE

100 NEW BRIDGE STREET
LONDON EC4V 6JA

Telephone: +44 20 7919 1000
Fax: +44 20 7919 1999
E-mail: london.info@bakernet.com
Website: www.bakernet.com

Languages
Afrikaans, Bulgarian, Chinese, Czech, French, German, Hebrew, Hindi, Italian, Japanese, Kiswahili, Korean, Portuguese, Russian, Spanish, Swedish

Other offices
Almaty, Amsterdam, Antwerp, Bahrain, Baku, Bangkok, Barcelona, Beijing, Berlin, Bogotá, Bologna, Brasilia, Brussels, Budapest, Buenos Aires, Cairo, Calgary, Caracas, Chicago, Dallas, Düsseldorf, Frankfurt, Geneva, Guadalajara, Hanoi, Ho Chi Minh City, Hong Kong, Houston, Juarez, Kyiv, Madrid, Manila, Melbourne, Mexico City, Miami, Milan, Monterrey, Moscow, Munich, New York, Palo Alto, Paris, Porto Alegré, Prague, Rio de Janeiro, Riyadh, Rome, St Petersburg, San Diego, San Francisco, Santiago, São Paulo, Shanghai, Singapore, Stockholm, Sydney, Taipei, Tijuana, Tokyo, Toronto, Valencia, Vienna, Warsaw, Washington DC, Zürich

Number of lawyers 3,380
at this office 358

Contact
Melanie Edge

CATEGORIES OF WORK

Banking and finance
Christopher Hogan

Civil fraud and insolvency
Nick Pearson, Jeremy Goldring

Corporate and commercial
Bernd Ratzke, Beatriz Araujo

Dispute resolution/insurance
Andrew Keltie, Peter Schwartz

EC competition and trade
Samantha Mobley

Employment and pensions
Christine O'Brien, Robert West

Intellectual property and media
Michael Hart, Paul Rawlinson

Information technology, e-commerce
Harry Small, Robbie Downing

Pharmaceutical and healthcare
Beatriz Araujo

Privatisations and securities
Tim Gee, Michael Caro

Projects and construction
Mike Webster, Jeremy Winter

Property and environment
Michael Smith, Christopher Norton

Structured and project finance
Annie Williams, Mike Webster

Tax
James macLachlan, Geoff Kay

Telecommunications
Peter Strivens

THE FIRM

Founded in Chicago in 1949, Baker & McKenzie is a leading law firm with 66 offices in 36 countries. A multinational network of over 4,400 legal professionals offers clients resources and knowledge in every area of business law in virtually every important financial and commercial centre in the world.

Baker & McKenzie has been established in Europe for over 45 years, having opened its first European offices in 1957. Since then, the European and Middle Eastern network has grown to 29 offices, giving it unparalleled geographical coverage.

The London office was founded in 1961. The office has grown by anticipating trade and capital flows around the world. Its strategy is to provide for its clients the best combination of local legal and commercial knowledge and international expertise and resources.

The London office offers 'hotline' arrangements and secondments of its lawyers to major clients. As an integral part of its services, clients are offered regular seminars and workshops, newsletters and bulletins on legal developments, magazines and publications. In addition, the London office offers access to its library services and to a number of commercial and legal databases, and rapid international and external communications through over 300 proprietary client extranets. Above all, the London office is a City firm of solicitors that aims to provide commercially oriented advice of the highest quality, which adds value to the client's business in relation to English, European and global law matters.

AREAS OF PRACTICE

Baker & McKenzie co-ordinates its core practice areas on local, regional and global levels, giving most of its lawyers experience in more than one jurisdiction, as well as providing multinational teams of specialists.

Utilising a global practice group structure and ground-breaking technology coupled with a personal, detailed understanding of a client's specific business, Baker & McKenzie is able to organise its extensive resources to provide focused and strategic counsel to clients.

The types of work undertaken in the London office include: international and domestic banking and finance; derivatives and related markets; privatisations, domestic and cross-border corporate and commercial transactions; the structuring of multinational groups; international equity and debt offerings; venture capital; privately financed projects; international tax; VAT and import/export questions; litigation; arbitration and ADR; civil fraud; insolvency; EU and competition law; trade law (WTO); energy; environmental; intellectual property; pharmaceuticals and biotechnology; patents and trade marks; information technology; online services and electronic commerce; telecommunications; entertainment and media; employment and pension matters; insurance; construction and engineering; commercial property, tax and trust planning and the legal aspects of lobbying.

BAKER BOTTS

99 GRESHAM STREET
LONDON EC2V 7BA

Telephone: +44 20 7726 3636
Fax: +44 20 7726 3637
Website: www.bakerbotts.com

Languages
Arabic, French, Hindi, Mandarin, Russian, Spanish

Other offices
Austin, Baku, Dallas, Houston, Moscow, New York, Riyadh, Washington

Number of lawyers 676
at this office 21

Member
Lex Mundi

In association with
Afridi & Angell

CATEGORIES OF WORK

Asset finance
John White

Banking
John White, Julie Sim

Chemicals
Paul Landen

Corporate, M&A
Paul Landen, Tony Higginson

Electricity
Samantha Hampshire, Steven Wardlaw

Energy
Antony Higginson, Samantha Hampshire

Energy regulatory
Samantha Hampshire, Steven Wardlaw

Litigation, arbitration and dispute resolution
Jennifer Smith, Joseph Tirado

Oil and gas
Antony Higginson, Stephen Wardlaw

Privatisation
Samantha Hampshire

Project finance
John White, Paul Landen

TMT
Paul Landen

BIRD & BIRD

90 FETTER LANE
LONDON EC4A 1JP

Telephone: +44 20 7415 6000
Fax: +44 20 7415 6111
E-mail: london@twobirds.com
Website: www.twobirds.com

Languages
Dutch, Flemish, French, German, Italian, Mandarin, Spanish, Swedish

Other offices
Brussels, Düsseldorf, Hong Kong, Milan, Munich, Paris, Stockholm, The Hague

Number of lawyers 358
at this office 165

CATEGORIES OF WORK

Aviation
Catherine Erkelens

Banking and financial services
Trystan Tether, Brett Israel

Commercial
Dominic Cook

Communications
David Kerr, Frederique Dupuis-Toubol

Corporate
Neil Blundell, Chris Barrett

Dispute resolution
Jane Player

E-commerce
Felicity Reeve, Nick Perry

Employment
Ian Hunter

EU and competition
Richard Eccles, Olivier Freget

Information technology
Hamish Sandison, Roger Bickerstaff

Intellectual property
Morag Macdonald, Wolfgang von Meibom

Life sciences
John Wilkinson, Trevor Cook

Media
Justin Walkey

Real estate
Jonathan Baker

Sport
Justin Walkey, Felicity Reeve

Tax
Trevor James

THE FIRM

Working with some of the world's most innovative and technologically advanced companies, Bird & Bird has established a formidable reputation for advice at the cutting edge of law.

Sectoral focus has been pivotal to Bird & Bird's success, borne out by the fact that the firm is among the market leaders in the sectors in which it is active. The firm's sectors of focus are aviation, banking and financial services, communications, e-commerce, information technology, life sciences, media and sport. Bird & Bird offers a fully comprehensive service across each of these sectors.

AREAS OF PRACTICE

Aviation: the firm provides pro-active, practical and commercially focused advice to airlines, ground-handlers and air traffic control service providers.

Banking and financial services: working with leading banks and financial institutions, the firm advises on a full range of banking issues including e-banking, project finance, PFI, secured and syndicated lending, insolvency, corporate reconstruction and litigation.

Communications: the firm advises telecom users and suppliers on a variety of domestic and international issues including major infrastructure projects, regulatory issues, joint ventures and strategic alliances, M&A, interconnection agreements, outsourcing arrangements and 3G licenses.

E-commerce: Bird & Bird is one of Europe's leading practices in e-commerce and advises on all aspects from VC and Incubators funds, dot-com start-ups, funding and IPOs to established businesses developing an Internet presence and e-banking.

IT: the firm has considerable experience gained in-house within the IT industry and specialist backgrounds. The firm advises both IT users and suppliers from the public, private and utilities sectors on a variety of major projects.

Life sciences: the firm offers wide-ranging advice on IP, corporate and commercial issues to diverse domestic and multinational companies within the life sciences sector.

Media: expertise spans all areas of the media, including broadcasting, music, film, TV, publishing and computer games, with a particular focus on negotiating and drafting finance and distribution agreements, publishing deals and issues of digital convergence.

Sport: the firm's sports lawyers have extensive experience of advising governing bodies, rights purchasers, broadcasters, sponsors and leading sportsmen and women.

Other services include:

Commercial: the firm provides practical professional advice and assistance on a wide range of commercial arrangements.

Corporate: the firm advises on M&A, joint ventures, strategic alliances, investment, equity financing, venture capital and public offerings.

Dispute resolution: the firm offers specialist advice, both domestically and internationally.

Employment: working with companies and individuals, the firm advises on non-contentious and litigation issues, ranging from employee contracts to agreements to regulation change.

EU and competition: the firm has a significant EU and competition capability, concentrating on antitrust enforcement and legislative developments.

Finance: the firm provides advice on a wide range of issues including contentious matters.

IP: one of the largest practices in Europe, covering all areas of IP. The firm has a strong reputation for conducting successful patent actions.

Real estate: the firm's expertise ranges from PFI structures and commercial agreements to pan-European regulatory issues.

Tax: the firm advises on a wide range of matters including transaction-related issues and internal restructuring.

CHIOMENTI STUDIO LEGALE

20 BERKELEY SQUARE
LONDON W1J 6HF

Telephone: +44 20 7569 1500
Fax: +44 20 7569 1501
E-mail: london@chiomenti.net

Languages
English, French, German, Italian, Spanish

Other offices
Brussels, Milan, New York, Rome, Turin

Number of lawyers 140
at this office 10

Member
Lex Mundi

CATEGORIES OF WORK	
Corporate and M&A	**IP, media and IT**
Banking and finance	**Litigation and arbitration**
Capital markets	**Insolvency and corporate restructuring**
Regulatory and financial services	**Employment and labour**
Tax	**Telecommunications**
European, competition and international law	**Energy**
Administrative and environmental law	**Real estate**

THE FIRM

Chiomenti Studio Legale continues the practice started by Pasquale Chiomenti in the late 1940s as one of the first Italian law firms with international capabilities, advising Italian and foreign clients in the progressive expansion of post-war economy.

Since then, Chiomenti Studio Legale has steadily consolidated its initial position as one of Italy's leading law firms, meeting the challenge of increasing globalisation of business. Today the firm is composed of more than 150 lawyers and tax advisers and has offices in Rome, Milan, Turin, London, Brussels and – since September 2003 – New York.

Chiomenti has always been a leader in tailoring legal techniques developed in an international context for implementation in Italy and specifically in developing Italian legal techniques in order to accommodate the requirements of international business clients. This is of increasing importance today when the majority of business transactions in Europe have a cross-border dimension and a growing proportion of legal disputes have an international aspect.

In 2001, Chiomenti Studio Legale and Skadden, Arps, Slate, Meagher & Flom entered into a strategic alliance that combines their respective strengths in US, Italian and English law.

AREAS OF PRACTICE

Corporate and M&A: friendly and hostile takeovers, leveraged and management buy-outs, privatisations, joint ventures, company restructuring, general corporate and commercial transactions.

Banking and finance: debt and equity instruments, international and domestic loans, real estate loans, debt restructuring and rescheduling etc.

Capital markets: IPOs and other public offerings, equity offerings, financial products private and public placements.

Regulatory and financial services: rules and regulations applying to banks, financial intermediaries, investment funds and insurance companies. Representing clients before Bank of Italy, CONSOB and ISVAP, formations, mergers, spin-offs, purchases and sales.

Tax: corporate and individual taxation, mergers and acquisitions and corporate reorganisation, international and EU taxation.

European law, competition and international law: advice in connection with antitrust matters, public subsidies, telecoms, power, transportation, free circulation of goods and services, agriculture, concentration and consolidation of joint ventures and unfair competition.

Administrative law and environmental law: contracts and concessions of public works, service and supply contracts, legal assistance to administrative authorities and to private and public entities operating in the utilities sector.

IP, media and IT: copyrights, trade marks, trade secrets, patents, new communication and transmission systems and media and communications rules and regulations.

Litigation and arbitration: financial and commercial disputes before civil and administrative courts and administrative authorities and national supervisory authorities.

Insolvency and corporate restructuring: assistance in connection with bankruptcy procedures, pre-packaged bankruptcies, bankruptcy administration and liquidations.

Employment and labour: national, European and international employment and labour law.

Telecommunications and energy: regulatory issues, licensing, interconnection, telecoms securities offering and project financing.

Energy: regulatory issues, project finance, mergers and acquisitions, sales and joint venture.

Real estate: acquisition and sale, mergers and spin-offs, rentals, construction, bids, development, asset management services, leasing, credit over pledge securitisation, and credits from rentals.

CLEARY GOTTLIEB STEEN & HAMILTON

CITY PLACE HOUSE
55 BASINGHALL STREET
LONDON EC2V 5EH

Telephone: +44 20 7614 2200
Fax: +44 20 7600 1698
Website: www.clearygottlieb.com

Languages
French, German, Italian, Japanese, Punjabi, Russian, Spanish, Swedish, Urdu

Other offices
Brussels, Cologne, Frankfurt, Paris, Milan, Moscow, Rome

Number of lawyers 937
at this office 72

CATEGORIES OF WORK

- **Capital markets/securities**
- **Commercial**
- **Competition**
- **Corporate**
- **Financial services**
- **Intellectual property**
- **Joint ventures**
- **Mergers and acquisitions**
- **US, UK and international tax**

CLYDE & CO

51 EASTCHEAP
LONDON EC3M 1JP

Telephone: +44 20 7623 1244
Fax: +44 20 7623 5427
E-mail: info@clyde.co.uk
Website: www.clydeco.com

Languages
Arabic, Cantonese, Danish, Finnish, French, German, Greek, Gujerati, Hebrew, Italian, Japanese, Malay, Mandarin, Norwegian, Portuguese, Punjabi, Russian, Spanish, Swedish, Turkish

Other offices
Belgrade, Caracas, Cardiff, Dubai, Guildford, Hong Kong, Nantes, Paris, Piraeus, St Petersburg, Singapore

Number of lawyers 386
at this office 201

Contact
John Whittaker

CATEGORIES OF WORK

ADR
Jane Andrewartha

Aviation
Jane Andrewartha, Colin Franke

Banking
David Page

Dispute resolution
Jonathan Wood, Stuart Macdonald

Corporate and commercial
James O'Shea, Andrew Holderness

EU, WTO and competition law
Stuart Macdonald, Philippe Ruttley

Employment
Paul Newdick, Chris Duffy

Energy
Simon Fletcher

Immigration
Paul Newdick

Insolvency
Mark Fennessy, Jonathan Wood

Insurance and reinsurance
Nigel Brook, Nigel Chapman

International trade
John Whittaker, Andrew Wells

IP/IT and telecoms
Philip Hooley

Property
Robert Pilcher, Paul Berry

Shipping and transport
Derek Hodgson, Brian Nash

Tax
Colin Masters, Susan Ball

THE FIRM

Clyde & Co was established in the City of London in 1933. Its roots are based in global commerce and transportation. It has expanded rapidly in recent years and is a dominant player in the insurance, reinsurance, international litigation, shipping, aviation, transport, international trade, energy and commodities sectors. Clyde & Co has one of the largest litigation practices in the UK. Through its network of foreign offices and correspondents, the firm services the needs of clients worldwide.

AREAS OF PRACTICE

Clyde & Co undertakes a wide variety of commercial work nationally and internationally. It has extensive experience in handling complex multi-party international actions. Its client base includes multinational companies, banks, insurance and trading companies.

Insurance and reinsurance: the firm advises on a range of areas including aviation, general liability, insolvency and recovery, marine and energy, political and credit risks, professional indemnity, property and construction. There is also a dedicated corporate insurance group that specialises in insurance-related corporate transactions and regulatory work.

Shipping and transport: the firm's expertise in this field is second to none. It advises all sectors of the maritime industry on an international basis on a wide range of work.

Corporate and commercial: experience in this area covers international and domestic financing arrangements.

Dispute resolution: the firm is involved in litigation, mediation and arbitration before courts and tribunals in the UK and worldwide.

Energy and natural resources: energy group clients include government state oil companies recognised regulatory bodies, privatised utilities, banks, independent companies, some of the world's largest commodity traders, mining, exploration and production companies.

Property: international developers, contractors, consultants, funders and investors are among the firm's property clients.

Employment and immigration: the firm's experience in these areas is extensive.

Taxation: highly regarded tax specialists advise all areas of the practice. They deal with all aspects of corporate and personal taxation including company reorganisations, re-financings, employer remuneration packages, estate planning and settlements.

COUDERT BROTHERS

60 CANNON STREET
LONDON EC4N 6JP

Telephone: +44 20 7248 3000
Fax: +44 20 7248 3001
E-mail: london@coudert.com
Website: www.coudert.com

Languages
French, German, Greek, Hungarian, Italian, Mandarin, Portuguese, Russian, Spanish, Swedish

Other offices
Almaty, Antwerp, Bangkok, Beijing, Berlin, Brussels, Budapest*, Frankfurt, Ghent, Hong Kong, Jakarta*, Los Angeles, Mexico City*, Milan, Moscow, New York, Palo Alto, Paris, Prague*, Rome, St Petersburg, San Francisco, Shanghai, Singapore, Stockholm, Sydney, Tokyo, Washington DC

Number of lawyers 650+
at this office 34

Contact
Dean Poster (managing partner)

CATEGORIES OF WORK

Corporate, mergers and acquisitions
Dean Poster

Banking and securities
Alexander Janes

Telecommunications, media, IT
Alastair Gorrie

Oil, gas, natural resources
Martin Byatt

Competition law
Alastair Gorrie

Project finance
Peter O'Driscoll

Real estate
Anne O'Neill

Funds
Alasdair Gordon

Litigation and arbitration
Maria Frangeskides, Simon Cockshutt

Employment
John Evans

THE FIRM

Coudert Brothers was established in 1853 by French émigrés and was the first US law firm to set up an international legal practice. The firm now has more than 650 lawyers worldwide, operating as one single partnership with a common emphasis on client service of the highest quality.

The firm has extensive experience in international investment, trade and finance. Cross-border commercial transactions are a major focus, as is international arbitration and other complex dispute resolution. Coudert Brothers also provides domestic advice in countries where the firm has offices.

Coudert Brothers has offices in 30 cities in 18 countries around the world. These offices are located in the major financial and business centres of Europe, the United States and Asia Pacific region. More than 300 Coudert Brothers professionals now practise in Europe, making it the largest region in the firm's worldwide network.

The London office was established in 1960, and in 1990 became one of the first multinational partnerships established under the Courts and Legal Services Act of 1990. This brought together into single partnership English solicitors and foreign lawyers engaged in international practice.

AREAS OF PRACTICE

The London office provides representation to UK companies, multinationals and financial institutions, and advises foreign investors on significant commercial and financial transactions in the UK.

Areas of practice include securities, capital markets, banking and finance, funds, mergers and acquisitions, competition law, telecommunications and media law, international commercial arbitration and international commercial litigation. The firm also specialises in the oil, gas and electricity industries, infrastructure projects, privatisations, and project finance.

UK corporate and international tax matters are also handled, as are international banking and finance, including transactions in the Euromarkets and the US capital markets.

The litigation and arbitration department deals with a broad range of commercial court matters and international arbitration under the auspices of the LCIA, ICC and other major arbitral institutions.

The real estate group deals with the full range of UK property work, with the emphasis on land acquisition and development and refurbishment projects, and acquisition development and management of investment properties. It is well known for its expertise in regional and town centre shopping centres.

The employment department advises national and multinational employers and senior executives on all aspects of the employment relationship.

The firm is particularly well known for its international capability. It has been recognised as a pioneer in representing the interests of British and other international businesses in such markets as China, the former Soviet Union and Vietnam, in addition to providing representation in the United States and European countries.

COVINGTON & BURLING

265 STRAND
LONDON WC2R 1BH

Telephone: +44 20 7067 2000
Fax: +44 20 7067 2222
E-mail: infolondon@cov.com
Website: www.cov.com

Languages
Azerbaijani, English, French, German, Hebrew, Hindi, Italian, Polish, Portuguese, Russian, Serbo-Croatian, Spanish, Turkish, Ukrainian

Other offices
Brussels, New York, San Francisco, Washington DC

Number of lawyers 520+
at this office 45

International groupings
Please see www.cov.com for firm affiliations

CATEGORIES OF WORK

Arbitration Charles Lister, John Rupp	**Data protection** Dan Cooper
Corporate and M&A Hilary Prescott, Edward Britton	**Litigation** Richard Mattick
Private equity and investment funds Simon Goodworth	**Life sciences** Richard Kingham
EU and competition David Hull	**Tax** David Hinds
Intellectual property Kurt Wimmer, Lisa Peets	**Employment** Christopher Walter
IT and e-commerce Louise Nash, Robert Stankey	**Financial services regulation** Simon Currie

THE FIRM

Covington & Burling is a leading international law firm with over 500 lawyers and offices in London, Washington, New York, San Francisco and Brussels.

AREAS OF PRACTICE

Corporate: the firm's corporate lawyers in London have particular expertise in mergers and acquisitions, venture capital and private equity, securities and finance, private equity and investment funds, financial services regulation, and joint ventures, licensing and other strategic alliances. The London corporate group acts for major public and private US and European companies (many of them multinationals), investment and commercial banks, private equity firms, investment managers, emerging companies, investment funds and other financial institutions on transactions and other matters ranging in value from several million pounds to several billion dollars. Most of the transactions on which the corporate group in London advises are international in nature, including cross-border acquisitions, investments and securities placements.

IT, IP and e-commerce: the London office works with the Brussels office on issues relating to technology law reform throughout the EU. From London, the firm oversees IP reform and enforcement in 40 countries in Europe, the Middle East and Africa. It routinely advises multinational clients on cross-border Internet jurisdictional issues and strategic, regulatory and other issues raised by efforts to enter the UK and European markets. In addition, the firm provides commercially oriented and forward-looking advice to clients involved in corporate, licensing and content-sharing transactions. The London office also advises US and European companies on issues relating to information transfer across borders, data storage and processing, and mobile location privacy. It works with the firm's Washington office to provide co-ordinated advice on safe harbour issues and the impact of US state and federal privacy schemes on European companies.

Life sciences: the London office advises biotechnology and pharmaceutical clients on regulatory, commercial, corporate and tax issues. The firm's life sciences regulatory practice is one of the largest and most comprehensive in the EU and the US. It has advised many of the major multinational pharmaceutical manufacturers, biotechnology companies, and medical devices, cosmetics, food, food packaging, pesticide, speciality chemicals and consumer product companies. The London office also advises life sciences clients on a range of commercial transactions, including standard research collaboration and licensing agreements and complex joint ventures. It also advises on transactions including evaluation and option agreements, co-marketing agreements and clinical site agreements.

Tax: the London office's tax practice covers a wide range of transactional and advisory work and includes advising private companies and multinational corporations on the tax effective structuring of cross-border transactions. The firm also assists multinational companies to plan and implement tax-efficient corporate and operational structures, and advises high-net-worth individuals in respect of their international tax and estate planning. The firm has particular expertise in transfer pricing associated with high-value intangible property, with new modes of business operations and sophisticated trading structures.

Litigation and arbitration: the London office represents clients before virtually all major international arbitral tribunals and the English courts. Lawyers handle a broad range of disputes, including disputes involving complex corporate transactions or commercial contracts, IP, life sciences, product liability, wrongful denials of insurance coverage, competition law, environmental torts and sovereign states.

Employment: the firm's UK and European labour and employment practice is co-ordinated from its London office. The employment group advises corporate clients on strategic and transaction-specific issues in the context of acquisitions and other corporate matters. The group also advises on day-to-day contentious and non-contentious employment matters.

CURTIS, MALLET-PREVOST, COLT & MOSLE LLP

53 NEW BROAD STREET
LONDON EC2M 1BB

Telephone: +44 20 7011 9500
Fax: +44 20 7011 9501
E-mail: info@cm-p.com
Website: www.cm-p.com

Languages
Arabic, French, Spanish

Other offices
Frankfurt, Houston, Mexico City, Milan, Muscat, New York, Newark, Paris, Stamford, Washington DC

Number of lawyers 178
at this office 4

Contacts
Charles LO Buderi, Tom Mackay, Bruce Palmer

Member
The Law Society, Quoted Companies Alliance; British Institute of International and Comparative Law; United Kingdom Middle East Association; American Society of International Law

CATEGORIES OF WORK

Infrastructure and project finance

Petroleum and petrochemicals

Power generation

Privatisation

Construction

General corporate and commercial

Mergers and acquisitions

Financial services law

Venture capital

Private equity

Joint ventures

Sales and distribution arrangements

Arbitration

DEBEVOISE & PLIMPTON LLP

TOWER 42
OLD BROAD STREET
LONDON EC2N 1HQ

Telephone: +44 20 7786 9000
Fax: +44 20 7588 4180
E-mail: alsommer@debevoise.com
Website: www.debevoise.com

Languages
Arabic, Dutch, Finnish, French, German, Hurgarian, Italian, Mandarin, Portuguese, Russian, Spanish, Swedish

Other offices
Hong Kong, Frankfurt, Moscow, New York, Paris, Shanghai, Washington DC

Number of lawyers 600+
at this office 56

CATEGORIES OF WORK

Mergers and acquisitions
James A Kiernan, Andrew L Sommer

Private equity
James A Kiernan, Andrew L Sommer

Capital markets
James C Scoville, Katherine Ashton

Financing
Peter Hockless, Katherine Ashton

Corporate tax
Richard Ward, Peter FG Schuur

International dispute resolution
Arthur L Marriott QC, Mark W Friedman

DLA

3 NOBLE STREET
LONDON EC2V 7EE

Telephone: +44 8700 111 111
Fax: +44 20 7796 6666
E-mail: info@dla.com
Website: www.dla.com

Languages
Czech, Danish, Dutch, English, French, German, Hungarian, Italian, Russian, Spanish, Swedish

Other offices
Amsterdam, Antwerp, Bangkok, Bergen, Berlin, Birmingham, Bradford, Bratislava, Brussels, Budapest, Cologne, Copenhagen, Edinburgh, Essen, Frankfurt, Glasgow, Hamburg, Hong Kong, Leeds, Liverpool, Madrid, Manchester, Milan, Moscow, Oslo, Paris, Prague, Rotterdam, Salzberg, Sarajevo, Shanghai, Sheffield, Singapore, Stockholm, Vienna, Zagreb

Number of lawyers 1,800+
at this office 379

Contact
Nigel Knowles (managing partner)

Member
DLA Group

CATEGORIES OF WORK

Banking
Michael Burton

Business services group
Andrew Bennett

Business support and restructuring
Andrew Darwin

Commercial and projects
Mark Swindell

Corporate
Alastair Da Costa

Human resources
David Bradley

Insurance
Mike Tinker

Litigation
David Gray

Marine, aviation and reinsurance
Nigel Montgomery

Real estate
David Taylor

Regulation
Neil Gerrard

Technology, media and communications
Julian Stait

THE FIRM

DLA is one of the only full-service law firms able to offer a truly integrated service throughout the UK. The firm also has a rapidly growing presence in Europe and Asia Pacific. It develops long-term, full-service client relationships and provides businesses with continuous support across all areas of corporate and commercial law. DLA also has non-legal specialist groups, such as DLA Consulting which provides consultancy advice on a range of employment issues; DLA Upstream, the firm's communications and public affairs arm; and DLA Advance, which runs approximately 140 public training seminars and conferences annually.

DLA has more than 3,600 staff worldwide. DLA's practice in Asia has grown at a phenomenal rate, expanding into first-class offices in the Bank of China Tower with significant offices in Singapore, Shanghai and Bangkok. This is matched by DLA's ability to provide a full range of legal services across Europe. DLA is successful in building long-term relationships with clients and is now well on its way to achieving its vision to be a 'top-five, full-service European law firm with a significant presence in Asia' by 2005.

DLA is the founding member of DLA Group – an exclusive alliance of international full-service law firms with a shared vision. Established in 1999, DLA Group now has over 2,200 lawyers across 21 countries, who deliver expert local know-how and international solutions. DLA Group provides legal advice in 37 major cities across Europe, Singapore, Thailand, Hong Kong and the People's Republic of China.

AREAS OF PRACTICE

The banking group represents major financial institutions including clearing and investment banks, building societies, monoline insurers, issuers, borrowers and institutional investors. The group works closely with real estate and corporate, and specialises in asset-based finance, infrastructure and project finance, leveraged finance, real estate finance, securitisation and capital markets.

The corporate group handles all types of transactional and advisory matters. The group advises mid-sized Plcs and top FTSE companies, combining the strength of its City and UK teams together with a growing international reputation to create a substantial presence in the corporate market. The commercial and projects group delivers services related to infrastructure and project finance and structured joint ventures, working with specialist lawyers from a number of disciplines, including finance, construction and competition. The group has over 100 lawyers across the UK and provides European delivery through the DLA Group.

DLA's human resources group works with clients on a strategic and operational level to help mould their people strategies and work practices in order to support wider business objectives. The team comprises over 90 lawyers and consultants.

DLA's insurance group is one of the largest in the country, and acts for insurers, reinsurers, self-insured corporates and public sector clients in the management of pre-litigation and litigated claims.

DLA's litigation group's approach is to minimise risk and maximise certainty in commercial disputes. Over 400 lawyers, experienced in all aspects of commercial dispute management, work in partnership with clients to manage the litigation process.

The real estate group provides top-quality, multi-disciplinary services, not only to institutions and property companies, but also to those businesses for which real estate is merely a resource required to deliver their main commercial output. The team works with corporate occupiers, developers, the public sector and rapidly changing industry areas such as construction, retail, hotel and leisure.

DLA's technology, media and communications group provides contentious and non-contentious advice to clients in the areas of IT, telecommunications and IP.

Other types of work include: business support, corporate recovery and restructuring; EU and competition; marine, aviation and regulatory.

DENTON WILDE SAPTE

FIVE CHANCERY LANE
CLIFFORD'S INN
LONDON EC4A 1BU

Telephone: +44 20 7242 1212
Fax: +44 20 7404 0087
E-mail: info@dentonwildesapte.com
Website: www.dentonwildesapte.com

Languages
Afrikaans, Arabic, Bulgarian, Cantonese, Chinese, Czech, Danish, Dutch, Flemish, French, German, Greek, Hebrew, Hindi, Italian, Japanese, Korean, Mandarin, Norwegian, Portuguese, Punjabi, Romanian, Russian, Spanish, Swedish, Urdu

Other offices
Abu Dhabi, Almaty, Beijing, Cairo, Dubai, Gibraltar, Hong Kong, Istanbul, Milton Keynes, Moscow, Muscat, Paris, Singapore, Tashkent, Tokyo

Number of lawyers 876
at this office 627

Contact
Virginia Glastonbury

CATEGORIES OF WORK

Banking and finance
Howard Morris

Corporate
Philip Goodwin

Dispute resolution
Mark Gill, Liz Tout

Employment
Stephanie Dale

Energy and infrastructure and transport
Christopher McGee-Osborne

EU and competition
Jonathan Tatten

Technology, media and telecommunications
Tony Grant

Real estate and retail
Martin Quicke

Tax
Charlotte Sallabank

THE FIRM

Denton Wilde Sapte is a leading international law firm based in the City of London offering a comprehensive range of the highest quality and affordable commercial legal advice. Denton Wilde Sapte has 19 offices across Europe, the Middle East and Asia.

AREAS OF PRACTICE

Denton Wilde Sapte offers a comprehensive range of commercial legal advice and is particularly known for its sector strengths in the financial institutions, energy, transport and infrastructure, TMT and real estate sectors. The network of offices enables the firm to serve clients in a number of different locations and to support them wherever their businesses take them. The firm works alongside its clients, to help them achieve their business objectives. To do this, it is essential that the firm understands their business and the environment in which they operate. With a combination of locally trained lawyers and sector specialists, all the firm's offices are able to provide this level of expertise.

The firm's international work is not just restricted to the private sector. Denton Wilde Sapte has worked with a large number of governments and government agencies, particularly in drafting and reworking of local legislation and regulations.

The firm's international clients include: Electricité de France, Shell, Premier Oil, Itochu Corporation, Sumitomo, Nissho Iwai, Sony, Standard Chartered Bank, Daiwa Bank, Royal Bank of Scotland, Barclays Bank, UIP, Warner Bros Pictures, Sony Pictures, Universal Studios, Pearson Plc, BBC, FA Premier League, Virgin, the UK Government and Westdeutsche Landesbank Girozentrale.

FRESHFIELDS BRUCKHAUS DERINGER

65 FLEET STREET
LONDON EC4Y 1HS

Telephone: +44 20 7936 4000
Fax: +44 20 7832 7001
E-mail: email@freshfields.com
Website: www.freshfields.com

Languages
Extensive language capabilities

Other offices
Amsterdam, Bangkok, Barcelona, Beijing, Berlin, Bratislava, Brussels, Budapest, Cologne, Düsseldorf, Frankfurt, Hamburg, Hanoi, Ho Chi Minh City, Hong Kong, Madrid, Milan, Moscow, Munich, New York, Paris, Rome, Shanghai, Singapore, Tokyo, Vienna, Washington

Number of lawyers 2,504
at this office 913

Contact
Peter Jeffcote

CATEGORIES OF WORK

Corporate

Dispute resolution (including environment, planning and regulatory)

Finance

Antitrust, competition and trade

Real estate

Tax

Intellectual property and IT

Employment, pensions and benefits

FRIED, FRANK, HARRIS, SHRIVER & JACOBSON (LONDON) LLP

99 CITY ROAD
LONDON EC1Y 1AX

Telephone: +44 20 7972 9600
Fax: +44 20 7972 9602
E-mail: info@ffhsj.com
Website: www.friedfrank.com

Languages
French, German, Italian, Spanish

Other offices
New York, Washington DC, Los Angeles, Paris

Number of lawyers 522
at this office 17

Contacts
Daniel Bursky, Robert Mollen, Timothy Peterson, Karen Wiedemann

A Delaware Limited Liability Partnership

CATEGORIES OF WORK

Cross-border mergers and acquisitions (public and private)

Private equity and venture capital investments

International capital markets (public and private)

Structured finance and securitisation

Financings (M&A, senior mezzanine, project, leasing and REIT)

Corporate and regulatory advice (including US securities law)

Restructurings

FRORIEP RENGGLI
SWISS LAWYERS

1 KNIGHTRIDER COURT
LONDON EC4V 5JP

Telephone: +44 20 7236 6000
Fax: +44 20 7248 0209
E-mail: london@froriep.ch
Website: www.froriep.com

Languages
English, French, German, Italian, Swedish

Other offices
Geneva, Madrid, Zug, Zürich

Number of lawyers 48
at this office 4

Contact
Bruno W Boesch

CATEGORIES OF WORK

Company and commercial
Dunja Koch

Aviation
Dunja Koch

Mergers and acquisitions
Bruno W Boesch, Dunja Koch

Litigation, arbitration
Bruno W Boesch

Securities
Dunja Koch

White-collar crime
Bruno W Boesch

Banking
Bruno W Boesch

Wealth management/estate planning
Bruno W Boesch

GIDE LOYRETTE NOUEL

CITY POINT
1 ROPEMAKER STREET
LONDON EC2Y 9HT

Telephone: +44 20 7153 1040
Fax: +44 20 7153 1140
E-mail: gln.london@gide.com
Website: www.gide.com

Other offices
Algiers, Beijing, Brussels, Bucharest, Budapest, Casablanca, Hanoi, Istanbul, Moscow, New York, Paris, Prague, Riyadh, Shanghai, Tunis, Warsaw

Number of lawyers 480
at this office 30

Contacts
Scott PF Cameron, Michael Doran, Arnaud Duhamel, Christopher B Mead, Colin Mercer

CATEGORIES OF WORK

Banking and finance

Structured finance

Securitisation

International capital markets

HAARMANN HEMMELRATH

TOWER 42, 28TH FLOOR
25 OLD BROAD STREET
LONDON EC2N 1HQ

Telephone: +44 20 7382 4800
Fax: +44 20 7382 4833
E-mail:
london@haarmannhemmelrath.com
Website:
www.haarmannhemmelrath.com

Languages
Bulgarian, Croatian, Czech, Dutch, French, Hungarian, Italian, Japanese, Mandarin, Norwegian, Polish, Portuguese, Romanian, Russian, Slovak, Spanish, Vietnamese

Other offices
Berlin, Bielefeld, Brussels, Bucharest, Budapest, Cologne, Dusseldorf, Frankfurt, Hamburg, Leipzig, Milan, Moscow, Munich, Paris, Prague, Rome, Shanghai, Singapore, Stuttgart, Tokyo, Vienna, Warsaw

Number of lawyers 281

CATEGORIES OF WORK

Corporate reorganisations
Andrew Visintin, Grant Jones

Mergers and acquisitions
Philip Newhouse

Corporate finance
David von Saucken, Philip Newhouse

Capital markets law
David von Saucken

Funds
Philip Newhouse

Capital gains tax
Peter Vaines

Intellectual property/IT
Michael Molineaux, Christopher Hubbard

German law
Prof Dr Wilhelm Haarmann, David von Saucken

International corporate tax law
Prof Dr Wilhem Haarmann

International private tax law
Prof Dr Wilhelm Haarmann, Peter Vaines

Private tax law
Peter Vaines

Private equity
Philip Newhouse

Dispute resolution
Christopher Hubbard

Distressed debt trading
Andrew Visintin, David von Saucken

Asset-based lending
Andrew Visintin

HARNEY WESTWOOD & RIEGELS LLP

24 OLD BUILDINGS
LINCOLN'S INN
LONDON WC2A 3UP

Telephone: +44 20 7440 8790
Fax: +44 20 7440 8791
E-mail: mail@harneys.com
Website: www.harneys.com

Languages
French, German, Spanish

Other offices
Anguilla, British Virgin Islands

Numbers of lawyers 38
at this office 2

CATEGORIES OF WORK

Admiralty and shipping
Sheila George

Banking and finance
Peter Tarn

Corporate and commercial
Peter Tarn, Ray Wearmouth

Insolvency
Leonard Birmingham, Phillip Kite

Intellectual property
Sheila George

Litigation
Phillip Kite

Local business, property and tax
Sheila George

Mutual funds and regulatory
Kieron O'Rourke

Private client fiduciary services
Sheila George

Trusts, wills and estates
Christopher McKenzie

THE FIRM

Harney Westwood & Riegels is one of the premier legal practices in the Caribbean and is one of the oldest and largest law firms in the British Virgin Islands. It was established in 1960 by Harold Harney and now has over 150 lawyers and staff, providing services from offices in the British Virgin Islands, Anguilla and London.

The firm's focus is British Virgin Islands and Anguillan law, and its team of legal experts, many of whom have been recruited from top City law firms and international financial centres, have an in-depth understanding of the commercial environment in which their clients operate. The firm's client base ranges from leading international businesses and banks to private individuals, and the firm's London office offers European and Far East-based clients time-zone sensitive advice on all aspects of British Virgin Islands and Anguillan law.

Members of the firm are active in a number of government advisory committees dedicated to the development of the BVI's financial services industry and related legislative developments.

AREAS OF PRACTICE

Practice areas include: banking and finance; corporate and commercial; mutual funds and regulatory; corporate and trust litigation; insolvency; trusts, wills and estates; intellectual property; admiralty and shipping; captive insurance; and local business, property and tax.

The firm offers expertise in a broad range of transactions, including: syndicated and bilateral loans; bond issues; derivatives; securitisations and other structured finance; project finance; initial public offerings; joint ventures; mergers and takeovers; private placements; corporate restructurings; continuations; sale and purchase of shares; special purpose vehicles; copyrights; trade marks; patents; intellectual property disputes; high-profile multi-jurisdictional disputes, as well as fraud, trusts, insolvency and shareholder disputes; and offshore collective investment schemes, with particular emphasis on hedge funds.

The firm's close affiliation with HWR Services Ltd and HWR Insurance Management Services Ltd also allows for the seamless provision of related corporate services management services, including company formation and administration, trust administration and captive insurance management services.

HERBERT SMITH

EXCHANGE HOUSE
PRIMROSE STREET
LONDON EC2A 2HS

Telephone: +44 20 7374 8000
Fax: +44 20 7374 0888
E-mail: contact@herbertsmith.com
Website: www.herbertsmith.com

Languages
Chinese (Cantonese, Putonghua), English, French, German, Russian, Spanish

Other offices
Bangkok, Beijing, Brussels, Hong Kong, Moscow, Paris, Shanghai, Singapore, Tokyo

Number of lawyers 1,108
at this office 833

CATEGORIES OF WORK

Arbitration
Michael Davis

EU and competition
Jonathan Scott

Corporate
Caroline Goodall

Corporate recovery
Stephen Gale

Employment and trusts
Colin Chamberlain

Energy, natural resources and utilities
Alan Jowett, Ted Greeno

Finance and banking
Clive Barnard

Financial institutions
David Willis

Intellectual property and information technology
Bill Moodie

International mergers and acquisitions
Michael Walter

Litigation
David Gold

Project finance
Nicholas Tott

Real estate
James Barnes

Tax
Heather Gething

THE FIRM

Herbert Smith is a leading international law firm with offices in Europe and Asia. Through its network of over 1,000 lawyers, the firm advises its clients on corporate, dispute resolution, finance and banking matters and also offers a range of specialist services.

A significant proportion of the firm's work is international, involving the co-ordination and management of clients' commercial activities across many jurisdictions. The firm's international capability is resourced from offices in London, Brussels, Moscow and Paris and in Asia through offices in Bangkok, Beijing, Hong Kong, Shanghai, Singapore and Tokyo.

In January 2002, Herbert Smith established a three-way alliance with German firm Gleiss Lutz (with offices in Berlin, Brussels, Frankfurt, Munich, Prague, Stuttgart and Warsaw) and Dutch and Belgian firm Stibbe (with offices in Amsterdam, Brussels, London and New York). The firm's formal associations with Hiswara Bunjamin & Tandjung in Jakarta, ASG Law Corporation in Singapore and LawPlus Limited in Bangkok provide further expertise in Asia.

AREAS OF PRACTICE

The London office offers a leading full-service capability in transactional and contentious matters, covering all areas of commercial law. It is organised into three divisions – corporate, dispute resolution, and finance and banking – and five specialist departments – employment and trusts, EU and competition, IP/IT, real estate and tax. The firm also has top-class US law advisory capabilities.

The majority of matters handled in London have an international aspect. They frequently involve other offices in the global network and other firms with which Herbert Smith has an association including Gleiss Lutz and Stibbe. The office acts as a storehouse of knowledge and expertise, for the worldwide firm and its clients, enabling its offices around the world to call on the support and input of specialist teams with specific regional, sector and language skills.

HOGAN & HARTSON
SOLICITORS AND REGISTERED FOREIGN LAWYERS

ONE ANGEL COURT
LONDON EC2R 7HJ

Telephone: +44 20 7367 0200
Fax: +44 20 7367 0220
E-mail: dhmaccoby@hhlaw.com
Website: www.hhlaw.com

Languages
Czech, French, German, Korean

Other offices
Baltimore, Beijing, Berlin, Boulder, Brussels, Budapest, Colorado Springs, Denver, Los Angeles, McLean, Miami, Moscow, Munich, New York, Paris, Prague, Tokyo, Warsaw, Washington DC

Number of lawyers 1,018
at this office 30

Contacts
Daniel Maccoby, Garry Pegg

CATEGORIES OF WORK

- Mergers, acquisitions and divestitures
- Joint ventures and strategic alliances
- Venture capital, private equity and strategic investments
- Energy
- Privatisation
- Corporate finance
- Project finance
- Capital markets
- Tax
- E-commerce
- Labour and employment
- Telecommunications

HOUTHOFF BURUMA

33 SUN STREET
LONDON EC2M 2PY

Telephone: +44 20 7422 5050
Fax: +44 20 7422 5055
E-mail: info@houthoff.com
Website: www.houthoff.com

Languages
Dutch

Other offices
Amsterdam, Brussels, Rotterdam, The Hague

Number of lawyers 323
at this office 3

Contact
Albert Dreese

CATEGORIES OF WORK

- Banking
- Finance
- Corporate
- Mergers and acquisitions
- Joint ventures
- Bankruptcy
- Securities
- Dutch law

HOLMAN FENWICK & WILLAN

MARLOW HOUSE
LLOYDS AVENUE
LONDON EC3N 3AL

Telephone: +44 20 7488 2300
Fax: +44 20 7481 0316
E-mail: holmans@hfw.co.uk
Website: www.hfw.com

Languages
Afrikaans, Arabic, Bengali, Bulgarian, Czech, Dutch, Farsi, Flemish, French, German, Greek, Hebrew, Hindi, Hungarian, Indonesian, Italian, Japanese, Korean, Malay, Mandarin, Norwegian, Polish, Portuguese, Punjabi, Russian, Sinhalese, Spanish, Swedish, Urdu

Other offices
Hong Kong, Nantes, Paris, Piraeus, Rouen, Shanghai, Singapore

Number of lawyers 176
at this office 113

Founding patron and member
European Maritime Law Organisation (EMLO)

CATEGORIES OF WORK

Admiralty and crisis management
James Gosling, Hugh Brown

Banking and insolvency
Noel Campbell

Commercial arbitration/litigation
Peter Bennett, Noel Campbell

Corporate and financial
Nick Hutton, Jay Tooker

EC and competition law
Philip Wareham

Employment
Andrew Dekany

Energy
Robin Byron, Diana France

Environmental
James Gosling, Hugh Brown

Information technology
George Eddings

Insurance and reinsurance
John Duff, Paul Wordley

International trade and commodities
Chris Swart, Simon Blows

Marine litigation
Hugh Livingstone, Richard Crump

Marine non-contentious
Stephen Drury, Jay Tooker

Personal injury
Paul Dean

Professional negligence
Paul Wordley, David Robinson

Property
Nick Barr

Reinsurance
John Duff, Andrew Bandurka

Transport: air, rail and road
Glenn Moore

THE FIRM

Holman Fenwick & Willan is an international law firm specialising in shipping and transport, trade and energy, insurance and reinsurance and commercial law. The firm has a reputation worldwide for excellence and innovation. It has one of the largest international arbitration and dispute resolution practices of its kind, with offices in Europe and Asia Pacific.

The firm's international practice is founded upon its principal offices in London, Paris, Piraeus, Hong Kong, Singapore and Shanghai and over 120 years' experience of working with other law firms in jurisdictions throughout the world.

AREAS OF PRACTICE

The firm is pre-eminent in maritime work and has one of the world's largest Admiralty and marine litigation practices. It is a recognised leader in dry shipping work including charter parties, bills of lading, other carriage contracts, marine insurance and related disputes. Renowned as leaders in Admiralty and crisis management and operates a 24-hour emergency service geared to providing an immediate response to maritime casualties worldwide. Specialists deal with all forms of contractual disputes, marine insurance claims, collisions, fire and explosions, salvage, towage, wreck removal and recovery, personal injury, damage to oil terminals, rigs and offshore structures, pollution, environmental damage and clean up.

The international trade and commodity practice provides the international trading and financial community with services including advising on sale, purchase and futures contracts, quality claims, damage and shortfall disputes, swaps and barter trade, trade finance, EU law and transportation agreements.

Energy is another specialist work area covering power generation, oil and gas, coal and liquid natural gas.

The firm's insurance and reinsurance practice is recognised internationally as an industry leader. It advises on contentious and non-contentious matters including: facultative insurance and reinsurance coverage issues and policy interpretation; captive insurance and reinsurance; errors and omissions and professional negligence; property damage, business interruption and liability insurance; insolvency and schemes of arrangement; contract drafting and regulatory issues.

Areas of considerable strength are commercial litigation, arbitration and disputes in the areas of financial disputes, technology, coal, oil and gas, environmental claims, professional negligence, sovereign debt and fraud and asset recovery.

The fraud and asset recovery work focuses on the civil side with an emphasis on asset tracing and recovery in overseas jurisdictions. Other methods of recovery are also pursued.

The full spread of insolvency work is undertaken including voluntary arrangements, receiverships, provisional liquidations, liquidations and administrations. Much of the work focuses on international aspects, fraud-related insolvency and the insurance industry.

The firm's company and finance department advises some of the world's largest shipowners and operators on a wide variety of contractual issues, ranging from shipbuilding, and other offshore and construction contracts, financing documentation, the raising of capital, corporate finance and acquisitions, project and asset finance and joint ventures, as well as advising banks and financial institutions. The department also advises on EC and competition law, intellectual property and commercial property matters.

Advice is given on every aspect of e-commerce and information technology.

Holman Fenwick & Willan has extensive experience of air, road and rail, advising operators, financiers and underwriters on transactions, litigation and regulatory issues. All aspects of employment law are covered.

HOWREY SIMON ARNOLD & WHITE

CITY POINT
ONE ROPEMAKER STREET
LONDON EC2Y 9HS

Telephone: +44 20 7628 3303
Fax: +44 20 7065 6650
Website: www.howrey.com

Languages
Dutch, French, German, Spanish

Other offices
Amsterdam, Brussels, Chicago, Houston, Irvine, Los Angeles, Menlo Park, San Francisco, Washington DC

Number of lawyers 543
at this office 28

Contact
Koos Rasser

CATEGORIES OF WORK

Intellectual property (portfolio management)
Noel Akers, Koos Rasser

Intellectual property (litigation and dispute resolution)
Koos Rasser, Isabel Davies

Intellectual property (patent prosecution)
Noel Akers, Jean-Benoit Busnel

Trade marks
Isabel Davies, David Stone

International commercial litigation and arbitration
Peter Fitzpatrick, James Irvine

Medical negligence
Peter Fitzpatrick

JONES DAY

21 TUDOR STREET
LONDON EC4Y 0DJ

Telephone: +44 20 7039 5959
Fax: +44 20 7039 5999
Website: www.jonesday.com

Languages
Cantonese, Chinese, French, German, Italian, Spanish, Turkish, Ukrainian

Other offices
Atlanta, Beijing, Brussels, Chicago, Cleveland, Columbus, Dallas, Frankfurt, Hong Kong, Houston, Irvine, London, Los Angeles, Madrid, Menlo Park, Milan, Munich, New Delhi*, New York, Paris, Pittsburgh, San Diego, San Francisco, Shanghai, Singapore, Sydney, Taipei, Tokyo, Washington DC

Number of lawyers 2,100
at this office 200

*In association with Pathak & Associates

CATEGORIES OF WORK

Corporate, M&A
Hilary Winter, Russell Carmedy

Corporate finance
John Clark, Hilary Winter

Litigation
Robert L Thomson, Craig Shuttleworth

Structured finance
Keith Featherstone

Property
David Roberts

Private equity
Adam Greaves, Daljit Singh

Intellectual property
Charters Macdonald-Brown, Simon Chalkley

Investment trusts
John Clark

Environmental
Clare Deanesly

Employment
Martin Piers, Richard Martin

Pensions
John Papadakis, Martin Scott

Private client
Lucy Johnson

UK tax
Keith Featherstone, Robert Gaut

US tax
Martin Rowley

Banking
Martin Bartlam, Tom Budd

Competition, EU
Greg Olsen

Insolvency
Adam Plainer

KILPATRICK STOCKTON LLP

ONE CANADA SQUARE
39TH FLOOR
LONDON E14 5NZ

Telephone: +44 20 7154 6000
Fax: +44 20 7154 6100
E-mail:
kboehner@kilpatrickstockton.com
Website: www.kilpatrickstockton.com

Languages
Arabic, Dutch, English, Finnish, French, German, Greek, Hebrew, Punjabi, Russian, Serbo-Croatian, Spanish, Swedish

Other offices
Atlanta, Augusta, Charlotte, Raleigh, Stockholm, Washington DC, Winston-Salem

Number of lawyers 475
at this office 40

Contact
R Kenneth Boehner

CATEGORIES OF WORK

Arbitration Per Runeland	**Mergers and acquisitions** R Kenneth Boehner
Commercial property Mark Johnstone	**Mining and minerals** Eero Rautalahti
Corporate finance Susan Breen	**Private equity** J Scott Nelson
Dispute resolution Patricia Martin	**Projects** Anthony Fine
Intellectual property Dean Russell	**Tax** Vishvas Kanji
Labour and employment Peter Holt	**Trade marks** Virginia Taylor

THE FIRM
Kilpatrick Stockton is a full-service corporate law firm composed of some 475 lawyers. The firm serves clients around the world from its offices in the south-eastern United States, Washington, DC and Europe in virtually all areas of business-related law.

AREAS OF PRACTICE
Through its offices in the US and Europe, Kilpatrick Stockton is able to advise clients on virtually all matters of US law and the laws of member states of the European Union. The breadth of the firm's practice is indicated by its various internal practice groups: corporate (encompassing general corporate and commercial, international business and trade, public and private finance, private equity, M&A, securities, bankruptcy and property practices); intellectual property (encompassing trade mark, copyright, and patent practices); labour (encompassing labour relations, general employment and immigration); litigation (encompassing corporate, tax and employee benefits); legislative and government contracts; and competition. The firm has particularly well-respected intellectual property and technology practice groups.

Kilpatrick Stocktons' London office opened in 1981 and now constitutes one of the 15 largest US law firms in London. This office is a hub for the firm's European services, which include a full-service English law capability. As the firm is a major US law firm, it is important to offer its American clients cost-efficient legal services in Europe at the standards that its clients have come to expect. Similarly, the firm offers the same high-quality services to its European clients in relation to US matters.

The London office has a highly skilled and experienced team of corporate and corporate finance lawyers in London, as well as a projects team and expert teams in litigation, employment and pensions, tax and property. The firm also handles private equity, M&A, and venture capital transactions for US and European clients in the UK and across Europe.

Whilst this work continues, the firm has been able to export successfully to Europe its expertise in intellectual property and technology. To this end, the firm provides full-service intellectual property capability in Europe including its strategic portfolio management service (intellectual asset management). The firm has a formidable reputation in trade mark work including procurement, litigation and advice in brand strategy and domain names. The firm also advises on pan-European patent litigation and conducts patent litigation in Europe.

Of its 40 London-based lawyers 33 are solicitors or barristers in England and Wales. In addition to English lawyers, the London office team comprises attorneys admitted in the US (New York, North Carolina and Georgia), France, Finland, India, Scotland, Ireland, New Zealand, Australia, Canada and Sweden.

The legal, linguistic and cultural diversity of the team allows its lawyers to assist the firm's clients throughout Europe. Where the firm requires assistance on matters of local law, it selects local lawyers and other professional advisers and co-ordinates their activities throughout Europe to achieve effective and efficient results for its clients. Kilpatrick Stockton prides itself on the diversity and talent of its lawyers who have a keen understanding of the commercial pressures facing business clients.

KIRKLAND & ELLIS INTERNATIONAL LLP

TOWER 42
25 OLD BROAD STREET
LONDON EC2N 1HQ

Telephone: +44 20 7816 8700
Fax: +44 20 7816 8800
E-mail: bwooster@kirkland.com
Website: www.kirkland.com

Languages
French, German, Spanish, Mandarin

Other offices
Chicago, Los Angeles, New York, San Fransisco, Washington DC

Number of lawyers 865
at this office 34

Contact
Brigitte C Wooster (office administrator)

CATEGORIES OF WORK

Capital markets/securities
Stuart L Mills

Private equity
James L Learner

Insolvency
Lyndon E Norley

UK practice
Dr Nigel P Dunmore

German practice
Dr Thomas O Verhoeven

Tax
Ian Taplin

Intellectual property
Pierre-André Dubois

THE FIRM

For nearly 100 years, Kirkland & Ellis LLP, one of America's premier law firms, has handled complicated transactional, intellectual property, litigation and counselling matters for major US and international clients. Today, Kirkland & Ellis LLP continues to work with a base of long-standing clients engaged in varied industries such as hi-tech, manufacturing, computers, transportation, private equity and venture capital, oil and gas, healthcare, real estate, chemicals, food products, finance, insurance, advertising and accounting.

The London office, with more than 34 attorneys focusing on private equity, mergers and acquisitions, capital markets, arbitration, intellectual property and financial restructuring matters, has been serving UK, European and US clients since 1994.

AREAS OF PRACTICE

Kirkland & Ellis LLP is known for its ability to negotiate and close highly sophisticated transactions, representing private equity investors and public and private companies in mergers and acquisitions, securities, spin-offs and split-offs, and private equity transactions. The firm has a premier private equity practice, having represented private investment funds, the private equity groups at several major money centre banks and other participants in this industry for more than 25 years. During the last five years, Kirkland & Ellis LLP's private equity practice has represented more than 50 different clients in leveraged acquisitions and other transactions and has been principal counsel in over $50bn in fund formations. In the M&A and securities area, Kirkland & Ellis LLP has represented clients including a number of the world's largest corporations, major banks and investment banks in some of the world's largest and most complex M&A transactions and securities offerings.

On the litigation and arbitration side, Kirkland & Ellis LLP's attorneys have a stellar reputation as trial lawyers (not just 'litigators') by successfully defending companies with business-threatening lawsuits and class actions in diverse legal areas such as commercial, intellectual property, product liability, insurance coverage, and many others, handling the trial, appellate, and other US Supreme Court phases. This trial-ready reputation has been the impetus for favourable and prompt results for the firm's clients through settlements as well as through the various alternative dispute resolution mechanisms (ADRs) employed whenever practicable and desired by the client.

Kirkland & Ellis LLP also represents some of the world's leading technology companies and brings its expertise to all areas of intellectual property, including biotechnology, semi-conductor processing, telecommunications, and Internet and e-commerce technology. With a dedicated practice dating from 1925, Kirkland & Ellis LLP has always been at the forefront of IP developments. Kirkland & Ellis LLP has adopted and adapted to the Internet and e-commerce, and its 150 intellectual property lawyers understand fully the intricacies, implications, legal issues and arguments surrounding today's and tomorrow's communication and emerging technologies.

On the financial restructuring side, Kirkland & Ellis LLP has in excess of 60 insolvency specialists providing a broad range of advice on international insolvency matters to a varied client base. Representation of clients includes complex financial restructurings, corporate insolvencies, liquidation of troubled businesses, debtor-in-possession financings, litigation of all contentious issues arising out of insolvency-related situatons, and equitable subordination of claims.

Kirkland & Ellis LLP bases its commitment to client service on developing an intimate knowledge of each client's needs and objectives. The firm seeks long-term relationships with clients, ensuring the best total solution to the client's multi-disciplined and industry-specific legal service needs. The firm 's goal is to be an instrumental part of each client's success.

KROMANN REUMERT

42 NEW BROAD STREET
LONDON EC2M 1JD

Telephone: + 44 20 7920 3000
Fax: + 44 20 7920 3099
E-mail: lon@kromannreumert.com
Website: www.kromannreumert.com

Languages
Dutch, French, German,
the Scandinavian languages

Other offices
Aarhus, Brussels, Copenhagen

Number of lawyers 232
at this office 1

Member
Lex Mundi; Scandinavian Law Alliance

CATEGORIES OF WORK

- Banking and finance
- Commercial and company
- Competition
- Employment and labour
- Energy
- Insolvency
- Insurance and tort law
- Intellectual property, media and marketing law
- IT and telecommunications
- Litigation and arbitration
- Maritime and transportation
- Mergers and acquisitions
- Real property, environmental and construction law
- Shipping
- Stock exchange regulation
- Tax law

LATHAM & WATKINS

99 BISHOPSGATE
LONDON
EC2M 3XF

Telephone: +44 20 7710 1000
Fax: +44 20 7374 44 60
E-mail: latham&watkins.london@lw.com
Website: www.lw.com

Languages
Danish, Dutch, French, German, Gujarati, Hindi, Italian, Japanese, Norwegian, Punjabi, Russian, Spanish, Swedish

Other offices
Boston, Brussels, Chicago, Frankfurt, Hamburg, Hong Kong, Los Angeles, Milan, Moscow, New Jersey, New York, Northern Virginia, Orange County, Paris, San Diego, San Francisco, Silicon Valley, Singapore, Tokyo, Washington DC

Number of lawyers 1,500
at this office 85

CATEGORIES OF WORK

- Banking
- Corporate finance
- Debt and equity capital markets
- EU, competition
- Litigation and arbitration
- Mergers and acquisitions, private equity
- Employment
- Intellectual property
- Real estate
- Restructuring, insolvency
- Venture capital, investment funds
- Telecoms and media
- Italian practice
- Scandinavian practice
- Tax
- Leveraged/structured finance
- Project development and finance
- IT and technology transactions/outsourcing

LEWIS SILKIN, member of ius laboris

12 GOUGH SQUARE
LONDON EC4A 3DW

Telephone: +44 20 7074 8000
Fax: +44 20 7832 1200
E-mail: info@lewissilkin.com
Website: www.lewissilkin.com

Languages
French, German, Italian, Spanish

Number of lawyers 115

Member
ius laboris, International Employment Law Pensions and Employee Benefits Alliance; EALA (European Advertising Lawyers' Alliance); GALA (Global Advertising Lawyers' Alliance)

CATEGORIES OF WORK

Advertising and marketing services
Roger Alexander, Brinsley Dresden

Company commercial
Trevor Watkins

Construction
Peter Morris

Corporate finance
Clare Grayston, Philip Lamb

Defamation
Rod Dadak

Employment
Michael Burd, James Davies

Employee incentives
Guy Abbiss

Housing and project finance
Gillian Bastow, Lynne Murray

Information technology
Gillian Cordall

Insolvency
Jo Evans, Amanda Milsom

Intellectual property
Ian Jeffery

Litigation and dispute resolution
Tom Coates, Clive Greenwood

Partnership
Clive Greenwood

Real estate, planning and environment
Len Goodrich, Adam Perry

Sports
Dominic Farnsworth

THE FIRM

Lewis Silkin is a thriving commercial law firm due to its commitment to delivering results for clients. Independent commentators recognise the firm as already among the 'top twenty law firms with best business lawyers'. In tone as well as substance, Lewis Silkin is distinctive; notably relaxed and unstuffy, with each individual contributing to successful, productive and friendly working relationships.

Lewis Silkin regularly offers international service through its network of contacts and alliances, including the Global and European Advertising Lawyers' Alliances, and ius laboris, the leading global network of employment, employee incentives and pensions lawyers.

Clients particularly value Lewis Silkin's cost-effectiveness, its personalised approach to the needs of their business and its distinctive approach to legal updating and training events (details on the firm's website).

AREAS OF PRACTICE

Service teams are based around the unique needs of each client, drawing on the following practice areas and industry sectors.

Corporate services: the firm is increasingly instructed not only in transactions, but plays an active role as a business adviser, helping clients to structure deals and conducting complex negotiations on their behalf. The range includes shareholder agreements, flotations, employee benefits, project finance, insolvency and regulatory advice, acting on behalf of venture capitalists, sponsors and growing companies and businesses. Commercial work includes publishing, franchising and outsourcing.

Litigation and dispute resolution: from sensitive mediation to High Court litigation, the firm works with clients to achieve their commercial objectives. Known for success in winning disputes as a result of a string of high-profile victories, but, increasingly, many problems are being resolved effectively with appropriate resolution techniques.

Employment and incentives: one of the highest-rated teams in London, with a reputation for straightforward practical advice when a sensitive, commercial approach is needed. Lewis Silkin is the UK member for employment and incentives in the ius laboris global network of employment and pensions specialists.

Property: a seamless approach to all property-related needs including leases, litigation, finance, planning, development, and environmental issues.

Housing and project finance: a recognised leader, innovation and experience have resulted in a strong record in social housing and grant-aided financing.

Construction: a comprehensive service, from new-building property to civil engineering, often working from the outset of the project.

Marketing services: from long-established advertising agencies to start-ups, clients value Lewis Silkin's understanding of their challenges, the result of over 30 years advising leading names on domestic and international matters.

Technology and communications: an active convergence practice advising a range of brand-owners, media and technology clients on rights exploitation, systems procurement, data protection, software development, and distribution. Also advises on IT projects and disputes.

Defamation: advice to corporations, firms, brand-owners or individuals whose reputation is put at risk by libel, slander or malicious falsehood.

Partnership: advice on issues affecting partnerships, especially employment and contentious matters.

Sports, partnership structures: combining strengths in employment, immigration, brands and marketing, publishing, IP, finance, licensing and property, the team focuses its expertise and passion on solutions to the wide range of issues facing businesses today.

LINKLATERS

ONE SILK STREET
LONDON EC2Y 8HQ

Telephone: +44 20 7456 2000
Fax: +44 20 7456 2222
Website: www.linklaters.com

Languages
All commercial and local languages in the countries where Linklaters operates

Other offices
Alicante, Amsterdam, Antwerp, Bangkok, Beijing, Berlin, Bratislava, Brussels, Bucharest, Budapest, Cologne, Frankfurt am Main, Hong Kong, Lisbon, Luxembourg, Madrid, Milan, Moscow, Munich, New York, Paris, Prague, Rome, São Paulo, Shanghai, Singapore, Stockholm, Tokyo, Warsaw

Number of lawyers 2,000 worldwide

Contacts
Tony Angel, Anthony Cann

CATEGORIES OF WORK

Asset finance
Ron Gibbs

Banking
John Tucker

Capital markets
Nick Eastwell

Corporate/M&A
David Cheyne

Employment
Raymond Jeffers

Pensions and incentives
Ruth Goldman (pensions), Janet Cooper (incentives)

Environment and planning
Ray Jackson, Vanessa Havard-Williams

EU and competition
Bill Allan, Gerwin van Gerven

Financial markets
Paul Nelson

Intellectual property
Nigel Jones

Investment management
Tim Shipton

IT and communications
Christopher Millard

Litigation and arbitration
Christopher Style, Klaus Saffenreuther

Projects
Alan Black

Real estate and construction
Patrick Plant

Restructuring and insolvency
Robert Elliott

Tax
Guy Brannan

THE FIRM

Linklaters advises the world's leading companies, financial institutions and governments on their most challenging transactions and assignments. With 2,000 lawyers, including 470 partners, and offices in major business and financial centres, its clients choose the firm for its distinctive combination of technical skill, commercial experience and outstanding service.

Linklaters has built a formidable global practice through organic growth and a series of mergers, joint ventures and co-operations with other respected law firms. In 2001 Linklaters merged with three of Europe's leading law firms to form Linklaters Oppenhoff & Rädler in Germany, Linklaters in Sweden, Linklaters De Bandt in Belgium and Linklaters Loesch in Luxembourg. In the same year, the firm formed a co-operation with Brazilian firm Goulart Penteado, Iervolino e Lefosse. This co-operation combines Linklaters' international capability with GPIL's extensive knowledge of the Brazilian market. In Singapore the firm practises as Linklaters Allen & Gledhill, a joint venture with the premier Singapore practice of Allen & Gledhill. While in Italy, Linklaters has a preferred relationship with the law firm Gianni, Origoni, Grippo & Partners.

LOVELLS

ATLANTIC HOUSE
HOLBORN VIADUCT
LONDON EC1A 2FG

Telephone: +44 20 7296 2000
Fax: +44 20 7296 2001
E-mail: information@lovells.com
Website: www.lovells.com

Languages
Chinese, Czech, Dutch, French, German, Italian, Japanese, Russian

Other offices
Alicante, Amsterdam, Beijing, Berlin, Brussels, Budapest*, Chicago, Düsseldorf, Frankfurt, Hamburg, Ho Chi Minh City, Hong Kong, Moscow, Milan, Munich, New York, Paris, Prague, Rome, Shanghai, Singapore, Tokyo, Vienna*, Warsaw, Zagreb*

Number of lawyers 1,600
at this office 774

CATEGORIES OF WORK

Banking
Andrew Gamble, Matthew Cottis

Business restructuring/insolvency
Robin Spencer

Capital markets
David Hudd

Commercial and trading law
Andrew Skipper

Competition and Brussels EC
Simon Polito

Corporate (including private equity)
Hugh Nineham, Marco Campagnoni

Dispute resolution
Patrick Sherrington

Employment
David Harper

Energy
David Moss

Financial services
Richard Stones

Insurance (corporate)
John Young

Insurance and reinsurance
John Powell

Intellectual property
Robert Anderson

International arbitration
Andrew Foyle

Pensions
Russell Strachan, Jane Samsworth

Project finance
Gavin McQuater

Projects/engineering/construction
Philip Capper

Property
Robert Kidby

Tax
Philip Gershuny, Keith Ashman

Technology, media and telecoms
Quentin Archer

THE FIRM

Lovells is one of a small number of truly international business law firms. Its European capabilities have expanded significantly, and its aim is to provide clear, concise and practical advice based on an in-depth knowledge of the legal, regulatory and commercial environments within which the firm's clients operate and a full understanding of their overall business objectives.

The practice is structured to offer a flexible balance between specialist legal and transactional expertise and broader market sector knowledge. Where necessary, the firm can provide a co-ordinated multi-jurisdictional service from its 26 offices in Europe, Asia and North America.

The firm's services are tailored to the needs of individual clients in a way that builds on the collective knowledge of the practice. The firm's size, experience and international strengths enable it to assemble expert teams of lawyers to advise on the issues that concern its clients. Lovells aims to add value at all stages of a project, from its initiation, through its planning, to its execution.

AREAS OF PRACTICE

Lovells has offices in many of the major commercial and financial centres of the world. The practice of each of its international offices reflects the requirements of clients and the nature of local and regional markets. The firm's largest office is in London, and offers the full range of the firm's specialist services. The firm's German practice mirrors the decentralised structure of Germany in the heart of the 'Euro-zone', with offices in Frankfurt, Düsseldorf, Hamburg, Munich and Berlin, from which it provides legal services in all business matters, whether domestic or international. Elsewhere in continental Europe, Lovells' Brussels, Budapest, Milan, Moscow, Paris, Prague, Rome, Warsaw, Vienna and Zagreb offices offer a combination of local and cross-border legal services covering the areas of banking, corporate finance, private equity, project finance, capital markets, tax, intellectual property, competition and trade regulation, financial services and property. The firm's office in Alicante specialises in trade mark matters with the European Trademark Office. The Asia practice, which is managed from Lovells' Hong Kong office, has been further developed with the opening of Lovells' Shanghai office in 2003, focusing on regional banking, project finance, capital markets, corporate transactions, restructuring and insolvency, construction, intellectual property, litigation and property.

The North America offices in New York and Chicago concentrate particularly on UK and EU advice on corporate transactions, US securities law advice, insurance and reinsurance litigation, insurance insolvency, consumer financial services including regulatory advice, and product liability.

Where the firm is undertaking large-scale or complex international transactions, its resources enable it to transfer teams of knowledgeable lawyers to the appropriate office or to establish temporary offices for the duration of the transaction.

In jurisdictions where the firm does not have its own local practice, Lovells manages transactions, building on its knowledge of client requirements and preferences, and its established relationships with leading firms of local lawyers.

LOYENS & LOEFF

26 THROGMORTON STREET
LONDON EC2N 2AN

Telephone: +44 20 7826 3070
Fax: +44 20 7826 3080
E-mail: marc.klerks@loyensloeff.com/ bas.vletter@loyensloeff.com
Website: www.loyensloeff.com

Languages
French, German, Dutch

Other offices
Amsterdam, Antwerp (Loyens), Arnhem, Aruba, Brussels (Loyens), Curaçao, Eindhoven, Frankfurt, Geneva, Luxembourg, New York, Paris, Rotterdam, Singapore, Tokyo

Number of lawyers 744
at this office 9

Contacts
Marc Klerks, Bas Vletter

CATEGORIES OF WORK

Capital markets	**Regulatory law**
Banking and security	**Structured finance**
Commercial law	**Project finance**
Corporate law, mergers and acquisitions, joint ventures	**Corporate taxation, international**
Corporate financial restructuring	

THE FIRM

Loyens & Loeff is an independent Benelux law firm with over 700 lawyers and offices in the main financial centres around the world.

AREAS OF PRACTICE

The London office of Loyens & Loeff combines an integrated corporate law, regulatory and tax practice. It focuses on capital markets, private equity and structured finance, including securitisations, repackaging, asset-backed finance transactions, IPOs, secondary offerings, public takeovers, public to private transactions, corporate financial restructuring, mergers and acquisitions and all related corporate and tax advice.

MACFARLANES

10 NORWICH STREET
LONDON EC4A 1BD

Telephone: +44 20 7831 9222
Fax: +44 20 7831 9607
Website: www.macfarlanes.com

Languages
Cantonese, Dutch/Flemish, French, German, Greek, Gujarati, Hebrew, Italian, Japanese, Portuguese, Punjabi, Spanish, Swedish, Urdu, Welsh, Yoruba

Number of lawyers 234

CATEGORIES OF WORK

Debt finance
Julian Howard

Company law
Simon Martin

Commercial law/ intellectual property
Jeremy Courtenay-Stamp

Commercial property
Chris Field

EU and competition law
Jane Whittaker

Construction
Tony Blackler

Litigation
Willie Manners

Mergers and acquisitions
Robert Sutton

Private equity
Charles Martin

Securities
Tim Lewis

Corporate tax
Mark Baldwin

Private client
John Rhodes

Pensions
Hugh Arthur

Employment
Seán Lavin

THE FIRM

Macfarlanes offers a remarkable concentration of excellence and experience. Its distinctive market position as a leading City law firm is built on a reputation for the quality of its advice and client service. Macfarlanes is one of a small (and diminishing) number of high-quality unaligned law firms in the UK.

Much of the firm's practice is international work, involving continental European and US corporate clients and investors in the UK and outbound M&A and private equity, cross-border litigation and wealthy international families. This work is driven by the firm's excellent relationships with leading independent law firms outside the UK. Macfarlanes invests heavily in building these relationships through secondments and technical know-how sharing to give clients a first-class and seamless service.

AREAS OF PRACTICE

Corporate: Macfarlanes is particularly highly regarded for its work in the areas of corporate finance and mergers and acquisitions, including private equity and takeovers. Together these represent over half the firm's work.

The firm's specialist areas, such as intellectual property, corporate tax, debt finance and employment benefits, enable Macfarlanes to provide its broad range of commercial clients with high-quality legal services, both in relation to corporate transactional work and at the clients' operational level. The firm has a particularly strong reputation for advertising and marketing work, as well as for its investment funds and financial services practice.

Property: By City standards, Macfarlanes' property practice is substantial in size. Property work accounts for 24% of the firm's work – unusual for a successful City firm. Work for the property sector covers all transactions involving the ownership, development, investment in, and financing of real estate. Commercial property investment and development transactions are at the core of the firm's property practice.

Litigation and dispute resolution: The wide range of Macfarlanes' business litigation and dispute resolution work includes: leading employment law cases; acting for insured and insurer, especially in advertising and surveying cases; IP cases and disputes over computer hardware and software; financial services regulatory issues and disputes; Lloyd's-related work; sovereign debt; securities and other banking cases; judicial review; breach of contract and professional negligence claims; major shipping and construction arbitration and jurisdictional disputes.

Private client: Macfarlanes' pre-eminent private client service commands a leading position and the practice continues to grow and flourish. Combined with the firm's strong corporate and property capability, this means that Macfarlanes is in a particularly strong position to advise high-net-wealth entrepreneurs. The firm's longstanding reputation is for work advising private clients and their family trusts, both domestically and internationally. Tax planning, including the creation and administration of trusts, the preparation of wills and the administration of estates, are central to this work. The international element to Macfarlanes' work is of special importance both for UK-based families and for overseas taxpayers seeking advice on tax and trust law. The firm is frequently instructed at the request of many of the largest US firms and private banks for this work.

MAPLES AND CALDER EUROPE

7 PRINCES STREET
LONDON EC2R 8AQ

Telephone: +44 20 7466 1600
Fax: +44 20 7466 1700
E-mail: ukinfo@maplesandcalder.com
Website: www.maplesandcalder.com

Languages
French, Italian, Malay, Spanish, Turkish

Other offices
Cayman Islands, Hong Kong

Number of lawyers 82
at this office 10

CATEGORIES OF WORK

Capital markets: securitisation, derivatives, preference shares, CBO/CLO/CDOs, repackaging and structured finance
Shaun Denton

Corporate: joint ventures, IPO, general partnership, banking and M&A
Gray Smith

Investment funds: hedge, mutual and private equity funds
Gray Smith, Richard Mansi

Asset finance: aircraft, ship and project finance
Shaun Denton

Litigation: trust, insolvency, advisory work, banking, fund and commercial litigation
Gray Smith

Trusts: commercial and private trust services and trust and estate planning
Tony Pursall

Insurance
Gray Smith

McDERMOTT, WILL & EMERY

7 BISHOPSGATE
LONDON
EC2N 3AR

Telephone: +44 20 7577 6900
Fax: +44 20 7577 6950
Website: www.mwe.com

Languages
All main business languages

Other offices
Boston, Chicago, Düsseldorf, Los Angeles, Miami, Milan, Munich, New York, Orange County, Rome, San Diego, Silicon Valley, Washington DC

Number of lawyers 1,000
at this office 67

CATEGORIES OF WORK

Banking and finance
Graham Rowbotham

Corporate and corporate finance
William Charnley

Employment
Fraser Younson

EU and competition
Scott Megregian

Financial services and funds
William Yonge

Insolvency and restructuring
Graham Rowbotham, Rick Mitchell

Intellectual property
Larry Cohen

Litigation and arbitration
John Reynolds

Mergers and acquisitions
William Charnley

Pensions and incentives
Steven Hull

Project finance
Andrew Watson

Taxation
Peter Nias

US securities
Rick Mitchell

THE FIRM

McDermott, Will & Emery was founded in Chicago in 1934 and is now one of the world's largest international law firms, with offices in 14 major cities.

The London office has quickly established a reputation as a full-service City and European practice, and complements the firm's capabilities in the US, Belgium, Germany and Italy. The firm regularly acts on highly complex, high-value cross-border transactions, assignments and litigation. The firm provides a complete multi-disciplinary legal service to a broad range of UK, European and international businesses including FTSE 250 and Fortune 1000 corporates; leading international banks and other financial institutions; governmental and regulatory authorities, and trade organisations.

The office is staffed by more than 67 lawyers, including 26 partners most of whom are acknowledged as leaders in their fields by leading directories and market commentators including the UK edition of *The Legal 500*. Unique among UK offices of US law firms, all of its London-based lawyers are UK-qualified except three US-qualified corporate and securities partners.

AREAS OF PRACTICE

McDermott, Will & Emery's core practice areas include corporate finance (including M&A, private equity and flotations); banking and finance (including capital markets, project finance, restructuring and insolvency); financial services and funds; communications and technology; employment; European competition; intellectual property and information technology, including e-commerce; litigation and dispute resolution; pensions and incentives; tax; and US securities.

To best understand and meet its clients' business needs, practice groups are broadly structured and many team members bring business acumen and an in-house perspective gained from industry experience. In addition to issue-focused and multi-disciplinary advice, the firm's clients benefit from an interactive approach with a host of client support services which add value to their business.

MORGAN LEWIS

2 GRESHAM STREET
LONDON EC2V 7PE

Telephone: +44 20 7710 5500
Fax: +44 20 7710 5600
E-mail: info@morganlewis.com
Website: www.morganlewis.com

Languages
French, German

Other offices
Boston, Brussels, Chicago, Frankfurt, Harrisburg, Irvine, Los Angeles, Miami, New York, Palo Alto, Philadelphia, Pittsburgh, Princeton, San Francisco, Tokyo, Washington DC

Number of lawyers 1,150+
at this office 26

CATEGORIES OF WORK

Corporate, finance, commercial
Peter Wallace, Ken Mildwaters

Life sciences
Anthony Warnock-Smith

Litigation, international arbitration
Robert Goldspink, Trevor Asserson

US and international taxation
Charles Lubar, Michael Cashman

THE FIRM

Morgan Lewis, with more than 1,150 lawyers in 17 offices in the US, Europe and Asia, ranks among the top ten law firms in the world.

Every area of the firm's practice – from antitrust to litigation – has a strong international component. Morgan Lewis represents clients in mergers and acquisitions, technology and emerging business all over the world, resolving differing and sometimes conflicting laws in a number of jurisdictions to produce optimum results. Additionally, the firm's lawyers understand the problems and complexities of transactional litigation and can advise on US and EU regulatory matters.

The firm's clients are diverse and include Fortune 250 companies, leading financial services and investment banking organisations, as well as pioneers in the e-commerce and Internet sector. The firm also represents high-net-worth individuals. All clients receive the same high level of care, and the firm recognises why clients choose Morgan Lewis – because they want a professional firm with experienced, quality people who are as internationally minded as they are.

The firm handles a vast diversity of legal work including antitrust, business and commercial litigation, business and finance, corporate transactions, employment, labour and benefits, energy and utilities, intellectual property, investment management, life sciences, personal law, mergers and acquisitions, real estate, securities, tax, and technology.

AREAS OF PRACTICE

The London office of Morgan Lewis is fully integrated with the firm's 16 other offices. In addition, the lawyers in the London office can offer clients worldwide legal representation through a comprehensive network of contacts and leading law firms in countries where the firm does not have offices.

From its inception in 1981, the office has had a leading international and US tax practice headed by Charles Lubar, which, as well as serving its own clients, provides creative tax structuring advice in support of the firm's international M&A and corporate practice.

Since the advent of multinational partnership in 1994, the office has had a fully dual US/UK corporate/commercial/financing capability advising major US and UK corporate clients on international M&A and joint venture transactions as well as capital raising transactions in both Europe and the US. The London office regularly acts for, among others, Cadbury Schweppes, Chase, Pearson and VerticalNet.

Unusual among offices of US firms in London, Morgan Lewis offers a top-rated English law litigation and international arbitration practice headed by Robert Goldspink, which has acted for clients in several high-profile matters. These include the biggest Commercial Court case of 1999; two recent Court of Appeal cases; and one House of Lords case, and two further Court of Appeal cases pending.

The life sciences practice in the London office is headed by Anthony Warnock-Smith, one of the most sought-after solicitors in the UK in this area, and is a fully integrated part of the firm's life sciences practice which, among many others, represents 15 of the world's 20 largest pharmaceutical companies.

MORRISON & FOERSTER MNP

21 GARLICK HILL
LONDON EC4V 2AU

Telephone: +44 20 7815 1150
Fax: +44 20 7815 1159
Website: www.mofo.com

Languages
French, Italian

Other offices
Beijing, Brussels, Century City, Denver, Hong Kong, Los Angeles, New York, Northern Virginia, Orange County, Palo Alto, Sacramento, San Diego, San Francisco, Shanghai, Singapore, Tokyo, Walnut Creek, Washington DC

Number of lawyers 975
at this office 15

Contact
Kristian Wiggert

CATEGORIES OF WORK

Corporate, M&A, venture capital/ private equity, capital markets
Kristian Wiggert, Neil Foster

Telecommunications, IT, Internet/e-commerce, entertainment and new media
David Naylor, Jane Thatcher-Browne

Debt and cross-border finance
Brian Bates, Neil Foster

Privacy/data protection
David Naylor, David Warner

Employment
David Warner, Ann Bevitt

Intellectual property
David Naylor, Tom Broadhurst

Litigation and dispute resolution
Tom Broadhurst,
Simeon Spencer (employment)

Biotechnology
Tom Broadhurst

THE FIRM

Morrison & Foerster was founded in 1883 and is now one of the world's largest international law firms, with approximately 1,000 attorneys located in 19 offices around the world. The firm takes pride in the talent of its employees, the depth of their expertise and the teamwork employed in assisting clients.

The London office was established in 1980. Its UK and US-qualified lawyers advise a broad range of clients on all aspects of corporate finance, including debt finance and venture capital; commercial technology, including biotechnology and telecoms; privacy; intellectual property and employment issues. The UK's position as a major gateway to and from Europe means that the firm's lawyers are continuously involved in leading-edge cross-border and multijurisdictional matters, enabling the firm to provide valuable advice to clients with well-established and developing European businesses.

AREAS OF PRACTICE

Corporate: the firm undertakes a full range of corporate finance work, including mergers and acquisitions; strategic alliances; joint ventures; spin-off and split-up transactions; venture capital; acquisition finance and buy-outs; and general corporate counselling. The firm's corporate attorneys have special expertise in transactions involving technology companies.

Capital markets: attorneys in the London office advise on securities transactions such as IPOs; public and private (including 144a and Regulation S); placings and other equity and institutional debt offerings.

Employment: the team (which formerly practised as Jones & Warner) integrates the skills and services of solicitors, barristers and human resources professionals to provide comprehensive advice on all areas of UK and international employment law. The team has capabilities in contentious and non-contentious employment matters. They also provide advice on the employment aspects of corporate and commercial transactions such as acquisitions, disposals and joint ventures.

IT, e-commerce and new media: the firm is one of only a few with a global capability focusing on technology transactions matters. The London office advises on all aspects of transactional work for technology-focused businesses, including online contracting and liability; website development and hosting; commercial arrangements with software, hardware and system providers and integrators; software and other technology licensing and transfer agreements; commercial arrangements with content and other service providers; and all aspects of IP protection and exploitation.

Privacy: the firm is a leader in advising on issues relating to privacy and trans-border data transfers around the world. The London office advises on issues such as complying with applicable privacy laws and regulations; developing and implementing privacy policies and training and awareness programmes; performing data audits; enforcing privacy policies against downstream users of information; and representing clients on privacy issues arising out of acquisitions, joint ventures and co-branding relationships.

Telecommunications: the firm's London attorneys have significant experience of advising telecommunications operators and services providers; Internet service providers; and providers and purchasers of telecommunications equipment in all matters from commercial contract negotiation to mergers and acquisitions and financings.

Biotechnology: the firm offers expertise for every phase of a biotech company's growth cycle and has one of the leading international biotechnology patent practices, with its multidisciplinary life sciences division representing a diverse group of participants in the biotechnology, medical technology and healthcare industries.

Litigation and dispute resolution: the firm represents clients in a wide range of disputes, with particular expertise in advising technology clients in patent litigation; copyright and trade mark disputes; passing off; and licensing and contractual disputes.

NAUTADUTILH

BOWMAN HOUSE
29 WILSON STREET
LONDON EC2M 2SJ

Telephone: +44 20 7786 9100
Fax: +44 20 7588 6888
E-mail: ndlondon@nautadutilh.com
Website: www.nautadutilh.com

Languages
Dutch, French, German

Other offices
Amsterdam, Brussels, Luxembourg, New York, Rotterdam

Number of lawyers 503
at this office 9

Contacts
Gijs Gerretsen, Joanne Kellermann

CATEGORIES OF WORK

Loan finance
Dirk Blaisse

Public M&A
Gijs Gerretsen

Private equity
Gijs Gerretsen

Structured finance and securitisation
Joanne Kellermann

Projects/project finance
Joanne Kellermann

Taxation
Pieter Elias

THE FIRM

NautaDutilh enjoys a strong reputation throughout the Benelux. With more than 500 attorneys, civil law notaries and tax advisers, and offices in Amsterdam and Rotterdam, NautaDutilh is one of the largest law firms in the Netherlands and its Brussels office has grown quickly to become a recognised player in the Belgian market. The firm's core businesses are corporate, banking, finance and tax law, but it has chosen to maintain a broader, market-focused practice than some of its peers.

The position established by the firm in its domestic market – and the interests of the clients it serves there – convinced it to resist the advances of global law firms and remain clearly and publicly independent. Nevertheless, it has invested in maintaining close but non-exclusive relationships with other market-leading (or specialist) law firms throughout the world, especially in the UK and the US. Today, over half of the firm's revenue comes from international business and it acts for many global corporations and (investment) banks. By nurturing its 'best friends' relationships, NautaDutilh has become the preferred Benelux referral firm for many leading overseas law firms, and it is convinced that it can offer each individual client a service tailor-made to their specific requirements. The firm's experience operating in the major financial centres of the world helps it to be even more effective in its domestic Benelux markets. Its offices in London and New York (which practise only Dutch and Belgian law) play an important role in supporting its corporate, banking and finance practice, and its Luxembourg office provides specialist support to its tax practice elsewhere.

AREAS OF PRACTICE

By listening carefully to its clients and studying the market place, NautaDutilh has recognised the need to focus its expertise in particular markets or business sectors. The firm has therefore organised itself in a range of market-driven practice groups, such as life sciences, energy and utilities, and shipping and logistics. Drawing their talents from throughout the firm, these groups offer clients a powerful concentration of legal and business skills tailored to their specific business needs and complement the firm's established areas of legal work.

Besides corporate, banking, finance and tax – NautaDutilh's core practices – the firm offers high-level advice on: construction/property; intellectual property and ICT; EU, regulatory and competition; employment; litigation; insurance and liability; and maritime law. The firm also offers its services to private clients.

NORTON ROSE

KEMPSON HOUSE
CAMOMILE STREET
LONDON EC3A 7AN

Telephone: +44 20 7283 6000
Fax: +44 20 7283 6500
Website: www.nortonrose.com

Languages
Afrikaans, Arabic, Bahasa Malay, Cantonese, Czech, Danish, Dutch, Flemish, English, French, German, Greek, Hebrew, Hindi, Italian, Japanese, Maltese, Mandarin, Norwegian, Polish, Russian, Shona, Spanish, Swahili, Swedish, Thai

Other offices
Amsterdam, Athens, Bahrain, Bangkok, Beijing, Brussels, Cologne, Dubai, Frankfurt, Hong Kong, Jakarta*, Milan, Moscow, Munich, Paris, Piraeus, Prague*, Singapore, Warsaw

Number of lawyers 1,102
at this office 605

*Associated offices

CATEGORIES OF WORK

Aviation	**Intellectual property and technology**
Banking, finance and capital markets	**Insurance**
Competition and EC	**Rail**
Corporate finance and general commercial	**Real property, planning and environemental**
Dispute resolution	**Shipping**
Employment, pensions and incentives	**Tax**
Energy and natural resources	

THE FIRM

Norton Rose services its clients through an international network of offices (see Other offices, above). The Dubai office became the latest addition to the network when it opened in 2003. The firm places emphasis on indutry expertise and focuses research and know-how on five key areas: international corporate finance, financial institutions, transportation, energy and infrastructure and technology, where the firm and its clients have particular interests.

The firm works for international corporates and financial institutions on complex cross-border transactions. The global nature of its client base and its strength in project and asset finance, international M&A and international dispute resolution means that much of its work is conducted across jurisditions. The firm has a top-ranking Islamic finance practice, which covers Europe, the Middle East and South East Asia. Norton Rose's major clients include ABN AMRO, BMW, Citigroup, Crédit Lyonnaise, easyGroup, ExxonMobil, GE Capital, HSBC, ING, Nestlé, P&O and Siemens.

AREAS OF PRACTICE

The firm is an acknowledged leader in the international corporate finance market, where specialisations include cross-border M&A, public offerings, private equity, investment funds, financial services and US corporate finance. Major deals include HSBC Holdings' US$15bn acquisition of Household International Inc, TX Logistik AG's joint venture with Trenitalia, and Malaysian International Shipping Corporation's acquisition of American Eagle Tankers from Neptune Orient Lines.

The firm's strong banking and finance practice includes top teams in bank lending, acquisition finance, Islamic finance and asset, structured and project finance. The firm also has a leading capital markets practice which advises clients on debt and equity securities, asset securitisation and derivatives. Major transactions on which the firm worked over the year include a US$500m international bond issue by the Kingdom of Bahrain, the largest ever QTE financing for SNCF, and the €665m debt financing of a power station in Spain for AES Energía Cartagena SRL.

Norton Rose has a large and varied dispute resolution practice, with extensive experience in resolving disputes worldwide through all forms of dispute resolution. The firm has worked on many high-profile litigation cases in recent years, including the winning of US$50m at a summary judgment at the Commercial Court in London, and acting for the Georgian government in a landmark arbitration.

With a team of 40 experienced competition lawyers, Norton Rose has excellent capability in competition and regulation, with outstanding understanding of regulatory bodies. In the past year, the team has advised clients in several high-profile merger filings and cartel investigations and has also been involved in cases relating to abuse of dominant position, commercial agreements, public procurement and state aids.

The award-winning employment, pensions and incentives team covers the full range of contentious and non-contentious work. The team has been active over the past year in training non-executive directors on their corporate governance responsibilities.

The firm offers first-class technical tax expertise, with a team experienced in structuring aspects of corporate acquisitions, joint ventures and investment funds advising numerous clients. The firm also handles tax issues arising from litigation cases.

The firm's leading IP and technology teams have particular experience in the UK and Germany. The firm offers a full service practice, advising on exploitation, enforcement of IP rights and the acquisition of IT products and services.

The firm's real estate, planning and environmental team attracts considerable recognition on an international level and has led projects in many countries throughout Europe and the Middle East.

OGIER & LE MASURIER

2 ROYAL EXCHANGE BUILDINGS
LONDON EC3V 31F

Telephone: +44 20 7220 1170
Fax: +44 20 7220 1199
E-mail: info@ogier.com
Website: www.ogier.com

Languages
English, French

Other offices
Cayman Islands (Ogier & Boxalls), Guernsey, Jersey

Number of lawyers 110
at this office 3

Member
Association of European Lawyers (AEL); STEP; EVCA; BVCA

CATEGORIES OF WORK

Banking
Aaron DeLacey

Capital markets: securitisation, derivatives, CBOs/CLOs/CDOs, repackagings and structured finance
Aaron DeLacey

Corporate and commercial: joint ventures, mergers and acquisitions
Aaron DeLacey

Trust and estate planning
Heather Tibbo

Private client
Heather Tibbo

Employee benefits and share plan administration
Heather Tibbo

Fiduciary services
Brian Lee

THE FIRM

Ogier is one of the leading and largest offshore providers of legal and administration services with approximately 370 employees across offices in Jersey, Guernsey, London and the Cayman Islands following its merger this year with Boxalls, a Cayman Islands law firm.

Ogier comprises Ogier & Le Masurier in the Channel Islands, Ogier & Boxalls in the Cayman Islands, and Ogier Fiduciary Services, its administration business. Ogier & Le Masurier continues to develop its strength in depth as one of the leading commercial law firms in the Channel Islands delivering practical commercial advice to clients with the highest possible client service.

Ogier has developed an extensive portfolio of international clients and intermediaries and continues to provide legal and administration services to them through its dedicated teams.

All work undertaken is managed by a team of specialists, led by a partner specifically selected to achieve the commercial objectives of the client. A large proportion of the firm's qualified lawyers have worked in some of the world's leading financial centres and bring to the firm exceptional experience and expertise sought by today's clients. The firm places a great importance and value on its relationships with intermediaries and professional advisers in other jurisdictions from whom it receives referrals. It seeks to work more closely with those advisers to deliver added value and commerical advantages to their clients' businesses and to exceed their expectations.

Ogier's London office provides its clients and intermediaries with easier access to Ogier's offshore legal and administration services across three of the world's leading offshore centres: Jersey, Guernsey and the Cayman Islands.

AREAS OF PRACTICE

Banking: Ogier & Le Masurier is widely regarded as a premier firm for banking and international finance. It specialises in advising on all areas of banking, security, structured finance, banking regulation and the establishment of banks.

Corporate and commercial: Ogier's highly experienced and extensive team covers mergers and acquisitions, employment and privacy laws, IT/IP and e-commerce.

Securitisation: Ogier has one of the leading and largest securitisation and capital markets teams, with particular expertise in asset-backed securities, CBOs, ABCP and structured notes.

Structured finance: The structured finance team covers structured equity, asset finance and tax neutral transactions.

Employee benefits: The employees benefits team is committed to providing an innovative and flexible approach to assist clients to achieve employee or clients' employee incentive requirements, tailored administration services, comprehensive advice and a quality, efficient and cost-effective service.

Trusts: The trust and estate planning group has one of the largest teams of trust lawyers dedicated to advising trust companies, intermediaries and individuals in matters of trust law.

Private client: Ogier continues to develop and grow its private client practice. The private client team can provide a full range of administration services to trusts, companies and limited partnerships established in the Channel Islands, as well as to entities established elsewhere.

Fiduciary services: Ogier Fiduciary Services provides professional administration and accounting services to trusts, companies and limited partnerships.

PINSENTS

DASHWOOD HOUSE
69 OLD BROAD STREET
LONDON EC2M 1NR

Telephone: +44 20 7418 7000
Fax: +44 20 7418 7050
E-mail: martin.lane@pinsents.com
Website: www.pinsents.com

Languages
Cantonese, Dutch, French, German, Greek, Hebrew, Hindi, Italian, Japanese, Mirpury, Punjabi, Shana, Spanish, Swedish, Ukrainian, Urdu, Welsh

Other offices
Birmingham, Brussels, Leeds, Manchester

Number of lawyers 552
at this office 144

Contacts
Julian Tonks, David Ryan

CATEGORIES OF WORK

Corporate
Martin Lane

Employment
John McMullen

Dispute resolution and litigation
Nigel Kissack

Insurance and reinsurance
Tim Burton

Pensions
Chris Mullen

Projects and commercial
Patrick Twist

Property
Nigel McClea

Tax
Judith Greaves

Technology and media
Michael Peeters

THE FIRM

Pinsents is distinguished as a full-service law firm by its ceaseless commitment to improving its service and sector offering to major UK and overseas companies, financial institutions and public sector organisations.

The firm, known as a blue-chip adviser, has expanded its UK and European operations over the past three years in pursuit of strategic sector growth. In the UK, the firm now has offices in London, Birmingham, Leeds and Manchester. In Europe, it has established a series of strategic alliances with firms in France, Germany, Scandinavia, Poland and Estonia. It also has long-established relations with leading US corporations and law firms.

Pinsents has more than 150 partners, a full legal team of more than 550 and total UK staff totalling more than 1,000.

AREAS OF PRACTICE

Pinsents is committed to strategic growth through six major sectors: financial services and insurance, government, manufacturing, real estate, services and technology. Within each sector, the firm further focuses its activity channelling expertise into areas such as electronics, automotive, food, construction, healthcare, banking, investment houses and support services.

The sector strategy is driven forward by specialist cross-discipline teams drawn from the firm's highly-rated legal practice groups in corporate, employment, dispute resolution and litigation, insurance and reinsurance, pensions, projects and commercial, property, tax and technology and media.

Pinsents' developing international profile builds on its extensive cross-border experience in advising UK and foreign controlled companies over many years. The firm has alliances with Granrut in Paris; Hoffman Liebs Fritsch & Partner in Düsseldorf and Berlin; and Magnusson Wahlin Qvist Stanbrook, which has offices in Stockholm, Gothenburg, Malmo, Copenhagen, Warsaw and Tallinn. The firm's US group is responsible for relationships with US corporations, including 18 Fortune 500 corporations, as well as with significant US law firms.

SJ BERWIN

222 GRAY'S INN ROAD
LONDON WC1X 8XF

Telephone: +44 20 7533 2222
Fax: +44 20 7533 2000
E-mail: info@sjberwin.com
Website: www.sjberwin.com

Languages
All principal languages are spoken

Other offices
Berlin, Brussels, Frankfurt, Madrid, Munich, Paris

Number of lawyers 411
at this office 285

Contact
David Harrel

Member
Interlaw – a worldwide association of independent law firms

CATEGORIES OF WORK

Banking and financial services
Gillian Smith, Bruce Gardner

Corporate finance , M&A
Robert Burrow, Steven Davis

IT and e-commerce
Andrew Shindler, Martin Bowen

EU, competition
Stephen Kon, Ralph Cohen

Employment, pensions
Nicola Kerr, Wyn Derbyshire

Insolvency and reconstruction
Stephen Maffey

Intellectual property
Ray Black, Jeremy Schrire

Leisure and sport
Perry Yam

Litigation, ADR, advocacy, public law
Tim Taylor, David Shapiro

Media and communications
Nigel Palmer, Tim Johnson

Pharmaceuticals and biotechnology
Jeremy Schrire, Stephen Kon

Private equity, MBOs, venture capital
Jonathan Blake, Steven Davis

Real estate, real estate funds, property litigation, construction, planning and environment
Bryan Pickup

Tax, VAT
Michael Trask, Simon Rose

THE FIRM

SJ Berwin is a leading corporate and commercial legal practice providing bright solutions, specialist advice and legal services to the UK and international business community.

As business demands have changed, so SJ Berwin has rapidly adapted, expanded, grown its client base and, at the same time, sought to maintain its individuality and commitment to excellence. The firm was named 'Law Firm of the Year' at 'The Lawyer' 2000 Awards.

AREAS OF PRACTICE

SJ Berwin has established a strong reputation among the leading corporate and commercial law firms as a European deals firm and acts for clients ranging from major multinational business corporations and financial institutions to high-net-worth individuals. SJ Berwin is especially favoured by entrepreneurial business clients who find the firm particularly well attuned to their outlook and needs. The firm's clients also include foreign governments, banks and institutional clients, particularly in highly specialised practice areas.

Increasingly, the firm is focusing on industry sectors including pharmaceuticals and biotechnology, fisheries and agrochemicals, e-commerce, telecommunications and IT, retailing, sport, leisure and media, publishing, and music. Specialist cross-departmental teams have been established to address the needs of these industry sectors.

The firm offers a full range of corporate finance services including mergers and acquisitions, capital markets, private equity, management buy-outs and venture capital and securities regulation, coupled with active international banking, financial services and insolvency and reconstruction practices.

The EU and competition department is highly regarded and advises on all aspects of EU and UK competition law especially in industry sectors highly regulated at Community and domestic levels. These include: pharmaceuticals, chemicals and agrochemicals, music and media; telecommunications; information technology; transport; banking and financial services, packaging and fishery law.

International trade mark, copyright and patent litigation, licensing and international trade mark registration is undertaken by a specialist intellectual property group.

Other significant areas of commercial work include media and communications, international commercial contracts, information technology and communications.

The real estate division provides a comprehensive service for UK and international public and private companies, including investors, developers, financial institutions, retailers, banks and local and health authorities. Specialist groups advise on real estate funds, property litigation, planning and environmental law and construction.

Taxation advice including the fiscal and financial structuring of international transactions and groups of companies is provided by the tax department. Estate planning and asset protection advice is given to private clients in the UK and abroad.

The firm's litigation and dispute resolution practice handles a broad range of international and domestic commercial litigation, arbitration and mediation.

The insolvency specialists deal with corporate insolvency, bankruptcy or reconstructions.

All aspects of employment law including employee benefits and pensions are handled.

SACKER & PARTNERS, member of ius laboris

29 LUDGATE HILL
LONDON EC4M 7NX

Telephone: +44 20 7329 6699
Fax: +44 20 7248 0552
E-mail: enquiries@sacker-partners.co.uk
Website: www.sacker-partners.co.uk

Languages
English, French, German, Spanish

Number of lawyers 46

Contacts
Peter Docking (ius laboris co-ordinating partner), Paul Phillips (partner), Joanna Matthews

Member
ius laboris, the International Employment Law Pensions and Employee Benefits Alliance; IPEBLA, Association of Pension Lawyers International Committee

CATEGORIES OF WORK

Pensions	Pensions litigation

THE FIRM

Sacker & Partners is one of the largest specialist pensions law practices under one roof in the UK. The firm comprises 20 partners and a total complement of 46 fee-earners who specialise solely in pensions law and its related areas.

The firm is the UK pensions member of ius laboris, the highly regarded international alliance of independent law firms providing specialist services in employment, pensions and employee benefits primarily for employers.

Peter Docking co-chairs the International Pensions Group within ius laboris and Joanna Matthews is an active member of the group and chairs its External Marketing Sub-Committee. Members of the International Pensions Group work closely together and meet regularly to discuss legal developments at national and international levels.

Sacker & Partners acts for a wide variety of clients including trustee boards, independent trustees, employers, members, trade unions, life offices, firms of consulting actuaries and benefit consultants. The firm is retained by over 800 pension schemes. Over 20 of its clients are FTSE-100 companies.

Specialist units exist within the firm to deal with key areas of pensions law. These include the firm's litigation unit, investment unit, services to other law firms unit and schemes in transition unit.

AREAS OF PRACTICE

The firm provides pro-active advice on all aspects of pension law including: pensions advice relating to the UK, including national compliance issues; setting up global pensions programs; pension provision for expatriates; pensions aspects of multinational transactions; new and forthcoming legislation; Pan-European pension funds; international investment pooling arrangements.

As a member of the ius laboris International Pensions Group of leading practitioners from each ius laboris member firm, Sacker & Partners has access to a unique pool of resources and specialist skills in other jurisdictions around the globe.

Clients can be reassured that the lawyers they are dealing with within ius laboris are all highly regarded in their own right, rather than being junior players in a large corporate firm.

Both Sacker & Partners and ius laboris are committed to providing value to their clients and provide additional services such as newsletters on the latest international developments, and organise seminars on hot topics and in-house training for clients.

SIMMONS & SIMMONS

CITYPOINT
ONE ROPEMAKER STREET
LONDON EC2Y 9SS

Telephone: +44 20 7628 2020
Fax: +44 20 7628 2070
E-mail: enquiries@simmons-simmons.com
Website: www.simmons-simmons.com

Languages
Afrikaans, Arabic, Cantonese, Czech, Dutch, French, German, Greek, Hindi, Hungarian, Italian, Japanese, Latvian, Mandarin, Polish, Portuguese, Russian, Slovakian, Spanish, Swedish, Vietnamese

Other offices
Rotterdam, Paris, Lisbon, Milan, Rome, Düsseldorf, Frankfurt, Brussels, Madrid, Padua, Oporto, Madeira, Abu Dhabi, Qatar, Hong Kong, Shanghai, Tokyo, New York

Number of lawyers 754
at this office 356

CATEGORIES OF WORK

Corporate
Jerry Walter, Damon Le Maître-George

Banking
Nick Fisher

Capital markets
Jeremy Hoyland

Taxation
Edward Troup

Projects, PFI
Richard Dyton

EU/competition
Martin Smith

Dispute resolution
Phillip Vaughan

Intellectual property
Kevin Mooney

Employment
William Dawson

Financial markets
Mark Dawkins

Pharmaceutical and biotechnology
Gerry Kamstra

Energy and utilities
Jerry Walter

TMT
David Barrett

Aerospace and defence
Richard Armitage

Transport
Juliet Reingold

Real estate and construction
Alan Butler

Consumer goods
Miles Alexander

THE FIRM

Simmons & Simmons is a world-class law firm providing advice to financial institutions, corporates, public and international bodies and private individuals through its international network of offices.

Simmons & Simmons has over 200 partners, of which over 100 are based in its offices outside the UK, and a total staff worldwide of over 1,900 across 19 offices. It provides a comprehensive range of legal services with strength and depth. It applies considerable expertise to all business sectors but focuses on those key to its clients. These are financial markets, energy and utilities, TMT, real estate and construction, aerospace and defence, pharmaceuticals and biotechnology, transport and consumer goods.

Simmons & Simmons is ranked in Global Counsel's 2004 Top 10 world rankings for client service. This ranking is significant as it is based solely on the views of in-house counsel at over 5,000 companies from 80 jurisdictions. Global Counsel comments that a firm's presence in the Top 10 is testament to both the breadth of practice it offers and to the quality of service it provides. In recognition of the success of its international network, Simmons & Simmons won a prestigious Queen's Award for Enterprise in the international trade category in 2003. The Queen's Awards are the leading awards for business performance. They recognise outstanding achievement in international trade and are awarded by Queen Elizabeth II on the advice of the Prime Minister. The awards are open to all industry sectors and only a small percentage of applicants actually win an award. Simmons & Simmons was the only law firm to win a Queen's Award in 2003.

In the past year, Simmons & Simmons has been awarded M&A Team of the Year at the *Legal Business* Awards 2004, Projects/ PFI Team of the Year at *The Lawyer* Awards 2003 and Employment Team of the Year at the *Asian Legal Business* Awards 2003.

Languages spoken in the firm include English, French, German, Spanish, Italian, Swedish, Portuguese, Dutch, Greek, Mandarin, Japanese, Russian, Czech, Slovakian, Polish, Cantonese, Afrikaans, Hungarian, Latvian, Hindi, Arabic and Vietnamese.

The recruitment of the very best candidates who are interested in a career at a leading international law firm is a priority for Simmons & Simmons. For further information, please see the firm's website, www.simmons-simmons.com.

AREAS OF PRACTICE

Simmons & Simmons was the only law firm in 2003 to create an entirely new structure for corporate finance work – the virtual bidder structure used for the £2.2bn acquisition of Northumbrian Water Group and the £285m acquisition of Center Parcs UK.

Simmons & Simmons' work has also included: advising INSA to provide the Spanish Ministry of Defence with satellite communications capacity for a value of €360m; advising BP in respect of its participation in the US$2.6bn Caspian Pipeline Consortium project (CPC); advising Vivendi Water UK on its £2bn acquisition of Southern Water; advising a bank syndicate on US$950m financing for an ABU Dhabi power plant; advising BNP Paribas on securitisation of €214.7m of Portuguese and Spanish consumer receivables; advising EIB in connection with a €740m loan to Wind Telecommunicazioni, as part of a €5.5bn financing; advising Nomura International on the listing of Zhejiang Glass Company, raising approximately HK$503.2m; advising PCCW on a series of financings totalling in excess of US$3.2bn.

SLAUGHTER AND MAY

ONE BUNHILL ROW
LONDON EC1Y 8YY

Telephone: +44 20 7600 1200
Fax: +44 20 7090 5000
Website: www.slaughterandmay.com

Other offices
Paris, Brussels, Singapore, Hong Kong, New York

Number of lawyers 569
at this office 481

CATEGORIES OF WORK

Mergers and acquisitions
Stephen Cooke

Corporate and commercial
Nigel Boardman

Financing/financial regulation
Richard Slater, Ruth Fox

Tax
Steve Edge

Competition
Malcolm Nicholson

IP and IT
Nigel Swycher

Technology, media and telecoms
William Underhill, Nigel Swycher

Real estate
Graham White, James Featherby

Environment
Ed Keeble

Dispute resolution
Elizabeth Barrett

Pensions and employment
Eddie Codrington, Philip Bennett

Asset management
James Cripps

Capital markets
Peter Brien, Sanjev Wama-Kula-Suriya

Corporate recovery and insolvency
Jonathan Rushworth

Energy and natural resources
Charles Randall, Christopher Saunders

Insurance
Glen James

Outsourcing
Nigel Swycher

Pharmaceuticals/biotechnology
Frances Murphy

Private equity
Christopher Saul

Projects, project finance, PFI & PPP
Christopher Saunders

Sport
Martin Hattrell, Robert Sumroy

Transport
Simon Robinson

THE FIRM

Slaughter and May is a leading international law firm with a worldwide corporate, commercial and financing practice comprising over 560 partners and associates. The firm provides its clients with a professional service of the highest calibre, combining technical excellence with commercial awareness and a practical, constructive approach to legal issues. The firm's lawyers are encouraged to handle a broad range of work in each of the firm's main practice areas.

International work is central to the firm's practice. Slaughter and May has a diverse and extensive international practice, advising on a wide range of corporate, commercial and financing matters for UK and international clients. The firm has close working relationships with leading independent law firms around the world, which enables it to provide clients with first-class and seamless legal advice worldwide.

AREAS OF PRACTICE

Slaughter and May provides a comprehensive range of legal services. Its main practice groups are corporate and financing (advising on mergers and acquisitions, other corporate and commercial transactions, capital markets, lending, other forms of debt finance, corporate recovery and insolvency and private equity); financial regulation; dispute resolution; technology, media and telecoms; intellectual property and information technology; commercial real estate; environment; corporate tax; competition and pensions and employment. Rather than developing single specialisms, lawyers in the core practice areas are encouraged to adopt a multi-disciplinary approach and the firm is well known for its innovative work.

SQUIRE, SANDERS & DEMPSEY

A MULTINATIONAL PARTNERSHIP OF FOREIGN LAWYERS AND SOLICITORS REGULATED BY THE LAW SOCIETY

ROYEX HOUSE
ALDERMANBURY SQUARE
LONDON EC2V 7HR

Telephone: +44 20 7776 5200
Fax: +44 20 7776 5233
E-mail: ssdinfo_london@ssd.com
Website: www.ssd.com

Languages
Croatian, French, German, Gujarati, Hungarian

Other offices
Beijing, Bratislava, Brussels, Budapest, Cincinnati, Cleveland, Columbus, Hong Kong, Houston, Los Angeles, Madrid, Miami, Milan, Moscow, New York, Palo Alto, Phoenix, Prague, Rio de Janeiro, San Francisco, Taipei, Tampa, Tokyo, Tysons Corner, Washington DC, Bucharest*, Dublin*, Kyiv*

Number of lawyers 710
at this office 19

Contact
Mara Babin

Member
American Chamber of Commerce

CATEGORIES OF WORK

Banking
Stephen Nelson

Capital markets
Martin Walsh

Computer technology, multimedia services
Andrew Wilkinson

Employment
Rebecca Emmet

EU competition law
Brian Hartnett, Andrew Wilkinson

Hospitality
Daniel Larkin, Stephen Nelson

Insolvency, corporate restructurings
Stephen Nelson, Paul Lewis

Intellectual property
Andrew Wilkinson

International dispute resolution
Carol Welu

International transactions
Mark Cusick, Carol Welu

Joint ventures
Mara Babin, Paul Lewis

Mergers and acquisitions
Mara Babin, Stephen Nelson

Private equity
Mara Babin, Daniel Larkin

Privatisations
Richard Surrey, Carol Welu

Project finance
Daniel Larkin

Real estate
Daniel Larkin

Telecoms
Antony Corel, Mark Cusick

THE FIRM

Founded in 1890, Squire, Sanders & Dempsey is a multi-jurisdictional law firm with 710 lawyers practising in offices in Europe, the Americas and Asia. The firm's practice covers most substantive areas of the law, with an emphasis on business and finance matters.

The firm operates as a single global partnership, which ensures client accountability and the seamless delivery of uniformly high-quality legal services throughout the world. The firm's lawyers come from many countries and cultures, are licensed to practise in both common law and civil law jurisdictions, and communicate with clients in their native languages. Today, the firm remains committed to the fundamental principles ordained by its founders: to serve clients effectively and maintain the professional standards that distinguish both the firm and its people.

AREAS OF PRACTICE

The firm is organised around four major practice areas: advocacy, business, capital markets and regulated industries. Within these practice areas, the firm's work can be divided into numerous areas of specialisation, including banking, bankruptcy and restructuring, biotechnology and pharmaceuticals, communications, competition law, converging technologies, corporate, energy, environmental, healthcare, intellectual property, international dispute resolution, labour and employment, litigation, mergers and acquisitions, privatisations, project finance, real estate, securities and taxation.

The London office advises clients on complex international and UK transactions in the communications, technology, real estate, transport, hospitality and leisure, private equity, energy and manufacturing sectors.

Opened in 1992, the London office offers a full set of services to clients investing or doing business in the UK, Europe or globally.

The London lawyers advise corporate and investment banking clients on transactional and commercial matters including cross-border international M&A, privatisations, joint ventures, project finance, real estate, securitisations, international capital markets, due diligence, management buy-outs, company restructuring, reorganisations, infrastructure, international dispute resolution and employment – often in multiple jurisdictions across the world.

An important centre of the firm's international practice, the London office serves the needs of clients with global businesses. Transactions with an international element are often centred in London and frequently require English or US law to govern key contractual relationships. Utilising experienced and sophisticated UK solicitors and US lawyers, the office is well positioned substantively and geographically to respond to the needs of the most complex and significant transactions in which globally-oriented clients engage.

The communications group provides advice on transactional and regulatory matters to cable broadband, telephony, satellite service providers, GSM and other wireless operators, data service and network companies, Internet service providers, private equity investors, investment banks, government agencies and multinational development organisations.

The London office has a particular focus on IT and e-business and handles cross-border IT M&A as well as all other IT and e-business related contracts and arrangements, systems integration, network management and project outsourcing and facilities management contracts.

The property and tourism group represents global corporate and financial groups, private equity investors, and governments in a wide variety of multi-jurisdictional transactions. The group is active with joint ventures, secured financings, acquisitions, disposals, privatisations, mergers and listings, as well as acting on pure real estate transactions involving single assets, new developments and property portfolios.

The employment group counsels clients on all aspects of UK and European employment law. Areas of particular advancement include domestic and international employment contracts, company handbooks, TUPE issues, secondment arrangements, large-scale redundancy programs, stock options and pensions.

STIBBE

EXCHANGE HOUSE
PRIMROSE STREET
LONDON EC2A 2ST

Telephone: +44 20 7466 6300
Fax: +44 20 7466 6311
E-mail: info@stibbe.co.uk
Website: www.stibbe.com

Languages
English, Dutch

Other offices
Amsterdam, Brussels, New York

Number of lawyers 309
at this office 5

Contact
Michael Molenaars

CATEGORIES OF WORK

Litigation and arbitration	Employment
Mergers and acquisitions	Tax
Equity capital markets	Administrative and public law, real estate
Finance and banking	EU, competition and regulation
Telecoms and IT	Intellectual property

STUDIO LEGALE SUTTI

19 PRINCES STREET
LONDON W1B 2LW

Telephone: +44 20 7409 1384
Fax: +44 20 7493 3395
E-mail: maildesk@sutti.com
Website: www.sutti.com

Languages
Bulgarian, Dutch, French, German, Italian, Japanese, Portuguese, Romanian, Serbian, Spanish

Other offices
Belgrade, Bucharest, Genoa, Milan, Rome, Sofia, Tokyo

Number of lawyers 130
at this office 3

Contact
Livia Oglio

CATEGORIES OF WORK

Company, commercial law	White-collar crime
Banking and finance	EC, competition and antitrust law
Mergers and acquisitions	IT and TLC law
Distribution, agency and franchising	Litigation and arbitration
Debt collection and insolvency	Employment, labour law
Commercial property law	Administrative law
Intellectual property	Environmental law
Patent and trade mark agency service	

TAYLOR WESSING

CARMELITE
50 VICTORIA EMBANKMENT
BLACKFRIARS
LONDON EC4Y 0DX

Telephone: +44 20 7300 7000
Fax: +44 20 7300 7100
E-mail: london@taylorwessing.com
Website: www.taylorwessing.com

Languages
Arabic, English, French, German, Greek, Gujarati, Hebrew, Indonesian, Italian, Malay, Portuguese, Punjabi, Spanish, Romanian, Russian

Number of lawyers 550
at this office 299

Contacts
Gary Moss (UK managing partner), Richard Marsh (senior partner)

Member
Interlex, Unilaw

CATEGORIES OF WORK

Corporate finance
Tim Eyles, Tim Stocks

Property, real estate
Adam Marks

Dispute resolution and arbitration
Michael Frawley

Banking, securities and finance
Rodney Dukes

Pharmaceuticals and biotechnology
David Kent, Mark Hodgson

Intellectual property
Gary Moss, Charles Lloyd

Entertainment, media
Paul Mitchell

Private equity
Simon Walker, Martin Winter

Competition, trade and regulation
Martin Baker

Tax and personal planning
Mark Buzzoni

Employment and pensions
Andrew Granger

Sport
Charles Lloyd

IT/Internet/e-commerce
Glyn Morgan, David Kent

Telecoms
Ted Mercer

Projects/PFI
Dominic Fitzpatrick, Hamid Yunis

Construction and engineering
Neil White

THE FIRM

Taylor Wessing is a powerful source of legal support for organisations doing business in or with Europe and is based primarily in the UK, Germany and France, with further offices in Brussels, Dubai, Shanghai and Alicante. A market leader in advising IP and technology-rich industries, Taylor Wessing boasts a strong reputation in the corporate, finance and real estate sectors alongside in-depth experience across the full range of legal services including tax, commercial disputes and employment.

Taylor Wessing has offices in Berlin, Brussels, Cambridge, Düsseldorf, Frankfurt, Hamburg, London, Munich and Paris, alongside representative offices in Alicante and Shanghai and an associated office in Dubai.

AREAS OF PRACTICE

Taylor Wessing offers a comprehensive list of legal services. Client matters are dealt with by specialist practice groups, which bring together expertise from a number of disciplines to speed response, explore opportunities, and reduce time and expense.

The firm operates through seven core areas, including:

Corporate/commercial, which places particular emphasis on corporate finance, M&A, environmental law, EC/EU law and corporate tax.

Intellectual property, one of the largest practices in Europe, where its highly regarded team includes specialists in entertainment, media, life sciences, telecoms, e-commerce, sports and information technology.

Finance and projects, which has particular expertise in project finance (advising leading sponsors and finance providers on project and structured finance in a wide range of sectors), energy, PFI, property finance, banking and bank lending.

Commercial litigation, with specialist groups advising on personal injury, fraud, construction and engineering, professional negligence and shipping, banking and corporate recoveries, advising clearing, merchant and foreign banks.

Employment, dealing with related contracts and disputes, pensions and employee benefits.

Real estate, including development and finance, incorporating specialist planning, property management and environmental teams.

Private client, providing advice on taxation, wills and settlements (including trusts and estates), matrimonial law and residential property.

TROWERS & HAMLINS

SCEPTRE COURT
40 TOWER HILL
LONDON EC3N 4DX

Telephone: +44 20 7423 8000
Fax: +44 20 7423 8001
E-mail: enquiries@trowers.com
Website: www.trowers.com

Languages
Arabic, French, German, Italian, Russian

Other offices
Abu Dhabi, Bahrain, Cairo, Dubai, Exeter, Manchester, Muscat

Number of lawyers 220
at this office 174

International groupings
Co-operation agreements with firms in Qatar (Hassan Al-Khater); Yemen (Dr Abdulla Maktari) and Jordan (Abdul Karim, J Al Fauri & Associates); The International Law Office Dr Behrooz Akhlagi & Associates (Iran); The firm works with Ledingham Chalmers in Azerbaijan and Istanbul; contacts in USA and Europe: Winstead Sechrest & Minnick (Texas); associated with Ann Tan & Associates (Singapore)

CATEGORIES OF WORK

Banking and finance
Andrew Rae, Neale Downes

Capital markets
Sean Angle, Majid Al Toky

Commercial agencies and distribution
Jennifer Bibbings, Nick White

Commercial law
Martin Amison, Nick White

Islamic finance
Nicholas Edmondes, Sarah Gooden

IT law
Adrian Creed, Majid Al Toky

Oil, gas, and petrochemicals
Edward Rose, Adrian Creed

Power and water
Martin Amison, Adrian Creed

Privatisation
Martin Amison

Project finance
Martin Amison, Andrew Rae

Tax
Nicholas Edmondes

Trade marks
Majid Al Toky

Litigation, arbitration
John Linwood, Majid Al Toky

THE FIRM

Trowers & Hamlins is an international law firm with its head office in the City of London and offices in the UK and overseas. Over the last 40 years it has developed a substantial international practice, with five offices in the Middle East – Abu Dhabi, Bahrain, Cairo, Dubai and Oman – as well as a number of active co-operation agreements with law firms in Qatar, Yemen and Jordan. The firm has been working in the Middle East region since 1959 and currently has 37 lawyers (including ten partners) working in its five regional offices. It also has an associated office in Singapore, contacts in the USA and in Europe, and works with Ledingham Chalmers in Azerbaijan and Istanbul. The firm's head office in London acts as the nucleus for the network of international offices and for the international projects, public international and private finance practice.

AREAS OF PRACTICE

The firm has been involved in a number of high-profile projects. Work handled includes a significant number of major projects, banking and finance (including Islamic finance), capital markets and commercial transactions. The firm is advising the government of Jordan on a large-scale gas pipeline project and continues to lead in the Middle East region in its participation in independent power and water projects; recently advising the developer of the latest IWPP in Abu Dhabi at Umm Al Nar and having also advised as sole external counsel the joint developers of the Shuweihat S1 IWPP (CMS Energy of the US and International Power of the UK) and the developer (CMS Energy) of the Taweelah A2 IWPP, as well as having advised upon all of the successful power projects in Oman at Manah (two phases), Barka, Al Kamil and Salalah; involvement in a number of major infrastructure projects in the region; advising the developer of a proposed water pipeline project between Iran and Kuwait; advising Salalah Port Services Company SAOG on the original concession agreement and related project documentation for the development of a strategic container trans-shipment terminal in the south of Oman (the initial private sector operated and financed project has been enhanced by a further 30-year concession agreement for the operation and management of the port's conventional cargo facilities); advising the project company sponsors on the establishment, a free trade zone adjacent to the port; acted as lead counsel (international and local) for Borealis A/S in all aspects of the development and financing of the Abu Dhabi Polymers Company (Borouge), a global scale petrochemicals joint venture with ADNOC valued in excess of US$1bn.

The firm has acted for the lenders on US$1.1bn Oman India Fertiliser Plant (OMIFCO) and on a considerable number of aircraft financings for regional carriers. The firm is retained as counsel by a regional airline. It also advises two of the region's central banks and has done considerable work for investment funds and institutions employing both Islamic and conventional finance. The firm has also acted during the year on major leisure sector acquisitions for a regional investor and has acted for a number of Islamic funds on property investments in Europe. The firm has considerably increased its business in the Middle East during 2003 and has expanded its complement of lawyers within the international department to 46.

ADVOKATFIRMAN VINGE

42 NEW BROAD STREET
LONDON EC2M 1JD

Telephone: +44 20 7920 3000
Fax: +44 20 7920 3099
Website: www.vinge.se

Languages
Spanish, Swedish

Other Offices
Brussels, Gothenburg, Helsingborg, Hong Kong, Malmö, Paris, Shanghai, Stockholm

Number of lawyers 262
at this office 3

Contact
Maria-Pia Midenbäck-Hope

Member
Scandinavian Law Alliance with Kromann & Reumert (Denmark) and Thommessen (Norway); Lex Mundi

CATEGORIES OF WORK	
Corporate finance	Telecoms
Mergers and acquisitions	Litigation
Corporate	Environmental
Capital markets	Real estate
EU and antitrust	Tax
Intellectual property	Insolvency and restructuring
IT	Insurance
Media	Employment
Marketing	Transport

THE FIRM

Established through a merger between leading Swedish firms in 1983, Vinge is today one of the largest firms in Scandinavia, with some 262 lawyers in nine Swedish and overseas offices. In 1991, the firm set up the Scandinavian Law Alliance together with the Danish law firm Kromann Reumert and the Norwegian firm Thommessen. Vinge is also a member of Lex Mundi.

AREAS OF PRACTICE

Vinge has a substantial international practice, with a strategic focus on M&A and corporate finance. The firm has acted in most of the major mergers and acquisitions in Sweden in recent years, and has consistently achieved top positions on *Merger Market*'s list of M&A advisers in the Nordic market. The firm regularly represents clients in connection with large international financing transactions, including project financing and structured finance arrangements. Vinge's competition law team is one of the most distinguished and experienced in the Nordic markets. A full-service firm, Vinge also advises domestic and international clients within a number of specialist areas such as employment, intellectual property, IT, media marketing, property, telecoms, litigation and arbitration, insolvency, insurance, tax, and transport. In addition to four offices in Sweden, the firm has a presence in London, Paris, Brussels, Hong Kong and Shanghai.

VINSON & ELKINS RLLP

**CITY POINT 33RD FLOOR
ONE ROPEMAKER STREET
LONDON EC2Y 9UE**

Telephone: +44 20 7065 6000
Fax: +44 20 7065 6001
Website: www.velaw.com

Languages
French, German, Russian, Spanish

Other offices
Austin, Beijing, Dallas, Dubai, Houston, Moscow, New York, Singapore, Washington DC

Number of lawyers 775

Member
International Bar Association; International Law Section of the American Bar Association; International Lawyers Group, Moscow; Law Society of England and Wales; The Bar of England and Wales; The State Bar of Texas International Law Section

CATEGORIES OF WORK

Asset finance/securitisation
Jeff Eldredge

Banking and finance
Christopher Clement-Davies, Lewis Jones

Capital markets
Jeff Eldredge

Construction
Doug Glass, Stephen York

Corporate and commercial
Jeff Eldredge, John LaMaster

Dispute resolution
Stephen York, Shai Wade

Energy and natural resources
Doug Glass, John LaMaster

Infrastructure/project finance
Christopher Clement-Davies, John LaMaster

Labour law
Chris Prior, Lewis Jones

Mergers and acquisitions
Jeff Eldredge, John LaMaster

Privatisation
Christopher Clement-Davies, Doug Glass

Telecommunications
Chris Prior, Lewis Jones

WEIL, GOTSHAL & MANGES

ONE SOUTH PLACE
LONDON EC2M 2WG

Telephone: + 44 20 7903 1000
Fax: + 44 20 7903 0990
E-mail: weil.london@weil.com
Website: www.weil.com

Other offices
Austin, Boston, Brussels, Budapest, Dallas, Frankfurt, Houston, Miami, Munich, New York, Paris, Prague, Silicon Valley, Singapore, Warsaw, Washington DC

Number of lawyers 1,000
at this office 108

Contacts
Mike Francies, Paul Claydon, Jacky Kelly

CATEGORIES OF WORK	
Acquisition finance	**IP, technology and communications**
Banking	**Litigation, arbitration**
Biotech and pharmaceuticals	**Private equity and venture capital**
Competition	**Property**
Consumer finance	**Restructuring**
Corporate finance and M&A	**Securitisation**
Debt and equity capital markets	**Taxation**

THE FIRM

Established in 1931 in New York, Weil, Gotshal & Manges combines lawyers worldwide to meet clients' needs in recognition of the benefits of broad industry and regional experience. The lawyers in the firm's practice groups work together to provide full-service legal advice to clients in sectors as diverse as energy, financial services and hi-tech.

The firm developed a network of offices across the US in the 1970s and 1980s to cater for its expanding client base, and was one of the first international law firms to establish a major presence in central Europe. The firm now has established offices in Brussels, Budapest, Frankfurt, London, Paris, Prague, Singapore and Warsaw.

The firm advises a broad and diverse group of clients, including many of the largest and most prominent corporations and government agencies around the globe, and leading financial institutions.

AREAS OF PRACTICE

The firm's US and European antitrust practice advises on international M&A regulatory notifications, antitrust distribution counselling, cartels, litigation and government and state competition policy. Expertise includes software and computer, healthcare, telecommunications and media, transportation, utilities, heavy industry, consumer goods, financial services and sports.

The corporate department is the firm's largest. The department advises international financial institutions and corporate clients in complex public and private M&As, private equity deals and strategic alliances.

The firm's corporate governance practice is recognised as one of the pre-eminent counsellors of corporate boards, management and institutional investors on the full range of governance issues, including board composition, structure and processes; executive and director compensation; director responsibilities; internal and governmental investigations of alleged accounting or other corporate misconduct; and shareholder initiatives. The firm has advised the World Bank, the OECD, the European Commission and various stock exchanges and regulatory bodies, and is a leader in providing director training programmes worldwide.

The firm advises on a wide range of financing activities and has particular expertise in acquisition finance, asset-based finance, debt restructuring and insolvency, debt and equity capital markets, derivatives, high-yield debt, securitisation, structured finance and telecoms and multimedia financing.

The firm has a leading IP and technology practice and advises some of the world's major technology, media and telecommunications companies. It also acts for investors in technology, media and communications entities. The practice handles patent infringements, outsourcing transactions, strategic alliances, cross-border mergers and acquisitions, investments and IPOs, and advises on the protection and exploitation of IP and on a wide range of e-commerce matters, including data protection. It has expertise in regulatory telecoms matters.

The litigation practice advises international clients on all major areas of the law and has extensive experience in all aspects of dispute resolution. It advises clients in jury trials and appeals, arbitration and alternative dispute forums.

The firm's real estate practice handles complex real estate transactions (including finance, securitisations, development, leasing, sales, acquisitions and debt restructurings) across the US and Europe. It also advises clients on real estate M&A transactions involving real estate investment trusts.

The firm has one of the largest bankruptcy and business reorganisation practices in the world. It includes attorneys in New York, Boston, Dallas, Frankfurt, Houston, London and Miami. The department has been involved in virtually all of the major chapter 11 reorganisation cases in the US and in major national and international out-of-court debt restructurings.

The tax department provides advice on international and domestic taxation, covering many different economic sectors. The department works with the firm's other departments to find innovative solutions to problems that present various and competing multi-disciplinary considerations.

WHITE & CASE

7-11 MOORGATE
LONDON EC2R 6HH

Telephone: + 44 20 7600 7300
Fax: +44 20 7600 7030
Website: www.whitecase.com

Languages
Extensive language capabilities

Other offices
Almaty, Ankara, Bangkok, Berlin, Bratislava, Brussels, Budapest, Dresden, Düsseldorf, Frankfurt, Hamburg, Helsinki, Ho Chi Minh City, Hong Kong, Istanbul, Johannesburg, Los Angeles, Mexico City, Miami, Milan, Moscow, New York, Palo Alto, Paris, Prague, Riyadh, Rome, San Francisco, São Paulo, Shanghai, Sinagpore, Stockholm, Tokyo, Warsaw, Washington DC

Number of lawyers 1,770
at this office 176

CATEGORIES OF WORK

Arbitration
John Bellhouse, Stephen Bond (Paris)

Asset financing and leasing
Justin Benson, Thomas McDonald (Paris)

Bank finance
Maurice Allen, Gilles Peigney (Paris)

Bankruptcy and workouts
Dan Hamilton, Klaus Pannen (Hamburg)

Capital markets
Francis Fritzherbert-Brockholes, Petri Haussila (Helsinki)

Commercial litigation
Alistair Graham

Construction
Ellis Baker, Christopher Seppala (Paris)

Corporate, M&A
Peter Finlay, Andreas Stilcken (Frankfurt)

Energy, infrastructure and project finance
Philip Stopford, Paule Biensan (Paris)

Employment
Oliver Brettle

EU and competition
Pontus Lindfelt (Brussels), Jacquelyn MacLennan (Brussels)

IP
David Llewelyn, Christian Rohnke (Hamburg)

Private equity
Peter Finlay, Vincent Morin (Paris)

Privatisation
Peter Finlay, David Eisenberg

Real estate
Lorraine Ufland, Endrick Lettau (Berlin)

Structured finance
Richard Reilly

Tax
Neil Woodgate, Josef Große Honebrink (Frankfurt)

Telecoms and technology
David Eisenberg, Rolf Olofsson (Stockholm)

THE FIRM

White & Case was founded in 1901 and now has over 1,700 lawyers – 820 in Europe, 750 in the Americas and 200 in Asia. The firm has 37 offices in 26 countries throughout Europe, the US, Middle East, Asia, Africa and Latin America. Its practice encompasses the full range of international finance and corporate law disciplines. The firm has offices in Almaty, Ankara, Bangkok, Berlin, Bombay, Bratislava, Brussels, Budapest, Dresden, Düsseldorf, Frankfurt, Hamburg, Helsinki, Ho Chi Minh City, Hong Kong, Istanbul, Jakarta, Johannesburg, London, Los Angeles, Mexico City, Miami, Milan, Moscow, New York, Palo Alto, Paris, Prague, Riyadh, Rome, San Francisco, São Paulo, Shanghai, Sinagpore, Stockholm, Tokyo, Warsaw and Washington DC.

AREAS OF PRACTICE

Antitrust: The firm has successfully defended mergers before the US Department of Justice, the Federal Trade Commission and the European Commission, as well as various regulatory bodies across Asia.

Arbitration: The firm has long-standing experience of arbitrations worldwide (including, in particular, ICC arbitrations), and has successfully concluded disputes in most arbitration forums around the globe.

Asset financing and leasing: White & Case has one of the strongest global asset finance practice of any law firm, with highly regarded teams across Europe, the Americas and Asia.

Bank finance: The firm is acknowledged to be a world leader in the field of bank finance, with a unique US, English, European and Asian legal capability.

Bankruptcy and workouts: The firm has wide experience in multinational insolvencies and a strong practice in restructurings.

Capital markets: White & Case has a formidable reputation in the field on international securities and finance.

Commercial litigation: Most of the firm's 37 offices offer leading commercial litigators who excel at both local and cross-border work.

Construction: White & Case has a full-service international practice covering all aspects of major corporate transactions from taxation to financings for both public and private businesses.

Employment: The firm has an experienced employment practice group with particular expertise in employee benefits law.

Energy, infrastructure and project finance: The firm is recognised as one of the world's leading providers of project finance, energy and infrastructure law advice in all the major jurisdictions.

EU and competition: The firm's EU law team is renowned for its expert handling of matters before the European Commission involving the full range of industry sectors.

IP: White & Case acts to protect the IP rights of its clients through the work of its IP law teams across the globe.

M&A and joint ventures: The firm has taken the lead in devising creative deal structures and acquisition programmes in the full range of domestic and cross-border transactions.

Privatisation: The global privatisation practice group has acted for governments, state-owned enterprises, multi-lateral institutions, international banks and investors.

Real estate: The firm advises on the assemblage, acquisition, development, ownership, operation and financing of all types of real estate assets.

Securitisation and structured finance: The firm played a leading role in the development of a range of structured products and the securitisations of a wide range of asset classes.

Sovereign: White & Case has represented an extremely large number of countries in sovereign-related projects.

Tax: The firm acts on a wide range of corporate and financial transactions, develops tax-advantaged financial products and helps multinational clients achieve worldwide tax efficiency.

Telecoms and technology: The firm offers a full service to clients in the e-commerce, media and technology sectors.

WIKBORG REIN

ONE KNIGHTRIDER COURT
LONDON EC4V 5JP

Telephone: +44 20 7236 4598
Fax: +44 20 7236 4599
E-mail: london@wr.no
Website: www.wr.no

Languages
English, the Scandinavian languages

Other offices
Bergen, Kobe, Oslo, Shanghai, Singapore

Number of lawyers 156
at this office 5

Contacts
Morten Lund Mathisen, Beate Mjaaland, Martin Nes

CATEGORIES OF WORK

Shipping/offshore

Marine law/transport/marine insurance

Ship financing/banking

Natural resources

Energy and petroleum law

Trade/industry

Corporate finance

Competition law (including EU and EEA law)

WILLKIE FARR & GALLAGHER LLP

1 ANGEL COURT
LONDON EC2R 7HJ

Telephone: +44 20 7696 5454
Fax: +44 20 7696 5455
Website: www.willkie.com

Other offices
New York, Washington DC, Paris, Milan, Rome, Frankfurt, Brussels

Number of lawyers 560
at this office 2

Contact
Gregory Astrachan

CATEGORIES OF WORK

Corporate and financial services
Gregory Astrachan

WILMER CUTLER PICKERING LLP

4 CARLTON GARDENS
LONDON SWIY 5AA

Telephone: +44 20 7872 1000
Fax: +44 20 7839 3537
E-mail: law@wilmer.com
Website: www.wilmer.com

Languages
Afrikaans, Farsi, French, German, Hindi, Italian, Persian, Russian, Sindhi, Spanish, Swedish

Other offices
Baltimore, Berlin, Brussels, New York, N Virginia, Washington DC

Number of lawyers 545
at this office 39

CATEGORIES OF WORK

Aviation
Dieter Lange, Michael Holter

Company and commercial
James Greig, Michael Holter

Corporate transactions
James Greig, Michael Holter

Competition, merger control and EU law
Suyong Kim

Investment funds
Simon Firth

International arbitration and litigation
Gary Born, David Capps

Private equity and venture capital
Gerry Cater

Telecommunications
Stephanie Liston, Paul von Hehn

Energy
Dieter Lange, Gerry Cater

Financial services regulation
James Greig, David Capps

Financial services investigations
David Capps

UNITED KINGDOM: NORTHERN IRELAND

Population	1.6 million
Number of lawyers	2,870 (2,300 solicitors; 570 barristers)
Professional title	barrister; solicitor
Currency	Pound Sterling (£)

Index

Northern Ireland's six counties are Down and Armagh in the south-east, Londonderry and Antrim in the north, and Tyrone and Fermanagh in the west. Two-thirds of the Province's population live within 50 kilometres of the capital, Belfast.

The Province has been ruled directly from London since the suspension of the Northern Ireland Assembly in October 2002. In the election which took place in November 2003, the Democratic Unionist Party overtook the Ulster Unionists to become the largest party in the assembly, with 30 seats out of 108. At the time of going to press, the DUP was expressing a desire to renegotiate the Good Friday Agreement and refusing to share power with Sinn Fein, and talks were underway in an effort to resolve the deadlock.

BILLING

Partner rates vary widely and peak at around £220 per hour. Though the hourly rate is still predominant, an increasing amount of work is awarded on a tender basis, and different fee bases, including fixed fees and capped fees, are becoming more common.

MARKETING

The majority of legal work in the Province continues to be gained through word-of-mouth, although beauty parades are increasingly common. Most firms have a website, as well as publishing brochures or newsletters.

IN-HOUSE LAWYERS

Of the few in-house lawyers in Northern Ireland, the majority are to be found in the public sector.

ECONOMIC CLIMATE

Northern Ireland's economy grew faster than any other region of the UK in the 1990s; the decade saw a 47.7% rise in manufacturing output and a huge rise in inward investment. The pace of investment has slowed significantly since 2001, in line with the global economic downturn, although the economy has managed to escape both recession and severe job losses. GDP is forecast to grow by around 2.5% in 2003, with an increase to around 3% as public and private sector investment and activity expand. Recent reports have identified an increasing 'east-west' gap between Greater Belfast and the rest of the Province, in terms of employment levels, job quality and general prosperity.

LEGAL SYSTEM

Northern Ireland is a distinct legal jurisdiction, and its laws are largely based on the laws of England and Wales. However, certain laws are directly applicable in the Province and in certain cases, for example in the area of property law, they differ significantly from their equivalents across the water.

LEGAL MARKET

A number of ties are in place between the larger Belfast and Dublin firms. **L'Estrange & Brett** has been allied with **McCann FitzGerald** since 1999 (the *North South Legal Alliance*), while **Tughans** is closely tied with **William Fry**. **Cleaver Fulton Rankin** established the *All Island Law Alliance* with **Matheson Ormsby Prentice** in 2002. The situation with the other two 'Big Five' Dublin firms - **A&L Goodbody** and **Arthur Cox** - is different; the former's alliance with **Elliott Duffy Garrett** was broken off in 2002, while **Arthur Cox** has a relatively hands-off relationship with its autonomously structured and managed Belfast counterpart, **Arthur Cox Northern Ireland**. The other Belfast-Dublin alliances are **C & H Jefferson**'s 'best friends' relationship with **Eugene F Collins**, in place since 2002, and **Carson McDowell**'s *i-law alliance* with **Mason Hayes & Curran.**

A number of English and Scottish firms have a profile in the market, alongside **A&L Goodbody**, which runs all of its Northern Ireland work from Dublin. **Travers Smith Braithwaite** runs a significant commercial property practice in the Province from its London office, while **Bird & Bird**, **Dickinson Dees** and **Berwin Leighton Paisner** have all been involved in the local PPP market.

English insurance specialist **Kennedys** has for many years had a litigation-based practice in Belfast, and **Thompsons McClure** is the associate office of English personal injury firm **Thompsons**. Scottish firm **McGrigors** has had an office in the capital since 2000; its initial focus was PFI work but the firm has since expanded its practice into other areas.

The largest firms

1	Carson McDowell	42
2	L'Estrange & Brett	36
3	Tughans	30
4	Elliott Duffy Garrett	26
5	McKinty and Wright	25
6	C & H Jefferson	24
	Cleaver Fulton Rankin	24
8	Arthur Cox Northern Ireland	20
9	Wilson Nesbitt	19
10	Mills Selig	18
11	John McKee & Sons	15
12	Diamond Heron	12
	McCartan Turkington & Breen	12
14	Babington & Croasdaile	11
	Hewitt & Gilpin	11
16	Johns Elliot	10
17	Kearney Sefton	8
18	Francis Hanna & Co	7
	Napier and Sons	7
20	Bigger & Strahan	6
	Comerton Hill	6
	McGrigors	6
23	Morrow & Wells	5
24	C & J Black	4
	Jones & Cassidy	4

These figures represent the total number of lawyers in this country only, and have been supplied by the firms themselves. The figures should be accurate as at 1 January 2004.

BANKING AND FINANCE

Arthur Cox Northern Ireland's banking group is headed by Angus Creed, who earlier in his career worked for over ten years as in-house counsel to the Bank of Ireland. The firm recently acted for a syndicate of banks in relation to the £32.5m refinancing of an international group of companies, and advised banks on a series of facilities relating to share purchases that involved financial assistance.

John McKee & Sons has an outstanding reputation for its banking work, with both Lex Ross and Avril McCammon highly recommended. The firm advises on the full range of secured lending for Northern Ireland's main clearing banks, as well as advising on the financing side of PFI work.

Brian Henderson is **L'Estrange & Brett**'s key banking specialist, while corporate partners Richard Gray and Paul McBride are also active in the field and Adrian Eakin, who specialises in banking and projects work, was made partner in March 2003. The firm advised nursing home provider BetterCare Group Ltd on its £33m bank debt refinancing and associated equity restructuring, and acted on the local aspects of Royal Bank of Canada's funding package for the acquisition of Belfast City Airport by Spanish group Ferrovial. The firm also has long-standing experience on securitisations, and regularly advises on the local aspects of programmes involving Northern Irish assets.

C & H Jefferson has developed a strong banking practice on the back of its property work, recently advising clients such as First Trust Bank, Bank of Ireland and Ulster Bank. It acted for a syndicate of banks on the financing of the Sprucefield Shopping Centre, which is the largest out-of-town shopping centre in Northern Ireland.

Carson McDowell has recently acted on a number of significant refinancings, including advising AES (NI) Ltd in relation to the £950m refinancing of the AES Group. Tom Adair, who heads the group, is recommended.

Cleaver Fulton Rankin's banking team is headed by Stephen Cross. Recent work includes advising, alongside **Matheson Ormsby Prentice**, IIB Bank plc and KBC Finance Ireland on the £19m refinancing of Altahullion Windfarm, County Londonderry, and acting for the issuer on the securitisation of a number of Rotch properties (including Riverside Tower in Belfast).

Elliott Duffy Garrett has a good reputation for its corporate lending work, and partner Kevin McVeigh is particularly recommended.

John Mills at **Tughans** is experienced in advising on secured and unsecured lending, and advises a range of financial institutions and borrowers.

BANKING AND FINANCE

ARTHUR COX NORTHERN IRELAND ✪
JOHN McKEE & SONS ✪
L'ESTRANGE & BRETT ✪

C & H Jefferson ✪
Carson McDowell
Cleaver Fulton Rankin
Elliott Duffy Garrett
Tughans

Babington & Croasdaile
Johns Elliot
McGrigors
McKinty and Wright
Mills Selig

Firms are listed A-Z in tiers which are ranked in order of priority
✪ Indicates firm displays contact details at the end of this chapter.

CORPORATE AND COMMERCIAL

Michael Johnston heads **Carson McDowell**'s corporate and commercial department, which advised Viridian on the sale of its majority shareholding in Shop Electric, and Montgomery Transport Ltd (a subsidiary of Ballyvesey Holdings Ltd) on its acquisition of Dukes Transport (Craigavon) Ltd. The firm also acted for Taiwanese listed company Ritek on its £28m investment in Remedia. Partner David Jamison is recommended for his M&A work.

L'Estrange & Brett's corporate team is headed by the highly regarded John Irvine. The firm advised Lakeland Dairies on its acquisition of LE Pritchitt & Company's milk manufacturing business, and Readymix plc on the Northern Irish element of its acquisition of Farrans' Breton and Breton Rocrete concrete products business. On the private equity side, recent clients include Amphion Semiconductor Ltd and EZ-DSP. The firm also advised leading healthcare technology provider Randox Laboratories on its expansion programme, which included funding from Invest Northern Ireland of £18m. Partners Richard Gray and Paul McBride are also recommended. The firm has nevertheless been depleted by the loss of four associates in 2003, including (on the corporate side) Mark Thompson to **Arthur Cox Northern Ireland** and Sarah Burrows to **John McKee & Sons**.

Kerry Canavan is the sole partner in **Arthur Cox Northern Ireland**'s corporate and commercial group, which was strengthened in March 2003 by the arrival of Mark Thompson as senior associate, from **L'Estrange & Brett**. The firm recently acted for the management team in the MBO of Tyrone Crystal, and advised the Musgrave Group on a significant range of acquisitions, disposals and franchises of supermarket businesses. On the private equity side, the firm acted for a local venture capital fund on investments in R&D and university spin-out companies in the IT sector.

Cleaver Fulton Rankin has a three-partner corporate and commercial team, headed by Jennifer Ebbage. On the commercial side, the firm advised Hewlett-Packard as main sub-contractor to Fujitsu on the Causeway Programme, a major

CORPORATE AND COMMERCIAL

CARSON MCDOWELL
L'ESTRANGE & BRETT ✪

ARTHUR COX NORTHERN IRELAND ✪
CLEAVER FULTON RANKIN
MILLS SELIG
TUGHANS

C & H JEFFERSON ✪
ELLIOTT DUFFY GARRETT

JOHN MCKEE & SONS ✪
JOHNS ELLIOT
McGRIGORS
McKINTY AND WRIGHT

Babington & Croasdaile
Dickson & McNulty
McCartan Turkington & Breen
Napier and Sons
R M Cullen & Son
Wilson Nesbitt

Bigger & Strahan
Comerton Hill
Fisher & Fisher
O'Reilly Stewart Solicitors
Thompson Mitchell

Firms are listed A-Z in tiers which are ranked in order of priority
✪ Indicates firm displays contact details at the end of this chapter.

government IT project (on which **Tughans** advised Fujitsu). The firm is on the panel of solicitors for Invest Northern Ireland, which it has recently advised on a number of equity investments in Northern Irish companies.

Mills Selig maintains a strong reputation for its corporate work, and has particular experience in the retail and pharmaceuticals sectors. Richard Fulton is recommended.

Tughans' recent headline corporate work includes advising Monaghan Mushrooms on its disposal of Pleroma Distribution Ltd, and advising the management team on the MBO of Smtek Europe Ltd. John-George Willis leads the group and has a strong reputation; it also includes a new partner in Neasa Quigley, who moved to **Tughans** from associate firm **William Fry** in Dublin in 2001 and was made up in April 2003.

C & H Jefferson's commercial work is handled by Mark Tinman. Clients include a number of banks and high street retailers, and the firm also receives some referral work from its association with Dublin firm **Eugene F Collins**.

Elliott Duffy Garrett's wide-ranging corporate and commercial practice advises both domestic and international clients, and partner Kevin McVeigh in particular is recommended.

Lex Ross and Avril McCammon at **John McKee & Sons** are both recommended.

Johns Elliot's corporate practice is headed by managing partner Maurice Butler and has extensive experience in company reconstructions, M&A and MBOs.

Scottish firm **McGrigors** has had a presence in Belfast since 2000 and has succeeded in establishing a good reputation for its corporate work on the back of its PFI experience for which it remains best known.

McKinty and Wright is primarily a defence litigation firm but also has a solid corporate and commercial practice headed by Eric Boyd.

DISPUTE RESOLUTION

C & H Jefferson has one of Northern Ireland's largest litigation teams, with five partners and nine other fee-earners. The department has strong experience on a wide range of litigation (including employer's liability, medical negligence and road traffic liability) and is largely focussed on insurance defence work, advising a number of leading UK composite insurers, international insurance companies and Lloyd's syndicates.

Carson McDowell's litigation practice is headed by Brian Turtle, who is very highly regarded for professional negligence and contentious employment work. The firm also has a strong reputation for construction litigation, in which partner Peter Davison specialises. Medical negligence expert Kenneth Gouk retired in early 2003.

Elliott Duffy Garrett has a strong commercial litigation practice, with experience in a range of areas including construction, product liability and defamation. The team is headed by Michael Lynch.

Kennedys is an English insurance specialist, which established a Belfast presence largely in response to the needs of London's insurance market. Sean Craig is the sole partner based at the Belfast office, and is highly regarded. Areas of expertise include professional indemnity, clinical negligence and construction.

L'Estrange & Brett's litigation group is led by three well-regarded partners in Adam Brett, Sam Beckett and David Kirkpatrick, and has experience on a wide range of matters, including agency, distribution and partnership disputes, corporate litigation, and professional negligence claims. The firm has recently been involved in a series of construction arbitrations and adjudications, and has some experience of handling mediation.

Senior partner John Cross heads **McKinty and Wright**'s ten-partner litigation team. The practice has experience in a wide range of areas, and is primarily focussed on insurance defence work.

Paul Spring at **Mills Selig** is a specialist in defamation defence work, while Adam Currie is an expert on contentious employment matters.

Tughans has five litigation partners in its Belfast office, including senior partner and department head Michael Gibson and managing partner Grahame Loughlin. The firm advises on a broad range of areas, including insurance defence litigation and construction and corporate disputes. Recent highlights include representing Axor (UK) Ltd in a major adjudication arising in relation to the development of Belfast City Airport. Defence litigation specialist Kathy McGillie and commercial litigator Michael McCord were both made up as partners in 2003.

DISPUTE RESOLUTION

C & H JEFFERSON ✪
CARSON MCDOWELL
ELLIOTT DUFFY GARRETT
KENNEDYS
L'ESTRANGE & BRETT ✪
McKINTY AND WRIGHT
MILLS SELIG
TUGHANS

Arthur Cox Northern Ireland ✪
Babington & Croasdaile
Cleaver Fulton Rankin
Fisher & Fisher
Johns Elliot

Napier and Sons
O'Reilly Stewart Solicitors
Thompsons McClure

Firms are listed A-Z in tiers which are ranked in order of priority
✪ Indicates firm displays contact details at the end of this chapter.

Arthur Cox Northern Ireland's two-partner group is headed by Peter Martin, and has experience in a variety of areas such as professional negligence (including medical defence) disputes, freight transport disputes and commercial litigation. The firm also acts for P&I clubs, and recently arbitrated for a substantial maritime insurer in relation to the complete loss of a vessel and injury to crew members.

Babington & Croasdaile is active on defence litigation and contentious employment work.

Cleaver Fulton Rankin's litigation team is headed by William Cross. It advises on a wide range of areas including employer's and public liability and commercial litigation. The other partners in the team are Patrick O'Driscoll and Brendan Fox, who has experience on professional negligence and construction claims.

Fisher & Fisher is a niche litigation firm that specialises in personal injury work, including handling asbestos claims.

Johns Elliot's litigation work reflects the firm's strong business and property focus, with areas of expertise including land disputes, mortgage repossessions and commercial litigation. Partner Ronnie Robertson leads the firm's niche defamation defence practice.

EMPLOYMENT

Carson McDowell's employment practice is led by the highly-regarded litigator Brian Turtle, while the firm is also strong on the transactional support side, including advising on TUPE and redundancy issues.

EMPLOYMENT

CARSON MCDOWELL
ELLIOTT DUFFY GARRETT
L'ESTRANGE & BRETT ✪

Arthur Cox Northern Ireland ✪
Cleaver Fulton Rankin
Jones & Cassidy
Mills Selig
Tughans

Babington & Croasdaile
C & H Jefferson ✪
John McKee & Sons ✪
Johns Elliot
McKinty and Wright
Napier and Sons

Firms are listed A-Z in tiers which are ranked in order of priority
✪ *Indicates firm displays contact details at the end of this chapter.*

ENVIRONMENT AND PLANNING

CARSON MCDOWELL
CLEAVER FULTON RANKIN
L'ESTRANGE & BRETT ✪
TUGHANS

Arthur Cox Northern Ireland ✪
C & H Jefferson ✪
Elliott Duffy Garrett
Johns Elliot
McKinty and Wright
Mills Selig
Napier and Sons

Firms are listed A-Z in tiers which are ranked in order of priority
✪ *Indicates firm displays contact details at the end of this chapter.*

IP AND IT

CARSON MCDOWELL
CLEAVER FULTON RANKIN
L'ESTRANGE & BRETT ✪
TUGHANS

Arthur Cox Northern Ireland ✪
Elliott Duffy Garrett

C & H Jefferson ✪
John McKee & Sons ✪
Johns Elliot
McKinty and Wright
Mills Selig
Napier and Sons
Wilson Nesbitt

Firms are listed A-Z in tiers which are ranked in order of priority
✪ *Indicates firm displays contact details at the end of this chapter.*

Elliott Duffy Garrett has an excellent employment practice, headed by managing partner Harry Coll. It advises on all aspects of employment law and practice, including the implementation and enforcement of anti-discrimination legislation.

Adam Brett is **L'Estrange & Brett**'s employment specialist, and leads a strong contentious and non-contentious team that has a particular niche in discrimination and TUPE advice. Clients include Queen's University and Sainsbury's, as well as a number of semi-public, financial and commercial entities. Recent transactional support work includes advising in relation to Lakeland Dairies' acquisition of LE Pritchitt and Co Ltd's milk manufacturing business.

Arthur Cox Northern Ireland's well-regarded employment team is led by litigator Peter Martin, and includes a second partner in Anna Beggan. Recent work includes successfully applying to the Court of Appeal to overturn a Tribunal decision that held a client employer liable for unlawful discrimination in an internal promotion exercise. The firm also enjoys a good reputation for its advisory work.

Cleaver Fulton Rankin's employment group advises on both contentious and non-contentious matters. It includes partners Rosalie Prytherch and Alyn Hicks, who act mainly for employers in defending cases in the Industrial and Fair Employment Tribunals and in bringing injunction proceedings to enforce restrictive covenants. Prytherch was a founder member of Northern Ireland's Employment Lawyer's Group.

Jones & Cassidy has a very strong reputation as a niche employment practice; its three partners, including Beverley Jones, undertake all aspects of employment, anti-discrimination and human rights law.

Mills Selig's team, headed by Adam Currie, acts for a number of well-known retailers and manufacturers, and has particular expertise in advising on injunctions for employers. Bill McCann is also recommended.

Eugene O'Loan heads **Tughans**' employment practice, which includes one other partner in Ursula Burns. The team acts in the defence of industrial tribunal claims, as well as advising on the employment aspects of corporate transactions and offering an audit service in relation to clients' employment procedures. Recent work includes acting on a significant judicial review case (relating to an Industrial Court decision), and successfully representing 'consultants' of a major UK financial institution in a claim that they were in fact employees and entitled to bring unfair dismissal claims.

ENVIRONMENT AND PLANNING

Commercial property partner Rosemary Carson heads **Carson McDowell**'s team, which includes associate Gary McGhee, a planning specialist who has advised clients such as Tesco and Belfast Harbour Commissioners. The firm's environmental experience includes commissioning audits and advising on impact assessments.

Planning specialist Karen Blair heads **Cleaver Fulton Rankin**'s environment and planning group, which was hit by the departure of leading environmental expert Neil Faris in 2003. The firm acts for Belfast City Airport in relation to its new terminal building, and for the Department for Regional Development's Water Service in relation to its proposed waste water treatment scheme in North Down/Ards, as well as advising numerous waste operators on licensing issues. Blair is the only legal associate of the Royal Town Planning Institute working in a commercial law firm.

L'Estrange & Brett's team is led by litigation partner Sam Beckett, who has acted on a number of high-profile planning enquiries, and commercial property partner Ian Huddleston, who advises on all aspects of property development, including planning and environmental issues. Recent work includes advising Bord Gais Eireann in relation to the new Belfast to Londonderry gas pipeline, and BG Group and Premier Power Ltd on clean-up obligations relating to contaminated land.

Tughans has a strong reputation in the field; head of property Phyllis Agnew has extensive experience on planning matters, while Deirdre Magill is recommended on the environmental side. The firm recently advised the principal objector at the public inquiry into the proposed Victoria Square Development Scheme.

IP AND IT

Carson McDowell advises a number of IT, communications and e-commerce businesses based in Northern Ireland and, on the IP side, has experience of advising a diverse client base on the full range of contentious and non-contentious matters. The firm's e-commerce, IT and IP team is led by Alan Taylor.

Jennifer Ebbage heads **Cleaver Fulton Rankin**'s IT team, which acted for Hewlett-Packard as the main sub-contractor to Fujitsu on the Causeway Programme, a major government IT project that aims to integrate the information systems of the Province's criminal justice organisations; the project is to run for ten years and is valued at £35m. Brendan Fox has a good reputation for his IP work and is experienced in contentious IP matters, including copyright, passing off and trade mark infringement, as well as on trade mark and design registration.

L'Estrange & Brett's IP and IT units are headed by Paul McBride. The IP unit, which includes litigation partner David Kirkpatrick, is particularly active in the biotechnology sector, and has recently advised clients such as Almac Sciences, Allhow Laboratories and Randox Laboratories. On the IT side, the firm has strong experience on financing matters, advising both start-ups and established clients on fundraising, and provides ongoing commercial advice to clients such as Viridian subsidiary Sx3, Ordnance Survey for Northern Ireland and UTV plc.

Tughans' team includes full-time IT specialist Adrian O'Connell, who is a senior associate at the firm. Recent work includes advising Fujitsu in relation to the Causeway Programme, and advising Consilium Technologies Ltd on the settlement of contracts in the local authority sector throughout the UK for its integrated financial management system solution. On the transactional side, the firm recently advised Xperience Group on its acquisition of Brikat Technical Services Ltd; corporate partner Ian Coulter has a strong reputation for his IT-related experience.

Arthur Cox Northern Ireland's recent work includes acting for a clearing bank in a major IT contract involving the provision of services to an ATM operator, and for Bank of Ireland on a system development and support agreement with Reuters. Kerry Canavan is recommended.

Elliott Duffy Garrett's commercial group advises on a range of IP, IT, e-commerce and data protection matters, and has a solid reputation.

INSOLVENCY

Napier and Sons is widely recognised as Northern Ireland's leading insolvency practice, and advises companies, partnerships and sole traders across the full range of insolvency matters. Managing partner John Gordon and Brigid Napier are both licensed insolvency practitioners. The firm also has a substantial debt recovery practice.

David Jamison heads **Carson McDowell**'s insolvency and corporate restructuring department, while Peter Davison is also active in the area. The firm has extensive experience in advising liquidators, receivers and administrators.

Litigation associate Michael Neill leads **Cleaver Fulton Rankin**'s growing insolvency practice and has experience in advising liquidators, receivers and administrators.

Elliott Duffy Garrett has a good reputation for its business recovery and insolvency advice, with Michael Wilson particularly recommended.

John McKee & Sons has a well-regarded insolvency and debt recovery practice; partner Lex Ross is a highly experienced practitioner and specialises in corporate receiverships.

L'Estrange & Brett's team, headed by Paul McBride, has been strengthened by the arrival of senior associate Kieran McGarrigle from **Eversheds LLP** in Newcastle, prior to which he worked with PwC in Belfast. As well as acting on several corporate restructurings, the firm is advising the liquidator of Irish Fertiliser Industries Ltd, a company registered in the Republic but with a substantial part of its business based in Northern Ireland.

Peter Martin at **Arthur Cox Northern Ireland** has strong experience in insolvency proceedings and, along with banking and finance specialist Angus Creed, has recently advised the administrators of Shop Electric Ltd. The firm also has a large debt recovery department.

INSOLVENCY

NAPIER AND SONS

Carson McDowell
Cleaver Fulton Rankin
Elliott Duffy Garrett
John McKee & Sons ✪
L'Estrange & Brett ✪

Arthur Cox Northern Ireland ✪
Babington & Croasdaile
C & H Jefferson ✪
Johns Elliot

McKinty and Wright
Mills Selig
Tughans
Wilson Nesbitt

Firms are listed A-Z in tiers which are ranked in order of priority
✪ *Indicates firm displays contact details at the end of this chapter.*

Babington & Croasdaile's insolvency and debt recovery practice advises a range of credit card companies.

Ken Rutherford handles **C & H Jefferson**'s insolvency work; the firm has particular experience in the manufacturing sector.

James Pringle at **Johns Elliot** has advised liquidators and trustees in bankruptcy, as well as nominees and supervisors in individual voluntary arrangements.

PROJECT FINANCE AND PFI

There continues to be significant investment in Northern Ireland, with a number of PPP/PFI projects earmarked for commencement of procurement in 2004. The projects are spread across a range of sectors, including water, roads, education/accommodation and health.

L'Estrange & Brett remains ahead of the field with its cross-disciplinary projects unit, which includes two corporate and commercial partners and two commercial property partners. The most active is corporate partner Adrian Eakin, who was made up in April 2003. Headline PFI work includes acting for Invest NI on its accommodation project (currently at bid stage), which is the first project to be sponsored by the government's Strategic Investment Board. The firm also advised Premier Power Ltd, Ireland's largest independent electricity generator, in relation to aspects of the draft Energy Bill in the context of the possible refinancing of Ireland's energy industry.

A&L Goodbody in Dublin has a strong presence in the sector, and continued to act in relation to the Omagh and East Tyrone Colleges of Further and Higher Education project (advising the college governing bodies), which completed in September 2003. The firm is advising either sponsors or authorities on a significant number of other projects in Northern Ireland, including acting for the Lanyon Consortium as bidder on Invest NI's accommodation project. Kevin Feeney heads the firm's projects department in Dublin, and has an excellent reputation.

PROJECT FINANCE AND PFI

L'ESTRANGE & BRETT ✪

A&L Goodbody
Masons

Arthur Cox Northern Ireland ✪
Carson McDowell
Elliott Duffy Garrett
John McKee & Sons ✪
McGrigors
Tughans

C & H Jefferson ✪
Cleaver Fulton Rankin
Mills Selig

Firms are listed A-Z in tiers which are ranked in order of priority
✪ *Indicates firm displays contact details at the end of this chapter.*

Masons' Dublin office has extensive PPP/PFI experience in Northern Ireland, advising across a wide range of sectors, and associate Tim Kinney has been based full time in Belfast since May 2003. Recent work includes advising the preferred bidder on the Belfast City Hospital Cancer Centre. The firm has also advised in relation to a number of accommodation projects and is acting for a bidding consortium for the M1 Westlink DBFO road projects (scheduled to commence in January 2004).

Arthur Cox Northern Ireland's PFI expert is Peter Stafford; the firm has advised in relation to a number of projects, particularly on the financing side.

Michael Johnston heads **Carson McDowell**'s projects and infrastructure team, which includes construction specialist Peter Davison. The firm has particular experience on the financing side, having acted for clients including Bank of Ireland on PFI projects, but has also advised at the consortium and authority level.

Elliott Duffy Garrett has considerable experience in PFI work, with Kevin McVeigh particularly recommended.

John McKee & Sons has niche expertise acting exclusively on the banking side of PFI work. Lex Ross is very highly regarded.

McGrigors has a strong reputation for PFI throughout the UK. Gregor Hamilton leads the practice in the firm's Belfast office, and has been involved in a range of projects representing both public and private sector parties in recent years.

John-George Willis heads **Tughans**' infrastructure and projects work. The firm has particular experience acting on healthcare PFI projects, and recently advised Fujitsu in relation to the Causeway Programme.

Partner Ken Rutherford at **C & H Jefferson** specialises in PFI work, and has recently acted for one of the bidders in relation to Invest NI's PFI accommodation project.

Cleaver Fulton Rankin recently advised the Electricity Supply Board in relation to its development of the Coolkeeragh power station, as well as acting alongside **Matheson Ormsby Prentice** in Dublin on the refinancing of Altahullion Windfarm, County Londonderry.

Mills Selig is recommended for its project finance work.

REAL ESTATE

REAL ESTATE

CARSON MCDOWELL
CLEAVER FULTON RANKIN
L'ESTRANGE & BRETT ✪
TUGHANS

ARTHUR COX NORTHERN IRELAND ✪
C & H JEFFERSON ✪
ELLIOTT DUFFY GARRETT
TRAVERS SMITH BRAITHWAITE

John McKee & Sons ✪
Johns Elliot
McGrigors
Mills Selig

Babington & Croasdaile
Bigger & Strahan
Fisher & Fisher
Kearney Sefton
McKinty and Wright
Napier and Sons
R M Cullen & Son
Wilson Nesbitt

Firms are listed A-Z in tiers which are ranked in order of priority
✪ Indicates firm displays contact details at the end of this chapter.

At **Carson McDowell**, department head Alan Reilly and Jeremy Hill are both highly regarded. Reilly is best known for his work on the landlord side and has been involved in the acquisition and/or development of a range of significant shopping centre sites in Northern Ireland. Rosemary Carson, the third partner in the group, specialises in the retail sector; she advised both national and local multiple retailers on the acquisition and disposal of sites, and also advises University of Ulster on property matters.

Cleaver Fulton Rankin is best known for its commercial property practice, although it has been hit by the departure of Neil Faris, one of Northern Ireland's leading environmental lawyers. Kathryn Collie has, since April 2003, headed the group, which also includes partner Jim Houston. Recent work includes acting for Harcourt Developments of Dublin on its acquisition of the Titanic Quarter development opportunity in Belfast's docklands, and for Dunnes Stores (Bangor) Ltd on the acquisition of its new flagship store in Belfast. The firm enjoys significant referral work from Dublin and London.

Of the five partners in **L'Estrange & Brett**'s commercial property group, Ian Huddleston and Graham Pierce are the most active. The firm recently advised Land Securities Trillium on the sale of the BT Tower in Belfast to the Tchenguiz Brothers Rotch Group, and Sainsbury's on the £15m sale of a large development site at Newtonabbey, County Antrim. Other significant clients include Laganside Corporation and McDonald's, along with a range of new retail clients including Matalan and Superdrug. Alan Hewitt heads the group.

Tughans' property department acts primarily for developers, and has recently advised in relation to a range of retail, leisure and business parks, including acting for Acquis Estates Ltd and Anglia and General Developments Ltd on the proposed £70m retail and leisure venture development at Belfast Harbour Estate. The firm also advised Reit Asset Management on the acquisition and subsequent disposal of two major shopping centres in the Province. Retail clients include Tesco. Department head Phyllis Agnew and John Mills are both highly regarded.

Arthur Cox Northern Ireland's two-partner commercial property practice is led by Rowan White. It advises a range of institutional clients, multiple retailers and developers. Recent highlights include acting for a Diageo subsidiary on the site acquisition for its new Baileys Irish Cream plant on the outskirts of Belfast, and advising a major financial institution on the disposal of a £10m property in the city centre.

C & H Jefferson's commercial property practice has a growing profile and reputation, and has particular strength in the retail sector, as well as acting for developers and institutional lenders. Having previously acted for the purchasers of Dunloe Ewart's Northern Ireland property portfolio, the firm has been involved in a number of related sales and joint venture projects, including the recent sale of Antrim Shopping Centre. Mark Tinman is widely recommended.

Elliott Duffy Garrett's clients include a range of developers, retailers, and private and institutional investors, both in Ireland and the UK. Laurence Mahood heads the practice and has an excellent reputation.

Travers Smith Braithwaite has a strong London-based practice; Andrew Barrow is the best known of four dual-qualified lawyers at the firm and is one of the leading commercial property lawyers in Northern Ireland, having been involved in many of the large-scale property developments undertaken in and around Belfast over the last 15 years. The firm is advising AM Development in relation to the capital's Victoria Square project, the total cost of which is likely to exceed £200m, and is also acting for Varo Estates on a project to reclaim and regenerate a large area within old Belfast (to be known as Cathedral Quarter).

John McKee & Sons has strong experience on the financing side of property transactions.

Johns Elliot's property department is headed by David Leitch, and has advised local and national clients on development projects. Partners Eric Kyle and James Pringle are recommended.

Alan McAlister heads **McGrigors**' commercial property practice in Belfast, which has particular experience in development work.

Mills Selig's team is headed by Brian Ham. The firm's clients include a range of developers, lenders and investors.

ARTHUR COX
NORTHERN IRELAND

CAPITAL HOUSE
3 UPPER QUEEN STREET
BELFAST BT1 6PU

Telephone: +44 28 9023 0007
Fax: +44 28 9023 3464
E-mail: belfast@arthurcox.com
Website: www.arthurcox.com

Languages
French, German, Italian, Spanish

Other offices
Dublin, London, New York

Number of lawyers 198
at this office 20

CATEGORIES OF WORK

Corporate and commercial
Kerry Canavan, Peter Stafford

Banking
Angus Creed, Judith Brown

Commercial property
Rowan White, Patricia Johnston

Financial services
Angus Creed, Judith Brown

Litigation
Peter Martin, Amanda Wylie

Employment
Peter Martin, Anna Beggan

EU and competition
John Meade

C & H JEFFERSON

NORWICH UNION HOUSE
7 FOUNTAIN STREET
BELFAST BT1 5EA

Telephone: +44 28 9032 9545
Fax: +44 28 9024 4644
E-mail: law@chjefferson.co.uk
Website: www.chjefferson.co.uk

Languages
French, Italian, Spanish

Number of lawyers 23

CATEGORIES OF WORK

Civil litigation/employers and public liability
David Lennon, Robin Johnston

Civil litigation/motor
Ian Jefferson, David Rocke

Commercial litigation
Gareth Jones

Insurance and professional indemnity
Gareth Jones

Banking and finance
Mark Tinman

Corporate and partnership
Ken Rutherford

Commercial property
Mark Tinman

Insolvency
Ken Rutherford

Employment
Liam Magill

Debt recovery
Ian Stanfield

Private finance initiative
Ken Rutherford

E-commerce and intellectual property
Julie Galbraith

Environmental and planning
Ken Rutherford, Gareth Jones

JOHN McKEE & SON SOLICITORS

HAMPDEN HOUSE
55 ROYAL AVENUE
BELFAST BT1 1FD

Telephone: +44 28 9023 2303
Fax: +44 28 9023 0081
E-mail: info@jmckee.co.uk
Website: www.jmckee.co.uk

Number of lawyers 14

CATEGORIES OF WORK

Banking and finance
Lex Ross, Avril McCammon

Project finance/PFI
Lex Ross, Avril McCammon

Property
Albert Jordan

Corporate
Lex Ross, Avril McCammon

Litigation
Leonard Edgar, Chris Ross

Insolvency
Lex Ross

L'ESTRANGE & BRETT

ARNOTT HOUSE
12-16 BRIDGE STREET
BELFAST BT1 1LS

Telephone: +44 2890 230 426
Fax: +44 2890 246 396
E-mail: law@lestrangeandbrett.com
Website: www.lestrangeandbrett.com

Languages
French, German, Spanish, Swedish

Number of lawyers 36

Member
North South Legal Alliance with McCann FitzGerald (Dublin)

CATEGORIES OF WORK

Companies, corporations
John Irvine, Richard Gray

Commercial and competition law
Richard Gray, Paul McBride

Mergers and acquisitions
John Irvine, Paul McBride

Commercial property
Alan Hewitt, Graham Pierce

Bankruptcy, insolvency
Paul McBride, David Kirkpatrick

Banking, securities and finance
Brian Henderson, Richard Gray

Projects, public private partnerships
Adrian Eakin, Richard Gray

Employment, labour
Adam Brett

Commercial litigation, intellectual property, maritime and shipping
Adam Brett, Samuel Beckett

Environment
Ian Huddleston, David Kirkpatrick

Wills, trusts, estate planning, financial services and private client
Ian Huddleston, Alan Hewitt

Construction and planning
Samuel Beckett, Andrea McIlroy-Rose

Information technology
Paul McBride

UNITED KINGDOM: SCOTLAND

Population	5.06 million
Number of lawyers	8,768
Professional title	Solicitor, advocate
Currency	Pound sterling (£)

Index

Scotland's central belt, which stretches between Edinburgh and Glasgow, is the engine room of the country's banking and corporate markets. Aberdeen, some 120 miles to the north, is an almost entirely separate market, focused heavily on the North Sea oil and gas industries.

BILLING

Clients are charged between £185 and £210 (€312 and €355) per hour for partners undertaking corporate/finance and litigation work and £155 and £160 (€262 and €270) per hour for assistant solicitors. The Law Society of Scotland provides guidance on billing.

MARKETING

There are no restrictions on lawyers advertising in Scotland. Most of the major firms have websites and produce brochures for clients. Details of transactions can be disclosed, provided clients' prior permission has been given.

IN-HOUSE LAWYERS

The Law Society of Scotland supports a specialist group which represents the interests of in-house lawyers. In-house lawyers are employed in all areas of industry and are particularly prevalent in the public sector.

THE LEGAL 500

For additional information on the law firms and legal practice in Scotland, see *The Legal 500* (UK edition) at www.legal500.com.

LEGAL MARKET

Five firms dominate the Scottish commercial legal market in Edinburgh and Glasgow. **Dundas & Wilson** withdrew from its accountancy link-up with *Andersen Legal* with managing partner Chris Campbell managing the exit superbly. The firm has emerged from a difficult period with a core team and a client base that is substantially intact. **McGrigors** is the only UK firm with offices in all three UK legal jurisdictions (Scotland, England and Wales and Northern Ireland). **Maclay Murray & Spens** is a blue-chip independent Scottish firm with a client base to match. Chief executive Magnus Swanson personifies the firm's ethos with his highly commercial approach to law. **Maclay Murray & Spens** is the only UK member of the global association of independent law firms, *Lex Mundi*. **Shepherd+ Wedderburn** completes the quintet of Scotland's dominant firms. The full-service firm has recognised strengths in property, planning, energy, corporate and technology. **Dickson Minto WS** is by common consent Scotland's leading corporate finance firm. The list of heavyweight transactional lawyers is lengthy and studded by some of the UK's M&A stars. The Anglo-Scottish firm, among the most profitable in the UK, has a market-leading investment funds practice.

Two Aberdeen-based firms are also strong. **Paull & Williamsons** scored a corporate triumph, advising longstanding client John Wood Group on its LSE float and oil and gas-focused **Ledingham Chalmers**' impressive international reach, which includes offices in Turkey, Azerbaijan and the Falklands.

BANKING AND FINANCE

The commercial group at **Dickson Minto WS** is smaller than its top-tier rivals, but its undisputed market-leading acquisition and structured finance practice justifies its ranking. Partners Colin McHale and Bruce Minto are two of the best-regarded operators in the market. The firm advised Bank of Scotland on debt facilities for the IBO of Swedish heat pump manufacturer IVT Industrier by ABN AMRO.

Dundas & Wilson boasts Scotland's largest dedicated banking team, featuring five partners, and headed by Stephen Phillips. Among a number of wide-ranging deals, the firm advised Bank of Scotland on the £335m financing of The Mall Limited Partnership for shopping centre acquisitions. Other clients include Barclays and Bank of America.

Maclay Murray & Spens has highlighted property finance as a key growth area to compensate for the downturn in M&A, though acquisition finance remains a core part of the team's business. Partner Susan Kelly heads the team which also features Graeme Sloan. Longstanding clients include Lloyds TSB, Bank of Scotland and RBS, with new clients including Barclays, Aviva and Rothschilds.

McGrigors is active in property finance and project finance deals. The firm recently advised the Bank of Scotland on two major financings, the

The largest firms

1	Dundas & Wilson	247
2	Shepherd+ Wedderburn	234
3	Bond Pearce	227
4	Maclay Murray & Spens	222
5	McGrigors	150
6	MacRoberts	136
7	Tods Murray WS	133
8	Biggart Baillie	129
9	Brodies	112
10	Henderson Boyd Jackson WS	93
11	Anderson Strathern	87
12	Burness	84
	McClure Naismith	84
14	Paull & Williamsons	81
15	Morton Fraser	80
16	DLA	77
17	Ledingham Chalmers	71
18	Simpson & Marwick	63
19	Thorntons WS	55
20	Harper Macleod	54
	Turcan Connell	54
	Wright Johnston & Mackenzie	54
23	Semple Fraser WS	53
24	Balfour & Manson	47
	Brechin Tindal Oatts	47

These figures represent the total number of lawyers in this country only, and have been supplied by the firms themselves. The figures should be accurate as at 1 January 2004.

BANKING AND FINANCE

DICKSON MINTO WS *Edinburgh, Glasgow*
DUNDAS & WILSON ✪ *Edinburgh, Glasgow*
MACLAY MURRAY & SPENS *Glasgow, Edinburgh*
McGRIGORS *Glasgow, Edinburgh*

SHEPHERD+ WEDDERBURN *Edinburgh, Glasgow*

BIGGART BAILLIE *Glasgow, Edinburgh*
BURNESS *Edinburgh*
TODS MURRAY WS *Edinburgh, Glasgow*

Brodies *Edinburgh*
MacRoberts *Glasgow, Edinburgh*
McClure Naismith *Glasgow, Edinburgh*
Morton Fraser *Edinburgh*

Anderson Strathern *Edinburgh*
Archibald Campbell & Harley WS *Edinburgh*
DLA *Glasgow, Edinburgh*
Golds *Glasgow*
Harper Macleod *Glasgow*
Henderson Boyd Jackson WS *Edinburgh, Glasgow*
Semple Fraser WS *Edinburgh*

Firms are listed A-Z in tiers which are ranked in order of priority
✪ *Indicates firm displays contact details at the end of this chapter.*

£193m Targetfollow property financing and the £200m Norwich Union PPP fund. Group head Michael Watson and Colin McKay are both well regarded.

Acquisition and project finance specialist Shona Sanders heads the banking team at **Shepherd+ Wedderburn**, which also features property finance expert Andrew Kinnes. Key deals include advising Adam Smith and the management team on the provision of debt for the Carlton Clubs-related secondary buy-out and advising Bank of Scotland on a major property acquisition.

Partner Derek Ellery of **Biggart Baillie**'s Glasgow office heads a team recommended for commercial property finance, where key clients include Anglo Irish Bank and Bank of Ireland. The firm acts for Scotland's three main clearing banks and an impressive mix of borrowers.

Bank of Scotland and RBS are both key lender clients of Scott Wilson's banking group at **Burness**. The team advised the former on the provision of £90m in debt and equity facilities to Lothian Fifty (I50), and on the reorganisation of debt to Semple Cochrane.

Tods Murray WS's five-partner team, led by group head Graham Burnside, advised on Abbey National's £4bn residential mortgage securitisation, the largest European deal of its kind to date. The firm regularly receives referrals from leading City firms, especially in the areas of structured finance and property finance.

Brodies handles a range of banking-related work, including acquisition finance, securitisation and derivatives. Major clients include RBS, HFC Bank and National Australia Group/Clydesdale Bank.

MacRoberts advised the EIB on the funding of a major housing stock transfer. Group head Norman Martin's team is particularly recommended for project finance.

McClure Naismith's banking team features former in-house lawyer John Blackwood. Clients include Bank of Scotland. Morag Campbell is an asset finance and property finance specialist.

Morton Fraser has a dedicated banking and finance unit headed by partner Susan Younger. Asset finance advice, to clients including Clydesdale Bank Asset Finance, remains the core strength of the team, with partner and corporate head Bruce Wood enjoying a national reputation.

CONSTRUCTION

MacRoberts has a superb construction practice. The team advises developers, contractors and consultants on all manner of construction projects and disputes. The firm recently acted for Network Rail on a major office and car park development at Waverley Station, Edinburgh.

Vincent Connor and Alastair Morrison jointly head **Masons**' construction practice, which remains at the forefront of Scottish construction law. Alongside a raft of quality non-contentious instructions, the team has seen a substantial increase in contentious work and acted on a number of high-profile Court of Session disputes.

Alistair McLean heads **Dundas & Wilson**'s well-regarded construction practice, which has solid expertise on both the contentious and non-contentious side. The group has dedicated teams for adjudications and boasts three solicitor advocates. The firm acted for Energy Power Resources and Enterprise Oil in two separate disputes. It has also been also instructed by EDI Group on a major ongoing office and mixed-use development in Haymarket, Edinburgh.

McGrigors' construction department is now split between the contentious and non-contentious practices, led by Colin Fraser and Gareth Parry, respectively. On the contentious side, which remains as busy as ever, rising star Scott Johnston has a depth of knowledge and experience which defies his young age. Meanwhile the non-contentious team is advising Royal Bank of Scotland on the construction of its new headquarters.

The three-partner construction group at **Biggart Baillie** continues to act on a number of adjudications, one involving a £4m claim for damages. Clients include Stannifer and Sainsbury's.

Chris Mackay heads **Burness**'s six fee-earner construction group. Clients such as Grosvenor Developments, BSkyB and Stadia Group produce a high volume of instructions.

CONSTRUCTION

MACROBERTS *Glasgow, Edinburgh*
MASONS *Glasgow, Edinburgh*

DUNDAS & WILSON ✪ *Edinburgh, Glasgow*
McGRIGORS *Glasgow, Edinburgh*

Biggart Baillie *Glasgow, Edinburgh*
Burness *Edinburgh, Glasgow*
Maclay Murray & Spens *Glasgow, Edinburgh*
Shepherd+ Wedderburn *Edinburgh, Glasgow*

Anderson Strathern *Edinburgh*
Bishops *Glasgow, Edinburgh*
Brodies *Edinburgh*
DLA *Glasgow, Edinburgh*
Harper Macleod *Glasgow*
Ledingham Chalmers *Aberdeen*
McClure Naismith *Glasgow, Edinburgh*
Paull & Williamsons *Aberdeen*
Semple Fraser WS *Glasgow, Edinburgh*
Tods Murray WS *Edinburgh, Glasgow*

Firms are listed A-Z in tiers which are ranked in order of priority
✪ Indicates firm displays contact details at the end of this chapter.

Maclay Murray & Spens' construction department includes three full-time partners, and recently advised on the construction of the Loch Lomond Shores Retail and Tourism development. Clients say department head Mark Macaulay is 'superb', while partner Kirsti Olson is 'extremely thorough and professional'.

Shepherd+ Wedderburn has an extremely well-regarded non-contentious practice, which remains busy with a number of sizeable instructions. The largest of these was the Greenside development for Pillar Projects in Edinburgh. Kevin Taylor heads the 14 fee-earner team.

CORPORATE AND COMMERCIAL

Premier firms: Dickson Minto WS is 'head and shoulders above everyone else' for corporate work say clients. Major highlights include advising Scottish Widows on its £225m listed property trust, and BC Partners on the £625m IBO of Galbani from Danone.

Dundas & Wilson's corporate team, headed by David Hardie, has unquestionable strength in depth. Deal highlights include advising Scottish and Southern Energy on its unsuccessful £1bn bid for TXU UK (led by Ewan Robertson) and on its acquisition of underground gas storage facility operator Dynegy Hornsea.

Maclay Murray & Spens boasts a prestigious group of corporate partners. Heading the roll call is chief executive Magnus Swanson. The firm advised on the sale of First Engineering to Peterhouse and the complex disposal of businesses at, and subsequent reconstruction of, Semple Cochrane. Partners Graeme Sloan and Kenneth Shand feature prominently in a robust team.

CORPORATE AND COMMERCIAL PREMIER FIRMS

DICKSON MINTO WS *Edinburgh, Glasgow*
DUNDAS & WILSON ✪ *Edinburgh, Glasgow*
MACLAY MURRAY & SPENS *Edinburgh, Glasgow*

McGRIGORS *Edinburgh, Glasgow*
SHEPHERD+ WEDDERBURN *Edinburgh, Glasgow*

Firms are listed A-Z in tiers which are ranked in order of priority
✪ Indicates firm displays contact details at the end of this chapter.

McGrigors advised on a number of solid deals including the acquisitive West Coast Capital as a new client. It acted for Burns Stewart Distillers on its takeover by CL Financial and advised Nomad Brewin Dolphin on the £47.75m reverse takeover of Berry Birch & Noble. Partner Morag McNeil and Paul Davidson are recommended.

At **Shepherd+ Wedderburn** partner Marian Glen has a 'wealth of experience', while group head James Will is a corporate finance expert. The team advised Teesland on the reverse takeover of engineering group Semple Cochrane, while the traditionally strong capital markets team advised on the £20m AIM listing of Highland Gold Mining.

Edinburgh and Glasgow: MacRoberts has the leading corporate practice outside Scotland's premier league. The group advised on a string of quality deals including acting for AWG in its joint venture with Edinburgh House Estates and CVC Capital Partners on the buy-out of Kwik-Fit from Ford.

Biggart Baillie has added significant resources to its commercial team in the last year. On the corporate side David Allan heads a team that includes corporate finance partner Catherine Feechan. The group advised AorTech International on its proposed acquisition of Becton Dickenson Critical Care Division, and Morrison Bowmore Distillers on its joint venture with Campari.

Brodies' impressive corporate team picked up the lead role advising the Strategic Rail Authority in the re-let of the ScotRail franchise, and advised the Ministry of Defence on its engineering and facilities management contract at the Faslane naval base.

Burness' corporate team continues to grow. The partner-led ethos attracts complex and high-profile deals. Highlights include advising Adam & Company Group on its acquisition of Stewart Ivory Wealth Management, a deal led by John Rafferty. Banking specialist Alan Soppitt heads the team together with pensions expert Andrew Sleigh.

A £500m subordinated step-up notes issue by HBOS was the highlight deal at **Tods Murray WS** last year. Partner William Simmons advised the bank on the Scottish law aspects of the mammoth transaction. Group head and investment funds specialist David Dunsire led a team that advised the Kenmore Group in its £45m property portfolio sale to Ashbourne Property Fund.

CORPORATE AND COMMERCIAL EDINBURGH AND GLASGOW

MACROBERTS *Glasgow, Edinburgh*

BIGGART BAILLIE *Edinburgh*
BRODIES *Edinburgh*
BURNESS *Edinburgh, Glasgow*
TODS MURRAY WS *Edinburgh, Glasgow*

McClure Naismith *Glasgow, Edinburgh*

Anderson Strathern *Edinburgh*
DLA *Glasgow*
Harper Macleod *Glasgow, Edinburgh*
Henderson Boyd Jackson WS *Edinburgh, Glasgow*
Morton Fraser *Edinburgh*
Semple Fraser WS *Edinburgh*

Boyds *Edinburgh*
Fyfe Ireland WS *Edinburgh*
Golds *Glasgow*
Wright Johnston & Mackenzie *Glasgow*

Firms are listed A-Z in tiers which are ranked in order of priority

Clients approve of **McClure Naismith**'s high-quality, price-competitive advice. Head of projects Steven Brown is recommended for power generation deals. Corporate head Dr Kenneth Chrystie led the team advising the vendor shareholders in the £66m sale of First Engineering to Peterhouse Group.

Two significant deals reflected the continuing strength of **Anderson Strathern**'s corporate team: Group head Simon Brown advised Kwik-Fit on its £350m sale to CVC Capital Partners; Jonathan MacQueen led the team that handled the Scottish aspects of Orb Estates' £600m acquisition of Thistle Hotels.

Harper Macleod partner Tom Thomas handled the purchase of one of the highest-profile Scottish companies of the last year, Semple Cochrane, by RTT (Holdings) Ltd. The firm also advised William Hill on the Scottish aspects of its flotation.

Semple Fraser WS's corporate team, headed by Dawn Davidson, advised the smart card technology business Aspects Software on a £5m investment, and the Kenmore Group on a property-related joint venture.

Boyds partner Calum Jones advised Gaelic Invoice Factors on its £10m MBI/MBO.

Elsewhere in Scotland: Ledingham Chalmers is best known for its oil and gas practice but also boasts a strong corporate team headed by Malcolm Laing.

CORPORATE AND COMMERCIAL ELSEWHERE IN SCOTLAND

LEDINGHAM CHALMERS *Aberdeen*
PAULL & WILLIAMSONS *Aberdeen*

Iain Smith & Co *Aberdeen*
Pagan Osborne *Cupar*
Stronachs *Aberdeen*

Raeburn Christie *Aberdeen*
The Commercial Law Practice *Aberdeen*
Thorntons WS *Dundee*

Firms are listed A-Z in tiers which are ranked in order of priority

Paull & Williamsons advised on the London Stock Exchange listing of oil services company John Wood Group. The firm's 11-partner team also features Alan McNiven and David Freeman and is recommended to oil and gas industry clients.

Iain Smith & Co continues to plough a lucrative furrow of agriculture-related corporate work for clients including Grampian Country Food Group. Partner Roy Roxburgh heads a solid team.

Law Firm of the Year at the Scottish Legal Awards, **Pagan Osborne** is recommended for asset management and property matters.

The 11-partner team at **Stronachs** is one of the largest in the north east of Scotland. Well-known partner David Rennie heads the team.

CORPORATE TAX

Maclay Murray & Spens' team features chartered accountant Gwen Souter. The ten-fee-earner group advised Stiell on its sale to Alfred McAlpine and Bank of Scotland on the sale and leaseback of Hilton Hotels.

MacRoberts' Isobel d'Inverno, who is well regarded for property and PFI deals, brings accountancy expertise to the tax group. Peter Trotter is also recommended.

McGrigors' team, headed by Ian Gordon, advised on several corporate reorganisations and reconstructions and excels in property-related structures such as stamp duty mitigation schemes.

Burness offers both stand-alone corporate tax advice, including stamp duty and VAT, or as part of a corporate or commercial property transaction. Partner John Finnick heads the dedicated in-house group.

Dickson Minto WS's leading M&A practice is supported by Nial Tosh.

Dundas & Wilson's team was strengthened by the arrival of chartered accountant and solicitor Carol Goodwin last year. Group head Susan Hoyle provided tax advice to SSE in the £130m acquisition of Dynegy Hornsea.

Shepherd+ Wedderburn is retained by HM Customs & Excise to handle all its Scottish matters. Group head Malcolm Rust has an expertise in advising on stamp duty aspects of commercial property deals.

CORPORATE TAX

MACLAY MURRAY & SPENS *Glasgow, Edinburgh*
MACROBERTS *Edinburgh*
McGRIGORS *Glasgow, Edinburgh*

Burness *Glasgow, Edinburgh*
Dickson Minto WS *Edinburgh, Glasgow*
Dundas & Wilson ✪ *Edinburgh, Glasgow*
Shepherd+ Wedderburn *Edinburgh, Glasgow*

Brodies *Edinburgh*
McClure Naismith *Glasgow*

Firms are listed A-Z in tiers which are ranked in order of priority
✪ Indicates firm displays contact details at the end of this chapter.

DISPUTE RESOLUTION

Brodies' David Williamson QC is among the best-regarded litigators in Scotland. The team's greatest strength, says one client, is its ability to 'advise us in our language and our terms rather than legal language'. The group head Joyce Cullen is highly rated for property litigation. The team advised a major insurance company on two £40m claims.

Dundas & Wilson's stellar client base provides a throughput of quality litigation. Lorna Sibbald heads the three-partner team. It advised Scottish and Southern Energy on its complex pricing dispute with British Energy and ScottishPower, and RBS on the insolvency of a Scottish shipping firm. Partner Colin McCleod is also prominent.

Maclay Murray & Spens group head Alayne Swanson appeared for Allied Domecq in the defence of a high-profile claim, while the team acted in a number of judicial reviews. Employment, property (primarily partner Ewan Easton), and recently, health and safety litigation are noted strengths of the strong team.

McGrigors boasts an extremely well-regarded litigation team that includes Craig Connal QC and Jim Cormack. A highlight was acting for William Grant in its ten-year passing off case against Glen Catrine over the 'Grants' brand, and its continuing involvement for Imperial Tobacco in the UK's leading tobacco litigation, with Jacqueline Harris leading. The team is particularly recommended for IP litigation and health and safety issues.

David Arnott continues to head the strong team at **MacRoberts** which acted for British Energy on its headline dispute with SSE and ScottishPower.

Partner David Anderson at **Shepherd+ Wedderburn** led the team advising ScottishPower on the Nuclear Energy agreement-related dispute. The team, headed by Kenny Cumming, is well regarded for a range of disputes advice, notably clinical negligence, aviation and insolvency.

According to a competitor, **Simpson & Marwick** has 'sharpened up its act' in recent years. The boutique litigation firm's partnership grew last year to 18, 16 of whom handle contentious matters. Senior partner Paul Wade is acting for Transco in a landmark corporate homicide criminal case relating to a gas explosion. The firm's core business is defendant insurance-related work for Zurich, Norwich Union, Iron Trades and many others.

Anderson Strathern's re-appointment in November 2002 to the Bank of Scotland's litigation panel and continued presence on the Royal Bank of Scotland's panel highlight its banking litigation expertise.

Burness' Glasgow office was recently boosted by the arrival of employment partners Ronald Mackay and David Morgan from **McGrigors**. Media clients include the BBC, while it also works for product liability clients such as Pfizer. The group is headed by Philip Rodney.

DISPUTE RESOLUTION

BRODIES *Edinburgh*
DUNDAS & WILSON ✪ *Edinburgh, Glasgow*
MACLAY MURRAY & SPENS *Glasgow, Edinburgh*
McGRIGORS *Glasgow, Edinburgh*

MACROBERTS *Glasgow, Edinburgh*
SHEPHERD+ WEDDERBURN *Edinburgh, Glasgow*
SIMPSON & MARWICK *Edinburgh*

ANDERSON STRATHERN *Edinburgh*
BURNESS *Edinburgh, Glasgow*

Biggart Baillie *Edinburgh*
DLA *Glasgow, Edinburgh*
Harper Macleod *Glasgow*
Lawford Kidd *Edinburgh*
McClure Naismith *Glasgow, Edinburgh*
Morton Fraser *Edinburgh*
Ross Harper *Glasgow*
Semple Fraser WS *Glasgow, Edinburgh*
Tods Murray WS *Edinburgh, Glasgow*

Archibald Campbell & Harley WS *Edinburgh*
Balfour & Manson *Edinburgh*
Bishops *Glasgow, Edinburgh*
Boyds *Glasgow, Edinburgh*
Fyfe Ireland WS *Edinburgh*
Golds *Glasgow*
Henderson Boyd Jackson WS *Edinburgh, Glasgow*
Iain Smith & Co *Aberdeen*
Ledingham Chalmers *Aberdeen, Edinburgh*
Miller Samuel LLP *Glasgow*
Morisons *Edinburgh*
Paull & Williamsons *Aberdeen, Edinburgh*

Firms are listed A-Z in tiers which are ranked in order of priority
✪ Indicates firm displays contact details at the end of this chapter.

Biggart Baillie's litigation team successfully secured DTI director disqualification work last year. Partner Brent Haywood joined from **Burness**. Elena Fry is now a partner.

Harper Macleod advised on a multi-million pound software liability claim and also acted for Shetland Sea Farms in relation to the Braer disaster. Partners Rod McKenzie and Michael Nicholson are both highly regarded.

McClure Naismith, particularly recommended for IP litigation, advised Glen Catrine on the major 'Grants' passing-off dispute with William Grant.

Morton Fraser gained the entire litigation and property teams from **Robson McLean WS** that included Duncan Murray, John Barrie, and Ewan McIntyre. They brought with them a number of key clients including the Ministry of Defence, the Scottish Secondary Teachers' Association, and Aberdeen City Council. Partner and contentious banking specialist Peter Braid remains group head.

The 'innovative' litigation head, Alison Gow at **Semple Fraser WS** advised SMG on a *Daily Mail* printing contract dispute. The broad practice features Kenneth Carruthers, who 'sticks to his guns'.

Tods Murray WS is active in commercial property, agricultural estates and forestry disputes. Partner Michael Simpson, principally a contentious construction expert, heads the team that was re-appointed as sole adviser to the Forestry Commission.

EU AND COMPETITION

Maclay Murray & Spens' market-leading competition group continues to go from strength to strength. The group headed by the respected Michael Dean counts Ofgem, Postcomm and Scottish Enterprise among its regular clients.

Burness' competition team, headed by James McLean, advises clients including Standard Life and the Area Tourist Boards on a range of issues including pricing, market practices, procurement and compliance.

Corporate group head David Hardie has now taken on the mantle as EU and competition group leader at **Dundas & Wilson**. Active sectors include utilities, TMT and financial services. Partner Graeme Henry led the team that recently advised Rangers Football Club and the Scottish Rugby Union, while Hardie advised the life and pensions trade association Origo on competition issues.

MacRoberts' two-partner competition group, headed by David Flint, handles all of British Energy's competition matters. During the year it has advised on dawn raids by the Office of Fair Trading (OFT).

Shepherd+ Wedderburn's Gordon Downie, competition group head, obtained the regulatory clearances necessary for the Nuclear Energy Agreement settlement in which the firm represented Scottish Power.

Biggart Baillie's team, headed by IP specialist Colin Miller, advised Scottish Care on competition issues related to procurement, and a major telecoms player on the competition issues relating to a £6m investment.

EU AND COMPETITION

MACLAY MURRAY & SPENS *Glasgow, Edinburgh*

BURNESS *Edinburgh, Glasgow*
DUNDAS & WILSON ✪ *Edinburgh, Glasgow*
MACROBERTS *Glasgow, Edinburgh*
SHEPHERD+ WEDDERBURN *Edinburgh, Glasgow*

Anderson Strathern *Edinburgh*
Biggart Baillie *Glasgow, Edinburgh*
Brodies *Edinburgh*
McClure Naismith *Glasgow, Edinburgh*
McGrigors *Glasgow, Edinburgh*

Firms are listed A-Z in tiers which are ranked in order of priority
✪ Indicates firm displays contact details at the end of this chapter.

EMPLOYMENT

Partner Eilidh Wiseman heads **Dundas & Wilson**'s 22-strong team, which advised Babcock International on the Faslane Naval Base outsourcing. The five-year project involved the transfer of almost 1,800 workers, in a deal estimated at £380m.

Headed by the renowned Malcolm Mackay, the group at **Maclay Murray & Spens** boasts 40 fee-earners and an impressive reputation in contentious and non-contentious matters. As well as its many corporate clients, the firm also acts for housing associations and clients in the care sector.

MacRoberts has an excellent reputation. The practice headed by Raymond Williamson boasts several recognised experts, including Emma Bell and Stephen Miller. The firm advises a wide selection of clients, including ScottishPower, Glasgow City Council and Boots.

Partner Alun Thomas heads **Anderson Strathern**'s highly recommended practice. It is currently acting on several high-profile disputes, such as Roddy Macdonald's ongoing sexual discrimination case against the MoD. The firm recently launched Spectrum, Scotland's first dedicated discrimination law service.

Brodies' employment team continues to grow. The practice, headed by Joan Cradden, has a strong litigation arm that acts for the Royal Bank of Scotland on all contentious matters. The firm also gained several important new clients, including Sainsbury's and Prudential.

Diane Nicol heads the team at **McGrigors**. Clients include the Royal Bank of Scotland, 3i and the Scottish Ambulance Service.

Under Sheila Gunn's experienced leadership, the department at **Shepherd+ Wedderburn** is carving itself out an impressive reputation. It boasts an array of blue-chip clients. The firm defended St Andrews University against a sex discrimination claim, and the US telecoms company, Convergys EMEA, in claims totalling £8.5m.

EMPLOYMENT

DUNDAS & WILSON ✪ *Edinburgh, Glasgow*
MACLAY MURRAY & SPENS *Glasgow, Edinburgh*
MACROBERTS *Glasgow, Edinburgh*

ANDERSON STRATHERN *Edinburgh*
BRODIES *Edinburgh*
McGRIGORS *Glasgow, Edinburgh*
SHEPHERD+ WEDDERBURN *Edinburgh, Glasgow*

BURNESS *Edinburgh*
HARPER MACLEOD *Glasgow*
MORTON FRASER *Edinburgh*

Biggart Baillie *Glasgow*
Brechin Tindal Oatts *Glasgow*
Burnside Kemp Fraser *Aberdeen*
Kidstons & Co *Glasgow*
Ledingham Chalmers *Aberdeen*
McClure Naismith *Glasgow*
Tods Murray WS *Edinburgh*
Wright Johnston & MacKenzie *Glasgow*

Firms are listed A-Z in tiers which are ranked in order of priority
✪ Indicates firm displays contact details at the end of this chapter.

New group head Ronald Mackay has considerably boosted **Burness**' contentious strength. Partner David Morgan is also highly recommended.

Rod McKenzie heads **Harper Macleod**'s well-regarded department. On top of gaining several new clients, including Whitbread and Optical Express, a recent highlight was advising Thus on all its employment matters.

Morton Fraser handles both contentious and non-contentious matters in the team headed by senior litigation partner David Stewart. Partner Duncan Murray led the team advising the Ministry of Defence in the high-profile *MacDonald v MoD* sexual orientation discrimination case.

ENERGY

Shepherd+ Wedderburn's energy practice is one of the jewels in the firm's crown. Its expertise lies primarily in electricity. Clients include ScottishPower, which instructed the team on the £6bn nuclear energy agreement and related litigation. It also advised ScottishPower on the groundbreaking British Electricity Transmission and Trading Arrangements (BETTA).

Biggart Baillie's primary energy client ScottishPower continues to provide the firm with a wide range of quality instructions Partner David Ross heads a heavyweight team that advised

ENERGY

SHEPHERD+ WEDDERBURN *Edinburgh, Glasgow*

BIGGART BAILLIE *Glasgow, Edinburgh*
CMS CAMERON McKENNA *Aberdeen*
LEDINGHAM CHALMERS *Aberdeen*
PAULL & WILLIAMSONS *Aberdeen*

DUNDAS & WILSON ✪ *Edinburgh, Glasgow*
MACLAY MURRAY & SPENS *Glasgow, Aberdeen*
MACROBERTS *Glasgow, Edinburgh*
WRIGHT JOHNSTON & MACKENZIE *Glasgow*

Anderson Strathern *Edinburgh*
Brodies *Edinburgh*
Burness *Edinburgh, Glasgow*
Harper Macleod *Glasgow*
Masons *Glasgow*
McGrigors *Glasgow, Edinburgh*
Tods Murray WS *Edinburgh*

Firms are listed A-Z in tiers which are ranked in order of priority
✪ *Indicates firm displays contact details at the end of this chapter.*

ScottishPower on a proposed underground gas storage project in Cheshire.

CMS Cameron McKenna continued to advise key client BP on completion issues relating to its £1.4bn sale of VEBA upstream assets. London and Aberdeen head Penelope Warne's impressive track record in major disposals for BP continued, with the £830m sale of interests in the Forties field to Apache and its £100m gas disposal in the southern North Sea.

Ledingham Chalmers' Robert Ruddiman is among the best-known names in upstream oil and gas circles. The firm advised the shareholders of Highland Energy, operator of the Windermere gas field, in its £100m sale to RWE, and Tuscan Energy in the £30m debt and equity funding for the redevelopment of the Ardmore oilfield. Ramco Energy, which the firm is advising on the Seven Heads gas development off Cork, is also a significant client.

Paull & Williamsons' dedicated upstream oil and gas team, in particular partner Gordon Buchan has an excellent reputation for corporate work in the sector. Oil clients include BP, Talisman Energy (UK) and Kerr McGee Oil (UK). Group head Sidney Barrie advised longstanding client John Wood Group on its London Stock Exchange listing, the biggest of a Scottish company for ten years.

Dundas & Wilson is particularly recommended for power and water-related matters but also regularly handles those in other sectors, notably oil and gas. The team, headed by water specialist Andrew Renton, acted for SSE in its dispute with Scottish Power and British Energy, and advised Scottish Water. Donald Cumming is an accomplished practitioner.

Maclay Murray & Spens was re-appointed in 2002 to Ofgem's panel, a client for which it has acted since 1999. The firm's new office opened in Aberdeen in 2003 will, no doubt, boost its energy work.

MacRoberts' energy team, headed by Ian Dickson, counts British Energy, AMEC, Vestas-Celtic, and TXU Europe Renewable Generation among its impressive client base.

Wright Johnston & Mackenzie's David Bone has built a deserved reputation for renewable energy matters, particularly major wind farm projects such as the 50MW Crystal Rig scheme (on which Bone advised Fred Olsen Renewables) and the 48MW Causeymire project (advising National Wind Power).

ENVIRONMENT

Brodies' well-respected environmental practice is headed by Charles Smith. The department spreads over the commercial property, corporate, litigation and private client practices. The team recently advised Dumfries & Galloway Council on pollution problems at a waste disposal facility managed by the Council, in which lawyers drafted a report for the Scottish Environment Protection agency.

The 'unrivalled' Karen Aitchison heads the environment group at **Dundas & Wilson**. The firm advised Lattice Property on its Granton Gas Works redevelopment, which eventually satisfied Edinburgh City Council's planning conditions.

Maclay Murray & Spens advised both Clyde Blowers and Hewden Stuart on environmental due diligence and liabilities, relating to the sale of divisions in their respective businesses. Chris Smylie leads the team, which works on an impressive range of environmental matters.

McGrigors' 'high-quality' environmental group is advising Lewis Windpower on environmental aspects of the Isle of Lewis Wind Energy Project. The team is also acting for the MOD on Project Aquatrine. Jennifer Ballantyne heads the department.

Nick Atkins heads the environment group at **Morton Fraser**. Atkins has particular experience in contaminated land issues. Recently the firm acted for South Lanarkshire Council on its flagship partnering arrangements for trade waste and civic amenity sites.

Semple Fraser WS's environment department is headed by Vincent Brown, one of the leading lights in UK environmental law. The firm has particularly strong expertise in remediation contracts and insurance packages. Highlights include acting for Cherokee Investment Partners, which specialises in the investment, remediation and development of polluted sites worldwide.

According to one client, **Burness**' environment team are all 'top-notch lawyers'. The group has very strong expertise in all aspects of waste management

MacRoberts' head of environment, Jamie Grant, is praised for his 'extremely high-quality advice and excellent project management skills'.

ENVIRONMENT

BRODIES *Edinburgh*

DUNDAS & WILSON ✪ *Edinburgh, Glasgow*
MACLAY MURRAY & SPENS *Glasgow, Edinburgh*
McGRIGORS *Glasgow, Edinburgh*
MORTON FRASER *Edinburgh*
SEMPLE FRASER WS *Glasgow, Edinburgh*

Burness *Edinburgh, Glasgow*
MacRoberts *Glasgow, Edinburgh*
Shepherd+ Wedderburn *Edinburgh, Glasgow*
Tods Murray WS *Edinburgh, Glasgow*

Anderson Strathern *Edinburgh*
Archibald Campbell & Harley WS *Edinburgh*
Biggart Baillie *Glasgow, Edinburgh*
Bishops *Glasgow*
DLA *Glasgow, Edinburgh*
Henderson Boyd Jackson WS *Edinburgh, Glasgow*
Ledingham Chalmers *Aberdeen*
McClure Naismith *Glasgow, Edinburgh*
Paull & Williamsons *Aberdeen*
Thorntons WS *Dundee*

Firms are listed A-Z in tiers which are ranked in order of priority
✪ *Indicates firm displays contact details at the end of this chapter.*

Major clients include GlaxoSmithKline, Amec Wind and British Energy.

Shepherd+ Wedderburn is acting for Kelly Fuels on a pending appeal against the Highland Council, regarding a noise abatement notice served to the company's coalyard in Wick. The highly regarded Colin Innes heads the department, which has a strong contentious practice.

IT AND IP

Maclay Murray & Spens continues to lead the way with across-the-board strengths in IP and IT. Partner Fiona Nicolson's team advised Microsoft on anti-piracy work and handled IP corporate support on a succession of weighty transactions. Partner Gill Grassie is recommended for IP litigation.

Dundas & Wilson's solid IP/IT team specialises in university spin-out work for clients such as the University of Glasgow. Well-regarded all-rounder Laurence Ward heads the team that handled a series of complex IP acquisitions by Ardana Bioscience and two major IT outsourcing deals for Standard Life Assurance.

McGrigors' senior partner Shonaig Macpherson continues to head an experienced team. It advises a range of clients including visitscotland.com, Vis Entertainment and PPL Therapeutics. The firm benefits from its association with KPMG Intellectual Property Services (KIPS) which allows it to offer new IP-related products. Director Matthew Godfrey-Faussett, a PFI-related technology specialist, has 'a pragmatic approach to problem resolution'.

IT AND IP

MACLAY MURRAY & SPENS *Glasgow*

DUNDAS & WILSON ✪ *Edinburgh*
McGRIGORS *Glasgow*
SHEPHERD+ WEDDERBURN *Edinburgh*

BIGGART BAILLIE *Glasgow*
MACROBERTS *Glasgow*
MASONS *Glasgow*
MORTON FRASER *Edinburgh*
TODS MURRAY WS *Edinburgh*
WRIGHT JOHNSTON & MACKENZIE *Glasgow*

Brechin Tindal Oatts *Glasgow*
Brodies *Edinburgh*
Burness *Edinburgh*
Dickson Minto WS *Edinburgh*

Anderson Strathern *Edinburgh*
DLA *Glasgow*
Harper Macleod *Glasgow*
Ledingham Chalmers *Aberdeen*
McClure Naismith *Glasgow*
Semple Fraser WS *Glasgow*
Thorntons WS *Dundee*

Firms are listed A-Z in tiers which are ranked in order of priority
✪ *Indicates firm displays contact details at the end of this chapter.*

Shepherd+ Wedderburn's media and technology practice is headed by the highly regarded Joanna Boag-Thomson. The group is primarily recommended for large-scale IT projects, such as the Disclosure Scotland PPP in which it advised the Scottish Executive, and a range of IP matters (including a growing niche in biotech and life sciences).

Biggart Baillie's IP partner Colin Miller led the team that advised ScottishPower on the procurement of its IT infrastructure, and acted for Web Broadcast Media on the funding and development of its interactive operator system product.

MacRoberts' partner David Flint is an accredited IP specialist and an expert in domain name disputes. The firm is particularly recommended for e-commerce matters where clients include Calligrafix and Scottish Internet Exchange.

Masons is best known for advising on major IT projects and complex IT litigation, although the Scottish team also handles IP, notably trade mark infringement matters. Partner John Salmon is a 'responsive and practical'. Major clients include the BBC and Scottish Life.

The arrival of former Voxar corporate counsel Lorne Byatt at **Morton Fraser** in was a catalyst for the group's resurgence and particularly useful in attracting early-stage companies to the firm. Other clients include National Australia Group and spin-out Librae.

Wright Johnston & Mackenzie has an excellent reputation for all aspects of IP, and is best known as legal adviser to the Edinburgh-based Roslin Institute, creator of Dolly the Sheep. The firm has advised on a number of spin-out deals as a result of this relationship. Partner Clare Neilson heads the 'IPcom' group.

Tods Murray WS's IP/IT group, which features non-contentious specialist Lynn Beaumont, advised SchlumbergerSema on the VisitScotland e-business project and advised on the Scottish National Photography Centre. The firm offers the full range of IP advice. New clients include Southern Water, AstraZeneca and Codefine.

Head of IP/IT Grant Campbell at **Brodies** is liked for his ability to advise on 'a sensible course of action from a commercial, as well as legal, perspective'. The firm advised RBS on the Law Society of Scotland's PKI project, *Lawseal*.

Burness's IP/IT team features the competition expert Jim McLean. The firm is particularly recommended for data protection advice. Clients appreciate the firm's emphasis on relationship building that, they say, leads to quick and effective problem solving.

Anderson Strathern is best known for IP matters. The firm was appointed in December 2002 to advise on Kwik-Fit's worldwide trade mark portfolio following its sale to CVC Capital Partners. Partner Simon Brown is praised for his ability to handle complex non-contentious IP work.

DLA launched a technology, media and communications practice in Scotland with the appointment of technology and IP specialist John McKinlay.

Harper Macleod is best known for sports-related IP matters, where clients include Celtic FC, the Scottish Premier League and Ice Hockey Services. Partner Tom Thomas adjudicates on domain name disputes for UK naming authority, Nominet.

Ledingham Chalmers' technology team, headed by corporate finance specialist Roger Connon, supports the firm's leading oil and gas practice and also advises the University of Aberdeen on spin-out work.

McClure Naismith is recommended for contentious IP and IP licensing. The firm acted for Glen Catrine in the high-profile passing-off case against William Grant (advised by **McGrigors**).

Semple Fraser WS's new IP/IT group, formed in 2002, is headed by Scott Kerr and provides support to the firm's corporate team.

INSOLVENCY AND CORPORATE RECOVERY

DUNDAS & WILSON ✪ *Edinburgh, Glasgow*

BURNESS *Edinburgh, Glasgow*
DLA *Glasgow, Edinburgh*
MACLAY MURRAY & SPENS *Glasgow, Edinburgh*
McGRIGORS *Glasgow, Edinburgh*
SEMPLE FRASER WS *Glasgow*
SHEPHERD+ WEDDERBURN *Glasgow, Edinburgh*

Anderson Strathern *Edinburgh*
Bennett & Robertson LLP *Edinburgh*
Biggart Baillie *Glasgow, Edinburgh*
Blackadders *Dundee*
Boyds *Glasgow*
Brodies *Edinburgh*
Harper Macleod *Glasgow*
Henderson Boyd Jackson WS *Edinburgh, Glasgow*
Iain Smith & Co *Aberdeen*
MacRoberts *Glasgow, Edinburgh*
McClure Naismith *Glasgow, Edinburgh*
Paull & Williamsons *Aberdeen*
Tods Murray WS *Edinburgh*

Firms are listed A-Z in tiers which are ranked in order of priority
✪ *Indicates firm displays contact details at the end of this chapter.*

Dundas & Wilson, Scotland's leading practice, boasts a full-time corporate recovery group of 16 fee-earners which acts for most of Scotland's major banks and accountants. Group head Ian Cuthbertson has an outstanding reputation, while Yvonne Brady is also highly regarded. Key instructions include acting for Bank of Scotland and RBS on the restructuring of Texstyle World, and Clydesdale Bank and PwC on the administration of J Stepek.

Burness advises most of Scotland's leading accountancy firms including PwC, Grant Thornton and KPMG, and reports a rise in instructions from Bank of Scotland and RBS. Group head Andrew Sleigh has a formidable reputation.

Partner Gordon Hollerin at **DLA** heads a highly regarded practice which advised on a number of headline receiverships and administrations, including those of Landmark Home Furnishing and Texstyle World.

Maclay Murray & Spens' insolvency practice, headed by Michael Hughes, has the resources and skills to handle high-end receiverships, liquidations and corporate work. The firm advised the administrators of Atlantic.

McGrigors is well regarded for restructurings, notably for financial institutions such as KPMG, Levy Gee, and Bank of Scotland. Partner Jim Cormack heads the team.

Semple Fraser WS's Rachel Grant was the first solicitor in Scotland to act for the DTI on disqualification cases. The firm also advised Finova Capital on the receivership of One Devonshire Gardens.

Shepherd+ Wedderburn picked up notable instructions on the restructuring of Semple Cochrane and Atlantic Telecom. Accredited insolvency specialist Gillian Carty heads the team.

Corporate partner John Kerr led the **Anderson Strathern** team advising the Danish IT company Aston Group on the insolvency of its Scottish subsidiary.

PENSIONS

SHEPHERD+ WEDDERBURN *Edinburgh*

BIGGART BAILLIE *Glasgow*
BURNESS *Edinburgh*
MACLAY MURRAY & SPENS *Glasgow*
MACROBERTS *Glasgow*

Dundas & Wilson ✪ *Edinburgh*
McGrigors *Glasgow*
Tods Murray WS *Edinburgh*

Firms are listed A-Z in tiers which are ranked in order of priority
✪ Indicates firm displays contact details at the end of this chapter.

REAL ESTATE
Edinburgh and Glasgow

DUNDAS & WILSON ✪ *Edinburgh, Glasgow*
MACLAY MURRAY & SPENS *Glasgow, Edinburgh*
McGRIGORS *Glasgow, Edinburgh*
SHEPHERD+ WEDDERBURN *Edinburgh, Glasgow*

BRODIES *Edinburgh*
BURNESS *Edinburgh, Glasgow*
MACROBERTS *Glasgow, Edinburgh*
SEMPLE FRASER WS *Glasgow, Edinburgh*

BIGGART BAILLIE *Glasgow, Edinburgh*
DLA *Glasgow, Edinburgh*
MORTON FRASER *Edinburgh*
TODS MURRAY WS *Edinburgh, Glasgow*

Fyfe Ireland WS *Edinburgh*
Masons *Glasgow*
McClure Naismith *Glasgow, Edinburgh*

Anderson Strathern *Edinburgh*
Archibald Campbell & Harley WS *Edinburgh*
Bell & Scott *Edinburgh*
Bishops *Glasgow*
Boyds *Edinburgh*
Brechin Tindal Oatts *Glasgow*
Golds *Glasgow*
Harper Macleod *Glasgow*
Henderson Boyd Jackson WS *Edinburgh, Glasgow*
Miller Samuel LLP *Glasgow*
Wright Johnston & Mackenzie *Glasgow, Edinburgh*

Firms are listed A-Z in tiers which are ranked in order of priority
✪ Indicates firm displays contact details at the end of this chapter.

REAL ESTATE
Elsewhere in Scotland

PAULL & WILLIAMSONS *Aberdeen*

LEDINGHAM CHALMERS *Aberdeen*

Iain Smith & Co *Aberdeen*
Stronachs *Aberdeen*
Thorntons WS *Dundee*

Blackadders *Dundee*
Clark & Wallace *Aberdeen*
Raeburn Christie *Aberdeen*

Firms are listed A-Z in tiers which are ranked in order of priority

Biggart Baillie also acts for the DTI on directors' disqualification cases. The firm is well connected with accountants, including KPMG, Tenon and James Macintyre & Co. Partner Murray Shaw is group head.

Tods Murray WS is involved in the restructuring of Scottish Media Group, advising the lending syndicate.

PENSIONS

Shepherd+ Wedderburn's much-vaunted team retains its position in the top tier. Andrew Holehouse leads eight specialists, including partner Louisa Knox. The UK-wide service is adviser to the Vivendi Universal Pension Scheme, following a competitive tender. Other clients include Morrison Group, Scottish Power and Virgin Group.

Biggart Baillie's highly experienced unit is headed by Iain Talman. The department has recently made a significant contribution, bringing in corporate work on the back of its considerable pensions expertise.

The well-respected pensions unit at **Burness** is headed by Andrew Fleming, who is very popular with his clients, and is praised for being 'thorough, down to earth, and extremely approachable'.

Pensions work at **Maclay Murray & Spens** is. headed by Gary Cullen, who has eight fee-earners at his disposal. The team is working on several significant pension schemes for HBOS and Coats, with a compound value of £1.5bn.

The **MacRoberts**' pension and employee benefits group is headed by Peter Trotter, and carries out support and stand-alone work in equal measure. A recent highlight was retaining its position as legal adviser to the Richards Group pension scheme, after Richards went into receivership.

REAL ESTATE

Edinburgh and Glasgow: Dundas & Wilson's impressive commercial property department claims 79 fee-earners, and is enjoying significant growth in London. One of the firm's top Scottish instructions was from the Industrial Property Investment Fund, the purchaser of a portfolio of industrial estates. Department head Iain Doran and partner David Steel are highly recommended.

Maclay Murray & Spens had a very fruitful year. Robin Garrett's team was boosted by the arrival of the highly experienced Ron Cole, while the firm's London office welcomed Nick Bird, formerly a partner at **Allen & Overy**. Significant highlights include acting for Wilson Bowden Developments in a joint venture to regenerate the former Ravenscraig Steelworks, and Southside Capital on the commercial redevelopment of the old Edinburgh Royal Infirmary.

McGrigors' 34 fee-earner property department benefited from the return of Scotland managing partner Kirk Murdoch to fee-earning duties two years ago. Among the firm's notable deals was advising the Co-operative Group on its acquisition of 160 stores and a distribution warehouse. It also continues to advise Glasgow Harbour on the Glasgow Harbour Development Project.

Shepherd+ Wedderburn's highly regarded group consists of 47 fee-earners, including 12 full-time partners. Significant instructions include advising Pillar Property and Parlison Properties on all aspects of their major Greenside development in Calton Square. Dorothy Boyd's department has gained several impressive new clients, including Regal Property Group, Credit Suisse First Boston, and Rosewood Hotels.

Brodies' property practice continues to enjoy a good reputation across a range of areas, thus ensuring a steady stream of top-notch instructions. The most high-profile of these was for Rolls-Royce, on its acquisition of a major new factory near Glasgow. This forward-funded project is the largest factory development in Scotland for several years.

Ian Wattie heads **Burness**'s 34-strong commercial property department. The firm acted for Grosvenor Developments on its £27m sale of the St John's Centre in Perth, and is also advising Chartwell Land. Partners Ken Ross and Richard Rennie are both credited for their commercial awareness.

MacRoberts' solid property team is jointly headed by Laurence Fraser and Allan MacKenzie. Key clients such as Network Rail Infrastructure provide the firm with numerous development instructions. The department also advised Haslemere on the securitisation of its Scottish property portfolio.

The nine-partner commercial property practice at **Semple Fraser WS** is highly recommended. The firm has gained several high-profile new clients, including JJ Gallagher and Amec Developments. It also acted for Royal & SunAlliance on its £50m redevelopment of Eastgate Phase II in Inverness.

Peter Cruickshank's commercial property department at **Biggart Baillie** is particularly well regarded for its expertise in the retail sector. Clients include Bhs, Sainsbury's and Debenhams.

DLA's commercial property team was boosted by the arrival of eight new fee-earners from **Archibald Campbell & Harley WS**, including partners Sheila Irvine and Drew Wallace, who joins Graeme Sunter as head of department. The firm is currently advising Selfridges on the development and acquisition of its new store site in Glasgow.

2002 was a year of considerable growth for **Morton Fraser** following the arrival of partners

Nick Atkins, Hugh Angus and three associates from **Robson McLean WS**. The practice brought in several impressive clients including the MoD. Partners Hugo Allan and Chris Harte are both described as excellent.

Douglas Moffat heads **Tods Murray WS**'s 12-partner commercial property team. A highlight was advising Kenmore Group in the sale to Eagle Holdings of a property portfolio worth £45m. Other clients include the Elphinstone Group and Heron International.

Elsewhere in Scotland: The commercial property department at **Paull & Williamsons** enjoyed a busy year, advising BAA on the development and letting of 60,000 square feet of office and warehouse space in Aberdeen. It also acted for Scotoil Group on its sale of a 200,000 square foot retail park. The practice is headed by Leslie Dalgarno.

Ledingham Chalmers' team continues to grow and now boasts 11 partners among its 20 fee-earners. Highlights include representing Cala Group on the real estate elements of its £50m property development joint venture with HBOS. John Curran heads the department.

Aberdeen's **Iain Smith & Co** is well regarded and advises on all aspects of commercial property.

Partner Duncan Campbell heads **Stronachs**' well-established commercial property practice. The department advises a wide range of clients on all aspects of property, from small lettings to large-scale industrial developments.

Partner Stewart Brymer heads **Thorntons WS**'s team. The practice acts for a number of high-profile clients, including the Bett Group, Grantchester and London & Amsterdam Developments.

TRANSPORT

Under the helm of James Lowe, the shipping practice at **Henderson Boyd Jackson WS** continues to chart an impressive course. The firm's client list reads like a Who's Who of the shipping industry and the department is extremely well regarded for contentious work.

Maclay Murray & Spens' shipping practice saw the retirement of department head, Bruce Patrick, in June 2003. But the recruitment of Andrew Meakin, and Patrick's continuing role as a consultant ensures that the group remains on an even keel. The firm has a strong contentious practice but at the same time continues to shine in shipping finance.

Based in Aberdeen, **Mackinnons** has one of Scotland's leading shipping practices. The firm has particularly strong expertise in the fishing industry and regularly advises on ship disposals, sales, and disputes. Keith MacRae is one of the firm's leading practitioners.

Neil Amner heads the transport group at **Biggart Baillie**, which has expertise in rail and aviation matters. Recently the firm advised ScotRail and its parent company, National Express Group, on the expiry and subsequent renewal of its franchise.

The transport group at **Brodies** is ably led by Julian Voge, and has been involved in Scottish rail restructure and franchising since 1994. The Strategic Rail Authority is one of the firm's major clients.

Dundas & Wilson's transport practice is led by John Watchman. The firm is extremely well experienced in road-related matters.

Partner Alistair Burrow is the main shipping contact at **Tods Murray WS**. The firm focuses largely on non-contentious work. Clients include Altnamara Shipping and Henry Abram & Sons.

TRANSPORT

HENDERSON BOYD JACKSON WS *Edinburgh, Glasgow*

MACLAY MURRAY & SPENS *Glasgow, Edinburgh*

MACKINNONS *Aberdeen*

Biggart Baillie *Edinburgh, Glasgow*

Brodies *Edinburgh*

Dundas & Wilson ✪ *Edinburgh, Glasgow*

Tods Murray WS *Edinburgh, Glasgow*

Firms are listed A-Z in tiers which are ranked in order of priority

✪ Indicates firm displays contact details at the end of this chapter.

DUNDAS & WILSON

SALTIRE COURT
20 CASTLE TERRACE
EDINBURGH EH1 2EN

Telephone: +44 131 228 8000
Fax: +44 131 228 8888
E-mail: dw-enquiries@dundas-wilson.com
Website: www.dundas-wilson.com

Languages
French, German, Italian, Spanish

Other offices
Glasgow, London

Number of lawyers 279
at this office 159

CATEGORIES OF WORK

Banking
Stephen Phillips

Corporate
David Hardie

Employment, pensions and incentives
Eilidh Wiseman

Infrastructure
Alan Campbell

Litigation
Colin Macleod

Property
Iain Doran

Technology
Gary Anderson

Industry sector focus:

Financial
Michael Stoneham

Government services
Michael McAuley

Real estate
Donald Shaw

Technology
Laurence Ward

Energy and utilities
Andrew Renton

WHO'S WHO IN THE LAW

Professional contacts

AUSTRIA

BARBIST, Johannes

Binder Grösswang Rechtsanwälte
Phone: Innsbruck (+43 512 579 973 0)
E-mail: barbist@bgnet.at
Unfair trade law, competition law, industrial property law, European law.
Position: Attorney-at-law.
Career: Foreign intern Patrick J Durcan & Co Solicitors, Ireland 1995; foreign intern European Commission, Brussels 1997-98; associate Binder Grösswang Rechtsanwälte 1998-2001, attorney-at-law 2001 to date. Publications: 'Die geplante Reform des österreichischen Kartellrechts', M&R 2001, 207; 'Hasta la vista Baby – Arnold(-stein) als Drehscheibe der Produktpiraterie in Österreich', ecolex 2001, 685 (with Rungg); 'Reform der EG-Wettbewerbsregeln für Unternehmenskooperationen, RdW 2001, 260 (with Rungg); 'Glosse zur KOG-Entschidung 16 Ok 6/00 – Abonnementpreise M&R', 2000, 391 (with Rungg); Glosse zur KOG-Entscheidung 16 Ok 4/00 – Hauszustellungssystem III', ÖBl 2001, 41; 'Schwere Zeiten für große Unternehmer', ecolex 2000, 367 (with Girsch); 'Neues in der österreichischen Fusionkontrolle auf Grund der Kartellgesetznovelle 1999', ecolex 2000, 51 (with Rungg); 'Renaissance des Verbotes von Verkäufen unter dem Einstandspreis', RdW 1999, 698 (with Rungg); 'Die Kartellgesetnovelle 1999 als Regierungsvorlage', ecolex 1999, 411 (with Girsch); Austrian contributor in Verloop (Ed), 'Merger Control in the EU', 3rd Ed, Kluwer 1999 (with Kutschera).
Languages: English, French, German.
Education: University of Innsbruck (1995 Mag iur, 2000 Dr iur); European Forum Alpbach (1996 Alpbach Summer School on European Integration); University of Limerick (1997 MA).
Personal: Born 1972.

BINDER, Michael

Binder Grösswang Rechtsanwälte
Phone: Vienna (+43 1 534 800)
E-mail: binder@bgnet.at
Takeover, corporate, financial services, investment funds, banking and finance, M&A.
Position: Partner.
Career: Admitted to the Bar, Austria 1985; lecturer and assistant at Institute for Commercial Law, University of Vienna Law School 1977-84; intern Chadbourne & Parke, New York 1982; associate Binder Grösswang Rechtsanwälte 1982-85, 1980-81; partner since 1986. Publications: the mandatory public offer in Austria's Takeover Act, M&A Yearbook 11/2000 (with Khol); 'Bankenehe HypoVereinsbank und Bank Austria – Kurzanalyse', ecolex 12/2000 (with Khol); 'Satellite to Cable Services in Austria, Intellectual Property in Business', Vol 2, Issue 1, 17, 1990; Article 11 bis of the Berne Convention and s59a of the Austrian Copyright Act, International Business Law 81, 1985; 'Bericht Handelsrecht', ÖZW 1983, 82.
Languages: English, French, German.
Member: International Bar Association.
Education: University of Vienna Law School (1978 Dr iur); Yale University Law School (1982 LLM, Fulbright Fellow).
Personal: Born 1955.

BUCHROITHNER, Hellmut

Binder Grösswang Rechtsanwälte
Phone: Innsbruck (+43 512 579 973 0)
E-mail: buchroithner@bgnet.at
Contract law, banking and finance, immaterial goods law, copyright, M&A.
Position: Attorney-at-law.
Career: Associate Binder Grösswang Rechtsanwälte 1996-2001, attorney-at-law 2001 to date. Publications: 'Markenartikel und Produktpiraterie', DHK Wirtschaftsspiegel 4/2000 (with Rungg).
Languages: English, German.
Education: University of Innsbruck (1994 Mag iur, 1997 Dr iur); Tulane University Law School, New Orleans (1999 LLM).
Personal: Born 1970.

FABIAN, Tibor

Binder Grösswang Rechtsanwälte
Phone: Vienna (+43 1 534 800)
E-mail: fabian@bgnet.at
Banking and finance, structured finance, capital markets, real estate and property.
Position: Partner.
Career: Assistant at the Institute for Roman Law – University of Vienna 1976-79; associate Exinger & Co (CPA) 1983; assistant to the chairman, Österr Kontrollbank AG 1984-86; assistant to the general manager Mayr Melnhof Karton 1987-88; head of international project finance, Österreichische Länderbank AG Vienna 1988-89; associate Binder Grösswang Rechtsanwälte 1990-96; partner since 1996.
Languages: Croatian, English, German.
Education: University of Vienna, Law School (1980 Dr iur); University of Economics and Business Administration Vienna (1981 Mag rer soc oec).
Personal: Born 1956.

FEYL, Peter

Schönherr Rechtsanwälte
Phone: Vienna (+43 1 53 43 70)
E-mail: p.feyl@schoenherr.at
Position: Partner dealing with banking, capital markets, corporate law, trusts, mergers and acquisitions.
Career: Admitted to the Austrian Bar 1990.
Languages: English, French, German.
Education: University of Vienna (1984 Dr iur); University of Virginia (1986 LLM).
Personal: Born 1961.

FROTZ, Stephan

Schönherr Rechtsanwälte
Phone: Vienna (+43 1 53 43 70)
E-mail: s.frotz@schoenherr.at
Position: Partner dealing with banking law, corporate restructurings, mergers and acquisitions, tax.
Career: Admitted to the Austrian Bar 1987.
Languages: English, French, German.
Education: University of Vienna (1981 Dr iur); research scholar, Max Planck-Institute for Foreign and International Patent.
Personal: Born 1957.

GRAF, Ferdinand

Graf, Maxl & Pitkowitz
Phone: Vienna (+43 1 401 17 40)
E-mail: graf@gmp.at
Position: Partner dealing with mergers and acquisitions, cartel and competition law, corporate law, general trade law, media law, telecommunications law.
Career: Assistant professor at University of Vienna, Institute of Civil Law 1988-89; internship at Arent, Fox, Kintner, Plotkin & Kahn, Washington DC 1991; associate Dr Ferdinand Graf and Preslmayr & Partners 1990-94; admitted to New York Bar 1993; admitted to Austrian Bar 1994; founding partner Graf, Maxl & Pitkowitz 1994.
Languages: English, German.
Member: Austrian Bar; American, New York State and International Bar Associations; Center for International Legal Studies, Salzburg.
Education: University of Vienna (1990 JD); New York University (1991 Master of Laws).
Personal: Born 1965; resides Vienna.

GRÖSSWANG, Klaus

Binder Grösswang Rechtsanwälte
Phone: Vienna (+43 1 534 800)
E-mail: groesswang@bgnet.at
Labour, real estate and tenancy, automobile trade.
Position: Partner.
Career: Associate Dr Martin Binder 1965-71; partner Binder Grösswang Rechtsanwälte since 1971.
Languages: English, German.
Member: International Bar Association; Disciplinary Board of the Bar of Vienna.
Education: University of Vienna (1963 Dr iur).
Personal: Born 1940.

HABLE, Andreas

Binder Grösswang Rechtsanwälte
Phone: Vienna (+43 1 534 800)
E-mail: hable@bgnet.at
Tax and corporate law, restructurings, M&A.
Position: Attorney-at-law.
Career: Associate/tax adviser Europa Treuhand Ernst & Young 1996-97; associate Haarmann Hemmelrath Hügel 1997-2001; attorney-at-law Binder Grösswang Rechtsanwälte 2001 to date. Publications: 'Fiscal Advancement of Broadband Internet Access', SWK August 2003; 'Stamp Duty Aspects of E-Commerce' in: 'Taxation of E-Commerce' (Toifl/Züger); numerous contributions to the Global Counsel journal.
Languages: English, French, German.
Member: International Fiscal Association.
Education: University of Innsbruck (1995 Mag iur, 1996 Dr iur); Université Paris XII – Val de Marne (1995); University of Economics and Business Administration, Vienna (2000 Postgraduate International Tax Law).
Personal: Born 1969.

HAUER, Christian

Schönherr Rechtsanwälte
Phone: Vienna (+43 1 53 43 70)
E-mail: ch.hauer@schoenherr.at
Position: Partner dealing with unfair competition law, trade marks, pharmaceuticals, food and drug law.
Career: Admitted to the Austrian Bar 1976.
Languages: English, French, German.
Member: Examining board for candidates for judgeship.
Education: University of Vienna (1967 Dr iur).
Personal: Born 1942.

HERBST, Christian

Schönherr Rechtsanwälte
Phone: Vienna (+43 1 53 43 70)
E-mail: ch.herbst@schoenherr.at
Position: Partner dealing with (international) mergers and acquisitions, takeovers, corporate law and telecoms.
Career: Admitted to the Bar 1988; foreign associate with a New York City law firm 1984. Lecturer on international business transactions at the University of Economics, Vienna, and on the MBL program at Salzburg University.
Languages: English, German.
Member: IBA; UIA; Forum Kartellrecht.
Education: Salzburg University (1982 Dr iur); School of Advanced International Studies JHU, Bologna (1983 Diploma); Harvard University (1984 LLM).
Personal: Born 1959.

HERMANN, Gerhard

Schönherr Rechtsanwälte
Phone: Vienna (+43 1 53 43 70)
E-mail: g.hermann@schoenherr.at
Position: Partner dealing with corporate, M&A.
Career: Admitted to the Bar 1996.
Languages: English, German.
Education: University of Vienna (1995 Dr iur); Cambridge University (1997 LLM).
Personal: Born 1968.

HOFFER, Raoul

Binder Grösswang Rechtsanwälte
Phone: Vienna (+43 1 534 800)
E-mail: hoffer@bgnet.at
Antitrust, procurement, state aid.
Position: Partner.
Career: Seminars and conferences in the field of public procurement law and antitrust law; associate Binder Grösswang Rechtsanwälte 1991-98; partner since 1999; summer associate Saul, Ewing, Remick & Saul, Philadelphia 1993; lecturer at the Fachhochschule for Finance, Accounting and Tax (FIRST), Chamber of Commerce Vienna 1998-2000. Publications (inter alia): Anmerkung zu BVA 14/6/2002, N-9/ – LKW-Mautsystem, RPA 2002, (with Schmölz); 'EuGH fordert verstärkten Bieterschutz', ecolex 2002, (with Schmölz); 'De-minimis-Bekanntmachung der Europäischen Kommission', ecolex 2002/360 (with Hornek); Kommentierung BVA 13/11/2001, N 69/01-32, 'Lieferung von Elektrizität für die Bundesdienststellen in Kärnten', RPA 2002/38 with Schmölz); 'Einstweilige Verfügungen gemäß' § 116 BVergG Teil II Fristen und Dauer, RPA 2002/27 (with Schmölz); 'Gründung von Gemeinschaftsunternehmen: Zulässige "Nebenabreden"', RdW 2002/65 (with Hornek); 'Nichtigkeit von freihändigen Vergaben', ecolex 2002/67 (with Schmölz); 'Umweltbelange und soziale Belange bei der Vergabe öffentlicher Aufträge', ecolex 2002/64 (with Schmölz). Permanent contributor to 'Recht und Praxis der öffentlichen Auftragsvergabe' (RPA) and 'Wirtschaft & Recht' ('Der Standard').
Languages: English, French, German, Spanish.
Member: Association Internationale des Jeunes Avocats (AIJA).
Education: University of Vienna (1990 Mag iur, 1992 Dr iur); London School of Economics and Political Science (1994 LLM).
Personal: Born 1967.

ISOLA, A

Graf, Maxl & Pitkowitz
Phone: Graz (+43 316 833 777)
E-mail: isola@gmp.at
Insolvency and corporate restructuring; banking.
Position: Partner.
Career: Partner RAe Hofstätter & Isola Kommandipartnerschaft, Graz, until 1998; partner Schönherr Rechtsanwälte OEG, until mid-2002; partner with Graf, Maxl & Pitkowitz, Vienna – Graz, since mid-2002. Co-author of 'The Handbook for Receivership' ('Handbuch des Masseverwalters'); author of several articles on bankruptcy law and corporate restructuring. Teaching positions, seminars in the field of corporate restructuring and insolvency law.
Languages: English, German.
Member: EIPA European Insolvency Practitioners Association; AIJA International Association of Young Lawyers; advisory board Zeitschrift für Insolvenzrecht und Kreditschutz (ZIK).
Education: University of Graz (1981 Dr iuris); traineeship European Council (1981); New York University (M1984 CJ).
Personal: Born 1957; resides in Graz and Vienna.
Leisure: Collecting modern art.

KHOL, Florian

Binder Grösswang Rechtsanwälte
Phone: Vienna (+43 1 534 800)
E-mail: khol@bgnet.at
Banking and capital markets law, takeover law, M&A, corporate law, international dispute settlement.
Position: Attorney-at-law.
Career: Associate Binder Grösswang Rechsanwälte 1998-2002, attorney-at-law 2002 to date; lecturer of commercial law, Fachhochschule der Wiener Wirtschaft (FIRST and MARS), Chamber of Commerce, Vienna 2000 to date. Publications: 'Bankenehe Hypo Vereinsbank und Bank Austria – Kurzanalyse', ecolex 12/2000 (with Binder); The mandatory public offer in Austria's Takeover Act, M&A Yearbook 11/2000 (with Binder); 'Die Umstellung von Kapitalgesellschaften auf den Euro – Änderungen im Gesellschaftsrecht' in WBL 1/1999; 'Option Neutralität', Khol/Ofner/Stirnemann (Hg), Österreichisches Jarbuch für Politik 1997.
Languages: English, German.
Education: University of Innsbruck Law School (1995 Mag iur, 1997 Dr iur); University of Saarbrücken, Institute for European Law, Germany (1998 Certificate).
Personal: Born 1971.

KLAUSEGGER, Christian

Binder Grösswang Rechtsanwälte
Phone: Vienna (+43 1 534 800)
E-mail: klausegger@bgnet.at
Structured finance, cross border leasing, banking, litigation and arbitration.
Position: Partner.
Career: System Engineer, IBM Austria 1981-83; independent ADP-consultant 1983-87; associate Binder Grösswang Rechtsanwälte 1988-95; partner since 1995.
Languages: English, French, German.
Member: Union International des Advocats.
Education: University of Vienna (1987 Dr iur); University of Vienna (1987 Mag rer soc oec).
Personal: Born 1962.

KONWITSCHKA, Peter

Schönherr Rechtsanwälte
Phone: Vienna (+43 1 53 43 70)
E-mail: p.konwitschka@schoenherr.at
Position: Partner dealing with commercial law, corporate, banking, M&A.
Career: Admitted to the Austrian Bar 1999.
Languages: English, French, German, Russian.
Education: University of Vienna (1991 Mag iur; 1998 Dr iur).
Personal: Born 1969.

KRAMER, Alexander

Binder Grösswang Rechtsanwälte
Phone: Vienna (+43 1 534 800)
E-mail: kramer@bgnet.at
M&A, banking markets, employment law.
Position: Attorney-at-law.
Career: Associate Dorda, Brugger & Jordis 1998-99; associate Binder Grösswang Rechtsanwälte 1999-2002, attorney-at-law 2002 to date. Publications: Austrian contributor in Neate-McCormick Ed, 'Bank Confidentiality', 3rd Ed, Butterworth 2003 (with Kutschera and Schirmer).
Languages: German, English, French.
Education: University of Vienna (1995 Mag iur); The University of Chicago Law School (1998 LLM).
Personal: Born 1969.

KUCSKO, Guido

Schönherr Rechtsanwälte
Phone: Vienna (+43 1 53 43 70)
E-mail: g.kucsko@schoenherr.at
Position: Partner dealing with unfair competition law, trade marks, copyright and information technology.
Career: Admitted to the Austrian Bar 1984. Adjunct professor in IP law, University of Vienna.
Languages: English, German.
Member: Executive Council of the Vienna Bar.
Education: University of Vienna (1979 Dr iur); university assistant, University of Vienna (1979-80); scholar, Max Planck Institute for Foreign and International Patent, Copyright and Competition Law, Munich (1979).
Personal: Born 1954, Austria.

KUTSCHERA, Michael

Binder Grösswang Rechtsanwälte
Phone: Vienna (+43 1 534 800)
E-mail: kutschera@bgnet.at

M&A, corporate, banking and finance, capital markets, arbitration.
Position: Partner.
Career: Assistant and lecturer, Institute of Commercial Law, University of Vienna Law School 1978-82; admitted to New York Bar 1985; Vienna Bar 1987; associate Dr Friedrich Mosing 1980-81; associate Binder Grösswang Rechtsanwälte 1987-89, 1984-85, 1981-82; foreign associate Shearman & Sterling – New York and Paris 1985-87; partner Binder Grösswang Rechtsanwälte since 1989. Publications: Austrian Contributor (together with Marianna Nitsch) in Axel Bösch (Ed), 'Provisional Remedies in International Commercial Arbitration', De Gruyter; Austrian Contributor (together with Christian Hoenig) in Emmanuel Gaillard (Ed), 'Insider Trading the Laws of Europe, the United States and Japan', Kluwer, 1992; Austrian Contributor (together with Johannes Barbist), 'Merger Control in the EU', 4th edition, Kluwer 2003; Gruson/Hutter/Kutschera, 'Legal Opinions in International Transactions', 3rd edition, 1997; Austrian Contributor (together with Thomas Schirmer) in Neate-McCormick (Ed), 'Bank Confidentiality', 3rd edition Butterworths 2003; Gruson/Kutschera, 'Opinion of Counsel on Agreements Governed by Foreign Law', 19 Vand. J. Transnat'IL 515, 1986; 'Zur Haftung des Geschäftsführers gemäß' § 25 GmbHG, GesRZ 1982, 243.
Languages: English, French, German.
Member: International Bar Association; board of the Vienna Bar; Austrian councillor of the International Bar Association; chairman of Committee E (Banking Law) of the International Bar Association.
Education: New York University Law School (1983 MCJ, Fulbright Fellow); University of Vienna (1979 Dr iur).
Personal: Born 1957.

LINDINGER, Christoph

Schönherr Rechtsanwälte
Phone: Vienna (+43 1 53 43 70)
E-mail: ch.hindinger@schoenherr.at
Position: Partner dealing with EU law, mergers and acquisitions, banking and antitrust.
Career: Admitted to the Austrian Bar 1991.
Languages: English, German.
Education: University of Salzburg (1984 Dr iur).
Personal: Born 1962.

LUKANEC, Horst

Binder Grösswang Rechtsanwälte
Phone: Vienna (+43 1 534 800)
E-mail: lukanec@bgnet.at
M&A, business, corporate, labour law.
Position: Partner.
Career: Associate, notary's office 1995; associate Binder Grösswang Rechtsanwälte 1996-2000; admitted to the Bar 2000; partner 2004 to date.
Languages: English, German.
Education: University of Vienna (1994 Mag iur); Tulane University Law School – New Orleans (1999 LLM).
Personal: Born 1964.

MADL, Peter

Schönherr Rechtsanwälte
Phone: Vienna (+43 1 53 43 70)
E-mail: p.madl@schoenherr.at
Position: Partner dealing with corporate law, construction, litigation and arbitration.
Career: Admitted to the Austrian Bar 1990.
Languages: English, German.
Education: University of Vienna (1983 Dr iur); University of Economics, Vienna (1987 Mag rer soc oec); university assistant at University of Vienna (1983-86).
Personal: Born 1960.

MAXL, Martin

Graf, Maxl & Pitkowitz
Phone: Vienna (+43 1 401 17 40)
E-mail: maxl@gmp.at
Corporate.
Position: Partner dealing with mergers and acquisitions, reorganisations, corporate and media law.
Career: Trained Weiss-Tessbach and Zeiner & Zeiner; Coca-Cola East Central Europe Division; admitted 1994; founding partner Graf, Maxl & Pitkowitz 1994.
Languages: English, French, German.
Member: Austrian Bar; IBA.
Education: University of Graz (1988 Mag iur; 1989 JD).
Personal: Born 1961; resides Vienna.
Leisure: Sports (running, cycling and skiing), collecting fine art and photography.

PITKOWITZ, Nikolaus

Graf, Maxl & Pitkowitz
Phone: Vienna (+43 1 401 17 40)
E-mail: pitkowitz@gmp.at
Real estate and arbitration.
Position: Partner dealing with corporate law, real estate law, arbitration, eastern Europe.
Career: Admitted to Austrian Bar 1990; partner with a major Austrian law firm 1990-94; university lecturer in Czech business law 1993-99; founding partner Graf, Maxl & Pitkowitz 1994; permanent arbitrator at Austrian Chamber of Commerce; permanent arbitrator at ICC.
Languages: English, German.
Member: Austrian Bar; IBA; American Foreign Lawyers Association.
Education: University of Vienna (1984 JD); Georgetown University (1991 Orientation in the US Legal System); University St Gallen (1999 Master of European and International Business Law).
Personal: Born 1961; resides Vienna.

RIEDEL, Laetizia

Binder Grösswang Rechtsanwälte
Phone: Innsbruck (+43 512 579 973 0)
E-mail: riedel@bgnet.at
Trusts and estates, privatisation, corporate law, M&A, contract law.
Position: Attorney-at-law.
Career: Associate Dorder, Brugger & Jordis 1999-2000; associate Binder Grösswang Rechtsanwälte 2001-03, attorney-at-law 2003 to date.
Languages: German, English.
Education: University of Innsbruck (1998 Mag iur); University of Vienna (2002 Bar Exam).
Personal: Born 1974.

RUNGG, Ivo

Binder Grösswang Rechtsanwälte
Phone: Innsbruck (+43 512 579 973 0)
E-mail: rungg@bgnet.at
Banking and capital markets, Internet law, M&A, European law, law against unfair competition, IP law.
Position: Partner.
Career: Foreign intern, Council of Europe Straßburg, 1992; associate Foglar-Deinhardstein & Brandstätter KEG Vienna (Law office) 1995-97; clerk European Court of Justice, Luxemburg 1998; partner Binder Grösswang Rechtsanwälte since 1998. Publications: 'Die jüngste Entscheidung der Kommission bei der Festsetzung der Höhe von Geldbußen in Kartellsachen', ecolex 2000, 171 (with Breit); 'Neues in der österreichischen Fusionskontrolle auf Grund der Kartellgesetznovelle' 1999, ecolex 2000, 51 (with Barbist); 'Renaissance des Verbotes von Verkäufen unter dem Einstandspreis', RdW 1999, 698 (with Barbist); 'Der einstweilige Rechtsschutz in der Rechtssprechungspraxis des EuG', Wbl 1999, 137 (with Breit); 'Verfahrensrechtliche Aspekte der Nichtigkeitsklage vor dem Gericht erster Instanz der EG', ecolex 1998, 745 (with Mair); as well as articles in newspapers and magazines.
Languages: English, French, German, Italian.
Member: Association Européenne des Avocats (AEA); British Honorary Vice-Consul, Innsbruck; Law Editor of business magazine 'Econova'.
Education: Centre International de Formation Européenne (Summer Academy, 1989); Universities of Innsbruck and Vienna (1992 Mag iur; 1994 Dr iur); University of Innsbruck (1993 Mag phil).
Personal: Born 1969.

SCHIRMER, Thomas

Binder Grösswang Rechtsanwälte
Phone: Vienna (+43 1 534 800)
E-mail: schirmer@bgnet.at
M&A, structured finance, cross-border leasing, banking law, capital markets, corporate law.
Position: Partner.
Career: Foreign intern, Deutsch, Kerrigan & Stiles – New Orleans, 1993; associate/attorney-at-law Binder Grösswang Rechtsanwälte 1995-99; partner since 2000; lecturer of commercial and company law at the Fachhochschule for Marketing and Sales and Tax and Finance, Chamber of Commerce, Vienna 1998-2000. Publications: Austrian Contributor in Neate-McCormick Ed, 'Bank Confidentiality', 3rd Ed Butterworths 2003 (with Kutschera and Kramer); 'Legal Opinions and Bankruptcy', IBA Newsletter on Banking Law, Vol 5 No 1, 1997; contributor in 'Liberalisierung Österreichischer Infrastrukturmärkte, Kurt P Nemec (Ed), LexisNexis Orac 2003; Austrian contributor in 'Corporate Governance 2002' (with Binder and Stark), 2002.
Languages: English, German.
Member: International Bar Association, Committee E (banking law); DACH – Europäische Anwaltsvereinigung; website coordinator, Committee E of IBA.
Education: Tulane University Law School, New Orleans (1993 LLM, Fulbright Fellow); University of Innsbruck (1989 Mag iur; 1994 Dr iur); University of Innsbruck (1991 Mag rer soc oec).
Personal: Born 1966.

SCHMELZ, Christian
Schönherr Rechtsanwälte
Phone: Vienna (+43 1 53 43 70)
E-mail: ch.schmelz@schoenherr.at
Position: Partner dealing with public law including environmental law, licensing, telecoms and information technology.
Career: University assistant, University of Vienna (1980-85); lecturer, University of Vienna (since 1982); admitted to the Austrian Bar 1987.
Languages: English, German.
Education: University of Vienna (1979 Dr iur).
Personal: Born 1955.

TIEFENTHALER, Stefan
Binder Grösswang Rechtsanwälte
Phone: Vienna (+43 1 534 800)
E-mail: tiefenthaler@bgnet.at
Structured finance, cross-border leasing, banking law, M&A, conflicts of laws and international jurisdiction.
Position: Partner.
Career: Intern Austrian Trade Commission, Washington DC 1995; intern, European Commission, Brussels legal service 1997; associate Dorda, Brugger & Jordis 1997-99; lecturer of commercial and company law at the Fachhochschule for Marketing & Sales and Tax and Finances, Chamber of Commerce, Vienna 1999-2002; associate Binder Grösswang Rechtsanwälte 1999-2000; admitted to the Bar 2000; secondment Slaughter and May 2002-03; partner Binder Grösswang Rechtsanwälte 2004 to date. Publications: 'Europäisches Gerichtsstands – und Vollstreckungsrecht – EuGVO und Übereinkommen', LexisNexis ARD Orac (with Czernich/Kodek); Art 16 EuGVÜ: 'Liegenschaftsstreitigkeiten mit Auslandsbezug', WoB1 1999, 255 (with Czernich); Neue Aspekte im internationalen Verfahrensrecht durch den Beitritt Österreichs zum EuGVÜ, JB1 1998, 745 (with Czernich); Innerstaatliche Gerichte als Hüter des europäischen Beihilfenrechts, WB1 1998, 509; LGVÜ: 'Gerichtsstand am "Erfüllungsort des Bereicherungsanspruchs"', ÖJZ 1998, 544; 'Die Streitanhängigkeit nach Art 21 Lugano-Übereinkommen', ZfRV 1997, 67.
Languages: English, French, German.
Education: University of Innsbruck (1994 Mag iur, 1996 Dr iur); University of Saarbrücken, Institute for European Law, Germany (1996 LLM Eur).
Personal: Born 1971.

TORGGLER, Hellwig
Schönherr Rechtsanwälte
Phone: Vienna (+43 1 53 43 70)
E-mail: h.torggler@schoenherr.at
Position: Partner dealing with corporate law, mergers and acquisitions, arbitration and tax.
Career: Admitted to the Austrian Bar 1969; adjunct professor, commercial law and taxation, University of Graz; visiting professor and lecturer, University of Economics, Vienna; arbitrator, ICC, International Arbitral Centre of the Austrian Federal Economic Chamber, and other institutional and ad hoc Courts of Arbitration.
Languages: English, French, German, Italian.
Member: Austrian Delegation to the Commission on International Arbitration, ICC International Court of Arbitration; Examining Board for the Austrian Bar Examination.
Education: Universities of Vienna, Graz, and St Gallen (1961 Dr iur; 1962 Dr rer pol); Southern Methodist University, Dallas (1963 LLM).
Personal: Born 1938.

WÄCHTER, Otto
Graf, Maxl & Pitkowitz
Phone: Vienna (+43 1 401 17 40)
E-mail: waechter@gmp.at
Finance and administrative law.
Position: Partner dealing with project finance, infrastructure, corporate, securities (3telecommunications and postal law), arbitration.
Career: Admitted in Austria 1994; in New York 1995; in California 1996; worked at law firms in Austria, New York and Adelaide, Australia; partner at Gabler & Gabler in Vienna 1996-99; partner at Graf, Maxl & Pitkowitz since 1999.
Languages: English, German.
Member: Austrian Bar; Australian Law Society; New York State and Californian Bar Associations.
Education: University of Vienna (1987 Dr); NYU School of Law (1994 LLM in Corporate Law); University St Gallen (1998 Master of European and International Business Law).
Personal: Born 1961; resides Vienna.

WENGER, Thomas
Schönherr Rechtsanwälte
Phone: Vienna (+43 1 53 43 70)
E-mail: t.wenger@schoenherr.at
Position: Partner dealing with corporate law, mergers and acquisitions, construction and litigation.
Career: Admitted to the Austrian Bar 1992.
Languages: English, German.
Education: University of Vienna (1983 Dr iur); University of Economics, Vienna (1987 Mag rer soc oec).
Personal: Born 1960.

WIESINGER, Norbert
Binder Grösswang Rechtsanwälte
Phone: Vienna (+43 1 534 800)
E-mail: wiesinger@bgnet.at
Telecommunications law, deregulation of infrastructure.
Position: Attorney-at-law.
Career: Associate Wolf Theiss & Partners 1996-99, partner 1999-2000; director legal and regulatory affairs and member of the company's executive board, European Telecom International AG (Telefonica Data Austria) 2000-02; attorney-at-law Binder Grösswang Rechtsanwälte 2002 to date. Publications: contributor in Kurt P Nemec (editor), 'Liberalising österreichischer Infrastrukturmärkte', LexisNexis ARD Orac, 2003; 'Partielle Gesamtrechtsnachfolge und Arbeitsvertrag', ecolex 1993, 619 ff; 'Haftung für Betriebspensionen und Abfertigungen beim Betriebsübergang', ecolex 1994, 702 ff; 'The Ukranian Law on Holding Companies', 1995 Parker Sch J E Eur L 142; co-author of the section on Austrain Telecommunications Law in SJ Berwin & Co, 'European Telecommunication Liberalisation'; 'Regulatory Handbook', edited by Phillips Tarifica 1998.
Languages: German, English, French, Italian.
Education: University of Vienna (1991 Mag iur, 1994 Dr iur); Colombia University School of Law (1995 LLM, Fulbright Fellow).
Personal: Born 1967.

WOLLMANN, Hanno
Schönherr Rechtsanwälte
Phone: Vienna (+43 1 53 43 70)
E-mail: h.wollmann@schoenherr.at
Position: Partner dealing with EU law, antitrust and corporate law.
Career: Admitted to the Austrian Bar 1995.
Languages: English, French, German.
Education: University of Vienna (1991 Dr iur); University of Economics, Vienna (1991 Mag rer soc oec.); University of Exeter (1992 LLM).
Personal: Born 1964.

ZEILER, Gerold
Schönherr Rechtsanwälte
Phone: Vienna (+43 1 53 43 70)
E-mail: g.zeiler@schoenherr.at
Position: Partner dealing with employment law and litigation.
Career: Admitted to the Austrian Bar 1993.
Languages: English, German, Italian.
Education: University of Vienna (1988 Mag iur; 1996 Dr iur).
Personal: Born 1964.

BELGIUM

COUMES, Jean-Michel
Hogan & Hartson L.L.P.
Phone: Brussels (+32 2 505 0911)
E-mail: jmcoumes@hhlaw.com
Antitrust, competition, consumer protection.
Position: Counsel focusing on EU and French competition law. This includes advice on Articles 81 and 82 on horizontal and vertical agreements as well as EU and French merger control.
Career: Qualified Paris 1994; Van Bael & Bellis 1991-95; Stanbrook & Hooper 1994 -99; Wilmer, Cutler & Pickering 1999-2002; Hogan & Hartson since 2002. Published articles on EU competition law topics (car distribution, modernisation proposal); EU and French merger control (last one in 'Global Competition Review', June 2002).
Languages: French, English.
Member: Paris Bar Association; ICC competition section.
Education: Europa College, Bruges; University of Toulouse (degree in High European Studies; LLM International Trade Law).
Personal: Born 1964; resides Brussels.
Leisure: Tennis (formerly an instructor).

CROSBY, Scott
Crosby Renouf
Phone: Brussels (+32 2 233 3747)
E-mail: crosby@renouf.be
Position: Scott Crosby has experience in most areas of EU law. His practice has become increasingly court-oriented over the years, and he has obtained a number of landmark

judgments against the European Commission. He now concentrates primarily on advocacy before the ECJ/CFI in Luxembourg and before the Belgian courts on European law issues and on the litigious aspects of EU law in general.
Career: Trained in Edinburgh with emphasis on court practice and pleading; admitted to the Law Society of Scotland 1979; moved to Brussels 1980; spent 20 years with Kemmler Rapp Böhlke & Crosby; partner for three years Stanbrook & Hooper; set up Crosby Renouf 2004. Publications include: many on various EU topics, including competition law, VAT law, excise duty law, community competence, access to documents, the rights of state-sharing nations under EU and international treaty law.
Languages: English, French, German, Italian, Dutch, passive Spanish.
Member: EU Committee of the Law Society of England and Wales; European Criminal Bar Association; International Criminal Law Association; European Air Law Association; Association of Former Students of the College of Europe; British Chamber of Commerce in Brussels.
Education: St Andrews (Hons degree in Modern Languages); University of Edinburgh (Law Degree); College of Europe (European Law).
Personal: Born 1951; resides Brussels.
Leisure: Skiing, sailing, literature, languages, history.

FIMOGNARI, Mariabruna

Hogan & Hartson L.L.P.
Phone: Brussels (+32 2 505 0911)
E-mail: mfimognari@hhlaw.com
Privacy, antitrust, competition, consumer protection.
Position: Counsel focusing on notification of cross-border and transatlantic operations to the European Commission and EU national authorities and on the coordination and review of merger filings outside the EU and the United States.
Career: Trained Italy and Belgium.
Languages: Italian, French, English.
Member: Amnesty International; Italian Bar; Brussels Bar.
Education: University of Bologna; University of Louvain-la-Neuve. Degrees in international law and European law.
Personal: Born 1970; resides Brussels.
Leisure: Classical and ethnical music; running and general fitness.

GOLDING, Jane

Crosby Renouf
Phone: Brussels (+32 2 233 3747)
E-mail: jane.golding@renouf.be
Position: Partner specialising in competition law, in particular merger control law, as well as public procurement law. Her main area of expertise is in advising corporate clients on EC competition law, and representing them before the European Commission. She has also worked as an adviser to governments on competition and regulatory issues, in particular advising the Estonian Competition Board from 1994-98 on competition issues. Her recent work has been particularly focused on the technology and media sectors.
Career: Called to the Bar (England and Wales) 1989; requalified as a solicitor 2002. Previous professional experience includes five years as the senior resident lawyer at Taylor Wessing's (formerly Taylor Joynson Garrett) Brussels office; assistant lawyer Brosio Casati e Associati Torino; assistant lawyer Cameron McKenna, Brussels (formerly McKenna & Co); worked for 18 months as an auxiliary fonctionnaire at the Directorate General for Competition of the Commission of the European Communities on a ground-breaking Article 82 case. Partner with Crosby Renouf 2004. Publications include: co-author of section on Article 81, 'The Laws of the European Communities' (Smit and Herzog 1998-2001).
Languages: English, French, Italian, German, basic Spanish.
Member: Member of the EU Committee of the Law Society and the Law Society's European Group.
Education: Kings' College, London (1983-85); Université de Paris I (Panthéon-Sorbonne) (1985-87 Maîtrise in English and French Law); Inns of Court School of Law (1988-89 Bar Finals).
Personal: Born 1965; resides Brussels.
Leisure: Literature, languages, playing the piano, travel, swimming, gardening.

HATTON, Catriona

Hogan & Hartson L.L.P.
Phone: Brussels (+32 2 505 0911)
E-mail: chatton@hhlaw.com
Antitrust, competition and consumer protection group, government regulation practice area.
Position: Partner specialising in EU competition law and data protection.
Career: Trained Mason Hayes & Curran, Dublin; Stanbrook & Hooper, Brussels; associate Stanbrook & Hopper, Brussels; partner Rowe & Maw, Brussels; managing partner Hogan & Hartson, Brussels. Publications: 'EU Enlargement, a Giant Step?' Plc Global Counsel (December 2003, January 2004); 'Multinational Merger Review' Global Competition Review (November 2002); 'EU Merger Regulation', National Law Journal (3 June 2002); 'Global Convergence in Merger Review Promoted', International Law Office (18 April 2002).
Languages: English, Dutch, Italian, French, Irish.
Member: American Chamber of Commerce subcommittee competition; Institute of European Affairs; Irish Centre for European Law; Law Society of Ireland; Law Society of England and Wales.
Education: Trinity College, Dublin; University of Brussels (VUB) (1985 Law degree hons; 1989 Masters in International Law).
Personal: Born 1963; resides Brussels.
Leisure: Piano, horseriding.

MAILLY, Jacqueline

Hogan & Hartson L.L.P.
Phone: Brussels (+32 2 505 0911)
E-mail: jmailly@hhlaw.com
Food, drug devices and agriculture; life sciences; government regulation practice area.
Position: European Regulatory Affairs Adviser with extensive experience in advising clients (both public and private) regarding the impact of EU policy and legislation in the areas of food, biotechnology, environment, trade and general pharmaceutical and consumer products regulation.
Career: Adviser, Stanbrook & Hooper, Brussels 1990-96; co-established and joined as EU Regulatory Affairs Adviser, O'Connor and Company, Brussels 1996-99; EU Regulatory Affairs Adviser, Hogan & Hartson LLP, Brussels since 1999.
Languages: Dutch, English, French, German.
Member: Vice Chair agro-food committee of the EU Committee of the American Chamber of Commerce in Belgium; policy group of the EU Committee of the American Chamber of Commerce; consumer affairs committee and the environment committee of the EU committee of the American Chamber of Commerce.
Education: University of Groningen, the Netherlands (1989 degree in French and English languages and in European and International Law); University of Amsterdam (1990 Masters in European integration (European law and economics)).
Personal: Born 1964; resides Brussels.
Leisure: Music, piano, swimming, horseriding.

METAXAS, George

Hogan & Hartson L.L.P.
Phone: Brussels (+32 2 505 0911)
E-mail: gmetaxas@hhlaw.com
Competition/antitrust, communications.
Position: Partner focusing on EU competition, communications, and intellectual property law.
Career: Qualified Athens Bar; partner Hogan & Hartson 2003. Publications: 'Intellectual Property Laws of Europe' (editor and co-author), Chancery Law Publishing, March 1995; 'Who's in Charge: Jurisdiction in European Merger Filings and the Sogecable Case' (with Hector Armengod), ABA Mergers and Acquisitions Newsletter, 2003 vol IV-I.
Languages: French, German, Greek, Spanish, Dutch.
Member: Athens Bar; Brussels Bar (List 'E').
Education: German School of Athens; University of Athens School of Law.
Personal: Born 1957; resides Brussels.

NAUWELAERTS, Wim

Hogan & Hartson L.L.P.
Phone: Brussels (+32 2 505 0911)
E-mail: wnauwelaerts@hhlaw.com
Competition, antitrust, data privacy.
Position: Counsel.
Career: Qualified Brussels Bar; counsel Hogan & Hartson 2004.
Languages: Dutch, English, French.
Member: Brussels Bar.
Education: Free University of Brussels; University of Georgia (LLM).

OBERST JR, Gerald E

Hogan & Hartson L.L.P.
Phone: Brussels (+32 2 505 0911)
E-mail: geoberst@hhlaw.com
International communications law, international telecommunications law, satellite communications, telecommunications regulation, radio spectrum regulation.
Position: Partner focusing on international telecommunications and satellite regulatory matters, European communications law and advises clients on international communications and radio spectrum matters.

Career: Managing editor, 'Virginia Journal of Natural Resources Law', 1980-81; regular columnist, 'Via Satellite Magazine' since 1992.
Languages: French.
Member: District of Columbia Bar; Federal Communications Bar Association (member, section of international law); vice-chairman European Satellite Action Plan Regulatory Group.
Education: University of Kentucky (1977 BA); University of Virginia (1981 JD).
Personal: Born 1954; resides Brussels.
Leisure: Outdoor activities, camping, hiking.

O'DWYER, Ursula

Crosby Renouf
Phone: Brussels (+32 2 233 3747)
E-mail: ursula.odwyer@renouf.be
Position: Partner specialising in competition law, particularly State aid, as well as regulatory law and anti-dumping. Has represented serveral importers and exporters in EC anti-dumping cases before the Commission; advised generally on trade issues and on competition and State aid issues in sectors such as telecommunications; air transport; rail transport; media; post; financial services; sport; pharmaceutical; automotive; tobacco and textiles.
Career: Admitted as Irish solicitor 1977; general practice in Ireland 1977-80, and 1985-86; joined Coopers & Lybrand 1987; responsible for EC law at Coopers & Lybrand, Belgium 1993-98; director in charge of EC law department Bogaert & Vandemeulebroeke, the Belgian member firm of Landwell 1998-2000; partner Renouf & Co 2000; partner Crosby Renouf 2004.
Languages: Dutch, French, English.
Member: EU Committee British Chamber of Commerce; American Chamber of Commerce to the European Union (competition committee); Irish Belgian Business Association; Irish Centre for European Law; Law Society of Ireland.
Education: Trinity College, University of Dublin (1975 BA Moderatorship in Legal Science); (1976 LLB; 1977 MA).
Personal: Born 1953; resides Brussels.

PAEMEN, Hugo

Hogan & Hartson L.L.P.
Phone: Brussels (+32 2 505 0911)
E-mail: hpaemen@hhlaw.com
Senior adviser.
Position: Ambassador Hugo Paemen is senior adviser with Hogan & Hartson LLP. He works with the firm's commercial and regulatory practice groups to advise US, European, and other companies concerning their dealings with European institutions. Ambassador Paemen also provides counsel on a wide variety of trade and investment matters involving the EU and the United States.
Career: Belgian Embassies in Geneva, Paris and Washington DC; Economic Minister, Washington DC; Chef de Cabinet to Commissioner Viscount Davignon 1978-85; official spokesman of the first Delors Commission 1978-85; European Commission's Deputy Director-General for External Relations, acted as the European Community's chief negotiator during the entire length of the Uruguay Round 1987-95; head of the European Commission's Washington delegation 1995-99; senior adviser Hogan & Hartson. Has been a distinguished visiting professor of the Catholic University of Leuven. Adjunct professor at Georgetown University and co-chairman of the European American Business Council. Co-author 'From the GATT to the WTO: The European Community in the Uruguay Round', Leuven University Press.
Member: Board of trustees, Catholic University of Leuven.
Education: Degrees in philosophy and classics and political and social science.
Personal: Resides Belgium and Washington DC.

RENOUF, Michael

Crosby Renouf
Phone: Brussels (+32 2 233 3747)
E-mail: michael.renouf@renouf.be
Position: Named partner of Brussels-based specialist EU law firm. His practice covers regulatory issues, especially environmental law (with particular emphasis on climate change and on ozone depleting substances); internal market law; and problem solving for industry and for individuals through European law including administrative advocacy. He is consultant to a number of regional UK firms on EU law matters. Frequent speaker on EU law subjects.
Career: Trainee, Legal Service European Commission (1984-85); professional experience with Belgian law firm (1985); articled Thomas Eggar, Sussex, England; responsible for the ground-breaking Cowan case (non-discrimination on the grounds of nationality) and others before the European Court of Justice; admitted as solicitor of Supreme Court of Judicature of England and Wales 1988; post-admission experience with Thomas Eggar, developing the firm's European practice 1988-90; associate Forrester Norall & Sutton, a niche EC and trade law practice in Brussels 1990-93; director of the Brussels office of the Legal Resources Group (LRG), a grouping of six major UK regional law firms 1993-98; established Renouf & Co 1998; established Crosby Renouf 2004.
Languages: English, French.
Member: Council of the Law Society of England and Wales (EU Matters seat); Chair of the Law Society's EU Committee; The British Institute of International and Comparative Law; The Law Society's European Group; Solicitors Pro Bono Group; Lawyers' Christian Fellowship; former member of National Committees of the Trainee Solicitors' Group (1985-88) and Solicitors' European Group (1986-88).
Education: Kingsdown School, Swindon; Manchester Metropolitan University (1983 BA Law with French; Law Society Finals); Vrije Universiteit Brussel (1984 LLM in International and Comparative law).
Personal: Born 1961; resides Brussels.
Leisure: Family, music, dramatic arts.

BOSNIA-HERZEGOVINA

KARABDIC, Kerim

Advokati Karabdic Salih & Kerim
Phone: Sarajevo (387 33 531 500)
E-mail: karabdic@bih.net.ba
Position: Lawyer and director of project co-ordination unit FBiH. Legal advisor for foreign companies and organisations in Bosnia and Herzegovina concerning questions of domestic law: local legal expert to the international consortium (PricewaterhouseCoopers, Atkins, CMS Cameron McKenna) working in the EU-funded project related to the development of Balkans Regional Electricty Market; counsel to a major Austrian bank in the successful privatisation of a leading Bosnian bank, including due diligence; counsel to a bank from the Netherlands concerning the privatisation of a Bosnian bank, including due diligence in Vienna; counsel to British and Austrian companies concerning the privatisation of a tobacco factory in Bosnia, including legal due diligence; counsel to an American company concerning the aircraft lease contract, legal review of the contract and bank guarantee; counsel to a Danish company with respect to the legal status of a company in Bosnia, capital transfer, work and lease contract preparations, purchase of assets etc; counsel to a Canadian company concerning foreign investment, including the domestic formation of a company and preparation of by-laws; counsel to an American organisation supporting the development of agricultural sectors in both entities of Bosnia and Herzegovina, including formation of an agricultural producers association, micro credit organisation, preparation of establishing acts, by-laws, contracts, legal opinions, negotiation with authorities related to the legal status etc; counsel to a British media company concerning commercial relations in Bosnia; and counsel to a Swiss company with respect to the sale of crude oil. Publications include: 'Doing Business in 2004, Understanding Regulation', World Bank, International Finance Corporation and Oxford University Press; 'The International Lawyer – Fall 2003, Central European Law', 2002 legislative report; 'The International Lawyer – Fall 2002, Central European Law', 2001 legislative report.
Career: Qualified 1987; lawyer, Bar Association of BiH 1988-93; counsellor consular, Ministry of Foreign Affairs RBiH 1993-94; counellor consular, Embassy BiH, London 1994-98; lawyer, Bar Assocation of BiH 1999 to date.
Languages: Bosnian, English, German.
Member: Bar Association of Bosnia and Herzegovina; Juritax Association; board member, JP PTT BiH, Sarajevo 2000-01; board member, BH TELECOM, Sarajevo 2000-01.
Education: University of Sarajevo, School of Law (1985 BA); Ministry for Justice and Administration RBiH (1987 Barrister Exam); University of Oxford, UK (1996 Certificate, Foreign Service Programme); Central European University, Budapest and Cardozo Law School, New York (2000 Certificate, Law of International Business Transactions); ILO Centre, Turin (2000 Diploma, Management of Technical Co-operation Projects).
Personal: Born 1958; married with one child.

BULGARIA

ANDONOVA, Lilia

Landwell Bulgaria
Phone: Sofia (+359 2 9355 100)
E-mail: lilia.andonova@bg.landwellglobal.com
Position: Executive counsel and attorney-at-law specialising in tax law, employment law, corporate

structuring, technology and telecommunications and real estate.
Career: Qualified 1999.
Languages: Bulgarian, English, German, Russian.
Member: Sofia Bar Association.
Education: Sofia University 'St Kliment Ohridski' (Master of Law); University of Hamburg.
Leisure: Travelling.

BEBOV, Nikolay

Landwell Bulgaria
Phone: Sofia (+359 2 9355 100)
E-mail: nikolay.bebov@bg.landwellglobal.com
Position: Executive counsel and attorney-at-law specialising in financial services law and banking, energy law, M&As, dispute resolution and litigation.
Career: Qualified 1999.
Languages: Bulgarian, English, French, Russian, Spanish.
Member: Sofia Bar Association; International Bar Association; British-Bulgarian Law Association.
Education: Sofia University 'St Kliment Ohridski' (Master of Law).
Leisure: Basketball, tall ships, aviation.

BORISSOV, Plamen M

Kambourov & Partners
Phone: Sofia (+359 2 986 9999)
E-mail: pborissov@kambourov.biz
Project finance.
Position: Senior consultant dealing with all areas of corporate law, finance, secured transactions, real estate and construction, and consumer law.
Career: Trained Sofia City Court; qualified 1997; chief legal counsel Trade and Consumer Protection Commission 1998-2000; associate Djingov, Gouginski, Kyutchukov & Velichkov 2000-02; senior consultant Kambourov & Partners 2002 to date; numerous publications in the area of international finance and consumer law.
Languages: English, Russian, Serbo-Croat.
Member: Sofia Bar Association; IBA; European Lawyers Association.
Education: Sofia University (1996 MA); Oxford University (1999); Edinburgh University (2000).
Personal: Born 1973; resides Sofia.
Leisure: Football, golf, Formula 1.

IVANOV, Ilian

Totev & Ivanov
Phone: Sofia (+359 2 981 43 31)
E-mail: ivanov@totevivanov.com
Position: Partner specialising in tax planning, labour law, social security levies, energy law, currency regime, litigation.
Career: ITL Group OOD, legal advisor. Legal and tax advice to local and international clients including Henkel Ecolal, Reemtsma, Sofregaz 1995-98; tax and legal consultant, PricewaterhouseCoopers Bulgaria. Tax advice and tax planning to international clients including Philip Morris, Kraft Foods, Socotab, The Coca-Cola Company; transaction support to a multinational bank in the acquisition of a Bulgarian pensions insurance company 1998-2001; partner, 'Totev & Ivanov'. Employment and tax advice to international clients including Entergy and Toyota since 2001. Publications: 'Deficiencies in Article 109 of the Tax Procedure Code', in Bulgarian Business, August 2001; 'Bulgarian Double Tax Treaties – Introduction', in Tax Practice, September 2001.
Languages: English, French, Serbian.
Member: Sofia Bar Association 1999.
Education: St Kliment Ohridsky University Law School (1997 LLM); Bulgarian Academy of Science (PhD Energy Law 2001).
Personal: Born 1971.

KAMBOUROV, Yavor

Kambourov & Partners
Phone: Sofia (+359 2 986 9999)
E-mail: ykambourov@kambourov.biz
Position: Managing partner, dealing with all areas of commercial law, including privatisation, telecommunications, banking and finance, and energy law.
Career: Trained Sofia Court; qualified 1988; partner Kambourov & Partners 1988.
Languages: English, French, Russian.
Member: International Bar Association (London); registered as a trustee in the Official List of Bulgarian Bank Trustees; Sofia Bar Association.
Education: University of Sofia (1987 MA).
Personal: Born 1962; resides Sofia.
Leisure: Rowing, travelling.

KARUSHKOV, Mitko

Kambourov & Partners
Phone: Sofia (+359 2 986 9999)
E-mail: karushkov@kambourov.biz
IP; corporate and commercial.
Position: Senior consultant in the IP and corporate and commercial departments.
Career: Trained Sofia City Court; qualified 1998; partner Kambourov & Partners 2001.
Languages: Bulgarian, English, Russian.
Member: Sofia Bar Association.
Education: University of Sofia (1996 MA).
Personal: Born 1971; resides Sofia.
Leisure: Sports, IT.

PENKOV, Vladimir

LIC-Penkov, Markov & Partners
Phone: Sofia (+359 2 971 3935)
E-mail: penkov@legainterconsult.com
Executive managing partner.
Position: Specialises in commercial and company law, foreign investments, licences and know-how, privatisation, mergers and acquisitions, taxation and customs law, international commercial arbitration. Has handled numerous acquisitions and joint venture establishment in breweries, banking, insurance, electronics, telecommunications, soft beverages etc. Recently represented Domaine Boyar AD for debt and equity financing by EBRD and Baring Central European Investments; TBI Holding for acquisition of DZI insurance; Gallagher Ltd in the bid for privatisation of Bulgartabac; Strabag AG for investment in construction; Koehne Group on infrastructure project for investment in railroad construction; and Advent International in the bid for Bulgarian Telecommunication Company (BTC).
Career: Qualified 1977; legal counsel and senior counsel Bulgarian Ministry of Foreign Economic Relations 1977-87; chief legal counsel Technica Foreign Trade Organisation 1987-89; founder and managing partner Lega InterConsult 1990 to date. Publications include: 'The Promotion and Protection of Foreign Investments in Bulgaria: some legal aspects' in 'International Relationships' magazine; articles in 'Foreign Trade', 'Bulgarisches Wirtschaftsblatt' and 'Business Opportunities in Bulgaria'; Rechtliche Grundlagen für ausländische Investoren in Bulgarien' in 'Südeuropa Mitteilungen'; 'Legal Aspects' in 'International Privatization Review' (Euromoney); 'Richtige Partnerauswahl hilft Vorteile zu gewinnen, interview in 'Bulgarische Wirtschaftsblatt'.
Languages: Bulgarian, English, German.
Member: Vice-president Bulgarian Chamber of Commerce and Industry (BCCI); Managing Board of Bulgarian International Business Association; arbitrator Arbitration Court at BCCI; Consultative Committee of International Association for Industrial Property Protection (AIPPI); member of the board and former CED Zagorka AD, Stara Zagora; chartered member and former president First Lions Club, Bulgaria.
Education: Economy University, Berlin (1970-72); Sofia University St Clement Ohridsky (1976 LLM).
Personal: Born 1952.

RANGELOFF, Vladimir

Kambourov & Partners
Phone: Sofia (+359 2 986 9999)
E-mail: vrangeloff@kambourov.biz
Foreign investments.
Position: Partner in the foreign investments department dealing with all areas of privatisation and foreign investments.
Career: Trained Sofia Court; qualified 1997; partner Kambourov & Partners 2001.
Languages: English, German, Russian.
Member: Sofia Bar Association; Institute for German Law with the Faculty of Law at Sofia University.
Education: University of Sofia (1996 MA).
Personal: Born 1972; resides Sofia.
Leisure: Reading.

TOTEV, Dimitar

Totev & Ivanov
Phone: Sofia (+359 2 981 43 31)
E-mail: totev@totevivanov.com
Position: Partner specialising in tax planning, corporate law, securities regulation, international payments, banking law, energy sector regulation and project finance, commercial contracts.
Career: Bulgarian National Bank, legal dept, trainee 1993; 'S Invest' financial-brokerage house, legal advisor 1994-95; Ministry of Trade and foreign economic relations, dept: 'agreements for promotion and protection of foreign investments'; Bulbank, documentary operations department, L/Cs, collections, guarantees, 1996-97; PricewaterhouseCoopers Legal and Tax Consultants, tax and legal advice, due diligence, and contract drafting for clients such as Danone, Ericsson, National Bank of Greece, Toyota, Societe Generale, 1997-2000; partner, 'Totev & Ivanov', working primarily on project finance, corporate

law, structuring and drafting of commercial transactions, since 2001. His experience in Totev & Ivanov includes the project between US Entergy and Natzionalna Electriceska Kompania for the rehabilitation and exploitation of the thermo-power plant Maritza East 3 and the project of the US company Horizon (part of National Fuel Gas Company) for development of the combined power and heat generation facilities with the Sofia heat supply company Toploficacia. Publications: 'Regulation of Clearing Houses in Bulgaria', in Bulgarian Business 1994; 'New Bulgarian Securities law', special report in 'World Securities Law Report', November 2000.
Languages: English.
Member: Sofia Bar Association.
Education: St Kliment Ohridsky University Law School (1996 LLM); Georgetown University Law School, Washington (specialisation in securities regulation).
Personal: Born 1971.

TSVETKOVA, Irina
Landwell Bulgaria
Phone: Sofia (+359 2 9355 100)
E-mail: irina.tsvetkova@bg.landwellglobal.com
Position: Partner and attorney-at-law specialising in privatisation and reorganisation of companies; bankruptcy; foreign direct investments; technology and telecommunications; legal regulation of the consumer goods industry; litigation in civil and commercial matters.
Career: Qualified 1991.
Languages: Bulgarian, English, French, Italian.
Member: Sofia Bar; International Bar Association.
Education: City College, New York (Literature and History); Sofia University 'St Kliment Ohridski' (Master of Law).
Leisure: Travelling, literature.

TZAKOV, Stefan
Kambourov & Partners
Phone: Sofia (+359 2 986 9999)
E-mail: tzakov@kambourov.biz
Corporate and commercial.
Position: Senior consultant dealing with all areas of commercial and corporate law, including contract law, security of debts and civil litigation.
Career: Trained Sofia City Court; qualified 2001; lawyer Lega InterConsult Law Offices 2000-03; partner Kambourov & Partners 2003; several publications in the areas of commercial law, security of debts and civil litigation.
Languages: German, English.
Member: Sofia Bar Association.
Education: University of Sofia (1999 MA).
Personal: Born 1975; resides Sofia.
Leisure: Tracking, mountaineering.

CYPRUS

DEMETRIOU, Andrew
Law Office of Andrew Demetriou & Co
Phone: Nicosia (+357 22 67 50 90)
E-mail: ad@ademetriou.com
Managing partner.
Position: Deals with all areas of litigation and arbitration, as well as legal services in the fields of commercial and construction law, administrative law, public infrastructure/BOT projects, joint ventures, M&A, energy and telecommunications law. For more information, see www.ademetriou.com.
Career: Barrister and Chartered Arbitrator; admitted to the Bar of England and Wales 1982; Cyprus Bar 1983; group legal counsel, DG Jones & Partners Group of Companies; adviser to a number of international and local companies and businesses, including state and public companies such as the Electricity Authority of Cyprus and The Cyprus Forrest Industries; represented the Republic of Cyprus in a number of cases; lecturer in both Cyprus and abroad on the topics of arbitration, commercial law, construction law, the Cyprus Stock Exchange, and business establishment; has served as chairman of the Cyprus branch of the Chartered Institute of Arbitrators; chairman of the Cyprus Alumni Association of his university.
Languages: English, Greek.
Member: Honorable Society of Gray's Inn; Cyprus Bar Association; Chartered Institute of Arbitrators; International Bar Association; Chartered Institute of Arbitrators; Institute of Directors.
Education: University of Liverpool (1980 LLB Hons); Inns of Court School of Law, Gray's Inn 1982.
Personal: Born Manchester, England 1959; resides Nicosia, Cyprus.
Leisure: Reading, music, sports.

NICOLAOU, Chrysostomos
Patrikios Pavlou & Co
Phone: Limassol (+357 25 87 15 99)
E-mail: cnicolaou@pavlaw.com
General litigation department.
Position: General litigation partner dealing with all aspects of: civil law; criminal law, mainly white-collar crime; construction law; commercial litigation; insurance law; administrative law; constitutional law; admiralty law; arbitration; labour law; tax law.
Career: Trained Patrikios Pavlou & Co; qualified 1997; partner 1996; promoted as general litigation partner. Published numerous articles in Cyprus on main practice areas. Successfully handled: for the plaintiff breach of contract claim to the value of US$4m; for the plaintiff personal injuries claim arising from a road traffic accident for an amount in excess of CYP250,000; on behalf of a Cyprus listed Plc a breach of contract; partnership dispute for an amount of CYP500,000; on behalf of developer handing an immovable property dispute between developer and purchaser for CYP1m; defended client against alleged claims of registration of property through false pretences, false entries in company books, and dishonoured cheques, abuse of power by public servant with intention to profit.
Languages: English, Greek.
Member: International Bar Association; Cyprus Bar Association.
Education: St Johns Lyceum; University of Athens (Law degree 1992).
Personal: Born 1967; resides Limassol.
Leisure: Music, table tennis.

PAVLOU, Patrikios
Patrikios Pavlou & Co
Phone: Limassol (+357 25 87 15 99)
E-mail: ppavlou@pavlaw.com
Companies department.
Position: Senior legal consultant dealing with all areas of: banking law; finance law; company law; corporate commercial law; administrative law; constitutional law; stock exchange law; capital markets; mergers and acquisitions; tax law; international tax planning; arbitration; travel and tourism law; intellectual property; trade marks.
Career: Trained Patrikios Pavlou & Co; qualified barrister-at-law 1962; founded Patrikios Pavlou & Co; partner 1963; as well as developing a successful practice, was elected as a member of the Cyprus parliament, a position he held between 1976 and 1981; served in several parliamentary committees and in this capacity represented the parliamentary committees on various international delegations, seminars and conferences; retired from partnership in 2002 and now acts as the senior legal consultant of the firm.
Languages: English, Greek.
Member: International Bar Association.
Personal: Born 1939; resides Limassol.
Leisure: Reading, swimming, walking.

PAVLOU, Stavros
Patrikios Pavlou & Co
Phone: Limassol (+357 25 87 15 99)
E-mail: spavlou@pavlaw.com
Senior and managing partner.
Position: Senior and managing partner dealing with all areas of: banking law; finance law; company law; corporate commercial law; stock exchange law; capital markets; mergers and acquisitions; civil law; criminal law; commercial litigation; international tax planning; arbitration; travel and tourism law; intellectual property; trade marks; information technology and Internet law; e-commerce law; European law.
Career: Trained Patrikios Pavlou & Co; barrister-at-law 1985; qualified 1986; partner 1988; litigation partner 1989; managing partner 1991; appointed managing and senior partner following the retirement of senior partner Patrikios Pavlou; 2002 publications of note: co-author of international publication on offshore companies in Cyprus; authored several articles in international law journals and periodicals on Cyprus tax structures and M&As, and Cyprus Stock Exchange. He has been a guest speaker in numerous international conferences, as well as a lecturer on company and business law, and on the stock market. Important cases/deals: multi-million pound M&As – local and international (eg acquisition of Sabre Airways; intended acquisition of Helios Airways); handling the following cases in conjunction with Soteris Pittas, commercial litigation partner: acting for Ukrainian respondents/counter-claimants in arbitration of US$75m filed by Daewoo of Korea before the London Court of International Arbitration against its Ukrainian partners in the Ukrainian joint venture of Ukrainian Rapid Systems; Nafta & Ruskiy Aluminium v Andrei Andriev; acting for OAA Nafta, Moscow & OAO Ruskiy

Aluminium in relation to Cyprus proceedings concerning control of Cyprus holding companies.
Languages: English, Greek.
Member: International Bar Association; Cyprus Bar Association; International Tax Planning Association.
Education: City University (Dip Law); Barrister (Gray's Inn); London School of Economics (BSc Economics).
Personal: Born 1960; resides Limassol.
Leisure: Reading, films, sports.

PITTAS, Soteris

Patrikios Pavlou & Co
Phone: Limassol (+357 25 87 15 99)
E-mail: spittas@pavlaw.com
Commercial litigation department.
Position: Commercial litigation partner dealing with all aspects of: banking law; finance law; Admiralty law; company law; international trade law; corporate commercial law; mergers and acquisitions; civil law; commercial litigation; arbitration.
Career: Trained Andreas Neocleous & Co; qualified 1989; partner 1994-2002 as leading litigation lawyer of that firm, dealing with international trade law; trusts and equity, company and partnership disputes and all insurance and Admiralty claims; partner Patrikios Pavlou & Co 2002. In conjunction with Stavros Pavlou, managing and senior partner, handling the following cases: acting for Ukrainian respondents/counter-claimants in arbitration of US$75m filed by Daewoo of Korea before the London Court of International Arbitration against its Ukrainian partners in the Ukrainian joint venture of Ukrainian Rapid Systems; Nafta & Ruskiy Aluminium v Andrei Andriev; acting for OAA Nafta Moscow and OAO Ruskiy Aluminium in relation to Cyprus proceedings concerning control of Cyprus holding companies; other cases include: Base Metal Ltd v Novokuznetsk Aluminium Plant, arbitration claim for US$40m (Uncitral Model Law); Darren Investments v Louis Tourist Agency, acting for plaintiff in relation to recovery of US$9m from sale of shareholding in Royal Cruises (NASDAQ-listed company) to Cyprus company Louis Tourist Agency; Russian Federation v Mechanov, handling of extradition proceedings against Valey Meschanov, a former general manager of a large Russian factory in order to be tried for misappropriation of the sum of US$50m. Publications of note: co-author of the Cyprus chapter on 'International Execution Against Judgment Debtors' by Sweet & Maxwell (1997); 'Encyclopaedia of Commercial Litigation' by Kluwer Law International (2000); co-author 'Introduction to Cyprus law' by Andreas Neocleous & Co (2000); Cyprus contribution in an international textbook concerning the extradition of fugitives (2001, to be published).
Languages: English, Greek.
Member: Cyprus Bar Association; Limassol Bar Association.
Education: Lanitium Gymnasium; University of Athens (Law degree 1984); University of London (LLM Commercial and Corporate Law 1988).
Personal: Born 1960; resides Limassol.
Leisure: Sports, reading.

CZECH REPUBLIC

Cermák JR, Karel

Cermák Horejs Myslil
Phone: Prague (+42 02 2494 6724)
E-mail: intelprop@apk.cz
Position: Partner, specialising in intellectual property, private international law, unfair competition, pharmaceuticals, trade marks, business law, mergers and acquisitions. Represents a number of national and international companies in proceedings before the Czech Industrial Property Office as well as in court litigation proceedings, in particular patent litigation matters. He has successfully dealt with a number of trade mark, patent and domain name infringement cases and provided legal support for a number of mergers and acquisitions by foreign companies in the Czech Republic (particulars on clients and cases may not be disclosed by virtue of local deontological rules).
Career: Legal trainee in Cermák Horejs Vrba 1996-99; traineeship with other domestic and foreign law firms, including Gaedertz Rechtsanwälte, Cologne 1997; admitted to Bar 1999; partner in Cermák Horejs Myslil Lawyers and Patent Attorneys 2000. Publications: 'The Problems of Conflict of Law in the Anglo-American Legal Orbit and Some Continental Jurisdictions'; publishes in a number of legal journals, in the field of industrial property among others. Co-author of 'Legal aspects of Domain Names', Linde Praha 2000 (in Czech); chapters on company law and contract law in 'Handbuch für Wirtschaft und Recht in Osteuropa' (Handbook on Economy and Law in Eastren Europe), CH Beck, Munich 2002 (in German).
Languages: English, French, German.
Member: Vice-president of the Czech National Group of AIPPI; committee member of the Czech National Group of International League of Competition Law (LIDC).
Education: Grammar School (Gymnasium) Sladkovského in Prague; Faculty of Law of the Charles University 1991-96 (1998 PhD); Université de Provence (Aix-en-Provence) 1994-95; European Academy of Legal Theory, Brussels (2000 LLM).
Personal: Born 1973; resides Prague.

LOVISEK, Milan

Hogan & Hartson Advokátní Kancelare, v.o.s.
Phone: Prague (+420 222 117 111)
E-mail: mlovisek@hhlaw.com
Corporate, securities and finance, Czech and Slovak corporate, commercial, real estate, regulatory and intellectual property matters.
Position: Partner, Hogan & Hartson, Prague; advises clients on privatisation transactions, cross-border mergers and acquisitions, corporate restructurings and secured financings in the region, representing Western multinational corporations, Czech businesses and multilateral institutions. Since joining Hogan & Hartson in 1992, has advised both Western and Czech clients in many different business sectors, including the automative, broadcasting, banking, telephone, cable television, glass, energy, transportation, cement, packaging and agriculture industries, property in secured financings, worked to create innovative bank escrow devices to secure loan transactions, restructured mortgages of Czech real estate, negotiated sales of enterprises and parts of enterprises under the Czech Commercial Code, and worked with the Czech Bar Association and Czech and Slovak American Enterprise Fund to create forms for loan and venture capital transactions in the region.
Career: Qualified as trial judge in Bratislava 1988; two years as assistant law professor at Comenius University earning a Fulbright Scholarship to study law and work in the US as a Congressional Fellow to Senator Mark O Hatfield of Oregon. Has been published in a number of law journals. Co-author of a book on human rights published in 1991 and 1995.
Languages: Slovak, Czech, English.
Member: Czech and Slovak Bar Association.
Education: Comenius University, Bratislava (1986 Dr iur with highest honours); George Washington University National Law Center in Washington (1992 LLM).
Personal: Born 1963; resides Prague.
Leisure: Theatre, music, travel.

MATEJKA, Jan

Cermák Horejs Myslil
Phone: Prague (+42 02 9616 7501)
E-mail: jmatejka@apk.cz
Patents, trade marks.
Position: Partner dealing with intellectual property law, patents, trade marks, commercial, corporate law, contracts, international law, unfair competition, arbitration. Represents in patent and trade mark matters including disputes in the Czech Republic. Takes an active part in the legislative process, namely in the field of intellectual property. Publishes in a number of legal journals.
Career: Legal trainee, Legal Consultancy in Pelhrimov 1971-75; attorney-at-law (advocate), head of law office in Pelhrimov 1975-83; Chairman of regional committee – Ceské Budejovice 1983-90; partner in Cermák Horejs Vrba 1991-2000; partner in Cermák Horejs Myslil Law and Patent Offices since 2000.
Languages: English, German, Russian.
Member: Czech National LES Committee; examination committee for Law Examinations and Acceptance Examinations; discipline commission of the Czech Bar Association.
Education: Academic Grammar School (Gymnasium) in Pelhrimov (1962-65); faculty of law, Charles University (1974 Dr Juris); University of California, School of Law – Orientation in American Law 1993.
Personal: Born 1946; resides Prague.

MYSLIL, Richard

Cermák Horejs Myslil
Phone: Prague (+42 02 2494 6724)
E-mail: intelprop@apk.cz
Position: Partner, specialising in commercial law, acquisitions, companies, competition law, agreements.
Career: Legal trainee, Bubník & Myslil 1995-97; partly practised in Coudert Brothers in New York 1996; Herbert Smith in London 1995; Laffili van Crombrugghe, Brussels 1995; management practice in chemical and pharmaceutical industry (1984-95); admitted to Bar 1997. Partner in Bubník & Myslil 1997; partner in Cermák Horejs Myslil 2001.

Languages: English, French.
Education: University of Chemistry Technology in Prague, specialisation economy and management (1980-84); Faculty of Law of Charles University (1990-95). Post-graduate studies at the University of Birmingham (1995).
Personal: Born 1962.

MYSLIL, Stanislav

Cermák Horejs Myslil
Phone: Prague (+42 02 4947 317)
E-mail: smyslil@apk.cz
Commercial law.
Position: Partner dealing with all areas of commercial/corporate law including mergers and acquisitions, investments, formation and restructuring of commercial companies and related fields.
Career: Former chief of section, legal department, Ministry for Foreign Affairs; United Nations legal staff; attorney at Law Office No 1, Prague; partner Bubnik Myslil 1991-2000; arbitrator, Arbitration Court, Prague; author of two books and many articles on international public and private law.
Languages: English, French, German, some Russian.
Member: Czech Bar; honorary member of Center for International Legal Studies, Salzburg.
Education: Charles University Prague (postgraduate studies); Charles University Prague (partly London University).
Personal: Born 1930; resides Prague.

TANZER, Jan

Hogan & Hartson Advokátní Kancelare, v.o.s.
Phone: Prague (+420 222 117 111)
E-mail: jtanzer@hhlaw.com
Corporate, securities and finance, international business transactions, project and international finance.
Position: Managing partner of Hogan & Hartson Prague Office, Czech Republic. Focuses on Czech corporate, commercial, real estate, regulatory and tax matters. Since joining Hogan & Hartson in 1992, has advised both Western and Czech clients on a wide range of business transactions in the manufacturing, telecommunications, and energy sectors, including privatisation, mergers and acquisitions, corporate restructuring, cross-border equity and debt investments, and international joint ventures. Has significant experience in advising clients on regulatory matters in the areas of radio and TV broadcasting, and food and consumer products. Was involved in the first project financing in Central and Eastern Europe, which closed without governmental credit or performance guarantees.
Career: Deputy Director General, International Finance and Foreign Exchange, Federal Ministry of Finance, Czechoslovakia. One of the principal draftsmen of the Foreign Exchange Act and was in charge of issues connected with Czechoslovakia's cooperation with multilateral financial institutions, such as the International Monetary Fund, the World Bank, the International Finance Corporation, the European Bank for Reconstruction and Development, and the European Investment Bank. Joined Hogan & Hartson 1992.
Languages: Czech, English, German.
Member: Czech Bar Association.
Education: Prague School of Economics; Charles University Faculty of Law, Prague (Dr iur).
Personal: Born 1950; resides Prague.
Leisure: Literature, theatre, gardening.

DENMARK

HALGREEN, Lars

Johan Schlüter Advokatfirma
Phone: Copenhagen (+45 33 63 96 50)
E-mail: lha@jschluter.com
Sports law.
Position: Partner.
Career: Qualified 1988; admitted to High Court 1992; author: report commission by Danish Sports Federation on commercial rights of athletes and sports federations (1999); first Danish book on commercial and EU aspects in Danish sports law (2000); book on sponsorship contracts (2003; comparative analysis between American and European models of sport (PhD thesis, published 2004); numerous articles in Danish and international legal journals on sports law and related sub-disciplines.
Languages: English, the Scandinavian languages.
Member: Danish Bar; Danish Copyright Society; Danish Sports Law Society; Society for Media and Entertainment.
Education: University of Copenhagen (1988).
Personal: Born 1964; resides Copenhagen.

SCHLÜTER, Johan

Johan Schlüter Advokatfirma
Phone: Copenhagen (+45 33 63 96 50)
E-mail: jos@jschluter.com
IPR, competition law, company law, M&A, arbitration.
Position: Partner and chairman of the board.
Career: Qualified 1970; admitted Danish Supreme Court 1979; former lecturer, University of Copenhagen; censor, University of Copenhagen; general secretary: IFPI Danmark; Danish Video Association; Association of Danish Film Distributers; Rights Holder Alliance; and film and record producers' rights management societies; board director for a number of commercial companies and rights organisations; author of books and articles on IPR, company law, e-commerce and competition law.
Languages: English, French, the Scandinavian languages.
Member: Danish Bar; board member, Danish Copyright Society; chairman of copyright committee, IBA Committee C and L.
Education: University of Aix-en-Provence; University of Copenhagen.
Personal: Born 1944; resides Copenhagen.

SCHLÜTER SCHIERBECK, Katrine

Johan Schlüter Advokatfirma
Phone: Copenhagen (+45 33 63 96 50)
E-mail: kas@jschluter.com
Intellectual property.
Position: Partner; specialises in entertainment law, including production, financing and distribution of feature films and sound recordings, license agreements.
Career: Qualifed 1995; teacher, Danish Film School and the Danish Rhythmic Conservatory.
Languages: English, the Scandinavian languages.
Member: Danish Bar; Danish Copyright Society; Danish Association for Entertainment and Media Law.
Education: University of Copenhagen; European Audio-Visual Entrepreneurs.
Personal: Born 1968; resides Copenhagen.

STEFFENSEN, Torben

Johan Schlüter Advokatfirma
Phone: Copenhagen (+45 33 63 96 50)
E-mail: tst@jschluter.com
Litigation.
Position: Partner; specialises in all areas of intellectual property rights and litigation, including copyright, trademarks and franchise.
Career: Qualified 1988; admitted Danish Supreme Court 2000; head of AntiPiracyGroup in Denmark; lecturer in intellectual property rights, University of Copenhagen; author of many articles on litigation matters, mediation, film industry and TV formats.
Languages: English, the Scandinavian languages.
Member: Danish Bar; Association of Supreme Court Lawyers; Danish Association for Industrial Rights Protection.
Education: University of Copenhagen (1988).
Personal: Born 1964; resides Copenhagen.

VALENTIN, Anders

Johan Schlüter Advokatfirma
Phone: Copenhagen (+45 33 63 96 55)
E-mail: anv@jschluter.com
Patents.
Position: Partner; specialises in patent litigation and strategic counseling, chiefly for clients in the pharmaceutical industry, as well as patent litigation involving various technologies; acts for several clients in the copyrights industry involving both litigation and strategic counseling.
Career: Qualified 2000; admitted Danish High Court 2003; partner Johan Schlüter Advokatfirma 2004; author of articles on corporate and patent issues.
Languages: English, the Scandinavian languages.
Member: Danish Bar; Danish Copyright Society; Danish Association for Industrial Right Protection.
Education: University of London (1989); University of Copenhagen (1997).
Personal: Born 1967; resides Copenhagen.

FINLAND

ALHO, Jari-Pekka

Krogerus & Co. Oy
Phone: Helsinki (+358 9 622 6520)
E-mail: jp.alho@krogerus.com
Corporate and commercial.
Position: Partner in the corporate and commercial practice group; specialises in dispute resolution, insolvency law, IT, technology and telecommunications, and contract law; work consists mainly of advising major companies on their operative legal issues, representing

companies in arbitration or litigation and assisting companies in establishing in Finland; additionally active in policy-related matters.
Career: Legal counsel Law Office Aaltonen, Alho & Untamala Oy 1995-98; Helsinki Chamber of Commerce 1998-2000; policy manager (IT, telecommunication and e-commerce) International Chamber of Commerce (ICC), Paris 2000-01; associate Matti Oksala Attorneys-at-Law 2001-02; associate Krogerus & Co Oy 2002-03; partner 2003.
Languages: English, Finnish, Swedish, Spanish.
Member: Finnish Bar Association; International Bar Association; ICC Commission E-Business, IT and Telecom.
Education: University of Helsinki (1996 LLM; 1998 Postgraduate Degree).
Personal: Born 1970; resides Espoo.
Leisure: Golf, sailing.

ELO, Hanna-Maija

Heinonen & Co, Attorneys-at-Law, Ltd
Phone: Helsinki (+358 9 25 300 600)
E-mail: hanna-maija.elo@heinonen.com
Position: Partner dealing with intellectual property, anti-counterfeiting, trade mark infringements, franchising and franchise agreements, advertising, marketing, consumer law, copyright and litigation.
Career: Admitted to practise as a judge 1996; admitted to Finnish Bar 1998.
Languages: English, German, Swedish, Italian.
Member: Finnish Bar Association; Finnish Anti-Counterfeiting Group (chairman); Finnish Association of Industrial Property; Finnish AIPPI Group; Finnish Copyright Association; International Association of Young Lawyers.
Education: University of Helsinki (1994 LLM).
Personal: Born 1970.
Leisure: Sports.

HÄKKÄNEN, Petteri

Heinonen & Co, Attorneys-at-Law, Ltd
Phone: Helsinki (+358 9 25 300 600)
E-mail: petteri.hakkanen@heinonen.com
Position: Partner dealing with intellectual property, trade marks, advertising, marketing, patent law and employee invention law.
Career: Admitted to Finnish Bar 2001.
Languages: English, Swedish, French.
Member: Finnish Bar Association; Finnish Association of Industrial Property; Finnish group of AIPPI.
Education: University of Helsinki (1996 LLM).
Personal: Born 1970.
Leisure: Sports, drawing.

JÄRVINEN, Marja-Liisa

Krogerus & Co. Oy
Phone: Jyväskylä (+358 14 333 0800)
E-mail: marja-liisa.jarvinen@krogerus.com
Jyväskylä office.
Position: Partner specialising in public procurement, EU projects and legal services for small- and medium-sized companies.
Career: Lawyer, Chamber of Commerce of Central Finland 1987-91; associate Attorneys-at-Law Hirvonen & Raivio 1991-93; partner Attorneys-at-Law Marja Liisa Järvinen Oy 1993-2002; partner Krogerus & Co. Oy 2003.
Languages: Finnish, English.
Member: Finnish Bar Association.
Education: University of Turku (1987 LLM); trained on the Bench 1990.
Personal: Born 1961; resides Jyväskylä.
Leisure: Motorcycling, gym.

JOENPOLVI, Katri

Krogerus & Co. Oy
Phone: Helsinki (+358 9 622 6520)
E-mail: katri.joenpolvi@krogerus.com
Transactions.
Position: Partner and head of EC and competition law competence group.
Career: Associate Procopé & Hornborg Attorneys-at-Law 1994-95; senior research officer, deputy head of division Finnish Competition Authority 1996-2000; legal counsel, manager Klegal Oy 2000-01; senior associate Krogerus & Co. Oy 2001-03; partner 2003. Publications: several articles on merger control; several publications of Ministry of Communications concerning the telesector.
Languages: Finnish, English, Swedish.
Member: Finnish Bar Association.
Education: University of Edinburgh (1993-94); University of Helsinki (1994 LLM); trained on the Bench 1996.
Personal: Born 1969; resides Helsinki.
Leisure: Reading, jogging, skiing.

KAIRO, Janne

Borenius & Kemppinen
Phone: Helsinki (+358 9 615 333)
E-mail: janne.kairo@borenius.com
EU and competition, dispute resolution, information technology.
Position: Partner responsible for Borenius & Kemppinen's competition practice, and also specialised in telecoms, public procurement and M&A. Head of telecommunications practice as well as EU and competition.
Career: Admitted to the Finnish Bar 2002; associate Borenius & Kemppinen 1996-2002; partner Borenius & Kemppinen 2003.
Languages: Finnish, English, Swedish, French.
Member: The Finnish Bar Association; The Finnish Competition Law Association; Finnish Industrial Property Society; International Alumni of Boalt Hall, UC Berkeley; country correspondent of the European Competition Law Review.
Education: University of Helsinki (1996 LLM); University of California, Berkeley, Boalt Hall, USA (2000 LLM).
Personal: Born 1967; resides Helsinki.

KAPANEN, Pasi

Krogerus & Co. Oy
Phone: Jyväskylä (+358 14 333 0800)
E-mail: pasi.kapanen@krogerus.com
Jyväskylä office.
Position: Partner and head of Jyväskylä office; specialises in mergers and acquisitions, contract law and commercial law.
Career: Associate at Krogerus & Co. Oy from 1994; partner since 1999.
Languages: Finnish, English.
Member: Finnish Bar Association; International Bar Association.
Education: University of Lapland (1990 LLM); trained on the Bench 1993.
Personal: Born 1966; resides Laukaa.
Leisure: Cross-country skiing, motorcycling.

KATAINEN, Juha Pekka

Krogerus & Co. Oy
Phone: Helsinki (+358 9 622 6520)
E-mail: jp.katainen@krogerus.com
Corporate and commercial.
Position: Partner and head of corporate and commercial practice group; dealing with IT, technology and telecommunications law, contract law, outsourcing arrangements, IT dispute resolution.
Career: Partner Law Office Katainen & Co from 1997 to 2001; partner Krogerus & Co. Oy 2001; frequently lectures on IT law.
Languages: Finnish, English, Swedish.
Member: Finnish Bar Association; International Bar Association.
Education: University of Helsinki (1997 LLM).
Personal: Born 1969; resides Helsinki.
Leisure: Golf, literature.

KAUTTU, Tuomo

Kauttu & Sainio
Phone: Helsinki (+358 9 6124 3933)
E-mail: tuomo.kauttu@kauttu-sainio.com
Corporate and commercial.
Position: Partner; practises in the areas of M&A, intellectual property, real estate and construction; has over 15 years' extensive experience by serving the business community as in-house and outside corporate counsel; has assisted Finnish corporations with their domestic and international activities and several foreign companies to establish business in Finland.
Career: Qualified 1988; author of articles and international publications in corporate and commercial law.
Languages: Finnish, English.
Member: Commission on international commercial practice and law, International Chamber of Commerce; vice-chair, Finnish-Canadian Trade Association; Finnish Bar Association; American Bar Association.
Education: University of Helsinki (LLB); University of Washington, Law School (1998 LLM Tax).
Personal: Born 1962; resides Espoo.

KEMPPINEN, Seppo

Borenius & Kemppinen
Phone: Helsinki (+358 9 615 333)
E-mail: seppo.kemppinen@borenius.com
Intellectual property rights, dispute resolution, associations and foundations.
Position: Partner specialising in industrial rights, patent litigation and arbitration. Group leader in technology and IP; head of practice in associations and foundations, arbitration, IP litigation, mediation, patents and utility models as well as private clients.

Career: Admitted to the Finnish Bar 1978; notary at Lapua judicial district 1975, Court of Appeal of Eastern Finland (Kuopio) 1976; associate Attorneys at Law Borenius & Kemppinen 1977-82; partner 1982; chairman of the board 2003.
Languages: Finnish, English, German, Swedish.
Member: The Finnish Bar Association (served as chairman of mediation committee 1998-2001 and chairman of the delegation 1993-96); Finnish Lawyers' Association (vice-chairman of the board, chairman of the economic committee and the legal policy committee); International Bar Association; Finnish Industrial Property Society; Association International pour la protection de la Propriété Industrielle (AIPPI).
Education: University of Helsinki (1975 LLM).
Personal: Born 1950; resides Espoo.
Leisure: Classical music, golf.

KOTIRANTA, Kai
Borenius & Kemppinen
Phone: Helsinki (+358 9 615 333)
E-mail: kai.kotiranta@borenius.com
Dispute resolution, M&A, private equity and venture capital, capital markets, shipping, associations and foundations.
Position: Partner specialising in the fields of litigation and arbitration at Borenius & Kemppinen's Helsinki office. Group leader in dispute resolution. Head of shipping practice.
Career: Admitted to the Finnish Bar 2001; associate, Borenius & Kemppinen 1997-2002; partner 2003.
Languages: Finnish, English, Swedish.
Member: The Finnish Bar Association; The Union of Finnish Lawyers; International Bar Association; Finnish Lawyers' Association.
Education: University of Lapland (1997 LLM).
Personal: Born 1968; resides Helsinki.

KROGERUS, Hannu
Krogerus & Co. Oy
Phone: Helsinki (+358 9 622 6520)
E-mail: hannu.krogerus@krogerus.com
Corporate advisory.
Position: Partner and head of corporate advisory practice group, CEO; specialising in company law, corporate law, commercial law, contracts, mergers and acquisitions, corporate restructuring, banking and finance, and commercial litigation and arbitration. Advises major companies in their global transactions and business development.
Career: Legal counsel, Finnish Export Credit Ltd, Kansallis-Osake-Pankki, and Lohja Oy Ab 1971-87; administrative director and general counsel, Lohja Oy Ab 1987-91; senior vice-president Oy Metra Ab 1991-92; partner Krogerus & Co. Oy since 1992.
Languages: Finnish, English, Swedish.
Member: Finnish Bar Association; International Bar Association.
Education: University of Helsinki (LLM 1971); trained on the Bench 1975.
Personal: Born in 1949; resides Helsinki.
Leisure: Golf, music.

LUOMARANTA, Ritva-Liisa
Borenius & Kemppinen
Phone: Helsinki (+358 9 615 333)
E-mail: ritva-liisa.luomaranta@borenius.com
Dispute resolution, associations and foundations, private clients.
Position: Partner dealing with labour and employment matters as well as litigation and arbitration.
Career: Admitted to the Finnish Bar 1975; partner Borenius & Kemppinen 1982.
Languages: Finnish, English, Swedish.
Member: Finnish Bar Association; The Union of Finnish Lawyers; International Bar Association; elected to Espoo City Counsel 2001-04.
Education: University of Helsinki (1972 LLM).
Personal: Born 1948; resides Espoo.

MAKKONEN, Jarmo
Krogerus & Co. Oy
Phone: Kuopio (+358 17 368 1800)
E-mail: jarmo.makkonen@krogerus.com
Kuopio office.
Position: Partner dealing with company law, contract law, acquisitions, capital markets, litigation, insolvency and general practice.
Career: Lawyer Finnvera Oyj 1990-96; partner Attorneys-at-Law Karvinen, Kuosmanen & Makkonen Ky 1996-2003; partner Krogerus & Co. Oy 2003.
Languages: Finnish, English.
Member: Finnish Bar Association.
Education: University of Lapland (1989 LLM).
Personal: Born 1966; resides Kuopio.
Leisure: Jogging, slalom skiing, badminton.

MALI, Mikko
Krogerus & Co. Oy
Phone: Helsinki (+358 9 622 6520)
E-mail: mikko.mali@krogerus.com
Transactions.
Position: Partner and head of transactions practice group; specialising in M&A and capital markets transactions such as venture capital investments, private placements and IPOs; work in 2003 has included advising in several multi-million euro M&A transactions as well as capital market transactions with venture capital investors.
Career: Lawyer at Helsinki Money Market Center Ltd 1990-94; associate at Castrén & Snellman Attorneys-at-Law 1994-2001; partner Krogerus & Co. Oy Attorneys-at-Law since 2001.
Languages: Finnish, English, Swedish.
Member: Finnish Bar Association; The Association of Finnish Lawyers; International Bar Association.
Education: University of Helsinki (1990 LLM); trained on the Bench 1991.
Personal: Born 1964; resides Espoo.
Leisure: Basketball, sailing.

OKKONEN, Vesa
Krogerus & Co. Oy
Phone: Kuopio (+358 17 368 1800)
E-mail: vesa.okkonen@krogerus.com
Kuopio office.
Position: Partner dealing with company law, contract law, arbitration, capital markets and insolvency.
Career: Lawyer and bank manager, OKO Bank Kuopio 1982-92; partner Aatos Sarvi Oy 1992-99; vice-president and president Oy Karelia Parketti Ltd 1999-2002; vice-president Karelia Corporation 2002-03; partner Krogerus & Co. Oy 2003.
Languages: Finnish, English.
Member: Finnish Bar Association.
Education: University of Turku (1981 LLM).
Personal: Born 1954; resides Kuopio.
Leisure: Motorcycling, downhill skiing.

PAANILA, Riku
Borenius & Kemppinen
Phone: Helsinki (+358 9 615 333)
E-mail: riku.paanila@borenius.com
Commercial contracts, dispute resolution, EU and competition, M&A.
Position: Partner specialising in M&A, contracts, international trade and competition. Head of practice in litigation.
Career: Admitted to the Finnish Bar 1991; admitted to the German Bar 1997; partner Borenius & Kemppinen 2000.
Languages: Finnish, German, English, Swedish.
Member: The Finnish Bar; The German Bar.
Education: Helsinki University (1986 LLM); University of Trier (1988 M Iur).
Personal: Born 1961; resides Espoo.
Leisure: Sports, golf, hunting.

PALSOLA, Hannu
Krogerus & Co. Oy
Phone: Kuopio (+358 17 368 1800)
E-mail: hannu.palsola@krogerus.com
Kuopio office.
Position: Partner dealing with corporate law, mergers and acquisitions, litigation, arbitration, mediation, company law, contracts, sports law and general practice.
Career: Attorney Procopé & Hornborg Attorneys-at-Law; partner Kolari, Heikinheimo & Palsola Oy; partner Kolari, Heikinheimo, Palsola & Reinikainen Oy; partner Krogerus & Co. Oy 2003.
Languages: Finnish, English, Swedish.
Member: Finnish Bar Association; IBA.
Education: University of Turku (1983 LLM).
Personal: Born 1956; resides Kuopio.
Leisure: Golf, ice hockey.

PELTOLA, Lauri
Waselius & Wist
Phone: Helsinki (+358 9 668 9520)
E-mail: ww@waseliuswist.fi
Mergers and acquisitions, finance law, capital markets.
Position: Partner dealing with all areas of corporate law: mergers and acquisitions, finance law, capital markets, banking law, securities law.
Career: Admitted 1978. Ministry of Trade and Industry 1975-76; Procope & Hornborg 1976-92 (partner 1980, head of London branch 1984, secondment SG Archibald, Paris 1980); Roschier-Holmberg & Waselius 1993-2002 (head of London branch 1993, partner 1995). Made partner at Waselius & Wist 2002. Numerous articles in Finnish and

international professional publications in the fields of corporate and financial law.
Languages: Finnish, Swedish, English, German.
Member: Finnish Bar Association; Legal Society of Finland; International Bar Association.
Education: University of Helsinki (1974 LLM); trained at the Bench (1977).
Personal: Born 1950.

PENTTILÄ, Kimmo

Krogerus & Co. Oy
Phone: Oulu (+358 8 534 4400)
E-mail: kimmo.penttila@krogerus.com
Oulu office.
Position: Partner and head of Oulu office, main fields of activities include technology law, M&A, litigation, general business law.
Career: Associate Procopé & Hornborg Attorneys-at-Law, Helsinki 1989-94; partner Jouko Penttilä Attorneys-at-Law, Oulu 1995-99; partner Krogerus & Co. Oy Attorneys-at-Law, Oulu, since 1999.
Languages: Finnish, English, Swedish.
Member: Finnish Bar Association; International Bar Association.
Education: University of Helsinki (1988 LLM); Master of Laws Diploma 1994.
Personal: Born 1963; resides Oulu.

RAMM-SCHMIDT, Marja

Krogerus & Co. Oy
Phone: Helsinki (+358 9 622 6520)
E-mail: marja.ramm-schmidt@krogerus.com
Corporate advisory.
Position: Partner specialising in corporate and commercial law, arbitration and mediation, inheritance and property law.
Career: Associate at Juhani Salmenkylä Ky, Attorneys-at-law 1974-78; Hannes Snellman Oy, Attorneys-at-law 1978-93, partner 1984-93; Ramm-Schmidt & Co. Oy, Attorneys-at-law 1993-2001; Krogerus & Co. Oy, Attorneys-at-law from 2001.
Languages: Finnish, Swedish, English, German.
Member: Member of the Finnish Bar Association since 1977; member International Bar Association; certified mediator Finnish Bar Association; member Board of Arbitration of the Central Chamber of Commerce since 2002; member Finnish Sports' Arbitration Panel since 1991; President of the Helsinki Bar 1992-96; AIJA Honorary Vice President 1996; AIJA Executive Committee 1987-90; member delegation of the Finnish Bar 1992-98; member Professional Board of the Finnish Bar 1998-2001; member Ethical Board of the Finnish Bar 1988-92; chairman Young Lawyers Board of the Finnish Bar 1998-2001; member Ethical Board of Advokaatti (magazine of the Finnish Bar) since 1996, chairman since 1999; member Association of Finnish Lawyers since 1974; member Juridiska Föreningen; member Deutsch-Nordische Juristenvereinigung; founding member Sports Law Federation, member of the Board 1994-99; member Medical Commission of International Orienteering Federation since 1998; member Board of Sports Institute Kisakallio 1994 to date, chairman 2001 to date.

Education: University of Helsinki (1974 LLM); trained on the Bench 1977.
Personal: Born 1949; resides Espoo.
Leisure: Cross-country skiing, sailing, orienteering.

SAANIO, Ari-Pekka

Borenius & Kemppinen
Phone: Helsinki (+358 9 615 333)
E-mail: ari-pekka.saanio@borenius.com
Capital markets, company law, M&A, private equity and venture capital.
Position: Partner specialising in securities law and corporate finance, general corporate law and M&A. Head of capital markets practice.
Career: Trainee Borenius & Kemppinen 1992-94; associate Borenius & Kemppinen 1994-97; associate, foreign lawyer Sullivan & Cromwell, New York, 1998-99; senior associate Borenius & Kemppinen 1999-2000; partner 2000. Admitted to the Bars of Finland and New York 1999.
Languages: Finnish, English, Swedish, French, German.
Member: Finnish Bar Association; New York Bar Association.
Education: University of Helsinki (1994 LLM); New York University School of Law (1998 LLM corporation law).
Personal: Born 1965; resides Helsinki.

SAARELAINEN, Minna

Borenius & Kemppinen
Phone: Helsinki (+358 9 615 333)
E-mail: minna.saarelainen@borenius.com
Labour law, employment, corporate governance, dispute resolution, insolvency.
Position: Partner specialising in the fields of labour law and employment, and also has extensive experience in handling litigation, arbitration and ADR matters. Head of insolvency and labour practice.
Career: Admitted to the Finnish Bar 1994; associate Borenius & Kemppinen 1992-2002; partner Borenius & Kemppinen 2003.
Languages: Finnish, English, Swedish.
Member: Finnish Bar Association; The Union of Finnish Lawyers; International Bar Association.
Education: University of Turku (1989 LLM); Helsinki School of Economics and Business Administration (1997 MBA).
Personal: Born 1964; resides Helsinki.

SALONEN, Mika

Borenius & Kemppinen
Phone: Helsinki (+358 9 615 333)
E-mail: mika.salonen@borenius.com
M&A, insolvency, corporate restructuring, dispute resolution.
Position: Partner dealing with M&A, corporate restructuring, general corporate law, entertainment law and litigation. Currently responsible for the firm's operations in the Baltic countries.
Career: Admitted to the Finnish Bar 1994; partner Borenius & Kemppinen 1997.
Languages: Finnish, English, French, Swedish.
Member: AIJA; board member Finnish Association of European Law; Finnish Bar Association; board member FinnishTrade Guild in Riga.

Education: University of Turku; University of Amsterdam (1992 LLM).
Personal: Born 1964; resides Helsinki and Riga.

SEPPÄLÄ, Timo

Borenius & Kemppinen
Phone: Tampere (+358 3 214 9111)
E-mail: timo.seppala@borenius.com
M&A, commercial contracts, insolvency, industrial rights.
Position: Partner responsible for Borenius & Kemppinen's office in Tampere. Special expertise in legal issues relating to the Baltic region.
Career: Admitted to Finnish Bar 1988; partner in own law office 1988; managing director KLegal 2000; partner Borenius & Kemppinen 2003.
Languages: Finnish, Swedish, English.
Member: Finnish Bar Association.
Education: University of Helsinki (1983, LLM); trained at the bench 1987.
Personal: Born 1957; resides Tampere.

STÅHLBERG, Mika

Krogerus & Co. Oy
Phone: Helsinki (+358 9 622 6520)
E-mail: mika.stahlberg@krogerus.com
Transactions.
Position: Member of the board of Krogerus & Co. Oy and partner in the transactions practice group; specialises in mergers and acquisitions, capital markets, venture capital investments, banking and finance, securities, as well as company and corporate law. Work consists mainly of advising major corporations in their capital market related transactions (including M&A activities), as well as advising Finnish and foreign venture capital investors relating to their investments in Finnish companies. In addition, he has been the legal adviser in several IPO's and mergers involving Finnish public listed companies.
Career: Legal Counsel at Okobank and Skandinaviska Enskilda Banken; associate at Krogerus & Co. Oy from 1997; partner since 2000.
Languages: Finnish, English, Swedish.
Member: Finnish Bar Association; International Bar Association.
Education: University of Helsinki (1995 LLM).
Personal: Born 1969; resides Helsinki.

TÄHTINEN, Jyrki

Borenius & Kemppinen
Phone: Helsinki (+358 9 615 333)
E-mail: jyrki.tahtinen@borenius.com
Private equity and venture capital, M&A, corporate governance, arbitration, insolvency.
Position: Managing partner dealing with private equity, M&A, capital markets, and restructuring. Group leader in finance as well as head of practice in private equity and venture capital, corporate governance and corporate restructuring.
Career: Admitted to the Finnish Bar 1990; partner Borenius & Kemppinen 1991; manaaging partner 1997.
Languages: Finnish, English, German, Swedish.
Member: Finnish Bar Association; Finnish European Law Association; AIJA; International Association of Young

Lawyers; The Union of Finnish Lawyers; Tax and Legal Committees of the Finnish and European Venure Capital Associations.
Education: University of Helsinki (1985 LLM); Helsinki School of Economics (1989 MBA).
Personal: Born 1961; resides Helsinki.

TARKELA, Pekka

Borenius & Kemppinen
Phone: Helsinki (+358 9 615 333)
E-mail: pekka.tarkela@borenius.com
IP litigation, information technology, intellectual property rights.
Position: Partner dealing with IP and IT; main practice areas are IP, communications, media and entertainment, IT, e-commerce and technology contract law. Head of practice in IT contracts and outsourcing, database protection and trade secrets.
Career: Admitted to the Bar 1999; general secretary of the Finnish State Copyright Commission 1992-97; governmental expert in WTO, WIPO and EU preparatory bodies 1992-97; joined Borenius & Kemppinen 1997; partner 2000 to date.
Languages: Finnish, Swedish, English, German.
Member: ICC Commission on IPR; member of the board NIR magazine; Finnish Bar Association.
Education: University of Helsinki (1992 LLM).
Personal: Born 1965; resides Helsinki.

TOMMILA, Kukka

Heinonen & Co, Attorneys-at-Law, Ltd
Phone: Helsinki (+358 9 25 300 600)
E-mail: kukka.tommila@heinonen.com
Position: Partner dealing with intellectual property, trade marks, Internet law (domain names), advertising, marketing and consumer law.
Career: Admitted to Finnish Bar 2002.
Languages: English, French, German, Spanish, Swedish.
Member: Finnish Bar Association; Association of Finnish Patent Attorneys (junior member); Finnish Anti-Counterfeiting Group (secretary); Finnish Association of Industrial Property; IT-Juridical Association; ISOC Finland (member of the board); Finnish AIPPI Group.
Education: University of Helsinki (1998 LLM).
Personal: Born 1974.
Leisure: Golf.

TOMMILA, Marja

Heinonen & Co, Attorneys-at-Law, Ltd
Phone: Helsinki (+358 9 25 300 600)
E-mail: marja.tommila@heinonen.com
Position: Managing partner dealing with intellectual property, trade marks, franchising, advertising, marketing, Internet law (domain names), copyright, patents, consumer law, and litigation.
Career: Admitted to practise as a judge 1978; admitted to Finnish Bar 1980.
Languages: English, Swedish, French.
Member: Finnish Bar Association; International Bar Association; Finnish AIPPI Group; WWF Finland (member of the board); Finnish Franchising Association (member of the law and advisory committee).
Education: University of Helsinki (1974 LLM).
Personal: Born 1950.
Leisure: Golf.

VIKIÖ, Jari

Borenius & Kemppinen
Phone: Helsinki (+358 9 615 333)
E-mail: jari.vikio@borenius.com
Banking and corporate finance, capital markets, M&A, private equity and venture capital.
Position: Partner dealing with venture capital, M&A, restructuring, the capital markets as well as various financing instruments. Head of practice in securitisation and structured finance.
Career: Admitted to the Finnish Bar 1998; partner, Borenius & Kemppinen 2000.
Languages: Finnish, English, Swedish.
Member: Finnish Association of Lawyers; Finnish Bar Association.
Education: 1994 LLM.
Personal: Born 1968; resides Helsinki.

WASELIUS, Jan

Waselius & Wist
Phone: Helsinki (+358 9 668 9520)
E-mail: ww@waseliuswist.fi
Mergers and acquisitions, finance law, banking law and capital markets.
Position: Partner practising in corporate law; finance law; banking law; mergers and acquisitions; commercial law; industrial property rights; labour law; litigation and arbitration; securities law.
Career: Admitted 1972, Finland, Roschier-Holmberg & Waselius 1968-97 (partner 1970-95, senior partner 1986-95, of-counsel 1996-97); numerous articles in Finnish and international professional publications in the field of corporate and financial law.
Languages: Finnish, Swedish, English.
Member: OBE, Knight of Dannebrogen; member Order of Oranje-Nassau; Officer First Class of The Royal Order of the Polar Star; honorary legal adviser to Her Britannic Majesty's Ambassador to Finland; honorary legal adviser to Her Danish Majesty's Ambassador to Finland; honorary legal adviser to Her Netherlands Majesty's Ambassador to Finland; honorary legal adviser to His Swedish Majesty's Ambassador to Finland; honorary legal adviser to the Ambassador of the Bolivarian Republic of Venezuela to Finland; honorary legal adviser to his Spanish Majesty's Ambassador to Finland; honorary Legal adviser to Mexico's Ambassador to Finland; board member of several Finnish Anglo-American and Nordic subsidiaries in Finland and abroad; Finnish Bar Association; Legal Society of Finland; International Bar Association; International Fiscal Association.
Education: University of Helsinki (1968 LLM); trained at the Bench 1972.
Personal: Born 1944.

WESSMAN, Juha

Krogerus & Co. Oy
Phone: Helsinki (+358 9 622 6520)
E-mail: juha.wessman@krogerus.com
Corporate and commercial.
Position: Leads the project and structured finance team of the firm; expertise includes project and infrastructure finance and public-private-partnerships (PPP), as well as equipment and real estate leasing and financing; continuously advises both domestic and international financial institutions and companies in project financing transactions, PPP projects and equipment and real estate financing transactions, being accustomed to drafting, reviewing and negotiating documentation relating to such transactions (including term sheets, shareholders' agreements, sponsor undertakings, financing and security documentations and legal opinions). He also posses experience in dealing with governmental and multinational financial institutions and organisations in relation to project financing, as well as multilateral development banks.
Career: Legal counsel at Finnish Fund for Industrial Cooperation Ltd (FINNFUND) and Kansallis Finance Ltd; senior associate at Krogerus & Co. Oy from 1998, partner since 2000.
Languages: Finnish, English, Swedish.
Member: Finnish Bar Association; International Bar Association.
Education: University of Helsinki (1987 LLM); trained on the Bench 1991.
Personal: Born 1962; resides Kerava.

WILKMAN, Nina

Borenius & Kemppinen
Phone: Helsinki (+358 9 615 333)
E-mail: nina.wilkman@borenius.com
Banking and corporate finance, company law, energy, environmental and real estate, M&A, private clients, private equity and venture capital, marketing law.
Position: Partner dealing with M&A, private equity, banking and finance and general corporate law. Group leader in M&A and corporate, as well as head of practice in M&A, company law, energy, environmental and real estate, and also unfair competition and marketing.
Career: Qualified 1985; trained at the bench 1987; admitted to the Bar 1991 and 1998. Attorneys at law Hannes Snellman 1987-92; Outokumpu Oyj 1992-96; Huhtamäki Oyj 1996-98; partner Borenius & Kemppinen 1998; director Müller Martini Oy.
Languages: Swedish, Finnish, English, German.
Member: Finnish Bar Association; Legal Society of Finland; International Bar Association.
Education: Helsinki University (1982 LLM).
Personal: Born 1958; resides Helsinki.
Leisure: Music, theatre.

WIST, Tarja

Waselius & Wist
Phone: Helsinki (+358 9 668 9520)
E-mail: ww@waseliuswist.fi
Capital markets, finance law, mergers and acquisitions.
Position: Partner whose principal practice areas are: finance law; securities law; banking law; corporate law; mergers and acquisitions.
Career: Admitted 1994. Roschier-Holmberg & Waselius 1989-97; secretary to the Legislative Commission for Securities Market Legislation 1990-93; trainee at Rechtsanwaltskanzlei Schmidt, Wiederman und

Hintermayer, Nürnberg 1988; publications: numerous articles in Finnish and international professional publications in the field of corporate and financial law.
Languages: Finnish, Swedish, English, German.
Member: Finnish Bar Association; Legal Society of Finland; International Bar Association; Association Internationale des Jeunes Avocats.
Education: University of Helsinki (1989 LLM).
Personal: Born 1965.

FRANCE

BOUGIS, Christine
Cariddi, Mee, Rué/Hogan & Hartson LLP
Phone: Paris (+33 1 42 61 57 71)
E-mail: cbougis@hhlaw.com
Business and finance, international business transactions..
Position: Partner focusing on corporate and commercial law, with particular emphasis on French and cross-border mergers, acquisitions, joint ventures and divestitures (stock and asset transactions), reorganisations and spin-offs.
Career: Mudge Rose Guthrie Alexander & Ferdon, Paris 1991-95; Hogan & Hartson, Paris since 1995, partner 2001.
Languages: French, English.
Member: Paris Bar; New York Bar.
Education: Lycee Clemenceau, Nantes; University of Paris II - Assas (Magistère de Juriste d'Affaires program; 1988 Master's degree Corporate and Tax Law (DESS)); University of Paris 1 – Panthéon – Sorbonne (post-graduate Master's Degree European Communities Law ('DEA'); University of Virginia (1990 LLM corporate, commercial and tax law).
Personal: Born 1966; resides Paris.

CAFRITZ, Eric
Fried, Frank, Harris, Shriver & Jacobson LLP
Phone: Paris (+33 1 45 55 16 30)
E-mail: eric.cafritz@friedfrank.com
Corporate.
Position: Partner, concentrating in corporate and securities matters and international transactions. Represents some of the world's largest European and US-based corporations and banks in a variety of transactions including cross-border mergers and acquisitions and structuring and financing of pan-European industrial ventures. Areas of expertise include corporate finance (M&A), capital markets, private equity and securities (financial services).
Career: Qualified 1980; partner Fried Frank 1993.
Education: University of California, Berkeley (1977 BA); Yale University (1980 JD).

CARIDDI, Alan F
Cariddi, Mee, Rué/Hogan & Hartson LLP
Phone: Paris (+33 1 42 61 57 71)
E-mail: afcariddi@hhlaw.com
Corporate, securities and finance, lending, international joint ventures, strategic alliances, commercial transactions.
Position: Partner focusing on corporate, international business transactions, banking and financial law, and commercial law. He also has in-depth knowledge of labour laws and EU law.
Career: Hogan & Hartson managing partner, Paris office since 1995; managing partner Mudge Rose Paris office 1982-1995.
Languages: English, French, Portuguese.
Member: Paris, New York and District of Columbia Bars; American Bar Association's sections on Business Law; International Law and Practice; International Bar Associations.
Education: Georgetown University (BA magna cum laude, Phi Beta Kappa); Columbia University (JD, Harlan Fiske Stone Scholar).
Personal: Born 1949; resides Paris.

CURTIN III, William J
Cariddi, Mee, Rué/Hogan & Hartson LLP
Phone: Paris (+33 1 42 61 57 71)
E-mail: wjcurtin@hhlaw.com
Corporate, securities, international business transactions.
Position: Partner focusing on a variety of corporate and securities matters, focusing primarily on international business transactions, private equity and venture capital transactions and compliance with US and international securities laws.
Career: One year fellowship from the French government to teach American political studies as a visiting professor at the Institut d'Etudes politiques in Paris.
Languages: French.
Member: Bars of the Districts of Columbia and Maryland. Not admitted in France.
Education: Duke University (cum laude History and French); University of Virginia School of Law (law degree).
Personal: Born 1969; resides Washington DC.
Leisure: The Vergennes Institute (Paris); The Metropolitan Club (Washington DC).

EGHBAL, Bijan E
Cariddi, Mee, Rué/Hogan & Hartson LLP
Phone: Paris (+33 1 42 61 57 71)
E-mail: beeghbal@hhlaw.com
Labour and employment.
Position: Partner focusing primarily in the area of French labour law, representing local and international clients doing business in France.
Career: Partner Hogan & Hartson 1998.
Languages: French, English.
Member: Paris Bar (Avocat).
Education: Université de Paris II – Assas (1986 Master in Business and Tax Law); George Washington University, National Law Center (1988 Master of Comparative Law).
Personal: Born 1963; resides Paris.

MAXWELL, Winston
Cariddi, Mee, Rué/Hogan & Hartson LLP
Phone: Paris (+33 1 42 61 57 71)
E-mail: wjmaxwell@hhlaw.com
Communications and media industry acquisitions, entertainment, French law (corporate, labour, commercial), telecommunications agreements, arbitration, venture capital.
Position: Partner concentrating on communications, privacy and media law, corporate transactions, entertainment and international arbitration.
Career: Trained Hughes Hubbard & Reed, qualified France, New York; associate Hughes Hubbard & Reed (Paris Office) 1985-95, partner 1995-2000; partner Hogan & Hartson (Paris office) since 2000. Publications: 'Moral rights clauses after Barbelivian' Entertainment Law Review December 2003; 'Europe Implements Anti-Spam Legislation', Communications and Strategies, Issue 51, September 2003; 'Electronic Communications: The New EU Framework' (Oceana Publications, 2003).
Languages: French.
Member: French Bar; New York Bar; co-chair American Chamber of Commerce in France's Communications and Technology Committee; International Association of Entertainment Lawyers.
Education: Cornell Law School (Ithaca, New York) (1985 JD).
Personal: Born 1960; resides Bourg-la-Reine.

MAZO, Mark E
Cariddi, Mee, Rué/Hogan & Hartson LLP
Phone: Paris (+33 1 42 61 84 14)
E-mail: memazo@hhlaw.com
International business transactions.
Position: Partner focusing on cross-border business transactions, with particular emphasis on strategic and financial investments, joint ventures and acquisitions for major international investors and for European and US companies. Can also be contacted on +1 202 637 56 73.
Career: Qualified US Supreme Court and US Court of Appeals for Washington DC, District of Columbia Bar; Partner Hogan & Hartson 1990. 'Foreign Investment in the US', International Financial Law Review, Legal Guide to Corporate Activity and Inward Investment (1995).
Member: Business Law and the International Law and Practice Sections of the American Bar Association. Not admitted in France.
Education: Princeton University (Woodrow Wilson School of Public and International Affairs) (1971 AB magna cum laude, Phi Beta Kappa; Distinguished Military Graduate (US army); Harvard Law School (1974 cum laude).
Personal: Born 1950; resides Chevy Chase, Maryland USA.
Leisure: Princeton Club of New York; Columbia Country Club; Colonial Club of Princeton.

MEE, Bruce
Cariddi, Mee, Rué/Hogan & Hartson LLP
Phone: Paris (+33 1 42 61 57 71)
E-mail: bcmee@hhlaw.com
Corporate, litigation/arbitration, intellectual property.
Position: Partner practises in the areas of industrial and intellectual property law, commercial law, litigation and arbitration. Intellectual property: has represented clients in the software, film, flat screen technology, television, textile, toy and video game areas, among others, in the drafting of licence and technology transfer agreements, anti-piracy enforcement and civil and criminal litigation relating to trade mark and copyright infringement and unfair trade practices. Litigation/arbitration: has represented clients in litigation before civil and commercial courts, including trial and appellate courts, throughout France, in

connection with disputes relating to distribution, supply, subcontracting, joint venture and project finance agreements, general contractual obligations, telecommunications law and regulations, insurance law and relations with foreign state-owned entities, among others. He has also represented clients in arbitration proceedings, notably before the ICC Court.
Career: Coudert Brothers, New York and Washington 1981-83; Mudge Rose Guthrie Alexander & Ferdon, Paris 1984-95 (partner 1991); partner Hogan & Hartson 1995.
Languages: French, German, Dutch.
Member: New York Bar; French Bar; New York State and American Bar Associations.
Education: Ludwig-Maximilians Universität, Munich 1974-75; Harvard University (1977 AB magna cum laude); Ecole Normale Supérieure de Paris 1977-78; Université de Paris I (1978 Maîtrise ès Lettres); Harlan Fiske Stone Scholar, Columbia University (JD).
Personal: Resides Saint-Germain-en-Laye.

RUE, Fabrice

Cariddi, Mee, Rué/Hogan & Hartson LLP
Phone: Paris (+33 1 42 61 57 71)
E-mail: frue@hhlaw.com
Tax, business and finance.
Position: Partner represents companies at all stages in a wide variety of tax transactions, in audits and controversies, with particular emphasis on international tax transactions.
Languages: French, English.
Member: Advisory board American Tax Institute in Europe; International Fiscal Association; tax committee of the French American Chamber of Commerce.
Education: University of Paris I (1979 DEA Public finance/tax); University of Michigan (1985 LLM).
Personal: Resides Paris.

TURCON, Rémi

Alexen Avocats
Phone: Paris (+33 1 56 69 50 00)
E-mail: remi.turcon@alexen.com
International practise group.
Position: French and US corporate law; French and US commercial law; commercial leases; real estate transactions; retail law; mergers and acquisitions; international transactions.
Career: Qualified 1988, Paris; 1989, California; trained and associate Graham & James, Los Angeles 1989-91; qualified 1991, New York; trained and associate Rogers & Wells, New York 1991-93; partner Alexen Avocats 1993 to date, in charge of the international department. Publications include: 'Foreign Direct Investment in the United States', Sweet & Maxwell, 1993; 'Investir aux Etats-Unis', Dalloz, 1994; 'Grundlagen des US-amerikanischen Gesellschafts-, Wirtschafts-, Steuer-und-Fremdenrechts', CH Beck, 1994; 'La LLC Américaine: étude de Droit compare', Petites Affiches, 1997.
Languages: English, French, Spanish.
Member: Paris Bar Association, State Bar of California, New York Bar Association, American Bar Association, International Bar Association.
Education: Aix en Provence Law School (Masters in Private Law; Diploma of Advanced Studies in Public Law; Diploma from the Institute of Litigation Studies; Doctorate Degree); University of California at Los Angeles (UCLA) (LLM in International Law).
Personal: Born 1963; resides London, Paris.

UMHOEFER, Carol AF

Cariddi, Mee, Rué/Hogan & Hartson LLP
Phone: Paris (+33 1 42 61 57 71)
E-mail: cafumhoefer@hhlaw.com
Corporate, commercial.
Position: Counsel focusing on corporate transactions and commercial matters in transnational contexts, with a particular emphasis on intellectual property matters.
Career: Author of articles for the Harvard International Law Journal and the Columbia Journal of Transnational Law.
Languages: French, English.
Member: New York Bar; Paris Bar membership pending.
Education: Harvard Law School (JD cum laude); Fulbright Scholar, University of Wisconsin (BA).

VUONG, Van Bac

Cariddi, Mee, Rué/Hogan & Hartson LLP
Phone: Paris (+33 1 42 61 57 71)
E-mail: vvanbac@hhlaw.com
Corporate, securities and finance, business finance.
Position: Counsel focusing on commercial law and corporate law matters, and on litigation (French court system).
Career: Admitted Hanoi Bar 1952, Saigon Bar 1954-75; admitted to practise in Paris 1977; counsel Hogan & Hartson 1977.
Languages: Vietnamese, French, English.
Member: Hanoi Bar; Saigon Bar; Paris Bar; treasurer Saigon Bar Council.
Education: Lycee Albert Sarraut, Hanoi; University of Hanoi (1952 Licence en Droit; 1953 DES de Droit Privé; 1954 DES de Droit Public).
Personal: Born 1927; resides Paris.

GERMANY

BALLEW, Steven E

Hogan & Hartson Raue L.L.P.
Phone: Munich (+49 89 2050 8880)
E-mail: seballew@hhlaw.com
International business transactions, capital markets, financial services.
Position: Partner focusing on international corporate finance projects, including equity and debt investments, and mergers and acquisitions.
Career: Pillsbury and Winthrop, San Francisco; Hogan & Hartson 1983 (managing partner Warsaw 1992-98; resident partner Berlin 2001). Author: 'Joint Ventures in Poland'; Corporate Finance 1992; 'Assignments of Rights, Franchises and Obligations of the Disappearing Corporation in a Merger', 'The Business Lawyer'.
Languages: German, English.
Member: Rechtsanwaltskammer Berlin; District of Columbia Bar; State Bar of California; American Bar Association; Order of the Coif.
Education: Duke University; Indiana University; University of Southern California (AB; PhD; JD).
Personal: Born 1945; resides Munich.
Leisure: Wagner Society of Washington; City Club of Washington.

BRAEUER, Dr Max

Hogan & Hartson Raue L.L.P.
Phone: Berlin (+49 30 726 115 312)
E-mail: mbraeuer@hhlaw.com
Real estate and tax law, notary, real estate transactions, real estate litigation, matrimonial law and family.
Position: Partner focusing on real estate transactions and on family law issues. Head of the notary with respect to all real estate matters counselled at the Berlin office. This has afforded him substantial experience in all matters and activities relating to real estate purchases and the real estate register. He counsels clients on tax-oriented real estate investments on a large scale, in particular with respect to real estate investment funds.
Languages: German, English, French.
Member: Berlin Bar Association.
Education: University of Hanover; Universities of Gottingen, Geneva and Heidelberg (First State Exam in Law; Second State Exam in Law).
Personal: Born 1950; resides Berlin.

BREMER, Dr Eckhard

Hogan & Hartson Raue L.L.P.
Phone: Berlin (+49 30 726 115 353)
E-mail: ebremer@hhlaw.com
Antitrust, German and European competition law, state aids, public procurement/government contracts, administrative law and regulation.
Position: Partner who counsels and represents private and public corporations as well as public corporate bodies and authorities in all fields of public commercial law and regulation. His practical experience covers numerous industry sectors: printed press, broadcasting and telecommunications, public and private transportation, energy, banking, municipal economy, as well as municipal, public and private infrastructure projects.
Career: Assessor (Hamburg) 1989; research fellow, Max Planck Institute for Foreign Private and Private International Law, Hamburg (department of antitrust and competition, director Prof Dr Ernst-Joachim Mestmaecker) 1989-96; counsel Wilmer Cutler Pickering, Berlin 1996-97; partner Richter Seiler Jenckel Bremer, Berlin 1997-2000; partner Hogan & Hartson 2001. Publications: 'Broadcast Content Regulation in the United States and the Policy of Deregulation' (Harvard University 1987); 'A Market Constitition for Broadcating' (1994); 'Freiheit Durch Organisation/Liberty and the Instrument of Organisation' (1995); 'Medienplanwirtschaft' (Planned Media Economy) in: ORDO 1995, p361-389; 'The Coordinated Exclusion of Competitors under German and European Procurement and Competition Law' (together with Ernst-Joachim Mestmäcker, 1995); Treuhandverwaltung und Jurisdiktionsbefugnis (Extraterritorial Reach and Application of National Regulation and Custodianship, 1997).
Languages: German, English.
Member: Berlin Bar Association; DAJV – German-American Lawyers' Society; German Society for

Comparative Law; Forum Vergabe – National Association for Public Procurement Law; Studenkreis Kartellrecht – National Association for Antitrust Law; Deutsche Verkehrswissenschaftliche Gesellschaft – German Society for Transport and Infrastructure Sciences.
Education: Domgymnasium Verden (Aller); Universitiy of Freiburg I Br; University of Gottingen (1983 Referendar; 1989 PhD); Harvard University (1987 LLM).
Personal: Born 1957; resides Berlin.
Leisure: Politics and economics; rowing, skiing.

GLAS, Holger

Maiwald Patentanwalts GmbH
Phone: Munich (+49 89 74 72 66 0)
E-mail: glas@maiwald.de
Position: Associate specialising in patent prosecution as well as opposition and litigation matters in the field of chemistry; chemical engineering and pharmaceuticals.
Career: Qualified in 2002; joined Maiwald Patentanwalts GmbH 1999.
Languages: English, German.
Education: Technical University of Munich; European Patent Attorney and European Trade Mark Attorney (2002).
Personal: Born 1969; resides Munich.

GOECKE, Klaus

Hogan & Hartson Raue L.L.P.
Phone: Berlin (+49 30 726 115 225)
E-mail: kgoecke@hhlaw.com
Real estate, healthcare, notary.
Position: Partner with a broad range of experience in real estate investment including real estate sales, purchases and donation, leases, sale and lease back transactions, developer's investment, and real estate funds and condominium structures, including the tax aspects of these transactions. His practice, secondly, focuses on advising hospitals and pharmaceutical companies in all areas of medical products and healthcare laws.
Career: Partner Hogan & Hartson Raue 2003.
Languages: German, English.
Member: Berlin Bar Association.
Education: University of Goettingen; University of Hanover; National University of Singapore (First State Exam in Law (top 2%); Second State Exam in Law (top 2%)).
Personal: Resides Berlin.

GOTTSCHALK, Matthias

Maiwald Patentanwalts GmbH
Phone: Munich (+49 89 74 72 66 0)
E-mail: gottschalk@maiwald.de
Position: Associate specialising in copyright law, unfair competition law, intellectual property law, including trade mark and design law; drafting and negotiation of all kinds of licensing agreements in the media, IT and communications industry; sport and event marketing; legal support of international TV and film productions; licensing of film, video, TV, music and publishing rights.
Career: Former positions include business and legal affairs associate, Universal Music, Germany; head of legal affairs, EM.TV and Merchandising AG; joined Maiwald Patentanwalts GmbH November 2003; various publications in 'Media Law'.
Languages: English, German.
Education: University of Hamburg, Germany (1994 Law); University of Tennessee, USA (Law); University of St Gallen, Switzerland; (MBA 2002).
Personal: Born 1962; resides Munich.

HAMM, Volker

Maiwald Patentanwalts GmbH
Phone: Hamburg (+49 40 555 89 50)
E-mail: hamm@maiwald.de
Position: Partner and managing director specialising in German and international intellectual property law; patent prosecution; trade mark prosecution; patent infringement; litigation; trade mark infringement; licensing; chemicals and chemistry; pharmaceutical sciences and engineering.
Career: Joined Maiwald Patentanwalts GmbH, Munich 1992; partner 1998; managing director, Hamburg 1999.
Languages: English, German.
Member: LES; GRUR; AIPPI; FICPI; INTA.
Education: University of Hamburg; German Patent Attorney; European Patent Attorney; European Trade Mark Attorney.
Personal: Born 1958; resides Hamburg.

HANSEN, Norbert

Maiwald Patentanwalts GmbH
Phone: Munich (+49 89 74 72 66 0)
E-mail: hansen@maiwald.de
Position: Associate specialising in German and international intellectual property law; patent prosecution and litigation in the field of chemistry, chemical engineering and pharmaceutical sciences; trade mark prosecution and litigation; design; licensing and German law relating to employee inventions.
Career: Qualified in 2002; joined Maiwald Patentanwalts GmbH 1998.
Languages: English, German.
Member: FICPI; GDCh.
Education: Technical University of Munich (1995 Diploma; 1997 Doctorate).
Personal: Born 1968; resides Munich.

HEGEMANN, Prof Dr Jan

Hogan & Hartson Raue L.L.P.
Phone: Munich (+49 89 2050 8880)
E-mail: jhegemann@hhlaw.com
Copyrights, intellectual property, press law, media law, entertainment and the arts, unfair competition.
Position: Partner focusing on intellectual property, information technology, press and media, the arts, and entertainment. His clients include numerous publishing companies, theatres, universities, and several internationally known artists and authors.
Career: Clerk at the Berlin High Court and at the German Chamber of Commerce in Tokyo/Japan; admitted to the Bar of Berlin 1992; associate Boden Oppenhoff Rasor Raue 1992; partner Oppenhoff & Rädler 2000; partner Hogan & Hartson Raue 2001. Publications: Exploitation Rights at the DEFA Film Stock, 1995.
Languages: German.
Member: Berlin Bar Association; German Association for Intellectual Property and Copyrights (GRUR); German Japanese Lawyers Association (DJJV).
Education: Collegium Augustinianum Gaesdonk; Universities of Bonn, Munich and Humboldt; University of Berlin (1989 First State Exam; 1992 Second State Exam; 1995 Doctor juris; 2001 Honorary Professor).
Personal: Born 1963; resides Munich.
Leisure: Mountain climbing, hunting; Corps Rhenania Bonn, Club von Berlin, Rotary.

HUENGES, Martin

Maiwald Patentanwalts GmbH
Phone: Munich (+49 89 74 72 66 0)
E-mail: huenges@maiwald.de
Position: Associate specialising in intellectual property law; patent prosecution and infringement in the field of chemistry, biochemistry and pharmaceutical sciences; trade mark prosecution and infringement.
Career: qualified in 2002; joined Maiwald Patentanwalts GmbH 1999.
Languages: English, French, German.
Education: Technical University of Munich (1995 Diploma; 1998 Doctorate); European Patent Attorney; German Patent Attorney; European Trade Mark Attorney.
Personal: Born 1971; resides Munich.

KIETZMANN, Lutz

Maiwald Patentanwalts GmbH
Phone: Düsseldorf (+49 211 669 698 40)
E-mail: kietzmann@maiwald.de
Position: Partner and managing director specialising in patent prosecution and infringement proceedings in the fields of mechanical engineering and electrical engineering; licensing, especially in the fields of hydraulic and pneumatic systems, gear technology, conversion technology, measurement and control technology and telecom technology.
Career: Qualified in 2002; patent engineer of the central patent department at Mannesmann AG (now Vodafone AG) 1996-2000; joined Maiwald Patentanwalts GmbH in 2002; became partner 2003.
Languages: English, German.
Member: INTA; VPP.
Education: Universities of Magdeburg and Berlin (1995 Diploma; 1996 LLM); Syväskyla Institute of Technology, Finland; European Patent Attorney (2002).
Personal: Born 1969; resides Düsseldorf.

KOPF, Korbinian Paul

Maiwald Patentanwalts GmbH
Phone: Munich (+49 89 74 72 66 0)
E-mail: kopf@maiwald.de
Position: Associate specialising in German and international intellectual property law; the prosecution and litigation of patent rights in all fields of electrical engineering, in particular in the field of telecommunications; automotive engineering and digital imaging; trade mark prosecution; trade mark litigation.
Career: Qualified in 2000; worked as a consultant with an American photo company and a German chemical

company in Hong Kong and southern China; trained at Hoffmann & Eitle, Munich; joined Kenyon & Kenyon, New York; joined Maiwald Patentanwalts GmbH 2002.
Languages: English, French, German.
Education: Technical University of Munich; ENST in Brest, France; Newcastle Business School, UK.
Personal: Born 1969; resides Munich.

KUHLA, Dr Wolfgang
Hogan & Hartson Raue L.L.P.
Phone: Berlin (+49 30 726 115 301)
E-mail: wkuhla@hhlaw.com
Healthcare, privatisation, zoning law, litigation, administrative litigation, constitutional litigation.
Position: Partner who focuses on the area of healthcare, zoning and environmental law. Specifically, he provides regulatory and policy advice both to German and international companies and governmental agencies.
Career: Partner Raue Braeuer Kuhla, Berlin 1987; partner Oppenhoff & Rädler 1991; chair of the German Bar's Institute for Administrative Law 1984-94. Publications: handbook on Legal Proceedings in Administrative Law Matters and several publications concerning Health Care Issues; 'Data Protection in Labour Law and for Civil Servants'.
Languages: German, English, French.
Member: Berlin Bar Association; Committee for Constitutional Law of the German Bar.
Education: Universities of Berlin, Lausanne and Tubingen (Dr jur).
Personal: Born 1953; resides Berlin.

MAIWALD, Walter
Maiwald Patentanwalts GmbH
Phone: Munich (+49 89 74 72 66 0)
E-mail: maiwald@maiwald.de
Position: Partner and managing director specialising in German and international intellectual property law; patent and trade mark prosecution; patent and trade mark infringement litigation; licensing; consulting.
Career: Qualified in 1985; member of a German patent attorney firm 1985-91; partner 1988; created own firm, 1991.
Languages: English, German; basic French.
Member: GRUR; AIPPI; FICPI; INTA.
Education: University of Hamburg; Imperial College, London; Dipl Chem (1978); Dr rer nat (1981); German Patent Attorney (1985); European Patent Attorney (1987); European Trade Mark Attorney.
Personal: Born 1951; resides Munich.

MEINEL, Dr Gernod
Hogan & Hartson Raue L.L.P.
Phone: Berlin (+49 30 726 115 314)
E-mail: gmeinel@hhlaw.com
Labour law.
Position: Partner focusing on labour law. Extensive experience in the areas of restructuring, collective bargaining, compensation plans, stock option plans, codetermination, and labour litigation.
Career: Research assistant at the Chair of Prof Dr Franz-Jürgen Säcker; teaching assistant at the Chair of Prof Dr Jürgen Prölss; attorney since 1988; Oppenhoff & Rädler and predecessors (partner 1994; Hogan & Hartson Raue (partner 2001). Co-author: Act on Part-Time Work and Fixed Term Contracts of Employment, Germany; author of numerous articles on labour and employment law.
Languages: German, English.
Member: Berlin Bar Association.
Education: Free University of Berlin (First State Exam in Law (top 2%); Second State Exam in Law (top 2%); Dr iur).
Personal: Born 1960; resides Berlin.
Leisure: Running.

MICHALSKI, Stefan
Maiwald Patentanwalts GmbH
Phone: Düsseldorf (+49 211 669 698 40)
E-mail: michalski@maiwald.de
Position: Partner and managing director specialising in German and international intellectual property law; patent prosecution; patent infringement; trade mark prosecution; trade mark infringement; design, licensing; chemicals and chemistry; pharmaceuticals; sciences and engineering; biochemistry; microbiology.
Career: Joined Maiwald Patentanwalts GmbH in Munich, 1993; Partner 1998; managing director, Düsseldorf 2001.
Languages: English, German.
Member: AIPPI; FICPI; INTA; GDCh.
Education: Universities of Hamburg; Göttingen; Paris; Berkeley, California; German Patent Attorney; European Trade Mark Attorney.
Personal: Born 1962; resides Düsseldorf.

NELLE, Dr Andreas
Hogan & Hartson Raue L.L.P.
Phone: Berlin (+49 30 726 115 352)
E-mail: anelle@hhlaw.com
Mergers and acquisitions, venture capital, corporate law, commercial law, litigation, arbitration.
Position: Partner focusing on mergers and acquisitions, venture capital, MBO/LBO, privatisations, joint ventures. As an attorney and a business consultant, he has gained extensive experience advising technology, media, telecommunications, and energy companies and entrepreneurs in planning, negotiating and executing corporate transactions. His litigation and arbitration practice focuses on international and transaction-related matters. He has been one of the pioneers of commercial mediation in Germany.
Career: Qualified Berlin, 1995; consultant, major US-based management consultancy firm 1992-94; attorney leading German law firm 1995-2000; partner specialised consulting and investment company 2000-02; author: 'Duties of Renegotiation'; 'Claim, Judgment or Award and Enforcement in International Commerce'; 'Exclusivity in Bidding Consortia and Remedies in Case of its Violation'.
Languages: German, English, French.
Member: German National Bar Association; Committee on Mediation German Association for the Advancement of Business Mediation (GWMK).
Education: University of Freiburg and Munich; University of Paris 2, France; John F Kennedy School of Government; Harvard University (1993 Dr iur; 1986 Licence en droit; 1991 MPA).
Personal: Born 1962; resides Berlin.
Leisure: Sailing (NRV/APC).

NEUEFEIND, Regina
Maiwald Patentanwalts GmbH
Phone: Munich (+49 89 74 72 66 0)
E-mail: neuefeind@maiwald.de
Position: Partner and head of biology and biochemistry department; main practice areas include intellectual property; patents; trade marks; pharmaceutical patents; biotechnology; biochemistry and genetics.
Career: Scientist positions at Max-Planck-Gesellschaft and Bayer AG; joined Maiwald Patentanwalts GmbH 1996; partner 1999.
Languages: English, German.
Member: GRUR; AIPPI; FICPI; INTA.
Education: Universities of Cologne; Sussex, UK; Hohenheim, Stuttgart; Diploma Biology (1991); Dr rer nat (1994); German Patent Attorney (1999); European Patent Attorney (2001); European Trade Mark Attorney.
Personal: Born 1966; resides Munich.

PLESSER, Dr Markus
Hogan & Hartson Raue L.L.P.
Phone: Berlin (+49 30 726 115 304)
E-mail: mplesser@hhlaw.com
Intellectual property, including trade marks, patents, unfair competition, secret know-how, licensing, IT and Internet law.
Position: Partner focusing on intellectual property, in particular trade marks, patents, unfair competition, and IT law. Clients include providers of hardware and software, a coffee shop chain, and various media industry companies.
Career: Düsseldorf Bar 1997; Berlin Bar 2000; associate von Rospatt – von der Osten – Pross 1997; associate Oppenhoff & Rädler Linklaters & Alliance 2000; Hogan & Hartson 2001.
Languages: German, French.
Member: Berlin Bar; Association for Intellectual Property and Copyrights (GRUR).
Education: German School of Paris; University of Bonn; University of Freiburg (1993 First State Exam); Temple University School of Law (1994 LLM); 1996 Doctor juris; 1997 Second State Exam in Berlin.
Personal: Born 1968; resides Berlin.

PREUSS, Udo
Maiwald Patentanwalts GmbH
Phone: Munich (+49 89 74 72 66 0)
E-mail: preuss@maiwald.de
Position: Partner specialising in patent and trade mark prosecution and litigation; licensing; mechanical; electrical and electronic engineering; aeronautical and aerospace engineering.
Career: Worked on voice-controlled automatic pilot systems at the University of the German Armed Forces; trained as patent attorney at a major German patent law firm 1992-96; joined Maiwald Patentanwalts GmbH 2000; partner 2003.
Languages: English, German.
Member: epi; VPP; FICPI.
Education: Technical University of Munich (1992 Diploma); Iowa State University (Scholarship); European Patent Attorney (1998).
Personal: Born 1965; resides Munich.

RAUE, Prof Dr Peter

Hogan & Hartson Raue L.L.P.
Phone: Berlin (+49 30 726 115 305)
E-mail: praue@hhlaw.com
Property rights (copyrights, publishers' right of publication, arts and entertainment, unfair competition law, law of foundations).
Position: Name partner of German office; practice involves representing high-profile clients such as publishers, theatres, operas, universities, museums, artistic directors, artists, actors, writers and cultural institutions of all kinds as well as providing advisory service for the German federal government and the Berlin government with regard to legal aspects of cultural politics.
Career: Founded own law office (Raue-Braeur-Kuhla) 1972; merged with Oppenhoff & Rädler; joined Hogan & Hartson Raue LLP 2001; notary public since 1981; lectures on intellectual property rights at Freie Universität Berlin.
Languages: German, English.
Member: Berlin Bar Association; German Association for Intellectual Property and Copyrights (GRUR); board member of several cultural institutions, among these the board of trustees of the Jewish Museum Berlin; chairman of the Association of the Friends of the National Gallery.
Education: Freie Universität Berlin (1965 First State Exam; 1970 Second State Exam); doctorate in law 1967; professor 1995.
Personal: Born 1941.
Leisure: Founder of the Association of the Friends of the National Gallery 1997, chairman for over 25 years.

SCHMIDT-OTT, Justus

Hogan & Hartson Raue L.L.P.
Phone: Berlin (+49 30 726 115 363)
E-mail: jschmidt-ott@hhlaw.com
Corporate law, mergers and acquisitions, securities (including IPOs) and litigation.
Position: Partner, has extensive experience in the fields of national and international transactions and corporate restructurings; has advised, inter alia, clients on privatisations in the utility sector, international venture capital funds holding interests in German entities, and joint ventures of federal and regional authorities; litigation and arbitration practice is focused on complex transactional and banking matters.
Career: Research fellow, department of history of law and historical comparison of law, Freiburg University; Berlin office of Frankfurt-based law firm 1993; corporate department, Pünder, Volhard, Weber & Axster 1994-99; partner Clifford Chance Pünder 1999-2001; partner Hogan & Hartson Raue; notary public since 2003.
Languages: German, French, English.
Member: Max Planck Institute for Human Development; German Bar Association; European Contract Law Association.
Education: Universities of Freiburg and Cologne (First State Exam in Law; doctorate in classical Roman law).
Personal: Born 1961; resides Berlin.

SCHNELLER, Stephan

Maiwald Patentanwalts GmbH
Phone: Munich (+49 89 74 72 66 0)
E-mail: schneller@maiwald.de
Position: Partner specialising in German and international intellectual property law; trade mark infringement; trade mark prosecution; unfair competition; copyright law; licensing; international commercial arbitration.
Career: Qualified in 1996; Joined Maiwald Patentanwalts GmbH 1998.
Languages: English, German.
Education: Universities of Konstanz; Cape Town, RSA; Stellenbosch, RSA; Referendar (1994); Assessor (1996); LLM (1998).
Personal: Born 1966; resides Munich.

SCHOENE, Friedrich Tobias

Hogan & Hartson Raue L.L.P.
Phone: Berlin (+49 30 726 115 208)
E-mail: ftschone@hhlaw.com
Litigation, arbitration, corporate law, commercial law, healthcare.
Position: Partner focusing on the representation of both German and international clients before civil courts and arbitral tribunals. He has extensive trial and appellate experience, and advises businesses on corporate and commercial law matters.
Languages: German, French, Hebrew.
Member: Berlin Bar Association; German-Israeli Lawyer's Association (board 1998-2001); Friends of Yad Vashem in Germany.
Education: Universities of Heidelberg, Muenster and Goettingen (First and Second State Exam in Law).
Personal: Born 1966; resides Berlin.

SCHULTE, Dr Johannes

Hogan & Hartson Raue L.L.P.
Phone: Berlin (+49 89 2050 8880)
E-mail: jschulte@hhlaw.com
Business and finance, corporate , M&A, private equity, venture capital.
Position: Counsels corporations on all legal issues of corporate law and on national and international transactions, with a focus on media, technology, telecoms, health care and transportation.
Career: Attorney since 1995; Linklaters, Oppenhoff & Rädler, Berlin 1998-2000; Hogan & Hartson Raue LLP 2000.
Languages: German, English.
Member: German Bar (since 1995).
Education: Studied in Freiburg, Bonn, Mainz; The Dickinson School of Law of The Pennsylvania State University, Carlisle, USA (LLM); University of Potsdam; Humboldt University (Dr iur).
Personal: Born 1968; resides Munich.
Leisure: Sailing, speedskating, opera.

SCHWEER, Carl-Stephan

Hogan & Hartson Raue L.L.P.
Phone: Berlin (+49 30 726 115 307)
E-mail: csschweer@hhlaw.com
Real estate, zoning and development, energy, environmental, water, waste, general administrative, constitutional.
Position: Partner who advises public bodies, governmental agencies, cities and municipalities, as well as private investors, in regulatory matters, privatisations, public-private-partnerships, and joint investments. His energy practice focuses on the water, renewable energy and utility industries. He also provides representation in regard to urban developments, including infrastructure and traffic projects, industrial projects, and large housing projects.
Career: Qualified 2001 Berlin; Boden Oppenhoff Rasor Raue (Berlin); Fulbright & Jaworski (Washington DC). Published numerous articles on administrative, environmental, and municipal law. Co-author of a standard-book on waterlaw.
Languages: German, English.
Member: Berlin Bar Association; German Bar Association.
Education: University of Freiburg; University of Berlin (1992 PhD; 1993 Special Admittance to Administrative Law).
Personal: Born 1963; resides Berlin.
Leisure: Mountain sports.

SEILER, Dr Hans M

Hogan & Hartson Raue L.L.P.
Phone: Berlin (+49 30 726 115 352)
E-mail: hseiler@hhlaw.com
Corporate law, mergers and acquisitions.
Position: Partner focusing on corporate law, mergers and acquistions, securities, privatisations, and real estate transactions.
Languages: German, English, French.
Member: Berlin and German Bar Association; International Bar Association; German-American Lawyers Association; German-British Jurists' Association.
Education: University of Bonn; University of Munster; Boalt Hall School of Law; University of California at Berkeley (Dr iur, second state exam).
Personal: Born 1957; resides Berlin.

TIEFBRUNNER, Vera

Maiwald Patentanwalts GmbH
Phone: Munich (+49 89 74 72 66 0)
E-mail: tiefbrunner@maiwald.de
Position: Associate specialising in German and international intellectual property law; prosecution and infringement in the field of chemistry; chemical engineering and pharmaceutical sciences; trade mark prosecution and infringement; design and German law relating to employee inventions.
Career: Qualified in 2003; joined Maiwald Patentanwalts GmbH 2000.
Languages: English, French, German.
Member: FICPI.
Education: University of Munich (1995 Diploma; 1999 Doctorate).
Personal: Born 1969; resides Munich.

TIMNER, Hanno

Hogan & Hartson Raue L.L.P.
Phone: Berlin (+49 30 726 115 332)
E-mail: htimner@hhlaw.com
Labour and employment, companies and securities.
Position: Partner, representing national and international employers in a broad range of labour law issues in and out

of court. Practice focuses on the counselling and representing of national and international corporations with regard to the employment of top executives, the acquisition of companies and employment consequences of company restructuring.
Career: Admitted Bar of Berlin 1997; associate Oppenhoff & Rädler 1997-2000; junior partner Hogan & Hartson Raue 2001; partner Hogan & Hartson Raue 2004. Publications: International Handbook on contracts of employment (jointly with Gernod Meinel; German chapter).
Languages: German, English.
Member: Berlin Bar Association.
Education: Gymnasium Ernestinum; Free University of Berlin (1993 First State Exam; 1997 Second State Exam).
Personal: Born 1965; resides Berlin.
Leisure: Family (children), reading.

VON HAMMERSTEIN, Christian
Hogan & Hartson Raue L.L.P.
Phone: Berlin (+49 30 726 115 107)
E-mail: cvhammerstein@hhlaw.com
Energy, telecommunications, antitrust, constitutional and administrative law, privatisation.
Position: Partner providing regulatory and policy advice to clients in regulated industries. Practice involves representing clients from the energy and telecoms sector on regulatory and antitrust issues as well as in national and trans-border transactions.
Languages: German, English.
Member: Berlin Bar Association; Berlin Society of Lawyers; certified as specialist in administrative law by Berlin Bar Association; Institut for Energy Law, Freie Universität Berlin.
Education: Universities of Heidelberg and Freiburg (First State Exam in Law; Second State Exam in Law; Certified Specialist for Administrative Law).
Personal: Born 1965; resides Berlin.

VON KROSIGK, Sigrid
Maiwald Patentanwalts GmbH
Phone: Hamburg (+49 40 555 89 50)
E-mail: krosigk@maiwald.de
Position: Associate specialising in German and international intellectual property law; patent prosecution and infringement in the field of chemistry; chemical engineering and pharmaceutical sciences; trade mark prosecution and infringement; design and German law.
Career: Qualified in 2003; joined Maiwald Patentanwalts GmbH 1999.
Languages: English, German.
Member: FICPI.
Education: University of Hamburg (1999 Doctorate).
Personal: Born 1969; resides Hamburg.

WAGNER, Christoph
Hogan & Hartson Raue L.L.P.
Phone: Berlin (+49 30 726 115 322)
E-mail: cwagner@hhlaw.com
Media and entertainment, telecommunications, transactions.
Position: Partner focusing on media and entertainment and telecommunications transactions and related competition and regulatory matters.
Career: Oppenhoff & Rädler, associate 1990-95, partner 1996-2000; partner Hogan & Hartson 2001. Director Communications Group Hogan & Hartson; author 'The Media Authorities of the German Lander'; 'Konzentrationskontrolle im privaten Rundfunk' Rundfunk und Fernsehen, Band 2/1990, page 165 (1990); 'Konzentrationskontrolle im Medien-Binnenmarkt der EG, Archiv für Presserecht, Band 1/1992 page 1 (1992); 'Rechtsfragen digitalen Kabelfernsehens, Untersuchung im Zusammenhang mit der Einführung on Digital Video Broadcasting', Vistas (1996); 'Vertragsrecht der TK-Anbieter', Dr Otto Schmidt Verlag 2000, Kapitel: 'Öffentlich-rechtliche Regulierung'; 'Wettbewerb in der Kabelkommunikation zwischen Transport- und Vermarktungsmodell' Multimedia & Recht (MMR, issue no 2/2001); 'Rechtsfragen auf dem Weg zu DVB-T Planungssicherheit beim Übergang zur digitalen Rundfunkübertragung', vistas September 2001; Beck'scher Kommentar zum Rundfunkrecht, Kommentierun, September 2002.
Languages: German, Italian.
Member: International Bar Association; German Media Ownership – Control Commission (KEK).
Education: University of Berlin (Dr jur).
Personal: Born 1962; resides Berlin.
Leisure: Surfing, chess.

ZIMMERMANN, Heinz
Hogan & Hartson Raue L.L.P.
Phone: Berlin (+49 30 726 115 326)
E-mail: hzimmermann@hhlaw.com
Taxation, trade, corporate, capital markets.
Position: Partner focusing on international and domestic tax matters. Counsels clients on varied matters such as mergers and acquisitions, restructurings, non-profit organisations, customs and VAT issues.
Career: Arthur Andersen, Düsseldorf and Mexico City, qualified as Certified Tax Adviser and CPA; partner with a major German law firm; director Lex Mundi; partner Hogan & Hartson, Berlin 2001. Contribution to a new commentary on German Double Taxation Treaties and the Foreign Tax Act.
Languages: German, Spanish, English.
Member: American Bar Association; International Bar Association; International Fiscal Association.
Education: University of Saarbrücken (1 and 2 Law degree).
Personal: Born 1947; resides Berlin.
Leisure: Running, golf.

GREECE

BERNITSAS, Panayotis M
M & P Bernitsas
Phone: Athens (+30 210 36 15 395)
E-mail: m&p.bernitsas@bernitsaslawoffices.gr
Position: Managing partner dealing with EU and competition law, international transactions, banking and finance, securities, investments and capital movement, mergers, acquisitions and privatisations, public tenders and public contracts, telecommunications, taxation (corporate and individual), aviation and arbitration.
Career: Admitted 1974 Athens Bar; Athens Court of Appeal and Supreme Court of Greece; Professional Representative before the European Patent Office; Associate Professor of International Economic Law and Law of International Business Transactions and European Community Law, University of Thrace; Counsel, Ministry of National Economy during negotiations for Greece's accession to European Communities (EEC) 1977-82; Legal Counsel, Hellenic Banks Association 1980-90; Counsel to Greek Commissioner for Common Market Transport Matters, Brussels 1983-84; Special Secretary for Public Investments, Regional Policy and Integrated Mediterranean Programmes, Ministry of National Economy 1989; Counsel to Greek Prime Minister Zolotas on EEC matters 1989-90; Counsel to Minister of Foreign Affairs 1989-90; Counsel to the Minister of National Economy on illegal state aids and privatisation issues 1990-91; Secretary-General of the Hellenic Centre for European Studies 1990-93; Ad Hoc Counsel to the Minister of National Economy on EEC matters; Ad Hoc Counsel to the Ministry of National Economy on the privatisation of state-owned enterprises (National Telecommunications Organisation (OTE) and Refineries) 1991-93; is or has been an active arbitrator in various ICC arbitrations. Publications include 'Securities in International Transactions', Athens, (1978); 'Transport Policy and Greece's Accession to the European Communities' Athens, (1980, 2nd ed 1985); 'ECC Maritime Policy and its Application in Greece', (1981); 'Exclusive Agency Agreements in European Community Law', Greek Review of European Law, (1981); 'Towards a new approach in the methodology of the choice of law on contractual obligations', Greek Review of European Law, (1986); 'Anti-Dumping Law', (1987); 'The 'Prinos' Case: The International Implications of the Nationalisation of Companies', (1987); 'European Community Competition Law and its Impact on the Enactment and Application of Law 703/1977 on Monopolies and Oligopolies and on the Protection of Free Competition', (1988); 'Free Movement of Capital in European and Greek Law', (2nd ed 1989); The adaptation of the Greek legislation to the EC Directive on the producer's liability for defective products, (1990); 'European Community Law', (2nd ed, 1990); 'Ailing Companies: Judicial Implications and the Distortion of Purposes' (article in 'National Administration and EC Law', a publication of the Greek Centre for European Studies and Research and the European Institute of Public Administration, 1993).
Languages: English, French, German, Greek, Italian.
Member: Athens Bar Association; International Bar Association (IBA); International Fiscal Association (IFA), Greek section; Fédération Internationale de Droit Européen (FIDE), Greek section; Greek Institute for International and Foreign Law; Hellenic Society for International Law and Relations; Société de Législation Comparée; International Law Association (ILA); American-Hellenic Chamber of Commerce; British-Hellenic Chamber of Commerce; Hellenic Society for Private International Law.
Education: University of Athens Law School (Degree in Law); University of Paris (1973 DES in Public Law); Hague International Law Academy (1973); Institute of Advanced Legal Studies, London (1975 Research); University of Thessaloniki (1979 PhD).

BERSIS, George

PI Partners
Phone: Athens (+30 210 28 86 550)
E-mail: giorgos.bersis@gr.eylaw.com
Banking, finance, capital markets.
Position: Partner dealing with securities, derivatives, syndicated loans, IPOs, investment services, banking and corporate transactions.
Career: Admitted New York 1997; Athens 1998; drafted the CSD rulebook for dematerialised securities in Greece; participated in the listing of Bank of Cyprus, the first foreign company in ATHEX; lecturer in the ATHEX training centre on securities and derivatives issues; has advised a number of IPOs, public offerings and share capital increases.
Languages: Greek, English, French, Spanish.
Member: New York Bar; Athens Bar.
Education: University of Athens (1994 LLB); School of Law, New York University, (1996 LLM).
Personal: Born 1970; resides Athens.

DRYLLERAKIS, John C

Dryllerakis & Associates
Phone: Athens (+30 210 36 28 159)
E-mail: lawoffice@dryllerakis.gr
Position: Senior partner.
Career: Admitted to Athens Bar 1964; qualified to represent clients before Greek Courts including Supreme Courts; actively practising litigation especially before the administrative courts and the Conseil d'Etat. Started in private practice in 1962 with a large law firm in Athens and subsequently returned to private practice, while at the same time joining Exxon Corporation in 1967; first counsel and senior counsel for six years; general counsel and general tax counsel of the Exxon Affiliates in Greece for ten years, operating a refinery, five chemical plants, an oil and chemicals marketing company and an LPG sector. Acted as primary negotiator for the free sale of those affiliates to the Greek government and withdrew in 1984 after the sale was successfully completed. Member of the management team of those affiliates; extensive experience in international transactions and decision-taking processes, having attended many seminars and training courses. Joined Shell affiliate in Greece in 1984 and became legal division manager and a member of its management team while continuing in private practice in the law firm, Therofanopoulos-Dryllerakis (now Dryllerakis & Associates). Experienced in public administration procedure, management and financial matters; maintains an excellent combination of legal culture and of entrepreneurial orientation, having taken part in the negotiation of major deals and acquisitions; director in Greek affiliates of multinational companies and other Greek companies listed in the Stock Exchange (Allatini AE, Hyatt Regency (Thessaloniki) AE, European Trust Insurance Company AE, Klonatex AE, Naoussa Spinning Mill AE (subsidiary of Danone), Misko Pasta Company AE (Barilla's subsidiary), Shell Hellas AE, Chemicals and Petroleum Products Company, TVX Hellas Mining and Gold Manufacturing Company AE). Author of specialised legal books including 'Law 2190/20 re corporations in practice' (1999), 'Investment Incentives' (L2601/98 and PD 456/95 for grants etc) (1999), 'The Protection of Free Competition: Codified Law 703/77 and other provisions of the Greek and European Law' (1995), 'The Liberation of Capital Movements' (1998), 'Incentives for Industrial and Handicraft Enterprises' (L849/78, 289/76, LD 1312/72) (1979), 'Protection of Foreign Investment after the New Constitution' (1976), 'Investments and Protection of Foreign Capital' (LD 2867/53) (1975); contributor to a number of collective legal works such as 'Sanctions in Violation of the Provisions of L703/1977 re concentrations' (1998), Investment Incentives in AHI edition 'Doing Business in Greece' (Washington 1996), 'International Agency & Distribution Law' (Mathew Bender 1996), 'The Law of the Limited Liability Company Interpretation of Articles 22, 24-25, 35, 48 & 50 of Law 3190/1955 Inventory taking and annual accounts, reserves, books, balance sheets, liquidation' (1994), 'Tax Law and Investment Incentives' Chapter XVII from the 'Introduction to the Greek Law' (Kluwer/Sakkoulas 1988 2nd edition 1993) and many others; lectures on Greek tax law in summer courses at the Temple University and has delivered many speeches in seminars at many international meetings and conferences both in Europe and the US.
Languages: Greek, English.
Member: Athens Bar Association; International Bar Association; International Fiscal Association; Independent Competition Committee and Capital Markets Committee; Griechische Gesellschaft für Gesetzgebung; director, Competition Law Society, the Hellenic Society of Tax Law and of Fiscal Studies; special secretary, board of the Hellenic Society of European Law.
Education: Athens University Law School (Law and Economics).

GEORGIADES, Apostolos

Apostolos Georgiades & Associates
Phone: Athens (+30 210 36 23 338)
E-mail: info@georgiades.com
Position: Senior partner dealing with all areas of commercial law including banking and finance, joint ventures, real estate, mergers and acquisitions. He also specialises in construction law as well as procurement and public contracts and has served as an arbitrator in numerous international disputes.
Career: Qualified 1959; partner Apostolos Georgiades & Asssociates 1969; professor at University of Munich 1970; professor in Civil Law at University of Athens 1976-2002; legal counsel to National Bank of Greece 1976-2000; Dean of the Law School of University of Athens 1987-89; governor of National Mortgage Bank of Greece 1989-93; legal counsel to Greek Telecommunications Company (OTE) 1996-2000; legal counsel to the Church of Greece 1999-present; legal counsel to the Hellenic Banks Association 2001-02. Editor-in-chief of 'Chronicles of Private Law' review; honourary president of the Greek Civil Law Association. Publications of note include: 'Die Eigentumsanwartschaft beim Vorbehaltskauf' (1963); 'Die Anspruchskonkurenz im Zivilrecht und Zivilprozessrecht' (1968); 'Option Agreement and Option Rights' (1970); 'Issues on Civil Liability' (1972); 'Property Law' (volume I-II, 1991-93); 'New Forms of Contracts in Modern Economy' (2000, 4th edition); 'General Principles of Civil Law' (2002, 3rd edition); 'Euro and Law' (1999); 'Law of Obligations' (general part) (1999); Credit and Security' (2001); editor/co-author, 'Commentary of Civil Code' (Vol I-X, 1978-2003); also numerous scientific studies in law reviews.
Languages: English, French, German, Greek.
Member: Academy of Athens; Athens Bar Association; German Civil Law Professors' Association; Greek Commercial Law Association.
Education: University of Athens Law Schoool (1956 LLB); University of Munich Law School (1963 Dr Jur).
Personal: Born 1935; resides Athens.

ILIADOU, Tati

PI Partners
Phone: Athens (+30 210 28 86 512)
E-mail: tati.iliadou@gr.eylaw.com
Corporate and labour law.
Position: Partner dealing with corporate, commercial and labour law.
Career: Admitted Athens 1989; associate, Karatzas & Perakis, Athens 1989-92; in-house counsel, Ernst & Young, Hellas 1992-95.
Languages: Greek, English, French.
Member: Athens Bar.
Education: University of Athens (1987 LLB); University of Paris I and II (1989 DEA Banking and Public Law).
Personal: Born 1964; resides Athens.

PAPACONSTANTINOU, Helen

Law Offices Papaconstantinou
Phone: Athens (+30 210 729 57 50)
E-mail: hpaplaw@ath.forthnet.gr
Position: Partner.
Career: Admitted 1982, Athens; 1982, New York; legal associate Phillips, Nizer, Benjamin, Krim and Ballon, New York 1980-81; 'The Extraterritorial effects of EEC Antitrust Law', 1981, Stagiaire at the European Commission in Brussels (Directorate-General of Competition) 1983; author of publications including 'Is the Greek State Monopoly of Petrol Consistent with EEC Laws?' Economikos Tahidromos, (Financial Courrier) 11.8.83; 'Is the Greek Policy on Public Supplies Consistent with EEC Laws?' Economikos Tahidromos, 12.1.84 English Translation in Greece's Weekly, 10.3.84; 'Greek Foreign Exchange Controls and Community Law' Economikos Tahidromos, 14.6.84; 'Is the Marketing Compaign "Buy Greek" consistent with EEC Laws?' Economikos Tahidromos, 9.8.84; 'Is it possible to protect the national interest without contravening EEC Laws?' Economikos Tahidromos, 26.12.85; 'Free Trade and Competition in the EEC: Law, Policy and Practice', 1988, published by Routledge; 'Corporate Law Recent Developments – Greece', International Business Lawyer 1988, 89, 90, 91; also contributor to the following publications: 'Commercial Agency and Distribution Agreements – Law and Practice in the Member States of the European Community' (Chapter on Greek law), published by Graham and Trotman on behalf of the Association Internationale des Jeunes Avocats; 'Mergers and Acquisitions in Europe' (Chapter on Greek Law), published by Professional Publishing Limited in conjunction with S.G. Warburg Group as editors; 'European Franchising – Law and Procedure in the European Community' (Chapter on Greek Law),

published by Waterlow's Publishers; 'Acquisition of shares in a foreign country – Substantive law and legal opinions' published by Graham and Trotman and International Bar Association; 'International Corporate Procedures', Chapter on Greek law, published by Jordans.
Languages: Greek, English, French.
Member: Association of European Lawyers (Greek branch) for the protection of the financial interests of the community; Association Internationale de Jeunes Avocats; American Bar Association; Greek Team Europe; Harvard Alumni Association of Greece (president of the Association); Hellenic Association for European Law; International Bar Association; Union Internationale des Avocats; Union des Avocats Européens.
Education: London School of Economics and Political Science (1979 LLB); Harvard Law School (1980 LLM); Université Libre de Bruxelles (1985 PhD).
Personal: Married to Symeon Sikiaridis; two children, 14 and 12 years old.

PAPARRIGOPOULOS, Xenophon
PI Partners
Phone: Athens (+30 210 28 86 550)
E-mail: xenophon.paparrigopoulos@gr.eylaw.com
Litigation and arbitration, EU Law and IP law.
Position: Partner dealing with dispute resolution, competition and intellectul property.
Career: Admitted Athens 1982; legal counsel, Greek Parliament 1989 to date; assistant professor of law and philosophy, University of Thessalia 1995 to date. Publications: author, 'Unger's System of Rights: A Defence' in European Journal of Law, Philosophy and Computer Science (1995); 'The Scientific Department of the Greek Parliament' in Issues of Administrative Transformation (1995); 'The John Rawls Theory on Justice in K Beys Book' (1994).
Languages: Greek, English, French, Italian, German.
Member: Athens Bar.
Education: University of Athens (1980 LLB); Harvard Law School (1981 LLM; 1984 SJD).
Personal: Born 1956; resides Athens.

POTAMITIS, Stathis
PI Partners
Phone: Athens (+30 210 28 86 550)
E-mail: stathis.potamitis@gr.eylaw.com
Banking, finance and M&A.
Position: Managing partner; recognised expert in securities, investment services, banking and corporate transactions.
Career: Admitted New York 1987, Thessaloniki 1992, Athens 2000; associate, Paul, Weiss, Rifkind, Wharton & Garrison, New York 1986-91; general counsel, Egnatia Bank 1991-94; deputy chairman, Athens Derivatives Exchange 1998-99; member, committee for the codification of securities exchange legislation; has drafted the Code of Conduct for investment services firms, regulations for licensing and reporting by investment services firms, as well as several laws. Publications: author, 'A Synopsis of Securities Exchange Legislation' (Athens Stock Exchange 1996).
Languages: Greek, English, French.
Member: New York Bar; Thessaloniki Bar; Athens Bar.
Education: University of Toronto (1979 BA; 1982 MA; 1986 LLB); Eleve Titulaire, University of Paris IV (1983).
Personal: Born 1956; resides Athens.

SPYROPOULOS, Philippos C
Dryllerakis & Associates
Phone: Athens (+30 210 36 28 159)
E-mail: lawoffice@dryllerakis.gr
Position: Specialises in litigation at the Supreme Administrative Court and in the provision of legal advice in public law matters.
Career: Qualified and joined Athens Bar 1976; licensed to practise before all Courts, including Supreme Courts; legal counsel at the office of the President of the Helenic Republic 1981-83; general secretary to the Prime Minister 1989, and subsequently to the Minister of Justice 1991-92; legal counsel to the intra-ministerial Committee on Privatisation 1992-93; president of the National Theatre 1993; has numerous publications in scientific works.
Languages: English, German, French.
Member: Athens Bar Association; Association of Greek Constitutionalists; Legal Counsel of the Church of Greece; National Telecommunications Committee 2000 to present day; Greek Human Rights Committee 2000 to present day.
Education: Law School of Athens University 1974 (LLM); University of London LSE 1979 (Dr iur); University of Freiburg (i Br).
Personal: Born 1952.

VEKRIS, Johnny
PI Partners
Phone: Athens (+30 210 28 86 549)
E-mail: ioannis.vekris@gr.eylaw.com
Corporate and commercial, M&A, shipping, and real estate.
Position: Partner dealing with corporate and commercial law, arbitrations, shipping law and real estate.
Career: Admitted Athens 1986, New York 1988; associated with major shipping operators in Greece and Bingham Dana & Gould, Boston 1985-86. Publications: co-author, chapter on Greece 'Modern Legal Systems' (University of Virginia 1985).
Languages: Greek, English, French.
Member: New York Bar; Athens Bar.
Education: University of Athens (1983 LLB); University College, London (1984 LLM); Harvard Law School (1985 LLM).
Personal: Born 1960; resides Athens.

GUERNSEY

LE TISSIER, Roger
Ogier & Le Masurier
Phone: St Peter Port (+44 1481 721672)
E-mail: roger.le_tissier@ogier.com
Business law.
Position: Partner specialising in investment funds, securitisation, banking, company and general commercial.
Career: Admitted English Bar 1986, Guernsey Bar 1987; general practice 1987-90; joined Guernsey International Fund Managers Ltd (GIFM); during this time was seconded to the Guernsey Financial Services Commission for 18 months; company secretary, compliance officer and head of corporate secretarial and legal departments; sole principal Ogier & Le Masurier 1998-2002; partner 2002.
Languages: English, French.
Member: Honourable Society of Gray's Inn; Guernsey Bar; IBA.
Education: Elizabeth College, Guernsey; De Montfort University, Leicester (1985 LLB); Inns of Court School of Law; Caen University, France (1987 Certificat d'Etudes Juridiques Francaises et Normandes).
Personal: Born 1964; resides Guernsey.
Leisure: Music, member of Guernsey Choral and Orchestral Society, and Guernsey Chamber Choir.

SIMPSON, William
Ogier & Le Masurier
Phone: St Peter Port (+44 1481 721672)
E-mail: william.simpson@ogier.com
Business law group.
Position: Partner and head of Guernsey office specialising in investment funds, banking and trusts.
Career: Qualified 1980, Lincoln's Inn; barrister England 1983-87; crown counsel, Cayman 1987-88; barrister and solicitor, British Virgin Islands 1989-90; associate lawyer, Guernsey 1991-95; partner and advocate, Guernsey 1996-2001; partner Ogier & Le Masurier 2002.
Languages: English.
Member: ITPA; STEP.
Education: Leeds University (1979 LLB).
Personal: Born 1956; resides Guernsey.

HUNGARY

NAGY-KOPPANY, Kornelia
Nagy & Pintér Hogan & Hartson
Phone: Budapest (+36 1 302 9050)
E-mail: knagykoppany@hhlaw.com
Corporate, securities and finance, life sciences, intellectual property, lending, bankruptcy and creditors' rights.
Position: Managing partner and a member of the firm's life sciences, corporate, securities and finance and bankruptcy and creditors' rights practice groups.
Career: Partner Hogan & Hartson 1996.
Languages: Hungarian.
Member: Chair, board of directors, American International School of Budapest; board of directors, American International School of Budapest; supervisory board member, Gyori Keksz (UB) Kft; supervisory board member, Colgate-Palmolive Hungary Kft; trustee First Presbyterian Church of Oceanside.
Education: New York University School of Law (LLM); Loránd Eötvös University School of Law, Budapest (JD); Faculté International de Droit Comparé, Strasbourg, France (international comparative law).
Personal: Born 1955; resides Hungary.

PINTER, Aurel
Nagy & Pintér Hogan & Hartson
Phone: Budapest (+36 1 302 9050)
E-mail: apinter@hhlaw.com
Corporate, securities and finance, intellectual property, entertainment.

Position: Counsel who practises in the areas of corporate law, tax law, media law, entertainment law and intellectual property law.
Career: Managing partner Hardy & Pinter; visiting attorney, Weil Gotschal & Manges Washington DC; partner, Budapest law firm; civil judge, Pest Central District Court, Budapest; partner Hogan & Hartson 1998. Publications: articles in newspapers about economic associations, articles in newspapers related to pension funds and tax regulations connected with those funds.
Languages: Hungarian, English.
Member: Budapest Bar Association.
Education: Loránd Eötvös University, School of Law, Budapest (1980 JD).
Personal: Born 1955; resides Hungary.
Leisure: Tennis, squash.

VARGA, Ildikó
Nagy és Trócsányi
Phone: Budapest (+36 1 487 8700)
E-mail: varga.ildiko@nagyestrocsanyi.hu
Corporate transactions group.
Position: Head of the corporate transactions group with significant experience and practice in M&A, structuring foreign direct investments and transnational transactions.
Career: Eötvös Lorànd Tudomànyegyetem qualified 1988. Joined White & Case, New York (1990) as foreign attorney; moved to Arent Fox, Washington (1991); Joined Nagy és Trócsànyi as partner in 1993. Publications: 'Comparative Study of Constitutional Courts of Europe and the USA' Vol I and II, published by the Law Institute of the Hungarian Academy of Sciences (1988).
Languages: English, Hungarian.
Member: New York Bar; Budapest Bar.
Education: Eötvös Lorànd Tudomànyegyetem, Faculty of Law (1985), Faculty of Arts (1986); Université de Strasbourg (1987); NYU, Graduate School of Arts and Sciences in New York (1989-90).
Personal: Born 1957; resides Budapest.

ISRAEL

BEN-NATHAN, Rami
Erdinast, Ben Nathan & Co
Phone: Tel Aviv (+972 3 621 2500)
E-mail: ben-nathan@ebnlaw.co.il
Position: Partner specialising in corporate law, securities law, hi-tech investments, antitrust law and communications law.
Career: Admitted to the Israel Bar Association in 1987; lecturer on contract law, University of Tel-Aviv (1987) and torts, Hebrew University of Jerusalem (1987-88); articled clerk to the Hon Judge S Netanyahu, the Supreme Court of Israel, 1986; chief editor of 'Mishpatim' Law Review, the Hebrew University of Jerusalem, 1986; author of 'Revision of the Implied Term Doctrine in Contemporary Israeli Law', Mishpatim 17, 571; established Erdinast, Ben-Nathan & Co, 1988.
Languages: English and Hebrew.
Member: Israel Bar Association.
Education: Hebrew University of Jerusalem (1986, LLB, cum laude).
Personal: Born 1956.

DANZIGER, Yoram
Danziger, Klagsbald, Rosen & Co
Phone: Ramat Gan (+972 3 611 0700)
E-mail: yoram@danklaw.co.il
Corporate department: company law, international commerce and M&A transactions.
Position: Managing partner and co-founder specialising in all areas of business law and has vast experience in corporate reconstructions, joint ventures and M&A activity. He often serves as legal counsel to international corporations operating in Israel and gained a considerable reputation in the representation of Israeli companies operating worldwide. He frequently uses his expertise by serving as an arbitrator and mediator resolving a wide variety of disputes.
Career: Awarded the Israeli Association for Parliamentarism's prize; appointed by the Minister of Justice to the official committee to review the structure and operations of the Official Receiver and General Custodian. Former member of Board of Editors, Tel Aviv University Law Review; vice-editor, Israeli Bar Law Review; author 'The Right to Information about the Company' 2000; author of various legal articles both in Israel and UK, focusing mainly on company law; lecturer in law, Tel Aviv University Faculty of Law from 1981 to date.
Languages: English, Hebrew.
Member: Israeli Bar Association.
Education: University of Tel Aviv Faculty of Law (LLB and LLM); London School of Economics 1983 (PhD in law).
Personal: Born 1953.

EPHRAT, Zvi
I Gornitzky & Co
Phone: Tel Aviv (+972 3 710 91 91)
E-mail: ephrat@gornitzky.co.il
Position: Partner specialising in corporate; commercial; international law; banking and finance.
Career: Admitted 1972; head of the International Law Department, Military Advocate General's Unit (participated in negotiations with Egypt for the signing of the Interim Agreement and the Camp David Peace Treaty); senior legal officer in the Office of Legal Affairs, Secretariat of the UN New York 1982-87; director Sonol, Ampal, Bank Hapoalim Switzerland; chairman of the newspaper Davar Rishon; director United Mizrahi Bank Ltd.
Languages: Hebrew, English.
Education: Hebrew University of Jerusalem (LLB).
Personal: Born 1943.

ERDINAST, Giora
Erdinast, Ben Nathan & Co
Phone: Tel Aviv (+972 3 621 2500)
E-mail: erdinast@ebnlaw.co.il
Position: Partner specialising in commercial litigation, securities law, mergers and acquisitions, competition law, hi-tech investments.
Career: Admitted to the Israel Bar Association in 1985; lecturer on constitutional law (1985) and logic (1983-85), University of Tel-Aviv; corporate department, Summit, Rovins & Feldesman (New York) 1986-87; established Erdinast, Ben-Nathan & Co, 1988.
Languages: English, French, Hebrew.
Member: Israel Bar Association.
Education: University of Tel-Aviv (1983, BA Philosophy; 1984, LLB, cum laude); Yale Law School (1986 LLM); Fulbright Fellowship for advanced studies.
Personal: Born 1956.

HACMUN, Amos
Heskia-Hacmun Law Firm
Phone: Tel Aviv (+972 3 608 1122)
E-mail: amos.hacmun@hh-law.co.il
Commercial and corporate.
Position: Managing partner in charge of corporate and transaction matters.
Career: Mr Hacmun negotiated and represented a European banking group in the sale of a 40% controlling interest in an Israeli bank. He was also nominated by an international banking group to serve as a board member at the Israel Continental Bank. Mr Hacmun headed a purchase transaction of a local company by an international group of companies specialising in the manufacture of hardware for the telecommunications industry, and also led the licensing of technology and know-how essential for the establishment of a semiconductor Fab project in northern Israel, at a cost of US$1.5bn.
Languages: English, German, Hebrew.
Education: Bar-Ilan University (1997 LLB).
Personal: Born 1972; resides Tel Aviv.

HESKIA, Dor
Heskia-Hacmun Law Firm
Phone: Tel Aviv (+972 3 608 1122)
E-mail: dor.heskia@hh-law.co.il
Corporate and litigation.
Position: Managing partner in charge of commercial and litigation matters.
Career: Mr Heskia has been nominated to represent a well-known European bank in its defence against a derivative lawsuit involving a claim for the amount of NIS152m from former directors and officers at a local bank. Mr Heskia was appointed by a well-known German telecom company to head its representation in a complex dispute with its Israeli partners. The dispute included a series of lawsuits, one of which involved a derivative lawsuit against the major shareholder and its board members. Mr Heskia's defence was successful, and the ruling set a precedent as it was the first time such a lawsuit was rejected on grounds of lack of good faith. Mr Heskia also represented a prominent singer, and former winner of The Eurovision Song Contest, in a lawsuit against the Israeli telecommunications company Bezek International. Mr Heskia claimed that the rights of his client, especially the right to publicity, were being compromised by the telecommunications company. The infringement was confirmed, and the parties came to a settlement, which included an apology from Bezek International before the singer. Mr Heskia is active in liquidation and insolvency proceedings. He was nominated as liquidator of a number of companies and successfully obtained protection from the court (stay of

proceedings) for clients that aimed to restructure their businesses to avoid bankruptcy.
Languages: English, Hebrew.
Education: Beer Sheva University (1989 BSc Electrical and Computer Engineering); Haifa University (1991 Advanced Management Studies); Bar Ilan University, Tel Aviv (1997 LLB).
Personal: Born 1964; resides Tel Aviv.

KHAYAT, Eyal

Eyal Khayat, Zolty & Co
Phone: Herzliya Pituach (+972 9 957 7171)
E-mail: eyal@khayatlaw.com
Position: Founding partner dealing with areas of corporate law, technology and biotech-related laws, including investment agreements, mergers and acquisitions, and corporate finance.
Career: Trained at Haim Zadok & Co Law Offices; qualified 1990; associate Haim Zadok & Co Law Offices 1990-92; associate Dan Ofer & Co 1992-94; partner Cohen, Khayat & Co 1995-98; partner in charge of hi-tech department Avital Dromi & Co 1999-2000; partner Eyal Khayat, Zolty & Co 2001.
Languages: English, Hebrew.
Member: Israeli Bar.
Education: Kingston University, London (1988 LLB).
Personal: Born 1961.

KLAGSBALD, Avigdor

Danziger, Klagsbald, Rosen & Co
Phone: Ramat Gan (+972 3 611 0700)
E-mail: dori@danklaw.co.il
Litigation department.
Position: Co-founder and head of litigation department; has vast experience handling high-profile and precedent-setting cases; has represented domestic and international individuals and business enterprises of all sizes, and has argued numerous cases before the Israeli Supreme Court, lower court, and other judicial and administrative tribunals and has set several notable precedents in the areas of company law, constitutional law, bids and tenders, antitrust, 'white-collar' and economic criminal law.
Career: Former member of Board of Editors, Tel Aviv University Law Review; author 'National Inquiry Commissions' 2001; author of various legal articles in both Israel and the UK focusing mainly on constitutional law and administrative law; lecturer in law in the Inter-disciplinary Center for the Studies of Business, Law and Technology, teaching courses in constitutional and administrative law.
Languages: English, Hebrew.
Member: Israeli Bar Association.
Education: University of Tel Aviv Faculty of Law (LLB and LLM); University of Tel Aviv 1988 (PhD in law).
Personal: Born 1953.

MATALON, Moriel

I Gornitzky & Co
Phone: Tel Aviv (+972 3 710 91 91)
E-mail: matalon@gornitzky.co.il
Managing partner.
Position: Managing partner specialising in commercial; corporate; mergers and acquisitions; tourism; hotel management; international business transactions; international project finance; public tenders and bids; energy project development; real estate; telecommunications.
Career: Admitted 1975; assistant to a minister, Israeli government 1969-70; senior legal adviser, international law department, Israel Defense Forces 1970-75; associate Amen, Weissman and Butler, New York 1975-78.
Languages: English, Hebrew.
Education: Admitted 1975; Faculty of Law, Hebrew University of Jerusalem (LLB; LLM cum laude).
Personal: Born 1948.

ROSEN, Ori

Danziger, Klagsbald, Rosen & Co
Phone: Ramat Gan (+972 3 611 0700)
E-mail: ori@danklaw.co.il
Hi-tech department.
Position: Work encompasses general corporate practice with focus on mergers and acquisitions, venture capital transactions, public offerings and intellectual property matters; clients include publicly traded and privately held companies, Israel's top venture capital funds and foreign funds investing in Israeli-related companies, multinational corporations seeking investments in Israel and numerous hi-tech and start-up companies in various fields. He is regarded by peers as one of the top two hi-tech lawyers in Israel (Maariv, March 27, 2002) and was elected as a leading attorney in Israel in e-commerce and Internet law, and highly recommended in company and corporate transactions and in mergers and acquisitions. The hi-tech practice tops the list of the 'European Legal 500's' recommended hi-tech law firms in Israel for three years in a row (2001-2003).
Career: Author: chapter on Israeli Cryptography Law and Policy in Baker & Hurst 'The Limits of Trust: Cryptography, Governments and Electronic Commerce' (Kluwer Law, 1998); has authored law review articles and numerous pieces of legal commentary in Israeli business newspapers.
Languages: English, Hebrew.
Member: Israeli Bar Association; New York Bar.
Education: Faculty of Law, Tel Aviv Univeristy (1984 LLB; 1990 LLM); University of Michigan Law School (1990 LLM).
Personal: Born 1963.

ROSENSWEIG, Joshua

I Gornitzky & Co
Phone: Tel Aviv (+972 3 710 91 91)
E-mail: rosensweig@gornitzky.co.il
Position: Partner specialising in corporate; local and international taxation; commercial; international business transactions; securities; mergers and acquisitions; international hi-tech; finance; venture capital.
Career: Admitted 1978; lecturer taxation, Bar Ilan University, School of Law 1980-94; Tel Aviv School of Business Management 1983-94; legal adviser, Finance Committee, Israeli Parliament 1983-85; member Somekh Committee on Mergers and Spin-Offs (Taxation) of Listed Companies 1993-94; member Rafael Committee on Reform of International Taxation 1990; member Rabinowitch Committee on Reform of Taxation 2002. Was ranked as one of the top five taxation lawyers in Israel, by Maariv (one of Israel's two largest newspapers by circulation). Recently nominated as chairman of The First International Bank, Israel's fifth-largest bank.
Languages: English, Hebrew.
Education: Yeshiva University (1973 BA); Bar Ilan University (1976 LLB); New York University (1979 LLM Taxation; 1981 JSD International Taxation).
Personal: Born Canada 1952.

RUBIN, Pinhas

I Gornitzky & Co
Phone: Tel Aviv (+972 3 710 91 91)
E-mail: rubin@gornitzky.co.il
Chairman.
Position: Chairman specialising in corporate; taxation; securities; international business transactions; litigation; antitrust; class actions; white-collar crimes; banks and banking; liquidation; bankruptcy.
Career: Admitted 1974; lectured tax law, business law and commercial law at Tel Aviv University, Faculty of Law and School of Business; was member of advisory committee on reform of the Israeli court system; chairman, Israel Bar Association taxation committee 1985-99; member Rabinowitch Committee on Reform of Taxation 2002. Was ranked as the best taxation lawyer in Israel and one of the top five commercial lawyers in Israel by Maariv (one of Israel's two largest newspapers by circulation); ranked as one of the top 100 influential persons in the Israeli economy by 'The Marker', a leading Israeli economic magazine, for the years 2000-03 (29th in 2003); ranked by the legal and accounting department of 'Ha'aretz', the third-largest Israeli newspaper, as the most successful lawyer in Israel 2003.
Languages: English, Hebrew.
Member: Rabinowitch Committee on Reform of Taxation 2002.
Education: Tel Aviv University (LLB).
Personal: Born Israel 1949.

ZELICHOV, Ariel

I Gornitzky & Co
Phone: Tel Aviv (+972 3 710 91 91)
E-mail: zelichov@gornitzky.co.il
Position: Partner specialising in commercial; corporate; securities; financing; real estate; international project finance; public tenders and bids; public finance.
Career: Admitted 1982.
Languages: English, Hebrew.
Member: Israel Bar Association.
Education: Faculty of Law, Hebrew University of Jerusalem (LLB).
Personal: Born 1955.

ZOLTY, Amir J

Eyal Khayat, Zolty & Co
Phone: Herzliya Pituach (+972 9 957 7171)
E-mail: amir@khayatlaw.com
Position: Partner dealing with all areas of corporate law, hi-tech and bio-tech law including investment agreements, mergers and acquisitions, corporate finance.
Career: Trained at Herzog, Fox & Neeman; qualified 1990; associate Herzog, Fox & Neeman 1990; senior assistant to

the Attorney General of the State of Israel 1993; lecturer in Tel Aviv University 1996-99; senior legal assistant to the president of the Supreme Court of the State of Israel 1997; registrar in the Supreme Court of the State of Israel, 2000; partner Eyal Khayat, Zolty & Co 2001.
Languages: English, Hebrew.
Member: Israeli Bar.
Education: Tel Aviv University (1989 LLB magna cum laude); Yale University, New Haven, CT (1992 LLM).
Personal: Born 1963.

ITALY

CAPELLI, Guido
Galgano
Phone: Milan (+39 02 777 2141)
E-mail: gcapelli@galgano.it
Corporate, M&A and private equity.
Position: Partner; head of the corporate practice; works in areas including M&A, corporate contracts, private equity, MBO and IPO.
Career: Qualified 1987; partner 1998.
Languages: English, French, Italian.
Member: IBA.
Education: University of Milan Law School.
Personal: Born 1962; resides Milan.

CONSONNI, Marco
Galgano
Phone: Milan (+39 02 777 2141)
E-mail: mconsonni@galgano.it
Technology and communication.
Position: Partner; head of the IT, telecoms and media practice; works in areas including the Internet, telecoms and e-commerce.
Career: Qualified 1989; partner 1998; co-author 'Fare Business in rete' (McGraw-Hill, 1999); 'Getting the Deal Through: E-Commerce' (Law Business Research, 2002).
Languages: English, French, Italian, Spanish.
Member: IBA.
Education: University of Milan Law School.
Personal: Born 1964; resides Milan.

CONTINI, Davide Giorgio
Galgano
Phone: Milan (+39 02 777 2141)
E-mail: dcontini@galgano.it
Capital markets.
Position: Partner; head of the banking and capital markets practice; works in areas including banking, securitisations, derivatives, IPOs and corporate law for financial institutions.
Career: Qualified 1988; partner 1998.
Languages: English, Italian.
Member: IBA.
Education: University of Milan Law School.
Personal: Born 1963; resides Milan.

GALGANO, Francesco
Galgano
Phone: Bologna (+39 051 232 622)
E-mail: bologna@galgano.it
Arbitration, corporate.
Position: Senior partner; head of the arbitration and corporate practice.
Career: Qualified 1974; founder partner of Galgano; author of several books and articles on contract, corporate and commercial law; professor of Civil Law at University of Bologna.
Languages: Italian, French, English.
Education: University of Bologna Law School; University of Seville (Doctor of Jurisprudence Honoris Causae).
Personal: Born 1933; resides Bologna.

GALGANO, Frederico
Galgano
Phone: Bologna (+39 051 232 622)
E-mail: fgalgano@galgano.it
Commercial and litigation.
Position: Partner; head of litigation practice; works in areas including commercial litigation, corporate litigation, international and national arbitration, commercial works.
Career: Qualified 1989; partner 1998; author of several articles and contributions on corporate and commercial law.
Languages: English, Italian.
Member: IBA.
Education: University of Bologna Law School.
Personal: Born 1965; resides Bologna.

GRIECO, Antonio
Grieco e Associati
Phone: Rome (+39 06 420 38 81)
E-mail: a.grieco@griecoassociati.it
Position: Partner specialising in corporate, competition, mergers and acquisitions, banking and public works and procurements.
Career: Called 1985, Rome; associate Bisconti Law Firm, New York 1985-86; associate Guerra Piga Law Firm, Rome 1987-88; lecturer on civil law, University of Rome, La Sapienza 1989-95; professor of international business law at the European School of Economics, Rome 2001.
Languages: English, French, Italian.
Member: Italian Bar Association (Rome); international associate Italian Arbitration Association; international associate American Bar Association; International Bar Association; NIAFF (North American Italian Foundation); Rotary Club of Rome.
Education: University of Rome, La Sapienza (1982 JD maxima cum laude); University of Illinois Law School (1984 MCJ; scholarship); New York University (1985 visiting scholar); CNR (Italian National Institute of Research (1985 scholarship); Harvard University Law School (1989 PIL).
Personal: Born 1960; resides Rome.

JERSEY

BERTRAM, Peter
Ogier & Le Masurier
Phone: St Helier (+44 1534 504110)
E-mail: peter.bertram@ogier.com
Property law.
Position: Partner; property and succession law, banking and security, general commercial matters.
Career: Trained Le Masurier Giffard & Poch; admitted English Bar 1980; legal assistant in property law 1981; admitted Jersey Bar 1984.
Languages: English.
Member: The Law Society of Jersey, chairman Bosdet (local charity providing sporting facilities and charitable assistance), Conveyancing Sub-committee of Jersey Law Society; The Honourable Society of Inner Temple.
Education: Victoria College, Jersey; Southampton University (1979 LLB).
Personal: Born 1957; resides Jersey.
Leisure: Music, reading, walking, fishing.

BINNINGTON, Alan
Mourant du Feu & Jeune
Phone: St Helier (+44 1534 609203)
E-mail: alan.binnington@mourant.com
Private wealth management.
Position: Partner and advocate; advises on structures for private wealth management.
Career: Admitted 1981 to English Bar (Middle Temple); Jersey Bar 1984; joined Mourant du Feu & Jeune 1981; partner 1985; editorial board of the Jersey Law Review; one of Jersey's Law Commissoners.
Languages: English, French.
Member: International Bar Association; Honorary Consul for Belgium in the Channel Islands; Association of Contentious Trust and Probate Specialists; Society of Trust and Estate Practitioners.
Education: Victoria College; St Catharine's College, Cambridge (1980 MA).
Personal: Born 1958.

BIRTWISTLE, Daniel
Mourant du Feu & Jeune
Phone: St Helier (+44 1534 609339)
E-mail: daniel.birtwistle@mourant.com
Jersey commercial law.
Position: Associate specialising in funds, financial services and mergers and acquisitions work.
Career: Admitted Jersey solicitor 1998; Jersey advocate 1999; associate Mourant du Feu & Jeune 2001.
Languages: English.
Member: Jersey Law Society.
Education: Victoria College, Jersey; Cardiff University (1994 Hons Law; BVC; 1995 ICSL).
Personal: Born 1972.

BREEN, Elizabeth
Mourant du Feu & Jeune
Phone: St Helier (+44 1534 609241)
E-mail: liz.breen@mourant.com
Property.
Position: Partner and head of the property group which deals with all matters of conveyancing together with development and joint venture agreements, JCT agreements and associated documents, commercial leases, mortgages, corporate and private relocation and property management.
Career: Admitted 1986 as Jersey solicitor; partner Mourant du Feu & Jeune 1993.
Languages: English, French.

Member: Society of Trust and Estate Practitioners; Whitely 90.
Education: Southampton University (1976-79).
Personal: Born 1953.

BYRNE, Christopher
Ogier & Le Masurier
Phone: St Helier (+44 1534 504264)
E-mail: chris.byrne@ogier.com
Business law.
Position: Partner; banking law, structured finance, investment funds, corporate law, commercial law, trusts and employee benefits.
Career: Trained Allen & Overy; qualified 1988; associate Allen & Overy; secondment from Allen & Overy to a London bank acting as bank's commercial in-house lawyer; posted to Asia to open Allen & Overy's Singapore office 1992; admitted Jersey Bar 1996; partner Ogier & Le Masurier 1997.
Languages: English.
Member: The Honourable Society of the Middle Temple; The English Law Society; The Law Society of Jersey; The International Bar Association.
Education: Leicester University (LLB).
Personal: Born 1965; resides Jersey.

CHAPLIN, Clive
Ogier & Le Masurier
Phone: St Helier (+44 1534 504250)
E-mail: clive.chaplin@ogier.com
Business law.
Position: Partner and head of group specialising in employee benefits, investment funds, limited partnerships, financial services regulation, trust law, company law, and with a wide experience of general company and commercial matters.
Career: Admitted English solicitor 1977, Jersey solicitor 1986; partner Ogier & Le Masurier 1994.
Languages: English, French, Spanish.
Member: The Law Society of England and Wales; The Law Society of Jersey; The Jersey Law Commission.
Education: Nottingham University (1974 BA Hons Law).
Personal: Born 1951; resides Jersey.
Leisure: Tennis, choral singing, music.

CHAPMAN, Julia
Mourant du Feu & Jeune
Phone: St Helier (+44 1534 609547)
E-mail: julia.chapman@mourant.com
Mourant International Finance Administration.
Position: Partner specialising primarily in the field of specialist collective investment structures and capital markets structures.
Career: Trained Simmons & Simmons, London; qualified England and Wales 1990; qualified Jersey 1995; Ogier & Le Cornu, Jersey 1990-94; joined Mourant du Feu & Jeune 1994; partner 1999; regularly makes contribution to professional publications; speaks at conferences and seminars.
Languages: English, French, Spanish.
Education: St Mary's Convent, Ascot; Queens' College, Cambridge (1986 BA Hons).
Personal: Born 1965.

CLYDE-SMITH, Julian
Ogier & Le Masurier
Phone: St Helier (+44 1534 504465)
E-mail: julian.clyde_smith@ogier.com
Trust and estate planning group.
Position: Partner; notary public; crown advocate.
Career: Trained Ogier & Le Cornu; admitted English Bar 1973, Jersey Bar 1974; partner Ogier & Le Masurier 1976.
Languages: English.
Member: The Honourable Society of the Middle Temple; The Law Society of Jersey.
Education: Worth School; Christ's College, Cambridge (1972 BA Hons Law).
Personal: Born 1950; resides Jersey.
Leisure: Sailing.

CRILL, James
Mourant du Feu & Jeune
Phone: St Helier (+44 1534 609232)
E-mail: james.crill@mourant.com
Private wealth management.
Position: Business development partner specialising in estate planning, trusts, private wealth administration, employee benefits and employee stock ownership plans.
Career: Admitted 1985, Jersey; partner Mourant du Feu & Jeune 1987; head of Mourant Equity Compensation Solutions until 2002; appointed Mourant's business development partner 2002; has regularly spoken at conferences and seminars in the UK, Europe and the USA on equity compensation solutions and trusts.
Languages: English.
Member: International Bar Association.
Education: Hailybury College, Hertfordshire.
Personal: Born 1954.

DAVIES, Claire
Mourant du Feu & Jeune
Phone: St Helier (+44 1534 609336)
E-mail: claire.deacon@mourant.com
Private client litigation.
Position: Associate specialising in all areas of private client litigation.
Career: Jersey solicitor and advocate 1997.
Languages: English.
Education: Coventry University (Business law).
Personal: Born 1970.

DAVIES, Cyman
Mourant du Feu & Jeune
Phone: St Helier (+44 1534 609346)
E-mail: cyman.davies@mourant.com
Jersey commercial law.
Position: Partner specialising in trust and mutual fund work including retail and private equity funds.
Career: Admitted 1987 to English Bar (Middle Temple); 1989 Jersey Bar; partner Mourant du Feu & Jeune 1993; frequent speaker at conferences and contributor of articles including 'Financial & Commercial Handbook of the Channel Islands'; editorial panel of 'Trusts & Trustees'; assisting formulating amendments to both the Trusts (Jersey) Law 1994 and the Companies (Jersey) Law 1991; contributor of articles to legal journals.
Languages: English, French.
Member: Law society; Society of Trust and Estate Practitioners; International Tax Planning Association.
Education: University College, Oxford (1983-86).
Personal: Born 1965.

DAVIES, Nicola
Mourant du Feu & Jeune
Phone: St Helier (+44 1534 609606)
E-mail: nicola.davies@mourant.com
International finance.
Position: Chief executive specialising in the establishment and administration of structured finance vehicles.
Career: Admitted English Bar (Middle Temple) 1989; Jersey Bar 1991; joined Mourant du Feu & Jeune 1988 in commercial department; also worked for Mourant & Co, the firm's wholly owned trust and company administration company; partner Mourant du Feu & Jeune 1995; deputy managing partner 2002-03; chief executive 2003; has spoken at numerous conferences across Europe; contributed to a number of professional journals.
Languages: English, French.
Member: Jersey Law Society; European Securitisation Forum; Jersey Capital Markets Working Group.
Education: Queen Elizabeth High School; St Hilda's College, Oxford (1985-88).
Personal: Born 1967; two children.
Leisure: Scuba diving, cooking, sailing.

DEVENPORT, Edward
Mourant du Feu & Jeune
Phone: St Helier (+44 1534 609243)
E-mail: edward.devenport@mourant.com
Jersey commercial law.
Position: Partner specialising in trusts, collective investment funds and banking.
Career: Admitted English Bar (Middle Temple) 1988; admitted as Jersey solicitor 1993; joined Mourant du Feu & Jeune 1990; partner 1996; regularly makes contributions to trust publications, including writing the Jersey chapter of 'Asset Protection: Domestic and International Law and Tactics'.
Languages: English, French.
Member: Society of Trust and Estate Practitioners.
Education: Birmingham University (1986 LLB Hons).
Personal: Born 1965.

FITZ, Sarah
Ogier & Le Masurier
Phone: St Helier (+44 1534 504180)
E-mail: sarah.fitz@ogier.com
Personal law group.
Position: Managing partner and head of personal law group; crown advocate; criminal law, drugs and narcotics, family law, children.
Career: Trained Ogier & Le Cornu; admitted English Bar 1986, Jersey Bar 1989; partner Ogier & Le Masurier 1991; head of the personal law group 1997.
Languages: English.
Member: The Honourable Society of the Middle Temple; The Law Society of Jersey.
Education: Convent FCJ, Jersey; Central London Polytechnic (1981 BA Hons Theology; 1985 Diploma in Law).
Personal: Born 1961; resides Jersey.

GOULD, Simon M
Mourant du Feu & Jeune
Phone: St Helier (+44 1534 609353)
E-mail: simon.gould@mourant.com
Jersey commercial law.
Position: Partner specialising in financial services, insurance, corporate, commercial and trust law.
Career: Pupillage 2 Gray's Inn Square, London 1992; joined Mourant du Feu & Jeune, Jersey 1992; joined commercial department 1994; associate 1997; partner 2000; regularly contributes to professional publications and speaks at conferences and seminars; member of Financial Services Commission working groups in relation to financial services business; chairman of industry working group on anti-money laundering procedures; member of industry working group on offshore insurance.
Languages: English, French.
Member: Law Society of Jersey; Society of Trust and Estate Practitioners.
Education: LLB Hons (1990); Inns of Court School of Law (1991); Jersey law professional exams (1994).
Personal: Born 1966.

GUILLAUME, Marc
Mourant du Feu & Jeune
Phone: St Helier (+44 1534 609245)
E-mail: marc.guillaume@mourant.com
Jersey commercial law.
Position: Associate specialising in offshore structures, trusts, pensions and employee share plans.
Career: Admitted English Bar 1993; Jersey Bar 1998.
Languages: English.
Education: Balliol College, Oxford.
Personal: Born 1968.

HAMEL, Nicole
Mourant du Feu & Jeune
Phone: St Helier (+44 1534 609579)
E-mail: nicole.hamel@mourant.com
Jersey commercial law.
Position: Associate specialising in legal advice on the creation and administration of trusts.
Career: Trained Mourant du Feu & Jeune, Jersey; qualified 1990; associate 1992.
Languages: English.
Member: Society of Trust and Estate Practitioners; Jersey Law Society.
Education: Convent FCJ, Jersey.
Personal: Born 1959.

HAMILTON, Michaela L
Mourant du Feu & Jeune
Phone: St Helier (+44 1534 609427)
E-mail: michaela.hamilton@mourant.com
International finance legal.
Position: Associate specialising in investment funds, securitisations and structured finance.
Career: Trained Bond Pearce, Plymouth; qualified 1997; admitted England and Wales 1997; Jersey advocate 2001; associate Mourant du feu & Jeune 2003.
Languages: French.
Member: Law Society of England and Wales; Law Society of Jersey.
Education: Beaulieu Convent School, Jersey; Exeter University (1993 BA French); College of Law, London (1994 Dip Law; 1995 Dip LP).
Personal: Born 1970; resides Jersey.

HERBERT, Tim
Mourant du Feu & Jeune
Phone: St Helier (+44 1534 609339)
E-mail: tim.herbert@mourant.com
Jersey commercial law.
Position: Partner specialising in corporate law, business affairs and investment fund work; has been involved in a number of significant mergers and acquisitions and investment funds; practice includes unit trust, corporate fund and limited partnership structures.
Career: Admitted 1982 to English Bar (Middle Temple); 1985 to Jersey Bar; joined Mourant du Feu & Jeune 1983; partner 1987; has spoken at conferences in the UK, US and Jersey and has contributed to a number of professional journals.
Languages: English, French.
Member: International Bar Association; Institute of Directors; Honorary Consul for Finland.
Education: Trinity College, Oxford (1978-81).
Personal: Born 1959.

HICKLING, Robert
Mourant du Feu & Jeune
Phone: St Helier (+44 1534 609396)
E-mail: robert.hickling@mourant.com
International finance.
Position: Partner specialising in capital markets, investment funds, structured finance, securitisation.
Career: Admitted as English solicitor 1987, Jersey solicitor 1998; partner 2000.
Languages: English, French.
Education: Birmingham University (1980-83).
Personal: Born 1962.

JAMES, Ian
Mourant du Feu & Jeune
Phone: St Helier (+44 1534 609337)
E-mail: ian.james@mourant.com
International finance.
Position: Senior partner; advises on a wide range of commercial matters, with a particular emphasis on structured finance, banking and partnership transactions.
Career: Admitted England and Wales 1976; Jersey solicitor 1986; joined Mourant du Feu & Jeune 1981; partner 1986.
Languages: English.
Member: International Bar Association.
Education: The Queen's College, Oxford (1969-73).
Personal: Born 1950.

JEUNE, Richard
Mourant du Feu & Jeune
Phone: St Helier (+44 1534 609262)
E-mail: richard.jeune@mourant.com
Position: Partner specialising in trust and company management, wealth management for private clients, and all aspects of employee share schemes.
Career: Admitted 1972, English Bar (Middle Temple); Jersey Bar 1975; trained and qualified with Mourant du Feu & Jeune; partner 1976; managing partner 1998-2003; has spoken at conferences in the UK and Europe on a variety of trust and company subjects, employee benefits and has written articles for a number of professional publications.
Languages: English, French.
Member: Honorary Consul for the Netherlands in Jersey.
Personal: Born 1949.

KERSHAW, Nick
Ogier & Le Masurier
Phone: St Helier (+44 1534 504235)
E-mail: nick.kershaw@ogier.com
Business law.
Position: Partner specialising in investment funds, real estate structuring, securitisation and general corporate work, including business acquisitions and disposals; investment funds clients include a number of leading international fund management groups for whom he's established open and closed ended corporate funds, unit trusts and limited partnerships, including in particular private equity funds; at the forefront of the growth in recent years of offshore property holding structures and acts for a range of property companies, private equity groups and insurance companies; involved in securitisation since its beginnings in Europe, advising on establishment of the first European securitisation conduit in 1993; acted for many leading investment banks on a number of the most high-profile securitisation transactions; heavily involved in general corporate/commercial advice.
Career: Called English Bar 1988, New South Wales Bar 1989, Jersey Bar 1996; corporate finance for UBS; corporate department Clifford Chance; joined Ogier & Le Masurier 1993; partner 1997.
Languages: English.
Member: The Honourable Society of the Middle Temple; The Law Society of Jersey; The International Bar Association; chairman Legal and Regulatory Sub-Committee Jersey Fund Managers Association.
Education: Bolton School; King's College, University of London (1986 LLB); Inns of Court School of Law.
Personal: Born 1963; resides Jersey.
Leisure: Golf, tennis, sailing.

LACEY, Beverley
Mourant du Feu & Jeune
Phone: St Helier (+44 1534 609371)
E-mail: beverley.lacey@mourant.com
Litigation and dispute resolution.
Position: Partner and advocate, specialising in commercial litigation and asset recovery, with particular specialism in directors' duties, shareholders' rights, insolvency and regulatory investigations and prosecutions for financial institutions.
Career: Admitted English Bar (Inner Temple) 1985; Chambers of NP Valios QC 1985-90 (general common and commercial law); admitted Jersey Bar 1994; joined Mourant du Feu & Jeune 1990; partner 1996.
Languages: English, French, German.
Education: Eastwood Hall Park School; Leeds University (1984 LLB Hons).
Personal: Born 1962.
Leisure: Sailing, family.

LAWRENCE, Kerry

Ogier & Le Masurier
Phone: St Helier (+44 1534 504376)
E-mail: kerry.lawrence@ogier.com
Commercial litigation.
Position: Partner, Jersey advocate and English barrister; majority of work is trust related, both litigation and contentious and non-contentious directions applications; advises on regulatory matters, particularly proceeds of crime; also practises in areas of professional negligence and corporate (directors duties), as well as undertaking general commercial litigation.
Career: Career in publishing (academic) 1988-93; admitted English Bar 1995, Jersey Bar 1999; general civil work 1995-97; commercial litigation group, Ogier & Le Masurier 1997 to date.
Member: International Bar Association.
Education: Royal Latin Grammar School; St Anne's College, Oxford (BA Hons Zoology, MA Zoology); CPE 1994.
Personal: Resides Jersey.

LE COCQ, Timothy

Ogier & Le Masurier
Phone: St Helier (+44 1534 504370)
E-mail: timothy.le_cocq@ogier.com
Litigation.
Position: Partner; senior counsel to the group; Crown Advocate; general litigation, trust litigation, commercial litigation, torts, crime; appears as counsel in all types of contentious work; on panel of legal advisers to Jersey Financial Services Commission.
Career: Admitted English Bar 1981, Jersey Bar 1985; litigation partner Bois Labesse, Jersey 1986-90; litigation partner Ogier & Le Cornu 1991 to date; publications include the Jersey entry in 'Encyclopaedia of International Commercial Litigation'.
Languages: English.
Member: The Honourable Society of the Inner Temple; The Law Society of Jersey; Association of Contentious Trusts & Probate Specialists; The International Bar Association.
Education: De La Salle College, Jersey; Keele University (1980 BA Hons Law and Psychology).
Personal: Born 1956; resides Jersey.
Leisure: Music, choral singing, equitation; member: United Club; Jersey Drag Hunt & Chase Club; Les Conteurs Singers (chairman).

LOMBARDI, Michael

Ogier & Le Masurier
Phone: St Helier (+44 1534 504280)
E-mail: michael.lombardi@ogier.com
Business law.
Position: Partner; securitisations, structured finance, investment funds, general commercial law.
Career: Trained Dundas & Wilson, Edinburgh; admitted Scottish solicitor 1984, Hong Kong solicitor 1986, called to the Bar in Bermuda 1989, English solicitor 1991, Jersey solicitor 1994; partner Ogier & Le Masurier 1996.
Languages: English.
Member: The Society of Writers to Her Majesty's Signet; The Law Society of England and Wales; The Law Society of Jersey; The International Bar Association.
Education: Fort Augustus Abbey School; University of Dundee (LLB); University of Exeter (LLM).
Personal: Born 1956; resides Jersey.
Leisure: Hockey, golf, skiing.

MALOREY, Wendy

Mourant du Feu & Jeune
Phone: St Helier (+44 1534 609483)
E-mail: wendy.malorey@mourant.com
Jersey commercial law.
Position: Partner specialising in employment law, mergers and acquisitions, and all aspects of local business advice, including regulatory and corporate matters.
Career: Admitted Jersey 1993; joined Mourant du Feu & Jeune 1985 (property law, both commercial and residential); joined commercial department 1996.
Languages: English.
Member: Law Society sub-committees on employment and competition laws.
Education: University of London.
Personal: Born 1967.

MEIKLEJOHN, Steven

Ogier & Le Masurier
Phone: St Helier (+44 1534 504462)
E-mail: steven.meiklejohn@ogier.com
Trust and estate planning group.
Position: Partner and head of group; notary public; trusts, tax and estate planning, wills and estates.
Career: Pupillage 1 Essex Court and Farrar's Building; admitted English Bar 1982; joined Ogier & Le Cornu 1983; admitted Jersey Bar 1985; partner Ogier & Le Masurier 1990; notary public 1991; head of trust and estate planning group 1996; assisted with current chapters on Jersey in 'European Succession Laws', 'Capital Taxes in Europe' and 'Planning and Administration of Onshore and Offshore Trusts'.
Languages: English.
Member: Gray's Inn; The Law Society of Jersey; The International Bar Association; The Society of Notaries; Society of Trust and Estate Practitioners.
Education: Manchester Polytechnic (1981 BA Hons 2(1)).
Personal: Born 1959; resides Jersey.

POLLANO, Gio

Mourant du Feu & Jeune
Phone: St Helier (+44 1534 609242)
E-mail: gio.pollano@mourant.com
Property.
Position: Associate specialising in property law; Notary Public.
Career: Trained Mourant du Feu & Jeune; qualified as a solicitor of the Royal Court of Jersey 1990; associate 1995; Notary Public 2001.
Languages: English, French, Italian.
Education: De La Salle College, Jersey.
Personal: Born 1960.

RENOUF, Christopher

Ogier & Le Masurier
Phone: St Helier (+44 1534 504104)
E-mail: christopher.renouf@ogier.com
Property law group.
Position: Partner and head of property law group; local commercial matters especially commercial property development, commercial leases, joint ventures and secured lendings and the property aspects of company acquisitions and insolvencies.
Career: Admitted English Bar 1978, Jersey Bar 1982; partner Ogier & Le Masurier 1984.
Languages: English.
Member: The Honourable Society of the Inner Temple; The Law Society of Jersey (committee member 1985-2000, treasurer 1995-2000); Topic Practitioner on the Jersey Law Commission reviewing the Law and Practice of Conveyancing in Jersey.
Education: Nottingham University (1977 BA Hons Law); Chancery Lane Law School (1978).
Personal: Born 1954; resides Jersey.
Leisure: Tennis, golf, photography.

RICHOMME, Jacqueline

Mourant du Feu & Jeune
Phone: St Helier (+44 1534 609341)
E-mail: jacqueline.richomme@mourant.com
International finance.
Position: Partner specialising in company, limited partnership and commercial law, with particular reference to capital markets work including securitisations, structured finance and investment funds; has worked on a number of innovative securitisations, asset-backed program financing and commercial property financing structures; collective investment funds practice focuses on specialised asset structures, private equity funds and property funds and it is in these areas that most recent work has been concentrated. Appointed as a Jersey Financial Services Commissioner in October 2001.
Career: Admitted 1982 as English solicitor; Farrer & Co London; joined Mourant du Feu & Jeune 1985; Jersey solicitor 1988; partner 1990; Jersey Financial Services Commissioner October 2001.
Languages: English, French.
Education: The Bar Convent; Durham University (1979 BA Law); Chester College of Law (1979-80).
Personal: Born 1957.

ROBINS, Ben

Mourant du Feu & Jeune
Phone: St Helier (+44 1534 609344)
E-mail: ben.robins@mourant.com
International finance.
Position: Partner specialising in structured finance, securitisations, repackagings and private equity funds.
Career: Trained Speechly Bircham; qualified English Solicitor 1996; Jersey Solicitor 2000; joined Mourant du Feu & Jeune 1997; associate 2001; partner 2002.
Languages: English, French.
Member: Jersey Law Society.
Education: Victoria College, Jersey; University of Reading (1992 English Degree); College of Law, Guildford (1994 CPE and LPC legal exams).
Personal: Born 1971; resides Jersey.

RUANE, James F

Mourant du Feu & Jeune
Phone: St Helier (+44 1534 609654)

E-mail: james.ruane@mourant.com
International finance.
Position: Member of the firm's international finance team, advising on a broad range of capital raising and structured finance transactions with a client base principally comprising global investment banks and FTSE 100 companies.
Career: Trained Pump Court Tax Chambers; called to the Bar 1994; worked in tax and public law chambers in London; Freshfields Bruckhaus Deringer; admitted as solicitor of the Royal Court of Jersey 2003; associate Mourant de Feu & Jeune 2003. Publications: co-author 'Accounting for the Private Finance Initiative' Butterworths Journal of International Banking and Finance Law.
Member: Middle Temple.
Education: Millfield School, Somerset; University of London (1992 BA (Hons)); College of Law, Guildford (1993 Dip Law); Inns of Court School of Law (1994).
Personal: Born 1970; resides Jersey.
Leisure: Skiing, surfing, sailing.

SCHOLFIELD, W Brian

Mourant du Feu & Jeune
Phone: St Helier (+44 1534 609 601)
E-mail: brian.scholfield@mourant.com
International finance.
Position: Specialises in capital markets; structured finance transactions; securitisations and investment funds. Involved in the application of Jersey laws to financial services/products offered via the Internet.
Career: Qualified as an Ontario, Canada barrister and solicitor 1986; Hong Kong solicitor 1997; English solicitor 1999; associate Goodmans, Toronto 1986; partner Goodmans, Toronto 1993; co-managing partner Goodmans, Hong Kong 1995-99; joined Mourant du Feu & Jeune 1999. Currently a director of CVC Capital Partners Asia Ltd.
Languages: English.
Member: Law Society of Upper Canada; Law Society of Hong Kong; Law Society of England; Canadian Bar Association.
Education: University of Toronto (BA of Arts - Commerce; Juris Doctor).
Personal: Born 1959.
Leisure: Skiing, trumpet, tennis, golf, Mustangs.

SCOTT, Emma

Mourant du Feu & Jeune
Phone: St Helier (+44 1534 609188)
E-mail: emma.scott@mourant.com
International finance.
Position: Associate specialising in capital markets, securities and structured finance transactions.
Career: Articled Vaudreys (now Beachcroft Wansbroughs); qualified England and Wales 1996; Jersey advocate 1999; associate Mourant du Feu & Jeune 2003.
Languages: English, French.
Member: Law Society of England and Wales; Jersey Law Society.
Education: Jersey College for Girls; University of Bath (1992 BSc Hons 2(1) Business Administration); College of Law, York (1993 CPE commendation; 1994 LPC distinction).
Personal: Born 1969; resides Jersey.

SPECK, Jonathan

Mourant du Feu & Jeune
Phone: St Helier (+44 1534 609256)
E-mail: jonathan.speck@mourant.com
Litigation and dispute resolution.
Position: Partner and advocate specialising in commercial litigation involving trust law, banking law and practice and all aspects of financial services regulation.
Career: Admitted to English Bar (Middle Temple) 1990; admitted as Jersey solicitor 1994; joined Mourant du Feu & Jeune 1991; partner 1996; has written and lectured widely on litigation and Jersey anti-money laundering legislation.
Languages: English, French.
Member: Association of Contentious Trust and Probate Specialists; Society of Trust and Estate Practitioners.
Education: Woodbridge School; Exeter University (1989 LLB Hons).
Personal: Born 1968.

SWAN, Matthew

Ogier & Le Masurier
Phone: St Helier (+44 1537 504238)
E-mail: matthew.swan@ogier.com
Business law group.
Position: Partner; head of banking group; member of securitisation group.
Career: Trained Baileys Shaw & Gillett; qualified 1995: assistant solicitor Baileys Shaw & Gillett 1995-96; lawyer, business law group Ogier & Le Masurier 1996 to date; advocate of Royal Court of Jersey 1999; partner Ogier & Le Masurier 2001.
Languages: English.
Member: Law Society of England and Wales; Jersey Law Society.
Education: Repton School; Gonville & Caius College, Cambridge (1990 BA); College of Law, York (1991 CPE, 1992 LSF).
Personal: Born 1968; resides Jersey.
Leisure: Hawks Club, Jersey United Banks RFC; United Club.

SYVRET, Alastair JR

Mourant du Feu & Jeune
Phone: St Helier (+44 1534 609322)
E-mail: alastair.syvret@mourant.com
International finance.
Position: Partner specialising in securitisations, structured finance and collective investment fund formation and advice.
Career: Admitted Jersey solicitor 1992; joined Mourant du Feu & Jeune 1989; partner 1995.
Languages: English.
Education: Victoria College; Exeter University (1989 LLB Hons).
Personal: Born 1968.

THOMAS, Richard

Ogier & Le Masurier
Phone: St Helier (+44 1534 504230)
E-mail: richard.thomas@ogier.com
Business law group.
Position: Partner specialising in offshore funds, structured finance and securitisation law, banking, trust, and general commercial matters.
Career: Trained College of Law, London; admitted as solicitor England and Wales 1976; Jersey Bar 1988; Slaughter and May 1974-78; in industry 1979-84; assistant commercial relations officer, financial regulation (mutual fund and banking supervisor) 1984-86; joined Ogier & Le Cornu 1986; partner 1990.
Languages: English.
Member: The Law Society of England and Wales; The Law Society of Jersey.
Education: Oundle School; St John's College, Oxford (MA Literae Humaniores).
Personal: Born 1950; resides Jersey.
Leisure: Jersey Symphony Orchestra.

THOMPSON, Matthew

Ogier & Le Masurier
Phone: St Helier (+44 1534 504311)
E-mail: matthew.thompson@ogier.com
Litigation.
Position: Partner and head of group specialising in commercial litigation, trust litigation, insolvency, employment, insurance, contentious regulatory matters.
Career: Trained Eversheds Hepworth & Chadwick; admitted English Bar 1988; assistant solicitor, Clyde & Co 1988-92; Ogier & Le Masurier litigation group 1993; admitted Jersey Bar 1996; partner 1997.
Languages: English, French.
Member: The English Law Society; The Law Society of Jersey; The International Bar Association; Association of Contentious Trust and Probate Specialists.
Education: Eirias High School; Stonyhurst College; Durham University (BA Hons Law 2(1)); University of Caen (1995 certicat d'etudes de Droit Français et Normand).
Personal: Born 1962; resides Jersey.
Leisure: Squash, tennis, golf, hill walking.

WALKER, Jonathan

Mourant du Feu & Jeune
Phone: St Helier (+44 1534 609608)
E-mail: jonathan.walker@mourant.com
International finance.
Position: Partner specialising in special purpose vehicles and financial structures for capital markets, corporate finance and banking transactions.
Career: Articled Bischoff & Co; qualified 1987; solicitor Bischoff & Co (company and commercial law) 1987-91; joined Mourant du Feu & Jeune 1991; admitted Jersey 1996; partner 1999.
Languages: English, French.
Member: Law Society Jersey.
Education: King's School, Canterbury; Hertford College, Oxford (MA (Oxon) Modern History); College of Law, Chancery Lane (1983-85).
Personal: Born 1961.

WESTON, Nigel

Mourant du Feu & Jeune
Phone: St Helier (+44 1534 609346)
E-mail: nigel.weston@mourant.com
International finance.
Position: Partner specialising in funds and private equity, corporate law, offshore structures, regulatory law and banking.

Career: Admitted English solicitor 1992; Jersey solicitor and advocate 1999.
Languages: English, French, Spanish.
Member: Law Society England and Wales; Jersey Law Society; committee of Jersey Funds Association; Society of Trust and Estate Practitioners; Institute of Directors.
Education: Charterhouse, Kings College; Guildford College of Law.
Personal: Born 1966.

WHITE, Jonathan
Ogier & Le Masurier
Phone: St Helier (+44 1534 504472)
E-mail: jonathan.white@ogier.com
Trust and estate planning.
Position: Chairman; trust law, general commercial matters, litigation, tax law; acted as lead advocate in the leading trust case of West v Lazard Brothers which determined important trust principles in Jersey; regularly advises both individuals and corporations on complex trust matters.
Career: Trained Bevan Ashford, Bristol; admitted England and Wales 1981, Jersey Bar 1986; partner Ogier & Le Cornu 1987; head of litigation 1987; managing partner 1995; has overseen merger of two Jersey firms of Ogier & Le Cornu and Le Masurier Giffard & Poch, and the establishment of their overseas affiliated office.
Languages: English, French.
Member: The Law Society of England and Wales; The Law Society of Jersey; Institute of Directors, Royal Academy.
Education: Cheltenham College; University of the West of England (1979 BA Hons).
Personal: Born 1955; resides Jersey.
Leisure: Golf, tennis, sailing, the arts; member of Royal Jersey Golf Club.

WILLING, Simon
Ogier & Le Masurier
Phone: St Helier (+44 1534 504457)
E-mail: simon.willing@ogier.com
Ogier Fiduciary Services.
Position: Partner and head of Ogier Fiduciary Services specialising in trust and estate planning, general commercial matters.
Career: Trained 4 Paper Buildings (Chambers of G Gray QC); admitted English Bar 1989, Jersey Bar 1992; associate, commercial litigation group Ogier & Le Masurier 1994; associate trust and estate planning group; partner 1998; managing director Ogier Fiduciary Services which provides trust and company administration services.
Languages: English.
Member: The Honourable Society of the Middle Temple; The Law Society of Jersey; The Society of Trust and Estate Practitioners.
Education: Victoria College; Stafford University (1988 LLB Hons); Inns of Court School of Law.
Personal: Born 1967; resides Jersey.
Leisure: Sailing, classic cars.

WILSON, David
Mourant du Feu & Jeune
Phone: St Helier (+44 1534 609381)
E-mail: david.wilson@mourant.com
Litigation and dispute resolution.
Position: Partner specialising in commercial litigation, with expertise in complex fraud, asset tracing, insolvency, financial services regulation, and trust, banking, corporate, professional negligence and employment disputes.
Career: Cameron McKenna 1989-93; English solicitor 1991; joined Mourant du Feu & Jeune 1993; Jersey solicitor 1996; Jersey advocate 1997; associate 1997; partner 2000.
Languages: English, French, German.
Member: The Law Society; Jersey Law Society; Society of Trust and Estate Practitioners; Association of Contentious Trust and Probate Specialists; honorary member Commercial Bar Association, North American Committee.
Education: Gillotts' School, Henley on Thames; King James' College, Henley; King's College, University of London (1987 LLB Hons).
Personal: Born 1965.
Leisure: Family, sports, reading, piano.

YATES, Marc
Ogier & Le Masurier
Phone: St Helier (+44 1534 504220)
E-mail: marc.yates@ogier.com
Business law.
Position: Partner specialising in banking law, structured finance, capital markets, insolvency, securitisation, general commercial and trust matters.
Career: Called Grays Inn 1982, Jersey Bar 1985; joined Ogier & Le Cornu 1983; partner 1989.
Languages: English, French.
Member: The Law Society of Jersey; The International Bar Association; Institute of Directors.
Education: Victoria College; Buckingham University (1981 Law Hons 2(1)).
Personal: Born 1960; resides Jersey.
Leisure: Motor racing participant, rifle shooting, gardening, classic sports cars.

LATVIA

KLAVINS, Filip K
Klavins & Slaidins
Phone: Riga (+371 703 5222)
E-mail: filips.klavins@klavinsslaidins.lv
Position: Founding partner of Klavins & Slaidins specialising in corporate and commercial law, mergers and acquisitions, corporate finance, securities and real estate.
Career: Attorney at Finley, Kumble, Wagner, Heine, Underberg, Manley, Myerson & Casey, New York; attorney Baker & McKenzie, New York; worked as lecturer in contract law, University of Latvia Law Faculty and Latvian Ministry of Foreign Affairs prior to beginning private practice in Latvia; founding partner Klavins & Slaidins 1992; has lectured on legal ethics, Stockholm School of Economics in Riga and University of Latvia Law Faculty; frequent speaker at numerous business and law conferences and events. Directorships: Arbitration of the Latvian Chamber of Commerce and Industry; Latvian National Opera Foundation; New Theatre of Riga Foundation.
Languages: English, Latvian.
Member: Latvian Bar; New York Bar; Connecticut Bar; International Bar Association; American Bar Association.
Education: Tufts University, Massachusetts (1983 BA cum laude); Duke University School of Law, North Carolina (1986 JD).

SLAIDINS, Raymond L
Klavins & Slaidins
Phone: Riga (+371 703 5222)
E-mail: raimonds.slaidins@klavinsslaidins.lv
Position: Founding partner of Klavins & Slaidins specialising in corporate and commercial law, mergers and acquisitions, corporate finance, securities and real estate.
Career: Attorney Carroll, Burdick & McDonough, San Francisco; senior corporate counsel Ingres Corporation, Alameda, California; worked as counsellor to the Foreign Minister of Latvia prior to beginning private practice in Latvia; founding partner Klavins & Slaidins 1992; registered trade mark agent in Latvia; has lectured on legal ethics, Riga Graduate School of Law and Stockholm School of Economics in Riga; frequent speaker at numerous business and law conferences and events, including IBA conferences.
Languages: English, Latvian.
Member: Latvian Bar; California Bar; International Bar Association; president American Chamber of Commerce in Latvia (board of directors since 1996).
Education: University of California at Berkeley (1980 BA); Santa Clara University, California (1984 JD).

LUXEMBOURG

OOSTVOGELS, Stef
Oostvogels & Pfister
Phone: Luxembourg (+352 46 83 83)
E-mail: stef.oostvogels@oostvogels.com
Position: Partner specialising in banking and finance, corporate, taxation, mergers and acquisitions and general business law.
Career: Admitted Brussels 1987; Luxembourg 1990; lecturer, Insitut de Formation Bancaire Luxembourg. Publications: co-author 'Participation Companies in the Grand-Duchy of Luxembourg' (International Business Lawyer 1991) and 'The Grand-Duchy of Luxembourg offers an alternative European Maritime Registry' (European Transport Law 1991); 'Luxembourg Banking Banking Secrecy' (International Business Lawyer 1993); 'Les Activités Professionelles Non Bancaires du Secteur Financier' (Droit Bancaire et Financier au Grand-Duché de Luxembourg 1994); 'De l'intérêt social à l'intérêt de groupe en droit des sociétés: perspectives luxembourgeoises' (Livre Jubilaire ALJB 2004, to be published); co-editor of tax committee newsletter of the IBA.
Languages: Dutch, English, French, German.
Member: Luxembourg Bar; Brussels Bar; International Bar Association; American Bar Association; Association Luxembourgeoise de Juristes de Banque; Association Luxembourgeoise d'Etudes Fiscales; International Fiscal Association; Association Luxembourgeoise pour l'Arbitrage; European Society for Banking and Financial Law; Chamber of Commerce of the Netherlands for Belgium and Luxembourg.

Education: University of Brussels UFSAL; University of Louvain KUL.
Personal: Born 1962.

PFISTER, François
Oostvogels & Pfister
Phone: Luxembourg (+352 46 83 83)
E-mail: fpfister@oostvogels.com
Position: Partner specialising in corporate, taxation, banking and investment funds, finance, mergers and acquisitions and general business law.
Career: Admitted Luxembourg 1991; KPMG; Svenska Handelsbanken; head of legal and tax, CLT – Group RTL; senior counsel continental Europe, Fidelity Investments.
Languages: French, English, German.
Member: Luxembourg Bar; International Bar Association; International Tax Planning Association; Association Luxembourgeoise d'Etudes Fiscales; International Fiscal Association; former member legal commission of Association Luxembourgeoise des Fonds d'Investissements.
Education: University of Strasbourg (1982 Institut d'Etudes Politiques; 1984 Maîtrise en Droit des Affaires; 1984 Maitrise en Sciences Politiques; 1985 DEA Droit Européen).
Personal: Born 1961.

NETHERLANDS

CORNEGOOR, Jacob
Spigthoff
Phone: Amsterdam (+31 20 305 1600)
E-mail: jacob.cornegoor@spigthoff.com
Corporate litigation.
Position: Partner specialising in litigation and arbitration, with a focus on securities-related disputes and disputes relating to M&A.
Career: Loeff Claeys Verbeke 1993-97; Smeets Thesseling van Bokhorst Spigt and Loyens & Loeff, Curaçao 1997-2001; partner Spigthoff 2001.
Languages: Dutch, English.
Member: Dutch Bar Association; Dutch Association for Corporate Litigation.
Education: University of Leiden (1992).
Personal: Born 1968; resides Amsterdam.
Leisure: Maserati.

HOFF, Jerry
Spigthoff
Phone: Amsterdam (+31 20 305 1600)
E-mail: jerry.hoff@spigthoff.com
Corporate department.
Position: Partner with a focus on corporate and securities law and litigation.
Career: Loeff Claeys Verbeke 1995-2000; Loyens & Loeff 2000-01; Spigthoff 2001; author of many articles and books on corporate and securities law.
Languages: English, Dutch.
Member: Dutch Bar Association; Dutch Securities Association.
Education: University of Leiden (1985).
Personal: Born 1962; resides The Netherlands.

LANGEREIS, Charles
Spigthoff
Phone: Amsterdam (+31 20 305 1600)
E-mail: charles.langereis@spigthoff.com
Tax.
Position: Advises on Dutch corporate, partnership and individual taxation (both domestic and international), with an emphasis on mergers and acquisitions, reorganisations, structured financing and tax litigation.
Career: Ministry of Finance until 1978; subsequently partner at Stibbe and Freshfields, Amsterdam. Part-time professor of law at the University of Leiden since 1986; has published numerous articles and handbooks on tax law, and is an editor of several tax law periodicals.
Languages: English, German, French, Dutch.
Member: International Fiscal Association; Dutch Bar Association; chairman Netherlands Association of Tax Lawyers.
Education: University of Leiden (degree 1971); University of Brabant (Doctorate 1986).
Personal: Born 1948; four children.
Leisure: Sailing, skiing, history.

PELINCK, Martien
Spigthoff
Phone: Amsterdam (+31 20 305 1600)
E-mail: martien.pelinck@spigthoff.com
Position: Partner specialising in litigation with a focus on tax litigation and related areas (white collar crime, tax-related civil litigation).
Career: Trained Houthoff 1993-96; associate Loyens & Loeff 1996-2000; partner Spigthoff 2001; lecturer in tax law, University of Amsterdam.
Languages: English, German, French, Dutch.
Member: Dutch Bar Association; Dutch Association of Tax Consultants.
Education: University of Groningen; University of Fribourg, Switzerland.
Personal: Born 1967; resides Amsterdam.

SPIGT, Leo
Spigthoff
Phone: Amsterdam (+31 20 305 1600)
E-mail: leo.spigt@spigthoff.com
Corporate law; insolvency.
Position: Partner dealing with corporate law, with an emphasis on corporate governance, directors' liabilty, and financial-economic criminal law/litigation.
Career: Active in the legal aid movement from its outset in the 1970s; involved in several community/service organisations; creator and host of radio and television programs about the law; former Dean of the Dutch Bar Association; founder of various law firms in The Netherlands and the Netherlands Antilles.
Languages: English, German, French, Dutch.
Member: Dutch Bar Association; International Bar Association; Insol Europe.
Education: University of Amsterdam (1975).
Personal: Born 1948; resides The Netherlands; married with four children.
Leisure: Golf.

VAN DER SMEEDE, Arnold
Spigthoff
Phone: Amsterdam (+31 20 305 1600)
E-mail: arnold.vandersmeede@spigthoff.com
Tax department.
Position: Tax partner with a focus on international tax planning.
Career: Coopers & Lybrand; Loeff Claeys Verbeke; Freshfields.
Member: International Fiscal Association; Dutch Bar Association; Dutch Association of Tax Advisers (NOB).
Education: Leiden University (1989).
Personal: Born 1965; married with one child.
Leisure: Rallying, classic cars, Italy, skiing.

VAN SOELEN, Albert-Jan
Spigthoff
Phone: Amsterdam (+31 20 305 1600)
E-mail: albert-jan.vansoelen@spigthoff.com
Position: Partner dealing with all areas of tax law; specialisations include tax law with emphasis on acquisitions and reorganisations, real estate transactions and IPOs.
Career: Tax consultant, Deloitte & Touche 1988-95; Loyens & Volkmaars 1995-99; Loyens & Loeff 1999-2000; Spigthoff 2000 to date; author of a number of publications and guest speaker at legal training courses.
Languages: Dutch, German, English.
Member: Dutch Association of Tax Advisers.
Education: University of Amsterdam (graduated cum laude in tax law).
Personal: Born 1965; resides Bilthoven.

NETHERLANDS ANTILLES

FRIELINK, Karel
Spigthoff
Phone: Curaçao (+599 9 461 8700)
E-mail: karel.frielink@spigthoff.com
Corporate department.
Position: Partner with a focus on corporate and securities law.
Career: Russell 1989-95; Loeff Claeys Verbeke 1995-98; Smeets Thesseling van Bokhorst Spigt 1998-2000; Loyens & Loeff 2000; partner Spigthoff 2001; author of many articles and books on corporate and securities law, including the laws of the Netherlands Antilles and Aruba.
Languages: English, Dutch.
Member: Dutch Bar Association; Dutch Securities Association; fellow of the Business & Law Research Centre, University of Nijmegen.
Education: Free University of Amsterdam (1989).
Personal: Born 1964; resides The Netherlands; married with two daughters.

KLEINE-VAN DIJK, Xandra
Spigthoff
Phone: Curaçao (+599 9 461 8700)
E-mail: xandra.kleine@spigthoff.com
Position: Tax partner dealing with international areas of tax law as well as local tax matters; speaker at seminars.
Career: Peat Marwick; Nobel & van Wierst, Amsterdam; Baker & McKenzie, Washington DC 1990-91, salaried partner

1996; PricewaterhouseCoopers 1998; partner Spigthoff, head of tax practice Spigthoff, Curaçao June 2003.
Languages: Dutch, English, German.
Member: Cifa; Ifa; Dutch Association of Tax Advisers (NOB); Association of Tax Academy.
Education: University of Amsterdam; several courses at Georgetown University, Washington DC.
Personal: Born 1959; married with two children.
Leisure: Rotary club, diving, reading.

WELTEN, Martijn
Spigthoff
Phone: Curaçao (+599 9 461 87 00)
E-mail: martijn.welten@spigthoff.com
Position: Partner acting for various national and international clients; specialises in corporate law, mergers and acquisitions and (corporate) litigation.
Career: AKD Prinsen Van Wijmen 1995-99; Smeets Thesseling Van Bokhorst Spigt; Loyens & Loeff; partner Spigthoff 2003.
Languages: Dutch, English.
Member: Curaçao Bar; Registered as attorney with Joint Court of Appeal of the Netherlands Antilles and Aruba.
Education: University of Tiburg (law).
Personal: Born 1969.
Leisure: Tennis, golf, sailing.

WESTERMANN, Kees
Spigthoff
Phone: Curaçao (+599 9 461 87 00)
E-mail: kees.westermann@spigthoff.com
Position: Partner acting for banks, companies and governments; specialises in project and asset financings, capital market transactions, takeovers, privatisations and other international transactions.
Career: Attorney at law since 1994; Clifford Chance, Amsterdam and Moscow 1994-99; thereafter Spigthoff, Curaçao and its predecessor Loyens & Loeff, Curaçao.
Languages: Dutch, English, Russian.
Member: Curaçao Bar; registered as an attorney with the Joint Court of Appeal of the Netherlands Antilles and Aruba.
Education: University of Leiden (law); University of London (LLM); winner of the Jenkins & Gilchrist prize for securites regulation (King's College, London), as well as of a Leiden scholarship.
Personal: Born 1968.
Leisure: Various ballsports, chess.

NORWAY

AABØ-EVENSEN, Ole Kristian
Aabø-Evensen & Co Advokatfirma
Phone: Oslo (+47 2415 9010)
E-mail: oka@aaboevensen.com
M&A, corporate finance, capital markets and securities, private equity, dispute resolution.
Position: Specialising in counseling and representation of clients, both corporate and individual, in connection with M&A, corporate reorganisations, international transactions, private equity, securitisation of assets, banking, securities and structured financing work and general legal services; also an experienced advocate, particularly within the fields of director's liability and white-collar crime.
Career: Attorney and associated partner, de Besche & Co, Oslo 1988-94; trainee at Sinclair Roche & Temperley (solicitors) and Four Essex Court (barristers, now Essex Court Chambers), London 1992; partner and head of Corporate Legal Services KPMG, Oslo 1995-2002; mentioned in the 'Guide to the World's leading White-Collar Crime Lawyer's'.
Languages: English, the Scandinavian languages.
Member: IBA; Norwegian Bar Association; International Fiscal Association; Honorably Member Center for International Legal Studies.
Education: University of Oslo (1988); King's College, London (1992 English Law and International Finance).
Personal: Born 1964.

AAS, Preben
Advokatfirmaet Steenstrup Stordrange DA
Phone: Oslo (+47 22 81 45 00)
E-mail: preben@steenstrup.no
Corporate/tax.
Position: Works primarily with contracts, negotiations, mergers and acquisitions and corporate/tax law in general as well as labour law.
Career: Admitted 1992; trained Smith, Grette & Meltvedt; broker in Scanbroker AS 1980-85; associate Smith Grette & Meltvedt 1992-93; partner Lyng & Co DA 1993-94; partner 1994-2002; partner Advokatfirmaet Steenstrup Stordrange DA 2002 to date; extensive experience from board positions and counselling from industry, trade and consultancy firms; previously worked within corporate finance.
Languages: English, the Scandinavian languages.
Member: Norwegian Bar Association.
Education: University of Oslo (1979 Cand Jur).
Personal: Born 1953; resides Oslo.

ANDREASSEN, Ole-Martin
Advokatfirmaet Steenstrup Stordrange DA
Phone: Tromsø (+47 77 61 78 00)
E-mail: oma@steenstrup.no
Fishery and aquaculture; EU law, competition and marketing law.
Position: Head of Tromsø office; works primarily with contract and corporate law, insolvency, restructuring and fishery licence law; works especially for clients within the fields of fishery, fish-farming and marine business; also advises clients with businesses in Russia; has extensive experience from contract negotiations, as well as restructuring and refinancing of businesses.
Career: Admitted 1992; partner Advokatfirmaet Steenstrup Stordrange DA 2002; former partner and head of Advokatfirmaet PricewaterhouseCoopers DA in Tromsø. Holds board positions within fisheries and insurance. Has written 'Legal Protection for Creditors' (Doctor's degree).
Languages: English, the Scandinavian languages.
Member: Norwegian Bar Association.
Education: University of Tromsø (1989 Cand jur; 1999 Dr jur).
Personal: Born 1958; resides Tromsø.

ÅRSETH, Nils Olav
Aabø-Evensen & Co Advokatfirma
Phone: Oslo (+47 2415 9020)
E-mail: noa@aaboevensen.com
M&A, corporate finance, capital markets, property finance.
Position: Partner specialising in international M&A, take private and MBO's, private equity and capital markets, reorganisations, contracts and contract negotiations, international transactions, agency and distribution; also experienced within legal issues relating to real estate, hereunder tenancy and construction law.
Career: Associated partner, Wiersholm, Mellbye & Bech; head of legal services, Unitor ASA; general manager, Unitor (Italy).
Languages: English, the Scandinavian languages.
Member: Norwegian Bar Association.
Education: University of Bergen (1988).
Personal: Born 1963.

BADE, Fredny
Advokatfirmaet Steenstrup Stordrange DA
Phone: Oslo (+47 22 81 45 00)
E-mail: bade@steenstrup.no
IT and intellectual property law; the press.
Position: Works primarily with intellectual property law, marketing law, IT law, contract law, negotiations, litigation and transactions.
Career: Admitted 1999; The Norwegian Patent Office 1993-96; Bryns Patentkontor AS 1996-98; BAHR 1998-2000; Kvale & Co 2000-02; partner Advokatfirmaet Steenstrup Stordrange DA 2002. Written several articles regarding IP Law issues.
Languages: English, some German, the Scandinavian languages.
Member: Norwegian Bar Association; NIR; AIPPI; Norwegian Association of Copyright; Norwegian Association of Female Lawyers.
Education: University of Oslo (1992 Cand Jur).
Personal: Born 1966; resides Oslo.

BANG, Joachim S
Advokatfirmaet Steenstrup Stordrange DA
Phone: Oslo (+47 22 81 45 00)
E-mail: joachim.bang@steenstrup.no
Corporate.
Position: Works primarily with contract law, negotiations, mergers and acquisitions, corporate law in general as well as labour law. Counsellor for several telecommunication and venture companies.
Career: Admitted 1983; Ministry of Agriculture 1979-81; associate Elektro Union AS 1981-83; general counsel, vice-president 1983-86; general counsel, senior vice-president of the EB Corporation (ABB, Norway) 1986-91; partner Smith, Grette & Meltvedt 1992-93; partner Lyng & Co 1993-2002; partner Advokatfirmaet Steenstrup Stordrange DA 2002; current directorships: chairman of the Board Noral ASA; Sealift AS.
Languages: English, the Scandinavian languages.
Member: Norwegian Bar Association.
Education: University of Oslo (1978 Cand Jur).
Personal: Born 1950; resides Oslo.

BERG, Arne Seemann

Kvale & Co
Phone: Oslo (+47 22 47 97 00)
E-mail: seemann@kvaleco.no
Media, intellectual property law, labour law, company law, acquisition and sale of business, negotiations and litigation.
Position: Partner.
Career: Admitted Norway 1982; legal officer, Defence Construction Directorate 1979-80; associate/salaried partner, de Bosche & Thune 1980-86; partner, Brokhus & Alo 1986-92; partner, Kvale & Co since 1992; lecturer Norwegian Law Society.
Languages: English, the Scandinavian languages.
Member: Norwegian Bar Association.
Education: University of Oslo (1979 Candidate in Jurisprudence).
Personal: Born 1953; resides Oslo.

BERGLI, Håvard

Advokatfirmaet Steenstrup Stordrange DA
Phone: Oslo (+47 22 81 45 00)
E-mail: haavard.bergli@steenstrup.no
Corporate.
Position: Particularly involved with corporate law, mergers and acquisitions, corporate finance and agency law as well as general contract law.
Career: Formerly an academic assistant at the Institute of Civil Law at the University of Oslo; admitted 1999; partner 2002.
Languages: English, the Scandinavian languages.
Member: Norwegian Bar Association.
Education: University of Oslo (1997 Cand Jur; 1993 Cand Mag, intellectual history and social science).
Personal: Born 1968; resides Oslo.
Leisure: Tennis, music, reading.

BREDE, Jens

Kvale & Co
Phone: Oslo (+47 22 47 97 00)
E-mail: brede@kvaleco.no
Petroleum and energy law, contracting law, company law, financing, aviation, capital markets, negotiations and litigation.
Position: Partner.
Career: Admitted Norway 1986; assistant judge Lofoten District Court 1984-86; associate Wikborg Rein & Co 1986-88; partner Kvale & Brede 1988-92; partner Kvale & Co since 1992.
Languages: English, the Scandinavian languages.
Member: Norwegian Bar Association.
Education: University of Oslo (1984 Candidate in Jurisprudence).
Personal: Born 1958; resides Oslo.

BRYNE, Eivind

Advokatfirmaet Steenstrup Stordrange DA
Phone: Oslo (+47 22 81 45 00)
E-mail: eivind.bryne@steenstrup.no
Tax.
Position: In charge of the firm's department of indirect tax issues; specialises in EU VAT and international transactions, VAT in telecoms, IT and finance.
Career: Stavanger tax office 1987; senior executive officer Rogaland County Tax Office 1988; admitted 1992; tax department Ernst & Young 1988-2002; partner 1998-2001; partner Advokatfirmaet Steenstrup Stordrange DA 2001; has been a member of the editing committee of the Norwegian tax newsletter 'Avgiftsnytt' and contributor to 'BFD Guide to European Taxation'; co-author of several international VAT publications.
Languages: English, the Scandinavian languages.
Member: Norwegian Bar Association.
Education: University of Bergen (1987 Cand jur).
Personal: Resides Oslo.

CHRISTOFFERSEN, Per Torp

Kvale & Co
Phone: Oslo (+47 22 47 97 00)
E-mail: christoffersen@kvaleco.no
Agency distribution/competition, company law, contract and marketing law, insurance and compensation law, labour law, telecommunications, media and IT.
Position: Partner.
Career: Admitted Norway 1986; legal adviser Ministry of Justice 1981-84; associate judge 1984-85; associate Nergaard, Mellbye, Schjoldager & Sejersted 1985-88; partner Langseth, Mår & Stake-Larsen; partner Kvale & Co, since 1992.
Languages: English, German, the Scandinavian languages.
Member: Norwegian Bar Association.
Education: University of Oslo (1981 Candidate in Jurisprudence).
Personal: Born 1955; resides Oslo.

ELLEFSEN, Harald

Advokatfirmaet Steenstrup Stordrange DA
Phone: Trondheim (+47 73 99 27 00)
E-mail: he@steenstrup.no
Public administration.
Position: Has particular experience in strategic counselling for companies, commercial law, consultations with government authorities, project development, corporate law and public administrative matters; Herald Ellefsen is in charge of the firm's Trondheim office, which was established in 2000.
Career: Admitted 1997; police lawyer 1977; assistant judge 1978-79; member of the Norwegian Parliament 1983-97; vice-chairman of the Justice Committee 1985-89; member of the Standing Committee on finance 1989-97; lawyer in Trondheim 1997-2001; partner Advokatfirmaet Steenstrup Stordrange DA 2000; published theses on topics in criminal law.
Languages: English, the Scandinavian languages.
Member: Norwegian Bar Association; board member National Social Security Fund and AS Anlegg.
Education: University of Oslo (1976 Cand Jur).
Personal: Born 1950; resides Trondheim.

ERSDAL, Hege Birkeland

Advokatfirmaet Steenstrup Stordrange DA
Phone: Oslo (+47 22 81 45 00)
E-mail: hege.ersdal@steenstrup.no
IT and intellectual property law; the press; civil disputes/litigation.
Position: Works primarily with litigation and contract law, especially within the fields of IT, property and labour law.
Career: Admitted 1999; partner Advokatfirmaet Steenstrup Stordrange DA 2002 to date.
Languages: English, the Scandinavian languages.
Member: Norwegian Bar Association.
Education: University of Bergen (1996 Cand jur).
Personal: Born 1972; resides Oslo.

FARHANG, Thomas S

Kvale & Co
Phone: Oslo (+47 22 47 97 00)
E-mail: farhang@kvaleco.no
Company law, acquisitions and sale of business, negotiations and litigation.
Position: Partner.
Career: Admitted Norway 1998; legal officer Headquarters Defence Command Norway 1996; associate Kvale & Co 1996-98; salaried partner Kvale & Co 1998-2000; partner Kvale & Co since 2001.
Languages: English, Farsi, the Scandinavian languages.
Member: Norwegian Bar Association.
Education: University of Oslo (1995 Candidate of Jurisprudence).
Personal: Born 1970; resides Oslo.

FINNØY, Frode

Advokatfirmaet Steenstrup Stordrange DA
Phone: Oslo (+47 22 81 45 00)
E-mail: frode.finnoy@steenstrup.no
Insolvency; IT and intellectual property law; the press.
Position: Partner specialising in general business and legal counselling; particularly involved with information technology and communications law, bankruptcy and insolvency issues, litigation, negotiations, contracts and corporate law; court-appointed bankruptcy trustee for many business estates; serves as an adviser to Norwegian companies that require working permits for foreign employees; holds several board positions.
Career: Admitted 1991; senior executive officer Directorate of Immigration, legal department 1988-89; associate Advokatfirmaet Flod & Gjerde ANS 1989-91; assistant judge, District Court of Sunnfjord 1991-93; partner Advokatfirmaet Flod & Co ANS 1993-98; partner Advokatfirmaet Steenstrup Stordrange DA 1998 to date.
Languages: English, some German, the Scandinavian languages.
Member: Norwegian Bar Association.
Education: University of Bergen (1988 Cand Jur).
Personal: Born 1962; resides Oslo.
Leisure: Telemark skiing.

GJERDE, Odd Magne

Advokatfirmaet Steenstrup Stordrange DA
Phone: Oslo (+47 22 81 45 00)
E-mail: odd.gjerde@steenstrup.no
Insolvency.
Position: In charge of the firm's department of insolvency and restructuring, advising companies on general corporate matters, bankruptcy and mortgage issues; handles a great deal of litigations and also works with banking and financial law, real estate law,

inheritance, contract law, general business and legal counselling.
Career: Admitted 1987; associate Advokatfirmaet Flod & Flod ANS 1986-88; assistant judge District Court of Nedre Romerike 1988-89; partner Advokatfirmaet Flod & Co ANS 1990-98; partner Advokatfirmaet Steenstrup Stordrange DA 1998.
Languages: English, the Scandinavian languages.
Member: Norwegian Bar Association.
Education: University of Oslo (1986 Cand Jur).
Personal: Born 1961; resides Oslo.

GRANLUND, Ove-Marthin
Advokatfirmaet Steenstrup Stordrange DA
Phone: Oslo (+47 22 81 45 00)
E-mail: ove@steenstrup.no
Corporate, tax.
Position: Particularly involved with issues concerning the taxation of businesses and corporate legislation, property financing, development and management.
Career: Executive officer and office manager, department of Taxes, Directorate of Taxes 1986-89; associate Steenstrup ANS 1989-91; admitted 1991; partner Advokatfirmaet Steenstrup ANS (now Advokatfirmaet Steenstrup Stordrange DA) 1991 to date; directorships in several representatives for foreign trade marks within textile and electronics; published several tax articles and comments on current tax issues.
Languages: English, Scandinavian languages.
Member: Norwegian Bar Association.
Education: University of Oslo (1986 Cand Jur).
Personal: Born 1959; resides Oslo.
Leisure: Open-air activities on- and offshore.

GRØNLAND, Karl-Anders
Advokatfirmaet Steenstrup Stordrange DA
Phone: Oslo (+47 22 81 45 00)
E-mail: kag@steenstrup.no
Corporate.
Position: Specialises in corporate issues, corporate finance, M&A and corporate law in general.
Career: Admitted 1998; research assistant, Institute of Private Law, University of Oslo 1993-94; legal secretary, The Committee for New Companies Act 1995-96; external examinator, Faculty of Law, University of Oslo 1997-; associate judge, Nedenes City Court (Arendal) 1997-98; attorney in the law firm BAHR 1995-96 and 1998-99; attorney Kvale & Co 1999-2002; partner Advokatfirmaet Steenstrup Stordrange DA 2002. Holds several directorships in Norway and the UK; has written a book regarding a company's access to acquire or receive pledges in its own shares (1998).
Languages: English, Scandinavian languages.
Member: Norwegian Bar Association.
Education: University of Oslo (1995 Cand Jur).
Personal: Born 1970; resides Oslo.

HAMAR, Espen R
Kvale & Co
Phone: Oslo (+47 22 47 97 00)
E-mail: hamar@kvaleco.no
Contracting law, property, restructuring, insolvency proceedings and credit security, contract and marketing law, negotiations and litigation, wills and probate, inheritance planning.
Position: Partner.
Career: Admitted Norway 1993; Supreme Court of Norway 1998; legal officer Directorate of Prices 1990-92; associate Kvale & Co 1992-94; assistant/acting judge Vardø District Court 1994-95; partner Hegg & Hamar 1995-99; partner Kvale & Co since 1999.
Languages: English, the Scandinavian languages.
Member: Norwegian Bar Association.
Education: University of Oslo (1989 Candidate in Jurisprudence).
Personal: Born 1964; resides Oslo.

HANSEN, Rode Stig Rønning
Aabø-Evensen & Co Advokatfirma
Phone: Oslo (+47 2415 9040)
E-mail: rsrh@aaboevensen.com
M&A, fishing and fish industry, corporations, project finance.
Position: Partner specialising in M&A, corporate law and project finance and reorganisations, contracts and contract negotiations; holds substantial industry experience in areas such as commercial fishery and fish farming and represents Norwegian and foreign seafood buyers and commercial fishing companies within red- and white fish, prawns etc; also represents businesses in fraud cases in the fishing industry.
Career: Attorney, KPMG, Oslo and Tromsø; attorney in the legal department of Postbanken (later merged with DnB), Oslo; the Norwegian Directorate of Taxes, Oslo.
Languages: English, the Scandinavian languages.
Member: Norwegian Bar Association.
Education: University of Tromsø (1996).
Personal: Born 1968.

JOHANNESSEN, Espen
Advokatfirmaet Steenstrup Stordrange DA
Phone: Tromsø (+47 77 61 78 00)
E-mail: ej@steenstrup.no
Labour law; real estate; energy and construction.
Position: Particularly works with contract law, labour law, real estate issues, mergers and acquisitions in addition to advising the public sector with regard to reorganisation. Also litigates, especially within the above mentioned fields. Lectures at the Faculty of Law at the University of Tromsø.
Career: Deputy judge 1995-97; assistant professor 1997-99; associate Wikborg, Rein & Co 1999-2000; admitted 2000; lawyer PricewaterhouseCoopers DA, Tromsø 2000-02; partner Advokatfirmaet Steenstrup Stordrange DA 2003 to date.
Languages: English, the Scandinavian languages.
Member: Norwegian Bar Association.
Education: University of Tromsø (1994 Cand Jur).
Personal: Born 1967; resides Tromsø.

JOHNSON, Ida Espolin
Advokatfirmaet Steenstrup Stordrange DA
Phone: Oslo (+47 22 81 45 00)
E-mail: ida@steenstrup.no
Corporate.
Position: Works primarily with mergers and acquisitions, general corporate and contract law; has extensive experience with all types of transactions, conversions and reorganisations, including strategic legal advice and negotiations.
Career: Scientific assistant, University of Oslo, Faculty of Law 1987-89; associate BAHR 1991-93; assistant judge District Court of Nedre Romerike 1993-94; attorney BAHR 1995-99; admitted 1996; partner Advokatfirmaet Steenstrup Stordrange DA 1999 to date; group managing director Itera Consulting Group ASA 2001.
Languages: English, the Scandinavian languages.
Member: Norwegian Bar Association.
Education: University of Oslo (1990 Cand jur).
Personal: Born 1964; resides Oslo.

KENWORTHY, Ian William
Advokatfirmaet Steenstrup Stordrange DA
Phone: Oslo (+47 22 81 45 00)
E-mail: ian.kenworthy@steenstrup.no
Banking and finance; litigation and arbitration; corporate.
Position: Particularly involved with banking, financial law and contract law as well as litigation.
Career: Admitted 1973; in-house lawyer Elkem 1973-81; general counsel and head of legal department, Union Bank of Norway 1981-89; executive vice-president of the Oslo Stock Exchange 1989-90; general counsel and head of legal department Den Norske Bank 1990-93; partner Advokatfirmaet Steenstrup Stordrange DA 1999 to date; formerly a member of the board of the Norwegian Bar Association and chairman of the law committee on trade, craft and industry 1991-99; member of the control committee of the Oslo Stock Exchange and chairman of the control committee of Oslo Forsikring (insurance).
Languages: English, the Scandinavian languages.
Member: Norwegian Bar Association.
Education: University of Oslo (1971 Cand Jur).
Personal: Born 1943; resides Oslo.
Leisure: Oslo Rotary Club.

KVALE, Anders
Kvale & Co
Phone: Oslo (+47 22 47 97 00)
E-mail: kvale@kvaleco.no
Petroleum and energy law, telecommunications, media and IT, company law, negotiations and litigation.
Position: Partner.
Career: Admitted Norway 1977; executive officer The Industrial Bank 1971-72, business manager 1972-76; lawyer in private practice 1976-83; lawyer Norsk Hydro 1983-85; own law practice 1985-88; partner Kvale & Brede 1988-92; partner Kvale & Co since 1992.
Languages: English, the Scandinavian languages.
Member: Norwegian Bar Association.
Education: Norwegian School of Economics and Business administration (1970 MBA); University of Oslo (1977 Candidate in Jurisprudence).
Personal: Born 1947; resides Oslo.

LOUS, Søren L
Advokatfirmaet Steenstrup Stordrange DA
Phone: Oslo (+47 22 81 45 00)
E-mail: soren.lous@steenstrup.no

IT and intellectual property law; the press; real estate, energy and construction.
Position: Particularly involved with all aspects of property law with substantial experience of public regulation and expropriation. Also works with intellectual property and media, particularly within the film business, and has been engaged in several major feature film productions.
Career: Admitted 1985; partner Lous, Hagemann & Arff-Pettersen 1986-92; partner Dalan, Sigmond, Hagemann & Lous DA 1992-2002; partner Advokatfirmaet Steenstrup Stordrange DA 2002; holds several board positions.
Languages: English, the Scandinavian languages.
Member: Norwegian Bar Association.
Education: University of Oslo (1983 Cand Jur).
Personal: Born 1954; resides Oslo.

MEINICH, Thomas
Advokatfirmaet Steenstrup Stordrange DA
Phone: Oslo (+47 22 81 45 00)
E-mail: thomas@steenstrup.no
Labour law; health and damages.
Position: Particularly involved with the law of torts and the law of damages; also deals with contracts and disputes concerning employment, general wage agreements, individual employment and dismissals.
Career: Deputy judge Ålesund County Court 1990-92; admitted 1992; associate Advokatfirmaet Steenstrup ANS 1992-94; lawyer 1994-99; partner from 1999.
Languages: English, the Scandinavian languages.
Member: Norwegian Bar Association.
Education: University of Oslo (1990 Cand jur).
Personal: Born 1964; resides Oslo.

MOE, Odd
Advokatfirmaet Steenstrup Stordrange DA
Phone: Oslo (+47 22 81 45 00)
E-mail: odd.moe@steenstrup.no
Corporate, banking and finance.
Position: Particularly involved with M&A, banking, securities and finance, real estate.
Career: Admitted 1988; tax law division Ministry of Finance 1984-86; associate lawyer Advokatfirmaet Haavind & Co 1986-89; in-house attorney for the Union Bank of Norway 1989-90; partner Advokatfirmaet Steenstrup Stordrange DA 1996.
Languages: English, the Scandinavian languages.
Member: Norwegian Bar Association.
Education: University of Oslo (1984 Cand Jur).
Personal: Born 1956; resides Oslo.

MYKSVOLL, Laila
Kvale & Co
Phone: Oslo (+47 22 47 97 00)
E-mail: myksvoll@kvaleco.no
Telecommunications, media and IT, contract and marketing law, company law, wills and probate, inheritance planning, labour law.
Position: Partner.
Career: Admitted Norway 1998; legal officer Sør-Trøndelag County Tax Office 1995-96; associate Giæver & Helge, Trondheim 1996-97; associate Kvale & Co 1997-99; salaried partner Kvale & Co 1999-2002; partner Kvale & Co since 2003.
Languages: English, the Scandinavian languages.
Member: Norwegian Bar Association.
Education: University of Bergen (1995 Candidate in Jurispudence).
Personal: Born 1964; resides Oslo.

NILSEN, Geir Johan
Aabø-Evensen & Co Advokatfirma
Phone: Oslo (+47 2415 9030)
E-mail: gin@aaboevensen.com
M&A, labour and employment, due diligence, dispute resolution.
Position: Partner specialising in M&A, labour law, reorganisations, contracts and contract negotiations, international transactions, director's liability, arbitration and negotiations.
Career: Nine years with the law firm Flod & Co; attorney and partner, KPMG Law Advokatfirma 1997-2002; lecturer in jurisprudence, University of Oslo.
Languages: English, the Scandinavian languages.
Member: Norwegian Bar Association; Norwegian Chartered Engineer's Group for Hearing of Legal Reforms on Business and Corporate law.
Education: University of Oslo (1987 company law, tax law).
Personal: Born 1960.

OTTESEN, Tom Hugo
Kvale & Co
Phone: Oslo (+47 22 47 97 00)
E-mail: ottesen@kvaleco.no
Restructuring, insolvency proceedings and credit security, wills and probate, inheritance planning.
Position: Partner specialising in descendant estates, insolvency.
Career: Admitted Norway 1986; associate Thune & Co 1984-89; partner Thune & Co 1989-96; partner Kvale & Co since 1996; lecturer Norwegian Law Society.
Languages: English, the Scandinavian languages.
Member: Norwegian Bar Association; International Bar Association.
Education: University of Oslo (1984 Candidate in Jurisprudence).
Personal: Born 1957; resides Oslo.

OVERHOLDT, Thorbjørn
Advokatfirmaet Steenstrup Stordrange DA
Phone: Oslo (+47 22 81 45 00)
E-mail: to@steenstrup.no
Business development and strategy department.
Position: Thorbjørn Overholdt is in charge of the build-up and development of the Business and Strategic Department; works across all practice areas and in the various cases being handled on behalf of the firm's clients, particularly in the field of commercial and strategic counselling.
Career: Admitted 1981; development director, Ministry of Labour and Government Administration; experience in own consultancy firms; partner and general manager Ernst & Young; development director SAS (Scandinavian Airlines System); first non-legal partner to joining the firm 2003; current directorships: Agendum Partner; Clean Soft.
Languages: English, the Scandinavian languages.
Education: University of Oslo (Master of Political Science).
Personal: Born 1953; resides Oslo.

RAVNAAS, Ernst
Advokatfirmaet Steenstrup Stordrange DA
Phone: Oslo (+47 22 81 45 00)
E-mail: ernst@steenstrup.no
Tax, corporate.
Position: Corporate tax and tax planning, financial derivatives and M&A. Ravnaas has been in charge of a comprehensive tax reform project on behalf of Norsk Investorforum (a membership organisation representing the largest private fortunes in Norway). The proposal is among the alternatives that are to be evaluated by The Ministry of Finance in connection with the prospected tax reform in 2004/2005. Ravnaas has assisted several companies on Oslo Stock Exchange in connection with merger and acquisitions and tax planning.
Career: Admitted 1978; associate professor Norwegian School of Economics 1983-2000; partner BAHR 1991-2003; partner Advokatfirmaet Steenstrup Stordrange DA; former chairman of the board in two companies at Oslo Stock Exchange; written several books and articles in the field of tax planning and accounting; current directorships: Start Toppfotball ASA 2002; Sector Management AS 2001.
Languages: English, the Scandinavian languages.
Education: University of Oslo (1978 Cand jur); NHH Bergen (1980 MBA).
Personal: Born 1955; resides Oslo.
Leisure: Football.

SCHNEIDER, Susanne
Advokatfirmaet Steenstrup Stordrange DA
Phone: Oslo (+47 22 81 45 00)
E-mail: susanne@steenstrup.no
Corporate; IT and intellectual property law.
Position: Partner specialising in M&A, private equity transactions, and securities and corporate law; has been involved in all aspects of acquisitions and has broad experience representing companies in their acquisitions, divestitures and capital markets activities. Schneider has been involved in M&A projects in Norway, Germany, UK, Iceland, Romania, US, Brazil, Venezuela and Egypt; areas of expertise include: M&A, demergers, joint ventures, securities and corporate law, corporate tax, commercial contracts and intellectual property rights.
Career: Associate Vogt & Co 1987-90; admitted 1990; attorney-at-law Vogt & Co 1990-93 and 1995-96; district judge Asker and Bærum 1993-95; attorney-at-law Elkem 1996-98; general counsel and vice president Aker Yards 1998-2000; vice president Business Development Tandberg Data 2001-03; partner Advokatfirmaet Steenstrup Stordrange DA 2003 to date.
Languages: English, German, the Scandinavian languages.
Member: Norwegian Bar Association.
Education: University of Oslo (1986 Cand jur); IMD, Lausanne, Switzerland (2000 MBA).
Personal: Born 1966; resides Oslo.

SOLHEIM, Ingar
Advokatfirmaet Steenstrup Stordrange DA
Phone: Oslo (+47 22 81 45 00)
E-mail: ingar@steenstrup.no
Corporate.
Position: Has extensive experience in a broad range of commercial law; has mainly been working on projects related to M&A, banking and financing, securities law, company law, negotiations, contract law, transformation of businesses, complex international transactions as well as follow-up of companies which he had assisted in purchases; his experience embraces a whole range of different business sectors, with a lion's share covering equity-funds investing in European enterprises with headquarters in Norway.
Career: BAHR 1994-97; Sinclair Roche & Temperley, London 1997; lawyer BAHR 1998-2001; senior lawyer 2002; partner Advokatfirmaet Steenstrup Stordrange DA.
Languages: English, the Scandinavian languages.
Member: Norwegian Bar Association.

STAALESEN, Ulf-Einar
Advokatfirmaet Steenstrup Stordrange DA
Phone: Stavanger (+47 51 51 00 70)
E-mail: ulf-einar@steenstrup.no
Offshore and petroleum.
Position: Company law, offshore contracts and litigation.
Career: Admitted 1974; assistant judge Onsøy County Court 1973-74; associate Rekve, Bull & Tvendt 1974-82; admitted Supreme Court 1984; partner Advokatene Våland, Staalesen & Maloney 1982-2003; partner Advokatfirmaet Steenstrup Stordrange DA 2003 to date; current directorship: board member Honorary Consul of Poland; published these on topics in criminal law.
Languages: English, the Scandinavian languages.
Member: Norwegian Bar Association.
Education: University of Oslo (1972 Cand jur).
Personal: Born 1945; resides Stavanger.

STAKE-LARSEN, Gunnar
Kvale & Co
Phone: Oslo (+47 22 47 97 00)
E-mail: stake-larsen@kvaleco.no
Acquisitions and sale of businesses, company law, capital markets, contract and marketing law, negotiation and litigation.
Position: Partner.
Career: Research assistant University of Oslo 1978-79; associate judge Sandnes 1980-81; assistant judge 1980-81; admitted Norway 1982; Supreme Court of Norway 1988; associate Nergaard, Mellbye, Schjoldager & Sejersted 1982-85; partner Langseth, Mår & Stake-Larsen 1985-1992; partner Kvale & Co since 1992.
Languages: English, German, the Scandinavian languages.
Member: Norwegian Bar Association; Norwegian Association for Protection of Industrial Property.
Education: University of Oslo (1980 Candidate in Jurisprudence).
Personal: Born 1953; resides Oslo.

STEENSTRUP, Morten
Advokatfirmaet Steenstrup Stordrange DA
Phone: Oslo (+47 22 81 45 00)
E-mail: morten@steenstrup.no
Corporate and public administration.
Position: Particularly involved with strategic counselling, corporate transactions, corporate law, negotiations, consultations with government authorities and litigation. He also has extensive experience in telecomunications law; senior partner to several of the major telecommunications companies in Norway; legal counsel to telecommunications companies in major legal cases.
Career: Member of Tønsberg City Council 1975-83; associate Advoaktfirmaet Hesselberg, Larvik; member of Parliament 1981-89; Standing Committee of Justice, MP 1981-83 and Standing Committee of Finance, MP 1983-89; Parliamentary Secretary to the Ministry of Finance 1985-86; Parliamentary Secretary to the Prime Minister's Office 1986; lawyer Gram Hambro Garman 1986-89; admitted 1987; founded Advokatfirmaet Steenstrup ANS (now Advokatfirmaet Steenstrup Stordrange DA) 1989; admitted to the Supreme Court 1993.
Languages: English, Scandinavian languages.
Member: Chairman: Board of Advokatfirmaet Steenstrup Stordrange DA; Board Continental Dekk Norge AS; Board Fabricom AS; Board City Parking AS; Board Varnamoss AS; Board Herføll Bygg AS; Ant.L.Zeiner AS. Board member: Supervisory Council of the Norwegian Central Bank; Oslo Konserthus AS. Norwegian Bar Association.
Education: University of Oslo (1976 BA Sociology and Political Science; 1980 Cand Jur).
Personal: Born 1953; resides Oslo.

STORDRANGE, Bjørn
Advokatfirmaet Steenstrup Stordrange DA
Phone: Oslo (+47 22 81 45 00)
E-mail: bjorn.stordrange@steenstrup.no
EU law; competition and marketing law; IT and intellectual property law; media; civil disputes.
Position: He is particularly involved with contract law, expropriation, white-collar crime and constitutional law.
Career: Member of Parliament 1981-83; admitted 1982; admitted to the Supreme Court 1988; District Court Judge, Flekkefjord 1988-92; Parliamentary Secretary to the Ministry of Justice 1989-90; Professor II University of Tromsø 1989-96; partner Advokatfirmaet Smith Grette Wille DA 1992-99; Professor II The Norwegian School of Management 1996; partner Advokatfirmaet Steenstrup Stordrange DA 1999; author of law books within each of his working fields, including books on: parliamnetary legislating, Expropriation Law, 'Lectures on the Sales Act', economic crime and fraud, Constitutional Law; and articles on: Public Information Law, the new Credit Sales Act, cooling-off period in consumers sales; consumer disputes; manuscript regarding consumer purchases and consumers' protection; leader regarding calculation of compensation; study report on new Consumer Purchases Act.
Languages: English, Russian, Scandinavian languages.
Member: Norwegian Bar Association.
Education: University of Oslo (1982 Cand Jur; 1988 Dr Jur).
Personal: Born 1956; resides Oslo.

STRØMSMOEN, Ola J
Advokatfirmaet Steenstrup Stordrange DA
Phone: Oslo (+47 22 81 45 00)
E-mail: ola@steenstrup.no
Litigation and arbitration; torts and compensation; health and damages; real estate; energy and construction.
Position: Particularly involved with issues relating to real estate, building and construction; also deals with torts, contract law and disputes concerning labour law, general wage agreements, individual employment and dismissals, and litigation.
Career: Admitted 1987; attorney Bech, Hirsch & Co 1987-90; attorney Steenstrup ANS 1990-92; partner Advokatfirmaet Steenstrup Stordrange DA 1992 to date.
Languages: English, the Scandinavian languages.
Member: Norwegian Bar Association.
Education: University of Bergen (1986 Cand Jur); Institute of Business Administration, Oslo (1987 BI); holds a Bachelors degree in Business Administration from the Norwegian School of Management.
Personal: Born 1959; resides Oslo and Copenhagen.
Leisure: Sport, outdoor activities.

STRØNSTAD, Dagfinn
Advokatfirmaet Steenstrup Stordrange DA
Phone: Tromsø (+47 77 61 78 00)
E-mail: ds@steenstrup.no
Real estate, energy and construction; insolvency and restructuring.
Position: Particularly involved with real estate, building, construction and litigation in addition to bankruptcy and insolvency. Has litigation case experience especially in representing contractors.
Career: Admitted 1982; own law practice 1981-2000; lawyer PricewaterhouseCoopers 2000-02; partner Advokatfirmaet Steenstrup Stordrange 2002. Administers the Norwegian Houseowner's Organisation in Tromsø.
Languages: English, Scandinavian languages.
Member: Norwegian Bar Association.
Education: University of Bergen (1975 Cand jur).
Personal: Born 1949; resides Tromsø.

SVANE, Henrik
Kvale & Co
Phone: Oslo (+47 22 47 97 00)
E-mail: svane@kvaleco.no
Competition and antitrust law, EU law, intellectual property, agency and distributorship.
Position: Partner.
Career: Admitted 1995; associate in legal department in Københavns Telefon Aktieselskab 1987-88; executive officer the Price Directorate (The Norwegian Competition Authority) 1988-91; attorney-at-law and partner Wiersholm, Mellbye & Beth 1991-2002; partner Kvale & Co since 2003.
Languages: English, the Scandinavian languages.
Member: Norwegian Bar Association.
Education: University of København (1987 Candidate of Jurispudence).
Personal: Born 1970; resides Oslo.

SVEEN, Robert

Advokatfirmaet Steenstrup Stordrange DA
Phone: Oslo (+47 22 81 45 00)
E-mail: robert@steenstrup.no
Corporate.
Position: Specialises in corporate finance, mergers and acquisitions, and listings, securities law, accounting legislation, and corporate law in general.
Career: Admitted 1995; legal assistant to the Judge Advocate General 1993-94; senior associate BAHR 1994-2000; partner Advokatfirmaet Steenstrup Stordrange DA 2000 to date.
Languages: English, the Scandinavian languages.
Member: Norwegian Bar Association.
Education: University of Oslo (1992 Cand jur).
Personal: Born 1968; resides Oslo.

TERKELSEN, Thor Ask

Advokatfirmaet Steenstrup Stordrange DA
Phone: Oslo (+47 22 81 45 00)
E-mail: thor.ask.terkelsen@streenstrup.no
Corporate and public administration.
Position: Particularly involved with corporate law, maritime law and insurance, including P&I as well as contract law.
Career: Competition authorities 1980-81; admitted 1983; associate Gram, Hambro & Garman 1981-96 (partner from 1986); partner Advokatfirmaet Steenstrup ANS (now Advokatfirmaet Steenstrup Stordrange DA) 1996 to date.
Languages: English, Scandinavian languages.
Member: Norwegian Bar Association.
Education: University of Oslo (1980 Cand Jur).
Personal: Born 1953; resides Oslo.
Leisure: Boating, skiing.

POLAND

DOBROWOLSKI, Tomasz

Hogan & Hartson M. Jamka, A. Galos, and Partners, LP
Phone: Warsaw (+48 22 653 4221)
E-mail: tdobrowolski@hhlaw.com
Energy, corporate, commercial, international trade, arbitration, investments.
Position: Partner focusing on the energy sector and energy law. He has also been involved in major privatisation and investment projects in the energy and telecom sectors (including eurobond and convertible bond issues and acquisitions).
Career: Apprenticeship in Legal Counsels' Bar in Warsaw. Qualified 1980. Legal counsel Pezetel Agromet-Motoimport, Elektrim; head of legal team, Elektrim; partner Nabarro Nathanson; partner Allen & Overy; partner Hogan & Hartson. Various publications on energy regulatory issues.
Languages: Polish, English.
Member: Legal Counsel's Bar; Advocates' Bar; Polish Association for Amicable Dispute Settlement (founder member).
Education: Nicolas Copernicus Lyceum; Warsaw University (1974 MA); Poznan University (1978 post-graduate course).
Personal: Born 1951; resides Warsaw.
Leisure: Farming.

GALOS, Aleksander

Hogan & Hartson M. Jamka, A. Galos, and Partners, LP
Phone: Warsaw (+48 22 653 4219)
E-mail: agalos@hhlaw.com
Project finance, infrastructure, anti-dumping, corporate, municipal investments.
Position: Partner focusing on corporate, administrative and civil law, with a particular emphasis on contract law, public finance, public procurement, and anti-dumping matters.
Career: Voivodeship Court in Krakow judge exam 1987; Regional Chamber of Legal Counsels legal adviser exam 1994. Assistant in the department of law at the Jagiellonian University 1984-92; co-founder and co-owner of the law office called 'Centrum Prawne' in Krakow 1991-92, later to become Warsaw Office of Hogan & Hartson, director of the Cabinet of Ministers – head of the Council of Ministers' office 1992-93; Hogan & Hartson since 1994. Managing partner Hogan & Hartson Warsaw office; Supervisory Board of Bank Zachodni WBK SA; Revisory Commission of Academy for Philanthropy in Poland; Actions Planning Board of Economic Forum at Krynica.
Languages: Polish, English, Slovenian.
Member: Warsaw Chamber of Legal Counselors.
Education: Jagiellonian University in Krakow (1984 LLM).
Personal: Born 1960; resides Krakow and Warsaw.

JAMKA, Maciej

Hogan & Hartson M. Jamka, A. Galos, and Partners, LP
Phone: Warsaw (+48 22 653 4204)
E-mail: mjamka@hhlaw.com
Commercial and corporate, finance, real estate, telecommunications.
Position: Partner and Polish advocate. Practises in all areas of Polish law, with particular emphasis on mergers and acquisitions, financial institutions and new technologies.
Career: Co-author: Mortgage.
Languages: Polish, English, German.
Member: Warsaw Bar of Advocates.
Education: Jagiellonian University (Magister of Law).
Personal: Born 1959; resides Warsaw.
Leisure: Sailing.

KARWOWSKI, Robert

Hogan & Hartson M. Jamka, A. Galos, and Partners, LP
Phone: Warsaw (+48 22 653 4218)
E-mail: rkarwowski@hhlaw.com
Broker-dealer regulation, initial public offerings, private placement, public offering, securities registration, corporate, EU regulations.
Position: Partner focuses on counselling companies on their obligations under the law, stock exchange rules and representing clients in public company takeovers. Recently he has been involved in litigation pertaining to a hostile takeover and shareholder control matters.
Career: Judge exam 1987; bar exam 1988; private law firm, Regional Court; general director and Undersecretary of State in Council of Ministers Office; counsel to management board; director of the legal office at Warsaw stock exchange; legal counsel and partner Hogan & Hartson since 1996. Chairman of the Supervisory Board of Centrum Bankowo-Finansowe 'Nowy Swiat' S.A. Co-author of legal acts regarding public trading in securities. Responsible for the creation of National Securities Deposit S.A and Centrum Gieldowe S.A.
Languages: Polish, English, Russian.
Member: Warsaw Chamber of Legal Counselors.
Education: Warsaw University (1984 LLM).
Personal: Born 1959; resides Warsaw.
Leisure: Boxing.

KORDASIEWICZ, Bogudar

Hogan & Hartson M. Jamka, A. Galos, and Partners, LP
Phone: Warsaw (+48 22 653 4206)
E-mail: bkordasiewicz@hhlaw.com
Commercial, secured transactions, mortgages, real estate transactions, intellectual property, mass media law.
Position: Counsel focusing on advising private clients on the Polish commercial and civil law aspects of international transactions as well as advising generally on commercial, corporate and financing matters, including company and debt restructuring.
Career: Max Planck Instytut, Hamburg 1980; Alexander von Humboldt Foundation 1989-90; professor at the Institute of Legal Studies of the Polish Academy of Sciences. Has taught at the University of Belgrade and the universities of Regensburg and Hamburg. Conducted research in Germany at the Max Planck Institute for International Private Law. Adviser to the Polish Ministry of Justice, Ministry of Foreign Affairs; Polish Parliament, and the governmental commission on the Codification of the Polish Civil Law. Of counsel Hogan & Hartson since 1995. Publications include three books and approximately 50 articles in various Polish and international professional journals.
Languages: Polish, English, German, Russian.
Member: Association of Polish Lawyers.
Education: Warsaw University (1972 Magister; 1975 PhD Civil Law; 1991 Doctor Jur Habilitatus Civil Law).
Personal: Born 1950; resides Warsaw.
Leisure: Tourism, skiing, bridge.

NAJBAUER, Lech

Hogan & Hartson M. Jamka, A. Galos, and Partners, LP
Phone: Warsaw (+48 22 653 4216)
E-mail: lnajbauer@hhlaw.com
Commercial, administration, anti-monopoly.
Position: Counsel focusing on the areas of commercial transactions and corporate and administrative law, with specific focus on anti-monopoly issues.
Career: Judge training program by the Vioivodhip Court in Warsaw (1994-96); Hogan & Hartson 1991; European counsel since 2001.
Languages: Polish, English.
Member: Warsaw District Bar of Legal Advisors.
Education: LO no. XXXIII named after Nicolaus Copernicus in Warsaw; Warsaw University (1993 LLM).
Personal: Born 1969; resides Warsaw.
Leisure: Tourism, movies, literature, music, dogs, cars.

RUTKOWSKI, Karol

Karol Rutkowski Law Office Sp. k.
Phone: Warsaw (48 607 302 609)
E-mail: karolrutkowski@op.pl
Position: Head of Karol Rutkowski Law Office Sp. k., which deals with litigation and arbitration, banking, capital markets and corporate matters. Mr Rutkowski has

significant experience in Polish securities law, banking law and litigation, including civil and criminal cases. He is an arbitrator of the Court of Arbitration at the National Chamber of Commerce in Warsaw. He is the author of many articles on dispute resolutions, banking and capital markets, and has participated in the drafting of the Polish 'Accounting Law', the 'Chartered Auditors Law' and the 'Act on the Organisation and Operation of Pension Funds'.
Career: Qualified as a prosecutor and judge 1988, as a legal adviser (solicitor) 1993, and as an advocate (barrister) 1996; head of financial crimes department, Regional Public Prosecutor's Office 1988; legal adviser, Bank Gospodarki Zywnosciowej 1992; vice-president, Coopers & Lybrand 1994; partner, Cameron McKenna, Warsaw 1996; partner London 1997; partner, Lovells 2001; founded Karol Rutkowski Law Office Sp. k. 2003. During his professional life, Karol Rutkowski has been responsible for the preparation and submission to the Polish Securities and Stock Exchange Commission of nine prospectuses for public offerings of shares, including the privatisation of one of the major commercial banks and two other banks listed on the Stock Exchange. He was also in charge of a team of lawyers, which conducted a due diligence exercise on five leading Polish commercial banks, and led the team which carried out the separation of the National Depository of Securities from the Warsaw Stock Exchange. He also led the legal team which put together the agreement establishing the only banking group in Poland during the consolidation of the Polish banking sector and which prepared a comprehensive report on the legal issues associated with this venture.
Languages: Polish, English.
Member: Distric Chamber of Barristers, Warsaw; District Chamber of Legal Advisers, Warsaw; Court of Arbitration, National Chamber of Commerce, Warsaw; Law Society of England and Wales.
Education: Faculty of Law, University of Gdansk; Faculty of Law and Administration, Warsaw University (1986 MA Law); Law Institute, Polish Academy of Sciences PAN (doctoral studies).
Leisure: Natural philosophy, sport.

TULODZIECKI, Oskar

Hogan & Hartson M. Jamka, A. Galos, and Partners, LP
Phone: Warsaw (+48 22 653 4211)
E-mail: otulodziecki@hhlaw.com
Intellectual property, media law, commercial law.
Position: Partner focusing on intellectual property and media, as well as general commercial and civil law. Has substantial experience in public procurement law.
Career: IT Poland SA member of legal department 1991-93; Wardynski & Partners 1994-2000; Hogan & Hartson since 2000. Appointed arbitrator of the Copyright Law Commission at the Ministry of Culture 2001.
Languages: Polish, English, Russian, basic German.
Member: District Chamber of Legal Advisors; IP Committee of the American Chamber of Commerce.
Education: Warsaw University (1991 LLM); 1998 post-graduate studies in copyright, publishing, and media law at Institute of Patents and Protection of Intellectual Property of the Jagiellonian University; Queen Mary and Westfield College of the University of London (1992).
Personal: Born 1965; resides Warsaw.
Leisure: Tennis, cooking.

PORTUGAL

BAIÃO DO NASCIMENTO, Felipe

Baião do Nascimento, Castro Nunes, Castro e Solla & Associados
Phone: Lisbon (351 21 319 0646)
E-mail: fbn@bcs.pt
Banking and capital markets, project finance.
Position: Partner.
Career: Qualified 1994; in-house lawyer BCP Investimento; Committee for the Reform of the Law on Portuguese Public Debt; lecturer University of Lisbon Faculty of Law (Tax law and Public Finance); partner Baião do Nascimento, Castro Nunes, Castro e Solla & Associados 1997 to date. Publications include 'Reforma da Dívida Pública – Legislação Anotada' (co-authored).
Languages: Portuguese, English, Italian, Spanish.
Member: Portuguese Bar Association; International Bar Association; Portuguese Securities Institute.
Education: University of Lisbon Faculty of Law (1992).
Personal: Born 1969; resides Lisbon.

CASTRO E SOLLA, José

Baião do Nascimento, Castro Nunes, Castro e Solla & Associados
Phone: Lisbon (351 21 319 0640)
E-mail: jcs@bcs.pt
Corporate and M&A, tax.
Position: Partner.
Career: Qualified 1993; in-house lawyer Tabaqueira; senior in-house lawyer Nutrinveste, SGPS; senior in-house lawyer Finibanco; parter Baião do Nascimento, Castro Nunes, Castro e Solla & Associados 1997 to date.
Languages: Portuguese, English, Spanish.
Member: Portuguese Bar Association.
Education: Portuguese Catholic University Faculty of Law (1990).
Personal: Born 1967; resides Lisbon.

CASTRO NUNES, Victor

Baião do Nascimento, Castro Nunes, Castro e Solla & Associados
Phone: Lisbon (351 21 319 0647)
E-mail: vcn@bcs.pt
Commercial and financial transactions, privatisations.
Position: Partner.
Career: Qualified 1993; senior in-house lawyer BCP Investimento; lawyer Miguel Galvão Teles, João Soares da Silva & Associados; lecturer University of Lisbon Faculty of Law (Tax Law and the Law of Economy); partner Baião do Nascimento, Castro Nunes, Castro e Solla & Associados 1997 to date.
Languages: Portuguese, English, French, Spanish.
Member: Portuguese Bar Association; International Bar Association; Portuguese Fiscal Association; International Fiscal Association.
Education: University of Lisbon Faculty of Law (1990); Queen Mary University of London (1994 LLM).
Personal: Born 1968; resides Lisbon.

DELGADO, Rita

Barros, Sobral, G Gomes & Associados
Phone: Lisbon ()
E-mail: rita.delgado@bsgg.pt
Corporate and commercial; mergers and acquisitions; IT and telecoms; real estate.
Position: Partner.
Career: Admitted to the Portuguese Bar 1986; partner Roquette, Vaz Pinto & Marques dos Santos 1996-98; partner Olavo Cunha, Franqueira Dias, Barros Figueiredo, Vaz Pinto 1998-2000; partner Barros, Sobral, G Gomes & Associados 2000 to date.
Languages: English, French, Spanish.
Member: IBA; Association Internationale des Jeunes Advocats (AIJA); jury of the Portuguese Bar Association exams board; National Political Commission of a political party 1999); National Jurisdictional Council of a political party (2000).
Education: Portuguese Catholic University, Lisbon.
Personal: Born 1963; resides Lisbon.
Leisure: Golf.

GOMES, João Pedro Marques Gonçalves

Barros, Sobral, G Gomes & Associados
Phone: Lisbon ()
E-mail: j.pedrogomes@bsgg.pt
International tax planning; banking and finance; privatisation.
Position: Founding and managing partner.
Career: Thompson McLitock & Co Chartered Accountants 1975-78; assistant lawyer Assis de Almeida & Associados 1983-87; admitted to the Portuguese Bar Association 1985, Brazilian Bar Association 1989; chairman of a management company in the Madeira International Business Centre; representative partner of Bomchill, Castro, Goodrich, Claro, Arosemena & Associates, Lisbon; presently also chairman of the Portuguese Law Firms Association (ASAP).
Languages: English, French, Italian, Spanish.
Member: International Bar Association; Association Internationale des Jeunes Avocats; International Tax Planning Association.
Education: Portuguese Catholic University, Lisbon (1983 LLB).
Personal: Born 1956; resides Lisbon.
Leisure: Sailing.

MATOS MARTINS, Ana Paula

Baião do Nascimento, Castro Nunes, Castro e Solla & Associados
Phone: Lisbon (351 21 319 0640)
E-mail: apmm@bcs.pt
Litigation and arbitration.
Position: Partner.
Career: Qualified 1994; lawyer José Miranda Dias (Law Office); partner Baião do Nascimento, Castro Nunes, Castro e Solla & Associados 2001 to date.
Languages: Portuguese, English, Spanish.
Member: Portuguese Bar Association; Portuguese Bar Association Examinations Board.
Education: University of Lisbon Faculty of Law (1992).
Personal: Born 1969; resides Lisbon.

QATAR

AL-NAIMI, Ali bin Nasser
Law Office of Ali bin Nasser Al-Naimi
Phone: Doha (+974 4432 959)
E-mail: theqatarifirm@yahoo.co.uk
Position: Researches in the fields of arbitration, advocacy and public administration.
Career: Assistant judge and judge in the Court of Justice 1975-79; director Land Department and legal research officer Ruler's Office, Doha 1979-81; advocate and legal consultant Qatar 1981-86; director Legal Department, the Ruler's Office 1986-89; director Legal Affairs Department, Ministry of Justice 1989-90; undersecretary Ministry of Justice 1990-94; chairman Permanent Committee on Legal Affairs 1990-94; member of Doha Municipal Council 1982-98.
Languages: Arabic, English, working French.
Member: International Bar Association.
Education: BA Qatar, 1971; LLB Cairo, 1975; holder of certificate of the Institute National Magistratur Ministry of Justice, Paris 1979.
Personal: Born 1951.

ROMANIA

BADESCU, Veronica
Wood Lupascu Dumitrescu & Associates SCPA
Phone: Bucharest (40 21 222 88 88)
E-mail: veronica.badescu@wldlaw.ro
Position: Associate, dealing with corporate and commercial matters, intellectual property law, real estate, trade mark legislation, litigation and succession.
Career: Junior lawyer, Mihaela Nistor Law Office 2000-02; associate WLD 2003 to date.
Languages: English, Romanian.
Member: Bucharest Bar Association.
Education: University of Bucharest, Faculty of Law (2000).
Personal: Born 1974.

DELEANU, Vasile
Deleanu Vasile – Lawyers
Phone: Bucharest (+40 21 312 45 36)
E-mail: office@deleanu.ro
Position: Co-ordinating partner of the law firm, working from the Bucharest office, specialising in corporate and commercial law, debt recovery, insolvency and corporate restructuring law.
Career: Barrister; PHARE expert; authorised evaluator of company's assets and insolvency practitioner; author of many articles in business magazines.
Languages: English, Italian.
Member: Insol Europe; Romanian National Union of Insolvency practitioners; National Lawyers' Union; Bucharest Bar Association; French Chamber of Commerce in Romania.
Education: University of Bucharest – Law School, post-academic courses in international trade.
Personal: Born 1948; resides Bucharest.
Leisure: Collects paintings.

DICULESCU-SOVA, Ana
Nestor Nestor Diculescu Kingston Petersen
Phone: Bucharest (+40 21 20 11 200)
E-mail: ana.diculescu@nnkp.ro
Position: Partner dealing with all aspects of the dispute resolution practice, specialising in litigation.
Career: Private practice in civil and commercial litigation from 1977; vice-president, Romanian International Union of Lawyers 1996; ad hoc judge, European Court for Human Rights 1999; partner Nestor Nestor Diculescu Kingston Petersen 2001.
Languages: French.
Member: Bucharest Bar Association, International Union of Lawyers.
Education: University of Bucharest, Law Faculty (1976 magna cum laudae; 1988 PhD).
Personal: Born 1954; resides Bucharest.
Leisure: Reading, theatre.

DUMITRESCU, Florentina
Wood Lupascu Dumitrescu & Associates SCPA
Phone: Bucharest (40 21 222 88 88)
E-mail: florentina.dumitrescu@wldlaw.ro
Position: Partner, dealing with corporate, commercial, banking and finance.
Career: Associate, Musat & Associates SCPA 1996-98; associate, Nestor & Nestor SCPA 1998-2000; associate, Hall, Dickler (Romania) 2000-02; partner WLD 2002 to date.
Languages: English, French, Italian, Romanian.
Member: Bucharest Bar Association.
Education: Ecologic University of Bucharest, School of Law (1996 magna cum laude).
Personal: Born 1970; resides Bucharest.

EFTIMIE, Cristian
Wood Lupascu Dumitrescu & Associates SCPA
Phone: Bucharest (40 21 222 88 88)
E-mail: cristian.eftimie@wldlaw.ro
Position: Associate, dealing with corporate and commercial matters, tax legislation, competition, bankruptcy, real estate, trade mark legislation and commercial litigation.
Career: Legal counsel, Cremer & Diaconescu 1998-99; associate, Cerveni & Cerveni 1999-2000; attorney-at-law, Cristian Eftimie Law Office 2000-03; associate WLD 2003 to date.
Languages: English, German, Romanian.
Member: Bucharest Bar Association.
Education: University of Bucharest, Faculty of Law (1998).
Personal: Born 1973.

GASPAR, Adriana
Nestor Nestor Diculescu Kingston Petersen
Phone: Bucharest (+40 21 20 11 200)
E-mail: adriana.gaspar@nnkp.ro
Position: Partner dealing with drafting of legislative items, regulated activities, direct investment, securities and financial markets.
Career: Judge, Bucharest Court – Sector 1 1993; associated professor, Bucharest University Law Faculty 1997; partner, Nestor Nestor Diculescu Kingston Petersen 2001.
Languages: English.
Member: Bucharest Bar Association.
Education: University of Bucharest, Faculty of Law (1993 magna cum laudae); Romanian Judicial College for Judges and Magistrates (1994 Honors Graduate).
Personal: Born 1970; resides Bucharest.
Leisure: Sport, theatre.

LUPASCU, Nicu
Wood Lupascu Dumitrescu & Associates SCPA
Phone: Bucharest (40 21 222 88 88)
E-mail: nicu.lupascu@wldlaw.ro
Position: Partner, dealing with all aspects of dispute resolution, specialised in commercial and criminal litigation, banking law and real estate.
Career: Prosecutor, Bucharest Court 1993-96; private practice 1996-98; associate, Hall, Dickler (Romania) 1998-2002; partner WLD 2002 to date.
Languages: English, Romanian.
Member: Bucharest Bar Association.
Education: University of Bucharest, Faculty of Law (1993).
Personal: Born 1967.

MONAC, Veronica
Wood Lupascu Dumitrescu & Associates SCPA
Phone: Bucharest (40 21 222 88 88)
E-mail: veronica.monac@wldlaw.ro
Position: Senior associate, dealing with corporate and commercial matters, mergers and acquisitions, privatisations, banking law, bankruptcy, real estate and commercial litigation.
Career: Associate, Hall, Dickler (Romania) 1998-2002; associate WLD 2002 to date; assistant, Romanian-British University.
Languages: English, Romanian.
Member: Bucharest Bar Association.
Education: University of Bucharest, Faculty of Law (1998).
Personal: Born 1976.

MUSAT, Gheorghe
Musat & Asociatii
Phone: Bucharest (+40 21 223 3717)
E-mail: musat@musat.ro
Senior partner.
Position: Apart from heading the management committee and overseeing the direction of the firm, he is still heavily involved in the practice. He has practised for over 21 years and counts a substantial amount of Supreme Court Hearings. He has an extensive wealth of experience both from the foreign investors' perspective in Romania, and a deep knowledge of the local market both in the private and state-owned sectors, and numbers important achievements as legal adviser in the privatisation and reorganisation of state-owned companies in Romania. He has been involved as team leader in various successful mergers and acquisitions, as well as in most of the major privatisation deals in Romania, acting either on the side of the Romanian government, or on the side of the buyer. His areas of practice include: corporate and commercial law, mergers and acquisitions/privatisation, project and corporate finance, banking and foreign investment law.
Languages: Romanian, English, French.
Member: Bucharest and Romanian Bar Associations.
Education: Law degree (RO).

NESTOR, Ion
Nestor Nestor Diculescu Kingston Petersen
Phone: Bucharest (+40 21 20 11 200)
E-mail: ion.nestor@nnkp.ro
Position: Partner dealing with privatisations, mergers and acquisitions, litigation.
Career: Legal adviser and chief legal counsel, Romanian Consulting Institute 1976; legal consultant Institute of Legal Research, Romanian Academy in Bucharest 1983; private practitioner 1984; partner Nestor Nestor Diculescu Kingston Petersen since formation in 1990.
Languages: English, French.
Member: Bucharest Bar Association.
Education: University of Bucharest, Law Faculty (1976 magna cum laudae).
Personal: Born 1953; resides Bucharest.
Leisure: Tennis, music, history.

NESTOR, Manuela
Nestor Nestor Diculescu Kingston Petersen
Phone: Bucharest (+40 21 20 11 200)
E-mail: manuela.nestor@nnkp.ro
Position: Partner dealing with direct investment, banking, project/corporate finance, bankruptcy, privatisation.
Career: Legal adviser and general counsel, Romanian Consulting Institute 1976; general counsel, University of Bucharest 1987; partner Nestor Nestor Diculescu Kingston Petersen since formation in 1990.
Languages: English, French.
Member: Bucharest Bar Association.
Education: University of Bucharest, Law faculty (1976 magna cum laudae).
Personal: Born 1953; resides Bucharest.
Leisure: Sport, music, reading.

SANDU, Andrei
Wood Lupascu Dumitrescu & Associates SCPA
Phone: Bucharest (40 21 222 88 88)
E-mail: andrei.sandu@wldlaw.ro
Position: Senior associate, dealing with corporate and commercial, mergers and acquisitions, banking law, intellectual property, bankruptcy and real estate.
Career: Associate, Hall, Dickler (Romania) 1997-2002; associate WLD 2002 to date; assistant with the Bucharest University Faculty of Law.
Languages: English, French, Romanian.
Member: Bucharest Bar Association.
Education: University of Bucharest, Faculty of Law (1996).
Personal: Born 1974.

STOICA, Cristiana I
STOICA & Asociatii Attorneys at Law
Phone: Bucharest (+40 21 40 20 930)
E-mail: sca@stoica-asociatii.ro
Commercial law, intellectual property law, taxation law, security and stock exchange regulation, international private law, privatisation, competition law, real estate, capital markets, international contracts.
Position: Senior partner.
Career: Qualified 1980; president of the Young Lawyers Association 1991-93; associated lecturer in international and commercial law, Bucharest University 1992-97; founding partner 1995; a leading Romanian lawyer in the company/commercial/M&A section of 'Chambers Global Guide' (1999-2000); publication of articles in various fields of law in Romania and abroad; author of a legal book concerning the international public underwriting of stocks and bonds.
Languages: English, French.
Member: Bucharest Bar Association; Romanian Union of Lawyers; Union Internationale des Avocats; Canadian Business Association in Romania; member of ICC Romania (working with the ICC Commission for competition and intellectual property).
Education: Bucharest University Law Faculty (1979); PhD International Commercial Law (2000); International Institute of Human Rights, Strasbourg (1990); European Commission of Human Rights, Council of Europe (1991); International Academy of Private Law – The Hague (1994); Agency for International Development Capital Markets Development (USA) 1998.
Personal: Born 1956; resides Bucharest.

STOICA, Valeriu
STOICA & Asociatii Attorneys at Law
Phone: Bucharest (+40 21 40 20 930)
E-mail: sca@stoica-asociatii.ro
Civil and commercial law, banking, financial and insurance law, foreign investments, security and stock exchange regulation, international private and public law, human rights law, administrative law, competition law.
Position: Senior partner.
Career: Qualified 1990; judge, Bucharest 1976-87; professor of law (civil) 1987 to date, University of Bucharest; initiated human rights programme, University of Bucharest 1990; professor and dean, Romanian National Institute of Magistracy 1991-93; European Commission Against Racism and Intolerance European Council 1994-96; arbitrator, Romanian Court of Arbitration; elected to Romanian Parliament 1996-2003; Minister of Justice 1996-2000; founding partner 1995; European Commision for Democracy through Law 1998-2002; over 60 publications in Romania and abroad in the fields of civil, commercial, international private, human rights and public law.
Languages: English, French.
Member: Bucharest Bar Association; Romanian Union of Lawyers; International Institute of Human Rights, Strasbourg.
Education: University of Bucharest Law Faculty (1976; 1997 PhD civil law); seminaries, international conferences, professional training in the USA, UK, France, Holland, Sweden, Egypt, Israel, Greece, Italy, Denmark, Norway, Austria.
Personal: Born 1953; resides Bucharest.

TUCA, Florentin
Musat & Asociatii
Phone: Bucharest (+40 21 223 3717)
E-mail: tuca@musat.ro
Managing partner.
Position: Florentin has been closely involved as a co-ordinator in the privatisation of several state-owned companies, supervising and controlling all the elements of the complex legal due diligence, drafting and negotiating the necessary transaction documentation including joint venture, shareholders and other related agreements. Most notably, he is instrumental in drafting laws and regulations including the elaboration and establishment of new legal and regulatory frameworks for the industry. His areas of practice cover: corporate and commercial law, banking, mergers and acquisitions, taxation, secured transactions and concessions, capital markets and litigation. He has published several articles on commercial law and is an author of several legal books.
Languages: Romanian, English, French.
Member: Member of the Bucharest and Romanian Bar Associations.
Education: Law degree (RO), PhD candidate in commercial law (RO).

WOOD, Douglas
Wood Lupascu Dumitrescu & Associates SCPA
Phone: Bucharest (40 21 222 88 88)
E-mail: douglas.wood@wldlaw.ro
Position: Partner with over 26 years' experience representing multinational companies in advertising and unfair competition, intellectual property, Internet matters, marketing and promotion law. Publications include: 'Please Be Advised – The Legal Reference Guide For The Advertising Executive'; co-author, 'Legal Problems In Advertising, The Internet and Advertising Law'; regular columnist for 'The Advertiser'; editor of the online news letter 'Adlaw By Request'.
Career: Associate, Hall, Dickler LLP 1977-85; partner 1985-2001; partner WLD 2001 to date.
Languages: English.
Member: New Jersey Bar Association; New York Bar Association; Bucharest Bar Association; general counsel, Association of National Advertisers and the Advertising Research Foundation; founder, chairman and member, the Global Advertising Lawyers' Alliance (GALA); chair of the Board of Trustees, Franklin Pierce Law Center (1998); member of the Board of Directors and past President, Touchdown Club of America.
Education: University of Rhode Island (1972 BA Political Science); Franklin Pierce Law Center (1976 Juris Doctor Degree); New York University School of Law (1977 MA Law, Trade Regulation; LLM Trade Regulation).
Personal: Born 1950.

RUSSIA AND THE CIS: KAZAKHSTAN

EMMOTT, John F
Michael Wilson & Partners
Phone: Almaty (+7 3272 58 48 90)
E-mail: john.emmott@mwp.kz
Oil and gas (upstream and downstream), foreign investments and joint ventures, international trade, banking and finance, litigation and arbitration.
Position: Partner, specialising in litigation and international arbitration, as well as all aspects of foreign investment throughout the region. Recently has been advising a number of governments, national oil and gas companies and foreign investors in the region on energy, investment and arbitration issues. Has a great deal of experience in international trade matters, and represents a number of large trading groups in Russia, Kazakhstan and Uzbekistan.

Career: Qualified 1977; lawyer at Johnson Stokes & Master, Hong Kong 1981-83; Richards Butler, UK 1983-86, partner 1986-2001; partner Michael Wilson & Partners Ltd since 2002. Current directorship: Michael Wilson & Partners, Limited.
Languages: English.
Member: Law Society of England and Wales; International Bar Association; admitted as a solicitor of the Supreme Court of England and Wales 1985; admitted as a solicitor, proctor and attorney of the Supreme Court of New South Wales and a solicitor of the High Court of Australia 1978.
Education: University of Sydney (1974 BA; 1977 LLB).
Personal: Born 1953; resides Almaty.
Leisure: Golf, classical music.

WILSON, Michael Earl

Michael Wilson & Partners
Phone: Almaty (+7 32 72 584 890)
E-mail: michael.wilson@mwp.kz
Corporate, commercial, major projects.
Position: Partner dealing with oil and gas; privatisation; power industry (generation, transmission and distribution); mining and natural resources; foreign investments and joint ventures; corporate, corporate finance and securities; banking, finance and project finance; tax; and engineering and construction. Michael Wilson has structured, documented and advised on almost all of the major transactions in Kazakhstan and the Central Asia region to date, including representing Marubeni Corporation/JGC Corporation in their dealings with CJSC NC KazMunaiGas as to the US$350m Atyrau Oil Refinery Modernisation Project, related sovereign guarantee, JBIC financing of US$200m and down payment financing, construction and licensing issues; advising TuranAlem Finance BV/Bank TuranAlem OJSC as to US$225m Eurobond issue – Issuers' and Guarantors' counsel – US$45m bridge facility with Citibank NA; advising as to an e-commerce-based Price Information and Customs Audit Programme System and related Joint Venture in the Republic of Kazakhstan, the first of its kind in the region; corporate litigation in Kazakhstan, Malaysia, the Cayman Islands and elsewhere relating to the Karaganda Cement Plant, as well as in the Supreme Court of Kazakhstan and its subsequent restructuring for OJSC Central Asian Cement Plant and its shareholders; advising CJSC NC KazMunaiGas, as well as the Ministries of Energy and Mineral Resources, of Finance and the Tax Committee (and the Republic of Kazakhstan generally) as to Tengizchevroil, the largest oil and gas producer in the Republic as to various issues, including the dispute over depreciation, the prepayment of US$600m in Royalties, payment of the outstanding US$210m Purchase Price, as to cash distributions of US$800m, as to the principles of the US$3.5bn financing of the SGI/SGP Expansion Project, as to the principles of the expansion of the Caspian Pipeline Consortium; advising Bovis Lend Lease on real estate acquisition and development issues as to the proposed new headquarters for the Karachagnak Production Organisation in Uralsk, and on various construction projects in Kazakhstan, including the City Palace Project and the new Transport Tower in Astana; advising Eurasian Financial and Industrial Group on various corporate and commercial matters to their enterprises comprising Kazchrome, Aluminy of Kazakhstan, SSGPO, and Eurasian Energy Corporation; advising Corrica AG as to privatisation of the balance of the State shareholding in Aluminium of Kazakhstan and as to the commitment to build an aluminium smelter of 250,000 tpy.
Career: Legal assistant Freehill, Hollingdate and Page, Sydney 1981-82; trainee solicitor and solicitor specialising in corporate, commercial, major projects, engineering and construction in a global law firm, London 1982-87; senior associate of a global law firm, London and Sydney 1987-91; international partner and local partner of a global law firm, London 1991-94; founding, managing partner and practice partner of an international law firm in Central Asia and the Caucasus, establishing offices in Almaty in 1995, Tashkent in 1996, Bishkek in 1997, Astana and Baku in 1998; founding and managing partner of Michael Wilson & Partners Ltd, Almaty 1998.
Languages: English.
Member: Law Society of England and Wales; Law Society of New South Wales; The Bar Association of Victoria, Australia; UK-based Major Projects Association; founding member and chairman, European Business Association of Kazakhstan; founding member Business Lawyers Association of Kazakhstan; member American Chamber of Commerce in Kazakhstan; selected by the EBRD as a member of the Foreign Investors Council in March 1998 as the leading foreign lawyer practising in Central Asia; Prospectors and Developers Association of Canada; associate member of the London Bullion Market Association.
Education: Manchester University (1980 LLB Hons 2(1)); Chester Law School (1981 Solicitor Final Examination).
Personal: Born 1958; resides Almaty since 1995; married with three children.
Leisure: Skiing, running, swimming, tennis, horse riding (Director of the Department of Show Jumping of the Equestrian Federation of the Republic of Kazakhstan).

RUSSIA AND THE CIS: RUSSIA

CHEROUTES, Michael L

Hogan & Hartson L.L.P.
Phone: Moscow (+7 095 797 9900)
E-mail: mlcheroutes@hhlaw.com
Public finance, project finance.
Position: Partner whose practice centers on public/project debt financings, with particular emphasis on major infrastructure construction and privatisation projects.
Member: National Association of Bond Lawyers; Colorado Bar; registered foreign lawyer with the Law Society of England and Wales.
Education: Harvard University (1962 AB); Stanford University (1965 LLB).
Personal: Born 1940.

GOLTSBLAT, Andrey

Pepeliaev, Goltsblat & Partners
Phone: Moscow (+7 095 258 5040)
E-mail: a.goltsblat@pgplaw.ru
Managing partner.
Position: Specialises in foreign investments, tax and customs law with a concentration on tax allowances and customs preferences. His practice also includes intellectual property. He has considerable experience in providing legal support to investment projects at all stages and rendering legal assistance to foreign investors carrying out commercial projects in Russia and the CIS. Practice areas include civil law, tax law, customs law, litigation, intellectual property, consumer law and antimonopoly legislation.
Career: Admitted 1987, Russia; former Chief of Staff of the Constitutional Commission of the Russian Parliament 1991-93; acted as chief adviser to the Legal Department of the State Duma, the lower house of the Russian Parliament; managing partner, Legal Practice LLC 1994-2002; managing partner, Pepeliaev, Goltsblat & Partners 2002 to date. Legislative expertise includes the drafting of the Russian Constitution and legislative initiatives to improve Russian product certification laws. Publications include 'Land Transactions' and numerous publications on tax issues and IP protection.
Languages: English.
Member: International Bar Association.
Education: Law School, Interior Ministry of the USSR (with honours 1987, JD 1994).
Personal: Born 1962; resides Moscow.

KOMOLOV, Sergey B

Hogan & Hartson L.L.P.
Phone: Moscow (+7 095 979 9900)
E-mail: sbkomolov@hhlaw.com
Finance, securities, mergers and acquisitions, investment banking, commercial banking, bankruptcy and restructuring, corporate, transactional.
Position: Partner who focuses on public and private finance, corporate acquisitions, investment and commercial banking, securities and derivatives trading, bank and corporate restructurings, and general corporate and transactional advice.
Career: Acting General Counsel of UNEXIM Bank, Moscow; consultant to the legal department of the World Bank, Washington DC 1996; career in the Russian diplomatic service (First Secretary); partner Hogan & Hartson 2003.
Languages: Russian, English, French.
Member: American Bar Association; Business Law Section.
Education: MGIMO Law School (1982 Diploma in International Law (hons)); Georgetown University Law Center (1996 LLM distinction).
Personal: Born 1960; resides Moscow.
Leisure: Classical music, books on history.

KOZYR, Olga

Hogan & Hartson L.L.P.
Phone: Moscow (+7 501 487 0609)
E-mail: okozyr@hhlaw.com
Corporate, real estate, environmental, litigation.
Position: Counsel who practises in the areas of corporate, commercial, real estate, and environmental law. Ms Kozyr's areas of practice also include privatisation issues, land reform, acquisitions, import and export of goods, construction issues, trade marks, and litigation.

Career: Trained Patterson, Belknap, Webb & Tyler LLP; professor (Moscow State University Law School); member of working groups of Duma on the Land Code and Urban Development Code. Has authored over 60 articles and publications, including 'Environmental Aspects of Legal Regulation of Chemical Pollution in Agriculture' Moscow 1989; 'Legal Regulation of the Protection of the Environment in Agriculture' (co-authored with Prof Kolbasov, Brinchuk and others), Moscow 1989; 'The Land Market and Legal Regulation of Land Relations' in 'Russia: Urban Development and Emerging Property Markets' Paris, ADEF 1995; 'Russia's Embattled Land Laws', AmCham News Vol 5 Number 24 1998; 'The Case Studies on Land Law. Manual for students' (co-authored with Prof Golichenkov, Volkov and others), Moscow 2001; comments to the Land Code of the Russian Federation (co-authored with Prof Golichenkov, Volkov), Moscow 2002.
Languages: Russian, English, French.
Member: Inter Republican Bar (Russian Federation); International Bar Association (London).
Education: Moscow State University (1982 JD summa cum laude; 1985 PhD); Harvard University (1996).
Personal: Born 1960; resides Moscow.
Leisure: Downhill skiing, swimming, travelling.

LAZAREV, Sergei L
Russin & Vecchi LLC
Phone: Moscow (+7 095 959 1288)
E-mail: sergei.lazarev@russinvecchi.ru
Russian practice group.
Position: Partner and executive director specialising in: civil law; corporate law; foreign investments; commercial law; labour law; international law; oil and gas law; trade marks; clients include: Dewey Ballantine; South African Breweries International; ExxonMobil; Credit Agricole Indosuez; Burson-Marsteller; General Dynamics; Bristol, Myers & Squibb; Landis & Gyr (Europe) Corp; Raytheon; Tidewater; Kaluga Brewing Company.
Career: Qualified Russian Bar 1983; research associate, academic secretary of the Institute of Scientific Information for Social Sciences (INION), Department of State and Law 1983-93; chief legal counsellor on international trade, Firma Melodiya (Russian record company) 1992; competitively selected for Muskie Fellowship, National Law Center, George Washington University 1992-93; senior Russian attorney, Russin & Vecchi LLP 1993-99; partner since 2000; publications: author 'International Arbitration' (Moscow International Affairs 1991); 'Ad Hoc Chambers of International Arbitration', Soviet State and Law (No 11, 1991); 'Topical Problems of International Arbitration', Soviet State and Law (No 2 1991); 'Arbitral Settlement of Disputes Arising Out of Bilateral Investment Treaties', Legislation and Economy (No 1/2, 1991).
Languages: English, Russian.
Member: Russian Association of International Law; International Bar Association.
Education: Law Faculty, Moscow State University (1983 LLB; 1990 PhD); The Hague Academy of International Law, Netherlands (1992); National Law Center, George Washington University, Washington DC (1992-93).
Personal: Born 1961; resides Moscow.
Leisure: Travelling, photography, reading, music.

MONASTYRSKY, Yuri
Monastyrsky, Zyuba, Stepanov & Partners
Phone: Moscow (+7 095 231 4222)
E-mail: monastyrsky@mzs.ru
Managing partner.
Position: Managing partner dealing with arbitration, litigation, intellectual property, securities, corporate law, insurance, insolvency, telecommunications, land law, foreign exchange regulations, antitrust law, investments, foreign trade, transportation law, taxation, criminal law.
Career: Qualified 1990; Monastysky, Zyuba, Stepanov & Partners 1991; arbitrator of the Court of Adjudication under the National Association of Stock Market Participants; arbitrator of the Court of Adjudication under the Central Transport Agency.
Languages: English.
Member: Moscow Bar.
Education: Moscow State Institute of International Relations (1990 law degree); Institute of State and Law of Russia's Academy of Sciences (1999); candidate of legal sciences.
Personal: Born 1964; resides Moscow.

PEPELIAEV, Sergey
Pepeliaev, Goltsblat & Partners
Phone: Moscow (+7 095 258 5040)
E-mail: s.pepeliaev@pgplaw.ru
Managing partner.
Position: Specialises in financial law, including budget law, tax law, banking law, exchange regulation and securities. Practice areas also include tax litigation and dispute resolution, and arbitration.
Career: Admitted 1987, Russia; lecturer, administrative and financial law, law department of Moscow State University 1989-95; former director of tax and law department of FBK, one of the leading auditing and consulting firms in Russia 1993-2002; former senior researcher for the Tax Law Sector at the Russian Academy of Sciences' Institute of State and Law 1995-2002; professor, financial law, State University Higher School of Economics 2001 to date; managing partner, Pepeliaev, Goltsblat & Partners 2002 to date. Sits on the panel of experts under the Federation Council Committee for Legal and Judicial Matters. Adviser, budget and finance committee of the State Duma, lower house of the Russian Parliament. Legislative drafting experience encompasses finalisation of the draft Russian Tax Code and participation in projects aimed to improve Russian tax legislation. Publications of note: 'Liability for Tax Violations'; 'Tax Laws: Elements of Structure'; 'The Tax Law Manual'; 'Entrepreneur – Taxpayer – Government'; 'Russian Constitutional Court Viewpoints' (co-authored with G.Gadzhiev). Awards: Themis Prize awarded by Moscow Lawyers' Club.
Member: Presidium of the Russian Tax Law Association.
Education: Moscow State University, law department (1987; JD 1991).
Personal: Born 1964; resides Moscow.

PETTIBONE, Peter J
Hogan & Hartson L.L.P.
Phone: Moscow (+7 501 487 0707)
E-mail: pipettibone@hhlaw.com
Corporate, international, securities regulation.
Position: Managaing partner of the Moscow office of Hogan & Hartson LLP. Mr Pettibone's practice focuses on general corporate advice to US and other Western companies engaging in business in the Russian market, as well as advice to Russian companies seeking to conduct transactions in the West. Mr Pettibone has extensive experience in cross-border transactions, including financing equipment sales and leases, ADR issuances, debt and equity financings, mergers and acquisitions and recapitalisations.
Career: Qualified New York, District of Columbia, Pennysylvania. Cravath, Swaine & Moore 1967-74; Lord Day & Lord, Barret Smith 1974-94; Patterson Belknap Webb & Tyler LLP 1994-99; Hogan & Hartson LLP since 2000.
Languages: English, Russian.
Member: US-Russia Business Council; International Tax and Investment Center.
Education: Princeton University (1961 AB summa cum lade, Phi Beta Kappa); Harvard University (1964 JD); New York University (1971 LLM).
Personal: Born 1939; resides New York, Moscow.
Leisure: Golf, skiing, fishing, sailing, Moscow Country Club, New York Yacht Club.

ROUBTSOV, Alexander
AR Consulting Law Firm
Phone: Moscow (+7 095 234 38 89)
E-mail: info@arconsulting.ru
Position: Managing partner dealing with corporate law, securities, joint ventures, international commercial contracts, information technology, oil and gas regulation, arbitration and civil litigation.
Career: Admitted 1976 to Russian Bar; legal adviser for the foreign trade organisations of the former USSR: Sovfracht, Machinoimport, Avtopromimport, Machinoexport 1976-89; vice president (legal affairs) of the Association for the Development of Information Technologies 1989-90; deputy general manager (legal affairs) of the West-East Consulting Company 1990-91; managing partner AR Consulting Law Firm 1991 to date; author of many articles on contract for supervision of erection; trial lawyer, pleased cases before all court jurisdictions in Russia and before national and international arbitral panels.
Languages: Russian, English.
Member: IBA.
Education: Moscow State Institute of International Relations (International Law Faculty); Institute of State and Law of the USSR Academy of Sciences.
Personal: Born 1953; resides Moscow.

RUSSIN, Jonathan
Russin & Vecchi LLC
Phone: Moscow (+7 095 959 1288)
E-mail: jonathan.russin@russinvecchi.ru
Russian practice group.
Position: Managing partner specialising in: investment in Russia; Russia trade; oil and gas law; international investment; international finance; emerging markets; international corporate law; international business law; clients include: Sakhalin Energy Investment Co; South African Breweries International; ExxonMobil; Burson-Marsteller; Samsung Corporation; ICN Pharmaceuticals;

Sun Capital Group; Moscow Norodny Bank; SHV Holdings; ITERA; Crowley.
Career: Qualified District of Columbia 1964; Office of the General Counsel, Agency for International Development, US Department of State 1964-69; regional legal adviser, Caribbean area 1967-69; founder and managing partner, Russin & Vecchi since 1969; directorships: chair, Advisory Council for European, Russian and Eurasian Studies 1991-93; general counsel, Orthodox Church in America; recipient, Order of Prince St Vladimir, Russian Orthodox Church, 1991. Publications: author, 'The Powers That Be: The Constitutional Court of the Russian Federation' AmCham (Russia) News (Vol 7, No 33 2000); 'Forming a Russian Company' sponsored by the Embassy of the Russian Federation in Washington DC (1994); 'Laws Affecting Franchise Operations in Spain' (American Bar Association, 1982).
Languages: English, Russian, Spanish.
Member: District of Columbia Bar; American Bar Association; Inter-American Bar Association; Russian Association of International Law; International Bar Association.
Education: Yale University (1959 BA; 1963 JD).
Personal: Born 1937; resides Moscow.
Leisure: Reading, music, golf, tennis.

SCHAFER, Todd D

Hogan & Hartson L.L.P.
Phone: Moscow (+7 095 797 9900)
E-mail: tdschafer@hhlaw.com
International corporate, international financial transactions and restructurings, cross-border mergers and acquisitions, international arbitration.
Position: Partner who focuses on major corporate and governmental entities of the Russian Federation in their dealings with United States and European counterparts. Mr Schafer also counsels some of the best known multinationals and public policy institutions. Mr Schafer's practice has focused on the banking, energy, mining and media/telecommunications sectors.
Career: Board of Stillwater Mining Company (a NYSE-listed company) and has sat on other boards, including Junior Achievement.
Languages: Russian, Spanish.
Member: The District of Columbia Bar; New York State Bar Association.
Education: Vassar College (1984 BA); Oxford University (1986 MPH); Harvard University (1989 JD).
Personal: Born 1962.

STEPANOV, Vladimir

Monastyrsky, Zyuba, Stepanov & Partners
Phone: Moscow (+7 095 231 4222)
E-mail: stepanov@mzs.ru
Position: Partner specialising in corporate law; antitrust law; securities; bankruptcy; arbitration; contracts; banking; investment; privatisation.
Career: Qualified 1990; partner Monastyrsky, Zyuba, Stepanov & Partners 1991; an arbitrator on the Court of Adjudication under the National Association of Stock Market Participants.
Languages: English.
Member: Moscow Bar.
Education: Moscow State Institute of International Relations (1990 Law degree).
Personal: Born 1968; resides Moscow.

TERENTIEV, Sergei V

Hogan & Hartson L.L.P.
Phone: Moscow (+7 095 487 0706)
E-mail: svterentiev@hhlaw.com
Projects and corporate.
Position: Mr Terentiev's practice focuses on corporate acquisitions; joint ventures, investment projects in Russia in mining, energy, real estate, telecommunication and consumer products manufacturing sectors.
Languages: Russian, English, Spanish.
Education: MIGIMO (1993 JD equivalent).
Personal: Born 1971.

ZYUBA, Alexander

Monastyrsky, Zyuba, Stepanov & Partners
Phone: Moscow (+7 095 231 4222)
E-mail: azyuba@mzs.ru
Corporate law, mergers and acquisitions.
Position: Partner specialising in corporate – general, M&A, antitrust law, securities, bankruptcy, privatisation, natural resources, telecommunications.
Career: Qualified 1991; partner Monastyrsky, Zyuba, Stepanov & Partners 2000. Associate Mannheimer Swartling, Moscow; tax and legal counsel for CIS and Baltic countries operations Tetra Laval International SA, Switzerland; senior associate Mannheimer Swartling, Moscow; senior Russian lawyer Patterson, Belknap, Webb & Tyler Ltd, Moscow.
Languages: English, Swedish, Ukrainian.
Member: Moscow Bar.
Education: Moscow State Institute of International Relations (1991 Law degree); licence to practice law.
Personal: Born 1965; resides Moscow.

SPAIN

ALCANTARA, José M

Abogados AMYA
Phone: Madrid (+34 91 548 83 28)
E-mail: jmalcantara@amya.es
Position: Director and senior partner dealing with all areas of shipping and Admiralty law, commercial law, arbitration, finance and environment law.
Career: Practiced in Madrid since 1973; founder and senior partner of Abogados AMYA; professor of maritime law; lecturer at numerous conferences worldwide; author of many articles.
Languages: Spanish, English, French.
Member: President, Spanish Maritime Law Association; executive councillor and titulary member, Comité Maritime International; titulary member, Association Internationale de Dispacheurs Européens; vice-president, Spanish Maritime Arbitration Association; ex-president, Iberoamerican Institute of Maritime Law; member IBA; board member, Spanish Committee of International Chamber of Commerce.
Education: University of Madrid (1965 Diploma on International Law of Sea); City of London College (1969-70 Fellowship course in Shipping and Shipbroking; 1970 Diploma in Shipping Law).
Personal: Born 1944; resides Madrid.

ALCARAZ, Miguel Angel

Ernst & Young Abogados, SL
Phone: Madrid (+34 91 572 7840)
E-mail: miguelangel.alcarazgarcia@es.ey.com
Labour.
Position: Managing partner of the labour practice of Ernst & Young Abogados Spain.
Career: Trained Universidad Complutense de Madrid. Responsible for employment and human resources TAL-PWC; partner responsible for the labour and social security department in Estudio Legal; human resources manager RJ Reynolds; permanent teacher in labour, Master Ceu. Partner Ernst & Young Abogados 2001.
Languages: English.
Member: Spanish Labour Lawyers Forum; European Employment Lawyers Association; BAR Association.
Education: Universidad Complutense de Madrid (degree in labour law school of legal practice; degree in HAY description appraisal system).
Personal: Born 1955; resides Madrid.
Leisure: Sailing, music.

ARENCIBIA RODRIGUEZ, Juan

Ernst & Young Abogados, SL
Phone: Madrid (+34 92 838 0984)
E-mail: juan.arencibiarodriguez@es.ey.com
Tax.
Position: Company law, corporate tax, international taxation, mergers and acquisitions.
Career: Trained Universidad Pontificia de Navarra. Partner Ernst & Young Abogados 1989.
Languages: English, French.
Education: Universidad Pontificia de Navarra, Esade (Barcelona), IMD Lausanne (law degree, MBA, Companies Management Diplome).
Personal: Born 1955; resides Tafira (Gran Canaria).
Leisure: Golf.

AYUSO, Mariano

Broseta Abogados
Phone: Valencia (+34 96 392 10 06)
E-mail: mayuso@broseta.com
Public law.
Position: Senior associate responsible for the public law department dealing with all areas of administrative law; advising both public bodies and private corporations on their relationships with local, regional, and state governments and public entities.
Career: Qualified 1980; joined Broseta Abogados 2003; member of the Military Judicial Body of the Spanish Jury 1981; various responsibilities in legal affairs; Ministry of Defence; professor, administrative law; member of many public and private institutions; magistrate, Superior Justice Tribunal of the Valencian Community 1991-2003; member editorial board of many relevant legal publications and other organisations dealing with tax and legal issues. Publications: numerous and relevant publications in recent years.
Languages: English.

Member: Judicial Career.
Education: Universities of San Pablo and Madrid (1975 Law Degree); Valencia University (1980 Doctor in Law).
Personal: Born 1958; resides Madrid.

BERROCAL, Javier

Santiago Mediano Abogados
Phone: Madrid (+34 91 310 63 63)
E-mail: jberrocal@santiagomediano.com
Information technology department.
Position: Senior partner and head of the information technology department; practice areas are entertainment, software, data protection, e-commerce, Internet media and unfair competition law. He specialises in counselling for negotiating agreements relating to production and exploitation of contents of all kinds (audiovisual, multimedia, software, publishing); developing protection strategies of company's intangible assets, negotating agreements, conflict-solving and intellectual property rights protection and exploitation strategies.
Career: Prior to joining the firm, worked on intellectual property, entertainment, software, data protection and media matters in local and international law firms; also worked in the copyright legal department of the Motion Picture Association (MPA).
Languages: English, Spanish.
Member: Madrid Bar Association.
Education: University of Salamanca (1991 Law Degree).
Personal: Born 1973.

BRINDLE, Pilar

Mullerat
Phone: Madrid (+34 91 399 51 89)
E-mail: p.brindle@mullerat.com
Litigation, criminal law, white-collar crime.
Position: Partner.
Career: Admitted 1985, Madrid.
Languages: Spanish, English.
Member: Madrid Bar Association; Young Women Association; Center of International Legal Studies; International Bar Association.
Education: Law School of Universidad Complutense de Madrid (1978-83).
Personal: Born 1960.

BRIZ PUERTAS, Nieves

Ernst & Young Abogados, SL
Phone: Madrid (+34 93 366 3800)
E-mail: marianieves.brizpuertas@es.ey.com
Corporate law, M&A.
Position: Specialising in commercial/mercantile/contracting law, professional background consolidated by experience in merger and acquisition projects.
Career: Trained Barcelona University, qualified 1986; 17 years' professional experience, 14 of which acquired at current firm. Has directed projects of considerable economic relevance and with multi-disciplinary professional teams, in terms of the specialisation of its members. Partner Ernst & Young Abogados 1986. Relevant projects participated in include: due diligence reports; participation in business association; teacher of M&A higher education course (ISDE) projects. Published several articles in relation to mergers and acquisitions.
Languages: English, Catalan, Spanish.
Member: Legal Firm Advisory Board (ESADE); Economic Circle; Commission of Mercantile Law of the Barcelona Bar.
Education: University of Barcelona (1986 law degree; Masters in European Community Law 1988).
Personal: Born 1963; resides Barcelona.

BROSETA, Manuel

Broseta Abogados
Phone: Valencia (+34 96 392 1006)
E-mail: mbroseta@broseta.com
Corporate.
Position: Partner since 1993 specialising in, among others, corporate law; mergers and acquisitions; company law; securities; arbitration.
Career: Qualified in 1991; former associate at Uria & Menédez 1991-93, associate professor of Business Law at the University of Valencia 1996-2000; regular lecturer on different masters courses and conferences. Patron of the International Fair of Valencia; Protector of the Investor in Valencia's Stock Exchange since 2000; Special Counsellor of the Local Government of Valencia for the high speed Madrid-Valencia train, (1999-2000).
Languages: English, French.
Member: Valencia and Madrid Bar Association; Valencia Court of Arbitration; Chamber of Commerce of France.
Education: University of Valencia (1990 Law degree Hons; Extraordinary Graduation Prize); Kings College London (1990 EEC Law); College of Europe, Bruges (1991 Master in European Law); Harvard Law School (1992 Negotiation Workshop); Georgetown University (1992 US Legal System).
Personal: Born 1967; resides Valencia.
Leisure: Golf.

COOKE, Chris

Santiago Mediano Abogados
Phone: Madrid (+34 91 310 63 63)
E-mail: ccooke@santiagomediano.com
International operations department.
Position: Senior associate specialising in international deals, negotation, finance and distribution agreements, logo and product clearances, production and international sales and operations; also dealt with anti-piracy matters and dispute resolution.
Career: Admitted to the Bar of England and Wales 1993; before joining the firm has worked in the UK for some of the most important film production companies and studios; also has experience as practising barrister, including appearances in the Court of Appeal; and ten years' experience working in the entertainment and media area.
Languages: English, Spanish.
Education: Bristol University (1991 LLB).
Personal: Born 1969.

DIAZ-GÁLVEZ, Javier

Ernst & Young Abogados, SL
Phone: Madrid (+34 93 572 7390)
E-mail: javier.diazgalvez@es.ey.com
Litigation.
Position: Procedural law, litigation strategy, commercial arbitration, litigation, dispute resolution, bankruptcies, restructuring, in-house counsel and claims manager. Participation in seminars and conferences on court proceedings, merchantile law, leases and real estate.
Career: Trained University of Madrid; qualified 1976; partner Alberto Oliart Abogados 1979-89; partner Ernst & Young Abogados since 1989; real estate agent; articles published in the business newspaper 'Expansion'.
Languages: English, French, Spanish.
Personal: Born 1952; resides Madrid.

ECHARRI, Alberto

Mullerat
Phone: Madrid (+34 91 399 5189)
E-mail: a.echarri@mullerat.com
Senior partner.
Position: Areas of specialisation include: mergers and acquisitions, general corporate/commercial and franchising, national and international arbitration in connection with the foregoing. Arbitration experience includes: counsel, mediator, chairman of arbitration panel and party-appointed arbitrator in several national and international cases on joint venture agreements, construction projects, share acquisition agreements, non-compete clauses and civil law matters involving parties from Spain, France, UK, Germany, Denmark, US, Canada and Colombia. Professor Instituto de Empresa and Universidad Alfonso X el Sabio; conference speaker in national and international forums; counsel to private and public companies; legal adviser to several governmental and private institutions; counsel to the Spanish Franchisors Association; counsel to ANEFRYC (National Freezing and Heating Industry Association); counsel to CONFMETAL (National Steel Industry Association); counsel to Chamber of Commerce of Madrid; counsel to several banking institutions, investment funds and institutional investers, counsel to the Western European Organisation (NATO; counsel to French government agencies; counsel to Canadian government by appointment of the Attorney General; counsel to the government of Québec; counsel to the University of Alcalá de Henares Foundation; counsel to the UCLES University of Cambridge Foundation; counsel to the Irish College Foundation; counsel to the Canadian Studies Foundation; approved counsel to the embassies of Canada, United States, France, Germany, Austria and UK; counsel to the economic newspaper expansion.
Career: Admitted to Bar 1983; junior partner Bufete Bertran y Musitu 1984-89; senior partner Echarri & Brindle 1989-2001; senior partner Mullerat 2001. Holds office as director in several public companies. Author of articles on international law and, in particular, versing on takeover acquisitions, foreign investments in Spain, international licensing, franchising and EU regulations; appeared in 'Contratos Internacionales' (Madrid, Confemetal 1998); chapter on 'Franchising in Spain', Mathew Bender 'International Franchising'; chapter on 'Licensing in Spain', 'International Licensing' BNA; permanent collaborater with business newspaper EXPANSION, member of advisery board of WLL Journal, BNA; 'Franchising' (Editorial Aranzadi, 2002).

Languages: Spanish, English, French.
Member: Member of the International Bar Association (Arbitration and ADR and Franchise Committees); member of the American Bar Association (International Law, Franchising and Arbitration Forum); Society of Franchising; member of the Association Internationale de Jeunes Avocats; Center for International Legal Studies (Arbitration Forum); International Business Law Consortium; chairman and co-founder of the Spanish Canadian Business Association; adviser to Spanish Franchisor's Association; supporting member of US-Spain Chamber of Commerce in New York; member of the Ireland Spain Economic Association. Panel of arbitrators: ICC, Spanish National Committee; Spanish Court of Arbitration; Madrid Court of Arbitration.
Education: University of Madrid (Law Graduate); Instituto Estudios Fiscales, Madrid (Master Tax Law); Instituto de Empresa, Madrid (Master Business Law).

FERNANDEZ, Arturo

Santiago Mediano Abogados
Phone: Madrid (+34 91 310 63 63)
E-mail: afernandez@santiagomediano.com
Dispute resolution and litigation department.
Position: Senior associate providing legal advice and represents national and international clients in all matters concerning civil and criminal law, especially in the non-fulfilment of agreements, claims for damages, intellectual property, copyright and related rights.
Career: Has a broad professional career regarding conflict solving both before Spanish courts and arbitration bodies on a national, European and international basis with regard to trade marks, parallel imports and designs; has lately offered his services on real property to a wide range of companies. Lectures on procedural and civil law in different relevant institutions.
Languages: English, Italian, Spanish.
Member: Madrid Bar Association; BLACA (London, UK); Institute of Advanced Legal Studies.
Education: University of Navarra (1994 Law Degree); Universidad Complutense of Madrid (1996 MA Corporate Legal Advice); University of London (2001 LLM Intellectual and Industrial Property field).
Personal: Born 1970.

GIMENEZ, Sergio

Mullerat
Phone: Barcelona (+34 93 405 93 00)
E-mail: s.gimenez@mullerat.com
Information and technology, media and telecommunications.
Position: Partner.
Career: Admitted 1989, Barcelona. Lecturer of Private International Law at the Law School of universitat de les Illes Balears 1998-2000; lecturer of International Contracting at 'Escuela Superior de Comercio Internacional' of the Universitat Pompeu Fabra since 2001. Author of different articles and publications on European interest groupings, banking law and foreign investments in Spain.
Languages: Spanish, Catalan, German, English.
Member: Barcelona Bar Association; Executive Committee of the Barcelona Young Lawyers Association; International Bar Association (IBA).
Education: Law School of Universitat de Barcelona (1984-89); Law School of the Freiburg University, Germany (EEC Law Certificate 1984-85; Patronat Catalá pro Europa 1985-86); Münster, Germany (LLM Master in Private International Law 1990).
Personal: Born 1966.

LÓPEZ-CHICHERI, Jaime

Ernst & Young Abogados, SL
Phone: Madrid (+34 91 572 7211)
E-mail: jaime.lopez-chicheri@es.ey.com
Tax, law.
Position: Managing partner of the tax and legal practice of Ernst & Young Abogados; partner, Cervelló, López-Chicheri y Aragón Abogados.
Career: Trained Universidad Complutense de Madrid. 27 years' experience of national and international tax advice. Arthur Andersen 1975-77; tax and legal department, Ernst & Young, since 1978. Collaboration and supervision of 'Guía Práctica de Sociedades Mercantiles' (Lexnova); 'Corporate Income Tax' (Aranzadi); 'Administración de Empresas, Factbook' (Aranzadi & Thompson).
Languages: English, French.
Member: Advisory Council of the Instituto de Empresa; BAR Association; Real Sociedad Hipica Española Club de Campo; director of the Country Club.
Education: Universidad Complutense de Madrid; ICADE. Law degree; master in fiscal affairs; several diplomas in accounting, international tax, and so on.
Personal: Born 1948; resides Madrid.
Leisure: Hunting, golf, sailing.

MEDIANO, Santiago

Santiago Mediano Abogados
Phone: Madrid (+34 91 310 63 63)
E-mail: smediano@santiagomediano.com
Intellectual property department.
Position: Senior partner, expert in media and intellectual property; leads a team of experts dealing with all areas of intellectual property and information technology.
Career: Was responsible for general advice in the legal department of the Spanish Authors and Publishers Society (SGAE); was the head of the IP department of international and national law firms in Spain; is a professor of intellectual property at the Autónoma University of Madrid; professor of civil law at the Complutense University of Madrid and professor of private law at the Ramon Carande University of Madrid; regular collaborator in courses, conferences and master programmes on intellectual property, at the Madrid Bar Association and the Carlos III University of Madrid; author of several publications on this subject.
Languages: English, German, French, Italian, Spanish.
Member: MMRC (Multimedia Rights Clearance System) Group of Experts; ALADDA (Literary and Artistic Association for the Defence of the Author).
Education: Universidad Autónoma de Madrid (1991).
Personal: Born 1968.

NAVARRO, Antonio

Broseta Abogados
Phone: Valencia (+34 96 392 10 06)
E-mail: ajnavarro@broseta.com
Commercial law department.
Position: Partner dealing with business law, commercial law, agency and distribution, international trade and finance.
Career: Qualified in 1992; former associate Uria & Menendez, Madrid and Barcelona; former associate Fox & Horan, New York.
Languages: English, Italian.
Member: Madrid and New York Bar Associations.
Education: University of Murcia (1991 Law Degree); Institute de Empresa, Madrid (1992 Master in Business Law); University of Edinburgh (1993 English Law); New York University (1995 Master of Laws LLM).
Personal: Born 1968; resides Valencia.
Leisure: Fishing.

PENDÁS, Angel

Mullerat
Phone: Madrid (+34 91 399 51 89)
E-mail: a.pendas@mullerat.com
Banking, finance, securitites, labour law, mergers and acquisitions.
Career: Admitted 1995, Madrid. Lecturer of mergers and acquisitions in Master of Business Law (MAJ), Instituto de Empresa, Madrid. Author of several books, articles, and conferences on joint ventures, limited liability companies, takeover bids, technology transfer and patents and trade marks licensing agreements.
Languages: Spanish, English, German.
Member: Madrid Bar Association; Center of International of Legal Studies.
Education: Law School of Fundación Universitaria San Pablo CEU; Instituto de Empresa, Madrid (Master of Business Law – MAJ).
Personal: Born 1971.

PRAT, Carles

Mullerat
Phone: Barcelona (+34 93 405 93 00)
E-mail: c.prat@mullerat.com
Intellectual property, EU competition and consumer law.
Position: Managing partner in the IP and competition group of Mullerat.
Career: Admitted to the Bar of Barcelona 1981; and subsequently in Madrid and Valencia, where he also practises. Visiting lecturer University of West England 1991-92; regular lecturer on competition and intellectual property at the Barcelona Bar and the University Ramon Llull (ESADE), Barcelona. Has written numerous articles on intellectual property and is a frequent lecturer on these topics at several national and international forums.
Languages: Spanish, Catalan, English, French.
Member: Previous board member of Marques, the European Trade Mark Owners Association since 1997; vice president of the Catalan Society of Legal Studies; member of IBA; INTA; AIPPI; LIDC; formerly Spanish vice president of the Association Internationale des Jeunes Avocats (AIJA); board member and legal adviser to the British Chamber of Commerce, Barcelona.
Education: Barcelona University (1981; Dip Law of the European Economic communities 1982).
Personal: Born 1959.

RODRIGUEZ-SAHAGUN, Miguel Angel

Ernst & Young Abogados, SL
Phone: Madrid (+34 91 572 7436)
E-mail: miguel.rodriguez-s@es.ey.com
Tax and legal.
Position: Corporate law, mergers and acquisitions, foreign investments, exchange control regulations, expert reports on economic fraud investigations.
Career: Trained Madrid University, qualified 1982; Fabregat Abogados 1983; tax and legal department of Arthur Young 1984-89; currently partner Ernst & Young Abogados (tax and legal practice) since.
Languages: English.
Member: Madrid Bar; Ernst & Young Law Practice; Merger and Acquisitions Cross Border Team.
Education: University of Madrid; Universidad Complutense (1982 law degree); 1983 Instituto de Empresa.
Personal: Born 1960; resides Madrid.

SAAVEDRA, Amalia

Santiago Mediano Abogados
Phone: Madrid (+34 91 310 63 63)
E-mail: asaavedra@santiagomediano.com
Tax and accountancy areas.
Position: Senior associate focusing her work on direct taxation, dealing with international restructurings, including mergers, branches and subsidiaries incorporations and day-to-day work, expatriates and transnational operations among others. With regard to indirect taxation, she advises on VAT and on double tax conventions.
Career: Has practised in well-known international consulting groups, representing the interests of national and multinational companies before the Spanish Tax Administration; has dealt with tax inspections and appeals before the Spanish authorities for both domestic and international operations; also works for the Industrial Organisation School in Madrid as tax professor for small and medium-sized entrepreneurs.
Languages: English, Spanish.
Member: Madrid Bar Association.
Education: Comillas Pontificial University (1992 Law Degree; Diploma Business Administration); Instituto de Empresa, Madrid (1993 MA Tax Law for Corporations).
Personal: Born 1968.

SALLARÈS, Joaquim

Mullerat
Phone: Barcelona (+34 93 405 93 00)
E-mail: jsallares@mullerat.com
Real estate and zoning law.
Position: Partner.
Career: Admitted 1990, Barcelona.
Languages: Spanish, Catalan, English.
Member: Barcelona Bar Association.
Education: Law School of Universitat de Barcelona (Post Graduate in Town Planning Technical 1990-94); Universitat Politècnica de Catalunya UPC (Taxation of Real Estate 1998).
Personal: Born 1961.

URRENGOECHEA, Juan Alberto

Mullerat
Phone: Madrid (+34 91 399 51 89)
E-mail: ja.urrengoechea@mullerat.com
Tax.
Position: Partner.
Career: Admitted 1989, Madrid. Author of several articles, publications and conferences on general tax law and e-business tax issues. Visiting lecturer, University of Dijon, France, Faculty of Law; professor of commercial and tax law, Instituto de Empresa, Madrid.
Languages: Spanish, English, French.
Member: Madrid Bar Association.
Education: Law School of Universidad de Deusto, Bilbao; Instituto de Empresa, Madrid (Master of Business Law 1988; Master of Tax Law 1989).
Personal: Born 1962.

VERARDINI, María José

Santiago Mediano Abogados
Phone: Madrid (+34 91 310 63 63)
E-mail: mjverardini@santiagomediano.com
Corporate and commercial department.
Position: Senior associate; as part of her legal assessment, Mariá José is in charge of the analysis, negotiation, preparation, wording, complaint, termination, etc of any commercial letter of intention, pre-contract, or contract, including but not limited to: shareholders' agreements, companies' sale, sale contracts in general, commercial representation and distribution contracts (agency, mediation, franchising, distribution, etc); contracts of an associative nature, such as joint ventures, commercial renting contracts (contract of works, services, engineering, technology transfer, outsourcing collaboration, consultancy contracts, merchandising, etc); advertising contracts, contracts of funding and confidentiality agreements. She works as general legal adviser in commercial law and, in particular, corporate law, commercial trading and contractual guarantees, international trading, law of exchange, mergers and acquisitions, MBOs, joint ventures, financial restructuring and corporate reorganisation as well as structured funding (project finance). Among other services, her work on due diligence is of utmost importance, considered as an initial step to an acquisition, in order to foresee and correct potential legal anomalies in whichever companies, or regarding the optimisation of resources from a legal point of view.
Career: Over the last 11 years, has developed her professional career in international law firms of great prestige, as well as in the legal department of international companies.
Languages: English, French, German, Russian, Spanish.
Member: Madrid Bar Association.
Education: University of Comillas (1991 Law Degree).
Personal: Born 1968.

SWEDEN

BIRKELAND, Sören

Advokatfirman Carler KB
Phone: Stockholm (+46 8 545 184 50)
E-mail: soren.birkeland@carler.se
Position: Partner specialising in real estate and tenancy rights.
Career: In-house lawyer, Swedish Homeowners Association 1983-87; in-house lawyer, the Swedish Association for Tenant-owners' Societies 1987-97; qualified 2001; associate Advokatfirman Carler KB 1997; partner 2003 to date.
Languages: English.
Education: University of Stockholm (1983 LLM).
Personal: Born 1953; resides Stockholm.

OLOFSON, Mats

Advokatfirman Carler KB
Phone: Stockholm (+46 8 545 184 57)
E-mail: mats.olofson@carler.se
Mergers and acquisitions.
Position: Partner specialising in mergers and acquisitions and general business transactions.
Career: Head of legal department of the Electrolux Group; secretary to the board of AB Electrolux; in-house counsel of the Facil Group, associate Swedbergs Advokatbyrå; clerk district court of Torna and Bara, Lund; secretary to the Swedish National Board of Trade, department for foreign trade; appointed expert in Swedish bilateral trade delegations; active in various national and international student bodies; board member of various corporations.
Languages: English, French.
Member: Swedish Bar Association.
Education: University of Uppsala (LLB); University of Toronto.
Personal: Born 1932; resides Stockholm.
Leisure: Skiing.

SWITZERLAND

BAJAN, Björn

Haymann & Baldi
Phone: Zurich (+41 1 250 25 25)
E-mail: bbajan@hblaw.ch
Position: Partner dealing with international commercial litigation and arbitration, compulsory enforcement and bankruptcy law, reconstructions, corporate and commercial, banking, contracts, employment, trusts and wills.
Career: Admitted 1986; advocacy 1989; publications: co-author contribution on Switzerland in Park & Cromie 'International Commercial Litigation', Butterworths (1997); co-author 'Dilemmas of a Withholding Agent' (June 1995); 'Handling a Tax Appeal' (March 1995) in 'Forum' (Tax Management International); co-author 'Dispute Resolution Methods in Switzerland' ('Comparative Law Yearbook of International Business', 1994).
Languages: English, German, French.
Member: Zürich Bar Association; member of various cantonal bars; Institute for Civil Procedure; Swiss Arbitration Association; Chartered Institute of Arbitrators (ACIArb) London.
Education: Zürich University (1986 lic iur, cum laude); Queen Mary and Westfield College, London (1994 LLM).
Personal: Born 1960; Biel.

BALDI, Peter

Haymann & Baldi
Phone: Zurich (+41 1 250 25 25)
E-mail: pbaldi@hblaw.ch

Position: Partner dealing with business law, banking law, arbitration, competition law, international civil procedure, international commercial litigation, intellectual property law, wills and trusts.
Career: Admitted 1977, Zürich Bar; previously corporate lawyer with bank; in advocacy since 1980, for own account since 1985; partner Haymann & Baldi; publications: 'Über die Gewährleistungspflicht des Verkäufers von Aktien, insbesondere beim Verkauf aller Aktien einer Gesellschaft' (1975); contribution on Switzerland in Park & Cromie 'International Commercial Litigation', Butterworths (1997); 'Switzerland, Double Taxation Treaties' (1992).
Languages: English, French, German, Italian.
Member: International Bar Association (Sections on Business and Banking Law); Swiss Bar Association; member of various cantonal bars; German Society for Banking Law.
Education: University of Zürich (1971 Lic iur magna cum laude; 1974 Dr iur summa cum laude).
Personal: Born 1946; Brunnen.

BOUZAGLO, James

Monfrini Crettol & Associés
Phone: Geneva (+41 22 310 22 66)
E-mail: jbouzaglo@mcswisslaw.com
Position: Associate active in: international contracts; agency and distributorship; copyrights; trade marks; television; debt collection and bankruptcy; company and corporate law; international assistance in penal matters; civil and commercial litigation; arbitration.
Career: Admitted Bern 1991, Geneva 1995; Steiner & Contini, Bienne 1991-93; Tribunal Cantonal de Bienne 1993; Hauchmann & Monfrini 1996-97; Monfrini Bottge & Associés 1998-2003; Monfrini Crettol & Associés 2004.
Languages: French, English, German, Italian, Spanish.
Member: Geneva Bar Association; Swiss Bar Association.
Education: University of Geneva (1990 Licence en droit); Graduate Institute of International Studies, Geneva (1998 Certificate of Internation Business Law).
Personal: Born 1966.

BUEHLER, Stefan

Rohner Rechtsanwälte
Phone: Zurich (+41 1 281 10 00)
E-mail: stefan.buehler@rohnerlaw.ch
Corporate and contract law; litigation.
Position: Partner dealing with all areas of corporate and contract law including mergers and acquisitions, banking and securities, and insolvency.
Career: Qualified 1994; admitted to the Bar 1998; partner Rohner Rechtsanwälte 2003; author and co-author of several publications on domestic and European corporate law.
Languages: English, French, German.
Member: Zurich Bar Association; Swiss Bar Association; IBA.
Education: University of Basel (1997 JD).
Personal: Born 1968; resides Zurich.
Leisure: Tennis, skiing, literature.

CARATSCH, Michele

Haymann & Baldi
Phone: Zurich (+41 1 250 25 25)
E-mail: mcaratsch@hblaw.ch
Position: Partner dealing with commercial and corporate law, Eastern European and CIS M&A, project finance and privatisations, Swiss and US securities law, initial public offerings, unfair competition law, intellectual property law, international commercial litigation and international arbitration.
Career: Admitted 1991, Zürich; admitted 1996, New York Bar; partner Haymann & Baldi, previously associate lawyer, Winston & Strawn, New York; publications: contribution on Switzerland in 'Worldwide Injunctions', in 'International Commercial Litigation' (June 1999); contribution on Tajikstan in 'International Privatisation Review' (2001-02).
Languages: English, German, Italian, Portuguese, Spanish.
Member: Zürich Bar Association; American Bar Association.
Education: New York University (1995 LLM Corporate Law); University of Zürich (1988 lic iur cum laude).
Personal: Born 1963; St Gall.

CRETTOL, Gilles

Monfrini Crettol & Associés
Phone: Geneva (+41 22 310 22 66)
E-mail: gcrettol@mcswisslaw.com
Position: Partner active in: corporate, tax and banking law; transportation law; air space law; family office services; arbitration.
Career: Admitted Geneva 1988; Python, Schifferli, Peters & Partners, Geneva 1990-91; Ch Projects Management Ltd, Tokyo 1991-93; partner Pestalozzi Lachenal Patry, Geneva 1993-2003; partner Monfrini Crettol & Associés 2004. Publications: correspondent for the 'Journal of International Taxation'.
Languages: French, English, German, Italian.
Member: Geneva Bar Association; Swiss Bar Association; Swiss Arbitration Association; Swiss Association for Air Space Law.
Education: University of Bern and Geneva (1987 Licence en droit).
Personal: Born 1963.

ECKERT, Martin K

Meyer Müller Eckert Partners – Attorneys at Law
Phone: Zurich (+41 1 254 99 66)
E-mail: eckert@mme-law.ch
Position: Partner, specialising in IT and technology law, mergers and acquisitions, IP, telecommunications and insurance law.
Career: High Court secretary at the Commercial Court of the Canton of Zurich 1991; qualified 1994; associate Carrard Paschoud Heim et Associés, Lausanne 1994-95; associate Hartmann, Meyer and Partner 1995-99; partner Meyer Müller Eckert 1999 to date; judge at the Swiss Federal Appeal Commission of Intellectual Property; lecturer on insurance and economic law at the University of Zurich; lecturer on contract and economic law at IFS Institute of Financial Services (Fachhochschule Luzern); publications: 'Basic Features of the Swiss Private Insurance Law', Zurich 2002; 'The Commercial Register, in Kommentar zum Schweizerischen Privatrecht' Basel/Frankfurt am Main 1994 (in German); 'Development of Law in the Area of Firm Names and Identification Marks' 1996-97, in Yearbook of the Commercial Register, Zurich 1997 (in German); 'Duty of Restoration and Cost Sharing Upon Restoration of Environmentally Damaged Sites Under New Art. 32d'; Environmental Protection Law and Ordinance Thereto, in 'Umweltrecht in der Praxis' Zurich 1998 (in German); 'Repetitorium Public International Law' Bern/Stuttgart/Wien 1999 (in German).
Languages: English, French, German.
Member: INGRES; Swiss Intellectual Property Institute; Swiss Interactive Media and Software Association (SIMSA); Licensing Executives Society; AIPPI; Computer Law Association; ASA (Swiss Arbitration Association); Swiss Sports Law Association; Ordre des Avocats (membre honoraire).
Education: University of Zurich (1992 Dr jur).
Personal: Born 1963; resides Zurich.

HAYMANN, Michel

Haymann & Baldi
Phone: Zurich (+41 1 250 25 25)
E-mail: mhaymann@hblaw.ch
Position: Partner dealing with business law, banking and securities, mergers and acquisitions, EC law, arbitration, competition law, international civil procedure, and international commercial litigation, wills and trusts.
Career: Admitted 1975, Zürich Bar; in advocacy since 1974; for own account since 1977; partner Haymann & Baldi; publications: 'Extraterritoriale Wirkung des EWG-Wettbewerbsrechtes' (1973); 'Extraterritorial Application of Antitrust Law, The Swiss Approach' in: 12 Revue Suisse du Droit International de la Concurrence (May 1981); 'Swiss to Outlaw Insider Trading' in: International Financial Law Review (October 1987); 'Contract Drafting Problems in the Light of the Lugano Convention' in: Bar European News, No 27; 'The Lugano Convention and the European Communities (May 1990)' in: Current ED Legal Developments Series, The Lugano and San Sebastian Conventions, Butterworths (1990); 'Joint Ventures and Mergers as a Test-Mark for a European Competition Law between EEC and EFTA: Switzerland as an Example' in: World Competition Law and Economics Review Vol 14 No. 1 (September 1990); 'Contribution on Switzerland' in: Cromie, Merger Control in Europe, IFR Publishing Limited (1991); 'Approaching Europe: Swiss Prospectives and Dilemmas' in: Legal Issues of European Integration (1992-1); contribution on Switzerland in: Stamp/Welsh (ed), 'International Insider Dealing', FT Law and Tax (1996); contribution on Switzerland in: Park & Cromie, 'International Commercial Litigation', second edition, Butterworths (1997).
Languages: English, French, German, Italian.
Member: American Society for International Law; International Bar Association (Antitrust and Banking Law Section); Swiss Association for International Law; Swiss Bar Association; member of various cantonal bars; Swiss Jurists Association; Union Internationale des Avocats (EEC Law Section); Association Suisse de l'Arbitrage.
Education: University of Zurich (1968 Lic iur magna cum laude; 1973 Dr iur summa cum laude).
Personal: Born Zürich; 1942.

KLEIN, Yves

Monfrini Crettol & Associés
Phone: Geneva (+41 22 310 22 66)

E-mail: yklein@mcswisslaw.com
Position: Associate active in: international commercial and business; tax; international tax planning; international contracts; company and corporate; banking law; international assistance in penal matters; international tracing of assets; international public law.
Career: Admitted Geneva 1995; International Trade Center UNCTAD/GATT, Geneva 1991; Directorate General for Development, European Commission, Brussels 1992; Lasa, Monroig & Veve, Washington DC 1994-95; Cabinet Mayor, Geneva 1995-98; Monfrini Bottge & Associés 1999-2003; Monfrini Crettol & Associés 2004. Publications: co-author of Swiss chapter 'International Tracing of Assests' (Sweet & Maxwell 1996, loose-leaf).
Languages: French, English, Spanish, Portuguese.
Member: Geneva Bar Association; Swiss Bar Association.
Education: University of Geneva (1989 Licence en droit); Graduate Institute of International Studies, Geneva (1993 Diploma of Higher Studies in International Law; 1998 Certificate of International Business Law).
Personal: Born 1967.

KUHN, Moritz W

Meyer Müller Eckert Partners – Attorneys at Law
Phone: Zurich (+41 1 254 99 66)
E-mail: kuhn@mme-law.ch
Position: Partner specialising in commercial law, private and public insurance law, economic law, EEC law, medical law, medical malpractice, mandate law, arbitration.
Career: Admitted to Zurich and Swiss Bars 1972; attorney at law, professor in law, Zurich University since 1986; expert activity in private, economic, insurance and commercial law; military investigating judge 1979-90; public prosecutor at Military Law Court 1991-95; president of the Supreme Court of the State (Kanton) Zurich since 2002; president of Swiss Insurance Brokers' Association since March 2001; executive vice-president/general secretary/head of legal and tax services, Swiss Life Insurance and Pension Company Group 1980-99; former judge at Commercial Law Court of Zurich (Chamber 'Banks and Insurances'); lecturer on insurance and economic law at the LLM post-graduate courses, University of Zurich; conference speaker (Symposiums, etc) on topics of insurance/banks; competition; financial services/bank insurance; restructuring; EEC; WTO/GATS; etc. Publications: Zurich habilitation paper, published by Peter Lang AG, Berne and Frankfurt am Main, November 1986 (habilitation theme: 'The Effects of EEC Harmonisation Endeavours and of Art. 31 Series BV on the Future Structure of the Swiss Insurance Contract Law (VVG)'); 'Basic features of the Swiss Private Insurance law', Zurich 1989, second edition, Zurich 2002; author of numerous articles on liability, commercial, economic and insurance law, law of obligation, corporation law, medical law, medical malpractice, financial services.
Languages: English, French, German, Italian.
Member: Committee 1986-88 and president 1993-98, Swiss Association of Insurance Law; member of the Presidential Council of AIDA (International Association of Insurance law); Swiss Arbitration Association since 1987.
Education: University of Zurich (1986 habilitation for Private and Insurance Law); University of Zurich (1970 Dr iur); Cambridge University (1970 introduction into Anglo-Saxon Law).
Personal: Born 1944; resides Zurich.

MEYER-HAUSER, Bernhard F

Meyer Müller Eckert Partners – Attorneys at Law
Phone: Zurich (+41 1 254 99 66)
E-mail: meyer-hauser@mme-law.ch
Position: Partner specialising in contracts, litigation, and arbitration.
Career: Qualified 1975; associate Baker & McKenzie 1978-82; partner Hartmann, Meyer and Partner 1983-99; partner Meyer Müller Eckert 1999 to date; Publications: 'Enforcement of a Money Claim in Switzerland – Outline of Procedure' Swiss American Chamber of Commerce, Zurich 1994; 'Ad hoc Arbitration and UNCITRAL Rules' (in German), in 'Schiedsgerichtsbarkeit', Schulthess Polygraphischer Verlag, Zurich 1997; 'Swiss Arbitration and Zurich Mini Trial Rules' Centre for International Legal Studies, Salzburg 1999; 'The Affiliate Contract – Agency and Brokerage Concepts on the Internet', Zurich 2000; 'Online Aid for Arbitrators and Arbitration Counsel (in German)' Basel 2000.
Languages: English, French, German, Italian.
Member: Chairman Emeritus Committee M of International Bar Association (International Sales and Related Transactions); member Chapter Board Doing Business in Switzerland and Legal Committee of Swiss-American Chamber of Commerce; Fellow Chartered Institute of Arbitrators (FCIArb) London; co-chairman Zürich Chamber of Commerce International Arbitration Court; member Swiss Arbitration Commission of the International Chamber of Commerce; WIPO arbitrator (World Intellectual Property Organisation); ICC arbitrator and arbitrator AAA.
Education: University of Zurich (1979 Dr jur); Northwestern University School of Law, Chicago (1977 LLM).
Personal: Born 1946; resides Zurich.

MONFRINI, Enrico

Monfrini Crettol & Associés
Phone: Geneva (+41 22 310 22 66)
E-mail: emonfrini@mcswisslaw.com
Position: Partner active in: international business; international taxation; banking; maritime; mergers and acquistions; antitrust and unfair competition; international art and entertainment; auction; media and television; intellectual property; bankruptcy; company and corporate law; white-collar crime and international assistance in penal matters; international and complex litigation; arbitration.
Career: Admitted Geneva 1970; Lalive Budin & Partners, Geneva 1970-72; Lachenal, Brechbuhl, Cottier & Partners, Geneva 1972-78; partner Hauchmann & Monfrini 1979-97; Monfrini Bottge & Associés 1998-2003; Monfrini Crettol & Associés 2004.
Languages: French, English, German, Italian, Swedish.
Member: Geneva Bar Association; Swiss Bar Association; International Bar Association.
Education: University of Geneva (1970 Licence en droit).
Personal: Born 1944.

MÜLLER-STUDER, R Luka

Meyer Müller Eckert Partners – Attorneys at Law
Phone: Zurich (+41 1 254 99 66)
E-mail: muller@mme-law.ch
Position: Partner, specialising in legal compliance for the financial sector.
Career: Qualified 1992; public prosecutor in 1993; associate Hartmann, Meyer and Partner 1995-99; member of several working groups of different Federal departments in the field of enforcement of money laundering control legislation 1997-98; member of task force to set up a self-regulating organisation 1997-98; partner Meyer Müller Eckert 1999 to date; publications: 'The Legal Discretion of Self-regulating Organisations under the Federal Money Laundering Law'; 'Journal of Insolvency Law' 4/1999; 'Outline of Interlocutory Injunctions under the Brussels and Lugano Conventions in Switzerland Taking into Account the Legal Systems of Germany and England' Basel 1999; 'Doing Business in Zug' Official Brochure of the Economic Department of the Canton of Zug 1998-2001.
Languages: English, French, German.
Member: Secretary of the Trade and Service Association of the Canton of Zug; lecturer at IFZ-Institute of Financial Services (University College of Central Switzerland).
Education: University of Zurich (1990 lic jur); London School of Economics and Political Science, London (1994 LLM); University of Basel (1999 Dr jur).
Personal: Born 1964; resides Zurich.

PRÉTÔT, Didier O

Monfrini Crettol & Associés
Phone: Geneva (+41 22 310 22 66)
E-mail: dpretot@mcswisslaw.com
Position: Associate active in: civil law; contract and corporate law; civil litigation; arbitration; legal advice; debt collection and insolvency; finance and international business.
Career: Admitted Geneva 2000; Python, Schifferli, Peters & Partners, Geneva 2000-02; Monfrini Crettol & Associés 2004.
Languages: French, Italian, English, German, Spanish.
Member: Geneva Bar Association; Swiss Bar Association.
Education: University of Fribourg (1999 Licence en Droit); University of Tübingen, Germany (2000 LLM).
Personal: Born 1975.

RAUCH, Men

Rohner Rechtsanwälte
Phone: Zurich (+41 1 281 10 00)
E-mail: men.rauch@rohnerlaw.ch
Tax and corporate; litigation.
Position: Attorney-at-law dealing with all areas of tax contract and corporate law including mergers and acquisitions, succession planning.
Career: Qualified 1980; admitted to the Bar 1983; attorney-at-law Rohner Rechtsanwälte 1995; author and co-author of several commentaries on tax law.
Languages: English, French, German, Italian.
Member: Zurich Bar Association; Swiss Bar Association; IPBA.
Education: University of Zurich (1985 JD).

Personal: Born 1954; resides Zurich.
Leisure: Mountaineering, biking, skiing, piano.

ROHNER, Louis
Rohner Rechtsanwälte
Phone: Zurich (+41 1 281 10 00)
E-mail: louis.rohner@rohnerlaw.ch
Banking and finance; litigation and arbitration.
Position: Partner dealing with all areas of banking and finance including trusts.
Career: Qualified 1974; admitted to the Bar 1977; partner Rohner & Partner 1982; author of several publications on computer law.
Languages: English, French, German, Italian, Spanish.
Member: Zurich Bar Association; Swiss Bar Association; IBA; Swiss Arbitration Association; International Fiscal Association; AIPPI.
Education: University of Zurich (1976 JD); Harvard Law School (1978 LLM).
Personal: Born 1949; resides Zurich.
Leisure: Golf, tennis, skiing.

TERRIER-HAGMANN, Isabelle
Monfrini Crettol & Associés
Phone: Geneva (+41 22 310 22 66)
E-mail: iterrier@mcswisslaw.com
Position: Associate active in: corporate and company law; contracts; labour law; media law; debt collection; bankruptcy; private international law; civil litigation; commercial litigation; arbitration.
Career: Admitted Geneva 1990; Ziegler Poncet Grumbach, Avocats, Geneva 1990-99; Monfrini Bottge & Associés 1999-2003; Monfrini Crettol & Associés 2004.
Languages: French, English, German.
Member: Geneva Bar Association; Swiss Bar Association.
Education: University of Geneva (1989 Licence en Droit; 1995 Diploma of Advanced Studies in European Law).
Personal: Born 1966.

TURKEY

INAL, Seyma
Inal Law Office
Phone: Istanbul (+90 212 339 0797)
E-mail: seyma@inal-law.com
Head of firm.
Position: Responsible for all aspects of the firm. Specialist areas – corporate law, project finance, commercial litigation, maritime law, death and personal injury.
Career: Qualified 1981 Ankara University; associate Metin Baran Law Firm 1981-90, partner 1990-94; partner Gur & Inal Attorneys-At-Law 1994-2003; founder/principal Inal Law Office 2003; frequent contributor to international maritime press 'Lloyds List', 'Maritime Advocate', 'P&I International'.
Languages: Turkish, English.
Member: Istanbul Bar Association; British Chamber of Commerce Turkey (honorary legal counsel); Turkish American Business Association; London Maritime Arbitrators' Association.
Education: Univerity of Ankara (1981 degree in law with distinction).
Personal: Born 1960; resides Istanbul.
Leisure: Walking, travelling, yoga, wine-tasting.

KARACA, Ali Zafer
Karaca & Associates
Phone: Istanbul (+90 212 347 10 31)
E-mail: z.karaca@karacalaw.com
Managing partner.
Position: Managing partner who has advised and worked for companies active in financial markets, trade and shipping, information technology, textile, iron and steel industry, oil and gas, project finance, banking and litigation. Areas of practice: corporate and company law; contract law and commercial disputes; competition and European law; employment law; foreign investment law; maritime and transportation law; property law; administrative and financial services law; privatisation and government tenders; international business transactions; project finance; mergers and acquisitions; international trade law; information technology law; litigation and commercial arbitration.
Career: Lawyer, Aybay & Aybay, Istanbul 1993-94; internship, European Commission DG XXI-Free Movement of Goods, Brussels 1994; partner Sakmar & Partners 1994-96; founded Karaca & Associates. Publications: author 'The Role of the Ankara Association Agreement in the Development of the Legal Relations Between the EC and Turkey'.
Languages: Turkish, English.
Member: Istanbul Bar Association; Turkish-Israel Business Council Board; Turkish-Finnish Business Council Board; Turkish-Swiss Business Council Board; vice-president (country), AIJA; Turkish Maritime Law Association; board member, Turkish Economic Law Research Foundation.
Education: University of Marmara, Istanbul (1990); Queen Mary College, University of London (1993 LLM Business Law); Centre of European Studies, Istanbul University (pending PhD studies in European and Turkish Competition Law).
Personal: Born 1967; resides Istanbul.

UK: ENGLAND AND WALES

ABBISS, Guy
Lewis Silkin, member of ius laboris
Phone: London (+44 20 7074 8000)
E-mail: guy.abbiss@lewissilkin.com
Employment and incentives.
Position: Partner specialising in equity-based incentives and tax efficient remuneration arrangements. Head of employee incentives. Joint head of ius laboris' international compensation and benefits practice group.
Career: Non-practising barrister Offenbach & Co 1990; solicitor Bevan Ashford 1992; solicitor Veale Wasbrough, Bristol 1995; head of employment and benefits Jones Day, Reavis & Pogue 1998; partner Lewis Silkin 2002; publications: contributing author 'International Stock Plans' (Browne Publishing).
Member: Share Scheme Lawyers Group; Global Equity Organisation; Chartered Institute of Personnel and Development; ProShare.
Education: Watford Boys Grammar School; Polytechnic of North London (1988 LLB Hons); Council of Legal Education (1990 Bar exams).
Personal: Born 1964; resides London.
Leisure: Motorcycling, flying, travel.

ALEXANDER, Roger
Lewis Silkin, member of ius laboris
Phone: London (+44 20 7074 8000)
E-mail: roger.alexander@lewissilkin.com
Corporate.
Position: Senior partner; head of marketing services law group and member of employment law group; acts for a raft of marketing services clients, UK and overseas, on flotations, acquisitions, disposals, mergers, joint ventures, corporate governance, employee incentivisation, including executive and other share schemes.
Career: Articled Lewis Silkin, qualified 1965; partner 1965; first head of corporate department, lead partner 1989-98; senior partner 1999; Campaign Magazine 'Number One Advertising Lawyer' (December 2001 and September 2002) and 'A List' (December 2003).
Languages: French.
Member: Society of Share Scheme Practitioners; freeman of the Worshipful Company of Marketors.
Education: Dulwich College.
Personal: Born 1942; resides London.
Leisure: Photography, travel, gardening, 20th Century literature (especially US), theatre.

BATLA, Raymond J
Hogan & Hartson
Phone: London (+44 20 7367 0202)
E-mail: rjbatla@hhlaw.com
Corporate, securities and finance, energy, project and international finance.
Position: Managing partner of the international offices of Hogan & Hartson LLP. Advises clients on a wide range of business transactions in the energy, telecom and manufacturing sectors, including privatisations, mergers and acquisitions, corporate restructurings, cross-border equity and debt investments, and international joint ventures. Nearly two decades of experience in energy matters – has been especially active in international energy project financings, including the first significant project financing undertaken without government guarantees or credit support in Central and Eastern Europe, and the $2.2bn financing of the Bolivia-Brazil gas pipeline, the largest public/private project undertaken to date in South America.
Career: Trained Hogan & Hartson, qualified 1973, partner 1983. Published over 30 articles and contributed to two books on a variety of subjects relating to energy matters. Admitted to practise before the US Supreme Court; registered foreign lawyer, Law Society of England and Wales.
Languages: Czech.
Member: International Bar Association; American Bar Association's Section on International Law; ABA Central and East European Law Institute Working Group; ABA Special Committee on Energy Finance; former chair International Energy Transactions Committee of the Federal Energy Bar Association in Washington; Bars of

Texas and the District of Columbia. London Capital Club. City Club of Washington DC.
Education: University of Texas (1970 BSc Civil Engineering, with Highest Honours, elected to engineering honorary societies Tau Beta Pi and Chi Epsilon; 1973 Doctor of Jurisprudence, with Honours, elected to th Order of the Coif).
Personal: Born 1947; resides London and Washington DC.
Leisure: Theatre, travel; London Capital Club; City Club of Washington.

BURD, Michael

Lewis Silkin, member of ius laboris
Phone: London (+44 20 7074 8000)
E-mail: michael.burd@lewissilkin.com
Employment and incentives.
Position: Joint head of employment and incentives dealing with full range of employment matters, particularly business transfers, contentious employment disputes, employment tribunal claims, severance negotiations and agreements, High Court litigation and employment documentation and policies.
Career: Articled Lewis Silkin; qualified 1986; partner 1988; head of employment; president, City of Westminster Law Society 1995-96; publications: editor Croner's 'Managing Termination of Employment'; Croner's 'Discrimination Law' looseleaf; frequent lecturer and writer on employment matters.
Member: Board of ius laboris; Employment Lawyers Association; International Bar Association; European Employment Lawyers Association; committee member London Solicitors Litigation Association.
Education: Tappan Zee High School, New York; Columbia University (1980 BA); Cambridge University (1982 MPhil).
Personal: Born 1958; resides London.
Leisure: Travel, fine food and wines, choral musician.

BURSKY, Daniel J

Fried, Frank, Harris, Shriver & Jacobson (London) LLP
Phone: London (+44 20 7972 9600)
E-mail: daniel.bursky@friedfrank.com
Corporate.
Position: Partner, concentrating in corporate finance and the US securities law representing both issuers and underwriters in a variety of financing transactions, including equity offerings, high-yield debt, Yankee bonds, eurobonds and private placements; M&A experience includes advising on the US implications of European transactions and acting for leveraged buy-out funds and their investment bankers in acquisition financings and management buy-outs, as well as advising investment banks in their role as financial advisers in M&A transactions; representations range from acting as designated underwriter's counsel for investment grade issuers to acting for growth companies in connection with venture capital financings and initial public offerings. Areas of expertise include: corporate finance, capital markets and high-yield debt.
Career: Qualified 1993; associate Fried Frank 1993; partner 2001.
Member: New York State Bar.
Education: Yale University (1990 BA); Columbia University Law School (1993 JD).
Personal: Born 1968; resides London.

CRAIK, Colin W

Hogan & Hartson
Phone: London (+44 20 7367 0209)
E-mail: cwcraik@hhlaw.com
Corporate, securities and finance lending, bankruptcy and creditors' rights, project and international finance.
Position: Partner who focuses on international mergers and acquisitions, joint ventures and corporate finance. He has extensive experience in representing US and foreign clients in structuring and executing complex acquisitions and investment strategies and in the development of joint operating and commercial arrangements among strategic partners.
Career: Admitted as a solicitor of England and Wales; New York Bar; member of the Czech Chamber of Advocates; partner Hogan & Hartson 1996.
Languages: English.
Member: New York State (sections on business law and international law); American (sections on business law, international law, committee on Central and Eastern European Law, International Law Section) and International Bar Associations; Law Society of England and Wales; Czech Chamber of Advocates.
Education: Bristol University (1977 LLB); College of Law (1979); King's College, University of London (1982 LLM).
Personal: Born 1956; resides Kew.
Leisure: Theatre, music, travel.

DAVIES, James

Lewis Silkin, member of ius laboris
Phone: London (+44 20 7074 8000)
E-mail: james.davies@lewissilkin.com
Employment and incentives.
Position: Partner and joint head of employment and incentives, specialising in all aspects of employment law with a special interest in European Community social law; discrimination law; TUPE; and sports law.
Career: Articled Denton Hall 1986; qualified 1988; solicitor Denton Hall London 1988-90; solicitor Denton Hall Hong Kong 1990-91; solicitor Lewis Silkin 1992-95; partner Lewis Silkin 1995 to date; director and management committee: Advice on Individual Rights in Europe (AIRE Centre); chair of Employment Lawyers Association working groups on TUPE, age discrimination and workplace privacy; publications: regular contributor to national, legal and personnel media; contribution to 'Croner's Discrimination Law' looseleaf and 'Sweet & Maxwell's TUPE' looseleaf; editorial board of Croner's 'Discrimination Law Briefing', and Members Advisory Panel of Employees Forum on Age.
Languages: English, French.
Member: European Employment Lawyers Association; Industrial Law Society; Institute of Employment Rights; Chartered Institute of Personnel and Development; Employment Lawyers Association; ius laboris.
Education: Ysgol Gyfun David Hughes, Menai Bridge; Leicester University (1985 LLB Law with French; 1995 LLM Law and Employment Relations); University of Strasbourg, France (1984 Diplome d'Etudes Juridiques Françaises).
Personal: Born 1962; resides London.
Leisure: Welsh rugby, Glamorgan County Cricket Club; sport, travel.

DOCKING, Peter

Sacker & Partners, member of ius laboris
Phone: London (+44 20 7615 9553)
E-mail: peter.docking@sacker-partners.co.uk
Pensions (niche practice).
Position: Partner specialising in all aspects of pensions law, acting for employers, trustees, members, and trade unions.
Career: Articled May, May & Merrimans; qualified 1987; partner Nicholson Graham & Jones 1991; partner Sacker & Partners since 1996; specialist in pensions law since 1987; former chairman of Education Committee of APL; frequent lecturer for many pension bodies; author of many articles in pensions and academic press; director Independent Trustee Limited.
Languages: German.
Member: Association of Pension Lawyers (APL); Association of Pension Lawyers International Committee; International Pensions and Employee Benefits Association; ius laboris (International Employment Law, Pensions and Employee Benefits Alliance).
Education: Sutton Manor High School for Boys; University of Exeter (1982 BA Hons).
Personal: Born 1961; resides London.
Leisure: Travel, walking, skiing, mountaineering; member British Mountaineering Council.

DRESDEN, Brinsley

Lewis Silkin, member of ius laboris
Phone: London (+44 20 7074 8000)
E-mail: brinsley.dresden@lewissilkin.com
Intellectual property group; litigation department.
Position: Partner; head of advertising law; specialises in intellectual property and increasingly involved in sport law; contributes to legal and industry journals.
Career: Trained Nabarro Nathanson; qualified 1991; three years in-house at BT working full-time on legal and regulatory issues relating to advertising and marketing; joined Lewis Silkin 1996; partner 1999.
Member: UK representative and managing director elect of the European Advertising Lawyers Association and the Global Advertising Lawyers Alliance; Advertising Law Group.
Education: King's College School, Wimbledon; Bristol University (1987 LLB Hons); College of Law, Guildford (1988 Law Society Finals); London University (1999 LLM Intellectual Property).
Personal: Born 1966; resides London.
Leisure: Sailing, skiing.

LORENZO, Toni

Lewis Silkin, member of ius laboris
Phone: London (+44 20 7074 8000)
E-mail: toni.lorenzo@lewissilkin.com
Employment and incentives.
Position: Partner specialising in contentious employment issues, including High Court litigation, advising on restrictive covenants and defending and bringing injunctive proceedings.
Career: Trained Lewis Silkin; qualified 1995; partner 2001; contributer to Gee's 'Employment Case Law: The Impact on Managers'.
Languages: Spanish, Italian.

Member: ELA (sub-committee drafting the pre-action protocol for breach of contract claims); European Employment Lawyers Association; ius laboris.
Education: Manchester University (1990 Spanish, Italian); College of Law, Guildford (1992 CPE; 1993 Finals).
Personal: Born 1966; resides London.
Leisure: Football, cricket, running.

MOLLEN, Robert P

Fried, Frank, Harris, Shriver & Jacobson (London) LLP
Phone: London (+44 20 7972 9600)
E-mail: robert.mollen@friedfrank.com
Corporate.
Position: Managing partner concentrating his practice in international corporate and securities matters and international legal crisis management; advises on M&A, securities offering, joint venture and privatisation matters, including particular experience with respect to regulated industries; frequently involved in the US aspects of UK public takeover matters, as well as the extraterritorial application of US federal securities laws, including the laws regulating takeovers and proxy solicitation, the issuance of securities, foreign private issuer compliance (including Sarbanes-Oxley issues) and audit, legal and other professional services. Areas of expertise include: corporate finance (M&A), capital markets, private equity, and securities (financial services).
Career: Qualified 1979; associate Fried Frank 1979; partner 1987.
Member: New York State Bar; District of Columbia Bar; International Bar Association.
Education: School of Foreign Service at Georgetown University (1976 BSFS summa cum laude); Harvard Law School (1979 JD magna cum laude).
Personal: Born 1955; resides London.

PETERSON, Timothy E

Fried, Frank, Harris, Shriver & Jacobson (London) LLP
Phone: London (+44 20 7972 9600)
E-mail: tim.peterson@friedfrank.com
Corporate.
Position: Partner concentrating his practice in public and private securities offerings and acquisitions, and acts as counsel to US and foreign companies and broker-dealers on securities and other regulatory issues. In addition, he has experience handling mezzanine financings, privatisations, Yankee bond offerings, high-yield debt offerings, MTN programs and acquisition financings. Areas of expertise include: capital markets, M&A, MBOs, corporate and commercial.
Career: Qualified 1986; associate Fried Frank 1985; partner 1992.
Member: New York and New Jersey State Bar.
Education: Rutgers University (1982 BA (Hons); 1985 JD (Hons)).
Personal: Born 1960; resides Surrey, England.

PHILLIPS, Paul

Sacker & Partners, member of ius laboris
Phone: London (+44 20 7615 9523)
E-mail: paul.phillips@sacker-partners.co.uk
Pensions (niche practice).
Position: Partner specialising in all aspects of pensions law, acting for employers, trustees, members and trade unions. He is a member of the firm's investment unit, with broad experience in advising pension schemes on the legal aspects of their investment arrangements, including investment reorganisations and the investment documentation for DB and DC schemes; has particular expertise in relation to contract negotiation with investment managers on behalf of both trustees and companies.
Career: Articled Wilde Sapte; qualified 1991; partner Sacker & Partners 1998; specialist in pensions law since 1991; frequent lecturer for many pensions bodies; author of many articles in pensions and academic press.
Member: Association of Pension Lawyers; ius laboris (International Employment Law, Pensions and Employee Benefits Alliance).
Education: Harvey Grammar School, Folkestone; Oxford University (1987 BA); College of Law, Guildford (1988 Common Professional Examination; 1989 Law Society Finals).
Personal: Born 1965; resides London.

RIGBY, Jonathan David

Mourant du Feu & Jeune
Phone: London (+44 20 7073 7863)
E-mail: jonathan.rigby@mourant.com
International finance.
Position: Partner based in the firm's London office specialising in structured finance and investment funds.
Career: Trained as an English barrister and called to the English Bar 1995; joined banking and international finance practice, CMS Cameron McKenna 1996; subsequently qualified as solicitor in England and Wales; joined Mourant du Feu & Jeune, Jersey 1998; Jersey advocate 2000; member of Mourant's international finance department; operational head of London office from April 2003; partner October 2003.
Languages: English, French.
Member: Jersey Law Society; Law Society of England and Wales; Chartered Institute of Bankers.
Education: Hautlieu School, Jersey; Kingston University (1994 BA Hons); Inns of Court School of Law (1995 Bar Vocational Course).
Personal: Born 1968; resides London.

WIEDEMANN, Karen

Fried, Frank, Harris, Shriver & Jacobson (London) LLP
Phone: London (+44 20 7972 9600)
E-mail: karen.wiedemann@friedfrank.com
Corporate.
Position: Partner specialising in private equity transactions, M&A and US securities and corporate law; private equity practice includes representing buyout groups in acquisitions of both public and private targets, as well as minority investments in startup and rollup companies; has been involved in all aspects of acquisition financing and has extensive experience representing portfolio companies in their acquisitions, divestitures and capital markets activities; practice also includes representing underwriters, purchasers, selling security holders and other parties in securities offerings and counselling on US antitakeover, proxy solicitation and corporate governance matters. Areas of expertise include: M&A takeovers, MBOs, capital markets, corporate and commercial.
Career: Qualified 1988 New Jersey; 1990 New York; joined Reboul, MacMurray, Hewitt, Maynard & Kristol, New York; associate 1989-95; partner 1996-99; partner Fried Frank 1999.
Member: New York and New Jersey State Bar.
Education: Yale College (1982 BA cum laude); New York University School of Law (1988 JD cum laude).
Personal: Born 1961; resides London.

UK: NORTHERN IRELAND

BECKETT, Samuel R

L'Estrange & Brett
Phone: Belfast (+44 2890 230 426)
E-mail: sam.beckett@lestrangeandbrett.com
Commercial litigation, including construction and professional indemnity.
Position: Partner in the firm's litigation department. Deals with commercial disputes including construction and professional indemnity cases. Also concerned with liquor licensing applications.
Career: Qualified 1980. John Johnson & Son 1980; L'Estrange & Brett 1984; made partner 1986; served on the Contentious Business Committee of the Incorporated Law Society of Northern Ireland.
Member: Chancery Division Liaison Committee; Commercial Court Liaison Committee.
Education: Bangor Grammar School; Queen's University of Belfast (1979 LLB); Certificate of Professional Legal Studies (1980).
Personal: Born 1957; resides Holywood, County Down.
Leisure: Cricket, rugby, golf and music.

BRETT, Adam TG

L'Estrange & Brett
Phone: Belfast (+44 2890 230 426)
E-mail: adam.brett@lestrangeandbrett.com
Litigation, including employment law, administrative law, professional negligence and intellectual property.
Position: Jointly heads litigation department; responsible for a wide range of commercial litigation including professional negligence, administrative law and judicial review, injunctive relief and intellectual property cases. Principal area of work is in relation to employment law and employee reward schemes. Personally involved in a considerable number of all the claims brought in Northern Ireland alleging discrimination on grounds of religious belief/political opinion. Dealt with a wide range of claims on other discriminatory grounds, including equal pay claims, disability claims and race claims. Has been involved in formal investigations brought by the Equal Opportunities Commission. Advises on the terms and conditions of employment, disciplinary and grievance procedures and issues relating to employee reward including bonus schemes and pensions. Advises in relation to restrictive covenants, European directives affecting employment law and trade union/strike action matters.
Career: Qualified 1981; partner at L'Estrange & Brett 1984. Contributor on Employment Law in Northern Ireland to

Encyclopaedia of 'Employment Law and Practice' (Gee) and 'Employment Forms and Precedents'.
Member: Employment Lawyers Association; committee member of the Employment Lawyers Group for Northern Ireland.
Education: Oxford University (MA); Queen's University of Belfast (Certificate of Professional Legal Studies).
Personal: Born 1957; resides Belfast.
Leisure: Council member, the Royal Society for the Protection of Birds; Chairman of the Society's Northern Ireland Committee.

EAKIN, Adrian D
L'Estrange & Brett
Phone: Belfast (+44 2890 230 426)
E-mail: adrian.eakin@lestrangeandbrett.com
Corporate department (projects unit).
Position: Partner in the corporate department specialising in project work and corporate finance.
Career: Goldman Sachs International, London (placement in legal department) 1995-96; Allen & Overy, London (two-year training contract) 1996-98; admitted 1998; assistant solicitor L'Estrange & Brett, Belfast 1998-2003, partner 2003 to date.
Member: Law Societies of England, Wales and Northern Ireland.
Education: Coleraine Academical Institution, University of Dundee (1993 LLB Hons); College of Law (1995 LPC).
Personal: Born 1970; resides Belfast.
Leisure: Watersports, motorsports, martial arts and walking.

GRAY, Richard
L'Estrange & Brett
Phone: Belfast (+44 2890 230 426)
E-mail: richard.gray@lestrangeandbrett.com
Corporate department, including corporate finance and banking work. Also project finance, PFI and inward investment work.
Position: Partner in the corporate and commercial department. Main areas of practice are in company, commercial and banking law, particularly in the areas of PFI/PPP and project finance.
Career: Called to the Northern Ireland Bar 1989; admitted as a solicitor in England and Wales and Northern Ireland 1992; joined the firm in 1992, having spent a number of years working with Cameron, Markby Hewitt (now CMS Cameron McKenna, London); course adviser and tutor at the Institute of Professional Legal Studies in Belfast (company law).
Member: Law societies of Northern Ireland and England and Wales.
Education: Methodist College, Belfast; Queen's University of Belfast, (LLM 1993).
Personal: Born 1966; resides in Belfast.
Leisure: Football, walking.

HENDERSON, Brian
L'Estrange & Brett
Phone: Belfast (+44 2890 230 426)
E-mail: brian.henderson@lestrangeandbrett.com
Commercial property – banking.
Position: Head of banking unit, advising on all aspects of banking and secured lending work; advises generally on commercial property matters.
Career: Administrative trainee in the European Commission 1978; qualified in 1976; partner L'Estrange & Brett 1979.
Languages: English, German.
Member: Non-Contentious Business Committee of the Law Society of Northern Ireland; Solicitor's European Group.
Education: Campbell College, Belfast; Trinity College, Dublin (BA Mod, 1973; 1973 LLB).
Personal: Born 1951; resides Belfast.
Leisure: Tennis.

HEWITT, V Alan
L'Estrange & Brett
Phone: Belfast (+44 2890 230 426)
E-mail: alan.hewitt@lestrangeandbrett
Commercial property and private client.
Position: Senior partner. Heads commercial property department, advising several major public and private companies and quasi-public corporations; retains an interest in trust law, including charitable trusts.
Career: Qualified 1967; L'Estrange & Brett since 1964; partner 1969; Council of the Law Society of Northern Ireland 1992-2003; President of the Law Society of Northern Ireland 2001-2002.
Languages: French.
Member: Society of Trust and Estate Practitioners; Society for Computers and Law; Law Reform Advisory Committee for Northern Ireland from 1997-2001.
Education: Belfast Royal Academical Institution; Queen's University of Belfast (1963 LLB); University of Michigan (1964 LLM).
Personal: Born 1941; resides Belfast.
Leisure: Golf (Royal County Down Golf Club and Malone Golf Club), reading and music.

HUDDLESTON, Ian W
L'Estrange & Brett
Phone: Belfast (+44 2890 230 426)
E-mail: ian.huddleston@lestrangeandbrett.com
Commercial property.
Position: Partner in commercial property department and advises in relation to all aspects of commercial property law, with emphasis on development work and the property aspects of PFI/PPP transactions. Advises on a number of public limited companies, national banks, and the Council of Mortgage Lenders on their lending policies and standard documentation for Northern Ireland.
Career: Qualified 1991; trained J Murland and Co; partner L'Estrange & Brett 1994. Part time lecturer and tutor at Queen's University, Belfast (conveyancing and secured lending); former member of the Parliamentary and Law reform committee.
Member: Land Registry Computerisation Working Group; Environmental and Planning Law Association for Northern Ireland; Society of Trust and Estate Practitioners.
Education: Down High School, Downpatrick; Queen's University of Belfast (1988 LLB); Bristol University (1989 LLM).
Personal: Born 1965; resides Belfast.
Leisure: Hill walking, cycling, equestrianism and farming.

IRVINE, John W
L'Estrange & Brett
Phone: Belfast (+44 2890 230 426)
E-mail: john.irvine@lestrangeandbrett.com
Corporate, including corporate finance and partnership.
Position: Head of corporate department. Considerable experience in all aspects of company and commercial law; has advised on many of the most significant and high-profile mergers and acquisitions projects in Northern Ireland in recent years.
Career: Lectured in Canada (employment law); lectured in England (commercial law subjects); joined L'Estrange & Brett 1985. Qualified 1986; partner 1988; head of the corporate department since 1994. Current directorships: Almac Sciences Ltd, Alhow Laboratories Ltd, Clinical Trial Services Ltd, Clinical Trial Services US Inc and Interactive Clinical Technologies Inc.
Member: Law Society of Northern Ireland.
Education: Portora Royal School, Enniskillen; Queen's University of Belfast (1980 LLB); Queen's University, Kingston, Ontario (1983 LLM).
Personal: Born 1957; resides Belfast.
Leisure: Football, fishing and running.

KIRKPATRICK, David J
L'Estrange & Brett
Phone: Belfast (+44 2890 230 426)
E-mail: david.kirkpatrick@lestrangeandbrett.com
Litigation including insolvency; agency/distributorship, contract, tort, debt and personal injury.
Position: Partner in the litigation department; specialises in commercial litigation including insolvency, contract, tort and debt. Deals with both plaintiff and defendant personal injury claims.
Career: Qualified 1990; partner 2001; worked with the European Commission in Brussels 1992-93.
Member: Northern Ireland Solicitors European Group; Association of Personal Injury Lawyers.
Education: Wallace High School, Lisburn; Queen's University of Belfast (1988 LLB); University of Edinburgh (1991 LLM).
Personal: Born 1965; resides Lisburn.

McBRIDE, Paul M
L'Estrange & Brett
Phone: Belfast (+44 2890 230 426)
E-mail: paul.mcbride@lestrangeandbrett.com
Corporate department, including corporate and commercial, project finance and inward investment.
Position: Partner in the corporate department. Advised in a number of significant mergers and acquisitions, management buy-outs and venture capital projects in Northern Ireland; experience in PFI and project finance transactions, advising both public and private sector clients; advised on a number of substantial inward investment projects.
Career: Called to the Bar 1990; admitted as a solicitor in Northern Ireland 1993; trained McKinty and Wright (Belfast); partner L'Estrange & Brett 1998.
Member: Law Society of Northern Ireland.
Education: Queen's University of Belfast (1989 LLB); Sidney Sussex College, University of Cambridge (LLM corporate law and finance 1991).

McILROY-ROSE, Andrea

L'Estrange & Brett
Phone: Belfast (+44 2890 230 426)
E-mail: andrea.mcilroy-rose@lestrangeandbrett.com
Commercial property and construction.
Position: Partner in the commercial property department; specialises in commercial leases and retail, investment and development work, and in particular shopping centres. Member of the construction group; with particular experience of PFI projects, advising on both property and construction matters.
Career: Qualified in England 1991; spent eight years working for Mayer, Brown, Rowe & Maw, (City of London firm); partner at L'Estrange & Brett 2000. Retains a practising certificate for England and Wales as well as Northern Ireland and acts for clients in both jurisdictions.
Member: Law Society of England and Wales; Law Society of Northern Ireland; Society of Construction Law.
Education: Victoria College, Belfast; University of Reading; The College of Law, Guildford (1987 LLB).
Personal: Born 1965; resides Belfast.

PIERCE, I Graham L

L'Estrange & Brett
Phone: Belfast (+44 2890 230 426)
E-mail: graham.pierce@lestrangeandbrett.com
Commercial property.
Position: Partner in commercial property department and advises on all aspects of commercial property work with particular emphasis on retail development and institutional investment; advises landlords and tenants on the impact of Business Tenancies legislation in Northern Ireland and writes on the subject. Sits on the firm's construction unit; advises developers, contractors and consultants on construction contracts, professional appointments and warranties.
Career: Qualified 1988; partner 1992; sits on the firm's training committee.
Member: Law Society of Northern Ireland.
Education: Portora Royal School, County Fermanagh; De Montfort University (1986 LLB).
Personal: Born 1965; resides Belfast.